PHILIP'S

WORLD ATLAS

IN ASSOCIATION WITH
THE ROYAL GEOGRAPHICAL SOCIETY
WITH THE INSTITUTE OF BRITISH GEOGRAPHERS

Contents

World Statistics

Countries	vi
Physical Dimensions	vii
User Guide	viii

The World in Focus

Planet Earth	2–3
Restless Earth	4–5
Landforms	6–7
Oceans	8–9
Climate	10–11
Water and Vegetation	12–13
Environment	14–15
Population	16–17
The Human Family	18–19
Wealth	20–21
Quality of Life	22–23
Energy	24–25
Production	26–27
Trade	28–29
Travel and Tourism	30–31

World Cities

Amsterdam	2
Athens	2
Atlanta	3
Baghdad	3
Bangkok	3
Barcelona	4
Beijing	4
Berlin	5
Boston	6
Brussels	6
Budapest	7
Buenos Aires	7
Cairo	7
Cape Town	8
Copenhagen	8
Chicago	9
Dubai	9
Delhi	10
Dublin	10
Edinburgh	11
Guangzhou (Canton)	11
Helsinki	11
Hong Kong	12
Istanbul	12
Jakarta	12
Jerusalem	13
Johannesburg	13
Karachi	13
Kolkata (Calcutta)	14
Lagos	14
Las Vegas	14
Lima	14
London	15
Lisbon	16
Los Angeles	16
Madrid	17
Manila	17
Melbourne	18
Mexico City	18
Milan	18
Miami	19
Moscow	19
Montréal	20
Mumbai (Bombay)	20
Munich	21
New Orleans	21
New York	22
Orlando	23
Osaka	23
Oslo	23
Paris	24
Prague	25
Rio de Janeiro	25
Rome	26
San Francisco	26
St Petersburg	27
Santiago	27
São Paulo	27
Seoul	27
Shanghai	28
Singapore	28
Stockholm	29
Sydney	29
Tokyo	30
Tehran	31
Toronto	31
Venice	32
Vienna	32
Warsaw	33
Washington	33
Index to City Maps	34–39
World Cities Satellite Images	40–48

World Maps

Map Symbols	1
The World: Political 1:95 000 000	2–3
Arctic Ocean 1:35 000 000	4
Antarctica 1:35 000 000	5

Europe

Europe: Physical 1:20 000 000	6
Europe: Political 1:20 000 000	7
Scandinavia 1:6 000 000 Iceland 1:6 000 000 Færoe Islands 1:6 000 000	8–9
Ireland 1:2 000 000	10
Scotland 1:2 000 000	11
England and Wales 1:2 000 000	12–13
British Isles 1:5 000 000	14

Netherlands, Belgium and Luxembourg 1:2 500 000	15
Central Europe 1:5 000 000	16–17
Eastern Europe and Turkey 1:10 000 000	18–19
France 1:5 000 000	20
Spain and Portugal 1:5 000 000	21
Italy and the Balkan States 1:5 000 000	22–23

Asia

Asia: Physical 1:47 000 000	24
Asia: Political 1:47 000 000	25
Russia and Northern Asia 1:20 000 000	26–27
Japan 1:5 000 000	28–29

China and the Far East 1:15 000 000 Hong Kong, Macau and Shenzhen 1:1 000 000	30–31
Northern China and Korea 1:6 000 000	32–33
Southern China 1:6 000 000	34–35
Indonesia and the Philippines 1:12 500 000 Java and Madura 1:7 500 000 Bali 1:2 000 000	36–37
Mainland South-east Asia 1:6 000 000 Ko Phuket 1:1 000 000 Ko Samui 1:1 000 000 Pinang 1:1 000 000 Singapore 1:1 000 000	38–39
South Asia 1:10 000 000	40–41
Northern India, Pakistan and Nepal 1:6 000 000 Jammu and Kashmir 1:6 000 000	42–43

Southern India and Sri Lanka
1:6 000 000
Andaman and Nicobar Islands
1:6 000 000

44–45

The Middle East
1:7 000 000

46–47

The Near East 1:2 500 000

48

Arabia and the Horn of Africa 1:15 000 000

49

Africa

Africa: Physical
1:42 000 000   50

Africa: Political
1:42 000 000   51

Northern Africa
1:15 000 000
Azores 1:15 000 000
Cape Verde Islands 1:10 000 000

52–53

Central and Southern Africa
1:15 000 000
Comoros 1:8 000 000
Seychelles 1:2 500 000
Réunion 1:2 500 000
Mauritius 1:2 500 000
Madagascar 1:15 000 000

54–55

Southern Africa
1:8 000 000

56–57

Australia and Oceania

Australia and Oceania: Physical and Political
1:50 000 000   58

New Zealand 1:6 000 000
Fiji 1:6 000 000
Samoan Islands 1:6 000 000
Tonga 1:6 000 000
Tahiti and Moorea 1:1 000 000

59

Western Australia
1:8 000 000

60–61

Eastern Australia
1:8 000 000
Torres Strait 1:8 000 000
Whitsunday Islands 1:2 500 000
Tasmania 1:8 000 000

62–63

Pacific Ocean
1:54 000 000   64–65

North America

North America: Physical
1:35 000 000   66

North America: Political
1:35 000 000   67

Canada 1:15 000 000

68–69

Western Canada 1:7 000 000

70–71

Eastern Canada 1:7 000 000

72–73

United States 1:15 000 000
Hawai'i 1:15 000 000
Alaska 1:15 000 000

74–75

United States – West
1:6 700 000

76–77

Central and Southern California and Western Washington
1:2 500 000

78–79

United States – Midwest and North-east
1:6 700 000

80–81

North-eastern United States
1:2 500 000

82–83

United States – South
1:6 700 000

84–85

Mexico 1:8 000 000

86–87

Central America and the West Indies 1:8 000 000
Jamaica 1:3 000 000
Guadeloupe 1:2 000 000
Martinique 1:2 000 000
Puerto Rico 1:3 000 000
Virgin Islands 1:2 000 000
St Lucia 1:1 000 000
Barbados 1:1 000 000

88–89

South America

South America: Physical
1:35 000 000   90

South America: Political
1:35 000 000   91

South America – North
1:16 000 000
Trinidad and Tobago 1:2 500 000

92–93

Central South America
1:8 000 000

94–95

South America – South
1:16 000 000

96

Index to World Maps
97–176

World Statistics: Countries

This alphabetical list includes the principal countries and territories of the world. If a territory is not completely independent, the country it is associated with is named. The area figures give the total area of land, inland water and ice. The population figures are 2014 estimates where available. The annual income is the Gross Domestic Product per capita in US dollars. The figures are the latest available, usually 2014 estimates.

Country/Territory	Area km² Thousands	Area miles² Thousands	Population Thousands	Capital	Annual Income US $
Afghanistan	652	252	31,823	Kabul	2,000
Albania	28.7	11.1	3,020	Tirana	11,100
Algeria	2,382	920	38,814	Algiers	14,300
American Samoa (US)	0.20	0.08	55	Pago Pago	8,000
Andorra	0.47	0.18	85	Andorra La Vella	37,200
Angola	1,247	481	19,088	Luanda	8,200
Anguilla (UK)	0.10	0.04	16	The Valley	12,200
Antigua & Barbuda	0.44	0.17	91	St John's	22,600
Argentina	2,780	1,074	43,024	Buenos Aires	22,100
Armenia	29.8	11.5	3,061	Yerevan	7,400
Aruba (Netherlands)	0.19	0.07	111	Oranjestad	25,300
Australia	7,741	2,989	22,508	Canberra	46,600
Austria	83.9	32.4	8,223	Vienna	45,400
Azerbaijan	86.6	33.4	9,686	Baku	17,900
Azores (Portugal)	2.2	0.86	246	Ponta Delgada	15,197
Bahamas	13.9	5.4	322	Nassau	25,100
Bahrain	0.69	0.27	1,314	Manama	51,400
Bangladesh	144	55.6	166,281	Dhaka	3,400
Barbados	0.43	0.17	290	Bridgetown	16,200
Belarus	208	80.2	9,608	Minsk	18,200
Belgium	30.5	11.8	10,449	Brussels	41,700
Belize	23.0	8.9	341	Belmopan	8,100
Benin	113	43.5	10,161	Porto-Novo	1,900
Bermuda (UK)	0.05	0.02	70	Hamilton	86,000
Bhutan	47.0	18.1	734	Thimphu	7,700
Bolivia	1,099	424	10,631	La Paz/Sucre	6,200
Bosnia-Herzegovina	51.2	19.8	3,872	Sarajevo	9,800
Botswana	582	225	2,156	Gaborone	16,000
Brazil	8,514	3,287	202,657	Brasília	15,200
Brunei	5.8	2.2	423	Bandar Seri Begawan	77,700
Bulgaria	111	42.8	6,925	Sofia	17,100
Burkina Faso	274	106	18,365	Ouagadougou	1,700
Burma (Myanmar)	677	261	55,746	Rangoon/Naypyidaw	4,800
Burundi	27.8	10.7	10,396	Bujumbura	900
Cabo Verde	4.0	1.6	539	Praia	6,300
Cambodia	181	69.9	15,458	Phnom Penh	3,300
Cameroon	475	184	23,131	Yaoundé	3,000
Canada	9,971	3,850	34,835	Ottawa	44,500
Canary Is. (Spain)	7.2	2.8	1,682	Las Palmas/Santa Cruz	19,900
Cayman Is. (UK)	0.26	0.10	55	George Town	43,800
Central African Republic	623	241	5,278	Bangui	600
Chad	1,284	496	11,412	Ndjaména	2,600
Chile	757	292	17,364	Santiago	23,200
China	9,597	3,705	1,355,693	Beijing	12,900
Colombia	1,139	440	46,245	Bogotá	13,500
Comoros	2.2	0.86	767	Moroni	1,700
Congo	342	132	4,662	Brazzaville	6,600
Congo (Dem. Rep. of the)	2,345	905	77,434	Kinshasa	700
Cook Is. (NZ)	0.24	0.09	10	Avarua	9,100
Costa Rica	51.1	19.7	4,755	San José	14,900
Croatia	56.5	21.8	4,471	Zagreb	20,400
Cuba	111	42.8	11,047	Havana	10,200
Curaçao (Netherlands)	0.44	0.17	147	Willemstad	15,000
Cyprus	9.3	3.6	1,172	Nicosia	28,000
Czech Republic	78.9	30.5	10,627	Prague	28,400
Denmark	43.1	16.6	5,569	Copenhagen	44,300
Djibouti	23.2	9.0	810	Djibouti	3,000
Dominica	0.75	0.29	73	Roseau	10,700
Dominican Republic	48.5	18.7	10,350	Santo Domingo	12,800
East Timor	14.9	5.7	1,202	Dili	6,800
Ecuador	284	109	15,654	Quito	11,400
Egypt	1,001	387	86,895	Cairo	11,100
El Salvador	21.0	8.1	6,126	San Salvador	8,000
Equatorial Guinea	28.1	10.8	722	Malabo	32,600
Eritrea	118	45.4	6,381	Asmara	1,200
Estonia	45.1	17.4	1,258	Tallinn	26,600
Ethiopia	1,104	426	96,633	Addis Ababa	1,500
Falkland Is. (UK)	12.2	4.7	3	Stanley	55,400
Faroe Is. (Denmark)	1.4	0.54	50	Tórshavn	30,500
Fiji	18.3	7.1	903	Suva	8,200
Finland	338	131	5,269	Helsinki	40,500
France	552	213	66,259	Paris	40,400
French Guiana (France)	90.0	34.7	250	Cayenne	8,300
French Polynesia (France)	4.0	1.5	280	Papeete	26,100
Gabon	268	103	1,673	Libreville	21,600
Gambia, The	11.3	4.4	1,926	Banjul	1,700
Georgia	69.7	26.9	4,936	Tbilisi	7,700
Germany	357	138	80,997	Berlin	44,700
Ghana	239	92.1	25,758	Accra	4,200
Gibraltar (UK)	0.006	0.002	29	Gibraltar Town	43,000
Greece	132	50.9	10,776	Athens	25,800
Greenland (Denmark)	2,176	840	58	Nuuk	38,400
Grenada	0.34	0.13	110	St George's	11,800
Guadeloupe (France)	1.7	0.66	406	Basse-Terre	7,900
Guam (US)	0.55	0.21	161	Agana	28,700
Guatemala	109	42.0	14,647	Guatemala City	7,500
Guinea	246	94.9	11,474	Conakry	1,300
Guinea-Bissau	36.1	13.9	1,693	Bissau	1,400
Guyana	215	83.0	736	Georgetown	6,900
Haiti	27.8	10.7	9,997	Port-au-Prince	1,800
Honduras	112	43.3	8,599	Tegucigalpa	4,700
Hungary	93.0	35.9	9,919	Budapest	24,300
Iceland	103	39.8	317	Reykjavik	42,600
India	3,287	1,269	1,236,345	New Delhi	5,800
Indonesia	1,905	735	253,610	Jakarta	10,200
Iran	1,648	636	80,841	Tehran	16,500
Iraq	438	169	32,586	Baghdad	14,100
Ireland	70.3	27.1	4,833	Dublin	46,800
Israel	20.6	8.0	7,822	Jerusalem	33,400
Italy	301	116	61,680	Rome	34,500
Ivory Coast (Côte d'Ivoire)	322	125	22,849	Yamoussoukro	2,900
Jamaica	11.0	4.2	2,930	Kingston	8,700
Japan	378	146	127,103	Tokyo	37,800
Jordan	89.3	34.5	7,930	Amman	11,900
Kazakhstan	2,725	1,052	17,949	Astana	24,100
Kenya	580	224	45,010	Nairobi	3,100
Kiribati	0.73	0.28	104	Tarawa	1,600
Korea, North	121	46.5	24,852	Pyŏngyang	1,800
Korea, South	99.3	38.3	49,040	Seoul	35,400
Kosovo	10.9	4.2	1,859	Pristina	8,000
Kuwait	17.8	6.9	2,743	Kuwait City	71,000
Kyrgyzstan	200	77.2	5,604	Bishkek	3,400

Country/Territory	Area km² Thousands	Area miles² Thousands	Population Thousands	Capital	Annual Income US $
Laos	237	91.4	6,804	Vientiane	5,000
Latvia	64.6	24.9	2,165	Riga	23,900
Lebanon	10.4	4.0	5,883	Beirut	17,900
Lesotho	30.4	11.7	1,942	Maseru	2,900
Liberia	111	43.0	4,092	Monrovia	900
Libya	1,760	679	6,244	Tripoli	16,600
Liechtenstein	0.16	0.06	37	Vaduz	89,400
Lithuania	65.2	25.2	3,506	Vilnius	26,700
Luxembourg	2.6	1.0	521	Luxembourg	92,400
Macedonia (FYROM)	25.7	9.9	2,092	Skopje	13,200
Madagascar	587	227	23,202	Antananarivo	1,400
Madeira (Portugal)	0.78	0.30	268	Funchal	25,800
Malawi	118	45.7	17,377	Lilongwe	800
Malaysia	330	127	30,073	Kuala Lumpur/Putrajaya	24,500
Maldives	0.30	0.12	394	Malé	12,400
Mali	1,240	479	16,456	Bamako	1,600
Malta	0.32	0.12	413	Valletta	31,700
Marshall Is.	0.18	0.07	71	Majuro	3,200
Martinique (France)	1.1	0.43	386	Fort-de-France	14,400
Mauritania	1,026	396	3,517	Nouakchott	3,400
Mauritius	2.0	0.79	1,331	Port Louis	17,900
Mayotte (France)	0.37	0.14	213	Mamoudzou	4,900
Mexico	1,958	756	120,287	Mexico City	17,900
Micronesia, Fed. States of	0.70	0.27	106	Palikir	3,200
Moldova	33.9	13.1	3,583	Kishinev	4,800
Monaco	0.001	0.0004	31	Monaco	78,700
Mongolia	1,567	605	2,953	Ulan Bator	10,200
Montenegro	14.0	5.4	650	Podgorica	15,200
Montserrat (UK)	0.10	0.39	5	Brades	8,500
Morocco	447	172	32,987	Rabat	7,700
Mozambique	802	309	24,692	Maputo	1,100
Namibia	824	318	2,198	Windhoek	10,800
Nauru	0.02	0.008	9	Yaren	5,000
Nepal	147	56.8	30,987	Katmandu	2,400
Netherlands	41.5	16.0	16,877	Amsterdam/The Hague	47,400
New Caledonia (France)	18.6	7.2	268	Nouméa	38,800
New Zealand	271	104	4,402	Wellington	35,000
Nicaragua	130	50.2	5,849	Managua	4,800
Niger	1,267	489	17,466	Niamey	1,000
Nigeria	924	357	177,156	Abuja	6,100
Northern Mariana Is. (US)	0.46	0.18	51	Saipan	13,600
Norway	324	125	5,148	Oslo	65,900
Oman	310	119	3,220	Muscat	44,100
Pakistan	796	307	196,174	Islamabad	4,700
Palau	0.46	0.18	21	Melekeok	15,100
Panama	75.5	29.2	3,608	Panamá	20,300
Papua New Guinea	463	179	6,553	Port Moresby	2,400
Paraguay	407	157	6,704	Asunción	8,400
Peru	1,285	496	30,148	Lima	12,000
Philippines	300	116	107,668	Manila	7,000
Poland	323	125	38,346	Warsaw	24,400
Portugal	88.8	34.3	10,814	Lisbon	26,300
Puerto Rico (US)	8.9	3.4	3,621	San Juan	16,300
Qatar	11.0	4.2	2,123	Doha	144,400
Réunion (France)	2.5	0.97	841	St-Denis	6,200
Romania	238	92.0	21,730	Bucharest	19,400
Russia	17,075	6,593	142,470	Moscow	24,800
Rwanda	26.3	10.2	12,337	Kigali	1,700
St Kitts & Nevis	0.26	0.10	52	Basseterre	20,300
St Lucia	0.54	0.21	163	Castries	11,100
St Vincent & Grenadines	0.39	0.15	103	Kingstown	10,900
Samoa	2.8	1.1	197	Apia	5,200
San Marino	0.06	0.02	33	San Marino	55,000
São Tomé & Príncipe	0.96	0.37	190	São Tomé	3,100
Saudi Arabia	2,150	830	27,346	Riyadh	52,800
Senegal	197	76.0	13,636	Dakar	2,300
Serbia	77.5	29.9	7,210	Belgrade	12,500
Seychelles	0.46	0.18	92	Victoria	24,500
Sierra Leone	71.7	27.7	5,744	Freetown	2,100
Singapore	0.68	0.26	5,567	Singapore City	81,300
Slovak Republic	49.0	18.9	5,444	Bratislava	27,700
Slovenia	20.3	7.8	1,988	Ljubljana	29,400
Solomon Is.	28.9	11.2	610	Honiara	1,800
Somalia	638	246	10,428	Mogadishu	600
South Africa	1,221	471	48,376	Cape Town/Pretoria	12,700
Spain	498	192	47,738	Madrid	33,000
Sri Lanka	65.6	25.3	21,866	Colombo	10,400
Sudan	1,886	728	35,482	Khartoum	4,500
Sudan, South	620	239	11,563	Juba	2,000
Suriname	163	63.0	573	Paramaribo	16,700
Swaziland	17.4	6.7	1,420	Mbabane	7,800
Sweden	450	174	9,724	Stockholm	44,700
Switzerland	41.3	15.9	8,062	Berne	55,200
Syria	185	71.5	17,952	Damascus	5,100
Taiwan	36.0	13.9	23,360	Taipei	43,600
Tajikistan	143	55.3	8,052	Dushanbe	2,700
Tanzania	945	365	49,639	Dodoma	1,900
Thailand	513	198	67,741	Bangkok	14,400
Togo	56.8	21.9	7,351	Lomé	1,500
Tonga	0.65	0.25	106	Nuku'alofa	5,000
Trinidad & Tobago	5.1	2.0	1,224	Port of Spain	31,300
Tunisia	164	63.2	10,938	Tunis	11,400
Turkey	775	299	81,619	Ankara	19,600
Turkmenistan	488	188	5,172	Ashkhabad	14,200
Turks & Caicos Is. (UK)	0.43	0.17	49	Cockburn Town	29,100
Tuvalu	0.03	0.01	11	Fongafale	3,200
Uganda	241	93.1	35,919	Kampala	1,800
Ukraine	604	233	44,291	Kiev	8,200
United Arab Emirates	83.6	32.3	5,629	Abu Dhabi	65,000
United Kingdom	242	93.4	63,743	London	37,700
United States of America	9,629	3,718	318,892	Washington, DC	54,800
Uruguay	175	67.6	3,333	Montevideo	20,500
Uzbekistan	447	173	28,930	Tashkent	5,600
Vanuatu	12.2	4.7	267	Port-Vila	2,500
Vatican City	0.0004	0.0002	0.842	Vatican City	
Venezuela	912	352	28,868	Caracas	17,900
Vietnam	332	128	93,422	Hanoi	5,600
Virgin Is. (UK)	0.15	0.06	28	Road Town	42,300
Virgin Is. (US)	0.35	0.13	104	Charlotte Amalie	14,500
Yemen	528	204	26,053	Sana'	3,900
Zambia	753	291	14,639	Lusaka	4,100
Zimbabwe	391	151	13,772	Harare	2,000

World Statistics: Physical Dimensions

Each topic list is divided into continents and within a continent the items are listed in order of size. The bottom part of many of the lists is selective in order to give examples from as many different countries as possible. The order of the continents is the same as in the atlas, beginning with Europe and ending with South America. The figures are rounded as appropriate.

World, Continents, Oceans

	km²	miles²	%
The World	509,450,000	196,672,000	–
Land	149,450,000	57,688,000	29.3
Water	360,000,000	138,984,000	70.7
Asia	44,500,000	17,177,000	29.8
Africa	30,302,000	11,697,000	20.3
North America	24,241,000	9,357,000	16.2
South America	17,793,000	6,868,000	11.9
Antarctica	14,100,000	5,443,000	9.4
Europe	9,957,000	3,843,000	6.7
Australia & Oceania	8,557,000	3,303,000	5.7
Pacific Ocean	155,557,000	60,061,000	46.4
Atlantic Ocean	76,762,000	29,638,000	22.9
Indian Ocean	68,556,000	26,470,000	20.4
Southern Ocean	20,327,000	7,848,000	6.1
Arctic Ocean	14,056,000	5,427,000	4.2

Ocean Depths

Atlantic Ocean		m	ft
Puerto Rico (Milwaukee) Deep		8,605	28,232
Cayman Trench		7,680	25,197
Gulf of Mexico		5,203	17,070
Mediterranean Sea		5,121	16,801
Black Sea		2,211	7,254
North Sea		660	2,165

Indian Ocean	m	ft
Java Trench	7,450	24,442
Red Sea	2,635	8,454

Pacific Ocean	m	ft
Mariana Trench	11,022	36,161
Tonga Trench	10,882	35,702
Japan Trench	10,554	34,626
Kuril Trench	10,542	34,587

Arctic Ocean	m	ft
Molloy Deep	5,608	18,399

Southern Ocean	m	ft
South Sandwich Trench	7,235	23,737

Mountains

Europe		m	ft
Elbrus	Russia	5,642	18,510
Dykh-Tau	Russia	5,205	17,076
Shkhara	Russia/Georgia	5,201	17,064
Koshtan-Tau	Russia	5,152	16,903
Kazbek	Russia/Georgia	5,047	16,558
Pushkin	Russia/Georgia	5,033	16,512
Katyn-Tau	Russia/Georgia	4,979	16,335
Shota Rustaveli	Russia/Georgia	4,860	15,945
Mont Blanc	France/Italy	4,808	15,774
Monte Rosa	Italy/Switzerland	4,634	15,203
Dom	Switzerland	4,545	14,911
Liskamm	Switzerland	4,527	14,852
Weisshorn	Switzerland	4,505	14,780
Taschorn	Switzerland	4,490	14,730
Matterhorn/Cervino	Italy/Switzerland	4,478	14,691
Grossglockner	Austria	3,797	12,457
Mulhacén	Spain	3,478	11,411
Zugspitze	Germany	2,962	9,718
Olympus	Greece	2,917	9,570
Galdhøpiggen	Norway	2,469	8,100
Ben Nevis	UK	1,344	4,409

Asia		m	ft
Everest	China/Nepal	8,850	29,035
K2 (Godwin Austen)	China/Kashmir	8,611	28,251
Kanchenjunga	India/Nepal	8,598	28,208
Lhotse	China/Nepal	8,516	27,939
Makalu	China/Nepal	8,481	27,824
Cho Oyu	China/Nepal	8,201	26,906
Dhaulagiri	Nepal	8,167	26,795
Manaslu	Nepal	8,156	26,758
Nanga Parbat	Kashmir	8,126	26,660
Annapurna	Nepal	8,078	26,502
Gasherbrum	China/Kashmir	8,068	26,469
Broad Peak	China/Kashmir	8,051	26,414
Xixabangma	China	8,012	26,286
Kangbachen	Nepal	7,858	25,781
Trivor	Pakistan	7,720	25,328
Pik Imeni Ismail Samani	Tajikistan	7,495	24,590
Demavend	Iran	5,604	18,386
Ararat	Turkey	5,165	16,945
Gunong Kinabalu	Malaysia (Borneo)	4,101	13,455
Fuji-San	Japan	3,776	12,388

Africa		m	ft
Kilimanjaro	Tanzania	5,895	19,340
Mt Kenya	Kenya	5,199	17,057
Ruwenzori (Margherita)	Ug./Congo (D.R.)	5,109	16,762
Meru	Tanzania	4,565	14,977
Ras Dashen	Ethiopia	4,553	14,937
Karisimbi	Rwanda/Congo (D.R.)	4,507	14,787
Mt Elgon	Kenya/Uganda	4,321	14,176
Batu	Ethiopia	4,307	14,130
Toubkal	Morocco	4,165	13,665
Mt Cameroun	Cameroon	4,070	13,353

Oceania		m	ft
Puncak Jaya	Indonesia	4,884	16,024
Puncak Trikora	Indonesia	4,730	15,518
Puncak Mandala	Indonesia	4,702	15,427
Mt Wilhelm	Papua New Guinea	4,508	14,790
Mauna Kea	USA (Hawai'i)	4,205	13,796
Mauna Loa	USA (Hawai'i)	4,169	13,678
Aoraki Mt Cook	New Zealand	3,724	12,218
Mt Kosciuszko	Australia	2,228	7,310

North America		m	ft
Mt McKinley (Denali)	USA (Alaska)	6,168	20,237
Mt Logan	Canada	5,959	19,551
Pico de Orizaba	Mexico	5,610	18,405
Mt St Elias	USA/Canada	5,489	18,008
Popocatépetl	Mexico	5,452	17,887
Mt Foraker	USA (Alaska)	5,304	17,401
Iztaccihuatl	Mexico	5,286	17,342
Mt Lucania	Canada	5,226	17,146
Mt Steele	Canada	5,073	16,644
Mt Bona	USA (Alaska)	5,005	16,420
Mt Whitney	USA	4,418	14,495
Tajumulco	Guatemala	4,220	13,845
Chirripó Grande	Costa Rica	3,837	12,589
Pico Duarte	Dominican Rep.	3,175	10,417

South America		m	ft
Aconcagua	Argentina	6,962	22,841
Bonete	Argentina	6,872	22,546
Ojos del Salado	Argentina/Chile	6,863	22,516
Pissis	Argentina	6,779	22,241
Mercedario	Argentina/Chile	6,770	22,211
Huascarán	Peru	6,768	22,204
Llullaillaco	Argentina/Chile	6,723	22,057
Nevado de Cachi	Argentina	6,720	22,047
Yerupaja	Peru	6,632	21,758
Sajama	Bolivia	6,520	21,391
Chimborazo	Ecuador	6,267	20,561
Pico Cristóbal Colón	Colombia	5,800	19,029
Pico Bolivar	Venezuela	5,007	16,427

Antarctica	m	ft
Vinson Massif	4,897	16,066
Mt Kirkpatrick	4,528	14,855

Rivers

Europe		km	miles
Volga	Caspian Sea	3,700	2,300
Danube	Black Sea	2,850	1,770
Ural	Caspian Sea	2,535	1,575
Dnieper	Black Sea	2,285	1,420
Kama	Volga	2,030	1,260
Don	Black Sea	1,990	1,240
Petchora	Arctic Ocean	1,790	1,110
Oka	Volga	1,480	920
Dniester	Black Sea	1,400	870
Vyatka	Kama	1,370	850
Rhine	North Sea	1,320	820
N. Dvina	Arctic Ocean	1,290	800
Elbe	North Sea	1,145	710

Asia		km	miles
Yangtse	Pacific Ocean	6,380	3,960
Yenisey–Angara	Arctic Ocean	5,550	3,445
Huang He	Pacific Ocean	5,464	3,395
Ob–Irtysh	Arctic Ocean	5,410	3,360
Mekong	Pacific Ocean	4,500	2,795
Amur	Pacific Ocean	4,442	2,760
Lena	Arctic Ocean	4,402	2,735
Irtysh	Ob	4,250	2,640
Yenisey	Arctic Ocean	4,090	2,540
Ob	Arctic Ocean	3,680	2,285
Indus	Indian Ocean	3,100	1,925
Brahmaputra	Indian Ocean	2,900	1,800
Syrdarya	Aralkum Desert	2,860	1,775
Salween	Indian Ocean	2,800	1,740
Euphrates	Indian Ocean	2,700	1,675
Amudarya	Aralkum Desert	2,540	1,575

Africa		km	miles
Nile	Mediterranean	6,695	4,160
Congo	Atlantic Ocean	4,670	2,900
Niger	Atlantic Ocean	4,180	2,595
Zambezi	Indian Ocean	3,540	2,200
Oubangi/Uele	Congo (D.R.)	2,250	1,400
Kasai	Congo (D.R.)	1,950	1,210
Shaballe	Indian Ocean	1,930	1,200
Orange	Atlantic Ocean	1,860	1,155
Cubango	Okavango Delta	1,800	1,120
Limpopo	Indian Ocean	1,770	1,100
Senegal	Atlantic Ocean	1,640	1,020

Australia		km	miles
Murray–Darling	Southern Ocean	3,750	2,330
Darling	Murray	3,070	1,905
Murray	Southern Ocean	2,575	1,600
Murrumbidgee	Murray	1,690	1,050

North America		km	miles
Mississippi–Missouri	Gulf of Mexico	5,971	3,710
Mackenzie	Arctic Ocean	4,240	2,630
Missouri	Mississippi	4,088	2,540
Mississippi	Gulf of Mexico	3,782	2,350
Yukon	Pacific Ocean	3,185	1,980
Rio Grande	Gulf of Mexico	3,030	1,880
Arkansas	Mississippi	2,340	1,450
Colorado	Pacific Ocean	2,330	1,445
Red	Mississippi	2,040	1,270
Columbia	Pacific Ocean	1,950	1,210
Saskatchewan	Lake Winnipeg	1,940	1,205

South America		km	miles
Amazon	Atlantic Ocean	6,450	4,010
Paraná–Plate	Atlantic Ocean	4,500	2,800
Purus	Amazon	3,350	2,080
Madeira	Amazon	3,200	1,990
São Francisco	Atlantic Ocean	2,900	1,800
Paraná	Plate	2,800	1,740
Tocantins	Atlantic Ocean	2,750	1,710
Orinoco	Atlantic Ocean	2,740	1,700
Paraguay	Paraná	2,550	1,580
Pilcomayo	Paraná	2,500	1,550
Araguaia	Tocantins	2,250	1,400

Lakes

Europe		km²	miles²
Lake Ladoga	Russia	17,700	6,800
Lake Onega	Russia	9,700	3,700
Saimaa system	Finland	8,000	3,100
Vänern	Sweden	5,500	2,100

Asia		km²	miles²
Caspian Sea	Asia	371,000	143,000
Lake Baikal	Russia	30,500	11,780
Tonlé Sap	Cambodia	20,000	7,700
Lake Balqash	Kazakhstan	18,500	7,100
Aral Sea	Kazakhstan/Uzbekistan	17,160	6,625

Africa		km²	miles²
Lake Victoria	East Africa	68,000	26,300
Lake Tanganyika	Central Africa	33,000	13,000
Lake Malawi/Nyasa	East Africa	29,600	11,430
Lake Chad	Central Africa	25,000	9,700
Lake Bangweulu	Zambia	9,840	3,800
Lake Turkana	Ethiopia/Kenya	8,500	3,290

Australia		km²	miles²
Lake Eyre	Australia	8,900	3,400
Lake Torrens	Australia	5,800	2,200
Lake Gairdner	Australia	4,800	1,900

North America		km²	miles²
Lake Superior	Canada/USA	82,350	31,800
Lake Huron	Canada/USA	59,600	23,010
Lake Michigan	USA	58,000	22,400
Great Bear Lake	Canada	31,800	12,280
Great Slave Lake	Canada	28,500	11,000
Lake Erie	Canada/USA	25,700	9,900
Lake Winnipeg	Canada	24,400	9,400
Lake Ontario	Canada/USA	19,500	7,500
Lake Nicaragua	Nicaragua	8,200	3,200

South America		km²	miles²
Lake Titicaca	Bolivia/Peru	8,300	3,200
Lake Poopo	Bolivia	2,800	1,100

Islands

Europe		km²	miles²
Great Britain	UK	229,880	88,700
Iceland	Atlantic Ocean	103,000	39,800
Ireland	Ireland/UK	84,400	32,600
Novaya Zemlya (N.)	Russia	48,200	18,600
Sicily	Italy	25,500	9,800
Corsica	France	8,700	3,400

Asia		km²	miles²
Borneo	Southeast Asia	744,360	287,400
Sumatra	Indonesia	473,600	182,860
Honshu	Japan	230,500	88,980
Celebes	Indonesia	189,000	73,000
Java	Indonesia	126,700	48,900
Luzon	Philippines	104,700	40,400
Hokkaido	Japan	78,400	30,300

Africa		km²	miles²
Madagascar	Indian Ocean	587,040	226,660
Socotra	Indian Ocean	3,600	1,400
Réunion	Indian Ocean	2,500	965

Oceania		km²	miles²
New Guinea	Indonesia/Papua NG	821,030	317,000
New Zealand (S.)	Pacific Ocean	150,500	58,100
New Zealand (N.)	Pacific Ocean	114,700	44,300
Tasmania	Australia	67,800	26,200
Hawai'i	Pacific Ocean	10,450	4,000

North America		km²	miles²
Greenland	Atlantic Ocean	2,175,600	839,800
Baffin Is.	Canada	508,000	196,100
Victoria Is.	Canada	212,200	81,900
Ellesmere Is.	Canada	212,000	81,800
Cuba	Caribbean Sea	110,860	42,800
Hispaniola	Dominican Rep./Haiti	76,200	29,400
Jamaica	Caribbean Sea	11,400	4,400
Puerto Rico	Atlantic Ocean	8,900	3,400

South America		km²	miles²
Tierra del Fuego	Argentina/Chile	47,000	18,100
Falkland Is. (E.)	Atlantic Ocean	6,800	2,600

User Guide

The reference maps which form the main body of this atlas have been prepared in accordance with the highest standards of international cartography to provide an accurate and detailed representation of the Earth. The scales and projections used have been carefully chosen to give balanced coverage of the world, while emphasizing the most densely populated and economically significant regions. A hallmark of Philip's mapping is the use of hill shading and relief colouring to create a graphic impression of landforms: this makes the maps exceptionally easy to read. However, knowledge of the key features employed in the construction and presentation of the maps will enable the reader to derive the fullest benefit from the atlas.

Map sequence

The atlas covers the Earth continent by continent: first Europe; then its land neighbour Asia (mapped north before south, in a clockwise sequence), then Africa, Australia and Oceania, North America and South America. This is the classic arrangement adopted by most cartographers since the 16th century. For each continent, there are maps at a variety of scales. First, physical relief and political maps of the whole continent; then a series of larger-scale maps of the regions within the continent, each followed, where required, by still larger-scale maps of the most important or densely populated areas. The governing principle is that by turning the pages of the atlas, the reader moves steadily from north to south through each continent, with each map overlapping its neighbours.

Map presentation

With very few exceptions (for example, for the Arctic and Antarctica), the maps are drawn with north at the top, regardless of whether they are presented upright or sideways on the page. In the borders will be found the map title; a locator diagram showing the area covered; continuation arrows showing the page numbers for maps of adjacent areas; the scale; the projection used; the degrees of latitude and longitude; and the letters and figures used in the index for locating place names and geographical features. Physical relief maps also have a height reference panel identifying the colours used for each layer of contouring.

Map symbols

Each map contains a vast amount of detail which can only be conveyed clearly and accurately by the use of symbols. Points and circles of varying sizes locate and identify the relative importance of towns and cities; different styles of type are employed for administrative, geographical and regional place names. A variety of pictorial symbols denote features such as glaciers and marshes, as well as man-made structures including roads, railways, airports and canals.

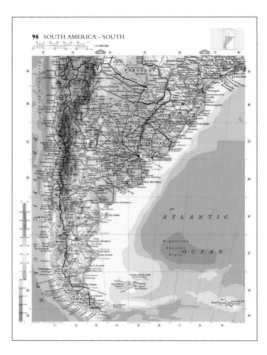

International borders are shown by red lines. Where neighbouring countries are in dispute, for example in the Middle East, the maps show the de facto boundary between nations, regardless of the legal or historical situation. The symbols are explained on the first page of the World Maps section of the atlas.

Map scales

The scale of each map is given in the numerical form known as the 'representative fraction'. The first figure is always one, signifying one unit of distance on the map; the second figure, usually in millions, is the number by which the map unit must be multiplied to give the equivalent distance on the Earth's surface. Calculations can easily be made in centimetres and kilometres, by dividing the Earth units figure by 100 000 (i.e. deleting the last five 0s). Thus 1:1 000 000 means 1 cm = 10 km. The calculation for inches and miles is more laborious, but 1 000 000 divided by 63 360 (the number of inches in a mile) shows that the ratio 1:1 000 000 means approximately 1 inch = 16 miles. The table below provides distance equivalents for scales down to 1:50 000 000.

LARGE SCALE		
1:1 000 000	1 cm = 10 km	1 inch = 16 miles
1:2 500 000	1 cm = 25 km	1 inch = 39.5 miles
1:5 000 000	1 cm = 50 km	1 inch = 79 miles
1:6 000 000	1 cm = 60 km	1 inch = 95 miles
1:8 000 000	1 cm = 80 km	1 inch = 126 miles
1:10 000 000	1 cm = 100 km	1 inch = 158 miles
1:15 000 000	1 cm = 150 km	1 inch = 237 miles
1:20 000 000	1 cm = 200 km	1 inch = 316 miles
1:50 000 000	1 cm = 500 km	1 inch = 790 miles
SMALL SCALE		

Measuring distances

Although each map is accompanied by a scale bar, distances cannot always be measured with confidence because of the distortions involved in portraying the curved surface of the Earth on a flat page. As a general rule, the larger the map scale (i.e. the lower the number of Earth units in the representative fraction), the more accurate and reliable will be the distance measured. On small-scale maps such as those of the world and of entire continents, measurement may only be accurate along the 'standard parallels', or central axes, and should not be attempted without considering the map projection.

Latitude and longitude

Accurate positioning of individual points on the Earth's surface is made possible by reference to the geometrical system of latitude and longitude. Latitude *parallels* are drawn west–east around the Earth and numbered by degrees north and south of the Equator, which is designated 0° of latitude. Longitude *meridians* are drawn north–south and numbered by degrees east and west of the *prime meridian*, 0° of longitude, which passes through Greenwich in England. By referring to these co-ordinates and their subdivisions of minutes ($1/60$th of a degree) and seconds ($1/60$th of a minute), any place on Earth can be located to within a few hundred metres. Latitude and longitude are indicated by blue lines on the maps; they are straight or curved according to the projection employed. Reference to these lines is the easiest way of determining the relative positions of places on different maps, and for plotting compass directions.

Name forms

For ease of reference, both English and local name forms appear in the atlas. Oceans, seas and countries are shown in English throughout the atlas; country names may be abbreviated to their commonly accepted form (for example, Germany, not The Federal Republic of Germany). Conventional English forms are also used for place names on the smaller-scale maps of the continents. However, local name forms are used on all large-scale and regional maps, with the English form given in brackets only for important cities – the large-scale map of Russia and Central Asia thus shows Moskva (Moscow). For countries which do not use a Roman script, place names have been transcribed according to the systems adopted by the British and US Geographic Names Authorities. For China, the Pin Yin system has been used, with some more widely known forms appearing in brackets, as with Beijing (Peking). Both English and local names appear in the index, the English form being cross-referenced to the local form.

THE WORLD IN FOCUS

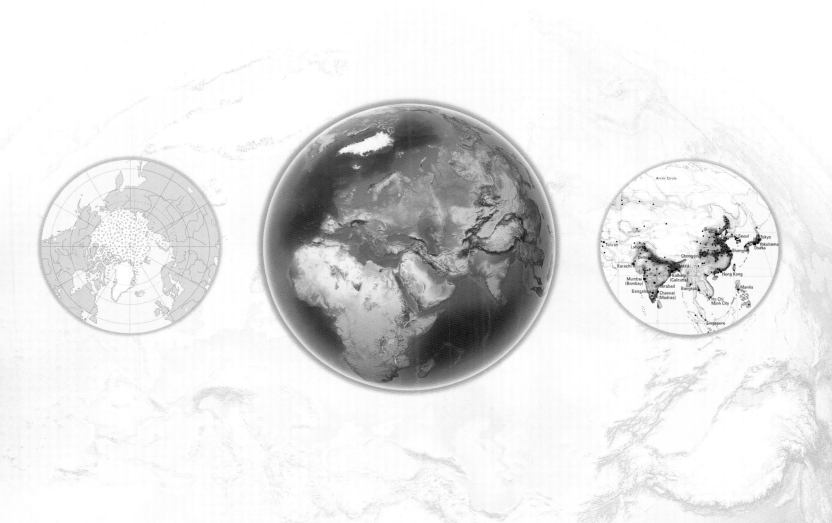

PLANET EARTH	2	WATER AND VEGETATION	12	QUALITY OF LIFE	22
RESTLESS EARTH	4	ENVIRONMENT	14	ENERGY	24
LANDFORMS	6	POPULATION	16	PRODUCTION	26
OCEANS	8	THE HUMAN FAMILY	18	TRADE	28
CLIMATE	10	WEALTH	20	TRAVEL AND TOURISM	30

Planet Earth

Sun · Mercury · Venus · Earth · Mars · Jupiter · Saturn · Uranus · Neptune

THE SOLAR SYSTEM

A minute part of one of the billions of galaxies (collections of stars) that populate the Universe, the Solar System lies about 26,000 light-years from the centre of our own Galaxy, the 'Milky Way'. Thought to be about 5 billion years old, it consists of a central Sun with eight planets and their moons revolving around it, attracted by its gravitational pull. The planets orbit the Sun in the same direction – anti-clockwise when viewed from above the Sun's north pole – and almost in the same plane. Their orbital distances, however, vary enormously.

The Sun's diameter is 109 times that of the Earth, and the temperature at its core – caused by continuous thermonuclear fusions of hydrogen into helium – is estimated to be 15 million degrees Celsius. It is the Solar System's source of light and heat.

PROFILE OF THE PLANETS

	Mean distance from Sun (million km)	Mass (Earth = 1)	Period of orbit (Earth days/years)	Period of rotation (Earth days)	Equatorial diameter (km)	Number of known satellites*
Mercury	57.9	0.06	87.97 days	58.65	4,879	0
Venus	108.2	0.82	224.7 days	243.02	12,104	0
Earth	149.6	1.00	365.3 days	1.00	12,756	1
Mars	227.9	0.11	687.0 days	1.029	6,792	2
Jupiter	778	317.8	11.86 years	0.411	142,984	67
Saturn	1,427	95.2	29.45 years	0.428	120,536	62
Uranus	2,871	14.5	84.02 years	0.720	51,118	27
Neptune	4,498	17.2	164.8 years	0.673	49,528	14

* Number of known satellites at mid-2015

All planetary orbits are elliptical in form, but only Mercury follows a path that deviates noticeably from a circular one. In 2006, Pluto was demoted from its former status as a planet and is now regarded as a member of the Kuiper Belt of icy bodies at the fringes of the Solar System.

THE SEASONS

Seasons occur because the Earth's axis is tilted at an angle of approximately 23½°. When the northern hemisphere is tilted to a maximum extent towards the Sun, on 21 June, the Sun is overhead at the Tropic of Cancer (latitude 23½° North). This is midsummer, or the summer solstice, in the northern hemisphere.

On 22 or 23 September, the Sun is overhead at the Equator, and day and night are of equal length throughout the world. This is the autumnal equinox in the northern hemisphere. On 21 or 22 December, the Sun is overhead at the Tropic of Capricorn (23½° South), the winter solstice in the northern hemisphere. The overhead Sun then tracks north until, on 21 March, it is overhead at the Equator. This is the spring (vernal) equinox in the northern hemisphere.

In the southern hemisphere, the seasons are the reverse of those in the north.

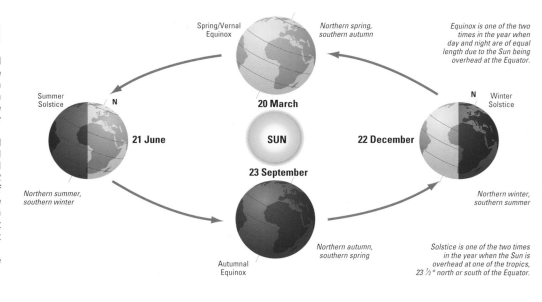

Spring/Vernal Equinox — Northern spring, southern autumn

Equinox is one of the two times in the year when day and night are of equal length due to the Sun being overhead at the Equator.

Summer Solstice — Northern summer, southern winter

20 March — 21 June — SUN — 22 December — 23 September

Winter Solstice — Northern winter, southern summer

Autumnal Equinox — Northern autumn, southern spring

Solstice is one of the two times in the year when the Sun is overhead at one of the tropics, 23 ½° north or south of the Equator.

DAY AND NIGHT

The Sun appears to rise in the east, reach its highest point at noon, and then set in the west, to be followed by night. In reality, it is not the Sun that is moving but the Earth rotating from west to east. The moment when the Sun's upper limb first appears above the horizon is termed sunrise; the moment when the Sun's upper limb disappears below the horizon is sunset.

At the summer solstice in the northern hemisphere (21 June), the Arctic has total daylight and the Antarctic total darkness. The opposite occurs at the winter solstice (21 or 22 December). At the Equator, the length of day and night are almost equal all year.

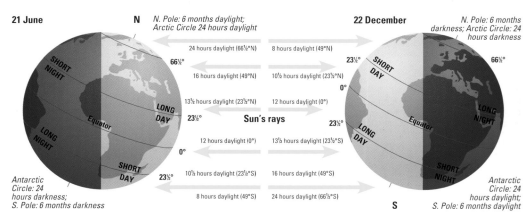

21 June — N. Pole: 6 months daylight; Arctic Circle 24 hours daylight

24 hours daylight (66½°N) — 8 hours daylight (49°N)
16 hours daylight (49°N) — 10½ hours daylight (23½°N)
13½ hours daylight (23½°N) — 12 hours daylight (0°)

Sun's rays

12 hours daylight (0°) — 13½ hours daylight (23½°S)
10½ hours daylight (23½°S) — 16 hours daylight (49°S)
8 hours daylight (49°S) — 24 hours daylight (66½°S)

Antarctic Circle: 24 hours darkness; S. Pole: 6 months darkness

22 December — N. Pole: 6 months darkness; Arctic Circle: 24 hours darkness

Antarctic Circle: 24 hours daylight; S. Pole: 6 months daylight

TIME

Year: The time taken by the Earth to revolve around the Sun, or 365.24 days.

Leap Year: A calendar year of 366 days, 29 February being the additional day. It offsets the difference between the calendar and the solar year.

Month: The 12 calendar months of the year are approximately equal in length to a lunar month.

Week: An artificial period of 7 days, not based on astronomical time.

Day: The time taken by the Earth to complete one rotation on its axis.

Hour: 24 hours make one day. The day is divided into hours a.m. (ante meridiem or before noon) and p.m. (post meridiem or after noon), although most timetables now use the 24-hour system, from midnight to midnight.

Sunrise

Sunset

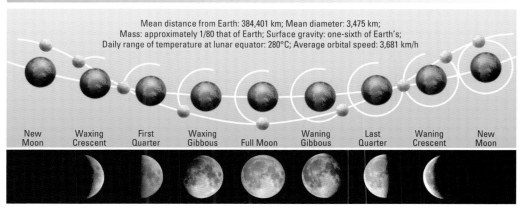

THE MOON

The Moon rotates more slowly than the Earth, taking just over 27 days to make one complete rotation on its axis. This corresponds to the Moon's orbital period around the Earth, and therefore the Moon always

PHASES OF THE MOON

Mean distance from Earth: 384,401 km; Mean diameter: 3,475 km;
Mass: approximately 1/80 that of Earth; Surface gravity: one-sixth of Earth's;
Daily range of temperature at lunar equator: 280°C; Average orbital speed: 3,681 km/h

| New Moon | Waxing Crescent | First Quarter | Waxing Gibbous | Full Moon | Waning Gibbous | Last Quarter | Waning Crescent | New Moon |

presents the same hemisphere towards us; some 41% of the Moon's far side is never visible from the Earth. The interval between one New Moon and the next is 29½ days – this is called a lunation, or lunar month.

The Moon shines only by reflected sunlight, and emits no light of its own. During each lunation the Moon displays a complete cycle of phases, caused by the changing angle of illumination from the Sun.

ECLIPSES

When the Moon passes between the Sun and the Earth, the Sun becomes partially eclipsed (1). A partial eclipse becomes a total eclipse if the Moon proceeds to cover the Sun completely (2) and the dark central part of the lunar shadow touches the Earth. The broad geographical zone covered by the Moon's outer shadow (P) has only a very small central area (often less than 100 km wide) that experiences totality. Totality can never last for more than 7½ minutes at maximum, but is usually much briefer than this. Lunar eclipses take place when the Moon moves through the shadow of the Earth, and can be partial or total. Any single location on Earth can experience a maximum of four solar and three lunar eclipses in any single year, while a total solar eclipse occurs an average of once every 360 years for any given location.

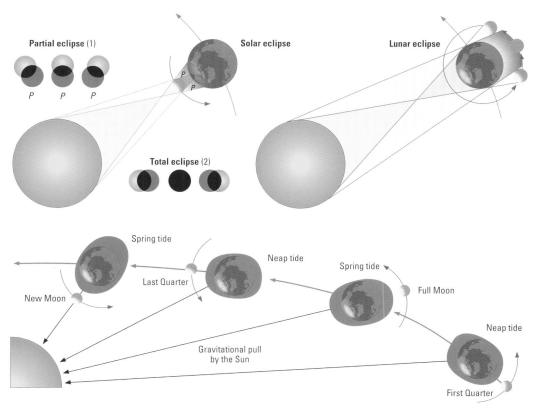

TIDES

The daily rise and fall of the ocean's tides are the result of the gravitational pull of the Moon and that of the Sun, though the effect of the latter is not as strong as that of the Moon. This effect is greatest on the hemisphere facing the Moon and causes a tidal 'bulge'.

Spring tides occur when the Sun, Earth and Moon are aligned; high tides are at their highest, and low tides fall to their lowest. When the Moon and Sun are furthest out of line (near the Moon's First and Last Quarters), neap tides occur, producing the smallest range between high and low tides.

Restless Earth

THE EARTH'S STRUCTURE

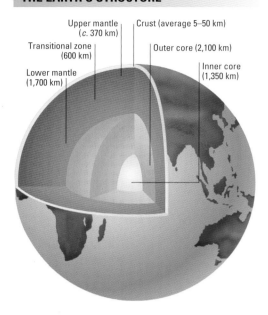

Upper mantle (c. 370 km)
Transitional zone (600 km)
Lower mantle (1,700 km)
Crust (average 5–50 km)
Outer core (2,100 km)
Inner core (1,350 km)

CONTINENTAL DRIFT

About 200 million years ago the original Pangaea landmass began to split into two continental groups, which further separated over time to produce the present-day configuration.

135 million years ago

Laurasia
Gondwanaland

180 million years ago

Present day

———— Trench
———— Rift
New ocean floor
———— Zones of slippage

NOTABLE EARTHQUAKES SINCE 1900

Year	Location	Richter Scale	Deaths
1906	San Francisco, USA	8.3	3,000
1906	Valparaiso, Chile	8.6	22,000
1908	Messina, Italy	7.5	83,000
1915	Avezzano, Italy	7.5	30,000
1920	Gansu (Kansu), China	8.6	180,000
1923	Yokohama, Japan	8.3	143,000
1927	Nan Shan, China	8.3	200,000
1932	Gansu (Kansu), China	7.6	70,000
1933	Sanriku, Japan	8.9	2,990
1934	Bihar, India/Nepal	8.4	10,700
1935	Quetta, India (now Pakistan)	7.5	60,000
1939	Chillan, Chile	8.3	28,000
1939	Erzincan, Turkey	7.9	30,000
1960	S. W. Chile	9.5	2,200
1960	Agadir, Morocco	5.8	12,000
1962	Khorasan, Iran	7.1	12,230
1964	Anchorage, USA	9.2	125
1970	N. Peru	7.8	70,000
1972	Managua, Nicaragua	6.2	5,000
1976	Guatemala	7.5	22,500
1976	Tangshan, China	8.2	255,000
1978	Tabas, Iran	7.7	25,000
1980	El Asnam, Algeria	7.3	20,000
1985	Mexico City, Mexico	8.1	4,200
1988	N.W. Armenia	6.8	55,000
1990	N. Iran	7.7	36,000
1993	Maharashtra, India	6.4	30,000
1994	Los Angeles, USA	6.6	51
1995	Kobe, Japan	7.2	5,000
1998	Rostaq, Afghanistan	7.0	5,000
1999	Izmit, Turkey	7.4	15,000
1999	Taipei, Taiwan	7.6	1,700
2001	Gujarat, India	7.7	14,000
2003	Bam, Iran	6.6	30,000
2004	Sumatra, Indonesia	9.0	250,000
2005	N. Pakistan	7.6	74,000
2006	Java, Indonesia	6.4	6,200
2008	Sichuan, China	7.9	70,000
2010	Haiti	7.0	230,000
2011	Christchurch, New Zealand	6.3	182
2011	N. Japan	9.0	28,000
2015	Nepal	7.8	8,500

EARTHQUAKES

Earthquake magnitude is usually rated according to either the Richter or the Modified Mercalli scale, both devised by seismologists in the 1930s. The Richter scale measures absolute earthquake power with mathematical precision: each step upwards represents a tenfold increase in shockwave amplitude. Theoretically, there is no upper limit, but most of the largest earthquakes measured have been rated at between 8.8 and 8.9. The 12–point Mercalli scale, based on observed effects, is often more meaningful, ranging from I (earthquakes noticed only by seismographs) to XII (total destruction); intermediate points include V (people awakened at night; unstable objects overturned), VII (collapse of ordinary buildings; chimneys and monuments fall), and IX (conspicuous cracks in ground; serious damage to reservoirs).

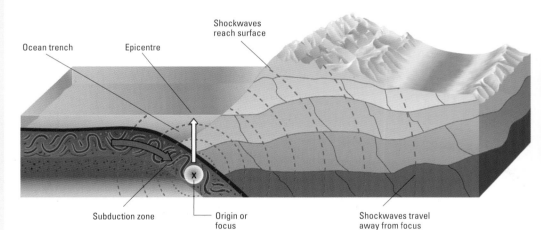

Ocean trench
Epicentre
Shockwaves reach surface
Subduction zone
Origin or focus
Shockwaves travel away from focus

DISTRIBUTION OF EARTHQUAKES

Mobile land areas
Submarine zones of mobile land areas
Stable land platforms
Submarine extensions of stable land platforms

• 1995 Principal earthquakes and dates (since 1900)

Earthquakes are a series of rapid vibrations originating from the slipping or faulting of parts of the Earth's crust when stresses within build up to breaking point. They usually happen at depths varying from 8 km to 30 km. Severe earthquakes cause extensive damage when they take place in populated areas, destroying structures and severing communications. Most initial loss of life occurs due to secondary causes such as falling masonry, fires and flooding.

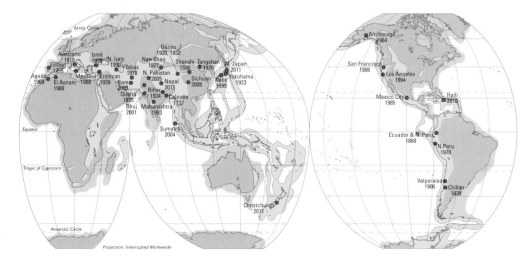

Projection: Interrupted Mollweide

PLATE TECTONICS

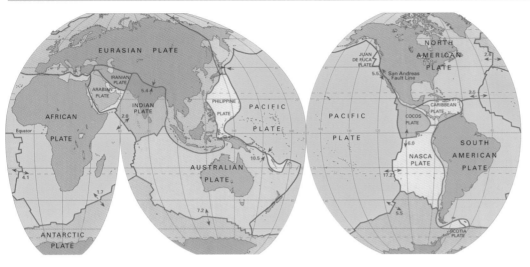

— Plate boundaries

⤧ Direction of plate movements and
rate of movement (cm/year)

The drifting of the continents is a feature that is unique to planet Earth. The complementary, almost jigsaw-puzzle fit of the coastlines on each side of the Atlantic Ocean inspired Alfred Wegener's theory of continental drift in 1915. The theory suggested that the ancient supercontinent, which Wegener named Pangaea, incorporated all of the Earth's landmasses and gradually split up to form today's continents.

The original debate about continental drift was a prelude to a more radical idea: plate tectonics. The basic theory is that the Earth's crust is made up of a series of rigid plates which float on a soft layer of the mantle and are moved about by continental convection currents within the Earth's interior. These plates diverge and converge along margins marked by seismic activity. Plates diverge from mid-ocean ridges where molten lava pushes upwards and forces the plates apart at rates of up to 40 mm [1.6 in] a year.

The three diagrams, left, give some examples of plate boundaries from around the world. Diagram (a) shows sea-floor spreading at the Mid-Atlantic Ridge as the American and African plates slowly diverge. The same thing is happening in (b) where sea-floor spreading at the Mid-Indian Ocean Ridge is forcing the Indian plate to collide into the Eurasian plate. In (c) oceanic crust (sima) is being subducted beneath lighter continental crust (sial).

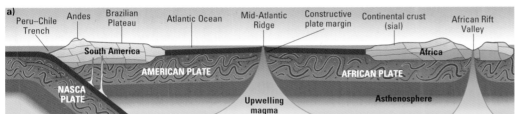

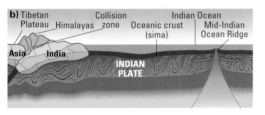

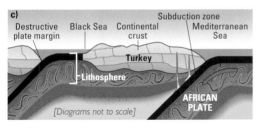

VOLCANOES

Volcanoes occur when hot liquefied rock beneath the Earth's crust is pushed up by pressure to the surface as molten lava. Some volcanoes erupt in an explosive way, throwing out rocks and ash, whilst others are effusive and lava flows out of the vent. There are volcanoes which are both, such as Mount Fuji. An accumulation of lava and cinders creates cones of variable size and shape. As a result of many eruptions over centuries, Mount Etna in Sicily has a circumference of more than 120 km [75 miles].

Climatologists believe that volcanic ash, if ejected high into the atmosphere, can influence temperature and weather for several years afterwards. The 1991 eruption of Mount Pinatubo in the Philippines ejected more than 20 million tonnes of dust and ash 32 km [20 miles] into the atmosphere and is believed to have accelerated ozone depletion over a large part of the globe.

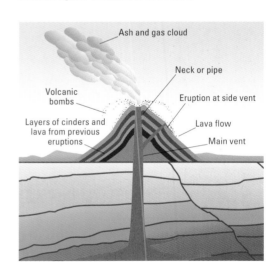

DISTRIBUTION OF VOLCANOES

Volcanoes today may be the subject of considerable scientific study but they remain both dramatic and unpredictable: in 1991 Mount Pinatubo, 100 km [62 miles] north of the Philippines capital Manila, suddenly burst into life after lying dormant for more than six centuries. Most of the world's active volcanoes occur in a belt around the Pacific Ocean, on the edge of the Pacific plate, called the 'ring of fire'. Indonesia has the greatest concentration with 90 volcanoes, 12 of which are active. The most famous, Krakatoa, erupted in 1883 with such force that the resulting tidal wave killed 36,000 people, and tremors were felt as far away as Australia.

▬▬ 'Ring of Fire'

° Submarine volcanoes

▲ Land volcanoes active since 1700

— Boundaries of tectonic plates

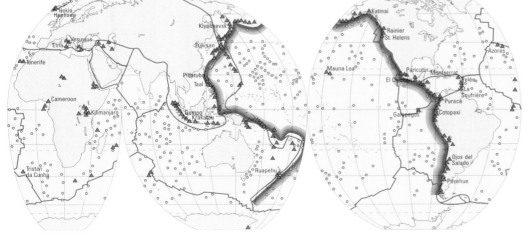

Landforms

THE ROCK CYCLE

James Hutton first proposed the rock cycle in the late 1700s after he observed the slow but steady effects of erosion.

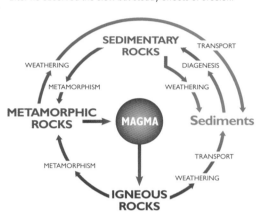

Above and below the surface of the oceans, the features of the Earth's crust are constantly changing. The phenomenal forces generated by convection currents in the molten core of our planet carry the vast segments or 'plates' of the crust across the globe in an endless cycle of creation and destruction. A continent may travel little more than 25 mm [1 in] per year, yet in the vast span of geological time this process throws up giant mountain ranges and creates new land.

Destruction of the landscape, however, begins as soon as it is formed. Wind, water, ice and sea, the main agents of erosion, mount a constant assault that even the most resistant rocks cannot withstand. Mountain peaks may dwindle by as little as a few millimetres each year, but if they are not uplifted by further movements of the crust they will eventually be reduced to rubble and transported away.

Water is the most powerful agent of erosion – it has been estimated that 100 billion tonnes of sediment are washed into the oceans every year.

Three Asian rivers account for 20% of this total: the Huang He, in China, and the Brahmaputra and the Ganges in Bangladesh.

Rivers and glaciers, like the sea itself, generate much of their effect through abrasion – pounding the land with the debris they carry with them. But as well as destroying they also create new landforms, many of them spectacular: vast deltas like those of the Mississippi and the Nile, or the deep fjords cut by glaciers in British Columbia, Norway and New Zealand.

Geologists once considered that landscapes evolved from 'young', newly uplifted mountainous areas, through a 'mature' hilly stage, to an 'old age' stage when the land was reduced to an almost flat plain, or peneplain. This theory, called the 'cycle of erosion', fell into disuse when it became evident that so many factors, including the effects of plate tectonics and climatic change, constantly interrupt the cycle, which takes no account of the highly complex interactions that shape the surface of our planet.

MOUNTAIN BUILDING

Mountains are formed when pressures on the Earth's crust caused by continental drift become so intense that the surface buckles or cracks. This happens where oceanic crust is subducted by continental crust or, more dramatically, where two tectonic plates collide: the Rockies, Andes, Alps, Urals and Himalayas resulted from such impacts. These are all known as fold mountains because they were formed by the compression of the rocks, forcing the surface to bend and fold like a crumpled rug. The Himalayas were formed from the folded former sediments of the Tethys Sea, which was trapped in the collision zone between the Indian and Eurasian plates.

The other main mountain-building process occurs when the crust fractures to create faults, allowing rock to be forced upwards in large blocks; or when the pressure of magma within the crust forces the surface to bulge into a dome, or erupts to form a volcano. Large mountain ranges may reveal a combination of these features; the Alps, for example, have been compressed so violently that the folds are fragmented by numerous faults and intrusions of molten igneous rock.

Over millions of years, even the greatest mountain ranges can be reduced by the agents of erosion (most notably rivers) to a low rugged landscape known as a peneplain.

Types of faults: Faults occur where the crust is being stretched or compressed so violently that the rock strata break in a horizontal or vertical movement. They are classified by the direction in which the blocks of rock have moved. A normal fault results when a vertical movement causes the surface to break apart; compression causes a reverse fault. Horizontal movement causes shearing, known as a strike-slip fault. When the rock breaks in two places, the central block may be pushed up in a horst fault, or sink (creating a rift valley) in a graben fault.

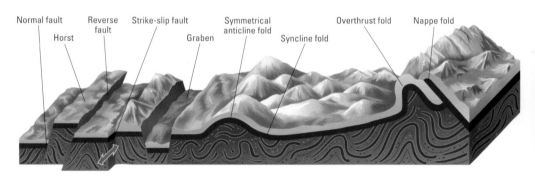

Types of fold: Folds occur when rock strata are squeezed and compressed. They are common, therefore, at destructive plate margins and where plates have collided, forcing the rocks to buckle into mountain ranges. Geographers give different names to the degrees of fold that result from continuing pressure on the rock. A simple fold may be symmetric, with even slopes on either side, but as the pressure builds up, one slope becomes steeper and the fold becomes asymmetric. Later, the ridge or 'anticline' at the top of the fold may slide over the lower ground or 'syncline' to form a recumbent fold. Eventually, the rock strata may break under the pressure to form an overthrust and finally a nappe fold.

CONTINENTAL GLACIATION

Ice sheets were at their greatest extent about 200,000 years ago. The maximum advance of the last Ice Age was about 18,000 years ago, when ice covered virtually all of Canada and reached as far south as the Bristol Channel in Britain.

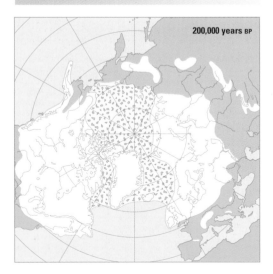

200,000 years BP

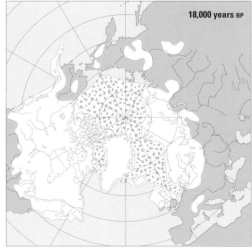

18,000 years BP

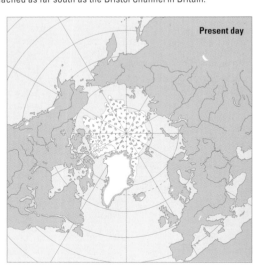

Present day

GLOBAL WARMING PROJECTIONS

Projected Change in Global Warming

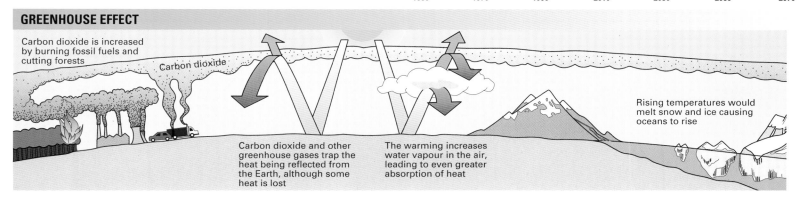

Rise in average temperatures assuming present trends in CO_2 emissions continue

Assuming some cuts are made in emissions

Assuming drastic cuts are made in emissions

Climate models are used to provide the best scientifically-based estimates of the future global climate. A typical method is to run the models for some decades ahead and then to compare the predicted average with a past 30-year period. A range of climate models are used, run with different scenarios that express the breadth of possibilities of, for example, industrial development and the degree of atmospheric pollution 'clean-up' by industrial nations.

The diagram on the right shows global observed and predicted surface mean temperature change from 1950 to 2070 with three prediction scenarios. The first (red) assumes rapid economic growth and continued population increases. The second (blue) assumes some attempts are made to cut greenhouse gas emissions, while the green line involves the greater use of cleaner technologies, with global population peaking mid-century then declining.

GREENHOUSE EFFECT

Carbon dioxide is increased by burning fossil fuels and cutting forests

Carbon dioxide

Rising temperatures would melt snow and ice causing oceans to rise

Carbon dioxide and other greenhouse gases trap the heat being reflected from the Earth, although some heat is lost

The warming increases water vapour in the air, leading to even greater absorption of heat

DESERTIFICATION AND DEFORESTATION

Existing deserts

Areas with a high risk of desertification

Areas with a moderate risk of desertification

Former areas of rainforest

Existing rainforest

FOREST CLEARANCE

Thousands of hectares of forest cleared annually, tropical countries surveyed 1980–85, 1990–95, 2000–2005 and 2005–10. Loss as a percentage of remaining stocks is shown in figures on each column. Gain is indicated as a minus figure.

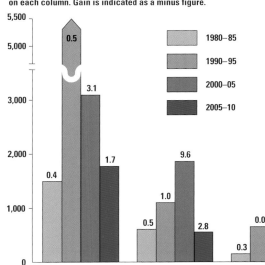

1980–85
1990–95
2000–05
2005–10

DEFORESTATION

The Earth's remaining forests are under attack from three directions: expanding agriculture, logging, and growing consumption of fuelwood, often in combination. Sometimes deforestation is the direct result of government policy, as in the efforts made to resettle the urban poor in some parts of Brazil; just as often, it comes about despite state attempts at conservation.

Loggers, licensed or unlicensed, blaze a trail into virgin forest, often destroying twice as many trees as they harvest. Landless farmers follow, burning away most of what remains to plant their crops, completing the destruction. However, some countries such as Vietnam, Philippines and Costa Rica have successfully implemented reafforestation programmes.

15

Population

DEMOGRAPHIC PROFILES

Developed nations such as the UK have populations evenly spread across the age groups and, usually, a growing proportion of elderly people. The great majority of the people in developing nations, however, are in the younger age groups, about to enter their most fertile years. In time, these population profiles should resemble the world profile (even Nigeria has made recent progress by reducing its birth rate), but the transition will come about only after a few more generations of rapid population growth.

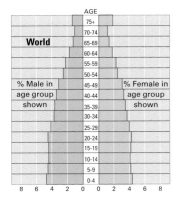

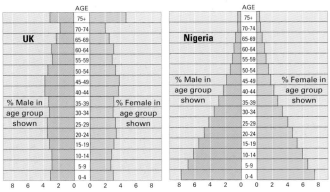

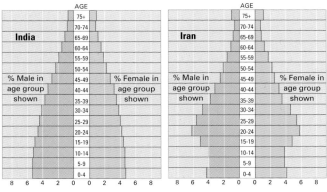

MOST POPULOUS NATIONS

Totals in millions (2014 estimates)

1. China	1,356	9. Russia	142	17. Germany	81
2. India	1,236	10. Japan	127	18. Iran	81
3. USA	319	11. Mexico	120	19. Congo (Dem. Rep.)	77
4. Indonesia	254	12. Philippines	108	20. Thailand	68
5. Brazil	203	13. Ethiopia	97	21. France	66
6. Pakistan	196	14. Vietnam	93	22. UK	64
7. Nigeria	177	15. Egypt	87	23. Italy	62
8. Bangladesh	166	16. Turkey	82	24. Burma (Myanmar)	56

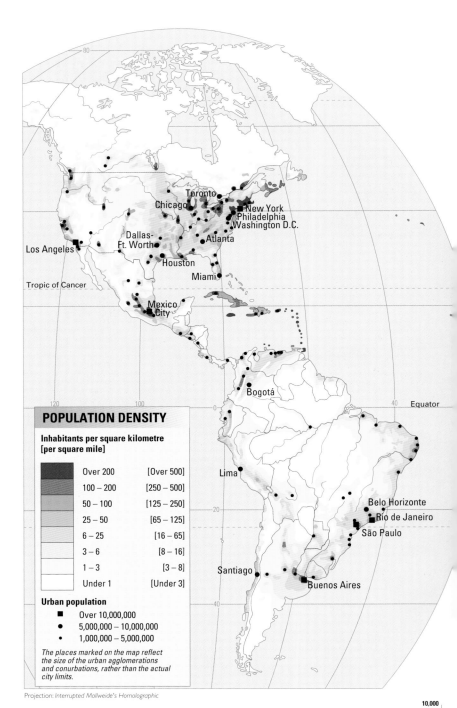

POPULATION DENSITY

Inhabitants per square kilometre [per square mile]

Over 200	[Over 500]
100 – 200	[250 – 500]
50 – 100	[125 – 250]
25 – 50	[65 – 125]
6 – 25	[16 – 65]
3 – 6	[8 – 16]
1 – 3	[3 – 8]
Under 1	[Under 3]

Urban population

■ Over 10,000,000
● 5,000,000 – 10,000,000
• 1,000,000 – 5,000,000

The places marked on the map reflect the size of the urban agglomerations and conurbations, rather than the actual city limits.

Projection: *Interrupted Mollweide's Homolographic*

CONTINENTAL COMPARISONS

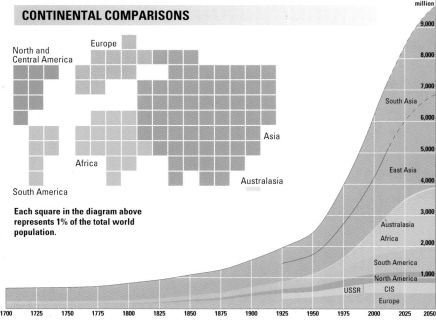

Each square in the diagram above represents 1% of the total world population.

COPYRIGHT PHILIP'S

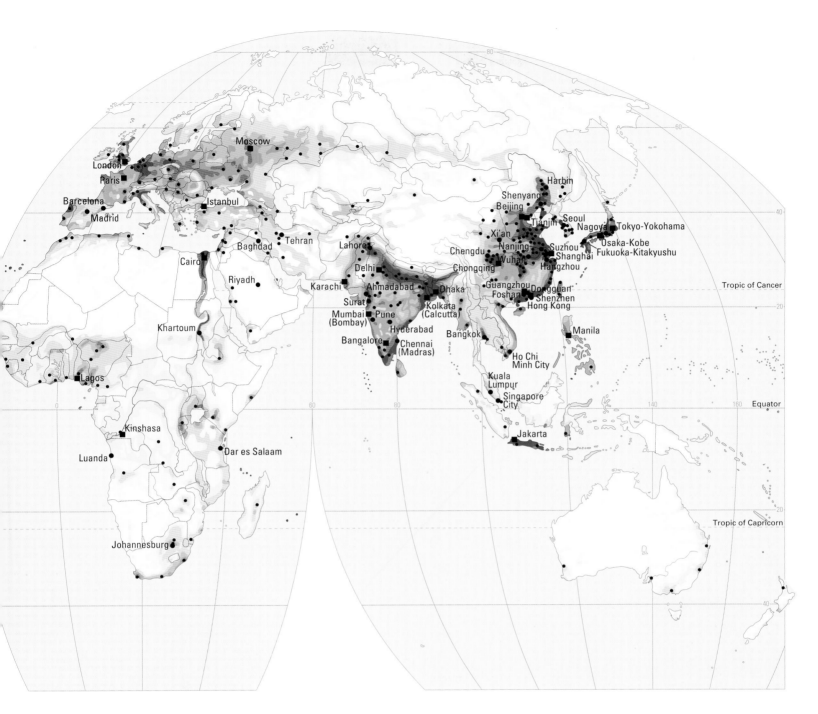

Moscow
London
Paris
Barcelona
Madrid
Istanbul
Baghdad Tehran
Cairo
Riyadh
Khartoum
Lahore
Delhi
Karachi Ahmadabad
Surat
Mumbai (Bombay) Pune
Bangalore
Hyderabad
Chennai (Madras)
Kolkata (Calcutta)
Dhaka
Bangkok
Harbin
Shenyang
Beijing
Tianjin Seoul
Xi'an
Nanjing
Chengdu Wuhan Suzhou
Chongqing Shanghai
Hangzhou
Guangzhou Dongguan
Foshan Shenzhen
Hong Kong
Nagoya Tokyo-Yokohama
Osaka-Kobe
Fukuoka-Kitakyushu
Manila
Ho Chi Minh City
Kuala Lumpur
Singapore City
Jakarta
Lagos
Kinshasa
Luanda
Dar es Salaam
Johannesburg

Tropic of Cancer
Equator
Tropic of Capricorn

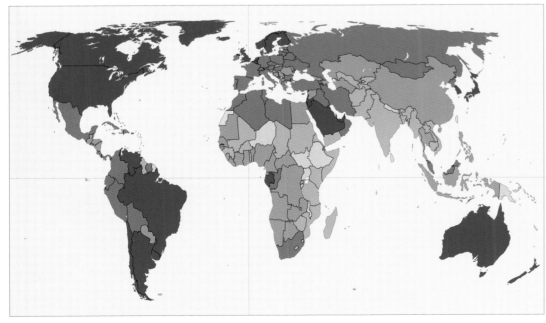

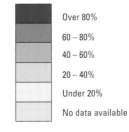

URBAN POPULATION

Percentage of total population living in towns and cities (2014)

- Over 80%
- 60 – 80%
- 40 – 60%
- 20 – 40%
- Under 20%
- No data available

Most urbanized

Singapore	100%
Qatar	99%
Belgium	98%
Kuwait	98%
Malta	95%

Least urbanized

Trinidad & Tobago	9%
Burundi	12%
Papua New Guinea	13%
Liechtenstein	14%
Sri Lanka	18%

17

The Human Family

PREDOMINANT LANGUAGES

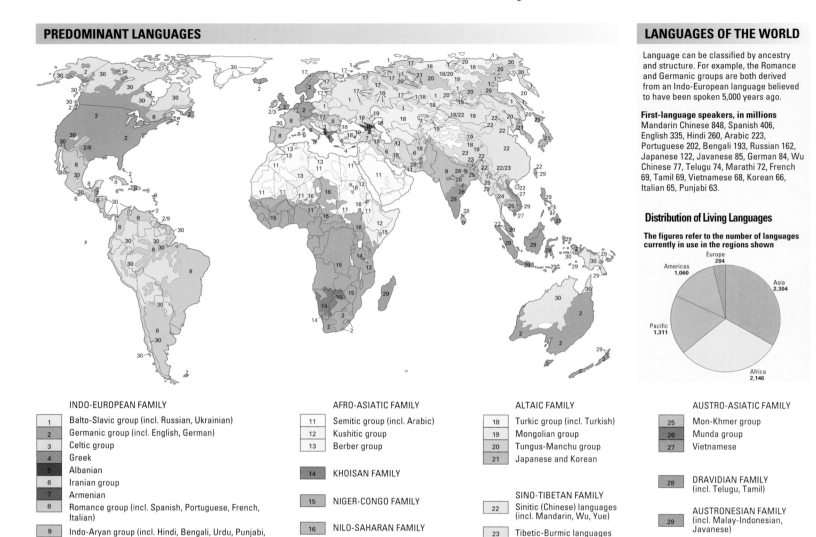

INDO-EUROPEAN FAMILY

1	Balto-Slavic group (incl. Russian, Ukrainian)
2	Germanic group (incl. English, German)
3	Celtic group
4	Greek
5	Albanian
6	Iranian group
7	Armenian
8	Romance group (incl. Spanish, Portuguese, French, Italian)
9	Indo-Aryan group (incl. Hindi, Bengali, Urdu, Punjabi, Marathi)
10	CAUCASIAN FAMILY

AFRO-ASIATIC FAMILY

11	Semitic group (incl. Arabic)
12	Kushitic group
13	Berber group
14	KHOISAN FAMILY
15	NIGER-CONGO FAMILY
16	NILO-SAHARAN FAMILY
17	URALIC FAMILY

ALTAIC FAMILY

18	Turkic group (incl. Turkish)
19	Mongolian group
20	Tungus-Manchu group
21	Japanese and Korean

SINO-TIBETAN FAMILY

22	Sinitic (Chinese) languages (incl. Mandarin, Wu, Yue)
23	Tibetic-Burmic languages
24	TAI FAMILY

AUSTRO-ASIATIC FAMILY

25	Mon-Khmer group
26	Munda group
27	Vietnamese
28	DRAVIDIAN FAMILY (incl. Telugu, Tamil)
29	AUSTRONESIAN FAMILY (incl. Malay-Indonesian, Javanese)
30	OTHER LANGUAGES

LANGUAGES OF THE WORLD

Language can be classified by ancestry and structure. For example, the Romance and Germanic groups are both derived from an Indo-European language believed to have been spoken 5,000 years ago.

First-language speakers, in millions
Mandarin Chinese 848, Spanish 406, English 335, Hindi 260, Arabic 223, Portuguese 202, Bengali 193, Russian 162, Japanese 122, Javanese 85, German 84, Wu Chinese 77, Telugu 74, Marathi 72, French 69, Tamil 69, Vietnamese 68, Korean 66, Italian 65, Punjabi 63.

Distribution of Living Languages

The figures refer to the number of languages currently in use in the regions shown

- Europe 284
- Americas 1,060
- Asia 2,304
- Pacific 1,311
- Africa 2,146

PREDOMINANT RELIGIONS

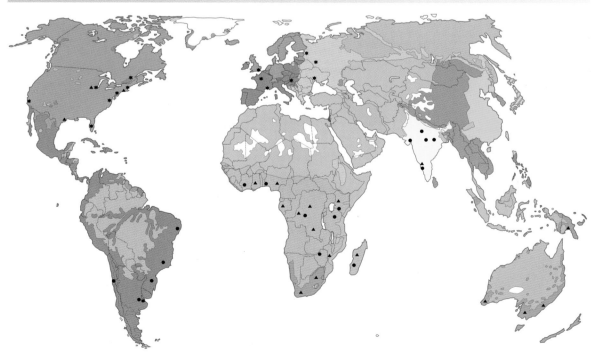

RELIGIOUS ADHERENTS

Religious adherents in millions

Christianity	2,000	Chinese traditional	394
Roman Catholic	*1,500*	Buddhism	360
Orthodox	*225*	Sikhism	23
Anglican	*70*	Taoism	20
Lutheran	*66*	Judaism	14
Methodist	*8*	Mormonism	12
Islam	1,300	Spiritism	11
Sunni	*940*	Baha'i	6
Shi'ite	*120*	Confucianism	5
Non-religious	1,100	Jainism	4
Hinduism	900	Shintoism	4

- Roman Catholicism
- Orthodox and other Eastern Churches
- Protestantism
- Sunni Islam
- Shi'ite Islam
- Buddhism
- Hinduism
- Confucianism
- Judaism
- Shintoism
- Tribal Religions

ILLITERACY

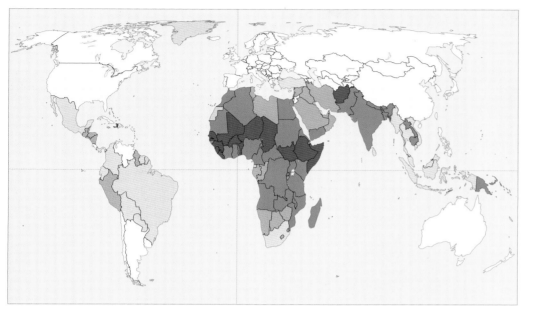

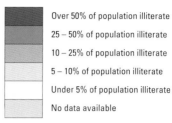

Percentage of the total adult population unable to read or write (2012)

- Over 50% of population illiterate
- 25 – 50% of population illiterate
- 10 – 25% of population illiterate
- 5 – 10% of population illiterate
- Under 5% of population illiterate
- No data available

Countries with the highest illiteracy rates as percentage of population

Guinea	75%	Niger	71%
South Sudan	73%	Mali	67%
Afghanistan	72%	Chad	65%
Benin	71%	Somalia	62%
Burkina Faso	71%	Ethiopia	61%

FERTILITY AND EDUCATION

Fertility rates compared with female education, selected countries

Percentage of females aged 12–17 in secondary education

Fertility rate: average number of children borne per woman

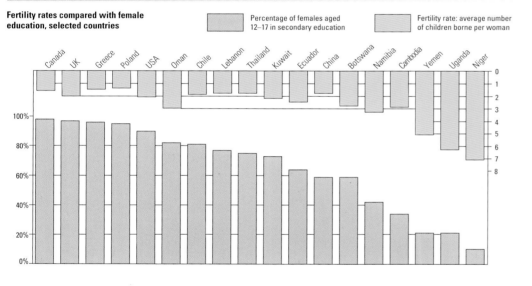

LIVING STANDARDS

At first sight, most international contrasts in living standards are swamped by differences in wealth. The rich not only have more money, they have more of everything, including years of life. Those with only a little money are obliged to spend most of it on food and clothing, the basic maintenance costs of their existence; air travel and tourism are unlikely to feature on their expenditure lists. However, poverty and wealth are both relative: slum dwellers living on social security payments in an affluent industrial country have far more resources at their disposal than an average African peasant, but feel their own poverty nonetheless. A middle-class Indian lawyer cannot command the earnings of a counterpart living in New York, London or Rome; nevertheless, he rightly sees himself as prosperous.

The rich not only live longer, on average, than the poor, they also die from different causes. Infectious and parasitic diseases, all but eliminated in the developed world, remain a scourge in the developing nations. On the other hand, more than two-thirds of the populations of OECD nations eventually succumb to cancer or circulatory disease.

HUMAN DEVELOPMENT INDEX

The Human Development Index (HDI), calculated by the UN Development Programme (UNDP), gives a value to countries using indicators of life expectancy, education and standards of living (2013). Higher values show more developed countries.

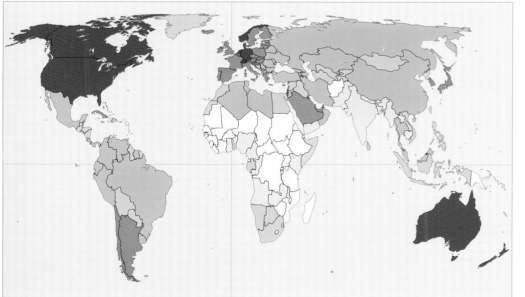

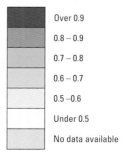

- Over 0.9
- 0.8 – 0.9
- 0.7 – 0.8
- 0.6 – 0.7
- 0.5 – 0.6
- Under 0.5
- No data available

Highest values		Lowest values	
Norway	0.944	Niger	0.337
Australia	0.933	Congo (Dem. Rep.)	0.338
Switzerland	0.917	Central African Rep.	0.341
Netherlands	0.915	Chad	0.372
USA	0.914	Sierra Leone	0.374

Energy

ENERGY PRODUCTION

Each square represents 1% of world primary energy production, by region

North America   Western Europe   Eastern Europe & Russia

Middle East

Africa

Asia

South America

Oceania

ENERGY CONSUMPTION

Each square represents 1% of world primary energy production, by region

North America   Western Europe   Eastern Europe & Russia

Middle East

Africa

Asia

South America

Oceania

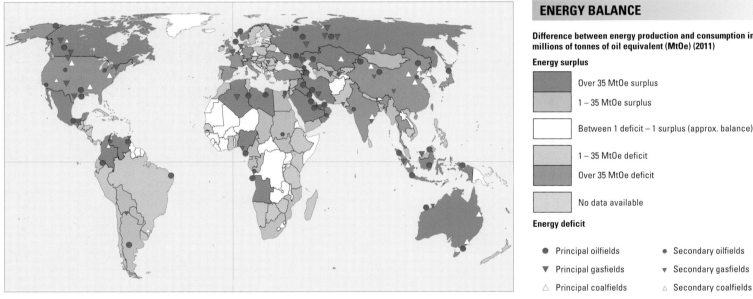

ENERGY BALANCE

Difference between energy production and consumption in millions of tonnes of oil equivalent (MtOe) (2011)

Energy surplus

- Over 35 MtOe surplus
- 1 – 35 MtOe surplus
- Between 1 deficit – 1 surplus (approx. balance)
- 1 – 35 MtOe deficit
- Over 35 MtOe deficit
- No data available

Energy deficit

- ● Principal oilfields   ● Secondary oilfields
- ▼ Principal gasfields   ▼ Secondary gasfields
- △ Principal coalfields   △ Secondary coalfields

WORLD ENERGY CONSUMPTION

Energy consumed by world regions, measured in million tonnes of oil equivalent (2013)
Total world consumption was 12,451 MtOe. Only energy from oil, natural gas, coal, nuclear and hydroelectric sources are included. Excluded are biomass fuels such as wood, peat and animal waste, and wind, solar and geothermal energy which, though important locally in some countries, are not always reliably documented statistically.

Oil   Gas   Coal   Nuclear   Hydro

Africa

South and Central America

Middle East

North America

Europe and Eurasia

Asia Pacific

0   500   1,000   1,500   2000   2,500   3000   3,500   4000   4,500   5000

million tonnes of oil equivalent

World energy consumption, by source (2013)

- 33.6%
- 24.3%
- 30.7%
- 4.5%
- 6.9%

Source: BP Statistical Review of World Energy 2014

ENERGY

Energy is used to keep us warm or cool, fuel our industries and our transport systems, and even feed us; high-intensity agriculture, with its use of fertilizers, pesticides and machinery, is heavily energy-dependent. Although we live in a high-energy society, there are vast discrepancies between rich and poor; for example, a North American consumes six times as much energy as a Chinese person. But even developing nations have more power at their disposal than was imaginable a century ago.

The distribution of energy supplies, most importantly fossil fuels (coal, oil and natural gas), is very uneven. In addition, the diagrams and map opposite show that the largest producers of energy are not necessarily the largest consumers. The movement of energy supplies around the world is therefore an important component of international trade.

As the finite reserves of fossil fuels are depleted, renewable energy sources, such as solar, hydro-thermal, wind, tidal and biomass, will become increasingly important around the world.

NUCLEAR POWER

Major producers by percentage of world total and by percentage of domestic electricity generation (2013)

Country	% of world total production	Country	% of nuclear as proportion of domestic electricity
1. USA	33.5%	1. France	73.3%
2. France	17.2%	2. Belgium	52.1%
3. Russia	6.9%	3. Slovak Republic	51.7%
4. South Korea	5.6%	4. Hungary	50.7%
5. China	4.4%	5. Ukraine	43.6%
6. Canada	4.0%	6. Sweden	42.7%
7. Germany	3.9%	7. Switzerland	36.4%
8. Ukraine	3.3%	8. Czech Republic	35.9%
9. UK	2.7%	9. Slovenia	33.6%
10. Sweden	2.7%	10. Finland	33.3%

Although the 1980s were a bad time for the nuclear power industry (fears of long-term environmental damage were heavily reinforced by the 1986 disaster at Chernobyl), the industry picked up in the early 1990s. Despite this, growth has recently been curtailed whilst countries review their energy mix, in light of the March 2011 Japanese earthquake and tsunami which seriously damaged the Fukushima nuclear power station.

HYDROELECTRICITY

Major producers by percentage of world total and by percentage of domestic electricity generation (2012)

Country	% of world total production	Country	% of hydroelectric as proportion of domestic electricity
1. China	19.8%	1. Albania	100.0%
2. Brazil	12.3%	2. Paraguay	100.0%
3. Canada	10.8%	3. Ethiopia	99.9%
4. USA	9.4%	4. Mozambique	99.9%
5. Russia	4.7%	5. Nepal	99.9%
6. India	3.8%	6. Zambia	99.7%
7. Norway	3.5%	7. Congo (Dem. Rep.)	99.6%
8. Japan	2.4%	8. Tajikistan	98.8%
9. Venezuela	2.4%	9. Namibia	98.2%
10. Sweden	1.9%	10. Norway	96.6%

Countries heavily reliant on hydroelectricity are usually small and non-industrial: a high proportion of hydroelectric power more often reflects a modest energy budget than vast hydroelectric resources. The USA, for instance, produces only 6% of its power requirements from hydroelectricity; yet that 6% amounts to almost half the hydropower generated by most of Africa.

ELECTRICITY PRODUCTION

Percentage of electricity generated by source (latest available data)

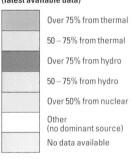

- Over 75% from thermal
- 50 – 75% from thermal
- Over 75% from hydro
- 50 – 75% from hydro
- Over 50% from nuclear
- Other (no dominant source)
- No data available

● Selected geothermal plants

◆ Selected hydroelectric plants

Conversion Rates

1 barrel = 0.136 tonnes or 159 litres or 35 Imperial gallons or 42 US gallons

1 tonne = 7.33 barrels or 1,185 litres or 256 Imperial gallons or 261 US gallons

1 tonne oil = 1.5 tonnes hard coal or 3.0 tonnes lignite or 12,000 kWh

1 Imperial gallon = 1.201 US gallons or 4.546 litres or 277.4 cubic inches

Measurements
For historical reasons, oil is traded in 'barrels'. The weight and volume equivalents (shown right) are all based on average-density 'Arabian light' crude oil.

The energy equivalents given for a tonne of oil are also somewhat imprecise: oil and coal of different qualities will have varying energy contents, a fact usually reflected in their price on world markets.

ENERGY RESERVES

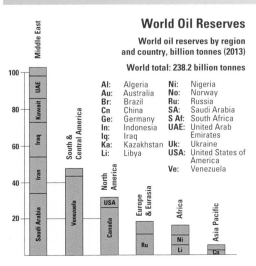

World Oil Reserves
World oil reserves by region and country, billion tonnes (2013)

World total: 238.2 billion tonnes

Al: Algeria	Ni: Nigeria
Au: Australia	No: Norway
Br: Brazil	Ru: Russia
Cn: China	SA: Saudi Arabia
Ge: Germany	S Af: South Africa
In: Indonesia	UAE: United Arab Emirates
Iq: Iraq	Uk: Ukraine
Ka: Kazakhstan	USA: United States of America
Li: Libya	Ve: Venezuela

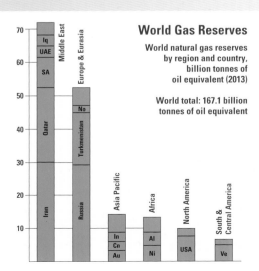

World Gas Reserves
World natural gas reserves by region and country, billion tonnes of oil equivalent (2013)

World total: 167.1 billion tonnes of oil equivalent

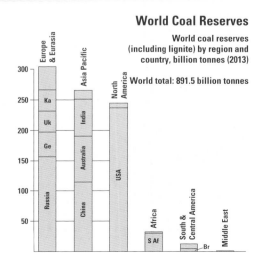

World Coal Reserves
World coal reserves (including lignite) by region and country, billion tonnes (2013)

World total: 891.5 billion tonnes

Production

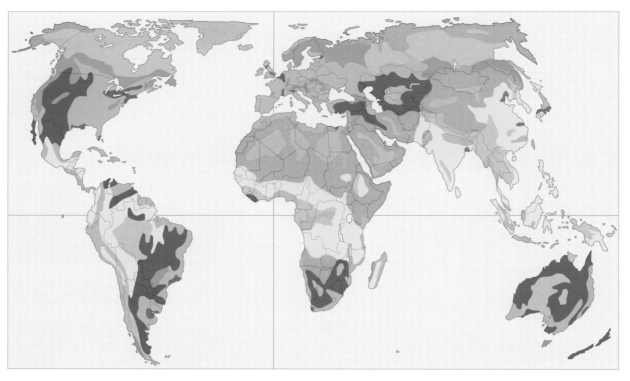

AGRICULTURE

Predominant type of farming or land use

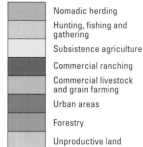

- Nomadic herding
- Hunting, fishing and gathering
- Subsistence agriculture
- Commercial ranching
- Commercial livestock and grain farming
- Urban areas
- Forestry
- Unproductive land

The development of agriculture has transformed human existence more than any other. The whole business of farming is constantly developing: due mainly to the new varieties of rice and wheat, world grain production has more than doubled since 1965. New machinery and modern agricultural techniques enable farmers to produce food for the world's developed economies, but the poorer third world relies very much on subsistence agriculture.

STAPLE CROPS

Wheat

China 18.0% | India 14.1% | USA 9.2% | France 6.0% | Russia 5.6% | Canada 4.0% | Germany 3.3%

World total (2012): 670,875,110 tonnes

Maize
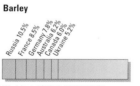
USA 31.4% | China 23.9% | Brazil 8.1%

World total (2012): 872,066,770 tonnes

Barley
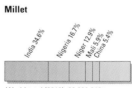
Russia 10.5% | France 8.5% | Germany 7.8% | Australia 6.2% | Canada 6.0% | Ukraine 5.2%

World total (2012): 132,886,519 tonnes

Millet
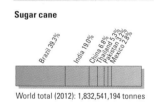
India 34.6% | Nigeria 16.7% | Niger 12.9% | Mali 5.9% | China 5.4%

World total (2012): 29,866,016 tonnes

Rice/Paddy

China 28.6% | India 21.2% | Indonesia 9.6% | Vietnam 6.1% | Thailand 5.3% | Bangladesh 4.7% | Burma (Myanmar) 4.6

World total (2012): 719,738,273 tonnes

Potatoes

China 23.6% | India 12.3% | Russia 8.1% | Ukraine 6.4% | USA 5.3%

World total (2012): 364,808,768 tonnes

Soybeans
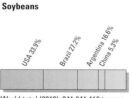
USA 33.9% | Brazil 27.2% | Argentina 16.6% | China 5.3%

World total (2012): 241,841,416 tonnes

Cassava
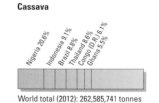
Nigeria 20.6% | Indonesia 9.1% | Brazil 8.8% | Thailand 8.6% | Congo (D.R.) 6.1% | Ghana 5.5%

World total (2012): 262,585,741 tonnes

SUGARS

Sugar cane
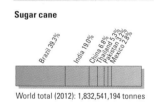
Brazil 39.5% | India 19.0% | China 6.8% | Thailand 5.3% | Pakistan 3.2% | Mexico 2.8%

World total (2012): 1,832,541,194 tonnes

Sugar beet
Russia 16.7% | France 12.5% | USA 11.8% | Germany 10.3% | Ukraine 6.8% | Turkey 5.6% | Poland 5.4% | UK 2.7%

World total (2012): 269,865,481 tonnes

EMPLOYMENT

The number of workers employed in manufacturing for every 100 workers engaged in agriculture (2013)

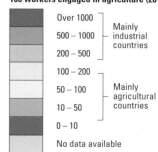

- Over 1000 ⎫
- 500 – 1000 ⎬ Mainly industrial countries
- 200 – 500 ⎭
- 100 – 200
- 50 – 100 ⎫
- 10 – 50 ⎬ Mainly agricultural countries
- 0 – 10 ⎭
- No data available

Countries with the highest number of workers employed in manufacturing per 100 workers engaged in agriculture (2013)

1. Bahrain 7,900
2. Qatar 5,400
3. Liechtenstein 3,900
4. Sweden 2,800
5. Malta 2,200
6. Singapore 2,200
7. Micronesia, Fed. States .. 2,100
8. USA 2,000
9. Guyana 1,900
10. Luxembourg 1,900

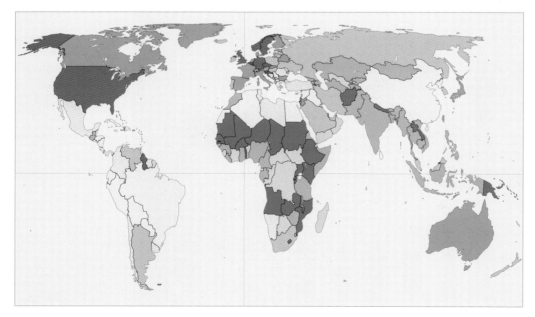

MINERAL PRODUCTION

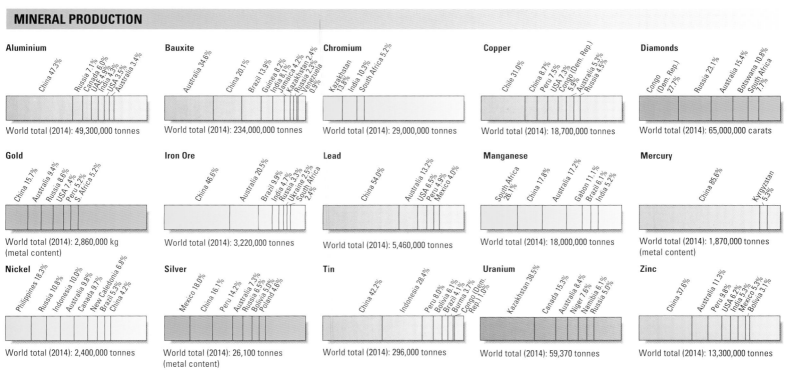

Aluminium
China 47.3% · Russia 7.1% · Canada 6.0% · UAE 4.9% · India 4.3% · USA 3.5% · Australia 3.4%
World total (2014): 49,300,000 tonnes

Bauxite
Australia 34.6% · China 20.1% · Brazil 13.9% · Guinea 8.2% · India 8.1% · Jamaica 4.2% · Kazakhstan 4.2% · Russia 2.4% · Venezuela 2.3% · 0.9%
World total (2014): 234,000,000 tonnes

Chromium
Kazakhstan 13.8% · India 10.3% · South Africa 5.2%
World total (2014): 29,000,000 tonnes

Copper
Chile 31.0% · China 8.7% · Peru 7.5% · USA 7.3% · Congo (Dem. Rep.) 5.9% · Russia 5.3% · Australia 4.5%
World total (2014): 18,700,000 tonnes

Diamonds
Congo (Dem. Rep.) 27.7% · Russia 23.1% · Australia 15.4% · Botswana 10.8% · South Africa 7.7%
World total (2014): 65,000,000 carats

Gold
China 15.7% · Australia 9.4% · Russia 8.6% · USA 7.4% · Peru 5.2% · S. Africa 5.2%
World total (2014): 2,860,000 kg (metal content)

Iron Ore
China 46.6% · Australia 20.5% · Brazil 9.9% · India 4.7% · Russia 3.3% · Ukraine 2.5% · South Africa 2.4%
World total (2014): 3,220,000 tonnes

Lead
China 54.0% · Australia 13.2% · USA 6.5% · Peru 4.9% · Mexico 4.0%
World total (2014): 5,460,000 tonnes

Manganese
South Africa 26.1% · China 17.8% · Australia 17.2% · Gabon 11.1% · Brazil 6.1% · India 5.2%
World total (2014): 18,000,000 tonnes

Mercury
China 85.6% · Kyrgyzstan 5.5%
World total (2014): 1,870,000 tonnes (metal content)

Nickel
Philippines 18.3% · Russia 10.8% · Indonesia 10.0% · Australia 9.8% · Canada 9.7% · New Caledonia 6.8% · Brazil 5.3% · China 4.2%
World total (2014): 2,400,000 tonnes

Silver
Mexico 18.0% · China 16.1% · Peru 14.2% · Australia 7.3% · Russia 6.5% · Bolivia 5.0% · Poland 4.6%
World total (2014): 26,100 tonnes (metal content)

Tin
China 42.2% · Indonesia 28.4% · Peru 8.0% · Bolivia 6.1% · Brazil 4.1% · Burma 3.7% · Congo (Dem. Rep.) 1.0%
World total (2014): 296,000 tonnes

Uranium
Kazakhstan 38.5% · Canada 15.3% · Australia 8.4% · Niger 7.6% · Namibia 6.1% · Russia 5.0%
World total (2014): 59,370 tonnes

Zinc
China 37.6% · Australia 11.3% · Peru 9.8% · USA 6.2% · India 5.3% · Mexico 5.3% · Bolivia 3.1%
World total (2014): 13,300,000 tonnes

MINERAL DISTRIBUTION

The map shows the richest sources of the most important minerals

Precious metals
◇ Diamonds
○ Gold
◉ Silver

Iron and ferro-alloys
◇ Chromium
◑ Cobalt
◇ Iron ore
◇ Manganese
◈ Molybdenum
◈ Nickel ore
◆ Tungsten

Non-ferrous metals
◈ Bauxite
(◈ Aluminium)
◇ Copper
◇ Lead
◆ Mercury
◇ Zinc

Fertilizers
▲ Phosphates
▲ Potash

The map does not show undersea deposits, most of which are currently inaccessible.

INDUSTRIAL PRODUCTION

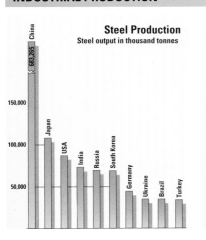

Steel Production
Steel output in thousand tonnes

China 683,265 · Japan · USA · India · Russia · South Korea · Germany · Ukraine · Brazil · Turkey

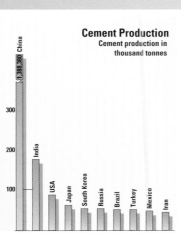

Cement Production
Cement production in thousand tonnes

China 1,388,380 · India · USA · Japan · South Korea · Russia · Brazil · Turkey · Mexico · Iran

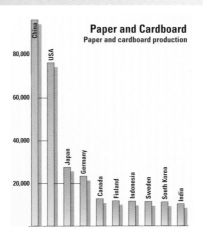

Paper and Cardboard
Paper and cardboard production

China · USA · Japan · Germany · Canada · Finland · Indonesia · Sweden · South Korea · India

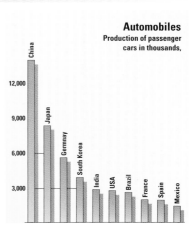

Automobiles
Production of passenger cars in thousands,

China · Japan · Germany · South Korea · India · USA · Brazil · France · Spain · Mexico

Trade

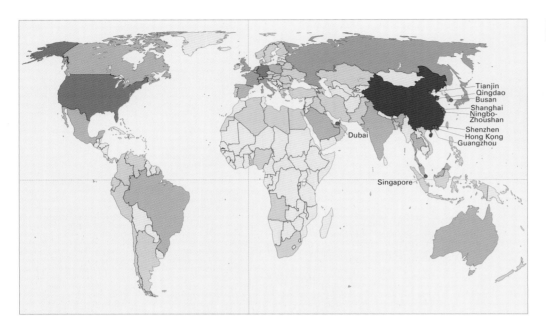

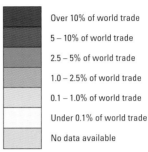

SHARE OF WORLD TRADE

Percentage share of total world exports by value (2013)

- Over 10% of world trade
- 5 – 10% of world trade
- 2.5 – 5% of world trade
- 1.0 – 2.5% of world trade
- 0.1 – 1.0% of world trade
- Under 0.1% of world trade
- No data available

● Top ten container ports

Countries with the largest share of world trade (2013)

1. China	11.0%	6. South Korea	3.0%
2. USA	8.5%	7. Netherlands	3.0%
3. Germany	8.1%	8. Russia	2.8%
4. Japan	3.8%	9. UK	2.6%
5. France	3.1%	10. Italy	2.6%

THE MAIN TRADING NATIONS

The imports and exports of the top ten trading nations as a percentage of world trade (2014). Each country's trade in manufactured goods is shown in dark blue

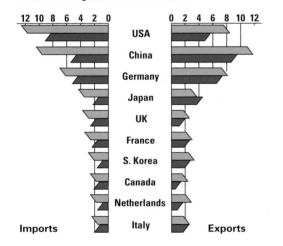

MAJOR EXPORTS

Leading manufactured items and their exporters

Motor Vehicles
World total (2013): US$ 4,068,895 million

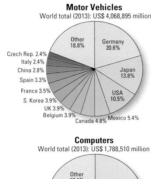

Computers
World total (2013): US$ 1,788,510 million

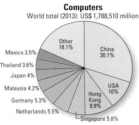

Telecommunications Gear
World total (2013): US$ 2,140,743 million

Electrical Components
World total (2013): US$ 6,742,402 million

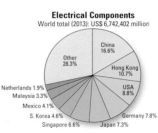

Petrol Products
World total (2013): US$ 2,510,843 million

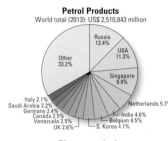

Pharmaceuticals
World total (2013): US$ 1,530,424 million

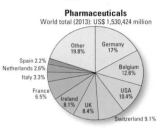

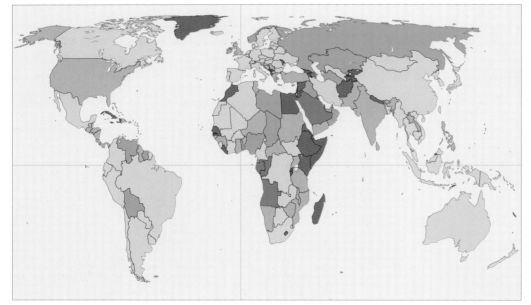

BALANCE OF TRADE

Value of exports in proportion to the value of imports (2013)

- More than 50%
- 25 – 50%
- 0 – 25%
- 0 – 25%
- 25 – 50%
- More than 50%
- No data available

Exports exceed imports

Imports exceed exports

The total world trade balance should amount to zero, since exports must equal imports on a global scale. In practice, at least $100 billion in exports go unrecorded, leaving the world with an apparent deficit and many countries in a better position than public accounting reveals. However, a favourable trade balance is not necessarily a sign of prosperity: many poorer countries must maintain a high surplus in order to service debts, and do so by restricting imports below the levels needed to sustain successful economies.

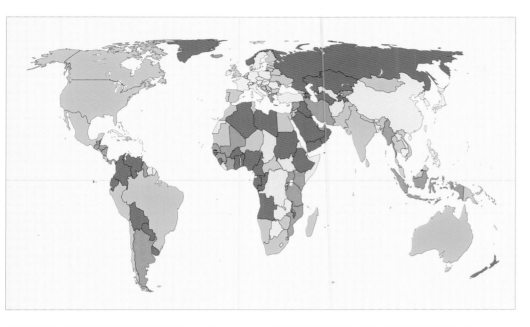

Primary exports as a percentage of total export value (2013)

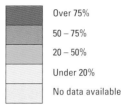

- Over 75%
- 50 – 75%
- 20 – 50%
- Under 20%
- No data available

Primary exports are raw materials or partly processed products that form the basis for manufacturing. They are the necessary requirements of industries and include agricultural products, minerals, fuels and timber, as well as many semi-manufactured goods such as cotton, which has been spun but not woven, wood pulp or flour. Many developed countries have few natural resources and rely on imports for the majority of their primary products. The countries of South-east Asia export hardwoods to the rest of the world, while some South American countries are heavily dependent on coffee exports.

MERCHANT FLEETS

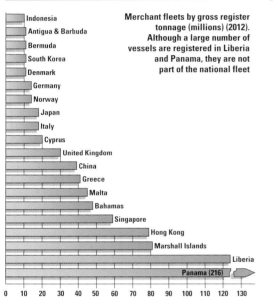

Merchant fleets by gross register tonnage (millions) (2012). Although a large number of vessels are registered in Liberia and Panama, they are not part of the national fleet

Indonesia
Antigua & Barbuda
Bermuda
South Korea
Denmark
Germany
Norway
Japan
Italy
Cyprus
United Kingdom
China
Greece
Malta
Bahamas
Singapore
Hong Kong
Marshall Islands
Liberia
Panama (216)

0 10 20 30 40 50 60 70 80 90 100 110 120 130

TOP TEN PORTS

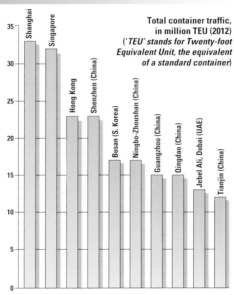

Total container traffic, in million TEU (2012) ('*TEU' stands for Twenty-foot Equivalent Unit, the equivalent of a standard container*)

Shanghai
Singapore
Hong Kong
Shenzhen (China)
Busan (S. Korea)
Ningbo-Zhoushan (China)
Guangzhou (China)
Qingdao (China)
Jebel Ali, Dubai (UAE)
Tianjin (China)

TYPES OF VESSELS

World fleet by type of vessel (2014)

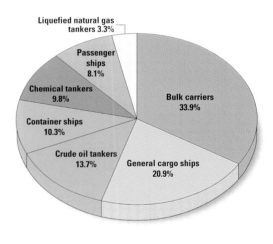

- Liquefied natural gas tankers 3.3%
- Passenger ships 8.1%
- Chemical tankers 9.8%
- Container ships 10.3%
- Crude oil tankers 13.7%
- Bulk carriers 33.9%
- General cargo ships 20.9%

IMPORTANCE OF SERVICE SECTOR

Percentage of total GDP from service sector (2013)

- Over 70%
- 60 – 70%
- 50 – 60%
- 40 – 50%
- Under 40%
- No data available

Countries with the highest and lowest percentage of GDP from services

Highest		Lowest	
1. Bahamas	91%	1. Paraguay	2%
2. Monaco	90%	2. Andorra	6%
3. Montenegro	88%	3. Equatorial Guinea	8%
4. Luxembourg	86%	4. East Timor	16%
5. Malta	85%	5. Liberia	18%

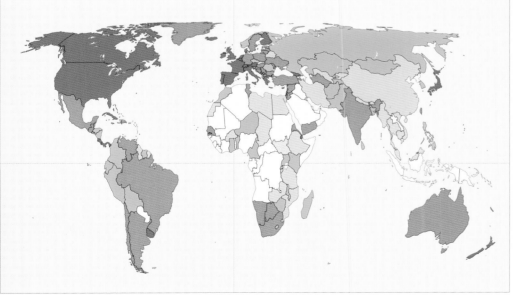

29

Travel and Tourism

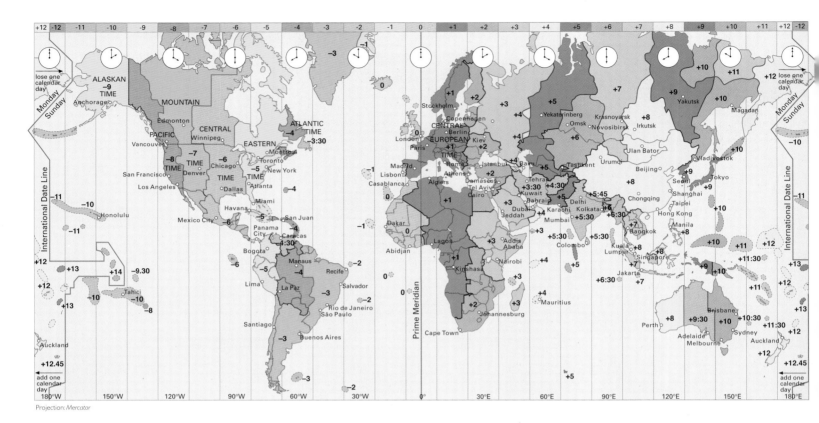

Projection: *Mercator*

TIME ZONES

▨ Zones using UT (GMT)		▥ Zones ahead of UT (GMT)	
▥ Zones behind UT (GMT)		▨ Half-hour zones	

— International boundaries

— Time-zone boundaries

10 Hours fast or slow of UT or Co-ordinated Universal Time

— International Date Line

Certain time zones are affected by the incidence of daylight saving time in countries where it is adopted.

Actual solar time, when it is noon at Greenwich, is shown along the top of the map.

The world is divided into 24 time zones, each centred on meridians at 15° intervals, which is the longitudinal distance the sun travels every hour. The meridian running through Greenwich, London, passes through the middle of the first zone.

RAIL AND ROAD: THE LEADING NATIONS

Total rail network ('000 km)		Passenger km per head per year		Total road network ('000 km)		Vehicle km per head per year		Number of vehicles per km of roads	
1. USA	228.5	Switzerland	2,258	USA	6,486.2	Peru	38,553	Kuwait	271
2. Russia	85.3	Japan	1,910	China	3,799.4	USA	34,560	Hong Kong	241
3. China	65.5	Slovakia	1,420	India	3,428.0	Tunisia	25,225	Macau	238
4. India	63.3	Denmark	1,322	Brazil	1,841.5	Pakistan	25,199	UAE	220
5. Canada	58.3	France	1,320	Canada	1,419.3	Ecuador	23,570	Singapore	218
6. Germany	33.7	Austria	1,227	Japan	1,201.3	Chile	22,671	Taiwan	170
7. France	33.6	Ukraine	1,097	France	1,030.2	South Korea	21,763	South Korea	157
8. UK	31.5	Russia	1,075	Russia	953.0	Singapore	21,563	ABC Islands	154
9. Brazil	29.8	Belgium	972	Australia	815.5	Morocco	18,455	Israel	128
10. Mexico	26.7	Germany	961	Sweden	697.8	Croatia	17,723	Malta	123
11. Argentina	25.0	Netherlands	922	Spain	680.3	Finland	17,639	Thailand	121
12. South Africa	22.1	UK	887	Germany	644.8	Canada	17,498	Bahrain	114
13. Ukraine	21.7	Kazakhstan	879	Italy	490.0	Denmark	16,903	Jordan	112
14. Japan	20.0	Belarus	779	Turkey	427.2	Thailand	16,823	Puerto Rico	110
15. Poland	19.7	Italy	735	Indonesia	404.3	Isreal	16,721	Dom. Rep.	105

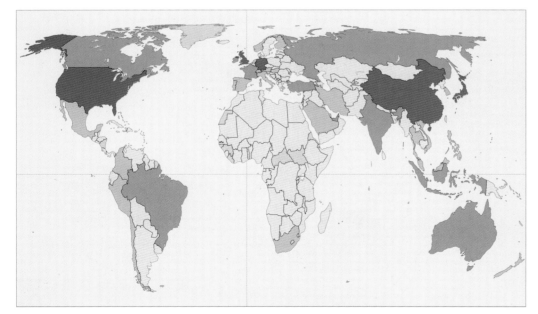

AIR TRAVEL

Number of air passengers carried (2013)

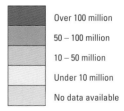

▨	Over 100 million
▨	50 – 100 million
▨	10 – 50 million
▢	Under 10 million
▨	No data available

World's busiest airports (2013) - total passengers in millions

1. Atlanta Hartsfield International (ATL) 94.4
2. Beijing Capital International (PEK) 83.7
3. London Heathrow (LHR) 72.4
4. Tokyo Haneda (HND) 68.9
5. Chicago O'Hare International (ORD) 66.9
6. Los Angeles International (LAX) 66.7
7. Dubai International (DXB) 66.4
8. Paris Charles de Gaulle (CDG) 62.1
9. Dallas/Fort Worth International (DFW) 60.4
10. Jakarta International (CGK) 59.7

TOURIST CENTRES

■ Cultural and historical centres
□ Coastal resorts
□ Ski resorts
■ Centres of entertainment
■ Places of pilgrimage
■ Places of great natural beauty
— Popular holiday cruise routes

VISITORS TO THE USA

Overseas arrivals to the USA, in thousands (2013)

1. Canada	23,387
2. Mexico	14,343
3. UK	3,835
4. Japan	3,730
5. Brazil	2,060
6. Germany	1,916
7. China	1,807
8. France	1,505
9. South Korea	1,360
10. Australia	1,205

TOURIST SPENDING

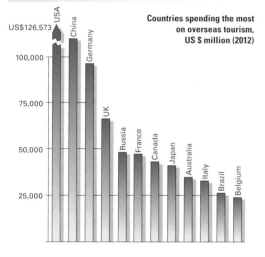

Countries spending the most on overseas tourism, US $ million (2012)

THE MAIN DESTINATIONS

		Arrivals from abroad millions (2013)	% of world total (2013)
1.	France	84.7	7.8%
2.	USA	69.8	6.4%
3.	Spain	60.7	5.6%
4.	China	55.7	5.1%
5.	Italy	47.7	4.4%
6.	Turkey	37.8	3.5%
7.	Germany	31.5	2.9%
8.	UK	31.2	2.9%
9.	Russia	28.4	2.6%
10.	Thailand	26.5	2.4%

The 1,087 million international arrivals in 2013 represented an additional 57 million over the 2012 level – a growth in numbers of 5%. Growth was common to all regions, except in the Middle East.

TOURIST EARNINGS

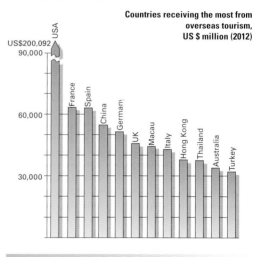

Countries receiving the most from overseas tourism, US $ million (2012)

IMPORTANCE OF TOURISM

Tourism receipts as a percentage of Gross National Income (2013)

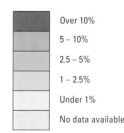

Over 10%
5 – 10%
2.5 – 5%
1 – 2.5%
Under 1%
No data available

Countries with the highest tourism receipts as % of GNI (2013)

1. Vanuatu	39	6. Samoa	24
2. Bahamas	32	7. Dominica	23
3. Cabo Verde	26	8. Montenegro	20
4. Barbados	25	9. Belize	19
5. Fiji	25	10. Malta	18

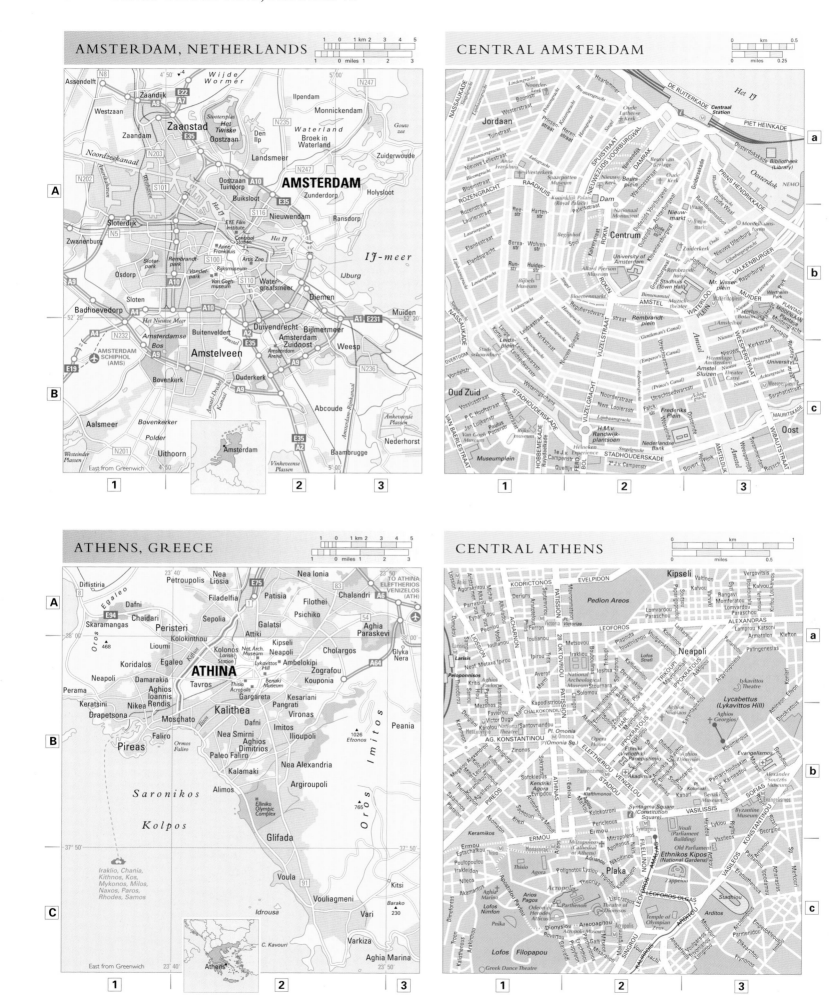

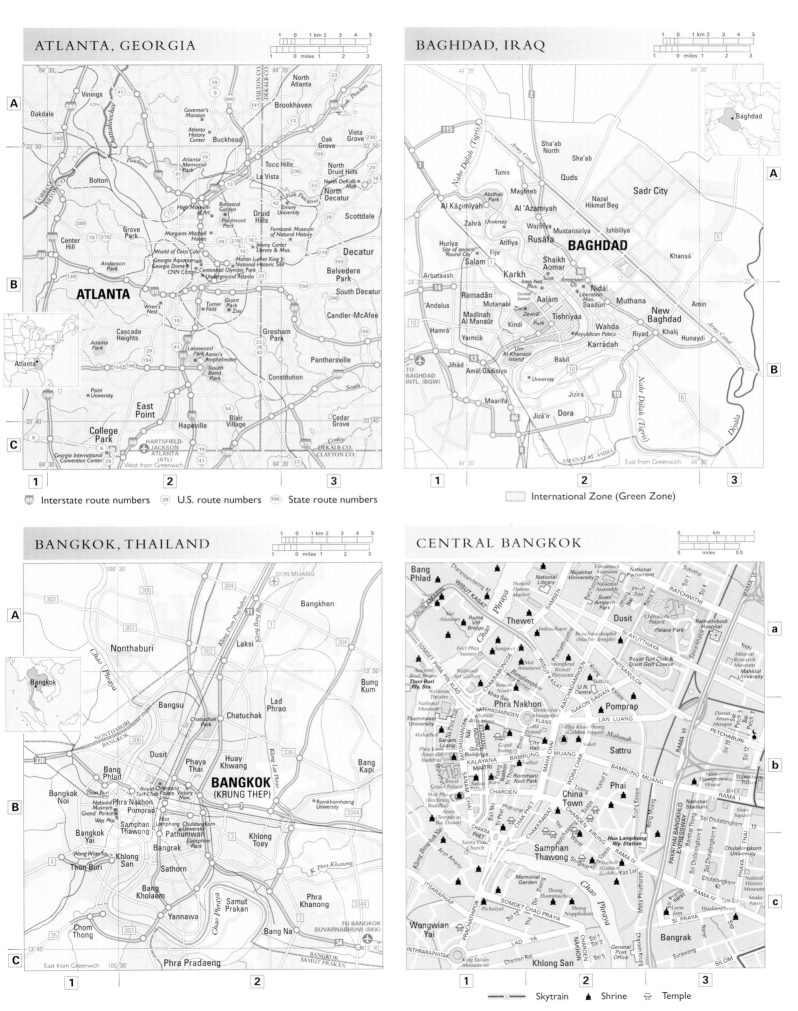

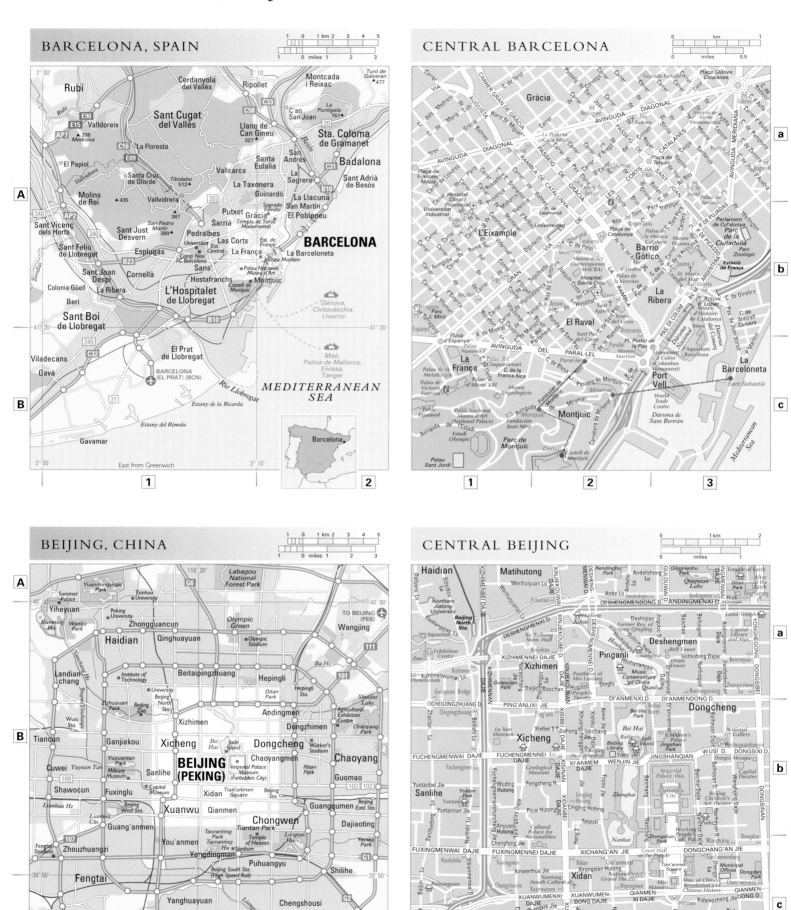

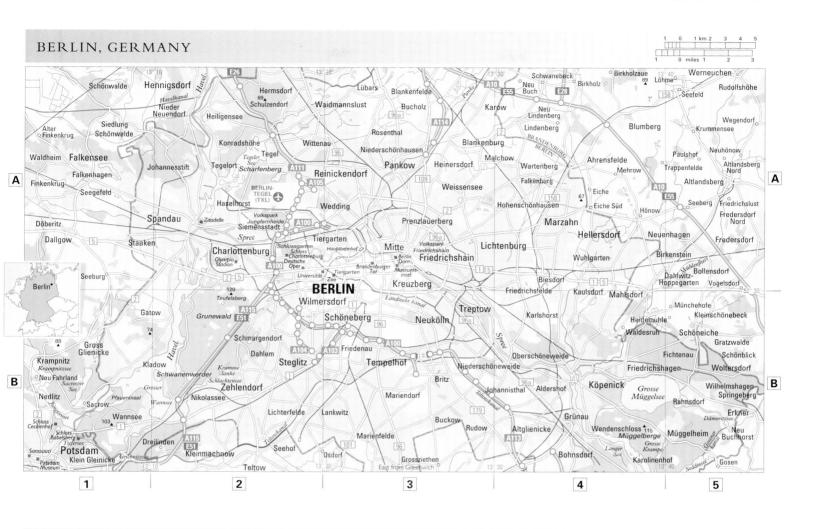

BERLIN, GERMANY

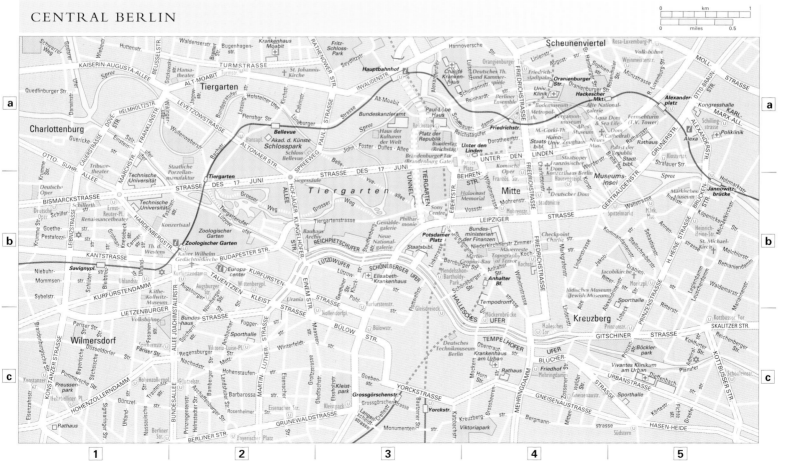

CENTRAL BERLIN

COPYRIGHT PHILIP'S

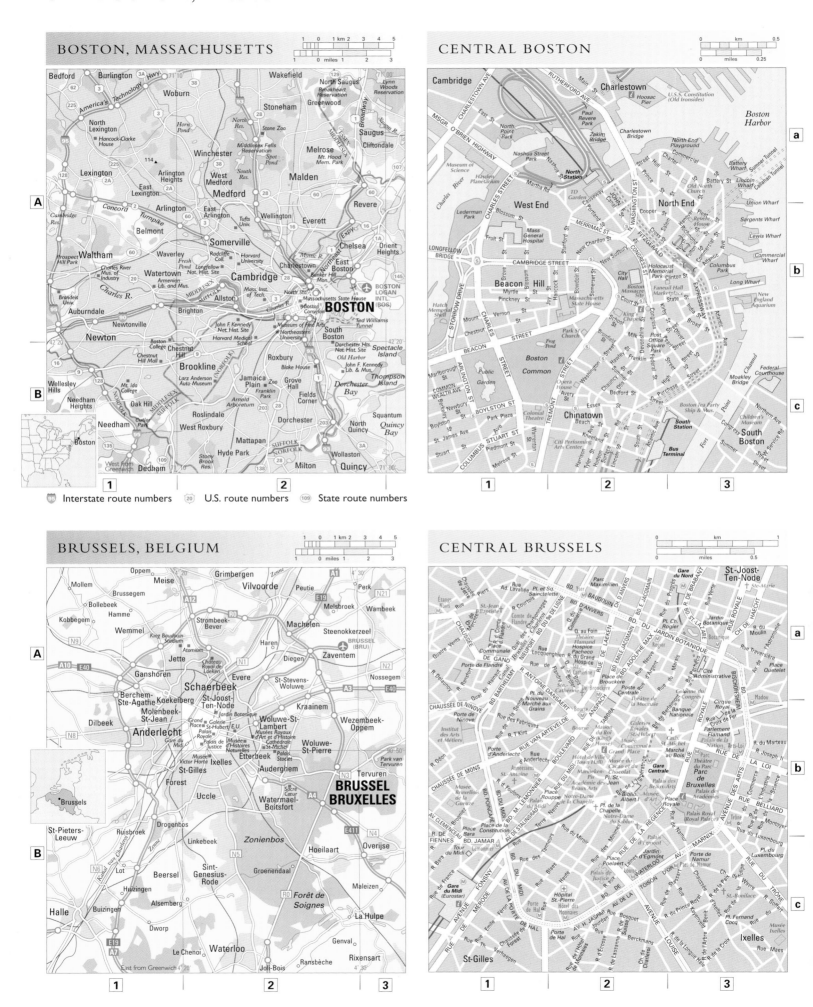

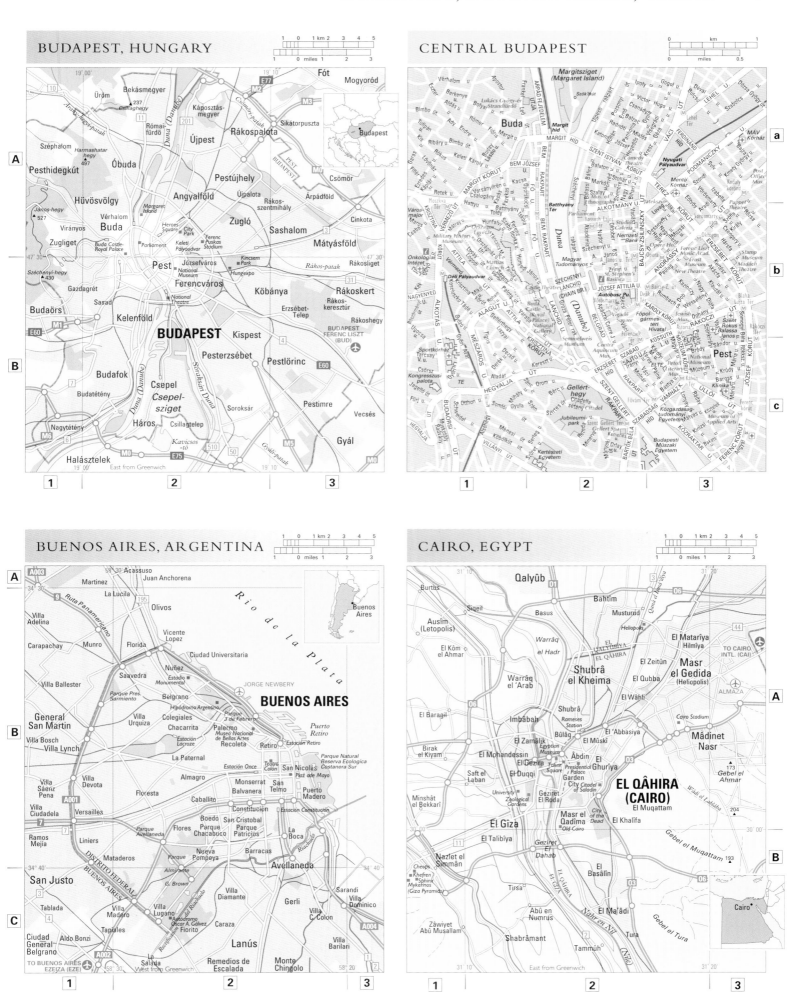

BUDAPEST, HUNGARY

CENTRAL BUDAPEST

BUENOS AIRES, ARGENTINA

CAIRO, EGYPT

COPYRIGHT PHILIP'S

CAPE TOWN, SOUTH AFRICA

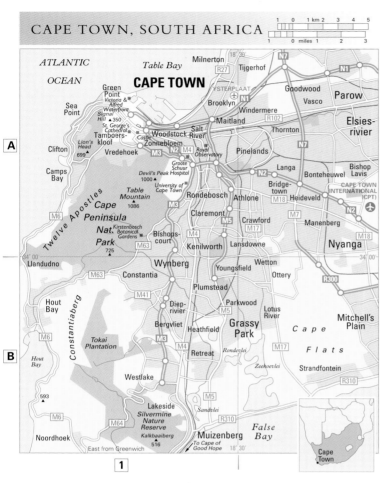

CENTRAL CAPE TOWN

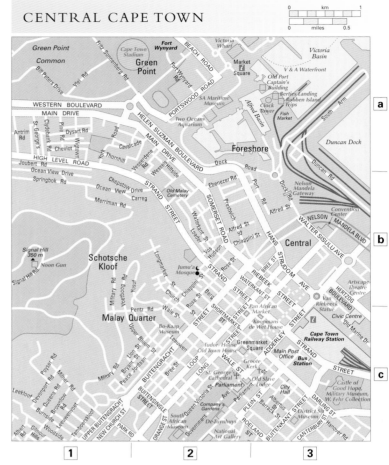

COPENHAGEN, DENMARK

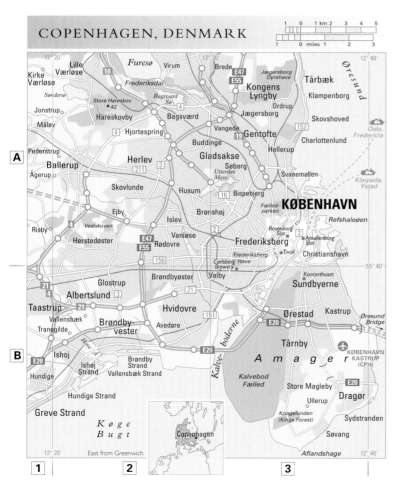

CENTRAL COPENHAGEN

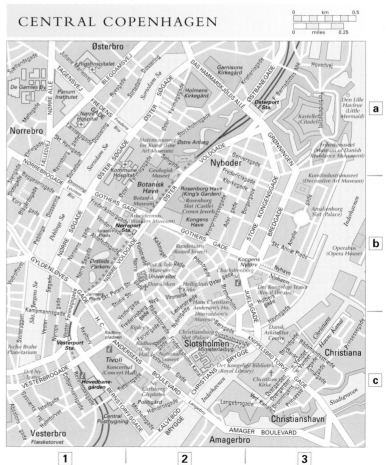

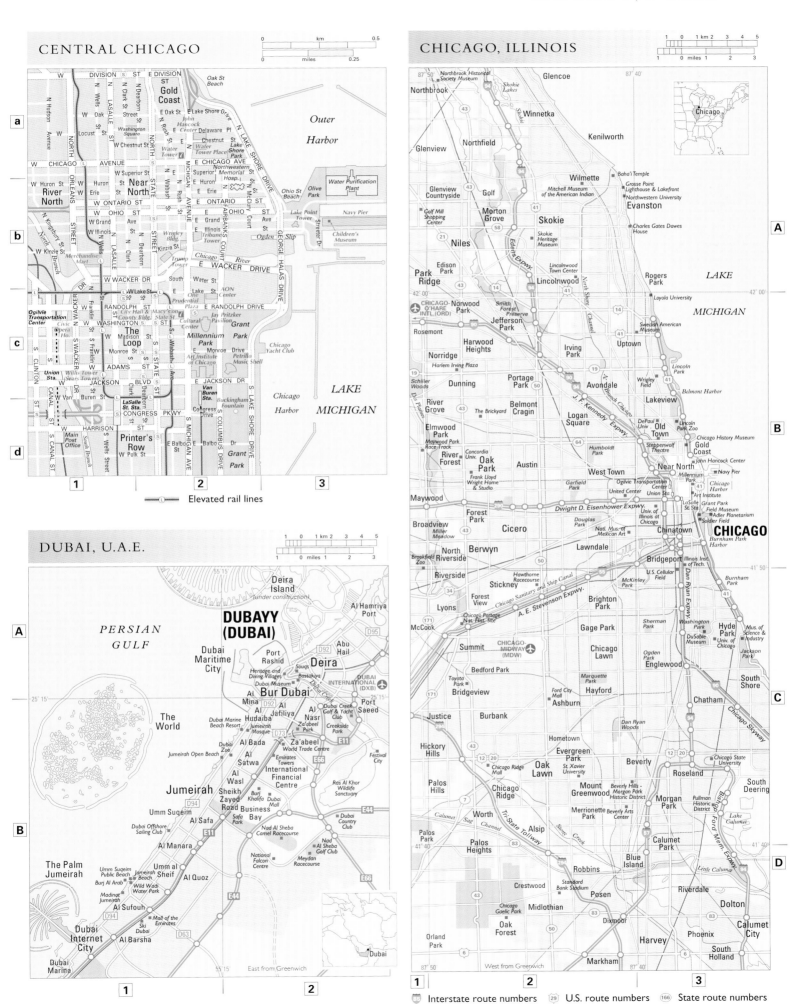

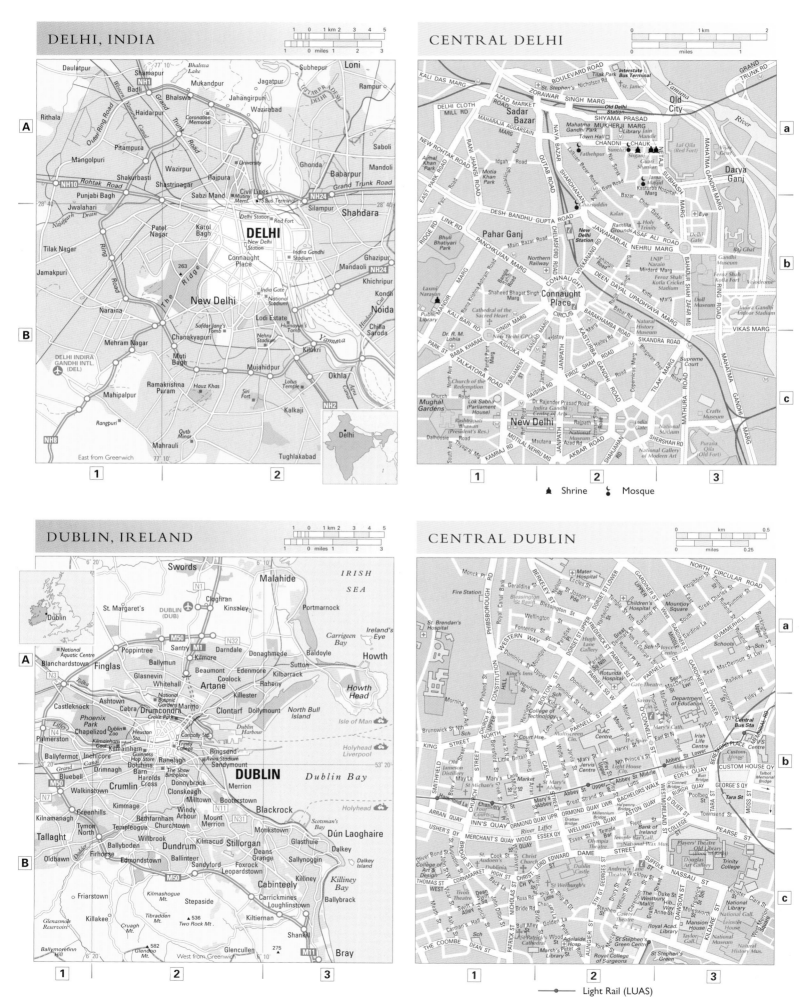

DELHI, INDIA

CENTRAL DELHI

▲ Shrine ⚱ Mosque

DUBLIN, IRELAND

CENTRAL DUBLIN

Light Rail (LUAS)

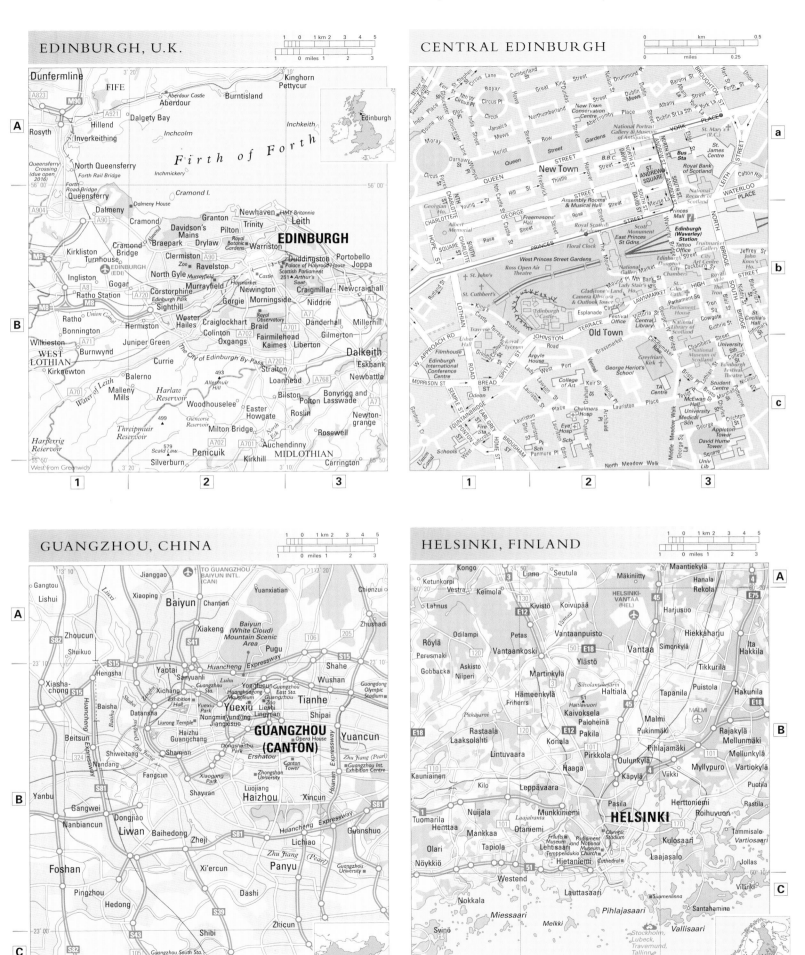

EDINBURGH, U.K.

Dunfermline
FIFE
Kinghorn
Pettycur
Aberdour Castle
Aberdour
Burntisland
A823
M90
A921
Inchkeith
A
Rosyth
Hillend
Dalgety Bay
Inchcolm
Edinburgh
Inverkeithing
North Queensferry
Firth of Forth
Queensferry Crossing (due open 2016)
Forth Rail Bridge
56° 00'
Forth Road Bridge
Queensferry
Cramond I.
Dalmeny
Dalmeny House
Newhaven
HMY Britannia
Leith
A904
A90
Cramond
Granton
Pilton
Trinity
M9
Kirkliston
Turnhouse
Cramond Bridge
Davidson's Mains
Braepark
Drylaw
Warriston
EDINBURGH
Portobello
Joppa
M8
Ingliston
Gogar
EDINBURGH (EDI)
Clermiston
Zoo
Ravelston
Palace of Holyrood House
Scottish Parliament
251 Arthur's Seat
Duddingston
Ratho Station
Corstorphine
North Gyle
Murrayfield
Castle
Haymarket
Newington
Craigmillar
Newcraighall
A8
A720
Murrayfield
Newington
A1
Ratho
Sighthill
Gorgie
Morningside
Niddrie
M8
Hermiston
Wester Hailes
Craiglockhart
Royal Observatory
A701
Danderhall
Millerhill
Bonnington
Colinton
Braid
A71
A702
Gilmerton
WEST LOTHIAN
Juniper Green
Oxgangs
Kaimes
Liberton
Wilkieston
Burnwynd
Kirknewton
Currie
The City of Edinburgh By-Pass
A720
Dalkeith
Eskbank
Newbattle
Balerno
Malleny Mills
Straiton
A768
493
Allermuir Hill
Loanhead
A768
A70
Water of Leith
Harlaw Reservoir
Woodhouselee
Bilston
Polton
Lasswade
Bonyrigg and
A7
Threipmuir Reservoir
499
Glencorse Reservoir
Easter Howgate
Roslin
Newton-grange
Harperrig Reservoir
Scald Law 579
Milton Bridge
Rosewell
56° 50'
West from Greenwich
Penicuik
Silverburn
A702
Auchendinny
A701
Kirkhill
MIDLOTHIAN
Carrington
55° 50'
3° 20'
3° 10'

1 2 3

CENTRAL EDINBURGH

New Town
Old Town

1 2 3
a b c

GUANGZHOU, CHINA

TO GUANGZHOU BAIYUN INTL. (CAN)
Gangtou
Lishui
Jianggao
Xiaoping
Yuanxiatian
Chienzui
113° 10'
112° 20'
Baiyun
Chantian
A
S82
Zhoucun
Shuikuo
Xiakeng
Baiyun (White Cloud) Mountain Scenic Area
Zhushadi
Pugu
106
205
S41
S15
S15
Hengsha
Yaotai
Huancheng Expressway
Shahe
Wushan
23° 10'
Xiashachong
Sanyuanli
Luhu
Yongtaicun
Guangzhou East Sta.
Guangdong Olympic Stadium
S15
Xichang
Exhibition Hall
Huanghuagang Mausoleum
Guangzhou Zoo
Baisha
Datansha
Yuexiu Park
Liede
Lingnan
Tianhe
Shipai
Beitsun
Liurong Temple
Nongminyundong
Jiangxisuo
Yuancun
Nandang
Haizhu Guangchang
Shamian
GUANGZHOU (CANTON)
Opera House
324
Shiweitang
Dongshankou Park
Ershatou
Zhu Jiang (Pearl)
Huanan Expressway
Yanbu
Gangwei
Fangcun
Xiaogang Park
Canton Tower
Guangzhou Int. Exhibition Centre
Nanbiancun
Dongjiao
Baihedong
Luojiang
Xincun
S81
Liwan
Zheji
Huancheng Expressway
Guanshuo
Foshan
Xi'ercun
Lichiao
Zhu Jiang (Pearl)
Panyu
Guangzhou University
Pingzhou
Dashi
Hedong
Zhicun
23° 00'
S43
Shibi
S82
105
Guangzhou South Sta. (High Speed Train)
East from Greenwich
Guangzhou
113° 10'

1 2

HELSINKI, FINLAND

Kongo
Linna
Seutula
Mäntiekylä
Maantiekylä
Hanala
Rekola
E75
A
Ketunkorpi
Vestra
Keimola
HELSINKI-VANTAA (HEL)
45
Harjusuo
60° 20'
24° 50'
3
130
Kivistö
Koivupää
E12
Lahnus
Odilampi
Petas
Vantaanpuisto
Hiekkaharju
Ita Hakkila
Röylä
Perusmäki
Vantaankoski
50
E18
Vantaa
Simonkylä
Tikkurila
Gobbacka
Askisto
Niiperi
Ylästö
Silvolant-kojärvi
Haltiala
Tapanila
Puistola
Hakunila
E18
Hämeenkylä
Friherrs
Haltiavuori
Kaivoksela
Paloheinä
Malmi
MALMI
Rajakylä
Mellunmäki
E18
E12
Pitäjärvi
Rastaala
Laaksolahti
120
Konala
Pakila
Pukinmäki
Pihlajamäki
B
Kauniainen
Lintuvaara
101
Pirkkola
Oulunkylä
101
Mellunkylä
Vartiokylä
110
Kilo
Haaga
Käpylä
Viikki
Puotila
1
Leppävaara
Munkkiniemi
Pasila
Herttoniemi
Roihuvuori
Rastila
Tuomarila
Nuijala
Laajalanta
HELSINKI
170
Henttaa
Mankkaa
Otaniemi
Olympic Stadium
Kulosaari
Tammisalo
Vartiosaari
Olari
Tapiola
Parliament Museum National Museum
Lehtisaari
Temppeliaukio Church
Cathedral
Laajasalo
Jollas
Nöykkiö
Hietaniemi
51
Westend
Lauttasaari
Suomenlinna
Villinki
60° 10'
C
Nokkala
Svinö
Miessaari
Melkki
Pihlajasaari
Vallisaari
Santahamina
Stockholm, Lübeck, Travemünd, Tallinn, Rostock
Harmaja
Helsinki
24° 50'
East from Greenwich
25° 00'

1 2 3

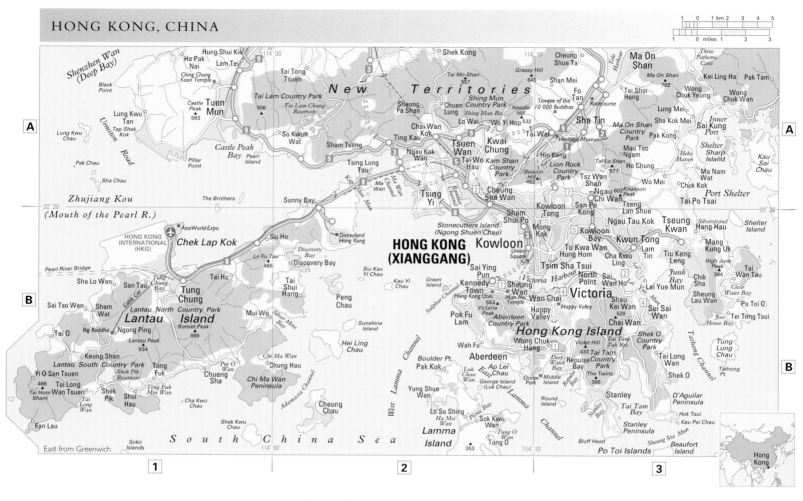

HONG KONG, CHINA

ISTANBUL, TURKEY

JAKARTA, INDONESIA

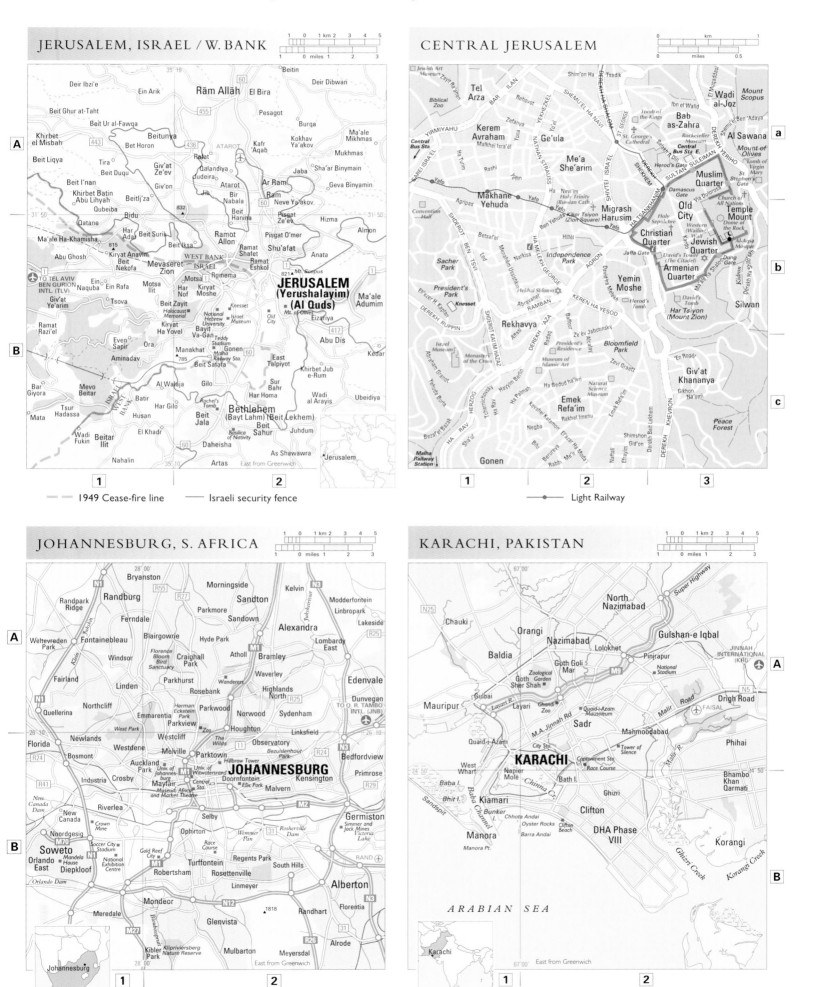

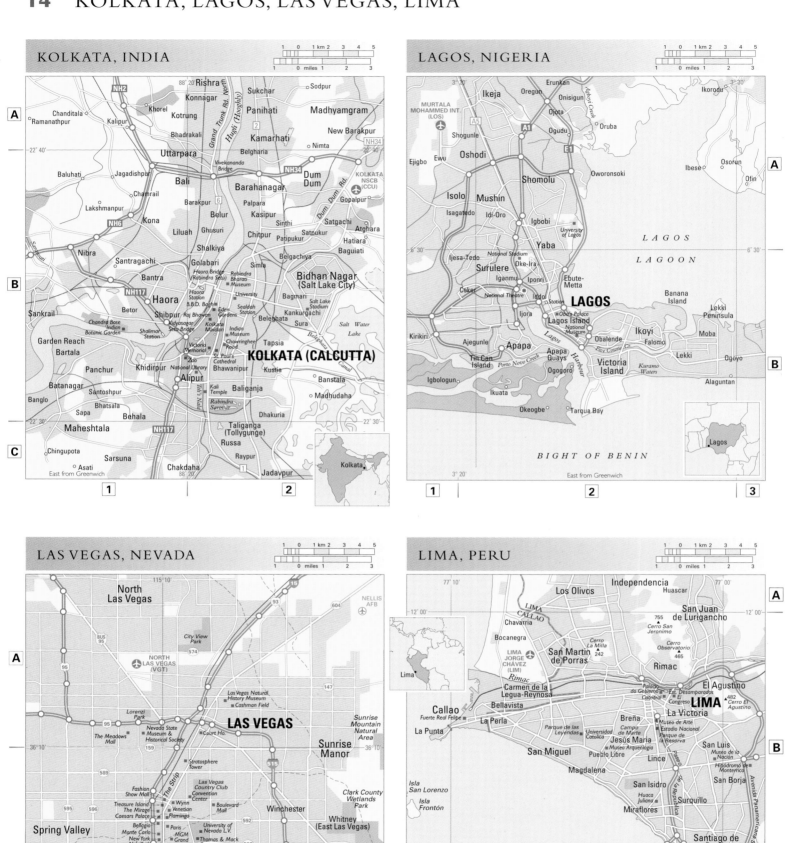

LONDON, U.K.

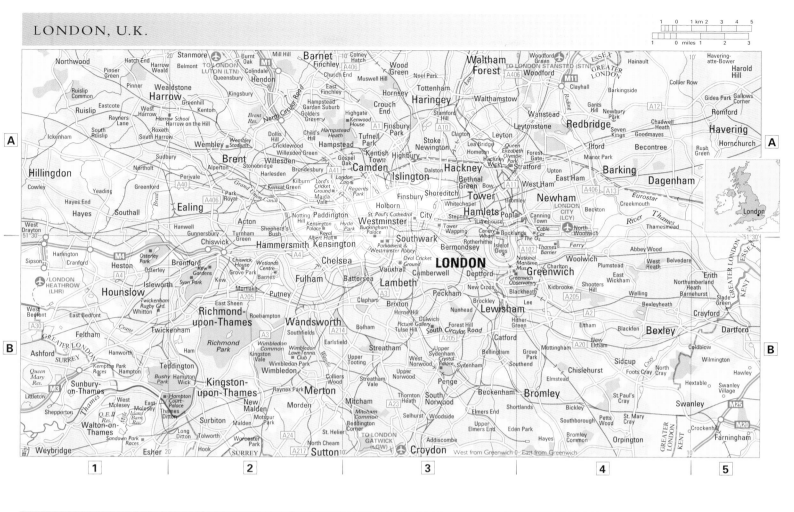

CENTRAL LONDON

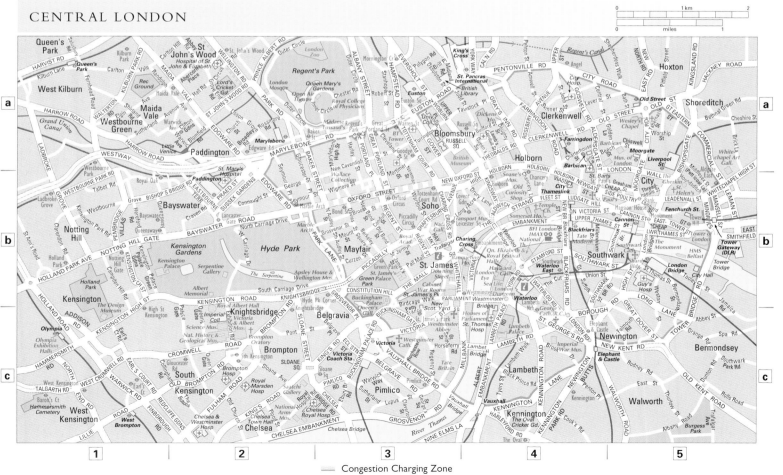

— Congestion Charging Zone

LISBON, PORTUGAL

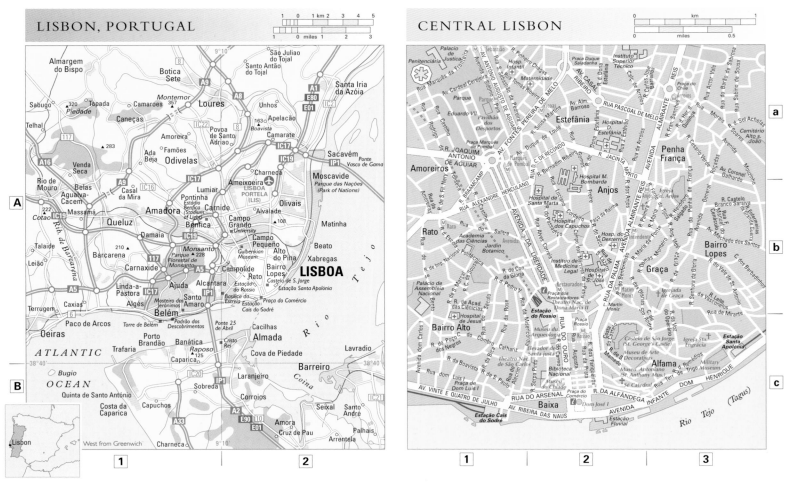

CENTRAL LISBON

LOS ANGELES, CALIFORNIA

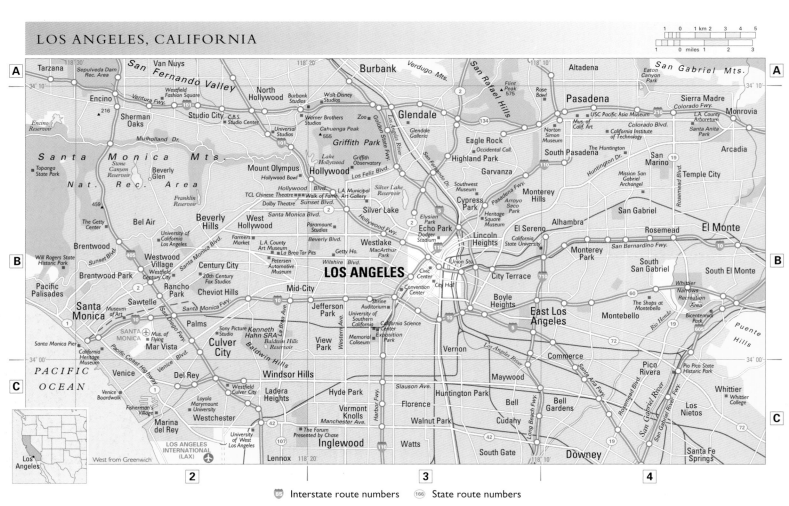

85 Interstate route numbers   166 State route numbers

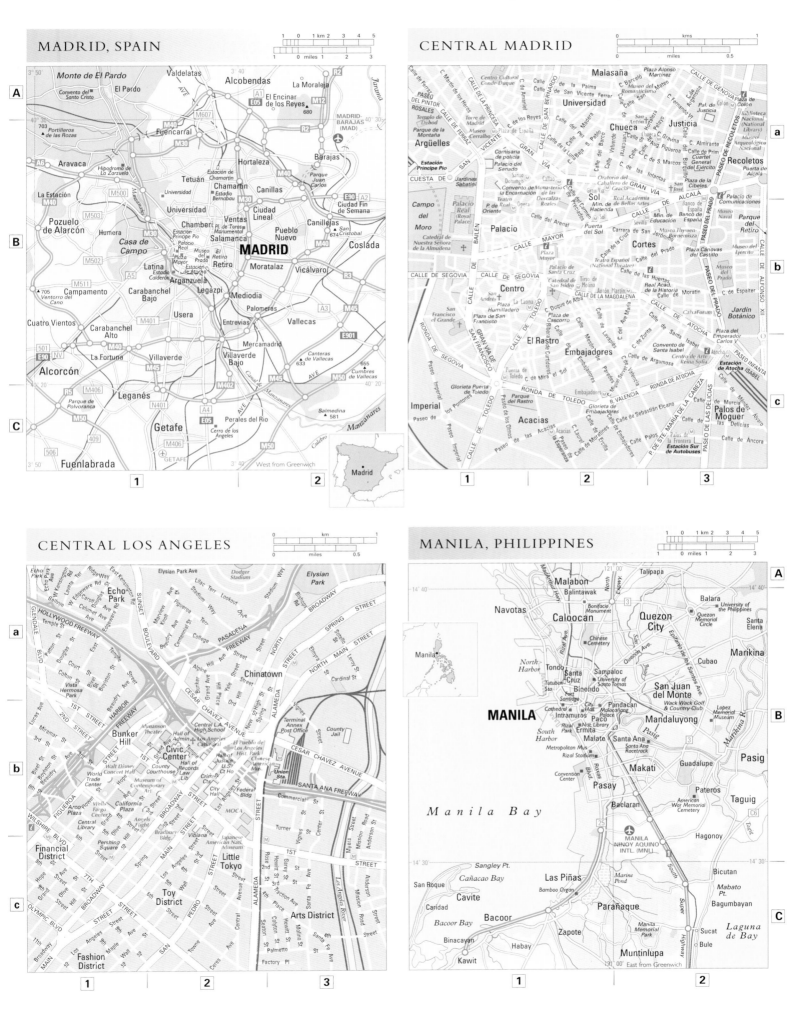

MADRID, SPAIN

CENTRAL MADRID

CENTRAL LOS ANGELES

MANILA, PHILIPPINES

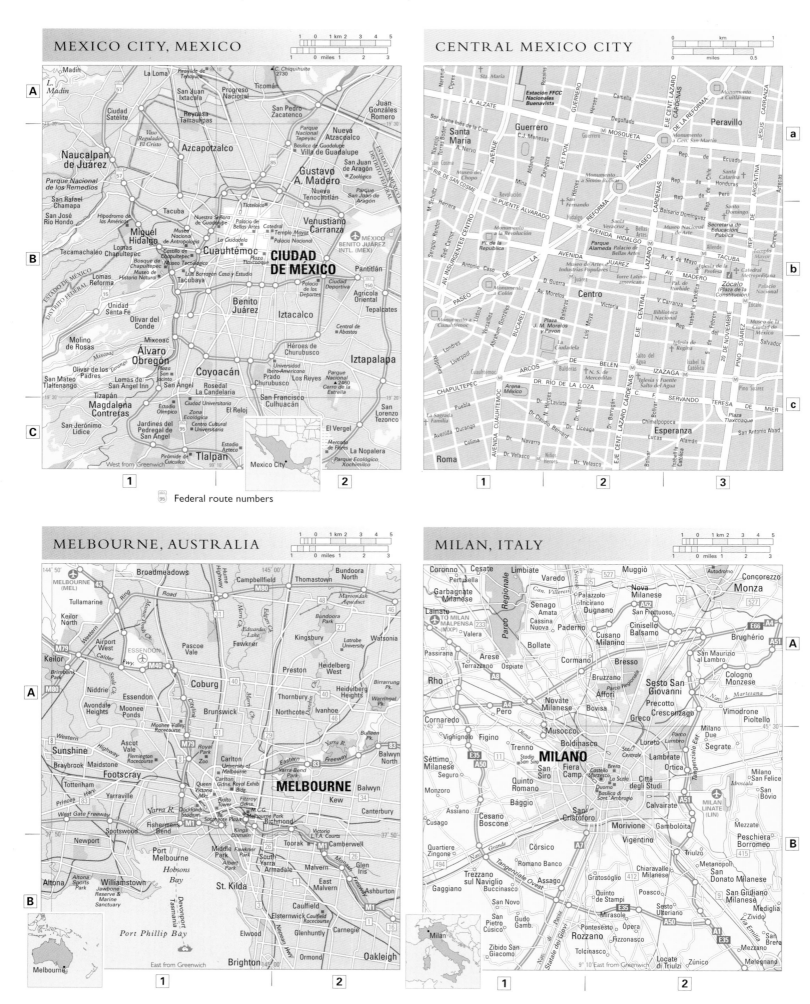

MEXICO CITY, MEXICO

Federal route numbers

CENTRAL MEXICO CITY

MELBOURNE, AUSTRALIA

MILAN, ITALY

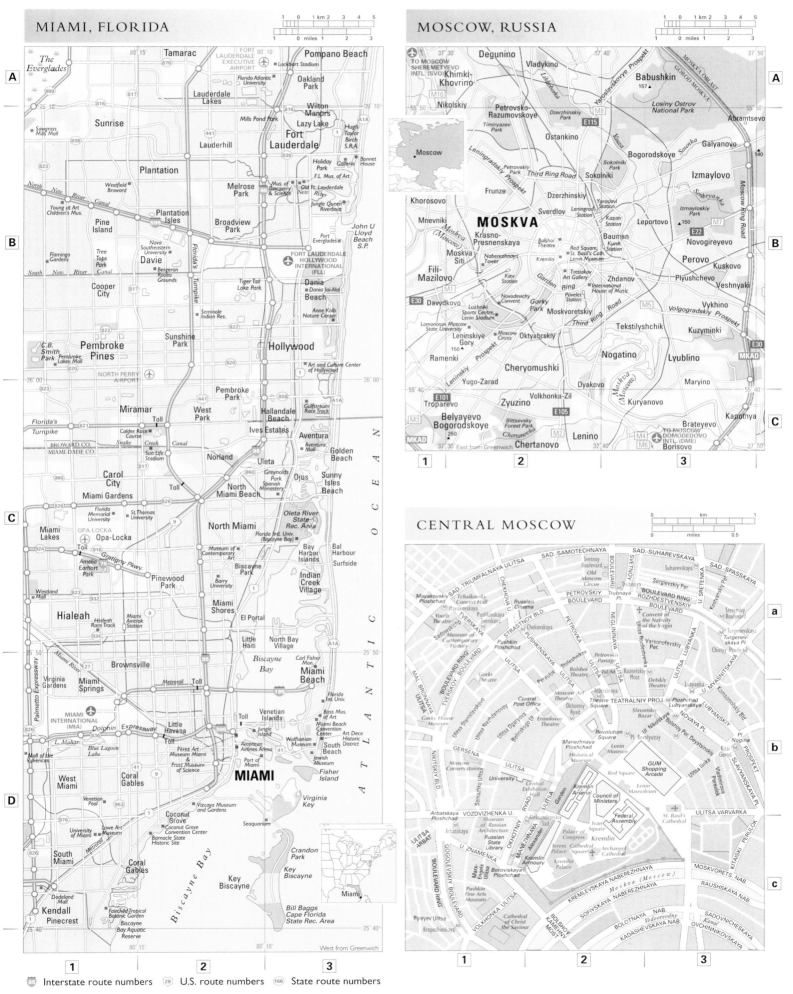

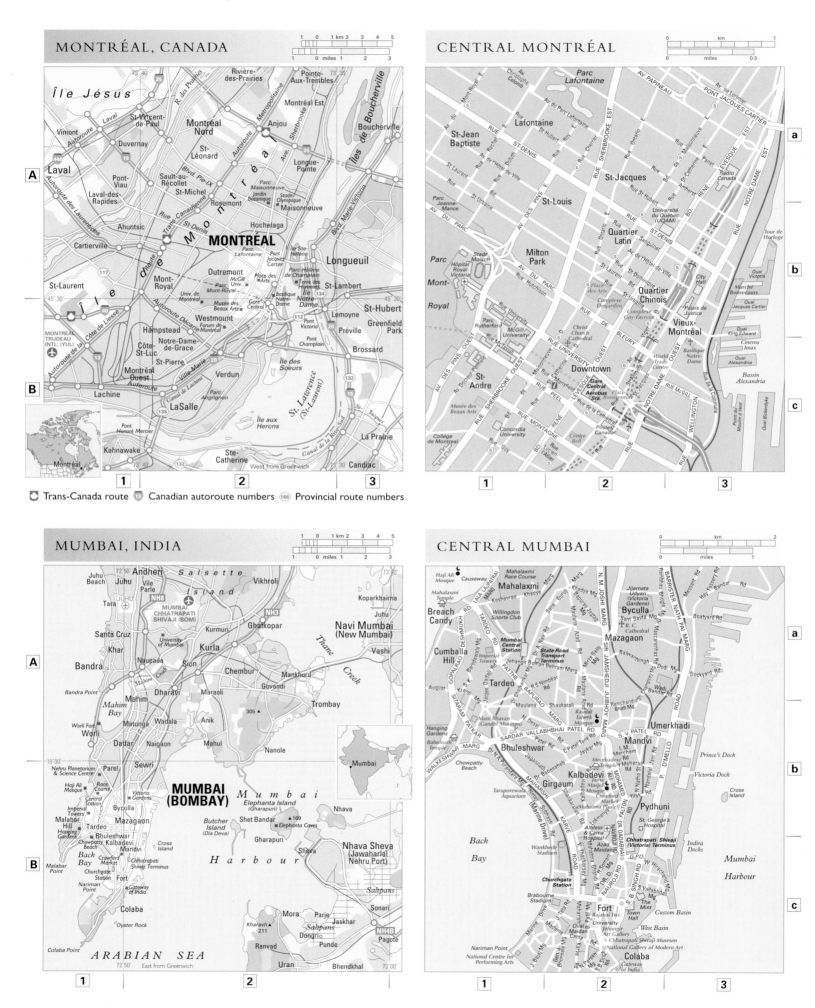

MONTRÉAL, CANADA

Trans-Canada route Canadian autoroute numbers Provincial route numbers

CENTRAL MONTRÉAL

MUMBAI, INDIA

CENTRAL MUMBAI

MUNICH, GERMANY

CENTRAL MUNICH

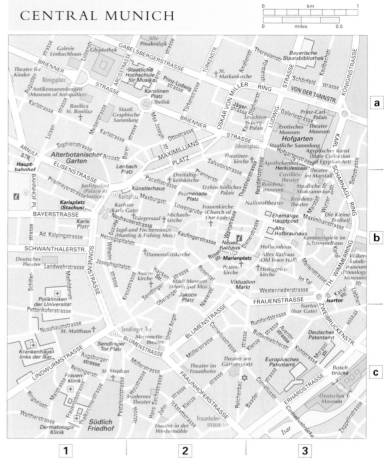

NEW ORLEANS, LOUISIANA

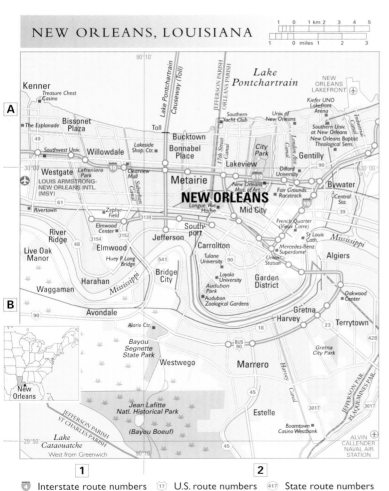

CENTRAL NEW ORLEANS

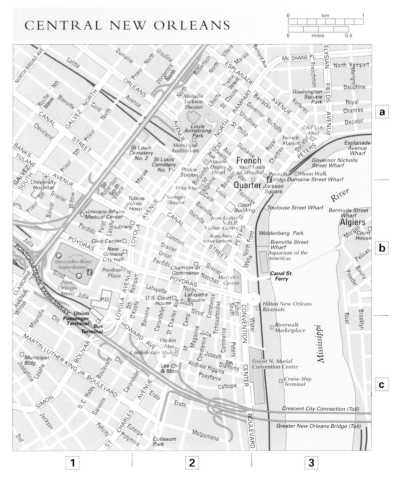

Interstate route numbers   U.S. route numbers   State route numbers

COPYRIGHT PHILIP'S

NEW YORK, NEW YORK

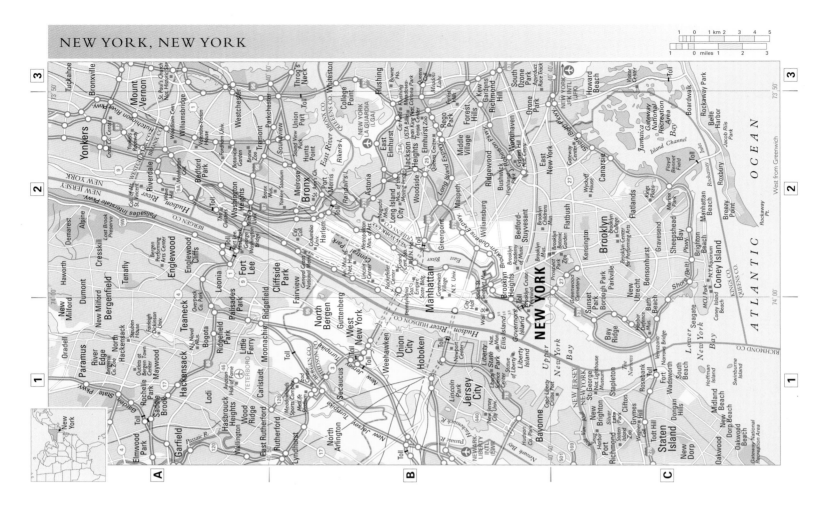

CENTRAL NEW YORK

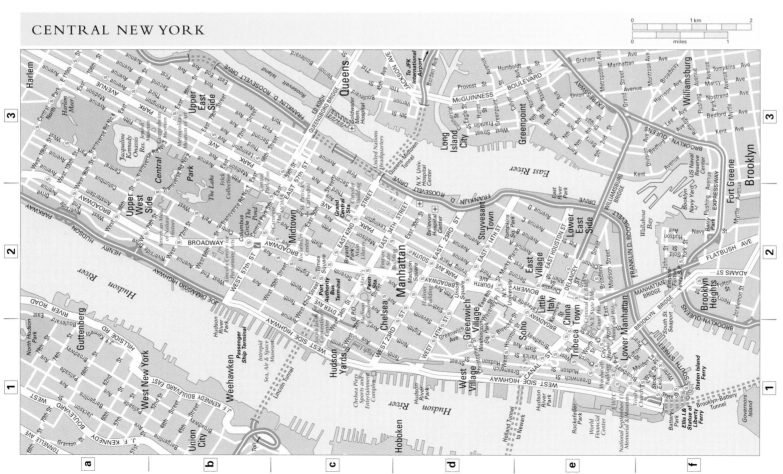

ORLANDO, FLORIDA

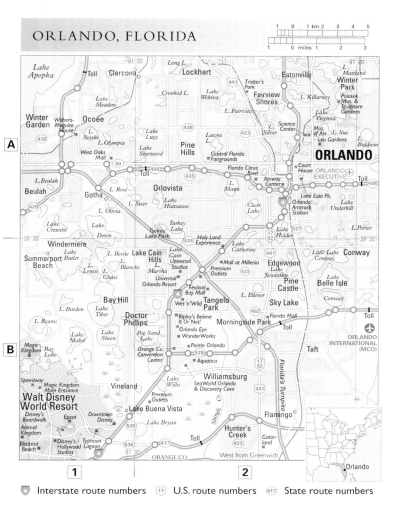

Interstate route numbers · U.S. route numbers · State route numbers

OSAKA, JAPAN

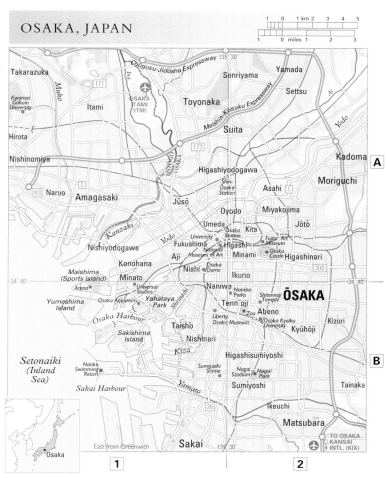

OSLO, NORWAY

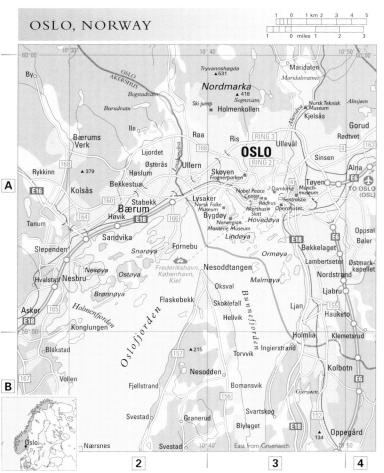

CENTRAL OSLO

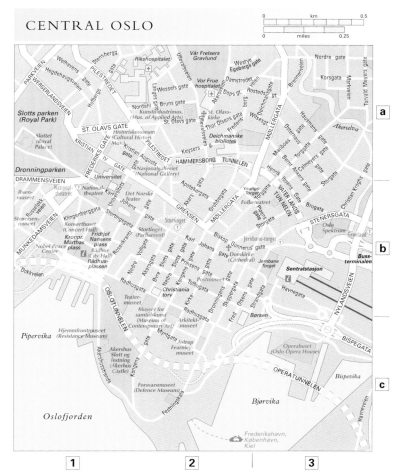

COPYRIGHT PHILIP'S

PARIS, FRANCE

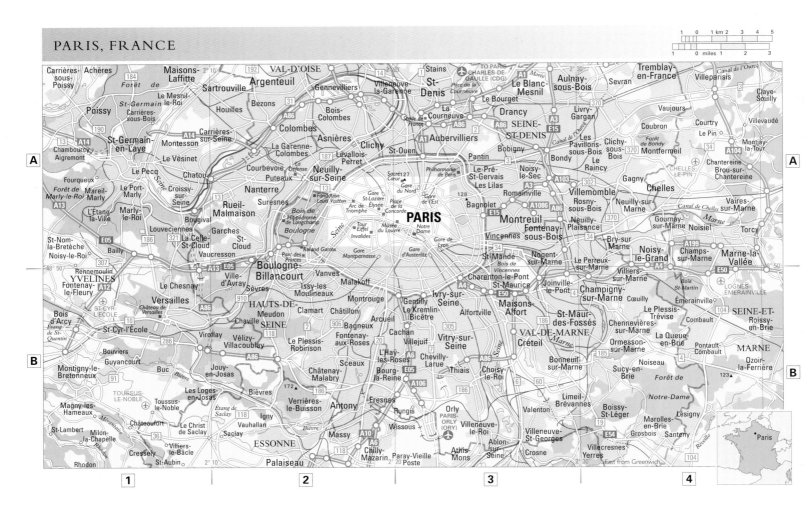

CENTRAL PARIS

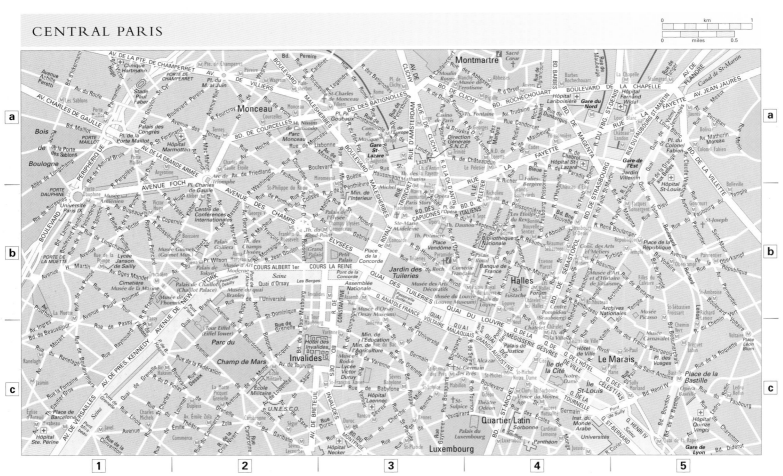

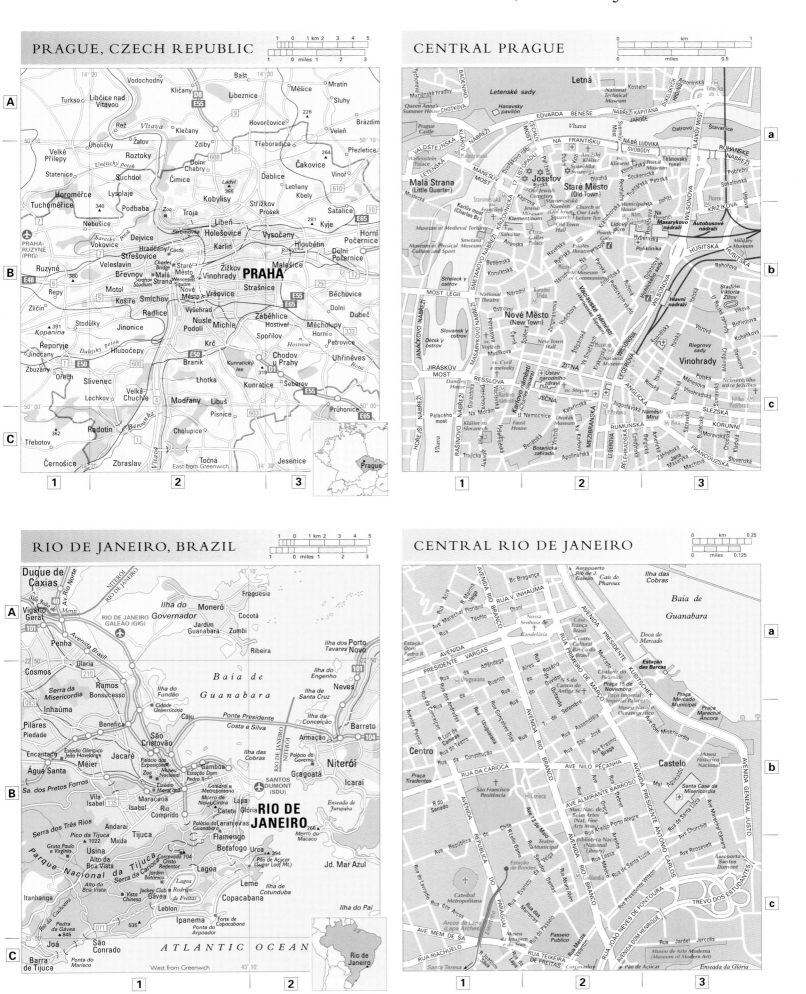

PRAGUE, CZECH REPUBLIC

0   1 km 2   3   4   5
1   0 miles 1   2   3

Vodochodny
Turkso
Libčice nad Vltavou
Kličany
Bašt
Mratín
Libeznice
Měšice
Sluhy
Rež
Vltava
Klečany
Hovorčovice
Veleň
Brázdim
Velké Přílepy
Žalov
Zdiby
Třeboradice
Statenice
Únětický potok
Dolní Chabry
Čakovice
Vinoř
Suchdol
Čimice
Ládví
Letňany
Kbely
Horoměřice
Lysolaje
Podbaba
Kobylisy
Satalice
Nebušice
Zoo
Troja
Libeň
Střížkov
Prosek
Kyje
Horní Počernice
Dejvice
Holešovice
Vysočany
Hloubětín
Dolní Počernice
Vokovice
Střešovice
Karlín
Maleśice
Veleslavín
Břevnov
Žižkov
Vinohrady
PRAHA
Motol
Malá Strana
Vršovice
Strašnice
Běchovice
Košíře
Smíchov
Nové Město
Dubeč
Radlice
Vyšehrad
Záběhlice
Dolní
Nusle
Michle
Hostivař
Měcholupy
Stodůlky
Jinonice
Podolí
Spořilov
Hostivař
Petrovice
Řeporyje
Hlubočepy
Krč
Braník
Kunratický les
Chodov u Prahy
Uhříněves
Zbuzany
Orech
Slivenec
Lhotka
Kunratice
Šeberov
Lochkov
Velká-Chuchle
Modřany
Libuš
Písnice
Průhonice
Radotín
Černošice
Zbraslav
Vltava
Točná
Jesenice

CENTRAL PRAGUE

0   km   1
0   miles   0.5

Letná
Malá Strana (Little Quarter)
Josefov
Staré Město (Old Town)
Nové Město (New Town)
Vinohrady

RIO DE JANEIRO, BRAZIL

0   1 km 2   3   4   5
1   0 miles 1   2   3

Duque de Caxias
Vigário Geral
Penha
Cosmos
Olaria
RIO DE JANEIRO GALEÃO (GIG)
Ilha do Governador
Moneró
Cocotá
Jardim Guanabara
Zumbi
Ribeira
Freguesia
Porto Novo
Ilha dos Tavares
Baía de Guanabara
Ramos
Bonsucesso
Ilha do Fundão
Ilha do Engenho
Neves
Ilha de Santa Cruz
Inhaúma
Cidade Universitária
Caju
Ilha da Conceição
Barreto
Pilares
Piedade
Benefica
Ponte Presidente Costa e Silva
São Cristóvão
Ilha das Cobras
Palácio do Governo
Niterói
Encantado
Jacaré
Gamboa
Gragoatá
Água Santa
Méier
Zoo
Estação Dom Pedro II
Icaraí
Vila Isabel
Maracanã
Catedral Metropolitana
Lapa
RIO DE JANEIRO
Andaraí
Tijuca
Rio Comprido
Flamengo
Botafogo
Urca
Usina
Corcovado
Redentor
Lagoa
Pão de Açúcar (Sugar Loaf Mt.)
Jd. Mar Azul
Itanhanga
Gávea
Leme
Copacabana
Ipanema
Leblon
Joá
São Conrado
Barra de Tijuca
ATLANTIC OCEAN

CENTRAL RIO DE JANEIRO

0   km   0.25
0   miles   0.125

Aeroporto Rio de J. Galeão
Ilha das Cobras
Baía de Guanabara
Centro
Castelo

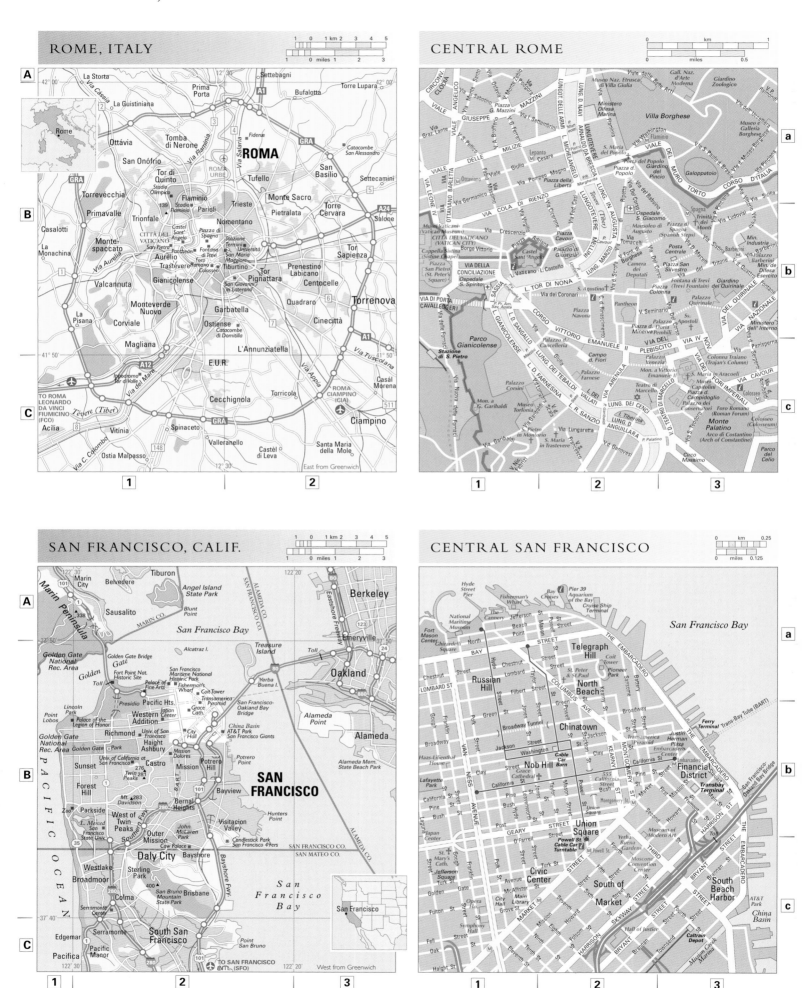

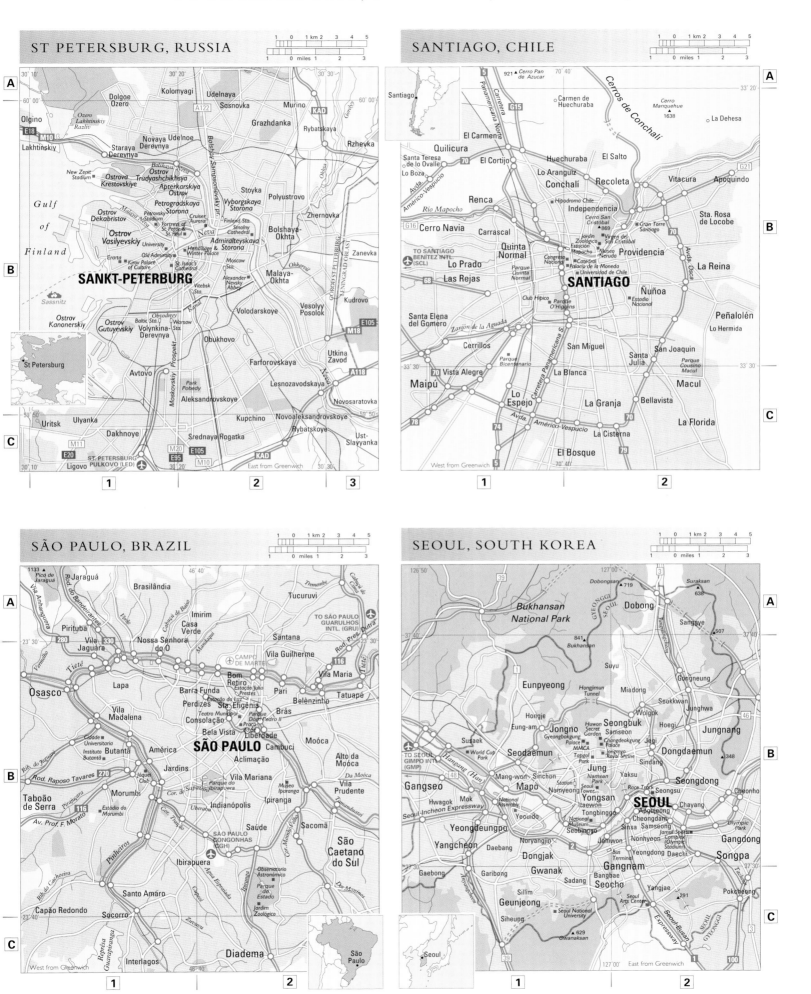

ST PETERSBURG, RUSSIA

SANTIAGO, CHILE

SÃO PAULO, BRAZIL

SEOUL, SOUTH KOREA

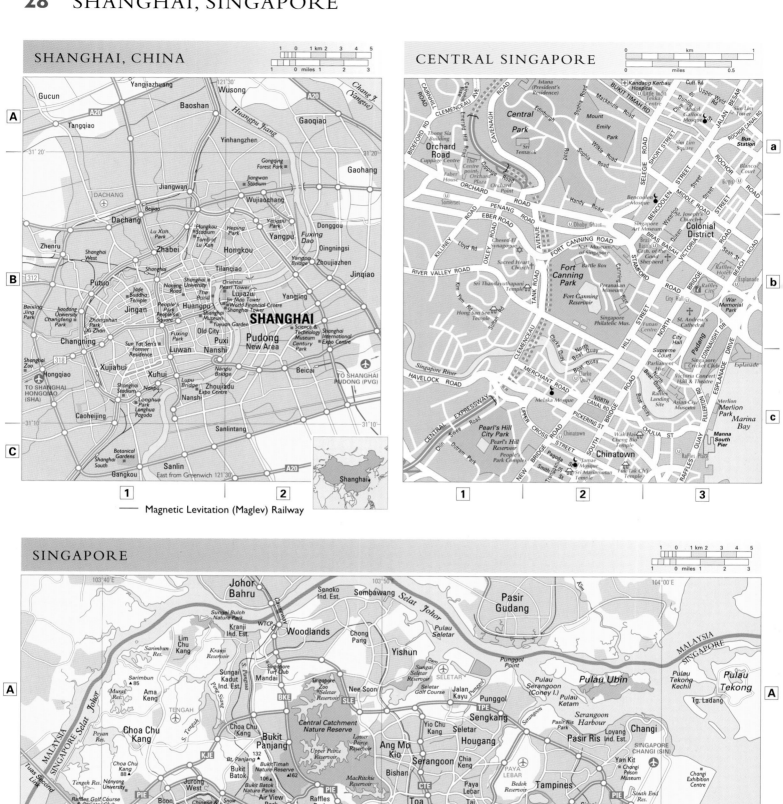

SHANGHAI, CHINA

— Magnetic Levitation (Maglev) Railway

CENTRAL SINGAPORE

SINGAPORE

STOCKHOLM, SWEDEN

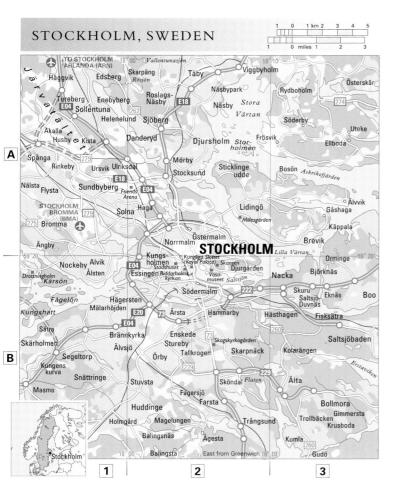

CENTRAL STOCKHOLM

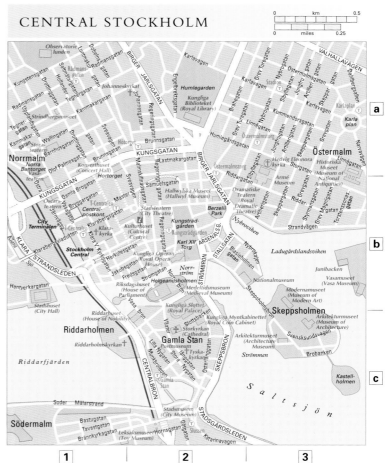

SYDNEY, AUSTRALIA

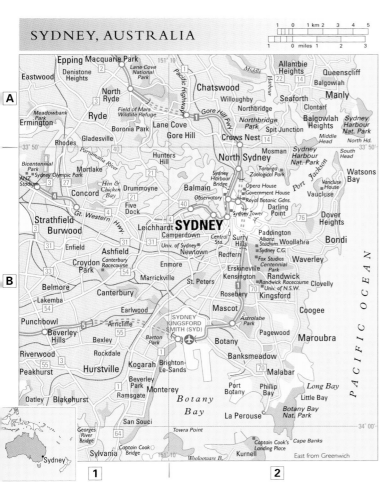

CENTRAL SYDNEY

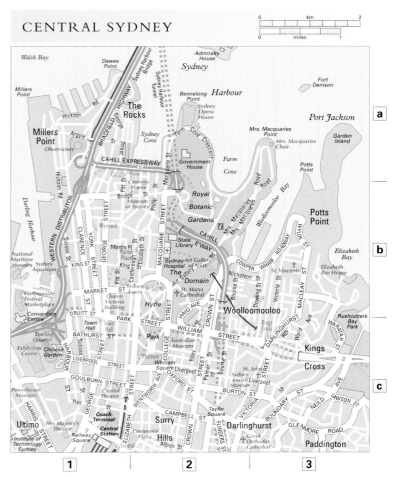

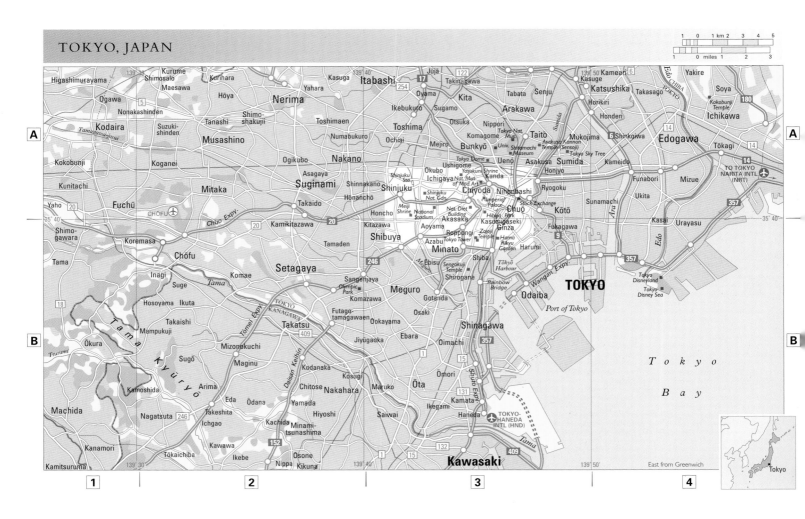

TOKYO, JAPAN

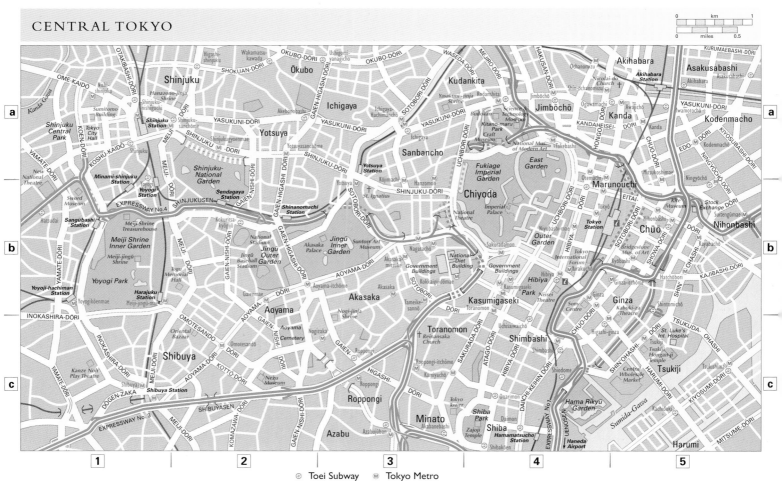

CENTRAL TOKYO

Ⓢ Toei Subway   Ⓜ Tokyo Metro

TEHRAN, IRAN

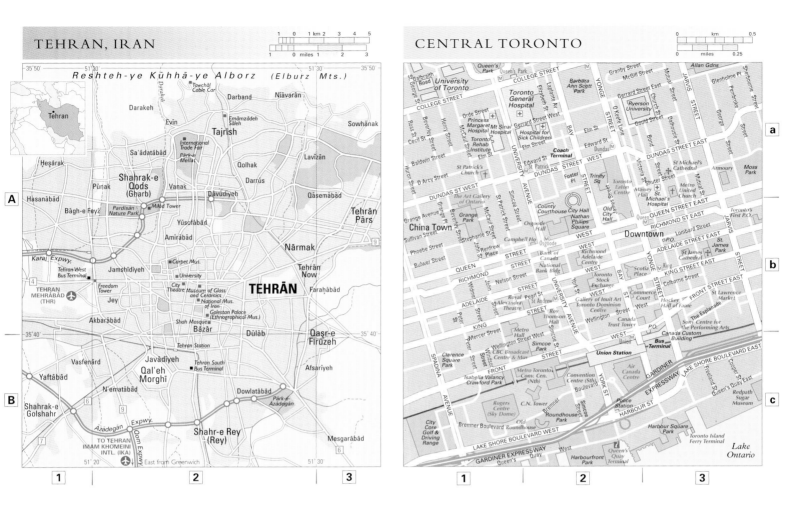

CENTRAL TORONTO

TORONTO, CANADA

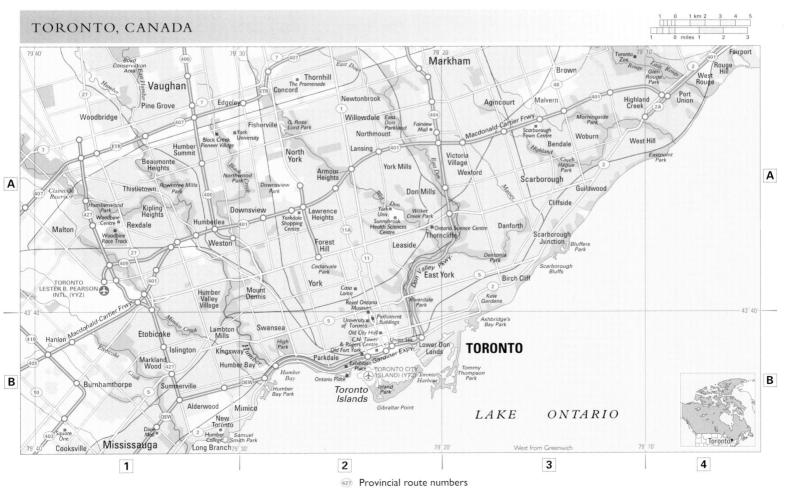

(427) Provincial route numbers

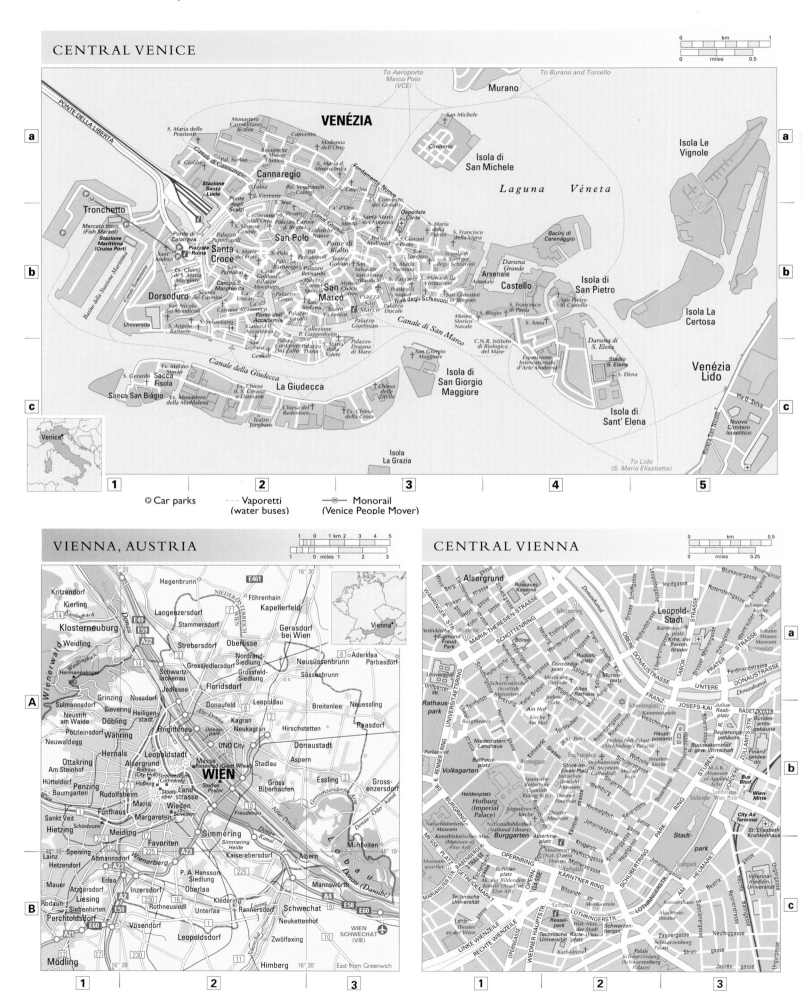

WARSAW, POLAND

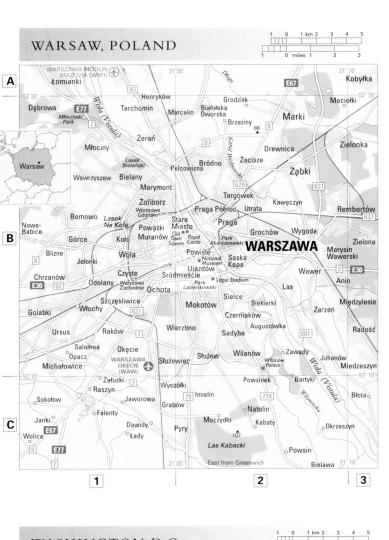

CENTRAL WARSAW

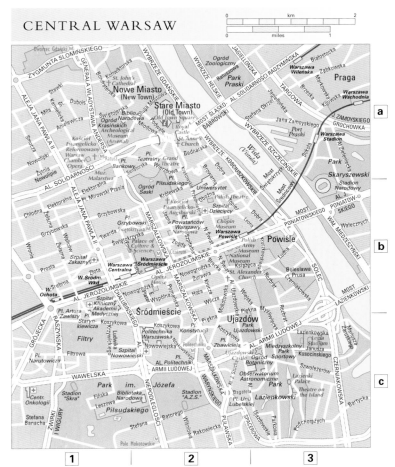

WASHINGTON D.C.

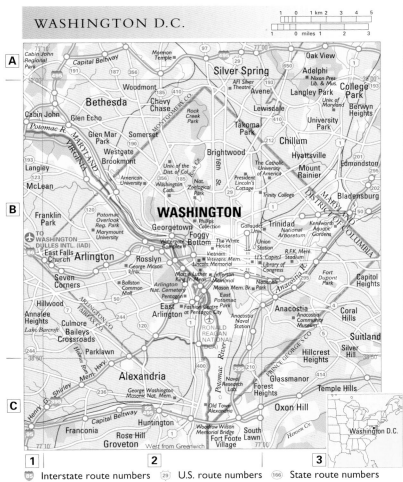

CENTRAL WASHINGTON

Interstate route numbers   U.S. route numbers   State route numbers

INDEX TO CITY MAPS

The index contains the names of all the principal places and features shown on the City Maps. Each name is followed by an additional entry in italics giving the name of the City Map within which it is located.

The number in bold type which follows each name refers to the number of the City Map page where that feature or place will be found.

The letter and figure which are immediately after the page number give the grid square on the map within which the feature or place is situated.

The letter represents the latitude and the figure the longitude. The full geographic reference is provided in the border of the City Maps.

The location given is the centre of the city, suburb or feature and is not necessarily the name. Rivers, canals and roads are indexed to their name. Rivers carry the symbol ➔ after their name.

An explanation of the alphabetical order rules and a list of the abbreviations used are to be found at the beginning of the World Map Index.

A

A.N.Z. Stadium *Sydney* **29** B1
Aalām *Baghdad* **3** B2
Aalsmeer *Amsterdam* **2** B1
Abbey Wood *London* **15** B4
Abcoude *Amsterdam* **2** B2
Âbdin *Cairo* **7** A2
Abeno *Osaka* **23** B2
Aberdeen *Hong Kong* **12** B2
Aberdeen Country Park △
Hong Kong **12** B2
Aberdour *Edinburgh* **11** A2
Aberdour Castle *Edinburgh* **11** A2
Abfanggraben ➔ *Munich* **21** A3
Ablon-sur-Seine *Paris* **24** B3
Abramtsevo *Moscow* **19** B3
Abu Dis *Jerusalem* **13** B2
Abû en Numrus *Cairo* **7** B2
Abu Ghosh *Jerusalem* **13** B1
Abu Hail *Dubai* **9** A2
Acassuso *Buenos Aires* **7** A2
Achères *Paris* **24** A1
Acilia *Rome* **26** C1
Aclimação *São Paulo* **27** B2
Acropolis *Athens* **2** B2
Acton *London* **15** A2
Açúcar, Pão de
Rio de Janeiro **25** B2
Ada Beja *Lisbon* **16** A1
Adamastra Channel
Hong Kong **12** A2
Adams Park *Atlanta* **3** B2
Addiscombe *London* **15** B3
Adelphi *Washington* **33** A3
Aderklaa *Vienna* **31** A2
Adler Planetarium *Chicago* **9** B3
Admiralteyskaya Storona
St. Petersburg **27** B2
Áffori *Milan* **18** A2
Aflandshage *Copenhagen* **8** B3
Afsarîyeh *Tehran* **31** B2
Agboyi Cr. ➔ *Lagos* **14** A2
Ágerup *Copenhagen* **8** A1
Ágesta *Stockholm* **29** B2
Aghia Marina *Athens* **2** C3
Aghia Paraskevi *Athens* **2** B2
Aghios Dimitrios *Athens* **2** B2
Aghios Ioannis Rendis
Athens **2** B2
Agincourt *Toronto* **31** A3
Agra Canal *Delhi* **10** B2
Agricola Oriental
Mexico City **18** B2
Água Espraiada ➔
São Paulo **27** B2
Agualva-Cacem *Lisbon* **16** A1
Ahrensfelde *Berlin* **5** A4
Ahuntsic *Montreal* **20** A1
Ai ➔ *Osaka* **23** A2
Aigremont *Paris* **24** A1
Air View Park *Singapore* **28** A2
Airport West *Melbourne* **18** A1
Ajegunle *Lagos* **14** B2
Aji *Osaka* **23** A1
Ajuda *Lisbon* **16** A1
Akalla *Stockholm* **29** A1
Akasaka *Tokyo* **30** A3
Akbarābād *Tehran* **31** A2
Akershus Slott *Oslo* **23** A3
Al 'Agamîyah *Baghdad* **3** A2
Al Bada *Dubai* **9** A2
Al Barsha *Dubai* **9** B2
Al Hamriya Port *Dubai* **9** A2
Al Hudaiba *Dubai* **9** B2
Al Jafiliya *Dubai* **9** B2
Al Manara *Dubai* **9** B1
Al Mina *Dubai* **9** B2
Al Nasr *Dubai* **9** B2
Al Quds = Jerusalem
Jerusalem **13** B2
Al Quoz *Dubai* **9** B1
Al Safa *Dubai* **9** B1
Al Satwa *Dubai* **9** B2
Al Sufouh *Dubai* **9** B1
Al Walaja *Jerusalem* **13** B1
Al Wasl *Dubai* **9** B2
Alaguntan *Lagos* **14** B2
Alameda *San Francisco* **26** B3
Alameda Memorial State
Beach Park *San Francisco* **26** B3
Albern *Vienna* **31** B2
Albert Park *Melbourne* **18** B1
Alberton *Johannesburg* **13** B2
Albertslund *Copenhagen* **8** B1
Alcantara *Lisbon* **16** A1
Alcatraz I. *San Francisco* **26** B2
Alcobendas *Madrid* **17** A2
Alcorcón *Madrid* **17** B1
Aldershof *Berlin* **5** B4
Alderwood *Toronto* **31** B1
Aldo Bonzi *Buenos Aires* **7** C1
Aleksandrovskoye
St. Petersburg **27** B2
Alexander Nevsky Abbey
St. Petersburg **27** B2
Alexandra *Johannesburg* **13** A2
Alexandra *Singapore* **28** B2
Alexandria *Washington* **33** C2
Alfortville *Paris* **24** B3
Algés *Lisbon* **16** A1
Algiers *New Orleans* **21** B2
Alhambra *Los Angeles* **16** B4
Alibey ➔ *Istanbul* **12** B1
Alibey Baraji *Istanbul* **12** B1
Alibeyköy *Istanbul* **12** B1
Alimos *Athens* **2** B2
Alipur *Kolkata* **14** B1
Allach *Munich* **21** A1
Allambie Heights *Sydney* **29** A2
Allermuir Hill *Edinburgh* **11** B2

Allianz Arena *Munich* **21** A2
Allston *Boston* **6** A3
Almada *Lisbon* **16** A2
Almagro *Buenos Aires* **7** B2
Almargem do Bispo *Lisbon* **16** A1
Almirante G. Brown,
Parque *Buenos Aires* **7** C2
Almon *Jerusalem* **13** B2
Almond ➔ *Edinburgh* **11** B2
Alna *Oslo* **23** A4
Ainsjoen *Oslo* **23** A4
Alperton *London* **15** A2
Alpine *New York* **22** A2
Alrode *Johannesburg* **13** B2
Alsemberg *Brussels* **6** B1
Alsergrund *Vienna* **32** A2
Alsip *Chicago* **9** C2
Älsten *Stockholm* **29** B1
Älta *Stockholm* **29** B3
Altadena *Los Angeles* **16** A4
Alte-Donau ➔ *Vienna* **32** A2
Alter Finkenkrug *Berlin* **5** A1
Altes Rathaus *Munich* **21** B2
Altglienicke *Berlin* **5** B4
Altlandsberg *Berlin* **5** A5
Altlandsberg Nord *Berlin* **5** A5
Altmannsdorf *Vienna* **32** B1
Alto da Boa Vista
Rio de Janeiro **25** B1
Alto da Moóca *São Paulo* **27** B2
Alto do Pina *Lisbon* **16** A2
Altona *Melbourne* **18** B1
Alvalade *Lisbon* **16** A2
Alvik *Stockholm* **29** B1
Alvin Callendar Naval Air
Station *New Orleans* **21** B2
Älvsjo *Stockholm* **29** B2
Älvvik *Stockholm* **29** A3
Am Hasenbergl *Munich* **21** A2
Am Steinhof *Vienna* **32** A1
Am Wald *Munich* **21** B2
Ama Keng *Singapore* **28** A2
Amadora *Lisbon* **16** A1
Amagasaki *Osaka* **23** A1
Amager *Copenhagen* **8** B3
Amâl Qâdisiya *Baghdad* **3** B2
Amalienborg Slot *Copenhagen* **8** A3
Amata *Milan* **18** A1
Ambelokipi *Athens* **2** B2
Ameixoeira *Lisbon* **16** A1
Amelia Earhart Park *Miami* **19** C1
América *São Paulo* **27** B2
American Univ. *Washington* **33** B2
Amin *Baghdad* **3** B2
Aminadav *Jerusalem* **13** B1
Amîrâbâd *Tehran* **31** A2
Amora *Lisbon* **16** B2
Amoreira *Lisbon* **16** A1
Amper ➔ *Munich* **21** A1
Amstel-Drecht-Kanaal
Amsterdam **2** B2
Amstelveen *Amsterdam* **2** B1
Amsterdam *Amsterdam* **2** A2
Amsterdam **2** B1
Amsterdam ✈ (AMS)
Amsterdam **2** B1
Amsterdam Arena
Amsterdam **2** B2
Amsterdam-Rijnkanaal
Amsterdam **2** B2
Amsterdam Zuidoost
Amsterdam **2** B2
Amsterdamse Bos
Amsterdam **2** B1
Anacostia *Washington* **33** B3
Anacostia ➔ *Washington* **33** B3
Anadoluhisarı *Istanbul* **12** B2
Anadolukavağı *Istanbul* **12** A2
Anata *Jerusalem* **13** B2
Ancol *Jakarta* **12** A1
'Andalus *Baghdad* **3** B1
Andarai *Rio de Janeiro* **25** B1
Anderlecht *Brussels* **6** A1
Anderson Park *Atlanta* **3** B2
Andingmen *Beijing* **4** B2
Ang Mo Kio *Singapore* **28** A3
Ângby *Stockholm* **29** A1
Angel I. *San Francisco* **26** A2
Angel Island State Park ⌒
San Francisco **26** A2
Angke, Kali ➔ *Jakarta* **12** A1
Angyalföld *Budapest* **7** A2
Anik *Mumbai* **20** A2
Anin *Warsaw* **33** B2
Anjou *Montreal* **20** A2
Annalee Heights
Washington **33** B2
Anne Frankhuis *Amsterdam* **2** A2
Antonio Carlos Jobim
Int. ✈ (GIG) *Rio de Janeiro* **25** A1
Antony *Paris* **24** B2
Aoyama *Tokyo* **30** B3
Ap Lei Chau *Hong Kong* **12** B2
Apapa *Lagos* **14** B2
Apapa Quays *Lagos* **14** B2
Apelacão *Lisbon* **16** A2
Apguejeong *Seoul* **27** B2
Apokka, L. *Orlando* **23** A1
Apoquindo *Santiago* **27** B2
Apterkarskiy Ostrov
St. Petersburg **27** B2
Ar Kazimiyah *Baghdad* **3** B1
Ar Ram *Jerusalem* **13** B2
Ara ➔ *Tokyo* **30** A3
Arakawa *Tokyo* **30** A3
Arany-hegyi-patak ➔
Budapest **7** A2
Aravaca *Madrid* **17** B1
Arbataash *Baghdad* **3** B1
Arc de Triomphe *Paris* **24** A2
Arcadia *Los Angeles* **16** B4
Arcueil *Paris* **24** B2
Arese *Milan* **18** A1
Arganzuela *Madrid* **17** B1

Argenteuil *Paris* **24** A2
Argiroupoli *Athens* **2** B2
Arima *Tokyo* **30** B2
Arlanda, Stockholm ✈
(ARN) *Stockholm* **29** A1
Arlington *Boston* **6** A1
Arlington *Washington* **33** B2
Arlington Heights *Boston* **6** A1
Arlington Nat. Cemetery
Washington **33** B2
Armação *Rio de Janeiro* **25** B2
Armadale *Melbourne* **18** B2
Armour Heights *Toronto* **31** A2
Arncliffe *Sydney* **29** B1
Arnold Arboretum *Boston* **6** B2
Árpádföld *Budapest* **7** A3
Arrentela *Lisbon* **16** B2
Arroyo Seco Park
Los Angeles **16** B3
Årsta *Stockholm* **29** B2
Artane *Dublin* **10** A2
Artas *Jerusalem* **13** B2
Arthur's Seat *Edinburgh* **11** B3
Arts, Place des *Montreal* **20** A2
As Shawawra *Jerusalem* **13** B2
Asagaya *Tokyo* **30** A2
Asahi *Osaka* **23** A2
Asakusa *Tokyo* **30** A3
Asati *Kolkata* **14** B1
Aschheim *Munich* **21** A3
Ascot Vale *Melbourne* **18** A1
Ashbridge's Bay Park
Toronto **31** B3
Ashburn *Chicago* **9** C2
Ashburton *Melbourne* **18** B2
Ashfield *Sydney* **29** B1
Ashford *London* **15** B1
Ashtown *Dublin* **10** A2
AsiaWorld-Expo *Hong Kong* **12** B1
Askisto *Helsinki* **31** B1
Askrikefjärden *Stockholm* **29** A3
Asnières *Paris* **24** A2
Aspern *Vienna* **32** A2
Assago *Milan* **18** B1
Assendelft *Amsterdam* **2** A1
Assiano *Milan* **18** B1
Astoria *New York* **22** B2
Astrolabe Park *Sydney* **29** B2
Atarot *Jerusalem* **13** B2
Atarot ✈ (JRS) *Jerusalem* **13** A2
Atghara *Kolkata* **14** B2
Athens = Athina *Athens* **2** B2
Athina *Athens* **2** B2
Athina ✈ (ATH) *Athens* **2** A3
Athinai = Athina *Athens* **2** B2
Athis-Mons *Paris* **24** B3
Athlone *Cape Town* **8** A2
Atholl *Johannesburg* **13** A2
Atiffya *Baghdad* **3** A2
Atisalen *Istanbul* **12** B1
Atlanta *Atlanta* **3** B2
Atlanta Hartsfield-Jackson
Int. ✈ (ATL) *Atlanta* **3** C2
Atlanta History Center
Atlanta **3** B2
Atlanta Zoo *Atlanta* **3** B2
Atomium *Brussels* **6** A2
Attiki *Athens* **2** B2
Atzgersdorf *Vienna* **32** B1
Aubervilliers *Paris* **24** A3
Aubing *Munich* **21** B1
Auburndale *Boston* **6** A1
Auchendinny *Edinburgh* **11** B2
Auckland Park
Johannesburg **13** B2
Auderghem *Brussels* **6** B2
Audubon Park *New Orleans* **21** B2
Augustówka *Warsaw* **33** B2
Aulnay-sous-Bois *Paris* **24** A3
Aurelio *Rome* **26** B1
Ausín *Paris* **24** A1
Austerlitz, Gare d' *Paris* **24** A3
Austin *Chicago* **9** B2
Avedøre *Copenhagen* **8** B2
Avellaneda *Buenos Aires* **7** C2
Avenel *Washington* **33** B1
Aventura *Miami* **19** C3
Aviva Stadium *Dublin* **10** A2
Avondale *Chicago* **9** B2
Avondale *New Orleans* **21** B1
Avondale Heights
Melbourne **18** A1
Avtovo *St. Petersburg* **27** B1
Ayazağa *Istanbul* **12** B1
Ayer Chawan, Pulau
Singapore **28** B2
Ayer Merbau, Pulau
Singapore **28** B2
Azabu *Tokyo* **30** B3
Azcapotzalco *Mexico City* **18** B1
Azteca, Estadia *Mexico City* **18** C2
Azucar, Cerro Pan de
Santiago **27** A1

B

Baambrugge *Amsterdam* **2** B2
Baba Channel *Karachi* **13** B1
Baba I. *Karachi* **13** B1
Babarpur *Delhi* **10** A2
Babushkin *Moscow* **19** A3
Back B. *Mumbai* **20** B1
Baclaran *Manila* **17** B2
Bacoor *Manila* **17** C1
Bacoor B. *Manila* **17** C1
Badalona *Barcelona* **4** A2
Badhoevedorp *Amsterdam* **2** A1
Badli *Delhi* **10** A1
Bägçlar *Istanbul* **12** B1
Bâggio *Milan* **18** B1
Bağcılar *Istanbul* **12** B1
Bâgh-e-Feyz *Tehran* **31** A1

Baghdâd *Baghdad* **3** A2
Baghdad Int. ✈ (BGW)
Baghdad **3** B1
Bagmari *Kolkata* **14** B2
Bagneux *Paris* **24** B2
Bagnolet *Paris* **24** A3
Bagsværd *Copenhagen* **8** A2
Bagsværd So *Copenhagen* **8** A2
Baguiati *Kolkata* **14** B2
Bagumbayan *Manila* **17** C2
Baha'i Temple *Chicago* **9** A2
Bahçeköy *Istanbul* **12** A1
Bahçehevler *Istanbul* **12** B1
Bahtîm *Cairo* **7** A2
Baihedong *Guangzhou* **11** B2
Baile Átha Cliath = Dublin
Dublin **10** A2
Baileys Crossroads
Washington **33** B2
Bailly *Paris* **24** A1
Bairro Lopes *Lisbon* **16** A2
Baisha *Guangzhou* **11** B2
Baiyun *Guangzhou* **11** A2
Baiyun Mountain Scenic
Area ⌒ *Guangzhou* **11** A2
Bakrköy *Istanbul* **12** C1
Bal Harbor *Miami* **19** C3
Balara *Manila* **17** B2
Baldia *Karachi* **13** B1
Baldoyle *Dublin* **10** A3
Baldwin, L. *Orlando* **23** A2
Baldwin Hills *Los Angeles* **16** B2
Baldwin Hills Res.
Los Angeles **16** B2
Balgowlah *Sydney* **29** A2
Balgowlah Heights *Sydney* **29** A2
Balham *London* **15** B3
Bali *Kolkata* **14** B1
Baliganja *Kolkata* **14** B2
Balingsnäs *Stockholm* **29** B2
Balingsta *Stockholm* **29** B2
Balintawak *Manila* **17** B1
Ballerup *Copenhagen* **8** A2
Ballinteer *Dublin* **10** B2
Ballyboden *Dublin* **10** B2
Ballybrack *Dublin* **10** B3
Ballyfermot *Dublin* **10** A1
Ballymorefinn Hill *Dublin* **10** B1
Ballymun *Dublin* **10** A2
Balmain *Sydney* **29** B2
Baluhati *Kolkata* **14** B1
Balvanera *Buenos Aires* **7** B2
Balwyn *Melbourne* **18** A2
Balwyn North *Melbourne* **18** A2
Banana Island *Lagos* **14** B2
Banática *Lisbon* **16** A1
Bandra *Mumbai* **20** A1
Bandra Pt. *Mumbai* **20** A1
Bang Kapi *Bangkok* **3** B2
Bang Na *Bangkok* **3** B2
Bangae *Seoul* **27** C1
Bangkhen *Bangkok* **3** A2
Bangkok *Bangkok* **3** B2
Bangkok Don Muang
Int. ✈ (BKK) *Bangkok* **3** A2
Bangkok Noi *Bangkok* **3** B1
Bangkok Yai *Bangkok* **3** B1
Banglo *Kolkata* **14** B1
Bangrak *Bangkok* **3** B2
Bangsu *Bangkok* **3** B2
Banks, C. *Sydney* **29** B2
Banksmeadow *Sydney* **29** B2
Banstala *Kolkata* **14** B2
Bantra *Kolkata* **14** B1
Baoshan *Shanghai* **28** A1
Bar Giyora *Jerusalem* **13** B1
Barahanagar *Kolkata* **14** B2
Barajas *Madrid* **17** B2
Barajas, Madrid ✈ (MAD)
Madrid **17** B2
Barakpur *Kolkata* **14** B2
Barcarena *Lisbon* **16** A1
Barcarena, Rib. de ➔
Lisbon **16** A1
Barcelona *Barcelona* **4** A2
Barcelona, El Prat ✈
(BCN) *Barcelona* **4** B1
Barcroft, L. *Washington* **33** B2
Barking *London* **15** A4
Barkingside *London* **15** A4
Barnes *London* **15** B2
Barnet *London* **15** A2
Barra Andai *Karachi* **13** B2
Barra Funda *São Paulo* **27** B2
Barracas *Buenos Aires* **7** B2
Barrackpur = Barakpur
Kolkata **14** B2
Barranco *Lima* **14** B2
Barreiro *Lisbon* **16** B2
Barreto *Rio de Janeiro* **25** B2
Bartala *Kolkata* **14** B2
Barton Park *Sydney* **29** B2
Bartyki *Warsaw* **33** C2
Basus *Cairo* **7** A2
Batanagar *Kolkata* **14** B1
Bath Beach *New York* **22** C2
Bath I. *Karachi* **13** B2
Batir *Jerusalem* **13** B1
Batok, Bukit *Singapore* **28** A2
Battersea *London* **15** B3
Bauman *Moscow* **19** B3
Baumgarten *Vienna* **32** A1
Bay, L. *Orlando* **23** B1
Bay Harbor Islands *Miami* **19** C3
Bay Hill *Orlando* **23** B1
Bay Ridge *New York* **22** C1
Bayit Va-Gan *Jerusalem* **13** B2
Bayonne *New York* **22** B1
Bayou Boeuf *New Orleans* **21** B1
Bayou Segnette State
Park ⌒ *New Orleans* **21** B1
Bayrampaşa *Istanbul* **12** B1
Bayshore *San Francisco* **26** B2

Bayt Lahm *Jerusalem* **13** B2
Bayview *San Francisco* **26** B2
Bâzâr *Tehran* **31** A2
Beacon Hill *Hong Kong* **12** A3
Beato *Lisbon* **16** A2
Beaumont *Dublin* **10** A2
Beaumonte Heights *Toronto* **31** A1
Bebek *Istanbul* **12** B2
Beckenham *London* **15** B3
Beckton *London* **15** A4
Becontree *London* **15** A4
Beddington Corner *London* **15** B3
Bedford *Boston* **6** A1
Bedford Park *Chicago* **9** C2
Bedford Park *New York* **22** A2
Bedford Stuyvesant
New York **22** B2
Bedford View *Johannesburg* **13** B2
Bedok *Singapore* **28** B3
Bedok, Res. *Singapore* **28** A3
Beersel *Brussels* **6** B1
Behala *Kolkata* **14** B1
Bei Hai *Beijing* **4** B2
Beicai *Shanghai* **28** B2
Beijing *Beijing* **4** B1
Beit Duqu *Jerusalem* **13** A1
Beit Ghur at-Taht *Jerusalem* **13** A1
Beit Ghur el-Fawqa
Jerusalem **13** A1
Beit Hanina *Jerusalem* **13** B2
Beit Ij'za *Jerusalem* **13** A1
Beit Iksa *Jerusalem* **13** B2
Beit I'nan *Jerusalem* **13** B2
Beit Jala *Jerusalem* **13** B2
Beit Lahm = Bayt Lahm
Jerusalem **13** B2
Beit Liqya *Jerusalem* **13** B1
Beit Nekofa *Jerusalem* **13** B1
Beit Sahur *Jerusalem* **13** B2
Beit Sofafa *Jerusalem* **13** B2
Beit Surik *Jerusalem* **13** B2
Beit Ur al-Fawqa *Jerusalem* **13** A1
Beit Zayit *Jerusalem* **13** B1
Beitaipingzhuan *Beijing* **4** B1
Beitar Ilit *Jerusalem* **13** B1
Beitin *Jerusalem* **13** A2
Beitsun *Guangzhou* **11** B2
Beitunya *Jerusalem* **13** B2
Beixing Jing Park *Shanghai* **28** B1
Birak el Kiyam *Cairo* **7** A1
Békásmegyer *Budapest* **7** A2
Bekkelaget *Oslo* **23** A3
Bekkestua *Oslo* **23** A2
Bel Air *Los Angeles* **16** B2
Bela Vista *São Paulo* **27** B2
Bélanger *Montreal* **20** A1
Belas *Lisbon* **16** A1
Beleghata *Kolkata* **14** B2
Belém *Lisbon* **16** A1
Belém, Torre de *Lisbon* **16** A1
Belénzinho *São Paulo* **27** B2
Belgachiya *Kolkata* **14** B2
Belgharia *Kolkata* **14** B2
Belgrano *Buenos Aires* **7** B2
Bell Los Angeles* **16** C4
Bell Gardens *Los Angeles* **16** C4
Bellavista *Lima* **14** B2
Bellavista *Santiago* **27** C2
Belle Harbor *New York* **22** C2
Bellingham *London* **15** B3
Belmont *Boston* **6** A1
Belmont *London* **15** A2
Belmont Cragin *Chicago* **9** B2
Belmont Harbor *Chicago* **9** B3
Belmore *Sydney* **29** B1
Belur *Kolkata* **14** B1
Belvedere *London* **15** B4
Belvedere *San Francisco* **26** A2
Belvedere Park *Atlanta* **3** B2
Belyayevo Bogorodskoye
Moscow **19** C3
Bemowo *Warsaw* **33** B1
Benaki Museum *Athens* **2** B2
Bendale *Toronto* **31** A3
Benefica *Rio de Janeiro* **25** B1
Benfica *Lisbon* **16** A1
Benitez Int. ✈ (SCL)
Santiago **27** B1
Benito Juárez Int. ✈
(MEX) *Mexico City* **18** B2
Bensonhurst *New York* **22** C2
Berchem-Ste-Agathe
Brussels **6** A1
Berg am Laim *Munich* **21** B2
Bergenfield *New York* **22** A2
Bergham *Munich* **21** B2
Bergvliet *Cape Town* **8** B1
Beri *Barcelona* **4** A1
Berkeley *San Francisco* **26** A3
Berlin *Berlin* **5** A3
Berlin Brandenburg ✈
(BER) *Berlin* **5** B4
Berlin Dom *Berlin* **5** A3
Berlin Tegel ✈ (TXL) *Berlin* **5** B3
Bermondsey *London* **15** B3
Bernabeu, Estadio *Madrid* **17** B1
Bernal Heights
San Francisco **26** B2
Berwick *Chicago* **9** B2
Berwyn *Chicago* **9** B2
Berwyn Heights *Washington* **33** B3
Besiktas *Istanbul* **12** B2
Besòs *Barcelona* **4** A2
Bessie, L. *Orlando* **23** B2
Bet Horon *Jerusalem* **13** A1
Bethesda *Washington* **33** B2
Bethlehem = Bayt Lahm
Jerusalem **13** B2
Bethnal Green *London* **15** A3
Betor *Kolkata* **14** B1
Beulah *Orlando* **23** A1
Beulah, L. *Orlando* **23** A1
Beverley Hills *Sydney* **29** B1
Beverley Park *Sydney* **29** B1

Beverly *Chicago* **9** C3
Beverly Arts Center *Chicago* **9** C2
Beverly Glen *Los Angeles* **16** B2
Beverly Hills *Los Angeles* **16** B2
Beverly Hills -Morgan
Park Historic District
Chicago **9** C2
Bexley *Sydney* **29** B1
Bexley □ *London* **15** B4
Bexleyheath *London* **15** B4
Beykoz *Istanbul* **12** A2
Beylerbeyi *Istanbul* **12** B2
Beyoğlu *Istanbul* **12** B1
Bezons *Paris* **24** A2
Bezuidenhout Park
Johannesburg **13** B2
Bhadrakali *Kolkata* **14** A2
Bhalswa *Delhi* **10** A2
Bhambo Khan Qarmati
Karachi **13** B2
Bhatsala *Kolkata* **14** B1
Bhawanipur *Kolkata* **14** B2
Bhendkhal *Mumbai* **20** B2
Bhit I. *Jerusalem* **13** B1
Bhuleshwar *Mumbai* **20** B1
Bialoleka Dworska *Warsaw* **33** B2
Bialany *Warsaw* **33** B1
Bicentennial Park
Los Angeles **16** B4
Bicentennial Park *Sydney* **29** B1
Bickley *London* **15** B4
Bicutan *Manila* **17** C2
Bidhan Nagar *Kolkata* **14** B2
Bidu *Jerusalem* **13** B1
Bielany *Warsaw* **33** B1
Bielawa *Warsaw* **33** C2
Biesdorf *Berlin* **5** A4
Bièvre ➔ *Paris* **24** B2
Bièvres *Paris* **24** B2
Big Buddha *Hong Kong* **12** B1
Big Sand L. *Orlando* **23** B2
Bijlmermeer *Amsterdam* **2** B2
Bilston *Edinburgh* **11** B2
Binacayan *Manila* **17** C1
Binondo *Manila* **17** B1
Bir Nabala *Jerusalem* **13** A2
Birak el Kiyam *Cairo* **7** A1
Birch Cliff *Toronto* **31** B3
Birkenstein *Berlin* **5** A5
Birkholz *Berlin* **5** A4
Birkholzaue *Berlin* **5** A4
Birrarrung Park *Melbourne* **18** A2
Biscayne Bay Aquatic
Reserve *Miami* **19** E2
Biscayne Park *Miami* **19** C3
Bishop Lavis *Cape Town* **8** A2
Bishopscourt *Cape Town* **8** A1
Bispebjerg *Copenhagen* **8** A3
Bissonet Plaza *New Orleans* **21** B1
Bittersvsky Forest Park
Moscow **19** C2
Björknas *Stockholm* **29** B3
Black Cr. ➔ *Toronto* **31** A2
Black Creek Pioneer
Village *Toronto* **31** A1
Blackfen *London* **15** B4
Blackheath *London* **15** B4
Blackrock *Dublin* **10** B2
Bladensburg *Washington* **33** B3
Blair Village *Atlanta* **3** C2
Blairgowrie *Johannesburg* **13** A2
Blake House *Boston* **6** B3
Blakehurst *Sydney* **29** B1
Blakstad *Oslo* **23** B1
Blanchardstown *Dublin* **10** A1
Blanche, L. *Orlando* **23** A2
Blankenburg *Berlin* **5** A3
Blankenfelde *Berlin* **5** A3
Blizne *Warsaw* **33** B1
Blota *Warsaw* **33** C2
Blue Island *Chicago* **9** D2
Blue Lagoon L. *Miami* **19** D1
Blue Mosque =
Sultanahme Camil
Istanbul **12** B1
Bluebell *Dublin* **10** B1
Bluff Hd. *Hong Kong* **12** B3
Bluffers Park *Toronto* **31** A3
Blumberg *Berlin* **5** A4
Blunt Pt. *San Francisco* **26** A2
Blutenberg *Munich* **21** B1
Blylaget *Oslo* **23** B3
Boa Vista, Alto do
Rio de Janeiro **25** B1
Boardwalk *New York* **22** C2
Boavista *Lisbon* **16** A2
Bobigny *Paris* **24** A3
Bocanegra *Lima* **14** B2
Boedo *Buenos Aires* **7** B2
Bogenhausen *Munich* **21** B2
Bogorodskoye *Moscow* **19** B3
Bogota *New York* **22** A1
Bogstadvatnet *Oslo* **23** A2
Bohnsdorf *Berlin* **5** B4
Bois-Colombes *Paris* **24** A2
Bois-d'Arcy *Paris* **24** B1
Boissy-St-Léger *Paris* **24** B4
Boldinvang *Oslo* **23** A2
Boldmonte *Milan* **18** A1
Boler *Oslo* **23** A4
Bollate *Milan* **18** A1
Bollebeek *Brussels* **6** A1
Bollendorf *Berlin* **5** B3
Bollmora *Stockholm* **29** B3
Boshaya Okhta
St. Petersburg **27** B2
Bolton *Milan* **18** A1
Bom Retiro *São Paulo* **27** B2
Bombay = Mumbai
Mumbai **20** B1
Bondi *Sydney* **29** B2

Bondy *Paris* **24** A3
Bondy, Forêt de *Paris* **24** A4
Bonifacio Monument
Manila **17** B1
Bonnabel Place *New Orleans* **21** A2
Bonneuil-sur-Marne *Paris* **24** B4
Bonnington *Edinburgh* **11** B1
Bonnyrigg and Lasswade
Edinburgh **11** B3
Bonsucesso *Rio de Janeiro* **25** B1
Bonteheuwel *Cape Town* **8** A2
Boo *Stockholm* **29** A3
Booterstown *Dublin* **10** B2
Borisovo *Moscow* **19** C3
Borle *Mumbai* **20** A2
Borola Park *Sydney* **29** B2
Boronia Park *Sydney* **29** A1
Bosmont *Johannesburg* **13** B1
Bosön *Stockholm* **29** A3
Bosporus = İstanbul
Boğazı *Istanbul* **12** B2
Bostancı *Istanbul* **12** C2
Boston *Boston* **6** A2
Boston Common *Boston* **6** A2
Boston Logan Int. ✈ (BOS)
Boston **6** A2
Botafogo *Rio de Janeiro* **25** B1
Botany *Sydney* **29** B2
Botany B. *Sydney* **29** B2
Botany Bay △ *Sydney* **29** B2
Botič ➔ *Prague* **25** B3
Botica Sete *Lisbon* **16** A1
Boucherville *Montreal* **20** A3
Boucherville, Îs. de
Montreal **20** A3
Bougival *Paris* **24** A1
Boulder Pt. *Hong Kong* **12** B2
Boulogne, Bois de *Paris* **24** A2
Boulogne-Billancourt *Paris* **24** B2
Bourg-la-Reine *Paris* **24** B2
Bouviers *Paris* **24** B1
Bovenkerk *Amsterdam* **2** B2
Bovenkerker Polder
Amsterdam **2** B2
Bovisa *Milan* **18** A2
Bow *London* **15** A3
Boyacıköy *Istanbul* **12** B2
Boyd Conservation Area
Toronto **31** A1
Boyle Heights *Los Angeles* **16** B3
Braepark *Edinburgh* **11** B2
Braid *Edinburgh* **11** B2
Bramley *Johannesburg* **13** A2
Brandeis Univ. *Boston* **6** A1
Brandenburger Tor *Berlin* **5** A3
Brani, Pulau *Singapore* **28** B3
Branik *Prague* **25** B2
Brännkyrka *Stockholm* **29** B2
Brás *São Paulo* **27** B2
Brasilândia *São Paulo* **27** A1
Brateyevo *Moscow* **19** C3
Braybrook *Melbourne* **18** A1
Brazdim *Prague* **25** A3
Breakheart Reservation
Boston **6** A2
Brede *Copenhagen* **8** A3
Breezy Point *New York* **22** C2
Breitenlee *Vienna* **32** A3
Breña *Lima* **14** B2
Brent □ *London* **15** A2
Brent Res. *London* **15** A2
Brentford *London* **15** B2
Brentwood *Los Angeles* **16** B2
Brentwood Park *Los Angeles* **16** B2
Brera *Milan* **18** B2
Bresso *Milan* **18** A2
Brevik *Stockholm* **29** A3
Břevnov *Prague* **25** B2
Brickyard, The *Chicago* **9** B2
Bridge City *New Orleans* **21** B1
Bridgeport *Chicago* **9** B3
Bridgetown *Cape Town* **8** A2
Bridgeview *Chicago* **9** C2
Brighton *Boston* **6** A2
Brighton *Melbourne* **18** B1
Brighton Beach *New York* **22** C2
Brighton-Le-Sands *Sydney* **29** B1
Brighton Park *Chicago* **9** C2
Brightwood *Washington* **33** B2
Brigittenau *Vienna* **32** A2
Brimbank Park *Melbourne* **18** A1
Brisbane *San Francisco* **26** B2
Britz *Berlin* **5** B3
Brixton *London* **15** B3
Broadmeadows *Melbourne* **18** A1
Broadmoor *San Francisco* **26** B2
Broadview *Chicago* **9** B1
Broadview Park *Miami* **19** B2
Brockley *London* **15** B3
Bródno *Warsaw* **33** B2
Bródnowski, Kanal *Warsaw* **33** B2
Broek *Amsterdam* **2** B1
Bromley □ *London* **15** B4
Bromley *London* **15** A4
Bromley Common *London* **15** B4
Bromma *Stockholm* **29** A1
Bromma ✈ (BMA)
Stockholm **29** A1
Brøndby Strand *Copenhagen* **8** B2
Brøndbyvester *Copenhagen* **8** B2
Brøndbyøster *Copenhagen* **8** B2
Brøndbysury *London* **15** B4
Brønnøya *Oslo* **23** B2
Brønshøj *Copenhagen* **8** A3
Bronxville *New York* **22** A3
Brookfield Zoo *Chicago* **9** C1
Brookhaven *Atlanta* **3** A2
Brookline *Boston* **6** A3
Brooklyn *Cape Town* **8** A1
Brooklyn *New York* **22** B2
Brooklyn Heights *New York* **22** B2

Brown *Toronto* **31** A3
Brownsville *Miami* **19** D1
Brughério *Milan* **18** A2
Brunswick *Melbourne* **18** A1
Brussegem *Brussels* **6** A1
Brussel *Brussels* **6** A1
Brussel ✈ (BRU) *Brussels* **6** A2
Brussels = Brussel *Brussels* **6** A2
Bruxelles = Brussel *Brussels* **6** A2
Bruzzano *Milan* **18** A2
Bry-sur-Marne *Paris* **24** A4
Bryan, L. *Orlando* **23** B2
Bryanston *Johannesburg* **13** A1
Brzeziny *Warsaw* **33** B2
Bubeneč *Prague* **25** B2
Buc *Paris* **24** B1
Buchenhain *Munich* **21** B1
Buckow *Berlin* **5** B3
Buckhead *Atlanta* **3** A2
Buckingham Palace *London* **15** A3
Buckow *Berlin* **5** B3
Bucktown *New Orleans* **21** A2
Buda *Budapest* **7** A2
Buda Castle =
Budaváripalota *Budapest* **7** A2
Budafok *Budapest* **7** B2
Budaörs *Budapest* **7** B1
Budapest *Budapest* **7** B2
Budapest Ferihegy ✈
(BUD) *Budapest* **7** B2
Budatétény *Budapest* **7** B2
Budaváripalota *Budapest* **7** A2
Buddinge *Copenhagen* **8** A3
Buenos Aires *Buenos Aires* **7** B2
Buenos Aires Ezeiza ✈
(EZE) *Buenos Aires* **7** C1
Bufalotta *Rome* **26** B2
Bugio *Lisbon* **16** B1
Buiksloot *Amsterdam* **2** A2
Buitenveldert *Amsterdam* **2** B2
Buizingen *Brussels* **6** B1
Bukhansan *Seoul* **27** B1
Bukit Batok *Singapore* **28** A2
Bukit Panjang *Singapore* **28** A2
Bukit Panjang Nature
Reserve ⌒ *Singapore* **28** A2
Bukit Timah Nature
Reserve ⌒ *Singapore* **28** A2
Bukum, Pulau *Singapore* **28** B2
Bûlâq *Cairo* **7** A2
Bule *Manila* **17** C2
Bullen Park *Melbourne* **18** A2
Bund, The *Shanghai* **28** B1
Bundoora North *Melbourne* **18** A2
Bundoora Park *Melbourne* **18** A2
Bunker Hill Memorial
Boston **6** A2
Bunker I. *Karachi* **13** B1
Bunkyô *Tokyo* **30** A3
Buona Vista Park *Singapore* **28** B2
Bur Dubai *Dubai* **9** A2
Burbank *Chicago* **9** C2
Burden, L. *Orlando* **23** B1
Burj Al Arab *Dubai* **9** B1
Burj Khalifa *Dubai* **9** B2
Burlington *Boston* **6** A1
Burnham Park *Chicago* **9** C3
Burnham Park Harbor
Chicago **9** B3
Burnhamthorpe *Toronto* **31** B1
Burnt Oak *London* **15** A2
Burntisland *Edinburgh* **11** A2
Burnwynd *Edinburgh* **11** B1
Burqa *Jerusalem* **13** A2
Burtus *Cairo* **7** A1
Burudvatn *Oslo* **23** A2
Burwood *Sydney* **29** B1
Bushwick *New York* **22** B2
Bushy Park *London* **15** B1
Business Bay *Dubai* **9** B2
Butantã *São Paulo* **27** B1
Butcher I. *Mumbai* **20** B2
Butler, L. *Orlando* **23** B1
Büyükdere *Istanbul* **12** B2
Byculla *Mumbai* **20** B2
Bygdøy *Oslo* **23** A3
Bywater *New Orleans* **21** B2

C

C.B.S. Fox Studios
Los Angeles **16** B2
C.N. Tower *Toronto* **31** B2
Caballito *Buenos Aires* **7** B2
Cabin John *Washington* **33** B1
Cabin John Regional
Park ⌒ *Washington* **33** B1
Cabinteely *Dublin* **10** B3
Cabra *Dublin* **10** A2
Cabuçu de Baixo ➔
São Paulo **27** A1
Cabuçu de Cima ➔
São Paulo **27** A2
Cachan *Paris* **24** B2
Cachoeira, Rib. da ➔
São Paulo **27** B2
Cacilhas *Lisbon* **16** A2
Cahuenga Pk. *Los Angeles* **16** B3
Cain, L. *Orlando* **23** B2
Cairo = El Qâhira *Cairo* **7** A2
Cairo ✈ (CAI) *Cairo* **7** A1
Caju *Rio de Janeiro* **25** B1
Calcutta = Kolkata *Kolkata* **14** B2
California Institute of
Technology *Los Angeles* **16** B4
California Univ. of Los Angeles,
Univ. of *Los Angeles* **16** B2
California State Univ.
Los Angeles **16** B3

Callao *Lima* 14 B2
Caloocan *Manila* 17 B1
Calumet, L. *Chicago* 9 C3
Calumet City *Chicago* 9 C3
Calumet Park *Chicago* 9 C3
Calumet Sag Channel → *Chicago* 9 C2
Calvarate *Milan* 18 B2
Camarate *Lisbon* 16 A2
Camaroes *Lisbon* 16 A1
Camberwell *London* 15 B3
Camberwell *Melbourne* 18 B2
Cambridge *Boston* 6 A2
Cambuci *São Paulo* 27 B2
Camden □ *London* 15 A3
Çamlıca *Istanbul* 12 B2
Camp Nou F.C. Barcelona *Barcelona* 4 A1
Camp Springs *Washington* 33 C3
Campamento *Madrid* 17 B1
Campbellfield *Melbourne* 18 A1
Camperdown *Sydney* 29 B1
Campo, Casa de *Madrid* 17 B1
Campo Grando *Lisbon* 16 A2
Campo Pequeño *Lisbon* 16 A2
Campolide *Lisbon* 16 A2
Camps Bay *Cape Town* 8 A1
C'an San Joan *Barcelona* 4 A2
Cañacao B. *Manila* 17 C1
Canarsie *New York* 22 C2
Canary Wharf *London* 15 A3
Candiac *Montreal* 20 B2
Candler-McAfee *Atlanta* 3 B3
Caneças *Lisbon* 16 A1
Canillas *Madrid* 17 B2
Canillejas *Madrid* 17 B2
Canning Town *London* 15 A4
Canteras de Vallecas *Madrid* 17 B2
Canterbury *Melbourne* 18 A2
Canterbury *Sydney* 29 B1
Canton = Guangzhou *Guangzhou* 11 B2
Canton Tower *Guangzhou* 11 B2
Caohejing *Shanghai* 28 B1
Capão Redondo *São Paulo* 27 B1
Caparica *Lisbon* 16 A2
Caparica, Costa da *Lisbon* 16 A2
Cape Flats *Cape Town* 8 B2
Cape Town *Cape Town* 8 A1
Cape Town Int. ✈ (CPT) *Cape Town* 8 B1
Capitol Heights *Washington* 33 B3
Captain Cook Bridge *Sydney* 29 C1
Captain Cook Landing Place Park *Sydney* 29 C2
Capuchos *Lisbon* 16 A1
Carabanchel Alto *Madrid* 17 B1
Carabanchel Bajo *Madrid* 17 B1
Carapachay *Buenos Aires* 7 B1
Caraza *Buenos Aires* 7 C2
Caridad *Manila* 17 C1
Carioca, Sa. da *Rio de Janeiro* 25 B1
Carlstadt *New York* 22 A1
Carlton *Melbourne* 18 A1
Carlton Gardens *Melbourne* 18 A1
Carmen de Huechuraba *Santiago* 27 B1
Carmen de la Legua -Reynosa *Lima* 14 B2
Carnaxide *Lisbon* 16 A1
Carnegie *Melbourne* 18 B2
Carnide *Lisbon* 16 A1
Carol City *Miami* 19 C1
Carollton *New Orleans* 21 B2
Carrascal *Santiago* 27 B1
Carrickmines *Dublin* 10 B3
Carrières-sous-Bois *Paris* 24 A1
Carrières-sous-Poissy *Paris* 24 A1
Carrières-sur-Seine *Paris* 24 A2
Carrigeen B. *Dublin* 10 A3
Cartierville *Montreal* 20 A1
Casa Loma *Toronto* 31 A2
Casa Verde *São Paulo* 27 A1
Casal da Mira *Lisbon* 16 A1
Casál Morena *Madrid* 26 C2
Casalotti *Rome* 26 B1
Cascade Heights *Atlanta* 3 B2
Castél de Leva *Rome* 26 C2
Castél Sant' Angelo *Rome* 26 B1
Castle Peak B. *Hong Kong* 12 A1
Castle Pk. *Hong Kong* 12 A1
Castleknock *Dublin* 10 A2
Castleton Corners *New York* 22 C1
Cataouatche, L. *New Orleans* 21 B1
Catete *Rio de Janeiro* 25 B2
Catford *London* 15 B3
Catherine, L. *Orlando* 23 B2
Caulfield *Melbourne* 18 B2
Cavite *Manila* 17 C1
Caxias *Lisbon* 16 A1
Cebecci *Istanbul* 12 B1
Cecchignola *Rome* 26 C2
Cecilienhof, Schloss *Berlin* 5 B1
Cedar Grove *Atlanta* 3 C3
Cedarvale Park *Toronto* 31 A2
Cempaka Putih *Jakarta* 12 A2
Çengelköy *Istanbul* 12 B2
Cengkareng *Jakarta* 12 A1
Centennial Olympic Park *Atlanta* 3 B2
Centennial Park *Sydney* 29 B2
Center Hill *Atlanta* 3 B2
Centocelle *Rome* 26 B2
Central, Gare *Montreal* 20 B2
Central Park *New York* 22 B2
Century City *Los Angeles* 16 B2
Cerdanyola del Vallès *Barcelona* 4 A1
Cerillos *Santiago* 27 B1
Cerro de la Estrella △ *Mexico City* 18 B2
Cerro de los Angeles *Madrid* 17 C1
Cerro Navia *Santiago* 27 B1
Cesano Boscone *Milan* 18 B1
Cesate *Milan* 18 A1
Cha Kwo Ling *Hong Kong* 12 B2
Chacarrita *Buenos Aires* 7 B2
Chadwell Heath *London* 15 A4
Chai Chee *Singapore* 28 B3
Chai Wan *Hong Kong* 12 B2
Chai Wan Kok *Hong Kong* 12 A1
Chaidari *Athens* 2 A1
Chakdaha *Kolkata* 14 C1
Chalandri *Athens* 2 A2
Chamartin *Madrid* 17 B1
Chamberi *Madrid* 17 B1
Chambourcy *Paris* 24 A1
Champigny-sur-Marne *Paris* 24 B4
Champlain, Pont *Montreal* 20 B2
Champs-Sur-Marne *Paris* 24 A4
Chamrail *Mumbai* 20 A2
Chanakyapuri *Delhi* 10 B2
Chanditala *Kolkata* 14 A1
Changfeng Park *Shanghai* 28 B1
Shanghai = Shanghai *Shanghai* 28 B1
Changning *Shanghai* 28 B1
Changi, Singapore ✈ (SIN) *Singapore* 28 A3
Chantereine *Paris* 24 A4
Chantian *Guangzhou* 11 A2

Chaoyang *Beijing* 4 B2
Chaoyangmen *Beijing* 4 B2
Chapelizod *Dublin* 10 A1
Chapultepec, Bosque de *Mexico City* 18 B1
Chapultepec, Castillo de *Mexico City* 18 B1
Charenton-le-Pont *Paris* 24 B3
Charleroi, Kanal de → *Brussels* 6 B1
Charles Bridge = Karlův most *Prague* 25 B2
Charles Gates Dawes House *Chicago* 9 B2
Charlestown *Boston* 6 A2
Charlottenburg *Berlin* 5 A2
Charlottenburg, Schloss *Berlin* 5 A2
Charlottenlund *Copenhagen* 8 A3
Charlton *London* 15 B4
Charneca *Lisbon* 16 A2
Charneca *Lisbon* 16 B1
Chase, L. *Orlando* 23 A2
Châteaufort *Paris* 24 B1
Châtenay-Malabry *Paris* 24 B2
Chatham *Chicago* 9 C3
Châtillon *Paris* 24 B2
Chatou *Paris* 24 A1
Chatpur *Kolkata* 14 B2
Chatswood *Sydney* 29 A2
Chatuchak *Bangkok* 3 B2
Chatuchak Park *Bangkok* 3 B2
Chauki *Karachi* 13 A1
Chavarria *Lima* 14 B2
Chaville *Paris* 24 B2
Chayang *Seoul* 27 B2
Chek Lap Kok *Hong Kong* 12 B1
Chek Lap Kok ✈ (HKG) *Hong Kong* 12 B1
Chelles *Paris* 24 A4
Chelles, Canal de *Paris* 24 A4
Chelles-le-Pin ✈ *Paris* 24 A4
Chelsea *London* 15 B2
Chelsea *New York* 22 B2
Chembur *Mumbai* 20 A2
Chengshousi *Beijing* 4 C2
Chennevières-sur-Marne *Paris* 24 B4
Cheongdam *Seoul* 27 B2
Cheonho *Seoul* 27 B2
Cheops *Cairo* 7 A1
Chertanovka → *Moscow* 19 C2
Chertanovo *Moscow* 19 B2
Cheryomushki *Moscow* 19 B2
Chestnut Hill *Boston* 6 A1
Cheung Chau *Hong Kong* 12 B1
Cheung Sha *Hong Kong* 12 B1
Cheung Sha Wan *Hong Kong* 12 B1
Cheung Shue Tan *Hong Kong* 12 B1
Cheverly *Washington* 33 B3
Chevilly-Larue *Paris* 24 B2
Cheviot Hills *Los Angeles* 16 B2
Chevy Chase *Washington* 33 B2
Chhatrapati Shivaji Int., Mumbai ✈ (BOM) *Mumbai* 20 A2
Chhatrapati Shivaji Terminus *Mumbai* 20 B2
Chi Ma Wan Pen. *Hong Kong* 12 B1
Chia Keng *Singapore* 28 A3
Chiaravalle Milanese *Milan* 18 B2
Chicago *Chicago* 9 C2
Chicago, Univ. of *Chicago* 9 C3
Chicago Harbor *Chicago* 9 B3
Chicago Lawn *Chicago* 9 C2
Chicago Ridge *Chicago* 9 C2
Chicago River, North Branch → *Chicago* 9 B2
Chicago Sanitary and Ship Canal *Chicago* 9 C2
Chicago State Univ. *Chicago* 9 C3
Chienzui *Guangzhou* 11 A3
Chik Sha *Hong Kong* 12 B3
Child's Hill *London* 15 A2
Chile, Univ. de *Santiago* 27 B2
Chilla Saroda *Delhi* 10 B2
Chillum *Washington* 33 B3
Chilly-Mazarin *Paris* 24 B2
Chinese Theatre *Los Angeles* 16 B2
Chingupota *Kolkata* 14 C1
Chinna Cr. → *Karachi* 13 B2
Chiquihuite, Cerro *Mexico City* 18 A2
Chislehurst *London* 15 B4
Chiswick *London* 15 B2
Chiswick House *London* 15 B2
Chitose *Tokyo* 30 B2
Chitralada Palace *Bangkok* 3 B2
Chiyoda *Tokyo* 30 A3
Choa Chu Kang *Singapore* 28 A2
Chodov u Prahy *Prague* 25 B3
Chōfu *Tokyo* 30 B2
Choisy-le-Roi *Paris* 24 B3
Cholargos *Athens* 2 A2
Cholupice *Prague* 25 C2
Chom Thong *Bangkok* 3 B1
Chong Pang *Singapore* 28 A2
Chongwen *Beijing* 4 B2
Chorrillos *Lima* 14 C2
Chowpatty Beach *Mumbai* 20 B1
Christianshavn *Copenhagen* 8 A3
Chrzanów *Warsaw* 33 B1
Chuen Lung *Hong Kong* 12 A1
Chuk Kok *Hong Kong* 12 A2
Chulalongkom Univ. *Bangkok* 3 B2
Chung Hau *Hong Kong* 12 B2
Chuō *Tokyo* 30 A3
Church End *London* 15 A2
Church of our Lady = Frauenkirche *Munich* 21 B2
Churchtown *Dublin* 10 B2
Ciampino *Rome* 26 B2
Ciampino ✈ (CIA) *Rome* 26 C2
Cicero *Chicago* 9 C2
Cilandak *Jakarta* 12 B1
Cilincing *Jakarta* 12 A2
Ciliwung → *Jakarta* 12 B2
Čímice *Prague* 25 B2
Cinecittà *Rome* 26 B2
Ciniselllo Bálsamo *Milan* 18 A2
Cinkota *Budapest* 7 A3
Cipete *Jakarta* 12 B1
Città degli Studi *Milan* 18 B2
Città del Vaticano = Vatican City ■ *Rome* 26 B1
City, The *London* 15 A3
City Hall = Rådhus *Oslo* 23 A3
City Hall = Stadshuset *Stockholm* 29 B2
City of the Dead *Cairo* 7 A2
City Park *New Orleans* 21 A2
City Terrace *Los Angeles* 16 B3
Ciudad de México *Mexico City* 18 B1
Ciudad Deportivo *Mexico City* 18 B2
Ciudad Fin de Semana *Madrid* 17 B2
Ciudad General Belgrano *Buenos Aires* 7 C1
Ciudad Lineál *Madrid* 17 B2

Ciudad Satélite *Mexico City* 18 A1
Ciudad Universitaria *Buenos Aires* 7 B2
Ciudad Universitaria *Mexico City* 18 C1
Claireville Res. *Toronto* 31 A1
Clamart *Paris* 24 B2
Clapham *London* 15 B3
Clapton *London* 15 A3
Claremont *Cape Town* 8 A1
Clayhall *London* 15 A4
Clear, L. *Orlando* 23 A2
Clear Water B. *Hong Kong* 12 B2
Clermiston *Edinburgh* 11 B2
Clichy *Paris* 24 A2
Clichy-sous-Bois *Paris* 24 A4
Cliffside *London* 15 A4
Cliffside Park *New York* 22 B2
Clifton *Boston* 6 A3
Clifton *Karachi* 13 B2
Clifton Beach *Karachi* 13 B1
Cliftondale *Boston* 6 A3
Cloghran *Dublin* 10 A2
Clonskeagh *Dublin* 10 B2
Clontarf *Dublin* 10 A2
Clontarf *Sydney* 29 A2
Clovelly *Sydney* 29 B2
CNN Center *Atlanta* 3 B2
Cobras, I. das *Rio de Janeiro* 25 B2
Coburg *Melbourne* 18 A1
Coconut Grove *Miami* 19 D2
Cocotá *Rio de Janeiro* 25 A2
Cœuilly *Paris* 24 B4
Coina *Lisbon* 16 B2
Coker *Sydney* 14 B2
Colaba *Mumbai* 20 B1
Colaba Pt. *Mumbai* 20 B1
Colegiales *Buenos Aires* 7 B2
Colindale *London* 15 A2
Colinton *Edinburgh* 11 B2
College Park *Washington* 33 B3
College Point *New York* 22 B2
Collégien *Paris* 24 A4
Collier Row *London* 15 A4
Colliers Wood *London* 15 B2
Colma *San Francisco* 26 B2
Colney Hatch *London* 15 A3
Cologno Monzese *Milan* 18 A2
Colombes *Paris* 24 A2
Colonia Güell *Barcelona* 4 A1
Colosseo *Rome* 26 B1
Colosseum = Colosseo *Rome* 26 B1
Combault *Paris* 24 B4
Comércio, Praça do *Lisbon* 16 A2
Commerce *Los Angeles* 16 B4
Conceição, I. da *Rio de Janeiro* 25 B2
Conchali *Santiago* 27 B2
Concord *Sydney* 29 B1
Concord *Toronto* 31 A1
Concorde, Place de la *Paris* 24 A2
Concorezzo *Milan* 18 A2
Condet *Jakarta* 12 A2
Coney I. = Serangoon, Pulau *Singapore* 28 A3
Coney Island *New York* 22 C2
Congonhas, São Paulo ✈ (CGH) *São Paulo* 27 B2
Conley → *Atlanta* 3 C3
Connaught Place *Delhi* 10 B2
Consolação *São Paulo* 27 B2
Constantia *Cape Town* 8 B1
Constitución *Buenos Aires* 7 B2
Constitution *Atlanta* 3 B2
Conway *Orlando* 23 B2
Conway, L. *Orlando* 23 B2
Coogee *Sydney* 29 B2
Cooksville *Toronto* 31 B1
Coolock *Dublin* 10 A2
Cooper City *Miami* 19 B1
Copacabana *Rio de Janeiro* 25 B2
Copenhagen = København *Copenhagen* 8 A3
Coral Gables *Miami* 19 D1
Coral Hills *Washington* 33 B3
Corcovado, Cristo Redentor *Rio de Janeiro* 25 B1
Cormano *Milan* 18 A2
Cornaredo *Milan* 18 A1
Córsico *Milan* 18 B1
Corstorphine *Edinburgh* 11 B2
Corviale *Rome* 26 B1
Coslada *Madrid* 17 B2
Cossigny *Paris* 24 B4
Cotao *Lisbon* 16 A1
Côte-St-Luc *Montreal* 20 B2
Cotunduba, I. de *Rio de Janeiro* 25 B2
Coubron *Paris* 24 A4
Courbevoie *Paris* 24 A2
Courtry *Paris* 24 A4
Cowley *London* 15 A1
Coyoacán *Mexico City* 18 B2
Craighall Park *Johannesburg* 13 A2
Craiglockhart *Edinburgh* 11 B2
Craigmillar *Edinburgh* 11 B3
Cramond *Edinburgh* 11 B2
Cramond Bridge *Edinburgh* 11 B1
Cramond I. *Edinburgh* 11 B2
Crandon Park *Miami* 19 D3
Cranford *London* 15 A1
Crawford *Cape Town* 8 A2
Crayford *London* 15 B5
Creekmouth *London* 15 A4
Crescent, L. *Orlando* 23 A1
Crescenzago *Milan* 18 A2
Cressely *Paris* 24 B1
Cresskill *New York* 22 A2
Crestwood *Chicago* 9 C2
Créteil *Paris* 24 B3
Cricklewood *London* 15 A2
Cristo Redentor, Corcovado *Rio de Janeiro* 25 B1
Crockenhill *London* 15 B5
Croissy-Beaubourg *Paris* 24 B4
Croissy-sur-Seine *Paris* 24 A1
Croke Park *Dublin* 10 A2
Crosby *Johannesburg* 13 B1
Crosne *Paris* 24 B3
Cross I. *Mumbai* 20 B2
Crouch End *London* 15 A3
Crown Mine *Johannesburg* 13 B1
Crows Nest *Sydney* 29 B2
Croydon □ *London* 15 B3
Croydon Park *Sydney* 29 B1
Cruagh Mt. *Dublin* 10 B1
Crumlin *Dublin* 10 B2
Cruz de Pau *Lisbon* 16 B2
Crystal Palace *London* 15 B3
Csepel *Budapest* 7 B2
Csepelsziget *Budapest* 7 B2
Csillaghegy *Budapest* 7 A2
Csillagtelep *Budapest* 7 B2
Csömör *Budapest* 7 A3
Csömöri-patak → *Budapest* 7 A3
Cuatro Vientos *Madrid* 17 B1
Cuauhtémoc *Mexico City* 18 B2
Cubao *Manila* 17 B2
Čubuklu *Istanbul* 12 B1
Cudham *London* 15 A2
Cuicuilco, Pirámide de *Mexico City* 18 C1

Culmore *Washington* 33 B2
Culver City *Los Angeles* 16 B2
Cupecê → *São Paulo* 27 B1
Currie *Edinburgh* 11 B2
Cusago *Milan* 18 B1
Cusano Milanino *Milan* 18 A2
Cutler Park *Boston* 6 A1
Çuvuşabaşı → *Istanbul* 12 B1
Cuwei *Beijing* 4 B2
Cypress Hills *New York* 22 B2
Cypress Park *Los Angeles* 16 B3
Czernriaków *Warsaw* 33 B2
Czyste *Warsaw* 33 B1

D

D.H.A. Phase VIII *Karachi* 13 B2
Da Mooca → *São Paulo* 27 B2
Ďáblice *Prague* 25 B2
Dąbrowa *Warsaw* 33 B1
Dachang *Shanghai* 28 B1
Dachau *Munich* 21 A1
Dachau-Ost *Munich* 21 A1
Dachauer Moos *Munich* 21 A1
Dadar *Mumbai* 20 A2
Daebang *Seoul* 27 B1
Daechi *Seoul* 27 B2
Dafni *Athens* 2 B2
Dagenham *London* 15 A4
Dagmarsgården *Stockholm* 29 A2
Daglfing *Munich* 21 A2
D'Aguilar Pen. *Hong Kong* 12 B2
Dahab, Gezîret el *Cairo* 7 B2
Daheisha *Jerusalem* 13 B2
Dahlem *Berlin* 5 B2
Dahlwitz-Hoppegarten *Berlin* 5 A5
Dahongmen *Beijing* 4 C2
Daiba = Odaiba *Tokyo* 30 B3
Dajiaoting *Beijing* 4 B2
Dakhnoye *St. Petersburg* 27 C1
Dalejsky potok → *Prague* 25 B2
Dalgety Bay *Edinburgh* 11 A1
Dalkeith *Edinburgh* 11 B3
Dalkey *Dublin* 10 B3
Dalkey I. *Dublin* 10 B3
Dalgow *Berlin* 5 A1
Dalmeny *Edinburgh* 11 B1
Dalston *London* 15 A3
Daly City *San Francisco* 26 B2
Damaia *Lisbon* 16 A1
Damarakia *Athens* 2 B1
Dämeritzsee *Berlin* 5 B5
Dan Ryan Woods *Chicago* 9 C2
Danderhall *Edinburgh* 11 B3
Danderyd *Stockholm* 29 A2
Danforth *Toronto* 31 A3
Dania Beach *Miami* 19 B3
Darakeh *Tehran* 31 A2
Darband *Tehran* 31 A2
Darling Point *Sydney* 29 B2
Darndale *Dublin* 10 A2
Darrûs *Tehran* 31 A2
Dartford *London* 15 B5
Dashi *Guangzhou* 11 B2
Datansha *Guangzhou* 11 B2
Datun *Beijing* 4 B2
Daulatpur *Delhi* 10 A1
Davidson, Mt. *San Francisco* 26 B2
Davidson's Mains *Edinburgh* 11 B2
Davie *Miami* 19 B2
Dāvūdiyeh *Tehran* 31 A2
Davydkovo *Moscow* 19 B2
Dawidy *Warsaw* 33 C1
Daxing *Beijing* 4 C1
Decatur *Atlanta* 3 B3
Dedham *Boston* 6 B1
Deep Water B. *Hong Kong* 12 B2
Degunino *Moscow* 19 A2
Deir Dibwan *Jerusalem* 13 A2
Deir Ibzi'e *Jerusalem* 13 A1
Deira *Dubai* 9 A2
Dejvice *Prague* 25 B2
Dekabristov, Ostrov *St. Petersburg* 27 B1
Del Rey *Los Angeles* 16 C2
Delhi *Delhi* 10 B2
Delhi Indira Gandhi Int. ✈ (DEL) *Delhi* 10 B1
Demarest *New York* 22 A2
Den Ilp *Amsterdam* 2 A2
Denistone Heights *Sydney* 29 A1
Dentonia Park *Toronto* 31 A3
DePaul Univ. *Chicago* 9 B3
Deptford *London* 15 B3
Desert Wetlands Park *Las Vegas* 14 B2
Deutsche Oper *Berlin* 5 A2
Deutsches Museum *Munich* 21 B2
Devil's Peak *Cape Town* 8 A1
Dhakuria *Kolkata* 14 B2
Dharavi *Mumbai* 20 A2
Dia Deva = Butcher I. *Mumbai* 20 B2
Diadema *São Paulo* 27 C2
Diegen *Brussels* 6 A2
Diemen *Amsterdam* 2 A2
Diepkloof *Johannesburg* 13 B1
Dieprivier *Cape Town* 8 B1
Dilbeek *Brussels* 6 A1
Dilli = Delhi *Delhi* 10 B2
Dirnismaning *Munich* 21 A2
Discovery B. *Hong Kong* 12 B1
Disney-M.G.M. Studios *Orlando* 23 B2
Disney Studios *Los Angeles* 16 B3
Disneyland Hong Kong *Hong Kong* 12 B1
Disneyland Tōkyō *Tokyo* 30 B4
Dixmoor *Chicago* 9 D3
Djakarta = Jakarta *Jakarta* 12 A1
Djursholm *Stockholm* 29 A2
Döberitz *Berlin* 5 A1
Döbling *Vienna* 32 A2
Dobong *Seoul* 27 A2
Dobongsan *Seoul* 27 A2
Docklands *London* 15 A3
Doctor Phillips *Orlando* 23 B2
Dodder → *Dublin* 10 B2
Dodger Stadium *Los Angeles* 16 B3
Dogs, Isle of *London* 15 B3
Dolgoe Ozero *St. Petersburg* 27 B1
Dollis Hill *London* 15 A2
Dollymount *Dublin* 10 A2
Dolni *Prague* 25 B2
Dolni Počernice *Prague* 25 B3
Dolphins Barn *Dublin* 10 B2
Dolton *Chicago* 9 D3
Dom Pedro II, Parque *São Paulo* 27 B1
Don Mills *Toronto* 31 A2
Don Muang Int. ✈ (BKK) *Bangkok* 3 A1
Donaghmede *Dublin* 10 A3
Donau-Oder Kanal *Vienna* 32 A3
Donaufeld *Vienna* 32 A2
Donaupark *Vienna* 32 A2
Donaustadt *Vienna* 32 A2
Dongan Hills *New York* 22 C1
Dongcheng *Beijing* 4 B2
Dongdaemun *Seoul* 27 B2
Donggou *Shanghai* 28 B2

Dongjak *Seoul* 27 B1
Dongjiao *Guangzhou* 11 B2
Dongri *Mumbai* 20 B2
Dongshanhu Park *Guangzhou* 11 B2
Dongzhimen *Beijing* 4 B2
Donnybrook *Dublin* 10 B2
Doornfontein *Johannesburg* 13 B2
Dora *Baghdad* 3 B2
Dorchester *Boston* 6 B2
Dorchester B. *Boston* 6 B2
Dorchester Heights Nat. Historical Site ☐ *Boston* 6 A2
Dornach *Munich* 21 B3
Dorval Int., Montréal ✈ (YUL) *Montreal* 20 B1
Dos Moninos → *São Paulo* 27 C1
Douglas Park *Chicago* 9 C2
Dover Heights *Sydney* 29 B2
Dowlatābād *Tehran* 31 A2
Down, L. *Orlando* 23 A1
Downey *Los Angeles* 16 C4
Downsview *Toronto* 31 A2
Downsview Park *Toronto* 31 A2
Dragør *Copenhagen* 8 B3
Drancy *Paris* 24 A3
Drapetsona *Athens* 2 B1
Dreilinden *Berlin* 5 B2
Drewnica *Warsaw* 33 B2
Drigh Road *Karachi* 13 A2
Drimnagh *Dublin* 10 B2
Drogenbos *Brussels* 6 B1
Drottningholm *Stockholm* 29 B1
Druid Hills *Atlanta* 3 B2
Drumcondra *Dublin* 10 A2
Drummoyne *Sydney* 29 B1
Drylaw *Edinburgh* 11 B2
Dubai *Dubai* 9 A2
Dubai = Dubayy *Dubai* 9 A2
Dubai Creek *Dubai* 9 A2
Dubai Int. ✈ (DXB) *Dubai* 9 A2
Dubai Int. Financial Centre *Dubai* 9 B1
Dubai Internet City *Dubai* 9 B1
Dubai Marina *Dubai* 9 B1
Dubai Maritime City *Dubai* 9 A2
Dubayy *Dubai* 9 A2
Dubeč *Prague* 25 B3
Dublin *Dublin* 10 A2
Dublin B. *Dublin* 10 A3
Dublin Harbour *Dublin* 10 A3
Duddingston *Edinburgh* 11 B3
Dugnano *Milan* 18 A2
Dülab *Tehran* 31 A2
Dulwich *London* 15 B3
Dum Dum *Kolkata* 14 B2
Dumont *New York* 22 A2
Dún Laoghaire *Dublin* 10 B3
Dunearn *Singapore* 28 B2
Dunleary = Dún Laoghaire *Dublin* 10 B3
Dunning *Chicago* 9 B2
Dunvegan *Johannesburg* 13 A2
Duomo *Milan* 18 B2
Duque de Caxias *Rio de Janeiro* 25 A1
Duren Sawit *Jakarta* 12 B2
Dusit *Baghdad* 3 B2
Dworp *Brussels* 6 B1
Dyakovo *Moscow* 19 B2
Dyker Beach Park *New York* 22 C1
Dzerzhinskiy *Moscow* 19 B3
Dzerzhinskiy Park *Moscow* 19 B2

E

E.U.R. = Esposizione Universale di Roma *Rome* 26 C1
Eagle Rock *Los Angeles* 16 B3
Ealing □ *London* 15 A2
Earlsfield *London* 15 B2
Earlwood *Sydney* 29 B1
East Arlington *Boston* 6 A2
East Bedfont *London* 15 B1
East Boston *Boston* 6 A2
East Don → *Toronto* 31 A2
East Don Parkland *Toronto* 31 A2
East Elmhurst *New York* 22 B2
East Falls Church *Washington* 33 B2
East Finchley *London* 15 A2
East Flatbush *New York* 22 C2
East Ham *London* 15 A4
East Humber → *Toronto* 31 A1
East Lexington *Boston* 6 A1
East Los Angeles *Los Angeles* 16 B3
East Molesey *London* 15 B1
East New York *New York* 22 B2
East Pines *Atlanta* 3 B3
East Point *Atlanta* 3 B2
East Potomac Park *Washington* 33 B2
East River → *New York* 22 B2
East Rutherford *New York* 22 A1
East Sheen *London* 15 B2
East Talpiot *Jerusalem* 13 B2
East Wickham *London* 15 B4
Eastcote *London* 15 A1
Easter Howgate *Edinburgh* 11 B2
Eastpoint Park *Toronto* 31 A3
Eastwood *Sydney* 29 A1
Eaton Canyon Park *Los Angeles* 16 B4
Ebara *Tokyo* 30 B3
Ebisu *Tokyo* 30 B3
Ebute-Metta *Lagos* 14 B2
Eda *Tokyo* 30 B2
Eden Gardens *Kolkata* 14 B2
Edendale *Johannesburg* 13 A2
Edenmore *Dublin* 10 A2
Edgars Cr. → *Melbourne* 18 A1
Edgbaston *Toronto* 31 A2
Edgecliff *Sydney* 29 B2
Edgemar *San Francisco* 26 C2
Edgewater *New York* 22 B2
Edgewood *Orlando* 23 B2
Edinburgh *Edinburgh* 11 B2
Edinburgh ✈ (EDI) *Edinburgh* 11 B1
Edinburgh Castle *Edinburgh* 11 B2
Edison Park *Chicago* 9 B2
Edmonds *Washington* 33 B2
Edmondstown *Dublin* 10 B2
Edo → *Tokyo* 30 B4
Edogawa *Tokyo* 30 A4
Edsberg *Stockholm* 29 A1
Edwards L. *Melbourne* 18 A1
Efzonos *Athens* 2 B1
Egaleo *Athens* 2 B2
Egaleo, Oros *Athens* 2 B1
Eiche *Berlin* 5 A5
Eiche Süd *Berlin* 5 A5
Eiffel, Tour *Paris* 24 B2
Ein Arik *Jerusalem* 13 A1
Ein Naquba *Jerusalem* 13 B1

Ein Rafa *Jerusalem* 13 B1
Eizariya *Jerusalem* 13 B2
Ejby *Copenhagen* 8 A2
Ejigbo *Lagos* 14 A1
Ekeberg *Oslo* 23 A3
Eknäs *Stockholm* 29 B3
El 'Abbasiya *Cairo* 7 A2
El Agustino *Lima* 14 B2
El Agustino, Cerro *Lima* 14 B3
El Baragil *Cairo* 7 A1
El Basâlîn *Cairo* 7 B2
El Bira *Jerusalem* 13 A2
El Bosque *Santiago* 27 B1
El Carmen *Santiago* 27 B1
El Cortijo *Santiago* 27 B1
El Cristo, Vaso Regulador *Mexico City* 18 B1
El Duqqi *Cairo* 7 A2
El Encinar de los Reyes *Madrid* 17 A2
El Gezira *Cairo* 7 A2
El Ghuriya *Cairo* 7 A2
El Gîza *Cairo* 7 A2
El Khadr *Jerusalem* 13 B1
El Khalifa *Cairo* 7 A2
El Kôm el Ahmar *Cairo* 7 A2
El Ma'âdi *Cairo* 7 B2
El Matarîya *Cairo* 7 A2
El Mohandessin *Cairo* 7 A2
El Monte *Los Angeles* 16 B4
El Muqattam *Cairo* 7 A2
El Mûski *Cairo* 7 A2
El Pardo *Madrid* 17 A1
El Pobleneau *Barcelona* 4 A2
El Portal *Miami* 19 C2
El Qâhira *Cairo* 7 A2
El Qubba *Cairo* 7 A2
El Reloj *Mexico City* 18 C2
El Retiro *Madrid* 17 B1
El Salto *Santiago* 27 B2
El Sereno *Los Angeles* 16 B3
El Talibiya *Cairo* 7 A1
El Vergel *Mexico City* 18 C2
El Wâhli *Cairo* 7 A2
El Zamâlik *Cairo* 7 A2
El Zeitûn *Cairo* 7 A2
Eleftherios Venizelos ✈ (ATH) *Athens* 2 B2
Elephanta Caves *Mumbai* 20 B2
Elephanta I. *Mumbai* 20 B2
Ellboda *Stockholm* 29 A3
Ellenor, L. *Orlando* 23 B2
Elliniko Olympic Complex *Athens* 2 B2
Ellis I. *New York* 22 B1
Elmers End *London* 15 B3
Elmhurst *New York* 22 B2
Elmstead *London* 15 B4
Elmwood *New Orleans* 21 B1
Elmwood Park *Chicago* 9 B2
Elmwood Park *New York* 22 A1
Elsiesrivier *Cape Town* 8 A2
Elsternwick *Melbourne* 18 B2
Eltham *London* 15 B4
Elwood *Melbourne* 18 B1
Élysée *Paris* 24 A2
Elysian Park *Los Angeles* 16 B3
Emämzädeh Sâleh *Tehran* 31 A2
Emerainville *Paris* 24 B4
Emeryville *San Francisco* 26 B2
Eminönü *Istanbul* 12 B1
Emirates, Mall of the *Dubai* 9 B1
Emirgan *Istanbul* 12 B2
Emmarentia *Johannesburg* 13 A2
Empire State Building *New York* 22 B2
Encantado *Rio de Janeiro* 25 B1
Encino *Los Angeles* 16 B2
Encino Res. *Los Angeles* 16 B2
Enebyberg *Stockholm* 29 A1
Enfield *Sydney* 29 B1
Englewood *Chicago* 9 C3
Englewood *New York* 22 A2
Englewood Cliffs *New York* 22 A2
Enmore *Sydney* 29 B1
Enskede *Stockholm* 29 A2
Enterprise *Las Vegas* 14 B1
Entrevías *Madrid* 17 B1
Epcot *Orlando* 23 B2
Epping *Sydney* 29 A1
Erenköy *Istanbul* 12 C2
Erith *London* 15 B5
Erlaa *Vienna* 32 B1
Ermita *Manila* 17 B1
Ershatou *Guangzhou* 11 B2
Erskineville *Sydney* 29 B2
Erunkan *Lagos* 14 A2
Erzsébet-Telep *Budapest* 7 B3
Eschenried *Munich* 21 A1
Esenler *Istanbul* 12 B1
Esher *London* 15 B1
Eskbank *Edinburgh* 11 B3
Esplanade *Shanghai* 28 c3
Esplugas *Barcelona* 4 A1
Esposizione Universale di Roma *Rome* 26 C1
Essendon *Melbourne* 18 A1
Essendon ✈ (MEB) *Melbourne* 18 A1
Essingen *Stockholm* 29 B2
Essling *Vienna* 32 A3
Est, Gare de l' *Paris* 24 A3
Estado, Parque do *São Paulo* 27 B2
Estelle *New Orleans* 21 B2
Estrela, Basilica da *Lisbon* 16 A2
Etobicoke *Toronto* 31 B1
Etobicoke Cr. → *Toronto* 31 B1
Etterbeek *Brussels* 6 B2
Euram *Seoul* 27 B1
Eunpyeong *Seoul* 27 B1
Evanston *Chicago* 9 A2
Even Sapir *Jerusalem* 13 B1
Evere *Brussels* 6 A2
Everett *Boston* 6 A2
Evergreen Park *Chicago* 9 C2
Evîn *Tehran* 31 A2
Ewu *Lagos* 14 A2
Exhibition Place *Toronto* 31 B2
Expo Centre *Shanghai* 28 c3
Exposições, Pálacio das *Rio de Janeiro* 25 B1
Eyüp *Istanbul* 12 B1
Ezeiza ✈ (EZE) *Buenos Aires* 7 C1

F

Faber, Mt. *Singapore* 28 B2
Fælledparken *Copenhagen* 8 A3
Fågelön *Stockholm* 29 B1
Fagersjö *Stockholm* 29 B2
Fairland *Johannesburg* 13 A1
Fairmilehead *Edinburgh* 11 B2
Fairport *Toronto* 31 A4
Fairview *New York* 22 B2
Fairview Park *Toronto* 31 A2
Faliro *Athens* 2 B2
Faliro, Ormos *Athens* 2 B2
Falkenberg *Berlin* 5 A4

Falkenhagen *Berlin* 5 A1
Falkensee *Berlin* 5 A1
Falomo *Lagos* 14 B2
False Bay *Cape Town* 8 B2
Famões *Lisbon* 16 A1
Fan Lau *Hong Kong* 12 B1
Fangcun *Guangzhou* 11 B2
Farahābād *Tehran* 31 A2
Farforovskaya *St. Petersburg* 27 B2
Farningham *London* 15 B5
Farsta *Stockholm* 29 B2
Fasanerie-Nord *Munich* 21 A2
Fasangarten *Munich* 21 B2
Fatih *Istanbul* 12 B1
Favoriten *Vienna* 32 B2
Fawkner *Melbourne* 18 A1
Fawkner Park *Melbourne* 18 B1
Feldkirchen *Munich* 21 B3
Feldmoching *Munich* 21 A2
Feltham *London* 15 B1
Fener *Istanbul* 12 B1
Fenerbahçe *Istanbul* 12 C2
Fengtai *Beijing* 4 C1
Fengtai Stadium *Beijing* 4 B1
Ferencváros *Budapest* 7 B2
Ferihegy, Budapest ✈ (BUD) *Budapest* 7 B3
Ferndale *Johannesburg* 13 A2
Fichtenau *Berlin* 5 B5
Field Museum of Natural History *Chicago* 9 C2
Fields Corner *Boston* 6 B2
Fiera Camp *Milan* 18 B1
Figino *Milan* 18 B1
Fijir *Baghdad* 3 A2
Filadelfia *Moscow* 19 B1
Fili-Mazilovo *Moscow* 19 B1
Filothei *Athens* 2 A2
Finchley *London* 15 A2
Fine Arts, Museum of *Boston* 6 A2
Finglas *Dublin* 10 A2
Finsbury *London* 15 A3
Finsbury Park *London* 15 A3
Fiorito *Buenos Aires* 7 C2
Firhouse *Dublin* 10 B2
Fischerhäuser *Munich* 21 A3
Fisher I. *Miami* 19 D3
Fishermans Bend *Melbourne* 18 A1
Fisherman's Village *Los Angeles* 16 C2
Fishersville *Toronto* 31 A2
Fisksätra *Stockholm* 29 B3
Fitzroy Gardens *Melbourne* 18 A1
Five Cowrie Cr. → *Lagos* 14 B2
Five Dock *Sydney* 29 B1
Fjellstrand *Oslo* 23 B2
Flamengo *Rio de Janeiro* 25 B2
Flamingo *Orlando* 23 B2
Flaminio *Rome* 26 B1
Fläskebäck *Oslo* 23 A2
Flatbush *New York* 22 C2
Flaten *Stockholm* 29 B2
Flatlands *New York* 22 C2
Flemington Racecourse *Melbourne* 18 A1
Flint Pk. *Los Angeles* 16 B3
Florence *Los Angeles* 16 C3
Florence Bloom Bird Sanctuary *Johannesburg* 13 A2
Florentia *Johannesburg* 13 B2
Flores *Buenos Aires* 7 B2
Flores, Mercado de *Mexico City* 18 B2
Floresta *Buenos Aires* 7 B2
Florida *Buenos Aires* 7 B2
Florida *Johannesburg* 13 B1
Floridsdorf *Vienna* 32 A2
Flushing *New York* 22 B3
Flushing Meadows Corona Park *New York* 22 B2
Flysta *Stockholm* 29 A1
Fo Tan *Hong Kong* 12 A2
Foggy Bottom *Washington* 33 B2
Föhrenhain *Vienna* 32 A2
Fontainebleau *Johannesburg* 13 A1
Fontenay-aux-Roses *Paris* 24 B2
Fontenay-le-Fleury *Paris* 24 A1
Fontenay-sous-Bois *Paris* 24 A3
Foots Cray *London* 15 B4
Footscray *Melbourne* 18 B1
Forbidden City = Imperial Palace Museum *Beijing* 4 B2
Forest *Brussels* 6 B1
Forest Gate *London* 15 A4
Forest Heights *Washington* 33 C2
Forest Hill *London* 15 B3
Forest Hills *New York* 22 B2
Forest Park *Chicago* 9 B2
Forest Park *New York* 22 B2
Forest View *Chicago* 9 C2
Fornebu *Oslo* 23 A2
Foro Romano *Rome* 26 B1
Forstenried *Munich* 21 B1
Forstenrieder Park *Munich* 21 B1
Fort *Mumbai* 20 B2
Fort Dupont Park *Washington* 33 B3
Fort Foote Village *Washington* 33 C2
Fort Lauderdale *Miami* 19 A2
Fort Lauderdale Executive ✈ (FXE) *Miami* 19 A2
Fort Lauderdale-Hollywood Int. ✈ (FLL) *Miami* 19 B3
Forth, Firth of *Edinburgh* 11 A3
Forth Rail Bridge *Edinburgh* 11 A1
Forth Road Bridge *Edinburgh* 11 A1
Forum, The *Los Angeles* 16 C2
Foshan *Guangzhou* 11 B1
Fôt *Budapest* 7 A3
Fourqueux *Paris* 24 A1
Fox Studios *Sydney* 29 B2
Foxrock *Dublin* 10 B3
Franconia *Washington* 33 C2
Frank Lloyd Wright Home *Chicago* 9 B2
Frankel *Singapore* 28 B3
Franklin Park *Boston* 6 B2
Franklin Park *Washington* 33 B2
Franklin Res. *Los Angeles* 16 B2
Franz Josef Strauss ✈ (MUC) *Munich* 21 A3
Frauenkirche *Munich* 21 B2
Frederiksberg *Copenhagen* 8 A3
Frederiksdal *Copenhagen* 8 A2
Fredersdorf *Berlin* 5 A5
Freguesia *Rio de Janeiro* 25 A1
Freimann *Munich* 21 A2
French Quarter *New Orleans* 21 B2
Fresh Pond *Boston* 6 A1
Fresnes *Paris* 24 B2
Friedrichsfelde *Berlin* 5 A4
Friedrichshagen *Berlin* 5 B4
Friedrichshain *Berlin* 5 A3
Friedrichslust *Berlin* 5 A5

Friends Arena *Stockholm* 29 A2
Friherrs *Helsinki* 11 B2
Friiufts Museum *Helsinki* 11 B2
Frontón, I. *Lima* 14 B1
Frunze *Moscow* 19 B2
Fuchū *Tokyo* 30 B1
Fuencarral *Madrid* 17 B1
Fuenlabrada *Madrid* 17 C1
Fukagawa *Tokyo* 30 B3
Fukushima *Osaka* 30 A1
Fulham *London* 15 B2
Funabori *Tokyo* 30 A4
Fundão, I. do *Rio de Janeiro* 25 B1
Fünfhaus *Vienna* 32 A2
Fureso *Copenhagen* 8 A2
Fürth *Munich* 21 A3
Futago-tamagawen *Tokyo* 30 B2
Fuxing Dao *Shanghai* 28 B2
Fuxing Park *Shanghai* 28 B1
Fuxinglu *Beijing* 4 B1

G

G. Ross Lord Park *Toronto* 31 A2
Gaebong *Seoul* 27 C1
Gage Park *Chicago* 9 C2
Gagny *Paris* 24 A4
Galata *Istanbul* 12 B1
Galata Tower *Istanbul* 12 B1
Galatsi *Athens* 2 A2
Galeão Int. ✈ (GIG) *Rio de Janeiro* 25 B1
Galyanovo *Moscow* 19 B3
Gambir *Jakarta* 12 A1
Gamboa *Rio de Janeiro* 25 B1
Gambòòita *Milan* 18 B2
Gamlebyen *Oslo* 23 A3
Gamngdong *Seoul* 27 B2
Gangnam *Seoul* 27 B2
Gangseo *Seoul* 27 B1
Gangtou *Guangzhou* 11 A1
Gangwei *Guangzhou* 11 B2
Ganjiakou *Beijing* 4 B1
Ganshoren *Brussels* 6 A1
Gants Hill *London* 15 A4
Gaohang *Shanghai* 28 B2
Gaoqiao *Shanghai* 28 B2
Garbagnate Milanese *Milan* 18 A1
Garbatella *Rome* 26 B1
Garches *Paris* 24 A2
Garching *Munich* 21 A3
Garden City *Paris* 7 A2
Garden District *New Orleans* 21 B2
Garden Reach *Kolkata* 14 B1
Garder *Oslo* 23 B2
Garfield *New York* 22 A1
Garfield Park *Chicago* 9 B2
Gargareta *Athens* 2 B1
Garibong *Seoul* 27 C1
Garvanza *Los Angeles* 16 B3
Gåshaga *Stockholm* 29 A3
Gateway → *New York* 22 C2
Gateway of India *Mumbai* 20 B2
Gatow *Berlin* 5 B1
Gavà *Barcelona* 4 B1
Gavamar *Barcelona* 4 B1
Gávea *Rio de Janeiro* 25 B1
Gávea, Pedra da *Rio de Janeiro* 25 B1
Gazdagrét *Budapest* 7 B1
Gaziosmanpaşa *Istanbul* 12 B1
Gebel el Ahmar *Cairo* 7 A2
Gebel el Muqattam *Cairo* 7 A2
Gebel el Tura *Cairo* 7 B2
Geiselgasteig *Munich* 21 B2
Gelora Bung Karno Stadium *Jakarta* 12 B1
General San Martin *Buenos Aires* 7 B1
Gennevilliers *Paris* 24 A2
Gentilly *New Orleans* 21 A2
Gentilly *Paris* 24 B2
Gentofte *Copenhagen* 8 A3
Genval *Brussels* 6 B2
George I. *Hong Kong* 12 B2
Georges River Bridge *Sydney* 29 C1
Georgetown *Washington* 33 B2
Georgia Aquarium *Atlanta* 3 B2
Georgia Dome *Atlanta* 3 B2
Gerasdorf bei Wien *Vienna* 32 A2
Gerberau *Munich* 21 A1
Gerli *Buenos Aires* 7 C2
Germiston *Johannesburg* 13 B2
Gern *Munich* 21 A2
Getafe *Madrid* 17 C1
Getty Center, The *Los Angeles* 16 B2
Geunjeong *Seoul* 27 B1
Geva Binyamin *Jerusalem* 13 A2
Geylang Serai *Singapore* 28 B3
Gharapuri = Elephanta I. *Mumbai* 20 B2
Gharb = Shahrak-e Qods *Tehran* 31 A2
Ghatkopar *Mumbai* 20 A2
Ghazipur *Delhi* 10 B2
Ghizri *Karachi* 13 B2
Ghizri Cr. → *Karachi* 13 B2
Ghonda *Delhi* 10 A2
Ghusuri *Kolkata* 14 B2
Gianicolense *Rome* 26 B1
Giant Wheel = Riesenrad *Vienna* 32 A2
Gibraltar Pt. *Toronto* 31 B2
Gidea Park *London* 15 A5
Gilmerton *Edinburgh* 11 B3
Gilo *Jerusalem* 13 B2
Gimmersta *Stockholm* 29 B3
Ginza *Tokyo* 30 A3
Giv'at Ram *Jerusalem* 13 B1
Giv'at Ye'arim *Jerusalem* 13 B1
Giv'at Ze'ev *Jerusalem* 13 A1
Giv'on *Jerusalem* 13 A2
Giza = El Gîza *Cairo* 7 A2
Giza Pyramids *Cairo* 7 A1
Gjersjøen *Oslo* 23 B3
Gladesville *Sydney* 29 B1
Gladsakse *Copenhagen* 8 A2
Glasnevin *Dublin* 10 A2
Glassmanor *Washington* 33 C2
Glasthule *Dublin* 10 B3
Glen Iris *Melbourne* 18 B2
Glen Mar Park *Washington* 33 B2
Glen Rouge Park *Toronto* 31 A4
Glenamsmole Reservoirs *Dublin* 10 B1
Glencoe *Chicago* 9 A2
Glencorse Res. *Edinburgh* 11 B2
Glencullen *Dublin* 10 B2
Glendale *Los Angeles* 16 B3
Glendoo Mt. *Dublin* 10 B2
Glenhuntly *Melbourne* 18 B2
Glenvista *Johannesburg* 13 B2
Glifada *Athens* 2 B2
Glostrup *Copenhagen* 8 B2
Glyfada = Glifada *Athens* 2 B2
Gogar *Edinburgh* 11 B2
Göktürk *Istanbul* 12 B1
Golabari *Kolkata* 14 B2
Golabki *Warsaw* 33 B1

Le Vésinet Paris 24 A1
Lea Bridge London 15 A3
Leaside Toronto 31 A2
Leblon Rio de Janeiro 25 B1
Lee London 15 B4
Leganés Madrid 17 C1
Legazpi Madrid 17 B1
Lehtisaari Helsinki 11 B2
Lei Yue Mun Hong Kong 12 B3
Leião Lisbon 16 A1
Leichhardt Sydney 29 B1
Leith Edinburgh 11 B3
Lekki Lagos 14 B2
Lekki Peninsula Lagos 14 B2
Leme Rio de Janeiro 25 B1
Lemoyne Montreal 20 B3
Lenino Moscow 19 C2
Leninskiye Gory Moscow 19 B2
Lennox Los Angeles 16 C2
Leonia New York 22 A2
Leopardstown Dublin 10 B2
Leopoldau Vienna 32 A2
Leopoldsdorf Vienna 32 B2
Leopoldstadt Vienna 32 A2
Leportovo Moscow 19 B3
Leppävaara Helsinki 11 B1
Les Lilas Paris 24 A3
Les Loges-en-Josas Paris 24 B1
Les Pavillons-sous-Bois Paris 24 A4
Lésigny Paris 24 B4
Lesnozavodskaya St. Petersburg 27 B2
Lester B. Pearson Int., Toronto ✕ (YYZ) Toronto 31 A1
L'Étang-la-Ville Paris 24 A1
Letňany Prague 25 B3
Letopolis = Ausim Cairo 7 A1
Levallois-Perret Paris 24 A2
Levent Istanbul 12 B2
Lewisdale Washington 33 B3
Lewisham □ London 15 B3
Lexington Boston 6 A1
Leyton London 15 A3
Leytonstone London 15 A4
L'Haÿ-les-Roses Paris 24 B3
L'Hospitalet de Llobregat Barcelona 4 A1
Lhotka Prague 25 B2
Liangshui He → Beijing 4 C2
Lianhua Chi Beijing 4 B1
Lianhua He → Beijing 4 B1
Libčice nad Vltavou Prague 25 A2
Libeň Prague 25 B2
Liberdade São Paulo 27 B2
Liberton Edinburgh 11 B3
Liberty I. New York 22 B1
Liberty Ōsaka Museum Osaka 23 B1
Liberty State Park ⌂ New York 22 B1
Libeznice Prague 25 A2
Libuš Prague 25 B2
Lichiao Guangzhou 11 B2
Lichtenburg Berlin 5 A4
Lichterfelde Berlin 5 B2
Lidingö Stockholm 29 A2
Lieshi Lingyuan Guangzhou 11 B2
Liesing Vienna 32 B1
Liesing → Vienna 32 B2
Ligovo St. Petersburg 27 C1
Lijordet Oslo 23 A2
Likhoborka → Moscow 19 A2
Lilla Värtan Stockholm 29 A3
Lille Værløse Copenhagen 8 A2
Liluah Kolkata 14 B1
Lim Chu Kang Singapore 28 A2
Lima Lima 14 B2
Lima Jorge Chavez Int. ✕ (LIM) Lima 14 B2
Limbiate Milan 18 A1
Limehouse London 15 A3
Limeil-Brévannes Paris 24 B3
Linate, Milano ✕ (LIN) Milan 18 B2
Linbropark Johannesburg 13 A2
Lincoln Center for Performing Arts New York 22 B2
Lincoln Heights Los Angeles 16 B3
Lincoln Memorial Washington 33 B2
Lincoln Park Chicago 9 B3
Lincoln Park New York 22 B1
Lincoln Park San Francisco 26 B1
Lincoln Park Zoo Chicago 9 B3
Lincolnwood Chicago 9 A2
Linda-a-Pastora Lisbon 16 A1
Linden Johannesburg 13 A2
Lindenberg Berlin 5 A4
Lindøya Oslo 23 A3
Liniers Buenos Aires 7 B1
Linkebeek Brussels 6 B2
Linksfield Johannesburg 13 A2
Linmeyer Johannesburg 13 B2
Linna Helsinki 11 A2
Lintuvaara Helsinki 11 B1
Lion Rock Country Park ⌂ Hong Kong 12 A3
Lion's Head Cape Town 8 A1
Lioumi Athens 2 B2
Lisboa Lisbon 16 A2
Lisboa ✕ (LIS) Lisbon 16 A2
Lisbon = Lisboa Lisbon 16 A2
Lishui Guangzhou 11 A1
Little B. Sydney 29 B2
Little Calumet → Chicago 9 D3
Little Ferry New York 22 A1
Little Haiti Miami 19 C2
Little Havana Miami 19 D1
Little India Singapore 28 B3
Little Lake Conway Orlando 23 B2
Little Rouge → Toronto 31 A4
Liuhang Shanghai 28 A1
Liurong Temple Guangzhou 11 B2
Live Oak Manor New Orleans 21 B1
Livry-Gargan Paris 24 A4
Liwan Guangzhou 11 B2
Ljan Oslo 23 A3
Llano de Can Gineu Barcelona 4 A2
Lo Aranguiz Santiago 27 B2
Lo Boza Santiago 27 B1
Lo Espejo Santiago 27 C1
Lo Hermida Santiago 27 B2
Lo Prado Santiago 27 B1
Lo So Shing Hong Kong 12 B2
Lo Wai Hong Kong 12 A2
Loanhead Edinburgh 11 B3
Lobau Vienna 32 A3
Lobos, Pt. San Francisco 26 B1
Locham Munich 21 B1
Lochkov Prague 25 B2
Lockhausen Munich 21 A1
Lodi New York 22 A1
Lodi Estate Delhi 10 B2
Logan Int., Boston ✕ (BOS) Boston 6 A2
Logan Square Chicago 9 B2
Lognes-Émerainville ✕ (XLG) Paris 24 B4
Löhme Berlin 5 A5
Lolokhet Karachi 13 A2
Lomas Chapultepec Mexico City 18 B1
Lomas de San Angel Inn Mexico City 18 B1
Lombardy East Johannesburg 13 A2
Lomianki Warsaw 33 A1
Lomus Reforma Mexico City 18 B1
London London 15 B3
London Avenue Canal New Orleans 21 A2
London City ✕ (LCY) London 15 A4
London Heathrow ✕ (LHR) London 15 B1
London Zoo London 15 A3
Long B. Sydney 29 B2
Long Branch Toronto 31 B1
Long Ditton London 15 B2
Long Island City New York 22 B2
Longchamp, Hippodrome de Paris 24 A2
Longhua Pagoda Shanghai 28 B1
Longhua Park Shanghai 28 B1
Longtan Hu → Beijing 4 B2
Longue-Pointe Montreal 20 A2
Longueuil Montreal 20 A3
Loni Delhi 10 A2
Lord's Cricket Ground London 15 A3
Loreto Milan 18 B2
Los Angeles Los Angeles 16 B3
Los Angeles Int. ✕ (LAX) Los Angeles 16 C2
Los Cerrillos ✕ (ULC) Santiago 27 B1
Los Nietos Los Angeles 16 C4
Los Olivos Lima 14 A2
Los Remedios △ Mexico City 18 B1
Los Reyes Mexico City 18 B2
Losiny Ostrov △ Moscow 19 A3
Lot Brussels 6 B1
Lotus River Cape Town 8 B2
Lotus Temple Delhi 10 B2
Loughlinstown Dublin 10 B3
Louis Armstrong New Orleans Int. ✕ (MSY) New Orleans 21 B1
Louise, L. Orlando 23 B1
Louisiana Superdome = Mercedes-Benz Superdome New Orleans 21 B2
Loures Lisbon 16 A1
Louveciennes Paris 24 A1
Louvre, Musée du Paris 24 A3
Lower B. New York 22 C1
Lower Don Lands Toronto 31 B2
Lower New York B. = Lower B. New York 22 C1
Lower Peirce Res. Singapore 28 A2
Loyola Univ. Chicago 9 B3
Lu Xun, Tomb of Shanghai 28 B1
Lu Xun Park Shanghai 28 B1
Lübars Berlin 5 A3
Lucy, L. Orlando 23 A2
Ludwigsfeld Munich 21 A1
Luhu Guangzhou 11 B2
Luk Chau = George I. Hong Kong 12 B2
Lumiar Lisbon 16 A2
Lundtofte Copenhagen 8 A3
Lung Kwu Chau Hong Kong 12 A1
Lung Kwu Tan Hong Kong 12 A1
Lung Mei Hong Kong 12 A3
Luojiang Guangzhou 11 B2
Lustheim Munich 21 A2
Luwan Shanghai 28 B1
Luz, Estádio da Lisbon 16 A1
Luzhniki Sports Centre Moscow 19 B2
Lyndhurst New York 22 B1
Lynn Woods Res. Boston 6 A2
Lyon, Gare de Paris 24 A3
Lyons Chicago 9 C2
Lysaker Oslo 23 A2
Lysakerselva → Oslo 23 A2
Lysolaje Prague 25 B2
Lyublino Moscow 19 B3

M

Ma Nam Wat Hong Kong 12 A3
Ma On Shan Hong Kong 12 A3
Ma On Shan Country Park ⌂ Hong Kong 12 A3
Ma Wan Hong Kong 12 A2
Ma Wan Channel Hong Kong 12 A2
Ma'ale Adumim Jerusalem 13 B2
Ma'ale Ha Khamisha Jerusalem 13 B1
Ma'ale Mikhmas Jerusalem 13 A2
Maantiekylä Helsinki 11 A3
Maarifa Baghdad 3 B2
Mabato Pt. Manila 17 C2
Mabel, L. Orlando 23 B1
Macaco, Morro do Rio de Janeiro 25 B2
McCarran Int., Las Vegas ✕ (LAS) Las Vegas 14 B2
McCook Chicago 9 C2
McGill Univ. Montreal 20 A2
Machelen Brussels 6 A2
Machida Tokyo 30 B1
Maciołki Warsaw 33 B2
McKinley Park Chicago 9 C2
McLean Washington 33 B1
Macopocho → Santiago 27 B1
MacRitchie Res. Singapore 28 A2
Macul Santiago 27 C2
Madhudaha Kolkata 14 B2
Madhyamgram Kolkata 14 A2
Madin Mexico City 18 A1
Madin, L. Mexico City 18 A1
Madīnah Al Manṣūr Baghdad 3 B2
Mâdinet Nasr Cairo 7 A2
Madrid Madrid 17 B1
Madrid Barajas ✕ (MAD) Madrid 17 B2
Madrona Barcelona 4 A1
Maesawa Tokyo 30 A2
Magdalena Lima 14 B2
Magdalena Contreras Mexico City 18 C1
Magelungen Stockholm 29 B2
Maghreb Baghdad 3 A2
Maginu Tokyo 30 B2
Magliana Rome 26 B1
Magny-les-Hameaux Paris 24 B1
Mahar, L. Miami 19 D1
Maheshtala Kolkata 14 C1
Mahim Mumbai 20 A2
Mahim B. Mumbai 20 A1
Mahipalpur Delhi 10 B1
Mahlsdorf Berlin 5 A4
Mahmoodabad Karachi 13 A2
Mahrauli Delhi 10 B2
Mahul Mumbai 20 A2
Maida Vale London 15 A2
Maidstone Melbourne 18 A1
Maipú Santiago 27 C1
Maisonneuve, Parc Montreal 20 A2
Maisons-Alfort Paris 24 B3
Maisons-Laffitte Paris 24 A1
Maissoneuve Montreal 20 A2
Maitland Cape Town 8 A1
Makasar Jakarta 12 B2
Makati Manila 17 B2
Mäkiniitty Helsinki 11 A2
Malá Strana Prague 25 B2
Malabar Sydney 29 B2
Malabar Hill Mumbai 20 B1
Malabar Pt. Mumbai 20 B1
Malabon Manila 17 B1
Malacañang Palace Manila 17 B1
Malahide Dublin 10 A3
Malakoff Paris 24 B2
Mälarhöjaen Stockholm 29 B1
Malate Manila 17 B1
Malaya Neva St. Petersburg 27 B1
Malaya Okhta St. Petersburg 27 B2
Malchow Berlin 5 A3
Malden Boston 6 A2
Malden London 15 B2
Maleizen Brussels 6 B3
Malešice Prague 25 B3
Malir → Karachi 13 B2
Malleny Mills Edinburgh 11 B2
Malmi Helsinki 11 B2
Malmøya Oslo 23 A3
Måløv Copenhagen 8 A1
Malpensa, Milano ✕ (MXP) Milan 18 A1
Malton Toronto 31 A1
Malvern Johannesburg 13 B2
Malvern Melbourne 18 B2
Malvern Toronto 31 A3
Mampang Prapatan Jakarta 12 B1
Mampukuji Tokyo 30 B2
Man Budrukh Mumbai 20 A2
Man Khurd Mumbai 20 A2
Manakhat Jerusalem 13 B2
Mandai Singapore 28 A2
Mandaluyong Manila 17 B2
Mandaoli Delhi 10 B2
Mandaqui → São Paulo 27 A2
Mandoli Delhi 10 A2
Mandvi Mumbai 20 B2
Manenberg Cape Town 8 A2
Mang Kung Uk Hong Kong 12 B3
Mang-won Seoul 27 B1
Mangolpuri Delhi 10 A1
Manhattan New York 22 B2
Manhattan Beach New York 22 C2
Manila Manila 17 B1
Manila Ninoy Aquino Int. ✕ (MNL) Manila 17 B2
Mankkaa Helsinki 11 B1
Manly Sydney 29 A2
Mann, L. Orlando 23 A2
Mannswörth Vienna 32 B3
Manor Park London 15 A4
Manora Karachi 13 B1
Manora Pt. Karachi 13 B1
Manquehue, Cerro Santiago 27 B2
Manzanares, Canal de Madrid 17 C2
Mapo Seoul 27 B1
Mar Vista Los Angeles 16 B2
Maracanã, Estádio Rio de Janeiro 25 B1
Maraoli Mumbai 20 A2
Marcelin Warsaw 33 B1
Mareil-Marly Paris 24 A1
Margaret I. = Margitsziget Budapest 7 A2
Margareten Vienna 32 A2
Margitsziget Budapest 7 A2
Maria Vienna 32 A2
Maridalen Oslo 23 A3
Maridalsvatnet Oslo 23 A3
Mariendorf Berlin 5 B3
Marienfelde Berlin 5 B3
Marikina Manila 17 B2
Marikina → Manila 17 B2
Marin City San Francisco 26 A1
Marin Pen. San Francisco 26 A1
Marina Bay Sands Singapore 28 B3
Marina del Rey Los Angeles 16 C2
Marino Dublin 10 A2
Marisco, Ponta do Rio de Janeiro 25 C1
Markham Chicago 9 D2
Markham Toronto 31 A2
Marki Warsaw 33 B2
Markland Wood Toronto 31 B1
Marly, Forêt de Paris 24 A1
Marly-le-Roi Paris 24 A1
Marne-la-Vallée Paris 24 A4
Marolles-en-Brie Paris 24 B4
Maroubra Sydney 29 B2
Marquette Park Chicago 9 C2
Marrero New Orleans 21 B2
Marrickville Sydney 29 B1
Marsfield Sydney 29 A1
Marsha, L. Orlando 23 B2
Marte, Campo de São Paulo 27 B2
Martesana, Naviglio della Milan 18 A2
Martin Luther King Nat. Historic Site ⌂ Atlanta 3 B2
Martinez Buenos Aires 7 A1
Martinkylä Helsinki 11 B2
Martinsried Munich 21 B1
Maruko Tokyo 30 B3
Maryino Moscow 19 B3
Maryland Singapore 28 B2
Marymont Warsaw 33 B1
Marysin Wawerski Warsaw 33 B2
Marzahn Berlin 5 A4
Mascot Sydney 29 B2
Masmo Stockholm 29 B1
Maspeth New York 22 B2
Masr el Gedida Cairo 7 A2
Masr el Qadîma Cairo 7 A2
Massachusetts Inst. of Tech. Boston 6 A2
Massamá Lisbon 16 A1
Massey → Toronto 31 A3
Massy Paris 24 B2
Mata Jerusalem 13 B1
Matinha Lisbon 16 A2
Matramam Jakarta 12 B2
Matsubara Osaka 23 B2
Mattapan Boston 6 B2
Mátyásföld Budapest 7 A3
Mau Tso Ngam Hong Kong 12 A3
Mauer Vienna 32 B1
Mauripur Karachi 13 A1
Maxhof Munich 21 B1
Mayfair Johannesburg 13 B2
Maywood Chicago 9 B1
Maywood Los Angeles 16 C3
Maywood New York 22 A1
Maywood Park Race Track Chicago 9 B1
Mazagaon Mumbai 20 B2
Meadowbank Park Sydney 29 A1
Meadowlands Sports Complex New York 22 B1
Měcholupy Prague 25 B3
Měčice Prague 25 A3
Mecidiyeköy Istanbul 12 B2
Medford Boston 6 A2
Mediodia Madrid 17 B2
Meguro Tokyo 30 B3
Meguro → Tokyo 30 B3
Mehrābād ✕ (THR) Tehran 31 A1
Mehram Nagar Delhi 10 B1
Mehrow Berlin 5 A4
Meidling Vienna 32 A2
Méier Rio de Janeiro 25 B1
Meiji Shrine Tokyo 30 A3
Meise Brussels 6 A1
Mejiro Tokyo 30 A3
Melbourne Melbourne 18 A1
Melbourne ✕ (MEL) Melbourne 18 A1
Melkki Helsinki 11 C2
Mellunkylä Helsinki 11 B3
Mellunmäki Helsinki 11 B3
Melrose Boston 6 A2
Melrose New York 22 B2
Melrose Park Miami 19 B3
Melsbroek Brussels 6 A2
Melville Johannesburg 13 B2
Menteng Jakarta 12 B1
Mérantaise → Paris 24 B1
Mercamadrid Madrid 17 B2
Merced, L. San Francisco 26 B2
Mercedes-Benz Superdome New Orleans 21 B2
Meredale Johannesburg 13 B1
Merlimau, Pulau Singapore 28 B2
Merri Cr. → Melbourne 18 A1
Merrion Dublin 10 B2
Merrionette Park Chicago 9 C2
Merton □ London 15 B2
Mesgarābād Tehran 31 B3
Messe Vienna 32 A2
Metairie New Orleans 21 A2
Metanòpoli Milan 18 B2
MetLife Stadium New York 22 B1
Metro Toronto Zoo Toronto 31 A3
Metropolitan Museum of Art New York 22 B2
Meudon Paris 24 B2
Mevaseret Zion Jerusalem 13 B1
Mevo Beitar Jerusalem 13 B1
México, Ciudad de Mexico City 18 B2
Mexico City Int. ✕ (MEX) Mexico City 18 B2
Meyersdal Johannesburg 13 B2
Mezzate Milan 18 B2
Miadong Seoul 27 B2
Miami Miami 19 D2
Miami → Miami 19 D1
Miami Beach Miami 19 D3
Miami Gardens Miami 19 C1
Miami Int. ✕ (MIA) Miami 19 D1
Miami Lakes Miami 19 C1
Miami Shores Miami 19 C2
Miami Springs Miami 19 D1
Miasto Warsaw 33 B2
Michałowice Warsaw 33 B1
Michle Prague 25 B2
Mid-City Los Angeles 16 B2
Mid City New Orleans 21 B2
Middle Harbour Sydney 29 A2
Middle Hd. Sydney 29 A2
Middle Park Melbourne 18 B1
Middle Village New York 22 B2
Middlesex Fells Reservation Boston 6 A2
Midland Beach New York 22 C1
Midlothian Chicago 9 D2
Midwood New York 22 C2
Miedzeszyn Warsaw 33 B3
Międzylesie Warsaw 33 B3
Miessaari Helsinki 11 C1
Miguel Hidalgo Mexico City 18 B1
Milan = Milano Milan 18 B1
Milanese, Parco Regionale ⌂ Milan 18 A1
Milano Milan 18 B1
Milano Due Milan 18 B2
Milano Linate ✕ (LIN) Milan 18 B2
Milano Malpense ✕ (MXP) Milan 18 A1
Milano San Felice Milan 18 B2
Milbertshofen Munich 21 A2
Mill Hill London 15 A2
Millennium Dome London 15 A4
Miller Meadow Chicago 9 B2
Millerhill Edinburgh 11 B3
Milltown Dublin 10 B2
Milnerton Cape Town 8 A1
Milon-la-Chapelle Paris 24 B1
Milton Boston 6 B2
Milton Bridge Edinburgh 11 B2
Mimico Toronto 31 B2
Mimico Creek → Toronto 31 B1
Minami Osaka 23 A2
Minamitsunashima Tokyo 30 B2
Minato Osaka 23 B1
Minato Tokyo 30 B3
Minshât el Bekkari Cairo 7 A1
Miraflores Lima 14 B2
Miramar Miami 19 C1
Misericordia, Sa. da Rio de Janeiro 25 B1
Mission San Francisco 26 B2
Mississauga Toronto 31 B1
Mitaka Tokyo 30 A2
Mitcham London 15 B2
Mitcham Common London 15 B3
Mitchell Museum of the American Indian Chicago 9 A2
Mitchell's Plain Cape Town 8 B2
Mitte Berlin 5 A3
Mittel Isarkanal → Munich 21 A3
Mixcoac Mexico City 18 B1
Miyakojima Osaka 23 A2
Mizonokuchi Tokyo 30 B2
Mizue Tokyo 30 A4
Młocinski, Park Warsaw 33 B1
Młociny Warsaw 33 B1
Mnevniki Moscow 19 B1
Moba Lagos 14 B2
Moczydło Warsaw 33 C2
Modderfontein Johannesburg 13 A2
Modřany Prague 25 B2
Mogyoród Budapest 7 A3
Moinho Velho, Cor. → São Paulo 27 B2
Mok Seoul 27 B1
Mokotów Warsaw 33 B2
Molenbeek-St-Jean Brussels 6 A1
Molino de Rosas Mexico City 18 B1
Mollem Brussels 6 A1
Mollins de Rey Barcelona 4 A1
Mondeor Johannesburg 13 B2
Moneda, Palacio de la Santiago 27 B2
Moneró Rio de Janeiro 25 A1
Mong Kok Hong Kong 12 B3
Monkstown Dublin 10 B3
Monnickendam Amsterdam 2 A3
Monrovia Los Angeles 16 B4
Monsanto Lisbon 16 A1
Monsanto, Parque Florestal de Lisbon 16 A1
Mont-Royal Montreal 20 A2
Mont-Royal, Parc Montreal 20 A2
Montcada i Reixac Barcelona 4 A2
Monte Chingolo Buenos Aires 7 C2
Montebello Los Angeles 16 B4
Montemor Lisbon 16 A1
Monterey Hills Los Angeles 16 B3
Monterey Park Los Angeles 16 B4
Montespaccato Rome 26 B1
Montesson Paris 24 A1
Monteverde Nuovo Rome 26 B1
Montigny-le-Bretonneux Paris 24 B1
Montjay-la-Tour Paris 24 A4
Montjuïc Barcelona 4 A2
Montparnasse, Gare Paris 24 A2
Montréal Montreal 20 A2
Montréal, Î. de Montreal 20 A2
Montréal, Univ. de Montreal 20 B2
Montréal Est Montreal 20 A2
Montréal Nord Montreal 20 A2
Montréal Ouest Montreal 20 B1
Montréal Trudeau Int. ✕ (YUL) Montreal 20 B1
Montreuil Paris 24 A3
Montrouge Paris 24 B2
Montserrat Buenos Aires 7 B2
Monza Milan 18 A2
Monzoro Milan 18 B1
Mooca São Paulo 27 B2
Moonachie New York 22 B1
Moonee Ponds Melbourne 18 A1
Moonee Valley Racecourse Melbourne 18 A1
Moosach Munich 21 A2
Mora Mumbai 20 B2
Moratalaz Madrid 17 B2
Mörby Stockholm 29 A2
Morden London 15 B2
Morée → Paris 24 A3
Morgan Park Chicago 9 C3
Moriguchi Osaka 23 A2
Morivione Milan 18 B2
Morningside Edinburgh 11 B2
Morningside Johannesburg 13 A2
Morningside Park New York 22 B2
Morningside Park Toronto 31 A3
Morro Solar, Cerro Lima 14 C2
Mortlake London 15 B2
Mortlake Sydney 29 B1
Morton Grove Chicago 9 A2
Morumbi São Paulo 27 B1
Moscavide Lisbon 16 A2
Moschato Athens 2 B2
Moscow = Moskva Moscow 19 B2
Moscow Sheremetyevo Int. ✕ (SVO) Moscow 19 A1
Moskva Moscow 19 B2
Moskvoretskiy Moscow 19 B2
Mosman Sydney 29 B2
Moti Bagh Delhi 10 B2
Motol Prague 25 B2
Motsa Jerusalem 13 B2
Motsa Illit Jerusalem 13 B1
Motspur Park London 15 B2
Mottingham London 15 B4
Mount Dennis Toronto 31 A2
Mount Greenwood Chicago 9 C2
Mount Hood Memorial Park ⌂ Boston 6 A2
Mount Merrion Dublin 10 B2
Mount Olympus Los Angeles 16 B2
Mount Rainier Washington 33 B3
Mount Vernon New York 22 A3
Müggelberge Berlin 5 B4
Müggelheim Berlin 5 B5
Muggiò Milan 18 A2
Mühleiten Vienna 32 A3
Mühlenfliess → Berlin 5 A5
Mui Wo Hong Kong 12 B1
Muiden Amsterdam 2 A3
Muizenberg Cape Town 8 B1
Mujahidpur Delhi 10 B2
Mukandpur Delhi 10 A2
Mukhmas Jerusalem 13 A2
Muko → Osaka 23 A1
Mukojima Tokyo 30 A3
Mulbarton Johannesburg 13 B2
Mullach Ide = Malahide Dublin 10 A3
Mumbai Mumbai 20 B2
Mumbai Chhatrapati Shivaji Int. ✕ (BOM) Mumbai 20 A2
Mumbai Harbour Mumbai 20 B2
Munch-museum Oslo 23 A3
Münchehofe Berlin 5 B5
München Munich 21 B2
München Franz Josef Strauss ✕ (MUC) Munich 21 A2
Munich = München Munich 21 B2
Munkkiniemi Helsinki 11 B2
Munro Buenos Aires 7 B1
Muntinlupa Manila 17 C2
Murai Res. Singapore 28 A2
Muranów Warsaw 33 B1
Murino St. Petersburg 27 B2
Murrayfield Edinburgh 11 B2
Murtala Mohammed Int. ✕ (LOS) Lagos 14 A1
Musashino Tokyo 30 A2
Museumsinsel Berlin 5 A3
Mushin Lagos 14 A2
Musocco Milan 18 B1
Mustansirīya Baghdad 3 A2
Musturud Cairo 7 A2
Muswell Hill London 15 A3
Mutanabi Baghdad 3 B2
Muthana Baghdad 3 B2
Myllypuro Helsinki 11 B3
Mystic → Boston 6 A2

N

N.S.C.B. Int. ✕ (CCU) Kolkata 14 B2
Naberezhnaya Tower Moscow 19 B2
Nacka Stockholm 29 B3
Næsnes Oslo 23 B1
Nagatsuta Tokyo 30 B2
Nagytétény Budapest 7 B1
Nahalin Jerusalem 13 B1
Najafgarh Drain → Delhi 10 B1
Nakahara Tokyo 30 B2
Nakano Tokyo 30 A2
Namsan Park Seoul 27 B1
Namyeong Seoul 27 B1
Nanbiancun Guangzhou 11 B1
Nanchang He → Beijing 4 B1
Nandang Guangzhou 11 B2
Nangal Dewat Delhi 10 B1
Naniwa Osaka 23 B1
Nanole Mumbai 20 A2
Nanpu Bridge Shanghai 28 B2
Nanshi Shanghai 28 B1
Nanterre Paris 24 A2
Napier Mole Karachi 13 B1
Naraina Delhi 10 B1
Nariman Pt. Mumbai 20 B1
Nārmak Tehran 31 A2
Naruo Osaka 23 A1
Näsby Stockholm 29 A2
Näsbypark Stockholm 29 A2
National Arboretum Washington 33 B2
National Maritime Museum London 15 B3
National September 11 Memorial and Museum New York 22 B1
National University (N.U.S.) Singapore 28 B2
National Zoological Park Washington 33 B2
Nationals Park Washington 33 B2
Nativity, Basilica of Jerusalem 13 B2
Natolin Warsaw 33 C2
Naucalpan de Juárez Mexico City 18 B1
Naupada Mumbai 20 A2
Navi Mumbai Mumbai 20 A2
Naviglio di Pavia Milan 18 B1
Naviglio Grande Milan 18 B1
Navotas Manila 17 B1
Navy Pier Chicago 9 B3
Nazal Hikmat Beg Baghdad 3 A2
Nazimabad Karachi 13 A2
Nazlet el Simmân Cairo 7 B1
Nea Alexandria Athens 2 B2
Nea Ionia Athens 2 A2
Nea Liosia Athens 2 A2
Nea Smirni Athens 2 B2
Neapoli Athens 2 B2
Near North Chicago 9 B3
Nebušice Prague 25 B1
Nederhorst Amsterdam 2 B3
Nedlitz Berlin 5 B1
Nee Soon Singapore 28 A2
Needham Boston 6 B1
Needham Heights Boston 6 B1
Nellis Air Force Base ✕ (LSV) Las Vegas 14 A2
N'ematābād Tehran 31 B2
Nerima Tokyo 30 A3
Nesodden Oslo 23 B3
Nesoddtangen Oslo 23 A3
Nesøya Oslo 23 A2
Netaji Subhash Chandra Bose Int. ✕ (CCU) Kolkata 14 B2
Neu Aubing Munich 21 B1
Neu Buch Berlin 5 A4
Neu Buchhorst Berlin 5 B5
Neu Fahrland Berlin 5 B1
Neu Lindenberg Berlin 5 A4
Neubiberg Munich 21 B3
Neuenhagen Berlin 5 A4
Neuessling Vienna 32 A3
Neuhausen Munich 21 B2
Neuherberg Munich 21 A2
Neuhönow Berlin 5 A5
Neuilly-Plaisance Paris 24 A4
Neuilly-sur-Marne Paris 24 A4
Neuilly-sur-Seine Paris 24 A2
Neukagran Vienna 32 A2
Neukettenhof Vienna 32 B2
Neukölln Berlin 5 B3
Neuperlach Munich 21 B2
Neuried Munich 21 B1
Neustift am Walde Vienna 32 A1
Neusüssenbrunn Vienna 32 A2
Neuwaldegg Vienna 32 A1
Neve Ya'akov Jerusalem 13 A2
Neves Rio de Janeiro 25 B2
New Baghdād Baghdad 3 B2
New Barakpur Kolkata 14 A2
New Brighton New York 22 C1
New Canada Johannesburg 13 B1
New Canada Dam Johannesburg 13 B1
New Cross London 15 B3
New Delhi Delhi 10 B2
New Dorp New York 22 C1
New Dorp Beach New York 22 C1
New Malden London 15 B2
New Milford New York 22 A1
New Mumbai = Navi Mumbai Mumbai 20 A2
New Orleans New Orleans 21 B2
New Orleans Int. ✕ (MSY) New Orleans 21 B1
New River → Miami 19 B3
New Territories Hong Kong 12 A2
New Toronto Toronto 31 B1
New Utrecht New York 22 C2
New York New York 22 B2
New York La Guardia ✕ (LGA) New York 22 B2
Newark B. New York 22 B1
Newbattle Edinburgh 11 B3
Newbury Park London 15 A4
Newcraighall Edinburgh 11 B3
Newham □ London 15 A4
Newhaven Edinburgh 11 B2
Newington Edinburgh 11 B2
Newlands Johannesburg 13 B1
Newport Melbourne 18 B1
Newton Boston 6 B1
Newtonbrook Toronto 31 A2
Newtongrange Edinburgh 11 B3
Newtonville Boston 6 A1
Newtown Sydney 29 B2
Ngau Chi Wan Hong Kong 12 A3
Ngau Tau Kok Hong Kong 12 B3
Ngong Ping Hong Kong 12 B1
Ngong Shuen Chau = Stonecutters I. Hong Kong 12 B2
Ngua Kok Wan Hong Kong 12 A2
Nhava Sheva Mumbai 20 B2
Niāvarān Tehran 31 A2
Nibra Kolkata 14 B1
Nīdāl Baghdad 3 B2
Niddrie Edinburgh 11 B3
Niddrie Melbourne 18 A1
Nieder Neuendorf Berlin 5 A2
Niederschönenweide Berlin 5 B3
Niederschönhausen Berlin 5 A3
Niemeyer Rio de Janeiro 25 B1
Nieuwendam Amsterdam 2 A2
Nihonbashi Tokyo 30 A3
Niipperi Helsinki 11 B1
Nikea Athens 2 B1
Nikolassee Berlin 5 B2
Nikolskiy Moscow 19 B1
Niles Chicago 9 A2
Nimta Kolkata 14 A2
Ninoy Aquino Int. ✕ (MNL) Manila 17 B2
Nippa Tokyo 30 B2
Nippori Tokyo 30 A3
Nishi Osaka 23 A1
Nishinari Osaka 23 B1
Nishinomiya Osaka 23 A1
Nishiyodogawa Osaka 23 A1
Niterói Rio de Janeiro 25 B2
Nockeby Stockholm 29 B1
Noel Park London 15 A3
Nogatino Moscow 19 B3
Nogent-sur-Marne Paris 24 A3
Noida Delhi 10 B2
Noiseau Paris 24 B4
Noisiel Paris 24 A4
Noisy-le-Grand Paris 24 A4
Noisy-le-Roi Paris 24 A1
Noisy-le-Sec Paris 24 A3
Nokkala Helsinki 11 C1
Nomentano Rome 26 B2
Nonakashinden Tokyo 30 A2
Nongminyundong Jiangxisuo Guangzhou 11 B2
Nonhyeon Seoul 27 B2
Nonthaburi Bangkok 3 A1
Noordgesig Johannesburg 13 B1
Noordzeekanaal Amsterdam 2 A1
Nord, Gare du Paris 24 A3
Nordmarka Oslo 23 A3
Nordrand-Siedlung Vienna 32 A2
Nordstrand Oslo 23 A3
Norland Miami 19 C2
Norridge Chicago 9 B2
Norrmalm Stockholm 29 A2
North Arlington New York 22 B1
North Atlanta Atlanta 3 A3
North Bay Village Miami 19 C3
North Bergen New York 22 B1
North Bull I. Dublin 10 A3
North Cheam London 15 B2
North Cray London 15 B4
North Druid Hills Atlanta 3 B3
North Esk → Edinburgh 11 B2
North Gyle Edinburgh 11 B2
North Hackensack New York 22 A1
North Harbor Manila 17 B1
North Hd. Sydney 29 A2
North Hollywood Los Angeles 16 B2
North Las Vegas Las Vegas 14 A1
North Las Vegas ✕ (VGT) Las Vegas 14 A1
North Lexington Boston 6 A1
North Miami Miami 19 C2
North Miami Beach Miami 19 C2
North Nazimabad Karachi 13 A2
North Perry ✕ (HWO) Miami 19 B2
North Point Hong Kong 12 B3
North Queensferry Edinburgh 11 A1
North Quincy Boston 6 B2
North Res. Boston 6 A2
North Riverside Chicago 9 B2
North Saugus Boston 6 A2
North Shore Channel → Chicago 9 B2
North Station Boston 6 A2
North Sydney Sydney 29 B2
North Woolwich London 15 A4
North York Toronto 31 A2
Northbridge Sydney 29 A2
Northbridge Park Sydney 29 A2
Northbrook Chicago 9 A2
Northcliff Johannesburg 13 A1
Northcote Melbourne 18 A2
Northeastern Univ. Boston 6 A2
Northfield Chicago 9 A2
Northmount Toronto 31 A2
Northolt London 15 A1
Northumberland Heath London 15 B5
Northwestern Univ. Chicago 9 A2
Northwood London 15 A1
Northwood Park Toronto 31 A1
Norwood Johannesburg 13 A2
Norwood Park Chicago 9 B2
Noryangjin Seoul 27 B1
Nossa Senhora do O São Paulo 27 B1
Nossegem Brussels 6 A3
Notre-Dame Paris 24 A3
Notre-Dame, Basilique Montreal 20 B2
Notre-Dame, Bois Paris 24 B4
Notre-Dame-de-Grace Montreal 20 B2
Notting Hill London 15 A2
Nova Milanese Milan 18 A2
Novate Milanese Milan 18 A1
Novaya Derevnya St. Petersburg 27 A1
Nové Město Prague 25 B2
Novoaleksandrovskoye St. Petersburg 27 B2
Novodevichy Convent Moscow 19 B2
Novogireyevo Moscow 19 B3
Novosaratovka St. Petersburg 27 B3
Nowe-Babice Warsaw 33 B1
Nöykkiö Helsinki 11 B1
Nueva Atzacoalco Mexico City 18 A2
Nueva Pompeya Buenos Aires 7 C2
Nueva Tenochtitlán Mexico City 18 B2
Nuijala Helsinki 11 B1
Numabukuro Tokyo 30 A2
Nuñez Buenos Aires 7 B2
Nunhead London 15 B3
Ñuñoa Santiago 27 B2
Nusle Prague 25 B2
Nussdorf Vienna 32 A2
Nyanga Cape Town 8 A2
Nymphenburg Munich 21 B2
Nymphenburg, Schloss Munich 21 B2

O

Oak Forest Chicago 9 D2
Oak Grove Atlanta 3 A3
Oak Hill Boston 6 B1
Oak Lawn Chicago 9 C2
Oak Park Chicago 9 B2
Oak View Washington 33 A3
Oakdale Atlanta 3 A2
Oakland San Francisco 26 B3
Oakland Park Miami 19 A3
Oaklawn Washington 33 C3
Oakleigh Melbourne 18 B2
Oakwood Beach New York 22 C1
Oatley Sydney 29 B1
Obalende Lagos 14 B2
Oba's Palace Lagos 14 B2
Oberföhring Munich 21 B2
Oberhaching Munich 21 B2
Oberlaa Vienna 32 B2
Oberlisse Vienna 32 A2
Obermenzing Munich 21 A1
Obermoos Schwaige Munich 21 A1
Oberschleissheim Munich 21 A2
Oberschöneweide Berlin 5 B4
Observatory Johannesburg 13 B2
Óbuda Budapest 7 A2
Obukhovo St. Petersburg 27 B2
Obvodnyy Kanal St. Petersburg 27 B1
Ocean Park Hong Kong 12 B3
Ochota Warsaw 33 B1
Ocoee Orlando 23 A1
Odaiba Tokyo 30 B3
Ōdana Tokyo 30 B2
Ōden-Stockach Munich 21 B3
Odilampi Helsinki 11 B1
Odivelas Lisbon 16 A1
Odolany Warsaw 33 B1
Oeiras Lisbon 16 A1
Ofin Lagos 14 A3
Ogawa Tokyo 30 A1
Ogden Park Chicago 9 C2
Ogikubo Tokyo 30 A2
Ogilvie Transportation Center Chicago 9 B3
Ogogoro Lagos 14 B2
Ogoyo Lagos 14 B2
Ogudu Lagos 14 A2
O'Higgins, Parque Santiago 27 B2
Ōimachi Tokyo 30 B3
Ojota Lagos 14 A2
Ojus Miami 19 C3
Oke-Ira Lagos 14 B2
Okęcie Warsaw 33 B1
Okęcie, Warszawa ✕ (WAW) Warsaw 33 B1
Okeogbe Lagos 14 B2
Okhla Delhi 10 B2
Okhta → St. Petersburg 27 B2
Okkervil → St. Petersburg 27 B2
Okrzeszyn Warsaw 33 C2
Oksval Oslo 23 A3
Oktyabrskiy Moscow 19 B2
Ōkubo Tokyo 30 A3
Ōkura Tokyo 30 B1
Olari Helsinki 11 B1
Olaria Rio de Janeiro 25 B1
Old Admiralty St. Petersburg 27 B1
Old City Jerusalem 13 B2
Old City Shanghai 28 B1
Old Fort York Toronto 31 B2
Old Harbor Boston 6 B2
Old Town = Stare Miasto Warsaw 33 B2
Old Town Chicago 9 B3
Old Town Hall = Altes Rathaus Munich 21 B2
Oldbawn Dublin 10 B1
Oleta River State Rec. Area Miami 19 C3
Olgino St. Petersburg 27 B1
Olímpico, Estadio Mexico City 18 C1
Olivais Lisbon 16 A2
Olivar de los Padres Mexico City 18 B1
Olivar del Conde Mexico City 18 B1
Olives, Mt. of Jerusalem 13 B2
Olivia, L. Orlando 23 A1
Olivos Buenos Aires 7 B2
Olona → Milan 18 B1
Olympia, L. Orlando 23 A1
Olympic Green Beijing 4 B2
Olympic Stadium = Turner Field Atlanta 3 B2
Olympic Stadium Beijing 4 B2
Olympic Stadium Helsinki 11 B2
Olympique, Stade Montreal 20 A2
Ōmori Tokyo 30 B3
One World Trade Center New York 22 e1
Onisigun Lagos 14 A2
Ontario Science Centre Toronto 31 A2
Ōokayama Tokyo 30 B3
Oostzaan Tuindorp Amsterdam 2 A2
Opa-Locka Miami 19 C1
Opa-Locka ✕ (OPF) Miami 19 C1
Opacz Warsaw 33 B1
Opera House Sydney 29 B2
Ophirton Johannesburg 13 B2
Oppegård Oslo 23 B3
Oppem Brussels 6 A1
Oppsal Oslo 23 A4
Ora Jerusalem 13 B1
Oradell New York 22 A1
Oradell Res. New York 22 A1
Orangi Karachi 13 A2
Ordrup Copenhagen 8 A3
Ořech Prague 25 B1
Oregun Lagos 14 A2
Ørestad Copenhagen 8 B3
Orient Heights Boston 6 A3
Oriental Pearl Tower Shanghai 28 B2
Orland Park Chicago 9 D2
Orlando Orlando 23 A2
Orlando Dam Johannesburg 13 B1
Orlando East Johannesburg 13 B1
Orlando Executive ✕ (ORL) Orlando 23 A2
Orlando Int. ✕ (MCO) Orlando 23 B3
Orlovista Orlando 23 A2
Orly Paris 24 B3
Orly, Paris ✕ (ORY) Paris 24 B3
Ormesson-sur-Marne Paris 24 B4
Ormond Melbourne 18 B2
Ormøya Oslo 23 A3
Orpington London 15 B4
Ortaköy Istanbul 12 B2
Ortica Milan 18 B2
Oruba Lagos 14 A2
Ōsaka Osaka 23 B2
Ōsaka Castle Osaka 23 A2
Ōsaka Harbour Osaka 23 B1
Ōsaka Itami Int. ✕ (ITM) Osaka 23 A1
Ōsaka Kansai Int. ✕ (KIX) Osaka 23 B2
Ōsaki Tokyo 30 B3
Osasco São Paulo 27 B1
Osdorf Berlin 5 B3
Osdorp Amsterdam 2 A1
Oshodi Lagos 14 A2
Oslo Oslo 23 A3
Oslo ✕ (OSL) Oslo 23 A4
Ōsone Tokyo 30 B2
Osorun Lagos 14 B2
Ospiate Milan 18 A1
Ostankino Moscow 19 B2
Osterley London 15 B1
Osterley Park London 15 B1
Östermalm Stockholm 29 A2
Österskär Stockholm 29 A3
Östia Malpasso Rome 26 C1
Ostiense Rome 26 B1
Østmarkkapellet Oslo 23 A4
Østøya Oslo 23 B2
Ōta Tokyo 30 B3
Otaniemi Helsinki 11 B1
Otsuka Tokyo 30 A3
Ottakring Vienna 32 A1
Ottávia Rome 26 B1
Ottery Cape Town 8 B2
Ottobrunn Munich 21 B3
Ouderkerk Amsterdam 2 B2
Oulunkylä Helsinki 11 B2
Ourcq, Canal de l' Paris 24 A3
Outer Mission San Francisco 26 B2
Outremont Montreal 20 A2
Overijse Brussels 6 B3
Oworonsoki Lagos 14 A2
Oxgangs Edinburgh 11 B2
Oxon Hill Washington 33 C3
Oyodo Osaka 23 A1
Oyster Rock Mumbai 20 B1
Oyster Rocks Karachi 13 B2
Ozoir-la-Ferrière Paris 24 B4
Ozone Park New York 22 B2

P

Pacific Heights San Francisco 26 B2
Pacific Manor San Francisco 26 C2
Pacific Palisades Los Angeles 16 B1
Pacifica San Francisco 26 C2
Paco Manila 17 B1
Paco de Arcos Lisbon 16 A1
Paddington London 15 A2

Paddington Sydney 29 B2
Paderno Milan 18 A1
Pagewood Sydney 29 B2
Pagote Mumbai 20 B2
Pai, I. do Rio de Janeiro 25 B2
Pak Kok Hong Kong 12 B2
Pak Kong Hong Kong 12 A3
Pak Tam Hong Kong 12 A3
Pakila Helsinki 11 B2
Palacio Real Madrid 17 B1
Palaiseau Paris 24 B2
Palazzolo Milan 18 A1
Paleo Faliro Athens 2 B2
Palermo Buenos Aires 7 B2
Palhais Lisbon 16 B2
Palisades Park New York 22 A1
Palm Deira, The Dubai 9 A2
Palm Jumeirah, The Dubai 9 B1
Palmerston Dublin 10 A1
Palms Los Angeles 16 B2
Paloheinä Helsinki 11 B2
Palomeras Madrid 17 B2
Palos Heights Chicago 9 D2
Palos Hills Chicago 9 C2
Palos Park Chicago 9 C1
Palpara Kolkata 14 B2
Panchur Kolkata 14 B1
Pandacan Manila 17 B2
Pandan, Selat Singapore 28 B2
Pandan Res. Singapore 28 B2
Pangrati Athens 2 B2
Pangsua, Sungei → Singapore 28 A2
Panihati Kolkata 14 A2
Panjang, Bukit Singapore 28 A2
Panke → Berlin 5 A3
Pankow Berlin 5 A3
Pantheon Rome 26 B1
Panthersville Atlanta 3 B3
Pantin Paris 24 A3
Pantitlán Mexico City 18 B2
Panyu Guangzhou 11 B2
Papiol Barcelona 4 A1
Paradise Las Vegas 14 B2
Paramount Studios Los Angeles 16 B3
Paramus New York 22 A1
Paranaque Manila 17 B1
Paray-Vieille-Poste Paris 24 B3
Parc des Princes Paris 24 A2
Pardisān Nature Park Tehran 31 A2
Parel Mumbai 20 B1
Pari São Paulo 27 B2
Parioli Rome 26 B1
Paris Paris 24 A3
Paris Orly ✈ (ORY) Paris 24 B3
Parje Mumbai 20 B2
Pārk-e Āzādegān Tehran 31 B2
Pārk-e Mellat Tehran 31 A2
Park Ridge Chicago 9 A1
Park Royal London 15 A2
Parkchester New York 22 B2
Parkdale Toronto 31 B2
Parkhurst Johannesburg 13 A2
Parklawn Washington 33 B2
Parkmore Johannesburg 13 A2
Parkside San Francisco 26 B2
Parktown Johannesburg 13 B2
Parkview Johannesburg 13 A2
Parkville New York 22 C2
Parkwood Cape Town 8 B1
Parkwood Johannesburg 13 A2
Parow Cape Town 8 A2
Parque Chacabuco Buenos Aires 7 B2
Parque Patricios Buenos Aires 7 B2
Parramatta → Sydney 29 A1
Paşabahçe Istanbul 12 B2
Pasadena Los Angeles 16 B4
Pasar Minggu Jakarta 12 B1
Pasay Manila 17 B1
Pascoe Vale Melbourne 18 A1
Pasig Manila 17 B2
Pasig → Manila 17 B2
Pasila Helsinki 11 B2
Pasing Munich 21 B1
Pasir Panjang Singapore 28 B2
Pasir Ris Singapore 28 A3
Passaic New York 22 A1
Passaic → New York 22 B1
Passirana Milan 18 A1
Patel Nagar Delhi 10 B1
Pateros Manila 17 B2
Pathumwan Bangkok 3 B2
Patipukur Kolkata 14 B2
Patisia Athens 2 A2
Paulo E. Virginia, Gruta Rio de Janeiro 25 B1
Paulshof Berlin 5 A5
Paya Lebar Singapore 28 A3
Peakhurst Sydney 29 B1
Peania Athens 2 B3
Pearson Int. Toronto ✈ (YYZ) Toronto 31 A1
Peckham London 15 B3
Pederstrup Copenhagen 8 A2
Pedralbes Barcelona 4 A1
Pedregal de San Angel, Jardines del Mexico City 18 C1
Peip'ing = Beijing Beijing 4 B1
Peking = Beijing Beijing 4 B1
Pelcowizna Warsaw 33 B2
Pembroke Park Miami 19 C2
Pembroke Pines Miami 19 B1
Peñalolén Santiago 27 B2
Peng Chau Hong Kong 12 B2
Peng Siang → Singapore 28 A2
Penge London 15 B3
Penha Rio de Janeiro 25 A1
Penicuik Edinburgh 11 B2
Penjaringan Jakarta 12 A1
Pentagon Washington 33 B2
Penzing Vienna 32 A1
People's Park Shanghai 28 B1
People's Square Shanghai 28 B1
Perales del Rio Madrid 17 C2
Perchtoldsdorf Vienna 32 B1
Perdizes São Paulo 27 B2
Peristeri Athens 2 A2
Perivale London 15 A2
Perk Brussels 6 A2
Perlach Munich 21 B2
Perlacher Forst Munich 21 B2
Pero Milan 18 A1
Peropok, Bukit Singapore 28 B2
Perovo Moscow 19 B3
Pertusella Milan 18 A1
Pesagot Jerusalem 13 A2
Pesanggrahag, Kali → Jakarta 12 B1
Peschiera Borromeo Milan 18 B2
Pesek, Pulau Singapore 28 B2
Pest Budapest 7 B2
Pesterzsébet Budapest 7 B2
Pesthidegkút Budapest 7 A1
Pestimre Budapest 7 B3
Pestlőrinc Budapest 7 B3
Pestújhely Budapest 7 A2
Petas Helsinki 11 B2
Petrogradskaya Storona St. Petersburg 27 B2
Petroupoli Athens 2 A2
Petrovice Prague 25 B3
Petrovskiy Park Moscow 19 B2
Petrovsko-Razumovskoye Moscow 19 B2
Petrovsky Stadium St. Petersburg 27 B1
Pettycur Edinburgh 11 A2
Peutie Brussels 6 A2
Pfaueninsel Berlin 5 B1
Phaya Thai Bangkok 3 B2
Phihai Karachi 13 A2
Phillip B. Sydney 29 B2
Phoenix Chicago 9 D3
Phoenix Park Dublin 10 A2
Phra Khanong Bangkok 3 B2
Phra Nakhon Bangkok 3 B2
Phra Pradaeng Bangkok 3 C2
Picnic B. Hong Kong 12 B2
Pico Rivera Los Angeles 16 C4
Piedade Lisbon 16 A1
Piedade Rio de Janeiro 25 B1
Piedade, Cova da Lisbon 16 A2
Piedmont Park Atlanta 3 B2
Pierre Elliott Trudeau Int. ✈ (YUL) Montreal 20 B1
Pietralata Rome 26 B2
Pihlajamäki Helsinki 11 B2
Pihlajasaari Helsinki 11 C2
Pilares Rio de Janeiro 25 B1
Pilton Edinburgh 11 B2
Pine Castle Orlando 23 B2
Pine Grove Toronto 31 A1
Pine Hills Orlando 23 A2
Pine Island Miami 19 B1
Pinecrest Miami 19 D1
Pinewood Park Miami 19 C2
Pingzhou Guangzhou 11 B2
Pinheiros → São Paulo 27 B1
Pinjrapur Karachi 13 A2
Pinner London 15 A1
Pinner Green London 15 A1
Pioltello Milan 18 A2
Piræus = Pireas Athens 2 B1
Piraiévs = Pireas Athens 2 B1
Pirajuçara → São Paulo 27 B1
Pireas Athens 2 B1
Pirinççi Istanbul 12 B1
Pirituba São Paulo 27 A1
Pirkkola Helsinki 11 B2
Pisgat O'mer Jerusalem 13 B2
Pisgat Ze'ev Jerusalem 13 B2
Pisnice Prague 25 C2
Pitampura Delhi 10 A1
Pitkäjärvi Helsinki 11 B1
Planegg Munich 21 B1
Plantation Miami 19 B2
Plantation Isles Miami 19 B2
Plaza Mayor Madrid 17 B1
Pleasure Island Orlando 23 B1
Plumstead Cape Town 8 B1
Plumstead London 15 B4
Plyushchevo Moscow 19 B3
Po Toi Is. Hong Kong 12 B3
Po Toi O Hong Kong 12 B3
Poasco Milan 18 B2
Podbaba Prague 25 B2
Podoli Prague 25 B2
Pointe-Aux-Trembles Montreal 20 A2
Poissy Paris 24 A1
Pok Fu Lam Hong Kong 12 B2
Pokcheong Seoul 27 C2
Polton Edinburgh 11 B3
Polvoranca, Parque de Madrid 17 C1
Polyustrovo St. Petersburg 27 B2
Pompano Beach Miami 19 A3
Pomprap Bangkok 3 B2
Pondok Gede Jakarta 12 A2
Pondok Indah Jakarta 12 B1
Pont-Viau Montreal 20 A1
Pontault-Combault Paris 24 B4
Pontinha Lisbon 16 A1
Poplar London 15 A3
Poppintree Dublin 10 A2
Port Botany Sydney 29 B2
Port Mearnóg = Portmarnock Dublin 10 A3
Port Melbourne Melbourne 18 B1
Port Rashid Dubai 9 A2
Port Richmond New York 22 C1
Port Saeed Dubai 9 B2
Port Shelter Hong Kong 12 A3
Port Union Toronto 31 A4
Portage Park Chicago 9 B2
Portela, Lisboa ✈ (LIS) Lisbon 16 A2
Porter, L. Orlando 23 A3
Portmarnock Dublin 10 A3
Porto Brandão Lisbon 16 A1
Pôrto Novo Rio de Janeiro 25 A2
Porto Novo Cr. → Lagos 14 B2
Portobello Edinburgh 11 B3
Portrero San Francisco 26 B3
Posen Chicago 9 D2
Potomac Overlook Reg. Park ⌂ Washington 33 B2
Potrero Pt. San Francisco 26 B2
Potsdam Berlin 5 B1
Potzham Munich 21 B2
Pötzleinsdorf Vienna 32 A1
Póvoa de Santo Adriao Lisbon 16 A2
Powązki Warsaw 33 B1
Powiśle Warsaw 33 B2
Powsin Warsaw 33 C2
Powsinek Warsaw 33 C2
Poyan Res. Singapore 28 A2
Pozuelo de Alarcón Madrid 17 B1
Prado, Museo del Madrid 17 B1
Prado Churubusco Mexico City 18 B2
Praga Warsaw 33 B2
Prague = Praha Prague 25 B2
Praha Prague 25 B2
Praha ✈ (PRG) Prague 25 B1
Praires, R. des → Montreal 20 A2
Prater Vienna 32 A2
Precotto Milan 18 A2
Prenestino Labicano Rome 26 B2
Prenzlauerberg Berlin 5 A3
Preston Melbourne 18 A1
Pretos Forros, Sa. dos Rio de Janeiro 25 B1
Préville Montreal 20 B3
Přezletice Prague 25 B3
Prima Porta Rome 26 B1
Primavalle Rome 26 B1
Primrose Johannesburg 13 B2
Progreso Nacional Mexico City 18 A2
Prosek Prague 25 B3
Prospect Hill Park Boston 6 A1
Providencia Santiago 27 B2
Průhonice Prague 25 C3
Psichiko Athens 2 A2
Pudong New Area Shanghai 28 B2
Pueblo Libre Lima 14 B2
Pueblo Nuevo = El Pobleneu Barcelona 4 A2
Pueblo Nuevo Madrid 17 B2
Puerto Madero Buenos Aires 7 B2
Pugu Guangzhou 11 A2
Puhuangyu Beijing 4 B2
Pui O Wan Hong Kong 12 B1
Puistola Helsinki 11 B3
Pukinmäki Helsinki 11 B2
Pulkovo Int. ✈ (LED) St. Petersburg 27 C1
Pullach Munich 21 B1
Pullman Historic District Chicago 9 C3
Pulo Gadung Jakarta 12 B2
Pūnak Tehran 31 A2
Punchbowl Sydney 29 B1
Punde Mumbai 20 B2
Punggol Singapore 28 A3
Punggol, Sungei → Singapore 28 A3
Punggol Pt. Singapore 28 A3
Punjabi Bagh Delhi 10 A1
Puotila Helsinki 11 B3
Puteaux Paris 24 A2
Putney London 15 B2
Putuo Shanghai 28 B1
Putxet Barcelona 4 A1
Puxi Shanghai 28 B1
Pyramids Cairo 7 B1
Pyry Warsaw 33 C1

Q

Qalandiya Jerusalem 13 A2
Qal'eh Morghī Tehran 31 B2
Qāsemābād Tehran 31 A3
Qasr-e Firūzeh Tehran 31 B3
Qatane Jerusalem 13 B1
Qianmen Beijing 4 B2
Qinghuayuan Beijing 4 B1
Qingningsi Shanghai 28 B2
Qolhak Tehran 31 A2
Quadraro Rome 26 B2
Quaid-i-Azam Karachi 13 A1
Quartiere Zingone Milan 18 B1
Qubeiba Jerusalem 13 A1
Quds Baghdad 3 A2
Queen Elizabeth Olympic Park London 15 A3
Queen Mary Res. London 15 B1
Queen Victoria Market Melbourne 18 A1
Queensbury London 15 A2
Queenscliffe Sydney 29 A2
Queensferry Edinburgh 11 B1
Queenstown Singapore 28 B2
Quellerina Johannesburg 13 A1
Queluz Lisbon 16 A1
Quezon City Manila 17 B2
Quilicura Santiago 27 B1
Quincy Boston 6 B2
Quincy B. Boston 6 B3
Quinta Normal Santiago 27 B1
Quinto de Stampi Milan 18 B2
Quinto Romano Milan 18 B1
Quirinale Rome 26 B1
Qutb Minar Delhi 10 B2

R

R.F.K. Memorial Stadium Washington 33 B3
Raasdorf Vienna 32 A3
Radcliffe College Boston 6 A2
Rådhus Oslo 23 A3
Radlice Prague 25 B2
Radość Warsaw 33 B3
Radotin Prague 25 C2
Rafat Jerusalem 13 A2
Raffles Park Singapore 28 B2
Raheny Dublin 10 A3
Rahnsdorf Berlin 5 B5
Rajakylä Helsinki 11 B3
Rajpura Delhi 10 A2
Rákos-patak → Budapest 7 B3
Rákoshegy Budapest 7 B3
Rákoskeresztúr Budapest 7 B3
Rákoskert Budapest 7 B3
Rákosliget Budapest 7 B3
Rákospalota Budapest 7 A2
Rákosszentmihály Budapest 7 A2
Raków Warsaw 33 B1
Ram Jerusalem 13 A2
Rām Allāh Jerusalem 13 A2
Ramadān Baghdad 3 B2
Ramakrishna Puram Delhi 10 B1
Rāmallāh = Rām Allāh Jerusalem 13 A2
Ramanathpur Kolkata 14 A1
Ramat Allon Jerusalem 13 B2
Ramat Eshkol Jerusalem 13 B2
Ramat Razi'el Jerusalem 13 B1
Ramat Shafet Jerusalem 13 B2
Rambler Channel Hong Kong 12 A2
Ramenki Moscow 19 B1
Ramersdorf Munich 21 B2
Rameses Station Cairo 7 A2
Ramos Rio de Janeiro 25 B1
Ramos Mejia Buenos Aires 7 B1
Ramot Jerusalem 13 B2
Rampur Delhi 10 A2
Ramsgate Sydney 29 B1
Rancho Park Los Angeles 16 B2
Rand ✈ (QRA) Johannesburg 13 B2
Randalls I. New York 22 B2
Randburg Johannesburg 13 A1
Randhart Johannesburg 13 B2
Randpark Ridge Johannesburg 13 A1
Randwick Sydney 29 B2
Ranelagh Dublin 10 A2
Rangpuri Delhi 10 B1
Rannersdorf Vienna 32 B2
Ransbèche Brussels 6 B2
Ransdorp Amsterdam 2 A2
Ranvad Mumbai 20 B2
Raposo Lisbon 16 A1
Rastaala Helsinki 11 B1
Rastila Helsinki 11 B3
Raszyn Warsaw 33 C1
Rathfarnham Dublin 10 B2
Ratho Edinburgh 11 B1
Ratho Station Edinburgh 11 B1
Rato Lisbon 16 A2
Ravelston Edinburgh 11 B2
Rawamangun Jakarta 12 B2
Rayners Lane London 15 A1
Raynes Park London 15 B2
Raypur Kolkata 14 B1
Real Felipe, Fuerte Lima 14 B2
Reams, L. Orlando 23 B1
Reclining Buddha = Wat Pho Bangkok 3 B1
Recoleta Buenos Aires 7 B2
Recoleta Santiago 27 B2
Red Fort = Lal Qila Delhi 10 B2
Red Square Moscow 19 B2
Redbridge □ London 15 A4
Redfern Sydney 29 B2
Refshaleøen Copenhagen 8 A3
Regents Park Johannesburg 13 B2
Regent's Park London 15 A3
Rego Park New York 22 B2
Reinickendorf Berlin 5 A3
Rekola Helsinki 11 B3
Rembertów Warsaw 33 B2
Rembrandtpark Amsterdam 2 A2
Remedios de Escalada Buenos Aires 7 C2
Rémola, Estany del Barcelona 4 B1
Renca Santiago 27 B1
Rennemoulin Paris 24 A1
Řeporyje Prague 25 B1
Repulse Bay Hong Kong 12 B3
Repy Prague 25 B1
Residenz Munich 21 B2
Retiro Buenos Aires 7 B2
Retiro Madrid 17 B1
Retiro, Puerto Buenos Aires 7 B2
Retreat Cape Town 8 B1
Reutov Moscow 19 B4
Réveillon → Paris 24 B4
Revere Boston 6 A2
Rexdale Toronto 31 A1
Reynosa Tamaulipas Mexico City 18 A1
Rho Milan 18 A1
Rhodes Sydney 29 A1
Rhodon Paris 24 B1
Rhodon → Paris 24 B1
Rialto Towers Melbourne 18 A1
Ribeira Rio de Janeiro 25 A1
Ricarda, Estany de la Barcelona 4 B1
Richmond Melbourne 18 A2
Richmond San Francisco 26 B2
Richmond Hill New York 22 B2
Richmond Park London 15 B2
Richmond-upon-Thames □ London 15 B2
Ridge, The Delhi 10 B2
Ridgefield New York 22 B1
Ridgefield Park New York 22 A1
Ridgewood New York 22 B2
Riem Munich 21 B3
Riesenrad Vienna 32 A2
Rijksmuseum Amsterdam 2 A2
Rikers I. New York 22 B2
Rimac Lima 14 B2
Ringsend Dublin 10 A2
Rinkeby Stockholm 29 A1
Rio Comprido Rio de Janeiro 25 B1
Rio de Janeiro Rio de Janeiro 25 B1
Rio de Janeiro Galeão ✈ (GIG) Rio de Janeiro 25 A1
Rio de Mouro Lisbon 16 A1
Ripollet Barcelona 4 A1
Ris Oslo 23 A3
Risby Copenhagen 8 A1
Rishra Kolkata 14 A2
Rithala Delhi 10 A1
Rive Sud, Canal de la Montreal 20 B2
River Edge New York 22 A1
River Forest Chicago 9 B2
River Grove Chicago 9 B1
River Ridge New Orleans 21 B1
Riverdale Chicago 9 D3
Riverdale New York 22 A2
Riverdale Washington 33 B3
Riverdale Park Toronto 31 A2
Riverlea Johannesburg 13 B1
Riverside Chicago 9 C2
Riverwood Sydney 29 B1
Rivière-des-Praires Montreal 20 A2
Rixensart Brussels 6 B3
Riyad Baghdad 3 B2
Rizal Park Manila 17 B1
Rizal Stadium Manila 17 B1
Røa Oslo 23 A2
Robbins Chicago 9 D2
Robertsham Johannesburg 13 B2
Rochelle Park New York 22 A1
Rock Cr. → Washington 33 B2
Rock Creek Park Washington 33 B2
Rockaway Beach New York 22 C3
Rockaway Pt. New York 22 C2
Rockdale Sydney 29 B1
Rockefeller Center New York 22 B2
Roda, Gezîret el Cairo 7 A2
Roda I. = Roda, Gezîret el Cairo 7 A2
Rodaon Vienna 32 B1
Rødovre Copenhagen 8 A2
Rodrigo de Freitas, L. Rio de Janeiro 25 B1
Roehampton London 15 B2
Rogers Park Chicago 9 A3
Roihuvuori Helsinki 11 B3
Roissy-en-Brie Paris 24 B4
Rokytka → Prague 25 B3
Roland Garros Paris 24 A2
Roma Rome 26 B1
Roma Urbe ✈ Rome 26 B2
Római-Fürdő Budapest 7 A2
Romainville Paris 24 A3
Roman Forum = Foro Romano Rome 26 B1
Romano Banco Milan 18 B1
Rome = Roma Rome 26 B1
Romema Jerusalem 13 B2
Romford London 15 A5
Ronald Reagan Nat. Washington ✈ (DCA) Washington 33 B2
Rondebosch Cape Town 8 A1
Roppongi Tokyo 30 B3
Rose, L. Orlando 23 A1
Rose Bowl Los Angeles 16 B4
Rose Hill Washington 33 C2
Rosebank Johannesburg 13 A2
Rosebank New York 22 C1
Rosebery Sydney 29 B2
Rosedal La Candelaria Mexico City 18 B2
Roseland Chicago 9 C3
Rosemead Los Angeles 16 B4
Rosemont Chicago 9 B1
Rosemont Montreal 20 A2
Rosenborg Slot Copenhagen 8 A3
Rosenthal Berlin 5 A3
Rosettenville Johannesburg 13 B2
Rosewell Edinburgh 11 B3
Rosherville Dam Johannesburg 13 B2
Rösjön Stockholm 29 A2
Roslags-Näsby Stockholm 29 A2
Roslin Edinburgh 11 B3
Roslindale Boston 6 B2
Rosny-sous-Bois Paris 24 A4
Rosslyn Washington 33 B2
Rosyth Edinburgh 11 A1
Rotherhithe London 15 B3
Rothneusiedl Vienna 32 B2
Rothschmaige Munich 21 A1
Rouge Hill Toronto 31 A4
Round I. Hong Kong 12 B3
Roxbury Boston 6 B2
Roxeth London 15 A1
Royal Botanic Gardens Edinburgh 11 B2
Royal Exhibition Building Melbourne 18 A1
Royal Observatory Edinburgh 11 B2
Royal Palace = Kungliga Slottet Stockholm 29 B2
Royal Palace = Palacio Real Madrid 17 B1
Royal Park Melbourne 18 A1
Röylä Helsinki 11 B1
Rozas, Portilleros de las Madrid 17 B1
Roztoky Prague 25 B2
Rozzano Milan 18 B1
Rubí → Barcelona 4 A1
Rudolfsheim Vienna 32 A2
Rudolfshöhe Berlin 5 A5
Rudow Berlin 5 B3
Rueil-Malmaison Paris 24 A2
Ruisbroek Brussels 6 B1
Ruislip London 15 A1
Rumelihisarı Istanbul 12 B2
Rungis Paris 24 B3
Rusāfa Baghdad 3 A2
Rush Green London 15 A5
Russa Kolkata 14 C2
Rutherford New York 22 B1
Ruzyně Prague 25 B1
Ruzyně, Praha ✈ (PRG) Prague 25 B1
Rybatskaya St. Petersburg 27 B2
Rydboholm Stockholm 29 A3
Ryde Sydney 29 A1
Ryogoku Tokyo 30 A3
Rzhevka St. Petersburg 27 B3

S

Sa'ādatābād Tehran 31 A2
Saadūn Baghdad 3 B2
Saavedra Buenos Aires 7 B2
Saboli Delhi 10 A2
Sabugo Lisbon 16 A1
Sabzi Mand Delhi 10 A2
Sacavém Lisbon 16 A2
Saclay Paris 24 B2
Saclay, Étang de Paris 24 B1
Sacomã São Paulo 27 B2
Sacré Cœur Paris 24 A3
Sacrow Berlin 5 B1
Sacrower See Berlin 5 B1
Sadang Seoul 27 C1
Saddle → New York 22 A1
Saddle Brook New York 22 A1
Sadr Karachi 13 A2
Sadr City Baghdad 3 A2
Sadyba Warsaw 33 B2
Safdar Jang's Tomb Delhi 10 B2
Saft el Laban Cairo 7 A2
Sagene Oslo 23 A3
Sagrada Familia, Templo de Barcelona 4 A2
Sahar, Mumbai ✈ (BOM) Mumbai 20 A2
Sai Kung Hong Kong 12 A3
Sai Tso Wan Hong Kong 12 B1
Sai Wan Ho Hong Kong 12 B3
Sai Ying Pun Hong Kong 12 B2
St-Aubin Paris 24 B1
St-Cloud Paris 24 A2
St-Cyr-l'École Paris 24 B1
St-Cyr-l'École ✈ Paris 24 B1
St-Denis Paris 24 A3
St-Germain, Forêt de Paris 24 A1
St-Germain-en-Laye Paris 24 A1
St-Gilles Brussels 6 B2
St. Helier London 15 B2
St-Hubert Montreal 20 B3
St-Hubert, Galeries Royales Brussels 6 A2
St. Isaac's Cathedral St. Petersburg 27 B1
St-Jacques → Montreal 20 B3
St-Joost-Ten-Node Brussels 6 A2
St. Kilda Melbourne 18 B1
St-Lambert Montreal 20 A3
St-Lambert Paris 24 B1
St-Laurent Montreal 20 A1
St-Léonard Montreal 20 A2
St-Mandé Paris 24 A3
St. Margaret's Dublin 10 A2
St-Martin, Bois Paris 24 B4
St. Mary Cray London 15 B4
St-Maur-des-Fossés Paris 24 B3
St-Maurice Paris 24 B3
St-Michel Montreal 20 A2
St-Ouen Paris 24 A3
St. Paul's Cray London 15 B4
St. Peters Sydney 29 B2
St. Peter's Square = San Pietro, Piazza Rome 26 B1
St. Petersburg = Sankt-Peterburg St. Petersburg 27 B1
St. Petersburg Pulkovo Int. ✈ (LED) St. Petersburg 27 C1
St-Pierre Montreal 20 B2
St-Pieters Leew Brussels 6 B1
St-Quentin, Étang de Paris 24 B1
St. Stephen's Cathedral = Stephansdom Vienna 32 A2
St-Stevens-Woluwe Brussels 6 A2
St-Vincent-de-Paul Montreal 20 A2
St. Xavier Univ. Chicago 9 C2
Ste-Catherine Montreal 20 B2
Ste-Hélène, Î. Montreal 20 A2
Saiwai Tokyo 30 B3
Sakai Osaka 23 B1
Sakai Harbour Osaka 23 B1
Sakra, Pulau Singapore 28 B2
Salam Baghdad 3 A2
Salamanca Madrid 17 B1
Sallynoggin Dublin 10 B3
Salmannsdorf Vienna 32 A1
Salmedina Madrid 17 C2
Salomea Warsaw 33 B1
Salsette I. Mumbai 20 A2
Salt Lake City = Bidhan Nagar Kolkata 14 B2
Salt Lake Stadium Kolkata 14 B2
Salt River Cape Town 8 A1
Salt Water L. Kolkata 14 B2
Saltsjö-Duvnäs Stockholm 29 B3
Samatya Istanbul 12 C1
Sampaloc Manila 17 B1
Samphan Thawong Bangkok 3 B2
Samseon Seoul 27 B2
Samseong Seoul 27 B2
Samuel Smith Park Toronto 31 B1
Samut Prakan Bangkok 3 B2
San Andrés Barcelona 4 A2
San Angel Mexico City 18 B1
San Basilio Rome 26 B2
San Borja Lima 14 B3
San Bóvio Milan 18 B2
San Bruno, Pt. San Francisco 26 C2
San Bruno Mountain State Park ⌂ San Francisco 26 B2
San Cristóbal Buenos Aires 7 B2
San Cristóbal Madrid 17 B2
San Cristóbal, Cerro Santiago 27 B2
San Cristóbal, Virgen del Santiago 27 B2
San Cristoforo Milan 18 B1
San Donato Milanese Milan 18 B2
San Francisco San Francisco 26 B2
San Francisco B. San Francisco 26 B3
San Francisco Culhuacán Mexico City 18 C2
San Fruttuoso Milan 18 A2
San Gabriel Los Angeles 16 B4
San Gabriel → Los Angeles 16 C4
San Giuliano Milanese Milan 18 B2
San Isidro Lima 14 B2
San Jerónimo Lídice Mexico City 18 C1
San Joaquín Santiago 27 B2
San José Río Hondo Mexico City 18 B1
San Juan → Manila 17 B2
San Juan de Aragón Mexico City 18 B2
San Juan de Aragón, Parque Mexico City 18 B2
San Juan de Lurigancho Lima 14 A2
San Juan del Monte Manila 17 B2
San Juan Ixtacala Mexico City 18 A1
San Just Desvern Barcelona 4 A1
San Justo Buenos Aires 7 C1
San Lorenzo Tezonco Mexico City 18 C2
San Luis Lima 14 B2
San Marino Los Angeles 16 B4
San Martín Barcelona 4 A2
San Martín de Porras Lima 14 B2
San Mateo Tlaltenango Mexico City 18 B1
San Miguel Lima 14 B2
San Miguel Santiago 27 B2
San Nicolás Buenos Aires 7 B2
San Onófrio Rome 26 B1
San Pedro Mártir Barcelona 4 A1
San Pedro Zacatenco Mexico City 18 A2
San Pietro, Piazza Rome 26 B1
San Po Kong Hong Kong 12 B3
San Rafael Chamapa Mexico City 18 B1
San Rafael Hills Los Angeles 16 A3
San Roque Manila 17 B2
San Siro Milan 18 B1
San Souci Sydney 29 B1
San Tau Hong Kong 12 B1
San Telmo Buenos Aires 7 B2
San Vicenç dels Horts Barcelona 4 A1
Sandown Johannesburg 13 A2
Sandown Park Races London 15 B1
Sandton Johannesburg 13 A2
Sandvika Oslo 23 A2
Sandyford Dublin 10 B2
Sandymount Dublin 10 B2
Sangenjaya Tokyo 30 B2
Sanggye Seoul 27 B2
Sangley Pt. Manila 17 C1
Sankrail Kolkata 14 B1
Sankt-Peterburg St. Petersburg 27 B1
Sankt Veit Vienna 32 A1
Sanlihe Beijing 4 B1
Sanlin Shanghai 28 C1
Sanlintang Shanghai 28 C1
Sans Barcelona 4 A1
Sanssouci Berlin 5 B1
Sant Ambrogio, Basilica di Milan 18 B2
Sant Boi de Llobregat Barcelona 4 A1
Sant Cugat Barcelona 4 A1
Sant Feliu de Llobregat Barcelona 4 A1
Sant Joan Despi Barcelona 4 A1
Santa Ana Manila 17 B2
Santa Anita Park Los Angeles 16 B4
Santa Coloma de Gramenet Barcelona 4 A2
Santa Cruz Manila 17 B1
Santa Cruz Mumbai 20 A1
Santa Cruz, I. de Rio de Janeiro 25 B2
Santa Cruz de Olorde Barcelona 4 A1
Santa Efigênia São Paulo 27 B2
Santa Elena Manila 17 B2
Santa Elena del Gomero Santiago 27 B1
Santa Eulalia Barcelona 4 A2
Santa Fe Springs Los Angeles 16 C4
Santa Iria da Azóia Lisbon 16 A2
Santa Julia Santiago 27 C2
Santa Monica Los Angeles 16 B2
Santa Monica Mts. Los Angeles 16 B2
Santa Rosa de Locobe Santiago 27 B2
Santa Teresa de la Ovalle Santiago 27 B1
Santahamina Helsinki 11 C3
Santana São Paulo 27 A2
Santeny Paris 24 B4
Santiago Santiago 27 B2
Santiago Benitez Int. ✈ (SCL) Santiago 27 B1
Santiago de Surco Lima 14 B2
Santo Amaro Lisbon 16 A1
Santo Amaro São Paulo 27 B1
Santo André Lisbon 16 B2
Santo Antão do Tojal Lisbon 16 A2
Santo Antônio, Qta. de Lisbon 16 B1
Santo Tomas, Univ. of Manila 17 B1
Santos Dumont ✈ (SDU) Rio de Janeiro 25 B2
Santoshpur Kolkata 14 B1
Santragachi Kolkata 14 B1
Santry Dublin 10 A2
Sanyuanli Guangzhou 11 B2
São Caetano do Sul São Paulo 27 B2
São Conrado Rio de Janeiro 25 B1
São Cristóvão Rio de Janeiro 25 B1
São Jorge, Castelo de Lisbon 16 A2
São Julião do Tojal Lisbon 16 A2
São Paulo São Paulo 27 B2
São Paulo Congonhas ✈ (CGH) São Paulo 27 B2
Sapa Kolkata 14 B1
Sapateiro, Cor. do → São Paulo 27 B1
Sarandi Buenos Aires 7 C2
Saraswati → Kolkata 14 A1
Sarecky potok → Prague 25 B2
Sarimbun Singapore 28 A2
Sarimbun Res. Singapore 28 A2
Sarıyer Istanbul 12 A2
Sarriá Barcelona 4 A1
Sarsuna Kolkata 14 C1
Sartrouville Paris 24 A2
Sasad Budapest 7 B2
Sashalom Budapest 7 A3
Saska Warsaw 33 B2
Satalice Prague 25 B3
Satgachi Kolkata 14 B2
Satpukur Kolkata 14 B2
Sätra Stockholm 29 B1
Saúde São Paulo 27 B2
Saugus Boston 6 A2
Saugus → Boston 6 A2
Sault-au-Récollet Montreal 20 A2
Sausalito San Francisco 26 A2
Sawah Besar Jakarta 12 A1
Sawtelle Los Angeles 16 B2
Scald Law Edinburgh 11 B2
Scarborough Toronto 31 A3
Scarborough Bluffs Toronto 31 A3
Scarborough Junction Toronto 31 A3
Sceaux Paris 24 B2
Schaerbeek Brussels 6 A2
Scharfenberg Berlin 5 A2
Schiller Woods Chicago 9 B1
Schiphol, Amsterdam ✈ (AMS) Amsterdam 2 B1
Schlachtensee Berlin 5 B2
Schlossgarten Berlin 5 A2
Schmargendorf Berlin 5 B2
Schönblick Berlin 5 B5
Schönbrunn Vienna 32 A1
Schöneberg Berlin 5 B3
Schönefeld Berlin 5 B4
Schöneiche Berlin 5 B5
Schönwalde Berlin 5 A1
Schulzendorf Berlin 5 A2
Schwabing Munich 21 B2
Schwanebeck Berlin 5 A4
Schwanenwerder Berlin 5 B2
Schwarzlackenau Vienna 32 A2
Schwechat Vienna 32 B2
Schwechat, Wien ✈ (VIE) Vienna 32 B3
Science and Industry, Museum of Chicago 9 C3
Scopus, Mt. Jerusalem 13 B2
Scottdale Atlanta 3 B3
Scottish Parliament Edinburgh 11 B2
Scutari = Üsküdar Istanbul 12 B2
Sea Point Cape Town 8 A1
Seacliff San Francisco 26 B2
Seaforth Sydney 29 A2
Seagate New York 22 C1
SeaWorld Orlando 23 B2
Šeberov Prague 25 B3
Secaucus New York 22 B1
Seddinsee Berlin 5 B5
Seeberg Berlin 5 A5
Seeburg Berlin 5 A1
Seefeld Berlin 5 A5
Seegefeld Berlin 5 A1
Seehof Berlin 5 B2
Segeltorp Stockholm 29 B1
Segrate Milan 18 B2
Seguro Milan 18 B1
Seixal Lisbon 16 B2
Selby Johannesburg 13 B2
Seletar Singapore 28 A3
Seletar, Pulau Singapore 28 A3
Seletar Hills Singapore 28 A3
Seletar Res. Singapore 28 A2
Selhurst London 15 B3
Sembawang Singapore 28 A2
Senago Milan 18 A1
Senayan Stadium = Gelora Bung Karno Stadium Jakarta 12 B1
Sendling Munich 21 B2
Senju Tokyo 30 A3
Senkang Singapore 28 A3
Senriyama Osaka 23 A2
Sentosa Singapore 28 B2
Seobinggo Seoul 27 B2
Seocho Seoul 27 C1
Seodaemun Seoul 27 B1
Seokkwan Seoul 27 B2
Seongbuk Seoul 27 B2
Seongdong Seoul 27 B2
Seongsu Seoul 27 B2
Seoul Seoul 27 B2
Seoul Nat. Univ. Seoul 27 C1
Seoul Tower Seoul 27 B1
Sepolia Athens 2 A2
Sepulveda Dam Rec. Area ⌂ Los Angeles 16 A2
Serangoon Singapore 28 A3
Serangoon, Pulau Singapore 28 A3
Serangoon, Sungei → Singapore 28 A3
Serangoon Harbour Singapore 28 A3
Seraya, Pulau Singapore 28 B2
Serebryanka → Moscow 19 B3
Serramonte San Francisco 26 C2
Sesto San Giovanni Milan 18 A2
Sesto Ulteriano Milan 18 B2
Setagaya Tokyo 30 B2
Seter Oslo 23 A3
Setia Budi Jakarta 12 B1
Settebagni Rome 26 A2
Settecamini Rome 26 B2
Séttimo Milanese Milan 18 B1
Settsu Osaka 23 A2
Seutula Helsinki 11 A2
Seven Corners Washington 33 B2
Seven Kings London 15 A4
Seventeenth Street Canal New Orleans 21 A2
Sévesco → Milan 18 A1
Sevran Paris 24 A4
Sèvres Paris 24 B2
Sewri Mumbai 20 B2
Sforzesco, Castello Milan 18 B2
Sha Chau Hong Kong 12 A1
Sha Kok Mei Hong Kong 12 A3
Sha Lo Wan Hong Kong 12 B1
Sha Tin Hong Kong 12 A3
Sha'ab Baghdad 3 A2
Sha'ab North Baghdad 3 A2
Sha'ar Binyamin Jerusalem 13 A2
Shabrâmant Cairo 7 B2
Shah Mosque Tehran 31 A2
Shahdara Delhi 10 A2
Shahe Guangzhou 11 B2
Shahr-e Rey Tehran 31 B2
Shahrak-e Golshahr Tehran 31 B1
Shahrak-e Qods Tehran 31 A2
Shaikh Aomar Baghdad 3 A2
Shakurbasti Delhi 10 A1
Shalkiya Kolkata 14 B2
Sham Shui Po Hong Kong 12 B2
Sham Tseng Hong Kong 12 A2
Sham Wat Hong Kong 12 B1
Shamapur Delhi 10 A1
Shamian Guangzhou 11 B2
Shan Mei Hong Kong 12 A3
Shanghai Shanghai 28 B2
Shanghai Hongqiao Int. ✈ (SHA) Shanghai 28 B1
Shanghai Pudong Int. ✈ (PVG) Shanghai 28 B2
Shankill Dublin 10 B3
Sharp I. Hong Kong 12 A3
Shastrinagar Delhi 10 A2
Shau Kei Wan Hong Kong 12 B3
Shawocun Beijing 4 B1
Shayuan Guangzhou 11 B2
Sheen, L. Orlando 23 B1
Sheepshead Bay New York 22 C2
Sheikh Zayed Road Dubai 9 B2
Shek Kong Hong Kong 12 A2
Shek Kwu Chau Hong Kong 12 B1
Shek O Hong Kong 12 B3
Shek O Country Park ⌂ Hong Kong 12 B3
Shek Pik Hong Kong 12 B1
Shek Pik Res. Hong Kong 12 B1
Shelter I. Hong Kong 12 B3
Shepherds Bush London 15 A2
Shepperton London 15 B1
Sheremetyevo Int., Moscow ✈ (SVO) Moscow 19 A1
Sherman Oaks Los Angeles 16 B2
Sherman Park Chicago 9 C2
Sherwood, L. Orlando 23 A2
Shet Bandar Mumbai 20 B2
Sheung Fa Shan Hong Kong 12 A2
Sheung Lau Wan Hong Kong 12 B3
Sheung Wan Hong Kong 12 B2
Sheva Mumbai 20 B2
Sheva Nhava Mumbai 20 B2
Shiba Tokyo 30 B3
Shibpur Kolkata 14 B1
Shibuya Tokyo 30 B3
Shilihe Beijing 4 B2
Shimogawara Tokyo 30 B1
Shimosalo Tokyo 30 A2
Shimoshakujii Tokyo 30 A2
Shinagawa Tokyo 30 B3
Shing Mun Country Park ⌂ Hong Kong 12 A2
Shing Mun Res. Hong Kong 12 A2
Shinjuku Tokyo 30 A3
Shinjuku Nat. Garden Tokyo 30 A3
Shinkoiwa Tokyo 30 A4
Shinnakano Tokyo 30 A3
Shipai Guangzhou 11 B3
Shirinashi → Osaka 23 B1
Shirogane Tokyo 30 B3
Shitennoji Temple Osaka 23 B2
Shiweitang Guangzhou 11 B2
Shogunle Lagos 14 A2
Shomolu Lagos 14 A2
Shooters Hill London 15 B4
Shoreditch London 15 A3
Shortlands London 15 B4
Shu'afat Jerusalem 13 B2
Shubrâ Cairo 7 A2
Shubrâ el Kheima Cairo 7 A2
Shui Hau Hong Kong 12 B1
Shuikuo Guangzhou 11 A2
Sidcup London 15 B4
Siebenhirten Vienna 32 B1
Siedlung Berlin 5 A1
Siekierki Warsaw 33 B2
Sielce Warsaw 33 B2
Siemensstadt Berlin 5 A2
Sierra Madre Los Angeles 16 B4
Sievering Vienna 32 A2
Sighthill Edinburgh 11 B2
Signal Hill Cape Town 8 A1
Siheung Seoul 27 C1
Sikátorpuszta Budapest 7 A3
Silampur Delhi 10 B2
Sillim Seoul 27 C1
Silver, L. Orlando 23 A2
Silver Hill Washington 33 B3
Silver Lake Los Angeles 16 B3
Silver Mine B. Hong Kong 12 B2
Silver Spring Washington 33 A2
Silvermine Nature Reserve Cape Town 8 B1
Silverstrand Hong Kong 12 B3
Silvolantekojärvi Helsinki 11 B2
Simei Singapore 28 A3
Simla Kolkata 14 B2
Simmering Vienna 32 A2
Simmering Heide Vienna 32 A2
Simonkylä Helsinki 11 B3
Sinchon Seoul 27 B1
Sindang Seoul 27 B2
Singapore ■ Singapore 28 B3
Singapore Changi ✈ (SIN) Singapore 28 A3
Sinki, Selat Singapore 28 B2
Sinsa Seoul 27 B2
Sint-Genesius-Rode Brussels 6 B2
Sion Mumbai 20 A2
Sipson London 15 B1
Siqeil Cairo 7 A1
Şişli Istanbul 12 B1
Siu Kau Yi Chau Hong Kong 12 B2
Skansen Stockholm 29 B2
Skärholmen Stockholm 29 B1
Skarpäng Stockholm 29 A2
Skarpnäck Stockholm 29 B2
Skaryszewski, Park Warsaw 33 B2
Skogskyrkogården Stockholm 29 B2
Skokie Chicago 9 A2
Skokie → Chicago 9 A2
Skokie Heritage Museum Chicago 9 A2
Skoklefall Oslo 23 A3
Sköndal Stockholm 29 B2
Skovlunde Copenhagen 8 A2
Skovshoved Copenhagen 8 A3
Skuru Stockholm 29 B3
Sky Lake Orlando 23 B2
Slade Green London 15 B5
Slependen Oslo 23 A2
Slipi Jakarta 12 B1
Slivenec Prague 25 B2
Sloten Amsterdam 2 A1
Sloterdijk Amsterdam 2 A1
Sloterpark Amsterdam 2 A1
Sluhy Prague 25 A3
Służew Warsaw 33 B2
Służewiec Warsaw 33 B2
Smíchov Prague 25 B2
Smith Forest Preserve Chicago 9 B2
Smolny St. Petersburg 27 B2
Smolny Cathedral St. Petersburg 27 B2
Snake Creek Canal Miami 19 C2
Snarøya Oslo 23 A2
Snättringe Stockholm 29 B1
So Kwun Wat Hong Kong 12 A2
Søborg Copenhagen 8 A2
Sobreda Lisbon 16 B1
Soccer City Stadium Johannesburg 13 B1
Söderby Stockholm 29 A3
Södermalm Stockholm 29 B2
Sodpur Kolkata 14 A2
Soeurs, Î. des Montreal 20 B2
Sognsvatn Oslo 23 A3
Soignes, Forêt de Brussels 6 B2
Sok Kwu Wan Hong Kong 12 B2
Soko Is. Hong Kong 12 B1
Sokolniki Moscow 19 B3
Sokolniki Park Moscow 19 B3
Sokołów Warsaw 33 C1
Solalinden Munich 21 B3
Sollentuna Stockholm 29 A1
Solln Munich 21 B2
Solna Stockholm 29 A1
Somerset Washington 33 B2
Somerville Boston 6 A2
Sonari Mumbai 20 B2
Søndersø Copenhagen 8 A2
Songpa Seoul 27 B2
Sony Picture Studio Los Angeles 16 B2
Sord = Swords Dublin 10 A2
Soroksár Budapest 7 B2
Soroksari Duna → Budapest 7 B2
Sosenka → Moscow 19 B3
Sosnovka St. Petersburg 27 B2
Sŏul = Seoul Seoul 27 B2

Soundview New York 22 B2
South Beach Miami 19 D3
South Beach New York 22 C1
South Bend Park Atlanta 3 B2
South Boston Boston 6 A2
South Decatur Atlanta 3 B3
South Deering Chicago 9 C3
South El Monte Los Angeles 16 B4
South Gate Los Angeles 16 C3
South Harbor Manila 17 B1
South Harrow London 15 A1
South Hd. Sydney 29 B2
South Hills Johannesburg 13 B2
South Holland Chicago 9 D3
South Lawn Washington 33 C2
South Miami Miami 19 D1
South Norwood London 15 B3
South of Market
San Francisco 26 B2
South Ozone Park
New York 22 B3
South Pasadena Los Angeles 16 B4
South Res. Boston 6 A2
South Ruislip London 15 A1
South San Francisco
San Francisco 26 C2
South San Gabriel
Los Angeles 16 B4
South Shore Chicago 9 C3
Southall London 15 A1
Southborough London 15 B4
Southend London 15 B3
Southern California, Univ.
of Los Angeles 16 B3
Southfields London 15 B2
Southport New Orleans 21 B2
Southwark □ London 15 B3
Southwest Museum
Los Angeles 16 B3
Søvang Copenhagen 8 B3
Soweto Johannesburg 13 B1
Sowhānak Tehran 31 A3
Soya Tokyo 30 A4
Spandau Berlin 5 A1
Spånga Stockholm 29 A1
Spectacle I. Boston 6 A3
Speicher-See Munich 21 A3
Speising Vienna 32 B1
Sphinx Cairo 7 B1
Spinaceto Rome 26 C1
Spit Junction Sydney 29 A2
Spořilov Prague 25 B3
Spot Pond Boston 6 A2
Spotswood Melbourne 18 B1
Spring Valley Las Vegas 14 B1
Springeberg Berlin 5 B5
Springfield Washington 33 C1
Squantum Boston 6 B2
Srednaya Rogatka
St. Petersburg 27 C2
Śródmieście Warsaw 33 B2
Staaken Berlin 5 A1
Stabekk Oslo 23 A2
Stade de France Paris 24 A3
Stadlau Vienna 32 A2
Stadshuset Stockholm 29 B2
Stains Paris 24 A3
Stamford Hill London 15 A3
Stammersdorf Vienna 32 A2
Stanley Hong Kong 12 B3
Stanley B. Hong Kong 12 B3
Stanley Pen. Hong Kong 12 B3
Stanmore London 15 A2
Stapleton New York 22 C1
Staraya Derevnya
St. Petersburg 27 B1
Staré Město Prague 25 B2
Stare Miasto Warsaw 33 B2
Starke, L. Orlando 23 A1
Staten Island Zoo New York 22 C1
Staten Islands Ferry
Terminal New York 22 C1
Statenice Prague 25 B1
Stedelijk Museum
Amsterdam 2 A2
Steele Creek Melbourne 18 A1
Steenokkerzeel Brussels 6 A2
Steer, L. Orlando 23 A2
Steglitz Berlin 5 B2
Stepaside Dublin 10 B2
Stephansdom Vienna 32 A2
Stepney London 15 A3
Sterling Park San Francisco 26 B2
Sticklinge udde Stockholm 29 A2
Stickney Chicago 9 C2
Stillorgan Dublin 10 B2
Stockholm Stockholm 29 B2
Stockholm Arlanda ✕
(ARN) Stockholm 29 A1
Stocksund Stockholm 29 A2
Stoclet, Palais Brussels 6 B2
Stodůlky Prague 25 B1
Stoke Newington London 15 A3
Stone Canyon Res.
Los Angeles 16 B2
Stone Zoo Boston 6 A2
Stonebridge London 15 A2
Stonecutters I. Hong Kong 12 B2
Stoneham Boston 6 A2
Stony Brook Res. Boston 6 B2
Stony Creek → Chicago 9 C2
Stora Värtan Stockholm 29 A2
Store Hareskov Copenhagen 8 A2
Store Magleby Copenhagen 8 B3
Storholmen Stockholm 29 A2
Stoyka St. Petersburg 27 B2
Straiton Edinburgh 11 B3
Strandfontein Cape Town 8 B2
Strašnice Prague 25 B2
Strasstrudering Munich 21 B3
Stratford London 15 A4
Strathfield Sydney 29 B1
Streatham London 15 B3
Streatham Vale London 15 B3
Strebersdorf Vienna 32 A2
Střešovice Prague 25 B2
Strip, The Las Vegas 14 B2
Střížkov Prague 25 B2
Strombeek-Bever Brussels 6 A2
Stromovka Prague 25 B2
Studio City Los Angeles 16 B2
Stureby Stockholm 29 B2
Stuvsta Stockholm 29 B2
Subhepur Delhi 10 A2
Suburban Canal
New Orleans 21 B1
Sucat Manila 17 C2
Suchdol Prague 25 B2
Sucy-en-Brie Paris 24 B4
Sue, L. Orlando 23 A2
Sugamo Tokyo 30 A3
Sugar Loaf Mt. = Açúcar,
Pão de Rio de Janeiro 25 B2
Suge Tokyo 30 B2
Suginami Tokyo 30 A2
Sugō Tokyo 30 B2
Sui Sai Wan Hong Kong 12 B3
Suita Osaka 23 A2
Suitland Washington 33 B3
Sukchar Kolkata 14 A2
Sulphur Channel
Hong Kong 12 B2
Sultanahme Camil Istanbul 12 B1
Sumida Tokyo 30 A3
Sumida → Tokyo 30 A3
Sumiyoshi Osaka 23 B2
Sumiyoshi Shrine Osaka 23 B1
Summerville Toronto 31 B1
Summit Chicago 9 C2
Sunamachi Tokyo 30 A4
Sunbury-on-Thames
London 15 B1
Sundbyberg Stockholm 29 A1
Sundbyerne Copenhagen 8 B3
Sungei Kadut Industrial
Estate Singapore 28 A2
Sungei Selatar Res.
Singapore 28 A3
Sunny Bay Hong Kong 12 B1
Sunny Isles Beach Miami 19 C3
Sunrise Miami 19 B2
Sunrise Manor Las Vegas 14 A2
Sunrise Mountain Natural
Area ⌓ Las Vegas 14 A2
Sunset Park Las Vegas 14 B2
Sunset Park New York 22 C2
Sunset Peak Hong Kong 12 B1
Sunshine I. Hong Kong 12 B2
Sunshine Park Miami 19 B2
Sunter Jakarta 12 A2
Sunter, Kali → Jakarta 12 B2
Suomenlinna Helsinki 11 C2
Sur Bahr Jerusalem 13 B2
Sura Kolkata 14 B2
Suraksan Seoul 27 A2
Surbiton London 15 B2
Suresnes Paris 24 A2
Surfside Miami 19 C3
Surquillo Lima 14 B2
Surrey Hills Sydney 29 B2
Surulere Lagos 14 B2
Susaek Seoul 27 B1
Süssenbrunn Vienna 32 A2
Sutton Dublin 10 A3
Sutton London 15 B2
Suyu Seoul 27 B2
Suzukishinden Tokyo 30 A2
Svanemøllen Copenhagen 8 A3
Sveaborg = Suomenlinna
Helsinki 11 C2
Sverdlov Moscow 19 B2
Svestad Oslo 23 B2
Svinö Helsinki 11 C1
Swanley London 15 B4
Swansea Toronto 31 B2
Swinburne I. New York 22 C1
Swords Dublin 10 A2
Sydenham Johannesburg 13 A2
Sydney Sydney 29 B2
Sydney, Univ. of Sydney 29 B2
Sydney Harbour △ Sydney 29 B2
Sydney Harbour Bridge
Sydney 29 B2
Sydney Kingsford Smith ✕
(SYD) Sydney 29 B2
Sydstranden Copenhagen 8 B3
Sylvania Sydney 29 C1
Syon Park London 15 B2
Szczęśliwice Warsaw 33 B1
Széchenyi-hegy Budapest 7 B1
Széphalom Budapest 7 A1

T

Taastrup Copenhagen 8 B1
Tabata Tokyo 30 A3
Tablada Buenos Aires 7 C1
Table B. Cape Town 8 A1
Table Mountain △
Cape Town 8 A1
Table Mt. Cape Town 8 A1
Taboão da Serra São Paulo 27 B1
Täby Stockholm 29 A2
Tacuba Mexico City 18 B1
Tacubaya Mexico City 18 B1
Tafelbaai = Table B.
Cape Town 8 A1
Taft Orlando 23 B2
Taguig → Manila 17 B2
Taguig Manila 17 B2
Tahrir Square Cairo 7 A2
Tai Ho Hong Kong 12 B1
Tai Lam Chung Res.
Hong Kong 12 A2
Tai Lam Country Park ⌓
Hong Kong 12 A2
Tai Long Wan Tsuen
Hong Kong 12 B2
Tai Mo Shan Hong Kong 12 A2
Tai O Hong Kong 12 B1
Tai Po Tsai Hong Kong 12 A3
Tai Seng Singapore 28 A3
Tai Shui Hang Hong Kong 12 A3
Tai Tam B. Hong Kong 12 B3
Tai Tam Country Park ⌓
Hong Kong 12 B3
Tai Tam Tuk Res.
Hong Kong 12 B3
Tai Wai Hong Kong 12 A3
Tai Wan Tau Hong Kong 12 B3
Tai Wo Hau Hong Kong 12 A2
Tai Yue Shan = Lantau I.
Hong Kong 12 B1
Tainaka Osaka 23 B2
Taishō Osaka 23 B1
Tajrish Tehran 31 A2
Takaido Tokyo 30 A2
Takaishi Tokyo 30 B2
Takarazuka Osaka 23 A1
Takasago Tokyo 30 A4
Takatsu Tokyo 30 B2
Takeshita Tokyo 30 B2
Takinegawa Tokyo 30 A3
Takoma Park Washington 33 B2
Taksim Istanbul 12 B1
Talaide Lisbon 16 A1
Taliganga Kolkata 14 B2
Talipapa Manila 17 A2
Tallaght Dublin 10 B1
Tallkrogen Stockholm 29 B2
Tama Tokyo 30 B1
Tama → Tokyo 30 B2
Tama Kyūryō Tokyo 30 B2
Tamaden Tokyo 30 B2
Tamagawa-josui → Tokyo 30 A1
Taman Sari Jakarta 12 A1
Tamanduateí → São Paulo 27 B2
Tamarac Miami 19 A1
Tamboerskloof Cape Town 8 A1
Tambora Jakarta 12 A1
Tammisalo Helsinki 11 B3
Tammūh Cairo 7 B2
Tampines Singapore 28 A3
Tanah Abang Jakarta 12 B1
Tanah Kusir Jakarta 12 B1
Tangelo Park Orlando 23 B2
Tanjung Duren Jakarta 12 B1
Tanjung Priok Jakarta 12 A2
Tanum Oslo 23 A1
Tap Shek Kok Hong Kong 12 A1
Tapada Lisbon 16 A1
Tapanila Helsinki 11 B3
Tapiales Buenos Aires 7 C1
Tapiola Helsinki 11 B1
Tapsia Kolkata 14 B2
Tara Mumbai 20 A1
Tarabya Istanbul 12 B2
Tårbæk Copenhagen 8 A3
Tarchomin Warsaw 33 B1
Tardeo Mumbai 20 B1
Targówek Warsaw 33 B2
Tårnby Copenhagen 8 B3
Tarqua Bay Lagos 14 B2
Tathong Channel
Hong Kong 12 B3
Tathong Pt. Hong Kong 12 B3
Tatuapé São Paulo 27 B2
Taufkirchen Munich 21 B2
Tavares, I. dos Rio de Janeiro 25 A2
Tavros Athens 2 B2
Teaneck New York 22 A1
Tebet Jakarta 12 B2
Tecamachalco Mexico City 18 B1
Ted Williams Tunnel Boston 6 A2
Teddington London 15 B1
Tegel Berlin 5 A2
Tegel, Berlin ✕ (TXL) Berlin 5 A2
Tegeler See Berlin 5 A2
Tegelort Berlin 5 A2
Teheran = Tehrān Tehran 31 A2
Tehrān Tehran 31 A2
Tehrān Mehrābād ✕
(THR) Tehran 31 A1
Tehrān Pārs Tehran 31 A3
Tei Tong Tsui Hong Kong 12 B3
Tejo, Rio → Lisbon 16 A2
Tekstilyshchik Moscow 19 B3
Telhal Lisbon 16 A1
Telok Blangah Singapore 28 B2
Teltow Berlin 5 B2
Teltow kanal Berlin 5 B3
Tempelhof Berlin 5 B3
Temple City Los Angeles 16 B4
Temple Hills Washington 33 C3
Temple of Heaven Beijing 4 B2
Templeogue Dublin 10 B2
Temppeliaukio Church
Helsinki 11 B2
Tenafly New York 22 A2
Tenayuca, Piramide de
Mexico City 18 A1
Tengah → Singapore 28 A2
Tennoji Osaka 23 B2
Tepalcates Mexico City 18 B2
Tepeyac △ Mexico City 18 B2
Terrazzano Milan 18 A1
Terre des Hommes Montreal 20 A2
Terrugem Lisbon 16 A1
Terrytown New Orleans 21 B2
Tervuren Brussels 6 B3
Tervuren, Park van Brussels 6 B3
Tetuán Madrid 17 B1
Teufelsberg Berlin 5 B2
Thalkirchen Munich 21 B2
Thames Ditton London 15 B1
Thamesmead London 15 A4
Thana Cr. → Mumbai 20 A2
Thiais Paris 24 B3
Thisio Athens 2 B2
Thistletown Toronto 31 A1
Thomastown Melbourne 18 A2
Thompson I. Boston 6 B3
Thon Buri Bangkok 3 B1
Thornbury Melbourne 18 A2
Thorncliffe Toronto 31 A2
Thornhill Toronto 31 A2
Thornton Cape Town 8 A2
Thornton Heath London 15 B3
Three Fathoms Cove
Hong Kong 12 A3
Threipmuir Res. Edinburgh 11 B2
Throg's Neck New York 22 B3
Tian Tan Buddha = Big
Buddha Hong Kong 12 B1
Tiancun Beijing 4 B1
Tianhe Guangzhou 11 B2
Tibet, L. Orlando 23 B1
Tibidabo Barcelona 4 A1
Tibradden Mt. Dublin 10 B2
Tiburon San Francisco 26 A2
Tiburtino Rome 26 B2
Ticomán Mexico City 18 A2
Tiefersee Berlin 5 B1
Tiergarten Berlin 5 A3
Tijgerhof Cape Town 8 A2
Tijuca Rio de Janeiro 25 B1
Tijuca, Pico da Rio de Janeiro 25 B1
Tijuca △ Rio de Janeiro 25 B1
Tikkurila Helsinki 11 B3
Tilak Nagar Delhi 10 B1
Tilanqiao Shanghai 28 B1
Timah, Bukit Singapore 28 A2
Timiryazev Park Moscow 19 B2
Tin Can I. Lagos 14 B2
Ting Kau Hong Kong 12 A2
Tira Jerusalem 13 A1
Tirsa Cairo 7 B2
Tishrīyaa Baghdad 3 B2
Tiu Keng Leng Hong Kong 12 B3
Tizapán Mexico City 18 C1
Tlalnepantla → Mexico City 18 A1
Tlalpan Mexico City 18 C2
To Kwa Wan Hong Kong 12 B2
Toa Payoh Singapore 28 A3
Točná Prague 25 C2
Toco Hills Atlanta 3 B2
Todt Hill New York 22 C1
Tōkagi Tokyo 30 A4
Tokai Plantation Cape Town 8 B1
Tōkaichiba Tokyo 30 B2
Tōkyō Tokyo 30 B3
Tōkyō B. = Tōkyō-Wan
Tokyo 30 B4
Tōkyō Haneda ✕ (HND)
Tokyo 30 B3
Tōkyō Harbour Tokyo 30 B3
Tōkyō Sky Tree Tokyo 30 A3
Tōkyō-Wan Tokyo 30 B4
Tolka → Dublin 10 A1
Tollygunge = Taliganga
Kolkata 14 B2
Tolo Harbour Hong Kong 12 A3
Tolworth London 15 B2
Tomba di Nerone Rome 26 B1
Tommy Thompson Park
Toronto 31 B3
Tondo Manila 17 B1
Tong Fuk Hong Kong 12 B1
Tongbinggo Seoul 27 B1
Tongqiao Shanghai 28 A1
Toorak Melbourne 18 B2
Topanga State Park ⌓
Los Angeles 16 B1
Topkapı Istanbul 12 B1
Topkapı Palaca Istanbul 12 B1
Tor di Quinto Rome 26 B1
Tor Pignattara Rome 26 B2
Tor Sapienza Rome 26 B2
Torcy Paris 24 A4
Toronto Toronto 31 B2
Toronto, Univ. of Toronto 31 B2
Toronto City Centre ✕
(YTZ) Toronto 31 B2
Toronto Harbour Toronto 31 B2
Toronto I. Toronto 31 B2
Toronto Lester B. Pearson
Int. ✕ (YYZ) Toronto 31 A1
Torre Lupara Rome 26 B2
Torre Nova Rome 26 B2
Torrellas → Barcelona 4 A1
Torrevécchia Rome 26 B1
Toshima Tokyo 30 A3
Toshimaen Tokyo 30 A2
Tottenham London 15 A3
Tottenham Melbourne 18 A1
Toussus-le-Noble Paris 24 B1
Toussus-le-Noble ✕ (TNF)
Paris 24 B1
Towchāl Cable Car Tehran 31 A2
Tower Hamlets □ London 15 A3
Tower of London London 15 A3
Towra Pt. Sydney 29 C2
Tøyen Oslo 23 A3
Toyonaka Osaka 23 A1
Trafaria Lisbon 16 A1
Traição, Cor. → São Paulo 27 B2
Tranegilde Copenhagen 8 B2
Trångsund Stockholm 29 B2
Trappenfelde Berlin 5 A4
Trastévere Rome 26 B1
Treasure I. San Francisco 26 B2
Třeboradice Prague 25 B3
Třebotov Prague 25 C1
Tree Tops Park Miami 19 B1
Tremblay-en-France Paris 24 A4
Tremembe → São Paulo 27 A2
Tremont New York 22 A2
Trenno Milan 18 B1
Treptow Berlin 5 B3
Três Rios, Sa. dos
Rio de Janeiro 25 B1
Trevi, Fontana di Rome 26 B1
Trezzano sul Naviglio Milan 18 B1
Trieste Rome 26 B2
Trinidad Washington 33 B3
Trinity Edinburgh 11 B2
Trinity College Dublin 10 A2
Trionfale Rome 26 B1
Triulzo Milan 18 B2
Troja Prague 25 B2
Trollbäcken Stockholm 29 B3
Trombay Mumbai 20 A2
Troparevo Moscow 19 C1
Trudeau Int., Montréal ✕
(YUL) Montreal 20 B1
Trudyashchikhsya,
Ostrov St. Petersburg 27 B1
Tryvasshøgda Oslo 23 A3
Tseng Lan Shue Hong Kong 12 B3
Tseung Kwan Hong Kong 12 B3
Tsim Sha Tsui Hong Kong 12 B2
Tsing Lung Tau Hong Kong 12 A2
Tsing Yi Hong Kong 12 A2
Tsova Jerusalem 13 B1
Tsuen Wan Hong Kong 12 A2
Tsur Hadassa Jerusalem 13 B1
Tsurumi → Tokyo 30 B3
Tsz Wan Shan Hong Kong 12 A3
Tuas Singapore 28 B1
Tuchoměřice Prague 25 B1
Tuckahoe New York 22 A3
Tucuruvi São Paulo 27 A2
Tuen Mun Hong Kong 12 A1
Tufello Rome 26 B2
Tufnell Park London 15 A3
Tufts Univ. Boston 6 A2
Tughlakabad Delhi 10 B2
Tullamarine Melbourne 18 A1
Tulse Hill London 15 B3
Tung Chung Hong Kong 12 B1
Tung Lung Chau Hong Kong 12 B3
Tung O Hong Kong 12 B2
Tunis Baghdad 3 A2
Tuomarila Helsinki 11 B1
Tureberg Stockholm 29 A1
Turffontein Johannesburg 13 B2
Türk Telekom Arena
Istanbul 12 B1
Turkey L. Orlando 23 A2
Turkey Lake Park Orlando 23 A2
Turner Field Atlanta 3 B2
Turnham Green London 15 B2
Turnhouse Edinburgh 11 B1
Tuscolana, Via Rome 26 B2
Twelve Apostles Cape Town 8 A1
Twentieth Century Fox
Studios Los Angeles 16 B2
Twickenham London 15 B1
Twickenham Rugby
Ground London 15 B1
Twin Peaks San Francisco 26 B2
Twins, The Hong Kong 12 B3
Two Rock Mt. Dublin 10 B2
Tymon North Dublin 10 B1

U

U.S. Capitol Washington 33 B2
U.S. Cellular Field Chicago 9 C3
Ubeidiya Jerusalem 13 B2
Uberaba → São Paulo 27 B2
Ubin, Pulau Singapore 28 A3
Uccle Brussels 6 B2
Udelnaya St. Petersburg 27 A2
Udelnoe St. Petersburg 27 B1
Üdlding Munich 21 A1
Ueno Tokyo 30 A3
Úholičky Prague 25 B1
Uhříněves Prague 25 B3
Uithoorn Amsterdam 2 B1
Ujazdów Warsaw 33 B2
Újpalota Budapest 7 A2
Újpest Budapest 7 A2
Ukita Tokyo 30 A4
Uleta Miami 19 C2
Ullerup Copenhagen 8 B3
Ullevål Oslo 23 A3
Ulriksdal Stockholm 29 A1
Ulyanka St. Petersburg 27 B1
Um Al Khanazir I. Baghdad 3 B2
Umeda Osaka 23 A1
Umm al Sheif Dubai 9 B1
Umm Suqeim Dubai 9 B1
Ümraniye Istanbul 12 B2
Underground Atlanta
Atlanta 3 B2
Underhill, L. Orlando 23 A3
Unětický potok → Prague 25 B2
Unhos Lisbon 16 A2
Unidad Santa Fe
Mexico City 18 B1
Union City New York 22 B1
Union Port New York 22 B2
Union Square Hong Kong 12 B2
Union Station Toronto 31 B2
United Center Chicago 9 B2
United Nations
Headquarters New York 22 B2
Universal Studios
Los Angeles 16 B2
Universal Studios Orlando 23 B2
Universidad Madrid 17 B1
University Park Washington 33 B3
Unterbiberg Munich 21 B2
Unterföhring Munich 21 A3
Unterhaching Munich 21 B2
Unterlaa Vienna 32 B2
Untermenzing Munich 21 A1
Upper B. New York 22 C1
Upper Elmers End London 15 B3
Upper New York B. =
Upper B. New York 22 C1
Upper Norwood London 15 B3
Upper Peirce Res. Singapore 28 A2
Upper Sydenham London 15 B3
Upper Tooting London 15 B3
Upton London 15 A4
Uptown Chicago 9 B2
Uran Mumbai 20 B2
Urayasu Tokyo 30 B4
Urbe ✕ Rome 26 B2
Urca Rio de Janeiro 25 B2
Uritsk St. Petersburg 27 C1
Urmston Road Hong Kong 12 A1
Üröm Budapest 7 A2
Ursus Warsaw 33 B1
Ursvik Stockholm 29 A1
Usera Madrid 17 B1
Ushigome Tokyo 30 A3
Usina Rio de Janeiro 25 B1
Üsküdar Istanbul 12 B2
Ust-Slavyanka
St. Petersburg 27 C3
Uteke Stockholm 29 A3
Utrata Warsaw 33 B2
Uttarpara Kolkata 14 B1
Utterslev Mose Copenhagen 8 A2

V

Vaclavské náměstí Prague 25 B2
Vadaul Mumbai 20 A2
Vaires-sur-Marne Paris 24 A4
Valby Copenhagen 8 B2
Valcannuta Rome 26 B1
Valdelatas Madrid 17 A1
Valenton Paris 24 B3
Valera Milan 18 A1
Vallcarca Barcelona 4 A1
Valldoreix Barcelona 4 A1
Vallecas Madrid 17 B2
Vallecas, Cumbres de
Madrid 17 B2
Vallensbæk Copenhagen 8 B2
Vallensbæk Strand
Copenhagen 8 B2
Vallentunasjön Stockholm 29 A2
Valleranello Rome 26 C1
Vallisaari Helsinki 11 C3
Vallvidrera Barcelona 4 A1
Valvidrera → Barcelona 4 A1
Van Gogh Museum
Amsterdam 2 A2
Vanak Tehran 31 A2
Vanda = Vantaa Helsinki 11 B2
Vangede Copenhagen 8 A3
Vaniköy Istanbul 12 B2
Vanløse Copenhagen 8 A2
Vantaa Helsinki 11 B2
Vantaankoski Helsinki 11 B2
Vantaanpuisto Helsinki 11 B2
Vanves Paris 24 B2
Varedo Milan 18 A1
Varkiza Athens 2 C2
Vartiokylä Helsinki 11 B3
Vartiosaari Helsinki 11 B3
Vasamuseet Stockholm 29 B2
Vasco Cape Town 8 A2
Vasfenārd Tehran 31 B2
Vashi Mumbai 20 A2
Vasilyevskiy, Ostrov
St. Petersburg 27 B1
Vatican City ■ Rome 26 B1
Vaucluse Sydney 29 B2
Vaucluse House Sydney 29 B2
Vaucresson Paris 24 A1
Vaughan Toronto 31 A1
Vauhallan Paris 24 B2
Vaujours Paris 24 A4
Vauxhall London 15 B3
Vecsés Budapest 7 B3
Veleň Prague 25 A3
Veleslavín Prague 25 B2
Vélizy-Villacoublay Paris 24 B2
Velka-Chuchle Prague 25 B2
Velké Přílepy Prague 25 B1
Venda Seca Lisbon 16 A1
Venetian Islands Miami 19 D3
Venice Los Angeles 16 C2
Ventas Madrid 17 B1
Ventorro del Cano Madrid 17 B1
Venustiano Carranza
Mexico City 18 B2
Verde → São Paulo 27 A1
Verdi Athens 2 A2
Verdugo Mts. Los Angeles 16 A2
Verdun Montreal 20 B2
Vérhalom Budapest 7 A2
Vermelho → São Paulo 27 B1
Vermont Knolls Los Angeles 16 C3
Vernon Los Angeles 16 B3
Verrières-le-Buisson Paris 24 B2
Versailles Buenos Aires 7 B1
Versailles Paris 24 B1
Veshnyaki Moscow 19 B3
Vesolyy Posolok
St. Petersburg 27 B2
Vestra Helsinki 11 B1
Vestskoven Copenhagen 8 A2
Vicálvaro Madrid 17 B2
Vicente Lopez Buenos Aires 7 B2
Victoria Hong Kong 12 B2
Victoria, Pont Montreal 20 B2
Victoria and Alfred
Waterfront Cape Town 8 A1
Victoria Gardens Mumbai 20 B2
Victoria Harbour Hong Kong 12 B3
Victoria Island Lagos 14 B2
Victoria, L. Johannesburg 13 B2
Victoria Lawn Tennis
Courts Melbourne 18 B2
Victoria Park Singapore 28 B2
Victoria Peak Hong Kong 12 B2
Victoria Terminus =
Chhatrapati Shivaji
Terminus Mumbai 20 B2
Victoria Village Toronto 31 A3
Vienna = Wien Vienna 32 A2
Vietnam Veterans
Memorial Washington 33 B2
Vieux Carré = French
Quarter New Orleans 21 B2
View Park Los Angeles 16 B3
Vigário Geral Rio de Janeiro 25 A1
Vigentino Milan 18 B2
Viggbyholm Stockholm 29 A2
Vighignolo Milan 18 B1
Viikki Helsinki 11 B3
Vikhroli Mumbai 20 A2
Vila Guilherme São Paulo 27 B2
Vila Isabel Rio de Janeiro 25 B1
Vila Jaguára São Paulo 27 B1
Vila Madalena São Paulo 27 B1
Vila Maria São Paulo 27 B2
Vila Mariana São Paulo 27 B2
Vila Prudente São Paulo 27 B2
Viladecans Barcelona 4 B1
Vile Parle Mumbai 20 A2
Villa Adelina Buenos Aires 7 B1
Villa Ballester Buenos Aires 7 B1
Villa Barilari Buenos Aires 7 C2
Villa Bosch Buenos Aires 7 B1
Villa C. Colon Buenos Aires 7 C2
Villa Ciudadela Buenos Aires 7 B1
Villa de Guadalupe
Mexico City 18 B2
Villa Devoto Buenos Aires 7 B1
Villa Diamante Buenos Aires 7 C2
Villa Dominico Buenos Aires 7 C3
Villa Lugano Buenos Aires 7 C2
Villa Lynch Buenos Aires 7 B1
Villa Madero Buenos Aires 7 C1
Villa Sáenz Pena
Buenos Aires 7 B1
Villa Urquiza Buenos Aires 7 B2
Villaverde Madrid 17 B1
Villaverde Bajo Madrid 17 B1
Ville-d'Avray Paris 24 B2
Villecresnes Paris 24 B4
Villejuif Paris 24 B3
Villemomble Paris 24 A4
Villeneuve-la-Garenne
Paris 24 A2
Villeneuve-le-Roi Paris 24 B3
Villeneuve-St-Georges Paris 24 B3
Villeparisis Paris 24 A4
Villevaudé Paris 24 A4
Villiers-le-Bâcle Paris 24 B1
Villiers-sur-Marne Paris 24 B4
Villinki Helsinki 11 C3
Villoresi, Canale Milan 18 A1
Vilvoorde Brussels 6 A2
Vimodrone Milan 18 A2
Vimont Montreal 20 A1
Vincennes Paris 24 A3
Vincennes, Bois de Paris 24 B3
Vineland Orlando 23 B1
Vinings Atlanta 3 A2
Vinohrady Prague 25 B2
Vinoř Prague 25 B3
Violet Hill Hong Kong 12 B3
Virányos Budapest 7 A1
Virginia, L. Orlando 23 A2
Virginia Gardens Miami 19 D1
Virginia Key Miami 19 D3
Viroflay Paris 24 B2
Vironas Athens 2 B2
Virum Copenhagen 8 A2
Visitacion Valley
San Francisco 26 B2
Vista Alegre Lima 14 B3
Vista Alegre Santiago 27 C1
Vista Grove Atlanta 3 A3
Vitacura Santiago 27 B2
Vitinia Rome 26 C1
Vitry-sur-Seine Paris 24 B3
Vladykino Moscow 19 A2
Vokovice Prague 25 B2
Volgelsdorf Berlin 5 B5
Volkhonka-Zil Moscow 19 C2
Vollen Oslo 23 B1
Volodarskoye St. Petersburg 27 B2
Volynkina-Derevnya
St. Petersburg 27 B1
Vondelpark Amsterdam 2 A2
Vösendorf Vienna 32 B2
Voula Athens 2 C2
Vouliagmeni Athens 2 C2
Vredehoek Cape Town 8 A1
Vršovice Prague 25 B2
Vyborgskaya Storona
St. Petersburg 27 B2
Vykhino Moscow 19 B3
Vyšehrad Prague 25 B2

W

Wachterhof Munich 21 B3
Wadala Mumbai 20 A2
Wadi al-Arayis Jerusalem 13 B2
Wadi Fukin Jerusalem 13 B1
Waduk Pluit Jakarta 12 A1
Waggaman New Orleans 21 B1
Wah Fu Hong Kong 12 B2
Wahda Baghdad 3 B2
Währing Vienna 32 A2
Waidmannslust Berlin 5 A3
Wakefield Boston 6 A2
Waldesruh Berlin 5 B4
Waldperlach Munich 21 B3
Waldtrudering Munich 21 B3
Walkinstown Dublin 10 B1
Wall Street New York 22 B1
Walt Disney World Resort
Orlando 23 B1
Waltham Boston 6 A1
Waltham Forest □ London 15 A3
Walthamstow London 15 A3
Walton-on-Thames London 15 B1
Wambeek Brussels 6 A3
Wan Chai Hong Kong 12 B3
Wandle → London 15 B2
Wandsworth □ London 15 B2
Wangjing Beijing 4 B2
Wannsee Berlin 5 B1
Wansdorf Berlin 5 A1
Wanstead London 15 A4
Wapping London 15 A3
Wards I. New York 22 B2
Warnberg Munich 21 B2
Warner Brothers Studios
Los Angeles 16 B2
Warrāq el 'Arab Cairo 7 A2
Warringal Park Melbourne 18 A2
Warriston Edinburgh 11 B2
Warsaw = Warszawa
Warsaw 33 B2
Warsaw Chopin ✕
(WAW) Warsaw 33 B1
Warszawa Warsaw 33 B2
Wartenberg Berlin 5 A4
Washington Washington 33 B2
Washington Heights
New York 22 A2
Washington Park Chicago 9 C3
Washington Ronald
Reagan Nat. ✕ (DCA)
Washington 33 B2
Wat Pho Bangkok 3 B1
Water of Leith → Edinburgh 11 B1
Watergraafsmeer Amsterdam 2 A2
Waterland Amsterdam 2 A2
Waterloo Brussels 6 B2
Watermael-Boitsfort Brussels 6 B2
Watertown Boston 6 A1
Watsonia Melbourne 18 A2
Watts Los Angeles 16 C3
Waverley Boston 6 A1
Waverley Johannesburg 13 A2
Waverley Sydney 29 B2
Wawer Warsaw 33 B2
Wawrzyszew Warsaw 33 B1
Wazirabad Delhi 10 A2
Wazīrīya Baghdad 3 A2
Wazirpur Delhi 10 A2
Wealdstone London 15 A1
Wedding Berlin 5 A3
Weehawken New York 22 B1
Weesp Amsterdam 2 B3
Weidling Vienna 32 A1
Weidlingbach Vienna 32 A1
Weissensee Berlin 5 A3
Wellesley Hills Boston 6 B1
Welling London 15 B4
Wellington Boston 6 A2
Weltevreden Park
Johannesburg 13 A1
Wembley London 15 A2
Wemmel Brussels 6 A1
Wemmer Pan Johannesburg 13 B2
Wenceslas Square =
Vaclavské náměstí
Prague 25 B2
Wendenschloss Berlin 5 B4
Wennington London 15 A5
Werneuchen Berlin 5 A5
West Don → Toronto 31 A2
West Drayton London 15 A1
West Ham London 15 A4
West Harrow London 15 A1
West Heath London 15 B4
West Hill Toronto 31 A3
West Hollywood Los Angeles 16 B2
West Lamma Channel
Hong Kong 12 B2
West Los Angeles, Univ. of
Los Angeles 16 C2
West Medford Boston 6 A2
West Miami Miami 19 D1
West Molesey London 15 B1
West New York New York 22 B1
West of Twin Peaks
San Francisco 26 B2
West Park Johannesburg 13 A1
West Park Miami 19 C2
West Rouge Toronto 31 A4
West Roxbury Boston 6 B2
West Town Chicago 9 B2
West Wharf Karachi 13 B1
Westchester Los Angeles 16 C2
Westchester New York 22 A2
Westcliff Johannesburg 13 B2
Westdene Johannesburg 13 B1
Westend Helsinki 11 C1
Wester Hailes Edinburgh 11 B2
Westerham Munich 21 B2
Western Addition
San Francisco 26 B2
Westgate New Orleans 21 A1
Westgate Washington 33 B2
Westlake Cape Town 8 B1
Westlake Los Angeles 16 B3
Westlake San Francisco 26 B2
Westminster London 15 A3
Westmount Montreal 20 B2
Weston Toronto 31 A1
Westwego New Orleans 21 B2
Westwood Village
Los Angeles 16 B2
Westzaan Amsterdam 2 A1
Wetton Cape Town 8 B2
Wexford Toronto 31 A3
Weybridge London 15 B1
Wezembeek-Oppem Brussels 6 A2
White Cloud Hill = Baiyun
Mountain Scenic
Area ⌓ Guangzhou 11 A2
White House, The
Washington 33 B2
Whitechapel London 15 A3
Whitehall Dublin 10 A2
Whitney Las Vegas 14 B2
Whittier Los Angeles 16 C4
Whittier Narrows
Recreation Area ⌓
Los Angeles 16 B4
Whitton London 15 B1
Wieden Vienna 32 A2
Wien Vienna 32 A2
Wien-Schwechat ✕ (VIE)
Vienna 32 B3
Wienerberg Vienna 32 B2
Wierzbno Warsaw 33 B2
Wijde Wormer Amsterdam 2 A2
Wilanów Warsaw 33 B2
Wilanówka → Warsaw 33 C2
Wilds, The Johannesburg 13 B2
Wilhelmshagen Berlin 5 B5
Wilket Creek Park Toronto 31 A2
Wilkieston Edinburgh 11 B1
Will Rogers State
Historical Park ⌓
Los Angeles 16 B1
Willbrook Dublin 10 B2
Willesden London 15 A2
Willesden Green London 15 A2
Williamsbridge New York 22 A2
Williamsburg New York 22 B2
Williamsburg Orlando 23 B2
Williamstown Melbourne 18 B1
Willis, L. Orlando 23 B2
Willoughby Sydney 29 A2
Willowdale New Orleans 21 A1
Willowdale Toronto 31 A2
Wilmersdorf Berlin 5 B2
Wilmette Chicago 9 A2
Wilmington London 15 B5
Wilton Manors Miami 19 B3
Wimbledon London 15 B2
Wimbledon Common
London 15 B2
Wimbledon Park London 15 B2
Wimbledon Tennis
Ground London 15 B2
Winchester Boston 6 A2
Winchester Las Vegas 14 B2
Windermere Cape Town 8 A2
Windermere Orlando 23 B1
Windsor Johannesburg 13 A1
Windsor, Gare Montreal 20 B2
Windsor Hills Los Angeles 16 C2
Windy Arbour Dublin 10 B2
Winnetka Chicago 9 A2
Winning Munich 21 B3
Wissous Paris 24 B2
Wittenau Berlin 5 A2
Witwatersrand, Univ. of
Johannesburg 13 B2
Włochy Warsaw 33 B1
Wo Mei Hong Kong 12 A3
Wo Yi Hop Hong Kong 12 A2
Woburn Boston 6 A2
Woburn Toronto 31 A3
Wola Warsaw 33 B1
Wolgok Seoul 27 B2
Wolica Warsaw 33 C1
Wollaston Boston 6 B2
Woltersdorf Berlin 5 B5
Woluwe-St-Lambert Brussels 6 A2
Woluwe-St-Pierre Brussels 6 A2
Wong Chuk Hang
Hong Kong 12 B3
Wong Chuk Wan
Hong Kong 12 A3
Wong Chuk Yeung
Hong Kong 12 A3
Wood Green London 15 A3
Wood Ridge New York 22 A1
Woodbine Race Track
Toronto 31 A1
Woodbridge Toronto 31 A1
Woodford London 15 A4
Woodford Bridge London 15 A4
Woodford Green London 15 A4
Woodhaven New York 22 B2
Woodhouselee Edinburgh 11 B2
Woodlands Singapore 28 A2
Woodmont Washington 33 B2
Woodside London 15 B3
Woodside New York 22 B2
Woodstock Cape Town 8 A1
Woollahra Sydney 29 B2
Woolooware B. Sydney 29 C1
Woolwich London 15 B4
Worker's Stadium Beijing 4 B2
World Financial Centre
Shanghai 28 B2
World Trade Center, Site
of former = National
September 11 Memorial
and Museum New York 22 B1
Worli Mumbai 20 A1
Worth Chicago 9 C2
Wren's Nest Atlanta 3 B2
Wrigley Field Chicago 9 B3
Wuhlgarten Berlin 5 A4
Wujiaochang Shanghai 28 B2
Würm → Munich 21 B1
Würm-kanal Munich 21 A1
Wushan Guangzhou 11 B3
Wusong Shanghai 28 A1
Wyczółki Warsaw 33 C1
Wygoda Warsaw 33 B2
Wynberg Cape Town 8 B1

X

Xabregas Lisbon 16 A2
Xiakeng Guangzhou 11 A2
Xiaogang Park Guangzhou 11 B2
Xiaoping Guangzhou 11 A2
Xiashachong Guangzhou 11 B1
Xichang Guangzhou 11 B2
Xicheng Beijing 4 B1
Xidan Beijing 4 B2
Xi'ercun Guangzhou 11 B2
Xincun Guangzhou 11 B2
Xizhimen Beijing 4 B1
Xochimilco, Parque
Ecológico Mexico City 18 C2
Xuanwu Beijing 4 B1
Xuhui Shanghai 28 B1
Xujiahui Shanghai 28 B1

Y

Yaba Lagos 14 A2
Yaftābād Tehran 31 B1
Yahara Tokyo 30 A2
Yaho Tokyo 30 A1
Yakire Tokyo 30 A4
Yaksu Seoul 27 B2
Yamada Osaka 23 A2
Yamada Tokyo 30 B2
Yamato → Osaka 23 B1
Yan Kit Singapore 28 A3
Yanbu Guangzhou 11 B1
Yangcheon Seoul 27 B1
Yanghuayuan Beijing 4 C1
Yangjae Seoul 27 C2
Yangjiazhuang Shanghai 28 A1
Yangjing Shanghai 28 B2
Yangpu Shanghai 28 B2
Yangpu Park Shanghai 28 B2
Yannawa Bangkok 3 B2
Yaotai Guangzhou 11 B2
Yarmūk Baghdad 3 B1
Yarra Bend Park Melbourne 18 A2
Yarraville Melbourne 18 A1
Yauza → Moscow 19 B4
Yeading London 15 A1
Yedikule Istanbul 12 C1
Yenikapı Istanbul 12 B1
Yeniköy Istanbul 12 B2
Yeongdeungpo Seoul 27 B1
Yeongdong Seoul 27 B2
Yeouido Seoul 27 B1
Yerba Buena I.
San Francisco 26 B2
Yerres Paris 24 B4
Yerushalayim =
Jerusalem Jerusalem 13 B2
Yi O San Tsuen Hong Kong 12 B1
Yiheyuan Beijing 4 B1
Yıldız Park Istanbul 12 B2
Yinhangzhen Shanghai 28 A2
Yishun Singapore 28 A3
Ylästö Helsinki 11 B2
Yodo → Osaka 23 A2
Yongdingman Beijing 4 B2
Yongfucun Guangzhou 11 B2
Yongsan Seoul 27 B1
Yonkers New York 22 A2
York Toronto 31 A2
York Mills Toronto 31 A2
York Univ. Toronto 31 A2
You'anmen Beijing 4 B1
Youngsfield Cape Town 8 B1
Yuancun Guangzhou 11 B3
Yuanmingyuan Park Beijing 4 A1
Yuanxiatian Guangzhou 11 A2
Yuexiu Guangzhou 11 B2
Yuexiu Park Guangzhou 11 B2
Yugo-Zarad Moscow 19 B2
Yung Shue Wan Hong Kong 12 B2
Yūsofābād Tehran 31 A2

Z

Za'abeel Dubai 9 B2
Zaandam Amsterdam 2 A1
Zaandijk Amsterdam 2 A1
Zaanstad Amsterdam 2 A1
Záběhlice Prague 25 B2
Zabki Warsaw 33 B2
Žacisze Warsaw 33 B2
Zahrā Baghdad 3 A1
Žalov Prague 25 A2
Załuski Warsaw 33 C1
Zamdorf Munich 21 B2
Zanevka St. Petersburg 27 B3
Zapote Manila 17 C1
Zaventem Brussels 6 A2
Zawady Warsaw 33 B2
Zāwiyet Abû Musallam
Cairo 7 B1
Zawrā' Park Baghdad 3 B2
Zbraslav Prague 25 C2
Zbuzany Prague 25 B1
Zdiby Prague 25 B2
Zeekoevlei Cape Town 8 B2
Zehlendorf Berlin 5 B2
Zenne → Brussels 6 A2
Zephyr Field New Orleans 21 B1
Żerań Warsaw 33 B1
Zerzeń Warsaw 33 B2
Zeytinburnu Istanbul 12 C1
Zhabei Shanghai 28 B1
Zhdanov Moscow 19 B3
Zheji Guangzhou 11 B2
Zhenru Shanghai 28 B1
Zhernovka St. Petersburg 27 B2
Zhicun Guangzhou 11 B2
Zhongguancun Beijing 4 B1
Zhongshan Park Shanghai 28 B1
Zhoucun Guangzhou 11 A2
Zhoujiadu Shanghai 28 B1
Zhoujiazhen Shanghai 28 B2
Zhouzhuangzi Beijing 4 B1
Zhulebino Moscow 19 B4
Zhushadi Guangzhou 11 A3
Zielona Warsaw 33 B3
Zielonka Warsaw 33 B2
Zizhuyuan Park Beijing 4 B1
Žižkov Prague 25 B2
Zličín Prague 25 B1
Zografou Athens 2 B2
Żoliborz Warsaw 33 B1
Zonnebloem Cape Town 8 A1
Zugliget Budapest 7 A1
Zuglö Budapest 7 A2
Zuiderwoude Amsterdam 2 A3
Zumbi Rio de Janeiro 25 A1
Zunderdorp Amsterdam 2 A2
Zuvuvu → São Paulo 27 C1
Zwanenburg Amsterdam 2 A1
Zwölfaxing Vienna 32 B2

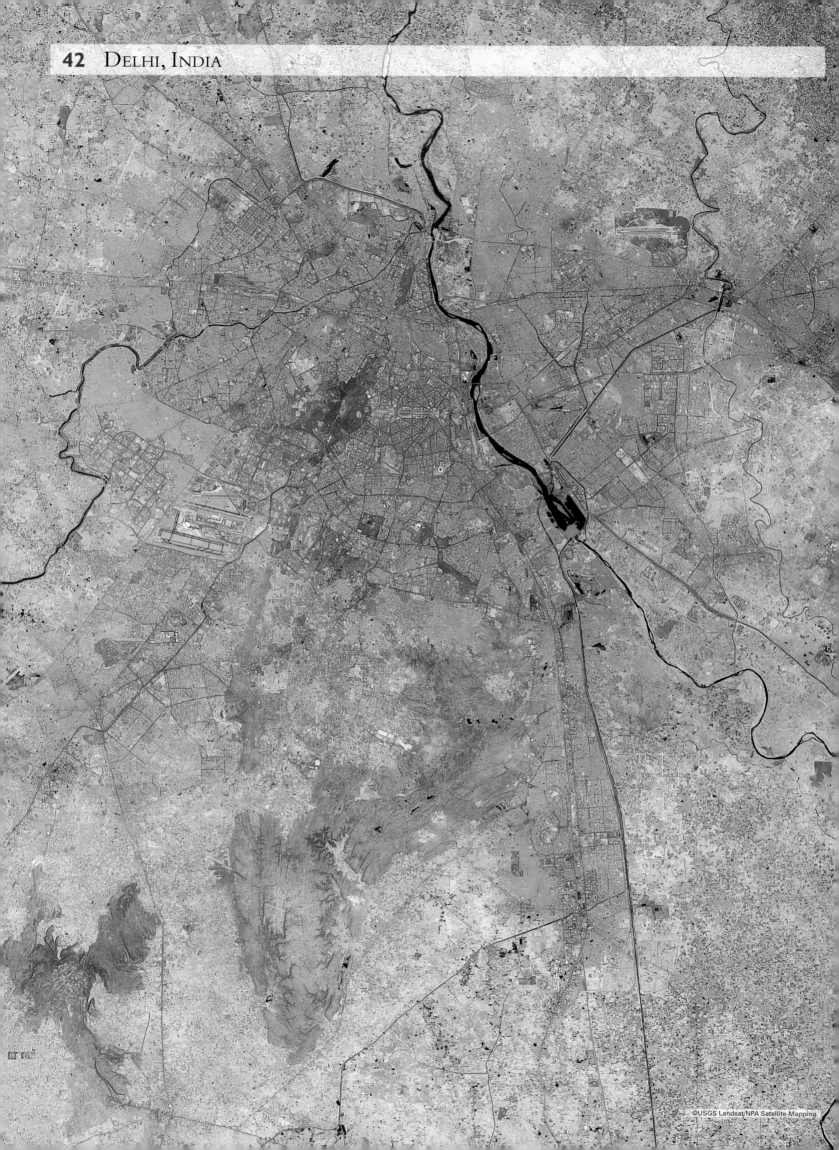

©USGS Landsat/NPA Satellite Mapping

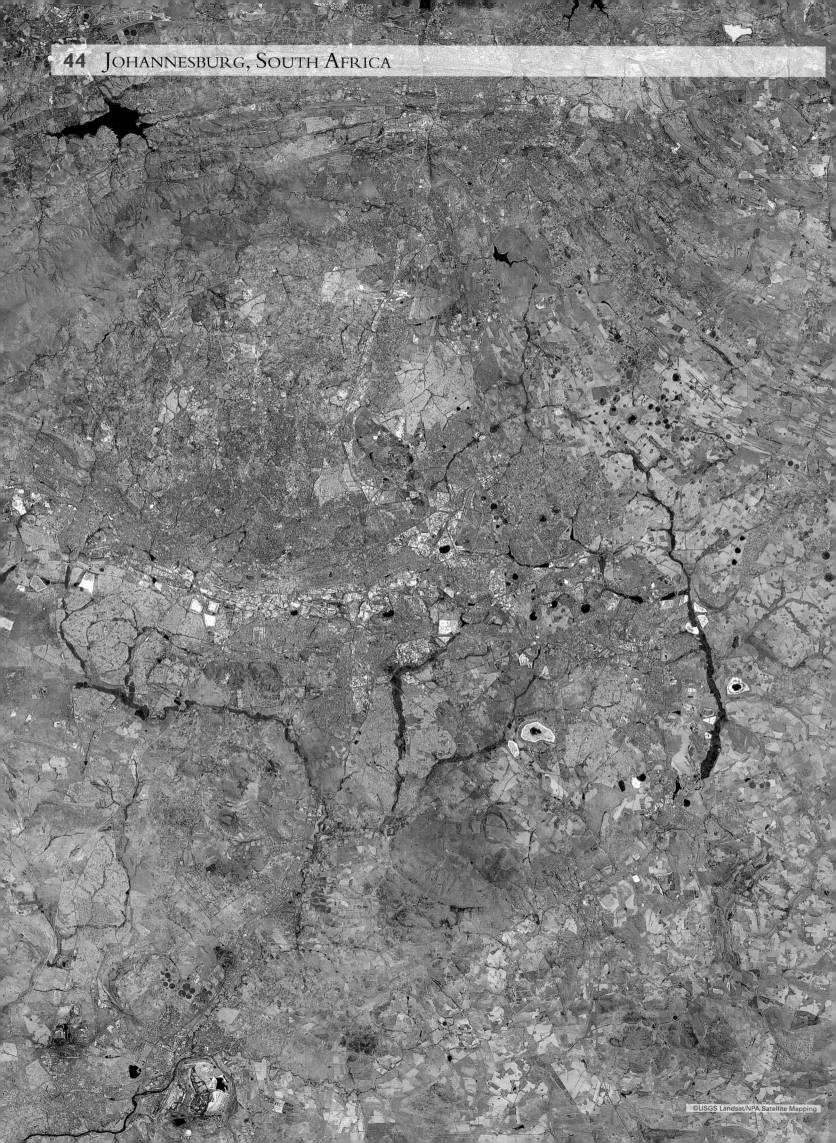

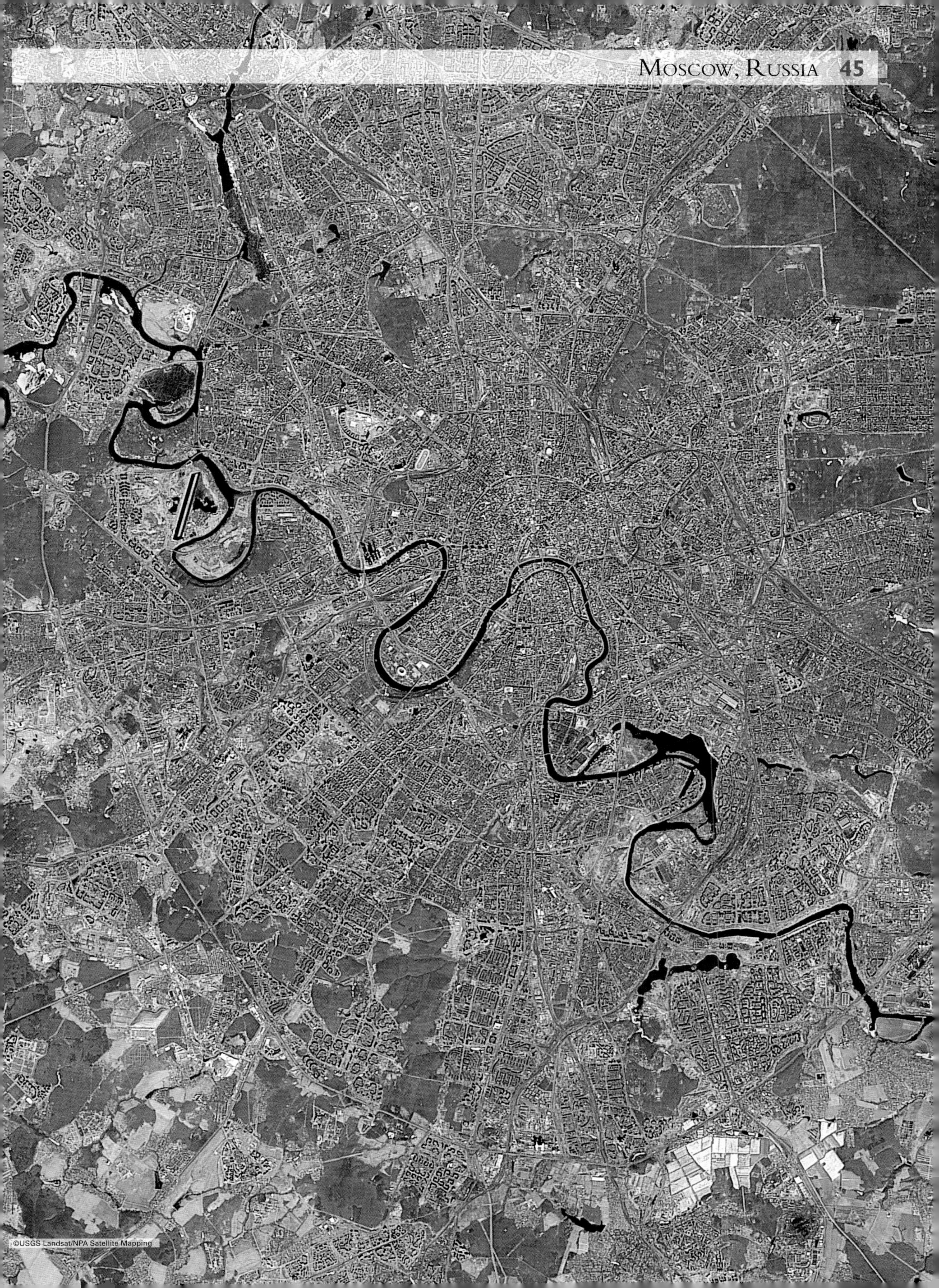

SYDNEY, AUSTRALIA

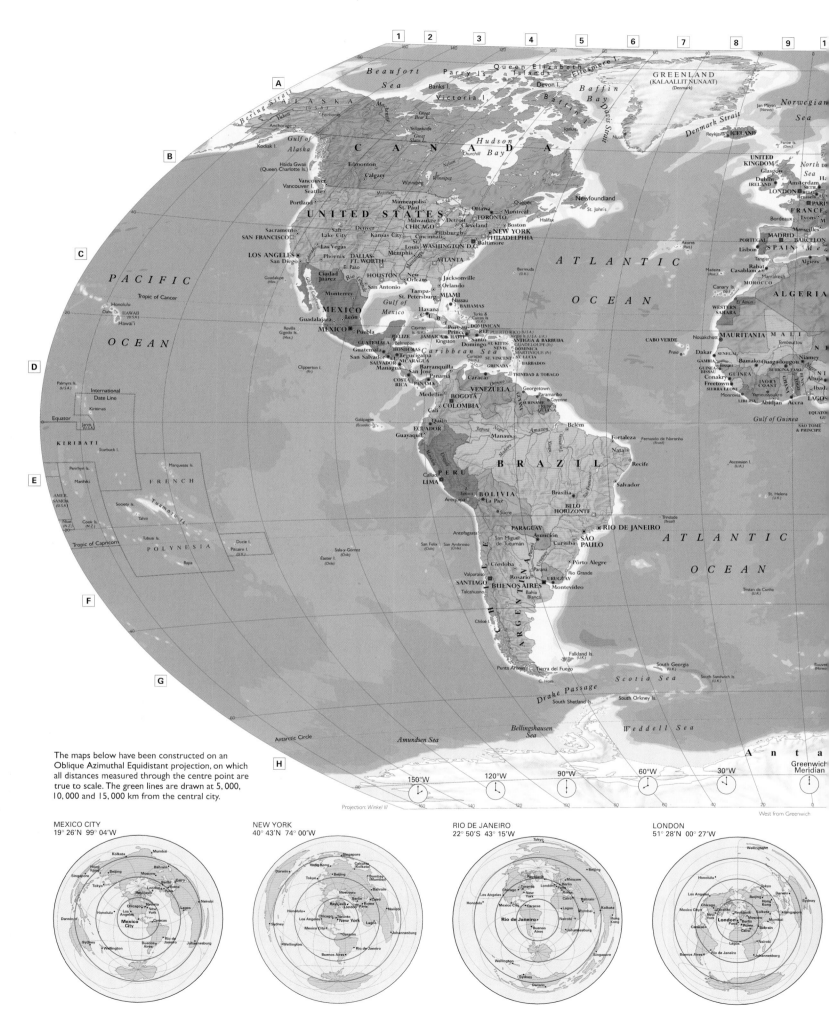

The maps below have been constructed on an Oblique Azimuthal Equidistant projection, on which all distances measured through the centre point are true to scale. The green lines are drawn at 5, 000, 10, 000 and 15, 000 km from the central city.

Projection: Winkel III

West from Greenwich

MEXICO CITY
19° 26'N 99° 04'W

NEW YORK
40° 43'N 74° 00'W

RIO DE JANEIRO
22° 50'S 43° 15'W

LONDON
51° 28'N 00° 27'W

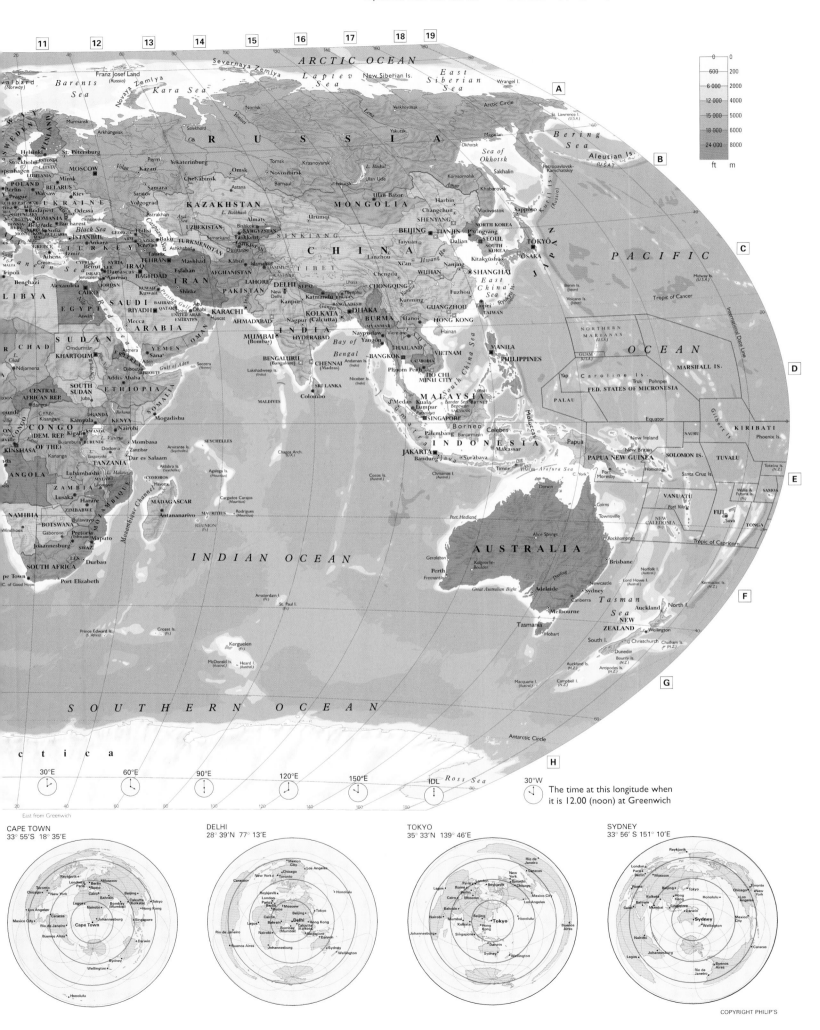

100 0 200 400 600 800 1000 1200 1400 km
100 0 200 400 600 800 1000 miles

1:35 000 000

18	17	16	15	

JAPAN

PACIFIC OCEAN

Tufts Abyssal Plain

Gilbert Seamounts

Aleutian Trench

Aleutian Islands (U.S.A.)

Bowers Basin

Near Is. (U.S.A.)

Kurilskiye Ostrova (Russia)

HOKKAIDŌ
SAPPORO

Dutch Harbor

Aleutian Basin

Bowers Ridge

Komandorskiye Ostrova

Mys Lopatka

La Perouse Str.

Kuril Basin

Yuzhno-Sakhalinsk

Bristol Bay

Unimak I.
2857

Bering Sea

Petropavlovsk-Kamchatskiy
Klyuchevskaya Sopka 4750

Poluostrov Kamchatka

Sakhalin (Russia)
1609

Vanino

Kodiak I.
1362

Pribilof Is. (U.S.A.)

42

St. Matthew (U.S.A.)

Mys Navarin

Ust-Kamchatsk
Ostrov Karaginskiy

Amur

Khabarovsk

G. of Alaska

Seward

Nunivak

St. Lawrence I. (U.S.A.)

2453

Penzhinskaya G.
Gizhiginskaya Guba

Tauiskaya Guba

Magadan

Nikolayevsk

Komsomolsk-na-Amure

Prince William Sd.
Anchorage
Cordova Mt. McKinley 6168

Yukon

Nome

Norton Sd.

Anadyrskiy Zaliv

Anadyr

S

Udskaya Guba

Okhotsk

Haida Gwaii (Queen Charlotte Is.)

Mt. St. Elias
44
5489

Fairbanks

Bering Str.

Providenskiy Mys Dezhneva

Chukotskoye Nagorye

e

Sea of Okhotsk

Prince Rupert

Skagway Mt. Logan
4949
5959

ALASKA (U.S.A.)

Kuskokwim

C. Prince of Wales

Kotzebue Sd.

Pt. Hope

C. Lisburne

Pevek

Kolymskoye Nagorye

v

Okhotsk

Stanovoy Khrebet

4019

Juneau

Whitehorse

Dawson

Koyukuk

Proliv Longa

Nizhne-Kolymsk

Kolyma
3147

Srednekolymsk

e

Yakutsk

Aldan

Chukchi Sea

Ostrov Vrangelya (Russia)

Indigirka

Verkhoyansk

2295

Olekma

Rocky Mountains

Dawson Creek

Stewart
2762

Peel

Porcupine

Fort Yukon

Prudhoe Bay
2761

Fort McPherson

C. Halkett
Pt. Barrow

1696

46

East Siberian Sea

Yana

Verkhoyansky Khrebet

Zhigansk

Kazachye
Lyakhovskiye Ostrova

Bulun

Lena
Olenek

Fort Simpson

Liard

Mackenzie

Fort Good Hope

Harrison Bay

Herschel I.

Beaufort Sea

Novosibirskiye Ostrova

Kotelnyy
374

Tiksi

Fort Vermilion

Peace

Great Bear Lake

Tulita

Mackenzie Bay
2882
Tuktoyaktuk

Canada Abyssal Plain

O. Delonga

Laptev Sea

Anabar

North

Athabasca

Yellowknife

Great Slave Lake

Coppermine

C. Bathurst

Canada Basin

A R C T I C

Nordvik

Ostrova Petra

Poluostrov Taymyr

Khatanga

America

Athabasca Lake

Kugluktuk

Banks I.

C. Kellett

C. Prince Alfred
371

Chukchi Plateau

3327

Mendeleyev Ridge

3546

O C E A N

3849

4100

Severnaya Zemlya

Mys Chelyuskin

Ozero Taymyr

Gory Putorana

Z

NUNAVUT

Victoria Island

Prince Albert Pen.

M'Clure Str.

Prince Patrick I.

North Magnetic Pole 2014
+

4007

Alpha Ridge

Makarov Basin

Amundsen Basin
4484

Oktyabrskoy Revolyutsii
965

Norilsk

Dudinka

Queen

Melville I.

Parry Is.

3700

Lomonosov Ridge
NORTH POLE

4346

Arctic Mid-Ocean Ridge

3741

3910

O. Ushakova

O. Uedineniya

Pyasina

Igarka

Yenisey

King William I.

M'Clintock Chan.

Viscount Melville Sd.

Borden I.

2104

Elizabeth

Islands

Eureka

Ellef Ringnes I.

Sverdrup Is.

Nansen Sd.

Nansen Basin

Zemlya Frantsa Iosifa (Russia)

O. Greem-Bell
Z. Vilcheka

90

O. Belyy

Dikson

Norilsk

Gydanskiy Poluostrov

Novyy Urengoy

Taz

Churchill

Boothia Pen.

Somerset I.

Resolute

Axel Heiberg I.

Devon I.

Ellesmere I. (Canada)
2616

C. Columbia

Lincoln Sea

5449

Z. Aleksandry

480

Novaya
1547

Kara Sea

Baydaratskaya Guba

Poluostrov Yamal

Ob

Nadym

Hudson Bay

Chesterfield Inlet

Prince of Wales I.

Alert

McKinley Sea

Zemlya

Novaya Zemlya

1342

Poluostrov Yamal

Novyy Port

Nizhnevartovsk

Surgut

Southampton I.

Coats I.

Melville Pen.

Foxe Basin

Prince Charles I.

K. Morris Jesup

Peary Land

Kronprins Frederik Land

Independence Fjord

A

Nordkapp

Nordaustlandet

1717

Barents Sea

Belushya Guba

Salekhard

Nefteyugansk

Mansel I.

Foxe Chan.

Iqaluit
2147

Bylot

Smith Sund

Qaanaaq

Kane Basin

Kong Frederik VIII's Land

2571

Spitsbergen
Svalbard (Norway)

Edgeøya

1894

Narodnaya

Vorkuta

Amderma

Berezovo

Tobolsk

Baffin Bay

Cumberland Sd.

C. Dyer

Upernavik

Uummannaq

Knud Rasmussen Land

Kong Frederik IX's Land
3238

Greenland Sea

Nordaustlandet

Longyearbyen

O. Kolguyev

Mys Kanin Nos

Naryan-Mar
Pechora

Ukhta

Uralskie Gory

YEKATERINBURG

C. Wolstenholme

Resolution I.

Hudson Str.

Frobisher Bay

Qeqertarsuaq

Nuuk

2276

GREENLAND (KALAALLIT NUNAAT) (Denmark)

Kong Christian IX's Land

Kejser Franz Joseph Fd.

Bjørnøya (Norway)

Vardø

Kirkenes

Mys Svyatoy Nos

Mezen

Perm

UFA

Labrador

Ungava Bay

Davis Str.

Qeqertarsuaq

Paamiut

Mt. Forel
3360

Kong Christian IX's Land
3693

Ittoqqortoormiit

Kong Oscar Fjord

Mohns Ridge

Jan Mayen (Norway)
2277

Nordkapp

Hammerfest

Tromsø

Murmansk

Kolskiy Poluostrov

Arkhangelsk
Sev. Dvina

Severodvinsk

Syktyvkar

Labrador Sea

Northwest Atlantic Mid-Ocean Canyon

Hamilton Inlet

Qaqortoq

Kong Frederik VI's Kyst
2850

Gunnbjørn Fjeld

Kangikajik

Icelandic Plateau

Lofoten

Narvik

Beloye More

Kandalaksha

Onega

Onezhskoye Ozero

Mid-Atlantic Ridge

Alluitsup Paa

Tasiilaq

Denmark Str.

Horn

Arctic Circle

Norwegian Sea

Trondheim

2469

N O R W A Y

S W E D E N

Gulf of Bothnia

Tornio

Oulu

Ladozhskoye Ozero

Kargopol

Volga

SAMARA

NIZHNIY NOVGOROD

Saratov

Nunap Isua (Kap Farvel)

Breiðafjörður

Fontur

Norwegian Basin

3800

Bergen

Oslo

STOCKHOLM

FINLAND

HELSINKI

Chudskoye Ozero

ST. PETERBURG

MOSKVA

VOLGOGRAD

Charlie Gibbs Fracture Zone

4563

A T L A N T I C

Reykjavik ICELAND

Ørafajökull
2119

Iceland Basin

ICELAND

Føroyar (Den.)

Shetland Is. (U.K.)

60

2469

Skagerrak

KØBENHAVN

DENMARK

Kaliningrad (Russia)

Riga

LATVIA

Tallinn

ESTONIA

Gulf of Finland

Gula of Finland

Baltic Sea

BELARUS

KYYIV

KHARKIV

ROSTOV

O C E A N

King's Trough

Rockall (U.K.)

Hebrides (U.K.)

Orkney Is. (U.K.)

North Sea

Edinburgh

GLASGOW

UNITED KINGDOM

Belfast

IRELAND

DUBLIN

NETH.

AMSTERDAM

LONDON

Rockall Trough

Lithuania

Vilnius

Wisła

WARSZAWA

POLAND

Kraków

Lviv

UKRAINE

ODESA

MOLDOVA

ROMANIA

Donetsk

Black Sea

HAMBURG

BERLIN

GERMANY

PRAHA

C. Clear

King's Trough

ft m
12 000 4000
6000 2000
4500 1500
3000 1000
400
200
0 0
600 200
1000 3000
2000 6000
3000 9000
4000 12 000
5000 15 000
m ft

	Maximum extent of sea ice
	Minimum extent of sea ice
	Ice caps and permanent ice shelf

Projection: *Zenithal Equidistant*

West from Greenwich 0 East from Greenwich

COPYRIGHT PHILIP'S

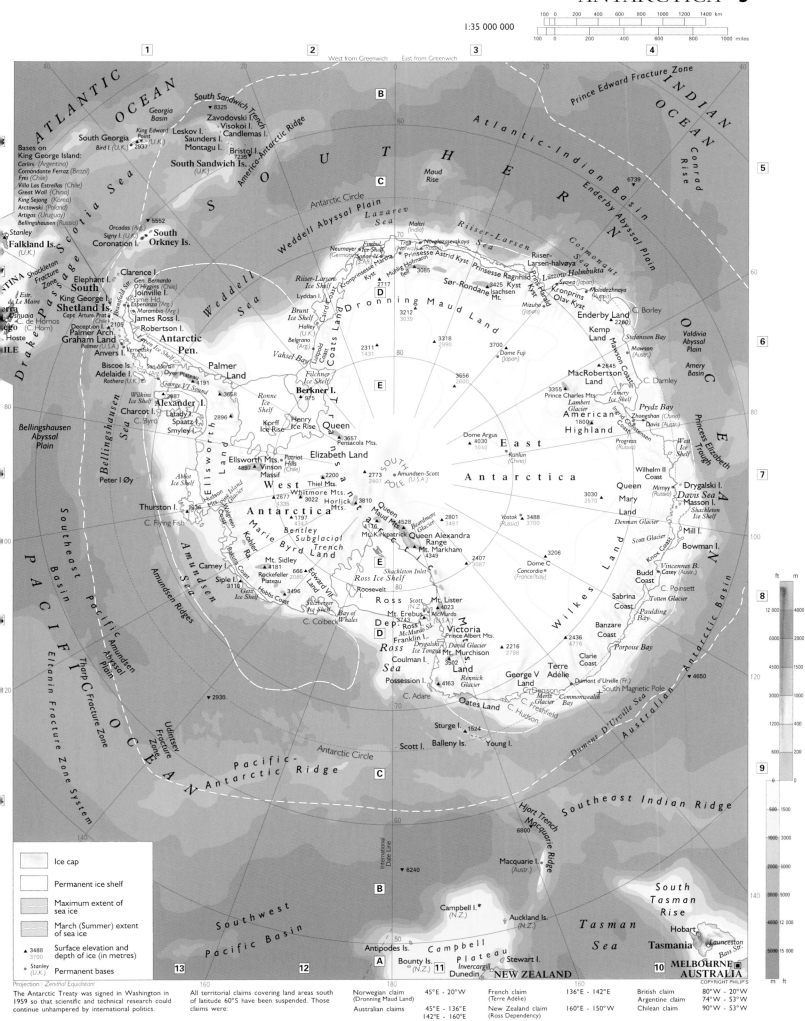

1:35 000 000

100   0   200   400   600   800   1000   1200   1400 km
100   0   200   400   600   800   1000 miles

ATLANTIC OCEAN

Bases on
King George Island:
Carlini (Argentina)
Comandante Ferraz (Brazil)
Frei (Chile)
Villa Las Estrellas (Chile)
Great Wall (China)
King Sejong (Korea)
Arctowski (Poland)
Artigas (Uruguay)
Bellingshausen (Russia)

Georgia Basin
South Sandwich Trench ▼8325
South Georgia
Bird I. (U.K.) ▲2937 King Edward Point (U.K.)
Leskov I. Zavodovski I. Visokoi I. Candlemas I.
Saunders I. Montagu I. Bristol I. ▼7235
South Sandwich Is. (U.K.)

SOUTHERN

South Sandwich Is. (U.K.)

West from Greenwich   East from Greenwich

Antarctic Circle

Maud Rise

Prince Edward Fracture Zone

INDIAN OCEAN

Atlantic-Indian Basin

Conrad Rise

▲6739

Enderby Abyssal Plain

Lazarev Sea

Weddell Abyssal Plain

America-Antarctic Ridge

Stanley
Falkland Is. (U.K.)

Orcadas (Arg.)
Signy I. (U.K.) ▼5552
Coronation I. South Orkney Is.

Clarence I.
Elephant I. (U.K.)
Gen. Bernardo O'Higgins (Chile)
Joinville I.
James Ross I.
Robertson I.

ARGENTINA Shackleton Fracture Zone
Estr. de Le Maire
Ushuaia
C. de Hornos (C. Horn)
Hoste
CHILE

South Shetland Is.
Capt. Arturo Prat (Chile)
Deception I. (Chile) ▲2105
Palmer Arch
Graham Land
Anvers I. Palmer (U.S.A.)
Vernadsky (Ukr.)

Maltri (India)
Neumayer (Germany)
Troll (Norway)
Novolazarevskaya (Russia)
Fimbul Ice Shelf
Sanae IV (S. Afr.)
Maud Land
Prinsesse Astrid Kyst
Mühlig Hofmann fjell ▲3085
Kronprinsesse Martha Kyst ▲2717

Riiser-Larsen Ice Shelf
Lyddan I.
Brunt Ice Shelf
Halley (U.K.)
Belgrano (Arg.)
Vahsel Bay

Coats Land

Dronning Maud Land

Sør-Rondane ▲3425 Isachsen Mt.
Prinsesse Ragnhild Kyst
Prins Harald Kyst
Kronprins Olav Kyst
Lützow Holmbukta
Syowa (Japan)
Molodezhnaya (Russia)
▲3212 3039
▲3318 2990
Dome Fuji (Japan) ▲3700

Enderby Land
C. Borley
Kemp Land
Mawson (Austr.)
Stefansson Bay
MacRobertson Land ▲2645
▲1800 Prince Charles Mts
Lambert Glacier
Amery Ice Shelf
C. Darnley
Zhongshan (China)
Davis (Austr.)

Valdivia Abyssal Plain
Prydz Bay
Amery Basin

INDIAN OCEAN

Scotia Sea

Drake Passage

Bellingshausen Sea

Biscoe Is.
Adelaide I.
Rothera (U.K.)
San Martín (Arg.)
Dyer Plateau
Palmer Land
George VI Sound

Alexander I. ▲2987
Charcot I.
Latady I.
Spaatz I.
Smyley I.

Wilkins Ice Shelf
▲3658
Korff Ice Rise
Henry Ice Rise

Ronne Ice Shelf

Filchner Ice Shelf

Berkner I. ▲975

Queen ▲3657
Pensacola Mts.
Ellsworth Mts. ▲4897 Vinson Massif
Patriot Hills (Chile)
Elizabeth Land

▲2311 1431

▲3318

South Pole ▲2773 2407
Amundsen-Scott (U.S.A.)

Dome Argus ▲4030 1040
Kunlun (China)

East Antarctica

▲3656 2600

▲3355

American Highland

Prince Charles Mts
Ingrid Christensen Coast
Progress (Russia)
Davis (Austr.)

West Ice Shelf

Princess Elizabeth Trough

Bellingshausen Abyssal Plain

Peter I Øy

Abbot Ice Shelf
Thurston I.
C. Flying Fish

Ellsworth Land
Hudson Mts. ▲1936 Pine Island Glacier
Bakutis Coast

West ▲2677 4335
Antarctica
Thiel Mts. ▲2200
Whitmore Mts. Horlick Mts. ▲3022 3496 ▲3810
▲1797 434

Marie Byrd Land
Kohler Ra.
Carney I.
Siple I. ▲3110
Getz Ice Shelf
Mt. Sidley ▲4181
Rockefeller Plateau ▲666 2080

Queen ▲4528
Maud Mts. ▲4176
Beardmore Glacier
Mt. Kirkpatrick ▲4528
Queen Alexandra Range
Mt. Markham ▲4349

▲2801 3491

Vostok (Russia) ▲3488 3700

Dome C ▲3206
Concordia (France/Italy)

▲3030 2570

Queen Mary Land

Wilhelm II Coast
Mirnyy (Russia)
Drygalski I.
Masson I.
Davis Sea
Shackleton Ice Shelf

Amundsen Sea

Amundsen Ridges

Walgreen Coast

Edward VII Land

Salzberger Ice Shelf
Bay of Whales
C. Colbeck

Roosevelt I.

Ross Ice Shelf

Shackleton Inlet

▲2407 3087

Dome C

Budd Coast
Casey (Austr.)
Vincennes B.
C. Poinsett
Sabrina Coast
Totten Glacier
Paulding Bay

Wilkes Land

Knox Coast
Scott Glacier
Mill I.
Bowman I.

Antarctic Basin

PACIFIC OCEAN

Southeast Pacific Basin

Eltanin Fracture Zone System

Udintsev Fracture Zone

Tharp Fracture Zone

Ross Dep.

Scott (N.Z.)
McMurdo (U.S.A.)
Mt. Erebus ▲3743
Franklin I.
Victoria
Prince Albert Mts. ▲4023
McMurdo Sd.
Drygalski Ice Tongue
Mt. Lister ▲4025
Mt. Murchison ▲2216 2798

Banzare Coast
▲2436 4776
Clarie Coast
Porpoise Bay

Terre Adélie
Dumont d'Urville (Fr.)
George V Land

South Magnetic Pole
▼4650

Ross Sea

Coulman I.
▲3502

Possession I. ▲4163

C. Adare

Oates Land

Denison
Mertz Glacier
Commonwealth Bay
C. Freshfield
C. Hudson
Dumont D'Urville Sea

Australian-Antarctic Basin

Antarctic Circle

Pacific-Antarctic Ridge

Southeast Indian Ridge

Hjort Trench
Macquarie Ridge ▼6800

International Date Line

▼2930

Sturge I. ▲1524
Scott I.
Balleny Is.
Young I.

▼6240

Macquarie I. (Austr.)

South Tasman Rise

Southwest Pacific Basin

Campbell I. (N.Z.)
Auckland Is. (N.Z.)

Tasman Sea

Hobart
Launceston
Bass Str.
Tasmania

Antipodes Is. (N.Z.)
Bounty Is. (N.Z.)
Campbell Plateau
Stewart I.
Invercargill
Dunedin

NEW ZEALAND

MELBOURNE AUSTRALIA

COPYRIGHT PHILIP'S

ft   m
12 000   4000
9000   3000
6000   2000
4500   1500
3000   1000
1200   400
600   200
0   0
500   1500
1000   3000
2000   6000
3000   9000
4000   12 000
5000   15 000
m   ft

Legend:
Ice cap
Permanent ice shelf
Maximum extent of sea ice
March (Summer) extent of sea ice
▲3488 3700 Surface elevation and depth of ice (in metres)
• Stanley (U.K.) Permanent bases

Projection: Zenithal Equidistant

The Antarctic Treaty was signed in Washington in 1959 so that scientific and technical research could continue unhampered by international politics.

All territorial claims covering land areas south of latitude 60°S have been suspended. Those claims were:

Norwegian claim (Dronning Maud Land)   45°E - 20°W
Australian claims   45°E - 136°E   142°E - 160°E

French claim (Terre Adélie)   136°E - 142°E
New Zealand claim (Ross Dependency)   160°E - 150°E

British claim   80°W - 20°W
Argentine claim   74°W - 53°W
Chilean claim   90°W - 53°W

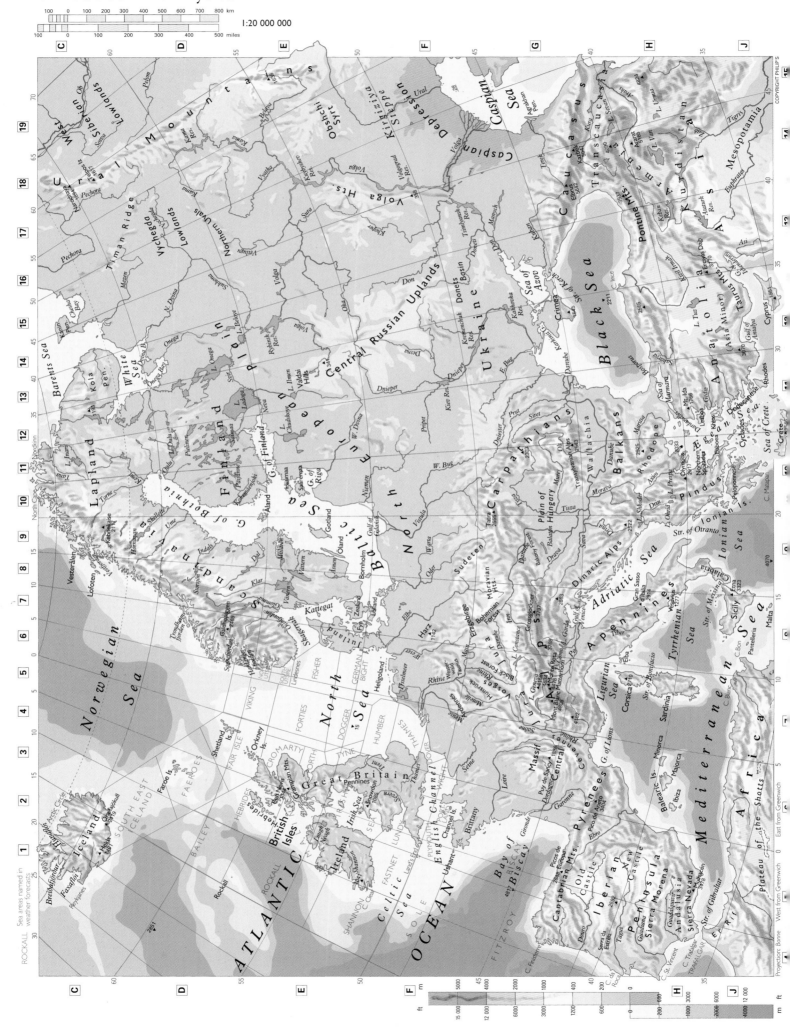

1:20 000 000

■ LONDON Capital Cities

COPYRIGHT PHILIP'S

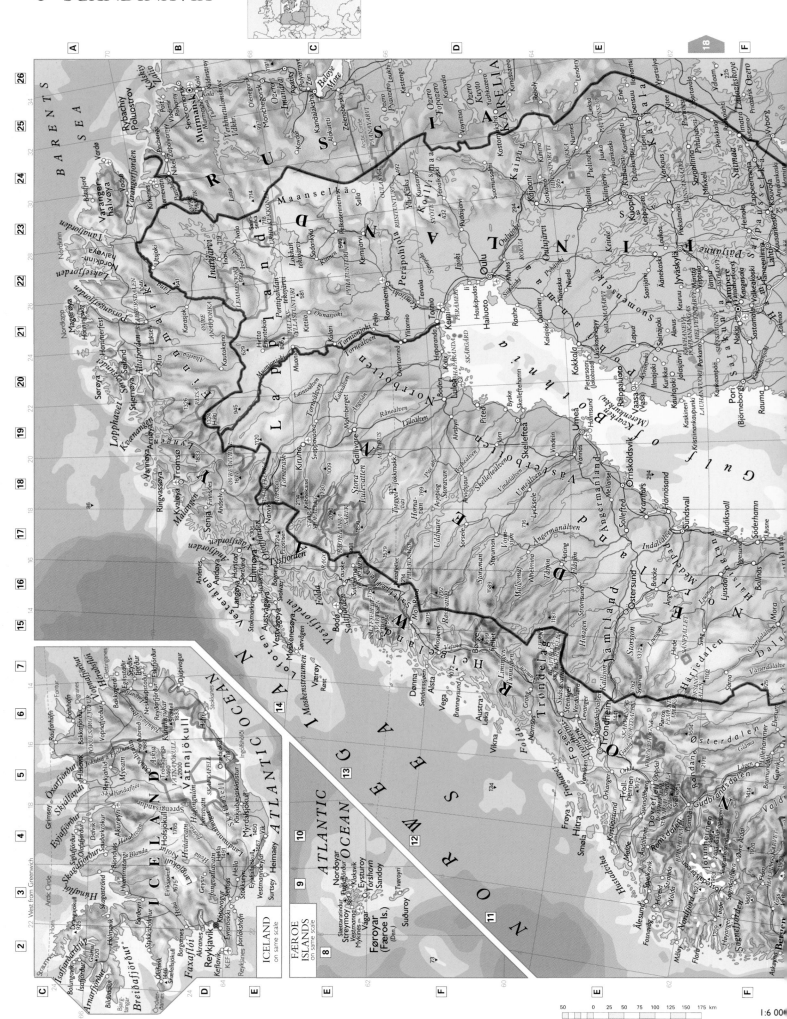

ICELAND
on same scale

FÆROE
ISLANDS
on same scale

1:6 000

50   0   25   50   75 100 125 150 175 km

50   0   25   50   75   100 125 miles

1:2 000 000

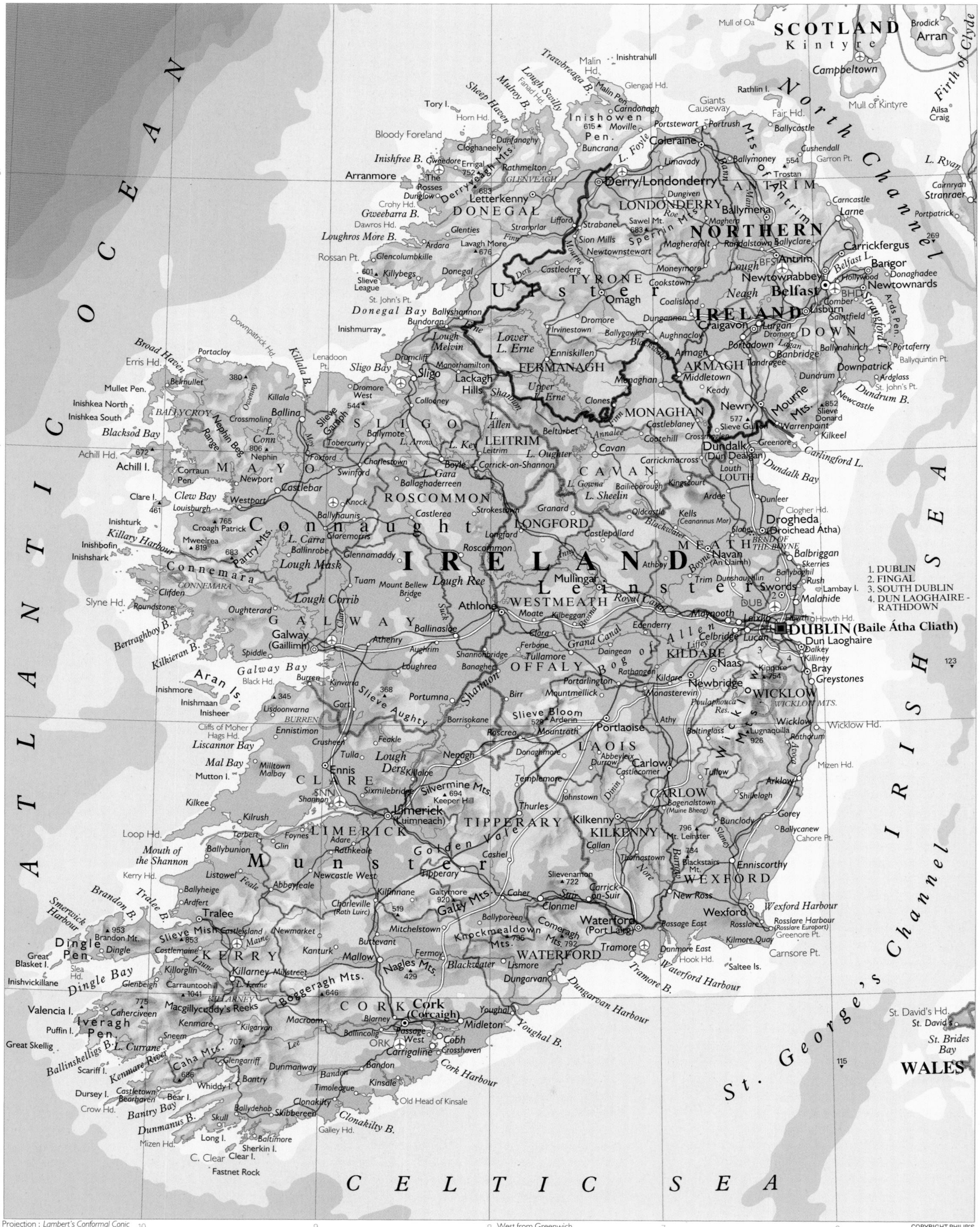

10 0 10 20 30 40 50 60 70 80 km
10 0 10 20 30 40 50 miles

SCOTLAND
Kintyre
Mull of Oa
Brodick
Arran
Campbeltown
Mull of Kintyre
Ailsa Craig
Firth of Clyde
Cairnryan
Stranraer
Portpatrick

North Channel

ATLANTIC OCEAN

Malin Hd.
Inishtrahull
Trawbreaga B.
Fanad Hd.
Malin Pen.
Carndonagh
Inishowen Pen.
Moville
Giants Causeway
Portstewart
Portrush
Ballycastle
Fair Hd.
Garron Pt.
Cushendall
Rathlin I.
Ballymoney
554
Trostan
Garron Pt.
Carncastle
Larne
Carrickfergus
269

Tory I.
Horn Hd.
Sheep Haven
Mulroy B.
Dunfanaghy
Lough Swilly
Buncrana
L. Foyle
Coleraine
Limavady
Ballymena
ANTRIM
Bloody Foreland
Cloghaneely
Gweedore
Errigal 752
Rathmelton
Letterkenny
Derry/Londonderry
Dunginen
LONDONDERRY
Roe
Mts. of Antrim
Inishfree B.
The Rosses
Duntoghan
GLENVEAGH
Strabane
683 Sawel Mt.
Sperrin Mts.
Magherafelt
Randalstown
Ballyclare
Newtownabbey
Belfast L.
Bangor
Donaghadee
Arranmore
Crohy Hd.
Killybegs
Glenties
Ardara
Lavagh More 676
601
Slieve League
St. John's Pt.
Donegal
DONEGAL
Sion Mills
Newtownstewart
Castlederg
Omagh
TYRONE
Cookstown
Moneymore
Coalisland
Dungannon
Lough Neagh
Antrim
BFS
Craigavon
Lurgan
Portadown
Belfast
Holywood
Newtownards
Ards Pen.
Lisburn
DOWN
Saintfield
Comber
Strangford L.
Portaferry

NORTHERN IRELAND

Donegal Bay
Ballyshannon
Bundoran
Lough Erne
Lower L. Erne
Dromore
Irvinestown
Enniskillen
FERMANAGH
Upper L. Erne
Clones
MONAGHAN
Ballygawley
Aughnacloy
Armagh
ARMAGH
Middletown
Keady
Monaghan
Castleblaney
Cootehill
Belturbet
577
Slieve Gullion
Newry
Crossmaglen
Mourne Mts.
852
Slieve Donard
Warrenpoint
Rostrevor
Kilkeel
Newcastle
Dundrum B.
Downpatrick
Clogher Hd.

Broad Haven
Erris Hd.
Portacloy
Belmullet
Mullet Pen.
Inishkea North
Inishkea South
BALLYCROY
Blacksod Bay
Achill Hd.
Achill I. 672
Clare I. 461
Clew Bay
Inishturk
Killary Harbour
Inishbofin
Inishshark
Portaloy
Downpatrick Hd.
Killala B.
Lenadoon Pt.
Killala
Ballina
Crossmolina
Nephin Beg Range
Slieve Gamph
544
SLIGO
Dromore West
Collooney
Sligo Bay
Sligo
Dromore West
Manorhamilton
Lackagh Hills
Dartry Mts.
Lough Melvin
Garrison
LEITRIM
L. Allen
L. Arrow
Tobercurry
Ballymote
Foxford
Charlestown
Swinford
MAYO
Nephin 806
Corraun Pen.
Newport
Westport
Castlebar
Knock
Ballyhaunis
Claremorris
Croagh Patrick 765
Louisburgh
Mweelrea 819
Partry Mts.
L. Carra
683
Ballinrobe
CONNAUGHT
Lough Mask
Connemara
Clifden
Slyne Hd.
Roundstone
Bertraghboy B.
Kilkieran B.
CONNEMARA
Oughterard
Lough Corrib
Galway (Gaillimh)
GALWAY
Spiddle
Galway Bay
Black Hd.
Aran Is.
Inishmore
Inishmaan
Inisheer
Cliffs of Moher
Hags Hd.
Liscannor Bay
BURREN
Lisdoonvarna
Ennistimon
Crusheen
Mal Bay
Mutton I.
Milltown Malbay
CLARE
Ennis
Kilkee
Loop Hd.
Kilrush
Larbert
Mouth of the Shannon
Foynes
Kerry Hd.
Ballybunion
Listowel
Abbeyfeale
Newcastle West
LIMERICK
Adare
Rathkeale
Limerick (Luimneach)
Sixmilebridge
SNN
Shannon
Feakle
Tulla
Nenagh
Silvermine Mts.
694
Keeper Hill
Roscommon
ROSCOMMON
Castlerea
Castlereagh
Strokestown
Frenchpark
Boyle
Carrick-on-Shannon
L. Key
Ballaghaderreen
L. Gara
LONGFORD
Longford
Granard
CAVAN
Cavan
L. Oughter
L. Sheelin
Oldcastle
Kells (Ceanannus Mor)
Kingscourt
Carrickmacross
Annalee
L. Gowna
MEATH
Navan (An Uaimh)
Trim
Athboy
WESTMEATH
Mullingar
Castlepollard
L. Derravaragh
Athlone
Moate
Kilbeggan
Tyrrellspass
Royal Canal
LEINSTER
Edenderry
Rhode
Daingean
KILDARE
Maynooth
Celbridge
Leixlip
Lucan
DUBLIN (Baile Átha Cliath)
Dún Laoghaire
Dalkey
Killiney
Bray
Greystones
754
Delgany
Balbriggan
Skerries
Rush
Lambay I.
Swords
Malahide
Howth Hd.
Drogheda (Droichead Átha)
Bend of the Boyne
LOUTH
Dundalk (Dún Dealgan)
Dundalk Bay
Ardee
Dunleer
Castlebellingham
Carlingford L.
Greenore
Carlingford

1. DUBLIN
2. FINGAL
3. SOUTH DUBLIN
4. DUN LAOGHAIRE-RATHDOWN

IRELAND

Tuam
Mount Bellew Bridge
Athenry
Loughrea
Aughrim
Ballinasloe
Shannonbridge
Banagher
Portumna
Lough Derg
Birr
OFFALY
Tullamore
Ferbane
Clara
Kilcormac
Slieve Bloom Mts.
Arderin 529
Mountmellick
Portarlington
Monasterevin
Newbridge
Naas
Kilcullen
Kildare
Athy
Carlow
Bog of Allen
Grand Canal
Barrow
LAOIS
Portlaoise
Mountrath
Abbeyleix
Durrow
Castlecomer
CARLOW
Bagenalstown (Muine Bheag)
Tullow
Bunclody
Borris
Gorey
Arklow
Avoca
WICKLOW
Wicklow
Wicklow Hd.
WICKLOW MTS.
Lugnaquilla 926
Rathdrum
Roundwood
Blessington
Poulaphouca Res.
Mizen Hd.
123
115

Roscrea
Borrisokane
Nenagh
Templemore
Thurles
TIPPERARY
Roscrea
Donaghmore
Johnstown
Kilkenny
KILKENNY
Callan
Thomastown
Graiguenamanagh
New Ross
Enniscorthy
WEXFORD
Wexford Harbour
Rosslare
Rosslare Harbour (Rosslare Europort)
Greenore Pt.
Carnsore Pt.
Saltee Is.
Hook Hd.
Waterford Harbour
Passage East
Dunmore East
Tramore
Tramore B.
WATERFORD
Waterford (Port Láirge)
Carrick-on-Suir
Clonmel
Suir
Comeragh Mts. 792
Knockmealdown Mts. 795
Lismore
Dungarvan
Dungarvan Harbour
Mitchelstown
Fermoy
Blackwater
MUNSTER
Golden Vale
Tipperary
Cashel
Caher
Slievenamon 722
Gaitymore 920
Galty Mts.
Galtymore
Ballyporeen
Kilfinnane
Charleville (Rath Luirc)
519
Buttevant
Mallow
Nagles Mts. 429
Midleton
Youghal
Youghal B.
Blackwater
CORK
Cork (Corcaigh)
Blarney
Carrigaline
Crosshaven
Cobh
Cork Harbour
Old Head of Kinsale
Kinsale
Bandon
Clonakilty
Clonakilty B.
Galley Hd.
Skibbereen
Baltimore
Sherkin I.
Clear I.
C. Clear
Fastnet Rock
Mizen Hd.
Long I.
Skull
Dunmanus B.
Crow Hd.
Bantry Bay
Bantry
Whiddy I.
Ballydehob
Timoleague
Dunmanway
Ballinspittle
Macroom
Ballyvourney
Inchigeelagh
Lee
Glengarriff
Caha Mts. 686
Bear I.
Bearhaven
Castletown
Dursey I.
Kenmare River
Sneem
Kenmare
707
Killarney
Iveragh Pen.
Macgillycuddy's Reeks
Carrauntoohil 1041
L. Leane
KILLARNEY
Boggeragh Mts. 646
Millstreet
Rathmore
Kanturk
Newmarket
Castleisland
Tralee
Tralee B.
Brandon B.
Brandon Mt. 953
Dingle 853
Slieve Mish
Dingle Pen.
Slea Hd.
Dingle Bay
Inishvickillane
Great Blasket I.
Smerwick Harbour
Ardfert
Ballyheige
Feale
Killorglin
Glenbeigh
Cahersiveen
775
Valentia I.
Puffin I.
Great Skellig
Ballinskelligs
B.L. Currane
L. Currane
Scariff I.
Castlemaine
Maine
Laune
Kilgarvan

D ft m
1500 500
600 200
300 100
0 0
50 150
100 300
200 600
500 1500
1000 3000
2000 6000
m ft

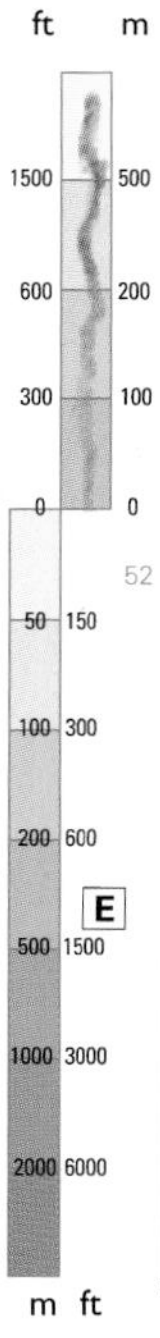

Projection: Lambert's Conformal Conic

West from Greenwich

CELTIC SEA

St. George's Channel
WALES
St. David's Hd.
St. David's
St. Brides Bay

IRISH SEA

COPYRIGHT PHILIP'S

1:2 000 000

Key to Scottish unitary
authorities on map

1 ABERDEEN CITY
2 DUNDEE CITY
3 WEST DUNBARTONSHIRE
4 EAST DUNBARTONSHIRE
5 GLASGOW CITY
6 INVERCLYDE
7 RENFREWSHIRE
8 EAST RENFREWSHIRE
9 NORTH LANARKSHIRE
10 FALKIRK
11 CLACKMANNANSHIRE
12 WEST LOTHIAN
13 CITY OF EDINBURGH
14 MIDLOTHIAN

ORKNEY IS.
on same scale

SHETLAND IS.
on same scale

Projection: Lambert's Conformal Conic

West from Greenwich

COPYRIGHT PHILIP'S

1:2 500 000

10 0 10 20 30 40 50 60 70 80 90 km
10 0 10 20 30 40 50 60 miles

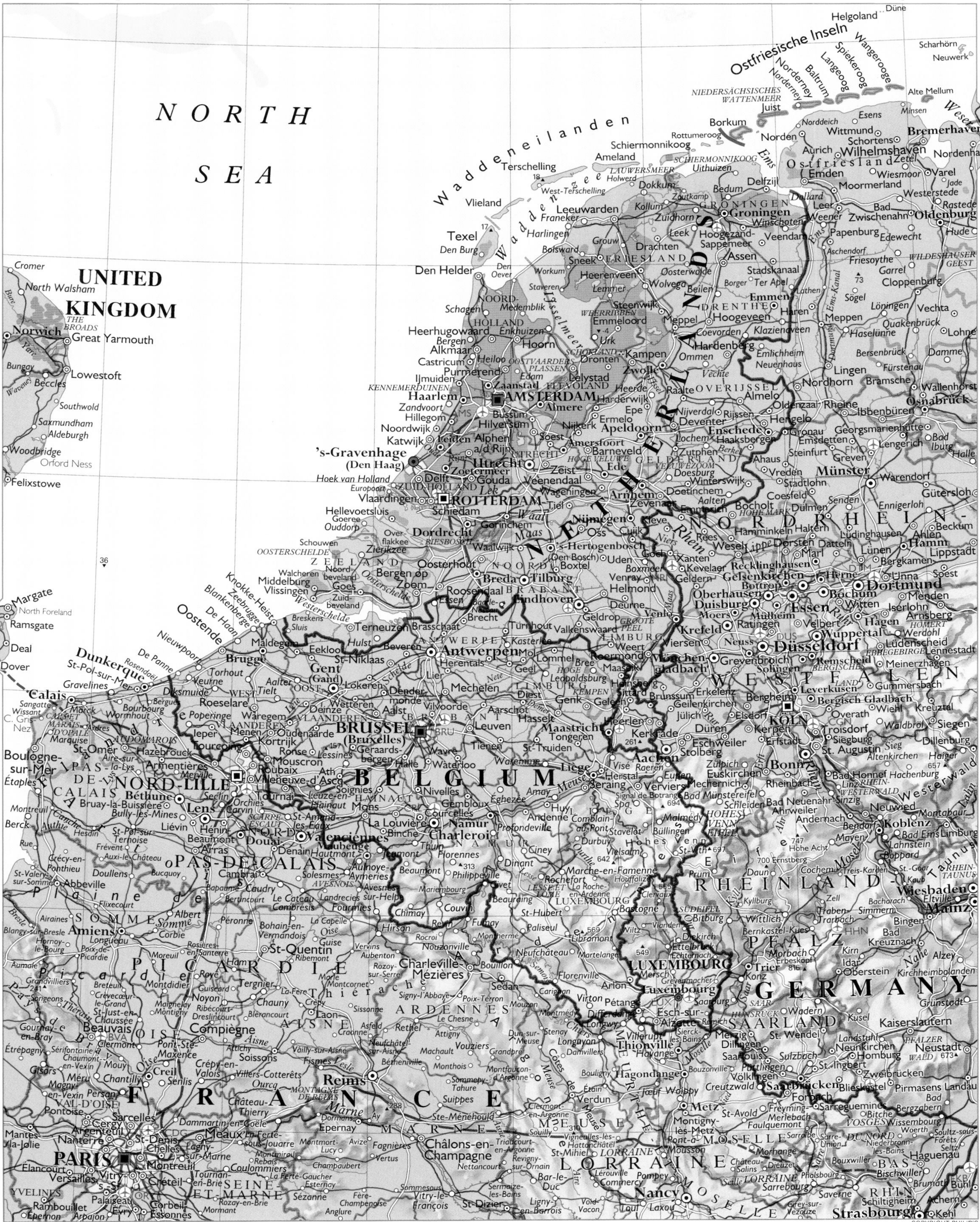

NORTH SEA

Waddeneilanden

NIEDERSÄCHSISCHES WATTENMEER

Ostfriesische Inseln

UNITED KINGDOM

THE BROADS

NETHERLANDS

AMSTERDAM

's-Gravenhage (Den Haag)

ROTTERDAM

ZEELAND

NOORD-BRABANT

LIMBURG

NORDRHEIN-WESTFALEN

BELGIUM

BRUSSEL (Bruxelles)

Antwerpen

Gent (Gand)

VLAANDEREN

HAINAUT

NAMUR

LUXEMBOURG

LUXEMBOURG

GERMANY

RHEINLAND-PFALZ

SAARLAND

FRANCE

NORD

PAS-DE-CALAIS

PICARDIE

SOMME

AISNE

ARDENNES

LORRAINE

PARIS

Reims

Nancy

Strasbourg

Projection: Lambert's Conformal Conic

COPYRIGHT PHILIP'S

—— High-speed rail routes

Underlined towns give their name to the administrative area in which they stand.

m ft
1500 500
600 200
0
50
m ft

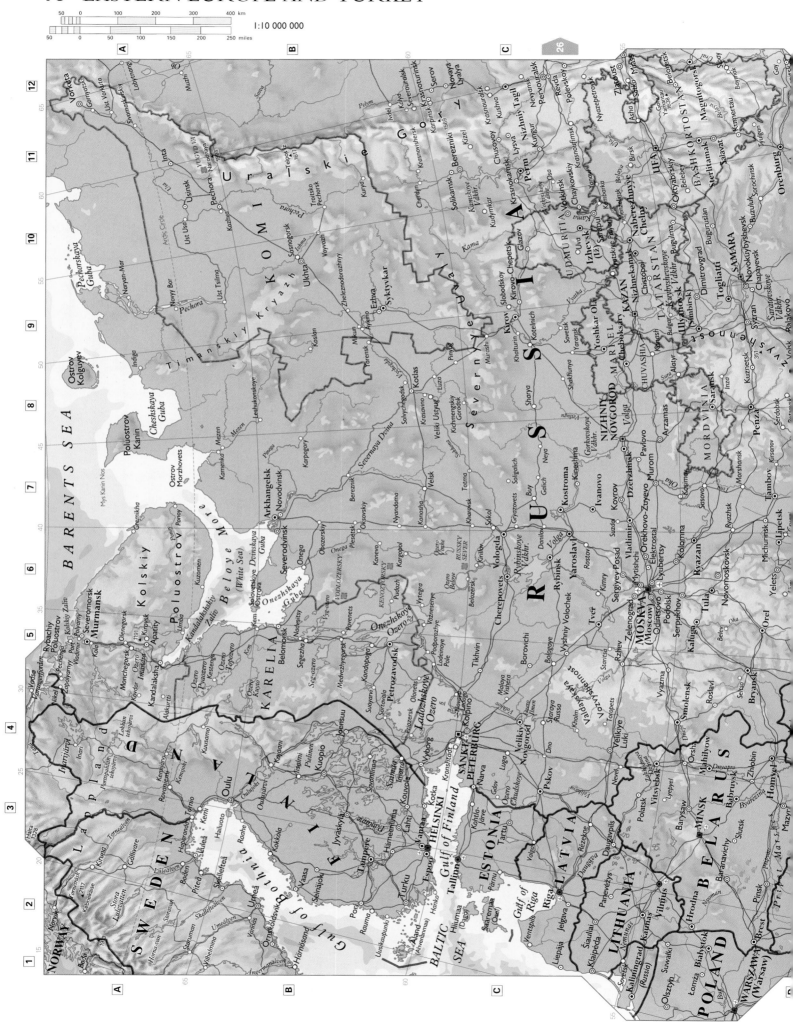

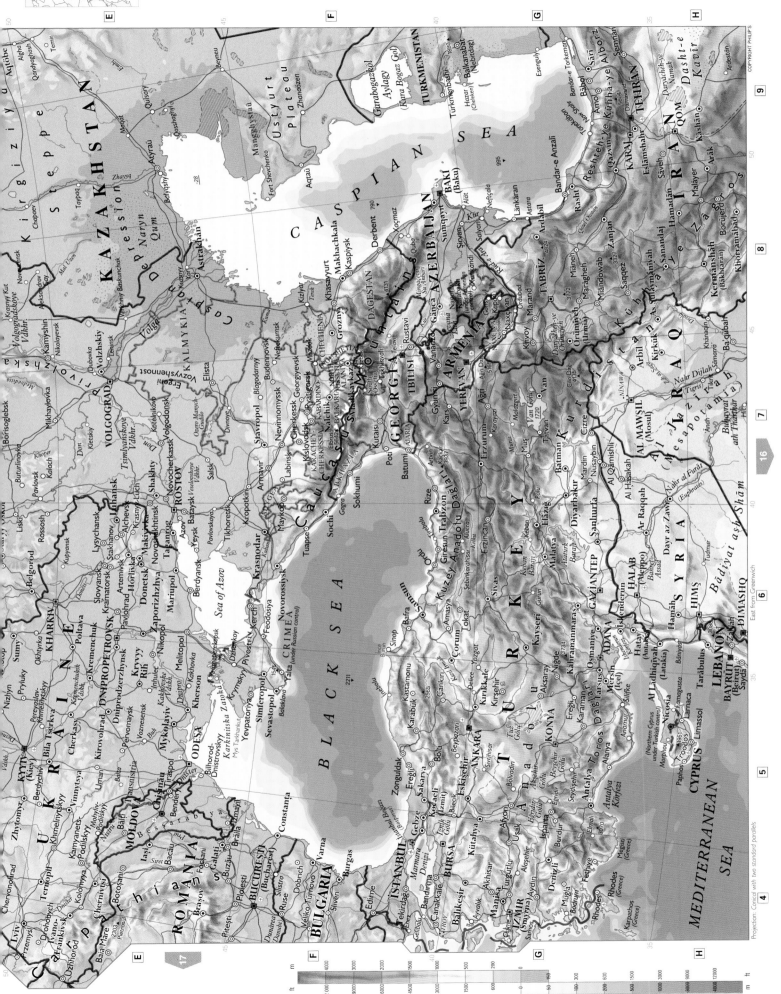

Projection: Conical with two standard parallels

East from Greenwich

COPYRIGHT PHILIP'S

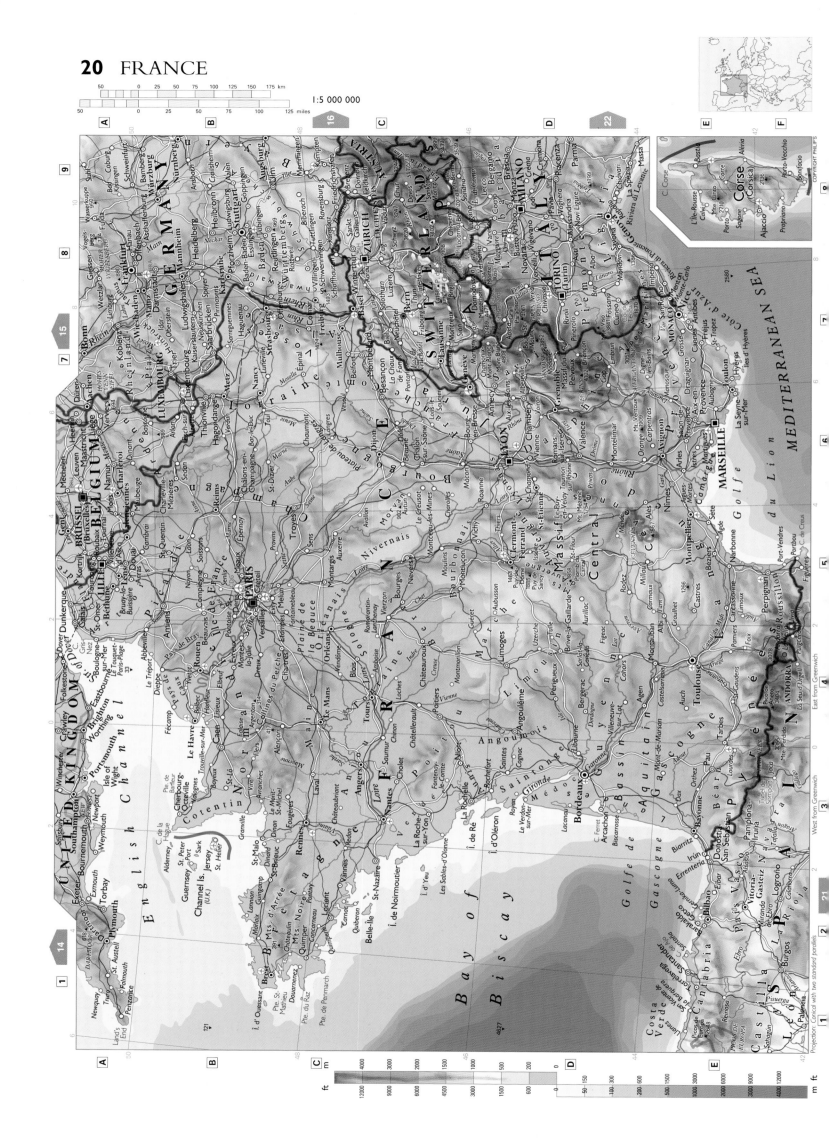

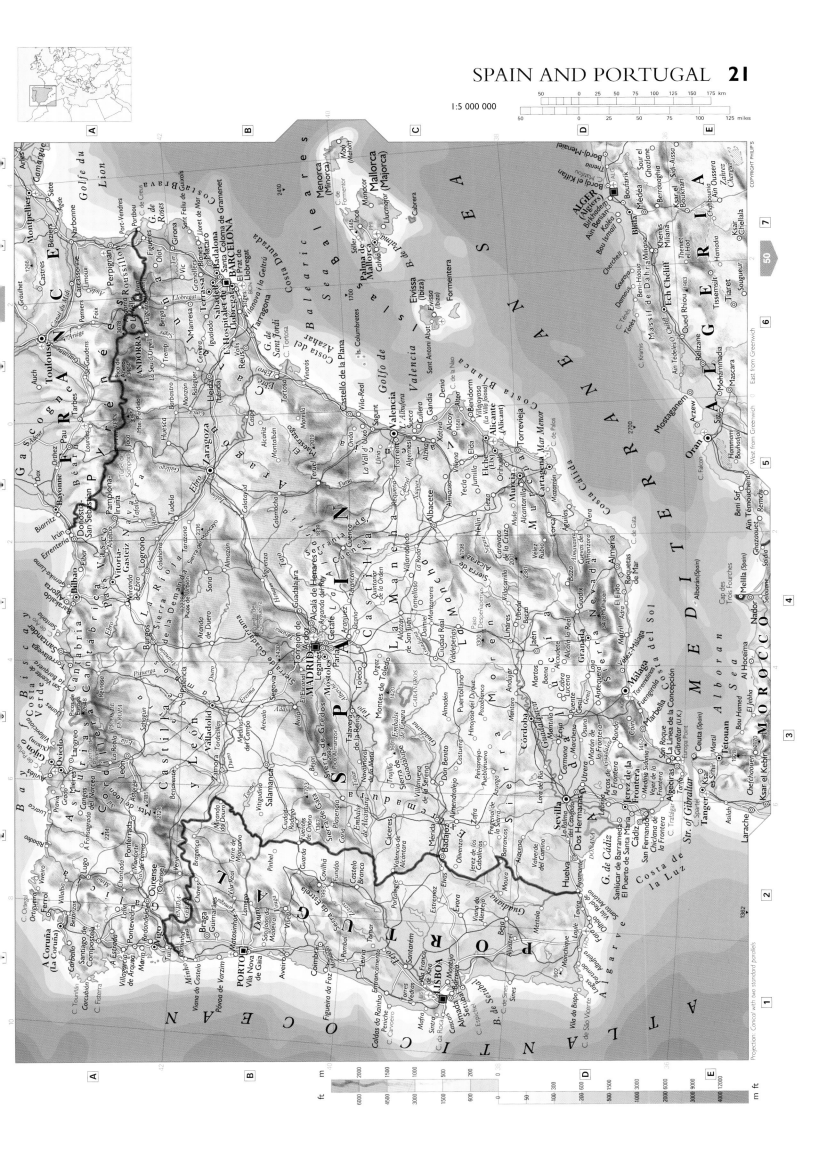

1:5 000 000

COPYRIGHT PHILIP'S

Projection: Conical with two standard parallels

1:47 000 000

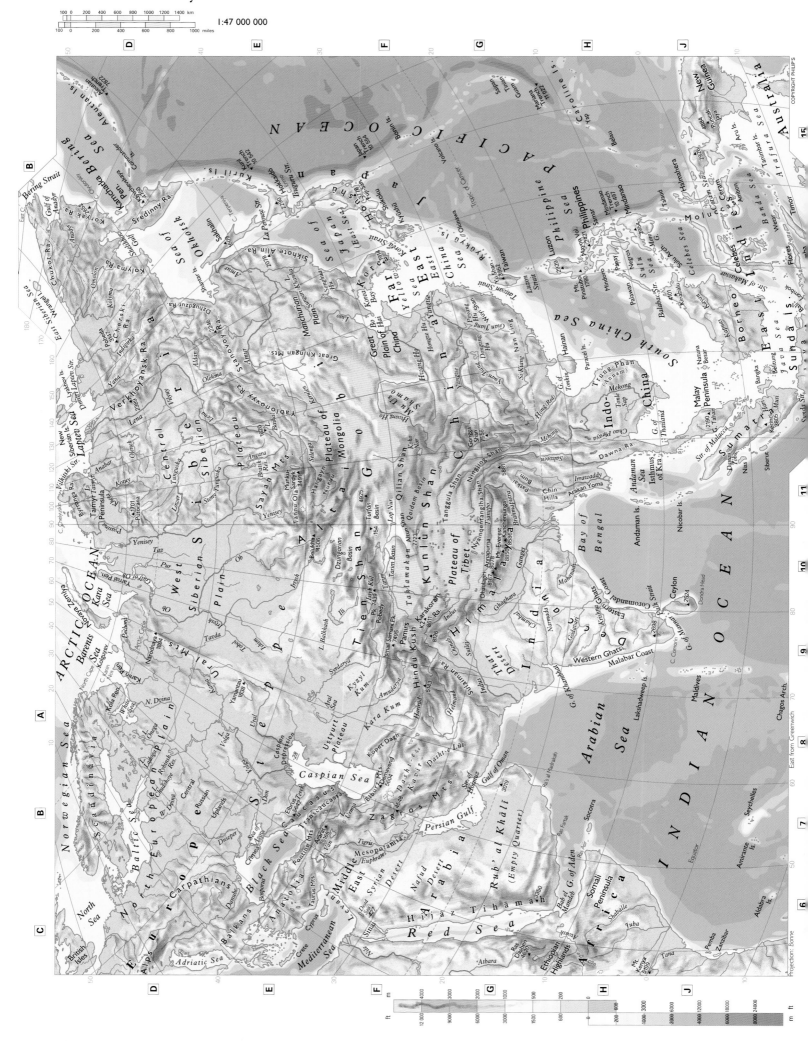

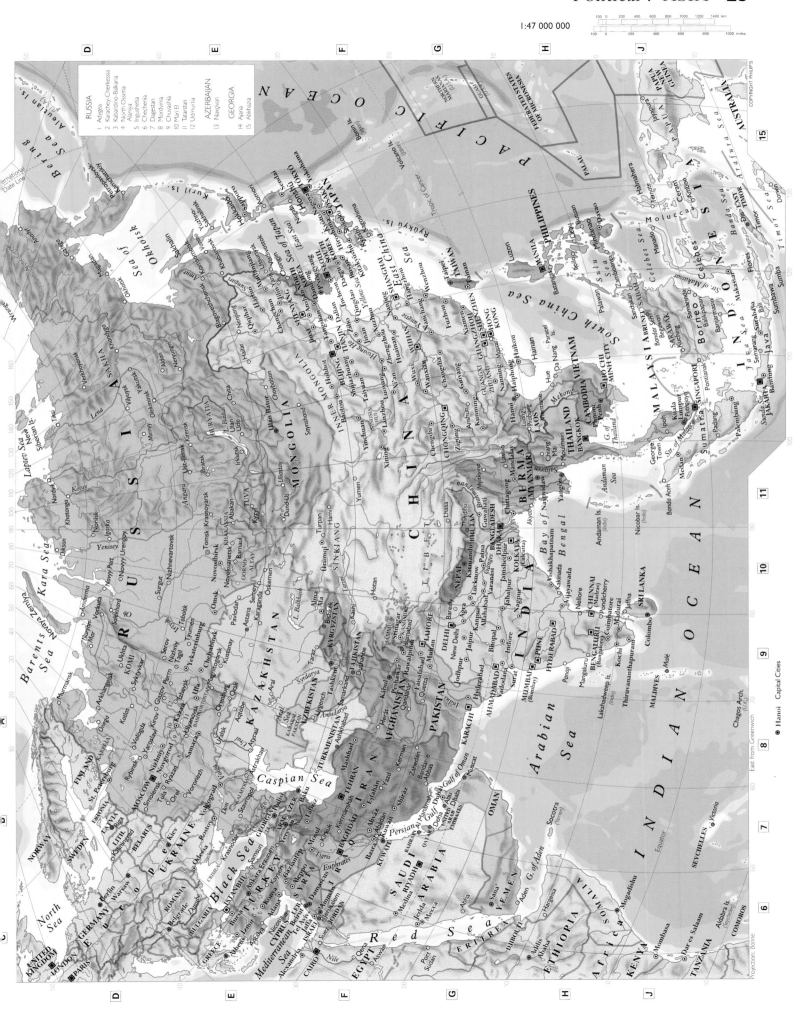

1:47 000 000

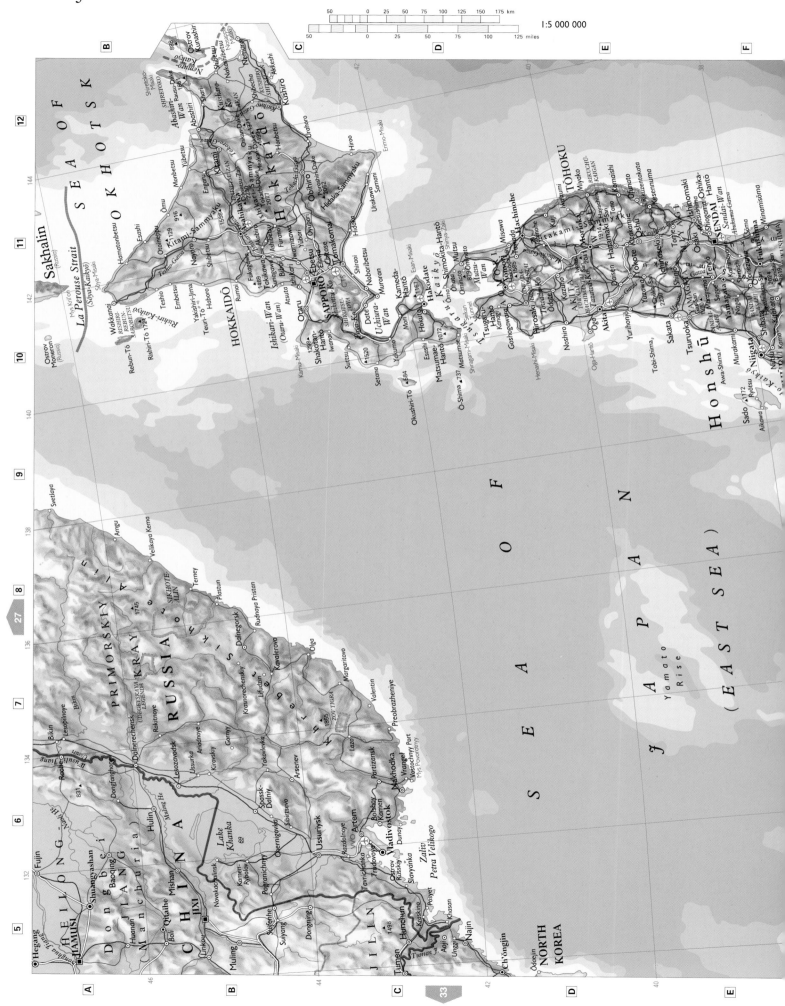

1:5 000 000

SEA OF OKHOTSK

Sakhalin

La Perouse Strait
(Sōya-Kaikyō)

HOKKAIDO

SAPPORO

TOHOKU

Honshū

SENDAI

SEA OF JAPAN

(EAST SEA)

Yamato Rise

RUSSIA

PRIMORSKY KRAY

SIKHOTE-ALIN

Vladivostok

CHINA

HEILONGJIANG

Manchuria

Dongbei

JILIN

Lake Khanka

NORTH KOREA

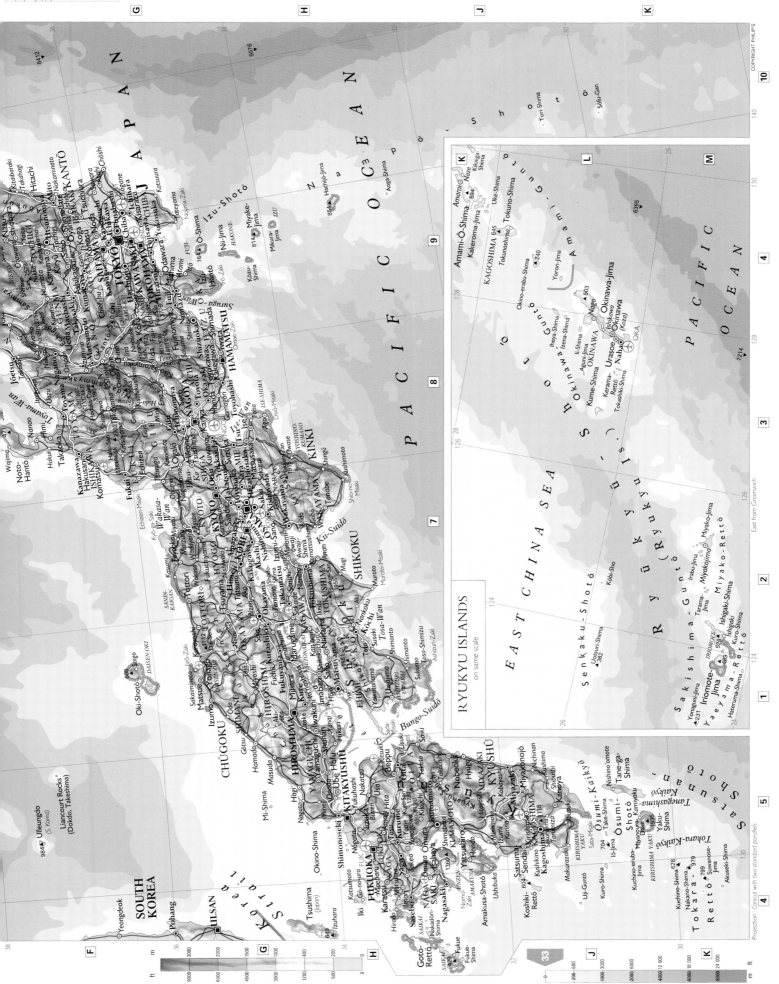

1:6 000 000

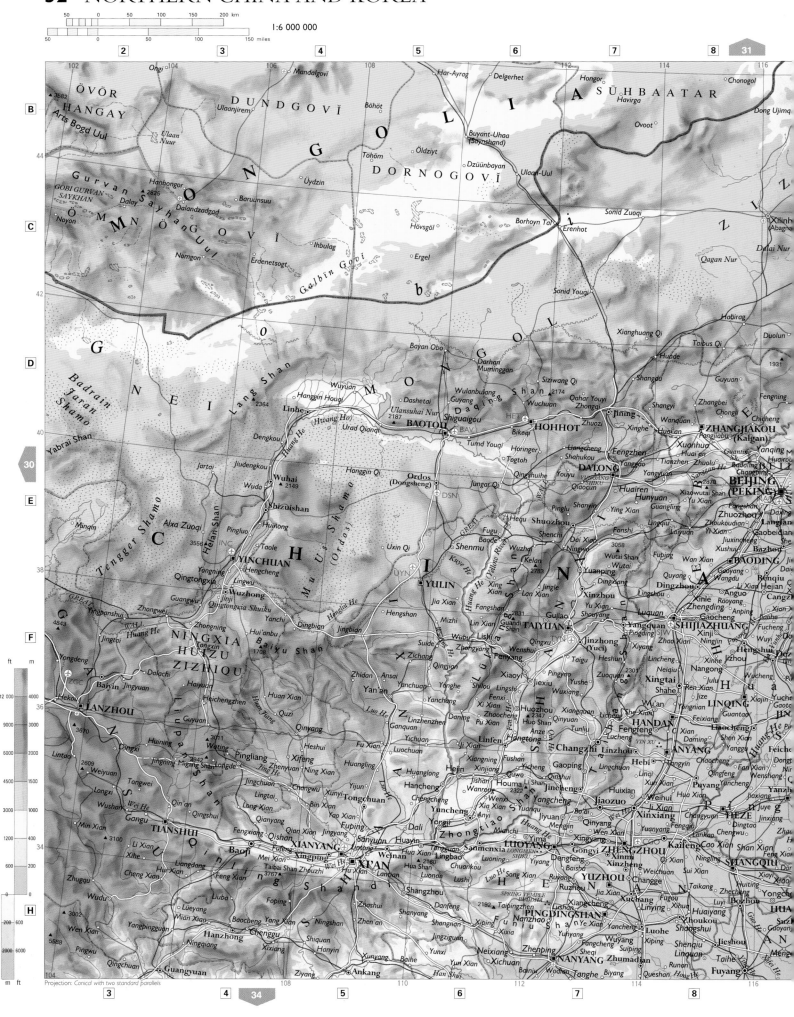

Projection: Conical with two standard parallels

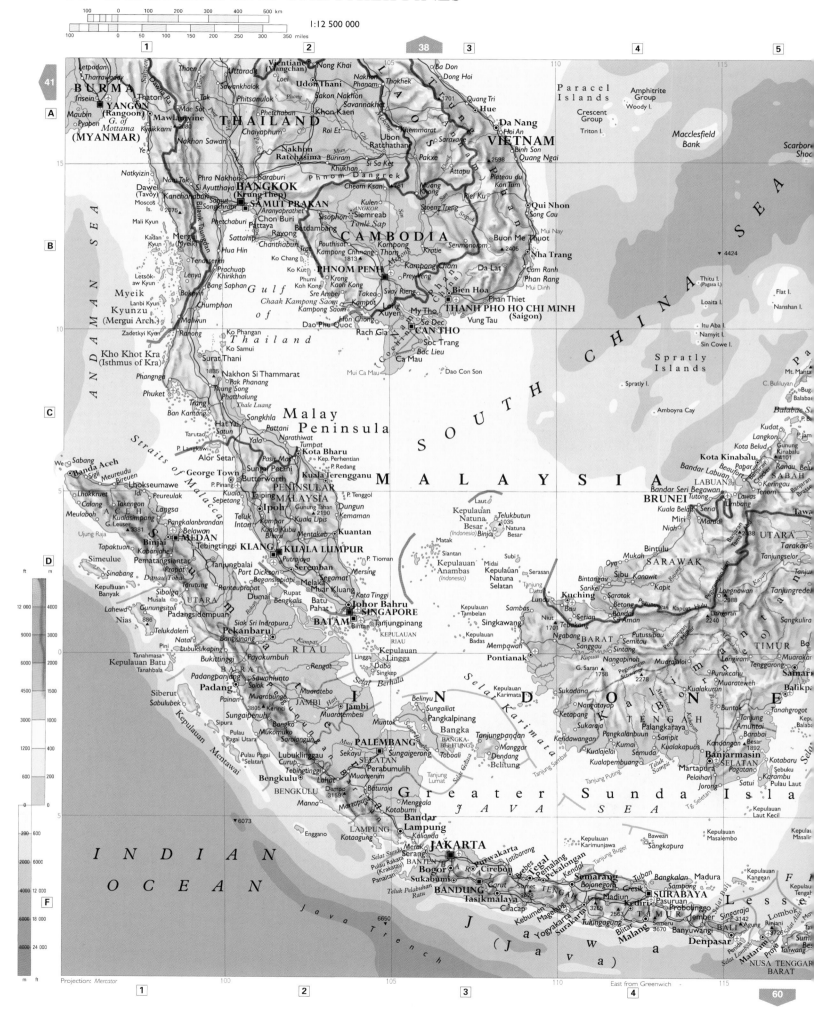

1:12 500 000

Projection: Mercator

East from Greenwich

JAVA AND MADURA

1:7 500 000

BALI

1:2 000 000

COPYRIGHT PHILIP'S

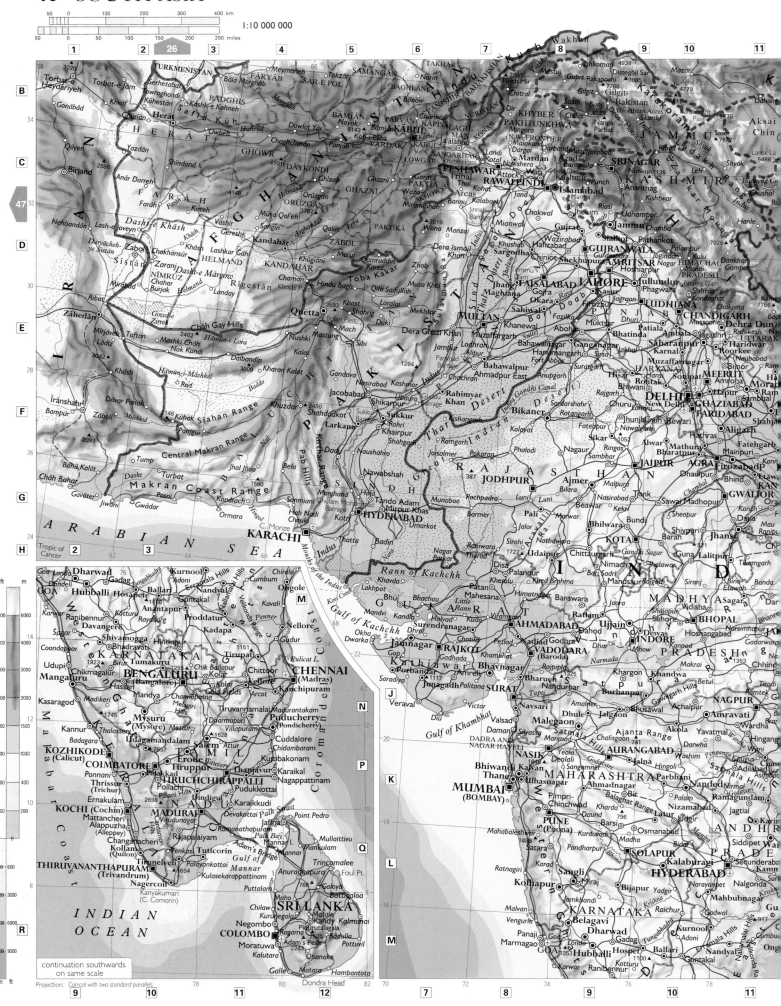

1:10 000 000

continuation southwards
on same scale

Projection: Conical with two standard parallels

1:6 000 000

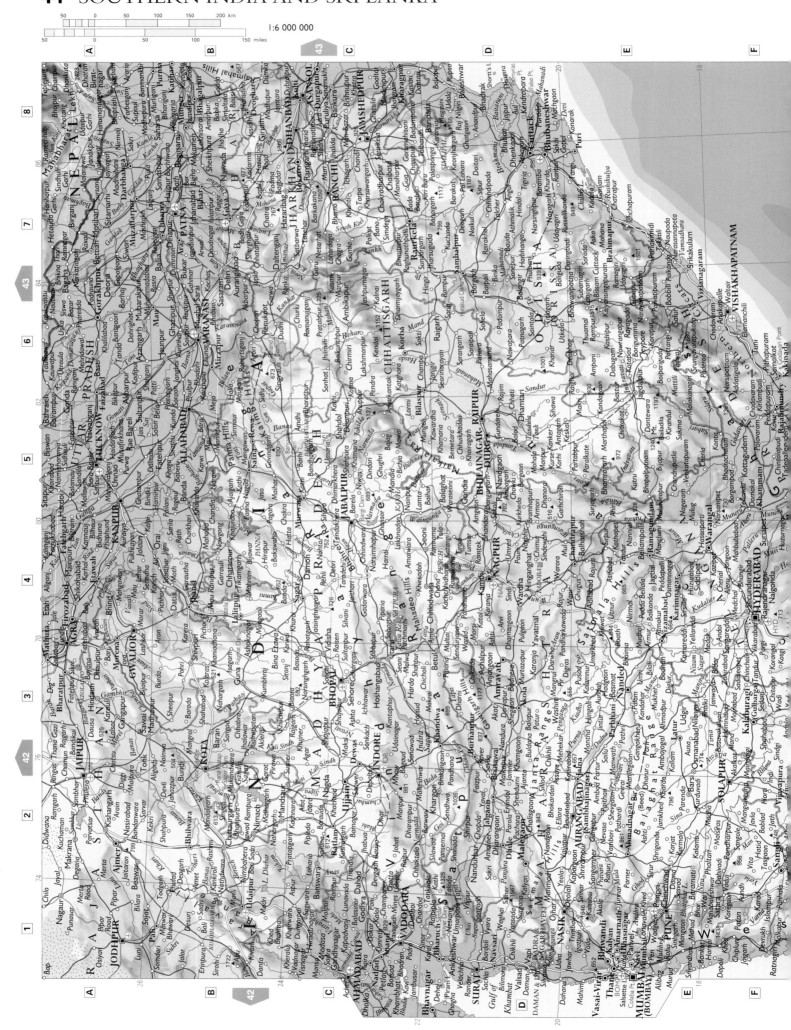

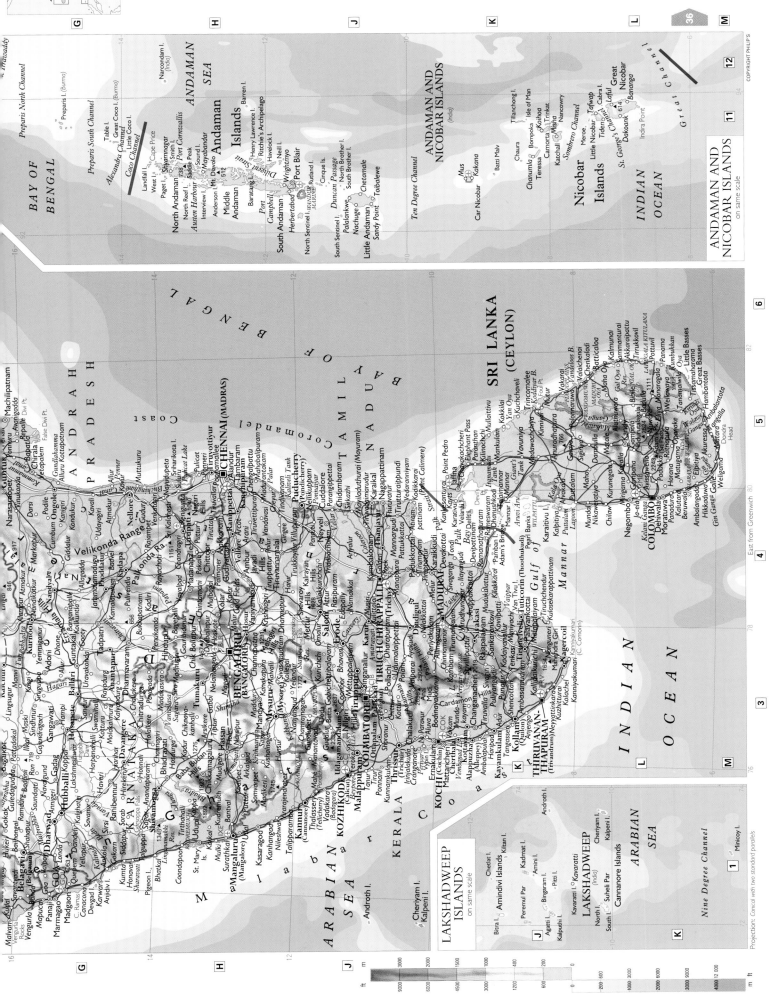

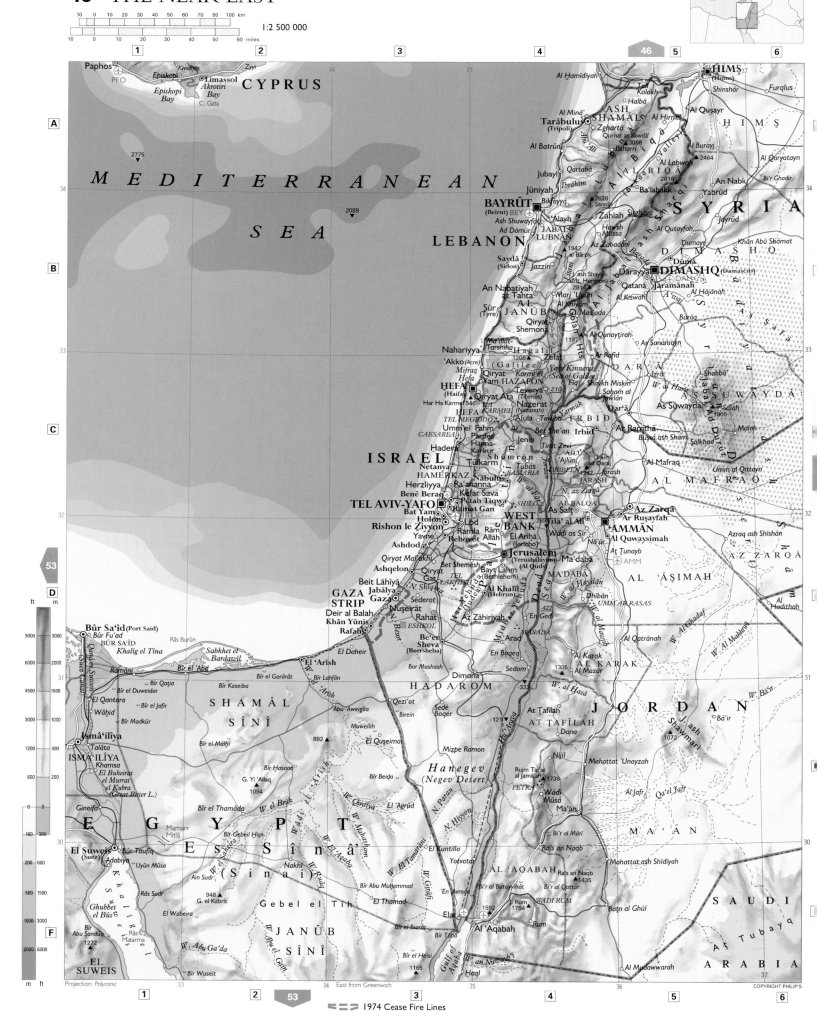

1:2 500 000

48

53

1974 Cease Fire Lines

Projection: Polyconic

East from Greenwich

COPYRIGHT PHILIP'S

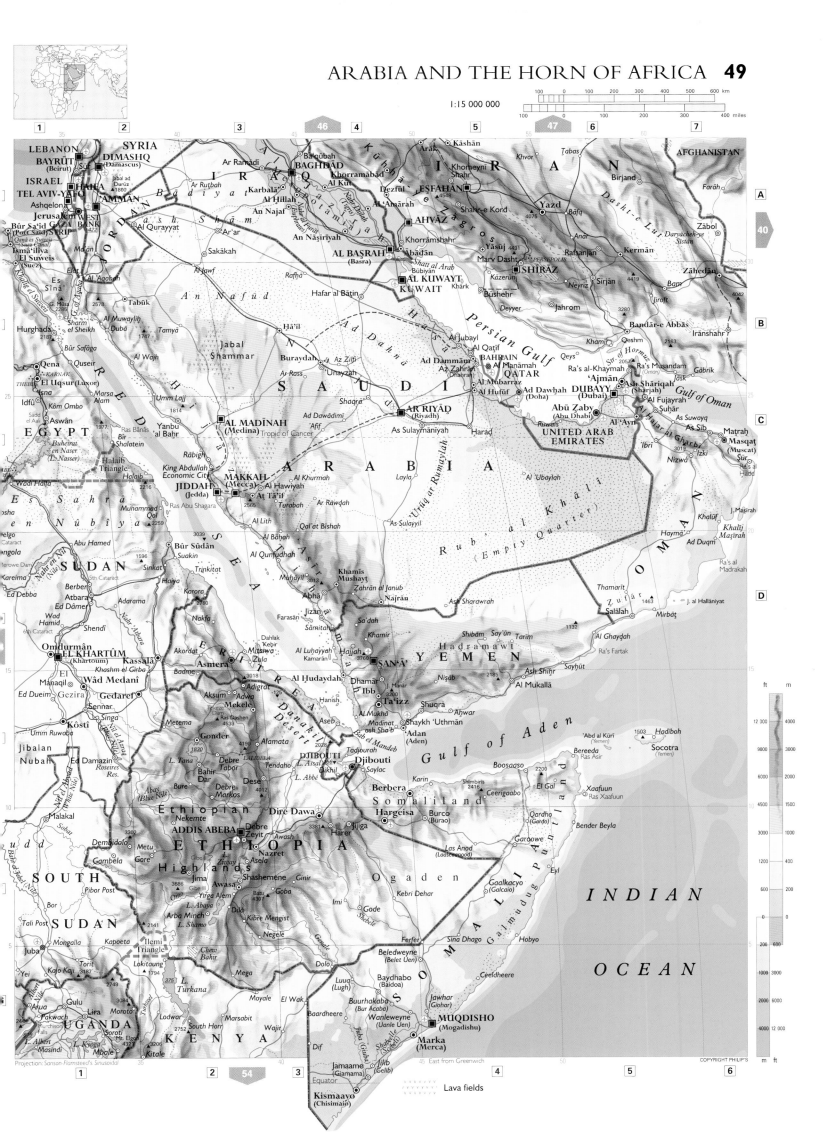

1:15 000 000

100 0 100 200 300 400 500 600 km
100 0 100 200 300 400 miles

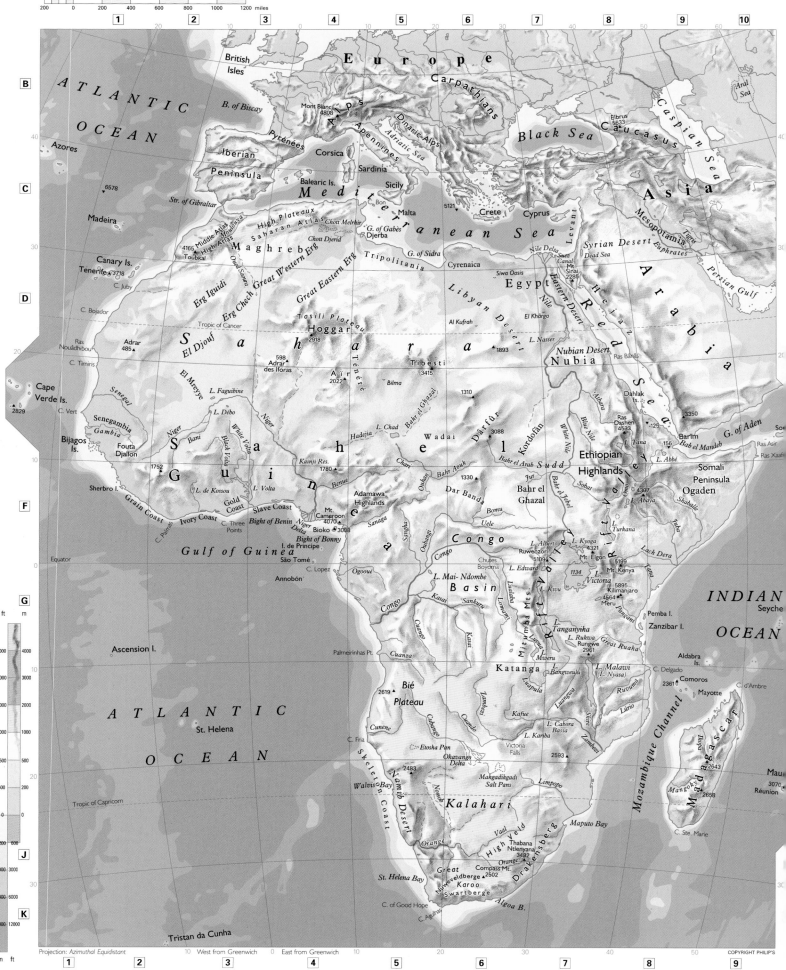

1:42 000 000

ATLANTIC OCEAN

Azores

Madeira

Canary Is.
Tenerife ▲3718
C. Juby

Cape Verde Is.
▲2829
C. Vert

Bijagos Is.

British Isles

B. of Biscay

Mont Blanc ▲4808
Pyrénées
Iberian Peninsula
Balearic Is.
Corsica
Sardinia
Str. of Gibraltar
6578 ▲

Europe
Carpathians
Alps
Apennines
Dinaric Alps
Adriatic Sea
Sicily
Bon
Malta
Crete
Cyprus

Elbrus 5633
Black Sea
Caucasus
Caspian Sea
Aral Sea
Asia
Mesopotamia

Mediterranean Sea

High Plateaux
Saharan Atlas
Chott Melrhir
Middle Atlas ▲4165 Moulouya
High Atlas
Toubkal
Maghreb
Oued Saoura
Erg Iguidi
Erg Chech Great Western Erg
Great Eastern Erg
Tripolitania
Chott Djerid
G. of Gabès
Djerba
G. of Sidra
Cyrenaica

Tasili Plateau
Hoggar 2918
Aïr 2022
Ténéré
Tibesti 3415
Bilma
598 Adrar des Iforas

Sahara

Egypt
Libyan Desert
Al Kufrah
El Khârga
Siwa Oasis
Nile Delta
Suez Canal
Mt. Sinai 2285
Dead Sea
Syrian Desert
Euphrates
Tigris
Persian Gulf
Arabia
Hejaz
Red Sea

Nubian Desert
Nubia
Ras Bânâs

Tropic of Cancer

Ras Nouâdhibou
C. Bojador
C. Timiris

S A H A R A
El Djouf
Adrar 485 ▲

1893

Dahlak Is.
3350 ▲
Ras Dashen 4533
Abhara
Blue Nile
L. Tana
Barîm
Bab el Mandeb
G. of Aden
Ras Asir
Ras Xaafun

Senegambia
Gambia
Fouta Djallon

Senegal
El Mreyye
L. Faguibine
L. Débo
Niger
Bani
White Volta
Black Volta
Niger

1310
Dârfûr 3088
Wadai
Kordofan
L. Chad
Bahr el Ghazal
Hadejia
Chari

Sahel
Bahr el Arab
White Nile
Sudd
Ethiopian Highlands
4307
Somali Peninsula
Ogaden
Shabelle

1752 ▲
Kainji Res. 1780

S U D A N
G U I N E A

L. de Kossou
L. Volta
Gold Coast
Benue
Adamawa Highlands
Bahr Aouk 1330
Dar Banda
Bahr el Ghazal
Jur
Sobat
L. Abbé
Turkana
Juba

Sherbro I.
Grain Coast
Ivory Coast
C. Palmas
C. Three Points
Slave Coast
Bight of Benin
Mt. Cameroon 4070
Bioko ▲3088
Niger Delta
Bight of Bonny
I. de Principe
São Tomé
Gulf of Guinea
C. Lopez
Annobón

Ntem
Ouham
Sanaga
Sangha
Uele
Bomu
Congo
Ubangi
Congo Basin
L. Mai-Ndombe
Kasai
Sankuru
Lomami
Lualaba
Mitumba Mts.
L. Albert 4321
Ruwenzori 5109
L. Edward
Chutes Boyoma
L. Kivu
L. Victoria
1134
Mt. Elgon
Mt. Kenya 5199
Meru 4564
Kilimanjaro 5895
Pemba I.
Zanzibar I.

Equator

INDIAN OCEAN
Seyche

Ascension I.

ATLANTIC OCEAN

St. Helena

Palmeirinhas Pt.

Ogooué
Cuanza
Cuango
Kasai
Cuanza

Katanga
L. Tanganyika
L. Rukwa
Rungwe 2961
L. Mweru
L. Bangweulu
Luapula
Lualaba
Bié Plateau 2619

Great Ruaha
Pangani
Ruvuma
Lúrio
L. Malawi (L. Nyasa)
C. Delgado
Comoros 2361
Aldabra Is.
Mayotte
C. d'Ambre

Mangoky
Madagascar 2643
Hopo
2658
Mau
3070
Réunion

Tropic of Capricorn

Cunene
Etosha Pan
Okavango Delta
Skeleton Coast
Namib Desert
Walvis Bay
2483
Nossob
Kalahari
Makgadikgadi Salt Pans
Victoria Falls 2593
Cubango
Zambezi
Kafue
Luangwa
L. Cabora Bassa
L. Kariba
Shire
Limpopo
Mozambique Channel
Maputo Bay
C. Ste. Marie

St. Helena Bay
Orange
Vaal
Orange
High Veld
Thabana Ntlenyana 3482
Compass Mt. 2502
Drakensberg
Algoa B.
Great Karoo
Nieuveldberge
Swartberge
C. of Good Hope
C. Agulhas

Tristan da Cunha

ft m
12000 4000
9000 3000
6000 2000
3000 1000
1500 500
600 200
0 0
200 600
1000 3000
2000 6000
4000 12000
m ft

1:42 000 000

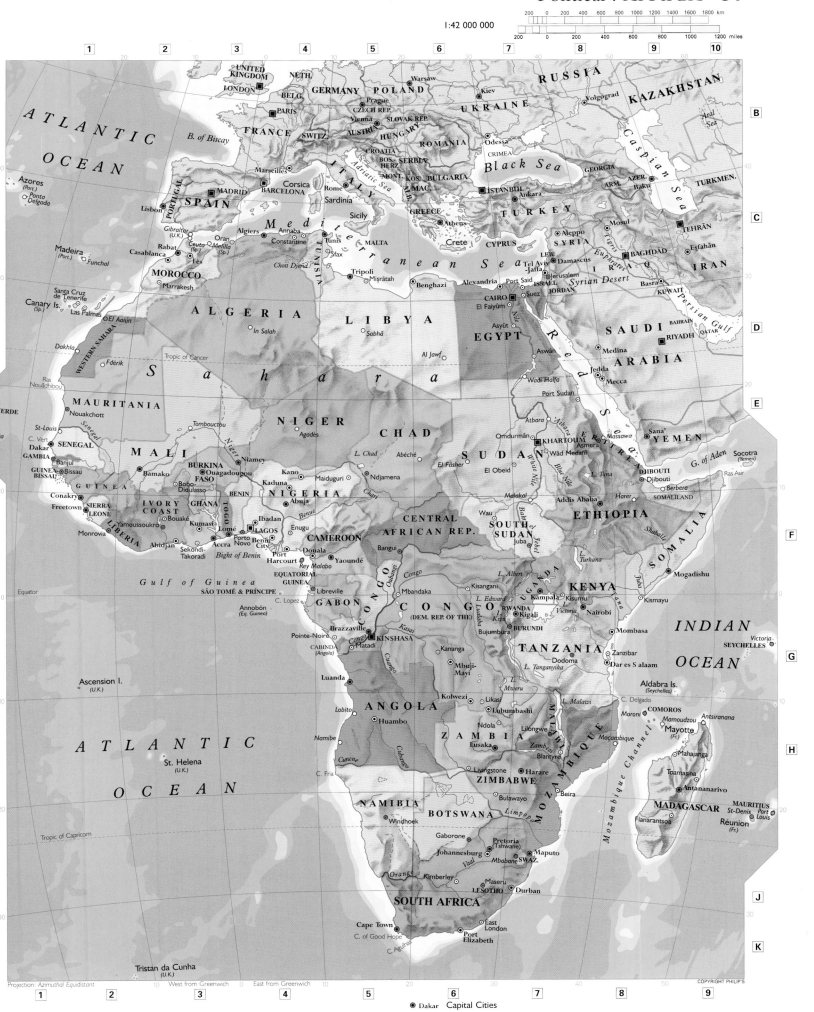

● Dakar Capital Cities

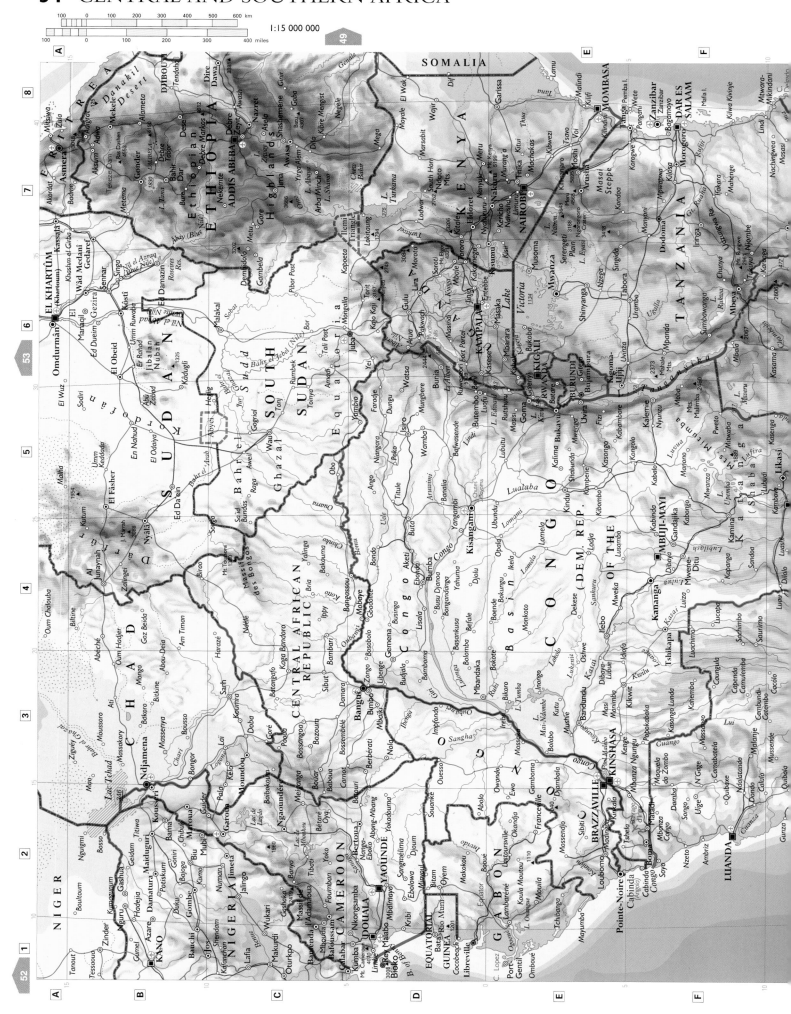

1:15 000 000

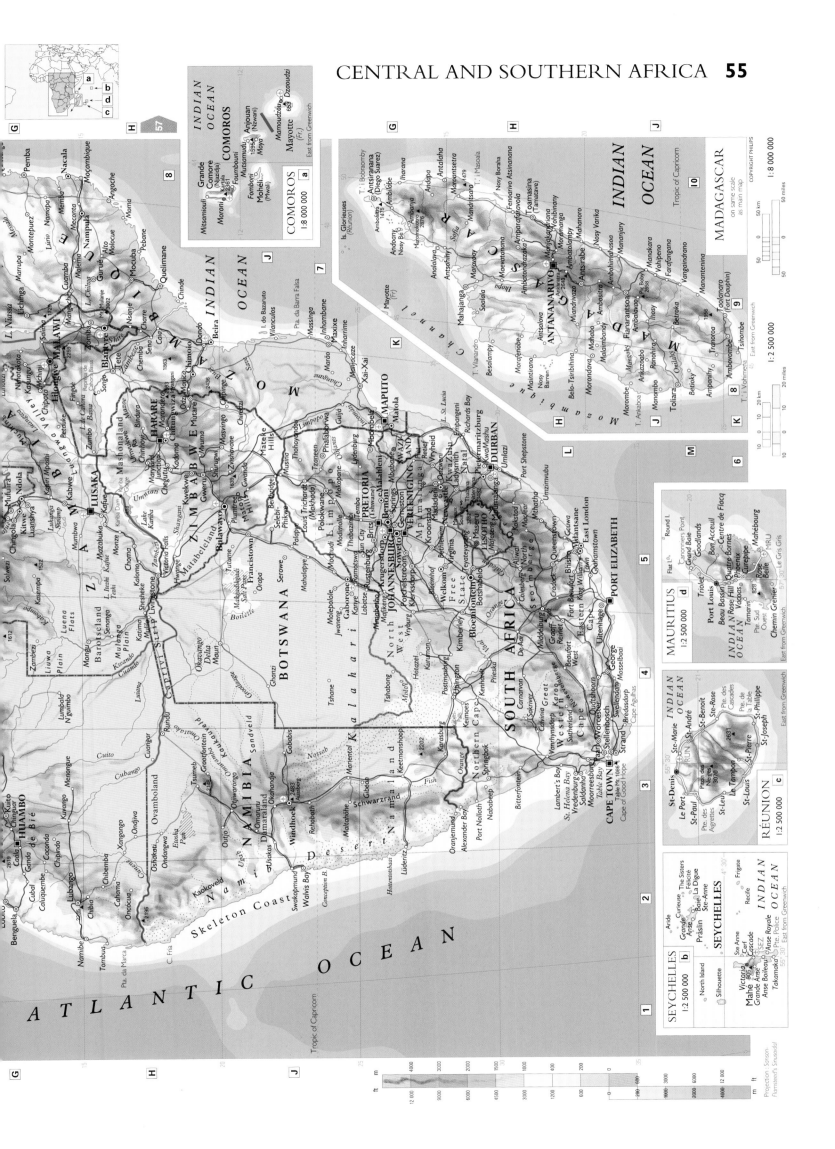

COMOROS
1:8 000 000 **a**

INDIAN OCEAN

COMOROS

Mitsamiouli Grande
Comore (Ngadja)
Moroni Karala
Foumbouni
Fomboni Mohéli
(Mwali)
Mutsamudu
Anjouan
(Nzwani) Mamoudzou
Moya Dzaoudzi
Mayotte
(Fr.)
East from Greenwich

Is. Glorieuses
(Réunion)

MADAGASCAR
on same scale
as main map
1:8 000 000

INDIAN OCEAN

Tropic of Capricorn

COPYRIGHT PHILIP'S

MAURITIUS
1:2 500 000 **d**

Round I.
Cap Malheureux Grand Baie
Goodlands
Port Louis Centre de Flacq
Beau Bassin Bon Accueil
Quatre Bornes
Curepipe Phoenix
Rose Belle
Mahébourg
Le Gris Gris

RÉUNION
1:2 500 000 **c**

INDIAN OCEAN

St-Denis Ste-Marie
Le Port St-André
St-Paul Pte. des
Cascades
Pte. des
Aigrettes Piton des
Neiges
3070 St-Benoît
St-Rose
St-Leu Le Tampon
St-Louis St-Pierre St-Philippe
St-Joseph
East from Greenwich

SEYCHELLES
1:2 500 000 **b**

North Island
Silhouette
Aride
Praslin Cureuse The Sisters
Anse Félicité
Baie La Digue
Ste-Anne
SEYCHELLES
Ste Anne
Victoria Cerf Frégate
Mahé 905 Recife
Grande Anse Cascade
Anse Boileau Anse Royale
Takamaka Pte. Police INDIAN OCEAN
East from Greenwich

ATLANTIC OCEAN

INDIAN OCEAN

Projection: Sanson-Flamsteed's Sinusoidal

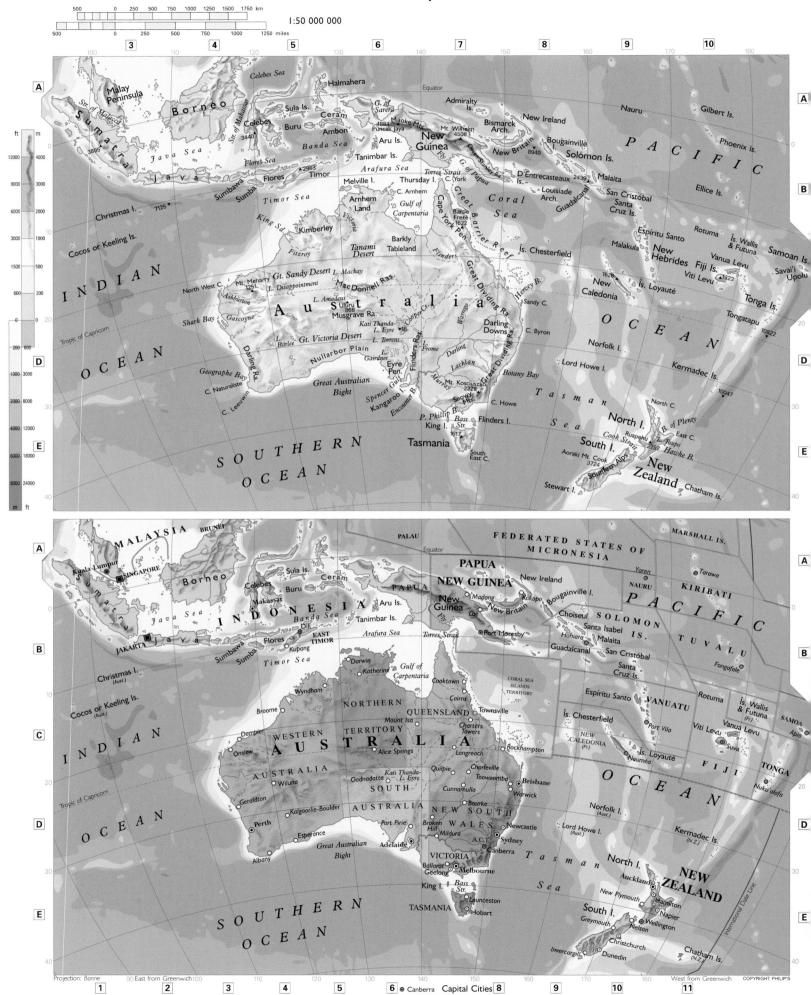

1:50 000 000

Physical Map (top):

PACIFIC OCEAN

Malay Peninsula · Borneo · Celebes Sea · Halmahera · Sumatra · Str. of Malacca · Sula Is. · Ceram · Buru · Ambon · Puncak Jaya 4884 · Maoke Mts. · Aru Is. · Tanimbar Is. · New Guinea · Mt. Wilhelm 4508 · Admiralty Is. · New Ireland · Bismarck Arch. · New Britain 8940 · Bougainville · Solomon Is. · Nauru · Gilbert Is. · Phoenix Is.

Christmas I. 7125 · Cocos or Keeling Is. · Java Sea · Java · Str. of Makassar 3440 · Flores Sea · Flores 2963 · Sumbawa · Sumba · Timor · Arafura Sea · Melville I. · C. Arnhem · Thursday I. · C. York · Torres Strait · G. of Papua · Great Stanley Ra. · D'Entrecasteaux 2439 · Malaita · San Cristóbal · Santa Cruz Is. · Espíritu Santo · Rotuma · Ís. Wallis & Futuna · Samoan Is.

INDIAN OCEAN · Timor Sea · Arnhem Land · Gulf of Carpentaria · Kimberley · King Sd. · Fitzroy · Victoria · Barkly Tableland · Cape York Pen. · Bartle Frere 1622 · Great Barrier Reef · Coral Sea · Ís. Chesterfield · Guadalcanal · Malakula · New Hebrides · Fiji Is. · Vanua Levu · Viti Levu · Savai'i · Upolu

North West C. · Mt. Meharry 1251 · Tanami Desert · Gt. Sandy Desert · L. Mackay · L. Disappointment · MacDonnell Ras. · Flinders Ra. · Hervey B. · New Caledonia · Ís. Loyauté · Tonga Is. · 1323

Ashburton · Shark Bay · Gascoyne · L. Amadeus · Uluru 868 · Musgrave Ra. · Australia · Sandy C. · 1628 · Tongatapu · 10822

Darling Ra. · Kati Thanda–L. Eyre 16 · Gt. Victoria Desert · L. Barlee · L. Torrens · L. Gairdner · L. Frome · Cooper Cr. · Warrego · Darling Downs · Great Dividing Ra. · C. Byron · Norfolk I. · Kermadec Is.

Geographe Bay · C. Naturaliste · Nullarbor Plain · Eyre Pen. · Flinders Ras. · Lachlan · Darling · Botany Bay · Lord Howe I. · 10047

C. Leeuwin · Great Australian Bight · Spencer Gulf · Kangaroo I. · Encounter B. · Murray · Mt. Kosciuszko 2228 · Snowy Mts. · Snowy · C. Howe · Tasman Sea · North C. · Ruapehu 2797 · L. Taupo · Hawke B.

SOUTHERN OCEAN · P. Phillip B. · King I. · Bass Str. · Flinders I. · 1617 · Tasmania · South East C. · Aoraki Mt. Cook 3724 · Southern Alps · North I. · B. of Plenty · East C. · South I. · New Zealand · Chatham Is. · Stewart I.

Elevation scale (left):

ft / m: 12000 / 4000 · 9000 / 3000 · 6000 / 2000 · 3000 / 1000 · 1500 / 500 · 600 / 200 · 0 / 0 · 600 / 200 · 3000 / 1000 · 6000 / 2000 · 12000 / 4000 · 18000 / 6000 · 24000 / 8000 · ft / m

Political Map (bottom):

MALAYSIA · BRUNEI · Kuala Lumpur · SINGAPORE · Borneo · Celebes · Buru · Ceram · PALAU · FEDERATED STATES OF MICRONESIA · MARSHALL IS.

Sumatra · Str. · Sula Is. · INDONESIA · Makassar · Aru Is. · PAPUA · PAPUA NEW GUINEA · New Ireland · New Guinea · Madang · New Britain · Rabaul · Bougainville I. · NAURU · Yaren · Tarawa · KIRIBATI · PACIFIC

JAKARTA · Java · Java Sea · Banda Sea · Tanimbar Is. · Arafura Sea · DILI · EAST TIMOR · Kupang · Flores · Sumbawa · Sumba · Timor Sea · Lae · Fly · Port Moresby · Torres Strait · Choiseul · Santa Isabel · Honiara · Malaita · Guadalcanal · San Cristóbal · SOLOMON IS. · TUVALU · Fongafale

Christmas I. (Aust.) · Cocos or Keeling Is. (Aust.) · INDIAN OCEAN · Darwin · Katherine · Gulf of Carpentaria · NORTHERN TERRITORY · Cooktown · Cairns · CORAL SEA ISLANDS TERRITORY · Santa Cruz Is. · Espíritu Santo · VANUATU · Rotuma · Ís. Wallis & Futuna (Fr.) · SAMOA · Apia

Wyndham · Broome · Dampier · Onslow · WESTERN AUSTRALIA · Mount Isa · QUEENSLAND · Townsville · Charters Towers · Rockhampton · Port Vila · NEW CALEDONIA (Fr.) · Ís. Chesterfield · Viti Levu · Vanua Levu · FIJI · Suva · TONGA · Nuku'alofa

Tropic of Capricorn · Wiluna · Alice Springs · Longreach · Charleville · Toowoomba · Quilpie · Oodnadatta · Kati Thanda–L. Eyre · SOUTH AUSTRALIA · Cunnamulla · Brisbane · Warwick · Norfolk I. (Aust.) · Nouméa · Ís. Loyauté

Geraldton · Kalgoorlie-Boulder · Perth · Esperance · AUSTRALIA · Port Pirie · Broken Hill · Mildura · NEW SOUTH WALES · Bourke · Newcastle · A.C.T. · Sydney · Canberra · Lord Howe I. (Aust.) · Kermadec Is. (N.Z.)

Albany · Great Australian Bight · Adelaide · VICTORIA · Ballarat · Geelong · Melbourne · King I. · Bass Str. · Launceston · Tasman Sea · North I. · Auckland · NEW ZEALAND · New Plymouth · Hamilton

SOUTHERN OCEAN · TASMANIA · Hobart · South I. · Greymouth · Nelson · Napier · Wellington · Invercargill · Christchurch · Dunedin · Chatham Is. (N.Z.) · International Date Line

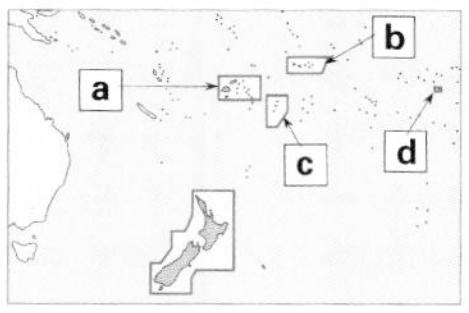

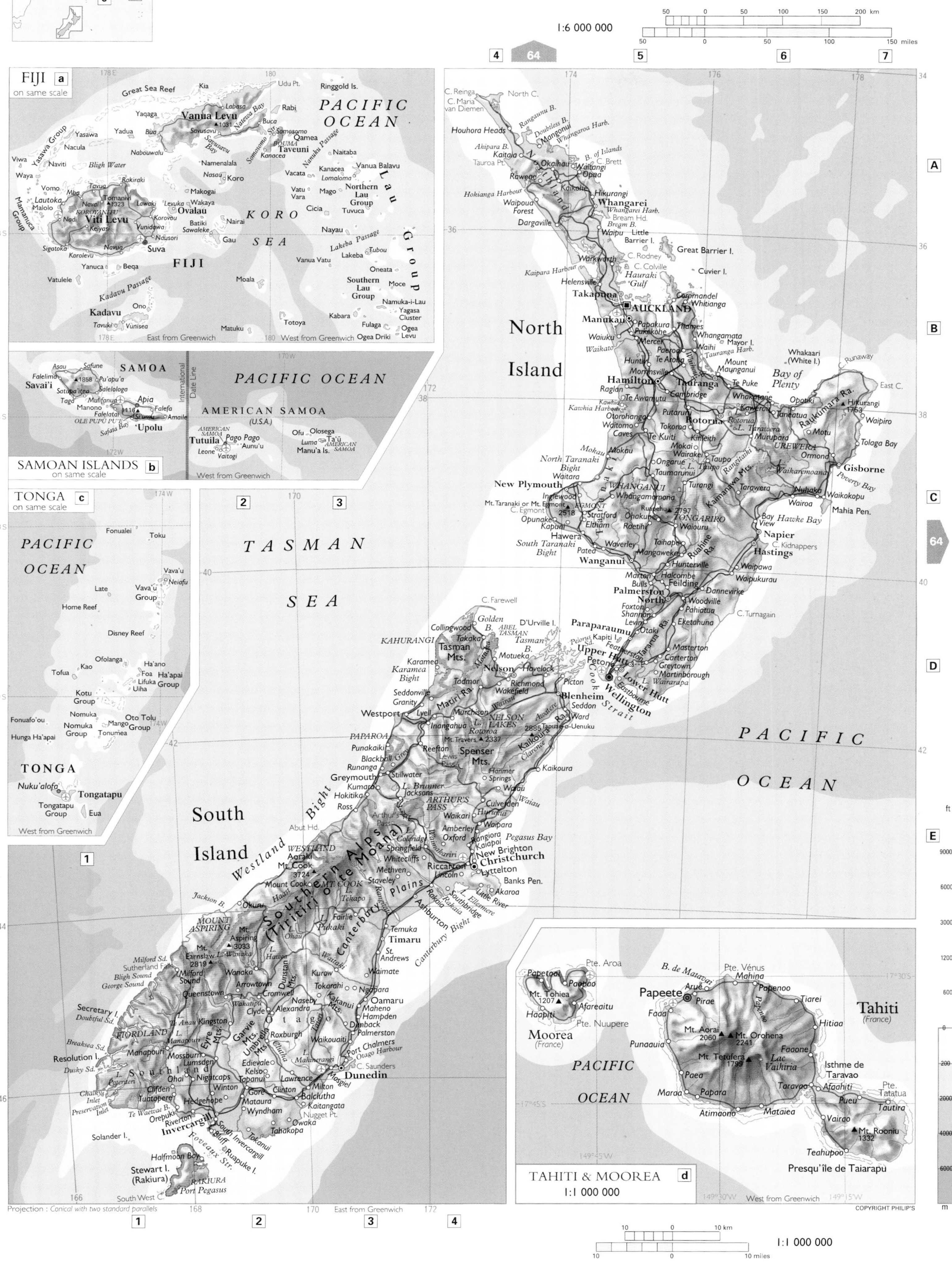

1:6 000 000

50 0 50 100 150 200 km
50 0 50 100 150 miles

FIJI
on same scale **a**

Great Sea Reef
Kia
Udu Pt.
Ringgold Is.
Yaqaga
Labasa
Rabi
Vanua Levu
Yasawa Group
Yasawa
Yadua
Bua
Buca
Somosomo
Qamea
Taveuni
Naitaba
Natewa Bay
BOUMA
Viwa
Nacula
Nabouwalu
Namenalala
Nasau
Koro
Vanua Balavu
Naviti
Vomo
Tavua
Lawaki
Makogai
Vatu
Vara
Mago
Cicia
Northern Lau Group
Waya
Malolo
Tomanivi
1323
Levuka
Ovalau
Vanua Vatu
Lakeba Passage
KORO SEA
Mamanuca Group
Lautoka
Nadi
Viti Levu
KOROYANITU
Keiyasi
Korovou
Vunidawa
Nausori
Nairai
Batiki
Sawaleke
Gau
Nayau
Lakeba
Sigatoka
Korolevu
Suva
Tubou
FIJI
Vanua Vatu
Moala
Oneata
Moce
Southern Lau Group
Namuka-i-Lau
Vatulele
Yanuca
Beqa
Kadavu Passage
Totoya
Matuku
Kabara
Yagasa Cluster
Ogea Levu
Kadavu
Ono
Tavuki
Vunisea
Fulaga
Ogea Driki

PACIFIC OCEAN

178 E East from Greenwich 180 West from Greenwich

SAMOA
on same scale

Asau
Safune
Sotupa Idea
Salelologa
1858
Savai'i
Taga
Mulifanua
Pu'apu'a
Falealupo
Manono
1118
Apia
Falefa
Upolu
OLE PUPU PU'E
Safata Bay
Amaile
Vaitogi

PACIFIC OCEAN

AMERICAN SAMOA (U.S.A.)
AMERICAN SAMOA
Tutuila
Leone
Pago Pago
Aunu'u I.
Ofu
Olosega
Luma
Ta'ū
Manu'a Is.
AMERICAN SAMOA

SAMOAN ISLANDS
on same scale **b**

172 E 172 W West from Greenwich

TONGA
on same scale **c**

Fonualei
Toku
PACIFIC OCEAN
Vava'u
Neiafu
Vava'u Group
Late
Home Reef
Disney Reef
Ha'ano
Foa
Lifuka
Uiha
Ha'apai Group
Tofua
Kao
Ofolanga
Kotu Group
Fonuafo'ou
Nomuka
Mango
Oto Tolu Group
Hunga Ha'apai
Nomuka Group
Tonumea
TONGA
Nuku'alofa
Tongatapu
Tongatapu Group
Eua

West from Greenwich

PACIFIC OCEAN

C. Reinga
C. Maria van Diemen
North C.
Rangaunu B.
Houhora Heads
Ahipara B.
Kaitaia
Tauroa Pt.
Rawene
Okaihau
Kaikohe
Waitangi
B. of Islands
C. Brett
Doubtless B.
Mangonui
Whangaroa Harb.
Opua
Hokianga Harbour
Waipoua Forest
Hikurangi
Whangarei
Whangarei Harb.
Bream Hd.
Dargaville
Waipu
Bream B.
Little Barrier I.
Great Barrier I.
North Island
Warkworth
Helensville
Kaipara Harbour
C. Rodney
C. Colville
Cuvier I.
Hauraki Gulf
Takapuna
Coromandel
Whitianga
AUCKLAND
Papakura
Thames
Whangapoa
Mayor I.
Manukau
Waiuku
Mercer
Paeroa
Waihi
Tauranga Harb.
Huntly
Te Aroha
Whangamata
Whakaari (White I.)
Runaway
Hamilton
Morrinsville
Raglan
Cambridge
Te Awamutu
Putaruru
Kawhia Harbour
Otorohanga
Tauranga
Te Puke
Bay of Plenty
East C.
Mount Maunganui
Whakatane
Kawerau
Te Kuiti
Mokai
Waiotapu
Rotorua
L. Rotorua
Taneatua
Motu
Hikurangi 1753
RAUKUMARA Ra.
Mokau
Waitomo Caves
Wairakei
Taupo
L. Taupo
Murupara
Waipiro
UREWERA
Waikaremoana
Tolaga Bay
North Taranaki Bight
Waitara
New Plymouth
Inglewood
Ongarue
Taumarunui
Turangi
WHANGANUI
Kaingaroa
Ruatahuna
Ormond
Gisborne
Mt. Taranaki or Mt. Egmont
C. Egmont 2518
EGMONT
Ohakune
TONGARIRO
Ruapehu 2797
Poverty Bay
Opunake
Stratford
Eltham
Raetihi
Waiouru
Nuhaka
Wairoa
Waikokopu
Mahia Pen.
Kaponga
Hawera
Taihape
Napier
Waverley
Mangaweka
Ohura
Mahia
Hawke Bay
C. Kidnappers
South Taranaki Bight
Patea
Hastings
Wanganui
Marton
Halcombe
Bulls
Feilding
Dannevirke
Waipukurau
Palmerston North
Foxton
Shannon
Pahiatua
Woodville
C. Turnagain
Levin
Otaki
Masterton
Carterton
Greytown
C. Farewell
D'Urville I.
Paraparaumu
Kapiti I.
Martinborough
Wairarapa
Collingwood
Golden B.
ABEL TASMAN
Tasman B.
Upper Hutt
Featherston
KAHURANGI
Takaka
Tasman Mts.
Nelson
Havelock
Petone
Lower Hutt
Wellington
Cook Strait
Karamea
Motueka
Picton
Richmond
Wakefield
Karamea Bight
Matiri Ra.
Blenheim
Seddon
Granity
Seddonville
Tadmor
Murchison
Ward
Westport
Lyell
Inangahua
NELSON LAKES
Wairau
PAPAROA
Rotoiti
Mt. Travers 2337
Kaikoura
PACIFIC OCEAN
Punakaiki
Blackball
Spenser Mts.
2885 Tapuae-o-Uenuku
Reefton
Lewis Pass
Hanmer Springs
Clarence
Runanga
Greymouth
Waiau
Kumara
L. Brunner
Jacksons
Culverden
Kaikoura
Hokitika
Ross
ARTHUR'S PASS
Waikari
Hurunui
Waipara
Arthur's
Oxford
Amberley
Rangiora
Kaiapoi
Pegasus Bay
Springfield
Whitecliffs
Kaiapoi
New Brighton
South Island
Westland Bight
Abut Hd.
Methven
Staveley
Darfield
Lincoln
Christchurch
Lyttelton
WESTLAND
Aoraki
Mt Cook
3724
MT COOK (Aoraki)
Rakaia
L. Ellesmere
Little River
Akaroa
Banks Pen.
Mount Cook
Tekapo
Fairlie
Ashburton
Canterbury Bight
Jackson B.
Haast
Okuru
Southern Alps (Tiritiri o te Moana)
MOUNT ASPIRING
Mt. Aspiring 3033
Pukaki
Temuka
Timaru
Milford Sd.
Sutherland Falls
Mt. Earnslaw 2819
Milford Sound
Wanaka
L. Hawea
Ohau
St. Andrews
Waimate
Bligh Sound
George Sound
Queenstown
Arrowtown
Cromwell
Clyde
Dunstan Mts.
Naseby
Kurow
Waitaki
Otematata
Duntroon
Maheno
Oamaru
Secretary I.
Doubtful Sd.
FIORDLAND
Te Anau
L. Te Anau
Kingston
Eyre Mts.
Garvie Mts.
Alexandra
Roxburgh
Waikouaiti
Breaksea Sd.
Manapouri
L. Manapouri
Mossburn
Lumsden
Otago
Ranfurly
Hampden
Palmerston
Resolution I.
Dusky Sd.
Clifden
Nightcaps
Winton
Gore
Mataura
Kaitangata
Port Chalmers
Otago Harbour
C. Saunders
Chalky Inlet
Tuatapere
Ohai
Edievale
Kelso
Lawrence
Milton
Dunedin
Mosgiel
Preservation Inlet
Riverton
Orepuki
Te Waewae B.
Invercargill
Bluff
South
Wyndham
Owaka
Balclutha
Nugget Pt.
Solander I.
Foveaux Str.
Ruapuke I.
Tokanui
Tahakopa
Halfmoon Bay
Stewart I. (Rakiura)
RAKIURA
South West
Port Pegasus

TASMAN SEA

South Island

Projection: Conical with two standard parallels

East from Greenwich

COPYRIGHT PHILIP'S

TAHITI & MOOREA **d**
1:1 000 000

Pte. Aroa
Papetoai
Paopao
B. de Matavai
Pte. Vênus
Mahina
Papeete
Arué
Pirae
Mt. Tohiea 1207
Haapiti
Afareaitu
Faaa
Papenoo
Tiarei
Moorea (France)
Tahiti (France)
Punaauia
Hitiaa
Mt. Aorai 2060
Mt. Orohena 2241
Faaone
PACIFIC OCEAN
Mt. Tetufera 1799
L. Vaihiria
Paea
Isthme de Taravao
Papara
Taravao
Afaahiti
Maraa
Atimaono
Mataiea
Pte. Tatata
Pueu
Vairao
Mt. Rooniu 1332
Tautira
Teahupoo
Presqu'île de Taiarapu

ft m
9000 3000
6000 2000
3000 1000
1200 400
600 200
0 0
200 600
1200
2000 6000
4000 12 000
6000 18 000
m ft

10 0 10 km
10 0 10 miles
1:1 000 000

1:8 000 000

50 0 50 100 150 200 250 300 km
50 0 50 100 150 200 miles

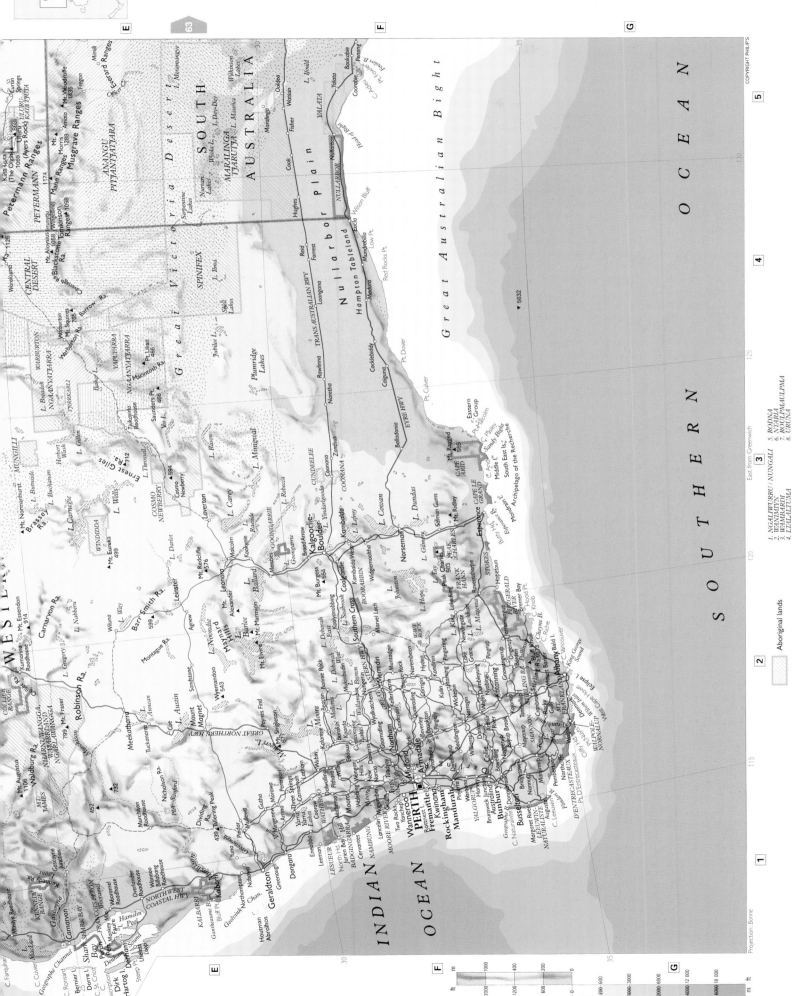

INDIAN

OCEAN

SOUTHERN

OCEAN

WESTERN

SOUTH

AUSTRALIA

Great Victoria Desert

Nullarbor Plain

Great Australian Bight

PERTH

Fremantle
Rockingham
Mandurah

Kalgoorlie
Boulder

Geraldton

Kalbarri

Carnarvon

Esperance

Albany

Busselton
Bunbury

Projection: Bonne

East from Greenwich

1. NGALIWURRU / NUNGALI
2. WINIMINY
3. WAMBARDI
4. LIHALITUMA
5. RODNA
6. NTARIA
7. ROULPMAULPMA
8. URUNA

Aboriginal lands

1 2 3 4 5

E F G

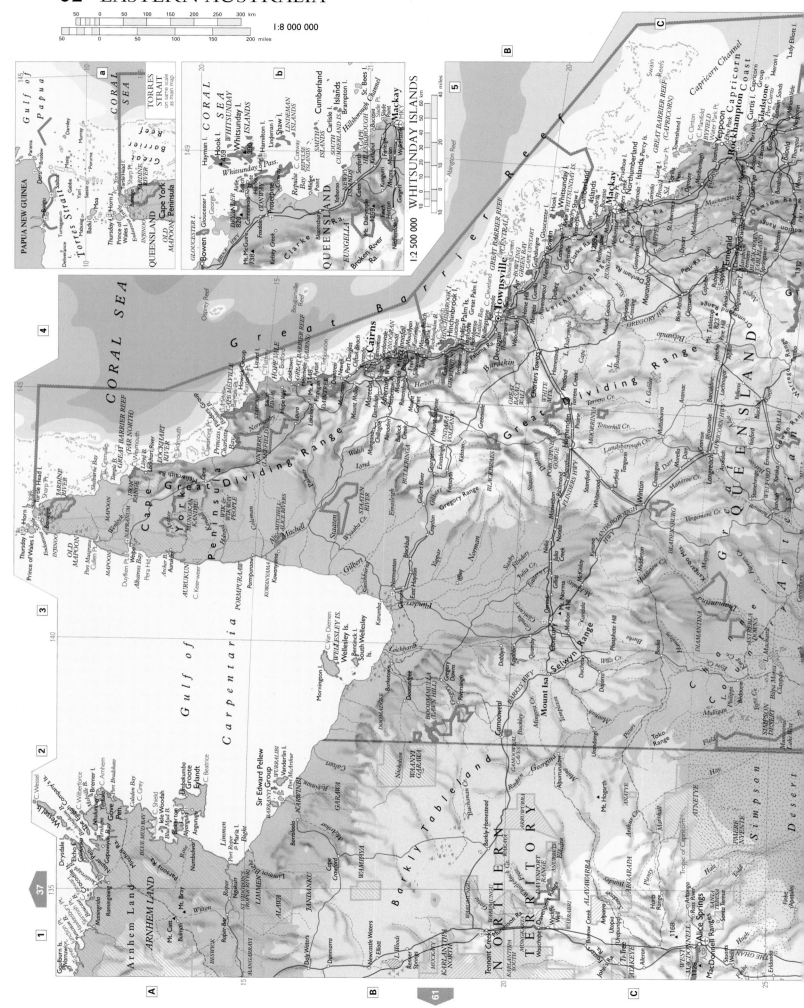

NEW SOUTH WALES

SOUTH AUSTRALIA

VICTORIA

TASMANIA

TASMAN SEA

Bass Strait

Major places: BRISBANE, SYDNEY, Canberra, MELBOURNE, ADELAIDE, Newcastle, Wollongong, Geelong, Hobart, Launceston

Gold Coast, Sunshine Coast, Coffs Harbour, Port Macquarie, Tamworth, Armidale, Toowoomba, Warwick, Dubbo, Orange, Bathurst, Parkes, Forbes, Wagga Wagga, Albury, Broken Hill, Bourke, Cobar, Mildura, Wentworth, Shepparton, Bendigo, Ballarat, Horsham, Mount Gambier, Warrnambool, Port Augusta, Port Pirie, Whyalla, Port Lincoln, Ceduna

Great Dividing Range, Darling Downs, Flinders Ranges, Barrier Range, Grampians, Gippsland, Murray River, Darling River, Lake Eyre, Lake Torrens, Lake Gairdner, Lake Frome, Lake Blanche

Simpson Desert, Sturt Stony Desert, Strzelecki Desert, Tirari Desert, Big Desert, Little Desert, Sunset Country, Mallee

Eyre Peninsula, Yorke Peninsula, Spencer Gulf, Gulf St Vincent, Kangaroo Island, King Island, Flinders Island, Cape Barren Island, Furneaux Group, Kent Group

Coorong Peninsula, Wilsons Promontory, Cooper Cr., Warrego Highway, Stuart Highway

Aboriginal lands

Projection: Bonne

East from Greenwich

on same scale

m ft

Equatorial Scale 1:54 000 000

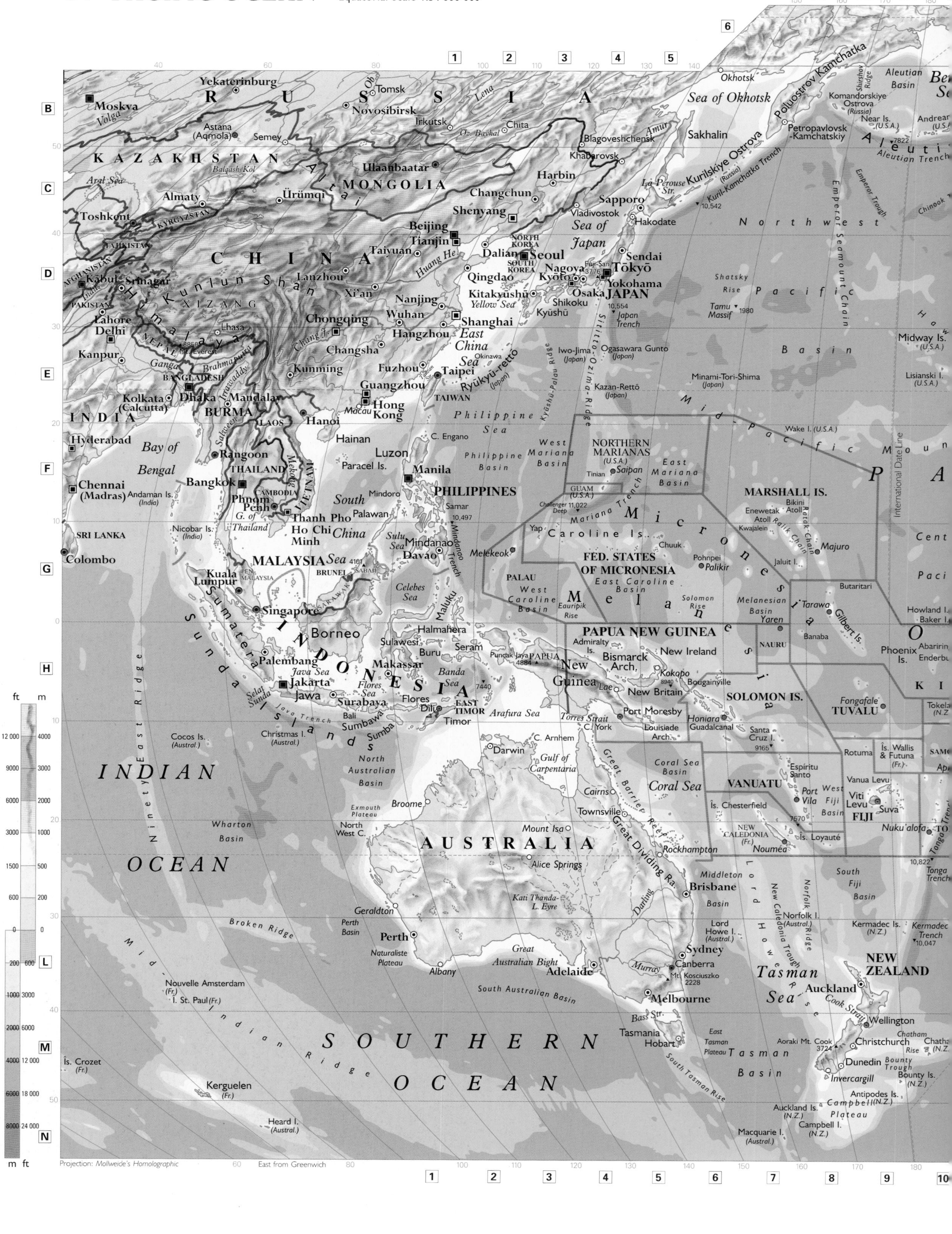

Oceans and Seas

Sea of Okhotsk
Northwest Pacific Basin
Sea of Japan
Yellow Sea
East China Sea
Philippine Sea
South China Sea
Bay of Bengal
Andaman Sea
Gulf of Thailand
Sulu Sea
Celebes Sea
Java Sea
Flores Sea
Banda Sea
Arafura Sea
Timor Sea
Coral Sea
Tasman Sea
Philippine Basin
West Mariana Basin
East Mariana Basin
Caroline Is.
West Caroline Basin
East Caroline Basin
North Australian Basin
Coral Sea Basin
South Fiji Basin
West Fiji Basin
Solomon Sea
Bismarck Sea
Melanesian Basin
South Australian Basin
Great Australian Bight
Gulf of Carpentaria
Exmouth Plateau
Wharton Basin
Broken Ridge
Mid-Indian Ridge
Ninetyeast Ridge
Sunda Trench
Java Trench
Mariana Trench
Challenger Deep 11,022
Mindanao Trench 10,497
Japan Trench 10,554
Kuril-Kamchatka Trench 10,542
Aleutian Trench
Tonga Trench 10,822
Kermadec Trench 10,047
East Tasman Plateau
South Tasman Rise
Tasman Basin
Naturaliste Plateau
Perth Basin
Broken Ridge

INDIAN OCEAN

SOUTHERN OCEAN

PACIFIC OCEAN

Countries and Regions

RUSSIA
KAZAKHSTAN
MONGOLIA
CHINA
XIZANG
KYRGYZSTAN
TAJIKISTAN
AFGHANISTAN
PAKISTAN
NEPAL
INDIA
BANGLADESH
BURMA
LAOS
THAILAND
CAMBODIA
VIETNAM
MALAYSIA
PEN. MALAYSIA
BRUNEI
SABAH
SARAWAK
INDONESIA
SRI LANKA
NORTH KOREA
SOUTH KOREA
JAPAN
TAIWAN
PHILIPPINES
PAPUA NEW GUINEA
PAPUA
EAST TIMOR
AUSTRALIA
NEW ZEALAND
NORTHERN MARIANAS (U.S.A.)
GUAM (U.S.A.)
MARSHALL IS.
FED. STATES OF MICRONESIA
PALAU
NAURU
SOLOMON IS.
TUVALU
VANUATU
NEW CALEDONIA (Fr.)
FIJI
TOKELAU (N.Z.)
Micronesia
Melanesia

Cities

Moskva
Yekaterinburg
Tomsk
Novosibirsk
Astana (Aqmola)
Semey
Irkutsk
Chita
Okhotsk
Blagoveshchensk
Khabarovsk
Sakhalin
Almaty
Ürümqi
Toshkent
Ulaanbaatar
Changchun
Shenyang
Vladivostok
Sapporo
Hakodate
Petropavlovsk-Kamchatskiy
Beijing
Tianjin
Taiyuan
Dalian
Seoul
Sendai
Nagoya
Tōkyō
Kyōto
Yokohama
Osaka
JAPAN
Kabul
Srinagar
Lanzhou
Qingdao
Kitakyūshū
Shikoku
Kyūshū
Lahore
Delhi
Xi'an
Nanjing
Shanghai
Hangzhou
Kanpur
Chongqing
Wuhan
Changsha
Lhasa
Kolkata (Calcutta)
Dhaka
Mandalay
Kunming
Fuzhou
Taipei
Hyderabad
Rangoon
Guangzhou
Macau
Hong Kong
Hainan
Hanoi
Chennai (Madras)
Bangkok
Luzon
Manila
Colombo
Phnom Penh
Thanh Pho Ho Chi Minh
Palawan
Mindoro
Samar
Mindanao
Davao
Kuala Lumpur
Singapore
Borneo
Makassar
Jakarta
Jawa
Surabaya
Bali
Flores
Sumbawa
Sumba
Dili
Timor
Palembang
Sumatera
Darwin
Broome
Mount Isa
Alice Springs
Cairns
Townsville
Rockhampton
Brisbane
Geraldton
Perth
Albany
Adelaide
Sydney
Canberra
Melbourne
Hobart
Tasmania
Auckland
Wellington
Christchurch
Dunedin
Invercargill
Port Moresby
Honiara
Port Vila
Nouméa
Suva
Nuku'alofa
Tarawa
Yaren
Majuro
Palikir
Melekeok
Saipan
Tinian
Hagåtña

Islands and Features

Aral Sea
Volga
Ob
Lena
Amur
Huang He
Chang
Ganga
Brahmaputra
Irrawaddy
Mekong
Salween
Murray
Darling
Balqash Köl
Altay
Kunlun Shan
Himalaya
Everest
K2
Fuji-San 3776
Kati Thanda-L. Eyre
Mt. Kosciuszko 2228
Aoraki Mt. Cook 3724
Mt. Arnhem
Puncak Jaya 4884
Fiji-San
Sakhalin
Kurilskiye Ostrova (Russia)
Poluostrov Kamchatka
Komandorskiye Ostrova (Russia)
Near Is. (U.S.A.)
Aleutian Is.
Shirshov Ridge
Emperor Seamount Chain
Emperor Trough
Midway Is. (U.S.A.)
Lisianski I. (U.S.A.)
Wake I. (U.S.A.)
Minami-Tori-Shima (Japan)
Kazan-Rettō (Japan)
Iwo-Jima (Japan)
Ogasawara Gunto (Japan)
Okinawa
Ryūkyū-rettō (Japan)
Kyūshū-Palau Ridge
Sitito-Ozima-Ridge
Shatsky Rise
Tamu Massif 1980
Pacific Basin
International Date Line
Bikini Atoll
Enewetak Atoll
Kwajalein
Ralik Chain
Ratak Chain
Yap
Chuuk
Pohnpei
Jaluit I.
Eauripik Rise
Butaritari
Tarawa
Banaba
Gilbert Is.
Phoenix Is.
Howland I. Baker I. (U.S.A.)
Abariringa Enderbury
Fongafale
Rotuma
Îs. Wallis & Futuna (Fr.)
Espíritu Santo
Vanua Levu
Viti Levu
Îs. Chesterfield
Îs. Loyauté
Norfolk I. (Austral.)
Lord Howe I. (Austral.)
Middleton
Kermadec Is. (N.Z.)
Chatham Is.
Chatham Rise
Bounty Is. (N.Z.)
Antipodes Is. (N.Z.)
Campbell I. (N.Z.)
Auckland Is. (N.Z.)
Macquarie I. (Austral.)
Campbell Plateau
Bounty Trough
Cook Strait
Îs. Crozet (Fr.)
Kerguelen (Fr.)
Heard I. (Austral.)
Nouvelle Amsterdam (Fr.)
Î. St. Paul (Fr.)
Cocos Is. (Austral.)
Christmas I. (Austral.)
Paracel Is.
Nicobar Is. (India)
Andaman Is. (India)
C. Engano
Halmahera
Sulawesi
Buru
Seram
Maluku
Admiralty Is.
Bismarck Arch.
New Ireland
New Britain
New Guinea
Kokopo
Lae
Bougainville
Guadalcanal
Santa Cruz Is. 9165
Louisiade Arch.
C. York
Torres Strait
New Caledonia Ridge
Norfolk Ridge
Lord Howe Rise
Great Barrier Reef
Great Dividing Ra.
Bass Str.
North West C.
Naturaliste Plateau
Naturaliste
Bungku
Samal
9840
7440
4101
7570
1980

Elevation / Depth scale

ft — m
12 000 — 4000
9000 — 3000
6000 — 2000
3000 — 1000
1500 — 500
600 — 200
0 — 0
200 — 600
1000 — 3000
2000 — 6000
4000 — 12 000
6000 — 18 000
8000 — 24 000
m — ft

Projection: Mollweide's Homolographic

East from Greenwich

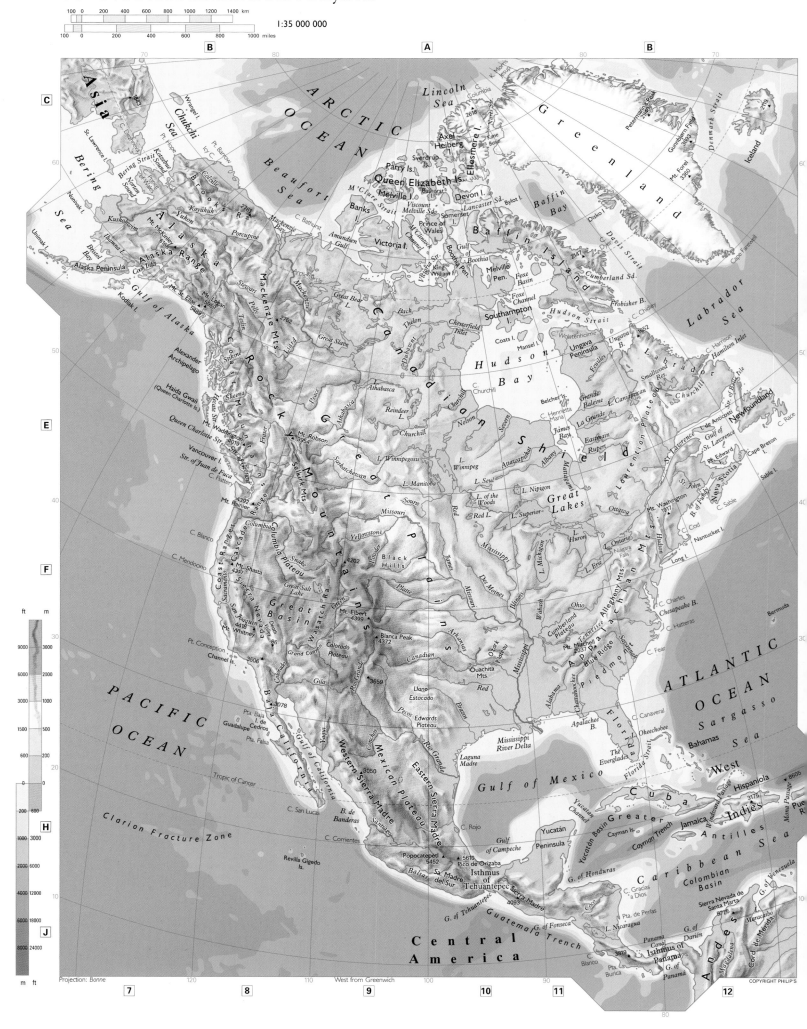

Projection: Bonne

West from Greenwich

COPYRIGHT PHILIP'S

1:35 000 000

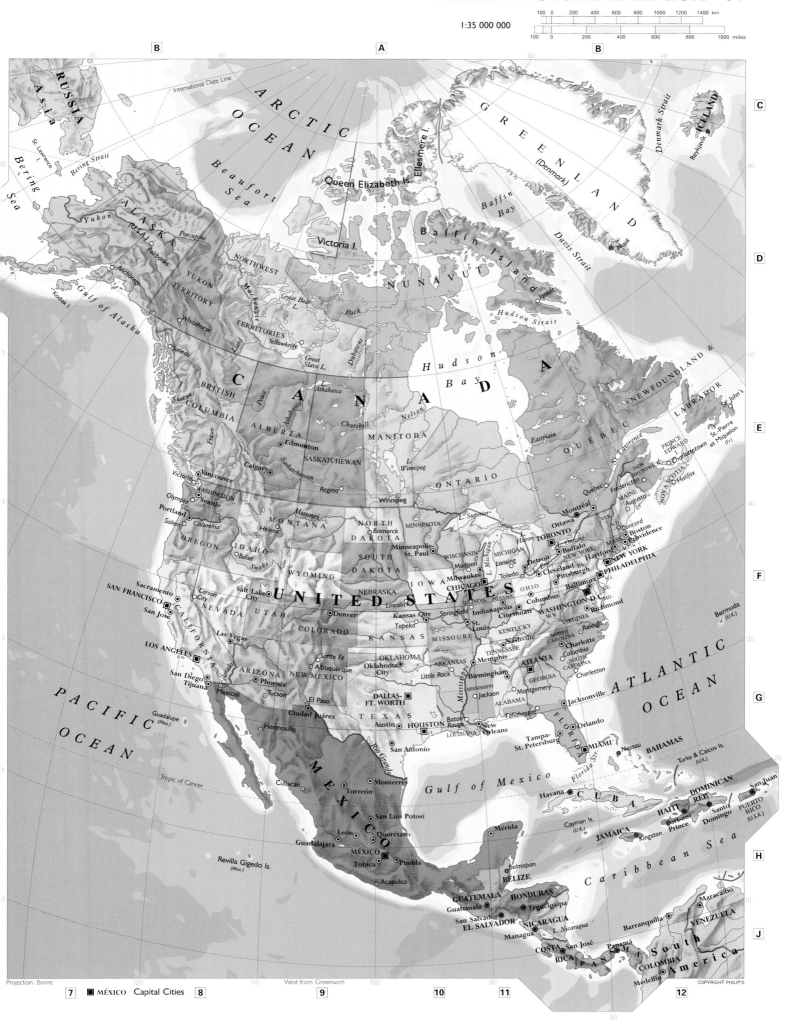

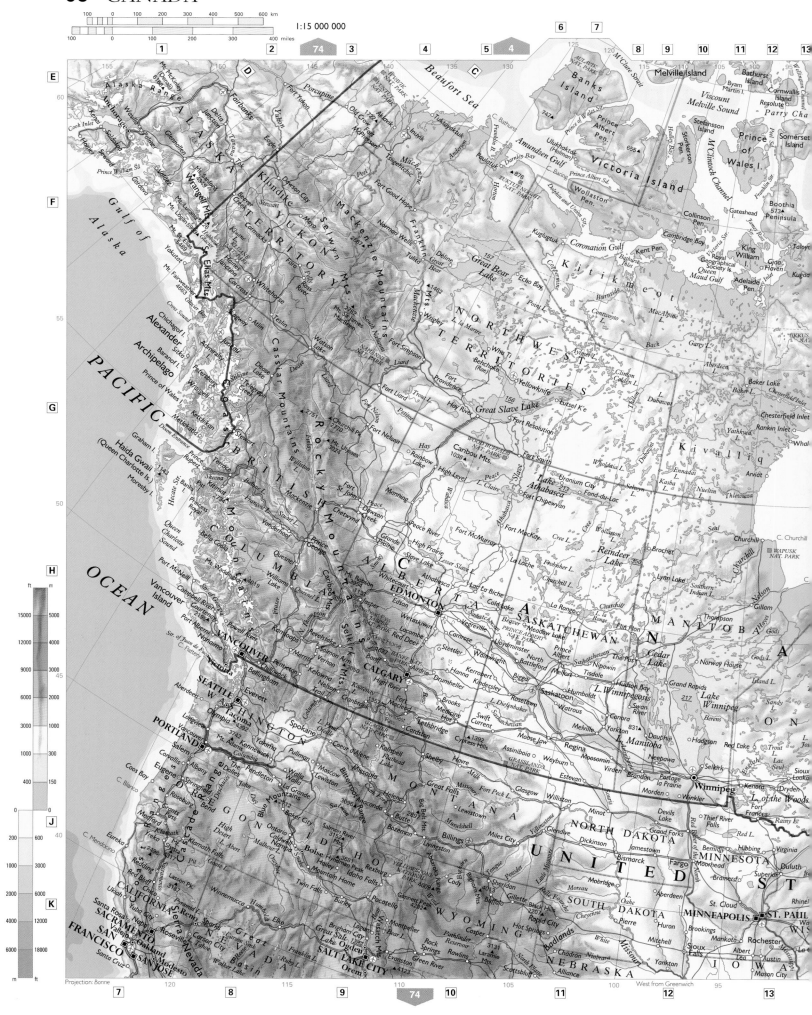

1:15 000 000

Projection: Bonne

West from Greenwich

NORTHERN CANADA
continuation northwards on same scale as main map

ARCTIC OCEAN

GREENLAND (KALAALLIT NUNAAT)
(Denmark)

Kronprins Frederik Land

Baffin Bay

Davis Strait

Baffin Island (Qikiqtaaluk)

NUNAVUT

Queen Elizabeth Islands

Parry Islands

Ellesmere Island

Devon Island

Lancaster Sound

Hudson Strait

Foxe Basin

Hudson Bay

James Bay

Labrador Sea

ATLANTIC OCEAN

QUÉBEC

Nunavik

Péninsule d'Ungava

Ungava Bay

ONTARIO

NEWFOUNDLAND & LABRADOR

Labrador

Newfoundland

Gulf of St. Lawrence

PRINCE EDWARD ISLAND

NOVA SCOTIA

NEW BRUNSWICK

MAINE

QUÉBEC

MONTRÉAL

OTTAWA

QUÉBEC

TORONTO

NEW YORK

BOSTON

VERMONT

NEW HAMPSHIRE

MASS.

CONN.

PENNSYLVANIA

DETROIT

CLEVELAND

BUFFALO

ROCHESTER

Lake Huron

Lake Ontario

Lake Erie

Lake Michigan

COPYRIGHT PHILIP'S

1:7 000 000

Projection: Lambert's Equivalent Azimuthal

LABRADOR SEA

Nunatsiavut

NEWFOUNDLAND &

Labrador

LABRADOR

Newfoundland

Smallwood Reservoir

QUÉBEC

GULF OF ST. LAWRENCE

Île d'Anticosti

St. Lawrence

Pén. de la Gaspésie

Mts. Chic-Chocs

NEW BRUNSWICK

PRINCE EDWARD ISLAND

Cape Breton Island

Cabot Strait

ST-PIERRE-ET-MIQUELON (France)

NOVA SCOTIA

Halifax

Dartmouth

Sable I. (Nova Scotia)

ATLANTIC OCEAN

MAINE

NEW HAMPSHIRE

BOSTON

UNITED STATES

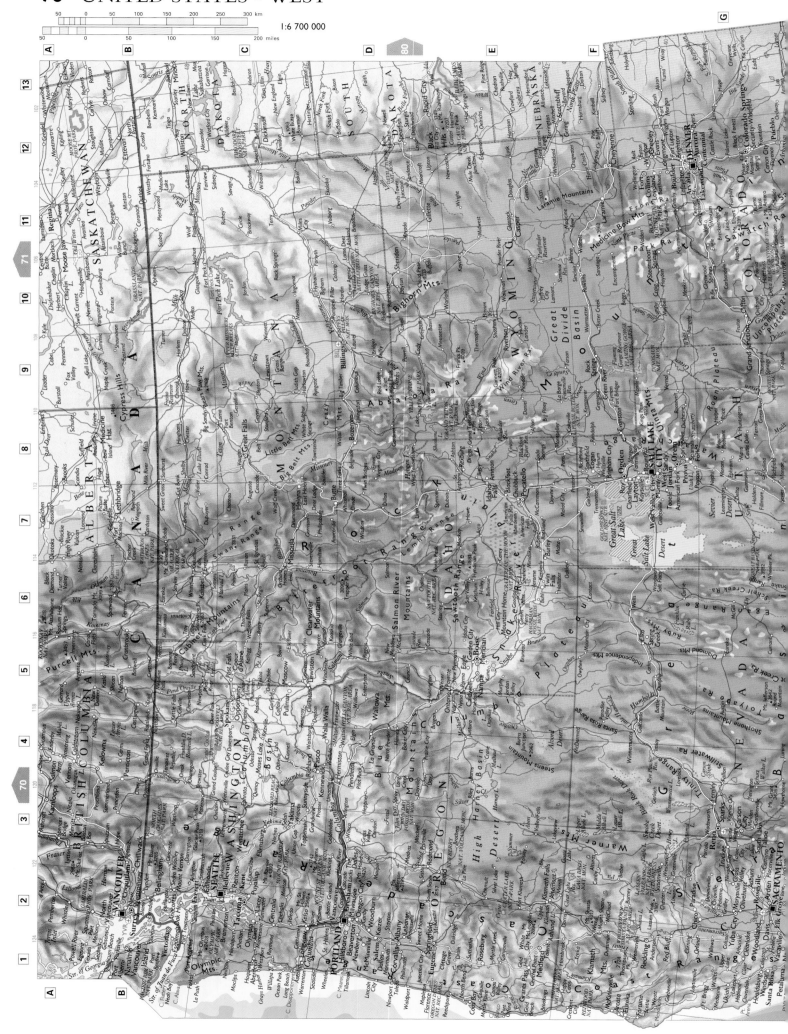

1:6 700 000

Projection: Albers' Equal Area with two standard parallels

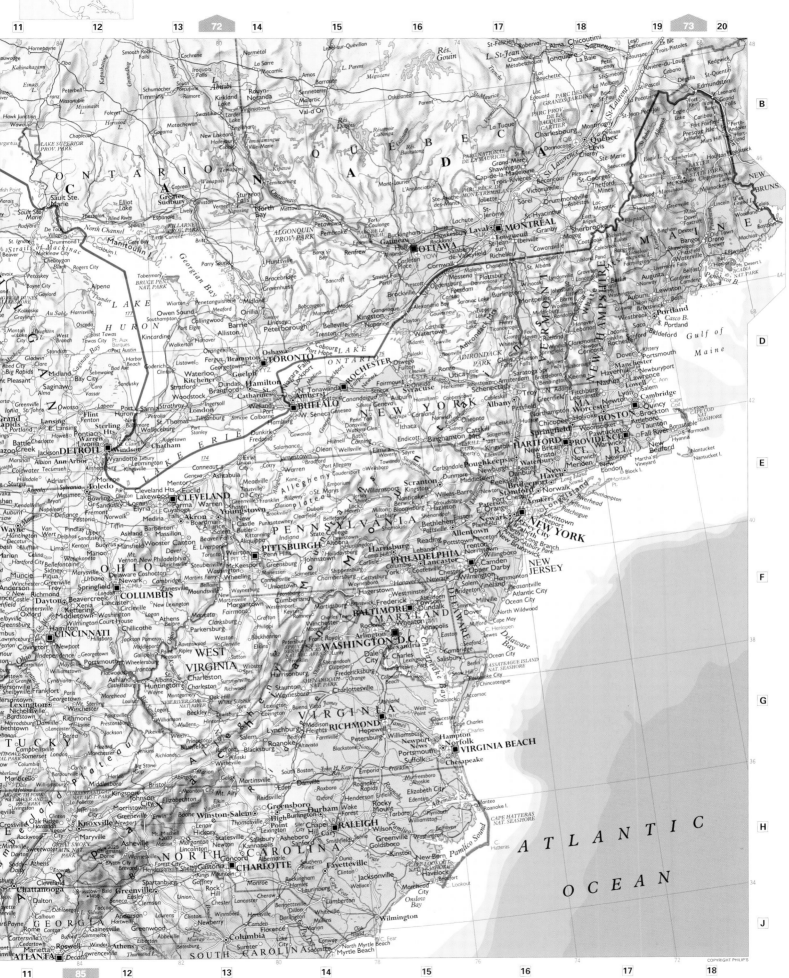

50 0 50 100 150 200 250 300 km
50 0 50 100 150 200 miles

1:8 000 000

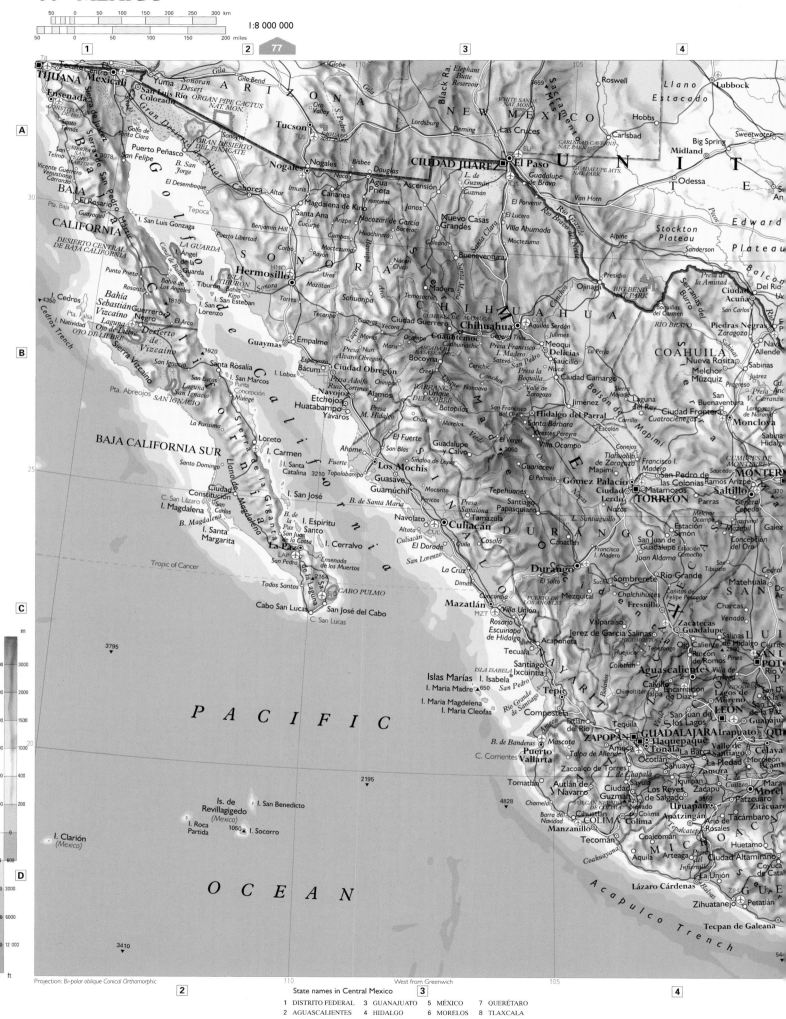

Projection: Bi-polar oblique Conical Orthomorphic

West from Greenwich

State names in Central Mexico

1 DISTRITO FEDERAL   3 GUANAJUATO   5 MÉXICO   7 QUERÉTARO
2 AGUASCALIENTES   4 HIDALGO   6 MORELOS   8 TLAXCALA

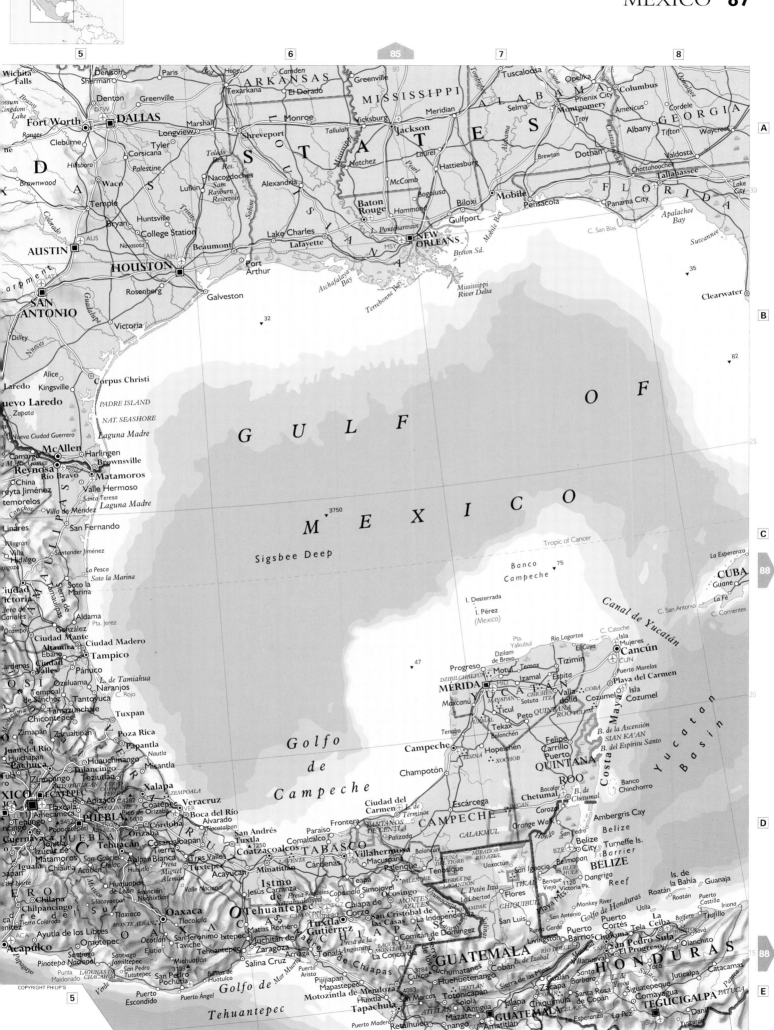

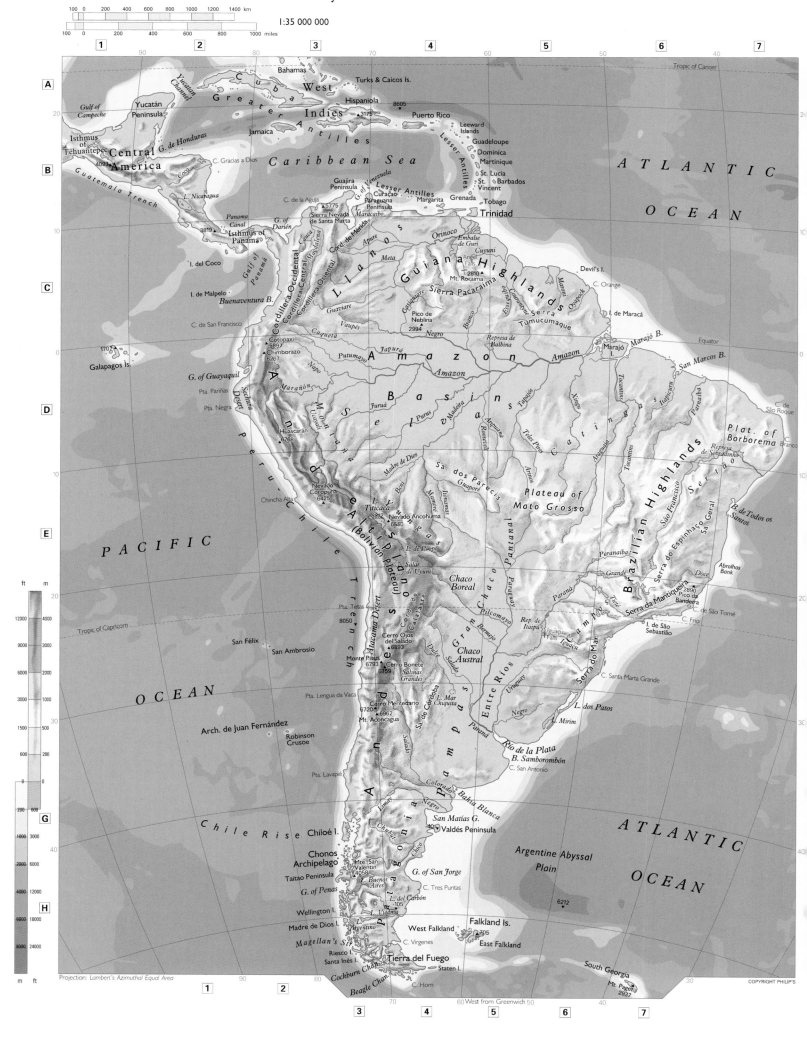

1:35 000 000

Projection: Lambert's Azimuthal Equal Area

COPYRIGHT PHILIP'S

1:35 000 000

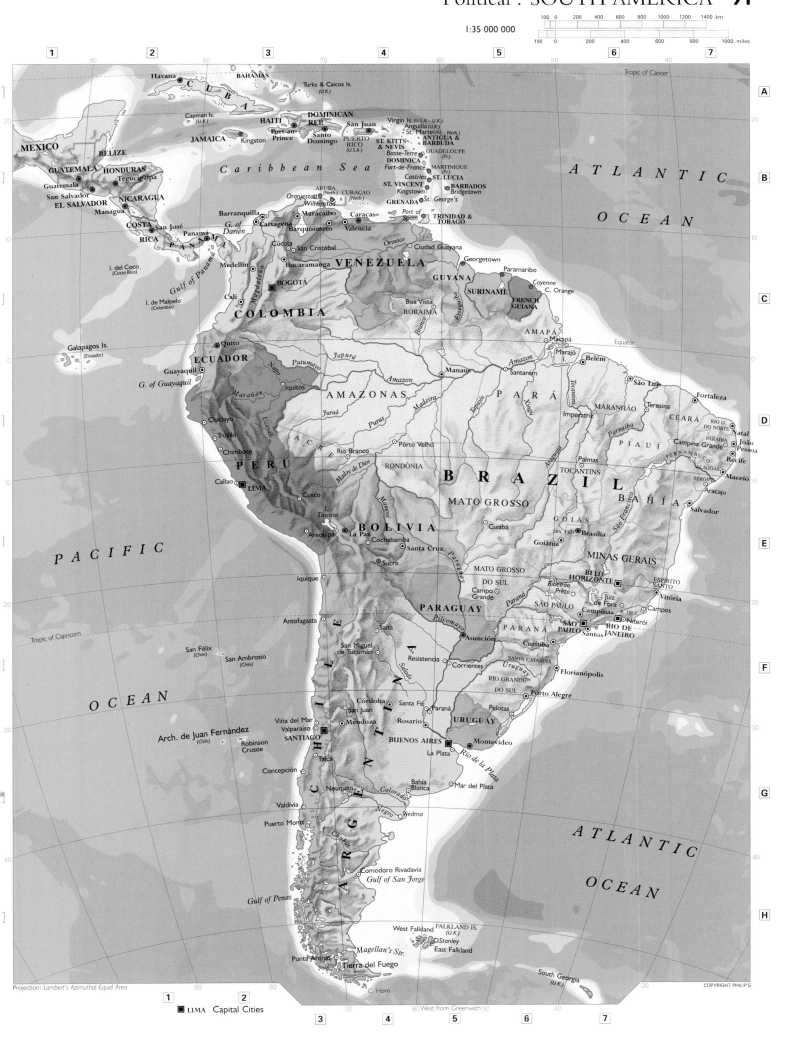

■ LIMA   Capital Cities

1:16 000 000

Projection: Sanson-Flamsteed's Sinusoidal

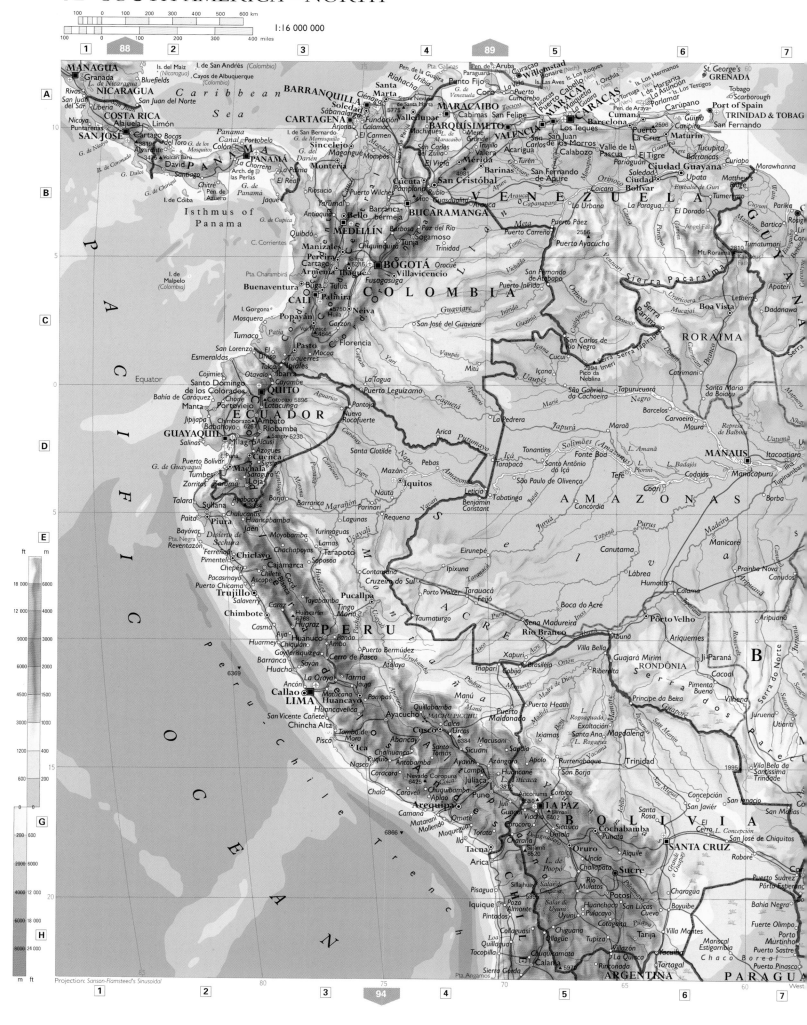

ATLANTIC

OCEAN

TRINIDAD AND
TOBAGO
1:2 500 000
10   0   10   20   30   40   50 km
10   0   10   20   30 miles

Tobago
Charlotteville · North Pt.
Castara · 565 Little
Plymouth · Main Ridge · Roxborough
Buccoo Reef · Tobago
Crown Pt. · Scarborough
Rocky Bay

VENEZUELA
Pen. de
Paria
Macuro
Güiria
Corozal Pt.
Dragon's Mouths
Maraval
Chupara Pt. Blanchisseuse
Las Cuevas
Maracas Bay
Morvant Village
Monos
Saut d'Eau
Matelot Sans Souci
Toco
Galera Pt.
Redhead
Salybia
Northern Range
936 ▲ ▲940 Mt. Aripo
**Port of
Spain**
San
Juan
Tunapuna
Arima
Valencia
Matura
Bay
ATLANTIC
OCEAN
Caroni
Guaico
Chaguanas
Golfo de Paria
Couva
Talparo
Sangre Grande
Upper Manzanilla
Nariva
Swamp
Cocos
Bay
Point Lisas
Otaheite Bay
San Fernando
Gasparillo
Rio Claro
Guatuaro Pt.
Trinidad
Brighton
La Brea
Penal
Princes Town
Mayaro
Mayaro Bay
Guapo Bay
Pitch
Lake
Basse Terre
Guayaguayare
Point Fortin
Cedros Bay
Palo Seco
Siparia
La Lune
304 ▲
Galeota Pt.
Bonasse
Icacos Pt.
Erin Pt.
Moruga
Trinity
Hills
VENEZUELA
Serpent's Mouth
Pta. Bombedor
West from Greenwich

São Pedro &
São Paulo
(Braz.)

Equator

Fernando de Noronha
(Braz.)
Atol
das Rocas
(Braz.)

SURINAME
Paramaribo
Nieuw Amsterdam
Nickerie
Moengo
Witness
Albina
St-Laurent du Maroni
Iracoubo
Sinnamary
Kourou
Cayenne
W. v. Van
Blommestein
Meer
FRENCH
GUIANA
C. Orange
St-Georges
Oiapoque
Kaw
Approuague
Camopi

AMAPÁ
Amapá
Serra do
Navio
Merirumã
Araguari
I. de Maracá

Macapá
I. Caviana
Mazagão
I. Mexiana
Afuá
Chaves
Curuçá
Salinópolis
C. Maguari
I. Grande
de Gurupá
I. de Soure
Vigia
Bragança
Óbidos
Monte
Alegre
Prainha
Breves
Marajó
BELÉM
Castanhal
Turiaçu
Viseu
Cururupu
Alenquer
Santarém
Almeirim
Porto de Moz
Cametá
Abaetetuba
B. de São Marcos
São Luís
Barreirinhas
Belterra
Aveiro
Gurupá
Baião
Capim
Alcântara
Pinheiro
Rosário
Tutóia
Luís Correia
Camocim
Brasília Legal
Porto
Curralinho
Itapecuru-
Mirim
Santa Inês
Viana
Brejo
Parnaíba
Granja
Itapipoca
Caucaia
Altamira
Baturité
Santa Ines
Acailândia
Bacabal
Coroatá
Piripiri
Piracuruca
Sobral
Maranguape
FORTALEZA
Itaituba
PARÁ
Tucurui
Represa de
Tucuruí
Codó
Caxias
Campo
Maior
Oiticica
Ipu
Quixadá
Cascavel
Aracati
Pedreiras
Teresina
Crateús
Russas
Macau
Ceará-Mirim
Santana do
Araguaia
Marabá
Imperatriz
Barra
do Corda
Colinas
Senador
Pompeu
CEARÁ
Mossoró
Caraúbas
RIO GRANDE
DO NORTE
NATAL
C. de São Roque
Parauapebas
Serra dos
Carajás
São João do
Araguaia
Porto Franco
Floriano
Amarante
Valença
do Piauí
Iguatu
Calcó
Currais
Novos
Carajás
Tocantinópolis
Estreito
Oeiras
Picos
Cajazeiras
Sousa
Patos
Cangaçaretama
Mamanguape
Cabedelo
Araguaína
Carolina
Loreto
Nova Iorque
Uruçuí
PIAUÍ
Crato
Juàzeiro
do Norte
PARAÍBA
Campina
Grande
JOÃO PESSOA
Conceição do
Araguaia
Riachão
São João
do Piauí
Ouricuri
Salgueiro
Caruaru
Olinda
RECIFE
Araguacema
Pedro Afonso
Remanso
Casa Nova
Juàzeiro
Petrolina
Garanhuns
Jaboatão
Serra
do Cachimbo
Caracol
Sa. Dois Irmãos
Petrolândia
Vitória de Santo Antão
Palmeira
dos Indios
Rio Largo
Palmares
Palmas
Porto Nacional
Parnaguá
Sta.
Filomena
Paulistana
Paulo Afonso
Arapiraca
MACEIÓ
BRAZIL
Santa Isabel
do Morro
I. do Banana
TOCANTINS
Barra
Senhor do
Bonfim
Própria
Penedo
ALAGOAS
SERGIPE
Gurupi
Peixe
Represa de
Sobradinho
Xique-Xique
Jacobina
Itapicuru
Capela
Aracaju
Serra Formosa
BAHÍA
Santa Maria
da Vitória
Paraná
Barreiras
Ibotirama
Mundo
Novo
Queimadas
Serrinho
São Cristóvão
Estância
Campos Belos
Posse
Carinhanha
Bom Jesus
da Lapa
Castro
Alves
**Feira de
Santana**
Alagoinhas
São Domingos
Santa Maria
da Vitória
Caetité
Itaberaba
Cachoeira
Santo Amaro
SALVADOR
MATO GROSSO
Planalto do
Mato Grosso
Uruaçu
Niquelândia
1678
Brumado
Condeúba
Valença
Nazaré
B. de Todas os Santos
Cuiabá
Barra do Garças
Aruanã
1840
Januária
Monte Azul
Vitória da Itabuna
Conquista
Jequié
Ubaitaba
Ilhéus
Santo Antônio
Rondonópolis
GOIÁS
Formosa
São Francisco
Salinas
Pedra Azul
Jaguaré
Canavieiras
MATO GROSSO
DO SUL
Goiás
Taguatinga
DIST.
FED.
BRASÍLIA
Luziânia
Montes
Claros
Araçuaí
Jequitinhonha
Belmonte
Campo
Grande
Alto Araguaia
GOIÂNIA
Vianópolis
Paracatu
Teófilo Otoni
Porto Seguro
Santo Antônio
Jataí
Rio Verde
Morrinhos
Ipameri
Diamantina
Itambacuri
Prado
Caravelas
Banco dos
Abrolhos
Quirinópolis
Itumbiara
Catalão
Patos de
Minas
Corinto
Araçuaí
Mucuri
Nanuque
Conceição
da Barra
Araguari
MINAS GERAIS
Patrocínio
Curvelo
Ipatinga
Nova
Venécia
São Mateus
Uberlândia
Araxá
Ibiá
Sête Lagoas
Itabira
Governador
Valadares
Linhares
Três Lagoas
Iturutaba
Prata
Frutal
Uberaba
BELO HORIZONTE
Sabará
Ponte
Nova
Catanguape
Colatina
VITÓRIA
Vila Velha
Trindade
(Braz.)
Martin Vaz
(Braz.)
São José do
Rio Preto
Barretos
Franca
Divinópolis
Conselheiro
Lafaiete
Ouro
Prêto
Poço da
Bandeira
Cachoeiro de Itapemirim
Araçatuba
Andradina
Catanduva
Araraquara
Ribeirão Prêto
Pocos de
Caldas
São João
del Rei
Ubá
Barbacena
Juiz de Fora
Campos
Presidente
Epitácio
Ponta Porã
Presidente
Prudente
Marília
Bauru
Jaú
SÃO
PAULO
Guaxupé
Mogi-Mirim
Três Rios
Nova Friburgo
Petrópolis
Assis
Piracicaba
Limeira
CAMPINAS
São Carlos
Volta
Redonda
RIO DE JANEIRO
Niterói
Cabo Frio
Botucatu

6059 ▼

6059

COPYRIGHT PHILIP'S

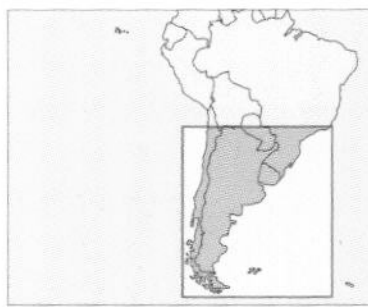

1:16 000 000

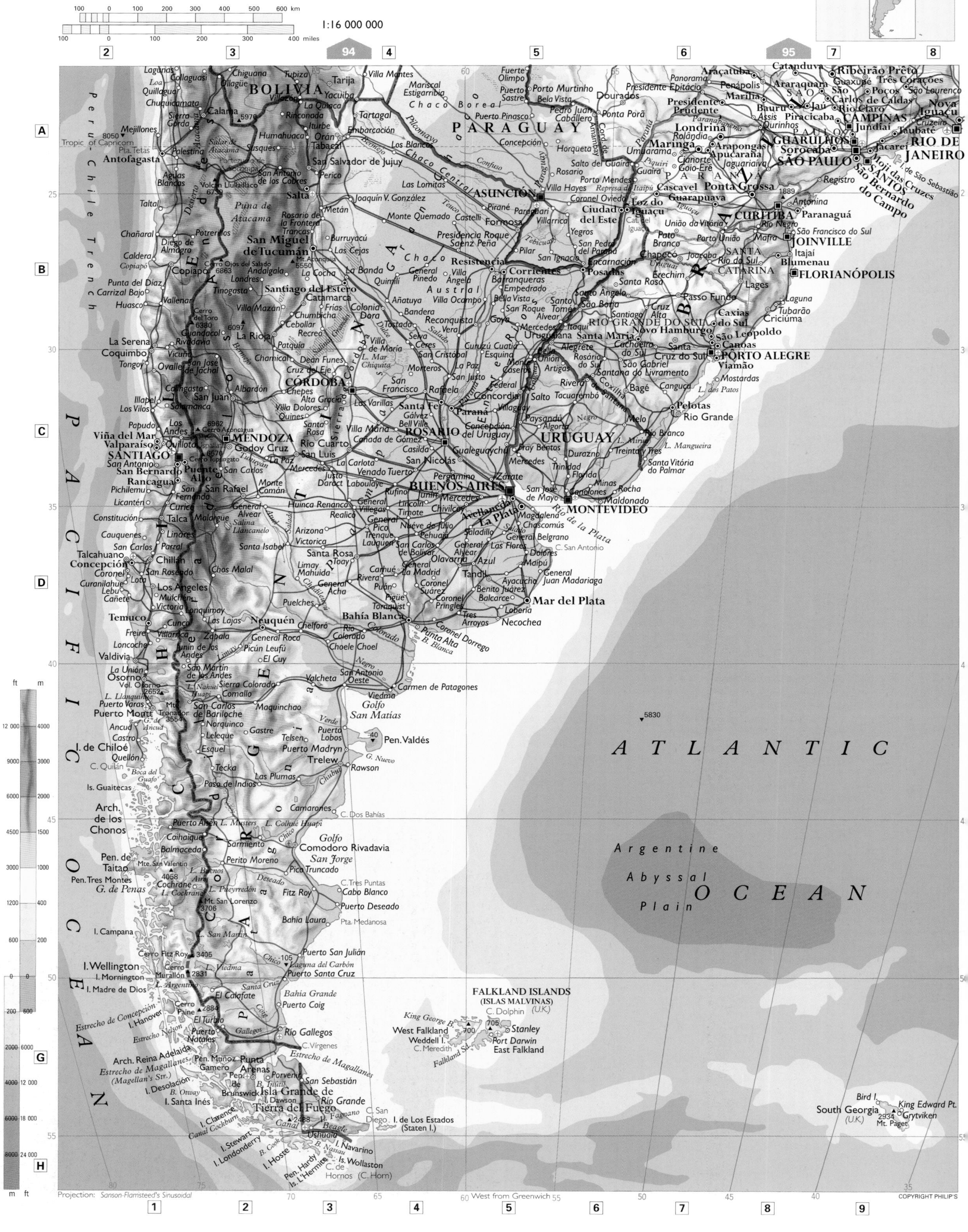

100 0 100 200 300 400 500 600 km
100 0 100 200 300 400 miles

94 95

ATLANTIC

Argentine
Abyssal
Plain OCEAN

PACIFIC OCEAN

BOLIVIA
PARAGUAY
Chaco Boreal
ASUNCIÓN
PARANÁ

BRASIL
São Paulo
RIO DE JANEIRO
CAMPINAS
CURITIBA
JOINVILLE
FLORIANÓPOLIS
Blumenau
SANTA CATARINA
RIO GRANDE DO SUL
PORTO ALEGRE
Pelotas
Rio Grande

A N D E S

Antofagasta
CHILE
San Miguel de Tucumán
CÓRDOBA
ROSARIO
SANTIAGO
Valparaíso
MENDOZA
BUENOS AIRES
La Plata
Mar del Plata
URUGUAY
MONTEVIDEO

A R G E N T I N A

P A T A G O N I A

Bahía Blanca
Neuquén
Pen. Valdés
Trelew
Comodoro Rivadavia
Golfo San Jorge

I. de Chiloé
Puerto Montt
Arch. de los Chonos

Puerto Deseado
Río Gallegos

FALKLAND ISLANDS
(ISLAS MALVINAS) (U.K.)
West Falkland
East Falkland
Stanley
Port Darwin

Estrecho de Magallanes (Magellan's Str.)
Punta Arenas
Isla Grande de Tierra del Fuego
Río Grande
Ushuaia
I. de Los Estados (Staten I.)
C. de Hornos (C. Horn)

South Georgia (U.K.)
Grytviken
Mt. Paget 2934

Tropic of Capricorn

Peru–Chile Trench

Projection: Sanson-Flamsteed's Sinusoidal

West from Greenwich

COPYRIGHT PHILIP'S

INDEX TO WORLD MAPS

The index contains the names of all the principal places and features shown on the World Maps. Each name is followed by an additional entry in italics giving the country or region within which it is located. The alphabetical order of names composed of two or more words is governed primarily by the first word, then by the second, and then by the country or region name that follows. This is an example of the rule:

Mīr Kūh *Iran*	26°22N 58°55E	**47** E8
Mīr Shahdād *Iran*	26°15N 58°29E	**47** E8
Mira *Italy*	45°26N 12°8E	**22** B5
Mira por vos Cay *Bahamas*	22°9N 74°30W	**89** B5

Physical features composed of a proper name (Erie) and a description (Lake) are positioned alphabetically by the proper name. The description is positioned after the proper name and is usually abbreviated:

Erie, L. *N. Amer.*	42°15N 81°0W	**82** D4

Where a description forms part of a settlement or administrative name, however, it is always written in full and put in its true alphabetical position:

Mount Morris *U.S.A.*	42°44N 77°52W	**82** D7

Names beginning with M' and Mc are indexed as if they were spelled Mac. Names beginning St. are alphabetized under Saint, but Sankt, Sint, Sant', Santa and San are all spelt in full and are alphabetized accordingly. If the same place name occurs two or more times in the index and all are in the same country, each is followed by the name of the administrative subdivision in which it is located.

The geographical co-ordinates which follow each name in the index give the latitude and longitude of each place. The first co-ordinate indicates latitude – the distance north or south of the Equator. The second co-ordinate indicates longitude – the distance east or west of the Greenwich Meridian. Both latitude and longitude are measured in degrees and minutes (there are 60 minutes in a degree).

The latitude is followed by N(orth) or S(outh) and the longitude by E(ast) or W(est).

The number in bold type which follows the geographical co-ordinates refers to the number of the map page where that feature or place will be found. This is usually the largest scale at which the place or feature appears.

The letter and figure that are immediately after the page number give the grid square on the map page, within which the feature is situated. The letter represents the latitude and the figure the longitude. A lower-case letter immediately after the page number refers to an inset map on that page.

In some cases the feature itself may fall within the specified square, while the name is outside. This is usually the case only with features that are larger than a grid square.

Rivers are indexed to their mouths or confluences, and carry the symbol ➤ after their names. The following symbols are also used in the index: ■ country, ☑ overseas territory or dependency, □ first-order administrative area, △ national park, ◠ other park (provincial park, nature reserve or game reserve), ✖ (LHR) principal airport (and location identifier), ۞ Australian aboriginal land.

Abbreviations used in the index

A.C.T. – Australian Capital Territory
A.R. – Autonomous Region
Afghan. – Afghanistan
Afr. – Africa
Ala. – Alabama
Alta. – Alberta
Amer. – America(n)
Ant. – Antilles
Arch. – Archipelago
Ariz. – Arizona
Ark. – Arkansas
Atl. Oc. – Atlantic Ocean
B. – Baie, Bahía, Bay, Bucht, Bugt
B.C. – British Columbia
Bangla. – Bangladesh
Barr. – Barrage
Bos.-H. – Bosnia-Herzegovina
C. – Cabo, Cap, Cape, Coast
C.A.R. – Central African Republic
C. Prov. – Cape Province
Calif. – California
Cat. – Catarata
Cent. – Central
Chan. – Channel
Colo. – Colorado
Conn. – Connecticut
Cord. – Cordillera
Cr. – Creek
Czech. – Czech Republic
D.C. – District of Columbia
Del. – Delaware
Dem. – Democratic
Dep. – Dependency
Des. – Desert
Dét. – Détroit
Dist. – District
Dj. – Djebel
Dom. Rep. – Dominican Republic

E. – East
El Salv. – El Salvador
Eq. Guin. – Equatorial Guinea
Est. – Estrecho
Falk. Is. – Falkland Is.
Fd. – Fjord
Fla. – Florida
Fr. – French
G. – Golfe, Golfo, Gulf, Guba, Gebel
Ga. – Georgia
Gt. – Great, Greater
Guinea-Biss. – Guinea-Bissau
H.K. – Hong Kong
H.P. – Himachal Pradesh
Hants. – Hampshire
Harb. – Harbor, Harbour
Hd. – Head
Hts. – Heights
I.(s). – Île, Ilha, Insel, Isla, Island, Isle
Ill. – Illinois
Ind. – Indiana
Ind. Oc. – Indian Ocean
Ivory C. – Ivory Coast
J. – Jabal, Jebel
Jaz. – Jazīrah
Junc. – Junction
K. – Kap, Kapp
Kans. – Kansas
Kep. – Kepulauan
Ky. – Kentucky
L. – Lac, Lacul, Lago, Lagoa, Lake, Limni, Loch, Lough
La. – Louisiana
Ld. – Land
Liech. – Liechtenstein
Lux. – Luxembourg
Mad. P. – Madhya Pradesh
Madag. – Madagascar
Man. – Manitoba
Mass. – Massachusetts

Md. – Maryland
Me. – Maine
Medit. S. – Mediterranean Sea
Mich. – Michigan
Minn. – Minnesota
Miss. – Mississippi
Mo. – Missouri
Mont. – Montana
Mozam. – Mozambique
Mt.(s) – Mont, Montaña, Mountain
Mte. – Monte
Mti. – Monti
N. – Nord, Norte, North, Northern, Nouveau, Nahal, Nahr
N.B. – New Brunswick
N.C. – North Carolina
N. Cal. – New Caledonia
N. Dak. – North Dakota
N.H. – New Hampshire
N.I. – North Island
N.J. – New Jersey
N. Mex. – New Mexico
N.S. – Nova Scotia
N.S.W. – New South Wales
N.W.T. – North West Territory
N.Y. – New York
N.Z. – New Zealand
Nac. – Nacional
Nat. – National
Nebr. – Nebraska
Neths. – Netherlands
Nev. – Nevada
Nfld & L. – Newfoundland and Labrador
Nic. – Nicaragua
O. – Oued, Ouadi
Occ. – Occidentale
Okla. – Oklahoma
Ont. – Ontario
Or. – Orientale

Oreg. – Oregon
Os. – Ostrov
Oz. – Ozero
P. – Pass, Passo, Pasul, Pulau
P.E.I. – Prince Edward Island
Pa. – Pennsylvania
Pac. Oc. – Pacific Ocean
Papua N.G. – Papua New Guinea
Pass. – Passage
Peg. – Pegunungan
Pen. – Peninsula, Péninsule
Phil. – Philippines
Pk. – Peak
Plat. – Plateau
Prov. – Province, Provincial
Pt. – Point
Pta. – Ponta, Punta
Pte. – Pointe
Qué. – Québec
Queens. – Queensland
R. – Rio, River
R.I. – Rhode Island
Ra. – Range
Raj. – Rajasthan
Recr. – Recreational, Récréatif
Reg. – Region
Rep. – Republic
Res. – Reserve, Reservoir
Rhld-Pfz. – Rheinland-Pfalz
S. – South, Southern, Sur
Si. Arabia – Saudi Arabia
S.C. – South Carolina
S. Dak. – South Dakota
S.I. – South Island
S. Leone – Sierra Leone
Sa. – Serra, Sierra
Sask. – Saskatchewan
Scot. – Scotland
Sd. – Sound
Sev. – Severnaya
Sib. – Siberia

Sprs. – Springs
St. – Saint
Sta. – Santa
Ste. – Sainte
Sto. – Santo
Str. – Strait, Stretto
Switz. – Switzerland
Tas. – Tasmania
Tenn. – Tennessee
Terr. – Territory, Territoire
Tex. – Texas
Tg. – Tanjung
Trin. & Tob. – Trinidad & Tobago
U.A.E. – United Arab Emirates
U.K. – United Kingdom
U.S.A. – United States of America
Ut. P. – Uttar Pradesh
Va. – Virginia
Vdkhr. – Vodokhranilishche
Vdskh. – Vodoskhovyshche
Vf. – Vírful
Vic. – Victoria
Vol. – Volcano
Vt. – Vermont
W. – Wadi, West
W. Va. – West Virginia
Wall. & F. Is. – Wallis and Futuna Is.
Wash. – Washington
Wis. – Wisconsin
Wlkp. – Wielkopolski
Wyo. – Wyoming
Yorks. – Yorkshire

A

A Coruña *Spain* 43°20N 8°25W **21** A1
A Estrada *Spain* 42°43N 8°27W **21** A1
A Fonsagrada *Spain* 43°8N 7°4W **21** A2
A Shau *Vietnam* 16°6N 107°22E **38** D6
Aabenraa *Denmark* 55°3N 9°25E **9** J13
Aachen *Germany* 50°45N 6°6E **16** C4
Aalborg *Denmark* 57°2N 9°54E **9** H13
Aalen *Germany* 48°51N 10°6E **16** D6
Aalst *Belgium* 50°56N 4°2E **15** D4
Aalten *Neths.* 51°56N 6°35E **15** C6
Aalter *Belgium* 51°5N 3°28E **15** C3
Äänekoski *Finland* 62°36N 25°44E **8** E21
Aarau *Switz.* 47°23N 8°4E **20** C8
Aare → *Switz.* 47°33N 8°14E **20** C8
Aarhus *Denmark* 56°8N 10°11E **9** H14
Aarschot *Belgium* 50°59N 4°49E **15** D4
Aba *China* 32°59N 101°42E **34** A3
Aba *Nigeria* 5°10N 7°19E **52** G7
Abaco I. *Bahamas* 26°25N 77°10W **88** A4
Ābādān *Iran* 30°22N 48°20E **47** D6
Ābādeh *Iran* 31°8N 52°40E **47** D7
Abadla *Algeria* 31°2N 2°45W **52** B5
Abaetetuba *Brazil* 1°40S 48°50W **93** D9
Abagnar Qi = Xilinhot *China* 43°52N 116°2E **32** C9
Abah, Tanjung *Indonesia* 8°46S 115°38E **37** K18
Abai *Paraguay* 25°58S 55°54W **95** B4
Abakan *Russia* 53°40N 91°10E **27** D10
Abancay *Peru* 13°35S 72°55W **92** F4
Abang, Gunung *Indonesia* 8°16S 115°25E **37** J18
Abariringa *Kiribati* 2°50S 171°40W **64** H10
Abarqū *Iran* 31°10N 53°20E **47** D7
Abashiri *Japan* 44°0N 144°15E **28** B12
Abashiri-Wan *Japan* 44°0N 144°30E **28** C12
Ābay = Nîl el Azraq → *Sudan* 15°38N 32°31E **53** E12
Abay *Kazakhstan* 49°38N 72°53E **26** E8
Abaya, L. *Ethiopia* 6°30N 37°50E **49** F2
Abaza *Russia* 52°39N 90°6E **26** D10
ʻAbbāsābād *Iran* 33°34N 58°23E **47** C8
Abbay = Nîl el Azraq → *Sudan* 15°38N 32°31E **53** E12
Abbaye, Pt. *U.S.A.* 46°58N 88°8W **80** B9
Abbé, L. *Ethiopia* 11°8N 41°47E **49** E3
Abbeville *France* 50°6N 1°49E **20** A4
Abbeville *Ala., U.S.A.* 31°34N 85°15W **85** F12
Abbeville *La., U.S.A.* 29°58N 92°8W **84** G8
Abbeville *S.C., U.S.A.* 34°11N 82°23W **85** D13
Abbeyfeale *Ireland* 52°23N 9°18W **10** D2
Abbeyleix *Ireland* 52°54N 7°22W **10** D4
Abbot Ice Shelf *Antarctica* 73°0S 92°0W **5** D16
Abbotsford *Canada* 49°5N 122°20W **70** D4
Abbottabad *Pakistan* 34°10N 73°15E **42** B5
ABC Islands *W. Indies* 12°15N 69°0W **89** D6
Abd al Kūrī *Yemen* 12°5N 52°20E **49** E5
Ābdar *Iran* 30°16N 55°19E **47** D7
ʻAbdolābād *Iran* 34°12N 56°30E **47** C8
Abdulpur *Bangla.* 24°15N 88°59E **43** G13
Abéché *Chad* 13°50N 20°35E **53** F10
Abel Tasman △ *N.Z.* 40°59S 173°3E **59** D4
Abengourou *Ivory C.* 6°42N 3°27W **52** G5
Åbenrå = Aabenraa *Denmark* 55°3N 9°25E **9** J13
Abeokuta *Nigeria* 7°3N 3°19E **52** G6
Aberaeron *U.K.* 52°15N 4°15W **13** E3
Aberayron = Aberaeron *U.K.* 52°15N 4°15W **13** E3
Aberchirder *U.K.* 57°34N 2°37W **11** D6
Abercorn *Australia* 25°12S 151°5E **63** D5
Aberdare *U.K.* 51°43N 3°27W **13** F4
Aberdaugleddau = Milford Haven *U.K.* 51°42N 5°7W **13** F2
Aberdeen *Australia* 32°9S 150°56E **63** E5
Aberdeen *Canada* 52°20N 106°8W **71** C7
Aberdeen *S. Africa* 32°28S 24°2E **56** D3
Aberdeen *U.K.* 57°9N 2°5W **11** D6
Aberdeen *Idaho, U.S.A.* 42°57N 112°50W **76** E7
Aberdeen *Md., U.S.A.* 39°31N 76°10W **81** F15
Aberdeen *Miss., U.S.A.* 33°49N 88°33W **85** E10
Aberdeen *S. Dak., U.S.A.* 45°28N 98°29W **80** C4
Aberdeen *Wash., U.S.A.* 46°59N 123°50W **78** D3
Aberdeen City □ *U.K.* 57°10N 2°10W **11** D6
Aberdeen L. *Canada* 64°30N 99°0W **68** E12
Aberdeenshire □ *U.K.* 57°17N 2°36W **11** D6
Aberdovey = Aberdyfi *U.K.* 52°33N 4°3W **13** E3
Aberdyfi *U.K.* 52°33N 4°3W **13** E3
Aberfeldy *U.K.* 56°37N 3°51W **11** E5
Aberfoyle *U.K.* 56°11N 4°23W **11** E4
Abergavenny *U.K.* 51°49N 3°1W **13** F4
Abergele *U.K.* 53°17N 3°35W **12** D4
Abergwaun = Fishguard *U.K.* 52°0N 4°58W **13** E3
Aberhonddu = Brecon *U.K.* 51°57N 3°23W **13** F4
Abermaw = Barmouth *U.K.* 52°44N 4°4W **12** E3
Abernathy *U.S.A.* 33°50N 101°51W **84** E4
Aberpennar = Mountain Ash *U.K.* 51°40N 3°23W **13** F4
Abert, L. *U.S.A.* 42°38N 120°14W **76** E3
Abertawe = Swansea *U.K.* 51°37N 3°57W **13** F4
Aberteifi = Cardigan *U.K.* 52°5N 4°40W **13** E3
Aberystwyth *U.K.* 52°25N 4°5W **13** E3
Abhā *Si. Arabia* 18°0N 42°34E **49** D3
Abhar *Iran* 36°9N 49°13E **47** B6
Abhayapuri *India* 26°24N 90°38E **43** F14
Abidjan *Ivory C.* 5°26N 3°58W **52** G5
Abilene *Kans., U.S.A.* 38°55N 97°13W **80** F5
Abilene *Tex., U.S.A.* 32°28N 99°43W **84** E5
Abingdon *U.S.A.* 36°43N 81°59W **81** G13
Abingdon-on-Thames *U.K.* 51°40N 1°17W **13** F6
Abington Reef *Australia* 18°0S 149°35E **62** B4
Abisko △ *Sweden* 68°18N 18°44E **8** B18
Abitau → *Canada* 59°53N 109°3W **71** B7
Abitibi → *Canada* 51°3N 80°55W **72** B3
Abitibi, L. *Canada* 48°40N 79°40W **72** C4
Abkhaz Republic = Abkhazia □ *Georgia* 43°12N 41°5E **19** F7
Abkhazia □ *Georgia* 43°12N 41°5E **19** F7
Abminga *Australia* 26°8S 134°51E **63** D1
Åbo = Turku *Finland* 60°30N 22°19E **9** F20
Abohar *India* 30°10N 74°10E **42** D6
Abomey *Benin* 7°10N 2°5E **52** G6
Abong-Mbang *Cameroon* 4°0N 13°8E **54** D2
Abou-Deïa *Chad* 11°20N 19°20E **53** F9
Aboyne *U.K.* 57°4N 2°47W **11** D6
Abra Pampa *Argentina* 22°43S 65°42W **94** A2
Abraham L. *Canada* 52°15N 116°35W **70** C5
Abreojos, Pta. *Mexico* 26°50N 113°40W **86** B2
Abrolhos, Banco dos *Brazil* 18°0S 38°0W **90** E7
Abrud *Romania* 46°19N 23°5E **17** E12
Absaroka Range *U.S.A.* 44°45N 109°50W **76** D9
Abu *India* 24°41N 72°50E **42** G5
Abū al Abyaḍ *U.A.E.* 24°11N 53°50E **47** E7
Abū al Khaṣīb *Iraq* 30°25N 48°0E **46** D5
Abū ʻAlī *Si. Arabia* 27°20N 49°27E **47** E6
Abū ʻAlī → *Lebanon* 34°25N 35°50E **48** A4
Abu Dhabi = Abū Ẓāby *U.A.E.* 24°28N 54°22E **47** E7
Abū Du'ān *Syria* 36°25N 38°15E **46** B3
Abu el Gaīn, W. → *Egypt* 29°35N 33°30E **48** F2
Abu Ga'da, W. → *Egypt* 29°15N 32°53E **48** F1
Abū Ḥadrīyah *Si. Arabia* 27°20N 48°58E **47** E6
Abu Hamed *Sudan* 19°32N 33°13E **53** E12
Abū Kamāl *Syria* 34°30N 41°0E **46** C4
Abū Madd, Ra's *Si. Arabia* 24°50N 37°7E **46** E3
Abū Mūsā *U.A.E.* 25°52N 55°3E **47** E7
Abū Qaṣr *Si. Arabia* 30°21N 38°34E **46** D3
Abu Shagara, Ras *Sudan* 21°4N 37°19E **53** D13
Abu Simbel *Egypt* 22°18N 31°40E **53** D12
Abū Şukhayr *Iraq* 31°54N 44°30E **46** D5
Abu Zabad *Sudan* 12°25N 29°10E **53** F11
Abū Ẓāby *U.A.E.* 24°28N 54°22E **47** E7
Abū Zeydābād *Iran* 33°54N 51°45E **47** C6
Abuja *Nigeria* 9°5N 7°32E **52** G7
Abukuma-Gawa → *Japan* 38°6N 140°52E **28** E10
Abukuma-Sammyaku *Japan* 37°30N 140°45E **28** F10
Abunã *Brazil* 9°40S 65°20W **92** E5
Abunã → *Brazil* 9°41S 65°20W **92** E5
Abut Hd. *N.Z.* 43°7S 170°15E **59** E3
Abyei ☑ *Sudan* 9°30N 28°30E **53** G11
Ābyek *Iran* 36°4N 50°33E **47** B6
Acadia △ *U.S.A.* 44°20N 68°13W **81** C19
Açailândia *Brazil* 4°57S 47°30W **93** D9
Acajutla *El Salv.* 13°36N 89°50W **88** D2
Acámbaro *Mexico* 20°2N 100°44W **86** D4
Acaponeta *Mexico* 22°30N 105°22W **86** C3
Acapulco *Mexico* 16°51N 99°55W **87** D5
Acapulco Trench *Pac. Oc.* 12°0N 88°0W **86** D4
Acarai, Serra *Brazil* 1°50N 57°50W **92** C7
Acarai Mts. = Acaraí, Serra *Brazil* 1°50N 57°50W **92** C7
Acarigua *Venezuela* 9°33N 69°12W **92** B5
Acatlán *Mexico* 18°12N 98°3W **87** D5
Acayucán *Mexico* 17°57N 94°55W **87** D6
Accomac *U.S.A.* 37°43N 75°40W **81** G16
Accra *Ghana* 5°35N 0°6W **52** G5
Accrington *U.K.* 53°45N 2°22W **12** D5
Acebal *Argentina* 33°20S 60°50W **94** C3
Aceh □ *Indonesia* 4°15N 97°30E **36** D1
Achalpur *India* 21°22N 77°32E **44** D3
Acharnes *Greece* 38°5N 23°44E **23** E10
Acheloos → *Greece* 38°19N 21°7E **23** E9
Acheng *China* 45°30N 126°58E **33** B14
Acher *India* 23°10N 72°32E **42** H5
Achill Hd. *Ireland* 53°58N 10°15W **10** C1
Achill I. *Ireland* 53°58N 10°1W **10** C1
Achinsk *Russia* 56°20N 90°20E **27** D10
Acireale *Italy* 37°37N 15°10E **22** F6
Ackerman *U.S.A.* 33°19N 89°11W **85** E10
Acklins I. *Bahamas* 22°30N 74°0W **89** B5
Acme *Canada* 51°33N 113°30W **70** C6
Acme *U.S.A.* 40°8N 79°26W **82** F5
Aconcagua, Cerro *Argentina* 32°39S 70°0W **94** C2
Aconquija, Mt. *Argentina* 27°0S 66°0W **94** B2
Açores, Is. dos *Atl. Oc.* 38°0N 27°0W **52** a
Acornhoek *S. Africa* 24°37S 31°2E **57** B5
Acraman, L. *Australia* 32°2S 135°23E **63** E2
Acre = ʻAkko *Israel* 32°55N 35°4E **48** C4
Acre □ *Brazil* 9°1S 71°0W **92** E4
Acre → *Brazil* 8°45S 67°22W **92** E5
Actinolite *Canada* 44°32N 77°19W **82** B7
Acton *Canada* 43°38N 80°3W **82** C4
Ad Dahnā *Si. Arabia* 24°30N 48°10E **49** C4
Ad Dammām *Si. Arabia* 26°20N 50°5E **47** E6
Ad Dāmūr *Lebanon* 33°43N 35°27E **48** B4
Ad Dawādimī *Si. Arabia* 24°35N 44°15E **46** E5
Ad Dawḥah *Qatar* 25°15N 51°35E **47** E6
Ad Dawr *Iraq* 34°27N 43°47E **46** C4
Ad Dhakhīrah *Qatar* 25°44N 51°33E **47** E6
Ad Dir'īyah *Si. Arabia* 24°44N 46°35E **46** E5
Ad Dīwānīyah *Iraq* 32°0N 45°0E **46** D5
Ad Dujayl *Iraq* 33°51N 44°14E **46** C5
Ad Duwayd *Si. Arabia* 30°15N 42°17E **46** D4
Ada *Minn., U.S.A.* 47°18N 96°31W **80** B5
Ada *Okla., U.S.A.* 34°46N 96°41W **84** D6
Adabiya *Egypt* 29°53N 32°28E **48** F1
Adair, C. *Canada* 71°30N 71°34W **69** C17
Adaja → *Spain* 41°32N 4°52W **21** B3
Adak *U.S.A.* 51°45N 176°45W **74** E4
Adak I. *U.S.A.* 51°45N 176°45W **74** E4
Adama = Nazret *Ethiopia* 8°32N 39°22E **49** F2
Adamaoua, Massif de l' *Cameroon* 7°20N 12°20E **53** G8
Adamawa Highlands = Adamaoua, Massif de l' *Cameroon* 7°20N 12°20E **53** G8
Adamello, Mte. *Italy* 46°9N 10°30E **20** C9
Adaminaby *Australia* 36°0S 148°45E **63** F4
Adams *Mass., U.S.A.* 42°38N 73°7W **83** D11
Adams *N.Y., U.S.A.* 43°49N 76°1W **83** C8
Adams *Wis., U.S.A.* 43°57N 89°49W **80** D9
Adams, Mt. *U.S.A.* 46°12N 121°30W **78** D5
Adam's Bridge *Sri Lanka* 9°15N 79°40E **45** K4
Adams L. *Canada* 51°10N 119°40W **70** C5
Adam's Peak *Sri Lanka* 6°48N 80°30E **45** L5
ʻAdan *Yemen* 12°45N 45°0E **49** E4
Adana *Turkey* 37°0N 35°16E **46** B2
Adang, Ko *Thailand* 6°33N 99°18E **39** J2
Adapazarı = Sakarya *Turkey* 40°48N 30°25E **19** F5
Adarama *Sudan* 17°10N 34°52E **53** E12
Adare *Ireland* 52°34N 8°47W **10** D3
Adare, C. *Antarctica* 71°0S 171°0E **5** D11
Adaut *Indonesia* 8°8S 131°7E **37** F8
Adavale *Australia* 25°52S 144°32E **63** D3
Adda → *Italy* 45°8N 9°53E **20** D8
Addatigala *India* 17°31N 82°3E **44** F6
Addis Ababa = Addis Abeba *Ethiopia* 9°2N 38°42E **49** F2
Addis Abeba *Ethiopia* 9°2N 38°42E **49** F2
Addison *U.S.A.* 42°1N 77°14W **82** D7
Addo *S. Africa* 33°32S 25°45E **56** D4
Addo △ *S. Africa* 33°30S 25°50E **56** D4
Ādeh *Iran* 37°42N 45°11E **46** B5
Adel *U.S.A.* 31°8N 83°25W **85** F13
Adelaide *Australia* 34°52S 138°30E **63** E2
Adelaide *S. Africa* 32°42S 26°20E **56** D4
Adelaide I. *Antarctica* 67°15S 68°30W **5** C17
Adelaide Pen. *Canada* 68°15N 97°30W **68** D12
Adelaide River *Australia* 13°15S 131°7E **60** B5
Adelaide Village *Bahamas* 25°0N 77°31W **88** A4
Adelanto *U.S.A.* 34°35N 117°22W **79** L9
Adele I. *Australia* 15°32S 123°9E **60** C3
Adélie, Terre *Antarctica* 68°0S 140°0E **5** C10
Adelie Land = Adélie, Terre *Antarctica* 68°0S 140°0E **5** C10
Aden = ʻAdan *Yemen* 12°45N 45°0E **49** E4
Aden, G. of *Ind. Oc.* 12°30N 47°30E **49** E4
Adendorp *S. Africa* 32°15S 24°30E **56** D3
Adh Dhayd *U.A.E.* 25°17N 55°53E **47** E7
Adhoi *India* 23°26N 70°32E **42** H4
Adi *Indonesia* 4°15S 133°30E **37** E8
Adieu, C. *Australia* 32°0S 132°10E **61** F5
Adieu Pt. *Australia* 15°14S 124°35E **60** C3
Adige → *Italy* 45°9N 12°20E **22** B5
Adigrat *Ethiopia* 14°20N 39°26E **49** E2
Adilabad *India* 19°33N 78°20E **44** E4
Adirondack ⌓ *U.S.A.* 44°0N 74°20W **83** C10
Adirondack Mts. *U.S.A.* 44°0N 74°0W **83** C10
Adis Abeba = Addis Abeba *Ethiopia* 9°2N 38°42E **49** F2
Adjuntas *Puerto Rico* 18°10N 66°43W **89** d
Adlavik Is. *Canada* 55°0N 58°40W **73** B8
Admiralty G. *Australia* 14°20S 125°55E **60** B4
Admiralty Gulf ✪ *Australia* 14°16S 125°52E **60** B4
Admiralty I. *U.S.A.* 57°30N 134°30W **70** B2
Admiralty Inlet *Canada* 72°30N 86°0W **69** C14
Admiralty Is. *Papua N. G.* 2°0S 147°0E **58** B7
Adolfo González Chaves *Argentina* 38°2S 60°5W **94** D3
Adolfo Ruiz Cortines, Presa *Mexico* 27°15N 109°6W **86** B3
Adonara *Indonesia* 8°15S 123°5E **37** F6
Adoni *India* 15°33N 77°18E **45** G3
Adour → *France* 43°32N 1°32W **20** E3
Adra *India* 23°30N 86°42E **43** H12
Adra *Spain* 36°43N 3°3W **21** D4
Adrano *Italy* 37°40N 14°50E **22** F6
Adrar *Algeria* 27°51N 0°19W **52** C6
Adrar *Mauritania* 20°30N 7°30W **52** D3
Adrar des Iforas *Africa* 19°40N 1°40E **52** E6
Adrian *Mich., U.S.A.* 41°54N 84°2W **81** E11
Adrian *Tex., U.S.A.* 35°16N 102°40W **84** D3
Adriatic Sea *Medit. S.* 43°0N 16°0E **22** C6
Adua *Indonesia* 1°45S 129°50E **37** E7
Adur *India* 9°8N 76°40E **45** K3
Adwa *Ethiopia* 14°15N 38°52E **49** E2
Adygea □ *Russia* 45°0N 40°0E **19** F7
Adzhar Republic = Ajaria □ *Georgia* 41°30N 42°0E **19** F7
Adzopé *Ivory C.* 6°7N 3°49W **52** G5
Ægean Sea *Medit. S.* 38°30N 25°0E **23** E11
Aerhtai Shan *Mongolia* 46°40N 92°45E **30** B7
Afaahiti *Tahiti* 17°45S 149°17W **59** d
ʻAfak *Iraq* 32°4N 45°15E **46** C5
Afareaitu *Moorea* 17°33S 149°47W **59** d
Afghanistan ■ *Asia* 33°0N 65°0E **40** C4
Aflou *Algeria* 34°7N 2°3E **52** B6
Afognak I. *U.S.A.* 58°15N 152°30W **74** D9
Africa 10°0N 20°0E **50** E6
ʻAfrīn *Syria* 36°32N 36°50E **46** B3
Afton *N.Y., U.S.A.* 42°14N 75°32W **83** D9
Afton *Wyo., U.S.A.* 42°44N 110°56W **76** E8
Afuá *Brazil* 0°15S 50°20W **93** D8
ʻAfula *Israel* 32°37N 35°17E **48** C4
Afyon *Turkey* 38°45N 30°33E **19** G5
Afyonkarahisar = Afyon *Turkey* 38°45N 30°33E **19** G5
Āgā Jarī *Iran* 30°42N 49°50E **47** D6
Agadés = Agadez *Niger* 16°58N 7°59E **52** E7
Agadez *Niger* 16°58N 7°59E **52** E7
Agadir *Morocco* 30°28N 9°55W **52** B4
Agalega Is. *Mauritius* 11°0S 57°0E **3** E12
Agar *India* 23°40N 76°2E **42** H7
Agar → *India* 21°0N 82°57E **44** D6
Agartala *India* 23°50N 91°23E **41** H17
Agassiz *Canada* 49°14N 121°46W **70** D4
Agassiz Icecap *Canada* 80°15N 76°0W **69** A16
Agats *Indonesia* 5°33S 138°0E **37** F9
Agatti I. *India* 10°50N 72°12E **45** J1
Agattu I. *U.S.A.* 52°25N 173°35E **74** E2
Agawam *U.S.A.* 42°5N 72°37W **83** D12
Agboville *Ivory C.* 5°55N 4°15W **52** G5
Ağdam *Azerbaijan* 40°0N 46°58E **46** B5
Agde *France* 43°19N 3°28E **20** E5
Agen *France* 44°12N 0°38E **20** D4
Āgh Kand *Iran* 37°15N 48°4E **47** B6
Aghios Efstratios *Greece* 39°34N 24°58E **23** E11
Aghiou Orous, Kolpos *Greece* 40°6N 24°0E **23** D11
Aginskoye *Russia* 51°6N 114°32E **27** D12
Agnew *Australia* 28°1S 120°31E **61** E3
Agori *India* 24°33N 82°57E **43** G10
Agra *India* 27°17N 77°58E **42** F7
Ağri *Turkey* 39°44N 43°3E **19** G7
Agri → *Italy* 40°13N 16°44E **22** D7
Ağrı Dağı *Turkey* 39°50N 44°15E **46** B5
Ağri Karakose = Ağri *Turkey* 39°44N 43°3E **19** G7
Agrigento *Italy* 37°19N 13°34E **22** F5
Agrinio *Greece* 38°37N 21°27E **23** E9
Agua Caliente *Mexico* 32°29N 116°59W **79** N10
Agua Caliente Springs *U.S.A.* 32°56N 116°19W **79** N10
Água Clara *Brazil* 20°25S 52°45W **93** H8
Agua Fria ⌓ *U.S.A.* 34°14N 112°0W **77** J8
Agua Hechicera *Mexico* 32°28N 116°15W **79** N10
Agua Prieta *Mexico* 31°18N 109°34W **86** A3
Aguadilla *Puerto Rico* 18°26N 67°10W **89** d
Aguadulce *Panama* 8°15N 80°32W **88** E3
Aguanga *U.S.A.* 33°27N 116°51W **79** M10
Aguanish *Canada* 50°14N 62°2W **73** B7
Aguanish → *Canada* 50°13N 62°5W **73** B7
Aguapey → *Argentina* 29°7S 56°36W **94** B4
Aguaray Guazú → *Paraguay* 24°47S 57°19W **94** A4
Aguarico → *Ecuador* 0°59S 75°11W **92** D3
Aguaro-Guariquito △ *Venezuela* 8°20N 66°35W **89** E6
Aguas Blancas *Chile* 24°15S 69°55W **94** A2
Aguas Calientes, Sierra de *Argentina* 25°26S 66°40W **94** B2
Aguascalientes *Mexico* 21°53N 102°18W **86** C4
Aguascalientes □ *Mexico* 22°0N 102°20W **86** C4
Aguila, Punta *Puerto Rico* 17°57N 67°13W **89** d
Aguilares *Argentina* 27°26S 65°35W **94** B2
Águilas *Spain* 37°23N 1°35W **21** D5
Aguja, C. de la *Colombia* 11°18N 74°12W **90** B3
Agujereada, Pta. *Puerto Rico* 18°30N 67°8W **89** d
Agulhas, C. *S. Africa* 34°52S 20°0E **56** D3
Agung, Gunung *Indonesia* 8°20S 115°28E **37** J18
Aguni-Jima *Japan* 26°30N 127°10E **29** L3
Agusan → *Phil.* 9°0N 125°30E **37** C7
Aha Mts. *Botswana* 19°45S 21°0E **56** A3
Ahaggar *Algeria* 23°0N 6°30E **52** D7
Ahai Dam *China* 27°21N 100°30E **34** D3
Ahar *Iran* 38°35N 47°0E **46** B5
Ahipara B. *N.Z.* 35°5S 173°5E **59** A4
Ahiri *India* 19°30N 80°0E **44** E5
Ahmad Wal *Pakistan* 29°18N 65°58E **42** E1
Ahmadabad *India* 23°0N 72°40E **42** H5
Aḥmadābād *Khorāsān, Iran* 35°3N 60°50E **47** C9
Aḥmadābād *Khorāsān, Iran* 35°49N 59°42E **47** C8
Aḥmadī *Iran* 27°56N 56°42E **47** E8
Ahmadnagar *India* 19°7N 74°46E **44** E2
Ahmadpur *India* 18°40N 76°57E **44** E3
Ahmadpur East *Pakistan* 29°12N 71°10E **42** E4
Ahmadpur Lamma *Pakistan* 28°19N 70°3E **42** E4
Ahmedabad = Ahmadabad *India* 23°0N 72°40E **42** H5
Ahmednagar = Ahmadnagar *India* 19°7N 74°46E **44** E2
Ahome *Mexico* 25°55N 109°11W **86** B3
Ahoskie *U.S.A.* 36°17N 76°59W **85** C16
Ahram *Iran* 28°52N 51°16E **47** D6
Ahuachapán *El Salv.* 13°54N 89°52W **88** D2
Ahvāz *Iran* 31°20N 48°40E **47** D6
Ahvenanmaa = Åland *Finland* 60°15N 20°0E **9** F19
Aḥwar *Yemen* 13°30N 46°40E **49** E4
Ai → *India* 26°26N 90°44E **43** F14
Ai-Ais *Namibia* 27°54S 17°59E **56** C2
Ai-Ais and Fish River Canyon △ *Namibia* 24°45S 17°15E **56** B2
Aichi □ *Japan* 35°0N 137°15E **29** G8
Aigrettes, Pte. des *Réunion* 21°3S 55°13E **55** c
Aiguá *Uruguay* 34°13S 54°46W **95** C5
Aigues-Mortes *France* 43°35N 4°12E **20** E6
Aihui = Heihe *China* 50°10N 127°30E **31** A14
Aija *Peru* 9°50S 77°45W **92** E3
Aikawa *Japan* 38°2N 138°15E **28** E9
Aiken *U.S.A.* 33°34N 81°43W **85** E14
Ailao Shan *China* 24°0N 101°20E **34** F3
Aileron *Australia* 22°39S 133°20E **62** C1
Aillik *Canada* 55°11N 59°18W **73** A8
Ailsa Craig *Canada* 43°8N 81°33W **82** C3
Ailsa Craig *U.K.* 55°15N 5°6W **11** F3
Aim *Russia* 59°0N 133°55E **27** D14
Aimogasta *Argentina* 28°33S 66°50W **94** B2
Aïn Ben Tili *Mauritania* 25°59N 9°27W **52** C4
Aïn Sefra *Algeria* 32°47N 0°37W **52** B5
Ain Sudr *Egypt* 29°50N 33°6E **48** F2
Aïn Témouchent *Algeria* 35°16N 1°8W **52** A5
Ainaži *Latvia* 57°50N 24°24E **9** H21
Ainsworth *U.S.A.* 42°33N 99°52W **80** D4
Aiquile *Bolivia* 18°10S 65°10W **92** G5
Aïr *Niger* 18°30N 8°0E **52** E7
Air Force I. *Canada* 67°58N 74°5W **69** D17
Air Hitam *Malaysia* 1°55N 103°11E **39** M4
Airdrie *Canada* 51°18N 114°2W **70** C6
Airdrie *U.K.* 55°52N 3°57W **11** F5
Aire → *U.K.* 53°43N 0°55W **12** D7
Airlie Beach *Australia* 20°16S 148°43E **62** b
Aisne → *France* 49°26N 2°50E **20** B5
Ait *India* 25°54N 79°14E **43** G8
Aitkin *U.S.A.* 46°32N 93°42W **80** B7
Aitutaki *Cook Is.* 18°52S 159°45W **65** J12
Aiud *Romania* 46°19N 23°44E **17** E12
Aix-en-Provence *France* 43°32N 5°27E **20** E6
Aix-la-Chapelle = Aachen *Germany* 50°45N 6°6E **16** C4
Aix-les-Bains *France* 45°41N 5°53E **20** D6
Aizawl *India* 23°40N 92°44E **41** H18
Aizkraukle *Latvia* 56°36N 25°11E **9** H21
Aizpute *Latvia* 56°43N 21°40E **9** H1…
Aizuwakamatsu *Japan* 37°30N 139°56E **28** F…
Ajaccio *France* 41°55N 8°40E **20** F…
Ajaigarh *India* 24°52N 80°16E **43** G…
Ajalpan *Mexico* 18°22N 97°15W **87** D…
Ajanta *India* 20°30N 75°48E **44** D…
Ajanta Ra. *India* 20°28N 75°50E **44** D…
Ajari Rep. = Ajaria □ *Georgia* 41°30N 42°0E **19** F…
Ajaria □ *Georgia* 41°30N 42°0E **19** F…
Ajax *Canada* 43°50N 79°1W **82** C…
Ajdābiyā *Libya* 30°54N 20°4E **53** B1…
Ajitgarh *India* 30°47N 76°41E **42** D…
Ajka *Hungary* 47°4N 17°31E **17** E…
ʻAjlūn *Jordan* 32°18N 35°47E **48** C…
ʻAjlūn □ *Jordan* 32°18N 35°47E **48** C…
ʻAjmān *U.A.E.* 25°25N 55°30E **47** E…
Ajmer *India* 26°28N 74°37E **42** F…
Ajnala *India* 31°50N 74°48E **42** D…
Ajo *U.S.A.* 32°22N 112°52W **77** K…
Ajo, C. de *Spain* 43°31N 3°35W **21** A…
Akabira *Japan* 43°33N 142°5E **28** C1…
Akalkot *India* 17°32N 76°13E **44** F…
Akan △ *Japan* 43°20N 144°20E **28** C1…
Akaroa *N.Z.* 43°49S 172°59E **59** E…
Akashi *Japan* 34°45N 134°58E **29** G…
Akbarpur *Bihar, India* 24°39N 83°58E **43** G1…
Akbarpur *Ut. P., India* 26°25N 82°32E **43** F1…
Akçakale *Turkey* 36°41N 38°56E **46** B…
Akelamo *Indonesia* 1°35N 129°40E **37** D…
Akeru → *India* 17°25N 80°5E **44** F…
Aketi *Dem. Rep. of the Congo* 2°38N 23°47E **54** D…
Akhisar *Turkey* 38°56N 27°48E **23** E1…
Akhnur *India* 32°52N 74°45E **43** C…
Akhtyrka = Okhtyrka *Ukraine* 50°25N 35°0E **19** D…
Aki *Japan* 33°30N 133°54E **29** H…
Akimiski I. *Canada* 52°50N 81°30W **72** B…
Akiōta *Japan* 34°36N 132°19E **29** G…
Akita *Japan* 39°45N 140°7E **28** E1…
Akita □ *Japan* 39°40N 140°30E **28** E1…
Akjoujt *Mauritania* 19°45N 14°15W **52** E…
Akkaraipattu *Sri Lanka* 7°13N 81°51E **45** L…
Akkeshi *Japan* 43°2N 144°51E **28** C1…
ʻAkko *Israel* 32°55N 35°4E **48** C…
Aklavik *Canada* 68°12N 135°0W **68** D…
Aklera *India* 24°26N 76°32E **42** G…
Akō *Japan* 34°45N 134°24E **29** G…
Akola *Maharashtra, India* 20°42N 77°2E **44** D…
Akola *Maharashtra, India* 19°32N 74°3E **44** E…
Akordat *Eritrea* 15°30N 37°40E **49** D…
Akot *India* 21°10N 77°10E **44** D…
Akpatok I. *Canada* 60°25N 68°8W **69** E1…
Åkrahamn *Norway* 59°15N 5°10E **9** G1…
Akranes *Iceland* 64°19N 22°5W **8** D…
Akron *Colo., U.S.A.* 40°10N 103°13W **76** F1…
Akron *Ohio, U.S.A.* 41°5N 81°31W **82** E…
Aksai Chin *China* 35°15N 79°55E **43** B…
Aksaray *Turkey* 38°25N 34°2E **46** B…
Aksay = Aqsay *Kazakhstan* 51°11N 53°0E **19** D…
Akşehir *Turkey* 38°18N 31°30E **46** B…
Akşehir Gölü *Turkey* 38°30N 31°25E **19** G…
Aksu *China* 41°5N 80°10E **30** C…
Aksum *Ethiopia* 14°5N 38°40E **49** E…
Aktsyabrski *Belarus* 52°38N 28°53E **17** B1…
Aktyubinsk = Aqtöbe *Kazakhstan* 50°17N 57°10E **19** D1…
Akure *Nigeria* 7°15N 5°5E **52** G…
Akuressa *Sri Lanka* 6°5N 80°29E **45** L…
Akureyri *Iceland* 65°40N 18°6W **8** D…
Akuseki-Shima *Japan* 29°27N 129°37E **29** K…
Akyab = Sittwe *Burma* 20°18N 92°45E **41** J1…
Al ʻAdan = ʻAdan *Yemen* 12°45N 45°0E **49** E…
Al Aḥsā = Hasa *Si. Arabia* 25°50N 49°0E **47** E…
Al Ajfar *Si. Arabia* 27°26N 43°0E **46** E…
Al Amādīyah *Iraq* 37°5N 43°30E **46** B…
Al ʻAmārah *Iraq* 31°55N 47°15E **46** D…
Al Anbār □ *Iraq* 33°25N 42°0E **46** C…
Al ʻAqabah *Jordan* 29°31N 35°0E **48** F…
Al ʻAqabah □ *Jordan* 29°30N 35°0E **48** F…
Al Arak *Syria* 34°38N 38°35E **46** C…
Al ʻAramah *Si. Arabia* 25°30N 46°0E **46** E…
Al ʻArṭāwīyah *Si. Arabia* 26°31N 45°20E **46** E…
Al ʻĀṣimah □ *Jordan* 31°40N 36°30E **48** D…
Al ʻAssāfiyah *Si. Arabia* 28°17N 38°59E **46** D…
Al ʻAwdah *Si. Arabia* 25°32N 45°41E **46** E…
Al ʻAyn *Si. Arabia* 25°4N 38°6E **46** E…
Al ʻAyn *U.A.E.* 24°15N 55°45E **47** E…
Al ʻAzīzīyah *Iraq* 32°54N 45°4E **46** C…
Al Bāb *Syria* 36°23N 37°29E **46** B…
Al Bad' *Si. Arabia* 28°28N 35°1E **46** D…
Al Bada'i' *Si. Arabia* 26°2N 43°33E **46** E…
Al Bādī *Iraq* 35°56N 41°32E **46** C…
Al Bāḥah *Si. Arabia* 20°1N 41°28E **49** C…
Al Baḥrah *Kuwait* 29°40N 47°52E **46** D…
Al Baḥral Mayyit = Dead Sea *Asia* 31°30N 35°30E **48** D…
Al Balqā' □ *Jordan* 32°5N 35°45E **48** C…
Al Bārūk, J. *Lebanon* 33°39N 35°40E **48** B…
Al Baṣrah *Iraq* 30°30N 47°50E **46** D…
Al Baṭḥā *Iraq* 31°6N 45°53E **46** D…
Al Batrūn *Lebanon* 34°15N 35°40E **48** A…
Al Bayḍā *Libya* 32°50N 21°44E **53** B1…
Al Biqā *Lebanon* 34°10N 36°10E **48** A…
Al Bi'r *Si. Arabia* 28°51N 36°16E **46** D…
Al Bukayrīyah *Si. Arabia* 26°9N 43°40E **46** E…
Al Burayj *Syria* 34°15N 36°46E **48** A…
Al Faḍīlī *Si. Arabia* 26°58N 49°10E **47** E…
Al Fallūjah *Iraq* 33°20N 43°55E **46** C…
Al Fāw *Iraq* 30°0N 48°30E **47** D…
Al Fujayrah *U.A.E.* 25°7N 56°18E **47** E…
Al Ghadaf, W. → *Jordan* 31°26N 36°43E **48** D…
Al Ghammās *Iraq* 31°45N 44°37E **46** D…
Al Ghazālah *Si. Arabia* 26°48N 41°19E **46** E…
Al Ghuwayfāt *U.A.E.* 24°10N 51°38E **47** E…
Al Ḥadīthah *Iraq* 34°0N 41°13E **46** C…
Al Ḥadīthah *Si. Arabia* 31°28N 37°8E **48** D…
Al Ḥaḍr *Iraq* 35°35N 42°44E **46** C…
Al Ḥājānah *Syria* 33°20N 36°33E **48** B…
Al Ḥajar al Gharbī *Oman* 24°10N 56°15E **47** E…

Al Hāmad Si. Arabia 31°30N 39°30E 46 D3
Al Ḩamdānīyah Syria 35°25N 36°50E 46 C3
Al Ḩamīdīyah Syria 34°42N 35°57E 48 A4
Al Ḩammār Iraq 30°57N 46°51E 46 D5
Al Ḩamrā' Si. Arabia 24°2N 38°55E 46 E3
Al Ḩamzah Iraq 31°43N 44°58E 46 D5
Al Ḩanākīyah Si. Arabia 24°51N 40°31E 46 E4
Al Harūj al Aswad Libya 27°0N 17°10E 53 C9
Al Ḩasakah Syria 36°35N 40°45E 46 B4
Al Ḩayy Iraq 32°5N 46°5E 46 C5
Al Ḩillah Iraq 32°30N 44°25E 46 C5
Al Hindīyah Iraq 32°30N 44°10E 46 C5
Al Hirmil Lebanon 34°26N 36°24E 48 A5
Al Hoceïma Morocco 35°8N 3°58W 52 A5
Al Ḩudaydah Yemen 14°50N 43°0E 49 E3
Al Ḩudūd ash Shamālīyah □ Si. Arabia 29°10N 42°30E 46 D4
Al Hufūf Si. Arabia 25°25N 49°45E 47 E6
Al Ḩumayḑah Si. Arabia 29°14N 34°56E 46 D2
Al Ḩunayy Si. Arabia 25°58N 48°45E 47 E6
Al Īsāwīyah Si. Arabia 30°43N 37°59E 46 D3
Al Jafr Jordan 30°18N 36°14E 48 E5
Al Jāfūrah Si. Arabia 25°0N 50°15E 47 E7
Al Jaghbūb Libya 29°42N 24°38E 53 C10
Al Jahrah Kuwait 29°25N 47°40E 46 D5
Al Jalāmīd Si. Arabia 31°20N 40°6E 46 D3
Al Jamalīyah Qatar 25°37N 51°5E 47 E6
Al Janūb □ Lebanon 33°20N 35°20E 48 B4
Al Jawf Libya 24°10N 23°24E 53 D10
Al Jawf □ Si. Arabia 29°30N 39°30E 46 D3
Al Jazair = Algeria ■ Africa 28°30N 2°0E 52 C6
Al Jazirah Iraq 33°30N 44°0E 46 C5
Al Jithāmīyah Si. Arabia 27°41N 41°43E 46 E4
Al Jubayl Si. Arabia 27°0N 49°50E 47 E6
Al Jubaylah Si. Arabia 24°55N 46°25E 46 E5
Al Jubb Si. Arabia 27°11N 42°17E 46 E4
Al Junaynah Sudan 13°27N 22°45E 53 F10
Al Kabā'ish Iraq 30°58N 47°0E 46 D5
Al Karak Jordan 31°11N 35°42E 48 D4
Al Karak □ Jordan 31°0N 36°0E 48 E5
Al Kāẓimīyah Iraq 33°22N 44°18E 46 C5
Al Khābūrah Oman 23°57N 57°5E 47 F8
Al Khafji Si. Arabia 28°24N 48°29E 47 E6
Al Khalīl West Bank 31°32N 35°6E 48 D4
Al Khāliṣ Iraq 33°49N 44°32E 46 C5
Al Kharsānīyah Si. Arabia 27°13N 49°18E 47 E6
Al Khaṣab Oman 26°14N 56°15E 47 E8
Al Khawr Qatar 25°41N 51°30E 47 E6
Al Khiḑr Iraq 31°12N 45°33E 46 D5
Al Khiyām Lebanon 33°20N 35°36E 48 B4
Al Khubar Si. Arabia 26°17N 50°12E 47 E6
Al Khums Libya 32°40N 14°17E 53 B8
Al Khurmah Si. Arabia 21°54N 42°3E 49 C3
Al Kiswah Syria 33°23N 36°14E 48 B5
Al Kūfah Iraq 32°2N 44°24E 46 C5
Al Kufrah Libya 24°17N 23°15E 53 D10
Al Kuhayfīyah Si. Arabia 27°12N 43°3E 46 E4
Al Kūt Iraq 32°30N 46°0E 46 C5
Al Kuwayt Kuwait 29°30N 48°0E 46 D5
Al Labwah Lebanon 34°11N 36°20E 48 A5
Al Lādhiqīyah Syria 35°30N 35°45E 46 C2
Al Līth Si. Arabia 20°9N 40°15E 49 C3
Al Liwā' Oman 24°31N 56°36E 47 E8
Al Luḩayyah Yemen 15°45N 42°40E 49 D3
Al Madīnah Iraq 30°57N 47°16E 46 D5
Al Madīnah Si. Arabia 24°35N 39°52E 46 E3
Al Mafraq Jordan 32°17N 36°14E 48 C5
Al Mafraq □ Jordan 32°17N 36°15E 48 C5
Al Maghreb = Morocco ■ N. Afr. 32°0N 5°50W 52 B4
Al Maḩmūdīyah Iraq 33°3N 44°21E 46 C5
Al Majma'ah Si. Arabia 25°57N 45°22E 46 E5
Al Makhruq, W. → Jordan 31°28N 37°0E 48 D6
Al Makḩūl Si. Arabia 26°37N 42°39E 46 E4
Al Manāmah Bahrain 26°10N 50°30E 47 E6
Al Maqwa' Kuwait 29°10N 47°59E 46 D5
Al Marāḩ Si. Arabia 25°35N 49°35E 47 E6
Al Marj Libya 32°25N 20°30E 53 B10
Al Maṭlā Kuwait 29°24N 47°40E 46 D5
Al Mawṣil Iraq 36°15N 43°5E 46 B4
Al Mayādin Syria 35°1N 40°27E 46 C4
Al Mazār Jordan 31°4N 35°41E 48 D4
Al Midhnab Si. Arabia 25°50N 44°18E 46 E5
Al Minā' Lebanon 34°24N 35°49E 48 A4
Al Miqdādīyah Iraq 34°0N 45°0E 46 C5
Al Mubarraz Si. Arabia 25°30N 49°40E 47 E6
Al Mudawwarah Jordan 29°19N 36°0E 48 F5
Al Mughayrā' U.A.E. 24°5N 53°32E 47 E7
Al Muḩarraq Bahrain 26°15N 50°40E 47 E6
Al Mukallā Yemen 14°33N 49°2E 49 E4
Al Mukhā Yemen 13°18N 43°15E 49 E3
Al Musayjīd Si. Arabia 24°5N 39°5E 46 E3
Al Musayyib Iraq 32°49N 44°20E 46 C5
Al Muthannā □ Iraq 30°30N 45°15E 46 D5
Al Muwayliḩ Si. Arabia 27°40N 35°30E 46 E2
Al Qādisīyah □ Iraq 32°0N 45°0E 46 D5
Al Qā'im Iraq 34°21N 41°7E 46 C4
Al Qalībah Si. Arabia 28°24N 37°42E 46 D3
Al Qāmishlī Syria 37°2N 41°14E 46 B4
Al Qaryatayn Syria 34°12N 37°13E 48 A6
Al Qaṣīm □ Si. Arabia 26°0N 43°0E 46 E4
Al Qaṭ'ā Syria 34°40N 40°48E 46 C4
Al Qaṭīf Si. Arabia 26°35N 50°0E 47 E6
Al Qatrānah Jordan 31°12N 36°6E 48 D5
Al Qaṭrūn Libya 24°56N 15°3E 53 D9
Al Qayṣūmah Si. Arabia 28°20N 46°7E 46 D5
Al Qunayṭirah Syria 33°5N 35°45E 48 B4
Al Qunfudhah Si. Arabia 19°3N 41°4E 49 D3
Al Qurayyāt Si. Arabia 31°20N 37°20E 46 D3
Al Qurnah Iraq 31°1N 47°25E 46 D5
Al Quṣayr Iraq 30°39N 45°50E 46 D5
Al Quṣayr Syria 34°31N 36°34E 48 A5
Al Qutayfah Syria 33°44N 36°36E 48 B5
Al Quwaysimah Jordan 31°55N 35°57E 48 D4
Al 'Ubaylah Si. Arabia 21°59N 50°57E 49 C5
Al 'Uḑaylīyah Si. Arabia 25°8N 49°18E 47 E6
Al 'Ulā Si. Arabia 26°35N 38°0E 46 E3
Al 'Uqayr Si. Arabia 25°40N 50°15E 47 E6
Al 'Uwaynid Si. Arabia 24°50N 46°0E 46 E5
Al 'Uwayqīlah Si. Arabia 30°30N 42°10E 46 D4
Al 'Uyūn Ḩijāz, Si. Arabia 24°33N 39°35E 46 E3
Al 'Uyūn Najd, Si. Arabia 26°30N 43°50E 46 E4
Al 'Uzayr Iraq 31°19N 47°25E 46 D5
Al Wajh Si. Arabia 26°10N 36°30E 46 E3
Al Wakrah Qatar 25°10N 51°40E 47 E6
Al Waqbah Si. Arabia 28°48N 45°33E 46 D5
Al Wari'āh Si. Arabia 27°51N 47°25E 46 E5
Al Yaman = Yemen ■ Asia 15°0N 44°0E 49 E3
Ala Dağ Turkey 37°44N 35°9E 46 B2
Ala Tau Asia 45°30N 80°40E 30 B5
Ala Tau Shankou = Dzungarian Gate Asia 45°10N 82°0E 30 B5
Alabama □ U.S.A. 33°0N 87°0W 85 E11
Alabama → U.S.A. 31°8N 87°57W 85 F11
Alabaster U.S.A. 33°15N 86°49W 85 E11
Alaçam Dağları Turkey 39°18N 28°49E 23 E13
Alacant = Alicante Spain 38°23N 0°30W 21 C5
Alachua U.S.A. 29°47N 82°30W 85 G13
Alagoa Grande Brazil 7°3S 35°35W 93 E11
Alagoas □ Brazil 9°0S 36°0W 93 E11
Alagoinhas Brazil 12°7S 38°20W 93 F11
Alaheaieatnu = Altaelva → Norway 69°54N 23°17E 8 B20
Alajuela Costa Rica 10°2N 84°8W 88 D3
Alaknanda → India 30°8N 78°36E 43 D8
Alakurtti Russia 66°58N 30°25E 8 C24
Alamarvdasht Iran 27°37N 52°59E 47 E7
Alameda U.S.A. 35°11N 106°37W 77 J10
Alamo U.S.A. 37°22N 115°10W 79 H11
Alamogordo U.S.A. 32°54N 105°57W 77 K11
Alamos Mexico 27°1N 108°56W 86 B3
Alamosa U.S.A. 37°28N 105°52W 77 H11
Alampur India 15°55N 78°6E 45 G4
Åland Finland 60°15N 20°0E 9 F19
Aland India 17°36N 76°35E 44 F3
Ålands hav Europe 60°0N 19°30E 9 G18
Alandur India 13°0N 80°15E 45 H5
Alaniya = North Ossetia-Alaniya □ Russia 43°30N 44°30E 19 F7
Alanya Turkey 36°38N 32°0E 46 B1
Alapayevsk Russia 57°52N 61°42E 26 D7
Alappuzha India 9°30N 76°28E 45 K3
Alaşehir Turkey 38°23N 28°30E 23 E13
Alaska □ U.S.A. 64°0N 154°0W 74 C9
Alaska, G. of Pac. Oc. 58°0N 145°0W 68 F3
Alaska Peninsula U.S.A. 56°0N 159°0W 74 D8
Alaska Range U.S.A. 62°50N 151°0W 68 E1
Älät Azerbaijan 39°58N 49°25E 47 B6
Alatau Shan = Ala Tau Asia 45°30N 80°40E 30 B5
Alatyr Russia 54°55N 46°35E 18 D8
Alausi Ecuador 2°0S 78°50W 92 D3
Alava, C. U.S.A. 48°10N 124°44W 78 B2
Alavo = Alavus Finland 62°35N 23°36E 8 E20
Alavus Finland 62°35N 23°36E 8 E20
Alawa ✪ Australia 15°42S 134°39E 62 B1
Alawoona Australia 34°45S 140°30E 63 E3
Alayawarra ✪ Australia 22°0S 134°30E 62 C1
'Alayh Lebanon 33°46N 35°33E 48 B4
Alba Italy 44°42N 8°2E 20 D8
Alba-Iulia Romania 46°8N 23°39E 17 E12
Albacete Spain 39°0N 1°50W 21 C5
Albacutya, L. Australia 35°45S 141°58E 63 F3
Albanel, L. Canada 50°55N 73°12W 72 B5
Albania ■ Europe 41°0N 20°0E 23 D9
Albany Australia 35°1S 117°58E 61 G2
Albany Ga., U.S.A. 31°35N 84°10W 85 F12
Albany N.Y., U.S.A. 42°39N 73°45W 83 D11
Albany Oreg., U.S.A. 44°38N 123°6W 76 D2
Albany Tex., U.S.A. 32°44N 99°18W 84 E5
Albany → Canada 52°17N 81°31W 72 B3
Albardón Argentina 31°20S 68°30W 94 C2
Albatross B. Australia 12°45S 141°30E 62 A3
Albemarle U.S.A. 35°21N 80°12W 85 D14
Albemarle Sd. U.S.A. 36°5N 76°0W 85 C16
Alberche → Spain 39°58N 4°46W 21 C3
Alberdi Paraguay 26°14S 58°20W 94 B4
Alberga → Australia 27°6S 135°33E 63 D2
Albert, L. Africa 1°30N 31°0E 54 D6
Albert, L. Australia 35°30S 139°10E 63 F2
Albert Edward Ra. Australia 18°17S 127°57E 60 C4
Albert Lea U.S.A. 43°39N 93°22W 80 D7
Albert Nile → Uganda 3°36N 32°2E 54 D6
Albert Town Bahamas 22°37N 74°33W 89 B5
Alberta □ Canada 54°40N 115°0W 70 C6
Alberti Argentina 35°1S 60°16W 94 D3
Albertinia S. Africa 34°11S 21°34E 56 D3
Alberton Canada 46°50N 64°0W 73 C7
Albertville France 45°40N 6°22E 20 D7
Albertville U.S.A. 34°16N 86°13W 85 D11
Albi France 43°56N 2°9E 20 E5
Albia U.S.A. 41°2N 92°48W 80 E7
Albina Suriname 5°37N 54°15W 93 B8
Albina, Ponta Angola 15°52S 11°44E 56 A1
Albion Mich., U.S.A. 42°15N 84°45W 81 D11
Albion Nebr., U.S.A. 41°42N 98°0W 80 E4
Albion Pa., U.S.A. 41°53N 80°22W 82 E4
Alborán Medit. S. 35°57N 3°0W 21 E4
Ålborg = Aalborg Denmark 57°2N 9°54E 9 H13
Alborz □ Iran 36°0N 50°50E 47 B6
Alborz, Reshteh-ye Kūhhā-ye Iran 36°0N 52°0E 47 C7
Albufeira Portugal 37°5N 8°15W 21 D1
Albuquerque U.S.A. 35°5N 106°39W 77 J10
Albuquerque, Cayos de Caribbean 12°10N 81°50W 88 D3
Alburg U.S.A. 44°59N 73°18W 83 B11
Albury Australia 36°3S 146°56E 63 F4
Alcalá de Henares Spain 40°28N 3°22W 21 B4
Alcalá la Real Spain 37°27N 3°57W 21 D4
Álcamo Italy 37°59N 12°55E 22 F5
Alcañiz Spain 41°2N 0°8W 21 B5
Alcântara Brazil 2°20S 44°30W 93 D10
Alcántara, Embalse de Spain 39°44N 6°50W 21 C2
Alcantarilla Spain 37°59N 1°12W 21 D5
Alcaraz, Sierra de Spain 38°40N 2°20W 21 C4
Alcaudete Spain 37°35N 4°5W 21 D3
Alcázar de San Juan Spain 39°24N 3°12W 21 C4
Alchevsk Ukraine 48°30N 38°45E 19 E6
Alcira = Alzira Spain 39°9N 0°30W 21 C5
Alcova U.S.A. 42°34N 106°43W 76 E10
Alcoy Spain 38°43N 0°30W 21 C5
Aldabra Is. Seychelles 9°22S 46°28E 51 G8
Aldama Mexico 22°55N 98°4W 87 C5
Aldan Russia 58°40N 125°30E 27 D13
Aldan → Russia 63°28N 129°35E 27 C13
Aldeburgh U.K. 52°10N 1°37E 13 E9
Alder Pk. U.S.A. 35°53N 121°22W 78 K5
Alderney U.K. 49°42N 2°11W 13 H5
Aldershot U.K. 51°15N 0°44W 13 F7
Aledo U.S.A. 41°12N 90°45W 80 E8
Aleg Mauritania 17°3N 13°55W 52 E3
Alegre Brazil 20°50S 41°30W 95 A7
Alegrete Brazil 29°40S 56°0W 95 B4
Aleksandriya = Oleksandriya Ukraine 50°37N 26°19E 17 C14
Aleksandrov Gay Russia 50°9N 48°34E 19 D8
Aleksandrovsk-Sakhalinskiy Russia 50°50N 142°20E 31 A17
Aleksandry, Zemlya Russia 80°25N 48°0E 26 A5
Além Paraíba Brazil 21°52S 42°41W 95 A7
Alemania Argentina 25°40S 65°30W 94 B2
Alemania Chile 25°10S 69°55W 94 B2
Alençon France 48°27N 0°4E 20 B4
Alenquer Brazil 1°56S 54°46W 93 D8
'Alenuihähä Channel U.S.A. 20°30N 156°0W 75 L8
Aleppo = Ḩalab Syria 36°10N 37°15E 46 B3
Aléria France 42°5N 9°26E 20 E9
Alert Canada 83°2N 60°0W 69 A20
Aleru India 17°39N 79°3E 44 F4
Alès France 44°9N 4°5E 20 D6
Alessándria Italy 44°54N 8°37E 20 D8
Ålesund Norway 62°28N 6°12E 8 E12
Aleutian Basin Pac. Oc. 57°0N 177°0E 64 B9
Aleutian Is. Pac. Oc. 52°0N 175°0W 64 B10
Aleutian Range U.S.A. 60°0N 154°0W 74 D9
Aleutian Trench Pac. Oc. 48°0N 180°0E 4 D17
Alexander U.S.A. 47°51N 103°39W 80 B2
Alexander, Mt. Australia 28°58S 120°16E 61 E3
Alexander Arch. U.S.A. 56°0N 136°0W 68 F4
Alexander Bay S. Africa 28°40S 16°30E 56 C2
Alexander City U.S.A. 32°56N 85°58W 85 E12
Alexander I. Antarctica 69°0S 70°0W 5 C17
Alexandra Australia 37°8S 145°40E 63 F4
Alexandra N.Z. 45°14S 169°25E 59 F2
Alexandra Channel Burma 14°7N 93°13E 45 G11
Alexandra Falls Canada 60°29N 116°18W 70 A5
Alexandria = El Iskandarîya Egypt 31°13N 29°58E 53 B11
Alexandria B.C., Canada 52°35N 122°27W 70 C4
Alexandria Ont., Canada 45°19N 74°38W 83 A10
Alexandria Romania 43°57N 25°24E 17 G13
Alexandria S. Africa 33°38S 26°28E 56 D4
Alexandria U.K. 55°59N 4°35W 11 F4
Alexandria La., U.S.A. 31°18N 92°27W 84 F8
Alexandria Minn., U.S.A. 45°53N 95°22W 80 C6
Alexandria S. Dak., U.S.A. 43°39N 97°47W 80 D5
Alexandria Bay U.S.A. 44°20N 75°55W 83 B9
Alexandrina, L. Australia 35°25S 139°10E 63 F2
Alexandroupoli Greece 40°50N 25°54E 23 D11
Alexis → Canada 52°33N 56°8W 73 B8
Alexis Creek Canada 52°10N 123°20W 70 C4
Aleysk Russia 52°40N 83°0E 26 D9
Alfenas Brazil 21°20S 46°10W 95 A6
Alford Aberds., U.K. 57°14N 2°41W 11 D6
Alford Lincs., U.K. 53°15N 0°10E 12 D8
Alfred Maine, U.S.A. 43°29N 70°43W 83 C14
Alfred N.Y., U.S.A. 42°16N 77°48W 82 D7
Alfreton U.K. 53°6N 1°24W 12 D6
Ålgård Norway 58°46N 5°53E 9 G11
Algarve Portugal 36°58N 8°20W 21 D1
Algeciras Spain 36°9N 5°28W 21 D3
Algemesí Spain 39°11N 0°27W 21 C5
Alger Algeria 36°42N 3°8E 52 A6
Algeria ■ Africa 28°30N 2°0E 52 C6
Algha Kazakhstan 49°53N 57°20E 19 E10
Alghero Italy 40°33N 8°19E 22 D3
Algiers = Alger Algeria 36°42N 3°8E 52 A6
Algoa B. S. Africa 33°50S 25°45E 56 D4
Algodones Dunes U.S.A. 32°50N 115°5W 79 N11
Algoma U.S.A. 44°36N 87°26W 80 C10
Algona U.S.A. 43°4N 94°14W 80 D6
Algonac U.S.A. 42°37N 82°32W 82 D2
Algonquin △ Canada 45°50N 78°30W 72 C4
Algorta Spain 43°21N 2°59W 21 A4
Algorta Uruguay 32°25S 57°24W 94 C4
Algorta Uruguay 32°25S 57°23W 96 C5
Alhucemas = Al Hoceïma Morocco 35°8N 3°58W 52 A5
'Alī al Gharbī Iraq 32°30N 46°45E 46 C5
'Alī ash Sharqī Iraq 32°7N 46°44E 46 C5
Äli Bayramlı = Şirvan Azerbaijan 39°59N 48°52E 47 B6
'Alī Khēl Afghan. 33°57N 69°43E 42 C3
Alī Shāh Iran 38°9N 45°50E 46 B5
'Alīābād Golestān, Iran 36°40N 54°33E 47 B7
'Alīābād Khorāsān, Iran 32°30N 57°30E 47 C8
'Alīābād Kordestān, Iran 35°4N 46°58E 46 C5
'Alīābād Yazd, Iran 31°41N 53°49E 47 D7
Aliağa Turkey 38°47N 26°59E 23 E12
Aliakmonas → Greece 40°30N 22°36E 23 D10
Alibag India 18°38N 72°56E 44 E1
Alicante Spain 38°23N 0°30W 21 C5
Alice S. Africa 32°48S 26°55E 56 D4
Alice U.S.A. 27°45N 98°5W 84 H5
Alice → Queens., Australia 24°2S 144°50E 62 C3
Alice → Queens., Australia 15°35S 142°20E 62 B3
Alice Arm Canada 55°29N 129°31W 70 B3
Alice Springs Australia 23°40S 133°50E 62 C1
Alicedale S. Africa 33°15S 26°4E 56 D4
Aliceville U.S.A. 33°8N 88°9W 85 E10
Aliganj India 27°30N 79°10E 43 F8
Aligarh Raj., India 25°55N 76°15E 42 G7
Aligarh Ut. P., India 27°55N 78°10E 42 F8
Alīgūdarz Iran 33°25N 49°45E 47 C6
Alingsås Sweden 57°55N 12°31E 9 H15
Alipur Pakistan 29°25N 70°55E 42 E4
Alipur Duar India 26°30N 89°35E 41 F16
Aliquippa U.S.A. 40°37N 80°15W 82 F4
Alishan Taiwan 23°31N 120°48E 35 F13
Alitus = Alytus Lithuania 54°24N 24°3E 9 J21
Aliwal North S. Africa 30°45S 26°45E 56 D4
Alix Canada 52°24N 113°11W 70 C6
Aljustrel Portugal 37°55N 8°10W 21 D1
Alkhanay △ Russia 51°0N 113°30E 27 D12
Alkmaar Neths. 52°37N 4°45E 15 B4
All American Canal U.S.A. 32°45N 115°15W 79 N11
Allagadda India 15°8N 78°30E 45 G4
Allagash → U.S.A. 47°5N 69°3W 81 B19
Allah Dad Pakistan 25°38N 67°34E 42 G2
Allahabad India 25°25N 81°58E 43 G9
Allan Canada 51°53N 106°4W 71 C7
Allanridge S. Africa 27°45S 26°40E 56 C4
Allegany U.S.A. 42°6N 78°30W 82 D6
Allegheny → U.S.A. 40°27N 80°1W 82 F5
Allegheny Mts. U.S.A. 38°15N 80°10W 81 F13
Allegheny Plateau U.S.A. 41°30N 78°30W 81 E14
Allegheny Res. U.S.A. 41°50N 79°0W 82 E6
Allègre, Pte. Guadeloupe 16°22N 61°46W 88 b
Allen, Bog of Ireland 53°15N 7°0W 10 C5
Allen, L. Ireland 54°8N 8°4W 10 B3
Allendale U.S.A. 33°1N 81°18W 85 E14
Allende Mexico 28°20N 100°51W 86 B4
Allentown U.S.A. 40°37N 75°29W 83 F9
Alleppey = Alappuzha India 9°30N 76°28E 45 K3
Aller → Germany 52°56N 9°12E 16 B5
Alleynes B. Barbados 13°13N 59°39W 89 g
Alliance Nebr., U.S.A. 42°6N 102°52W 80 D2
Alliance Ohio, U.S.A. 40°55N 81°6W 82 F3
Allier → France 46°57N 3°4E 20 C5
Alliford Bay Canada 53°12N 131°58W 70 C2
Alligator Pond Jamaica 17°52N 77°34W 88 a
Allinagaram India 10°2N 77°30E 45 J3
Alliston Canada 44°9N 79°52W 82 B5
Alloa U.K. 56°7N 3°47W 11 E5
Allora Australia 28°2S 152°0E 63 D5
Alluitsup Paa Greenland 60°30N 45°35W 4 C5
Allur India 14°40N 80°4E 45 G5
Alluru Kottapatnam India 15°24N 80°7E 45 G5
Alma Canada 48°35N 71°40W 73 C5
Alma Ga., U.S.A. 31°33N 82°28W 85 F13
Alma Kans., U.S.A. 39°1N 96°17W 80 F5
Alma Mich., U.S.A. 43°23N 84°39W 81 D11
Alma Nebr., U.S.A. 40°6N 99°22W 80 E4
Alma Wis., U.S.A. 44°20N 91°55W 80 C8
Alma Ata = Almaty Kazakhstan 43°15N 76°57E 30 C4
Alma Hill U.S.A. 42°2N 78°0W 82 D7
Almaden Australia 17°22S 144°40E 62 B3
Almadén Spain 38°49N 4°52W 21 C3
Almalyk = Olmaliq Uzbekistan 40°50N 69°35E 26 E7
Almanor, L. U.S.A. 40°14N 121°9W 76 F3
Almansa Spain 38°51N 1°5W 21 C5
Almanzor, Pico Spain 40°15N 5°18W 21 B3
Almanzora → Spain 37°14N 1°46W 21 D5
Almaty Kazakhstan 43°15N 76°57E 30 C4
Almazán Spain 41°30N 2°30W 21 B4
Almeirim Brazil 1°30S 52°34W 93 D8
Almelo Neths. 52°22N 6°42E 15 B6
Almendralejo Spain 38°41N 6°26W 21 C2
Almere Neths. 52°20N 5°15E 15 B5
Almería Spain 36°52N 2°27W 21 D4
Almirante Panama 9°10N 82°30W 88 E3
Almond U.S.A. 42°19N 77°44W 82 D7
Almont U.S.A. 42°55N 83°3W 82 D1
Almonte Canada 45°14N 76°12W 83 A8
Almora India 29°38N 79°40E 43 E8
Alness U.K. 57°41N 4°16W 11 D4
Alnmouth U.K. 55°24N 1°37W 12 B6
Alnwick U.K. 55°24N 1°42W 12 B6
Alon Burma 22°12N 95°5E 41 H19
Alor Indonesia 8°15S 124°30E 37 F6
Alor Setar Malaysia 6°7N 100°22E 39 J3
Alot India 23°56N 75°40E 42 H6
Aloysius, Mt. Australia 26°0S 128°38E 61 E4
Alpaugh U.S.A. 35°53N 119°29W 78 K7
Alpena U.S.A. 45°4N 83°27W 82 A1
Alpha Australia 23°39S 146°37E 62 C4
Alpha Ridge Arctic 84°0N 118°0W 4 A2
Alphen aan den Rijn Neths. 52°7N 4°40E 15 B4
Alpine Ariz., U.S.A. 33°51N 109°9W 77 K9
Alpine Calif., U.S.A. 32°50N 116°46W 79 N10
Alpine Tex., U.S.A. 30°22N 103°40W 84 F3
Alps Europe 46°30N 9°30E 16 E5
Alpurrurulam Australia 20°59S 137°50E 62 C2
Alsace □ France 48°15N 7°25E 20 B7
Alsask Canada 51°21N 109°59W 71 C7
Alsasua Spain 42°54N 2°10W 21 A4
Alsek → U.S.A. 59°10N 138°12W 70 B1
Alsta Norway 65°58N 12°40E 8 D15
Alston U.K. 54°49N 2°25W 12 C5
Alta Norway 69°57N 23°10E 8 B20
Alta Gracia Argentina 31°40S 64°30W 94 C3
Alta Sierra U.S.A. 35°42N 118°33W 79 K8
Altaelva → Norway 69°54N 23°17E 8 B20
Altafjorden Norway 70°5N 23°5E 8 A20
Altai = Aerhtai Shan Mongolia 46°40N 92°45E 30 B7
Altai = Gorno-Altay □ Russia 51°0N 86°0E 26 D9
Altamaha → U.S.A. 31°20N 81°20W 85 F14
Altamira Brazil 3°12S 52°10W 93 D8
Altamira Chile 25°47S 69°51W 94 B2
Altamira Mexico 22°24N 97°55W 87 C5
Altamont U.S.A. 42°42N 74°2W 83 D10
Altamura Italy 40°49N 16°33E 22 D7
Altanbulag Mongolia 50°16N 106°30E 30 A10
Altar Mexico 30°43N 111°44W 86 A2
Altar, Gran Desierto de Mexico 31°50N 114°10W 86 B2
Altata Mexico 24°40N 107°55W 86 C3
Altavista U.S.A. 37°6N 79°17W 81 G14
Altay China 47°48N 88°10E 30 B6
Altay Mongolia 46°22N 96°15E 30 B8
Altea Spain 38°38N 0°2W 21 C5
Altiplano Bolivia 17°0S 68°0W 92 G5
Alto Araguaia Brazil 17°15S 53°20W 93 G8
Alto Cuchumatanes = Cuchumatanes, Sierra de los Guatemala 15°35N 91°25W 88 C1
Alto del Carmen Chile 28°46S 70°30W 94 B1
Alto Molocue Mozam. 15°50S 37°35E 55 H7
Alto Paraguay □ Paraguay 21°0S 58°30W 94 A4
Alto Paraná □ Paraguay 25°30S 54°50W 95 B5
Alton Canada 43°54N 80°5W 82 C4
Alton U.K. 51°9N 0°59W 13 F7
Alton Ill., U.S.A. 38°53N 90°11W 80 F8
Alton N.H., U.S.A. 43°27N 71°13W 83 C13
Altona Canada 49°6N 97°33W 71 D9
Altoona U.S.A. 40°31N 78°24W 82 F6
Altsasu = Alsasua Spain 42°54N 2°10W 21 A4
Altun Kupri Iraq 35°45N 44°9E 46 C5
Altun Shan China 38°30N 88°0E 30 D6
Alturas U.S.A. 41°29N 120°32W 76 F3
Altus U.S.A. 34°38N 99°20W 84 D5
Alucra Turkey 40°22N 38°47E 19 F6
Alūksne Latvia 57°24N 27°3E 9 H22
Alunite U.S.A. 35°59N 114°55W 79 K12
Alur India 15°24N 77°15E 45 G3
Alusi Indonesia 7°35S 131°40E 37 F8
Alutgama Sri Lanka 6°26N 79°59E 45 L4
Alutnuwara Sri Lanka 7°19N 80°59E 45 L5
Aluva India 10°8N 76°24E 45 J3
Alva U.S.A. 36°48N 98°40W 84 C5
Alvarado Mexico 18°46N 95°46W 87 D5
Alvarado U.S.A. 32°24N 97°13W 84 E6
Alvaro Obregón, Presa Mexico 27°52N 109°52W 86 B3
Alvear Argentina 29°5S 56°30W 94 B4
Alvesta Sweden 56°54N 14°35E 9 H16
Alvinston Canada 42°49N 81°52W 82 D3
Älvkarleby Sweden 60°34N 17°26E 9 F17
Alvord Desert U.S.A. 42°30N 118°25W 76 E4
Älvsbyn Sweden 65°40N 21°0E 8 D19
Alwar India 27°38N 76°34E 42 F7
Alwaye = Aluva India 10°8N 76°24E 45 J3
Alxa Zuoqi China 38°50N 105°40E 32 E3
Alyangula Australia 13°55S 136°30E 62 A2
Alyata = Älät Azerbaijan 39°58N 49°25E 47 B6
Alyth U.K. 56°38N 3°13W 11 E5
Alytus Lithuania 54°24N 24°3E 9 J21
Alzada U.S.A. 45°2N 104°25W 76 D11
Alzamay Russia 55°33N 98°39E 27 D10
Alzira Spain 39°9N 0°30W 21 C5
Am Timan Chad 11°0N 20°10E 53 F10
Amadeus, L. Australia 24°54S 131°0E 61 D5
Amadi South Sudan 5°29N 30°25E 53 G12
Amadjuak L. Canada 65°0N 71°8W 69 E17
Amagansett U.S.A. 40°59N 72°9W 83 F12
Amagi Japan 33°25N 130°39E 29 H5
Amahai Indonesia 3°20S 128°55E 37 E7
Amaile Samoa 13°59S 171°22W 59 b
Amakusa = Hondo Japan 32°27N 130°12E 29 H5
Amakusa-Shotō Japan 32°15N 130°10E 29 H5
Åmål Sweden 59°3N 12°42E 9 G15
Amalapuram India 16°35N 81°55E 45 F5
Amaliada Greece 37°47N 21°22E 23 F9
Amalner India 21°5N 75°5E 44 D2
Amamapare Indonesia 4°53S 136°38E 37 E9
Amambaí Brazil 23°5S 55°13W 95 A4
Amambaí → Brazil 23°22S 53°56W 95 A5
Amambay □ Paraguay 23°0S 56°0W 95 A4
Amambay, Cordillera de S. Amer. 23°0S 55°45W 95 A4
Amami Japan 28°22N 129°27E 29 K4
Amami-Guntō Japan 27°16N 129°21E 29 L4
Amami-Ō-Shima Japan 28°16N 129°21E 29 K4
Aman, Pulau Malaysia 5°16N 100°24E 39 c
Amaná, L. Brazil 2°35S 64°40W 92 D6
Amanat → India 24°7N 84°4E 43 G11
Amanda Park U.S.A. 47°28N 123°55W 78 C3
Amankeldi Kazakhstan 50°10N 65°10E 26 D7
Amapá Brazil 2°5N 50°50W 93 C8
Amapá □ Brazil 1°40N 52°0W 93 C8
Amarante Brazil 6°14S 42°50W 93 E10
Amaranth Canada 50°36N 98°43W 71 C9
Amaravati → India 11°0N 78°15E 45 J4
Amargosa → U.S.A. 36°14N 116°51W 79 J10
Amargosa Desert U.S.A. 36°40N 116°30W 79 J10
Amargosa Range U.S.A. 36°20N 116°45W 79 J10
Amarillo U.S.A. 35°13N 101°50W 84 D4
Amarkantak India 22°40N 81°45E 43 H9
Amarnath India 19°12N 73°22E 44 E1
Amaro, Mte. Italy 42°5N 14°5E 22 C6
Amarpur India 25°5N 87°0E 43 G12
Amarwara India 22°18N 79°10E 43 H8
Amasya Turkey 40°40N 35°50E 19 F6
Amata Australia 26°9S 131°9E 61 E5
Amatikulu S. Africa 29°3S 31°33E 57 C5
Amatitlán Guatemala 14°29N 90°38W 88 D1
Amay Belgium 50°33N 5°19E 15 D5
Amazon = Amazonas → S. Amer. 0°5S 50°0W 93 D8
Amazonas □ Brazil 5°0S 65°0W 92 E6
Amazonas → S. Amer. 0°5S 50°0W 93 D8
Ambad India 19°38N 75°50E 44 E2
Ambagarh Chowki India 20°47N 80°43E 44 D5
Ambah India 26°43N 78°13E 42 F8
Ambajogal India 18°44N 76°23E 44 E3
Ambala India 30°23N 76°56E 42 D7
Ambalangoda Sri Lanka 6°15N 80°5E 45 L5
Ambalantota Sri Lanka 6°7N 81°1E 45 L5

Ambalapulai *India* 9°25N 76°25E **45** K3
Ambalavao *Madag.* 21°50S 46°56E **55** J9
Ambanja *Madag.* 13°40S 48°27E **55** G9
Ambarchik *Russia* 69°40N 162°20E **27** C17
Ambasamudram *India* 8°43N 77°25E **45** K3
Ambato *Ecuador* 1°5S 78°42W **92** D3
Ambato, Sierra de
  Argentina 28°25S 66°10W **94** B2
Ambatolampy *Madag.* 19°20S 47°35E **55** H9
Ambatondrazaka *Madag.* 17°55S 48°28E **55** H9
Amberg *Germany* 49°26N 11°52E **16** D6
Ambergris Cay *Belize* 18°0N 87°55W **87** D7
Amberley *Canada* 44°2N 81°42W **82** D3
Amberley *N.Z.* 43°9S 172°44E **59** E4
Ambikapur *India* 23°15N 83°15E **43** H10
Ambilobé *Madag.* 13°10S 49°3E **55** G9
Amble *U.K.* 55°20N 1°36W **12** B6
Ambleside *U.K.* 54°26N 2°58W **12** C5
Ambo *Peru* 10°5S 76°10W **92** F3
Ambohitra *Madag.* 12°30S 49°10E **55** G9
Amboise *France* 47°24N 1°2E **20** C4
Ambon *Indonesia* 3°43S 128°12E **37** E7
Ambositra *Madag.* 20°31S 47°25E **55** J9
Ambovombe *Madag.* 25°11S 46°5E **55** K9
Amboy *U.S.A.* 34°33N 115°45W **79** L11
Amboyna Cay
  S. China Sea 7°50N 112°50E **36** C4
Ambridge *U.S.A.* 40°36N 80°14W **82** F4
Ambriz *Angola* 7°48S 13°8E **54** F2
Ambur *India* 12°48N 78°43E **45** H4
Amchitka I. *U.S.A.* 51°32N 179°0E **74** E3
Amderma *Russia* 69°45N 61°30E **26** C7
Amdhi *India* 23°51N 81°27E **43** H9
Amdo *China* 32°20N 91°40E **30** E7
Ameca *Mexico* 20°33N 104°2W **86** C4
Ameca → *Mexico* 20°41N 105°18W **86** C3
Amecameca de Juárez
  Mexico 19°8N 98°46W **87** D5
Amed *Indonesia* 8°19S 115°39E **37** J18
Ameland *Neths.* 53°27N 5°45E **15** A5
Amenia *U.S.A.* 41°51N 73°33W **83** E11
America-Antarctica Ridge
  S. Ocean 59°0S 16°0W **5** B2
American Falls *U.S.A.* 42°47N 112°51W **76** E7
American Falls Res.
  U.S.A. 42°47N 112°52W **76** E7
American Fork *U.S.A.* 40°23N 111°48W **76** F8
American Highland
  Antarctica 73°0S 75°0E **5** D6
American Samoa ☒
  Pac. Oc. 14°20S 170°0W **59** b
American Samoa △
  Amer. Samoa 14°15S 170°28W **59** b
Americana *Brazil* 22°45S 47°20W **95** A6
Americus *U.S.A.* 32°4N 84°14W **85** E12
Amersfoort *Neths.* 52°9N 5°23E **15** B5
Amersfoort *S. Africa* 26°59S 29°53E **57** C4
Amery Basin *S. Ocean* 68°15S 74°30E **5** C6
Amery Ice Shelf *Antarctica* 69°30S 72°0E **5** C6
Ames *U.S.A.* 42°2N 93°37W **80** D7
Amesbury *U.S.A.* 42°51N 70°56W **83** D14
Amet *India* 25°18N 73°56E **42** G5
Amga *Russia* 60°50N 132°0E **27** C14
Amga → *Russia* 62°38N 134°32E **27** C14
Amgaon *India* 21°22N 80°22E **44** D5
Amgu *Russia* 45°45N 137°15E **28** B8
Amgun → *Russia* 52°56N 139°38E **27** D14
Amherst *Canada* 45°48N 64°8W **73** C7
Amherst *Mass., U.S.A.* 42°23N 72°31W **83** D12
Amherst *N.Y., U.S.A.* 42°59N 78°48W **82** D6
Amherst *Ohio, U.S.A.* 41°24N 82°14W **82** E2
Amherst I. *Canada* 44°8N 76°43W **83** B8
Amherstburg *Canada* 42°6N 83°6W **72** D3
Amiata, Mte. *Italy* 42°53N 11°37E **22** C4
Amidon *U.S.A.* 46°29N 103°19W **80** B2
Amiens *France* 49°54N 2°16E **20** B5
Amindivi Is. *India* 11°23N 72°23E **45** J1
Amini I. *India* 11°6N 72°45E **45** J1
Aminuis *Namibia* 23°43S 19°21E **56** B2
Amīrābād *Iran* 33°20N 46°16E **46** C5
Amirante Is. *Seychelles* 6°0S 53°0E **24** J7
Amisk → *Canada* 56°43N 98°0W **71** B9
Amisk L. *Canada* 54°35N 102°15W **71** C8
Amistad, Presa de la
  Mexico 29°26N 101°3W **86** B4
Amistad △ *U.S.A.* 29°32N 101°12W **84** G4
Amite *U.S.A.* 30°44N 90°30W **85** F9
Amla *India* 21°56N 78°7E **42** J8
Amlapura *Indonesia* 8°27S 115°37E **37** J18
Amlia I. *U.S.A.* 52°4N 173°30W **74** E5
Amlwch *U.K.* 53°24N 4°20W **12** D3
'Ammān *Jordan* 31°57N 35°52E **48** D4
Ammanford *U.S.A.* 51°48N 3°59W **13** F4
Ammassalik = Tasiilaq
  Greenland 65°40N 37°20W **4** C6
Ammochostos = Famagusta
  Cyprus 35°8N 33°55E **46** C2
Ammon *U.S.A.* 43°28N 111°58W **76** E8
Amnat Charoen
  Thailand 15°51N 104°38E **38** E5
Amnura *Bangla.* 24°37N 88°25E **43** G13
Amo Jiang → *China* 23°0N 101°50E **34** F3
Āmol *Iran* 36°23N 52°20E **47** B7
Amorgós *Greece* 36°50N 25°57E **23** F11
Amory *U.S.A.* 33°59N 88°29W **85** E10
Amos *Canada* 48°35N 78°5W **72** C4
Åmot *Norway* 59°57N 9°54E **9** G13
Amoy = Xiamen *China* 24°25N 118°4E **35** E12
Ampang *Malaysia* 3°8N 101°45E **39** L3
Ampani *India* 19°35N 82°38E **44** E6
Ampanihy *Madag.* 24°40S 44°45E **55** J8
Ampenan *Indonesia* 8°34S 116°4E **37** K19
Amper → *Germany* 48°29N 11°55E **16** D6
Amphitrite Group
  S. China Sea 16°50N 112°20E **36** A4
Amphoe Kathu *Thailand* 7°55N 98°21E **39** a
Amphoe Thalang *Thailand* 8°1N 98°20E **39** a
Amqui *Canada* 48°28N 67°27W **73** C6
Amrabad *India* 16°23N 78°50E **45** E4

Amravati *India* 20°55N 77°45E **44** D3
Amreli *India* 21°35N 71°17E **42** J4
Amritsar *India* 31°35N 74°57E **42** D6
Amroha *India* 28°53N 78°30E **43** E8
Amsterdam *Neths.* 52°23N 4°54E **15** B4
Amsterdam *U.S.A.* 42°56N 74°11W **83** D10
Amsterdam I. = Nouvelle
  Amsterdam, Î. *Ind. Oc.* 38°30S 77°30E **3** F13
Amstetten *Austria* 48°7N 14°51E **16** D8
Amudarya → *Uzbekistan* 43°58N 59°34E **26** E6
Amukta Pass *U.S.A.* 52°0N 171°0W **74** E5
Amund Ringnes I.
  Canada 78°20N 96°25W **69** B12
Amundsen Abyssal Plain
  S. Ocean 65°0S 125°0W **5** C14
Amundsen Basin *Arctic* 87°30N 80°0E **4** A
Amundsen Gulf *Canada* 71°0N 124°0W **68** C7
Amundsen Ridges
  S. Ocean 69°15S 123°0W **5** C14
Amundsen-Scott *Antarctica* 90°0S 166°0E **5** E
Amundsen Sea *Antarctica* 72°0S 115°0W **5** D15
Amuntai *Indonesia* 2°28S 115°25E **36** E5
Amur → *Russia* 52°56N 141°10E **27** D15
Amurang *Indonesia* 1°5N 124°40E **37** D6
Amursk *Russia* 50°14N 136°54E **27** D14
Amyderya = Amudarya →
  Uzbekistan 43°58N 59°34E **26** E6
An Bang, Dao = Amboyna Cay
  S. China Sea 7°50N 112°50E **36** C4
An Bien *Vietnam* 9°45N 105°0E **39** H5
An Hoa *Vietnam* 15°40N 108°5E **38** E7
An Khe *Vietnam* 13°57N 108°51E **38** F7
An Nabatīyah at Tahta
  Lebanon 33°23N 35°27E **48** B4
An Nabk *Syria* 34°2N 36°44E **48** A5
An Nafūd *Si. Arabia* 28°15N 41°0E **46** D4
An Najaf *Iraq* 32°3N 44°15E **46** D5
An Nāşirīyah *Iraq* 31°0N 46°15E **46** D5
An Nhon = Binh Dinh
  Vietnam 13°55N 109°7E **38** F7
An Nu'ayrīyah *Si. Arabia* 27°30N 48°30E **47** E6
An Nu'mānīyah *Iraq* 32°32N 45°25E **46** C5
An Ros = Rush *Ireland* 53°31N 6°6W **10** C5
An Thoi, Quan Dao
  Vietnam 9°58N 104°0E **39** H5
Anabar → *Russia* 73°8N 113°36E **27** B12
Anaconda *U.S.A.* 46°8N 112°57W **76** C7
Anacortes *U.S.A.* 48°30N 122°37W **78** B4
Anadarko *U.S.A.* 35°4N 98°15W **84** D5
Anadolu *Turkey* 39°0N 30°0E **19** G5
Anadyr *Russia* 64°35N 177°20E **27** C18
Anadyr → *Russia* 64°55N 176°5E **27** C18
Anadyrskiy Zaliv *Russia* 64°0N 180°0E **27** C19
'Ānah *Iraq* 34°25N 42°0E **46** C4
Anaheim *U.S.A.* 33°50N 117°55W **79** M9
Anahim Lake *Canada* 52°28N 125°18W **70** C3
Anai Mudi *India* 10°12N 77°4E **45** J3
Anaimalai Hills *India* 10°20N 76°40E **45** J3
Anakapalle *India* 17°42N 83°6E **44** F6
Anakie *Australia* 23°32S 147°45E **62** C4
Analalava *Madag.* 14°35S 48°0E **55** G9
Anambar → *Pakistan* 30°15N 68°50E **42** D3
Anambas, Kepulauan
  Indonesia 3°20N 106°30E **36** D3
Anambas Is. = Anambas,
  Kepulauan *Indonesia* 3°20N 106°30E **36** D3
Anamosa *U.S.A.* 42°7N 91°17W **80** D8
Anamur *Turkey* 36°8N 32°58E **46** B2
Anan *Japan* 33°54N 134°40E **29** H7
Anand *India* 22°32N 72°59E **42** H5
Anandapuram *India* 14°5N 75°12E **45** G2
Anandpur *India* 21°16N 86°13E **44** D8
Anangu Pitjantjatjara ⬡
  Australia 27°0S 132°0E **61** E5
Anantapur *India* 14°39N 77°42E **45** G3
Anantnag *India* 33°45N 75°10E **43** C6
Ananyiv *Ukraine* 47°44N 29°58E **17** E15
Anápolis *Brazil* 16°15S 48°50W **93** G9
Anapu → *Brazil* 1°53S 50°53W **93** D8
Anār *Iran* 30°55N 55°13E **47** D7
Anārak *Iran* 33°25N 53°40E **47** C7
Anas → *India* 23°26N 74°0E **42** H5
Anatolia = Anadolu *Turkey* 39°0N 30°0E **19** G5
Añatuya *Argentina* 28°20S 62°50W **94** B3
Anatye ⬡ *Australia* 22°29S 137°3E **62** C2
Anbyŏn *N. Korea* 39°1N 127°35E **33** E14
Ancaster *Canada* 43°13N 79°59W **82** C5
Anchor Bay *U.S.A.* 38°48N 123°34W **78** G3
Anchorage *U.S.A.* 61°13N 149°54W **68** E2
Anchuthengu *India* 8°40N 76°46E **45** K3
Anci *China* 39°20N 116°40E **32** E9
Ancohuma, Nevado
  Bolivia 16°0S 68°50W **92** G5
Ancón *Peru* 11°50S 77°10W **92** F3
Ancona *Italy* 43°38N 13°30E **22** C5
Ancud *Chile* 42°0S 73°50W **96** E2
Ancud, G. de *Chile* 42°0S 73°0W **96** E2
Anda *China* 46°24N 125°19E **31** B14
Andacollo *Argentina* 37°10S 70°42W **94** D1
Andacollo *Chile* 30°14S 71°6W **94** C1
Andalgalá *Argentina* 27°40S 66°30W **94** B2
Åndalsnes *Norway* 62°35N 7°43E **8** E12
Andalucía □ *Spain* 37°35N 5°0W **21** D3
Andalusia = Andalucía □
  Spain 37°35N 5°0W **21** D3
Andalusia *U.S.A.* 31°18N 86°29W **85** F11
Andaman & Nicobar Is. □
  India 10°0N 93°0E **45** K11
Andaman Is. *Ind. Oc.* 12°30N 92°45E **45** H11
Andaman Sea *Ind. Oc.* 13°0N 96°0E **36** B1
Andamooka *Australia* 30°27S 137°9E **63** E2
Andapa *Madag.* 14°39S 49°39E **55** G9
Andara *Namibia* 18°2S 21°9E **56** B3
Andenes *Norway* 69°19N 16°18E **8** B17
Andenne *Belgium* 50°28N 5°5E **15** D5
Anderson *Alaska,*
  U.S.A. 64°25N 149°15W **74** C10
Anderson *Calif., U.S.A.* 40°27N 122°18W **76** F2
Anderson *Ind., U.S.A.* 40°10N 85°41W **81** E11
Anderson *Mo., U.S.A.* 36°39N 94°27W **80** G6

Anderson *S.C., U.S.A.* 34°31N 82°39W **85** D13
Anderson → *Canada* 69°42N 129°0W **68** D6
Anderson I. *India* 12°46N 92°43E **45** H11
Andes *U.S.A.* 42°12N 74°47W **83** D10
Andes, Cord. de los
  S. Amer. 20°0S 68°0W **92** H5
Andfjorden *Norway* 69°10N 16°20E **8** B17
Andhra, L. *India* 18°54N 73°32E **44** E1
Andhra Pradesh □ *India* 18°0N 79°0E **44** F4
Andijon *Uzbekistan* 41°10N 72°15E **30** C3
Andikíthira = Antikythira
  Greece 35°52N 23°15E **23** G10
Andīmeshk *Iran* 32°27N 48°21E **47** C6
Andizhan = Andijon
  Uzbekistan 41°10N 72°15E **30** C3
Andoany *Madag.* 13°25S 48°16E **55** G9
Andol *India* 17°51N 78°4E **44** F4
Andola *India* 16°57N 76°50E **44** F3
Andong *S. Korea* 36°40N 128°43E **33** F15
Andorra ■ *Europe* 42°30N 1°30E **20** E4
Andorra La Vella *Andorra* 42°31N 1°32E **20** E4
Andover *U.K.* 51°12N 1°29W **13** F6
Andover *Kans., U.S.A.* 37°43N 97°7W **80** G5
Andover *Maine, U.S.A.* 44°38N 70°45W **83** B14
Andover *Mass., U.S.A.* 42°40N 71°8W **83** D13
Andover *N.J., U.S.A.* 40°59N 74°45W **83** F10
Andover *N.Y., U.S.A.* 42°10N 77°48W **82** D7
Andover *Ohio, U.S.A.* 41°36N 80°34W **82** E4
Andøya *Norway* 69°10N 15°50E **8** B16
Andradina *Brazil* 20°54S 51°23W **93** H8
Andreanof Is. *U.S.A.* 51°30N 176°0W **74** E4
Andrews *S.C., U.S.A.* 33°27N 79°34W **85** E15
Andrews *Tex., U.S.A.* 32°19N 102°33W **84** E3
Ándria *Italy* 41°13N 16°17E **22** D7
Andros *Greece* 37°50N 24°57E **23** F11
Andros I. *Bahamas* 24°30N 78°0W **88** B4
Andros Town *Bahamas* 24°43N 77°47W **88** B4
Androth I. *India* 10°50N 73°41E **45** J1
Andselv *Norway* 69°4N 18°34E **8** B18
Andújar *Spain* 38°3N 4°5W **21** C3
Andulo *Angola* 11°25S 16°45E **54** G3
Anegada *Br. Virgin Is.* 18°45N 64°20W **89** e
Anegada Passage
  W. Indies 18°15N 63°45W **89** C7
Aneto, Pico de *Spain* 42°37N 0°40E **21** A6
Anfu *China* 27°21N 114°40E **35** D10
Ang Thong *Thailand* 14°35N 100°31E **38** E3
Ang Thong, Ko *Thailand* 9°37N 99°41E **39** b
Ang Thong, Mu Ko △
  Thailand 9°40N 99°43E **39** b
Angamos, Punta *Chile* 23°1S 70°32W **94** A1
Angara → *Russia* 58°5N 94°20E **27** D10
Angarsk *Russia* 52°30N 104°0E **30** A9
Angas Hills *Australia* 23°0S 127°50E **60** D4
Angaston *Australia* 34°30S 139°8E **63** E2
Ånge *Sweden* 62°31N 15°35E **8** E16
Ángel, Salto = Angel Falls
  Venezuela 5°57N 62°30W **92** B6
Ángel de la Guarda, I.
  Mexico 29°20N 113°25W **86** B2
Angel Falls *Venezuela* 5°57N 62°30W **92** B6
Angeles *Phil.* 15°9N 120°33E **37** A6
Ängelholm *Sweden* 56°15N 12°58E **9** H15
Angels Camp *U.S.A.* 38°4N 120°32W **78** G6
Ångermanälven →
  Sweden 63°0N 17°20E **8** E17
Ångermanland *Sweden* 63°36N 17°45E **8** E17
Angers *Canada* 45°31N 75°29W **83** A9
Angers *France* 47°30N 0°35W **20** C3
Ängesån → *Sweden* 66°16N 22°47E **8** C20
Angikuni L. *Canada* 62°12N 99°59W **71** A9
Angkor *Cambodia* 13°22N 103°50E **38** F4
Angledool *Australia* 29°5S 147°55E **63** D4
Anglesey *U.K.* 53°17N 4°20W **12** D3
Anglesey, Isle of □ *U.K.* 53°16N 4°18W **12** D3
Angleton *U.S.A.* 29°10N 95°26W **84** G7
Angmagssalik = Tasiilaq
  Greenland 65°40N 37°20W **4** C6
Ango *Dem. Rep. of the Congo* 4°10N 26°5E **54** D5
Angoche *Mozam.* 16°8S 39°55E **55** H7
Angol *Chile* 37°56S 72°45W **94** D1
Angola *Ind., U.S.A.* 41°38N 85°0W **81** E11
Angola *N.Y., U.S.A.* 42°38N 79°2W **82** D5
Angola ■ *Africa* 12°0S 18°0E **55** G3
Angoulême *France* 45°39N 0°10E **20** D4
Angoumois *France* 45°50N 0°25E **20** D3
Angra do Heroísmo
  Azores 38°39N 27°13W **52** a
Angra dos Reis *Brazil* 23°0S 44°10W **95** A7
Angtassom *Cambodia* 11°1N 104°41E **39** G5
Anguang *China* 45°15N 123°45E **33** B12
Anguilla ☒ *W. Indies* 18°14N 63°5W **89** C7
Angul *India* 20°51N 85°6E **44** D7
Anguo *China* 38°28N 115°15E **32** E8
Angurugu *Australia* 14°0S 136°25E **62** A2
Angus *Canada* 44°19N 79°53W **82** B5
Angus □ *U.K.* 56°46N 2°56W **11** E6
Angwa → *Zimbabwe* 16°0S 30°23E **57** A5
Anhanduí → *Brazil* 21°46S 52°9W **95** A5
Anholt *Denmark* 56°42N 11°33E **9** H14
Anhua *China* 28°23N 111°12E **35** C8
Anhui □ *China* 32°0N 117°0E **35** B11
Anhwei = Anhui □
  China 32°0N 117°0E **35** B11
Anichab *Namibia* 21°0S 14°46E **56** B1
Animas → *U.S.A.* 36°43N 108°13W **77** H9
Anin *Burma* 15°36N 97°50E **38** E1
Anjalankoski *Finland* 60°45N 26°51E **8** F22
Anjangaon *India* 21°10N 77°20E **44** D3
Anjar = Hawsh Mūssá
  Lebanon 33°45N 35°55E **48** B4
Anjar *India* 23°6N 70°10E **42** H4
Anjengo = Anchuthengu
  India 8°40N 76°46E **45** K3
Anji *China* 30°46N 119°40E **35** B12
Anjidiv I. *India* 14°40N 74°10E **45** M9
Anjou *France* 47°20N 0°15W **20** C3
Anjouan *Comoros Is.* 12°15S 44°20E **55** a
Anju *N. Korea* 39°36N 125°40E **33** E13
Ankaboa, Tanjona
  Madag. 21°58S 43°20E **55** J8

Ankang *China* 32°40N 109°1E **32** H5
Ankara *Turkey* 39°57N 32°54E **19** G5
Ankaratra *Madag.* 19°25S 47°12E **55** H9
Ankazoabo *Madag.* 22°18S 44°31E **55** J8
Ankeny *U.S.A.* 41°44N 93°36W **80** E7
Ankleshwar *India* 21°38N 73°3E **44** D1
Ankola *India* 14°40N 74°18E **45** G2
Anlong *China* 25°2N 105°27E **34** E5
Anlong Veng *Cambodia* 14°14N 104°5E **38** E5
Anlu *China* 31°15N 113°45E **35** B9
Anmyeondo *S. Korea* 36°25N 126°25E **33** F14
Ann, C. *U.S.A.* 42°38N 70°35W **83** D14
Ann Arbor *U.S.A.* 42°17N 83°45W **81** D12
Anna *U.S.A.* 37°28N 89°15W **80** G9
Annaba *Algeria* 36°50N 7°46E **52** A7
Annalee → *Ireland* 54°2N 7°24W **10** B4
Annam = Trung Phan
  Vietnam 17°0N 109°0E **38** D6
Annamitique, Chaîne
  Asia 17°0N 106°40E **38** D6
Annan *U.K.* 54°59N 3°16W **11** G5
Annan → *U.K.* 54°58N 3°16W **11** G5
Annapolis *U.S.A.* 38°59N 76°30W **81** F15
Annapolis Royal *Canada* 44°44N 65°32W **73** D6
Annapurna *Nepal* 28°34N 83°50E **43** E10
Annean, L. *Australia* 26°54S 118°14E **61** E2
Annecy *France* 45°55N 6°8E **20** D7
Annette I. *U.S.A.* 55°9N 131°28W **70** D2
Anning *China* 24°55N 102°26E **34** E4
Anniston *U.S.A.* 33°39N 85°50W **85** E12
Annobón *Atl. Oc.* 1°25S 5°36E **51** G4
Annotto B. *Jamaica* 18°17N 76°45W **88** a
Annville *U.S.A.* 40°20N 76°31W **83** F8
Anping *Hebei, China* 38°15N 115°30E **32** E8
Anping *Liaoning, China* 41°5N 123°30E **33** D12
Anpu Gang *China* 21°25N 109°56E **34** G7
Anqing *China* 30°30N 117°3E **35** B11
Anqiu *China* 36°25N 119°10E **33** F10
Anren *China* 26°43N 113°18E **35** D9
Ansai *China* 36°50N 109°20E **32** F5
Ansan *S. Korea* 37°21N 126°52E **33** F14
Ansbach *Germany* 49°28N 10°34E **16** D6
Anse la Raye *St. Lucia* 13°55N 61°3W **89** f
Anse Royale *Seychelles* 4°44S 55°31E **55** b
Anshan *China* 41°5N 122°58E **33** D12
Anshun *China* 26°18N 105°57E **34** D5
Ansley *U.S.A.* 41°18N 99°23W **80** E4
Anson *U.S.A.* 32°45N 99°54W **84** E5
Anson B. *Australia* 13°20S 130°6E **60** B5
Ansongo *Mali* 15°25N 0°35E **52** E6
Ansonia *U.S.A.* 41°21N 73°5W **83** E11
Anstruther *U.K.* 56°14N 2°41W **11** E6
Ansudu *Indonesia* 2°11S 139°22E **37** E9
Antabamba *Peru* 14°40S 73°0W **92** F4
Antalaha *Madag.* 14°57S 50°20E **55** G10
Antalya *Turkey* 36°52N 30°45E **19** G5
Antalya Körfezi *Turkey* 36°15N 31°30E **19** G5
Antananarivo *Madag.* 18°55S 47°31E **55** H9
Antarctic Pen. *Antarctica* 67°0S 60°0W **5** C18
Antarctica 90°0S 0°0 **5** E
Antep = Gaziantep *Turkey* 37°6N 37°23E **46** B3
Antequera *Paraguay* 24°8S 57°7W **94** A4
Antequera *Spain* 37°5N 4°33W **21** D3
Antero, Mt. *U.S.A.* 38°41N 106°15W **76** G10
Anthony *Kans., U.S.A.* 37°9N 98°2W **80** G4
Anthony *N. Mex.,*
  U.S.A. 32°0N 106°36W **77** K10
Anti Atlas *Morocco* 30°0N 8°30W **52** C4
Anti-Lebanon = Sharqi, Al Jabal
  ash *Lebanon* 33°40N 36°10E **48** B5
Antibes *France* 43°34N 7°6E **20** E7
Anticosti, Î. d' *Canada* 49°30N 63°0W **73** C7
Antigo *U.S.A.* 45°9N 89°9W **80** C9
Antigonish *Canada* 45°38N 61°58W **73** C7
Antigua *Guatemala* 14°34N 90°41W **88** D1
Antigua *W. Indies* 17°0N 61°50W **89** C7
Antigua & Barbuda ■
  W. Indies 17°20N 61°48W **89** C7
Antikythira *Greece* 35°52N 23°15E **23** G10
Antilla *Cuba* 20°40N 75°50W **88** B4
Antilles = West Indies
  Cent. Amer. 15°0N 65°0W **89** D7
Antioch *U.S.A.* 38°1N 121°48W **78** G5
Antioquia *Colombia* 6°40N 75°55W **92** B3
Antipodes Is. *Pac. Oc.* 49°45S 178°40E **64** M9
Antlers *U.S.A.* 34°14N 95°37W **84** D7
Antofagasta *Chile* 23°50S 70°30W **94** A1
Antofagasta □ *Chile* 24°0S 69°0W **94** A2
Antofagasta de la Sierra
  Argentina 26°5S 67°20W **94** B2
Antofalla *Argentina* 25°30S 68°5W **94** B2
Antofalla, Salar de
  Argentina 25°40S 67°45W **94** B2
Anton *U.S.A.* 33°49N 102°10W **84** E3
Antonina *Brazil* 25°26S 48°42W **95** B6
Antrim *U.K.* 54°43N 6°14W **10** B5
Antrim *U.S.A.* 40°7N 81°21W **82** F3
Antrim □ *U.K.* 54°56N 6°25W **10** B5
Antrim, Mts. of *U.K.* 55°3N 6°14W **10** A5
Antrim Plateau *Australia* 18°8S 128°20E **60** C4
Antsalova *Madag.* 18°40S 44°37E **55** H8
Antsirabe *Madag.* 19°55S 47°2E **55** H9
Antsiranana *Madag.* 12°25S 49°20E **55** G9
Antsohihy *Madag.* 14°50S 47°59E **55** G9
Antu *China* 42°30N 128°20E **33** C15
Antwerp = Antwerpen
  Belgium 51°13N 4°25E **15** C4
Antwerp *U.S.A.* 44°12N 75°37W **83** B9
Antwerpen *Belgium* 51°13N 4°25E **15** C4
Antwerpen □ *Belgium* 51°15N 4°40E **15** C4
Anupgarh *India* 29°10N 73°10E **42** E5
Anuppur *India* 23°6N 81°41E **43** H9
Anuradhapura *Sri Lanka* 8°22N 80°28E **45** K5
Anurrete ⬡ *Australia* 20°50S 135°38E **62** C2
Anveh *Iran* 27°23N 54°11E **47** E7
Anvers = Antwerpen
  Belgium 51°13N 4°25E **15** C4

Anvers I. *Antarctica* 64°30S 63°40W **5** C17
Anwen *China* 29°4N 120°26E **35** C13
Anxi *Fujian, China* 25°2N 118°12E **35** E12
Anxi *Gansu, China* 40°30N 95°43E **30** C8
Anxian *China* 31°40N 104°25E **34** B5
Anxiang *China* 29°27N 112°11E **35** C9
Anxious B. *Australia* 33°24S 134°45E **63** E1
Anyang *China* 36°5N 114°21E **32** F8
Anyang *S. Korea* 37°23N 126°55E **33** F14
Anyer *Indonesia* 6°4S 105°53E **37** G11
Anyi *Jiangxi, China* 28°49N 115°25E **35** C10
Anyi *Shanxi, China* 35°2N 111°2E **32** G6
Anyuan *China* 25°9N 115°21E **35** E10
Anyue *China* 30°9N 105°50E **34** B5
Anza *U.S.A.* 33°35N 116°39W **79** M10
Anze *China* 36°10N 112°12E **32** F7
Anzhero-Sudzhensk
  Russia 56°10N 86°0E **26** D9
Ânzio *Italy* 41°27N 12°37E **22** D5
Ao Makham *Thailand* 7°50N 98°24E **39** a
Ao Phangnga △ *Thailand* 8°10N 98°32E **39** a
Aoga-Shima *Japan* 32°28N 139°46E **29** H9
Aohan Qi *China* 43°18N 119°43E **33** C10
Aoji *N. Korea* 42°31N 130°23E **33** C16
Aomen = Macau *China* 22°12N 113°33E **35** F9
Aomori *Japan* 40°45N 140°45E **28** D10
Aomori □ *Japan* 40°45N 140°40E **28** D10
†Aonach, An = Nenagh
  Ireland 52°52N 8°11W **10** D3
Aonla *India* 28°16N 79°11E **43** E8
Aorai, Mt. *Tahiti* 17°34S 149°30W **59** d
Aoraki Mount Cook *N.Z.* 43°36S 170°9E **59** E3
Aoral, Phnum *Cambodia* 12°0N 104°15E **39** G5
Aosta *Italy* 45°45N 7°20E **20** D7
Aotearoa = New Zealand ■
  Oceania 40°0S 176°0E **59** D6
Aoukâr *Mauritania* 17°40N 10°0W **52** E4
Aozou, Couloir d' *Chad* 22°0N 19°0E **53** D9
Apá → *S. Amer.* 22°6S 58°2W **94** A4
Apache *U.S.A.* 34°54N 98°22W **84** D5
Apache Junction *U.S.A.* 33°25N 111°33W **77** K8
Apalachee B. *U.S.A.* 30°0N 84°0W **85** G3
Apalachicola *U.S.A.* 29°43N 84°59W **85** G12
Apalachicola → *U.S.A.* 29°43N 84°58W **85** G12
Apaporis → *Colombia* 1°23S 69°25W **92** D5
Aparados da Serra △
  Brazil 29°10S 50°8W **95** B5
Aparri *Phil.* 18°22N 121°38E **37** A6
Apatity *Russia* 67°34N 33°22E **8** C25
Apatula = Finke
  Australia 25°34S 134°35E **62** D1
Apatzingán *Mexico* 19°5N 102°21W **86** D4
Apeldoorn *Neths.* 52°13N 5°57E **15** B5
Apennines = Appennini
  Italy 44°30N 10°0E **22** B4
Api *Nepal* 30°0N 80°57E **30** D5
Apia *Samoa* 13°50S 171°50W **59** b
Apiacás, Serra dos *Brazil* 9°50S 57°0W **92** E7
Apies → *S. Africa* 25°15S 28°8E **57** C4
Apizaco *Mexico* 19°25N 98°8W **87** D5
Aplao *Peru* 16°0S 72°40W **92** G4
Apo, Mt. *Phil.* 6°53N 125°14E **37** C7
Apollonia = Sūsah *Libya* 32°52N 21°59E **53** B10
Apolo *Bolivia* 14°30S 68°30W **92** F5
Apopa *El Salv.* 13°48N 89°10W **88** D2
Aporé → *Brazil* 19°27S 50°57W **93** G8
Apostle Is. *U.S.A.* 47°0N 90°40W **80** B8
Apostle Islands △ *U.S.A.* 46°55N 91°0W **80** B8
Apóstoles *Argentina* 28°0S 56°0W **95** B4
Apostolos Andreas, C.
  Cyprus 35°42N 34°35E **46** C3
Apoteri *Guyana* 4°2N 58°32W **92** C7
Appalachian Mts. *U.S.A.* 38°0N 80°0W **81** G14
Appennini *Italy* 44°30N 10°0E **22** B4
Apple Hill *Canada* 45°13N 74°46W **83** A10
Apple Valley *U.S.A.* 34°32N 117°14W **79** L9
Appleby-in-Westmorland
  U.K. 54°35N 2°29W **12** C5
Appledore *U.K.* 51°3N 4°13W **13** F3
Appleton *U.S.A.* 44°16N 88°25W **80** C9
Approuague →
  Fr. Guiana 4°30N 51°57W **93** C8
Aprília *Italy* 41°36N 12°39E **22** D5
Apsley *Canada* 44°45N 78°6W **82** B6
Apucarana *Brazil* 23°55S 51°33W **95** A5
Apure → *Venezuela* 7°37N 66°25W **92** B5
Apurímac → *Peru* 12°17S 73°56W **92** F4
Āq Qālā *Iran* 37°10N 54°30E **47** B7
Aqaba = Al 'Aqabah
  Jordan 29°31N 35°0E **48** F4
Aqaba, G. of *Red Sea* 29°0N 34°40E **46** D2
'Aqabah, Khalīj al = Aqaba, G. of
  Red Sea 29°0N 34°40E **46** D2
'Aqdā *Iran* 32°26N 53°37E **47** C7
'Aqrah *Iraq* 36°46N 43°45E **46** B4
Aqsay *Kazakhstan* 51°11N 53°0E **19** D9
Aqtaū *Kazakhstan* 43°39N 51°12E **19** F9
Aqtoghay *Kazakhstan* 46°57N 79°40E **26** E8
Aqtöbe *Kazakhstan* 50°17N 57°10E **19** D10
Aquidauana *Brazil* 20°30S 55°50W **93** H7
Aquila *Mexico* 18°36N 103°30W **86** D4
Aquiles Serdán *Mexico* 28°36N 105°53W **86** B3
Aquin *Haiti* 18°16N 73°24W **89** C5
Aquitain, Bassin *France* 44°0N 0°30W **20** D3
Ar Horqin Qi *China* 43°45N 120°0E **33** C11
Ar Rafid *Syria* 32°57N 35°52E **48** C4
Ar Raḩḩālīyah *Iraq* 32°44N 43°23E **46** C4
Ar Ramādī *Iraq* 33°25N 43°20E **46** C4
Ar Ramthā *Jordan* 32°34N 36°0E **48** C5
Ar Raqqah *Syria* 35°59N 39°8E **46** C3
Ar Rashidiya = Er Rachidia
  Morocco 31°58N 4°20W **52** B5
Ar Rass *Si. Arabia* 25°50N 43°40E **46** E4
Ar Rawḑah *Si. Arabia* 21°45N 42°50E **49** C4
Ar Rayyan *Qatar* 25°23N 51°20E **47** E6
Ar Rifā'ī *Iraq* 31°50N 46°10E **46** D5
Ar Riyāḑ *Si. Arabia* 24°41N 46°42E **46** E5
Ar Ru'ays *Qatar* 26°8N 51°12E **47** E6
Ar Rukhaymīyah *Iraq* 29°22N 45°38E **46** D5

Ar Rumaythah Iraq 31°31N 45°12E 46 D5
Ar Ruşāfah Syria 35°45N 38°49E 46 C3
Ar Ruţbah Iraq 33°0N 40°15E 46 C4
Ara India 25°35N 84°32E 43 G11
Arab U.S.A. 34°19N 86°30W 85 D11
Arab, Bahr el →
  South Sudan 9°0N 29°30E 53 G11
Arab, Shatt al → Asia 29°57N 48°34E 47 D6
Arabābād Iran 33°2N 57°41E 47 C8
Arabia Asia 25°0N 45°0E 24 F6
Arabian Desert = Sharqîya, Es
  Sahrâ esh Egypt 27°30N 32°30E 53 C12
Arabian Gulf = Persian Gulf
  Asia 27°0N 50°0E 47 E6
Arabian Sea Ind. Oc. 16°0N 65°0E 24 G8
Aracaju Brazil 10°55S 37°4W 93 F11
Aracati Brazil 4°30S 37°44W 93 D11
Araçatuba Brazil 21°10S 50°30W 95 A5
Aracena Spain 37°53N 6°38W 21 D2
Araçuaí Brazil 16°52S 42°4W 93 G10
Arad Israel 31°15N 35°12E 48 D4
Arad Romania 46°10N 21°20E 17 E11
Arādān Iran 35°21N 52°30E 47 C7
Arafura Sea E. Indies 9°0S 135°0E 58 B6
Aragón □ Spain 41°25N 0°40W 21 B5
Aragón → Spain 42°13N 1°44W 21 A5
Araguacema Brazil 8°50S 49°20W 93 E9
Araguaia → Brazil 5°21S 48°41W 93 E9
Araguaína Brazil 7°12S 48°12W 93 E9
Araguari Brazil 18°38S 48°11W 93 G9
Araguari → Brazil 1°15N 49°55W 93 C9
Arain India 26°27N 75°2E 42 F6
Arāk Algeria 25°20N 3°45E 52 C6
Arāk Iran 34°0N 49°40E 47 C6
Arakan = Rakhine □
  Burma 19°0N 94°15E 41 K18
Arakan Coast Burma 19°0N 94°0E 41 K19
Arakan Yoma Burma 20°0N 94°40E 41 K19
Arakkonam India 13°7N 79°43E 45 H4
Araks = Aras, Rūd-e →
  Asia 40°5N 48°29E 46 B5
Aral Kazakhstan 46°41N 61°45E 26 E7
Aral Sea Asia 45°0N 58°20E 26 E7
Aral Tengizi = Aral Sea
  Asia 45°0N 58°20E 26 E7
Aralsk = Aral Kazakhstan 46°41N 61°45E 26 E7
Aralskoye More = Aral Sea
  Asia 45°0N 58°20E 26 E7
Aramac Australia 22°58S 145°14E 62 C4
Aran → India 19°55N 78°12E 44 E4
Aran I. = Arranmore
  Ireland 55°0N 8°30W 10 A3
Aran Is. Ireland 53°6N 9°38W 10 C2
Aranda de Duero Spain 41°39N 3°42W 21 B4
Arandān Iran 35°23N 46°55E 46 C5
Arani India 12°43N 79°19E 45 H4
Aranjuez Spain 40°1N 3°40W 21 B4
Aranos Namibia 24°9S 19°7E 56 B2
Aransas Pass U.S.A. 27°55N 97°9W 84 H6
Aranyaprathet Thailand 13°41N 102°30E 38 F4
Arapahoe U.S.A. 40°18N 99°54W 80 E4
Arapey Grande →
  Uruguay 30°55S 57°49W 94 C4
Arapgir Turkey 39°5N 38°30E 46 B3
Arapiraca Brazil 9°45S 36°39W 93 E11
Arapongas Brazil 23°29S 51°28W 95 A5
Ar'ar Si. Arabia 30°59N 41°2E 46 D4
Araranguá Brazil 29°0S 49°30W 95 B6
Araraquara Brazil 21°50S 48°0W 93 H9
Ararás, Serra das Brazil 25°0S 53°10W 95 B5
Ararat Australia 37°16S 142°58E 63 F3
Ararat, Mt. = Ağrı Dağı
  Turkey 39°50N 44°15E 46 B5
Araria India 26°9N 87°33E 43 F12
Araripe, Chapada do
  Brazil 7°20S 40°0W 93 E11
Araruama, L. de Brazil 22°53S 42°12W 95 A7
Aras, Rūd-e → Asia 40°5N 48°29E 46 B5
Arauca Colombia 7°0N 70°40W 92 B4
Arauca → Venezuela 7°24N 66°35W 92 B5
Arauco Chile 37°16S 73°25W 94 D1
Aravalli Range India 25°0N 73°30E 42 G5
Araxá Brazil 19°35S 46°55W 93 G9
Araya, Pen. de Venezuela 10°40N 64°0W 92 A6
Arba Minch Ethiopia 6°0N 37°30E 49 F2
Arbat Iraq 35°25N 45°35E 46 C5
Árbatax Italy 39°56N 9°42E 22 E3
Arbīl Iraq 36°15N 44°5E 46 B5
Arborfield Canada 53°6N 103°39W 71 C8
Arborg Canada 50°54N 97°13W 71 C9
Arbroath U.K. 56°34N 2°35W 11 E6
Arbuckle U.S.A. 39°1N 122°3W 78 F4
Arcachon France 44°40N 1°10W 20 D3
Arcade U.S.A. 42°32N 78°25W 82 D6
Arcadia Fla., U.S.A. 27°13N 81°52W 85 H14
Arcadia La., U.S.A. 32°33N 92°55W 84 E8
Arcadia Pa., U.S.A. 40°47N 78°51W 82 F6
Arcata U.S.A. 40°52N 124°5W 76 F1
Archangel = Arkhangelsk
  Russia 64°38N 40°36E 18 B7
Archbald U.S.A. 41°30N 75°32W 83 E9
Archer → Australia 13°28S 141°41E 62 A3
Archer B. Australia 13°20S 141°30E 62 A3
Archer Bend = Mungkan
  Kandju △ Australia 13°35S 142°52E 62 A3
Arches △ U.S.A. 38°45N 109°25W 76 G9
Archipel-de-Mingan △
  Canada 50°13N 63°10W 73 B7
Archipiélago Los Roques △
  Venezuela 11°50N 66°44W 89 D6
Arckaringa Cr. →
  Australia 28°10S 135°22E 63 D2
Arco U.S.A. 43°38N 113°18W 76 E7
Arcos de la Frontera
  Spain 36°45N 5°49W 21 D3
Arcot India 12°53N 79°20E 45 H4
Arctic Bay Canada 73°1N 85°7W 69 C14
Arctic Mid-Ocean Ridge
  87°0N 90°0E 4 A
Arctic Ocean Arctic 78°0N 160°0W 4 B18

Arctic Red River = Tsiigehtchic
  Canada 67°15N 134°0W 68 B5
Arctowski Antarctica 62°30S 58°0W 5 C18
Arda → Bulgaria 41°40N 26°30E 23 D12
Ardabīl Iran 38°15N 48°18E 47 B6
Ardabīl □ Iran 38°15N 48°20E 47 B6
Ardakān = Sepīdān Iran 30°20N 52°5E 47 D7
Ardakān Iran 32°19N 53°59E 47 C7
Ardara Ireland 54°46N 8°25W 10 B3
Ardee Ireland 53°52N 6°33W 10 C5
Arden Canada 44°43N 76°56W 82 B8
Arden Calif., U.S.A. 38°36N 121°33W 78 G5
Arden Nev., U.S.A. 36°1N 115°14W 79 J11
Ardenne Belgium 49°50N 5°5E 15 E5
Ardennes = Ardenne
  Belgium 49°50N 5°5E 15 E5
Arderin Ireland 53°2N 7°39W 10 C4
Ardestān Iran 33°20N 52°25E 47 C7
Ardfert Ireland 52°20N 9°47W 10 D2
Ardglass U.K. 54°16N 5°36W 10 B6
Ardivachar Pt. U.K. 57°23N 7°26W 11 D1
Ardlethan Australia 34°22S 146°53E 63 E4
Ardmore Okla., U.S.A. 34°10N 97°8W 84 D6
Ardmore Pa., U.S.A. 40°2N 75°17W 83 F9
Ardnamurchan, Pt. of
  U.K. 56°43N 6°14W 11 E2
Ardnave Pt. U.K. 55°53N 6°20W 11 F2
Ardrossan Australia 34°26S 137°53E 63 E2
Ardrossan U.K. 55°39N 4°49W 11 F4
Ards Pen. U.K. 54°33N 5°34W 10 B6
Arecibo Puerto Rico 18°29N 66°43W 89 d
Areia Branca Brazil 5°0S 37°0W 93 E11
Arena, Pt. U.S.A. 38°57N 123°44W 78 G3
Arenal Honduras 15°21N 86°50W 88 C2
Arendal Norway 58°28N 8°46E 9 G13
Arequipa Peru 16°20S 71°30W 92 G4
Arévalo Spain 41°3N 4°43W 21 B3
Arezzo Italy 43°25N 11°53E 22 C4
Arga Turkey 38°21N 37°59E 46 B3
Argamasilla del Rey Spain 40°19N 3°26W 21 B4
Argarapa ☉ Australia 22°20S 134°58E 62 C1
Argenta Canada 50°11N 116°56W 70 C5
Argentan France 48°45N 0°1W 20 B3
Argentário, Mte. Italy 42°24N 11°9E 22 C4
Argentia Canada 47°18N 53°58W 73 C9
Argentina ■ S. Amer. 35°0S 66°0W 96 D3
Argentine Basin Atl. Oc. 45°0S 45°0W 96 F6
Argentino, L. Argentina 50°10S 73°0W 96 G2
Arges → Romania 44°5N 26°38E 17 F14
Arghandab → Afghan. 31°30N 64°15E 42 D1
Argolikos Kolpos Greece 37°20N 22°52E 23 F10
Argos Greece 37°40N 22°43E 23 F10
Argostoli Greece 38°11N 20°29E 23 E9
Arguello, Pt. U.S.A. 34°35N 120°39W 79 L6
Argun → Russia 53°20N 121°28E 31 A13
Argungu Nigeria 12°40N 4°31E 52 F6
Argus Pk. U.S.A. 35°52N 117°26W 79 K9
Argyle, L. Australia 16°20S 128°40E 60 C4
Argyll & Bute □ U.K. 56°13N 5°28W 11 E3
Århus = Aarhus Denmark 56°8N 10°11E 9 H14
Ariadnoye Russia 45°8N 134°25E 28 B7
Ariamsvlei Namibia 28°9S 19°51E 56 C2
Ariana, L' Tunisia 36°52N 10°12E 53 A8
Arica Chile 18°32S 70°20W 92 G4
Arica Colombia 2°0S 71°50W 92 D4
Arid, C. Australia 34°1S 123°10E 61 F3
Arida Japan 34°5N 135°8E 29 G7
Aride Seychelles 4°13S 55°40E 55 b
Ariège → France 43°30N 1°25E 20 E4
Arima Trin. & Tob. 10°38N 61°17W 93 K15
Arinos → Brazil 10°25S 58°20W 92 F7
Ario de Rosales Mexico 19°12N 101°43W 86 D4
Aripo, Mt. Trin. & Tob. 10°45N 61°15W 93 K15
Aripuanã Brazil 9°25S 60°30W 92 E6
Aripuanã → Brazil 5°7S 60°25W 92 E6
Ariquemes Brazil 9°55S 63°6W 92 E6
Arisaig U.K. 56°55N 5°51W 11 E3
Aristazabal I. Canada 52°40N 129°10W 70 C3
Ariyalur India 11°8N 79°8E 45 J4
Arizaro, Salar de
  Argentina 24°40S 67°50W 94 A2
Arizona Argentina 35°45S 65°25W 94 D2
Arizona □ U.S.A. 34°0N 112°0W 77 J8
Arizpe Mexico 30°20N 110°10W 86 A2
'Arjah Si. Arabia 24°43N 44°17E 46 E5
Arjeplog Sweden 66°3N 17°54E 8 C17
Arjepluovve = Arjeplog
  Sweden 66°3N 17°54E 8 C17
Arjona Colombia 10°14N 75°22W 92 A3
Arjuna Indonesia 7°49S 112°34E 37 G15
Arka Russia 60°15N 142°0E 27 C15
Arkadelphia U.S.A. 34°7N 93°4W 84 D8
Arkaig, L. U.K. 56°59N 5°10W 11 E3
Arkalgud India 12°46N 76°3E 45 H3
Arkalyk = Arqalyk
  Kazakhstan 50°13N 66°50E 26 D7
Arkansas □ U.S.A. 35°0N 92°30W 84 D8
Arkansas → U.S.A. 33°47N 91°4W 84 E9
Arkansas City U.S.A. 37°4N 97°2W 80 G5
Arkaroola Australia 30°20S 139°22E 63 E2
Arkhangelsk Russia 64°38N 40°36E 18 B7
Arki India 31°9N 76°58E 42 D7
Arklow Ireland 52°48N 6°10W 10 D5
Arkport U.S.A. 42°24N 77°42W 82 D7
Arkticheskiy, Mys Russia 81°10N 95°0E 27 A10
Arkville U.S.A. 42°9N 74°37W 83 D10
Arlanzón → Spain 42°3N 4°17W 21 A3
Arlbergpass Austria 47°9N 10°12E 16 E6
Arlbergtunnel Austria 47°9N 10°12E 16 E6
Arles France 43°41N 4°40E 20 E6
Arlington S. Africa 28°1S 27°53E 57 D4
Arlington N.Y., U.S.A. 41°42N 73°54W 83 E11
Arlington Oreg., U.S.A. 45°43N 120°12W 76 D3
Arlington S. Dak., U.S.A. 44°22N 97°8W 80 C5
Arlington Tex., U.S.A. 32°44N 97°6W 84 E6
Arlington Vt., U.S.A. 43°5N 73°9W 83 C11
Arlington Wash., U.S.A. 48°12N 122°8W 78 B4
Arlington Heights
  U.S.A. 42°5N 87°59W 80 D10
Arlit Niger 19°0N 7°38E 52 E7

Arlon Belgium 49°42N 5°49E 15 E5
Arlparra Australia 22°11S 134°30E 62 C1
Arltunga Australia 23°26S 134°41E 62 C1
Armadale Australia 32°9S 116°0E 61 F2
Armagh U.K. 54°21N 6°39W 10 B5
Armagh □ U.K. 54°18N 6°37W 10 B5
Armando Bermudez △
  Dom. Rep. 19°3N 71°0W 89 C5
Armavir Russia 45°2N 41°7E 19 E7
Armenia Colombia 4°35N 75°45W 92 C3
Armenia ■ Asia 40°20N 45°0E 19 F7
Armidale Australia 30°30S 151°40E 63 E5
Armori India 20°28N 79°59E 44 D4
Armour U.S.A. 43°19N 98°21W 80 D4
Armstrong B.C., Canada 50°25N 119°10W 70 C5
Armstrong Ont., Canada 50°18N 89°4W 72 B2
Armur India 18°48N 78°16E 44 E4
Arnarfjörður Iceland 65°48N 23°40W 8 D2
Arnaud → Canada 59°59N 69°46W 69 F18
Arnauti, C. Cyprus 35°6N 32°17E 46 C2
Arnett U.S.A. 36°8N 99°46W 84 C5
Arnhem Neths. 51°58N 5°55E 15 C5
Arnhem, C. Australia 12°20S 137°30E 62 A2
Arnhem B. Australia 12°20S 136°10E 62 A2
Arnhem Land Australia 13°10S 134°30E 62 A1
Arnhem Land ☉
  Australia 12°50S 134°50E 62 A1
Arno → Italy 43°41N 10°17E 22 C4
Arno Bay Australia 33°54S 136°34E 63 E2
Arnold U.K. 53°1N 1°7W 12 D6
Arnold Calif., U.S.A. 38°15N 120°21W 78 G6
Arnold Mo., U.S.A. 38°26N 90°23W 80 F9
Arnøya Norway 70°9N 20°40E 8 A19
Arnprior Canada 45°26N 76°21W 83 A8
Arnsberg Germany 51°24N 8°5E 16 C5
Aroa, Pte. Moorea 17°28S 149°46W 59 d
Aroab Namibia 26°41S 19°39E 56 C2
Aron → India 25°57N 77°56E 42 G6
Aros → Mexico 29°9N 107°57W 86 B3
Arqalyk Kazakhstan 50°13N 66°50E 26 D7
Arrah = Ara India 25°35N 84°32E 43 G11
Arrah Ivory C. 6°40N 3°58W 52 G5
Arran U.K. 55°34N 5°12W 11 F3
Arranmore Ireland 55°0N 8°30W 10 A3
Arras France 50°17N 2°46E 20 A5
Arrecife Canary Is. 28°57N 13°37W 52 C3
Arrecifes Argentina 34°6S 60°9W 94 C3
Arrée, Mts. d' France 48°26N 3°55W 20 B2
Arriaga Mexico 16°14N 93°54W 87 D6
Arrilalah Australia 23°43S 143°54E 62 C3
Arrino Australia 29°30S 115°40E 61 E2
Arrow, L. Ireland 54°3N 8°19W 10 B3
Arrowtown N.Z. 44°57S 168°50E 59 F2
Arroyo Grande U.S.A. 35°7N 120°35W 79 K6
Ars Iran 37°9N 47°46E 46 B5
Arsenault L. Canada 55°6N 108°32W 71 B7
Arsenev Russia 44°10N 133°15E 28 B6
Arsikere India 13°15N 76°15E 45 H3
Arta Greece 39°8N 21°2E 23 E9
Arteaga Mexico 18°28N 102°25W 86 D4
Artem Russia 43°22N 132°13E 28 C6
Artemivsk Ukraine 48°35N 38°0E 19 E6
Artemovsk Russia 54°45N 93°35E 27 D10
Artesia = Mosomane
  Botswana 24°2S 26°19E 56 B4
Artesia U.S.A. 32°51N 104°24W 77 K11
Arthur Canada 43°50N 80°32W 82 C4
Arthur → Australia 41°2S 144°40E 63 G3
Arthur Cr. → Australia 22°30S 136°25E 62 C2
Arthur Pt. Australia 22°7S 150°3E 62 C5
Arthur River Australia 33°20S 117°2E 61 F2
Arthur's Pass N.Z. 42°54S 171°35E 59 E3
Arthur's Pass △ N.Z. 42°53S 171°42E 59 E3
Arthur's Town Bahamas 24°38N 75°42W 89 B4
Artigas Antarctica 62°30S 58°0W 5 C18
Artigas Uruguay 30°20S 56°30W 94 C4
Artillery L. Canada 63°9N 107°52W 71 A7
Artois France 50°20N 2°30E 20 A5
Arts Bogd Uul Mongolia 44°40N 102°20E 32 B2
Artsyz Ukraine 46°4N 29°26E 17 E15
Artux China 39°40N 76°10E 30 D4
Artvin Turkey 41°14N 41°44E 19 F7
Artyk Russia 64°12N 145°6E 27 C15
Aru, Kepulauan Indonesia 6°0S 134°30E 37 F8
Aru Is. = Aru, Kepulauan
  Indonesia 6°0S 134°30E 37 F8
Arua Uganda 3°1N 30°58E 54 D6
Aruanã Brazil 14°54S 51°10W 93 F8
Aruba ☑ W. Indies 12°30N 70°0W 89 D6
Arué Tahiti 17°31S 149°30W 59 d
Arun → Nepal 26°55N 87°10E 43 F12
Arun → U.K. 50°49N 0°33W 13 G7
Arunachal Pradesh □
  India 28°0N 95°0E 41 F19
Aruppukkottai India 9°31N 78°8E 45 K4
Arusha Tanzania 3°20S 36°40E 54 E7
Aruvi → Sri Lanka 8°48N 79°53E 45 K4
Aruwimi →
  Dem. Rep. of the Congo 1°13N 23°36E 54 D4
Arvada Colo., U.S.A. 39°48N 105°5W 76 G11
Arvada Wyo., U.S.A. 44°39N 106°8W 76 D10
Arvakalu Sri Lanka 8°20N 79°58E 45 K4
Arvayheer Mongolia 46°15N 102°48E 30 B9
Arvi India 20°59N 78°12E 44 D4
Arviat Canada 61°6N 93°59W 71 A10
Arvidsjaur Sweden 65°35N 19°10E 8 D18
Arvika Sweden 59°40N 12°36E 9 G15
Arvin U.S.A. 35°12N 118°50W 79 K8
Arwal India 25°15N 84°41E 43 G11
Arxan China 47°11N 119°57E 33 B6
Arys Kazakhstan 42°26N 68°48E 26 E7
Arzamas Russia 55°27N 43°55E 18 C7
Arzanah U.A.E. 24°47N 52°34E 47 E7
As Safā Syria 33°10N 37°0E 48 B6
As Saffānīyah Si. Arabia 27°55N 48°50E 47 E6
As Safīrah Syria 36°5N 37°21E 46 B3
Aş Şahm Oman 24°10N 56°53E 47 E8
As Sājir Si. Arabia 25°11N 44°36E 46 E5
As Salamīyah Syria 35°1N 37°2E 46 C3

As Salmān Iraq 30°30N 44°32E 46 D5
As Salt Jordan 32°2N 35°43E 48 C4
As Sal'w'a Qatar 24°23N 50°50E 47 E6
As Samāwah Iraq 31°15N 45°15E 46 D5
As Sanamayn Syria 33°3N 36°10E 48 B5
As Sila' U.A.E. 24°4N 51°45E 47 E6
As Sukhnah Syria 34°52N 38°52E 46 C3
As Sulaymānīyah Iraq 35°35N 45°29E 46 C5
As Sulaymī Si. Arabia 26°17N 41°21E 46 E4
As Sulayyil Si. Arabia 20°27N 45°34E 49 C4
As Summān Si. Arabia 25°0N 47°0E 46 E5
As Suwaydā Syria 32°40N 36°30E 48 C5
As Suwaydā □ Syria 32°45N 36°45E 48 C5
As Suwayq Oman 23°51N 57°26E 47 F8
Aş Şuwayrah Iraq 32°55N 45°0E 46 C5
Asab Namibia 25°30S 18°0E 56 C2
Asad, Buḩayrat al Syria 36°0N 38°15E 46 C3
Asahi Japan 35°43N 140°39E 29 G10
Asahi-Gawa → Japan 34°36N 133°58E 29 G6
Asahigawa = Asahikawa
  Japan 43°46N 142°22E 28 C11
Asahikawa Japan 43°46N 142°22E 28 C11
Asaluyeh Iran 27°29N 52°37E 47 E7
Asamankese Ghana 5°50N 0°40W 52 G5
Asan → India 26°37N 78°24E 43 F8
Asansol India 23°40N 87°1E 43 H12
Asau Samoa 13°27S 172°33W 59 b
Asbesberge S. Africa 29°0S 23°0E 56 C3
Asbestos Canada 45°47N 71°58W 73 C5
Asbury Park U.S.A. 40°13N 74°1W 83 F10
Ascensión Mexico 31°6N 107°59W 86 A3
Ascensión, B. de la
  Mexico 19°40N 87°30W 87 D7
Ascension I. Atl. Oc. 7°57S 14°23W 51 G2
Aschaffenburg Germany 49°58N 9°6E 16 D5
Aschersleben Germany 51°45N 11°29E 16 C6
Áscoli Piceno Italy 42°51N 13°34E 22 C5
Ascope Peru 7°46S 79°8W 92 E3
Ascotán Chile 21°45S 68°17W 94 A2
Aseb Eritrea 13°0N 42°40E 49 E3
Asela Ethiopia 8°0N 39°0E 49 F2
Asenovgrad Bulgaria 42°1N 24°51E 23 C11
Aşgabat = Ashgabat
  Turkmenistan 37°58N 58°24E 47 B8
Ash Fork U.S.A. 35°13N 112°29W 77 J7
Ash Grove U.S.A. 37°19N 93°35W 80 G7
Ash Shabakah Iraq 30°49N 43°39E 46 D4
Ash Shamāl □ Lebanon 34°25N 36°0E 48 A5
Ash Shāmīyah Iraq 31°55N 44°35E 46 D5
Ash Shāriqah U.A.E. 25°23N 55°26E 47 E7
Ash Sharmah Si. Arabia 28°1N 35°16E 46 D2
Ash Sharqāt Iraq 35°27N 43°16E 46 C4
Ash Shaţrah Iraq 31°30N 46°10E 46 D5
Ash Shawbak Jordan 30°32N 35°34E 46 D2
Ash Shiḩr Yemen 14°45N 49°36E 49 E4
Ash Shināfīyah Iraq 31°35N 44°39E 46 D5
Ash Shu'bah Si. Arabia 28°54N 44°44E 46 D5
Ash Shumlūl Si. Arabia 26°31N 47°20E 46 E5
Ash Shūr'a Iraq 35°58N 43°13E 46 C4
Ash Shurayf Si. Arabia 25°43N 39°14E 46 E3
Ash Shuwayfāt Lebanon 33°45N 35°30E 48 B4
Asha Russia 55°0N 57°16E 18 D10
Ashbourne U.K. 53°2N 1°43W 12 D6
Ashburn U.S.A. 31°43N 83°39W 85 F13
Ashburton N.Z. 43°53S 171°48E 59 E3
Ashburton → Australia 21°40S 114°56E 60 D1
Ashcroft Canada 50°40N 121°20W 70 C4
Ashdod Israel 31°49N 34°35E 48 D3
Ashdown U.S.A. 33°40N 94°8W 84 E7
Asheboro U.S.A. 35°43N 79°49W 85 D15
Ashern Canada 51°11N 98°21W 71 C9
Asherton U.S.A. 28°27N 99°46W 84 G5
Asheville U.S.A. 35°36N 82°33W 85 D13
Asheweig → Canada 54°17N 87°12W 72 B2
Ashford Australia 29°15S 151°3E 63 D5
Ashford U.K. 51°8N 0°53E 13 F8
Ashgabat Turkmenistan 37°58N 58°24E 47 B8
Ashibetsu Japan 43°31N 142°11E 28 C11
Ashikaga Japan 36°28N 139°29E 29 F9
Ashington U.K. 55°11N 1°33W 12 B6
Ashizuri-Uwakai △
  Japan 32°56N 132°32E 29 H6
Ashizuri-Zaki Japan 32°44N 133°0E 29 H6
Ashkarkot Afghan. 33°3N 67°58E 42 C2
Ashkhabad = Ashgabat
  Turkmenistan 37°58N 58°24E 47 B8
Āshkhāneh Iran 37°26N 56°55E 47 B8
Ashland Kans., U.S.A. 37°11N 99°46W 80 G4
Ashland Ky., U.S.A. 38°28N 82°38W 81 F12
Ashland Maine, U.S.A. 46°38N 68°24W 81 B19
Ashland Mont., U.S.A. 45°36N 106°16W 76 D10
Ashland Ohio, U.S.A. 40°52N 82°19W 82 F2
Ashland Oreg., U.S.A. 42°12N 122°43W 76 E2
Ashland Va., U.S.A. 37°46N 77°29W 81 G15
Ashland Wis., U.S.A. 46°35N 90°53W 80 B8
Ashley N. Dak., U.S.A. 46°2N 99°22W 80 B4
Ashley Pa., U.S.A. 41°12N 75°55W 83 E9
Ashmore and Cartier Is.
  Ind. Oc. 12°15S 123°0E 60 B3
Ashmore Reef Australia 12°14S 123°5E 60 B3
Ashmyany Belarus 54°26N 25°52E 17 A13
Ashokan Res. U.S.A. 41°56N 74°13W 83 E10
Ashoknagar India 24°34N 77°43E 42 G7
Ashqelon Israel 31°42N 34°35E 48 D3
Ashta India 23°1N 76°43E 42 H7
Ashtabula U.S.A. 41°52N 80°47W 82 E4
Ashti Maharashtra, India 21°12N 78°11E 44 D4
Ashti Maharashtra, India 18°50N 75°15E 44 E2
Āshtīyan Iran 34°31N 50°0E 47 C6
Ashton S. Africa 33°50S 20°5E 56 D3
Ashton U.S.A. 44°4N 111°27W 76 D8
Ashuanipi, L. Canada 52°45N 66°15W 73 B6
Ashuapmushuan →
  Canada 48°37N 72°20W 72 C5
Ashur = Assur Iraq 35°27N 43°15E 46 C4
Ashville U.S.A. 40°34N 78°33W 82 F6
Asia 45°0N 75°0E 24 E9
Asia, Kepulauan Indonesia 1°0N 131°13E 37 D8

Asifabad India 19°20N 79°24E 44 E4
Asinara Italy 41°4N 8°16E 22 D3
Asinara, G. dell' Italy 41°0N 8°30E 22 D3
Asino Russia 57°0N 86°0E 26 D9
Asipovichy Belarus 53°19N 28°33E 17 B15
'Asīr Si. Arabia 18°40N 42°30E 49 D3
Asir, Ras Somalia 11°55N 51°10E 49 E5
Aska India 19°2N 84°42E 44 K14
Askham S. Africa 26°59S 20°47E 56 C3
Askim Norway 59°35N 11°10E 9 G14
Askja Iceland 65°3N 16°48W 8 D5
Askøyna Norway 60°29N 5°10E 8 F11
Asmara = Asmera
  Eritrea 15°19N 38°55E 49 D2
Asmera Eritrea 15°19N 38°55E 49 D2
Åsnen Sweden 56°37N 14°45E 9 H16
Aso Kujū △ Japan 32°53N 131°6E 29 H5
Aspatria U.K. 54°47N 3°19W 12 C4
Aspen U.S.A. 39°11N 106°49W 76 G10
Aspermont U.S.A. 33°8N 100°14W 84 E4
Aspiring, Mt. N.Z. 44°23S 168°46E 59 F2
Aspur India 23°58N 74°7E 42 H6
Asquith Canada 52°8N 107°13W 71 C7
Assab = Aseb Eritrea 13°0N 42°40E 49 E3
Assal, L. Djibouti 11°40N 42°26E 49 E3
Assam □ India 26°0N 93°0E 41 G18
Assateague Island △
  U.S.A. 38°15N 75°10W 81 F16
Assaye India 20°15N 75°53E 44 D2
Asse Belgium 50°24N 4°10E 15 D4
Assen Neths. 53°0N 6°35E 15 A6
Assiniboia Canada 49°40N 105°59W 71 D7
Assiniboine → Canada 49°53N 97°8W 71 D9
Assiniboine, Mt. Canada 50°52N 115°39W 70 C5
Assis Brazil 22°40S 50°20W 95 A5
Assisi Italy 43°4N 12°37E 22 C5
Assur Iraq 35°27N 43°15E 46 C4
Assynt, L. U.K. 58°10N 5°3W 11 C3
Astana Kazakhstan 51°10N 71°30E 30 A3
Āstāneh Iran 37°17N 49°59E 47 B6
Astara Azerbaijan 38°30N 48°50E 47 B6
Astarabad = Gorgān Iran 36°55N 54°30E 47 B7
Asti Italy 44°54N 8°12E 20 D8
Astipalaia Greece 36°32N 26°22E 23 F12
Astorga Spain 42°29N 6°8W 21 A2
Astoria U.S.A. 46°11N 123°50W 78 D3
Astrakhan Russia 46°25N 48°5E 19 E8
Astrebla Downs
  Australia 24°12S 140°34E 62 C3
Asturias □ Spain 43°15N 6°0W 21 A3
Asunción Paraguay 25°10S 57°30W 94 B4
Asunción Nochixtlán
  Mexico 17°28N 97°14W 87 D5
Aswân Egypt 24°4N 32°57E 53 D12
Aswân High Dam = Sadd el Aali
  Egypt 23°54N 32°54E 53 D12
Asyût Egypt 27°11N 31°4E 53 C12
Aţ Ţafīlah Jordan 30°45N 35°30E 48 E4
Aţ Ţafīlah □ Jordan 30°45N 35°30E 48 E4
Aţ Ţā'if Si. Arabia 21°5N 40°27E 49 C3
Aţ Ta'mīm □ Iraq 35°30N 44°20E 46 C5
Aţ Ţīrāq Si. Arabia 27°19N 44°33E 46 E5
Aţ Tubayq Si. Arabia 29°30N 37°0E 46 D3
Aţ Ţunayb Jordan 31°48N 35°57E 48 D4
Atacama □ Chile 27°30S 70°0W 94 B2
Atacama, Desierto de
  Chile 24°0S 69°20W 94 A2
Atacama, Salar de Chile 23°30S 68°20W 94 A2
Atakeye ☉ Australia 22°30S 133°45E 60 D5
Atakpamé Togo 7°31N 1°13E 52 G6
Atalaya Peru 10°45S 73°50W 92 F4
Atami Japan 35°5N 139°4E 29 G9
Atamyrat Turkmenistan 37°50N 65°12E 28 F7
Atapupu Indonesia 9°0S 124°51E 37 F6
Atâr Mauritania 20°30N 13°5W 52 D3
Atari Pakistan 30°56N 74°2E 42 D6
Atascadero U.S.A. 35°29N 120°40W 78 K6
Atasu Kazakhstan 48°30N 71°0E 26 E8
Atatürk Barajı Turkey 37°28N 38°30E 19 G6
Atauro E. Timor 8°10S 125°30E 37 F7
Atbara Sudan 17°42N 33°59E 53 E12
'Atbara, Nahr → Sudan 17°40N 33°56E 53 E12
Atbasar Kazakhstan 51°48N 68°20E 26 D7
Atchafalaya B. U.S.A. 29°25N 91°25W 84 G9
Atchison U.S.A. 39°34N 95°7W 80 F6
Āteshān Iran 35°35N 52°37E 47 C7
Ath Belgium 50°38N 3°47E 15 D3
Athabasca Canada 54°45N 113°20W 70 C6
Athabasca → Canada 58°40N 110°50W 71 B6
Athabasca, L. Canada 59°15N 109°15W 71 B7
Athabasca Sand Dunes △
  Canada 59°4N 108°43W 71 B7
Athagarh India 20°32N 85°37E 44 D7
Athboy Ireland 53°36N 6°56E 10 C5
Athenry Ireland 53°18N 8°44W 10 C3
Athens Ala., U.S.A. 34°48N 86°58W 85 D11
Athens Ga., U.S.A. 33°57N 83°23W 85 E13
Athens N.Y., U.S.A. 42°16N 73°49W 83 D11
Athens Ohio, U.S.A. 39°20N 82°6W 81 F12
Athens Pa., U.S.A. 41°57N 76°31W 83 E8
Athens Tenn., U.S.A. 35°27N 84°36W 85 D12
Athens Tex., U.S.A. 32°12N 95°51W 84 E7
Atherley Canada 44°37N 79°20W 82 B5
Atherton Australia 17°17S 145°30E 62 B4
Athlone Ireland 53°25N 7°56W 10 C4
Athmallik India 20°43N 84°32E 44 D7
Athni India 16°44N 75°6E 44 F2
Athol U.S.A. 42°36N 72°14W 83 D12
Atholl, Forest of U.K. 56°51N 3°50W 11 E5
Atholville Canada 47°59N 66°43W 73 C6
Athos Greece 40°9N 24°22E 23 D11
Athy Ireland 53°0N 7°0W 10 C5
Ati Chad 13°13N 18°20E 53 F9
Atik L. Canada 55°15N 96°0W 71 B9
Atikaki △ Canada 51°30N 95°31W 71 C9
Atikameg → Canada 52°30N 82°46W 72 B3
Atikokan Canada 48°45N 91°37W 72 C1
Atikonak L. Canada 52°40N 64°32W 73 B7
Atimaono Tahiti 17°46S 149°28W 59 d
Atirampattinam India 10°28N 79°20E 45 J4

Atiu *Cook Is.* 20°0S 158°10W **65** J12
Atka *Russia* 60°50N 151°48E **27** C16
Atka I. *U.S.A.* 52°7N 174°30W **74** E5
Atkinson *U.S.A.* 42°32N 98°59W **80** D4
Atlanta *U.S.A.* 33°7N 94°10W **84** D7
Atlantic *U.S.A.* 41°24N 95°1W **80** E6
Atlantic City *U.S.A.* 39°21N 74°27W **81** F16
Atlantic-Indian Basin
  Antarctica 60°0S 30°0E **5** B4
Atlantic Ocean 0°0 20°0W **2** D8
Atlantis *S. Africa* 33°34S 18°29E **56** D2
Atlas Mts. = Haut Atlas
  Morocco 32°30N 5°0W **52** B4
Atlin *Canada* 59°31N 133°41W **70** B2
Atlin, L. *Canada* 59°26N 133°45W **70** B2
Atlin △ *Canada* 59°10N 134°30W **70** B2
Atmakur *Andhra Pradesh,*
  India 14°37N 79°40E **45** G4
Atmakur *Andhra Pradesh,*
  India 15°53N 78°35E **45** G4
Atmakur *Telangana, India* 18°45N 78°39E **44** H4
Atmore *U.S.A.* 31°2N 87°29W **85** F11
Atoka *U.S.A.* 34°23N 96°8W **84** D6
Atolia *U.S.A.* 35°19N 117°37W **79** K9
Atqasuk *U.S.A.* 70°28N 157°24W **74** A8
Atrai → *Bangla.* 24°7N 89°22E **43** G13
Atrak = Atrek →
  Turkmenistan 37°35N 53°58E **47** B8
Atrauli *India* 28°2N 78°20E **42** E8
Atrek → *Turkmenistan* 37°35N 53°58E **47** B8
Atsuta *Japan* 43°24N 141°26E **28** C10
Attalla *U.S.A.* 34°1N 86°6W **85** D11
Attapeu *Laos* 14°48N 106°50E **38** E6
Attawapiskat *Canada* 52°56N 82°24W **72** B3
Attawapiskat → *Canada* 52°57N 82°18W **72** B3
Attawapiskat L. *Canada* 52°18N 87°54W **72** B2
Attica *Ind., U.S.A.* 40°18N 87°15W **80** E10
Attica *Ohio, U.S.A.* 41°4N 82°53W **82** E2
Attikamagen L. *Canada* 55°0N 66°30W **73** B6
Attleboro *U.S.A.* 41°57N 71°17W **83** E13
Attock *Pakistan* 33°52N 72°20E **42** C5
Attopeu = Attapeu *Laos* 14°48N 106°50E **38** E6
Attu I. *U.S.A.* 52°55N 172°55E **74** E2
Attur *India* 11°35N 78°30E **45** H4
Atuel → *Argentina* 36°17S 66°50W **94** D2
Åtvidaberg *Sweden* 58°12N 16°0E **9** G17
Atwater *U.S.A.* 37°21N 120°37W **78** H6
Atwood *Canada* 43°40N 81°1W **82** C3
Atwood *U.S.A.* 39°48N 101°3W **80** F3
Atyraū *Kazakhstan* 47°5N 52°0E **19** E9
Au Sable → *U.S.A.* 44°25N 83°20W **81** C12
Au Sable Forks *U.S.A.* 44°27N 73°41W **83** B11
Au Sable Pt. *U.S.A.* 44°20N 83°20W **82** B1
Auas *Honduras* 15°29N 84°20W **88** D3
Auasberg *Namibia* 22°37S 17°13E **56** B2
Aubagne *France* 43°17N 5°37E **20** E6
Aube □ *France* 48°34N 3°43E **20** B5
Auberry *U.S.A.* 37°7N 119°29W **78** H7
Auburn *Ala., U.S.A.* 32°36N 85°29W **85** E12
Auburn *Calif., U.S.A.* 38°54N 121°4W **78** G5
Auburn *Ind., U.S.A.* 41°22N 85°4W **81** E11
Auburn *Maine, U.S.A.* 44°6N 70°14W **81** C18
Auburn *N.Y., U.S.A.* 42°56N 76°34W **83** D8
Auburn *Nebr., U.S.A.* 40°23N 95°51W **80** E7
Auburn *Pa., U.S.A.* 40°36N 76°6W **83** F8
Auburn *Wash., U.S.A.* 47°18N 122°14W **78** C4
Auburn Ra. *Australia* 25°15S 150°30E **63** D5
Auburndale *U.S.A.* 28°4N 81°48W **85** G14
Aubusson *France* 45°57N 2°11E **20** D5
Auch *France* 43°39N 0°36E **20** E4
Auchterarder *U.K.* 56°18N 3°41W **11** E5
Auchtermuchty *U.K.* 56°18N 3°13W **11** E5
Auckland *N.Z.* 36°52S 174°46E **59** B5
Auckland Is. *Pac. Oc.* 50°40S 166°5E **64** N8
Aude → *France* 43°13N 3°14E **20** E5
Auden *Canada* 50°14N 87°53W **72** B2
Audubon *U.S.A.* 41°43N 94°56W **80** E6
Augathella *Australia* 25°48S 146°35E **63** D4
Aughnacloy *U.K.* 54°25N 6°59W **10** B5
Aughrim *Ireland* 53°18N 8°19W **10** C3
Augrabies Falls *S. Africa* 28°35S 20°20E **56** C3
Augrabies Falls △
  S. Africa 28°40S 20°22E **56** C3
Augsburg *Germany* 48°25N 10°52E **16** D6
Augusta *Australia* 34°19S 115°9E **61** F2
Augusta *Italy* 37°13N 15°13E **22** F6
Augusta *Ark., U.S.A.* 35°17N 91°22W **84** D9
Augusta *Ga., U.S.A.* 33°28N 81°58W **85** E14
Augusta *Kans., U.S.A.* 37°41N 96°59W **80** G6
Augusta *Maine, U.S.A.* 44°19N 69°47W **81** C19
Augusta *Mont., U.S.A.* 47°30N 112°24W **76** C7
Augustów *Poland* 53°51N 23°0E **17** B12
Augustus, Mt. *Australia* 24°20S 116°50E **61** D2
Augustus I. *Australia* 15°20S 124°30E **60** C3
Aujuittuq = Grise Fiord
  Canada 76°25N 82°57W **69** B15
Aukštaitija △ *Lithuania* 55°15N 26°0E **9** J22
Aukum *U.S.A.* 38°34N 120°43W **78** G6
Aul *India* 20°41N 86°39E **44** D8
Aulavik △ *Canada* 73°42N 119°55W **68** C8
Auld, L. *Australia* 22°25S 123°50E **60** D3
Ault *U.S.A.* 40°35N 104°44W **76** F11
Aundah *India* 19°32N 77°3E **44** E3
Aundh *India* 17°33N 74°23E **44** F2
Aunis *France* 46°5N 0°50W **20** C3
Aunu'u *Amer. Samoa* 14°20S 170°31W **59** b
Auponhia *Indonesia* 1°58S 125°27E **37** E7
Aur, Pulau *Malaysia* 2°35N 104°10E **39** L5
Auraiya *India* 26°28N 79°33E **43** F8
Aurangabad *Bihar, India* 24°45N 84°18E **43** G11
Aurangabad *Maharashtra,*
  India 19°50N 75°23E **44** E2
Aurich *Germany* 53°28N 7°28E **16** B4
Aurillac *France* 44°55N 2°26E **20** D5
Aurora *Canada* 44°0N 79°28W **82** C5
Aurora *S. Africa* 32°40S 18°29E **56** C2
Aurora *Colo., U.S.A.* 39°42N 104°49W **76** G11
Aurora *Ill., U.S.A.* 41°45N 88°19W **80** E9
Aurora *Mo., U.S.A.* 36°58N 93°43W **80** G7

Aurora *N.Y., U.S.A.* 42°45N 76°42W **83** D8
Aurora *Nebr., U.S.A.* 40°52N 98°0W **80** E5
Aurora *Ohio, U.S.A.* 41°21N 81°20W **82** E3
Aurukun *Australia* 13°20S 141°45E **62** A3
Aurukun ○ *Australia* 13°36S 141°48E **62** A3
Aus *Namibia* 26°35S 16°12E **56** C2
Ausa *India* 18°15N 76°30E **44** E3
Ausable → *Canada* 43°19N 81°46W **82** C3
Auschwitz = Oświęcim
  Poland 50°2N 19°11E **17** C10
Austen Harbour *India* 12°55N 92°45E **45** H11
Austin *Minn., U.S.A.* 43°40N 92°58W **80** D7
Austin *Nev., U.S.A.* 39°30N 117°4W **76** G5
Austin *Pa., U.S.A.* 41°38N 78°6W **82** E6
Austin, L. *Australia* 27°40S 118°0E **61** E2
Austin I. *Canada* 61°10N 94°0W **71** A10
Austra *Norway* 65°8N 11°55E **8** D14
Austral Is. = Tubuaï, Îs.
  French Polynesia 25°0S 150°0W **65** K13
Austral Seamount Chain
  Pac. Oc. 24°0S 150°0W **65** K13
Australia ■ *Oceania* 23°0S 135°0E **58** D6
Australian-Antarctic Basin
  S. Ocean 60°0S 120°0E **5** C9
Australian Capital Territory □
  Australia 35°30S 149°0E **63** F4
Australind *Australia* 33°17S 115°42E **61** F2
Austria ■ *Europe* 47°0N 14°0E **16** E8
Austvågøya *Norway* 68°20N 14°40E **8** B16
Autlán de Navarro
  Mexico 19°46N 104°22W **86** D4
Autun *France* 46°58N 4°17E **20** C6
Auvergne □ *France* 45°20N 3°15E **20** D5
Auvergne, Mts. d' *France* 45°20N 2°55E **20** D5
Auxerre *France* 47°48N 3°32E **20** C5
Auyuittuq △ *Canada* 67°30N 66°0W **69** B13
Av-Dovurak *Russia* 51°17N 91°35E **27** D10
Ava *U.S.A.* 36°57N 92°40W **80** G7
Avachinskaya Sopka
  Russia 53°15N 158°50E **27** D16
Avallon *France* 47°30N 3°53E **20** C5
Avalon *U.S.A.* 33°21N 118°20W **79** M8
Avanigadda *India* 16°0N 80°56E **45** G5
Avanos *Turkey* 38°43N 34°51E **46** B2
Avaré *Brazil* 23°4S 48°58W **95** A6
Avawatz Mts. *U.S.A.* 35°40N 116°30W **79** K10
Aveiro *Brazil* 3°10S 55°5W **93** D7
Aveiro *Portugal* 40°37N 8°38W **21** B1
Åvej *Iran* 35°40N 49°15E **47** C6
Avellaneda *Italy* 40°54N 14°47E **22** D6
Avellino *Italy* 40°54N 14°46E **22** D6
Avenal *U.S.A.* 36°0N 120°8W **78** K6
Aversa *Italy* 40°58N 14°12E **22** D6
Avery *U.S.A.* 47°15N 115°49W **76** C6
Aves, I. de *W. Indies* 15°45N 63°55W **89** C7
Aves, Is. las *Venezuela* 12°0N 67°30W **89** D6
Avesta *Sweden* 60°9N 16°10E **9** F17
Aveyron □ *France* 44°5N 1°16E **20** D4
Avezzano *Italy* 42°2N 13°25E **22** C5
Aviá Terai *Argentina* 26°45S 60°50W **94** B3
Aviemore *U.K.* 57°12N 3°50W **11** D5
Avignon *France* 43°57N 4°50E **20** E6
Ávila *Spain* 40°39N 4°43W **21** B3
Avila Beach *U.S.A.* 35°11N 120°44W **79** K6
Avilés *Spain* 43°35N 5°57W **21** A3
Avis *U.S.A.* 41°11N 77°19W **82** E7
Avissawella *Sri Lanka* 6°56N 80°11E **45** L5
Avoca *U.S.A.* 42°25N 77°25W **82** D7
Avoca → *Australia* 35°40S 143°43E **63** F3
Avoca → *Ireland* 52°48N 6°10W **10** D5
Avola *Canada* 51°45N 119°19W **70** C5
Avola *Italy* 36°56N 15°7E **22** F6
Avon *U.S.A.* 42°55N 77°45W **82** D7
Avon → *Australia* 31°40S 116°7E **61** F2
Avon → *Bristol, U.K.* 51°29N 2°41W **13** F5
Avon → *Dorset, U.K.* 50°44N 1°46W **13** G6
Avon → *Warks., U.K.* 52°0N 2°8W **13** E5
Avon Park *U.S.A.* 27°36N 81°31W **85** H14
Avonlea *Canada* 50°0N 105°0W **71** D8
Avonmore *Canada* 45°10N 74°58W **83** A10
Avonmouth *U.K.* 51°30N 2°42W **13** F5
Avranches *France* 48°40N 1°20W **20** B3
Awa-Shima *Japan* 38°27N 139°14E **28** E9
A'waj → *Syria* 33°23N 36°20E **48** B5
Awaji-Shima *Japan* 34°30N 134°50E **29** G7
'Awālī *Bahrain* 26°0N 50°30E **47** E6
Awantipur *India* 33°55N 75°3E **43** C6
Awarja → *India* 17°5N 76°15E **44** F3
Awasa *Ethiopia* - 7°2N 38°28E **49** F2
Awash *Ethiopia* 9°1N 40°10E **49** F3
Awatere → *N.Z.* 41°37S 174°10E **59** D5
Awbārī *Libya* 26°46N 12°57E **53** C8
Awbārī, Idehan *Libya* 27°10N 11°30E **53** C8
Awe, L. *U.K.* 56°17N 5°16W **11** E3
Awjilah *Libya* 29°8N 21°7E **53** C10
Axe → *U.K.* 50°42N 3°4W **13** F5
Axel Heiberg I. *Canada* 80°0N 90°0W **69** B14
Axim *Ghana* 4°51N 2°15W **52** H5
Axios → *Greece* 40°57N 22°35E **23** D10
Axminster *U.K.* 50°46N 3°0W **13** G4
Ayabaca *Peru* 4°40S 79°53W **92** D3
Ayabe *Japan* 35°20N 135°20E **29** G7
Ayacucho *Argentina* 37°5S 58°20W **94** D4
Ayacucho *Peru* 13°0S 74°0W **92** F4
Ayaguz = Ayaköz
  Kazakhstan 48°10N 80°10E **30** B5
Ayakkum Hu *China* 37°30N 89°20E **30** D6
Ayaköz *Kazakhstan* 48°10N 80°10E **30** B5
Ayakudi *India* 10°28N 77°56E **45** J3
Ayamonte *Spain* 37°12N 7°24W **21** D2
Ayan *Russia* 56°30N 138°16E **27** D14
Ayaviri *Peru* 14°50S 70°35W **92** F4
Aydın *Turkey* 37°51N 27°51E **23** F12
Aydingkol Hu *China* 42°40N 89°15E **30** C6
Ayer *U.S.A.* 42°34N 71°35W **83** D13
Ayer Hitam *Malaysia* 1°55N 103°11E **39** d
Ayer's Cliff *Canada* 45°10N 72°3W **83** A12

Ayers Rock = Uluru
  Australia 25°23S 131°5E **61** E5
Ayeyarwady = Ayeyawadi →
  Burma 15°50N 95°6E **41** M19
Ayeyawadi → *Burma* 15°50N 95°6E **41** M19
Aykhal *Russia* 66°0N 111°30E **27** C12
Aykino *Russia* 62°15N 49°56E **18** B8
Aylesbury *U.K.* 51°49N 0°49W **13** F7
Aylmer *Canada* 42°46N 80°59W **82** D3
Aylmer, L. *Canada* 64°5N 108°30W **68** E10
Ayn Dār *Si. Arabia* 25°55N 49°10E **47** E7
Ayn Zālah *Iraq* 36°45N 42°35E **46** B4
Ayolas *Paraguay* 27°10S 56°59W **94** B4
Ayon, Ostrov *Russia* 69°50N 169°0E **27** C17
'Ayoûn el 'Atroûs
  Mauritania 16°38N 9°37W **52** E4
Ayr *Australia* 19°35S 147°25E **62** B4
Ayr *Canada* 43°17N 80°27W **82** C4
Ayr *U.K.* 55°28N 4°38W **11** F4
Ayr → *U.K.* 55°28N 4°38W **11** F4
Ayre, Pt. of *I. of Man* 54°25N 4°21W **12** C3
Ayteke Bi *Kazakhstan* 45°48N 62°6E **26** E7
Ayton *Australia* 15°56S 145°22E **62** B4
Aytos *Bulgaria* 42°42N 27°16E **23** C12
Ayu, Kepulauan *Indonesia* 0°35N 131°5E **37** D8
Ayutla *Guatemala* 14°40N 92°10W **88** D1
Ayutla de los Libres
  Mexico 16°54N 99°13W **87** D5
Ayutthaya = Phra Nakhon Si
  Ayutthaya *Thailand* 14°25N 100°30E **38** E3
Ayvacık *Turkey* 39°36N 26°24E **23** E12
Ayvalık *Turkey* 39°20N 26°46E **23** E12
Az Zabadānī *Syria* 33°43N 36°5E **48** B5
Az Z̧āhirīyah *West Bank* 31°25N 34°58E **48** D3
Az Z̧ahrān *Si. Arabia* 26°10N 50°7E **47** E6
Az Zarqā *Jordan* 32°5N 36°4E **48** C5
Az Zarqā *U.A.E.* 24°53N 53°4E **47** E7
Az Zarqā' □ *Jordan* 32°5N 36°4E **48** C5
Az Zāwiyah *Libya* 32°52N 12°56E **53** B8
Az Zībār *Iraq* 36°52N 44°4E **46** B5
Az Zilfī *Si. Arabia* 26°12N 44°52E **46** E5
Az Zubayr *Iraq* 30°26N 47°40E **46** D5
Azad Kashmir □ *Pakistan* 33°50N 73°50E **43** C5
Azamgarh *India* 26°5N 83°13E **43** F10
Azangaro *Peru* 14°55S 70°13W **92** F4
Azaouad *Mali* 19°0N 3°0W **52** E5
Āzār Shahr *Iran* 37°45N 45°59E **46** B5
Azarān *Iran* 37°25N 47°16E **46** B5
Azbine = Aïr *Niger* 18°30N 8°0E **52** E7
Azerbaijan ■ *Asia* 40°20N 48°0E **19** F8
Azogues *Ecuador* 2°35S 78°0W **92** D3
Azores = Açores, Is. dos
  Atl. Oc. 38°0N 27°0W **52** a
Azov *Russia* 47°3N 39°25E **19** E6
Azov, Sea of *Europe* 46°0N 36°30E **19** E6
Azovskoye More = Azov, Sea of
  Europe 46°0N 36°30E **19** E6
Azraq ash Shīshān *Jordan* 31°50N 36°49E **48** D5
Aztec *U.S.A.* 36°49N 107°59W **77** H10
Azua de Compostela
  Dom. Rep. 18°25N 70°44W **89** C5
Azuaga *Spain* 38°16N 5°39W **21** C3
Azuero, Pen. de *Panama* 7°30N 80°30W **88** E3
Azul *Argentina* 36°42S 59°43W **94** D4
Azumino *Japan* 36°20N 137°50E **29** F8
Azur, Côte d' *France* 43°25N 7°10E **20** E7
Azusa *U.S.A.* 34°8N 117°52W **79** L9
Azzel Matti, Sebkra
  Algeria 26°10N 0°43E **52** C6

B

Ba Be △ *Vietnam* 22°25N 105°37E **38** A5
Ba Don *Vietnam* 17°45N 106°26E **38** D6
Ba Dong *Vietnam* 9°40N 106°33E **39** H6
Ba Ngoi *Vietnam* 11°54N 109°10E **39** G7
Ba Ria *Vietnam* 10°30N 107°10E **39** G6
Ba Tri *Vietnam* 10°2N 106°36E **39** G6
Ba Vì △ *Vietnam* 21°1N 105°22E **38** B5
Ba Xian = Bazhou *China* 39°8N 116°22E **32** E9
Baa *Indonesia* 10°50S 123°0E **60** B3
Baalbek = Ba'labakk
  Lebanon 34°0N 36°10E **48** B5
Baardheere *Somalia* 2°20N 42°27E **49** G3
Baarle-Nassau *Belgium* 51°27N 4°56E **15** C4
Bab el Mandeb *Red Sea* 12°35N 43°25E **49** E3
Bābā, Koh-i- *Afghan.* 34°30N 67°0E **40** B5
Baba Budan Hills *India* 13°30N 75°44E **45** H2
Baba Burnu *Turkey* 39°29N 26°2E **23** E12
Bābā Kalū *Iran* 30°7N 50°49E **47** D6
Babadag *Romania* 44°53N 28°44E **17** F15
Babaeski *Turkey* 41°26N 27°6E **23** D12
Babahoyo *Ecuador* 1°40S 79°30W **92** D3
Babai = Sarju → *India* 27°21N 81°23E **43** F9
Babai *Nepal* 28°10N 81°23E **43** E10
Babar *Indonesia* 8°0S 129°30E **37** F7
Babar *India* 31°7N 69°32E **42** D3
Babarkach *Pakistan* 29°45N 68°0E **42** E3
Babb *U.S.A.* 48°51N 113°27W **76** B7
Babelthuap *Palau* 7°30N 134°30E **36** C4
Babi Besar, Pulau
  Malaysia 2°25N 103°59E **39** L4
Babian Jiang → *China* 22°55N 101°47E **34** F3
Bābil □ *Iraq* 32°30N 44°30E **46** C5
Babinda *Australia* 17°20S 145°56E **62** B4
Babine *Canada* 55°22N 126°37W **70** B3
Babine → *Canada* 55°45N 127°44W **70** B3
Babine L. *Canada* 54°48N 126°0W **70** C3
Babo *Indonesia* 2°30S 133°30E **37** E8
Bābol *Iran* 36°40N 52°50E **47** B7
Bābol Sar *Iran* 36°45N 52°45E **47** B7

Babruysk *Belarus* 53°10N 29°15E **17** B15
Babuhri *India* 26°49N 69°43E **42** F3
Babusar Pass *Pakistan* 35°12N 73°59E **43** B5
Babuyan Chan. *Phil.* 18°40N 121°30E **37** A6
Babylon *Iraq* 32°34N 44°22E **46** C5
Bac Can *Vietnam* 22°8N 105°49E **34** F5
Bac Giang *Vietnam* 21°16N 106°11E **34** G6
Bac Lieu *Vietnam* 9°17N 105°43E **39** H5
Bac Ninh *Vietnam* 21°13N 106°4E **34** G6
Bac Phan *Vietnam* 22°0N 105°0E **34** G5
Bacabal *Brazil* 4°15S 44°45W **93** D10
Bacalar *Mexico* 18°43N 88°27W **87** D7
Bacan, Kepulauan
  Indonesia 0°35S 127°30E **37** E7
Bacarra *Phil.* 18°15N 120°37E **37** A6
Bacău *Romania* 46°35N 26°55E **17** E14
Bacerac *Mexico* 30°18N 108°50W **86** A3
Bach Long Vi, Dao
  Vietnam 20°10N 107°40E **38** C6
Bach Ma △ *Vietnam* 16°11N 107°49E **38** D6
Bachhwara *India* 25°35N 85°54E **43** G11
Back → *Canada* 65°10N 104°0W **68** D11
Bacolod *Phil.* 10°40N 122°57E **37** B6
Bacuk *Malaysia* 6°4N 102°25E **39** J4
Bácum *Mexico* 27°33N 110°5W **86** B2
Bad → *U.S.A.* 44°21N 100°22W **80** C3
Bad Axe *U.S.A.* 43°48N 83°0W **82** C2
Bad Ischl *Austria* 47°44N 13°38E **16** E7
Bad Kissingen *Germany* 50°11N 10°4E **16** C6
Bada Barabil *India* 22°7N 85°24E **43** H11
Badagara = Vadakara
  India 11°35N 75°40E **45** J2
Badain Jaran Shamo
  China 40°23N 102°0E **30** D9
Badajós, L. *Brazil* 3°15S 62°50W **92** D6
Badajoz *Spain* 38°50N 6°59W **21** C2
Badakhshān □ *Afghan.* 36°30N 71°0E **40** A7
Badaling *China* 40°20N 116°0E **32** D9
Badalona *Spain* 41°26N 2°15E **21** B7
Badalzai *Afghan.* 29°50N 65°35E **42** E1
Badami *India* 15°55N 75°41E **45** G2
Badampahar *India* 22°10N 86°10E **44** D8
Badanah *Si. Arabia* 30°58N 41°30E **46** D4
Badarinath *India* 30°45N 79°30E **43** D8
Badas, Kepulauan
  Indonesia 0°45N 107°5E **36** D3
Baddo → *Pakistan* 28°0N 64°20E **40** F4
Bade *Indonesia* 7°10S 139°35E **37** F9
Baden *Austria* 48°1N 16°13E **16** D9
Baden *U.S.A.* 40°38N 80°14W **82** F4
Baden-Baden *Germany* 48°44N 8°13E **16** D5
Baden-Württemberg □
  Germany 48°20N 8°40E **16** D5
Badgam *India* 34°1N 74°45E **43** B6
Badgastein *Austria* 47°7N 13°9E **16** E7
Badger *Canada* 49°0N 56°4W **73** C8
Badger *U.S.A.* 36°38N 119°1W **78** J7
Bādghīs □ *Afghan.* 35°0N 63°0E **40** B3
Badgingarra △ *Australia* 30°23S 115°22E **61** F2
Badin *Pakistan* 24°38N 68°54E **42** G3
Badlands *U.S.A.* 43°55N 102°30W **80** D2
Badlands △ *U.S.A.* 43°38N 102°56W **80** D2
Badme *Africa* 14°43N 37°48E **46** G4
Badnera *India* 20°48N 77°44E **44** D3
Badrah *Iraq* 33°6N 45°58E **46** C5
Badrain Jaran Shamo
  China 40°40N 103°20E **32** D2
Badrinath *India* 30°44N 79°29E **43** D8
Badu *Australia* 10°7S 142°11E **62** a
Badulla *Sri Lanka* 7°1N 81°7E **45** L5
Badung, Bukit *Indonesia* 8°49S 115°10E **37** K18
Badung, Selat *Indonesia* 8°37S 115°20E **37** K18
Badvel *India* 14°45N 79°3E **45** G4
Baena *Spain* 37°37N 4°20W **21** D3
Baengnyeongdo
  S. Korea 37°57N 124°40E **33** F13
Baeza *Spain* 37°57N 3°25W **21** D4
Bafatá *Guinea-Biss.* 12°8N 14°40W **52** F3
Baffin B. *N. Amer.* 72°0N 64°0W **66** B3
Baffin I. *Canada* 68°0N 75°0W **69** D17
Bafing → *Mali* 13°49N 10°50W **52** F3
Bafliyūn *Syria* 36°37N 36°59E **46** B3
Bafoulabé *Mali* 13°50N 10°55W **52** F3
Bafoussam *Cameroon* 5°28N 10°25E **54** C2
Bāfq *Iran* 31°40N 55°25E **47** D7
Bafra *Turkey* 41°34N 35°54E **19** F6
Bāft *Iran* 29°15N 56°38E **47** D8
Bafwasende
  Dem. Rep. of the Congo 1°3N 27°5E **54** D5
Bagaha *India* 27°6N 84°5E **44** A7
Bagalkot *India* 16°10N 75°40E **45** F2
Bagamoyo *Tanzania* 6°28S 38°55E **54** F7
Bagan Datoh *Malaysia* 3°59N 100°47E **39** L3
Bagan Serai *Malaysia* 5°1N 100°32E **39** K3
Baganga *Phil.* 7°34N 126°33E **37** C7
Bagani *Namibia* 18°7S 21°41E **56** A3
Bagansiapiapi *Indonesia* 2°12N 100°50E **36** D2
Bagasra *India* 21°30N 71°0E **42** J4
Bagaud *India* 22°19N 75°53E **42** H6
Bagdad *U.S.A.* 34°35N 115°53W **79** L11
Bagdarin *Russia* 54°26N 113°36E **27** D12
Bagé *Brazil* 31°20S 54°15W **95** C5
Bagenalstown *Ireland* 52°42N 6°58W **10** D5
Bagepalli *India* 13°47N 77°47E **45** H3
Bageshwar *India* 29°51N 79°46E **43** E8
Bagevadi *India* 16°35N 75°58E **44** F2
Baggs *U.S.A.* 41°2N 107°39W **76** F10
Bagh *Pakistan* 33°59N 73°45E **43** C5
Baghain → *India* 25°32N 81°1E **43** G9
Bagheria *Italy* 38°5N 13°30E **22** E5
Baghlān *Afghan.* 32°12N 68°46E **40** B6
Baghlān □ *Afghan.* 36°0N 68°30E **40** B6
Bagley *U.S.A.* 47°32N 95°24W **80** B6
Baglung *Nepal* 28°16N 83°36E **43** E10
Bago *Burma* 17°20N 96°29E **41** L20
Bagodar *India* 24°5N 85°52E **43** G11
Bagrationovsk *Russia* 54°23N 20°39E **9** J19
Baguio *Phil.* 16°26N 120°34E **37** A6
Bahadurganj *India* 26°16N 87°49E **43** F12
Bahadurgarh *India* 28°40N 76°57E **42** E7

Bahama, Canal Viejo de
  W. Indies 22°10N 77°30W **88** B4
Bahamas ■ *N. Amer.* 24°0N 75°0W **89** B5
Bahār *Iran* 34°54N 48°26E **47** C6
Baharampur *India* 24°2N 88°27E **43** G13
Baharu Pandan = Pandan
  Malaysia 1°32N 103°46E **39** d
Bahawalnagar *Pakistan* 30°0N 73°15E **42** E5
Bahawalpur *Pakistan* 29°24N 71°40E **42** E4
Bäherden *Turkmenistan* 38°25N 57°26E **47** B8
Baheri *India* 28°45N 79°34E **43** E8
Bahía = Salvador *Brazil* 13°0S 38°30W **93** F11
Bahía □ *Brazil* 12°0S 42°0W **93** F10
Bahía, Is. de la *Honduras* 16°45N 86°15W **88** C2
Bahía Blanca *Argentina* 38°35S 62°13W **94** D3
Bahía de Caráquez
  Ecuador 0°40S 80°27W **92** D2
Bahía de Los Angeles
  Mexico 28°56N 113°34W **86** B2
Bahía Honda *Cuba* 22°54N 83°10W **88** B3
Bahía Kino *Mexico* 28°47N 111°58W **86** B2
Bahía Laura *Argentina* 48°10S 66°30W **96** F3
Bahía Negra *Paraguay* 20°5S 58°5W **92** H7
Bahir Dar *Ethiopia* 11°37N 37°10E **49** E2
Bahmanzād *Iran* 31°15N 51°47E **47** D6
Bahraich *India* 27°38N 81°37E **43** F9
Bahrain ■ *Asia* 26°0N 50°35E **47** E6
Bahror *India* 27°51N 76°20E **42** F7
Bāhū Kalāt *Iran* 25°43N 61°25E **47** E9
Bai Bung, Mui = Ca Mau, Mui
  Vietnam 8°38N 104°44E **39** H5
Bai Thuong *Vietnam* 19°54N 105°23E **38** C5
Baia Mare *Romania* 47°40N 23°35E **17** E12
Baião *Brazil* 2°40S 49°40W **93** D9
Baïbokoum *Chad* 7°46N 15°43E **53** G9
Baidoa = Baydhabo
  Somalia 3°8N 43°30E **49** G3
Baie-Comeau *Canada* 49°12N 68°10W **73** C6
Baie-St-Paul *Canada* 47°28N 70°32W **73** C5
Baie Ste-Anne *Seychelles* 4°18S 55°45E **55** b
Baie-Trinité *Canada* 49°25N 67°20W **73** C6
Baie Verte *Canada* 49°55N 56°12W **73** C8
Baihar *India* 22°6N 80°33E **43** H9
Baihe *Hubei, China* 32°50N 110°5E **32** H6
Baihe *Jilin, China* 42°27N 128°8E **33** C15
Baihetan Dam *China* 27°11N 102°54E **34** D4
Ba'ījī *Iraq* 35°0N 43°30E **46** C4
Baijnath *India* 29°55N 79°37E **43** E8
Baikal, L. = Baykal, Oz.
  Russia 53°0N 108°0E **27** D11
Baikonur = Bayqonyr
  Kazakhstan 45°40N 63°20E **26** E7
Baikunthpur *India* 23°15N 82°33E **43** H10
Bailadila, Mt. *India* 18°43N 81°15E **44** E5
Baile Átha Fhirdhia = Ardee
  Ireland 53°52N 6°33W **10** C5
Baile Átha Í = Athy *Ireland* 53°0N 7°0W **10** C5
Baile Átha Luain = Athlone
  Ireland 53°25N 7°56W **10** C4
Baile Átha Troim = Trim
  Ireland 53°33N 6°48W **10** C5
Bailešti *Romania* 44°1N 23°20E **17** F12
Bailhongal *India* 15°55N 74°53E **45** G2
Bailieborough *Ireland* 53°56N 6°59W **10** C5
Baile Sear = Baleshare
  U.K. 57°31N 7°22W **11** D1
Baine *China* 42°0N 128°0E **31** C14
Baing *Indonesia* 10°14S 120°34E **37** F6
Bainiu *China* 32°50N 112°15E **32** H7
Bains *K. of Jordan* 28°40N 81°8W **85** G14
Baird Mts. *U.S.A.* 67°0N 160°0W **74** B8
Bairiki = Tarawa *Kiribati* 1°30N 173°0E **64** G9
Bairin Youqi *China* 43°30N 118°35E **33** C10
Bairin Zuoqi *China* 43°58N 119°15E **33** C10
Bairnsdale *Australia* 37°48S 147°36E **63** F4
Baisha *China* 34°20N 112°32E **32** G7
Baisha Li *China* 19°12N 109°20E **38** C7
Baishan = Hunjiang
  China 41°54N 126°26E **33** D14
Baitadi *Nepal* 29°35N 80°25E **43** E9
Baitarani → *India* 20°45N 86°48E **44** D8
Baiyin *China* 36°45N 104°14E **32** F3
Baiyü *China* 31°16N 98°50E **34** B2
Baiyu Shan *China* 37°15N 107°30E **32** F4
Baj Baj *India* 22°30N 88°5E **43** H13
Baja *Hungary* 46°12N 18°59E **17** E10
Baja, Pta. *Mexico* 29°58N 115°49W **86** B1
Baja California *Mexico* 31°10N 115°12W **86** A1
Baja California □ *Mexico* 30°0N 115°0W **86** B2
Baja California Sur □
  Mexico 25°50N 111°50W **86** B2
Bajag *India* 22°40N 81°21E **43** H9
Bajatrejo *Indonesia* 8°29S 114°19E **37** J17
Bajawa *Indonesia* 8°47S 120°59E **37** F6
Bajera *Indonesia* 8°31S 115°2E **37** J18
Bājgīrān *Iran* 37°36N 58°24E **47** B8
Bajimba, Mt. *Australia* 29°17S 152°6E **63** D5
Bajo Boquete *Panama* 8°46N 82°27E **88** E3
Bajo Nuevo *Caribbean* 15°40N 78°50W **88** C4
Bajoga *Nigeria* 10°57N 11°20E **53** F8
Bajool *Australia* 23°40S 150°35E **62** C5
Bakel *Senegal* 14°56N 12°20W **52** F3
Baker *Calif., U.S.A.* 35°16N 116°4W **79** K10
Baker *Mont., U.S.A.* 46°22N 104°17W **76** C11
Baker, L. *Canada* 64°0N 95°0W **68** E12
Baker, Mt. *U.S.A.* 48°50N 121°49W **76** B3
Baker City *U.S.A.* 44°47N 117°50W **76** D5
Baker I. *Pac. Oc.* 0°10N 176°35W **64** G10
Baker I. *U.S.A.* 55°20N 133°40W **70** B2

Baker L. *Australia* 26°54S 126°5E **61** E4
Baker Lake *Canada* 64°20N 96°3W **68** E12
Bakers Creek *Australia* 21°13S 149°7E **62** C4
Bakersfield *Calif., U.S.A.* 35°23N 119°1W **79** K8
Bakersfield *Vt., U.S.A.* 44°45N 72°48W **83** B12
Bakharden = Bäherden
  Turkmenistan 38°25N 57°26E **47** B8
Bākhtarān = Kermānshāh
  Iran 34°23N 47°0E **46** C5
Bākhtarān = Kermānshāh □
  Iran 34°0N 46°30E **46** C5
Bakhtegān, Daryācheh-ye
  Iran 29°40N 53°50E **47** D7
Bakhtegān △ *Iran* 29°51N 53°40E **47** D7
Bakı *Azerbaijan* 40°29N 49°56E **47** A6
Bakkafjörður *Iceland* 66°2N 14°48W **8** C6
Bakkagerði *Iceland* 65°31N 13°49W **8** D7
Bakony *Hungary* 47°10N 17°30E **17** E9
Bakony Forest = Bakony
  Hungary 47°10N 17°30E **17** E9
Bakouma *C.A.R.* 5°40N 22°56E **54** C4
Bakswaho *India* 24°15N 79°18E **43** G8
Baku = Bakı *Azerbaijan* 40°29N 49°56E **47** A6
Bakutis Coast *Antarctica* 74°0S 120°0W **5** D15
Baky = Bakı *Azerbaijan* 40°29N 49°56E **47** A6
Bala *Canada* 45°1N 79°37W **82** A5
Bala *U.K.* 52°54N 3°36W **12** E4
Bala, L. *U.K.* 52°53N 3°37W **12** E4
Balabac I. *Phil.* 8°0N 117°0E **36** C5
Balabac Str. *E. Indies* 7°53N 117°5E **36** C5
Balabagh *Afghan.* 34°25N 70°12E **42** B4
Ba'labakk *Lebanon* 34°0N 36°10E **48** B5
Balabalangan, Kepulauan
  Indonesia 2°20S 117°30E **36** E5
Balad *Iraq* 34°0N 44°9E **46** C5
Balad Rūz *Iraq* 33°42N 45°5E **46** C5
Balādeh *Fārs, Iran* 29°17N 51°56E **47** D6
Balādeh *Māzandaran, Iran* 36°12N 51°48E **47** B6
Balaghat *India* 21°49N 80°12E **44** E3
Balaghat Ra. *India* 18°50N 76°30E **44** E3
Balaguer *Spain* 41°50N 0°50E **21** B6
Balaklava *Ukraine* 44°30N 33°30E **19** F5
Balakovo *Russia* 52°4N 47°55E **18** D8
Balamau *India* 27°10N 80°21E **43** F9
Balancán *Mexico* 17°48N 91°32W **87** D6
Balangir *India* 20°43N 83°35E **44** D6
Balapur *India* 20°40N 76°45E **44** D3
Balashov *Russia* 51°30N 43°10E **19** D7
Balasinor *India* 22°57N 73°23E **42** H5
Balasore = Baleshwar
  India 21°35N 87°3E **44** D8
Balaton *Hungary* 46°50N 17°40E **17** E9
Balbina, Represa de *Brazil* 2°0S 59°30W **92** D7
Balboa *Panama* 8°57N 79°34W **88** E4
Balbriggan *Ireland* 53°37N 6°11W **10** C5
Balcarce *Argentina* 38°0S 58°10W **94** D4
Balcarres *Canada* 50°50N 103°35W **71** C8
Balchik *Bulgaria* 43°28N 28°11E **23** C13
Balclutha *N.Z.* 46°15S 169°45E **59** G2
Balcones Escarpment
  U.S.A. 29°30N 99°15W **84** G5
Bald I. *Australia* 34°57S 118°27E **61** F2
Bald Knob *U.S.A.* 35°19N 91°34W **84** D9
Baldock L. *Canada* 56°33N 97°57W **71** B9
Baldwin *Mich., U.S.A.* 43°54N 85°51W **81** D11
Baldwin *Pa., U.S.A.* 40°21N 79°58W **82** F5
Baldwinsville *U.S.A.* 43°10N 76°20W **83** C8
Baldy Peak *U.S.A.* 33°54N 109°34W **77** K9
Baleares, Is. *Spain* 39°30N 3°0E **21** C7
Balearic Is. = Baleares, Is.
  Spain 39°30N 3°0E **21** C7
Balearic Sea *Spain* 40°0N 2°0E **21** B6
Baleine → *Canada* 58°15N 67°40W **73** A6
Baleine, Petite R. de la →
  Canada 56°0N 76°45W **72** A4
Baleshare *U.K.* 57°31N 7°22W **11** D1
Baleshwar *India* 21°35N 87°3E **44** D8
Baley *Russia* 51°36N 116°37E **27** D12
Balfate *Honduras* 15°48N 86°25W **88** C2
Balgo *Australia* 20°9S 127°58E **60** D4
Balharshah *India* 19°50N 79°23E **44** E4
Bali *India* 25°11N 73°17E **42** G5
Bali *Indonesia* 8°20S 115°0E **37** J18
Bali □ *Indonesia* 8°20S 115°0E **37** J17
Bali, Selat *Indonesia* 8°18S 114°25E **37** J17
Bali Barat △ *Indonesia* 8°12S 114°35E **37** J17
Bali Sea *Indonesia* 8°0S 115°0E **37** J17
Baliapal *India* 21°40N 87°17E **43** J12
Baliguda *India* 20°12N 83°55E **44** D6
Balik Pulau *Malaysia* 5°21N 100°14E **39** c
Balikeşir *Turkey* 39°39N 27°53E **23** E12
Balikpapan *Indonesia* 1°10S 116°55E **36** E5
Balimbing *Phil.* 5°5N 119°58E **37** C5
Baling *Malaysia* 5°41N 100°55E **39** K3
Balkan Mts. = Stara Planina
  Bulgaria 43°15N 23°0E **23** C10
Balkanabat *Turkmenistan* 39°30N 54°22E **47** B7
Balkhash = Balqash
  Kazakhstan 46°50N 74°50E **26** E8
Balkhash, Ozero = Balqash Köli
  Kazakhstan 46°0N 74°50E **30** B3
Balkonda *India* 18°52N 78°21E **44** E4
Ballachulish *U.K.* 56°41N 5°8W **11** E3
Balladonia *Australia* 32°27S 123°51E **61** F3
Ballaghaderreen *Ireland* 53°55N 8°34W **10** C3
Ballarat *Australia* 37°33S 143°50E **63** F3
Ballard, L. *Australia* 29°20S 120°40E **61** E3
Ballari *India* 15°10N 76°56E **45** G3
Ballater *U.K.* 57°3N 3°3W **11** D5
Ballenas, Canal de
  Mexico 29°10N 113°29W **86** B2
Balleny Is. *Antarctica* 66°30S 163°0E **5** C11
Ballia *India* 25°46N 84°12E **43** G11
Ballina *Australia* 28°50S 153°31E **63** D5
Ballina *Ireland* 54°7N 9°9W **10** B2
Ballinasloe *Ireland* 53°20N 8°13W **10** C3
Ballincollig *Ireland* 51°53N 8°33W **10** E3
Ballinger *U.S.A.* 31°45N 99°57W **84** F5

Ballinrobe *Ireland* 53°38N 9°13W **10** C2
Ballinskelligs B. *Ireland* 51°48N 10°13W **10** E1
Ballston Spa *U.S.A.* 43°0N 73°51W **83** D11
Ballybofey *Ireland* 53°32N 6°16W **10** C5
Ballybunion *Ireland* 52°31N 9°40W **10** D2
Ballycanew *Ireland* 52°37N 6°19W **10** D5
Ballycastle *U.K.* 55°12N 6°15W **10** A5
Ballyclare *U.K.* 54°46N 6°0W **10** B5
Ballycroy △ *Ireland* 54°5N 9°50W **10** B2
Ballydehob *Ireland* 51°34N 9°28W **10** E2
Ballygawley *U.K.* 54°27N 7°2W **10** B4
Ballyhaunis *Ireland* 53°46N 8°46W **10** C3
Ballyheige *Ireland* 52°23N 9°49W **10** D2
Ballymena *U.K.* 54°52N 6°17W **10** B5
Ballymoney *U.K.* 55°5N 6°31W **10** A5
Ballymote *Ireland* 54°5N 8°31W **10** B3
Ballynahinch *U.K.* 54°24N 5°54W **10** B6
Ballyporeen *Ireland* 52°16N 8°6W **10** D3
Ballyquintin Pt. *U.K.* 54°20N 5°30W **10** B6
Ballyshannon *Ireland* 54°30N 8°11W **10** B3
Balmaceda *Chile* 46°0S 71°50W **96** F2
Balmertown *Canada* 51°4N 93°41W **71** C10
Balmoral *Australia* 37°15S 141°48E **63** F3
Balmorhea *U.S.A.* 30°59N 103°45W **84** F3
Balneário Camboriú
  Brazil 26°59S 48°38W **95** B6
Balochistan = Baluchistan □
  Pakistan 27°30N 65°0E **40** F4
Balod *India* 20°44N 81°13E **44** D5
Balonne → *Australia* 28°47S 147°56E **63** D4
Balotra *India* 25°50N 72°14E **42** G5
Balqash *Kazakhstan* 46°50N 74°50E **26** E8
Balqash Köli *Kazakhstan* 46°0N 74°50E **30** B3
Balrampur *India* 27°30N 82°20E **43** F10
Balranald *Australia* 34°38S 143°33E **63** E3
Balsas → *Brazil* 7°15S 44°35W **93** E9
Balsas → *Mexico* 17°55N 102°10W **86** D4
Balsas del Norte *Mexico* 18°0N 99°46W **87** D5
Balta *Ukraine* 47°56N 29°45E **17** D15
Bălți *Moldova* 47°48N 27°58E **17** E14
Baltic Sea *Europe* 57°0N 19°0E **9** H18
Baltimore *Ireland* 51°29N 9°22W **10** E2
Baltimore *Md., U.S.A.* 39°17N 76°36W **81** F15
Baltimore *Ohio, U.S.A.* 39°51N 82°36W **82** G2
Baltimore-Washington Int. ✈
  (BWI) *U.S.A.* 39°10N 76°40W **81** F15
Baltinglass *Ireland* 52°56N 6°43W **10** D5
Baltit *Pakistan* 36°15N 74°40E **43** A6
Baltiysk *Russia* 54°41N 19°58E **9** J18
Baluchistan □ *Pakistan* 27°30N 65°0E **40** F4
Balurghat *India* 25°15N 88°44E **43** G13
Balvi *Latvia* 57°8N 27°15E **9** H22
Balya *Turkey* 39°44N 27°35E **23** E12
Balykchy *Kyrgyzstan* 42°26N 76°12E **30** C4
Balyqshy *Kazakhstan* 47°4N 51°52E **19** E9
Bam *Iran* 29°7N 58°14E **47** D8
Bama *China* 24°8N 107°12E **34** E6
Bama *Nigeria* 11°33N 13°41E **53** F8
Bamaga *Australia* 10°50S 142°25E **62** A3
Bamaji L. *Canada* 51°9N 91°25W **72** B1
Bamako *Mali* 12°34N 7°55W **52** F4
Bambari *C.A.R.* 5°40N 20°35E **54** C4
Bambaroo *Australia* 18°50S 146°10E **62** B4
Bamberg *Germany* 49°54N 10°54E **16** D6
Bamberg *U.S.A.* 33°18N 81°2W **85** E14
Bamburgh *U.K.* 55°37N 1°43W **12** B6
Bamfield *Canada* 48°45N 125°10W **70** D3
Bāmīān □ *Afghan.* 35°0N 67°0E **40** B5
Bamiancheng *China* 43°15N 124°2E **33** C13
Bamou → *China* 29°45N 52°35E **47** D7
Bampūr *Iran* 27°15N 60°21E **47** E9
Bampūr → *Iran* 27°24N 59°0E **47** E8
Ban Ao Tu Khun *Thailand* 8°9N 98°20E **39** a
Ban Ban *Laos* 19°31N 103°30E **38** C4
Ban Bang Hin *Thailand* 9°32N 98°35E **39** H2
Ban Bang Khu *Thailand* 7°57N 98°23E **39** a
Ban Bang Rong *Thailand* 8°3N 98°25E **39** a
Ban Bo Phut *Thailand* 9°33N 100°2E **39** b
Ban Chaweng *Thailand* 9°32N 100°3E **39** b
Ban Chiang *Thailand* 17°23N 103°10E **38** D4
Ban Chiang Klang
  Thailand 19°25N 100°55E **38** C3
Ban Choho *Thailand* 15°2N 102°9E **38** E4
Ban Dan Lan Hoi *Thailand* 17°0N 99°35E **38** D2
Ban Don = Surat Thani
  Thailand 9°6N 99°20E **39** H2
Ban Don *Vietnam* 12°53N 107°48E **38** F6
Ban Don, Ao → *Thailand* 9°20N 99°25E **39** H2
Ban Dong *Thailand* 19°30N 100°59E **38** C3
Ban Hong *Thailand* 18°18N 98°50E **38** C2
Ban Hua Thanon *Thailand* 9°26N 100°1E **39** b
Ban Kantang *Thailand* 7°25N 99°31E **39** J2
Ban Karon *Thailand* 7°51N 98°18E **39** a
Ban Kata *Thailand* 7°50N 98°18E **39** a
Ban Keun *Laos* 18°22N 102°35E **38** C4
Ban Khai *Thailand* 12°46N 101°18E **38** F3
Ban Kheun *Laos* 20°13N 101°7E **38** B3
Ban Khlong Khian *Thailand* 8°10N 98°26E **39** a
Ban Khlong Kua *Thailand* 6°57N 100°8E **39** J3
Ban Khuan *Thailand* 8°20N 98°25E **39** a
Ban Ko Yai Chim
  Thailand 11°17N 99°26E **39** G2
Ban Laem *Thailand* 13°13N 99°59E **38** F2
Ban Lamai *Thailand* 9°28N 100°3E **39** b
Ban Lao Ngam *Laos* 15°28N 106°10E **38** E6
Ban Le Kathe *Thailand* 15°49N 98°53E **38** E2
Ban Lo Po Noi *Thailand* 8°1N 98°34E **39** a
Ban Mae Chedi *Thailand* 19°11N 99°31E **38** C2
Ban Mae Nam *Thailand* 9°34N 100°0E **39** b
Ban Mae Sariang
  Thailand 18°10N 97°56E **38** C1
Ban Mê Thuột = Buon Ma Thuot
  Vietnam 12°40N 108°3E **38** F7
Ban Mi *Thailand* 15°3N 100°32E **38** E3
Ban Muang Mo *Laos* 19°4N 103°58E **38** C4
Ban Na Bo *Thailand* 9°19N 99°41E **39** b
Ban Na San *Thailand* 8°53N 99°52E **39** H2
Ban Na Tong *Laos* 20°56N 101°47E **38** B3
Ban Nam Bac *Laos* 20°38N 102°20E **38** B4

Ban Nammi *Laos* 17°7N 105°40E **38** D5
Ban Nong Bok *Laos* 17°5N 104°48E **38** D5
Ban Nong Pling *Thailand* 15°40N 100°10E **38** E3
Ban Pak Chan *Thailand* 10°32N 98°51E **39** G2
Ban Patong *Thailand* 7°54N 98°18E **39** a
Ban Phai *Thailand* 16°4N 102°44E **38** D4
Ban Phak Chit *Thailand* 8°0N 98°24E **39** a
Ban Pong *Thailand* 13°50N 99°55E **38** F2
Ban Rawai *Thailand* 7°47N 98°20E **39** a
Ban Ron Phibun *Thailand* 8°9N 99°51E **39** H2
Ban Sakhu *Thailand* 8°4N 98°18E **39** a
Ban Sanam Chai *Thailand* 7°33N 100°25E **39** J3
Ban Tak *Thailand* 17°2N 99°4E **38** D2
Ban Tako *Thailand* 14°5N 102°40E **38** E4
Ban Tha Nun *Thailand* 8°12N 98°18E **39** a
Ban Tha Rua *Thailand* 7°59N 98°22E **39** a
Ban Tha Yu *Thailand* 8°17N 98°22E **39** a
Ban Thong Krut *Thailand* 9°25N 99°57E **39** b
Ban Xien Kok *Laos* 20°54N 100°39E **38** B3
Ban Yen Nhan *Vietnam* 20°57N 106°2E **38** B6
Banaba *Kiribati* 0°45S 169°50E **64** H8
Banagher *Ireland* 53°11N 7°59W **10** C4
Banalia
  Dem. Rep. of the Congo 1°32N 25°5E **54** D5
Banam *Cambodia* 11°20N 105°17E **39** G5
Bananal, I. do *Brazil* 11°30S 50°30W **93** F8
Banana *India* 6°57N 93°54E **45** L11
Banaras = Varanasi *India* 25°22N 83°0E **43** G10
Banas → *Gujarat, India* 23°45N 71°25E **42** H4
Banas → *Mad. P., India* 24°15N 81°30E **43** G9
Bânâs, Ras *Egypt* 23°57N 35°59E **53** D13
Banbridge *U.K.* 54°22N 6°16W **10** B5
Banbury *U.K.* 52°4N 1°20W **13** E6
Banchory *U.K.* 57°3N 2°29W **11** D6
Bancroft *Canada* 45°3N 77°51W **82** A7
Band Bonī *Iran* 25°30N 59°33E **47** E8
Band Qīr *Iran* 31°39N 48°53E **47** D6
Banda *Mad. P., India* 24°3N 78°57E **43** G8
Banda *Maharashtra, India* 15°49N 73°52E **45** G1
Banda *Ut. P., India* 25°30N 80°26E **43** G9
Banda, Kepulauan
  Indonesia 4°37S 129°50E **37** E7
Banda Aceh *Indonesia* 5°35N 95°20E **36** C1
Banda Banda, Mt.
  Australia 31°10S 152°28E **63** E5
Banda Elat *Indonesia* 5°40S 133°5E **37** F8
Banda Is. = Banda, Kepulauan
  Indonesia 4°37S 129°50E **37** E7
Banda Sea *Indonesia* 6°0S 130°0E **37** F8
Bandai-Asahi △ *Japan* 37°38N 140°5E **28** F10
Bandai-San *Japan* 37°36N 140°4E **28** F10
Bandān *Iran* 31°23N 60°44E **47** D9
Bandanaira *Indonesia* 4°32S 129°54E **37** E7
Bandanwara *India* 26°9N 74°38E **42** F6
Bandar = Machilipatnam
  India 16°12N 81°8E **45** F5
Bandar-e Abbās *Iran* 27°15N 56°15E **47** E8
Bandar-e Anzalī *Iran* 37°30N 49°30E **47** B6
Bandar-e'Bushehr = Büshehr
  Iran 28°55N 50°55E **47** D6
Bandar-e Chārak *Iran* 26°45N 54°20E **47** E7
Bandar-e Deylam *Iran* 30°5N 50°10E **47** D6
Bandar-e Emām Khomeynī
  Iran 30°30N 49°5E **47** D6
Bandar-e Lengeh *Iran* 26°35N 54°58E **47** E7
Bandar-e Maqām *Iran* 26°56N 53°29E **47** E7
Bandar-e Ma'shur *Iran* 30°35N 49°10E **47** D6
Bandar-e Rīg *Iran* 29°29N 50°38E **47** D6
Bandar-e Torkeman *Iran* 37°0N 54°10E **47** B7
Bandar Labuan *Malaysia* 5°20N 115°14E **36** C5
Bandar Lampung
  Indonesia 5°20S 105°10E **36** F3
Bandar Maharani = Muar
  Malaysia 2°3N 102°34E **39** L4
Bandar Penggaram = Batu Pahat
  Malaysia 1°50N 102°56E **39** M4
Banzare Coast *Antarctica* 68°0S 125°0E **5** C9
Bandar Seri Begawan
  Brunei 4°52N 115°0E **36** D5
Bandar Shahid Rajaee *Iran* 27°7N 56°4E **47** E8
Bandar Sri Aman
  Malaysia 1°15N 111°32E **36** D4
Bandeira, Pico da *Brazil* 20°26S 41°47W **95** A7
Bandera *Argentina* 28°55S 62°20W **94** B3
Banderas, B. de *Mexico* 20°40N 105°25W **86** C3
Bandhavgarh *India* 23°40N 81°2E **43** H9
Bandhavgarh △ *India* 23°45N 81°10E **44** C5
Bandi → *India* 26°12N 75°47E **42** F6
Bandia → *India* 19°2N 80°28E **44** E5
Bandikui *India* 27°3N 76°34E **42** F7
Bandipur △ *India* 11°45N 76°30E **45** J3
Bandırma *Turkey* 40°20N 28°0E **23** D13
Bandjarmasin = Banjarmasin
  Indonesia 3°20S 114°35E **36** E4
Bandon *Ireland* 51°44N 8°44W **10** E3
Bandon → *Ireland* 51°43N 8°37W **10** E3
Bandundu
  Dem. Rep. of the Congo 3°15S 17°22E **54** E3
Bandung *Indonesia* 6°54S 107°36E **37** G12
Bāneh *Iran* 35°59N 45°53E **46** C5
Banes *Cuba* 21°0N 75°42W **89** B4
Banff *Canada* 51°10N 115°34W **70** C5
Banff *U.K.* 57°40N 2°33W **11** D6
Banff △ *Canada* 51°30N 116°15W **70** C5
Bang Fai → *Laos* 16°57N 104°45E **38** D5
Bang Hieng → *Laos* 16°10N 105°10E **38** D5
Bang Krathum *Thailand* 16°34N 100°18E **38** D3
Bang Lang △ *Thailand* 5°58N 101°19E **39** K3
Bang Lang Res. *Thailand* 6°6N 101°17E **39** J3
Bang Mun Nak *Thailand* 16°2N 100°23E **38** D3
Bang Pa In *Thailand* 14°14N 100°35E **38** E3
Bang Rakam *Thailand* 16°45N 100°7E **38** D3
Bang Saphan *Thailand* 11°14N 99°28E **39** G2
Bang Thao *Thailand* 8°1N 98°18E **39** a
Banganduni I. *India* 21°34N 88°52E **43** J13
Bangalore = Bengaluru
  India 12°59N 77°40E **45** H3
Banganapalle *India* 15°19N 78°14E **45** G4
Banganga → *India* 27°6N 77°25E **42** F6
Bangaon *India* 23°0N 88°47E **43** H13
Bangassou *C.A.R.* 4°55N 23°7E **54** D4

Banggai *Indonesia* 1°34S 123°30E **37** E6
Banggai, Kepulauan
  Indonesia 1°40S 123°30E **37** E6
Banggai Arch. = Banggai,
  Kepulauan *Indonesia* 1°40S 123°30E **37** E6
Banggi, Pulau *Malaysia* 7°17N 117°12E **36** C5
Banghāzī *Libya* 32°11N 20°3E **53** B10
Bangka *Sulawesi, Indonesia* 1°50N 125°5E **37** D7
Bangka *Sumatera, Indonesia* 2°0S 105°50E **36** E3
Bangka, Selat *Indonesia* 2°30S 105°30E **36** E3
Bangka-Belitung □
  Indonesia 2°30S 107°0E **36** E3
Bangkalan *Indonesia* 7°2S 112°46E **37** G15
Bangkang *Burma* 22°4N 99°1E **34** F2
Bangkinang *Indonesia* 0°18N 101°5E **36** D2
Bangko *Indonesia* 2°5S 102°9E **36** E2
Bangkok, Bight of
  Thailand 12°55N 100°30E **38** F3
Bangla = Paschimbanga □
  India 23°0N 88°0E **43** H13
Bangladesh ■ *Asia* 24°0N 90°0E **41** H17
Bangli *Indonesia* 8°27S 115°21E **37** J18
Bangong Co *China* 33°45N 78°43E **43** C8
Bangor *Down, U.K.* 54°40N 5°40W **10** B6
Bangor *Gwynedd, U.K.* 53°14N 4°8W **12** D3
Bangor *Maine, U.S.A.* 44°48N 68°46W **81** C19
Bangor *Pa., U.S.A.* 40°52N 75°13W **83** F9
Bangued *Phil.* 17°40N 120°37E **37** A6
Bangui *C.A.R.* 4°23N 18°35E **54** D3
Bangweulu, L. *Zambia* 11°0S 30°0E **54** G6
Banhine △ *Mozam.* 22°49S 32°55E **57** B5
Banī *Dom. Rep.* 18°16N 70°22W **89** C5
Banī Sa'd *Iraq* 33°34N 44°32E **46** C5
Banihal Pass *India* 33°30N 75°12E **43** C6
Banja → *India* 22°36N 80°22E **43** H9
Banjar *Indonesia* 7°24S 108°30E **37** G13
Banjar → *India* 22°36N 80°22E **43** H9
Banjarmasin *Indonesia* 3°20S 114°35E **36** E4
Banjul *Gambia* 13°28N 16°40W **52** F2
Banka *India* 24°53N 86°55E **43** G12
Bankipore *India* 25°35N 85°10E **41** G14
Bankot *India* 17°58N 73°2E **44** F1
Banks I. = Moa *Australia* 10°11S 142°16E **62** a
Banks I. *B.C., Canada* 53°20N 130°0W **70** C3
Banks I. *N.W.T., Canada* 73°15N 121°30W **68** C7
Banks Pen. *N.Z.* 43°45S 173°15E **59** E4
Banks Str. *Australia* 40°40S 148°10E **63** G4
Bankura *India* 23°11N 87°18E **43** H12
Bann → *Armagh, U.K.* 54°30N 6°31W **10** B5
Bann → *L'derry., U.K.* 55°8N 6°41W **10** A5
Bannang Sata *Thailand* 6°16N 101°16E **39** J3
Banning *U.S.A.* 33°56N 116°53W **79** M10
Bannockburn *Canada* 44°39N 77°33W **82** B7
Bannockburn *U.K.* 56°5N 3°55W **11** E5
Bannu *Pakistan* 33°0N 70°18E **40** C7
Bano *India* 22°40N 84°55E **43** H11
Bansagar Dam *India* 24°11N 81°17E **44** B5
Bansgaon *India* 26°33N 83°21E **43** F10
Banská Bystrica
  Slovak Rep. 48°46N 19°14E **17** D10
Banswara *India* 23°32N 74°24E **42** H6
Bantaeng *Indonesia* 5°32S 119°56E **37** F5
Banteay Prei Nokor
  Cambodia 11°56N 105°40E **39** G5
Banten □ *Indonesia* 6°30S 106°0E **37** G11
Bantry *Ireland* 51°41N 9°27W **10** E2
Bantry B. *Ireland* 51°37N 9°44W **10** E2
Bantva *India* 21°29N 70°12E **42** J4
Bantval *India* 12°55N 75°0E **45** H2
Banyak, Kepulauan
  Indonesia 2°10N 97°10E **36** D1
Banyo *Cameroon* 6°52N 11°45E **54** C2
Banyuwangi *Indonesia* 8°13S 114°21E **37** J17
Banzare Coast *Antarctica* 68°0S 125°0E **5** C9
Bao Ha *Vietnam* 22°11N 104°21E **38** A5
Bao Lac *Vietnam* 22°57N 105°40E **38** A5
Bao Loc *Vietnam* 11°32N 107°48E **39** G6
Bao'an *China* 22°34N 113°52E **31** a
Baocheng *China* 33°12N 106°56E **34** A5
Baode *China* 39°1N 111°5E **32** E6
Baodi *China* 39°38N 117°20E **33** E9
Baoding *China* 38°50N 115°28E **32** E8
Baoji *China* 34°20N 107°5E **32** G4
Baojing *China* 28°45N 109°41E **34** C7
Baokang *China* 31°54N 111°5E **35** B8
Baoshan *China* 25°10N 99°5E **34** E2
Baotou *China* 40°32N 110°2E **32** D6
Baoxing *China* 30°24N 102°50E **34** B4
Baoying *China* 33°17N 119°20E **33** H10
Baoyou = Ledong *China* 18°41N 109°5E **38** C7
Bap *India* 27°23N 72°18E **42** F5
Bapatla *India* 15°55N 80°30E **45** G5
Bāqerābād *Iran* 33°2N 51°58E **47** C6
Ba'qubah *Iraq* 33°45N 44°50E **46** C5
Baquedano *Chile* 23°20S 69°52W **94** A2
Bar *Montenegro* 42°8N 19°6E **23** C8
Bar *Ukraine* 49°4N 27°40E **17** D14
Bar Bigha *India* 25°21N 85°47E **43** G11
Bar Harbor *U.S.A.* 44°23N 68°13W **81** C19
Bar-le-Duc *France* 48°47N 5°10E **20** B6
Bara *India* 25°16N 81°43E **43** G9
Bara Banki *India* 26°55N 81°12E **43** F9
Barabai *Indonesia* 2°32S 115°34E **36** E5
Baraboo *U.S.A.* 43°28N 89°45W **80** D9
Baracoa *Cuba* 20°20N 74°30W **89** B5
Baradā → *Syria* 33°33N 36°34E **48** B5
Baradero *Argentina* 33°52S 59°29W **94** C4
Baraga *U.S.A.* 46°47N 88°30W **80** B9
Barah → *India* 27°42N 77°5E **42** F6
Barahona *Dom. Rep.* 18°13N 71°7W **89** C5
Barail Range *India* 25°15N 93°20E **41** G18
Barakaldo *Spain* 43°18N 2°59W **21** A4
Barakar → *India* 24°7N 86°14E **43** G12
Barakot *India* 21°33N 84°59E **43** J11
Baralaba *Australia* 24°13S 149°50E **62** C4
Baralzon L. *Canada* 60°0N 98°3W **71** B9
Baramati *India* 18°11N 74°33E **44** F2
Baramba *India* 20°25N 85°23E **44** D7

Baramula *India* 34°15N 74°20E **43** B6
Baran *India* 25°9N 76°40E **42** G7
Baran → *Pakistan* 25°13N 68°17E **42** G3
Baranavichy *Belarus* 53°10N 26°0E **17** B14
Baranof *U.S.A.* 57°5N 134°50W **70** B2
Baranof I. *U.S.A.* 57°0N 135°0W **68** F4
Barapasi *Indonesia* 2°15S 137°5E **37** E9
Barasat *India* 22°46N 88°31E **43** H13
Barat Daya, Kepulauan
  Indonesia 7°30S 128°0E **37** F7
Baratang I. *India* 12°13N 92°45E **45** H11
Barataria B. *U.S.A.* 29°20N 89°55W **85** G10
Barauda *India* 23°33N 75°15E **42** H6
Baraut *India* 29°13N 77°7E **42** E7
Barbacena *Brazil* 21°15S 43°56W **95** A7
Barbados ■ *W. Indies* 13°10N 59°30W **89** g
Barbas, C. *W. Sahara* 22°20N 16°42W **52** D2
Barbastro *Spain* 42°2N 0°5E **21** A6
Barberton *S. Africa* 25°42S 31°2E **57** D5
Barberton *U.S.A.* 41°1N 81°39W **82** E3
Barbosa *Colombia* 5°57N 73°37W **92** B4
Barbourville *U.S.A.* 36°52N 83°53W **81** G12
Barbuda *W. Indies* 17°30N 61°40W **89** C7
Barcaldine *Australia* 23°43S 145°6E **62** C4
Barcellona Pozzo di Gotto
  Italy 38°9N 15°13E **22** E6
Barcelona *Venezuela* 10°10N 64°40W **92** A6
Barcelona *Spain* 41°21N 2°10E **21** B7
Barceloneta *Puerto Rico* 18°27N 66°32W **89** d
Barcelos *Brazil* 1°0S 63°0W **92** D6
Barcoo → *Australia* 25°30S 142°50E **62** D3
Bardaï *Chad* 21°25N 17°0E **53** D9
Bardas Blancas *Argentina* 35°49S 69°45W **94** D2
Bardawīl, Sabkhet el
  Egypt 31°10N 33°15E **48** D2
Barddhaman *India* 23°14N 87°39E **43** H12
Bardejov *Slovak Rep.* 49°18N 21°15E **17** D11
Bardera = Baardheere
  Somalia 2°20N 42°27E **49** G3
Bardīyah *Libya* 31°45N 25°5E **53** B10
Bardoli *India* 21°12N 73°5E **44** D1
Bardsey I. *U.K.* 52°45N 4°47W **12** E3
Bardstown *U.S.A.* 37°49N 85°28W **81** G11
Bareilly *India* 28°22N 79°27E **43** E8
Barela *India* 23°6N 80°3E **43** H9
Barents Sea *Arctic* 73°0N 39°0E **4** B9
Barfleur, Pte. de *France* 49°42N 1°16W **20** B3
Bargara *Australia* 24°50S 152°25E **62** C5
Bargarh *India* 21°20N 83°37E **44** D6
Bargi Dam *India* 22°59N 80°0E **44** C5
Barguzin *Russia* 53°37N 109°37E **27** D11
Barh *India* 25°29N 85°46E **43** G11
Barhaj *India* 26°18N 83°44E **43** F10
Barharwa *India* 24°52N 87°47E **43** G12
Barhi *India* 24°15N 85°25E **43** G11
Bari *India* 26°39N 77°39E **42** F7
Bari *Italy* 41°8N 16°51E **22** D7
Bari Doab *Pakistan* 30°20N 73°0E **42** D5
Bari Sadri *India* 24°28N 74°30E **42** G6
Barīdī, Ra's *Si. Arabia* 24°17N 37°31E **46** E3
Barīm *Yemen* 12°39N 43°25E **50** E8
Barinas *Venezuela* 8°36N 70°15W **92** B4
Baring, C. *Canada* 70°0N 117°30W **68** D8
Baripada *India* 21°57N 86°45E **44** D8
Barisal *Bangla.* 22°45N 90°20E **41** H17
Barisal □ *Bangla.* 22°45N 90°20E **41** H17
Barisan, Pegunungan
  Indonesia 3°30S 102°15E **36** E2
Barito → *Indonesia* 4°0S 114°50E **36** E4
Barjüj, Wadi → *Libya* 25°26N 12°12E **53** C8
Bark L. *Canada* 45°27N 77°51W **82** A7
Barkakana *India* 23°37N 85°29E **43** H11
Barkam *China* 31°51N 102°28E **34** B4
Barker *U.S.A.* 43°20N 78°33W **82** C6
Barkley, L. *U.S.A.* 37°1N 88°14W **85** C10
Barkley Sound *Canada* 48°50N 125°10W **70** D3
Barkly East *S. Africa* 30°58S 27°33E **56** E4
Barkly Homestead
  Australia 19°52S 135°50E **62** B2
Barkly Tableland
  Australia 17°50S 136°40E **62** B2
Barkly West *S. Africa* 28°5S 24°31E **56** D3
Barkol Kazak Zizhixian
  China 43°37N 93°2E **30** C7
Bârlad *Romania* 46°15N 27°38E **17** E14
Bârlad → *Romania* 45°38N 27°32E **17** F14
Barlee, L. *Australia* 29°15S 119°30E **61** E2
Barlee, Mt. *Australia* 24°38S 128°13E **61** D4
Barletta *Italy* 41°19N 16°17E **22** D7
Barlovento *C. Verde Is.* 17°0N 25°0W **52** b
Barlow L. *Canada* 62°0N 103°0W **71** A8
Barmedman *Australia* 34°9S 147°21E **63** E4
Barmer *India* 25°45N 71°20E **42** G4
Barmera *Australia* 34°15S 140°28E **63** E3
Barmouth *U.K.* 52°44N 4°4W **12** E3
Barna → *India* 25°21N 83°3E **43** G10
Barnagar *India* 23°7N 75°19E **42** H6
Barnala *India* 30°23N 75°33E **42** D6
Barnard Castle *U.K.* 54°33N 1°55W **12** C6
Barnaul *Russia* 53°20N 83°40E **26** D9
Barnesville *Ga., U.S.A.* 33°3N 84°9W **85** E12
Barnesville *Minn., U.S.A.* 46°43N 96°28W **80** B5
Barnet □ *U.K.* 51°38N 0°9W **13** F7
Barneveld *Neths.* 52°7N 5°36E **15** B5
Barnhart *U.S.A.* 31°8N 101°10W **84** F4
Barnsley *U.K.* 53°34N 1°27W **12** D6
Barnstable *U.S.A.* 41°42N 70°18W **81** E18
Barnstaple *U.K.* 51°5N 4°4W **13** F3
Barnstaple Bay = Bideford Bay
  U.K. 51°5N 4°20W **13** F3
Barnwell *U.S.A.* 33°15N 81°23W **85** E14
Baro *Nigeria* 8°35N 6°18E **52** G7
Baroda = Vadodara *India* 22°20N 73°10E **42** H5
Baroda *India* 25°29N 76°35E **42** G7
Baroe *S. Africa* 33°13S 24°33E **56** E3
Baron Ra. *Australia* 23°30S 127°45E **60** D4
Barong *China* 31°3N 99°0E **34** B2
Barotseland *Zambia* 15°0S 24°0E **55** H4
Barpali *India* 21°11N 83°35E **44** D6

Barpeta *India* 26°20N 91°10E **41 F17**
Barqa *Libya* 27°0N 23°0E **53 C10**
Barques, Pt. Aux *U.S.A.* 44°4N 82°58W **82 B2**
Barquisimeto *Venezuela* 10°4N 69°19W **92 A5**
Barr Smith Range *Australia* 27°4S 120°20E **61 E3**
Barra *Brazil* 11°5S 43°10W **93 F10**
Barra *U.K.* 57°0N 7°29W **11 E1**
Barra, Pta. *Mozam.* 23°48S 35°32E **57 B6**
Barra, Sd. of *U.K.* 57°4N 7°25W **11 D1**
Barra de Navidad *Mexico* 19°12N 104°41W **86 D4**
Barra do Corda *Brazil* 5°30S 45°10W **93 E9**
Barra do Garças *Brazil* 15°54S 52°16W **93 G8**
Barra do Piraí *Brazil* 22°30S 43°50W **95 A7**
Barra Falsa, Pta. da *Mozam.* 22°58S 35°37E **57 B6**
Barra Hd. *U.K.* 56°47N 7°40W **11 E1**
Barra Mansa *Brazil* 22°35S 44°12W **95 A7**
Barraba *Australia* 30°21S 150°35E **63 E5**
Barranca *Lima, Peru* 10°45S 77°50W **92 F3**
Barranca *Loreto, Peru* 4°50S 76°50W **92 D3**
Barranca del Cobre △ *Mexico* 27°18N 107°40W **86 B3**
Barrancabermeja *Colombia* 7°0N 73°50W **92 B4**
Barrancas *Venezuela* 8°55N 62°5W **92 B6**
Barrancos *Portugal* 38°10N 6°58W **21 C2**
Barranqueras *Argentina* 27°30S 59°0W **94 B4**
Barranquilla *Colombia* 11°0N 74°50W **92 A4**
Barraute *Canada* 48°26N 77°38W **72 C4**
Barre *Mass., U.S.A.* 42°25N 72°6W **83 D12**
Barre *Vt., U.S.A.* 44°12N 72°30W **83 B12**
Barreal *Argentina* 31°33S 69°28W **94 C2**
Barreiras *Brazil* 12°8S 45°0W **93 F10**
Barreirinhas *Brazil* 2°30S 42°50W **93 D10**
Barren, Nosy *Madag.* 18°25S 43°40E **57 C7**
Barren I. *India* 12°16N 93°51E **45 H11**
Barretos *Brazil* 20°30S 48°35W **93 H9**
Barrhead *Canada* 54°10N 114°24W **70 C6**
Barrie *Canada* 44°24N 79°40W **82 B5**
Barrier Ra. *Australia* 31°0S 141°30E **63 E3**
Barrière *Canada* 51°12N 120°7W **70 C4**
Barrington *U.S.A.* 41°44N 71°18W **83 E13**
Barrington L. *Canada* 56°55N 100°15W **71 B8**
Barrington Tops *Australia* 32°6S 151°28E **63 E5**
Barringun *Australia* 29°1S 145°41E **63 D4**
Barron *U.S.A.* 45°24N 91°51W **80 C8**
Barrow *U.S.A.* 71°18N 156°47W **74 A8**
Barrow → *Ireland* 52°25N 6°58W **10 D5**
Barrow, Pt. *U.S.A.* 71°23N 156°29W **74 A8**
Barrow Creek *Australia* 21°30S 133°55E **62 C1**
Barrow I. *Australia* 20°45S 115°20E **60 D2**
Barrow-in-Furness *U.K.* 54°7N 3°14W **12 C4**
Barrow Pt. *Australia* 14°20S 144°40E **62 A3**
Barrow Ra. *Australia* 26°0S 127°40E **61 E4**
Barrow Str. *Canada* 74°20N 95°0W **69 C13**
Barry *U.K.* 51°24N 3°16W **13 F4**
Barry's Bay *Canada* 45°29N 77°41W **82 A7**
Barsat *Pakistan* 36°10N 72°45E **43 A5**
Barsi *India* 18°10N 75°50E **44 E2**
Barsoi *India* 25°48N 87°57E **41 G15**
Barstow *U.S.A.* 34°54N 117°1W **79 L9**
Bartica *Guyana* 6°25N 58°40W **92 B7**
Bartle Frere *Australia* 17°27S 145°50E **62 B4**
Bartlesville *U.S.A.* 36°45N 95°59W **84 C7**
Bartlett *Calif., U.S.A.* 36°29N 118°2W **78 J8**
Bartlett *Tenn., U.S.A.* 35°12N 89°52W **85 D10**
Bartlett, L. *Canada* 63°5N 118°20W **70 A5**
Barton *U.S.A.* 44°45N 72°11W **83 B12**
Barton-upon-Humber *U.K.* 53°41N 0°25W **12 D7**
Bartow *U.S.A.* 27°54N 81°50W **85 H14**
Barú, Volcan *Panama* 8°55N 82°35W **88 E3**
Barung, Nusa *Indonesia* 8°30S 113°30E **37 H15**
Baruun Urt *Mongolia* 46°46N 113°15E **31 B11**
Baruunsuu *Mongolia* 43°43N 105°35E **32 C3**
Barwani *India* 22°2N 74°57E **42 H6**
Barysaw *Belarus* 54°17N 28°28E **17 A15**
Barzán *Iraq* 36°55N 44°3E **46 B5**
Bāsa'idū *Iran* 26°35N 55°20E **47 E7**
Basal *Pakistan* 33°33N 72°13E **42 C5**
Basankusu *Dem. Rep. of the Congo* 1°5N 19°50E **54 D3**
Basarabeasca *Moldova* 46°21N 28°58E **17 E15**
Basarabia = Bessarabiya *Moldova* 47°0N 28°10E **17 E15**
Basavakalyan *India* 17°52N 76°57E **44 F3**
Basawa *Afghan.* 34°15N 70°50E **42 B4**
Bascuñán, C. *Chile* 28°52S 71°35W **94 B1**
Basel *Switz.* 47°35N 7°35E **20 C7**
Bashākerd, Kūhhā-ye *Iran* 26°42N 58°35E **47 E8**
Bashaw *Canada* 52°35N 112°58W **70 C6**
Bāshī *Iran* 28°41N 51°4E **47 D6**
Bashkir Republic = Bashkortostan □ *Russia* 54°0N 57°0E **18 D10**
Bashkortostan □ *Russia* 54°0N 57°0E **18 D10**
Basilan I. *Phil.* 6°35N 122°0E **37 C6**
Basilan Str. *Phil.* 6°50N 122°0E **37 C6**
Basildon *U.K.* 51°34N 0°28E **13 F8**
Basim = Washim *India* 20°3N 77°0E **44 D3**
Basin *U.S.A.* 44°23N 108°2W **76 D9**
Basingstoke *U.K.* 51°15N 1°5W **13 F6**
Baskatong, Rés. *Canada* 46°46N 75°50W **72 C4**
Basle = Basel *Switz.* 47°35N 7°35E **20 C7**
Basmat *India* 19°15N 77°12E **44 E3**
Basoda *India* 23°52N 77°54E **42 H7**
Basque Provinces = País Vasco □ *Spain* 42°50N 2°45W **21 A4**
Basra = Al Başrah *Iraq* 30°30N 47°50E **46 D5**
Bass Str. *Australia* 39°15S 146°30E **63 F4**
Bassano *Canada* 50°48N 112°20W **70 C6**
Bassano del Grappa *Italy* 45°46N 11°44E **22 B4**
Bassas da India *Ind. Oc.* 22°0S 39°0E **57 B6**
Basse-Pointe *Martinique* 14°52N 61°8W **88 c**
Basse-Terre *Trin. & Tob.* 10°7N 61°19W **93 K15**
Bassein = Pathein *Burma* 16°45N 94°30E **41 L19**

Basses, Pte. des *Guadeloupe* 15°52N 61°17W **88 b**
Basseterre *St. Kitts & Nevis* 17°17N 62°43W **89 C7**
Bassett *U.S.A.* 42°35N 99°32W **80 D4**
Bassi *India* 30°44N 76°21E **42 D7**
Bastak *Iran* 27°15N 54°25E **47 E7**
Baştām *Iran* 36°29N 55°4E **47 B7**
Bastar *India* 19°15N 81°40E **44 E5**
Basti *India* 26°52N 82°55E **43 F10**
Bastia *France* 42°40N 9°30E **20 E8**
Bastogne *Belgium* 50°1N 5°43E **15 D5**
Bastrop *La., U.S.A.* 32°47N 91°55W **84 E9**
Bastrop *Tex., U.S.A.* 30°7N 97°19W **84 F6**
Basuo = Dongfang *China* 18°50N 108°33E **38 C7**
Bat Yam *Israel* 32°2N 34°44E **48 C3**
Bata *Eq. Guin.* 1°57N 9°50E **54 D1**
Bataan □ *Phil.* 14°40N 120°25E **37 B6**
Batabanó *Cuba* 22°41N 82°18W **88 B3**
Batabanó, G. de *Cuba* 22°30N 82°30W **88 B3**
Batac *Phil.* 18°3N 120°34E **37 A6**
Batagai *Russia* 67°38N 134°38E **27 C14**
Batala *India* 31°48N 75°12E **42 D6**
Batamay *Russia* 63°30N 129°15E **27 C13**
Batang *China* 30°1N 99°0E **34 B2**
Batang *Indonesia* 6°55S 109°45E **37 G13**
Batangafo *C.A.R.* 7°25N 18°20E **54 C3**
Batangas *Phil.* 13°35N 121°10E **37 B6**
Batanta *Indonesia* 0°55S 130°40E **37 E8**
Batatais *Brazil* 20°54S 47°37W **95 A6**
Batavia *U.S.A.* 43°0N 78°11W **82 D6**
Batchelor *Australia* 13°4S 131°1E **60 B5**
Batdambang *Cambodia* 13°7N 103°12E **38 F4**
Batemans B. *Australia* 35°40S 150°12E **63 F5**
Batemans Bay *Australia* 35°44S 150°11E **63 F5**
Batesburg-Leesville *U.S.A.* 33°54N 81°33W **85 E14**
Batesville *Ark., U.S.A.* 35°46N 91°39W **84 D9**
Batesville *Miss., U.S.A.* 34°19N 89°57W **85 D10**
Batesville *Tex., U.S.A.* 28°58N 99°37W **84 G5**
Bath *Canada* 44°11N 76°47W **83 B8**
Bath *U.K.* 51°23N 2°22W **13 F5**
Bath *Maine, U.S.A.* 43°55N 69°49W **81 D19**
Bath *N.Y., U.S.A.* 42°20N 77°19W **82 D7**
Bath & North East Somerset □ *U.K.* 51°21N 2°27W **13 F5**
Batheay *Cambodia* 11°59N 104°57E **39 G5**
Bathsheba *Barbados* 13°13N 59°32W **89 g**
Bathurst *Australia* 33°25S 149°31E **63 E4**
Bathurst *Canada* 47°37N 65°43W **73 C6**
Bathurst *S. Africa* 33°30S 26°50E **56 E4**
Bathurst, C. *Canada* 70°34N 128°0W **68 B7**
Bathurst B. *Australia* 14°16S 144°25E **62 A3**
Bathurst Harb. *Australia* 43°15S 146°10E **63 G4**
Bathurst I. *Australia* 11°30S 130°10E **60 B5**
Bathurst I. *Canada* 76°0N 100°30W **69 B11**
Bathurst Inlet *Canada* 66°50N 108°1W **68 D10**
Bati *Ethiopia* 6°55N 39°45E **49 F2**
Batlow *Australia* 35°31S 148°9E **63 F4**
Batman *Turkey* 37°55N 41°5E **46 B4**
Batn al Ghūl *Jordan* 29°36N 35°56E **48 F4**
Batna *Algeria* 35°34N 6°15E **52 A7**
Baton Rouge *U.S.A.* 30°27N 91°11W **84 F9**
Batong, Ko *Thailand* 6°32N 99°12E **39 J2**
Batopilas *Mexico* 27°1N 107°44W **86 B3**
Batouri *Cameroon* 4°30N 14°25E **54 D2**
Båtsfjord *Norway* 70°38N 29°39E **8 A23**
Battambang = Batdambang *Cambodia* 13°7N 103°12E **38 F4**
Batti Malv *India* 8°50N 92°51E **45 K11**
Batticaloa *Sri Lanka* 7°43N 81°45E **45 L5**
Battipáglia *Italy* 40°37N 14°58E **22 D6**
Battle *U.K.* 50°55N 0°30E **13 G8**
Battle → *Canada* 52°43N 108°15W **71 C7**
Battle Creek *U.S.A.* 42°19N 85°11W **81 D11**
Battle Ground *U.S.A.* 45°47N 122°32W **78 E4**
Battle Harbour *Canada* 52°16N 55°35W **73 B8**
Battle Lake *U.S.A.* 46°17N 95°43W **80 B6**
Battle Mountain *U.S.A.* 40°38N 116°56W **76 F5**
Battleford *Canada* 52°45N 108°15W **71 C7**
Batu *Ethiopia* 6°55N 39°45E **49 F2**
Batu *Malaysia* 3°15N 101°40E **39 L3**
Batu, Kepulauan *Indonesia* 0°30S 98°25E **36 E1**
Batu Ferringhi *Malaysia* 5°28N 100°15E **39 c**
Batu Gajah *Malaysia* 4°28N 101°3E **39 K3**
Batu Is. = Batu, Kepulauan *Indonesia* 0°30S 98°25E **36 E1**
Batu Pahat *Malaysia* 1°50N 102°56E **39 M4**
Batu Puteh, Gunung *Malaysia* 4°15N 101°31E **39 K3**
Batuata *Indonesia* 6°12S 122°42E **37 F6**
Batugondang, Tanjung *Indonesia* 8°6S 114°29E **37 J17**
Batukaru, Gunung *Indonesia* 8°20S 115°5E **37 J18**
Batumi *Georgia* 41°39N 41°44E **19 F7**
Batur, Gunung *Indonesia* 8°14S 115°23E **37 J18**
Batura Sar *Pakistan* 36°30N 74°31E **43 A6**
Baturaja *Indonesia* 4°11S 104°15E **36 E2**
Baturité *Brazil* 4°28S 38°45W **93 D11**
Baturiti *Indonesia* 8°9S 115°11E **37 J18**
Bau *Malaysia* 1°25N 110°9E **36 D4**
Baubau *Indonesia* 5°25S 122°38E **37 F6**
Bauchi *Nigeria* 10°22N 9°48E **52 F7**
Bauda *India* 20°50N 84°25E **44 D7**
Baudette *U.S.A.* 48°43N 94°36W **80 A6**
Bauer, C. *Australia* 32°44S 134°4E **63 E1**
Bauhinia *Australia* 24°35S 149°18E **62 C4**
Baukau = Baucau *E. Timor* 8°27S 126°27E **37 F7**
Bauld, C. *Canada* 51°38N 55°26W **69 G20**
Bauru *Brazil* 22°10S 49°0W **95 A6**
Bausi *India* 24°48N 87°1E **43 G12**
Bauska *Latvia* 56°24N 24°15E **9 H21**
Bautzen *Germany* 51°10N 14°26E **16 C8**
Bavānāt *Iran* 30°28N 53°27E **47 D7**
Bavaria = Bayern □ *Germany* 48°50N 12°0E **16 D6**

Bavispe → *Mexico* 29°15N 109°11W **86 B3**
Bawdwin *Burma* 23°5N 97°20E **41 H20**
Bawean *Indonesia* 5°46S 112°35E **36 F4**
Bawku *Ghana* 11°3N 0°19W **52 F5**
Bawlake *Burma* 19°11N 97°21E **41 K20**
Bawolung *China* 28°50N 101°16E **34 C3**
Baxley *U.S.A.* 31°47N 82°21W **85 F13**
Baxter *U.S.A.* 46°21N 94°17W **80 B6**
Baxter Springs *U.S.A.* 37°2N 94°44W **80 G6**
Baxter State ○ *U.S.A.* 46°5N 68°57W **81 B19**
Bay City *Mich., U.S.A.* 43°36N 83°54W **81 D12**
Bay City *Tex., U.S.A.* 28°59N 95°58W **84 G7**
Bay Is. = Bahía, Is. de la *Honduras* 16°45N 86°15W **88 C2**
Bay Minette *U.S.A.* 30°53N 87°46W **85 F11**
Bay Roberts *Canada* 47°36N 53°16W **73 C9**
Bay St. Louis *U.S.A.* 30°19N 89°20W **85 F10**
Bay Springs *U.S.A.* 31°59N 89°17W **85 F10**
Bay View *N.Z.* 39°25S 176°50E **59 C6**
Bayamo *Cuba* 20°20N 76°40W **88 B4**
Bayamón *Puerto Rico* 18°24N 66°9W **89 d**
Bayan Har Shan *China* 34°0N 98°0E **30 E8**
Bayan Hot = Alxa Zuoqi *China* 38°50N 105°40E **32 E3**
Bayan Lepas *Malaysia* 5°17N 100°16E **39 c**
Bayan Obo *China* 41°52N 109°59E **32 D5**
Bayan-Ovoo = Erdenetsogt *Mongolia* 42°55N 106°5E **32 C4**
Bayana *India* 26°55N 77°18E **42 F7**
Bayanaüyl *Kazakhstan* 50°45N 75°45E **26 D8**
Bayanhongor *Mongolia* 46°8N 102°43E **30 B9**
Bayard *N. Mex., U.S.A.* 32°46N 108°8W **77 K9**
Bayard *Nebr., U.S.A.* 41°45N 103°20W **80 E2**
Baybay *Phil.* 10°40N 124°55E **37 B6**
Baydaratskaya Guba *Russia* 69°0N 67°30E **26 C7**
Baydhabo *Somalia* 3°8N 43°30E **49 G3**
Bayern □ *Germany* 48°50N 12°0E **16 D6**
Bayeux *France* 49°17N 0°42W **20 B3**
Bayfield *Canada* 43°34N 81°42W **82 C3**
Bayfield *U.S.A.* 46°49N 90°49W **80 B8**
Bayındır *Turkey* 38°13N 27°39E **23 E12**
Baykal, Oz. *Russia* 53°0N 108°0E **27 D11**
Baykan *Turkey* 38°7N 41°44E **46 B4**
Baymak *Russia* 52°36N 58°19E **18 D10**
Baynes Mts. *Namibia* 17°15S 13°0E **56 A1**
Bayombong *Phil.* 16°30N 121°10E **37 A6**
Bayonne *France* 43°30N 1°28W **20 E3**
Bayonne *U.S.A.* 40°40N 74°6W **83 F10**
Bayovar *Peru* 5°50S 81°0W **92 E2**
Bayqongyr *Kazakhstan* 45°40N 63°20E **26 E7**
Bayram-Ali = Baýramaly *Turkmenistan* 37°37N 62°10E **47 B9**
Baýramaly *Turkmenistan* 37°37N 62°10E **47 B9**
Bayramiç *Turkey* 39°48N 26°36E **23 E12**
Bayreuth *Germany* 49°56N 11°35E **16 D6**
Bayrūt *Lebanon* 33°53N 35°31E **48 B4**
Bays, L. of *Canada* 45°15N 79°4W **82 A5**
Baysville *Canada* 45°9N 79°7W **82 A5**
Baytown *U.S.A.* 29°43N 94°59W **84 G7**
Bayuquan *China* 40°16N 122°8E **33 D12**
Baza *Spain* 37°30N 2°47W **21 D4**
Bazaruto, I. do *Mozam.* 21°40S 35°28E **57 B6**
Bazaruto △ *Mozam.* 21°42S 35°26E **57 B6**
Bazhong *China* 31°52N 106°46E **34 B6**
Bazhou *China* 39°8N 116°22E **32 E9**
Bazmān, Kūh-e *Iran* 28°4N 60°1E **47 D9**
Bé, Nosy *Madag.* 13°25S 48°15E **55 G9**
Beach *U.S.A.* 46°58N 104°0W **80 B2**
Beach City *U.S.A.* 40°39N 81°35W **82 F3**
Beachport *Australia* 37°29S 140°0E **63 F3**
Beachville *Canada* 43°5N 80°49W **82 C4**
Beachy Hd. *U.K.* 50°44N 0°15E **13 G8**
Beacon *Australia* 30°26S 117°52E **61 F2**
Beacon *U.S.A.* 41°30N 73°58W **83 E11**
Beaconsfield *Australia* 41°11S 146°48E **63 G4**
Beagle, Canal *S. Amer.* 55°0S 68°30W **96 H3**
Beagle Bay *Australia* 16°58S 122°40E **60 C3**
Beagle G. *Australia* 12°15S 130°25E **60 B5**
Béal an Átha = Ballina *Ireland* 54°7N 9°9W **10 B2**
Béal Átha na Sluaighe = Ballinasloe *Ireland* 53°20N 8°13W **10 C3**
Beals Cr. → *U.S.A.* 32°10N 100°51W **84 E4**
Beamsville *Canada* 43°12N 79°28W **82 C5**
Bear → *Calif., U.S.A.* 38°56N 121°36W **78 G5**
Bear → *Utah, U.S.A.* 41°30N 112°8W **74 G17**
Bear I. = Bjørnøya *Arctic* 74°30N 19°0E **4 B8**
Bear I. *Ireland* 51°38N 9°50W **10 E2**
Bear L. *Canada* 55°8N 96°0W **71 B9**
Bear L. *U.S.A.* 41°59N 111°21W **76 F8**
Bear Lake *Canada* 45°27N 79°35W **82 A5**
Beardmore *Canada* 49°36N 87°57W **72 C2**
Beardmore Glacier *Antarctica* 84°30S 170°0E **5 E11**
Beardstown *U.S.A.* 40°1N 90°26W **80 E8**
Bearma → *India* 24°20N 79°51E **43 G8**
Béarn *France* 43°20N 0°30W **20 E3**
Bearpaw Mts. *U.S.A.* 48°12N 109°30W **76 B9**
Bearskin Lake *Canada* 53°58N 91°2W **72 B1**
Beas → *India* 31°10N 74°59E **42 D6**
Beata, C. *Dom. Rep.* 17°40N 71°30W **89 C5**
Beata, I. *Dom. Rep.* 17°34N 71°31W **89 C5**
Beatrice *U.S.A.* 40°16N 96°45W **80 E5**
Beatrice, C. *Australia* 14°20S 136°55E **62 A2**
Beatton → *Canada* 56°15N 120°45W **70 B4**
Beatton River *Canada* 57°26N 121°20W **70 B4**
Beatty *U.S.A.* 36°54N 116°46W **78 J10**
Beau Bassin *Mauritius* 20°13S 57°27E **55 d**
Beauce, Plaine de la *France* 48°10N 1°45E **20 B4**
Beauceville *Canada* 46°13N 70°46W **73 C5**
Beaudesert *Australia* 27°59S 153°0E **63 D5**
Beaufort *Malaysia* 5°30N 115°40E **36 C5**
Beaufort *N.C., U.S.A.* 34°43N 76°40W **85 D16**
Beaufort *S.C., U.S.A.* 32°26N 80°40W **85 E14**
Beaufort Sea *Arctic* 72°0N 140°0W **66 B5**
Beaufort West *S. Africa* 32°18S 22°36E **56 E3**
Beauharnois *Canada* 45°20N 73°52W **83 A11**
Beaulieu → *Canada* 62°3N 113°11W **70 A6**

Beauly *U.K.* 57°30N 4°28W **11 D4**
Beauly → *U.K.* 57°29N 4°27W **11 D4**
Beaumaris *U.K.* 53°16N 4°6W **12 D3**
Beaumont *Belgium* 50°15N 4°14E **15 D4**
Beaumont *Calif., U.S.A.* 33°57N 116°59W **79 M9**
Beaumont *Tex., U.S.A.* 30°5N 94°6W **84 F7**
Beaune *France* 47°2N 4°50E **20 C6**
Beaupré *Canada* 47°3N 70°54W **73 C5**
Beauraing *Belgium* 50°7N 4°57E **15 D4**
Beausejour *Canada* 50°5N 96°35W **71 C9**
Beauvais *France* 49°25N 2°8E **20 B5**
Beauval *Canada* 55°9N 107°37W **71 B7**
Beaver *Okla., U.S.A.* 36°49N 100°31W **84 C4**
Beaver *Pa., U.S.A.* 40°42N 80°19W **82 F4**
Beaver *Utah, U.S.A.* 38°17N 112°38W **76 G7**
Beaver → *B.C., Canada* 59°52N 124°20W **70 B4**
Beaver → *Ont., Canada* 55°55N 87°48W **72 A2**
Beaver → *Sask., Canada* 55°26N 107°45W **71 B7**
Beaver City *U.S.A.* 40°8N 99°50W **80 E4**
Beaver Creek *Canada* 63°0N 141°0W **68 E3**
Beaver Dam *U.S.A.* 43°28N 88°50W **80 D9**
Beaver Falls *U.S.A.* 40°46N 80°20W **82 F4**
Beaver Hill L. *Canada* 54°5N 94°50W **71 C10**
Beaver I. *U.S.A.* 45°40N 85°33W **81 C11**
Beavercreek *U.S.A.* 39°43N 84°11W **81 F11**
Beaverhill L. *Canada* 53°27N 112°32W **70 C6**
Beaverlodge *Canada* 55°11N 119°29W **70 B5**
Beaverstone → *Canada* 54°59N 89°25W **72 B2**
Beaverton *Canada* 44°26N 79°9W **82 B5**
Beaverton *U.S.A.* 45°29N 122°48W **78 E4**
Beawar *India* 26°3N 74°18E **42 F6**
Bebedouro *Brazil* 21°0S 48°25W **95 A6**
Bebington *U.K.* 53°22N 3°0W **12 D4**
Becán *Mexico* 18°34N 89°31W **87 D7**
Bécancour *Canada* 46°20N 72°26W **81 B17**
Beccles *U.K.* 52°27N 1°35E **13 E9**
Bečej *Serbia* 45°36N 20°3E **23 B9**
Béchar *Algeria* 31°38N 2°18W **52 B5**
Becharof L. *U.S.A.* 57°56N 156°23W **74 D8**
Beckley *U.S.A.* 37°47N 81°11W **81 G13**
Beddouza, C. *Morocco* 32°33N 9°9W **52 B4**
Bedford *Canada* 45°7N 72°59W **83 A12**
Bedford *S. Africa* 32°40S 26°10E **56 E4**
Bedford *U.K.* 52°8N 0°28W **13 E7**
Bedford *Ind., U.S.A.* 38°52N 86°29W **80 F10**
Bedford *Iowa, U.S.A.* 40°40N 94°44W **80 E6**
Bedford *Ohio, U.S.A.* 41°23N 81°32W **82 E3**
Bedford *Pa., U.S.A.* 40°1N 78°30W **82 F6**
Bedford *Va., U.S.A.* 37°20N 79°31W **81 G14**
Bedford □ *U.K.* 52°4N 0°28W **13 E7**
Bedford, C. *Australia* 15°14S 145°21E **62 B4**
Bedourie *Australia* 24°30S 139°30E **62 C2**
Bedti → *India* 14°50N 74°44E **45 G2**
Bedugul *Indonesia* 8°17S 115°10E **37 J18**
Bedum *Neths.* 53°18N 6°36E **15 A6**
Beebe Plain *Canada* 45°1N 72°9W **83 A12**
Beech Creek *U.S.A.* 41°5N 77°36W **82 E7**
Beechy *Canada* 50°53N 107°24W **71 C7**
Beed = Bir *India* 19°4N 75°46E **44 E2**
Beef I. *Br. Virgin Is.* 18°26N 64°30W **89 e**
Beenleigh *Australia* 27°43S 153°10E **63 D5**
Be'er Sheva *Israel* 31°15N 34°48E **48 D3**
Beersheba = Be'er Sheva *Israel* 31°15N 34°48E **48 D3**
Beestekraal *S. Africa* 25°23S 27°38E **57 C4**
Beeston *U.K.* 52°56N 1°14W **12 E6**
Beeton *Canada* 44°5N 79°47W **82 B5**
Beeville *U.S.A.* 28°24N 97°45W **84 G6**
Befale *Dem. Rep. of the Congo* 0°25N 20°45E **54 D4**
Bega *Australia* 36°41S 149°51E **63 F4**
Begusarai *India* 25°24N 86°9E **43 G12**
Behābād *Iran* 31°30N 56°30E **47 D8**
Behbehān *Iran* 30°30N 50°15E **47 D6**
Behchoko *Canada* 62°50N 116°3W **70 A5**
Behm Canal *U.S.A.* 55°10N 131°0W **70 B2**
Behshahr *Iran* 36°45N 53°35E **47 B7**
Bei Jiang → *China* 23°2N 112°58E **35 F9**
Bei Shan *China* 41°30N 96°0E **30 C8**
Bei'an *China* 48°10N 126°20E **31 B14**
Beibei *China* 29°47N 106°22E **34 C6**
Beichuan *China* 31°55N 104°39E **34 B5**
Beihai *China* 21°28N 109°6E **34 G7**
Beijing *China* 39°55N 116°20E **32 D9**
Beijing Capital Int. ✈ (PEK) *China* 40°5N 116°35E **32 D9**
Beijing Shi □ *China* 39°55N 116°20E **32 D9**
Beilen *Neths.* 52°52N 6°27E **15 B6**
Beiliu *China* 22°41N 110°21E **35 F8**
Beilpajah *Australia* 32°54S 143°52E **63 E3**
Beinn na Faoghla = Benbecula *U.K.* 57°26N 7°21W **11 D1**
Beipan Jiang → *China* 24°55S 106°5E **34 E6**
Beipiao *China* 41°52N 120°32E **33 D11**
Beira *Mozam.* 19°50S 34°52E **55 H6**
Beirut = Bayrūt *Lebanon* 33°53N 35°31E **48 B4**
Beiseker *Canada* 51°23N 113°32W **70 C6**
Beit Lāhīyā *Gaza Strip* 31°33N 34°32E **48 D3**
Beitaolaizhao *China* 44°58N 125°58E **33 B13**
Beitbridge *Zimbabwe* 22°12S 30°0E **55 J6**
Beizhen = Binzhou *China* 37°20N 118°2E **33 F10**
Beizhen *China* 41°38N 121°54E **33 D11**
Beizhengzhen *China* 44°31N 123°30E **33 B12**
Beja *Portugal* 38°2N 7°53W **21 C2**
Béja *Tunisia* 36°43N 9°12E **53 A7**
Bejaïa *Algeria* 36°42N 5°2E **52 A7**
Béjar *Spain* 40°23N 5°46W **21 B3**
Bejestān *Iran* 34°30N 58°5E **47 C8**
Bekaa Valley = Al Biqā *Lebanon* 34°10N 36°10E **48 A5**
Bekasi *Indonesia* 6°14S 106°59E **37 G12**
Békéscsaba *Hungary* 46°40N 21°5E **17 E11**
Bekok *Malaysia* 2°20N 103°7E **39 b**
Bela *India* 25°50N 82°0E **43 G10**
Bela *Pakistan* 26°12N 66°20E **42 F2**

Bela Bela *S. Africa* 24°51S 28°19E **57 B4**
Bela Crkva *Serbia* 44°55N 21°27E **23 B9**
Bela Vista *Brazil* 22°12S 56°20W **94 A4**
Bela Vista *Mozam.* 26°10S 32°44E **57 C5**
Belagavi *India* 15°55N 74°35E **45 G2**
Belan → *India* 24°2N 81°45E **43 G9**
Belarus ■ *Europe* 53°30N 27°0E **17 B14**
Belau = Palau ■ *Palau* 7°30N 134°30E **64 G5**
Belawan *Indonesia* 3°33N 98°32E **36 D1**
Belaya → *Russia* 54°40N 56°0E **18 C10**
Belaya Tserkov = Bila Tserkva *Ukraine* 49°45N 30°10E **17 D16**
Belaya Zemlya, Ostrova *Russia* 81°36N 62°18E **26 A7**
Belcher Is. *Canada* 56°15N 78°45E **72 A4**
Belden *U.S.A.* 40°2N 121°17W **78 E5**
Belebey *Russia* 54°7N 54°7E **18 D9**
Beledweyne *Somalia* 4°30N 45°5E **49 G4**
Belém *Brazil* 1°20S 48°30W **93 D9**
Belén *Argentina* 27°40S 67°5W **94 B2**
Belén *Paraguay* 23°30S 57°6W **94 A4**
Belen *U.S.A.* 34°40N 106°46W **77 J10**
Belet Uen = Beledweyne *Somalia* 4°30N 45°5E **49 G4**
Belev *Russia* 53°50N 36°5E **18 D6**
Belfast = eMakhazeni *S. Africa* 25°42S 30°2E **57 C5**
Belfast *U.K.* 54°37N 5°56W **10 B6**
Belfast *Maine, U.S.A.* 44°26N 69°1W **81 D19**
Belfast *N.Y., U.S.A.* 42°21N 78°7W **82 D6**
Belfast L. *U.K.* 54°40N 5°50W **10 B6**
Belfield *U.S.A.* 46°53N 103°12W **80 B2**
Belfort *France* 47°38N 6°50E **20 C7**
Belfry *U.S.A.* 45°9N 109°1W **76 D9**
Belgaum = Belagavi *India* 15°55N 74°35E **45 G2**
Belgium ■ *Europe* 50°30N 5°0E **15 D4**
Belgorod *Russia* 50°35N 36°35E **19 D6**
Belgorod-Dnestrovskiy = Bilhorod-Dnistrovskyy *Ukraine* 46°11N 30°23E **19 E5**
Belgrade = Beograd *Serbia* 44°50N 20°37E **23 B9**
Belgrade *U.S.A.* 45°47N 111°11W **76 D8**
Belgrano *Antarctica* 77°52S 34°37W **5 D1**
Belhaven *U.S.A.* 35°33N 76°37W **85 D16**
Beli Drim → *Europe* 42°6N 20°25E **23 C9**
Belimbing *Indonesia* 8°24S 115°2E **37 J18**
Belinyu *Indonesia* 1°35S 105°50E **36 E3**
Beliton Is. = Belitung *Indonesia* 3°10S 107°50E **36 E3**
Belitung *Indonesia* 3°10S 107°50E **36 E3**
Belize ■ *Cent. Amer.* 17°0N 88°30W **87 D7**
Belize Barrier Reef *Belize* 17°9N 88°3W **87 D7**
Belize City *Belize* 17°25N 88°10W **87 D7**
Belkovskiy, Ostrov *Russia* 75°32N 135°44E **27 B14**
Bell → *Canada* 49°48N 77°38W **72 C4**
Bell I. *Canada* 50°46N 55°35W **73 B8**
Bell-Irving → *Canada* 56°12N 129°5W **70 B3**
Bell Peninsula *Canada* 63°50N 82°0W **69 E15**
Bell Ville *Argentina* 32°40S 62°40W **94 C3**
Bella Bella *Canada* 52°10N 128°10W **70 C3**
Bella Coola *Canada* 52°25N 126°40W **70 C3**
Bella Unión *Uruguay* 30°15S 57°40W **94 C4**
Bella Vista *Corrientes, Argentina* 28°33S 59°0W **94 B4**
Bella Vista *Tucuman, Argentina* 27°10S 65°25W **94 B2**
Bella Vista *U.S.A.* 36°28N 94°16W **80 G6**
Bellaire *U.S.A.* 40°1N 80°45W **82 F4**
Bellata *Australia* 29°53S 149°46E **63 D4**
Belle Fourche *U.S.A.* 44°40N 103°51W **80 C2**
Belle Fourche → *U.S.A.* 44°26N 102°18W **80 C2**
Belle Glade *U.S.A.* 26°41N 80°40W **85 H14**
Belle-Île *France* 47°20N 3°10W **20 C2**
Belle Isle *Canada* 51°57N 55°25W **73 B8**
Belle Isle, Str. of *Canada* 51°30N 56°30W **73 B8**
Belle Plaine *Canada* 41°54N 92°17W **80 E7**
Belle River *Canada* 42°18N 82°43W **82 D2**
Bellefontaine *U.S.A.* 40°22N 83°46W **81 E12**
Bellefonte *U.S.A.* 40°55N 77°47W **82 F7**
Belleoram *Canada* 47°31N 55°25W **73 C8**
Belleplaine *Barbados* 13°15N 59°34W **89 g**
Belleville *Canada* 44°10N 77°23W **82 B7**
Belleville *Ill., U.S.A.* 38°31N 89°59W **80 F9**
Belleville *Kans., U.S.A.* 39°50N 97°38W **80 F5**
Belleville *N.J., U.S.A.* 40°47N 74°9W **83 F10**
Belleville *N.Y., U.S.A.* 43°46N 76°10W **83 C8**
Bellevue *Canada* 49°35N 114°22W **70 D6**
Bellevue *Idaho, U.S.A.* 43°28N 114°16W **76 E6**
Bellevue *Nebr., U.S.A.* 41°9N 95°54W **80 E6**
Bellevue *Ohio, U.S.A.* 41°17N 82°51W **82 E2**
Bellevue *Wash., U.S.A.* 47°37N 122°12W **78 C4**
Bellin = Kangirsuk *Canada* 60°0N 70°0W **69 F18**
Bellingen *Australia* 30°25S 152°50E **63 E5**
Bellingham *U.S.A.* 48°46N 122°29W **78 B4**
Bellingshausen Abyssal Plain *S. Ocean* 64°0S 90°0W **5 C16**
Bellingshausen Sea *Antarctica* 66°0S 80°0W **5 C17**
Bellinzona *Switz.* 46°11N 9°1E **20 C8**
Bello *Colombia* 6°20N 75°33W **92 B3**
Bellows Falls *U.S.A.* 43°8N 72°27W **83 C12**
Bellpat *Pakistan* 29°0N 68°5E **42 E3**
Belluno *Italy* 46°9N 12°13E **22 A5**
Bellwood *U.S.A.* 40°36N 78°20W **82 F6**
Belmont *Australia* 33°4S 151°42E **63 E5**
Belmont *Canada* 42°53N 81°5W **82 D3**
Belmont *S. Africa* 29°28S 24°22E **56 D3**
Belmont *U.S.A.* 42°14N 78°2W **82 D6**
Belmonte *Brazil* 16°0S 39°0W **93 G11**
Belmopan *Belize* 17°18N 88°30W **87 D7**
Belmullet *Ireland* 54°14N 9°58W **10 B2**
Belo Horizonte *Brazil* 19°55S 43°56W **93 G10**
Belo-Tsiribihina *Madag.* 19°40S 44°30E **55 H8**
Belogorsk *Russia* 51°0N 128°20E **27 D13**
Beloit *Kans., U.S.A.* 39°28N 98°6W **80 F4**
Beloit *Wis., U.S.A.* 42°31N 89°2W **80 D9**
Belokorovichi *Ukraine* 51°7N 28°2E **17 C15**
Belomorsk *Russia* 64°35N 34°54E **18 B5**

Belonia India 23°15N 91°30E 41 H17
Beloretsk Russia 53°58N 58°24E 18 D10
Belorussia = Belarus ■
  Europe 53°30N 27°0E 17 B14
Belovo Russia 54°30N 86°0E 26 D9
Beloyarskiy Russia 63°42N 66°40E 26 C7
Beloye, Ozero Russia 60°10N 37°35E 18 B6
Beloye More Russia 66°30N 38°0E 18 A6
Belozersk Russia 60°1N 37°45E 18 B6
Belpre U.S.A. 39°17N 81°34W 81 F13
Belrain India 28°23N 80°55E 43 E9
Belt U.S.A. 47°23N 110°55W 76 C8
Beltana Australia 30°48S 138°25E 63 E2
Belterra Brazil 2°45S 55°0W 93 D8
Belton U.S.A. 31°3N 97°28W 84 F6
Belton L. U.S.A. 31°6N 97°28W 84 F6
Belţsy = Bălţi Moldova 47°48N 27°58E 17 E14
Belturbet Ireland 54°6N 7°26W 10 B4
Belukha Russia 49°50N 86°50E 30 B6
Beluran Malaysia 5°48N 117°35E 36 C5
Belushya Guba Russia 71°32N 52°19E 26 B6
Belvidere Ill., U.S.A. 42°15N 88°50W 80 D9
Belvidere N.J., U.S.A. 40°50N 75°5W 83 F9
Belyando → Australia 21°38S 146°50E 62 C4
Belyando Crossing
  Australia 21°32S 146°51E 62 C4
Belyuen Australia 12°34S 130°42E 60 B5
Belyy, Ostrov Russia 73°30N 71°0E 26 B8
Belyy Yar Russia 58°26N 84°39E 26 D9
Belzoni U.S.A. 33°11N 90°29W 85 E9
Bembéréke Benin 10°11N 2°43E 52 F6
Bemetara India 21°42N 81°32E 43 J9
Bemidji U.S.A. 47°28N 94°53W 80 B6
Ben Iran 32°32N 50°45E 47 C6
Ben Cruachan U.K. 56°26N 5°8W 11 E3
Ben Dearg U.K. 57°47N 4°56W 11 D4
Ben En △ Vietnam 19°37N 105°30E 38 C5
Ben Gardane Tunisia 33°11N 11°11E 53 B8
Ben Hope U.K. 58°25N 4°36W 11 C4
Ben Lawers U.K. 56°32N 4°14W 11 E4
Ben Lomond N.S.W.,
  Australia 30°1S 151°43E 63 E5
Ben Lomond Tas.,
  Australia 41°38S 147°42E 63 G4
Ben Lomond U.K. 56°11N 4°38W 11 E4
Ben Lomond △ Australia 41°33S 147°39E 63 G4
Ben Luc Vietnam 10°39N 106°29E 39 G6
Ben Macdhui U.K. 57°4N 3°40W 11 D5
Ben Mhor U.K. 57°15N 7°18W 11 D1
Ben More Argyll & Bute,
  U.K. 56°26N 6°1W 11 E2
Ben More Stirling, U.K. 56°23N 4°32W 11 E4
Ben More Assynt U.K. 58°8N 4°52W 11 C4
Ben Nevis U.K. 56°48N 5°1W 11 E3
Ben Quang Vietnam 17°3N 106°55E 38 D6
Ben Tre Vietnam 10°14N 106°23E 39 G6
Ben Vorlich U.K. 56°21N 4°14W 11 E4
Ben Wyvis U.K. 57°40N 4°35W 11 D4
Bena Nigeria 11°20N 5°50E 52 F7
Benaco, L. di = Garda, L. di
  Italy 45°40N 10°41E 22 B4
Benalla Australia 36°30S 146°0E 63 F4
Benares = Varanasi India 25°22N 83°0E 43 G10
Benavente Spain 42°2N 5°43W 21 A3
Benavides U.S.A. 27°36N 98°25W 84 H5
Benbecula U.K. 57°26N 7°21W 11 D1
Benbonyathe Hill
  Australia 30°25S 139°11E 63 E2
Bend U.S.A. 44°4N 121°19W 76 D3
Bender Beyla Somalia 9°30N 50°48E 49 F5
Bendery Moldova 46°50N 29°30E 17 E15
Bendigo Australia 36°40S 144°15E 63 F3
Bene Beraq Israel 32°6N 34°51E 48 C3
Benevento Italy 41°8N 14°45E 22 D6
Beng Mealea Cambodia 13°28N 104°14E 38 F5
Bengal, Bay of Ind. Oc. 15°0N 90°0E 41 M17
Bengaluru India 12°59N 77°40E 45 H3
Bengbu China 32°58N 117°20E 33 H9
Benghazi = Banghāzī
  Libya 32°11N 20°3E 53 B10
Bengkalis Indonesia 1°30N 102°10E 39 M4
Bengkulu Indonesia 3°50S 102°12E 36 E2
Bengkulu □ Indonesia 3°48S 102°16E 36 E2
Bengough Canada 49°25N 105°10W 71 D7
Benguela Angola 12°37S 13°25E 55 G2
Benguérua, I. Mozam. 21°58S 35°28E 57 B6
Beni Dem. Rep. of the Congo 0°30N 29°27E 54 D5
Beni → Bolivia 10°23S 65°24W 92 F5
Beni Mellal Morocco 32°21N 6°21W 52 B4
Beni Suef Egypt 29°5N 31°6E 53 C12
Beniah L. Canada 63°23N 112°17W 70 A6
Benidorm Spain 38°33N 0°9W 21 C5
Benin ■ Africa 10°0N 2°0E 52 G6
Benin, Bight of W. Afr. 5°0N 3°0E 52 H6
Benin City Nigeria 6°20N 5°31E 52 G7
Benito Juárez Argentina 37°40S 59°43W 94 D4
Benjamin Aceval
  Paraguay 24°58S 57°34W 94 A4
Benjamin Constant Brazil 4°40S 70°15W 92 D4
Benjamin Hill Mexico 30°9N 111°7W 86 A2
Benkelman U.S.A. 40°3N 101°32W 80 E3
Bennett Canada 59°51N 135°0W 70 B2
Bennett, L. Australia 22°50S 131°2E 60 D5
Bennetta, Ostrov
  Russia 76°21N 148°56E 27 B15
Bennettsville U.S.A. 34°37N 79°41W 85 D15
Bennington N.H., U.S.A. 43°0N 71°55W 83 D13
Bennington Vt., U.S.A. 42°53N 73°12W 83 D11
Benom Malaysia 3°50N 102°6E 39 L4
Benoni S. Africa 26°11S 28°18E 57 D4
Benque Viejo del Carmen
  Belize 17°5N 89°8W 87 D7
Benson Ariz., U.S.A. 31°58N 110°18W 77 L8
Benson Minn., U.S.A. 45°19N 95°36W 80 C6
Bent Iran 26°20N 59°31E 47 E8
Benteng Indonesia 6°10S 120°30E 37 F6
Bentinck I. Australia 17°3S 139°35E 62 B2
Bentinck I. Burma 11°45N 98°3E 39 G2
Bentley Subglacial Trench
  Antarctica 80°0S 115°0W 5 E15

Bento Gonçalves Brazil 29°10S 51°31W 95 B5
Benton Ark., U.S.A. 34°34N 92°35W 84 D8
Benton Calif., U.S.A. 37°48N 118°32W 78 H8
Benton Ill., U.S.A. 38°0N 88°55W 80 F9
Benton Pa., U.S.A. 41°12N 76°23W 83 E8
Benton Harbor U.S.A. 42°6N 86°27W 80 D10
Bentong Malaysia 3°31N 101°55E 39 L3
Bentonville U.S.A. 36°22N 94°13W 84 C7
Benue → Nigeria 7°48N 6°46E 52 G7
Benxi China 41°20N 123°48E 33 D12
Beo Indonesia 4°25N 126°50E 37 D7
Beograd Serbia 44°50N 20°37E 23 B9
Beolgyo S. Korea 34°51N 127°21E 33 G14
Beppu Japan 33°15N 131°30E 29 H5
Beqa Fiji 18°23S 178°8E 59 a
Beqaa Valley = Al Biqâ
  Lebanon 34°10N 36°10E 48 A5
Ber Mota India 23°27N 68°34E 42 H3
Bera, Tasik Malaysia 3°5N 102°38E 39 L4
Berach → India 25°15N 75°2E 42 G6
Berastagi Indonesia 3°11N 98°31E 39 L2
Berat Albania 40°43N 19°59E 23 D8
Berau = Tanjungredeb
  Indonesia 2°9N 117°29E 36 D5
Berau, Teluk Indonesia 2°30S 132°30E 37 E8
Berber Sudan 18°0N 34°0E 53 E12
Berbera Somalia 10°30N 45°2E 49 E4
Berbérati C.A.R. 4°15N 15°40E 54 D3
Berbice → Guyana 6°20N 57°32W 92 B7
Berdichev = Berdychiv
  Ukraine 49°57N 28°30E 17 D15
Berdsk Russia 54°47N 83°2E 26 D9
Berdyansk Ukraine 46°45N 36°50E 19 E6
Berdychiv Ukraine 49°57N 28°30E 17 D15
Berea U.S.A. 37°34N 84°17W 81 G11
Berebere Indonesia 2°25N 128°45E 37 D7
Bereeda Somalia 11°45N 51°0E 49 E5
Berehove Ukraine 48°15N 22°35E 17 D12
Berekum Ghana 7°29N 2°34W 52 G5
Berens → Canada 52°25N 97°2W 71 C9
Berens I. Canada 52°18N 97°18W 71 C9
Berens River Canada 52°25N 97°0W 71 C9
Beresford U.S.A. 43°5N 96°47W 80 D6
Berestechko Ukraine 50°22N 25°5E 17 C13
Bereza = Byaroza
  Belarus 52°31N 24°51E 17 B13
Berezhany Ukraine 49°26N 24°58E 17 D13
Berezina = Byarezina
  Belarus 52°33N 30°14E 17 B16
Bereznik Russia 62°51N 42°40E 18 B7
Berezniki Russia 59°24N 56°46E 18 C10
Berezovo Russia 64°0N 65°0E 26 C7
Berga Spain 42°6N 1°48E 21 A6
Bergama Turkey 39°8N 27°11E 23 E12
Bérgamo Italy 45°41N 9°43E 20 D8
Bergaon India 20°41N 80°27E 44 D5
Bergen Neths. 52°40N 4°43E 15 B4
Bergen Norway 60°20N 5°20E 8 F11
Bergen op Zoom Neths. 51°28N 4°18E 15 C4
Bergerac France 44°51N 0°30E 20 D4
Bergholz U.S.A. 40°31N 80°53W 82 F4
Berhala, Selat Indonesia 1°0S 104°15E 36 E2
Berhampore = Baharampur
  India 24°2N 88°27E 43 G13
Berhampur = Brahmapur
  India 19°15N 84°54E 44 E7
Bering Glacier U.S.A. 60°20N 143°0W 74 C11
Bering Sea Pac. Oc. 58°0N 171°0W 66 D2
Bering Strait Pac. Oc. 65°30N 169°0W 74 B6
Beringovskiy Russia 63°3N 179°19E 27 C18
Berisso Argentina 34°56S 57°50W 94 C4
Berja Spain 36°50N 2°56W 21 D4
Berkner I. Antarctica 79°30S 50°0W 5 D18
Berkshire U.S.A. 42°19N 76°11W 83 D8
Berkshire Downs U.K. 51°33N 1°29W 13 F6
Berlin Md., U.S.A. 38°20N 75°13W 81 F16
Berlin N.H., U.S.A. 44°28N 71°11W 83 B13
Berlin N.Y., U.S.A. 42°42N 73°23W 83 D11
Berlin Wis., U.S.A. 43°58N 88°57W 80 D9
Berlin L. U.S.A. 41°3N 81°0W 82 E4
Bermejo → Formosa,
  Argentina 26°51S 58°23W 94 B4
Bermejo → San Juan,
  Argentina 32°30S 67°30W 94 C2
Bermejo, Paso = Uspallata, P. de
  Argentina 32°37S 70°25W 94 C2
Bermen, L. Canada 53°35N 68°55W 73 B6
Bermuda ☑ Atl. Oc. 32°18N 64°45W 67 F13
Bern Switz. 46°57N 7°28E 20 C7
Bernalillo U.S.A. 35°18N 106°33W 77 J10
Bernardo de Irigoyen
  Argentina 26°15S 53°40W 95 B5
Bernardsville U.S.A. 40°43N 74°34W 83 F10
Bernasconi Argentina 37°55S 63°44W 94 D3
Bernburg Germany 51°47N 11°44E 16 C6
Berne = Bern Switz. 46°57N 7°28E 20 C7
Berneray U.K. 57°43N 7°11W 11 D1
Bernier I. Australia 24°50S 113°12E 61 D1
Bernina, Piz Switz. 46°20N 9°54E 20 C8
Beroun Czech Rep. 49°57N 14°5E 16 D8
Berri Australia 34°14S 140°35E 63 E3
Berriane Algeria 32°50N 3°26E 52 B6
Berry Australia 34°46S 150°43E 63 E5
Berry France 46°50N 2°0E 20 C5
Berry Is. Bahamas 25°40N 77°50W 88 A4
Berryessa, L. U.S.A. 38°31N 122°6W 78 G4
Berryville U.S.A. 36°22N 93°34W 84 C8
Berséba Namibia 26°0S 17°46E 56 C2
Bershad Ukraine 48°22N 29°31E 17 D15
Berthold U.S.A. 48°19N 101°44W 80 A3
Berthoud U.S.A. 40°19N 105°5W 76 F11
Bertoua Cameroon 4°30N 13°45E 54 D2
Bertraghboy B. Ireland 53°22N 9°54W 10 C2
Beruwala Sri Lanka 6°30N 80°0E 45 L4
Berwick U.S.A. 41°3N 76°14W 83 E8
Berwick-upon-Tweed U.K. 55°46N 2°0W 12 B6
Berwyn Mts. U.K. 52°54N 3°26W 12 E4

Besal Pakistan 35°4N 73°56E 43 B5
Besalampy Madag. 16°43S 44°29E 55 H8
Besançon France 47°15N 6°2E 20 C7
Besar Indonesia 2°40S 116°0E 36 E5
Besni Turkey 37°41N 37°52E 46 B3
Besor, N. → Egypt 31°28N 34°22E 48 D3
Bessarabiya Moldova 47°0N 28°10E 17 E15
Bessarabka = Basarabeasca
  Moldova 46°21N 28°58E 17 E15
Bessemer Ala., U.S.A. 33°24N 86°58W 85 E11
Bessemer Mich., U.S.A. 46°29N 90°3W 80 B8
Bessemer Pa., U.S.A. 40°59N 80°30W 82 F4
Beswick Australia 14°34S 132°53E 60 B5
Beswick ۞ Australia 14°31S 132°51E 60 B5
Bet She'an Israel 32°30N 35°30E 48 C4
Bet Shemesh Israel 31°44N 35°0E 48 D4
Betanzos Spain 43°15N 8°12W 21 A1
Bétaré Oya Cameroon 5°40N 14°5E 54 C2
Bethal S. Africa 26°27S 29°28E 57 D4
Bethanien Namibia 26°31S 17°8E 56 C2
Bethany Canada 44°11N 78°34W 82 B6
Bethany Mo., U.S.A. 40°16N 94°2W 80 E6
Bethany Okla., U.S.A. 35°31N 97°38W 84 D6
Bethel Alaska, U.S.A. 60°48N 161°45W 74 C7
Bethel Conn., U.S.A. 41°22N 73°25W 83 E11
Bethel Maine, U.S.A. 44°25N 70°47W 83 B14
Bethel Vt., U.S.A. 43°50N 72°38W 83 C12
Bethel Park U.S.A. 40°19N 80°2W 82 F4
Bethlehem S. Africa 28°14S 28°18E 57 C4
Bethlehem U.S.A. 40°37N 75°23W 83 F9
Bethulie S. Africa 30°30S 25°59E 56 D4
Béthune France 50°30N 2°38E 20 A5
Betioky Madag. 23°48S 44°20E 55 J8
Betong Malaysia 1°24N 111°31E 36 D4
Betong Thailand 5°45N 101°5E 39 K3
Betoota Australia 25°45S 140°42E 62 D3
Betpaqdala Kazakhstan 45°45N 70°30E 30 E8
Betroka Madag. 23°16S 46°0E 55 J9
Betsiamites Canada 48°56N 68°40W 73 C6
Betsiamites → Canada 48°56N 68°38W 73 C6
Bettendorf U.S.A. 41°32N 90°30W 80 E8
Bettiah India 26°48N 84°33E 43 F11
Betul India 21°58N 77°59E 44 D3
Betws-y-Coed U.K. 53°5N 3°48W 12 D4
Beulah Mich., U.S.A. 44°38N 86°6W 80 C10
Beulah N. Dak., U.S.A. 47°16N 101°47W 80 B3
Beveren Belgium 51°12N 4°16E 15 C4
Beverley Australia 32°9S 116°56E 61 F2
Beverley U.K. 53°51N 0°26W 12 D7
Beverly U.S.A. 42°33N 70°53W 83 D14
Beverly Hills U.S.A. 28°55N 82°28W 85 G13
Bewas → India 23°59N 79°21E 43 H8
Bewdley Canada 44°5N 78°19W 82 B6
Bexhill U.K. 50°51N 0°29E 13 G8
Beyānlū Iran 36°0N 47°51E 46 C5
Beyneu Kazakhstan 45°18N 55°9E 19 E10
Beypazarı Turkey 40°10N 31°56E 19 F5
Beypore India 11°10N 75°47E 45 J1
Beyşehir Turkey 37°41N 31°33E 46 B1
Beyşehir Gölü Turkey 37°41N 31°45E 46 B1
Béziers France 43°20N 3°12E 20 E5
Bezwada = Vijayawada
  India 16°31N 80°39E 44 F5
Bhabua India 25°3N 83°37E 43 G10
Bhachau India 23°20N 70°16E 42 H4
Bhadar → Gujarat, India 22°17N 72°20E 42 H5
Bhadar → Gujarat, India 21°27N 69°47E 42 J3
Bhadarwah India 32°58N 75°46E 43 C6
Bhadgaon = Bhaktapur
  Nepal 27°38N 85°24E 43 F11
Bhadohi India 25°25N 82°34E 43 G10
Bhadra India 29°8N 75°14E 42 E6
Bhadra → India 14°0N 75°20E 45 H2
Bhadrachalam India 17°40N 80°53E 44 F5
Bhadrak India 21°10N 86°30E 44 D8
Bhadran India 22°19N 72°6E 42 H5
Bhadravati India 13°49N 75°40E 45 H2
Bhag Pakistan 29°2N 67°49E 42 E2
Bhagalpur India 25°10N 87°0E 43 G12
Bhagirathi → Paschimbanga,
  India 23°25N 88°23E 43 H13
Bhagirathi → Uttarakhand,
  India 30°8N 78°35E 43 D8
Bhainsa India 19°10N 77°58E 44 E3
Bhakkar Pakistan 31°40N 71°5E 42 D4
Bhakra Dam India 31°30N 76°45E 42 D7
Bhaktapur Nepal 27°38N 85°24E 43 F11
Bhalki India 18°2N 77°13E 44 E3
Bhamo Burma 24°15N 97°15E 41 G20
Bhamragarh India 19°30N 80°40E 44 E5
Bhandara India 21°5N 79°42E 44 D4
Bhanpura India 24°31N 75°44E 42 G6
Bhanrer Ra. India 23°40N 79°45E 43 H8
Bhaptiahi India 26°19N 86°44E 43 F12
Bharat = India ■ Asia 20°0N 78°0E 40 K11
Bharatpur Chhattisgarh,
  India 23°44N 81°46E 43 H9
Bharatpur Raj., India 27°15N 77°30E 42 F7
Bharatpur Nepal 27°34N 84°10E 43 H11
Bharno India 23°14N 84°53E 43 H11
Bharraig = Barra U.K. 57°0N 7°29W 11 E1
Bharraig, Caolas = Barra, Sd. of
  U.K. 57°4N 7°25W 11 D1
Bharuch India 21°47N 73°0E 44 J1
Bhatarsaigh = Vatersay
  U.K. 56°55N 7°32W 11 E1
Bhatghar L. India 18°10N 73°48E 44 E1
Bhatinda India 30°15N 74°57E 42 D6
Bhatkal India 13°58N 74°35E 45 H2
Bhatpara India 22°50N 88°25E 43 H13
Bhattu India 29°36N 75°19E 42 E6
Bhaun Pakistan 32°55N 72°40E 42 C5
Bhaunagar = Bhavnagar
  India 21°45N 72°10E 44 D1
Bhavnagar India 21°45N 72°10E 44 D1
Bhawanipatna India 19°55N 83°10E 44 E5
Bhawari India 25°31N 73°4E 42 G5
Bhayavadar India 21°51N 70°15E 42 J4
Bhearnaraigh = Berneray
  U.K. 57°43N 7°11W 11 D1

Bhera Pakistan 32°29N 72°57E 42 C5
Bheri → Nepal 28°47N 81°18E 43 E9
Bhikangaon India 21°52N 75°57E 42 J6
Bhilai = Bhilainagar-Durg
  India 21°13N 81°26E 44 D5
Bhilainagar-Durg India 21°13N 81°26E 44 D5
Bhilsa = Vidisha India 23°28N 77°53E 42 H7
Bhilwara India 25°25N 74°38E 42 G6
Bhima → India 16°25N 77°17E 44 F3
Bhimavaram India 16°30N 81°30E 45 F5
Bhimbar Pakistan 32°59N 74°3E 43 C6
Bhind India 26°30N 78°46E 43 F8
Bhinga India 27°43N 81°56E 43 F9
Bhinmal India 25°0N 72°15E 42 G5
Bhisho S. Africa 32°50S 27°23E 56 D4
Bhiwandi India 19°20N 73°0E 44 E1
Bhiwani India 28°50N 76°9E 42 E7
Bhogava → India 22°26N 72°20E 42 H5
Bhojpur Nepal 27°10N 87°3E 43 F12
Bhokardan India 20°16N 75°46E 44 D2
Bhola Bangla. 22°45N 90°35E 41 H17
Bholari Pakistan 25°19N 68°13E 42 G3
Bhongir India 17°30N 78°56E 44 F4
Bhopal India 23°20N 77°30E 42 H7
Bhopalpatnam India 18°52N 80°23E 44 E5
Bhor India 18°12N 73°53E 44 E1
Bhuban India 20°53N 85°50E 44 D7
Bhubaneshwar India 20°15N 85°50E 44 D7
Bhuj India 23°15N 69°49E 42 H3
Bhumiphol Res. Thailand 17°20N 98°40E 38 D2
Bhusawal India 21°3N 75°46E 44 D2
Bhutan ■ Asia 27°25N 90°30E 41 F17
Biafra, B. of = Bonny, Bight of
  Africa 3°30N 9°20E 54 D1
Biak Indonesia 1°10S 136°6E 37 E9
Biała Podlaska Poland 52°4N 23°6E 17 B12
Białogard Poland 54°2N 15°58E 16 A8
Białystok Poland 53°10N 23°10E 17 B12
Biaora India 23°56N 76°56E 42 H7
Biārjmand Iran 36°6N 55°53E 47 B7
Biaro Indonesia 2°5N 125°26E 37 D7
Biarritz France 43°29N 1°33W 20 E3
Bibai Japan 43°19N 141°52E 28 C10
Bibby I. Canada 61°55N 93°0W 71 A10
Biberach Germany 48°5N 9°47E 16 D5
Bibile Sri Lanka 7°10N 81°25E 45 L5
Bicester U.K. 51°54N 1°9W 13 F6
Bicheno Australia 41°52S 148°18E 63 G4
Bichia India 22°27N 80°42E 43 H9
Bickerton I. Australia 13°45S 136°10E 62 A2
Bid = Bir India 19°4N 75°46E 44 E2
Bida Nigeria 9°3N 5°58E 52 G7
Bidar India 17°55N 77°35E 44 F3
Biddeford U.S.A. 43°30N 70°28W 81 D18
Bideford U.K. 51°1N 4°13W 13 F3
Bideford Bay U.K. 51°5N 4°20W 13 F3
Bidhuna India 26°49N 79°31E 43 F8
Bidokht Iran 34°20N 58°46E 47 C8
Bidor Malaysia 4°6N 101°15E 39 K3
Bidyadanga Australia 18°45S 121°43E 60 C3
Bié, Planalto de Angola 12°0S 16°0E 55 G3
Bieber U.S.A. 41°7N 121°8W 76 F3
Biel Switz. 47°8N 7°14E 20 C7
Bielefeld Germany 52°1N 8°33E 16 B5
Biella Italy 45°34N 8°3E 20 D7
Bielsk Podlaski Poland 52°47N 23°12E 17 B12
Bielsko-Biała Poland 49°50N 19°2E 17 D10
Bien Hoa Vietnam 10°57N 106°49E 39 G6
Bienne = Biel Switz. 47°8N 7°14E 20 C7
Bienville, L. Canada 55°5N 72°40W 72 A5
Biesbosch △ Neths. 51°45N 4°48E 15 C4
Biesiesfontein S. Africa 30°57S 17°58E 56 D2
Big → Canada 54°50N 58°55W 73 B8
Big B. Canada 55°43N 60°35W 73 A7
Big Bear City U.S.A. 34°16N 116°51W 79 L10
Big Bear Lake U.S.A. 34°15N 116°56W 79 L10
Big Belt Mts. U.S.A. 46°30N 111°25W 76 C8
Big Bend Swaziland 26°50S 31°58E 57 D5
Big Bend △ U.S.A. 29°20N 103°5W 84 G3
Big Black → U.S.A. 32°3N 91°4W 85 E9
Big Blue → U.S.A. 39°35N 96°34W 80 F6
Big Buddha
  Hong Kong, China 22°15N 113°54E 31 a
Big Creek U.S.A. 37°11N 119°14W 78 H7
Big Creek △ Canada 51°18N 123°10W 70 C4
Big Cypress △ U.S.A. 26°0N 81°10W 85 H13
Big Desert Australia 35°45S 141°10E 63 F3
Big Falls U.S.A. 48°12N 93°48W 80 A7
Big Fork → U.S.A. 48°31N 93°43W 80 A7
Big Horn Mts. = Bighorn Mts.
  U.S.A. 44°25N 107°0W 76 D10
Big I. Canada 61°7N 116°45W 70 A5
Big Lake U.S.A. 31°12N 101°28W 84 F4
Big Moose U.S.A. 43°49N 74°58W 83 C10
Big Muddy Cr. →
  U.S.A. 48°8N 104°36W 76 B11
Big Pine U.S.A. 37°10N 118°17W 78 H8
Big Piney U.S.A. 42°32N 110°7W 76 E8
Big Quill L. Canada 51°55N 104°50W 71 C8
Big Rapids U.S.A. 43°42N 85°29W 81 D11
Big Rideau L. Canada 44°40N 76°15W 83 B8
Big River Canada 53°50N 107°0W 71 C7
Big Run U.S.A. 40°57N 78°55W 82 F6
Big Sable Pt. U.S.A. 44°3N 86°1W 80 C10
Big Salmon → Canada 61°52N 134°55W 70 A2
Big Sand L. Canada 57°45N 99°45W 71 B9
Big Sandy U.S.A. 48°11N 110°7W 76 B8
Big Sandy → U.S.A. 38°25N 82°36W 81 F12
Big Sandy Cr. = Sandy Cr. →
  U.S.A. 41°51N 109°47W 76 F9
Big Sandy Cr. → U.S.A. 38°7N 102°29W 76 G12
Big Sioux → U.S.A. 42°29N 96°27W 80 D5
Big South Fork △
  U.S.A. 36°27N 84°47W 85 C12
Big Spring U.S.A. 32°15N 101°28W 84 E4
Big Stone City U.S.A. 45°18N 96°28W 80 C5
Big Stone Gap U.S.A. 36°52N 82°47W 81 G12
Big Stone L. U.S.A. 45°30N 96°35W 80 C5
Big Sur U.S.A. 36°15N 121°48W 78 J5
Big Timber U.S.A. 45°50N 109°57W 76 D9

Big Trout L. Canada 53°40N 90°0W 72 B2
Big Trout Lake Canada 53°45N 90°0W 72 B2
Biğa Turkey 40°13N 27°14E 23 D12
Bigadiç Turkey 39°22N 28°7E 23 E13
Biggar Canada 52°4N 108°0W 71 C7
Biggar U.K. 55°38N 3°32W 11 F5
Bigge I. Australia 14°35S 125°10E 60 B4
Biggenden Australia 25°31S 152°4E 63 D5
Biggleswade U.K. 52°5N 0°14W 13 E7
Biggs U.S.A. 39°25N 121°43W 78 F5
Bighorn U.S.A. 46°10N 107°27W 76 C10
Bighorn → U.S.A. 46°10N 107°28W 76 C10
Bighorn Canyon △
  U.S.A. 45°10N 108°0W 76 D10
Bighorn L. U.S.A. 44°55N 108°15W 76 D9
Bighorn Mts. U.S.A. 44°30N 107°30W 76 D10
Bigstone L. Canada 53°42N 95°44W 71 C9
Bihać Bos.-H. 44°49N 15°57E 16 F8
Bihar India 25°5N 85°40E 43 G11
Bihar □ India 25°0N 86°0E 43 G12
Bihariganj India 25°44N 86°59E 43 G12
Bihor, Munţii Romania 46°29N 22°47E 17 E12
Bijagós, Arquipélago dos
  Guinea-Biss. 11°15N 16°10W 52 F2
Bijaipur India 26°2N 77°20E 42 F7
Bijapur = Vijayapura
  India 16°50N 75°55E 44 F2
Bijapur India 18°50N 80°50E 44 E5
Bijār Iran 35°52N 47°35E 46 C5
Bijauri Nepal 28°6N 82°20E 43 E10
Bijawar India 24°38N 79°30E 43 G8
Bijeljina Bos.-H. 44°46N 19°14E 23 B8
Bijie China 27°20N 105°16E 34 D5
Bijnor India 29°27N 78°11E 42 E8
Bikaner India 28°2N 73°18E 42 E5
Bikapur India 26°30N 82°7E 43 F10
Bikeqi China 40°43N 111°20E 32 D6
Bikfayyā Lebanon 33°55N 35°41E 48 B4
Bikin Russia 46°50N 134°20E 28 A7
Bikin → Russia 46°51N 134°2E 28 A7
Bikini Atoll Marshall Is. 12°0N 167°30E 64 F8
Bikita Zimbabwe 20°6S 31°41E 57 B5
Bīkkū Bīttī Libya 22°0N 19°12E 53 D9
Bila Tserkva Ukraine 49°45N 30°10E 17 D16
Bilara India 26°14N 73°53E 42 F5
Bilaspur Chhattisgarh,
  India 22°2N 82°15E 43 H10
Bilaspur Punjab, India 31°19N 76°50E 42 D7
Bilauk Taungdan Thailand 13°0N 99°0E 38 F2
Bilauri Nepal 28°41N 80°21E 43 E9
Bilbao Spain 43°16N 2°56W 21 A4
Bilbo = Bilbao Spain 43°16N 2°56W 21 A4
Bildudalur Iceland 65°41N 23°36W 8 D2
Bílé Karpaty Europe 49°5N 18°0E 17 D9
Bilecik Turkey 40°5N 30°5E 19 F5
Bilgram India 27°11N 80°2E 43 F9
Bilhaur India 26°51N 80°5E 43 F9
Bilhorod-Dnistrovskyy
  Ukraine 46°11N 30°23E 19 E5
Bilibino Russia 68°3N 166°20E 27 C17
Bilimora India 20°45N 72°57E 44 D1
Bililuna Australia 19°37S 127°41E 60 C4
Billings U.S.A. 45°47N 108°30W 76 D9
Billiton Is. = Belitung
  Indonesia 3°10S 107°50E 36 E3
Bilma Niger 18°50N 13°30E 53 E8
Bilma, Grand Erg de Niger 18°30N 14°0E 53 E8
Biloela Australia 24°24S 150°31E 62 C5
Biloli India 18°46N 77°44E 44 E3
Biloxi U.S.A. 30°24N 88°53W 85 F10
Bilpa Morea Claypan
  Australia 25°0S 140°0E 62 D3
Biltine Chad 14°40N 20°50E 53 F10
Bim Son Vietnam 20°4N 105°51E 38 B5
Bima Indonesia 8°22S 118°49E 37 F5
Bimbo C.A.R. 4°15N 18°33E 54 D3
Bimini Is. Bahamas 25°42N 79°25W 88 A4
Bin Xian Heilongjiang,
  China 45°42N 127°32E 33 B14
Bin Xian Shaanxi, China 35°2N 108°4E 32 G5
Bina-Etawah India 24°13N 78°14E 42 G8
Binalong Australia 34°40S 148°39E 63 E4
Bīnālūd, Kūh-e Iran 36°30N 58°30E 47 B8
Binatang = Bintangau
  Malaysia 2°10N 111°40E 36 D4
Binche Belgium 50°26N 4°10E 15 D4
Binchuan China 25°40N 100°38E 34 E3
Bindki India 26°2N 80°36E 43 F9
Bindura Zimbabwe 17°18S 31°18E 55 H6
Bingara Australia 29°52S 150°36E 63 D5
Bingham U.S.A. 45°3N 69°53W 81 C19
Binghamton U.S.A. 42°6N 75°55W 83 D9
Bingöl Turkey 38°53N 40°29E 46 B4
Binh Dinh Vietnam 13°55N 109°7E 38 F7
Binh Son Vietnam 15°20N 108°40E 38 E7
Binhai China 34°2N 119°49E 33 G10
Binjai Indonesia 3°20N 98°30E 39 L2
Binka India 21°2N 83°48E 44 D6
Binnaway Australia 31°28S 149°24E 63 E4
Binongko Indonesia 5°57S 124°2E 37 F6
Binscarth Canada 50°37N 101°17W 71 C8
Bintan Indonesia 1°0N 104°0E 36 D2
Bintangau Malaysia 2°10N 111°40E 36 D4
Bintuni Indonesia 2°7S 133°32E 37 E8
Binyang China 23°12N 108°47E 34 F7
Binzert = Bizerte Tunisia 37°15N 9°50E 53 A7
Binzhou China 37°20N 118°2E 33 F10
Biobío □ Chile 37°35S 72°0W 94 D1
Biobío → Chile 36°49S 73°10W 94 D1
Bioko Eq. Guin. 3°30N 8°40E 54 D1
Bir India 19°4N 75°46E 44 E2
Bîr Abu Muḩammad
  Egypt 29°44N 34°14E 48 F3
Bi'r al Butayyihāt Jordan 29°47N 35°20E 48 F4
Bi'r al Mārī Jordan 30°4N 35°33E 48 E4
Bi'r al Qaṭṭār Jordan 30°4N 35°29E 48 E4
Bir Atrun Sudan 18°15N 26°40E 53 E11
Bîr Beiḑa Egypt 30°25N 34°29E 48 E3

Bîr el 'Abd Egypt 31°2N 33°0E 48 D2
Bîr el Biarât Egypt 29°30N 34°43E 48 F3
Bîr el Duweidar Egypt 30°56N 32°32E 48 E1
Bîr el Garârât Egypt 31°3N 33°34E 48 D2
Bîr el Heisi Egypt 29°22N 34°36E 48 F3
Bîr el Jafir Egypt 30°50N 32°41E 48 E1
Bîr el Mâlḥi Egypt 30°38N 33°19E 48 E2
Bîr el Thamâda Egypt 30°12N 33°27E 48 E2
Bîr Gebeil Ḥisn Egypt 30°2N 33°18E 48 E2
Bi'r Ghaḍîr Syria 34°6N 37°3E 48 A6
Bîr Ḥasana Egypt 30°29N 33°46E 48 E2
Bîr Kaseiba Egypt 31°0N 33°17E 48 E2
Bîr Lahfân Egypt 31°0N 33°51E 48 E2
Bîr Madkûr Egypt 30°44N 32°33E 48 E1
Bi'r Muṭribah Kuwait 29°54N 47°17E 46 D5
Bîr Qaṭia Egypt 30°58N 32°45E 48 E1
Bîr Shalatein Egypt 23°5N 35°25E 53 D13
Birâk Libya 27°31N 14°20E 53 C8
Biratnagar Nepal 26°27N 87°17E 43 F12
Birch → Canada 58°28N 112°17W 70 B6
Birch Hills Canada 52°59N 105°25W 71 C7
Birch I. Canada 52°26N 99°54W 71 C9
Birch L. N.W.T., Canada 62°4N 116°33W 70 A5
Birch L. Ont., Canada 51°23N 92°18W 72 B1
Birch Mts. Canada 57°30N 113°10W 70 B6
Birch River Canada 52°24N 101°6W 71 C8
Birchip Australia 35°56S 142°55E 63 F3
Bird Canada 56°30N 94°13W 71 B10
Bird I. = Aves, I. de W. Indies 15°45N 63°55W 89 C7
Bird I. S. Georgia 54°0S 38°3W 96 G9
Birds Creek Canada 45°6N 77°52W 82 A7
Birdsville Australia 25°51S 139°20E 62 D2
Birdum Cr. → Australia 15°14S 133°0E 60 C5
Birecik Turkey 37°2N 38°0E 46 B3
Birein Israel 30°50N 34°28E 48 E3
Bireuen Indonesia 5°14N 96°39E 36 C1
Birganj Nepal 27°1N 84°52E 43 F11
Birigüi Brazil 21°18S 50°16W 95 A5
Bîrjand Iran 32°53N 59°13E 47 C8
Birkenhead U.K. 53°23N 3°2W 12 D4
Bîrlad = Bârlad Romania 46°15N 27°38E 17 E14
Birmingham U.K. 52°29N 1°52W 13 E6
Birmingham U.S.A. 33°31N 86°48W 85 E11
Birmingham Int. ✈ (BHX) U.K. 52°26N 1°45W 13 E6
Birmitrapur India 22°24N 84°46E 44 C7
Birni Nkonni Niger 13°55N 5°15E 52 F7
Birnin Kebbi Nigeria 12°32N 4°12E 52 F6
Birobidzhan Russia 48°50N 132°50E 31 B15
Birr Ireland 53°6N 7°54W 10 C4
Birrie → Australia 29°43S 146°37E 63 D4
Birsilpur India 28°11N 72°15E 42 E5
Birsk Russia 55°25N 55°30E 18 C10
Birtle Canada 50°30N 101°5W 71 C8
Birur India 13°30N 75°55E 40 N9
Biržai Lithuania 56°11N 24°45E 9 H21
Bisa Indonesia 1°15S 127°28E 37 E7
Bisalpur India 28°14N 79°48E 43 E8
Bisbee U.S.A. 31°27N 109°55W 77 L9
Biscarrosse France 44°22N 1°20W 20 D3
Biscay, B. of Atl. Oc. 45°0N 2°0W 20 D1
Biscayne B. U.S.A. 25°40N 80°12W 85 J14
Biscoe Is. Antarctica 66°0S 67°0W 5 C17
Biscotasing Canada 47°18N 82°9W 72 C3
Bishan China 29°33N 106°12E 34 C6
Bishkek Kyrgyzstan 42°54N 74°46E 30 C3
Bishnupur India 23°8N 87°20E 43 H12
Bisho = Bhisho S. Africa 32°50S 27°23E 56 D4
Bishoftu = Debre Zeyit Ethiopia 8°50N 39°0E 49 F2
Bishop Calif., U.S.A. 37°22N 118°24W 78 H8
Bishop Tex., U.S.A. 27°35N 97°48W 84 H6
Bishop Auckland U.K. 54°39N 1°40W 12 C6
Bishop's Falls Canada 49°2N 55°30W 73 C8
Bishop's Stortford U.K. 51°52N 0°10E 13 F8
Biskra Algeria 34°50N 5°44E 52 B7
Bismarck U.S.A. 46°48N 100°47W 80 B3
Bismarck Arch. Papua N. G. 2°30S 150°0E 58 B7
Bison U.S.A. 45°31N 102°28W 80 C2
Bîsotûn Iran 34°23N 47°26E 46 C5
Bissagos = Bijagós, Arquipélago dos Guinea-Biss. 11°15N 16°10W 52 F2
Bissam Cuttack India 19°31N 83°31E 44 E6
Bissau Guinea-Biss. 11°45N 15°45W 52 F2
Bistcho L. Canada 59°45N 118°50W 70 B5
Bistrița Romania 47°9N 24°35E 17 E13
Bistrița → Romania 46°30N 26°57E 17 E14
Biswan India 27°29N 81°2E 43 F9
Bitam Gabon 2°5N 11°25E 54 D2
Bitkine Chad 11°59N 18°13E 53 F9
Bitlis Turkey 38°20N 42°3E 46 B4
Bitola Macedonia 41°1N 21°20E 23 D9
Bitolj = Bitola Macedonia 41°1N 21°20E 23 D9
Bitra I. India 11°33N 72°9E 45 J1
Bitter Creek U.S.A. 41°33N 108°33W 76 F9
Bitterfontein S. Africa 31°1S 18°32E 56 D2
Bitterroot → U.S.A. 46°52N 114°7W 76 C6
Bitterroot Range U.S.A. 46°0N 114°20W 76 C6
Bitterwater U.S.A. 36°23N 121°0W 78 J6
Biu Nigeria 10°40N 12°3E 53 F8
Biwa-Ko Japan 35°15N 136°10E 29 G8
Biwabik U.S.A. 47°32N 92°21W 80 B7
Bixby U.S.A. 35°57N 95°53W 84 D7
Biyang China 32°38N 113°21E 32 H7
Biysk Russia 52°40N 85°0E 26 D9
Bizana S. Africa 30°50S 29°52E 57 D4
Bizen Japan 34°43N 134°8E 29 G7
Bizerte Tunisia 37°15N 9°50E 53 A7
Bjargtangar Iceland 65°30N 24°30W 8 D1
Bjelovar Croatia 45°56N 16°49E 22 B7
Bjørneborg = Pori Finland 61°29N 21°48E 8 F19
Bjørnevatn Norway 69°40N 30°0E 8 B24
Bjørnøya Arctic 74°30N 19°0E 4 B8
Black = Da → Vietnam 21°15N 105°20E 34 G5
Black → Canada 49°29N 79°19W 82 A3
Black → Ariz., U.S.A. 33°44N 110°13W 77 K8
Black → Ark., U.S.A. 35°38N 91°20W 84 D9

Black → La., U.S.A. 31°16N 91°50W 84 F9
Black → Mich., U.S.A. 42°59N 82°27W 82 D2
Black → N.Y., U.S.A. 43°59N 76°4W 83 C8
Black → Wis., U.S.A. 43°57N 91°22W 80 D8
Black Bay Pen. Canada 48°38N 88°21W 72 C2
Black Birch L. Canada 56°53N 107°45W 71 B7
Black Canyon of the Gunnison △ U.S.A. 38°40N 107°35W 76 G10
Black Diamond Canada 50°45N 114°14W 70 C6
Black Duck → Canada 56°51N 89°2W 72 A2
Black Forest = Schwarzwald Germany 48°30N 8°20E 16 D5
Black Forest U.S.A. 39°0N 104°43W 76 G11
Black Hd. Ireland 53°9N 9°16W 10 C2
Black Hills U.S.A. 44°0N 103°45W 80 D2
Black I. Canada 51°12N 96°30W 71 C9
Black L. Canada 59°12N 105°15W 71 B7
Black L. Mich., U.S.A. 45°28N 84°16W 81 C11
Black L. N.Y., U.S.A. 44°31N 75°36W 83 B9
Black Lake Canada 59°11N 105°20W 71 B7
Black Mesa U.S.A. 36°58N 102°58W 84 C3
Black Mt. = Mynydd Du U.K. 51°52N 3°50W 13 F4
Black Mts. U.K. 51°55N 3°7W 13 F4
Black Range U.S.A. 33°15N 107°50W 77 K10
Black River Jamaica 18°0N 77°50W 88 a
Black River U.S.A. 44°0N 75°47W 83 C9
Black River Falls U.S.A. 44°18N 90°51W 80 C8
Black Rock Barbados 13°7N 59°37W 89 g
Black Rock Desert U.S.A. 41°10N 118°50W 76 F4
Black Sea Eurasia 43°30N 35°0E 19 F6
Black Tickle Canada 53°28N 55°45W 73 B8
Black Volta → Africa 8°41N 1°33W 52 G5
Black Warrior → U.S.A. 32°32N 87°51W 85 E11
Blackall Australia 24°25S 145°45E 62 C4
Blackball N.Z. 42°22S 171°26E 59 E3
Blackbraes △ Australia 19°10S 144°10E 62 B3
Blackbull Australia 17°55S 141°45E 62 B3
Blackburn U.K. 53°45N 2°29W 12 D5
Blackburn, Mt. U.S.A. 61°44N 143°26W 74 C11
Blackburn with Darwen □ U.K. 53°45N 2°29W 12 D5
Blackdown Tableland △ Australia 23°52S 149°8E 62 C4
Blackfoot U.S.A. 43°11N 112°21W 76 E7
Blackfoot → U.S.A. 46°52N 113°53W 76 C7
Blackfoot Res. U.S.A. 42°55N 111°39W 76 E8
Blackpool U.K. 53°49N 3°3W 12 D4
Blackpool □ U.K. 53°49N 3°3W 12 D4
Blackriver U.S.A. 44°46N 83°17W 82 B1
Blacks Harbour Canada 45°3N 66°49W 73 C6
Blacksburg U.S.A. 37°14N 80°25W 81 G13
Blacksod B. Ireland 54°6N 10°0W 10 B1
Blackstairs Mt. Ireland 52°33N 6°48W 10 D5
Blackstone U.S.A. 37°5N 78°0W 81 G14
Blackstone Ra. Australia 26°0S 128°30E 61 E4
Blackwater = West Road → Canada 53°18N 122°53W 70 C4
Blackwater Australia 23°35S 148°53E 62 C4
Blackwater → Meath, Ireland 53°39N 6°41W 10 C5
Blackwater → Waterford, Ireland 52°4N 7°52W 10 D4
Blackwater → U.K. 54°31N 6°35W 10 B5
Blackwell U.S.A. 36°48N 97°17W 84 C6
Blackwells Corner U.S.A. 35°37N 119°47W 79 K7
Blackwood → U.K. 51°39N 3°12W 13 F4
Bladensburg △ Australia 22°30S 142°59E 62 C3
Blaenau Ffestiniog U.K. 53°0N 3°56W 12 E4
Blaenau Gwent □ U.K. 51°48N 3°12W 13 F4
Blâfjella-Skjækerfjella △ Norway 64°15N 13°8E 8 D15
Blagodarnyy Russia 45°7N 43°37E 19 E7
Blagoevgrad Bulgaria 42°2N 23°5E 23 C10
Blagoveshchensk Russia 50°20N 127°30E 31 A14
Blahkiuh Indonesia 8°31S 115°12E 37 J18
Blain U.S.A. 40°20N 77°31W 82 F7
Blaine Minn., U.S.A. 45°10N 93°13W 80 C7
Blaine Wash., U.S.A. 48°59N 122°45W 78 B4
Blaine Lake Canada 52°51N 106°52W 71 C7
Blair U.S.A. 41°33N 96°8W 80 E5
Blair Athol Australia 22°42S 147°31E 62 C4
Blair Atholl U.K. 56°46N 3°50W 11 E5
Blairgowrie U.K. 56°35N 3°21W 11 E5
Blairsden U.S.A. 39°47N 120°37W 78 F6
Blairsville U.S.A. 40°26N 79°16W 82 F5
Blakang Mati, Pulau Singapore 1°15N 103°50E 39 d
Blake Pt. U.S.A. 48°11N 88°25W 80 A9
Blakely Ga., U.S.A. 31°23N 84°56W 85 F12
Blakely Pa., U.S.A. 41°28N 75°37W 83 E9
Blambangan, Semenanjung Indonesia 8°42S 114°29E 37 K17
Blanc, Mont Europe 45°48N 6°50E 20 D7
Blanca, B. Argentina 39°10S 61°30W 96 D4
Blanca, Cord. Peru 9°10S 77°35W 92 E3
Blanca, Costa Spain 38°25N 0°10W 21 C5
Blanca Peak U.S.A. 37°35N 105°29W 77 H11
Blanche, C. Australia 33°1S 134°9E 63 E1
Blanche, L. S. Austral., Australia 29°15S 139°40E 63 D2
Blanche, L. W. Austral., Australia 22°25S 123°17E 60 D3
Blanchisseuse Trin. & Tob. 10°48N 61°18W 93 K15
Blanco S. Africa 33°55S 22°23E 56 D3
Blanco U.S.A. 30°6N 98°25W 84 F5
Blanco → Argentina 30°20S 68°42W 94 C2
Blanco, C. Costa Rica 9°34N 85°8W 88 E7
Blanco, C. Spain 39°21N 2°51E 24 B9
Blanco, C. U.S.A. 42°51N 124°34W 76 E1
Bland → Australia 33°42S 147°30E 63 E4
Blanda → Iceland 65°37N 20°9W 8 D3
Blandford Forum U.K. 50°51N 2°9W 13 G5
Blanding U.S.A. 37°37N 109°29W 77 H9
Blanes Spain 41°40N 2°48E 21 B7
Blankenberge Belgium 51°20N 3°9E 15 C3
Blanquilla, I. Venezuela 11°51N 64°37W 89 D7

Blanquillo Uruguay 32°53S 55°37W 95 C4
Blantyre Malawi 15°45S 35°0E 55 H7
Blarney Ireland 51°56N 8°33W 10 E3
Blasdell U.S.A. 42°48N 78°50W 82 D6
Blåvands Huk Denmark 55°33N 8°4E 9 J13
Blaydon U.K. 54°58N 1°42W 12 C6
Blayney Australia 33°32S 149°14E 63 E4
Blaze, Pt. Australia 12°56S 130°11E 60 B5
Blekinge Sweden 56°25N 15°20E 9 H16
Blenheim Canada 42°20N 82°0W 82 D3
Blenheim N.Z. 41°38S 173°57E 59 D4
Bletchley U.K. 51°59N 0°44W 13 F7
Blida Algeria 36°30N 2°49E 52 A6
Bligh Sound N.Z. 44°47S 167°32E 59 F1
Bligh Water Fiji 17°0S 178°0E 59 a
Blind River Canada 46°10N 82°58W 72 C3
Bliss Idaho, U.S.A. 42°56N 114°57W 76 E6
Bliss N.Y., U.S.A. 42°34N 78°15W 82 D6
Blissfield U.S.A. 41°50N 83°52W 82 F3
Blitar Indonesia 8°5S 112°11E 37 H15
Block I. U.S.A. 41°11N 71°35W 83 E13
Block Island Sd. U.S.A. 41°15N 71°40W 83 E13
Bloemfontein S. Africa 29°6S 26°7E 56 D4
Bloemhof S. Africa 27°38S 25°32E 56 D4
Blois France 47°35N 1°20E 20 C4
Blönduós Iceland 65°40N 20°12W 8 D3
Blongas Indonesia 8°53S 116°2E 37 K19
Bloodvein → Canada 51°47N 96°43W 71 C9
Bloody Foreland Ireland 55°10N 8°17W 10 A3
Bloomer U.S.A. 45°6N 91°29W 80 C8
Bloomfield Canada 43°59N 77°14W 82 C7
Bloomfield Iowa, U.S.A. 40°45N 92°25W 80 E7
Bloomfield N. Mex., U.S.A. 36°43N 107°59W 77 H10
Bloomfield Nebr., U.S.A. 42°36N 97°39W 80 D5
Bloomington Ill., U.S.A. 40°28N 89°0W 80 E9
Bloomington Ind., U.S.A. 39°10N 86°32W 80 F10
Bloomington Minn., U.S.A. 44°50N 93°17W 80 C7
Bloomsburg U.S.A. 41°0N 76°27W 83 F8
Bloomsbury Australia 20°48S 148°38E 62 b
Blora Indonesia 6°57S 111°25E 37 G14
Blossburg U.S.A. 41°41N 77°4W 82 E7
Blouberg S. Africa 23°8S 28°59E 57 B4
Blountstown U.S.A. 30°27N 85°3W 85 F12
Blue Earth U.S.A. 43°38N 94°6W 80 D6
Blue Hole △ Belize 17°19N 88°40W 88 C2
Blue Mesa Res. U.S.A. 38°28N 107°20W 76 G10
Blue Mountain Lake U.S.A. 43°51N 74°27W 83 C10
Blue Mountain Pk. Jamaica 18°3N 76°36W 88 a
Blue Mt. U.S.A. 40°30N 76°30W 83 F8
Blue Mts. Jamaica 18°3N 76°36W 88 a
Blue Mts. Maine, U.S.A. 44°50N 70°35W 83 B14
Blue Mts. Oreg., U.S.A. 45°0N 118°20W 76 D4
Blue Mud B. Australia 13°30S 136°0E 62 A2
Blue Nile = Nîl el Azraq → Sudan 15°38N 32°31E 53 E12
Blue Rapids U.S.A. 39°41N 96°39W 80 F5
Blue Ridge U.S.A. 36°40N 80°50W 81 G13
Blue River Canada 52°6N 119°18W 70 C5
Bluefield U.S.A. 37°15N 81°17W 81 G13
Bluefields Nic. 12°20N 83°50W 88 D3
Bluevale Canada 43°51N 81°15W 82 C3
Bluff Australia 23°35S 149°4E 62 C4
Bluff N.Z. 46°37S 168°20E 59 G2
Bluff U.S.A. 37°17N 109°33W 77 H9
Bluff Knoll Australia 34°24S 118°15E 61 F2
Bluff Pt. Australia 27°50S 114°5E 61 E1
Bluffton U.S.A. 40°44N 85°11W 81 E11
Bluffton S.C., U.S.A. 32°14N 80°52W 85 E14
Blumenau Brazil 27°0S 49°0W 95 B6
Blunt U.S.A. 44°31N 99°59W 80 C4
Blyde River Canyon △ S. Africa 24°37S 31°2E 57 B5
Blyth Canada 43°44N 81°26W 82 C3
Blyth U.K. 55°8N 1°31W 12 B6
Blythe U.S.A. 33°37N 114°36W 79 M12
Blytheville U.S.A. 35°56N 89°55W 85 D10
Bo S. Leone 7°55N 11°50W 52 G3
Bo Duc Vietnam 11°58N 106°50E 39 G6
Bo Hai China 39°0N 119°0E 33 E10
Bo Hai Haixia Asia 38°25N 121°8E 33 E11
Bo Xian = Bozhou China 33°55N 115°41E 32 H8
Boa Vista Brazil 2°48N 60°30W 92 C6
Boaco Nic. 12°29N 85°35W 88 D2
Bo'ai China 35°10N 113°3E 32 G7
Boalsburg U.S.A. 40°47N 77°49W 82 F7
Boane Mozam. 26°6S 32°19E 57 C5
Boao China 19°8N 110°34E 38 C8
Boardman U.S.A. 41°2N 80°40W 82 E4
Boath India 19°20N 78°20E 44 E4
Bobadah Australia 32°19S 146°41E 63 E4
Bobai China 22°17N 109°59E 34 F7
Bobbili India 18°35N 83°30E 44 E6
Bobcaygeon Canada 44°33N 78°33W 82 B6
Boblad India 17°13N 75°26E 44 F2
Bobo-Dioulasso Burkina Faso 11°8N 4°13W 52 F5
Bobonong Botswana 21°58S 28°20E 57 B4
Bóbr → Poland 52°4N 15°4E 16 B8
Bobraomby, Tanjon' i Madag. 12°40S 49°10E 55 G9
Bobruysk = Babruysk Belarus 53°10N 29°15E 17 B15
Boby, Pic Madag. 22°12S 46°55E 55 J9
Boca del Río Mexico 19°5N 96°4W 87 D5
Boca do Acre Brazil 8°50S 67°27W 92 E5
Boca Raton U.S.A. 26°21N 80°5W 85 H14
Bocas del Dragón = Dragon's Mouths Trin. & Tob. 11°0N 61°50W 93 K15
Bocas del Toro Panama 9°15N 82°20W 88 E3
Bochnia Poland 49°58N 20°27E 17 D11
Bochum = Senwabarana S. Africa 23°17S 29°7E 57 B4
Bochum Germany 51°28N 7°13E 16 C4

Bocoyna Mexico 27°52N 107°35W 86 B3
Bodaybo Russia 57°50N 114°0E 27 D12
Boddam U.K. 59°56N 1°17W 11 B7
Boddington Australia 32°50S 116°30E 61 F2
Bodega Bay U.S.A. 38°20N 123°3W 78 G3
Boden Sweden 65°50N 21°42E 8 D19
Bodensee Europe 47°35N 9°25E 20 C8
Bodh Gaya India 24°41N 84°58E 43 G11
Bodhan India 18°40N 77°44E 44 E3
Bodinayakkanur India 10°2N 77°10E 45 J3
Bodmin U.K. 50°28N 4°43W 13 G3
Bodmin Moor U.K. 50°33N 4°36W 13 G3
Bodø Norway 67°17N 14°24E 8 C16
Bodrog → Hungary 48°11N 21°22E 17 D11
Bodrum Turkey 37°3N 27°30E 23 F12
Boende Dem. Rep. of the Congo 0°24S 21°12E 54 E4
Boerne U.S.A. 29°47N 98°44W 84 G5
Boesmans → S. Africa 33°42S 26°39E 56 D4
Bogalusa U.S.A. 30°47N 89°52W 85 F10
Bogan → Australia 30°20S 146°50E 63 E4
Bogan Gate Australia 33°7S 147°49E 63 E4
Bogantungan Australia 23°41S 147°17E 62 C4
Bogata U.S.A. 33°28N 95°13W 84 E7
Bogda Shan China 43°35N 89°40E 30 C6
Boggabilla Australia 28°36S 150°24E 63 D5
Boggabri Australia 30°45S 150°5E 63 E5
Boggeragh Mts. Ireland 52°2N 8°55W 10 D3
Boglan = Solhan Turkey 38°57N 41°3E 46 B4
Bognes Norway 68°13N 16°5E 8 B17
Bognor Regis U.K. 50°47N 0°40W 13 G7
Bogo Phil. 11°3N 124°0E 37 B6
Bogong, Mt. Australia 36°47S 147°17E 63 F4
Bogor Indonesia 6°36S 106°48E 37 G12
Bogotá Colombia 4°34N 74°0W 92 C4
Bogotol Russia 56°15N 89°50E 26 D9
Bogra Bangla. 24°51N 89°22E 41 G16
Boguchanskoye Vdkhr. Russia 58°42N 99°9E 27 D10
Boguchany Russia 58°40N 97°30E 27 D10
Bogué Mauritania 16°45N 14°10W 52 E3
Bohemian Forest = Böhmerwald Germany 49°8N 13°14E 16 D7
Böhmerwald Germany 49°8N 13°14E 16 D7
Bohol □ Phil. 9°50N 124°10E 37 C6
Bohol Sea Phil. 9°0N 124°0E 37 C6
Bohorok Indonesia 3°30N 98°12E 39 L2
Böhöt Mongolia 45°13N 108°16E 32 B7
Bohuslän Sweden 58°25N 12°0E 9 G15
Boi, Pta. do Brazil 23°55S 45°15W 95 A6
Boiaçu Brazil 0°27S 61°46W 92 D6
Boigu Australia 9°16S 142°13E 62 a
Boileau, C. Australia 17°40S 122°7E 60 C3
Boise U.S.A. 43°37N 116°13W 76 E5
Boise City U.S.A. 36°44N 102°31W 84 C3
Boissevain Canada 49°15N 100°5W 71 D8
Bojador, C. W. Sahara 26°0N 14°30W 52 C3
Bojana → Albania 41°52N 19°22E 23 D8
Bojnūrd Iran 37°30N 57°20E 47 B8
Bojonegoro Indonesia 7°11S 111°54E 37 G14
Bokaro India 23°46N 85°55E 43 H11
Boké Guinea 10°56N 14°17W 52 F3
Bokhara → Australia 29°55S 146°42E 63 D4
Boknafjorden Norway 59°14N 5°40E 9 G11
Bokor △ Cambodia 10°50N 104°1E 39 G5
Bokoro Chad 12°25N 17°14E 53 F9
Bokpyin Burma 11°18N 98°42E 39 G2
Bokungu Dem. Rep. of the Congo 0°35S 22°50E 54 E4
Bolan → Pakistan 28°38N 67°42E 42 E2
Bolan Pass Pakistan 29°50N 67°20E 40 E5
Bolaños → Mexico 21°12N 104°5W 86 C4
Bolbec France 49°30N 0°30E 20 B4
Bole China 44°55N 81°37E 30 C5
Bolekhiv Ukraine 49°0N 23°57E 17 D12
Bolesławiec Poland 51°17N 15°37E 16 C8
Bolgatanga Ghana 10°44N 0°53W 52 F5
Bolgrad = Bolhrad Ukraine 45°40N 28°32E 17 F15
Bolhrad Ukraine 45°40N 28°32E 17 F15
Bolinao Phil. 16°23N 119°54E 37 A5
Bolivar Mo., U.S.A. 37°37N 93°25W 80 G7
Bolivar N.Y., U.S.A. 42°4N 78°10W 82 D6
Bolivar Tenn., U.S.A. 35°12N 89°0W 85 D10
Bolívar, Pico Venezuela 8°32N 71°2W 92 B4
Bolivia ■ S. Amer. 17°6S 64°0W 92 G6
Bolivian Plateau = Altiplano Bolivia 17°0S 68°0W 92 G5
Bollnäs Sweden 61°21N 16°24E 8 F17
Bollon Australia 28°2S 147°29E 63 D4
Bolmen Sweden 56°55N 13°40E 9 H15
Bolobo Dem. Rep. of the Congo 2°6S 16°20E 54 E3
Bologna Italy 44°29N 11°20E 22 B4
Bologoye Russia 57°55N 34°5E 18 C5
Bolomba Dem. Rep. of the Congo 0°35N 19°0E 54 D3
Bolonchén Mexico 20°1N 89°45W 87 D7
Boloven, Cao Nguyen Laos 15°10N 106°30E 38 E6
Bolpur India 23°40N 87°45E 43 H12
Bolsena, L. di Italy 42°36N 11°56E 22 C4
Bolshevik, Ostrov Russia 78°30N 102°0E 27 B11
Bolshoy Anyuy → Russia 68°30N 160°49E 27 C17
Bolshoy Begichev, Ostrov Russia 74°20N 112°30E 27 B12
Bolshoy Kamen Russia 43°7N 132°19E 28 C6
Bolshoy Kavkaz = Caucasus Mountains Eurasia 42°50N 44°0E 19 F7
Bolshoy Lyakhovskiy, Ostrov Russia 73°35N 142°0E 27 B15
Bolshoy Tyuters, Ostrov Russia 59°51N 27°13E 9 G22
Bolsward Neths. 53°3N 5°32E 15 A5
Bolt Head U.K. 50°12N 3°48W 13 G4
Bolton Canada 43°54N 79°45W 82 C5
Bolton U.K. 53°35N 2°26W 12 D5

Bolton Landing U.S.A. 43°32N 73°35W 83 C11
Bolu Turkey 40°45N 31°35E 19 F5
Bolungavík Iceland 66°9N 23°15W 8 C2
Boluo China 23°3N 114°21E 35 F10
Bolvadin Turkey 38°45N 31°4E 46 B5
Bolzano Italy 46°31N 11°22E 22 A4
Bom Jesus da Lapa Brazil 13°15S 43°25W 93 F10
Boma Dem. Rep. of the Congo 5°50S 13°4E 54 F2
Bombala Australia 36°56S 149°15E 63 F4
Bombay = Mumbai India 18°56N 72°50E 44 E1
Bombedor, Pta. Venezuela 9°53N 61°37W 93 L15
Bomberai, Semenanjung Indonesia 3°0S 133°0E 37 E8
Bomboma Dem. Rep. of the Congo 2°25N 18°55E 54 D3
Bomi China 29°50N 95°45E 30 F8
Bomlo Norway 59°37N 5°13E 9 G11
Bompoka India 8°15N 93°13E 45 K11
Bomu → C.A.R. 4°40N 22°30E 54 D4
Bon, C. = Ra's aṭ Ṭib Tunisia 37°1N 11°2E 22 F4
Bon Acceuil Mauritius 20°10S 57°39E 55 d
Bon Echo △ Canada 44°55N 77°16W 82 F7
Bon Sar Pa Vietnam 12°24N 107°35E 38 F6
Bonāb Iran 36°35N 48°41E 47 B6
Bonaigarh India 21°50N 84°57E 43 J11
Bonaire W. Indies 12°10N 68°15W 89 D6
Bonampak Mexico 16°44N 91°5W 87 D6
Bonang Australia 37°11S 148°41E 63 F4
Bonanza Nic. 13°54N 84°35W 88 D3
Bonaparte Arch. Australia 14°0S 124°30E 60 B3
Bonar Bridge U.K. 57°54N 4°20W 11 D4
Bonasse Trin. & Tob. 10°5N 61°54W 93 K15
Bonaventure Canada 48°5N 65°32W 73 C6
Bonavista Canada 48°40N 53°5W 73 C9
Bonavista, C. Canada 48°42N 53°5W 73 C9
Bonavista B. Canada 48°45N 53°25W 73 C9
Bondo Dem. Rep. of the Congo 3°55N 23°53E 54 D4
Bondokodi Indonesia 9°35S 119°0E 60 A1
Bondoukou Ivory C. 8°2N 2°47W 52 G5
Bondowoso Indonesia 7°55S 113°49E 37 G15
Bone, Teluk Indonesia 4°10S 120°50E 37 E6
Bonerate Indonesia 7°25S 121°5E 37 F6
Bonerate, Kepulauan Indonesia 6°30S 121°10E 37 F6
Bo'ness U.K. 56°1N 3°37W 11 E5
Bonete, Cerro Argentina 27°55S 68°40W 94 B2
Bong Son = Hoai Nhon Vietnam 14°28N 109°1E 38 E7
Bongaigaon India 26°28N 90°34E 30 F7
Bongandanga Dem. Rep. of the Congo 1°24N 21°3E 54 D4
Bongor Chad 10°35N 15°20E 53 F9
Bongos, Massif des C.A.R. 8°40N 22°25E 54 C4
Bonham U.S.A. 33°35N 96°11W 84 E6
Bonifacio France 41°24N 9°10E 20 F8
Bonifacio, Bouches de Medit. S. 41°12N 9°15E 22 D3
Bonin Is. = Ogasawara Gunto Pac. Oc. 27°0N 142°0E 64 E6
Bonn Germany 50°46N 7°6E 16 C4
Bonners Ferry U.S.A. 48°42N 116°19W 76 B5
Bonney, L. Australia 37°50S 140°20E 63 F3
Bonnie Rock Australia 30°29S 118°22E 61 F2
Bonny, Bight of Africa 3°30N 9°20E 52 H6
Bonnyrigg U.K. 55°53N 3°6W 11 F5
Bonnyville Canada 54°20N 110°45W 71 C6
Bonoi Indonesia 1°45S 137°41E 37 E9
Bonsall U.S.A. 33°16N 117°14W 79 M9
Bontang Indonesia 0°10N 117°30E 36 D5
Bonthe S. Leone 7°30N 12°33W 52 G3
Bonython Ra. Australia 23°40S 128°45E 60 D4
Boodjamulla △ Australia 18°15S 138°6E 62 B2
Bookabie Australia 31°50S 132°41E 61 F5
Booker U.S.A. 36°27N 100°32W 84 C4
Booligal Australia 33°58S 144°53E 63 E3
Böön Tsagaan Nuur Mongolia 45°35N 99°9E 30 B8
Boonah Australia 27°58S 152°41E 63 D5
Boone Iowa, U.S.A. 42°4N 93°53W 80 D7
Boone N.C., U.S.A. 36°13N 81°41W 85 C14
Booneville Ark., U.S.A. 35°8N 93°55W 84 D8
Booneville Miss., U.S.A. 34°39N 88°34W 85 D10
Boonville Calif., U.S.A. 39°1N 123°22W 78 F3
Boonville Ind., U.S.A. 38°3N 87°16W 80 F10
Boonville Mo., U.S.A. 38°58N 92°44W 80 F7
Boonville N.Y., U.S.A. 43°29N 75°20W 83 C9
Boorabbin △ Australia 31°30S 120°10E 61 F3
Boorindal Australia 30°22S 146°11E 63 E4
Boorowa Australia 34°28S 148°44E 63 E4
Boosaaso Somalia 11°12N 49°18E 49 E4
Boothia, Gulf of Canada 71°0N 90°0W 68 B11
Boothia Pen. Canada 71°0N 94°0W 68 B11
Bootle U.K. 53°28N 3°1W 12 D4
Booué Gabon 0°5S 11°55E 54 E2
Boquilla, Presa de la Mexico 27°31N 105°30W 86 B3
Boquillas del Carmen Mexico 29°11N 102°58W 86 B4
Bor Serbia 44°5N 22°7E 23 B10
Bor South Sudan 6°10N 31°40E 53 G12
Bor Mashash Israel 31°7N 34°50E 48 D3
Bora Bora French Polynesia 16°30S 151°45W 65 J12
Borah Peak U.S.A. 44°8N 113°47W 76 D7
Boraha, Nosy Madag. 16°50S 49°55E 55 H9
Borås Sweden 57°43N 12°56E 9 H15
Borāzjān Iran 29°22N 51°10E 47 D6
Borba Brazil 4°12S 59°34W 92 D7
Borborema, Planalto da Brazil 7°0S 37°0W 90 D7
Bord Khūn-e Now Iran 28°3N 51°28E 47 D6
Borda, C. Australia 35°45S 136°34E 63 F2
Bordeaux France 44°50N 0°36W 20 D3
Borden Australia 34°3S 118°12E 61 F2

Borden-Carleton Canada 46°18N 63°47W 73 C7
Borden I. Canada 78°30N 111°30W 69 B9
Borden Pen. Canada 73°0N 83°0W 69 C15
Border Ranges △ Australia 28°24S 152°56E 63 D5
Borders = Scottish Borders □ U.K. 55°35N 2°50W 11 F6
Bordertown Australia 36°19S 140°45E 63 F3
Borðeyri Iceland 65°12N 21°6W 8 D3
Bordj Flye Ste-Marie Algeria 27°19N 2°32W 52 C5
Bordj in Eker Algeria 24°9N 5°3E 52 D7
Bordj Mokhtar Algeria 21°20N 0°56E 52 D6
Bordj Omar Driss Algeria 28°10N 6°40E 52 C7
Borehamwood U.K. 51°40N 0°15W 13 F7
Borgampad India 17°39N 80°52E 44 F5
Borgarnes Iceland 64°32N 21°55W 8 D3
Børgefjellet Norway 65°20N 13°45E 8 D15
Borger Neths. 52°54N 6°44E 15 B6
Borger U.S.A. 35°39N 101°24W 84 D4
Borgholm Sweden 56°52N 16°39E 9 H17
Borhoyn Tal Mongolia 43°50N 111°58E 32 C6
Borigumma India 19°3N 82°33E 44 E6
Borikhane Laos 18°33N 103°43E 38 C4
Borisoglebsk Russia 51°27N 42°5E 19 D7
Borisov = Barysaw Belarus 54°17N 28°28E 17 A15
Borja Peru 4°20S 77°40W 92 D3
Borkou Chad 18°15N 18°50E 53 E9
Borkum Germany 53°34N 6°40E 16 B4
Borlänge Sweden 60°29N 15°26E 9 F16
Borley, C. Antarctica 66°15S 52°30E 5 C5
Borneo E. Indies 1°0N 115°0E 36 D5
Bornholm Denmark 55°10N 15°0E 9 J16
Borobudur △ Indonesia 7°36S 110°12E 37 G14
Borogontsy Russia 62°42N 131°8E 27 C14
Borohoro Shan China 44°6N 83°10E 30 C5
Boron U.S.A. 35°0N 117°39W 79 L9
Borongan Phil. 11°37N 125°26E 37 B7
Borovichi Russia 58°25N 33°55E 18 C5
Borrego Springs U.S.A. 33°15N 116°23W 79 M10
Borrisokane Ireland 53°0N 8°7W 10 D3
Borroloola Australia 16°4S 136°17E 62 B2
Borşa Romania 47°41N 24°50E 17 E13
Borsad India 22°25N 72°54E 42 H5
Bortala = Bole China 44°55N 81°37E 30 C5
Borth U.K. 52°29N 4°2W 13 E3
Borūjerd Iran 33°55N 48°50E 47 C6
Boryeong S. Korea 36°21N 126°36E 33 F14
Boryslav Ukraine 49°18N 23°28E 17 D12
Borzya Russia 50°24N 116°31E 31 A12
Bosa Italy 40°18N 8°30E 22 D3
Bosanska Gradiška = Gradiška Bos.-H. 45°10N 17°15E 22 B7
Boscastle U.K. 50°41N 4°42W 13 G3
Boscobelle Barbados 13°17N 59°35W 89 g
Bose China 23°53N 106°35E 34 F6
Boseong S. Korea 34°46N 127°5E 33 G14
Boshan China 36°28N 117°49E 33 F9
Boshof S. Africa 28°31S 25°13E 56 C4
Boshrūyeh Iran 33°50N 57°30E 47 C8
Bosna → Bos.-H. 45°4N 18°29E 23 B8
Bosna i Hercegovina = Bosnia-Herzegovina ■ Europe 44°0N 18°0E 22 B7
Bosnia-Herzegovina ■ Europe 44°0N 18°0E 22 B7
Bosnik Indonesia 1°5S 136°10E 37 E9
Bosobolo Dem. Rep. of the Congo 4°15N 19°50E 54 D3
Bosque Farms U.S.A. 35°51N 106°42W 77 J10
Bosra = Buşra ash Shām Syria 32°30N 36°25E 48 C5
Bossangoa C.A.R. 6°35N 17°30E 54 C3
Bossier City U.S.A. 32°31N 93°44W 84 E8
Bossiesvlei Namibia 25°1S 16°44E 56 C2
Bosso Niger 13°43N 13°19E 53 F8
Bostan Pakistan 30°26N 67°2E 42 D2
Bostānābād Iran 37°50N 46°50E 46 B5
Bosten Hu China 41°55N 87°40E 30 C6
Boston U.K. 52°59N 0°2W 12 E7
Boston Bar Canada 49°52N 121°30W 70 D4
Boston Mts. U.S.A. 35°42N 93°15W 84 D8
Boswell Canada 49°28N 116°45W 70 D5
Boswell U.S.A. 40°10N 79°2W 82 F5
Botad India 22°15N 71°40E 42 H4
Botene Laos 17°35N 101°12E 38 D3
Bothaville S. Africa 27°23S 26°34E 56 C4
Bothnia, G. of Europe 62°0N 20°0E 8 F19
Bothwell Australia 42°20S 147°1E 63 G4
Bothwell Canada 42°38N 81°52W 82 D3
Botletle → Botswana 20°10S 23°15E 56 B3
Botoşani Romania 47°42N 26°41E 17 E14
Botou Burkina Faso 12°42N 1°59E 52 F6
Botou China 38°4N 116°34E 32 E9
Botshabelo S. Africa 29°14S 26°44E 56 C4
Botswana ■ Africa 22°0S 24°0E 56 B3
Bottineau U.S.A. 48°50N 100°27W 80 A3
Botucatu Brazil 22°55S 48°30W 95 A6
Botum Sakor △ Cambodia 11°5N 103°15E 39 G4
Botwood Canada 49°6N 55°23W 73 C8
Bou Saâda Algeria 35°11N 4°9E 52 A6
Bouaflé Ivory C. 7°1N 5°47W 52 G4
Bouaké Ivory C. 7°40N 5°2W 52 G4
Bouar C.A.R. 6°0N 15°40E 54 C3
Bouârfa Morocco 32°32N 1°58W 52 B5
Boucaut B. Australia 12°0S 134°25E 62 A1
Bouctouche Canada 46°30N 64°45W 73 C7
Bougainville, C. Australia 13°57S 126°4E 60 B4
Bougainville I. Papua N. G. 6°0S 155°0E 58 B8
Bougainville Reef Australia 15°30S 147°5E 62 B4
Bougie = Bejaïa Algeria 36°42N 5°2E 52 A7
Bougouni Mali 11°30N 7°20W 52 F4
Bouillon Belgium 49°44N 5°3E 15 E5
Boulder Colo., U.S.A. 40°1N 105°17W 76 F11
Boulder Mont., U.S.A. 46°14N 112°7W 76 C7
Boulder City U.S.A. 35°58N 114°49W 79 K12
Boulder Creek U.S.A. 37°7N 122°7W 78 H4
Boulder Dam = Hoover Dam U.S.A. 36°1N 114°44W 79 K12
Boulia Australia 22°52S 139°51E 62 C2
Boulogne-sur-Mer France 50°42N 1°36E 20 A4
Boulsa Burkina Faso 12°39N 0°34W 52 F5
Boultoum Niger 14°45N 10°25E 53 F8
Bouma △ Fiji 16°50S 179°52W 59 a
Boun Neua Laos 21°38N 101°54E 38 B3
Boun Tai Laos 21°23N 101°58E 38 B3
Bouna Ivory C. 9°10N 3°0W 52 G5
Boundary Peak U.S.A. 37°51N 118°21W 78 H8
Boundiali Ivory C. 9°30N 6°20W 52 G4
Bountiful U.S.A. 40°53N 111°52W 76 F8
Bounty Is. Pac. Oc. 48°0S 178°30E 64 M9
Bounty Trough Pac. Oc. 46°0S 178°0E 64 M9
Bourbonnais France 46°28N 3°0E 20 C5
Bourdel L. Canada 56°43N 74°10W 72 A5
Bourem Mali 17°0N 0°24W 52 E5
Bourg-en-Bresse France 46°13N 5°12E 20 C6
Bourg-St-Maurice France 45°35N 6°46E 20 D7
Bourgas = Burgas Bulgaria 42°33N 27°29E 23 C12
Bourges France 47°9N 2°25E 20 C5
Bourget Canada 45°26N 75°9W 83 A9
Bourgogne □ France 47°0N 4°50E 20 C6
Bourke Australia 30°8S 145°55E 63 E4
Bourne U.K. 52°47N 0°22W 12 E7
Bournemouth U.K. 50°43N 1°52W 13 G6
Bournemouth □ U.K. 50°43N 1°52W 13 G6
Bouse U.S.A. 33°56N 114°0W 79 M13
Bousso Chad 10°34N 16°52E 53 F9
Bouvet I. = Bouvetøya Antarctica 54°26S 3°24E 2 G10
Bouvetøya Antarctica 54°26S 3°24E 2 G10
Bovanenkovo Russia 70°22N 68°40E 26 B7
Bovill U.S.A. 46°51N 116°24W 76 C5
Bovril Argentina 31°21S 59°26W 94 C4
Bow → Canada 49°57N 111°41W 70 C6
Bow Island Canada 49°50N 111°23W 76 B8
Bowbells U.S.A. 48°48N 102°15W 80 A2
Bowdle U.S.A. 45°27N 99°39W 80 C4
Bowelling Australia 33°25S 116°30E 61 F2
Bowen Argentina 35°0S 67°31W 94 D2
Bowen Australia 20°0S 148°16E 62 J6
Bowen Mts. Australia 37°0S 147°50E 63 F4
Bowers Basin Pac. Oc. 53°45N 176°0E 4 D16
Bowers Ridge Pac. Oc. 54°0N 180°0E 4 D17
Bowie Ariz., U.S.A. 32°19N 109°29W 77 K9
Bowie Tex., U.S.A. 33°34N 97°51W 84 E6
Bowkān Iran 36°31N 46°12E 46 B5
Bowland, Forest of U.K. 54°0N 2°30W 12 D5
Bowling Green Ky., U.S.A. 36°59N 86°27W 80 G10
Bowling Green Ohio, U.S.A. 41°23N 83°39W 81 E12
Bowling Green, C. Australia 19°19S 147°25E 62 B4
Bowling Green Bay △ Australia 19°26S 146°57E 62 B4
Bowman U.S.A. 46°11N 103°24W 80 B2
Bowman I. Antarctica 65°0S 104°0E 5 C8
Bowmanville = Clarington Canada 43°55N 78°41W 82 C6
Bowmore U.K. 55°45N 6°17W 11 F2
Bowral Australia 34°26S 150°27E 63 E5
Bowraville Australia 30°37S 152°52E 63 E5
Bowron → Canada 54°3N 121°50W 70 C4
Bowron Lake ⌂ Canada 53°10N 121°5W 70 C4
Bowser L. Canada 56°30N 129°30W 70 B3
Bowsman Canada 52°14N 101°12W 71 C8
Box Cr. → Australia 34°10S 143°50E 63 E3
Boxmeer Neths. 51°38N 5°56E 15 C5
Boxtel Neths. 51°36N 5°20E 15 C5
Boyang China 29°0N 116°38E 35 C11
Boyce U.S.A. 31°23N 92°40W 84 F8
Boyd L. Canada 52°46N 76°42W 72 B4
Boyle Canada 54°35N 112°49W 70 C6
Boyle Ireland 53°59N 8°18W 10 C3
Boyne → Ireland 53°43N 6°15W 10 C5
Boyne, Bend of the Ireland 53°41N 6°27W 10 C5
Boyne City U.S.A. 45°13N 85°1W 81 C11
Boynton Beach U.S.A. 26°32N 80°4W 85 H14
Boyoma, Chutes Dem. Rep. of the Congo 0°35N 25°23E 50 F6
Boysen Res. U.S.A. 43°25N 108°11W 76 E9
Boyuibe Bolivia 20°25S 63°17W 92 G6
Boyup Brook Australia 33°50S 116°23E 61 F2
Boz Dağları Turkey 38°20N 28°0E 23 E13
Bozburun Turkey 36°43N 28°4E 23 F13
Bozcaada Turkey 39°49N 26°3E 23 E12
Bozdoğan Turkey 37°40N 28°17E 23 F13
Bozeman U.S.A. 45°41N 111°2W 76 D8
Bozen = Bolzano Italy 46°31N 11°22E 22 A4
Bozhou China 33°55N 115°41E 32 H8
Bozoum C.A.R. 6°25N 16°35E 54 C3
Bozyazı Turkey 36°6N 33°0E 46 B2
Bra Italy 44°42N 7°51E 20 D7
Brabant □ Belgium 50°46N 4°30E 15 D4
Brabant L. Canada 55°58N 103°43W 71 B8
Brač Croatia 43°20N 16°40E 22 C7
Bracadale, L. U.K. 57°20N 6°30W 11 D2
Bracciano, L. di Italy 42°7N 12°14E 22 C5
Bracebridge Canada 45°2N 79°19W 82 A5
Bräcke Sweden 62°45N 15°26E 8 E16
Brackettville U.S.A. 29°19N 100°25W 84 G4
Bracknell U.K. 51°25N 0°43W 13 F7
Bracknell Forest □ U.K. 51°25N 0°44W 13 F7
Brad Romania 46°10N 22°50E 17 E12
Bradenton U.S.A. 27°30N 82°34W 85 H13
Bradford Canada 44°7N 79°34W 82 B5
Bradford U.K. 53°47N 1°45W 12 D6
Bradford Pa., U.S.A. 41°58N 78°38W 82 E6
Bradford Vt., U.S.A. 43°59N 72°9W 83 C12
Bradley Ark., U.S.A. 33°6N 93°39W 84 E8
Bradley Calif., U.S.A. 35°52N 120°48W 78 K6
Brady U.S.A. 31°9N 99°20W 84 F5
Braeside Canada 45°28N 76°24W 83 A8
Braga Portugal 41°35N 8°25W 21 B1
Bragado Argentina 35°2S 60°27W 94 D3
Bragança Brazil 1°0S 47°2W 93 D9
Bragança Portugal 41°48N 6°50W 21 B2
Bragança Paulista Brazil 22°55S 46°32W 95 A6
Brahestad = Raahe Finland 64°40N 24°28E 8 D21
Brahmanbaria Bangla. 23°58N 91°15E 41 H17
Brahmani → India 20°39N 86°46E 44 D8
Brahmapur India 19°15N 84°54E 44 E7
Brahmaputra → Asia 23°40N 90°35E 43 H13
Braich-y-pwll U.K. 52°47N 4°46W 12 E3
Braidwood Australia 35°27S 149°49E 63 F4
Brăila Romania 45°19N 27°59E 17 F14
Brainerd U.S.A. 46°22N 94°12W 80 B6
Braintree U.K. 51°53N 0°34E 13 F8
Braintree U.S.A. 42°13N 71°0W 83 D14
Brak → S. Africa 29°35S 22°55E 56 C3
Brakwater Namibia 22°28S 17°3E 56 B2
Bramhapuri India 20°36N 79°52E 44 D4
Brampton Canada 43°45N 79°45W 82 C5
Brampton U.K. 54°57N 2°44W 12 C5
Brampton I. Australia 20°49S 149°16E 62 b
Branco → Brazil 1°20S 61°50W 92 D6
Branco, C. Brazil 7°9S 34°47W 90 D7
Brandberg Namibia 21°10S 14°33E 56 B1
Brandberg ⌂ Namibia 21°10S 14°30E 56 B1
Brandenburg = Neubrandenburg Germany 53°33N 13°15E 16 B7
Brandenburg Germany 52°25N 12°33E 16 B7
Brandenburg □ Germany 52°50N 13°0E 16 B6
Brandfort S. Africa 28°40S 26°30E 56 C4
Brandon Canada 49°50N 99°57W 71 D9
Brandon U.S.A. 43°48N 73°6W 83 C11
Brandon B. Ireland 52°17N 10°8W 10 D1
Brandon Mt. Ireland 52°15N 10°15W 10 D1
Brandsen Argentina 35°10S 58°15W 94 D4
Brandvlei S. Africa 30°25S 20°30E 56 D3
Branford U.S.A. 41°17N 72°49W 83 E12
Braniewo Poland 54°25N 19°50E 17 A10
Bransfield Str. Antarctica 63°0S 59°0W 5 C18
Branson U.S.A. 36°39N 93°13W 80 G7
Brantford Canada 43°10N 80°15W 82 C4
Bras d'Or L. Canada 45°50N 60°50W 73 C7
Brasher Falls U.S.A. 44°49N 74°47W 83 B10
Brasil = Brazil ■ S. Amer. 12°0S 50°0W 93 F9
Brasil, Planalto Brazil 18°0S 46°30W 90 E6
Brasiléia Brazil 11°0S 68°45W 92 F5
Brasília Brazil 15°47S 47°55W 93 G9
Brasília Legal Brazil 3°49S 55°36W 93 D7
Braslaw Belarus 55°38N 27°0E 9 J22
Braşov Romania 45°38N 25°35E 17 F13
Brasschaat Belgium 51°19N 4°27E 15 C4
Brassey, Banjaran Malaysia 5°0N 117°15E 36 D5
Brassey Ra. Australia 25°8S 122°15E 61 E3
Brasstown Bald U.S.A. 34°53N 83°49W 85 D13
Brastad Sweden 58°23N 11°30E 9 G14
Bratislava Slovak Rep. 48°10N 17°7E 17 D9
Bratsk Russia 56°10N 101°30E 27 D11
Bratskoye Vdkhr. Russia 56°0N 101°40E 27 D11
Brattleboro U.S.A. 42°51N 72°34W 83 D12
Braunau am Inn Austria 48°15N 13°3E 16 D7
Braunschweig Germany 52°15N 10°31E 16 B6
Braunton U.K. 51°7N 4°10W 13 F3
Brava C. Verde Is. 15°0N 24°40W 52 b
Brava, Costa Spain 41°30N 3°0E 21 B7
Bravo del Norte, Rio = Grande, Rio → N. Amer. 25°58N 97°9W 84 J6
Brawley U.S.A. 32°59N 115°31W 79 N11
Bray Ireland 53°13N 6°7W 10 C5
Bray, Mt. Australia 14°0S 134°30E 62 A1
Bray, Pays de France 49°46N 1°26E 20 B4
Brazeau → Canada 52°55N 115°14W 70 C5
Brazil U.S.A. 39°32N 87°8W 80 F10
Brazil ■ S. Amer. 12°0S 50°0W 93 F9
Brazilian Highlands = Brasil, Planalto Brazil 18°0S 46°30W 90 E6
Brazo Sur → S. Amer. 25°21S 57°42W 94 B4
Brazos → U.S.A. 28°53N 95°23W 84 G7
Brazzaville Congo 4°9S 15°12E 54 E3
Brčko Bos.-H. 44°54N 18°46E 23 B8
Bré = Bray Ireland 53°13N 6°7W 10 C5
Breaden, L. Australia 25°51S 125°28E 61 E4
Breaksea Sd. N.Z. 45°35S 166°35E 59 F1
Bream B. N.Z. 35°56S 174°28E 59 A5
Bream Hd. N.Z. 35°51S 174°36E 59 A5
Breas Chile 25°29S 70°24W 94 B1
Brebes Indonesia 6°52S 109°3E 37 G13
Brechin Canada 44°32N 79°10W 82 B5
Brechin U.K. 56°44N 2°39W 11 E6
Brecht Belgium 51°21N 4°38E 15 C4
Breckenridge Colo., U.S.A. 39°29N 106°3W 76 G10
Breckenridge Minn., U.S.A. 46°16N 96°35W 80 B5
Breckenridge Tex., U.S.A. 32°45N 98°54W 84 E5
Breckland U.K. 52°30N 0°40E 13 E8
Brecon U.K. 51°57N 3°23W 13 F4
Brecon Beacons U.K. 51°53N 3°26W 13 F4
Brecon Beacons △ U.K. 51°50N 3°30W 13 F4
Breda Neths. 51°35N 4°45E 15 C4
Bredasdorp S. Africa 34°33S 20°2E 56 D3
Bree Belgium 51°8N 5°35E 15 C5
Bregenz Austria 47°30N 9°45E 16 E5
Breiðafjörður Iceland 65°15N 23°15W 8 D2
Brejo Brazil 3°41S 42°47W 93 D10
Bremen Germany 53°4N 8°47E 16 B5
Bremer Bay Australia 34°21S 119°20E 61 F2
Bremer I. Australia 12°5S 136°45E 62 A2
Bremerhaven Germany 53°33N 8°36E 16 B5
Bremerton U.S.A. 47°34N 122°37W 78 C4
Brenham U.S.A. 30°10N 96°24W 84 F6
Brennerpass Austria 47°2N 11°30E 16 E6
Brent U.S.A. 32°56N 87°10W 85 E11
Brentwood U.K. 51°37N 0°19E 13 F8
Brentwood Calif., U.S.A. 37°56N 121°42W 78 H5
Brentwood N.Y., U.S.A. 40°47N 73°15W 83 F11
Bréscia Italy 45°33N 10°15E 20 D9
Breskens Neths. 51°23N 3°33E 15 C3
Breslau = Wrocław Poland 51°5N 17°5E 17 C9
Bressanone Italy 46°43N 11°39E 22 A4
Bressay U.K. 60°9N 1°6W 11 A7
Brest Belarus 52°10N 23°40E 17 B12
Brest France 48°24N 4°31W 20 B1
Brest □ Belarus 52°30N 26°10E 17 B13
Brest-Litovsk = Brest Belarus 52°10N 23°40E 17 B12
Bretagne □ France 48°10N 3°0W 20 B2
Breton Canada 53°7N 114°28W 70 C6
Breton Sd. U.S.A. 29°35N 89°15W 85 G10
Brett, C. N.Z. 35°10S 174°20E 59 A5
Brevard U.S.A. 35°14N 82°44W 85 D13
Breves Brazil 1°40S 50°29W 93 D8
Brewarrina Australia 30°0S 146°51E 63 E4
Brewer U.S.A. 44°48N 68°46W 81 C19
Brewer, Mt. U.S.A. 36°44N 118°28W 78 J8
Brewster N.Y., U.S.A. 41°24N 73°36W 83 E11
Brewster Ohio, U.S.A. 40°43N 81°36W 82 F3
Brewster Wash., U.S.A. 48°6N 119°47W 76 B4
Brewster, Kap = Kangikajik Greenland 70°7N 22°0W 4 B6
Brewton U.S.A. 31°7N 87°4W 85 F11
Breyten S. Africa 26°16S 30°0E 57 C5
Bria C.A.R. 6°30N 21°58E 54 C4
Briançon France 44°54N 6°39E 20 D7
Bribie I. Australia 27°0S 153°10E 63 D5
Bribri Costa Rica 9°38N 82°50W 88 E3
Bridgefield Barbados 13°9N 59°36W 89 g
Bridgehampton U.S.A. 40°56N 72°19W 83 F12
Bridgend U.K. 51°30N 3°34W 13 F4
Bridgend □ U.K. 51°36N 3°36W 13 F4
Bridgenorth Canada 44°23N 78°23W 82 B6
Bridgeport Calif., U.S.A. 38°15N 119°14W 78 G7
Bridgeport Conn., U.S.A. 41°11N 73°12W 83 E11
Bridgeport N.Y., U.S.A. 43°9N 75°58W 83 C9
Bridgeport Nebr., U.S.A. 41°40N 103°6W 80 E2
Bridgeport Tex., U.S.A. 33°13N 97°45W 84 E6
Bridger U.S.A. 45°18N 108°55W 76 D9
Bridgeton U.S.A. 39°26N 75°14W 81 F16
Bridgetown Australia 33°58S 116°7E 61 F2
Bridgetown Barbados 13°6N 59°37W 89 g
Bridgetown Canada 44°55N 65°18W 73 D6
Bridgewater Australia 42°44S 147°14E 63 G4
Bridgewater Canada 44°25N 64°31W 73 D7
Bridgewater Mass., U.S.A. 41°59N 70°58W 83 E14
Bridgewater N.Y., U.S.A. 42°53N 75°15W 83 D9
Bridgewater, C. Australia 38°23S 141°23E 63 F3
Bridgnorth U.K. 52°32N 2°25W 13 E5
Bridgton U.S.A. 44°3N 70°42W 83 B14
Bridgwater U.K. 51°8N 2°59W 13 F5
Bridgwater B. U.K. 51°15N 3°15W 13 F4
Bridlington U.K. 54°5N 0°12W 12 C7
Bridlington B. U.K. 54°4N 0°10W 12 C7
Bridport Australia 40°59S 147°23E 63 G4
Bridport U.K. 50°44N 2°45W 13 G5
Brig Switz. 46°18N 7°59E 20 C7
Brigg U.K. 53°34N 0°28W 12 D7
Brigham City U.S.A. 41°31N 112°1W 76 F7
Bright Australia 36°42S 146°56E 63 F4
Brighton Australia 35°5S 138°30E 63 F2
Brighton Canada 44°2N 77°44W 82 B7
Brighton Trin. & Tob. 10°15N 61°39W 93 K15
Brighton U.K. 50°49N 0°7W 13 G7
Brighton U.S.A. 43°8N 77°34W 82 C7
Brightside Canada 45°7N 76°29W 83 A8
Brilliant U.S.A. 40°15N 80°39W 82 F4
Bríndisi Italy 40°39N 17°55E 23 D7
Brinkley U.S.A. 34°53N 91°12W 84 D9
Brinnon U.S.A. 47°41N 122°54W 78 C4
Brion, Î. Canada 47°46N 61°26W 73 C7
Brisay Canada 54°26N 70°31W 73 B5
Brisbane Australia 27°25S 153°2E 63 D5
Brisbane → Australia 27°24S 153°9E 63 D5
Brisbane ✕ (BNE) Australia 27°35S 153°7E 63 D5
Bristol U.K. 51°26N 2°35W 13 F5
Bristol Conn., U.S.A. 41°40N 72°57W 83 E12
Bristol Pa., U.S.A. 40°6N 74°51W 83 F10
Bristol R.I., U.S.A. 41°40N 71°16W 83 E13
Bristol Tenn., U.S.A. 36°36N 82°11W 85 C13
Bristol Vt., U.S.A. 44°8N 73°4W 83 B11
Bristol, City of □ U.K. 51°27N 2°36W 13 F5
Bristol B. U.S.A. 58°0N 160°0W 74 D8
Bristol Channel U.K. 51°18N 4°30W 13 F3
Bristol I. Antarctica 58°45S 28°0W 5 B1
Bristol L. U.S.A. 34°28N 115°41W 79 L11
Bristow U.S.A. 35°50N 96°23W 84 D6
Britain = Great Britain Europe 54°0N 2°15W 6 E5
British Columbia □ Canada 55°0N 125°15W 70 C3
British Indian Ocean Terr. = Chagos Arch. ⧄ Ind. Oc. 6°0S 72°0E 3 E13
British Isles Europe 54°0N 4°0W 14 D5
British Mts. N. Amer. 68°50N 140°0W 74 B12
British Virgin Is. ⧄ W. Indies 18°30N 64°30W 89 e
Brits S. Africa 25°37S 27°48E 57 C4
Britstown S. Africa 30°37S 23°30E 56 D3
Britt Canada 45°46N 80°34W 72 C3
Brittany = Bretagne □ France 48°10N 3°0W 20 B2
Britton U.S.A. 45°48N 97°45W 80 C5
Brive-la-Gaillarde France 45°10N 1°32E 20 D4
Brixen = Bressanone Italy 46°43N 11°39E 22 A4
Brixham U.K. 50°23N 3°31W 13 G4
Brno Czech Rep. 49°10N 16°35E 17 D9
Broach = Bharuch India 21°47N 73°0E 44 D1
Broad → U.S.A. 34°1N 81°4W 85 D14
Broad Arrow Australia 30°23S 121°15E 61 F3
Broad B. U.K. 58°14N 6°18W 11 C2
Broad Haven Ireland 54°20N 9°55W 10 B2
Broad Law U.K. 55°30N 3°21W 11 F5
Broad Pk. = Faichan Kangri India 35°48N 76°34E 43 B7
Broad Sd. Australia 22°0S 149°45E 62 C4
Broadalbin U.S.A. 43°4N 74°12W 83 C10
Broadback → Canada 51°21N 78°52W 72 B4
Broadhurst Ra. Australia 22°30S 122°30E 60 D3
Broads, The U.K. 52°45N 1°30E 12 E9
Broadus U.S.A. 45°27N 105°25W 76 D11
Brochet Canada 57°53N 101°40W 71 B8
Brochet, L. Canada 58°36N 101°35W 71 B8
Brock I. Canada 77°52N 114°19W 69 B9
Brocken Germany 51°47N 10°37E 16 C6
Brockport U.S.A. 43°13N 77°56W 82 C7
Brockton U.S.A. 42°5N 71°1W 83 D13
Brockville Canada 44°35N 75°41W 83 B9
Brockway Mont., U.S.A. 47°18N 105°45W 76 C11
Brockway Pa., U.S.A. 41°15N 78°47W 82 E6
Brocton U.S.A. 42°23N 79°26W 82 D5
Brodeur Pen. Canada 72°30N 88°10W 69 C14
Brodick U.K. 55°35N 5°9W 11 F3
Brodnica Poland 53°15N 19°25E 17 B10
Brody Ukraine 50°5N 25°10E 17 C13
Brogan U.S.A. 44°15N 117°31W 76 D5
Broken Arrow U.S.A. 36°3N 95°48W 84 C7
Broken Bow Nebr., U.S.A. 41°24N 99°38W 80 E4
Broken Bow Okla., U.S.A. 34°2N 94°44W 84 D7
Broken Bow Lake U.S.A. 34°9N 94°40W 84 D7
Broken Hill Australia 31°58S 141°29E 63 E3
Broken Ridge Ind. Oc. 30°0S 94°0E 64 L1
Broken River Ra. Australia 21°0S 148°22E 62 b
Bromo, Gunung Indonesia 7°56N 112°57E 37 H15
Bromo Tengger Semeru △ Indonesia 7°56S 112°57E 37 H15
Bromsgrove U.K. 52°21N 2°2W 13 E5
Brønderslev Denmark 57°16N 9°57E 9 H13
Bronkhorstspruit S. Africa 25°46S 28°45E 57 C4
Brønnøysund Norway 65°28N 12°14E 8 D15
Brook Park U.S.A. 41°23N 81°48W 82 E4
Brookhaven U.S.A. 31°35N 90°26W 85 F9
Brookings Oreg., U.S.A. 42°3N 124°17W 76 E1
Brookings S. Dak., U.S.A. 44°19N 96°48W 80 C5
Brooklin Canada 43°55N 78°55W 82 C6
Brooklyn Park U.S.A. 45°6N 93°23W 80 C7
Brooks Canada 50°35N 111°55W 70 C6
Brooks Range U.S.A. 68°0N 152°0W 74 B9
Brooksville U.S.A. 28°33N 82°23W 85 G13
Brookton Australia 32°22S 117°0E 61 F2
Brookville U.S.A. 41°10N 79°5W 82 E5
Broom, L. U.K. 57°55N 5°15W 11 D3
Broome Australia 18°0S 122°15E 60 C3
Brora U.K. 58°0N 3°52W 11 C5
Brora → U.K. 58°0N 3°51W 11 C5
Brosna → Ireland 53°14N 7°58W 10 C4
Brothers U.S.A. 43°49N 120°36W 76 E3
Brough U.K. 54°32N 2°18W 12 C5
Brough Hd. U.K. 59°8N 3°20W 11 B5
Broughton Island = Qikiqtarjuaq Canada 67°33N 63°0W 69 D19
Brown, L. Australia 31°5S 118°15E 61 F2
Brown, Pt. Australia 32°32S 133°50E 63 E1
Brown City U.S.A. 43°13N 82°59W 82 C2
Brown Willy U.K. 50°35N 4°37W 13 G3
Brownfield U.S.A. 33°11N 102°17W 84 E3
Browning U.S.A. 48°34N 113°1W 76 B7
Brownsville Oreg., U.S.A. 44°24N 122°59W 76 D2
Brownsville Pa., U.S.A. 40°1N 79°53W 82 F5
Brownsville Tenn., U.S.A. 35°36N 89°16W 85 D10
Brownsville Tex., U.S.A. 25°54N 97°30W 84 J6
Brownville U.S.A. 44°0N 75°59W 83 C9
Brownwood U.S.A. 31°43N 98°59W 84 F5
Browse I. Australia 14°7S 123°33E 60 B3
Bruas Malaysia 4°30N 100°47E 39 K3
Bruay-la-Buissière France 50°29N 2°33E 20 A5
Bruce, Mt. Australia 22°37S 118°8E 60 D2
Bruce Pen. Canada 45°0N 81°30W 82 B3
Bruce Peninsula △ Canada 45°14N 81°36W 82 A3
Bruce Rock Australia 31°52S 118°8E 61 F2
Bruck an der Leitha Austria 48°1N 16°47E 17 D9
Bruck an der Mur Austria 47°24N 15°16E 16 E8
Brue → U.K. 51°13N 2°59W 13 F5
Bruges = Brugge Belgium 51°13N 3°13E 15 C3
Brugge Belgium 51°13N 3°13E 15 C3
Bruin U.S.A. 41°3N 79°43W 82 E5
Brûk, W. el → Egypt 30°15N 33°50E 48 E2
Brûlé Canada 53°15N 117°58W 70 C5
Brûlé, L. Canada 53°35N 64°4W 73 B7
Brumado Brazil 14°14S 41°40W 93 F10
Brumunddal Norway 60°53N 10°56E 8 F14
Bruneau U.S.A. 42°53N 115°48W 76 E6
Bruneau → U.S.A. 42°56N 115°57W 76 E6
Brunei = Bandar Seri Begawan Brunei 4°52N 115°0E 36 D5
Brunei ■ Asia 4°50N 115°0E 36 D5
Brunner, L. N.Z. 42°37S 171°27E 59 E3
Brunssum Neths. 50°57N 5°59E 15 D5
Brunswick = Braunschweig Germany 52°15N 10°31E 16 B6
Brunswick Ga., U.S.A. 31°10N 81°30W 85 F14
Brunswick Maine, U.S.A. 43°55N 69°58W 81 D19
Brunswick Md., U.S.A. 39°19N 77°38W 81 F15
Brunswick Mo., U.S.A. 39°26N 93°8W 80 F7
Brunswick Ohio, U.S.A. 41°14N 81°51W 82 E3
Brunswick, Pen. de Chile 53°30S 71°30W 96 G2
Brunswick B. Australia 15°15S 124°50E 60 C3
Brunswick Junction Australia 33°15S 115°50E 61 F2
Brunt Ice Shelf Antarctica 75°30S 25°0W 5 D2
Brus Laguna Honduras 15°47N 84°35W 88 C3
Brush U.S.A. 40°15N 103°37W 76 F12
Brushton U.S.A. 44°50N 74°31W 83 B10
Brusque Brazil 27°5S 49°0W 95 B6
Brussels Canada 43°44N 81°15W 82 C3
Bruthen Australia 37°42S 147°50E 63 F4
Bryan Ohio, U.S.A. 41°28N 84°33W 81 E11
Bryan Tex., U.S.A. 30°40N 96°22W 84 F6
Bryan, Mt. Australia 33°30S 139°5E 63 E2
Bryansk Russia 53°13N 34°25E 18 D4
Bryce Canyon △ U.S.A. 37°30N 112°10W 77 H7
Bryne Norway 58°44N 5°38E 9 G11

Bryson City U.S.A. 35°26N 83°27W 85 D13
Bsharri Lebanon 34°15N 36°0E 48 A5
Bū Baqarah U.A.E. 25°35N 56°25E 47 E8
Bu Craa W. Sahara 26°45N 12°50W 52 C3
Bū Ḩasā U.A.E. 23°30N 53°20E 47 F7
Bua Fiji 16°48S 178°37E 59 a
Bua Yai Thailand 15°33N 102°26E 38 E4
Buan S. Korea 35°44N 126°44E 33 G14
Buapinang Indonesia 4°40S 121°30E 37 E6
Bubi → Zimbabwe 22°20S 31°7E 57 B5
Būbiyān Kuwait 29°45N 48°15E 47 D6
Buca Fiji 16°38S 179°52E 59 a
Bucaramanga Colombia 7°0N 73°0W 92 B4
Bucasia Australia 21°2S 149°10E 62 b
Buccaneer Arch. Australia 16°7S 123°20E 60 C3
Buccoo Reef Trin. & Tob. 11°10N 60°51W 93 J16
Buchach Ukraine 49°5N 25°25E 17 D13
Buchan U.K. 57°32N 2°21W 11 D6
Buchan Ness U.K. 57°29N 1°46W 11 D7
Buchanan Canada 51°40N 102°45W 71 C8
Buchanan Liberia 5°57N 10°2W 52 G3
Buchanan, L. Queens., Australia 21°35S 145°52E 62 C4
Buchanan, L. W. Austral., Australia 25°33S 123°2E 61 E3
Buchanan, L. U.S.A. 30°45N 98°25W 84 F5
Buchanan Cr. → Australia 19°13S 136°33E 62 B2
Buchans Canada 48°50N 56°52W 73 C8
Bucharest = Bucureşti Romania 44°27N 26°10E 17 F14
Bucheon S. Korea 37°28N 126°45E 33 F14
Buchon, Pt. U.S.A. 35°15N 120°54W 78 K6
Buck Hill Falls U.S.A. 41°11N 75°16W 83 E9
Buckeye Lake U.S.A. 39°55N 82°29W 82 G2
Buckhannon U.S.A. 39°0N 80°8W 81 F13
Buckhaven U.K. 56°11N 3°3W 11 E5
Buckhorn L. Canada 44°29N 78°23W 82 B6
Buckie U.K. 57°41N 2°58W 11 D6
Buckingham Canada 45°37N 75°24W 72 C4
Buckingham U.K. 51°59N 0°57W 13 F7
Buckingham B. Australia 12°10S 135°40E 62 A2
Buckingham Canal India 14°0N 80°5E 45 H5
Buckinghamshire □ U.K. 51°53N 0°55W 13 F7
Buckle Hd. Australia 14°26S 127°52E 60 B4
Buckleboo Australia 32°54S 136°12E 63 E2
Buckley U.K. 53°10N 3°5W 12 D4
Buckley → Australia 20°10S 138°49E 62 C2
Bucklin U.S.A. 37°33N 99°38W 80 G4
Bucks L. U.S.A. 39°54N 121°12W 78 F5
Bucureşti Romania 44°27N 26°10E 17 F14
Bucyrus U.S.A. 40°48N 82°59W 81 E12
Budalin Burma 22°20N 95°10E 41 H19
Budaun India 28°5N 79°10E 43 E8
Budd Coast Antarctica 68°0S 112°0E 5 C8
Bude U.K. 50°49N 4°34W 13 G3
Budennovsk Russia 44°50N 44°10E 19 F7
Budge Budge = Baj Baj India 22°30N 88°5E 43 H13
Budgewoi Australia 33°13S 151°34E 63 E5
Budjala Dem. Rep. of the Congo 2°50N 19°40E 54 D3
Budo-Sungai Padi △ Thailand 6°19N 101°42E 39 J3
Buellton U.S.A. 34°37N 120°12W 79 L6
Buena Esperanza Argentina 34°45S 65°15W 94 C2
Buena Park U.S.A. 33°52N 117°59W 79 M9
Buena Vista Colo., U.S.A. 38°51N 106°8W 76 G10
Buena Vista Va., U.S.A. 37°44N 79°21W 81 G14
Buena Vista Lake Bed U.S.A. 35°12N 119°18W 79 K7
Buenaventura Colombia 3°53N 77°4W 92 C3
Buenaventura Mexico 29°51N 107°29W 86 B3
Buenos Aires Costa Rica 9°10N 83°20W 88 E3
Buenos Aires □ Argentina 36°30S 60°0W 94 D4
Buenos Aires, L. = General Carrera, L. S. Amer. 46°35S 72°0W 96 F2
Buffalo Mo., U.S.A. 37°39N 93°6W 80 G7
Buffalo N.Y., U.S.A. 42°53N 78°53W 82 D6
Buffalo Okla., U.S.A. 36°50N 99°38W 84 C5
Buffalo S. Dak., U.S.A. 45°35N 103°33W 80 C2
Buffalo Wyo., U.S.A. 44°21N 106°42W 76 D10
Buffalo → Canada 60°5N 115°5W 70 A5
Buffalo → S. Africa 28°43S 30°37E 57 C5
Buffalo ⌂ U.S.A. 36°14N 92°36W 84 C8
Buffalo Head Hills Canada 57°25N 115°55W 70 B5
Buffalo L. Alta., Canada 52°27N 112°54W 70 C6
Buffalo L. N.W.T., Canada 60°12N 115°25W 70 A5
Buffalo Narrows Canada 55°51N 108°29W 71 B7
Buffels → S. Africa 29°36S 17°3E 56 C2
Buford U.S.A. 34°7N 83°59W 85 D12
Bug = Buh → Ukraine 46°59N 31°58E 19 E5
Bug → Poland 52°31N 21°5E 17 B11
Buga Colombia 4°0N 76°15W 92 C3
Bugel, Tanjung Indonesia 6°26S 111°3E 37 G14
Bugsuk I. Phil. 8°12N 117°18E 36 C5
Bugulma Russia 54°33N 52°48E 18 D9
Buguruslan Russia 53°39N 52°26E 18 D9
Buh → Ukraine 46°59N 31°58E 19 E5
Buhera Zimbabwe 19°18S 31°29E 57 A5
Buhl U.S.A. 42°36N 114°46W 76 E6
Builth Wells U.K. 52°9N 3°25W 13 E4
Buir Nur Mongolia 47°50N 117°42E 31 B12
Buji China 22°37N 114°5E 31 a
Bujumbura Burundi 3°16S 29°18E 54 E5
Bukachacha Russia 52°55N 116°50E 27 D12
Bukavu Dem. Rep. of the Congo 2°20S 28°52E 54 E5
Bukhara = Buxoro Uzbekistan 39°48N 64°25E 26 F7
Bukhoro = Buxoro Uzbekistan 39°48N 64°25E 26 F7
Bukhtarma Res. = Zaysan Köli Kazakhstan 48°0N 83°0E 26 E9
Bukit Bendera Malaysia 5°25N 100°15E 39 c
Bukit Mertajam Malaysia 5°22N 100°28E 39 c
Bukit Nil Malaysia 1°22N 104°12E 39 d
Bukit Tengah Malaysia 5°22N 100°25E 39 c
Bukittinggi Indonesia 0°20S 100°20E 36 E2
Bukkapatnam India 14°14N 77°46E 45 G3
Bukoba Tanzania 1°20S 31°49E 54 E6
Būl, Kuh-e Iran 30°48N 52°45E 47 D7
Bula Indonesia 3°6S 130°30E 37 E8
Bulahdelah Australia 32°23S 152°13E 63 E5
Bulan Phil. 12°40N 123°52E 37 B6
Bulawayo Zimbabwe 20°7S 28°32E 55 J5
Buldan Turkey 38°2N 28°50E 23 E13
Buldana India 20°30N 76°18E 44 D3
Buldir I. U.S.A. 52°21N 175°56E 74 E3
Bulgan Mongolia 48°45N 103°34E 30 B9
Bulgar Russia 54°57N 49°4E 18 D8
Bulgaria ■ Europe 42°35N 25°30E 23 C11
Buli, Teluk Indonesia 0°48N 128°25E 37 D7
Buliluyan, C. Phil. 8°20N 117°15E 36 C5
Bulkley → Canada 55°15N 127°40W 70 B3
Bull Shoals L. U.S.A. 36°22N 92°35W 84 C8
Bullering △ Australia 17°39S 143°56E 62 B3
Bullhead City U.S.A. 35°8N 114°32W 79 K12
Büllingen Belgium 50°25N 6°16E 15 D6
Bullock Creek Australia 17°43S 144°31E 62 B3
Bulloo → Australia 28°43S 142°30E 63 D3
Bulloo L. Australia 28°43S 142°25E 63 D3
Bulls N.Z. 40°10S 175°24E 59 D5
Bulman Australia 13°39S 134°20E 62 A1
Bulnes Chile 36°42S 72°19W 94 D1
Bulsar = Valsad India 20°40N 72°58E 44 D1
Bultfontein S. Africa 28°18S 26°10E 56 C4
Bulukumba Indonesia 5°33S 120°11E 37 F6
Bulun Russia 70°37N 127°30E 27 B13
Bumba Dem. Rep. of the Congo 2°13N 22°30E 54 D4
Bumbah, Khalīj Libya 32°20N 23°15E 53 B10
Bumhpa Bum Burma 26°51N 97°14E 41 F20
Bunaken Indonesia 1°37N 124°46E 37 D6
Bunbury Australia 33°20S 115°35E 61 F2
Bunclody Ireland 52°39N 6°40W 10 D5
Buncrana Ireland 55°8N 7°27W 10 A4
Bundaberg Australia 24°54S 152°22E 63 C5
Bundey → Australia 21°46S 135°37E 62 C2
Bundi India 25°30N 75°35E 42 G6
Bundjalung △ Australia 29°16S 153°21E 63 D5
Bundoran Ireland 54°28N 8°18W 10 B3
Bung Kan Thailand 18°23N 103°37E 38 C4
Bungay U.K. 52°27N 1°28E 13 E9
Bungil Cr. → Australia 27°5S 149°5E 63 D4
Bungle Bungle = Purnululu △ Australia 17°20S 128°20E 60 C4
Bungo-Suidō Japan 33°0N 132°15E 29 H6
Bungotakada Japan 33°35N 131°25E 29 H5
Bunia Dem. Rep. of the Congo 1°35N 30°20E 54 D6
Bunji Pakistan 35°45N 74°40E 43 B6
Bunkie U.S.A. 30°57N 92°11W 84 F8
Bunnell U.S.A. 29°28N 81°16W 85 G14
Buntok Indonesia 1°40S 114°58E 36 E4
Bunya Mts. △ Australia 26°51S 151°34E 63 D5
Bunyu Indonesia 3°35N 117°50E 36 D5
Buol Indonesia 1°15N 121°32E 37 D6
Buon Brieng Vietnam 13°9N 108°12E 38 F7
Buon Ho Vietnam 12°57N 108°18E 38 F7
Buon Ma Thuot Vietnam 12°40N 108°3E 38 F7
Buong Long Cambodia 13°44N 106°59E 38 F6
Buorkhaya, Mys Russia 71°50N 132°40E 27 B14
Buqayq Si. Arabia 26°0N 49°45E 47 E6
Bur Acaba = Buurhakaba Somalia 3°12N 44°20E 49 G3
Bûr Safâga Egypt 26°43N 33°57E 46 E2
Bûr Sa'îd Egypt 31°16N 32°18E 53 B12
Bûr Sûdân Sudan 19°32N 37°9E 53 E13
Burakin Australia 30°31S 117°10E 61 F2
Burang China 30°15N 81°10E 30 E5
Burao = Burco Somalia 9°32N 45°32E 49 F4
Burāq Syria 33°11N 36°29E 48 B5
Burathum Nepal 28°4N 84°50E 43 E11
Buraydah Si. Arabia 26°20N 43°59E 46 E4
Burco Somalia 9°32N 45°32E 49 F4
Burda India 25°50N 77°35E 42 G7
Burdekin → Australia 19°38S 147°25E 62 B4
Burdur Turkey 37°45N 30°17E 19 G5
Burdwan = Barddhaman India 23°14N 87°39E 43 H12
Bure Ethiopia 10°40N 37°4E 49 E2
Bure → U.K. 52°38N 1°43E 12 E9
Bureskoye Vdkhr. Russia 50°16N 130°20E 27 D14
Bureya → Russia 49°27N 129°30E 27 E13
Burford Canada 43°7N 80°27W 82 C4
Burgas Bulgaria 42°33N 27°29E 23 C12
Burgeo Canada 47°37N 57°38W 73 C8
Burgersdorp S. Africa 31°0S 26°20E 56 D4
Burgess, Mt. Australia 30°50S 121°5E 61 F3
Burghead U.K. 57°43N 3°30W 11 D5
Burgos Spain 42°21N 3°41W 21 A4
Burgsvik Sweden 57°3N 18°19E 9 H18
Burgundy = Bourgogne □ France 47°0N 4°50E 20 C6
Burhaniye Turkey 39°30N 26°58E 23 E12
Burhanpur India 21°18N 76°14E 44 D3
Burhi Gandak → India 25°20N 86°37E 43 G12
Burhner → India 22°43N 80°31E 43 H9
Burias I. Phil. 12°55N 123°5E 37 B6
Burica, Pta. Costa Rica 8°3N 82°51W 88 E3
Burien U.S.A. 47°28N 122°20W 78 C4
Burin Canada 47°1N 55°14W 73 C8
Buriram Thailand 15°0N 103°0E 38 E4
Burkburnett U.S.A. 34°6N 98°34W 84 D5
Burke → Australia 23°12S 139°33E 62 C2
Burke Chan. Canada 52°10N 127°30W 70 C3
Burketown Australia 17°45S 139°33E 62 B2
Burkina Faso ■ Africa 12°0N 1°0W 52 F5
Burk's Falls Canada 45°37N 79°24W 72 C4
Burleigh Falls Canada 44°33N 78°12W 82 B6
Burley U.S.A. 42°32N 113°48W 76 E7
Burlingame U.S.A. 37°35N 122°21W 78 H4
Burlington Canada 43°18N 79°45W 82 C5
Burlington Colo., U.S.A. 39°18N 102°16W 76 G12
Burlington Iowa, U.S.A. 40°49N 91°14W 80 E8
Burlington Kans., U.S.A. 38°12N 95°45W 80 F6
Burlington N.C., U.S.A. 36°6N 79°26W 85 C15
Burlington N.J., U.S.A. 40°4N 74°51W 83 F10
Burlington Vt., U.S.A. 44°29N 73°12W 83 B11
Burlington Wash., U.S.A. 48°28N 122°20W 78 B4
Burlington Wis., U.S.A. 42°41N 88°17W 80 D9
Burma ■ Asia 21°0N 96°30E 41 J20
Burnaby I. Canada 52°25N 131°19W 70 C2
Burnet U.S.A. 30°45N 98°14W 84 F5
Burney U.S.A. 40°53N 121°40W 76 F3
Burnham U.S.A. 40°38N 77°34W 82 F7
Burnham-on-Sea U.K. 51°14N 3°0W 13 F5
Burnie Australia 41°4S 145°56E 63 G4
Burnley U.K. 53°47N 2°14W 12 D5
Burns U.S.A. 43°35N 119°3W 76 E4
Burns Junction U.S.A. 42°47N 117°51W 76 E5
Burns Lake Canada 54°14N 125°45W 70 C3
Burnside → Canada 66°51N 108°4W 68 D10
Burnside, L. Australia 25°22S 123°0E 61 E3
Burnsville U.S.A. 44°47N 93°17W 80 C7
Burnt River Canada 44°41N 78°42W 82 B6
Burntwood → Canada 56°8N 96°34W 71 B9
Burntwood L. Canada 55°22N 100°26W 71 B8
Burqān Kuwait 29°0N 47°57E 46 D5
Burqin China 47°43N 87°0E 30 B6
Burra Australia 33°40S 138°55E 63 E2
Burray U.K. 58°51N 2°54W 11 C6
Burren △ Ireland 53°9N 9°5W 10 C2
Burren Junction Australia 30°7S 148°58E 63 E4
Burrinjuck, L. Australia 35°0S 148°36E 63 F4
Burro, Serranías del Mexico 28°56N 102°5W 86 B4
Burrow Hd. U.K. 54°41N 4°24W 11 G4
Burrum Coast △ Australia 25°13S 152°36E 63 D5
Burruyacú Argentina 26°30S 64°40W 94 B3
Burry Port U.K. 51°41N 4°15W 13 F3
Bursa Turkey 40°15N 29°5E 23 D13
Burstall Canada 50°39N 109°54W 71 C7
Burton Ohio, U.S.A. 41°28N 81°8W 82 E3
Burton S.C., U.S.A. 32°26N 80°43W 85 E14
Burton, L. Canada 54°45N 78°20W 72 B4
Burton upon Trent U.K. 52°48N 1°38W 12 E6
Buru Indonesia 3°30S 126°30E 37 E7
Burûn, Râs Egypt 31°14N 33°7E 48 D2
Burundi ■ Africa 3°15S 30°0E 54 E6
Burutu Nigeria 5°20N 5°29E 52 G7
Burwell U.S.A. 41°47N 99°8W 80 E4
Burwick U.K. 58°45N 2°58W 11 C5
Bury U.K. 53°35N 2°17W 12 D5
Bury St. Edmunds U.K. 52°15N 0°43E 13 E8
Buryatia □ Russia 53°0N 110°0E 27 D12
Busan S. Korea 35°5N 129°0E 33 G15
Busaso = Boosaaso Somalia 11°12N 49°18E 49 E4
Buşayrah Syria 35°9N 40°26E 46 C4
Būshehr Iran 28°55N 50°55E 47 D6
Būshehr □ Iran 28°20N 51°45E 47 D6
Bushire = Būshehr Iran 28°55N 50°55E 47 D6
Businga Dem. Rep. of the Congo 3°16N 20°59E 54 D4
Buşra ash Shām Syria 32°30N 36°25E 48 C5
Busselton Australia 33°42S 115°15E 61 F2
Bussol, Proliv Russia 46°30N 151°0E 27 E16
Bussum Neths. 52°16N 5°10E 15 B5
Busto Arsízio Italy 45°37N 8°51E 20 D8
Busu Djanoa Dem. Rep. of the Congo 1°43N 21°23E 54 D4
Busuanga I. Phil. 12°10N 120°0E 37 B6
Busungbiu Indonesia 8°16S 114°58E 37 J17
Buta Dem. Rep. of the Congo 2°50N 24°53E 54 D4
Butare Rwanda 2°31S 29°52E 54 E5
Butaritari Kiribati 3°30N 174°0E 64 G9
Bute U.K. 55°48N 5°2W 11 F3
Bute Inlet Canada 50°40N 124°53W 70 C4
Butembo Dem. Rep. of the Congo 0°9N 29°18E 54 D5
Butha-Buthe Lesotho 28°47S 28°14E 57 C4
Butler Mo., U.S.A. 38°16N 94°20W 80 F6
Butler Pa., U.S.A. 40°52N 79°54W 82 F5
Buton Indonesia 5°0S 122°45E 37 E6
Butte Mont., U.S.A. 46°0N 112°32W 76 C7
Butte Nebr., U.S.A. 42°58N 98°51W 80 D4
Butte Creek → U.S.A. 39°12N 121°56W 78 F5
Butterworth = Gcuwa S. Africa 32°20S 28°11E 57 D4
Butterworth Malaysia 5°24N 100°23E 39 c
Buttevant Ireland 52°14N 8°40W 10 D3
Buttfield, Mt. Australia 24°45S 128°9E 61 D4
Button B. Canada 58°45N 94°23W 71 B10
Buttonwillow U.S.A. 35°24N 119°28W 79 K7
Butty Hd. Australia 33°54S 121°39E 61 F3
Butuan Phil. 8°57N 125°33E 37 C7
Butung = Buton Indonesia 5°0S 122°45E 37 E6
Buturlinovka Russia 50°50N 40°35E 19 D7
Butwal Nepal 27°33N 83°31E 43 F10
Buurhakaba Somalia 3°12N 44°20E 49 G3
Buxa Duar India 27°45N 89°35E 43 F13
Buxar India 25°34N 83°58E 43 G10
Buxoro Uzbekistan 39°48N 64°25E 26 F7
Buxtehude Germany 53°28N 9°39E 16 B5
Buxton U.K. 53°16N 1°54W 12 D6
Buy Russia 58°28N 41°28E 18 C7
Buyant-Uhaa Mongolia 44°55N 110°11E 32 B6
Buyo, L. de Ivory C. 6°16N 7°10W 52 G4
Büyük Menderes → Turkey 37°28N 27°11E 23 F12
Büyükçekmece Turkey 41°2N 28°35E 23 D13
Buyun Shan China 40°4N 122°43E 33 D12
Buzău Romania 45°10N 26°50E 17 F14
Buzău → Romania 45°26N 27°44E 17 F14
Buzen Japan 33°35N 131°5E 29 H5
Buzi → Mozam. 19°50S 34°43E 55 H6
Büzmeyin Turkmenistan 38°3N 58°12E 47 B8
Buzuluk Russia 52°48N 52°12E 18 D9
Buzzards Bay U.S.A. 41°45N 70°37W 83 E14
Byam Martin I. Canada 75°15N 104°15W 69 B11
Byarezina → Belarus 52°33N 30°14E 17 B16
Byaroza Belarus 52°31N 24°51E 17 B13
Byblos = Jubayl Lebanon 34°5N 35°39E 48 A4
Bydgoszcz Poland 53°10N 18°0E 17 B9
Byelorussia = Belarus ■ Europe 53°30N 27°0E 17 B14
Byers U.S.A. 39°43N 104°14W 76 G11
Byesville U.S.A. 39°58N 81°32W 82 G3
Byfield △ Australia 22°52S 150°45E 62 C5
Bykhaw Belarus 53°31N 30°14E 17 B16
Bykhov = Bykhaw Belarus 53°31N 30°14E 17 B16
Bylas U.S.A. 33°8N 110°7W 77 K8
Bylot Canada 58°25N 94°8W 71 B10
Bylot I. Canada 73°13N 78°34W 69 C16
Byram U.S.A. 32°11N 90°15W 85 E9
Byrd, C. Antarctica 69°38S 76°7W 5 C17
Byrock Australia 30°40S 146°27E 63 E4
Byron, C. Australia 28°43S 153°38E 63 D5
Byron Bay Australia 28°43S 153°37E 63 D5
Byrranga, Gory Russia 75°0N 100°0E 27 B11
Byrranga Mts. = Byrranga, Gory Russia 75°0N 100°0E 27 B11
Byske Sweden 64°57N 21°11E 8 D19
Byskeälven → Sweden 64°57N 21°13E 8 D19
Bytom Poland 50°25N 18°54E 17 C10
Bytów Poland 54°10N 17°30E 17 A9

C

C.W. McConaughy, L. U.S.A. 41°14N 101°40W 80 E3
Ca → Vietnam 18°45N 105°45E 38 C5
Ca Mau Vietnam 9°7N 105°8E 39 H5
Ca Mau, Mui Vietnam 8°38N 104°44E 39 H5
Ca Na Vietnam 11°20N 108°54E 39 G7
Caacupé Paraguay 25°23S 57°5W 94 B4
Caaguazú △ Paraguay 26°5S 55°31W 95 B4
Caála Angola 12°46S 15°30E 55 G3
Caamaño Sd. Canada 52°55N 129°25W 70 C3
Caazapá Paraguay 26°8S 56°19W 94 B4
Caazapá □ Paraguay 26°10S 56°0W 95 B4
Cabanatuan Phil. 15°30N 120°58E 37 A6
Cabano Canada 47°40N 68°56W 73 C6
Cabazon U.S.A. 33°55N 116°47W 79 M10
Cabedelo Brazil 7°0S 34°50W 93 E12
Cabhán, An = Cavan Ireland 54°0N 7°22W 10 B4
Cabildo Chile 32°30S 71°5W 94 C1
Cabimas Venezuela 10°23N 71°25W 92 A4
Cabinda Angola 5°33S 12°11E 54 F2
Cabinda □ Angola 5°0S 12°30E 54 F2
Cabinet Mts. U.S.A. 48°10N 115°50W 76 B6
Cabo Blanco Argentina 47°15S 65°47W 96 F3
Cabo Frio Brazil 22°51S 42°3W 95 A7
Cabo Pantoja Peru 1°0S 75°10W 92 D3
Cabo Pulmo △ Mexico 23°20N 109°28W 86 C3
Cabo San Lucas Mexico 22°53N 109°54W 86 C3
Cabo Verde ■ Atl. Oc. 16°0N 24°0W 52 b
Cabonga, Réservoir Canada 47°20N 76°40W 72 C4
Cabool U.S.A. 37°7N 92°6W 80 G7
Caboolture Australia 27°5S 152°58E 63 D5
Cabora Bassa Dam = Cahora Bassa, Lago de Mozam. 15°20S 32°50E 55 H6
Caborca Mexico 30°37N 112°6W 86 A2
Cabot, Mt. U.S.A. 44°30N 71°25W 83 B13
Cabot Hd. Canada 45°14N 81°17W 82 A3
Cabot Str. Canada 47°15N 59°40W 73 C8
Cabra Spain 37°30N 4°28W 21 D3
Cabra I. India 7°18N 93°50E 45 L11
Cabrera Spain 39°8N 2°57E 21 C7
Cabri Canada 50°35N 108°25W 71 C7
Cabriel → Spain 39°14N 1°3W 21 C5
Caçador Brazil 26°47S 51°0W 95 B5
Čačak Serbia 43°54N 20°20E 23 C9
Caçapava do Sul Brazil 30°30S 53°30W 95 C5
Cáceres Brazil 16°5S 57°40W 92 G7
Cáceres Spain 39°26N 6°23W 21 C2
Cache Bay Canada 46°22N 80°0W 72 C4
Cache Cr. → U.S.A. 38°42N 121°42W 78 G5
Cache Creek Canada 50°48N 121°19W 70 C4
Cachi Argentina 25°5S 66°10W 94 B2
Cachimbo, Serra do Brazil 9°30S 55°30W 93 E7
Cachinal de la Sierra Chile 24°58S 69°32W 94 A2
Cachoeira Brazil 12°30S 39°0W 93 F11
Cachoeira do Sul Brazil 30°3S 52°53W 95 C5
Cachoeiro de Itapemirim Brazil 20°51S 41°7W 95 A7
Cacoal Brazil 11°32S 61°18W 92 F6
Cacólo Angola 10°9S 19°21E 54 G3
Caconda Angola 13°48S 15°8E 55 G3
Caddo U.S.A. 34°7N 96°16W 84 D6
Cader Idris U.K. 52°42N 3°53W 13 E4
Cadereyta de Jiménez Mexico 25°36N 100°0W 86 B5
Cadibarrawirracanna, L. Australia 28°52S 135°27E 63 D2
Cadillac U.S.A. 44°15N 85°24W 81 C11
Cadiz Phil. 10°57N 123°15E 37 B6
Cádiz Spain 36°30N 6°20W 21 D2
Cadiz Calif., U.S.A. 34°30N 115°28W 79 L11
Cadiz Ohio, U.S.A. 40°22N 81°0W 82 F4
Cádiz, G. de Spain 36°40N 7°0W 21 D2
Cadiz L. U.S.A. 34°18N 115°24W 79 L11
Cadney Park Australia 27°55S 134°3E 63 D1
Cadomin Canada 53°2N 117°20W 70 C5
Cadotte Lake Canada 56°26N 116°23W 70 B5
Cadoux Australia 30°46S 117°7E 61 F2
Caen France 49°10N 0°22W 20 B3
Caerdydd = Cardiff U.K. 51°29N 3°10W 13 F4
Caerfyrddin = Carmarthen U.K. 51°52N 4°19W 13 F3
Caergybi = Holyhead U.K. 53°18N 4°38W 12 D3
Caernarfon U.K. 53°8N 4°16W 12 D3
Caernarfon B. U.K. 53°4N 4°40W 12 D3
Caernarvon = Caernarfon U.K. 53°8N 4°16W 12 D3
Caerphilly U.K. 51°35N 3°13W 13 F4
Caerphilly □ U.K. 51°37N 3°12W 13 F4
Caesarea Israel 32°30N 34°53E 48 C3
Caetité Brazil 13°50S 42°32W 93 F10
Cafayate Argentina 26°2S 66°0W 94 B2
Cafu Angola 16°30S 15°8E 56 A2
Cagayan de Oro Phil. 8°30N 124°40E 37 C6
Cágliari Italy 39°13N 9°7E 22 E3
Cágliari, G. di Italy 39°8N 9°11E 22 E3
Caguán → Colombia 0°8S 74°18W 92 D4
Caguas Puerto Rico 18°14N 66°2W 89 d
Caha Mts. Ireland 51°45N 9°40W 10 E2
Cahama Angola 16°17S 14°19E 56 A1
Caherciveen Ireland 51°56N 10°14W 10 E1
Cahir Ireland 52°22N 7°56W 10 D4
Cahora Bassa, Lago de Mozam. 15°20S 32°50E 55 H6
Cahore Pt. Ireland 52°33N 6°12W 10 D5
Cahors France 44°27N 1°27E 20 D4
Cahul Moldova 45°50N 28°15E 17 F15
Cai Bau, Dao Vietnam 21°10N 107°27E 34 G6
Cai Be Vietnam 10°20N 106°2E 39 G6
Cai Nuoc Vietnam 8°56N 105°1E 39 H5
Caia Mozam. 17°51S 35°24E 55 H7
Caianda Angola 11°2S 23°31E 54 G4
Caibarién Cuba 22°30N 79°30W 88 B4
Caicara Venezuela 7°38N 66°10W 92 B5
Caicó Brazil 6°20S 37°0W 93 E11
Caicos Is. Turks & Caicos 21°40N 71°40W 89 B5
Caicos Passage W. Indies 22°45N 72°45W 89 B5
Caidian China 30°35N 114°2E 35 B10
Caiguna Australia 32°16S 125°29E 61 F4
Caird Coast Antarctica 75°0S 25°0W 5 D1
Cairn Gorm U.K. 57°7N 3°39W 11 D5
Cairngorm Mts. U.K. 57°6N 3°42W 11 D5
Cairngorms △ U.K. 57°10N 3°50W 11 D5
Cairnryan U.K. 54°59N 5°1W 11 G3
Cairns Australia 16°57S 145°45E 62 B4
Cairns L. Canada 51°42N 94°30W 71 C10
Cairo Ga., U.S.A. 30°52N 84°13W 85 F12
Cairo Ill., U.S.A. 37°0N 89°11W 80 G9
Cairo N.Y., U.S.A. 42°18N 74°0W 83 D10
Caiseal = Cashel Ireland 52°30N 7°53W 10 D4
Caisleán an Bharraigh = Castlebar Ireland 53°52N 9°18W 10 C2
Caithness U.K. 58°25N 3°35W 11 C5
Caithness, Ord of U.K. 58°8N 3°36W 11 C5
Caja de Muertos, I. Puerto Rico 17°54N 66°32W 89 d
Cajamarca Peru 7°5S 78°28W 92 E3
Cajazeiras Brazil 6°52S 38°30W 93 E11
Calabar Nigeria 4°57N 8°20E 52 H7
Calabogie Canada 45°18N 76°43W 83 A8
Calabozo Venezuela 9°0N 67°28W 92 B5
Calábria □ Italy 39°0N 16°30E 22 E7
Calahorra Spain 42°18N 1°59W 21 A5
Calais France 50°57N 1°56E 20 A4
Calais U.S.A. 45°11N 67°17W 81 C20
Calakmul ⌂ Mexico 18°14N 89°48W 87 D7
Calalaste, Cord. de Argentina 25°0S 67°0W 94 B2
Calama Brazil 8°0S 62°50W 92 E6
Calama Chile 22°30S 68°55W 94 A2
Calamar Colombia 10°15N 74°55W 92 A4
Calamian Group Phil. 11°50N 119°55E 37 B5
Calamocha Spain 40°50N 1°17W 21 B5
Calang Indonesia 4°37N 95°37E 36 D1
Calanscio, Sarīr Libya 27°30N 22°30E 53 C10
Calapan Phil. 13°25N 121°7E 37 B6
Călăraşi Romania 44°12N 27°20E 17 F14
Calatayud Spain 41°20N 1°40W 21 B5
Calauag Phil. 13°55N 122°15E 37 B6
Calavite, C. Phil. 13°26N 120°20E 37 B6
Calbayog Phil. 12°4N 124°38E 37 B6
Calca Peru 13°22S 72°0W 92 F4
Calcasieu L. U.S.A. 29°55N 93°18W 84 G8
Calcium U.S.A. 44°1N 75°50W 83 B9
Calcutta U.S.A. 40°40N 80°34W 82 F4
Caldas da Rainha Portugal 39°24N 9°8W 21 C1
Calder → U.K. 53°44N 1°22W 12 D6
Caldera Chile 27°5S 70°55W 94 B1
Caldwell Idaho, U.S.A. 43°40N 116°41W 76 E5
Caldwell Kans., U.S.A. 37°2N 97°37W 80 G5
Caldwell Tex., U.S.A. 30°32N 96°42W 84 F6
Caledon Canada 43°51N 79°51W 82 C5
Caledon S. Africa 34°14S 19°26E 56 D2
Caledon → S. Africa 30°31S 26°5E 56 D4
Caledon B. Australia 12°45S 137°0E 62 A2
Caledonia Canada 43°7N 79°58W 82 C5
Caledonia U.S.A. 42°58N 77°51W 82 D7
Calemba Angola 16°0S 15°44E 56 A2
Calen Australia 20°56S 148°48E 62 b
Caletones Chile 34°6S 70°27W 94 C1
Calexico U.S.A. 32°40N 115°30W 79 N11
Calf of Man I. of Man 54°3N 4°48W 12 C3
Calgary Canada 51°0N 114°10W 70 C6
Calhoun U.S.A. 34°30N 84°57W 85 D12
Cali Colombia 3°25N 76°35W 92 C3
Calicut = Kozhikode India 11°15N 75°43E 45 J2
Cálida, Costa Spain 37°30N 1°30W 21 D5
Caliente U.S.A. 37°37N 114°31W 77 H6
California Mo., U.S.A. 38°38N 92°34W 80 F7
California Pa., U.S.A. 40°4N 79°54W 82 F5
California □ U.S.A. 37°30N 119°30W 78 H7
California, Baja, T.N. = Baja California □ Mexico 30°0N 115°0W 86 B2
California, Baja, T.S. = Baja California Sur □ Mexico 25°50N 111°50W 86 B2
California, G. de Mexico 27°0N 111°0W 86 B2
California City U.S.A. 35°10N 117°55W 79 K9
California Hot Springs U.S.A. 35°51N 118°41W 79 K8
Calilegua △ Argentina 25°36S 64°50W 94 B3
Calingasta Argentina 31°15S 69°30W 94 C2
Calipatria U.S.A. 33°8N 115°31W 79 M11

Calistoga *U.S.A.* 38°35N 122°35W **78** G4
Calitzdorp *S. Africa* 33°33S 21°42E **56** D3
Callabonna, L. *Australia* 29°40S 140°5E **63** D3
Callan *Ireland* 52°32N 7°24W **10** D4
Callander *U.K.* 56°15N 4°13W **11** E4
Callicoon *U.S.A.* 41°46N 75°3W **83** E9
Calling Lake *Canada* 55°15N 113°12W **70** B6
Calliope *Australia* 24°0S 151°16E **62** C5
Calne *U.K.* 51°26N 2°0W **13** F6
Calola *Angola* 16°25S 17°48E **56** A2
Caloundra *Australia* 26°45S 153°10E **63** D5
Calpella *U.S.A.* 39°14N 123°12W **78** F3
Calpine *U.S.A.* 39°40N 120°27W **78** F6
Calstock *Canada* 49°47N 84°9W **72** C3
Caltagirone *Italy* 37°14N 14°31E **22** F6
Caltanissetta *Italy* 37°29N 14°4E **22** F6
Calulo *Angola* 10°1S 14°56E **54** G2
Calvert → *Australia* 16°17S 137°44E **62** B2
Calvert I. *Canada* 51°30N 128°0W **70** C3
Calvert Ra. *Australia* 24°0S 122°30E **60** D3
Calvi *France* 42°34N 8°45E **20** E8
Calvià *Spain* 39°34N 2°31E **21** C7
Calvillo *Mexico* 21°51N 102°43W **86** C4
Calvinia *S. Africa* 31°28S 19°45E **56** D2
Calwa *U.S.A.* 36°42N 119°46W **78** J7
Cam → *U.K.* 52°21N 0°16E **13** E8
Cam Lam = Ba Ngoi
Vietnam 11°54N 109°10E **39** G7
Cam Pha *Vietnam* 21°7N 107°18E **34** G6
Cam Ranh *Vietnam* 11°54N 109°12E **39** G7
Cam Xuyen *Vietnam* 18°15N 106°0E **38** C6
Camabatela *Angola* 8°20S 15°26E **54** F3
Camacupa *Angola* 11°58S 17°22E **55** G3
Camagüey *Cuba* 21°20N 77°55W **88** B4
Camaná *Peru* 16°30S 72°50W **92** G4
Camanche Res. *U.S.A.* 38°14N 121°1W **78** G6
Camaquã *Brazil* 30°51S 51°49W **95** C5
Camaquã → *Brazil* 31°17S 51°47W **95** C5
Camargo *Mexico* 26°19N 98°50W **87** B5
Camarillo *U.S.A.* 34°13N 119°2W **79** L7
Camarón, C. *Honduras* 16°0N 85°5W **88** C2
Camarones *Argentina* 44°50S 65°40W **96** E3
Camas *U.S.A.* 45°35N 122°24W **78** E4
Camas Valley *U.S.A.* 43°2N 123°40W **76** E2
Camballin *Australia* 17°59S 124°12E **60** C3
Cambará *Brazil* 23°2S 50°5W **95** A5
Cambay = Khambhat
India 22°23N 72°33E **42** H5
Cambay, G. of = Khambhat, G. of
India 20°45N 72°30E **40** J8
Cambodia ■ *Asia* 12°15N 105°0E **38** F5
Camborne *U.K.* 50°12N 5°19W **13** G2
Cambrai *France* 50°11N 3°14E **20** A5
Cambria *U.S.A.* 35°34N 121°5W **78** K5
Cambrian Mts. *U.K.* 52°3N 3°57W **13** E4
Cambridge *Canada* 43°23N 80°15W **82** C4
Cambridge *Jamaica* 18°18N 77°54W **88** a
Cambridge *N.Z.* 37°54S 175°29E **59** B5
Cambridge *U.K.* 52°12N 0°8E **13** E8
Cambridge *Minn., U.S.A.* 45°34N 93°13W **80** C7
Cambridge *N.Y., U.S.A.* 43°2N 73°22W **83** C11
Cambridge *Nebr., U.S.A.* 40°17N 100°10W **80** E3
Cambridge *Ohio, U.S.A.* 40°2N 81°35W **82** F3
Cambridge Bay *Canada* 69°10N 105°0W **68** D11
Cambridge G. *Australia* 14°55S 128°15E **60** B4
Cambridge Springs *U.S.A.* 41°48N 80°4W **82** E4
Cambridgeshire □ *U.K.* 52°25N 0°7W **13** E7
Cambuci *Brazil* 21°35S 41°55W **95** A7
Cambundi-Catembo
Angola 10°10S 17°35E **54** G3
Camdeboo △ *S. Africa* 32°28S 24°25E **56** D3
Camden *Australia* 34°1S 150°43E **63** B5
Camden *Ala., U.S.A.* 31°59N 87°17W **85** F11
Camden *Ark., U.S.A.* 33°35N 92°50W **84** E8
Camden *Maine, U.S.A.* 44°13N 69°4W **81** C19
Camden *N.J., U.S.A.* 39°55N 75°7W **83** G9
Camden *N.Y., U.S.A.* 43°20N 75°45W **83** C9
Camden *S.C., U.S.A.* 34°16N 80°36W **85** D14
Camden Sd. *Australia* 15°27S 124°25E **60** C3
Camdenton *U.S.A.* 38°1N 92°45W **80** F7
Camelford *U.K.* 50°37N 4°42W **13** G3
Cameron *Ariz., U.S.A.* 35°53N 111°25W **77** J8
Cameron *La., U.S.A.* 29°48N 93°20W **84** G8
Cameron *Mo., U.S.A.* 39°44N 94°14W **80** F6
Cameron *Tex., U.S.A.* 30°51N 96°59W **84** F6
Cameron Highlands
Malaysia 4°27N 101°22E **39** K3
Cameron Hills *Canada* 59°48N 118°0W **70** B5
Cameroon ■ *Africa* 6°0N 12°30E **53** G7
Cameroun, Mt. *Cameroon* 4°13N 9°10E **54** D1
Cametá *Brazil* 2°12S 49°30W **93** D9
Camilla *U.S.A.* 31°14N 84°12W **85** F12
Caminha *Portugal* 41°50N 8°50W **21** B1
Camino *U.S.A.* 38°44N 120°41W **78** G6
Cammal *U.S.A.* 41°24N 77°28W **82** E7
Camocim *Brazil* 2°55S 40°50W **93** D10
Camooweal *Australia* 19°56S 138°7E **62** B2
Camooweal Caves △
Australia 20°1S 138°11E **62** C2
Camopi *Fr. Guiana* 3°12N 52°17W **93** C8
Camorta *India* 8°8N 93°30E **45** K11
Camp Hill *U.S.A.* 40°14N 76°55W **82** F8
Camp Nelson *U.S.A.* 36°8N 118°39W **79** J8
Camp Pendleton *U.S.A.* 33°13N 117°24W **79** M9
Camp Verde *U.S.A.* 34°34N 111°51W **77** J8
Camp Wood *U.S.A.* 29°40N 100°1W **84** G4
Campana *Argentina* 34°10S 58°55W **94** C4
Campana, I. *Chile* 48°20S 75°20W **96** F1
Campánia □ *Italy* 41°0N 14°30E **22** D6
Campas del Tuyú △
Argentina 36°17S 56°50W **94** D4
Campbell *S. Africa* 28°48S 23°44E **56** C3
Campbell *Calif., U.S.A.* 37°17N 121°57W **78** H5
Campbell *Ohio, U.S.A.* 41°5N 80°37W **82** E4
Campbell I. *Pac. Oc.* 52°30S 169°0E **64** N8
Campbell L. *Canada* 63°14N 106°55W **71** A7
Campbell Plateau *S. Ocean* 50°0S 170°0E **5** A11
Campbell River *Canada* 50°5N 125°20W **70** C3
Campbellford *Canada* 44°18N 77°48W **82** B7
Campbellpur *Pakistan* 33°46N 72°26E **42** C5
Campbellsville *U.S.A.* 37°21N 85°20W **81** G11
Campbellton *Canada* 47°57N 66°43W **73** C6
Campbelltown *Australia* 34°4S 150°49E **63** E5
Campbeltown *U.K.* 55°26N 5°36W **11** F3
Campeche *Mexico* 19°51N 90°32W **87** D6
Campeche □ *Mexico* 19°0N 90°30W **87** D6
Campeche, Banco *Mexico* 22°30N 88°0W **87** C7
Campeche, Golfo de
Mexico 19°30N 93°0W **87** D6
Camperdown *Australia* 38°14S 143°9E **63** F3
Camperville *Canada* 51°59N 100°9W **71** C8
Câmpina *Romania* 45°10N 25°45E **17** F13
Campina Grande *Brazil* 7°20S 35°47W **93** E11
Campinas *Brazil* 22°50S 47°0W **95** A6
Campo de los Alisos △
Argentina 27°15S 66°0W **94** B2
Campo Grande *Brazil* 20°25S 54°40W **93** H8
Campo Maior *Brazil* 4°50S 42°12W **93** D10
Campo Mourão *Brazil* 24°3S 52°22W **95** A5
Campobasso *Italy* 41°34N 14°39E **22** D6
Campos *Brazil* 21°50S 41°20W **95** A7
Campos Belos *Brazil* 13°10S 47°3W **93** F9
Campos Novos *Brazil* 27°21S 51°50W **95** B5
Camptonville *U.S.A.* 39°27N 121°3W **78** F5
Camptown *U.S.A.* 41°44N 76°14W **83** E8
Câmpulung *Romania* 45°17N 25°3E **17** F13
Camrose *Canada* 53°0N 112°50W **70** C6
Camsell Portage *Canada* 59°37N 109°15W **71** B7
Çan *Turkey* 40°2N 27°3E **23** D12
Can Gio *Vietnam* 10°25N 106°58E **39** G6
Can Tho *Vietnam* 10°2N 105°46E **39** G5
Canaan *U.S.A.* 42°2N 73°20W **83** D11
Canacona *India* 15°1N 74°4E **45** G2
Canada ■ *N. Amer.* 60°0N 100°0W **68** G11
Canada Abyssal Plain
Arctic 80°0N 140°0W **4** B18
Canada Basin *Arctic* 75°0N 145°0W **4** B18
Cañada de Gómez
Argentina 32°40S 61°30W **94** C3
Canadian *U.S.A.* 35°55N 100°23W **84** D4
Canadian → *U.S.A.* 35°28N 95°3W **84** D7
Canadian Shield *Canada* 53°0N 75°0W **66** D12
Canajoharie *U.S.A.* 42°54N 74°35W **83** D10
Çanakkale *Turkey* 40°8N 26°24E **23** D12
Çanakkale Boğazı
Turkey 40°17N 26°32E **23** D12
Canal Flats *Canada* 50°10N 115°48W **70** C5
Canalejas *Argentina* 35°15S 66°34W **94** D2
Canals *Argentina* 33°35S 62°53W **94** C3
Canandaigua *U.S.A.* 42°54N 77°17W **82** D7
Canandaigua L. *U.S.A.* 42°47N 77°19W **82** D7
Cananea *Mexico* 31°0N 110°18W **86** A2
Canarias, Is. *Atl. Oc.* 28°30N 16°0W **52** C2
Canaries *St. Lucia* 13°55N 61°4W **89** f
Canarreos, Arch. de los
Cuba 21°35N 81°40W **88** B3
Canary Is. = Canarias, Is.
Atl. Oc. 28°30N 16°0W **52** C2
Canaseraga *U.S.A.* 42°27N 77°45W **82** D7
Canatlán *Mexico* 24°31N 104°47W **86** C4
Canaveral, C. *U.S.A.* 28°27N 80°32W **85** G14
Canaveral ⌓ *U.S.A.* 28°28N 80°34W **85** G14
Canavieiras *Brazil* 15°39S 39°0W **93** G11
Canberra *Australia* 35°15S 149°8E **63** F4
Canby *Calif., U.S.A.* 41°27N 120°52W **76** F3
Canby *Minn., U.S.A.* 44°43N 96°16W **80** C5
Canby *Oreg., U.S.A.* 45°16N 122°42W **78** E4
Cancún *Mexico* 21°8N 86°44W **87** C7
Candelaria *Argentina* 27°29S 55°44W **95** B4
Candelo *Australia* 36°47S 149°43E **63** F4
Candi Dasa *Indonesia* 8°30S 115°34E **37** J18
Candia = Iraklio *Greece* 35°20N 25°12E **23** G11
Candle L. *Canada* 53°50N 105°18W **71** C7
Candlemas I. *Antarctica* 57°3S 26°40W **5** B1
Cando *U.S.A.* 48°32N 99°12W **80** A4
Canea = Chania *Greece* 35°30N 24°4E **23** G11
Canelones *Uruguay* 34°32S 56°17W **95** C4
Cañete *Chile* 37°50S 73°30W **94** D1
Cangas del Narcea *Spain* 43°10N 6°32W **21** A2
Cangnan *China* 27°30N 120°23E **35** D13
Cangshan *China* 34°50N 118°2E **33** G10
Canguaretama *Brazil* 6°20S 35°5W **93** E11
Canguçu *Brazil* 31°22S 52°43W **95** C5
Canguçu, Serra do *Brazil* 31°20S 52°40W **95** C5
Cangxi *China* 31°47N 105°59E **34** B5
Cangyuan *China* 23°12N 99°14E **34** F2
Cangzhou *China* 38°19N 116°52E **32** E9
Caniapiscau → *Canada* 56°40N 69°30W **73** A6
Caniapiscau, L. *Canada* 54°10N 69°55W **73** B6
Canicattì *Italy* 37°21N 13°51E **22** F5
Canim Lake *Canada* 51°47N 120°54W **70** C4
Canindeyu □ *Paraguay* 24°10S 55°0W **95** A5
Canisteo *U.S.A.* 42°16N 77°36W **82** D7
Canisteo → *U.S.A.* 42°7N 77°8W **82** D7
Cañitas de Felipe Pescador
Mexico 23°36N 102°43W **86** C4
Çankırı *Turkey* 40°40N 33°37E **19** F5
Canmore *Canada* 51°7N 115°18W **70** C5
Cann River *Australia* 37°35S 149°7E **63** F4
Canna *U.K.* 57°3N 6°33W **11** D2
Cannanore = Kannur
India 11°53N 75°27E **45** J2
Cannanore Is. *India* 10°30N 72°30E **45** J1
Cannes *France* 43°32N 7°1E **20** E7
Canning Town = Port Canning
India 22°23N 88°40E **43** H13
Cannington *Canada* 44°20N 79°2W **82** B5
Cannock *U.K.* 52°41N 2°1W **13** E5
Cannonball → *U.S.A.* 46°26N 100°35W **80** B3
Cannondale Mt.
Australia 25°13S 148°57E **62** D4
Cannonsville Res. *U.S.A.* 42°4N 75°22W **83** D9
Cannonvale *Australia* 20°17S 148°43E **62** b
Canoas *Brazil* 29°56S 51°11W **95** B5
Canoe L. *Canada* 55°10N 108°15W **71** B7
Cañon City *U.S.A.* 38°27N 105°14W **76** G11
Cañón de Río Blanco △
Mexico 18°43N 97°15W **87** D5
Canonniers Pt. *Mauritius* 20°2S 57°32E **55** d
Canora *Canada* 51°40N 102°30W **71** C8
Canowindra *Australia* 33°35S 148°38E **63** E4
Canso *Canada* 45°20N 61°0W **73** C7
Canso, Str. of *Canada* 45°37N 61°22W **73** C7
Cantabria □ *Spain* 43°10N 4°0W **21** A4
Cantabrian Mts. = Cantábrica, Cordillera *Spain* 43°0N 5°10W **21** A3
Cantábrica, Cordillera
Spain 43°0N 5°10W **21** A3
Cantal, Plomb du *France* 45°3N 2°45E **20** D5
Canterbury *Australia* 25°23S 141°53E **62** D3
Canterbury *U.K.* 51°16N 1°6E **13** F9
Canterbury Bight *N.Z.* 44°16S 171°55E **59** F3
Canterbury Plains *N.Z.* 43°55S 171°22E **59** E3
Cantil *U.S.A.* 35°18N 117°58W **79** K9
Canton *Ga., U.S.A.* 34°14N 84°29W **85** D12
Canton *Ill., U.S.A.* 40°33N 90°2W **80** E8
Canton *Miss., U.S.A.* 32°37N 90°2W **85** E9
Canton *Mo., U.S.A.* 40°8N 91°32W **80** E8
Canton *N.Y., U.S.A.* 44°36N 75°10W **83** B9
Canton *Ohio, U.S.A.* 40°48N 81°23W **82** F3
Canton *Pa., U.S.A.* 41°39N 76°51W **82** E8
Canton *S. Dak., U.S.A.* 43°18N 96°35W **80** D5
Canton L. *U.S.A.* 36°6N 98°35W **84** C5
Canudos *Brazil* 7°13S 58°5W **92** E7
Canumã → *Brazil* 3°55S 59°10W **92** D7
Canutama *Brazil* 6°30S 64°20W **92** E6
Canutillo *U.S.A.* 31°55N 106°36W **84** F1
Canvey Island *U.K.* 51°31N 0°37E **13** F8
Canyon *U.S.A.* 34°59N 101°55W **84** D4
Canyon De Chelly ⌓
U.S.A. 36°10N 109°20W **77** H9
Canyonlands △ *U.S.A.* 38°15N 110°0W **77** G9
Canyons of the Ancients ⌓
U.S.A. 37°30N 108°55W **77** H9
Canyonville *U.S.A.* 42°56N 123°17W **76** E2
Cao Bang *Vietnam* 22°40N 106°15E **34** F6
Cao He → *China* 40°10N 124°32E **33** D13
Cao Lanh *Vietnam* 10°27N 105°38E **39** G5
Cao Xian *China* 34°50N 115°35E **32** G8
Caofeidian *China* 38°56N 118°32E **33** E10
Cap-aux-Meules *Canada* 47°23N 61°52W **73** C7
Cap-Chat *Canada* 49°6N 66°40W **73** C6
Cap-de-la-Madeleine
Canada 46°22N 72°31W **72** C5
Cap-Haïtien *Haiti* 19°40N 72°20W **89** C5
Cap Pt. *St. Lucia* 14°7N 60°57W **89** f
Capac *U.S.A.* 43°1N 82°56W **82** C2
Capanaparo → *Venezuela* 7°1N 67°7W **92** B5
Cape → *Australia* 20°59S 146°51E **62** C4
Cape Arid △ *Australia* 33°58S 123°13E **61** F3
Cape Barren I. *Australia* 40°25S 148°15E **63** G4
Cape Breton Highlands △
Canada 46°50N 60°40W **73** C7
Cape Breton I. *Canada* 46°0N 60°30W **73** C7
Cape Charles *U.S.A.* 37°16N 76°1W **81** G15
Cape Coast *Ghana* 5°5N 1°15W **52** G5
Cape Cod ⌓ *U.S.A.* 41°56N 70°6W **81** E18
Cape Coral *U.S.A.* 26°33N 81°57W **85** H14
Cape Crawford *Australia* 16°41S 135°43E **62** B2
Cape Dorset = Kinngait
Canada 64°14N 76°32W **69** E16
Cape Fear → *U.S.A.* 33°53N 78°1W **85** E15
Cape Girardeau *U.S.A.* 37°19N 89°32W **80** G9
Cape Hatteras ⌓ *U.S.A.* 35°30N 75°28W **85** D17
Cape Hillsborough △
Australia 20°54S 149°2E **62** b
Cape Lambert *Australia* 20°36S 117°11E **60** D2
Cape Le Grand △
Australia 33°54S 122°26E **61** F3
Cape Lookout ⌓ *U.S.A.* 35°45N 76°25W **85** D16
Cape May *U.S.A.* 38°56N 74°56W **81** F16
Cape May Point *U.S.A.* 38°56N 74°58W **81** F16
Cape Melville △
Australia 14°26S 144°28E **62** A3
Cape Range △ *Australia* 22°3S 114°0E **60** D1
Cape St. George *Canada* 48°28N 59°14W **73** C8
Cape Tormentine *Canada* 46°8N 63°47W **73** C7
Cape Upstart △ *Australia* 19°45S 147°48E **62** B4
Cape Verde Is. = Cabo Verde ■
Atl. Oc. 16°0N 24°0W **52** b
Cape Vincent *U.S.A.* 44°8N 76°20W **83** B8
Cape York Peninsula
Australia 12°0S 142°30E **62** A3
Capela *Brazil* 10°30S 37°0W **93** F11
Capella *Australia* 23°2S 148°1E **62** C4
Capesterre-Belle-Eau
Guadeloupe 16°4N 61°36W **88** b
Capesterre-de-Marie-Galante
Guadeloupe 15°53N 61°14W **88** b
Capim → *Brazil* 1°40S 47°47W **93** D9
Capitan *U.S.A.* 33°35N 105°35W **77** K11
Capitán Arturo Prat
Antarctica 63°0S 61°0W **5** C17
Capitol Reef △ *U.S.A.* 38°15N 111°10W **77** G8
Capitola *U.S.A.* 36°59N 121°57W **78** J5
Capodistria = Koper
Slovenia 45°31N 13°44E **16** F7
Caporetto = Kobarid
Slovenia 46°15N 13°30E **16** E7
Capraia *Italy* 43°2N 9°50E **20** E8
Capri *Italy* 40°33N 14°14E **22** D6
Capricorn Coast
Australia 23°16S 150°49E **62** C5
Capricorn Group
Australia 23°30S 151°55E **62** C5
Capricorn Ra. *Australia* 23°20S 116°50E **60** D2
Caprivi ⌓ *Namibia* 17°55S 22°37E **56** A3
Caprivi Strip *Namibia* 18°0S 23°0E **56** A3
Captains Flat *Australia* 35°35S 149°27E **63** F4
Capulin Volcano ⌓
U.S.A. 36°47N 103°58W **84** C3
Caquetá → *Colombia* 1°15S 69°15W **92** D5
Car Nicobar *India* 9°10N 92°47E **45** K11
Caracal *Romania* 44°8N 24°22E **17** F13
Caracas *Venezuela* 10°30N 66°55W **92** A5
Caracol *Belize* 16°45N 89°6W **88** C2
Caracol *Mato Grosso do Sul, Brazil* 22°18S 57°1W **94** A4
Caracol *Piauí, Brazil* 9°15S 43°22W **93** E10
Carajas *Brazil* 6°5S 50°23W **93** E8
Carajás, Serra dos *Brazil* 6°0S 51°30W **93** E8
Carangola *Brazil* 20°44S 42°5W **95** A7
Caransebeş *Romania* 45°28N 22°18E **17** F12
Caraquet *Canada* 47°48N 64°57W **73** C6
Caratasca, L. de
Honduras 15°20N 83°40W **88** C3
Caratinga *Brazil* 19°50S 42°10W **93** G10
Caraúbas *Brazil* 5°43S 37°33W **93** E11
Caravaca de la Cruz *Spain* 38°8N 1°52W **21** C5
Caravelas *Brazil* 17°45S 39°15W **93** G11
Caraveli *Peru* 15°45S 73°25W **92** G4
Caravelle, Presqu'île de la
Martinique 14°46N 60°48W **88** c
Caraz *Peru* 9°3S 77°47W **92** E3
Carazinho *Brazil* 28°16S 52°46W **95** B5
Carballo *Spain* 43°13N 8°41W **21** A1
Carberry *Canada* 49°50N 99°25W **71** D9
Carbó *Mexico* 29°42N 110°58W **86** B2
Carbón, L. del *Argentina* 49°35S 68°21W **90** G3
Carbonara, C. *Italy* 39°6N 9°31E **22** E3
Carbondale *Colo., U.S.A.* 39°24N 107°13W **76** G10
Carbondale *Ill., U.S.A.* 37°44N 89°13W **80** G9
Carbondale *Pa., U.S.A.* 41°35N 75°30W **83** E9
Carbonear *Canada* 47°42N 53°13W **73** C9
Carbónia *Italy* 39°10N 8°30E **22** E3
Carcajou *Canada* 57°47N 117°6W **70** B5
Carcarana → *Argentina* 32°27S 60°48W **94** C3
Carcasse, C. *Haiti* 18°30N 74°28W **89** C5
Carcassonne *France* 43°13N 2°20E **20** E5
Carcross *Canada* 60°13N 134°45W **70** A2
Cardamon Hills *India* 9°30N 77°15E **45** K3
Cardamon Mts. = Kravanh, Chuor Phnum *Cambodia* 12°0N 103°32E **39** G4
Cárdenas *Cuba* 23°0N 81°30W **88** B3
Cárdenas *San Luis Potosí, Mexico* 22°0N 99°38W **87** C5
Cárdenas *Tabasco, Mexico* 17°59N 93°22W **87** D6
Cardiff *U.K.* 51°29N 3°10W **13** F4
Cardiff □ *U.K.* 51°31N 3°12W **13** F4
Cardiff-by-the-Sea
U.S.A. 33°1N 117°17W **79** M9
Cardigan *U.K.* 52°5N 4°40W **13** E3
Cardigan B. *U.K.* 52°30N 4°30W **13** E3
Cardinal *Canada* 44°47N 75°23W **83** B9
Cardona *Uruguay* 33°53S 57°18W **94** C4
Cardoso, Ilha do *Brazil* 25°8S 47°58W **95** B5
Cardston *Canada* 49°15N 113°20W **70** D6
Cardwell *Australia* 18°14S 146°2E **62** B4
Careen L. *Canada* 57°0N 108°11W **71** B7
Carei *Romania* 47°40N 22°29E **17** E12
Carey *U.S.A.* 43°19N 113°57W **76** E7
Carey, L. *Australia* 29°0S 122°15E **61** E3
Carey L. *Canada* 62°12N 102°55W **71** A8
Carhué *Argentina* 37°10S 62°50W **94** D3
Caria *Turkey* 37°20N 28°10E **23** F13
Cariacica *Brazil* 20°16S 40°25W **93** H10
Caribbean Sea *W. Indies* 15°0N 75°0W **89** D5
Cariboo Mts. *Canada* 53°0N 121°0W **70** C4
Caribou *U.S.A.* 46°52N 68°1W **81** B19
Caribou → *Man., Canada* 59°20N 94°44W **71** B10
Caribou → *N.W.T., Canada* 61°27N 125°45W **70** A3
Caribou I. *Canada* 47°22N 85°49W **72** C2
Caribou Is. *Canada* 61°55N 113°15W **70** A6
Caribou L. *Man., Canada* 59°21N 96°10W **71** B9
Caribou L. *Ont., Canada* 50°25N 89°5W **72** B2
Caribou Mts. *Canada* 59°12N 115°40W **70** B5
Caribou River ⌓ *Canada* 59°35N 96°35W **71** B9
Carichic *Mexico* 27°56N 107°3W **86** B3
Carinda *Australia* 30°28S 147°41E **63** E4
Carinhanha *Brazil* 14°15S 44°46W **93** F10
Carinhanha → *Brazil* 14°20S 43°47W **93** F10
Carinthia = Kärnten □
Austria 46°52N 13°30E **16** E8
Caripito *Venezuela* 10°8N 63°6W **92** A6
Carleton, Mt. *Canada* 47°23N 66°53W **73** C6
Carleton Place *Canada* 45°8N 76°9W **83** A8
Carletonville *S. Africa* 26°23S 27°22E **56** C4
Carlin *U.S.A.* 40°43N 116°7W **76** F5
Carlingford L. *U.K.* 54°3N 6°9W **10** B5
Carlini Base *Antarctica* 62°30S 58°0W **5** C18
Carlinville *U.S.A.* 39°17N 89°53W **80** F9
Carlisle *U.K.* 54°54N 2°56W **12** C5
Carlisle *U.S.A.* 40°12N 77°12W **82** F7
Carlisle B. *Barbados* 13°5N 59°37W **89** g
Carlisle I. *Australia* 20°49S 149°18E **62** b
Carlos Casares *Argentina* 35°32S 61°20W **94** D3
Carlos Tejedor *Argentina* 35°25S 62°25W **94** D3
Carlow *Ireland* 52°50N 6°56W **10** D5
Carlow □ *Ireland* 52°43N 6°50W **10** D5
Carlsbad *Calif., U.S.A.* 33°10N 117°21W **79** M9
Carlsbad *N. Mex., U.S.A.* 32°25N 104°14W **77** K11
Carlsbad Caverns △
U.S.A. 32°10N 104°35W **77** K11
Carluke *U.K.* 55°45N 3°50W **11** F5
Carlyle *Canada* 49°40N 102°20W **71** D8
Carmacks *Canada* 62°5N 136°16W **68** E4
Carman *Canada* 49°30N 98°0W **71** D9
Carmarthen *U.K.* 51°52N 4°19W **13** F3
Carmarthen B. *U.K.* 51°40N 4°30W **13** F3
Carmarthenshire □ *U.K.* 51°55N 4°13W **13** F3
Carmaux *France* 44°3N 2°10E **20** D5
Carmel *U.S.A.* 41°26N 73°41W **83** E11
Carmel, Mt. = Ha Karmel, Har
Israel 32°44N 35°3E **48** C4
Carmel-by-the-Sea
U.S.A. 36°33N 121°55W **78** J5
Carmel Valley *U.S.A.* 36°29N 121°43W **78** J5
Carmelo *Uruguay* 34°0S 58°20W **94** C4
Carmen *Paraguay* 27°13S 56°12W **95** B4
Carmen, I. *Mexico* 25°57N 111°12W **86** B2
Carmen de Patagones
Argentina 40°50S 63°0W **96** E4
Carmensa *Argentina* 35°15S 67°40W **94** D2
Carmi *Canada* 49°36N 119°8W **70** D5
Carmi *U.S.A.* 38°5N 88°10W **80** F9
Carmila *Australia* 21°55S 149°24E **62** C4
Carmona *Costa Rica* 10°0N 85°15W **88** E2
Carmona *Spain* 37°28N 5°42W **21** D3
Carn Ban *U.K.* 57°7N 4°15W **11** D4
Carn Eige *U.K.* 57°17N 5°8W **11** D3
Carnamah *Australia* 29°41S 115°53E **61** E2
Carnarvon *Australia* 24°51S 113°42E **61** D1
Carnarvon *Canada* 45°3N 78°41W **82** A6
Carnarvon *S. Africa* 30°56S 22°8E **56** D3
Carnarvon △ *Australia* 24°54S 148°2E **62** C4
Carnarvon Ra. *Queens., Australia* 25°15S 148°30E **62** D4
Carnarvon Ra. *W. Austral., Australia* 25°20S 120°45E **61** E3
Carnatic *India* 9°40N 77°50E **45** K3
Carnation *U.S.A.* 47°39N 121°55W **78** C5
Carncastle *U.K.* 54°54N 5°53W **10** B6
Carndonagh *Ireland* 55°16N 7°15W **10** A4
Carnduff *Canada* 49°10N 101°50W **71** D8
Carnegie *U.S.A.* 40°24N 80°5W **82** F4
Carnegie, L. *Australia* 26°5S 122°30E **61** E3
Carnegie Ridge *Pac. Oc.* 1°0S 87°0W **65** H19
Carney I. *Antarctica* 74°0S 121°0W **5** D14
Carnic Alps = Karnische Alpen
Europe 46°36N 13°0E **16** E7
Carniche Alpi = Karnische Alpen
Europe 46°36N 13°0E **16** E7
Carnot *C.A.R.* 4°59N 15°56E **54** D3
Carnot, C. *Australia* 34°57S 135°38E **63** E2
Carnot B. *Australia* 17°20S 122°15E **60** C3
Carnoustie *U.K.* 56°30N 2°42W **11** E6
Carnsore Pt. *Ireland* 52°10N 6°22W **10** D5
Caro *U.S.A.* 43°29N 83°24W **81** D12
Caroga Lake *U.S.A.* 43°8N 74°28W **83** C10
Carolina *Brazil* 7°10S 47°30W **93** E9
Carolina *Puerto Rico* 18°23N 65°58W **89** d
Carolina *S. Africa* 26°5S 30°6E **57** C5
Caroline I. *Kiribati* 9°58S 150°13W **65** H12
Caroline Is. *Micronesia* 8°0N 150°0E **64** G6
Caroni *Trin. & Tob.* 10°34N 61°23W **93** K15
Caroní → *Venezuela* 8°21N 62°43W **92** B6
Caronie = Nébrodi, Monti
Italy 37°54N 14°35E **22** F6
Caroona *Australia* 31°24S 150°26E **63** E5
Carpathians *Europe* 49°30N 21°0E **17** D11
Carpaţii Meridionali
Romania 45°30N 25°0E **17** F13
Carpentaria, G. of *Australia* 14°0S 139°0E **62** A2
Carpentras *France* 44°3N 5°2E **20** D6
Carpi *Italy* 44°47N 10°53E **22** B4
Carpinteria *U.S.A.* 34°24N 119°31W **79** L7
Carr Boyd Ra. *Australia* 16°15S 128°35E **60** C4
Carra, L. *Ireland* 53°41N 9°14W **10** C2
Carrabelle *U.S.A.* 29°51N 84°40W **85** G12
Carraig Mhachaire Rois = Carrickmacross *Ireland* 53°59N 6°43W **10** C5
Carraig na Siúire = Carrick-on-Suir *Ireland* 52°21N 7°24W **10** D4
Carranya ☼ *Australia* 19°13S 127°46E **60** C4
Carrara *Italy* 44°5N 10°6E **20** D9
Carrauntoohill *Ireland* 52°0N 9°45W **10** D2
Carrick-on-Shannon
Ireland 53°57N 8°7W **10** C3
Carrick-on-Suir *Ireland* 52°21N 7°24W **10** D4
Carrickfergus *U.K.* 54°43N 5°49W **10** B6
Carrickmacross *Ireland* 53°59N 6°43W **10** C5
Carrieton *Australia* 32°25S 138°31E **63** E2
Carrigaline *Ireland* 51°48N 8°23W **10** E3
Carrillo *Mexico* 26°54N 103°55W **86** B4
Carrington *U.S.A.* 47°27N 99°8W **80** B4
Carrizal Bajo *Chile* 28°5S 71°20W **94** B1
Carrizalillo *Chile* 29°5S 71°30W **94** B1
Carrizo Cr. → *U.S.A.* 36°55N 103°55W **77** H12
Carrizo Plain ⌓ *U.S.A.* 35°11N 119°47W **78** K7
Carrizo Springs *U.S.A.* 28°31N 99°52W **84** G5
Carrizozo *U.S.A.* 33°38N 105°53W **77** K11
Carroll *U.S.A.* 42°4N 94°52W **80** D6
Carrollton *Ga., U.S.A.* 33°35N 85°5W **85** E12
Carrollton *Ill., U.S.A.* 39°18N 90°24W **80** F8
Carrollton *Ky., U.S.A.* 38°41N 85°11W **81** F11
Carrollton *Mo., U.S.A.* 39°22N 93°30W **80** F7
Carrollton *Ohio, U.S.A.* 40°34N 81°5W **82** F3
Carron → *U.K.* 57°53N 4°22W **11** D4
Carron, L. *U.K.* 57°22N 5°35W **11** D3
Carrot → *Canada* 53°50N 101°17W **71** C8
Carrot River *Canada* 53°17N 103°35W **71** C8
Carruthers *Canada* 52°52N 109°16W **71** C7
Carson *Calif., U.S.A.* 33°49N 118°16W **79** M8
Carson *N. Dak., U.S.A.* 46°25N 101°34W **80** B3
Carson → *U.S.A.* 39°45N 118°40W **78** F8
Carson City *U.S.A.* 39°10N 119°46W **78** F7
Carson Sink *U.S.A.* 39°50N 118°25W **76** G4
Cartagena *Colombia* 10°25N 75°33W **92** A3
Cartagena *Spain* 37°38N 0°59W **21** D5
Cartago *Colombia* 4°45N 75°55W **92** C3
Cartago *Costa Rica* 9°50N 83°55W **88** E3
Carter Bar *U.K.* 55°21N 2°29W **11** F6
Cartersville *U.S.A.* 34°10N 84°48W **85** D12
Carterton *N.Z.* 41°2S 175°31E **59** D5
Carthage *Tunisia* 36°52N 10°20E **22** F4
Carthage *Ill., U.S.A.* 40°25N 91°8W **80** E8
Carthage *Mo., U.S.A.* 37°11N 94°19W **80** G6
Carthage *N.Y., U.S.A.* 43°59N 75°37W **83** C9
Carthage *Tex., U.S.A.* 32°9N 94°20W **84** E7
Cartier I. *Australia* 12°31S 123°29E **60** B3
Cartwright *Canada* 53°41N 56°58W **73** B8
Caruaru *Brazil* 8°15S 35°55W **93** E11
Carúpano *Venezuela* 10°39N 63°15W **92** A6
Caruthersville *U.S.A.* 36°11N 89°39W **80** G9
Carvoeiro *Brazil* 1°30S 61°59W **92** D6
Carvoeiro, C. *Portugal* 39°21N 9°24W **21** C1
Cary *U.S.A.* 35°47N 78°46W **85** D15
Cas-gwent = Chepstow
U.K. 51°38N 2°41W **13** F5
Casa de Piedra *Argentina* 38°5S 67°28W **94** D2
Casa de Piedra, Embalse
Argentina 38°5S 67°32W **94** D2
Casa Grande *U.S.A.* 32°53N 111°45W **77** K8
Casa Nova *Brazil* 9°25S 41°5W **93** E10
Casablanca *Chile* 33°20S 71°25W **94** C1
Casablanca *Morocco* 33°36N 7°36W **52** B4

Cascada de Basaseachic △
   Mexico   28°9N 108°15W **86 B3**
Cascade *Seychelles*   4°39S 55°29E **55 b**
Cascade *Idaho, U.S.A.*   44°31N 116°2W **76 D5**
Cascade *Mont., U.S.A.*   47°16N 111°42W **76 C8**
Cascade Locks *U.S.A.*   45°40N 121°54W **78 E5**
Cascade Ra. *U.S.A.*   47°0N 121°30W **78 D5**
Cascade Res. *U.S.A.*   44°32N 116°3W **76 D5**
Cascades, Pte. des *Réunion*   21°9S 55°51E **55 c**
Cascais *Portugal*   38°41N 9°25W **21 C1**
Cascavel *Brazil*   24°57S 53°28W **95 A5**
Cáscina *Italy*   43°41N 10°33E **22 C4**
Casco B. *U.S.A.*   43°45N 70°0W **81 D19**
Caserta *Italy*   41°4N 14°20E **22 D6**
Casey *Antarctica*   66°0S 76°0E **5 C8**
Caseyr, Raas = Asir, Ras
   Somalia   11°55N 51°10E **49 E5**
Cashel *Ireland*   52°30N 7°53W **10 D4**
Casiguran *Phil.*   16°22N 122°7E **37 A6**
Casilda *Argentina*   33°10S 61°10W **94 C3**
Casino *Australia*   28°52S 153°3E **63 D5**
Casiquiare → *Venezuela*   2°1N 67°7W **92 C5**
Casma *Peru*   9°30S 78°20W **92 E3**
Casmalia *U.S.A.*   34°50N 120°32W **79 L6**
Casnewydd = Newport
   U.K.   51°35N 3°0W **13 F5**
Caspe *Spain*   41°14N 0°1W **21 B5**
Casper *U.S.A.*   42°51N 106°19W **76 E10**
Caspian Depression *Eurasia*   47°0N 48°0E **19 E8**
Caspian Sea *Eurasia*   43°0N 50°0E **19 F9**
Cass City *U.S.A.*   43°36N 83°10W **82 C1**
Cass Lake *U.S.A.*   47°23N 94°37W **80 B6**
Cassadaga *U.S.A.*   42°20N 79°19W **82 D5**
Casselman *Canada*   45°19N 75°5W **83 A9**
Casselton *U.S.A.*   46°54N 97°13W **80 B5**
Cassiar Mts. *Canada*   59°30N 130°30W **70 B2**
Cassino *Italy*   41°30N 13°49E **22 D5**
Cassville *U.S.A.*   36°41N 93°52W **80 G7**
Castaic *U.S.A.*   34°30N 118°38W **79 L8**
Castalia *U.S.A.*   41°24N 82°49W **82 E2**
Castanhal *Brazil*   1°18S 47°55W **93 D9**
Castara *Trin. & Tob.*   11°17N 60°42W **93 J16**
Casteddu = Cágliari *Italy*   39°13N 9°7E **22 E3**
Castell-Nedd = Neath
   U.K.   51°39N 3°48W **13 F4**
Castellammare di Stábia
   Italy   40°42N 14°29E **22 D6**
Castelli *Argentina*   36°7S 57°47W **94 D4**
Castelló de la Plana *Spain*   39°58N 0°3W **21 C5**
Castelo *Brazil*   20°33S 41°14W **95 A7**
Castelo Branco *Portugal*   39°50N 7°31W **21 C2**
Castelsarrasin *France*   44°2N 1°7E **20 E4**
Castelvetrano *Italy*   37°41N 12°47E **22 F5**
Casterton *Australia*   37°30S 141°30E **63 F3**
Castile *U.S.A.*   42°38N 78°3W **82 D6**
Castilla-La Mancha □
   Spain   39°30N 3°30W **21 C4**
Castilla y Leon □ *Spain*   42°0N 5°0W **21 B3**
Castillos *Uruguay*   34°12S 53°52W **95 C5**
Castle Dale *U.S.A.*   39°13N 111°1W **76 G8**
Castle Douglas *U.K.*   54°56N 3°56W **11 G5**
Castle Rock *Colo.,*
   U.S.A.   39°22N 104°51W **76 G11**
Castle Rock *Wash.,*
   U.S.A.   46°17N 122°54W **78 D4**
Castlebar *Ireland*   53°52N 9°18W **10 C2**
Castlebay *U.K.*   56°57N 7°31W **11 E1**
Castleblayney *Ireland*   54°7N 6°44W **10 B5**
Castlecomer *Ireland*   52°48N 7°14W **10 D4**
Castlederg *U.K.*   54°42N 7°36W **10 B4**
Castleford *U.K.*   53°43N 1°21W **12 D6**
Castlegar *Canada*   49°20N 117°40W **70 D5**
Castleisland *Ireland*   52°14N 9°28W **10 D2**
Castlemaine *Australia*   37°2S 144°12E **63 F3**
Castlemaine *Ireland*   52°10N 9°42W **10 D2**
Castlepollard *Ireland*   53°41N 7°19W **10 C4**
Castlerea *Ireland*   53°46N 8°29W **10 C3**
Castlereagh → *Australia*   30°12S 147°32E **63 E4**
Castlereagh B. *Australia*   12°10S 135°10E **62 A2**
Castleton *U.S.A.*   43°37N 73°11W **83 C11**
Castleton-on-Hudson
   U.S.A.   42°31N 73°45W **83 D11**
Castletown *I. of Man*   54°5N 4°38W **12 C3**
Castletown Bearhaven
   Ireland   51°39N 9°55W **10 E2**
Castor *Canada*   52°15N 111°50W **70 C6**
Castor → *Canada*   53°24N 78°58W **72 B4**
Castorland *U.S.A.*   43°53N 75°31W **83 C9**
Castres *France*   43°37N 2°13E **20 E5**
Castricum *Neths.*   52°33N 4°40E **15 B4**
Castries *St. Lucia*   14°2N 60°58W **89 f**
Castro *Brazil*   24°45S 50°0W **95 A6**
Castro *Chile*   42°30S 73°50W **96 E2**
Castro Alves *Brazil*   12°46S 39°33W **93 F11**
Castro Valley *U.S.A.*   37°41N 122°5W **78 H4**
Castuera *Spain*   38°43N 5°37W **21 C3**
Cat Ba, Dao *Vietnam*   20°50N 107°0E **38 B6**
Cat Ba → *Vietnam*   20°47N 107°3E **38 B6**
Cat I. *Bahamas*   24°30N 75°30W **89 B4**
Cat L. *Canada*   51°40N 91°50W **72 B1**
Cat Lake *Canada*   51°40N 91°50W **72 B1**
Cat Tien △ *Vietnam*   11°25N 107°17E **39 G6**
Catacamas *Honduras*   14°54N 85°56W **88 D2**
Cataguases *Brazil*   21°23S 42°39W **95 A7**
Catalão *Brazil*   18°10S 47°57W **93 G9**
Çatalca *Turkey*   41°8N 28°27E **23 D13**
Catalina *Canada*   48°31N 53°4W **73 C9**
Catalina *Chile*   25°13S 69°43W **94 B2**
Catalina *U.S.A.*   32°30N 110°50W **77 K8**
Catalonia = Cataluña □
   Spain   41°40N 1°15E **21 B6**
Cataluña □ *Spain*   41°40N 1°15E **21 B6**
Catamarca *Argentina*   28°30S 65°50W **94 B2**
Catamarca □ *Argentina*   27°0S 65°50W **94 B2**
Catanduanes □ *Phil.*   13°50N 124°20E **37 B6**
Catanduva *Brazil*   21°5S 48°58W **95 A6**
Catánia *Italy*   37°30N 15°6E **22 F6**
Catanzaro *Italy*   38°54N 16°35E **22 E7**
Catarman *Phil.*   12°28N 124°35E **37 B6**

Catatumbo-Bari △
   Colombia   9°3N 73°12W **89 E5**
Catchacoma *Canada*   44°44N 78°19W **82 B6**
Catembe *Mozam.*   26°0S 32°33E **57 C5**
Caterham *U.K.*   51°15N 0°4W **13 F7**
Cathair na Mart = Westport
   Ireland   53°48N 9°31W **10 C2**
Cathcart *S. Africa*   32°18S 27°10E **56 D4**
Cathedral City *U.S.A.*   33°47N 116°28W **79 M10**
Cathlamet *U.S.A.*   46°12N 123°23W **78 D3**
Catlettsburg *U.S.A.*   38°25N 82°36W **81 F12**
Catoche, C. *Mexico*   21°35N 87°5W **87 C7**
Catril *Argentina*   36°26S 63°24W **94 D3**
Catrimani *Brazil*   0°27N 61°41W **92 C6**
Catrimani → *Brazil*   0°28N 61°44W **92 C6**
Catskill *U.S.A.*   42°14N 73°52W **83 D11**
Catskill □ *U.S.A.*   42°8N 74°39W **83 D10**
Catskill Mts. *U.S.A.*   42°10N 74°25W **83 D10**
Catt, Mt. *Australia*   13°49S 134°23E **62 A1**
Cattaraugus *U.S.A.*   42°20N 78°52W **82 D6**
Catterick *U.K.*   54°23N 1°37W **12 C6**
Catuala *Angola*   16°25S 19°2E **56 A2**
Catuane *Mozam.*   26°48S 32°18E **57 C5**
Caubvick, Mt. = Iberville, Mt. d'
   Canada   58°50N 63°50W **69 F19**
Cauca → *Colombia*   8°54N 74°28W **92 B4**
Caucaia *Brazil*   3°40S 38°35W **93 D11**
Caucasus Mountains
   Eurasia   42°50N 44°0E **19 F7**
Caucete *Argentina*   31°38S 68°20W **94 C2**
Caungula *Angola*   8°26S 18°38E **54 F3**
Caura → *Venezuela*   7°38N 64°53W **92 B6**
Causapscal *Canada*   48°19N 67°12W **73 C6**
Cauvery → *India*   11°9N 78°52E **45 J4**
Caux, Pays de *France*   49°38N 0°35E **20 B4**
Cavalier *U.S.A.*   48°48N 97°37W **80 A5**
Cavan *Ireland*   54°0N 7°22W **10 B4**
Cavan □ *Ireland*   54°1N 7°16W **10 C4**
Cave Creek *U.S.A.*   33°50N 111°57W **77 K8**
Cavenagh Ra. *Australia*   26°12S 127°55E **61 E4**
Cavendish *Australia*   37°31S 142°2E **63 F3**
Caviana, I. *Brazil*   0°10N 50°10W **93 C8**
Cawndilla L. *Australia*   32°30S 142°15E **63 E3**
Cawnpore = Kanpur
   India   26°28N 80°20E **43 F9**
Caxias *Brazil*   4°55S 43°20W **93 D10**
Caxias do Sul *Brazil*   29°10S 51°10W **95 B5**
Cay Sal Bank *Bahamas*   23°45N 80°0W **88 B4**
Cayambe *Ecuador*   0°3N 78°8W **92 C3**
Cayenne *Fr. Guiana*   5°5N 52°18W **93 B8**
Cayey *Puerto Rico*   18°7N 66°10W **89 d**
Cayman Brac *Cayman Is.*   19°43N 79°49W **88 C4**
Cayman Is. ☑ *W. Indies*   19°40N 80°30W **88 C3**
Cayman Trench *Caribbean*   17°0N 83°0W **66 H11**
Cayuga *Canada*   42°59N 79°50W **82 D5**
Cayuga *U.S.A.*   42°54N 76°44W **83 D8**
Cayuga Heights *U.S.A.*   42°27N 76°29W **83 D8**
Cayuga L. *U.S.A.*   42°41N 76°41W **83 D8**
Cazenovia *U.S.A.*   42°56N 75°51W **83 D9**
Cazombo *Angola*   11°54S 22°56E **55 G4**
Ceadîr-Lunga *Moldova*   46°3N 28°51E **17 E15**
Ceanannus Mor = Kells
   Ireland   53°44N 6°53W **10 C5**
Ceará = Fortaleza *Brazil*   3°45S 38°35W **93 D11**
Ceará □ *Brazil*   5°0S 40°0W **93 E11**
Ceará-Mirim *Brazil*   5°38S 35°25W **93 E11**
Ceatharlach = Carlow
   Ireland   52°50N 6°56W **10 D5**
Cébaco, I. de *Panama*   7°33N 81°9W **88 E3**
Cebollar *Argentina*   29°10S 66°35W **94 B2**
Cebu *Phil.*   10°18N 123°54E **37 B6**
Cecil Plains *Australia*   27°30S 151°11E **63 D5**
Cedar → *U.S.A.*   41°17N 91°21W **80 E8**
Cedar City *U.S.A.*   37°41N 113°4W **77 H7**
Cedar Creek Res. *U.S.A.*   32°11N 96°4W **84 E6**
Cedar Falls *Iowa, U.S.A.*   42°32N 92°27W **80 D7**
Cedar Falls *Wash.,*
   U.S.A.   47°25N 121°45W **78 C5**
Cedar Key *U.S.A.*   29°8N 83°2W **85 G13**
Cedar L. *Canada*   53°10N 100°0W **71 C9**
Cedar Park *U.S.A.*   30°30N 97°49W **84 F6**
Cedar Rapids *U.S.A.*   41°59N 91°40W **80 E9**
Cedartown *U.S.A.*   34°1N 85°15W **85 D12**
Cedarvale *Canada*   55°1N 128°22W **70 B3**
Cedarville *S. Africa*   30°23S 29°3E **57 D4**
Cedral *Mexico*   23°50N 100°45W **86 C4**
Cedro *Brazil*   6°34S 39°3W **93 E11**
Cedros, I. *Mexico*   28°12N 115°15W **86 B1**
Cedros B. *Trin. & Tob.*   10°16N 61°54W **93 K15**
Ceduna *Australia*   32°7S 133°46E **63 E1**
Ceel Gaal *Somalia*   10°58N 50°20E **49 E5**
Ceel Waaq *Kenya*   2°49N 40°56E **54 D8**
Ceeldheere *Somalia*   3°50N 47°8E **49 G4**
Ceerigaabo *Somalia*   10°35N 47°20E **49 E4**
Cefalù *Italy*   38°2N 14°1E **22 E6**
Ceglédi *Hungary*   47°11N 19°47E **17 E10**
Ceheng *China*   24°58N 105°48E **34 E5**
Cekik *Indonesia*   8°12S 114°37E **37 J17**
Celaque △ *Honduras*   14°30N 88°43W **88 D2**
Celaya *Mexico*   20°31N 100°37W **86 C4**
Celbridge *Ireland*   53°20N 6°32W **10 C5**
Celebes = Sulawesi □
   Indonesia   2°0S 120°0E **37 E6**
Celebes Sea *Indonesia*   3°0N 123°0E **37 D6**
Celina *U.S.A.*   40°33N 84°35W **81 E11**
Celje *Slovenia*   46°16N 15°18E **16 E8**
Celle *Germany*   52°37N 10°4E **16 B6**
Celtic Sea *Atl. Oc.*   50°9N 9°34W **14 F2**
Cenderawasih, Teluk
   Indonesia   3°0S 135°20E **37 E9**
Cengong *China*   27°13N 108°44E **34 D7**
Centennial *U.S.A.*   39°34N 104°52W **76 G11**
Center *N. Dak., U.S.A.*   47°7N 101°18W **80 B3**
Center *Tex., U.S.A.*   31°48N 94°11W **84 F7**
Centerburg *U.S.A.*   40°18N 82°42W **82 F2**
Centerville *Calif., U.S.A.*   36°44N 119°30W **78 J7**
Centerville *Iowa, U.S.A.*   40°44N 92°52W **80 E8**
Centerville *Pa., U.S.A.*   40°3N 79°59W **82 F5**

Centerville *Tenn., U.S.A.*   35°47N 87°28W **85 D11**
Centerville *Tex., U.S.A.*   31°16N 95°59W **84 F7**
Central = Tsentralnyy □
   Russia   52°0N 40°0E **26 D4**
Central □ *Botswana*   25°0S 26°30E **56 B4**
Central, Cordillera *Colombia*   5°0N 75°0W **92 C4**
Central, Cordillera
   Costa Rica   10°10N 84°5W **88 D3**
Central, Cordillera
   Dom. Rep.   19°15N 71°0W **89 C5**
Central, Cordillera
   Puerto Rico   18°8N 66°35W **89 d**
Central African Rep. ■
   Africa   7°0N 20°0E **53 G9**
Central America *America*   12°0N 85°0W **66 H11**
Central Australia ◇
   Australia   22°30S 128°30E **60 D4**
Central Bedfordshire □
   U.K.   52°5N 0°20W **13 E7**
Central Butte *Canada*   50°48N 106°31W **71 C7**
Central City *Colo.,*
   U.S.A.   39°48N 105°31W **76 G11**
Central City *Ky., U.S.A.*   37°18N 87°7W **80 G10**
Central City *Nebr., U.S.A.*   41°7N 98°0W **80 E4**
Central Desert ◇
   Australia   19°56S 130°46E **60 C5**
Central Japan Int. ✈ **(NGO)**
   Japan   34°53N 136°45E **29 G8**
Central Kalahari △
   Botswana   22°36S 23°58E **56 B3**
Central Makran Range
   Pakistan   26°30N 64°15E **40 F4**
Central Pacific Basin
   Pac. Oc.   8°0N 175°0W **64 G10**
Central Patricia *Canada*   51°30N 90°9W **72 B1**
Central Point *U.S.A.*   42°23N 122°55W **76 E2**
Central Russian Uplands
   Europe   54°0N 36°0E **6 E13**
Central Siberian Plateau
   Russia   65°0N 105°0E **24 B12**
Central Square *U.S.A.*   43°17N 76°9W **83 C8**
Centralia *Canada*   43°17N 81°28W **82 C3**
Centralia *Ill., U.S.A.*   38°32N 89°8W **80 F9**
Centralia *Mo., U.S.A.*   39°13N 92°8W **80 F7**
Centralia *Wash., U.S.A.*   46°43N 122°58W **78 D4**
Centre de Flacq *Mauritius*   20°12S 57°43E **55 d**
Centreville *N.Y., U.S.A.*   42°28N 78°14W **82 D6**
Centreville *Pa., U.S.A.*   41°44N 79°45W **82 E5**
Cenxi *China*   22°57N 110°57E **35 F8**
Cephalonia = Kefalonia
   Greece   38°15N 20°30E **23 E9**
Cepu *Indonesia*   7°9S 111°35E **37 G14**
Ceram = Seram *Indonesia*   3°10S 129°0E **37 E7**
Ceram Sea = Seram Sea
   Indonesia   2°30S 128°30E **37 E7**
Ceredigion □ *U.K.*   52°16N 4°15W **13 E3**
Ceres *Argentina*   29°55S 61°55W **94 B3**
Ceres *S. Africa*   33°21S 19°18E **56 D2**
Ceres *U.S.A.*   37°35N 120°57W **78 H6**
Cerf *Seychelles*   4°38S 55°40E **55 b**
Cerignola *Italy*   41°17N 15°53E **22 D6**
Cerigo = Kythira *Greece*   36°8N 23°0E **23 F10**
Çerkezköy *Turkey*   41°17N 28°0E **23 D12**
Cerralvo, I. *Mexico*   24°15N 109°55W **86 C3**
Cerritos *Mexico*   22°25N 100°16W **86 C4**
Cerro Chato *Uruguay*   33°6S 55°8W **95 C4**
Cerro Cofre de Perote △
   Mexico   19°29N 97°8W **87 D5**
Cerro Corá △ *Paraguay*   22°35S 56°2W **95 A4**
Cerro de Pasco *Peru*   10°45S 76°10W **92 F3**
Cerro el Copey △
   Venezuela   10°59N 63°53W **89 D7**
Cerro Hoya △ *Panama*   7°17N 80°45W **88 E3**
Cerro Saroche △
   Venezuela   10°8N 69°38W **89 D6**
Cerventes *Australia*   30°31S 115°3E **61 F2**
Cervera *Spain*   41°40N 1°16E **21 B6**
Cesena *Italy*   44°8N 12°15E **22 B5**
Cēsis *Latvia*   57°18N 25°15E **9 H21**
Česká Rep. = Czech Rep. ■
   Europe   50°0N 15°0E **16 D8**
České Budějovice
   Czech Rep.   48°55N 14°25E **16 D8**
Českomoravská Vrchovina
   Czech Rep.   49°30N 15°40E **16 D8**
Çeşme *Turkey*   38°20N 26°23E **23 E12**
Cessnock *Australia*   32°50S 151°21E **63 E5**
Cetinje *Montenegro*   42°23N 18°59E **23 C8**
Cetraro *Italy*   39°31N 15°55E **22 E6**
Ceuta *N. Afr.*   35°52N 5°18W **21 E3**
Cévennes *France*   44°10N 3°50E **20 D5**
Ceyhan *Turkey*   37°4N 35°47E **46 B2**
Ceylanpınar *Turkey*   36°50N 40°2E **46 B4**
Ceylon = Sri Lanka ■ *Asia*   7°30N 80°50E **45 L5**
Cha-am *Thailand*   12°48N 99°58E **38 F2**
Chacabuco *Argentina*   34°40S 60°27W **94 C3**
Chachapoyas *Peru*   6°15S 77°50W **92 E3**
Chachoengsao *Thailand*   13°42N 101°5E **38 F3**
Chachran *Pakistan*   28°55N 70°30E **42 E4**
Chachro *Pakistan*   25°5N 70°15E **42 G4**
Chaco □ *Argentina*   26°30S 61°0W **94 B3**
Chaco □ *Paraguay*   26°0S 60°0W **94 B4**
Chaco → *U.S.A.*   36°46N 108°39W **77 H9**
Chaco Austral *S. Amer.*   27°0S 61°30W **96 B4**
Chaco Boreal *S. Amer.*   22°0S 60°0W **96 A4**
Chaco Central *S. Amer.*   24°0S 61°0W **96 A4**
Chaco Culture △ *U.S.A.*   36°3N 107°58W **77 H10**
Chacon, C. *U.S.A.*   54°42N 132°0W **70 C2**
Chad ■ *Africa*   15°0N 17°15E **53 F8**
Chad, L. = Tchad, L. *Chad*   13°30N 14°30E **53 F8**
Chadileuvú → *Argentina*   37°46S 66°0W **94 D2**
Chadron *U.S.A.*   42°50N 103°0W **80 D2**
Chadyr-Lunga = Ceadîr-Lunga
   Moldova   46°3N 28°51E **17 E15**
Chae Hom *Thailand*   18°43N 99°35E **38 C2**
Chae Son △ *Thailand*   18°42N 99°20E **38 C2**
Chaem → *Thailand*   18°11N 98°38E **38 C2**
Chaeryong *N. Korea*   38°24N 125°36E **33 E13**
Chagai Hills = Chāh Gay Hills
   Afghan.   29°30N 64°0E **40 E3**

Chagda *Russia*   58°45N 130°38E **27 D14**
Chaghcharān *Afghan.*   34°31N 65°15E **40 B4**
Chagos Arch. ☑ *Ind. Oc.*   6°0S 72°0E **3 E13**
Chagres △ *Panama*   9°33N 79°37W **88 E4**
Chaguanas *Trin. & Tob.*   10°30N 61°26W **93 K15**
Chāh Ākhvor *Iran*   32°41N 59°40E **47 C8**
Chāh Bahar *Iran*   25°20N 60°40E **47 E9**
Chāh-e Kavīr *Iran*   34°29N 56°52E **47 C8**
Chāh Gay Hills *Afghan.*   29°30N 64°0E **40 E3**
Chahār Borjak *Afghan.*   30°17N 62°3E **40 D3**
Chahār Mahāll va Bakhtīārī □
   Iran   32°0N 49°0E **47 C6**
Chai Badan *Thailand*   15°12N 101°8E **38 E3**
Chaibasa *India*   22°42N 85°49E **43 H11**
Chainat *Thailand*   15°11N 100°8E **38 E3**
Chainpur *Nepal*   27°17N 87°19E **43 F12**
Chaiya *Thailand*   9°23N 99°14E **39 H2**
Chaiyaphum *Thailand*   15°48N 102°2E **38 E3**
Chaj Doab *Pakistan*   32°15N 73°0E **42 C5**
Chajari *Argentina*   30°42S 58°0W **94 C4**
Chak Amru *Pakistan*   32°22N 75°11E **42 C6**
Chakar → *Pakistan*   29°29N 68°2E **42 E3**
Chakari *Zimbabwe*   18°5S 29°51E **57 A4**
Chakhānsūr *Afghan.*   31°10N 62°0E **40 D3**
Chakonipau, L. *Canada*   56°18N 68°30W **73 A6**
Chakradharpur *India*   22°45N 85°40E **43 H11**
Chakrata *India*   30°42N 77°51E **42 D7**
Chakwal *Pakistan*   32°56N 72°53E **42 C5**
Chala *Peru*   15°48S 74°20W **92 G4**
Chalakudi *India*   10°18N 76°20E **45 J3**
Chalchihuites *Mexico*   23°29N 103°53W **86 C4**
Chalcis = Chalkida
   Greece   38°27N 23°42E **23 E10**
Chaleur B. *Canada*   47°55N 65°30W **73 C6**
Chalfant *U.S.A.*   37°32N 118°21W **78 H8**
Chalhuanca *Peru*   14°15S 73°15W **92 F4**
Chaling *China*   26°58N 113°30E **35 D9**
Chalisgaon *India*   20°30N 75°10E **44 J2**
Chalk River *Canada*   46°1N 77°27W **72 C4**
Chalkida *Greece*   38°27N 23°42E **23 E10**
Chalky Inlet *N.Z.*   46°3S 166°31E **59 G1**
Challakere *India*   14°19N 76°39E **45 G3**
Challapata *Bolivia*   18°53S 66°50W **92 G5**
Challenger Deep *Pac. Oc.*   11°30N 142°0E **64 F6**
Challenger Fracture Zone
   Pac. Oc.   35°0S 105°0W **65 L17**
Challis *U.S.A.*   44°30N 114°14W **76 D6**
Chalmette *U.S.A.*   29°56N 89°57W **85 G10**
Chaloem Rattanakosin △
   Thailand   14°40N 99°17E **38 E2**
Chalon-sur-Saône *France*   46°48N 4°50E **20 C6**
Chalong *Thailand*   7°50N 98°22E **39 a**
Châlons-en-Champagne
   France   48°58N 4°20E **20 B6**
Chálten, Cerro = Fitz Roy, Cerro
   Argentina   49°17S 73°5W **96 F2**
Chālūs *Iran*   36°38N 51°26E **47 B6**
Cham, Cu Lao *Vietnam*   15°57N 108°30E **38 E7**
Chama *U.S.A.*   36°54N 106°35W **77 H10**
Chamaicó *Argentina*   35°3S 64°58W **94 D3**
Chaman *Pakistan*   30°58N 66°25E **40 D5**
Chamba *India*   32°35N 76°10E **42 C7**
Chamba → *India*   26°29N 79°15E **43 F8**
Chamberlain *U.S.A.*   43°49N 99°20W **80 D4**
Chamberlain →
   Australia   15°30S 127°54E **60 C4**
Chamberlain L. *U.S.A.*   46°14N 69°19W **81 B19**
Chambers *U.S.A.*   35°11N 109°26W **77 J9**
Chambersburg *U.S.A.*   39°56N 77°40W **81 F15**
Chambéry *France*   45°34N 5°55E **20 D6**
Chambeshi → *Zambia*   11°53S 29°48E **54 G6**
Chambly *Canada*   45°27N 73°17W **83 A11**
Chambord *Canada*   48°25N 72°6W **73 C5**
Chamchamal *Iraq*   35°32N 44°50E **46 C5**
Chamela *Mexico*   19°32N 105°5W **86 D3**
Chamical *Argentina*   30°22S 66°27W **94 C2**
Chamkar Luong
   Cambodia   11°0N 103°45E **39 G4**
Chamoli *India*   30°24N 79°21E **43 D8**
Chamonix-Mont Blanc
   France   45°55N 6°51E **20 D7**
Chamouchuane =
Ashuapmushuan →
   Canada   48°37N 72°20W **72 C5**
Champa *India*   22°2N 82°43E **43 H10**
Champagne *Canada*   60°49N 136°30W **70 A1**
Champagne *France*   48°40N 4°20E **20 B6**
Champaign *U.S.A.*   40°7N 88°15W **80 E9**
Champaner *India*   22°29N 73°32E **42 H5**
Champassak *Laos*   14°53N 105°52E **38 E5**
Champawat *India*   29°20N 80°6E **43 E9**
Champdoré, L. *Canada*   55°55N 65°49W **73 A6**
Champion *U.S.A.*   41°19N 80°51W **82 E4**
Champlain *U.S.A.*   44°59N 73°27W **83 B11**
Champlain, L. *U.S.A.*   44°40N 73°20W **83 B11**
Champotón *Mexico*   19°21N 90°43W **87 D6**
Champua *India*   22°5N 85°40E **43 H11**
Chamrajnagar *India*   11°52N 76°52E **45 J3**
Chana *Thailand*   6°55N 100°44E **39 J3**
Chañaral *Chile*   26°23S 70°40W **94 B1**
Chanārān *Iran*   36°39N 59°6E **47 B8**
Chanasma *India*   23°44N 72°5E **42 H5**
Chancery Lane *Barbados*   13°3N 59°30W **89 g**
Chanco *Chile*   35°44S 72°32W **94 D1**
Chandan *India*   24°38N 72°21E **42 G5**
Chandan Chauki *India*   28°33N 80°47E **43 E9**
Chandannagar *India*   22°52N 88°24E **43 H13**
Chandausi *India*   28°27N 78°49E **43 E8**
Chandeleur Is. *U.S.A.*   29°55N 88°57W **85 G10**
Chandeleur Sd. *U.S.A.*   29°55N 89°0W **85 G10**
Chandigarh *India*   30°43N 76°47E **42 D7**
Chandil *India*   22°58N 86°3E **43 H12**
Chandler *Canada*   48°18N 64°46W **73 C7**
Chandler *Ariz., U.S.A.*   33°18N 111°50W **77 K8**
Chandler *Okla., U.S.A.*   35°42N 96°53W **84 H6**
Chandod *India*   21°59N 73°28E **42 J5**
Chandpur *Bangla.*   23°8N 90°45E **41 H17**
Chandragiri *India*   13°35N 79°19E **45 H4**
Chandrapur *India*   19°57N 79°25E **44 K4**

Chandrupatla *India*   18°33N 80°24E **44 E5**
Chānf *Iran*   26°38N 60°29E **47 E9**
Chang *Pakistan*   26°59N 68°30E **42 F3**
Chang, Ko *Thailand*   12°0N 102°23E **39 G4**
Chang, Ko *Thailand*   9°50N 98°27E **39 H1**
Ch'ang Chiang = Chang Jiang →
   China   31°48N 121°10E **35 B13**
Chang Jiang → *China*   31°48N 121°10E **35 B13**
Changan *China*   22°48N 113°48E **34 G1**
Changanacheri *India*   9°25N 76°31E **45 K3**
Changanassery = Changanacheri
   India   9°25N 76°31E **45 K3**
Changane → *Mozam.*   24°30S 33°30E **57 B5**
Changbai *China*   41°25N 128°0E **33 D15**
Changbai Shan *China*   42°20N 129°0E **33 C15**
Changchiak'ou = Zhangjiakou
   China   40°48N 114°55E **32 D6**
Ch'angchou = Changzhou
   China   31°47N 119°58E **35 B12**
Changchun *China*   43°57N 125°17E **33 C13**
Changchunling *China*   45°18N 125°27E **33 B13**
Changde *China*   29°4N 111°35E **35 C8**
Changdo-ri *N. Korea*   38°30N 127°40E **33 E14**
Changfeng *China*   32°28N 117°10E **35 A11**
Changge *China*   34°13N 113°46E **32 G7**
Changhua *China*   30°12N 119°12E **35 B12**
Changhūngni *N. Korea*   40°24N 128°19E **33 D14**
Changji *China*   44°1N 87°19E **30 C6**
Changjiang *China*   19°20N 108°55E **38 C7**
Changjiang Shuiku
   China   22°29N 113°27E **31**
Changjin *N. Korea*   40°23N 127°15E **33 D14**
Changjin-ho *N. Korea*   40°30N 127°15E **33 D14**
Changle *China*   25°59N 119°27E **35 E12**
Changli *China*   39°40N 119°13E **33 E10**
Changling *China*   44°20N 123°58E **33 B12**
Changlun *Malaysia*   6°25N 100°26E **39 J3**
Changning *Hunan, China*   26°28N 112°22E **35 D9**
Changning *Sichuan,*
   China   28°40N 104°56E **34 C5**
Changning *Yunnan, China*   24°45N 99°30E **34 E2**
Changping *China*   40°14N 116°12E **32 D9**
Changsha *China*   28°12N 113°0E **35 C9**
Changshan *China*   28°55N 118°27E **35 C12**
Changshou *China*   29°50N 107°4E **34 C6**
Changshu *China*   31°38N 120°43E **35 B13**
Changshun *China*   26°3N 106°25E **34 D6**
Changtai *China*   24°35N 117°42E **35 E11**
Changting *China*   25°50N 116°22E **35 E11**
Changtu *China*   42°46N 124°6E **33 C13**
Changuinola *Panama*   9°26N 82°31W **88 E3**
Changwu *China*   23°25N 111°17E **35 F8**
Changwu *Shaanxi, China*   35°10N 107°45E **32 G4**
Changxing *China*   31°0N 119°55E **35 B12**
Changyang *China*   30°30N 111°10E **35 B8**
Changyi *China*   36°40N 119°30E **33 F10**
Changyŏn *N. Korea*   38°15N 125°6E **33 E13**
Changyuan *China*   35°15N 114°42E **32 G8**
Changzhi *China*   36°10N 113°6E **32 F7**
Changzhou *China*   31°47N 119°58E **35 B12**
Chanhanga *Angola*   16°0S 14°8E **56 A1**
Chania *Greece*   35°30N 24°4E **23 G11**
Chanion, Kolpos *Greece*   35°33N 23°55E **23 G10**
Channagiri *India*   14°2N 75°56E **45 G3**
Channapatna *India*   12°40N 77°15E **45 H3**
Channel Is. *U.K.*   49°19N 2°24W **13 H5**
Channel Is. *U.S.A.*   33°40N 119°15W **79 M7**
Channel Islands △
   U.S.A.   34°0N 119°24W **79 L7**
Channel-Port aux Basques
   Canada   47°30N 59°9W **73 C8**
Channel Tunnel *Europe*   51°0N 1°30E **13 F9**
Channing *U.S.A.*   35°41N 102°20W **84 D3**
Chantada *Spain*   42°36N 7°46W **21 A2**
Chanthaburi *Thailand*   12°38N 102°12E **38 F4**
Chantrey Inlet *Canada*   67°48N 96°20W **68 D13**
Chanute *U.S.A.*   37°41N 95°27W **80 G6**
Chao Hu *China*   31°30N 117°30E **35 B11**
Chao Phraya →
   Thailand   13°40N 100°31E **38 F3**
Chao Phraya Lowlands
   Thailand   15°30N 100°0E **38 E3**
Chaocheng *China*   36°4N 115°37E **32 F8**
Chaohu *China*   31°38N 117°50E **35 B11**
Chaoyang *Guangdong,*
   China   23°17N 116°30E **35 F11**
Chaoyang *Liaoning,*
   China   41°35N 120°22E **33 D11**
Chaozhou *China*   23°42N 116°32E **35 F11**
Chapaev *Kazakhstan*   50°25N 51°10E **19 D9**
Chapais *Canada*   49°47N 74°51W **72 C5**
Chapala, L. de *Mexico*   20°15N 103°0W **86 C4**
Chapayevsk *Russia*   53°0N 49°40E **18 D9**
Chapecó *Brazil*   27°14S 52°41W **95 B5**
Chapel Hill *U.S.A.*   35°55N 79°4W **85 D15**
Chapleau *Canada*   47°50N 83°24W **72 C3**
Chaplin *Canada*   50°28N 106°40W **71 C7**
Chaplin L. *Canada*   50°22N 106°36W **71 C7**
Chappell *U.S.A.*   41°6N 102°28W **80 E2**
Chapra = Chhapra *India*   25°48N 84°44E **43 G11**
Chara *Russia*   56°54N 118°20E **27 D12**
Charadai *Argentina*   27°35S 59°55W **94 B4**
Charagua *Bolivia*   19°45S 63°10W **92 G6**
Charambirá, Punta
   Colombia   4°16N 77°32W **92 C3**
Charaña *Bolivia*   17°30S 69°25W **92 G5**
Charanwala *India*   27°51N 72°10E **42 F5**
Charata *Argentina*   27°13S 61°14W **94 B3**
Charcas *Mexico*   23°8N 101°7W **86 C4**
Charcot I. *Antarctica*   70°0S 75°0W **5 C17**
Chard *U.K.*   50°52N 2°58W **13 G5**
Chardon *U.S.A.*   41°35N 81°12W **82 E3**
Chardzhou = Türkmenabat
   Turkmenistan   39°6N 63°34E **47 B9**

Charente → *France* 45°57N 1°5W **20** D3
Chari → *Chad* 12°58N 14°31E **53** F8
Chārīkār *Afghan.* 35°0N 69°10E **40** B6
Chariton *U.S.A.* 41°1N 93°19W **80** E7
Chariton → *U.S.A.* 39°19N 92°58W **80** F7
Chärjew = Türkmenabat
Turkmenistan 39°6N 63°34E **47** B9
Charkhari *India* 25°24N 79°45E **43** G8
Charkhi Dadri *India* 28°37N 76°17E **42** E7
Charleroi *Belgium* 50°24N 4°27E **15** D4
Charleroi *U.S.A.* 40°9N 79°57W **82** F5
Charles, C. *U.S.A.* 37°7N 75°58W **81** G16
Charles, Peak *Australia* 32°52S 121°11E **61** F3
Charles City *U.S.A.* 43°4N 92°41W **80** D7
Charles I. *Canada* 62°39N 74°15W **69** E17
Charles L. *Canada* 59°50N 110°33W **71** B6
Charlesbourg *Canada* 46°51N 71°16W **81** B18
Charleston *Ill., U.S.A.* 39°30N 88°10W **80** F9
Charleston *Miss., U.S.A.* 34°1N 90°4W **85** D9
Charleston *Mo., U.S.A.* 36°55N 89°21W **80** G9
Charleston *S.C., U.S.A.* 32°46N 79°56W **85** E15
Charleston *W. Va.,
U.S.A.* 38°21N 81°38W **81** F13
Charleston L. *Canada* 44°32N 76°0W **83** B9
Charleston Peak
U.S.A. 36°16N 115°42W **79** J11
Charlestown *Ireland* 53°58N 8°48W **10** C3
Charlestown *S. Africa* 27°26S 29°53E **57** C4
Charlestown *Ind.,
U.S.A.* 38°27N 85°40W **81** F11
Charlestown *N.H.,
U.S.A.* 43°14N 72°25W **83** C12
Charlestown of Aberlour
U.K. 57°28N 3°14W **11** D5
Charleville *Australia* 26°24S 146°15E **63** D4
Charleville *Ireland* 52°21N 8°40W **10** D3
Charleville-Mézières
France 49°44N 4°40E **20** B6
Charlevoix *U.S.A.* 45°19N 85°16W **81** C11
Charlotte *Mich., U.S.A.* 42°34N 84°50W **81** D11
Charlotte *N.C., U.S.A.* 35°13N 80°50W **85** D14
Charlotte *Vt., U.S.A.* 44°19N 73°16W **83** B11
Charlotte Amalie
U.S. Virgin Is. 18°21N 64°56W **89** e
Charlotte-Douglas Int. ✈ (CLT)
U.S.A. 35°12N 80°56W **85** D14
Charlotte Harbor *U.S.A.* 26°57N 82°4W **85** H13
Charlotte L. *Canada* 52°12N 125°19W **70** C3
Charlottesville *U.S.A.* 38°2N 78°30W **81** F14
Charlottetown *Nfld. & L.,
Canada* 52°46N 56°7W **73** B8
Charlottetown *P.E.I.,
Canada* 46°14N 63°8W **73** C7
Charlotteville
Trin. & Tob. 11°20N 60°33W **93** J16
Charlton *Australia* 36°16S 143°24E **63** F3
Charlton I. *Canada* 52°0N 79°20W **72** B4
Charny *Canada* 46°43N 71°15W **73** C5
Charolles *France* 46°27N 4°16E **20** C6
Charre *Mozam.* 17°13S 35°10E **55** H7
Charsadda *Pakistan* 34°7N 71°45E **42** B4
Charters Towers *Australia* 20°5S 146°13E **62** C4
Chartres *France* 48°29N 1°30E **20** B4
Chascomús *Argentina* 35°30S 58°0W **94** D4
Chase *Canada* 50°50N 119°41W **70** C5
Chashma Barrage
Pakistan 32°27N 71°20E **42** C4
Chāt *Iran* 37°59N 55°16E **47** B7
Châteaubriant *France* 47°43N 1°23W **20** C3
Chateauguay, L. *Canada* 56°26N 70°3W **73** A5
Châteaulin *France* 48°11N 4°8W **20** B1
Châteauroux *France* 46°50N 1°40E **20** C4
Châteaux, Pte. des
Guadeloupe 16°15N 61°10W **88** b
Châtellerault *France* 46°50N 0°30E **20** C4
Chatham = Miramichi
Canada 47°2N 65°28W **73** C6
Chatham *Canada* 42°24N 82°11W **82** D2
Chatham *U.K.* 51°22N 0°32E **13** F8
Chatham *U.S.A.* 42°21N 73°36W **83** D11
Chatham Is. *Pac. Oc.* 44°0S 176°40W **64** M10
Chatham Rise *Pac. Oc.* 43°30S 180°0E **64** M10
Chatmohar *Bangla.* 24°15N 89°15E **43** G13
Chatrapur *India* 19°22N 85°2E **44** E7
Chats, L. des *Canada* 45°30N 76°20W **83** A8
Chatsu *India* 26°36N 75°57E **42** F6
Chatsworth *Canada* 44°27N 80°54W **82** B4
Châttagâm = Chittagong
Bangla. 22°19N 91°48E **41** H17
Chattahoochee *U.S.A.* 30°42N 84°51W **85** F12
Chattahoochee →
U.S.A. 30°54N 84°57W **85** F12
Chattanooga *U.S.A.* 35°3N 85°19W **85** D12
Chatteris *U.K.* 52°28N 0°2E **13** E8
Chatturat *Thailand* 15°40N 101°51E **38** E3
Chau Doc *Vietnam* 10°42N 105°7E **39** G5
Chaukan Pass *Burma* 27°8N 97°10E **41** F20
Chaumont *France* 48°7N 5°8E **20** B6
Chaumont *U.S.A.* 44°4N 76°8W **83** B8
Chaunskaya G. *Russia* 69°0N 169°0E **27** C17
Chaura *India* 8°27N 93°2E **45** K11
Chautara *Nepal* 27°46N 85°42E **43** F11
Chautauqua L. *U.S.A.* 42°10N 79°24W **82** D5
Chauvin *Canada* 52°45N 110°10W **71** C6
Chaves *Brazil* 0°15S 49°55W **93** D9
Chaves *Portugal* 41°45N 7°32W **21** B2
Chawang *Thailand* 8°25N 99°30E **39** H2
Chaykovskiy *Russia* 56°47N 54°9E **18** C9
Chazy *U.S.A.* 44°53N 73°26W **83** B11
Cheb *Czech Rep.* 50°9N 12°28E **16** C7
Cheboksary *Russia* 56°8N 47°12E **18** C8
Cheboygan *U.S.A.* 45°39N 84°29W **81** C11
Chech, Erg *Africa* 25°0N 2°15W **52** D5
Chechenia ☐ *Russia* 43°30N 45°29E **19** F8
Checheno-Ingush Republic =
Chechenia ☐ *Russia* 43°30N 45°29E **19** F8

Chechnya = Chechenia ☐
Russia 43°30N 45°29E **19** F8
Checotah *U.S.A.* 35°28N 95°31W **84** D7
Chedabucto B. *Canada* 45°25N 61°8W **73** C7
Cheduba I. *Burma* 18°45N 93°40E **41** K18
Cheektowaga *U.S.A.* 42°54N 78°45W **82** D6
Cheepie *Australia* 26°33S 145°1E **63** D4
Chegdomyn *Russia* 51°7N 133°1E **27** D14
Chegga *Mauritania* 25°27N 5°40W **52** C4
Cheguto *Zimbabwe* 18°10S 30°14E **55** H6
Chehalis *U.S.A.* 46°40N 122°58W **78** D4
Chehalis → *U.S.A.* 46°57N 123°50W **78** D3
Cheju = Jeju *S. Korea* 33°31N 126°32E **33** H14
Cheju Str. = Jeju Haehyop
S. Korea 33°50N 126°30E **33** H14
Cheju-do = Jeju-do
S. Korea 33°29N 126°34E **33** H14
Chekiang = Zhejiang ☐
China 29°0N 120°0E **35** C13
Chela, Sa. da *Angola* 16°20S 13°20E **56** A1
Chelan *U.S.A.* 47°51N 120°1W **76** C3
Chelan, L. *U.S.A.* 48°11N 120°30W **76** B3
Cheleken = Hazar
Turkmenistan 39°34N 53°16E **19** G9
Cheleken Yarymadasy
Turkmenistan 39°30N 53°15E **47** B7
Chelforó *Argentina* 39°0S 66°33W **96** D3
Chelkar = Shalqar
Kazakhstan 47°48N 59°39E **26** E6
Chełm *Poland* 51°8N 23°30E **17** C12
Chełmno *Poland* 53°20N 18°30E **17** B10
Chelmsford *U.K.* 51°44N 0°29E **13** F8
Chelsea *Australia* 38°5S 145°8E **63** F4
Chelsea *U.S.A.* 43°59N 72°27W **83** C12
Cheltenham *U.K.* 51°54N 2°4W **13** F5
Chelyabinsk *Russia* 55°10N 61°24E **26** D7
Chelyuskin, C. = Chelyuskin, Mys
Russia 77°30N 103°0E **27** B11
Chelyuskin, Mys *Russia* 77°30N 103°0E **27** B11
Chemainus *Canada* 48°55N 123°42W **78** B3
Chemba *Mozam.* 17°9S 34°53E **55** H6
Chemin Grenier *Mauritius* 20°29S 57°28E **55** d
Chemnitz *Germany* 50°51N 12°54E **16** C7
Chemult *U.S.A.* 43°14N 121°47W **76** E3
Chen, Gora *Russia* 65°16N 141°50E **27** C15
Chenab → *Pakistan* 30°23N 71°2E **42** D4
Chenab Nagar *Pakistan* 31°45N 72°55E **42** D5
Chenango Forks *U.S.A.* 42°15N 75°51W **83** D9
Chenchiang = Zhenjiang
China 32°11N 119°26E **35** A12
Cheney *U.S.A.* 47°30N 117°35W **76** C5
Cheng Xian *China* 33°43N 105°42E **32** H3
Chengalpattu *India* 12°42N 79°58E **45** H4
Chengbu *China* 26°18N 110°16E **35** D8
Chengcheng *China* 35°8N 109°56E **32** G5
Chengchou = Zhengzhou
China 34°45N 113°34E **32** G7
Chengde *China* 40°59N 117°58E **33** D9
Chengdong Hu *China* 32°15N 116°20E **35** A11
Chengdu *China* 30°38N 104°2E **34** B5
Chengdu Shuangliu Int. ✈ (CTU)
China 30°35N 103°57E **34** B4
Chenggong *China* 24°52N 102°56E **34** E4
Chenggu *China* 33°10N 107°21E **34** A6
Chenghai *China* 23°30N 116°42E **35** F11
Chengjiang *China* 24°39N 103°0E **34** E4
Chengkou *China* 31°54N 108°31E **34** B7
Chengmai *China* 19°50N 109°58E **38** C7
Chengshan Jiao *China* 37°25N 122°44E **33** F12
Ch'engtu = Chengdu
China 30°38N 104°2E **34** B5
Chengwu *China* 34°58N 115°50E **32** G8
Chengxi Hu *China* 32°15N 116°10E **35** A11
Chengyang *China* 36°18N 120°21E **33** F11
Chenjiagang *China* 34°23N 119°47E **33** G10
Chenkaladi *Sri Lanka* 7°47N 81°35E **45** L5
Chennai *India* 13°8N 80°19E **45** H5
Chenxi *China* 28°2N 110°12E **35** C8
Chenzhou *China* 25°47N 113°1E **35** E9
Cheò, Eilean a' = Skye
U.K. 57°15N 6°10W **11** D2
Cheo Reo *Vietnam* 13°20N 108°25E **38** F7
Cheom Ksan *Cambodia* 14°13N 104°56E **38** E5
Cheonan *S. Korea* 36°48N 127°9E **33** F14
Cheongdo *S. Korea* 35°38N 128°42E **33** G15
Cheongju *S. Korea* 36°39N 127°27E **33** F14
Cheorwon *S. Korea* 38°15N 127°10E **33** E14
Chepén *Peru* 7°15S 79°23W **92** E3
Chepes *Argentina* 31°20S 66°35W **94** C2
Chepo *Panama* 9°10N 79°6W **88** E4
Chepstow *U.K.* 51°38N 2°41W **13** F5
Chequamegon B. *U.S.A.* 46°39N 90°51W **80** B8
Cher → *France* 47°21N 0°29E **20** C4
Cheraw *U.S.A.* 34°42N 79°53W **85** D15
Cherbourg-Octeville
France 49°39N 1°40W **20** B3
Cherdyn *Russia* 60°24N 56°29E **18** B10
Cheremkhovo *Russia* 53°8N 103°1E **30** A9
Cherepovets *Russia* 59°5N 37°55E **18** C6
Chergui, Chott ech *Algeria* 34°21N 0°25E **52** B6
Cherial *India* 17°55N 78°59E **44** F4
Cherikov = Cherykaw
Belarus 53°32N 31°20E **17** B16
Cheriyam I. *India* 10°9N 73°40E **45** J1
Cherkasy *Ukraine* 49°27N 32°4E **19** E5
Cherkessk *Russia* 44°15N 42°5E **19** F7
Cherla *India* 18°5N 80°49E **44** E5
Cherlak *Russia* 54°15N 74°55E **26** D8
Chernaya *Russia* 70°30N 89°10E **27** B9
Chernigov = Chernihiv
Ukraine 51°28N 31°20E **18** D5
Chernigovka *Russia* 44°19N 132°34E **28** B6
Chernihiv *Ukraine* 51°28N 31°20E **18** D5
Chernivtsi *Ukraine* 48°15N 25°52E **17** D13
Chernobyl = Chornobyl
Ukraine 51°20N 30°15E **17** C16
Chernogorsk *Russia* 53°49N 91°18E **27** D10
Chernovtsy = Chernivtsi
Ukraine 48°15N 25°52E **17** D13
Chernyakhovsk *Russia* 54°36N 21°48E **9** J19

Chernysheyskiy *Russia* 63°0N 112°30E **27** C12
Cherokee *Iowa, U.S.A.* 42°45N 95°33W **80** D6
Cherokee *Okla., U.S.A.* 36°45N 98°21W **84** C5
Cherokee Village *U.S.A.* 36°18N 91°31W **84** C9
Cherokees, Grand Lake O' The
U.S.A. 36°34N 94°55W **84** C7
Cherrapunji *India* 25°17N 91°47E **41** G17
Cherry Valley *U.S.A.* 42°48N 74°45W **83** D10
Cherskiy *Russia* 68°45N 161°18E **27** C17
Cherskogo Khrebet
Russia 65°0N 143°0E **27** C15
Cherthala *India* 9°42N 76°20E **45** K3
Cherven *Belarus* 53°45N 28°28E **17** B15
Chervonohrad *Ukraine* 50°25N 24°10E **17** C13
Cherwell → *U.K.* 51°44N 1°14W **13** F6
Cherykaw *Belarus* 53°32N 31°20E **17** B16
Chesapeake *U.S.A.* 36°49N 76°16W **81** G15
Chesapeake B. *U.S.A.* 38°0N 76°10W **81** F15
Cheshire East ☐ *U.K.* 53°15N 2°15W **12** D5
Cheshire West and Chester ☐
U.K. 53°15N 2°40W **12** D5
Cheshskaya Guba *Russia* 67°20N 47°0E **18** A8
Cheshunt *U.K.* 51°43N 0°1W **13** F7
Chesil Beach *U.K.* 50°37N 2°33W **13** G5
Chesley *Canada* 44°17N 81°5W **82** B3
Chester *U.K.* 53°12N 2°53W **12** D5
Chester *Calif., U.S.A.* 40°19N 121°14W **76** F3
Chester *Ill., U.S.A.* 37°55N 89°49W **80** G9
Chester *Mont., U.S.A.* 48°31N 110°58W **76** B8
Chester *Pa., U.S.A.* 39°51N 75°22W **81** F16
Chester *S.C., U.S.A.* 34°43N 81°12W **85** D14
Chester *Vt., U.S.A.* 43°16N 72°36W **83** C12
Chester *W. Va., U.S.A.* 40°37N 80°34W **82** F4
Chester-le-Street *U.K.* 54°51N 1°34W **12** C6
Chesterfield *U.K.* 53°15N 1°25W **12** D6
Chesterfield, Îs. *N. Cal.* 19°52S 158°15E **58** C8
Chesterfield Inlet
Canada 63°30N 90°45W **68** E12
Chesterton Ra. *Australia* 25°30S 147°27E **63** D4
Chesterton Range △
Australia 26°16S 147°22E **63** D4
Chestertown *U.S.A.* 43°40N 73°48W **83** C11
Chesterville *Canada* 45°6N 75°14W **83** A9
Chesuncook L. *U.S.A.* 46°0N 69°21W **81** C19
Chetamale *India* 10°43N 92°33E **45** J11
Chéticamp *Canada* 46°37N 60°59W **73** C7
Chetlat I. *India* 11°42N 72°42E **45** J1
Chetumal *Mexico* 18°30N 88°20W **87** D7
Chetumal, B. de
Cent. Amer. 18°40N 88°10W **87** D7
Chetwynd *Canada* 55°45N 121°36W **70** B4
Cheviot, The *U.K.* 55°29N 2°9W **12** B5
Cheviot Hills *U.K.* 55°20N 2°30W **12** B5
Cheviot Ra. *Australia* 25°20S 143°45E **62** D3
Chew Bahir *Ethiopia* 4°40N 36°50E **49** G2
Chewelah *U.S.A.* 48°17N 117°43W **76** B5
Cheyenne *Okla., U.S.A.* 35°37N 99°40W **84** D5
Cheyenne *Wyo., U.S.A.* 41°8N 104°49W **76** F11
Cheyenne → *U.S.A.* 44°41N 101°18W **80** C3
Cheyenne Wells
U.S.A. 38°49N 102°21W **76** G12
Cheyne B. *Australia* 34°35S 118°50E **61** F2
Cheyur *India* 12°21N 80°0E **45** H5
Chhabra *India* 24°40N 76°54E **42** G7
Chhaktala *India* 22°6N 74°11E **42** H6
Chhapra *India* 25°48N 84°44E **43** G11
Chhata *India* 27°42N 77°30E **42** F7
Chhatarpur *Jharkhand,
India* 24°23N 84°11E **43** G11
Chhatarpur *Mad. P., India* 24°55N 79°35E **43** G8
Chhati *India* 20°47N 81°40E **44** D5
Chhep *Cambodia* 13°45N 105°24E **38** F5
Chhindwara *Mad. P., India* 22°3N 79°29E **43** H8
Chhindwara *Mad. P., India* 22°2N 78°59E **43** H8
Chhlong *Cambodia* 12°15N 105°58E **39** F5
Chhota Tawa → *India* 22°14N 76°36E **42** H7
Chhoti Kali Sindh →
India 24°2N 75°31E **42** G6
Chhuikhadan *India* 21°32N 80°59E **43** J9
Chhuk *Cambodia* 10°46N 104°28E **39** G5
Chi → *Thailand* 15°11N 104°43E **38** E5
Chi Thanh *Vietnam* 13°17N 109°16E **38** F7
Chiai *Taiwan* 23°29N 120°25E **35** F13
Chiali *Taiwan* 23°9N 120°10E **35** F13
Chiang Dao *Thailand* 19°22N 98°58E **38** C2
Chiang Dao, Doi *Thailand* 19°23N 98°54E **38** C2
Chiang Kham *Thailand* 19°32N 100°18E **38** C3
Chiang Khan *Thailand* 17°52N 101°36E **38** D3
Chiang Khong *Thailand* 20°17N 100°24E **34** G3
Chiang Mai *Thailand* 18°47N 98°59E **38** C2
Chiang Rai *Thailand* 19°52N 99°50E **34** H2
Chiang Saen *Thailand* 20°16N 100°5E **34** G3
Chiapa de Corzo *Mexico* 16°42N 93°0W **87** D6
Chiapas ☐ *Mexico* 16°30N 92°30W **87** D6
Chiapas, Sa. Madre de
Mexico 15°40N 93°0W **87** D6
Chiatla de Tapia
Mexico 18°18N 98°36W **87** D5
Chiávari *Italy* 44°19N 9°19E **20** D8
Chiavenna *Italy* 46°19N 9°24E **20** C8
Chiba *Japan* 35°30N 140°7E **29** G10
Chiba ☐ *Japan* 35°30N 140°20E **29** G10
Chibabava *Mozam.* 20°17S 33°35E **57** B5
Chibemba *Cunene, Angola* 15°48S 14°8E **55** H2
Chibemba *Huila, Angola* 16°20S 15°20E **56** A2
Chibi *Zimbabwe* 20°18S 30°25E **57** B5
Chibia *Angola* 15°10S 13°42E **55** H2
Chibougamau *Canada* 49°56N 74°24W **72** C5
Chibougamau, L. *Canada* 49°50N 74°20W **72** C5
Chibuk *Nigeria* 10°52N 12°50E **53** F8
Chibuto *Mozam.* 24°40S 33°33E **57** B5
Chic-Chocs, Mts. *Canada* 48°55N 66°0W **73** C6
Chicacole = Srikakulam
India 18°14N 83°58E **44** E6
Chicago Heights *U.S.A.* 41°30N 87°38W **80** E10
Chichagof I. *U.S.A.* 57°30N 135°30W **68** F4
Chichaoua *Morocco* 31°32N 8°44W **52** B4
Chichawatni *Pakistan* 30°42N 72°42E **42** D5

Chichén-Itzá *Mexico* 20°37N 88°35W **87** C7
Chicheng *China* 40°55N 115°55E **32** D8
Chichester *U.K.* 50°50N 0°47W **13** G7
Chichester Ra. *Australia* 22°12S 119°15E **60** D2
Chichibu *Japan* 35°59N 139°10E **29** F9
Chichibu-Tama-Kai △
Japan 35°52N 138°42E **29** G9
Ch'ich'ihaerh = Qiqihar
China 47°26N 124°0E **31** B13
Chicholi *India* 22°1N 77°40E **42** H8
Chichón *Mexico* 27°23N 108°32W **86** B3
Chiclana de la Frontera
Spain 36°26N 6°9W **21** D2
Chiclayo *Peru* 6°42S 79°50W **92** E3
Chico *U.S.A.* 39°44N 121°50W **78** F5
Chico → *Chubut, Argentina* 44°0S 67°0W **96** E3
Chico → *Santa Cruz,
Argentina* 50°0S 68°30W **96** G3
Chicoa *Mozam.* 15°36S 32°20E **57** A5
Chicomo *Mozam.* 24°31S 34°6E **57** B5
Chicomostoc *Mexico* 22°28N 102°46W **86** C4
Chicontepec *Mexico* 20°58N 98°10W **87** C5
Chicopee *U.S.A.* 42°9N 72°37W **83** D12
Chicoutimi *Canada* 48°28N 71°5W **73** C5
Chicualacuala *Mozam.* 22°6S 31°42E **57** B5
Chidambaram *India* 11°20N 79°45E **45** J4
Chidenguele *Mozam.* 24°55S 34°11E **57** B5
Chidley, C. *Canada* 60°23N 64°26W **69** E19
Chiducuane *Mozam.* 24°35S 34°25E **57** B5
Chiede *Angola* 17°15S 16°22E **56** A2
Chiefs Pt. *Canada* 44°41N 81°18W **82** B3
Chiem Hoa *Vietnam* 22°12N 105°17E **38** A5
Chiemsee *Germany* 47°53N 12°28E **16** E7
Chiengmai = Chiang Mai
Thailand 18°47N 98°59E **38** C2
Chiese → *Italy* 45°8N 10°25E **20** D9
Chieti *Italy* 42°21N 14°10E **22** C6
Chifeng *China* 42°18N 118°58E **33** C10
Chignecto B. *Canada* 45°30N 64°40W **73** C7
Chiguana *Bolivia* 21°0S 67°58W **94** A2
Chigwell *U.K.* 51°37N 0°6E **13** F8
Chihli, G. of = Bo Hai
China 39°0N 119°0E **33** E10
Chihuahua *Mexico* 28°38N 106°5W **86** B3
Chihuahua ☐ *Mexico* 28°30N 106°0W **86** B3
Chiili = Shïeli *Kazakhstan* 44°20N 66°15E **26** E7
Chik Bollapur *India* 13°25N 77°45E **45** H3
Chikhli *Ahmadabad, India* 20°45N 73°4E **44** D1
Chikhli *Maharashtra, India* 20°20N 76°18E **44** D3
Chikkamagaluru *India* 13°15N 75°45E **45** H2
Chiknayakanhalli *India* 13°26N 76°37E **45** H3
Chikodi *India* 16°26N 74°38E **45** F2
Chilapa *Mexico* 17°36N 99°10W **87** D5
Chilas *Pakistan* 35°25N 74°5E **43** B6
Chilaw *Sri Lanka* 7°30N 79°50E **45** L4
Chilcotin → *Canada* 51°44N 122°23W **70** C4
Childers *Australia* 25°15S 152°17E **63** D5
Childress *U.S.A.* 34°25N 100°13W **84** D4
Chile ■ *S. Amer.* 35°0S 72°0W **96** D2
Chile Rise *Pac. Oc.* 38°0S 92°0W **65** L18
Chilecito *Argentina* 29°10S 67°30W **94** B2
Chilete *Peru* 7°10S 78°50W **92** E3
Chililabombwe *Zambia* 12°18S 27°43E **55** G5
Chilin = Jilin *China* 43°44N 126°30E **33** C14
Chilka L. *India* 19°40N 85°25E **44** E7
Chilko → *Canada* 52°0N 123°40W **70** C4
Chilko L. *Canada* 51°20N 124°10W **70** C4
Chillagoe *Australia* 17°7S 144°33E **62** B3
Chillán *Chile* 36°40S 72°10W **94** D1
Chillicothe *Ill., U.S.A.* 40°55N 89°29W **80** E9
Chillicothe *Mo., U.S.A.* 39°48N 93°33W **80** F7
Chillicothe *Ohio, U.S.A.* 39°20N 82°59W **81** F12
Chilliwack *Canada* 49°10N 121°54W **70** D4
Chilo *India* 27°25N 73°32E **42** F5
Chiloane, I. *Mozam.* 20°40S 34°55E **57** B5
Chiloé, I. de *Chile* 42°30S 73°50W **96** E2
Chilpancingo *Mexico* 17°33N 99°30W **87** D5
Chiltern Hills *U.K.* 51°40N 0°53W **13** F7
Chilton *U.S.A.* 44°2N 88°10W **80** C9
Chilung *Taiwan* 25°3N 121°45E **35** E13
Chilwa, L. *Malawi* 15°15S 35°40E **55** H7
Chimaltitán *Mexico* 21°35N 103°50W **86** C4
Chimán *Panama* 8°45N 78°40W **88** E4
Chimanimani *Zimbabwe* 19°48S 32°52E **57** A5
Chimanimani △ *Zimbabwe* 19°48S 33°0E **57** A5
Chimay *Belgium* 50°3N 4°20E **15** D4
Chimayo *U.S.A.* 36°0N 105°56W **77** J11
Chimborazo *Ecuador* 1°29S 78°55W **92** D3
Chimbote *Peru* 9°0S 78°35W **92** E3
Chimboy *Uzbekistan* 42°57N 59°47E **26** E6
Chimkent = Shymkent
Kazakhstan 42°18N 69°36E **26** E7
Chimoio *Mozam.* 19°4S 33°30E **55** H6
Chimur *India* 20°30N 79°23E **44** D4
Chin ☐ *Burma* 22°0N 93°0E **41** J18
Chin Hills *Burma* 22°30N 93°30E **41** H18
Chin Ling Shan = Qinling Shandi
China 33°50N 108°10E **32** H5
China *Mexico* 25°42N 99°14W **87** B5
China ■ *Asia* 30°0N 110°0E **31** E11
China, Great Plain of
Asia 35°0N 115°0E **24** E13
China Lake *U.S.A.* 35°44N 117°37W **79** K9
Chinan = Jinan *China* 36°38N 117°1E **32** F9
Chinandega *Nic.* 12°35N 87°12E **88** D2
Chinati Peak *U.S.A.* 29°57N 104°29W **84** G2
Chincha Alta *Peru* 13°25S 76°7W **92** F3
Chinchaga → *Canada* 58°53N 118°20W **70** B5
Chinchilla *Australia* 26°45S 150°38E **63** D5
Chincholi *India* 17°28N 77°26E **44** F3
Chinchorro, Banco
Mexico 18°35N 87°22W **87** D7
Chinchou = Jinzhou
China 41°5N 121°3E **33** D11
Chincoteague *U.S.A.* 37°56N 75°23W **81** G16
Chinde *Mozam.* 18°35S 36°30E **55** H7
Chindwin → *Burma* 21°26N 95°15E **41** J19

Chineni *India* 33°2N 75°15E **43** C6
Chingola *Zambia* 12°31S 27°53E **55** G5
Ch'ingtao = Qingdao
China 36°5N 120°20E **33** F11
Chinguetti *Mauritania* 20°25N 12°24W **52** D3
Chingune *Mozam.* 20°33S 34°58E **57** B5
Chinhanguanine *Mozam.* 25°21S 32°30E **57** C5
Chinhoyi *Zimbabwe* 17°20S 30°8E **55** H6
Chiniot *Pakistan* 31°45N 73°0E **42** D5
Chinipas *Mexico* 27°23N 108°32W **86** B3
Chinji *Pakistan* 32°42N 72°22E **42** C5
Chinju = Jinju *S. Korea* 35°12N 128°2E **33** G15
Chinko → *C.A.R.* 4°50N 23°53E **54** D4
Chinle *U.S.A.* 36°9N 109°33W **77** H9
Chinmen *Taiwan* 24°26N 118°19E **35** E12
Chinmen Tao *Taiwan* 24°26N 118°22E **35** E12
Chinnamanur *India* 9°50N 77°24E **45** K3
Chinnampo = Namp'o
N. Korea 38°52N 125°10E **33** E13
Chino *Japan* 35°59N 138°9E **29** G9
Chino *U.S.A.* 34°1N 117°41W **79** L9
Chino Valley *U.S.A.* 34°45N 112°27W **77** J7
Chinon *France* 47°10N 0°15E **20** C4
Chinook *U.S.A.* 48°35N 109°14W **76** B9
Chinook Trough *Pac. Oc.* 44°0N 175°0W **64** C10
Chinsura = Chunchura
India 22°53N 88°27E **43** H13
Chintalapudi *India* 17°4N 80°59E **44** F5
Chintamani *India* 13°26N 78°3E **45** H4
Chióggia *Italy* 45°13N 12°17E **22** B5
Chios *Greece* 38°27N 26°9E **23** E12
Chipata *Zambia* 13°38S 32°28E **55** G6
Chipindo *Angola* 13°49S 15°48E **55** G3
Chipinge *Zimbabwe* 20°13S 32°28E **55** J6
Chipley *U.S.A.* 30°47N 85°32W **85** F12
Chiplun *India* 17°31N 73°34E **44** F1
Chipman *Canada* 46°6N 65°53W **73** C6
Chippenham *U.K.* 51°27N 2°6W **13** F5
Chippewa → *U.S.A.* 44°25N 92°5W **80** C7
Chippewa Falls *U.S.A.* 44°56N 91°24W **80** C8
Chipping Norton *U.K.* 51°56N 1°32W **13** F6
Chiputneticook Lakes
N. Amer. 45°35N 67°35W **81** C20
Chiquián *Peru* 10°10S 77°0W **92** F3
Chiquibul △ *Belize* 16°49N 88°52W **88** C2
Chiquimula *Guatemala* 14°51N 89°37W **88** D2
Chiquinquira *Colombia* 5°37N 73°50W **92** B4
Chirala *India* 15°50N 80°26E **45** G5
Chirawa *India* 28°14N 75°42E **42** E6
Chirchiq *Uzbekistan* 41°29N 69°35E **26** E7
Chiredzi *Zimbabwe* 21°0S 31°38E **57** B5
Chiricahua △ *U.S.A.* 32°0N 109°20W **77** L9
Chiricahua Peak *U.S.A.* 31°51N 109°18W **77** L9
Chirikof I. *U.S.A.* 55°50N 155°40W **74** D7
Chiriquí, G. de *Panama* 8°0N 82°10W **88** E3
Chiriquí, L. de *Panama* 9°10N 82°0W **88** E3
Chirmiri *India* 23°15N 82°20E **43** H10
Chirripó Grande, Cerro
Costa Rica 9°29N 83°29W **88** E3
Chirundu *Zimbabwe* 16°3S 28°50E **57** A4
Chisapani *Nepal* 28°37N 81°16E **43** E9
Chisasibi *Canada* 53°50N 79°0W **72** B4
Ch'ishan *Taiwan* 22°44N 120°31E **35** F13
Chisholm *Canada* 54°55N 114°10W **70** C6
Chisholm *U.S.A.* 47°29N 92°53W **80** B7
Chishtian Mandi *Pakistan* 29°50N 72°55E **42** E5
Chishui *China* 28°30N 105°42E **34** C5
Chishui He → *China* 28°49N 105°50E **34** C5
Chisimaio = Kismaayo
Somalia 0°22S 42°32E **49** H3
Chişinău *Moldova* 47°2N 28°50E **17** E15
Chisos Mts. *U.S.A.* 29°5N 103°15W **84** G3
Chistopol *Russia* 55°25N 50°38E **18** C9
Chita *Russia* 52°0N 113°35E **31** A11
Chitapur *India* 17°10N 77°5E **44** F3
Chitose *Japan* 42°49N 141°39E **28** C10
Chitradurga *India* 14°14N 76°24E **45** G3
Chitrakot *India* 19°10N 81°40E **44** E5
Chitral *Pakistan* 35°50N 71°56E **40** B7
Chitravati → *India* 14°45N 78°15E **45** G4
Chitré *Panama* 7°59N 80°27W **88** E3
Chittagong *Bangla.* 22°19N 91°48E **41** H17
Chittagong ☐ *Bangla.* 24°5N 91°0E **41** G17
Chittaurgarh *India* 24°52N 74°38E **42** G6
Chittoor *India* 13°15N 79°5E **45** H4
Chittur *India* 10°40N 76°45E **45** J3
Chitungwiza *Zimbabwe* 18°0S 31°6E **55** H6
Chiusi *Italy* 43°1N 11°57E **22** C4
Chivasso *Italy* 45°11N 7°53E **20** D7
Chivilcoy *Argentina* 34°55S 60°0W **94** C4
Chixi *China* 22°0N 112°58E **35** G9
Chkalov = Orenburg
Russia 51°45N 55°6E **18** D10
Chloride *U.S.A.* 35°25N 114°12W **79** K12
Cho-do *N. Korea* 38°30N 124°40E **33** E13
Cho Phuoc Hai *Vietnam* 10°26N 107°18E **39** G6
Chobe △ *Botswana* 18°37S 24°23E **56** A4
Chocolate Mts. *U.S.A.* 33°15N 115°15W **79** M11
Choctawhatchee →
U.S.A. 30°25N 86°8W **85** F11
Chodavaram *Andhra Pradesh,
India* 17°50N 82°57E **44** F6
Chodavaram *Andhra Pradesh,
India* 17°27N 81°46E **44** F5
Choele Choel *Argentina* 39°11S 65°40W **96** D3
Choghā Zanbīl *Iran* 32°1N 48°32E **47** D6
Choiseul *St. Lucia* 13°47N 61°3W **89** f
Choiseul *Solomon Is.* 7°0S 156°40E **58** B8
Choix *Mexico* 26°43N 108°17W **86** B3
Chojnice *Poland* 53°42N 17°32E **17** B9
Chok Chai *Thailand* 14°44N 102°10E **38** E4
Chōkai-San *Japan* 39°6N 140°3E **28** E10
Choke Canyon Res.
U.S.A. 28°30N 98°20W **84** G5
Chokurdakh *Russia* 70°38N 147°55E **27** B15
Chokwé *Mozam.* 24°32S 32°59E **57** B5
Cholame *U.S.A.* 35°44N 120°18W **78** K6
Cholet *France* 47°4N 0°52W **20** C3
Cholguan *Chile* 37°10S 72°3W **94** D1
Choloma *Honduras* 15°37N 87°57W **88** C2

Choluteca Honduras 13°20N 87°14W 88 D2
Choluteca → Honduras 13°0N 87°20W 88 D2
Chom Bung Thailand 13°37N 99°36E 38 F2
Chom Thong Thailand 18°25N 98°41E 38 C2
Choma Zambia 16°48S 26°59E 55 H5
Chomolungma = Everest, Mt.
  Nepal 28°5N 86°58E 43 E12
Chomun India 27°15N 75°40E 42 F6
Chomutov Czech Rep. 50°28N 13°23E 16 C7
Chon Buri Thailand 13°21N 101°1E 38 F3
Chon Thanh Vietnam 11°24N 106°36E 39 G6
Chone Ecuador 0°40S 80°0W 92 D3
Chong Kai Cambodia 13°57N 103°35E 38 F4
Chong Mek Thailand 15°10N 105°27E 38 E5
Chong Phangan Thailand 9°39N 100°0E 39 b
Chong Samui Thailand 9°21N 99°50E 39 b
Chongde China 30°32N 120°26E 35 B13
Ch'ŏngjin N. Korea 41°47N 129°50E 33 D15
Chŏngju N. Korea 39°40N 125°5E 33 E13
Chongli China 40°58N 115°15E 32 D8
Chongming China 31°38N 121°23E 35 B13
Chongming Dao China 31°40N 121°30E 35 B13
Chŏngp'yŏng N. Korea 39°47N 127°23E 33 E14
Chongqing Chongqing,
  China 29°35N 106°25E 34 C6
Chongqing Sichuan,
  China 30°38N 103°40E 34 B4
Chongqing Jiangbei Int. ✈ (CKG)
  China 29°43N 106°38E 34 C6
Chongqing Shi □ China 30°0N 108°0E 34 C6
Chongren China 27°46N 116°3E 35 D11
Chonguene Mozam. 25°3S 33°49E 57 C5
Chongyi China 25°45N 114°29E 35 E10
Chongzuo China 22°23N 107°20E 34 F6
Chonogol Mongolia 45°54N 115°22E 32 B8
Chonos, Arch. de los Chile 45°0S 75°0W 96 F2
Chop Ukraine 48°26N 22°12E 17 D12
Chopda India 21°20N 75°15E 44 D2
Chopim → Brazil 25°35S 53°5W 95 B5
Chor Pakistan 25°31N 69°46E 42 G3
Chora Sfakion Greece 35°15N 24°9E 23 G11
Chorbat La India 34°42N 76°37E 43 B7
Chorley U.K. 53°39N 2°38W 12 D5
Chornobyl Ukraine 51°20N 30°15E 17 C16
Chorolque, Cerro Bolivia 20°59S 66°5W 94 A2
Chorregon Australia 22°40S 143°32E 62 C3
Chorro el Indio △
  Venezuela 7°43N 72°9W 89 E5
Chortkiv Ukraine 49°2N 25°46E 17 D13
Chorzów Poland 50°18N 18°57E 17 C10
Chos-Malal Argentina 37°20S 70°15W 94 D1
Ch'osan N. Korea 40°50N 125°47E 33 D13
Choszczno Poland 53°7N 15°25E 16 B8
Choteau U.S.A. 47°49N 112°11W 76 C7
Chotila India 22°23N 71°15E 42 H4
Chotta Udepur India 22°19N 74°1E 42 H6
Chowchilla U.S.A. 37°7N 120°16W 78 H6
Choybalsan Mongolia 48°4N 114°30E 31 B11
Choyr Mongolia 46°24N 108°30E 31 B10
Christchurch N.Z. 43°33S 172°47E 59 E4
Christchurch U.K. 50°44N 1°47W 13 G6
Christian I. Canada 44°50N 80°12W 82 B4
Christian Sd. U.S.A. 55°56N 134°40W 75 D13
Christiana S. Africa 27°52S 25°8E 56 C4
Christiansted
  U.S. Virgin Is. 17°45N 64°42W 89 C7
Christie B. Canada 62°32N 111°10W 71 A6
Christina → Canada 56°40N 111°3W 71 B6
Christmas Cr. →
  Australia 18°29S 125°23E 60 C4
Christmas I. = Kiritimati
  Kiribati 1°58N 157°27W 65 G12
Christmas I. Ind. Oc. 10°30S 105°40E 64 J2
Christopher, L. Australia 24°49S 127°42E 61 D4
Chū = Shū Kazakhstan 43°36N 73°42E 26 E8
Chu → Vietnam 19°53N 105°45E 38 C5
Chu Lai Vietnam 15°28N 108°45E 38 E7
Chu Mom Ray △
  Vietnam 14°29N 107°38E 38 E6
Chu Se Vietnam 13°40N 108°8E 38 F7
Chuadanga Bangla. 23°38N 88°51E 43 H13
Chuak, Ko Thailand 9°28N 99°41E 39 b
Chumar India 32°40N 78°35E 43 C8
Chumbicha Argentina 29°0S 66°10W 94 B2
Chumikan Russia 54°40N 135°10E 27 D14
Chumphon Thailand 10°35N 99°14E 39 G2
Chun'an China 29°35N 119°3E 35 C12
Chuna → Russia 57°47N 94°37E 27 D10
Chuncheon S. Korea 37°58N 127°44E 33 F14
Chunchura India 22°53N 88°27E 43 H13

Chunggang-ŭp
  N. Korea 41°48N 126°48E 33 D14
Chunghwa N. Korea 38°52N 125°47E 33 E13
Chungju S. Korea 36°58N 127°58E 33 F14
Chungking = Chongqing
  China 29°35N 106°25E 34 C6
Chungli Taiwan 24°57N 121°13E 35 E13
Chungt'iaoshan = Zhongtiao Shan
  China 35°0N 111°10E 32 G6
Chungyang Shanmo
  Taiwan 23°10N 121°0E 35 F13
Chunian Pakistan 30°57N 74°0E 42 D6
Chunya Tanzania 8°30S 33°27E 54 F6
Chunyang China 43°38N 129°23E 33 C15
Chupara Pt. Trin. & Tob. 10°49N 61°22W 93 K15
Chuquibamba Peru 15°47S 72°44W 92 G4
Chuquicamata Chile 22°15S 69°0W 94 A2
Churachandpur India 24°20N 93°40E 41 G18
Church Stretton U.K. 52°32N 2°48W 13 E5
Churchill Canada 58°47N 94°11W 71 B10
Churchill → Man.,
  Canada 58°47N 94°12W 71 B10
Churchill → Nfld. & L.,
  Canada 53°19N 60°10W 73 B7
Churchill, C. Canada 58°46N 93°12W 71 B10
Churchill Falls Canada 53°36N 64°19W 73 B7
Churchill L. Canada 55°55N 108°20W 71 B7
Churchill Pk. Canada 58°10N 125°10W 70 B3
Churki India 23°50N 83°12E 43 H10
Churu India 28°20N 74°50E 42 E6
Churún Merú = Angel Falls
  Venezuela 5°57N 62°30W 92 B6
Chushal India 33°40N 78°40E 43 C8
Chuska Mts. U.S.A. 36°15N 108°50W 77 H9
Chusovoy Russia 58°22N 57°50E 18 C10
Chute-aux-Outardes
  Canada 49°7N 68°24W 73 C6
Chuuk = Truk Micronesia 7°25N 151°46E 64 G7
Chuvash Republic = Chuvashia □
  Russia 55°30N 47°0E 18 C8
Chuvashia □ Russia 55°30N 47°0E 18 C8
Chuwārtah Iraq 35°43N 45°34E 46 C5
Chuxiong China 25°2N 101°28E 34 D3
Chuy Uruguay 33°41S 53°27W 95 C5
Chuzhou China 32°19N 118°20E 35 A12
Ci Xian China 36°20N 114°25E 32 G8
Ciamis Indonesia 7°20S 108°21E 37 G13
Cianjur Indonesia 6°49S 107°8E 37 G12
Cianorte Brazil 23°37S 52°37W 95 A5
Cibola U.S.A. 33°17N 114°42W 79 M12
Cicia Fiji 17°45S 179°18W 59 a
Ciénaga del Cataumbo △
  Venezuela 9°25N 71°54W 89 E5
Ciechanów Poland 52°52N 20°38E 17 B11
Ciego de Ávila Cuba 21°50N 78°50W 88 B4
Ciénaga Colombia 11°1N 74°15W 92 A4
Cienfuegos Cuba 22°10N 80°30W 88 B3
Cieszyn Poland 49°45N 18°35E 17 D10
Cieza Spain 38°17N 1°23W 21 C5
Cihuatlán Mexico 19°14N 104°35W 86 D4
Cijara, Embalse de Spain 39°18N 4°52W 21 C3
Cijulang Indonesia 7°42S 108°27E 37 G13
Cilacap Indonesia 7°43S 109°0E 37 G13
Cili China 29°30N 111°8E 35 C8
Cill Airne = Killarney
  Ireland 52°4N 9°30W 10 D2
Cill Chainnigh = Kilkenny
  Ireland 52°39N 7°15W 10 D4
Cill Dara = Kildare Ireland 53°9N 6°55W 10 C5
Cill Droichid = Celbridge
  Ireland 53°20N 6°32W 10 C5
Cill Mhantáin = Wicklow
  Ireland 52°59N 6°3W 10 D5
Cilo Dağı Turkey 37°28N 43°55E 19 G7
Cima U.S.A. 35°14N 115°30W 79 K11
Cimarron Kans., U.S.A. 37°48N 100°21W 80 G3
Cimarron N. Mex.,
  U.S.A. 36°31N 104°55W 77 H11
Cimarron → U.S.A. 36°10N 96°16W 84 C6
Cimişlia Moldova 46°34N 28°44E 17 E15
Cimone, Mte. Italy 44°12N 10°42E 22 B4
Cinca → Spain 41°26N 0°21E 21 B6
Cincar Bos.-H. 43°55N 17°5E 22 C7
Cincinnati U.S.A. 39°9N 84°27W 81 F11
Cincinnatus U.S.A. 42°33N 75°54W 83 D9
Çine Turkey 37°37N 28°2E 23 F13
Ciney Belgium 50°18N 5°5E 15 D5
Cinque I. India 11°16N 92°42E 45 J11
Cinto, Mte. France 42°24N 8°54E 20 E8
Circle Alaska, U.S.A. 65°50N 144°4W 74 B11
Circle Mont., U.S.A. 47°25N 105°35W 76 C11
Circleville U.S.A. 39°36N 82°57W 81 F12
Cirebon Indonesia 6°45S 108°32E 37 G13
Cirencester U.K. 51°43N 1°57W 13 F6
Cisco U.S.A. 32°23N 98°59W 84 E5
Citlaltépetl = Orizaba, Pico de
  Mexico 18°58N 97°15W 87 D5
Citrus Heights U.S.A. 38°42N 121°17W 78 G5
Citrusdal S. Africa 32°35S 19°0E 56 D2
Città di Castello Italy 43°27N 12°14E 22 C5
Ciudad Acuña Mexico 29°18N 100°55W 86 B4
Ciudad Altamirano
  Mexico 18°20N 100°40W 86 D4
Ciudad Anáhuac Mexico 27°14N 100°7W 86 B4
Ciudad Bolívar Venezuela 8°5N 63°36W 92 B6
Ciudad Camargo
  Mexico 27°40N 105°10W 86 B3
Ciudad Cortés Costa Rica 8°55N 84°0W 88 E3
Ciudad del Carmen
  Mexico 18°38N 91°50W 87 D6
Ciudad del Este Paraguay 25°30S 54°50W 95 B5
Ciudad Delicias = Delicias
  Mexico 28°13N 105°28W 86 B3
Ciudad Frontera Mexico 26°56N 101°27W 86 B4
Ciudad Guayana Venezuela 8°0N 62°30W 92 B6
Ciudad Guerrero
  Mexico 28°33N 107°30W 86 B3
Ciudad Guzmán Mexico 19°41N 103°29W 86 D4
Ciudad Juárez Mexico 31°44N 106°29W 86 A3

Ciudad Lerdo Mexico 25°32N 103°32W 86 B4
Ciudad Madero Mexico 22°19N 97°50W 87 C5
Ciudad Mante Mexico 22°44N 98°59W 87 C5
Ciudad Obregón Mexico 27°29N 109°56W 86 B3
Ciudad Real Spain 38°59N 3°55W 21 C4
Ciudad Rodrigo Spain 40°35N 6°32W 21 B2
Ciudad Valles Mexico 21°59N 99°1W 87 C5
Ciudad Victoria Mexico 23°44N 99°8W 87 C5
Civitanova Marche Italy 43°18N 13°44E 22 C5
Civitavécchia Italy 42°6N 11°48E 22 C4
Cixi China 30°17N 121°9E 35 B13
Cizre Turkey 37°19N 42°10E 46 B4
Clackmannanshire □
  U.K. 56°10N 3°43W 11 E5
Clacton-on-Sea U.K. 51°47N 1°11E 13 F9
Claire, L. Canada 58°35N 112°5W 70 B6
Clairton U.S.A. 40°18N 79°53W 82 F5
Clallam Bay U.S.A. 48°15N 124°16W 78 B2
Clanton U.S.A. 32°51N 86°38W 85 E11
Clanwilliam S. Africa 32°11S 18°52E 56 D2
Clara Ireland 53°21N 7°37W 10 C4
Claraville U.S.A. 35°24N 118°20W 79 K8
Clare Australia 33°50S 138°37E 63 E2
Clare U.S.A. 43°49N 84°46W 81 D11
Clare □ Ireland 52°45N 9°0W 10 D3
Clare → Ireland 53°20N 9°2W 10 C2
Clare I. Ireland 53°47N 10°0W 10 C1
Claremont Calif., U.S.A. 34°6N 117°43W 79 L9
Claremont N.H., U.S.A. 43°23N 72°20W 83 C12
Claremont Pt. Australia 14°1S 143°41E 62 A3
Claremore U.S.A. 36°19N 95°36W 84 C7
Claremorris Ireland 53°45N 9°0W 10 C3
Clarence → Australia 29°25S 153°22E 63 D5
Clarence → N.Z. 42°10S 173°56E 59 E4
Clarence, I. Chile 54°0S 72°0W 96 G2
Clarence I. Antarctica 61°10S 54°0W 5 C18
Clarence Str. Australia 12°0S 131°0E 60 B5
Clarence Town Bahamas 23°6N 74°59W 89 B5
Clarendon Pa., U.S.A. 41°47N 79°6W 82 E5
Clarendon Tex., U.S.A. 34°56N 100°53W 84 D4
Clarenville Canada 48°10N 54°1W 73 C9
Claresholm Canada 50°2N 113°33W 70 D6
Clarie Coast Antarctica 68°0S 135°0E 5 C9
Clarinda U.S.A. 40°44N 95°2W 80 E6
Clarington Canada 43°55N 78°41W 82 D6
Clarion Iowa, U.S.A. 42°44N 93°44W 80 D7
Clarion Pa., U.S.A. 41°13N 79°23W 82 E5
Clarion → U.S.A. 41°7N 79°41W 82 E5
Clarion Fracture Zone
  Pac. Oc. 20°0N 120°0W 66 H7
Clark U.S.A. 44°53N 97°44W 80 C5
Clark, Pt. Canada 44°4N 81°45W 82 B3
Clark Fork U.S.A. 48°9N 116°11W 76 B5
Clark Fork → U.S.A. 48°9N 116°15W 76 B5
Clarkdale U.S.A. 34°46N 112°3W 77 J7
Clarke City Canada 50°12N 66°38W 73 B6
Clarke I. Australia 40°32S 148°10E 63 G4
Clarke Ra. Australia 20°40S 148°30E 62 b
Clarks Fork Yellowstone →
  U.S.A. 45°39N 108°43W 76 D9
Clark's Harbour Canada 43°25N 65°38W 73 D6
Clarks Hill L. = J. Strom Thurmond
  L. U.S.A. 33°40N 82°12W 85 E13
Clarks Summit U.S.A. 41°30N 75°42W 83 E9
Clarksburg U.S.A. 39°17N 80°30W 81 F13
Clarksdale U.S.A. 34°12N 90°35W 85 D9
Clarkston U.S.A. 46°25N 117°3W 76 C5
Clarksville Ark., U.S.A. 35°28N 93°28W 84 D8
Clarksville Tenn., U.S.A. 36°32N 87°21W 85 C11
Clarksville Tex., U.S.A. 33°37N 95°3W 84 E7
Clatskanie U.S.A. 46°6N 123°12W 78 D3
Claude U.S.A. 35°7N 101°22W 84 D4
Claveria Phil. 18°37N 121°4E 37 A6
Clay U.S.A. 38°17N 121°10W 78 G5
Clay Center U.S.A. 39°23N 97°8W 80 F5
Claypool U.S.A. 33°25N 110°51W 77 K8
Claysburg U.S.A. 40°17N 78°27W 82 F6
Claysville U.S.A. 40°7N 80°25W 82 F4
Clayton N. Mex., U.S.A. 36°27N 103°11W 77 H12
Clayton N.Y., U.S.A. 44°14N 76°5W 83 B8
Clear, C. Ireland 51°25N 9°32W 10 E2
Clear, L. Canada 45°26N 77°12W 82 A7
Clear Hills Canada 56°40N 119°30W 70 B5
Clear I. Ireland 51°26N 9°30W 10 E2
Clear L. U.S.A. 39°2N 122°47W 78 F4
Clear Lake Iowa, U.S.A. 43°8N 93°23W 80 D7
Clear Lake S. Dak., U.S.A. 44°45N 96°41W 80 C5
Clear Lake Res. U.S.A. 41°56N 121°5W 76 F3
Clearfield Pa., U.S.A. 41°2N 78°27W 82 E6
Clearfield Utah, U.S.A. 41°7N 112°2W 76 F7
Clearlake U.S.A. 38°57N 122°38W 78 G4
Clearwater Canada 51°38N 120°2W 70 C4
Clearwater U.S.A. 27°59N 82°48W 85 H13
Clearwater → Alta.,
  Canada 52°22N 114°57W 70 C6
Clearwater → Alta.,
  Canada 56°44N 111°23W 71 B6
Clearwater L. Canada 53°34N 99°49W 71 C9
Clearwater Lake ○
  Canada 54°0N 101°0W 71 C8
Clearwater Mts. U.S.A. 46°5N 115°20W 76 C6
Clearwater River ○
  Canada 56°55N 109°10W 71 B7
Cleburne U.S.A. 32°21N 97°23W 84 E6
Clee Hills U.K. 52°26N 2°35W 13 E5
Cleethorpes U.K. 53°33N 0°3W 12 D7
Cleeve Cloud U.K. 51°56N 2°0W 13 F6
Clemson U.S.A. 34°41N 82°50W 85 D13
Clerke Reef Australia 17°22S 119°20E 60 C2
Clermont Australia 22°49S 147°39E 62 C4
Clermont U.S.A. 28°33N 81°46W 85 G14
Clermont-Ferrand France 45°46N 3°4E 20 D5
Clervaux Lux. 50°4N 6°2E 15 D6
Clevedon U.K. 51°26N 2°52W 13 F5
Cleveland Miss., U.S.A. 33°45N 90°43W 85 E9
Cleveland Ohio, U.S.A. 41°29N 81°41W 82 E3
Cleveland Okla., U.S.A. 36°19N 96°28W 84 C6
Cleveland Tenn., U.S.A. 35°10N 84°53W 85 D12
Cleveland Tex., U.S.A. 30°21N 95°5W 84 F7

Cleveland, C. Australia 19°11S 147°1E 62 B4
Cleveland, Mt. U.S.A. 48°56N 113°51W 76 B7
Cleveland Heights U.S.A. 41°31N 81°33W 82 E3
Clevelândia Brazil 26°24S 52°23W 95 B5
Clew B. Ireland 53°50N 9°49W 10 C2
Clewiston U.S.A. 26°45N 80°56W 85 H14
Clifden Ireland 53°29N 10°1W 10 C1
Clifden N.Z. 46°1S 167°42E 59 G1
Cliffdell U.S.A. 46°56N 121°5W 78 D5
Cliffy Hd. Australia 35°1S 116°29E 61 G2
Clifton Australia 27°59S 151°53E 63 D5
Clifton Ariz., U.S.A. 33°3N 109°18W 77 K9
Clifton Colo., U.S.A. 39°7N 108°25W 76 G9
Clifton Tex., U.S.A. 31°47N 97°35W 84 F6
Clifton Beach Australia 16°46S 145°39E 62 B4
Clinch → U.S.A. 35°53N 84°29W 85 D12
Clingmans Dome
  U.S.A. 35°34N 83°30W 85 D13
Clint U.S.A. 31°35N 106°14W 84 F1
Clinton B.C., Canada 51°6N 121°35W 70 C4
Clinton Ont., Canada 43°37N 81°32W 82 C3
Clinton N.Z. 46°12S 169°23E 59 G2
Clinton Ark., U.S.A. 35°36N 92°28W 84 D8
Clinton Conn., U.S.A. 41°17N 72°32W 83 E12
Clinton Ill., U.S.A. 40°9N 88°57W 80 E9
Clinton Ind., U.S.A. 39°40N 87°24W 80 F10
Clinton Iowa, U.S.A. 41°51N 90°12W 80 E8
Clinton Mass., U.S.A. 42°25N 71°41W 83 D13
Clinton Miss., U.S.A. 32°20N 90°20W 85 E9
Clinton Mo., U.S.A. 38°22N 93°46W 80 F7
Clinton N.C., U.S.A. 35°0N 78°22W 85 D15
Clinton Okla., U.S.A. 35°31N 98°58W 84 D5
Clinton S.C., U.S.A. 34°29N 81°53W 85 D14
Clinton Tenn., U.S.A. 36°6N 84°8W 85 C12
Clinton Wash., U.S.A. 47°59N 122°21W 78 C4
Clinton, C. Australia 22°30S 150°45E 62 C5
Clinton Colden L.
  Canada 63°58N 107°27W 68 E10
Clipperton, Î. Pac. Oc. 10°18N 109°13W 65 F17
Clipperton Fracture Zone
  Pac. Oc. 19°0N 122°0W 65 G16
Clisham U.K. 57°58N 6°49W 11 D2
Clitheroe U.K. 53°53N 2°22W 12 D5
Clo-oose Canada 48°39N 124°49W 78 B2
Cloates, Pt. Australia 22°43S 113°40E 60 D1
Clocolan S. Africa 28°55S 27°34E 57 C4
Clodomira Argentina 27°35S 64°14W 94 B3
Cloghaneely Ireland 55°8N 8°5W 10 A3
Clogher Hd. Ireland 53°48N 6°14W 10 C5
Clonakilty Ireland 51°37N 8°53W 10 E3
Clonakilty B. Ireland 51°35N 8°51W 10 E3
Cloncurry Australia 20°40S 140°28E 62 C3
Cloncurry Ireland 53°26N 6°48W 10 C5
Cloncurry → Australia 18°37S 140°40E 62 B3
Clondalkin Ireland 53°19N 6°25W 10 C5
Clones Ireland 54°11N 7°15W 10 B4
Clonmel Ireland 52°21N 7°42W 10 D4
Cloquet U.S.A. 46°43N 92°28W 80 B7
Clorinda Argentina 25°16S 57°45W 94 B4
Cloud Peak U.S.A. 44°23N 107°11W 76 D10
Cloudcroft U.S.A. 32°58N 105°45W 77 K11
Cloverdale U.S.A. 38°48N 123°1W 78 G4
Clovis Calif., U.S.A. 36°49N 119°42W 78 J7
Clovis N. Mex., U.S.A. 34°24N 103°12W 77 J12
Cloyne Canada 44°49N 77°11W 82 B7
Cluain Meala = Clonmel
  Ireland 52°21N 7°42W 10 D4
Cluj-Napoca Romania 46°47N 23°38E 17 E12
Clunes Australia 37°20S 143°45E 63 F3
Clutha → N.Z. 46°20S 169°49E 59 G2
Clwyd → U.K. 53°19N 3°31W 12 D4
Clyde Canada 54°9N 113°39W 70 C6
Clyde N.Z. 45°12S 169°20E 59 F2
Clyde → U.K. 55°55N 4°30W 11 F4
Clyde, Firth of U.K. 55°22N 5°1W 11 F3
Clyde River Canada 70°30N 68°30W 69 C18
Clydebank U.K. 55°54N 4°23W 11 F4
Clymer N.Y., U.S.A. 42°1N 79°37W 82 D5
Clymer Pa., U.S.A. 40°40N 79°1W 82 D5
Coachella U.S.A. 33°41N 116°10W 79 M10
Coachella Canal
  U.S.A. 32°43N 114°57W 79 N12
Coahoma U.S.A. 32°18N 101°18W 84 E4
Coahuayana → Mexico 18°41N 103°45W 86 D4
Coahuila □ Mexico 27°20N 102°0W 86 B4
Coal → Canada 59°39N 126°57W 70 B3
Coalcomán Mexico 18°47N 103°9W 86 D4
Coaldale Canada 49°45N 112°35W 70 D6
Coalgate U.S.A. 34°32N 96°13W 84 D6
Coalinga U.S.A. 36°9N 120°21W 78 J6
Coalisland U.K. 54°33N 6°42W 10 B5
Coalville U.K. 52°44N 1°23W 12 E6
Coalville U.S.A. 40°55N 111°24W 76 F8
Coamo Puerto Rico 18°5N 66°22W 89 d
Coari Brazil 4°8S 63°7W 92 D6
Coast Mts. Canada 55°0N 129°20W 70 C3
Coast Ranges U.S.A. 39°0N 123°0W 78 G4
Coatbridge U.K. 55°52N 4°6W 11 F4
Coatepec Mexico 19°27N 96°58W 87 D5
Coatepeque Guatemala 14°46N 91°55W 88 D1
Coatesville U.S.A. 39°59N 75°50W 81 F16
Coaticook Canada 45°10N 71°46W 83 A13
Coats I. Canada 62°30N 83°0W 69 E15
Coats Land Antarctica 77°0S 25°0W 5 D1
Coatzacoalcos Mexico 18°7N 94°25W 87 D6
Cobá Mexico 20°31N 87°45W 87 C7
Cobalt Canada 47°25N 79°42W 72 C4
Cobán Guatemala 15°30N 90°21W 88 C1
Cobar Australia 31°27S 145°48E 63 E4
Cobh Ireland 51°51N 8°17W 10 E3
Cóbh, An = Cobh Ireland 51°51N 8°17W 10 E3
Cobija Bolivia 11°0N 68°50W 92 F5
Cobleskill U.S.A. 42°41N 74°29W 83 D10
Coboconk Canada 44°39N 78°48W 82 B6
Cobourg Canada 43°58N 78°10W 82 C6
Cobourg Pen. Australia 11°20S 132°15E 60 B5
Cobram Australia 35°54S 145°40E 63 F4
Coburg Germany 50°15N 10°58E 16 C6
Coburg I. Canada 75°57N 79°26W 69 B16

Cocanada = Kakinada
  India 16°57N 82°11E 44 F6
Cochabamba Bolivia 17°26S 66°10W 92 G5
Cochin = Kochi India 9°58N 76°20E 45 K3
Cochin China = Nam Phan
  Vietnam 10°30N 106°0E 39 G6
Cochran U.S.A. 32°23N 83°21W 85 E13
Cochrane Alta., Canada 51°11N 114°30W 70 C6
Cochrane Ont., Canada 49°0N 81°0W 72 C3
Cochrane Chile 47°15S 72°33W 96 F2
Cochrane → Canada 59°0N 103°40W 71 B8
Cochrane, L. Chile 47°10S 72°0W 96 F2
Cochranton U.S.A. 41°31N 80°3W 82 E4
Cockburn Australia 32°5S 141°0E 63 E3
Cockburn, Canal Chile 54°30S 72°0W 96 G2
Cockburn I. Canada 45°55N 83°22W 72 C3
Cockburn Ra. Australia 15°46S 128°0E 60 C4
Cockermouth U.K. 54°40N 3°22W 12 C4
Cockpit Country, The
  Jamaica 18°15N 77°45W 88 a
Coco → Cent. Amer. 15°0N 83°8W 88 D3
Coco, I. del Pac. Oc. 5°25N 87°55W 65 G19
Coco Channel Asia 13°45N 93°10E 45 H11
Cocoa U.S.A. 28°21N 80°44W 85 G14
Cocobeach Gabon 0°59N 9°34E 54 D1
Cocos B. Trin. & Tob. 10°24N 61°2W 93 K15
Cocos I. = Coco, I. del
  Pac. Oc. 5°25N 87°55W 65 G19
Cocos Is. Ind. Oc. 12°10S 96°55E 64 J1
Cocos Ridge Pac. Oc. 4°0N 88°0W 65 G19
Cod, C. U.S.A. 42°5N 70°10W 81 D18
Codajás Brazil 3°55S 62°0W 92 D6
Codó Brazil 4°30S 43°55W 93 D10
Cody U.S.A. 44°32N 109°3W 76 D9
Coe Hill Canada 44°52N 77°50W 82 B7
Coelemu Chile 36°30S 72°48W 94 D1
Coen Australia 13°52S 143°12E 62 A3
Coeur d'Alene U.S.A. 47°41N 116°46W 76 C5
Coeur d'Alene L. U.S.A. 47°32N 116°49W 76 C5
Coevorden Neths. 52°40N 6°44E 15 B6
Coffeyville U.S.A. 37°2N 95°37W 80 G6
Coffin B. Australia 34°38S 135°28E 63 E2
Coffin Bay Australia 34°37S 135°19E 63 E2
Coffin Bay △ Australia 34°34S 135°19E 63 E2
Coffin Bay Peninsula
  Australia 34°32S 135°15E 63 E2
Coffs Harbour Australia 30°16S 153°5E 63 E5
Cognac France 45°41N 0°20W 20 D3
Cohocton U.S.A. 42°30N 77°30W 82 D7
Cohocton → U.S.A. 42°9N 77°6W 82 D7
Cohoes U.S.A. 42°46N 73°42W 83 D11
Cohuna Australia 35°45S 144°15E 63 F3
Coiba, I. de Panama 7°30N 81°40W 88 E3
Coig → Argentina 51°0S 69°10W 96 G3
Coigach, Rubha U.K. 58°6N 5°26W 11 C3
Coihaique Chile 45°35S 72°8W 96 F2
Coimbatore India 11°2N 76°59E 45 J3
Coimbra Brazil 19°55S 57°48W 92 G7
Coimbra Portugal 40°15N 8°27W 21 B1
Coín Spain 36°40N 4°48W 21 D3
Coipasa, Salar de Bolivia 19°26S 68°9W 92 G5
Cojimies Ecuador 0°20N 80°0W 92 C3
Cojutepeque El Salv. 13°41N 88°54W 88 D2
Cokeville U.S.A. 42°5N 110°57W 76 E8
Colac Australia 38°21S 143°35E 63 F3
Colachel = Kolachel India 8°10N 77°15E 45 K3
Colatina Brazil 19°32S 40°37W 93 G10
Colbeck, C. Antarctica 77°6S 157°48W 5 D13
Colborne Canada 44°0N 77°53W 82 C7
Colby U.S.A. 39°24N 101°3W 80 F3
Colca → Peru 15°55S 72°43W 92 G4
Colchester U.K. 51°54N 0°55E 13 F8
Colchester U.S.A. 41°35N 72°20W 83 E12
Cold L. Canada 54°33N 110°5W 71 C7
Cold Lake Canada 54°27N 110°10W 71 C6
Coldstream Canada 50°13N 119°11W 70 C5
Coldstream U.K. 55°39N 2°15W 11 F6
Coldwater Kans., U.S.A. 37°16N 99°20W 80 G4
Coldwater Mich., U.S.A. 41°57N 85°0W 81 E11
Colebrook U.S.A. 44°54N 71°30W 83 B13
Coleman Canada 49°40N 114°30W 70 D6
Coleman U.S.A. 31°50N 99°26W 84 F5
Coleman → Australia 15°6S 141°38E 62 B3
Colenso S. Africa 28°44S 29°50E 57 D4
Coleraine Australia 37°36S 141°40E 63 F3
Coleraine U.K. 55°8N 6°41W 10 A5
Coleridge, L. N.Z. 43°17S 171°30E 59 E3
Coleroon → India 11°25N 79°50E 45 J4
Colesberg S. Africa 30°45S 25°5E 56 D4
Coleville U.S.A. 38°34N 119°30W 78 G7
Colfax Calif., U.S.A. 39°6N 120°57W 78 F6
Colfax La., U.S.A. 31°31N 92°42W 84 F8
Colfax Wash., U.S.A. 46°53N 117°22W 76 C5
Colhué Huapi, L.
  Argentina 45°30S 69°0W 96 F3
Coligny S. Africa 26°17S 26°15E 57 C4
Colima Mexico 19°14N 103°43W 86 D4
Colima □ Mexico 19°10N 104°0W 86 D4
Colima, Nevado de
  Mexico 19°33N 103°38W 86 D4
Colina Chile 33°13N 70°45W 94 C1
Colinas Brazil 6°0S 44°10W 93 E10
Coll U.K. 56°39N 6°34W 11 E2
Collahuasi Chile 21°5S 68°45W 94 A2
Collarenebri Australia 29°33S 148°34E 63 D4
College U.S.A. 64°52N 147°49W 74 C10
College Station U.S.A. 30°37N 96°21W 84 F6
Collie Australia 33°22S 116°8E 61 F2
Collier B. Australia 16°10S 124°15E 60 C3
Collier Ra. Australia 24°45S 119°10E 61 D2
Collier Range △ Australia 24°39S 119°7E 61 D2
Collierville U.S.A. 35°3N 89°40W 85 D10
Collina, Passo di Italy 44°2N 10°56E 22 B4
Collingwood Canada 44°29N 80°13W 82 B4
Collingwood N.Z. 40°41S 172°40E 59 D4
Collins Canada 50°17N 89°27W 72 B2
Collins Bay Canada 58°50N 103°34W 71 B8
Collinson Pen. Canada 69°58N 101°24W 68 D11

Collinsville Australia 20°30S 147°56E 62 C4
Collipulli Chile 37°55S 72°30W 94 D1
Collooney Ireland 54°11N 8°29W 10 B3
Colmar France 48°5N 7°20E 20 B7
Colo → Australia 33°25S 150°52E 63 E5
Cologne = Köln Germany 50°56N 6°57E 16 C4
Coloma U.S.A. 38°48N 120°53W 78 G6
Colomb-Béchar = Béchar
   Algeria 31°38N 2°18W 52 B5
Colombia ■ S. Amer. 3°45N 73°0W 92 C4
Colombian Basin Caribbean 14°0N 76°0W 88 D4
Colombo Sri Lanka 6°56N 79°58E 45 L4
Colón B. Aires, Argentina 33°53S 61°7W 94 C3
Colón Entre Rios.
   Argentina 32°12S 58°10W 94 C4
Colón Cuba 22°42N 80°54W 88 B3
Colón Panama 9°20N 79°54W 88 E4
Colón, Arch. de Ecuador 0°1'90W 90 D1
Colonia del Sacramento
   Uruguay 34°25S 57°50W 94 C4
Colonia Dora Argentina 28°34S 62°59W 94 B3
Colonial Beach U.S.A. 38°15N 76°58W 81 F15
Colonie U.S.A. 42°43N 73°50W 83 D11
Colonsay Canada 51°59N 105°52W 71 C7
Colonsay U.K. 56°5N 6°12W 11 E2
Colorado → Argentina 39°50S 62°8W 96 D4
Colorado □ U.S.A. 39°30N 105°30W 76 G11
Colorado → N. Amer. 31°45N 114°40W 77 L6
Colorado → U.S.A. 28°36N 95°59W 84 G7
Colorado City U.S.A. 32°24N 100°52W 84 E4
Colorado Plateau U.S.A. 37°0N 111°0W 77 H8
Colorado River Aqueduct
   U.S.A. 33°50N 117°23W 79 L12
Colorado Springs
   U.S.A. 38°50N 104°49W 76 G11
Colotlán Mexico 22°6N 103°16W 86 C4
Colstrip U.S.A. 45°53N 106°38W 76 D10
Colton U.S.A. 44°33N 74°56W 83 B10
Columbia Ky., U.S.A. 37°6N 85°18W 81 G11
Columbia La., U.S.A. 32°6N 92°5W 84 E8
Columbia Miss., U.S.A. 31°15N 89°50W 85 F10
Columbia Mo., U.S.A. 38°57N 92°20W 80 F7
Columbia Pa., U.S.A. 40°2N 76°30W 83 F8
Columbia S.C., U.S.A. 34°0N 81°2W 85 D11
Columbia Tenn., U.S.A. 35°37N 87°2W 85 D11
Columbia → N. Amer. 46°15N 124°5W 78 D2
Columbia, C. Canada 83°6N 69°57W 69 A18
Columbia, District of □
   U.S.A. 38°55N 77°0W 81 F15
Columbia, Mt. Canada 52°8N 117°20W 70 C5
Columbia Basin U.S.A. 46°45N 119°5W 76 C4
Columbia Falls U.S.A. 48°23N 114°11W 76 B6
Columbia Mts. Canada 52°0N 119°0W 70 C5
Columbia Plateau U.S.A. 44°0N 117°30W 76 E5
Columbiana U.S.A. 40°53N 80°42W 82 F4
Columbretes, Is. Spain 39°50N 0°50E 21 C6
Columbus Ga., U.S.A. 32°28N 84°59W 85 E12
Columbus Ind., U.S.A. 39°13N 85°55W 81 F11
Columbus Kans., U.S.A. 37°10N 94°50W 80 G6
Columbus Miss., U.S.A. 33°30N 88°25W 85 E10
Columbus Mont., U.S.A. 45°38N 109°15W 76 D9
Columbus N. Mex.,
   U.S.A. 31°50N 107°38W 77 L10
Columbus Nebr., U.S.A. 41°26N 97°22W 80 E5
Columbus Ohio, U.S.A. 39°58N 83°0W 81 F12
Columbus Tex., U.S.A. 29°42N 96°33W 84 G6
Colusa U.S.A. 39°13N 122°1W 78 F4
Colville U.S.A. 48°33N 117°54W 76 B5
Colville → U.S.A. 70°25N 150°30W 74 A9
Colville, C. N.Z. 36°29S 175°21E 59 B5
Colwood Canada 48°26N 123°29W 78 B3
Colwyn Bay U.K. 53°18N 3°44W 12 D4
Comácchio Italy 44°42N 12°11E 22 B5
Comalcalco Mexico 18°16N 93°13W 87 D6
Comallo Argentina 41°0S 70°5W 96 E2
Comanche U.S.A. 31°54N 98°36W 84 F5
Comandante Ferraz
   Antarctica 62°30S 58°0W 5 C18
Comayagua Honduras 14°25N 87°37W 88 D2
Combahee → U.S.A. 32°31N 80°31W 85 E14
Combarbalá Chile 31°11S 71°2W 94 C1
Combe Martin U.K. 51°12N 4°3W 13 F3
Comber Canada 42°14N 82°33W 82 D2
Comber U.K. 54°33N 5°45W 10 B6
Combermere Canada 45°22N 77°37W 82 A7
Comblain-au-Pont
   Belgium 50°29N 5°35E 15 D5
Comeragh Mts. Ireland 52°18N 7°34W 10 D4
Comet Australia 23°36S 148°38E 62 C4
Comilla Bangla. 23°28N 91°10E 41 H17
Comino, C. Italy 40°32N 9°49E 22 D3
Comitán de Domínguez
   Mexico 16°15N 92°8W 87 D6
Commerce Ga., U.S.A. 34°12N 83°28W 85 D13
Commerce Tex., U.S.A. 33°15N 95°54W 84 E7
Committee B. Canada 68°30N 86°30W 69 D14
Commodore, C. Canada 44°47N 80°54W 82 B4
Commonwealth B.
   Antarctica 67°0S 144°0E 5 C10
Commoron Cr. →
   Australia 28°22S 150°8E 63 D5
Communism Pk. = imeni Ismail
   Samani, Pik Tajikistan 39°0N 72°2E 26 F8
Como Italy 45°47N 9°5E 20 D8
Como, L. di Italy 46°0N 9°11E 20 D8
Comodoro Rivadavia
   Argentina 45°50S 67°40W 96 F3
Comorin, C. = Kannyakumari
   India 8°4N 77°40E 45 K3
Comoros ■ Ind. Oc. 12°10S 44°15E 55 a
Comox Canada 49°42N 124°55W 70 D4
Compiègne France 49°24N 2°50E 20 B5
Compostela Mexico 21°14N 104°55W 86 C4
Comprida, I. Brazil 24°50S 47°42W 95 A6
Compton Canada 45°14N 71°49W 83 A13
Compton U.S.A. 33°53N 118°13W 79 M8
Con Cuong Vietnam 19°2N 104°54E 38 C5
Con Dao △ Vietnam 8°42N 106°35E 39 H6
Con Son, Dao Vietnam 8°41N 106°37E 39 H6

Conakry Guinea 9°29N 13°49W 52 G3
Conara Australia 41°50S 147°26E 63 G4
Concarneau France 47°52N 3°56W 20 C2
Conceição da Barra
   Brazil 18°35S 39°45W 93 G11
Conceição do Araguaia
   Brazil 8°0S 49°2W 93 E9
Concepción Argentina 27°20S 65°35W 94 B2
Concepción Bolivia 16°15S 62°8W 92 G6
Concepción Chile 36°50S 73°0W 94 D1
Concepción Paraguay 23°22S 57°26W 94 A4
Concepción □ Chile 37°0S 72°30W 94 D1
Concepción, Est. de Chile 50°30S 74°55W 96 G2
Concepción, L. Bolivia 17°20S 61°20W 92 G6
Concepción, Pta.
   Mexico 26°53N 111°50W 86 B2
Concepción del Oro
   Mexico 24°38N 101°25W 86 C4
Concepción del Uruguay
   Argentina 32°35S 58°20W 94 C4
Conception, Pt. U.S.A. 34°27N 120°28W 79 L6
Conception B. Canada 47°45N 53°0W 73 C9
Conception B. Namibia 23°55S 14°22E 56 B1
Conception I. Bahamas 23°52N 75°9W 89 B4
Conchas Dam U.S.A. 35°22N 104°11W 77 J11
Concho U.S.A. 34°28N 109°36W 77 J9
Concho → U.S.A. 31°34N 99°43W 84 F5
Conchos → Chihuahua,
   Mexico 29°35N 104°25W 86 B4
Conchos → Tamaulipas,
   Mexico 24°55N 97°38W 87 B5
Concord Calif., U.S.A. 37°59N 122°2W 78 H4
Concord N.C., U.S.A. 35°25N 80°35W 85 D14
Concord N.H., U.S.A. 43°12N 71°32W 83 D13
Concordia Antarctica 75°6S 123°23E 5 D9
Concordia Argentina 31°20S 58°2W 94 C4
Concórdia Amazonas,
   Brazil 4°36S 66°36W 92 D5
Concórdia Sta. Catarina,
   Brazil 27°14S 52°1W 95 B5
Concordia Mexico 23°17N 106°4W 86 C3
Concordia U.S.A. 39°34N 97°40W 80 F5
Concrete U.S.A. 48°32N 121°45W 76 B3
Condamine Australia 26°56S 150°9E 63 D5
Conde U.S.A. 45°9N 98°6W 80 C4
Condeúba Brazil 14°52S 42°0W 93 F10
Condobolin Australia 33°4S 147°6E 63 E4
Condon U.S.A. 45°14N 120°11W 76 D3
Conegliano Italy 45°53N 12°18E 22 B5
Conejos Mexico 26°14N 103°53W 86 B4
Confuso → Paraguay 25°9S 57°34W 94 B4
Conghua China 23°36N 113°31E 35 F9
Congjiang China 25°43N 108°52E 34 E7
Congleton U.K. 53°10N 2°13W 12 D5
Congo (Brazzaville) = Congo ■
   Africa 1°0S 16°0E 54 E3
Congo (Kinshasa) = Congo, Dem.
   Rep. of the ■ Africa 3°0S 23°0E 54 E4
Congo ■ Africa 1°0S 16°0E 54 E3
Congo → Africa 6°4S 12°24E 54 F2
Congo, Dem. Rep. of the ■
   Africa 3°0S 23°0E 54 E4
Congo Basin Africa 0°10S 24°30E 54 E4
Congonhas Brazil 20°30S 43°52W 95 A7
Congress U.S.A. 34°9N 112°51W 77 J7
Coniston Canada 46°29N 80°51W 72 C3
Conjeeveram = Kanchipuram
   India 12°52N 79°45E 45 H4
Conklin Canada 55°38N 111°5W 71 B6
Conklin U.S.A. 42°2N 75°49W 83 D9
Conn, L. Ireland 54°3N 9°15W 10 B2
Connacht □ Ireland 53°43N 9°12W 10 C2
Conneaut U.S.A. 41°57N 80°34W 82 E4
Conneautville U.S.A. 41°45N 80°22W 82 E4
Connecticut □ U.S.A. 41°30N 72°45W 83 E12
Connecticut → U.S.A. 41°16N 72°20W 83 E12
Connell U.S.A. 46°40N 118°52W 76 C4
Connellsville U.S.A. 40°1N 79°35W 82 F5
Connemara Ireland 53°29N 9°45W 10 C2
Connemara △ Ireland 53°32N 9°52W 10 C2
Connersville U.S.A. 39°39N 85°8W 81 F11
Connors Ra. Australia 21°40S 149°10E 62 C4
Conquest Canada 51°32N 107°14W 71 C7
Conrad U.S.A. 48°10N 111°57W 76 B8
Conran, C. Australia 37°49S 148°44E 63 F4
Conroe U.S.A. 30°19N 95°27W 84 F7
Consecon Canada 44°0N 77°31W 82 C7
Conselheiro Lafaiete
   Brazil 20°40S 43°48W 95 A7
Conselheiro Pena
   Brazil 19°10S 41°30W 93 G10
Consett U.K. 54°51N 1°50W 12 C6
Consort Canada 52°1N 110°46W 71 C6
Constance = Konstanz
   Germany 47°40N 9°10E 16 E5
Constance, L. = Bodensee
   Europe 47°35N 9°25E 20 C8
Constanța Romania 44°14N 28°38E 17 F15
Constantine Algeria 36°25N 6°42E 52 A7
Constitución Chile 35°20S 72°30W 94 D1
Constitución Uruguay 31°0S 57°50W 94 C4
Constitución de 1857 △
   Mexico 32°4N 115°55W 86 A1
Consul Canada 49°20N 109°30W 71 D7
Contact U.S.A. 41°46N 114°45W 76 F6
Contai India 21°54N 87°46E 43 J12
Contamana Peru 7°19S 74°55W 92 E4
Contas → Brazil 14°17S 39°1W 93 F11
Contoocook U.S.A. 43°13N 71°45W 83 C13
Contra Costa Mozam. 25°9S 33°30E 57 C5
Contwoyto L. Canada 65°42N 110°50W 68 D9
Conway = Conwy U.K. 53°17N 3°50W 12 D4
Conway = Conwy →
   U.K. 53°17N 3°50W 12 D4
Conway Australia 20°24S 148°41E 62 b
Conway Canada 44°6N 76°54W 82 B5
Conway Ark., U.S.A. 35°5N 92°26W 84 D8
Conway N.H., U.S.A. 43°59N 71°7W 83 C13
Conway S.C., U.S.A. 33°51N 79°3W 85 E15
Conway, C. Australia 20°34S 148°46E 62 b

Conway, L. Australia 28°17S 135°35E 63 D2
Conway U.K. 53°17N 3°50W 12 D4
Conwy □ U.K. 53°10N 3°44W 12 D4
Conwy → U.K. 53°17N 3°50W 12 D4
Coober Pedy Australia 29°1S 134°43E 63 D1
Cooch Behar = Koch Bihar
   India 26°22N 89°29E 41 F16
Cooinda Australia 13°15S 130°5E 60 B5
Cook Australia 30°37S 130°25E 61 F5
Cook U.S.A. 47°51N 92°41W 80 B7
Cook, B. Chile 55°10S 70°0W 96 H3
Cook, C. Canada 50°8N 127°55W 70 C3
Cook, Mt. = Aoraki Mount Cook
   N.Z. 43°36S 170°9E 59 E3
Cook Inlet U.S.A. 60°0N 152°0W 68 F1
Cook Is. ☑ Pac. Oc. 17°0S 160°0W 65 J12
Cook Strait N.Z. 41°15S 174°29E 59 D5
Cookeville U.S.A. 36°10N 85°30W 85 C12
Cookhouse S. Africa 32°44S 25°47E 56 D4
Cooks Harbour Canada 51°36N 55°52W 73 B8
Cookshire Canada 45°25N 71°38W 83 A13
Cookstown Canada 44°11N 79°42W 82 B5
Cookstown U.K. 54°38N 6°45W 10 B5
Cooktown Australia 15°30S 145°16E 62 B4
Coolabah Australia 31°1S 146°43E 63 E4
Cooladdi Australia 26°37S 145°23E 63 D4
Coolah Australia 31°48S 149°41E 63 E4
Coolamon Australia 34°46S 147°8E 63 E4
Coolgardie Australia 30°55S 121°8E 61 F3
Coolidge U.S.A. 32°59N 111°31W 77 K8
Coolidge Dam U.S.A. 33°10N 110°32W 77 K8
Cooma Australia 36°12S 149°8E 63 F4
Coon Rapids U.S.A. 45°9N 93°19W 80 C7
Coonabarabran
   Australia 31°14S 149°18E 63 E4
Coonamble Australia 30°56S 148°27E 63 E4
Coonana Australia 31°0S 123°0E 61 F3
Coonana ۞ Australia 30°51S 122°53E 61 F3
Coondapoor India 13°42N 74°40E 45 H2
Cooninnie, L. Australia 26°4S 139°59E 63 D2
Coonoor India 11°21N 76°45E 45 J3
Cooper U.S.A. 33°23N 95°42W 84 E7
Cooper Cr. → Australia 28°29S 137°46E 63 D2
Cooper Ridge Pac. Oc. 10°0N 150°30W 65 G12
Cooperstown N. Dak.,
   U.S.A. 47°27N 98°8W 80 B4
Cooperstown N.Y.,
   U.S.A. 42°42N 74°56W 83 D10
Coorabie Australia 31°54S 132°18E 61 F5
Coorong, The Australia 35°50S 139°20E 63 F2
Coorow Australia 29°53S 116°2E 61 E2
Cooroy Australia 26°22S 152°54E 63 D5
Coos Bay U.S.A. 43°22N 124°13W 76 E1
Coosa → U.S.A. 32°30N 86°16W 85 E11
Cootamundra Australia 34°36S 148°1E 63 E4
Cootehill Ireland 54°4N 7°5W 10 B4
Copahue Paso Argentina 37°49S 71°8W 94 D1
Copainalá Mexico 17°4N 93°18W 87 D6
Copake U.S.A. 42°7N 73°31W 83 D11
Copán Honduras 14°50N 89°9W 88 D2
Cope U.S.A. 39°40N 102°51W 76 G12
Copenhagen U.S.A. 43°54N 75°41W 83 C9
Copiapó Chile 27°30S 70°20W 94 B1
Copiapó → Chile 27°19S 70°56W 94 B1
Copley Australia 30°33S 138°26E 63 E2
Copo △ Argentina 25°53S 61°41W 94 B3
Copp L. Canada 60°14N 114°40W 70 A6
Coppename → Suriname 5°48N 55°55W 93 B7
Copper Canyon = Barranca del
   Cobre ≏ Mexico 27°18N 107°40W 86 B3
Copper Center U.S.A. 61°58N 145°18W 74 C10
Copper Harbor U.S.A. 47°28N 87°53W 80 B10
Copperas Cove U.S.A. 31°8N 97°54W 84 F6
Coppermine = Kugluktuk
   Canada 67°50N 115°5W 68 D8
Coppermine → Canada 67°49N 116°4W 68 D8
Copperopolis U.S.A. 37°58N 120°38W 78 H6
Coquet → U.K. 55°20N 1°32W 12 B6
Coquille U.S.A. 43°11N 124°11W 76 E1
Coquimbo Chile 30°0S 71°20W 94 C1
Coquimbo □ Chile 31°0S 71°0W 94 C1
Coquitlam Canada 49°17N 122°45W 78 A4
Corabia Romania 43°48N 24°30E 17 G13
Coracora Peru 15°5S 73°45W 92 G4
Coraki Australia 28°59S 153°17E 63 D5
Coral U.S.A. 40°29N 79°10W 82 F5
Coral Bay Australia 23°8S 113°46E 60 D1
Coral Harbour Canada 64°8N 83°10W 69 E15
Coral Sea Pac. Oc. 15°0S 150°0E 58 C8
Coral Sea Basin Pac. Oc. 14°0S 152°0E 64 J7
Coral Sea Islands Terr. □
   Australia 20°0S 155°0E 58 C8
Coral Springs U.S.A. 26°16N 80°16W 85 H14
Corantijn = Courantyne →
   S. Amer. 5°50N 57°8W 92 B7
Coraopolis U.S.A. 40°31N 80°10W 82 F4
Corato Italy 41°9N 16°25E 22 D7
Corbett △ India 29°20N 79°0E 43 E8
Corbin U.S.A. 36°57N 84°6W 81 G11
Corby U.K. 52°30N 0°41W 13 E7
Corcaigh = Cork Ireland 51°54N 8°29W 10 E3
Corcoran U.S.A. 36°6N 119°33W 78 J7
Corcovado △ Costa Rica 8°33N 83°35W 88 E3
Corcubión Spain 42°56N 9°12W 21 A1
Cordele U.S.A. 31°58N 83°47W 85 F13
Cordell U.S.A. 35°17N 98°59W 84 D5
Córdoba Argentina 31°20S 64°10W 94 C3
Córdoba Mexico 18°53N 96°56W 87 D5
Córdoba Spain 37°50N 4°50W 21 D3
Córdoba □ Argentina 31°22S 64°15W 94 C3
Córdoba, Sierra de
   Argentina 31°10S 64°25W 94 C3
Cordova U.S.A. 60°33N 145°45W 74 C10
Corella → Australia 19°34S 140°47E 62 B3
Corentyne = Courantyne →
   S. Amer. 5°50N 57°8W 92 B7
Corfield Australia 21°40S 143°21E 62 C3
Corfu = Kerkyra Greece 39°38N 19°50E 23 E8
Corfu U.K. 42°57N 78°24W 82 D6
Coria Spain 39°58N 6°33W 21 C2

Corigliano Cálabro Italy 39°36N 16°31E 22 E7
Coringa Is. Australia 16°58S 149°58E 62 B4
Corinth = Korinthos
   Greece 37°56N 22°55E 23 F10
Corinth Miss., U.S.A. 34°56N 88°31W 85 D10
Corinth N.Y., U.S.A. 43°15N 73°49W 83 C11
Corinth, G. of = Korinthiakos
   Kolpos Greece 38°16N 22°30E 23 E10
Corinto Brazil 18°20S 44°30W 93 G10
Corinto Nic. 12°30N 87°10W 88 D2
Cork Ireland 51°54N 8°29W 10 E3
Cork □ Ireland 51°57N 8°40W 10 E3
Cork Harbour Ireland 51°47N 8°16W 10 E3
Çorlu Turkey 41°11N 27°49E 23 D12
Cormack L. Canada 60°56N 121°37W 70 A4
Cormorant Canada 54°14N 100°35W 71 C8
Cormorant L. Canada 54°15N 100°50W 71 C8
Corn Is. = Maíz, Is. del
   Nic. 12°15N 83°4W 88 D3
Cornélio Procópio Brazil 23°7S 50°40W 95 A5
Corner Brook Canada 48°57N 57°58W 73 C8
Corneşti Moldova 47°21N 28°1E 17 E15
Corning Ark., U.S.A. 36°25N 90°35W 85 C9
Corning Calif., U.S.A. 39°56N 122°11W 76 G2
Corning Iowa, U.S.A. 40°59N 94°44W 80 E6
Corning N.Y., U.S.A. 42°9N 77°3W 82 D7
Cornwall Canada 45°2N 74°44W 83 A10
Cornwall U.S.A. 40°17N 76°25W 83 F8
Cornwall □ U.K. 50°26N 4°40W 13 G3
Cornwall I. Canada 77°37N 94°38W 69 B13
Cornwallis I. Canada 75°8N 95°0W 69 B13
Corny Pt. Australia 34°55S 137°0E 63 E2
Coro Venezuela 11°25N 69°41W 92 A5
Coroatá Brazil 4°8S 44°0W 93 D10
Corocoro Bolivia 17°15S 68°28W 92 G5
Coroico Bolivia 16°0S 67°50W 92 G5
Coromandel N.Z. 36°45S 175°31E 59 B5
Coromandel Coast India 12°30N 81°0E 45 H5
Corona Calif., U.S.A. 33°53N 117°34W 79 M9
Corona N. Mex., U.S.A. 34°15N 105°36W 77 J11
Coronado U.S.A. 32°41N 117°10W 79 N9
Coronado, B. de Costa Rica 9°0N 83°40W 88 E3
Coronados, Is. Los
   Mexico 32°26N 117°19W 79 N9
Coronation Canada 52°5N 111°27W 70 C6
Coronation Gulf Canada 68°25N 110°0W 68 D10
Coronation I. Antarctica 60°45S 46°0W 5 C18
Coronation Is. Australia 14°57S 124°55E 60 B3
Coronda Argentina 31°58S 60°56W 94 C3
Coronel Chile 37°0S 73°10W 94 D1
Coronel Bogado
   Paraguay 27°11S 56°18W 94 B4
Coronel Dorrego
   Argentina 38°40S 61°10W 94 D3
Coronel Oviedo Paraguay 25°24S 56°30W 94 B4
Coronel Pringles
   Argentina 38°0S 61°30W 94 D3
Coronel Suárez Argentina 37°30S 61°52W 94 D3
Coronel Vidal Argentina 37°28S 57°45W 94 D4
Coropuna, Nevado Peru 15°30S 72°41W 92 G4
Corowa Australia 35°58S 146°21E 63 F4
Corozal □ Belize 18°23N 88°23W 87 D7
Corozal Pt. Trin. & Tob. 10°45N 61°37W 93 K15
Corpus Argentina 27°10S 55°30W 94 B4
Corpus Christi U.S.A. 27°47N 97°24W 84 H6
Corpus Christi, L. U.S.A. 28°2N 97°52W 84 G6
Corraun Pen. Ireland 53°54N 9°54W 10 C2
Correntes, C. das Mozam. 24°6S 35°34E 57 B6
Corrib, L. Ireland 53°27N 9°16W 10 C2
Corrientes Argentina 27°30S 58°45W 94 B4
Corrientes □ Argentina 28°0S 57°0W 94 B4
Corrientes → Argentina 30°42S 59°38W 94 C4
Corrientes → Peru 3°43S 74°35W 92 D4
Corrientes, C. Colombia 5°30N 77°34W 92 B3
Corrientes, C. Cuba 21°43N 84°30W 88 B3
Corrientes, C. Mexico 20°25N 105°42W 86 C3
Corrigan U.S.A. 31°0N 94°52W 84 F7
Corrigin Australia 32°20S 117°53E 61 F2
Corriverton Guyana 5°55N 57°20W 92 B7
Corry U.S.A. 41°55N 79°39W 82 E5
Corse □ France 42°0N 9°0E 20 F8
Corse, C. France 43°1N 9°25E 20 E8
Corsica = Corse □ France 42°0N 9°0E 20 F8
Corsicana U.S.A. 32°6N 96°28W 84 E6
Corte France 42°19N 9°11E 20 E8
Cortés, Mar de = California, G. de
   Mexico 27°0N 111°0W 86 B2
Cortez U.S.A. 37°21N 108°35W 77 H9
Córthaidh, Inis = Enniscorthy
   Ireland 52°30N 6°34W 10 D5
Cortland N.Y., U.S.A. 42°36N 76°11W 83 D8
Cortland Ohio, U.S.A. 41°20N 80°44W 82 E4
Çorum Turkey 40°30N 34°57E 19 F5
Corumbá Brazil 19°0S 57°30W 92 G7
Corunna = A Coruña
   Spain 43°20N 8°25W 21 A1
Corvallis U.S.A. 44°34N 123°16W 76 D2
Corvette, L. de la Canada 53°25N 74°3W 72 B5
Corvo Azores 39°43N 31°8W 52 a
Corydon U.S.A. 40°46N 93°19W 80 E7
Cosalá Mexico 24°23N 106°41W 86 C3
Cosamaloapan de Carpio
   Mexico 18°22N 95°48W 87 D5
Cosenza Italy 39°18N 16°15E 22 E7
Coshocton U.S.A. 40°16N 81°51W 82 F3
Cosmo Newberry
   Australia 28°0S 122°54E 61 E3
Cosmo Newberry ۞
   Australia 27°59S 122°53E 61 E3
Cosmonaut Sea S. Ocean 66°30S 40°0E 5 C5
Coso Junction U.S.A. 36°3N 117°57W 79 J9
Coso Pk. U.S.A. 36°13N 117°44W 79 J9
Cosquín Argentina 31°15S 64°30W 94 C3
Costa de la Luz Spain 36°15N 5°58W 21 D2
Costa del Azahar Spain 39°39N 0°13E 21 B6
Costa Mesa U.S.A. 33°38N 117°55W 79 M9
Costa Rica ■ Cent. Amer. 10°0N 84°0W 88 E3
Costa Verde Spain 43°25N 5°30W 21 A3
Cosumnes → U.S.A. 38°16N 121°26W 78 G5
Cotabato Phil. 7°14N 124°15E 37 C6

Cotagaita Bolivia 20°45S 65°40W 94 A2
Côte-d'Ivoire = Ivory Coast ■
   Africa 7°30N 5°0W 52 G4
Coteau des Prairies
   U.S.A. 45°20N 97°50W 80 C5
Coteau du Missouri
   U.S.A. 47°0N 100°0W 80 B4
Cotentin France 49°15N 1°30W 20 B3
Cotonou Benin 6°20N 2°25E 52 G6
Cotopaxi Ecuador 0°40S 78°30W 92 D3
Cotswold Hills U.K. 51°42N 2°10W 13 F5
Cottage Grove U.S.A. 43°48N 123°3W 76 E2
Cottam Canada 42°8N 82°45W 82 D2
Cottbus Germany 51°45N 14°20E 16 C8
Cottingham U.K. 53°48N 0°25W 12 D7
Cottonwood U.S.A. 34°45N 112°1W 77 J7
Cotulla U.S.A. 28°26N 99°14W 84 G5
Coudersport U.S.A. 41°46N 78°1W 82 E6
Couedic, C. du Australia 36°5S 136°40E 63 F2
Coulee City U.S.A. 47°37N 119°17W 76 C4
Coulee Dam Nat. Recr. Area =
   Lake Roosevelt ≏
   U.S.A. 48°5N 118°14W 76 B4
Coulman I. Antarctica 73°35S 170°0E 5 D11
Coulonge → Canada 45°52N 76°46W 72 C4
Coulterville U.S.A. 37°43N 120°12W 78 H6
Council Alaska, U.S.A. 64°53N 163°41W 74 C7
Council Idaho, U.S.A. 44°44N 116°26W 76 D5
Council Bluffs U.S.A. 41°16N 95°52W 80 E6
Council Grove U.S.A. 38°40N 96°29W 80 F5
Coupeville U.S.A. 48°13N 122°41W 78 B4
Courantyne → S. Amer. 5°50N 57°8W 92 B7
Courcelles Belgium 50°28N 4°22E 15 D4
Courtenay Canada 49°45N 125°0W 70 D4
Courtland Canada 42°51N 80°38W 82 D4
Courtland U.S.A. 38°20N 121°34W 78 G5
Courtrai = Kortrijk
   Belgium 50°50N 3°17E 15 D3
Courtright Canada 42°49N 82°28W 82 D2
Coushatta U.S.A. 32°1N 93°21W 84 E8
Coutts Crossing
   Australia 29°49S 152°55E 63 D5
Couva Trin. & Tob. 10°25N 61°27W 93 K15
Couvin Belgium 50°3N 4°29E 15 D4
Cove I. Canada 45°17N 81°44W 82 A3
Coventry U.K. 52°25N 1°28W 13 E6
Covilhã Portugal 40°17N 7°31W 21 B2
Covington Ga., U.S.A. 33°36N 83°51W 85 E13
Covington Ky., U.S.A. 39°5N 84°30W 81 F11
Covington Tenn., U.S.A. 35°34N 89°39W 85 D10
Covington Va., U.S.A. 37°47N 79°59W 81 G14
Cowal, L. Australia 33°40S 147°25E 63 E4
Cowan, L. Australia 31°45S 121°45E 61 F3
Cowan L. Canada 54°0N 107°15W 71 C7
Cowangie Australia 35°12S 141°26E 63 F3
Cowansville Canada 45°14N 72°46W 83 A12
Coward Springs
   Australia 29°24S 136°49E 63 D2
Cowcowing Lakes
   Australia 30°55S 117°20E 61 F2
Cowdenbeath U.K. 56°7N 3°21W 11 E5
Cowell Australia 33°39S 136°56E 63 E2
Cowes U.K. 50°45N 1°18W 13 G6
Cowichan L. Canada 48°53N 124°17W 78 B2
Cowlitz → U.S.A. 46°6N 122°55W 78 D4
Cowra Australia 33°49S 148°42E 63 E4
Coxilha Grande Brazil 28°18S 51°30W 95 B5
Coxim Brazil 18°30S 54°55W 93 G8
Cox's Bazar Bangla. 21°26N 91°59E 41 J17
Coyote Wells U.S.A. 32°44N 115°58W 79 N11
Coyuca de Benítez Mexico 17°2N 100°4W 87 D4
Coyuca de Catalán
   Mexico 18°20N 100°39W 86 D4
Cozad U.S.A. 40°52N 99°59W 80 E4
Cozumel Mexico 20°31N 86°55W 87 C7
Cozumel, Isla Mexico 20°30N 86°40W 87 C7
Crab Hill Barbados 13°19N 59°38W 89 g
Cracow = Kraków
   Poland 50°4N 19°57E 17 C10
Cracow Australia 25°17S 150°17E 63 D5
Cradle Mt.-Lake St. Clair △
   Australia 41°49S 147°56E 63 G4
Cradock Australia 32°6S 138°31E 63 E2
Cradock S. Africa 32°8S 25°36E 56 D4
Craig U.S.A. 40°31N 107°33W 76 F10
Craigavon U.K. 54°27N 6°23W 10 B5
Craik Canada 51°3N 105°49W 71 C7
Crailsheim Germany 49°8N 10°5E 16 D6
Craiova Romania 44°21N 23°48E 17 F12
Cramsie Australia 23°20S 144°15E 62 C3
Cranberry L. U.S.A. 44°11N 74°50W 83 B10
Cranberry Portage
   Canada 54°35N 101°23W 71 C8
Cranbrook Australia 34°18S 117°33E 61 F2
Cranbrook Canada 49°30N 115°46W 70 D5
Crandon U.S.A. 45°34N 88°54W 80 C9
Crane Oreg., U.S.A. 43°25N 118°35W 76 E4
Crane Tex., U.S.A. 31°24N 102°21W 84 F3
Crane, The Barbados 13°6N 59°27W 89 g
Cranganore India 10°13N 76°13E 45 J3
Cranston U.S.A. 41°47N 71°26W 83 E13
Crater L. U.S.A. 42°56N 122°6W 76 E2
Crater Lake △ U.S.A. 42°55N 122°10W 76 E2
Craters of the Moon ≏
   U.S.A. 43°25N 113°30W 76 E7
Crateús Brazil 5°10S 40°39W 93 E10
Crato Brazil 7°10S 39°25W 93 E11
Craven, L. Canada 54°20N 76°56W 72 B4
Crawford U.S.A. 42°41N 103°25W 80 D2
Crawfordsville U.S.A. 40°2N 86°54W 80 E10
Crawley U.K. 51°7N 0°11W 13 F7
Crazy Mts. U.S.A. 46°12N 110°20W 76 C8
Crean L. Canada 54°5N 106°9W 71 C7
Crediton Canada 43°17N 81°33W 82 C3
Crediton U.K. 50°47N 3°40W 13 G4
Cree → Canada 58°57N 105°47W 71 B7
Cree → U.K. 54°55N 4°25W 11 G4
Cree L. Canada 57°30N 106°30W 71 B7
Creede U.S.A. 37°51N 106°56W 77 H10
Creekside U.S.A. 40°40N 79°11W 82 F5

Creel Mexico 27°45N 107°38W 86 B3
Creemore Canada 44°19N 80°6W 82 B4
Creighton Canada 54°45N 101°54W 71 C8
Creighton U.S.A. 42°28N 97°54W 80 D5
Crema Italy 45°22N 9°41E 20 D8
Cremona Italy 45°7N 10°2E 20 D9
Cres Croatia 44°58N 14°25E 16 F8
Crescent City U.S.A. 41°45N 124°12W 76 F1
Crescent Group
  S. China Sea 16°30N 111°40E 36 A4
Crespo Argentina 32°2S 60°19W 94 C3
Cresson U.S.A. 40°28N 78°36W 82 F6
Crestline Calif., U.S.A. 34°14N 117°18W 79 L9
Crestline Ohio, U.S.A. 40°47N 82°44W 82 F2
Creston Canada 49°10N 116°31W 70 D5
Creston Calif., U.S.A. 35°32N 120°33W 78 K6
Creston Iowa, U.S.A. 41°4N 94°22W 80 E6
Crestview Calif., U.S.A. 37°46N 118°58W 78 H8
Crestview Fla., U.S.A. 30°46N 86°34W 85 F11
Crete = Kriti Greece 35°15N 25°0E 23 G11
Crete U.S.A. 40°38N 96°58W 80 E5
Creus, C. de Spain 42°20N 3°19E 21 A7
Creuse → France 47°0N 0°34E 20 C4
Crewe U.K. 53°6N 2°26W 12 D5
Crewkerne U.K. 50°53N 2°48W 13 G5
Crianlarich U.K. 56°24N 4°37W 11 E4
Criciúma Brazil 28°40S 49°23W 95 B6
Crieff U.K. 56°22N 3°50W 11 E5
Crimea □ Ukraine 45°30N 33°10E 19 E5
Crimean Pen. = Krymskyy
  Pivostriv Ukraine 45°0N 34°0E 19 F5
Crişul Alb → Romania 46°42N 21°17E 17 E11
Crişul Negru →
  Romania 46°42N 21°16E 17 E11
Crna → Macedonia 41°33N 21°59E 23 D9
Crna Gora = Montenegro ■
  Europe 42°40N 19°20E 23 C8
Crna Gora Macedonia 42°10N 21°30E 23 C9
Crna Reka = Crna →
  Macedonia 41°33N 21°59E 23 D9
Croagh Patrick Ireland 53°46N 9°40W 10 C2
Croatia ■ Europe 45°20N 16°0E 16 F9
Crocker, Banjaran
  Malaysia 5°40N 116°30E 36 C5
Crockett U.S.A. 31°19N 95°27W 84 F7
Crocodile = Umgwenya →
  Mozam. 25°14S 32°18E 57 C5
Crocodile → S. Africa 24°12S 26°53E 56 B4
Crocodile Is. Australia 12°3S 134°58E 62 A1
Crohy Hd. Ireland 54°55N 8°26W 10 B3
Croix, L. la Canada 48°20N 92°15W 72 C1
Croker, C. Australia 10°58S 132°35E 60 B5
Croker, C. Canada 44°58N 80°59W 82 B4
Croker I. Australia 11°12S 132°32E 60 B5
Croker Islands Seas ○
  Australia 11°20S 132°30E 60 B5
Cromarty U.K. 57°40N 4°2W 11 D4
Cromer U.K. 52°56N 1°17E 12 E9
Cromwell N.Z. 45°3S 169°14E 59 F2
Cromwell U.S.A. 41°36N 72°39W 83 E12
Crook U.K. 54°43N 1°45W 12 C6
Crooked → Canada 54°50N 122°54W 70 C4
Crooked → U.S.A. 44°32N 121°16W 76 D3
Crooked I. Bahamas 22°50N 74°10W 89 B5
Crooked Island Passage
  Bahamas 22°55N 74°35W 89 B5
Crookston Minn., U.S.A. 47°47N 96°37W 80 B5
Crookston Nebr., U.S.A. 42°56N 100°45W 80 D3
Crookwell Australia 34°28S 149°24E 63 E4
Crosby U.K. 53°30N 3°3W 12 D4
Crosby N. Dak., U.S.A. 48°55N 103°18W 80 A2
Crosby Pa., U.S.A. 41°45N 78°23W 82 E6
Crosbyton U.S.A. 33°40N 101°14W 84 E4
Cross City U.S.A. 29°38N 83°7W 85 G13
Cross Fell U.K. 54°43N 2°28W 12 C5
Cross L. Canada 54°45N 97°30W 71 C9
Cross Lake Canada 54°37N 97°47W 71 C9
Cross Sound U.S.A. 58°0N 135°0W 68 F4
Crossett U.S.A. 33°8N 91°58W 84 E9
Crosshaven Ireland 51°47N 8°17W 10 E3
Crossmaglen U.K. 54°5N 6°36W 10 B5
Crossmolina Ireland 54°6N 9°20W 10 B2
Crossville U.S.A. 35°57N 85°2W 85 D12
Croswell U.S.A. 43°16N 82°37W 82 C2
Croton-on-Hudson
  U.S.A. 41°12N 73°55W 83 E11
Crotone Italy 39°5N 17°8E 22 E7
Crow → Canada 59°41N 124°20W 70 B4
Crow Agency U.S.A. 45°36N 107°28W 76 D10
Crow Hd. Ireland 51°35N 10°9W 10 E1
Crowell U.S.A. 33°59N 99°43W 84 E5
Crowley U.S.A. 30°13N 92°22W 84 F8
Crowley, L. U.S.A. 37°35N 118°42W 78 H8
Crown Point Ind., U.S.A. 41°25N 87°22W 80 E10
Crown Point N.Y.,
  U.S.A. 43°57N 73°26W 83 C11
Crown Pt. Trin. & Tob. 11°18N 60°51W 93 J16
Crownpoint U.S.A. 35°41N 108°9W 77 J9
Crows Landing U.S.A. 37°23N 121°6W 78 H5
Crows Nest Australia 27°16S 152°4E 63 D5
Croydon Australia 18°13S 142°14E 62 B3
Croydon □ U.K. 51°22N 0°5W 13 F7
Crozet, Îs. Ind. Oc. 46°27S 52°0E 3 G12
Crushen Ireland 52°57N 8°53W 10 D3
Cruz, C. Cuba 19°50N 77°50W 88 C4
Cruz Alta Brazil 28°45S 53°40W 95 B5
Cruz Bay U.S. Virgin Is. 18°20N 64°48W 89 e
Cruz del Eje Argentina 30°45S 64°50W 94 C3
Cruzeiro Brazil 22°33S 45°0W 95 A7
Cruzeiro do Oeste Brazil 23°46S 53°4W 95 A5
Cruzeiro do Sul Brazil 7°35S 72°35W 92 E4
Cry L. Canada 58°45N 129°0W 70 B3
Crystal Bay U.S.A. 39°15N 120°0W 78 F7
Crystal Brook Australia 33°21S 138°12E 63 E2
Crystal City U.S.A. 28°41N 99°50W 84 G5
Crystal Falls U.S.A. 46°5N 88°20W 80 B9
Crystal River U.S.A. 28°54N 82°35W 85 G13
Crystal Springs U.S.A. 31°59N 90°21W 85 F9
Csongrád Hungary 46°43N 20°12E 17 E11

Cu Lao Hon Vietnam 10°54N 108°18E 39 G7
Cua Rao Vietnam 19°16N 104°27E 38 C5
Cuamato Angola 17°2S 15°7E 56 A2
Cuamba Mozam. 14°45S 36°22E 55 G7
Cuando → Angola 17°30S 23°15E 55 H4
Cuando Cubango □
  Angola 16°25S 20°0E 56 B3
Cuangar Angola 17°36S 18°39E 56 A2
Cuango = Kwango →
  Dem. Rep. of the Congo 3°14S 17°22E 54 E3
Cuanza → Angola 9°21S 13°9E 54 F2
Cuarto → Argentina 33°25S 63°2W 94 C3
Cuatrociénegas Mexico 26°59N 102°5W 86 B4
Cuba N. Mex., U.S.A. 36°1N 107°4W 77 H10
Cuba N.Y., U.S.A. 42°13N 78°17W 82 D6
Cuba ■ W. Indies 22°0N 79°0W 88 B4
Cubango → Africa 18°50S 22°25E 56 B3
Cuc Phuong △ Vietnam 20°17N 105°38E 38 B5
Cuchumatanes, Sierra de los
  Guatemala 15°35N 91°25W 88 C1
Cuckfield U.K. 51°1N 0°8W 13 F7
Cucuí Brazil 1°12N 66°50W 92 C5
Cucurpé Mexico 30°20N 110°43W 86 A2
Cúcuta Colombia 7°54N 72°31W 92 B4
Cuddalore India 11°46N 79°45E 45 J4
Cuddapah = Kadapa
  India 14°30N 78°47E 45 G4
Cuddapan, L. Australia 25°45S 141°26E 62 D3
Cue Australia 27°25S 117°54E 61 E2
Cuenca Ecuador 2°50S 79°9W 92 D3
Cuenca Spain 40°5N 2°10W 21 B4
Cuenca, Serranía de Spain 39°55N 1°50W 21 C5
Cuernavaca Mexico 18°55N 99°15W 87 D5
Cuero U.S.A. 29°6N 97°17W 84 G6
Cueva de la Quebrada del Toro △
  Venezuela 10°46N 69°3W 89 D6
Cuevas del Almanzora
  Spain 37°18N 1°58W 21 D5
Cuevo Bolivia 20°15S 63°30W 92 H6
Cuiabá Brazil 15°30S 56°0W 93 G7
Cuiabá → Brazil 17°5S 56°36W 93 G7
Cuihangcun China 22°27N 113°32E 31 a
Cuijk Neths. 51°44N 5°50E 15 C5
Cuilco Guatemala 15°24N 91°58W 88 C1
Cuillin Hills U.K. 57°13N 6°15W 11 D2
Cuillin Sd. U.K. 57°4N 6°20W 11 D2
Cuilo = Kwilu →
  Dem. Rep. of the Congo 3°22S 17°22E 54 E3
Cuito → Angola 18°1S 20°48E 56 A3
Cuitzeo, L. de Mexico 19°55N 101°5W 86 D4
Cukai Malaysia 4°13N 103°25E 39 K4
Culbertson U.S.A. 48°9N 104°31W 76 B11
Culcairn Australia 35°41S 147°3E 63 F4
Culebra Puerto Rico 18°19N 65°18W 89 d
Culgoa → Australia 29°56S 146°20E 63 D4
Culgoa Flood Plain △
  Australia 28°58S 147°5E 63 D4
Culiacán Mexico 24°50N 107°23W 86 C3
Culiacán → Mexico 24°30N 107°42W 86 C3
Culik Indonesia 8°21S 115°37E 37 J18
Culion Phil. 11°54N 119°58E 37 B6
Cullarin Ra. Australia 34°30S 149°30E 63 E4
Cullen U.K. 57°42N 2°49W 11 D6
Cullen Pt. Australia 11°57S 141°54E 62 A3
Cullera Spain 39°9N 0°17W 21 C5
Cullman U.S.A. 34°11N 86°51W 85 D11
Cullompton U.K. 50°51N 3°24W 13 G4
Culpeper U.S.A. 38°30N 78°0W 81 F14
Culuene → Brazil 12°56S 52°51W 93 F8
Culver, Pt. Australia 32°54S 124°43E 61 F3
Culverden N.Z. 42°47S 172°49E 59 E4
Cumaná Venezuela 10°30N 64°5W 92 A6
Cumberland B.C., Canada 49°40N 125°0W 70 D4
Cumberland Ont., Canada 45°29N 75°24W 83 A9
Cumberland Wis., U.S.A. 45°30N 91°30W 80 C8
Cumberland → U.S.A. 37°9N 88°25W 80 G9
Cumberland, L. U.S.A. 36°52N 85°9W 81 G11
Cumberland Gap
  U.S.A. 36°36N 83°40W 81 G12
Cumberland I. U.S.A. 30°50N 81°25W 85 F14
Cumberland Is. Australia 20°35S 149°10E 62 b
Cumberland Island ○
  U.S.A. 30°12N 81°24W 85 F14
Cumberland L. Canada 54°3N 102°18W 71 C8
Cumberland Pen. Canada 67°0N 64°0W 69 D13
Cumberland Plateau
  U.S.A. 36°0N 85°0W 85 D12
Cumberland Sd. Canada 65°30N 66°0W 69 D13
Cumbernauld U.K. 55°57N 3°58W 11 F5
Cumborah Australia 29°40S 147°45E 63 D4
Cumbres de Majalca △
  Mexico 28°48N 106°30W 86 B3
Cumbres de Monterrey △
  Mexico 25°26N 100°25W 86 B4
Cumbria □ U.K. 54°42N 2°52W 12 C5
Cumbrian Mts. U.K. 54°30N 3°0W 12 C5
Cumbum India 15°40N 79°10E 45 G4
Cuminá → Brazil 1°30S 56°0W 93 D7
Cummings Mt. U.S.A. 35°2N 118°34W 79 K8
Cummins Australia 34°16S 135°43E 63 E2
Cumnock Australia 32°59S 148°46E 63 E4
Cumnock U.K. 55°28N 4°17W 11 F4
Cumpas Mexico 30°2N 109°48W 86 B3
Cunco Chile 38°55S 72°2W 94 D1
Cuncumén Chile 31°53S 70°38W 94 C1
Cundeelee ○ Australia 30°43S 123°25E 61 F3
Cunderdin Australia 31°37S 117°12E 61 F2
Cunene → Angola 17°20S 11°50E 56 A1
Cúneo Italy 44°23N 7°32E 20 D7
Cung Son Vietnam 13°2N 108°58E 38 F7
Çüngüş Turkey 38°13N 39°17E 46 B3
Cunnamulla Australia 28°2S 145°38E 63 D4
Cupar Canada 50°57N 104°10W 71 C8
Cupar U.K. 56°19N 3°1W 11 E5
Cupertino U.S.A. 37°19N 122°2W 78 H4
Cupica, G. de Colombia 6°25N 77°30W 92 B3
Curaçao ○ W. Indies 12°10N 69°0W 89 D6
Curanilahue Chile 37°29S 73°28W 94 D1
Curaray → Peru 2°20S 74°5W 92 D4

Curepipe Mauritius 20°19S 57°31E 55 d
Curepto Chile 35°8S 72°1W 94 D1
Curiapo Venezuela 8°33N 61°5W 92 B6
Curicó Chile 34°55S 71°20W 94 C1
Curieuse Seychelles 4°15S 55°44E 55 h
Curitiba Brazil 25°20S 49°10W 95 B6
Curitibanos Brazil 27°18S 50°36W 95 B5
Curonian Lagoon = Kurshskiy
  Zaliv Russia 55°9N 21°6E 9 J19
Currabubula Australia 31°16S 150°44E 63 E5
Currais Novos Brazil 6°13S 36°30W 93 E11
Curral Velho C. Verde Is. 16°8N 22°48W 52 b
Curralinho Brazil 1°45S 49°46W 93 D9
Currane, L. Ireland 51°49N 10°4W 10 E1
Currant → U.S.A. 36°50N 43°1E 46 B3
Currawinya △ Australia 28°55S 144°27E 63 D3
Current → U.S.A. 36°15N 90°55W 84 C9
Currie Australia 39°56S 143°53E 63 F3
Currie U.S.A. 40°16N 114°45W 76 F6
Curtea de Argeş
  Romania 45°12N 24°42E 17 F13
Curtin Springs Australia 25°20S 131°45E 61 E5
Curtis U.S.A. 40°38N 100°31W 80 E3
Curtis Group Australia 39°35S 146°37E 63 F4
Curtis I. Australia 23°35S 151°10E 62 C5
Curuápanema → Brazil 2°25S 55°2W 93 D7
Curuçá Brazil 0°43S 47°50W 93 D9
Curuguaty Paraguay 24°31S 55°42W 95 A4
Çürüksu Çayı = Büyük
  Menderes → Turkey 37°28N 27°11E 23 F12
Curup Indonesia 3°26S 102°13E 36 E2
Cururupu Brazil 1°50S 44°50W 93 D10
Curuzú Cuatiá Argentina 29°50S 58°5W 94 B4
Curvelo Brazil 18°45S 44°27W 93 G10
Cushendall U.K. 55°5N 6°4W 10 A5
Cushing U.S.A. 35°59N 96°46W 84 D6
Cushing, Mt. Canada 57°35N 126°57W 70 B3
Cusihuiriáchic Mexico 28°14N 106°50W 86 B3
Custer U.S.A. 43°46N 103°36W 80 D2
Cut Bank U.S.A. 48°38N 112°20W 76 B7
Cut Nhe Vietnam 15°28N 107°48E 38 E6
Cuthbert U.S.A. 31°46N 84°48W 85 F12
Cutler U.S.A. 36°31N 119°17W 78 J7
Cuttaburra → Australia 29°43S 144°22E 63 D3
Cuttack India 20°25N 85°57E 44 D7
Cuvier, C. Australia 23°14S 113°22E 61 D1
Cuvier I. N.Z. 36°27S 175°50E 59 B5
Cuxhaven Germany 53°51N 8°41E 16 B5
Cuyahoga Falls U.S.A. 41°8N 81°29W 82 E3
Cuyahoga Valley △
  U.S.A. 41°24N 81°33W 82 E3
Cuyo Phil. 10°51N 121°2E 37 B6
Cuyuni → Guyana 6°23N 58°41W 92 B7
Cuzco = Cusco Peru 13°32S 72°0W 92 F4
Cuzco Bolivia 20°0S 66°50W 92 H5
Cwmbran U.K. 51°39N 3°2W 13 F4
Cyclades = Kyklades
  Greece 37°0N 24°30E 23 F11
Cygnet Australia 43°8S 147°1E 63 G4
Cynthiana U.S.A. 38°23N 84°18W 81 F11
Cypress Hills Canada 49°40N 109°30W 71 D7
Cypress Hills △ Canada 49°40N 109°30W 71 D7
Cyprus ■ Asia 35°0N 33°0E 46 C2
Cyrenaica = Barqa Libya 25°0N 22°0E 53 C10
Cyrene Libya 32°53N 21°52E 53 B10
Czar Canada 52°27N 110°50W 71 C6
Czech Rep. ■ Europe 50°0N 15°0E 16 D8
Częstochowa Poland 50°49N 19°7E 17 C10

D

Da → Vietnam 21°15N 105°20E 34 G5
Da Hinggan Ling China 48°0N 121°0E 31 B13
Da Lat Vietnam 11°56N 108°25E 39 G7
Da Nang Vietnam 16°4N 108°13E 38 D7
Da Qaidam China 37°50N 95°15E 30 D8
Da Yunhe → Hopei,
  China 39°10N 117°10E 33 E9
Da Yunhe → Jiangsu,
  China 34°25N 120°5E 33 H10
Da'an China 45°30N 124°7E 33 B13
Daan Viljoen △ Namibia 22°2S 16°45E 56 B2
Daba Shan China 32°0N 109°0E 34 B7
Dabbagh, Jabal Si. Arabia 27°52N 35°45E 46 E2
Dabhoi India 22°10N 73°20E 42 H5
Dabie Shan China 31°20N 115°20E 35 B10
Dabola Guinea 10°50N 11°5W 52 F3
Dabu China 24°22N 116°41E 35 E11
Dabung Malaysia 5°23N 102°1E 39 K4
Dacca = Dhaka Bangla. 23°43N 90°26E 43 H14
Dachang China 38°44N 115°29E 34 E8
Dachaoshan Dam China 24°11N 100°22E 34 E3
Dachigam △ India 34°10N 75°0E 42 B6
Dacre Canada 45°22N 76°57W 82 A8
Dadanawa Guyana 2°50N 59°30W 92 C7
Dade City U.S.A. 28°22N 82°11W 85 G13
Dadhar Pakistan 29°28N 67°39E 42 E2
Dadnah U.A.E. 25°32N 56°22E 47 E8
Dadra & Nagar Haveli □
  India 20°5N 73°0E 44 D1
Dadri = Charkhi Dadri
  India 28°37N 76°17E 42 E7
Dadu Pakistan 26°45N 67°45E 42 F2
Dadu He → China 29°31N 103°46E 34 C4
Daegu S. Korea 35°50N 128°37E 33 G15
Daejeon S. Korea 36°20N 127°28E 33 F14
Daejeong S. Korea 33°8N 126°17E 33 H14
Daet Phil. 14°2N 122°55E 37 B6
Dafang China 27°9N 105°39E 34 D5
Dafeng China 33°3N 120°45E 33 H11
Dagana Senegal 16°30N 15°35W 52 E2
Dagestan □ Russia 42°30N 47°0E 19 F8
Daggett U.S.A. 34°52N 116°52W 79 L10
Daghestan Republic = Dagestan □
  Russia 42°30N 47°0E 19 F8
Dağlıq Qarabağ = Nagorno-
  Karabakh ◇ Azerbaijan 39°55N 46°45E 46 B5
Dagö = Hiiumaa Estonia 58°50N 22°45E 9 G20

Dagu China 38°59N 117°40E 33 E9
Daguan China 27°43N 103°56E 34 D4
Dagupan Phil. 16°3N 120°20E 37 A6
Daguragu Australia 17°33S 130°30E 60 C5
Daguragu ○ Australia 17°24S 130°48E 60 C5
Dahab Egypt 28°31N 34°31E 46 D2
Dahanu India 19°58N 72°44E 44 E1
Dahlak Kebir Eritrea 15°50N 40°10E 49 D3
Dahlonega U.S.A. 34°32N 83°59W 85 D13
Dahod India 22°50N 74°15E 42 H6
Dahong Shan China 31°25N 113°0E 35 B9
Dahongliutan China 35°45N 79°20E 43 B8
Dahra Libya 29°30N 17°50E 53 C9
Dahük Iraq 36°50N 43°1E 46 B3
Dai Hao Vietnam 18°1N 106°25E 38 C6
Dai-Sen Japan 35°22N 133°32E 29 G6
Dai Shan China 30°25N 122°10E 33 E7
Dai Xian China 39°4N 112°58E 32 E7
Daicheng China 38°42N 116°38E 32 E9
Daingean Ireland 53°18N 7°17W 10 C4
Daingean, An = Dingle
  Ireland 52°9N 10°17W 10 D1
Dainkog China 32°30N 97°58E 34 A1
Daintree Australia 16°20S 145°20E 62 B4
Daintree △ Australia 16°8S 145°2E 62 B4
Daiō-Misaki Japan 34°15N 136°45E 29 G8
Daisen Japan 39°27N 140°29E 28 E10
Daisen-Oki △ Japan 35°23N 133°34E 29 G6
Daisetsu-Zan Japan 43°30N 142°57E 28 C11
Daisetsu-Zan △ Japan 43°30N 142°52E 28 C11
Daitari India 21°10N 85°46E 44 D7
Dajin Shan China 25°50N 118°15E 35 E12
Dajarra Australia 21°42S 139°30E 62 C2
Dajin Chuan → China 31°16N 101°59E 34 B3
Dak Dam Cambodia 12°20N 107°21E 38 F6
Dak Nhe Vietnam 15°28N 107°48E 38 E6
Dak Pek Vietnam 15°4N 107°44E 38 E6
Dak Song Vietnam 12°19N 107°35E 39 F6
Dak Sui Vietnam 14°55N 107°43E 38 E6
Dakar Senegal 14°34N 17°29W 52 F2
Dakhla W. Sahara 23°50N 15°53W 52 D2
Dakhla, El Wâhât el
  Egypt 25°30N 28°50E 53 C11
Dakoank India 7°2N 93°43E 45 L11
Dakor India 22°45N 73°11E 42 H5
Dakota City U.S.A. 42°25N 96°25W 80 D5
Đakovica = Gjakovë
  Kosovo 42°22N 20°26E 23 C9
Dalachi China 36°48N 105°0E 32 F3
Dalai Nur China 43°20N 116°45E 32 C9
Dālaki Iran 29°26N 51°17E 47 D6
Dälälven → Sweden 60°12N 16°43E 9 F17
Dalaman → Turkey 36°41N 28°43E 23 F13
Dalandzadgad Mongolia 43°27N 104°30E 32 C3
Dalap-Uliga-Darrit = Majuro
  Marshall Is. 7°9N 171°12E 64 G9
Dalarna Sweden 61°0N 14°0E 8 F16
Dalay Mongolia 43°28N 103°30E 32 C2
Dālbandin Pakistan 29°0N 64°23E 40 E4
Dalbeattie U.K. 54°56N 3°50W 11 G5
Dalbeg Australia 20°16S 147°18E 62 C4
Dalby Australia 27°10S 151°17E 63 D5
Dale City U.S.A. 38°38N 77°19W 81 F15
Dale Hollow L. U.S.A. 36°32N 85°27W 85 C12
Dalgán Iran 27°31N 59°19E 47 E8
Dalhart U.S.A. 36°4N 102°31W 84 C1
Dalhousie Canada 48°5N 66°26W 73 C6
Dalhousie India 32°38N 75°58E 42 C6
Dali Shaanxi, China 34°48N 109°58E 34 G5
Dali Yunnan, China 25°40N 100°10E 34 E3
Dalian China 38°50N 121°40E 33 E11
Daliang Shan China 28°0N 102°45E 34 D4
Daliang Shan China 40°55N 121°40E 33 D11
Dāliyat el Karmel Israel 32°43N 35°2E 48 C4
Dallas Oreg., U.S.A. 44°55N 123°19W 76 D2
Dallas Tex., U.S.A. 32°47N 96°48W 84 E6
Dallas-Fort Worth Int. ✈ (DFW)
  U.S.A. 32°54N 97°2W 84 E6
Dalles, The U.S.A. 45°36N 121°10W 76 D3
Dalmã U.A.E. 24°30N 52°20E 47 E7
Dalmacija Croatia 43°20N 17°0E 22 C7
Dalmas, L. Canada 53°30N 71°50W 73 B5
Dalmatia = Dalmacija
  Croatia 43°20N 17°0E 22 C7
Dalmau India 26°4N 81°2E 43 F9
Dalmellington U.K. 55°19N 4°23W 11 F4
Dalnegorsk Russia 44°32N 135°33E 28 B7
Dalnerechensk Russia 45°50N 133°40E 28 B6
Dalnevostochnyy □
  Russia 67°0N 140°0E 27 C14
Daloa Ivory C. 7°0N 6°30W 52 G4
Dalou Shan China 28°15N 107°0E 34 C6
Dalry U.K. 55°42N 4°43W 11 F4
Dalrymple, L. Australia 20°40S 147°0E 62 C4
Dalrymple, Mt. Australia 21°1S 148°39E 62 b
Dalsland Sweden 58°50N 12°15E 9 G15
Daltenganj India 24°0N 84°4E 43 H11
Dalton Ga., U.S.A. 34°46N 84°58W 85 D12
Dalton Mass., U.S.A. 42°28N 73°11W 83 D11
Dalton Nebr., U.S.A. 41°25N 102°58W 80 E2
Dalton-in-Furness U.K. 54°10N 3°11W 12 C4
Dalvík Iceland 65°58N 18°32W 8 D4
Dálvvadis = Jokkmokk
  Sweden 66°35N 19°50E 8 C18
Dalwallinu Australia 30°17S 116°40E 61 F2
Daly → Australia 13°35S 130°19E 60 B5
Daly L. Canada 56°32N 105°39W 71 B7
Daly River Australia 13°46S 130°42E 60 B5
Daly River-Port Keats ◇
  Australia 14°13S 129°36E 60 B4
Daly Waters Australia 16°15S 133°24E 62 B1

Dāmaneh Iran 33°1N 50°29E 47 C6
Damanganga → India 20°25N 72°56E 44 D1
Damanhûr Egypt 31°0N 30°30E 53 B12
Damar Indonesia 7°7S 128°40E 37 F7
Damaraland Namibia 20°0S 15°0E 56 B2
Damascus = Dimashq
  Syria 33°30N 36°18E 48 B5
Damaturu Nigeria 11°45N 11°55E 54 B2
Damāvand Iran 35°47N 52°0E 47 C7
Damāvand, Qolleh-ye
  Iran 35°56N 52°10E 47 C7
Damba Angola 6°44S 15°20E 54 F3
Dâmbovita → Romania 44°12N 26°26E 17 F14
Dambulla Sri Lanka 7°51N 80°39E 45 L5
Dame Marie Haiti 18°36N 74°26W 89 C5
Dämghän Iran 36°10N 54°17E 47 C7
Damiel Spain 39°4N 3°37W 21 C4
Damietta = Dumyât
  Egypt 31°24N 31°48E 53 B12
Daming China 36°15N 115°6E 32 F8
Damīr Qābū Syria 36°58N 41°51E 46 B4
Dammam = Ad Dammām
  Si. Arabia 26°20N 50°5E 47 E6
Damodar → India 23°17N 87°35E 43 H12
Damoh India 23°50N 79°28E 43 H8
Dampier Australia 20°41S 116°42E 60 D2
Dampier, Selat Indonesia 0°40S 131°0E 37 E8
Dampier Arch. Australia 20°38S 116°32E 60 D2
Damrei, Chuor Phnum
  Cambodia 11°30N 103°0E 39 G4
Damyang S. Korea 35°19N 126°59E 33 G14
Dana Indonesia 11°0S 121°15E 37 F6
Dana Jordan 30°41N 35°37E 48 E4
Dana Nepal 28°32N 83°37E 43 E10
Dana, L. Canada 50°53N 77°20W 72 B4
Dana, Mt. U.S.A. 37°54N 119°12W 78 H7
Danakil Desert Ethiopia 12°45N 41°0E 49 E3
Danané Ivory C. 7°16N 8°9W 52 G4
Danba China 30°54N 101°48E 34 B3
Danbury U.S.A. 41°24N 73°28W 83 E11
Danby L. U.S.A. 34°13N 115°5W 79 L11
Dand Afghan. 31°28N 65°32E 42 D1
Dandeldhura Nepal 29°20N 80°35E 43 E9
Dandeli India 15°5N 74°30E 45 G2
Dandenong Australia 38°0S 145°15E 63 F4
Dandong China 40°10N 124°20E 33 D13
Danfeng China 33°45N 110°25E 32 H6
Dangan Liedao China 22°2N 114°8E 35 F10
Danger Is. = Pukapuka
  Cook Is. 10°53S 165°49W 65 J11
Danger Pt. S. Africa 34°40S 19°17E 56 E2
Dangla Shan = Tanggula Shan
  China 32°40N 92°10E 30 C7
Dangrek, Mts. = Dangrek, Phnom
  Thailand 14°20N 104°0E 38 E5
Dangrek, Phnom
  Thailand 14°20N 104°0E 38 E5
Dangriga Belize 17°0N 88°13W 87 D7
Dangshan China 34°27N 116°22E 32 G9
Dangtu China 31°32N 118°25E 35 B12
Dangyang China 30°52N 111°44E 35 B8
Daniel U.S.A. 42°52N 110°4W 76 E8
Daniel's Harbour Canada 50°13N 57°35W 73 B8
Danielskuil S. Africa 28°11S 23°33E 56 C3
Danielson U.S.A. 41°48N 71°53W 83 E13
Danilov Russia 58°16N 40°13E 18 C7
Daning China 36°28N 110°45E 32 F6
Danjiangkou China 32°31N 111°30E 35 A8
Danjiangkou Shuiku
  China 32°37N 111°30E 35 A8
Dank Oman 23°33N 56°16E 47 F8
Dankhar Gompa India 32°10N 78°10E 42 C8
Danleng China 30°1N 103°31E 34 B4
Danli Honduras 14°4N 86°35W 88 D2
Danmark = Denmark ■
  Europe 55°45N 10°0E 9 J14
Dannemora U.S.A. 44°43N 73°44W 83 B11
Dannevirke N.Z. 40°12S 176°8E 59 D6
Dannhauser S. Africa 28°0S 30°3E 57 D5
Dansville U.S.A. 42°34N 77°42W 82 D7
Danta India 24°11N 72°46E 42 G5
Dantan India 21°57N 87°20E 43 J12
Dante = Xaafuun Somalia 10°25N 51°16E 49 E5
Dantewara India 18°54N 81°21E 44 E5
Danube = Dunărea →
  Europe 45°20N 29°40E 17 F15
Danvers U.S.A. 42°34N 70°56W 83 D14
Danville Ill., U.S.A. 40°8N 87°37W 80 E10
Danville Ky., U.S.A. 37°39N 84°46W 81 G11
Danville Pa., U.S.A. 40°58N 76°37W 83 F8
Danville Va., U.S.A. 36°36N 79°23W 81 G14
Danville Vt., U.S.A. 44°25N 72°9W 83 B12
Danyang China 32°0N 119°31E 35 B12
Danzhai China 26°11N 107°48E 34 D6
Danzig = Gdańsk Poland 54°22N 18°40E 17 A10
Dao Xian China 25°36N 111°35E 35 D8
Daocheng China 29°0N 100°14E 34 C3
Dapaong Togo 10°55N 0°16E 52 F6
Dapoli India 17°45N 73°11E 44 E1
Daqing China 46°35N 125°0E 31 B13
Daqing Shan China 40°40N 111°0E 32 D6
Daqq-e Sorkh, Kavīr Iran 34°35N 52°55E 47 C7
Daqu Shan China 30°25N 122°20E 35 B14
Dar Banda Africa 8°0N 23°0E 50 F6
Dar el Beida = Casablanca
  Morocco 33°36N 7°36W 52 B4
Dar es Salaam Tanzania 6°50S 39°12E 54 F7
Dar Mazār Iran 29°14N 57°20E 47 D8
Dar'ā Syria 32°36N 36°7E 48 C5
Dar'ā □ Syria 32°36N 36°7E 48 C5
Dārāb Iran 28°50N 54°30E 47 D7
Daraban Pakistan 31°44N 70°20E 42 D4
Darband Pakistan 34°20N 72°50E 42 B5
Dārān Iran 32°59N 50°24E 47 C6
Dārayyā Syria 33°28N 36°15E 48 B5
Darband Pakistan 34°20N 72°50E 42 B5
Darband, Kūh-e Iran 31°34N 57°8E 47 D8

Darbhanga *India* 26°15N 85°55E **43 F11**
D'Arcy *Canada* 50°33N 122°29W **70 C4**
Dardanelle *Ark., U.S.A.* 35°13N 93°9W **84 D8**
Dardanelle *Calif., U.S.A.* 38°20N 119°50W **78 G7**
Dardanelles = Çanakkale Boğazı
  Turkey 40°17N 26°32E **23 D12**
Dārestān *Iran* 29°9N 58°42E **47 D8**
Dârfûr *Sudan* 13°40N 24°0E **53 F10**
Dargai *Pakistan* 34°25N 71°55E **42 B4**
Dargaville *N.Z.* 35°57S 173°52E **59 A4**
Darhan *Mongolia* 49°37N 106°21E **30 B10**
Darhan Muminggan
  China 41°40N 110°28E **32 D6**
Darıca *Turkey* 40°45N 29°23E **23 D13**
Darién, G. del *Caribbean* 9°0N 77°0W **92 B3**
Darién △ *Panama* 7°36N 77°57W **88 E4**
Dariganga = Ovoot
  Mongolia 45°21N 113°45E **32 B7**
Daringbadi *India* 19°54N 84°8E **44 E7**
Darjeeling = Darjiling
  India 27°3N 88°18E **43 F13**
Darjiling *India* 27°3N 88°18E **43 F13**
Darkan *Australia* 33°20S 116°43E **61 F2**
Darkhana *Pakistan* 30°39N 72°11E **42 D5**
Darkhazineh *Iran* 31°54N 48°39E **47 D6**
Darkot Pass *Pakistan* 36°45N 73°26E **43 A5**
Darling → *Australia* 34°4S 141°54E **63 E3**
Darling Downs *Australia* 27°30S 150°30E **63 D5**
Darling Ra. *Australia* 32°30S 116°20E **61 F2**
Darlington *U.K.* 54°32N 1°33W **12 C6**
Darlington *U.S.A.* 34°18N 79°52W **85 D15**
Darlington □ *U.K.* 54°32N 1°33W **12 C6**
Darlington, L. *S. Africa* 33°10S 25°9E **56 D4**
Darlot, L. *Australia* 27°48S 121°35E **61 E3**
Darlowo *Poland* 54°25N 16°25E **16 A9**
Darmstadt *Germany* 49°51N 8°39E **16 D5**
Darnah *Libya* 32°45N 22°45E **53 B10**
Darnall *S. Africa* 29°23S 31°18E **57 C5**
Darnley *Australia* 9°35S 143°46E **62 a**
Darnley, C. *Antarctica* 68°0S 69°0E **5 C6**
Darnley B. *Canada* 69°30N 123°30W **68 D7**
Darr → *Australia* 23°39S 143°50E **62 C3**
Darra Pezu *Pakistan* 32°19N 70°44E **42 C4**
Darregueira *Argentina* 37°42S 63°10W **94 D3**
Darrington *U.S.A.* 48°15N 121°36W **76 B3**
Darsi *India* 15°46N 79°44E **45 G4**
Dart → *U.K.* 50°24N 3°39W **13 G4**
Dartmoor *U.K.* 50°38N 3°57W **13 G4**
Dartmoor △ *U.K.* 50°37N 3°59W **13 G4**
Dartmouth *Canada* 44°40N 63°30W **73 D7**
Dartmouth *U.K.* 50°21N 3°36W **13 G4**
Dartmouth, L. *Australia* 26°4S 145°18E **63 D4**
Darvel, Teluk = Lahad Datu, Telok
  Malaysia 4°50N 118°20E **37 D5**
Darwen *U.K.* 53°42N 2°29W **12 D5**
Darwendale *Zimbabwe* 17°41S 30°33E **57 A5**
Darwha *India* 20°15N 77°45E **44 D3**
Darwin *Australia* 12°25S 130°51E **60 B5**
Darwin *U.S.A.* 36°15N 117°35W **79 J9**
Darya Khan *Pakistan* 31°48N 71°6E **42 D4**
Daryapur *India* 20°55N 77°20E **44 D3**
Daryoi Amu = Amudarya →
  Uzbekistan 43°58N 59°34E **26 E6**
Dās *U.A.E.* 25°20N 53°30E **47 E7**
Dashen, Ras *Ethiopia* 13°8N 38°26E **49 E2**
Dashetai *China* 41°0N 109°5E **32 D5**
Dashiqiao *China* 40°38N 122°30E **33 D12**
Dashköpri *Turkmenistan* 36°16N 62°8E **47 B9**
Dasht → *Pakistan* 25°10N 61°40E **40 G2**
Daska *Pakistan* 32°20N 74°20E **42 C6**
Daşoguz *Turkmenistan* 41°49N 59°58E **26 E6**
Dasuya *India* 31°49N 75°38E **42 D6**
Datça *Turkey* 36°46N 27°40E **23 F12**
Date *Japan* 42°28N 140°52E **28 C10**
Datia *India* 25°39N 78°27E **43 G8**
Datian *China* 25°40N 117°50E **35 E11**
Datong *Anhui, China* 30°48N 117°44E **35 B11**
Datong *Qinghai, China* 36°20N 102°50E **30 D9**
Datong *Shanxi, China* 40°6N 113°18E **32 D7**
Dattakhel *Pakistan* 32°54N 69°46E **42 C3**
Dattapur = Dhamangaon
  India 20°48N 78°9E **44 D4**
Datu, Tanjung *Indonesia* 2°5N 109°39E **36 D3**
Datu Piang *Phil.* 7°2N 124°30E **37 C6**
Datuk, Tanjong = Datu, Tanjung
  Indonesia 2°5N 109°39E **36 D3**
Daud Khel *Pakistan* 32°53N 71°34E **42 C4**
Daudnagar *India* 25°2N 84°24E **43 G11**
Daugava → *Latvia* 57°4N 24°3E **9 H21**
Daugavpils *Latvia* 55°53N 26°32E **9 J22**
Daulatabad *India* 19°57N 75°15E **44 E2**
Daulpur *India* 26°45N 77°59E **42 F7**
Daund *India* 18°26N 74°40E **44 D2**
Daung Kyun *Burma* 12°13N 98°4E **39 F1**
Dauphin *Canada* 51°9N 100°5W **71 C8**
Dauphin *U.S.A.* 40°22N 76°56W **82 F8**
Dauphin I. *Canada* 51°20N 99°45W **71 C9**
Dauphiné *France* 45°15N 5°25E **20 D6**
Daurada, Costa *Spain* 41°12N 1°15E **21 B6**
Dausa *India* 26°52N 76°20E **42 F7**
Davangere *India* 14°25N 75°55E **45 G2**
Davao *Phil.* 7°0N 125°40E **37 C7**
Davao G. *Phil.* 6°30N 125°48E **37 C7**
Dāvar Panāh = Sarāvān
  Iran 27°25N 62°15E **47 E9**
Davenport *Calif., U.S.A.* 37°1N 122°12W **78 H4**
Davenport *Iowa, U.S.A.* 41°32N 90°35W **80 E8**
Davenport *Wash., U.S.A.* 47°39N 118°9W **76 C4**
Davenport Ra. *Australia* 20°28S 134°0E **62 C1**
Davenport Range △
  Australia 20°36S 134°22E **62 C1**
Daventry *U.K.* 52°16N 1°10W **13 E6**
David *Panama* 8°30N 82°30W **88 E3**
David City *U.S.A.* 41°15N 97°8W **80 E5**
Dāvid Gorodok = Davyd Haradok
  Belarus 52°4N 27°8E **17 B14**
Davidson *Canada* 51°16N 105°59W **71 C7**
Davidson Mts. *U.S.A.* 68°41N 142°22W **74 B11**
Davis *Antarctica* 68°34S 77°55E **5 C6**

Davis *U.S.A.* 38°33N 121°44W **78 G5**
Davis Dam *U.S.A.* 35°12N 114°34W **79 K12**
Davis Mts. *U.S.A.* 30°50N 103°55W **84 F3**
Davis Sea *Antarctica* 66°0S 92°0E **5 C7**
Davis Str. *N. Amer.* 65°0N 58°0W **69 D19**
Davos *Switz.* 46°48N 9°49E **20 C8**
Davy L. *Canada* 58°53N 108°18W **71 B7**
Davyd Haradok *Belarus* 52°4N 27°8E **17 B14**
Dawei *Burma* 14°2N 98°12E **38 E2**
Dawes Ra. *Australia* 24°40S 150°40E **62 C5**
Dawlish *U.K.* 50°35N 3°28W **13 G4**
Dawmat al Jandal
  Si. Arabia 29°55N 39°40E **46 D3**
Dawna Ra. *Burma* 16°30N 98°30E **38 D2**
Dawros Hd. *Ireland* 54°50N 8°33W **10 B3**
Dawson, I. *Chile* 31°46N 84°27W **85 F12**
Dawson, I. *Chile* 53°50S 70°50W **96 G2**
Dawson B. *Canada* 52°53N 100°49W **71 C8**
Dawson City *Canada* 64°10N 139°30W **68 E4**
Dawson Creek *Canada* 55°45N 120°15W **70 B4**
Dawson Inlet *Canada* 61°50N 93°25W **71 A10**
Dawson Ra. *Australia* 24°30S 149°48E **62 C4**
Dawu *Hubei, China* 31°34N 114°7E **35 B10**
Dawu *Sichuan, China* 30°55N 101°10E **34 B3**
Dax *France* 43°44N 1°3W **20 E3**
Daxian *China* 31°15N 107°23E **34 B6**
Daxin *China* 22°50N 107°11E **34 F6**
Daxindian *China* 37°30N 120°50E **33 F11**
Daxinggou *China* 43°25N 129°40E **33 C15**
Daxue Shan *Sichuan, China* 30°30N 101°30E **34 B3**
Daxue Shan *Yunnan, China* 23°42N 99°48E **34 F2**
Dayao *China* 25°43N 101°20E **34 E3**
Daye *China* 30°6N 114°58E **35 B10**
Dayi *China* 30°41N 103°29E **34 B4**
Dāykondī □ *Afghan.* 34°0N 66°0E **40 C5**
Daylesford *Australia* 37°21S 144°9E **63 F3**
Dayong = Zhangjiajie
  China 29°11N 110°30E **35 C8**
Dayr az Zawr *Syria* 35°20N 40°5E **46 C4**
Daysland *Canada* 52°50N 112°20W **70 C6**
Dayton *Nev., U.S.A.* 39°14N 119°36W **78 F7**
Dayton *Ohio, U.S.A.* 39°45N 84°12W **81 F11**
Dayton *Pa., U.S.A.* 40°53N 79°15W **82 F5**
Dayton *Tenn., U.S.A.* 35°30N 85°1W **85 D12**
Dayton *Wash., U.S.A.* 46°19N 117°59W **76 C5**
Dayton *Wyo., U.S.A.* 44°53N 107°16W **76 D10**
Daytona Beach *U.S.A.* 29°13N 81°1W **85 G14**
Dayu *China* 25°24N 114°22E **35 E10**
Dazhu *China* 30°41N 107°15E **34 B6**
Dazu *China* 29°40N 105°42E **34 C5**
De Aar *S. Africa* 30°39S 24°0E **56 D3**
De Funiak Springs
  U.S.A. 30°43N 86°7W **85 F11**
De Grey → *Australia* 20°12S 119°13E **60 D2**
De Haan *Belgium* 51°16N 3°2E **15 C3**
De Hoop ○ *S. Africa* 34°30S 20°28E **56 D3**
De Kalb Junction *U.S.A.* 44°30N 75°16W **83 B9**
De Land *U.S.A.* 29°2N 81°18W **85 G14**
De Leon *U.S.A.* 32°7N 98°32W **84 E5**
De Long Mts. *U.S.A.* 68°10N 163°30W **74 B7**
De Panne *Belgium* 51°6N 2°34E **15 C2**
De Pere *U.S.A.* 44°27N 88°4W **80 C9**
De Queen *U.S.A.* 34°2N 94°21W **84 D7**
De Quincy *U.S.A.* 30°27N 93°26W **84 F8**
De Ruyters *U.S.A.* 42°45N 75°53W **83 D9**
De Smet *U.S.A.* 44°23N 97°33W **80 C5**
De Soto *U.S.A.* 38°8N 90°34W **80 F8**
De Tour Village *U.S.A.* 46°0N 83°56W **81 B12**
De Witt *U.S.A.* 34°18N 91°20W **84 D9**
Dead Sea *Asia* 31°30N 35°30E **48 D4**
Deadwood *U.S.A.* 44°23N 103°44W **80 C2**
Deadwood L. *Canada* 59°10N 128°30W **70 B3**
Deal *U.K.* 51°13N 1°25E **13 F9**
Deal I. *Australia* 39°30S 147°20E **63 F4**
Dealesville *S. Africa* 28°41S 25°44E **56 C4**
De'an *China* 29°21N 115°46E **35 C10**
Dean → *Canada* 52°49N 126°58W **70 C3**
Dean, Forest of *U.K.* 51°45N 2°33W **13 F5**
Dean Chan. *Canada* 52°30N 127°15W **70 C3**
Deán Funes *Argentina* 30°20S 64°20W **94 C3**
Dease → *Canada* 59°56N 128°32W **70 B3**
Dease L. *Canada* 58°40N 130°5W **70 B2**
Dease Lake *Canada* 58°25N 130°6W **70 B2**
Death Valley *U.S.A.* 36°15N 116°50W **79 J10**
Death Valley △ *U.S.A.* 36°29N 117°6W **79 J9**
Death Valley Junction
  U.S.A. 36°20N 116°25W **79 J10**
Deatnu = Tana →
  Norway 70°30N 28°14E **8 A23**
Debagram *India* 23°41N 88°18E **43 H13**
Debao *China* 23°21N 106°46E **34 F6**
Debar *Macedonia* 41°31N 20°30E **23 D9**
Debden *Canada* 53°30N 106°50W **71 C7**
Dębica *Poland* 50°2N 21°25E **17 C11**
DeBolt *Canada* 55°12N 118°1W **70 B5**
Deborah East, L.
  Australia 30°45S 119°30E **61 F2**
Deborah West, L.
  Australia 30°45S 119°5E **61 F2**
Debre Markos *Ethiopia* 10°20N 37°40E **49 E2**
Debre Tabor *Ethiopia* 11°50N 38°26E **49 E2**
Debre Zeyit *Ethiopia* 8°50N 39°0E **49 F2**
Debrecen *Hungary* 47°33N 21°42E **17 E11**
Decatur, A. *U.S.A.* 34°36N 86°59W **85 D11**
Decatur *Ill., U.S.A.* 39°51N 88°57W **80 F9**
Decatur *Ind., U.S.A.* 40°50N 84°56W **81 E11**
Decatur *Tex., U.S.A.* 33°14N 97°35W **84 E6**
Deccan *India* 18°0N 79°0E **44 F4**
Deception Bay *Australia* 27°10S 153°3E **63 D5**
Deception I. *Antarctica* 63°0S 60°15W **5 C17**
Deception L. *Canada* 56°33N 104°13W **71 B8**
Dechang *China* 27°25N 102°11E **34 D4**
Dechhu *India* 26°46N 72°20E **42 F5**
Děčín *Czech Rep.* 50°47N 14°12E **16 C8**
Deckerville *U.S.A.* 43°32N 82°44W **82 C2**
Decorah *U.S.A.* 43°18N 91°48W **80 D8**
Dedéagach = Alexandroupoli
  Greece 40°50N 25°54E **23 D11**

Dee → *Aberds., U.K.* 57°9N 2°5W **11 D6**
Dee → *Dumf. & Gall., U.K.* 54°51N 4°3W **11 G4**
Dee → *Wales, U.K.* 53°22N 3°17W **12 D4**
Deep B. *Canada* 61°15N 116°35W **70 A5**
Deep Bay = Shenzhen Wan
  China 22°27N 113°55E **31 a**
Deepwater *Australia* 29°25S 151°51E **63 D5**
Deer → *Canada* 58°23N 94°13W **71 B10**
Deer L. *Canada* 52°40N 94°20W **71 C10**
Deer Lake *Nfld. & L.,*
  Canada 49°11N 57°27W **73 C8**
Deer Lake *Ont., Canada* 52°36N 94°20W **71 C10**
Deer Lodge *U.S.A.* 46°24N 112°44W **76 C7**
Deer Park *U.S.A.* 47°57N 117°28W **76 C5**
Deer River *U.S.A.* 47°20N 93°48W **80 B7**
Deeragun *Australia* 19°16S 146°33E **62 B4**
Defiance *U.S.A.* 41°17N 84°22W **81 E11**
Degana *India* 26°50N 74°20E **42 F6**
Dêgê *China* 31°44N 98°39E **34 B2**
Dêgelis *Canada* 47°30N 68°35W **73 C6**
Deggendorf *Germany* 48°50N 12°57E **16 D7**
Degh → *Pakistan* 31°3N 73°21E **42 D5**
Deh Bīd *Iran* 30°39N 53°11E **47 D7**
Deh Dasht *Iran* 30°47N 50°33E **47 D6**
Deh-e Shīr *Iran* 31°29N 53°45E **47 D7**
Dehaj *Iran* 30°42N 54°53E **47 D7**
Dehaj *Iran* 27°11N 62°37E **47 E9**
Dehdez *Iran* 31°43N 50°17E **47 D6**
Dehej *India* 21°44N 72°40E **42 J5**
Dehestān *Iran* 28°30N 55°35E **47 D7**
Dehgolān *Iran* 35°17N 47°25E **46 C5**
Dehibat *Tunisia* 32°0N 10°47E **53 B8**
Dehlorān *Iran* 32°41N 47°16E **46 C5**
Dehnow-e Kūhestān *Iran* 27°58N 58°32E **47 E8**
Dehra Dun *India* 30°20N 78°4E **42 D8**
Dehri *India* 24°50N 84°15E **43 G11**
Dehua *China* 25°26N 118°14E **35 E12**
Dehui *China* 44°30N 125°40E **33 B13**
Deinze *Belgium* 50°59N 3°32E **15 D3**
Deir al Balah *Gaza Strip* 31°25N 34°21E **48 D3**
Dej *Romania* 47°10N 23°52E **17 E12**
Dejiang *China* 28°18N 108°7E **34 C7**
Deka → *Zimbabwe* 18°4S 26°42E **56 A4**
DeKalb *U.S.A.* 41°56N 88°46W **80 E9**
Dekese
  Dem. Rep. of the Congo 3°24S 21°24E **54 E4**
Del Mar *U.S.A.* 32°58N 117°16W **79 N9**
Del Norte *U.S.A.* 37°41N 106°21W **77 H10**
Del Rio *U.S.A.* 29°22N 100°54W **84 G4**
Delambre I. *Australia* 20°26S 117°5E **60 D2**
Delano *U.S.A.* 35°46N 119°15W **79 K7**
Delano Peak *U.S.A.* 38°22N 112°22W **76 G7**
Delareyville *S. Africa* 26°41S 25°26E **56 C4**
Delaronde L. *Canada* 54°3N 107°3W **71 C7**
Delavan *U.S.A.* 42°38N 88°39W **80 D9**
Delaware *U.S.A.* 40°18N 83°4W **81 E12**
Delaware □ *U.S.A.* 39°0N 75°20W **81 F8**
Delaware → *U.S.A.* 39°20N 75°25W **83 G9**
Delaware B. *U.S.A.* 39°0N 75°10W **81 F16**
Delaware Water Gap
  U.S.A. 41°10N 74°55W **83 E10**
Delay → *Canada* 56°56N 71°28W **73 A5**
Delegate *Australia* 37°4S 148°56E **63 F4**
Delevan *U.S.A.* 42°29N 78°29W **82 D6**
Delft *Neths.* 52°1N 4°22E **15 B4**
Delft I. *Sri Lanka* 9°30N 79°40E **45 K4**
Delfzijl *Neths.* 53°20N 6°55E **15 A6**
Delgado, C. *Mozam.* 10°45S 40°40E **54 G8**
Delgerhet *Mongolia* 45°50N 110°30E **32 B6**
Delgo *Sudan* 20°6N 30°40E **53 D12**
Delhi *Canada* 42°51N 80°30W **82 D4**
Delhi *La., U.S.A.* 32°28N 91°30W **84 E9**
Delhi *N.Y., U.S.A.* 42°17N 74°55W **83 D10**
Delia *Canada* 51°38N 112°23W **70 C6**
Delice *Turkey* 39°54N 34°2E **19 G5**
Delicias *Mexico* 28°13N 105°28W **86 B3**
Delījān *Iran* 33°59N 50°40E **47 C6**
Déline *Canada* 65°11N 123°25W **68 D7**
Delingha *China* 37°23N 97°23E **30 D8**
Delisle *Canada* 51°55N 107°8W **71 C7**
Deliverance I. *Australia* 9°31S 141°34E **62 a**
Dell City *U.S.A.* 31°56N 105°12W **84 F2**
Dell Rapids *U.S.A.* 43°50N 96°43W **80 D5**
Delmar *U.S.A.* 42°37N 73°47W **83 D11**
Delmenhorst *Germany* 53°3N 8°37E **16 B5**
Delonga, Ostrova
  Russia 76°40N 149°20E **27 B15**
Deloraine *Australia* 41°30S 146°40E **63 G4**
Deloraine *Canada* 49°15N 100°29W **71 D8**
Delphi *U.S.A.* 40°36N 86°41W **80 E10**
Delphos *U.S.A.* 40°51N 84°21W **81 E11**
Delportshoop *S. Africa* 28°22S 24°20E **56 C3**
Delray Beach *U.S.A.* 26°28N 80°4W **85 H14**
Delta *Colo., U.S.A.* 38°44N 108°4W **76 G9**
Delta *Utah, U.S.A.* 39°21N 112°35W **76 G7**
Delta Dunărea △
  Romania 45°15N 29°25E **17 F15**
Delta Junction *U.S.A.* 64°2N 145°44W **68 E2**
Deltona *U.S.A.* 28°54N 81°16W **85 G14**
Delungra *Australia* 29°39S 150°51E **63 D5**
Delvada *India* 20°46N 71°2E **42 J4**
Delvinë *Albania* 39°59N 20°6E **23 E9**
Demak *Indonesia* 6°53S 110°38E **37 G14**
Demanda, Sierra de la
  Spain 42°15N 3°0W **21 A4**
Demavend = Damāvand,
  Qolleh-ye *Iran* 35°56N 52°10E **47 C7**
Dembidolo *Ethiopia* 8°34N 34°50W **49 F1**
Demchok *India* 32°42N 79°29E **43 C8**
Demer → *Belgium* 50°57N 4°42E **15 D4**
Deming *N. Mex.,*
  U.S.A. 32°16N 107°46W **77 K10**
Deming *Wash., U.S.A.* 48°50N 122°13W **78 B4**
Demini → *Brazil* 0°46S 62°56W **92 D6**
Demirci *Turkey* 39°2N 28°38E **23 E13**
Demirköy *Turkey* 41°49N 27°45E **23 D12**
Demopolis *U.S.A.* 32°31N 87°50W **85 E11**
Dempo *Indonesia* 4°2S 103°15E **36 E2**
Den Bosch = 's-Hertogenbosch
  Neths. 51°42N 5°17E **15 C5**

Den Burg *Neths.* 53°3N 4°47E **15 A4**
Den Chai *Thailand* 17°59N 100°4E **38 D3**
Den Haag = 's-Gravenhage
  Neths. 52°7N 4°17E **15 B4**
Den Helder *Neths.* 52°57N 4°45E **15 B4**
Den Oever *Neths.* 52°56N 5°2E **15 B5**
Denair *U.S.A.* 37°32N 120°48W **78 H6**
Denali = McKinley, Mt.
  U.S.A. 63°4N 151°0W **68 E1**
Denau = Denov
  Uzbekistan 38°16N 67°54E **26 F7**
Denbigh *Canada* 45°8N 77°15W **82 A7**
Denbigh *U.K.* 53°12N 3°25W **12 D4**
Denbighshire □ *U.K.* 53°8N 3°22W **12 D4**
Dendang *Indonesia* 3°7S 107°56E **36 E3**
Dendermonde *Belgium* 51°2N 4°5E **15 C4**
Dengchuan *China* 25°59N 100°3E **34 E3**
Dengfeng *China* 34°25N 113°2E **34 G7**
Dengkou *China* 40°18N 106°55E **32 D4**
Dengzhou *China* 32°34N 112°4E **35 A9**
Denham *Australia* 25°56S 113°31E **61 E1**
Denham, Mt. *Jamaica* 18°13N 77°32W **88 a**
Denham Ra. *Australia* 21°55S 147°46E **62 C4**
Denham Sd. *Australia* 25°45S 113°15E **61 E1**
Denholm *Canada* 52°39N 108°1W **71 C7**
Denia *Spain* 38°49N 0°8E **21 C6**
Denial B. *Australia* 32°14S 133°32E **63 E1**
Deniliquin *Australia* 35°30S 144°58E **63 F3**
Denimoo = Fort Resolution
  Canada 61°10N 113°40W **70 A6**
Denison *Iowa, U.S.A.* 42°1N 95°21W **80 D6**
Denison *Tex., U.S.A.* 33°45N 96°33W **84 E6**
Denison, C. *Antarctica* 67°0S 142°40E **5 C10**
Denison Plains *Australia* 18°35S 128°0E **60 C4**
Deniyaya *Sri Lanka* 6°21N 80°33E **45 L5**
Denizli *Turkey* 37°42N 29°2E **19 G4**
Denman Glacier *Antarctica* 66°45S 100°0E **5 C8**
Denmark *Australia* 34°59S 117°25E **61 F2**
Denmark ■ *Europe* 55°45N 10°0E **9 J14**
Denmark Str. *Atl. Oc.* 66°0N 30°0W **66 C17**
Dennery *St. Lucia* 13°55N 60°54W **89 f**
Dennison *U.S.A.* 40°24N 81°19W **82 F3**
Denny *U.K.* 56°1N 3°55W **11 E5**
Denov *Uzbekistan* 38°16N 67°54E **26 F7**
Denpasar *Indonesia* 8°39S 115°13E **37 K18**
Denpasar ✈ (DPS)
  Indonesia 8°44S 115°10E **37 K18**
Denton *Mont., U.S.A.* 47°19N 109°57W **76 C9**
Denton *Tex., U.S.A.* 33°13N 97°8W **84 E6**
D'Entrecasteaux, Pt.
  Australia 34°50S 115°57E **61 F2**
D'Entrecasteaux △
  Australia 34°20S 115°33E **61 F2**
D'Entrecasteaux Is.
  Papua N. G. 9°0S 151°0E **58 B8**
Denver *Colo., U.S.A.* 39°42N 104°59W **76 G11**
Denver *Pa., U.S.A.* 40°14N 76°8W **83 F8**
Denver City *U.S.A.* 32°58N 102°50W **84 E3**
Denver Int. ✈ (DEN)
  U.S.A. 39°52N 104°40W **76 G11**
Deoband *India* 29°42N 77°43E **42 E7**
Deobhog *India* 19°53N 82°44E **44 E6**
Deodrug *India* 16°26N 76°55E **45 F3**
Deogarh *Odisha, India* 21°32N 84°45E **44 D7**
Deogarh *Raj., India* 25°32N 73°54E **42 G5**
Deoghar *India* 24°30N 86°42E **43 G12**
Deolali *India* 19°58N 73°50E **44 E1**
Deoli = Devli *India* 25°50N 75°20E **42 G6**
Deoli *India* 26°22N 70°55E **42 F4**
Deoria *India* 26°31N 83°48E **43 F10**
Deoria *India* 26°46N 90°29E **43 F14**
Deosai Mts. *Pakistan* 35°40N 75°0E **43 B6**
Deosri *India* 26°46N 90°29E **43 F14**
Depalpur *India* 22°51N 75°33E **42 H6**
Deposit *U.S.A.* 42°4N 75°25W **83 D9**
Depuch I. *Australia* 20°37S 117°44E **60 D2**
Deputatskiy *Russia* 69°18N 139°54E **27 C14**
Dêqên *China* 28°34N 98°51E **34 C2**
Deqing *China* 23°8N 111°42E **35 F8**
Dera Ghazi Khan *Pakistan* 30°5N 70°43E **42 D4**
Dera Ismail Khan
  Pakistan 31°50N 70°50E **42 D4**
Derabugti *Pakistan* 29°2N 69°9E **42 E3**
Derawar Fort *Pakistan* 28°46N 71°20E **42 E4**
Derby *Australia* 17°18S 123°38E **60 C3**
Derby *U.K.* 52°56N 1°28E **12 E6**
Derby *Conn., U.S.A.* 41°19N 73°5W **83 E11**
Derby *Kans., U.S.A.* 37°33N 97°16W **80 G6**
Derby *N.Y., U.S.A.* 42°41N 78°58W **82 D6**
Derby City □ *U.K.* 52°56N 1°28W **12 E6**
Derby Line *U.S.A.* 45°0N 72°6W **83 B12**
Derbyshire □ *U.K.* 53°11N 1°38W **12 D6**
Derdepoort *S. Africa* 24°38S 26°24E **56 B4**
Dereham *U.K.* 52°41N 0°57E **13 E8**
Derg → *U.K.* 54°44N 7°26W **10 B4**
Derg, L. *Ireland* 53°0N 8°20W **10 D3**
Deridder *U.S.A.* 30°51N 93°17W **84 F8**
Dermott *U.S.A.* 33°32N 91°26W **84 E9**
Dêrong *China* 28°44N 99°9E **34 C2**
Derry = Londonderry *U.K.* 55°0N 7°20W **10 B4**
Derry = Londonderry □
  U.K. 55°0N 7°20W **10 B4**
Derry *N.H., U.S.A.* 42°53N 71°19W **83 D13**
Derry *Pa., U.S.A.* 40°20N 79°18W **82 F5**
Derryveagh Mts. *Ireland* 54°56N 8°11W **10 B3**
Derwent → *Cumb., U.K.* 54°39N 3°33W **12 C4**
Derwent → *Derby, U.K.* 52°57N 1°28E **12 E6**
Derwent → *N. Yorks.,*
  U.K. 53°45N 0°58W **12 D7**
Derwent Water *U.K.* 54°35N 3°9W **12 C4**
Des Moines *Iowa, U.S.A.* 41°35N 93°37W **80 E7**
Des Moines *N. Mex.,*
  U.S.A. 36°46N 103°50W **77 H12**
Des Moines *Wash.,*
  U.S.A. 47°24N 122°19W **78 C4**
Des Moines → *U.S.A.* 40°23N 91°25W **80 E8**
Desaguadero →
  Argentina 34°30S 66°46W **94 C2**
Desaguadero → *Bolivia* 16°35S 69°5W **92 G5**

Desaru *Malaysia* 1°31N 104°17E **39 d**
Descanso, Pta. *Mexico* 32°21N 117°3W **79 N9**
Deschaillons-sur-St-Laurent
  Canada 46°32N 72°7W **73 C5**
Deschambault L.
  Canada 54°50N 103°30W **71 C8**
Deschutes → *U.S.A.* 45°38N 120°55W **76 D3**
Dese *Ethiopia* 11°5N 39°40E **49 E2**
Deseado → *Argentina* 47°45S 65°54W **96 F3**
Deseronto *Canada* 44°12N 77°3W **82 B7**
Desert Center *U.S.A.* 33°43N 115°24W **79 M11**
Desert Hot Springs
  U.S.A. 33°58N 116°30W **79 M10**
Deshnok *India* 27°48N 73°21E **42 F5**
Desierto Central de Baja
  California ○ Mexico 29°40N 114°50W **86 B2**
Desna → *Ukraine* 50°33N 30°32E **17 C16**
Desolación, I. *Chile* 53°0S 74°0W **96 G2**
Despeñaperros, Paso
  Spain 38°24N 3°30W **21 C4**
Dessau *Germany* 51°51N 12°14E **16 C7**
Dessye = Dese *Ethiopia* 11°5N 39°40E **49 E2**
D'Estrees B. *Australia* 35°55S 137°45E **63 F2**
Desuri *India* 25°18N 73°35E **42 G5**
Det Udom *Thailand* 14°54N 105°5E **38 E5**
Dete *Zimbabwe* 18°38S 26°50E **56 A4**
Detmold *Germany* 51°56N 8°52E **16 C5**
Detour, Pt. *U.S.A.* 45°40N 86°40W **80 C10**
Detroit *U.S.A.* 42°19N 83°12W **82 D1**
Detroit Lakes *U.S.A.* 46°49N 95°51W **80 B6**
Deua △ *Australia* 35°32S 149°46E **63 F4**
Deurne *Neths.* 51°27N 5°49E **15 C5**
Deutsche Bucht *Germany* 54°15N 8°0E **16 A5**
Deutschland = Germany ■
  Europe 51°0N 10°0E **16 C6**
Deva *Romania* 45°53N 22°55E **17 F12**
Devakottai *India* 9°55N 78°45E **45 K4**
Devaprayag *India* 30°13N 78°35E **43 D8**
Devarkonda *India* 16°42N 78°56E **44 F4**
Deventer *Neths.* 52°15N 6°10E **15 B6**
Deveron → *U.K.* 57°41N 2°32W **11 D6**
Devgad I. *Canada* 44°18N 74°5E **45 G2**
Devgadh Bariya *India* 22°40N 73°55E **42 H5**
Devgarh *India* 16°23N 73°23E **45 F1**
Devi → *India* 19°59N 86°24E **44 E8**
Devikot *India* 26°42N 71°12E **42 F4**
Devils Den *U.S.A.* 35°46N 119°58W **78 K7**
Devils Hole = Death Valley △
  U.S.A. 36°29N 117°6W **79 J9**
Devils Lake *U.S.A.* 48°7N 98°52W **80 A4**
Devils Paw *Canada* 58°47N 134°0W **70 B2**
Devils Postpile ○ *U.S.A.* 37°37N 119°5W **78 H7**
Devil's Pt. *Sri Lanka* 9°26N 80°6E **45 K5**
Devils Tower △ *U.S.A.* 44°35N 104°42W **76 D11**
Devils Tower △ *U.S.A.* 44°48N 104°55W **76 D11**
Devine *U.S.A.* 29°8N 98°54W **84 G5**
Devizes *U.K.* 51°22N 1°58W **13 F6**
Devli *India* 25°50N 75°20E **42 G6**
Devon □ *U.K.* 50°50N 3°40W **13 G4**
Devon I. *Canada* 75°10N 85°0W **69 B15**
Devonport *Australia* 41°10S 146°22E **63 G4**
Devonport *N.Z.* 36°49S 174°49E **59 B5**
Devrukh *India* 17°3N 73°37E **44 F1**
Dewas *India* 22°59N 76°3E **42 H7**
Dewetsdorp *S. Africa* 29°33S 26°39E **56 C4**
Dewey *Puerto Rico* 18°18N 65°18W **89 d**
Dexing *China* 28°46N 117°30E **35 C11**
Dexter *Maine, U.S.A.* 45°1N 69°18W **81 C19**
Dexter *Mo., U.S.A.* 36°48N 89°57W **80 G9**
Dexter *N. Mex., U.S.A.* 33°12N 104°22W **77 K11**
Dey-Dey, L. *Australia* 29°12S 131°4E **61 E5**
Deyang *China* 31°3N 104°27E **34 B5**
Deyhūk *Iran* 33°15N 57°30E **47 C8**
Deyyer *Iran* 27°55N 51°55E **47 E6**
Dez → *Iran* 31°39N 48°52E **47 D6**
Dezadeash L. *Canada* 60°28N 136°58W **70 A1**
Dezfūl *Iran* 32°20N 48°30E **47 C6**
Dezhneva, Mys *Russia* 66°5N 169°40W **27 C19**
Dezhou *China* 37°26N 116°18E **32 F9**
Dhadhar → *India* 24°56N 85°24E **43 G11**
Dhahiriya = Aẓ Ẓāhirīyah
  West Bank 31°25N 34°58E **48 D3**
Dhahran = Aẓ Ẓahrān
  Si. Arabia 26°10N 50°7E **47 E6**
Dhak *Pakistan* 32°25N 72°33E **42 C5**
Dhaka *Bangla.* 23°43N 90°26E **43 H14**
Dhaka □ *Bangla.* 24°25N 90°25E **43 G14**
Dhamangaon *India* 20°48N 78°9E **44 D4**
Dhamār *Yemen* 14°30N 44°20E **49 E3**
Dhampur *India* 29°19N 78°33E **43 E8**
Dhamra → *India* 20°47N 86°58E **44 D8**
Dhamtari *India* 20°42N 81°35E **44 D5**
Dhanbad *India* 23°50N 86°30E **43 H12**
Dhangarhi *Nepal* 28°55N 80°40E **43 E9**
Dhankuta *Nepal* 26°55N 87°40E **43 F12**
Dhanora *India* 20°20N 80°22E **44 D5**
Dhanpuri *India* 23°13N 81°30E **44 C5**
Dhanushkodi *India* 9°11N 79°24E **45 K4**
Dhar *India* 22°35N 75°26E **42 H6**
Dharampur *India* 22°13N 75°18E **42 H6**
Dharamsala = Dharmsala
  India 32°16N 76°23E **42 C7**
Dharan *Nepal* 26°49N 87°17E **43 F12**
Dharangaon *India* 21°1N 75°15E **44 D2**
Dharapuram *India* 10°45N 77°34E **45 J3**
Dhariwal *India* 31°57N 75°19E **42 D6**
Dharla → *Bangla.* 25°46N 89°42E **43 G13**
Dharmapuri *India* 12°10N 78°10E **45 H4**
Dharmavaram *India* 14°29N 77°44E **45 G3**
Dharmjaygarh *India* 22°28N 83°13E **43 H10**
Dharmsala *India* 32°16N 76°23E **42 C7**
Dharni *India* 21°33N 76°53E **42 J7**
Dharur *India* 18°3N 76°58E **44 E3**
Dharwad *India* 15°30N 75°4E **45 G2**
Dhasan → *India* 25°48N 79°24E **43 G8**
Dhaulagiri *Nepal* 28°39N 83°28E **43 E10**
Dhebar, L. *India* 24°10N 74°0E **42 G6**
Dhenkanal *India* 20°45N 85°35E **44 D7**

Dhī Qār □ *Iraq* 31°0N 46°15E **46** D5
Dhībān *Jordan* 31°30N 35°46E **48** D4
Dhilwan *India* 31°31N 75°21E **42** D6
Dhimarkhera *India* 23°28N 80°22E **43** H9
Dholka *India* 22°44N 72°29E **42** H5
Dhond = Daund *India* 18°26N 74°40E **44** E2
Dhone *India* 15°25N 77°53E **45** E3
Dhoraji *India* 21°45N 70°37E **42** J4
Dhorpatan *Nepal* 28°29N 83°4E **43** E10
Dhrangadhra *India* 22°59N 71°31E **42** H4
Dhrol *India* 22°33N 70°25E **42** H4
Dhuburi *India* 26°2N 89°59E **41** F16
Dhule *India* 20°58N 74°50E **44** D2
Di Linh *Vietnam* 11°35N 108°4E **39** G7
Di Linh, Cao Nguyen
  Vietnam 11°30N 108°0E **39** G7
Diablo Range *U.S.A.* 37°20N 121°25W **78** J5
Diafarabé *Mali* 14°9N 4°57W **52** F5
Diamante *Argentina* 32°5S 60°40W **94** C3
Diamante → *Argentina* 34°30S 66°46W **94** C2
Diamantina *Brazil* 18°17S 43°40W **93** G10
Diamantina →
  Australia 26°45S 139°10E **63** D2
Diamantina △ *Australia* 23°33S 141°23E **62** C3
Diamantino *Brazil* 14°30S 56°30W **93** F7
Diamond Bar *U.S.A.* 34°1N 117°48W **79** L9
Diamond Harbour *India* 22°11N 88°14E **43** H13
Diamond Is. *Australia* 17°25S 151°5E **62** B5
Diamond Mts. *U.S.A.* 39°40N 115°50W **76** G6
Diamond Springs
  U.S.A. 38°42N 120°49W **78** G6
Dian Chi *China* 24°50N 102°43E **34** E4
Dianbai *China* 21°33N 111°0E **35** G8
Diancheng *China* 21°30N 111°4E **35** G8
Dianjiang *China* 30°24N 107°20E **34** B6
Diaoyu Dao = Senkaku-Shotō
  E. China Sea 25°45N 123°30E **29** M1
Diaoyu Tai = Senkaku-Shotō
  E. China Sea 25°45N 123°30E **29** M1
Diavolo, Mt. *India* 12°40N 92°56E **45** H11
Diba = Dibbā al Ḩiṣn
  U.A.E. 25°45N 56°16E **47** E8
Dibai *India* 28°13N 78°15E **42** E8
Dibaya
  Dem. Rep. of the Congo 6°30S 22°57E **54** F4
Dibaya-Lubue
  Dem. Rep. of the Congo 4°12S 19°54E **54** E3
Dibbā al Ḩiṣn *U.A.E.* 25°45N 56°16E **47** E8
Dibbeen △ *Jordan* 32°20N 35°45E **48** C4
D'Iberville, Lac *Canada* 55°55N 73°15W **72** A5
Dibete *Botswana* 23°45S 26°32E **56** B4
Dibrugarh *India* 27°29N 94°55E **41** F19
Dickens *U.S.A.* 33°37N 100°50W **84** E4
Dickinson *U.S.A.* 46°53N 102°47W **80** B2
Dickson *U.S.A.* 36°5N 87°23W **85** C11
Dickson City *U.S.A.* 41°28N 75°36W **83** E9
Didiéni *Mali* 13°53N 8°6W **52** F4
Didsbury *Canada* 51°35N 114°10W **70** C6
Didwana *India* 27°23N 74°36E **42** F6
Diefenbaker, L. *Canada* 51°0N 106°55W **71** C7
Diego de Almagro *Chile* 26°22S 70°3W **94** B1
Diego Suarez = Antsiranana
  Madag. 12°25S 49°20E **55** G9
Diekirch *Lux.* 49°52N 6°10E **15** E6
Dien Ban *Vietnam* 15°53N 108°16E **38** E7
Dien Bien Phu *Vietnam* 21°20N 103°0E **34** G4
Dien Chau, Vinh *Vietnam* 19°0N 105°55E **38** C5
Dien Khanh *Vietnam* 12°15N 109°6E **39** F7
Dieppe *France* 49°54N 1°4E **20** B4
Dierks *U.S.A.* 34°7N 94°1W **84** D7
Diest *Belgium* 50°58N 5°4E **15** D5
Dif *Somalia* 0°59N 40°58E **49** G3
Differdange *Lux.* 49°31N 5°54E **15** E5
Dig *India* 27°28N 77°20E **42** F7
Digby *Canada* 44°38N 65°50W **73** D6
Digges Is. *Canada* 62°40N 77°50W **69** E16
Diggi *India* 26°22N 75°26E **42** F6
Dighinala *Bangla.* 23°15N 92°5E **41** H18
Dighton *U.S.A.* 38°29N 100°28W **80** F3
Diglur *India* 18°34N 77°33E **44** E3
Digne-les-Bains *France* 44°5N 6°12E **20** D7
Digos *Phil.* 6°45N 125°20E **37** C7
Digranes *Iceland* 66°4N 14°44W **8** C6
Digras *India* 20°6N 77°45E **44** D3
Digul → *Indonesia* 7°7S 138°42E **37** F9
Dihang = Brahmaputra →
  Asia 23°40N 90°35E **43** H13
Dijlah, Nahr → *Asia* 31°0N 47°25E **46** D5
Dijon *France* 47°20N 5°3E **20** C6
Dikhil *Djibouti* 11°8N 42°20E **49** E3
Diksmuide *Belgium* 51°2N 2°52E **15** C2
Dikson *Russia* 73°40N 80°5E **26** B9
Dikti Oros *Greece* 35°8N 25°30E **23** G11
Dila *Ethiopia* 6°21N 38°22E **49** F2
Dili *E. Timor* 8°39S 125°34E **37** F7
Diligent Strait *India* 12°11N 92°57E **45** H11
Dilley *U.S.A.* 28°40N 99°10W **84** G5
Dillingham *U.S.A.* 59°3N 158°28W **74** D8
Dillon *Canada* 55°56N 108°35W **71** B7
Dillon *Mont., U.S.A.* 45°13N 112°38W **76** D7
Dillon *S.C., U.S.A.* 34°25N 79°22W **85** D15
Dillon → *Canada* 55°56N 108°56W **71** B7
Dillsburg *U.S.A.* 40°7N 77°2W **82** F7
Dilolo
  Dem. Rep. of the Congo 10°28S 22°18E **54** G4
Dimapur *India* 25°54N 93°45E **30** F7
Dimas *Mexico* 23°43N 106°47W **86** C3
Dimashq *Syria* 33°30N 36°18E **48** B5
Dimashq □ *Syria* 33°30N 36°30E **48** B5
Dimbaza *S. Africa* 32°50S 27°14E **57** D4
Dimboola *Australia* 36°28S 142°7E **63** F3
Dimbovița = Dâmbovița →
  Romania 44°12N 26°26E **17** F14
Dimbulah *Australia* 17°8S 145°4E **62** B4
Dimitrovgrad *Bulgaria* 42°5N 25°35E **23** C11
Dimitrovgrad *Russia* 54°14N 49°39E **18** D8
Dimitrovo = Pernik
  Bulgaria 42°35N 23°2E **23** C10
Dimmitt *U.S.A.* 34°33N 102°19W **84** D3
Dimona *Israel* 31°2N 35°1E **48** D4

Dinagat I. *Phil.* 10°10N 125°40E **37** B7
Dinajpur *Bangla.* 25°33N 88°43E **41** G16
Dinan *France* 48°28N 2°2W **20** B2
Dinant *Belgium* 50°16N 4°55E **15** D4
Dinapur *India* 25°38N 85°5E **43** G11
Dīnār, Kūh-e *Iran* 30°42N 51°46E **47** D6
Dinara Planina *Croatia* 44°0N 16°30E **22** C7
Dinard *France* 48°38N 2°6W **20** B2
Dinaric Alps = Dinara Planina
  Croatia 44°0N 16°30E **22** C7
Dinbych-y-Pysgod = Tenby
  U.K. 51°40N 4°42W **13** F3
Dindi → *India* 16°24N 78°15E **45** F4
Dindigul *India* 10°25N 78°0E **45** J4
Dindori *India* 22°57N 81°5E **43** H9
Ding Xian = Dingzhou
  China 38°30N 114°59E **32** E8
Dinga *Pakistan* 25°26N 67°10E **42** G2
Ding'an *China* 19°42N 110°19E **38** C8
Dingbian *China* 37°35N 107°32E **32** F4
Dingle *Ireland* 52°9N 10°17W **10** D1
Dingle B. *Ireland* 52°3N 10°20W **10** D1
Dingle Pen. *Ireland* 52°12N 10°5W **10** D1
Dingmans Ferry *U.S.A.* 41°13N 74°55W **83** E10
Dingnan *China* 24°45N 115°0E **35** E10
Dingo *Australia* 23°38S 149°19E **62** C4
Dingtao *China* 35°5N 115°35E **32** G8
Dingwall *U.K.* 57°36N 4°26W **11** D4
Dingxi *China* 35°30N 104°33E **32** G3
Dingxiang *China* 38°30N 112°58E **32** E7
Dingyuan *China* 32°32N 117°41E **35** A11
Dingzhou *China* 38°30N 114°59E **32** E8
Dinh, Mui *Vietnam* 11°22N 109°1E **39** G7
Dinh Lap *Vietnam* 21°33N 107°6E **34** G6
Dinin → *Ireland* 52°43N 7°18W **10** D4
Dinira △ *Venezuela* 9°57N 70°6W **89** E6
Dinokwe *Botswana* 23°29S 26°37E **56** B4
Dinorwic *Canada* 49°41N 92°30W **71** D10
Dinosaur △ *Canada* 50°47N 111°30W **70** C6
Dinosaur ○ *U.S.A.* 40°30N 108°45W **76** F9
Dinuba *U.S.A.* 36°32N 119°23W **78** J7
Diourbel *Senegal* 14°39N 16°12W **52** F2
Dipalpur *Pakistan* 30°40N 73°39E **42** D5
Diplo *Pakistan* 24°35N 69°35E **42** G3
Dipolog *Phil.* 8°36N 123°20E **37** C6
Dipperu △ *Australia* 21°56S 148°42E **62** C4
Dir *Pakistan* 35°8N 71°59E **40** B7
Dire Dawa *Ethiopia* 9°35N 41°45E **49** F3
Dirfis Oros *Greece* 38°40N 23°54E **23** E10
Dirk Hartog I. *Australia* 25°50S 113°5E **61** E1
Dirranbandi *Australia* 28°33S 148°17E **63** D4
Disa *India* 24°18N 72°10E **42** G5
Disappointment, C.
  U.S.A. 46°18N 124°5W **78** D2
Disappointment, L.
  Australia 23°20S 122°40E **60** D3
Disaster B. *Australia* 37°15S 149°58E **63** F4
Discovery B. *Australia* 38°10S 140°40E **63** F3
Disko = Qeqertarsuaq
  Greenland 69°45N 53°30W **4** C5
Disney Reef *Tonga* 19°17S 174°7W **59** c
Diss *U.K.* 52°23N 1°7E **13** E9
Disteghil Sar *Pakistan* 36°20N 75°12E **43** A6
District of Columbia □
  U.S.A. 38°55N 77°0W **81** F15
Distrito Federal □ *Brazil* 15°45S 47°45W **93** G9
Distrito Federal □
  Mexico 19°15N 99°10W **87** D5
Diu *India* 20°45N 70°58E **42** J4
Dīvāndarreh *Iran* 35°55N 47°2E **46** C5
Divi Pt. *India* 15°59N 81°9E **45** G5
Divide *U.S.A.* 45°45N 112°45W **76** D7
Dividing Ra. *Australia* 27°45S 116°0E **61** E2
Divinópolis *Brazil* 20°10S 44°54W **93** H10
Divnoye *Russia* 45°55N 43°21E **19** E7
Divo *Ivory C.* 5°48N 5°15W **52** G4
Dīwāl Kol *Afghan.* 34°23N 67°52E **42** B2
Dixie Mt. *U.S.A.* 39°55N 120°16W **78** F6
Dixon *Calif., U.S.A.* 38°27N 121°49W **78** G5
Dixon *Ill., U.S.A.* 41°50N 89°29W **80** E9
Dixon Entrance *U.S.A.* 54°30N 132°0W **68** G5
Dixville *Canada* 45°4N 71°46W **83** A13
Diyālá □ *Iraq* 33°45N 44°50E **46** C5
Diyālá → *Iraq* 33°13N 44°30E **46** C5
Diyarbakır *Turkey* 37°55N 40°18E **46** B4
Diyodar *India* 24°8N 71°50E **42** G4
Djakarta = Jakarta *Indonesia* 6°9S 106°49E **37** G12
Djamba *Angola* 16°45S 13°58E **56** A1
Djambala *Congo* 2°32S 14°30E **54** E2
Djanet *Algeria* 24°35N 9°32E **52** D7
Djawa = Jawa *Indonesia* 7°0S 110°0E **36** F3
Djelfa *Algeria* 34°40N 3°15E **52** B6
Djerba, Î. de *Tunisia* 33°50N 10°48E **53** B8
Djerid, Chott *Tunisia* 33°42N 8°30E **52** B7
Djibouti *Djibouti* 11°30N 43°5E **49** E3
Djibouti ■ *Africa* 12°0N 43°0E **49** E3
Djolu *Dem. Rep. of the Congo* 0°35N 22°5E **54** D4
Djougou *Benin* 9°40N 1°45E **52** G6
Djoum *Cameroon* 2°41N 12°35E **54** D2
Djourab, Erg du *Chad* 16°40N 18°50E **53** E9
Djukbinj △ *Australia* 12°11S 131°2E **60** B5
Djúpivogur *Iceland* 64°39N 14°17W **8** D6
Dmitriya Lapteva, Proliv
  Russia 73°0N 140°0E **27** B15
Dnepr = Dnipro →
  Ukraine 46°30N 32°18E **19** E5
Dneprodzerzhinsk =
  Dniprodzerzhynsk
  Ukraine 48°32N 34°37E **19** E5
Dnepropetrovsk =
  Dnipropetrovsk
  Ukraine 48°30N 35°0E **19** E6
Dnestr = Dnister →
  Europe 46°18N 30°17E **17** E16
Dnieper = Dnipro →
  Ukraine 46°30N 32°18E **19** E5
Dniester = Dnister →
  Europe 46°18N 30°17E **17** E16
Dnipro → *Ukraine* 46°30N 32°18E **19** E5
Dniprodzerzhynsk
  Ukraine 48°32N 34°37E **19** E5

Dnipropetrovsk *Ukraine* 48°30N 35°0E **19** E6
Dnister → *Europe* 46°18N 30°17E **17** E16
Dno *Russia* 57°50N 29°58E **9** H23
Dnyapro = Dnipro →
  Ukraine 46°30N 32°18E **19** E5
Do Gonbadān = Gachsārān
  Iran 30°15N 50°45E **47** D6
Doaktown *Canada* 46°33N 66°8W **73** C6
Doan Hung *Vietnam* 21°30N 105°10E **34** G5
Doba *Chad* 8°40N 16°50E **53** G9
Dobandi *Pakistan* 31°13N 66°50E **42** D2
Dobbyn *Australia* 19°44S 140°2E **62** B3
Dobele *Latvia* 56°37N 23°16E **9** H20
Doberai, Jazirah *Indonesia* 1°25S 133°0E **37** E8
Doblas *Argentina* 37°5S 64°0W **94** D3
Dobo *Indonesia* 5°45S 134°15E **37** F8
Doboj *Bos.-H.* 44°46N 18°4E **23** B8
Dobrich *Bulgaria* 43°37N 27°49E **23** C12
Dobruja *Europe* 44°30N 28°15E **17** F15
Dobrush *Belarus* 52°25N 31°22E **17** B16
Doc, Mui *Vietnam* 17°58N 106°30E **38** D6
Docker River = Kaltukatjara
  Australia 24°52S 129°5E **61** D4
Doctor Arroyo *Mexico* 23°40N 100°11W **86** C4
Doctor Pedro P. Peña
  Paraguay 22°27S 62°21W **94** A3
Doda *India* 33°10N 75°34E **43** C6
Doda, L. *Canada* 49°25N 75°13W **72** C4
Doda Betta *India* 11°24N 76°44E **45** J3
Dodballapur *India* 13°18N 77°32E **45** H3
Dodecanese = Dodekanisa
  Greece 36°35N 27°0E **23** F12
Dodekanisa *Greece* 36°35N 27°0E **23** F12
Dodge City *U.S.A.* 37°45N 100°1W **80** G3
Dodge L. *Canada* 59°50N 105°36W **71** B7
Dodgeville *U.S.A.* 42°58N 90°8W **80** D8
Dodoma *Tanzania* 6°8S 35°45E **54** F7
Dodsland *Canada* 51°50N 108°45W **71** C7
Dodson *U.S.A.* 48°24N 108°15W **76** B9
Doesburg *Neths.* 52°1N 6°9E **15** B6
Doetinchem *Neths.* 51°59N 6°18E **15** C6
Dog Creek *Canada* 51°35N 122°14W **70** C4
Dog L. *Man., Canada* 51°2N 98°31W **71** C9
Dog L. *Ont., Canada* 48°48N 89°30W **72** C2
Dogran *Pakistan* 31°48N 73°35E **42** D5
Doğubayazıt *Turkey* 39°31N 44°5E **46** B5
Doha = Ad Dawḩah
  Qatar 25°15N 51°35E **47** E6
Doha Int. ✈ (DOH) *Qatar* 25°16N 51°34E **47** E6
Dohazari *Bangla.* 22°10N 92°5E **41** H18
Dohrighat *India* 26°16N 83°31E **43** F10
Doi *Indonesia* 2°14N 127°49E **37** D7
Doi Inthanon *Thailand* 18°35N 98°29E **38** C2
Doi Inthanon △ *Thailand* 18°33N 98°34E **38** C2
Doi Khuntan △ *Thailand* 18°33N 99°14E **38** C2
Doi Luang *Thailand* 18°30N 101°0E **38** C3
Doi Luang △ *Thailand* 19°22N 99°35E **38** C2
Doi Phukha △ *Thailand* 19°8N 101°9E **38** C3
Doi Saket *Thailand* 18°52N 99°9E **38** C2
Doi Suthep Pui △
  Thailand 18°49N 98°53E **38** C2
Doi Toa *Thailand* 17°55N 98°30E **38** D2
Dois Irmãos, Sa. *Brazil* 9°0S 42°30W **93** E10
Dokdo = Liancourt Rocks
  Asia 37°15N 131°52E **29** F5
Dokkum *Neths.* 53°20N 5°59E **15** A5
Dokri *Pakistan* 27°25N 68°7E **42** F3
Dolak, Pulau *Indonesia* 8°0S 138°30E **37** F9
Dolbeau-Mistassini
  Canada 48°53N 72°14W **73** C5
Dole *France* 47°7N 5°31E **20** C6
Dolgellau *U.K.* 52°45N 3°53W **12** E4
Dolgelley = Dolgellau
  U.K. 52°45N 3°53W **12** E4
Dolinsk *Russia* 47°21N 142°48E **27** E15
Dollard *Neths.* 53°20N 7°10E **15** A7
Dolo *Ethiopia* 4°11N 42°3E **49** G3
Dolomites = Dolomiti
  Italy 46°23N 11°51E **22** A4
Dolomiti *Italy* 46°23N 11°51E **22** A4
Dolores *Argentina* 36°20S 57°40W **94** D4
Dolores *Uruguay* 33°34S 58°15W **94** C4
Dolores *U.S.A.* 37°28N 108°30W **77** H9
Dolores → *U.S.A.* 38°49N 109°17W **76** G9
Dolphin, C. *Falk. Is.* 51°10S 59°0W **96** G5
Dolphin and Union Str.
  Canada 69°5N 114°45W **68** D8
Dom Pedrito *Brazil* 31°0S 54°40W **95** C5
Domariaganj → *India* 26°17N 83°44E **43** F10
Dombarovskiy *Russia* 50°46N 59°32E **26** D6
Dombås *Norway* 62°4N 9°8E **8** E13
Dome Argus *Antarctica* 80°50S 76°30E **5** D6
Dome C. *Antarctica* 75°12S 123°37E **5** D9
Dome Fuji *Antarctica* 77°20S 39°45E **5** D5
Domel I. = Letsôk-aw Kyun
  Burma 11°30N 98°25E **39** G2
Domeyko *Chile* 29°0S 71°0W **94** B1
Domeyko, Cordillera
  Chile 24°30S 69°0W **94** A2
Dominador *Chile* 24°21S 69°20W **94** A2
Dominica ■ *W. Indies* 15°20N 61°20W **89** C7
Dominica Passage
  W. Indies 15°10N 61°20W **89** C7
Dominican Rep. ■
  W. Indies 19°0N 70°30W **89** C5
Domodóssola *Italy* 46°7N 8°17E **20** C8
Domville, Mt. *Australia* 28°1S 151°15E **63** D5
Don → *India* 16°20N 76°15E **45** F3
Don → *Russia* 47°4N 39°18E **19** E6
Don → *Aberds., U.K.* 57°11N 2°5W **11** D6
Don → *S. Yorks., U.K.* 53°41N 0°52W **12** D7
Don, C. *Australia* 11°18S 131°46E **60** B5
Don Benito *Spain* 38°53N 5°51W **21** C3
Don Figuereoa Mts.
  Jamaica 18°5N 77°36W **88** a
Don Sak *Thailand* 9°18N 99°41E **39** b
Donaghadee *U.K.* 54°39N 5°33W **10** B6
Donaghmore *Ireland* 52°52N 7°36W **10** D4
Donald *Australia* 36°23S 143°0E **63** F3
Donaldsonville *U.S.A.* 30°6N 90°59W **84** F9

Donalsonville *U.S.A.* 31°3N 84°53W **85** F12
Donau = Dunărea →
  Europe 45°20N 29°40E **17** F15
Donauwörth *Germany* 48°43N 10°47E **16** D6
Doncaster *U.K.* 53°32N 1°6W **12** D6
Dondo *Angola* 9°45S 14°25E **54** F2
Dondo, Teluk *Indonesia* 0°50N 120°30E **37** D6
Dondra Head *Sri Lanka* 5°55N 80°40E **45** M5
Donegal *Ireland* 54°39N 8°5W **10** B3
Donegal □ *Ireland* 54°53N 8°0W **10** B4
Donegal B. *Ireland* 54°31N 8°49W **10** B3
Donets → *Russia* 47°33N 40°55E **19** E7
Donets Basin *Ukraine* 49°0N 38°0E **6** F13
Donetsk *Ukraine* 48°0N 37°45E **19** E6
Dong Ba Thin *Vietnam* 12°8N 109°13E **39** F7
Dong Dang *Vietnam* 21°54N 106°42E **34** G6
Dong Giam *Vietnam* 19°25N 105°31E **38** C5
Dong Ha *Vietnam* 16°55N 107°8E **38** D6
Dong Hene *Laos* 16°40N 105°18E **38** D5
Dong Hoi *Vietnam* 17°29N 106°36E **38** D6
Dong Jiang → *China* 23°6N 114°0E **35** F10
Dong Khe *Vietnam* 22°26N 106°27E **38** A6
Dong Phayayen
  Thailand 14°20N 101°22E **38** E3
Dong Ujimqin Qi *China* 45°32N 116°55E **32** B9
Dong Van *Vietnam* 23°16N 105°22E **38** A5
Dong Xoai *Vietnam* 11°32N 106°55E **39** G6
Dong'an *China* 26°23N 111°12E **35** D8
Dongara *Australia* 29°14S 114°57E **61** E1
Dongbei *China* 45°0N 125°0E **33** D13
Dongchuan *China* 26°8N 103°1E **34** D4
Dongfang *China* 18°50N 108°33E **38** C7
Dongfeng *China* 42°40N 125°34E **33** C13
Donggala *Indonesia* 0°30S 119°40E **37** E5
Donggan *China* 23°22N 105°9E **34** F5
Donggang *China* 39°52N 124°10E **33** E13
Dongguan *China* 22°58N 113°44E **35** F9
Dongguang *China* 37°50N 116°30E **32** F9
Donghae *S. Korea* 37°29N 129°7E **33** F15
Donghai Dao *China* 21°0N 110°15E **35** G8
Dongjingcheng *China* 44°5N 129°10E **33** B15
Dongkou *China* 27°6N 110°35E **35** D8
Donglan *China* 24°30N 107°21E **34** E6
Dongliao He → *China* 42°58N 123°32E **33** C12
Dongliu *China* 30°13N 116°55E **35** B11
Dongmen *China* 22°20N 107°48E **34** F6
Dongning *China* 44°2N 131°5E **33** B16
Dongnyi *China* 28°3N 100°15E **34** C3
Dongola *Sudan* 19°9N 30°22E **53** E12
Dongou *Congo* 2°0N 18°5E **54** D3
Dongping *China* 35°55N 116°20E **32** G9
Dongsha Dao
  S. China Sea 20°45N 116°43E **35** G11
Dongshan *China* 23°43N 117°30E **35** F11
Dongsheng = Ordos
  China 39°50N 110°0E **32** E6
Dongtai *China* 32°51N 120°21E **33** H11
Dongting Hu *China* 29°18N 112°45E **35** C9
Dongtou *China* 27°51N 121°10E **35** D13
Dongxiang *China* 28°11N 116°34E **35** C11
Dongxing *China* 21°34N 108°0E **34** G7
Dongyang *China* 29°13N 120°15E **35** C13
Dongying *China* 37°9N 118°37E **33** F10
Dongyinggang *China* 37°55N 118°58E **33** F10
Dongzhi *China* 30°9N 117°0E **35** B11
Donington, C. *Australia* 34°45S 136°0E **63** E2
Doniphan *U.S.A.* 36°37N 90°50W **80** G8
Dønna *Norway* 66°6N 12°30E **8** C15
Donna *U.S.A.* 26°9N 98°4W **84** H5
Donnaconna *Canada* 46°41N 71°41W **73** C5
Donnelly's Crossing
  N.Z. 35°42S 173°38E **59** A4
Donner Pass *U.S.A.* 39°19N 120°20W **78** F6
Donnybrook *Australia* 33°34S 115°48E **61** F2
Donnybrook *S. Africa* 29°59S 29°48E **57** C4
Donora *U.S.A.* 40°11N 79°52W **82** F5
Donostia = Donostia-San
  Sebastián *Spain* 43°17N 1°58W **21** A5
Donostia-San Sebastián
  Spain 43°17N 1°58W **21** A5
Donwood *Canada* 44°19N 78°16W **82** B6
Doomadgee *Australia* 17°56S 138°49E **62** B2
Doomadgee ○ *Australia* 17°56S 138°49E **62** B2
Doon → *U.K.* 55°27N 4°39W **11** F4
Doon Doon ○ *Australia* 16°18S 128°14E **60** C4
Dora, L. *Australia* 22°0S 123°0E **60** D3
Dora Báltea → *Italy* 45°11N 8°3E **20** D8
Doran L. *Canada* 61°13N 108°6W **71** A7
Dorchester, C. *Canada* 65°27N 77°27W **69** D16
Dorchester, C. *Canada* 50°42N 2°27W **13** G5
Dordabis *Namibia* 22°52S 17°38E **56** C2
Dordogne → *France* 45°2N 0°36W **20** D3
Dordrecht *Neths.* 51°48N 4°39E **15** C4
Dordrecht *S. Africa* 31°20S 27°3E **56** E4
Doré L. *Canada* 54°46N 107°17W **71** C7
Dori *Burkina Faso* 14°3N 0°2W **52** F5
Doring → *S. Africa* 31°54S 18°39E **56** E2
Doringbos *S. Africa* 31°59S 19°16E **56** E2
Dorking *U.K.* 51°14N 0°19W **13** F7
Dornakal *India* 17°27N 80°10E **44** F5
Dornbirn *Austria* 47°25N 9°45E **16** E5
Dornie *U.K.* 57°17N 5°31W **11** D3
Dornoch *U.K.* 57°52N 4°2W **11** D4
Dornoch *U.K.* 57°53N 4°2W **11** D4
Dornoch Firth *U.K.* 57°51N 4°4W **11** D4
Dornogovĭ □ *Mongolia* 44°0N 110°0E **32** C6
Dorohoi *Romania* 47°56N 26°23E **17** E14
Döröö Nuur *Mongolia* 48°0N 93°0E **30** B7
Dorr *Iran* 33°17N 50°38E **47** C6
Dorre I. *Australia* 25°13S 113°12E **61** E1
Dorrigo *Australia* 30°20S 152°44E **63** E5
Dorris *U.S.A.* 41°58N 121°55W **76** F3
Dorset *Canada* 45°14N 78°54W **82** A6
Dorset *Ohio, U.S.A.* 41°40N 80°40W **82** E4
Dorset *Vt., U.S.A.* 43°15N 73°5W **83** C11
Dorset □ *U.K.* 50°45N 2°26W **13** G5
Dortmund *Germany* 51°30N 7°28E **16** C4
Dörtyol *Turkey* 36°50N 36°13E **46** B3
Dorūneh *Iran* 35°10N 57°18E **47** C8

Dos Bahías, C. *Argentina* 44°58S 65°32W **96** E3
Dos Hermanas *Spain* 37°16N 5°55W **21** D3
Dos Palos *U.S.A.* 36°59N 120°37W **78** J6
Dosso *Niger* 13°0N 3°13E **52** F6
Dothan *U.S.A.* 31°13N 85°24W **85** F12
Douai *France* 50°21N 3°4E **20** A5
Douala *Cameroon* 4°0N 9°45E **54** D1
Douarnenez *France* 48°6N 4°21W **20** B1
Double Island Pt.
  Australia 25°56S 153°11E **63** D5
Double Mountain Fork →
  U.S.A. 33°16N 100°0W **84** E4
Doubs → *France* 46°53N 5°1E **20** C6
Doubtful Sd. *N.Z.* 45°20S 166°49E **59** F1
Doubtless B. *N.Z.* 34°55S 173°26E **59** A4
Douglas *Canada* 45°31N 76°56W **82** A7
Douglas *I. of Man* 54°10N 4°28W **12** C3
Douglas *S. Africa* 29°4S 23°46E **56** D3
Douglas *Ariz., U.S.A.* 31°21N 109°33W **77** L9
Douglas *Ga., U.S.A.* 31°31N 82°51W **85** F13
Douglas *Wyo., U.S.A.* 42°45N 105°24W **76** E11
Douglas Apsley △
  Australia 41°45S 148°11E **63** G4
Douglas Chan. *Canada* 53°40N 129°20W **70** C3
Douglas Pt. *Canada* 44°19N 81°37W **82** B3
Douglasville *U.S.A.* 33°45N 84°45W **85** E12
Doumen *China* 22°10N 113°18E **35** F9
Dounreay *U.K.* 58°35N 3°44W **11** C5
Dourada, Serra *Brazil* 13°10S 48°45W **93** F9
Dourados *Brazil* 22°9S 54°50W **95** A5
Dourados → *Brazil* 21°58S 54°18W **95** A5
Dourados, Serra dos
  Brazil 23°30S 53°30W **95** A5
Douro → *Europe* 41°8N 8°40W **21** B1
Dove → *U.K.* 52°51N 1°36W **12** E6
Dove Creek *U.S.A.* 37°46N 108°54W **77** H9
Dover *Australia* 43°18S 147°2E **63** G4
Dover *U.K.* 51°7N 1°19E **13** F9
Dover *Del., U.S.A.* 39°10N 75°32W **81** F16
Dover *N.H., U.S.A.* 43°12N 70°56W **83** C14
Dover *N.J., U.S.A.* 40°53N 74°34W **83** F10
Dover *Ohio, U.S.A.* 40°32N 81°29W **82** F3
Dover, Pt. *Australia* 32°32S 125°32E **61** F4
Dover, Str. of *Europe* 51°0N 1°30E **13** G9
Dover-Foxcroft *U.S.A.* 45°11N 69°13W **81** C19
Dover Plains *U.S.A.* 41°43N 73°35W **83** E11
Dovey = Dyfi → *U.K.* 52°32N 4°3W **13** E3
Dovrefjell *Norway* 62°15N 9°33E **8** E13
Dovrefjell-Sunndalsfjella △
  Norway 62°23N 9°11E **8** E13
Dow Rūd *Iran* 33°28N 49°4E **47** C6
Dowagiac *U.S.A.* 41°59N 86°6W **80** E10
Dowerin *Australia* 31°12S 117°2E **61** F2
Dowgha'i *Iran* 36°54N 58°32E **47** B8
Dowlatābād *Kermān, Iran* 28°20N 56°40E **47** D8
Dowlatābād *Khorāsān,
  Iran* 35°16N 59°29E **47** C8
Down □ *U.K.* 54°23N 6°2W **10** B5
Downey *U.S.A.* 42°26N 112°7W **76** E7
Downham Market *U.K.* 52°37N 0°23E **13** E8
Downieville *U.S.A.* 39°34N 120°50W **78** F6
Downpatrick *U.K.* 54°20N 5°43W **10** B6
Downpatrick Hd. *Ireland* 54°20N 9°21W **10** B2
Downsville *U.S.A.* 42°5N 75°0W **83** D10
Downton, Mt. *Canada* 52°42N 124°52W **70** C4
Dowsārī *Iran* 28°25N 57°59E **47** D8
Doyle *U.S.A.* 40°2N 120°6W **78** E6
Doylestown *U.S.A.* 40°21N 75°10W **83** F9
Dozois, Rés. *Canada* 47°30N 77°5W **72** C4
Dra Khel *Pakistan* 27°58N 66°45E **42** F2
Drâa, C. *Morocco* 28°47N 11°0W **52** C3
Drâa, Hamada du *Algeria* 28°0N 7°0W **52** C4
Drâa, Oued → *Morocco* 28°40N 11°10W **52** C3
Drachten *Neths.* 53°7N 6°5E **15** A6
Drăgăşani *Romania* 44°39N 24°17E **17** F13
Dragichyn *Belarus* 52°15N 25°8E **17** B13
Dragoman, Prokhod
  Bulgaria 42°58N 22°53E **23** C10
Dragon's Mouths
  Trin. & Tob. 11°0N 61°50W **93** K15
Draguignan *France* 43°32N 6°27E **20** E7
Drain *U.S.A.* 43°40N 123°19W **76** E2
Drake *U.S.A.* 47°55N 100°23W **80** B3
Drake Passage *S. Ocean* 58°0S 68°0W **5** B17
Drakensberg *S. Africa* 31°0S 28°0E **57** D4
Drama *Greece* 41°9N 24°10E **23** D11
Drammen *Norway* 59°42N 10°12E **9** G14
Drangajökull *Iceland* 66°9N 22°15W **8** C2
Dras *India* 34°25N 75°48E **43** B6
Drau = Drava → *Croatia* 45°33N 18°55E **23** B8
Drava → *Croatia* 45°33N 18°55E **23** B8
Drayton *Canada* 43°46N 80°40W **82** C4
Drayton Valley *Canada* 53°12N 114°58W **70** C6
Drenthe □ *Neths.* 52°52N 6°40E **15** B6
Dresden *Canada* 42°35N 82°11W **82** D2
Dresden *Germany* 51°3N 13°44E **16** C7
Dresden *U.S.A.* 42°41N 76°57W **82** D8
Dreux *France* 48°44N 1°23E **20** B4
Driffield *U.K.* 54°0N 0°26W **12** C7
Driftwood *U.S.A.* 41°20N 78°8W **82** E6
Driggs *U.S.A.* 43°44N 111°6W **76** E8
Drin → *Albania* 42°1N 19°38E **23** C8
Drina → *Bos.-H.* 44°53N 19°21E **23** B8
Drøbak *Norway* 59°39N 10°39E **9** G14
Drobeta-Turnu Severin
  Romania 44°39N 22°41E **17** F12
Drochia *Moldova* 48°2N 27°48E **17** D14
Drogheda *Ireland* 53°43N 6°22W **10** C5
Drogichin = Dragichyn
  Belarus 52°15N 25°8E **17** B13
Drogobych = Drohobych
  Ukraine 49°20N 23°30E **17** D12
Drohobych *Ukraine* 49°20N 23°30E **17** D12
Droichead Átha = Drogheda
  Ireland 53°43N 6°22W **10** C5
Droichead na Bandan = Bandon
  Ireland 51°44N 8°44W **10** E3
Droichead Nua = Newbridge
  Ireland 53°11N 6°48W **10** C5

Droitwich U.K. 52°16N 2°8W 13 E5
Drôme → France 44°46N 4°46E 20 D6
Dromedary, C. Australia 36°17S 150°10E 63 F5
Dromore Down, U.K. 54°25N 6°9W 10 B5
Dromore Tyrone, U.K. 54°31N 7°28W 10 B4
Dromore West Ireland 54°15N 8°52W 10 B3
Dronfield U.K. 53°19N 1°27W 12 D6
Dronning Maud Land Antarctica 72°30S 12°0E 5 D3
Dronten Neths. 52°32N 5°43E 15 B5
Druk Yul = Bhutan ■ Asia 27°25N 90°30E 41 F17
Drumbo Canada 43°16N 80°35W 82 C4
Drumcliff Ireland 54°20N 8°29W 10 B3
Drumheller Canada 51°25N 112°40W 70 C6
Drummond U.S.A. 46°40N 113°9W 76 C7
Drummond I. U.S.A. 46°1N 83°39W 81 B12
Drummond Pt. Australia 34°9S 135°16E 63 E2
Drummond Ra. Australia 23°45S 147°10E 62 C4
Drummondville Canada 45°55N 72°25W 72 C5
Drumright U.S.A. 35°59N 96°36W 84 D6
Druskininkai Lithuania 54°3N 23°58E 9 J20
Drut → Belarus 53°8N 30°5E 17 B16
Druzhina Russia 68°14N 145°18E 27 C15
Dry Harbour Mts. Jamaica 18°19N 77°24W 88 a
Dry Tortugas U.S.A. 24°38N 82°55W 85 J13
Dryander △ Australia 20°13S 148°34E 62 b
Dryden Canada 49°47N 92°50W 71 D10
Dryden U.S.A. 42°30N 76°18W 83 D8
Drygalski I. Antarctica 66°0S 92°0E 5 C7
Drygalski Ice Tongue Antarctica 75°24S 163°30E 5 D11
Drysdale → Australia 13°59S 126°51E 60 B4
Drysdale I. Australia 11°41S 136°0E 62 A2
Drysdale River △ Australia 14°56S 127°2E 60 B4
Du Gué → Canada 57°21N 70°45W 72 A5
Du He → China 32°48N 110°40E 35 A8
Du Quoin U.S.A. 38°1N 89°14W 80 F9
Du'an China 23°59N 108°3E 34 F7
Duanesburg U.S.A. 42°45N 74°11W 83 D10
Duaringa Australia 23°42S 149°42E 62 C4
Duarte, Pico Dom. Rep. 19°2N 70°59W 89 D5
Dubăsari Moldova 47°15N 29°10E 17 E15
Dubăsari Vdkhr. Moldova 47°30N 29°0E 17 E15
Dubawnt → Canada 64°33N 100°6W 71 A8
Dubawnt L. Canada 63°8N 101°28W 71 A8
Dubbo Australia 32°11S 148°35E 63 E4
Dublin Ga., U.S.A. 32°32N 82°54W 85 E13
Dublin Tex., U.S.A. 32°5N 98°21W 84 E5
Dublin □ Ireland 53°24N 6°20W 10 C5
Dubno Ukraine 50°25N 25°45E 17 C13
Dubois Idaho, U.S.A. 44°10N 112°14W 76 D7
DuBois Pa., U.S.A. 41°7N 78°46W 82 E6
Dubossary = Dubăsari Moldova 47°15N 29°10E 17 E15
Dubovka Russia 49°5N 44°50E 19 E7
Dubrajpur India 23°48N 87°25E 43 H12
Dubréka Guinea 9°46N 13°31W 52 G3
Dubrovitsa = Dubrovytsya Ukraine 51°31N 26°35E 17 C14
Dubrovnik Croatia 42°39N 18°6E 23 C8
Dubrovytsya Ukraine 51°31N 26°35E 17 C14
Dubuque U.S.A. 42°30N 90°41W 80 D8
Duc Tho Vietnam 18°32N 105°35E 38 C5
Duchang China 29°18N 116°12E 35 C11
Duchesne U.S.A. 40°10N 110°24W 76 F8
Duchess Australia 21°20S 139°50E 62 C2
Ducie I. Pac. Oc. 24°40S 124°48W 65 K15
Duck → U.S.A. 36°2N 87°52W 85 C11
Duck Cr. → Australia 22°37S 116°53E 60 D2
Duck Lake Canada 52°50N 106°16W 71 C7
Duck Mountain ⌂ Canada 51°45N 101°0W 71 C8
Duckwall, Mt. U.S.A. 37°58N 120°7W 78 H6
Dudhi India 24°15N 83°10E 43 G10
Dudinka Russia 69°30N 86°13E 27 C9
Dudley U.K. 52°31N 2°5W 13 E5
Dudna → India 19°17N 76°54E 44 E3
Dudwa India 28°30N 80°41E 43 E9
Dudwa △ India 28°30N 80°40E 43 E9
Duero = Douro → Europe 41°8N 8°40W 21 B1
Dufftown U.K. 57°27N 3°8W 11 D5
Dugi Otok Croatia 44°0N 15°3E 16 G8
Duisburg Germany 51°26N 6°45E 16 C4
Duiwelskloof = Modjadjiskloof S. Africa 23°42S 30°10E 57 B5
Dujiangyan China 31°2N 103°38E 34 B4
Dūkdamīn Iran 35°59N 57°43E 47 C8
Dukelský Průsmyk Slovak Rep. 49°25N 21°42E 17 D11
Dukhān Qatar 25°25N 50°50E 47 E6
Duki Pakistan 30°14N 68°25E 40 D6
Duku Nigeria 10°43N 10°43E 53 F8
Dukuza = Stanger S. Africa 29°27S 31°14E 57 C5
Dulan China 36°0N 97°11E 30 D8
Dulce U.S.A. 36°56N 107°0W 77 H10
Dulce → Argentina 30°32S 62°33W 94 C3
Dulce, G. Costa Rica 8°40N 83°20W 88 E3
Dulf Iraq 35°7N 45°51E 46 C5
Duliu China 39°2N 116°55E 32 E9
Dulles Int. ✈ (IAD) U.S.A. 38°57N 77°27W 81 F15
Dullewala Pakistan 31°50N 71°25E 42 D4
Dullstroom S. Africa 25°27S 30°7E 57 C5
Dulq Maghār Syria 36°22N 38°39E 46 B3
Duluth U.S.A. 46°47N 92°6W 80 B7
Dum Duma India 27°40N 95°40E 41 F19
Dūmā Syria 33°34N 36°24E 48 B5
Dumaguete Phil. 9°17N 123°15E 37 C6
Dumai Indonesia 1°35N 101°28E 36 D2
Dumaran Phil. 10°33N 119°50E 37 B5
Dumas Ark., U.S.A. 33°53N 91°29W 84 E9
Dumas Tex., U.S.A. 35°52N 101°58W 84 D4
Dumayr Syria 33°39N 36°42E 48 B5
Dumbarton U.K. 55°57N 4°33W 11 F4
Dumbleyung Australia 33°17S 117°42E 61 F2
Dumfries U.K. 55°4N 3°37W 11 F5
Dumfries & Galloway □ U.K. 55°9N 3°58W 11 F5
Dumka India 24°12N 87°15E 43 G12
Dumoine → Canada 46°13N 77°51W 72 C4
Dumoine, L. Canada 46°55N 77°55W 72 C4
Dumont d'Urville Antarctica 66°40S 140°0E 5 C10
Dumont d'Urville Sea S. Ocean 63°30S 138°0E 5 C9
Dumyât Egypt 31°24N 31°48E 53 B12
Dún Dealgan = Dundalk Ireland 54°1N 6°24W 10 B5
Dún Garbhán = Dungarvan Ireland 52°5N 7°37W 10 D4
Dun Laoghaire-Rathdown □ Ireland 53°14N 6°11W 10 C5
Duna = Dunărea → Europe 45°20N 29°40E 17 F15
Dunagiri India 30°31N 79°52E 43 D8
Dunaj = Dunărea → Europe 45°20N 29°40E 17 F15
Dunakeszi Hungary 47°37N 19°8E 17 E10
Dunărea → Europe 45°20N 29°40E 17 F15
Dunaújváros Hungary 46°58N 18°57E 17 E10
Dunav = Dunărea → Europe 45°20N 29°40E 17 F15
Dunay Russia 42°52N 132°22E 28 C6
Dunback N.Z. 45°23S 170°36E 59 F3
Dunbar U.K. 56°0N 2°31W 11 E6
Dunblane U.K. 56°11N 3°58W 11 E5
Duncan Canada 48°45N 123°40W 78 B3
Duncan Ariz., U.S.A. 32°43N 109°6W 77 K9
Duncan Okla., U.S.A. 34°30N 97°57W 84 D6
Duncan, L. Canada 53°29N 77°58W 72 B4
Duncan L. Canada 62°51N 113°58W 70 A6
Duncan Passage India 11°0N 92°0E 45 J11
Duncan Town Bahamas 22°15N 75°45W 88 B4
Duncannon U.S.A. 40°23N 77°2W 82 F7
Duncansby Head U.K. 58°38N 3°1W 11 C5
Duncansville U.S.A. 40°25N 78°26W 82 F6
Dund-Us Mongolia 48°1N 91°38E 30 B7
Dundalk Canada 44°10N 80°24W 82 B4
Dundalk Ireland 54°1N 6°24W 10 B5
Dundalk U.S.A. 39°15N 76°31W 81 F15
Dundalk Bay Ireland 53°55N 6°15W 10 C5
Dundas = Uummannaq Greenland 77°33N 68°52W 69 B18
Dundas Canada 43°17N 79°59W 82 C5
Dundas, L. Australia 32°35S 121°50E 61 F3
Dundas I. Canada 54°30N 130°50W 70 C2
Dundas Str. Australia 11°15S 131°35E 60 B5
Dundee S. Africa 28°11S 30°15E 57 C5
Dundee U.K. 56°28N 2°59W 11 E6
Dundee U.S.A. 42°32N 76°59W 82 D8
Dundee City □ U.K. 56°30N 2°58W 11 E6
Dundgovĭ □ Mongolia 45°10N 106°0E 32 B4
Dundrum U.K. 54°16N 5°52W 10 B6
Dundrum B. U.K. 54°13N 5°47W 10 B6
Dunedin N.Z. 45°50S 170°33E 59 F3
Dunedin U.S.A. 28°1N 82°46W 85 G13
Dunfanaghy Ireland 55°11N 7°58W 10 A4
Dunfermline U.K. 56°5N 3°27W 11 E5
Dungannon Canada 43°51N 81°36W 82 C3
Dungannon U.K. 54°31N 6°46W 10 B5
Dungarpur India 23°52N 73°45E 42 H5
Dungarvan Ireland 52°5N 7°37W 10 D4
Dungarvan Harbour Ireland 52°4N 7°35W 10 D4
Dungeness U.K. 50°54N 0°59E 13 G8
Dungiven U.K. 54°56N 6°56W 10 B5
Dunglow Ireland 54°57N 8°21W 10 B3
Dungo, L. do Angola 17°15S 19°0E 56 A2
Dungog Australia 32°22S 151°46E 63 E5
Dungu Dem. Rep. of the Congo 3°40N 28°32E 54 D5
Dungun Malaysia 4°45N 103°25E 39 K4
Dunhua China 43°20N 128°14E 33 C15
Dunhuang China 40°8N 94°36E 30 C7
Dunk I. Australia 17°59S 146°29E 62 B4
Dunkeld Australia 33°25S 149°29E 63 E4
Dunkeld U.K. 56°34N 3°35W 11 E5
Dunkerque France 51°2N 2°20E 20 A5
Dunkery Beacon U.K. 51°9N 3°36W 13 F4
Dunkirk = Dunkerque France 51°2N 2°20E 20 A5
Dunkirk U.S.A. 42°29N 79°20W 82 D5
Dunleer Ireland 53°50N 6°24W 10 C5
Dunmanus B. Ireland 51°31N 9°50W 10 E2
Dunmanway Ireland 51°43N 9°6W 10 E2
Dunmarra Australia 16°42S 133°25E 62 B1
Dunmore U.S.A. 41°25N 75°38W 83 E9
Dunmore East Ireland 52°9N 7°0W 10 D5
Dunmore Town Bahamas 25°30N 76°39W 88 A4
Dunn U.S.A. 35°19N 78°37W 85 D15
Dunnellon U.S.A. 29°3N 82°28W 85 G13
Dunnet Hd. U.K. 58°40N 3°21W 11 C5
Dunning U.S.A. 41°50N 100°6W 80 E3
Dunnville Canada 42°54N 79°36W 82 D5
Dunolly Australia 36°51S 143°44E 63 F3
Dunoon U.K. 55°57N 4°56W 11 F4
Duns U.K. 55°47N 2°20W 11 F6
Dunseith U.S.A. 48°50N 100°3W 80 A3
Dunshaughlin Ireland 53°31N 6°33W 10 C5
Dunsmuir U.S.A. 41°13N 122°16W 76 F2
Dunstable U.K. 51°53N 0°32W 13 F7
Dunstan Mts. N.Z. 44°53S 169°35E 59 F2
Dunster Canada 53°8N 119°50W 70 C5
Dunvegan U.K. 57°27N 6°35W 11 D2
Dunvegan L. Canada 60°8N 107°10W 71 A7
Duolun China 42°12N 116°28E 32 C9
Duong Dong Vietnam 10°13N 103°58E 39 G4
Dupree U.S.A. 45°4N 101°35W 80 C3
Dupuyer U.S.A. 48°13N 112°30W 76 B7
Durack → Australia 15°33S 127°52E 60 C4
Durack Ra. Australia 16°50S 127°40E 60 C4
Durack River Australia 15°32S 127°39E 60 C4
Durance → France 43°55N 4°45E 20 E6
Durand U.S.A. 44°38N 91°58W 80 C8
Durango Mexico 24°3N 104°39W 86 C4
Durango U.S.A. 37°16N 107°53W 77 H10
Durango □ Mexico 24°50N 105°20W 86 C4
Durant Miss., U.S.A. 33°4N 89°51W 85 E10
Durant Okla., U.S.A. 33°59N 96°25W 84 E6
Durazno Uruguay 33°25S 56°31W 94 C4
Durazzo = Durrës Albania 41°19N 19°28E 23 D8
Durban S. Africa 29°49S 31°1E 57 C5
Durban ✈ (DUR) S. Africa 29°37S 31°7E 57 C5
Durbuy Belgium 50°21N 5°28E 15 D5
Düren Germany 50°48N 6°29E 16 C4
Durg = Bhilainagar-Durg India 21°13N 81°26E 44 D5
Durgapur India 23°30N 87°20E 43 H12
Durham Canada 44°10N 80°49W 82 B4
Durham U.K. 54°47N 1°34W 12 C6
Durham Calif., U.S.A. 39°39N 121°48W 78 F5
Durham N.C., U.S.A. 35°59N 78°54W 85 D15
Durham N.H., U.S.A. 43°8N 70°56W 83 C14
Durham □ U.K. 54°42N 1°45W 12 C6
Durlas = Thurles Ireland 52°41N 7°49W 10 D4
Ḑurmā Si. Arabia 24°37N 46°8E 46 E5
Durmitor Montenegro 43°10N 19°0E 23 C8
Durness U.K. 58°34N 4°45W 11 C4
Durrës Albania 41°19N 19°28E 23 D8
Durrow Ireland 52°51N 7°24W 10 D4
Dursey I. Ireland 51°36N 10°12W 10 E1
Dursley U.K. 51°40N 2°21W 13 F5
Dursunbey Turkey 39°35N 28°37E 23 E13
Durūz, Jabal ad Jordan 32°35N 36°40E 48 C5
D'Urville, Tanjung Indonesia 1°28S 137°54E 37 E9
D'Urville I. N.Z. 40°50S 173°55E 59 D4
Duryea U.S.A. 41°20N 75°45W 83 E9
Dushak Turkmenistan 37°13N 60°1E 47 B9
Dushan China 25°48N 107°30E 34 E6
Dushanbe Tajikistan 38°33N 68°48E 26 F7
Dushore U.S.A. 41°31N 76°24W 83 E8
Dusky Sd. N.Z. 45°47S 166°30E 59 F1
Dussejour, C. Australia 14°45S 128°13E 60 B4
Düsseldorf Germany 51°14N 6°47E 16 C4
Dutch Harbor U.S.A. 53°53N 166°32W 74 E6
Dutlwe Botswana 23°58S 23°46E 56 B3
Dutton Canada 42°39N 81°30W 82 D3
Dutton → Australia 20°44S 143°10E 62 C3
Dutywa S. Africa 32°8S 28°18E 57 D4
Duwayhin, Khawr U.A.E. 24°20N 51°25E 47 E6
Duyfken Pt. Australia 12°33S 141°38E 62 A3
Duyun China 26°18N 107°29E 34 D6
Dvina, Severnaya → Russia 64°32N 40°30E 18 B7
Dvinsk = Daugavpils Latvia 55°53N 26°32E 9 J22
Dvinskaya Guba Russia 65°0N 39°0E 18 B6
Dwarka India 22°18N 69°8E 42 H3
Dwellingup Australia 32°43S 116°4E 61 F2
Dwight Canada 45°20N 79°1W 82 A5
Dwight U.S.A. 41°5N 88°26W 80 E9
Dyatlovo = Dzyatlava Belarus 53°28N 25°28E 17 B13
Dyce U.K. 57°13N 2°12W 11 D6
Dyer, C. Canada 66°37N 61°16W 69 D19
Dyer Bay Canada 45°10N 81°20W 82 A3
Dyer Plateau Antarctica 70°45S 65°30W 5 D17
Dyersburg U.S.A. 36°3N 89°23W 85 C10
Dyfi → U.K. 52°32N 4°3W 13 E3
Dymer Ukraine 50°47N 30°18E 17 C16
Dysart Australia 22°32S 148°23E 62 C4
Dzaoudzi Mayotte 12°47S 45°16E 55 a
Dzavhan Gol → Mongolia 48°54N 93°23E 30 B7
Dzerzhinsk Russia 56°14N 43°30E 18 C7
Dzhalinda Russia 53°26N 124°0E 27 D13
Dzhambul = Taraz Kazakhstan 42°54N 71°22E 30 C3
Dzhankoy Ukraine 45°40N 34°20E 19 E5
Dzhezkazgan = Zhezqazghan Kazakhstan 47°44N 67°40E 26 E7
Dzhizak = Jizzax Uzbekistan 40°6N 67°50E 26 E7
Dzhugdzur, Khrebet Russia 57°30N 138°0E 27 D14
Dzhungarskiye Vorota = Dzungarian Gate Asia 45°10N 82°0E 30 B5
Działdowo Poland 53°15N 20°15E 17 B11
Dzibilchaltún Mexico 21°10N 89°35W 87 C7
Dzierżoniów Poland 50°45N 16°39E 17 C9
Dzilam de Bravo Mexico 21°24N 88°53W 87 C7
Dzūkija △ Lithuania 54°10N 24°30E 9 J21
Dzungarian Basin = Junggar Pendi China 44°30N 86°0E 30 C6
Dzungarian Gate Asia 45°10N 82°0E 30 B5
Dzüünbayan Mongolia 44°29N 110°2E 32 B6
Dzüünharaa Mongolia 48°52N 106°28E 30 B10
Dzüünmod Mongolia 47°45N 106°58E 30 B10
Dzyarzhynsk Belarus 53°40N 27°1E 17 B14
Dzyatlava Belarus 53°28N 25°28E 17 B13

E

E.C. Manning ⌂ Canada 49°5N 120°45W 70 D4
Eabamet L. Canada 51°30N 87°46W 72 B2
Eabametoong Canada 51°30N 88°0W 72 B2
Éadan Doire = Edenderry Ireland 53°21N 7°4W 10 C4
Eads U.S.A. 38°29N 102°47W 76 G12
Eagar U.S.A. 34°6N 109°17W 77 J9
Eagle Alaska, U.S.A. 64°47N 141°12W 68 E3
Eagle Colo., U.S.A. 39°39N 106°50W 76 G10
Eagle → Canada 53°36N 57°26W 73 B8
Eagle Butte U.S.A. 45°0N 101°10W 80 C3
Eagle Grove U.S.A. 42°40N 93°54W 80 D7
Eagle L. Canada 49°42N 93°13W 71 D10
Eagle L. Calif., U.S.A. 40°39N 120°45W 76 F3
Eagle L. Maine, U.S.A. 46°20N 69°22W 81 B19
Eagle Lake Canada 45°8N 78°29W 82 A6
Eagle Lake Maine, U.S.A. 47°3N 68°36W 81 B19
Eagle Lake Tex., U.S.A. 29°35N 96°20W 84 G6
Eagle Mountain U.S.A. 33°49N 115°27W 79 M11
Eagle Nest U.S.A. 36°33N 105°16W 77 H11
Eagle Pass U.S.A. 28°43N 100°30W 84 G4
Eagle Pk. U.S.A. 38°10N 119°25W 78 G7
Eagle Pt. Australia 16°11S 124°23E 60 C3
Eagle River Mich., U.S.A. 47°25N 88°18W 80 B9
Eagle River Wis., U.S.A. 45°55N 89°15W 80 C9
Eaglehawk Australia 36°44S 144°15E 63 F3
Eagles Mere U.S.A. 41°25N 76°33W 83 E8
Ear Falls Canada 50°38N 93°13W 71 C10
Earlimart U.S.A. 35°53N 119°16W 79 K7
Earlville U.S.A. 42°44N 75°32W 83 D9
Earn → U.K. 56°21N 3°18W 11 E5
Earn, L. U.K. 56°23N 4°13W 11 E4
Earnslaw, Mt. N.Z. 44°32S 168°27E 59 F2
Earth U.S.A. 34°14N 102°24W 84 D3
Easley U.S.A. 34°50N 82°36W 85 D13
East Anglia U.K. 52°50N 1°0E 12 E9
East Angus Canada 45°30N 71°40W 73 C5
East Antarctica Antarctica 80°0S 90°0E 5 D7
East Aurora U.S.A. 42°46N 78°37W 82 D6
East Ayrshire □ U.K. 55°26N 4°11W 11 F4
East Bengal Bangla. 24°0N 90°0E 41 G17
East Beskids = Vychodné Beskydy Europe 49°20N 22°0E 17 D11
East Brady U.S.A. 40°59N 79°37W 82 F5
East Branch Clarion River L. U.S.A. 41°35N 78°35W 82 E6
East C. = Dezhneva, Mys Russia 66°5N 169°40W 27 C19
East C. N.Z. 37°42S 178°35E 59 B7
East Caroline Basin Pac. Oc. 4°0N 146°45E 64 G6
East Chicago U.S.A. 41°38N 87°27W 80 E10
East China Sea Asia 30°0N 126°0E 31 F14
East Coulee Canada 51°23N 112°27W 70 C6
East Dereham = Dereham U.K. 52°41N 0°57E 13 E8
East Dunbartonshire □ U.K. 55°57N 4°13W 11 F4
East Falkland Falk. Is. 51°30S 58°30W 96 G5
East Grand Forks U.S.A. 47°56N 97°1W 80 B5
East Greenwich U.S.A. 41°40N 71°27W 83 E13
East Grinstead U.K. 51°7N 0°0 13 F8
East Hartford U.S.A. 41°46N 72°39W 83 E12
East Haydon Australia 18°0S 141°30E 62 B3
East Helena U.S.A. 46°35N 111°56W 76 C8
East Indies Asia 0°0 120°0E 24 J14
East Kavango □ Namibia 18°0S 20°15E 56 A3
East Kilbride U.K. 55°47N 4°11W 11 F4
East Lansing U.S.A. 42°44N 84°29W 81 D11
East Liverpool U.S.A. 40°37N 80°35W 82 F4
East London S. Africa 33°0S 27°55E 57 D4
East Lothian □ U.K. 55°58N 2°44W 11 F6
East Main = Eastmain Canada 52°10N 78°30W 72 B4
East Mariana Basin Pac. Oc. 12°0N 153°0E 64 F7
East Northport U.S.A. 40°53N 73°19W 83 F11
East Orange U.S.A. 40°46N 74°12W 83 F10
East Pacific Rise Pac. Oc. 15°0S 110°0W 65 J17
East Palestine U.S.A. 40°50N 80°33W 82 F4
East Pine Canada 55°48N 120°12W 70 B4
East Providence U.S.A. 41°49N 71°23W 83 E13
East Pt. Br. Virgin Is. 18°40N 64°18W 89 e
East Pt. Canada 46°27N 61°58W 73 C7
East Renfrewshire □ U.K. 55°46N 4°21W 11 F4
East Retford = Retford U.K. 53°19N 0°56W 12 D7
East Riding of Yorkshire □ U.K. 53°55N 0°30W 12 D7
East Rochester U.S.A. 43°7N 77°29W 82 C7
East St. Louis U.S.A. 38°37N 90°9W 80 F8
East Schelde = Oosterschelde → Neths. 51°33N 4°0E 15 C4
East Sea = Japan, Sea of Asia 40°0N 135°0E 28 E7
East Siberian Sea Russia 73°0N 160°0E 27 B17
East Stroudsburg U.S.A. 41°1N 75°11W 83 E9
East Sussex □ U.K. 50°56N 0°19E 13 G8
East Tasman Plateau Pac. Oc. 43°30S 152°0E 64 M7
East Tawas U.S.A. 44°17N 83°29W 81 C12
East Timor ■ Asia 8°50S 126°0E 37 F7
East Toorale Australia 30°27S 145°28E 63 E4
East Walker → U.S.A. 38°52N 119°10W 78 G7
East Windsor U.S.A. 40°17N 74°34W 83 F10
Eastbourne N.Z. 41°19S 174°55E 59 D5
Eastbourne U.K. 50°46N 0°18E 13 G8
Eastend Canada 49°32N 108°50W 71 D7
Easter Fracture Zone Pac. Oc. 25°0S 115°0W 65 K16
Easter I. = Pascua, I. de Chile 27°7S 109°23W 65 K17
Eastern Cape □ S. Africa 32°0S 26°0E 56 D4
Eastern Cr. → Australia 20°40S 141°35E 62 C3
Eastern Desert = Sharqîya, Es Sahrâ esh Egypt 27°30N 32°30E 53 C12
Eastern Ghats India 14°0N 78°50E 45 H4
Eastern Group = Lau Group Fiji 17°0S 178°30W 59 a
Eastern Group Australia 33°30S 124°30E 61 F3
Eastern Guruma ☼ Australia 22°0S 117°30E 60 D2
Eastern Transvaal = Mpumalanga □ S. Africa 26°0S 30°0E 57 C5
Easterville Canada 53°8N 99°49W 71 C9
Easthampton U.S.A. 42°16N 72°40W 83 D12
Eastlake U.S.A. 41°40N 81°26W 82 E3
Eastland U.S.A. 32°24N 98°49W 84 E5
Eastleigh U.K. 50°58N 1°21W 13 G6
Eastmain Canada 52°10N 78°30W 72 B4
Eastmain → Canada 52°27N 78°26W 72 B4
Eastman Canada 45°18N 72°19W 83 A12
Eastman U.S.A. 32°12N 83°11W 85 E13
Easton Md., U.S.A. 38°47N 76°5W 81 F15
Easton Pa., U.S.A. 40°41N 75°13W 83 F9
Easton Wash., U.S.A. 47°14N 121°11W 78 C5
Eastport U.S.A. 44°56N 67°0W 81 C20
Eastsound U.S.A. 48°42N 122°55W 78 B4
Eaton U.S.A. 40°32N 104°42W 76 F11
Eatonia Canada 51°13N 109°25W 71 C7
Eatonton U.S.A. 33°20N 83°23W 85 E13
Eatontown U.S.A. 40°19N 74°4W 83 F10
Eatonville U.S.A. 46°52N 122°16W 78 D4
Eau Claire U.S.A. 44°49N 91°30W 80 C8
Eau Claire, L. à l' Canada 56°10N 74°25W 72 A5
Eauripik Rise Pac. Oc. 2°0N 142°0E 64 G6
Ebano Mexico 22°13N 98°24W 87 C5
Ebbw Vale U.K. 51°46N 3°12W 13 F4
Ebeltoft Denmark 56°12N 10°41E 9 H14
Ebensburg U.S.A. 40°29N 78°44W 82 F6
Eberswalde-Finow Germany 52°50N 13°49E 16 B7
Ebetsu Japan 43°7N 141°34E 28 C10
Ebey's Landing ⌂ U.S.A. 48°12N 122°41W 78 B4
Ebian China 29°11N 103°13E 34 C4
Ebinur Hu China 44°55N 82°55E 30 C5
Ebolowa Cameroon 2°55N 11°10E 54 D2
Ebonda Dem. Rep. of the Congo 2°12N 22°21E 54 D4
Ebre = Ebro → Spain 40°43N 0°54E 21 B6
Ebro → Spain 40°43N 0°54E 21 B6
Ecatepec de Morelos Mexico 19°36N 99°3W 87 D5
Ecbatana = Hamadān Iran 34°52N 48°32E 47 C6
Eceabat Turkey 40°11N 26°21E 23 D12
Ech Chéliff Algeria 36°10N 1°20E 52 A6
Echigo-Sammyaku Japan 36°50N 139°50E 29 F9
Echizen Japan 35°50N 136°10E 29 G8
Echizen-Misaki Japan 35°59N 135°57E 29 G7
Echo Bay N.W.T., Canada 66°5N 117°55W 68 D8
Echo Bay Ont., Canada 46°29N 84°4W 72 C3
Echoing → Canada 55°51N 92°5W 72 B1
Echternach Lux. 49°49N 6°25E 15 E6
Echuca Australia 36°10S 144°45E 63 F3
Écija Spain 37°30N 5°10W 21 D3
Eclipse I. Australia 35°5S 117°58E 61 G2
Eclipse Is. Australia 13°54S 126°19E 60 B4
Eclipse Sd. Canada 72°38N 79°0W 69 C16
Ecuador ■ S. Amer. 2°0S 78°0W 92 D3
Ed Da'ein Sudan 11°26N 26°9E 54 B5
Ed Damazin Sudan 11°46N 34°21E 53 F12
Ed Dâmer Sudan 17°27N 34°0E 53 E12
Ed Dar el Beida = Casablanca Morocco 33°36N 7°36W 52 B4
Ed Debba Sudan 18°0N 30°51E 53 E12
Ed Déffa Egypt 30°40N 26°30E 53 B11
Ed Dueim Sudan 14°0N 32°10E 53 F12
Edam Canada 53°11N 108°46W 71 C7
Edam Neths. 52°31N 5°3E 15 B5
Edapally India 11°19N 78°3E 45 J4
Eday U.K. 59°11N 2°47W 11 B6
Eddrachillis B. U.K. 58°17N 5°14W 11 C3
Eddystone U.K. 50°11N 4°16W 13 G3
Eddystone Pt. Australia 40°59S 148°20E 63 G4
Ede Neths. 52°4N 5°40E 15 B5
Edehon L. Canada 60°25N 97°15W 71 A9
Eden Australia 37°3S 149°55E 63 F4
Eden N.C., U.S.A. 36°29N 79°53W 85 C15
Eden N.Y., U.S.A. 42°39N 78°55W 82 D6
Eden Tex., U.S.A. 31°13N 99°51W 84 F5
Eden → U.K. 54°57N 3°1W 12 C4
Edenburg S. Africa 29°43S 25°58E 56 C4
Edendale S. Africa 29°39S 30°18E 57 C5
Edenderry Ireland 53°21N 7°4W 10 C4
Edenton U.S.A. 36°4N 76°39W 85 C16
Edenville S. Africa 27°37S 27°34E 57 C4
Eder → Germany 51°12N 9°28E 16 C5
Edessa Greece 40°48N 22°5E 23 D10
Edfu = Idfû Egypt 24°55N 32°49E 53 D12
Edgar U.S.A. 40°22N 97°58W 80 E5
Edgartown U.S.A. 41°23N 70°31W 83 E14
Edge Hill U.K. 52°8N 1°26W 13 E6
Edgefield U.S.A. 33°47N 81°56W 85 E14
Edgeley U.S.A. 46°22N 98°43W 80 B4
Edgemont U.S.A. 43°18N 103°50W 80 D2
Edgeøya Svalbard 77°45N 22°30E 4 B9
Édhessa = Edessa Greece 40°48N 22°5E 23 D10
Edievale N.Z. 45°49S 169°22E 59 F2
Edina U.S.A. 40°10N 92°11W 80 E7
Edinboro U.S.A. 41°52N 80°8W 82 E4
Edinburg U.S.A. 26°18N 98°10W 84 H5
Edinburgh, City of □ U.K. 55°57N 3°17W 11 F5
Edineţ Moldova 48°9N 27°18E 17 D14
Edirne Turkey 41°40N 26°34E 23 D12
Edison U.S.A. 48°33N 122°27W 78 B4
Edithburgh Australia 35°5S 137°43E 63 F2
Edmeston U.S.A. 42°42N 75°15W 83 D9
Edmond U.S.A. 35°39N 97°29W 84 D6
Edmonds U.S.A. 47°48N 122°22W 78 C4
Edmonton Australia 17°2S 145°46E 62 B4
Edmonton Canada 53°30N 113°30W 70 C6
Edmund L. Canada 54°45N 93°17W 72 B1
Edmundston Canada 47°23N 68°20W 73 C6
Edna U.S.A. 28°59N 96°39W 84 G6
Edremit Turkey 39°34N 27°0E 23 E12
Edremit Körfezi Turkey 39°30N 26°45E 23 E12
Edson Canada 53°35N 116°28W 70 C5
Eduardo Castex Argentina 35°50S 64°18W 94 D3
Eduardo Frei Montalva = Frei Antarctica 62°30S 58°0W 5 C18
Edward → Australia 35°5S 143°30E 63 F3
Edward, L. Africa 0°25S 29°40E 54 E5
Edward VII Land Antarctica 80°0S 150°0W 5 E13
Edwards Calif., U.S.A. 34°50N 117°40W 79 L9
Edwards N.Y., U.S.A. 44°20N 75°15W 83 B9
Edwards Plateau U.S.A. 30°45N 101°20W 84 F4
Edwardsville U.S.A. 41°15N 75°56W 83 E9
Edzná Mexico 19°39N 90°19W 87 D6
Edzo = Behchoko Canada 62°50N 116°3W 70 A5
Eeklo Belgium 51°11N 3°33E 15 C3
Eenhana Namibia 17°30S 16°23E 56 A2
Eesti = Estonia ■ Europe 58°30N 25°30E 9 G21
Effigy Mounds ⌂ U.S.A. 43°5N 91°11W 80 D8
Effingham U.S.A. 39°7N 88°33W 80 F9

Égadi, Ísole *Italy* 37°55N 12°16E **22 F5**
Egan Range *U.S.A.* 39°35N 114°55W **76 G6**
Eganville *Canada* 45°32N 77°5W **82 A7**
Eger = Cheb *Czech Rep.* 50°9N 12°28E **16 C7**
Eger *Hungary* 47°53N 20°27E **17 E11**
Egersund *Norway* 58°26N 6°1E **9 G12**
Egg L. *Canada* 55°5N 105°30W **71 B7**
Éghezée *Belgium* 50°35N 4°55E **15 D4**
Egilsstaðir *Iceland* 65°16N 14°25W **8 D6**
Egio *Greece* 38°15N 22°5E **23 E10**
Eglinton I. *Canada* 75°48N 118°30W **69 B8**
Egmont *Canada* 49°45N 123°56W **70 D4**
Egmont, C. *N.Z.* 39°16S 173°45E **59 C4**
Egmont, Mt. = Taranaki, Mt.
  N.Z. 39°17S 174°5E **59 C5**
Egmont △ *N.Z.* 39°17S 174°4E **59 C5**
Egra *India* 21°54N 87°32E **43 J12**
Eğridir *Turkey* 37°52N 30°51E **46 B1**
Eğridir Gölü *Turkey* 37°53N 30°50E **46 B1**
Egvekinot *Russia* 66°19N 179°50W **27 C19**
Egypt ■ *Africa* 28°0N 31°0E **53 C12**
Ehime □ *Japan* 33°30N 132°40E **29 H6**
Ehrenberg *U.S.A.* 33°36N 114°31W **79 M12**
Eibar *Spain* 43°11N 2°28W **21 A4**
Eidsvold *Australia* 25°25S 151°12E **63 D5**
Eidsvoll *Norway* 60°19N 11°14E **9 F14**
Eielson *U.S.A.* 64°40N 147°4W **74 C10**
Eifel *Germany* 50°15N 6°50E **16 C4**
Eigg *U.K.* 56°54N 6°10W **11 E2**
Eighty Mile Beach
  Australia 19°30S 120°40E **60 C3**
Eil, L. *U.K.* 56°51N 5°16W **11 E3**
Eildon, L. *Australia* 37°10S 146°0E **63 F4**
Eilean Siar □ *U.K.* 57°30N 7°10W **11 D1**
Einasleigh *Australia* 18°32S 144°5E **62 B3**
Einasleigh → *Australia* 17°30S 142°17E **62 B3**
Eindhoven *Neths.* 51°26N 5°28E **15 C5**
Eire = Ireland ■ *Europe* 53°50N 7°52W **10 C4**
Eiríksjökull *Iceland* 64°46N 20°24W **8 D3**
Eiriosgaigh = Eriskay *U.K.* 57°4N 7°18W **11 D1**
Eirunepé *Brazil* 6°35S 69°53W **92 E5**
Eiseb → *Namibia* 20°33S 20°59E **56 B2**
Eisenach *Germany* 50°58N 10°19E **16 C6**
Eisenerz *Austria* 47°32N 14°54E **16 E8**
Eivissa *Spain* 38°54N 1°26E **21 C6**
Ejutla *Mexico* 16°34N 96°44W **87 D5**
Ekalaka *U.S.A.* 45°53N 104°33W **76 D11**
Ekaterinburg = Yekaterinburg
  Russia 56°50N 60°30E **26 D7**
Ekenäs = Raasepori
  Finland 60°0N 23°26E **9 G20**
Eketahuna *N.Z.* 40°38S 175°43E **59 D5**
Ekibastuz *Kazakhstan* 51°50N 75°10E **26 D8**
Eksjö *Sweden* 57°40N 14°58E **9 H16**
Ekuma → *Namibia* 18°40S 16°2E **56 A2**
Ekwan → *Canada* 53°12N 82°15W **72 B3**
Ekwan Pt. *Canada* 53°16N 82°7W **72 B3**
El Aaiún *W. Sahara* 27°9N 13°12W **52 C3**
El Abanico *Chile* 37°20S 71°31W **94 D1**
El 'Agrûd *Egypt* 30°14N 34°24E **48 E3**
El Alamein *Egypt* 30°48N 28°58E **53 B11**
El 'Aqaba, W. → *Egypt* 30°7N 33°54E **48 E2**
El Ariha *West Bank* 31°52N 35°27E **48 D4**
El 'Arîsh *Egypt* 31°8N 33°50E **48 D2**
El 'Arîsh, W. → *Egypt* 31°8N 33°47E **48 D2**
El Asnam = Ech Chéliff
  Algeria 36°10N 1°20E **52 A6**
El Bayadh *Algeria* 33°40N 1°1E **52 B6**
El Bluff *Nic.* 11°59N 83°40W **88 D3**
El Cajon *U.S.A.* 32°48N 116°58W **79 N10**
El Calafate *Argentina* 50°19S 72°15W **96 G2**
El Campo *U.S.A.* 29°12N 96°16W **84 G6**
El Capitan *U.S.A.* 37°44N 119°38E **78 H7**
El Carbón *Honduras* 15°25N 85°32W **88 C2**
El Carmen *Colombia* 9°43N 75°8W **92 B3**
El Centro *U.S.A.* 32°48N 115°34W **79 N11**
El Cerro *Bolivia* 17°30S 61°40W **92 G6**
El Compadre *Mexico* 32°20N 116°14W **79 N10**
El Cuy *Argentina* 39°55S 68°25W **96 D3**
El Cuyo *Mexico* 21°31N 87°41W **87 C7**
El Daheir *Egypt* 31°13N 34°10E **48 D3**
El Descanso *Mexico* 32°12N 116°58W **79 N10**
El Desemboque *Mexico* 30°33N 113°1W **86 A2**
El Diviso *Colombia* 1°22N 78°14W **92 C3**
El Djouf *Mauritania* 20°0N 9°0W **52 D4**
El Dorado *Mexico* 24°17N 107°21W **86 C3**
El Dorado *Ark., U.S.A.* 33°12N 92°40W **84 E8**
El Dorado *Kans., U.S.A.* 37°49N 96°52W **80 G5**
El Dorado *Venezuela* 6°55N 61°37W **92 B6**
El Dorado Springs *U.S.A.* 37°52N 94°1W **80 G6**
El Escorial *Spain* 40°35N 4°7W **21 B3**
El Faiyûm *Egypt* 29°19N 30°50E **53 C12**
El Fâsher *Sudan* 13°33N 25°26E **53 F11**
El Ferrol = Ferrol *Spain* 43°29N 8°15W **21 A1**
El Fuerte *Mexico* 26°25N 108°39W **86 B3**
El Geneina = Al Junaynah
  Sudan 13°27N 22°45E **53 F10**
El Gezira □ *Sudan* 15°0N 33°0E **53 F12**
El Gogorrón △ *Mexico* 21°49N 100°57W **86 C4**
El Goléa *Algeria* 30°30N 2°50E **52 B6**
El Guácharo △ *Venezuela* 10°8N 63°21W **89 D7**
El Guache △ *Venezuela* 9°45N 69°30W **89 E6**
El Iskandarîya *Egypt* 31°13N 29°58E **53 B11**
El Istiwa'îya *Sudan* 5°0N 28°0E **53 G11**
El Jadida *Morocco* 33°11N 8°17W **52 B4**
El Jardal *Honduras* 14°54N 88°50W **88 D2**
El Kef □ *Tunisia* 36°0N 9°0E **53 A7**
El Khârga *Egypt* 25°30N 30°33E **53 C12**
El Khartûm *Sudan* 15°31N 32°35E **53 E12**
El Khartûm Bahri *Sudan* 15°40N 32°31E **53 E12**
El Kuntilla *Egypt* 30°1N 34°45E **48 E3**
El Leoncito △ *Argentina* 31°48S 69°15W **94 C2**
El Lucero *Mexico* 30°37N 106°34W **86 A3**
El Maestrazgo *Spain* 40°30N 0°25E **21 B5**
El Mahalla el Kubra *Egypt* 31°0N 31°0E **53 B12**
El Malpais △ *U.S.A.* 34°53N 108°0W **77 J10**
El Mansûra *Egypt* 31°0N 31°19E **53 B12**
El Ménia = El Goléa
  Algeria 30°30N 2°50E **52 B6**

El Milagro *Argentina* 30°59S 65°59W **94 C2**
El Minyâ *Egypt* 28°7N 30°33E **53 C12**
El Obeid *Sudan* 13°8N 30°10E **53 F12**
El Odaiya *Sudan* 12°8N 28°12E **53 F11**
El Oro *Mexico* 19°51N 100°7W **87 D4**
El Oued *Algeria* 33°20N 6°58E **52 B7**
El Palmar △ *Argentina* 32°10S 58°31W **94 C4**
El Paso *U.S.A.* 31°45N 106°29W **84 F1**
El Paso de Robles = Paso Robles
  U.S.A. 35°38N 120°41W **78 K6**
El Pinacate y Gran Desierto de
  Altar = Gran Desierto del
  Pinacate ☐ *Mexico* 31°51N 113°32W **86 A2**
El Portal *U.S.A.* 37°41N 119°47W **78 H7**
El Porvenir *Mexico* 31°15N 105°51W **86 A3**
El Progreso *Honduras* 15°26N 87°51W **88 C2**
El Puerto de Santa María
  Spain 36°36N 6°13W **21 D2**
El Qantara *Egypt* 30°51N 32°20E **48 E1**
El Quseima *Egypt* 30°40N 34°15E **48 E3**
El Real de Santa María
  Panama 8°0N 77°40W **92 B3**
El Reno *U.S.A.* 35°32N 97°57W **75 H20**
El Rey △ *Argentina* 24°40S 64°34W **94 A3**
El Río *U.S.A.* 34°14N 119°10W **79 L7**
El Rosario *Mexico* 30°1N 115°45W **86 A1**
El Salto *Mexico* 23°47N 105°22W **86 C3**
El Salvador ■ *Cent. Amer.* 13°50N 89°0W **88 D2**
El Sauce *Nic.* 13°0N 86°40W **88 D2**
El Suweis *Egypt* 29°58N 32°31E **53 C12**
El Tamarâni, W. → *Egypt* 30°7N 34°43E **48 E3**
El Thamad *Egypt* 29°40N 34°28E **48 F3**
El Tigre *Venezuela* 8°44N 64°15W **92 B6**
El Tîh, Gebel *Egypt* 29°40N 33°50E **48 F2**
El Tofo *Chile* 29°22S 71°18W **94 B1**
El Tránsito *Chile* 28°52S 70°17W **94 B1**
El Tûr *Egypt* 28°14N 33°36E **46 D2**
El Turbio *Argentina* 51°45S 72°5W **96 G2**
El Uqsur *Egypt* 25°41N 32°38E **53 C12**
El Vergel *Mexico* 26°28N 106°22W **86 B3**
El Vigía *Venezuela* 8°38N 71°39W **92 B4**
El Wabeira *Egypt* 29°34N 33°6E **48 F2**
El Wuz *Sudan* 15°5N 30°7E **53 E12**
Elamanchili *India* 17°33N 82°50E **44 F6**
Elat *Israel* 29°30N 34°56E **48 F3**
Elâzığ *Turkey* 38°37N 39°14E **46 B3**
Elba *Italy* 42°46N 10°17E **22 C4**
Elba *U.S.A.* 31°25N 86°4W **85 F11**
Elbasan *Albania* 41°9N 20°9E **23 D9**
Elbe → *Europe* 53°50N 9°0E **16 B5**
Elbert, Mt. *U.S.A.* 39°7N 106°27W **76 G10**
Elberton *U.S.A.* 34°7N 82°52W **85 D13**
Elbeuf *France* 49°17N 1°2E **20 B4**
Elbląg = Elbląg *Poland* 54°10N 19°25E **17 A10**
Elbistan *Turkey* 38°13N 37°15E **46 B3**
Elbląg *Poland* 54°10N 19°25E **17 A10**
Elbow *Canada* 51°7N 106°35W **71 C7**
Elbrus *Russia* 43°21N 42°30E **19 F7**
Elburz Mts. = Alborz, Reshteh-ye
  Kūhhā-ye *Iran* 36°0N 52°0E **47 C7**
Elche *Spain* 38°15N 0°42W **21 C5**
Elcho I. *Australia* 11°55S 135°45E **62 A2**
Elda *Spain* 38°29N 0°47W **21 C5**
Elde → *Germany* 53°7N 11°15E **16 B6**
Eldon *Mo., U.S.A.* 38°21N 92°35W **80 F7**
Eldon *Wash., U.S.A.* 47°33N 123°3W **78 C3**
Eldora *U.S.A.* 42°22N 93°5W **80 D7**
Eldorado *Argentina* 26°28S 54°43W **95 B5**
Eldorado *Canada* 44°35N 77°31W **82 B7**
Eldorado *Ill., U.S.A.* 37°49N 88°26W **80 G9**
Eldorado *Tex., U.S.A.* 30°52N 100°36W **84 F4**
Eldoret *Kenya* 0°30N 35°17E **54 D7**
Eldred *U.S.A.* 41°58N 78°23W **82 E6**
Eleanora, Pk. *Australia* 32°57S 121°9E **61 F3**
Elefantes → *Africa* 24°10S 32°40E **57 C5**
Elektrostal *Russia* 55°41N 38°32E **18 C6**
Elemi Triangle = Ilemi Triangle
  Africa 5°0N 35°20E **54 D7**
Elephant Butte Res.
  U.S.A. 33°9N 107°11W **77 K10**
Elephant I. *Antarctica* 61°0S 55°0W **5 C18**
Elephant Pass *Sri Lanka* 9°35N 80°25E **45 K5**
Eleuthera I. *Bahamas* 25°0N 76°20W **88 B4**
Elgin *Canada* 44°36N 76°13W **83 B8**
Elgin *U.K.* 57°39N 3°19W **11 D5**
Elgin *Ill., U.S.A.* 42°2N 88°17W **80 D9**
Elgin *N. Dak., U.S.A.* 46°24N 101°51W **80 B3**
Elgin *Oreg., U.S.A.* 45°34N 117°55W **76 D5**
Elgin *Tex., U.S.A.* 30°21N 97°22W **84 F6**
Elgon, Mt. *Africa* 1°10N 34°50E **54 D6**
Eliase *Indonesia* 8°21S 130°48E **37 F8**
Elim *Namibia* 17°48S 15°31E **56 A2**
Elim *S. Africa* 34°35S 19°45E **56 E2**
Elista *Russia* 46°16N 44°14E **19 E7**
Elizabeth *Australia* 34°42S 138°41E **63 E2**
Elizabeth *U.S.A.* 40°39N 74°12W **83 F10**
Elizabeth City *U.S.A.* 36°18N 76°14W **85 C16**
Elizabethton *U.S.A.* 36°21N 82°13W **85 C13**
Elizabethtown *Ky.,*
  U.S.A. 37°42N 85°52W **81 G11**
Elizabethtown *N.Y.,*
  U.S.A. 44°13N 73°36W **83 B11**
Elizabethtown *Pa., U.S.A.* 40°9N 76°36W **83 F8**
Elk *Poland* 53°50N 22°21E **17 B12**
Elk → *Canada* 49°11N 115°14W **70 C5**
Elk → *U.S.A.* 34°46N 87°16W **85 D11**
Elk City *U.S.A.* 35°25N 99°25W **84 D5**
Elk Creek *U.S.A.* 39°36N 122°32W **78 F4**
Elk Grove *U.S.A.* 38°25N 121°22W **78 G5**
Elk Island △ *Canada* 53°35N 112°59W **70 C6**
Elk Lake *Canada* 47°40N 80°25W **72 C3**
Elk Point *Canada* 53°54N 110°55W **71 C6**
Elk River *Idaho, U.S.A.* 46°47N 116°11W **76 C5**
Elk River *Minn., U.S.A.* 45°18N 93°35W **80 C7**
Elkedra → *Australia* 21°8S 136°22E **62 C2**
Elkhart *Ind., U.S.A.* 41°41N 85°58W **81 E11**
Elkhart *Kans., U.S.A.* 37°0N 101°54W **84 G3**
Elkhorn *Canada* 49°59N 101°14W **71 D8**
Elkhorn → *U.S.A.* 41°8N 96°19W **80 E5**

Elkhovo *Bulgaria* 42°10N 26°35E **23 C12**
Elkin *U.S.A.* 36°15N 80°51W **85 C14**
Elkins *U.S.A.* 38°55N 79°51W **81 F14**
Elkland *U.S.A.* 41°59N 77°19W **82 E7**
Elko *Canada* 49°20N 115°10W **70 D5**
Elko *U.S.A.* 40°50N 115°46W **76 F6**
Elkton *U.S.A.* 43°49N 83°11W **82 C1**
Ellas = Greece ■ *Europe* 40°0N 23°0E **23 E9**
Ellef Ringnes I. *Canada* 78°30N 102°2W **69 B11**
Ellen, Mt. *U.S.A.* 44°9N 72°56W **83 B12**
Ellenburg *U.S.A.* 44°54N 73°48W **83 B11**
Ellendale *U.S.A.* 46°0N 98°32W **80 B4**
Ellensburg *U.S.A.* 46°59N 120°34W **76 C3**
Ellenville *U.S.A.* 41°43N 74°24W **83 E10**
Ellerton *Barbados* 13°7N 59°33E **89 g**
Ellery, Mt. *Australia* 37°28S 148°47E **63 F4**
Ellesmere, L. *N.Z.* 43°47S 172°28E **59 G4**
Ellesmere I. *Canada* 79°30N 80°0W **69 B5**
Ellesmere Port *U.K.* 53°17N 2°54W **12 D5**
Ellice Is. = Tuvalu ■
  Pac. Oc. 8°0S 178°0E **58 B10**
Ellicottville *U.S.A.* 42°17N 78°40W **82 D6**
Ellington *U.S.A.* 42°13N 79°6W **82 D5**
Elliot *Australia* 17°33S 133°32E **62 B1**
Elliot *S. Africa* 31°22S 27°48E **57 D4**
Elliot Lake *Canada* 46°25N 82°35W **72 C3**
Elliotdale = Xhora
  S. Africa 31°55S 28°38E **57 D4**
Ellis *U.S.A.* 38°56N 99°34W **80 F4**
Elliston *Australia* 33°39S 134°53E **63 E1**
Ellisville *U.S.A.* 31°36N 89°12W **85 F10**
Ellon *U.K.* 57°22N 2°4W **11 D6**
Ellora *India* 20°1N 75°10E **44 D2**
Ellore = Eluru *India* 16°48N 81°8E **44 F5**
Ellsworth *Kans., U.S.A.* 38°44N 98°14W **80 F4**
Ellsworth *Maine, U.S.A.* 44°33N 68°25W **81 C19**
Ellsworth Land *Antarctica* 76°0S 89°0W **5 D16**
Ellsworth Mts. *Antarctica* 78°30S 85°0W **5 D16**
Ellwood City *U.S.A.* 40°52N 80°17W **82 F4**
Elma *Canada* 49°52N 95°55W **71 D9**
Elma *U.S.A.* 47°0N 123°25W **78 D3**
Elmalı *Turkey* 36°44N 29°56E **19 G4**
Elmhurst *U.S.A.* 41°53N 87°56W **80 E10**
Elmira *Canada* 43°36N 80°33W **82 C4**
Elmira *U.S.A.* 42°6N 76°48W **82 D8**
Elmira Heights *U.S.A.* 42°8N 76°50W **82 D8**
Elmore *Australia* 36°30S 144°37E **63 F3**
Elmshorn *Germany* 53°43N 9°40E **16 B5**
Elmvale *Canada* 44°35N 79°52W **82 B5**
Elora *Canada* 43°41N 80°26W **82 C4**
Eloy *U.S.A.* 32°45N 111°33W **77 K8**
Elphin *Canada* 44°55N 76°37W **83 B8**
Elpitiya *Sri Lanka* 6°17N 80°10E **45 L5**
Elrose *Canada* 51°12N 108°0W **71 C7**
Elsby △ *Australia* 14°55S 133°10E **60 B5**
Elsie *U.S.A.* 45°52N 123°36W **78 E3**
Elsinore = Helsingør
  Denmark 56°2N 12°35E **9 H15**
Eltanin Fracture Zone System
  S. Ocean 54°0S 130°0W **5 B14**
Eltham *N.Z.* 39°26S 174°19E **59 C5**
Eluru *India* 16°48N 81°8E **44 F5**
Elvas *Portugal* 38°50N 7°10E **21 C2**
Elverum *Norway* 60°53N 11°34E **8 F14**
Elvire → *Australia* 17°51S 128°11E **60 C4**
Elvire, Mt. *Australia* 29°22S 119°36E **61 E2**
Elwell, L. = Tiber Res.
  U.S.A. 48°19N 111°6W **76 B8**
Elwood *Ind., U.S.A.* 40°17N 85°50W **81 E11**
Elwood *Nebr., U.S.A.* 40°36N 99°52W **80 E4**
Elx = Elche *Spain* 38°15N 0°42W **21 C5**
Ely *U.K.* 52°24N 0°16E **13 E8**
Ely *Minn., U.S.A.* 47°55N 91°51W **80 B8**
Ely *Nev., U.S.A.* 39°15N 114°54W **76 G6**
Elyria *U.S.A.* 41°22N 82°7W **82 E2**
eMakhazeni *S. Africa* 25°42S 30°2E **57 C5**
eMalahleni *S. Africa* 25°51S 29°14E **57 C4**
Emāmrūd *Iran* 36°30N 55°0E **47 B7**
eMbalenhle *S. Africa* 26°32S 29°5E **57 C4**
Embarcación *Argentina* 23°10S 64°0W **94 A3**
Embetsu *Japan* 44°44N 141°47E **28 B10**
Embi *Kazakhstan* 48°50N 58°8E **26 E6**
Embi = Kazakhstan* 46°55N 53°28E **19 E9**
Embro *Canada* 43°9N 80°54W **82 C4**
Embrun *France* 44°34N 6°30E **20 D7**
Emden *Germany* 53°21N 7°12E **16 B4**
Emei Shan *China* 29°32N 103°46E **34 C4**
Emeishan *China* 29°31N 103°23E **34 C4**
Emerald *Australia* 23°32S 148°10E **62 C4**
Emerald I. *Canada* 76°48N 114°10W **69 B9**
Emerson *Canada* 49°0N 97°10W **71 D9**
Emet *Turkey* 39°20N 29°15E **23 E13**
Emgwenya *S. Africa* 25°40S 30°18E **57 C5**
Emi Koussi *Chad* 19°45N 18°55E **53 E9**
Eminabad *Pakistan* 32°2N 74°8E **42 C6**
Emine, Nos *Bulgaria* 42°40N 27°56E **23 C12**
Emissi, Tarso *Chad* 21°27N 18°36E **53 D9**
eMkhondo = Piet Retief
  S. Africa 27°1S 30°50E **57 D5**
Emlenton *U.S.A.* 41°11N 79°43W **82 E5**
Emmaus *S. Africa* 29°2S 25°15E **56 C4**
Emmeloord *Neths.* 52°44N 5°46E **15 B5**
Emmen *Neths.* 52°48N 6°57E **15 B6**
Emmetsburg *U.S.A.* 43°7N 94°41W **80 D6**
Emmett *Idaho, U.S.A.* 43°52N 116°30W **76 E5**
Emmett *Mich., U.S.A.* 42°59N 82°46W **82 D2**
Emmiganuru = Yemmiganur
  India 15°44N 77°29E **45 G3**
Emmonak *U.S.A.* 62°47N 164°31W **74 C7**
Emo *Canada* 48°38N 93°50W **71 D10**
Empalme *Mexico* 27°58N 110°51W **86 B2**
Empangeni *S. Africa* 28°50S 31°52E **57 D5**
Empedrado *Argentina* 28°0S 58°46W **94 B4**
Emperor Seamount Chain
  Pac. Oc. 40°0N 170°0E **64 D9**
Emperor Trough *Pac. Oc.* 43°0N 175°30E **64 C9**
Emporia *Kans., U.S.A.* 38°25N 96°11W **80 F5**
Emporia *Va., U.S.A.* 36°42N 77°32W **81 G15**

Emporium *U.S.A.* 41°31N 78°14W **82 E6**
Empress *Canada* 50°57N 110°0W **71 C7**
Empty Quarter = Rub' al Khālī
  Si. Arabia 19°0N 48°0E **49 D4**
Ems → *Germany* 53°20N 7°12E **16 B4**
Emsdale *Canada* 45°32N 79°19W **82 A5**
Emu *China* 43°40N 128°6E **33 C15**
Emu Park *Australia* 23°13S 150°50E **62 C5**
En 'Avrona *Israel* 29°43N 35°0E **48 F3**
'En Boqeq *Israel* 31°12N 35°21E **47 D4**
'En Gedi *Israel* 31°28N 35°25E **47 D4**
En Nahud *Sudan* 12°45N 28°25E **53 F11**
Ena *Japan* 35°25N 137°25E **29 G8**
Enard B. *U.K.* 58°5N 5°20W **11 C3**
Enare träsk = Inarijärvi
  Finland 69°0N 28°0E **8 B23**
Enarotali *Indonesia* 3°55S 136°21E **37 E9**
Encampment *U.S.A.* 41°12N 106°47W **76 F10**
Encantadas, Serra *Brazil* 30°40S 53°0W **95 C5**
Encarnación *Paraguay* 27°15S 55°50W **95 B4**
Encarnación de Díaz
  Mexico 21°31N 102°14W **86 C4**
Encinitas *U.S.A.* 33°3N 117°17W **79 M9**
Encino *U.S.A.* 34°39N 105°28W **77 J11**
Encounter B. *Australia* 35°45S 138°45E **63 F2**
Endako *Canada* 54°6N 125°2W **70 C3**
Endau Rompin △
  Malaysia 2°27N 103°45E **39 L4**
Ende *Indonesia* 8°45S 121°40E **37 F6**
Endeavour Str. *Australia* 10°45S 142°0E **62 A3**
Enderbury *Kiribati* 3°8S 171°5W **64 H10**
Enderby *Canada* 50°35N 119°10W **70 C5**
Enderby Abyssal Plain
  S. Ocean 60°0S 40°0E **5 C5**
Enderby I. *Australia* 20°35S 116°30E **60 D2**
Enderby Land *Antarctica* 66°0S 53°0E **5 C5**
Enderlin *U.S.A.* 46°38N 97°36W **80 B5**
Endicott *U.S.A.* 42°6N 76°4W **83 D8**
Endicott Mts. *U.S.A.* 68°0N 152°0W **74 B9**
Endwell *U.S.A.* 42°6N 76°2W **83 D8**
Endyalgout I. *Australia* 11°40S 132°35E **60 B5**
Eneabba *Australia* 29°49S 115°16E **61 E2**
Enewetak Atoll
  Marshall Is. 11°30N 162°15E **64 F8**
Enez *Turkey* 40°45N 26°5E **23 D12**
Enfer, Pte. d' *Martinique* 14°22N 60°54W **88 c**
Enfield *Canada* 44°56N 63°32W **73 D7**
Enfield *Conn., U.S.A.* 41°58N 72°36W **83 E12**
Enfield *N.C., U.S.A.* 36°11N 77°41W **85 C16**
Enfield *N.H., U.S.A.* 43°39N 72°9W **83 C12**
Engadin *Switz.* 46°45N 10°10E **20 C9**
Engaño, C. *Dom. Rep.* 18°30N 68°20W **89 C6**
Engaño, C. *Phil.* 18°35N 122°23E **37 A6**
Engaru *Japan* 44°3N 143°31E **28 B11**
Engcobo = Ngcobo
  S. Africa 31°37S 28°0E **57 D4**
Engels *Russia* 51°28N 46°6E **19 D8**
Engemann L. *Canada* 58°0N 106°55W **71 B7**
Enggano *Indonesia* 5°20S 102°40E **36 F2**
England *U.S.A.* 34°33N 91°58W **84 D9**
England □ *U.K.* 53°0N 2°0W **13 E5**
Englee *Canada* 50°45N 56°5W **73 B8**
Englehart *Canada* 47°49N 79°52W **72 C4**
English → *Canada* 49°12N 91°5W **71 C10**
English Bazar = Ingraj Bazar
  India 24°58N 88°10E **43 G13**
English Channel *Europe* 50°0N 2°0W **13 G6**
English Company's Is., The
  Australia 11°50S 136°32E **62 A2**
English River *Canada* 49°14N 91°0W **72 C1**
Enid *U.S.A.* 36°24N 97°53W **84 C6**
Eniwa *Japan* 43°0N 141°30E **28 C10**
Enkhuizen *Neths.* 52°42N 5°17E **15 B5**
Enle *China* 24°0N 101°9E **34 F3**
Enna *Italy* 37°34N 14°16E **22 F6**
Ennadai L. *Canada* 60°58N 101°20W **71 A8**
Ennedi *Chad* 17°15N 22°0E **53 E10**
Enngonia *Australia* 29°21S 145°50E **63 D4**
Ennis *Ireland* 52°51N 8°59W **10 D3**
Ennis *Mont., U.S.A.* 45°21N 111°44W **76 D8**
Ennis *Tex., U.S.A.* 32°20N 96°38W **84 E6**
Enniscorthy *Ireland* 52°30N 6°34W **10 D5**
Enniskillen *U.K.* 54°21N 7°39W **10 B4**
Ennistimon *Ireland* 52°57N 9°17W **10 D2**
Enns → *Austria* 48°14N 14°32E **16 D8**
Eno *Finland* 62°47N 30°10E **8 E24**
Enosburg Falls *U.S.A.* 44°55N 72°48W **83 B12**
Enping *China* 22°16N 112°21E **35 F9**
Enriquillo, L. *Dom. Rep.* 18°20N 71°10W **89 C5**
Enschede *Neths.* 52°13N 6°53E **15 B6**
Ensenada *Argentina* 34°55S 57°55W **94 C4**
Ensenada *Mexico* 31°52N 116°37W **86 A1**
Ensenada de los Muertos
  Mexico 23°59N 109°50W **86 C3**
Enshi *China* 30°18N 109°29E **34 B7**
Entebbe *Uganda* 0°4N 32°28E **54 D6**
Enterprise *Canada* 60°47N 115°45W **70 A5**
Enterprise *Ala., U.S.A.* 31°19N 85°51W **85 F12**
Enterprise *Oreg., U.S.A.* 45°25N 117°17W **76 D5**
Entiako △ *Canada* 53°15N 125°26W **70 C3**
Entre Ríos *Bolivia* 21°30S 64°25W **94 A3**
Entre Ríos □ *Argentina* 30°30S 58°30W **94 C4**
Entroncamento *Portugal* 39°28N 8°28W **21 C1**
Enugu *Nigeria* 6°20N 7°30E **52 G7**
Enumclaw *U.S.A.* 47°12N 121°59W **78 C5**
Eochaill = Youghal
  Ireland 51°56N 7°52W **10 E4**
Eólie, Ís. *Italy* 38°30N 14°57E **22 E6**
Epe *Neths.* 52°21N 5°59E **15 B5**
Épernay *France* 49°3N 3°56E **20 B5**
Ephesus *Turkey* 37°55N 27°22E **23 F12**
Ephraim *U.S.A.* 39°22N 111°35W **76 G8**
Ephrata *Pa., U.S.A.* 40°11N 76°11W **83 F8**
Ephrata *Wash., U.S.A.* 47°19N 119°33W **76 C4**
Epidaurus *Greece* 37°38N 23°10E **23 F10**
Épinal *France* 48°10N 6°27E **20 B7**
Epsom *U.K.* 51°19N 0°16W **13 F7**
Epukiro *Namibia* 21°40S 19°9E **56 B2**
Equatoria = El Istiwa'iya
  Sudan 5°0N 28°0E **53 G11**

Equatorial Guinea ■ *Africa* 2°0N 8°0E **54 D1**
Er Hai *China* 25°48N 100°11E **34 E3**
Er Rachidia *Morocco* 31°58N 4°20W **52 B5**
Er Rahad *Sudan* 12°45N 30°32E **53 F12**
Er Rif *Morocco* 35°1N 4°1W **52 A5**
Erandol *India* 20°56N 75°20E **44 D2**
Erāwadi Myit = Ayeawady →
  Burma 15°50N 95°6E **41 M19**
Erāwadi Myitwanya = Irrawaddy,
  Mouths of the *Burma* 15°30N 95°0E **41 M19**
Erawan △ *Thailand* 14°25N 98°58E **38 E2**
Erçek *Turkey* 38°39N 43°36E **46 B4**
Erciyaş Dağı *Turkey* 38°30N 35°30E **46 B2**
Érd *Hungary* 47°22N 18°56E **17 E10**
Erdao Jiang → *China* 42°37N 128°0E **33 C14**
Erdek *Turkey* 40°23N 27°47E **23 D12**
Erdene = Ulaan-Uul
  Mongolia 46°4N 100°49E **32 B9**
Erdenet *Mongolia* 49°2N 104°5E **30 B9**
Erdenetsogt *Mongolia* 46°56N 102°6E **32 C4**
Erebus, Mt. *Antarctica* 77°35S 167°0E **5 D11**
Erechim *Brazil* 27°35S 52°15W **95 B5**
Ereğli *Konya, Turkey* 37°31N 34°4E **46 B2**
Ereğli *Zonguldak, Turkey* 41°15N 31°24E **19 F5**
Erenhot *China* 43°48N 112°2E **32 C7**
Eresma → *Spain* 41°26N 4°45W **21 B3**
Erfenisdam *S. Africa* 28°30S 26°50E **56 C4**
Erfurt *Germany* 50°58N 11°2E **16 C6**
Ergani *Turkey* 38°17N 39°49E **46 B3**
Ergel *Mongolia* 43°8N 109°5E **32 C5**
Ergeni Vozvyshennost
  Russia 47°0N 44°0E **19 E7**
Ērgli *Latvia* 56°54N 25°38E **9 H21**
Ergun He = Argun →
  Russia 53°20N 121°28E **31 A13**
Ergun Youqi *China* 50°15N 120°11E **31 A13**
Erhlin *Taiwan* 23°54N 120°22E **35 F13**
Eriboll, L. *U.K.* 58°30N 4°42W **11 C4**
Érice *Italy* 38°2N 12°35E **22 E5**
Erie *U.S.A.* 42°8N 80°5W **82 D4**
Erie, L. *N. Amer.* 42°15N 81°0W **82 D4**
Erie Canal *U.S.A.* 43°5N 78°43W **82 D6**
Erieau *Canada* 42°16N 81°57W **82 D3**
Erigavo = Ceerigaabo
  Somalia 10°35N 47°20E **49 E4**
Eriksdale *Canada* 50°52N 98°7W **71 C9**
Erimanthos *Greece* 37°57N 21°50E **23 F9**
Erimo-Misaki *Japan* 41°50N 143°15E **28 D11**
Erin *Canada* 43°45N 80°7W **82 C4**
Erin Pt. *Trin. & Tob.* 10°3N 61°39W **93 K15**
Erinpura *India* 25°9N 73°3E **42 G5**
Eriskay *U.K.* 57°4N 7°18W **11 D1**
Eritrea ■ *Africa* 14°0N 38°30E **49 D2**
Erlangen *Germany* 49°36N 11°0E **16 D6**
Erldunda *Australia* 25°14S 133°12E **62 D1**
Ermelo *Neths.* 52°18N 5°35E **15 B5**
Ermelo *S. Africa* 26°31S 29°59E **57 C4**
Ermenek *Turkey* 36°38N 33°0E **46 B2**
Ermoupoli *Greece* 37°28N 24°57E **23 F11**
Ernakulam *India* 9°59N 76°22E **45 K3**
Erne → *Ireland* 54°30N 8°16W **10 B3**
Erne, Lower L. *U.K.* 54°28N 7°47W **10 B4**
Erne, Upper L. *U.K.* 54°14N 7°32W **10 B4**
Ernest Giles Ra. *Australia* 27°0S 123°45E **61 E3**
Erode *India* 11°24N 77°45E **45 J3**
Eromanga *Australia* 26°40S 143°11E **63 D3**
Erongo *Namibia* 21°39S 15°58E **56 B2**
Erongo □ *Namibia* 22°0S 15°0E **56 B2**
Erramala Hills *India* 15°30N 78°15E **45 G4**
Errenteria *Spain* 43°19N 1°54W **21 A5**
Errigal *Ireland* 55°2N 8°6W **10 A3**
Errinundra △ *Australia* 37°20S 148°45E **63 F4**
Erris Hd. *Ireland* 54°17N 10°0W **10 B1**
Erskine *U.S.A.* 47°40N 96°0W **80 B6**
Ertan Shuiku *China* 27°5N 101°52E **34 D3**
Ertis = Irtysh → *Russia* 61°4N 68°52E **26 C7**
Erwin *U.S.A.* 36°9N 82°25W **85 C13**
Eryuan *China* 26°7N 99°57E **34 D3**
Erzgebirge *Germany* 50°27N 12°55E **16 C7**
Erzin *Russia* 50°15N 95°10E **27 D10**
Erzincan *Turkey* 39°46N 39°30E **46 B3**
Erzurum *Turkey* 39°57N 41°15E **46 B4**
Es Sînâ' *Egypt* 29°0N 34°0E **48 F2**
Esan-Misaki *Japan* 41°40N 141°10E **28 D10**
Esashi *Hokkaidō, Japan* 44°56N 142°35E **28 B11**
Esashi *Hokkaidō, Japan* 41°52N 140°7E **28 D10**
Esbjerg *Denmark* 55°29N 8°29E **9 J13**
Esbo = Espoo *Finland* 60°12N 24°40E **9 F21**
Escalante *U.S.A.* 37°47N 111°36W **77 H8**
Escalante → *U.S.A.* 37°24N 110°57W **77 H8**
Escalón *Mexico* 26°45N 104°20W **86 B4**
Escambia → *U.S.A.* 30°32N 87°11W **85 F11**
Escanaba *U.S.A.* 45°45N 87°4W **80 C10**
Escárcega *Mexico* 18°37N 90°43W **87 D6**
Esch-sur-Alzette *Lux.* 49°32N 6°0E **15 E6**
Escondido *U.S.A.* 33°7N 117°5W **79 M9**
Escuinapa de Hidalgo
  Mexico 22°50N 105°50W **86 C3**
Escuintla *Guatemala* 14°20N 90°48W **88 D1**
Esenguly *Turkmenistan* 37°37N 53°59E **26 F6**
Eşfahān *Iran* 32°39N 51°43E **47 C6**
Eşfahān □ *Iran* 32°50N 51°30E **47 C6**
Esfarāyen *Iran* 37°4N 57°30E **47 B8**
Esfideh *Iran* 33°39N 59°46E **47 C8**
Esh Sham = Dimashq
  Syria 33°30N 36°18E **48 B5**
Esha Ness *U.K.* 60°29N 1°38W **11 A7**
Eshan *China* 24°11N 102°24E **34 E4**
Eshkol △ *Israel* 31°20N 34°30E **48 D3**
Eshowe *S. Africa* 28°50S 31°30E **57 D5**
Esigodini *Zimbabwe* 20°18S 28°56E **57 B4**
Esil = Ishim → *Russia* 57°45N 71°10E **26 D8**
Esk → *Dumf. & Gall., U.K.* 54°58N 3°2W **11 G5**
Esk → *N. Yorks., U.K.* 54°30N 0°37W **12 C7**
Eskån *Iran* 26°48N 63°9E **47 E9**
Esker Siding *Canada* 53°53N 66°25E **73 B6**
Eskilstuna *Sweden* 59°22N 16°32E **9 G17**
Eskimo Point = Arviat
  Canada 61°6N 93°59W **71 A10**

Eskişehir Turkey 39°50N 30°30E 19 G5
Esla → Spain 41°29N 6°3W 21 B2
Eslāmābād-e Gharb Iran 34°10N 46°30E 46 C5
Eslāmshahr Iran 35°40N 51°10E 47 C6
Eşme Turkey 38°23N 28°58E 23 E13
Esmeraldas Ecuador 1°0N 79°40W 92 C3
Esna = Isna Egypt 25°17N 32°30E 53 C12
Esnagi L. Canada 48°36N 84°33W 72 C3
España = Spain ■ Europe 39°0N 4°0W 21 B4
Espanola Canada 46°15N 81°46W 72 C3
Espanola U.S.A. 35°59N 106°5W 77 J10
Esparza Costa Rica 9°59N 84°40W 88 E3
Esperance Australia 33°45S 121°55E 61 F3
Esperance B. Australia 33°48S 121°55E 61 F3
Esperance Harbour St. Lucia 14°4N 60°55W 89 f
Esperanza Antarctica 65°0S 55°0W 5 C18
Esperanza Argentina 31°29S 61°3W 94 C3
Esperanza Puerto Rico 18°6N 65°28W 89 d
Espichel, C. Portugal 38°22N 9°16W 21 C1
Espigão, Serra do Brazil 26°35S 50°30W 95 B5
Espinazo, Sierra del = Espinhaço, Serra do Brazil 17°30S 43°30W 93 G10
Espinhaço, Serra do Brazil 17°30S 43°30W 93 G10
Espinilho, Serra do Brazil 28°30S 55°0W 95 B5
Espírito Santo □ Brazil 20°0S 40°45W 93 H10
Espírito Santo do Pinhal Brazil 22°10S 46°46W 95 A6
Espíritu Santo Vanuatu 15°15S 166°50E 58 C9
Espíritu Santo, B. del Mexico 19°20N 87°35W 87 D7
Espíritu Santo, I. Mexico 24°30N 110°22W 86 C2
Espita Mexico 21°1N 88°19W 87 C7
Espoo Finland 60°12N 24°40E 9 F21
Espungabera Mozam. 20°29S 32°45E 57 B5
Esquel Argentina 42°55S 71°20W 96 E2
Esquimalt Canada 48°26N 123°25W 78 B3
Esquina Argentina 30°0S 59°30W 94 C4
Essaouira Morocco 31°32N 9°42W 52 B4
Essen Belgium 51°28N 4°28E 15 C4
Essen Germany 51°28N 7°2E 16 C4
Essendon, Mt. Australia 25°0S 120°29E 61 E3
Essequibo → Guyana 6°50N 58°30W 92 B7
Essex Canada 42°10N 82°49W 82 D2
Essex Calif., U.S.A. 34°44N 115°15W 79 L11
Essex N.Y., U.S.A. 44°19N 73°21W 83 B11
Essex □ U.K. 51°54N 0°27E 13 F8
Essex Junction U.S.A. 44°29N 73°7W 83 B11
Esslingen Germany 48°44N 9°18E 16 D5
Estación Camacho Mexico 24°25N 102°18W 86 C4
Estación Simón Mexico 24°42N 102°35W 86 C4
Estados, I. de Los Argentina 54°40S 64°30W 96 G4
Eşţahbānāt Iran 29°8N 54°4E 47 D7
Estância Brazil 11°16S 37°26W 93 F11
Estancia U.S.A. 34°46N 106°4W 77 J10
Estārm Iran 28°21N 58°21E 47 D8
Estcourt S. Africa 29°0S 29°53E 57 C4
Este △ Dom. Rep. 18°14N 68°42W 89 C6
Estelí Nic. 13°9N 86°22W 88 D2
Esterhazy Canada 50°37N 102°5W 71 C8
Estevan Canada 49°10N 102°59W 71 D8
Estevan Group Canada 53°3N 129°38W 70 C3
Estherville U.S.A. 43°24N 94°50W 80 D6
Eston Canada 51°8N 108°40W 71 C7
Estonia ■ Europe 58°30N 25°30E 9 G21
Estreito Brazil 6°32S 47°25W 93 E9
Estrela, Serra da Portugal 40°10N 7°45W 21 B2
Estremoz Portugal 38°51N 7°39W 21 C2
Estrondo, Serra do Brazil 7°20S 48°0W 93 E9
Esztergom Hungary 47°47N 18°44E 17 E10
Et Tîdra Mauritania 19°45N 16°20W 52 E2
Etah India 27°35N 78°40E 43 F8
Étampes France 48°26N 2°10E 20 B5
Etanga Namibia 17°55S 13°0E 56 A1
Etawah India 26°48N 79°6E 43 F8
Etawney L. Canada 57°50N 96°50W 71 B9
Etchojoa Mexico 26°55N 109°38W 86 B3
eThekwini = Durban S. Africa 29°49S 31°1E 57 C5
Ethel U.S.A. 46°32N 122°46W 78 D4
Ethelbert Canada 51°32N 100°25W 71 C8
Ethiopia ■ Africa 8°0N 40°0E 49 F3
Ethiopian Highlands Ethiopia 10°0N 37°0E 49 F2
Etive, L. U.K. 56°29N 5°10W 11 E3
Etna Italy 37°50N 14°55E 22 F6
Etolin Strait U.S.A. 60°20N 165°15W 74 C6
Etosha △ Namibia 19°0S 16°0E 56 A2
Etosha Pan Namibia 18°40S 16°30E 56 A2
Etowah U.S.A. 35°20N 84°32W 85 D12
Etrek Turkmenistan 37°36N 54°46E 47 B7
Ettelbruck Lux. 49°51N 6°5E 15 E6
Ettrick Water → U.K. 55°31N 2°55W 11 F6
Etzná-Tixmucuy = Edzná Mexico 19°39N 90°19W 87 D6
Eua Tonga 21°22S 174°56W 59 c
Euboea = Evia Greece 38°30N 24°0E 23 E11
Eucla Australia 31°41S 128°52E 61 F4
Euclid U.S.A. 41°34N 81°32W 82 E3
Eucumbene, L. Australia 36°2S 148°40E 63 F4
Eudora U.S.A. 33°7N 91°16W 84 E9
Eufaula Ala., U.S.A. 31°54N 85°9W 85 F12
Eufaula Okla., U.S.A. 35°17N 95°35W 84 D7
Eufaula L. U.S.A. 35°18N 95°21W 84 D7
Eugene U.S.A. 44°5N 123°4W 76 D2
Eugowra Australia 33°22S 148°24E 63 E4
Eulo Australia 28°10S 145°3E 63 D4
Eungella △ Australia 20°57S 148°40E 62 b
Eunice La., U.S.A. 30°30N 92°25W 84 F8
Eunice N. Mex., U.S.A. 32°26N 103°10W 77 K12
Eupen Belgium 50°37N 6°3E 15 D6
Euphrates = Furāt, Nahr al → Asia 31°0N 47°25E 46 D5
Eureka Canada 80°0N 85°56W 69 B14
Eureka Calif., U.S.A. 40°47N 124°9W 76 F1
Eureka Kans., U.S.A. 37°49N 96°17W 80 G5
Eureka Mont., U.S.A. 48°53N 115°3W 76 B6
Eureka Nev., U.S.A. 39°31N 115°58W 76 G6
Eureka S. Dak., U.S.A. 45°46N 99°38W 80 C4
Eureka, Mt. Australia 26°35S 121°35E 61 E3
Eureka Sd. Canada 79°0N 85°0W 69 B15
Euroa Australia 36°44S 145°35E 63 F4
Europa, Île Ind. Oc. 22°20S 40°22E 57 B7
Europa, Picos de Spain 43°10N 4°49W 21 A3
Europa, Pt. Gib. 36°3N 5°21W 21 D3
Europe 50°0N 20°0E 6 E10
Europoort Neths. 51°57N 4°10E 15 C4
Euskadi = País Vasco □ Spain 42°50N 2°45W 21 A4
Eustis U.S.A. 28°51N 81°41W 85 G14
Eutsuk L. Canada 53°20N 126°45W 70 C3
Evale Angola 16°33S 15°44E 56 A2
Evans U.S.A. 40°23N 104°41W 76 F11
Evans, L. Canada 50°50N 77°0W 72 B4
Evans City U.S.A. 40°46N 80°4W 82 F4
Evans Head Australia 29°7S 153°27E 63 D5
Evansburg Canada 53°36N 114°59W 70 C5
Evanston U.S.A. 41°16N 110°58W 76 F8
Evansville U.S.A. 37°58N 87°35W 80 G10
Evaz Iran 27°46N 53°59E 47 E7
Eveleth U.S.A. 47°28N 92°32W 80 B7
Evensk Russia 62°12N 159°30E 27 C16
Everard, L. Australia 31°30S 135°0E 63 E2
Everard Ranges Australia 27°5S 132°28E 61 E5
Everest, Mt. Nepal 28°5N 86°58E 43 E12
Everett Pa., U.S.A. 40°1N 78°23W 82 F6
Everett Wash., U.S.A. 47°59N 122°12W 78 C4
Everglades, The U.S.A. 25°50N 81°0W 85 J14
Everglades △ U.S.A. 25°30N 81°0W 85 J14
Everglades City U.S.A. 25°52N 81°23W 85 J14
Evergreen Ala., U.S.A. 31°26N 86°57W 85 F11
Evergreen Mont., U.S.A. 48°14N 114°17W 76 B6
Evesham U.K. 52°6N 1°56W 13 E6
Evia Greece 38°30N 24°0E 23 E11
Evje Norway 58°36N 7°51E 9 G12
Évora Portugal 38°33N 7°57W 21 C2
Evowghlī Iran 38°43N 45°13E 46 B5
Évreux France 49°3N 1°8E 20 B4
Evros → Greece 41°40N 26°34E 23 D12
Évry France 48°38N 2°27E 20 B5
Évvoia = Evia Greece 38°30N 24°0E 23 E11
Ewe, L. U.K. 57°49N 5°38W 11 D3
Ewing U.S.A. 42°16N 98°21W 80 D4
Ewo Congo 0°48S 14°45E 54 E2
Exaltación Bolivia 13°10S 65°20W 92 F5
Excelsior Springs U.S.A. 39°20N 94°13W 80 F6
Exe → U.K. 50°41N 3°29W 13 G4
Exeter Canada 43°21N 81°29W 82 C3
Exeter U.K. 50°43N 3°31W 13 G4
Exeter Calif., U.S.A. 36°18N 119°9W 78 J7
Exeter N.H., U.S.A. 42°59N 70°57W 83 D14
Exmoor U.K. 51°12N 3°45W 13 F4
Exmoor △ U.K. 51°8N 3°42W 13 F4
Exmouth Australia 21°54S 114°10E 60 D1
Exmouth U.K. 50°37N 3°25W 13 G4
Exmouth G. Australia 22°15S 114°15E 60 D1
Exmouth Plateau Ind. Oc. 19°0S 114°0E 64 J3
Expedition △ Australia 25°41S 149°7E 63 D4
Expedition Ra. Australia 24°30S 149°12E 62 C4
Extremadura □ Spain 39°30N 6°5W 21 C2
Exuma Sound Bahamas 24°30N 76°20W 88 B4
Eyasi, L. Tanzania 3°30S 35°0E 54 E7
Eye Pen. U.K. 58°13N 6°10W 11 C2
Eyemouth U.K. 55°52N 2°5W 11 F6
Eyjafjallajökull Iceland 63°38N 19°36W 8 E4
Eyjafjörður Iceland 66°15N 18°30W 8 C4
Eyl Somalia 8°0N 49°50E 49 F4
Eyre, L. = Kati Thanda-Lake Eyre Australia 29°30S 137°26E 58 D6
Eyre Mts. N.Z. 45°25S 168°25E 59 F2
Eyre Pen. Australia 33°30S 136°17E 63 E2
Eysturoy Færoe Is. 62°13N 6°54W 8 E9
Eyvān = Jūy Zar Iran 33°50N 46°18E 46 C5
Eyvānkī Iran 35°24N 51°56E 47 C6
Ezhou China 30°23N 114°50E 35 B10
Ezhva Russia 61°48N 50°35E 18 B9
Ezine Turkey 39°48N 26°20E 23 E12

F

F.Y.R.O.M. = Macedonia ■ Europe 41°53N 21°40E 23 D9
Faaa Tahiti 17°34S 149°35W 59 d
Faaone Tahiti 17°40S 149°21W 59 d
Fabala Guinea 9°44N 9°5W 52 G4
Fabens U.S.A. 31°30N 106°10W 84 F1
Fabius U.S.A. 42°50N 75°59W 83 D9
Fabriano Italy 43°20N 12°54E 22 C5
Fachi Niger 18°6N 11°34E 53 E8
Fada Chad 17°13N 21°34E 53 E10
Fada-n-Gourma Burkina Faso 12°10N 0°30E 52 F6
Faddeyevskiy, Ostrov Russia 76°0N 144°0E 27 B15
Fadghāmī Syria 35°53N 40°52E 46 C4
Faenza Italy 44°17N 11°53E 22 B4
Færoe Is. = Føroyar ⊠ Atl. Oc. 62°0N 7°0W 8 F9
Făgăraş Romania 45°48N 24°58E 17 F13
Fagersta Sweden 60°1N 15°46E 9 F16
Fagnano, L. Argentina 54°30S 68°0W 96 G3
Fahlīān Iran 30°11N 51°28E 47 D6
Fahraj Kermān, Iran 29°0N 59°0E 47 D8
Fahraj Yazd, Iran 31°46N 54°36E 47 D7
Fai Tsi Long Vietnam 21°0N 107°30E 34 G6
Faial Azores 38°34N 28°42W 52 a
Faichan Kangri India 35°48N 76°34E 43 B7
Fair Haven N.Y., U.S.A. 43°18N 76°42W 83 C8
Fair Haven Vt., U.S.A. 43°36N 73°16W 83 C11
Fair Hd. U.K. 55°14N 6°9W 10 A5
Fair Isle U.K. 59°32N 1°38W 14 B6
Fair Oaks U.S.A. 38°39N 121°16W 78 G5
Fairbanks U.S.A. 64°51N 147°43W 68 E2
Fairbury U.S.A. 40°8N 97°11W 80 E5
Fairfax U.S.A. 44°40N 73°1W 83 B11
Fairfield Calif., U.S.A. 38°15N 122°3W 78 G4
Fairfield Conn., U.S.A. 41°9N 73°16W 83 E11
Fairfield Idaho, U.S.A. 43°21N 114°44W 76 E6
Fairfield Ill., U.S.A. 38°23N 88°22W 80 F9
Fairfield Iowa, U.S.A. 40°56N 91°57W 80 E8
Fairfield Tex., U.S.A. 31°44N 96°10W 84 F6
Fairford Canada 51°37N 98°38W 71 C9
Fairhope U.S.A. 30°31N 87°54W 85 F11
Fairlie N.Z. 44°5S 170°49E 59 F3
Fairmead U.S.A. 37°5N 120°10W 78 H6
Fairmont Minn., U.S.A. 43°39N 94°28W 80 D6
Fairmont W. Va., U.S.A. 39°29N 80°9W 81 F13
Fairmount Calif., U.S.A. 34°45N 118°26W 79 L8
Fairmount N.Y., U.S.A. 43°5N 76°12W 83 C8
Fairplay U.S.A. 39°15N 106°2W 76 G10
Fairport U.S.A. 43°6N 77°27W 82 C7
Fairport Harbor U.S.A. 41°45N 81°17W 82 E3
Fairview Canada 56°5N 118°25W 70 B5
Fairview Mont., U.S.A. 47°51N 104°3W 76 C11
Fairview Okla., U.S.A. 36°16N 98°29W 84 C5
Fairweather, Mt. U.S.A. 58°55N 137°32W 70 B1
Faisalabad Pakistan 31°30N 73°5E 42 D5
Faith U.S.A. 45°2N 102°2W 80 C2
Faizabad India 26°45N 82°10E 43 F10
Faizpur India 21°14N 75°49E 44 D2
Fajardo Puerto Rico 18°20N 65°39W 89 d
Fajr, W. → Si. Arabia 29°10N 38°10E 46 D3
Fakenham U.K. 52°51N 0°51E 12 E8
Fakfak Indonesia 2°55S 132°18E 37 E8
Faku China 42°32N 123°21E 33 C12
Falaise France 48°54N 0°12W 20 B3
Falam Burma 23°0N 93°45E 41 H18
Falcón, Presa Mexico 26°35N 99°10W 87 B5
Falcon Lake Canada 49°42N 95°15W 71 D9
Falcon Res. U.S.A. 26°34N 99°10W 84 H5
Falconara Marittima Italy 43°37N 13°24E 22 C5
Falcone, C. del Italy 40°58N 8°12E 22 D3
Falconer U.S.A. 42°7N 79°12W 82 D5
Falefa Samoa 13°54S 171°31W 59 b
Falelatai Samoa 13°55S 171°59W 59 b
Falelima Samoa 13°32S 172°41W 59 b
Faleshty = Făleşti Moldova 47°32N 27°44E 17 E14
Făleşti Moldova 47°32N 27°44E 17 E14
Falfurrias U.S.A. 27°14N 98°9W 84 H5
Falher Canada 55°44N 117°15W 70 B5
Falkenberg Sweden 56°54N 12°30E 9 H15
Falkirk U.K. 56°0N 3°47W 11 F5
Falkirk □ U.K. 55°58N 3°49W 11 F5
Falkland U.K. 56°16N 3°12W 11 E5
Falkland Is. ⊠ Atl. Oc. 51°30S 59°0W 96 G5
Falkland Sd. Falk. Is. 52°0S 60°0W 96 G5
Fall River U.S.A. 41°43N 71°10W 83 E13
Fallbrook U.S.A. 33°23N 117°15W 79 M9
Fallon U.S.A. 39°28N 118°47W 76 G4
Falls City U.S.A. 40°3N 95°36W 80 E6
Falls Creek U.S.A. 41°9N 78°48W 82 E6
Falmouth Jamaica 18°30N 77°40W 88 a
Falmouth U.K. 50°9N 5°5W 13 G2
Falmouth U.S.A. 41°33N 70°37W 83 E14
Falsa, Pta. Mexico 27°51N 115°3W 86 B1
False B. S. Africa 34°15S 18°40E 56 D2
False Divi Pt. India 15°43N 80°50E 45 G5
False Pt. India 20°18N 86°48E 44 D8
Falso, C. Honduras 15°12N 83°21W 88 C3
Falster Denmark 54°45N 11°55E 9 J14
Fălticeni Romania 47°21N 26°20E 17 E14
Falun Sweden 60°37N 15°37E 8 F16
Famagusta Cyprus 35°8N 33°55E 46 C2
Famatina, Sierra de Argentina 27°30S 68°0W 94 B2
Family L. Canada 51°54N 95°27W 71 C9
Famoso U.S.A. 35°37N 119°12W 79 K7
Fan Xian China 35°55N 115°38E 32 G8
Fanad Hd. Ireland 55°17N 7°38W 10 A4
Fang Thailand 19°55N 99°13E 38 C2
Fang Xian China 32°3N 110°40E 35 A8
Fangchang China 31°5N 118°4E 35 B12
Fangcheng China 33°18N 112°59E 32 H7
Fangchenggang China 21°42N 108°21E 34 G7
Fangliao Taiwan 22°22N 120°38E 35 F13
Fangshan Beijing, China 39°41N 116°0E 32 E9
Fangshan Shanxi, China 38°3N 111°25E 32 E6
Fangzi China 36°33N 119°10E 33 F10
Fanjiatun China 43°40N 125°15E 33 C13
Fanling China 22°30N 114°8E 31 a
Fannich, L. U.K. 57°38N 4°59W 11 D4
Fannūj Iran 26°35N 59°38E 47 E8
Fanø Denmark 55°25N 8°25E 9 J13
Fano Italy 43°50N 13°1E 22 C5
Fanshi China 39°12N 113°20E 32 E7
Fao = Al Fāw Iraq 30°0N 48°30E 47 D6
Faqirwali Pakistan 29°27N 73°0E 42 E5
Far East = Dalnevostochnyy □ Russia 67°0N 140°0E 27 C14
Far East Asia 40°0N 130°0E 24 E14
Faradje Dem. Rep. of the Congo 3°50N 29°45E 54 D5
Farafangana Madag. 22°49S 47°50E 55 J9
Farāh Afghan. 32°20N 62°7E 40 C3
Farāh □ Afghan. 32°25N 62°10E 40 C3
Farasān, Jazā'ir Si. Arabia 16°45N 41°55E 49 D3
Farasan Is. = Farasān, Jazā'ir Si. Arabia 16°45N 41°55E 49 D3
Fareham U.K. 50°51N 1°11W 13 G6
Farewell, C. = Nunap Isua Greenland 59°48N 43°55W 66 D15
Farewell, C. N.Z. 40°29S 172°43E 59 D4
Fargo U.S.A. 46°53N 96°48W 80 B5
Farg'ona Uzbekistan 40°23N 71°19E 26 E8
Fār'iah, W. al → West Bank 32°12N 35°27E 48 C4
Faribault U.S.A. 44°18N 93°16W 80 C7
Faridabad India 28°26N 77°19E 42 E6
Faridkot India 30°44N 74°45E 42 D6
Faridpur Bangla. 23°15N 89°55E 43 H13
Faridpur India 28°13N 79°33E 43 E8
Farīmān Iran 35°40N 59°49E 47 C8
Farleigh Australia 21°4S 149°8E 62 b
Farmerville U.S.A. 32°47N 92°24W 84 E8
Farmingdale U.S.A. 40°12N 74°10W 83 F10
Farmington Canada 55°54N 120°30W 70 B4
Farmington Calif., U.S.A. 37°55N 120°59W 78 H6
Farmington Maine, U.S.A. 44°40N 70°9W 81 C18
Farmington Mo., U.S.A. 37°47N 90°25W 80 G8
Farmington N.H., U.S.A. 43°24N 71°4W 83 C13
Farmington N. Mex., U.S.A. 36°44N 108°12W 77 H9
Farmington Utah, U.S.A. 40°59N 111°53W 76 F8
Farmington → U.S.A. 41°51N 72°38W 83 E12
Farmville U.S.A. 37°18N 78°24W 81 G14
Farne Is. U.K. 55°38N 1°37W 12 B6
Farnham Canada 45°17N 72°59W 83 A12
Farnham, Mt. Canada 50°29N 116°30W 70 C5
Faro Brazil 2°10S 56°39W 93 D7
Faro Canada 62°11N 133°22W 68 E5
Faro Portugal 37°2N 7°55W 21 D2
Fårö Sweden 57°55N 19°5E 9 H18
Farquhar, C. Australia 23°50S 113°36E 61 D1
Farrars Cr. → Australia 25°35S 140°43E 62 D3
Farrāshband Iran 28°57N 52°5E 47 D7
Farrell U.S.A. 41°13N 80°30W 82 E4
Farrokhī Iran 33°50N 59°31E 47 C8
Farrukhabad India 27°24N 79°34E 44 A4
Fārs □ Iran 29°30N 55°0E 47 D7
Farsala Greece 39°17N 22°23E 23 E10
Fārsī Iran 27°58N 50°11E 47 E6
Farson U.S.A. 42°7N 109°26W 76 E9
Farsund Norway 58°5N 6°55E 9 G12
Fartak, Râs Si. Arabia 28°5N 34°34E 46 D2
Fartak, Ra's Yemen 15°38N 52°15E 49 D5
Fartura, Serra da Brazil 26°21S 52°52W 95 B5
Fārūj Iran 37°14N 58°14E 47 B8
Farvel, Kap = Nunap Isua Greenland 59°48N 43°55W 66 D15
Farwell U.S.A. 34°23N 103°2W 84 D3
Faryāb □ Afghan. 36°0N 65°0E 40 B4
Fasā Iran 29°0N 53°39E 47 D7
Fasano Italy 40°50N 17°22E 22 D7
Fastiv Ukraine 50°7N 29°57E 17 C15
Fastnet Rock Ireland 51°22N 9°37W 10 E2
Fastov = Fastiv Ukraine 50°7N 29°57E 17 C15
Fatagartuting, Tanjung Indonesia 2°46S 131°57E 37 E8
Fatehabad Haryana, India 29°31N 75°27E 42 E6
Fatehabad Ut. P., India 27°1N 78°19E 42 F8
Fatehgarh India 27°25N 79°35E 43 F8
Fatehpur Bihar, India 24°38N 85°14E 43 G11
Fatehpur Raj., India 28°0N 74°40E 42 F6
Fatehpur Ut. P., India 25°56N 81°13E 43 G9
Fatehpur Ut. P., India 27°10N 81°13E 43 F9
Fatehpur Sikri India 27°6N 77°40E 42 F6
Fathom Five ⌂ Canada 45°17N 81°40W 82 A3
Fatima Canada 47°24N 61°53W 73 C7
Faulkton U.S.A. 45°2N 99°8W 80 C4
Faure I. Australia 25°52S 113°50E 61 E1
Fauresmith S. Africa 29°44S 25°17E 56 C4
Fauske Norway 67°17N 15°25E 8 C16
Favara Italy 37°19N 13°39E 22 F5
Favignana Italy 37°56N 12°20E 22 F5
Fawcett, Pt. Australia 11°46S 130°2E 60 B5
Fawn → Canada 55°20N 87°35W 72 A2
Fawnskin U.S.A. 34°16N 116°56W 79 L10
Faxaflói Iceland 64°29N 23°0W 8 D2
Faya-Largeau Chad 17°58N 19°6E 53 E9
Fayd Si. Arabia 27°1N 42°52E 46 E4
Fayette Ala., U.S.A. 33°41N 87°50W 85 E11
Fayette Mo., U.S.A. 39°9N 92°41W 80 F7
Fayette N.Y., U.S.A. 42°48N 76°48W 83 D8
Fayetteville Ark., U.S.A. 36°4N 94°10W 84 C7
Fayetteville N.C., U.S.A. 35°3N 78°53W 85 D15
Fayetteville N.Y., U.S.A. 43°1N 76°0W 83 C9
Fayetteville Tenn., U.S.A. 35°9N 86°34W 85 D11
Faylakah Kuwait 29°27N 48°20E 47 D6
Fazilka India 30°27N 74°2E 42 D6
Fazilpur Pakistan 29°18N 70°29E 42 E4
Fdérik Mauritania 22°40N 12°45W 52 D3
Feakle Ireland 52°56N 8°40W 10 D3
Feale → Ireland 52°27N 9°37W 10 D2
Fear, C. U.S.A. 33°50N 77°58W 85 E16
Feather → U.S.A. 38°47N 121°36W 78 G5
Feather Falls U.S.A. 39°36N 121°16W 78 F5
Featherston N.Z. 41°6S 175°20E 59 D5
Fécamp France 49°45N 0°22E 20 B4
Fedala = Mohammedia Morocco 33°44N 7°21W 52 B4
Federación Argentina 31°0S 57°55W 94 C4
Féderal Argentina 30°57S 58°48W 94 C4
Féderal Argentina 30°57S 58°48W 96 C5
Federal Way U.S.A. 47°18N 122°19W 78 C4
Fedeshkūh Iran 28°49N 53°50E 47 D7
Fehmarn Germany 54°27N 11°7E 16 A6
Fehmarn Bælt Europe 54°35N 11°20E 9 J14
Fehmarn Belt = Fehmarn Bælt Europe 54°35N 11°20E 9 J14
Fei Xian China 35°18N 117°59E 33 G9
Feicheng China 36°14N 116°45E 32 F9
Feidong China 32°0N 117°35E 35 B11
Feijó Brazil 8°9S 70°21W 92 E4
Feilding N.Z. 40°13S 175°35E 59 D5
Feira de Santana Brazil 12°15S 38°57W 93 F11
Feixi China 31°43N 117°59E 35 B11
Feixiang China 36°30N 114°45E 32 F8
Feldkirch Austria 47°15N 9°37E 16 E5
Félicité Seychelles 4°19S 55°52E 55 b
Felipe Carrillo Puerto Mexico 19°38N 88°3W 87 D7
Felixburg Zimbabwe 19°29S 30°51E 57 A5
Felixstowe U.K. 51°58N 1°23E 13 F9
Felton U.S.A. 37°3N 122°4W 78 H4
Femer Bælt = Fehmarn Bælt Europe 54°35N 11°20E 9 J14
Femunden Norway 62°10N 11°53E 8 E14
Femundsmarka △ Norway 62°18N 12°6E 8 E15
Fen He → China 35°36N 110°42E 32 G6
Fenelon Falls Canada 44°32N 78°45W 82 B6
Feng Xian Jiangsu, China 34°43N 116°35E 32 G9
Feng Xian Shaanxi, China 33°54N 106°40E 32 H4
Fengcheng Jiangxi, China 28°12N 115°48E 35 C10
Fengcheng Liaoning, China 40°28N 124°5E 33 D13
Fengdu China 29°55N 107°48E 34 C6
Fengfeng China 36°28N 114°8E 32 F8
Fenggang China 27°57N 107°47E 34 D6
Fenghua China 29°40N 121°25E 35 C13
Fenghuang China 27°57N 109°29E 34 D7
Fengjie China 31°3N 109°31E 34 B7
Fengkai China 23°24N 111°30E 35 F8
Fengkang Taiwan 22°12N 120°41E 35 F13
Fengle China 31°29N 112°29E 35 B9
Fenglin Taiwan 23°45N 121°26E 35 F13
Fengning China 41°10N 116°33E 32 D9
Fengqing China 24°38N 99°55E 34 E2
Fengqiu China 35°2N 114°25E 32 G8
Fengrun China 39°48N 118°8E 33 E10
Fengshan Guangxi Zhuangzu, China 24°39N 109°15E 34 E7
Fengshan Guangxi Zhuangzu, China 24°31N 107°3E 34 E6
Fengshan Taiwan 22°38N 120°21E 35 F13
Fengshun China 23°46N 116°10E 35 F11
Fengtai China 32°50N 116°40E 35 A11
Fengtongzhai △ China 30°32N 102°54E 34 B4
Fengxiang China 34°29N 107°25E 32 G4
Fengxin China 28°41N 115°18E 35 C10
Fengyang China 32°51N 117°29E 33 H9
Fengyi China 25°37N 100°20E 34 E3
Fengyüan Taiwan 24°15N 120°35E 35 E13
Fengzhen China 40°25N 113°2E 32 D7
Fenoarivo Atsinanana Madag. 17°22S 49°25E 55 H9
Fens, The U.K. 52°38N 0°2W 12 E7
Fenton U.S.A. 42°48N 83°42W 81 D12
Fenxi China 36°40N 111°31E 32 F6
Fenyang China 37°18N 111°48E 32 F6
Fenyi China 27°45N 114°47E 35 D10
Feodosiya Ukraine 45°2N 35°16E 19 E6
Ferbane Ireland 53°16N 7°50W 10 C4
Ferdows Iran 33°58N 58°2E 47 C8
Ferfer Somalia 5°4N 45°9E 49 F4
Fergana = Farg'ona Uzbekistan 40°23N 71°19E 26 E8
Fergus Canada 43°43N 80°24W 82 C4
Fergus Falls U.S.A. 46°17N 96°4W 80 B5
Ferizaj Kosovo 42°23N 21°10E 23 C9
Ferkéssédougou Ivory C. 9°35N 5°6W 52 G4
Ferland Canada 50°19N 88°27W 72 B2
Ferlo, Vallée du Senegal 15°15N 14°15W 52 E3
Fermanagh □ U.K. 54°21N 7°40W 10 B4
Fermo Italy 43°9N 13°43E 22 C5
Fermont Canada 52°47N 67°5W 73 B6
Fermoy Ireland 52°9N 8°16W 10 D3
Fernández Argentina 27°55S 63°50W 94 B3
Fernandina Beach U.S.A. 30°40N 81°27W 85 F14
Fernando de Noronha Brazil 4°0S 33°10W 93 D12
Fernando Póo = Bioko Eq. Guin. 3°30N 8°40E 54 D1
Ferndale Canada 44°58N 81°17W 82 B3
Ferndale U.S.A. 48°51N 122°36W 78 B4
Fernie Canada 49°30N 115°5W 70 D5
Fernlees Australia 23°51S 148°7E 62 C4
Fernley U.S.A. 39°36N 119°14W 76 G4
Fernwood U.S.A. 43°16N 73°38W 83 C11
Feroke India 11°9N 75°46E 45 J2
Ferozepore = Firozpur India 30°55N 74°40E 42 D6
Ferrara Italy 44°50N 11°35E 22 B4
Ferreñafe Peru 6°42S 79°50W 92 E3
Ferret, C. France 44°38N 1°15W 20 D3
Ferriday U.S.A. 31°38N 91°33W 84 F9
Ferrol Spain 43°29N 8°15W 21 A1
Ferron U.S.A. 39°5N 111°8W 76 G8
Ferryland Canada 47°2N 52°53W 73 C9
Fertile U.S.A. 47°32N 96°17W 80 B5
Fès Morocco 34°0N 5°0W 52 B5
Fessenden U.S.A. 47°39N 99°38W 80 B4
Festus U.S.A. 38°13N 90°24W 80 F8
Feteşti Romania 44°22N 27°51E 17 F14
Fethiye Turkey 36°36N 29°6E 19 G4
Fetlar U.K. 60°36N 0°52W 11 A8
Feuilles → Canada 58°47N 70°4W 69 F17
Fez = Fès Morocco 34°0N 5°0W 52 B5
Fezzan Libya 27°0N 13°0E 53 C8
Fiambalá Argentina 27°45S 67°37W 94 B2
Fianarantsoa Madag. 21°26S 47°5E 55 J9
Ficksburg S. Africa 28°51S 27°53E 57 C4
Field → Australia 23°48S 138°0E 62 C2
Field I. Australia 12°5S 132°23E 60 B5
Fier Albania 40°43N 19°33E 23 D8
Fife □ U.K. 56°16N 3°1W 11 E5
Fife Ness U.K. 56°17N 2°35W 11 E6
Fifth Cataract Sudan 18°22N 33°50E 53 E12
Figeac France 44°37N 2°2E 20 D5
Figueira da Foz Portugal 40°7N 8°54W 21 B1
Figueres Spain 42°18N 2°58E 21 A7
Figuig Morocco 32°5N 1°11W 52 B5
Fiji ■ Pac. Oc. 17°20S 179°0E 59 a
Filabusi Zimbabwe 20°34S 29°20E 57 B4
Filadelfia Paraguay 22°21S 60°2W 94 A3
Filchner Ice Shelf Antarctica 79°0S 40°0W 5 D1
Filey U.K. 54°12N 0°18W 12 C7
Filey B. U.K. 54°12N 0°15W 12 C7
Filiatra Greece 37°9N 21°35E 23 F9
Filingué Niger 14°21N 3°22E 52 F6
Filipstad Sweden 59°43N 14°9E 9 G16
Fillmore Calif., U.S.A. 34°24N 118°55W 79 L8
Fillmore Utah, U.S.A. 38°58N 112°20W 77 G7
Fimbul Ice Shelf S. Ocean 69°30S 1°0W 5 C2
Finch Canada 45°11N 75°7W 83 A9
Finch Hatton Australia 20°25S 148°39E 62 b
Findhorn → U.K. 57°38N 3°38W 11 D5
Findlay U.S.A. 41°2N 83°39W 81 E12
Fine U.S.A. 44°14N 75°8W 83 B9
Fingal □ Ireland 53°29N 6°14W 10 C5

Finger L. Canada 53°33N 93°30W 72 B1
Finger Lakes U.S.A. 42°40N 76°30W 83 D8
Fíngoè Mozam. 15°55S 31°50E 55 G6
Finisterre, C. = Fisterra, C.
  Spain 42°50N 9°19W 21 A1
Finke Australia 25°34S 134°35E 62 D1
Finke Gorge △ Australia 24°8S 132°49E 60 D5
Finland ■ Europe 63°0N 27°0E 8 E22
Finland, G. of Europe 60°0N 26°0E 9 G22
Finlay → Canada 57°0N 125°10W 70 B3
Finley Australia 35°38S 145°35E 63 F4
Finley U.S.A. 47°31N 97°50W 80 B5
Finn → Ireland 54°51N 7°28W 10 B4
Finnigan, Mt. Australia 15°49S 145°17E 62 B4
Finniss, C. Australia 33°8S 134°51E 63 E1
Finnmark Norway 69°37N 23°57E 8 B20
Finnsnes Norway 69°14N 18°0E 8 B18
Finspång Sweden 58°43N 15°47E 9 G16
Fiora → Italy 42°20N 11°34E 22 C4
Fiordland △ N.Z. 45°46S 167°0E 59 F1
Fíq Syria 32°46N 35°41E 48 C4
Firat = Furāt, Nahr al →
  Asia 31°0N 47°25E 46 D5
Fire Island △ U.S.A. 40°38N 73°8W 83 F11
Firebag → Canada 57°45N 111°21W 71 B6
Firebaugh U.S.A. 36°52N 120°27W 78 J6
Firenze Italy 43°46N 11°15E 22 C4
Firk, Sha'ib → Iraq 30°59N 44°34E 46 D5
Firozabad India 27°10N 78°25E 43 F8
Firozpur India 30°55N 74°40E 42 D6
Firozpur-Jhirka India 27°48N 76°57E 42 F7
Fīrūzābād Iran 28°52N 52°35E 47 D7
Fīrūzkūh Iran 35°50N 52°50E 47 C7
Firvale Canada 52°27N 126°13W 70 C3
Fish → Namibia 28°7S 17°10E 56 D2
Fish → S. Africa 31°30S 20°16E 56 D3
Fish River Canyon
  Namibia 27°40S 17°35E 56 C2
Fisher B. Canada 51°35N 97°13W 71 C9
Fishers I. U.S.A. 41°15N 72°0W 83 E13
Fishguard U.K. 52°0N 4°58W 13 E3
Fishing L. Canada 52°10N 95°24W 71 C9
Fishkill U.S.A. 41°32N 73°54W 83 E11
Fisterra, C. Spain 42°50N 9°19W 21 A1
Fitchburg Mass., U.S.A. 42°35N 71°48W 83 D13
Fitchburg Wis., U.S.A. 42°58N 89°28W 80 D9
Fitz Roy Argentina 47°0S 67°0W 96 F3
Fitz Roy, Cerro Argentina 49°17S 73°5W 96 F2
Fitzgerald Canada 59°51N 111°36W 70 B6
Fitzgerald U.S.A. 31°43N 83°15W 85 F13
Fitzgerald River △
  Australia 33°53S 119°55E 61 F3
Fitzmaurice → Australia 14°45S 130°5E 60 B5
Fitzroy → Queens.,
  Australia 23°32S 150°52E 62 C5
Fitzroy → W. Austral.,
  Australia 17°31S 123°35E 60 C3
Fitzroy Crossing Australia 18°9S 125°38E 60 C4
Fitzwilliam I. Canada 45°30N 81°45W 82 A3
Fiume = Rijeka Croatia 45°20N 14°21E 16 F8
Five Points U.S.A. 36°26N 120°6W 78 J6
Fizi Dem. Rep. of the Congo 4°17S 28°55E 54 E5
Flagstaff U.S.A. 35°12N 111°39W 77 J8
Flagstaff L. U.S.A. 45°12N 70°18W 83 A14
Flaherty I. Canada 56°15N 79°15W 72 A4
Flåm Norway 60°50N 7°7E 8 F12
Flambeau → U.S.A. 45°18N 91°14W 80 C8
Flamborough Hd. U.K. 54°7N 0°5W 12 C7
Flaming Gorge
  U.S.A. 41°10N 109°25W 76 F9
Flaming Gorge Res.
  U.S.A. 41°10N 109°25W 76 F9
Flamingo, Teluk Indonesia 5°30S 138°0E 37 F9
Flanders = Flandre Europe 50°50N 2°30E 15 B9
Flandre Europe 50°50N 2°30E 15 B9
Flandre-Occidentale = West-
  Vlaanderen □ Belgium 51°0N 3°0E 15 D2
Flandre-Orientale = Oost-
  Vlaanderen □ Belgium 51°5N 3°50E 15 C3
Flandreau U.S.A. 44°3N 96°36W 80 C5
Flanigan U.S.A. 40°10N 119°53W 78 F7
Flannan Is. U.K. 58°17N 7°36W 11 C1
Flåsjön Sweden 64°5N 15°40E 8 D16
Flat → Canada 61°33N 125°18W 70 A3
Flat I. Mauritius 19°53S 57°35E 55 d
Flat I. S. China Sea 10°49N 115°49E 36 B5
Flathead L. U.S.A. 47°51N 114°8W 76 C7
Flattery, C. Australia 14°58S 145°21E 62 A4
Flattery, C. U.S.A. 48°23N 124°29W 78 B2
Flatwoods U.S.A. 38°31N 82°43W 81 F12
Fleetwood U.K. 53°55N 3°1W 12 D4
Fleetwood U.S.A. 40°27N 75°49W 83 F9
Flekkefjord Norway 58°18N 6°39E 9 G12
Flemington U.S.A. 41°7N 77°28W 82 E7
Flensburg Germany 54°47N 9°27E 16 A5
Flers France 48°47N 0°33W 20 B3
Flesherton Canada 44°16N 80°33W 82 B4
Flesko, Tanjung Indonesia 0°29N 124°30E 37 D6
Fleurieu Pen. Australia 35°40S 138°5E 63 F2
Flevoland □ Neths. 52°30N 5°30E 15 B5
Flin Flon Canada 54°46N 101°53W 71 C8
Flinders → Australia 17°36S 140°36E 62 B3
Flinders B. Australia 34°19S 115°19E 61 F2
Flinders Group Australia 14°11S 144°15E 62 A3
Flinders I. S. Austral.,
  Australia 33°44S 134°41E 63 E1
Flinders I. Tas., Australia 40°0S 148°0E 63 G4
Flinders Ranges
  Australia 31°30S 138°30E 63 E2
Flinders Reefs Australia 17°37S 148°31E 62 B4
Flint U.K. 53°15N 3°8W 12 D4
Flint U.S.A. 43°1N 83°41W 81 D12
Flint → U.S.A. 30°57N 84°34W 85 F12
Flint I. Kiribati 11°26S 151°48W 65 J12
Flintshire □ U.K. 53°17N 3°17W 12 D4
Flodden U.K. 55°37N 2°8W 12 B5
Floodplains △ Sri Lanka 8°10N 81°10E 45 K5
Floodwood U.S.A. 46°56N 92°55W 80 B7
Flora → Italy 38°40N 88°29W 80 F9
Florala U.S.A. 31°0N 86°20W 85 F11

Florence = Firenze Italy 43°46N 11°15E 22 C4
Florence Ala., U.S.A. 34°48N 87°41W 85 D11
Florence Ariz., U.S.A. 33°2N 111°23W 77 K8
Florence Colo., U.S.A. 38°23N 105°8W 76 G11
Florence Oreg., U.S.A. 43°58N 124°7W 76 D1
Florence S.C., U.S.A. 34°12N 79°46W 85 D15
Florence, L. Australia 28°53S 138°9E 63 D2
Florencia Colombia 1°36N 75°36W 92 C3
Florennes Belgium 50°15N 4°35E 15 D4
Florenville Belgium 49°40N 5°19E 15 E5
Flores Azores 39°26N 31°13W 52 a
Flores Guatemala 16°59N 89°50W 88 C2
Flores Indonesia 8°35S 121°0E 37 F6
Flores I. Canada 49°20N 126°10W 70 D3
Flores Sea Indonesia 6°30S 120°0E 37 F6
Floreşti Moldova 47°53N 28°17E 17 E15
Floresville U.S.A. 29°8N 98°10W 84 G5
Floriano Brazil 6°50S 43°0W 93 E10
Florianópolis Brazil 27°30S 48°30W 95 B6
Florida Cuba 21°32N 78°14W 88 B4
Florida Uruguay 34°7S 56°10W 95 C4
Florida □ U.S.A. 28°0N 82°0W 85 G14
Florida, Straits of U.S.A. 25°0N 80°0W 88 B4
Florida B. U.S.A. 25°0N 80°45W 88 B3
Florida Keys U.S.A. 24°40N 81°0W 85 K4
Florin U.S.A. 38°30N 121°24W 78 G5
Florina Greece 40°48N 21°26E 23 D9
Florissant U.S.A. 38°47N 90°19W 80 F8
Florø Norway 61°35N 5°1E 8 F11
Flower Station Canada 45°10N 76°41W 83 A8
Flowerpot I. Canada 45°18N 81°38W 82 A3
Floydada U.S.A. 33°59N 101°20W 84 E4
Fluk Indonesia 1°42S 127°44E 37 E7
Flushing = Vlissingen
  Neths. 51°26N 3°34E 15 C3
Fly → Papua N. G. 8°25S 143°0E 58 B7
Flying Fish, C. Antarctica 72°6S 102°29W 5 D15
Foa Tonga 19°45S 174°19W 59 c
Foam Lake Canada 51°40N 103°32W 71 C8
Foça Turkey 38°39N 26°46E 23 E12
Fochabers U.K. 57°37N 3°6W 11 D5
Focşani Romania 45°41N 27°15E 17 F14
Fogang China 23°52N 113°30E 35 F9
Fóggia Italy 41°27N 15°34E 22 D6
Fogo Canada 49°43N 54°17W 73 C9
Fogo C. Verde Is. 15°5N 24°20W 52 b
Fogo I. Canada 49°40N 54°5W 73 C9
Föhr Germany 54°43N 8°30E 16 A5
Foix France 42°58N 1°38E 20 E4
Folda Nord-Trøndelag,
  Norway 64°32N 10°30E 8 D14
Folda Nordland, Norway 67°38N 14°50E 8 C16
Foley Botswana 21°34S 27°21E 56 B4
Foley U.S.A. 30°24N 87°41W 85 F11
Foleyet Canada 48°15N 82°25W 72 C3
Folgefonna Norway 60°3N 6°23E 9 F12
Foligno Italy 42°57N 12°42E 22 C5
Folkestone U.K. 51°5N 1°12E 13 F9
Folkston U.S.A. 30°50N 82°0W 85 F13
Follansbee U.S.A. 40°19N 80°35W 82 F4
Folsom U.S.A. 38°40N 121°9W 78 G5
Folsom L. U.S.A. 38°42N 121°9W 78 G5
Fomboni Comoros Is. 12°18S 43°46E 55 a
Fond-du-Lac Canada 59°19N 107°12W 71 B7
Fond du Lac U.S.A. 43°47N 88°27W 80 D9
Fond-du-Lac → Canada 59°17N 106°0W 71 B7
Fonda U.S.A. 42°57N 74°22W 83 D10
Fondi Italy 41°21N 13°25E 22 D5
Fongafale Tuvalu 8°31S 179°13E 58 B10
Fonsagrada = A Fonsagrada
  Spain 43°8N 7°4W 21 A2
Fonseca, G. de
  Cent. Amer. 13°10N 87°40W 88 D2
Fontainebleau France 48°24N 2°40E 20 B5
Fontana U.S.A. 34°6N 117°26W 79 L9
Fontas → Canada 58°14N 121°48W 70 B4
Fonte Boa Brazil 2°33S 66°0W 92 D5
Fontenay-le-Comte
  France 46°28N 0°48W 20 C3
Fontenelle Res. U.S.A. 42°1N 110°3W 76 E8
Fontur Iceland 66°23N 14°32W 8 C6
Fonuafo'ou Tonga 20°19S 175°25W 59 c
Fonualei Tonga 18°1S 174°19W 59 c
Foochow = Fuzhou
  China 26°5N 119°16E 35 D12
Foping China 33°41N 108°0E 32 H5
Foraker, Mt. U.S.A. 62°58N 151°24W 74 C9
Forbes Australia 33°22S 148°5E 63 E4
Forbesganj India 26°17N 87°18E 43 F12
Ford City Calif., U.S.A. 35°9N 119°27W 79 K7
Ford City Pa., U.S.A. 40°46N 79°32W 82 F5
Førde Norway 61°27N 5°53E 8 F11
Fords Bridge Australia 29°41S 145°29E 63 D4
Fordyce U.S.A. 33°49N 92°25W 84 E8
Forel, Mt. Greenland 66°52N 36°55W 4 C6
Foremost Canada 49°26N 111°34W 70 D6
Forest Canada 43°6N 82°0W 82 C3
Forest U.S.A. 32°22N 89°29W 85 E10
Forest City Iowa, U.S.A. 43°16N 93°39W 80 D7
Forest City N.C., U.S.A. 35°20N 81°52W 85 D14
Forest City Pa., U.S.A. 41°39N 75°28W 83 E9
Forest Grove U.S.A. 45°31N 123°7W 78 E3
Forestburg Canada 52°35N 112°1W 70 C6
Foresthill U.S.A. 39°1N 120°49W 78 F6
Forestier Pen. Australia 43°0S 148°0E 63 G4
Forestville Canada 48°48N 69°2W 73 C6
Forestville Calif., U.S.A. 38°28N 122°54W 78 G4
Forestville N.Y., U.S.A. 42°28N 79°10W 82 D5
Forfar U.K. 56°39N 2°53W 11 E6
Forillon △ Canada 48°46N 64°12W 73 C7
Forks U.S.A. 47°57N 124°23W 78 C2
Forksville U.S.A. 41°29N 76°35W 83 E8
Forlì Italy 44°13N 12°3E 22 B5
Forman U.S.A. 46°7N 97°38W 80 B5
Formby Pt. U.K. 53°33N 3°6W 12 D4
Formentera Spain 38°43N 1°27E 21 C6
Formentor, C. de Spain 39°58N 3°13E 21 C7
Former Yugoslav Republic of
  Macedonia = Macedonia ■
  Europe 41°53N 21°40E 23 D9
Fórmia Italy 41°15N 13°37E 22 D5

Formosa = Taiwan ■
  Asia 23°30N 121°0E 35 F13
Formosa Argentina 26°15S 58°10W 94 B4
Formosa Brazil 15°32S 47°20W 93 G9
Formosa □ Argentina 25°0S 60°0W 94 B4
Formosa, Serra Brazil 12°0S 55°0W 93 F8
Forollhogna △ Norway 62°39N 10°41E 8 E14
Foroyar ☑ Atl. Oc. 62°0N 7°0W 8 F9
Forres U.K. 57°37N 3°37W 11 D5
Forrest Australia 30°51S 128°6E 61 F4
Forrest, Mt. Australia 24°48S 127°45E 61 D4
Forrest City U.S.A. 35°1N 90°47W 85 D9
Forsayth Australia 18°33S 143°34E 62 B3
Forssa Finland 60°49N 23°38E 8 F20
Forst Germany 51°45N 14°37E 16 C8
Forster Australia 32°12S 152°31E 63 E5
Forsyth U.S.A. 46°16N 106°41W 76 C10
Fort Abbas Pakistan 29°12N 72°52E 42 E5
Fort Albany Canada 52°15N 81°35W 72 B3
Fort Assiniboine Canada 54°20N 114°45W 70 C6
Fort Augustus U.K. 57°9N 4°42W 11 D4
Fort Beaufort S. Africa 32°46S 26°40E 56 D4
Fort Benton U.S.A. 47°49N 110°40W 76 C8
Fort Bragg U.S.A. 39°26N 123°48W 76 G2
Fort Bridger U.S.A. 41°19N 110°23W 76 F8
Fort Chipewyan Canada 58°42N 111°8W 71 B6
Fort Clatsop = Lewis and Clark △
  U.S.A. 46°8N 123°53W 78 D3
Fort Collins U.S.A. 40°35N 105°5W 76 F11
Fort-Coulonge Canada 45°50N 76°45W 72 C4
Fort Covington U.S.A. 44°59N 74°29W 83 B10
Fort Dauphin = Taolanaro
  Madag. 25°2S 47°0E 55 K9
Fort Davis U.S.A. 30°35N 103°54W 84 F3
Fort-de-France Martinique 14°36N 61°5W 88 c
Fort Defiance U.S.A. 35°45N 109°5W 77 J9
Fort Dodge U.S.A. 42°30N 94°11W 80 D6
Fort Edward U.S.A. 43°16N 73°35W 83 C11
Fort Erie Canada 42°54N 78°56W 82 D6
Fort Fairfield U.S.A. 46°46N 67°50W 81 B20
Fort Frances Canada 48°36N 93°24W 71 D10
Fort Franklin = Déline
  Canada 65°11N 123°25W 68 B7
Fort Garland U.S.A. 37°26N 105°26W 77 H11
Fort George = Chisasibi
  Canada 53°50N 79°0W 72 B4
Fort Good Hope Canada 66°14N 128°40W 68 B6
Fort Hancock U.S.A. 31°18N 105°51W 84 F2
Fort Hope = Eabametoong
  Canada 51°30N 88°0W 72 B2
Fort Irwin U.S.A. 35°16N 116°41W 79 K10
Fort Kent U.S.A. 47°15N 68°36W 81 B19
Fort Klamath U.S.A. 42°42N 122°0W 76 D3
Fort Laramie U.S.A. 42°13N 104°31W 76 E11
Fort Liard Canada 60°14N 123°30W 70 A4
Fort Liberté Haiti 19°42N 71°51W 89 C5
Fort Lupton U.S.A. 40°5N 104°49W 76 F11
Fort MacKay Canada 57°12N 111°41W 70 B6
Fort Macleod Canada 49°45N 113°30W 70 D6
Fort McMurray Canada 56°44N 111°7W 70 B6
Fort McPherson Canada 67°30N 134°55W 68 B5
Fort Madison U.S.A. 40°38N 91°27W 80 E8
Fort Meade U.S.A. 27°45N 81°48W 85 H14
Fort Morgan U.S.A. 40°15N 103°48W 76 F12
Fort Myers U.S.A. 26°39N 81°52W 85 H14
Fort Nelson Canada 58°50N 122°44W 70 B4
Fort Nelson → Canada 59°32N 124°0W 70 B4
Fort Norman = Tulita
  Canada 64°57N 125°30W 68 B6
Fort Payne U.S.A. 34°26N 85°43W 85 D12
Fort Peck U.S.A. 48°1N 106°27W 76 B10
Fort Peck Dam U.S.A. 48°0N 106°26W 76 C10
Fort Peck L. U.S.A. 48°0N 106°26W 76 C10
Fort Pierce U.S.A. 27°27N 80°20W 85 H14
Fort Pierre U.S.A. 44°21N 100°22W 80 C3
Fort Plain U.S.A. 42°56N 74°37W 83 D10
Fort Portal Uganda 0°40N 30°20E 54 D6
Fort Providence Canada 61°3N 117°40W 70 A5
Fort Qu'Appelle Canada 50°45N 103°50W 71 C8
Fort Resolution Canada 61°10N 113°40W 70 A6
Fort Ross U.S.A. 38°32N 123°13W 78 G3
Fort Rupert = Waskaganish
  Canada 51°30N 78°40W 72 B4
Fort St. James Canada 54°30N 124°10W 70 C4
Fort St. John Canada 56°15N 120°50W 70 B4
Fort Saskatchewan
  Canada 53°40N 113°15W 70 C6
Fort Scott U.S.A. 37°50N 94°42W 80 G6
Fort Severn Canada 56°0N 87°40W 72 A2
Fort Shevchenko
  Kazakhstan 44°35N 50°23E 19 F9
Fort Simpson Canada 61°45N 121°15W 70 A4
Fort Smith Canada 60°0N 111°51W 70 B6
Fort Smith U.S.A. 35°23N 94°25W 84 D7
Fort Stockton U.S.A. 30°53N 102°53W 84 F3
Fort Sumner U.S.A. 34°28N 104°15W 77 J11
Fort Thompson U.S.A. 44°3N 99°26W 80 C4
Fort Union △ U.S.A. 35°54N 105°1W 77 J11
Fort Valley U.S.A. 32°33N 83°53W 85 E13
Fort Vermilion Canada 58°24N 116°0W 70 B5
Fort Walton Beach
  U.S.A. 30°25N 86°36W 85 F11
Fort Ware Canada 57°26N 125°41W 70 B3
Fort Wayne U.S.A. 41°4N 85°9W 81 E11
Fort William U.K. 56°49N 5°7W 11 E3
Fort Worth U.S.A. 32°43N 97°19W 84 E6
Fort Yates U.S.A. 46°5N 100°38W 80 B3
Fort Yukon U.S.A. 66°34N 145°16W 68 B5
Fortaleza Brazil 3°45S 38°35W 93 D11
Forteau Canada 51°28N 56°58W 73 B8
Fortescue → Australia 21°0S 116°4E 60 D2
Fortescue River Roadhouse
  Australia 21°17S 116°8E 60 D2
Forth → U.K. 56°9N 3°50W 11 E5
Forth, Firth of U.K. 56°5N 2°55W 11 E6
Fortrose U.K. 57°35N 4°9W 11 D4
Fortuna Calif., U.S.A. 40°36N 124°9W 76 F1
Fortuna N. Dak., U.S.A. 48°55N 103°47W 80 A2
Fortune Canada 47°4N 55°50W 73 C8
Fortune B. Canada 47°30N 55°22W 73 C8
Forūr Iran 26°17N 54°32E 47 E7
Fosen Norway 63°50N 10°20E 8 E14

Fosnavåg Norway 62°22N 5°38E 8 E11
Fossano Italy 44°33N 7°43E 20 D7
Fossil U.S.A. 45°0N 120°9W 76 D3
Fossil Butte △ U.S.A. 41°50N 110°27W 76 F8
Foster Canada 45°17N 72°30W 83 A12
Foster → Canada 55°47N 105°49W 71 B7
Fosters Ra. Australia 21°35S 133°48E 62 C1
Fostoria U.S.A. 41°10N 83°25W 81 E12
Fougères France 48°21N 1°14W 20 B3
Foul Pt. Sri Lanka 8°35N 81°18E 45 K5
Foula U.K. 60°10N 2°5W 11 A6
Foulness I. U.K. 51°36N 0°55E 13 F8
Foumban Cameroon 5°45N 10°50E 54 C2
Foumbouni Comoros Is. 11°51S 43°29E 55 a
Fountain U.S.A. 38°41N 104°42W 76 G11
Fountain Hills U.S.A. 33°37N 111°43W 77 K8
Fountain Springs
  U.S.A. 35°54N 118°51W 79 K8
Four Mountains, Is. of
  U.S.A. 53°0N 170°0W 74 E5
Fouriesburg S. Africa 28°38S 28°14E 57 C4
Fourni Greece 37°36N 26°32E 23 F12
Fourth Cataract Sudan 18°47N 32°3E 53 E12
Fouta Djallon Guinea 11°20N 12°10W 52 F3
Foux, Cap-à- Haiti 19°43N 73°27W 89 C5
Foveaux Str. N.Z. 46°42S 168°10E 59 G2
Fowey U.K. 50°20N 4°39W 13 G3
Fowler Calif., U.S.A. 36°38N 119°41W 78 J7
Fowler Colo., U.S.A. 38°8N 104°2W 76 G11
Fowler, Pt. Australia 32°2S 132°3E 61 F5
Fowlers B. Australia 31°59S 132°34E 61 F5
Fowman Iran 37°13N 49°19E 47 B6
Fox → Canada 56°3N 93°18W 71 B10
Fox Creek Canada 54°24N 116°48W 70 C5
Fox Is. U.S.A. 53°0N 168°0W 74 E6
Fox Lake Canada 58°28N 114°31W 70 B6
Fox Valley Canada 50°30N 109°25W 71 C7
Foxboro Canada 44°14N 77°26W 82 B7
Foxboro U.S.A. 42°4N 71°16W 83 D13
Foxdale Australia 20°22S 148°35E 62 b
Foxe Basin Canada 66°0N 77°0W 69 E16
Foxe Chan. Canada 65°0N 80°0W 69 E16
Foxe Pen. Canada 65°0N 76°0W 69 E16
Foxford Ireland 53°59N 9°7W 10 C2
Foxton N.Z. 40°29S 175°18E 59 D5
Foyle, Lough U.K. 55°7N 7°4W 10 A4
Foynes Ireland 52°37N 9°7W 10 D2
Foz do Cunene Angola 17°15S 11°48E 56 A1
Foz do Iguaçu Brazil 25°30S 54°30W 95 B5
Frackville U.S.A. 40°47N 76°14W 83 F8
Fraile Muerto Uruguay 32°31S 54°32W 95 C5
Framingham U.S.A. 42°18N 71°24W 83 D13
Franca Brazil 20°33S 47°30W 93 H9
Francavilla Fontana
  Italy 40°32N 17°35E 23 D7
Frances Australia 36°41S 140°55E 63 F3
Frances → Canada 60°16N 129°10W 70 A3
Frances L. Canada 61°23N 129°30W 70 A3
Franceville Gabon 1°40S 13°32E 54 E2
Franche-Comté □ France 46°50N 5°55E 20 C6
Francis Case, L. U.S.A. 43°4N 98°34W 80 D4
Francisco Beltrão Brazil 26°5S 53°4W 95 B5
Francisco Ignacio Madero Coahuila,
  Mexico 25°48N 103°18W 86 B4
Francisco Ignacio Madero Durango,
  Mexico 24°32N 104°18W 86 C4
Francisco Ignacio Madero, Presa
  Mexico 28°10N 105°37W 86 B3
Francistown Botswana 21°7S 27°33E 57 B4
François Canada 47°35N 56°45W 73 C8
François L. Canada 54°0N 125°30W 70 C3
Francois Peron △
  Australia 25°42S 113°33E 61 E1
Francs Pk. U.S.A. 43°58N 109°20W 76 E9
Franeker Neths. 53°12N 5°33E 15 A5
Frank Hann △ Australia 32°52S 120°19E 61 F3
Frankford Canada 44°12N 77°36W 82 B7
Frankfort S. Africa 27°17S 28°30E 57 C4
Frankfort Ind., U.S.A. 40°17N 86°31W 80 E10
Frankfort Kans., U.S.A. 39°42N 96°25W 80 F5
Frankfort Ky., U.S.A. 38°12N 84°52W 81 F11
Frankfort N.Y., U.S.A. 43°2N 75°4W 83 C9
Frankfurt Brandenburg,
  Germany 52°20N 14°32E 16 B8
Frankfurt Hessen, Germany 50°7N 8°41E 16 C5
Fränkische Alb Germany 49°10N 11°23E 16 D6
Frankland → Australia 35°0S 116°48E 61 G2
Franklin Ky., U.S.A. 36°43N 86°35W 80 G10
Franklin La., U.S.A. 29°48N 91°30W 84 G9
Franklin Mass., U.S.A. 42°5N 71°24W 83 D13
Franklin N.H., U.S.A. 43°27N 71°39W 83 C13
Franklin N.Y., U.S.A. 42°20N 75°9W 83 D9
Franklin Nebr., U.S.A. 40°6N 98°57W 80 E4
Franklin Pa., U.S.A. 41°24N 79°50W 82 E5
Franklin Va., U.S.A. 36°41N 76°56W 81 G15
Franklin W. Va., U.S.A. 38°39N 79°20W 81 F14
Franklin B. Canada 69°45N 126°0W 68 B6
Franklin D. Roosevelt L.
  U.S.A. 48°18N 118°9W 76 B4
Franklin-Gordon Wild Rivers △
  Australia 42°19S 145°51E 63 G4
Franklin I. Antarctica 76°10S 168°30E 5 D11
Franklin I. Canada 45°24N 80°20W 82 A4
Franklin L. U.S.A. 40°25N 115°22W 76 F6
Franklin Mts. Canada 65°0N 125°0W 68 C6
Franklin Str. Canada 72°0N 96°0W 68 A12
Franklinton U.S.A. 30°51N 90°9W 85 F9
Franklinville U.S.A. 42°20N 78°27W 82 D6
Frankston Australia 38°8S 145°8E 63 F4
Fransfontein Namibia 20°12S 15°1E 56 B2
Frantsa Iosifa, Zemlya
  Arctic 82°0N 55°0E 26 A6
Franz Canada 48°25N 84°30W 72 C3
Franz Josef Land = Frantsa Iosifa,
  Zemlya Arctic 82°0N 55°0E 26 A6
Fraser → B.C., Canada 49°7N 123°11W 78 A3
Fraser → Nfld. & L.,
  Canada 56°39N 62°10W 73 A7

Fraser, Mt. Australia 25°35S 118°20E 61 E2
Fraser I. Australia 25°15S 153°10E 63 D5
Fraser Lake Canada 54°0N 124°50W 70 C4
Fraserburg S. Africa 31°55S 21°30E 56 E3
Fraserburgh U.K. 57°42N 2°1W 11 D6
Fraserdale Canada 49°55N 81°37W 72 C3
Fray Bentos Uruguay 33°10S 58°15W 94 C4
Fray Jorge △ Chile 30°42S 71°40W 94 C1
Fredericia Denmark 55°34N 9°45E 9 J13
Frederick Md., U.S.A. 39°25N 77°25W 81 F15
Frederick Okla., U.S.A. 34°23N 99°1W 84 H5
Frederick S. Dak., U.S.A. 45°50N 98°31W 80 C4
Fredericksburg Pa.,
  U.S.A. 40°27N 76°26W 83 F8
Fredericksburg Tex.,
  U.S.A. 30°16N 98°52W 84 G5
Fredericksburg Va.,
  U.S.A. 38°18N 77°28W 81 F15
Fredericktown Mo.,
  U.S.A. 37°34N 90°18W 80 G8
Fredericktown Ohio,
  U.S.A. 40°29N 82°33W 82 F2
Frederico Westphalen
  Brazil 27°22S 53°24W 95 B5
Fredericton Canada 45°57N 66°40W 73 C6
Fredericton Junction
  Canada 45°41N 66°40W 73 C6
Frederikshåb = Paamiut
  Greenland 62°0N 49°43W 4 C5
Frederikshamn = Hamina
  Finland 60°34N 27°12E 8 F22
Frederikshavn Denmark 57°28N 10°31E 9 H14
Frederiksted
  U.S. Virgin Is. 17°43N 64°53W 89 C7
Fredonia Ariz., U.S.A. 36°57N 112°32W 77 H7
Fredonia Kans., U.S.A. 37°32N 95°49W 80 G6
Fredonia N.Y., U.S.A. 42°26N 79°20W 82 D5
Fredrikstad Norway 59°13N 10°57E 9 G14
Free State □ S. Africa 28°30S 27°0E 56 C4
Freehold U.S.A. 40°16N 74°17W 83 F10
Freeland U.S.A. 41°1N 75°54W 83 E9
Freels, C. Nfld. & L.,
  Canada 49°15N 53°30W 73 C9
Freels, C. Nfld. & L.,
  Canada 46°37N 53°32W 73 C9
Freeman Calif., U.S.A. 35°35N 117°53W 79 K9
Freeman S. Dak., U.S.A. 43°21N 97°26W 80 D5
Freeport Bahamas 26°30N 78°47W 88 A4
Freeport Ill., U.S.A. 42°17N 89°36W 80 D9
Freeport N.Y., U.S.A. 40°39N 73°35W 83 F11
Freeport Ohio, U.S.A. 40°12N 81°15W 82 F3
Freeport Pa., U.S.A. 40°41N 79°41W 82 F5
Freeport Tex., U.S.A. 28°57N 95°21W 84 G7
Freetown S. Leone 8°30N 13°17W 52 G3
Frégate, L. de la Canada 53°15N 74°45W 72 B5
Fregenal de la Sierra
  Spain 38°10N 6°39W 21 C2
Fregon Australia 26°45S 132°1E 61 E5
Frei Antarctica 62°30S 58°0W 5 C18
Freibourg = Fribourg
  Switz. 46°49N 7°9E 20 C7
Freiburg Germany 47°59N 7°51E 16 E4
Freire Chile 38°54S 72°38W 96 D2
Freirina Chile 28°30S 71°10W 94 B1
Freising Germany 48°24N 11°45E 16 D6
Freistadt Austria 48°30N 14°30E 16 D8
Fréjus France 43°25N 6°44E 20 E7
Fremantle Australia 32°7S 115°47E 61 F2
Fremont Calif., U.S.A. 37°32N 121°57W 78 H4
Fremont Mich., U.S.A. 43°28N 85°57W 81 D11
Fremont Nebr., U.S.A. 41°26N 96°30W 80 E5
Fremont Ohio, U.S.A. 41°21N 83°7W 81 E12
Fremont → U.S.A. 38°24N 110°42W 76 G8
Fremont L. U.S.A. 42°57N 109°48W 76 E9
French Camp U.S.A. 37°53N 121°16W 78 H5
French Cays = Plana Cays
  Bahamas 22°38N 73°30W 89 B5
French Creek → U.S.A. 41°24N 79°50W 82 E5
French Frigate Shoals
  U.S.A. 23°45N 166°10W 75 L6
French Guiana □ S. Amer. 4°0N 53°0W 93 C8
French Polynesia ☑
  Pac. Oc. 20°0S 145°0W 65 J13
French Riviera = Azur, Côte d'
  France 43°25N 7°10E 20 E7
Frenchman Cr. →
  N. Amer. 48°31N 107°10W 76 B10
Frenchman Cr. →
  U.S.A. 40°14N 100°50W 80 E3
Fresco → Brazil 7°15S 51°30W 93 E8
Freshfield, C. Antarctica 68°25S 151°10E 5 C10
Fresnillo Mexico 23°10N 102°53W 86 C4
Fresno U.S.A. 36°44N 119°47W 78 J7
Fresno Res. U.S.A. 48°36N 109°57W 76 B9
Frew → Australia 20°0S 135°38E 62 C2
Frewsburg U.S.A. 42°3N 79°10W 82 D5
Freycinet △ Australia 42°11S 148°19E 63 G4
Freycinet Pen. Australia 42°10S 148°25E 63 G4
Fria Guinea 10°27N 13°38W 52 F3
Fria, C. Namibia 18°0S 12°0E 56 B1
Frías Argentina 28°40S 65°5W 94 B2
Fribourg Switz. 46°49N 7°9E 20 C7
Friday Harbor U.S.A. 48°32N 123°1W 78 B3
Friedens U.S.A. 40°3N 78°59W 82 F6
Friedrichshafen Germany 47°39N 9°30E 16 E5
Friendship U.S.A. 42°12N 78°8W 82 D6
Friesland □ Neths. 53°5N 5°50E 15 A5
Frio → U.S.A. 28°26N 98°11W 84 G5
Frio, C. Brazil 22°50S 41°50W 90 F6
Friona U.S.A. 34°38N 102°43W 84 D3
Frisco U.S.A. 33°8N 96°49W 84 E6
Fritch U.S.A. 35°38N 101°36W 84 D4
Friza, Proliv Russia 45°0N 149°0E 27 E15
Frobisher B. Canada 62°30N 66°0W 69 E18
Frobisher Bay = Iqaluit
  Canada 63°44N 68°31W 69 E18

Frobisher L. Canada 56°20N 108°15W 71 B7
Frohavet Norway 64°0N 9°30E 8 E13
Frome U.K. 51°14N 2°19W 13 F5
Frome → U.K. 50°41N 2°6W 13 G5
Frome, L. Australia 30°45S 139°45E 63 E2
Front Range U.S.A. 40°25N 105°45W 76 F11
Front Royal U.S.A. 38°55N 78°12W 81 F14
Frontenac ⌂ Canada 44°32N 76°30W 83 B8
Frontera Mexico 18°32N 92°38W 87 D6
Fronteras Mexico 30°56N 109°31W 86 A3
Frosinone Italy 41°38N 13°19E 22 D5
Frostburg U.S.A. 39°39N 78°56W 81 F14
Frostisen Norway 68°14N 17°10E 8 B17
Frøya Norway 63°43N 8°40E 8 E13
Fruita Brazil 39°9N 108°44W 76 G9
Frunze = Bishkek
  Kyrgyzstan 42°54N 74°46E 30 C3
Frutal Brazil 20°0S 49°0W 93 H9
Frýdek-Místek
  Czech Rep. 49°40N 18°20E 17 D10
Fryeburg U.S.A. 44°1N 70°59W 83 B14
Fu Xian = Wafangdian
  China 39°38N 121°58E 33 E11
Fu'an China 36°0N 109°20E 32 G5
Fu'an China 27°11N 119°36E 35 D12
Fubian China 31°17N 102°22E 34 B4
Fucheng China 37°50N 116°10E 32 F9
Fuchou = Fuzhou China 26°5N 119°16E 35 D12
Fuchū Japan 34°34N 133°14E 29 G6
Fuchuan China 24°50N 111°5E 35 E8
Fuchun Jiang → China 30°5N 120°5E 35 B13
Fuding China 27°20N 120°12E 35 D13
Fuengirola Spain 36°32N 4°41W 21 D3
Fuentes de Oñoro Spain 40°33N 6°52W 21 B2
Fuerte → Mexico 25°54N 109°22W 86 B3
Fuerte Olimpo Paraguay 21°0S 57°51W 94 A4
Fuerteventura Canary Is. 28°30N 14°0W 52 C3
Fufeng China 34°22N 108°0E 32 G5
Fugong China 27°5N 98°47E 34 D2
Fugou China 34°3N 114°25E 32 G8
Fugu China 39°2N 111°3E 32 E6
Fuhai China 47°2N 87°25E 30 B6
Fuḥaymī Iraq 34°16N 42°10E 46 C4
Fuidhaigh = Wiay U.K. 57°24N 7°13W 11 D1
Fuji Japan 35°9N 138°39E 29 G9
Fuji-Hakone-Izu △
  Japan 35°15N 138°45E 29 G9
Fuji-San Japan 35°22N 138°44E 29 G9
Fuji-Yoshida Japan 35°30N 138°46E 29 G9
Fujian □ China 26°0N 118°0E 35 E12
Fujin China 47°16N 132°1E 31 B15
Fujinomiya Japan 35°10N 138°40E 29 G9
Fujisawa Japan 35°22N 139°29E 29 G9
Fujiyama, Mt. = Fuji-San
  Japan 35°22N 138°44E 29 G9
Fukagawa Japan 43°43N 142°2E 28 C11
Fukien = Fujian □ China 26°0N 118°0E 35 E12
Fukuchiyama Japan 35°19N 135°9E 29 G7
Fukue Japan 32°41N 128°51E 29 H4
Fukue-Shima Japan 32°40N 128°45E 29 H4
Fukui Japan 36°5N 136°10E 29 F8
Fukui □ Japan 36°0N 136°12E 29 G8
Fukuoka Japan 33°39N 130°21E 29 H5
Fukuoka □ Japan 33°30N 131°0E 29 H5
Fukushima Japan 37°44N 140°28E 28 F10
Fukushima □ Japan 37°30N 140°15E 28 F10
Fukuyama Japan 34°35N 133°20E 29 G6
Fulaga Fiji 19°8S 178°33W 59 a
Fulda Germany 50°32N 9°40E 16 C5
Fulda → Germany 51°25N 9°39E 16 C5
Fulford Harbour Canada 48°47N 123°27W 78 B3
Fuliang China 29°23N 117°14E 35 C11
Fuling China 29°29N 107°17E 34 C6
Fullerton Calif., U.S.A. 33°53N 117°56W 79 M9
Fullerton Nebr., U.S.A. 41°22N 97°58W 80 E5
Fulongquan China 44°20N 124°42E 33 B13
Fulton Mo., U.S.A. 38°52N 91°57W 80 F8
Fulton N.Y., U.S.A. 43°19N 76°25W 83 C8
Fumin China 25°0N 102°20E 34 E4
Funabashi Japan 35°45N 140°0E 29 G10
Funan China 32°39N 115°42E 35 A10
Funchal Madeira 32°38N 16°54W 52 B2
Fundación Colombia 10°31N 74°11W 92 A4
Fundão Portugal 40°8N 7°30W 21 B2
Fundy, B. of Canada 45°0N 66°0W 73 D6
Fundy △ Canada 45°35N 65°10W 73 D6
Funhalouro Mozam. 23°3S 34°25E 57 B5
Funing Hebei, China 39°53N 119°12E 33 E10
Funing Jiangsu, China 33°45N 119°50E 33 H10
Funing Yunnan, China 23°35N 105°45E 34 F5
Funiu Shan China 33°30N 112°20E 32 H7
Funtua Nigeria 11°30N 7°18E 52 F7
Fuping Hebei, China 38°48N 114°12E 32 E8
Fuping Shaanxi, China 34°42N 109°10E 32 G5
Fuqing China 25°41N 119°21E 35 E12
Fuquan China 26°40N 107°27E 34 D6
Furano Japan 43°21N 142°23E 28 C11
Furāt, Nahr al → Asia 31°0N 47°25E 46 D5
Fürg Iran 28°18N 55°13E 47 D7
Furnas, Represa de
  Brazil 20°50S 45°30W 95 A6
Furneaux Group
  Australia 40°10S 147°50E 63 G4
Furqlus Syria 34°36N 37°8E 48 A6
Fürstenwalde Germany 52°22N 14°3E 16 B8
Fürth Germany 49°28N 10°59E 16 D6
Furukawa = Ōsaki
  Japan 38°34N 140°58E 28 E10
Fury and Hecla Str.
  Canada 69°56N 84°0W 69 D15
Fusagasugá Colombia 4°21N 74°22W 92 C4
Fushan Shandong, China 37°30N 121°15E 33 F11
Fushan Shanxi, China 35°58N 111°51E 32 G6
Fushun Liaoning, China 41°50N 123°56E 33 D12
Fushun Sichuan, China 29°13N 104°52E 34 C5
Fusong China 42°20N 127°15E 33 C14
Fustic Barbados 13°16N 59°38W 89 g
Fusui China 22°40N 107°56E 34 F6
Futian China 22°32N 114°4E 31 a

Fuxian Hu China 24°30N 102°53E 34 E4
Fuxin China 42°5N 121°48E 33 C11
Fuyang Anhui, China 33°0N 115°48E 32 H8
Fuyang Zhejiang, China 30°5N 119°57E 35 B12
Fuyang He → China 38°12N 117°0E 32 E9
Fuying Dao China 26°34N 120°9E 35 D13
Fuyong China 22°40N 113°49E 31 a
Fuyu Heilongjiang, China 47°49N 124°27E 31 B13
Fuyu Jilin, China 45°12N 124°43E 33 B13
Fuyuan China 25°40N 104°16E 34 E5
Fuyun China 47°0N 89°28E 30 B6
Fuzhou = Linchuan
  China 27°57N 116°15E 35 D11
Fuzhou China 26°5N 119°16E 35 D12
Fyn Denmark 55°20N 10°30E 9 J14
Fyne, L. U.K. 55°59N 5°23W 11 F3

G

Gaalkacyo Somalia 6°30N 47°30E 49 F4
Gabba Australia 9°45S 142°38E 62 a
Gabela Angola 11°0S 14°24E 54 G2
Gabès Tunisia 33°53N 10°2E 53 B8
Gabès, G. de Tunisia 34°0N 10°30E 53 B8
Gabon ■ Africa 0°10S 10°0E 54 E2
Gaborone Botswana 24°45S 25°57E 56 B4
Gabriels U.S.A. 44°26N 74°12W 83 B10
Gäbrīk Iran 25°44N 58°28E 47 E8
Gabrovo Bulgaria 42°52N 25°19E 23 C11
Gāch Sār Iran 36°7N 51°19E 47 B6
Gachsārān Iran 30°15N 50°45E 47 D6
Gad Hinglaj India 16°14N 74°21E 45 F2
Gadag India 15°30N 75°45E 45 G2
Gadap Pakistan 25°5N 67°28E 42 G2
Gadarwara India 22°50N 78°50E 43 H8
Gadhada India 22°0N 71°35E 42 J4
Gadra Pakistan 25°40N 70°38E 42 G4
Gadsden U.S.A. 34°1N 86°1W 85 D11
Gadwal India 16°10N 77°50E 45 F3
Gaffney U.S.A. 35°5N 81°39W 85 D14
Gafsa Tunisia 34°24N 8°43E 53 B7
Gagaria India 25°43N 70°46E 42 G4
Găgăuzia □ Moldova 46°10N 28°40E 17 E15
Gagnoa Ivory C. 6°56N 6°16W 52 G4
Gagnon Canada 51°50N 68°5W 73 B6
Gagnon, L. Canada 62°3N 110°27W 71 A6
Gahmar India 25°27N 83°49E 43 G10
Gahnpa = Ganta Liberia 7°15N 8°59W 52 G4
Gai Xian = Gaizhou
  China 40°22N 122°20E 33 D12
Gail U.S.A. 32°46N 101°27W 84 E4
Gaillimh = Galway Ireland 53°17N 9°3W 10 C2
Gaines U.S.A. 41°46N 77°35W 82 E7
Gainesville Fla., U.S.A. 29°40N 82°20W 85 G13
Gainesville Ga., U.S.A. 34°18N 83°50W 85 D13
Gainesville Mo., U.S.A. 36°36N 92°26W 80 G7
Gainesville Tex., U.S.A. 33°38N 97°8W 84 E6
Gainsborough U.K. 53°24N 0°46W 12 D7
Gairdner, L. Australia 31°30S 136°0E 63 E2
Gairloch U.K. 57°43N 5°41W 11 D3
Gairloch, L. U.K. 57°43N 5°45W 11 D3
Gaizhou China 40°22N 122°20E 33 D12
Gaj → Pakistan 26°26N 67°21E 42 F2
Gajendragarh India 15°44N 75°59E 45 G2
Gakuch Pakistan 36°7N 73°45E 43 A5
Gal Oya → Sri Lanka 7°0N 81°30E 45 L5
Gal Oya Res. Sri Lanka 7°5N 81°30E 45 L5
Galán, Cerro Argentina 25°55S 66°52W 94 B2
Galápagos = Colón, Arch. de
  Ecuador 0°0 91°0W 90 D1
Galapagos Fracture Zone
  Pac. Oc. 3°0N 110°0W 65 G17
Galapagos Rise Pac. Oc. 15°0S 95°0W 65 J18
Galashiels U.K. 55°37N 2°49W 11 F6
Galați Romania 45°27N 28°2E 17 F15
Galatina Italy 40°10N 18°10E 23 D8
Galax U.S.A. 36°40N 80°56W 81 G13
Galbīn Govĭ Mongolia 43°0N 107°0E 32 C4
Galcaio = Gaalkacyo
  Somalia 6°30N 47°30E 49 F4
Galdhøpiggen Norway 61°38N 8°18E 8 F13
Galeana Chihuahua,
  Mexico 30°7N 107°38W 86 A3
Galeana Nuevo León,
  Mexico 24°50N 100°4W 86 B3
Galela Indonesia 1°50N 127°49E 37 D7
Galeota Pt. Trin. & Tob. 10°8N 60°59W 93 K16
Galera Pt. Trin. & Tob. 10°49N 60°54W 93 K16
Galesburg U.S.A. 40°57N 90°22W 80 E8
Galestan △ Iran 37°30N 56°0E 47 B8
Galeton U.S.A. 41°44N 77°39W 82 E7
Galich Russia 58°22N 42°24E 18 C7
Galicia □ Spain 42°43N 7°45W 21 A2
Galilee = Hagalil Israel 32°53N 35°18E 48 C4
Galilee, L. Australia 22°20S 145°50E 62 C4
Galilee, Sea of = Yam Kinneret
  Israel 32°45N 35°35E 48 C4
Galina Pt. Jamaica 18°24N 76°58W 88 a
Galion U.S.A. 40°44N 82°47W 82 F2
Galiuro Mts. U.S.A. 32°30N 110°20W 77 K8
Galiwinku Australia 12°2S 135°34E 62 A2
Gallan Hd. U.K. 58°15N 7°2W 11 D1
Gallatin U.S.A. 36°24N 86°27W 85 C11
Galle Sri Lanka 6°5N 80°10E 45 L5
Gállego → Spain 41°39N 0°51W 21 B5
Gallegos → Argentina 51°35S 69°0W 96 G3
Galley Hd. Ireland 51°32N 8°55W 10 E3
Gallinas, Pta. Colombia 12°28N 71°40W 92 A4
Gallipoli = Gelibolu
  Turkey 40°28N 26°43E 23 D12
Gallípoli Italy 40°3N 17°58E 23 D8
Gallipolis U.S.A. 38°49N 82°12W 81 F12
Gällivare Sweden 67°9N 20°40E 8 C19
Galloo I. U.S.A. 43°55N 76°25W 83 C8
Galloway U.K. 55°1N 4°29W 11 F4
Galloway, Mull of U.K. 54°39N 4°52W 11 G4
Gallup U.S.A. 35°32N 108°45W 77 J9
Galmudug Somalia 6°30N 48°0E 49 F4
Galoya Sri Lanka 8°10N 80°55E 45 K5
Galt U.S.A. 38°15N 121°18W 78 G5

Galty Mts. Ireland 52°22N 8°10W 10 D3
Galtymore Ireland 52°21N 8°11W 10 D3
Galugāh Iran 36°43N 53°48E 47 B7
Galva U.S.A. 41°10N 90°3W 80 E8
Galveston U.S.A. 29°18N 94°48W 84 G7
Galveston B. U.S.A. 29°36N 94°50W 84 G7
Gálvez Argentina 32°0S 61°14W 94 C3
Galway Ireland 53°17N 9°3W 10 C2
Galway □ Ireland 53°22N 9°1W 10 C2
Galway B. Ireland 53°13N 9°10W 10 C2
Gam → Vietnam 21°55N 105°12E 38 B5
Gamagōri Japan 34°50N 137°14E 29 G8
Gambat Pakistan 27°17N 68°26E 42 F3
Gambhir → India 26°58N 77°27E 42 F6
Gambia ■ W. Afr. 13°25N 16°0W 52 F2
Gambia → W. Afr. 13°28N 16°34W 52 F2
Gambier U.S.A. 40°22N 82°23W 82 F2
Gambier, C. Australia 11°56S 130°57E 60 B5
Gambier, Îs.
  French Polynesia 23°8S 134°58W 65 K14
Gambier Is. Australia 35°3S 136°30E 63 F2
Gambo Canada 48°47N 54°13W 73 C9
Gamboli Pakistan 29°53N 68°24E 42 E3
Gamboma Congo 1°55S 15°52E 54 E3
Gamka → S. Africa 33°18S 21°39E 56 E3
Gamkab → Namibia 28°4S 17°54E 56 C2
Gamlakarleby = Kokkola
  Finland 63°50N 23°8E 8 E20
Gammon → Canada 51°24N 95°44W 71 C9
Gammon Ranges △
  Australia 30°38S 139°8E 63 E2
Gampaha Sri Lanka 7°5N 79°59E 45 L4
Gampola Sri Lanka 7°10N 80°34E 45 L5
Gamtoos → S. Africa 33°58S 25°1E 56 D4
Gamzigrad-Romuliana
  Serbia 43°53N 22°11E 23 C10
Gan Jiang → China 29°15N 116°0E 35 C11
Ganado U.S.A. 35°43N 109°33W 77 J9
Gananoque Canada 44°20N 76°10W 83 B8
Ganāveh Iran 29°35N 50°35E 47 D6
Gäncä Azerbaijan 40°45N 46°20E 19 F8
Gancheng China 18°51N 108°37E 38 C7
Gand = Gent Belgium 51°2N 3°42E 15 C3
Ganda Angola 13°3S 14°35E 55 G2
Gandajika
  Dem. Rep. of the Congo 6°46S 23°58E 54 F4
Gandak → India 25°39N 85°13E 43 G11
Gandava Pakistan 28°32N 67°32E 42 E2
Gander Canada 48°58N 54°35W 73 C9
Gander L. Canada 48°58N 54°35W 73 C9
Gandhi Sagar India 24°40N 75°40E 42 G6
Gandhinagar India 23°15N 72°45E 42 H5
Gandia Spain 38°58N 0°9W 21 C5
Ganedidalem = Gani
  Indonesia 0°48S 128°14E 37 E7
Ganga → India 23°20N 90°30E 43 H14
Ganga Sagar India 21°38N 88°5E 43 J13
Gangakher India 18°57N 76°45E 44 E3
Gangan → India 28°38N 78°58E 43 E8
Ganganagar India 29°56N 73°56E 42 E5
Gangapur Maharashtra,
  India 19°41N 75°1E 44 E2
Gangapur Raj., India 26°32N 76°49E 42 F7
Gangaw Burma 22°5N 94°5E 41 H19
Gangawati India 15°30N 76°36E 45 G3
Gangdisê Shan China 31°20N 81°0E 43 D9
Ganges = Ganga →
  India 23°20N 90°30E 43 H14
Ganges Canada 48°51N 123°31W 70 D4
Ganges, Mouths of the
  India 21°30N 90°0E 43 J14
Ganggyeong S. Korea 36°10N 127°0E 33 F14
Gangneung S. Korea 37°45N 128°54E 33 F15
Gangoh India 29°46N 77°18E 42 E7
Gangotri India 30°50N 79°10E 43 D8
Gangotri △ India 30°50N 79°10E 43 D8
Gangseong S. Korea 38°24N 128°30E 33 E15
Gangtok India 27°20N 88°37E 41 F16
Gangu China 34°40N 105°15E 32 G3
Gangyao China 44°12N 126°37E 33 B14
Gani Indonesia 0°48S 128°14E 37 E7
Ganj India 27°45N 78°57E 43 F8
Ganjam India 19°23N 85°4E 44 K14
Ganluo China 28°58N 102°59E 34 C4
Ganquan China 36°20N 109°20E 32 F5
Gansu □ China 36°0N 104°0E 32 G3
Ganta Liberia 7°15N 8°59W 52 G4
Gantheaume, C. Australia 36°4S 137°32E 63 F2
Gantheaume B. Australia 27°40S 114°10E 61 E1
Gantsevichi = Hantsavichy
  Belarus 52°49N 26°30E 17 B14
Ganyem = Genyem
  Indonesia 2°46S 140°12E 37 E10
Ganyu China 34°50N 119°8E 33 G10
Ganzhou China 25°51N 114°56E 35 E10
Gao Mali 16°15N 0°5W 52 E5
Gao Xian China 28°21N 104°32E 34 C5
Gao'an China 28°26N 115°17E 35 C10
Gaobeidian China 39°19N 115°51E 32 E8
Gaocheng China 38°2N 114°49E 32 E8
Gaochun China 31°20N 118°49E 35 B12
Gaohebu China 30°43N 117°18E 35 B11
Gaokeng China 27°40N 113°58E 35 D9
Gaolan Dao China 21°55N 113°10E 35 G9
Gaoligong Shan China 24°45N 98°45E 34 E2
Gaoming China 22°55N 112°55E 32 G2
Gaoping China 35°45N 112°55E 32 G7
Gaotang China 36°50N 116°15E 32 F9
Gaoua Burkina Faso 10°20N 3°8W 52 F5
Gaoual Guinea 11°45N 13°25W 52 F3
Gaoyang China 38°40N 115°45E 32 E8
Gaoyao China 23°3N 112°27E 35 F9
Gaoyou China 32°47N 119°26E 35 A12
Gaoyou Hu China 32°45N 119°20E 33 H10
Gaoyuan China 37°8N 117°58E 33 F9
Gap France 44°33N 6°5E 20 D7
Gapat → India 24°30N 82°28E 43 G10

Gapuwiyak Australia 12°25S 135°43E 62 A2
Gar China 32°10N 79°58E 30 E4
Gara, L. Ireland 53°57N 8°26W 10 C3
Garabogazköl Aylagy
  Turkmenistan 41°0N 53°30E 19 F9
Garachiné Panama 8°0N 78°12W 88 E4
Garagum Turkmenistan 39°30N 60°0E 47 B9
Garah Australia 29°5S 149°38E 63 D4
Garanhuns Brazil 8°50S 36°30W 93 E11
Garautha India 25°34N 79°18E 43 G8
Garawa → Australia 16°43S 136°51E 62 B2
Garberville U.S.A. 40°6N 123°48W 76 F2
Garbiyang India 30°8N 80°54E 43 D9
Gard → France 43°51N 4°37E 20 E6
Garda, L. di Italy 45°40N 10°41E 22 B4
Garde L. Canada 62°50N 106°13W 71 A7
Garden City Ga., U.S.A. 32°6N 81°9W 85 E14
Garden City Kans.,
  U.S.A. 37°58N 100°53W 80 G3
Garden Grove U.S.A. 33°47N 117°55W 79 M9
Gardēz Afghan. 33°37N 69°9E 42 C3
Gardiner Maine, U.S.A. 44°14N 69°47W 81 C19
Gardiner Mont., U.S.A. 45°2N 110°22W 76 D8
Gardiners I. U.S.A. 41°6N 72°6W 83 E12
Gardner U.S.A. 42°34N 71°59W 83 D13
Gardner Canal Canada 53°27N 128°8W 70 C3
Gardner Pinnacles
  U.S.A. 25°0N 167°55W 75 L6
Gardnerville U.S.A. 38°56N 119°45W 78 G7
Gardo = Qardho Somalia 9°30N 49°6E 49 F4
Garey U.S.A. 34°53N 120°19W 79 L6
Garfield U.S.A. 47°1N 117°9W 76 C5
Garforth U.K. 53°47N 1°24W 12 D6
Gargantua, C. Canada 47°36N 85°2W 81 B11
Gargett Australia 21°9S 148°46E 62 b
Garhchiroli India 20°10N 80°0E 44 D5
Garibaldi △ Canada 49°50N 122°40W 70 D4
Gariep, L. S. Africa 30°40S 25°40E 56 D4
Garies S. Africa 30°32S 17°59E 56 D2
Garig Gunak Barlu △
  Australia 11°26S 131°58E 60 B5
Garigliano → Italy 41°13N 13°45E 22 D5
Garissa Kenya 0°25S 39°40E 54 E7
Garland Tex., U.S.A. 32°54N 96°38W 84 E6
Garland Utah, U.S.A. 41°45N 112°10W 76 F7
Garmāb Iran 35°25N 56°45E 47 C8
Garmisch-Partenkirchen
  Germany 47°30N 11°6E 16 E6
Garmsār Iran 35°20N 52°25E 47 C7
Garner U.S.A. 43°6N 93°36W 80 D7
Garnett U.S.A. 38°17N 95°14W 80 F6
Garo Hills India 25°30N 90°30E 43 G14
Garoe = Garoowe Somalia 8°25N 48°33E 49 F4
Garonne → France 45°2N 0°36W 20 D3
Garoowe Somalia 8°25N 48°33E 49 F4
Garot India 24°19N 75°41E 42 G6
Garoua Cameroon 9°19N 13°21E 53 G8
Garrauli India 25°5N 79°22E 43 G8
Garrison Mont., U.S.A. 46°31N 112°49W 76 C7
Garrison N. Dak., U.S.A. 47°40N 101°25W 80 B3
Garrison Res. = Sakakawea, L.
  U.S.A. 47°30N 101°25W 80 B3
Garron Pt. U.K. 55°3N 5°59W 10 A6
Garry → U.K. 56°44N 3°47W 11 E5
Garry, L. Canada 65°58N 100°18W 68 D11
Garrygala Turkmenistan 38°31N 56°29E 47 B8
Garson L. Canada 56°19N 110°2W 71 B6
Garstang U.K. 53°55N 2°46W 12 D5
Garu India 23°40N 84°14E 43 H11
Garub Namibia 26°37S 16°0E 56 D2
Garut Indonesia 7°14S 107°53E 37 G12
Garvie Mts. N.Z. 45°30S 168°50E 59 F2
Garwa = Garoua
  Cameroon 9°19N 13°21E 53 G8
Garwa India 24°11N 83°47E 43 G10
Gary U.S.A. 41°36N 87°20W 80 E10
Garzê China 31°38N 100°1E 34 B3
Garzón Colombia 2°10N 75°40W 92 C3
Gas-San Japan 38°32N 140°1E 28 E10
Gasan Kuli = Esenguly
  Turkmenistan 37°37N 53°59E 26 F6
Gascogne France 43°45N 0°20E 20 E4
Gascogne, G. de Europe 44°0N 2°0W 20 D2
Gascony = Gascogne
  France 43°45N 0°20E 20 E4
Gascoyne → Australia 24°52S 113°37E 61 D1
Gascoyne Junction
  Australia 25°2S 115°17E 61 E2
Gashaka Nigeria 7°20N 11°29E 53 G8
Gasherbrum Pakistan 35°40N 76°40E 43 B7
Gashua Nigeria 12°54N 11°0E 53 F8
Gaspar Str. = Gelasa, Selat
  Indonesia 2°50S 107°0E 36 E3
Gasparillo Trin. & Tob. 10°18N 61°26W 93 K15
Gaspé Canada 48°52N 64°30W 73 C7
Gaspé, C. de Canada 48°48N 64°7W 73 C7
Gaspé Pen. = Gaspésie, Pén. de la
  Canada 48°45N 65°40W 73 C6
Gaspésie, Pén. de la
  Canada 48°45N 65°40W 73 C6
Gaspésie △ Canada 48°55N 66°10W 73 C6
Gasteiz = Vitoria-Gasteiz
  Spain 42°50N 2°41W 21 A4
Gastonia U.S.A. 35°16N 81°11W 85 D14
Gastre Argentina 42°20S 69°15W 96 E3
Gata, C. de Spain 36°41N 2°13W 21 D4
Gata, Sierra de Spain 40°20N 6°45W 21 B2
Gataga → Canada 58°35N 126°59W 70 B3
Gatchina Russia 59°35N 30°9E 9 G6
Gatehouse of Fleet U.K. 54°53N 4°12W 11 G4
Gates U.S.A. 43°9N 77°42W 82 C7
Gateshead U.K. 54°57N 1°35W 12 C6
Gateshead I. Canada 70°36N 100°26W 68 C11
Gatesville U.S.A. 31°26N 97°45W 84 F6
Gateway U.S.A. 38°41N 108°59W 76 G9
Gatineau Canada 45°29N 75°39W 83 A9
Gatineau → Canada 45°27N 75°42W 72 C4
Gatineau △ Canada 45°40N 76°0W 72 C4
Gatton Australia 27°32S 152°17E 63 D5
Gatún, L. Panama 9°7N 79°56W 88 E4

Gatwick, London ✈ (LGW)
  U.K. 51°10N 0°11W 13 F7
Gatyana S. Africa 32°16S 28°31E 57 D4
Gau Fiji 18°2S 179°18E 59 a
Gauer L. Canada 57°0N 97°50W 71 B9
Gauhati = Guwahati
  India 26°10N 91°45E 41 F17
Gauja → Latvia 57°10N 24°16E 9 H21
Gaujas △ Latvia 57°10N 24°50E 9 H21
Gaula → Norway 63°21N 10°14E 8 E14
Gauri Phanta India 28°41N 80°36E 43 E9
Gauribidanur India 13°37N 77°32E 45 H3
Gaustatoppen Norway 59°48N 8°40E 9 G13
Gauteng □ S. Africa 26°0S 28°0E 57 C4
Gāv Koshī Iran 28°38N 57°12E 47 D8
Gāvakān Iran 29°37N 53°10E 47 D7
Gavāter Iran 25°10N 61°31E 47 E9
Gāvbandī Iran 27°12N 53°4E 47 E7
Gavdos Greece 34°50N 24°5E 23 G11
Gaviota U.S.A. 34°29N 120°13W 79 L6
Gävkhūnī, Bāţlāq-e Iran 32°6N 52°52E 47 C7
Gävle Sweden 60°40N 17°9E 8 F17
Gawachab Namibia 27°4S 17°55E 56 C2
Gawilgarh Hills India 21°15N 76°45E 44 D3
Gawler Australia 34°30S 138°42E 63 E2
Gawler Ranges Australia 32°30S 135°45E 63 E2
Gaxun Nur China 42°22N 100°30E 30 C9
Gay Russia 51°27N 58°27E 18 D10
Gaya India 24°47N 85°4E 43 G11
Gaya Niger 11°52N 3°28E 52 F6
Gaylord U.S.A. 45°2N 84°41W 81 C11
Gayndah Australia 25°35S 151°32E 63 D5
Gaysin = Haysyn
  Ukraine 48°57N 29°25E 17 D15
Gayvoron = Hayvoron
  Ukraine 48°22N 29°52E 17 D15
Gaza Gaza Strip 31°30N 34°28E 48 D3
Gaza □ Mozam. 23°10S 32°45E 57 B5
Gaza Strip ■ Asia 31°29N 34°25E 48 D3
Gazanjyk = Bereket
  Turkmenistan 39°16N 55°32E 47 B7
Gāzbor Iran 28°5N 58°51E 47 D8
Gaziantep Turkey 37°6N 37°23E 46 B3
Gazimağusa = Famagusta
  Cyprus 35°8N 33°55E 46 C2
Gbadolite
  Dem. Rep. of the Congo 4°17N 21°1E 54 D4
Gbarnga Liberia 7°19N 9°13W 52 G4
Gcoverega Botswana 19°8S 24°18E 56 A3
Gcuwa S. Africa 32°20S 28°11E 57 D4
Gdańsk Poland 54°22N 18°40E 17 A10
Gdansk B. = Gdańska, Zatoka
  Poland 54°30N 19°20E 17 A10
Gdańska, Zatoka Poland 54°30N 19°20E 17 A10
Gdov Russia 58°48N 27°55E 9 G22
Gdynia Poland 54°35N 18°33E 17 A10
Gebe Indonesia 0°5N 129°25E 37 D7
Gebze Turkey 40°47N 29°25E 23 D13
Gedaref Sudan 14°2N 35°28E 53 F13
Gede, Tanjung Indonesia 6°46S 105°12E 37 G11
Gediz → Turkey 38°35N 26°48E 23 E12
Gedser Denmark 54°35N 11°55E 9 J14
Gedung, Pulau Malaysia 5°17N 100°23E 39 c
Geegully Cr. →
  Australia 18°32S 123°41E 60 C3
Geel Belgium 51°10N 4°59E 15 C4
Geelong Australia 38°10S 144°22E 63 F3
Geelvink B. = Cenderawasih,
  Teluk Indonesia 3°0S 135°20E 37 E9
Geelvink Chan. Australia 28°30S 114°0E 61 E1
Geesthacht Germany 53°26N 10°22E 16 B6
Geidam Nigeria 12°57N 11°57E 53 F8
Geikie → Canada 57°45N 103°52W 71 B8
Geikie Gorge △ Australia 18°3S 125°41E 60 C4
Geistown U.S.A. 40°18N 78°52W 82 F6
Gejiu China 23°20N 103°10E 34 F4
Gel, Meydān-e Iran 29°4N 54°50E 47 D7
Gela Italy 37°4N 14°15E 22 F6
Gelang Patah Malaysia 1°27N 103°35E 39 d
Gelasa, Selat Indonesia 2°50S 107°0E 36 E3
Gelderland □ Neths. 52°5N 6°10E 15 B6
Geldrop Neths. 51°25N 5°32E 15 C5
Geleen Neths. 50°57N 5°49E 15 D5
Gelib = Jilib Somalia 0°29N 42°46E 49 G3
Gelibolu Turkey 40°28N 26°43E 23 D12
Gelsenkirchen Germany 51°32N 7°6E 16 C4
Gelugur Malaysia 5°22N 100°18E 39 c
Gemas Malaysia 2°37N 102°36E 39 L4
Gembloux Belgium 50°34N 4°43E 15 D4
Gemena
  Dem. Rep. of the Congo 3°13N 19°48E 54 D3
Gemerek Turkey 39°15N 36°10E 46 B3
Gemlik Turkey 40°26N 29°9E 23 D13
Gemsbok △ Botswana 25°5S 21°1E 56 C3
Genale → Ethiopia 6°2N 39°1E 49 F2
General Acha Argentina 37°20S 64°38W 94 D3
General Alvear B. Aires,
  Argentina 36°0S 60°0W 94 D4
General Alvear Mendoza,
  Argentina 35°0S 67°40W 94 D2
General Artigas
  Paraguay 26°52S 56°16W 94 B4
General Belgrano
  Argentina 36°35S 58°47W 94 D4
General Bernardo O'Higgins
  Antarctica 63°0S 58°3W 5 C18
General Cabrera
  Argentina 32°53S 63°52W 94 C3
General Carrera, L.
  S. Amer. 46°35S 72°0W 96 F2
General Cepeda Mexico 25°21N 101°22W 86 B4
General Guido Argentina 36°40S 57°50W 94 D4
General Juan Madariaga
  Argentina 37°0S 57°0W 94 D4
General La Madrid
  Argentina 37°17S 61°20W 94 D3
General MacArthur
  Phil. 11°18N 125°28E 37 B7
General Martin Miguel de Güemes
  Argentina 24°50S 65°0W 94 A3

General Pico *Argentina* 35°45S 63°50W **94** D3
General Pinedo *Argentina* 27°15S 61°20W **94** B3
General Pinto *Argentina* 34°45S 61°50W **94** C3
General Roca *Argentina* 39°2S 67°35W **96** D3
General Santos *Phil.* 6°5N 125°14E **37** C7
General Treviño *Mexico* 26°14N 99°29W **87** B5
General Trías *Mexico* 28°21N 106°22W **86** B3
General Viamonte *Argentina* 35°1S 61°3W **94** D3
General Villegas *Argentina* 35°5S 63°0W **94** D3
Genesee *Idaho, U.S.A.* 46°33N 116°56W **76** C5
Genesee *Pa., U.S.A.* 41°59N 77°54W **82** E7
Genesee → *U.S.A.* 43°16N 77°36W **82** C7
Geneseo *Ill., U.S.A.* 41°27N 90°9W **80** E8
Geneseo *N.Y., U.S.A.* 42°48N 77°49W **82** D7
Geneva = Genève *Switz.* 46°12N 6°9E **20** C7
Geneva *Ala., U.S.A.* 31°2N 85°52W **85** F12
Geneva *N.Y., U.S.A.* 42°52N 76°59W **82** D8
Geneva *Nebr., U.S.A.* 40°32N 97°36W **80** E5
Geneva *Ohio, U.S.A.* 41°48N 80°57W **82** E4
Geneva, L. = Léman, L. *Europe* 46°26N 6°30E **20** C7
Genève *Switz.* 46°12N 6°9E **20** C7
Gengma *China* 23°32N 99°20E **34** F2
Genhe *China* 50°47N 121°31E **31** A13
Genil → *Spain* 37°42N 5°19W **21** D3
Genk *Belgium* 50°58N 5°32E **15** D5
Gennargentu, Mti. del *Italy* 40°1N 9°19E **22** D3
Genoa = Génova *Italy* 44°25N 8°57E **20** D8
Genoa *Australia* 37°29S 149°35E **63** F4
Genoa *N.Y., U.S.A.* 42°40N 76°32W **83** D8
Genoa *Nebr., U.S.A.* 41°27N 97°44W **80** E5
Genoa *Nev., U.S.A.* 39°2N 119°50W **78** F7
Génova *Italy* 44°25N 8°57E **20** D8
Génova, G. di *Italy* 44°0N 9°0E **22** C3
Genriyetty, Ostrov *Russia* 77°6N 156°30E **27** B16
Gent *Belgium* 51°2N 3°42E **15** C3
Genteng *Jawa Barat, Indonesia* 7°22S 106°24E **37** G12
Genteng *Jawa Timur, Indonesia* 8°22S 114°9E **37** J17
Genyem *Indonesia* 2°46S 140°12E **37** E10
Geochang *S. Korea* 35°41N 127°55E **33** G14
Geographe B. *Australia* 33°30S 115°15E **61** F2
Geographe Chan. *Australia* 24°30S 113°0E **61** D1
Geoje *S. Korea* 34°51N 128°35E **33** G15
Georga, Zemlya *Russia* 80°30N 49°0E **26** A5
George *S. Africa* 33°58S 22°29E **56** D3
George → *Canada* 58°49N 66°10W **73** A6
George, L. *N.S.W., Australia* 35°10S 149°25E **63** F4
George, L. *S. Austral., Australia* 37°25S 140°0E **63** F3
George, L. *W. Austral., Australia* 22°45S 123°40E **60** D3
George, L. *Fla., U.S.A.* 29°17N 81°36W **85** G14
George, L. *N.Y., U.S.A.* 43°37N 73°33W **83** C11
George Bush Intercontinental, Houston ✈ (IAH) *U.S.A.* 29°59N 95°20W **84** G7
George Gill Ra. *Australia* 24°22S 131°45E **60** D5
George Pt. *Australia* 20°6S 148°36E **62** b
George River = Kangiqsualujjuaq *Canada* 58°30N 65°59W **69** F18
George Sound *N.Z.* 44°52S 167°25E **59** F1
George Town *Australia* 41°6S 146°49E **63** G4
George Town *Bahamas* 23°33N 75°47W **88** B4
George Town *Cayman Is.* 19°20N 81°24W **88** C3
George Town *Malaysia* 5°25N 100°20E **39** c
George V Land *Antarctica* 69°0S 148°0E **5** C10
George VI Sound *Antarctica* 71°0S 68°0W **5** D17
George West *U.S.A.* 28°20N 98°7W **84** G5
Georgetown = Janjanbureh *Gambia* 13°30N 14°47W **52** F3
Georgetown *Australia* 18°17S 143°33E **62** B3
Georgetown *Ont., Canada* 43°40N 79°56W **82** C5
Georgetown *P.E.I., Canada* 46°13N 62°24W **73** C7
Georgetown *Guyana* 6°50N 58°12W **92** B7
Georgetown *Calif., U.S.A.* 38°54N 120°50W **78** G6
Georgetown *Colo., U.S.A.* 39°42N 105°42W **76** G11
Georgetown *Ky., U.S.A.* 38°13N 84°33W **81** F11
Georgetown *N.Y., U.S.A.* 42°46N 75°44W **83** D9
Georgetown *Ohio, U.S.A.* 38°52N 83°54W **81** F12
Georgetown *S.C., U.S.A.* 33°23N 79°17W **85** E15
Georgetown *Tex., U.S.A.* 30°38N 97°41W **84** F6
Georgia □ *U.S.A.* 32°50N 83°15W **85** E13
Georgia ■ *Asia* 42°0N 43°0E **19** F7
Georgia, Str. of *N. Amer.* 49°25N 124°0W **78** A3
Georgia Basin *S. Ocean* 50°45S 35°30W **5** B1
Georgian B. *Canada* 45°15N 81°0W **82** A4
Georgian Bay Islands △ *Canada* 44°53N 79°52W **82** B5
Georgīevka *Kazakhstan* 49°19N 84°34E **26** E9
Georgina → *Australia* 23°30S 139°47E **62** C2
Georgina I. *Canada* 44°22N 79°17W **82** B5
Georgiyevsk *Russia* 44°12N 43°28E **19** F7
Gera *Germany* 50°53N 12°4E **16** C7
Geraardsbergen *Belgium* 50°45N 3°53E **15** D3
Geral, Serra *Brazil* 26°25S 50°0W **95** B6
Geral de Goiás, Serra *Brazil* 12°0S 46°0W **93** F9
Geraldine *U.S.A.* 47°36N 110°16W **76** C8
Geraldton *Australia* 28°48S 114°32E **61** E1
Geraldton *Canada* 49°44N 87°10W **72** C2
Gerdine, Mt. *U.S.A.* 61°35N 152°27W **74** C9
Gereshk *Afghan.* 31°47N 64°35E **40** D4
Gerik *Malaysia* 5°50N 101°15E **39** K3
Gering *U.S.A.* 41°50N 103°40W **80** E2
Gerlach *U.S.A.* 40°39N 119°21W **76** F4
German Bight = Deutsche Bucht *Germany* 54°15N 8°0E **16** A5
Germansen Landing *Canada* 55°43N 124°40W **70** B4
Germantown *U.S.A.* 35°5N 89°49W **85** D10
Germany ■ *Europe* 51°0N 10°0E **16** C6
Germī *Iran* 39°1N 48°3E **47** B6
Gernika-Lumo *Spain* 43°19N 2°40W **21** A4
Gero *Japan* 35°48N 137°14E **29** G8
Gerokgak *Indonesia* 8°11S 114°27E **37** J17
Gerona = Girona *Spain* 41°58N 2°46E **21** B7
Gerrard *Canada* 50°30N 117°17W **70** C5
Gersoppa Falls *India* 14°12N 74°46E **45** G2
Gertak Sanggul *Malaysia* 5°17N 100°12E **39** c
Gertak Sanggul, Tanjung *Malaysia* 5°16N 100°11E **39** c
Gerung *Indonesia* 8°43S 116°7E **37** K19
Geser *Indonesia* 3°50S 130°54E **37** E8
Gettysburg *Pa., U.S.A.* 39°50N 77°14W **81** F15
Gettysburg *S. Dak., U.S.A.* 45°1N 99°57W **80** C4
Getxo = Algorta *Spain* 43°21N 2°59W **21** A4
Getz Ice Shelf *Antarctica* 75°0S 130°0W **5** D14
Gevrai *India* 19°16N 75°45E **44** E2
Geyser *U.S.A.* 47°16N 110°30W **76** C8
Geyserville *U.S.A.* 38°42N 122°54W **78** G4
Gezhouba Dam *China* 30°40N 111°20E **35** B8
Ghadāf, W. al → *Iraq* 32°56N 43°30E **46** C4
Ghadāmis *Libya* 30°11N 9°29E **53** B8
Ghaggar → *India* 29°30N 74°53E **42** E6
Ghaghara → *India* 25°45N 84°40E **43** G11
Ghaghat → *Bangla.* 25°19N 89°38E **43** G13
Ghagra *India* 23°17N 84°33E **43** H11
Ghallamane *Mauritania* 23°15N 10°0W **52** D4
Ghana ■ *W. Afr.* 8°0N 1°0W **52** G5
Ghanpokhara *Nepal* 28°17N 84°14E **43** E11
Ghansor *India* 22°39N 80°1E **43** H9
Ghanzi *Botswana* 21°50S 21°34E **56** B3
Ghanzi □ *Botswana* 22°30S 22°30E **56** B3
Ghardaïa *Algeria* 32°20N 3°37E **52** B6
Gharm *Tajikistan* 39°0N 70°20E **26** F8
Gharyān *Libya* 32°10N 13°0E **53** B8
Ghāt *Libya* 24°59N 10°11E **53** D8
Ghatal *India* 22°40N 87°46E **43** H12
Ghatampur *India* 26°8N 80°13E **43** F9
Ghatgaon *India* 21°24N 85°53E **44** D7
Ghatprabha → *India* 16°15N 75°20E **45** F2
Ghats, Eastern *India* 14°0N 78°50E **45** H4
Ghats, Western *India* 14°0N 75°0E **45** H2
Ghatsila *India* 22°36N 86°29E **43** H12
Ghaṭṭī *Si. Arabia* 31°16N 37°31E **46** D3
Ghawdex = Gozo *Malta* 36°3N 14°15E **22** F6
Ghazal, Bahr el → *Chad* 13°0N 15°47E **53** F9
Ghazal, Bahr el → *South Sudan* 9°31N 30°25E **53** G12
Ghaziabad *India* 28°42N 77°26E **42** E7
Ghazipur *India* 25°38N 83°35E **43** G10
Ghaznī *Afghan.* 33°30N 68°28E **42** C3
Ghaznī □ *Afghan.* 32°10N 68°20E **40** C6
Ghent = Gent *Belgium* 51°2N 3°42E **15** C3
Gheorghe Gheorghiu-Dej = Oneşti *Romania* 46°17N 26°47E **17** E14
Ghīnah, Wādī al → *Si. Arabia* 30°27N 38°14E **46** D3
Ghizar → *Pakistan* 36°15N 73°43E **43** A5
Ghod → *India* 18°30N 74°35E **44** E2
Ghogha *India* 21°40N 72°20E **44** D1
Ghotaru *India* 27°20N 70°1E **42** F4
Ghotki *Pakistan* 28°5N 69°21E **42** E3
Ghowr □ *Afghan.* 34°0N 64°20E **40** C4
Ghughri *India* 22°39N 80°41E **43** H9
Ghugus *India* 19°58N 79°12E **44** E4
Ghulam Mohammad Barrage *Pakistan* 25°30N 68°20E **42** G3
Ghūrīān *Afghan.* 34°17N 61°25E **40** B2
Gia Dinh *Vietnam* 10°49N 106°42E **39** G6
Gia Lai = Plei Ku *Vietnam* 13°57N 108°0E **38** F7
Gia Nghia *Vietnam* 11°58N 107°42E **39** G6
Gia Ngoc *Vietnam* 14°50N 108°58E **38** E7
Gia Vuc *Vietnam* 14°42N 108°34E **38** E7
Giamama = Jamaame *Somalia* 0°4N 42°44E **49** G3
Gianitsa *Greece* 40°46N 22°24E **23** D10
Giant Forest *U.S.A.* 36°36N 118°43W **78** J8
Giant Sequoia ⌂ *U.S.A.* 36°10N 118°35W **78** K8
Giants Causeway *U.K.* 55°16N 6°29W **10** A5
Giant's Tank *Sri Lanka* 8°51N 80°2E **45** K5
Gianyar *Indonesia* 8°32S 115°20E **37** K18
Giarabub = Al Jaghbūb *Libya* 29°42N 24°38E **53** C10
Giarre *Italy* 37°43N 15°11E **22** F6
Gibara *Cuba* 21°9N 76°11W **88** B4
Gibbon *U.S.A.* 40°45N 98°51W **80** E4
Gibe II *Ethiopia* 8°0N 37°30E **49** F2
Gibe III *Ethiopia* 7°0N 37°30E **49** F2
Gibeon *Namibia* 25°9S 17°43E **56** C2
Gibraltar ☒ *Europe* 36°7N 5°22W **21** D3
Gibraltar, Str. of *Medit. S.* 35°55N 5°40W **21** E3
Gibraltar Range △ *Australia* 29°31S 152°19E **63** D5
Gibson Desert *Australia* 24°0S 126°0E **60** D4
Gibsons *Canada* 49°24N 123°32W **70** D4
Gibsonville *U.S.A.* 39°46N 120°54W **78** F6
Giddalur *India* 15°20N 78°57E **45** G4
Giddings *U.S.A.* 30°11N 96°56W **84** F6
Giebnegáisi = Kebnekaise *Sweden* 67°53N 18°33E **8** C18
Giessen *Germany* 50°34N 8°41E **16** C5
Gīfān *Iran* 37°54N 57°28E **47** B8
Gift Lake *Canada* 55°53N 115°49W **70** B5
Gifu *Japan* 35°30N 136°45E **29** G8
Gifu □ *Japan* 35°40N 137°0E **29** G8
Giganta, Sa. de la *Mexico* 26°0N 111°39W **86** B2
Gigha *U.K.* 55°42N 5°44W **11** F3
Giglio *Italy* 42°20N 10°52E **22** C4
Gijón *Spain* 43°32N 5°42W **21** A3
Gil I. *Canada* 53°12N 129°15W **70** C3
Gila → *U.S.A.* 32°43N 114°33W **77** K6
Gila Bend *U.S.A.* 32°57N 112°43W **77** K7
Gila Bend Mts. *U.S.A.* 33°10N 113°0W **77** K7
Gila Cliff Dwellings ⌂ *U.S.A.* 33°12N 108°16W **77** K9
Gīlān □ *Iran* 37°0N 50°0E **47** B6
Gilbert → *Australia* 16°35S 141°15E **62** B3
Gilbert Is. *Kiribati* 1°0N 172°0E **58** A10
Gilbert River *Australia* 18°9S 142°52E **62** B3
Gilbert Seamounts *Pac. Oc.* 52°50N 150°10W **4** D18
Gilead *U.S.A.* 44°24N 70°59W **83** B14
Gilf el Kebîr, Hadabat el *Egypt* 23°50N 25°50E **53** D11
Gilford I. *Canada* 50°40N 126°30W **70** C3
Gilgandra *Australia* 31°43S 148°39E **63** E4
Gilgit *India* 35°50N 74°15E **43** B6
Gilgit → *Pakistan* 35°44N 74°37E **43** B6
Gilgit-Baltistan □ *Pakistan* 36°30N 73°0E **43** A5
Gilimanuk *Indonesia* 8°10S 114°26E **37** J17
Gillam *Canada* 56°20N 94°40W **71** B10
Gillen, L. *Australia* 26°11S 124°38E **61** E3
Gilles, L. *Australia* 32°50S 136°45E **63** E2
Gillette *U.S.A.* 44°18N 105°30W **76** D11
Gilliat *Australia* 20°40S 141°28E **62** C3
Gillingham *U.K.* 51°23N 0°33E **13** F8
Gilmer *U.S.A.* 32°44N 94°57W **84** E7
Gilmore, L. *Australia* 32°29S 121°37E **61** F3
Gilmour *Canada* 44°48N 77°37W **82** B7
Gilroy *U.S.A.* 37°1N 121°34W **78** H5
Gimcheon *S. Korea* 36°11N 128°4E **33** F15
Gimhae *S. Korea* 35°14N 128°53E **33** G15
Gimhwa *S. Korea* 38°17N 127°28E **33** E14
Gimie, Mt. *St. Lucia* 13°54N 61°0W **89** f
Gimje *S. Korea* 35°48N 126°45E **33** G14
Gimli *Canada* 50°40N 97°0W **71** C9
Gin → *Sri Lanka* 6°5N 80°7E **45** L5
Gin Gin *Australia* 25°0S 151°58E **63** D5
Gingee *India* 12°15N 79°25E **45** H4
Gingin *Australia* 31°22S 115°54E **61** F2
Gingindlovu *S. Africa* 29°2S 31°30E **57** C5
Ginir *Ethiopia* 7°6N 40°40E **49** F3
Giohar = Jawhar *Somalia* 2°48N 45°30E **49** G4
Giona, Oros *Greece* 38°38N 22°14E **23** E10
Gir △ *India* 21°0N 71°0E **42** J4
Gir Hills *India* 21°0N 71°0E **42** J4
Girab *India* 26°2N 70°38E **42** F4
Girâfi, W. → *Egypt* 29°58N 34°39E **48** F3
Girard *St. Lucia* 13°59N 60°57W **89** D7
Girard *Kans., U.S.A.* 37°31N 94°51W **80** G6
Girard *Ohio, U.S.A.* 41°9N 80°42W **82** E4
Girard *Pa., U.S.A.* 42°0N 80°19W **82** E4
Girdle Ness *U.K.* 57°9N 2°3W **11** D6
Giresun *Turkey* 40°55N 38°30E **19** F6
Girga *Egypt* 26°17N 31°55E **53** C12
Giri → *India* 30°28N 77°41E **42** D7
Giridih *India* 24°10N 86°21E **43** G12
Girne = Kyrenia *Cyprus* 35°20N 33°20E **46** C2
Giron = Kiruna *Sweden* 67°52N 20°15E **8** C19
Girona *Spain* 41°58N 2°46E **21** B7
Gironde → *France* 45°32N 1°7W **20** D3
Girraween △ *Australia* 28°46S 151°54E **63** D5
Girringun △ *Australia* 18°15S 145°32E **62** B4
Giru *Australia* 19°30S 147°5E **62** B4
Girvan *U.K.* 55°14N 4°51W **11** F4
Gisborne *N.Z.* 38°39S 178°5E **59** C7
Gisenyi *Rwanda* 1°41S 29°15E **54** E5
Gislaved *Sweden* 57°19N 13°32E **9** H15
Gitega *Burundi* 3°26S 29°56E **54** E5
Githio *Greece* 36°46N 22°34E **23** F10
Giuba = Juba → *Somalia* 1°30N 42°35E **49** G3
Giurgiu *Romania* 43°52N 25°57E **17** G13
Giyani *S. Africa* 23°19S 30°43E **57** B5
Gizab *Afghan.* 33°22N 66°17E **42** C1
Gizhiga *Russia* 62°3N 160°30E **27** C17
Gizhiginskaya Guba *Russia* 61°0N 158°0E **27** C16
Giżycko *Poland* 54°2N 21°48E **17** A11
Gjakovë *Kosovo* 42°22N 20°26E **23** C9
Gjirokastër *Albania* 40°7N 20°10E **23** D9
Gjoa Haven *Canada* 68°38N 95°53W **68** D12
Gjøvik *Norway* 60°47N 10°43E **8** F14
Glace Bay *Canada* 46°11N 59°58W **73** C8
Glacier △ *Canada* 51°15N 117°30W **70** C5
Glacier △ *U.S.A.* 48°42N 113°48W **76** B7
Glacier Bay *U.S.A.* 58°40N 136°0W **68** F4
Glacier Bay ⌂ *U.S.A.* 58°45N 136°30W **70** B1
Glacier Peak *U.S.A.* 48°7N 121°7W **76** B3
Gladewater *U.S.A.* 32°33N 94°56W **84** E7
Gladstone *Queens., Australia* 23°52S 151°16E **62** C5
Gladstone *S. Austral., Australia* 33°15S 138°22E **63** E2
Gladstone *Canada* 50°13N 98°57W **71** C9
Gladstone *U.S.A.* 45°51N 87°1W **80** C10
Gladwin *U.S.A.* 43°59N 84°29W **81** D11
Glagah *Indonesia* 8°13S 114°18E **37** J17
Glåma = Glomma → *Norway* 59°12N 10°57E **9** G14
Gláma *Iceland* 65°48N 23°0W **8** D2
Glamis *U.S.A.* 32°55N 115°5W **79** N11
Glamorgan, Vale of □ *U.K.* 51°28N 3°25W **13** F4
Glasco *Kans., U.S.A.* 39°22N 97°50W **80** F5
Glasco *N.Y., U.S.A.* 42°3N 73°57W **83** D11
Glasgow *U.K.* 55°51N 4°15W **11** F4
Glasgow *Ky., U.S.A.* 37°0N 85°55W **81** G11
Glasgow *Mont., U.S.A.* 48°12N 106°38W **76** B10
Glasgow City □ *U.K.* 55°51N 4°12W **11** F4
Glasgow Int. ✈ (GLA) *U.K.* 55°51N 4°21W **11** F4
Glaslyn *Canada* 53°22N 108°21W **71** C7
Glastonbury *U.K.* 51°9N 2°43W **13** F5
Glastonbury *U.S.A.* 41°43N 72°37W **83** E12
Glazov *Russia* 58°9N 52°40E **18** C9
Gleichen *Canada* 50°52N 113°3W **70** C6
Gleiwitz = Gliwice *Poland* 50°22N 18°41E **17** C10
Glen *U.S.A.* 44°7N 71°11W **83** B13
Glen Affric *U.K.* 57°17N 5°1W **11** D3
Glen Canyon *U.S.A.* 37°30N 110°40W **77** H8
Glen Canyon ⌂ *U.S.A.* 37°15N 111°0W **77** H8
Glen Canyon Dam *U.S.A.* 36°57N 111°29W **77** H8
Glen Coe *U.K.* 56°40N 5°0W **11** E3
Glen Cove *U.S.A.* 40°52N 73°38W **83** F11
Glen Garry *U.K.* 57°3N 5°7W **11** D3
Glen Innes *Australia* 29°44S 151°44E **63** D5
Glen Lyon *U.S.A.* 41°10N 76°5W **83** E8
Glen Mor *U.K.* 57°9N 4°37W **11** D4
Glen Moriston *U.K.* 57°11N 4°52W **11** D4
Glen Robertson *Canada* 45°22N 74°30W **83** A10
Glen Spean *U.K.* 56°53N 4°40W **11** E4
Glen Ullin *U.S.A.* 46°49N 101°50W **80** B3
Glenbeigh *Ireland* 52°3N 9°58W **10** D2
Glencoe *Canada* 42°45N 81°43W **82** D3
Glencoe *S. Africa* 28°11S 30°11E **57** C5
Glencoe *U.S.A.* 44°46N 94°9W **80** C6
Glencolumbkille *Ireland* 54°43N 8°42W **10** B3
Glendale *U.S.A.* 33°32N 112°11W **77** K7
Glendive *U.S.A.* 47°7N 104°43W **76** C11
Glendo *U.S.A.* 42°30N 105°2W **76** E11
Glenelg → *Australia* 38°4S 140°59E **63** F3
Glenfield *U.S.A.* 43°43N 75°24W **83** C9
Glengad Hd. *Ireland* 55°20N 7°10W **10** A4
Glengarriff *Ireland* 51°45N 9°34W **10** E2
Glenmont *U.S.A.* 40°31N 82°6W **82** F2
Glenmorgan *Australia* 27°14S 149°42E **63** D4
Glenn *U.S.A.* 39°31N 122°1W **78** F4
Glennallen *U.S.A.* 62°7N 145°33W **68** E2
Glennamaddy *Ireland* 53°37N 8°33W **10** C3
Glenns Ferry *U.S.A.* 42°57N 115°18W **76** E6
Glenora *Canada* 44°2N 77°3W **82** B7
Glenorchy *Australia* 42°49S 147°18E **63** G4
Glenore *Australia* 17°50S 141°12E **62** B3
Glenreagh *Australia* 30°2S 153°1E **63** E5
Glenrock *U.S.A.* 42°52N 105°52W **76** E11
Glenrothes *U.K.* 56°12N 3°10W **11** E5
Glens Falls *U.S.A.* 43°19N 73°39W **83** C11
Glenside *U.S.A.* 40°6N 75°9W **83** F9
Glenties *Ireland* 54°48N 8°17W **10** B3
Glenveagh △ *Ireland* 55°3N 8°1W **10** A3
Glenville *U.S.A.* 38°56N 80°50W **81** F13
Glenwood *Canada* 49°0N 54°58W **73** C9
Glenwood *Ark., U.S.A.* 34°20N 93°33W **84** D8
Glenwood *Iowa, U.S.A.* 41°3N 95°45W **80** E6
Glenwood *Minn., U.S.A.* 45°39N 95°23W **80** C6
Glenwood *Wash., U.S.A.* 46°1N 121°17W **78** D5
Glenwood Springs *U.S.A.* 39°33N 107°19W **76** G10
Glettinganes *Iceland* 65°30N 13°37W **8** D7
Glin *Ireland* 52°34N 9°17W **10** D2
Gliwice *Poland* 50°22N 18°41E **17** C10
Globe *U.S.A.* 33°24N 110°47W **77** K8
Głogów *Poland* 51°37N 16°5E **16** C9
Glomma → *Norway* 59°12N 10°57E **9** G14
Glorieuses, Îs. *Ind. Oc.* 11°30S 47°20E **55** G9
Glossop *U.K.* 53°27N 1°56W **12** D6
Gloucester *Australia* 32°0S 151°59E **63** E5
Gloucester *U.K.* 51°53N 2°15W **13** F5
Gloucester *U.S.A.* 42°37N 70°40W **83** D14
Gloucester I. *Australia* 20°0S 148°30E **62** b
Gloucester Island △ *Australia* 20°2S 148°30E **62** b
Gloucester Point *U.S.A.* 37°15N 76°30W **81** G15
Gloucestershire □ *U.K.* 51°46N 2°15W **13** F5
Gloversville *U.S.A.* 43°3N 74°21W **83** C10
Glovertown *Canada* 48°40N 54°3W **73** C9
Glusk *Belarus* 52°53N 28°41E **17** B15
Glyn Ebwy = Ebbw Vale *U.K.* 51°46N 3°12W **13** F4
Gmünd *Austria* 48°45N 15°0E **16** D8
Gmunden *Austria* 47°55N 13°48E **16** E7
Gniezno *Poland* 52°30N 17°35E **17** B9
Gnowangerup *Australia* 33°58S 117°59E **61** F2
Go Cong *Vietnam* 10°22N 106°40E **39** G6
Gō-no-ura *Japan* 33°44N 129°40E **29** H4
Goa *India* 15°33N 73°59E **45** G1
Goa □ *India* 15°33N 73°59E **45** G1
Goalen Hd. *Australia* 36°33S 150°4E **63** F5
Goalpara *India* 26°10N 90°40E **41** F17
Goaltor *India* 22°43N 87°10E **43** H12
Goalundo Ghat *Bangla.* 23°50N 89°47E **43** H13
Goat Fell *U.K.* 55°38N 5°11W **11** F3
Goba *Ethiopia* 7°1N 39°59E **49** F2
Goba *Mozam.* 26°15S 32°13E **57** C5
Gobabis *Namibia* 22°30S 19°0E **56** B2
Gobi *Asia* 44°0N 110°0E **32** C6
Gobi Gurvan Saykhan △ *Mongolia* 43°24N 101°24E **32** C2
Gobichettipalayam *India* 11°31N 77°21E **45** J3
Gobō *Japan* 33°53N 135°10E **29** H7
Gochas *Namibia* 24°59S 18°55E **56** B2
Godalming *U.K.* 51°11N 0°36W **13** F7
Godavari → *India* 16°25N 82°18E **44** F6
Godavari Pt. *India* 17°0N 82°20E **44** F6
Godbout *Canada* 49°20N 67°38W **73** C6
Godda *India* 24°50N 87°13E **43** G12
Goderich *Canada* 43°45N 81°41W **82** C3
Godfrey Ra. *Australia* 24°0S 117°0E **61** D2
Godhavn = Qeqertarsuaq *Greenland* 69°15N 53°38W **4** C5
Godhra *India* 22°49N 73°40E **42** H5
Godoy Cruz *Argentina* 32°56S 68°52W **94** C2
Gods → *Canada* 56°22N 92°51W **72** A1
Gods L. *Canada* 54°40N 94°15W **72** B1
Gods River *Canada* 54°50N 94°5W **71** C10
Godthåb = Nuuk *Greenland* 64°10N 51°35W **67** C14
Goeie Hoop, Kaap die = Good Hope, C. of *S. Africa* 34°24S 18°30E **56** D2
Goéland, L. au *Canada* 49°50N 76°48W **72** C4
Goélands, L. aux *Canada* 55°27N 64°17W **73** A7
Goeree *Neths.* 51°50N 4°0E **15** C3
Goes *Neths.* 51°30N 3°55E **15** C3
Goffstown *U.S.A.* 43°1N 71°36W **83** C13
Gogama *Canada* 47°35N 81°43W **72** C3
Gogebic, L. *U.S.A.* 46°30N 89°35W **80** B9
Gogra = Ghaghara → *India* 25°45N 84°40E **43** G11
Gogrial *South Sudan* 8°30N 28°8E **53** G11
Gohana *India* 29°8N 76°42E **42** E7
Goharganj *India* 23°1N 77°41E **42** H7
Goi → *India* 22°4N 74°46E **42** H6
Goiânia *Brazil* 16°43S 49°20W **93** G9
Goiás *Brazil* 15°55S 50°10W **93** G8
Goiás □ *Brazil* 12°10S 48°0W **93** F9
Goio-Erê *Brazil* 24°12S 53°1W **95** A5
Gojō *Japan* 34°21N 135°42E **29** G7
Gojra *Pakistan* 31°10N 72°40E **42** D5
Gokak *India* 16°11N 74°52E **45** F2
Gokarn *India* 14°33N 74°17E **45** G2
Gökçeada *Turkey* 40°10N 25°50E **23** D11
Gökova Körfezi *Turkey* 36°55N 27°50E **23** F12
Göksu → *Turkey* 36°19N 34°5E **46** B2
Gokteik *Burma* 22°26N 97°0E **41** H20
Gokurt *Pakistan* 29°40N 67°26E **42** E2
Gokwe *Zimbabwe* 18°7S 28°58E **57** A4
Gola *India* 28°3N 80°32E **43** E9
Golakganj *India* 26°8N 89°52E **43** F13
Golan Heights = Hagolan *Syria* 33°0N 35°45E **48** C4
Golāshkerd *Iran* 27°59N 57°16E **47** E8
Golconda *India* 17°24N 78°23E **44** F4
Golconda *U.S.A.* 40°58N 117°30W **76** F5
Gold *U.S.A.* 41°52N 77°50W **82** E7
Gold Beach *U.S.A.* 42°25N 124°25W **76** E1
Gold Coast *W. Afr.* 4°0N 1°40W **52** H5
Gold Hill *U.S.A.* 42°26N 123°3W **76** E2
Gold River *Canada* 49°46N 126°3W **70** D3
Golden *Canada* 51°20N 116°59W **70** C5
Golden B. *N.Z.* 40°40S 172°50E **59** D4
Golden Gate Highlands △ *S. Africa* 28°40S 28°40E **57** C4
Golden Hinde *Canada* 49°40N 125°44W **70** D3
Golden Lake *Canada* 45°34N 77°21W **82** A7
Golden Rock *India* 10°45N 78°48E **45** J4
Golden Spike ⌂ *U.S.A.* 41°37N 112°33W **76** F7
Golden Vale *Ireland* 52°33N 8°17W **10** D3
Goldendale *U.S.A.* 45°49N 120°50W **76** D3
Goldfield *U.S.A.* 37°42N 117°14W **77** H5
Goldsand L. *Canada* 57°2N 101°8W **71** B8
Goldsboro *U.S.A.* 35°23N 77°59W **85** D16
Goldsmith *U.S.A.* 31°59N 102°37W **84** F3
Goldthwaite *U.S.A.* 31°27N 98°34W **84** F5
Goleniów *Poland* 53°35N 14°50E **16** B8
Golestān □ *Iran* 37°20N 55°25E **47** B7
Golestānak *Iran* 30°36N 54°14E **47** D7
Goleta *U.S.A.* 34°27N 119°50W **79** L7
Golfito *Costa Rica* 8°41N 83°5W **88** E3
Golfo Aranci *Italy* 40°59N 9°38E **22** D3
Golfo de Santa Clara *Mexico* 31°42N 114°30W **86** A2
Goliad *U.S.A.* 28°40N 97°23W **84** G6
Golmud *China* 36°25N 94°53E **30** D7
Golpāyegān *Iran* 33°27N 50°18E **47** C6
Golra *Pakistan* 33°37N 72°56E **42** C5
Golspie *U.K.* 57°58N 3°59W **11** D5
Goma *Dem. Rep. of the Congo* 1°37S 29°10E **54** E5
Gomal Pass *Pakistan* 31°56N 69°20E **42** D3
Gomati → *India* 25°32N 83°11E **43** G10
Gombe *Nigeria* 10°19N 11°2E **53** F8
Gomel = Homyel *Belarus* 52°28N 31°0E **17** B16
Gomera *Canary Is.* 28°7N 17°14W **52** C2
Gómez Palacio *Mexico* 25°34N 103°30W **86** B4
Gomīshān *Iran* 37°4N 54°6E **47** B7
Gomogomo *Indonesia* 6°39S 134°43E **37** F8
Gomoh *India* 23°52N 86°10E **43** H12
Gompa = Ganta *Liberia* 7°15N 8°59W **52** G4
Gonābād *Iran* 34°15N 58°45E **47** C8
Gonaïves *Haiti* 19°20N 72°42W **89** C5
Gonâve, G. de la *Haiti* 19°29N 72°42W **89** C5
Gonâve, Île de la *Haiti* 18°51N 73°3W **89** C5
Gonbad-e Kāvūs *Iran* 37°20N 55°25E **47** B7
Gonda *India* 27°9N 81°58E **43** F9
Gondal *India* 21°58N 70°52E **42** J4
Gonder *Ethiopia* 12°39N 37°30E **49** E2
Gondia *India* 21°23N 80°10E **44** D5
Gönen *Turkey* 40°6N 27°39E **23** D12
Gong Xian *China* 28°23N 104°47E **34** C5
Gong'an *China* 30°7N 112°12E **35** B9
Gongbei *China* 22°12N 113°32E **31** a
Gongchangling *China* 41°7N 123°27E **33** D12
Gongcheng *China* 24°50N 110°49E **35** E8
Gongga Shan *China* 29°40N 101°55E **34** C3
Gonggar *China* 29°23N 91°7E **30** F7
Gongguan *China* 21°48N 109°36E **34** G7
Gonghe *China* 36°18N 100°32E **30** D9
Gongju *S. Korea* 36°27N 127°7E **33** F14
Gongming *China* 22°47N 113°53E **31** a
Gongolgon *Australia* 30°21S 146°54E **63** E4
Gongshan *China* 27°43N 98°29E **34** D2
Gongtan *China* 28°55N 108°20E **34** C7
Gongyi *China* 34°45N 112°58E **32** G7
Gongzhuling *China* 43°30N 124°40E **33** C13
Goniri *Nigeria* 11°30N 12°15E **53** F8
Gonjo *China* 30°52N 98°17E **34** B2
Gonzales *Calif., U.S.A.* 36°30N 121°26W **78** J5
Gonzales *Tex., U.S.A.* 29°30N 97°27W **84** G6
González *Mexico* 22°48N 98°25W **87** C5
Good Hope, C. of *S. Africa* 34°24S 18°30E **56** D2
Good Hope Lake *Canada* 59°16N 129°18W **70** B3
Gooderham *Canada* 44°54N 78°21W **82** B6
Goodhouse *S. Africa* 28°57S 18°13E **56** C2
Gooding *U.S.A.* 42°56N 114°43W **76** E6
Goodland *U.S.A.* 39°21N 101°43W **80** F3
Goodlands *Mauritius* 20°2S 57°39E **55** d
Goodlow *Canada* 56°20N 120°8W **70** B4
Goodooga *Australia* 29°3S 147°28E **63** D4
Goodsprings *U.S.A.* 35°49N 115°27W **79** K11
Goole *U.K.* 53°42N 0°53W **12** D7
Goolgowi *Australia* 33°58S 145°41E **63** E4
Goomalling *Australia* 31°15S 116°49E **61** F2
Goomeri *Australia* 26°12S 152°6E **63** D5
Goondiwindi *Australia* 28°30S 150°21E **63** D5
Goongarrie, L. *Australia* 30°3S 121°9E **61** F3
Goongarrie △ *Australia* 30°7S 121°30E **61** F3
Goonyella *Australia* 21°47S 147°58E **62** C4
Goose → *Canada* 53°20N 60°35W **73** B7
Goose Creek *U.S.A.* 32°59N 80°2W **85** E14
Goose L. *U.S.A.* 41°56N 120°26W **76** F3
Gooty *India* 15°7N 77°41E **45** G3
Gop *India* 22°5N 69°50E **42** H3
Gopalganj *India* 26°28N 84°30E **43** F11
Göppingen *Germany* 48°42N 9°39E **16** D5
Gorakhpur *India* 26°47N 83°23E **43** F10
Goražde *Bos.-H.* 43°38N 18°58E **23** C8
Gorda, Pta. *Nic.* 14°20N 83°10W **88** D3
Gordan B. *Australia* 11°35S 130°10E **60** B5
Gordon *U.S.A.* 42°48N 102°12W **80** D2
Gordon → *Australia* 42°27S 145°30E **63** G4

Gordon Bay *Canada* 45°12N 79°47W **82** A5
Gordon L. *Alta., Canada* 56°30N 110°25W **71** B6
Gordon L. *N.W.T., Canada* 63°5N 113°11W **70** A6
Gordonvale *Australia* 17°5S 145°50E **62** B4
Goré *Chad* 7°59N 16°31E **53** G9
Gore *Ethiopia* 8°12N 35°32E **49** F2
Gore *N.Z.* 46°5S 168°58E **59** G2
Gore Bay *Canada* 45°57N 82°28W **72** C3
Gorey *Ireland* 52°41N 6°18W **10** D5
Gorg *Iran* 29°29N 59°43E **47** D8
Gorgān *Iran* 36°55N 54°30E **47** B7
Gorgona, I. *Colombia* 3°0N 78°10W **92** C3
Gorham *U.S.A.* 44°23N 71°10W **83** B13
Goribidnur = Gauribidanur
India 13°37N 77°32E **45** H3
Goriganga → *India* 29°45N 80°23E **43** E9
Gorinchem *Neths.* 51°50N 4°59E **15** C4
Goris *Armenia* 39°31N 46°22E **19** G8
Gorizia *Italy* 45°56N 13°37E **22** B5
Gorkiy = Nizhniy Novgorod
Russia 56°20N 44°0E **18** C7
Gorkovskoye Vdkhr.
Russia 57°2N 43°4E **18** C7
Gorleston-on-Sea *U.K.* 52°35N 1°44E **13** E9
Görlitz *Germany* 51°9N 14°58E **16** C8
Gorlovka = Horlivka
Ukraine 48°19N 38°5E **19** E6
Gorman *U.S.A.* 34°47N 118°51W **79** L8
Gorna Dzhumayo = Blagoevgrad
Bulgaria 42°2N 23°5E **23** C10
Gorna Oryakhovitsa
Bulgaria 43°7N 25°40E **23** C11
Gorno-Altay □ *Russia* 51°0N 86°0E **26** D9
Gorno-Altaysk *Russia* 51°50N 86°5E **26** D9
Gornozavodsk *Russia* 46°33N 141°50E **27** E15
Gornyatski *Russia* 67°32N 64°3E **18** A11
Gornyy *Russia* 44°57N 133°59E **28** B6
Gorodenka = Horodenka
Ukraine 48°41N 25°29E **17** D13
Gorodok = Horodok
Ukraine 49°46N 23°32E **17** D12
Gorokhov = Horokhiv
Ukraine 50°30N 24°45E **17** C13
Gorong, Kepulauan
Indonesia 3°59S 131°25E **37** E8
Gorongose → *Mozam.* 20°30S 34°40E **57** B5
Gorongoza △ *Mozam.* 18°50S 34°29E **57** A5
Gorontalo *Indonesia* 0°35N 123°5E **37** D6
Gorontalo □ *Indonesia* 0°50N 122°20E **37** D6
Gort *Ireland* 53°3N 8°49W **10** C3
Gorumahisani *India* 22°20N 86°24E **44** C8
Goryeong *S. Korea* 35°44N 128°15E **33** G15
Gorzów Wielkopolski
Poland 52°43N 15°15E **16** B8
Gosford *Australia* 33°23S 151°18E **63** E5
Goshen *Calif., U.S.A.* 36°21N 119°25W **78** J7
Goshen *Ind., U.S.A.* 41°35N 85°50W **81** E11
Goshen *N.Y., U.S.A.* 41°24N 74°20W **83** E10
Goshogawara *Japan* 40°48N 140°27E **28** D10
Goslar *Germany* 51°54N 10°25E **16** C6
Gospič *Croatia* 44°35N 15°23E **16** F8
Gosport *U.K.* 50°48N 1°9W **13** G6
Gosse → *Australia* 19°32S 134°37E **62** B1
Göta älv → *Sweden* 57°42N 11°54E **9** H14
Göta kanal *Sweden* 58°30N 15°58E **9** G16
Götaland *Sweden* 57°30N 14°30E **9** H16
Göteborg *Sweden* 57°43N 11°59E **9** H14
Gotha *Germany* 50°56N 10°42E **16** C6
Gothenburg = Göteborg
Sweden 57°43N 11°59E **9** H14
Gothenburg *U.S.A.* 40°56N 100°10W **80** E3
Gotland *Sweden* 57°30N 18°33E **9** H18
Gotō = Fukue *Japan* 32°41N 128°51E **29** H4
Gotska Sandön *Sweden* 58°24N 19°15E **9** G18
Gōtsu *Japan* 35°0N 132°14E **29** G6
Göttingen *Germany* 51°31N 9°55E **16** C5
Gottwaldov = Zlin
Czech Rep. 49°14N 17°40E **17** D9
Gouda *Neths.* 52°1N 4°42E **15** B4
Gouin, Rés. *Canada* 48°35N 74°40W **72** C5
Goulburn *Australia* 34°44S 149°44E **63** E4
Goulburn Is. *Australia* 11°40S 133°20E **62** A1
Goundam *Mali* 16°27N 3°40W **52** E5
Gourits → *S. Africa* 34°21S 21°52E **56** D3
Gourock *U.K.* 55°57N 4°49W **11** F4
Gouverneur *U.S.A.* 44°20N 75°28W **83** B9
Gove Peninsula
Australia 12°17S 136°49E **62** A2
Governador Valadares
Brazil 18°15S 41°57W **93** G10
Governor's Harbour
Bahamas 25°10N 76°14W **88** A4
Govindgarh *India* 24°23N 81°18E **43** G9
Gowan Ra. *Australia* 25°0S 145°0E **62** D4
Gowanda *U.S.A.* 42°28N 78°56W **82** D6
Gower *U.K.* 51°35N 4°10W **13** F3
Gowna, L. *Ireland* 53°51N 7°34W **10** C4
Goya *Argentina* 29°10S 59°10W **94** B4
Goyang *S. Korea* 37°39N 126°50E **33** F14
Goyder Lagoon *Australia* 27°3S 138°58E **63** D2
Goyllarisquizga *Peru* 10°31S 76°24W **92** F3
Goz Beïda *Chad* 12°10N 21°20E **53** F10
Gozo *Malta* 36°3N 14°15E **25** C1
Graaff-Reinet *S. Africa* 32°13S 24°32E **56** D3
Gračac *Croatia* 44°18N 15°57E **16** F8
Gracias a Dios, C.
Honduras 15°0N 83°10W **88** D3
Graciosa *Azores* 39°4N 28°0W **52** a
Gradiška *Bos.-H.* 45°10N 17°15E **22** B7
Grado *Spain* 43°23N 6°4W **21** A2
Grady *U.S.A.* 34°49N 103°19W **77** J12
Grafham Water *U.K.* 52°19N 0°18W **13** E7
Grafton *Australia* 29°38S 152°58E **63** D5
Grafton *N. Dak., U.S.A.* 48°25N 97°25W **80** A5
Grafton *W. Va., U.S.A.* 39°21N 80°2W **81** F13
Graham *Canada* 49°20N 90°30W **72** C1
Graham *U.S.A.* 33°6N 98°35W **84** E5
Graham, Mt. *U.S.A.* 32°42N 109°52W **77** K9

Graham Bell, Ostrov = Greem-Bell,
Ostrov *Russia* 81°0N 62°0E **26** A7
Graham I. *B.C., Canada* 53°40N 132°30W **70** C2
Graham I. *Nunavut,
Canada* 77°25N 90°30W **69** B13
Graham Land *Antarctica* 65°0S 64°0W **5** C17
Grahamstown *S. Africa* 33°19S 26°31E **56** D4
Grahamsville *U.S.A.* 41°51N 74°33W **83** E10
Grain Coast *W. Afr.* 4°20N 10°0W **52** H3
Grajagan *Indonesia* 8°35S 114°13E **37** K17
Grajaú *Brazil* 5°50S 46°4W **93** E9
Grajaú → *Brazil* 3°41S 44°48W **93** D10
Grampian *U.S.A.* 40°58N 78°37W **82** F6
Grampian Highlands = Grampian
Mts. *U.K.* 56°50N 4°0W **11** E5
Grampian Mts. *U.K.* 56°50N 4°0W **11** E5
Grampians, The
Australia 37°15S 142°20E **63** F3
Gran Canaria *Canary Is.* 27°55N 15°35W **52** C2
Gran Chaco *S. Amer.* 25°0S 61°0W **94** B3
Gran Desierto del Pinacate △
Mexico 31°51N 113°32W **86** A2
Gran Paradiso *Italy* 45°33N 7°17E **20** D7
Gran Sasso d'Itália *Italy* 42°27N 13°42E **22** C5
Granada *Nic.* 11°58N 86°0W **88** D2
Granada *Spain* 37°10N 3°35W **21** D4
Granada *U.S.A.* 38°4N 102°19W **76** G12
Granard *Ireland* 53°47N 7°30W **10** C4
Granbury *U.S.A.* 32°27N 97°47W **84** E6
Granby *Canada* 45°25N 72°45W **83** A12
Granby *U.S.A.* 40°5N 105°56W **76** F11
Grand → *Canada* 42°51N 79°34W **82** D5
Grand → *Mo., U.S.A.* 39°23N 93°7W **80** F7
Grand → *S. Dak., U.S.A.* 45°40N 100°45W **80** C3
Grand-Anse = Portsmouth
Dominica 15°34N 61°27W **89** C7
Grand Bahama I.
Bahamas 26°40N 78°30W **88** A4
Grand Baie *Mauritius* 20°0S 57°35E **55** d
Grand Bank *Canada* 47°6N 55°48W **73** C8
Grand Bassam *Ivory C.* 5°10N 3°49W **52** G5
Grand Bend *Canada* 43°18N 81°45W **82** C3
Grand-Bourg *Guadeloupe* 15°53N 61°19W **88** b
Grand Canal = Da Yunhe →
China 34°25N 120°5E **33** H10
Grand Canyon *U.S.A.* 36°3N 112°9W **77** H7
Grand Canyon △
U.S.A. 36°15N 112°30W **77** H7
Grand Canyon-Parashant △
U.S.A. 36°30N 113°45W **77** H7
Grand Cayman
Cayman Is. 19°20N 81°20W **88** C3
Grand Coulee *U.S.A.* 47°57N 119°0W **76** C4
Grand Coulee Dam
U.S.A. 47°57N 118°59W **76** C4
Grand Falls *Canada* 47°3N 67°44W **73** C6
Grand Falls-Windsor
Canada 48°56N 55°40W **73** C8
Grand Forks *Canada* 49°0N 118°30W **70** D5
Grand Forks *U.S.A.* 47°55N 97°3W **80** B6
Grand Gorge *U.S.A.* 42°21N 74°29W **83** D10
Grand Haven *U.S.A.* 43°4N 86°13W **80** D10
Grand I. *Mich., U.S.A.* 46°31N 86°40W **80** B10
Grand I. *N.Y., U.S.A.* 43°0N 78°58W **82** D6
Grand Island *U.S.A.* 40°55N 98°21W **80** E4
Grand Isle *La., U.S.A.* 29°14N 90°0W **85** G9
Grand Isle *Vt., U.S.A.* 44°43N 73°18W **83** B11
Grand Junction *U.S.A.* 39°4N 108°33W **76** G9
Grand L. *N.B., Canada* 45°57N 66°7W **73** C6
Grand L. *Nfld. & L., Canada* 49°0N 57°30W **73** C8
Grand L. *Nfld. & L.,
Canada* 53°40N 60°30W **73** B7
Grand L. *U.S.A.* 29°55N 92°47W **84** G8
Grand Lake *U.S.A.* 40°15N 105°49W **76** F11
Grand Manan I. *Canada* 44°45N 66°52W **73** D6
Grand Marais *Mich.,
U.S.A.* 46°40N 85°59W **81** B11
Grand Marais *Minn.,
U.S.A.* 47°45N 90°25W **72** C1
Grand-Mère *Canada* 46°36N 72°40W **72** C5
Grand Portage *U.S.A.* 47°58N 89°41W **80** B9
Grand Prairie *U.S.A.* 32°44N 96°59W **84** E6
Grand Rapids *Canada* 53°12N 99°19W **71** C9
Grand Rapids *Mich.,
U.S.A.* 42°58N 85°40W **81** D11
Grand Rapids *Minn.,
U.S.A.* 47°14N 93°31W **80** B7
Grand St-Bernard, Col du
Europe 45°50N 7°10E **20** D7
Grand Staircase-Escalante △
U.S.A. 37°25N 111°33W **77** H8
Grand Teton *U.S.A.* 43°54N 110°50W **76** E8
Grand Teton △ *U.S.A.* 43°50N 110°50W **76** E8
Grand Union Canal *U.K.* 52°7N 0°53W **13** E7
Grande → *Jujuy, Argentina* 24°20S 65°2W **94** A2
Grande → *Mendoza,
Argentina* 36°52S 69°45W **94** D2
Grande → *Bolivia* 15°51S 64°39W **92** G6
Grande → *Bahia, Brazil* 11°30S 44°30W **93** F10
Grande → *Minas Gerais,
Brazil* 20°6S 51°4W **93** H8
Grande, B. *Argentina* 50°30S 68°20W **96** G3
Grande, Rio → *N. Amer.* 25°58N 97°9W **84** J6
Grande Anse *Seychelles* 4°18S 55°45E **55** b
Grande Baleine →
Canada 55°16N 77°47W **72** A4
Grande Cache *Canada* 53°53N 119°8W **70** C5
Grande Comore
Comoros Is. 11°35S 43°20E **55** a
Grande-Entrée *Canada* 47°30N 61°40W **73** C7
Grande Prairie *Canada* 55°10N 118°50W **70** B5
Grande-Rivière *Canada* 48°26N 64°30W **73** C7
Grande-Terre *Guadeloupe* 16°20N 61°25W **88** b
Grande-Vallée *Canada* 49°14N 65°8W **73** C6
Grande Vigie, Pte. de la
Guadeloupe 16°32N 61°27W **88** b
Grandfalls *U.S.A.* 31°20N 102°51W **84** F3
Grands-Jardins △
Canada 47°41N 70°51W **73** C5
Grandview *Canada* 51°10N 100°42W **71** C8

Grandview *U.S.A.* 46°15N 119°54W **76** C4
Graneros *Chile* 34°5S 70°45W **94** C1
Grangemouth *U.K.* 56°1N 3°42W **11** E5
Granger *U.S.A.* 41°35N 109°58W **76** F9
Grangeville *U.S.A.* 45°56N 116°7W **76** D5
Granisle *Canada* 54°53N 126°13W **70** C3
Granite City *U.S.A.* 38°42N 90°8W **80** F8
Granite Falls *U.S.A.* 44°49N 95°33W **80** C6
Granite L. *Canada* 48°8N 57°5W **73** C8
Granite Mt. *U.S.A.* 33°5N 116°28W **79** M10
Granite Pk. *U.S.A.* 45°10N 109°48W **76** D9
Graniteville *U.S.A.* 44°8N 72°29W **83** B12
Granity *N.Z.* 41°39S 171°51E **59** D3
Granja *Brazil* 3°7S 40°50W **93** D10
Granollers *Spain* 41°39N 2°18E **21** B7
Grant *U.S.A.* 40°50N 101°43W **80** E3
Grant, Mt. *U.S.A.* 38°34N 118°48W **76** G4
Grant City *U.S.A.* 40°29N 94°25W **80** E6
Grant I. *Australia* 11°10S 132°52E **60** B5
Grant Range *U.S.A.* 38°30N 115°25W **76** G6
Grantham *U.K.* 52°55N 0°38W **12** E7
Grants *U.S.A.* 35°9N 107°52W **77** J10
Grants Pass *U.S.A.* 42°26N 123°19W **76** E2
Grantsville *U.S.A.* 40°36N 112°28W **76** F7
Granville *France* 48°50N 1°35W **20** B3
Granville *N. Dak., U.S.A.* 48°16N 100°47W **80** A3
Granville *N.Y., U.S.A.* 43°24N 73°16W **83** C11
Granville *Ohio, U.S.A.* 40°4N 82°31W **82** F2
Granville L. *Canada* 56°18N 100°30W **71** B8
Graskop *S. Africa* 24°56S 30°49E **57** B5
Grass → *Canada* 56°3N 96°33W **71** B9
Grass Range *U.S.A.* 47°2N 108°48W **76** C9
Grass River △ *Canada* 54°40N 100°50W **71** C8
Grass Valley *Calif., U.S.A.* 39°13N 121°4W **78** F6
Grass Valley *Oreg.,
U.S.A.* 45°22N 120°47W **76** D3
Grasse *France* 43°38N 6°56E **20** E7
Grassflat *U.S.A.* 41°0N 78°6W **82** E6
Grasslands △ *Canada* 49°11N 107°38W **71** D7
Grassy *Australia* 40°3S 144°5E **63** G3
Graulhet *France* 43°45N 1°59E **20** E4
Gravelbourg *Canada* 49°50N 106°35W **71** D7
's-Gravenhage *Neths.* 52°7N 4°17E **15** B4
Gravenhurst *Canada* 44°52N 79°20W **82** B5
Gravesend *Australia* 29°35S 150°20E **63** D5
Gravesend *U.K.* 51°26N 0°22E **13** F8
Gravois, Pointe-à- *Haiti* 18°2N 73°56W **89** C5
Grayling *U.S.A.* 44°40N 84°43W **81** C11
Grays *U.K.* 51°28N 0°21E **13** F8
Grays Harbor *U.S.A.* 46°59N 124°1W **78** D2
Grays L. *U.S.A.* 43°4N 111°26W **76** E8
Grays River *U.S.A.* 46°21N 123°37W **78** D3
Graz *Austria* 47°4N 15°27E **16** E8
Greasy L. *Canada* 62°55N 122°12W **70** A4
Great Abaco I. = Abaco I.
Bahamas 26°25N 77°10W **88** A4
Great Artesian Basin
Australia 23°0S 144°0E **62** C3
Great Australian Bight
Australia 33°30S 130°0E **61** F5
Great Bahama Bank
Bahamas 23°15N 78°0W **88** B4
Great Barrier I. *N.Z.* 36°11S 175°25E **59** B5
Great Barrier Reef
Australia 18°0S 146°50E **62** B4
Great Barrier Reef △
Australia 20°0S 150°0E **62** B4
Great Barrington
U.S.A. 42°12N 73°22W **83** D11
Great Basalt Wall △
Australia 19°52S 145°43E **62** B4
Great Basin *U.S.A.* 40°0N 117°0W **76** G5
Great Basin △ *U.S.A.* 38°56N 114°15W **76** G6
Great Basses *Sri Lanka* 6°11N 81°29E **45** L5
Great Bear → *Canada* 65°0N 126°0W **68** C7
Great Bear L. *Canada* 65°30N 120°0W **68** C8
Great Belt = Store Bælt
Denmark 55°20N 11°0E **9** J14
Great Bend *Kans., U.S.A.* 38°22N 98°46W **80** F4
Great Bend *Pa., U.S.A.* 41°58N 75°45W **83** E9
Great Blasket I. *Ireland* 52°6N 10°32W **10** D1
Great Britain *Europe* 54°0N 2°15W **6** E5
Great Camanoe
Br. Virgin Is. 18°30N 64°35W **89** e
Great Channel *Asia* 6°0N 94°0E **45** L11
Great Coco I. = Koko Kyunzu
Burma 14°7N 93°22E **45** G11
Great Codroy *Canada* 47°51N 59°16W **73** C8
Great Divide, The = Great Dividing
Ra. *Australia* 23°0S 146°0E **62** C4
Great Divide Basin *U.S.A.* 42°0N 108°0W **76** E9
Great Dividing Ra.
Australia 23°0S 146°0E **62** C4
Great Driffield = Driffield
U.K. 54°0N 0°26W **12** C7
Great Exuma I. *Bahamas* 23°30N 75°50W **88** B4
Great Falls *U.S.A.* 47°30N 111°17W **76** C8
Great Fish = Groot-Vis →
S. Africa 33°28S 27°5E **56** D4
Great Guana Cay
Bahamas 24°0N 76°20W **88** B4
Great Himalayan △ *India* 31°30N 77°30E **42** D7
Great Inagua I. *Bahamas* 21°0N 73°20W **89** B5
Great Indian Desert = Thar Desert
India 28°0N 72°0E **42** F5
Great Karoo *S. Africa* 31°55S 21°0E **56** D3
Great Khingan Mts. = Da Hinggan
Ling *China* 48°0N 121°0E **31** B13
Great Lake *Australia* 41°50S 146°40E **63** G4
Great Lakes *N. Amer.* 46°0N 84°0W **66** E11
Great Limpopo Transfrontier △
Africa 23°0S 31°45E **57** B5
Great Malvern *U.K.* 52°7N 2°18W **13** E5
Great Miami → *U.S.A.* 39°7N 84°49W **81** F11
Great Nicobar *India* 7°0N 93°50E **45** L11
Great Ormes Head *U.K.* 53°20N 3°52W **12** D4
Great Ouse → *U.K.* 52°48N 0°21E **12** E8
Great Palm I. *Australia* 18°45S 146°40E **62** B4
Great Pedro Bluff *Jamaica* 17°51N 77°44W **88** a

Great Pee Dee →
U.S.A. 33°21N 79°10W **85** E15
Great Plains *N. Amer.* 47°0N 105°0W **66** E9
Great Ruaha → *Tanzania* 7°56S 37°52E **54** F7
Great Sacandaga L.
U.S.A. 43°6N 74°16W **83** C10
Great Saint Bernard Pass = Grand
St-Bernard, Col du
Europe 45°50N 7°10E **20** D7
Great Salt Desert = Kavīr, Dasht-e
Iran 34°30N 55°0E **47** C7
Great Salt L. *U.S.A.* 41°15N 112°40W **76** F7
Great Salt Lake Desert
U.S.A. 40°50N 113°30W **76** F7
Great Sand Dunes △
U.S.A. 37°48N 105°45W **77** H11
Great Sandy △ *Australia* 26°13S 153°2E **63** D5
Great Sandy Desert
Australia 21°0S 124°0E **60** D3
Great Sangi = Sangihe, Pulau
Indonesia 3°35N 125°30E **37** D7
Great Sea Reef *Fiji* 16°15S 179°0E **59** a
Great Sitkin I. *U.S.A.* 52°3N 176°6W **74** E4
Great Skellig *Ireland* 51°47N 10°33W **10** E1
Great Slave L. *Canada* 61°23N 115°38W **70** A5
Great Smoky Mts. △
U.S.A. 35°40N 83°40W **85** D13
Great Stour = Stour →
U.K. 51°18N 1°22E **13** F9
Great Victoria Desert
Australia 29°30S 126°30E **61** E4
Great Wall *Antarctica* 62°30S 58°0W **5** C18
Great Wall *China* 38°30N 109°30E **32** E5
Great Whernside *U.K.* 54°10N 1°58W **12** C6
Great Yarmouth *U.K.* 52°37N 1°44E **13** E9
Great Zab = Zāb al Kabīr →
Iraq 36°1N 43°24E **46** B4
Greater Antilles *W. Indies* 17°40N 74°0W **89** C5
Greater London □ *U.K.* 51°31N 0°6W **13** F7
Greater Manchester □
U.K. 53°30N 2°15W **12** D5
Greater Sudbury *Canada* 46°30N 81°0W **72** C3
Greater Sunda Is. *Indonesia* 7°0S 112°0E **36** F4
Gredos, Sierra de *Spain* 40°20N 5°0W **21** B3
Greece *U.S.A.* 43°13N 77°41W **82** C7
Greece ■ *Europe* 40°0N 23°0E **23** E9
Greeley *Colo., U.S.A.* 40°25N 104°42W **76** F11
Greeley *Nebr., U.S.A.* 41°33N 98°32W **80** E4
Greely Fd. *Canada* 80°30N 85°0W **69** A15
Greem-Bell, Ostrov *Russia* 81°0N 62°0E **26** A7
Green → *Ky., U.S.A.* 37°54N 87°30W **80** G10
Green → *Utah, U.S.A.* 38°11N 109°53W **76** G9
Green B. *U.S.A.* 45°0N 87°30W **80** C10
Green C. *Australia* 37°13S 150°1E **63** F5
Green Cove Springs
U.S.A. 29°59N 81°42W **85** G14
Green I. = Lütao
Taiwan 22°40N 121°30E **35** F13
Green Lake *Canada* 54°17N 107°47W **71** C7
Green Mts. *U.S.A.* 43°45N 72°45W **83** C12
Green River *Utah,
U.S.A.* 38°59N 110°10W **76** G8
Green River *Wyo.,
U.S.A.* 41°32N 109°28W **76** F9
Green Valley *U.S.A.* 31°52N 110°56W **77** L8
Greenbank *U.S.A.* 48°6N 122°34W **78** B4
Greenbush *Mich., U.S.A.* 44°35N 83°19W **82** B1
Greenbush *Minn., U.S.A.* 48°42N 96°11W **80** A5
Greencastle *U.S.A.* 39°38N 86°52W **80** F10
Greene *U.S.A.* 42°20N 75°46W **83** D9
Greeneville *U.S.A.* 36°10N 82°50W **85** C13
Greenfield *Calif., U.S.A.* 36°19N 121°15W **78** J5
Greenfield *Calif., U.S.A.* 35°15N 119°0W **79** K8
Greenfield *Ind., U.S.A.* 39°47N 85°46W **81** F11
Greenfield *Iowa, U.S.A.* 41°18N 94°28W **80** E6
Greenfield *Mass., U.S.A.* 42°35N 72°36W **83** D12
Greenfield *Mo., U.S.A.* 37°25N 93°51W **80** G7
Greenland ☑ *N. Amer.* 66°0N 45°0W **67** C15
Greenland Sea *Arctic* 73°0N 10°0W **4** B7
Greenock *U.K.* 55°57N 4°46W **11** F4
Greenore *Ireland* 54°1N 6°9W **10** B5
Greenore Pt. *Ireland* 52°14N 6°19W **10** D5
Greenough *Australia* 28°58S 114°43E **61** E1
Greenough → *Australia* 28°51S 114°38E **61** E1
Greenough Pt. *Canada* 44°58N 81°26W **82** B3
Greenport *U.S.A.* 41°6N 72°22W **83** E12
Greensboro *Ga., U.S.A.* 33°35N 83°11W **85** E13
Greensboro *N.C., U.S.A.* 36°4N 79°48W **85** C15
Greensboro *Vt., U.S.A.* 44°36N 72°18W **83** B12
Greensburg *Ind., U.S.A.* 39°20N 85°29W **81** F11
Greensburg *Kans., U.S.A.* 37°36N 99°18W **80** G4
Greensburg *Pa., U.S.A.* 40°18N 79°33W **82** F5
Greenstone = Geraldton
Canada 49°44N 87°10W **72** C2
Greenstone Pt. *U.K.* 57°55N 5°37W **11** D3
Greenvale *Australia* 18°59S 145°7E **62** B4
Greenville *Liberia* 5°1N 9°6W **52** G4
Greenville *Ala., U.S.A.* 31°50N 86°38W **85** F11
Greenville *Calif., U.S.A.* 40°8N 120°57W **78** E6
Greenville *Maine, U.S.A.* 45°28N 69°35W **81** C19
Greenville *Mich., U.S.A.* 43°11N 85°15W **81** D11
Greenville *Miss., U.S.A.* 33°24N 91°4W **85** E9
Greenville *Mo., U.S.A.* 37°8N 90°27W **80** G8
Greenville *N.C., U.S.A.* 35°37N 77°23W **85** D16
Greenville *N.H., U.S.A.* 42°46N 71°49W **83** D13
Greenville *N.Y., U.S.A.* 42°25N 74°1W **83** D10
Greenville *Ohio, U.S.A.* 40°6N 84°38W **81** E11
Greenville *Pa., U.S.A.* 41°24N 80°23W **82** E4
Greenville *S.C., U.S.A.* 34°51N 82°24W **85** D13
Greenville *Tex., U.S.A.* 33°8N 96°7W **84** E6
Greenwater Lake △
Canada 52°32N 103°30W **71** C8
Greenwich *Conn., U.S.A.* 41°2N 73°38W **83** E11
Greenwich *N.Y., U.S.A.* 43°5N 73°30W **83** C11
Greenwich *Ohio, U.S.A.* 41°2N 82°31W **82** E2
Greenwood *Canada* 49°10N 118°40W **70** D5
Greenwood *Ark., U.S.A.* 35°13N 94°16W **84** D7
Greenwood *Ind., U.S.A.* 39°37N 86°7W **80** F10

Greenwood *Miss., U.S.A.* 33°31N 90°11W **85** E9
Greenwood *S.C., U.S.A.* 34°12N 82°10W **85** D13
Greenwood, Mt. *Australia* 13°48S 130°4E **60** B5
Gregory *U.S.A.* 43°14N 99°26W **80** D4
Gregory → *Australia* 17°53S 139°17E **62** B2
Gregory, L. *S. Austral.,
Australia* 28°55S 139°0E **63** D2
Gregory, L. *W. Austral.,
Australia* 20°0S 127°40E **60** D4
Gregory, L. *W. Austral.,
Australia* 25°38S 119°58E **61** E2
Gregory △ *Australia* 15°38S 131°15E **60** C5
Gregory Downs
Australia 18°35S 138°45E **62** B2
Gregory Ra. *Queens.,
Australia* 19°30S 143°40E **62** B3
Gregory Ra. *W. Austral.,
Australia* 21°20S 121°12E **60** D3
Greifswald *Germany* 54°5N 13°23E **16** A7
Greiz *Germany* 50°39N 12°10E **16** C7
Gremikha *Russia* 67°59N 39°47E **18** A6
Grenaa *Denmark* 56°25N 10°53E **9** H14
Grenada *U.S.A.* 33°47N 89°49W **85** E10
Grenada ■ *W. Indies* 12°10N 61°40W **89** D7
Grenadier I. *U.S.A.* 44°3N 76°22W **83** B8
Grenadines, The
St. Vincent 12°40N 61°20W **89** D7
Grenen *Denmark* 57°44N 10°40E **9** H14
Grenfell *Australia* 33°52S 148°8E **63** E4
Grenfell *Canada* 50°30N 102°56W **71** C8
Grenoble *France* 45°12N 5°42E **20** D6
Grenville, C. *Australia* 12°0S 143°13E **62** A3
Grenville Chan. *Canada* 53°40N 129°46W **70** C3
Gresham *U.S.A.* 45°30N 122°25W **78** E4
Gresik *Indonesia* 7°13S 112°38E **37** G15
Gretna *U.K.* 55°0N 3°3W **11** F5
Grevenmacher *Lux.* 49°41N 6°26E **15** E6
Grey → *Canada* 47°34N 57°6W **73** C8
Grey → *N.Z.* 42°27S 171°12E **59** E3
Grey, C. *Australia* 13°0S 136°35E **62** A2
Grey Is. *Canada* 50°50N 55°35W **69** G20
Grey Ra. *Australia* 27°0S 143°30E **63** D3
Greybull *U.S.A.* 44°30N 108°3W **76** D9
Greymouth *N.Z.* 42°29S 171°13E **59** E3
Greystones *Ireland* 53°9N 6°5W **10** C5
Greytown *N.Z.* 41°5S 175°29E **59** D5
Greytown *S. Africa* 29°1S 30°36E **57** C5
Gribbell I. *Canada* 53°23N 129°0W **70** C3
Gridley *U.S.A.* 39°22N 121°42W **78** F5
Griekwastad *S. Africa* 28°49S 23°15E **56** C3
Griffin *U.S.A.* 33°15N 84°16W **85** E12
Griffith *Australia* 34°18S 146°2E **63** E4
Griffith *Canada* 45°15N 77°10W **82** A7
Griffith I. *Canada* 44°50N 80°55W **82** B4
Grimari = Hrymayliv
Ukraine 49°20N 26°5E **17** D14
Grimes *U.S.A.* 39°4N 121°54W **78** F5
Grimsay *U.K.* 57°29N 7°14W **11** D1
Grimsby *Canada* 43°12N 79°34W **82** C5
Grimsby *U.K.* 53°34N 0°5W **12** D7
Grimsey *Iceland* 66°33N 17°58W **8** C5
Grimshaw *Canada* 56°10N 117°40W **70** B5
Grimstad *Norway* 58°20N 8°35E **9** G13
Grindstone I. *U.S.A.* 44°17N 76°27W **83** B8
Grinnell *U.S.A.* 41°45N 92°43W **80** E7
Grinnell Pen. *Canada* 76°40N 95°0W **69** B13
Griomasaigh = Grimsay
U.K. 57°29N 7°14W **11** D1
Gris-Nez, C. *France* 50°52N 1°35E **20** A4
Grise Fiord *Canada* 76°25N 82°57W **69** B15
Groais I. *Canada* 50°55N 55°35W **73** B8
Groblersdal *S. Africa* 25°15S 29°25E **57** C4
Grodno = Hrodna
Belarus 53°42N 23°52E **17** B12
Grodzyanka = Hrodzyanka
Belarus 53°31N 28°42E **17** B15
Groesbeck *U.S.A.* 31°31N 96°32W **84** F6
Grójec *Poland* 51°50N 20°58E **17** C11
Grong *Norway* 64°25N 12°8E **8** D15
Groningen *Neths.* 53°15N 6°35E **15** A6
Groningen □ *Neths.* 53°16N 6°40E **15** A6
Groom *U.S.A.* 35°12N 101°6W **84** D4
Groot → *S. Africa* 33°45S 24°36E **56** D3
Groot-Berg → *S. Africa* 32°47S 18°8E **56** D2
Groot-Brakrivier *S. Africa* 34°2S 22°18E **56** D3
Groot Karasberge
Namibia 27°20S 18°40E **56** D2
Groot-Kei → *S. Africa* 32°41S 28°22E **57** D4
Groot-Vis → *S. Africa* 33°28S 27°5E **56** D4
Grootdrink *S. Africa* 28°33S 21°42E **56** C3
Groote Eylandt *Australia* 14°0S 136°40E **62** A2
Groote Peel △ *Neths.* 51°20N 5°48E **15** C5
Grootfontein *Namibia* 19°31S 18°6E **56** A2
Grootlaagte → *Africa* 20°55S 21°27E **56** B3
Grootvloer → *S. Africa* 30°0S 20°40E **56** D3
Gros C. *Canada* 61°59N 113°32W **70** A6
Gros Islet *St. Lucia* 14°5N 60°58W **89** f
Gros Morne △ *Canada* 49°40N 57°50W **73** C8
Gros Piton *St. Lucia* 13°49N 61°5W **89** f
Gros Piton Pt. *St. Lucia* 13°49N 61°5W **89** f
Grosse Point *U.S.A.* 42°23N 82°54W **82** D2
Grosser Arber *Germany* 49°6N 13°8E **16** D7
Grosseto *Italy* 42°46N 11°8E **22** C4
Grossglockner *Austria* 47°5N 12°40E **16** E7
Groswater B. *Canada* 54°20N 57°40W **73** B8
Groton *Conn., U.S.A.* 41°21N 72°5W **83** E12
Groton *N.Y., U.S.A.* 42°36N 76°22W **83** D8
Groton *S. Dak., U.S.A.* 45°27N 98°6W **80** C4
Grouard Mission *Canada* 55°33N 116°9W **70** B5
Groulx, Mts. *Canada* 51°27N 68°41W **73** B6
Groundhog → *Canada* 48°45N 82°58W **72** C3
Grouw *Neths.* 53°5N 5°51E **15** A5
Grove City *U.S.A.* 41°10N 80°5W **82** E4
Grove Hill *U.S.A.* 31°42N 87°47W **85** F11
Groveland *U.S.A.* 37°50N 120°14W **78** H6
Grover Beach *U.S.A.* 35°7N 120°37W **79** K6
Groves *U.S.A.* 29°57N 93°54W **84** D8
Groveton *U.S.A.* 44°36N 71°31W **83** B13
Grovetown *U.S.A.* 33°27N 82°12W **85** E13
Groznyy *Russia* 43°20N 45°45E **19** F8

Grudziądz *Poland* 53°30N 18°47E **17** B10
Gruinard B. *U.K.* 57°56N 5°35W **11** D3
Grundy Center *U.S.A.* 42°22N 92°47W **80** D7
Gruver *U.S.A.* 36°16N 101°24W **84** C4
Gryazi *Russia* 52°30N 39°58E **18** D6
Gryazovets *Russia* 58°50N 40°12E **18** C7
Grytviken *S. Georgia* 54°19S 36°33W **96** G9
Gua *India* 22°18N 85°20E **43** H11
Gua Musang *Malaysia* 4°53N 101°58E **39** K3
Guacanayabo, G. de
  Cuba 20°40N 77°20W **88** B4
Guachípas → *Argentina* 25°40S 65°30W **94** B2
Guadalajara *Mexico* 20°40N 103°20W **86** C4
Guadalajara *Spain* 40°37N 3°12W **21** B4
Guadalaviar = Turia →
  Spain 39°27N 0°19W **21** C5
Guadalcanal *Solomon Is.* 9°32S 160°12E **58** B9
Guadales *Argentina* 34°30S 67°55W **94** C2
Guadalete → *Spain* 36°35N 6°13W **21** D2
Guadalquivir → *Spain* 36°47N 6°22W **21** D2
Guadalupe = Guadeloupe ☑
  W. Indies 16°15N 61°40W **88** b
Guadalupe *Mexico* 22°45N 102°31W **86** C4
Guadalupe *U.S.A.* 34°58N 120°34W **79** L6
Guadalupe → *U.S.A.* 28°27N 96°47W **84** G6
Guadalupe, Sierra de
  Spain 39°28N 5°30W **21** C3
Guadalupe de Bravo
  Mexico 31°23N 106°7W **86** A3
Guadalupe I. *Pac. Oc.* 29°0N 118°50W **66** G8
Guadalupe Mts. △
  U.S.A. 31°40N 104°30W **84** F2
Guadalupe Peak *U.S.A.* 31°50N 104°52W **84** F2
Guadalupe y Calvo
  Mexico 26°6N 106°58W **86** B3
Guadarrama, Sierra de
  Spain 41°0N 4°0W **21** B4
Guadeloupe ☑ *W. Indies* 16°15N 61°40W **88** b
Guadeloupe △ *Guadeloupe* 16°10N 61°40W **88** b
Guadeloupe Passage
  W. Indies 16°50N 62°15W **89** C7
Guadiana → *Portugal* 37°14N 7°22W **21** D2
Guadix *Spain* 37°18N 3°11W **21** D4
Guafo, Boca del *Chile* 43°35S 74°0W **96** E2
Guáhán = Guam ☑
  Pac. Oc. 13°27N 144°45E **64** F6
Guaico *Trin. & Tob.* 10°35N 61°9W **93** K15
Guainía → *Colombia* 2°1N 67°7W **92** C5
Guaíra *Brazil* 24°5S 54°10W **95** A5
Guaíra □ *Paraguay* 25°45S 56°30W **94** B4
Guaire = Gorey *Ireland* 52°41N 6°18W **10** D5
Guaitecas, Is. *Chile* 44°0S 74°30W **96** E2
Guajará-Mirim *Brazil* 10°50S 65°20W **92** F5
Guajira, Pen. de la
  Colombia 12°0N 72°0W **92** A4
Gualán *Guatemala* 15°8N 89°22W **88** C2
Gualeguay *Argentina* 33°10S 59°14W **94** C4
Gualeguaychú *Argentina* 33°3S 59°31W **94** C4
Gualequay → *Argentina* 33°19S 59°39W **94** C4
Guam ☑ *Pac. Oc.* 13°27N 144°45E **64** F6
Guamini *Argentina* 37°1S 62°28W **94** D3
Guamúchil *Mexico* 25°28N 108°6W **86** B3
Guana I. *Br. Virgin Is.* 18°30N 64°30W **89** e
Guanabacoa *Cuba* 23°8N 82°18W **88** B3
Guanacaste, Cordillera de
  Costa Rica 10°40N 85°4W **88** D2
Guanacaste △ *Costa Rica* 10°57N 85°30W **88** D2
Guanacevi *Mexico* 25°56N 105°57W **86** B3
Guanahani = San Salvador I.
  Bahamas 24°0N 74°30W **89** B5
Guanaja *Honduras* 16°30N 85°55W **88** C2
Guanajay *Cuba* 22°56N 82°42W **88** B3
Guanajuato *Mexico* 21°1N 101°15W **86** C4
Guanajuato □ *Mexico* 21°1N 101°0W **86** C4
Guandacol *Argentina* 29°30S 68°40W **94** B2
Guandi Shan *China* 37°53N 111°29E **32** F6
Guane *Cuba* 22°10N 84°7W **88** B3
Guang'an *China* 30°28N 106°35E **34** B6
Guangchang *China* 26°50N 116°21E **35** D11
Guangde *China* 30°54N 119°25E **35** B12
Guangdong □ *China* 23°0N 113°0E **35** F9
Guangfeng *China* 28°20N 118°15E **35** C12
Guanghan *China* 30°58N 104°17E **34** B5
Guangling *China* 39°47N 114°22E **32** E8
Guangnan *China* 24°5N 105°4E **34** E5
Guangning *China* 23°40N 112°22E **35** F9
Guangrao *China* 37°5N 118°25E **33** F10
Guangshui *China* 31°37N 114°0E **35** B10
Guangshun *China* 26°8N 106°21E **34** D6
Guangwu *China* 37°48N 105°57E **32** F3
Guangxi Zhuangzu Zizhiqu □
  China 24°0N 109°0E **34** F7
Guangyuan *China* 32°26N 105°51E **32** H3
Guangze *China* 27°30N 117°12E **35** D11
Guanica *Puerto Rico* 17°58N 66°55W **89** d
Guanipa → *Venezuela* 9°56N 62°26W **92** B6
Guanling *China* 25°56N 105°35E **34** E5
Guannan *China* 34°8N 119°21E **33** G10
Guantánamo *Cuba* 20°10N 75°14W **89** B4
Guantánamo B. *Cuba* 19°59N 75°0W **89** C4
Guantao *China* 36°42N 115°25E **32** F8
Guanting Shuiku *China* 40°14N 115°35E **32** D8
Guanyang *China* 25°30N 111°8E **35** E8
Guanyun *China* 34°20N 119°18E **33** G10
Guapay = Grande →
  Bolivia 15°51S 64°39W **92** G6
Guápiles *Costa Rica* 10°10N 83°46W **88** D3
Guapo B. *Trin. & Tob.* 10°12N 61°41W **93** K15
Guaporé *Brazil* 28°51S 51°54W **95** B5
Guaporé → *Brazil* 11°55S 65°4W **92** F5
Guaqui *Bolivia* 16°41S 68°54W **92** G5
Guaramacal △ *Venezuela* 9°13N 70°12W **89** E5
Guarapari *Brazil* 20°40S 40°30W **95** A7
Guarapuava *Brazil* 25°20S 51°30W **95** B5
Guaratinguetá *Brazil* 22°49S 45°9W **95** A6
Guaratuba *Brazil* 25°53S 48°38W **95** B6
Guarda *Portugal* 40°32N 7°20W **21** B2
Guardafui, C. = Asir, Ras
  Somalia 11°55N 51°10E **49** E5
Guárico □ *Venezuela* 8°40N 66°35W **92** B5

Guarujá *Brazil* 24°2S 46°25W **95** A6
Guarulhos *Brazil* 23°29S 46°33W **95** A6
Guasave *Mexico* 25°34N 108°27W **86** B3
Guasdualito *Venezuela* 7°15N 70°44W **92** B4
Guatemala *Guatemala* 14°40N 90°22W **88** C1
Guatemala ■ *Cent. Amer.* 15°40N 90°30W **88** C1
Guatemala Basin *Pac. Oc.* 11°0N 95°0W **65** F18
Guatemala Trench
  Pac. Oc. 14°0N 95°0W **66** H10
Guatopo △ *Venezuela* 10°5N 66°30W **89** D6
Guatuaro Pt.
  Trin. & Tob. 10°19N 60°59W **93** K16
Guaviare → *Colombia* 4°3N 67°44W **92** C5
Guaxupé *Brazil* 21°10S 47°5W **95** A6
Guayaguayare
  Trin. & Tob. 10°8N 61°2W **93** K15
Guayama *Puerto Rico* 17°59N 66°7W **89** d
Guayaquil *Ecuador* 2°15S 79°52W **92** D3
Guayaquil *Mexico* 29°59N 115°4W **86** B1
Guayaquil, G. de *Ecuador* 3°10S 81°0W **92** D2
Guaymas *Mexico* 27°56N 110°54W **86** B2
Gubbi *India* 13°19N 76°56E **45** H3
Gubkin *Russia* 51°17N 37°32E **19** D6
Gubkinskiy *Russia* 64°27N 76°36E **26** C8
Gucheng *China* 32°20N 111°30E **35** A8
Gudalur *India* 11°30N 76°29E **45** J3
Gudbrandsdalen *Norway* 61°33N 10°10E **8** F14
Gudu Barrage *Pakistan* 28°30N 69°50E **42** E3
Gudivada *India* 16°30N 81°3E **45** F5
Gudiyattam *India* 12°57N 78°55E **45** H4
Gudur *India* 14°12N 79°55E **45** G4
Guecho = Algorta *Spain* 43°21N 2°59W **21** A4
Guékédou *Guinea* 8°40N 10°5W **52** G3
Guelmim *Morocco* 28°56N 10°0W **52** C3
Guelph *Canada* 43°35N 80°20W **82** C4
Guéret *France* 46°11N 1°51E **20** C4
Guerneville *U.S.A.* 38°30N 123°0W **78** G4
Guernica = Gernika-Lumo
  Spain 43°19N 2°40W **21** A4
Guernsey *U.S.A.* 42°16N 104°45W **76** E11
Guernsey *U.K.* 49°26N 2°35W **13** H5
Guerrara *Algeria* 32°51N 4°22E **52** B6
Guerrero □ *Mexico* 17°40N 100°0W **87** D5
Güğher *Iran* 29°28N 56°27E **47** D8
Gui Jiang → *China* 23°30N 111°15E **35** F8
Guia Lopes da Laguna
  Brazil 21°26S 56°7W **95** A4
Guiana Highlands
  S. Amer. 5°10N 60°40W **90** C4
Guichi *China* 30°39N 117°27E **35** B11
Guiding *China* 26°34N 107°11E **34** D6
Guidong *China* 26°7N 113°57E **35** D9
Guidónia-Montecélio *Italy* 42°1N 12°45E **22** C5
Guigang *China* 23°8N 109°35E **34** F7
Guijá *Mozam.* 24°27S 33°0E **57** B5
Guildford *U.K.* 51°14N 0°34W **13** F7
Guilford *U.S.A.* 41°17N 72°41W **83** E12
Guilin *China* 25°18N 110°15E **35** E8
Guillaume-Delisle, L.
  Canada 56°15N 76°17W **72** A4
Guimarães *Portugal* 41°28N 8°24W **21** B1
Guimaras □ *Phil.* 10°35N 122°37E **37** B6
Guinda *U.S.A.* 38°50N 122°12W **78** G4
Guinea ■ *W. Afr.* 10°20N 11°30W **52** F3
Guinea, Gulf of *Atl. Oc.* 3°0N 2°30E **51** F4
Guinea-Bissau ■ *Africa* 12°0N 15°0W **52** F3
Güines *Cuba* 22°50N 82°0W **88** B3
Guingamp *France* 48°34N 3°10W **20** B2
Guiping *China* 23°21N 110°2E **35** F8
Güiria *Venezuela* 10°32N 62°18W **93** K14
Guiuan *Phil.* 11°5N 125°55E **37** B7
Guixi *China* 28°16N 117°15E **35** C11
Guiyang *Guizhou, China* 26°32N 106°40E **34** D6
Guiyang *Hunan, China* 25°46N 112°42E **35** E9
Guizhou □ *China* 27°0N 107°0E **34** D6
Gujar Khan *Pakistan* 33°16N 73°19E **42** C5
Gujarat □ *India* 23°20N 71°0E **42** H4
Gujiang *China* 27°11N 114°47E **35** D10
Gujō *Japan* 35°45N 136°57E **29** G8
Gujranwala *Pakistan* 32°10N 74°12E **42** C6
Gujrat *Pakistan* 32°40N 74°2E **42** C6
Gulbarga = Kalaburagi
  India 17°20N 76°50E **44** F3
Gulbene *Latvia* 57°8N 26°52E **9** H22
Guledagudda *India* 16°3N 75°48E **45** F2
Gulf, The = Persian Gulf
  Asia 27°0N 50°0E **47** E6
Gulf Islands ⌐ *U.S.A.* 30°10N 87°10W **85** F11
Gulfport *U.S.A.* 30°22N 89°6W **85** F10
Gulgong *Australia* 32°20S 149°49E **63** E4
Gulian *China* 52°56N 122°21E **31** A13
Gulin *China* 28°1N 105°50E **34** C5
Gulistan *Pakistan* 30°30N 66°35E **42** D2
Gulja = Yining *China* 43°58N 81°10E **30** C5
Gull Lake *Canada* 50°10N 108°29W **71** C7
Güllük *Turkey* 37°14N 27°35E **23** F12
Gulmarg *India* 34°3N 74°25E **43** B6
Gulong → *Australia* 19°53S 147°41E **62** B4
Gulu *Uganda* 2°48N 32°17E **54** D6
Gumal → *Pakistan* 31°40N 71°50E **42** D4
Gumbaz *Pakistan* 30°2N 69°0E **42** D3
Gumel *Nigeria* 12°39N 9°22E **52** F7
Gumi *S. Korea* 36°10N 128°12E **33** F15
Gumla *India* 23°3N 84°33E **43** H11
Gumlu *Australia* 19°53S 147°41E **62** B4
Gumzai *Indonesia* 5°28S 134°42E **37** F8
Guna *India* 24°40N 77°19E **42** G7
Gunbalanya *Australia* 12°20S 133°4E **60** B5
Gundarehi *India* 20°57N 81°17E **44** D5
Gundlakamma → *India* 15°30N 80°15E **45** G5
Gundlupet *India* 11°48N 76°41E **45** J3
Gunisao → *Canada* 53°56N 97°53W **71** C9
Gunisao L. *Canada* 53°33N 96°15W **71** C9
Gunjyal *Pakistan* 32°20N 71°55E **42** C4
Gunma □ *Japan* 36°30N 138°20E **29** F9
Gunnbjørn Fjeld
  Greenland 68°55N 29°47W **4** C6

Gunnedah *Australia* 30°59S 150°15E **63** E5
Gunnewin *Australia* 25°59S 148°33E **63** D4
Gunningbar Cr. →
  Australia 31°14S 147°6E **63** E4
Gunnison *Colo., U.S.A.* 38°33N 106°56W **76** G10
Gunnison *Utah, U.S.A.* 39°9N 111°49W **76** G8
Gunnison → *U.S.A.* 39°4N 108°35W **76** G9
Gunsan *S. Korea* 35°59N 126°45E **33** G14
Gunter *Canada* 44°52N 77°32W **82** B7
Guntersville *U.S.A.* 34°21N 86°18W **85** D11
Guntong *Malaysia* 4°36N 101°3E **39** K3
Guntur *India* 16°23N 80°30E **45** F5
Gunung Ciremay △
  Indonesia 6°53S 108°24E **37** G13
Gunungapi *Indonesia* 6°45S 126°30E **37** F7
Gunungsitoli *Indonesia* 1°15N 97°30E **36** D1
Gunupur *India* 19°5N 83°50E **44** E6
Guo He → *China* 32°59N 117°10E **33** H9
Guoyang *China* 33°32N 116°12E **32** H9
Gupis *Pakistan* 36°15N 73°20E **43** A5
Gurbantünggüt Shamo
  China 45°8N 87°20E **30** B6
Gurdaspur *India* 32°5N 75°31E **42** C6
Gurdon *U.S.A.* 33°55N 93°9W **84** E8
Gurgaon *India* 28°27N 77°1E **42** E7
Gurgueia → *Brazil* 6°50S 43°24W **93** E10
Gurha *India* 25°12N 71°39E **42** G4
Guri, Embalse de
  Venezuela 7°50N 62°52W **92** B6
Gurkha *Nepal* 28°5N 84°40E **43** E11
Gurla Mandhata = Naimona'nyi
  Feng *China* 30°26N 81°18E **43** D9
Gurley *Australia* 29°45S 149°48E **63** D4
Gurnet Point *U.S.A.* 42°1N 70°34W **83** D14
Gurun *Malaysia* 5°49N 100°27E **39** K3
Gürün *Turkey* 38°43N 37°15E **19** G6
Gurupá *Brazil* 1°25S 51°35W **93** D8
Gurupá, I. Grande de
  Brazil 1°25S 51°45W **93** D8
Gurupi *Brazil* 11°43S 49°4W **93** F9
Gurupi → *Brazil* 1°13S 46°6W **93** D9
Guruwe *Zimbabwe* 16°40S 30°42E **57** A5
Gurvan Sayhan Uul
  Mongolia 43°50N 104°0E **32** C3
Guryev = Atyraū
  Kazakhstan 47°5N 52°0E **19** E9
Gusau *Nigeria* 12°12N 6°40E **52** F7
Gushan *China* 39°50N 123°35E **33** E12
Gushgy = Serhetabat
  Turkmenistan 35°20N 62°18E **47** C9
Gushi *China* 32°11N 115°41E **35** A10
Gusinoozersk *Russia* 51°16N 106°27E **27** D11
Gustavus *U.S.A.* 58°25N 135°44W **70** B1
Gustine *U.S.A.* 37°16N 121°0W **78** H6
Güstrow *Germany* 53°47N 12°10E **16** B7
Gütersloh *Germany* 51°54N 8°24E **16** C5
Gutha *Australia* 28°58S 115°55E **61** E2
Guthalungra *Australia* 19°52S 147°50E **62** B4
Guthrie *Canada* 44°28N 79°32W **82** B5
Guthrie *Okla., U.S.A.* 35°53N 97°25W **84** D6
Guthrie *Tex., U.S.A.* 33°37N 100°19W **84** E4
Gutian *China* 26°32N 118°43E **35** D12
Guttenberg *U.S.A.* 42°47N 91°6W **80** D8
Gutu *Zimbabwe* 19°41S 31°9E **57** A5
Guwahati *India* 26°10N 91°45E **41** F17
Guy Fawkes River △
  Australia 30°0S 152°20E **63** D5
Guyana ■ *S. Amer.* 5°0N 59°0W **92** C7
Guyane française = French
  Guiana ☑ *S. Amer.* 4°0N 53°0W **93** C8
Guyang *China* 41°0N 110°5E **32** D6
Guyenne *France* 44°30N 0°40E **20** D4
Guymon *U.S.A.* 36°41N 101°29W **84** C4
Guyra *Australia* 30°15S 151°40E **63** E5
Guyuan *Hebei, China* 41°37N 115°40E **32** D8
Guyuan *Ningxia Huizu,
  China* 36°0N 106°20E **32** F4
Güzelyurt = Morphou
  Cyprus 35°12N 32°59E **46** C2
Guzhang *China* 28°42N 109°58E **34** C7
Guzhen *China* 33°22N 117°18E **33** H9
Guzmán, L. de *Mexico* 31°20N 107°30W **86** A3
Gwa *Burma* 17°36N 94°34E **41** L19
Gwabegar *Australia* 30°37S 148°59E **63** E4
Gwādar *Pakistan* 25°10N 62°18E **40** G3
Gwaii Haanas △
  Canada 52°21N 131°26W **70** C2
Gwalior *India* 26°12N 78°10E **42** F8
Gwanda *Zimbabwe* 20°55S 29°0E **55** J5
Gwangju *S. Korea* 35°9N 126°54E **33** G14
Gwangyang *S. Korea* 34°56N 127°41E **33** G14
Gwanju = Gwangju
  S. Korea 35°9N 126°54E **33** G14
Gweebarra B. *Ireland* 54°51N 8°23W **10** B3
Gweedore *Ireland* 55°3N 8°14W **10** A3
Gweru *Zimbabwe* 19°28S 29°45E **55** H5
Gwinn *U.S.A.* 46°19N 87°27W **80** B10
Gwydir → *Australia* 29°27S 149°48E **63** D4
Gwynedd □ *U.K.* 52°52N 4°10W **12** E3
Gyandzha = Gäncä
  Azerbaijan 40°45N 46°20E **19** F8
Gyangzê *China* 29°N 89°47E **30** F6
Gyaring Hu *China* 34°50N 97°40E **30** D8
Gydanskiy Poluostrov
  Russia 70°0N 78°0E **26** C8
Gyeonggi-man *S. Korea* 37°0N 125°30E **33** F13
Gyeongju *S. Korea* 35°51N 129°14E **33** G15
Gympie *Australia* 26°11S 152°38E **63** D5
Gyöngyös *Hungary* 47°48N 19°56E **17** E10
Győr *Hungary* 47°41N 17°40E **17** E9
Gypsum Pt. *Canada* 61°53N 114°35W **70** A6
Gypsumville *Canada* 51°45N 98°40W **71** C9
Gyula *Hungary* 46°38N 21°17E **17** E11
Gyumri *Armenia* 40°47N 43°50E **19** F7
Gyzylarbat = Serdar
  Turkmenistan 39°4N 56°23E **47** B8
Gyzyletrek = Etrek
  Turkmenistan 37°36N 54°46E **47** B7

H

Ha 'Arava → *Israel* 30°50N 35°20E **48** E4
Ha Coi *Vietnam* 21°26N 107°46E **34** G6
Ha Dong *Vietnam* 20°58N 105°46E **34** G5
Ha Giang *Vietnam* 22°50N 104°59E **34** F5
Ha Karmel, Har *Israel* 32°44N 35°3E **48** C4
Ha Karmel △ *Israel* 32°45N 35°5E **48** C4
Ha Long = Hong Gai
  Vietnam 20°57N 107°5E **34** G6
Ha Long, Vinh *Vietnam* 20°56N 107°3E **38** B6
Ha Tien *Vietnam* 10°23N 104°29E **39** G5
Ha Tinh *Vietnam* 18°20N 105°54E **38** C5
Ha Trung *Vietnam* 19°58N 105°50E **38** C5
Haaksbergen *Neths.* 52°9N 6°45E **15** B6
Ha'ano *Tonga* 19°41S 174°18W **59** c
Ha'apai Group *Tonga* 19°47S 174°27W **59** c
Haapiti *Moorea* 17°34S 149°52W **59** d
Haapsalu *Estonia* 58°56N 23°30E **9** G20
Haarlem *Neths.* 52°23N 4°39E **15** B4
Haast → *N.Z.* 43°50S 169°2E **59** E2
Haast Bluff *Australia* 23°22S 132°0E **60** D5
Haasts Bluff ◌ *Australia* 23°39S 130°34E **60** D5
Hab → *Pakistan* 24°53N 66°41E **42** G3
Hab Nadi Chauki *Pakistan* 25°0N 66°50E **42** G2
Habahe *China* 48°3N 86°23E **30** B6
Habay *Canada* 58°50N 118°44W **70** B5
Habbānīyah *Iraq* 33°17N 43°29E **46** C4
Habirag *China* 42°17N 115°42E **32** C8
Haboro *Japan* 44°22N 141°42E **28** B10
Habshān *U.A.E.* 23°50N 53°37E **47** F7
Hachijō-Jima *Japan* 33°5N 139°45E **29** H9
Hachiman = Gujō *Japan* 35°45N 136°57E **29** G8
Hachinohe *Japan* 40°30N 141°29E **28** D10
Hachiōji *Japan* 35°40N 139°20E **29** G9
Hackettstown *U.S.A.* 40°51N 74°50W **83** F10
Hadali *Pakistan* 32°16N 72°11E **42** C5
Hadarba, Ras *Sudan* 22°4N 36°51E **53** D13
Hadarom □ *Israel* 31°0N 35°0E **48** E4
Hadd, Ra's al *Oman* 22°35N 59°50E **49** C6
Haddington *U.K.* 55°57N 2°47W **11** F6
Hadejia *Nigeria* 12°30N 10°5E **52** F7
Hadera *Israel* 32°27N 34°55E **48** C3
Hadera, N. → *Israel* 32°28N 34°52E **48** C3
Haderslev *Denmark* 55°15N 9°30E **9** J13
Hadgaon *India* 19°30N 77°40E **44** E3
Hadhramaut = Ḥaḍramawt □
  Yemen 15°30N 49°30E **49** D4
Ḥadīboh *Yemen* 12°39N 54°2E **49** E5
Hadley B. *Canada* 72°31N 108°12W **68** C10
Hadong *S. Korea* 35°5N 127°44E **33** G14
Ḥaḍramawt □ *Yemen* 15°30N 49°30E **49** D4
Ḥadrāniyah *Iraq* 35°38N 43°14E **46** C4
Hadrian's Wall *U.K.* 55°0N 2°30W **12** B5
Hae, Ko *Thailand* 7°44N 98°22E **39** a
Haeju *N. Korea* 38°3N 125°45E **33** E13
Ha'ena *U.S.A.* 22°14N 159°34W **75** L8
Haenam *S. Korea* 34°34N 126°35E **33** G14
Haenertsburg *S. Africa* 24°0S 29°50E **57** B4
Haerhpin = Harbin
  China 45°48N 126°40E **33** B14
Hafar al Bāṭin *Si. Arabia* 28°32N 45°52E **46** D5
Ḥafirat al 'Aydā *Si. Arabia* 26°26N 39°12E **46** E3
Hafit *Oman* 23°59N 55°49E **47** F7
Hafizabad *Pakistan* 32°5N 73°40E **42** C5
Haflong *India* 25°10N 93°5E **41** G18
Haft Gel *Iran* 31°30N 49°32E **47** D6
Hagalil *Israel* 32°53N 35°18E **48** C4
Hagari → *India* 15°40N 77°0E **45** G3
Hagemeister I. *U.S.A.* 58°39N 160°54W **74** D7
Hagen *Germany* 51°21N 7°27E **16** C4
Hagerman *U.S.A.* 33°7N 104°20W **77** K11
Hagerman Fossil Beds ⌐
  U.S.A. 42°48N 114°57W **76** E6
Hagerstown *U.S.A.* 39°39N 77°43W **81** F15
Hagersville *Canada* 42°58N 80°3W **82** D4
Hagfors *Sweden* 60°3N 13°45E **9** F15
Hagi *Japan* 34°30N 131°22E **29** G5
Hagolan *Syria* 33°0N 35°45E **48** C4
Hagondange *France* 49°16N 6°11E **20** B7
Hags Hd. *Ireland* 52°57N 9°28W **10** D2
Hague, C. de la *France* 49°44N 1°56W **20** B3
Hague, The = 's-Gravenhage
  Neths. 52°7N 4°17E **15** B4
Haguenau *France* 48°49N 7°47E **20** B7
Hai Duong *Vietnam* 20°56N 106°19E **34** G6
Hai'an *Guangdong, China* 20°18N 110°11E **35** G8
Hai'an *Jiangsu, China* 32°37N 120°27E **35** A13
Haicheng *China* 40°50N 122°45E **33** D12
Haida Gwaii *Canada* 53°20N 132°10W **70** C2
Haidar Khel *Afghan.* 33°58N 68°38E **42** C3
Haidarābād = Hyderabad
  India 17°22N 78°29E **44** F4
Haidargarh *India* 26°37N 81°22E **43** F9
Haifa = Ḥefa *Israel* 32°46N 35°0E **48** C4
Haifeng *China* 22°58N 115°10E **35** F10
Haikou *China* 20°1N 110°16E **38** B8
Ḥā'il *Si. Arabia* 27°28N 41°45E **46** E4
Ḥā'il □ *Si. Arabia* 26°40N 41°40E **46** E4
Hailar *China* 49°10N 119°38E **31** B12
Hailey *U.S.A.* 43°31N 114°19W **76** E6
Haileybury *Canada* 47°30N 79°38W **72** C4
Hailin *China* 44°37N 129°30E **33** B15
Hailing Dao *China* 21°35N 111°47E **35** G8
Hailuoto *Finland* 65°3N 24°45E **8** D21
Haimen *Guangdong,
  China* 23°15N 116°38E **35** F11
Haimen *Jiangsu, China* 31°52N 121°10E **35** B13
Hainan □ *China* 19°0N 109°30E **38** C7
Hainan Dao *China* 19°0N 109°30E **38** C7
Hainan Str. = Qiongzhou Haixia
  China 20°10N 110°15E **38** B8
Hainaut □ *Belgium* 50°30N 4°0E **15** D4
Haines *Alaska, U.S.A.* 59°14N 135°26W **70** B1
Haines *Oreg., U.S.A.* 44°55N 117°56W **76** D5
Haines City *U.S.A.* 28°7N 81°38W **85** G14
Haines Junction *Canada* 60°45N 137°30W **70** A1
Haining *China* 30°28N 120°40E **35** B13
Haiphong *Vietnam* 20°47N 106°41E **34** G6

Haitan Dao *China* 25°30N 119°45E **35** E12
Haiti ■ *W. Indies* 19°0N 72°30W **89** C5
Haiya *Sudan* 18°20N 36°21E **53** E13
Haiyan *Qinghai, China* 36°53N 100°59E **30** D9
Haiyan *Zhejiang, China* 30°28N 120°58E **35** B13
Haiyang *China* 36°47N 121°9E **33** F11
Haiyuan *Guangxi Zhuangzu,
  China* 22°8N 107°35E **34** F6
Haiyuan *Ningxia Huizu,
  China* 36°35N 105°52E **32** F3
Haizhou *China* 34°37N 119°7E **33** G10
Haizhou Wan *China* 34°50N 119°20E **33** G10
Hajdúböszörmény
  Hungary 47°40N 21°30E **17** E11
Haji Ibrahim *Iraq* 36°40N 44°30E **46** B5
Hajipur *India* 25°45N 85°13E **43** G11
Ḥājj Ali Qolī, Kavīr-e
  Iran 35°55N 54°50E **47** C7
Ḥajjah *Yemen* 15°42N 43°36E **49** D3
Ḥājjīābād *Hormozgān, Iran* 28°19N 55°55E **47** D7
Ḥājjīābād *Khorāsān, Iran* 33°37N 60°0E **47** C9
Ḥājjīābād-e Zarrīn *Iran* 33°9N 54°51E **47** C7
Hajnówka *Poland* 52°47N 23°35E **17** B12
Hakansson, Mts.
  Dem. Rep. of the Congo 8°40S 25°45E **54** F5
Hakkâri *Turkey* 37°34N 43°44E **46** B4
Hakken-Zan *Japan* 34°10N 135°54E **29** G7
Hakkōda San *Japan* 40°50N 141°0E **28** D10
Hakodate *Japan* 41°45N 140°44E **28** D10
Hakos *Namibia* 23°13S 16°21E **56** C2
Hakskeenpan *S. Africa* 26°48S 20°13E **56** D3
Haku-San *Japan* 36°9N 136°46E **29** F8
Haku-San △ *Japan* 36°15N 136°45E **29** F8
Hakui *Japan* 36°53N 136°47E **29** F8
Hakusan *Japan* 36°31N 136°24E **29** F8
Hala *Pakistan* 25°43N 68°20E **40** G6
Ḥalab *Syria* 36°10N 37°15E **46** B3
Ḥalabjah *Iraq* 35°10N 45°58E **46** C5
Halaib *Sudan* 22°12N 36°30E **53** D13
Halaib Triangle *Africa* 22°30N 35°20E **53** D13
Ḥalat 'Ammār *Si. Arabia* 29°10N 36°4E **46** D3
Halba *Lebanon* 34°34N 36°6E **48** A5
Halberstadt *Germany* 51°54N 11°3E **16** C6
Halcombe *N.Z.* 40°8S 175°30E **59** D5
Halcon, Mt. *Phil.* 13°16N 121°0E **37** B6
Halden *Norway* 59°9N 11°23E **9** G14
Haldia *Bangla.* 22°1N 88°3E **43** H13
Haldwani *India* 29°31N 79°30E **43** E8
Hale → *Australia* 24°56S 135°53E **62** C2
Halesowen *U.K.* 52°27N 2°3W **13** E5
Halesworth *U.K.* 52°20N 1°31E **13** E9
Haleyville *U.S.A.* 34°14N 87°37W **85** D11
Half Dome *U.S.A.* 37°44N 119°32E **78** H7
Halfmoon Bay *N.Z.* 46°50S 168°5E **59** G2
Halfway → *Canada* 56°12N 121°32W **70** B4
Halia *India* 24°50N 82°19E **43** G10
Haliburton *Canada* 45°3N 78°30W **82** A6
Halifax *Australia* 18°32S 146°22E **62** B4
Halifax *Canada* 44°38N 63°35W **73** D7
Halifax *U.K.* 53°43N 1°52W **12** D6
Halifax *U.S.A.* 40°25N 76°55W **82** F8
Halifax B. *Australia* 18°50S 147°0E **62** B4
Halifax I. *Namibia* 26°38S 15°4E **56** D2
Halik Shan *China* 42°20N 81°22E **30** C5
Ḥalīl → *Iran* 27°40N 58°30E **47** E8
Halimun △ *Indonesia* 6°42S 106°26E **37** G11
Halkida = Chalkida
  Greece 38°27N 23°42E **23** E10
Halkirk *U.K.* 58°30N 3°29W **11** C5
Hall Beach *Canada* 68°46N 81°12W **69** D15
Hall Pen. *Canada* 63°30N 66°0W **69** E18
Hall Pt. *Australia* 15°40S 124°23E **60** C3
Halland *Sweden* 57°8N 12°47E **9** H15
Ḥallāniyat, Jazā'ir al
  Oman 17°30N 55°58E **49** D6
Hallasan *S. Korea* 33°22N 126°32E **33** H14
Halle *Germany* 51°30N 11°56E **16** C6
Hällefors *Sweden* 59°47N 14°31E **9** G16
Hallett *Australia* 33°25S 138°55E **63** E2
Hallettsville *U.S.A.* 29°27N 96°57W **84** G6
Halley *Antarctica* 75°35S 26°39W **5** D1
Hallia → *India* 16°55N 79°20E **44** F4
Hallim *S. Korea* 33°24N 126°15E **33** H14
Hallingdalselva →
  Norway 60°23N 9°35E **8** F13
Hallingskarvet △ *Norway* 60°37N 7°45E **8** F13
Hallock *U.S.A.* 48°47N 96°57W **80** A5
Halls Creek *Australia* 18°16S 127°38E **60** C4
Halls Gap *Australia* 37°8S 142°34E **63** F3
Halls Lake *Canada* 45°7N 78°45W **82** A6
Hallsberg *Sweden* 59°5N 15°7E **9** G16
Hallstead *U.S.A.* 41°58N 75°45W **83** E9
Halmahera *Indonesia* 0°40N 128°0E **37** D7
Halmahera Sea *Indonesia* 2°0N 130°0E **37** D7
Halmstad *Sweden* 56°41N 12°52E **9** H15
Halong Bay = Ha Long, Vinh
  Vietnam 20°56N 107°3E **38** B6
Hälsingborg = Helsingborg
  Sweden 56°3N 12°42E **9** H15
Hälsingland *Sweden* 61°40N 16°5E **8** F17
Halstead *U.K.* 51°57N 0°40E **13** F8
Haltiatunturi *Finland* 69°17N 21°18E **8** B19
Halton □ *U.K.* 53°22N 2°45W **12** D5
Haltwhistle *U.K.* 54°58N 2°26W **12** C5
Halvad *India* 23°1N 71°11E **42** H4
Halvān *Iran* 33°57N 56°15E **47** C8
Hamab *Namibia* 28°7S 19°16E **56** D2
Hamada *Japan* 34°56N 132°4E **29** G6
Hamadān *Iran* 34°52N 48°32E **46** C6
Hamadān □ *Iran* 35°0N 49°0E **46** C6
Ḥamāh *Syria* 35°5N 36°40E **46** C3
Hamamatsu *Japan* 34°45N 137°45E **29** G8
Hamar *Norway* 60°48N 11°7E **8** F14
Hamâta, Gebel *Egypt* 24°17N 35°0E **53** C13
Hamatonbetsu *Japan* 45°10N 142°20E **28** B11
Hambantota *Sri Lanka* 6°10N 81°10E **45** L5
Hamber △ *Canada* 52°20N 118°0W **70** C5
Hamburg *Germany* 53°33N 9°59E **16** B5
Hamburg *Ark., U.S.A.* 33°14N 91°48W **84** E9

Hamburg *N.Y., U.S.A.* 42°43N 78°50W **82** D6
Hamburg *Pa., U.S.A.* 40°33N 75°59W **83** F9
Ḥamḍ, W. al → *Si. Arabia* 24°55N 36°20E **46** E3
Hamden *U.S.A.* 41°23N 72°54W **83** E12
Häme *Finland* 61°38N 25°10E **8** F21
Hämeenlinna *Finland* 61°0N 24°28E **8** F21
Hamelin Pool *Australia* 26°22S 114°20E **61** E1
Hameln *Germany* 52°6N 9°21E **16** B5
Hamerkaz □ *Israel* 32°15N 34°55E **48** C3
Hamersley Ra. *Australia* 22°0S 117°45E **60** D2
Hamhŭng *N. Korea* 39°54N 127°30E **33** E14
Hami *China* 42°55N 93°25E **30** C7
Hamilton *Australia* 37°45S 142°2E **63** F3
Hamilton *Canada* 43°15N 79°50W **82** C5
Hamilton *N.Z.* 37°47S 175°19E **59** B5
Hamilton *U.K.* 55°46N 4°2W **11** F4
Hamilton *Ala., U.S.A.* 34°9N 87°59W **85** D11
Hamilton *Mont., U.S.A.* 46°15N 114°10W **76** C6
Hamilton *N.Y., U.S.A.* 42°50N 75°33W **83** D9
Hamilton *Ohio, U.S.A.* 39°24N 84°34W **81** F11
Hamilton *Tex., U.S.A.* 31°42N 98°7W **84** F5
Hamilton → *Queens., Australia* 23°30S 139°47E **62** C2
Hamilton → *S. Austral., Australia* 26°40S 135°19E **63** D2
Hamilton City *U.S.A.* 39°45N 122°1W **78** F4
Hamilton I. *Australia* 20°21S 148°56E **62** b
Hamilton Inlet *Canada* 54°0N 57°30W **73** B8
Hamilton Mt. *U.S.A.* 43°25N 74°22W **83** C10
Hamina *Finland* 60°34N 27°12E **8** F22
Hamirpur *H.P., India* 31°41N 76°31E **42** D7
Hamirpur *Ut. P., India* 25°57N 80°9E **43** G9
Hamlet *U.S.A.* 34°53N 79°42W **85** D15
Hamley Bridge *Australia* 34°17S 138°35E **63** E2
Hamlin = Hameln *Germany* 52°6N 9°21E **16** B5
Hamlin *N.Y., U.S.A.* 43°17N 77°55W **82** C7
Hamlin *Tex., U.S.A.* 32°53N 100°8W **84** E4
Hamm *Germany* 51°40N 7°50E **16** C4
Ḥammār, Hawr al *Iraq* 30°50N 47°10E **46** D5
Hammerfest *Norway* 70°39N 23°41E **8** A20
Hammond *Ind., U.S.A.* 41°38N 87°30W **80** E10
Hammond *La., U.S.A.* 30°30N 90°28W **85** F9
Hammond *N.Y., U.S.A.* 44°27N 75°42W **83** B9
Hammondsport *U.S.A.* 42°25N 77°13W **82** D7
Hammonton *U.S.A.* 39°39N 74°48W **81** F16
Hampden *N.Z.* 45°18S 170°50E **59** F3
Hampi *India* 15°18N 76°28E **45** G3
Hampshire □ *U.K.* 51°7N 1°23W **13** F6
Hampshire Downs *U.K.* 51°15N 1°10W **13** F6
Hampton *N.B., Canada* 45°32N 65°51W **73** C6
Hampton *Ont., Canada* 43°58N 78°45W **82** C6
Hampton *Ark., U.S.A.* 33°32N 92°28W **84** E8
Hampton *Iowa, U.S.A.* 42°45N 93°13W **80** D7
Hampton *N.H., U.S.A.* 42°57N 70°50W **83** D14
Hampton *S.C., U.S.A.* 32°52N 81°7W **85** E14
Hampton *Va., U.S.A.* 37°2N 76°21W **81** G15
Hampton Bays *U.S.A.* 40°53N 72°30W **83** F12
Hampton Tableland *Australia* 32°0S 127°0E **61** F4
Hamyang *S. Korea* 35°32N 127°42E **33** G14
Han = Hangang → *S. Korea* 37°50N 126°30E **33** F14
Han Jiang → *China* 23°25N 116°40E **35** F11
Han Pijesak *Bos.-H.* 44°5N 18°57E **23** B8
Han Shui → *China* 30°34N 114°17E **35** B10
Hanak *Si. Arabia* 25°32N 37°0E **46** E3
Hanamaki *Japan* 39°23N 141°7E **28** E10
Hanau *Germany* 50°7N 8°56E **16** C5
Hanbogd = Ihbulag *Mongolia* 43°11N 107°10E **32** C4
Hancheng *China* 35°31N 110°25E **32** G6
Hanchuan *China* 30°40N 113°50E **35** B9
Hancock *Mich., U.S.A.* 47°8N 88°35W **80** B9
Hancock *N.Y., U.S.A.* 41°57N 75°17W **83** E9
Hancock *Vt., U.S.A.* 43°55N 72°50W **83** C12
Handa *Japan* 34°53N 136°55E **29** G8
Handa I. *U.K.* 58°23N 5°11W **11** C3
Handan *China* 36°35N 114°28E **32** F8
Handwara *India* 34°21N 74°20E **43** B6
Hanegev *Israel* 30°50N 35°0E **48** E4
Hanford *U.S.A.* 36°20N 119°39W **78** J7
Hanford Reach △ *U.S.A.* 46°40N 119°30W **76** C4
Hang Chat *Thailand* 18°20N 99°21E **38** C2
Hangang → *S. Korea* 37°50N 126°30E **33** F14
Hangayn Nuruu *Mongolia* 47°30N 99°0E **30** B8
Hangchou = Hangzhou *China* 30°18N 120°11E **35** B13
Hanggin Houqi *China* 40°58N 107°4E **32** D4
Hanggin Qi *China* 39°52N 108°50E **32** E5
Hangu *China* 39°18N 117°53E **33** E9
Hangzhou *China* 30°18N 120°11E **35** B13
Hangzhou Wan *China* 30°15N 120°45E **35** B13
Hanh *Mongolia* 51°32N 100°35E **30** A9
Hanhongor *Mongolia* 43°55N 104°28E **32** C3
Hania = Chania *Greece* 35°30N 24°4E **23** G11
Ḥanīdh *Si. Arabia* 26°35N 48°38E **47** E6
Ḥanīsh *Yemen* 13°45N 42°46E **49** E3
Hanjiang *China* 25°26N 119°6E **35** E12
Hankinson *U.S.A.* 46°4N 96°54W **80** B6
Hankö *Finland* 59°50N 22°57E **9** G20
Hanksville *U.S.A.* 38°22N 110°43W **76** G8
Hanle *India* 32°42N 79°4E **43** C8
Hanmer Springs *N.Z.* 42°32S 172°50E **59** E4
Hann → *Australia* 17°26S 126°17E **60** C4
Hann, Mt. *Australia* 15°45S 126°0E **60** C4
Hanna *Canada* 51°40N 111°54W **70** C6
Hanna *U.S.A.* 41°52N 106°34W **76** F10
Hannah B. *Canada* 51°40N 80°0W **72** B4
Hannibal *Mo., U.S.A.* 39°42N 91°22W **80** F8
Hannibal *N.Y., U.S.A.* 43°19N 76°35W **83** C8
Hannover *Germany* 52°22N 9°46E **16** B5
Hanoi *Vietnam* 21°5N 105°55E **34** G5
Hanover = Hannover *Germany* 52°22N 9°46E **16** B5
Hanover *Canada* 44°9N 81°2W **82** B3
Hanover *S. Africa* 31°4S 24°29E **56** D3
Hanover *N.H., U.S.A.* 43°42N 72°17W **83** C12
Hanover *Ohio, U.S.A.* 40°4N 82°16W **82** F2

Hanover *Pa., U.S.A.* 39°48N 76°59W **81** F15
Hanover, I. *Chile* 51°0S 74°50W **96** G2
Hans Lollik I. *U.S. Virgin Is.* 18°24N 64°53W **89** e
Hansdiha *India* 24°36N 87°5E **43** G12
Hanshou *China* 28°56N 111°50E **35** C8
Hansi *H.P., India* 32°27N 77°50E **42** C7
Hansi *Haryana, India* 29°10N 75°57E **42** E6
Hanting *China* 36°46N 119°12E **33** F10
Hantsavichy *Belarus* 52°49N 26°30E **17** B14
Hanumangarh *India* 29°35N 74°19E **42** E6
Hanyin *China* 32°54N 108°28E **32** H5
Hanyuan *China* 29°21N 102°40E **34** C4
Hanzhong *China* 33°10N 107°1E **34** A6
Hanzhuang *China* 34°33N 117°23E **33** G9
Haoxue *China* 30°3N 112°24E **35** B9
Haparanda *Sweden* 65°52N 24°8E **8** D21
Haparanda Skärgård △ *Sweden* 65°35N 23°44E **8** D20
Happy *U.S.A.* 34°45N 101°52W **84** D4
Happy Camp *U.S.A.* 41°48N 123°23W **76** F2
Happy Valley-Goose Bay *Canada* 53°15N 60°20W **73** B7
Hapsu *N. Korea* 41°13N 128°51E **33** D15
Hapur *India* 28°45N 77°45E **42** E7
Ḥaql *Si. Arabia* 29°10N 34°58E **48** F3
Har *Indonesia* 5°16S 133°14E **37** F8
Har-Ayrag *Mongolia* 45°47N 109°16E **32** B5
Har Hu *China* 38°20N 97°38E **30** D8
Har Us Nuur *Mongolia* 48°0N 92°0E **30** B7
Har Yehuda *Israel* 31°35N 34°57E **48** D3
Ḥaraḍ *Si. Arabia* 24°22N 49°0E **49** C4
Haramosh *Pakistan* 35°50N 74°54E **43** B6
Haranomachi = Minamisōma *Japan* 37°38N 140°58E **28** F10
Harar = Harer *Ethiopia* 9°20N 42°8E **49** F3
Harare *Zimbabwe* 17°43S 31°2E **55** H6
Harazé *Chad* 9°57N 20°48E **53** G10
Harbhanga *India* 20°38N 84°36E **44** D7
Harbin *China* 45°48N 126°40E **33** B14
Harbor Beach *U.S.A.* 43°51N 82°39W **82** C2
Harborcreek *U.S.A.* 42°9N 79°57W **82** D5
Harbour Breton *Canada* 47°29N 55°50W **73** C8
Harbour Deep *Canada* 50°25N 56°32W **73** B8
Harda *India* 22°27N 77°5E **42** H7
Hardangerfjorden *Norway* 60°5N 6°0E **9** F12
Hardangervidda *Norway* 60°7N 7°20E **9** F12
Hardap □ *Namibia* 24°0S 17°0E **56** B2
Hardap △ *Namibia* 24°29S 17°45E **56** B2
Hardap Dam *Namibia* 24°32S 17°50E **56** B2
Hardenberg *Neths.* 52°34N 6°37E **15** B6
Harderwijk *Neths.* 52°21N 5°38E **15** B5
Hardey → *Australia* 22°45S 116°8E **60** D2
Hardin *U.S.A.* 45°44N 107°37W **76** D10
Harding *S. Africa* 30°35S 29°55E **57** D4
Harding Ra. *Australia* 16°17S 124°55E **60** C3
Hardisty *Canada* 52°40N 111°18W **70** C6
Hardoi *India* 27°26N 80°6E **43** F9
Hardwar = Haridwar *India* 29°58N 78°9E **42** E8
Hardwick *U.S.A.* 44°30N 72°22W **83** B12
Hardwood Lake *Canada* 45°12N 77°26W **82** A7
Hardy, Pen. *Chile* 55°30S 68°20W **96** H3
Hardy, Pte. *St. Lucia* 14°6N 60°56W **89** f
Hare B. *Canada* 51°15N 55°45W **73** B8
Hareid *Norway* 62°22N 6°1E **8** E12
Harer *Ethiopia* 9°20N 42°8E **49** F3
Hargeisa *Somalia* 9°30N 44°2E **49** F3
Hari → *Indonesia* 1°16S 104°5E **36** E2
Haridwar *India* 29°58N 78°9E **42** E8
Harihar *India* 14°32N 75°44E **45** G2
Hariharpur Garhi *Nepal* 27°19N 85°29E **43** F11
Harim, Jabal al *Oman* 25°58N 56°14E **47** E8
Haringhata → *Bangla.* 22°0N 89°58E **41** J16
Haripad *India* 9°14N 76°28E **45** K3
Ḥarīr, W. al → *Syria* 32°44N 35°59E **48** C4
Ḥarīrūd → *Asia* 37°24N 60°38E **47** B9
Härjedalen *Sweden* 62°22N 13°5E **8** E15
Harlan *Iowa, U.S.A.* 41°39N 95°19W **80** E6
Harlan *Ky., U.S.A.* 36°51N 83°19W **81** G12
Harlech *U.K.* 52°52N 4°6W **12** E3
Harlem *U.S.A.* 48°32N 108°47W **76** B9
Harlingen *Neths.* 53°11N 5°25E **15** A5
Harlingen *U.S.A.* 26°12N 97°42W **84** H6
Harlow *U.K.* 51°46N 0°8E **13** F8
Harlowton *U.S.A.* 46°26N 109°50W **76** C9
Harnai *India* 17°48N 73°6E **44** F1
Harnai *Pakistan* 30°6N 67°56E **42** D2
Harney Basin *U.S.A.* 43°0N 119°30W **76** E4
Harney L. *U.S.A.* 43°14N 119°8W **76** E4
Harney Peak *U.S.A.* 43°52N 103°32W **80** D2
Härnösand *Sweden* 62°38N 17°55E **8** E17
Haroldswick *U.K.* 60°48N 0°50W **11** A8
Harp L. *Canada* 55°5N 61°50W **73** A7
Harpanahalli *India* 14°47N 76°2E **45** G3
Harper *Liberia* 4°25N 7°43W **52** H4
Harper, Mt. *U.S.A.* 64°14N 143°51W **74** C11
Harrai *India* 22°37N 79°13E **43** H8
Harrand *Pakistan* 29°28N 70°3E **42** E4
Harricana → *Canada* 50°56N 79°32W **72** B4
Harriman *U.S.A.* 35°56N 84°33W **85** D12
Harrington Harbour *Canada* 50°31N 59°30W **73** B8
Harris *U.K.* 57°50N 6°55W **11** D2
Harris, L. *Australia* 31°10S 135°10E **63** E2
Harris, Sd. of *U.K.* 57°44N 7°6W **11** D1
Harris Pt. *Canada* 43°6N 82°9W **82** C2
Harrisburg *Ill., U.S.A.* 37°44N 88°32W **80** G9
Harrisburg *Nebr., U.S.A.* 41°33N 103°44W **80** E2
Harrisburg *Pa., U.S.A.* 40°16N 76°53W **82** F8
Harrismith *S. Africa* 28°15S 29°8E **57** D4
Harrison *Ark., U.S.A.* 36°14N 93°7W **84** C8
Harrison *Maine, U.S.A.* 44°7N 70°39W **83** B14
Harrison *Nebr., U.S.A.* 42°41N 103°53W **80** D2
Harrison, C. *Canada* 54°55N 57°55W **73** B8
Harrison Bay *U.S.A.* 70°40N 151°0W **74** A9
Harrison L. *Canada* 49°33N 121°50W **70** D4
Harrisonburg *U.S.A.* 38°27N 78°52W **81** F14
Harrisonville *U.S.A.* 38°39N 94°21W **80** F6

Harriston *Canada* 43°57N 80°53W **82** C4
Harrisville *Mich., U.S.A.* 44°39N 83°17W **82** B1
Harrisville *N.Y., U.S.A.* 44°9N 75°19W **83** B9
Harrisville *Pa., U.S.A.* 41°8N 80°0W **82** E5
Harrodsburg *U.S.A.* 37°46N 84°51W **81** G11
Harrogate *U.K.* 54°0N 1°33W **12** C6
Harrow *Canada* 42°2N 82°55W **82** D2
Harrowsmith *Canada* 44°24N 76°40W **83** B8
Harry S. Truman Res. *U.S.A.* 38°16N 93°24W **80** F7
Harsīn *Iran* 34°18N 47°33E **46** C5
Harstad *Norway* 68°48N 16°30E **8** B17
Harsud *India* 22°6N 76°44E **42** H7
Hart *U.S.A.* 43°42N 86°22W **80** D10
Hart, L. *Australia* 31°10S 136°25E **63** E2
Hartbees → *S. Africa* 28°45S 20°32E **56** D3
Hartford *Conn., U.S.A.* 41°46N 72°41W **83** E12
Hartford *Ky., U.S.A.* 37°27N 86°55W **80** G10
Hartford *S. Dak., U.S.A.* 43°38N 96°57W **80** D5
Hartford *Vt., U.S.A.* 43°40N 72°20W **83** C12
Hartford *Wis., U.S.A.* 43°19N 88°22W **80** D9
Hartford City *U.S.A.* 40°27N 85°22W **81** E11
Hartland *Canada* 46°20N 67°32W **73** C6
Hartland Pt. *U.K.* 51°1N 4°32W **13** F3
Hartlepool *U.K.* 54°42N 1°13W **12** C6
Hartley Bay *Canada* 53°25N 129°15W **70** C3
Hartmannberge *Namibia* 17°0S 13°0E **56** A1
Hartney *Canada* 49°30N 100°35W **71** D8
Harts → *S. Africa* 28°24S 24°17E **56** D3
Harts Range *Australia* 23°6S 134°55E **62** C1
Hartselle *U.S.A.* 34°27N 86°56W **85** D11
Hartshorne *U.S.A.* 34°51N 95°34W **84** D7
Hartstown *U.S.A.* 41°33N 80°23W **82** E4
Hartsville *U.S.A.* 34°23N 80°4W **85** D14
Hartswater *S. Africa* 27°34S 24°43E **56** C3
Hartwell *U.S.A.* 34°21N 82°56W **85** D13
Harunabad *Pakistan* 29°35N 73°8E **42** E5
Harur *India* 12°3N 78°29E **45** H4
Harvand *Iran* 28°25N 55°43E **47** D7
Harvey *Australia* 33°5S 115°54E **61** F2
Harvey *Ill., U.S.A.* 41°36N 87°50W **80** E2
Harvey *N. Dak., U.S.A.* 47°47N 99°56W **80** B4
Harwich *U.K.* 51°56N 1°17E **13** F9
Haryana □ *India* 29°0N 76°10E **42** E7
Haryn → *Belarus* 52°7N 27°17E **17** B14
Harz *Germany* 51°38N 10°44E **16** C6
Hasa *Si. Arabia* 25°50N 49°0E **47** E6
Ḥasā, W. al → *Jordan* 31°4N 35°29E **48** D4
Ḩasanābād *Iran* 32°8N 52°44E **47** C7
Hasanparti *India* 18°4N 79°32E **44** E4
Ḩasb, W. → *Iraq* 31°45N 44°17E **46** D5
Hasdo → *India* 21°44N 82°44E **43** J10
Hashimoto *Japan* 34°19N 135°37E **29** G7
Hashtjerd *Iran* 35°52N 50°40E **47** C6
Hashtpur = Tālesh *Iran* 37°58N 48°58E **46** B6
Haskell *U.S.A.* 33°10N 99°44W **84** E5
Haskovo = Khaskovo *Bulgaria* 41°56N 25°30E **23** D11
Haslemere *U.K.* 51°5N 0°43W **13** F7
Hassan *India* 13°0N 76°5E **45** H3
Hasselt *Belgium* 50°56N 5°21E **15** D5
Hassi Messaoud *Algeria* 31°51N 6°1E **52** B7
Hässleholm *Sweden* 56°10N 13°46E **9** H15
Hastings *N.Z.* 39°39S 176°52E **59** C6
Hastings *U.K.* 50°51N 0°35E **13** G8
Hastings *Mich., U.S.A.* 42°39N 85°17W **81** D11
Hastings *Minn., U.S.A.* 44°44N 92°51W **80** C7
Hastings *Nebr., U.S.A.* 40°35N 98°23W **80** E4
Hastings Ra. *Australia* 31°15S 152°14E **63** E5
Hat Lot *Vietnam* 21°15N 104°7E **38** B5
Hat Yai *Thailand* 7°1N 100°27E **39** J3
Hatanbulag = Ergel *Mongolia* 43°8N 109°5E **32** C5
Hatay *Turkey* 36°14N 36°10E **46** B3
Hatch *U.S.A.* 32°40N 107°9W **77** K10
Hatchet L. *Canada* 58°36N 103°40W **71** B8
Hateruma-Shima *Japan* 24°3N 123°47E **29** M1
Hatfield *Australia* 33°54S 143°49E **63** E3
Hatgal *Mongolia* 50°26N 100°9E **30** A9
Hathras *India* 27°36N 78°6E **42** F8
Hatia *Bangla.* 22°30N 91°5E **41** H17
Hatia *Nepal* 27°43N 87°21E **43** F12
Hato Mayor *Dom. Rep.* 18°46N 69°15W **89** C6
Hatra = Al Ḩaḍr *Iraq* 35°35N 42°44E **46** C4
Hatta *India* 24°7N 79°36E **43** G8
Hatta *U.A.E.* 24°45N 56°4E **47** E8
Hattah *Australia* 34°48S 142°17E **63** E3
Hattah Kulkyne △ *Australia* 34°16S 142°33E **63** E3
Hatteras, C. *U.S.A.* 35°14N 75°32W **85** D17
Hattiesburg *U.S.A.* 31°20N 89°17W **85** F10
Hatvan *Hungary* 47°40N 19°45E **17** E10
Hau → *Vietnam* 9°30N 106°13E **39** H6
Haugesund *Norway* 59°23N 5°13E **9** G11
Hauraki G. *N.Z.* 36°35S 175°5E **59** B5
Haut Atlas *Morocco* 32°30N 5°0W **52** B4
Hautes-Fagnes = Hohes Venn *Belgium* 50°30N 6°5E **15** D6
Hauts Plateaux *Algeria* 35°0N 1°0E **52** B6
Havana = La Habana *Cuba* 23°8N 82°22W **88** B3
Havana *U.S.A.* 40°18N 90°4W **80** E8
Havant *U.K.* 50°51N 0°58W **13** G7
Havasu, L. *U.S.A.* 34°18N 114°28W **79** L12
Havelian *Pakistan* 34°2N 73°10E **42** B5
Havelock *Canada* 44°26N 77°53W **82** B7
Havelock *N.Z.* 41°17S 173°48E **59** D4
Havelock *U.S.A.* 34°53N 76°54W **85** D16
Haverfordwest *U.K.* 51°48N 4°58W **13** F3
Haverhill *U.S.A.* 42°47N 71°5W **83** D13
Haveri *India* 14°53N 75°24E **45** G2
Haverstraw *U.S.A.* 41°12N 73°58W **83** E11
Havirga *Mongolia* 45°41N 113°5E **32** B7
Havířov *Czech Rep.* 49°46N 18°20E **17** D10

Havlíčkův Brod *Czech Rep.* 49°36N 15°33E **16** D8
Havre *U.S.A.* 48°33N 109°41W **76** B9
Havre-Aubert *Canada* 47°12N 61°56W **73** C7
Havre-St.-Pierre *Canada* 50°18N 63°33W **73** B7
Haw → *U.S.A.* 35°36N 79°3W **85** D15
Hawai'i *U.S.A.* 19°30N 155°30W **75** M8
Hawai'i □ *U.S.A.* 19°30N 156°30W **75** M8
Hawaiian Is. *Pac. Oc.* 20°30N 156°0W **65** E12
Hawaiian Ridge *Pac. Oc.* 24°0N 165°0W **65** E11
Hawarden *U.S.A.* 43°0N 96°29W **80** D5
Hawea, L. *N.Z.* 44°28S 169°19E **59** F2
Hawera *N.Z.* 39°35S 174°19E **59** C5
Hawick *U.K.* 55°26N 2°47W **11** F6
Hawk Junction *Canada* 48°5N 84°38W **72** C3
Hawke B. *N.Z.* 39°25S 177°20E **59** C6
Hawker *Australia* 31°59S 138°22E **63** E2
Hawke's Bay *Canada* 50°36N 57°10W **73** B8
Hawkesbury *Canada* 45°37N 74°37W **72** C5
Hawkesbury I. *Canada* 53°37N 129°3W **70** C3
Hawkesbury Pt. *Australia* 11°55S 134°5E **62** A1
Hawkinsville *U.S.A.* 32°17N 83°28W **85** E13
Hawley *Minn., U.S.A.* 46°53N 96°19W **80** B5
Hawley *Pa., U.S.A.* 41°28N 75°11W **83** E9
Ḩawrān, W. → *Iraq* 33°58N 42°34E **46** C4
Hawsh Mūssá *Lebanon* 33°45N 35°55E **48** B4
Hawthorne *U.S.A.* 38°32N 118°38W **76** G4
Hay *Australia* 34°30S 144°51E **63** E3
Hay → *Australia* 24°50S 138°0E **62** C2
Hay → *Canada* 60°50N 116°26W **70** A5
Hay, C. *Australia* 14°5S 129°29E **60** B4
Hay I. *Canada* 44°53N 80°58W **82** B4
Hay L. *Canada* 58°50N 118°50W **70** B5
Hay-on-Wye *U.K.* 52°5N 3°8W **13** E4
Hay Point *Australia* 21°18S 149°17E **62** C4
Hay River *Canada* 60°51N 115°44W **70** A5
Hay Springs *U.S.A.* 42°41N 102°41W **80** D2
Hayachine-San *Japan* 39°34N 141°29E **28** E10
Hayastan = Armenia ■ *Asia* 40°20N 45°0E **19** F7
Haydān, W. al → *Jordan* 31°29N 35°34E **48** D4
Hayden *U.S.A.* 40°30N 107°16W **76** F10
Hayes → *U.S.A.* 44°23N 101°1W **80** C3
Hayes → *Canada* 57°3N 92°12W **72** A1
Hayes, Mt. *U.S.A.* 63°37N 146°43W **74** C10
Hayes Creek *Australia* 13°43S 131°22E **60** B5
Hayle *U.K.* 50°11N 5°26W **13** G2
Hayling I. *U.K.* 50°48N 0°59W **13** G7
Hayman I. *Australia* 20°4S 148°53E **62** b
Hayrabolu *Turkey* 41°12N 27°5E **23** D12
Hays *Canada* 50°6N 111°48W **70** C6
Hays *U.S.A.* 38°53N 99°20W **80** F4
Haysyn *Ukraine* 48°57N 29°25E **17** D15
Hayvoron *Ukraine* 48°22N 29°52E **17** D15
Hayward *Calif., U.S.A.* 37°40N 122°4W **78** H4
Hayward *Wis., U.S.A.* 46°1N 91°29W **80** B8
Haywards Heath *U.K.* 51°0N 0°5W **13** G7
Hazafon □ *Israel* 32°40N 35°20E **48** C4
Hazar *Turkmenistan* 39°34N 53°16E **19** G9
Hazārān, Kūh-e *Iran* 29°35N 57°20E **47** D8
Hazard *U.S.A.* 37°15N 83°12W **81** G12
Hazaribag *India* 23°58N 85°26E **43** H11
Hazaribag Road *India* 24°12N 85°57E **43** G11
Hazelton *Canada* 55°20N 127°42W **70** B3
Hazelton *U.S.A.* 46°29N 100°17W **80** B3
Hazen *U.S.A.* 47°18N 101°38W **80** B3
Hazen, L. *Canada* 81°47N 71°1W **69** A17
Hazlehurst *Ga., U.S.A.* 31°52N 82°36W **85** F13
Hazlehurst *Miss., U.S.A.* 31°52N 90°24W **85** F9
Hazlet *U.S.A.* 40°25N 74°12W **83** F10
Hazleton *U.S.A.* 40°57N 75°59W **83** F9
Hazlett, L. *Australia* 21°30S 128°48E **60** D4
Hazro *Turkey* 38°15N 40°47E **46** B4
He Xian = Hezhou *China* 24°27N 111°30E **35** E8
He Xian *China* 31°45N 118°20E **35** B12
Head of Bight *Australia* 31°30S 131°25E **61** F5
Head-Smashed-In Buffalo Jump *Canada* 49°44N 113°37W **70** D6
Healdsburg *U.S.A.* 38°37N 122°52W **78** G4
Healdton *U.S.A.* 34°14N 97°29W **84** D6
Healesville *Australia* 37°35S 145°30E **63** F4
Healy *U.S.A.* 63°52N 148°58W **74** C10
Heany Junction *Zimbabwe* 20°6S 28°54E **57** B4
Heard I. *Ind. Oc.* 53°6S 72°36E **3** G13
Hearne *U.S.A.* 30°53N 96°36W **84** F6
Hearst *Canada* 49°40N 83°41W **72** C3
Heart → *U.S.A.* 46°46N 100°50W **80** B3
Heart's Content *Canada* 47°54N 53°27W **73** C9
Heath, Pte. *Canada* 49°8N 61°40W **73** C7
Heavener *U.S.A.* 34°53N 94°36W **84** D7
Hebbronville *U.S.A.* 27°18N 98°41W **84** H5
Hebei □ *China* 39°0N 116°0E **32** E9
Hebel *Australia* 28°58S 147°47E **63** D4
Heber *U.S.A.* 34°30N 110°35W **77** J8
Heber Springs *U.S.A.* 35°30N 92°2W **84** D8
Hebgen L. *U.S.A.* 44°52N 111°20W **76** D8
Hebi *China* 35°57N 114°7E **32** G8
Hebrides *U.K.* 57°30N 7°0W **6** D4
Hebrides, Sea of the *U.K.* 57°5N 7°0W **11** D2
Hebron = Al Khalīl *West Bank* 31°32N 35°6E **48** D4
Hebron *Canada* 58°5N 62°30W **69** F19
Hebron *N. Dak., U.S.A.* 46°54N 102°3W **80** B2
Hebron *Nebr., U.S.A.* 40°10N 97°35W **80** E5
Hecate Str. *Canada* 53°10N 130°30W **70** C2
Heceta I. *U.S.A.* 55°46N 133°40W **70** B2
Hechi *China* 24°40N 108°2E **34** E7
Hechuan *China* 30°2N 106°12E **34** B6
Hecla *U.S.A.* 45°53N 98°9W **80** C4
Hecla I. *Canada* 51°10N 96°43W **71** C9
Hede *Sweden* 62°23N 13°30E **8** E15
Hedemora *Sweden* 60°18N 15°58E **9** F16
Heerde *Neths.* 52°24N 6°2E **15** B6
Heerenveen *Neths.* 52°57N 5°55E **15** B5
Heerhugowaard *Neths.* 52°40N 4°51E **15** B4
Heerlen *Neths.* 50°55N 5°58E **15** D5
Ḩefa *Israel* 32°46N 35°0E **48** C4
Ḩefa □ *Israel* 32°40N 35°0E **48** C4
Hefei *China* 31°52N 117°18E **35** B11

Hefeng *China* 29°55N 109°52E **34** C7
Hegang *China* 47°20N 130°19E **31** B15
Heglig *Sudan* 10°0N 29°24E **53** G11
Heichengzhen *China* 36°24N 106°3E **32** F4
Heidelberg *Germany* 49°24N 8°42E **16** D5
Heidelberg *S. Africa* 34°6S 20°59E **56** D3
Heidelberg *S. Africa* 26°30S 28°21E **57** D4
Heihe *China* 50°10N 127°30E **31** A14
Heijing *China* 25°22N 101°44E **34** E3
Heilbron *S. Africa* 27°16S 27°59E **57** D4
Heilongjiang □ *China* 48°0N 126°0E **31** B14
Heiloo *Neths.* 52°36N 4°42E **15** B4
Heilunkiang = Heilongjiang □ *China* 48°0N 126°0E **31** B14
Heimaey *Iceland* 63°26N 20°17W **8** E3
Heinola *Finland* 61°13N 26°2E **8** F22
Heinze Chaung *Burma* 14°42N 97°52E **38** E1
Heinze Kyun *Burma* 14°25N 97°45E **38** E1
Heishan *China* 41°40N 122°5E **33** D12
Heishui *Liaoning, China* 42°8N 119°30E **33** C10
Heishui *Sichuan, China* 32°4N 103°2E **34** A4
Hejaz = Ḩijāz *Si. Arabia* 24°0N 40°0E **46** E3
Hejian *China* 38°25N 116°5E **32** E9
Hejiang *China* 28°43N 105°46E **34** C5
Hejin *China* 35°35N 110°42E **32** G6
Hekimhan *Turkey* 38°50N 37°55E **46** B3
Hekla *Iceland* 63°56N 19°35W **8** E4
Hekou *Gansu, China* 36°10N 103°26E **32** F2
Hekou *Guangdong, China* 23°13N 112°45E **35** F9
Hekou *Yunnan, China* 22°30N 103°59E **34** F4
Helan Shan *China* 38°30N 105°55E **32** E3
Helen Atoll *Palau* 2°40N 132°0E **37** D8
Helena *U.S.A.* 46°36N 112°2W **76** C7
Helena -West Helena *U.S.A.* 34°32N 90°36W **85** D9
Helendale *U.S.A.* 34°44N 117°19W **79** L9
Helensburgh *U.K.* 56°1N 4°43W **11** E4
Helensville *N.Z.* 36°41S 174°29E **59** B5
Helenvale *Australia* 15°43S 145°14E **62** B4
Helgeland *Norway* 66°7N 13°29E **8** C15
Helgoland *Germany* 54°10N 7°53E **16** A4
Heligoland = Helgoland *Germany* 54°10N 7°53E **16** A4
Heligoland B. = Deutsche Bucht *Germany* 54°15N 8°0E **16** A5
Hell Hole Gorge △ *Australia* 25°31S 144°12E **62** D3
Hella *Iceland* 63°50N 20°24W **8** E3
Hellas = Greece ■ *Europe* 40°0N 23°0E **23** E9
Hellertown *U.S.A.* 40°35N 75°21W **83** F9
Hellespont = Çanakkale Boğazı *Turkey* 40°17N 26°32E **23** D12
Hellevoetsluis *Neths.* 51°50N 4°8E **15** C4
Hellín *Spain* 38°31N 1°40W **21** C5
Hells Canyon △ *U.S.A.* 45°30N 117°45W **76** D5
Helmand □ *Afghan.* 31°20N 64°0E **40** D4
Helmand → *Afghan.* 31°12N 61°34E **40** D2
Helmeringhausen *Namibia* 25°54S 16°57E **56** C2
Helmond *Neths.* 51°29N 5°41E **15** C5
Helmsdale *U.K.* 58°7N 3°39W **11** C5
Helmsdale → *U.K.* 58°8N 3°43W **11** C5
Helong *China* 42°40N 129°0E **33** C15
Helper *U.S.A.* 39°41N 110°51W **76** G8
Helsingborg *Sweden* 56°3N 12°42E **9** H15
Helsingør *Denmark* 56°2N 12°35E **9** H15
Helston *U.K.* 50°6N 5°17W **13** G2
Helvellyn *U.K.* 54°32N 3°1W **12** C4
Helvetinjärvi △ *Finland* 62°55N 23°47E **8** E20
Helwân *Egypt* 29°50N 31°20E **53** C12
Hemavati → *India* 12°30N 76°20E **45** H3
Hemel Hempstead *U.K.* 51°44N 0°28W **13** F7
Hemet *U.S.A.* 33°45N 116°58W **79** M10
Hemingford *U.S.A.* 42°19N 103°4W **80** D2
Hemis △ *India* 34°10N 77°15E **42** B7
Hemmingford *Canada* 45°3N 73°35W **83** A11
Hempstead *N.Y., U.S.A.* 40°42N 73°37W **83** F11
Hempstead *Tex., U.S.A.* 30°6N 96°5W **84** F6
Hemse *Sweden* 57°15N 18°22E **9** H18
Henan □ *China* 34°0N 114°0E **32** H8
Henares → *Spain* 40°24N 3°30W **21** B4
Henashi-Misaki *Japan* 40°37N 139°51E **28** D9
Henderson *Argentina* 36°18S 61°43W **94** D3
Henderson *Ky., U.S.A.* 37°50N 87°35W **80** G10
Henderson *N.C., U.S.A.* 36°20N 78°25W **85** C15
Henderson *N.Y., U.S.A.* 43°50N 76°10W **83** C8
Henderson *Tenn., U.S.A.* 35°26N 88°38W **85** D10
Henderson *Tex., U.S.A.* 32°9N 94°48W **84** E7
Henderson I. *Pac. Oc.* 24°22S 128°19W **65** K15
Hendersonville *N.C., U.S.A.* 35°19N 82°28W **85** D13
Hendersonville *Tenn., U.S.A.* 36°18N 86°37W **85** C11
Hendījān *Iran* 30°14N 49°43E **47** D6
Hendorābī *Iran* 26°40N 53°37E **47** E7
Heng Jiang → *China* 28°40N 104°25E **34** C5
Heng Xian *China* 22°40N 109°17E **34** F7
Hengām *Iran* 26°38N 55°53E **47** E7
Hengcheng *China* 38°18N 106°28E **32** E4
Hengch'un *Taiwan* 22°0N 120°44E **35** F13
Hengdaohezi *China* 44°52N 129°0E **33** B15
Hengduan Shan *China* 25°30N 99°20E **34** E2
Hengelo *Neths.* 52°16N 6°48E **15** B6
Henggang *China* 22°39N 114°12E **31** a
Hengmen *China* 22°33N 113°35E **31** a
Hengshan *Hunan, China* 27°16N 112°45E **35** D9
Hengshan *Shaanxi, China* 37°58N 109°5E **32** F5
Hengshui *China* 37°41N 115°40E **32** F8
Hengyang *China* 26°59N 112°22E **35** D9
Henley-on-Thames *U.K.* 51°32N 0°54W **13** F7
Henlopen, C. *U.S.A.* 38°48N 75°6W **81** F16
Hennenman *S. Africa* 27°59S 27°1E **56** C4
Hennessey *U.S.A.* 36°6N 97°54W **84** C6
Henri Pittier △ *Venezuela* 10°26N 67°37W **89** D6
Henrietta *N.Y., U.S.A.* 43°4N 77°37W **82** D7
Henrietta *Tex., U.S.A.* 33°49N 98°12W **84** E5
Henrietta, Ostrov = Genriyetty, Ostrov *Russia* 77°6N 156°30E **27** B16
Henrietta Maria, C. *Canada* 55°9N 82°20W **72** A3

Henry U.S.A. 41°7N 89°22W 80 E9
Henry Ice Rise Antarctica 80°35S 62°0W 5 E17
Henry Lawrence I. India 12°9N 93°5E 45 H11
Henryetta U.S.A. 35°27N 95°59W 84 D7
Henryville Canada 45°8N 73°11W 83 A11
Hensall Canada 43°26N 81°30W 82 C3
Hentiesbaai Namibia 22°8S 14°18E 56 B1
Hentiyn Nuruu Mongolia 48°30N 108°30E 31 B10
Henty Australia 35°30S 147°3E 63 F4
Henzada = Hinthada Burma 17°38N 95°26E 41 L19
Heping China 24°29N 115°0E 35 E10
Heppner U.S.A. 45°21N 119°33W 76 D4
Hepworth Canada 44°37N 81°9W 82 B3
Hequ China 39°20N 111°15E 32 E6
Heqing China 26°37N 100°1E 34 D3
Héraðsflói Iceland 65°42N 14°12W 8 D6
Héraðsvötn → Iceland 65°45N 19°25W 8 D4
Heraklion = Iraklio Greece 35°20N 25°12E 23 G11
Herald Cays Australia 16°58S 149°9E 62 B4
Herāt Afghan. 34°20N 62°7E 40 B3
Herāt □ Afghan. 35°0N 62°0E 40 B3
Herbert Canada 50°30N 107°10W 71 C7
Herbert → Australia 18°31S 146°17E 62 B4
Herberton Australia 17°20S 145°25E 62 B4
Herbertsdale S. Africa 34°1S 21°46E 56 D3
Herceg-Novi Montenegro 42°30N 18°33E 23 C8
Herchmer Canada 57°22N 94°10W 71 B10
Herðubreið Iceland 65°11N 16°21W 8 D5
Hereford U.K. 52°4N 2°43W 13 E5
Hereford U.S.A. 34°49N 102°24W 84 D3
Herefordshire □ U.K. 52°8N 2°40W 13 E5
Herentals Belgium 51°12N 4°51E 15 C4
Herford Germany 52°7N 8°39E 16 B5
Herington U.S.A. 38°40N 96°57W 80 F6
Herkimer U.S.A. 43°2N 74°59W 83 D10
Herlen → Asia 48°48N 117°0E 31 B12
Herlong U.S.A. 40°8N 120°8W 78 E6
Herm U.K. 49°30N 2°28W 13 H5
Hermann U.S.A. 38°42N 91°27W 80 F8
Hermannsburg Australia 23°57S 132°45E 60 D5
Hermanus S. Africa 34°27S 19°12E 56 D2
Hermidale Australia 31°30S 146°42E 63 E4
Hermiston U.S.A. 45°51N 119°17W 76 D4
Hermon Canada 45°6N 77°37W 82 A7
Hermon U.S.A. 44°28N 75°14W 83 B9
Hermon, Mt. = Shaykh, J. ash Lebanon 33°25N 35°50E 48 B4
Hermosillo Mexico 29°10N 111°0W 86 B2
Hernád → Hungary 47°56N 21°8E 17 D11
Hernandarias Paraguay 25°20S 54°40W 95 B5
Hernandez U.S.A. 36°24N 120°46W 78 J6
Hernando Argentina 32°28S 63°40W 94 C3
Hernando U.S.A. 34°50N 90°0W 85 D9
Herndon U.S.A. 40°43N 76°51W 82 F8
Herne Germany 51°32N 7°14E 15 C7
Herne Bay U.K. 51°21N 1°8E 13 F9
Herning Denmark 56°8N 8°58E 9 H13
Heroica Caborca = Caborca Mexico 30°37N 112°6W 86 A2
Heroica Nogales = Nogales Mexico 31°19N 110°56W 86 A2
Heron Bay Canada 48°40N 86°25W 72 C2
Heron I. Australia 23°27S 151°55E 62 C5
Herreid U.S.A. 45°50N 100°4W 80 C3
Herrin U.S.A. 37°48N 89°2W 80 G9
Herriot Canada 56°22N 101°16W 71 B8
Herschel I. Canada 69°35S 139°4W 4 C1
Hershey U.S.A. 40°17N 76°39W 83 F8
Herstal Belgium 50°40N 5°38E 15 D5
Hertford U.K. 51°48N 0°4W 13 F7
Hertfordshire □ U.K. 51°51N 0°5W 13 F7
's-Hertogenbosch Neths. 51°42N 5°17E 15 C5
Hertzogville S. Africa 28°9S 25°30E 56 C4
Hervey B. Australia 25°0S 152°52E 62 C5
Herzliyya Israel 32°10N 34°50E 48 C3
Heşar Fārs, Iran 29°52N 50°16E 47 D6
Heşar Markazī, Iran 35°50N 49°12E 47 C6
Heshan Guangdong, China 22°34N 113°4E 35 F9
Heshan Guangxi Zhuangzu, China 23°50N 108°53E 34 F7
Heshui China 35°48N 108°0E 32 G5
Heshun China 37°22N 113°32E 32 F7
Hesperia U.S.A. 34°25N 117°18W 79 L9
Hesse = Hessen □ Germany 50°30N 9°0E 16 C5
Hessen □ Germany 50°30N 9°0E 16 C5
Hessle U.K. 53°44N 0°24W 12 D7
Hetauda Nepal 27°25N 85°2E 43 F11
Hetch Hetchy Aqueduct U.S.A. 37°29N 122°19W 78 H5
Hetta Enontekiö Finland 68°23N 23°37E 8 B20
Hettinger U.S.A. 46°0N 102°42W 80 B2
Heuksando S. Korea 34°40N 125°30E 33 G13
Heunghae S. Korea 36°12N 129°21E 33 F15
Heuvelton U.S.A. 44°37N 75°25W 83 B9
Hewitt U.S.A. 31°28N 97°12W 84 F6
Hexham U.K. 54°58N 2°4W 12 C5
Hexi Yunnan, China 24°9N 102°38E 34 E4
Hexi Zhejiang, China 27°58N 119°38E 35 D12
Hexigten Qi China 43°18N 117°30E 33 C9
Heydarābād Iran 30°33N 55°38E 47 D7
Heysham U.K. 54°3N 2°53W 12 C5
Heyuan China 23°39N 114°40E 35 F10
Heywood Australia 38°8S 141°37E 63 F3
Heze China 35°14N 115°20E 32 G8
Hezhang China 27°8N 104°41E 34 D5
Hezhou China 24°29N 111°32E 35 E8
Hi Vista U.S.A. 34°45N 117°46W 79 L9
Hiawatha U.S.A. 39°51N 95°32W 80 F6
Hibbing U.S.A. 47°25N 92°56W 80 B7
Hibernia Reef Australia 12°0S 123°23E 60 B3
Hickman U.S.A. 36°34N 89°11W 80 G9
Hickory U.S.A. 35°44N 81°21W 85 D14
Hicks, Pt. Australia 37°49S 149°17E 63 F4
Hicks L. Canada 61°25N 100°0W 71 A9
Hicksville U.S.A. 40°46N 73°32W 83 F11
Hida-Gawa → Japan 35°26N 137°3E 29 G8

Hida-Sammyaku Japan 36°30N 137°40E 29 F8
Hidaka Japan 42°30N 142°10E 28 C11
Hidaka-Sammyaku Japan 42°35N 142°45E 28 C11
Hidalgo □ Mexico 20°30N 99°0W 87 C5
Hidalgo del Parral Mexico 26°56N 105°40W 86 B3
Hierro Canary Is. 27°44N 18°0W 52 C2
Higashiajima-San Japan 37°40N 140°12E 28 F10
Higashiōsaka Japan 34°39N 135°37E 29 G7
Higgins U.S.A. 36°7N 100°2W 84 C4
Higgins Corner U.S.A. 39°2N 121°5W 78 F5
High Bridge U.S.A. 40°40N 74°54W 83 F10
High Desert U.S.A. 43°40N 120°20W 76 E3
High Island Res. China 22°22N 114°21E 31 a
High Level Canada 58°31N 117°8W 70 B5
High Point U.S.A. 35°57N 80°0W 85 D15
High Prairie Canada 55°30N 116°30W 70 B5
High River Canada 50°30N 113°50W 70 C6
High Tatra = Tatry Slovak Rep. 49°20N 20°0E 17 D11
High Veld Africa 27°0S 27°0E 50 J6
High Wycombe U.K. 51°37N 0°45W 13 F7
Highland □ U.K. 57°17N 4°21W 11 D4
Highland Park U.S.A. 42°11N 87°48W 80 D10
Highmore U.S.A. 44°31N 99°27W 80 C4
Higüey Dom. Rep. 18°37N 68°42W 89 C6
Hiidenportti △ Finland 63°53N 29°0E 8 E23
Hiiumaa Estonia 58°50N 22°45E 9 G20
Hijārah, Şahrā' al Iraq 30°25N 44°30E 46 D5
Hijāz Si. Arabia 24°0N 40°0E 46 E3
Hijo → Tagum Phil. 7°33N 125°53E 37 C7
Hikari Japan 33°58N 131°58E 29 H5
Hikkaduwa Sri Lanka 6°8N 80°6E 45 L5
Hiko U.S.A. 37°32N 115°14W 78 H11
Hikone Japan 35°15N 136°10E 29 G8
Hikurangi Gisborne, N.Z. 37°55S 178°4E 59 C6
Hikurangi Northland, N.Z. 35°36S 174°17E 59 A5
Hildesheim Germany 52°9N 9°56E 16 B5
Hill → Australia 30°23S 115°3E 61 F2
Hill City Idaho, U.S.A. 43°18N 115°3W 76 E6
Hill City Kans., U.S.A. 39°22N 99°51W 80 F4
Hill City Minn., U.S.A. 46°59N 93°36W 80 B7
Hill City S. Dak., U.S.A. 43°56N 103°35W 80 D2
Hill Island L. Canada 60°30N 109°50W 71 A7
Hillaby, Mt. Barbados 13°12N 59°35W 89 g
Hillcrest Barbados 13°13N 59°31W 89 g
Hillegom Neths. 52°18N 4°35E 15 B4
Hillsboro Kans., U.S.A. 38°21N 97°12W 80 F5
Hillsboro N. Dak., U.S.A. 47°26N 97°3W 80 B5
Hillsboro Ohio, U.S.A. 39°12N 83°37W 81 F12
Hillsboro Oreg., U.S.A. 45°31N 122°59W 78 E4
Hillsboro Tex., U.S.A. 32°1N 97°8W 84 E6
Hillsborough Grenada 12°28N 61°28W 89 D7
Hillsborough Channel Australia 20°56S 149°15E 62 b
Hillsdale Mich., U.S.A. 41°56N 84°38W 81 E11
Hillsdale N.Y., U.S.A. 42°11N 73°32W 83 D11
Hillsport Canada 49°27N 85°34W 72 C2
Hillston Australia 33°30S 145°31E 63 E4
Hilo U.S.A. 19°44N 155°5W 75 M8
Hilton U.S.A. 43°17N 77°48W 82 C7
Hilton Head Island U.S.A. 32°13N 80°45W 85 E14
Hilversum Neths. 52°14N 5°10E 15 B5
Himachal Pradesh □ India 31°30N 77°0E 42 D7
Himalaya Asia 29°0N 84°0E 43 E11
Himalchuli Nepal 28°27N 84°38E 43 E11
Himatnagar India 23°37N 72°57E 42 H5
Himeji Japan 34°50N 134°40E 29 G7
Himi Japan 36°50N 136°55E 29 F8
Himş Syria 34°40N 36°45E 48 A5
Himş □ Syria 34°30N 37°0E 48 A6
Hin Khom, Laem Thailand 9°25N 99°56E 39 b
Hinche Haiti 19°9N 72°1W 89 C5
Hinchinbrook I. Australia 18°20S 146°15E 62 B4
Hinchinbrook Island △ Australia 18°14S 146°6E 62 B4
Hinckley U.K. 52°33N 1°22W 13 E6
Hinckley U.S.A. 46°1N 92°56W 80 B7
Hindaun India 26°44N 77°5E 42 F7
Hindmarsh, L. Australia 36°5S 141°55E 63 F3
Hindol India 20°40N 85°10E 44 D7
Hindu Bagh Pakistan 30°56N 67°50E 42 D2
Hindu Kush Asia 36°0N 71°0E 40 B7
Hindupur India 13°49N 77°32E 45 H3
Hines Creek Canada 56°20N 118°40W 70 B5
Hinesville U.S.A. 31°51N 81°36W 85 F14
Hinganghat India 20°30N 78°52E 44 D4
Hingham U.S.A. 48°33N 110°25W 76 B8
Hingir India 21°57N 83°41E 43 J10
Hingoli India 19°41N 77°15E 44 E3
Hinna = Imi Ethiopia 6°28N 42°10E 49 F3
Hinnøya Norway 68°35N 15°50E 8 B16
Hinojosa del Duque Spain 38°30N 5°9W 21 C3
Hinsdale U.S.A. 42°47N 73°23D D12
Hinthada Burma 17°38N 95°26E 41 L19
Hinton Canada 53°26N 117°34W 70 C5
Hinton U.S.A. 37°40N 80°54W 81 G13
Hios = Chios Greece 38°27N 26°9E 23 E12
Hirado Japan 33°22N 129°33E 29 H4
Hirakud Dam India 21°32N 83°45E 44 D6
Hiran → India 23°6N 79°21E 43 H8
Hirapur India 24°22N 79°13E 43 G8
Hirara = Miyakojima Japan 24°48N 125°17E 29 M2
Hiratsuka Japan 35°19N 139°21E 29 G9
Hirekerur India 14°28N 75°39E 45 G2
Hiroo Japan 42°17N 143°19E 28 C11
Hirosaki Japan 40°34N 140°28E 28 D10
Hiroshima Japan 34°24N 132°30E 29 G6
Hiroshima □ Japan 34°50N 133°0E 29 G6
Hisar India 29°12N 75°45E 42 E6
Hisb, Sha'ib → Iraq 31°45N 44°17E 46 D5

Ḥismā Si. Arabia 28°30N 36°0E 46 D3
Hispaniola W. Indies 19°0N 71°0W 89 C5
Hīt Iraq 33°38N 42°49E 46 C4
Hita Japan 33°20N 130°58E 29 H5
Hitachi Japan 36°36N 140°39E 29 F10
Hitchin U.K. 51°58N 0°16W 13 F7
Hitiaa Tahiti 17°36S 149°18W 59 d
Hitoyoshi Japan 32°13N 130°45E 29 H5
Hitra Norway 63°30N 8°45E 8 E13
Hiva Oa French Polynesia 9°45S 139°0W 65 H14
Hixon Canada 53°25N 122°35W 70 C4
Hiyyon, N. → Israel 30°25N 35°10E 48 E4
Hjalmar L. Canada 61°33N 109°25W 71 A7
Hjälmaren Sweden 59°18N 15°40E 9 G16
Hjørring Denmark 57°29N 9°59E 9 H13
Hjort Trench S. Ocean 58°0S 157°30E 5 B10
Hkakabo Razi Burma 28°25N 97°23E 34 C1
Hkamti Burma 26°0N 95°39E 41 G19
Hlobane S. Africa 27°42S 31°0E 57 C5
Hluhluwe S. Africa 28°1S 32°15E 57 C5
Hluhluwe △ S. Africa 22°10S 32°5E 57 B5
Hlyboka Ukraine 48°5N 25°56E 17 D13
Ho Ghana 6°30N 0°27E 52 G6
Ho Chi Minh City = Thanh Pho Ho Chi Minh Vietnam 10°58N 106°40E 39 G6
Ho Hoa Binh Vietnam 20°50N 105°0E 34 G5
Ho Thac Ba Vietnam 21°42N 105°1E 38 A5
Ho Thuong Vietnam 19°32N 105°48E 38 C5
Hoa Binh Vietnam 20°50N 105°20E 34 G5
Hoa Hiep Vietnam 11°34N 105°51E 39 G5
Hoai Nhon Vietnam 14°28N 109°1E 38 E7
Hoang Lien △ Vietnam 22°20N 103°30E 34 F4
Hoang Lien Son Vietnam 22°0N 104°0E 34 F4
Hoang Sa, Dao = Paracel Is. S. China Sea 15°50N 112°0E 36 A4
Hoanib → Namibia 19°27S 12°46E 56 A2
Hoare B. Canada 65°17N 62°30W 69 D19
Hoarusib → Namibia 19°3S 12°36E 56 A2
Hobart Australia 42°50S 147°21E 63 G4
Hobart U.S.A. 35°1N 99°6W 84 D5
Hobbs U.S.A. 32°42N 103°8W 77 K12
Hobbs Coast Antarctica 74°50S 131°0W 5 D14
Hobe Sound U.S.A. 27°4N 80°8W 85 H14
Hobro Denmark 56°39N 9°46E 9 H13
Hoburgen Sweden 56°55N 18°7E 9 H18
Hobyo Somalia 5°25N 48°30E 49 F4
Hochfeld Namibia 21°28S 17°58E 56 C2
Hodaka-Dake Japan 36°17N 137°39E 29 F8
Hodeida = Al Ḩudaydah Yemen 14°50N 43°0E 49 E3
Hodgeville Canada 50°7N 106°58W 71 C7
Hodgson Canada 51°13N 97°36W 71 C9
Hódmezővásárhely Hungary 46°28N 20°22E 17 E11
Hodna, Chott el Algeria 35°26N 4°43E 52 A6
Hodonín Czech Rep. 48°50N 17°10E 17 D9
Hoek van Holland Neths. 52°0N 4°7E 15 C4
Hoengseong S. Korea 37°29N 127°59E 33 F14
Hoeryong N. Korea 42°30N 129°45E 33 C15
Hoeyang N. Korea 38°43N 127°36E 33 E14
Hof Germany 50°19N 11°55E 16 C6
Hofmeyr S. Africa 31°39S 25°50E 56 D4
Höfn Iceland 64°15N 15°13W 8 D6
Hofors Sweden 60°31N 16°15E 9 F17
Hofsjökull Iceland 64°49N 18°48W 8 D4
Hōfu Japan 34°3N 131°34E 29 G5
Hogan Group Australia 39°13S 147°1E 63 F4
Hogarth, Mt. Australia 21°48S 136°58E 62 C2
Hoge Kempen △ Belgium 51°6N 5°35E 15 C5
Hoge Veluwe △ Neths. 52°5N 5°46E 15 B5
Hogenakal Falls India 12°6N 77°50E 45 H3
Hoggar = Ahaggar Algeria 23°0N 6°30E 52 D7
Hogsty Reef Bahamas 21°41N 73°48W 89 B5
Hoh → U.S.A. 47°45N 124°29W 78 C2
Hoh Xil Shan China 36°30N 89°0E 30 D6
Hohenwald U.S.A. 35°33N 87°33W 85 D11
Hoher Rhön = Rhön Germany 50°24N 9°58E 16 C5
Hohes Venn Belgium 50°30N 6°5E 15 D6
Hohhot China 40°52N 111°40E 32 D6
Hoi An Vietnam 15°30N 108°19E 38 E7
Hoi Xuan Vietnam 20°25N 105°9E 34 G5
Hoisington U.S.A. 38°31N 98°47W 80 F4
Hōjō Japan 33°58N 132°46E 29 H6
Hokianga Harbour N.Z. 35°31S 173°22E 59 A4
Hokitika N.Z. 42°42S 171°0E 59 E3
Hokkaidō □ Japan 43°30N 143°0E 28 C11
Hokuto Japan 41°49N 140°39E 28 D10
Holalkere India 14°2N 76°11E 45 G3
Holbrook Australia 35°42S 147°18E 63 F4
Holbrook U.S.A. 34°54N 110°10W 77 J8
Holcomb U.S.A. 42°54N 77°25W 82 D7
Holden U.S.A. 39°6N 112°16W 76 G7
Holdenville U.S.A. 35°5N 96°24W 84 D6
Holdrege U.S.A. 40°26N 99°23W 80 E4
Hole-Narsipur India 12°48N 76°16E 45 H3
Holetown Barbados 13°11N 59°38W 89 g
Holguín Cuba 20°50N 76°20W 88 B4
Hollams Bird I. Namibia 24°40S 14°30E 56 B1
Holland = Netherlands ■ Europe 52°0N 5°30E 15 C5
Holland Mich., U.S.A. 42°47N 86°7W 80 D10
Holland N.Y., U.S.A. 42°38N 78°32W 82 D6
Holland Centre Canada 44°23N 80°47W 82 B4
Holland Patent U.S.A. 43°14N 75°15W 83 C9
Hollandale U.S.A. 33°10N 90°51W 85 E9
Holley U.S.A. 43°14N 78°2W 82 C6
Hollidaysburg U.S.A. 40°26N 78°24W 82 F6
Hollis U.S.A. 34°41N 99°55W 84 D5
Hollister Calif., U.S.A. 36°51N 121°24W 78 J5
Hollister Idaho, U.S.A. 42°21N 114°35W 76 E6
Holly Hill U.S.A. 29°16N 81°3W 85 G14
Holly Springs U.S.A. 34°46N 89°27W 85 D10
Hollywood Ireland 53°6N 6°35W 10 B6
Holman = Ulukhaktok Canada 70°44N 117°44W 68 C8
Hólmavík Iceland 65°42N 21°40W 8 D3
Holmen U.S.A. 43°58N 91°15W 80 D8
Holmes Reefs Australia 16°27S 148°0E 62 B4
Holmsund Sweden 63°41N 20°20E 8 E19

Holon Israel 32°2N 34°46E 48 C3
Holroyd → Australia 14°10S 141°36E 62 A3
Holstebro Denmark 56°22N 8°37E 9 H13
Holsworthy U.K. 50°48N 4°22W 13 G3
Holton Canada 54°31N 57°12W 73 B8
Holton U.S.A. 39°28N 95°44W 80 F6
Holtville U.S.A. 32°49N 115°23W 79 N11
Holwerd Neths. 53°22N 5°54E 15 A5
Holy Cross U.S.A. 62°12N 159°46W 74 C8
Holy I. Anglesey, U.K. 53°17N 4°37W 12 D3
Holy I. Northumberland, U.K. 55°40N 1°47W 12 B6
Holyhead U.K. 53°18N 4°38W 12 D3
Holyoke Colo., U.S.A. 40°35N 102°18W 76 F12
Holyoke Mass., U.S.A. 42°12N 72°37W 83 D12
Holyrood Canada 47°27N 53°8W 73 C9
Homalin Burma 24°55N 95°0E 41 G19
Homand Iran 32°28N 59°37E 47 C8
Homathko → Canada 51°0N 124°56W 70 C4
Hombori Mali 15°20N 1°38W 52 E5
Home B. Canada 68°40N 67°10W 69 D18
Home Hill Australia 19°43S 147°25E 62 B4
Home Reef Tonga 18°59S 174°47W 59 c
Homedale U.S.A. 43°37N 116°56W 76 E5
Homer Alaska, U.S.A. 59°39N 151°33W 68 F1
Homer La., U.S.A. 32°48N 93°4W 84 E8
Homer N.Y., U.S.A. 42°38N 76°10W 83 D8
Homer City U.S.A. 40°32N 79°10W 82 F5
Homestead Australia 20°20S 145°40E 62 C4
Homestead U.S.A. 25°28N 80°29W 85 J14
Homewood U.S.A. 40°17N 96°50W 80 E5
Homnabad India 17°45N 77°11E 44 F3
Homoine Mozam. 23°55S 35°8E 57 B6
Homs = Ḩimş Syria 34°40N 36°45E 48 A5
Homyel Belarus 52°28N 31°0E 17 B16
Hon Chong Vietnam 10°25N 104°30E 39 G5
Hon Hai Vietnam 10°10N 109°0E 39 H7
Hon Me Vietnam 19°23N 105°56E 38 C5
Honan = Henan □ China 34°0N 114°0E 32 H8
Honavar India 14°17N 74°27E 45 G2
Honbetsu Japan 43°7N 143°37E 28 C11
Honcut U.S.A. 39°20N 121°32W 78 F5
Hondeklipbaai S. Africa 30°19S 17°17E 56 D2
Hondo Japan 32°27N 130°12E 29 H5
Hondo U.S.A. 29°21N 99°9W 84 G5
Hondo, Río → Belize 18°25N 88°21W 87 D7
Honduras ■ Cent. Amer. 14°40N 86°30W 88 D2
Honduras, G. de Caribbean 16°50N 87°0W 88 C2
Hønefoss Norway 60°10N 10°18E 9 F14
Honesdale U.S.A. 41°34N 75°16W 83 E9
Honey Harbour Canada 44°52N 79°49W 82 B5
Honey L. U.S.A. 40°15N 120°19W 78 E6
Honfleur France 49°25N 0°13E 20 B4
Hong → Asia 20°16N 106°34E 38 B5
Hong Gai Vietnam 20°57N 107°5E 34 G6
Hong He → China 32°25N 115°35E 32 H8
Hong Hu China 29°54N 113°24E 35 C9
Hong Kong □ China 22°11N 114°14E 31 a
Hong'an China 31°20N 114°40E 35 B10
Hongcheon S. Korea 37°44N 127°53E 33 F14
Honghai Wan China 22°40N 115°0E 35 F10
Honghe China 23°25N 102°25E 34 F4
Honghu China 29°50N 113°30E 35 C9
Hongjiang China 27°7N 109°59E 34 D7
Hongliu He → China 38°0N 109°50E 32 E5
Hongor Mongolia 45°45N 112°50E 32 B7
Hongseong S. Korea 36°37N 126°38E 33 F14
Hongshan China 36°38N 117°58E 33 F9
Hongshui He → China 23°48N 109°30E 34 F7
Hongtong China 36°16N 111°40E 32 F6
Honguedo, Détroit d' Canada 49°15N 64°0W 73 C7
Hongwon N. Korea 40°0N 127°56E 33 E14
Hongya China 29°57N 103°22E 34 C4
Hongyuan China 32°51N 102°34E 34 A4
Hongze China 33°15N 118°35E 33 H10
Honiara Solomon Is. 9°27S 159°57E 58 B8
Honiton U.K. 50°47N 3°11W 13 G4
Honjō = Yurihonjō Japan 39°23N 140°3E 28 E10
Honnali India 14°15N 75°40E 45 G2
Honningsvåg Norway 70°59N 25°59E 8 A21
Honolulu U.S.A. 21°19N 157°52W 75 L8
Honshū Japan 36°0N 138°0E 29 F9
Hood, Mt. U.S.A. 45°23N 121°41W 78 E5
Hood, Pt. Australia 34°23S 119°34E 61 F2
Hood River U.S.A. 45°43N 121°31W 78 E5
Hoodsport U.S.A. 47°24N 123°9W 78 C3
Hoogeveen Neths. 52°44N 6°28E 15 B6
Hoogezand-Sappemeer Neths. 53°9N 6°45E 15 A6
Hooghly = Hugli → India 21°56N 88°4E 43 J13
Hooghly-Chinsura = Chunchura India 22°53N 88°27E 43 H13
Hook Hd. Ireland 52°7N 6°56W 10 D5
Hook I. Australia 20°4S 149°0E 62 b
Hook of Holland = Hoek van Holland Neths. 52°0N 4°7E 15 C4
Hooker U.S.A. 36°52N 101°13W 84 C4
Hooker Creek = Lajamanu Australia 18°23S 130°38E 60 C5
Hooker Creek ☆ Australia 18°30S 130°0E 60 C5
Hoonah U.S.A. 58°7N 135°27W 70 B1
Hooper Bay U.S.A. 61°32N 166°6W 74 C6
Hoopeston U.S.A. 40°28N 87°40W 80 E10
Hoopstad S. Africa 27°50S 25°55E 56 C4
Hoorn Neths. 52°38N 5°4E 15 B5
Hoover U.S.A. 33°24N 86°49W 85 E11
Hoover Dam U.S.A. 36°1N 114°44W 79 K12
Hooversville U.S.A. 40°9N 78°55W 82 F6
Hop Bottom U.S.A. 41°42N 75°46W 83 E9
Hope Canada 49°25N 121°25W 70 D4
Hope Ariz., U.S.A. 33°43N 113°42W 79 M13
Hope Ark., U.S.A. 33°40N 93°36W 84 E8
Hope, L. S. Austral., Australia 28°24S 139°18E 63 D2
Hope, L. W. Austral., Australia 32°35S 120°15E 61 F3
Hope, Pt. U.S.A. 68°21N 166°47W 66 C3
Hope I. Canada 44°55N 80°11W 82 B4

Hope Town Bahamas 26°35N 76°57W 88 A4
Hope Vale Australia 15°16S 145°20E 62 B4
Hope Vale ☆ Australia 15°8S 145°15E 62 B4
Hopedale Canada 55°28N 60°13W 73 A7
Hopefield S. Africa 33°3S 18°22E 56 D2
Hopei = Hebei □ China 39°0N 116°0E 32 E9
Hopetoun Vic., Australia 35°42S 142°22E 63 F3
Hopetoun W. Austral., Australia 33°57S 120°7E 61 F3
Hopetown S. Africa 29°34S 24°3E 56 C3
Hopewell U.S.A. 37°18N 77°17W 81 G15
Hopkins, L. Australia 24°15S 128°35E 60 D4
Hopkinsville U.S.A. 36°52N 87°29W 80 G10
Hopland U.S.A. 38°58N 123°7W 78 G3
Hoquiam U.S.A. 46°59N 123°53W 78 D3
Horana Sri Lanka 6°43N 80°4E 45 L5
Horden Hills Australia 20°15S 130°0E 60 D5
Horinger China 40°28N 111°48E 32 D6
Horizontina Brazil 27°37S 54°19W 95 B5
Horlick Mts. Antarctica 84°0S 102°0W 5 E15
Horlivka Ukraine 48°19N 38°5E 19 E6
Hormak Iran 29°58N 60°51E 47 D9
Hormoz Iran 27°35N 55°0E 47 E8
Hormoz, Jaz.-ye Iran 27°8N 56°28E 47 E8
Hormozgān □ Iran 27°30N 56°0E 47 E8
Hormuz, Kūh-e Iran 27°27N 55°10E 47 E7
Hormuz, Str. of The Gulf 26°30N 56°30E 47 E8
Horn Austria 48°39N 15°40E 16 D8
Horn → Canada 61°30N 118°1W 70 A5
Horn, Cape = Hornos, C. de Chile 55°50S 67°30W 96 H3
Horn Head Ireland 55°14N 8°0W 10 A3
Horn I. Australia 10°37S 142°17E 62 A3
Horn Plateau Canada 62°15N 119°15W 70 A5
Hornavan Sweden 66°15N 17°30E 8 C17
Hornbeck U.S.A. 31°20N 93°24W 84 F8
Hornbrook U.S.A. 41°55N 122°33W 76 F2
Horncastle U.K. 53°13N 0°7W 12 D7
Hornell U.S.A. 42°20N 77°40W 82 D7
Hornell L. Canada 62°20N 119°25W 70 A5
Hornepayne Canada 49°14N 84°48W 72 C3
Hornitos U.S.A. 37°30N 120°14W 78 H6
Hornos, C. de Chile 55°50S 67°30W 96 H3
Hornsby Australia 33°42S 151°2E 63 B5
Hornsea U.K. 53°55N 0°11W 12 D7
Horobetsu = Noboribetsu Japan 42°24N 141°6E 28 C10
Horodenka Ukraine 48°41N 25°29E 17 D13
Horodok Khmelnytskyy, Ukraine 49°10N 26°34E 17 D14
Horodok Lviv, Ukraine 49°46N 23°32E 17 D12
Horokhiv Ukraine 50°30N 24°45E 17 C13
Horqin Youyi Qianqi China 46°5N 122°3E 33 B12
Horqin Zuoyi Zhongqi China 44°8N 123°18E 33 B12
Horqueta Paraguay 23°15S 56°55W 94 A4
Horse Cr. → U.S.A. 41°57N 103°58W 76 F12
Horse I. Canada 53°20N 99°6W 71 C9
Horse Is. Canada 50°15N 55°50W 73 B8
Horsefly L. Canada 52°25N 121°0W 70 C4
Horseheads U.S.A. 42°10N 76°49W 82 D8
Horsens Denmark 55°52N 9°51E 9 J13
Horseshoe Lake Canada 45°17N 79°51W 82 A5
Horsham Australia 36°44S 142°13E 63 F3
Horsham U.K. 51°4N 0°20W 13 F7
Horta Azores 38°32N 28°38W 52 d
Horten Norway 59°25N 10°32E 9 G14
Horti India 17°7N 75°47E 44 F2
Horton U.S.A. 39°40N 95°32W 80 F6
Horton → Canada 69°56N 126°52W 68 D6
Horwood L. Canada 48°5N 82°20W 72 C3
Hosanna India 15°16N 76°20E 45 G3
Hosdrug = Kanhangad India 12°21N 74°58E 45 H2
Hosdurga India 13°49N 76°17E 45 H3
Ḩoseynābād Khuzestān, Iran 32°45N 48°20E 47 C6
Ḩoseynābād Kordestān, Iran 35°33N 47°8E 46 C5
Hoshangabad India 22°45N 77°45E 42 H7
Hoshiarpur India 31°30N 75°58E 42 D6
Hoskote India 13°4N 77°46E 45 H4
Hospet = Hosapete India 15°15N 76°20E 45 G3
Hoste, I. Chile 55°0S 69°0W 96 H3
Hosur India 12°43N 77°49E 45 H3
Hot Thailand 18°8N 98°29E 38 C2
Hot Creek Range U.S.A. 38°40N 116°20W 76 G5
Hot Springs Ark., U.S.A. 34°31N 93°3W 84 D8
Hot Springs S. Dak., U.S.A. 43°26N 103°29W 80 D2
Hot Springs △ U.S.A. 34°31N 93°3W 84 D8
Hotagen Sweden 63°59N 14°12E 8 E16
Hotan China 37°25N 79°55E 30 D4
Hotan He → China 40°22N 80°56E 30 C5
Hotazel S. Africa 27°17S 22°58E 56 D3
Hotchkiss U.S.A. 38°48N 107°43W 76 G10
Hotham, C. Australia 12°2S 131°18E 60 B5
Hoting Sweden 64°8N 16°15E 8 D17
Hotte, Massif de la Haiti 18°30N 73°45W 89 C5
Hottentotsbaai Namibia 26°8S 14°59E 56 D1
Hou Hai China 22°32N 113°56E 31 a
Houei Sai Laos 20°18N 100°26E 34 G3
Houffalize Belgium 50°8N 5°48E 15 D5
Houghton Mich., U.S.A. 47°7N 88°34W 80 B9
Houghton N.Y., U.S.A. 42°25N 78°10W 82 D6
Houghton L. U.S.A. 44°21N 84°44W 81 C11
Houghton-le-Spring U.K. 54°51N 1°28W 12 C6
Houhora Heads N.Z. 34°49S 173°9E 59 A4
Houlton U.S.A. 46°8N 67°51W 81 B20
Houma China 35°36N 111°20E 32 G6
Houma U.S.A. 29°36N 90°43W 85 G9
Housatonic → U.S.A. 41°10N 73°7W 83 E11
Houston Canada 54°25N 126°39W 70 C3
Houston Mo., U.S.A. 37°22N 91°58W 80 G8
Houston Tex., U.S.A. 29°45N 95°21W 84 G7

Houston George Bush
Intercontinental ✕ (IAH)
  U.S.A. 29°59N 95°20W **84** G7
Hout = Mogwadi ➤
  S. Africa 23°4S 29°36E **57** B4
Houtkraal S. Africa 30°23S 24°5E **56** D3
Houtman Abrolhos
  Australia 28°43S 113°48E **61** E1
Hovd = Dund-Us Mongolia 48°1N 91°38E **30** B7
Hove U.K. 50°50N 0°10W **13** G7
Hovenweep ◠ U.S.A. 37°20N 109°0W **77** H9
Hoveyzeh Iran 31°27N 48°4E **47** D6
Hövsgöl Mongolia 43°37N 109°39E **32** C5
Hövsgöl Nuur Mongolia 51°0N 100°30E **30** A9
Howar, Wadi ➤ Sudan 17°30N 27°8E **53** E11
Howard Australia 25°16S 152°32E **63** D5
Howard Pa., U.S.A. 41°1N 77°40W **82** F7
Howard S. Dak., U.S.A. 44°1N 97°32W **80** C5
Howe U.K. 43°48N 113°0W **76** E7
Howe, C. Australia 37°30S 150°0E **63** F5
Howe, West Cape
  Australia 35°8S 117°36E **61** G2
Howe I. Canada 44°16N 76°17W **83** B8
Howell U.S.A. 42°36N 83°56W **81** D12
Howick Canada 45°11N 73°51W **83** A11
Howick S. Africa 29°28S 30°14E **57** C5
Howick Group Australia 14°20S 145°30E **62** A4
Howitt, L. Australia 27°40S 138°40E **63** D2
Howland I. Pac. Oc. 0°48N 176°38W **64** G10
Höxter Germany 51°46N 9°22E **16** C5
Hoy U.K. 58°50N 3°15W **11** C5
Høyanger Norway 61°13N 6°4E **8** F12
Hoyerswerda Germany 51°26N 14°14E **16** C8
Hpa-an = Pa-an Burma 16°51N 97°40E **41** L20
Hpunan Pass Asia 27°30N 96°55E **41** F20
Hpyu = Pyu Burma 18°30N 96°28E **41** K20
Hradec Králové
  Czech Rep. 50°15N 15°50E **16** C8
Hrodna Belarus 53°42N 23°52E **17** B12
Hrodzyanka Belarus 53°31N 28°42E **17** B15
Hron ➤ Slovak Rep. 47°49N 18°45E **17** E10
Hrvatska = Croatia ■
  Europe 45°20N 16°0E **16** F9
Hrymayliv Ukraine 49°20N 26°5E **17** D14
Hsenwi Burma 23°22N 97°55E **41** H20
Hsiamen = Xiamen
  China 24°25N 118°4E **35** E12
Hsian = Xi'an China 34°15N 109°0E **32** G5
Hsinchu Taiwan 24°48N 120°58E **35** E13
Hsinhailien = Lianyungang
  China 34°40N 119°11E **33** G10
Hsinkai = Bhamo
  Burma 24°15N 97°15E **41** G20
Hsinying Taiwan 23°21N 120°17E **35** F13
Hsopket Burma 23°11N 98°26E **34** F2
Hsüchou = Xuzhou
  China 34°18N 117°10E **33** G9
Htawei = Dawei Burma 14°2N 98°12E **38** E2
Hu Xian China 34°8N 108°42E **32** G5
Hua Hin Thailand 12°34N 99°58E **38** F2
Hua Muang Laos 20°13N 103°52E **38** B4
Hua Shan China 34°28N 110°4E **32** G6
Hua Xian Henan, China 35°30N 114°30E **32** G8
Hua Xian Shaanxi, China 34°30N 109°48E **32** G5
Hua'an China 25°1N 117°32E **35** E11
Huab ➤ Namibia 20°52S 13°25E **56** A2
Huacheng China 24°4N 115°37E **35** E10
Huachinera Mexico 30°9N 108°55W **86** A3
Huacho Peru 11°10S 77°35W **92** F3
Huade China 41°55N 113°59E **32** D7
Huadian China 43°0N 126°40E **33** C14
Huadu China 23°22N 113°12E **35** F9
Huahine, Î.
  French Polynesia 16°46S 150°58W **65** J12
Huai He ➤ China 33°0N 118°30E **35** A12
Huai Kha Khaeng ◠
  Thailand 15°30N 98°55E **38** E2
Huai Nam Dang △
  Thailand 19°30N 98°30E **38** C2
Huai Yot Thailand 7°45N 99°37E **39** J12
Huai'an Hebei, China 40°30N 114°20E **32** D8
Huai'an Jiangsu, China 33°30N 119°10E **33** H10
Huaibei China 34°0N 116°48E **32** G9
Huaibin China 32°32N 115°27E **35** A10
Huaide = Gongzhuling
  China 43°30N 124°40E **33** C13
Huaidezhen China 43°48N 124°50E **33** C13
Huaihua China 27°32N 109°57E **34** D7
Huaiji China 23°55N 112°12E **35** F9
Huainan China 32°38N 116°58E **35** A11
Huaining China 30°24N 116°40E **35** B11
Huairen China 39°48N 113°20E **32** E7
Huairou China 40°20N 116°35E **32** D9
Huaiyang China 33°40N 114°52E **32** H8
Huaiyin China 33°30N 119°2E **33** H10
Huaiyuan Anhui, China 32°55N 117°10E **33** H9
Huaiyuan Guangxi Zhuangzu,
  China 24°31N 108°22E **34** E7
Huajuapán de León
  Mexico 17°48N 97°46W **87** D5
Hualapai Peak U.S.A. 35°5N 113°54W **79** K13
Hualien Taiwan 23°59N 121°36E **35** F13
Huallaga ➤ Peru 5°15S 75°30W **92** E3
Huambo Angola 12°42S 15°54E **55** G3
Huan Jiang ➤ China 34°28N 109°0E **32** G5
Huan Xian China 36°33N 107°7E **32** F4
Huancabamba Peru 5°10S 79°15W **92** E3
Huancane Peru 15°10S 69°44W **92** G5
Huancavelica Peru 12°50S 75°5W **92** F3
Huancayo Peru 12°5S 75°12W **92** F3
Huanchaca Bolivia 20°15S 66°40W **92** H5
Huang Hai = Yellow Sea
  China 35°0N 123°0E **33** G12
Huang He ➤ China 37°55N 118°50E **33** F10
Huang Xian China 37°38N 120°30E **33** F11
Huangchuan China 32°15N 115°10E **35** A10
Huanggang China 30°29N 114°52E **35** B10
Huangguoshu China 26°0N 105°40E **34** E5

Huanghua China 38°22N 117°20E **33** E9
Huanghuagang China 40°45N 117°54E **33** E9
Huangling China 35°34N 109°15E **32** G5
Huanglong China 35°30N 109°59E **32** G5
Huanglong ◠ China 32°44N 103°50E **34** A4
Huangmei China 30°5N 115°56E **35** B10
Huangpi China 30°50N 114°22E **35** B10
Huangping China 26°52N 107°54E **34** D6
Huangshan Anhui, China 30°8N 118°9E **35** B12
Huangshan Anhui,
  China 29°42N 118°25E **35** C12
Huangshi China 30°10N 115°3E **35** B10
Huangsongdian China 43°45N 127°25E **33** C14
Huangyan China 28°38N 121°19E **35** C13
Huangyangsi China 26°33N 111°39E **35** D8
Huaning China 24°17N 102°56E **34** E4
Huanjiang China 24°50N 108°18E **34** E7
Huantai China 41°23N 125°20E **33** D13
Huánuco Peru 9°55S 76°15W **92** E3
Huaping China 26°46N 101°25E **34** D3
Huaraz Peru 9°30S 77°32W **92** E3
Huarmey Peru 10°5S 78°5W **92** F3
Huarong China 29°29N 112°30E **35** C9
Huascarán, Nevado Peru 9°7S 77°37W **92** E3
Huasco Chile 28°30S 71°15W **94** B1
Huasco ➤ Chile 28°27S 71°13W **94** B1
Huasna U.S.A. 35°6N 120°24W **79** K6
Huatabampo Mexico 26°50N 109°38W **86** B3
Huauchinango Mexico 20°12N 98°3W **87** C5
Huautla de Jiménez
  Mexico 18°8N 96°51W **87** D5
Huaxi China 26°25N 106°40E **34** D6
Huayin China 34°35N 110°5E **32** G6
Huaying China 30°8N 106°44E **34** B6
Huayuan China 28°37N 109°29E **34** C7
Huazhou China 21°33N 110°33E **35** G8
Hubballi China 15°22N 75°15E **45** G2
Hubbard Ohio, U.S.A. 41°9N 80°34W **82** E4
Hubbard Tex., U.S.A. 31°51N 96°48W **84** F6
Hubbard Glacier Canada 60°18N 139°22W **68** E4
Hubbart Pt. Canada 59°21N 94°41W **71** B10
Hubei □ China 31°0N 112°0E **35** B9
Hubli = Hubballi India 15°22N 75°15E **45** G2
Huch'ang N. Korea 41°25N 127°2E **33** D14
Hucknall U.K. 53°3N 1°13W **12** D6
Huddersfield U.K. 53°39N 1°47W **12** D6
Hudiksvall Sweden 61°43N 17°10E **8** F17
Hudson Canada 50°6N 92°9W **72** B1
Hudson Mass., U.S.A. 42°23N 71°34W **83** D13
Hudson N.Y., U.S.A. 42°15N 73°46W **83** D11
Hudson Wis., U.S.A. 44°58N 92°45W **80** C7
Hudson Wyo., U.S.A. 42°54N 108°35W **76** E9
Hudson ➤ U.S.A. 40°42N 74°2W **83** F10
Hudson, C. Antarctica 68°21S 153°45E **5** C10
Hudson Bay Nunavut,
  Canada 60°0N 86°0W **69** F14
Hudson Bay Sask.,
  Canada 52°51N 102°23W **71** C8
Hudson Falls U.S.A. 43°18N 73°35W **83** C11
Hudson Mts. Antarctica 74°32S 99°20W **5** D16
Hudson Str. Canada 62°0N 70°0W **69** E18
Hudson's Hope Canada 56°0N 121°54W **70** B4
Hue Vietnam 16°30N 107°35E **38** D6
Huehuetenango
  Guatemala 15°20N 91°28W **88** C1
Huejúcar Mexico 22°21N 103°13W **86** C4
Huelva Spain 37°18N 6°57W **21** D2
Huentelauquén Chile 31°38S 71°33W **94** C1
Huerta, Sa. de la
  Argentina 31°10S 67°30W **94** C2
Huesca Spain 42°8N 0°25W **21** A5
Huetamo Mexico 18°35N 100°53W **86** D4
Hugh ➤ Australia 25°1S 134°1E **62** D1
Hughenden Australia 20°52S 144°10E **62** C3
Hughesville U.S.A. 41°14N 76°44W **83** E8
Hugli ➤ India 21°56N 88°4E **43** J13
Hugo Colo., U.S.A. 39°8N 103°28W **76** G12
Hugo Okla., U.S.A. 34°1N 95°31W **84** D7
Hui Xian = Huixian
  China 35°27N 113°12E **32** G7
Hui Xian China 33°50N 106°4E **32** H4
Hui'an China 25°1N 118°43E **35** E12
Hui'anbu China 37°28N 106°38E **32** F4
Huichang China 25°32N 115°45E **35** E10
Huichapan Mexico 20°23N 99°39W **87** C5
Huichon N. Korea 40°10N 126°16E **33** D14
Huidong Guangdong,
  China 22°58N 114°43E **35** F10
Huidong Sichuan, China 26°34N 102°35E **34** D4
Huifa He ➤ China 43°0N 127°50E **33** C14
Huila, Nevado del Colombia 3°0N 76°0W **92** C3
Huilai China 23°0N 116°18E **35** F11
Huili China 26°35N 102°17E **34** D4
Huimin China 37°27N 117°28E **33** F9
Huinan China 42°40N 126°2E **33** C14
Huinca Renancó
  Argentina 34°51S 64°22W **94** C3
Huining China 35°38N 105°0E **32** G3
Huinong China 39°5N 106°35E **32** E4
Huishui China 26°7N 106°38E **34** D6
Huiting China 34°5N 116°5E **32** G9
Huitong China 26°51N 109°45E **34** D7
Huixian China 35°27N 113°12E **32** G7
Huixtla Mexico 15°9N 92°28W **87** D6
Huize Mexico 26°24N 103°15E **34** D4
Huizhou China 23°0N 114°23E **35** F10
Hukawng Valley Burma 26°30N 96°30E **41** F20
Hukeri India 16°14N 74°36E **45** F2
Hukou China 29°45N 116°21E **35** C11
Hukuntsi Botswana 23°58S 21°45E **56** B3
Hulayfa' Si. Arabia 25°58N 40°45E **46** E4
Hulin China 45°48N 132°59E **31** B15
Hulin He ➤ China 45°0N 122°10E **33** B12
Hull = Kingston upon Hull
  U.K. 53°45N 0°21W **12** D7
Hull Canada 45°26N 75°43W **83** A9
Hull ➤ U.K. 53°44N 0°20W **12** D7

Hulst Neths. 51°17N 4°2E **15** C4
Huludao China 40°45N 120°50E **33** D11
Hulun Nur China 49°0N 117°30E **31** B12
Hulunbuir = Hailar
  China 49°10N 119°38E **31** B12
Huma, Tanjung Malaysia 5°29N 100°16E **39** c
Humacao Puerto Rico 18°9N 65°50W **89** d
Humahuaca Argentina 23°10S 65°25W **94** A2
Humaitá Brazil 7°35S 63°1W **92** E6
Humaitá Paraguay 27°2S 58°31W **94** B4
Humansdorp S. Africa 34°2S 24°46E **56** D3
Humbe Angola 16°40S 14°55E **56** A1
Humber ➤ U.K. 53°42N 0°27W **12** D7
Humboldt Canada 52°15N 105°9W **71** C7
Humboldt Iowa, U.S.A. 42°44N 94°13W **80** D6
Humboldt Tenn., U.S.A. 35°50N 88°55W **85** D10
Humboldt ➤ U.S.A. 39°59N 118°36W **76** G4
Humboldt Gletscher = Sermersuaq
  Greenland 79°30N 62°0W **69** B19
Hume U.S.A. 36°48N 118°54W **78** J8
Hume, L. Australia 36°0S 147°5E **63** F4
Humen China 22°50N 113°40E **31** a
Humenné Slovak Rep. 48°55N 21°50E **17** D11
Humphreys, Mt. U.S.A. 37°17N 118°40W **78** H8
Humphreys Peak
  U.S.A. 35°21N 111°41W **77** J8
Humptulips U.S.A. 47°14N 123°57W **78** C3
Hûn Libya 29°2N 16°0E **53** C9
Húnaflói Iceland 65°50N 20°50W **8** D3
Hunan □ China 27°30N 112°0E **35** D9
Hunchun China 42°52N 130°28E **33** C16
Hundewali Pakistan 31°55N 72°38E **42** D5
Hundred Mile House
  Canada 51°38N 121°18W **70** C4
Hunedoara Romania 45°40N 22°50E **17** F12
Hung Yen Vietnam 20°39N 106°4E **34** G6
Hunga Ha'apai Tonga 20°41S 175°7W **59** c
Hungary ■ Europe 47°20N 19°20E **17** E10
Hungary, Plain of Europe 47°0N 20°0E **6** F10
Hungerford Australia 28°58S 144°24E **63** D3
Hüngnam N. Korea 39°49N 127°45E **33** E14
Hungt'ou Hsü = Lan Yü
  Taiwan 22°4N 121°25E **35** F13
Hunjiang China 41°54N 126°26E **33** D14
Hunsberge Namibia 27°45S 17°12E **56** C2
Hunsrück Germany 49°56N 7°27E **16** D4
Hunstanton U.K. 52°56N 0°29E **12** E8
Hunsur India 12°16N 76°16E **45** H3
Hunter ➤ U.S.A. 42°13N 74°13W **83** D10
Hunter I. Australia 40°30S 144°45E **63** G3
Hunter I. Canada 51°55N 128°0W **70** C3
Hunter Ra. Australia 32°45S 150°15E **63** E5
Hunterville N.Z. 39°56S 175°35E **59** C5
Huntingburg U.S.A. 38°18N 86°57W **80** F10
Huntingdon U.K. 52°20N 0°11W **13** E7
Huntingdon U.S.A. 40°30N 78°1W **82** F6
Huntington Ind., U.S.A. 40°53N 85°30W **81** E11
Huntington N.Y., U.S.A. 40°52N 73°26W **83** F11
Huntington Oreg.,
  U.S.A. 44°21N 117°16W **76** D5
Huntington Utah,
  U.S.A. 39°20N 110°58W **76** G8
Huntington W. Va.,
  U.S.A. 38°25N 82°27W **81** F12
Huntington Beach
  U.S.A. 33°40N 118°5W **79** M9
Huntly N.Z. 37°34S 175°11E **59** B5
Huntly U.K. 57°27N 2°47W **11** D6
Huntsville Canada 45°20N 79°14W **82** A5
Huntsville Ala., U.S.A. 34°44N 86°35W **85** D11
Huntsville Tex., U.S.A. 30°43N 95°33W **84** F7
Hunyuan China 39°42N 113°42E **32** E7
Hunza ➤ India 35°54N 74°20E **43** B6
Huo Shan China 36°26N 111°52E **32** F6
Huo Xian = Huozhou
  China 36°36N 111°42E **32** F6
Huolin Gol China 45°32N 119°38E **33** B10
Huong Khe Vietnam 18°13N 105°41E **38** C5
Huonville Australia 43°0S 147°5E **63** G4
Huoqiu China 32°20N 116°12E **35** A11
Huoshan China 31°25N 116°20E **35** B11
Huoshao Dao = Lütao
  Taiwan 22°40N 121°30E **35** F13
Huozhou China 36°36N 111°42E **32** F6
Hupeh = Hubei □ China 31°0N 112°0E **35** B9
Hūr Iran 30°50N 57°7E **47** D8
Huränd Iran 38°51N 47°22E **46** B5
Ḥuraymīla Si. Arabia 25°8N 46°8E **46** E5
Hurd, C. Canada 45°13N 81°44W **82** A3
Hure Qi China 42°45N 121°45E **33** C11
Hurghada Egypt 27°15N 33°50E **53** C12
Hurley N. Mex., U.S.A. 32°42N 108°8W **77** K9
Hurley Wis., U.S.A. 46°27N 90°11W **80** B8
Huron Calif., U.S.A. 36°12N 120°6W **78** J6
Huron Ohio, U.S.A. 41°24N 82°33W **82** E2
Huron S. Dak., U.S.A. 44°22N 98°13W **80** C4
Huron, L. U.S.A. 44°30N 82°40W **82** B2
Huron East Canada 43°37N 81°18W **82** C3
Hurricane U.S.A. 37°11N 113°17W **77** H7
Hurunui ➤ N.Z. 42°54S 173°18E **59** E4
Húsavík Iceland 66°3N 17°21W **8** C5
Huşi Romania 46°41N 28°7E **17** E15
Hustadvika Norway 63°0N 7°0E **8** E12
Hustontown U.S.A. 40°3N 78°2W **82** F6
Hutchinson Kans., U.S.A. 38°5N 97°56W **80** F5
Hutchinson Minn.,
  U.S.A. 44°54N 94°22W **80** C6
Hutiao Xia China 27°13N 100°9E **34** D3
Hutte Sauvage, L. de la
  Canada 56°15N 64°45W **73** A7
Hutton, Mt. Australia 25°51S 148°20E **63** D4
Huwaki Indonesia 7°55S 126°30E **37** F7
Huy Belgium 50°31N 5°15E **15** D5
Huzhou China 30°51N 120°8E **35** B13
Huzurabad India 18°20N 79°32E **45** K4
Huzurnagar India 16°54N 79°53E **44** L4
Hvammstangi Iceland 65°24N 20°57W **8** D3
Hvar Croatia 43°11N 16°28E **22** C7
Hvítá ➤ Iceland 64°30N 21°58W **8** D3

Hwacheon-Cheosuji
  S. Korea 38°5N 127°50E **33** E14
Hwang Ho = Huang He ➤
  China 37°55N 118°50E **33** F10
Hwange Zimbabwe 18°18S 26°30E **55** F2
Hwange △ Zimbabwe 19°0S 26°30E **56** A4
Hwllfordd = Haverfordwest
  U.K. 51°48N 4°58W **13** F3
Hyannis Mass., U.S.A. 41°39N 70°17W **81** E18
Hyannis Nebr., U.S.A. 42°0N 101°46W **80** E3
Hyargas Nuur Mongolia 49°0N 93°0E **30** B7
Hydaburg U.S.A. 55°15N 132°50W **70** B2
Hyde Park U.S.A. 41°47N 73°56W **83** E11
Hyden Australia 32°24S 118°53E **61** F2
Hyderabad India 17°22N 78°29E **44** F4
Hyderabad Pakistan 25°23N 68°24E **42** G3
Hyères France 43°8N 6°9E **20** E7
Hyères, Îs. d' France 43°0N 6°20E **20** E7
Hyesan N. Korea 41°20N 128°10E **33** D15
Hyland ➤ Canada 59°52N 128°12W **70** B3
Hyndman Peak U.S.A. 43°45N 114°8W **76** E6
Hyōgo □ Japan 35°15N 134°50E **29** G7
Hyrum U.S.A. 41°38N 111°51W **76** F8
Hysham U.S.A. 46°18N 107°14W **76** C10
Hythe U.K. 51°4N 1°5E **13** F9
Hyūga Japan 32°25N 131°35E **29** H5
Hyvinge = Hyvinkää
  Finland 60°38N 24°50E **8** F21
Hyvinkää Finland 60°38N 24°50E **8** F21

I

I-n-Gall Niger 16°51N 7°1E **52** E7
Iaco ➤ Brazil 9°3S 68°34W **92** E5
Ialomița ➤ Romania 44°42N 27°51E **17** F14
Iași Romania 47°10N 27°40E **17** E14
Ib ➤ India 21°34N 83°48E **43** J10
Iba Phil. 15°22N 120°0E **37** A6
Ibadan Nigeria 7°22N 3°58E **52** G6
Ibagué Colombia 4°20N 75°20W **92** C3
Ibar ➤ Serbia 43°43N 20°45E **23** C9
Ibaraki □ Japan 36°10N 140°10E **29** F10
Ibarra Ecuador 0°21N 78°7W **92** C3
Ibb Yemen 14°2N 44°10E **49** E3
Ibenga ➤ Congo 2°9N 18°9E **54** D3
Ibera, L. Argentina 28°30S 57°9W **94** B4
Iberian Peninsula Europe 40°0N 5°0W **6** H5
Iberville Canada 45°19N 73°17W **83** A11
Iberville, Mt. d' Canada 58°50N 63°50W **69** F19
Ibiá Brazil 19°30S 46°30W **93** G9
Ibiapaba, Sa. da Brazil 4°0S 41°30W **93** D10
Ibicuí ➤ Brazil 29°25S 56°47W **95** B4
Ibicuy Argentina 33°55S 59°10W **94** C4
Ibiza = Eivissa Spain 38°54N 1°26E **21** C6
Ibonma Indonesia 3°29S 133°31E **37** E8
Ibotirama Brazil 12°13S 43°12W **93** F10
Ibrāhīm ➤ Lebanon 34°4N 35°38E **48** A4
'Ibrī Oman 23°14N 56°30E **49** C6
Ibu Indonesia 1°35N 127°33E **37** D7
Ibusuki Japan 31°12N 130°40E **29** J5
Ica Peru 14°0S 75°48W **92** F3
Içá ➤ Brazil 2°55S 67°58W **92** D5
Icacos Pt. Trin. & Tob. 10°3N 61°57W **93** K15
Içana Brazil 0°21N 67°19W **92** C5
Içana ➤ Brazil 0°26N 67°19W **92** C5
İçel = Mersin Turkey 36°51N 34°36E **46** B2
Iceland ■ Europe 64°45N 19°0W **8** D4
Iceland Basin Atl. Oc. 61°0N 19°0W **4** C7
Icelandic Plateau Arctic 64°10N 10°0W **4** C7
Ichalkaranji India 16°40N 74°33E **44** F2
Ich'ang = Yichang
  China 30°40N 111°20E **35** B8
Ichchapuram India 19°10N 84°40E **44** E7
Ichhawar India 23°1N 77°1E **42** H7
Ichihara Japan 35°28N 140°5E **29** G10
Ichilo ➤ Bolivia 15°57S 64°50W **92** G6
Ichinohe Japan 40°13N 141°17E **28** D10
Ichinomiya Japan 35°18N 136°48E **29** G8
Ichinoseki Japan 38°55N 141°8E **28** E10
Içoguz Turkmenistan 40°11N 58°24E **26** E6
Icy C. U.S.A. 70°20N 161°52W **66** B3
Ida Grove U.S.A. 42°21N 95°28W **80** D6
Idabel U.S.A. 33°54N 94°50W **84** E7
Idaho □ U.S.A. 45°0N 115°0W **76** D6
Idaho City U.S.A. 43°50N 115°50W **76** E6
Idaho Falls U.S.A. 43°30N 112°2W **76** E7
Idalia △ Australia 24°49S 144°36E **62** C3
Idar-Oberstein Germany 49°43N 7°16E **16** D4
Idensalmi = Iisalmi
  Finland 63°32N 27°10E **8** E22
Idfû Egypt 24°55N 32°49E **53** D12
Idi Indonesia 5°2N 97°37E **36** C1
Idi, Oros = Psiloritis, Oros
  Greece 35°15N 24°45E **23** G11
Idiofa Dem. Rep. of the Congo 4°55S 19°42E **54** E3
Idlib Syria 35°55N 36°36E **46** C3
Idra = Hydra Greece 37°20N 23°28E **23** F10
Idria U.S.A. 36°25N 120°41W **78** J6
Idutywa = Dutywa
  S. Africa 32°8S 28°18E **57** D4
Ieper Belgium 50°51N 2°53E **15** D2
Ierapetra Greece 35°1N 25°44E **23** G11
Iesi Italy 43°31N 13°14E **22** C5
Ifakara Tanzania 8°8S 36°41E **54** F7
'Ifâl, W. al ➤ Si. Arabia 28°7N 35°3E **46** D2
Ife Nigeria 7°30N 4°31E **52** G6
Iffley Australia 18°53S 141°12E **62** B3
Iforas, Adrar des Africa 19°40N 1°40E **52** E6
Ifould, L. Australia 30°52S 132°6E **61** F5
Igarapava Brazil 20°3S 47°47W **93** H9
Igarka Russia 67°30N 86°33E **26** C9
Igatpuri India 19°40N 73°27E **44** E1
Iggesund Sweden 61°39N 17°10E **8** F17
Iglésias Italy 39°19N 8°32E **22** E3
Igloolik = Iglulik
  Canada 69°20N 81°49W **69** D15
Iglulik Canada 69°20N 81°49W **69** D15
Igluligaarjuk = Chesterfield Inlet
  Canada 63°30N 90°45W **68** E13

Iglulik Canada 69°20N 81°49W **69** D15
Ignace Canada 49°30N 91°40W **72** C1
İğneada Burnu Turkey 41°53N 28°2E **23** D13
Igoumenitsa Greece 39°32N 20°18E **23** E9
Igrim Russia 63°12N 64°30E **26** C7
Iguaçu ➤ Brazil 25°36S 54°36W **95** B5
Iguaçu, Cat. del Brazil 25°41S 54°26W **95** B5
Iguaçu △ Brazil 25°30S 54°0W **95** B5
Iguaçu Falls = Iguaçu, Cat. del
  Brazil 25°41S 54°26W **95** B5
Iguala Mexico 18°21N 99°32W **87** D5
Igualada Spain 41°37N 1°37E **21** B6
Iguassu = Iguaçu ➤
  Brazil 25°36S 54°36W **95** B5
Iguatu Brazil 6°20S 39°18W **93** E11
Iguazú △ Argentina 25°42S 54°22W **95** B5
Iguidi, Erg Africa 27°0N 6°0W **52** C4
Iharana Madag. 13°25S 50°0E **55** G10
Ihbulag Mongolia 43°11N 107°10E **32** C4
Iheya-Shima Japan 27°4N 127°58E **29** L3
Ihosy Madag. 22°24S 46°8E **55** J9
Ii Finland 65°19N 25°22E **8** D21
Ii-Shima Japan 26°43N 127°47E **29** L3
Iida Japan 35°35N 137°50E **29** G8
Iijoki ➤ Finland 65°20N 25°20E **8** D21
Iisalmi Finland 63°32N 27°10E **8** E22
Iiyama Japan 36°51N 138°22E **29** F9
Iizuka Japan 33°38N 130°42E **29** H5
Ijâfene Mauritania 20°40N 8°0W **52** D4
Ijebu-Ode Nigeria 6°47N 3°58E **52** G6
IJmuiden Neths. 52°28N 4°35E **15** B4
Ijo älv = Iijoki ➤ Finland 65°20N 25°20E **8** D21
IJssel ➤ Neths. 52°35N 5°50E **15** B5
IJsselmeer Neths. 52°45N 5°20E **15** B5
Ijuí Brazil 28°23S 53°55W **95** B5
Ijuí ➤ Brazil 27°58S 55°20W **95** B4
Ikare Nigeria 7°32N 5°40E **52** G7
Ikaria Greece 37°35N 26°10E **23** F12
Ikeda Japan 34°1N 133°48E **29** G6
Ikela Dem. Rep. of the Congo 1°6S 23°6E **54** E4
Iki Japan 33°45N 129°42E **29** H4
Ikopa ➤ Madag. 16°45S 46°40E **55** H9
Ikparjuk = Arctic Bay
  Canada 73°1N 85°7W **69** C14
Iksan S. Korea 35°59N 127°0E **33** G14
Ikuntji = Haasts Bluff
  Australia 23°22S 132°0E **60** D5
Ilagan Phil. 17°7N 121°53E **37** A6
Īlām Iran 33°36N 46°36E **46** C5
Ilam Nepal 26°58N 87°58E **43** F12
Īlām □ Iran 33°0N 47°0E **46** C5
Ilan Taiwan 24°45N 121°44E **35** E13
Ilanskiy Russia 56°14N 96°3E **27** D10
Iława Poland 53°36N 19°34E **17** B10
Ilayangudi India 9°34N 78°37E **45** K4
Ile ➤ Kazakhstan 45°53N 77°10E **26** E8
Île-à-la-Crosse Canada 55°27N 107°53W **71** B7
Île-à-la-Crosse, Lac
  Canada 55°40N 107°45W **71** B7
Île-de-France □ France 49°0N 2°20E **20** B5
Ilebo Dem. Rep. of the Congo 4°17S 20°55E **54** E4
Ilek Russia 51°32N 53°21E **26** D6
Ilek ➤ Russia 51°30N 53°22E **18** D9
Ilemi Triangle Africa 5°0N 35°20E **54** D7
Ilesha Nigeria 7°37N 4°40E **52** G6
Ilford Canada 56°4N 95°35W **71** B9
Ilfracombe Australia 23°30S 144°30E **62** C3
Ilfracombe U.K. 51°12N 4°8W **13** F3
Ilha Grande, Represa
  Brazil 23°10S 53°5W **95** A5
Ilha Grande △ Brazil 23°10S 53°20W **95** A5
Ilhéus Brazil 14°49S 39°2W **93** F11
Ili = Ile ➤ Kazakhstan 45°53N 77°10E **26** E8
Iliamna L. U.S.A. 59°30N 155°0W **74** D8
Iligan Phil. 8°12N 124°13E **37** C6
Ilkal India 15°57N 76°8E **45** G3
Ilkeston U.K. 52°58N 1°19W **12** E6
Ilkley U.K. 53°56N 1°48W **12** D6
Illampu = Ancohuma, Nevado
  Bolivia 16°0S 68°50W **92** G5
Illana B. Phil. 7°35S 123°45E **37** C6
Illapel Chile 32°0S 71°10W **94** C1
Iller ➤ Germany 48°23N 9°58E **16** D6
Illes Balears = Baleares, Is.
  Spain 39°30N 3°0E **21** C7
Illimani, Nevado Bolivia 16°30S 67°50W **92** G5
Illinois □ U.S.A. 40°15N 89°30W **80** E8
Illinois ➤ U.S.A. 38°58N 90°28W **80** F8
Illizi Algeria 26°31N 8°32E **52** C7
Ilma, L. Australia 29°13S 127°46E **61** E4
Ilmajoki Finland 62°44N 22°34E **8** E20
Ilmen, Ozero Russia 58°15N 31°10E **18** C5
Ilo Peru 17°40S 71°20W **92** G4
Iloilo Phil. 10°45N 122°33E **37** B6
Ilomantsi Finland 62°38N 30°57E **8** E24
Ilorin Nigeria 8°30N 4°35E **52** G6
Ilwaco U.S.A. 46°19N 124°3W **78** D2
Imabari Japan 34°4N 133°0E **29** G6
Imandra, Ozero Russia 67°30N 33°0E **8** C25
Imari Japan 33°15N 129°52E **29** H4
Imatra Finland 61°12N 28°48E **8** F23
imeni 26 Bakinskikh Komissarov
  = Neftçala Azerbaijan 39°19N 49°12E **47** B6
imeni 26 Bakinskikh Komissarov
  Turkmenistan 39°22N 54°10E **47** B7
imeni Ismail Samani, Pik
  Tajikistan 39°0N 72°2E **26** F8
Imeri, Serra Brazil 0°50N 65°25W **92** C5
Imfolozi ➤ S. Africa 28°18S 32°0E **57** C5
Imi Ethiopia 6°28N 42°10E **49** F3
Imlay U.S.A. 40°40N 118°9W **76** F4
Imlay City U.S.A. 43°2N 83°5W **82** D1
Immingham U.K. 53°37N 0°13W **12** D7
Immokalee U.S.A. 26°25N 81°25W **85** H14
Ímola Italy 44°20N 11°42E **22** B4
Imperatriz Brazil 5°30S 47°29W **93** E9
Impéria Italy 43°53N 8°3E **20** E8
Imperial Canada 51°21N 105°28W **71** C7
Imperial Calif., U.S.A. 32°51N 115°34W **79** N11

Imperial Nebr., U.S.A. 40°31N 101°39W 80 E3
Imperial Beach U.S.A. 32°35N 117°6W 79 N9
Imperial Dam U.S.A. 32°55N 114°25W 79 N12
Imperial Res. U.S.A. 32°53N 114°28W 79 N12
Imperial Valley U.S.A. 33°0N 115°30W 79 N11
Imperieuse Reef
  Australia 17°36S 118°50E 60 C2
Impfondo Congo 1°40N 18°0E 54 D3
Imphal India 24°48N 93°56E 41 G18
İmroz = Gökçeada
  Turkey 40°10N 25°50E 23 D11
Imuris Mexico 30°47N 110°52W 86 A2
Imuruan B. Phil. 10°40N 119°10E 37 B5
In Amenas Algeria 28°5N 9°33E 53 C7
In Guezzam Algeria 19°37N 5°52E 52 E7
In Salah Algeria 27°10N 2°32E 52 C6
Ina Japan 35°50N 137°55E 29 G8
Inagua △ Bahamas 21°5N 73°24W 89 B5
Inangahua N.Z. 41°52S 171°59E 59 D3
Inanwatan Indonesia 2°8S 132°10E 37 E8
Iñapari Peru 11°0S 69°40W 92 F5
Inari Finland 68°54N 27°1E 8 B22
Inarijärvi Finland 69°0N 28°0E 8 B23
Inawashiro-Ko Japan 37°29N 140°6E 28 F10
tInbhear Mór, An = Arklow
  Ireland 52°48N 6°10W 10 D5
Inca Spain 39°43N 2°54E 21 C7
Inca de Oro Chile 26°45S 69°54W 94 B2
Incahuasi Argentina 27°2S 68°18W 94 B2
Incahuasi Chile 29°12S 71°5W 94 B1
İnce Burun Turkey 42°7N 34°56E 19 F5
İncesu Turkey 38°38N 35°11E 46 B2
Incheon S. Korea 37°27N 126°40E 33 F14
İncirliova Turkey 37°50N 27°41E 23 F12
Incline Village U.S.A. 39°10N 119°58W 78 F7
Incomáti → Mozam. 25°46S 32°43E 57 C5
Indalsälven → Sweden 62°36N 17°30E 8 E17
Indaw Burma 24°15N 96°5E 41 G20
Independence Calif.,
  U.S.A. 36°48N 118°12W 78 J8
Independence Iowa,
  U.S.A. 42°28N 91°54W 80 D8
Independence Kans.,
  U.S.A. 37°14N 95°42W 80 G6
Independence Ky.,
  U.S.A. 38°57N 84°33W 81 F11
Independence Mo., U.S.A. 39°6N 94°25W 80 F6
Independence Fjord
  Greenland 82°10N 29°0W 4 A6
Independence Mts.
  U.S.A. 41°20N 116°0W 76 F5
Index U.S.A. 47°50N 121°33W 78 C5
Indi India 17°10N 75°58E 44 F2
India ■ Asia 20°0N 78°0E 40 K11
Indian → U.S.A. 27°59N 80°34W 85 H14
Indian Cabins Canada 59°52N 117°40W 70 B5
Indian Harbour Canada 54°27N 57°13W 73 B8
Indian Head Canada 50°30N 103°41W 71 C8
Indian L. U.S.A. 43°46N 74°16W 83 C10
Indian Lake U.S.A. 43°47N 74°16W 83 C10
Indian Springs U.S.A. 36°35N 115°40W 79 J11
Indiana U.S.A. 40°37N 79°9W 82 F5
Indiana □ U.S.A. 40°0N 86°0W 81 F11
Indianapolis U.S.A. 39°46N 86°9W 80 F10
Indianola Iowa, U.S.A. 41°22N 93°34W 80 E7
Indianola Miss., U.S.A. 33°27N 90°39W 85 E9
Indiga Russia 67°38N 49°9E 18 A8
Indigirka → Russia 70°48N 148°54E 27 B15
Indio U.S.A. 33°43N 116°13W 79 M10
Indira Gandhi Canal India 28°0N 72°0E 42 F5
Indira Pt. India 6°44N 93°49E 45 L11
Indira Sagar India 22°15N 76°40E 42 H7
Indo-China India 15°0N 102°0E 24 G2
Indonesia ■ Asia 5°0S 115°0E 36 F5
Indore India 22°42N 75°53E 42 H6
Indramayu Indonesia 6°20S 108°19E 37 G13
Indravati → India 19°20N 80°20E 44 E5
Indre → France 47°16N 0°11E 20 C4
Indulkana Australia 26°58S 133°5E 63 D1
Indus → Pakistan 24°20N 67°47E 42 G2
Indus, Mouths of the
  Pakistan 24°0N 68°0E 42 H3
İnebolu Turkey 41°55N 33°40E 19 F5
Infiernillo, Presa del
  Mexico 18°35N 101°50W 86 D4
Inga, Barrage d'
  Dem. Rep. of the Congo 5°39S 13°39E 54 F2
Ingenio Santa Ana
  Argentina 27°25S 65°40W 94 B2
Ingersoll Canada 43°4N 80°55W 82 C4
Ingham Australia 18°43S 146°10E 62 B4
Ingleborough U.K. 54°10N 2°22W 12 C5
Inglewood Queens.,
  Australia 28°25S 151°2E 63 D5
Inglewood Vic., Australia 36°29S 143°53E 63 F3
Inglewood N.Z. 39°9S 174°14E 59 C5
Ingólfshöfði Iceland 63°48N 16°39W 8 E5
Ingolstadt Germany 48°46N 11°26E 16 D6
Ingomar U.S.A. 46°35N 107°23W 76 C10
Ingonish Canada 46°42N 60°18W 73 C7
Ingraj Bazar India 24°58N 88°10E 43 G13
Ingrid Christensen Coast
  Antarctica 69°30S 76°0E 5 C6
Ingulec = Inhulec
  Ukraine 47°42N 33°14E 19 E5
Ingushetia □ Russia 43°20N 44°50E 19 F8
Ingwavuma S. Africa 27°9S 31°59E 57 C5
Inhaca Mozam. 26°1S 32°57E 57 C5
Inhaca Pen. Mozam. 26°13S 32°57E 57 C5
Inhafenga Mozam. 20°36S 33°53E 57 B5
Inhambane Mozam. 23°54S 35°30E 57 B6
Inhambane □ Mozam. 22°30S 34°20E 57 B5
Inharrime Mozam. 24°30S 35°0E 57 B6
Inharrime → Mozam. 24°30S 35°0E 57 B6
Inhulec Ukraine 47°42N 33°14E 19 E5
Ining = Yining China 43°58N 81°10E 30 C5
Inírida → Colombia 3°55N 67°52W 92 C5
Inis = Ennis Ireland 52°51N 8°59E 10 D3
Inishbofin Ireland 53°37N 10°13W 10 C1
Inisheer Ireland 53°3N 9°32W 10 C2

Inishfree B. Ireland 55°4N 8°23W 10 A3
Inishkea North Ireland 54°9N 10°11W 10 B1
Inishkea South Ireland 54°7N 10°12W 10 B1
Inishmaan Ireland 53°5N 9°35W 10 C2
Inishmore Ireland 53°8N 9°45W 10 C2
Inishmurray Ireland 54°26N 8°39W 10 B3
Inishowen Pen. Ireland 55°14N 7°15W 10 A4
Inishshark Ireland 53°37N 10°16W 10 C1
Inishturk Ireland 53°42N 10°7W 10 C1
Inishvickillane Ireland 52°3N 10°37W 10 D1
Injinoo ◎ Australia 10°56S 142°15E 62 A3
Injune Australia 25°53S 148°32E 63 D4
Inklin → N. Amer. 58°50N 133°10W 70 B2
Inland Kaikoura Ra.
  N.Z. 41°59S 173°41E 59 D4
Inland Sea = Setonaikai
  Japan 34°20N 133°30E 29 G6
Inle L. Burma 20°30N 96°58E 41 J20
Inlet U.S.A. 43°45N 74°48W 83 C10
Inn → Austria 48°35N 13°28E 16 D7
Innamincka Australia 27°44S 140°46E 63 D3
Inner Hebrides U.K. 57°0N 6°30W 11 E2
Inner Mongolia = Nei Mongol
  Zizhiqu □ China 42°0N 112°0E 32 D7
Inner Sound U.K. 57°30N 5°55W 11 D3
Innerkip Canada 43°13N 80°42W 82 C4
Innerleithen U.K. 55°37N 3°4W 11 F5
Innetalling I. Canada 56°0N 79°0W 72 A4
Innisfail Australia 17°33S 146°5E 62 B4
Innisfail Canada 52°2N 113°57W 70 C6
In'noshima Japan 34°19N 133°10E 29 G6
Innsbruck Austria 47°16N 11°23E 16 E6
Inny → Ireland 53°32N 7°51W 10 C4
Inongo
  Dem. Rep. of the Congo 1°55S 18°30E 54 E3
Inowrocław Poland 52°50N 18°12E 17 B10
Inscription, C. Australia 25°29S 112°59E 61 E1
Insein Burma 16°50N 96°5E 41 L20
Inta Russia 66°5N 60°8E 18 A11
Intendente Alvear
  Argentina 35°12S 63°32W 94 D3
Interlaken Switz. 46°41N 7°50E 20 C7
Interlaken U.S.A. 42°37N 76°44W 83 D8
International Falls
  U.S.A. 48°36N 93°25W 80 A7
Interview I. India 12°55N 92°43E 45 H11
Intiyaco Argentina 28°43S 60°5W 94 B3
Inukjuak Canada 58°25N 78°15W 69 F16
Inútil, B. Chile 53°30S 70°15W 96 G2
Inuvik Canada 68°16N 133°40W 68 D5
Inveraray U.K. 56°14N 5°5W 11 E3
Inverbervie U.K. 56°51N 2°17W 11 E6
Invercargill N.Z. 46°24S 168°24E 59 G2
Inverclyde □ U.K. 55°55N 4°49W 11 F4
Inverell Australia 29°45S 151°8E 63 D5
Invergordon U.K. 57°41N 4°10W 11 D4
Inverloch Australia 38°38S 145°45E 63 F4
Invermere Canada 50°30N 116°2W 70 C5
Inverness Canada 46°15N 61°19W 73 C7
Inverness U.K. 57°29N 4°13W 11 D4
Inverness U.S.A. 28°50N 82°20W 85 G13
Inverurie U.K. 57°17N 2°23W 11 D6
Investigator Group
  Australia 34°45S 134°20E 63 E1
Investigator Str. Australia 35°30S 137°0E 63 F2
Inya Russia 50°28N 86°37E 26 D9
Inyangani Zimbabwe 18°5S 32°50E 55 H6
Inyantue Zimbabwe 18°33S 26°39E 56 A4
Inyo Mts. U.S.A. 36°40N 118°0W 78 J9
Inyokern U.S.A. 35°39N 117°49W 79 K9
Inza Russia 53°55N 46°25E 18 D8
Iō-Jima Japan 30°48N 130°18E 29 J5
Ioannina Greece 39°42N 20°47E 23 E9
Iola U.S.A. 37°55N 95°24W 80 G6
Iona U.K. 56°20N 6°25W 11 E2
Ione U.S.A. 38°21N 120°56W 78 G6
Ionia U.S.A. 42°59N 85°4W 81 D11
Ionian Is. = Ionioi Nisoi
  Greece 38°40N 20°0E 23 E9
Ionian Sea Medit. S. 37°30N 17°30E 23 E7
Ionioi Nisoi Greece 38°40N 20°0E 23 E9
Ios Greece 36°41N 25°20E 23 F11
Iony, Ostrov Russia 56°24N 143°22E 27 D15
Ios Greece 36°41N 25°20E 23 F11
Iowa □ U.S.A. 42°18N 93°30W 80 D7
Iowa → U.S.A. 41°10N 91°1W 80 E8
Iowa City U.S.A. 41°40N 91°32W 80 E8
Iowa Falls U.S.A. 42°31N 93°16W 80 D7
Iowa Park U.S.A. 33°57N 98°40W 84 E5
Ipameri Brazil 17°44S 48°9W 93 G9
Ipatinga Brazil 19°32S 42°30W 93 G10
Ipiales Colombia 0°50N 77°37W 92 C3
Ipin = Yibin China 28°45N 104°32E 34 C5
Ipixuna Brazil 7°0S 71°40W 92 E4
Ipoh Malaysia 4°35N 101°5E 39 K3
Ippy C.A.R. 6°5N 21°7E 54 C4
İpsala Turkey 40°55N 26°23E 23 D12
Ipswich Australia 27°35S 152°40E 63 D5
Ipswich U.K. 52°4N 1°10E 13 E9
Ipswich Mass., U.S.A. 42°41N 70°50W 83 D14
Ipswich S. Dak., U.S.A. 45°27N 99°2W 80 C4
Ipu Brazil 4°23S 40°44W 93 D10
Iqaluit Canada 63°44N 68°31W 69 E18
Iqaluktuutiaq = Cambridge Bay
  Canada 69°10N 105°0W 68 D11
Iquique Chile 20°19S 70°5W 92 H4
Iquitos Peru 3°45S 73°10W 92 D4
Irabu-Jima Japan 24°50N 125°10E 29 M2
Iracoubo Fr. Guiana 5°30N 53°10W 93 B8
Irafshān Iran 26°42N 61°56E 47 E9
Iráklio Greece 35°20N 25°12E 23 G11
Iráklion = Iráklio Greece 35°20N 25°12E 23 G11
Irala Paraguay 25°55S 54°35W 95 B5
Iran ■ Asia 33°0N 53°0E 47 C7
Iran, Pegunungan
  Malaysia 2°20N 114°50E 36 D4
Iran Ra. = Iran, Pegunungan
  Malaysia 2°20N 114°50E 36 D4
Iranamadu Tank Sri Lanka 9°23N 80°29E 45 K5
Īrānshahr Iran 27°15N 60°40E 47 E9

Irapuato Mexico 20°41N 101°28W 86 C4
Iraq ■ Asia 33°0N 44°0E 46 C5
Irati Brazil 25°25S 50°38W 95 B5
Irazú, Volcan Costa Rica 9°59N 83°51W 88 D3
Irbid Jordan 32°35N 35°48E 48 C4
Irbid □ Jordan 32°30N 35°50E 48 C5
Irbil = Arbil Iraq 36°15N 44°5E 46 B5
Irebu Dem. Rep. of the Congo 0°40S 17°46E 54 E3
Ireland ■ Europe 53°50N 7°52W 10 C4
Iri = Iksan S. Korea 35°59N 127°0E 33 G14
Irian Jaya = Papua □
  Indonesia 4°0S 137°0E 37 E9
Irian Jaya Barat □
  Indonesia 2°5S 132°50E 37 E8
Iringa Tanzania 7°48S 35°43E 54 F7
Irinjalakuda India 10°21N 76°14E 45 J3
Iriomote △ Japan 24°29N 123°53E 29 M1
Iriomote-Jima Japan 24°19N 123°48E 29 M1
Iriona Honduras 15°57N 85°11W 88 C2
Iriri → Brazil 3°52S 52°37W 93 D8
Irish Sea Europe 53°38N 4°48W 12 D3
Irkutsk Russia 52°18N 104°20E 30 D9
Irō-Zaki Japan 34°36N 138°51E 29 G9
Iron Baron Australia 32°58S 137°11E 63 E2
Iron Gate = Portile de Fier
  Europe 44°44N 22°30E 17 F12
Iron Knob Australia 32°46S 137°8E 63 E2
Iron Mountain U.S.A. 45°49N 88°4W 80 C9
Iron Range △ Australia 12°34S 143°18E 62 A3
Iron River U.S.A. 46°6N 88°39W 80 B9
Irondequoit U.S.A. 43°13N 77°35W 82 C7
Ironton Mo., U.S.A. 37°36N 90°38W 80 G8
Ironton Ohio, U.S.A. 38°32N 82°41W 81 F12
Ironwood U.S.A. 46°27N 90°9W 80 B8
Ironwood Forest ○
  U.S.A. 32°32N 111°28W 77 K8
Iroquois Canada 44°51N 75°19W 83 B9
Iroquois Falls Canada 48°46N 80°41W 72 C3
Irpin Ukraine 50°30N 30°15E 17 C16
Irrara Cr. → Australia 29°35S 145°31E 63 D4
Irrawaddy = Ayeyarwady →
  Burma 15°50N 95°6E 41 M19
Irrawaddy □ Burma 17°0N 95°0E 41 L19
Irrawaddy, Mouths of the
  Burma 15°30N 95°0E 41 M19
Irricana Canada 51°19N 113°37W 70 C6
Irrunytju Australia 26°3S 128°56E 61 E4
Irtysh → Russia 61°4N 68°52E 26 C7
Irún Spain 43°20N 1°52W 21 A5
Irunea = Pamplona-Iruña
  Spain 42°48N 1°38W 21 A5
Irvine Canada 49°57N 110°16W 71 D6
Irvine U.K. 55°37N 4°41W 11 F4
Irvine Calif., U.S.A. 33°41N 117°46W 79 M9
Irvine Ky., U.S.A. 37°42N 83°58W 81 G12
Irvinestown U.K. 54°28N 7°39W 10 B4
Irving U.S.A. 32°48N 96°56W 84 E6
Irvona U.S.A. 40°46N 78°33W 82 F6
Irwin → Australia 29°15S 114°54E 61 E1
Irymple Australia 34°14S 142°8E 63 E3
Isa Khel Pakistan 32°41N 71°17E 42 C4
Isaac → Australia 22°55S 149°20E 62 C4
Isabel U.S.A. 45°24N 101°26W 80 C3
Isabel, I. Mexico 21°51N 105°55W 86 C3
Isabela Phil. 6°40N 121°59E 37 C6
Isabela Puerto Rico 18°30N 67°2W 89 d
Isabella, Cord. Nic. 13°30N 85°25W 88 D2
Isabella Ra. Australia 21°0S 121°4E 60 D3
Isachsen, C. Canada 79°20N 105°28W 69 B10
Isachsen Mt. Antarctica 72°8S 26°5E 5 D4
Ísafjarðardjúp Iceland 66°10N 23°0W 8 C2
Ísafjörður Iceland 66°5N 23°9W 8 C2
Isagarh India 24°48N 77°51E 42 G7
Isahaya Japan 32°52N 130°2E 29 H5
Isan → India 26°51N 80°7E 43 F9
Isana = Içana → Brazil 0°26N 67°19W 92 C5
Isar → Germany 48°48N 12°57E 16 D7
İschia Italy 40°44N 13°57E 22 D5
Ischigualasto △ Argentina 30°0S 68°0W 94 B2
Isdell → Australia 16°27S 124°51E 60 C3
Ise Japan 34°25N 136°45E 29 G8
Ise-Shima △ Japan 34°30N 136°48E 29 G8
Ise-Wan Japan 34°43N 136°43E 29 G8
Isère → France 44°59N 4°51E 20 D6
Isérnia Italy 41°36N 14°14E 22 D6
Isfahan = Eşfahān Iran 32°39N 51°43E 47 C6
Ishigaki Japan 24°26N 124°10E 29 M2
Ishigaki-Shima Japan 24°20N 124°10E 29 M2
Ishikari Japan 43°20N 141°15E 28 C10
Ishikari-Gawa →
  Japan 43°15N 141°23E 28 C10
Ishikari-Sammyaku
  Japan 43°30N 143°0E 28 C11
Ishikari-Wan Japan 43°25N 141°1E 28 C10
Ishikawa Japan 26°25N 127°49E 29 L3
Ishikawa □ Japan 36°30N 136°30E 29 F8
Ishim Russia 56°10N 69°30E 26 D7
Ishim → Russia 57°45N 71°10E 26 D8
Ishinomaki Japan 38°32N 141°20E 28 E10
Ishioka Japan 36°11N 140°16E 29 F10
Ishkoman Pakistan 36°30N 73°50E 43 A5
Ishpeming U.S.A. 46°29N 87°40W 80 B10
Isil Kul Russia 54°55N 71°16E 26 D8
İsimangaliso △ S. Africa 27°50S 32°32E 57 D5
Isiro Dem. Rep. of the Congo 2°53N 27°40E 54 D5
Isisford Australia 24°15S 144°21E 62 C3
İskenderun Turkey 36°32N 36°10E 46 B3
İskenderun Körfezi
  Turkey 36°40N 35°50E 19 G6
İskür → Bulgaria 43°45N 24°25E 23 C11
Iskut → Canada 56°45N 131°49W 70 B2
Isla → U.K. 56°32N 3°20W 11 E5
Isla Coiba △ Panama 7°33N 81°36W 88 E3
Isla de Salamanca △
  Colombia 10°59N 74°40W 89 D5
Isla Gorge △ Australia 25°10S 149°57E 62 D4
Isla Isabel △ Mexico 21°54N 105°58W 86 C3
Isla Tiburón y San Estebán ○
  Mexico 29°0N 112°27W 86 B2

Isla Vista U.S.A. 34°25N 119°53W 79 L7
Islam Headworks
  Pakistan 29°49N 72°33E 42 E5
Islamabad Pakistan 33°40N 73°10E 42 C5
Islamgarh Pakistan 27°51N 70°48E 42 F4
Islamkot Pakistan 24°42N 70°13E 42 G4
Islampur Bihar, India 25°9N 85°12E 43 G11
Islampur Maharashtra,
  India 17°2N 74°20E 44 F2
Islampur Paschimbanga,
  India 26°16N 88°12E 43 F13
Island = Iceland ■ Europe 64°45N 19°0W 8 D4
Island L. Canada 53°47N 94°25W 71 C10
Island Lagoon Australia 31°30S 136°40E 63 E2
Island Pond U.S.A. 44°49N 71°53W 83 B13
Islands, B. of Canada 49°11N 58°15W 73 C8
Islands, B. of N.Z. 35°15S 174°6E 59 A5
Islay U.K. 55°46N 6°10W 11 F2
Isle → France 44°55N 0°15W 20 D3
Isle aux Morts Canada 47°35N 59°0W 73 C8
Isle of Wight □ U.K. 50°41N 1°17W 13 G6
Isle Royale △ U.S.A. 48°0N 88°55W 80 B9
Isleton U.S.A. 38°10N 121°37W 78 G5
Ismail = Izmayil Ukraine 45°22N 28°46E 17 F15
Ismâ'ilîya Egypt 30°37N 32°18E 53 B12
Isna Egypt 25°17N 32°30E 53 C12
Isojärvi △ Finland 61°40N 25°0E 8 F21
Isparta Turkey 37°47N 30°30E 19 G5
İspica Italy 36°47N 14°55E 22 F6
Israel ■ Asia 32°0N 34°50E 48 D3
Issoire France 45°32N 3°15E 20 D5
Issyk-Kul = Balykchy
  Kyrgyzstan 42°26N 76°12E 30 C8
Issyk-Kul, Ozero = Ysyk-Köl
  Kyrgyzstan 42°25N 77°15E 26 E8
Istiea Greece 38°57N 23°9E 23 E10
Isto, Mt. U.S.A. 69°12N 143°48W 74 B11
Istokpoga, L. U.S.A. 27°23N 81°17W 85 H14
Istra Croatia 45°10N 14°0E 16 F7
Istres France 43°31N 4°59E 20 E6
Istria = Istra Croatia 45°10N 14°0E 16 F7
Itá Paraguay 25°29S 57°21W 94 B4
Itaberaba Brazil 12°32S 40°18W 93 F11
Itabira Brazil 19°37S 43°13W 93 G10
Itabirito Brazil 20°15S 43°48W 95 A7
Itabuna Brazil 14°48S 39°16W 93 F11
Itacaunas → Brazil 5°21S 49°8W 93 E9
Itacoatiara Brazil 3°8S 58°25W 92 D7
Itaguaí Brazil 22°15S 43°46W 95 A7
Itaipú, Represa de Brazil 25°30S 54°30W 95 B5
Itaituba Brazil 4°10S 55°50W 93 D7
Itajaí Brazil 27°50S 48°39W 95 B6
Itajubá Brazil 22°24S 45°30W 95 A6
Itala △ S. Africa 27°30S 31°7E 57 C5
Italy ■ Europe 42°0N 13°0E 22 C5
Itamaraju Brazil 17°4S 39°32W 93 G11
Itapecuru Mirim Brazil 3°24S 44°20W 93 D10
Itaperuna Brazil 21°10S 41°54W 95 A7
Itapetininga Brazil 23°36S 48°7W 95 A6
Itapeva Brazil 23°59S 48°59W 95 A6
Itapicuru → Bahia,
  Brazil 11°47S 37°32W 93 F11
Itapicuru → Maranhão,
  Brazil 2°52S 44°12W 93 D10
Itapipoca Brazil 3°30S 39°35W 93 D11
Itapuá □ Paraguay 26°40S 55°40W 95 B4
Itaquí Brazil 29°8S 56°30W 94 B4
Itararé Brazil 24°6S 49°23W 95 A6
Itarsi India 22°36N 77°51E 42 H7
Itati Argentina 27°16S 58°15W 94 B4
Itatiaia △ Brazil 22°22S 44°38W 95 A7
Itchen → U.K. 50°55N 1°22W 13 G6
Itezhi Tezhi, L. Zambia 15°30S 25°30E 55 H5
Ithaca = Ithaki Greece 38°25N 20°40E 23 E9
Ithaca U.S.A. 42°27N 76°30W 83 D8
Ithaki Greece 38°25N 20°40E 23 E9
Itiquira → Brazil 17°18S 56°44W 93 G7
Itiyuro → Argentina 22°40S 63°50W 94 A3
Itō Japan 34°58N 139°5E 29 G9
Itoigawa Japan 37°2N 137°51E 29 F8
Itonamas → Bolivia 12°28S 64°24W 92 F6
Ittoqqortoormiit Greenland 70°20N 23°0W 4 B6
Itu Brazil 23°17S 47°15W 95 A6
Itu Aba I. S. China Sea 10°23N 114°21E 36 B4
Ituiutaba Brazil 19°0S 49°25W 93 G9
Itumbiara Brazil 18°20S 49°10W 93 G9
Ituna Canada 51°10N 103°24W 71 C8
Iturbe Argentina 23°0S 65°25W 94 A2
Iturup, Ostrov Russia 45°0N 148°0E 27 E15
Ituxi → Brazil 7°18S 64°51W 92 E6
Itzehoe Germany 53°55N 9°31E 16 B5
Ivaí → Brazil 23°18S 53°42W 95 A5
Ivalo Finland 68°38N 27°35E 8 B22
Ivalojoki → Finland 68°40N 27°40E 8 B22
Ivanava Belarus 52°7N 25°29E 17 B13
Ivanhoe Australia 32°56S 144°20E 63 E3
Ivanhoe Canada 44°23N 77°28W 82 B7
Ivanhoe Minn., U.S.A. 44°28N 96°15W 80 C5
Ivano-Frankivsk
  Ukraine 48°40N 24°40E 17 D13
Ivanovo = Ivanava
  Belarus 52°7N 25°29E 17 B13
Ivanovo Russia 57°5N 41°0E 18 C7
Ivatsevichy Belarus 52°43N 25°21E 17 B13
Ivdel Russia 60°42N 60°24E 18 B11
Iveragh Pen. Ireland 51°52N 10°15E 10 E1
Ivinheima → Brazil 23°14S 53°42W 95 A5
Ivinhema Brazil 22°10S 53°37W 95 A5
Ivory Coast W. Afr. 4°20N 7°0W 52 H4
Ivory Coast ■ Africa 7°30N 5°0W 52 G4
Ivrea Italy 45°28N 7°52E 20 D7
Ivujivik Canada 62°24N 77°55W 69 E16
Ivvavik △ Canada 69°6N 139°30W 68 D4
Ivybridge U.K. 50°23N 3°56W 13 G4
Iwaizumi Japan 39°50N 141°45E 28 E10

Iwaki Japan 37°3N 140°55E 29 F10
Iwakuni Japan 34°15N 132°8E 29 G6
Iwamizawa Japan 43°12N 141°46E 28 C10
Iwanai Japan 42°58N 140°30E 28 C10
Iwata Japan 34°42N 137°51E 29 G8
Iwate □ Japan 39°30N 141°30E 28 E10
Iwate-San Japan 39°51N 141°0E 28 E10
Iwo Nigeria 7°39N 4°9E 52 G6
Iwŏn N. Korea 40°19N 128°39E 33 D15
Ixiamas Bolivia 13°50S 68°5W 92 F5
Ixopo S. Africa 30°11S 30°5E 57 C5
Ixtepec Mexico 16°34N 95°6W 87 D5
Ixtlán del Río Mexico 21°2N 104°22W 86 C4
Iyo Japan 33°45N 132°45E 29 H6
Izabal, L. de Guatemala 15°30N 89°10W 88 C2
Izamal Mexico 20°56N 89°1W 87 C7
Izena-Shima Japan 26°56N 127°56E 29 L3
Izhevsk Russia 56°51N 53°14E 18 C9
Izhma → Russia 65°19N 52°54E 18 A9
Izmayil Ukraine 45°22N 28°46E 17 F15
İzmir Turkey 38°25N 27°8E 23 E12
İzmit = Kocaeli Turkey 40°45N 29°50E 19 F4
İznik Gölü Turkey 40°27N 29°30E 23 D13
Izra Syria 32°51N 36°15E 48 C5
Izu-Hantō Japan 34°45N 139°0E 29 G9
Izu-Shotō Japan 34°30N 140°0E 29 G10
Izúcar de Matamoros
  Mexico 18°36N 98°28W 87 D5
Izumi Japan 32°5N 130°22E 29 H5
Izumi-Sano Japan 34°23N 135°18E 29 G7
Izumo Japan 35°20N 132°46E 29 G6
Izyaslav Ukraine 50°5N 26°50E 17 C14

J

J.F.K. Int. ✈ (JFK)
  U.S.A. 40°38N 73°47W 83 F11
J. Strom Thurmond L.
  U.S.A. 33°40N 82°12W 85 E13
Ja-ela Sri Lanka 7°5N 79°53E 45 L4
Jabalpur India 23°9N 79°58E 43 H8
Jabālya Gaza Strip 31°32N 34°29E 48 D3
Jabbūl Syria 36°4N 37°30E 46 B3
Jabiru Australia 12°40S 132°53E 60 B5
Jablah Syria 35°20N 36°0E 46 C3
Jablonec nad Nisou
  Czech Rep. 50°43N 15°10E 16 C8
Jaboatão Brazil 8°7S 35°1W 93 E11
Jaboticabal Brazil 21°15S 48°17W 95 A6
Jaca Spain 42°35N 0°33W 21 A5
Jacarei Brazil 23°20S 46°0W 95 A6
Jacarèzinho Brazil 23°5S 49°58W 95 A6
Jack River △ Australia 14°58S 144°19E 62 A3
Jackman U.S.A. 45°37N 70°15W 81 C18
Jacksboro U.S.A. 33°13N 98°10W 84 E5
Jackson Barbados 13°7N 59°36W 89 g
Jackson Ala., U.S.A. 31°31N 87°53W 85 F11
Jackson Calif., U.S.A. 38°21N 120°46W 78 G6
Jackson Ky., U.S.A. 37°33N 83°23W 81 G12
Jackson Mich., U.S.A. 42°15N 84°24W 81 D11
Jackson Minn., U.S.A. 43°37N 95°1W 80 D6
Jackson Miss., U.S.A. 32°18N 90°12W 85 E9
Jackson Mo., U.S.A. 37°23N 89°40W 80 G9
Jackson Ohio, U.S.A. 39°3N 82°39W 81 F12
Jackson Tenn., U.S.A. 35°37N 88°49W 85 D10
Jackson Wyo., U.S.A. 43°29N 110°46W 76 E8
Jackson B. N.Z. 43°58S 168°42E 59 E2
Jackson L. U.S.A. 43°52N 110°36W 76 E8
Jacksons N.Z. 42°46S 171°32E 59 E3
Jackson's Arm Canada 49°52N 56°47W 73 C8
Jacksonville Ala., U.S.A. 33°49N 85°46W 85 E12
Jacksonville Ark., U.S.A. 34°52N 92°7W 84 D8
Jacksonville Calif.,
  U.S.A. 37°52N 120°24W 78 H6
Jacksonville Fla., U.S.A. 30°20N 81°39W 85 F14
Jacksonville Ill., U.S.A. 39°44N 90°14W 80 F8
Jacksonville N.C.,
  U.S.A. 34°45N 77°26W 85 D16
Jacksonville Tex., U.S.A. 31°58N 95°17W 84 F7
Jacksonville Beach
  U.S.A. 30°17N 81°24W 85 F14
Jacmel Haiti 18°14N 72°32W 89 C5
Jacob Lake U.S.A. 36°43N 112°13W 77 H7
Jacobabad Pakistan 28°20N 68°29E 42 E3
Jacobina Brazil 11°11S 40°30W 93 F10
Jacques-Cartier, Dét. de
  Canada 50°0N 63°30W 73 C7
Jacques-Cartier, Mt.
  Canada 48°57N 66°0W 73 C6
Jacques-Cartier △
  Canada 47°15N 71°33W 73 C5
Jacuí → Brazil 30°2S 51°15W 95 C5
Jacumba U.S.A. 32°37N 116°11W 79 N10
Jacundá → Brazil 1°57S 50°26W 93 D8
Jadcherla India 16°46N 78°9E 44 F4
Jade Dragon Snow Mt. = Yulong
  Xueshan China 27°6N 100°10E 34 D3
Jade Mt. = Yü Shan
  Taiwan 23°25N 120°52E 35 F13
Jaén Peru 5°25S 78°40W 92 E3
Jaén Spain 37°44N 3°43W 21 D4
Jafarabad India 20°52N 71°22E 42 J4
Jaffa = Tel Aviv-Yafo
  Israel 32°4N 34°48E 48 C3
Jaffa, C. Australia 36°58S 139°40E 63 F2
Jaffna Sri Lanka 9°45N 80°2E 45 K5
Jaffrey U.S.A. 42°49N 72°2W 83 D12
Jagadhri India 30°10N 77°20E 42 D7
Jagadishpur India 25°30N 84°21E 43 G11
Jagat Nepal 28°19N 84°53E 43 E11
Jagdalpur India 19°3N 82°0E 44 E6
Jagdaqi China 50°25N 124°7E 31 A13
Jagersfontein S. Africa 29°44S 25°27E 56 D4
Jaghīn → Iran 27°17N 57°13E 47 E8
Jagodina Serbia 44°5N 21°15E 23 C9
Jagraon India 30°50N 75°25E 42 D6
Jagtial India 18°50N 79°0E 44 E4
Jaguariaíva Brazil 24°10S 49°50W 95 A6

aguaribe → *Brazil* 4°25S 37°45W **93** D11
agüey Grande *Cuba* 22°35N 81°7W **88** B3
ahanabad *India* 25°13N 84°59E **43** G11
ahazpur *India* 25°37N 75°17E **42** G6
ahrom *Iran* 28°30N 53°31E **47** D7
aigarh *India* 17°17N 73°13E **44** F1
aijon *India* 31°21N 76°9E **42** D7
ailolo *Indonesia* 1°5N 127°30E **37** D7
ailolo, Selat *Indonesia* 0°5N 129°5E **37** D7
aipur *India* 27°0N 75°50E **42** F6
ais *India* 26°15N 81°32E **43** F9
aisalmer *India* 26°55N 70°54E **42** F4
aisinghnagar *India* 23°38N 78°34E **43** H8
aitaran *India* 26°12N 73°56E **42** F5
aithari *India* 23°14N 78°37E **43** H8
ajarkot *Nepal* 28°42N 82°14E **43** E10
ajarm *Iran* 36°58N 56°27E **47** B8
ajpur *India* 20°53N 86°22E **44** D8
akam → *India* 23°54N 74°13E **42** H6
akarta Sukarno-Hatta Int. ✈
  (CGK) *Indonesia* 6°7S 106°40E **37** G12
akhal *India* 29°48N 75°50E **42** E6
akhau *India* 23°13N 68°43E **42** H3
akobstad = Pietarsaari
  Finland 63°40N 22°43E **8** E20
al *U.S.A.* 32°7N 103°12W **77** K12
alãjil *Si. Arabia* 25°40N 45°27E **46** E5
alãlãbãd *Afghan.* 34°30N 70°29E **42** B4
alalabad *India* 27°41N 79°42E **43** F8
alalpur Jattan *Pakistan* 32°38N 74°11E **42** C6
alama *U.S.A.* 34°29N 120°29W **79** L6
alandhar *India* 31°20N 75°40E **42** D6
alapa *Guatemala* 14°39N 89°59W **88** D2
alapa Enríquez = Xalapa
  Mexico 19°32N 96°55W **87** D5
alasjärvi *Finland* 62°29N 22°47E **8** E20
alaun *India* 26°8N 79°25E **43** F8
aldhaka → *Bangla.* 26°16N 89°16E **43** F13
alesar *India* 27°29N 78°19E **42** F8
aleswar *Nepal* 26°38N 85°48E **43** F11
algaon *India* 21°0N 75°42E **44** D2
alibah → *India* 30°35N 46°32E **46** D5
alingo *Nigeria* 8°55N 11°25E **53** G8
alisco → *Mexico* 20°20N 103°40W **86** D4
alkot *Pakistan* 35°14N 73°24E **43** B5
alna *India* 19°48N 75°38E **44** E2
alón → *Spain* 41°47N 1°4W **21** B5
alor *India* 25°21N 72°37E **42** G5
alpa *Mexico* 21°38N 102°58W **86** C4
alpaiguri *India* 26°32N 88°46E **41** F16
alpan *Mexico* 21°14N 99°29W **87** C5
aluit I. *Marshall Is.* 6°0N 169°30E **64** G8
alūlã *Iraq* 34°16N 45°10E **46** C5
amaame *Somalia* 0°4N 42°44E **49** G3
amaica ■ *W. Indies* 18°10N 77°30W **88** a
amalpur *Bangla.* 24°52N 89°56E **41** G16
amalpur *India* 25°18N 86°28E **43** G12
amalpurganj *India* 23°2N 87°59E **43** H13
amanxim → *Brazil* 4°43S 56°18W **93** D7
ambewangi *Indonesia* 8°17S 114°7E **37** J17
ambi *Indonesia* 1°38S 103°30E **36** E2
ambi □ *Indonesia* 1°30S 102°30E **36** E2
ambongan, Pulau
  Malaysia 6°45N 117°20E **36** C5
ambusar *India* 22°3N 72°51E **42** H5
ames → *S. Dak., U.S.A.* 42°52N 97°18W **80** D5
ames → *Va., U.S.A.* 36°56N 76°27W **81** G15
ames B. *Canada* 54°0N 80°0W **72** B3
ames Ranges *Australia* 24°10S 132°30E **60** D5
ames Ross I. *Antarctica* 63°58S 57°50W **5** C18
ames Ross Str. *Canada* 69°40N 96°10W **68** D12
amesabad *Pakistan* 25°17N 69°15E **42** G3
amestown *Australia* 33°10S 138°32E **63** E2
amestown *S. Africa* 31°6S 26°45E **56** D4
amestown N. Dak.,
  U.S.A. 46°54N 98°42W **80** B4
amestown N.Y., U.S.A. 42°6N 79°14W **82** D5
amestown Pa., U.S.A. 41°29N 80°27W **82** E5
amîlãbãd *Iran* 34°24N 48°28E **47** C6
amira → *India* 21°35N 82°28E **43** J13
amkhandi *India* 16°30N 75°15E **44** F2
amkhed *India* 18°43N 75°19E **44** E2
ammalamadugu *India* 14°51N 78°25E **45** G4
ammu *India* 32°43N 74°54E **42** C6
ammu & Kashmir □
  India 34°25N 77°0E **43** B7
amnagar *India* 22°30N 70°6E **42** H4
amner *India* 20°45N 75°52E **44** D2
amni → *India* 25°13N 78°35E **43** G8
ampur *Pakistan* 29°39N 70°40E **42** E4
amrud *Pakistan* 33°59N 71°24E **42** C4
amsä *Finland* 61°53N 25°10E **8** F21
amshedpur *India* 22°44N 86°12E **43** H12
amtara *India* 23°59N 86°49E **43** H12
amtland *Sweden* 63°31N 14°0E **8** E16
an L. *Canada* 54°56N 102°55W **71** C8
an Mayen *Arctic* 71°0N 9°0W **4** B7
anakpur *Nepal* 26°42N 85°55E **44** A7
anaúba *Brazil* 15°48S 43°19W **93** G10
and *Pakistan* 33°30N 72°6E **42** C5
andanku ✪ *Australia* 16°20S 135°45E **62** B2
andaq *Iran* 34°3N 54°22E **47** C7
andola *Pakistan* 32°20N 70°9E **42** C4
andowae *Australia* 26°45S 151°7E **63** D5
anesville *U.S.A.* 42°41N 89°1W **80** D9
angamo *Mozam.* 24°6S 35°21E **57** B6
anghai *India* 25°33N 82°19E **43** G10
angheung *S. Korea* 34°41N 126°52E **33** G14
angipur *India* 24°28N 88°4E **43** G12
angoon *India* 17°44N 79°5E **44** F4
anjanbureh *Gambia* 13°30N 14°47W **52** F3
anjgir *India* 22°1N 82°34E **43** J10
anos *Mexico* 21°54N 101°10W **86** A3
anuária *Brazil* 15°25S 44°25W **93** G10
anûb Sînî □ *Egypt* 29°30N 33°50E **48** F2
anwada *India* 23°40N 75°10E **42** H6
aora *India* 26°10N 136°0E **29** G8
apan ■ *Asia* 36°0N 136°0E **28** F7
apan, Sea of *Asia* 40°0N 135°0E **28** E7
apan Trench *Pac. Oc.* 32°0N 142°0E **64** D6

Japen = Yapen *Indonesia* 1°50S 136°0E **37** E9
Japla *India* 24°33N 84°1E **43** G11
Japurá → *Brazil* 3°8S 65°46W **92** D5
Jaquarão *Brazil* 32°34S 53°23W **95** C5
Jaqué *Panama* 7°27N 78°8W **88** E4
Jarãbulus *Syria* 36°49N 38°1E **46** B3
Jaraguá do Sul *Brazil* 26°29S 49°4W **95** B6
Jarama → *Spain* 40°24N 3°32W **21** B4
Jaranwala *Pakistan* 31°15N 73°26E **42** D5
Jarash *Jordan* 32°17N 35°54E **48** C4
Jarash □ *Jordan* 32°17N 35°54E **48** C4
Jardim *Brazil* 21°28S 56°2W **94** A4
Jardin América *Argentina* 27°3S 55°14W **95** B4
Jardine River △ *Australia* 11°9S 142°21E **62** A3
Jardines de la Reina, Arch. de los
  Cuba 20°50N 78°50W **88** B4
Jargalang *China* 43°5N 122°55E **33** C12
Jari → *Brazil* 1°9S 51°54W **93** D8
Jarir, W. al → *Si. Arabia* 25°38N 42°30E **46** E4
Jarosław *Poland* 50°2N 22°42E **17** C12
Jarrahdale *Australia* 32°24S 116°5E **61** F2
Jarrahi → *Iran* 30°49N 48°48E **47** D6
Jartai *China* 39°45N 105°48E **32** E3
Jarud Qi *China* 44°28N 120°50E **33** B11
Järvenpää *Finland* 60°29N 25°5E **8** F21
Jarvis *Canada* 42°53N 80°6W **82** D4
Jarvis I. *Pac. Oc.* 0°15S 160°5W **65** H11
Jarwa *India* 27°38N 82°30E **43** F10
Jasdan *India* 22°2N 71°12E **42** H4
Jashpurnagar *India* 22°54N 84°9E **43** H11
Jasidih *India* 24°31N 86°39E **43** G12
Jãsimîyah *Iraq* 33°45N 44°41E **46** C5
Jasin *Malaysia* 2°20N 102°26E **39** L4
Jãsk *Iran* 25°38N 57°45E **47** E8
Jaslo *Poland* 49°45N 21°30E **17** D11
Jaso *India* 24°30N 80°29E **43** G9
Jasper *Alta., Canada* 52°55N 118°5W **70** C5
Jasper *Ont., Canada* 44°52N 75°57W **83** B9
Jasper *Ala., U.S.A.* 33°50N 87°17W **85** E11
Jasper *Fla., U.S.A.* 30°31N 82°57W **85** F13
Jasper *Ind., U.S.A.* 38°24N 86°56W **80** F10
Jasper *Tex., U.S.A.* 30°56N 94°1W **84** F8
Jasper △ *Canada* 52°50N 118°8W **70** C5
Jasrasar *India* 27°43N 73°49E **42** F5
Jászberény *Hungary* 47°30N 19°55E **17** E10
Jataí *Brazil* 17°58S 51°48W **93** G8
Jath *India* 17°3N 75°13E **44** F2
Jati *Pakistan* 24°20N 68°19E **42** G3
Jatibarang *Indonesia* 6°28S 108°18E **37** G13
Jatiluwih *Indonesia* 8°23S 115°8E **37** J18
Játiva = Xàtiva *Spain* 38°59N 0°32W **21** C5
Jaú *Brazil* 22°10S 48°30W **95** A6
Jauja *Peru* 11°45S 75°15W **92** F3
Jaunpur *India* 25°46N 82°44E **43** G10
Java = Jawa *Indonesia* 7°0S 110°0E **36** F3
Java Sea *Indonesia* 4°35S 107°15E **36** E3
Java Trench *Ind. Oc.* 9°0S 105°0E **36** F3
Javadi Hills *India* 12°40N 78°40E **45** H4
Javla *India* 17°18N 75°9E **44** F2
Jawa *Indonesia* 7°0S 110°0E **36** F3
Jawa Barat □ *Indonesia* 7°0S 107°0E **37** G12
Jawa Tengah □ *Indonesia* 7°0S 110°0E **37** G14
Jawa Timur □ *Indonesia* 8°0S 113°0E **37** G15
Jawad *India* 24°36N 74°51E **42** G6
Jawhar *India* 19°55N 73°14E **44** E1
Jawhar *Somalia* 2°48N 45°30E **49** G4
Jawoyn ✪ *Australia* 14°16S 132°28E **60** B5
Jay Peak *U.S.A.* 44°55N 72°32W **83** B12
Jaya, Puncak *Indonesia* 3°57S 137°17E **37** E9
Jayanti *India* 26°45N 89°40E **41** F16
Jayapura *Indonesia* 2°28S 140°38E **37** E10
Jayawijaya, Pegunungan
  Indonesia 5°0S 139°0E **37** F9
Jaynagar *India* 26°43N 86°9E **43** F12
Jaypur = Jeypore *India* 18°50N 82°38E **44** E6
Jayrûd *Syria* 33°49N 36°44E **46** C3
Jayton *U.S.A.* 33°15N 100°34W **84** E4
Jãz Mûrîãn, Hãmûn-e
  Iran 27°20N 58°55E **47** E8
Jazîreh-ye Shîf *Iran* 29°4N 50°54E **47** D6
Jazminal *Mexico* 24°52N 101°24W **86** C4
Jazzîn *Lebanon* 33°31N 35°35E **48** B4
Jean *U.S.A.* 35°47N 115°20W **79** K11
Jean Marie River
  Canada 61°32N 120°38W **70** A4
Jean-Rabel *Haiti* 19°50N 73°5W **89** C5
Jeanerette *U.S.A.* 29°55N 91°40W **84** G9
Jeanette, Ostrov = Zhannetty,
  Ostrov *Russia* 76°43N 158°0E **27** B16
Jeannette *U.S.A.* 40°20N 79°36W **82** F5
Jebâl Bârez, Kûh-e *Iran* 28°30N 58°20E **47** D8
Jebel, Bahr el →
  South Sudan 9°30N 30°25E **53** G12
Jebel Ali = Minâ' Jabal 'Alī
  U.A.E. 25°2N 55°8E **47** E7
Jecheon *S. Korea* 37°8N 128°12E **33** F15
Jedburgh *U.K.* 55°29N 2°33W **11** F6
Jedda = Jiddah *Si. Arabia* 21°29N 39°10E **46** G4
Jeddore L. *Canada* 48°3N 55°55W **73** C8
Jędrzejów *Poland* 50°35N 20°15E **17** C11
Jefferson *Iowa, U.S.A.* 42°1N 94°23W **80** D6
Jefferson *Ohio, U.S.A.* 41°44N 80°46W **82** E4
Jefferson *Tex., U.S.A.* 32°46N 94°21W **84** E7
Jefferson, Mt. *Nev.,*
  U.S.A. 38°47N 116°56W **76** G5
Jefferson, Mt. *Oreg.,*
  U.S.A. 44°41N 121°48W **76** D3
Jefferson City *Mo., U.S.A.* 38°34N 92°10W **80** F7
Jefferson City *Tenn.,*
  U.S.A. 36°7N 83°30W **85** C13
Jeffersontown *U.S.A.* 38°12N 85°35W **81** F11
Jeffersonville *U.S.A.* 38°17N 85°44W **81** F11
Jeffrey City *U.S.A.* 42°30N 107°49W **76** E10
Jega *Nigeria* 12°15N 4°23E **52** F6
Jeju *S. Korea* 33°31N 126°32E **33** H14
Jeju-do *S. Korea* 33°29N 126°34E **33** H14
Jeju Haehyop *S. Korea* 33°50N 126°0E **33** H14
Jēkabpils *Latvia* 56°29N 25°57E **9** H21
Jekyll I. *U.S.A.* 31°4N 81°25W **85** F14
Jelenia Góra *Poland* 50°50N 15°45E **16** C8

Jelgava *Latvia* 56°41N 23°49E **9** H20
Jemaluang *Malaysia* 2°16N 103°52E **39** L4
Jember *Indonesia* 8°11S 113°41E **37** H15
Jena *Germany* 50°54N 11°35E **16** C6
Jena *U.S.A.* 31°41N 92°8W **84** F8
Jengish Chokusu = Pobedy, Pik
  Asia 42°0N 79°58E **30** C4
Jenin *West Bank* 32°28N 35°18E **48** C4
Jenkins *U.S.A.* 37°10N 82°38W **81** G12
Jenner *U.S.A.* 38°27N 123°7W **78** G3
Jennings *U.S.A.* 30°13N 92°40W **84** F8
Jeong-eup *S. Korea* 35°35N 126°50E **33** G14
Jeongseon *S. Korea* 37°20N 128°45E **33** F15
Jeonju *S. Korea* 35°50N 127°4E **33** G14
Jepara *Indonesia* 7°40S 109°14E **37** G14
Jeparit *Australia* 36°8S 142°1E **63** F3
Jequié *Brazil* 13°51S 40°5W **93** F10
Jequitinhonha *Brazil* 16°30S 41°0W **93** G10
Jequitinhonha →
  Brazil 15°51S 38°53W **93** G11
Jerada *Morocco* 34°17N 2°10W **52** B5
Jerantut *Malaysia* 3°56N 102°22E **39** L4
Jerejak, Pulau *Malaysia* 5°19N 100°19E **39** c
Jérémie *Haiti* 18°40N 74°10W **89** C5
Jerez, Pta. *Mexico* 22°58N 97°40W **87** C5
Jerez de García Salinas
  Mexico 22°39N 103°0W **86** C4
Jerez de la Frontera *Spain* 36°41N 6°7W **21** D2
Jerez de los Caballeros
  Spain 38°20N 6°45W **21** C2
Jericho = El Arîhã
  West Bank 31°52N 35°27E **48** D4
Jericho *Australia* 23°38S 146°6E **62** C4
Jerid, Chott el = Djerid, Chott
  Tunisia 33°42N 8°30E **52** B7
Jerilderie *Australia* 35°20S 145°41E **63** F4
Jermyn *U.S.A.* 41°32N 75°33E **83** E9
Jerome *U.S.A.* 42°44N 114°31W **76** E6
Jerramungup *Australia* 33°55S 118°55E **61** F2
Jersey *U.K.* 49°11N 2°7W **13** H5
Jersey Shore *U.S.A.* 41°12N 77°15W **82** E7
Jerseyville *U.S.A.* 39°7N 90°20W **80** F8
Jervis B. *Australia* 35°8S 150°46E **63** F5
Jervis Inlet *Canada* 50°0N 123°57W **70** C4
Jesi = Iesi *Italy* 43°31N 13°14E **22** C5
Jesup *U.S.A.* 31°36N 81°53W **85** F14
Jesús Carranza *Mexico* 17°26N 95°2W **87** D5
Jesús María *Argentina* 30°59S 64°5W **94** C3
Jetmore *U.S.A.* 38°4N 99°54W **80** F4
Jetpur *India* 21°45N 70°10E **42** J4
Jevnaker *Norway* 60°15N 10°26E **9** F14
Jewett *U.S.A.* 40°22N 81°2W **82** F3
Jewett City *U.S.A.* 41°36N 71°59W **83** E13
Jeyhûnābād *Iran* 34°58N 48°59E **47** C6
Jeypore *India* 18°50N 82°38E **44** E6
Jha Jha *India* 24°46N 86°22E **43** G12
Jhaarkand = Jharkhand □
  India 24°0N 85°50E **43** H11
Jhabua *India* 22°46N 74°36E **42** H6
Jhajjar *India* 28°37N 76°42E **42** E7
Jhal *Pakistan* 28°17N 67°27E **42** E2
Jhal Jhao *Pakistan* 26°20N 65°35E **40** F4
Jhalawar *India* 24°40N 76°10E **42** G7
Jhalida *India* 23°22N 85°58E **43** H11
Jhalrapatan *India* 24°33N 76°10E **42** G7
Jhang Maghiana
  Pakistan 31°15N 72°22E **42** D5
Jhang Sadr = Jhang Maghiana
  Pakistan 31°15N 72°22E **42** D5
Jhansi *India* 25°30N 78°36E **43** G8
Jhargram *India* 22°27N 86°59E **43** H12
Jharia *India* 23°45N 86°26E **43** H11
Jharkhand □ *India* 24°0N 85°50E **43** H11
Jharsuguda *India* 21°56N 84°5E **44** D7
Jhelum *Pakistan* 33°0N 73°45E **42** C5
Jhelum → *Pakistan* 31°20N 72°10E **42** D5
Jhilmilli *India* 23°24N 82°51E **43** H10
Jhudo *Pakistan* 24°58N 69°18E **42** G3
Jhunjhunu *India* 28°10N 75°30E **42** E6
Ji-Paraná *Brazil* 10°52S 62°57W **92** F6
Ji Xian *China* 36°7N 110°40E **32** F6
Jia Xian *Henan, China* 33°59N 113°12E **32** H7
Jia Xian *Shaanxi, China* 38°12N 110°28E **32** E6
Jiahe *China* 25°38N 112°19E **35** E9
Jiaji = Qionghai *China* 19°15N 110°26E **38** C8
Jialing Jiang → *China* 30°2N 106°20E **34** C6
Jiamusi *China* 46°40N 130°26E **31** B15
Jian *Jiangxi, China* 27°6N 114°59E **35** D10
Ji'an *Jilin, China* 41°5N 126°10E **33** D14
Jianchang *China* 40°55N 120°35E **33** D11
Jianchuan *China* 26°38N 99°55E **34** D2
Jiande *China* 29°23N 119°15E **35** C12
Jiang'an *China* 28°40N 105°3E **34** C5
Jiangbei *China* 29°40N 106°34E **34** C6
Jiangcheng *China* 22°36N 101°52E **34** F3
Jiangchuan *China* 24°28N 102°50E **34** D4
Jiangdi *China* 26°57N 103°37E **34** D4
Jiangdu *China* 32°27N 119°36E **35** A12
Jiange *China* 32°4N 105°25E **34** A5
Jianghua *China* 25°0N 111°47E **35** E8
Jiangjin *China* 29°14N 106°10E **34** C6
Jiangkou *China* 27°40N 108°49E **34** D7
Jiangle *China* 26°42N 117°23E **35** D11
Jiangmen *China* 22°32N 113°0E **35** F9
Jiangning *China* 31°55N 118°50E **35** B12
Jiangsu □ *China* 33°0N 120°0E **35** H11
Jiangxi □ *China* 27°30N 116°0E **35** D11
Jiangyan *China* 32°30N 120°17E **35** B13
Jiangyin *China* 31°54N 120°17E **35** B13
Jiangyong *China* 25°20N 111°22E **35** E8
Jiangyou *China* 31°44N 104°43E **34** B5
Jiangyuan *China* 42°2N 126°34E **33** C14
Jianhe *China* 26°40N 108°34E **34** D7
Jianli *China* 29°46N 112°56E **35** C9
Jianning *China* 26°50N 116°50E **35** D11
Jian'ou *China* 27°3N 118°17E **35** D12
Jianping *China* 41°53N 119°42E **33** D10
Jianshi *China* 30°37N 109°38E **34** B7

Jianshui *China* 23°36N 102°43E **34** F4
Jianyang *Fujian, China* 27°20N 118°5E **35** D12
Jianyang *Sichuan, China* 30°24N 104°33E **34** B5
Jiao Xian = Jiaozhou
  China 36°18N 120°1E **33** F11
Jiaohe *Hebei, China* 38°2N 116°20E **32** E9
Jiaohe *Jilin, China* 43°40N 127°22E **33** C14
Jiaoling *China* 24°41N 116°12E **35** E11
Jiaonan *China* 35°52N 119°58E **33** G10
Jiaozhou *China* 36°18N 120°1E **33** F11
Jiaozhou Wan *China* 36°5N 120°10E **33** F11
Jiaozuo *China* 35°16N 113°12E **32** G7
Jiawang *China* 34°28N 117°26E **33** G9
Jiaxiang *China* 35°25N 116°20E **32** G9
Jiaxing *China* 30°49N 120°45E **35** B13
Jiayu *China* 29°55N 113°55E **35** C9
Jiayuguan *China* 39°49N 98°18E **30** D8
Jibuti = Djibouti ■ *Africa* 12°0N 43°0E **49** E3
Jicarón, I. *Panama* 7°10N 81°50W **88** E3
Jiddah *Si. Arabia* 21°29N 39°10E **49** C2
Jido *India* 29°2N 94°58E **41** E19
Jieshou *China* 33°18N 115°22E **32** H8
Jiexiu *China* 37°2N 111°55E **32** F6
Jieyang *China* 23°35N 116°21E **35** F11
Jigalong *Australia* 23°21S 120°47E **60** D3
Jigalong ✪ *Australia* 23°21S 120°46E **60** D3
Jigni *India* 25°45N 79°25E **43** G8
Jihlava *Czech Rep.* 49°28N 15°35E **16** D8
Jihlava → *Czech Rep.* 48°55N 16°36E **17** D9
Jijiga *Ethiopia* 9°20N 42°50E **49** F3
Jilib *Somalia* 0°29N 42°46E **49** G3
Jilin *China* 43°44N 126°30E **33** C14
Jilin □ *China* 44°0N 127°0E **33** C14
Jim Thorpe *U.S.A.* 40°52N 75°44W **83** F9
Jima *Ethiopia* 7°40N 36°47E **49** F2
Jimbaran, Teluk *Indonesia* 8°46S 115°9E **37** K18
Jiménez *Mexico* 27°8N 104°54W **86** B4
Jimeta *Nigeria* 9°17N 12°28E **54** C2
Jimo *China* 36°23N 120°30E **33** F11
Jin Jiang → *China* 28°24N 115°48E **35** C10
Jin Xian = Jinzhou
  China 38°55N 121°42E **33** E11
Jinan *China* 36°38N 117°1E **32** F9
Jinchang *China* 38°30N 102°10E **30** D9
Jincheng *China* 35°29N 112°50E **32** G7
Jinchuan *China* 31°30N 102°3E **34** B4
Jind *India* 29°19N 76°22E **42** E7
Jindabyne *Australia* 36°25S 148°35E **63** F4
Jinding *China* 22°22N 113°33E **31** a
Jindo *S. Korea* 34°28N 126°15E **33** G14
Jindřichův Hradec
  Czech Rep. 49°10N 15°2E **16** D8
Jing He → *China* 34°27N 109°42E **32** G5
Jing Shan *China* 31°20N 111°35E **35** B8
Jing Xian *China* 30°38N 118°25E **35** B12
Jing'an *China* 28°50N 115°17E **35** C10
Jingbian *China* 37°20N 108°30E **32** F5
Jingchuan *China* 35°20N 107°20E **32** G4
Jingde *China* 30°15N 118°27E **35** B12
Jingdezhen *China* 29°20N 117°11E **35** C11
Jingdong *China* 24°25N 100°47E **34** E3
Jinggangshan *China* 26°58N 114°15E **35** D10
Jinggu *China* 23°35N 100°41E **34** F3
Jinghai *Guangdong,*
  China 23°5N 116°31E **35** F11
Jinghai *Tianjin, China* 38°55N 116°55E **32** E9
Jinghong *China* 22°0N 100°45E **34** F3
Jinghong Dam *China* 22°10N 100°46E **34** F3
Jingjiang *China* 32°2N 120°12E **35** A13
Jingle *China* 38°20N 111°55E **32** E6
Jingmen *China* 31°0N 112°10E **35** B9
Jingning *China* 35°30N 105°43E **32** G3
Jingpo Hu *China* 43°55N 128°55E **33** C15
Jingshan *China* 31°1N 113°7E **35** B9
Jingtai *China* 37°10N 104°6E **32** F3
Jingtang *China* 39°8N 119°0E **33** E10
Jingxi *China* 23°8N 106°27E **34** F6
Jingyang *China* 34°30N 108°50E **32** G5
Jingyu *China* 42°25N 126°45E **33** C14
Jingyuan *China* 36°30N 104°40E **32** F3
Jingzhou *Hubei, China* 30°21N 112°11E **35** B9
Jingzhou *Hunan, China* 26°33N 109°40E **34** D7
Jingziguan *China* 33°15N 111°0E **32** H6
Jinhua *China* 29°8N 119°38E **35** C12
Jining *Nei Monggol Zizhiqu,*
  China 41°5N 113°0E **32** D7
Jining *Shandong, China* 35°22N 116°34E **32** G9
Jinja *Uganda* 0°25N 33°12E **54** D6
Jinjang *Malaysia* 3°13N 101°39E **39** L3
Jinji *China* 37°58N 106°8E **32** F4
Jinjiang *Fujian, China* 24°43N 118°33E **35** E12
Jinjiang *Yunnan, China* 26°14N 100°34E **34** D3
Jinju *S. Korea* 35°12N 128°2E **33** G15
Jinkou *China* 30°20N 114°8E **35** B10
Jinkouhe *China* 29°18N 103°4E **34** C4
Jinmu Jiao *China* 18°9N 109°34E **38** C7
Jinnah Barrage *Pakistan* 32°58N 71°33E **42** C4
Jinning *China* 24°38N 102°37E **34** D4
Jinotega *Nic.* 13°6N 85°59W **88** D2
Jinotepe *Nic.* 11°50N 86°10W **88** D2
Jinping *Guizhou, China* 26°41N 109°10E **34** D7
Jinping *Yunnan, China* 22°48N 103°22E **34** F4
Jinping Bend Dams *China* 28°1N 101°39E **34** C3
Jinsha *China* 27°29N 106°12E **34** D6
Jinsha Jiang → *China* 28°46N 104°50E **34** C5
Jinshi *China* 29°40N 111°50E **35** C8
Jintur *India* 19°36N 76°42E **44** E3
Jinxi *Jiangxi, China* 27°30N 116°50E **35** D11
Jinxi *Liaoning, China* 40°52N 120°50E **33** D11
Jinxian *China* 28°26N 116°17E **35** C11
Jinxiang *China* 35°5N 116°22E **32** G9
Jinyang *China* 28°5N 103°2E **34** C4
Jinyun *China* 28°37N 120°8E **35** C13
Jinzhou *Liaoning, China* 38°55N 121°42E **33** E11
Jinzhou *Liaoning, China* 41°5N 121°3E **33** D11
Jiparaná → *Brazil* 8°3S 62°52W **92** E6
Jipijapa *Ecuador* 1°0S 80°40W **92** D2

Jiquilpan *Mexico* 19°59N 102°43W **86** D4
Jirisan *S. Korea* 35°20N 127°44E **33** G14
Jiroft *Iran* 28°45N 57°50E **47** D8
Jishan *China* 35°34N 110°58E **32** G6
Jishou *China* 28°21N 109°43E **34** C7
Jishui *China* 27°12N 115°8E **35** D10
Jisr ash Shughūr *Syria* 35°49N 36°18E **46** C3
Jitarning *Australia* 32°48S 117°57E **61** F2
Jitra *Malaysia* 6°16N 100°25E **39** J3
Jiu → *Romania* 43°47N 23°48E **17** F12
Jiudengkou *China* 39°56N 106°40E **32** E4
Jiujiang *Guangdong, China* 22°50N 113°0E **35** F9
Jiujiang *Jiangxi, China* 29°42N 115°58E **35** C10
Jiuling Shan *China* 28°40N 114°40E **35** C10
Jiulong *China* 28°57N 101°31E **34** C3
Jiuquan *China* 39°50N 98°20E **30** D8
Jiutai *China* 44°10N 125°50E **33** B13
Jiuxincheng *China* 39°17N 115°59E **32** E8
Jiuzhaigou △ *China* 33°15N 104°0E **34** A5
Jiwani *Pakistan* 25°1N 61°44E **40** G2
Jixi *Anhui, China* 30°5N 118°34E **35** B12
Jixi *Heilongjiang, China* 45°20N 130°50E **33** B16
Jixian *China* 37°0N 117°12E **33** F9
Jiyuan *China* 35°7N 112°57E **32** G7
Jīzān *Si. Arabia* 17°0N 42°20E **49** D3
Jize *China* 36°54N 114°56E **32** F8
Jizhou *China* 37°35N 115°30E **32** F8
Jizl, Wādī al → *Si. Arabia* 25°39N 38°25E **46** E3
Jizō-Zaki *Japan* 35°34N 133°20E **29** G6
Jizzax *Uzbekistan* 40°6N 67°50E **26** E7
Joaçaba *Brazil* 27°5S 51°31W **95** B5
João Pessoa *Brazil* 7°10S 34°52W **93** E12
Joaquín V. González
  Argentina 25°10S 64°0W **94** B3
Jobat *India* 22°25N 74°34E **42** H6
Jodhpur *India* 26°23N 73°8E **42** F5
Jodiya *India* 22°42N 70°18E **42** H4
Joensuu *Finland* 62°37N 29°49E **8** E23
Jõetsu *Japan* 37°12N 138°10E **29** F9
Jofane *Mozam.* 21°15S 34°18E **57** B5
Jog Falls = Gersoppa Falls
  India 14°12N 74°46E **45** G2
Jogbani *India* 26°25N 87°15E **43** F12
Jõgeva *Estonia* 58°45N 26°24E **9** G22
Jogjakarta = Yogyakarta
  Indonesia 7°49S 110°22E **37** G14
Johannesburg *U.S.A.* 35°22N 117°38W **79** K9
Johilla → *India* 23°37N 81°14E **43** H9
John Crow Mts. *Jamaica* 18°5N 76°25W **88** a
John Day *U.S.A.* 44°25N 118°57W **76** D4
John Day → *U.S.A.* 45°44N 120°39W **76** D3
John Day Fossil Beds △
  U.S.A. 44°33N 119°38W **76** D4
John D'or Prairie *Canada* 58°30N 115°8W **70** B5
John H. Kerr Res.
  U.S.A. 36°36N 78°18W **85** C15
John o' Groats *U.K.* 58°38N 3°4W **11** C5
Johnnie *U.S.A.* 36°25N 116°5W **79** J10
John's Ra. *Australia* 21°55S 133°23E **62** C1
Johnson *U.S.A.* 44°38N 72°41W **83** B12
Johnson City *Kans.,*
  U.S.A. 37°34N 101°45W **80** G3
Johnson City *N.Y., U.S.A.* 42°7N 75°58W **83** D9
Johnson City *Tenn.,*
  U.S.A. 36°19N 82°21W **85** C13
Johnson City *Tex., U.S.A.* 30°17N 98°25W **84** F5
Johnsonburg *U.S.A.* 41°29N 78°41W **82** E6
Johnsondale *U.S.A.* 35°58N 118°32W **79** K8
Johnsons Crossing
  Canada 60°29N 133°18W **70** A2
Johnston, L. *Australia* 32°25S 120°30E **61** F3
Johnston Atoll *Pac. Oc.* 17°10N 169°8W **65** F11
Johnston Falls = Mambilima Falls
  Zambia 10°31S 28°45E **54** G5
Johnstone Str. *Canada* 50°28N 126°0W **70** C3
Johnstown *Ireland* 52°45N 7°33W **10** D4
Johnstown *N.Y., U.S.A.* 43°0N 74°22W **83** D10
Johnstown *Ohio, U.S.A.* 40°9N 82°41W **82** F2
Johnstown *Pa., U.S.A.* 40°20N 78°55W **82** F6
Johor □ *Malaysia* 2°5N 103°20E **39** M4
Johor, Selat *Asia* 1°28N 103°47E **39** d
Johor Bahru *Malaysia* 1°28N 103°46E **39** d
Johor Port *Malaysia* 1°26N 103°53E **39** d
Jõhvi *Estonia* 59°22N 27°27E **9** G22
Joinville *Brazil* 26°15S 48°55W **95** B6
Joinville I. *Antarctica* 65°0S 55°30W **5** C18
Jojutla *Mexico* 18°37N 99°11W **87** D5
Jokkmokk *Sweden* 66°35N 19°50E **8** C18
Jökulsá á Bru → *Iceland* 65°40N 14°16W **8** D6
Jökulsá á Fjöllum →
  Iceland 66°10N 16°30W **8** C5
Jökulsárgljúfur △ *Iceland* 65°56N 16°31W **8** C5
Jolfã *Āzarbājān-e Sharqī,*
  Iran 38°57N 45°38E **46** B5
Jolfã *Esfahan, Iran* 32°58N 51°37E **47** C6
Joliet *U.S.A.* 41°32N 88°5W **80** E9
Joliette *Canada* 46°3N 73°24W **72** C5
Jolo *Phil.* 6°0N 121°0E **37** C6
Jolon *U.S.A.* 35°58N 121°9W **78** K5
Jomalig *Phil.* 14°43N 122°15E **37** B6
Jombang *Indonesia* 7°33S 112°14E **37** G15
Jomda *China* 31°28N 98°12E **34** B2
Jonava *Lithuania* 55°8N 24°12E **9** J21
Jones Sound *Canada* 76°0N 85°0W **69** B15
Jonesboro *Ark., U.S.A.* 35°50N 90°42W **85** D9
Jonesboro *La., U.S.A.* 32°15N 92°43W **84** E8
Joniškis *Lithuania* 56°13N 23°35E **9** H20
Jönköping *Sweden* 57°45N 14°8E **9** H16
Jonquière *Canada* 48°27N 71°14W **73** C5
Joplin *U.S.A.* 37°6N 94°31W **80** G6
Jora *India* 26°20N 77°49E **42** F6
Jordan *Mont., U.S.A.* 47°19N 106°55W **76** C10
Jordan *N.Y., U.S.A.* 43°4N 76°29W **83** C8
Jordan ■ *Asia* 31°0N 36°0E **48** E5
Jordan → *Asia* 31°48N 35°32E **48** D3
Jordan Valley *U.S.A.* 42°59N 117°3W **76** E5
Jorhat *India* 26°45N 94°12E **41** F19
Jörn *Sweden* 65°4N 20°1E **8** D19
Jorong *Indonesia* 3°58S 114°56E **36** E4
Jørpeland *Norway* 59°3N 6°1E **9** G12
Jorquera → *Chile* 28°3S 69°58W **94** B2

Jos *Nigeria* 9°53N 8°51E **52 G7**
José Batlle y Ordóñez
   Uruguay 33°20S 55°10W **95 C4**
Joseph, L. *Canada* 45°10N 79°44W **82 A5**
Joseph Bonaparte G.
   Australia 14°35S 128°50E **60 B4**
Joseph L. *Canada* 52°45N 65°18W **73 B6**
Joshinath *India* 30°34N 79°34E **43 D8**
Joshinetsu-Kōgen △
   Japan 36°42N 138°32E **29 F9**
Joshua Tree *U.S.A.* 34°8N 116°19W **79 L10**
Joshua Tree △ *U.S.A.* 33°55N 116°0W **79 M10**
Jost Van Dyke I.
   Br. Virgin Is. 18°29N 64°47W **89 e**
Jostedalsbreen *Norway* 61°40N 6°59E **8 F12**
Jotunheimen *Norway* 61°35N 8°25E **8 F13**
Joubertberge *Namibia* 18°30S 14°0E **56 A1**
Jourdanton *U.S.A.* 28°55N 98°33W **84 G5**
Jovellanos *Cuba* 22°40N 81°10W **88 B3**
Ju Xian *China* 35°35N 118°20E **33 G10**
Juan Aldama *Mexico* 24°19N 103°21W **86 C4**
Juan Bautista Alberdi
   Argentina 34°26S 61°48W **94 C3**
Juan de Fuca, Str of.
   N. Amer. 48°15N 124°0W **78 B3**
Juan de Nova *Ind. Oc.* 17°3S 43°45E **57 A7**
Juan Fernández, Arch. de
   Pac. Oc. 33°50S 80°0W **90 G2**
Juan José Castelli
   Argentina 25°27S 60°57W **94 B3**
Juan L. Lacaze *Uruguay* 34°26S 57°25W **94 C4**
Juankoski *Finland* 63°3N 28°19E **8 E23**
Juárez *Mexico* 27°37N 100°44W **86 B4**
Juárez, Sa. de *Mexico* 32°0N 115°50W **86 A1**
Juàzeiro *Brazil* 9°30S 40°30W **93 E10**
Juàzeiro do Norte *Brazil* 7°10S 39°18W **93 E11**
Juba *South Sudan* 4°50N 31°35E **53 H12**
Juba → *Somalia* 1°30N 42°35E **49 G3**
Jubail = Al Jubayl
   Si. Arabia 27°0N 49°50E **47 E6**
Jubany = Carlini Base
   Antarctica 62°30S 58°0W **5 C18**
Jubayl *Lebanon* 34°5N 35°39E **48 A4**
Jubbah *Si. Arabia* 28°2N 40°56E **46 D4**
Jubbal *India* 31°5N 77°40E **42 D7**
Jubbulpore = Jabalpur
   India 23°9N 79°58E **43 H8**
Jubilee L. *Australia* 29°0S 126°50E **61 E4**
Juby, C. *Morocco* 28°0N 12°59W **52 C3**
Júcar = Xúquer → *Spain* 39°5N 0°10W **21 C5**
Júcaro *Cuba* 21°37N 78°51W **88 B4**
Juchitán de Zaragoza
   Mexico 16°26N 95°1W **87 D5**
Judea = Har Yehuda
   Israel 31°35N 34°57E **48 D3**
Judith → *U.S.A.* 47°44N 109°39W **76 C9**
Judith, Pt. *U.S.A.* 41°22N 71°29W **83 E13**
Judith Gap *U.S.A.* 46°41N 109°45W **76 C9**
Juigalpa *Nic.* 12°6N 85°26W **88 D2**
Juiz de Fora *Brazil* 21°43S 43°19W **95 A7**
Juju *Argentina* 23°20S 65°40W **94 A2**
Jujuy □ *Argentina* 23°20S 65°40W **94 A2**
Julesburg *U.S.A.* 40°59N 102°16W **76 F12**
Juli *Peru* 16°10S 69°25W **92 G5**
Julia Cr. → *Australia* 20°0S 141°11E **62 C3**
Julia Creek *Australia* 20°39S 141°44E **62 C3**
Juliaca *Peru* 15°25S 70°10W **92 G4**
Julian *U.S.A.* 33°4N 116°38W **79 M10**
Julian, L. *Canada* 54°25N 77°57W **72 B4**
Julianatop *Suriname* 3°40N 56°30W **93 C7**
Julianehåb = Qaqortoq
   Greenland 60°43N 46°0W **4 C5**
Julimes *Mexico* 28°25N 105°27W **86 B3**
Jullundur = Jalandhar
   India 31°20N 75°40E **42 D6**
Julu *China* 37°15N 115°2E **32 F8**
Jumbo Pk. *U.S.A.* 36°12N 114°11W **79 J12**
Jumentos Cays *Bahamas* 23°0N 75°40W **88 B4**
Jumilla *Spain* 38°28N 1°19W **21 C5**
Jumla *Nepal* 29°15N 82°13E **43 E10**
Jumna = Yamuna →
   India 25°30N 81°53E **43 G9**
Jumunjin *S. Korea* 37°55N 128°54E **33 F15**
Junagadh *India* 21°30N 70°30E **42 J4**
Junan *China* 35°12N 118°53E **33 G10**
Junction *Tex., U.S.A.* 30°29N 99°46W **84 F5**
Junction *Utah, U.S.A.* 38°14N 112°13W **77 G7**
Junction B. *Australia* 11°52S 133°55E **62 A1**
Junction City *Kans., U.S.A.* 39°2N 96°50W **80 F5**
Junction City *Oreg.,*
   U.S.A. 44°13N 123°12W **76 D2**
Junction Pt. *Australia* 11°45S 133°50E **62 A1**
Jundah *Australia* 24°46S 143°2E **62 C3**
Jundiaí *Brazil* 24°30S 47°0W **95 A6**
Juneau *U.S.A.* 58°18N 134°25W **70 B2**
Junee *Australia* 34°53S 147°35E **63 E4**
Jungar Qi *China* 39°49N 110°57E **32 E6**
Jungfrau *Switz.* 46°32N 7°58E **20 C7**
Junggar Pendi *China* 44°30N 86°0E **30 C6**
Jungshahi *Pakistan* 24°52N 67°44E **42 G2**
Juniata → *U.S.A.* 40°24N 77°1W **82 F7**
Junín *Argentina* 34°33S 60°57W **94 C3**
Junín de los Andes
   Argentina 39°45S 71°0W **96 D2**
Jūniyah *Lebanon* 33°59N 35°38E **48 B4**
Junkerdal △ *Norway* 66°50N 15°0E **8 C16**
Junlian *China* 28°8N 104°29E **34 C5**
Junnar *India* 19°12N 73°58E **44 E1**
Juntas *Chile* 28°24S 69°58W **94 B2**
Juntura *U.S.A.* 43°45N 118°5W **76 E4**
Jur → *South Sudan* 8°45N 29°15E **53 G11**
Jura = Jura, Mts. du *Europe* 46°40N 6°5E **20 C7**
Jura = Schwäbische Alb
   Germany 48°20N 9°30E **16 D5**
Jura *U.K.* 56°0N 5°50W **11 F3**
Jura, Mts. du *Europe* 46°40N 6°5E **20 C7**
Jura, Sd. of *U.K.* 55°57N 5°45W **11 F3**
Jurassic Coast *U.K.* 50°42N 2°50W **13 G5**
Jurbarkas *Lithuania* 55°4N 22°46E **9 J20**
Jurien Bay *Australia* 30°18S 115°2E **61 F2**
Jūrmala *Latvia* 56°58N 23°34E **9 H20**

Jurong *China* 31°57N 119°9E **35 B12**
Juruá → *Brazil* 2°37S 65°44W **92 D5**
Juruena *Brazil* 13°0S 58°10W **92 F7**
Juruena → *Brazil* 7°20S 58°3W **92 E7**
Juruti *Brazil* 2°9S 56°4W **93 D7**
Justo Daract *Argentina* 33°52S 65°12W **94 C2**
Jutaí → *Brazil* 2°43S 66°57W **92 D5**
Juticalpa *Honduras* 14°40N 86°12W **88 D2**
Jutland = Jylland *Denmark* 56°25N 9°30E **9 H13**
Juuka *Finland* 63°13N 29°17E **8 E23**
Juventud, I. de la *Cuba* 21°40N 82°40W **88 B3**
Jūy Zar *Iran* 33°50N 46°18E **46 C5**
Jwaneng *Botswana* 24°45S 24°50E **55 J4**
Jylland *Denmark* 56°25N 9°30E **9 H13**
Jyväskylä *Finland* 62°14N 25°50E **8 E21**

K

K2 *Pakistan* 35°58N 76°32E **43 B7**
Kaakha = Kaka
   Turkmenistan 37°21N 59°36E **47 B8**
Kaap Plateau *S. Africa* 28°30S 24°0E **56 C3**
Kaapkruis *Namibia* 21°55S 13°57E **56 B1**
Kabaena *Indonesia* 5°15S 122°0E **37 F6**
Kabala *S. Leone* 9°38N 11°37W **52 G3**
Kabale *Uganda* 1°15S 30°0E **54 E6**
Kabalo
   Dem. Rep. of the Congo 6°0S 27°0E **54 F5**
Kabambare
   Dem. Rep. of the Congo 4°41S 27°39E **54 E5**
Kabanjahe *Indonesia* 3°6N 98°30E **36 D1**
Kabankalan *Phil.* 9°59N 122°49E **37 C6**
Kabara *Fiji* 18°59S 178°56W **59 a**
Kabardino-Balkaria □
   Russia 43°30N 43°30E **19 F7**
Kabarega Falls = Murchison Falls
   Uganda 2°15N 31°30E **54 D6**
Kabasalan *Phil.* 7°47N 122°44E **37 C6**
Kabat *Indonesia* 8°16S 114°19E **37 J17**
Kabbani → *India* 12°13N 76°54E **45 H3**
Kabin Buri *Thailand* 13°57N 101°43E **38 F3**
Kabinakagami L. *Canada* 48°54N 84°25W **72 C3**
Kabinda
   Dem. Rep. of the Congo 6°19S 24°20E **54 F4**
Kabompo → *Zambia* 14°11S 23°11E **55 G4**
Kabongo
   Dem. Rep. of the Congo 7°22S 25°33E **54 F5**
Kabrît, G. el *Egypt* 29°42N 33°16E **48 F2**
Kabūd Gonbad *Iran* 37°5N 59°45E **47 B8**
Kābul *Afghan.* 34°28N 69°11E **42 B3**
Kābul □ *Afghan.* 34°30N 69°0E **40 B6**
Kābul → *Pakistan* 33°55N 72°14E **42 C5**
Kaburuang *Indonesia* 3°50N 126°30E **37 D7**
Kabwe *Zambia* 14°30S 28°29E **55 G5**
Kachchh, Gulf of *India* 22°50N 69°15E **42 H3**
Kachchh, Rann of *India* 24°0N 70°0E **42 H4**
Kachchhidhana *India* 21°44N 78°46E **43 J8**
Kachikau *Botswana* 18°8S 24°26E **56 A3**
Kachin □ *Burma* 26°0N 97°30E **34 D1**
Kachīry *Kazakhstan* 53°10N 75°50E **26 D8**
Kachnara *India* 23°50N 75°6E **42 H6**
Kachot *Cambodia* 11°30N 103°3E **39 G4**
Kaçkar *Turkey* 40°45N 41°10E **19 F7**
Kadaiyanallur *India* 9°3N 77°22E **45 K3**
Kadan Kyun *Burma* 12°30N 98°20E **38 F2**
Kadanai → *Afghan.* 31°22N 65°45E **42 D1**
Kadapa *India* 14°30N 78°47E **45 G4**
Kadavu *Fiji* 19°0S 178°15E **59 a**
Kadavu Passage *Fiji* 18°45S 178°0E **59 a**
Kade *Ghana* 6°7N 0°56W **52 G5**
Kadhimain = Al Kāẓimīyah
   Iraq 33°22N 44°18E **46 C5**
Kadi *India* 23°18N 72°23E **42 H5**
Kadina *Australia* 33°55S 137°43E **63 E2**
Kadipur *India* 26°10N 82°23E **43 F10**
Kadirabad *India* 19°51N 75°54E **44 E2**
Kadiri *India* 14°12N 78°13E **45 G4**
Kadirli *Turkey* 37°23N 36°5E **46 B3**
Kadiyevka = Stakhanov
   Ukraine 48°35N 38°40E **19 E6**
Kadmat I. *India* 11°14N 72°47E **45 J1**
Kadoka *U.S.A.* 43°50N 101°31W **80 D3**
Kadoma *Zimbabwe* 18°20S 29°52E **55 H5**
Kādugli *Sudan* 11°0N 29°45E **53 F11**
Kaduna *Nigeria* 10°30N 7°21E **52 F7**
Kadur *India* 13°34N 76°1E **45 H3**
Kaédi *Mauritania* 16°9N 13°28W **52 E3**
Kaeng Khoi *Thailand* 14°35N 101°0E **38 E3**
Kaeng Krachan △
   Thailand 12°57N 99°23E **38 F2**
Kaeng Krung △ *Thailand* 9°30N 98°50E **39 H2**
Kaeng Tana △ *Thailand* 15°25N 105°32E **38 E5**
Kaesŏng *N. Korea* 37°58N 126°35E **33 F14**
Kāf *Si. Arabia* 31°25N 37°29E **46 D3**
Kafan = Kapan *Armenia* 39°18N 46°27E **46 B5**
Kafanchan *Nigeria* 9°40N 8°20E **52 G7**
Kafue *Zambia* 15°46S 28°9E **55 H5**
Kafue → *Zambia* 15°30S 29°0E **55 H5**
Kaga *Afghan.* 34°14N 70°10E **42 B4**
Kaga Bandoro *C.A.R.* 7°0N 19°10E **54 C3**
Kagawa □ *Japan* 34°15N 134°0E **29 G7**
Kagera → *Uganda* 0°57S 31°47E **54 C6**
Kağızman *Turkey* 40°5N 43°10E **46 B4**
Kagoshima *Japan* 31°35N 130°33E **29 J5**
Kagoshima □ *Japan* 31°30N 130°30E **29 J5**
Kagul = Cahul *Moldova* 45°50N 28°15E **17 F15**
Kahak *Iran* 36°6N 49°46E **47 B6**
Kahan *Pakistan* 29°18N 65°48E **42 E3**
Kahang *Malaysia* 2°12N 103°32E **39 L4**
Kahayan → *Indonesia* 3°40S 114°0E **36 E4**
Kahemba
   Dem. Rep. of the Congo 7°18S 18°55E **54 F3**
Kahnūj *Iran* 27°55N 57°40E **47 E8**
Kahoka *U.S.A.* 40°25N 91°44W **80 E8**
Kaho'olawe *U.S.A.* 20°33N 156°37W **75 L8**
Kahramanmaraş *Turkey* 37°37N 36°53E **46 B3**
Kâhta *Turkey* 37°46N 38°36E **46 B3**
Kahugani △ *N.Z.* 41°10S 172°32E **59 D4**
Kahuta *Pakistan* 33°35N 73°24E **42 C5**

Kai, Kepulauan *Indonesia* 5°55S 132°45E **37 F8**
Kai Besar *Indonesia* 5°35S 133°0E **37 F8**
Kai Is. = Kai, Kepulauan
   Indonesia 5°55S 132°45E **37 F8**
Kai Kecil *Indonesia* 5°45S 132°40E **37 F8**
Kai Xian *China* 31°11N 108°21E **34 B7**
Kaiapoi *N.Z.* 43°24S 172°40E **59 E4**
Kaidu He → *China* 41°46N 86°31E **30 C6**
Kaieteur Falls *Guyana* 5°1N 59°10W **92 B7**
Kaifeng *China* 34°48N 114°21E **32 G8**
Kaihua *China* 29°12N 118°20E **35 C12**
Kaijiang *China* 31°7N 107°55E **34 B6**
Kaikohe *N.Z.* 35°25S 173°49E **59 A4**
Kaikoura *N.Z.* 42°25S 173°43E **59 E4**
Kailash = Kangrinboqe Feng
   China 31°0N 81°25E **43 D9**
Kaili *China* 26°33N 107°59E **34 D6**
Kailu *China* 43°38N 121°18E **33 C11**
Kailua Kona *U.S.A.* 19°39N 155°59W **75 M8**
Kaimana *Indonesia* 3°39S 133°45E **37 E8**
Kaimanawa Mts. *N.Z.* 39°15S 175°56E **59 C5**
Kaimganj *India* 27°33N 79°24E **43 F8**
Kaimur Hills *India* 24°30N 82°0E **43 G10**
Kainab → *Namibia* 28°32S 19°34E **56 C2**
Kainji Res. *Nigeria* 10°1N 4°40E **52 F6**
Kainuu □ *Finland* 64°30N 29°7E **8 D23**
Kaipara Harbour *N.Z.* 36°25S 174°14E **59 B5**
Kaiping *China* 22°23N 112°42E **35 F9**
Kaipokok B. *Canada* 54°54N 59°47W **73 B8**
Kaira *India* 22°45N 72°50E **42 H5**
Kairana *India* 29°24N 77°15E **42 E7**
Kaironi *Indonesia* 0°47S 133°40E **37 E8**
Kairouan *Tunisia* 35°45N 10°5E **53 A8**
Kaiserslautern *Germany* 49°26N 7°45E **16 D4**
Kaitaia *N.Z.* 35°8S 173°17E **59 A4**
Kaitangata *N.Z.* 46°17S 169°51E **59 G2**
Kaithal *India* 29°48N 76°26E **42 E7**
Kaitu → *Pakistan* 33°10N 70°30E **42 C4**
Kaiwi Channel *U.S.A.* 21°15N 157°30W **75 L8**
Kaiyang *China* 27°4N 106°59E **34 D6**
Kaiyuan *Liaoning, China* 42°28N 124°1E **33 C13**
Kaiyuan *Yunnan, China* 23°40N 103°12E **34 F4**
Kaiyuh Mts. *U.S.A.* 64°30N 158°0W **74 C8**
Kajaani *Finland* 64°17N 27°46E **8 D22**
Kajabbi *Australia* 20°0S 140°1E **62 C3**
Kajana = Kajaani
   Finland 64°17N 27°46E **8 D22**
Kajang *Malaysia* 2°59N 101°48E **39 L3**
Kajo Kaji *South Sudan* 3°58N 31°40E **53 H12**
Kaka *Turkmenistan* 37°21N 59°36E **47 B8**
Kakabeka Falls *Canada* 48°24N 89°37W **72 C2**
Kakadu △ *Australia* 12°0S 132°3E **60 B5**
Kakamas *S. Africa* 28°45S 20°33E **56 C3**
Kakamega *Kenya* 0°20N 34°46E **54 D6**
Kakana *India* 9°7N 92°48E **45 K11**
Kakanui Mts. *N.Z.* 45°10S 170°30E **59 F3**
Kakdwip *India* 21°53N 88°11E **43 J13**
Kake *= Akiōta *Japan* 34°36N 132°19E **29 G6**
Kake *U.S.A.* 56°59N 133°57W **70 B2**
Kakegawa *Japan* 34°45N 138°1E **29 G9**
Kakeroma-Jima *Japan* 28°8N 129°14E **29 K4**
Kakhovka *Ukraine* 46°45N 33°30E **19 E5**
Kakhovske Vdskh. *Ukraine* 47°5N 34°0E **19 E5**
Kakinada *India* 16°57N 82°11E **44 F6**
Kakisa *Canada* 60°56N 117°25W **70 A5**
Kakisa → *Canada* 61°3N 118°10W **70 A5**
Kakisa L. *Canada* 60°56N 117°43W **70 A5**
Kakogawa *Japan* 34°46N 134°51E **29 G7**
Kakwa → *Canada* 54°37N 118°28W **70 C5**
Kāl Gūdām = Kadavu *Fiji* 19°0S 178°15E **59 a**
Kal Sefid *Iran* 34°52N 47°23E **46 C5**
Kala Oya → *Sri Lanka* 8°20N 79°45E **45 K4**
Kalaallit Nunaat = Greenland ☑
   N. Amer. 66°0N 45°0W **67 C15**
Kalabagh *Pakistan* 33°0N 71°28E **42 C4**
Kalabahi *Indonesia* 8°13S 124°31E **37 F6**
Kalaburagi *India* 17°20N 76°50E **44 F3**
Kalach *Russia* 50°22N 41°0E **19 D7**
Kaladan → *Burma* 20°20N 93°5E **41 J18**
Kaladar *Canada* 44°37N 77°5W **82 B7**
Kalahari *Africa* 24°0S 21°30E **56 B3**
Kalahari Gemsbok △
   S. Africa 25°30S 20°30E **56 C3**
Kalajoki *Finland* 64°12N 24°10E **8 D21**
Kalakamati *Botswana* 20°40S 27°25E **57 B4**
Kalakan *Russia* 55°15N 116°45E **27 D12**
K'alak'unlun Shank'ou =
   Karakoram Pass *Asia* 35°33N 77°50E **43 B7**
Kalam *Pakistan* 35°34N 72°30E **43 B5**
Kalama *U.S.A.* 46°1N 122°51W **78 E4**
Kalámata *Greece* 37°3N 22°10E **23 F10**
Kalamazoo *U.S.A.* 42°17N 85°35W **81 D11**
Kalamazoo → *U.S.A.* 42°40N 86°10W **80 D10**
Kalamb *India* 18°3N 74°48E **44 E2**
Kalamnuri *India* 19°40N 77°20E **44 E3**
Kalan = Tunceli *Turkey* 39°6N 39°31E **46 B3**
Kalannie *Australia* 30°22S 117°5E **61 F2**
Kalāntarī *Iran* 32°10N 54°8E **47 C7**
Kalao *Indonesia* 7°21S 121°0E **37 F6**
Kalaotoa *Indonesia* 7°20S 121°50E **37 F6**
Kalasin *Thailand* 16°26N 103°30E **38 D4**
Kalāt *Iran* 25°29N 59°22E **47 E9**
Kalat *Pakistan* 29°8N 66°31E **40 E4**
Kalāteh *Iran* 36°33N 55°41E **47 B7**
Kalāteh-ye Ganj *Iran* 27°31N 57°55E **47 E8**
Kalbā *U.A.E.* 25°5N 56°22E **47 E8**
Kalbarri *Australia* 27°40S 114°10E **61 E1**
Kalbarri △ *Australia* 27°51S 114°30E **61 E1**
Kalce *Slovenia* 45°54N 14°13E **16 F8**
Kale *Turkey* 37°27N 28°49E **23 F13**
Kalegauk Kyun *Burma* 15°33N 97°35E **38 E1**
Kalemie
   Dem. Rep. of the Congo 5°55S 29°9E **54 F5**
Kalewa *Burma* 23°10N 94°15E **41 H19**
Kaleybar *Iran* 38°47N 47°2E **46 B5**
Kalghatgi *India* 15°11N 74°58E **45 G2**
Kalgoorlie-Boulder
   Australia 30°40S 121°22E **61 F3**
Kali → *India* 27°6N 79°55E **43 F8**

Kali Sindh → *India* 25°32N 76°17E **42 G6**
Kaliakra, Nos *Bulgaria* 43°21N 28°30E **23 C13**
Kalianda *Indonesia* 5°50S 105°45E **36 F3**
Kalibo *Phil.* 11°43N 122°22E **37 B6**
Kalimantan *Indonesia* 0°0 114°0E **36 E4**
Kalimantan Barat □
   Indonesia 0°0 110°30E **36 E4**
Kalimantan Selatan □
   Indonesia 2°30S 115°30E **36 E5**
Kalimantan Tengah □
   Indonesia 2°0S 113°30E **36 E4**
Kalimantan Timur □
   Indonesia 1°30N 116°30E **36 D5**
Kálimnos *Greece* 37°0N 27°0E **23 F12**
Kalimpong *India* 27°4N 88°35E **43 F13**
Kalinadi → *India* 14°50N 74°7E **45 G2**
Kaliningrad *Russia* 54°42N 20°32E **9 J19**
Kalinkovichi = Kalinkavichy
   Belarus 52°12N 29°20E **17 B15**
Kalisher *U.S.A.* 48°12N 114°19W **76 B6**
Kalisz *Poland* 51°45N 18°8E **17 C10**
Kaliveli Tank *India* 12°5N 79°50E **45 H4**
Kalix *Sweden* 65°53N 23°12E **8 D20**
Kalixälven → *Sweden* 65°50N 23°11E **8 D20**
Kalka *India* 30°46N 76°57E **42 D7**
Kalkaska *U.S.A.* 44°44N 85°11W **81 C11**
Kalkfeld *Namibia* 20°57S 16°14E **56 B2**
Kalkfontein *Botswana* 22°4S 20°57E **56 B3**
Kalkrand *Namibia* 24°1S 17°35E **56 B2**
Kallakurichchi *India* 11°44N 79°1E **45 J4**
Kallam *India* 18°36N 76°2E **44 E3**
Kallavesi *Finland* 62°58N 27°10E **8 E22**
Kallidaikurichi *India* 8°38N 77°31E **45 K3**
Kallsjön *Sweden* 63°38N 13°0E **8 E15**
Kalmar *Sweden* 56°40N 16°20E **9 H17**
Kalmykia □ *Russia* 46°5N 46°1E **19 E8**
Kalna *India* 23°13N 88°25E **43 H13**
Kalnai *India* 22°46N 83°30E **43 H10**
Kalocsa *Hungary* 46°32N 19°0E **17 E10**
Kalol *Gujarat, India* 22°37N 73°31E **42 H5**
Kalol *Gujarat, India* 23°15N 72°33E **42 H5**
Kalpeni I. *India* 10°5N 73°38E **45 J1**
Kalpi *India* 26°8N 79°47E **43 F8**
Kalpitiya *Sri Lanka* 8°14N 79°46E **45 K4**
Kalputhi I. *India* 10°49N 72°10E **45 J1**
Kalrayan Hills *India* 11°45N 78°40E **45 J4**
Kalsubai *India* 19°35N 73°45E **44 E1**
Kaltag *U.S.A.* 64°20N 158°43W **74 C8**
Kaltukatjara *Australia* 24°52S 129°5E **61 D4**
Kalu *Pakistan* 25°5N 67°39E **42 G2**
Kaluga *Russia* 54°35N 36°10E **18 D6**
Kalumburu *Australia* 13°55S 126°35E **60 B4**
Kalumburu ◎ *Australia* 14°17S 126°38E **60 B4**
Kalush *Ukraine* 49°3N 24°23E **17 D13**
Kalutara *Sri Lanka* 6°35N 80°0E **45 L5**
Kalwakurti *India* 16°41N 78°30E **44 F4**
Kalya *Russia* 60°15N 59°59E **18 B10**
Kalyan = Basavakalyan
   India 17°52N 76°57E **44 F3**
Kalyan *Maharashtra, India* 20°30N 74°3E **44 D2**
Kalyan *Maharashtra, India* 19°15N 73°9E **44 E1**
Kalyansingapuram *India* 19°30N 83°19E **44 E6**
Kama *Japan* 33°33N 130°49E **29 H5**
Kama → *Russia* 55°45N 52°0E **18 C9**
Kamaishi *Japan* 39°16N 141°53E **28 E10**
Kamalapuram *India* 14°35N 78°39E **45 G4**
Kamalia *Pakistan* 30°44N 72°42E **42 D5**
Kaman *India* 27°39N 77°16E **42 F6**
Kamanjab *Namibia* 19°35S 14°51E **56 B2**
Kamapanda *Zambia* 12°5S 24°0E **55 G4**
Kamarān *Yemen* 15°21N 42°35E **49 D3**
Kamareddi *India* 18°19N 78°21E **44 E4**
Kamativi *Zimbabwe* 18°20S 27°6E **56 A4**
Kambalda West
   Australia 31°10S 121°37E **61 F3**
Kambam *India* 9°45N 77°16E **45 K3**
Kambangan, Nusa
   Indonesia 7°40S 108°10E **37 G13**
Kambar *Pakistan* 27°37N 68°1E **42 F3**
Kambarka *Russia* 56°15N 54°11E **18 C9**
Kambove
   Dem. Rep. of the Congo 10°51S 26°33E **54 G5**
Kamchatka, Poluostrov
   Russia 57°0N 160°0E **27 D17**
Kamchatka Pen. = Kamchatka,
   Poluostrov *Russia* 57°0N 160°0E **27 D17**
Kamchiya → *Bulgaria* 43°4N 27°44E **23 C12**
Kameda-Hantō *Japan* 41°50N 141°0E **28 D10**
Kamen *Russia* 53°50N 81°30E **26 D9**
Kamen-Rybolov *Russia* 44°46N 132°2E **28 B5**
Kamenjak, Rt *Croatia* 44°47N 13°55E **16 F7**
Kamenka *Russia* 65°58N 44°0E **18 A7**
Kamenka Bugskaya =
   Kamyanka-Buzka
   Ukraine 50°8N 24°16E **17 C13**
Kamensk Uralskiy *Russia* 56°25N 62°2E **26 D7**
Kamenskoye *Russia* 62°45N 165°30E **27 C17**
Kameoka *Japan* 35°0N 135°35E **29 G7**
Kamiah *U.S.A.* 46°14N 116°2W **76 C5**
Kamieskroon *S. Africa* 30°9S 17°56E **56 D2**
Kamilukuak L. *Canada* 62°22N 101°40W **71 A8**
Kamin-Kashyrskyy
   Ukraine 51°39N 24°56E **17 C13**
Kamina
   Dem. Rep. of the Congo 8°45S 25°0E **54 F5**
Kaminak L. *Canada* 62°10N 95°0W **71 A10**
Kaminoyama *Japan* 38°9N 140°17E **28 E10**
Kamla → *India* 25°35N 86°36E **43 G12**
Kamloops *Canada* 50°40N 120°20W **70 C4**
Kamo *Japan* 37°39N 139°3E **28 F9**
Kamoke *Pakistan* 32°4N 74°4E **42 C6**
Kampala *Uganda* 0°20N 32°32E **54 D6**
Kampar *Malaysia* 4°18N 101°9E **39 K3**
Kampar → *Indonesia* 0°30N 103°8E **36 D2**
Kampen *Neths.* 52°33N 5°53E **15 B5**

Kamphaeng Phet
   Thailand 16°28N 99°30E **38 D2**
Kampong Cham
   Cambodia 12°0N 105°30E **38 F5**
Kampong Chhnang
   Cambodia 12°20N 104°35E **39 F5**
Kampong Pengerang
   Malaysia 1°22N 104°7E **39 d**
Kampong Punggai
   Malaysia 1°27N 104°18E **39 d**
Kampong Saom
   Cambodia 10°38N 103°30E **39 G4**
Kampong Saom, Chaak
   Cambodia 10°50N 103°32E **39 G4**
Kampong Tanjong Langsat
   Malaysia 1°28N 104°11E **39 d**
Kampong Telok Ramunia
   Malaysia 1°22N 104°15E **39 d**
Kampot *Cambodia* 10°36N 104°10E **39 G5**
Kampuchea = Cambodia ■
   Asia 12°15N 105°0E **38 F5**
Kampung Air Putih
   Malaysia 4°15N 103°10E **39 K4**
Kampung Jerangau
   Malaysia 4°50N 103°10E **39 K4**
Kampung Raja *Malaysia* 5°45N 102°35E **39 K4**
Kampungbaru = Tolitoli
   Indonesia 1°5N 120°50E **37 D6**
Kamrau, Teluk *Indonesia* 3°30S 133°36E **37 E8**
Kamsack *Canada* 51°34N 101°54W **71 C9**
Kamsar *Guinea* 10°40N 14°36W **52 F3**
Kamskoye Vdkhr. *Russia* 58°41N 56°7E **18 C10**
Kamthi *India* 21°9N 79°19E **44 D4**
Kamui-Misaki *Japan* 43°20N 140°21E **28 C10**
Kamyanets-Podilskyy
   Ukraine 48°45N 26°40E **17 D14**
Kamyanka-Buzka
   Ukraine 50°8N 24°16E **17 C13**
Kāmyārān *Iran* 34°47N 46°56E **46 C5**
Kamyshin *Russia* 50°10N 45°24E **19 D8**
Kanaaupscow → *Canada* 54°2N 76°30E **72 B4**
Kanab *U.S.A.* 37°3N 112°32W **77 H7**
Kanab Cr. → *U.S.A.* 36°24N 112°38W **77 H7**
Kanacea *Lau Group, Fiji* 17°15S 179°6W **59 a**
Kanacea *Taveuni, Fiji* 16°59S 179°56E **59 a**
Kanagi *Japan* 40°54N 140°27E **28 D10**
Kanairiktok → *Canada* 55°2N 60°18W **73 A7**
Kanakapura *India* 12°33N 77°28E **45 H3**
Kananga
   Dem. Rep. of the Congo 5°55S 22°18E **54 F4**
Kanash *Russia* 55°30N 47°32E **18 C8**
Kanaskat *U.S.A.* 47°19N 121°54W **78 C5**
Kanastraíon, Ákra = Paliouri,
   Akra *Greece* 39°57N 23°45E **23 E10**
Kanawha → *U.S.A.* 38°50N 82°9W **81 F12**
Kanazawa *Japan* 36°30N 136°38E **29 F8**
Kanchanaburi *Thailand* 14°2N 99°31E **38 E2**
Kanchenjunga *Nepal* 27°50N 88°10E **43 F13**
Kanchenjunga △ *India* 27°42N 88°8E **43 F13**
Kanchipuram *India* 12°52N 79°45E **45 H4**
Kandaghat *India* 30°59N 77°7E **42 D7**
Kandahar *India* 18°52N 77°12E **44 E3**
Kandahar *Afghan.* 31°32N 65°43E **40 D4**
Kandahār □ *Afghan.* 31°0N 65°0E **40 D4**
Kandalaksha *Russia* 67°9N 32°30E **8 C25**
Kandalakshkiy Zaliv
   Russia 66°0N 35°0E **18 A6**
Kandangan *Indonesia* 2°50S 115°20E **36 E5**
Kandavu = Kadavu *Fiji* 19°0S 178°15E **59 a**
Kandavu Passage =
   Kadavu Passage *Fiji* 18°45S 178°0E **59 a**
Kandhkot *Pakistan* 28°16N 69°8E **42 E3**
Kandhla *India* 29°18N 77°19E **42 E7**
Kandi *Benin* 11°7N 2°55E **52 F6**
Kandiaro *Pakistan* 27°4N 68°13E **42 F3**
Kandla *India* 23°0N 70°10E **42 H4**
Kandos *Australia* 32°45S 149°58E **63 E4**
Kandy *Sri Lanka* 7°18N 80°43E **45 L5**
Kane *U.S.A.* 41°40N 78°49W **82 E6**
Kane Basin *Greenland* 79°1N 70°0W **69 B18**
Kang *Botswana* 23°41S 22°50E **56 B3**
Kangān *Fārs, Iran* 27°50N 52°3E **47 E7**
Kangān *Hormozgān, Iran* 25°48N 57°28E **47 E8**
Kangar *Malaysia* 6°27N 100°12E **39 c**
Kangaroo I. *Australia* 35°45S 137°0E **63 F2**
Kangaroo Mts. *Australia* 23°29S 141°51E **62 C3**
Kangasala *Finland* 61°28N 24°4E **8 F21**
Kangāvar *Iran* 34°40N 48°0E **47 C6**
Kangdong *N. Korea* 39°9N 126°5E **33 E14**
Kangean, Kepulauan
   Indonesia 6°55S 115°23E **36 F5**
Kangean Is. = Kangean,
   Kepulauan *Indonesia* 6°55S 115°23E **36 F5**
Kanggye *N. Korea* 41°0N 126°35E **33 D14**
Kangikajik *Greenland* 70°7N 22°0W **4 B7**
Kangiqliniq = Rankin Inlet
   Canada 62°30N 93°0W **68 E13**
Kangiqsualujjuaq
   Canada 58°30N 65°59W **69 F18**
Kangiqsujuaq *Canada* 61°30N 72°0W **69 E17**
Kangirsuk *Canada* 60°0N 70°0W **69 F18**
Kangkar Chemaran
   Malaysia 1°34N 104°12E **39 d**
Kangkar Sungai Tiram
   Malaysia 1°35N 103°51E **39 d**
Kangkar Teberau
   Malaysia 1°32N 103°51E **39 d**
Kangping *China* 42°43N 123°18E **33 C12**
Kangra *India* 32°6N 76°16E **42 C7**
Kangrinboqe Feng *China* 31°0N 81°25E **43 D9**
Kangto *China* 27°50N 92°35E **41 F18**
Kanha △ *India* 22°15N 80°40E **43 H9**
Kanhan → *India* 21°4N 79°34E **44 D4**
Kanhangad *India* 12°21N 74°58E **45 G2**

Kanhar → India 24°28N 83°8E 43 G10
Kaniapiskau = Caniapiscau →
  Canada 56°40N 69°30W 73 A6
Kaniapiskau, L. = Caniapiscau, L.
  Canada 54°10N 69°55W 73 B6
Kanigiri India 15°24N 79°31E 45 G4
Kanin, Poluostrov Russia 68°0N 45°0E 18 A8
Kanin Nos, Mys Russia 68°39N 43°32E 18 A7
Kanin Pen. = Kanin, Poluostrov
  Russia 68°0N 45°0E 18 A8
Kaniva Australia 36°22S 141°18E 63 F3
Kanjut Sar Pakistan 36°7N 75°25E 43 A6
Kankaanpää Finland 61°44N 22°50E 8 E20
Kankakee U.S.A. 41°7N 87°52W 80 E10
Kankakee → U.S.A. 41°23N 88°15W 80 E9
Kankan Guinea 10°23N 9°15W 52 F4
Kankendy = Xankändi
  Azerbaijan 39°52N 46°49E 46 B5
Kanker India 20°10N 81°40E 44 D5
Kankesanturai Sri Lanka 9°49N 80°2E 45 K5
Kankroli India 25°4N 73°53E 42 G5
Kanmaw Kyun Burma 11°40N 98°28E 39 G2
Kannapolis U.S.A. 35°30N 80°37W 85 D14
Kannauj India 27°3N 79°56E 43 F8
Kanniyakumari India 8°5N 77°34E 45 K3
Kannod India 22°45N 76°40E 40 H10
Kannur India 11°53N 75°27E 45 J2
Kannyakumari India 8°3N 77°40E 45 K3
Kano Nigeria 12°2N 8°30E 52 F7
Kan'onji Japan 34°7N 133°39E 29 G6
Kanowit Malaysia 2°14N 112°20E 36 D4
Kanoya Japan 31°25N 130°50E 29 J5
Kanpetlet Burma 21°10N 93°59E 41 J18
Kanpur India 26°28N 80°20E 43 F9
Kansas □ U.S.A. 38°30N 99°0W 80 F4
Kansas → U.S.A. 39°7N 94°37W 80 F6
Kansas City Kans., U.S.A. 39°7N 94°38W 80 F6
Kansas City Mo., U.S.A. 39°6N 94°35W 80 F6
Kansk Russia 56°20N 95°37E 27 D10
Kansu = Gansu □ China 36°0N 104°0E 32 G3
Kantaphor India 22°35N 76°34E 42 H7
Kantharalak Thailand 14°39N 104°39E 38 E5
Kanthi = Contai India 21°54N 87°46E 43 J12
Kantli → India 28°20N 75°30E 42 E6
Kantō □ Japan 36°15N 139°30E 29 F9
Kantō-Sanchi Japan 35°59N 138°50E 29 G9
Kanturk Ireland 52°11N 8°54W 10 D3
Kanuma Japan 36°34N 139°42E 29 F9
Kanus Namibia 27°50S 18°39E 56 C2
Kanye Botswana 24°55S 25°28E 56 C4
Kao Tonga 19°40S 175°1W 59 c
Kao Phara Thailand 8°3N 98°22E 39 a
Kaohsiung Taiwan 22°35N 120°16E 35 F13
Kaokoveld Namibia 19°15S 14°30E 56 A1
Kaolack Senegal 14°5N 16°8W 52 F2
Kaoshan China 44°38N 124°50E 33 B13
Kapa'a U.S.A. 22°5N 159°19W 75 L8
Kapadvanj India 23°5N 73°0E 42 H5
Kapan Armenia 39°18N 46°27E 46 B5
Kapanga
  Dem. Rep. of the Congo 8°30S 22°40E 54 F4
Kapchagai = Qapshaghay
  Kazakhstan 43°51N 77°14E 26 E8
Kapela = Velika Kapela
  Croatia 45°10N 15°5E 16 F8
Kapfenberg Austria 47°26N 15°18E 16 E8
Kapiri Mposhi Zambia 13°59S 28°43E 55 G5
Kāpīsā □ Afghan. 35°0N 69°20E 40 B6
Kapiskau → Canada 52°47N 81°55W 72 B3
Kapit Malaysia 2°0N 112°55E 36 D4
Kapiti I. N.Z. 40°50S 174°56E 59 D5
Kaplan U.S.A. 30°0N 92°17W 84 F8
Kapoe Thailand 9°34N 98°32E 39 H2
Kapoeta South Sudan 4°50N 33°35E 53 H12
Kaposvár Hungary 46°25N 17°47E 17 E9
Kapowsin U.S.A. 46°59N 122°13W 78 D4
Kapps Namibia 22°32S 17°18E 56 B2
Kapsan N. Korea 41°4N 128°19E 33 D15
Kapsukas = Marijampolė
  Lithuania 54°33N 23°19E 9 J20
Kaptai L. Bangla. 22°40N 92°20E 41 H18
Kapuas → Indonesia 0°25S 109°20E 36 E3
Kapuas Hulu, Pegunungan
  Malaysia 1°30N 113°30E 36 D4
Kapuas Hulu Ra. = Kapuas Hulu,
  Pegunungan Malaysia 1°30N 113°30E 36 D4
Kapunda Australia 34°20S 138°56E 63 E2
Kapuni N.Z. 39°29S 174°8E 59 C5
Kapurthala India 31°23N 75°25E 42 D6
Kapuskasing Canada 49°25N 82°30W 72 C3
Kapuskasing → Canada 49°49N 82°0W 72 C3
Kaputar, Mt. Australia 30°15S 150°10E 63 E5
Kaputir Kenya 2°5N 35°28E 54 B4
Kara Russia 69°10N 65°0E 26 C7
Kara Bogaz Gol, Zaliv =
  Garabogazköl Aylagy
  Turkmenistan 41°0N 53°30E 19 F9
Kara Kala = Garrygala
  Turkmenistan 38°31N 56°29E 47 B8
Kara Kalpak Republic =
  Qoraqalpog'iston □
  Uzbekistan 43°0N 58°0E 26 E6
Kara Kum = Garagum
  Turkmenistan 39°30N 60°0E 47 B8
Kara Sea Russia 75°0N 70°0E 26 B8
Karabiğa Turkey 40°23N 27°17E 23 D12
Karabük Turkey 41°12N 32°37E 19 F5
Karaburun Turkey 38°41N 26°28E 23 E12
Karabutak = Qarabutaq
  Kazakhstan 50°0N 60°14E 26 E7
Karacabey Turkey 40°12N 28°21E 23 D13
Karacasu Turkey 37°43N 28°35E 23 F13
Karachey-Cherkessia □
  Russia 43°40N 41°30E 19 F7
Karad India 17°15N 74°10E 44 F2
Karaganda = Qaraghandy
  Kazakhstan 49°50N 73°10E 30 B3
Karagayly = Qaraghayly
  Kazakhstan 49°26N 76°0E 26 E8
Karaginskiy, Ostrov
  Russia 58°45N 164°0E 27 D17

Karagiye, Vpadina
  Kazakhstan 43°27N 51°45E 19 F9
Karagiye Depression = Karagiye,
  Vpadina Kazakhstan 43°27N 51°45E 19 F9
Karagola Road India 25°29N 87°23E 43 G12
Karaikal India 10°59N 79°50E 45 J4
Karaikkudi India 10°5N 78°45E 45 J4
Karaitivu I. Sri Lanka 9°45N 79°52E 45 K4
Karaj Iran 35°48N 51°0E 47 C6
Karajarri ☺ Australia 19°0S 122°30E 60 C3
Karak Malaysia 3°25N 102°2E 39 L4
Karakalpakstan =
  Qoraqalpog'iston □
  Uzbekistan 43°0N 58°0E 26 E6
Karakelong Indonesia 4°35N 126°50E 37 D7
Karakitang Indonesia 3°14N 125°28E 37 D7
Karakol Kyrgyzstan 42°30N 78°20E 30 C4
Karakoram Pass Asia 35°33N 77°50E 43 B7
Karakoram Ra. Pakistan 35°30N 77°0E 43 B7
Karakuwisa Namibia 18°56S 19°40E 56 A2
Karalon Russia 57°5N 115°50E 27 D12
Karama Jordan 31°57N 35°35E 48 D4
Karaman Turkey 37°14N 33°13E 46 B2
Karamay China 45°30N 84°58E 30 B5
Karambu Indonesia 3°53S 116°6E 36 E5
Karamea Bight N.Z. 41°22S 171°40E 59 D3
Karamnasa → India 25°31N 83°52E 43 G10
Karān Si. Arabia 27°43N 49°49E 47 E6
Karand Iran 34°16N 46°15E 46 C5
Karanganyar Indonesia 7°38S 109°37E 37 G13
Karangasem = Amlapura
  Indonesia 8°27S 115°37E 37 J18
Karanja Maharashtra,
  India 21°11N 78°24E 44 D4
Karanja Maharashtra,
  India 20°29N 77°31E 44 D3
Karanjia India 21°47N 85°58E 43 J11
Karas □ Namibia 27°0S 17°30E 56 C2
Karasburg Namibia 28°0S 18°44E 56 C2
Karasino Russia 66°50N 86°50E 26 C9
Karasjok Norway 69°27N 25°30E 8 B21
Karasuk Russia 53°44N 78°2E 26 D8
Karasuyama Japan 36°39N 140°9E 29 F10
Karatau, Khrebet = Qarataū
  Kazakhstan 43°30N 69°30E 26 E7
Karatax Shan China 35°57N 81°0E 30 D5
Karativu Sri Lanka 8°22N 79°47E 45 K4
Karatsu Japan 33°26N 129°58E 29 H5
Karaul Russia 70°6N 82°15E 26 B9
Karauli India 26°30N 77°4E 42 F7
Karawang Indonesia 6°30S 107°15E 37 G12
Karawanken Europe 46°30N 14°40E 16 E8
Karayazı Turkey 39°41N 42°9E 19 G7
Karazhal = Qarazhal
  Kazakhstan 48°2N 70°49E 26 E8
Karbalā' Iraq 32°36N 44°3E 46 C5
Karcag Hungary 47°19N 20°57E 17 E11
Karcha → Pakistan 34°45N 76°10E 43 B7
Karchana India 25°17N 81°56E 43 G9
Karditsa Greece 39°23N 21°54E 23 E9
Kärdla Estonia 59°0N 22°45E 9 G20
Kardzhali = Kürdzhali
  Bulgaria 41°38N 25°21E 23 D11
Kareeberge S. Africa 30°59S 21°50E 56 D3
Kareha → India 25°44N 86°21E 43 G12
Kareima Sudan 18°30N 31°49E 53 E12
Karelia □ Russia 65°30N 32°30E 18 A5
Karelian Republic = Karelia □
  Russia 65°30N 32°30E 18 A5
Karera India 25°32N 78°9E 42 G8
Kārevāndar Iran 27°53N 60°44E 47 E9
Kargasok Russia 59°3N 80°53E 26 D9
Kargat Russia 55°10N 80°15E 26 D9
Kargil India 34°32N 76°12E 43 B7
Kargopol Russia 61°30N 38°58E 18 B6
Kariān Iran 26°57N 57°14E 47 E8
Kariba, L. Zimbabwe 16°40S 28°25E 55 H5
Kariba Dam Zimbabwe 16°30S 28°35E 55 H5
Kariba Gorge Zambia 16°30S 28°50E 55 H5
Karibib Namibia 22°0S 15°56E 56 B2
Karijini △ Australia 23°8S 118°15E 60 D2
Karimata, Kepulauan
  Indonesia 1°25S 109°0E 36 E3
Karimata, Selat Indonesia 2°0S 108°40E 36 E3
Karimata Is. = Karimata,
  Kepulauan Indonesia 1°25S 109°0E 36 E3
Karimnagar India 18°26N 79°10E 44 E4
Karimun, Pulau Indonesia 1°3N 103°22E 39 d
Karimun Kecil, Pulau
  Indonesia 1°8N 103°22E 39 d
Karimunjawa, Kepulauan
  Indonesia 5°50S 110°30E 36 F4
Karin Somalia 10°50N 45°52E 49 E4
Kariti Iran 33°29N 56°55E 47 C8
Kariya Japan 34°58N 137°1E 29 G8
Kariyangwe Zimbabwe 18°0S 27°38E 57 A4
Karjala Finland 62°0N 30°25E 8 F24
Karjat India 18°33N 75°0E 44 E2
Karkal India 13°15N 74°56E 45 H2
Karkaralinsk = Qarqaraly
  Kazakhstan 49°26N 75°30E 30 B4
Karkheh → Iran 31°2N 47°29E 46 D5
Karkinitska Zatoka
  Ukraine 45°56N 33°0E 19 E5
Karkinitskiy Zaliv = Karkinitska
  Zatoka Ukraine 45°56N 33°0E 19 E5
Karkuk = Kirkūk Iraq 35°30N 44°21E 46 C5
Karlantijpa North ☺
  Australia 19°27S 133°33E 60 C5
Karlantijpa South ☺
  Australia 20°31S 133°9E 60 D5
Karleby = Kokkola
  Finland 63°50N 23°8E 8 E20
Karlovac Croatia 45°31N 15°36E 16 F8
Karlovo Bulgaria 42°38N 24°47E 23 C11
Karlovy Vary Czech Rep. 50°13N 12°51E 16 C7
Karlsbad = Karlovy Vary
  Czech Rep. 50°13N 12°51E 16 C7
Karlsborg Sweden 58°33N 14°33E 9 G16
Karlsena, Mys Russia 77°0N 67°42E 26 B7
Karlshamn Sweden 56°10N 14°51E 9 H16

Karlskoga Sweden 59°28N 14°33E 9 G16
Karlskrona Sweden 56°10N 15°35E 9 H16
Karlsruhe Germany 49°0N 8°23E 16 D5
Karlstad Sweden 59°23N 13°30E 9 G15
Karlstad U.S.A. 48°35N 96°31W 80 A5
Karmala India 18°25N 75°12E 44 E2
Karmi'el Israel 32°55N 35°18E 48 C4
Karnak Egypt 25°43N 32°39E 53 C12
Karnal India 29°42N 77°2E 42 E7
Karnali = Ghaghara →
  India 25°45N 84°40E 43 G11
Karnali → Nepal 28°45N 81°16E 43 E9
Karnaphuli Res. = Kaptai L.
  Bangla. 22°40N 92°20E 41 H18
Karnaprayag India 30°16N 79°15E 43 D8
Karnataka □ India 13°15N 77°0E 45 H3
Karnes City U.S.A. 28°53N 97°54W 84 G6
Karnische Alpen Europe 46°36N 13°0E 16 E7
Kärnten □ Austria 46°52N 13°30E 16 E8
Karon, Ao Thailand 7°51N 98°17E 39 a
Karonga Malawi 9°57S 33°55E 54 F6
Karoo △ S. Africa 32°18S 22°27E 56 D3
Karoonda Australia 35°1S 139°59E 63 F2
Karor Pakistan 31°15N 70°59E 42 D4
Karora Sudan 17°44N 38°15E 53 E13
Karpathos Greece 35°37N 27°10E 23 G12
Karpinsk Russia 59°45N 60°1E 18 C11
Karpogory Russia 64°0N 44°27E 18 B7
Karpuz Burnu = Apostolos
  Andreas, C. Cyprus 35°42N 34°35E 46 C2
Karratha Australia 20°44S 116°52E 60 D2
Kars Turkey 40°40N 43°5E 19 F7
Karsakpay Kazakhstan 47°55N 66°40E 26 E7
Karshi = Qarshi
  Uzbekistan 38°53N 65°48E 26 F7
Karsiyang India 26°56N 88°18E 43 F13
Karsog India 31°23N 77°12E 42 D7
Kartala Comoros Is. 11°45S 43°21E 55 a
Kartaly Russia 53°3N 60°40E 26 D7
Kartapur India 31°27N 75°32E 42 D6
Karthaus U.S.A. 41°8N 78°9W 82 E6
Karufa Indonesia 3°50S 133°20E 37 E8
Karumba Australia 17°31S 140°50E 62 B3
Kārūn → Iran 30°26N 48°10E 47 D6
Karungu Kenya 0°50S 34°10E 54 E6
Karur India 10°59N 78°2E 45 J4
Karviná Czech Rep. 49°53N 18°31E 17 D10
Karwan → India 27°26N 78°4E 42 F8
Karwar India 14°55N 74°13E 45 G2
Karwi India 25°12N 80°57E 43 G9
Karymskoye Russia 51°36N 114°21E 27 D12
Kasai →
  Dem. Rep. of the Congo 3°30S 16°10E 54 E3
Kasama Zambia 10°16S 31°9E 54 G6
Kasan-dong N. Korea 41°18N 126°55E 33 D14
Kasane Namibia 17°34S 24°50E 56 A3
Kasaragod India 12°30N 74°58E 45 H2
Kasba L. Canada 60°20N 102°10W 71 A8
Kāseh Garān Iran 34°5N 46°2E 46 C5
Kasempa Zambia 13°30S 25°44E 55 G5
Kasenga
  Dem. Rep. of the Congo 10°20S 28°45E 54 G5
Kasese Uganda 0°13N 30°3E 54 D6
Kasganj India 27°48N 78°42E 43 F8
Kashabowie Canada 48°40N 90°26W 72 C1
Kashaf Iran 35°58N 61°7E 47 C9
Kāshān Iran 34°5N 51°30E 47 C6
Kashechewan Canada 52°18N 81°37W 72 B3
Kashgar = Kashi China 39°30N 76°2E 30 D4
Kashi China 39°30N 76°2E 30 D4
Kashipur Odisha, India 19°16N 83°3E 44 K6
Kashipur Uttarakhand,
  India 29°15N 79°0E 43 E8
Kashiwazaki Japan 37°22N 138°33E 29 F9
Kashk-e Kohneh Afghan. 34°55N 62°30E 40 B3
Kashkū'īyeh Iran 30°31N 55°40E 47 D7
Kāshmar Iran 35°16N 58°0E 47 C8
Kashmir Asia 34°0N 76°0E 43 C7
Kashmor Pakistan 28°28N 69°32E 42 E3
Kashun Noerh = Gaxun Nur
  China 42°22N 100°30E 30 C9
Kasiari India 22°8N 87°14E 43 H12
Kasimov Russia 54°55N 41°20E 18 D7
Kasiruta Indonesia 0°25S 127°12E 37 E7
Kaskaskia → U.S.A. 37°58N 89°57W 80 G9
Kaskinen Finland 62°22N 21°15E 8 E19
Kaskö = Kaskinen
  Finland 62°22N 21°15E 8 E19
Kaslo Canada 49°55N 116°55W 70 D5
Kasmere L. Canada 59°34N 101°10W 71 B8
Kasongo
  Dem. Rep. of the Congo 4°30S 26°33E 54 E5
Kasongo Lunda
  Dem. Rep. of the Congo 6°35S 16°49E 54 F3
Kasos Greece 35°20N 26°55E 23 G12
Kassalâ Sudan 15°30N 36°0E 53 E13
Kassandra Kolpos Greece 40°5N 23°30E 23 D10
Kassel Germany 51°18N 9°26E 16 C5
Kasson U.S.A. 44°2N 92°45W 80 C7
Kastamonu Turkey 41°25N 33°43E 19 F5
Kasterlee Belgium 51°15N 4°59E 15 C4
Kastoria Greece 40°30N 21°19E 23 D9
Kastrom Mefa'a = Umm al Rasas
  Jordan 31°30N 35°55E 48 D4
Kasumi Japan 35°38N 134°38E 29 G7
Kasur Pakistan 31°5N 74°25E 42 D6
Kata, Ao Thailand 7°48N 98°18E 39 a
Kata Tjuta Australia 25°20S 130°50E 61 E5
Katahdin, Mt. U.S.A. 45°54N 68°56W 81 C19
Kataka = Cuttack India 20°25N 85°57E 44 D7
Katanga
  Dem. Rep. of the Congo 8°0S 25°0E 54 F4
Katangi India 21°56N 79°50E 44 D4
Katanning Australia 33°40S 117°33E 61 F2
Katchall India 7°57N 93°22E 45 L11
Katerini Greece 40°18N 22°37E 23 D10
Katghora India 22°30N 82°33E 43 H10
Katha Burma 24°10N 96°30E 41 G20
Katherîna, Gebel Egypt 28°30N 33°57E 46 D2

Katherine Australia 14°27S 132°20E 60 B5
Katherine Gorge = Nitmiluk △
  Australia 14°6S 132°15E 60 B5
Kathi India 21°47N 74°3E 42 J6
Kathiawar India 22°20N 71°0E 42 H4
Kathmandu Nepal 27°45N 85°20E 43 F11
Kathua India 32°23N 75°34E 42 C6
Kati Thanda-Lake Eyre
  Australia 29°30S 137°26E 58 D6
Kati Thanda-Lake Eyre (North)
  Australia 28°30S 137°20E 63 D2
Kati Thanda-Lake Eyre (South)
  Australia 29°18S 137°25E 63 D2
Katihar India 25°34N 87°36E 43 G12
Katima Mulilo Namibia 17°28S 24°13E 56 A3
Katingan = Mendawai →
  Indonesia 3°30S 113°0E 36 E4
Katiola Ivory C. 8°10N 5°10W 52 G4
Katiti ☺ Australia 25°1S 131°11E 61 E5
Katmandu = Kathmandu
  Nepal 27°45N 85°20E 43 F11
Katni India 23°51N 80°24E 43 H9
Katol India 21°17N 78°38E 44 D4
Katoomba Australia 33°41S 150°19E 63 E5
Katowice Poland 50°17N 19°5E 17 C10
Katrine, L. U.K. 56°15N 4°30W 11 E4
Katrineholm Sweden 59°0N 16°12E 9 G17
Katsina Nigeria 13°0N 7°32E 52 F7
Katsumoto Japan 33°51N 129°42E 29 H4
Katsuura Japan 35°10N 140°20E 29 G10
Katsuyama Japan 36°3N 136°30E 29 F8
Kattegat Denmark 56°40N 11°20E 9 H14
Katwa India 23°30N 88°5E 43 H13
Katwijk Neths. 52°12N 4°24E 15 B4
Kau-Ye Kyun Burma 11°1N 98°32E 39 G2
Kaua'i U.S.A. 22°3N 159°30W 75 L8
Kaudom △ Namibia 18°45S 20°51E 56 A3
Kaufman U.S.A. 32°35N 96°19W 84 E6
Kauhajoki Finland 62°25N 22°10E 8 E20
Kauhaneva-Pohjankangas △
  Finland 62°13N 22°20E 8 E20
Kaukauna U.S.A. 44°17N 88°17W 80 C9
Kaukauveld Namibia 20°0S 20°15E 56 B3
Ka'ula I. U.S.A. 21°40N 160°33W 75 L7
Kaunas Lithuania 54°54N 23°54E 9 J20
Kaunia Bangla. 25°46N 89°26E 43 G13
Kautokeino Norway 69°0N 23°4E 8 B20
Kauwapur India 27°31N 82°18E 43 F10
Kavacha Russia 60°16N 169°51E 27 C17
Kavala Greece 40°57N 24°28E 23 D11
Kavalerovo Russia 44°15N 135°4E 28 B7
Kavali India 14°55N 80°1E 45 G5
Kavango = Cubango →
  Africa 18°50S 22°25E 56 A3
Kavār Iran 29°11N 52°44E 47 D7
Kavaratti India 10°34N 72°37E 45 J1
Kavaratti I. India 10°33N 72°38E 45 J1
Kaveri = Cauvery → India 11°9N 78°52E 45 J4
Kavimba Botswana 18°2S 24°38E 56 A3
Kavīr, Dasht-e Iran 34°30N 55°0E 47 C7
Kavīr △ Iran 34°40N 52°0E 47 C7
Kaw Fr. Guiana 4°30N 52°15W 93 C8
Kawagoe Japan 35°55N 139°29E 29 G9
Kawaguchi Japan 35°52N 139°45E 29 G9
Kawah Ijen △ Indonesia 8°3S 114°14E 37 H15
Kawanoe = Shikokuchūō
  Japan 34°1N 133°34E 29 G6
Kawardha India 22°0N 81°17E 43 J9
Kawasi Indonesia 1°38S 127°28E 37 E7
Kawawachikamach
  Canada 54°48N 66°50W 73 B6
Kawerau N.Z. 38°7S 176°42E 59 C6
Kawhia N.Z. 38°4S 174°49E 59 C5
Kawhia Harbour N.Z. 38°5S 174°51E 59 C5
Kawio, Kepulauan
  Indonesia 4°30N 125°30E 37 D7
Kawthaung Burma 10°5N 98°36E 39 H2
Kawthoolei = Kayin □
  Burma 18°0N 97°30E 41 L20
Kawthule = Kayin □
  Burma 18°0N 97°30E 41 L20
Kaya Burkina Faso 13°4N 1°10W 52 F5
Kayah □ Burma 19°15N 97°15E 41 K20
Kayak I. U.S.A. 59°56N 144°23W 74 D11
Kayamkulam India 9°10N 76°33E 45 K3
Kayan → Indonesia 2°55N 117°35E 36 D5
Kaycee U.S.A. 43°43N 106°38W 76 E10
Kayeli Indonesia 3°20S 127°10E 37 E7
Kayenta U.S.A. 36°44N 110°15W 77 H8
Kayes Mali 14°25N 11°30W 52 F3
Kayin □ Burma 18°0N 97°30E 41 L20
Kayoa Indonesia 0°1N 127°28E 37 D7
Kayseri Turkey 38°45N 35°30E 46 B3
Kaysville U.S.A. 41°2N 111°56W 76 F8
Kayts Sri Lanka 9°42N 79°51E 45 K4
Kazachye Russia 70°52N 135°58E 27 B14
Kazakhstan ■ Asia 50°0N 70°0E 26 E7
Kazan Russia 55°50N 49°10E 18 C8
Kazan → Canada 64°2N 95°29W 71 A9
Kazan-Rettō Pac. Oc. 25°0N 141°0E 64 E6
Kazanlŭk Bulgaria 42°38N 25°20E 23 C11
Kazatin = Kozyatyn
  Ukraine 49°45N 28°50E 17 D15
Kāzerūn Iran 29°38N 51°40E 47 D6
Kazi Magomed = Qazımämmäd
  Azerbaijan 40°3N 49°0E 47 A6
Kazipet India 17°58N 79°30E 44 F4
Kazo Japan 40°10N 140°45E 28 D10
Kazym → Russia 63°54N 65°50E 26 C7
Kea Greece 37°35N 24°22E 23 F11
Keady U.K. 54°15N 6°42W 10 B5
Kearney U.S.A. 40°42N 99°5W 80 E4
Kearney ☺ Australia 20°10S 128°4E 60 D4
Kearny U.S.A. 33°3N 110°55W 77 K8
Kearsarge, Mt. U.S.A. 43°22N 71°50W 83 C13
Keban Baraji Turkey 38°41N 38°33E 46 B3
Kebnekaise Sweden 67°53N 18°33E 8 C18

Kebri Dehar Ethiopia 6°45N 44°17E 49 F3
Kebumen Indonesia 7°42S 109°40E 37 G13
Kechika → Canada 59°41N 127°12W 70 B3
Kecskemét Hungary 46°57N 19°42E 17 E10
Kedah □ Malaysia 5°50N 100°40E 39 K3
Kėdainiai Lithuania 55°15N 24°2E 9 J21
Kedarnath India 30°44N 79°4E 43 D8
Kedgwick Canada 47°40N 67°20W 73 C6
Kediri Indonesia 7°51S 112°1E 37 G15
Keeler U.S.A. 36°29N 117°52W 78 J9
Keeley L. Canada 54°54N 108°8W 71 C7
Keeling Is. = Cocos Is.
  Ind. Oc. 12°10S 96°55E 64 J1
Keelung = Chilung
  Taiwan 25°3N 121°45E 35 E13
Keene Canada 44°15N 78°10W 82 B6
Keene Calif., U.S.A. 35°13N 118°33W 79 K8
Keene N.H., U.S.A. 42°56N 72°17W 83 D12
Keene N.Y., U.S.A. 44°16N 73°46W 83 B11
Keep River △ Australia 15°49S 129°8E 60 C4
Keeper Hill Ireland 52°45N 8°16W 10 D3
Keerweer, C. Australia 14°0S 141°32E 62 A3
Keeseville U.S.A. 44°29N 73°30W 83 B11
Keetmanshoop Namibia 26°35S 18°8E 56 D2
Keewatin Canada 49°46N 94°34W 71 D10
Keewatin → Canada 56°29N 100°46W 71 B8
Kefalonia Greece 38°15N 20°30E 23 E9
Kefamenanu Indonesia 9°28S 124°29E 37 F6
Kefar Sava Israel 32°11N 34°54E 48 C3
Keffi Nigeria 8°55N 7°43E 52 G7
Keflavík Iceland 64°2N 22°35W 8 D2
Keg River Canada 57°54N 117°55W 70 B5
Kegalla Sri Lanka 7°15N 80°21E 45 L5
Kegaska Canada 50°9N 61°18W 73 B7
Keighley U.K. 53°52N 1°54W 12 D6
Keila Estonia 59°18N 24°25E 9 G21
Keimoes S. Africa 28°41S 20°59E 56 D3
Keitele Finland 63°10N 26°20E 8 E22
Keith Australia 36°6S 140°20E 63 F3
Keith U.K. 57°32N 2°57W 11 D6
Keiyasi Fiji 17°53S 177°46E 59 a
Keizer U.S.A. 44°57N 123°1W 76 D2
Kejimkujik △ Canada 44°25N 65°25W 73 D6
Kejserr Franz Joseph Fd.
  Greenland 73°30N 24°30W 4 B6
Kekri India 26°0N 75°10E 42 G6
Kelan China 38°43N 111°31E 32 E6
Kelang = Klang Malaysia 3°2N 101°26E 39 L3
Kelani Ganga → Sri Lanka 6°58N 79°50E 45 L4
Kelantan □ Malaysia 5°10N 102°0E 39 K3
Kelantan → Malaysia 6°13N 102°14E 39 K4
Kelkit → Turkey 40°45N 36°32E 19 F6
Kellerberrin Australia 31°36S 117°38E 61 F2
Kellett, C. Canada 72°0N 126°0W 4 B1
Kelleys I. U.S.A. 41°36N 82°42W 82 E2
Kellogg U.S.A. 47°32N 116°7W 76 C5
Kells Ireland 53°44N 6°53W 10 C5
Kélo Chad 9°10N 15°45E 53 G9
Kelowna Canada 49°50N 119°25W 70 D5
Kelsey Creek Australia 20°26S 148°31E 62 b
Kelseyville U.S.A. 38°59N 122°50W 78 G4
Kelso N.Z. 45°54S 169°15E 59 F2
Kelso U.K. 55°36N 2°26W 11 F6
Kelso U.S.A. 46°9N 122°54W 78 D4
Keluang = Kluang
  Malaysia 2°3N 103°18E 39 L4
Kelud Indonesia 7°56N 112°18E 37 H15
Kelvington Canada 52°10N 103°30W 71 C8
Kem Russia 65°0N 34°38E 18 B5
Kem → Russia 64°57N 34°41E 18 B5
Kemah Turkey 39°32N 39°5E 46 B3
Kemaman Malaysia 4°12N 103°18E 39 K4
Kemano Canada 53°35N 128°0W 70 C3
Kemasik Malaysia 4°25N 103°27E 39 K4
Kemerovo Russia 55°20N 86°5E 26 D9
Kemi Finland 65°44N 24°34E 8 D21
Kemi älv = Kemijoki →
  Finland 65°47N 24°32E 8 D21
Kemi träsk = Kemijärvi
  Finland 66°43N 27°22E 8 C22
Kemijärvi Finland 66°43N 27°22E 8 C22
Kemijoki → Finland 65°47N 24°32E 8 D21
Kemmerer U.S.A. 41°48N 110°32W 76 F8
Kemp, L. U.S.A. 33°46N 99°9W 84 E5
Kemp Land Antarctica 69°0S 55°0E 5 C5
Kempas Malaysia 1°33N 103°42E 39 d
Kempsey Australia 31°1S 152°50E 63 E5
Kempt, L. Canada 47°25N 74°22W 72 C5
Kempten Germany 47°45N 10°17E 16 E6
Kempton Australia 42°31S 147°12E 63 G4
Kemptville Canada 45°0N 75°38W 83 B9
Ken → India 25°13N 80°27E 43 G9
Kenai U.S.A. 60°33N 151°16W 68 E1
Kenai Mts. U.S.A. 60°0N 150°0W 74 D9
Kendai India 22°45N 82°37E 43 H10
Kendal Indonesia 6°56S 110°14E 37 G14
Kendal U.K. 54°20N 2°44W 12 C5
Kendall Australia 31°35S 152°44E 63 E5
Kendall → Australia 14°4S 141°35E 62 A3
Kendallville U.S.A. 41°27N 85°16W 81 E11
Kendari Indonesia 3°50S 122°30E 37 E6
Kendawangan Indonesia 2°32S 110°17E 36 E4
Kendi, Pulau Malaysia 5°13N 100°11E 39 c
Kendrapara India 20°35N 86°30E 44 D8
Kendrew S. Africa 32°32S 24°30E 56 D3
Kene Thao Laos 17°44N 101°10E 38 D3
Kenedy U.S.A. 28°49N 97°51W 84 G6
Kenema S. Leone 7°50N 11°14W 52 G3
Keng Kok Laos 16°26N 105°12E 38 D5
Keng Tawng Burma 20°45N 98°18E 41 J21
Keng Tung Burma 21°18N 99°39E 38 B2
Kenhardt S. Africa 29°19S 21°12E 56 D3
Kenitra Morocco 34°15N 6°40W 52 B4
Kenli China 37°30N 118°20E 33 F10
Kenmare Ireland 51°53N 9°36W 10 E2
Kenmare U.S.A. 48°41N 102°5W 80 A2
Kenmare River → Ireland 51°48N 9°51W 10 E2
Kennebec U.S.A. 43°54N 99°52W 80 D4
Kennebec → U.S.A. 45°4N 70°40W 83 A14
Kennebec U.S.A. 43°54N 99°52W 80 D4

Kennebec → *U.S.A.* 43°45N 69°46W **81** D19
Kennebunk *U.S.A.* 43°23N 70°33W **83** C14
Kennedy *Zimbabwe* 18°52S 27°10E **56** A4
Kennedy Ra. *Australia* 24°45S 115°10E **61** D2
Kennedy Channel *Arctic* 80°50N 66°0W **69** A18
Kennedy Range △
  Australia 24°34S 115°2E **61** D2
Kennemerduinen △
  Neths. 52°27N 4°33E **15** B4
Kennet → *U.K.* 51°27N 0°57W **13** F7
Kenneth Ra. *Australia* 23°50S 117°8E **61** D2
Kennett *U.S.A.* 36°14N 90°3W **80** G8
Kennewick *U.S.A.* 46°12N 119°7W **76** C4
Kennisis Lake *Canada* 45°13N 78°36W **82** A6
Kenogami → *Canada* 51°6N 84°28W **72** B3
Kenora *Canada* 49°47N 94°29W **71** D10
Kenosha *U.S.A.* 42°35N 87°49W **80** D10
Kenozersky △ *Russia* 62°5S 38°10E **26** C1
Kensington *Canada* 46°28N 63°34W **73** C7
Kent *Ohio, U.S.A.* 41°9N 81°22W **82** E3
Kent *Tex., U.S.A.* 31°4N 104°13W **84** F2
Kent *Wash., U.S.A.* 47°22N 122°14W **78** C4
Kent □ *U.K.* 51°12N 0°40E **13** F8
Kent Group *Australia* 39°30S 147°20E **63** F4
Kent Pen. *Canada* 68°30N 107°0W **68** D10
Kentau *Kazakhstan* 43°32N 68°36E **26** E7
Kentland *U.S.A.* 40°46N 87°27W **80** E10
Kenton *U.S.A.* 40°39N 83°37W **81** E12
Kentucky □ *U.S.A.* 37°0N 84°0W **81** G11
Kentucky → *U.S.A.* 38°41N 85°11W **81** F11
Kentucky L. *U.S.A.* 37°1N 88°16W **80** G9
Kentville *Canada* 45°6N 64°29W **73** C7
Kentwood *U.S.A.* 30°56N 90°31W **85** F9
Kenya ■ *Africa* 1°0N 38°0E **54** D7
Kenya, Mt. *Kenya* 0°10S 37°18E **54** E7
Kenyir, Tasik *Malaysia* 5°1N 102°54E **39** K4
Keo Neua, Deo *Vietnam* 18°23N 105°10E **38** C5
Keokuk *U.S.A.* 40°24N 91°24W **80** E8
Keoladeo △ *India* 27°0N 77°20E **42** F7
Keonjhargarh *India* 21°28N 85°35E **43** J11
Kep *Cambodia* 10°29N 104°19E **39** G5
Kep *Vietnam* 21°24N 106°16E **38** B6
Kep △ *Cambodia* 10°30N 104°18E **39** G5
Kepala Batas *Malaysia* 5°31N 100°26E **39** c
Kepi *Indonesia* 6°32S 139°19E **37** F9
Kerala □ *India* 11°0N 76°15E **45** J3
Kerama-Rettō *Japan* 26°5N 127°15E **29** L3
Keran *Pakistan* 34°35N 73°59E **43** B5
Kerang *Australia* 35°40S 143°55E **63** F3
Keraudren, C. *Australia* 19°58S 119°45E **60** C2
Kerch *Ukraine* 45°20N 36°20E **19** E6
Kerepakupai-Meru = Angel Falls
  Venezuela 5°57N 62°30W **92** B6
Kerguelen *Ind. Oc.* 49°15S 69°10E **3** G13
Kerian, Kuala *Malaysia* 5°10N 100°25E **39** c
Kericho *Kenya* 0°22S 35°15E **54** E7
Kerinci *Indonesia* 1°40S 101°15E **36** E2
Kerki = Atamyrat
  Turkmenistan 37°50N 65°12E **26** F7
Kerkrade *Neths.* 50°53N 6°4E **15** D6
Kerkyra *Greece* 39°38N 19°50E **23** E8
Kermadec Is. *Pac. Oc.* 30°0S 178°15W **58** E11
Kermadec Trench
  Pac. Oc. 30°30S 176°0W **64** L10
Kermān *Iran* 30°15N 57°1E **47** D8
Kerman *U.S.A.* 36°43N 120°4W **78** J6
Kermān □ *Iran* 30°0N 57°0E **47** D8
Kermān, Biābān-e *Iran* 28°45N 59°45E **47** D8
Kermānshāh *Iran* 34°23N 47°0E **46** C5
Kermānshāh □ *Iran* 34°0N 46°30E **46** C5
Kermit *U.S.A.* 31°52N 103°6W **84** F3
Kern → *U.S.A.* 35°16N 119°18W **79** K7
Kernow = Cornwall □
  U.K. 50°26N 4°40W **13** G3
Kernville *U.S.A.* 35°45N 118°26W **79** K8
Keroh *Malaysia* 5°43N 101°1E **39** K3
Kerrera *U.K.* 56°24N 5°33W **11** E3
Kerrobert *Canada* 51°56N 109°8W **71** C7
Kerrville *U.S.A.* 30°3N 99°8W **84** F5
Kerry □ *Ireland* 52°7N 9°35W **10** D2
Kerry Hd. *Ireland* 52°25N 9°56W **10** D2
Kerulen = Herlen →
  Asia 48°48N 117°0E **31** B12
Kerzaz *Algeria* 29°29N 1°37W **52** C5
Kesagami → *Canada* 51°40N 79°45W **72** B4
Kesagami L. *Canada* 50°23N 80°15W **72** B3
Keşan *Turkey* 40°49N 26°38E **23** D12
Kesennuma *Japan* 38°54N 141°35E **28** E10
Keshit *Iran* 29°43N 58°17E **47** D8
Kesgi = Kosgi *India* 15°51N 77°16E **45** G3
Keskal *India* 20°5N 81°35E **44** D5
Kestenga *Russia* 65°50N 31°45E **8** D24
Keswick *U.K.* 54°36N 3°9W **12** C4
Ket → *Russia* 58°55N 81°32E **26** D9
Ketapang *Jawa Timur,*
  Indonesia 8°9S 114°23E **37** J17
Ketapang *Kalimantan Barat,*
  Indonesia 1°55S 110°0E **36** E4
Ketchikan *U.S.A.* 55°21N 131°39W **70** B2
Ketchum *U.S.A.* 43°41N 114°22W **76** E6
Keti Bandar *Pakistan* 24°8N 67°27E **42** G2
Ketri *India* 28°1N 75°50E **42** E6
Kętrzyn *Poland* 54°7N 21°22E **17** A11
Kettering *U.K.* 52°24N 0°43W **13** E7
Kettering *U.S.A.* 39°41N 84°10W **81** F11
Kettle → *Canada* 56°40N 89°34W **71** B11
Kettle Falls *U.S.A.* 48°37N 118°3W **76** B4
Kettle Point *Canada* 43°13N 82°1W **82** C2
Kettle Pt. *Canada* 43°13N 82°1W **82** C2
Kettleman City *U.S.A.* 36°1N 119°58W **78** J7
Keuka L. *U.S.A.* 42°30N 77°9W **82** D7
Keuruu *Finland* 62°16N 24°41E **8** E21
Kewanee *U.S.A.* 41°14N 89°56W **80** E9
Kewanee *Nepal* 27°57N 83°47E **43** F10
Kewaunee *U.S.A.* 44°27N 87°31W **80** C10
Keweenaw B. *U.S.A.* 47°0N 88°15W **80** B9
Keweenaw Pen. *U.S.A.* 47°15N 88°15W **80** B9
Keweenaw Pt. *U.S.A.* 47°25N 87°43W **80** B10
Key, L. *Ireland* 54°0N 8°15W **10** C3
Key Lake Mine *Canada* 57°5N 105°32W **71** B7

Key Largo *U.S.A.* 25°5N 80°27W **85** J14
Key West *U.S.A.* 24°33N 81°48W **88** B3
Keynsham *U.K.* 51°24N 2°29W **13** F5
Keyser *U.S.A.* 39°26N 78°59W **81** F14
Kezhma *Russia* 58°59N 101°9E **27** D11
Kezi *Zimbabwe* 20°58S 28°32E **57** B4
Kgalagadi □ *Botswana* 24°30S 22°0E **56** B3
Kgalagadi Transfrontier □
  Africa 25°10S 21°0E **56** C3
Khabarovsk *Russia* 48°30N 135°5E **31** B16
Khabr △ *Iran* 28°51N 56°22E **47** D8
Khābūr → *Syria* 35°17N 40°35E **46** C4
Khachmas = Xaçmaz
  Azerbaijan 41°31N 48°42E **19** F8
Khachrod *India* 23°25N 75°20E **42** H6
Khadro *Pakistan* 26°11N 68°50E **42** F3
Khadzhilyangar = Dahongliutan
  China 35°45N 79°20E **43** B8
Khaga *India* 25°47N 81°7E **43** G9
Khagaria *India* 25°30N 86°32E **43** G12
Khaipur *Pakistan* 29°34N 72°17E **42** E5
Khair *India* 27°57N 77°46E **42** F7
Khairabad *India* 27°33N 80°47E **43** F9
Khairagarh *India* 21°27N 81°2E **43** J9
Khairpur *Pakistan* 27°32N 68°49E **42** F3
Khairpur Nathan Shah
  Pakistan 27°6N 67°44E **42** F2
Khairwara *India* 23°58N 73°38E **42** H5
Khaisor → *Pakistan* 31°17N 68°59E **42** D3
Khajuraho *India* 24°51N 79°55E **43** G8
Khajuri Kach *Pakistan* 32°4N 69°51E **42** C3
Khakassia □ *Russia* 53°0N 90°0E **26** D9
Khakhea *Botswana* 24°48S 23°22E **56** B3
Khalafābād *Iran* 30°54N 49°24E **47** D6
Khalilabad *India* 26°48N 83°5E **43** F10
Khalīlī *Iran* 27°38N 53°17E **47** E7
Khalkhāl *Iran* 37°37N 48°32E **47** B6
Khalkís = Chalkida
  Greece 38°27N 23°42E **23** E10
Khalmer Yu *Russia* 67°58N 65°1E **26** C7
Khalturin *Russia* 58°40N 48°50E **18** C8
Khalūf *Oman* 20°30N 58°13E **49** C6
Kham Keut *Laos* 18°15N 104°43E **38** C5
Khamaria *India* 23°5N 80°48E **43** H9
Khambhaliya *India* 22°14N 69°41E **42** H3
Khambhat *India* 22°23N 72°33E **42** H5
Khambhat, G. of *India* 20°45N 72°30E **40** J8
Khamgaon *India* 20°42N 76°37E **44** J10
Khamir *Iran* 26°57N 55°36E **47** E7
Khamir *Yemen* 16°2N 44°0E **49** D3
Khamīs Mushayţ
  Si. Arabia 18°18N 42°44E **49** D3
Khammam *India* 17°11N 80°6E **44** F5
Khamsa *Egypt* 30°27N 32°23E **48** E1
Khan → *Namibia* 22°37S 14°56E **56** B2
Khān Abū Shāmat *Syria* 33°39N 36°53E **48** B5
Khān Azād *Iraq* 33°7N 44°22E **46** C5
Khān Mujiddah *Iraq* 32°21N 43°48E **46** C4
Khān Shaykhūn *Syria* 35°26N 36°38E **46** C4
Khan Tengri, Pik *Asia* 42°12N 80°10E **30** C5
Khān Yūnis *Gaza Strip* 31°21N 34°18E **48** D3
Khanai *Pakistan* 30°30N 67°8E **42** D2
Khānaqīn *Iraq* 34°23N 45°25E **46** C5
Khānbāghī *Iran* 36°10N 55°25E **47** B7
Khandwa *India* 21°49N 76°22E **44** D3
Khandyga *Russia* 62°42N 135°35E **27** C14
Khanewal *Pakistan* 30°20N 71°55E **42** D4
Khangah Dogran
  Pakistan 31°50N 73°37E **42** D5
Khangchendzonga =
  Kanchenjunga △ *India* 27°42N 88°8E **43** F13
Khaniá = Chania *Greece* 35°30N 24°4E **23** G11
Khaniadhana *India* 25°1N 78°8E **42** G8
Khanka, L. *Asia* 45°0N 132°24E **28** B6
Khankendy = Xankändi
  Azerbaijan 39°52N 46°49E **46** B5
Khanna *India* 30°42N 76°16E **42** D7
Khanozai *Pakistan* 30°37N 67°19E **42** D2
Khanpur *Pakistan* 28°42N 70°35E **42** E4
Khanty-Mansiysk *Russia* 61°0N 69°0E **26** C7
Khao Khitchakut △
  Thailand 12°50N 102°10E **38** F4
Khao Laem △ *Thailand* 14°56N 98°31E **38** E2
Khao Laem Res. *Thailand* 14°50N 98°30E **38** E2
Khao Lak = *Malaysia* 8°38N 98°18E **39** H2
Khao Luang △ *Thailand* 8°34N 99°42E **39** H2
Khao Nam Khang △
  Thailand 6°32N 100°35E **39** J3
Khao Phlu *Thailand* 9°29N 99°59E **39** b
Khao Pu -Khao Ya △
  Thailand 7°26N 99°57E **39** J2
Khao Sam Roi Yot △
  Thailand 12°13N 99°57E **39** F2
Khao Sok △ *Thailand* 8°55N 98°38E **39** H2
Khao Yai △ *Thailand* 14°21N 101°29E **38** E3
Khaoen Si Nakarin △
  Thailand 14°47N 99°0E **38** E2
Khapalu *Pakistan* 35°10N 76°20E **43** B7
Khapcheranga *Russia* 49°42N 112°24E **27** E12
Khaptao △ *Nepal* 29°20N 81°10E **43** E9
Kharagoda *India* 23°11N 71°46E **42** H4
Kharagpur *India* 22°20N 87°25E **43** H12
Kharan Kalat *Pakistan* 28°34N 65°21E **40** E4
Kharānaq *Iran* 32°20N 54°45E **47** C7
Kharda *India* 18°40N 75°34E **44** E2
Khardung La *India* 34°20N 77°43E **43** B7
Kharg = Khārk, Jazīreh-ye
  Iran 29°15N 50°28E **47** D6
Khârga, El Wâhât el
  Egypt 25°10N 30°35E **53** C12
Khargon *India* 21°45N 75°40E **44** D2
Khari → *India* 25°54N 74°31E **42** G6
Kharian *Pakistan* 32°49N 73°52E **42** C5
Khariar *India* 20°17N 82°46E **44** D6
Khārk, Jazīreh-ye *Iran* 29°15N 50°28E **47** D6
Kharkiv *Ukraine* 49°58N 36°20E **19** E6
Kharkov = Kharkiv
  Ukraine 49°58N 36°20E **19** E6
Kharovsk *Russia* 59°56N 40°13E **18** C7

Kharsawangarh *India* 22°48N 85°50E **43** H11
Kharta *Turkey* 40°55N 29°7E **23** D13
Khartoum = El Khartûm
  Sudan 15°31N 32°35E **53** E12
Khartum *Canada* 45°15N 77°5W **82** A7
Khasan *Russia* 42°25N 130°40E **28** C5
Khāsh *Iran* 28°15N 61°15E **47** D9
Khashm el Girba *Sudan* 14°59N 35°58E **53** F13
Khaskovo *Bulgaria* 41°56N 25°30E **23** D11
Khat, Laem *Thailand* 8°6N 98°26E **39** a
Khatanga *Russia* 72°0N 102°20E **27** B11
Khatanga → *Russia* 72°55N 106°0E **27** B11
Khatauli *India* 29°17N 77°43E **42** E7
Khatra *India* 22°59N 86°51E **43** H12
Khavda *India* 23°51N 69°43E **42** H3
Khawr Fakkān *U.A.E.* 25°21N 56°22E **47** E8
Khaybar, Ḩarrat
  Si. Arabia 25°30N 39°45E **46** E4
Khāzimīyah *Iraq* 34°46N 43°37E **46** C4
Khe Bo *Vietnam* 19°8N 104°41E **38** C5
Khe Long *Vietnam* 21°29N 104°46E **38** B5
Khe Sanh *Vietnam* 16°37N 106°45E **38** D6
Khed *Maharashtra, India* 17°43N 73°27E **44** F1
Khed *Maharashtra, India* 18°51N 73°56E **44** E1
Khed Brahma *India* 24°7N 73°5E **42** G5
Khekra *India* 28°52N 77°20E **42** E7
Khemarak Phouminville = Krong
  Kaoh Kong *Cambodia* 11°37N 102°59E **39** G4
Khemisset *Morocco* 33°50N 6°1W **52** B4
Khemmarat *Thailand* 16°10N 105°15E **38** D5
Khenāmān *Iran* 30°27N 56°29E **47** D8
Khenchela *Algeria* 35°28N 7°11E **52** A7
Khersān → *Iran* 31°33N 50°22E **47** D6
Kheta → *Russia* 71°54N 102°6E **27** B11
Khewari *Pakistan* 26°36N 68°52E **42** F3
Khilchipur *India* 24°2N 76°34E **42** G7
Khilok *Russia* 51°30N 110°45E **27** D12
Khíos = Chios *Greece* 38°27N 26°9E **23** E12
Khirsadoh *India* 22°11N 78°47E **43** H8
Khiuma = Hiiumaa
  Estonia 58°50N 22°45E **9** G20
Khiva = Xiva *Uzbekistan* 41°30N 60°18E **26** E7
Khiwa = Xiva *Uzbekistan* 41°30N 60°18E **26** E7
Khlong Khlung *Thailand* 16°12N 99°43E **38** D2
Khlong Lan △ *Thailand* 16°12N 99°11E **38** D2
Khlong Phanom △
  Thailand 8°45N 98°38E **39** H2
Khmelnik *Ukraine* 49°33N 27°58E **17** D14
Khmelnytskyy *Ukraine* 49°23N 27°0E **17** D14
Khmelnytskyy □
  Ukraine 49°50N 26°40E **17** D14
Khmer Rep. = Cambodia ■
  Asia 12°15N 105°0E **38** F5
Khoai, Hon *Vietnam* 8°26N 104°50E **39** H5
Khobar = Al Khubar
  Si. Arabia 26°17N 50°12E **47** E6
Khodoriv *Ukraine* 49°24N 24°19E **17** D13
Khodzent = Khŭjand
  Tajikistan 40°17N 69°37E **26** E7
Khojak Pass *Afghan.* 30°51N 66°34E **42** D2
Khok Kloi *Thailand* 8°17N 98°19E **39** a
Khok Pho *Thailand* 6°43N 101°6E **39** J3
Khok Samrong *Thailand* 15°3N 100°43E **38** E3
Kholm *Russia* 57°10N 31°15E **18** C5
Kholmsk *Russia* 47°40N 142°5E **27** E15
Khomas □ *Namibia* 22°30S 17°0E **56** B2
Khomas Hochland
  Namibia 22°40S 16°0E **56** B2
Khomeyn *Iran* 33°40N 50°7E **47** C6
Khomeynī Shahr *Iran* 32°41N 51°31E **47** C6
Khomodino *Botswana* 22°46S 23°52E **56** B3
Khon Kaen *Thailand* 16°30N 102°47E **38** D4
Khong → *Cambodia* 13°32N 105°58E **38** F5
Khong Sedone *Laos* 15°34N 105°49E **38** E5
Khonuu *Russia* 66°30N 143°12E **27** C15
Khoper → *Russia* 49°30N 42°20E **19** D6
Khorāsān-e Janūb □ *Iran* 32°0N 59°0E **47** C8
Khorāsān-e Razavī □ *Iran* 34°0N 58°0E **47** C8
Khorāsān-e Shemālī □
  Iran 37°0N 57°0E **47** B8
Khorat = Nakhon Ratchasima
  Thailand 14°59N 102°12E **38** E4
Khorat, Cao Nguyen
  Thailand 15°30N 102°50E **38** E4
Khorixas *Namibia* 20°16S 14°59E **56** B1
Khorramābād *Khorāsān,*
  Iran 35°6N 57°57E **47** C8
Khorramābād *Lorestān,*
  Iran 33°30N 48°25E **47** C6
Khorramshahr *Iran* 30°29N 48°15E **47** D6
Khorugh *Tajikistan* 37°30N 71°36E **26** F8
Khosravī *Iran* 30°48N 51°28E **47** D6
Khosrowābād *Khuzestān,*
  Iran 30°10N 48°25E **47** D6
Khosrowābād *Kordestān,*
  Iran 35°31N 47°38E **46** C5
Khost *Pakistan* 30°13N 67°35E **42** D2
Khosūyeh *Iran* 28°32N 54°26E **47** D7
Khotang *Nepal* 27°1N 86°51E **43** F12
Khotyn *Ukraine* 48°31N 26°27E **17** D14
Khouribga *Morocco* 32°58N 6°57W **52** B4
Khowst *Afghan.* 33°22N 69°58E **40** C6
Khowst □ *Afghan.* 33°20N 70°0E **40** C6
Khoyniki *Belarus* 51°54N 29°55E **17** C15
Khrysokhou B. *Cyprus* 35°6N 32°25E **25** D11
Khu Khan *Thailand* 14°42N 104°12E **38** E5
Khudzhand = Khŭjand
  Tajikistan 40°17N 69°37E **26** E7
Khuff *Si. Arabia* 24°55N 44°53E **46** E5
Khūgiāni *Afghan.* 31°34N 66°32E **42** D2
Khuis *Botswana* 26°40S 21°49E **56** C3
Khuiyala *India* 27°9N 70°25E **42** F4
Khujand *Tajikistan* 40°17N 69°37E **26** E7
Khujner *India* 23°47N 76°36E **42** H7
Khukhan *Thailand* 14°42N 104°12E **38** E5
Khulna *Bangla.* 22°45N 89°34E **41** H16
Khulna □ *Bangla.* 22°25N 89°35E **41** H16

Khumago *Botswana* 20°26S 24°32E **56** B3
Khunjerab △ *Pakistan* 36°40N 75°30E **43** A6
Khunjerab Pass = Kinjirap Daban
  Asia 36°40N 75°25E **40** A9
Khŭnsorkh *Iran* 27°9N 56°7E **47** E8
Khunti *India* 23°5N 85°17E **43** H11
Khūr *Iran* 32°55N 58°18E **47** C8
Khurai *India* 24°3N 78°23E **42** G8
Khurayş *Si. Arabia* 25°6N 48°2E **47** E6
Khurda *India* 20°11N 85°37E **44** D7
Khurja *India* 28°15N 77°58E **42** E7
Khūrmāl *Iraq* 35°18N 46°2E **46** C5
Khurr, Wādī al *Iraq* 32°3N 43°52E **46** C4
Khūsf *Iran* 32°46N 58°53E **47** C8
Khushab *Pakistan* 32°20N 72°20E **42** C5
Khust *Ukraine* 48°10N 23°18E **17** D12
Khutse △ *Botswana* 23°31S 24°12E **56** B3
Khuzdar *Pakistan* 27°52N 66°30E **42** F2
Khūzestān □ *Iran* 31°0N 49°0E **47** D6
Khvāf *Iran* 34°33N 60°8E **47** C9
Khvājeh *Iran* 38°9N 46°35E **46** B5
Khvānsār *Iran* 29°56N 54°8E **47** D7
Khvor *Iran* 33°45N 55°0E **47** C7
Khvorgū *Iran* 27°34N 56°27E **47** E8
Khvormūj *Iran* 28°40N 51°30E **47** D6
Khvoy *Iran* 38°35N 45°0E **46** B5
Khwae Noi → *Thailand* 14°1N 99°32E **38** E2
Khyber Pakhtunkhwa □
  Pakistan 34°0N 72°0E **42** B5
Khyber Pass *Afghan.* 34°10N 71°8E **42** B4
Kia *Fiji* 16°16S 179°8E **59** a
Kiadho → *India* 19°37N 77°40E **44** E3
Kiama *Australia* 34°40S 150°50E **63** E5
Kiamba *Phil.* 6°2N 124°46E **37** C6
Kiangsi = Jiangxi □
  China 27°30N 116°0E **35** D11
Kiangsu = Jiangsu □
  China 33°0N 120°0E **33** H11
Kibombo
  Dem. Rep. of the Congo 3°57S 25°53E **54** E5
Kibre Mengist *Ethiopia* 5°54N 38°59E **49** F2
Kıbrıs = Cyprus ■ *Asia* 35°0N 33°0E **46** C2
Kibwezi *Kenya* 2°27S 37°57E **54** E7
Kichha → *India* 28°41N 79°18E **43** E8
Kichmengsky Gorodok
  Russia 59°59N 45°48E **18** B8
Kicking Horse Pass
  Canada 51°28N 116°16W **70** C5
Kidal *Mali* 18°26N 1°22E **52** E6
Kidderminster *U.K.* 52°24N 2°15W **13** E5
Kidnappers, C. *N.Z.* 39°38S 177°5E **59** C6
Kidsgrove *U.K.* 53°5N 2°14W **12** D5
Kidston *Australia* 18°52S 144°8E **62** B3
Kiel *Germany* 54°19N 10°8E **16** A6
Kiel Canal = Nord-Ostsee-Kanal
  Germany 54°12N 9°32E **16** A5
Kielce *Poland* 50°52N 20°42E **17** C11
Kielder Water *U.K.* 55°11N 2°31W **12** B5
Kieler Bucht *Germany* 54°35N 10°25E **16** A6
Kiev = Kyyiv *Ukraine* 50°30N 30°28E **17** C16
Kiffa *Mauritania* 16°37N 11°24W **52** E3
Kifrī *Iraq* 34°45N 45°0E **46** C5
Kigali *Rwanda* 1°59S 30°4E **54** E6
Kigoma-Ujiji *Tanzania* 4°55S 29°36E **54** E5
Kığzı *Turkey* 38°18N 43°25E **46** B4
Kihnu *Estonia* 58°9N 24°1E **9** G21
Kii-Sanchi *Japan* 34°20N 136°0E **29** G8
Kii-Suidō *Japan* 33°40N 134°45E **29** H7
Kikaiga-Shima *Japan* 28°19N 129°59E **29** K4
Kikiak = Rigolet *Canada* 54°10N 58°23W **73** B8
Kikinda *Serbia* 45°50N 20°30E **23** B9
Kikládhes = Kyklades
  Greece 37°0N 24°30E **23** F11
Kikuchi *Japan* 32°59N 130°47E **29** H5
Kikwit *Dem. Rep. of the Congo* 5°0S 18°45E **54** F3
Kilakkarai *India* 9°12N 78°47E **45** K4
Kilar *India* 33°6N 76°25E **42** C7
Kilbeggan *Ireland* 53°22N 7°30E **10** C4
Kilbrannan Sd. *U.K.* 55°37N 5°26W **11** F3
Kilbuck Mts. *U.S.A.* 60°36N 159°53W **74** C8
Kilchu *N. Korea* 40°57N 129°25E **33** D15
Kilcoy *Australia* 26°59S 152°30E **63** D5
Kildare *Ireland* 53°9N 6°55W **10** C5
Kildare □ *Ireland* 53°10N 6°50W **10** C5
Kildinstroy *Russia* 68°48N 33°6E **8** B25
Kilfinnane *Ireland* 52°21N 8°28W **10** D3
Kilgarvan *Ireland* 51°54N 9°27W **10** E2
Kilgore *U.S.A.* 32°23N 94°53W **84** E7
Kilifi *Kenya* 3°40S 39°48E **54** E7
Kilimanjaro *Tanzania* 3°7S 37°20E **54** E7
Kilindini *Kenya* 4°4S 39°40E **54** E7
Kilinochchi *Sri Lanka* 9°24N 80°25E **45** K5
Kilis *Turkey* 36°42N 37°6E **46** B3
Kiliya *Ukraine* 45°28N 29°16E **17** F15
Kilkee *Ireland* 52°41N 9°39W **10** D2
Kilkeel *U.K.* 54°4N 5°59W **10** B5
Kilkenny *Ireland* 52°39N 7°15W **10** D4
Kilkenny □ *Ireland* 52°35N 7°15W **10** D4
Kilkieran B. *Ireland* 53°20N 9°41W **10** C2
Kilkis *Greece* 40°58N 22°57E **23** D10
Killala *Ireland* 54°13N 9°13W **10** B2
Killala B. *Ireland* 54°16N 9°8W **10** B2
Killaloe *Ireland* 52°48N 8°28W **10** D3
Killaloe *Canada* 45°33N 77°25W **82** A7
Killarney *Canada* 45°55N 81°30W **72** C3
Killarney *Ireland* 52°4N 9°30W **10** D2
Killarney *Australia* 28°20S 152°18E **63** D5
Killarney △ *Ireland* 52°0N 9°33W **10** D2
Killary Harbour *Ireland* 53°38N 9°52W **10** C2
Killdeer *Canada* 49°6N 106°22W **71** D7
Killeen *U.S.A.* 31°7N 97°44W **84** F6
Killin *U.K.* 56°28N 4°19W **11** E4
Killini *Greece* 37°54N 22°25E **23** F10
Killiniq I. *Canada* 60°24N 64°37W **69** E19
Killorglin *Ireland* 52°6N 9°47W **10** D2
Killybegs *Ireland* 54°38N 8°26W **10** B3
Kilmarnock *U.K.* 55°37N 4°29W **11** F4
Kilmore *Australia* 37°25S 144°53E **63** F3

Kilmore Quay *Ireland* 52°10N 6°36W **10** D5
Kilosa *Tanzania* 6°48S 37°0E **54** F7
Kilrush *Ireland* 52°38N 9°29W **10** D2
Kiltan I. *India* 11°29N 73°0E **45** J1
Kilwa Kivinje *Tanzania* 8°45S 39°25E **54** F7
Kilwinning *U.K.* 55°39N 4°43W **11** F4
Kim *U.S.A.* 37°15N 103°21W **77** H11
Kimaam *Indonesia* 7°58S 138°53E **37** F9
Kimba *Australia* 33°8S 136°23E **63** E2
Kimball *Nebr., U.S.A.* 41°14N 103°40W **80** E2
Kimball *S. Dak., U.S.A.* 43°45N 98°57W **80** D4
Kimberley *Australia* 16°20S 127°0E **60** C4
Kimberley *B.C., Canada* 49°40N 115°59W **70** D5
Kimberley *Ont., Canada* 44°23N 80°32W **82** B4
Kimberley *S. Africa* 28°43S 24°46E **56** D3
Kimberly *U.S.A.* 42°32N 114°22W **76** E6
Kimch'aek *N. Korea* 40°40N 129°10E **33** D15
Kimhae = Gimhae
  S. Korea 35°14N 128°53E **33** G15
Kimmirut *Canada* 62°50N 69°50W **69** E18
Kimpese
  Dem. Rep. of the Congo 5°35S 14°26E **54** F2
Kimry *Russia* 56°55N 37°15E **18** C6
Kinabalu, Gunung
  Malaysia 6°3N 116°14E **36** C5
Kinaskan L. *Canada* 57°38N 130°8W **70** B2
Kinbasket L. *Canada* 52°0N 118°10W **70** C5
Kincardine *Canada* 44°10N 81°40W **82** B3
Kincolith *Canada* 55°0N 129°57W **70** C3
Kinde *U.S.A.* 43°56N 83°0W **82** C2
Kinder Scout *U.K.* 53°24N 1°52W **12** D6
Kindersley *Canada* 51°30N 109°10W **71** C7
Kindia *Guinea* 10°0N 12°52W **52** F2
Kindu
  Dem. Rep. of the Congo 2°55S 25°50E **54** E5
Kineshma *Russia* 57°30N 42°5E **18** C7
King, L. *Australia* 33°10S 119°35E **61** F2
King, Mt. *Australia* 25°10S 147°30E **62** D
King Abdullah Economic City
  Si. Arabia 22°54N 39°5E **49** C2
King Christian I.
  Canada 77°48N 101°40W **69** B11
King City *U.S.A.* 36°13N 121°8W **78** J5
King Cr. → *Australia* 24°35S 139°30E **62** C2
King Edward →
  Australia 14°14S 126°35E **60** B4
King Edward Point
  S. Georgia 54°17S 36°30W **96** G9
King Frederick VI Land = Kong
  Frederik VI.s Kyst
  Greenland 63°0N 43°0W **4** C5
King George B. *Falk. Is.* 51°30S 60°30W **96** G4
King George I. *Antarctica* 60°0S 60°0W **5** C18
King George Is. *Canada* 57°20N 80°30W **69** F15
King George Sd. *Australia* 35°5S 118°0E **61** G2
King I. = Kadan Kyun
  Burma 12°30N 98°20E **38** F2
King I. *Australia* 39°50S 144°0E **63** F3
King I. *Canada* 52°10N 127°40W **70** C3
King Khalid Int. ✈ (RUH)
  Si. Arabia 24°57N 46°42E **46** E5
King Khalid Military City =
  Madinat al Malik Khālid al
  Askarīyah *Si. Arabia* 27°54N 45°31E **46** E5
King Leopold Ranges
  Australia 17°30S 125°45E **60** C4
King of Prussia *U.S.A.* 40°5N 75°23W **83** F9
King Sd. *Australia* 16°50S 123°20E **60** C3
King Sejong *Antarctica* 62°13S 58°44W **5** C18
King Shaka Int. ✈ (DUR)
  S. Africa 29°37S 31°7E **57** C5
King William I. *Canada* 69°10N 97°25W **68** D12
King William's Town
  S. Africa 32°51S 27°22E **56** E4
Kingaok = Bathurst Inlet
  Canada 66°50N 108°1W **68** D12
Kingaroy *Australia* 26°32S 151°51E **63** D5
Kingfisher *U.S.A.* 35°52N 97°56W **84** D6
Kingirbān *Iraq* 34°40N 44°54E **46** C5
Kingisepp = Kuressaare
  Estonia 58°15N 22°30E **9** G20
Kingisepp *Russia* 59°25N 28°40E **9** G23
Kingoonya *Australia* 30°55S 135°19E **63** E2
Kingri *Pakistan* 30°27N 69°49E **42** D3
Kings → *U.S.A.* 36°3N 119°50W **78** J7
Kings Canyon *Australia* 24°15S 131°34E **60** D5
Kings Canyon △ *U.S.A.* 36°50N 118°40W **78** J8
King's Lynn *U.K.* 52°45N 0°24E **12** E8
Kings Park *U.S.A.* 40°53N 73°16W **83** F11
Kings Peak *U.S.A.* 40°46N 110°23W **76** F8
Kingsbridge *U.K.* 50°17N 3°47W **13** G4
Kingsburg *U.S.A.* 36°31N 119°33W **78** J7
Kingscote *Australia* 35°40S 137°38E **63** F2
Kingscourt *Ireland* 53°54N 6°48W **10** C5
Kingsford *U.S.A.* 45°48N 88°4W **80** C9
Kingsland *U.S.A.* 30°48N 81°41W **85** F14
Kingsport *U.S.A.* 36°33N 82°33W **85** C13
Kingston *Canada* 44°14N 76°30W **83** B8
Kingston *Jamaica* 17°55N 76°50W **88** a
Kingston *N.Z.* 45°20S 168°43E **59** F2
Kingston *N.H., U.S.A.* 42°56N 71°3W **83** D13
Kingston *N.Y., U.S.A.* 41°56N 73°59W **83** E11
Kingston *Pa., U.S.A.* 41°16N 75°54W **83** E9
Kingston *R.I., U.S.A.* 41°29N 71°30W **83** E13
Kingston Pk. *U.S.A.* 35°44N 115°55W **79** K11
Kingston South East
  Australia 36°51S 139°55E **63** F2
Kingston upon Hull *U.K.* 53°45N 0°21W **12** D7
Kingston upon Hull □
  U.K. 53°45N 0°21W **12** D7
Kingstown St. Vincent *St. Vincent* 13°10N 61°10W **89** D7
Kingstree *U.S.A.* 33°40N 79°50W **85** E15
Kingsville *Canada* 42°2N 82°45W **82** D2
Kingsville *U.S.A.* 27°31N 97°52W **84** H6
Kingussie *U.K.* 57°6N 4°2W **11** D4
Kingwood *U.S.A.* 30°2N 95°16W **84** F7
Kınık *Turkey* 39°6N 27°24E **23** E12
Kinistino *Canada* 52°57N 105°2W **71** C7

njirap Daban Asia 36°40N 75°25E 40 A9
nkala Congo 4°18S 14°49E 54 E2
nki □ Japan 33°45N 136°0E 29 H8
nleith N.Z. 38°20S 175°56E 59 C5
nlochleven U.K. 56°43N 5°0W 11 E4
nmount Canada 44°48N 78°45W 82 B6
nna Sweden 57°32N 12°42E 9 H15
nnairds Hd. U.K. 57°43N 2°1W 11 D6
nnarodden = Nordkinn
  Norway 71°8N 27°40E 8 A22
nngait Canada 64°14N 76°32W 69 E16
nniyai Sri Lanka 8°29N 81°11E 45 K5
no Nuevo Mexico 28°52N 112°3W 86 B2
noje ⬅ Canada 52°8N 81°25W 72 B3
nomoto Japan 35°30N 136°13E 29 G8
noosao Canada 57°5N 102°1W 71 B8
nross U.K. 56°13N 3°25W 11 E5
nsale Ireland 51°37N 8°33W 10 E3
nsale, Old Hd. of Ireland 51°37N 8°33W 10 E3
nsha = Chang Jiang ⬅
  China 31°48N 121°10E 35 B13
nshasa
  Dem. Rep. of the Congo 4°20S 15°15E 54 E3
nsley U.S.A. 37°55N 99°20W 80 G4
nsman U.S.A. 41°26N 80°35W 82 E4
nston U.S.A. 35°16N 77°35W 85 D16
ntamani Indonesia 8°14S 115°19E 37 J18
ntore U.K. 57°14N 2°20W 11 D6
ntore Ra. Australia 23°15S 128°47E 60 D4
ntyre U.K. 55°30N 5°35W 11 F3
ntyre, Mull of U.K. 55°17N 5°47W 11 F3
nushseo ⬅ Canada 55°15N 83°45W 72 A3
nvarra Ireland 53°8N 8°56W 10 C3
nwat India 19°38N 78°12E 44 E4
nzua U.S.A. 41°52N 78°58W 82 E6
osk Canada 46°6N 78°53W 72 C4
iowa Kans., U.S.A. 37°1N 98°29W 80 G4
iowa Okla., U.S.A. 34°43N 95°54W 81 H7
pahigan L. Canada 52°0N 101°55W 71 B8
parissia Greece 37°15N 21°40E 23 F9
parissiakos Kolpos
  Greece 37°25N 21°25E 23 F9
pawa, L. Canada 46°50N 79°0W 72 C4
pling Canada 50°6N 102°38W 71 C8
ppure Ireland 53°11N 6°21W 10 C5
pushi
  Dem. Rep. of the Congo 11°48S 27°12E 55 G5
irandul India 18°33N 81°10E 44 E5
irensk Russia 57°50N 107°55E 27 D11
irghiz Range Asia 42°40N 73°40E 30 C3
irghizia = Kyrgyzstan ■
  Asia 42°0N 75°0E 26 E8
irgiziya Steppe Eurasia 50°0N 55°0E 19 E10
iri Buru India 22°0N 85°0E 44 D7
iribati ■ Pac. Oc. 3°0S 180°0E 58 B10
irikkale Turkey 39°51N 33°32E 19 G5
irikkurra Australia 22°49S 127°45E 60 D4
irikkurra Australia 22°49S 127°45E 60 D4
irin = Jilin China 43°44N 126°30E 33 C14
irindi Oya ⬅ Sri Lanka 6°15N 81°20E 45 L5
irinyaga = Kenya, Mt.
  Kenya 0°10S 37°18E 54 E7
irirom △ Cambodia 11°18N 104°5E 39 G5
irishima Japan 31°44N 130°46E 29 J5
irishima Yaku △ Japan 31°24N 130°32E 29 J5
iritimati Kiribati 1°58N 157°27W 65 G12
irkby U.K. 53°30N 2°54W 12 D5
irkby-in-Ashfield U.K. 53°6N 1°14W 12 D6
irkby Lonsdale U.K. 54°12N 2°36W 12 C5
irkby Stephen U.K. 54°29N 2°21W 12 C5
irkcaldy U.K. 56°7N 3°9W 11 E5
irkcudbright U.K. 54°50N 4°2W 11 G4
irkenes Norway 69°40N 30°5E 8 B24
irkfield Canada 44°34N 78°59W 82 B6
irkintilloch U.K. 55°56N 4°8W 11 F4
irkjubæjarklaustur
  Iceland 63°47N 18°4W 8 E4
irkkonummi Finland 60°8N 24°26E 9 F21
irkland U.K. 47°40N 122°12W 78 C4
irkland Lake Canada 48°9N 80°2W 72 C3
irklareli Turkey 41°44N 27°15E 23 D12
irkpatrick, Mt.
  Antarctica 84°20S 166°25E 5 E11
irksville U.S.A. 40°12N 92°35W 80 E7
irkūk Iraq 35°30N 44°21E 46 C5
irkwall U.K. 58°59N 2°58W 11 C6
irkwood S. Africa 33°22S 25°15E 56 D4
irlampudi India 17°12N 82°12E 44 F6
irov Russia 58°35N 49°40E 18 C8
irovabad = Gäncä
  Azerbaijan 40°45N 46°20E 19 F8
irovo-Chepetsk Russia 58°28N 50°0E 18 C9
irovograd = Kirovohrad
  Ukraine 48°35N 32°20E 19 E5
irovohrad Ukraine 48°35N 32°20E 19 E5
irovsk Russia 67°32N 33°41E 18 A5
irovskiy Kamchatka,
  Russia 54°27N 155°42E 27 D16
irovskiy Primorsk,
  Russia 45°7N 133°30E 28 B6
irriemuir U.K. 56°41N 3°1W 11 E5
irsanov Russia 52°35N 42°40E 18 D7
irşehir Turkey 39°14N 34°5E 46 B2
irthar △ Pakistan 25°45N 67°30E 42 F2
irthar Range Pakistan 27°0N 67°0E 42 F2
irtland U.S.A. 36°44N 108°21W 77 H9
iruna Sweden 67°52N 20°15E 8 C19
iryū □ Japan 36°24N 139°20E 29 F9
isangani
  Dem. Rep. of the Congo 0°35N 25°15E 54 D5
isar Indonesia 8°5S 127°10E 37 F7
isarazu Japan 35°23N 139°55E 29 G9
iselevsk Russia 54°5N 86°39E 26 D9
ish = Qeys Iran 26°32N 53°58E 47 E7
ishanganga ⬅ Pakistan 34°18N 73°28E 43 B5
ishanganj India 26°3N 87°14E 43 F13
ishangarh Raj., India 26°34N 74°52E 42 F6
ishangarh Raj., India 27°50N 70°30E 42 F4
ishinev = Chişinău
  Moldova 47°2N 28°50E 17 E15

Kishiwada Japan 34°28N 135°22E 29 G7
Kishtwar India 33°20N 75°48E 42 C6
Kisii Kenya 0°40S 34°45E 54 E6
Kiska I. U.S.A. 51°59N 177°30E 74 E3
Kiskőrös Hungary 46°37N 19°20E 17 E10
Kiskunfélegyháza
  Hungary 46°42N 19°53E 17 E10
Kiskunhalas Hungary 46°28N 19°37E 17 E10
Kiso-Gawa ⬅ Japan 35°20N 136°45E 29 G8
Kiso-Sammyaku Japan 35°45N 137°45E 29 G8
Kisofukushima Japan 35°52N 137°43E 29 G8
Kissidougou Guinea 9°5N 10°5W 52 G3
Kissimmee U.S.A. 28°18N 81°24W 85 G14
Kissimmee ⬅ U.S.A. 27°9N 80°52W 85 H14
Kississing L. Canada 55°10N 101°20W 71 B8
Kisumu Kenya 0°3S 34°45E 54 E6
Kit Carson U.S.A. 38°46N 102°48W 76 G12
Kita Mali 13°5N 9°25W 52 F4
Kitaibaraki Japan 36°50N 140°45E 29 F10
Kitakami Japan 39°20N 141°10E 28 E10
Kitakami-Gawa ⬅
  Japan 38°25N 141°19E 28 E10
Kitakami-Sammyaku
  Japan 39°30N 141°30E 28 E10
Kitakata Japan 37°39N 139°52E 28 F9
Kitakyūshū Japan 33°50N 130°50E 29 H5
Kitale Kenya 1°0N 35°0E 54 D7
Kitami Japan 43°48N 143°54E 28 C11
Kitami-Sammyaku
  Japan 44°22N 142°43E 28 B11
Kitchener Canada 43°27N 80°29W 82 C4
Kitee Finland 62°5N 30°8E 8 E24
Kitega = Gitega Burundi 3°26S 29°56E 54 E5
Kithira = Kythira Greece 36°8N 23°0E 23 F10
Kithnos = Kythnos
  Greece 37°26N 24°27E 23 F11
Kitikmeot Canada 67°0N 110°0W 68 D9
Kitimat Canada 54°3N 128°38W 70 C3
Kitinen ⬅ Finland 67°14N 27°27E 8 C22
Kitsuki Japan 33°25N 131°37E 29 H5
Kittakittaooloo, L.
  Australia 28°3S 138°14E 63 D2
Kittanning U.S.A. 40°49N 79°31W 82 F5
Kittatinny Mt. U.S.A. 41°19N 74°39W 83 F10
Kittery U.S.A. 43°5N 70°45W 83 C14
Kittilä Finland 67°40N 24°51E 8 C21
Kitui Kenya 1°17S 38°0E 54 E7
Kitwanga Canada 55°6N 128°4W 70 B3
Kitwe Zambia 12°54S 28°13E 55 G5
Kivalliq Canada 62°0N 97°30W 68 E12
Kivarli India 24°33N 72°46E 42 G5
Kivertsi Ukraine 50°50N 25°28E 17 C13
Kivu, L.
  Dem. Rep. of the Congo 1°48S 29°0E 54 E5
Kiwirrkurra Australia 22°49S 127°45E 60 D4
Kiwirrkurra Australia 22°49S 127°45E 60 D4
Kiyev = Kyyiv Ukraine 50°30N 30°28E 17 C16
Kiyevskoye Vdkhr. = Kyyivske
  Vdskh. Ukraine 51°0N 30°25E 17 C16
Kizel Russia 59°3N 57°40E 18 C10
Kızıl Irmak ⬅ Turkey 41°44N 35°58E 19 F6
Kizil Jilga China 35°26N 78°50E 43 B8
Kızıldağ △ Turkey 38°5N 31°20E 46 B1
Kızıltepe Turkey 37°12N 40°35E 46 B4
Kizlyar Russia 43°51N 46°40E 19 F8
Kizyl-Arvat = Serdar
  Turkmenistan 39°4N 56°23E 47 B8
Kjölur Iceland 64°50N 19°25E 8 D4
Kladno Czech Rep. 50°10N 14°7E 16 C8
Klaeng Thailand 12°47N 101°39E 38 F3
Klagenfurt Austria 46°38N 14°20E 16 E8
Klaipėda Lithuania 55°43N 21°10E 9 J19
Klaksvík Færoe Is. 62°14N 6°35W 8 E9
Klamath ⬅ U.S.A. 41°33N 124°5W 76 F1
Klamath Falls U.S.A. 42°13N 121°46W 76 E3
Klamath Mts. U.S.A. 41°50N 123°20W 76 F2
Klamono Indonesia 1°8S 131°30E 37 E8
Klang Malaysia 3°2N 101°26E 39 L3
Klappan ⬅ Canada 58°0N 129°43W 70 B3
Klarälven ⬅ Sweden 59°23N 13°32E 9 G15
Klatovy Czech Rep. 49°23N 13°18E 16 D7
Klawer S. Africa 31°44S 18°36E 56 D2
Klazienaveen Neths. 52°44N 7°0E 15 B6
Kleena Kleene Canada 52°0N 124°59W 70 C4
Klein-Karas Namibia 27°33S 18°7E 56 D2
Kleinbegin S. Africa 28°54S 21°40E 56 D3
Klerksdorp S. Africa 26°53S 26°38E 56 D4
Kletsk = Klyetsk Belarus 53°5N 26°45E 17 B14
Kletskiy Russia 49°16N 43°11E 19 E7
Klickitat U.S.A. 45°49N 121°9W 76 D3
Klickitat ⬅ U.S.A. 45°42N 121°17W 78 E5
Klinaklini ⬅ Canada 51°21N 125°40W 70 C3
Klip ⬅ S. Africa 27°3S 29°3E 57 C4
Klipdale S. Africa 34°19S 19°57E 56 D2
Klipplaat S. Africa 33°1S 24°22E 56 D3
Kłodzko Poland 50°28N 16°38E 17 C9
Klondike Canada 64°0N 139°26W 68 E4
Klong Wang Chao △
  Thailand 16°20N 99°9E 38 D2
Kluane L. Canada 60°45N 139°30W 70 A1
Kluane L. Canada 61°15N 138°40W 68 E4
Kluang Malaysia 2°3N 103°18E 39 L4
Klukwan U.S.A. 59°24N 135°54W 70 B1
Klyuqing Indonesia 8°32S 115°24E 37 K18
Klyetsk Belarus 53°5N 26°45E 17 B14
Klyuchi Russia 56°18N 160°51E 27 D17
Knaresborough U.K. 54°1N 1°28W 12 C6
Knee L. Man., Canada 55°3N 94°45W 72 A1
Knee L. Sask., Canada 55°51N 107°0W 71 B7
Knight Inlet Canada 50°45N 125°40W 70 C3
Knighton U.K. 52°21N 3°3W 13 E4
Knights Ferry U.S.A. 37°50N 120°40W 78 H6
Knights Landing U.S.A. 38°48N 121°43W 78 G5
Knob, C. Australia 34°32S 119°16E 61 F2
Knock Ireland 53°48N 8°55W 10 C3

Knockmealdown Mts.
  Ireland 52°14N 7°56W 10 D4
Knokke-Heist Belgium 51°21N 3°17E 15 C3
Knossos Greece 35°16N 25°10E 23 G11
Knowlton Canada 45°13N 72°31W 83 A12
Knox U.S.A. 41°18N 86°37W 80 E10
Knox Coast Antarctica 66°30S 108°0E 5 C8
Knoxville Iowa, U.S.A. 41°19N 93°6W 80 E7
Knoxville Pa., U.S.A. 41°57N 77°27W 82 E7
Knoxville Tenn., U.S.A. 35°58N 83°55W 85 D13
Knud Rasmussen Land
  Greenland 78°0N 60°0W 69 B20
Knysna S. Africa 34°2S 23°2E 56 D3
Ko Kha Thailand 18°11N 99°24E 38 C2
Ko Tarutao △ Thailand 6°31N 99°26E 39 J2
Ko Yao Thailand 8°7N 98°35E 39 a
Koartac = Quaqtaq
  Canada 60°55N 69°40W 69 E18
Koba Indonesia 6°37S 134°37E 37 F8
Kobarid Slovenia 46°15N 13°30E 16 E7
Kobayashi Japan 31°56N 130°59E 29 J5
Kōbe Japan 34°41N 135°13E 29 G7
Kōbi-Sho E. China Sea 25°56N 123°41E 29 M1
Koblenz Germany 50°21N 7°36E 16 C4
Kobryn Belarus 52°15N 24°22E 17 B13
Kobuk ⬅ U.S.A. 66°54N 160°38W 74 B7
Kocaeli Turkey 40°45N 29°50E 19 F4
Kočani Macedonia 41°55N 22°25E 23 D10
Koch Bihar India 26°22N 89°29E 41 F16
Kochas India 25°15N 83°56E 43 G10
Kochi India 9°58N 76°20E 45 K3
Kōchi Japan 33°30N 133°35E 29 H6
Kōchi □ Japan 33°40N 133°30E 29 H6
Kochiu = Gejiu China 23°20N 103°10E 34 F4
Kodala India 19°38N 84°57E 44 E7
Kodarma India 24°28N 85°36E 43 G11
Koddiyar B. Sri Lanka 8°33N 81°15E 45 K5
Kodiak U.S.A. 57°47N 152°24W 74 D9
Kodiak I. U.S.A. 57°30N 152°45W 74 D9
Kodikkarai = Point Calimere
  India 10°17N 79°49E 45 J4
Kodinar India 20°46N 70°46E 42 J4
Kodinsk Russia 58°40N 99°10E 27 D10
Kodlipet India 12°48N 75°53E 45 H2
Kodungallur = Cranganore
  India 10°13N 76°13E 45 J3
Koedoesberge S. Africa 32°40S 20°11E 56 D3
Koes Namibia 26°0S 19°15E 56 C2
Koffiefontein S. Africa 29°30S 25°0E 56 C4
Kofiau Indonesia 1°11S 129°50E 37 E7
Koforidua Ghana 6°3N 0°17W 52 G5
Kōfu Japan 35°40N 138°30E 29 G9
Koga Japan 36°11N 139°43E 29 F9
Kogaluc ⬅ Canada 56°12N 61°44W 73 A7
Køge Denmark 55°27N 12°11E 9 J15
Kogon Uzbekistan 39°43N 64°33E 26 F7
Koh-i-Khurd Afghan. 33°30N 65°59E 42 C1
Koh-i-Maran Pakistan 29°18N 66°50E 42 E2
Koh Ker Cambodia 13°47N 104°32E 38 F5
Koh Wai Thailand 11°54N 102°25E 39 H4
Kohat Pakistan 33°40N 71°29E 42 C4
Kohima India 25°35N 94°10E 41 G19
Kohkīlūyeh va Būyer Aḥmadī □
  Iran 31°30N 50°30E 47 D6
Kohler Ra. Antarctica 77°0S 110°0W 5 D15
Kohlu Pakistan 29°54N 69°15E 42 E3
Kohtla-Järve Estonia 59°20N 27°20E 9 G22
Koi Sanjaq Iraq 36°5N 44°38E 46 B5
Koihoa India 8°12N 93°29E 45 K11
Koilkuntla India 15°14N 78°19E 45 M11
Koillismaa Finland 65°44N 28°36E 8 D23
Koin N. Korea 40°28N 126°18E 33 D14
Kojō N. Korea 38°58N 127°58E 33 E14
Kojonup Australia 33°48S 117°10E 61 F2
Kojūr Iran 36°23N 51°43E 47 B6
Kokand = Qo'qon
  Uzbekistan 40°31N 70°56E 26 E8
Kokang Burma 23°45N 98°30E 34 F2
Kokas Indonesia 2°42S 132°26E 37 E8
Kokchetav = Kökshetaū
  Kazakhstan 53°20N 69°25E 26 D7
Kokemäenjoki ⬅
  Finland 61°32N 21°44E 8 F19
Kokkilai Sri Lanka 9°0N 80°57E 45 K5
Kokkola Finland 63°50N 23°8E 8 E20
Koko Kyunzu Burma 14°7N 93°22E 45 G11
Koko Nur = Qinghai Hu
  China 36°40N 100°10E 30 D9
Kokomo U.S.A. 40°29N 86°8W 80 E10
Kokopo Papua N. G. 4°22S 152°19E 64 H7
Koksan N. Korea 38°46N 126°40E 33 E14
Kökshetaū Kazakhstan 53°20N 69°25E 26 D7
Koksoak ⬅ Canada 58°30N 68°10W 69 F18
Kokstad S. Africa 30°32S 29°29E 57 D4
Kokubu = Kirishima
  Japan 31°44N 130°46E 29 J5
Kola Indonesia 5°35S 134°30E 37 F8
Kola Russia 68°45N 33°8E 8 B25
Kola Pen. = Kolskiy Poluostrov
  Russia 67°30N 38°0E 18 A6
Kolachel India 8°10N 77°15E 45 K3
Kolachi ⬅ Pakistan 27°8N 67°2E 42 F2
Kolahoi India 34°12N 75°22E 43 B6
Kolaka Indonesia 4°3S 121°46E 37 E6
Kolar India 13°12N 78°15E 45 H4
Kolaras India 25°14N 77°36E 42 G6
Kolari Finland 67°20N 23°48E 8 C20
Kolasib India 24°15N 92°45E 41 G18
Kolayat India 27°50N 72°50E 42 F5
Kolda Senegal 12°55N 14°57W 52 F3
Kolding Denmark 55°30N 9°29E 9 J13
Kolepom = Dolak, Pulau
  Indonesia 8°0S 138°30E 37 F9
Kolguyev, Ostrov Russia 69°20N 48°30E 18 A8
Kolhapur India 16°43N 74°15E 44 F2
Kolín Czech Rep. 50°2N 15°9E 16 C8
Kolkas rags Latvia 57°46N 22°37E 9 H20
Kollam India 8°50N 76°38E 45 K3
Kollegal India 12°9N 77°9E 45 H3

Kolleru L. India 16°40N 81°10E 44 F5
Kollum Neths. 53°17N 6°10E 15 A6
Kolmanskop Namibia 26°45S 15°14E 56 C2
Köln Germany 50°56N 6°57E 16 C4
Kolo Poland 52°14N 18°40E 17 B10
Kołobrzeg Poland 54°10N 15°35E 16 A8
Kolokani Mali 13°35N 7°45W 52 F4
Kolomna Russia 55°8N 38°45E 18 C6
Kolomyya Ukraine 48°31N 25°2E 17 D13
Kolonodale Indonesia 2°0S 121°19E 37 E6
Kolpashevo Russia 58°20N 83°5E 26 D9
Kolpino Russia 59°44N 30°39E 18 C5
Kolskiy Poluostrov Russia 67°30N 38°0E 18 A6
Kolskiy Zaliv Russia 69°23N 34°0E 8 B26
Kolwezi
  Dem. Rep. of the Congo 10°40S 25°25E 54 G5
Kolyma ⬅ Russia 69°30N 161°0E 27 C17
Kolymskoye Nagorye
  Russia 63°0N 157°0E 27 C16
Kôm Ombo Egypt 24°25N 32°52E 53 D12
Komandorskiye Is. =
  Komandorskiye Ostrova
  Russia 55°0N 167°0E 27 D17
Komandorskiye Ostrova
  Russia 55°0N 167°0E 27 D17
Komárno Slovak Rep. 47°49N 18°5E 17 E10
Komatipoort S. Africa 25°25S 31°55E 57 C5
Komatsu Japan 36°25N 136°30E 29 F8
Komatsushima Japan 34°0N 134°35E 29 H7
Komi □ Russia 64°0N 55°0E 18 B10
Kommamur Canal India 16°0N 80°25E 45 G5
Kommunarsk = Alchevsk
  Ukraine 48°30N 38°45E 19 E6
Kommunizma, Pik = imeni Ismail
  Samani, Pik Tajikistan 39°0N 72°2E 26 F8
Komodo Indonesia 8°37S 119°20E 37 F5
Komoran, Pulau
  Indonesia 8°18S 138°45E 37 F9
Komoro Japan 36°19N 138°26E 29 F9
Komotini Greece 41°9N 25°26E 23 D11
Kompasberg S. Africa 31°45S 24°32E 56 D3
Kompong Chhnang = Kampong
  Chhnang Cambodia 12°20N 104°35E 38 F5
Kompong Chikreng
  Cambodia 13°5N 104°18E 38 F5
Kompong Kleang
  Cambodia 13°6N 104°8E 38 F5
Kompong Luong
  Cambodia 11°49N 104°48E 39 G5
Kompong Pranak
  Cambodia 13°35N 104°55E 38 F5
Kompong Som = Kampong Saom
  Cambodia 10°38N 103°30E 39 G4
Kompong Som, Chhung =
  Kampong Saom, Chaak
  Cambodia 10°50N 103°32E 39 G4
Kompong Speu
  Cambodia 11°26N 104°32E 39 G5
Kompong Sralau
  Cambodia 14°5N 105°46E 38 E5
Kompong Thom
  Cambodia 12°35N 104°51E 38 F5
Kompong Trabeck
  Cambodia 13°6N 105°14E 38 F5
Kompong Trach
  Cambodia 11°25N 105°48E 39 G5
Kompong Tralach
  Cambodia 11°54N 104°47E 39 G5
Komrat = Comrat
  Moldova 46°18N 28°40E 17 E15
Komsberg S. Africa 32°40S 20°45E 56 D3
Komsomolets, Ostrov
  Russia 80°30N 95°0E 27 A10
Komsomolsk-na-Amur
  Russia 50°30N 137°0E 31 A16
Kon Ka Kinh △ Vietnam 14°19N 107°23E 38 E7
Kon Tum Vietnam 14°24N 108°0E 38 E7
Kon Tum, Plateau du
  Vietnam 14°30N 108°30E 38 E7
Konar □ Afghan. 34°30N 71°3E 40 B7
Konarak India 19°54N 86°7E 44 F8
Konārak Iran 25°21N 60°23E 47 E9
Konārī Iran 28°13N 51°36E 47 D6
Konch India 26°0N 79°10E 43 G8
Kondagaon India 19°35N 81°35E 44 E5
Kondinin Australia 32°34S 118°8E 61 F2
Kondoa Tanzania 4°55S 35°50E 54 E7
Kondopoga Russia 62°12N 34°17E 18 B5
Kondratyevo Russia 57°22N 98°15E 27 D10
Kondukur India 15°12N 79°57E 45 G4
Köneürgench
  Turkmenistan 42°19N 59°10E 26 E6
Konevo Russia 62°8N 39°20E 18 B6
Kong = Khong ⬅
  Cambodia 13°32N 105°58E 38 F5
Kong Ivory C. 8°54N 4°36W 52 G5
Kong, Koh Cambodia 11°20N 103°0E 39 G4
Kong Christian IX.s Land
  Greenland 68°0N 36°0W 4 C6
Kong Christian X.s Land
  Greenland 74°0N 29°0W 4 B6
Kong Frederik IX.s Land
  Greenland 67°0N 52°0W 4 C5
Kong Frederik VI.s Kyst
  Greenland 63°0N 43°0W 4 C5
Kong Frederik VIII.s Land
  Greenland 78°30N 26°0W 4 B6
Kong Oscar Fjord
  Greenland 72°20N 24°0W 4 B6
Konglu Burma 27°13N 97°57E 41 F20
Kongola Namibia 17°45S 23°20E 56 A3
Kongolo
  Dem. Rep. of the Congo 5°22S 27°0E 54 F5
Kongsberg Norway 59°39N 9°39E 9 G13
Kongsvinger Norway 60°12N 12°2E 9 F15
Kongur Shan China 38°34N 75°18E 30 D4
Konin Poland 52°12N 18°15E 17 B10
Konjic Bos.-H. 43°42N 17°58E 23 C7
Konkiep Namibia 26°49S 17°15E 56 D2
Konnur India 16°14N 74°49E 45 F2

Konosha Russia 61°0N 40°5E 18 B7
Kōnosu Japan 36°3N 139°31E 29 F9
Konotop Ukraine 51°12N 33°7E 19 D5
Konqi He ⬅ China 40°45N 90°10E 30 C6
Końskie Poland 51°15N 20°23E 17 C11
Konstanz Germany 47°40N 9°10E 16 E5
Kont Iran 26°55N 61°50E 47 E9
Konta India 17°48N 81°23E 44 F5
Kontagora Nigeria 10°23N 5°27E 52 F7
Kontiolahti Finland 62°46N 29°50E 8 E23
Konya Turkey 37°52N 32°35E 46 B2
Koocanusa, L. Canada 49°20N 115°15W 76 B6
Kookynie Australia 29°17S 121°22E 61 E3
Koolyanobbing Australia 30°48S 119°36E 61 F2
Koonibba Australia 31°54S 133°25E 63 E1
Koorawatha Australia 34°2S 148°33E 63 E4
Koorda Australia 30°48S 117°35E 61 F2
Kooskia U.S.A. 46°9N 115°59W 76 C6
Kootenay ⬅ U.S.A. 49°19N 117°39W 70 D5
Kootenay △ Canada 51°0N 116°0W 70 C5
Kootenay L. Canada 49°45N 116°50W 76 B5
Kootjieskolk S. Africa 31°15S 20°21E 56 D3
Kopaonik Serbia 43°10N 20°50E 23 C9
Kopargaon India 19°51N 74°28E 44 E2
Koper Slovenia 45°31N 13°44E 16 F7
Kopervik Norway 59°17N 5°17E 9 G11
Kopet Dagh Asia 38°0N 58°0E 47 B8
Kopeysk Russia 55°7N 61°37E 26 D7
Kopi Australia 33°24S 135°40E 63 E2
Köping Sweden 59°31N 16°3E 9 G17
Koppa India 13°33N 75°21E 45 H2
Koppal India 15°23N 76°5E 45 G3
Koppeh Dāgh = Kopet Dagh
  Asia 38°0N 58°0E 47 B8
Koppies S. Africa 27°20S 27°30E 57 D4
Koprivnica Croatia 46°12N 16°45E 22 A7
Köprülü △ Turkey 37°30N 31°5E 46 B1
Kopychyntsi Ukraine 49°7N 25°58E 17 D13
Korab Macedonia 41°44N 20°40E 23 D9
Koral India 21°50N 73°12E 42 J5
Korangal India 17°6N 77°38E 44 E3
Koraput India 18°50N 82°40E 44 E6
Korba India 22°20N 82°45E 43 H10
Korbu, Gunung Malaysia 4°41N 101°18E 39 K3
Korçë Albania 40°37N 20°50E 23 D9
Korčula Croatia 42°56N 16°57E 22 C7
Kord Kūy Iran 36°48N 54°7E 47 B7
Kord Sheykh Iran 28°31N 52°53E 47 D7
Kordestān □ Iran 36°0N 47°0E 46 C5
Kordofân Sudan 13°0N 29°0E 53 F11
Korea, North ■ Asia 40°0N 127°0E 33 E14
Korea, South ■ Asia 36°0N 128°0E 33 G15
Korea Bay Korea 39°0N 124°0E 33 E13
Korea Strait Asia 34°0N 129°30E 33 H15
Koregaon India 17°40N 74°10E 44 F2
Korets Ukraine 50°40N 27°5E 17 C14
Korff Ice Rise Antarctica 79°0S 69°30W 5 D17
Korhogo Ivory C. 9°29N 5°28W 52 G4
Korinthiakos Kolpos
  Greece 38°16N 22°30E 23 E10
Korinthos Greece 37°56N 22°55E 23 F10
Kōriyama Japan 37°24N 140°23E 28 F10
Korla China 41°45N 86°4E 30 C6
Korneshty = Corneşti
  Moldova 47°21N 28°1E 17 E15
Koro Fiji 17°19S 179°23E 59 a
Koro Ivory C. 8°32N 7°30W 52 G4
Koro Sea Fiji 17°30S 179°45W 59 a
Korogwe Tanzania 5°5S 38°25E 54 F7
Korolevu Fiji 18°12S 177°46E 59 a
Koronadal Phil. 6°12N 124°51E 37 C6
Körös ⬅ Hungary 46°43N 20°12E 17 E11
Korosten Ukraine 50°54N 28°36E 17 C15
Korostyshev Ukraine 50°19N 29°4E 17 C15
Korovou Fiji 17°47S 178°32E 59 a
Koroyanitu △ Fiji 17°40S 177°35E 59 a
Korsakov Russia 46°36N 142°42E 27 E15
Korshunovo Russia 58°37N 110°10E 27 D12
Korsør Denmark 55°20N 11°9E 9 J14
Kortrijk Belgium 50°50N 3°17E 15 D3
Korwai India 24°7N 78°5E 42 G8
Koryakskoye Nagorye
  Russia 61°0N 171°0E 27 C18
Kos Greece 36°50N 27°15E 23 F12
Kosan N. Korea 38°52N 127°25E 33 E14
Kościan Poland 52°5N 16°40E 17 B9
Kosciusko U.S.A. 33°4N 89°35W 85 E10
Kosciuszko, Mt.
  Australia 36°27S 148°16E 63 F4
Kosgi Andhra Pradesh,
  India 16°58N 77°43E 44 F3
Kosgi Andhra Pradesh,
  India 15°51N 77°16E 45 G3
Kosha Sudan 20°50N 30°30E 53 D12
K'oshih = Kashi China 39°30N 76°2E 30 D4
Koshiki-Rettō Japan 31°45N 129°49E 29 J4
Kosi India 27°48N 77°29E 42 F7
Kosi ⬅ India 28°41N 78°57E 43 E8
Košice Slovak Rep. 48°42N 21°15E 17 D11
Koslan Russia 63°34N 49°14E 18 B8
Košöng N. Korea 38°40N 128°22E 33 E15
Kosovo ■ Europe 42°30N 21°0E 23 C9
Kosovska Mitrovica = Mitrovicë
  Kosovo 42°54N 20°52E 23 C9
Kossou, L. de Ivory C. 6°59N 5°31W 52 G4
Koster S. Africa 25°52S 26°54E 56 D4
Kôstî Sudan 13°8N 32°43E 53 F12
Kostomuksha Russia 64°41N 30°49E 8 D24
Kostopil Ukraine 50°51N 26°22E 17 C14
Kostroma Russia 57°50N 40°58E 18 C7
Kostrzyn Poland 52°35N 14°39E 16 B8
Koszalin Poland 54°11N 16°8E 16 A9
Kot Addu Pakistan 30°30N 71°0E 42 D4
Kot Kapura India 30°35N 74°50E 42 D6
Kot Moman Pakistan 32°13N 73°0E 42 C5
Kot Sultan Pakistan 30°46N 70°56E 42 D4
Kota India 25°14N 75°49E 42 G6
Kota Barrage India 25°6N 75°51E 42 G6
Kota Belud Malaysia 6°21N 116°26E 36 C5

Kota Bharu *Malaysia* 6°7'N 102°14E **39 J4**
Kota I. = Loaita I.
  S. China Sea 10°41'N 114°25'E **36 B4**
Kota Kinabalu *Malaysia* 6°0'N 116°4E **36 C5**
Kota Tinggi *Malaysia* 1°44'N 103°53'E **39 M4**
Kotaagung *Indonesia* 5°38'S 104°29'E **36 F2**
Kotabaru *Indonesia* 3°20'S 116°20'E **36 E5**
Kotabumi *Indonesia* 4°49'S 104°54'E **36 E2**
Kotapad *India* 19°9'N 82°21'E **44 H6**
Kotapinang *Indonesia* 1°53'N 100°5E **39 M3**
Kotcho L. *Canada* 59°7'N 121°12'W **70 B4**
Kotdwara *India* 29°45'N 78°32'E **43 E8**
Kotelnikovo *Russia* 58°22'N 48°24E **18 C8**
Kotelnich *Russia* 47°38'N 43°8E **19 E7**
Kotelnyy, Ostrov *Russia* 75°10'N 139°0E **27 B14**
Kothapet *India* 19°21'N 79°28E **44 E4**
Kothari → *India* 25°20'N 75°4E **42 G6**
Kothi *Chhattisgarh, India,* 23°21'N 82°3E **43 H10**
Kothi *Mad. P., India* 24°45'N 80°40E **43 G9**
Kotiro *Pakistan* 26°17'N 67°13E **42 F2**
Kotka *Finland* 60°28'N 26°58E **8 F22**
Kotlas *Russia* 61°17'N 46°43E **18 B8**
Kotli *Pakistan* 33°30'N 73°55E **42 C5**
Kotma *India* 23°12'N 81°58E **43 H9**
Kotor *Montenegro* 42°25'N 18°47E **23 C8**
Kotovsk *Ukraine* 47°45'N 29°35E **17 E15**
Kotputli *India* 27°43'N 76°12E **42 F7**
Kotri *Pakistan* 25°22'N 68°22E **42 G3**
Kotri → *India* 19°15'N 80°35E **44 E5**
Kottagudem *India* 17°30'N 80°40E **44 F5**
Kottayam *India* 9°35'N 76°33E **45 K3**
Kotto → *C.A.R.* 4°14'N 22°2E **54 D4**
Kottur *India* 10°34'N 76°56E **45 J3**
Kotturu *India* 14°45'N 76°10E **45 G3**
Kotu Group *Tonga* 20°0'S 174°45'W **59 c**
Kotuy → *Russia* 71°54'N 102°6E **27 B11**
Kotzebue *U.S.A.* 66°53'N 162°39'W **74 B7**
Kotzebue Sound *U.S.A.* 66°20'N 163°0'W **74 B7**
Kouchibouguac △
  Canada 46°50'N 65°0'W **73 C6**
Koudougou *Burkina Faso* 12°10'N 2°20'W **52 F5**
Kougaberge *S. Africa* 33°48'S 23°50'E **56 D3**
Kouilou → *Congo* 4°10'S 12°5E **54 E2**
Koukdjuak → *Canada* 66°43'N 73°0'W **69 D17**
Koula Moutou *Gabon* 1°15'S 12°25E **54 E2**
Koulen = Kulen
  Cambodia 13°50'N 104°40E **38 F5**
Koumala *Australia* 21°38'S 149°15E **62 C4**
Koumra *Chad* 8°50'N 17°35E **53 G9**
Kountze *U.S.A.* 30°22'N 94°19'W **84 F7**
Kourou *Fr. Guiana* 5°9'N 52°39'W **93 B8**
Kouroussa *Guinea* 10°45'N 9°45'W **52 F4**
Kousseri *Cameroon* 12°0'N 14°55E **53 F8**
Koutiala *Mali* 12°25'N 5°23'W **52 F4**
Kouvola *Finland* 60°52'N 26°43E **8 F22**
Kovdor *Russia* 67°34'N 30°24E **8 C24**
Kovel *Ukraine* 51°11'N 24°38E **17 C13**
Kovilpatti *India* 9°10'N 77°50E **45 K3**
Kovrov *Russia* 56°25'N 41°25E **18 C7**
Kovur *Andhra Pradesh, India* 17°3'N 81°39E **44 F5**
Kovur *Andhra Pradesh,*
  India 14°30'N 80°1E **45 G5**
Kowanyama *Australia* 15°29'S 141°44E **62 B3**
Kowanyama ◎ *Australia* 15°20'S 141°47E **62 B3**
Kowŏn *N. Korea* 39°26'N 127°14E **33 E14**
Koyampattur = Coimbatore
  India 11°2'N 76°59E **45 J3**
Köyceğiz *Turkey* 36°57'N 28°40E **23 F13**
Koyukuk → *U.S.A.* 64°55'N 157°32'W **74 C8**
Koza = Okinawa *Japan* 26°19'N 127°46E **29 L3**
Kozan *Turkey* 37°26'N 35°50E **46 B2**
Kozani *Greece* 40°19'N 21°47E **23 D9**
Kozhikode *India* 11°15'N 75°43E **45 J2**
Kozhva *Russia* 65°10'N 57°0E **18 A10**
Kōzu-Shima *Japan* 34°13'N 139°10E **29 G9**
Kozyatyn *Ukraine* 49°45'N 28°50E **17 D15**
Kozyrevsk *Russia* 56°3'N 159°51E **27 D16**
Kpalimé *Togo* 6°57'N 0°44E **52 G6**
Kra, Isthmus of = Kra, Kho Khot
  Thailand 10°15'N 99°30E **39 G2**
Kra, Kho Khot *Thailand* 10°15'N 99°30E **39 G2**
Kra Buri *Thailand* 10°22'N 98°46E **39 G2**
Kraai → *S. Africa* 30°40'S 26°45E **56 D4**
Krabi *Thailand* 8°4'N 98°55E **39 H2**
Kracheh = Kratie
  Cambodia 12°32'N 106°10E **38 F6**
Kragan *Indonesia* 6°43'S 111°38E **37 G14**
Kragero *Norway* 58°52'N 9°25E **9 G13**
Kragujevac *Serbia* 44°2'N 20°56E **23 B9**
Krakatau = Rakata, Pulau
  Indonesia 6°10'S 105°20E **37 G11**
Krakatoa = Rakata, Pulau
  Indonesia 6°10'S 105°20E **37 G11**
Krakor *Cambodia* 12°32'N 104°12E **38 F5**
Kraków *Poland* 50°4'N 19°57E **17 C10**
Kraksaan *Indonesia* 7°43'S 113°23E **37 G16**
Kralanh *Cambodia* 13°35'N 103°25E **38 F4**
Kraljevo *Serbia* 43°44'N 20°41E **23 C9**
Kramatorsk *Ukraine* 48°50'N 37°30E **19 E6**
Kramfors *Sweden* 62°55'N 17°48E **8 E17**
Kranj *Slovenia* 46°16'N 14°22E **16 E8**
Krankskop *S. Africa* 28°0'S 30°47E **57 C5**
Krasavino *Russia* 60°58'N 46°29E **18 B8**
Krasieo Res. *Thailand* 14°49'N 99°30E **38 E2**
Kraskino *Russia* 42°44'N 130°48E **28 C5**
Kraśnik *Poland* 50°55'N 22°15E **17 C12**
Krasnoarmeysk *Russia* 51°0'N 45°42E **26 D5**
Krasnodar *Russia* 45°5'N 39°0E **19 E6**
Krasnokamensk *Russia* 50°3'N 118°0E **27 D12**
Krasnokamsk *Russia* 58°4'N 55°48E **18 C10**
Krasnoperekopsk *Ukraine* 46°0'N 33°54E **19 E5**
Krasnorechenskiy
  Russia 44°41'N 135°14E **28 B7**
Krasnoselkup *Russia* 65°20'N 82°10E **26 C9**
Krasnoturinsk *Russia* 59°46'N 60°12E **18 C11**
Krasnoufimsk *Russia* 56°36'N 57°38E **18 C10**
Krasnouralsk *Russia* 58°21'N 60°3E **18 C11**
Krasnovishersk *Russia* 60°23'N 57°3E **18 B10**

Krasnoyarsk *Russia* 56°8'N 93°0E **27 D10**
Krasnoyarskoye Vdkhr.
  Russia 56°0'N 92°30E **27 D10**
Krasnyy Kut *Russia* 50°50'N 47°0E **19 D8**
Krasnyy Luch *Ukraine* 48°13'N 39°0E **19 E6**
Krasnyy Yar *Russia* 46°43'N 48°23E **19 E8**
Kratie *Cambodia* 12°32'N 106°10E **38 F6**
Krau *Indonesia* 3°19'S 140°5E **37 E10**
Kravanh, Chuor Phnum
  Cambodia 12°0'N 103°32E **39 G4**
Krefeld *Germany* 51°20'N 6°33E **16 C4**
Kremen *Croatia* 44°28'N 15°53E **16 F8**
Kremenchuk *Ukraine* 49°5'N 33°25E **19 E5**
Kremenchuksk Vdskh.
  Ukraine 49°20'N 32°30E **19 E5**
Kremenets *Ukraine* 50°8'N 25°43E **17 C13**
Kremmling *U.S.A.* 40°4'N 106°24'W **76 F10**
Krems an der Donau
  Austria 48°25'N 15°36E **16 D8**
Kretinga *Lithuania* 55°53'N 21°15E **9 J19**
Krichev = Krychaw
  Belarus 53°40'N 31°41E **17 B16**
Kril'on, Mys *Russia* 45°53'N 142°5E **28 B11**
Krishna → *India* 15°57'N 80°59E **45 G5**
Krishnagiri *India* 12°32'N 78°16E **45 H4**
Krishnanagar *India* 23°24'N 88°33E **43 H13**
Krishnaraja Sagar *India* 12°20'N 76°30E **45 H3**
Kristiansand *Norway* 58°8'N 8°1E **9 G13**
Kristianstad *Sweden* 56°2'N 14°9E **9 H16**
Kristiansund *Norway* 63°7'N 7°45E **8 E12**
Kristiinankaupunki
  Finland 62°16'N 21°21E **8 E19**
Kristinehamn *Sweden* 59°18'N 14°7E **9 G16**
Kristinestad = Kristiinankaupunki
  Finland 62°16'N 21°21E **8 E19**
Kriti *Greece* 35°15'N 25°0E **23 G11**
Krivoy Rog = Kryvyy Rih
  Ukraine 47°51'N 33°20E **19 E5**
Krk *Croatia* 45°8'N 14°40E **16 F8**
Krokodil → Umgwenya →
  Mozam. 25°14'S 32°18E **57 C5**
Krong Kaoh Kong
  Cambodia 11°37'N 102°59E **39 G4**
Kronprins Frederik Land
  Greenland 81°0'N 45°0'W **4 B5**
Kronprins Olav Kyst
  Antarctica 69°0'S 42°0E **5 C5**
Kronprinsesse Märtha Kyst
  Antarctica 73°30'S 10°0'W **5 D2**
Kronshtadt *Russia* 59°57'N 29°51E **18 B4**
Kroonstad *S. Africa* 27°43'S 27°19E **56 C4**
Kropotkin *Russia* 45°28'N 40°28E **19 E7**
Krosno *Poland* 49°42'N 21°46E **17 D11**
Krotoszyn *Poland* 51°42'N 17°23E **17 C9**
Kruger △ *S. Africa* 24°50'S 26°10E **57 B4**
Krugersdorp *S. Africa* 26°5'S 27°46E **57 B4**
Kruisfontein *S. Africa* 33°59'S 24°43E **56 D3**
Krupki *Belarus* 54°19'N 29°8E **17 A15**
Kruševac *Serbia* 43°35'N 21°28E **23 C9**
Kruzenshterna, Proliv
  Russia 48°0'N 154°0E **27 E16**
Krychaw *Belarus* 53°40'N 31°41E **17 B16**
Krymskiy Poluostrov = Krymskyy
  Pivostriv *Ukraine* 45°0'N 34°0E **19 F5**
Krymskyy Pivostriv
  Ukraine 45°0'N 34°0E **19 F5**
Kryvyy Rih *Ukraine* 47°51'N 33°20E **19 E5**
Ksar el Kebir *Morocco* 35°0'N 6°0'W **52 B4**
Ksar es Souk = Er Rachidia
  Morocco 31°58'N 4°20'W **52 B5**
Kuah *Malaysia* 6°19'N 99°51E **39 J2**
Kuala Belait *Malaysia* 4°35'N 114°11E **36 D4**
Kuala Berang *Malaysia* 5°5'N 103°1E **39 K4**
Kuala Dungun = Dungun
  Malaysia 4°45'N 103°25E **39 K4**
Kuala Kangsar *Malaysia* 4°46'N 100°56E **39 K3**
Kuala Kelawang *Malaysia* 2°56'N 102°5E **39 L4**
Kuala Kerai *Malaysia* 5°30'N 102°12E **39 K4**
Kuala Kubu Bharu
  Malaysia 3°34'N 101°39E **39 L3**
Kuala Lipis *Malaysia* 4°10'N 102°3E **39 K4**
Kuala Lumpur *Malaysia* 3°9'N 101°41E **39 L3**
Kuala Lumpur Int. ✈ (KUL)
  Malaysia 2°44'N 101°42E **39 L3**
Kuala Nerang *Malaysia* 6°16'N 100°37E **39 J3**
Kuala Pilah *Malaysia* 2°45'N 102°15E **39 L4**
Kuala Rompin *Malaysia* 2°49'N 103°29E **39 L4**
Kuala Selangor *Malaysia* 3°20'N 101°15E **39 L3**
Kuala Sepetang *Malaysia* 4°49'N 100°28E **39 K3**
Kuala Terengganu
  Malaysia 5°20'N 103°8E **39 K4**
Kualajelai *Indonesia* 2°58'S 110°46E **36 E4**
Kualakapuas *Indonesia* 2°55'S 114°20E **36 E4**
Kualakurun *Indonesia* 1°10'S 113°50E **36 E4**
Kualapembuang
  Indonesia 3°14'S 112°38E **36 E4**
Kualasimpang *Indonesia* 4°17'N 98°3E **36 D1**
Kuancheng *China* 40°37'N 118°30E **33 D10**
Kuandang *Indonesia* 0°56'N 123°1E **37 D6**
Kuandian *China* 40°45'N 124°45E **33 D13**
Kuanshan *Taiwan* 23°3'N 121°9E **35 F13**
Kuantan *Malaysia* 3°49'N 103°20E **39 L4**
Kuba = Quba *Azerbaijan* 41°21'N 48°32E **19 F8**
Kuban → *Russia* 45°20'N 37°30E **19 E6**
Kubokawa = Shimanto
  Japan 33°12'N 133°8E **29 H6**
Kuba *Indonesia* 8°16'S 115°35E **37 J18**
Kubutambahan *Indonesia* 8°5'S 115°10E **37 J18**
Kucar, Tanjung
  Indonesia 8°39'S 114°34E **37 K18**
Kuchaman *India* 27°13'N 74°47E **42 F6**
Kuchchaveli *Sri Lanka* 8°50'N 81°6E **45 K5**
Kuchinda *India* 21°44'N 84°21E **43 J11**
Kuching *Malaysia* 1°33'N 110°25E **36 D4**
Kuchino-eruba-Jima
  Japan 30°28'N 130°12E **29 J5**
Kuchino-Shima *Japan* 29°57'N 129°55E **29 K4**
Kuchinotsu *Japan* 32°36'N 130°11E **29 H5**
Kucing = Kuching
  Malaysia 1°33'N 110°25E **36 D4**

Kud → *Pakistan* 26°5'N 66°20E **42 F2**
Kuda *India* 23°10'N 71°15E **42 H4**
Kudal *India* 16°2'N 73°41E **45 F1**
Kudalier → *India* 18°35'N 79°48E **44 E4**
Kudat *Malaysia* 6°55'N 116°55E **36 C5**
Kudremukh *India* 13°15'N 75°20E **45 H2**
Kudus *Indonesia* 6°48'S 110°51E **37 G14**
Kudymkar *Russia* 59°1'N 54°39E **18 C9**
Kueiyang = Guiyang
  China 26°32'N 106°40E **34 D6**
Kufra Oasis = Al Kufrah
  Libya 24°17'N 23°15E **53 D10**
Kufstein *Austria* 47°35'N 12°11E **16 E7**
Kugaaruk = Pelly Bay
  Canada 68°38'N 89°50'W **69 D14**
Kugluktuk *Canada* 67°50'N 115°5'W **68 D8**
Kugong I. *Canada* 56°18'N 79°50'W **72 A4**
Kūh Dasht *Iran* 33°32'N 47°36E **46 C5**
Kūhak *Iran* 27°12'N 63°10E **47 E9**
Kuhan *Pakistan* 28°19'N 67°14E **42 E2**
Kūhbonān *Iran* 31°23'N 56°19E **47 D8**
Kūhestak *Iran* 26°47'N 57°2E **47 E8**
Kuhin *Iran* 36°22'N 49°40E **47 B6**
Kūhīrī *Iran* 26°55'N 61°2E **47 E9**
Kui Buri *Thailand* 12°3'N 99°52E **39 F2**
Kuiburi △ *Thailand* 12°10'N 99°37E **39 F2**
Kuichong *China* 22°38'N 114°25E **31 a**
Kuiseb → *Namibia* 22°59'S 14°31E **56 B1**
Kuito *Angola* 12°22'S 16°55E **55 G3**
Kuiu I. *U.S.A.* 57°45'N 134°10'W **70 B2**
Kujang *N. Korea* 39°57'N 126°1E **33 E14**
Kuji *Japan* 40°11'N 141°46E **28 D10**
Kujū-San *Japan* 33°5'N 131°15E **29 H5**
Kukës *Albania* 42°5'N 20°27E **23 C9**
Kukup *Malaysia* 1°20'N 103°27E **39 d**
Kukup, Pulau *Malaysia* 1°18'N 103°25E **39 d**
Kula *Turkey* 38°32'N 28°40E **23 E13**
K'ula Shan *Bhutan* 28°14'N 90°36E **30 F7**
Kulachi *Pakistan* 31°56'N 70°27E **42 D4**
Kulai *Malaysia* 1°44'N 103°35E **39 M4**
Kulasekarappattinam *India* 8°20'N 78°5E **45 K4**
Kuldiga *Latvia* 56°58'N 21°59E **9 H19**
Kulen *Cambodia* 13°50'N 104°40E **38 F5**
Kulgam *India* 33°36'N 75°2E **43 C6**
Kulgera *Australia* 25°50'S 133°18E **62 D1**
Kulim *Malaysia* 5°22'N 100°34E **39 K3**
Kulikuta ◎ *Australia* 24°0'S 127°5E **60 D4**
Kulittalai *India* 10°55'N 78°25E **45 J4**
Kulkayu = Hartley Bay
  Canada 53°25'N 129°15'W **70 C3**
Kullu *India* 31°58'N 77°6E **42 D7**
Kŭlob *Tajikistan* 37°55'N 69°50E **26 F7**
Kulsary = Qulsary
  Kazakhstan 46°59'N 54°1E **19 E9**
Kulti *India* 23°43'N 86°50E **43 H12**
Kulunda *Russia* 52°35'N 78°57E **26 D8**
Kulungar *Afghan.* 34°0'N 69°2E **42 C3**
Kŭlvand *Iran* 31°21'N 54°35E **47 D7**
Kulwin *Australia* 35°2'S 142°42E **63 F3**
Kulyab = Kŭlob *Tajikistan* 37°55'N 69°50E **26 F7**
Kuma → *Russia* 44°55'N 47°0E **19 F8**
Kumaganum *Nigeria* 13°8'N 10°38E **53 F8**
Kumagaya *Japan* 36°9'N 139°22E **29 F9**
Kumai *Indonesia* 2°44'S 111°43E **36 E4**
Kumamba, Kepulauan
  Indonesia 1°36'S 138°45E **37 E9**
Kumamoto *Japan* 32°45'N 130°45E **29 H5**
Kumamoto □ *Japan* 32°55'N 130°55E **29 H5**
Kumanovo *Macedonia* 42°9'N 21°42E **23 C9**
Kumara *N.Z.* 42°37'S 171°12E **59 E3**
Kumarina Roadhouse
  Australia 24°41'S 119°32E **61 D2**
Kumasi *Ghana* 6°41'N 1°38'W **52 G5**
Kumba *Cameroon* 4°36'N 9°24E **54 D1**
Kumbakonam *India* 10°58'N 79°25E **45 J4**
Kumbarilla *Australia* 27°15'S 150°55E **63 D5**
Kumbhalgarh △ *India* 25°10'N 73°35E **42 G5**
Kumbhraj *India* 24°22'N 77°3E **42 G7**
Kumbia *Australia* 26°41'S 151°39E **63 D5**
Kumbukkan Oya →
  Sri Lanka 6°35'N 81°40E **45 L5**
Kŭmch'on *N. Korea* 38°10'N 126°29E **33 E14**
Kume-Shima *Japan* 26°20'N 126°47E **29 L3**
Kumertau *Russia* 52°45'N 55°57E **18 D10**
Kumharsain *India* 31°19'N 77°27E **42 D7**
Kumo *Nigeria* 10°1'N 11°12E **53 F8**
Kumo älv = Kokemäenjoki →
  Finland 61°32'N 21°44E **8 F19**
Kumon Bum *Burma* 26°30'N 97°15E **41 F20**
Kumta *India* 14°29'N 74°25E **45 G2**
Kumtag Shamo *China* 39°40'N 92°0E **30 D7**
Kumul = Hami *China* 42°55'N 93°25E **30 E7**
Kuna *U.S.A.* 43°30'N 116°25'W **76 E5**
Kunashir, Ostrov *Russia* 44°0'N 146°0E **27 E15**
Kunchha *Nepal* 28°8'N 84°20E **43 E11**
Kunda *Estonia* 59°30'N 26°34E **9 G22**
Kunda *India* 25°43'N 81°31E **43 G9**
Kundar → *Pakistan* 31°56'N 69°19E **42 D3**
Kundian *Pakistan* 32°27'N 71°28E **42 C4**
Kundla *India* 21°21'N 71°25E **42 J4**
Kunene → *Namibia* 17°20'S 11°50E **56 B1**
Kung, Ao *Thailand* 8°5'N 98°24E **39 a**
Kunga → *Bangla.* 21°46'N 89°30E **43 J13**
Kunghit I. *Canada* 52°6'N 131°3'W **70 C2**
Kungrad = Qŭnghirot
  Uzbekistan 43°2'N 58°50E **26 E6**
Kungsbacka *Sweden* 57°30'N 12°5E **9 H15**
Kungur *Russia* 57°25'N 56°57E **18 C10**
Kungurri *Australia* 21°4'S 148°45E **62 b**
Kuningan *Indonesia* 6°59'S 108°29E **37 G13**
Kunlong *Burma* 23°20'N 98°50E **34 F2**
Kunlun Shan *Asia* 36°0'N 86°30E **30 D6**
Kunlun Shankou *China* 35°35'N 94°4E **30 D7**

Kunming *China* 25°1'N 102°41E **34 E4**
Kunming Changshui Int. ✈ (KMG)
  China 24°59'N 102°45E **34 E4**
Kunmunya ◎ *Australia* 15°26'S 124°42E **60 C3**
Kunnamkulam *India* 10°38'N 76°7E **45 J3**
Kunshan *China* 31°22'N 120°58E **35 B13**
Kununurra *Australia* 15°40'S 128°50E **60 C4**
Kunwari → *India* 26°26'N 79°11E **43 F8**
Kunya-Urgench = Köneürgench
  Turkmenistan 42°19'N 59°10E **26 E6**
Kuopio *Finland* 62°53'N 27°35E **8 E22**
Kupa → *Croatia* 45°28'N 16°24E **16 F9**
Kupang *Indonesia* 10°19'S 123°39E **37 F6**
Kupreanof I. *U.S.A.* 56°50'N 133°30'W **70 B2**
Kupyansk-Uzlovoi
  Ukraine 49°40'N 37°43E **19 E6**
Kuqa *China* 41°35'N 82°30E **30 C5**
Kür = Kür → *Azerbaijan* 39°29'N 49°15E **19 G8**
Kür Dili *Azerbaijan* 39°3'N 49°13E **47 B6**
Kura = Kür → *Azerbaijan* 39°29'N 49°15E **19 G8**
Kuranda *Australia* 16°48'S 145°35E **62 B4**
Kuranga *India* 22°4'N 69°10E **42 H3**
Kurashiki *Japan* 34°40'N 133°50E **29 G6**
Kurayn *Si. Arabia* 27°39'N 49°50E **47 E6**
Kurayoshi *Japan* 35°26'N 133°50E **29 G6**
Kŭrchatov *Kazakhstan* 50°45'N 78°32E **26 D8**
Kurduvadi *India* 18°8'N 75°29E **44 E2**
Kŭrdzhali *Bulgaria* 41°38'N 25°21E **23 D11**
Kure *Japan* 34°14'N 132°32E **29 G6**
Kure I. *U.S.A.* 28°25'N 178°25'W **75 K4**
Kuressaare *Estonia* 58°15'N 22°30E **9 G20**
Kurgan *Russia* 55°26'N 65°18E **26 D7**
Kuri *India* 26°37'N 70°43E **42 F4**
Kuria Maria Is. = Ḩallāniyat,
  Jazā'ir al *Oman* 17°30'N 55°58E **49 D6**
Kurichchi *India* 11°36'N 77°35E **45 J3**
Kuridala *Australia* 21°16'S 140°29E **62 C3**
Kurigram *Bangla.* 25°49'N 89°39E **41 G16**
Kurikka *Finland* 62°36'N 22°24E **8 E20**
Kuril Basin *Pac. Oc.* 47°0'N 150°0E **4 E15**
Kuril Is. = Kurilskiye Ostrova
  Russia 45°0'N 150°0E **27 E16**
Kuril-Kamchatka Trench
  Pac. Oc. 44°0'N 153°0E **64 C7**
Kurilsk *Russia* 45°14'N 147°53E **27 E15**
Kurilskiye Ostrova
  Russia 45°0'N 150°0E **27 E16**
Kurino *Japan* 31°57'N 130°43E **29 J5**
Kurinskaya Kosa = Kür Dili
  Azerbaijan 39°3'N 49°13E **47 B6**
Kurkheda *India* 20°37'N 80°12E **44 D5**
Kurlkuta ◎ *Australia* 24°5'S 127°5E **60 D4**
Kurnool *India* 15°45'N 78°0E **45 G4**
Kuro-Shima *Kagoshima,*
  Japan 30°50'N 129°57E **29 J4**
Kuro-Shima *Okinawa,*
  Japan 24°14'N 124°1E **29 M2**
Kurow *N.Z.* 44°44'S 170°29E **59 F3**
Kurram → *Pakistan* 32°36'N 71°20E **42 C4**
Kurri Kurri *Australia* 32°50'S 151°28E **63 E5**
Kurrimine *Australia* 17°47'S 146°6E **62 B4**
Kurse Korhi *India* 20°14'N 80°46E **44 D5**
Kurseong = Karsiyang
  India 26°56'N 88°18E **43 F13**
Kurshskiy Zaliv *Russia* 55°9'N 21°6E **9 J19**
Kursk *Russia* 51°42'N 36°11E **18 D6**
Kuruçay *Turkey* 39°39'N 38°29E **46 B3**
Kurukshetra = Thanesar
  India 30°1'N 76°52E **42 D7**
Kuruktag *China* 41°0'N 89°0E **30 C6**
Kuruman *S. Africa* 27°28'S 23°28E **56 C3**
Kuruman → *S. Africa* 26°56'S 20°39E **56 C3**
Kurume *Japan* 33°15'N 130°30E **29 H5**
Kurunegala *Sri Lanka* 7°30'N 80°23E **45 L5**
Kurya *Russia* 61°42'N 57°9E **18 B10**
Kus Gölü *Turkey* 40°10'N 27°55E **23 D12**
Kuşadası *Turkey* 37°52'N 27°15E **23 F12**
Kusamba *Indonesia* 8°34'S 115°27E **37 K18**
Kusatsu *Japan* 36°37'N 138°36E **29 F9**
Kusawa L. *Canada* 60°20'N 136°13'W **70 A1**
Kushalgarh *India* 23°10'N 74°27E **42 H6**
Kushalnagar *India* 12°14'N 75°57E **45 H2**
Kushikino *Japan* 31°44'N 130°16E **29 J5**
Kushima *Japan* 31°29'N 131°14E **29 J5**
Kushimoto *Japan* 33°28'N 135°47E **29 H7**
Kushiro *Japan* 43°0'N 144°25E **28 C12**
Kushiro-Gawa →
  Japan 42°59'N 144°23E **28 C12**
Kushiro Shitsugen △
  Japan 43°9'N 144°26E **28 C12**
Kŭshk *Iran* 28°46'N 56°51E **47 D8**
Kushka = Serhetabat
  Turkmenistan 35°20'N 62°18E **47 C9**
Kushol *India* 33°40'N 76°36E **43 C7**
Kushtia *Bangla.* 23°55'N 89°5E **41 H16**
Kushva *Russia* 58°18'N 59°45E **18 C10**
Kuskokwim → *U.S.A.* 60°5'N 162°25'W **74 C7**
Kuskokwim B. *U.S.A.* 59°45'N 162°25'W **74 D7**
Kuskokwim Mts. *U.S.A.* 62°30'N 156°0'W **74 C8**
Kusmi *India* 23°17'N 83°55E **43 H10**
Kusŏng *N. Korea* 39°59'N 125°15E **33 E13**
Kussharo-Ko *Japan* 43°38'N 144°21E **28 C12**
Kustanay = Qostanay
  Kazakhstan 53°10'N 63°35E **26 D7**
Kut, Ko *Thailand* 11°40'N 102°35E **39 G4**
Kütahya *Turkey* 39°30'N 30°2E **19 G5**
Kutaisi *Georgia* 42°19'N 42°40E **19 F7**
Kutaraja = Banda Aceh
  Indonesia 5°35'N 95°20E **36 C1**
Kutch, Gulf of = Kachchh, Gulf of
  India 22°50'N 69°15E **42 H3**
Kutch, Rann of = Kachchh, Rann
  of *India* 24°0'N 70°0E **42 H4**
Kutiyana *India* 21°36'N 70°2E **42 J4**
Kutno *Poland* 52°15'N 19°23E **17 B10**
Kutru *India* 19°5'N 80°46E **44 E5**
Kutse *Botswana* 21°7'S 22°16E **56 B3**
Kuttabul *Australia* 21°1'S 148°54E **62 b**
Kutu *Dem. Rep. of the Congo* 2°40'S 18°11E **54 E3**
Kutum *Sudan* 14°10'N 24°40E **53 F10**

Kuujjuaq *Canada* 58°6'N 68°15'W **69 F18**
Kuujjuarapik *Canada* 55°20'N 77°35'W **72 A4**
Kuusamo *Finland* 65°57'N 29°8E **8 D23**
Kuusankoski *Finland* 60°55'N 26°38E **8 F22**
Kuwait = Al Kuwayt
  Kuwait 29°30'N 48°0E **46 D5**
Kuwait ■ *Asia* 29°30'N 47°30E **46 D5**
Kuwana *Japan* 35°5'N 136°43E **29 G8**
Kuwana → *India* 26°25'N 83°15E **43 F10**
Kuybyshev = Samara
  Russia 53°8'N 50°6E **18 D9**
Kuybyshev *Russia* 55°27'N 78°19E **26 D8**
Kuybyshevskoye Vdkhr.
  Russia 55°2'N 49°30E **18 C8**
Kuye He → *China* 38°23'N 110°46E **32 E6**
Kūyeh *Iran* 38°45'N 47°57E **46 B5**
Kuyto, Ozero *Russia* 65°6'N 31°20E **8 D24**
Kuytun *China* 44°25'N 85°0E **30 C5**
Kuyumba *Russia* 60°58'N 96°59E **27 C10**
Kuzey Anadolu Dağları
  Turkey 41°30'N 36°45E **19 F6**
Kuzhitturai *India* 8°18'N 77°11E **45 K3**
Kuznetsk *Russia* 53°12'N 46°40E **18 D8**
Kuzomen *Russia* 66°22'N 36°50E **18 A6**
Kvænangen *Norway* 70°5'N 21°15E **8 A19**
Kvaløya *Norway* 69°40'N 18°30E **8 B18**
Kvarner *Croatia* 44°50'N 14°10E **16 F8**
Kvarnerič *Croatia* 44°43'N 14°37E **16 F8**
Kwabhaca *S. Africa* 30°51'S 29°0E **57 D4**
Kwai = Khwae Noi →
  Thailand 14°1'N 99°32E **38 E2**
Kwajalein *Marshall Is.* 9°5'N 167°20E **64 G8**
Kwakhanai *Botswana* 21°39'S 21°16E **56 C3**
Kwakoegron *Suriname* 5°12'N 55°25'W **93 B7**
KwaMashu *S. Africa* 29°45'S 30°58E **57 C5**
Kwando → *Botswana* 24°0'S 25°0E **56 B3**
Kwangdaeri *N. Korea* 40°34'N 127°33E **33 D14**
Kwango →
  Dem. Rep. of the Congo 3°14'S 17°22E **54 E3**
Kwangsi-Chuang = Guangxi
  Zhuangzu Zizhiqu □
  China 24°0'N 109°0E **34 F7**
Kwangtung = Guangdong □
  China 23°0'N 113°0E **35 F9**
Kwataboahegan →
  Canada 51°9'N 80°50'W **72 B3**
Kwatisore *Indonesia* 3°18'S 134°50E **37 E8**
KwaZulu Natal □ *S. Africa* 29°0'S 30°0E **57 C5**
Kweichow = Guizhou □
  China 27°0'N 107°0E **34 D6**
Kwekwe *Zimbabwe* 18°58'S 29°48E **55 H5**
Kweneng □ *Botswana* 24°0'S 25°0E **56 B3**
Kwidzyn *Poland* 53°44'N 18°55E **17 B10**
Kwilu →
  Dem. Rep. of the Congo 3°22'S 17°22E **54 E3**
Kwinana *Australia* 32°15'S 115°47E **61 F2**
Kwoka *Indonesia* 0°31'S 132°27E **37 E8**
Kyabra Cr. → *Australia* 25°36'S 142°55E **63 D3**
Kyabram *Australia* 36°19'S 145°4E **63 F4**
Kyaikto *Burma* 17°20'N 97°3E **38 D1**
Kyaing Tong = Keng Tung
  Burma 21°18'N 99°39E **38 B2**
Kyakhta *Russia* 50°30'N 106°25E **27 D11**
Kyancutta *Australia* 33°8'S 135°33E **63 E2**
Kyaukpadaung *Burma* 20°52'N 95°8E **41 J19**
Kyaukpyu *Burma* 19°28'N 93°30E **41 K18**
Kyaukse *Burma* 21°36'N 96°10E **41 J20**
Kyburz *U.S.A.* 38°47'N 120°18'W **78 G6**
Kyelang *India* 32°35'N 77°2E **42 C7**
Kyklades *Greece* 37°0'N 24°30E **23 F11**
Kyle *Canada* 50°50'N 108°2'W **71 C7**
Kyle L. *U.S.A.* 29°59'N 97°53'W **84 F6**
Kyle of Lochalsh *U.K.* 57°17'N 5°44'W **11 D3**
Kymijoki → *Finland* 60°30'N 26°55E **8 F22**
Kymmene älv = Kymijoki →
  Finland 60°30'N 26°55E **8 F22**
Kyneton *Australia* 37°10'S 144°29E **63 F3**
Kynuna *Australia* 21°37'S 141°55E **62 C3**
Kyō-ga-Saki *Japan* 35°45'N 135°15E **29 G7**
Kyoga, L. *Uganda* 1°35'N 33°0E **54 D6**
Kyogle *Australia* 28°40'S 153°0E **63 D5**
Kyŏngju = Gyeongju
  S. Korea 35°51'N 129°14E **33 G15**
Kyŏngsŏng *N. Korea* 41°35'N 129°36E **33 D15**
Kyonpyaw *Burma* 17°12'N 95°10E **41 L19**
Kyōto *Japan* 35°0'N 135°45E **29 G7**
Kyōto □ *Japan* 35°15'N 135°45E **29 G7**
Kypros = Cyprus ■ *Asia* 35°0'N 33°0E **46 C2**
Kyrenia *Cyprus* 35°20'N 33°20E **46 C2**
Kyrgyzstan ■ *Asia* 42°0'N 75°0E **26 E8**
Kyro älv = Kyrönjoki →
  Finland 63°14'N 21°45E **8 E19**
Kyrönjoki → *Finland* 63°14'N 21°45E **8 E19**
Kystatyam *Russia* 67°20'N 123°10E **27 C13**
Kythira *Greece* 36°8'N 23°0E **23 F10**
Kythnos *Greece* 37°26'N 24°27E **23 F11**
Kyunhla *Burma* 23°25'N 95°15E **41 H19**
Kyuquot Sound *Canada* 50°2'N 127°22'W **70 D3**
Kyūshū *Japan* 33°0'N 131°0E **29 H5**
Kyūshū □ *Japan* 33°0'N 131°0E **29 H5**
Kyūshū-Palau Ridge
  Pac. Oc. 20°0'N 136°0E **64 E5**
Kyūshū-Sanchi *Japan* 32°35'N 131°17E **29 H5**
Kyustendil *Bulgaria* 42°16'N 22°41E **23 C10**
Kyusyur *Russia* 70°19'N 127°30E **27 B13**
Kyyiv *Ukraine* 50°30'N 30°28E **17 C16**
Kyyivske Vdskh. *Ukraine* 51°0'N 30°25E **17 C16**
Kyzyl *Russia* 51°50'N 94°30E **30 A7**
Kyzyl Kum *Uzbekistan* 42°30'N 65°0E **26 E7**
Kyzyl-Kyya *Kyrgyzstan* 40°16'N 72°8E **26 E8**
Kyzyl Orda = Qyzylorda
  Kazakhstan 44°48'N 65°28E **26 E7**

L

La Alcarria *Spain* 40°31'N 2°45'W **21 B4**
La Amistad △ *Cent. Amer.* 9°28'N 83°18'W **88 E3**
La Asunción *Venezuela* 11°2'N 63°53'W **92 A6**
La Baie *Canada* 48°19'N 70°53'W **73 B5**
La Banda *Argentina* 27°45'S 64°10'W **94 B3**
La Barca *Mexico* 20°17'N 102°34'W **86 C4**

La Barge U.S.A. 42°16N 110°12W 76 E8
La Barra Nic. 12°54N 83°33W 88 D3
La Belle U.S.A. 26°46N 81°26W 85 H14
La Biche → Canada 59°57N 123°50W 70 B4
La Biche, L. Canada 54°50N 112°3W 70 C6
La Brea Trin. & Tob. 10°15N 61°37W 93 K15
La Calera Chile 32°50S 71°10W 94 C1
La Campana △ Chile 32°58S 71°14W 94 C1
La Carlota Argentina 33°30S 63°20W 94 C3
La Ceiba Honduras 15°40N 86°50W 88 C2
La Chaux-de-Fonds Switz. 47°7N 6°50E 20 C7
La Chorrera Panama 8°53N 79°47W 88 E4
La Cocha Argentina 27°50S 65°40W 94 B2
La Concepción Panama 8°31N 82°37W 88 E3
La Concordia Mexico 16°5N 92°38W 87 D6
La Coruña = A Coruña Spain 43°20N 8°25W 21 A1
La Crescent U.S.A. 43°50N 91°18W 80 D8
La Crete Canada 58°11N 116°24W 70 B5
La Crosse Kans., U.S.A. 38°32N 99°18W 80 F4
La Crosse Wis., U.S.A. 43°48N 91°15W 80 D8
La Cruz Costa Rica 11°4N 85°39W 88 D2
La Cruz Mexico 23°55N 106°54W 86 C3
La Désirade Guadeloupe 16°18N 61°3W 88 b
La Digue Seychelles 4°20S 55°51E 55 b
La Esperanza Cuba 22°46N 83°44W 88 B3
La Esperanza Honduras 14°15N 88°10W 88 D2
La Estrada = A Estrada Spain 42°43N 8°27W 21 A1
La Fayette U.S.A. 34°42N 85°17W 85 D12
La Fé Cuba 22°2N 84°15W 88 B3
La Follette U.S.A. 36°23N 84°7W 85 C12
La Gi Vietnam 10°40N 107°45E 39 G6
La Grande U.S.A. 45°20N 118°5W 76 D4
La Grande → Canada 53°50N 79°0W 72 B5
La Grande 3, Rés. Canada 53°40N 75°10W 72 B4
La Grande 4, Rés. Canada 54°0N 73°15W 72 B5
La Grange Calif., U.S.A. 37°42N 120°27W 78 H6
La Grange Ga., U.S.A. 33°2N 85°2W 85 E12
La Grange Ky., U.S.A. 38°24N 85°22W 81 F11
La Grange Tex., U.S.A. 29°54N 96°52W 84 G6
La Guaira Venezuela 10°36N 66°56W 92 A5
La Guarda △ Mexico 29°20N 113°27W 86 B2
La Habana Cuba 23°8N 82°22W 88 B3
La Independencia Mexico 16°15N 92°1W 87 D6
La Isabela Dom. Rep. 19°58N 71°2W 89 C5
La Junta U.S.A. 37°59N 103°33W 76 H12
La Libertad = Puerto Libertad Mexico 29°55N 112°43W 86 B2
La Libertad Guatemala 16°47N 90°7W 88 C1
La Ligua Chile 32°30S 71°16W 94 C1
La Línea de la Concepción Spain 36°15N 5°23W 21 D3
La Loche Canada 56°29N 109°26W 71 B7
La Louvière Belgium 50°27N 4°10E 15 D4
La Lune Trin. & Tob. 10°3N 61°22W 93 K15
La Malbaie Canada 47°40N 70°10W 73 C5
La Malinche △ Mexico 19°15N 98°3W 87 D5
La Mancha Spain 39°10N 2°54W 21 C4
La Martre, L. Canada 63°15N 117°55W 70 A5
La Mercy ✕ (DUR) S. Africa 29°37S 31°7E 57 C5
La Mesa Mexico 32°30N 116°57W 79 N10
La Mesa U.S.A. 32°46N 117°1W 79 N9
La Mesilla U.S.A. 32°16N 106°48W 77 K10
La Moure U.S.A. 46°21N 98°18W 80 B4
La Negra Chile 23°46S 70°18W 94 A1
La Oroya Peru 11°32S 75°54W 92 F3
La Palma Canary Is. 28°40N 17°50W 52 C2
La Palma Panama 8°15N 78°0W 88 E4
La Palma del Condado Spain 37°21N 6°38W 21 D2
La Paloma Chile 30°35S 71°0W 94 C1
La Pampa □ Argentina 36°50S 66°0W 94 D2
La Paragua Venezuela 6°50N 63°20W 92 B6
La Paz Entre Ríos, Argentina 30°50S 59°45W 94 C4
La Paz San Luis, Argentina 33°30S 67°20W 94 C2
La Paz Bolivia 16°20S 68°10W 92 G5
La Paz Honduras 14°20N 87°47W 88 D2
La Paz Mexico 24°10N 110°18W 86 C2
La Paz Centro Nic. 12°20N 86°41W 88 D2
La Pedrera Colombia 1°18S 69°43W 92 D5
La Pérade Canada 46°35N 72°12W 73 C5
La Perla Mexico 28°18N 104°32W 86 B4
La Perouse Str. Asia 45°40N 142°0E 28 B11
La Pesca Mexico 23°46N 97°47W 87 C5
La Piedad Mexico 20°21N 102°0W 86 C4
La Pine U.S.A. 43°40N 121°30W 76 E3
La Plata Argentina 35°0S 57°55W 94 C4
La Pocatière Canada 47°22N 70°2W 73 C5
La Porte U.S.A. 29°40N 95°1W 84 G7
La Purísima Mexico 26°10N 112°4W 86 B2
La Push U.S.A. 47°55N 124°38W 78 C2
La Quiaca Argentina 22°5S 65°35W 94 A2
La Rioja Argentina 29°20S 67°0W 94 B2
La Rioja □ Argentina 29°30S 67°0W 94 B2
La Rioja □ Spain 42°20N 2°20W 21 A4
La Robla Spain 42°50N 5°41W 21 A3
La Roche-en-Ardenne Belgium 50°11N 5°35E 15 D5
La Roche-sur-Yon France 46°40N 1°25W 20 C3
La Rochelle France 46°10N 1°9W 20 C3
La Roda Spain 39°13N 2°15W 21 C4
La Romaine Canada 50°13N 60°40W 73 B7
La Romana Dom. Rep. 18°27N 68°57W 89 C6
La Ronge Canada 55°5N 105°20W 71 B7
La Rumorosa Mexico 32°34N 116°6W 79 N10
La Salle U.S.A. 41°20N 89°6W 80 E9
La Sarre Canada 48°45N 79°15W 72 C4
La Scie Canada 49°57N 55°36W 73 C8
La Selva Beach U.S.A. 36°56N 121°51W 78 J5
La Serena Chile 29°55S 71°10W 94 B1
La Seu d'Urgell Spain 42°22N 1°23E 21 A6
La Seyne-sur-Mer France 43°7N 5°52E 20 E6
La Soufrière St. Vincent 13°20N 61°11W 89 D7
La Spézia Italy 44°7N 9°50E 20 D8
La Tagua Colombia 0°3N 74°40W 92 C4
La Tortuga, I. Venezuela 11°0N 65°22W 89 D6
La Trinité Martinique 14°45N 60°58W 88 c
La Tuque Canada 47°30N 72°50W 72 C5
La Unión Chile 40°10S 73°0W 96 E2
La Unión El Salv. 13°20N 87°50W 88 D2
La Unión Mexico 17°58N 101°49W 86 D4
La Urbana Venezuela 7°8N 66°56W 92 B5
La Vache Pt. Trin. & Tob. 10°47N 61°28W 93 K15
La Vall d'Uixó Spain 39°49N 0°15W 21 C5
La Vega Dom. Rep. 19°20N 70°30W 89 C5
La Vela de Coro Venezuela 11°27N 69°34W 92 A5
La Venta Mexico 18°5N 94°3W 87 D6
La Vergne U.S.A. 36°1N 86°35W 85 C11
La Villa Joiosa = Villajoyosa Spain 38°30N 0°12W 21 C5
Laascaanood = Las Anod Somalia 8°26N 47°19E 49 F4
Labasa Fiji 16°30S 179°27E 59 a
Labdah = Leptis Magna Libya 32°40N 14°12E 53 B8
Labe = Elbe → Europe 53°50N 9°0E 16 B5
Labé Guinea 11°24N 12°16W 52 F3
Laberge, L. Canada 61°11N 135°12W 70 A1
Labinsk Russia 44°40N 40°48E 19 F7
Labis Malaysia 2°22N 103°2E 39 L4
Laborie St. Lucia 13°45N 61°2W 89 f
Laboulaye Argentina 34°10S 63°30W 94 C3
Labrador Canada 53°20N 61°0W 73 B7
Labrador City Canada 52°57N 66°55W 73 B6
Labrador Sea Atl. Oc. 57°0N 54°0W 69 F21
Lábrea Brazil 7°15S 64°51W 92 E6
Labuan □ Malaysia 5°20N 115°12E 36 C4
Labuha Indonesia 0°30S 127°30E 37 E7
Labuhan Indonesia 6°22S 105°50E 37 G11
Labuhanbajo Indonesia 8°28S 119°54E 37 F6
Labuhanbilik Indonesia 2°31N 100°10E 39 L3
Labuk, Telok Malaysia 6°10N 117°50E 36 C5
Labyrinth, L. Australia 30°40S 135°11E 63 E2
Labytnangi Russia 66°39N 66°21E 18 A12
Lac-Bouchette Canada 48°16N 72°11W 73 C5
Lac-Édouard Canada 47°40N 72°16W 73 C5
Lac La Biche Canada 54°45N 111°58W 70 C6
Lac la Martre = Wha Ti Canada 63°8N 117°16W 68 E8
Lac La Ronge ⌓ Canada 55°9N 104°41W 71 B7
Lac-Mégantic Canada 45°35N 70°53W 73 C5
Lac Thien Vietnam 12°25N 108°11E 38 F7
Lacanau France 44°58N 1°5W 20 D3
Lacantún → Mexico 16°36N 90°39W 87 D6
Laccadive Is. = Lakshadweep Is. India 10°0N 72°30E 45 J1
Lacepede B. Australia 36°40S 139°40E 63 F2
Lacepede Is. Australia 16°55S 122°0E 60 C3
Lacey U.S.A. 47°7N 122°49W 78 C4
Lachhmangarh India 27°50N 75°4E 42 F6
Lachi Pakistan 33°25N 71°20E 42 C4
Lachlan → Australia 34°22S 143°55E 63 E3
Lachute Canada 45°39N 74°21W 72 C5
Lackagh Hills Ireland 54°16N 8°10W 10 B3
Lackawanna U.S.A. 42°50N 78°50W 82 D6
Lackawaxen U.S.A. 41°29N 74°59W 83 E10
Lacolle Canada 45°5N 73°22W 83 A11
Lacombe Canada 52°30N 113°44W 70 C6
Lacona U.S.A. 43°39N 76°10W 83 C8
Laconia U.S.A. 43°32N 71°28W 83 C13
Ladakh Ra. India 34°0N 78°0E 43 C8
Ladismith S. Africa 33°28S 21°15E 56 D3
Lādīz Iran 28°55N 61°15E 47 D9
Ladnun India 27°38N 74°25E 42 F6
Ladoga, L. = Ladozhskoye Ozero Russia 61°15N 30°30E 8 F24
Ladozhskoye Ozero Russia 61°15N 30°30E 8 F24
Lady Elliott I. Australia 24°7S 152°42E 62 C5
Lady Frere S. Africa 31°42S 27°14E 56 D4
Lady Grey S. Africa 30°43S 27°13E 56 D4
Ladybrand S. Africa 29°9S 27°29E 56 C4
Ladysmith Canada 49°0N 123°49W 78 B3
Ladysmith S. Africa 28°32S 29°46E 57 C4
Ladysmith U.S.A. 45°28N 91°12W 80 C8
Lae Papua N. G. 6°40S 147°2E 58 B7
Laem Chabang Thailand 13°5N 100°53E 38 F3
Laem Ngop Thailand 12°10N 102°26E 39 F4
Laem Son △ Thailand 9°29N 98°24E 39 H2
Læsø Denmark 57°15N 11°5E 9 H14
Lafayette Ind., U.S.A. 40°25N 86°54W 80 E10
Lafayette La., U.S.A. 30°14N 92°1W 84 F8
Lafayette Tenn., U.S.A. 36°31N 86°2W 85 C11
Laferte → Canada 61°53N 117°44W 70 A5
Lafia Nigeria 8°30N 8°34E 52 G7
Lafleche Canada 49°45N 106°40W 71 D7
Laful India 7°10N 93°52E 45 L11
Lagan → U.K. 54°36N 5°55W 10 B6
Lagarfljót → Iceland 65°40N 14°18W 8 D6
Lagdo, L. de Cameroon 8°40N 14°0E 53 G8
Lågen → Oppland, Norway 61°8N 10°25E 8 F14
Lågen → Vestfold, Norway 59°3N 10°3E 9 G14
Lages Brazil 27°48S 50°20W 95 B5
Laghouat Algeria 33°50N 2°59E 52 B6
Lagoa do Peixe △ Brazil 31°12S 50°55W 95 C5
Lagoa Vermelha Brazil 28°13S 51°32W 95 B5
Lagonoy G. Phil. 13°35N 123°50E 37 B6
Lagos Portugal 37°5N 8°41W 21 D1
Lagos de Moreno Mexico 21°21N 101°55W 86 C4
Lagrange = Bidyadanga Australia 18°45S 121°43E 60 C3
Lagrange B. Australia 18°38S 121°42E 60 C3
Laguna Brazil 28°30S 48°50W 95 B6
Laguna U.S.A. 35°2N 107°25W 77 J10
Laguna, Sa. de la Mexico 23°35N 109°55W 86 C3
Laguna Beach U.S.A. 33°33N 117°47W 79 M9
Laguna de la Restinga △ Venezuela 10°58N 64°0W 89 D6
Laguna de Lachuá △ Guatemala 15°55N 90°40W 88 C1
Laguna del Laja △ Chile 37°27S 71°20W 94 D1
Laguna del Tigre △ Guatemala 17°32N 90°56W 88 C1
Laguna Limpia Argentina 26°32S 59°45W 94 B4
Lagunas Chile 21°0S 69°45W 94 A2
Lagunas Peru 5°10S 75°35W 92 E3
Lagunas de Chacahua △ Mexico 16°0N 97°43W 87 D5
Lagunas de Montebello △ Mexico 16°4N 91°42W 87 D6
Lahad Datu Malaysia 5°0N 118°20E 37 D5
Lahad Datu, Telok Malaysia 4°50N 118°20E 37 D5
Lahan Sai Thailand 14°25N 102°52E 38 E4
Lahanam Laos 16°16N 105°16E 38 D5
Lahar India 26°12N 78°57E 43 F8
Laharpur India 27°43N 80°56E 43 F9
Lahat Indonesia 3°45S 103°30E 36 E2
Lahewa Indonesia 1°22N 97°12E 36 D1
Lāhījān Iran 37°10N 50°6E 47 B6
Lahn → Germany 50°19N 7°37E 16 C4
Laholm Sweden 56°30N 13°2E 9 H15
Lahore Pakistan 31°32N 74°22E 42 D6
Lahri Pakistan 29°11N 68°13E 42 E3
Lāhrūd Iran 38°30N 47°52E 46 B5
Lahti Finland 60°58N 25°40E 8 F21
Lahtis = Lahti Finland 60°58N 25°40E 8 F21
Lahugala Kitulana △ Sri Lanka 6°50N 81°40E 45 L5
Laï Chad 9°25N 16°18E 53 G9
Lai Chau Vietnam 22°5N 103°3E 34 F4
Lai'an China 32°28N 118°30E 35 A12
Laibin China 23°42N 109°14E 34 F7
Laifeng China 29°27N 109°20E 34 C7
Laila = Layla Si. Arabia 22°10N 46°40E 49 C4
Laingsburg S. Africa 33°9S 20°52E 56 D3
Lainioälven → Sweden 67°35N 22°40E 8 C20
Lairg U.K. 58°2N 4°24W 11 C4
Laiwu China 36°15N 117°40E 33 F9
Laixi China 36°50N 120°31E 33 F11
Laiyang China 36°59N 120°45E 33 F11
Laiyuan China 39°20N 114°40E 32 E8
Laizhou China 37°8N 119°57E 33 F10
Laizhou Wan China 37°30N 119°30E 33 F10
Lajamanu Australia 18°23S 130°38E 60 C5
Lak Sao Laos 18°11N 104°59E 38 C5
Lakaband Pakistan 31°2N 69°15E 42 D3
Lake U.S.A. 44°33N 110°24W 76 D8
Lake Alpine U.S.A. 38°29N 120°0W 78 G7
Lake Andes U.S.A. 43°9N 98°32W 80 D4
Lake Arthur U.S.A. 30°5N 92°41W 84 F8
Lake Bindegolly △ Australia 28°0S 144°12E 63 D3
Lake Cargelligo Australia 33°15S 146°22E 63 E4
Lake Charles U.S.A. 30°14N 93°13W 84 F8
Lake City Colo., U.S.A. 38°2N 107°19W 76 G10
Lake City Fla., U.S.A. 30°11N 82°38W 85 F13
Lake City Mich., U.S.A. 44°20N 85°13W 81 C11
Lake City Minn., U.S.A. 44°27N 92°16W 80 C7
Lake City Pa., U.S.A. 42°1N 80°21W 82 D4
Lake City S.C., U.S.A. 33°52N 79°45W 85 E15
Lake Cowichan Canada 48°49N 124°3W 70 D4
Lake District △ U.K. 54°30N 3°21W 12 C4
Lake Elsinore U.S.A. 33°38N 117°20W 79 M9
Lake Eyre △ Australia 28°40S 137°31E 63 D2
Lake Gairdner △ Australia 31°41S 135°51E 63 E2
Lake George U.S.A. 43°26N 73°43W 83 C11
Lake Grace Australia 33°7S 118°28E 61 F2
Lake Gregory ☼ Australia 20°12S 127°27E 60 D4
Lake Harbour = Kimmirut Canada 62°50N 69°50W 69 E18
Lake Havasu City U.S.A. 34°27N 114°22W 79 L12
Lake Hughes U.S.A. 34°41N 118°26W 79 L8
Lake Isabella U.S.A. 35°38N 118°28W 79 K8
Lake Jackson U.S.A. 29°3N 95°27W 84 G7
Lake King Australia 33°5S 119°45E 61 F2
Lake Lenore Canada 52°24N 104°59W 71 C8
Lake Louise Canada 51°30N 116°10W 70 C5
Lake Mackay ☼ Australia 21°48S 129°46E 60 D4
Lake Mead ⌓ U.S.A. 36°30N 114°22W 79 K12
Lake Meredith ⌓ U.S.A. 35°50N 101°50W 84 D4
Lake Mills U.S.A. 43°25N 93°32W 80 D7
Lake Placid U.S.A. 44°17N 73°59W 83 B11
Lake Pleasant U.S.A. 43°28N 74°25W 83 C10
Lake Providence U.S.A. 32°48N 91°10W 84 E9
Lake Roosevelt ⌓ U.S.A. 48°5N 118°14W 76 B4
Lake St. Peter Canada 45°18N 78°2W 82 A6
Lake Stevens U.S.A. 48°1N 122°4W 78 B4
Lake Superior ⌓ Canada 47°45N 84°45W 72 C3
Lake Torrens △ Australia 30°55S 137°40E 63 E2
Lake Village U.S.A. 33°20N 91°17W 84 E9
Lake Wales U.S.A. 27°54N 81°35W 85 H14
Lake Worth U.S.A. 26°37N 80°3W 85 H14
Lakeba Fiji 18°13S 178°47W 59 a
Lakeba Passage Fiji 18°0S 178°45W 59 a
Lakefield = Rinyirru △ Australia 15°24S 144°26E 62 B3
Lakefield Canada 44°25N 78°16W 82 B6
Lakehurst U.S.A. 40°1N 74°19W 83 F10
Lakeland Australia 15°49S 144°57E 62 B3
Lakeland U.S.A. 28°3N 81°57W 85 G14
Lakemba = Lakeba Fiji 18°13S 178°47W 59 a
Lakeport Calif., U.S.A. 39°3N 122°55W 78 F4
Lakeport Mich., U.S.A. 43°7N 82°30W 82 C2
Lakes Entrance Australia 37°50S 148°0E 63 F4
Lakeside Calif., U.S.A. 32°52N 116°55W 79 N10
Lakeside Nebr., U.S.A. 42°3N 102°26W 80 D2
Lakeview U.S.A. 42°11N 120°21W 76 E3
Lakeville U.S.A. 44°39N 93°14W 80 C7
Lakewood Colo., U.S.A. 39°42N 105°4W 76 G11
Lakewood N.J., U.S.A. 40°6N 74°13W 83 F10
Lakewood N.Y., U.S.A. 42°6N 79°19W 82 D5
Lakewood Ohio, U.S.A. 41°28N 81°47W 82 E3
Lakewood Wash., U.S.A. 47°11N 122°32W 78 C4
Lakha India 26°9N 70°54E 42 F4
Lakhimpur India 27°57N 80°46E 43 F9
Lakhisarai India 25°11N 86°5E 43 G12
Lakhnadon India 22°36N 79°36E 43 H8
Lakhnau = Lucknow India 26°50N 81°0E 43 F9
Lakhonpheng Laos 15°54N 105°34E 38 E5
Lakhpat India 23°48N 68°47E 42 H3
Lakin U.S.A. 37°57N 101°15W 80 G3
Lakitusaki → Canada 54°21N 82°25W 72 B3
Lakki Pakistan 32°36N 70°55E 42 C4
Lakonikos Kolpos Greece 36°40N 22°40E 23 F10
Lakor Indonesia 8°15S 128°17E 37 F7
Lakota Ivory C. 5°50N 5°30W 52 G4
Lakota U.S.A. 48°2N 98°21W 80 A4
Laksar India 29°46N 78°3E 42 E8
Laksefjorden Norway 70°45N 26°50E 8 A22
Lakselv Norway 70°2N 25°0E 8 A21
Laksettipet India 18°52N 79°13E 44 E4
Lakshadweep □ India 10°0N 72°30E 45 J1
Lakshadweep Is. India 10°0N 72°30E 45 J1
Lakshmanpur India 22°58N 83°3E 43 H10
Lakshmeshwar India 15°9N 75°28E 45 G2
Lakshmikantapur India 22°5N 88°20E 43 H13
Lala Musa Pakistan 32°40N 73°57E 42 C5
Lalaghat India 24°30N 92°40E 41 G18
L'Albufera Spain 39°20N 0°27W 21 C5
Lalganj India 25°52N 85°13E 43 G11
Lalgola India 24°25N 88°15E 43 G13
Lālī Iran 32°21N 49°6E 47 C6
Lalibela Ethiopia 12°3N 39°0E 49 E2
Lalin China 45°12N 127°0E 33 B14
Lalín Spain 42°40N 8°5W 21 A1
Lalin He → China 45°32N 125°40E 33 B13
Lalitpur India 24°42N 78°28E 43 G8
Lalitpur Nepal 27°40N 85°20E 43 F11
Lalkua India 29°5N 79°31E 43 E8
Lalsot India 26°34N 76°20E 42 F7
Lam Nam Nan △ Thailand 17°55N 100°28E 38 D3
Lam Pao Res. Thailand 16°50N 103°15E 38 D4
Lama Kara Togo 9°30N 1°15E 52 G6
Lamae Thailand 9°51N 99°5E 39 H2
Lamaing Burma 15°25N 97°53E 38 E1
Lamar Colo., U.S.A. 38°5N 102°37W 76 G12
Lamar Mo., U.S.A. 37°30N 94°16W 80 G6
Lamas Peru 6°28S 76°31W 92 E3
Lamayuru India 34°25N 76°56E 43 B7
Lambaréné Gabon 0°41S 10°12E 54 E2
Lambasa = Labasa Fiji 16°30S 179°27E 59 a
Lambay I. Ireland 53°29N 6°1W 10 C5
Lambert's Bay S. Africa 32°5S 18°17E 56 D2
Lambeth Canada 42°54N 81°18W 82 D3
Lame Deer U.S.A. 45°37N 106°40W 76 D10
Lamego Portugal 41°5N 7°52W 21 B2
Lamèque Canada 47°45N 64°38W 73 C7
Lameroo Australia 35°19S 140°33E 63 F3
Lamesa U.S.A. 32°44N 101°58W 84 E4
Lamia Greece 38°55N 22°26E 23 E10
Lamington △ Australia 28°13S 153°12E 63 D5
Lammermuir Hills U.K. 55°50N 2°40W 11 F6
Lamoille → U.S.A. 44°38N 73°13W 83 B11
Lamon B. Phil. 14°30N 122°20E 37 B6
Lamont Canada 53°46N 112°50W 70 C6
Lamont Calif., U.S.A. 35°15N 118°55W 79 K8
Lamont Wyo., U.S.A. 42°13N 107°29W 76 E10
Lampa Peru 15°22S 70°22W 92 G4
Lampang Thailand 18°16N 99°32E 38 C2
Lampasas U.S.A. 31°4N 98°11W 84 F5
Lampazos de Naranjo Mexico 27°1N 100°31W 86 B4
Lampedusa Medit. S. 35°36N 12°40E 22 G5
Lampeter U.K. 52°7N 4°4W 13 E3
Lamphun Thailand 18°40N 99°2E 38 C2
Lampione Medit. S. 35°33N 12°20E 22 G5
Lampman Canada 49°25N 102°50W 71 D8
Lampung □ Indonesia 5°30S 104°30E 36 F2
Lamta India 22°8N 80°7E 43 H9
Lamu Kenya 2°16S 40°55E 54 E8
Lamy U.S.A. 35°29N 105°53W 77 J11
Lan Xian China 38°15N 111°35E 32 E6
Lan Yü Taiwan 22°4N 121°25E 35 F13
Lāna'i U.S.A. 20°50N 156°55W 75 L8
Lanak La China 34°27N 79°32E 43 B8
Lanak'o Shank'ou = Lanak La China 34°27N 79°32E 43 B8
Lanark Canada 45°1N 76°22W 83 A8
Lanark U.K. 55°40N 3°47W 11 F5
Lanbi Kyun Burma 10°50N 98°20E 39 G2
Lancang China 22°36N 99°58E 34 F2
Lancang Jiang → China 21°40N 101°10E 34 G3
Lancashire □ U.K. 53°50N 2°48W 12 D5
Lancaster Canada 45°10N 74°30W 83 A10
Lancaster U.K. 54°3N 2°48W 12 C5
Lancaster Calif., U.S.A. 34°42N 118°8W 79 L8
Lancaster Ky., U.S.A. 37°37N 84°35W 81 G11
Lancaster N.H., U.S.A. 44°29N 71°34W 83 B13
Lancaster Ohio, U.S.A. 39°43N 82°36W 81 F12
Lancaster Pa., U.S.A. 40°2N 76°19W 83 F8
Lancaster S.C., U.S.A. 34°43N 80°46W 85 D14
Lancaster Wis., U.S.A. 42°51N 90°43W 80 D8
Lancaster Sd. Canada 74°13N 84°0W 69 C15
Lancelin Australia 31°0S 115°18E 61 F2
Lanchow = Lanzhou China 36°1N 103°52E 32 F2
Lanciano Italy 42°14N 14°23E 22 C6
Lancun China 36°25N 120°10E 33 F11
Land Between the Lakes ⌓ U.S.A. 36°25N 88°0W 85 C11
Landeck Austria 47°9N 10°34E 16 E6
Lander U.S.A. 42°50N 108°44W 76 E9
Lander → Australia 22°0S 132°0E 60 D5
Landes France 44°0N 1°0W 20 D3
Landfall I. India 13°40N 93°2E 45 H11
Landi Kotal Pakistan 34°7N 71°6E 42 B4
Landisburg U.S.A. 40°21N 77°19W 82 F7
Landmannalaugar Iceland 63°59N 19°4W 8 E4
Land's End U.K. 50°4N 5°44W 13 G2
Landsborough Cr. → Australia 22°28S 144°35E 62 C3
Landshut Germany 48°34N 12°8E 16 D7
Lanesboro U.S.A. 41°57N 75°34W 83 E9
Lanett U.S.A. 32°52N 85°12W 85 E12
Lang Shan China 41°0N 106°30E 32 D4
Lang Son Vietnam 21°52N 106°42E 34 G6
Lang Suan Thailand 9°57N 99°4E 39 H2
La'nga Co China 30°45N 81°15E 43 D9
Langar Iran 35°23N 60°25E 47 C9
Langara I. Canada 54°14N 133°1W 70 C2
Langarūd Iran 37°11N 50°8E 47 B6
Langdai China 26°6N 105°21E 34 D5
Langdon U.S.A. 48°45N 98°22W 80 A4
Langeberg S. Africa 33°55S 21°0E 56 D3
Langeberge S. Africa 28°15S 22°33E 56 C3
Langeland Denmark 54°56N 10°48E 9 J14
Langenburg Canada 50°51N 101°43W 71 C8
Langfang China 39°30N 116°41E 32 E9
Langholm U.K. 55°9N 3°0W 11 F5
Langjökull Iceland 64°39N 20°12W 8 D3
Langkawi, Pulau Malaysia 6°25N 99°45E 39 J2
Langklip S. Africa 28°12S 20°20E 56 C3
Langkon Malaysia 6°30N 116°40E 36 C5
Langley Canada 49°7N 122°39W 78 A4
Langøya Norway 68°45N 14°50E 8 B16
Langreo Spain 43°18N 5°40W 21 A3
Langres France 47°52N 5°20E 20 C6
Langres, Plateau de France 47°45N 5°3E 20 C6
Langsa Indonesia 4°30N 97°57E 36 D1
Langtang △ Nepal 28°10N 85°30E 43 E11
Langtou China 40°1N 124°19E 33 D13
Langtry U.S.A. 29°49N 101°34W 84 G4
Langu Thailand 6°53N 99°47E 39 J2
Languedoc France 43°58N 3°55E 20 E5
Langwang China 22°38N 113°27E 31 a
Langxi China 31°10N 119°12E 35 B12
Langzhong China 31°38N 105°58E 34 B5
Lanigan Canada 51°51N 105°2W 71 C7
Lanjigarh India 19°43N 83°23E 44 E6
Lankao China 34°48N 114°50E 32 G8
Länkäran Azerbaijan 38°48N 48°52E 47 B6
Lannion France 48°46N 3°29W 20 B2
L'Annonciation Canada 46°25N 74°55W 72 C5
Lanping China 26°28N 99°15E 34 D2
Lansang △ Thailand 16°45N 99°0E 38 D2
Lansdale U.S.A. 40°14N 75°17W 83 F9
Lansdowne Australia 31°48S 152°30E 63 E5
Lansdowne Canada 44°24N 76°1W 83 B8
Lansdowne India 29°50N 78°41E 43 E8
Lansdowne House = Neskantaga Canada 52°14N 87°53W 72 B2
L'Anse U.S.A. 46°45N 88°27W 80 B9
L'Anse au Loup Canada 51°32N 56°50W 73 B8
L'Anse aux Meadows Canada 51°36N 55°32W 73 B8
Lansford U.S.A. 40°50N 75°53W 83 F9
Lanshan China 25°24N 112°10E 35 E9
Lanshantou China 35°5N 119°20E 33 G10
Länsi-Turunmaa Finland 60°18N 22°18E 9 F20
Lansing U.S.A. 42°44N 84°33W 81 D11
Lanta, Ko Thailand 7°35N 99°3E 39 J2
Lantian China 34°11N 109°20E 32 G5
Lanusei Italy 39°52N 9°34E 22 E3
Lanxi China 29°13N 119°28E 35 C12
Lanzarote Canary Is. 29°0N 13°40W 52 C3
Lanzhou China 36°1N 103°52E 32 F2
Lao Cai Vietnam 22°30N 103°57E 34 F4
Laoag Phil. 18°7N 120°34E 37 A6
Laoang Phil. 12°32N 125°8E 37 B7
Laoha He → China 43°25N 120°35E 33 C11
Laohekou China 32°22N 111°38E 35 A8
Laois □ Ireland 52°57N 7°27W 10 D4
Laon France 49°33N 3°35E 20 B5
Laona U.S.A. 45°34N 88°40W 80 C9
Laos ■ Asia 17°45N 105°0E 38 D5
Lapa Brazil 25°46S 49°44W 95 B6
Lapeer U.S.A. 43°3N 83°19W 81 D12
Lapland = Lappland Europe 68°7N 24°0E 8 B21
LaPorte Ind., U.S.A. 41°36N 86°43W 80 E10
Laporte Pa., U.S.A. 41°25N 76°30W 83 E8
Lappeenranta Finland 61°3N 28°12E 8 F23
Lappland Europe 68°7N 24°0E 8 B21
Lappo = Lapua Finland 62°58N 23°0E 8 E20
Laprida Argentina 37°34S 60°45W 94 D3
Lâpseki Turkey 40°20N 26°41E 23 D12
Laptev Sea Russia 76°0N 125°0E 27 B13
Lapua Finland 62°58N 23°0E 8 E20
L'Aquila Italy 42°22N 13°22E 22 C5
Lār Iran 27°40N 54°14E 47 E7
Lārak Iran 26°51N 56°21E 47 E8
Laramie U.S.A. 41°19N 105°35W 76 F11
Laramie Mts. U.S.A. 42°0N 105°30W 76 F11
Laranda = Karaman Turkey 37°14N 33°13E 46 B2
Laranjeiras do Sul Brazil 25°23S 52°23W 95 B5
Larantuka Indonesia 8°21S 122°55E 37 F6
Larat Indonesia 7°0S 132°0E 37 F8
Larder Lake Canada 48°5N 79°40W 72 C4
Laredo U.S.A. 27°30N 99°30W 84 H5
Laredo Sd. Canada 52°30N 128°53W 70 C3
Largo U.S.A. 27°54N 82°47W 85 H13
Largs U.K. 55°47N 4°52W 11 F4
Lariang Indonesia 1°26S 119°17E 37 E5
Larimore U.S.A. 47°54N 97°38W 80 B5
Lario, Il = Como, L. di Italy 46°0N 9°11E 20 D8
Larisa Greece 39°36N 22°27E 23 E10
Larkana Pakistan 27°32N 68°2E 42 F3
Larnaca Cyprus 34°55N 33°38E 46 C2
Larne U.K. 54°51N 5°51W 10 B6
Larned U.S.A. 38°11N 99°6W 80 F4
Larose U.S.A. 29°34N 90°23W 85 G9
Larrimah Australia 15°35S 133°12E 60 C5
Larsen Ice Shelf Antarctica 67°0S 62°0W 5 C17
Larvik Norway 59°4N 10°2E 9 G14
Las Animas U.S.A. 38°4N 103°13W 76 G12
Las Anod Somalia 8°26N 47°19E 49 F4
Las Brenãs Argentina 27°5S 61°7W 94 B3
Las Cejas Argentina 26°53S 64°44W 94 B3
Las Cejas Argentina 26°53S 64°44W 96 B4
Las Chimeneas Mexico 32°8N 116°5W 79 N10
Las Cruces U.S.A. 32°19N 106°47W 77 K10
Las Flores Argentina 36°10S 59°7W 94 D4
Las Heras Argentina 32°51S 68°49W 94 C2

Las Lajas *Argentina* 38°30S 70°25W **96** D2
Las Lomitas *Argentina* 24°43S 60°35W **94** A3
Las Palmas *Argentina* 27°8S 58°45W **94** B4
Las Palmas ➤ *Mexico* 32°31N 116°58W **79** N10
Las Palmas de Gran Canaria
  Canary Is. 28°7N 15°26W **52** C2
Las Piedras *Uruguay* 34°44S 56°14W **95** C4
Las Pipinas *Argentina* 35°30S 57°19W **94** D4
Las Plumas *Argentina* 43°40S 67°15W **96** E3
Las Rosas *Argentina* 32°30S 61°35W **94** C3
Las Tablas *Panama* 7°49N 80°14W **88** E3
Las Toscas *Argentina* 28°21S 59°18W **94** B4
Las Tunas *Cuba* 20°58N 76°59W **88** B4
Las Varillas *Argentina* 31°50S 62°50W **94** C3
Las Vegas *U.S.A.* 36°10N 115°9W **77** J11
Lascano *Uruguay* 33°35S 54°12W **95** C5
Lash-e Joveyn *Afghan.* 31°45N 61°30E **40** D2
Lashburn *Canada* 53°10N 109°40W **71** C7
Lashio *Burma* 22°56N 97°45E **41** H20
Lashkar *India* 26°10N 78°10E **42** F8
Lāsjerd *Iran* 35°24N 53°4E **47** C7
Lassen Pk. *U.S.A.* 40°29N 121°30W **76** F3
Lassen Volcanic △
  U.S.A. 40°30N 121°20W **76** F3
Last Mountain L. *Canada* 51°5N 105°14W **71** C7
Lastchance Cr. ➤
  U.S.A. 40°2N 121°15W **78** E5
Lastoursville *Gabon* 0°55S 12°38E **54** E2
Lastovo *Croatia* 42°46N 16°55E **22** C7
Lat Yao *Thailand* 15°45N 99°48E **38** E2
Latacunga *Ecuador* 0°50S 78°35W **92** D3
Latady I. *Antarctica* 70°45S 74°35W **5** D17
Latakia = Al Lādhiqīyah
  Syria 35°30N 35°45E **46** C2
Latchford *Canada* 47°20N 79°50W **72** C4
Late *Tonga* 18°48S 174°39W **59** c
Latehar *India* 23°45N 84°30E **43** H11
Latham *Australia* 29°44S 116°20E **61** E2
Lathi *India* 27°43N 71°23E **42** F4
Lathrop Wells *U.S.A.* 36°39N 116°24W **79** J10
Latina *Italy* 41°28N 12°52E **22** D5
Latium = Lazio □ *Italy* 42°10N 12°30E **22** C5
Laton *U.S.A.* 36°26N 119°41W **78** J7
Latouche Treville, C.
  Australia 18°27S 121°49E **60** C3
Latrobe *Australia* 41°14S 146°30E **63** G4
Latrobe *U.S.A.* 40°19N 79°23W **82** F5
Latur *India* 18°25N 76°40E **44** E3
Latvia ■ *Europe* 56°50N 24°0E **9** H21
Lau Group *Fiji* 17°0S 178°30W **59** a
Lauchhammer *Germany* 51°29N 13°47E **16** C7
Lauge Koch Kyst
  Greenland 75°45N 57°45W **69** B20
Laughlin *U.S.A.* 35°10N 114°34W **79** K12
Lauhanvuori △ *Finland* 62°8N 22°4E **8** E20
Laukaa *Finland* 62°24N 25°56E **8** E21
Launceston *Australia* 41°24S 147°8E **63** G4
Launceston *U.K.* 50°38N 4°22W **13** G3
Laune ➤ *Ireland* 52°7N 9°47W **10** D2
Launglon Bok *Burma* 13°50N 97°54E **38** F1
Laura *Australia* 15°32S 144°32E **62** B3
Laurel *Miss., U.S.A.* 31°41N 89°8W **85** F10
Laurel *Mont., U.S.A.* 45°40N 108°46W **76** D9
Laurel Hill *U.S.A.* 40°14N 79°6W **82** F5
Laurencekirk *U.K.* 56°50N 2°28W **11** E6
Laurens *U.S.A.* 34°30N 82°1W **85** D13
Laurentian Plateau *Canada* 52°0N 70°0W **73** B6
Lauria *Italy* 40°2N 15°50E **22** E6
Laurie L. *Canada* 56°35N 101°57W **71** B8
Laurinburg *U.S.A.* 34°47N 79°28W **85** D15
Laurium *U.S.A.* 47°14N 88°27W **80** B9
Lausanne *Switz.* 46°32N 6°38E **20** C7
Laut *Indonesia* 4°45N 108°0E **36** D3
Laut, Pulau *Indonesia* 3°40S 116°10E **36** E5
Laut Kecil, Kepulauan
  Indonesia 4°45S 115°40E **36** E5
Lautoka *Fiji* 17°37S 177°27E **59** a
Lauwersmeer △ *Neths.* 53°22N 6°11E **15** A6
Lava Beds △ *U.S.A.* 41°40N 121°30W **76** F3
Lavagh More *Ireland* 54°46N 8°6W **10** B3
Laval *France* 48°4N 0°48W **20** B3
Lavalle *Argentina* 28°15S 65°15W **94** B2
Lāvān *Iran* 26°48S 53°22E **47** E7
Lavant *Canada* 45°3N 76°42W **83** A8
Lāvar Meydān *Iran* 30°20N 54°30E **47** D7
Laverton *Australia* 28°44S 122°29E **61** E3
Lavras *Brazil* 21°20S 45°0W **95** A7
Lavrio *Greece* 37°40N 24°4E **23** F11
Lavumisa *Swaziland* 27°20S 31°55E **57** C5
Lawas *Malaysia* 4°55N 115°25E **36** D5
Lawele *Indonesia* 5°13S 122°57E **37** F6
Lawn Hill = Boodjamulla △
  Australia 18°15S 138°6E **62** B2
Lawqah *Si. Arabia* 29°49N 42°45E **46** D4
Lawrence *N.Z.* 45°55S 169°41E **59** F2
Lawrence *Ind., U.S.A.* 39°50N 86°2W **80** F10
Lawrence *Kans., U.S.A.* 38°58N 95°14W **80** F7
Lawrence *Mass., U.S.A.* 42°43N 71°10W **83** D13
Lawrenceburg *Ind.,
  U.S.A.* 39°6N 84°52W **81** F11
Lawrenceburg *Tenn.,
  U.S.A.* 35°14N 87°20W **85** D11
Lawrenceville *Ga.,
  U.S.A.* 33°57N 83°59W **85** E13
Lawrenceville *Pa., U.S.A.* 41°59N 77°8W **82** E7
Laws *U.S.A.* 37°24N 118°20W **78** H8
Lawton *U.S.A.* 34°37N 98°25W **84** H5
Lawu *Indonesia* 7°40S 111°13E **37** G14
Laxford, L. *U.K.* 58°24N 5°6W **11** C3
Laxiwa Dam *China* 36°4N 101°11E **30** D9
Layla *Si. Arabia* 22°10N 46°40E **49** C4
Laylān *Iraq* 35°18N 44°31E **46** C5
Laysan I. *U.S.A.* 25°50N 171°50W **75** K5
Layton *U.S.A.* 41°4N 111°58W **76** F8
Laytonville *U.S.A.* 39°41N 123°29W **76** G2
Lazarev *Russia* 52°13N 141°30E **27** D15
Lazarev Sea *S. Ocean* 76°0S 3°0W **5** C2

Lázaro Cárdenas
  Mexico 17°55N 102°11W **86** D4
Lazio □ *Italy* 42°10N 12°30E **22** C5
Lazo *Russia* 43°25N 133°55E **28** C6
Le Bic *Canada* 48°20N 68°41W **73** C6
Le Creusot *France* 46°48N 4°24E **20** C6
Le François *Martinique* 14°38N 60°57W **88** c
Le Gosier *Guadeloupe* 16°14N 61°29W **88** b
Le Gris Gris *Mauritius* 20°31S 57°32E **55** d
Le Havre *France* 49°30N 0°5E **20** B4
Le Lamentin *Martinique* 14°35N 61°2W **88** c
Le Mans *France* 48°0N 0°10E **20** C4
Le Marin *Martinique* 14°27N 60°55W **88** c
Le Mars *U.S.A.* 42°47N 96°10W **80** D5
Le Mont-St-Michel *France* 48°40N 1°30W **20** B3
Le Moule *Guadeloupe* 16°20N 61°22W **88** b
Le Moyne, L. *Canada* 56°45N 68°47W **73** A6
Le Port *Réunion* 20°56S 55°18E **55** c
Le Prêcheur *Martinique* 14°50N 61°12W **88** c
Le Puy-en-Velay *France* 45°3N 3°52E **20** D5
Le Raysville *U.S.A.* 41°50N 76°10W **83** E8
Le Robert *Martinique* 14°40N 60°56W **88** c
Le Roy *U.S.A.* 42°58N 77°59W **82** D7
Le St-Esprit *Martinique* 14°34N 60°56W **88** c
Le Sueur *U.S.A.* 44°28N 93°55W **80** C7
Le Tampon *Réunion* 21°16S 55°32E **55** c
Le Thuy *Vietnam* 17°14N 106°49E **38** D6
Le Touquet-Paris-Plage
  France 50°30N 1°36E **20** A4
Le Tréport *France* 50°3N 1°20E **20** A4
Le Verdon-sur-Mer *France* 45°33N 1°4W **20** D3
Lea ➤ *U.K.* 51°31N 0°1E **13** F8
Leach *Cambodia* 12°21N 103°46E **39** F4
Lead *U.S.A.* 44°21N 103°46W **80** C2
Leader *Canada* 50°50N 109°30W **71** C7
Leadville *U.S.A.* 39°15N 106°18W **76** G10
Leaf ➤ *U.S.A.* 30°59N 88°44W **85** F10
Leaf Rapids *Canada* 56°30N 99°59W **71** B9
League City *U.S.A.* 29°31N 95°6W **84** G7
Leamington *Canada* 42°3N 82°36W **82** D2
Leamington *U.S.A.* 39°32N 112°17W **76** G7
Leamington Spa = Royal
  Leamington Spa *U.K.* 52°18N 1°31W **13** E6
Le'an *China* 27°22N 115°48E **35** D10
Leander *U.S.A.* 30°34N 97°52W **84** F5
Leandro Norte Alem
  Argentina 27°34S 55°15W **95** B4
Leane, L. *Ireland* 52°2N 9°32W **10** D2
Learmonth *Australia* 22°13S 114°10E **60** D1
Leask *Canada* 53°5N 106°45W **71** C7
Leatherhead *U.K.* 51°18N 0°20W **13** F7
Leavdnjá = Lakselv *Norway* 70°2N 25°0E **8** A21
Leavenworth *Kans.,
  U.S.A.* 39°19N 94°55W **80** F6
Leavenworth *Wash.,
  U.S.A.* 47°36N 120°40W **76** C3
Leawood *U.S.A.* 38°58N 94°37W **80** F6
Lebak *Phil.* 6°32N 124°5E **37** C6
Lebam *U.S.A.* 46°34N 123°33W **78** D3
Lebanon *Ind., U.S.A.* 40°3N 86°28W **80** E10
Lebanon *Kans., U.S.A.* 39°49N 98°33W **80** F4
Lebanon *Ky., U.S.A.* 37°34N 85°15W **81** G11
Lebanon *Mo., U.S.A.* 37°41N 92°40W **80** G7
Lebanon *N.H., U.S.A.* 43°39N 72°15W **83** C12
Lebanon *Oreg., U.S.A.* 44°32N 122°55W **76** D2
Lebanon *Pa., U.S.A.* 40°20N 76°26W **83** F8
Lebanon *Tenn., U.S.A.* 36°12N 86°18W **85** C11
Lebanon ■ *Asia* 34°0N 36°0E **48** B5
Lebec *U.S.A.* 34°51N 118°52W **79** L8
Lebel-sur-Quévillon
  Canada 49°3N 76°59W **72** C4
Lebomboberge *S. Africa* 24°30S 32°0E **57** B5
Lebork *Poland* 54°33N 17°46E **17** A9
Lebowakgomo *S. Africa* 24°12S 29°30E **57** B4
Lebrija *Spain* 36°53N 6°5W **21** D2
Lebu *Chile* 37°40S 73°47W **94** D1
Lecce *Italy* 40°23N 18°11E **23** D8
Lecco *Italy* 45°51N 9°23E **20** D8
Lech ➤ *Germany* 48°43N 10°56E **16** D6
Lechang *China* 25°10N 113°20E **35** E9
Lecontes Mills *U.S.A.* 41°5N 78°17W **82** E6
Łęczyca *Poland* 52°5N 19°15E **17** B10
Ledang, Gunung
  Malaysia 2°22N 102°37E **39** L4
Ledong *China* 18°41N 109°5E **38** C7
Leduc *Canada* 53°15N 113°30W **70** C6
Lee ➤ *Ireland* 51°53N 8°56W **10** E3
Lee Vining *U.S.A.* 37°58N 119°7W **78** H7
Leech L. *U.S.A.* 47°10N 94°24W **80** B6
Leechburg *U.S.A.* 40°37N 79°36W **82** F5
Leeds *U.K.* 53°48N 1°33W **12** D6
Leeds *U.S.A.* 33°33N 86°33W **85** E11
Leek *Neths.* 53°10N 6°24E **15** A6
Leek *U.K.* 53°7N 2°1W **12** D5
Leeman *Australia* 29°57S 114°58E **61** E1
Leeper *U.S.A.* 41°22N 79°18W **82** E5
Leer *Germany* 53°13N 7°26E **16** B4
Leesburg *U.S.A.* 28°49N 81°53W **85** G14
Leesville *U.S.A.* 31°8N 93°16W **84** F8
Leeton *Australia* 34°33S 146°23E **63** E4
Leetonia *U.S.A.* 40°53N 80°45W **82** F4
Leeu Gamka *S. Africa* 32°47S 21°59E **56** D3
Leeuwarden *Neths.* 53°15N 5°48E **15** A5
Leeuwin, C. *Australia* 34°20S 115°9E **61** F2
Leeuwin Naturaliste △
  Australia 34°6S 115°3E **61** F2
Leeward Is. *Atl. Oc.* 16°30N 63°30W **89** C7
Lefka *Cyprus* 35°6N 32°51E **25** D11
Lefkada *Greece* 38°40N 20°43E **23** E9
Lefkosia = Nicosia
  Cyprus 35°10N 33°25E **46** C2
Lefroy *Canada* 44°16N 79°34W **82** B5
Lefroy, L. *Australia* 31°21S 121°40E **61** F3
Legazpi *Phil.* 13°10N 123°45E **37** B6
Legendre I. *Australia* 20°22S 116°55E **60** D2
Leghorn = Livorno *Italy* 43°33N 10°19E **22** C4
Legian *Indonesia* 8°42S 115°10E **37** K18
Legionowo *Poland* 52°25N 20°50E **17** B11
Legnago *Italy* 45°11N 11°18E **22** B4
Legnica *Poland* 51°12N 16°10E **16** C9

Leh *India* 34°9N 77°35E **43** B7
Lehigh Acres *U.S.A.* 26°36N 81°39W **85** H14
Lehighton *U.S.A.* 40°50N 75°43W **83** F9
Lehututu *Botswana* 23°54S 21°55E **56** B3
Lei Shui ➤ *China* 26°55N 112°35E **35** D9
Leibo *China* 28°11N 103°34E **34** C4
Leicester *U.K.* 52°38N 1°8W **13** E6
Leicester City □ *U.K.* 52°38N 1°8W **13** E6
Leicestershire □ *U.K.* 52°41N 1°17W **13** E6
Leichhardt ➤ *Australia* 17°35S 139°48E **62** B2
Leichhardt Ra. *Australia* 20°46S 147°40E **62** C4
Leiden *Neths.* 52°9N 4°30E **15** B4
Leie ➤ *Belgium* 51°2N 3°45E **15** C3
Leimus *Nic.* 14°40N 84°3W **88** D3
Leine ➤ *Germany* 52°43N 9°36E **16** B5
Leinster *Australia* 27°51S 120°36E **61** E3
Leinster □ *Ireland* 53°3N 7°8W **10** C4
Leinster, Mt. *Ireland* 52°37N 6°46W **10** D5
Leipzig *Germany* 51°18N 12°22E **16** C7
Leiria *Portugal* 39°46N 8°53W **21** C1
Leirvik *Norway* 59°47N 5°28E **9** G11
Leishan *China* 26°15N 108°20E **34** D7
Leisler, Mt. *Australia* 23°23S 129°20E **60** D4
Leith *U.K.* 55°59N 3°11W **11** F5
Leith Hill *U.K.* 51°11N 0°22W **13** F7
Leitir Ceanainn = Letterkenny
  Ireland 54°57N 7°45W **10** B4
Leitrim *Ireland* 54°0N 8°5W **10** B3
Leitrim □ *Ireland* 54°8N 8°0W **10** B4
Leixlip *Ireland* 53°22N 6°30W **10** C5
Leiyang *China* 26°27N 112°45E **35** D9
Leizhou *China* 20°52N 110°8E **35** G8
Leizhou Bandao *China* 21°0N 110°0E **34** G7
Leizhou Wan *China* 20°50N 110°20E **34** G8
Lek ➤ *Neths.* 51°54N 4°35E **15** C4
Leka *Norway* 65°5N 11°35E **8** D14
Leland *Mich., U.S.A.* 45°1N 85°45W **81** C11
Leland *Miss., U.S.A.* 33°24N 90°54W **85** E9
Leleque *Argentina* 42°28S 71°0W **96** E2
Leling *China* 37°44N 117°13E **33** F9
Lelystad *Neths.* 52°30N 5°25E **15** B5
Léman, L. *Europe* 46°26N 6°30E **20** C7
Lembar *Indonesia* 8°45S 116°4E **37** K19
Lembongan, Nusa
  Indonesia 8°40S 115°27E **37** K18
Lembuak *Indonesia* 8°36S 116°11E **37** K19
Lemesós = Limassol
  Cyprus 34°42N 33°1E **46** C2
Lemhi Ra. *U.S.A.* 44°0N 113°0W **76** D7
Lemmenjoki △ *Finland* 68°40N 25°30E **8** B21
Lemmer *Neths.* 52°51N 5°43E **15** B5
Lemmon *U.S.A.* 45°57N 102°10W **80** C2
Lemon Grove *U.S.A.* 32°44N 117°1W **79** N9
Lemoore *U.S.A.* 36°18N 119°46W **78** J7
Lemvig *Denmark* 56°33N 8°20E **9** H13
Lena ➤ *Russia* 72°52N 126°40E **27** B13
Lena Pillars = Lenskiy Stolby
  Russia 60°55N 126°0E **27** C13
Lenadoon Pt. *Ireland* 54°18N 9°3W **10** B2
Lenggong *Malaysia* 5°6N 100°58E **39** K3
Lengshuijiang *China* 27°40N 111°26E **35** D8
Lengshuitan *China* 26°27N 111°35E **35** D8
Lengua de Vaca, Pta.
  Chile 30°14S 71°38W **94** C1
Leningorsk = Ridder
  Kazakhstan 50°20N 83°30E **26** D9
Leninsk *Russia* 48°40N 45°15E **19** E8
Leninsk-Kuznetskiy
  Russia 54°44N 86°10E **26** D9
Lenkoran = Länkäran
  Azerbaijan 38°48N 48°52E **47** B6
Lenmalu *Indonesia* 1°45S 130°15E **37** E8
Lennox *U.S.A.* 43°21N 96°53W **80** D5
Lennoxville *Canada* 45°22N 71°51W **83** A13
Lenoir *U.S.A.* 35°55N 81°32W **85** D14
Lenoir City *U.S.A.* 35°48N 84°16W **85** D12
Lenore L. *Canada* 52°30N 104°59W **71** C8
Lenox *U.S.A.* 42°22N 73°17W **83** D11
Lens *France* 50°26N 2°50E **20** A5
Lensk *Russia* 60°48N 114°55E **27** C12
Lenskiy Stolby *Russia* 60°55N 126°0E **27** C13
Lentini *Italy* 37°17N 15°0E **22** F6
Lenwood *U.S.A.* 34°53N 117°7W **79** L9
Lenya *Burma* 11°33N 98°57E **39** G2
Leoben *Austria* 47°22N 15°5E **16** E8
Leodhais = Lewis *U.K.* 58°9N 6°40W **11** C2
Leola *U.S.A.* 45°43N 98°56W **80** C4
Leominster *U.K.* 52°14N 2°43W **13** E5
Leominster *U.S.A.* 42°32N 71°46W **83** D13
León *Mexico* 21°6N 101°41W **86** C4
León *Nic.* 12°27N 86°51W **88** D2
León *Spain* 42°38N 5°34W **21** A3
Leon *U.S.A.* 40°44N 93°45W **80** E7
León, Montes de *Spain* 42°30N 6°18W **21** A2
Leonardtown *U.S.A.* 38°17N 76°38W **81** F15
Leonardville *Namibia* 23°29S 18°49E **56** B2
Leone *Amer. Samoa* 14°23S 170°48W **59** b
Leongatha *Australia* 38°30S 145°58E **63** F4
Leonora *Australia* 28°49S 121°19E **61** E3
Leopoldina *Brazil* 21°28S 42°40W **95** A7
Leopoldsburg *Belgium* 51°7N 5°13E **15** C5
Leoti *U.S.A.* 38°29N 101°21W **80** F3
Leova *Moldova* 46°28N 28°15E **17** E15
Leoville *Canada* 53°39N 107°33W **71** C7
Lepel = Lyepyel *Belarus* 54°50N 28°4E **9** J23
Leping *China* 28°47N 117°7E **35** C11
Lépo, L. do *Angola* 17°0S 19°0E **56** A2
Leppävirta *Finland* 62°29N 27°46E **8** E22
Leptis Magna *Libya* 32°40N 14°12E **53** B8
Leribe *Lesotho* 28°51S 28°3E **57** C4
Lérida = Lleida *Spain* 41°37N 0°39E **21** B6
Lerwick *U.K.* 60°9N 1°9W **11** A7
Les Cayes *Haiti* 18°15N 73°46W **89** C5
Les Coteaux *Canada* 45°15N 74°13W **83** A10
Les Escoumins *Canada* 48°21N 69°24W **73** C6
Les Sables-d'Olonne
  France 46°30N 1°45W **20** C3
Lesbos *Greece* 39°10N 26°20E **23** E12
Leshan *China* 29°33N 103°41E **34** C4

Leshukonskoye *Russia* 64°54N 45°46E **18** B8
Leskov I. *Antarctica* 56°0S 28°0W **5** B1
Leskovac *Serbia* 43°0N 21°58E **23** C9
Lesopilnoye *Russia* 46°44N 134°20E **28** A7
Lesotho ■ *Africa* 29°40S 28°0E **57** C4
Lesozavodsk *Russia* 45°30N 133°29E **28** B6
Lesse ➤ *Belgium* 50°15N 4°54E **15** D4
Lesser Antilles *W. Indies* 15°0N 61°0W **89** D7
Lesser Slave L. *Canada* 55°30N 115°25W **70** B5
Lesser Sunda Is. *Indonesia* 8°0S 120°0E **37** F6
Lessines *Belgium* 50°42N 3°50E **15** D3
Lestock *Canada* 51°19N 103°59W **71** C8
Lesuer I. *Australia* 13°50S 127°17E **60** B4
Lesueur △ *Australia* 30°11S 115°10E **61** F2
Lésvos = Lesbos *Greece* 39°10N 26°20E **23** E12
Leszno *Poland* 51°50N 16°30E **17** C9
Letaba *S. Africa* 23°59S 31°50E **57** B5
Letchworth Garden City
  U.K. 51°59N 0°13W **13** F7
Lethbridge *Canada* 49°45N 112°45W **70** D6
Lethem *Guyana* 3°20N 59°50W **92** C7
Leti, Kepulauan *Indonesia* 8°10S 128°0E **37** F7
Leti Is. = Leti, Kepulauan
  Indonesia 8°10S 128°0E **37** F7
Letiahau ➤ *Botswana* 21°16S 24°0E **56** B3
Leticia *Colombia* 4°9S 70°0W **92** D5
Leting *China* 39°23N 118°55E **33** E10
Letjiesbos *S. Africa* 32°34S 22°16E **56** D3
Letlhakane *Botswana* 21°27S 25°30E **56** C4
Letlhakeng *Botswana* 24°0S 24°59E **56** C3
Letpadan *Burma* 17°45N 95°45E **41** L19
Letpan *Burma* 19°28N 94°10E **41** K19
Letsôk-aw Kyun *Burma* 11°30N 98°25E **39** G2
Letterkenny *Ireland* 54°57N 7°45W **10** B4
Leucadia *U.S.A.* 33°4N 117°18W **79** M9
Leuchars *U.K.* 56°24N 2°53W **11** E6
Leuser, Gunung *Indonesia* 3°46N 97°12E **36** D1
Leuven *Belgium* 50°52N 4°42E **15** D4
Leuze-en-Hainaut *Belgium* 50°36N 3°37E **15** D3
Levanger *Norway* 63°45N 11°19E **8** E14
Levelland *U.S.A.* 33°35N 102°23W **84** E3
Leven *U.K.* 56°12N 3°0W **11** E6
Leven, L. *U.K.* 56°12N 3°22W **11** E5
Leveque C. *Australia* 16°20S 123°0E **60** C3
Levice *Slovak Rep.* 48°13N 18°35E **17** D10
Levin *N.Z.* 40°37S 175°18E **59** D5
Lévis *Canada* 46°48N 71°9W **73** C5
Levis, L. *Canada* 62°37N 117°58W **70** A5
Levittown *N.Y., U.S.A.* 40°44N 73°31W **83** F11
Levittown *Pa., U.S.A.* 40°9N 74°51W **83** F10
Levka Oros *Greece* 35°18N 24°3E **23** G11
Levkás = Lefkada *Greece* 38°40N 20°43E **23** E9
Levkosia = Nicosia
Levski *Bulgaria* 43°21N 25°10E **23** C11
Levskigrad = Karlovo
  Bulgaria 42°38N 24°47E **23** C11
Levuka *Fiji* 17°34S 179°0E **59** a
Lewes *U.K.* 50°52N 0°1E **13** G8
Lewes *U.S.A.* 38°46N 75°9W **81** F16
Lewis *U.K.* 58°9N 6°40W **11** C2
Lewis ➤ *U.S.A.* 45°51N 122°48W **78** E4
Lewis, Butt of *U.K.* 58°31N 6°16W **11** C2
Lewis and Clark △
  U.S.A. 46°8N 123°53W **78** D3
Lewis Ra. *Australia* 20°3S 128°50E **60** D4
Lewis Range *U.S.A.* 48°5N 113°5W **76** B7
Lewis Run *U.S.A.* 41°52N 78°40W **82** E6
Lewisburg *Pa., U.S.A.* 40°58N 76°54W **82** F8
Lewisburg *Tenn., U.S.A.* 35°27N 86°48W **85** D11
Lewisburg *W. Va.,
  U.S.A.* 37°48N 80°27W **81** G13
Lewisporte *Canada* 49°15N 55°3W **73** C8
Lewiston *Idaho, U.S.A.* 46°25N 117°1W **76** C5
Lewiston *Maine, U.S.A.* 44°6N 70°13W **81** C18
Lewiston *N.Y., U.S.A.* 43°11N 79°3W **82** C5
Lewistown *Mont., U.S.A.* 47°4N 109°26W **76** C9
Lewistown *Pa., U.S.A.* 40°36N 77°34W **82** F7
Lexington *Ill., U.S.A.* 40°39N 88°47W **80** E9
Lexington *Ky., U.S.A.* 38°3N 84°30W **81** F11
Lexington *Mich., U.S.A.* 43°16N 82°32W **82** C2
Lexington *Mo., U.S.A.* 39°11N 93°52W **80** F7
Lexington *N.C., U.S.A.* 35°49N 80°15W **85** D14
Lexington *Nebr., U.S.A.* 40°47N 99°45W **80** E4
Lexington *Ohio, U.S.A.* 40°41N 82°35W **82** F2
Lexington *S.C., U.S.A.* 33°59N 81°11W **85** E14
Lexington *Tenn., U.S.A.* 35°39N 88°24W **85** D10
Lexington *Va., U.S.A.* 37°47N 79°27W **81** G14
Lexington Park *U.S.A.* 38°16N 76°27W **81** F15
Leyburn *U.K.* 54°19N 1°48W **12** C6
Leye *China* 24°48N 106°29E **34** E6
Leyland *U.K.* 53°42N 2°43W **12** D5
Leyte □ *Phil.* 11°0N 125°0E **37** B7
Lezhë *Albania* 41°47N 19°39E **23** D8
Lezhi *China* 30°19N 104°58E **34** B5
Lhasa *China* 29°25N 90°58E **30** F7
Lhazê *China* 29°5N 87°38E **30** F6
L'Hermite, I. *Chile* 55°50S 68°0W **96** H3
Lhokkruet *Indonesia* 4°55N 95°24E **36** D1
Lhokseumawe *Indonesia* 5°10N 97°10E **36** C1
Li *Thailand* 17°48N 98°57E **38** D2
Li Jiang ➤ *China* 24°0N 110°40E **35** E8
Li Shan *China* 35°30N 111°56E **32** G6
Li Shui ➤ *China* 29°24N 112°1E **35** C9
Li Xian *Gansu, China* 34°10N 105°5E **34** A5
Li Xian *Hebei, China* 38°30N 115°35E **32** E8
Li Xian *Hunan, China* 29°36N 111°42E **35** C8
Liancheng *China* 25°42N 116°40E **35** E11
Liancourt Rocks *Asia* 37°15N 131°52E **29** F5
Lianga *China* 30°38N 107°47E **34** B6
Liangcheng *Nei Monggol Zizhiqu,
  China* 40°28N 112°25E **32** D7
Liangcheng *Shandong,
  China* 35°32N 119°37E **33** G10
Liangdang *China* 33°56N 106°18E **34** H4
Lianghe *China* 24°50N 98°20E **34** E2
Lianghekou *China* 29°11N 108°44E **34** C7
Liangping *China* 30°38N 107°47E **34** B6
Liangpran *Indonesia* 1°4N 114°23E **36** D4
Lianhua *China* 27°3N 113°54E **35** D9

Lianhua Shan *China* 23°40N 115°48E **35** F10
Lianjiang *Fujian, China* 26°12N 119°27E **35** D12
Lianjiang *Guangdong,
  China* 21°40N 110°20E **35** G8
Lianping *China* 24°26N 114°30E **35** E10
Lianshan *China* 24°38N 112°8E **35** E9
Lianshanguan *China* 40°53N 123°43E **33** D12
Lianshui *China* 33°42N 119°20E **33** H10
Lianyuan *China* 27°40N 111°38E **35** D8
Lianyungang *China* 34°40N 119°11E **35** G10
Lianzhou *China* 24°51N 112°22E **35** E9
Liao He ➤ *China* 41°0N 121°50E **33** D11
Liaocheng *China* 36°28N 115°58E **32** F8
Liaodong Bandao *China* 40°0N 122°30E **33** E12
Liaodong Wan *China* 40°20N 121°10E **33** D11
Liaoning □ *China* 41°40N 122°30E **33** D12
Liaotung, G. of = Liaodong Wan
  China 40°20N 121°10E **33** D11
Liaoyang *China* 41°15N 122°58E **33** D12
Liaoyuan *China* 42°58N 125°2E **33** C13
Liaozhong *China* 41°23N 122°50E **33** D12
Liard ➤ *Canada* 61°51N 121°18W **70** A4
Liard River *Canada* 59°25N 126°5W **70** B3
Liari *Pakistan* 25°37N 66°30E **42** G2
Libanggaon *Nepal* 28°18N 82°38E **43** E10
Libau = Liepāja *Latvia* 56°30N 21°0E **9** H19
Libby *U.S.A.* 48°23N 115°33W **76** B6
Libenge
  Dem. Rep. of the Congo 3°40N 18°55E **54** D3
Liberal *U.S.A.* 37°3N 100°55W **80** G3
Liberec *Czech Rep.* 50°47N 15°7E **16** C8
Liberia *Costa Rica* 10°40N 85°30W **88** D2
Liberia ■ *W. Afr.* 6°30N 9°30W **52** G4
Libertador □ *Chile* 34°15S 70°45W **94** C1
Liberty *Mo., U.S.A.* 39°15N 94°25W **80** F6
Liberty *N.Y., U.S.A.* 41°48N 74°45W **83** E10
Liberty *Pa., U.S.A.* 41°34N 77°6W **82** E7
Liberty *Tex., U.S.A.* 30°3N 94°48W **84** F7
Liberty-Newark Int. ✈ (EWR)
  U.S.A. 40°42N 74°10W **83** F10
Lībīya, Sahrā' *Africa* 25°0N 25°0E **53** C10
Libo *China* 25°22N 107°53E **34** E6
Libobo, Tanjung *Indonesia* 0°54S 128°28E **37** E7
Libode *S. Africa* 31°33S 29°2E **57** D4
Libong, Ko *Thailand* 7°15N 99°23E **39** J2
Libourne *France* 44°55N 0°14W **20** D3
Libramont *Belgium* 49°55N 5°23E **15** E5
Libreville *Gabon* 0°25N 9°26E **54** D1
Libya ■ *N. Afr.* 27°0N 17°0E **53** C9
Libyan Desert = Lībīya, Sahrā'
  Africa 25°0N 25°0E **53** C10
Libyan Plateau = Ed Déffa
  Egypt 30°40N 26°30E **53** B11
Licantén *Chile* 35°55S 72°0W **94** D1
Licata *Italy* 37°6N 13°56E **22** F5
Licheng *China* 36°28N 113°20E **32** F7
Lichfield *U.K.* 52°41N 1°49W **13** E6
Lichinga *Mozam.* 13°13S 35°11E **55** G7
Lichtenburg *S. Africa* 26°8S 26°8E **56** C4
Lichuan *Hubei, China* 30°18N 108°57E **34** B7
Lichuan *Jiangxi, China* 27°18N 116°55E **35** D11
Licking ➤ *U.S.A.* 39°6N 84°30W **81** F11
Lida *Belarus* 53°53N 25°15E **17** B13
Lidköping *Sweden* 58°31N 13°7E **9** G15
Liebig, Mt. *Australia* 23°18S 131°22E **60** D5
Liechtenstein ■ *Europe* 47°8N 9°35E **20** C8
Liège *Belgium* 50°38N 5°35E **15** D5
Liège □ *Belgium* 50°32N 5°35E **15** D5
Liegnitz = Legnica *Poland* 51°12N 16°10E **16** C9
Lieksa *Finland* 63°18N 30°2E **8** E24
Lienyünchiangshih =
  Lianyungang *China* 34°40N 119°11E **33** G10
Lienz *Austria* 46°50N 12°46E **16** E7
Liepāja *Latvia* 56°30N 21°0E **9** H19
Lier *Belgium* 51°7N 4°34E **15** C4
Lierne △ *Norway* 64°20N 13°50E **8** D15
Liesua = Lithuania ■
  Europe 55°30N 24°0E **9** J21
Lièvre ➤ *Canada* 45°31N 75°26W **72** C4
Liffey ➤ *Ireland* 53°21N 6°13W **10** C5
Lifford *Ireland* 54°51N 7°29W **10** B4
Lifudzin *Russia* 44°21N 134°58E **28** B7
Lightning Ridge *Australia* 29°22S 148°0E **63** D4
Ligonier *U.S.A.* 40°15N 79°14W **82** F5
Liguria □ *Italy* 44°30N 8°50E **20** D8
Ligurian Sea *Medit. S.* 43°20N 9°0E **22** C3
Lihou Reefs and Cays
  Australia 17°25S 151°40E **62** B5
Lihué Calel △ *Argentina* 38°0S 65°0W **94** D2
Lijiang *China* 26°55N 100°0E **34** D3
Lik ➤ *Laos* 18°31N 102°30E **38** C4
Likasi
  Dem. Rep. of the Congo 10°55S 26°48E **54** G5
L'Île-Rousse *France* 42°38N 8°57E **20** E8
Liling *China* 27°42N 113°29E **35** D9
Lille *France* 50°38N 3°3E **20** A5
Lille Bælt *Denmark* 55°20N 9°45E **9** J13
Lillehammer *Norway* 61°8N 10°30E **8** F14
Lillesand *Norway* 58°15N 8°23E **9** G13
Lillian Pt. *Australia* 27°40S 126°6E **61** E4
Lillooet *Canada* 50°44N 121°57W **70** C4
Lillooet ➤ *Canada* 49°15N 121°57W **70** D4
Lilongwe *Malawi* 14°0S 33°48E **55** G6
Liloy *Phil.* 8°4N 122°39E **37** C6
Lim ➤ *Europe* 43°45N 19°15E **23** C8
Lima *Indonesia* 3°39S 127°58E **37** E7
Lima *Mont., U.S.A.* 44°38N 112°36W **76** D7
Lima *Ohio, U.S.A.* 40°44N 84°6W **81** E11
Lima ➤ *Portugal* 41°41N 8°50W **21** B1
Lima *Peru* 12°3S 77°0W **92** F3
Limassol *Cyprus* 34°42N 33°1E **46** C2
Limavady *U.K.* 55°3N 6°56W **10** A5
Limay ➤ *Argentina* 39°0S 68°0W **96** D3
Limay Mahuida
  Argentina 37°10S 66°45W **94** D2
Limbang *Malaysia* 4°42N 115°6E **36** D5
Limbaži *Latvia* 57°31N 24°42E **9** H21
Limbdi *India* 22°34N 71°51E **42** H4
Limbe *Cameroon* 4°1N 9°10E **54** D1
Limburg *Germany* 50°22N 8°4E **16** C5

Limburg □ Belgium 51°2N 5°25E 15 C5
Limburg □ Neths. 51°20N 5°55E 15 C5
Limeira Brazil 22°35S 47°28W 95 A6
Limenas = Thasos Greece 40°40N 24°40E 23 D11
Limerick Ireland 52°40N 8°37W 10 D3
Limerick U.S.A. 43°41N 70°48W 83 C14
Limerick □ Ireland 52°30N 8°50W 10 D3
Limestone U.S.A. 42°2N 78°38W 82 D6
Limestone → Canada 56°31N 94°7W 71 B10
Limfjorden Denmark 56°55N 9°0E 9 H13
Limia = Lima → Portugal 41°41N 8°50W 21 B1
Limingen Norway 64°48N 13°35E 8 D15
Limmen ○ Australia 15°15S 135°30E 62 B2
Limmen Bight Australia 14°40S 135°35E 62 A2
Limmen Bight → Australia 15°7S 135°44E 62 B2
Limnos Greece 39°50N 25°5E 23 E11
Limoges Canada 45°20N 75°16W 83 A9
Limoges France 45°50N 1°15E 20 D4
Limón Costa Rica 10°0N 83°2W 88 E3
Limon U.S.A. 39°16N 103°41W 76 G12
Limousin □ France 45°30N 1°30E 20 D4
Limoux France 43°4N 2°12E 20 E5
Limpopo □ S. Africa 24°5S 29°0E 57 C4
Limpopo → Africa 25°5S 33°30E 57 C5
Limuru Kenya 1°2S 36°35E 54 E7
Lin Xian China 37°57N 110°58E 32 F6
Lin'an China 30°15N 119°42E 35 B12
Linares Chile 35°50S 71°40W 94 D1
Linares Mexico 24°52N 99°34W 87 C5
Linares Spain 38°10N 3°40W 21 C4
Lincang China 23°58N 100°1E 34 F3
Lincheng China 37°25N 114°30E 32 F8
Linchuan China 27°57N 116°15E 35 D11
Lincoln = Beamsville Canada 43°12N 79°28W 82 C5
Lincoln Argentina 34°55S 61°30W 94 C3
Lincoln N.Z. 43°38S 172°30E 59 E4
Lincoln U.K. 53°14N 0°32W 12 D7
Lincoln Calif., U.S.A. 38°54N 121°17W 78 G5
Lincoln Ill., U.S.A. 40°9N 89°22W 80 E9
Lincoln Kans., U.S.A. 39°3N 98°9W 80 F4
Lincoln Maine, U.S.A. 45°22N 68°30W 81 C19
Lincoln N.H., U.S.A. 44°3N 71°40W 83 B13
Lincoln N. Mex., U.S.A. 33°30N 105°23W 77 K11
Lincoln Nebr., U.S.A. 40°49N 96°41W 80 E6
Lincoln City U.S.A. 44°57N 124°1W 76 D1
Lincoln Hav = Lincoln Sea Arctic 84°0N 55°0W 69 A21
Lincoln Sea Arctic 84°0N 55°0W 69 A21
Lincolnshire □ U.K. 53°14N 0°32W 12 D7
Lincolnshire Wolds U.K. 53°26N 0°13W 12 D7
Lincolnton U.S.A. 35°29N 81°16W 85 D14
Lind U.S.A. 46°58N 118°37W 76 C4
Linda U.S.A. 39°8N 121°34W 78 F5
Lindeman I. Australia 20°27S 149°3E 62 b
Lindeman Islands △ Australia 20°28S 149°5E 62 b
Linden Guyana 6°0N 58°10W 92 B7
Linden Ala., U.S.A. 32°18N 87°48W 85 E11
Linden Calif., U.S.A. 38°1N 121°5W 78 G5
Linden Tex., U.S.A. 33°1N 94°22W 84 E7
Lindenhurst U.S.A. 40°41N 73°23W 83 F11
Lindesnes Norway 57°58N 7°3E 9 H12
Lindi Tanzania 9°58S 39°38E 54 F7
Lindi □ Dem. Rep. of the Congo 0°33N 25°5E 54 D5
Lindley U.S.A. 42°1N 77°8W 82 D7
Lindos Greece 36°6N 28°4E 23 F13
Lindsay Canada 44°22N 78°43W 82 B6
Lindsay Calif., U.S.A. 36°12N 119°5W 78 J7
Lindsay Okla., U.S.A. 34°50N 97°38W 84 H6
Lindsborg U.S.A. 38°35N 97°40W 80 F5
Line Islands Pac. Oc. 7°0N 160°0W 65 H12
Linesville U.S.A. 41°39N 80°26W 82 E4
Linfen China 36°3N 111°30E 32 F6
Ling Xian Hunan, China 26°29N 113°48E 35 D9
Ling Xian Shandong, China 37°22N 116°30E 32 F9
Lingal India 16°17N 78°31E 45 F4
Linganamakki Res. India 14°6N 74°52E 45 G2
Lingao China 19°56N 109°42E 38 C7
Lingayen Phil. 16°1N 120°14E 37 A6
Lingayen G. Phil. 16°10N 120°15E 37 A6
Lingbao China 34°31N 110°51E 32 G6
Lingbi China 33°33N 117°33E 33 H9
Lingchuan Guangxi Zhuangzu, China 25°26N 110°21E 35 E8
Lingchuan Shanxi, China 35°45N 113°12E 32 G7
Lingding Yang China 22°25N 113°44E 31 a
Lingen Germany 52°31N 7°19E 16 B4
Lingga Indonesia 0°12S 104°37E 36 E2
Lingga, Kepulauan Indonesia 0°10S 104°30E 36 E2
Lingga Arch. = Lingga, Kepulauan Indonesia 0°10S 104°30E 36 E2
Linghai China 41°11N 121°22E 33 D11
Lingle U.S.A. 42°8N 104°21W 76 E11
Lingqiu China 39°28N 114°22E 32 E8
Lingshan China 22°25N 109°18E 34 F7
Lingshi China 36°48N 111°48E 32 F6
Lingshou China 38°20N 114°20E 32 E8
Lingshui China 18°27N 110°0E 38 C8
Lingsugur India 16°10N 76°31E 45 F3
Lingtai China 35°0N 107°40E 32 G4
Linguère Senegal 15°25N 15°5W 52 E2
Lingui China 25°12N 110°8E 35 E8
Lingwu China 38°6N 106°20E 32 E4
Lingyuan China 41°10N 119°15E 33 D10
Lingyun China 25°2N 106°35E 34 E6
Linhai China 28°50N 121°8E 35 C13
Linhares Brazil 19°25S 40°4W 93 G10
Linhe China 40°48N 107°20E 32 D4
Linjiang China 41°50N 127°0E 33 D14
Linköping Sweden 58°28N 15°36E 9 G16
Linkou China 45°15N 130°18E 33 B16
Linli China 29°27N 111°30E 35 C8
Linnansaari △ Finland 62°3N 28°40E 8 E23
Linnhe, L. U.K. 56°36N 5°25W 11 E3

Linosa Medit. S. 35°51N 12°50E 22 G5
Linqi China 35°45N 113°52E 32 G7
Linqing China 36°50N 115°42E 32 F8
Linqu China 36°25N 118°30E 33 F10
Linquan China 33°5N 115°17E 35 A10
Lins Brazil 21°40S 49°44W 95 A6
Linshu China 34°53N 118°38E 33 G10
Linshui China 30°21N 106°57E 34 B6
Lintao China 35°26N 103°58E 32 G2
Linton Ind., U.S.A. 39°2N 87°10W 80 F10
Linton N. Dak., U.S.A. 46°16N 100°14W 80 B3
Lintong China 34°20N 109°10E 32 G5
Linwood Canada 43°35N 80°43W 82 C4
Linwu China 25°19N 112°31E 35 E9
Linxi Hebei, China 39°42N 118°26E 33 E10
Linxi Liaoning, China 43°36N 118°2E 33 C10
Linxia China 35°36N 103°10E 30 D9
Linxiang China 29°28N 113°23E 35 C9
Linyanti → Africa 17°50S 25°5E 56 A4
Linyi Shandong, China 37°13N 116°54E 32 F9
Linyi Shandong, China 35°5N 118°21E 33 G10
Linying China 33°48N 113°56E 32 H7
Linz Austria 48°18N 14°18E 16 D8
Linzhenzhen China 36°30N 109°59E 32 F5
Linzhou China 36°4N 113°49E 32 F7
Linzi China 36°50N 118°20E 33 F10
Lions, G. du France 43°10N 4°0E 20 E6
Lions, G. of = Lion, G. du France 43°10N 4°0E 20 E6
Lion's Head Canada 44°58N 81°15W 82 B3
Lipa Phil. 13°57N 121°10E 37 B6
Lípari Italy 38°26N 14°58E 22 E6
Lípari, Is. = Eólie, Ís. Italy 38°30N 14°57E 22 E6
Lipcani Moldova 48°14N 26°48E 17 D14
Liperi Finland 62°31N 29°24E 8 E23
Lipetsk Russia 52°37N 39°35E 18 D6
Liping China 26°15N 109°7E 34 D7
Lipkany = Lipcani Moldova 48°14N 26°48E 17 D14
Lipovets Ukraine 49°12N 29°1E 17 D15
Lippe → Germany 51°39N 6°36E 16 C4
Lipscomb U.S.A. 36°14N 100°16W 84 C4
Liptrap, C. Australia 38°50S 145°55E 63 F4
Lipu China 24°30N 110°22E 35 E8
Lira Uganda 2°17N 32°57E 54 D6
Liria = Lliria Spain 39°37N 0°35W 21 C5
Lisala Dem. Rep. of the Congo 2°12N 21°38E 54 D4
Lisbon N. Dak., U.S.A. 46°27N 97°41W 80 B5
Lisbon N.H., U.S.A. 44°13N 71°55W 83 B13
Lisbon N.Y., U.S.A. 44°43N 75°19W 83 B9
Lisbon Ohio, U.S.A. 40°46N 80°46W 82 F4
Lisbon Falls U.S.A. 44°0N 70°4W 81 D18
Lisburn U.K. 54°31N 6°3W 10 B5
Lisburne, C. U.S.A. 68°53N 166°13W 74 B6
Liscannor B. Ireland 52°55N 9°24W 10 D2
Lisdoonvarna Ireland 53°2N 9°18W 10 C2
Lishe Jiang → China 24°15N 101°35E 34 E3
Lishi China 37°31N 111°8E 32 F6
Lishu China 43°20N 124°18E 33 C13
Lishui Jiangsu, China 31°38N 119°2E 35 B12
Lishui Zhejiang, China 28°28N 119°54E 35 C12
Lisianski I. U.S.A. 26°2N 174°0W 75 K5
Lisichansk = Lysychansk Ukraine 48°55N 38°30E 19 E6
Lisieux France 49°10N 0°12E 20 B4
Liski Russia 51°3N 39°30E 19 D6
Lismore Australia 28°44S 153°21E 63 D5
Lismore Ireland 52°8N 7°55W 10 D4
Lista Norway 58°7N 6°39E 9 G12
Lister, Mt. Antarctica 78°0S 162°0E 5 D11
Liston Australia 28°39S 152°6E 63 D5
Listowel Canada 43°44N 80°58W 82 C4
Listowel Ireland 52°27N 9°29W 10 D2
Litang Guangxi Zhuangzu, China 23°12N 109°8E 34 F7
Litang Sichuan, China 30°1N 100°17E 34 B3
Litang Qu → China 28°4N 101°32E 34 C3
Litani → Lebanon 33°20N 35°15E 48 B4
Litchfield Calif., U.S.A. 40°24N 120°23W 78 E6
Litchfield Conn., U.S.A. 41°45N 73°11W 83 E11
Litchfield Ill., U.S.A. 39°11N 89°39W 80 F9
Litchfield Minn., U.S.A. 45°8N 94°32W 80 C8
Litchfield △ Australia 13°14S 131°1E 60 B5
Lithgow Australia 33°25S 150°8E 63 E5
Lithino, Akra Greece 34°55N 24°44E 23 G11
Lithuania ■ Europe 55°30N 24°0E 9 J21
Lititz U.S.A. 40°9N 76°18W 83 F8
Litoměřice Czech Rep. 50°33N 14°10E 16 C8
Little Abaco Bahamas 26°50N 77°30W 88 A4
Little Andaman I. India 10°45N 92°30E 45 J11
Little Barrier I. N.Z. 36°12S 175°8E 59 B5
Little Basses Sri Lanka 6°24N 81°43E 45 L5
Little Belt Mts. U.S.A. 46°40N 110°45W 76 C8
Little Bighorn Battlefield △ U.S.A. 45°34N 107°25W 76 D10
Little Blue → U.S.A. 39°42N 96°41W 80 F5
Little Buffalo → Canada 61°0N 113°46W 70 A6
Little Cayman Cayman Is. 19°41N 80°3W 88 C3
Little Churchill → Canada 57°30N 95°22W 71 B9
Little Coco I. Burma 14°0N 93°13E 45 H11
Little Colorado → U.S.A. 36°12N 111°48W 77 H8
Little Current Canada 45°55N 82°0W 72 C3
Little Current → Canada 50°57N 84°36W 72 B3
Little Diomede I. U.S.A. 65°45N 168°56W 74 B6
Little Falls Minn., U.S.A. 45°59N 94°22W 80 C7
Little Falls N.Y., U.S.A. 43°3N 74°51W 83 C10
Little Fork → U.S.A. 48°31N 93°35W 80 A7
Little Grand Rapids Canada 52°0N 95°29W 71 C9
Little Humboldt → U.S.A. 41°1N 117°43W 76 F5
Little Inagua I. Bahamas 21°40N 73°50W 89 B5
Little Karoo S. Africa 33°45S 21°0E 56 D3
Little Khingan Mts. = Xiao Hinggan Ling China 49°0N 127°0E 31 B14
Little Lake U.S.A. 35°56N 117°55W 79 K9

Little Mecatina = Petit-Mécatina → Canada 50°40N 59°30W 73 B8
Little Minch U.K. 57°35N 6°45W 11 D1
Little Missouri → U.S.A. 47°36N 102°25W 80 B2
Little Nicobar India 7°20N 93°40E 45 L11
Little Ouse → U.K. 52°22N 1°12E 13 E9
Little Rann India 23°25N 71°25E 42 H4
Little Red → U.S.A. 35°11N 91°27W 84 D9
Little River N.Z. 43°45S 172°49E 59 E4
Little Rock U.S.A. 34°45N 92°17W 84 D8
Little Sable Pt. U.S.A. 43°38N 86°33W 80 D10
Little Sioux → U.S.A. 41°48N 96°4W 80 E5
Little Smoky → Canada 54°44N 117°11W 70 C5
Little Snake → U.S.A. 40°27N 108°26W 76 F9
Little Tobago Trin. & Tob. 11°18N 60°30W 93 J16
Little Valley U.S.A. 42°15N 78°48W 82 D6
Little Wabash → U.S.A. 37°55N 88°5W 80 G9
Little White → U.S.A. 43°40N 100°40W 80 D3
Little Zab = Zāb aş Şaghīr → Iraq 35°17N 43°29E 46 C4
Littlefield U.S.A. 33°55N 102°20W 84 E3
Littlehampton U.K. 50°49N 0°32W 13 G7
Littleton U.S.A. 44°18N 71°46W 83 B13
Liu He → China 40°55N 121°35E 33 D11
Liu Jiang → China 23°55N 109°30E 34 F7
Liuba China 33°38N 106°55E 34 A6
Liucheng China 24°38N 109°14E 34 E7
Liugou China 40°57N 118°15E 33 D10
Liuhe China 42°17N 125°43E 33 C13
Liuheng Dao China 29°40N 122°5E 35 C14
Liujiang China 24°26N 109°11E 34 E7
Liukang Tenggaja = Sabalana, Kepulauan Indonesia 6°45S 118°50E 37 F5
Liupan Shan China 35°39N 106°12E 32 G4
Liupanshui China 26°38N 104°48E 34 D5
Liuwa Plain Zambia 14°20S 22°30E 55 G4
Liuyang China 28°10N 113°37E 35 C9
Liuzhou China 24°22N 109°22E 34 E7
Liuzhuang China 33°12N 120°18E 33 H11
Livadia Greece 38°27N 22°54E 23 E10
Live Oak Calif., U.S.A. 39°17N 121°40W 78 F5
Live Oak Fla., U.S.A. 30°18N 82°59W 85 F13
Lively Canada 46°26N 81°9W 81 B13
Livermore U.S.A. 37°41N 121°47W 78 H5
Livermore, Mt. U.S.A. 30°38N 104°11W 84 F2
Livermore Falls U.S.A. 44°29N 70°11W 81 C18
Liverpool Australia 33°54S 150°58E 63 B5
Liverpool Canada 44°5N 64°41W 73 D7
Liverpool U.K. 53°25N 3°0W 12 D4
Liverpool U.S.A. 43°6N 76°13W 83 C8
Liverpool Bay U.K. 53°30N 3°20W 12 D4
Liverpool Ra. Australia 31°50S 150°30E 63 E5
Livingston Guatemala 15°50N 88°50W 88 C2
Livingston U.K. 55°54N 3°30W 11 F5
Livingston Ala., U.S.A. 32°35N 88°11W 85 E10
Livingston Calif., U.S.A. 37°23N 120°43W 78 H6
Livingston Mont., U.S.A. 45°40N 110°34W 76 D8
Livingston S.C., U.S.A. 33°38N 81°7W 85 E14
Livingston Tenn., U.S.A. 36°23N 85°19W 85 C12
Livingston Tex., U.S.A. 30°43N 94°56W 84 F7
Livingston, L. U.S.A. 30°50N 95°10W 84 F7
Livingston Manor U.S.A. 41°54N 74°50W 83 E10
Livingstone Zambia 17°46S 25°52E 55 H5
Livny Russia 52°30N 37°30E 18 D6
Livonia Mich., U.S.A. 42°23N 83°23W 81 D12
Livonia N.Y., U.S.A. 42°49N 77°40W 82 D7
Livorno Italy 43°33N 10°19E 22 C4
Livramento Brazil 30°55S 55°30W 95 C4
Lixi China 26°23N 101°59E 34 D3
Lixian China 31°23N 103°13E 34 B4
Lixin China 33°8N 116°13E 35 A11
Liyang China 31°26N 119°28E 35 B12
Lizard I. Australia 14°42S 145°30E 62 A4
Lizard Pt. U.K. 49°57N 5°13W 13 H2
Ljubljana Slovenia 46°4N 14°33E 16 E8
Ljungan → Sweden 62°18N 17°23E 8 E17
Ljungby Sweden 56°49N 13°55E 9 H15
Ljusdal Sweden 61°46N 16°3E 8 F17
Ljusnan → Sweden 61°12N 17°8E 8 F17
Ljusne Sweden 61°13N 17°7E 8 F17
Llancanelo, Salina Argentina 35°40S 69°8W 94 D2
Llandeilo U.K. 51°53N 3°59W 13 F4
Llandovery U.K. 51°59N 3°48W 13 F4
Llandrindod Wells U.K. 52°14N 3°22W 13 E4
Llandudno U.K. 53°19N 3°50W 12 D4
Llanelli U.K. 51°41N 4°10W 13 F3
Llanes Spain 43°25N 4°50W 21 A3
Llanfair-ym-Muallt = Builth Wells U.K. 52°9N 3°25W 13 E4
Llangollen U.K. 52°58N 3°11W 12 E4
Llanidloes U.K. 52°27N 3°31W 13 E4
Llano U.S.A. 30°45N 98°41W 84 F5
Llano → U.S.A. 30°39N 98°26W 84 F5
Llano Estacado U.S.A. 33°30N 103°0W 84 E3
Llanos S. Amer. 5°0N 71°35W 92 C4
Llanos de Challe △ Chile 28°8S 71°1W 94 B1
Llanquihue, L. Chile 41°10S 72°50W 96 E1
Llanwrtyd Wells U.K. 52°7N 3°38W 13 E4
Lleida Spain 41°37N 0°39E 21 B6
Llera de Canales Mexico 23°19N 99°1W 87 C5
Lleyn Peninsula U.K. 52°51N 4°36W 12 E3
Llico Chile 34°46S 72°5W 94 C1
Lliria Spain 39°37N 0°35W 21 C5
Llobregat → Spain 41°19N 2°5E 21 B7
Lloret de Mar Spain 41°41N 2°53E 21 B7
Lloyd B. Australia 12°45S 143°27E 62 A3
Lloyd L. Canada 57°22N 108°57W 71 B7
Lloydminster Canada 53°17N 110°0W 71 C7
Llucmajor Spain 39°29N 2°53E 21 C7
Llullaillaco, Volcán S. Amer. 24°43S 68°30W 94 A3
Llullaillaco △ Chile 24°50S 68°51W 94 A2
Lo, Ko Thailand 7°47N 98°23E 39 a
Lo → Vietnam 21°18N 105°25E 38 B5
Loa U.S.A. 38°24N 111°39W 76 G8
Loa → Chile 21°26S 70°41W 94 A1

Loaita I. S. China Sea 10°41N 114°25E 36 B4
Loange → Dem. Rep. of the Congo 4°17S 20°2E 54 E4
Lobamba Swaziland 26°28S 31°12E 57 C5
Lobatse Botswana 25°12S 25°40E 56 C4
Lobería Argentina 38°10S 58°40W 94 D4
Lobito Angola 12°18S 13°35E 55 G2
Lobos Argentina 35°10S 59°0W 94 D4
Lobos, I. Mexico 27°20N 110°36W 86 B2
Loc Binh Vietnam 21°46N 106°54E 38 B6
Loc Ninh Vietnam 11°50N 106°34E 39 G6
Locarno Switz. 46°10N 8°47E 20 C8
Loch Garman = Wexford Ireland 52°20N 6°28W 10 D5
Loch Lomond and the Trossachs △ U.K. 56°10N 4°40W 11 E4
Lochaber U.K. 56°59N 5°1W 11 E3
Locharbriggs U.K. 55°7N 3°35W 11 F5
Lochboisdale U.K. 57°9N 7°20W 11 D1
Loche, L. La Canada 56°30N 109°30W 71 B7
Lochem Neths. 52°9N 6°26E 15 B6
Loches France 47°7N 1°0E 20 C4
Lochgilphead U.K. 56°2N 5°26W 11 E3
Lochinver U.K. 58°9N 5°14W 11 C3
Lochmaddy U.K. 57°36N 7°10W 11 D1
Lochnagar Australia 23°33S 145°38E 62 C4
Lochnagar U.K. 56°57N 3°15W 11 E5
Lochy, L. U.K. 57°0N 4°53W 11 E4
Lock Australia 33°34S 135°46E 63 E2
Lock Haven U.S.A. 41°8N 77°28W 82 E7
Lockeford U.S.A. 38°10N 121°9W 78 G5
Lockeport Canada 43°47N 65°4W 73 D6
Lockerbie U.K. 55°7N 3°21W 11 F5
Lockhart U.S.A. 29°53N 97°40W 84 G6
Lockhart, L. Australia 33°15S 119°3E 61 F2
Lockhart River Australia 12°58S 143°30E 62 A3
Lockhart River ○ Australia 12°47S 143°20E 62 A3
Lockney U.S.A. 34°7N 101°27W 84 D4
Lockport U.S.A. 43°10N 78°42W 82 C6
Lod Israel 31°57N 34°54E 48 D3
Lodeinoye Pole Russia 60°44N 33°33E 18 B5
Lodge Bay Canada 52°14N 55°51W 73 B8
Lodge Grass U.S.A. 45°19N 107°22W 76 D10
Lodhran Pakistan 29°32N 71°30E 42 E4
Lodi Italy 45°19N 9°30E 20 D8
Lodi Calif., U.S.A. 38°8N 121°16W 78 G5
Lodi Ohio, U.S.A. 41°2N 82°1W 82 E3
Lodja Dem. Rep. of the Congo 3°30S 23°23E 54 E4
Lodwar Kenya 3°7N 35°36E 54 D7
Łódź Poland 51°45N 19°27E 17 C10
Loei Thailand 17°29N 101°35E 38 D3
Loeriesfontein S. Africa 31°0S 19°26E 56 D2
Lofoten Norway 68°30N 13°59E 8 B16
Logan Iowa, U.S.A. 41°39N 95°47W 80 E6
Logan Ohio, U.S.A. 39°32N 82°25W 81 F12
Logan Utah, U.S.A. 41°44N 111°50W 76 F8
Logan W. Va., U.S.A. 37°51N 81°59W 81 G13
Logan, Mt. Canada 60°34N 140°23W 68 E3
Logandale U.S.A. 36°36N 114°29W 79 J12
Logansport Ind., U.S.A. 40°45N 86°22W 80 E10
Logansport La., U.S.A. 31°58N 94°0W 84 F8
Logone → Chad 12°6N 15°2E 53 F9
Logroño Spain 42°28N 2°27W 21 A4
Lohardaga India 23°27N 84°45E 43 H11
Loharia India 23°45N 74°14E 42 H6
Lohri Wah → Pakistan 27°3N 67°37E 42 F2
Loikaw Burma 19°40N 97°17E 41 K20
Loimaa Finland 60°50N 23°5E 8 F20
Loir → France 47°33N 0°32W 20 C3
Loire → France 47°16N 2°10W 20 C2
Loja Ecuador 3°59S 79°16W 92 D3
Loja Spain 37°10N 4°10W 21 D3
Loji = Kawasi Indonesia 1°38S 127°28E 37 E7
Lojung China 24°27N 109°36E 34 E7
Lokeren Belgium 51°6N 3°59E 15 C3
Lokgwabe Botswana 24°10S 21°50E 56 B3
Lokitaung Kenya 4°12N 35°48E 54 D7
Lokkan tekojärvi Finland 67°55N 27°35E 8 C22
Lokoja Nigeria 7°47N 6°45E 52 G7
Lokolo → Dem. Rep. of the Congo 1°43S 18°23E 54 E3
Lola, Mt. U.S.A. 39°26N 120°22W 78 F6
Lolland Denmark 54°45N 11°30E 9 J14
Lolo U.S.A. 46°45N 114°5W 76 C6
Lom Bulgaria 43°48N 23°12E 23 C10
Lom Kao Thailand 16°53N 101°14E 38 D3
Lom Sak Thailand 16°47N 101°15E 38 D3
Loma U.S.A. 47°56N 110°30W 76 C8
Loma Linda U.S.A. 34°3N 117°16W 79 L9
Lomaloma Fiji 17°17S 178°59W 59 a
Lomami → Dem. Rep. of the Congo 0°46N 24°16E 54 D4
Lomas de Zamora Argentina 34°45S 58°24W 94 C4
Lombadina Australia 16°31S 122°54E 60 C3
Lombárdia □ Italy 45°40N 9°30E 20 D8
Lombardy = Lombárdia □ Italy 45°40N 9°30E 20 D8
Lomblen Indonesia 8°30S 123°32E 37 F6
Lombok Indonesia 8°45S 116°30E 37 K19
Lombok, Selat Indonesia 8°30S 115°50E 37 K18
Lomé Togo 6°9N 1°20E 52 G6
Lomela Dem. Rep. of the Congo 2°19S 23°15E 54 E4
Lomela → Dem. Rep. of the Congo 0°15S 20°40E 54 E4
Lommel Belgium 51°14N 5°19E 15 C5
Lomond Canada 50°24N 112°36W 70 C6
Lomond, L. U.K. 56°8N 4°38W 11 E4
Lomonosov Ridge Arctic 88°0N 140°0E 4 A
Lomphat Cambodia 13°30N 106°59E 38 F6
Lompobatang Indonesia 5°24S 119°56E 37 F5
Lompoc U.S.A. 34°38N 120°28W 79 L6
Łomża Poland 53°10N 22°2E 17 B12
Lon, Ko Thailand 7°47N 98°23E 39 a
Lonavale India 18°46N 73°29E 44 E1
Loncoche Chile 39°20S 72°50W 96 D2
Londa India 15°30N 74°30E 45 G2

London Canada 42°59N 81°15W 82 D3
London Ky., U.S.A. 37°8N 84°5W 81 G11
London Ohio, U.S.A. 39°53N 83°27W 81 F12
London, Greater □ U.K. 51°36N 0°5W 13 F7
London Gateway U.K. 51°31N 0°29E 13 F8
London Gatwick ✈ (LGW) U.K. 51°10N 0°11W 13 F7
London Stansted ✈ (STN) U.K. 51°54N 0°14E 13 F8
Londonderry U.K. 55°0N 7°20W 10 B4
Londonderry □ U.K. 55°0N 7°20W 10 B4
Londonderry, C. Australia 13°45S 126°55E 60 B4
Londonderry, I. Chile 55°0S 71°0W 96 H2
Londres Argentina 27°46S 67°7W 94 B2
Londres Argentina 27°43S 67°7W 94 B2
Londrina Brazil 23°18S 51°10W 95 A5
Lone Pine U.S.A. 36°36N 118°4W 78 J8
Lonely Mine Zimbabwe 19°30S 28°49E 57 A4
Long B. U.S.A. 33°35N 78°45W 85 E15
Long Beach Calif., U.S.A. 33°46N 118°11W 79 M8
Long Beach N.Y., U.S.A. 40°35N 73°39W 83 F11
Long Beach Wash., U.S.A. 46°21N 124°3W 78 D2
Long Branch U.S.A. 40°18N 74°0W 83 F11
Long Creek U.S.A. 44°43N 119°6W 76 D4
Long Eaton U.K. 52°53N 1°15E 12 E6
Long I. Australia 20°22S 148°51E 62 b
Long I. Bahamas 23°20N 75°10W 89 B4
Long I. Canada 54°50N 79°20W 72 B4
Long I. Ireland 51°30N 9°34W 10 E2
Long I. U.S.A. 40°45N 73°30W 83 F11
Long Island Sd. U.S.A. 41°10N 73°0W 83 E12
Long L. Canada 49°30N 86°50W 72 C2
Long L. U.S.A. 44°0N 74°23W 83 C10
Long Lake U.S.A. 43°58N 74°25W 83 C10
Long Point Canada 42°34N 80°25W 82 D4
Long Point B. Canada 42°40N 80°10W 82 D4
Long Prairie U.S.A. 45°59N 94°52W 80 C6
Long Prairie → U.S.A. 46°20N 94°36W 80 B6
Long Pt. Ont., Canada 42°35N 80°2W 82 D4
Long Pt. Ont., Canada 43°56N 76°53W 83 C8
Long Range Mts. Canada 49°30N 57°30W 73 C8
Long Reef Australia 14°1S 125°48E 60 B4
Long Sault Canada 45°2N 74°53W 83 A10
Long Str. = Longa, Proliv Russia 70°0N 175°0E 27 C18
Long Thanh Vietnam 10°47N 106°57E 39 G6
Long Xian China 34°55N 106°55E 32 G4
Long Xuyen Vietnam 10°19N 105°28E 39 G5
Longa, Proliv Russia 70°0N 175°0E 27 C18
Long'an China 23°10N 107°40E 34 F6
Longbenton U.K. 55°1N 1°31W 12 B6
Longboat Key U.S.A. 27°23N 82°39W 85 H13
Longchang China 29°18N 105°23E 34 C5
Longchuan Guangdong, China 24°5N 115°17E 35 E10
Longchuan Yunnan, China 24°23N 97°58E 34 E1
Longde China 35°30N 106°20E 32 G4
Longeau Canada 45°45N 86°25W 72 C2
Longford Australia 41°32S 147°3E 63 G4
Longford Ireland 53°43N 7°49W 10 C4
Longford □ Ireland 53°42N 7°45W 10 C4
Longfort, An = Longford Ireland 53°43N 7°49W 10 C4
Longhai China 24°25N 117°46E 35 E11
Longhua Guangdong, China 22°39N 114°0E 31 a
Longhua Hebei, China 41°18N 117°45E 33 D9
Longhui China 27°7N 111°2E 35 D8
Longiram Indonesia 0°5S 115°45E 36 E5
Longjiang China 47°20N 123°12E 33 B13
Longjing Jiangxi, China 26°8N 115°10E 35 D10
Longkou Shandong, China 37°40N 120°18E 33 F11
Longlac Canada 49°45N 86°25W 72 C2
Longli China 26°25N 106°58E 34 D6
Longlin China 24°47N 105°20E 34 E5
Longling China 24°37N 98°39E 34 E2
Longmeadow U.S.A. 42°3N 72°34W 83 D12
Longmen China 23°40N 114°18E 35 F10
Longmen Shiku China 34°28N 112°28E 32 G7
Longming China 22°59N 107°7E 34 F6
Longmont U.S.A. 40°10N 105°6W 76 F11
Longnan China 24°55N 114°47E 35 E10
Longnawan Indonesia 1°51N 114°55E 36 D4
Longquan China 28°7N 119°10E 35 C12
Longreach Australia 23°28S 144°14E 62 C3
Longshan China 29°29N 109°25E 34 C7
Longsheng China 25°48N 110°0E 35 E8
Longtan Dam China 25°0N 107°0E 34 E6
Longtan Shuiku China 25°10N 106°50E 34 E6
Longview Tex., U.S.A. 32°30N 94°44W 84 E7
Longview Wash., U.S.A. 46°8N 122°57W 78 D4
Longxi China 34°53N 104°40E 32 G3
Longxue Dao China 22°41N 113°38E 31 a
Longyan China 25°10N 117°0E 35 E11
Longyearbyen Svalbard 78°13N 15°40E 4 B8
Longyou China 29°1N 119°8E 35 C12
Longzhou China 22°22N 106°50E 34 F6
Lonoke U.S.A. 34°47N 91°54W 84 D9
Lonquimay Chile 38°26S 71°14W 96 D2
Lons-le-Saunier France 46°40N 5°31E 20 C6
Lookout, C. Canada 50°22N 4°28W 13 G3
Lookout, C. U.S.A. 52°18N 83°56W 72 A3
Lookout, C. U.S.A. 34°35N 76°32W 85 D16
Loon → Alta., Canada 57°8N 115°3W 70 B5
Loon → Man., Canada 55°53N 101°59W 71 B8
Loon Lake Canada 54°2N 109°10W 71 C7
Loongana Australia 30°52S 127°5E 61 F4
Loop Hd. Ireland 52°34N 9°56W 10 D2
Lop China 37°3N 80°11E 30 D5
Lop Nor = Lop Nur China 40°20N 90°10E 30 C7
Lop Nur China 40°20N 90°10E 30 C7
Lopatina, Gora Russia 50°47N 143°10E 27 D15
Lopatka, Mys Russia 50°52N 156°40E 27 D16
Lopburi Thailand 14°48N 100°37E 38 E3
Lopez U.S.A. 41°27N 76°20W 83 E8
Lopez, C. Gabon 0°47S 8°40E 54 E1
Lopphavet Norway 70°27N 21°15E 8 A19
Lora → Afghan. 31°35N 66°32E 40 D4

138 Lora, Hāmūn-i- INDEX TO WORLD MAPS

Lora, Hāmūn-i- *Pakistan* 29°38N 64°58E **40** E4
Lora Cr. → *Australia* 28°10S 135°22E **63** D2
Lora del Río *Spain* 37°39N 5°33W **21** D3
Lorain *U.S.A.* 41°28N 82°11W **82** E2
Loralai *Pakistan* 30°20N 68°41E **42** D3
Lorca *Spain* 37°41N 1°42W **21** D5
Lord Howe I. *Pac. Oc.* 31°33S 159°6E **58** E8
Lord Howe Rise *Pac. Oc.* 30°0S 162°30E **64** L8
Lord Loughborough I. *Burma* 10°25N 97°54E **39** G1
Lordsburg *U.S.A.* 32°21N 108°43W **77** K9
Lorestān □ *Iran* 33°30N 48°40E **47** C6
Loreto *Brazil* 7°5S 45°10W **93** E9
Loreto *Mexico* 26°0N 111°21W **86** B2
Lorient *France* 47°45N 3°23W **20** C2
Lormi *India* 22°17N 81°41E **43** H9
Lorn *U.K.* 56°26N 5°10W **11** E3
Lorn, Firth of *U.K.* 56°20N 5°40W **11** E3
Lorne *Australia* 38°33S 143°59E **63** F3
Lorraine □ *France* 48°53N 6°0E **20** B7
Los Alamos *Calif., U.S.A.* 34°44N 120°17W **79** L6
Los Alamos *N. Mex., U.S.A.* 35°53N 106°19W **77** J10
Los Altos *U.S.A.* 37°23N 122°7W **78** H4
Los Andes *Chile* 32°50S 70°40W **94** C1
Los Angeles *Chile* 37°28S 72°23W **94** D1
Los Angeles Aqueduct *U.S.A.* 35°22N 118°5W **79** K9
Los Banos *U.S.A.* 37°4N 120°51W **78** H6
Los Blancos *Argentina* 23°40S 62°30W **94** A3
Los Cabos Int. ✈ **(SJD)** *Mexico* 23°9N 109°43W **86** C3
Los Cardones △ *Argentina* 25°8S 65°55W **94** B2
Los Chiles *Costa Rica* 11°2N 84°43W **88** D3
Los Gatos *U.S.A.* 37°14N 121°59W **78** H5
Los Haïtises △ *Dom. Rep.* 19°4N 69°36W **89** C6
Los Hermanos, Is. *Venezuela* 11°45N 64°25W **89** D7
Los Loros *Chile* 27°50S 70°6W **94** B1
Los Lunas *U.S.A.* 34°48N 106°44W **77** J10
Los Mochis *Mexico* 25°45N 108°57W **86** B3
Los Olivos *U.S.A.* 34°40N 120°7W **79** L6
Los Palacios *Cuba* 22°35N 83°15W **88** B3
Los Queñes *Chile* 35°1S 70°48W **94** D1
Los Reyes de Salgado *Mexico* 19°35N 102°29W **86** D4
Los Roques, Is. *Venezuela* 11°50N 66°45W **89** D6
Los Teques *Venezuela* 10°21N 67°2W **92** A5
Los Testigos, Is. *Venezuela* 11°23N 63°6W **92** A6
Los Vilos *Chile* 32°10S 71°30W **94** C1
Lošinj *Croatia* 44°30N 14°30E **16** F8
Loskop Dam *S. Africa* 25°23S 29°20E **57** C4
Lossiemouth *U.K.* 57°42N 3°17W **11** D5
Lostwithiel *U.K.* 50°24N 4°41W **13** G3
Lot → *France* 44°18N 0°20E **20** D4
Lota *Chile* 37°5S 73°10W **94** D1
Loṭfābād *Iran* 37°32N 59°20E **47** B8
Lothair *S. Africa* 26°22S 30°27E **57** C5
Lotta → *Europe* 68°42N 31°6E **8** B24
Lotung *Taiwan* 24°41N 121°46E **35** E13
Loubomo *Congo* 4°9S 12°47E **54** E2
Loudi *China* 27°42N 111°59E **35** D8
Loudonville *U.S.A.* 40°38N 82°14W **82** F2
Louga *Senegal* 15°45N 16°5W **52** E2
Loughborough *U.K.* 52°47N 1°11W **12** E6
Lougheed I. *Canada* 77°26N 105°6W **69** B10
Loughrea *Ireland* 53°12N 8°33W **10** C3
Loughros More B. *Ireland* 54°48N 8°32W **10** B3
Louis Trichardt *S. Africa* 23°1S 29°43E **57** B4
Louis XIV, Pte. *Canada* 54°37N 79°45W **72** B4
Louisa *U.S.A.* 38°7N 82°36W **81** F12
Louisbourg *Canada* 45°55N 60°0W **73** C8
Louisburgh *Ireland* 53°46N 9°49W **10** C2
Louise I. *Canada* 52°55N 131°50W **70** C2
Louiseville *Canada* 46°20N 72°56W **72** C5
Louisiade Arch. *Papua N. G.* 11°10S 153°0E **58** C8
Louisiana *U.S.A.* 39°27N 91°3W **80** F8
Louisiana □ *U.S.A.* 30°50N 92°0W **84** F9
Louisville *Ky., U.S.A.* 38°15N 85°46W **81** F11
Louisville *Miss., U.S.A.* 33°7N 89°3W **85** E10
Louisville *Ohio, U.S.A.* 40°50N 81°16W **82** F3
Louisville Ridge *Pac. Oc.* 31°0S 172°30W **64** L10
Loulé *Portugal* 37°9N 8°0W **21** D1
Loup City *U.S.A.* 41°17N 98°58W **80** E4
Loups Marins, Lacs des *Canada* 56°30N 73°45W **72** A5
Lourdes *France* 43°6N 0°3W **20** E3
Lourdes-de-Blanc-Sablon *Canada* 51°24N 57°12W **73** B8
Louth *Australia* 30°30S 145°8E **63** E4
Louth *Ireland* 53°58N 6°32W **10** C5
Louth *U.K.* 53°22N 0°1W **12** D7
Louth □ *Ireland* 53°56N 6°34W **10** C5
Louvain = Leuven *Belgium* 50°52N 4°42E **15** D4
Louwsburg *S. Africa* 27°37S 31°7E **57** C5
Lovech *Bulgaria* 43°8N 24°42E **23** C11
Loveland *U.S.A.* 40°24N 105°5W **76** F11
Lovell *U.S.A.* 44°50N 108°24W **76** D9
Lovelock *U.S.A.* 40°11N 118°28W **76** F4
Loviisa *Finland* 60°28N 26°12E **8** F22
Lovina *Indonesia* 8°9S 115°1E **37** J18
Loving *U.S.A.* 32°17N 104°6W **77** K11
Lovington *U.S.A.* 32°57N 103°21W **77** K12
Lovisa = Loviisa *Finland* 60°28N 26°12E **8** F22
Low, L. *Canada* 52°29N 76°17W **72** B4
Low Pt. *Australia* 32°25S 127°25E **61** F4
Low Tatra = Nízké Tatry *Slovak Rep.* 48°55N 19°30E **17** D10
Lowell *U.S.A.* 42°38N 71°19W **83** D13
Lowellville *U.S.A.* 41°2N 80°32W **82** E4
Löwen → *Namibia* 26°51S 18°17E **56** C2
Lower Alkali L. *U.S.A.* 41°16N 120°2W **76** F3
Lower Arrow L. *Canada* 49°40N 118°5W **70** D5
Lower California = Baja California *Mexico* 31°10N 115°12W **86** A1
Lower Hutt *N.Z.* 41°10S 174°55E **59** D5
Lower Lake *U.S.A.* 38°55N 122°37W **78** G4
Lower Manitou L. *Canada* 49°15N 93°0W **71** D10
Lower Post *Canada* 59°58N 128°30W **70** B3
Lower Red L. *U.S.A.* 47°58N 95°0W **80** B6
Lower Saxony = Niedersachsen □ *Germany* 52°50N 9°0E **16** B5
Lower Tunguska = Tunguska, Nizhnyaya → *Russia* 65°48N 88°4E **27** C9
Lowestoft *U.K.* 52°29N 1°45E **13** E9
Lowgar □ *Afghan.* 34°0N 69°0E **40** B6
Łowicz *Poland* 52°6N 19°55E **17** B10
Lowther I. *Canada* 74°33N 97°30W **69** C12
Lowville *U.S.A.* 43°47N 75°29W **83** C9
Loxton *Australia* 34°28S 140°31E **63** E3
Loxton *S. Africa* 31°30S 22°22E **56** D3
Loyalton *U.S.A.* 39°41N 120°14W **78** F6
Loyalty Is. = Loyauté, Îs. *N. Cal.* 20°50S 166°30E **58** D9
Loyang = Luoyang *China* 34°40N 112°26E **32** G7
Loyauté, Îs. *N. Cal.* 20°50S 166°30E **58** D9
Loyev = Loyew *Belarus* 51°56N 30°46E **17** C16
Loyew *Belarus* 51°56N 30°46E **17** C16
Ltalaltuma ⌂ *Australia* 23°57S 132°25E **60** D5
Lü Shan *China* 29°30N 115°55E **35** C10
Lü Shan △ *China* 29°26N 115°52E **35** C10
Lu Wo *China* 22°33N 114°6E **31** a
Luachimo *Angola* 7°23S 20°48E **54** F4
Luajan → *India* 24°44N 85°1E **43** G11
Lualaba → *Dem. Rep. of the Congo* 0°26N 25°20E **54** D5
Lu'an *China* 31°45N 116°29E **35** B11
Luan Chau *Vietnam* 21°38N 103°24E **34** G4
Luan He → *China* 39°20N 119°5E **33** E10
Luan Xian *China* 39°40N 118°40E **33** E10
Luancheng *Guangxi Zhuangzu, China* 22°48N 108°55E **34** F7
Luancheng *Hebei, China* 37°53N 114°40E **32** F8
Luanda *Angola* 8°50S 13°15E **54** F2
Luang, Doi *Thailand* 18°30N 101°15E **38** C3
Luang, Thale *Thailand* 7°30N 100°15E **39** J3
Luang Nam Tha *Laos* 20°58N 101°30E **34** G3
Luang Prabang *Laos* 19°52N 102°10E **34** H4
Luangwa → *Zambia* 14°25S 30°25E **55** G6
Luangwa Valley *Zambia* 13°30S 31°30E **55** G6
Luangwe = Loange → *Dem. Rep. of the Congo* 4°17S 20°2E **54** E4
Luanne *China* 40°55N 117°40E **33** D9
Luanping *China* 40°53N 117°23E **33** D9
Luanshya *Zambia* 13°3S 28°28E **55** G5
Luapula → *Africa* 9°26S 28°33E **54** F5
Luarca *Spain* 43°32N 6°32W **21** A2
Luashi *Dem. Rep. of the Congo* 10°50S 23°36E **54** G4
Luau *Angola* 10°40S 22°10E **54** G4
Lubana, Ozero = Lubānas Ezers *Latvia* 56°45N 27°0E **9** H22
Lubānas Ezers *Latvia* 56°45N 27°0E **9** H22
Lubang Is. *Phil.* 13°50N 120°12E **37** B6
Lubango *Angola* 14°55S 13°30E **55** G2
Lubbock *U.S.A.* 33°35N 101°51W **84** E4
Lübeck *Germany* 53°52N 10°40E **16** B6
Lubero = Luofu *Dem. Rep. of the Congo* 0°10S 29°15E **54** E5
Lubicon L. *Canada* 56°23N 115°56W **70** B5
Lubilash → *Dem. Rep. of the Congo* 6°2S 23°45E **54** F4
Lubin *Poland* 51°24N 16°11E **16** C9
Lublin *Poland* 51°12N 22°38E **17** C12
Lubnān = Lebanon ■ *Asia* 34°0N 36°0E **48** B5
Lubnān, Jabal *Lebanon* 33°45N 35°40E **48** B4
Lubny *Ukraine* 50°3N 32°58E **26** D4
Lubudi *Dem. Rep. of the Congo* 9°57S 25°58E **54** F5
Lubuklinggau *Indonesia* 3°15S 102°55E **36** E2
Lubuksikaping *Indonesia* 0°10N 100°15E **36** D2
Lubumbashi *Dem. Rep. of the Congo* 11°40S 27°28E **55** G5
Lubutu *Dem. Rep. of the Congo* 0°45S 26°30E **54** E5
Lucan *Canada* 43°11N 81°24W **82** C3
Lucan *Ireland* 53°22N 6°28W **10** C5
Lucania, Mt. *Canada* 61°1N 140°27W **68** E3
Lucas Channel = Main Channel *Canada* 45°21N 81°45W **82** A3
Lucca *Italy* 43°50N 10°29E **22** C4
Luce Bay *U.K.* 54°45N 4°48W **11** G4
Lucea *Jamaica* 18°27N 78°10W **88** a
Lucedale *U.S.A.* 30°56N 88°35W **85** F10
Lucena *Phil.* 13°56N 121°37E **37** B6
Lucena *Spain* 37°27N 4°31W **21** D3
Lučenec *Slovak Rep.* 48°18N 19°42E **17** D10
Lucerne = Luzern *Switz.* 47°3N 8°18E **20** C8
Lucerne *U.S.A.* 39°6N 122°48W **78** F4
Lucerne Valley *U.S.A.* 34°27N 116°57W **79** L10
Lucheng *China* 36°20N 113°11E **32** F7
Luchuan *China* 22°21N 110°12E **35** F8
Lucia *U.S.A.* 36°2N 121°33W **78** J5
Lucinda *Australia* 18°32S 146°20E **62** B4
Luckenwalde *Germany* 52°5N 13°10E **16** B7
Luckhoff *S. Africa* 29°44S 24°43E **56** C3
Lucknow *Canada* 43°57N 81°31W **82** C3
Lucknow *India* 26°50N 81°0E **43** F9
Lüda = Dalian *China* 38°50N 121°40E **33** E11
Lüderitz *Namibia* 26°41S 15°8E **56** C2
Lüderitzbaai *Namibia* 26°36S 15°8E **56** C2
Ludhiana *India* 30°57N 75°56E **42** D6
Ludian *China* 27°10N 103°33E **34** D4
Luding Qiao *China* 29°53N 102°12E **34** C4
Ludington *U.S.A.* 43°57N 86°27W **80** D10
Ludlow *U.K.* 52°22N 2°42W **13** E5
Ludlow *Calif., U.S.A.* 34°43N 116°10W **79** L10
Ludlow *Pa., U.S.A.* 41°43N 78°56W **82** E6
Ludlow *Vt., U.S.A.* 43°24N 72°42W **83** C12
Ludvika *Sweden* 60°8N 15°14E **9** F16
Ludwigsburg *Germany* 48°53N 9°11E **16** D5
Ludwigshafen *Germany* 49°29N 8°26E **16** D5
Luena Flats *Zambia* 14°47S 23°17E **55** G4
Lüeyang *China* 33°22N 106°10E **34** A6
Lufeng *Guangdong, China* 22°57N 115°38E **35** F10
Lufeng *Yunnan, China* 25°0N 102°5E **34** E4
Lufira → *Dem. Rep. of the Congo* 9°30S 27°0E **54** F5
Lufkin *U.S.A.* 31°21N 94°44W **84** F7
Luga *Russia* 58°40N 29°55E **9** G23
Lugano *Switz.* 46°1N 8°57E **20** C8
Lugansk = Luhansk *Ukraine* 48°38N 39°15E **19** E6
Lugard's Falls *Kenya* 3°6S 38°41E **54** E7
Lugenda → *Mozam.* 11°25S 38°33E **55** G7
Lugh = Luuq *Somalia* 3°48N 42°34E **49** G3
Lugnaquilla *Ireland* 52°58N 6°28W **10** D5
Lugo *Italy* 44°25N 11°54E **22** B4
Lugo *Spain* 43°2N 7°35W **21** A2
Lugoj *Romania* 45°42N 21°57E **17** F11
Lugovoy = Qulan *Kazakhstan* 42°55N 72°43E **26** E8
Luhansk *Ukraine* 48°38N 39°15E **19** E6
Luhe *China* 32°19N 118°50E **35** A12
Luhuo *China* 31°21N 100°48E **34** B3
Lui → *Angola* 8°21S 17°33E **54** F3
Luiana *Angola* 17°25S 22°59E **56** A3
Luiana → *Angola* 17°24S 23°3E **55** H4
Luichow Pen. = Leizhou Bandao *China* 21°0N 110°0E **34** G7
Luimneach = Limerick *Ireland* 52°40N 8°37W **10** D3
Luing *U.K.* 56°14N 5°39W **11** E3
Luís Correia *Brazil* 3°0S 41°35W **93** D10
Luitpold Coast *Antarctica* 78°30S 32°0W **5** D1
Luiza *Dem. Rep. of the Congo* 7°40S 22°30E **54** F4
Luján *Argentina* 34°45S 59°5W **94** C4
Lujiang *China* 31°20N 117°15E **35** B11
Lukang *Taiwan* 24°1N 120°22E **35** E13
Lukanga Swamp *Zambia* 14°30S 27°40E **55** G5
Lukenie → *Dem. Rep. of the Congo* 3°0S 18°50E **54** E3
Lukla *Nepal* 27°42N 86°43E **43** F12
Łuków *Poland* 51°55N 22°23E **17** C12
Lülang Shan *China* 38°0N 111°15E **32** F6
Luleå *Sweden* 65°35N 22°10E **8** D20
Luleälven → *Sweden* 65°35N 22°10E **8** D20
Lüleburgaz *Turkey* 41°23N 27°22E **23** D12
Luliang *China* 25°0N 103°40E **34** E4
Luling *U.S.A.* 29°41N 97°39W **84** G6
Lulong *China* 39°53N 118°51E **33** E10
Lulonga → *Dem. Rep. of the Congo* 1°0N 18°10E **54** D3
Lulua → *Dem. Rep. of the Congo* 4°30S 20°30E **54** E4
Luma *Amer. Samoa* 14°16S 169°33W **59** b
Lumajang *Indonesia* 8°8S 113°13E **37** H15
Lumbala N'guimbo *Angola* 14°18S 21°18E **55** G4
Lumberton *N.C., U.S.A.* 34°37N 79°0W **85** D15
Lumberton *Tex., U.S.A.* 30°16N 94°12W **84** F7
Lumsden *Canada* 50°39N 104°52W **71** C8
Lumsden *N.Z.* 45°44S 168°27E **59** F2
Lumut *Malaysia* 4°13N 100°37E **39** K3
Lumut, Tanjung *Indonesia* 3°50S 105°58E **36** E3
Luna *India* 23°43N 69°16E **42** H3
Lunan *China* 24°40N 103°18E **34** E4
Lunavada *India* 23°8N 73°37E **42** H5
Lund *Sweden* 55°44N 13°12E **9** J15
Lundazi *Zambia* 12°20S 33°7E **55** G6
Lundu *Malaysia* 1°40N 109°50E **36** D3
Lundy *U.K.* 51°10N 4°41W **13** F3
Lune → *U.K.* 54°0N 2°51W **12** C5
Lüneburg *Germany* 53°15N 10°24E **16** B6
Lüneburg Heath = Lüneburger Heide *Germany* 53°10N 10°12E **16** B6
Lüneburger Heide *Germany* 53°10N 10°12E **16** B6
Lunenburg *Canada* 44°22N 64°18W **73** D7
Lunéville *France* 48°36N 6°30E **20** B7
Lunglei *India* 22°55N 92°45E **41** H18
Luni *India* 26°0N 73°6E **42** G5
Luni → *India* 24°41N 71°14E **42** G4
Luninets = Luninyets *Belarus* 52°15N 26°50E **17** B14
Luning *U.S.A.* 38°30N 118°11W **76** G4
Luninyets *Belarus* 52°15N 26°50E **17** B14
Lunkaransar *India* 28°29N 73°44E **42** E5
Luo He → *China* 34°35N 110°20E **32** G6
Luocheng *China* 24°48N 108°53E **34** E7
Luochuan *China* 35°45N 109°26E **32** G5
Luoci *China* 25°19N 102°18E **34** E4
Luodian *China* 25°24N 106°43E **34** E6
Luoding *China* 22°45N 111°40E **35** F8
Luofu *Dem. Rep. of the Congo* 0°10S 29°15E **54** E5
Luohe *China* 33°32N 114°2E **32** H8
Luojiang *China* 31°18N 104°33E **34** B5
Luonan *China* 34°5N 110°10E **32** G6
Luoning *China* 34°35N 111°40E **32** G6
Luoshan *China* 32°13N 114°30E **35** A10
Luotian *China* 30°46N 115°22E **35** B10
Luoxiao Shan *China* 26°30N 114°1E **35** D10
Luoyang *China* 34°40N 112°26E **32** G7
Luoyuan *China* 26°28N 119°30E **35** D12
Luozigou *China* 43°42N 130°18E **33** C16
Lupingu *China* 24°53N 104°21E **34** E5
Luquan *Hebei, China* 38°4N 114°17E **32** E8
Luquan *Yunnan, China* 25°35N 102°25E **34** E4
Luque *Paraguay* 25°19S 57°25W **94** B4
Luquillo, Sierra de *Puerto Rico* 18°20N 65°47W **89** d
Luray *U.S.A.* 38°40N 78°28W **81** F14
Lurgan *U.K.* 54°27N 6°20W **10** B5
Lusaka *Zambia* 15°28S 28°16E **55** H5
Lusambo *Dem. Rep. of the Congo* 4°58S 23°28E **54** E4
Luseland *Canada* 52°5N 109°24W **71** C7
Lushan *Henan, China* 33°45N 112°55E **32** H7
Lushan *Sichuan, China* 30°12N 102°52E **34** B4
Lushi *China* 34°3N 111°3E **32** G6
Lushnjë *Albania* 40°55N 19°41E **23** D8
Lushui *China* 25°58N 98°44E **34** E2
Lüshun *China* 38°45N 121°15E **33** E11
Lusk *U.S.A.* 42°46N 104°27W **76** E11
Lūt, Dasht-e *Iran* 31°30N 58°0E **47** D8
Luta = Dalian *China* 38°50N 121°40E **33** E11
Lütao *Taiwan* 22°40N 121°30E **35** F13
Lutherstadt Wittenberg *Germany* 51°53N 12°39E **16** C7
Luton *U.K.* 51°53N 0°24W **13** F7
Luton □ *U.K.* 51°53N 0°24W **13** F7
Lutsel K'e *Canada* 62°24N 110°44W **71** A6
Lutsk *Ukraine* 50°50N 25°15E **17** C13
Lutto = Lotta → *Europe* 68°42N 31°6E **8** B24
Lützow Holmbukta *Antarctica* 69°10S 37°30E **5** C4
Lutzputs *S. Africa* 28°3S 20°40E **56** C3
Luuq *Somalia* 3°48N 42°34E **49** G3
Luverne *Ala., U.S.A.* 31°43N 86°16W **85** F11
Luverne *Minn., U.S.A.* 43°39N 96°13W **80** D5
Luvua → *Dem. Rep. of the Congo* 6°50S 27°30E **54** F5
Luvuvhu → *S. Africa* 22°25S 31°18E **57** B5
Luwuk *Indonesia* 0°56S 122°47E **37** E6
Luxembourg *Lux.* 49°37N 6°9E **15** E6
Luxembourg □ *Belgium* 49°58N 5°30E **15** E5
Luxembourg ■ *Europe* 49°45N 6°0E **15** E5
Luxembourg ✈ **(LUX)** *Lux.* 49°37N 6°10E **15** E6
Luxi *Hunan, China* 28°20N 110°7E **35** C8
Luxi *Yunnan, China* 24°40N 103°55E **34** E4
Luxi *Yunnan, China* 24°27N 98°36E **34** E2
Luxian *China* 29°9N 105°24E **34** C5
Luxor = El Uqsur *Egypt* 25°41N 32°38E **53** C12
Luyi *China* 33°50N 115°35E **32** H8
Luykau = Loikaw *Burma* 19°40N 97°17E **41** K20
Luza *Russia* 60°39N 47°10E **18** B8
Luzern *Switz.* 47°3N 8°18E **20** C8
Luzhai *China* 24°29N 109°42E **34** E7
Luzhi *China* 26°21N 105°16E **34** D5
Luzhou *China* 28°52N 105°20E **34** C5
Luziânia *Brazil* 16°20S 48°0W **93** G9
Luzon *Phil.* 16°0N 121°0E **37** A6
Luzon Strait *Asia* 21°0N 120°40E **35** G13
Lviv *Ukraine* 49°50N 24°0E **17** D13
Lviv □ *Ukraine* 49°30N 23°45E **17** D12
Lvov = Lviv *Ukraine* 49°50N 24°0E **17** D13
Lyakhavichy *Belarus* 53°2N 26°32E **17** B14
Lyakhovskiye, Ostrova *Russia* 73°40N 141°0E **27** B15
Lyal I. *Canada* 44°57N 81°24W **82** B3
Lybster *U.K.* 58°18N 3°15W **11** C5
Lycksele *Sweden* 64°38N 18°40E **8** D18
Lydda = Lod *Israel* 31°57N 34°54E **48** D3
Lyddan I. *Antarctica* 74°0S 21°0W **5** D2
Lydenburg *S. Africa* 25°10S 30°29E **57** C5
Lydia *Turkey* 38°48N 28°19E **23** E13
Lyell *N.Z.* 41°48S 172°4E **59** D4
Lyell I. *Canada* 52°40N 131°35W **70** C2
Lyepyel *Belarus* 54°50N 28°40E **9** J23
Lykens *U.S.A.* 40°34N 76°42W **83** F8
Lyman *U.S.A.* 41°20N 110°18W **76** F8
Lyme B. *U.K.* 50°42N 2°53W **13** G4
Lyme Regis *U.K.* 50°43N 2°57W **13** G5
Lymington *U.K.* 50°45N 1°32W **13** G6
Łyna → *Poland* 54°37N 21°14E **17** A11
Lynchburg *U.S.A.* 37°25N 79°9W **81** G14
Lynd → *Australia* 16°28S 143°18E **62** B3
Lynd Ra. *Australia* 25°30S 149°20E **63** D4
Lynden *Canada* 43°14N 80°9W **82** C4
Lynden *U.S.A.* 48°57N 122°27W **78** B4
Lyndhurst *Australia* 30°15S 138°18E **63** E2
Lyndon → *Australia* 23°29S 114°6E **61** D1
Lyndonville *N.Y., U.S.A.* 43°20N 78°23W **82** C6
Lyndonville *Vt., U.S.A.* 44°31N 72°1W **83** B12
Lyngen *Norway* 69°45N 20°30E **8** B19
Lynher Reef *Australia* 15°27S 121°55E **60** C3
Lynn *U.S.A.* 42°28N 70°57W **83** D14
Lynn Canal *U.S.A.* 58°50N 135°15W **74** D12
Lynn Haven *U.S.A.* 30°15N 85°39W **85** F12
Lynn Lake *Canada* 56°51N 101°3W **71** B8
Lynnwood *U.S.A.* 47°49N 122°18W **78** C4
Lynton *U.K.* 51°13N 3°50W **13** F4
Lyntupy *Belarus* 55°4N 26°23E **9** J22
Lynx L. *Canada* 62°25N 106°15W **71** A7
Lyon *France* 45°46N 4°50E **20** D6
Lyonnais *France* 45°45N 4°15E **20** D6
Lyons = Lyon *France* 45°46N 4°50E **20** D6
Lyons *Ga., U.S.A.* 32°12N 82°19W **85** E13
Lyons *Kans., U.S.A.* 38°21N 98°12W **80** F4
Lyons *N.Y., U.S.A.* 43°5N 77°0W **82** C8
Lyons → *Australia* 25°2S 115°9E **61** E2
Lyons Falls *U.S.A.* 43°37N 75°22W **83** C9
Lys = Leie → *Belgium* 51°2N 3°45E **15** C3
Lysva *Russia* 58°7N 57°49E **18** C10
Lysychansk *Ukraine* 48°55N 38°30E **19** E6
Lytham St. Anne's *U.K.* 53°45N 3°0W **12** D4
Lyttelton *N.Z.* 43°35S 172°44E **59** E4
Lytton *Canada* 50°13N 121°31W **70** C4
Lyubertsy *Russia* 55°40N 37°51E **18** C6
Lyuboml *Ukraine* 51°11N 24°4E **17** C13

M

Ma → *Vietnam* 19°47N 105°56E **34** H5
Ma'adaba *Jordan* 31°43N 35°47E **48** D4
Ma'alot-Tarshiha *Israel* 33°1N 35°17E **48** B4
Maamba *Zambia* 17°17S 26°28E **56** A4
Ma'ān *Jordan* 30°12N 35°44E **48** E4
Ma'ān □ *Jordan* 30°0N 36°0E **48** F5
Maanselkä *Finland* 63°52N 28°32E **8** C23
Ma'anshan *China* 31°44N 118°29E **35** B12
Maarianhamina = Mariehamn *Finland* 60°5N 19°55E **9** F18
Ma'arrat an Nu'mān *Syria* 35°43N 36°43E **46** C3
Maas → *Neths.* 51°45N 4°32E **15** C4
Maaseik *Belgium* 51°6N 5°45E **15** C5
Maasin *Phil.* 10°8N 124°50E **37** B6
Maastricht *Neths.* 50°50N 5°40E **15** D5
Maave *Mozam.* 21°4S 34°47E **57** B5
Mababe Depression *Botswana* 18°50S 24°15E **56** A3
Mabalane *Mozam.* 23°37S 32°31E **57** B5
Mabel L. *Canada* 50°35N 118°43W **70** C5
Maberly *Canada* 44°50N 76°32W **83** B8
Mabian *China* 28°47N 103°37E **34** C4
Mablethorpe *U.K.* 53°20N 0°15E **12** D8
Mabuasehube ⌂ *Botswana* 25°5S 21°10E **56** C3
Mabuiag *Australia* 9°57S 142°11E **62** a
Mac Bac *Vietnam* 9°46N 106°7E **39** H6
Macachín *Argentina* 37°10S 63°43W **94** D3
Macaé *Brazil* 22°20S 41°43W **95** A7
McAlester *U.S.A.* 34°56N 95°46W **84** D7
McAllen *U.S.A.* 26°12N 98°14W **84** H5
MacAlpine L. *Canada* 66°32N 102°45W **68** D11
Macamic *Canada* 48°45N 79°0W **72** C4
Macao = Macau *China* 22°12N 113°33E **35** F9
Macapá *Brazil* 0°5N 51°4W **93** C8
Macarao △ *Venezuela* 10°22N 67°7W **89** D6
McArthur → *Australia* 15°54S 136°40E **62** B2
McArthur, Port *Australia* 16°4S 136°23E **62** B2
Macau *Brazil* 5°15S 36°40W **93** E11
Macau *China* 22°12N 113°33E **35** F9
McBride *Canada* 53°20N 120°19W **70** C4
McCall *U.S.A.* 44°55N 116°6W **76** D5
McCamey *U.S.A.* 31°8N 102°14W **84** F3
McCammon *U.S.A.* 42°39N 112°12W **76** E7
McCauley I. *Canada* 53°40N 130°15W **70** C2
McCleary *U.S.A.* 47°3N 123°16W **78** C3
Macclenny *U.S.A.* 30°17N 82°7W **85** F13
Macclesfield *U.K.* 53°15N 2°8W **12** D5
Macclesfield Bank *S. China Sea* 16°0N 114°30E **36** A4
M'Clintock Chan. *Canada* 72°0N 102°0W **68** C11
McClintock Ra. *Australia* 18°44S 127°38E **60** C4
McCloud *U.S.A.* 41°15N 122°8W **76** F2
McCluer I. *Australia* 11°5S 133°0E **60** B5
McClure *U.S.A.* 40°42N 77°19W **82** F7
McClure, L. *U.S.A.* 37°35N 120°16W **78** H6
M'Clure Str. *Canada* 75°0N 119°0W **69** C8
McClusky *U.S.A.* 47°29N 100°27W **80** B3
McComb *U.S.A.* 31°15N 90°27W **85** F9
McCook *U.S.A.* 40°12N 100°38W **80** E3
McCreary *Canada* 50°47N 99°29W **71** C9
McCullough Mt. *U.S.A.* 35°35N 115°13W **79** K11
McCusker → *Canada* 55°32N 108°39W **71** B7
McDermitt *U.S.A.* 41°59N 117°43W **76** F5
McDonald *U.S.A.* 40°22N 80°14W **82** F4
Macdonald, L. *Australia* 23°30S 129°0E **60** D4
McDonald Is. *Ind. Oc.* 53°0S 73°0E **3** G13
MacDonnell Ranges *Australia* 23°40S 133°0E **60** D5
MacDowell L. *Canada* 52°15N 92°45W **72** B1
Macduff *U.K.* 57°40N 2°31W **11** D6
Macedonia *U.S.A.* 41°19N 81°31W **82** E3
Macedonia □ *Greece* 40°39N 22°0E **23** D10
Macedonia ■ *Europe* 41°53N 21°40E **23** D9
Maceió *Brazil* 9°40S 35°41W **93** E11
Macerata *Italy* 43°18N 13°27E **22** C5
McFarland *U.S.A.* 35°41N 119°14W **79** K7
McFarlane → *Canada* 59°12N 107°58W **71** B7
Macfarlane, L. *Australia* 32°0S 136°40E **63** E2
McGehee *U.S.A.* 33°38N 91°24W **84** E9
McGill *U.S.A.* 39°23N 114°47W **76** G6
Macgillycuddy's Reeks *Ireland* 51°58N 9°45W **10** E2
McGraw *U.S.A.* 42°36N 76°8W **83** D8
McGregor *U.S.A.* 43°1N 91°11W **80** D8
McGregor Ra. *Australia* 27°0S 142°45E **63** D3
McGuire, Mt. *Australia* 20°18S 148°23E **62** b
Mach *Pakistan* 29°50N 67°20E **42** E2
Māch Kowr *Iran* 25°48N 61°28E **47** E9
Machado = Jiparaná → *Brazil* 8°3S 62°52W **92** E6
Machagai *Argentina* 26°56S 60°2W **94** B3
Machakos *Kenya* 1°30S 37°15E **54** E7
Machala *Ecuador* 3°20S 79°57W **92** D3
Machanga *Mozam.* 20°59S 35°0E **57** B6
Machattie, L. *Australia* 24°50S 139°48E **62** C2
Machava *Mozam.* 25°54S 32°28E **57** C5
Macheke *Zimbabwe* 18°5S 31°51E **57** A5
Macheng *China* 31°12N 115°2E **35** B10
Macherla *India* 16°29N 79°26E **44** F4
Machgaon *India* 20°5N 86°17E **44** D8
Machhu → *India* 23°6N 70°46E **42** H4
Machiara △ *Pakistan* 34°40N 73°30E **42** B5
Machias *Maine, U.S.A.* 44°43N 67°28W **81** C20
Machias *N.Y., U.S.A.* 42°25N 78°29W **82** D6
Machichi → *Canada* 57°3N 92°6W **71** B10
Machilipatnam *India* 16°12N 81°8E **45** F5
Machiques *Venezuela* 10°4N 72°34W **92** A4
Machu Picchu *Peru* 13°8S 72°30W **92** F4
Machynlleth *U.K.* 52°35N 3°50W **13** E4
Macia *Mozam.* 25°2S 33°8E **57** C5
McIlwraith Ra. *Australia* 13°50S 143°20E **62** A3
McInnes L. *Canada* 52°13N 93°45W **71** C10
McIntosh *U.S.A.* 45°55N 101°21W **80** C3
McIntosh L. *Canada* 55°45N 105°0W **71** B8
Macintosh Ra. *Australia* 27°39S 125°32E **61** E4
Macintyre → *Australia* 28°37S 150°47E **63** D5
Mackay *Australia* 21°8S 149°11E **62** K4
Mackay *U.S.A.* 43°55N 113°37W **76** E7
MacKay → *Canada* 57°10N 111°38W **70** B6
Mackay, L. *Australia* 22°30S 129°0E **60** D4
McKay Ra. *Australia* 23°0S 122°30E **60** D3
McKeesport *U.S.A.* 40°20N 79°51W **82** F5
McKellar *Canada* 45°30N 79°55W **82** A5
McKenna *U.S.A.* 46°56N 122°33W **78** D4
Mackenzie = Linden *Guyana* 6°0N 58°10W **92** B7
Mackenzie *Canada* 55°20N 123°5W **70** B4
McKenzie *U.S.A.* 36°8N 88°31W **85** C10
Mackenzie → *Australia* 23°38S 149°46E **62** C4
Mackenzie → *Canada* 69°10N 134°20W **68** D5
McKenzie → *U.S.A.* 44°7N 123°6W **76** D2
Mackenzie Bay *Canada* 69°0N 137°30W **66** C6
Mackenzie King I. *Canada* 77°45N 111°0W **69** B9
Mackenzie Mts. *Canada* 64°0N 130°0W **66** C6
Mackinac, Straits of *U.S.A.* 45°50N 84°40W **81** C11
Mackinaw City *U.S.A.* 45°47N 84°44W **81** C11

McKinlay Australia 21°16S 141°18E 62 C3
McKinlay → Australia 20°50S 141°28E 62 C3
McKinley, Mt. U.S.A. 63°4N 151°0W 68 E1
McKinley Sea Arctic 82°0N 0°0 4 A7
McKinney U.S.A. 33°12N 96°37W 84 E6
McKittrick U.S.A. 35°18N 119°37W 79 K7
Macklin Canada 52°20N 109°56W 71 C7
Macksville Australia 30°40S 152°56E 63 E5
McLaughlin U.S.A. 45°49N 100°49W 80 C3
Maclean Australia 29°26S 153°16E 63 D5
McLean U.S.A. 35°14N 100°36W 84 D4
McLeansboro U.S.A. 38°6N 88°32W 80 F9
Maclear S. Africa 31°2S 28°23E 57 D4
Macleay → Australia 30°56S 153°0E 63 E5
McLennan Canada 55°42N 116°50W 70 B5
McLeod → Canada 54°9N 115°44W 70 C5
MacLeod, L. Australia 24°9S 113°47E 61 D1
MacLeod B. Canada 62°53N 110°0W 71 A7
MacLeod Lake Canada 54°58N 123°0W 70 C4
McLoughlin, Mt. U.S.A. 42°27N 122°19W 76 E2
McMechen U.S.A. 39°57N 80°44W 82 G4
McMinnville Oreg., U.S.A. 45°13N 123°12W 76 D2
McMinnville Tenn., U.S.A. 35°41N 85°46W 85 D12
McMurdo Antarctica 77°51S 166°37E 5 D11
McMurdo Sd. Antarctica 77°0S 170°0E 5 D11
McMurray = Fort McMurray Canada 56°44N 111°7W 70 B6
McMurray U.S.A. 48°19N 122°14W 78 B4
Maçobere Mozam. 21°13S 32°47E 57 B5
Macodoene Mozam. 23°32S 35°5E 57 B6
Macomb U.S.A. 40°27N 90°40W 80 E8
Mâcon France 46°19N 4°50E 20 C6
Macon Ga., U.S.A. 32°51N 83°38W 85 E13
Macon Miss., U.S.A. 33°7N 88°34W 85 E10
Macon Mo., U.S.A. 39°44N 92°28W 80 F7
Macoun L. Canada 56°32N 103°40W 71 B8
Macovane Mozam. 21°30S 35°2E 57 B6
McPherson U.S.A. 38°22N 97°40W 80 F5
McPherson Pk. U.S.A. 34°53N 119°53W 79 L7
McPherson Ra. Australia 28°15S 153°15E 63 D5
Macquarie → Australia 30°7S 147°24E 63 E4
Macquarie Harbour Australia 42°15S 145°23E 63 G4
Macquarie I. Pac. Oc. 54°36S 158°55E 64 N7
Macquarie Ridge S. Ocean 57°0S 159°0E 5 B10
MacRobertson Land Antarctica 71°0S 64°0E 5 D6
Macroom Ireland 51°54N 8°57W 10 E3
MacTier Canada 45°8N 79°47W 82 A5
Macuira △ Colombia 12°9N 71°21W 89 D5
Macumba → Australia 27°52S 137°12E 63 D2
Macuro Venezuela 10°42N 61°55W 93 K15
Macusani Peru 14°4S 70°29W 92 F4
Macuspana Mexico 17°46N 92°36W 87 D6
Macusse Angola 17°48S 20°23E 56 A3
Ma'dabā □ Jordan 31°43N 35°47E 48 D4
Madadeni S. Africa 27°43S 30°3E 57 C5
Madagascar ■ Africa 20°0S 47°0E 55 J9
Madā'in Sālih Si. Arabia 26°46N 37°57E 46 E3
Madakasira India 13°56N 77°16E 45 H3
Madama Niger 22°0N 13°40E 53 D8
Madame, I. Canada 45°30N 60°58W 73 C7
Madanapalle India 13°33N 78°28E 45 H4
Madang Papua N. G. 5°12S 145°49E 58 B7
Madaripur Bangla. 23°19N 90°15E 41 H17
Madauk Burma 17°56N 96°52E 41 L20
Madawaska Canada 45°30N 78°0W 82 A7
Madawaska → Canada 45°27N 76°21W 82 A7
Madaya Burma 22°12N 96°10E 41 H20
Maddalena Italy 41°16N 9°23E 22 D3
Maddur India 12°36N 77°4E 45 H3
Madeira Atl. Oc. 32°50N 17°0W 52 B2
Madeira → Brazil 3°22S 58°45W 92 D7
Madeleine, Îs. de la Canada 47°30N 61°40W 73 C7
Madera Mexico 29°12N 108°7W 86 B3
Madera Calif., U.S.A. 36°57N 120°3W 78 J6
Madera Pa., U.S.A. 40°49N 78°26W 82 F6
Madgaon India 15°12N 73°58E 45 G1
Madha India 18°0N 75°30E 44 F2
Madhavpur India 21°15N 69°58E 42 J3
Madhepura India 26°11N 86°23E 43 F12
Madhira India 16°55N 80°22E 44 F5
Madhubani India 26°21N 86°7E 43 F12
Madhugiri India 13°40N 77°12E 45 H3
Madhupur India 24°16N 86°39E 43 G12
Madhya Pradesh □ India 22°50N 78°0E 42 J8
Madidi → Bolivia 12°32S 66°52W 92 F5
Madikeri India 12°30N 75°45E 45 H2
Madikwe ⌓ S. Africa 27°38S 32°15E 57 C5
Madill U.S.A. 34°6N 96°46W 84 D6
Madimba Dem. Rep. of the Congo 4°58S 15°5E 54 E3
Ma'din Syria 35°45N 39°36E 46 C3
Madinat al Malik Khālid al Askarīyah Si. Arabia 27°54N 45°31E 46 E5
Madīnat Masdar U.A.E. 24°26N 54°37E 47 E7
Madingou Congo 4°10S 13°33E 54 E2
Madison Calif., U.S.A. 38°41N 121°59W 78 G5
Madison Fla., U.S.A. 30°28N 83°25W 85 F13
Madison Ind., U.S.A. 38°44N 85°23W 81 F11
Madison Nebr., U.S.A. 41°50N 97°27W 80 E5
Madison Ohio, U.S.A. 41°46N 81°3W 82 E3
Madison S. Dak., U.S.A. 44°0N 97°7W 80 C5
Madison Wis., U.S.A. 43°4N 89°24W 80 D9
Madison → U.S.A. 45°56N 111°31W 76 D8
Madison Heights U.S.A. 37°25N 79°8W 81 G14
Madisonville Ky., U.S.A. 37°20N 87°30W 80 G10
Madisonville Tex., U.S.A. 30°57N 95°55W 84 F7
Madista Botswana 21°15S 25°6E 56 B4
Madiun Indonesia 7°38S 111°32E 37 G14
Madoc Canada 44°30N 77°28W 82 B7
Madoi China 34°46N 98°18E 30 E8
Madona Latvia 56°53N 26°5E 9 H22
Madrakah, Ra's al Oman 19°0N 57°50E 49 D6
Madras = Chennai India 13°8N 80°19E 45 H5
Madras = Tamil Nadu □ India 11°0N 77°0E 45 J3
Madras U.S.A. 44°38N 121°8W 76 D3
Madre, L. U.S.A. 26°50N 97°30W 84 J6
Madre, Sierra Phil. 17°0N 122°0E 37 A6
Madre de Dios → Bolivia 10°59S 66°8W 92 F5
Madre de Dios, I. Chile 50°20S 75°10W 96 G1
Madre del Sur, Sierra Mexico 17°30N 100°0W 87 D5
Madre Occidental, Sierra Mexico 27°0N 107°0W 86 B3
Madre Oriental, Sierra Mexico 25°0N 100°0W 86 C5
Madri India 24°16N 73°32E 42 G5
Madrid U.S.A. 44°45N 75°8W 83 B9
Madura Australia 31°55S 127°0E 61 F4
Madura Indonesia 7°30S 114°0E 37 G15
Madura, Selat Indonesia 7°30S 113°20E 37 G15
Madura Oya △ Sri Lanka 7°20N 81°10E 45 L5
Madurai India 9°55N 78°10E 45 K4
Madurantakam India 12°30N 79°50E 45 H4
Mae Chan Thailand 20°9N 99°52E 38 B2
Mae Charim △ Thailand 18°17N 100°59E 38 C3
Mae Hong Son Thailand 19°16N 97°56E 38 C2
Mae Khlong → Thailand 13°24N 100°0E 38 F3
Mae Moei △ Thailand 17°26N 98°7E 38 D2
Mae Phang △ Thailand 19°7N 99°13E 38 C2
Mae Phrik Thailand 17°27N 99°7E 38 D2
Mae Ping △ Thailand 17°37N 98°51E 38 D2
Mae Ramat Thailand 16°58N 98°31E 38 D2
Mae Rim Thailand 18°54N 98°57E 38 C2
Mae Sai Thailand 20°20N 99°55E 34 G2
Mae Sot Thailand 16°43N 98°34E 38 D2
Mae Suai Thailand 19°39N 99°33E 34 H2
Mae Tha Thailand 18°28N 99°8E 38 C2
Mae Tup Res. Thailand 17°52N 98°45E 38 D2
Mae Wa △ Thailand 17°23N 99°16E 38 D2
Mae Wong △ Thailand 15°54N 99°12E 38 E2
Mae Yom △ Thailand 18°43N 100°15E 38 C3
Maebaru Japan 33°33N 130°12E 29 H5
Maebashi Japan 36°24N 139°4E 29 F9
Maelpaeg L. Canada 48°20N 56°30W 73 C8
Maestra, Sierra Cuba 20°15N 77°0W 88 B4
Maevatanana Madag. 16°56S 46°49E 55 H9
Mafadi S. Africa 29°12S 29°21E 57 C4
Mafeking = Mafikeng S. Africa 25°50S 25°38E 56 C4
Mafeking Canada 52°40N 101°10W 71 C8
Mafeteng Lesotho 29°51S 27°15E 56 C4
Maffra Australia 37°53S 146°58E 63 F4
Mafia I. Tanzania 7°45S 39°50E 54 F7
Mafikeng S. Africa 25°50S 25°38E 56 C4
Mafra Brazil 26°10S 49°55W 95 B6
Mafra Portugal 38°55N 9°20W 21 C1
Magadan Russia 59°38N 150°50E 27 D16
Magadi India 12°58N 77°14E 45 H3
Magaliesburg S. Africa 26°0S 27°32E 57 C4
Magallanes, Estrecho de Chile 52°30S 75°0W 96 G2
Magangué Colombia 9°14N 74°45W 92 B4
Magdagachi Russia 53°27N 125°48E 27 D13
Magdalen Is. = Madeleine, Îs. de la Canada 47°30N 61°40W 73 C7
Magdalena Argentina 35°5S 57°30W 94 D4
Magdalena Bolivia 13°13S 63°57W 92 F6
Magdalena U.S.A. 34°7N 107°15W 77 J10
Magdalena → Colombia 11°6N 74°51W 92 A4
Magdalena, B. Mexico 24°35N 112°0W 86 C2
Magdalena, I. Mexico 24°40N 112°15W 86 C2
Magdalena, Llano de Mexico 25°0N 111°25W 86 C2
Magdalena de Kino Mexico 30°38N 110°57W 86 A2
Magdeburg Germany 52°7N 11°38E 16 B6
Magdelaine Cays Australia 16°33S 150°18E 62 B5
Magee U.S.A. 31°52N 89°44W 85 F10
Magelang Indonesia 7°29S 110°13E 37 G14
Magellan's Str. = Magallanes, Estrecho de Chile 52°30S 75°0W 96 G2
Magenta, L. Australia 33°30S 119°2E 61 F2
Magerøya Norway 71°3N 25°40E 8 A21
Maggiore, L. Italy 45°57N 8°39E 20 D8
Maggotty Jamaica 18°9N 77°46W 88 a
Maghâgha Egypt 28°38N 30°50E 53 C12
Maghera U.K. 54°51N 6°41W 10 B5
Magherafelt U.K. 54°45N 6°37W 10 B5
Maghreb N. Afr. 32°0N 4°0W 50 C3
Magistralnyy Russia 56°16N 107°36E 27 D11
Magnetic Pole (North) Arctic 85°9N 149°0W 4 A1
Magnetic Pole (South) Antarctica 64°8S 138°8E 5 C9
Magnitogorsk Russia 53°27N 59°4E 18 D10
Magnolia Ark., U.S.A. 33°16N 93°14W 84 E8
Magnolia Miss., U.S.A. 31°9N 90°28W 85 F9
Mago Fiji 17°26S 179°8W 59 a
Magog Canada 45°18N 72°9W 83 A12
Magpie, L. Canada 51°0N 64°41W 73 B7
Magrath Canada 49°25N 112°50W 70 D6
Maguan China 23°0N 104°21E 34 F5
Maguarinho, C. Brazil 0°15S 48°30W 93 D9
Magude Mozam. 25°2S 32°40E 57 C5
Mağusa = Famagusta Cyprus 35°8N 33°55E 46 C2
Maguse L. Canada 61°37N 95°10W 71 A9
Maguse Pt. Canada 61°20N 93°50W 71 A10
Magvana India 23°13N 69°22E 42 H3
Magway Burma 20°10N 95°0E 41 J19
Magyarorszag = Hungary ■ Europe 47°20N 19°20E 17 E10
Maha Oya Sri Lanka 7°31N 81°22E 45 L5
Maha Sarakham Thailand 16°12N 103°16E 38 D4
Mahābād Iran 36°50N 45°45E 46 B5
Mahabaleshwar India 17°58N 73°43E 44 F1
Mahabalipuram India 12°37N 80°11E 45 H5
Mahabharat Lekh Nepal 28°30N 82°0E 43 E10
Mahabo Madag. 20°23S 44°40E 55 J8
Mahad India 18°6N 73°29E 44 E1
Mahadeo Hills India 22°20N 78°30E 43 H8
Mahadeopur India 18°48N 80°0E 44 E5
Mahaffey U.S.A. 40°53N 78°44W 82 F6
Mahajan India 28°48N 73°56E 42 E5
Mahajanga Madag. 15°40S 46°25E 55 H9
Mahakam → Indonesia 0°35S 117°17E 36 E5
Mahalapye Botswana 23°1S 26°51E 56 B4
Mahale Mts. Tanzania 6°20S 30°0E 54 F6
Maḥallāt Iran 33°55N 50°30E 47 C6
Māhān Iran 30°5N 57°18E 47 D8
Mahan → India 23°30N 82°50E 43 H10
Mahanadi → India 20°20N 86°25E 44 D8
Mahananda → India 25°12N 87°52E 43 G12
Mahanoro Madag. 19°54S 48°48E 55 H9
Mahanoy City U.S.A. 40°49N 76°9W 83 F8
Maharashtra □ India 20°30N 75°30E 44 D2
Mahasamund India 21°6N 82°6E 44 D6
Mahasham, W. → Egypt 30°15N 34°10E 48 E3
Mahattat ash Shīdīyah Jordan 29°55N 35°55E 48 F4
Mahattat 'Unayzah Jordan 30°30N 35°47E 48 E4
Mahaweli Ganga → Sri Lanka 8°27N 81°13E 45 K5
Mahaxay Laos 17°22N 105°12E 38 D5
Mahbubabad India 17°42N 80°2E 44 F5
Mahbubnagar India 16°45N 77°59E 44 F3
Mahda U.A.E. 25°20N 56°15E 47 E8
Maḥḍah Oman 24°24N 55°59E 47 E7
Mahdia Tunisia 35°28N 11°0E 53 A8
Mahe Jammu & Kashmir, India 33°10N 78°32E 43 C8
Mahé Pondicherry, India 11°42N 75°34E 45 J2
Mahé Seychelles 5°0S 55°30E 55 b
Mahé ✈ (SEZ) Seychelles 4°40S 55°31E 55 b
Mahébourg Mauritius 20°24S 57°42E 55 d
Mahendra Giri India 8°20N 77°30E 45 K3
Mahendragarh India 28°17N 76°14E 42 E7
Mahendranagar Nepal 28°55N 80°20E 43 E9
Mahenge Tanzania 8°45S 36°41E 54 F7
Maheno N.Z. 45°10S 170°50E 59 F3
Mahesana India 23°39N 72°26E 42 H5
Maheshwar India 22°11N 75°35E 42 H6
Mahgawan India 26°29N 78°37E 43 F8
Mahi → India 22°15N 72°55E 42 H5
Mahia Pen. N.Z. 39°9S 177°55E 59 C6
Mahikeng = Mafikeng S. Africa 25°50S 25°38E 56 C4
Mahilyow Belarus 53°55N 30°18E 17 B16
Mahim India 19°39N 72°44E 44 E1
Mahina Tahiti 17°30S 149°27W 59 d
Mahinerangi, L. N.Z. 45°50S 169°56E 59 F2
Mahmud Kot Pakistan 30°16N 71°0E 42 D4
Mahnomen U.S.A. 47°19N 95°58W 80 B6
Maho Sri Lanka 7°49N 80°16E 45 L5
Mahoba India 25°15N 79°55E 43 G8
Mahón = Maó Spain 39°53N 4°16E 21 C8
Mahone Bay Canada 44°27N 64°23W 73 D7
Mahongo ⌓ Namibia 18°0S 23°15E 56 B3
Mahopac U.S.A. 41°22N 73°45W 83 E11
Mahuva India 21°5N 71°48E 42 J4
Mai-Ndombe, L. Dem. Rep. of the Congo 2°0S 18°20E 54 E3
Mai Thon, Ko Thailand 7°40N 98°28E 39 a
Maicuru → Brazil 2°14S 54°17W 93 D8
Maidan Khula Afghan. 33°36N 69°50E 42 C3
Maidenhead U.K. 51°31N 0°42W 13 F7
Maidstone Canada 53°5N 109°20W 71 C7
Maidstone U.K. 51°16N 0°32E 13 F8
Maiduguri Nigeria 12°0N 13°20E 53 F8
Maigh Nuad = Maynooth Ireland 53°23N 6°34W 10 C5
Maihar India 24°16N 80°45E 43 G9
Maikala Ra. India 22°0N 81°0E 44 D5
Mailani India 28°17N 80°21E 43 E9
Mailsi Pakistan 29°48N 72°15E 42 E5
Main → Germany 50°0N 8°18E 16 C5
Main → U.K. 54°48N 6°18W 10 B5
Main Channel Canada 45°21N 81°45W 82 A3
Main Range △ Australia 28°11S 152°27E 63 D5
Main Ridge Trin. & Tob. 11°16N 60°40W 93 J16
Maindargi India 17°28N 76°18E 44 F3
Maine France 48°20N 0°15W 20 C3
Maine □ U.S.A. 45°20N 69°0W 81 C19
Maine → Ireland 52°9N 9°45W 10 D2
Maine, G. of U.S.A. 43°0N 68°30W 75 G26
Maingkwan Burma 26°15N 96°37E 41 F20
Mainistir na Corann = Midleton Ireland 51°55N 8°10W 10 E3
Mainit, L. Phil. 9°31N 125°30E 37 C7
Mainland Orkney, U.K. 58°59N 3°8W 11 C5
Mainland Shet., U.K. 60°15N 1°22W 11 A7
Mainpuri India 27°18N 79°4E 43 F8
Maintirano Madag. 18°3S 44°1E 55 H8
Mainz Germany 50°1N 8°14E 16 C5
Maio C. Verde Is. 15°10N 23°10W 52 b
Maipú Argentina 36°52S 57°50W 94 D4
Maiquetía Venezuela 10°36N 66°57W 92 A5
Mairabari India 26°30N 92°22E 41 F18
Maisi Cuba 20°17N 74°9W 89 B5
Maisi, Pta. de Cuba 20°10N 74°10W 89 B5
Maitland N.S.W., Australia 32°33S 151°36E 63 E5
Maitland S. Austral., Australia 34°23S 137°40E 63 E2
Maitland → Canada 43°45N 81°43W 82 C3
Maitri Antarctica 70°0S 3°0W 5 D3
Maiyuan China 25°34N 117°28E 35 E11
Maíz, Is. del Nic. 12°15N 83°4W 88 D3
Maizuru Japan 35°25N 135°22E 29 G7
Majalengka Indonesia 6°50S 108°13E 37 G13
Majene Indonesia 3°38S 118°57E 37 E5
Majiang China 26°28N 107°32E 34 D6
Majorca = Mallorca Spain 39°30N 3°0E 21 C7
Majuro Marshall Is. 7°9N 171°12E 64 G9
Mak, Ko Thailand 11°49N 102°29E 39 G4
Maka Senegal 13°40N 14°10W 52 F3
Makaha Zimbabwe 17°20S 32°39E 57 A5
Makalamabedi Botswana 20°19S 23°51E 56 B3
Makale Indonesia 3°6S 119°51E 37 E5
Makalu Nepal 27°55N 87°8E 43 F12
Makalu-Barun △ Nepal 27°45N 87°10E 43 F12
Makarikari = Makgadikgadi Salt Pans Botswana 20°40S 25°45E 56 B4
Makarov Basin Arctic 87°0N 150°0W 4 A
Makarovo Russia 57°40N 107°45E 27 D11
Makassar Indonesia 5°10S 119°20E 37 F5
Makassar, Selat Indonesia 1°0S 118°20E 37 E5
Makassar, Str. of = Makassar, Selat Indonesia 1°0S 118°20E 37 E5
Makat = Maqat Kazakhstan 47°39N 53°19E 19 E9
Makedonija = Macedonia ■ Europe 41°53N 21°40E 23 D9
Makeni S. Leone 8°55N 12°5W 52 G3
Makeyevka = Makiyivka Ukraine 48°0N 38°0E 19 E6
Makgadikgadi △ Botswana 20°27S 24°47E 56 B3
Makgadikgadi Salt Pans Botswana 20°40S 25°45E 56 B4
Makhachkala Russia 43°0N 47°30E 19 F8
Makhado = Louis Trichardt S. Africa 23°1S 29°43E 57 B4
Makham, Ao Thailand 7°51N 98°25E 39 a
Makhfar al Buşayyah Iraq 30°0N 46°10E 46 D5
Makhmūr Iraq 35°46N 43°35E 46 C4
Makhtal India 16°30N 77°31E 45 E3
Makian Indonesia 0°20N 127°20E 37 D7
Makīnsk Kazakhstan 52°37N 70°26E 26 D8
Makira = San Cristóbal Solomon Is. 10°30S 161°0E 58 C9
Makiyivka Ukraine 48°0N 38°0E 19 E6
Makkah Si. Arabia 21°30N 39°54E 49 C2
Makkovik Canada 55°10N 59°10W 73 A8
Makó Hungary 46°14N 20°33E 17 E11
Makogai Fiji 17°28S 179°0E 59 a
Makokou Gabon 0°40N 12°50E 54 D2
Makrai India 22°2N 77°0E 42 H7
Makran Coast Range Pakistan 25°40N 64°0E 40 G4
Makrana India 27°2N 74°46E 42 F6
Makri India 19°46N 81°55E 44 E5
Mākū Iran 39°15N 44°31E 46 B5
Makunda Botswana 22°30S 20°7E 56 B3
Makung Taiwan 23°34N 119°34E 35 F12
Makurazaki Japan 31°15N 130°20E 29 J5
Makurdi Nigeria 7°43N 8°35E 52 G7
Makushin Volcano U.S.A. 53°53N 166°55W 74 E6
Makūyeh Iran 28°7N 53°9E 47 D7
Makwassie S. Africa 27°17S 26°0E 56 C4
Makwiro Zimbabwe 17°58S 30°25E 57 A5
Mal B. Ireland 52°50N 9°30W 10 D2
Mala = Mallow Ireland 52°8N 8°39W 10 D3
Mala ❂ Australia 21°39S 130°45E 60 D5
Mala, Pta. Panama 7°28N 80°2W 88 E3
Malabar Coast India 11°0N 75°0E 45 J2
Malacca, Straits of Indonesia 3°0N 101°0E 39 L3
Malad City U.S.A. 42°12N 112°15W 76 E7
Maladzyechna Belarus 54°20N 26°50E 17 A14
Málaga Spain 36°43N 4°23W 21 D3
Malagasy Rep. = Madagascar ■ Africa 20°0S 47°0E 55 J9
Malaimbandy Madag. 20°20S 45°36E 55 J9
Malaita Solomon Is. 9°0S 161°0E 58 B9
Malakal South Sudan 9°33N 31°40E 53 G12
Malakanagiri India 18°21N 81°54E 44 E5
Malakand Pakistan 34°40N 71°55E 42 B4
Malakula Vanuatu 16°15S 167°30E 58 C9
Malakwal Pakistan 32°34N 73°13E 42 C5
Malamala Indonesia 3°21S 120°55E 37 E6
Malanda Australia 17°22S 145°35E 62 B4
Malang Indonesia 7°59S 112°45E 37 G15
Malangen Norway 69°24N 18°37E 8 B18
Malangwa Nepal 26°52N 85°34E 43 F11
Malanje Angola 9°36S 16°17E 54 F3
Malappuram India 11°7N 76°11E 45 J3
Mälaren Sweden 59°30N 17°10E 9 G17
Malargüe Argentina 35°32S 69°30W 94 D2
Malartic Canada 48°9N 78°9W 72 C4
Malaryta Belarus 51°50N 24°3E 17 C13
Malaspina Glacier U.S.A. 59°50N 140°30W 74 D11
Malatya Turkey 38°25N 38°20E 46 B3
Malawi ■ Africa 11°55S 34°0E 55 G6
Malawi, L. Africa 12°30S 34°30E 55 G6
Malay Pen. Asia 7°25N 100°0E 39 J3
Malaya Vishera Russia 58°55N 32°25E 18 C5
Malaybalay Phil. 8°5N 125°7E 37 C7
Malāyer Iran 34°19N 48°51E 47 C6
Malaysia ■ Asia 5°0N 110°0E 36 D4
Malazgirt Turkey 39°10N 42°33E 46 B4
Malbon Australia 21°5S 140°17E 62 C3
Malbooma Australia 30°41S 134°11E 63 E1
Malbork Poland 54°3N 19°1E 17 B10
Malcolm Australia 28°51S 121°25E 61 E3
Malcolm, Pt. Australia 33°48S 123°45E 61 F3
Maldah India 25°2N 88°9E 43 G13
Maldegem Belgium 51°14N 3°26E 15 C3
Malden U.S.A. 36°34N 89°57W 80 G9
Malden I. Kiribati 4°3S 155°1W 65 H12
Maldives ■ Ind. Oc. 5°0N 73°0E 25 H9
Maldon U.K. 51°44N 0°42E 13 F8
Maldonado Uruguay 34°59S 55°0W 95 C5
Maldonado, Pta. Mexico 16°20N 98°33W 87 D5
Malé Karpaty Slovak Rep. 48°30N 17°20E 17 D9
Maleas, Akra Greece 36°28N 23°7E 23 F10
Malebo, Pool Africa 4°17S 15°20E 54 E3
Malegaon India 20°30N 74°38E 44 D2
Malek Kandī Iran 37°9N 46°6E 46 B5
Malema Mozam. 14°57S 37°20E 55 G7
Maler Kotla India 30°32N 75°58E 42 D6
Malgomaj Sweden 64°40N 16°30E 8 D17
Malha Sudan 15°8N 25°10E 53 E11
Malhargarh India 24°17N 74°59E 42 G6
Malheur → U.S.A. 44°4N 116°59W 76 D5
Malheur L. U.S.A. 43°20N 118°48W 76 E4
Mali ■ Africa 17°0N 3°0W 52 E5
Mali → Burma 25°42N 97°30E 41 G20
Mali Kyun Burma 13°0N 98°20E 38 F2
Malibu U.S.A. 34°2N 118°41W 79 L8
Maliku = Minicoy I. India 8°17N 73°2E 45 K1
Maliku Indonesia 0°39S 123°16E 37 E6
Malili Indonesia 2°42S 121°6E 37 E6
Malimba, Mts. Dem. Rep. of the Congo 7°30S 29°30E 54 F5
Malin Hd. Ireland 55°23N 7°23W 10 A4
Malin Pen. Ireland 55°20N 7°17W 10 A4
Malindi Kenya 3°12S 40°5E 54 E8
Malines = Mechelen Belgium 51°2N 4°29E 15 C4
Malino Indonesia 1°0N 121°0E 37 D6
Malipo China 23°7N 104°42E 34 F5
Malita Phil. 6°19N 125°39E 37 C7
Maliwun Burma 10°17N 98°40E 39 G2
Maliya India 23°5N 70°46E 42 H4
Malkapur India 20°53N 76°12E 44 D3
Malkara Turkey 40°53N 26°53E 23 D12
Malkhangiri = Malakanagiri India 18°21N 81°54E 44 E5
Mallacoota Inlet Australia 37°34S 149°40E 63 F4
Mallaig U.K. 57°0N 5°50W 11 D3
Mallawan India 27°4N 80°12E 43 F9
Mallawi Egypt 27°44N 30°44E 53 C12
Mallicolo = Malakula Vanuatu 16°15S 167°30E 58 C9
Mallorca Spain 39°30N 3°0E 21 C7
Mallorytown Canada 44°29N 75°53W 83 B9
Mallow Ireland 52°8N 8°39W 10 D3
Malmberget Sweden 67°11N 20°40E 8 C19
Malmédy Belgium 50°25N 6°2E 15 D6
Malmesbury S. Africa 33°28S 18°41E 56 D2
Malmivaara = Malmberget Sweden 67°11N 20°40E 8 C19
Malmö Sweden 55°36N 12°59E 9 J15
Malolo Fiji 17°45S 177°11E 59 a
Malolos Phil. 14°50N 120°49E 37 B6
Malolotja ⌓ Swaziland 26°4S 31°6E 57 C5
Malone U.S.A. 44°51N 74°18W 83 B10
Malong China 25°24N 103°34E 34 E4
Maloti Mts. = Drakensberg S. Africa 31°0S 28°0E 57 D4
Måløy Norway 61°57N 5°6E 8 F11
Malpaso, Presa = Netzahualcóyotl, Presa Mexico 17°8N 93°35W 87 D6
Malpelo, I. de Colombia 4°3N 81°35W 92 C2
Malprabha → India 16°20N 76°5E 45 F3
Malpur India 23°21N 73°27E 42 H5
Malpura India 26°17N 75°23E 42 F6
Malsiras India 17°52N 74°55E 44 F2
Malta Idaho, U.S.A. 42°18N 113°22W 76 E7
Malta Mont., U.S.A. 48°21N 107°52W 76 B10
Malta ■ Europe 35°55N 14°26E 22 G6
Malta Freeport Malta 35°49N 14°32E 22 a
Maltahöhe Namibia 24°55S 17°0E 56 B2
Malton U.K. 54°8N 0°49W 12 C7
Maluku Indonesia 1°0S 127°0E 37 E7
Maluku □ Indonesia 3°0S 128°0E 37 E7
Maluku Sea = Molucca Sea Indonesia 0°0 125°0E 37 E6
Malur India 13°0N 77°55E 45 H3
Malvalli India 12°28N 77°8E 45 H3
Malvan India 16°2N 73°30E 45 F1
Malvern U.S.A. 34°22N 92°49W 84 D8
Malvern Hills U.K. 52°0N 2°19W 13 E5
Malvinas, Is. = Falkland Is. ⊠ Atl. Oc. 51°30S 59°0W 96 G5
Malyn Ukraine 50°46N 29°3E 17 C15
Malyy Lyakhovskiy, Ostrov Russia 74°7N 140°36E 27 B15
Malyy Taymyr, Ostrov Russia 78°6N 107°15E 27 B11
Mama Russia 58°18N 112°54E 27 D12
Mamanguape Brazil 6°50S 35°4W 93 E11
Mamanuca Group Fiji 17°35S 177°5E 59 a
Mamarr Mitlā Egypt 30°2N 32°54E 48 E1
Mamasa Indonesia 2°55S 119°20E 37 E5
Mamberamo → Indonesia 2°0S 137°50E 37 E9
Mambilima Falls Zambia 10°31S 28°45E 54 G5
Mamburao Phil. 13°13N 120°39E 37 B6
Mameigwess L. Canada 52°35N 87°50W 72 B2
Mamili △ Namibia 18°2S 24°1E 56 A3
Mammoth U.S.A. 32°43N 110°39W 77 K8
Mammoth Cave △ U.S.A. 37°8N 86°13W 80 G10
Mammoth Lakes U.S.A. 37°39N 118°59W 78 H8
Mamoré → Bolivia 10°23S 65°53W 92 F5
Mamou Guinea 10°15N 12°0W 52 F3
Mamoudzou Mayotte 12°48S 45°14E 55 a
Mamuju Indonesia 2°41S 118°50E 37 E5
Mamuno Botswana 22°16S 20°1E 56 B3
Man Ivory C. 7°30N 7°40W 52 G4
Man → India 17°31N 75°32E 44 F2
Man, I. of India 8°28N 93°36E 45 K11
Man, I. of U.K. 54°15N 4°30W 12 C3
Man-Bazar India 23°4N 86°39E 43 H12
Man Na Burma 23°27N 97°19E 41 H20
Mänä U.S.A. 22°2N 159°47W 75 L8
Mana → Fr. Guiana 5°45N 53°55W 93 B8
Manaar, G. of = Mannar, G. of Asia 8°30N 79°0E 45 K4
Manacapuru Brazil 3°16S 60°37W 92 D6
Manacor Spain 39°34N 3°13E 21 C7
Manado Indonesia 1°29N 124°51E 37 D6
Managua Nic. 12°6N 86°20W 88 D2
Managua, L. de Nic. 12°20N 86°30W 88 D2
Manakara Madag. 22°8S 48°1E 55 J9
Manali India 32°16N 77°10E 42 C7
Manama = Al Manāmah Bahrain 26°10N 50°30E 47 E6
Mananjary Madag. 21°13S 48°20E 55 J9
Manantavadi India 11°49N 76°1E 45 J3
Manantenina Madag. 24°17S 47°19E 55 J9
Manaos = Manaus Brazil 3°0S 60°0W 92 D7
Manapire → Venezuela 7°42N 66°7W 92 B5
Manapouri N.Z. 45°34S 167°39E 59 F1
Manapouri, L. N.Z. 45°32S 167°32E 59 F1
Manapparai India 10°36N 78°25E 45 J4
Manar → India 18°50N 77°20E 44 E3

Manār, Jabal *Yemen* 14°2N 44°17E **49** E3
Manas *China* 44°17N 86°10E **30** C6
Manas → *India* 26°12N 90°40E **41** F17
Manas He → *China* 45°38N 85°12E **30** B6
Manaslu *Nepal* 28°33N 84°33E **43** E11
Manasquan *U.S.A.* 40°8N 74°3W **83** F10
Manassa *U.S.A.* 37°11N 105°56W **77** H11
Manatí *Puerto Rico* 18°26N 66°29W **89** d
Manaus *Brazil* 3°0S 60°0W **92** D7
Manawan L. *Canada* 55°24N 103°14W **71** B8
Manbij *Syria* 36°31N 37°57E **46** B3
Manchegorsk *Russia* 67°54N 32°58E **26** C4
Manchester *U.K.* 53°29N 2°12W **12** D5
Manchester *Calif.,*
  U.S.A. 38°58N 123°41W **78** G3
Manchester *Conn.,*
  U.S.A. 41°47N 72°31W **83** E12
Manchester *Ga., U.S.A.* 32°51N 84°37W **85** E12
Manchester *Iowa, U.S.A.* 42°29N 91°27W **80** D8
Manchester *Ky., U.S.A.* 37°9N 83°46W **81** G12
Manchester *N.H.,*
  U.S.A. 42°59N 71°28W **83** D13
Manchester *N.Y., U.S.A.* 42°56N 77°16W **82** D7
Manchester *Pa., U.S.A.* 40°4N 76°43W **83** F8
Manchester *Tenn., U.S.A.* 35°29N 86°5W **85** D11
Manchester *Vt., U.S.A.* 43°10N 73°5W **83** C11
Manchester Int. ✈ (MAN)
  U.K. 53°21N 2°17W **12** D5
Manchester L. *Canada* 61°28N 107°29W **71** A7
Manchhar L. *Pakistan* 26°25N 67°39E **42** F2
Manchuria = Dongbei
  China 45°0N 125°0E **33** D13
Manchurian Plain *China* 47°0N 124°0E **24** D14
Mand → *India* 21°42N 83°15E **43** J10
Mand → *Iran* 28°20N 52°30E **47** D7
Mandaguari *Brazil* 23°32S 51°42W **95** A5
Mandah = Töhöm
  Mongolia 44°27N 108°2E **32** B5
Mandal *Norway* 58°2N 7°25E **9** G12
Mandala, Puncak
  Indonesia 4°44S 140°20E **37** E10
Mandalay *Burma* 22°0N 96°4E **41** J20
Mandale = Mandalay
  Burma 22°0N 96°4E **41** J20
Mandalgarh *India* 25°12N 75°6E **42** G6
Mandalgovĭ *Mongolia* 45°45N 106°10E **32** B4
Mandalī *Iraq* 33°43N 45°28E **46** C5
Mandan *U.S.A.* 46°50N 100°54W **80** B3
Mandar, Teluk *Indonesia* 3°32S 119°21E **37** E5
Mandaue *Phil.* 10°20N 123°56E **37** B6
Mandeville *Jamaica* 18°2N 77°31W **88** a
Mandi *India* 31°39N 76°58E **42** D7
Mandi Burewala *Pakistan* 30°9N 72°41E **42** D5
Mandi Dabwali *India* 29°58N 74°42E **42** E6
Mandimba *Mozam.* 14°20S 35°40E **55** E7
Mandioli *Indonesia* 0°40S 127°20E **37** E7
Mandla *India* 22°39N 80°30E **43** H9
Mandorah *Australia* 12°32S 130°42E **60** B5
Mandra *Pakistan* 33°23N 73°12E **42** C5
Mandritsara *Madag.* 15°50S 48°49E **55** H9
Mandsaur *India* 24°3N 75°8E **42** G6
Mandurah *Australia* 32°36S 115°48E **61** F2
Mandvi *India* 22°51N 69°22E **42** H3
Mandya *India* 12°30N 77°0E **45** H3
Mandzai *Pakistan* 30°55N 67°6E **42** D2
Maneh *Iran* 37°39N 57°7E **47** B8
Maner → *India* 18°30N 79°40E **44** E4
Maneroo Cr. →
  Australia 23°21S 143°53E **62** C3
Manfalūt *Egypt* 27°20N 30°52E **53** C12
Manfredónia *Italy* 41°38N 15°55E **22** D6
Mangabeiras, Chapada das
  Brazil 10°0S 46°30W **93** F9
Mangaia *Cook Is.* 21°55S 157°55W **65** K12
Mangalagiri *India* 16°26N 80°36E **45** F5
Mangalia *Romania* 43°50N 28°35E **17** G15
Mangalore = Mangaluru
  India 12°55N 74°47E **45** H2
Mangaluru *India* 12°55N 74°47E **45** H2
Mangalvedha *India* 17°31N 75°28E **44** F2
Mangan *India* 27°31N 88°32E **43** F13
Mangaon *India* 18°15N 73°20E **44** E1
Mangarrayi ◇ *Australia* 15°5S 133°10E **62** B1
Mangawan *India* 24°41N 81°33E **43** G9
Mangaweka *N.Z.* 39°48S 175°47E **59** C5
Mangetti △ *Namibia* 18°43S 19°8E **56** A2
Manggar *Indonesia* 2°50S 108°10E **36** E3
Manggawitu *Indonesia* 4°8S 133°32E **37** E8
Mangghystaū Tübegi
  Kazakhstan 44°30N 52°30E **26** E6
Manggis *Indonesia* 8°29S 115°31E **37** J18
Mangkalihat, Tanjung
  Indonesia 1°2N 118°59E **37** D5
Mangkururrpa ◇
  Australia 20°35S 129°43E **60** D4
Mangla *Pakistan* 33°7N 73°39E **42** C5
Mangla Dam *Pakistan* 33°9N 73°44E **43** C5
Manglaur *India* 29°44N 77°49E **42** E7
Mangnai *China* 37°52N 91°43E **30** D7
Mangnai Zhen *China* 38°24N 90°14E **30** D7
Mango *Togo* 10°20N 0°30E **52** F6
Mango *Tonga* 20°17S 174°29W **59** c
Mangoche *Malawi* 14°25S 35°16E **55** E7
Mangoky → *Madag.* 21°29S 43°41E **55** J8
Mangole *Indonesia* 1°50S 125°55E **37** E7
Mangonui *N.Z.* 35°1S 173°32E **59** A4
Mangrol *Mad. P., India* 21°7N 70°7E **42** J4
Mangrol *Raj., India* 25°20N 76°31E **42** G6
Mangrul Pir *India* 20°19N 77°21E **44** D3
Mangshi = Luxi *China* 24°27N 98°36E **34** E2
Mangueira, L. da *Brazil* 33°0S 52°50W **95** C5
Mangum *U.S.A.* 34°53N 99°30W **84** D5
Manguri *India* 28°58S 134°22E **63** A1
Mangyshlak, Poluostrov =
  Mangghystaū Tübegi
  Kazakhstan 44°30N 52°30E **26** E6
Manhattan *U.S.A.* 39°11N 96°35W **80** F5
Manhiça *Mozam.* 25°23S 32°49E **57** C5
Manica *Mozam.* 18°58S 32°59E **57** A5
Manica □ *Mozam.* 19°10S 33°45E **57** A5

Manicoré *Brazil* 5°48S 61°16W **92** E6
Manicouagan → *Canada* 49°30N 68°30W **73** C6
Manicouagan, Rés.
  Canada 51°5N 68°40W **73** B6
Manīfah *Si. Arabia* 27°44N 49°0E **47** E6
Manifold, C. *Australia* 22°41S 150°50E **62** C5
Maniganggo *China* 31°56N 99°10E **34** B2
Manigotagan *Canada* 51°6N 96°18W **71** C9
Manigotagan → *Canada* 51°7N 96°20W **71** C9
Manihari *India* 25°21N 87°38E **43** G12
Manihiki *Cook Is.* 10°24S 161°1W **65** J11
Manihiki Plateau
  Pac. Oc. 11°0S 164°0W **65** J11
Manikpur *India* 25°4N 81°7E **43** G9
Manila *U.S.A.* 40°59N 109°43W **76** F9
Manila *Phil.* 14°40N 120°35E **37** B6
Manila B. *Phil.* 14°40N 120°35E **37** B6
Manilla *Australia* 30°45S 150°43E **63** E5
Maningrida *Australia* 12°3S 134°13E **62** A1
Manipa, Selat *Indonesia* 3°20S 127°25E **37** E7
Manipur □ *India* 25°0N 94°0E **41** G19
Manipur → *Burma* 23°45N 94°20E **41** H19
Manisa *Turkey* 38°38N 27°30E **23** E12
Manistee *U.S.A.* 44°15N 86°19W **80** C10
Manistee → *U.S.A.* 44°15N 86°21W **80** C10
Manistique *U.S.A.* 45°57N 86°15W **80** C10
Manitoba □ *Canada* 53°30N 97°0W **71** B9
Manitoba, L. *Canada* 51°0N 98°45W **71** C9
Manitou *Canada* 49°15N 98°32W **71** D9
Manitou, L. *U.S.A.* 50°55N 65°17W **73** B6
Manitou Is. *U.S.A.* 45°8N 86°0W **80** C10
Manitou L. *Canada* 52°43N 109°43W **71** C7
Manitou Springs
  U.S.A. 38°52N 104°55W **76** G11
Manitoulin I. *Canada* 45°40N 82°30W **72** C3
Manitouwadge *Canada* 49°8N 85°48W **72** C2
Manitowoc *U.S.A.* 44°5N 87°40W **80** C10
Maniyachi *India* 8°51N 77°55E **45** K3
Manizales *Colombia* 5°5N 75°32W **92** B3
Manjacaze *Mozam.* 24°45S 34°0E **57** B5
Manjakandriana *Madag.* 18°55S 47°47E **55** H9
Manjhand *Pakistan* 25°50N 68°10E **42** G3
Manjimup *Australia* 34°15S 116°6E **61** F2
Manjlegaon *India* 19°9N 76°14E **44** E3
Manjra → *India* 18°49N 77°52E **44** E3
Mankato *Kans., U.S.A.* 39°47N 98°13W **80** F5
Mankato *Minn., U.S.A.* 44°10N 94°0W **80** C6
Mankayane *Swaziland* 26°40S 31°4E **57** C5
Mankera *Pakistan* 31°23N 71°26E **42** D4
Mankota *Canada* 49°25N 107°5W **71** D7
Mankulam *Sri Lanka* 9°8N 80°26E **45** K5
Manlay = Üydzin *Mongolia* 44°9N 107°0E **32** B4
Manmad *India* 20°18N 74°28E **44** D2
Mann Ranges *Australia* 26°6S 130°5E **61** E5
Manna *Indonesia* 4°25S 102°55E **36** E2
Mannahill *Australia* 32°25S 139°59E **63** E3
Mannar *Sri Lanka* 9°1N 79°54E **45** K4
Mannar, G. of *Asia* 8°30N 79°0E **45** K4
Mannar I. *Sri Lanka* 9°5N 79°45E **45** K4
Mannargudi *India* 10°45N 79°51E **45** J4
Mannheim *Germany* 49°29N 8°29E **16** D5
Manning *Canada* 56°53N 117°39W **70** B5
Manning *Oreg., U.S.A.* 45°45N 123°13W **78** E3
Manning *S.C., U.S.A.* 33°42N 80°13W **85** E14
Mannum *Australia* 34°50S 139°20E **63** E2
Manohar *India* 22°23N 85°12E **43** H11
Manokwari *Indonesia* 0°54S 134°0E **37** E8
Manombo *Madag.* 22°57S 43°28E **55** J8
Manono
  Dem. Rep. of the Congo 7°15S 27°25E **54** F5
Manono *Samoa* 13°50S 172°5W **59** b
Manorhamilton *Ireland* 54°18N 8°11W **10** B3
Manosque *France* 43°49N 5°47E **20** E6
Manotick *Canada* 45°13N 75°41W **83** A9
Manouane → *Canada* 49°30N 71°10W **73** C5
Manouane, L. *Canada* 50°45N 70°45W **73** B5
Manp'o *N. Korea* 41°6N 126°24E **33** D14
Manpojin = Manp'o
  N. Korea 41°6N 126°24E **33** D14
Manpur *Chhattisgarh,*
  India 23°17N 83°35E **43** H10
Manpur *Chhattisgarh,*
  India 20°22N 80°43E **44** D5
Manpur *Mad. P., India* 22°26N 75°37E **42** H6
Manresa *Spain* 41°48N 1°50E **21** B6
Mansa *Gujarat, India* 23°27N 72°45E **42** H5
Mansa *Punjab, India* 30°0N 75°27E **42** E6
Mansa *Zambia* 11°13S 28°55E **54** G5
Mansehra *Pakistan* 34°20N 73°15E **42** B5
Mansel I. *Canada* 62°0N 80°0W **69** E15
Mansfield *Australia* 37°4S 146°6E **63** F4
Mansfield *U.K.* 53°9N 1°11W **12** D6
Mansfield *La., U.S.A.* 32°2N 93°43W **84** E8
Mansfield *Ohio, U.S.A.* 40°45N 82°31W **82** F2
Mansfield *Pa., U.S.A.* 41°48N 77°5W **82** E7
Mansfield *Tex., U.S.A.* 32°33N 97°8W **84** E6
Mansfield, Mt. *U.S.A.* 44°33N 72°49W **83** B12
Manson Creek *Canada* 55°37N 124°32W **70** B4
Manta *Ecuador* 1°0S 80°40W **92** D2
Mantalingajan, Mt. *Phil.* 8°55N 117°45E **36** C5
Manteca *U.S.A.* 37°48N 121°13W **78** H5
Manteo *U.S.A.* 35°55N 75°40W **85** D17
Mantes-la-Jolie *France* 48°58N 1°41E **20** B4
Mantha *India* 19°40N 76°23E **44** E3
Manthani *India* 18°40N 79°35E **44** E4
Manti *U.S.A.* 39°16N 111°38W **76** G8
Mantiqueira, Serra da
  Brazil 22°0S 44°0W **95** A7
Manton *U.S.A.* 44°25N 85°24W **81** C11
Mántova *Italy* 45°9N 10°48E **22** B4
Mänttä Vilppula *Finland* 62°2N 24°40E **8** E21
Mantua = Mántova *Italy* 45°9N 10°48E **22** B4
Manú *Peru* 12°10S 70°51W **92** F4
Manú → *Peru* 12°16S 70°55W **92** F4
Manu'a Is. *Amer. Samoa* 14°13S 169°35W **59** b
Manuel Alves → *Brazil* 11°19S 48°28W **93** F9
Manui *Indonesia* 3°35S 123°5E **37** E6
Manukau *N.Z.* 37°0S 174°52E **59** B5
Manuripi → *Bolivia* 11°6S 67°36W **92** F5
Manvi *India* 15°57N 76°59E **45** G3

Manwan Dam *China* 24°44N 100°20E **34** E3
Manwath *India* 19°19N 76°32E **44** E3
Many *U.S.A.* 31°34N 93°29W **84** F8
Manyallaluk ◇
  Australia 14°16S 132°49E **60** B5
Manych-Gudilo, Ozero
  Russia 46°24N 42°38E **19** E7
Manyoni *Tanzania* 5°45S 34°55E **54** F6
Manzai *Pakistan* 32°12N 70°15E **42** C4
Manzanar △ *U.S.A.* 36°44N 118°9W **78** J7
Manzanares *Spain* 39°2N 3°22W **21** C4
Manzanillo *Cuba* 20°20N 77°31W **88** B4
Manzanillo *Mexico* 19°3N 104°20W **86** D4
Manzanillo, Pta. *Panama* 9°30N 79°40W **88** E4
Manzano Mts. *U.S.A.* 34°40N 106°20W **77** J10
Manẓarīyeh *Iran* 34°53N 50°50E **47** C6
Manzhouli *China* 49°35N 117°25E **31** B12
Manzini *Swaziland* 26°30S 31°25E **57** C5
Manzouli = Manzhouli
  China 49°35N 117°25E **31** B12
Manzur Vadisi △ *Turkey* 39°10N 39°30E **46** B3
Mao *Chad* 14°4N 15°19E **53** F9
Maó *Spain* 39°53N 4°16E **21** C8
Maoke, Pegunungan
  Indonesia 3°40S 137°30E **37** E9
Maolin *China* 43°58N 123°30E **33** C12
Maoming *China* 21°50N 110°54E **35** G8
Maopi T'ou *China* 21°56N 120°43E **35** G13
Maoxian *China* 31°41N 103°49E **34** B4
Maoxing *China* 45°28N 124°40E **33** B13
Mapam Yumco *China* 30°45N 81°28E **43** D9
Mapastepec *Mexico* 15°26N 92°54W **87** D6
Maphrao, Ko *Thailand* 7°56N 98°26E **39** a
Mapia, Kepulauan
  Indonesia 0°50N 134°20E **37** D8
Mapimí *Mexico* 25°49N 103°51W **86** B4
Mapimí, Bolsón de
  Mexico 27°0N 104°15W **86** B4
Maping *China* 31°34N 113°32E **35** B9
Mapinhane *Mozam.* 22°20S 35°0E **57** B6
Maple Creek *Canada* 49°55N 109°29W **71** D7
Maple Valley *U.S.A.* 47°25N 122°3W **78** C4
Mapleton *U.S.A.* 44°2N 123°52W **76** D2
Mapoon ◇ *Australia* 11°44S 142°8E **62** A3
Mapuca *India* 15°36N 73°46E **45** G1
Mapuera → *Brazil* 1°5S 57°2W **92** D7
Mapulanguene *Mozam.* 24°29S 32°6E **57** B5
Mapungubwe △ *S. Africa* 22°12S 29°22E **57** B4
Maputo *Mozam.* 25°58S 32°32E **57** C5
Maputo □ *Mozam.* 26°0S 32°25E **57** C5
Maputo, B. de *Mozam.* 25°50S 32°45E **57** C5
Maputo △ *Mozam.* 26°23S 32°48E **57** C5
Maqat *Kazakhstan* 47°39N 53°19E **19** E9
Maqên *China* 34°24N 100°6E **30** E9
Maqên Gangri *China* 34°55N 99°18E **34** A3
Maqiaoshi *China* 44°40N 130°30E **33** B16
Maqnā *Si. Arabia* 28°25N 34°50E **46** D2
Maqteïr *Mauritania* 21°50N 11°40W **52** D3
Maqu *China* 33°52N 101°42E **30** E9
Maquan He = Brahmaputra →
  Asia 23°40N 90°35E **43** H13
Maquela do Zombo *Angola* 6°0S 15°15E **54** F3
Maquinchao *Argentina* 41°15S 68°50W **96** E3
Maquoketa *U.S.A.* 42°4N 90°40W **80** D8
Mar *Canada* 44°49N 81°12W **82** B3
Mar, Serra do *Brazil* 25°30S 49°0W **95** B6
Mar Chiquita, L.
  Argentina 30°40S 62°50W **94** C3
Mar del Plata *Argentina* 38°0S 57°30W **94** D4
Mar Menor *Spain* 37°40N 0°45W **21** D5
Maraã *Brazil* 1°52S 65°25W **92** D5
Maraa *Tahiti* 17°46S 149°34W **59** d
Marabá *Brazil* 5°20S 49°5W **93** E9
Maraboon, L. *Australia* 23°41S 148°0E **62** C4
Maracá, I. de *Brazil* 2°10N 50°30W **93** C8
Maracaibo *Venezuela* 10°40N 71°37W **92** A4
Maracaibo, L. de
  Venezuela 9°40N 71°30W **92** B4
Maracaju *Brazil* 21°38S 55°9W **95** A4
Maracas Bay Village
  Trin. & Tob. 10°46N 61°28W **93** K15
Maracay *Venezuela* 10°15N 67°28W **92** A5
Marādah *Libya* 29°15N 19°15E **53** C9
Maradi *Niger* 13°29N 7°20E **52** F7
Marāgheh *Iran* 37°30N 46°12E **46** B5
Marāh *Si. Arabia* 25°0N 45°35E **46** E5
Marajó, I. de *Brazil* 1°0S 49°30W **93** D9
Marākand *Iran* 38°51N 45°16E **46** B5
Marakele △ *S. Africa* 24°30S 25°30E **57** D4
Maralinga *Australia* 30°13S 131°32E **61** F5
Maralinga Tjarutja ◇
  Australia 29°30S 131°0E **61** E5
Marambio *Antarctica* 64°0S 56°0W **5** C18
Maran *Malaysia* 3°35N 102°45E **39** L4
Marana *U.S.A.* 32°27N 111°13W **77** K8
Maranboy *Australia* 14°40S 132°39E **60** B5
Marand *Iran* 38°30N 45°45E **46** B5
Marang *Malaysia* 5°12N 103°13E **39** K4
Maranguape *Brazil* 3°55S 38°50W **93** D11
Maranhão = São Luís
  Brazil 2°39S 44°15W **93** D10
Maranhão □ *Brazil* 5°0S 46°0W **93** E9
Maranoa → *Australia* 27°50S 148°37E **63** D4
Marañón → *Peru* 4°30S 73°35W **92** D4
Marão *Mozam.* 24°18S 34°2E **57** B5
Maraş = Kahramanmaraş
  Turkey 37°37N 36°53E **46** B3
Marathasa *Australia* 20°51S 143°32E **62** C3
Marathon *Canada* 48°44N 86°23W **72** C2
Marathon *N.Y., U.S.A.* 42°27N 76°2W **83** D8
Marathon *Tex., U.S.A.* 30°12N 103°15W **84** F3
Maratua *Indonesia* 2°10N 118°35E **37** D5
Maraval *Trin. & Tob.* 10°42N 61°31W **93** K15
Maravatío *Mexico* 19°54N 100°27W **86** D4
Marāwih *U.A.E.* 24°18N 53°18E **47** E7
Marbella *Spain* 36°30N 4°57W **21** D3
Marble Bar *Australia* 21°9S 119°44E **60** D2
Marblehead *Mass.,*
  U.S.A. 42°30N 70°51W **83** D14
Marblehead *Ohio, U.S.A.* 41°32N 82°44W **82** E2

Marburg *Germany* 50°47N 8°46E **16** C5
Marca, Pta. do *Angola* 16°31S 11°43E **55** H2
March *U.K.* 52°33N 0°5E **13** E8
Marche *France* 46°5N 1°20E **20** C4
Marche-en-Famenne
  Belgium 50°14N 5°19E **15** D5
Marchena *Spain* 37°18N 5°23W **21** D3
Marco Island *U.S.A.* 25°58N 81°44W **85** H14
Marcos Juárez *Argentina* 32°42S 62°5W **94** C3
Marcus Baker, Mt.
  U.S.A. 61°26N 147°45W **74** C10
Marcus I. = Minami-Tori-Shima
  Pac. Oc. 24°20N 153°58E **64** E7
Marcy, Mt. *U.S.A.* 44°7N 73°56W **83** B11
Mardan *Pakistan* 34°20N 72°0E **42** B5
Mardie *Australia* 21°12S 115°59E **60** D2
Mardin *Turkey* 37°20N 40°43E **46** B4
Maree, L. *U.K.* 57°40N 5°26E **11** D3
Mareeba *Australia* 16°59S 145°28E **62** B4
Mareetsane *S. Africa* 26°9S 25°25E **56** C4
Marek = Stanke Dimitrov
  Bulgaria 42°17N 23°9E **23** C10
Marengo *U.S.A.* 41°48N 92°4W **80** E7
Marfa *U.S.A.* 30°19N 104°1W **84** F2
Margao = Madgaon
  India 15°12N 73°58E **45** G1
Margaret → *Australia* 18°9S 125°41E **60** C4
Margaret Bay *Canada* 51°20N 127°35W **70** C3
Margaret L. *Canada* 58°56N 115°25W **70** B5
Margaret River *Australia* 33°57S 115°4E **61** F2
Margarita, I. de *Venezuela* 11°0N 64°0W **92** A6
Margaritovo *Russia* 43°25N 134°45E **28** C7
Margate *S. Africa* 30°50S 30°20E **57** D5
Margate *U.K.* 51°23N 1°23E **13** F9
Marg'ilon *Uzbekistan* 40°27N 71°42E **26** E8
Mārgow, Dasht-e *Afghan.* 30°40N 62°30E **40** D3
Marguerite *Canada* 52°30N 122°25W **70** C4
Mari El □ *Russia* 56°30N 48°0E **18** C8
Mari Indus *Pakistan* 32°57N 71°34E **42** C4
Mari Republic = Mari El □
  Russia 56°30N 48°0E **18** C8
María Elena *Chile* 22°18S 69°40W **94** A2
María Grande *Argentina* 31°45S 59°55W **94** C4
Maria I. *N. Terr.,*
  Australia 14°52S 135°45E **62** A2
Maria I. *Tas., Australia* 42°35S 148°0E **63** G4
Maria Island △ *Australia* 42°38S 148°5E **63** G4
Maria van Diemen, C.
  N.Z. 34°29S 172°40E **59** A4
Mariala △ *Australia* 25°57S 145°2E **63** D4
Marian *Australia* 21°9S 148°57E **62** b
Marian L. *Canada* 63°0N 116°15W **70** A5
Mariana Trench *Pac. Oc.* 13°0N 145°0E **64** F6
Marianna *Ark., U.S.A.* 34°46N 90°46W **85** D9
Marianna *Fla., U.S.A.* 30°46N 85°14W **85** F12
Marias → *U.S.A.* 47°56N 110°30W **76** C8
Marías, Is. *Mexico* 21°25N 106°28W **86** C3
Mariato, Punta *Panama* 7°12N 80°52W **88** E3
Maribor *Slovenia* 46°36N 15°40E **16** E8
Marico → *Africa* 23°35S 26°57E **56** B4
Maricopa *Ariz., U.S.A.* 33°4N 112°3W **77** K7
Maricopa *Calif., U.S.A.* 35°4N 119°24W **79** K7
Marié → *Brazil* 0°27S 66°26W **92** D5
Marie Byrd Land
  Antarctica 79°30S 125°0W **5** D14
Marie-Galante *Guadeloupe* 15°56N 61°16W **88** b
Mariecourt = Kangiqsujuaq
  Canada 61°30N 72°0W **69** E17
Mariehamn *Finland* 60°5N 19°55E **9** F18
Mariembourg *Belgium* 50°6N 4°31E **15** D4
Mariental *Namibia* 24°36S 18°0E **56** B2
Marienville *U.S.A.* 41°28N 79°8W **82** E5
Mariestad *Sweden* 58°43N 13°50E **9** G15
Marietta *Ga., U.S.A.* 33°57N 84°33W **85** E12
Marietta *Ohio, U.S.A.* 39°25N 81°27W **81** F13
Marieville *Canada* 45°26N 73°10W **83** A11
Mariinsk *Russia* 56°10N 87°20E **26** D9
Marijampolė *Lithuania* 54°33N 23°19E **9** J20
Marília *Brazil* 22°13S 50°0W **95** A6
Marín *Spain* 42°23N 8°42W **21** A1
Marina *U.S.A.* 36°41N 121°48W **78** J5
Marinduque *Phil.* 13°25N 122°0E **37** B6
Marine City *U.S.A.* 42°43N 82°30W **82** D2
Marinette *U.S.A.* 45°6N 87°38W **80** C10
Maringá *Brazil* 23°26S 52°2W **95** A5
Marion *Ala., U.S.A.* 32°38N 87°19W **85** E11
Marion *Ark., U.S.A.* 35°13N 90°12W **80** H8
Marion *Ill., U.S.A.* 37°44N 88°56W **80** G9
Marion *Ind., U.S.A.* 40°32N 85°40W **81** E11
Marion *Iowa, U.S.A.* 42°2N 91°36W **80** D8
Marion *Kans., U.S.A.* 38°21N 97°1W **80** F5
Marion *N.C., U.S.A.* 35°41N 82°1W **85** D13
Marion *Ohio, U.S.A.* 40°35N 83°8W **81** E12
Marion *S.C., U.S.A.* 34°11N 79°24W **85** D15
Marion *Va., U.S.A.* 36°50N 81°31W **81** G13
Marion, L. *U.S.A.* 33°28N 80°10W **85** E14
Mariposa *U.S.A.* 37°29N 119°58W **78** H7
Mariscal Estigarribia
  Paraguay 22°3S 60°40W **94** A3
Maritime Alps = Maritimes, Alpes
  Europe 44°10N 7°10E **20** D7
Maritimes, Alpes *Europe* 44°10N 7°10E **20** D7
Maritsa = Evros →
  Greece 41°40N 26°34E **23** D12
Mariupol *Ukraine* 47°5N 37°31E **19** E6
Mariusa △ *Venezuela* 9°24N 61°27W **89** D7
Marīvān *Iran* 35°30N 46°25E **46** C5
Marj 'Uyūn *Lebanon* 33°21N 35°34E **48** B4
Marka *Somalia* 1°48N 44°50E **49** G3
Markam *China* 29°42N 98°38E **34** C2
Markapur *India* 15°44N 79°19E **45** G4
Markazī □ *Iran* 34°0N 49°30E **47** C6
Markdale *Canada* 44°19N 80°39W **82** B4
Marked Tree *U.S.A.* 35°32N 90°25W **85** D9
Market Drayton *U.K.* 52°54N 2°29W **12** E5
Market Harborough *U.K.* 52°29N 0°55W **13** E7
Market Rasen *U.K.* 53°24N 0°20W **12** D7
Markham, Mt. *Antarctica* 83°0S 164°0E **5** E11
Markleeville *U.S.A.* 38°42N 119°47W **78** G7
Markovo *Russia* 64°40N 170°24E **27** C17

Marks *Russia* 51°45N 46°50E **18** D8
Marksville *U.S.A.* 31°8N 92°4W **84** F8
Marla *Australia* 27°19S 133°33E **63** D1
Marlbank *Canada* 44°26N 77°6W **82** B7
Marlboro *U.S.A.* 41°36N 73°59W **83** E11
Marlborough *Australia* 22°46S 149°52E **62** C4
Marlborough *U.K.* 51°25N 1°43W **13** F6
Marlborough □ *N.Z.* 41°30S 173°33W **59** D4
Marlborough Downs
  U.K. 51°27N 1°53W **13** F6
Marlin *U.S.A.* 31°18N 96°54W **84** F6
Marlow = Minami-Tori-Shima
  Pac. Oc. 24°20N 153°58E **64** E7
Marlow *U.K.* 51°34N 0°46W **13** F7
Marlow *U.S.A.* 34°39N 97°58W **84** D6
Marmagao *India* 15°25N 73°56E **45** G1
Marmara *Turkey* 40°35N 27°34E **23** D12
Marmara, Sea of = Marmara
  Denizi *Turkey* 40°45N 28°15E **23** D13
Marmara Denizi *Turkey* 40°45N 28°15E **23** D13
Marmaris *Turkey* 36°50N 28°14E **23** F13
Marmion, Mt. *Australia* 29°16S 119°50E **61** E2
Marmion L. *Canada* 48°55N 91°20W **72** C1
Marmolada, Mte. *Italy* 46°26N 11°51E **22** A4
Marmora *Canada* 44°28N 77°41W **82** B7
Marne □ *France* 48°48N 4°45E **20** B6
Marne → *France* 48°47N 2°29E **20** B5
Maro Reef *U.S.A.* 25°25N 170°35W **75** K5
Maroantsetra *Madag.* 15°26S 49°44E **55** H9
Maroelaboom *Namibia* 19°15S 18°53E **56** A2
Maroni → *Fr. Guiana* 5°30N 54°0W **93** B8
Maroochydore *Australia* 26°29S 153°5E **63** D5
Maroona *Australia* 37°27S 142°54E **63** F3
Maroua *Cameroon* 10°40N 14°20E **53** F8
Marovoay *Madag.* 16°6S 46°39E **55** H9
Marquard *S. Africa* 28°40S 27°28E **56** C4
Marquesas Fracture Zone
  Pac. Oc. 9°0S 125°0W **65** H15
Marquesas Is. = Marquises, Îs.
  French Polynesia 9°30S 140°0W **65** H14
Marquette *U.S.A.* 46°33N 87°24W **80** B10
Marquis *St. Lucia* 14°2N 60°54W **89** f
Marquises, Îs.
  French Polynesia 9°30S 140°0W **65** H14
Marra, Djebel *Sudan* 13°10N 24°22E **53** F10
Marracuene *Mozam.* 25°45S 32°35E **57** C5
Marrakech *Morocco* 31°9N 8°0W **52** B4
Marrawah *Australia* 40°55S 144°42E **63** G3
Marree *Australia* 29°39S 138°1E **63** D2
Marrimane *Mozam.* 22°58S 33°34E **57** B5
Marromeu *Mozam.* 18°15S 36°25E **57** A6
Marrowie Cr. →
  Australia 33°23S 145°40E **63** E4
Marrupa *Mozam.* 13°8S 37°30E **55** E7
Mars Hill *U.S.A.* 46°31N 67°52W **81** B20
Marsá 'Alam *Egypt* 25°5N 34°54E **47** F8
Marsá Matrûh *Egypt* 31°19N 27°9E **53** B11
Marsabit *Kenya* 2°18N 38°0E **54** D7
Marsala *Italy* 37°48N 12°26E **22** F5
Marsden *Australia* 33°47S 147°32E **63** E4
Marseille *France* 43°18N 5°23E **20** E6
Marseilles = Marseille
  France 43°18N 5°23E **20** E6
Marsh I. *U.S.A.* 29°34N 91°53W **84** G9
Marshall *Ark., U.S.A.* 35°55N 92°38W **84** D8
Marshall *Mich., U.S.A.* 42°16N 84°58W **81** D11
Marshall *Minn., U.S.A.* 44°27N 95°47W **80** C6
Marshall *Mo., U.S.A.* 39°7N 93°12W **80** F7
Marshall *Tex., U.S.A.* 32°33N 94°23W **84** E7
Marshall → *Australia* 22°59S 136°59E **62** C2
Marshall Is. ■ *Pac. Oc.* 9°0N 171°0E **64** G9
Marshalltown *U.S.A.* 42°3N 92°55W **80** D7
Marshbrook *Zimbabwe* 18°33S 31°9E **57** B5
Marshfield *Mo., U.S.A.* 37°15N 92°54W **80** G7
Marshfield *Vt., U.S.A.* 44°20N 72°20W **83** B12
Marshfield *Wis., U.S.A.* 44°40N 90°10W **80** C8
Mārsta *Sweden* 59°37N 17°52E **9** G17
Mart *U.S.A.* 31°33N 96°50W **84** F6
Martaban *Burma* 16°30N 97°35E **41** L20
Martaban, G. of = Mottama, G. of
  Burma 16°5N 96°30E **41** L20
Martapura *Kalimantan Selatan,*
  Indonesia 3°22S 114°47E **36** E4
Martapura *Sumatera Selatan,*
  Indonesia 4°19S 104°22E **36** E2
Marte R. Gómez, Presa
  Mexico 26°10N 99°0W **87** B5
Martelange *Belgium* 49°49N 5°43E **15** E5
Marthapal *India* 19°24N 81°37E **44** E5
Martha's Vineyard
  U.S.A. 41°25N 70°38W **83** E14
Martigny *Switz.* 46°6N 7°3E **20** C7
Martigues *France* 43°24N 5°4E **20** E6
Martin *Slovak Rep.* 49°6N 18°58E **17** D10
Martin *S. Dak., U.S.A.* 43°11N 101°44W **80** D3
Martin *Tenn., U.S.A.* 36°21N 88°51W **85** C10
Martin L. *U.S.A.* 32°41N 85°55W **85** E12
Martina Franca *Italy* 40°42N 17°20E **22** D7
Martinborough *N.Z.* 41°14S 175°29E **59** D5
Martínez *Calif., U.S.A.* 38°1N 122°8W **78** G4
Martínez *Ga., U.S.A.* 33°31N 82°5W **85** E13
Martinique ☑ *W. Indies* 14°40N 61°0W **88** c
Martinique Passage
  W. Indies 15°15N 61°0W **89** C7
Martinópolis *Brazil* 22°11S 51°12W **95** A5
Martins Bay *Barbados* 13°12N 59°29E **89** g
Martins Ferry *U.S.A.* 40°6N 80°44W **82** F4
Martinsburg *Pa., U.S.A.* 40°19N 78°20W **82** F6
Martinsburg *W. Va.,*
  U.S.A. 39°27N 77°58W **81** F15
Martinsville *Ind., U.S.A.* 39°26N 86°25W **80** F10
Martinsville *Va., U.S.A.* 36°41N 79°52W **81** G14
Marton *N.Z.* 40°4S 175°23E **59** D5
Martos *Spain* 37°44N 3°58W **21** D4
Martu ◇ *Australia* 23°0S 122°30E **60** D3
Marudi *Malaysia* 4°11N 114°19E **36** D4
Maruf *Afghan.* 31°30N 67°6E **40** D5
Marugame *Japan* 34°15N 133°40E **29** G6
Marunga *Angola* 17°28S 20°2E **56** A3
Maruwa ◇ *Australia* 22°30S 127°30E **60** D4

Marv Dasht *Iran* 29°50N 52°40E **47** D7
Marvast *Iran* 30°30N 54°15E **47** D7
Marvel Loch *Australia* 31°28S 119°29E **61** F2
Mary *Turkmenistan* 37°40N 61°50E **47** B9
Maryborough = Portlaoise
　Ireland 53°2N 7°18W **10** C4
Maryborough *Queens.,*
　Australia 25°31S 152°37E **63** D5
Maryborough *Vic.,*
　Australia 37°3S 143°44E **63** F3
Maryfield *Canada* 49°50N 101°35W **71** D8
Maryland □ *U.S.A.* 39°00N 76°30W **81** F15
Maryland Junction
　Zimbabwe 17°45S 30°31E **55** H6
Maryport *U.K.* 54°44N 3°28W **12** C4
Mary's Harbour *Canada* 52°18N 55°51W **73** B8
Marystown *Canada* 47°10N 55°10W **73** C8
Marysville *Calif., U.S.A.* 39°09N 121°35W **78** F5
Marysville *Kans., U.S.A.* 39°51N 96°39W **80** F5
Marysville *Mich., U.S.A.* 42°54N 82°29W **82** D2
Marysville *Ohio, U.S.A.* 40°14N 83°22W **81** E12
Marysville *Wash., U.S.A.* 48°3N 122°11W **78** B4
Maryville *Mo., U.S.A.* 40°21N 94°52W **80** E6
Maryville *Tenn., U.S.A.* 35°46N 83°58W **85** D13
Masada *Israel* 31°18N 35°21E **48** D4
Masai *Malaysia* 1°29N 103°55E **39** d
Masai Steppe *Tanzania* 4°30S 36°30E **54** E7
Masaka *Uganda* 0°21S 31°45E **54** E6
Masalembo, Kepulauan
　Indonesia 5°35S 114°30E **36** F4
Masalima, Kepulauan
　Indonesia 5°4S 117°5E **36** F5
Masamba *Indonesia* 2°30S 120°15E **37** E6
Masan *S. Korea* 35°11N 128°32E **33** G15
Masandam, Ra's *Oman* 26°30N 56°30E **47** E8
Masasi *Tanzania* 10°45S 38°52E **54** G7
Masaya *Nic.* 12°0N 86°7W **88** D2
Masbate *Phil.* 12°21N 123°36E **37** B6
Mascara *Algeria* 35°26N 0°6E **52** A6
Mascarene Is. *Ind. Oc.* 22°0S 55°0E **50** J9
Mascota *Mexico* 20°32N 104°49W **86** C4
Masdar City = Madīnat Masdar
　U.A.E. 24°26N 54°37E **47** E7
Masela *Indonesia* 8°9S 129°51E **37** F7
Maseru *Lesotho* 29°18S 27°30E **56** C4
Mashābih *Si. Arabia* 25°35N 36°30E **46** E3
Mashan *China* 23°40N 108°11E **34** F7
Mashang *China* 36°48N 117°57E **33** F9
Mashatu □ *Botswana* 22°45S 29°5E **57** B4
Masherbrum *Pakistan* 35°38N 76°18E **43** B7
Mashhad *Iran* 36°20N 59°35E **47** B8
Mashīz *Iran* 29°56N 54°24E **47** D8
Māshkel, Hāmūn-i-
　Pakistan 28°20N 62°56E **47** D9
Mashki Chāh *Pakistan* 29°5N 62°30E **40** E3
Mashonaland *Zimbabwe* 16°30S 31°0E **55** H6
Mashonaland Central □
　Zimbabwe 17°30S 31°0E **57** A5
Mashonaland East □
　Zimbabwe 18°0S 32°0E **57** A5
Mashonaland West □
　Zimbabwe 17°30S 29°30E **57** A4
Mashrakh *India* 26°7N 84°48E **43** F11
Masi Manimba
　Dem. Rep. of the Congo 4°40S 17°54E **54** E3
Masig *Australia* 9°45S 143°24E **62** a
Masindi *Uganda* 1°40N 31°43E **54** D6
Maşīrah, Jazīrat *Oman* 21°0N 58°50E **49** C6
Maşīrah, Khalīj *Oman* 20°10N 58°10E **49** C6
Masisi
　Dem. Rep. of the Congo 1°23S 28°49E **54** E5
Masjed Soleyman *Iran* 31°55N 49°18E **47** D6
Mask, L. *Ireland* 53°36N 9°22W **10** C2
Maski *India* 15°56N 76°46E **45** G3
Maskin *Oman* 23°44N 56°52E **47** F8
Masoala, Tanjon' i
　Madag. 15°59S 50°13E **55** H10
Masohi = Amahai
　Indonesia 3°20S 128°55E **37** E7
Mason *Nev., U.S.A.* 38°56N 119°8W **78** G4
Mason *Tex., U.S.A.* 30°45N 99°14W **84** F5
Mason City *U.S.A.* 43°9N 93°12W **80** D7
Masqat *Oman* 23°37N 58°36E **49** C6
Massa *Italy* 44°1N 10°9E **20** D9
Massachusetts □ *U.S.A.* 42°30N 72°0W **83** D13
Massachusetts B.
　U.S.A. 42°25N 70°50W **83** D14
Massakory *Chad* 13°0N 15°49E **53** F9
Massangena *Mozam.* 21°34S 33°0E **57** B5
Massango *Angola* 8°2S 16°21E **54** F3
Massawa = Mitsiwa
　Eritrea 15°35N 39°25E **49** D2
Massena *U.S.A.* 44°56N 74°54W **83** B10
Massenya *Chad* 11°21N 16°9E **53** F9
Masset *Canada* 54°2N 132°10W **70** C2
Massiah Street *Barbados* 13°9N 59°29W **89** g
Massif Central *France* 44°55N 3°0E **20** D5
Massillon *U.S.A.* 40°48N 81°32W **82** F3
Massinga *Mozam.* 23°15S 35°22E **57** B6
Massingir *Mozam.* 23°51S 32°4E **57** B5
Masson-Angers *Canada* 45°32N 75°25W **83** A9
Masson I. *Antarctica* 66°10S 93°20E **5** C7
Mastanli = Momchilgrad
　Bulgaria 41°33N 25°23E **23** D11
Masterton *N.Z.* 40°56S 175°39E **59** D5
Mastic *U.S.A.* 40°47N 72°54W **83** F12
Mastuj *Pakistan* 36°20N 72°36E **43** A5
Mastung *Pakistan* 29°50N 66°56E **40** E5
Masty *Belarus* 53°27N 24°38E **17** B13
Masuda *Japan* 34°40N 131°51E **29** G5
Masuku = Franceville
　Gabon 1°40S 13°32E **54** E2
Masurian Lakes = Mazurski,
　Pojezierze *Poland* 53°50N 21°0E **17** B11
Masvingo *Zimbabwe* 20°8S 30°49E **55** G3
Maşyāf *Syria* 35°4N 36°20E **46** C3
Mata-au = Clutha →
　N.Z. 46°20S 169°49E **59** G2
Matabeleland *Zimbabwe* 18°0S 27°0E **55** H5

Matachewan *Canada* 47°56N 80°39W **72** C3
Matadi
　Dem. Rep. of the Congo 5°52S 13°31E **54** F2
Matagalpa *Nic.* 13°0N 85°58W **88** D2
Matagami *Canada* 49°45N 77°34W **72** C4
Matagami, L. *Canada* 49°50N 77°40W **72** C4
Matagorda B. *U.S.A.* 28°40N 96°12W **84** G6
Matagorda I. *U.S.A.* 28°15N 96°30W **84** G6
Mataiea *Tahiti* 17°46S 149°25W **59** d
Matak *Indonesia* 3°18N 106°16E **36** D3
Matale *Sri Lanka* 7°30N 80°37E **45** L5
Matam *Senegal* 15°34N 13°17W **52** E3
Matamoros *Coahuila,*
　Mexico 25°32N 103°15W **86** B4
Matamoros *Tamaulipas,*
　Mexico 25°53N 97°30W **87** B5
Ma'ṭan as Sarra *Libya* 21°45N 22°0E **53** D10
Matane *Canada* 48°50N 67°33W **73** C6
Matang *China* 23°30N 104°7E **34** F5
Matanomadh *India* 23°33N 68°57E **42** H3
Matanzas *Cuba* 23°0N 81°40W **88** B3
Matapa *Botswana* 23°11S 24°39E **56** B3
Matapan, C. = Tenaro, Akra
　Greece 36°22N 22°27E **23** F10
Matapédia *Canada* 48°0N 66°59W **73** C6
Matara *Sri Lanka* 5°58N 80°30E **45** M5
Mataram *Indonesia* 8°35S 116°7E **37** K19
Matarani *Peru* 17°0S 72°10W **92** G4
Mataranka *Australia* 14°55S 133°4E **60** B5
Matarma, Râs *Egypt* 30°27N 32°44E **48** E1
Mataró *Spain* 41°32N 2°29E **21** B7
Matatiele *S. Africa* 30°20S 28°49E **57** D4
Mataura *N.Z.* 46°11S 168°51E **59** G2
Matatila Dam *India* 25°0N 78°22E **44** B4
Matavai, B. de *Tahiti* 17°30S 149°23W **59** d
Matehuala *Mexico* 23°39N 100°39W **86** C4
Mateke Hills *Zimbabwe* 21°48S 31°0E **55** H6
Matelot *Trin. & Tob.* 10°50N 61°7W **93** K15
Matera *Italy* 40°40N 16°36E **22** D7
Mathis *U.S.A.* 28°6N 97°50W **84** G6
Mathraki *Greece* 39°48N 19°31E **23** E8
Mathura *India* 27°30N 77°40E **42** F7
Mati *Phil.* 6°55N 126°15E **37** C7
Matiali *India* 26°56N 88°49E **43** F13
Matías Romero *Mexico* 16°53N 95°2W **87** D5
Matiri Ra. *N.Z.* 41°38S 172°20E **59** D4
Matjiesfontein *S. Africa* 33°14S 20°35E **56** E3
Matla → *India* 21°40N 88°40E **43** J13
Matlamanyane *Botswana* 19°33S 25°57E **56** A4
Matli *Pakistan* 25°2N 68°39E **42** G3
Matlock *U.K.* 53°9N 1°33W **12** D6
Mato Grosso □ *Brazil* 14°0S 55°0W **93** F8
Mato Grosso, Planalto do
　Brazil 15°0S 55°0W **93** G8
Mato Grosso do Sul □
　Brazil 18°0S 55°0W **93** G8
Matochkin Shar, Proliv
　Russia 73°23N 55°12E **26** B6
Matola *Mozam.* 25°57S 32°27E **57** C5
Matopo Hills *Zimbabwe* 20°36S 28°20E **55** J5
Matosinhos *Portugal* 41°11N 8°42W **21** B1
Matroosberg *S. Africa* 33°23S 19°40E **56** D2
Maṭruḥ *Oman* 23°37N 58°30E **49** C6
Matsu Tao *Taiwan* 26°8N 119°56E **35** D12
Matsue *Japan* 35°25N 133°10E **29** G6
Matsum, Ko *Thailand* 9°22N 99°59E **39** b
Matsumae *Japan* 41°26N 140°7E **28** D10
Matsumae-Hantō
　Japan 41°30N 140°15E **28** D10
Matsumoto *Japan* 36°15N 138°0E **29** F9
Matsusaka *Japan* 34°34N 136°32E **29** G8
Matsushima *Japan* 38°20N 141°10E **28** E10
Matsuura *Japan* 33°20N 129°49E **29** H4
Matsuyama *Japan* 33°45N 132°45E **29** H6
Mattagami → *Canada* 50°43N 81°29W **72** B3
Mattancheri *India* 9°50N 76°15E **45** K3
Mattawa *Canada* 46°20N 78°45W **72** C4
Matterhorn *Switz.* 45°58N 7°39E **20** D7
Matthew Town *Bahamas* 20°57N 73°40W **89** B5
Matthews Ridge *Guyana* 7°37N 60°10W **92** B6
Mattice *Canada* 49°40N 83°20W **72** C3
Mattili *India* 18°33N 82°12E **44** E6
Mattituck *U.S.A.* 40°59N 72°32W **83** F12
Mattō = Hakusan *Japan* 36°31N 136°34E **29** F8
Mattoon *U.S.A.* 39°29N 88°23W **80** F9
Matuba *Mozam.* 24°28S 32°49E **57** B5
Matucana *Peru* 11°55S 76°25W **92** F3
Matugama *Sri Lanka* 6°31N 80°7E **45** L5
Matuku *Fiji* 19°10S 179°44E **59** a
Matún = Khowst *Afghan.* 33°22N 69°58E **42** C3
Matura B. *Trin. & Tob.* 10°39N 61°1W **93** K15
Maturín *Venezuela* 9°45N 63°11W **92** B6
Mau *Mad. P., India* 26°17N 78°41E **43** F8
Mau *Ut. P., India* 25°56N 83°33E **43** G10
Mau *Ut. P., India* 25°17N 81°23E **43** G9
Mau Ranipur *India* 25°16N 79°8E **43** G8
Maubeuge *France* 50°17N 3°57E **20** A6
Maubin *Burma* 16°44N 95°39E **41** L19
Maud, Pt. *Australia* 23°6S 113°45E **60** D1
Maud Rise *S. Ocean* 65°0S 3°0E **5** C3
Maude *Australia* 34°29S 144°18E **63** E3
Maudin Sun *Burma* 16°0N 94°30E **41** M19
Maués *Brazil* 3°20S 57°45W **92** D7
Mauganj *India* 24°50N 81°55E **43** G9
Maughold Hd. *I. of Man* 54°18N 4°18W **12** C3
Maui *U.S.A.* 20°48N 156°20W **75** L8
Maulamyaing = Mawlamyine
　Burma 16°30N 97°40E **41** L20
Maule □ *Chile* 36°5S 72°30W **94** D1
Maumee *U.S.A.* 41°34N 83°39W **81** E12
Maumee → *U.S.A.* 41°42N 83°28W **81** E12
Maumere *Indonesia* 8°38S 122°13E **37** F6
Maun *Botswana* 20°0S 23°26E **56** B3
Mauna Kea *U.S.A.* 19°50N 155°28W **75** M8
Mauna Loa *U.S.A.* 19°30N 155°35W **75** M8
Maunath Bhanjan = Mau
　India 25°56N 83°33E **43** G10
Maungmagan Kyunzu
　Burma 14°0N 97°48E **38** E1
Maupin *U.S.A.* 45°11N 121°5W **76** D3

Maurepas, L. *U.S.A.* 30°15N 90°30W **85** F9
Maurice, L. *Australia* 29°30S 131°0E **61** E5
Mauricie △ *Canada* 46°45N 73°0W **72** C5
Maurienne *France* 45°15N 6°20E **20** D7
Mauritania ■ *Africa* 20°50N 10°0W **52** E3
Mauritius ■ *Ind. Oc.* 20°0S 57°0E **55** d
Mauston *U.S.A.* 43°48N 90°5W **80** D8
Mavli *India* 24°45N 73°55E **42** G5
Mawai *India* 22°30N 81°4E **43** H9
Mawana *India* 29°6N 77°58E **42** E7
Mawand *Pakistan* 29°33N 68°38E **42** E3
Mawjib, W. al → *Jordan* 31°28N 35°36E **48** D4
Mawkmai *Burma* 20°14N 97°37E **41** J20
Mawlaik *Burma* 23°40N 94°26E **41** H19
Mawlamyine *Burma* 16°30N 97°40E **41** L20
Mawqaq *Si. Arabia* 27°25N 41°8E **46** E4
Mawson Coast *Antarctica* 68°30S 63°0E **5** C6
Max *U.S.A.* 47°49N 101°18W **80** B3
Maxcanú *Mexico* 20°35N 90°0W **87** C6
Maxesibeni *S. Africa* 30°49S 29°23E **57** D4
Maxhamish L. *Canada* 59°50N 123°17W **70** B4
Maxixe *Mozam.* 23°54S 35°17E **57** B6
Maxville *Canada* 45°17N 74°51W **83** A10
Maxwell *U.S.A.* 39°17N 122°11W **78** F4
Maxwelton *Australia* 20°43S 142°41E **62** C3
May, C. *U.S.A.* 38°56N 74°58W **81** F16
May Pen *Jamaica* 17°58N 77°15W **88** a
Maya → *Russia* 60°28N 134°28E **27** D14
Maya Mexico *Mexico* 18°44N 87°42W **87** D7
Maya Mts. *Belize* 16°30N 89°0W **87** D7
Mayabandar *India* 12°56N 92°56E **45** H11
Mayaguana *I. Bahamas* 22°30N 72°44W **89** B5
Mayaguana Passage
　Bahamas 22°32N 73°15W **89** B5
Mayagüez *Puerto Rico* 18°12N 67°9W **89** d
Mayāmey *Iran* 36°24N 55°42E **47** B7
Mayang *China* 27°53N 109°49E **34** D7
Mayanup *Australia* 33°57S 116°27E **61** F2
Mayapan *Mexico* 20°29N 89°11W **87** C7
Mayarí *Cuba* 20°40N 75°41W **89** B4
Mayaro *Trin. & Tob.* 10°17N 61°1W **93** K15
Mayaya *B. Trin. & Tob.* 10°16N 60°59W **93** K16
Mayavaram = Mayiladuthurai
　India 11°3N 79°42E **45** J4
Maybell *U.S.A.* 40°31N 108°5W **76** F9
Maybole *U.K.* 55°21N 4°42W **11** F4
Maydän *Iraq* 34°55N 45°37E **46** C5
Mayen *Germany* 50°19N 7°8E **16** C4
Mayenne → *France* 47°30N 0°32W **20** C3
Mayer *U.S.A.* 34°24N 112°14W **77** J7
Mayerthorpe *Canada* 53°57N 115°8W **70** C5
Mayfield *Ky., U.S.A.* 36°44N 88°38W **80** G9
Mayfield *N.Y., U.S.A.* 43°6N 74°16W **83** C10
Mayhill *U.S.A.* 32°53N 105°29W **77** K11
Mayiladuthurai *India* 11°3N 79°42E **45** J4
Maykop *Russia* 44°35N 40°10E **19** F7
Maymyo = Pyin-U-Lwin
　Burma 22°2N 96°28E **38** A1
Maynard *Mass., U.S.A.* 42°26N 71°27W **83** D13
Maynard *Wash., U.S.A.* 47°59N 122°55W **78** C4
Maynard Hills *Australia* 28°28S 119°49E **61** E2
Mayne → *Australia* 23°40S 141°55E **62** C3
Maynooth *Canada* 45°13N 77°56W **82** A7
Maynooth *Ireland* 53°23N 6°34W **10** C5
Mayo *Canada* 63°38N 135°57W **68** E4
Mayo □ *Ireland* 53°53N 9°3W **10** C2
Mayon Volcano *Phil.* 13°15N 123°41E **37** B6
Mayor I. *N.Z.* 37°16S 176°17E **59** B6
Mayotte ☐ *Ind. Oc.* 12°50S 45°10E **55** a
Maysān □ *Iraq* 31°55N 47°15E **46** D5
Maysville *U.S.A.* 38°39N 83°46W **81** F12
Mayu *Indonesia* 1°30N 126°30E **37** D7
Mayuram = Mayiladuthurai
　India 11°3N 79°42E **45** J4
Mayville *N. Dak., U.S.A.* 47°30N 97°20W **80** B5
Mayville *N.Y., U.S.A.* 42°15N 79°30W **82** D5
Mazabuka *Zambia* 15°52S 27°44E **55** H5
Mazagán = El Jadida
　Morocco 33°11N 8°17W **52** B4
Mazagão *Brazil* 0°7S 51°16W **93** D8
Mazán *Peru* 3°30S 73°0W **92** D4
Māzandarān □ *Iran* 36°30N 52°0E **47** B7
Mazapil *Mexico* 24°39N 101°34W **86** C4
Mazar *China* 36°32N 77°1E **30** D4
Mazara del Vallo *Italy* 37°39N 12°35E **22** F5
Mazarrón *Spain* 37°38N 1°19W **21** D5
Mazaruni → *Guyana* 6°25N 58°35W **92** B7
Mazatán *Mexico* 29°0N 110°8W **86** B2
Mazatenango *Guatemala* 14°35N 91°30W **88** D1
Mazatlán *Mexico* 23°13N 106°25W **86** C3
Mažeikiai *Lithuania* 56°20N 22°20E **9** H20
Māzhān *Iran* 32°30N 59°0E **47** C8
Mazinän *Iran* 36°19N 56°56E **47** B8
Mazoe → *Mozam.* 16°20S 33°30E **55** H6
Mazurski, Pojezierze
　Poland 53°50N 21°0E **17** B11
Mazyr *Belarus* 51°59N 29°15E **17** B15
Mba *Fiji* 17°33S 177°41E **59** a
Mbabane *Swaziland* 26°18S 31°6E **57** D5
Mbaïki *C.A.R.* 3°53N 18°1E **54** D3
Mbala *Zambia* 8°46S 31°24E **54** F6
Mbale *Uganda* 1°8N 34°12E **54** D6
Mbalmayo *Cameroon* 3°33N 11°33E **54** D2
Mbandaka
　Dem. Rep. of the Congo 0°1N 18°18E **54** D3
Mbanza Ngungu
　Dem. Rep. of the Congo 5°12S 14°53E **54** F2
Mbarara *Uganda* 0°35S 30°40E **54** E6
Mbengga = Beqa *Fiji* 18°23S 178°8E **59** a
Mbeya *Tanzania* 8°54S 33°29E **54** F6
Mbhashe → *S. Africa* 32°15S 28°54E **57** D4
Mbini = Río Muni □
　Eq. Guinea 1°30N 10°0E **54** D2
Mbizi *Zimbabwe* 21°23S 31°1E **57** B5
Mbombela *S. Africa* 25°29S 30°59E **57** D5
Mbomou = Bomu →
　C.A.R. 4°40N 22°30E **54** D4
Mboro *Senegal* 15°9N 16°54E **52** E2
Mbou *Cameroon* 38°18N 10°15E **52** D2
M'boukou, L. de *Cameroon* 6°23N 12°50E **54** C2

Mbour *Senegal* 14°22N 16°54W **52** F2
Mbuji-Mayi
　Dem. Rep. of the Congo 6°9S 23°40E **54** F4
Mburucuyá *Argentina* 28°1S 58°14W **94** B4
Mburucuyá △ *Argentina* 28°1S 58°12W **94** B4
Mchinji *Malawi* 13°47S 32°58E **55** G6
Mdantsane *S. Africa* 32°56S 27°46E **57** D4
Mead, L. *U.S.A.* 36°0N 114°44W **79** J12
Meade *U.S.A.* 37°17N 100°20W **80** G3
Meade River = Atqasuk
　U.S.A. 70°28N 157°24W **74** A8
Meadow Lake *Canada* 54°10N 108°26W **71** C7
Meadow Lake △ *Canada* 54°27N 109°0W **71** C7
Meadow Valley Wash →
　U.S.A. 36°40N 114°34W **79** J12
Meadville *U.S.A.* 41°39N 80°9W **82** E4
Meaford *Canada* 44°36N 80°35W **82** B4
Meakan Dake *Japan* 45°15N 144°0E **28** C11
Mealy Mts. *Canada* 53°10N 58°0W **73** B8
Meander River *Canada* 59°2N 117°42W **70** B5
Meares, C. *U.S.A.* 45°37N 124°0W **76** D1
Mearim → *Brazil* 3°4S 44°35W **93** D10
Meath □ *Ireland* 53°40N 6°57W **10** C5
Meath Park *Canada* 53°27N 105°22W **71** C7
Meaux *France* 48°58N 2°50E **20** B5
Mebechi-Gawa →
　Japan 40°31N 141°31E **28** D10
Mebulu, Tanjung
　Indonesia 8°50S 115°5E **37** K18
Mecca = Makkah
　Si. Arabia 21°30N 39°54E **49** C2
Mecca *U.S.A.* 33°34N 116°5W **79** M10
Mechanicsburg *U.S.A.* 40°13N 77°1W **82** F8
Mechanicville *U.S.A.* 42°54N 73°41W **83** D11
Mechelen *Belgium* 51°2N 4°29E **15** C4
Mecheria *Algeria* 33°35N 0°18W **52** B5
Mecklenburg *Germany* 53°33N 11°40E **16** B7
Mecklenburger Bucht
　Germany 54°20N 11°40E **16** A6
Meconta *Mozam.* 14°59S 39°50E **55** G7
Medan *Indonesia* 3°40N 98°38E **36** D1
Medanosa, Pta. *Argentina* 48°8S 66°0W **96** F3
Medawachchiya *Sri Lanka* 8°30N 80°30E **45** K5
Medchal *India* 17°37N 78°29E **44** F4
Médéa *Algeria* 36°12N 2°50E **52** A6
Medellín *Colombia* 6°15N 75°35W **92** B3
Medelpad *Sweden* 62°33N 16°30E **8** E17
Medemblik *Neths.* 52°46N 5°8E **15** B5
Medford *Oreg., U.S.A.* 42°19N 122°52W **76** E2
Medford *Wis., U.S.A.* 45°9N 90°20W **80** C8
Medgidia *Romania* 44°15N 28°19E **17** F15
Media Agua *Argentina* 31°58S 68°25W **94** C2
Media Luna *Argentina* 34°45S 66°44W **94** C2
Medianeira *Brazil* 25°17S 54°5W **95** B5
Mediaș *Romania* 46°9N 24°22E **17** E13
Medicine Bow *U.S.A.* 41°54N 106°12W **76** F10
Medicine Bow Mts.
　U.S.A. 40°40N 106°0W **76** F10
Medicine Hat *Canada* 50°0N 110°45W **71** D6
Medicine Lake *U.S.A.* 48°30N 104°30W **76** B11
Medicine Lodge *U.S.A.* 37°17N 98°35W **80** G4
Medina = Al Madīnah
　Si. Arabia 24°35N 39°52E **46** E3
Medina *N. Dak., U.S.A.* 46°54N 99°18W **80** B4
Medina *N.Y., U.S.A.* 43°13N 78°23W **82** C6
Medina *Ohio, U.S.A.* 41°8N 81°52W **82** E3
Medina → *U.S.A.* 29°16N 98°29W **84** G5
Medina del Campo *Spain* 41°18N 4°55W **21** B3
Medina Sidonia *Spain* 36°28N 5°57W **21** D3
Medinipur *India* 22°25N 87°21E **43** H12
Médoc *France* 45°10N 0°50W **20** D3
Medveditsa → *Russia* 49°35N 42°41E **19** E7
Medvezhi, Ostrava
　Russia 71°0N 161°0E **27** B17
Medvezhyegorsk *Russia* 63°0N 34°25E **18** B5
Medway □ *U.K.* 51°25N 0°32E **13** F8
Medway → *U.K.* 51°27N 0°46E **13** F8
Meekatharra *Australia* 26°32S 118°29E **61** E2
Meeker *U.S.A.* 40°2N 107°55W **76** F10
Meerut *India* 29°1N 77°42E **42** E7
Meeteetse *U.S.A.* 44°9N 108°52W **76** D9
Mega *Ethiopia* 3°57N 38°19E **49** G2
Megara *Greece* 37°58N 23°22E **23** F10
Megasini *India* 21°38N 86°21E **43** J12
Meghalaya □ *India* 25°50N 91°0E **41** G17
Meghna → *Bangla.* 22°50N 90°50E **41** H17
Megion *Russia* 61°3N 76°6E **26** C8
Mégiscane, L. *Canada* 48°35N 75°55W **72** C4
Mehar *Pakistan* 27°23S 118°35E **60** D2
Mehekar *India* 20°9N 76°34E **44** D3
Mehlville *U.S.A.* 38°31N 90°19W **80** F8
Mehndawal *India* 26°58N 83°5E **43** F10
Mehr Jän *Iran* 33°50N 55°6E **47** C7
Mehrābād *Iran* 36°53N 47°55E **46** B5
Mehrān *Iran* 33°7N 46°10E **46** C5
Mehrän → *Iran* 26°45N 55°26E **47** E7
Mehrgarh *Pakistan* 29°30N 67°30E **42** E2
Mehrīz *Iran* 31°35N 54°28E **47** D7
Mei Jiang → *China* 24°25N 116°35E **35** E11
Mei Xian *China* 34°18N 107°55E **32** G4
Meicheng *China* 29°29N 119°16E **35** C8
Meichengzhen *China* 28°9N 111°40E **35** C8
Meichuan *China* 30°8N 115°31E **35** B10
Meighen I. *Canada* 80°0N 99°30W **69** B12
Meigu *China* 28°16N 103°20E **34** C4
Meihekou *China* 42°32N 125°40E **33** C13
Meiktila *Burma* 20°53N 95°54E **41** J19
Meili Xue Shan *China* 28°30N 98°39E **34** C2
Meimu = Pyin-U-Lwin
　Burma 22°2N 96°28E **38** A1
Meishan *China* 30°3N 103°23E **34** C4
Meissen *Germany* 51°9N 13°29E **16** C7
Meitan *China* 27°45N 107°29E **34** D6
Meizhou *China* 24°16N 116°6E **35** E11
Meja *India* 25°9N 82°7E **43** G10

Mejillones *Chile* 23°10S 70°30W **94** A1
Mekele *Ethiopia* 13°33N 39°30E **49** E2
Mekerghene, Sebkra
　Algeria 26°21N 1°30E **52** C6
Mekhtar *Pakistan* 30°30N 69°15E **40** D6
Meknès *Morocco* 33°57N 5°33W **52** B4
Mekong → *Asia* 9°30N 106°15E **39** H6
Mekongga *Indonesia* 3°39S 121°15E **37** E6
Mekvari = Kür →
　Azerbaijan 39°29N 49°15E **19** G8
Melagiri Hills *India* 12°20N 77°30E **45** H3
Melaka *Malaysia* 2°15N 102°15E **39** L4
Melaka □ *Malaysia* 2°15N 102°15E **39** L4
Melanesia *Pac. Oc.* 4°0S 155°0E **64** H7
Melanesian Basin *Pac. Oc.* 0°5N 160°35E **64** G8
Melapalaiyam *India* 8°39N 77°44E **45** K3
Melaya *Indonesia* 8°17S 114°30E **37** J17
Melbourne *U.S.A.* 28°5N 80°37W **85** G14
Melchor Múzquiz
　Mexico 27°53N 101°31W **86** B4
Melchor Ocampo
　Mexico 24°51N 101°39W **86** C4
Melekeok *Palau* 7°27N 134°38E **64** G5
Mélèzes → *Canada* 57°40N 69°29W **72** A5
Melfort *Canada* 52°50N 104°37W **71** C8
Melhus *Norway* 63°17N 10°18E **8** E14
Melilla *N. Afr.* 35°21N 2°57W **21** E4
Melipilla *Chile* 33°42S 71°15W **94** C1
Melissa *Canada* 45°24N 79°14W **82** A5
Melita *Canada* 49°15N 101°0W **71** D8
Melitopol *Ukraine* 46°50N 35°22E **19** E6
Melk *Austria* 48°13N 15°20E **16** D8
Mellansel *Sweden* 63°26N 18°19E **8** E18
Mellen *U.S.A.* 46°20N 90°40W **80** B8
Mellerud *Sweden* 58°41N 12°28E **9** G15
Mellette *U.S.A.* 45°9N 98°30W **80** C4
Melo *Uruguay* 32°20S 54°10W **95** C5
Melolo *Indonesia* 9°53S 120°40E **37** F6
Meloupey *Cambodia* 13°48N 105°16E **38** F5
Melrhir, Chott *Algeria* 34°13N 6°30E **52** B7
Melrose *Australia* 32°42S 146°57E **63** E4
Melrose *U.K.* 55°36N 2°43W **11** F6
Melrose *Minn., U.S.A.* 45°40N 94°49W **80** C6
Melrose *N. Mex., U.S.A.* 34°26N 103°38W **77** J12
Melstone *U.S.A.* 46°36N 107°52W **76** C10
Melton Mowbray *U.K.* 52°47N 0°54W **12** E7
Melun *France* 48°32N 2°39E **20** B5
Melung *Nepal* 27°31N 86°3E **43** F12
Melur *India* 10°2N 78°23E **45** J4
Melville *Canada* 50°55N 102°50W **71** C8
Melville, C. *Australia* 14°11S 144°30E **62** A3
Melville, L. *Canada* 53°30N 60°0W **73** B8
Melville B. *Australia* 12°0S 136°45E **62** A2
Melville B. *Greenland* 75°30N 63°0W **69** B19
Melville I. *Australia* 11°30S 131°0E **60** B5
Melville I. *Canada* 75°30N 112°0W **69** B8
Melville Pen. *Canada* 68°0N 84°0W **69** C15
Melvin, Lough *Ireland* 54°26N 8°10W **10** B3
Memba *Mozam.* 14°11S 40°30E **55** G8
Memboro *Indonesia* 9°30S 119°30E **60** A2
Memel = Klaipėda
　Lithuania 55°43N 21°10E **9** J19
Memel *S. Africa* 27°38S 29°36E **57** C4
Memmingen *Germany* 47°58N 10°10E **16** E6
Mempawah *Indonesia* 0°30N 109°5E **36** D3
Memphis *Mich., U.S.A.* 42°54N 82°46W **82** D2
Memphis *Tenn., U.S.A.* 35°8N 90°2W **85** D9
Memphis *Tex., U.S.A.* 34°44N 100°33W **84** D4
Memphrémagog, L.
　N. Amer. 45°8N 72°17W **83** B12
Mena *U.S.A.* 34°35N 94°15W **84** D7
Menado = Manado
　Indonesia 1°29N 124°51E **37** D6
Menai Strait *U.K.* 53°11N 4°13W **12** D3
Ménaka *Mali* 15°59N 2°18E **52** E6
Menan = Chao Phraya →
　Thailand 13°40N 100°31E **38** F3
Menard *U.S.A.* 30°55N 99°47W **84** F5
Menard Fracture Zone
　Pac. Oc. 43°0S 97°0W **65** M18
Mendaña Fracture Zone
　Pac. Oc. 16°0S 91°0W **65** J18
Mendawai → *Indonesia* 3°30S 113°0E **36** E4
Mende *France* 44°31N 3°30E **20** D5
Mendhar *India* 33°35N 74°10E **43** C6
Mendip Hills *U.K.* 51°17N 2°40W **13** F5
Mendocino *U.S.A.* 39°19N 123°48W **76** G2
Mendocino, C. *U.S.A.* 40°26N 124°25W **76** F1
Mendocino Fracture Zone
　Pac. Oc. 40°0N 142°0W **65** D13
Mendota *Calif., U.S.A.* 36°45N 120°23W **78** J6
Mendota *Ill., U.S.A.* 41°33N 89°7W **80** E9
Mendoyo *Indonesia* 8°23S 114°42E **37** J17
Mendoza *Argentina* 32°50S 68°52W **94** C2
Mendoza □ *Argentina* 33°0S 69°0W **94** C2
Mene Grande *Venezuela* 9°49N 70°56W **92** B4
Menemen *Turkey* 38°34N 27°3E **23** E12
Menen *Belgium* 50°47N 3°7E **15** D3
Mengcheng *China* 33°12N 116°36E **32** H9
Mengdingjie *China* 23°31N 98°58E **34** F2
Menggala *Indonesia* 4°30S 105°15E **36** E3
Menghai *China* 21°49N 100°20E **34** F3
Mengjin *China* 34°55N 112°45E **32** G7
Mengla *China* 21°20N 101°25E **34** G3
Menglian *China* 22°21N 99°27E **34** F2
Mengshan *China* 24°14N 110°55E **35** E8
Mengyin *China* 35°40N 117°58E **33** G9
Mengzhe *China* 22°2N 100°15E **34** F3
Mengzi *China* 23°20N 103°22E **34** F4
Menifee *U.S.A.* 33°41N 117°10W **79** M9
Menihek *Canada* 54°28N 56°36W **73** B6
Menihek L. *Canada* 54°0N 66°35W **73** B6
Menin = Menen *Belgium* 50°47N 3°7E **15** D3
Menindee *Australia* 32°20S 142°25E **63** E3
Menindee L. *Australia* 32°20S 142°25E **63** E3
Meningie *Australia* 35°50S 139°18E **63** F2
Menjangan, Pulau
　Indonesia 8°7S 114°31E **37** J17
Menlo Park *U.S.A.* 37°27N 122°12W **78** H4

Menngen ☼ *Australia* 15°21S 131°16E **60 C5**
Menominee *U.S.A.* 45°6N 87°37W **80 C10**
Menominee → *U.S.A.* 45°6N 87°35W **80 C10**
Menomonie *U.S.A.* 44°53N 91°55W **80 C8**
Menongue *Angola* 14°48S 17°52E **55 G3**
Menorca *Spain* 40°0N 4°0E **21 C8**
Mentakab *Malaysia* 3°29N 102°21E **39 L4**
Mentawai, Kepulauan *Indonesia* 2°0S 99°0E **36 E1**
Menton *France* 43°50N 7°29E **20 E7**
Mentor *U.S.A.* 41°40N 81°21W **82 E3**
Menzelinsk *Russia* 55°47N 53°11E **18 C9**
Menzies *Australia* 29°40S 121°2E **61 E3**
Meob B. *Namibia* 24°25S 14°34E **56 B1**
Meoqui *Mexico* 28°17N 105°29W **86 B3**
Meppel *Neths.* 52°42N 6°12E **15 B6**
Merak *Indonesia* 6°10N 106°26E **37 F12**
Meramangye, L. *Australia* 28°25S 132°13E **61 E5**
Meran = Merano *Italy* 46°40N 11°9E **22 A4**
Merano *Italy* 46°40N 11°9E **22 A4**
Merauke *Indonesia* 8°29S 140°24E **37 F10**
Merbein *Australia* 34°10S 142°2E **63 E3**
Merca = Marka *Somalia* 1°48N 44°50E **49 G3**
Merced *U.S.A.* 37°18N 120°29W **78 H6**
Merced → *U.S.A.* 37°21N 120°59W **78 H6**
Merced Pk. *U.S.A.* 37°36N 119°24W **78 H7**
Mercedes *B. Aires, Argentina* 34°40S 59°30W **94 C4**
Mercedes *Corrientes, Argentina* 29°10S 58°5W **94 B4**
Mercedes *San Luis, Argentina* 33°40S 65°21W **94 C2**
Mercedes *Uruguay* 33°12S 58°0W **94 C4**
Merceditas *Chile* 28°20S 70°35W **94 B1**
Mercer *N.Z.* 37°16S 175°5E **59 B5**
Mercer *U.S.A.* 41°14N 80°15W **82 E4**
Mercer Island *U.S.A.* 47°34N 122°13W **78 C4**
Mercury *U.S.A.* 36°40N 115°59W **79 J11**
Mercy, C. *Canada* 65°0N 63°30W **69 E19**
Mere *U.K.* 51°6N 2°16W **13 F5**
Merebuk, Gunung *Indonesia* 8°13S 114°39E **37 J17**
Meredith, C. *Falk. Is.* 52°15S 60°40W **96 G4**
Meredith, L. *U.S.A.* 35°43N 101°33W **84 D4**
Mergui *Burma* 12°26N 98°34E **38 F2**
Mergui Arch. = Myeik Kyunzu *Burma* 11°30N 97°30E **39 G1**
Mérida *Mexico* 20°58N 89°37W **87 C7**
Mérida *Spain* 38°55N 6°25W **21 C2**
Mérida *Venezuela* 8°24N 71°8W **92 B4**
Mérida, Cord. de *Venezuela* 9°0N 71°0W **92 B4**
Meriden *U.K.* 52°26N 1°38W **13 E6**
Meriden *U.S.A.* 41°32N 72°48W **83 E12**
Meridian *Calif., U.S.A.* 39°9N 121°55W **78 F5**
Meridian *Idaho, U.S.A.* 43°37N 116°24W **76 E5**
Meridian *Miss., U.S.A.* 32°22N 88°42W **85 E10**
Merinda *Australia* 20°2S 148°11E **62 C4**
Merir *Palau* 4°10N 132°30E **37 D8**
Meriruma *Brazil* 1°15N 54°50W **93 C8**
Merkel *U.S.A.* 32°28N 100°1W **84 E4**
Mermaid Reef *Australia* 17°6S 119°36E **60 C2**
Meroe *India* 7°33N 93°33E **45 L11**
Merowe Dam *Sudan* 18°35N 31°56E **53 E12**
Merredin *Australia* 31°28S 118°18E **61 F2**
Merrick *U.K.* 55°8N 4°28W **11 F4**
Merrickville *Canada* 44°55N 75°50W **83 B9**
Merrill *Oreg., U.S.A.* 42°1N 121°36W **76 E3**
Merrill *Wis., U.S.A.* 45°11N 89°41W **80 C9**
Merrimack → *U.S.A.* 42°49N 70°49W **83 D14**
Merriman *U.S.A.* 42°55N 101°42W **80 D3**
Merritt *Canada* 50°10N 120°45W **70 C4**
Merritt Island *U.S.A.* 28°21N 80°42W **85 G14**
Merriwa *Australia* 32°6S 150°22E **63 E5**
Merry I. *Canada* 55°29N 77°31W **72 A4**
Merryville *U.S.A.* 30°45N 93°33W **84 F8**
Mersch *Lux.* 49°44N 6°7E **15 E6**
Mersea I. *U.K.* 51°47N 0°58E **13 F8**
Merseburg *Germany* 51°22N 11°59E **16 C6**
Mersey → *U.K.* 53°25N 3°1W **12 D4**
Merseyside □ *U.K.* 53°31N 3°2W **12 D4**
Mersin *Turkey* 36°51N 34°36E **46 B2**
Mersing *Malaysia* 2°25N 103°50E **39 L4**
Merta *India* 26°39N 74°4E **42 F6**
Merta Road *India* 26°43N 73°55E **42 F5**
Merthyr Tydfil *U.K.* 51°45N 3°22W **13 F4**
Merthyr Tydfil □ *U.K.* 51°46N 3°21W **13 F4**
Mértola *Portugal* 37°40N 7°40W **21 D2**
Mertz Glacier *Antarctica* 67°30S 144°45E **5 C10**
Mertzon *U.S.A.* 31°16N 100°49W **84 F4**
Meru *Kenya* 0°3N 37°40E **54 D7**
Meru *Tanzania* 3°15S 36°46E **54 E7**
Meru Betiri △ *Indonesia* 8°27S 113°51E **37 H15**
Mesa *U.S.A.* 33°25N 111°50W **77 K8**
Mesa Verde △ *U.S.A.* 37°11N 108°29W **77 H9**
Mesada = Masada *Israel* 31°18N 35°21E **48 D4**
Mesgouez, L. *Canada* 51°20N 75°0W **72 B5**
Meshed = Mashhad *Iran* 36°20N 59°35E **47 B8**
Meshgin Shahr *Iran* 38°30N 47°45E **46 B5**
Meshoppen *U.S.A.* 41°36N 76°3W **83 E8**
Mesilinka → *Canada* 56°6N 124°30W **70 B4**
Mesolongi *Greece* 38°21N 21°28E **23 E9**
Mesopotamia = Al Jazirah *Iraq* 33°30N 44°0E **46 C5**
Mesopotamia *U.S.A.* 41°27N 80°57W **82 E4**
Mesquite *Nev., U.S.A.* 36°48N 114°4W **77 H6**
Mesquite *Tex., U.S.A.* 32°47N 96°36W **84 E6**
Messaad *Algeria* 34°8N 3°30E **52 B6**
Messalo → *Mozam.* 12°25S 39°15E **55 G7**
Messene *Greece* 37°4N 22°1E **23 F10**
Messina = Musina *S. Africa* 22°20S 30°5E **57 B5**
Messina *Italy* 38°11N 15°34E **22 E6**
Messina, Str. di *Italy* 38°15N 15°35E **22 F6**
Messiniakos Kolpos *Greece* 36°45N 22°5E **23 F10**
Mesta = Nestos → *Europe* 40°54N 24°49E **23 D11**
Meta → *S. Amer.* 6°12N 67°28W **92 B5**
Meta Incognita Pen. *Canada* 62°45N 68°30W **69 E18**
Metabetchouan *Canada* 48°26N 71°52W **73 C5**
Metaline Falls *U.S.A.* 48°52N 117°22W **76 B5**
Metán *Argentina* 25°30S 65°0W **94 B3**
Metcalfe *Canada* 45°14N 75°28W **83 A9**
Metema *Ethiopia* 12°58N 36°12E **49 E2**
Methven *N.Z.* 43°38S 171°40E **59 E3**
Metlakatla *U.S.A.* 55°8N 131°35W **68 F5**
Metropolis *U.S.A.* 37°9N 88°44W **80 G9**
Metropolitana □ *Chile* 33°30S 70°50W **94 C1**
Mettuppalaiyam *India* 11°18N 76°59E **45 J3**
Mettur *India* 11°48N 77°47E **45 J3**
Metu *Ethiopia* 8°18N 35°35E **49 F2**
Metz *France* 49°8N 6°10E **20 B7**
Meulaboh *Indonesia* 4°11N 96°3E **36 D1**
Meureudu *Indonesia* 5°19N 96°10E **36 C1**
Meuse → *Europe* 50°45N 5°41E **15 D5**
Mexia *U.S.A.* 31°41N 96°29W **84 F6**
Mexiana, I. *Brazil* 0°0 49°30W **93 D9**
Mexicali *Mexico* 32°40N 115°30W **79 N11**
Mexican Plateau *Mexico* 25°0N 104°0W **66 G9**
Mexican Water *U.S.A.* 36°57N 109°32W **77 H9**
Mexico *Maine, U.S.A.* 44°34N 70°33W **83 B14**
Mexico *Mo., U.S.A.* 39°10N 91°53W **80 F8**
Mexico *N.Y., U.S.A.* 43°28N 76°14W **83 C8**
México □ *Mexico* 19°20N 99°30W **87 D5**
Mexico ■ *Cent. Amer.* 25°0N 105°0W **86 C4**
Mexico, G. of *Cent. Amer.* 25°0N 90°0W **87 C7**
Mexico B. *U.S.A.* 43°35N 76°20W **83 C8**
Meydān-e Naftūn *Iran* 31°56N 49°18E **47 D6**
Meydani, Ra's-e *Iran* 25°24N 59°6E **47 E8**
Meyers Chuck *U.S.A.* 55°45N 132°15W **70 B2**
Meymaneh *Afghan.* 35°53N 64°38E **40 B4**
Mezen *Russia* 65°50N 44°20E **18 A7**
Mezen → *Russia* 65°44N 44°22E **18 A7**
Mézenc, Mt. *France* 44°54N 4°11E **20 D6**
Mezhdurechensk *Russia* 53°41N 88°3E **26 D9**
Mezhdurechenskiy *Russia* 59°36N 65°56E **26 D7**
Mezőkövesd *Hungary* 47°49N 20°35E **17 E11**
Mezőtúr *Hungary* 47°1N 20°41E **17 E11**
Mezquital *Mexico* 23°29N 104°23W **86 C4**
Mfolozi → *S. Africa* 28°25S 32°26E **57 C5**
Mhow *India* 22°33N 75°50E **42 H6**
Miahuatlán *Mexico* 16°20N 96°36W **87 D5**
Miami *Okla., U.S.A.* 36°53N 94°53W **84 C7**
Miami *Tex., U.S.A.* 35°42N 100°38W **84 D4**
Mian Xian *China* 33°10N 106°32E **34 A6**
Mianchi *China* 34°48N 111°48E **32 G6**
Mīāndarreh *Iran* 35°37N 53°39E **47 C7**
Mīāndowāb *Iran* 37°0N 46°5E **46 B5**
Miandrivazo *Madag.* 19°31S 45°29E **55 H9**
Mīāneh *Iran* 37°30N 47°40E **46 B5**
Mianning *China* 28°32N 102°9E **34 C4**
Mianwali *Pakistan* 32°38N 71°28E **42 C4**
Mianyang *China* 31°22N 104°47E **34 B5**
Mianzhu *China* 31°22N 104°7E **34 B5**
Miao Ling *China* 26°5N 107°30E **34 D6**
Miaodao Qundao *China* 38°10N 120°45E **33 E11**
Miaoli *Taiwan* 24°37N 120°49E **35 E13**
Miass *Russia* 54°59N 60°6E **18 D11**
Mica *S. Africa* 24°10S 30°48E **57 B5**
Michalovce *Slovak Rep.* 48°47N 21°58E **17 D11**
Michigan □ *U.S.A.* 44°0N 85°0W **81 C11**
Michigan, L. *U.S.A.* 44°0N 87°0W **80 D10**
Michigan City *U.S.A.* 41°43N 86°54W **80 E10**
Michipicoten I. *Canada* 47°40N 85°40W **72 C2**
Michoacán □ *Mexico* 19°10N 101°50W **86 D4**
Michurin *Bulgaria* 42°9N 27°51E **23 C12**
Michurinsk *Russia* 52°58N 40°27E **18 D7**
Micoud *St. Lucia* 13°49N 60°54W **89 f**
Micronesia *Pac. Oc.* 11°0N 160°0E **64 G7**
Micronesia, Federated States of ■ *Pac. Oc.* 9°0N 150°0E **64 G7**
Mid-Indian Ridge *Ind. Oc.* 30°0S 75°0E **64 M1**
Mid-Oceanic Ridge *Ind. Oc.* 42°0S 90°0E **64 M1**
Mid-Pacific Seamounts *Pac. Oc.* 18°0N 177°0W **64 F10**
Midai *Indonesia* 3°0N 107°47E **36 D3**
Midale *Canada* 49°25N 103°20W **71 D8**
Middelburg *Neths.* 51°30N 3°36E **15 C3**
Middelburg *Eastern Cape, S. Africa* 31°30S 25°0E **56 D4**
Middelburg *Mpumalanga, S. Africa* 25°49S 29°28E **57 C4**
Middelpos *S. Africa* 31°55S 20°13E **56 D3**
Middelwit *S. Africa* 24°51S 27°3E **56 B4**
Middle Alkali L. *U.S.A.* 41°27N 120°5W **76 F3**
Middle America Trench = Guatemala Trench *Pac. Oc.* 14°0N 95°0W **66 H10**
Middle Andaman I. *India* 12°30N 92°50E **45 H11**
Middle Bass I. *U.S.A.* 41°41N 82°48W **82 E2**
Middle East *Asia* 35°0N 40°0E **24 E5**
Middle Fork Feather → *U.S.A.* 38°33N 121°30W **78 F5**
Middle I. *Australia* 34°6S 123°11E **61 F3**
Middle Loup → *U.S.A.* 41°17N 98°24W **80 E4**
Middleboro *U.S.A.* 41°54N 70°55W **83 E14**
Middleburg *Fla., U.S.A.* 30°4N 81°52W **85 F14**
Middleburg *Pa., U.S.A.* 40°47N 77°3W **82 F7**
Middleburgh *U.S.A.* 42°36N 74°20W **83 D10**
Middlebury *U.S.A.* 44°1N 73°10W **83 B11**
Middlefield *U.S.A.* 41°27N 81°4W **82 E3**
Middlemount *Australia* 22°50S 148°40E **62 C4**
Middleport *N.Y., U.S.A.* 43°13N 78°29W **82 C6**
Middleport *Ohio, U.S.A.* 39°0N 82°3W **81 F12**
Middlesboro *U.S.A.* 36°36N 83°43W **81 G12**
Middlesbrough *U.K.* 54°35N 1°13W **12 C6**
Middlesbrough □ *U.K.* 54°28N 1°13W **12 C6**
Middlesex *Belize* 17°2N 88°31W **88 C2**
Middlesex *N.J., U.S.A.* 40°36N 74°30W **83 F10**
Middlesex *N.Y., U.S.A.* 42°42N 77°16W **82 D7**
Middleton *Australia* 22°22S 141°32E **62 C3**
Middleton *Canada* 44°57N 65°4W **73 D6**
Middleton Cr. → *Australia* 22°35S 141°51E **62 C3**
Middleton I. *U.S.A.* 59°26N 146°20W **74 D10**
Middletown *U.K.* 54°17N 6°51W **10 B5**
Middletown *Calif., U.S.A.* 38°45N 122°37W **78 G4**
Middletown *Conn., U.S.A.* 41°34N 72°39W **83 E12**
Middletown *N.Y., U.S.A.* 41°27N 74°25W **83 E10**
Middletown *Ohio, U.S.A.* 39°31N 84°24W **81 F11**
Middletown *Pa., U.S.A.* 40°12N 76°44W **83 F8**
Midge Point *Australia* 20°39S 148°43E **62 b**
Midhurst *Canada* 44°26N 79°43W **82 B5**
Midhurst *U.K.* 50°59N 0°44W **13 G7**
Midi, Canal du → *France* 43°45N 1°21E **20 E4**
Midland *Australia* 31°54S 116°1E **61 F2**
Midland *Canada* 44°45N 79°50W **82 B5**
Midland *Calif., U.S.A.* 33°52N 114°48W **79 M12**
Midland *Mich., U.S.A.* 43°37N 84°14W **81 D11**
Midland *Pa., U.S.A.* 40°39N 80°27W **82 F4**
Midland *Tex., U.S.A.* 32°0N 102°3W **84 F3**
Midleton *Ireland* 51°55N 8°10W **10 E3**
Midlothian □ *U.K.* 55°51N 3°5W **11 F5**
Midnapore = Medinipur *India* 22°25N 87°21E **43 H12**
Midu *China* 25°18N 100°30E **34 E3**
Midway Is. *Pac. Oc.* 28°13N 177°22W **75 K4**
Midway Wells *U.S.A.* 32°41N 115°7W **79 N11**
Midwest *U.S.A.* 42°0N 90°0W **75 G22**
Midwest *Wyo., U.S.A.* 43°25N 106°16W **76 E10**
Midwest City *U.S.A.* 35°27N 97°24W **84 D6**
Midyat *Turkey* 37°25N 41°23E **46 B4**
Midžor *Bulgaria* 43°24N 22°40E **23 C10**
Mie □ *Japan* 34°30N 136°10E **29 G8**
Międzychód *Poland* 52°35N 15°53E **16 B8**
Międzyrzec Podlaski *Poland* 51°58N 22°45E **17 C12**
Mielec *Poland* 50°15N 21°25E **17 C11**
Mienga *Angola* 17°12S 19°48E **56 A2**
Miercurea-Ciuc *Romania* 46°21N 25°48E **17 E13**
Mieres *Spain* 43°18N 5°48W **21 A3**
Mifflintown *U.S.A.* 40°34N 77°24W **82 F7**
Mifraz Hefa *Israel* 32°52N 35°0E **48 C4**
Migang Shan *China* 35°32N 106°13E **32 G4**
Miguasha △ *Canada* 48°5N 66°26W **73 C6**
Miguel Alemán, Presa *Mexico* 18°15N 96°32W **87 D5**
Miguel Hidalgo, Presa *Mexico* 26°30N 108°34W **86 B3**
Mihara *Japan* 34°24N 133°5E **29 G6**
Mikhaylovgrad = Montana *Bulgaria* 43°27N 23°16E **23 C10**
Mikhaylovka *Russia* 50°3N 43°5E **19 D7**
Mikkeli *Finland* 61°43N 27°15E **8 F22**
Mikkwa → *Canada* 58°25N 114°46W **70 B6**
Mikonos = Mykonos *Greece* 37°30N 25°25E **23 F11**
Mikun *Russia* 62°20N 50°0E **18 B9**
Milaca *U.S.A.* 45°45N 93°39W **80 C7**
Milagro *Ecuador* 2°11S 79°36W **92 D3**
Milan *Mo., U.S.A.* 40°12N 93°7W **80 E7**
Milan *Tenn., U.S.A.* 35°55N 88°46W **85 D10**
Milâs *Turkey* 37°20N 27°50E **23 F12**
Milazzo *Italy* 38°13N 15°15E **22 E6**
Milbank *U.S.A.* 45°13N 96°38W **80 C5**
Milbanke Sd. *Canada* 52°19N 128°33W **70 C3**
Milden *Canada* 51°29N 107°32W **71 C7**
Mildenhall *U.K.* 52°21N 0°32E **13 E8**
Mildmay *Canada* 44°3N 81°7W **82 B3**
Mildura *Australia* 34°13S 142°9E **63 E3**
Mile *China* 24°28N 103°20E **34 E4**
Miles *Australia* 26°40S 150°9E **63 D5**
Miles City *U.S.A.* 46°25N 105°51W **76 C11**
Milestone *Canada* 49°59N 104°31W **71 D8**
Miletus *Turkey* 37°30N 27°18E **23 F12**
Milford *Calif., U.S.A.* 40°10N 120°22W **78 E6**
Milford *Conn., U.S.A.* 41°14N 73°3W **83 E11**
Milford *Del., U.S.A.* 38°55N 75°26W **81 F16**
Milford *Mass., U.S.A.* 42°8N 71°31W **83 D13**
Milford *N.H., U.S.A.* 42°50N 71°39W **83 D13**
Milford *N.Y., U.S.A.* 42°35N 74°56W **83 D10**
Milford *Pa., U.S.A.* 41°19N 74°48W **83 E10**
Milford *Utah, U.S.A.* 38°24N 113°1W **76 G7**
Milford Haven *U.K.* 51°42N 5°7W **13 F2**
Milford Sd. *N.Z.* 44°41S 167°47E **59 F1**
Milford Sound *N.Z.* 44°41S 167°55E **59 F1**
Milḥ, Baḥr al = Razāzah, Buḥayrat ar *Iraq* 32°40N 43°35E **46 C4**
Milikapiti *Australia* 11°26S 130°40E **60 B5**
Miling *Australia* 30°30S 116°17E **61 F2**
Milk River *Canada* 49°10N 112°5W **70 D6**
Mill → *U.S.A.* 42°57N 83°23W **82 D1**
Mill I. *Antarctica* 66°0S 101°30E **5 C8**
Mill I. *Canada* 63°58N 77°47W **69 E16**
Mill Valley *U.S.A.* 37°54N 122°32W **78 H4**
Millau *France* 44°8N 3°4E **20 D5**
Millbridge *Canada* 44°41N 77°36W **82 B7**
Millbrook *Canada* 44°10N 78°29W **82 B6**
Millbrook *Ala., U.S.A.* 32°29N 86°22W **85 E11**
Millbrook *N.Y., U.S.A.* 41°47N 73°42W **83 E11**
Mille Lacs, L. des *Canada* 48°45N 90°35W **72 C1**
Mille Lacs L. *U.S.A.* 46°15N 93°39W **80 B7**
Milledgeville *U.S.A.* 33°5N 83°14W **85 E13**
Millen *U.S.A.* 32°48N 81°57W **85 E14**
Millennium I. = Caroline I. *Kiribati* 9°58S 150°13W **65 H12**
Miller *U.S.A.* 44°31N 98°59W **80 C4**
Miller Lake *Canada* 45°6N 81°26W **82 A3**
Millersburg *Ohio, U.S.A.* 40°33N 81°55W **82 F3**
Millersburg *Pa., U.S.A.* 40°32N 76°58W **82 F8**
Millerton *U.S.A.* 41°57N 73°31W **83 E11**
Millerton L. *U.S.A.* 37°1N 119°41W **78 J7**
Millet *St. Lucia* 13°55N 60°59W **89 f**
Millheim *U.S.A.* 40°54N 77°29W **82 F7**
Millicent *Australia* 37°34S 140°21E **63 F3**
Millington *U.S.A.* 35°20N 89°53W **85 D10**
Millinocket *U.S.A.* 45°39N 68°43W **81 C19**
Millmerran *Australia* 27°53S 151°16E **63 D5**
Millom *U.K.* 54°13N 3°16W **12 C4**
Mills L. *Canada* 61°30N 118°20W **70 A5**
Millsboro *U.S.A.* 40°0N 80°0W **82 G5**
Millstream Chichester △ *Australia* 21°35S 117°6E **60 D2**
Millstreet *Ireland* 52°4N 9°4W **10 D2**
Milltown Malbay *Ireland* 52°52N 9°24W **10 D2**
Millville *N.J., U.S.A.* 39°24N 75°2W **81 F16**
Millville *Pa., U.S.A.* 41°7N 76°32W **83 E8**
Millwood L. *U.S.A.* 33°42N 93°58W **84 E8**
Milne → *Australia* 21°10S 137°33E **62 C2**
Milo *U.S.A.* 45°15N 68°59W **81 C19**
Milos *Greece* 36°44N 24°25E **23 F11**
Milparinka *Australia* 29°46S 141°57E **63 D3**
Milpitas *U.S.A.* 37°26N 121°55W **78 H5**
Milton *N.S., Canada* 44°4N 64°45W **73 D7**
Milton *Ont., Canada* 43°31N 79°53W **82 C5**
Milton *N.Z.* 46°7S 169°59E **59 G2**
Milton *Calif., U.S.A.* 38°3N 120°51W **78 G6**
Milton *Fla., U.S.A.* 30°38N 87°3W **85 F11**
Milton *Pa., U.S.A.* 41°1N 76°51W **82 F8**
Milton *Vt., U.S.A.* 44°38N 73°7W **83 B11**
Milton-Freewater *U.S.A.* 45°56N 118°23W **76 D4**
Milton Keynes *U.K.* 52°1N 0°44W **13 E7**
Milton Keynes □ *U.K.* 52°1N 0°44W **13 E7**
Miluo *China* 29°0N 112°59E **35 C9**
Milverton *Canada* 43°34N 80°55W **82 C4**
Milwaukee *U.S.A.* 43°2N 87°54W **80 D10**
Milwaukee Deep *Atl. Oc.* 19°50N 68°0W **89 C6**
Milwaukie *U.S.A.* 45°26N 122°38W **78 E4**
Mimili *Australia* 27°0S 132°42E **61 E5**
Min Jiang → *Fujian, China* 26°0N 119°35E **35 E12**
Min Jiang → *Sichuan, China* 28°45N 104°40E **34 C5**
Min Xian *China* 34°25N 104°5E **32 G3**
Mīnā' al Aḥmadī *Kuwait* 29°5N 48°10E **47 D6**
Mīnā' Jabal 'Alī *U.A.E.* 25°2N 55°8E **47 E7**
Mina Pirquitas *Argentina* 22°40S 66°30W **94 A2**
Mīnā Su'ud *Si. Arabia* 28°45N 48°28E **47 D6**
Minago → *Canada* 54°33N 98°59W **71 C9**
Minaki *Canada* 49°59N 94°40W **71 D10**
Minamata *Japan* 32°10N 130°30E **29 H5**
Minami-Arapusa △ *Japan* 35°30N 138°9E **29 G9**
Minami-Tori-Shima *Pac. Oc.* 24°20N 153°58E **64 E7**
Minamiaizu *Japan* 37°12N 139°46E **29 F9**
Minamiawaji *Japan* 34°10N 134°42E **29 G7**
Minamisōma *Japan* 37°38N 140°58E **28 F10**
Minas *Uruguay* 34°20S 55°10W **95 C4**
Minas, Sierra de las *Guatemala* 15°9N 89°31W **88 C2**
Minas Basin *Canada* 45°20N 64°12W **73 C7**
Minas Gerais □ *Brazil* 18°50S 46°0W **93 G9**
Minatitlán *Mexico* 17°59N 94°31W **87 D6**
Minbu *Burma* 20°10N 94°52E **41 J19**
Minchinabad *Pakistan* 30°10N 73°34E **42 D5**
Mindanao *Phil.* 8°0N 125°0E **37 C7**
Mindanao Sea = Bohol Sea *Phil.* 9°0N 124°0E **37 C6**
Mindanao Trench *Pac. Oc.* 12°0N 126°6E **37 B7**
Mindelo *C. Verde Is.* 16°24N 25°0W **52 b**
Minden *Canada* 44°55N 78°43W **82 B6**
Minden *Germany* 52°17N 8°55E **16 B5**
Minden *La., U.S.A.* 32°37N 93°17W **84 E8**
Minden *Nev., U.S.A.* 38°57N 119°46W **78 G7**
Mindibungu = Billiluna *Australia* 19°37S 127°41E **60 C4**
Mindiptana *Indonesia* 5°55S 140°22E **37 F10**
Mindoro *Phil.* 13°0N 121°0E **37 B6**
Mindoro Str. *Phil.* 12°30N 120°30E **37 B6**
Mine *Japan* 34°12N 131°7E **29 G5**
Minehead *U.K.* 51°12N 3°29W **13 F4**
Mineola *N.Y., U.S.A.* 40°44N 73°38W **83 F11**
Mineola *Tex., U.S.A.* 32°40N 95°29W **84 E7**
Mineral King *U.S.A.* 36°27N 118°36W **78 J8**
Mineral Wells *U.S.A.* 32°48N 98°7W **84 E5**
Miners Bay *Canada* 44°49N 78°46W **82 B6**
Minersville *U.S.A.* 40°41N 76°16W **83 F8**
Minerva *N.Y., U.S.A.* 43°47N 73°59W **83 C11**
Minerva *Ohio, U.S.A.* 40°44N 81°6W **82 F3**
Minetto *U.S.A.* 43°24N 76°28W **83 C8**
Minfeng *China* 37°4N 82°46E **30 D5**
Mingäçevir Su Anbarı *Azerbaijan* 40°57N 46°50E **19 F8**
Mingan *Canada* 50°20N 64°0W **73 B7**
Mingechaurskoye Vdkhr. = Mingäçevir Su Anbarı *Azerbaijan* 40°57N 46°50E **19 F8**
Mingela *Australia* 19°52S 146°38E **62 B4**
Mingenew *Australia* 29°12S 115°21E **61 E2**
Mingera Cr. → *Australia* 20°38S 137°45E **62 C2**
Minggang *China* 32°24N 114°3E **35 A10**
Mingguang *China* 32°46N 117°59E **35 A11**
Mingin *Burma* 22°50N 94°30E **41 H19**
Minglun *China* 25°10N 108°21E **34 E7**
Mingo Junction *U.S.A.* 40°19N 80°37W **82 F4**
Mingora *Pakistan* 34°48N 72°22E **43 B5**
Mingshan *China* 30°6N 103°10E **34 B4**
Mingteke Daban = Mintaka Pass *Pakistan* 37°0N 74°58E **43 A6**
Mingxi *China* 26°18N 117°12E **35 D11**
Mingyuegue *China* 43°2N 128°50E **33 C15**
Minhe *China* 36°9N 102°45E **30 D9**
Minho = Miño → *Spain* 41°52N 8°40W **21 A2**
Minho *Portugal* 41°25N 8°20W **21 B1**
Minhou *China* 26°0N 119°15E **35 E12**
Minicoy I. *India* 8°17N 73°2E **45 K1**
Minidoka *U.S.A.* 42°45N 113°29W **76 E7**
Minigwal, L. *Australia* 29°31S 123°14E **61 E3**
Minilya → *Australia* 23°45S 114°0E **61 D1**
Minilya Roadhouse *Australia* 23°55S 114°0E **61 D1**
Minipi L. *Canada* 52°25N 60°45W **73 B7**
Minjilang *Australia* 11°8S 132°33E **60 B5**
Mink L. *Canada* 61°54N 117°40W **70 A5**
Minna *Nigeria* 9°37N 6°30E **52 G7**
Minneapolis *Kans., U.S.A.* 39°8N 97°42W **80 F5**
Minneapolis *Minn., U.S.A.* 44°57N 93°16W **80 C7**
Minneapolis-St. Paul Int. ✈ **(MSP)** *U.S.A.* 44°53N 93°13W **80 C7**
Minnedosa *Canada* 50°14N 99°50W **71 C9**
Minnesota □ *U.S.A.* 46°0N 94°15W **80 B6**
Minnesota → *U.S.A.* 44°54N 93°9W **80 C7**
Minnewaukan *U.S.A.* 48°4N 99°15W **80 A4**
Minnipa *Australia* 32°51S 135°9E **63 E2**
Minnitaki L. *Canada* 49°57N 92°10W **72 C1**
Mino *Japan* 35°32N 136°55E **29 G8**
Miño → *Spain* 41°52N 8°40W **21 A2**
Minorca = Menorca *Spain* 40°0N 4°0E **21 C8**
Minot *U.S.A.* 48°14N 101°18W **80 A3**
Minqin *China* 38°38N 103°20E **32 E2**
Minqing *China* 26°15N 118°50E **35 D12**
Minsk *Belarus* 53°52N 27°30E **17 B14**
Mińsk Mazowiecki *Poland* 52°10N 21°33E **17 B11**
Mintabie *Australia* 27°15S 133°7E **63 D1**
Mintaka Pass *Pakistan* 37°0N 74°58E **43 A6**
Minto *Canada* 46°5N 66°5W **73 C6**
Minto, L. *Canada* 57°13N 75°0W **72 A5**
Minton *Canada* 49°10N 104°35W **71 D8**
Minturn *U.S.A.* 39°35N 106°26W **76 G10**
Minudasht *Iran* 37°17N 56°7E **47 B8**
Minusinsk *Russia* 53°43N 91°20E **27 D10**
Minutang *India* 28°15N 96°30E **41 E20**
Minvoul *Gabon* 2°9N 12°8E **54 D2**
Minya Konka = Gongga Shan *China* 29°40N 101°55E **34 C3**
Minzhong *China* 22°37N 113°30E **31 a**
Miquelon *Canada* 49°25N 76°27W **72 C4**
Miquelon *St-P. & M.* 47°8N 56°22W **73 C8**
Mir *Belarus* 53°27N 26°28E **17 B14**
Mīr Kūh *Iran* 26°22N 58°55E **47 E8**
Mīr Shahdād *Iran* 26°15N 58°29E **47 E8**
Mira *Italy* 45°26N 12°8E **22 B5**
Mira por vos Cay *Bahamas* 22°9N 74°30W **89 B5**
Mirabello, Kolpos *Greece* 35°10N 25°50E **23 G11**
Mirador-Río Azul △ *Guatemala* 17°45N 89°50W **88 C2**
Miraj *India* 16°50N 74°45E **44 F2**
Miram Shah *Pakistan* 33°0N 70°2E **42 C4**
Miramar *Argentina* 38°15S 57°50W **94 D4**
Miramar *Mozam.* 23°50S 35°35E **57 B6**
Miramichi *Canada* 47°2N 65°28W **73 C6**
Miramichi B. *Canada* 47°15N 65°0W **73 C7**
Miranda *Brazil* 20°10S 56°15W **93 H7**
Miranda → *Brazil* 19°25S 57°20W **92 G7**
Miranda de Ebro *Spain* 42°41N 2°57W **21 A4**
Miranda do Douro *Portugal* 41°30N 6°16W **21 B2**
Mirandópolis *Brazil* 21°9S 51°6W **95 A5**
Mirani *Australia* 21°8S 148°53E **62 b**
Mirassol *Brazil* 20°46S 49°28W **95 A6**
Mirbāṭ *Oman* 17°0N 54°45E **49 D5**
Miri *Malaysia* 4°23N 113°59E **36 D4**
Mirialguda *India* 16°52N 79°35E **44 F4**
Miriam Vale *Australia* 24°20S 151°33E **62 C5**
Mirigama *Sri Lanka* 7°15N 80°8E **45 L5**
Mirim, L. *S. Amer.* 32°45S 52°50W **95 C5**
Miriuwung Gajerrong ☼ *Australia* 15°0S 128°45E **60 C4**
Mīrjāveh *Iran* 29°1N 61°30E **47 D9**
Mirnyy *Antarctica* 66°50S 92°30E **5 C14**
Mirnyy *Russia* 62°33N 113°53E **27 C12**
Mirokhan *Pakistan* 27°46N 68°6E **42 F3**
Mirond L. *Canada* 55°6N 102°47W **71 B8**
Mirpur *Pakistan* 33°32N 73°56E **43 C5**
Mirpur Batoro *Pakistan* 24°44N 68°16E **42 G3**
Mirpur Bibiwari *Pakistan* 28°33N 67°44E **42 E2**
Mirpur Khas *Pakistan* 25°30N 69°0E **42 G3**
Mirpur Sakro *Pakistan* 24°33N 67°41E **42 G2**
Mirs Bay = Tai Pang Wan *China* 22°33N 114°24E **31 a**
Mirtağ *Turkey* 38°23N 41°56E **46 B4**
Mirtoo Sea *Greece* 37°0N 23°20E **23 F10**
Miryang *S. Korea* 35°31N 128°44E **33 G15**
Mirzapur *India* 25°10N 82°34E **43 G10**
Mirzapur-cum-Vindhyachal = Mirzapur *India* 25°10N 82°34E **43 G10**
Misantla *Mexico* 19°56N 96°50W **87 D5**
Misawa *Japan* 40°41N 141°24E **28 D10**
Miscou I. *Canada* 47°57N 64°31W **73 C7**
Misha *India* 7°59N 93°20E **45 L10**
Mish'āb, Ra's al *Si. Arabia* 28°15N 48°43E **47 D6**
Mishan *China* 45°37N 131°48E **28 B5**
Mishawaka *U.S.A.* 41°40N 86°11W **80 E10**
Mishima *Japan* 35°10N 138°52E **29 G9**
Misión *Mexico* 32°6N 116°53W **79 N10**
Misiones □ *Argentina* 27°0S 55°0W **95 B5**
Misiones □ *Paraguay* 27°0S 56°0W **94 B4**
Miskah *Si. Arabia* 24°49N 42°56E **46 E4**
Miskitos, Cayos *Nic.* 14°26N 82°50W **88 D3**
Miskolc *Hungary* 48°7N 20°50E **17 D11**
Misool *Indonesia* 1°52S 130°10E **37 E8**
Mişr = Egypt ■ *Africa* 28°0N 31°0E **53 C12**
Mişrātah *Libya* 32°24N 15°3E **53 B9**
Missanabie *Canada* 48°20N 84°6W **72 C3**
Missinaibi → *Canada* 50°43N 81°29W **72 B3**
Missinaibi L. *Canada* 48°23N 83°40W **72 C3**
Mission *Canada* 49°10N 122°15W **70 D4**
Mission *S. Dak., U.S.A.* 43°18N 100°39W **80 D3**
Mission *Tex., U.S.A.* 26°13N 98°20W **84 H5**
Mission Beach *Australia* 17°53S 146°6E **62 B4**
Mission Viejo *U.S.A.* 33°36N 117°40W **79 M9**
Missisa L. *Canada* 52°20N 85°7W **72 B2**
Missisicabi → *Canada* 51°14N 79°31W **72 B4**
Mississagi → *Canada* 46°15N 83°9W **72 C3**
Mississippi □ *U.S.A.* 33°0N 90°0W **85 E10**
Mississippi → *U.S.A.* 29°9N 89°15W **85 G10**
Mississippi L. *Canada* 45°5N 76°10W **83 A8**
Mississippi River Delta *U.S.A.* 29°10N 89°15W **85 G10**
Mississippi Sd. *U.S.A.* 30°20N 89°0W **85 F10**
Missoula *U.S.A.* 46°52N 114°1W **76 C6**
Missouri □ *U.S.A.* 38°25N 92°30W **80 F7**
Missouri → *U.S.A.* 38°49N 90°7W **80 F8**
Missouri City *U.S.A.* 29°37N 95°32W **84 G7**
Missouri Valley *U.S.A.* 41°34N 95°53W **80 E6**
Mist *U.S.A.* 45°59N 123°15W **78 E3**
Mistassibi → *Canada* 48°53N 72°13W **73 B5**

Mistassini _Canada_ 48°53N 72°12W **73** C5
Mistassini → _Canada_ 48°42N 72°20W **73** C5
Mistassini, L. _Canada_ 51°0N 73°30W **72** B5
Mistastin L. _Canada_ 55°57N 63°20W **73** A7
Mistinibi, L. _Canada_ 55°56N 64°17W **73** A7
Mistissini _Canada_ 48°53N 72°12W **73** C5
Misty L. _Canada_ 58°53N 101°40W **71** B8
Misurata = Miṣrātah
  Libya 32°24N 15°3E **53** B9
Mitchell _Australia_ 26°29S 147°58E **63** D4
Mitchell _Canada_ 43°28N 81°12W **82** C3
Mitchell _Nebr., U.S.A._ 41°57N 103°49W **80** E2
Mitchell _Oreg., U.S.A._ 44°34N 120°9W **76** D3
Mitchell _S. Dak., U.S.A._ 43°43N 98°2W **80** D4
Mitchell → _Australia_ 15°12S 141°35E **62** B3
Mitchell-Alice Rivers △
  Australia 15°28S 142°5E **62** B3
Mitchell Ra. _Australia_ 12°49S 135°36E **62** A2
Mitchelstown _Ireland_ 52°15N 8°16W **10** D3
Mitha Tiwana _Pakistan_ 32°13N 72°6E **42** C5
Mithi _Pakistan_ 24°44N 69°48E **42** G3
Mithrao _Pakistan_ 27°28N 69°40E **42** F3
Mitilini _Greece_ 39°6N 26°35E **23** E12
Mitla Pass = Mamarr Mitlā
  Egypt 30°2N 32°54E **48** E1
Mito _Japan_ 36°20N 140°30E **29** F10
Mitrovicë _Kosovo_ 42°54N 20°52E **23** C9
Mitsamiouli _Comoros Is._ 11°20S 43°16E **55** a
Mitsiwa _Eritrea_ 15°35N 39°25E **49** D2
Mitsukaidō _Japan_ 36°1N 139°59E **29** F9
Mittagong _Australia_ 34°28S 150°29E **63** E5
Mittimatalik = Pond Inlet
  Canada 72°40N 77°0W **69** C16
Mitú _Colombia_ 1°15N 70°13W **92** C4
Mitumba, Mts.
  Dem. Rep. of the Congo 7°0S 27°30E **54** F5
Mitwaba
  Dem. Rep. of the Congo 8°2S 27°17E **54** F5
Mixteco → _Mexico_ 18°11N 98°30W **87** D5
Miyagi □ _Japan_ 38°15N 140°45E **28** E10
Miyah, W. el → _Syria_ 34°44N 39°57E **46** C3
Miyake-Jima _Japan_ 34°5N 139°30E **29** G9
Miyako _Japan_ 39°40N 141°59E **28** E10
Miyako-Jima _Japan_ 24°45N 125°20E **29** M2
Miyako-Rettō _Japan_ 24°24N 125°0E **29** M2
Miyakojima _Japan_ 24°48N 125°17E **29** M2
Miyakonojō _Japan_ 31°40N 131°5E **29** J5
Miyani _India_ 21°50N 69°26E **42** J3
Miyanoura-Dake _Japan_ 30°20N 130°31E **29** J5
Miyazaki _Japan_ 31°56N 131°30E **29** J5
Miyazaki □ _Japan_ 32°30N 131°30E **29** H5
Miyazu _Japan_ 35°35N 135°10E **29** G7
Miyet, Bahr el = Dead Sea
  Asia 31°30N 35°30E **48** D4
Miyi _China_ 26°47N 102°9E **34** D4
Miyoshi _Japan_ 34°48N 132°51E **29** G6
Miyun _China_ 40°28N 116°50E **32** D9
Miyun Shuiku _China_ 40°30N 117°0E **33** D9
Mizdah _Libya_ 31°30N 13°0E **53** B8
Mizen Hd. _Cork, Ireland_ 51°27N 9°50W **10** E2
Mizen Hd. _Wicklow, Ireland_ 52°51N 6°4W **10** D5
Mizhi _China_ 37°47N 110°12E **32** F6
Mizoram □ _India_ 23°30N 92°40E **41** H18
Mizpe Ramon _Israel_ 30°34N 34°49E **48** E3
Mizuho _Antarctica_ 70°30S 41°0E **5** D5
Mizusawa = Ōshū _Japan_ 39°8N 141°8E **28** E10
Mjölby _Sweden_ 58°20N 15°10E **9** G16
Mjosa _Norway_ 60°40N 11°0E **8** F14
Mkhaya △ _Swaziland_ 26°34S 31°45E **57** C5
Mkhuze → _S. Africa_ 29°27S 29°30E **57** C4
Mkomazi → _S. Africa_ 30°12S 30°50E **57** D5
Mkuze _S. Africa_ 27°10S 32°0E **57** D5
Mladá Boleslav _Czech Rep._ 50°27N 14°53E **16** C8
Mlange = Mulanje, Mt.
  Malawi 16°2S 35°33E **55** H7
Mława _Poland_ 53°9N 20°25E **17** B11
Mlawula △ _Swaziland_ 26°12S 32°2E **57** C5
Mljet _Croatia_ 42°43N 17°30E **22** C7
Mmabatho _S. Africa_ 25°49S 25°30E **56** C4
Mo i Rana _Norway_ 66°20N 14°7E **8** C16
Moa _Australia_ 10°11S 142°16E **62** a
Moa _Cuba_ 20°40N 74°56W **89** B4
Moa _Indonesia_ 8°0S 128°0E **37** F7
Moa → _S. Leone_ 6°59N 11°36W **52** G3
Moab _U.S.A._ 38°35N 109°33W **76** G9
Moala _Fiji_ 18°36S 179°53E **59** a
Moama _Australia_ 36°7S 144°46E **63** F3
Moamba _Mozam._ 25°36S 32°15E **57** D5
Moapa _U.S.A._ 36°40N 114°37W **79** J12
Moate _Ireland_ 53°24N 7°44W **10** C4
Mobārakābād _Iran_ 28°24N 53°20E **47** D7
Mobaye _C.A.R._ 4°25N 21°5E **54** D4
Moberly _U.S.A._ 39°25N 92°26W **80** F7
Moberly Lake _Canada_ 55°50N 121°44W **70** B4
Mobile _U.S.A._ 30°41N 88°3W **85** F11
Mobile B. _U.S.A._ 30°30N 88°0W **85** F11
Mobridge _U.S.A._ 45°32N 100°26W **80** C3
Moc Chau _Vietnam_ 20°50N 104°38E **38** B5
Moc Hoa _Vietnam_ 10°46N 105°56E **39** G5
Moçambique = Mozambique ■
  Africa 19°0S 35°0E **55** H7
Moçâmedes _Mozam._ 15°3S 40°42E **54** G8
Mocanaqua _U.S.A._ 41°9N 76°8W **83** E8
Moce _Fiji_ 18°40S 178°29W **59** a
Mochima △ _Venezuela_ 10°30N 64°5W **89** D7
Mochudi _Botswana_ 24°27S 26°7E **56** B4
Mocimboa da Praia
  Mozam. 11°25S 40°20E **54** G8
Moclips _U.S.A._ 47°14N 124°13W **78** C2
Mocoa _Colombia_ 1°7N 76°35W **92** C3
Mococa _Brazil_ 21°28S 47°0W **95** A6
Mocorito _Mexico_ 25°29N 107°55W **86** B3
Moctezuma _Mexico_ 29°48N 109°42W **86** B3
Moctezuma → _Mexico_ 21°59N 98°34W **87** C5
Mocuba _Mozam._ 16°54S 36°57E **55** H7
Modane _France_ 45°12N 6°40E **20** D7
Modasa _India_ 23°30N 73°21E **42** H5
Modder → _S. Africa_ 29°2S 24°37E **56** D3
Modderrivier _S. Africa_ 29°2S 24°38E **56** C3

Módena _Italy_ 44°40N 10°55E **22** B4
Modena _U.S.A._ 37°48N 113°56W **77** H7
Modesto _U.S.A._ 37°39N 121°0W **78** H6
Módica _Italy_ 36°52N 14°46E **22** F6
Modimolle _S. Africa_ 24°42S 28°22E **57** B4
Modjadjiskloof _S. Africa_ 23°42S 30°10E **57** B5
Moe _Australia_ 38°12S 146°19E **63** F4
Moengo _Suriname_ 5°45N 54°20W **93** B8
Moenjodaro = Mohenjodaro
  Pakistan 27°19N 68°7E **42** F3
Moffat _U.K._ 55°21N 3°27W **11** F5
Moga _India_ 30°48N 75°8E **42** D6
Mogadisho = Muqdisho
  Somalia 2°2N 45°25E **49** G4
Mogador = Essaouira
  Morocco 31°32N 9°42W **52** B4
Mogalakwena →
  S. Africa 22°38S 28°40E **57** B4
Mogami-Gawa → _Japan_ 38°45N 140°0E **28** E10
Mogi-Mirim _Brazil_ 22°29S 47°0W **93** H9
Mogilev = Mahilyow
  Belarus 53°55N 30°18E **17** B16
Mogilev-Podolskiy = Mohyliv-
  Podilskyy _Ukraine_ 48°26N 27°48E **17** D14
Mogocha _Russia_ 53°40N 119°50E **27** D12
Mogoditshane _Botswana_ 24°37S 25°51E **56** B4
Mogok _Burma_ 23°0N 96°40E **41** H20
Mogollon Rim _U.S.A._ 34°10N 110°50W **77** J8
Mogumber _Australia_ 31°2S 116°3E **61** F2
Mogwadi → _S. Africa_ 23°4S 29°36E **57** B4
Mohács _Hungary_ 45°58N 18°41E **17** F10
Mohala _India_ 20°35N 80°44E **44** D5
Mohales Hoek _Lesotho_ 30°7S 27°26E **56** D4
Mohali = Ajitgarh _India_ 30°47N 76°41E **42** D7
Mohall _U.S.A._ 48°46N 101°31W **80** A3
Moḥammadābād _Iran_ 37°52N 59°5E **47** B8
Mohammedia _Morocco_ 33°44N 7°21W **52** B4
Mohana _India_ 19°27N 84°16E **44** E7
Mohana → _India_ 24°43N 85°0E **43** G11
Mohave, L. _U.S.A._ 35°12N 114°34W **79** K12
Mohawk → _U.S.A._ 42°47N 73°41W **83** D11
Mohéli _Comoros Is._ 12°20S 43°40E **55** a
Mohenjodaro _Pakistan_ 27°19N 68°7E **42** F3
Moher, Cliffs of _Ireland_ 52°58N 9°27W **10** D2
Mohicanville Res. _U.S.A._ 40°45N 82°9W **82** F2
Mohns Ridge _Arctic_ 72°30N 5°0W **4** B7
Mohsenābād _Iran_ 36°40N 59°35E **47** B8
Mohyliv-Podilskyy
  Ukraine 48°26N 27°48E **17** D14
Moidart, L. _U.K._ 56°47N 5°52W **11** E3
Moinabad _India_ 17°44N 77°16E **44** F3
Moira → _Canada_ 44°21N 77°24W **82** B7
Moisaküla _Estonia_ 58°3N 25°12E **9** G21
Moisie _Canada_ 50°12N 66°1W **73** B6
Moisie → _Canada_ 50°14N 66°5W **73** B6
Mojave _U.S.A._ 35°3N 118°10W **79** K8
Mojave _U.S.A._ 35°7N 115°32W **79** K11
Mojave Desert _U.S.A._ 35°0N 116°30W **79** L10
Moji das Cruzes _Brazil_ 23°31S 46°11W **95** A6
Moji-Guaçu → _Brazil_ 20°53S 48°10W **95** A6
Mojiang _China_ 23°37N 101°35E **34** F3
Mojo _Bolivia_ 21°48S 65°33W **94** A2
Mojokerto _Indonesia_ 7°28S 112°26E **37** G15
Mokai _N.Z._ 38°32S 175°56E **59** C5
Mokala △ _S. Africa_ 29°10S 24°10E **56** C3
Mokameh _India_ 25°24N 85°55E **43** G11
Mokau _N.Z._ 38°42S 174°39E **59** C5
Mokelumne → _U.S.A._ 38°13N 121°28W **78** G5
Mokelumne Hill _U.S.A._ 38°18N 120°43W **78** G6
Mokhotlong _Lesotho_ 29°22S 29°2E **57** C4
Mokoan, L. _Australia_ 36°27S 146°5E **63** C4
Mokokchung _India_ 26°15N 94°30E **41** F19
Mokolo → _S. Africa_ 23°14S 27°43E **57** B4
Mokopane _S. Africa_ 24°10S 28°55E **57** B4
Mokpo _S. Korea_ 34°50N 126°25E **33** G14
Mokra Gora _Europe_ 42°50N 20°30E **23** C9
Mol _Belgium_ 51°11N 5°5E **15** C5
Molakalmuru _India_ 14°55N 76°50E **45** G3
Molchanovo _Russia_ 57°40N 83°50E **26** D9
Mold _U.K._ 53°9N 3°8W **12** D4
Moldavia = Moldova ■
  Europe 47°0N 28°0E **17** E15
Moldavia _Romania_ 46°30N 27°0E **17** E14
Molde _Norway_ 62°45N 7°9E **8** E12
Moldova ■ _Europe_ 47°0N 28°0E **17** E15
Moldoveanu, Vf.
  Romania 45°36N 24°45E **17** F13
Mole → _U.K._ 51°24N 0°21W **13** F7
Molepolole _Botswana_ 24°28S 25°28E **56** C4
Molfetta _Italy_ 41°12N 16°36E **22** D7
Moline _U.S.A._ 41°30N 90°31W **80** E8
Molinos _Argentina_ 25°28S 66°15W **94** B2
Mollendo _Peru_ 17°0S 72°0W **92** G4
Mollerin, L. _Australia_ 30°30S 117°35E **61** F2
Molodechno = Maladzyechna
  Belarus 54°20N 26°50E **17** A14
Molodezhnaya _Antarctica_ 67°40S 45°51E **5** C9
Moloka'i _U.S.A._ 21°8N 157°0W **75** L8
Molokai Fracture Zone
  Pac. Oc. 28°0N 125°0W **65** E15
Molong _Australia_ 33°5S 148°54E **63** E4
Molopo → _Africa_ 28°30S 20°12E **56** D3
Molson L. _Canada_ 54°22N 96°40W **71** C9
Molteno _S. Africa_ 31°22S 26°22E **56** D4
Molu _Indonesia_ 6°45S 131°40E **37** F8
Molucca Sea _Indonesia_ 0°0 125°0E **37** E6
Moluccas = Maluku
  Indonesia 1°0S 127°0E **37** E7
Moma _Mozam._ 16°47S 39°4E **55** H7
Mombasa _Kenya_ 4°3S 39°40E **54** E7
Mombetsu _Japan_ 44°21N 143°22E **28** B11
Momchilgrad _Bulgaria_ 41°33N 25°23E **23** D11
Mompós _Colombia_ 9°14N 74°26W **92** B4
Møn _Denmark_ 54°57N 12°20E **9** J15
Mon □ _Burma_ 16°0N 97°30E **41** L20
Mona, Canal de la = Mona
  Passage _W. Indies_ 18°30N 67°45W **89** C6
Mona, Isla _Puerto Rico_ 18°5N 67°54W **89** C6

Mona, Pta. _Costa Rica_ 9°37N 82°36W **88** E3
Mona Passage _W. Indies_ 18°30N 67°45W **89** C6
Monaca _U.S.A._ 40°41N 80°17W **82** F4
Monaco ■ _Europe_ 43°46N 7°23E **20** E7
Monadhliath Mts. _U.K._ 57°10N 4°4W **11** D4
Monadnock, Mt. _U.S.A._ 42°52N 72°7W **83** D12
Monaghan _Ireland_ 54°15N 6°57W **10** B5
Monaghan □ _Ireland_ 54°11N 6°56W **10** B5
Monahans _U.S.A._ 31°36N 102°54W **84** F3
Monar, L. _U.K._ 57°26N 5°8W **11** D3
Monaragala _Sri Lanka_ 6°52N 81°2E **45** L5
Monarch Mt. _Canada_ 51°55N 125°57W **70** C3
Monashee Mts. _Canada_ 51°0N 118°43W **70** C5
Monasterevin _Ireland_ 53°8N 7°4W **10** C4
Monastir = Bitola
  Macedonia 41°1N 21°20E **23** D9
Monastir _Tunisia_ 35°50N 10°49E **53** A8
Monbetsu = Hidaka
  Japan 42°30N 142°10E **28** C11
Moncayo, Sierra del _Spain_ 41°48N 1°50W **21** B5
Monchegorsk _Russia_ 67°54N 32°58E **8** C25
Mönchengladbach
  Germany 51°11N 6°27E **16** C4
Monchique _Portugal_ 37°19N 8°38W **21** D1
Moncks Corner _U.S.A._ 33°12N 80°1W **85** E14
Monclova _Mexico_ 26°54N 101°25W **86** B4
Moncton _Canada_ 46°7N 64°51W **73** C7
Mondego → _Portugal_ 40°9N 8°52W **21** B1
Mondeodo _Indonesia_ 3°34S 122°9E **37** E6
Mondlo _S. Africa_ 27°59S 30°43E **57** C5
Mondoví _Italy_ 44°23N 7°49E **20** D7
Mondrain I. _Australia_ 34°9S 122°14E **61** F3
Moneague _Jamaica_ 18°16N 77°7W **88** a
Moneron, Ostrov
  Russia 46°15N 141°16E **28** A10
Monessen _U.S.A._ 40°9N 79°54W **82** F5
Monett _U.S.A._ 36°55N 93°55W **80** G7
Moneymore _U.K._ 54°41N 6°40W **10** B5
Monforte de Lemos _Spain_ 42°31N 7°33W **21** A2
Mong Hpayak _Burma_ 20°52N 99°55E **38** B2
Mong Hsat _Shan, Burma_ 21°54N 98°30E **34** G2
Mong Hsat _Burma_ 20°31N 99°15E **38** B2
Mong Kung _Burma_ 21°35N 97°35E **41** J20
Mong Nai _Burma_ 20°32N 97°46E **41** J20
Mong Ping _Burma_ 21°22N 99°2E **34** G2
Mong Tai = Shan □
  Burma 21°30N 98°30E **41** J21
Mong Ton _Burma_ 20°17N 98°45E **41** J21
Mong Yai _Burma_ 22°21N 98°3E **41** H21
Mong Yang _Burma_ 21°50N 99°41E **38** B2
Mongalla _South Sudan_ 5°8N 31°42E **53** G12
Mongers, L. _Australia_ 29°25S 117°5E **61** E2
Monghyr = Munger
  India 25°23N 86°30E **43** G12
Mongibello = Etna _Italy_ 37°50N 14°55E **22** F6
Mongo _Chad_ 12°14N 18°43E **53** F9
Mongolia ■ _Asia_ 47°0N 103°0E **30** B9
Mongolia, Plateau of
  Asia 45°0N 105°0E **24** D12
Mongu _Zambia_ 15°16S 23°12E **55** H4
Môngua _Angola_ 16°43S 15°20E **56** A2
Monifieth _U.K._ 56°30N 2°48W **11** E6
Monkey Mia _Australia_ 25°48S 113°43E **61** E1
Monkey River _Belize_ 16°22N 88°29W **87** D7
Monkland _Canada_ 45°11N 74°52W **83** A10
Monkoto
  Dem. Rep. of the Congo 1°38S 20°35E **54** E4
Monkton _Canada_ 43°35N 81°5W **82** C3
Monmouth _U.K._ 51°48N 2°42W **13** F5
Monmouth _Ill., U.S.A._ 40°55N 90°39W **80** E8
Monmouth _Oreg.,
  U.S.A._ 44°51N 123°14W **76** D2
Monmouthshire □ _U.K._ 51°48N 2°54W **13** F5
Mono, Pta. _Nic._ 12°0N 83°30W **88** D3
Mono L. _U.S.A._ 38°1N 119°1W **78** H7
Monolith _U.S.A._ 35°7N 118°22W **79** K8
Monongahela _U.S.A._ 40°12N 79°56W **82** F5
Monópoli _Italy_ 40°57N 17°18E **22** D7
Monos I. _Trin. & Tob._ 10°42N 61°44W **93** K15
Monroe _Ga., U.S.A._ 33°47N 83°43W **85** E13
Monroe _La., U.S.A._ 32°30N 92°7W **84** E8
Monroe _Mich., U.S.A._ 41°55N 83°24W **81** E12
Monroe _N.C., U.S.A._ 34°59N 80°33W **85** D14
Monroe _N.Y., U.S.A._ 41°20N 74°11W **83** E10
Monroe _Utah, U.S.A._ 38°38N 112°7W **76** G7
Monroe _Wash., U.S.A._ 47°51N 121°58W **78** C5
Monroe _Wis., U.S.A._ 42°36N 89°38W **80** D9
Monroe City _U.S.A._ 39°39N 91°44W **80** F8
Monroeton _U.S.A._ 41°43N 76°29W **83** E8
Monroeville _Ala., U.S.A._ 31°31N 87°20W **85** F11
Monroeville _Pa., U.S.A._ 40°26N 79°45W **82** F5
Monrovia _Liberia_ 6°18N 10°47W **52** G3
Mons _Belgium_ 50°27N 3°58E **15** D3
Monse _Indonesia_ 4°7S 123°15E **37** E6
Mont-de-Marsan _France_ 43°54N 0°31W **20** E3
Mont-Joli _Canada_ 48°37N 68°10W **73** C6
Mont-Laurier _Canada_ 46°35N 75°30W **72** C4
Mont-Louis _Canada_ 49°15N 65°44W **73** C6
Mont-St-Michel, Le
  France 48°40N 1°30W **20** B3
Mont-Tremblant △
  Canada 46°30N 74°30W **72** C5
Montagu _S. Africa_ 33°45S 20°8E **56** D3
Montagu I. _Antarctica_ 58°25S 26°20W **5** B1
Montague _Canada_ 46°10N 62°39W **73** C7
Montague, I. _Mexico_ 31°45N 114°48W **86** A2
Montague I. _U.S.A._ 60°0N 147°30W **74** D10
Montague Ra. _Australia_ 27°15S 119°30E **61** E2
Montague Sd. _Australia_ 14°28S 125°20E **60** B4
Montalbán _Spain_ 40°50N 0°45W **21** B5
Montalvo _U.S.A._ 34°15N 119°12W **79** L7
Montana _Bulgaria_ 43°27N 23°16E **23** C10
Montaña _Peru_ 6°0S 73°0W **92** E4
Montana □ _U.S.A._ 47°0N 110°0W **76** C9
Montargis _France_ 47°59N 2°43E **20** C5
Montauban _France_ 44°2N 1°21E **20** D4
Montauk _U.S.A._ 41°3N 71°57W **83** E13
Montauk Pt. _U.S.A._ 41°4N 71°51W **83** E13
Montbéliard _France_ 47°31N 6°48E **20** C7
Montceau-les-Mines
  France 46°40N 4°23E **20** C6

Montclair _U.S.A._ 40°49N 74°12W **83** F10
Monte Albán _Mexico_ 17°2N 96°46W **87** D5
Monte Alegre _Brazil_ 2°0S 54°0W **93** D8
Monte Azul _Brazil_ 15°9S 42°53W **93** G10
Monte-Carlo _Monaco_ 43°44N 7°25E **20** E7
Monte Caseros _Argentina_ 30°10S 57°50W **94** C4
Monte Comán _Argentina_ 34°40S 67°53W **94** C2
Monte Cristi _Dom. Rep._ 19°52N 71°39W **89** C5
Monte Lindo →
  Paraguay 23°56S 57°12W **94** A4
Monte Patria _Chile_ 30°42S 70°58W **94** C1
Monte Quemado
  Argentina 25°53S 62°41W **94** B3
Monte Rio _U.S.A._ 38°28N 123°0W **78** G4
Monte Santu, C. di _Italy_ 40°5N 9°44E **22** D3
Monte Vista _U.S.A._ 37°35N 106°9W **77** H10
Monteagudo _Argentina_ 27°14S 54°8W **95** B5
Montebello _Canada_ 45°40N 74°55W **72** C5
Montebello Is. _Australia_ 20°30S 115°45E **60** D2
Montecarlo _Argentina_ 26°34S 54°47W **95** B5
Montecito _U.S.A._ 34°26N 119°40W **79** L7
Montecristo _Italy_ 42°20N 10°19E **22** C4
Montego Bay _Jamaica_ 18°28N 77°55W **88** a
Montélimar _France_ 44°33N 4°45E **20** D6
Montello _U.S.A._ 43°48N 89°20W **80** D9
Montemorelos _Mexico_ 25°12N 99°49W **87** B5
Montenegro _Brazil_ 29°39S 51°29W **95** B5
Montenegro ■ _Europe_ 42°40N 19°20E **23** C8
Montepuez _Mozam._ 13°8S 38°59E **55** G7
Monterey _U.S.A._ 36°37N 121°55W **78** J5
Monterey B. _U.S.A._ 36°45N 122°0W **78** J5
Montería _Colombia_ 8°46N 75°53W **92** B3
Monteros _Argentina_ 27°11S 65°30W **94** B2
Monterrey _Mexico_ 25°40N 100°19W **86** B4
Montes Azules △ _Mexico_ 16°21N 91°3W **87** D6
Montes Claros _Brazil_ 16°30S 43°50W **93** G10
Montesano _U.S.A._ 46°59N 123°36W **78** D3
Montesilvano _Italy_ 42°29N 14°8E **22** C6
Montevideo _Uruguay_ 34°50S 56°11W **95** C4
Montezuma _U.S.A._ 44°57N 95°43W **80** C6
Montezuma _U.S.A._ 41°35N 92°32W **80** E7
Montezuma Castle △
  _U.S.A._ 34°39N 111°45W **77** J8
Montgomery _U.K._ 52°34N 3°8W **13** E4
Montgomery _Ala.,
  U.S.A._ 32°23N 86°19W **85** E11
Montgomery _Pa., U.S.A._ 41°10N 76°53W **82** E8
Montgomery _W. Va.,
  U.S.A._ 38°11N 81°19W **81** F13
Montgomery City _U.S.A._ 38°59N 91°30W **80** F8
Monticello _Ark., U.S.A._ 33°38N 91°47W **84** E9
Monticello _Fla., U.S.A._ 30°33N 83°52W **85** F13
Monticello _Ind., U.S.A._ 40°45N 86°46W **81** E10
Monticello _Iowa, U.S.A._ 42°15N 91°12W **80** E8
Monticello _Ky., U.S.A._ 36°50N 84°51W **81** G11
Monticello _Minn., U.S.A._ 45°18N 93°48W **80** C7
Monticello _Miss., U.S.A._ 31°33N 90°7W **85** F9
Monticello _N.Y., U.S.A._ 41°39N 74°42W **83** E10
Monticello _Utah, U.S.A._ 37°52N 109°21W **77** H9
Montijo _Portugal_ 38°41N 8°54W **21** C1
Montilla _Spain_ 37°36N 4°40W **21** D3
Montluçon _France_ 46°22N 2°36E **20** C5
Montmagny _Canada_ 46°58N 70°34W **73** C5
Montmartre _Canada_ 50°14N 103°27W **71** C8
Montmorillon _France_ 46°26N 0°50E **20** C4
Monto _Australia_ 24°52S 151°6E **62** C5
Montongbuwoh _Indonesia_ 8°33S 116°4E **37** K19
Montoro _Spain_ 38°1N 4°27W **21** C3
Montour Falls _U.S.A._ 42°21N 76°51W **82** D8
Montoursville _U.S.A._ 41°15N 76°55W **82** E8
Montpelier _Idaho, U.S.A._ 42°19N 111°18W **76** E8
Montpelier _Vt., U.S.A._ 44°16N 72°35W **83** B12
Montpellier _France_ 43°37N 3°52E **20** E5
Montréal → _Canada_ 47°14N 84°39W **72** C3
Montréal L. _Canada_ 54°20N 105°45W **71** C7
Montreal Lake _Canada_ 54°3N 105°46W **71** C7
Montreux _Switz._ 46°26N 6°55E **20** D7
Montrose _U.K._ 56°44N 2°27W **11** E6
Montrose _Colo., U.S.A._ 38°29N 107°53W **76** G10
Montrose _Pa., U.S.A._ 41°50N 75°53W **83** E9
Monts, Pte. des _Canada_ 49°20N 67°12W **73** C6
Montserrat ■ _W. Indies_ 16°40N 62°10W **89** C7
Monywa _Burma_ 22°7N 95°11E **41** H19
Monze _Zambia_ 16°17S 27°29E **55** H5
Monze, C. _Pakistan_ 24°47N 66°37E **42** G2
Monzón _Spain_ 41°52N 0°10E **21** B6
Mooers _U.S.A._ 44°58N 73°35W **83** B11
Mooi → _S. Africa_ 28°45S 30°34E **57** C5
Mooi River _S. Africa_ 29°13S 29°50E **57** C4
Mookgopong _S. Africa_ 24°31S 28°44E **57** B4
Moomba _Australia_ 28°6S 140°12E **63** A3
Moonah → _Australia_ 22°3S 138°33E **62** C2
Moonda, L. _Australia_ 25°52S 140°25E **62** D3
Moonie _Australia_ 27°46S 150°20E **63** D5
Moonie → _Australia_ 29°19S 148°43E **63** D4
Moonta _Australia_ 34°6S 137°32E **63** E2
Moora _Australia_ 30°37S 115°58E **61** F2
Moorcroft _U.S.A._ 44°16N 104°57W **76** D11
Moore → _Australia_ 31°22S 115°30E **61** F2
Moore, L. _Australia_ 29°50S 117°35E **61** E2
Moore Falls _Canada_ 44°48N 78°48E **82** B6
Moore Park _Australia_ 24°43S 152°17E **62** C5
Moore Res. _U.S.A._ 44°20N 71°53W **83** B13
Moore River △ _U.S.A._ 31°12N 83°13E **61** F2
Moorea _French Polynesia_ 17°30S 149°50W **59** d
Moorefield _U.S.A._ 39°4N 78°58W **81** F14
Moorfoot Hills _U.K._ 55°44N 3°8W **11** F5
Moorhead _U.S.A._ 46°53N 96°45W **80** B5
Moorpark _U.S.A._ 34°17N 118°53W **79** L8
Mooreesburg _S. Africa_ 33°6S 18°38E **56** D2
Moorrinya △ _Australia_ 21°42S 144°58E **62** C3
Moose → _Canada_ 51°20N 80°25W **72** B3
Moose → _U.S.A._ 43°38N 75°24W **83** C9
Moose Creek _Canada_ 45°15N 74°58W **83** A10
Moose Factory _Canada_ 51°16N 80°32W **72** B3
Moose Jaw _Canada_ 50°24N 105°30W **71** C7
Moose Jaw → _Canada_ 50°34N 105°18W **71** C7
Moose Lake _Canada_ 53°46N 100°8W **71** C8
Moose Lake _U.S.A._ 46°27N 92°46W **80** B7
Moose Mountain
  Canada 49°48N 102°25W **71** D8

Moosehead L. _U.S.A._ 45°38N 69°40W **81** C19
Mooselookmeguntic L.
  _U.S.A._ 44°55N 70°49W **83** B14
Moosilauke, Mt. _U.S.A._ 44°3N 71°40W **83** B13
Moosomin _Canada_ 50°9N 101°40W **71** C8
Moosonee _Canada_ 51°17N 80°39W **72** B3
Moosup _U.S.A._ 41°43N 71°53W **83** E13
Mopane _S. Africa_ 22°37S 29°52E **57** B4
Mopipi _Botswana_ 21°6S 24°55E **56** B3
Mopti _Mali_ 14°30N 4°0W **52** F5
Moqor _Afghan._ 32°50N 67°42E **42** C2
Moquegua _Peru_ 17°15S 70°46W **92** G4
Mora _Sweden_ 61°2N 14°38E **8** F16
Mora _Minn., U.S.A._ 45°53N 93°18W **80** C7
Mora _N. Mex., U.S.A._ 35°58N 105°20W **77** J11
Moradabad _India_ 28°50N 78°50E **43** E8
Morafenobe _Madag._ 17°50S 44°53E **55** H8
Moramanga _Madag._ 18°56S 48°12E **55** H9
Moran _Kans., U.S.A._ 37°55N 95°10W **80** G6
Moran _Wyo., U.S.A._ 43°50N 110°31W **76** E8
Moranbah _Australia_ 22°1S 148°6E **62** C4
Morang = Biratnagar
  Nepal 26°27N 87°17E **43** F12
Morant Bay _Jamaica_ 17°53N 76°25W **88** a
Morant Cays _Jamaica_ 17°22N 76°0W **88** C4
Morant Pt. _Jamaica_ 17°55N 76°12W **88** a
Morar _India_ 26°14N 78°14E **42** F8
Morar, L. _U.K._ 56°57N 5°40W **11** E3
Moratuwa _Sri Lanka_ 6°45N 79°55E **45** L4
Morava → _Serbia_ 44°36N 21°4E **23** B9
Morava → _Slovak Rep._ 48°10N 16°59E **17** D9
Moravia _U.S.A._ 42°43N 76°25W **83** D8
Moravian Hts. = Českomoravská
  Vrchovina _Czech Rep._ 49°30N 15°40E **16** D8
Morawa _Australia_ 29°13S 116°0E **61** E2
Morawhanna _Guyana_ 8°30N 59°40W **92** B7
Moray □ _U.K._ 57°31N 3°18W **11** D5
Moray Firth _U.K._ 57°40N 3°52W **11** D5
Morbi _India_ 22°37N 70°37E **42** H4
Morden _Canada_ 49°15N 98°10W **71** D9
Mordovian Republic =
  Mordvinia □ _Russia_ 54°20N 44°30E **18** D7
Mordvinia □ _Russia_ 54°20N 44°30E **18** D7
Moreau → _U.S.A._ 45°18N 100°43W **80** C3
Morebeng _S. Africa_ 23°30S 29°55E **57** B4
Morecambe _U.K._ 54°5N 2°52W **12** C5
Morecambe B. _U.K._ 54°7N 3°0W **12** C5
Moree _Australia_ 29°28S 149°54E **63** D4
Morehead _U.S.A._ 38°11N 83°26W **81** F12
Morehead City _U.S.A._ 34°43N 76°43W **85** D16
Morel → _India_ 26°13N 76°36E **42** F7
Morelia _Mexico_ 19°42N 101°7W **86** D4
Morella _Australia_ 23°0S 143°52E **62** C3
Morella _Spain_ 40°35N 0°5W **21** B5
Morelos _Mexico_ 26°42N 107°40W **86** B3
Morelos □ _Mexico_ 18°45N 99°0W **87** D5
Moremi △ _Botswana_ 19°18S 23°10E **56** A3
Morena _India_ 26°30N 78°4E **42** F8
Morena, Sierra _Spain_ 38°20N 4°0W **21** C3
Moreno Valley _U.S.A._ 33°56N 117°14W **79** M10
Moresby I. _Canada_ 52°30N 131°40W **70** C2
Moreton I. _Australia_ 27°10S 153°25E **63** D5
Moreton Island △
  Australia 27°2S 153°24E **63** D5
Morgan _U.S.A._ 41°2N 111°41W **76** F8
Morgan City _U.S.A._ 29°42N 91°12W **84** G9
Morgan Hill _U.S.A._ 37°8N 121°39W **78** H5
Morganfield _U.S.A._ 37°41N 87°55W **80** G10
Morgan's Port _U.S.A._ 29°40N 95°0W **84** G7
Morganton _U.S.A._ 35°45N 81°41W **85** D14
Morgantown _U.S.A._ 39°38N 79°57W **81** F14
Morgenzon _S. Africa_ 26°45S 29°36E **57** C4
Morghak _Iran_ 29°7N 57°54E **47** D8
Morhar → _India_ 25°29N 85°11E **43** G11
Mori _Japan_ 42°6N 140°35E **28** C10
Moriarty _U.S.A._ 34°59N 106°3W **77** J10
Morice L. _Canada_ 53°50N 127°40W **70** C3
Morinville _Canada_ 53°49N 113°41W **70** C6
Morioka _Japan_ 39°45N 141°8E **28** E10
Moris _Mexico_ 28°10N 108°32E **86** B3
Morlaix _France_ 48°36N 3°52W **20** B2
Mormugao = Marmagao
  India 15°25N 73°56E **45** G1
Mornington _Australia_ 38°15S 145°5E **63** F4
Mornington, I. _Chile_ 49°50S 75°30W **96** F1
Mornington I. _Australia_ 16°30S 139°30E **62** B2
Moro _Pakistan_ 26°40N 68°0E **42** F2
Moro → _Pakistan_ 29°42N 67°22E **42** E2
Moro G. _Phil._ 6°30N 123°0E **37** C6
Morocco ■ _N. Afr._ 32°0N 5°50W **52** B4
Morogoro _Tanzania_ 6°50S 37°40E **54** F7
Moroleón _Mexico_ 20°8N 101°12W **86** C4
Morombe _Madag._ 21°45S 43°22E **55** J8
Moron _Argentina_ 34°39S 58°37W **94** C4
Morón _Cuba_ 22°8N 78°39W **88** B4
Mörön _Mongolia_ 49°38N 100°9E **30** B9
Morón de la Frontera
  Spain 37°6N 5°28W **21** D3
Morona → _Peru_ 4°40S 77°10W **92** D3
Morondava _Madag._ 20°17S 44°17E **55** J8
Morongo Valley _U.S.A._ 34°3N 116°37W **79** L10
Moroni _Comoros Is._ 11°40S 43°16E **55** a
Moroni _U.S.A._ 39°32N 111°35W **76** G8
Morotai _Indonesia_ 2°10N 128°30E **37** D7
Moroto _Uganda_ 2°28N 34°42E **54** D6
Morpeth _Canada_ 42°23N 81°50W **82** D3
Morpeth _U.K._ 55°10N 1°41W **12** B6
Morphou _Cyprus_ 35°12N 32°59E **46** C2
Morrilton _U.S.A._ 35°9N 92°44W **84** D8
Morrinhos _Brazil_ 17°45S 49°10W **93** G9
Morrinsville _N.Z._ 37°40S 175°32E **59** B5
Morris _Canada_ 49°25N 97°22W **71** D9
Morris _Ill., U.S.A._ 41°22N 88°26W **80** E9
Morris _Minn., U.S.A._ 45°35N 95°55W **80** C6
Morris _N.Y., U.S.A._ 42°33N 75°15W **83** D9
Morris _Pa., U.S.A._ 41°35N 77°17W **82** E7
Morris, Mt. _Australia_ 26°9S 131°4E **61** E5
Morris Jesup, Kap
  Greenland 83°40N 34°0W **66** A16
Morrisburg _Canada_ 44°55N 75°7W **83** B9

144 Morristown INDEX TO WORLD MAPS

Morristown *Ariz., U.S.A.* 33°51N 112°37W **77** K7
Morristown *N.J., U.S.A.* 40°48N 74°29W **83** F10
Morristown *N.Y., U.S.A.* 44°35N 75°39W **83** B9
Morristown *Tenn., U.S.A.* 36°13N 83°18W **85** C13
Morrisville *N.Y., U.S.A.* 42°53N 75°35W **83** D9
Morrisville *Pa., U.S.A.* 40°13N 74°47W **83** F10
Morrisville *Vt., U.S.A.* 44°34N 72°36W **83** B12
Morro, Pta. *Chile* 27°6S 71°0W **94** B1
Morro Bay *U.S.A.* 35°22N 120°51W **78** K6
Morrocoy △ *Venezuela* 10°48N 68°13W **89** D6
Morrosquillo, G. de *Colombia* 9°35N 75°40W **88** E4
Morrumbene *Mozam.* 23°31S 35°16E **57** B6
Morshansk *Russia* 53°28N 41°50E **18** D7
Morsi *India* 21°21N 78°0E **44** D4
Morteros *Argentina* 30°50S 62°0W **94** C3
Mortlach *Canada* 50°27N 106°4W **71** C7
Mortlake *Australia* 38°5S 142°50E **63** F3
Morton *Tex., U.S.A.* 33°44N 102°46W **84** E3
Morton *Wash., U.S.A.* 46°34N 122°17W **78** D4
Moruga *Trin. & Tob.* 10°4N 61°16W **93** K15
Morundah *Australia* 34°57S 146°19E **63** E4
Moruya *Australia* 35°58S 150°3E **63** F5
Morvan *France* 47°5N 4°3E **20** C6
Morven *Australia* 26°22S 147°5E **63** D4
Morvern *U.K.* 56°38N 5°44W **11** E3
Morwell *Australia* 38°10S 146°22E **63** F4
Morzhovets, Ostrov *Russia* 66°44N 42°35E **18** A7
Mosakahiken = Moose Lake *Canada* 53°46N 100°8W **71** C8
Moscos Is. *Burma* 14°0N 97°30E **38** F1
Moscow *Idaho, U.S.A.* 46°44N 117°0W **76** C5
Moscow *Pa., U.S.A.* 41°20N 75°31W **83** E9
Mosel → *Europe* 50°22N 7°36E **20** A7
Moselle = Mosel → *Europe* 50°22N 7°36E **20** A7
Moses Lake *U.S.A.* 47°8N 119°17W **76** C4
Mosgiel *N.Z.* 45°53S 170°21E **59** F3
Moshaweng → *S. Africa* 26°35S 22°50E **56** C3
Moshchnyy, Ostrov *Russia* 60°1N 27°50E **9** F22
Moshi *Tanzania* 3°22S 37°18E **54** E7
Moshupa *Botswana* 24°46S 25°29E **56** B4
Mosi-oa-Tunya = Victoria Falls *Zimbabwe* 17°58S 25°52E **55** H5
Mosjøen *Norway* 65°51N 13°12E **8** D15
Moskenesøya *Norway* 67°58N 13°0E **8** C15
Moskenstraumen *Norway* 67°47N 12°45E **8** C15
Mosomane *Botswana* 24°2S 26°19E **56** B4
Mosonmagyaróvár *Hungary* 47°52N 17°18E **17** E9
Mosquera *Colombia* 2°35N 78°24W **92** C3
Mosquero *U.S.A.* 35°47N 103°58W **77** J12
Mosquitia *Honduras* 15°20N 84°10W **88** C3
Mosquito Creek L. *U.S.A.* 41°18N 80°46W **82** E4
Mosquito L. *Canada* 62°35N 103°20W **71** A8
Mosquitos, G. de los *Panama* 9°15N 81°10W **88** E3
Moss *Norway* 59°27N 10°40E **9** G14
Moss Vale *Australia* 34°32S 150°25E **63** E5
Mossaka *Congo* 1°15S 16°45E **54** E3
Mossbank *Canada* 49°56N 105°56W **71** D7
Mossburn *N.Z.* 45°41S 168°15E **59** F2
Mosselbaai *S. Africa* 34°11S 22°8E **56** D3
Mossendjo *Congo* 2°55S 12°42E **54** E2
Mossgiel *Australia* 33°15S 144°5E **63** E3
Mossman *Australia* 16°21S 145°15E **62** B4
Mossoró *Brazil* 5°10S 37°15W **93** E11
Most *Czech Rep.* 50°31N 13°38E **16** C7
Mostaganem *Algeria* 35°54N 0°5E **52** A6
Mostar *Bos.-H.* 43°22N 17°50E **23** C7
Mostardas *Brazil* 31°2S 50°51W **95** C5
Mostiska = Mostyska *Ukraine* 49°48N 23°4E **17** D12
Mosty = Masty *Belarus* 53°27N 24°38E **17** B13
Mostyska *Ukraine* 49°48N 23°4E **17** D12
Mosul = Al Mawşil *Iraq* 36°15N 43°5E **46** B4
Motagua → *Guatemala* 15°44N 88°14W **88** C2
Motala *Sweden* 58°32N 15°1E **9** G16
Motaze *Mozam.* 24°48S 32°52E **57** B5
Moth *India* 25°43N 78°57E **43** G8
Motherwell *U.K.* 55°47N 3°58W **11** F5
Motihari *India* 26°30N 84°55E **43** F11
Motozintla de Mendoza *Mexico* 15°22N 92°14W **87** D6
Motril *Spain* 36°31N 3°37W **21** D4
Mott *U.S.A.* 46°23N 102°20W **80** B2
Mottama, G. of *Burma* 16°5N 96°30E **41** L20
Motueka *N.Z.* 41°7S 173°1E **59** D4
Motueka → *N.Z.* 41°5S 173°1E **59** D4
Motul *Mexico* 21°6N 89°17W **87** C7
Mouchalagane → *Canada* 50°56N 68°41W **73** B6
Mouding *China* 25°20N 101°28E **34** E3
Moudros *Greece* 39°50N 25°18E **23** E11
Mouhoun = Black Volta → *Africa* 8°41N 1°33W **52** G5
Mouila *Gabon* 1°50S 11°0E **54** E2
Moulamein *Australia* 35°3S 144°1E **63** F3
Moule à Chique, C. *St. Lucia* 13°43N 60°57W **89** f
Moulins *France* 46°35N 3°19E **20** C5
Moulmein = Mawlamyine *Burma* 16°30N 97°40E **41** L20
Moulouya, O. → *Morocco* 35°5N 2°25W **52** B5
Moultrie *U.S.A.* 31°11N 83°47W **85** F13
Moultrie, L. *U.S.A.* 33°20N 80°5W **85** E14
Mound City *Mo., U.S.A.* 40°7N 95°14W **80** E6
Mound City *S. Dak., U.S.A.* 45°44N 100°4W **80** C3
Moundou *Chad* 8°40N 16°10E **53** G9
Moundsville *U.S.A.* 39°55N 80°44W **82** G4
Moung *Cambodia* 12°46N 103°27E **38** F4
Mount Airy *U.S.A.* 36°31N 80°37W **85** C14
Mount Albert *Canada* 44°8N 79°19W **82** B5
Mount Aspiring △ *N.Z.* 44°19S 168°47E **59** F2
Mount Barker *S. Austral., Australia* 35°5S 138°52E **63** F2
Mount Barker *W. Austral., Australia* 34°38S 117°40E **61** F2
Mount Barnett Roadhouse *Australia* 16°39S 125°57E **60** C4
Mount Brydges *Canada* 42°54N 81°29W **82** D3
Mount Burr *Australia* 37°34S 140°26E **63** F3
Mount Carleton ⌓ *Canada* 47°25N 66°55W **73** C6
Mount Carmel = Ha Karmel △ *Israel* 32°45N 35°5E **48** C4
Mount Carmel *Ill., U.S.A.* 38°25N 87°46W **80** F10
Mount Carmel *Pa., U.S.A.* 40°47N 76°26W **83** F8
Mount Clemens *U.S.A.* 42°35N 82°53W **82** D2
Mount Coolon *Australia* 21°25S 147°25E **62** C4
Mount Desert I. *U.S.A.* 44°21N 68°20W **81** C19
Mount Dora *U.S.A.* 28°48N 81°38W **85** G14
Mount Ebenezer *Australia* 25°6S 132°34E **61** E5
Mount Edziza ⌓ *Canada* 57°30N 130°45W **70** B2
Mount Field △ *Australia* 42°39S 146°35E **63** G4
Mount Fletcher *S. Africa* 30°40S 28°30E **57** D4
Mount Forest *Canada* 43°59N 80°43W **82** C4
Mount Frankland △ *Australia* 31°47S 116°37E **61** F2
Mount Frederick ☼ *Australia* 19°39S 129°18E **60** C4
Mount Gambier *Australia* 37°50S 140°46E **63** F3
Mount Garnet *Australia* 17°37S 145°6E **62** B4
Mount Holly *U.S.A.* 39°59N 74°47W **83** G10
Mount Holly Springs *U.S.A.* 40°7N 77°12W **82** F7
Mount Hope *N.S.W., Australia* 32°51S 145°51E **63** E4
Mount Hope *S. Austral., Australia* 34°7S 135°23E **63** E2
Mount Isa *Australia* 20°42S 139°26E **62** C2
Mount James ☼ *Australia* 24°51S 116°54E **61** D2
Mount Jewett *U.S.A.* 41°44N 78°39W **82** E6
Mount Kaputar △ *Australia* 30°16S 150°10E **63** E5
Mount Kisco *U.S.A.* 41°12N 73°44W **83** E11
Mount Laguna *U.S.A.* 32°52N 116°25W **79** N10
Mount Larcom *Australia* 23°48S 150°59E **62** C5
Mount Lofty Ranges *Australia* 34°35S 139°5E **63** E2
Mount Magnet *Australia* 28°2S 117°47E **61** E2
Mount Maunganui *N.Z.* 37°40S 176°14E **59** B6
Mount Molloy *Australia* 16°42S 145°20E **62** B4
Mount Morgan *Australia* 23°40S 150°25E **62** C5
Mount Morris *U.S.A.* 42°44N 77°52W **82** D7
Mount Pearl *Canada* 47°31N 52°47W **73** C9
Mount Penn *U.S.A.* 40°20N 75°54W **83** F9
Mount Perry *Australia* 25°13S 151°42E **63** D5
Mount Pleasant *Iowa, U.S.A.* 40°58N 91°33W **80** E8
Mount Pleasant *Mich., U.S.A.* 43°36N 84°46W **81** D11
Mount Pleasant *Pa., U.S.A.* 40°9N 79°33W **82** F5
Mount Pleasant *S.C., U.S.A.* 32°47N 79°52W **85** E15
Mount Pleasant *Tenn., U.S.A.* 35°32N 87°12W **85** D11
Mount Pleasant *Tex., U.S.A.* 33°9N 94°58W **84** E7
Mount Pleasant *Utah, U.S.A.* 39°33N 111°27W **76** G8
Mount Pocono *U.S.A.* 41°7N 75°22W **83** E9
Mount Rainier △ *U.S.A.* 46°55N 121°50W **78** D5
Mount Revelstoke △ *Canada* 51°5N 118°30W **70** C5
Mount Robson ⌓ *Canada* 53°0N 119°0W **70** C5
Mount St. Helens ⌓ *U.S.A.* 46°14N 122°11W **78** D4
Mount Selinda *Zimbabwe* 20°24S 32°43E **57** B5
Mount Shasta *U.S.A.* 41°19N 122°19W **76** F2
Mount Signal *U.S.A.* 32°39N 115°37W **79** N11
Mount Sterling *Ill., U.S.A.* 39°59N 90°45W **80** F8
Mount Sterling *Ky., U.S.A.* 38°4N 83°56W **81** F12
Mount Surprise *Australia* 18°10S 144°17E **62** B3
Mount Union *U.S.A.* 40°23N 77°53W **82** F7
Mount Upton *U.S.A.* 42°26N 75°23W **83** D9
Mount Vernon *Ill., U.S.A.* 38°19N 88°55W **80** F9
Mount Vernon *Ind., U.S.A.* 37°56N 87°54W **75** H22
Mount Vernon *Ohio, U.S.A.* 40°23N 82°29W **82** F2
Mount Vernon *Wash., U.S.A.* 48°25N 122°20W **78** B4
Mount William △ *Australia* 40°56S 148°14E **63** G4
Mountain Ash *U.K.* 51°40N 3°23W **13** F4
Mountain Center *U.S.A.* 33°42N 116°44W **79** M10
Mountain City *Nev., U.S.A.* 41°50N 115°58W **76** F6
Mountain City *Tenn., U.S.A.* 36°29N 81°48W **85** C14
Mountain Dale *U.S.A.* 41°41N 74°32W **83** E10
Mountain Grove *U.S.A.* 37°8N 92°16W **80** G7
Mountain Home *Ark., U.S.A.* 36°20N 92°23W **84** C8
Mountain Home *Idaho, U.S.A.* 43°8N 115°41W **76** E6
Mountain Iron *U.S.A.* 47°32N 92°37W **80** B7
Mountain Pass *U.S.A.* 35°29N 115°35W **79** K11
Mountain View *Ark., U.S.A.* 35°52N 92°7W **84** D8
Mountain View *Calif., U.S.A.* 37°23N 122°5W **78** H4
Mountain Zebra △ *S. Africa* 32°14S 25°27E **56** D4
Mountainair *U.S.A.* 34°31N 106°15W **77** J10
Mountbellew *Ireland* 53°28N 8°31W **10** C3
Mountlake Terrace *U.S.A.* 47°47N 122°18W **78** C4
Mountmellick *Ireland* 53°7N 7°20W **10** C4
Mountrath *Ireland* 53°0N 7°28W **10** D4
Moura *Australia* 24°35S 149°58E **62** C4
Moura *Brazil* 1°32S 61°38W **92** D6
Moura *Portugal* 38°7N 7°30W **21** C2
Mourdi, Dépression du *Chad* 18°10N 23°0E **53** E10
Mourilyan *Australia* 17°35S 146°3E **62** B4
Mourne → *U.K.* 54°52N 7°26W **10** B4
Mourne Mts. *U.K.* 54°10N 6°0W **10** B5
Mouscron *Belgium* 50°45N 3°12E **15** D3
Moussoro *Chad* 13°41N 16°35E **53** F9
Moutong *Indonesia* 0°28N 121°13E **37** D6
Movas *Mexico* 28°10N 109°25W **86** B3
Moville *Ireland* 55°11N 7°3W **10** A4
Mowandjum *Australia* 17°22S 123°40E **60** C3
Moy → *Ireland* 54°8N 9°8W **10** B2
Moya *Comoros Is.* 12°18S 44°18E **55** a
Moyale *Kenya* 3°30N 39°4E **54** D7
Moyen Atlas *Morocco* 33°0N 5°0W **52** B4
Moyo *Indonesia* 8°10S 117°40E **36** F5
Moyobamba *Peru* 6°0S 77°0W **92** E3
Møysalen △ *Norway* 68°32N 15°29E **8** B16
Moyyero → *Russia* 68°44N 103°42E **27** C11
Moyynqum *Kazakhstan* 44°12N 71°0E **30** C3
Moyynty *Kazakhstan* 47°10N 73°18E **26** E8
Mozambique = Moçambique *Mozam.* 15°3S 40°42E **55** H8
Mozambique ■ *Africa* 19°0S 35°0E **55** H7
Mozambique Chan. *Africa* 17°30S 42°30E **57** A7
Mozdok *Russia* 43°45N 44°48E **19** F7
Mozdūrān *Iran* 36°9N 60°35E **47** B9
Mozhnābād *Iran* 34°7N 60°6E **47** C9
Mozyr = Mazyr *Belarus* 51°59N 29°15E **17** B15
Mpanda *Tanzania* 6°23S 31°1E **54** F6
Mphoeng *Zimbabwe* 21°10S 27°51E **57** B4
Mpika *Zambia* 11°51S 31°25E **55** G6
Mpumalanga *S. Africa* 29°50S 30°33E **57** C5
Mpumalanga □ *S. Africa* 26°0S 30°0E **57** C5
Mpwapwa *Tanzania* 6°23S 36°30E **54** F7
Mqanduli *S. Africa* 31°49S 28°45E **57** D4
Msaken *Tunisia* 35°49N 10°33E **53** A8
M'sila *Algeria* 35°46N 4°30E **52** A6
Mstislavl = Mstsislaw *Belarus* 54°0N 31°50E **17** A16
Mstsislaw *Belarus* 54°0N 31°50E **17** A16
Mtamvuna = Mthamvuna → *S. Africa* 31°6S 30°12E **57** D5
Mthamvuna → *S. Africa* 31°6S 30°12E **57** D5
Mthatha *S. Africa* 31°36S 28°49E **57** D4
Mtubatuba *S. Africa* 28°30S 32°8E **57** C5
Mtwalume *S. Africa* 30°30S 30°38E **57** D5
Mtwara-Mikindani *Tanzania* 10°20S 40°20E **54** G8
Mu Gia, Deo *Vietnam* 17°40N 105°47E **38** D5
Mu Ko Chang △ *Thailand* 11°59N 102°22E **39** G4
Mu Ko Surin *Thailand* 9°30N 97°55E **39** H1
Mu Us Shamo *China* 39°0N 109°0E **32** E5
Muang Beng *Laos* 20°23N 101°46E **34** G3
Muang Chiang Rai = Chiang Rai *Thailand* 19°52N 99°50E **34** H2
Muang Et *Laos* 20°49N 104°1E **38** B5
Muang Hiam *Laos* 20°5N 103°22E **38** B4
Muang Hongsa *Laos* 19°43N 101°20E **38** C3
Muang Houn *Laos* 20°8N 101°23E **34** G3
Muang Kau *Laos* 15°6N 105°47E **38** E5
Muang Khao *Laos* 19°38N 103°32E **38** C4
Muang Khong *Laos* 14°7N 105°51E **38** E5
Muang Khoua *Laos* 21°5N 102°31E **34** G4
Muang Liap *Laos* 18°29N 101°40E **38** C3
Muang Mai *Thailand* 8°5N 98°21E **39** a
Muang May *Laos* 14°49N 106°56E **38** E6
Muang Na Mo *Laos* 21°3N 101°49E **34** G3
Muang Ngeun *Laos* 20°36N 101°3E **34** G3
Muang Ngoi *Laos* 20°43N 102°41E **34** G4
Muang Nong *Laos* 16°22N 106°30E **38** D6
Muang Ou Neua *Laos* 22°18N 101°48E **34** F3
Muang Ou Tay *Laos* 22°7N 101°48E **34** F3
Muang Pak Beng *Laos* 19°54N 101°8E **34** H3
Muang Phalane *Laos* 16°39N 105°34E **38** D5
Muang Phiang *Laos* 19°6N 101°32E **38** C3
Muang Phine *Laos* 16°32N 106°2E **38** D6
Muang Phonhong *Laos* 18°30N 102°25E **38** C4
Muang Saiapoun *Laos* 18°24N 101°31E **38** C3
Muang Sing *Laos* 21°11N 101°9E **34** G3
Muang Son *Laos* 20°27N 103°19E **38** B4
Muang Soui *Laos* 19°33N 102°52E **38** C4
Muang Va *Laos* 21°53N 102°19E **34** G4
Muang Va *Laos* 18°18N 101°20E **38** C3
Muang Xai *Laos* 20°42N 101°59E **34** G3
Muang Xamteu *Laos* 19°59N 104°38E **38** C5
Muar *Malaysia* 2°3N 102°34E **39** L4
Muarabungo *Indonesia* 1°28S 102°52E **36** E2
Muaraenim *Indonesia* 3°40S 103°50E **36** E2
Muarajuloi *Indonesia* 0°12S 114°3E **36** E4
Muarakaman *Indonesia* 0°2S 116°45E **36** E5
Muaratebo *Indonesia* 1°30S 102°26E **36** E2
Muaratembesi *Indonesia* 1°42S 103°8E **36** E2
Muarateweh *Indonesia* 0°58S 114°52E **36** E4
Mubarakpur *India* 26°6N 83°18E **43** F10
Mubarraz = Al Mubarraz *Si. Arabia* 25°30N 49°40E **47** E6
Mubi *Nigeria* 10°18N 13°16E **53** F8
Mucajaí → *Brazil* 2°25N 60°52W **92** C6
Muchinga Mts. *Zambia* 11°30S 31°30E **55** G6
Muchuan *China* 28°57N 103°55E **34** C5
Muck *U.K.* 56°50N 6°15W **11** E2
Muckadilla *Australia* 26°35S 148°23E **63** D4
Muckaty ☼ *Australia* 18°37S 133°52E **62** B1
Muckle Flugga *U.K.* 60°51N 0°54W **11** A8
Mucuri *Brazil* 18°0S 39°36W **93** G11
Mucusso *Angola* 18°1S 21°25E **56** A3
Mudanjiang *China* 44°38N 129°30E **33** B15
Mudanya *Turkey* 40°25N 28°50E **23** D13
Muddebihal *India* 16°20N 76°8E **45** F3
Muddus △ *Sweden* 66°58N 20°15E **8** C19
Muddy Cr. → *U.S.A.* 38°24N 110°42W **76** G8
Mudgee *Australia* 32°32S 149°31E **63** E4
Mudhol *Karnataka, India* 16°21N 75°17E **45** F2
Mudhol *Telangana, India* 18°58N 77°55E **44** E3
Mudigere *India* 13°8N 75°38E **45** H2
Mudjatik → *Canada* 56°1N 107°36W **71** B7
Mudukulattur *India* 9°21N 78°31E **45** K4
Mudumu △ *Namibia* 18°5S 23°29E **56** A3
Mueller Ranges *Australia* 18°18S 126°46E **60** C4
Muerto, Mar *Mexico* 16°10N 94°10W **87** D6
Mufu Shan *China* 29°20N 114°30E **35** C10
Mufulira *Zambia* 12°32S 28°15E **55** G5
Mughal Sarai *India* 25°18N 83°7E **43** G10
Mughayrā' *Si. Arabia* 29°17N 37°41E **46** D3
Mugi *Japan* 33°40N 134°25E **29** H7
Muğla *Turkey* 37°15N 28°22E **23** F13
Mugu *Nepal* 29°45N 82°30E **43** E10
Mugu Karnali → *Nepal* 29°38N 81°51E **43** E9
Muhammad, Râs *Egypt* 27°44N 34°16E **46** E2
Muhammad Qol *Sudan* 20°53N 37°9E **53** D13
Muhammadabad *India* 26°4N 83°25E **43** F10
Muḩāyil *Si. Arabia* 18°33N 42°3E **49** D3
Mühlhausen *Germany* 51°12N 10°27E **16** C6
Mühlig Hofmann fjell *Antarctica* 72°30S 5°0E **5** D3
Muhos *Finland* 64°47N 25°59E **8** D21
Muhu *Estonia* 58°36N 23°11E **9** G20
Muileann gCearr, An = Mullingar *Ireland* 53°31N 7°21W **10** C4
Muine Bheag = Bagenalstown *Ireland* 52°42N 6°58W **10** D5
Muineachán = Monaghan *Ireland* 54°15N 6°57W **10** B5
Muir, L. *Australia* 34°30S 116°40E **61** F2
Muir of Ord *U.K.* 57°32N 4°28W **11** D4
Mujeres, I. *Mexico* 21°13N 86°43W **88** B2
Muka, Tanjung *Malaysia* 5°28N 100°11E **39** c
Mukacheve *Ukraine* 48°27N 22°45E **17** D12
Mukachevo = Mukacheve *Ukraine* 48°27N 22°45E **17** D12
Mukah *Malaysia* 2°55N 112°5E **36** D4
Mukandwara *India* 24°49N 75°59E **42** G6
Mukdahan *Thailand* 16°32N 104°43E **38** D5
Mukdahan △ *Thailand* 16°26N 104°45E **38** D5
Mukden = Shenyang *China* 41°48N 123°27E **33** D12
Mukerian *India* 31°57N 75°37E **42** D6
Mukher *India* 18°42N 77°22E **44** E3
Mukinbudin *Australia* 30°55S 118°5E **61** F2
Muko Phetra △ *Thailand* 6°57N 99°33E **39** J2
Mukomuko *Indonesia* 2°30S 101°10E **36** E2
Muktinath *Nepal* 28°49N 83°53E **43** E10
Muktsar *India* 30°30N 74°30E **42** D6
Mukur = Moqor *Afghan.* 32°50N 67°42E **42** C2
Mukutuwa → *Canada* 53°10N 97°24W **71** C9
Mul *India* 20°4N 79°40E **44** D4
Mula *Spain* 38°3N 1°33W **21** C5
Mula → *India* 18°34N 74°21E **44** E2
Mula → *Pakistan* 27°57N 67°36E **42** F2
Mulanje, Mt. *Malawi* 16°2S 35°33E **55** H7
Mulbagal *India* 13°10N 78°24E **45** H4
Mulchatna → *U.S.A.* 59°40N 157°7W **74** D8
Mulchén *Chile* 37°45S 72°20W **94** D1
Mulde → *Germany* 51°53N 12°15E **16** C7
Mule Creek Junction *U.S.A.* 43°23N 104°13W **76** E11
Mulegé *Mexico* 26°53N 111°59W **86** B2
Muleshoe *U.S.A.* 34°13N 102°43W **84** D3
Mulgrave *Canada* 45°38N 61°31W **73** C7
Mulgrave I. = Badu *Australia* 10°7S 142°11E **62** a
Mulhacén *Spain* 37°4N 3°20W **21** D4
Mulhouse *France* 47°40N 7°20E **20** C7
Muli *China* 27°52N 101°8E **34** D3
Mulifanua *Samoa* 13°50S 171°59W **59** b
Muling *China* 44°35N 130°10E **33** B16
Mulki *India* 13°6N 74°48E **45** H2
Mull *U.K.* 56°25N 5°56W **11** E3
Mull, Sound of *U.K.* 56°30N 5°50W **11** E3
Mullaittivu *Sri Lanka* 9°15N 80°49E **45** K5
Mullen *U.S.A.* 42°3N 101°1W **80** D3
Mullengudgery *Australia* 31°43S 147°23E **63** B4
Mullens *U.S.A.* 37°35N 81°23W **81** G13
Muller, Pegunungan *Indonesia* 0°30N 113°30E **36** D4
Mullet Pen. *Ireland* 54°13N 10°2W **10** B1
Mullewa *Australia* 28°29S 115°30E **61** E2
Mulligan → *Australia* 25°0S 139°0E **62** D2
Mullingar *Ireland* 53°31N 7°21W **10** C4
Mullins *U.S.A.* 34°12N 79°15W **85** D15
Mullumbimby *Australia* 28°30S 153°30E **63** D5
Mulonga Plain *Zambia* 16°20S 22°40E **55** H4
Mulroy B. *Ireland* 55°15N 7°46W **10** A4
Mulshi L. *India* 18°30N 73°48E **44** E1
Multai *India* 21°50N 78°21E **44** D4
Multan *Pakistan* 30°15N 71°36E **42** D4
Mulug *India* 18°11N 79°57E **44** E4
Mulvane *U.S.A.* 37°29N 97°15W **80** G5
Mulwala, L. *Australia* 35°59S 146°1E **63** C4
Mun → *Thailand* 15°19N 105°30E **38** E5
Muna *Indonesia* 5°0S 122°30E **37** F6
Munabao *India* 25°45N 70°17E **42** G4
Munamagi *Estonia* 57°43N 27°4E **9** H22
Munaung *Burma* 18°45N 93°40E **41** K18
Munaung I. = Cheduba I. *Burma* 18°45N 93°40E **41** K18
Muncan *Indonesia* 8°34S 115°11E **37** K18
Muncar *Indonesia* 8°26S 114°20E **37** J17
Munchen-Gladbach = Mönchengladbach *Germany* 51°11N 6°27E **16** C4
Muncho Lake *Canada* 59°0N 125°50W **70** B3
Munch'ŏn *N. Korea* 39°14N 127°19E **33** E14
Muncie *U.S.A.* 40°12N 85°23W **81** E11
Muncoonie L. West *Australia* 25°12S 138°40E **62** D2
Mundabbera *Australia* 25°36S 151°18E **63** D5
Mundakayam *India* 9°30N 76°50E **45** K3
Mundal *Sri Lanka* 7°48N 79°48E **45** L4
Munday *U.S.A.* 33°27N 99°38W **84** E5
Münden *Germany* 51°25N 9°38E **16** C5
Mundiwindi *Australia* 23°47S 120°9E **60** D3
Mundo Novo *Brazil* 11°50S 40°29W **93** F10
Mundra *India* 22°54N 69°48E **42** H3
Mundrabilla *Australia* 31°52S 127°51E **61** F4
Muneru → *India* 16°45N 80°3E **44** F5
Mungallala *Australia* 26°28S 147°34E **63** D4
Mungallala Cr. → *Australia* 28°53S 147°5E **63** D4
Mungana *Australia* 17°8S 144°27E **62** B3
Mungaoli *India* 24°24N 78°7E **42** G8
Mungbere *Dem. Rep. of the Congo* 2°36N 28°28E **54** D5
Mungeli *India* 22°4N 81°41E **43** H9
Munger *India* 25°23N 86°30E **43** G12
Mungerannie *Australia* 28°1S 138°39E **63** A2
Mungilli ☼ *Australia* 25°14S 124°17E **61** E3
Mungkan Kandju △ *Australia* 13°35S 142°52E **62** A3
Mungkarta ☼ *Australia* 20°22S 134°2E **62** C1
Munising *U.S.A.* 46°25N 86°40W **80** B10
Munku-Sardyk *Russia* 51°45N 100°20E **27** D11
Munnsville *U.S.A.* 42°58N 75°35W **83** D9
Muñoz Gamero, Pen. *Chile* 52°30S 73°5W **96** G2
Munroe L. *Canada* 59°13N 98°35W **71** B9
Munsan *S. Korea* 37°51N 126°48E **33** F14
Münster *Germany* 51°58N 7°37E **16** C4
Munster □ *Ireland* 52°18N 8°44W **10** D3
Muntadgin *Australia* 31°45S 118°33E **61** F2
Muntok *Indonesia* 2°5S 105°10E **36** E3
Muong Nhie *Vietnam* 22°12N 102°28E **34** F4
Muong Sen *Vietnam* 19°24N 104°8E **38** C5
Muong Te *Vietnam* 22°24N 102°49E **34** F4
Muong Xia *Vietnam* 20°19N 104°50E **38** B5
Muonio *Finland* 67°57N 23°40E **8** C20
Muonio älv = Muonionjoki → *Finland* 67°11N 23°34E **8** C20
Muonioälven = Muonionjoki → *Finland* 67°11N 23°34E **8** C20
Muonionjoki → *Finland* 67°11N 23°34E **8** C20
Mupa → *Mozam.* 18°58S 35°54E **57** A6
Muping *China* 37°22N 121°36E **33** F11
Muqdisho *Somalia* 2°2N 45°25E **49** G4
Mur → *Austria* 47°18N 16°52E **17** E9
Murakami *Japan* 38°14N 139°29E **28** E9
Muralag = Prince of Wales I. *Australia* 10°40S 142°10E **62** A3
Murallón, Cerro *Chile* 49°48S 73°30W **96** F2
Murang'a *Kenya* 0°45S 37°9E **54** E7
Murashi *Russia* 59°30N 49°0E **18** C8
Murat → *Turkey* 38°46N 40°0E **19** G7
Muratlı *Turkey* 41°10N 27°29E **23** D12
Murayama *Japan* 38°30N 140°25E **28** E10
Murchison → *Australia* 27°45S 114°0E **61** E1
Murchison, Mt. *Antarctica* 73°25S 166°20E **5** D11
Murchison Falls *Uganda* 2°15N 31°30E **54** D6
Murchison Ra. *Australia* 20°0S 134°10E **62** C1
Murchison Roadhouse *Australia* 27°39S 116°14E **61** E2
Murcia *Spain* 38°5N 1°10W **21** D5
Murcia □ *Spain* 37°50N 1°30W **21** D5
Murdo *U.S.A.* 43°53N 100°43W **80** D3
Murdoch Pt. *Australia* 14°37S 144°55E **62** A3
Mureş → *Romania* 46°15N 20°13E **17** E11
Mureşul = Mureş → *Romania* 46°15N 20°13E **17** E11
Murewa *Zimbabwe* 17°39S 31°47E **57** A5
Murfreesboro *N.C., U.S.A.* 36°27N 77°6W **85** C16
Murfreesboro *Tenn., U.S.A.* 35°51N 86°24W **85** D11
Murgap *Tajikistan* 38°10N 74°2E **26** F8
Murgap → *Turkmenistan* 38°18N 61°12E **47** B9
Murgenella *Australia* 11°34S 132°56E **60** B5
Murgha Kibzai *Pakistan* 30°44N 69°25E **42** D3
Murghob = Murgap *Tajikistan* 38°10N 74°2E **26** F8
Murgon *Australia* 26°15S 151°54E **63** D5
Muri *India* 23°22N 85°52E **43** H11
Muria *Indonesia* 6°36S 110°53E **37** G14
Muriaé *Brazil* 21°8S 42°23W **95** A7
Müritz *Germany* 53°25N 12°42E **16** B7
Murliganj *India* 25°54N 86°59E **43** G12
Murmansk *Russia* 68°57N 33°10E **8** B25
Murmashi *Russia* 68°47N 32°42E **8** B25
Murom *Russia* 55°35N 42°3E **18** C7
Muroran *Japan* 42°25N 141°0E **28** C10
Muroto *Japan* 33°18N 134°9E **29** H7
Muroto-Misaki *Japan* 33°15N 134°10E **29** H7
Murphy *U.S.A.* 43°13N 116°33W **76** E5
Murphys *U.S.A.* 38°8N 120°28W **78** G6
Murray *Australia* 9°56S 144°2E **62** a
Murray *Ky., U.S.A.* 36°37N 88°19W **80** G9
Murray *Utah, U.S.A.* 40°40N 111°53W **76** F8
Murray → *Australia* 35°20S 139°22E **63** F2
Murray, L. *U.S.A.* 34°3N 81°13W **85** D14
Murray Bridge *Australia* 35°6S 139°14E **63** F2
Murray Fracture Zone *Pac. Oc.* 35°0N 130°0W **65** D14
Murray Harbour *Canada* 46°0N 62°28W **73** C7
Murray River △ *Australia* 34°23S 140°32E **63** E3
Murraysburg *S. Africa* 31°58S 23°47E **56** D3
Murree *Pakistan* 33°56N 73°28E **42** C5
Murrieta *U.S.A.* 33°33N 117°13W **79** M9
Murrumbidgee → *Australia* 34°43S 143°12E **63** E3
Murrumburrah *Australia* 34°32S 148°22E **63** E4
Murrurundi *Australia* 31°42S 150°51E **63** E5
Murshidabad *India* 24°11N 88°19E **43** G13
Murtazapur *India* 20°40N 77°25E **44** D3
Murtle L. *Canada* 52°8N 119°38W **70** C5
Murtoa *Australia* 36°35S 142°28E **63** F3

Murud India 18°19N 72°58E 44 E1
Mururoa
French Polynesia 21°52S 138°55W 65 K14
Murwara India 23°46N 80°28E 43 H9
Murwillumbah Australia 28°18S 153°27E 63 D5
Murzūq Libya 25°53N 13°57E 53 C8
Murzūq, Idehān Libya 24°50N 13°51E 53 D5
Mürzzuschlag Austria 47°36N 15°41E 16 E8
Mus India 9°14N 92°47E 45 K11
Muş Turkey 38°45N 41°30E 46 B4
Mûsa, Gebel Egypt 28°33N 33°59E 46 D2
Musa Khel Pakistan 30°59N 69°52E 42 D3
Mûsa Qal'eh Afghan. 32°20N 64°50E 40 C4
Musafirkhana India 26°22N 81°48E 43 F9
Musala Bulgaria 42°13N 23°37E 23 C10
Musala Indonesia 1°41N 98°28E 36 D1
Muscat = Masqaṭ Oman 23°37N 58°36E 49 C6
Muscatine U.S.A. 41°25N 91°3W 80 E8
Muscle Shoals U.S.A. 34°45N 87°40W 85 D11
Musgrave Harbour
Canada 49°27N 53°58W 73 C9
Musgrave Ranges
Australia 26°0S 132°0E 61 E5
Mushie
Dem. Rep. of the Congo 2°56S 16°55E 54 E3
Musi → India 16°41N 79°40E 44 F4
Musi → Indonesia 2°20S 104°56E 36 E2
Musina S. Africa 22°20S 30°5E 57 B5
Musiri India 10°56N 78°27E 45 J4
Muskeg → Canada 60°20N 123°20W 70 A4
Muskegon U.S.A. 43°14N 86°16W 80 D10
Muskegon → U.S.A. 43°14N 86°21W 80 D10
Muskegon Heights
U.S.A. 43°12N 86°16W 80 D10
Muskogee U.S.A. 35°45N 95°22W 84 D7
Muskoka, L. Canada 45°0N 79°25W 82 B5
Muskoka Falls Canada 44°59N 79°17W 82 B5
Muskwa → Canada 58°47N 122°48W 70 B4
Muslīmiyah Syria 36°19N 37°12E 46 B3
Musoma Tanzania 1°30S 33°48E 54 E6
Musquaro, L. Canada 50°38N 61°5W 73 B7
Musquodoboit Harbour
Canada 44°50N 63°9W 73 D7
Musselburgh U.K. 55°57N 3°2W 11 F5
Musselshell → U.S.A. 47°21N 107°57W 76 C10
Mussende Angola 10°32S 16°5E 54 G3
Mussoorie India 30°27N 78°6E 42 D8
Mussuco Angola 17°2S 19°3E 56 A2
Mustafakemalpaşa
Turkey 40°2N 28°24E 23 D13
Mustang Nepal 29°10N 83°55E 43 E10
Musters, L. Argentina 45°20S 69°25W 96 F3
Musudan N. Korea 40°50N 129°43E 33 D15
Muswellbrook Australia 32°16S 150°56E 63 E5
Mût Egypt 25°28N 28°58E 53 C11
Mut Turkey 36°40N 33°28E 46 B2
Mutanda Mozam. 21°0S 33°34E 57 B5
Mutare Zimbabwe 18°58S 32°38E 55 H6
Mutawintji △ Australia 31°10S 142°30E 63 E3
Muting Indonesia 7°23S 140°20E 37 F10
Mutki = Mirtağ Turkey 38°23N 41°56E 46 B4
Mutoko Zimbabwe 17°24S 32°13E 55 H6
Mutoray Russia 60°56N 101°0E 27 C11
Mutsamudu Comoros Is. 12°10S 44°25E 55 a
Mutsu Japan 41°5N 140°55E 28 D10
Mutsu-Wan Japan 41°5N 140°55E 28 D10
Muttaburra Australia 22°38S 144°29E 62 C3
Mutton I. Ireland 52°49N 9°32W 10 D2
Muttukuru India 14°16N 80°6E 45 G5
Mutur Sri Lanka 8°27N 81°16E 45 K5
Muweilih Egypt 30°42N 34°19E 48 E3
Muy Muy Nic. 12°39N 85°36W 88 D2
Muyinga Burundi 3°14S 30°33E 54 C3
Muyunkum, Peski = Moyynqum
Kazakhstan 44°12N 71°0E 30 C3
Muz Tag China 36°25N 87°25E 30 D6
Muzaffarabad Pakistan 34°25N 73°30E 43 B5
Muzaffargarh Pakistan 30°5N 71°14E 42 D4
Muzaffarnagar India 29°26N 77°40E 42 E7
Muzaffarpur India 26°7N 85°23E 43 F11
Muzafirpur Pakistan 30°58N 69°9E 42 D3
Muzhi Russia 65°25N 64°40E 18 A11
Muztagh-Ata China 38°17N 75°7E 30 D4
Mvuma Zimbabwe 19°16S 30°30E 55 H6
Mwali = Mohéli
Comoros Is. 12°20S 43°40E 55 a
Mwanza
Dem. Rep. of the Congo 7°55S 26°43E 54 F5
Mwanza Tanzania 2°30S 32°58E 54 E6
Mweelrea Ireland 53°39N 9°49W 10 C2
Mweka
Dem. Rep. of the Congo 4°50S 21°34E 54 E4
Mwene-Ditu
Dem. Rep. of the Congo 6°35S 22°27E 54 F4
Mwenga
Dem. Rep. of the Congo 3°1S 28°28E 54 E5
Mweru, L. Zambia 9°0S 28°40E 54 F5
Mwinilunga Zambia 11°43S 24°25E 55 G4
My Son Vietnam 15°48N 108°7E 38 E7
My Tho Vietnam 10°29N 106°23E 39 G6
Myajlar India 26°15N 70°20E 42 F4
Myanaung Burma 18°18N 95°22E 41 K19
Myanmar = Burma ■
Asia 21°0N 96°30E 41 J20
Myaungmya Burma 16°30N 94°40E 41 L19
Mycenæ = Mykenes
Greece 37°43N 22°46E 23 F10
Myeik = Mergui Burma 12°26N 98°34E 38 F2
Myeik Kyunzu Burma 11°30N 97°30E 38 G1
Myerstown U.S.A. 40°22N 76°19W 83 F8
Myingyan Burma 21°30N 95°20E 41 J19
Myitkyina Burma 25°24N 97°26E 41 G20
Mykenes Greece 37°43N 22°46E 23 F10
Mykines Færoe Is. 62°7N 7°35W 8 E9
Mykolayiv Ukraine 46°58N 32°0E 19 E5
Mykonos Greece 37°30N 25°25E 23 F11
Mymensingh Bangla. 24°45N 90°24E 41 G17
Mynydd Du U.K. 51°52N 3°50W 13 F4
Mýrdalsjökull Iceland 63°40N 19°6W 8 E4

Myrtle Beach U.S.A. 33°42N 78°53W 85 E15
Myrtle Creek U.S.A. 43°1N 123°17W 76 E2
Myrtle Point U.S.A. 43°4N 124°8W 76 E1
Myrtoan Sea = Mirtoo Sea
Greece 37°0N 23°20E 23 F10
Mysia Turkey 39°50N 27°0E 23 E12
Mysore = Karnataka □
India 13°15N 77°0E 45 H3
Mysore = Mysuru India 12°17N 76°41E 45 H3
Mystic U.S.A. 41°21N 71°58W 83 E13
Mysuru India 12°17N 76°41E 45 H3
Myszków Poland 50°45N 19°22E 17 C10
Mytilene = Mitilini
Greece 39°6N 26°35E 23 E12
Mytishchi Russia 55°50N 37°50E 18 C6
Mývatn Iceland 65°36N 17°0W 8 D5
Mzimkulu → S. Africa 30°44S 30°28E 57 D5
Mzimvubu → S. Africa 31°38S 29°33E 57 E4
Mzuzu Malawi 11°30S 33°55E 54 G6

N

Na Clocha Liatha = Greystones
Ireland 53°9N 6°5W 10 C5
Na Haeo △ Thailand 17°31N 100°58E 38 D3
Na Hearadh = Harris
U.K. 57°50N 6°55W 11 D2
Na Hearadh, Caolas = Harris, Sd.
of U.K. 57°44N 7°6W 11 D1
Na Noi Thailand 18°19N 100°43E 38 C3
Na Phao Laos 17°35N 105°44E 38 D5
Na Sam Vietnam 22°3N 106°37E 34 F6
Na Sceirí = Skerries Ireland 53°35N 6°8W 10 C5
Na Thon Thailand 9°32N 99°56E 39 b
Naab → Germany 49°1N 12°2E 16 D6
Naantali Finland 60°29N 22°2E 9 F20
Naas Ireland 53°12N 6°40W 10 C5
Nababeep S. Africa 29°36S 17°46E 56 C2
Nabadwip = Navadwip
India 23°34N 88°20E 43 H13
Nabawa Australia 28°30S 114°48E 61 E1
Nabberu, L. Australia 25°50S 120°30E 61 E3
Naberezhnyye Chelny
Russia 55°42N 52°19E 18 C9
Nabeul Tunisia 36°30N 10°44E 53 A8
Nabha India 30°26N 76°14E 42 D7
Nabīd Iran 29°40N 57°38E 47 D8
Nabire Indonesia 3°15S 135°26E 37 E9
Nabisar Pakistan 25°8N 69°40E 42 G3
Nabisipi → Canada 50°14N 62°13W 73 B7
Nāblus = Nābulus
West Bank 32°14N 35°15E 48 C4
Naboomspruit S. Africa 24°32S 28°40E 57 B4
Nabouwalu Fiji 17°0S 178°45E 59 a
Nābulus West Bank 32°14N 35°15E 48 C4
Nacala Mozam. 14°32S 40°34E 55 G8
Nacaome Honduras 13°31N 87°30W 88 D2
Naches U.S.A. 46°44N 120°42W 78 D5
Naches → U.S.A. 46°38N 120°31W 78 D6
Nachicapau, L. Canada 56°40N 68°5W 73 A6
Nachingwea Tanzania 10°23S 38°49E 54 G7
Nachna India 27°34N 71°41E 42 F4
Nachuge India 10°47N 92°21E 45 J11
Nacimiento, L. U.S.A. 35°46N 120°53W 78 K6
Nacogdoches U.S.A. 31°36N 94°39W 84 F7
Nácori Chico Mexico 29°40N 108°57W 86 B3
Nacozari de García
Mexico 30°25N 109°38W 86 A3
Nacula Fiji 16°54S 177°27E 59 a
Nada = Danzhou China 19°31N 109°33E 38 D5
Nādendal = Naantali
Finland 60°29N 22°2E 9 F20
Nadi Fiji 17°42S 177°20E 59 a
Nadiad India 22°41N 72°56E 42 H5
Nador Morocco 35°14N 2°58W 52 E5
Nadūshan Iran 32°2N 53°35E 47 C7
Nadvirna Ukraine 48°37N 24°30E 17 D13
Nadvoitsy Russia 63°52N 34°14E 18 B5
Nadvornaya = Nadvirna
Ukraine 48°37N 24°30E 17 D13
Nadym Russia 65°35N 72°42E 26 C8
Nadym → Russia 66°12N 72°0E 26 C8
Nærbo Norway 58°40N 5°39E 9 G11
Næstved Denmark 55°13N 11°44E 9 J14
Nafarroa = Navarra □
Spain 42°40N 1°40W 21 A5
Nafpaktos Greece 38°24N 21°50E 23 E9
Nafplio Greece 37°33N 22°50E 23 F10
Naft-e Safid Iran 31°40N 49°17E 47 D6
Naftshahr Iran 34°0N 45°30E 46 C5
Nafud Desert = An Nafūd
Si. Arabia 28°15N 41°0E 46 D4
Naga Phil. 13°38N 123°15E 37 B6
Nagagami Canada 50°23N 84°20W 72 B3
Nagahama Japan 35°23N 136°16E 29 G8
Nagai Japan 38°6N 140°2E 28 E10
Nagaland □ India 26°0N 94°30E 41 G19
Nagano Japan 36°40N 138°10E 29 F9
Nagano □ Japan 36°15N 138°0E 29 F9
Nagaoka Japan 37°27N 138°51E 29 F9
Nagaon India 26°20N 92°50E 41 F18
Nagappattinam India 10°46N 79°51E 45 J4
Nagar → Bangla. 24°27N 89°12E 43 G13
Nagar Karnul India 16°29N 78°20E 45 F11
Nagar Parkar Pakistan 24°28N 70°46E 42 G4
Nagari Hills India 13°3N 79°45E 45 H4
Nagarjuna Sagar India 16°30N 79°13E 45 F4
Nagasaki Japan 32°47N 129°50E 29 H4
Nagasaki □ Japan 32°50N 129°40E 29 H4
Nagato Japan 34°19N 131°5E 29 G5
Nagaur India 27°15N 73°45E 42 F5
Nagbhir India 20°34N 79°55E 44 D4
Nagda India 23°27N 75°25E 42 H6
Nagercoil India 8°12N 77°26E 45 K3
Nagina India 29°30N 78°30E 43 E8
Nagīneh Iran 34°20N 57°15E 47 C8
Nagir Pakistan 36°12N 74°42E 43 A6

Nagles Mts. Ireland 52°8N 8°30W 10 D3
Nagod India 24°34N 80°36E 43 G9
Nagoorin Australia 24°17S 151°15E 62 C5
Nagorno-Karabakh □
Azerbaijan 39°55N 46°45E 46 B5
Nagornyy Russia 55°58N 124°57E 27 D13
Nagoya Japan 35°10N 136°50E 29 G8
Nagoya ✈ (NGO) Japan 34°53N 136°45E 29 G8
Nagpur India 21°8N 79°10E 44 D4
Nagqu China 31°29N 92°3E 30 E7
Nagua Dom. Rep. 19°23N 69°50W 89 C6
Naguabo Puerto Rico 18°13N 65°44W 89 d
Nagurunguru ◌
Australia 16°45S 129°45E 60 C4
Nagykanizsa Hungary 46°28N 17°0E 17 E9
Nagykőrös Hungary 47°5N 19°48E 17 E10
Naha Japan 26°13N 127°42E 29 L3
Nahan India 30°33N 77°18E 42 D7
Nahanni △ Canada 61°36N 125°41W 70 A4
Nahanni Butte Canada 61°2N 123°31W 70 A4
Nahargarh Mad. P., India 24°10N 75°14E 42 G6
Nahargarh Raj., India 24°55N 76°50E 42 G7
Nahariyya Israel 33°1N 35°5E 48 C4
Nahāvand Iran 34°10N 48°22E 47 C6
Nahuel Huapi, L.
Argentina 41°0S 71°32W 96 E2
Nahuelbuta △ Chile 37°44S 72°57W 94 D1
Nai Yong Thailand 8°14N 98°22E 39 a
Naicá Mexico 27°53N 105°31W 86 B3
Naicam Canada 52°30N 104°30W 71 C8
Naikoon △ Canada 53°55N 131°55W 70 C2
Naikul India 21°20N 84°58E 44 D7
Naimisharanya India 27°21N 80°30E 43 F9
Naimo'nyi Feng China 30°26N 81°18E 43 D9
Nain Canada 56°34N 61°40W 73 A7
Nā'īn Iran 32°54N 53°0E 47 C7
Naini Tal India 29°30N 79°30E 43 E8
Nainpur India 22°30N 80°10E 43 H9
Nainwa India 25°46N 75°51E 42 G6
Nairai Fiji 17°49S 179°15E 59 a
Nairn U.K. 57°35N 3°53W 11 D5
Nairobi Kenya 1°17S 36°48E 54 E7
Naissaar Estonia 59°34N 24°29E 9 G21
Naitaba Fiji 17°0S 179°16W 59 a
Naivasha Kenya 0°40S 36°30E 54 E7
Najaf = An Najaf Iraq 32°3N 44°15E 46 C5
Najafābād Iran 32°40N 51°15E 47 C6
Najd Si. Arabia 26°30N 42°0E 49 B3
Najibabad India 29°40N 78°20E 42 E8
Najin N. Korea 42°12N 130°15E 33 C16
Najmah Si. Arabia 26°42N 50°6E 47 E6
Najrān Si. Arabia 17°34N 44°18E 49 D3
Naju S. Korea 35°3N 126°43E 33 G14
Nakadōri-Shima Japan 32°57N 129°4E 29 H4
Nakaminato Japan 36°21N 140°36E 29 F10
Nakamura = Shimanto
Japan 32°59N 132°56E 29 H6
Nakano Japan 36°45N 138°22E 29 F9
Nakano-Shima Japan 29°51N 129°52E 29 K4
Nakashibetsu Japan 43°33N 144°59E 28 C12
Nakfa Eritrea 16°40N 38°32E 49 D2
Nakha Yai, Ko Thailand 8°3N 98°28E 39 a
Nakhichevan = Naxçıvan
Azerbaijan 39°12N 45°15E 46 B5
Nakhichevan Rep. = Naxçıvan □
Azerbaijan 39°25N 45°26E 46 B5
Nakhl Egypt 29°55N 33°43E 48 F2
Nakhl-e Taqī Iran 27°28N 52°36E 47 E7
Nakhodka Russia 42°53N 132°54E 28 C6
Nakhon Nayok Thailand 14°12N 101°13E 38 E3
Nakhon Pathom Thailand 13°49N 100°3E 38 F3
Nakhon Phanom
Thailand 17°23N 104°43E 38 D5
Nakhon Ratchasima
Thailand 14°59N 102°12E 38 E4
Nakhon Sawan Thailand 15°35N 100°10E 38 E3
Nakhon Si Thammarat
Thailand 8°29N 100°0E 39 H3
Nakhon Thai Thailand 17°5N 100°44E 38 D3
Nakhtarana India 23°20N 69°15E 42 H3
Nakina Canada 50°10N 86°40W 72 B2
Nakodar India 31°8N 75°31E 42 D6
Naktong → S. Korea 35°7N 128°57E 33 G15
Nakuru Kenya 0°15S 36°4E 54 E7
Nakusp Canada 50°20N 117°45W 70 C5
Nal → Pakistan 27°40N 66°12E 42 F2
Nal → Pakistan 25°20N 65°30E 42 G1
Nalázi Mozam. 24°3S 33°20E 57 B5
Nalchik Russia 43°30N 43°33E 19 F7
Nalgonda India 17°6N 79°15E 44 F4
Nalhati India 24°17N 87°52E 43 G12
Naliya India 23°16N 68°50E 42 H3
Nallamalai Hills India 15°30N 78°50E 45 G4
Nam Can Vietnam 8°46N 104°59E 39 H5
Nam-ch'on N. Korea 38°15N 126°26E 33 E14
Nam Co China 30°30N 90°45E 30 E7
Nam Dinh Vietnam 20°25N 106°5E 34 G6
Nam Du, Quan Dao
Vietnam 9°41N 104°21E 39 H5
Nam Hka → Burma 21°34N 95°41E 34 G2
Nam Loi → Burma 21°3N 98°27E 34 G3
Nam Nao △ Thailand 17°18S 101°34E 38 D3
Nam Ngum Res. Laos 18°35N 102°34E 38 C4
Nam Phan Vietnam 10°30N 106°0E 39 G6
Nam Phong Thailand 16°42N 102°52E 38 D4
Nam Theun Res. Laos 17°51N 105°12E 38 D5
Nam Tok Thailand 14°21N 99°4E 38 E2
Nam Un Res. Thailand 17°13N 103°45E 38 D4
Namacurra Mozam. 17°30S 36°50E 57 B6
Namak, Daryācheh-ye
Iran 34°30N 52°0E 47 C7
Namak, Kavir-e Iran 34°30N 57°30E 47 C8
Namakkal India 11°13N 78°13E 45 J4
Namakzār, Daryācheh-ye
Iran 34°0N 60°30E 47 C9
Namaland Namibia 26°0S 17°0E 56 C2
Namangan Uzbekistan 41°0N 71°40E 30 C3
Namapa Mozam. 13°43S 39°50E 55 G7
Namaqua △ S. Africa 30°0S 17°30E 56 D1

Namaqualand S. Africa 30°0S 17°25E 56 D2
Namber Indonesia 1°2S 134°49E 37 E8
Nambour Australia 26°32S 152°58E 63 D5
Nambouwalu = Nabouwalu
Fiji 17°0S 178°45E 59 a
Nambucca Heads
Australia 30°37S 153°0E 63 E5
Nambung △ Australia 30°30S 115°5E 61 F2
Namcha Barwa China 29°40N 95°10E 30 F8
Namche Bazar Nepal 27°51N 86°47E 43 F12
Namchonjŏm = Nam-ch'on
N. Korea 38°15N 126°26E 33 E14
Namenalala Fiji 17°8S 179°9E 59 a
Namew L. Canada 54°14N 101°56W 71 C8
Namgia India 31°48N 78°40E 43 D8
Namhkam Burma 23°50N 97°41E 34 E1
Namib Desert Namibia 22°30S 15°0E 56 B2
Namib-Naukluft □
Namibia 24°40S 15°16E 56 B2
Namibe Angola 15°7S 12°11E 55 H2
Namibe □ Angola 16°35S 12°30E 56 A1
Namibia ■ Africa 22°0S 18°9E 56 B2
Namibwoestyn = Namib Desert
Namibia 22°30S 15°0E 56 B2
Naminús = Lubango
Angola 14°55S 13°30E 55 G2
Naminús = Lüderitz
Namibia 26°41S 15°8E 56 C2
Namjeu S. Korea 33°14N 126°33E 33 H14
Namlea Indonesia 3°18S 127°5E 37 E7
Namoi → Australia 30°12S 149°30E 63 E4
Nampa U.S.A. 43°34N 116°34W 76 E5
Nampo N. Korea 38°52N 125°10E 33 E13
Nampō-Shotō Japan 32°0N 140°0E 29 J10
Nampula Mozam. 15°6S 39°15E 55 H7
Namrole Indonesia 3°46S 126°46E 37 E7
Namse Shankou China 30°0N 82°25E 43 E10
Namsen → Norway 64°28N 11°37E 8 D14
Namsos Norway 64°29N 11°30E 8 D14
Namtok Chat Trakan △
Thailand 17°17N 100°40E 38 D3
Namtok Huay Yang △
Thailand 11°35N 99°30E 39 G2
Namtok Mae Surin △
Thailand 18°55N 98°2E 38 C2
Namtok Ngao △ Thailand 9°58N 98°46E 39 H2
Namtok Phlew △
Thailand 12°32N 102°13E 38 F4
Namtok Yong △ Thailand 8°53N 99°44E 39 H2
Namtsy Russia 62°43N 129°37E 27 C13
Namtu Burma 23°5N 97°28E 41 H20
Namu Canada 51°52N 127°50W 70 C3
Namuka-i-Lau Fiji 18°53S 178°37W 59 a
Namur Belgium 50°27N 4°52E 15 D4
Namur □ Belgium 50°17N 5°0E 15 D4
Namutoni Namibia 18°49S 16°55E 56 A2
Namwon S. Korea 35°23N 127°23E 33 G14
Namyang N. Korea 42°57N 129°52E 33 C15
Namyit I. S. China Sea 10°11N 114°22E 36 C4
Nan Thailand 18°48N 100°46E 38 C3
Nan → Thailand 15°42N 100°9E 38 E3
Nan Ling China 25°0N 112°30E 35 E9
Nan Xian China 29°20N 112°22E 35 C9
Nanaimo Canada 49°10N 124°0W 70 D4
Nanam N. Korea 41°44N 129°40E 33 D15
Nan'an China 24°59N 118°21E 35 E12
Nanango Australia 26°40S 152°0E 63 D5
Nan'ao China 23°28N 117°5E 35 F11
Nanao Japan 37°0N 137°0E 29 F8
Nanbu China 31°18N 106°3E 34 B6
Nanchang China 28°42N 115°55E 35 C10
Nancheng China 27°33N 116°35E 35 D11
Nanching = Nanjing
China 32°2N 118°47E 35 A12
Nanchong China 30°43N 106°2E 34 B6
Nanchuan China 29°9N 107°6E 34 C6
Nancowry India 7°59N 93°32E 45 L11
Nancy France 48°42N 6°12E 20 B7
Nanda Devi India 30°23N 79°59E 43 D8
Nanda Devi △ India 30°30N 79°50E 43 D8
Nanda Kot India 30°17N 80°5E 43 D9
Nandan = Minamiawaji
Japan 34°10N 134°42E 29 G7
Nandan China 24°58N 107°29E 34 E6
Nanded India 19°10N 77°20E 44 E3
Nandewar Ra. Australia 30°15S 150°35E 63 E5
Nandgaon India 20°19N 74°39E 44 D2
Nandi = Nadi Fiji 17°42S 177°20E 59 a
Nandi Zimbabwe 16°58S 34°44E 57 B5
Nandigama India 16°47N 80°18E 44 F5
Nandigram India 22°1N 87°58E 43 H12
Nandikotkur India 15°52N 78°18E 45 G4
Nandura India 20°52N 76°25E 44 D3
Nandurbar India 21°20N 74°15E 44 D2
Nandyal India 15°30N 78°30E 45 G4
Nanfeng Guangdong,
China 23°45N 111°47E 35 F8
Nanfeng Jiangxi, China 27°12N 116°28E 35 D11
Nang Rong Thailand 14°38N 102°48E 38 E4
Nanga-Eboko Cameroon 4°41N 12°22E 54 D2
Nanga Parbat Pakistan 35°10N 74°35E 43 B6
Nangapinoh Indonesia 0°20S 111°44E 36 E4
Nangarhār □ Afghan. 34°20N 70°0E 40 B7
Nangatayap Indonesia 1°32S 110°34E 36 E4
Nangeya Mts. Uganda 3°30N 33°30E 54 B6
Nangong China 37°23N 115°22E 34 F8
Nanguneri India 8°29N 77°40E 45 K3
Nanhua China 25°13N 101°21E 34 E3
Nanhuang China 31°14N 121°44E 35 B13
Nanhui China 31°5N 121°44E 35 B13
Nanisivik Canada 73°2N 84°33W 69 C15
Nanjangud India 12°6N 76°43E 45 H3
Nanji Shan China 27°27N 121°4E 35 D13
Nanjian China 25°2N 100°25E 34 E3
Nanjiang China 32°28N 106°51E 34 A6
Nanjing Fujian, China 24°25N 117°20E 35 E11
Nanjing Jiangsu, China 32°2N 118°47E 35 A12
Nankana Sahib Pakistan 31°27N 73°38E 42 D5

Nankoku Japan 33°39N 133°44E 29 H6
Nanlang China 22°30N 113°32E 31 a
Nanling China 30°55N 118°20E 35 B12
Nannial India 19°4N 79°38E 44 E4
Nanning China 22°48N 108°20E 34 F7
Nannup Australia 33°59S 115°48E 61 F2
Nanpan Jiang → China 25°10N 106°5E 34 E6
Nanpara India 27°52N 81°33E 43 F9
Nanping Fujian, China 26°38N 118°10E 35 D12
Nanping Henan, China 33°55N 112°3E 35 C9
Nanri Dao China 25°15N 119°25E 35 E12
Nansei-Shotō = Ryūkyū-Rettō
Japan 26°0N 126°0E 29 M3
Nansen Basin Arctic 84°0N 50°0E 4 A10
Nansen Sd. Canada 81°0N 91°0W 69 A13
Nansha China 22°45N 113°34E 31 a
Nansha Port China 22°40N 113°42E 31 a
Nanshan China 18°19N 109°12E 38 D5
Nanshan I. S. China Sea 10°45N 115°49E 36 B5
Nantawarrinna ◌
Australia 30°49S 138°58E 63 B2
Nantes France 47°12N 1°33W 20 C3
Nanticoke U.S.A. 41°12N 76°0W 83 E8
Nanton Canada 50°21N 113°46W 70 C6
Nantong China 32°1N 120°52E 35 A13
Nantou China 22°32N 113°55E 31 a
Nant'ou Taiwan 23°55N 120°41E 35 F13
Nantucket U.S.A. 41°17N 70°6W 81 E18
Nantucket I. U.S.A. 41°16N 70°5W 81 E18
Nantwich U.K. 53°4N 2°31W 12 D5
Nanty Glo U.S.A. 40°28N 78°50W 82 F6
Nanuku Passage Fiji 16°45S 179°15W 59 a
Nanuque Brazil 17°50S 40°21W 93 G10
Nanusa, Kepulauan
Indonesia 4°45N 127°1E 37 D7
Nanutarra Roadhouse
Australia 22°32S 115°30E 60 D2
Nanxi China 28°54N 104°59E 34 C5
Nanxiong China 25°6N 114°15E 35 E10
Nanyang China 33°11N 112°30E 32 H7
Nanyuan China 39°47N 116°24E 32 E9
Nanyuki Kenya 0°2N 37°4E 54 D7
Nanzhang China 31°45N 111°50E 35 B8
Nanzhao China 33°30N 112°20E 32 H7
Nao, C. de la Spain 38°44N 0°14E 21 C6
Naococane, L. Canada 52°50N 70°45W 73 B5
Naozhou Dao China 20°55N 110°54E 34 G8
Napa U.S.A. 38°18N 122°17W 78 G4
Napa → U.S.A. 38°10N 122°19W 78 G4
Napanee Canada 44°15N 77°0W 82 B8
Napanoch U.S.A. 41°44N 74°22W 83 E10
Nape Laos 18°18N 105°6E 38 C5
Nape Pass = Keo Neua, Deo
Vietnam 18°23N 105°10E 38 C5
Napier N.Z. 39°30S 176°56E 59 C6
Napier Broome B.
Australia 14°2S 126°37E 60 B4
Napier Pen. Australia 12°4S 135°43E 62 A2
Napierville Canada 45°11N 73°25W 83 A11
Naples = Nápoli Italy 40°50N 14°15E 22 D6
Naples U.S.A. 26°8N 81°48W 85 H14
Napo China 23°22N 105°50E 34 F5
Napo → Peru 3°20S 72°40W 92 D4
Napoleon N. Dak., U.S.A. 46°30N 99°46W 80 B4
Napoleon Ohio, U.S.A. 41°23N 84°8W 81 E11
Nápoli Italy 40°50N 14°15E 22 D6
Naqadeh Iran 36°57N 45°23E 46 B5
Naqb, Ra's an Jordan 29°48N 35°44E 48 F4
Naqqāsh Iran 35°40N 49°6E 47 C6
Nara Mali 15°10N 7°20W 52 E4
Nara Japan 34°30N 136°0E 29 G8
Nara □ Japan 34°30N 136°0E 29 G8
Nara Canal Pakistan 24°30N 69°20E 42 G3
Nara Visa U.S.A. 35°37N 103°6W 77 J12
Naracoorte Australia 36°58S 140°45E 63 F3
Naradhan Australia 33°34S 146°17E 63 E4
Naraini India 25°11N 80°29E 43 G9
Naranjos Mexico 21°21N 97°41W 87 C5
Narasannapeta India 18°25N 84°4E 44 E7
Narasapur India 16°26N 81°40E 45 F5
Narasaraopet India 16°14N 80°4E 45 F5
Narathiwat Thailand 6°30N 101°48E 39 J3
Narayangadh = Bharatpur
Nepal 27°34N 84°10E 43 F11
Narayanganj Bangla. 23°40N 90°33E 41 H17
Narayanpet India 16°45N 77°30E 44 F3
Narberth U.K. 51°47N 4°44W 13 F3
Narbonne France 43°11N 3°0E 20 E5
Narcondam I. India 13°20N 94°16E 45 H12
Nardin Iran 37°3N 55°59E 47 B7
Nardò Italy 40°11N 18°2E 23 D8
Narembeen Australia 32°7S 118°24E 61 F2
Nares Str. Arctic 80°0N 70°0W 69 B18
Narew → Poland 52°26N 20°41E 17 B11
Nari → Pakistan 28°0N 67°40E 42 F2
Narin Afghan. 36°5N 69°0E 40 A6
Narita Japan 35°47N 140°19E 29 G10
Nariva Swamp
Trin. & Tob. 10°26N 61°4W 93 K15
Narmada → India 21°38N 72°36E 42 J5
Narmada Canal India 22°20N 73°45E 44 C1
Narnaul India 28°5N 76°11E 42 E7
Narodnaya Russia 65°5N 59°58E 18 A10
Narooma Australia 36°14S 150°4E 63 F5
Narowal Pakistan 32°6N 74°52E 42 C6
Narrabri Australia 30°19S 149°46E 63 E4
Narran → Australia 34°42S 146°31E 63 E4
Narrandera Australia 34°42S 146°31E 63 E4
Narromine Australia 32°12S 148°12E 63 E4
Narrogin Australia 32°58S 117°14E 61 F2
Narrow Hills △ Canada 54°0N 104°37W 71 C8
Narsampet India 17°57N 79°58E 44 F4
Narsimhapur India 22°54N 79°14E 43 H8
Narsinghgarh India 23°45N 76°40E 42 H7
Narsinghpur India 22°54N 79°14E 43 H8
Narsipatnam India 17°40N 82°37E 44 F6
Narutō = Sanmu Japan 34°11N 134°37E 29 G7

Narva Estonia 59°23N 28°12E 18 C4
Narva → Russia 59°27N 28°2E 9 G23
Narva Bay = Narva Laht Estonia 59°35N 27°35E 9 G22
Narva Laht Estonia 59°35N 27°35E 9 G22
Narvik Norway 68°28N 17°26E 8 B17
Narwana India 29°39N 76°6E 42 E7
Narwinbi ✪ Australia 16°7S 136°17E 62 B2
Naryan-Mar Russia 67°42N 53°12E 18 A9
Narym Russia 59°0N 81°30E 26 D9
Naryn Kyrgyzstan 41°26N 75°58E 30 C4
Naryn Qum Kazakhstan 47°30N 49°0E 26 E5
Nás, An = Naas Ireland 53°12N 6°40W 10 C5
Nasa Norway 66°29N 15°23E 8 C16
Nasau Fiji 17°19S 179°27E 59 a
Nasca Peru 14°50S 74°57W 92 F4
Nasca Ridge Pac. Oc. 20°0S 80°0W 65 K19
Naseby N.Z. 45°1S 170°10E 59 F3
Naselle U.S.A. 46°22N 123°49W 78 D3
Naser, Buheirat en Egypt 23°0N 32°30E 53 D12
Nashik = Nasik India 19°58N 73°50E 44 E1
Nashua Mont., U.S.A. 48°8N 106°22W 76 B10
Nashua N.H., U.S.A. 42°45N 71°28W 83 D13
Nashville Ark., U.S.A. 33°57N 93°51W 84 E8
Nashville Ga., U.S.A. 31°12N 83°15W 85 F13
Nashville Tenn., U.S.A. 36°10N 86°47W 85 C11
Nasik India 19°58N 73°50E 44 E1
Nasirabad India 26°15N 74°45E 42 F6
Nasirabad Pakistan 28°23N 68°24E 42 E3
Nasiri = Ahvāz Iran 31°20N 48°40E 47 D6
Nasiriyah = An Nāşirīyah Iraq 31°0N 46°15E 46 D5
Naskaupi → Canada 53°47N 60°51W 73 B7
Naşrābād Iran 34°8N 51°26E 47 C6
Naşriān-e Pā'īn Iran 32°52N 46°52E 46 C5
Nass → Canada 55°0N 129°40W 70 C3
Nassau Bahamas 25°5N 77°20W 88 A4
Nassau U.S.A. 42°31N 73°37W 83 D11
Nassau, B. Chile 55°20S 68°0W 96 H3
Nasser, L. = Naser, Buheirat en Egypt 23°0N 32°30E 53 D12
Nässjö Sweden 57°39N 14°42E 9 H16
Nastapoka → Canada 56°55N 76°33W 72 A4
Nastapoka, Is. Canada 56°55N 76°50W 72 A4
Nasushiobara Japan 36°58N 140°3E 29 F10
Nata Botswana 20°12S 26°12E 56 B4
Nata → Botswana 20°14S 26°10E 56 B4
Natal Brazil 5°47S 35°13W 93 E11
Natal Indonesia 0°35N 99°7E 36 D1
Natal Drakensberg = uKhahlamba Drakensberg ⌓ S. Africa 29°27S 29°30E 57 C4
Naṭanz Iran 33°30N 51°55E 47 C6
Natashquan Canada 50°14N 61°46W 73 B7
Natashquan → Canada 50°7N 61°50W 73 B7
Natchez U.S.A. 31°34N 91°24W 84 F9
Natchitoches U.S.A. 31°46N 93°5W 84 F8
Natewa B. Fiji 16°35S 179°40E 59 a
Nathalia Australia 36°1S 145°13E 63 F4
Nathdwara India 24°55N 73°50E 42 G5
Natimuk Australia 36°42S 142°0E 63 F3
Nation → Canada 55°30N 123°32W 70 B4
National City U.S.A. 32°40N 117°5W 79 N9
Natitingou Benin 10°20N 1°26E 52 F6
Natividad, I. Mexico 27°52N 115°11W 86 B1
Natkyizin Burma 14°57N 97°59E 38 E1
Natron, L. Tanzania 2°20S 36°0E 54 E7
Natrona Heights U.S.A. 40°37N 79°44W 82 F5
Natuashish Canada 55°55N 61°8W 73 A7
Natukanaoka Pan Namibia 18°40S 15°45E 56 A2
Natuna Besar, Kepulauan Indonesia 4°0N 108°15E 36 D3
Natuna Is. = Natuna Besar, Kepulauan Indonesia 4°0N 108°15E 36 D3
Natuna Selatan, Kepulauan Indonesia 2°45N 109°0E 36 D3
Natural Bridge U.S.A. 44°5N 75°30W 83 B9
Natural Bridges ⌓ U.S.A. 37°36N 110°0W 77 H9
Naturaliste, C. Tas., Australia 40°50S 148°15E 63 G4
Naturaliste, C. W. Austral., Australia 33°32S 115°0E 61 F2
Naturaliste Plateau Ind. Oc. 34°0S 112°0E 64 L3
Nau Qala Afghan. 34°5N 68°5E 42 B3
Naugatuck U.S.A. 41°30N 73°3W 83 E11
Naujaat = Repulse Bay Canada 66°30N 86°30W 69 D14
Naumburg Germany 51°9N 11°47E 16 C6
Naupada India 18°34N 84°18E 44 E7
Nauru ■ Pac. Oc. 1°0S 166°0E 58 B9
Naushahra = Nowshera Pakistan 34°0N 72°0E 40 C8
Naushahro Pakistan 26°50N 68°7E 42 F3
Naushon I. U.S.A. 41°29N 70°45W 83 E14
Nausori Fiji 18°2S 178°32E 59 a
Nauta Peru 4°31S 73°35W 92 D4
Nautanwa India 27°20N 83°25E 43 F10
Naute ⌓ Namibia 26°55S 17°57E 56 C2
Nautla Mexico 20°13N 96°47W 87 C5
Nava Mexico 28°25N 100°45W 86 B4
Navadwip India 23°34N 88°20E 43 H13
Navahrudak Belarus 53°40N 25°50E 17 B13
Navajo Res. U.S.A. 36°48N 107°36W 77 H10
Navalgund India 15°34N 75°22E 45 G2
Navalmoral de la Mata Spain 39°52N 5°33W 21 C3
Navan Ireland 53°39N 6°41W 10 C5
Navarin, Mys Russia 62°15N 179°5E 27 C18
Navarino, I. Chile 55°0S 67°40W 96 H3
Navarra □ Spain 42°40N 1°40W 21 A5
Navarre U.S.A. 40°43N 81°31W 82 F3
Navarro → U.S.A. 39°11N 123°45W 78 F3
Navasota U.S.A. 30°23N 96°5W 84 F6
Navassa I. W. Indies 18°30N 75°0W 89 C5
Naver → U.K. 58°32N 4°14W 11 C4
Navibandar India 21°26N 69°48E 42 J3
Navidad Chile 33°57S 71°50W 94 C1
Naviraí Brazil 23°8S 54°13W 95 A5
Naviti Fiji 17°7S 177°15E 59 a
Navlakhi India 22°58N 70°28E 42 H4
Năvodari Romania 44°19N 28°36E 17 F15
Navoiy Uzbekistan 40°9N 65°22E 26 E7
Navojoa Mexico 27°6N 109°26W 86 B3
Navolato Mexico 24°47N 107°42W 86 C3
Navsari India 20°57N 72°59E 44 D1
Navua Fiji 18°12S 178°11E 59 a
Nawa Kot Pakistan 28°21N 71°24E 42 E4
Nawab Khan Pakistan 30°17N 69°12E 42 D3
Nawabganj Ut. P., India 26°56N 81°14E 43 F9
Nawabganj Ut. P., India 28°32N 79°40E 43 E8
Nawabshah Pakistan 26°15N 68°25E 42 F3
Nawada India 24°50N 85°33E 43 G11
Nawakot Nepal 27°55N 85°10E 43 F11
Nawalgarh India 27°50N 75°15E 42 F6
Nawanshahr India 32°33N 74°48E 43 C6
Nawapara India 20°46N 82°33E 44 D6
Nawar, Dasht-i- Afghan. 33°52N 68°0E 42 C3
Nawoiy = Navoiy Uzbekistan 40°9N 65°22E 26 E7
Naxçıvan Azerbaijan 39°12N 45°15E 46 B5
Naxçıvan □ Azerbaijan 39°25N 45°26E 46 B5
Naxos Greece 37°8N 25°25E 23 F11
Nay, Mui Vietnam 12°54N 109°26E 38 F7
Nāy Band Būshehr, Iran 27°20N 52°40E 47 E7
Nāy Band Khorāsān, Iran 32°20N 57°34E 47 C8
Nay Pyi Taw = Naypyidaw Burma 19°44N 96°12E 30 H8
Nayagarh India 20°8N 85°6E 44 D7
Nayakhan Russia 61°56N 159°0E 27 C16
Nayarit □ Mexico 22°0N 105°0W 86 C4
Nayau Fiji 18°6S 178°10E 59 a
Nayong China 26°50N 105°20E 34 D5
Nayoro Japan 44°21N 142°28E 28 B11
Naypyidaw Burma 19°44N 96°12E 30 H8
Nayudupeta India 13°54N 79°54E 45 H4
Nayyāl, W. → Si. Arabia 28°35N 39°4E 46 D3
Nazaré Brazil 13°2S 39°0W 93 F11
Nazareth = Naẓerat Israel 32°42N 35°17E 48 C4
Nazareth U.S.A. 40°44N 75°19W 83 F9
Nazarovo Russia 57°2N 90°40E 27 D10
Nazas Mexico 25°14N 104°8W 86 B4
Nazas → Mexico 25°12N 104°12W 86 B4
Nazca = Nasca Peru 14°50S 74°57W 92 F4
Naze, The U.K. 51°53N 1°18E 13 F9
Naẓerat Israel 32°42N 35°17E 48 C4
Nāzīk Iran 39°1N 45°4E 46 B5
Nazilli Turkey 37°55N 28°15E 23 F13
Nazko Canada 53°1N 123°37W 70 C4
Nazko → Canada 53°7N 123°34W 70 C4
Nazret Ethiopia 8°32N 39°22E 49 F2
Ndalatando Angola 9°12S 14°48E 54 F2
Ndélé C.A.R. 8°25N 20°36E 54 C4
Ndjamena Chad 12°10N 15°0E 53 F8
Ndola Zambia 13°0S 28°34E 55 G5
Ndomo ⌓ S. Africa 26°52S 32°15E 57 C5
Ndoto Mts. Kenya 2°0N 37°0E 54 D7
Neagh, Lough U.K. 54°37N 6°25W 10 B5
Neah Bay U.S.A. 48°22N 124°37W 78 B2
Neale, L. Australia 24°15S 130°0E 60 D5
Neales → Australia 28°8S 136°47E 63 D2
Near Is. U.S.A. 52°30N 174°0E 74 E2
Neath U.K. 51°39N 3°48W 13 F4
Neath Port Talbot □ U.K. 51°42N 3°45W 13 F4
Nebine Cr. → Australia 29°27S 146°56E 63 D4
Nebitdag = Balkanabat Turkmenistan 39°30N 54°22E 47 B7
Nebo Australia 21°42S 148°42E 62 C4
Nebraska □ U.S.A. 41°30N 99°30W 80 E4
Nebraska City U.S.A. 40°41N 95°52W 80 E6
Nébrodi, Monti Italy 37°54N 14°35E 22 F6
Necedah U.S.A. 44°2N 90°4W 80 C8
Nechako → Canada 53°55N 122°42W 70 C4
Neches → U.S.A. 29°58N 93°51W 84 G8
Neckar → Germany 49°27N 8°29E 16 D5
Necker I. U.S.A. 23°35N 164°42W 75 L7
Necochea Argentina 38°30S 58°50W 94 D4
Nederland = Netherlands ■ Europe 52°0N 5°30E 15 C5
Needles Canada 49°53N 118°7W 70 D5
Needles U.S.A. 34°51N 114°37W 79 L12
Needles, The U.K. 50°39N 1°35W 13 G6
Neembucú □ Paraguay 27°0S 58°0W 94 B4
Neemuch = Nimach India 24°30N 74°56E 42 G6
Neenah U.S.A. 44°11N 88°28W 80 C9
Neepawa Canada 50°15N 99°30W 71 C9
Neftçala Azerbaijan 39°19N 49°12E 47 B6
Neftegorsk Russia 53°1N 142°58E 27 D15
Neftekumsk Russia 44°46N 44°50E 19 F7
Nefteyugansk Russia 61°5N 72°42E 26 C8
Nefyn U.K. 52°56N 4°31W 12 E3
Negapatam = Nagappattinam India 10°46N 79°51E 45 J4
Negara Indonesia 8°22S 114°37E 37 J17
Negaunee U.S.A. 46°30N 87°36W 80 B10
Negele Ethiopia 5°20N 39°36E 49 F2
Negeri Sembilan □ Malaysia 2°45N 102°10E 39 L4
Negev Desert = Hanegev Israel 30°50N 35°0E 48 E4
Negombo Sri Lanka 7°12N 79°50E 45 L4
Negotin Serbia 44°16N 22°37E 23 B10
Negra, Pta. Mauritania 22°54N 16°18W 52 D2
Negra, Pta. Peru 6°6S 81°10W 92 E2
Negrais, C. = Maudin Sun Burma 16°0N 94°30E 41 M19
Negril Jamaica 18°22N 78°20W 88 a
Negro → Argentina 41°2S 62°47W 96 E4
Negro → Brazil 3°0S 60°0W 92 D7
Negro → Uruguay 33°24S 58°22W 94 C4
Negros Phil. 9°30N 122°40E 37 C6
Neguac Canada 47°15N 65°5W 73 C6
Nehalem → U.S.A. 45°40N 123°56W 78 E3
Nehāvand Iran 35°56N 49°31E 47 C6
Nehbandān Iran 31°35N 60°5E 47 D9
Nehe China 48°29N 124°50E 31 B13
Nei Mongol Zizhiqu □ China 42°0N 112°0E 32 D7
Neiafu Tonga 18°39S 173°59W 59 c
Neiges, Piton des Réunion 21°5S 55°29E 55 c
Neijiang China 29°35N 104°55E 34 C5
Neilingding Dao China 22°25N 113°48E 31 a
Neill I. India 11°50N 93°3E 45 J11
Neillsville U.S.A. 44°34N 90°36W 80 C8
Neilton U.S.A. 47°25N 123°53W 78 C3
Neiqiu China 37°15N 114°30E 32 F8
Neiva Colombia 2°56N 75°18W 92 C3
Neixiang China 33°10N 111°52E 32 H6
Nejanilini L. Canada 59°33N 97°48W 71 B9
Nejd = Najd Si. Arabia 26°30N 42°0E 49 B3
Nekā Iran 36°39N 53°19E 47 B7
Nekemte Ethiopia 9°4N 36°30E 49 F2
Neksø Denmark 55°4N 15°8E 9 J16
Nelamangala India 13°6N 77°24E 45 H3
Nelia Australia 20°39S 142°12E 62 C3
Neligh U.S.A. 42°8N 98°2W 80 D4
Nelkan Russia 57°40N 136°4E 27 D14
Nellikuppam India 11°46N 79°43E 45 J4
Nellore India 14°27N 79°59E 45 G4
Nelson Canada 49°30N 117°20W 70 D5
Nelson N.Z. 41°18S 173°16E 59 D4
Nelson U.K. 53°50N 2°13W 12 D5
Nelson Ariz., U.S.A. 35°31N 113°19W 77 J7
Nelson Nev., U.S.A. 35°42N 114°49W 79 K12
Nelson → Canada 54°33N 98°2W 71 C9
Nelson, C. Australia 38°26S 141°32E 63 F3
Nelson, Estrecho Chile 51°30S 75°0W 96 G2
Nelson Forks Canada 59°30N 124°0W 70 B4
Nelson House Canada 55°47N 98°51W 71 B9
Nelson L. Canada 55°48N 100°7W 71 B8
Nelson Lakes △ N.Z. 41°55S 172°44E 59 D4
Nelspoort S. Africa 32°7S 23°0E 56 D3
Nelspruit = Mbombela S. Africa 25°29S 30°59E 57 C5
Néma Mauritania 16°40N 7°15W 52 E4
Neman = Nemunas → Lithuania 55°25N 21°10E 9 J19
Nembrala Indonesia 10°53S 122°50E 60 B3
Nemeiben L. Canada 55°20N 105°20W 71 B7
Nemiscau Canada 51°18N 76°54W 72 B4
Nemiscau, L. Canada 51°25N 76°40W 72 B4
Nemunas → Lithuania 55°25N 21°10E 9 J19
Nemuro Japan 43°20N 145°35E 28 C12
Nemuro-Kaikyō Japan 43°30N 145°30E 28 C12
Nen Jiang → China 45°28N 124°30E 33 B13
Nenagh Ireland 52°52N 8°11W 10 D3
Nenana U.S.A. 64°34N 149°5W 74 C10
Nenasi Malaysia 3°9N 103°23E 39 L4
Nene → U.K. 52°49N 0°11E 13 E8
Nenjiang China 49°10N 125°10E 31 B14
Neodesha U.S.A. 37°25N 95°41W 80 G6
Neora Valley △ India 27°0N 88°45E 43 F13
Neosho U.S.A. 36°52N 94°22W 80 G6
Neosho → U.S.A. 36°48N 95°18W 84 C7
Nepal ■ Asia 28°0N 84°30E 43 F11
Nepalganj Nepal 28°5N 81°40E 43 E9
Nepalganj Road India 28°1N 81°41E 43 E9
Nephi U.S.A. 39°43N 111°50W 76 G8
Nephin Ireland 54°1N 9°22W 10 B2
Nephin Beg Range Ireland 54°0N 9°40W 10 C2
Neptune U.S.A. 40°13N 74°2W 83 F10
Neqāb Iran 36°42N 57°25E 47 B8
Nerang Australia 27°58S 153°20E 63 D5
Nerchinsk Russia 52°0N 116°39E 27 D12
Néret, L. Canada 54°45N 70°44W 73 B5
Neretva → Croatia 43°1N 17°27E 23 C7
Neringa Lithuania 55°20N 21°5E 9 J19
Neris → Lithuania 55°8N 24°16E 9 J21
Neryungri Russia 57°38N 124°28E 27 D13
Nescopeck U.S.A. 41°3N 76°12W 83 E8
Neskantaga Canada 52°14N 87°53W 72 B2
Neskaupstaður Iceland 65°9N 13°42W 8 D7
Ness, L. U.K. 57°15N 4°32W 11 D4
Ness City U.S.A. 38°27N 99°54W 80 F4
Nesterov = Zhovkva Ukraine 50°4N 23°58E 17 C12
Nestos → Europe 40°54N 24°49E 23 D11
Nesvizh = Nyasvizh Belarus 53°14N 26°38E 17 B14
Netanya Israel 32°20N 34°51E 48 C3
Netarhat India 23°29N 84°16E 43 H11
Nete → Belgium 51°7N 4°14E 15 C4
Netherdale Australia 21°10S 148°33E 62 b
Netherlands ■ Europe 52°0N 5°30E 15 C5
Netherlands Antilles = ABC Islands W. Indies 12°15N 69°0W 89 D6
Netrang India 21°39N 73°21E 42 J5
Nettilling L. Canada 66°30N 71°0W 69 D17
Netzahualcóyotl, Presa Mexico 17°8N 93°35W 87 D6
Neubrandenburg Germany 53°33N 13°15E 16 B7
Neuchâtel Switz. 47°0N 6°55E 20 C7
Neuchâtel, Lac de Switz. 46°53N 6°50E 20 C7
Neufchâteau Belgium 49°50N 5°25E 15 E5
Neumayer Antarctica 71°0S 68°30W 5 D17
Neumünster Germany 54°4N 9°58E 16 A5
Neunkirchen Germany 49°20N 7°9E 16 D4
Neuquén Argentina 38°55S 68°0W 96 D3
Neuquén □ Argentina 38°0S 69°50W 94 D2
Neuruppin Germany 52°55N 12°48E 16 B7
Neuse → U.S.A. 35°6N 76°29W 85 D16
Neusiedler See Austria 47°50N 16°47E 17 E9
Neustrelitz Germany 53°21N 13°4E 16 B7
Neva → Russia 59°56N 30°20E 18 C5
Nevada Iowa, U.S.A. 42°1N 93°27W 80 D7
Nevada Mo., U.S.A. 37°51N 94°22W 80 G6
Nevada □ U.S.A. 39°0N 117°0W 76 G5
Nevada City U.S.A. 39°16N 121°1W 78 F6
Nevado, Cerro Argentina 35°30S 68°32W 94 D2
Nevado de Colima = Volcán de Colima △ Mexico 19°30N 103°40W 86 D4
Nevado de Tres Cruces △ Chile 27°13S 69°5W 94 B2
Nevasa India 19°34N 75°0E 44 E2
Nevel Russia 56°0N 29°55E 18 C4
Nevelsk Russia 46°40N 141°51E 27 E15
Nevers France 47°0N 3°9E 20 C5
Nevertire Australia 31°50S 147°44E 63 E4
Neville Canada 49°58N 107°39W 71 D7
Nevinnomyssk Russia 44°40N 42°0E 19 F7
Nevis St. Kitts & Nevis 17°0N 62°30W 89 C7
Nevşehir Turkey 38°33N 34°40E 46 B2
Nevyansk Russia 57°30N 60°13E 18 C11
New → U.S.A. 38°10N 81°12W 81 F13
New Aiyansh Canada 55°12N 129°4W 70 B3
New Albany Ind., U.S.A. 38°18N 85°49W 81 F11
New Albany Miss., U.S.A. 34°29N 89°0W 85 D10
New Albany Pa., U.S.A. 41°36N 76°27W 83 E8
New Amsterdam Guyana 6°15N 57°36W 92 B7
New Baltimore U.S.A. 42°41N 82°44W 82 D2
New Bedford U.S.A. 41°38N 70°56W 83 E14
New Berlin N.Y., U.S.A. 42°37N 75°20W 83 D9
New Berlin Pa., U.S.A. 40°50N 76°57W 82 F8
New Bern U.S.A. 35°7N 77°3W 85 D16
New Bethlehem U.S.A. 41°0N 79°20W 82 F5
New Bight Bahamas 24°19N 75°24W 89 B4
New Bloomfield U.S.A. 40°25N 77°11W 82 F7
New Boston U.S.A. 33°28N 94°25W 84 E7
New Braunfels U.S.A. 29°42N 98°8W 84 G5
New Brighton N.Z. 43°29S 172°43E 59 E4
New Brighton U.S.A. 40°42N 80°19W 82 F4
New Britain Papua N. G. 5°50S 150°20E 58 B8
New Britain U.S.A. 41°40N 72°47W 83 E12
New Brunswick U.S.A. 40°30N 74°27W 83 F10
New Brunswick □ Canada 46°50N 66°30W 73 C6
New Caledonia ⊠ Pac. Oc. 21°0S 165°0E 58 D9
New Caledonia Trough Pac. Oc. 30°0S 165°0E 64 L8
New Castile = Castilla-La Mancha □ Spain 39°30N 3°30W 21 C4
New Castle Ind., U.S.A. 39°55N 85°22W 81 F11
New Castle Pa., U.S.A. 41°0N 80°21W 82 F4
New Chitose ✈ (CTS) Japan 42°46N 141°41E 28 C10
New City U.S.A. 41°9N 73°59W 83 E11
New Concord U.S.A. 39°59N 81°54W 82 G3
New Cumberland U.S.A. 40°30N 80°36W 82 F4
New Cuyama U.S.A. 34°57N 119°38W 79 L7
New Denver Canada 50°0N 117°25W 70 D5
New Don Pedro Res. U.S.A. 37°43N 120°24W 78 H6
New England U.S.A. 43°0N 71°0W 75 G25
New England N. Dak., U.S.A. 46°32N 102°52W 80 B2
New England Ra. Australia 30°20S 151°45E 63 E5
New Forest △ U.K. 50°53N 1°34W 13 G6
New Galloway U.K. 55°5N 4°9W 11 F4
New Glasgow Canada 45°35N 62°36W 73 C7
New Guinea Oceania 4°0S 136°0E 58 B6
New Hamburg Canada 43°23N 80°42W 82 C4
New Hampshire □ U.S.A. 44°0N 71°30W 83 C13
New Hampton U.S.A. 43°3N 92°19W 80 D7
New Hanover S. Africa 29°22S 30°31E 57 C5
New Hartford U.S.A. 43°4N 75°18W 83 C9
New Haven Conn., U.S.A. 41°18N 72°55W 83 E12
New Haven Mich., U.S.A. 42°44N 82°48W 82 D2
New Haven N.Y., U.S.A. 43°28N 76°18W 83 C8
New Hazelton Canada 55°20N 127°30W 70 B3
New Hebrides = Vanuatu ■ Pac. Oc. 15°0S 168°0E 58 C9
New Holland U.S.A. 40°6N 76°5W 83 F8
New Iberia U.S.A. 30°1N 91°49W 84 F9
New Ireland Papua N. G. 3°20S 151°50E 58 B8
New Jersey □ U.S.A. 40°0N 74°30W 81 F16
New Kensington U.S.A. 40°34N 79°46W 82 F5
New Lexington U.S.A. 39°43N 82°13W 81 F12
New Liskeard Canada 47°31N 79°41W 72 C4
New London Conn., U.S.A. 41°22N 72°6W 83 E12
New London Ohio, U.S.A. 41°5N 82°24W 82 E2
New London Wis., U.S.A. 44°23N 88°45W 80 C9
New Madrid U.S.A. 36°36N 89°32W 80 G9
New Martinsville U.S.A. 39°39N 80°52W 81 F13
New Meadows U.S.A. 44°58N 116°18W 76 D5
New Melones L. U.S.A. 37°57N 120°31W 78 H6
New Mexico □ U.S.A. 34°30N 106°0W 77 J11
New Milford Conn., U.S.A. 41°35N 73°25W 83 E11
New Milford Pa., U.S.A. 41°52N 75°44W 83 E9
New Norcia Australia 30°57S 116°13E 61 F2
New Norfolk Australia 42°46S 147°2E 63 G4
New Philadelphia U.S.A. 40°30N 81°27W 82 F3
New Plymouth N.Z. 39°4S 174°5E 59 C5
New Plymouth U.S.A. 43°58N 116°49W 76 E5
New Port Richey U.S.A. 28°16N 82°43W 85 G13
New Providence Bahamas 25°25N 77°35W 88 A4
New Quay U.K. 52°13N 4°21W 13 E3
New Radnor U.K. 52°15N 3°9W 13 E4
New Richmond Canada 48°15N 65°45W 73 C6
New Richmond U.S.A. 45°7N 92°32W 80 C7
New River Gorge ⌓ U.S.A. 37°53N 81°5W 81 G13
New Roads U.S.A. 30°42N 91°26W 84 F9
New Rochelle U.S.A. 40°55N 73°46W 83 F11
New Rockford U.S.A. 47°41N 99°8W 80 B4
New Romney U.K. 50°59N 0°57E 13 G8
New Ross Ireland 52°23N 6°57W 10 D5
New Salem U.S.A. 46°51N 101°25W 80 B3
New Scone = Scone U.K. 56°25N 3°24W 11 E5
New Siberian I. = Novaya Sibir, Ostrov Russia 75°10N 150°0E 27 B16
New Siberian Is. = Novosibirskiye Ostrova Russia 75°0N 142°0E 27 B15
New Smyrna Beach U.S.A. 29°1N 80°56W 85 G14
New South Wales □ Australia 33°0S 146°0E 63 E4
New Tecumseth = Alliston Canada 44°9N 79°52W 82 B5
New Town U.S.A. 47°59N 102°30W 80 B2
New Ulm U.S.A. 44°19N 94°28W 80 C6
New Waterford Canada 46°13N 60°4W 73 C7
New Westminster Canada 49°13N 122°55W 78 A4
New York □ U.S.A. 43°0N 75°0W 83 D9
New York J.F. Kennedy Int. ✈ (JFK) U.S.A. 40°38N 73°47W 83 F11
New Zealand ■ Oceania 40°0S 176°0E 59 D6
Newaj → India 24°24N 76°49E 42 G7
Newark Del., U.S.A. 39°41N 75°46W 81 F16
Newark N.J., U.S.A. 40°44N 74°10W 83 F10
Newark N.Y., U.S.A. 43°3N 77°6W 82 C7
Newark Ohio, U.S.A. 40°3N 82°24W 82 F2
Newark Liberty Int. ✈ (EWR) U.S.A. 40°42N 74°10W 83 F10
Newark-on-Trent U.K. 53°5N 0°48W 12 D7
Newark Valley U.S.A. 42°14N 76°11W 83 D8
Newberg U.S.A. 45°18N 122°58W 76 D2
Newberry Mich., U.S.A. 46°21N 85°30W 81 B11
Newberry S.C., U.S.A. 34°17N 81°37W 85 D14
Newberry Springs U.S.A. 34°50N 116°41W 79 L10
Newboro L. Canada 44°38N 76°20W 83 B8
Newbridge Ireland 53°11N 6°48W 10 C5
Newburgh Canada 44°19N 76°52W 82 B8
Newburgh U.S.A. 41°30N 74°1W 83 E10
Newbury U.K. 51°24N 1°20W 13 F6
Newbury N.H., U.S.A. 43°19N 72°3W 83 B12
Newbury Vt., U.S.A. 44°5N 72°4W 83 B12
Newburyport U.S.A. 42°49N 70°53W 83 D14
Newcastle Australia 33°0S 151°46E 63 E5
Newcastle N.B., Canada 47°1N 65°38W 73 C6
Newcastle Ont., Canada 43°55N 78°35W 72 D4
Newcastle Ireland 52°27N 9°3W 10 D2
Newcastle S. Africa 27°45S 29°58E 57 C4
Newcastle U.K. 54°13N 5°54W 10 B6
Newcastle Calif., U.S.A. 38°53N 121°8W 78 G5
Newcastle Wyo., U.S.A. 43°50N 104°11W 76 E11
Newcastle Emlyn U.K. 52°2N 4°28W 13 E3
Newcastle Ra. Australia 15°45S 130°15E 60 C5
Newcastle-under-Lyme U.K. 53°1N 2°14W 12 D5
Newcastle-upon-Tyne U.K. 54°58N 1°36W 12 C6
Newcastle Waters Australia 17°30S 133°28E 62 B1
Newcomb U.S.A. 43°58N 74°10W 83 C10
Newcomerstown U.S.A. 40°16N 81°36W 82 F3
Newdegate Australia 33°6S 119°0E 61 F2
Newell Australia 16°20S 145°16E 62 B4
Newell U.S.A. 44°43N 103°25W 80 C2
Newenham, C. U.S.A. 58°39N 162°11W 74 D7
Newfane U.S.A. 43°17N 78°43W 82 C6
Newfield U.S.A. 42°18N 76°33W 83 D8
Newfound L. U.S.A. 43°40N 71°47W 83 C13
Newfoundland Canada 49°0N 55°0W 73 C8
Newfoundland U.S.A. 41°18N 75°19W 83 E9
Newfoundland & Labrador □ Canada 52°0N 58°0W 73 B8
Newhaven U.K. 50°47N 0°3E 13 G8
Newkirk U.S.A. 36°53N 97°3W 84 C6
Newlyn U.K. 50°6N 5°34W 13 G2
Newman Australia 23°18S 119°45E 60 D2
Newman U.S.A. 37°19N 121°1W 78 H5
Newmarket Canada 44°3N 79°28W 82 B5
Newmarket Ireland 52°13N 9°0W 10 D2
Newmarket U.K. 52°15N 0°25E 13 E8
Newmarket U.S.A. 43°5N 70°56W 83 C14
Newnan U.S.A. 33°23N 84°48W 85 E12
Newport Ireland 53°53N 9°33W 10 C2
Newport I. of W., U.K. 50°42N 1°17W 13 G6
Newport Newport, U.K. 51°35N 3°0W 13 F5
Newport Ark., U.S.A. 35°37N 91°16W 84 D9
Newport Ky., U.S.A. 39°5N 84°29W 81 F11
Newport N.H., U.S.A. 43°22N 72°10W 83 C12
Newport N.Y., U.S.A. 43°11N 75°1W 83 C9
Newport Oreg., U.S.A. 44°39N 124°3W 76 D1
Newport Pa., U.S.A. 40°29N 77°8W 82 F7
Newport R.I., U.S.A. 41°29N 71°19W 83 E13
Newport Tenn., U.S.A. 35°58N 83°11W 85 D13
Newport Vt., U.S.A. 44°56N 72°13W 83 B12
Newport Wash., U.S.A. 48°11N 117°3W 76 B5
Newport □ U.K. 51°33N 3°1W 13 F4
Newport Beach U.S.A. 33°37N 117°56W 79 M9
Newport News U.S.A. 36°58N 76°25W 81 G15
Newport Pagnell U.K. 52°5N 0°43W 13 E7
Newquay U.K. 50°25N 5°6W 13 G2
Newry U.K. 54°11N 6°21W 10 B5
Newry Islands △ Australia 20°51S 148°56E 62 b
Newton Ill., U.S.A. 38°59N 88°10W 80 F9
Newton Iowa, U.S.A. 41°42N 93°3W 80 E7
Newton Kans., U.S.A. 38°3N 97°21W 80 F5
Newton Miss., U.S.A. 32°19N 89°10W 85 E10
Newton N.C., U.S.A. 35°40N 81°13W 85 D14
Newton N.J., U.S.A. 41°3N 74°45W 83 E10
Newton Tex., U.S.A. 30°51N 93°46W 84 F8
Newton Abbot U.K. 50°32N 3°37W 13 G4
Newton Aycliffe U.K. 54°37N 1°34W 12 C6
Newton Falls N.Y., U.S.A. 44°12N 74°59W 83 B10
Newton Falls Ohio, U.S.A. 41°11N 80°59W 82 E4
Newton Stewart U.K. 54°57N 4°30W 11 G4
Newtonmore U.K. 57°4N 4°8W 11 D4
Newtown U.K. 52°31N 3°19W 13 E4
Newtownabbey U.K. 54°40N 5°56W 10 B6
Newtownards U.K. 54°36N 5°42W 10 B6
Newtownbarry = Bunclody Ireland 52°39N 6°40W 10 D5
Newtownstewart U.K. 54°43N 7°23W 10 B4
Newville U.S.A. 40°10N 77°24W 82 F7
Neya Russia 58°21N 43°49E 18 C7
Neyrīz Iran 29°15N 54°19E 47 D7
Neyshābūr Iran 36°10N 58°50E 47 B8
Neyveli India 11°32N 79°29E 45 J4
Neyyattinkara India 8°26N 77°5E 45 K3
Nezhin = Nizhyn Ukraine 51°5N 31°55E 19 D5

Nezperce *U.S.A.* 46°14N 116°14W **76** C5
Nga, Laem *Thailand* 7°55N 98°27E **39** a
Ngaanyatjarra ○
 Australia 22°40S 127°0E **60** D4
Ngabang *Indonesia* 0°23N 109°55E **36** D3
Ngabordamlu, Tanjung
 Indonesia 6°56S 134°11E **37** F8
Ngalia *Australia* 15°42S 130°4E **60** C5
Ngalurrtju ○ *Australia* 22°44S 132°55E **60** D5
Ngami Depression
 Botswana 20°30S 22°46E **56** B3
Ngamring *China* 29°14N 87°10E **30** D6
Nganglong Kangri *China* 33°0N 81°0E **43** C9
Ngao *Thailand* 18°46N 99°59E **38** C2
Ngaoundéré *Cameroon* 7°15N 13°35E **54** C2
Ngapara *N.Z.* 44°57S 170°46E **59** F3
Ngarluma ○ *Australia* 21°30S 118°30E **60** D2
Ngawi *Indonesia* 7°24S 111°26E **37** G14
Ngcobo *S. Africa* 31°37S 28°0E **57** D4
Ngerulmud = Melekeok
 Palau 7°27N 134°38E **64** G5
Nghia Lo *Vietnam* 21°33N 104°28E **34** G5
Ngoring Hu *China* 34°55N 97°5E **30** E8
Ngorongoro *Tanzania* 3°11S 35°32E **54** E7
Nguigmi *Niger* 14°20N 13°20E **53** F8
Nguiu *Australia* 11°46S 130°38E **60** B5
Ngukurr *Australia* 14°44S 134°44E **62** A1
Ngum → *Laos* 18°31N 102°32E **38** C4
Ngundu *Zimbabwe* 18°11S 31°15E **57** A5
Nguru *Nigeria* 12°56N 10°29E **53** F8
Nguyen Binh *Vietnam* 22°39N 105°56E **34** F5
Ngwaketse ○ *Botswana* 25°0S 25°0E **56** C4
Nha Bang *Vietnam* 10°37N 105°0E **39** G5
Nha Trang *Vietnam* 12°16N 109°10E **39** F7
Nhacoongo *Mozam.* 24°18S 35°14E **57** B6
Nhamundá → *Brazil* 2°12S 56°41W **93** D7
Nhangulaze, L. *Mozam.* 24°0S 34°30E **57** B5
Nharnuwangga, Wajarri and
 Ngarlawangga ○
 Australia 24°50S 118°0E **61** D2
Nhill *Australia* 36°18S 141°40E **63** F3
Nho Quan *Vietnam* 20°18N 105°45E **34** G5
Nhulunbuy *Australia* 12°10S 137°20E **62** A2
Niafounké *Mali* 16°0N 4°5W **52** E5
Niagara Falls *Canada* 43°7N 79°5W **82** C5
Niagara Falls *U.S.A.* 43°5N 79°4W **82** C6
Niagara-on-the-Lake
 Canada 43°15N 79°4W **82** C5
Niah *Malaysia* 3°58N 113°46E **36** D4
Niamey *Niger* 13°27N 2°6E **52** F6
Niangara
 Dem. Rep. of the Congo 3°42N 27°50E **54** D5
Niantic *U.S.A.* 41°20N 72°11W **83** E12
Nias *Indonesia* 1°0N 97°30E **36** D1
Niassa, L. = Malawi, L.
 Africa 12°30S 34°30E **55** G6
Nibāk *Si. Arabia* 24°25N 50°50E **47** E7
Nicaragua ■ *Cent. Amer.* 11°40N 85°30W **88** D2
Nicaragua, L. de *Nic.* 12°0N 85°30W **88** D2
Nicastro *Italy* 38°59N 16°19E **22** E7
Nice *France* 43°42N 7°14E **20** E7
Niceville *U.S.A.* 30°31N 86°30W **85** F11
Nichicun, L. *Canada* 53°5N 71°0W **73** B5
Nichinan *Japan* 31°38N 131°23E **29** J5
Nicholás, Canal *Caribbean* 23°30N 80°5W **88** B3
Nicholas Channel = Nicholás,
 Canal *Caribbean* 23°30N 80°5W **88** B3
Nicholasville *U.S.A.* 37°53N 84°34W **81** G11
Nichols *U.S.A.* 42°1N 76°22W **83** D8
Nicholson *Australia* 18°2S 128°54E **60** C4
Nicholson *U.S.A.* 41°37N 75°47W **83** E9
Nicholson → *Australia* 17°31S 139°36E **62** B2
Nicholson L. *Canada* 62°40N 102°40W **71** A8
Nicholson Ra. *Australia* 27°15S 116°45E **61** E2
Nicholville *U.S.A.* 44°41N 74°39W **83** B10
Nicobar Is. *Ind. Oc.* 8°0N 93°30E **45** L11
Nicola *Canada* 50°12N 120°40W **70** C4
Nicolls Town *Bahamas* 25°8N 78°0W **88** A4
Nicosia *Cyprus* 35°10N 33°25E **46** C2
Nicoya *Costa Rica* 10°9N 85°27W **88** D2
Nicoya, G. de *Costa Rica* 10°0N 85°0W **88** E3
Nicoya, Pen. de *Costa Rica* 9°45N 85°40W **88** E2
Nidd → *U.K.* 53°59N 1°23W **12** D6
Niedersachsen □ *Germany* 52°50N 9°0E **16** B5
Niekerkshoop *S. Africa* 29°19S 22°51E **56** D3
Niemen = Nemunas →
 Lithuania 55°25N 21°10E **9** J19
Nienburg *Germany* 52°39N 9°13E **16** B5
Nieu Bethesda *S. Africa* 31°51S 24°34E **56** D3
Nieuw Amsterdam
 Suriname 5°53N 55°5W **93** B7
Nieuw Nickerie *Suriname* 6°0N 56°59W **93** B7
Nieuwoudtville *S. Africa* 31°23S 19°7E **56** D2
Nieuwpoort *Belgium* 51°8N 2°45E **15** C2
Niğde *Turkey* 37°58N 34°40E **46** C6
Nigel *S. Africa* 26°27S 28°25E **57** C4
Niger ■ *W. Afr.* 17°30N 10°0E **52** E7
Niger → *W. Afr.* 5°33N 6°33E **52** G7
Nigeria ■ *W. Afr.* 8°30N 8°0E **52** G7
Nighasin *India* 28°14N 80°52E **43** E9
Nightcaps *N.Z.* 45°57S 168°2E **59** F2
Nihoa *U.S.A.* 23°6N 161°58W **75** L7
Nihon = Japan ■ *Asia* 36°0N 136°0E **29** G8
Nii-Jima *Japan* 34°20N 139°15E **29** G9
Niigata *Japan* 37°58N 139°0E **28** F9
Niigata □ *Japan* 37°15N 138°45E **29** F9
Niihama *Japan* 33°55N 133°16E **29** H6
Ni'ihau *U.S.A.* 21°54N 160°9W **75** L7
Niimi *Japan* 34°59N 133°28E **29** G6
Niitsu *Japan* 37°48N 139°7E **28** F9
Nijil *Jordan* 30°32N 35°33E **48** E4
Nijkerk *Neths.* 52°13N 5°30E **15** B5
Nijmegen *Neths.* 51°50N 5°52E **15** C5
Nijverdal *Neths.* 52°22N 6°28E **15** B6
Nīk Pey *Iran* 36°50N 48°10E **47** B6
Nikaweratiya *Sri Lanka* 7°45N 80°7E **45** L5
Nikel *Russia* 69°24N 30°13E **8** B24
Nikiniki *Indonesia* 9°49S 124°30E **60** A3

Nikkō *Japan* 36°45N 139°35E **29** F9
Nikkō △ *Japan* 36°56N 139°37E **29** F9
Nikolayev = Mykolayiv
 Ukraine 46°58N 32°0E **19** E5
Nikolayevsk *Russia* 50°0N 45°35E **19** E8
Nikolayevsk-na-Amur
 Russia 53°8N 140°44E **27** D15
Nikolskoye *Russia* 55°12N 166°0E **27** D17
Nikopol *Ukraine* 47°35N 34°25E **19** E5
Nikshahr *Iran* 26°15N 60°10E **47** E9
Nikšić *Montenegro* 42°50N 18°57E **23** C8
Nîl, Nahr en → *Africa* 30°10N 31°6E **53** B12
Nîl el Abyad → *Sudan* 15°38N 32°31E **53** E12
Nîl el Azraq → *Sudan* 15°38N 32°31E **53** E12
Nila *Indonesia* 6°44S 129°31E **37** F7
Nilakkottai *India* 10°10N 77°52E **45** J3
Nilanga *India* 18°6N 76°46E **44** E3
Nile = Nîl, Nahr en →
 Africa 30°10N 31°6E **53** B12
Niles *Mich., U.S.A.* 41°50N 86°15W **80** E10
Niles *Ohio, U.S.A.* 41°11N 80°46W **82** E4
Nileshwar *India* 12°15N 75°6E **45** H2
Nilgiri Hills *India* 11°30N 76°30E **45** J3
Nim Ka Thana *India* 27°44N 75°48E **42** F6
Nimach *India* 24°30N 74°56E **42** G6
Nimbahera *India* 24°37N 74°45E **42** G6
Nîmes *France* 43°50N 4°23E **20** E6
Nimfaíon, Ákra = Pines, Akra
 Greece 40°5N 24°20E **23** D11
Nimmitabel *Australia* 36°29S 149°15E **63** F4
Nīnawá *Iraq* 36°25N 43°0E **46** B4
Nīnawá □ *Iraq* 36°15N 43°0E **46** B4
Nindigully *Australia* 28°21S 148°50E **63** D4
Nine Degree Channel *India* 9°0N 73°0E **45** K1
Ninepin Group *China* 22°16N 114°21E **31** a
Nineveh = Nīnawá *Iraq* 36°25N 43°10E **46** B4
Ning Xian *China* 35°30N 107°58E **32** G4
Ningaloo Marine △
 Australia 22°23S 113°32E **60** D1
Ning'an *China* 44°22N 129°20E **33** B15
Ningbo *China* 29°51N 121°28E **35** D13
Ningcheng *China* 41°32N 119°53E **33** D10
Ningde *China* 26°38N 119°23E **35** D12
Ningdu *China* 26°25N 115°59E **35** D10
Ninggang *China* 26°42N 113°55E **35** D9
Ningguo *China* 30°35N 119°0E **35** B12
Ninghai *China* 29°15N 121°27E **35** C13
Ninghua *China* 26°14N 116°45E **35** D11
Ningjin *China* 37°35N 114°57E **32** F8
Ningjing Shan *China* 31°0N 98°20E **34** C2
Ninglang *China* 27°20N 100°55E **34** D3
Ningling *China* 34°25N 115°22E **32** G8
Ningming *China* 22°8N 107°4E **34** F6
Ningnan *China* 27°0N 102°36E **34** D4
Ningpo = Ningbo
 China 29°51N 121°28E **35** C13
Ningqiang *China* 32°47N 106°15E **32** H4
Ningshan *China* 33°21N 108°21E **34** A7
Ningsia Hui A.R. = Ningxia Huizu
 Zizhiqu □ *China* 38°0N 106°0E **32** F4
Ningwu *China* 39°0N 112°18E **32** E7
Ningxia Huizu Zizhiqu □
 China 38°0N 106°0E **32** F4
Ningxiang *China* 28°15N 112°30E **35** C9
Ningyang *China* 35°47N 116°45E **32** G9
Ningyuan *China* 25°37N 111°57E **35** E8
Ninh Binh *Vietnam* 20°15N 105°55E **34** G5
Ninh Giang *Vietnam* 20°44N 106°24E **38** B6
Ninh Hoa *Vietnam* 12°30N 109°7E **38** F7
Ninh Ma *Vietnam* 12°48N 109°21E **38** F7
Ninove *Belgium* 50°51N 4°2E **15** D4
Nioaque *Brazil* 21°5S 55°50W **95** A4
Niobrara *U.S.A.* 42°45N 98°2W **80** D4
Niobrara → *U.S.A.* 42°46N 98°3W **80** D4
Nioro du Sahel *Mali* 15°15N 9°30E **52** E4
Niort *France* 46°19N 0°29W **20** C3
Nipani *India* 16°20N 74°25E **45** F2
Nipawin *Canada* 53°20N 104°0W **71** C8
Nipigon *Canada* 49°0N 88°17W **72** C2
Nipigon, L. *Canada* 49°50N 88°30W **72** C2
Nipishish L. *Canada* 54°12N 60°45W **73** B7
Nipissing, L. *Canada* 46°20N 80°0W **72** C4
Nipomo *U.S.A.* 35°3N 120°29W **79** K6
Nippon = Japan ■ *Asia* 36°0N 136°0E **29** G8
Nipton *U.S.A.* 35°28N 115°16W **79** K11
Niquelândia *Brazil* 14°33S 48°23W **93** F9
Nira → *India* 17°58N 75°8E **44** F2
Nirasaki *Japan* 35°42N 138°27E **29** G9
Nirmal *India* 19°3N 78°20E **44** E4
Nirmali *India* 26°20N 86°35E **43** F12
Niš *Serbia* 43°19N 21°58E **23** C9
Nisa *Turkmenistan* 37°59N 58°11E **47** B8
Nişāb *Si. Arabia* 29°11N 44°43E **46** D5
Nişāb *Yemen* 14°25N 46°29E **49** E4
Nishino'omote *Japan* 30°43N 130°59E **29** J5
Nishiwaki *Japan* 34°59N 134°58E **29** G7
Niskibi → *Canada* 56°29N 88°9W **72** A2
Nisqually → *U.S.A.* 47°7N 122°42W **78** C4
Nissum Bredning *Denmark* 56°40N 8°20E **9** H13
Nistru = Dnister →
 Europe 46°18N 30°17E **17** E16
Nisutlin → *Canada* 60°14N 132°34W **70** A2
Nitchequon *Canada* 53°10N 70°58W **73** B5
Nith → *Canada* 43°12N 80°23W **82** C4
Nith → *U.K.* 55°14N 3°33W **11** F5
Nitmiluk △ *Australia* 14°6S 132°15E **60** B5
Nitra *Slovak Rep.* 48°19N 18°4E **17** D10
Nitra → *Slovak Rep.* 47°46N 18°10E **17** E10
Niue ☑ *Pac. Oc.* 19°2S 169°54W **65** J11
Niulan Jiang → *China* 27°30N 103°35E **34** D4
Niut *Indonesia* 0°55N 109°54E **36** D4
Niutou Shan *China* 29°51N 121°59E **35** C13
Niuzhuang *China* 40°58N 122°28E **33** D12
Nivala *Finland* 63°56N 24°57E **8** E21
Nivelles *Belgium* 50°35N 4°20E **15** D4
Nivernais *France* 47°15N 3°30E **20** C5
Niverville *Canada* 49°36N 97°3W **71** D9
Niwas *India* 23°3N 80°26E **43** H9

Nixa *U.S.A.* 37°3N 93°18W **80** G7
Nixon *U.S.A.* 29°16N 97°46W **84** G6
Nizam Sagar *India* 18°10N 77°58E **44** E3
Nizamabad *India* 18°45N 78°7E **44** E4
Nizamghat *India* 28°20N 95°45E **41** E19
Nizhne-Kolymsk
 Russia 68°34N 160°55E **27** C17
Nizhnekamsk *Russia* 55°38N 51°49E **18** C9
Nizhneudinsk *Russia* 54°54N 99°3E **27** D10
Nizhnevartovsk *Russia* 60°56N 76°38E **26** C8
Nizhniy Bestyakh
 Russia 61°57N 129°54E **27** C13
Nizhniy Novgorod *Russia* 56°20N 44°0E **18** C7
Nizhniy Tagil *Russia* 57°55N 59°57E **18** C10
Nizhyn *Ukraine* 51°5N 31°55E **19** D5
Nizip *Turkey* 37°5N 37°50E **46** B3
Nízké Tatry *Slovak Rep.* 48°55N 19°30E **17** D10
Nizwá *Oman* 22°56N 57°32E **49** C6
Njazidja = Grande Comore
 Comoros Is. 11°35S 43°20E **55** a
Njombe *Tanzania* 9°20S 34°50E **54** F6
Nkandla *S. Africa* 28°37S 31°5E **57** C5
Nkawkaw *Ghana* 6°36N 0°49W **52** G5
Nkhotakota *Malawi* 12°56S 34°15E **55** G6
Nkongsamba *Cameroon* 4°55N 9°55E **54** D1
Nkurenkuru *Namibia* 17°42S 18°32E **56** A2
Nmai → *Burma* 25°30N 97°25E **34** F2
Noakhali *Bangla.* 22°48N 91°10E **41** H17
Nobel *Canada* 45°25N 80°6W **86** A2
Nobeoka *Japan* 32°36N 131°41E **29** H5
Noblesville *U.S.A.* 40°3N 86°1W **80** E10
Noboribetsu *Japan* 42°24N 141°6E **28** C10
Noccundra *Australia* 27°50S 142°36E **63** D3
Nocera Inferiore *Italy* 40°44N 14°38E **22** D6
Nocona *U.S.A.* 33°47N 97°44W **84** E6
Noda *Japan* 35°56N 139°52E **29** G9
Nogales *Mexico* 31°19N 110°56W **86** A2
Nogales *U.S.A.* 31°21N 110°56W **77** L8
Nōgata *Japan* 33°48N 130°44E **29** H5
Noggerup *Australia* 33°32S 116°5E **61** F2
Noginsk *Russia* 64°30N 90°50E **27** C10
Nogliki *Russia* 51°50N 143°10E **27** D15
Nogoa → *Australia* 23°40S 147°55E **62** C4
Nogoyá *Argentina* 32°24S 59°48W **94** C4
Nohar *India* 29°11N 74°49E **42** E6
Nohta *India* 23°40N 79°34E **43** H8
Noirmoutier, Î. de *France* 46°58N 2°10W **20** C2
Nojane *Botswana* 23°15S 20°14E **56** B3
Nojima-Zaki *Japan* 34°54N 139°53E **29** G9
Nok Kundi *Pakistan* 28°50N 62°45E **40** E3
Nok Ta Phao, Ko *Thailand* 9°23N 99°42E **39** b
Nokaneng *Botswana* 19°40S 22°17E **56** A3
Nokia *Finland* 61°30N 23°30E **8** F20
Nokomis *Canada* 51°35N 105°0W **71** C8
Nokomis L. *Canada* 57°0N 103°0W **71** B8
Nola *C.A.R.* 3°35N 16°4E **54** D3
Noma Omuramba →
 Namibia 18°52S 20°53E **56** A3
Nombre de Dios *Panama* 9°34N 79°28W **88** E4
Nome *U.S.A.* 64°30N 165°25W **74** C6
Nomgon *Mongolia* 42°50N 105°8E **32** C3
Nomo-Zaki *Japan* 32°35N 129°44E **29** H4
Nomuka *Tonga* 20°17S 174°48W **59** c
Nomuka Group *Tonga* 20°20S 174°48W **59** c
Nonacho L. *Canada* 61°42N 109°40W **71** A7
Nonda *Australia* 20°40S 142°28E **62** C3
Nong Chang *Thailand* 15°23N 99°51E **38** E2
Nong Han Res. *Thailand* 17°11N 104°9E **38** D5
Nong Het *Laos* 19°29N 103°59E **38** C4
Nong Khai *Thailand* 17°50N 102°46E **38** D4
Nong'an *China* 44°25N 125°5E **33** B13
Nongoma *S. Africa* 27°58S 31°35E **57** C5
Nongsa *Indonesia* 1°11N 104°8E **39** d
Nonoava *Mexico* 27°28N 106°44W **86** B3
Nonsan *S. Korea* 36°12N 127°5E **33** F14
Noonamah *Australia* 12°40S 131°4E **60** B5
Noondie, L. *Australia* 28°30S 119°30E **61** E2
Noonkanbah ○
 Australia 18°30S 124°50E **60** C3
Noord Brabant □ *Neths.* 51°40N 5°0E **15** C5
Noord Holland □ *Neths.* 52°30N 4°45E **15** B4
Noordbeveland *Neths.* 51°35N 3°50E **15** C3
Noordoostpolder *Neths.* 52°45N 5°45E **15** B5
Noordwijk *Neths.* 52°14N 4°26E **15** B4
Noosa Heads *Australia* 26°25S 153°6E **63** D5
Nootka I. *Canada* 49°32N 126°42W **70** D3
Nopiming △ *Canada* 50°30N 95°37W **71** C9
Noralee *Canada* 53°59N 126°26W **70** C3
Noranda = Rouyn-Noranda
 Canada 48°20N 79°0W **72** C4
Norco *U.S.A.* 33°56N 117°33W **79** M9
Nord-Ostsee-Kanal
 Germany 54°12N 9°32E **16** A5
Nordaustlandet *Svalbard* 79°14N 23°0E **4** B9
Nordegg *Canada* 52°29N 116°5W **70** C5
Norderney *Germany* 53°42N 7°9E **16** B4
Norderstedt *Germany* 53°42N 10°1E **16** B5
Nordfjord *Norway* 61°55N 5°30E **8** F11
Nordfriesische Inseln
 Germany 54°40N 8°20E **16** A5
Nordhausen *Germany* 51°30N 10°47E **16** C6
Nordkapp *Norway* 71°10N 25°50E **8** A21
Nordkapp *Svalbard* 80°31N 20°0E **4** A9
Nordkinn *Norway* 71°8N 27°40E **8** A22
Nordkinnhalvøya
 Norway 70°55N 27°40E **8** A22
Nordrhein-Westfalen □
 Germany 51°45N 7°30E **16** C4
Nordvik *Russia* 74°2N 111°32E **27** B12
Nore → *Ireland* 52°25N 6°58W **10** D4
Noreland *Canada* 44°43N 78°48W **82** B6
Norfolk = Simcoe
 Canada 42°50N 80°23W **82** D4
Norfolk *Nebr., U.S.A.* 42°2N 97°25W **80** D5
Norfolk *Va., U.S.A.* 36°50N 76°17W **81** G15
Norfolk □ *U.K.* 52°39N 0°54E **13** E8
Norfolk Broads △ *U.K.* 52°45N 1°30E **13** E9

Norfolk I. *Pac. Oc.* 28°58S 168°3E **58** D9
Norfolk Ridge *Pac. Oc.* 29°0S 168°0E **64** K8
Norfork L. *U.S.A.* 36°15N 92°14W **84** C8
Norge = Norway ■ *Europe* 63°0N 11°0E **8** E14
Norilsk *Russia* 69°20N 88°6E **27** C9
Norma, Mt. *Australia* 20°55S 140°42E **62** C3
Normal *U.S.A.* 40°31N 88°59W **80** E9
Norman *U.S.A.* 35°13N 97°26W **84** H6
Norman → *Australia* 19°18S 141°51E **62** B3
Norman Wells *Canada* 65°17N 126°51W **68** D6
Normanby → *Australia* 14°23S 144°10E **62** A3
Normandie *France* 48°45N 0°10E **20** B4
Normandin *Canada* 48°49N 72°31W **72** C5
Normandy = Normandie
 France 48°45N 0°10E **20** B4
Normanhurst, Mt.
 Australia 25°4S 122°30E **61** E3
Normanton *Australia* 17°40S 141°10E **62** B3
Normétal *Canada* 49°0N 79°22W **72** C4
Norquay *Canada* 51°53N 102°5W **71** C8
Norquinco *Argentina* 41°51S 70°55W **96** E2
Norrbottens län □ *Sweden* 66°50N 20°0E **8** C19
Norris Point *Canada* 49°31N 57°53E **73** C8
Norristown *U.S.A.* 40°7N 75°21W **83** F9
Norrköping *Sweden* 58°37N 16°11E **9** G17
Norrland *Sweden* 62°15N 15°45E **8** E16
Norrtälje *Sweden* 59°46N 18°42E **9** G18
Norseman *Australia* 32°8S 121°43E **61** F3
Norsk *Russia* 52°30N 130°5E **27** D14
Norte, Serra do *Brazil* 11°20S 59°0W **92** F7
Norte, C. *Brazil* 1°40N 49°30W **93** C9
North, C. *Canada* 47°2N 60°20W **73** C7
North Adams *U.S.A.* 42°42N 73°7W **83** D11
North America 40°0N 100°0W **66** F10
North Andaman I. *India* 13°15N 92°55E **45** H11
North Arm *Canada* 62°0N 114°30W **70** A5
North Augusta *U.S.A.* 33°30N 81°59W **85** E14
North Australian Basin
 Ind. Oc. 14°30S 116°30E **64** J3
North Ayrshire □ *U.K.* 55°45N 4°44W **11** F4
North Bass I. *U.S.A.* 41°40N 82°56W **82** E2
North Battleford *Canada* 52°50N 108°17W **71** C7
North Bay *Canada* 46°20N 79°30W **72** C4
North Belcher Is. *Canada* 56°50N 79°50W **72** A4
North Bend *Oreg.,
 U.S.A.* 43°24N 124°14W **76** E1
North Bend *Pa., U.S.A.* 41°20N 77°42W **82** E7
North Bend *Wash.,
 U.S.A.* 47°30N 121°47W **78** C5
North Bennington
 U.S.A. 42°56N 73°15W **83** D11
North Berwick *U.K.* 56°4N 2°42W **11** E6
North Berwick *U.S.A.* 43°18N 70°44W **83** C14
North Brother I. *India* 10°59N 92°40E **45** J11
North Bruce *Canada* 44°22N 81°26W **82** B3
North C. *Canada* 47°5N 64°0W **73** C7
North C. *N.Z.* 34°23S 173°4E **59** A4
North Canadian →
 U.S.A. 35°22N 95°37W **84** D7
North Canton *U.S.A.* 40°53N 81°24W **82** F3
North Cape = Nordkapp
 Norway 71°10N 25°50E **8** A21
North Caribou L. *Canada* 52°50N 90°40W **72** B1
North Carolina □ *U.S.A.* 35°30N 80°0W **85** D15
North Cascades △
 U.S.A. 48°45N 121°10W **76** B3
North Channel *Canada* 46°0N 83°0W **72** C3
North Channel *U.K.* 55°13N 5°52W **11** F3
North Charleston
 U.S.A. 32°53N 79°58W **85** E15
North Chicago *U.S.A.* 42°19N 87°51W **80** D10
North Collins *U.S.A.* 42°35N 78°56W **82** D6
North Creek *U.S.A.* 43°42N 73°59W **83** C11
North Dakota □ *U.S.A.* 47°30N 100°15W **80** B4
North Downs *U.K.* 51°19N 0°21E **13** F8
North East □ *Botswana* 20°45S 27°30E **57** B4
North East Frontier Agency =
 Arunachal Pradesh □
 India 28°0N 95°0E **41** F19
North East Lincolnshire □
 U.K. 53°34N 0°2W **12** D7
North Esk → *U.K.* 56°46N 2°24W **11** E6
North European Plain
 Europe 55°0N 25°0E **6** E10
North Foreland *U.K.* 51°22N 1°28E **13** F9
North Fork *U.S.A.* 37°14N 119°21W **78** H7
North Fork American →
 U.S.A. 38°57N 120°59W **78** G5
North Fork Feather →
 U.S.A. 38°33N 121°30W **78** F5
North Fork Grand →
 U.S.A. 45°47N 102°16W **80** C2
North Fork Red →
 U.S.A. 34°24N 99°14W **84** D5
North Frisian Is. = Nordfriesische
 Inseln *Germany* 54°40N 8°20E **16** A5
North Gower *Canada* 45°8N 75°43W **83** A9
North Hd. *Australia* 30°14S 114°59E **61** E1
North Henik L. *Canada* 61°45N 97°40W **71** A9
North Highlands *U.S.A.* 38°40N 121°23W **78** G5
North I. *N.Z.* 38°0N 175°0E **59** C5
North I. *Seychelles* 4°25S 55°13E **55** b
North Kingsville *U.S.A.* 41°54N 80°42W **82** E4
North Knife → *Canada* 58°53N 94°45W **71** B10
North Koel → *India* 24°45N 83°50E **43** G10
North Korea ■ *Asia* 40°0N 127°0E **33** E14
North Lakhimpur *India* 27°14N 94°7E **41** F19
North Lanarkshire □
 U.K. 55°52N 3°56W **11** F5
North Lincolnshire □
 U.K. 53°36N 0°30W **12** D7
North Little Rock *U.S.A.* 34°45N 92°16W **84** D8
North Loup → *U.S.A.* 41°17N 98°24W **80** E4
North Magnetic Pole
 Canada
 Arctic 85°9N 149°0W **4** A1
North Mankato *U.S.A.* 44°10N 94°2W **80** C6
North Minch *U.K.* 58°5N 5°55W **11** C3
North Moose L. *Canada* 54°4N 100°12W **71** C8
North Myrtle Beach
 U.S.A. 33°48N 78°42W **85** E15

North Nahanni →
 Canada 62°15N 123°20W **70** A4
North Olmsted *U.S.A.* 41°25N 81°56W **82** E3
North Ossetia-Alaniya □
 Russia 43°30N 44°30E **19** F7
North Pagai, I. = Pagai Utara,
 Pulau *Indonesia* 2°35S 100°0E **36** E2
North Palisade *U.S.A.* 37°6N 118°31W **78** H8
North Paravar *India* 10°13N 76°14E **45** J3
North Platte *U.S.A.* 41°8N 100°46W **80** E3
North Platte → *U.S.A.* 41°7N 100°42W **80** E3
North Pole *Arctic* 90°0N 0°0 **4** A
North Portal *Canada* 49°0N 102°33W **71** D8
North Powder *U.S.A.* 45°2N 117°55W **76** D5
North Pt. *Barbados* 13°20N 59°37W **89** g
North Pt. *Trin. & Tob.* 11°21N 60°31W **93** J16
North Pt. *U.S.A.* 45°2N 83°16W **82** A1
North Reef I. *India* 13°5N 92°43E **45** H11
North Rhine Westphalia =
 Nordrhein-Westfalen □
 Germany 51°45N 7°30E **16** C4
North River *Canada* 53°49N 57°6W **73** B8
North Rona *Atl. Oc.* 59°7N 5°49W **14** B4
North Ronaldsay *U.K.* 59°22N 2°26W **11** B6
North Saskatchewan →
 Canada 53°15N 105°5W **71** C7
North Sea *Europe* 56°0N 4°0E **6** D6
North Seal → *Canada* 58°50N 98°7W **71** B9
North Sentinel I. *India* 11°33N 92°15E **45** J11
North Slope ☆ *U.S.A.* 69°15N 152°0W **74** B9
North Somerset □ *U.K.* 51°24N 2°45W **13** F5
North Sydney *Canada* 46°12N 60°15W **73** C7
North Syracuse *U.S.A.* 43°8N 76°7W **83** C8
North Taranaki Bight
 N.Z. 38°50S 174°15E **59** C5
North Thompson →
 Canada 50°40N 120°20W **70** C4
North Tonawanda *U.S.A.* 43°2N 78°53W **82** C6
North Troy *U.S.A.* 45°0N 72°24W **83** B12
North Twin I. *Canada* 53°20N 80°0W **72** B4
North Tyne → *U.K.* 55°0N 2°8W **12** B5
North Uist *U.K.* 57°40N 7°15W **11** D1
North Vancouver *Canada* 49°19N 123°4W **78** A3
North Vernon *U.S.A.* 39°0N 85°38W **81** F11
North Wabasca L.
 Canada 56°0N 113°55W **70** B6
North Walsham *U.K.* 52°50N 1°22E **12** E9
North West = Severo-Zapadnyy □
 Russia 65°0N 40°0E **26** C4
North West □ *Botswana* 19°0S 22°30E **56** A3
North-West □ *S. Africa* 27°0S 25°0E **56** C4
North West C. *Australia* 21°45S 114°9E **60** D1
North West Christmas I. Ridge
 Pac. Oc. 6°30N 165°0W **65** F11
North West Frontier = Khyber
 Pakhtunkhwa □
 Pakistan 34°0N 72°0E **42** B4
North West Highlands
 U.K. 57°33N 4°58W **11** D4
North West River *Canada* 53°30N 60°10W **73** B7
North Wildwood *U.S.A.* 39°0N 74°48W **81** F16
North York Moors *U.K.* 54°23N 0°53W **12** C7
North York Moors △
 U.K. 54°27N 0°51W **12** C7
North Yorkshire □ *U.K.* 54°15N 1°25W **12** C6
Northallerton *U.K.* 54°20N 1°26W **12** C6
Northam *Australia* 31°35S 116°42E **61** F2
Northam *S. Africa* 24°56S 27°18E **56** B4
Northampton *Australia* 28°27S 114°33E **61** E1
Northampton *U.K.* 52°15N 0°53W **13** E7
Northampton *Mass.,
 U.S.A.* 42°19N 72°38W **83** D12
Northampton *Pa., U.S.A.* 40°41N 75°30W **83** F9
Northamptonshire □
 U.K. 52°16N 0°55W **13** E7
Northbridge *U.S.A.* 42°9N 71°39W **83** D13
Northbrook *Canada* 44°44N 77°9W **82** B7
Northcliffe *Australia* 34°39S 116°7E **61** F2
Northeast Pacific Basin
 Pac. Oc. 32°0N 145°0W **65** D13
Northeast Providence Channel
 W. Indies 26°0N 76°0W **88** A4
Northern = Limpopo □
 S. Africa 24°5S 29°0E **57** B4
Northern Areas = Gilgit-
 Baltistan □ *Pakistan* 36°30N 73°0E **43** A5
Northern Cape □ *S. Africa* 30°0S 20°0E **56** C3
Northern Circars *India* 17°30N 82°30E **44** F6
Northern Dvina = Dvina,
 Severnaya → *Russia* 64°32N 40°30E **18** B7
Northern Indian L.
 Canada 57°20N 97°20W **71** B9
Northern Ireland □ *U.K.* 54°45N 7°0W **10** B5
Northern Lau Group *Fiji* 17°30S 178°59W **59** a
Northern Light L. *Canada* 48°15N 90°39W **72** C1
Northern Marianas ☑
 Pac. Oc. 17°0N 145°0E **64** F6
Northern Province □
 S. Africa 24°0S 29°0E **57** B4
Northern Range
 Trin. & Tob. 10°46N 61°15W **93** K15
Northern Sporades = Voreíoi
 Sporádes *Greece* 39°15N 23°30E **23** E10
Northern Territory □
 Australia 20°0S 133°0E **60** D5
Northfield *Minn., U.S.A.* 44°27N 93°9W **80** C7
Northfield *Vt., U.S.A.* 44°9N 72°40W **83** B12
Northgate *Canada* 49°0N 102°16W **71** D8
Northland □ *N.Z.* 35°30S 173°30E **59** A4
Northome *U.S.A.* 47°52N 94°17W **80** B6
Northport *Ala., U.S.A.* 33°14N 87°35W **85** E11
Northport *N.Y., U.S.A.* 40°54N 73°21W **83** F11
Northport *Wash., U.S.A.* 48°55N 117°48W **76** B5
Northumberland □ *U.K.* 55°12N 2°0W **12** B6
Northumberland, C.
 Australia 38°5S 140°40E **63** F3
Northumberland Is.
 Australia 21°30S 149°50E **62** C4
Northumberland Str.
 Canada 46°20N 64°0W **73** C7

Northville Canada 43°10N 81°56W 82 C3
Northville U.S.A. 43°13N 74°11W 83 C10
Northwest Pacific Basin
  Pac. Oc. 32°N 165°0E 64 D8
Northwest Providence Channel
  W. Indies 26°0N 78°0W 88 A4
Northwest Territories □
  Canada 63°0N 118°0W 68 E8
Northwich U.K. 53°15N 2°31W 12 D5
Northwood Iowa, U.S.A. 43°27N 93°13W 80 D7
Northwood N. Dak.,
  U.S.A. 47°44N 97°34W 80 B5
Norton U.S.A. 39°50N 99°53W 80 F4
Norton Sd. U.S.A. 63°50N 164°0W 74 C7
Norwalk Calif., U.S.A. 33°54N 118°4W 79 M8
Norwalk Conn., U.S.A. 41°7N 73°22W 83 E11
Norwalk Iowa, U.S.A. 41°29N 93°41W 80 E7
Norwalk Ohio, U.S.A. 41°15N 82°37W 82 E2
Norway Maine, U.S.A. 44°13N 70°32W 81 C18
Norway Mich., U.S.A. 45°47N 87°55W 80 C10
Norway ■ Europe 63°0N 11°0E 8 E14
Norway House Canada 53°59N 97°50W 71 C9
Norwegian B. Canada 77°30N 90°0W 69 B14
Norwegian Basin Atl. Oc. 68°0N 2°0W 4 C7
Norwegian Sea Atl. Oc. 66°0N 1°0E 8 B6
Norwich Canada 42°59N 80°36W 82 D4
Norwich U.K. 52°38N 1°18E 13 E9
Norwich Conn., U.S.A. 41°31N 72°5W 83 E12
Norwich N.Y., U.S.A. 42°32N 75°32W 83 D9
Norwood Canada 44°23N 77°59W 82 B7
Norwood U.S.A. 42°45N 75°6W 83 D9
Nosappu-Misaki Japan 45°26N 141°39E 28 C12
Noshiro Japan 40°12N 140°0E 28 D10
Noṣratābād Iran 29°55N 60°0E 47 D8
Noss Hd. U.K. 58°28N 3°3W 11 C5
Nossob → S. Africa 26°55S 20°45E 56 D3
Nosy Varika Madag. 20°35S 48°32E 55 J9
Noteć → Poland 52°44N 15°26E 16 B8
Notikewin → Canada 57°2N 117°38W 70 B5
Noto-Hantō Japan 37°15N 136°40E 29 F8
Notodden Norway 59°35N 9°17E 9 G13
Notre Dame B. Canada 49°45N 55°30W 73 C8
Notre-Dame-de-Koartac =
  Quaqtaq Canada 60°55N 69°40W 69 E18
Notre-Dame-des-Bois
  Canada 45°24N 71°4W 83 A13
Notre-Dame-d'Ivugivic = Ivujivik
  Canada 62°24N 77°55W 69 E16
Notre-Dame-du-Nord
  Canada 47°36N 79°30W 72 C4
Nottawasaga B. Canada 44°35N 80°15W 82 B4
Nottaway → Canada 51°22N 78°55W 72 B4
Nottingham U.K. 52°58N 1°10W 12 E6
Nottingham, City of □
  U.K. 52°58N 1°10W 12 E6
Nottingham I. Canada 63°20N 77°55W 69 E16
Nottinghamshire □ U.K. 53°10N 1°3W 12 E6
Nottoway → U.S.A. 36°33N 76°55W 81 G15
Notwane → Botswana 23°35S 26°58E 56 B4
Nouâdhibou Mauritania 20°54N 17°0W 52 D2
Nouâdhibou, Râs
  Mauritania 20°50N 17°0W 52 D2
Nouakchott Mauritania 18°9N 15°58W 52 E2
Nouméa N. Cal. 22°17S 166°30E 58 D9
Noupoort S. Africa 31°10S 24°57E 56 D3
Nouveau Comptoir = Wemindji
  Canada 53°0N 78°49W 72 B4
Nouvelle Amsterdam, Î.
  Ind. Oc. 38°30S 77°30E 3 F13
Nouvelle-Calédonie = New
  Caledonia ☑ Pac. Oc. 21°0S 165°0E 58 D9
Nova Esperança Brazil 23°8S 52°24W 95 A5
Nova Friburgo Brazil 22°16S 42°30W 95 A7
Nova Iguaçu Brazil 22°45S 43°28W 95 A7
Nova Iorque Brazil 7°0S 44°5W 93 E10
Nova Lamego
  Guinea-Biss. 12°19N 14°11W 52 F3
Nova Mambone Mozam. 21°0S 35°3E 57 B6
Nova Scotia □ Canada 45°10N 63°0W 73 C7
Nova Sofala Mozam. 20°7S 34°42E 57 B5
Nova Venécia Brazil 18°45S 40°24W 93 G10
Nova Zagora Bulgaria 42°32N 26°1E 23 C11
Novar Canada 45°27N 79°15W 82 A5
Novara Italy 45°28N 8°38E 20 D8
Novato U.S.A. 38°6N 122°35W 78 G4
Novaya Ladoga Russia 60°7N 32°16E 18 B5
Novaya Lyalya Russia 59°4N 60°45E 18 C11
Novaya Sibir, Ostrov
  Russia 75°10N 150°0E 27 B16
Novaya Zemlya Russia 75°0N 56°0E 26 B6
Nové Zámky Slovak Rep. 48°2N 18°8E 17 D10
Novgorod = Velikiy Novgorod
  Russia 58°30N 31°25E 18 C5
Novgorod-Severskiy = Novhorod-
  Siverskyy Ukraine 52°2N 33°10E 18 D5
Novhorod-Siverskyy
  Ukraine 52°2N 33°10E 18 D5
Novi Lígure Italy 44°46N 8°47E 20 D8
Novi Pazar Serbia 43°12N 20°28E 23 C9
Novi Sad Serbia 45°18N 19°52E 23 B8
Novo Hamburgo Brazil 29°37S 51°7W 95 B5
Novo Mesto Slovenia 45°47N 15°12E 22 B6
Novoaltaysk Russia 53°30N 84°0E 26 D9
Novocherkassk Russia 47°27N 40°15E 19 E7
Novodvinsk Russia 64°25N 40°42E 18 B7
Novogrudok = Navahrudak
  Belarus 53°40N 25°50E 17 B13
Novohrad-Volynskyy
  Ukraine 50°34N 27°35E 17 C14
Novokachalinsk Russia 45°5N 132°0E 28 B5
Novokuybyshevsk Russia 53°7N 49°58E 18 D8
Novokuznetsk Russia 53°45N 87°10E 26 D9
Novolazarevskaya Antarctica 71°0N 12°0E 5 D3
Novomoskovsk Russia 54°5N 38°15E 18 D6
Novorossiysk Russia 44°43N 37°46E 19 F6
Novorybnoye Russia 72°50N 105°50E 27 B11
Novoselytsya Ukraine 48°14N 26°15E 17 D14
Novoshakhtinsk Russia 47°46N 39°58E 19 E6
Novosibirsk Russia 55°0N 83°5E 26 D9
Novosibirskiye Ostrova
  Russia 75°0N 142°0E 27 B15

Novotroitsk Russia 51°10N 58°15E 18 D10
Novouzensk Russia 50°32N 48°17E 19 D8
Novovolynsk Ukraine 50°45N 24°4E 17 C13
Novska Croatia 45°19N 17°0E 22 B7
Novyy Bor Russia 66°43N 52°19E 18 A9
Novyy Port Russia 67°40N 72°30E 26 C8
Nowa Sól Poland 51°48N 15°44E 16 C8
Nowata U.S.A. 36°42N 95°38W 84 C7
Nowbarān Iran 35°8N 49°42E 47 C6
Nowghāb Iran 33°53N 59°4E 47 C8
Nowgong = Nagaon
  India 26°20N 92°50E 41 F18
Nowgong India 25°4N 79°27E 43 G8
Nowra Australia 34°53S 150°35E 63 E5
Nowrangapur India 19°14N 82°33E 44 E6
Nowshera Pakistan 34°0N 72°0E 40 C8
Nowy Sącz Poland 49°40N 20°41E 17 D11
Nowy Targ Poland 49°29N 20°2E 17 D11
Nowy Tomyśl Poland 52°19N 16°10E 16 B9
Noxen U.S.A. 41°25N 76°4W 83 E8
Noyabr'sk Russia 64°34N 76°21E 26 C8
Noyon France 49°34N 2°59E 20 B5
Noyon Mongolia 43°2N 102°4E 32 C2
Nqutu S. Africa 28°13S 30°32E 57 C5
Nsanje Malawi 16°55S 35°12E 55 H7
Nsawam Ghana 5°50N 0°24W 52 G5
Ntaria ◎ Australia 24°0S 132°41E 60 D5
Nu Jiang → China 29°58N 97°25E 34 C2
Nu Shan China 26°0N 99°20E 34 E2
Nuba Mts. = Nubah, Jibalan
  Sudan 12°0N 31°0E 53 F12
Nubah, Jibalan Sudan 12°0N 31°0E 53 F12
Nubia Africa 21°0N 32°0E 50 D7
Nubian Desert = Nûbîya, Es Sahrâ
  en Sudan 21°30N 33°30E 53 D12
Nûbîya, Es Sahrâ en
  Sudan 21°30N 33°30E 53 D12
Nuboai Indonesia 2°10S 136°30E 37 E9
Nubra → India 34°35N 77°35E 43 B7
Nueltin L. Canada 60°30N 99°30W 71 A9
Nuestra Señora del Rosario de
  Caá-Catí Argentina 27°45S 57°36W 94 B4
Nueva Ciudad Guerrero
  Mexico 26°34N 99°12W 87 B5
Nueva Gerona Cuba 21°53N 82°49W 88 B3
Nueva Palmira Uruguay 33°52S 58°20W 94 C4
Nueva Rosita Mexico 27°57N 101°13W 86 B4
Nueva San Salvador
  El Salv. 13°40N 89°18W 88 D2
Nuéve de Julio Argentina 35°30S 61°0W 94 D3
Nuevitas Cuba 21°30N 77°20W 88 B4
Nuevo, G. Argentina 43°0S 64°30W 96 E4
Nuevo Casas Grandes
  Mexico 30°25N 107°55W 86 A3
Nuevo Laredo Mexico 27°30N 99°31W 87 B5
Nuevo León □ Mexico 25°20N 100°0W 86 C5
Nuevo Rocafuerte
  Ecuador 0°55S 75°27W 92 D3
Nugget Pt. N.Z. 46°27S 169°50E 59 G2
Nuhaka N.Z. 39°3S 177°45E 59 C6
Nukey Bluff Australia 32°26S 135°29E 63 E2
Nukhayb Iraq 32°4N 42°3E 46 C4
Nuku Hiva
  French Polynesia 8°54S 140°6W 65 H13
Nuku'alofa Tonga 21°10S 175°12W 59 c
Nukus Uzbekistan 42°27N 59°41E 26 E6
Nulato U.S.A. 64°43N 158°6W 74 C8
Nullagine Australia 21°53S 120°7E 60 D3
Nullagine → Australia 21°20S 120°20E 60 D3
Nullarbor Australia 31°28S 130°55E 61 F5
Nullarbor △ Australia 32°39S 130°0E 61 F2
Nullarbor Plain Australia 31°10S 129°0E 61 F4
Numalla, L. Australia 28°43S 144°20E 63 D3
Numan Nigeria 9°29N 12°3E 53 G8
Numata Japan 36°45N 139°4E 29 F9
Numaykoos Lake △
  Canada 57°52N 95°58W 71 B9
Numazu Japan 35°7N 138°51E 29 G9
Numbulwar Australia 14°15S 135°45E 62 A2
Numfoor Indonesia 1°0S 134°50E 37 E8
Numurkah Australia 36°5S 145°26E 63 F4
Nunaksaluk I. Canada 55°49N 60°20W 73 A7
Nunap Isua Greenland 59°48N 43°55W 66 D15
Nunatsiavut Canada 55°50N 62°0W 73 A7
Nunavik Greenland 71°50N 54°25W 69 C21
Nunavut □ Canada 66°0N 85°0W 69 D15
Nunda U.S.A. 42°35N 77°56W 82 D7
Nuneaton U.K. 52°32N 1°27W 13 E6
Nungarin Australia 31°12S 118°6E 61 F2
Nunivak I. U.S.A. 60°10N 166°30W 74 C6
Nunkun India 33°57N 76°2E 43 C7
Núoro Italy 40°20N 9°20E 22 D3
Nuozhadu Dam China 22°39N 100°25E 34 F3
Nur Iran 36°33N 52°1E 47 B7
Nûrābād Hormozgān, Iran 27°47N 57°12E 47 E8
Nûrābād Lorestān, Iran 34°4N 47°58E 46 C5
Nuremberg = Nürnberg
  Germany 49°27N 11°3E 16 D6
Nuri Mexico 28°5N 109°22W 86 B3
Nuriootpa Australia 34°27S 139°0E 63 E2
Nuristān □ Afghan. 35°20N 71°0E 40 B7
Nurmes Finland 63°33N 29°10E 8 E23
Nürnberg Germany 49°27N 11°3E 16 D6
Nurpur Pakistan 31°53N 71°54E 42 D4
Nurran, L. = Terewah, L.
  Australia 29°52S 147°35E 63 D4
Nurrari Lakes Australia 29°1S 130°5E 61 E5
Nusa Dua Indonesia 8°48S 115°14E 37 K18
Nusa Tenggara Barat □
  Indonesia 8°50S 117°30E 36 F5
Nusa Tenggara Timur □
  Indonesia 9°30S 122°0E 37 F6
Nusaybin Turkey 37°3N 41°10E 19 G7
Nuşeirat Gaza Strip 31°27N 34°24E 48 D3
Nushki Pakistan 29°35N 66°0E 42 E2
Nuuk Greenland 64°10N 51°35W 67 C14
Nuupere, Pte. Moorea 17°36S 149°47W 59 d

Nuwakot Nepal 28°10N 83°55E 43 E10
Nuwara Eliya Sri Lanka 6°58N 80°48E 45 L5
Nuwaybi', W. an →
  Si. Arabia 29°18N 34°57E 48 F3
Nuweiba' Egypt 28°59N 34°39E 46 D2
Nuwerus S. Africa 31°8S 18°24E 56 E2
Nuweveldberge S. Africa 32°10S 21°45E 56 D3
Nuyts, Pt. Australia 35°4S 116°38E 61 G2
Nuyts Arch. Australia 32°35S 133°20E 63 E1
Nxai Pan △ Botswana 19°50S 24°46E 56 A3
Nxaunxau Botswana 18°57S 21°4E 56 A3
Nyabing Australia 33°33S 118°9E 61 F2
Nyack U.S.A. 41°5N 73°55W 83 E11
Nyagan Russia 62°30N 65°38E 26 C7
Nyahururu Kenya 0°2N 36°27E 54 D7
Nyaingêntanglha Shan
  China 30°0N 90°0E 30 F7
Nyâlâ Sudan 12°2N 24°58E 53 F10
Nyalam China 28°32N 86°4E 30 F6
Nyandoma Russia 61°40N 40°12E 18 B7
Nyangana Namibia 18°0S 20°40E 56 A3
Nyasa, L. = Malawi, L.
  Africa 12°30S 34°30E 55 G6
Nyasvizh Belarus 53°14N 26°38E 17 B14
Nyaungdon = Yandoon
  Burma 17°0N 95°40E 41 L19
Nyazepetrovsk Russia 56°3N 59°36E 18 C10
Nybro Sweden 56°44N 15°55E 9 H16
Nyda Russia 66°40N 72°58E 26 C8
Nyeboe Land Greenland 82°0N 57°0W 69 A20
Nyingchi China 29°32N 94°25E 30 F7
Nyíregyháza Hungary 47°58N 21°47E 17 E11
Nykarleby = Uusikaarlepyy
  Finland 63°32N 22°31E 8 E20
Nykøbing Nordjylland,
  Denmark 56°48N 8°51E 9 H13
Nykøbing Sjælland,
  Denmark 54°56N 11°52E 9 J14
Nykøbing Sjælland,
  Denmark 55°55N 11°40E 9 J14
Nyköping Sweden 58°45N 17°1E 9 G17
Nylstroom = Modimolle
  S. Africa 24°42S 28°22E 57 B4
Nymagee Australia 32°7S 146°20E 63 E4
Nymboida → Australia 29°39S 152°7E 63 D5
Nynäshamn Sweden 58°54N 17°57E 9 G17
Nyngan Australia 31°30S 147°8E 63 E4
Nyoma Rap India 33°10N 78°40E 43 C8
Nyoman = Nemunas →
  Lithuania 55°25N 21°10E 9 J19
Nysa Poland 50°30N 17°22E 17 C9
Nysa → Europe 52°4N 14°46E 16 B8
Nyslott = Savonlinna
  Finland 61°52N 28°53E 8 F23
Nyssa U.S.A. 43°53N 117°0W 76 E5
Nystad = Uusikaupunki
  Finland 60°47N 21°25E 8 F19
Nyunzu
  Dem. Rep. of the Congo 5°57S 27°58E 54 F5
Nyurba Russia 63°17N 118°28E 27 C12
Nzega Tanzania 4°10S 33°12E 54 E6
Nzérékoré Guinea 7°49N 8°48W 52 G4
Nzeto Angola 7°10S 12°52E 54 F2
Nzwani = Anjouan
  Comoros Is. 12°15S 44°20E 55 a

O

O Le Pupū Puʻe △ Samoa 13°59S 171°43W 59 b
Ō-Shima Hokkaidō, Japan 41°30N 139°22E 28 D9
Ō-Shima Shizuoka, Japan 34°44N 139°24E 29 G9
O.R. Tambo Int. ✈ (JNB)
  S. Africa 26°8S 28°15E 57 C4
Oa, Mull of U.K. 55°35N 6°20W 11 F2
Oacoma U.S.A. 43°48N 99°24W 80 D4
Oahe, L. U.S.A. 44°27N 100°24W 80 C3
Oahe Dam U.S.A. 44°27N 100°24W 80 C3
Oʻahu U.S.A. 21°28N 157°58W 75 L8
Oak Harbor U.S.A. 48°18N 122°39W 78 B4
Oak Hill U.S.A. 37°59N 81°9W 81 G13
Oak Island U.S.A. 33°55N 78°10W 85 E15
Oak Ridge U.S.A. 36°1N 84°16W 85 D12
Oak View U.S.A. 34°24N 119°18W 79 L7
Oakan-Dake Japan 43°27N 144°10E 28 C12
Oakdale Calif., U.S.A. 37°46N 120°51W 78 H6
Oakdale La., U.S.A. 30°49N 92°40W 84 F8
Oakes U.S.A. 46°8N 98°6W 80 B4
Oakesdale U.S.A. 47°8N 117°15W 76 C5
Oakey Australia 27°25S 151°43E 63 D5
Oakfield U.S.A. 43°4N 78°16W 82 C6
Oakham U.K. 52°40N 0°43W 13 E7
Oakhurst U.S.A. 37°19N 119°40W 78 H7
Oakland U.S.A. 37°48N 122°16W 78 H4
Oakley Idaho, U.S.A. 42°15N 113°53W 76 E7
Oakley Kans., U.S.A. 39°8N 100°51W 80 F3
Oakover → Australia 21°0S 120°40E 60 D3
Oakridge U.S.A. 43°45N 122°28W 76 E2
Oakville Canada 43°27N 79°41W 82 C5
Oakville U.S.A. 46°51N 123°14W 78 D3
Oamaru N.Z. 45°5S 170°59E 59 F3
Oasis Calif., U.S.A. 37°29N 117°55W 78 H9
Oasis Calif., U.S.A. 33°28N 116°6W 79 M10
Oates Land Antarctica 69°0S 160°0E 5 C11
Oatman U.S.A. 35°1N 114°19W 79 K12
Oaxaca Mexico 17°3N 96°43W 87 D5
Oaxaca □ Mexico 17°0N 96°30W 87 D5
Ob → Russia 66°45N 69°30E 26 C7
Oba Canada 49°4N 84°7W 72 C3
Obama Japan 35°30N 135°45E 29 G7
Oban U.K. 56°25N 5°29W 11 E3
Obbia = Hobyo Somalia 5°25N 48°30E 49 F4
Oberá Argentina 27°21S 55°2W 95 B4
Oberhausen Germany 51°28N 6°51E 16 C4
Oberlin Kans., U.S.A. 39°49N 100°32W 80 F3
Oberlin La., U.S.A. 30°37N 92°46W 84 F8
Oberlin Ohio, U.S.A. 41°18N 82°13W 82 E2
Oberon Australia 33°45S 149°52E 63 E4
Obi, Kepulauan Indonesia 1°23S 127°45E 37 E7
Óbidos Brazil 1°50S 55°30W 93 D7
Obihiro Japan 42°56N 143°12E 28 C11

Obilatu Indonesia 1°25S 127°20E 37 E7
Obluchye Russia 49°1N 131°4E 27 E14
Obo C.A.R. 5°20N 26°32E 54 C5
Oboyan Russia 51°15N 36°21E 26 D4
Obozerskaya = Obozerskiy
  Russia 63°34N 40°21E 18 B7
Obozerskiy Russia 63°34N 40°21E 18 B7
Observatory Inlet
  Canada 55°10N 129°54W 70 B3
Obshchi Syrt Russia 52°0N 53°0E 6 E16
Obskaya Guba Russia 69°0N 73°0E 26 C8
Obuasi Ghana 6°17N 1°40W 52 G5
Ocala U.S.A. 29°11N 82°8W 85 G13
Ocampo Chihuahua,
  Mexico 28°11N 108°23W 86 B3
Ocampo Tamaulipas,
  Mexico 22°50N 99°20W 87 C5
Ocaña Spain 39°55N 3°30W 21 C4
Occidental, Cordillera
  Colombia 5°0N 76°0W 92 C3
Occidental, Grand Erg
  Algeria 30°20N 1°0E 52 B6
Ocean City Md., U.S.A. 38°20N 75°5W 81 F16
Ocean City N.J., U.S.A. 39°17N 74°35W 81 F16
Ocean City Wash., U.S.A. 47°4N 124°10W 78 C2
Ocean Falls Canada 52°18N 127°48W 70 C3
Ocean I. = Banaba
  Kiribati 0°45S 169°50E 64 H8
Ocean Park U.S.A. 46°30N 124°3W 78 D2
Oceano U.S.A. 35°6N 120°37W 79 K6
Oceanport U.S.A. 40°19N 74°3W 83 F10
Oceanside U.S.A. 33°12N 117°23W 79 M9
Ochil Hills U.K. 56°14N 3°40W 11 E5
Ocho Rios Jamaica 18°24N 77°6W 88 a
Ocilla U.S.A. 31°36N 83°15W 85 F13
Ocmulgee → U.S.A. 31°58N 82°33W 85 F13
Ocniţa Moldova 48°25N 27°30E 17 D14
Oconee → U.S.A. 31°58N 82°33W 85 F13
Oconomowoc U.S.A. 43°7N 88°30W 80 D9
Oconto U.S.A. 44°53N 87°52W 80 C10
Oconto Falls U.S.A. 44°52N 88°9W 80 C9
Ocosingo Mexico 16°53N 92°15W 87 D6
Ocotal Nic. 13°41N 86°31W 88 D2
Ocotlán Jalisco, Mexico 20°21N 102°46W 86 C4
Ocotlán Oaxaca, Mexico 16°48N 96°40W 87 D5
Ōda Japan 35°11N 132°30E 29 G6
Ódáðahraun Iceland 65°5N 17°0W 8 D5
Ōdaejin N. Korea 41°34N 129°40E 28 D2
Odate Japan 40°16N 140°34E 28 D10
Odawara Japan 35°20N 139°6E 29 G9
Odda Norway 60°3N 6°35E 9 F12
Odei → Canada 56°6N 96°54W 71 B9
Ödemiş Turkey 38°15N 28°0E 23 E13
Odendaalsrus S. Africa 27°48S 26°45E 56 C4
Odense Denmark 55°22N 10°23E 9 J14
Oder → Europe 53°33N 14°38E 16 B8
Odesa Ukraine 46°30N 30°45E 19 E5
Odessa = Odesa Ukraine 46°30N 30°45E 19 E5
Odessa Canada 44°17N 76°43W 83 B8
Odessa Tex., U.S.A. 31°52N 102°23W 84 F3
Odessa Wash., U.S.A. 47°20N 118°41W 76 C4
Odiakwe Botswana 20°12S 25°17E 56 A4
Odienné Ivory C. 9°30N 7°34W 52 G4
Odintsovo Russia 55°40N 37°16E 18 C6
Odisha □ India 20°0N 84°0E 44 E7
O'Donnell U.S.A. 32°58N 101°50W 84 E4
O'Donnell Pt. Canada 45°5N 80°5W 82 A4
Odorheiu Secuiesc
  Romania 46°21N 25°21E 17 E13
Odra = Oder → Europe 53°33N 14°38E 16 B8
Odzi Zimbabwe 19°0S 32°20E 57 B5
Odzi → Zimbabwe 19°45S 32°23E 57 B5
Oecussi = Pante Macassar
  E. Timor 9°30S 123°58E 37 F6
Oeiras Brazil 7°0S 42°8W 93 E10
Oelrichs U.S.A. 43°11N 103°14W 80 D2
Oelwein U.S.A. 42°41N 91°55W 80 D8
Oeno I. Pac. Oc. 24°0S 131°0W 65 K14
Oenpelli = Gunbalanya
  Australia 12°20S 133°4E 60 B5
Ofanto → Italy 41°22N 16°13E 22 D7
Offa Nigeria 8°13N 4°42E 52 G6
Offaly □ Ireland 53°15N 7°30W 10 C4
Offenbach Germany 50°6N 8°44E 16 C5
Offenburg Germany 48°28N 7°56E 16 D4
Officer Cr. → Australia 27°46S 132°30E 61 E5
Ofolanga Tonga 19°38S 174°27W 59 c
Ofotfjorden Norway 68°27N 17°0E 8 B17
Ofu Amer. Samoa 14°11S 169°41W 59 b
Oga Japan 39°55N 139°50E 28 E9
Oga-Hantō Japan 39°58N 139°47E 28 E9
Ogaden Ethiopia 7°30N 45°30E 49 F3
Ōgaki Japan 35°21N 136°37E 29 G8
Ogallala U.S.A. 41°8N 101°43W 80 E3
Ogasawara Gunto Pac. Oc. 27°0N 142°0E 64 E6
Ogbomosho Nigeria 8°1N 4°11E 52 G6
Ogden U.S.A. 41°13N 111°58W 76 F8
Ogdensburg U.S.A. 44°42N 75°30W 83 B9
Ogea Driki Fiji 19°12S 178°27W 59 a
Ogea Levu Fiji 19°8S 178°24W 59 a
Ogeechee → U.S.A. 31°50N 81°3W 85 F14
Ogilby U.S.A. 32°49N 114°50W 79 N12
Òglio → Italy 45°2N 10°39E 22 B4
Ogmore Australia 22°37S 149°35E 62 C4
Ogoki Canada 51°38N 85°58W 72 B2
Ogoki → Canada 51°38N 85°57W 72 B2
Ogoki L. Canada 50°50N 87°10W 72 B2
Ogoki Res. Canada 50°45N 88°15W 72 B2
Ogooué → Gabon 1°0S 9°0E 54 E1
Ogowe = Ogooué → Gabon 1°0S 9°0E 54 E1
Ogre Latvia 56°49N 24°36E 9 H21
Ogurja Ada Turkmenistan 38°55N 53°2E 47 B7
Ohai N.Z. 45°55S 168°0E 59 F1
Ohakune N.Z. 39°24S 175°24E 59 C5
Ohangwena □ Namibia 17°25S 16°50E 56 B2
Ohata Japan 41°24N 141°10E 28 D10
Ohau, L. N.Z. 44°15S 169°53E 59 F2
Ohio □ U.S.A. 40°15N 82°45W 82 F2
Ohio → U.S.A. 36°59N 89°8W 80 G9

Ohře → Czech Rep. 50°30N 14°10E 16 C8
Ohrid Macedonia 41°8N 20°52E 23 D9
Ohridsko Jezero Macedonia 41°8N 20°52E 23 D9
Ohrigstad S. Africa 24°39S 30°36E 57 B5
Oi Qu → China 28°57N 98°16E 34 C1
Oil City U.S.A. 41°26N 79°42W 82 E5
Oil Springs Canada 42°47N 82°7W 82 D2
Oildale U.S.A. 35°25N 119°1W 79 K7
Oise → France 49°0N 2°4E 20 B5
Oistins Barbados 13°4N 59°33W 89 g
Oistins B. Barbados 13°4N 59°33W 89 g
Ōita Japan 33°14N 131°36E 29 H5
Ōita □ Japan 33°15N 131°30E 29 H5
Oiticica Brazil 5°3S 41°5W 93 E10
Ojai U.S.A. 34°27N 119°15W 79 L7
Ojhar India 20°6N 73°48E 44 D1
Ojinaga Mexico 29°34N 104°25W 86 B4
Ojiya Japan 37°18N 138°48E 29 F9
Ojo Caliente Mexico 22°34N 102°15W 86 C4
Ojo de Liebre, L. Mexico 27°45N 114°15W 86 B2
Ojos del Salado, Cerro
  Argentina 27°0S 68°40W 94 B2
Oka → Russia 56°20N 43°59E 18 C7
Okaba Indonesia 8°6S 139°42E 37 F9
Okahandja Namibia 22°0S 16°59E 56 B2
Okakarara Namibia 20°35S 17°27E 56 B2
Okanagan L. Canada 50°0N 119°30W 70 D5
Okandja Gabon 0°35S 13°45E 54 E2
Okanogan → U.S.A. 48°22N 119°35W 76 B4
Okanogan → U.S.A. 48°6N 119°44W 76 B4
Okanogan Range
  N. Amer. 49°0N 119°55W 70 D5
Okaputa Namibia 20°5S 17°0E 56 B2
Okara Pakistan 30°50N 73°31E 42 D5
Okarukambe = Steinhausen
  Namibia 21°49S 18°20E 56 B2
Okaukuejo Namibia 19°10S 16°0E 56 B2
Okavango = Cubango →
  Africa 18°50S 22°25E 56 A3
Okavango Delta
  Botswana 18°45S 22°45E 56 A3
Okavango Swamp = Okavango
  Delta Botswana 18°45S 22°45E 56 A3
Okaya Japan 36°5N 138°10E 29 F9
Okayama Japan 34°40N 133°54E 29 G6
Okayama □ Japan 35°0N 133°50E 29 G6
Okazaki Japan 34°57N 137°10E 29 G8
Okeechobee U.S.A. 27°15N 80°50W 85 H14
Okeechobee, L. U.S.A. 27°0N 80°50W 85 H14
Okefenokee △ U.S.A. 30°45N 82°18W 85 F13
Okefenokee Swamp
  U.S.A. 30°40N 82°20W 85 F13
Okehampton U.K. 50°44N 4°0W 13 G4
Okha India 22°27N 69°4E 42 H3
Okha Russia 53°40N 143°0E 27 D15
Okhotsk Russia 59°20N 143°10E 27 D15
Okhotsk, Sea of Asia 55°0N 145°0E 27 D15
Okhotskiy Perevoz
  Russia 61°52N 135°35E 27 C14
Okhtyrka Ukraine 50°25N 35°0E 19 D5
Oki-Shotō Japan 36°5N 133°15E 29 F5
Okiep S. Africa 29°39S 17°53E 56 D2
Okinawa Japan 26°19N 127°46E 29 L3
Okinawa □ Japan 26°40N 128°0E 29 L4
Okinawa-Guntō Japan 26°40N 128°0E 29 L4
Okinawa-Jima Japan 26°32N 128°0E 29 L4
Okino-erabu-Shima
  Japan 27°21N 128°33E 29 L4
Oklahoma □ U.S.A. 35°20N 97°30W 84 D6
Oklahoma City U.S.A. 35°30N 97°30W 84 D6
Okmulgee U.S.A. 35°37N 95°58W 84 D7
Oknitsa = Ocniţa
  Moldova 48°25N 27°30E 17 D14
Okolona U.S.A. 34°0N 88°45W 85 E10
Okombahe Namibia 21°23S 15°22E 56 B2
Okotoks Canada 50°43N 113°58W 70 C6
Oksovskiy Russia 62°33N 39°57E 18 B6
Oktyabrsk = Qandyaghash
  Kazakhstan 49°28N 57°25E 19 E10
Oktyabrskiy = Aktsyabrski
  Belarus 52°38N 28°53E 17 B15
Oktyabrskiy Bashkortostan,
  Russia 54°28N 53°28E 18 D9
Oktyabrskiy Kamchatka,
  Russia 52°39N 156°14E 27 D16
Oktyabrskoy Revolyutsii, Ostrov
  Russia 79°30N 97°0E 27 B10
Okuru N.Z. 43°55S 168°55E 59 F1
Okushiri-Tō Japan 42°15N 139°30E 28 C9
Okwa → Botswana 22°30S 23°0E 56 B3
Ola Russia 59°35N 151°17E 27 D16
Ola U.S.A. 35°2N 93°13W 84 D8
Ólafsfjörður Iceland 66°4N 18°39W 8 C4
Ólafsvík Iceland 64°53N 23°43W 8 D2
Olancha U.S.A. 36°17N 118°1W 79 J8
Olancha Pk. U.S.A. 36°16N 118°7W 79 J8
Olanchito Honduras 15°30N 86°30W 88 C2
Öland Sweden 56°45N 16°38E 9 H17
Olary Australia 32°18S 140°19E 63 E3
Olascoaga Argentina 35°15S 60°39W 94 D3
Olavarría Argentina 36°55S 60°20W 94 D3
Oława Poland 50°57N 17°20E 17 C9
Ólbia Italy 40°55N 9°31E 22 D3
Olcott U.S.A. 43°20N 78°42W 82 C6
Old Bahama Chan. = Bahama,
  Canal Viejo de
  W. Indies 22°10N 77°30W 88 B4
Old Baldy Pk. = San Antonio, Mt.
  U.S.A. 34°17N 117°38W 79 L9
Old Bridge U.S.A. 40°25N 74°22W 83 F10
Old Castile = Castilla y León □
  Spain 42°0N 5°0W 21 B3
Old Crow Canada 67°30N 139°55W 68 D4
Old Dale U.S.A. 34°8N 115°47W 79 L11
Old Forge N.Y., U.S.A. 43°43N 74°58W 83 C10
Old Forge Pa., U.S.A. 41°22N 75°45W 83 E9
Old Mapoon ◎ Australia 11°5S 142°22E 62 A3

Old Perlican *Canada* 48°5N 53°1W **73** C9
Old Speck Mt. *U.S.A.* 44°34N 70°57W **83** B14
Old Town *U.S.A.* 44°56N 68°39W **81** C19
Old Washington *U.S.A.* 40°2N 81°27W **82** F3
Oldbury *U.K.* 51°38N 2°33W **13** F5
Oldcastle *Ireland* 53°46N 7°10W **12** D5
Oldenburg *Germany* 53°9N 8°13E **16** B5
Oldenzaal *Neths.* 52°19N 6°53E **15** B6
Oldham *U.K.* 53°33N 2°7W **12** D5
Oldman → *Canada* 49°57N 111°42W **70** D6
Oldmeldrum *U.K.* 57°20N 2°19W **11** D6
Olds *Canada* 51°50N 114°10W **70** C6
Olean *U.S.A.* 42°5N 78°26W **82** D6
Olekma → *Russia* 60°22N 120°42E **27** C13
Olekminsk *Russia* 60°25N 120°30E **27** C13
Oleksandriya *Ukraine* 50°37N 26°19E **17** C14
Olema *U.S.A.* 38°3N 122°47W **78** G4
Olenegorsk *Russia* 68°9N 33°18E **8** B25
Olenek *Russia* 68°28N 112°18E **27** C12
Olenek → *Russia* 73°0N 120°10E **27** B13
Oléron, Î. d' *France* 45°55N 1°15W **20** D3
Olesnica *Poland* 51°13N 17°22E **17** C9
Olesvk *Ukraine* 51°12N 27°39E **17** C14
Olga, L. *Canada* 49°47N 77°15W **72** C4
Olgas, The = Kata Tjuta
   Australia 25°20S 130°50E **61** E5
Ölgiy *Mongolia* 48°56N 89°57E **30** B6
Olhão *Portugal* 37°3N 7°48W **21** D2
Olifants = Elefantes →
   Africa 24°10S 32°40E **57** B5
Olifants → *Namibia* 25°30S 19°30E **56** B2
Olifantshoek *S. Africa* 27°57S 22°42E **56** C3
Ólimbos, Óros = Olympos Oros
   Greece 40°6N 22°23E **23** D10
Olímpia *Brazil* 20°44S 48°54W **95** A6
Olinda *Brazil* 8°1S 34°51W **93** E12
Oliva *Argentina* 32°0S 63°38W **94** C3
Olivares, Cerro los
   Argentina 30°18S 69°55W **94** C2
Olive Branch *U.S.A.* 34°57N 89°49W **85** D10
Olivehurst *U.S.A.* 39°6N 121°34W **78** F5
Olivenza *Spain* 38°41N 7°9W **21** C2
Oliver *Canada* 49°13N 119°37W **70** D5
Oliver L. *Canada* 56°56N 103°22W **71** B8
Ollagüe *Chile* 21°15S 68°10W **94** A2
Olmaliq *Uzbekistan* 40°50N 69°35E **26** E7
Olney *Ill., U.S.A.* 38°44N 88°5W **80** F9
Olney *Tex., U.S.A.* 33°22N 98°45W **84** E5
Olomane → *Canada* 50°14N 60°37W **73** B7
Olomouc *Czech Rep.* 49°38N 17°12E **17** D9
Olonets *Russia* 61°0N 32°54E **18** B5
Olongapo *Phil.* 14°50N 120°18E **37** B6
Olosega *Amer. Samoa* 14°10S 169°37W **59** b
Olosenga = Swains I.
   Amer. Samoa 11°11S 171°4W **65** J11
Olot *Spain* 42°11N 2°30E **21** A7
Olovyannaya *Russia* 50°58N 115°35E **27** D12
Oloy → *Russia* 66°29N 159°29E **27** C16
Olsztyn *Poland* 53°48N 20°29E **17** B11
Olt → *Romania* 43°43N 24°51E **17** G13
Oltenita *Romania* 44°7N 26°42E **17** F14
Olton *U.S.A.* 34°11N 102°8W **84** D3
Oluan Pi *Taiwan* 21°53N 120°51E **35** G13
Olymbos Oros *Greece* 40°6N 22°23E **23** D10
Olympia *Greece* 37°39N 21°39E **23** F9
Olympia *U.S.A.* 47°3N 122°53W **78** C4
Olympic △ *U.S.A.* 47°45N 123°43W **78** C3
Olympic Dam *Australia* 30°30S 136°55E **63** E2
Olympic Mts. *U.S.A.* 47°55N 123°45W **78** C3
Olympus *Cyprus* 34°56N 32°52E **46** C2
Olympus, Mt. = Olymbos Oros
   Greece 40°6N 22°23E **23** D10
Olympus, Mt. = Uludağ
   Turkey 40°4N 29°13E **23** D13
Olympus, Mt. *U.S.A.* 47°48N 123°43W **78** C3
Olyphant *U.S.A.* 41°27N 75°36W **83** E9
Olyutorskiy, Mys
   Russia 59°55N 170°27E **27** D18
Om → *Russia* 54°59N 73°22E **26** D8
Om Koi *Thailand* 17°48N 98°22E **38** D2
Ōma *Japan* 41°45N 141°5E **28** D10
Ōmachi *Japan* 36°30N 137°50E **29** F8
Omae-Zaki *Japan* 34°36N 138°14E **29** G9
Ōmagari = Daisen
   Japan 39°27N 140°29E **28** E10
Omagh *U.K.* 54°36N 7°19W **10** B4
Omagh □ *U.K.* 54°35N 7°15W **10** B4
Omaha *U.S.A.* 41°17N 95°58W **80** E6
Omaheke □ *Namibia* 21°30S 19°0E **56** B2
Omak *U.S.A.* 48°25N 119°31W **76** B4
Omalur *India* 11°44N 78°4E **45** J4
Oman ■ *Asia* 23°0N 58°0E **49** C6
Oman, G. of *Asia* 24°30N 58°30E **47** E8
Omaruru *Namibia* 21°26S 16°0E **56** B2
Omaruru → *Namibia* 22°7S 14°15E **56** B1
Omate *Peru* 16°45S 71°0W **92** G4
Ombai, Selat *Indonesia* 8°30S 124°50E **37** F6
Omboué *Gabon* 1°35S 9°15E **54** E1
Ombrone → *Italy* 42°42N 11°5E **22** C4
Omdurmân *Sudan* 15°40N 32°28E **53** E12
Omemee *Canada* 44°18N 78°33W **82** B6
Ometepe, I. de *Nic.* 11°32N 85°35W **88** D2
Ometepec *Mexico* 16°41N 98°25W **87** D5
Ominato *Japan* 41°17N 141°10E **28** D10
Omineca → *Canada* 56°3N 124°16W **70** B4
Omineca Mts. *Canada* 56°30N 125°30W **70** B3
Omitara *Namibia* 22°16S 18°2E **56** B2
Ōmiya = Saitama *Japan* 35°54N 139°38E **29** G9
Ommen *Neths.* 52°31N 6°26E **15** B6
Omnögovi □ *Mongolia* 43°15N 104°0E **32** C3
Omo → *Ethiopia* 6°25N 36°10E **49** F2
Omolon → *Russia* 68°42N 158°36E **27** C16
Omono-Gawa → *Japan* 39°46N 140°3E **28** E10
Ompha *Canada* 45°0N 76°50W **83** B8
Omsk *Russia* 55°0N 73°12E **26** D8
Omsukchan *Russia* 62°32N 155°48E **27** C16
Omu *Japan* 44°34N 142°58E **28** B11
Ōmul, Vf. *Romania* 45°27N 25°29E **17** F13

Ōmura *Japan* 32°56N 129°57E **29** H4
Omuramba Omatako →
   Namibia 17°45S 20°25E **56** A2
Omuramba Ovambo →
   Namibia 18°45S 16°59E **56** A2
Omusati □ *Namibia* 18°30S 15°0E **56** A1
Ōmuta *Japan* 33°5N 130°26E **29** H5
Omuthiya *Namibia* 17°43S 16°13E **56** A2
Onaga *U.S.A.* 39°29N 96°10W **80** F5
Onalaska *U.S.A.* 43°53N 91°14W **80** D8
Onancock *U.S.A.* 37°43N 75°45W **81** G16
Onangue, L. *Gabon* 0°57S 10°4E **54** E2
Onaping L. *Canada* 47°3N 81°30W **72** C3
Onavas *Mexico* 28°31N 109°35W **86** B3
Onawa *U.S.A.* 42°2N 96°6W **80** D5
Oncócua *Angola* 16°30S 13°25E **56** A1
Onda *Spain* 39°55N 0°17W **21** C5
Ondangwa *Namibia* 17°57S 16°4E **56** A2
Ondjiva *Angola* 16°48S 15°50E **56** A2
Öndörhaan *Mongolia* 47°19N 110°39E **31** B11
Öndverðarnes *Iceland* 64°52N 24°0W **8** D2
One Arm Point *Australia* 16°26S 123°3E **60** C3
One Arm Point ◇
   Australia 16°31S 122°53E **60** C3
One Tree *Australia* 34°11S 144°43E **63** E3
Oneata *Fiji* 18°26S 178°25W **59** a
Onega *Russia* 64°0N 38°10E **18** B6
Onega → *Russia* 63°58N 38°2E **18** B6
Onega, G. of = Onezhskaya Guba
   Russia 64°24N 36°38E **18** B6
Onega, L. = Onezhskoye Ozero
   Russia 61°44N 35°22E **18** B6
Oneida *U.S.A.* 43°6N 75°39W **83** C9
Oneida L. *U.S.A.* 43°12N 75°54W **83** C9
O'Neill *U.S.A.* 42°27N 98°39W **80** D4
Onekotan, Ostrov
   Russia 49°25N 154°45E **27** E16
Oneonta *U.S.A.* 42°27N 75°4W **83** D9
Onesti *Romania* 46°17N 26°47E **17** E14
Onezhskaya Guba *Russia* 64°24N 36°38E **18** B6
Onezhskoye Ozero *Russia* 61°44N 35°22E **18** B6
Ongarue *N.Z.* 38°42S 175°19E **59** C5
Ongea Levu = Ogea Levu
   Fiji 19°8S 178°24W **59** a
Ongers → *S. Africa* 31°4S 23°13E **56** D3
Ongerup *Australia* 33°58S 118°28E **61** F2
Ongi *Mongolia* 45°27N 103°54E **32** B2
Ongkharak *Thailand* 14°8N 101°1E **38** E3
Ongniud Qi *China* 43°0N 118°38E **33** C10
Ongole *India* 15°33N 80°2E **45** G5
Ongon = Havirga
   Mongolia 45°41N 113°5E **32** B7
Ongwediva *Namibia* 17°47S 15°46E **56** A2
Onida *U.S.A.* 44°42N 100°4W **80** C3
Onilahy → *Madag.* 23°34S 43°45E **55** J8
Onitsha *Nigeria* 6°6N 6°42E **52** G7
Ono *Fiji* 18°55S 178°29E **59** a
Onoda *Japan* 33°59N 131°11E **29** G5
Onslow *Australia* 21°40S 115°12E **60** D2
Onslow B. *U.S.A.* 34°20N 77°15W **85** D16
Ontake-San *Japan* 35°53N 137°29E **29** G8
Ontario *Calif., U.S.A.* 34°4N 117°39W **79** L9
Ontario *Oreg., U.S.A.* 44°2N 116°58W **76** D5
Ontario □ *Canada* 48°0N 83°0W **72** B2
Ontario, L. *N. Amer.* 43°20N 78°0W **82** C7
Ontonagon *U.S.A.* 46°52N 89°19W **80** B9
Onyx *U.S.A.* 35°41N 118°14W **79** K8
Oodnadatta *Australia* 27°33S 135°30E **63** D2
Ooldea *Australia* 30°27S 131°50E **61** F5
Oombulgurri *Australia* 15°15S 127°45E **60** C4
Oombulgurri ◇
   Australia 15°10S 127°50E **60** C4
Oorindi *Australia* 20°40S 141°1E **62** C3
Oost-Vlaanderen □
   Belgium 51°5N 3°50E **15** C3
Oostende *Belgium* 51°15N 2°54E **15** C2
Oosterhout *Neths.* 51°39N 4°47E **15** C4
Oosterschelde → *Neths.* 51°33N 4°0E **15** C4
Oosterwolde *Neths.* 53°0N 6°17E **15** B6
Oostvaardersplassen ◇
   Neths. 52°27N 5°22E **15** B5
Ootacamund = Udagamandalam
   India 11°30N 76°44E **45** J3
Ootsa L. *Canada* 53°50N 126°2W **70** C3
Ooty = Udagamandalam
   India 11°30N 76°44E **45** J3
Op Luang △ *Thailand* 18°12N 98°32E **38** C2
Opala *Dem. Rep. of the Congo* 0°40S 24°20E **54** E4
Opanake *Sri Lanka* 6°35N 80°40E **45** L5
Opasatika *Canada* 49°30N 82°50W **72** C3
Opasquia *Canada* 53°33N 93°5W **72** B1
Opava *Czech Rep.* 49°57N 17°58E **17** D9
Opelika *U.S.A.* 32°39N 85°23W **85** E12
Opelousas *U.S.A.* 30°32N 92°5W **84** F8
Opémisca, L. *Canada* 49°56N 74°52W **72** C5
Opheim *U.S.A.* 48°51N 106°24W **76** B10
Ophthalmia Ra.
   Australia 23°15S 119°30E **60** D2
Opinaca → *Canada* 52°15N 78°2W **72** B4
Opinaca, Rés. *Canada* 52°39N 76°20W **72** B4
Opinnagau → *Canada* 54°12N 82°25W **72** B3
Opiscotéo, L. *Canada* 53°10N 68°10W **73** B6
Opobo *Nigeria* 4°35N 7°34E **52** H7
Opole *Poland* 50°42N 17°58E **17** C9
Oponono L. *Namibia* 18°8S 15°45E **56** A2
Oporto = Porto *Portugal* 41°8N 8°40W **21** B1
Opotiki *N.Z.* 38°1S 177°19E **59** C6
Opp *U.S.A.* 31°17N 86°16W **85** F11
Oppdal *Norway* 62°35N 9°41E **8** E13
Opportunity *U.S.A.* 47°39N 117°15W **76** C5
Opua *N.Z.* 35°19S 174°9E **59** A5
Opunake *N.Z.* 39°26S 173°52E **59** C4
Opuwo *Namibia* 18°3S 13°45E **56** A1
Oracle *U.S.A.* 32°37N 110°46W **77** K8
Oradea *Romania* 47°2N 21°58E **17** E11
Öræfajökull *Iceland* 64°2N 16°39E **8** D5
Orai *India* 25°58N 79°30E **43** G8
Oral = Zhayyq →
   Kazakhstan 47°0N 51°48E **19** E9

Oral *Kazakhstan* 51°20N 51°20E **19** D9
Oran *Algeria* 35°45N 0°39W **52** A5
Orange *Australia* 33°15S 149°7E **63** E4
Orange *France* 44°8N 4°47E **20** D6
Orange *Calif., U.S.A.* 33°47N 117°51W **79** M9
Orange *Mass., U.S.A.* 42°35N 72°19W **83** D12
Orange *Tex., U.S.A.* 30°6N 93°44W **84** F8
Orange *Va., U.S.A.* 38°15N 78°7W **81** F14
Orange → *S. Africa* 28°41S 16°28E **56** C2
Orange, C. *Brazil* 4°20N 51°30W **93** C8
Orange Cove *U.S.A.* 36°38N 119°19W **78** J7
Orange Free State = Free State □
   S. Africa 28°30S 27°0E **56** C4
Orange Grove *U.S.A.* 27°58N 97°56W **84** H6
Orange Walk *Belize* 18°6N 88°33W **87** D7
Orangeburg *U.S.A.* 33°30N 80°52W **85** E14
Orangeville *Canada* 43°55N 80°5W **82** C4
Orango *Guinea-Biss.* 11°5N 16°0W **52** F2
Oranienburg *Germany* 52°45N 13°14E **16** B7
Oranje = Orange →
   S. Africa 28°41S 16°28E **56** C2
Oranjemund *Namibia* 28°38S 16°29E **56** C2
Oranjerivier *S. Africa* 29°40S 24°12E **56** D3
Oranjestad *Aruba* 12°33N 70°2W **89** D5
Orapa *Botswana* 21°15S 25°30E **55** J5
Oras *Phil.* 12°9N 125°28E **37** B7
Orbetello *Italy* 42°27N 11°13E **22** C4
Orbisonia *U.S.A.* 40°15N 77°54W **82** F7
Orbost *Australia* 37°40S 148°29E **63** F4
Orcadas *Antarctica* 60°44S 44°37W **5** C18
Orcas I. *U.S.A.* 48°42N 122°56W **78** B4
Orchard City *U.S.A.* 38°50N 107°58W **76** G10
Orchard Homes *U.S.A.* 46°55N 114°4W **76** C6
Orchid I. = Lan Yü
   Taiwan 22°4N 121°25E **35** F13
Orchila, I. *Venezuela* 11°48N 66°10W **89** D6
Orcutt *U.S.A.* 34°52N 120°27W **79** L6
Ord *U.S.A.* 41°36N 98°56W **80** E4
Ord → *Australia* 15°33S 128°15E **60** C4
Ord, Mt. *Australia* 17°20S 125°34E **60** C4
Ord Mts. *U.S.A.* 34°39N 116°45W **79** L10
Orderville *U.S.A.* 37°17N 112°38W **77** H7
Ordos = Mu Us Shamo
   China 39°0N 109°0E **32** E5
Ordos *China* 39°50N 110°0E **32** E6
Ordu *Turkey* 40°55N 37°53E **19** F6
Ordway *U.S.A.* 38°13N 103°46W **76** G12
Ore Mts. = Erzgebirge
   Germany 50°27N 12°55E **16** C7
Örebro *Sweden* 59°20N 15°18E **9** G16
Oregon *U.S.A.* 42°1N 89°20W **80** D9
Oregon □ *U.S.A.* 44°0N 121°0W **76** E3
Oregon City *U.S.A.* 45°21N 122°36W **78** E4
Oregon Dunes △ *U.S.A.* 43°40N 124°10W **76** E1
Orekhovo-Zuyevo *Russia* 55°50N 38°55E **18** C6
Orel *Russia* 52°57N 36°3E **18** D6
Orem *U.S.A.* 40°19N 111°42W **76** F8
Ören *Turkey* 37°3N 27°57E **23** F12
Orenburg *Russia* 51°45N 55°6E **18** D10
Orense = Ourense *Spain* 42°19N 7°55W **21** A2
Orepuki *N.Z.* 46°19S 167°46E **59** G1
Orestes Pereyra *Mexico* 26°30N 105°39W **86** B3
Orestiada *Greece* 41°30N 26°33E **23** D12
Orfanos Kolpos *Greece* 40°33N 24°0E **23** D11
Orford Ness *U.K.* 52°5N 1°35E **13** E9
Organ Pipe Cactus △
   U.S.A. 32°0N 112°52W **77** K7
Orgaz *Spain* 39°39N 3°53W **21** C4
Orgeyev = Orhei
   Moldova 47°24N 28°50E **17** E15
Orhaneli *Turkey* 39°54N 28°59E **23** E13
Orhangazi *Turkey* 40°29N 29°18E **23** D13
Orhei *Moldova* 47°24N 28°50E **17** E15
Orhon Gol → *Mongolia* 50°21N 106°0E **30** A10
Oriental, Cordillera
   Colombia 6°0N 73°0W **92** B4
Oriental, Grand Erg *Algeria* 30°0N 6°30E **52** B7
Oriente *Argentina* 38°44S 60°37W **94** D3
Orihuela *Spain* 38°7N 0°55W **21** C5
Orillia *Canada* 44°40N 79°24W **82** B5
Orinoco → *Venezuela* 9°15N 61°30W **92** B6
Orion *Canada* 49°27N 110°49W **71** D6
Oriskany *U.S.A.* 43°10N 75°20W **83** C9
Orissa = Odisha □ *India* 20°0N 84°0E **44** E7
Orissaare *Estonia* 58°34N 23°5E **9** G20
Oristano *Italy* 39°54N 8°36E **22** E3
Oristano, G. di *Italy* 39°50N 8°29E **22** E3
Orizaba *Mexico* 18°51N 97°6W **87** D5
Orizaba, Pico de *Mexico* 18°58N 97°15W **87** D5
Orkanger *Norway* 63°18N 9°52E **8** E13
Orkhon = Orhon Gol →
   Mongolia 50°21N 106°0E **30** A10
Orkla → *Norway* 63°18N 9°51E **8** E13
Orkney *S. Africa* 26°58S 26°40E **56** C4
Orkney □ *U.K.* 59°2N 3°13W **11** B5
Orkney Is. *U.K.* 59°0N 3°0W **11** B6
Orland *U.S.A.* 39°45N 122°12W **78** F4
Orléanais *France* 48°0N 2°0E **20** C5
Orléans *France* 47°54N 1°52E **20** C4
Orleans *U.S.A.* 44°49N 72°12W **83** B12
Orléans, Î. d' *Canada* 46°54N 70°58W **73** C5
Ormara *Pakistan* 25°16N 64°33E **40** G4
Ormoc *Phil.* 11°0N 124°37E **37** B6
Ormond *N.Z.* 38°33S 177°56E **59** C6
Ormond Beach *U.S.A.* 29°17N 81°3W **85** G14
Ormskirk *U.K.* 53°35N 2°54W **12** D5
Örnsköldsvik *Sweden* 63°10N 18°38E **8** E18
Oro *N. Korea* 40°1N 127°27E **33** D14
Oro → *Mexico* 25°35N 105°2W **86** B3
Oro Grande *U.S.A.* 34°36N 117°20W **79** L9
Oro Valley *U.S.A.* 32°26N 110°55W **77** K8
Orocué *Colombia* 4°48N 71°20W **92** C4
Orofino *U.S.A.* 46°29N 116°15W **76** C5
Orohena, Mt. *Tahiti* 17°37S 149°28W **59** d
Orol Dengizi = Aral Sea
   Asia 45°0N 58°20E **26** E7
Oromocto *Canada* 45°54N 66°29W **73** C6
Orono *Canada* 43°59N 78°37W **82** C6
Orono *U.S.A.* 44°53N 68°40W **81** C19

Oronsay *U.K.* 56°1N 6°15W **11** E2
Oroquieta *Phil.* 8°32N 123°44E **37** C6
Orosei *Italy* 40°23N 9°42E **22** D3
Orosháza *Hungary* 46°32N 20°42E **17** E11
Orotukan *Russia* 62°16N 151°42E **27** C16
Oroville *Calif., U.S.A.* 39°31N 121°33W **78** F5
Oroville *Wash., U.S.A.* 48°56N 119°26W **76** B4
Oroville, L. *U.S.A.* 39°33N 121°29W **78** F5
Orroroo *Australia* 32°43S 138°38E **63** E2
Orrville *U.S.A.* 40°50N 81°46W **82** F3
Orsha *Belarus* 54°30N 30°25E **18** D5
Orsk *Russia* 51°12N 58°34E **26** D6
Orşova *Romania* 44°41N 22°25E **17** F12
Ortaca *Turkey* 36°49N 28°45E **23** F13
Ortegal, C. *Spain* 43°43N 7°52W **21** A2
Orthez *France* 43°29N 0°48W **20** E3
Ortigueira *Spain* 43°40N 7°50W **21** A2
Orting *U.S.A.* 47°6N 122°12W **78** C4
Ortles *Italy* 46°31N 10°33E **20** C9
Ortón → *Bolivia* 10°50S 67°0W **92** F5
Ortonville *U.S.A.* 45°19N 96°27W **80** C5
Orūmīyeh *Iran* 37°40N 45°0E **46** B5
Orūmīyeh, Daryācheh-ye
   Iran 37°50N 45°30E **46** B5
Oruro *Bolivia* 18°0S 67°9W **92** G5
Orust *Sweden* 58°10N 11°40E **9** G14
Oruzgān □ *Afghan.* 33°0N 66°0E **40** C5
Orvieto *Italy* 42°43N 12°7E **22** C5
Orwell N.Y., *U.S.A.* 43°35N 75°50W **83** C9
Orwell *Ohio, U.S.A.* 41°32N 80°52W **82** E4
Orwell → *U.K.* 51°59N 1°18E **13** F9
Orwigsburg *U.S.A.* 40°38N 76°6W **83** F8
Oryakhovo *Bulgaria* 43°40N 23°57E **23** C10
Oryol = Orel *Russia* 52°57N 36°3E **18** D6
Osa *Russia* 57°17N 55°26E **18** C10
Osa, Pen. de *Costa Rica* 8°0N 84°0W **88** E3
Osage *U.S.A.* 43°17N 92°49W **80** D7
Osage → *U.S.A.* 38°36N 91°57W **80** F8
Osage City *U.S.A.* 38°38N 95°50W **80** F6
Ōsaka *Japan* 34°42N 135°30E **29** G7
Osawatomie *U.S.A.* 38°31N 94°57W **80** F6
Osborne *U.S.A.* 39°26N 98°42W **80** F5
Osceola *Ark., U.S.A.* 35°42N 89°58W **85** D10
Osceola *Iowa, U.S.A.* 41°2N 93°46W **80** E7
Oscoda *U.S.A.* 44°26N 83°20W **82** B1
Ösel = Saaremaa *Estonia* 58°30N 22°30E **9** G20
Osgoode *Canada* 45°8N 75°36W **83** A9
Osh *Kyrgyzstan* 40°37N 72°49E **30** C3
Oshakati *Namibia* 17°45S 15°40E **55** H3
Oshana □ *Namibia* 17°50S 15°40E **56** A2
Oshawa *Canada* 43°50N 78°50W **82** C6
Oshigambo *Namibia* 17°45S 16°5E **56** A2
Oshika-Hantō *Japan* 38°20N 141°30E **28** E10
Oshkosh *Nebr., U.S.A.* 41°24N 102°21W **80** E2
Oshkosh *Wis., U.S.A.* 44°1N 88°33W **80** C9
Oshmyany = Ashmyany
   Belarus 54°26N 25°52E **17** A13
Oshnovīyeh *Iran* 37°2N 45°6E **46** B5
Oshogbo *Nigeria* 7°48N 4°37E **52** G6
Oshtorīnān *Iran* 34°1N 48°38E **47** C6
Ōshū *Japan* 39°8N 141°8E **28** E10
Oshwe
   Dem. Rep. of the Congo 3°25S 19°28E **54** E3
Osijek *Croatia* 45°34N 18°41E **23** B8
Osipovichi = Asipovichy
   Belarus 53°19N 28°33E **17** B15
Osiyan *India* 26°43N 72°55E **42** F5
Osizweni *S. Africa* 27°49S 30°7E **57** C5
Oskaloosa *U.S.A.* 41°18N 92°39W **80** E7
Oskarshamn *Sweden* 57°15N 16°27E **9** H17
Oskélanéo *Canada* 48°5N 75°15W **72** C4
Öskemen *Kazakhstan* 50°0N 82°36E **26** D9
Oslo *Norway* 59°54N 10°43E **9** G14
Oslofjorden *Norway* 59°20N 10°35E **9** G14
Osmanabad *India* 18°5N 76°10E **44** E3
Osmaniye *Turkey* 37°5N 36°10E **46** B3
Osmannagar *India* 18°30N 79°20E **44** E4
Osnabrück *Germany* 52°17N 8°3E **16** B5
Osogbo = Oshogbo *Nigeria* 7°48N 4°37E **52** G6
Osório *Brazil* 29°53S 50°17W **95** B5
Osorno *Chile* 40°25S 73°0W **96** E2
Osorno, Vol. *Chile* 41°0S 72°30W **96** D2
Osoyoos *Canada* 49°0N 119°30W **70** D5
Osøyro *Norway* 60°9N 5°30E **8** F11
Ospika → *Canada* 56°20N 124°0W **70** B4
Osprey Reef *Australia* 13°52S 146°36E **62** A4
Oss *Neths.* 51°46N 5°32E **15** C5
Ossa, Mt. *Australia* 41°52S 146°3E **63** G4
Ossa, Oros *Greece* 39°47N 22°42E **23** E10
Ossabaw I. *U.S.A.* 31°50N 81°5W **85** F14
Ossining *U.S.A.* 41°10N 73°55W **83** E11
Ossipee *U.S.A.* 43°41N 71°7W **83** C13
Ossokmanuan L. *Canada* 53°25N 65°0W **73** B7
Ossora *Russia* 59°20N 163°13E **27** D17
Ostend = Oostende
   Belgium 51°15N 2°54E **15** C2
Oster *Ukraine* 50°57N 30°53E **17** C16
Österbotten = Pohjanmaa □
   Finland 62°58N 22°50E **8** E20
Osterdalälven → *Sweden* 60°30N 15°7E **8** F15
Österdalen *Norway* 61°40N 10°50E **8** F14
Östermyra = Seinäjoki
   Finland 62°40N 22°51E **8** E20
Österreich = Austria ■
   Europe 47°0N 14°0E **16** E8
Östersund *Sweden* 63°10N 14°38E **8** E16
Ostfriesische Inseln
   Germany 53°42N 7°0E **16** B4
Ostrava *Czech Rep.* 49°51N 18°18E **17** D10
Ostróda *Poland* 53°42N 19°58E **17** B10
Ostroh *Ukraine* 50°20N 26°30E **17** C14
Ostrołęka *Poland* 53°4N 21°32E **17** B11
Ostrów Mazowiecka
   Poland 52°50N 21°51E **17** B11
Ostrów Wielkopolski
   Poland 51°36N 17°44E **17** C9
Ostrowiec-Świętokrzyski
   Poland 50°55N 21°22E **17** C11

Ostuni *Italy* 40°44N 17°35E **23** D7
Ōsumi-Kaikyō *Japan* 30°55N 131°0E **29** J5
Ōsumi-Shotō *Japan* 30°30N 130°0E **29** J5
Osuna *Spain* 37°14N 5°8W **21** D3
Oswegatchie → *U.S.A.* 44°42N 75°30W **83** B9
Oswego *U.S.A.* 43°27N 76°31W **83** C8
Oswego → *U.S.A.* 43°27N 76°30W **83** C8
Oswestry *U.K.* 52°52N 3°3W **12** E4
Oświęcim *Poland* 50°2N 19°11E **17** C10
Otago □ *N.Z.* 45°15S 170°0E **59** F2
Otago Harbour *N.Z.* 45°47S 170°42E **59** F3
Otaheite B. *Trin. & Tob.* 10°15N 61°30W **93** K15
Ōtake *Japan* 34°12N 132°13E **29** G6
Otaki *N.Z.* 40°45S 175°10E **59** D5
Otaru *Japan* 43°10N 141°0E **28** C10
Otaru-Wan = Ishikari-Wan
   Japan 43°25N 141°1E **28** C10
Otavalo *Ecuador* 0°13N 78°20W **92** C3
Otavi *Namibia* 19°40S 17°24E **56** A2
Ōtawara *Japan* 36°50N 140°5E **29** F10
Otchinjau *Angola* 16°30S 13°56E **56** A1
Otego *U.S.A.* 42°23N 75°10W **83** D9
Otelnuk, L. *Canada* 56°9N 68°12W **73** A6
Othello *U.S.A.* 46°50N 119°10W **76** C4
Otish, Mts. *Canada* 52°22N 70°30W **73** B5
Otjinene *Namibia* 21°8S 18°46E **56** B2
Otjiwarongo *Namibia* 20°30S 16°33E **56** B2
Otjozondjupa □ *Namibia* 21°0S 17°0E **56** B2
Oto Tolu Group *Tonga* 20°21S 174°32W **59** c
Otoineppu *Japan* 44°44N 142°16E **28** B11
Otorohanga *N.Z.* 38°12S 175°14E **59** C5
Otoskwin → *Canada* 52°13N 88°6W **72** B2
Otra → *Norway* 58°9N 8°1E **9** G13
Otranto *Italy* 40°9N 18°28E **23** D8
Otranto, C. d' *Italy* 40°7N 18°30E **23** D8
Otranto, Str. of *Italy* 40°15N 18°40E **23** D8
Otse *S. Africa* 25°2S 25°45E **56** C4
Otsego L. *U.S.A.* 42°45N 74°53W **83** D10
Ōtsu *Japan* 35°0N 135°50E **29** G7
Ōtsuki *Japan* 35°36N 138°57E **29** G9
Ottappalam *India* 10°46N 76°23E **45** J3
Ottawa = Outaouais →
   Canada 45°27N 74°8W **72** C5
Ottawa *Canada* 45°26N 75°42W **83** A9
Ottawa *Ill., U.S.A.* 41°21N 88°51W **80** E9
Ottawa *Kans., U.S.A.* 38°37N 95°16W **80** F6
Ottawa Is. *Canada* 59°35N 80°10W **69** C15
Otter Cr. → *U.S.A.* 44°13N 73°17W **83** B11
Otter Lake *Canada* 45°17N 79°56W **82** A5
Otterville *Canada* 42°55N 80°36W **82** D4
Ottery St. Mary *U.K.* 50°44N 3°17W **13** G4
Ottosdal *S. Africa* 26°46S 25°59E **56** C4
Ottumwa *U.S.A.* 41°1N 92°25W **80** E7
Oturkpo *Nigeria* 7°16N 8°8E **52** G7
Otway, B. *Chile* 53°30S 74°0W **96** G2
Otway, C. *Australia* 38°52S 143°30E **63** F3
Otwock *Poland* 52°5N 21°20E **17** B11
Ou → *Laos* 20°4N 102°13E **38** B4
Ou-Sammyaku *Japan* 39°20N 140°35E **28** E10
Ouachita → *U.S.A.* 31°38N 91°49W **84** F9
Ouachita, L. *U.S.A.* 34°34N 93°12W **84** D8
Ouachita Mts. *U.S.A.* 34°30N 94°30W **84** D7
Ouagadougou
   Burkina Faso 12°25N 1°30W **52** F5
Ouahigouya *Burkina Faso* 13°31N 2°25W **52** F5
Ouahran = Oran *Algeria* 35°45N 0°39W **52** A5
Ouallene *Algeria* 24°41N 1°11E **52** D6
Ouarâne *Mauritania* 21°0N 10°30W **52** D3
Ouargla *Algeria* 31°59N 5°16E **52** B7
Ouarra → *C.A.R.* 5°5N 24°26E **54** C4
Ouarzazate *Morocco* 30°55N 6°50W **52** B4
Oubangi →
   Dem. Rep. of the Congo 0°30S 17°50E **54** E3
Ouddorp *Neths.* 51°50N 3°57E **15** C3
Oude Rijn → *Neths.* 52°12N 4°24E **15** B4
Oudenaarde *Belgium* 50°50N 3°37E **15** D3
Oudtshoorn *S. Africa* 33°35S 22°14E **56** D3
Ouessant, Î. d' *France* 48°28N 5°6W **20** B1
Ouesso *Congo* 1°37N 16°5E **54** D3
Ouest, Pte. de l' *Canada* 49°52N 64°40W **73** C7
Ouezzane *Morocco* 34°51N 5°35W **52** B4
Oughter, L. *Ireland* 54°1N 7°28W **10** B4
Oughterard *Ireland* 53°26N 9°18E **10** C2
Ouidah *Benin* 6°25N 2°0E **52** G6
Oujda *Morocco* 34°41N 1°55W **52** B5
Oulainen *Finland* 64°17N 24°47E **8** D21
Oulanka △ *Finland* 66°26N 29°25E **8** C23
Oulu *Finland* 65°1N 25°29E **8** D21
Oulujärvi *Finland* 64°25N 27°15E **8** D22
Oulujoki → *Finland* 65°1N 25°30E **8** D21
Oum Chalouba *Chad* 15°48N 20°46E **53** E10
Oum Hadjer *Chad* 13°18N 19°41E **53** F9
Ounasjoki → *Finland* 66°31N 25°40E **8** C21
Ounguati *Namibia* 22°0S 15°46E **56** B2
Ounianga Kébir *Chad* 19°4N 20°29E **53** E10
Our → *Lux.* 49°55N 6°5E **15** E6
Ouray *U.S.A.* 38°1N 107°40W **77** G10
Ourense *Spain* 42°19N 7°55W **21** A2
Ouricuri *Brazil* 7°53S 40°5W **93** E10
Ourinhos *Brazil* 23°0S 49°54W **95** A6
Ouro Fino *Brazil* 22°16S 46°25W **95** A6
Ouro Prêto *Brazil* 20°20S 43°30W **95** A7
Ourthe → *Belgium* 50°29N 5°35E **15** D5
Ouse → *E. Susx, U.K.* 50°47N 0°4E **13** G8
Ouse → *N. Yorks., U.K.* 53°44N 0°55W **12** D7
Outaouais → *Canada* 45°27N 74°8W **72** C5
Outardes → *Canada* 49°24N 69°30W **73** C6
Outer Hebrides *U.K.* 57°30N 7°15W **11** D1
Outjo *Namibia* 20°5S 16°7E **56** B2
Outlook *Canada* 51°30N 107°0W **71** C7
Outokumpu *Finland* 62°43N 29°1E **8** E23
Ouyen *Australia* 35°1S 142°22E **63** F3
Ovalau *Fiji* 17°40S 178°48E **59** a
Ovalle *Chile* 30°33S 71°18W **94** C1
Ovamboland *Namibia* 18°30S 16°0E **56** A2
Overflakkee □ *Neths.* 51°44N 4°10E **15** C4
Overijssel □ *Neths.* 52°25N 6°35E **15** B6
Overland Park *U.S.A.* 38°58N 94°40W **80** F6
Overlander Roadhouse
   Australia 26°19S 114°28E **61** E1

Overton *U.S.A.* 36°33N 114°27W **79** J12
Övertorneå *Sweden* 66°23N 23°38E **8** C20
Ovid *U.S.A.* 42°41N 76°49W **83** D8
Oviedo *Spain* 43°25N 5°50W **21** A3
Ovišrags *Latvia* 57°33N 21°44E **9** H19
Övör Hangay □ *Mongolia* 45°0N 102°30E **32** B2
Øvör Anárjohka △
  Norway 68°30N 24°40E **8** B21
Øvre Årdal *Norway* 61°19N 7°48E **8** F12
Øvre Dividal △ *Norway* 68°43N 19°50E **8** B18
Øvre Pasvik △ *Norway* 69°6N 28°54E **8** B23
Ovruch *Ukraine* 51°25N 28°45E **17** C15
Owaka *N.Z.* 46°27S 169°40E **59** G2
Owambo = Ovamboland
  Namibia 18°30S 16°0E **56** A2
Owasco L. *U.S.A.* 42°50N 76°31W **83** D8
Owase *Japan* 34°7N 136°12E **29** G8
Owatonna *U.S.A.* 44°5N 93°14W **80** C7
Owbeh *Afghan.* 34°28N 63°10E **40** B3
Owego *U.S.A.* 42°6N 76°16W **83** D8
Owen Sound *Canada* 44°35N 80°55W **82** B4
Owen Stanley Ra.
  Papua N. G. 8°30S 147°0E **58** B7
Oweniny → *Ireland* 54°8N 9°34W **10** B2
Owens → *U.S.A.* 36°32N 117°59W **79** J9
Owens L. *U.S.A.* 36°26N 117°57W **79** J9
Owensboro *U.S.A.* 37°46N 87°7W **80** G10
Owl → *Canada* 57°51N 92°44W **71** B10
Owo *Nigeria* 7°10N 5°39E **52** G7
Owosso *U.S.A.* 43°0N 84°10W **81** D11
Owyhee *U.S.A.* 41°57N 116°6W **76** F5
Owyhee → *U.S.A.* 43°49N 117°2W **76** E5
Owyhee, L. *U.S.A.* 43°38N 117°14W **76** E5
Ox Mts. = Slieve Gamph
  Ireland 54°6N 9°0W **10** B3
Öxarfjörður *Iceland* 66°15N 16°45W **8** C5
Oxbow *Canada* 49°14N 102°10W **71** D8
Oxelösund *Sweden* 58°43N 17°5E **9** G17
Oxford *N.Z.* 43°18S 172°11E **59** E4
Oxford *U.K.* 51°46N 1°15W **13** F6
Oxford *Mass., U.S.A.* 42°7N 71°52W **83** D13
Oxford *Miss., U.S.A.* 34°22N 89°31W **85** D10
Oxford *N.C., U.S.A.* 36°19N 78°35W **85** C15
Oxford *N.Y., U.S.A.* 42°27N 75°36W **83** D9
Oxford *Ohio, U.S.A.* 39°31N 84°45W **81** F11
Oxford L. *Canada* 54°51N 95°37W **71** C9
Oxfordshire □ *U.K.* 51°48N 1°16W **13** F6
Oxnard *U.S.A.* 34°12N 119°11W **79** L7
Oxus = Amudarya →
  Uzbekistan 43°58N 59°34E **26** E6
Oya *Malaysia* 2°55N 111°55E **36** D4
Oyama *Japan* 36°18N 139°48E **29** F9
Oyem *Gabon* 1°34N 11°31E **54** D2
Oyen *Canada* 51°22N 110°28W **71** C6
Oykel → *U.K.* 57°56N 4°26W **11** D4
Oymyakon *Russia* 63°25N 142°44E **27** C15
Oyo *Nigeria* 7°46N 3°56E **52** G6
Ōyūbari *Japan* 43°1N 142°5E **28** C11
Ozamiz *Phil.* 8°15N 123°50E **37** C6
Ozar = Ojhar *India* 20°6N 73°56E **44** D1
Ozark *Ala., U.S.A.* 31°28N 85°39W **85** F12
Ozark *Ark., U.S.A.* 35°29N 93°50W **84** D8
Ozark *Mo., U.S.A.* 37°1N 93°12W **80** G7
Ozark Plateau *U.S.A.* 37°20N 91°40W **80** G8
Ozarks, L. of the *U.S.A.* 38°12N 92°38W **80** F7
Ózd *Hungary* 48°14N 20°15E **17** D11
Ozernovskiy *Russia* 51°30N 156°31E **27** D16
Ozette, L. *U.S.A.* 48°6N 124°38W **78** B2
Ozieri *Italy* 40°35N 9°0E **22** D3
Ozona *U.S.A.* 30°43N 101°12W **84** F4
Ozuluama *Mexico* 21°40N 97°50W **87** C5

P

Pa-an *Burma* 16°51N 97°40E **41** L20
Pa Mong Dam *Thailand* 18°0N 102°22E **38** D4
Pa Sak → *Thailand* 15°30N 101°0E **38** E3
Paamiut *Greenland* 62°0N 49°43W **4** C5
Paanayarvi △ *Russia* 66°16N 30°12E **8** C24
Paarl *S. Africa* 33°45S 18°56E **56** D2
Pab Hills *Pakistan* 26°30N 66°45E **42** F2
Pabaidh = Pabbay *U.K.* 57°46N 7°14W **11** D1
Pabbay *U.K.* 57°46N 7°14W **11** D1
Pabianice *Poland* 51°40N 19°20E **17** C10
Pabna *Bangla.* 24°1N 89°18E **41** G16
Pacaja → *Brazil* 1°56S 50°50W **93** D8
Pacaraima, Sa. *S. Amer.* 4°0N 62°30W **92** C6
Pacasmayo *Peru* 7°20S 79°35W **92** E3
Pachitea → *Peru* 8°46S 74°33W **92** E4
Pachmarhi *India* 22°28N 78°26E **43** H8
Pachora *India* 20°38N 75°29W **44** E2
Pachpadra *India* 25°58N 72°10E **42** G5
Pachuca *Mexico* 20°7N 98°44W **87** C5
Pacific Antarctic Ridge
  Pac. Oc. 43°0S 115°0W **5** B13
Pacific Grove *U.S.A.* 36°38N 121°56W **78** J5
Pacific Ocean 10°0N 140°0W **65** G14
Pacific Rim △ *Canada* 48°40N 124°45W **78** B2
Pacitan *Indonesia* 8°12S 111°7E **37** H14
Packwood *U.S.A.* 46°36N 121°40W **78** D5
Padaido, Kepulauan
  Indonesia 1°15S 136°30E **37** E9
Padampur *India* 20°59N 83°4E **44** D6
Padang *Riau, Indonesia* 1°0N 102°30E **39** M4
Padang *Sumatera Barat,*
  Indonesia 1°0S 100°20E **36** E2
Padang Endau *Malaysia* 2°40N 103°38E **39** L4
Padangpanjang *Indonesia* 0°40S 100°20E **36** E2
Padangsidempuan
  Indonesia 1°30N 99°15E **36** D1
Paddle Prairie *Canada* 57°57N 117°29W **70** B5
Paderborn *Germany* 51°42N 8°45E **16** C5
Paderoo *India* 18°5N 82°40E **44** E6
Padjelanta △ *Sweden* 67°20N 16°35E **8** C17
Padma *India* 24°12N 85°22E **43** G11
Padra *India* 22°15N 73°7E **42** H5
Padrauna *India* 26°54N 83°59E **43** F10
Padre I. *U.S.A.* 27°10N 97°25W **84** H6

Padre Island △ *U.S.A.* 27°0N 97°25W **84** H6
Padstow *U.K.* 50°33N 4°58W **13** G3
Padua = Pádova *Italy* 45°25N 11°53E **22** B4
Paducah *Ky., U.S.A.* 37°5N 88°37W **80** G9
Paducah *Tex., U.S.A.* 34°1N 100°18W **84** D4
Padukka *Sri Lanka* 6°50N 80°5E **45** L5
Padwa *India* 18°27N 82°47E **44** E6
Paea *Tahiti* 17°41S 149°35W **59** d
Paektu-san *N. Korea* 41°59N 128°4E **33** D15
Paeroa *N.Z.* 37°23S 175°41E **59** B5
Pafúri *Mozam.* 22°28S 31°17E **57** B5
Pag *Croatia* 44°25N 15°3E **16** F8
Pagadian *Phil.* 7°55N 123°30E **37** C6
Pagai Selatan, Pulau
  Indonesia 3°0S 100°15E **36** E2
Pagai Utara, Pulau
  Indonesia 2°35S 100°0E **36** E2
Pagalu = Annobón *Atl. Oc.* 1°25S 5°36E **51** G4
Pagara *India* 24°22N 80°1E **43** G9
Pagasa I. = Thitu I.
  S. China Sea 11°3N 114°17E **36** B4
Pagastikos Kolpos *Greece* 39°15N 23°0E **23** E10
Pagatan *Indonesia* 3°33S 115°59E **36** E5
Page *U.S.A.* 36°57N 111°27W **77** H8
Paget, Mt. *S. Georgia* 54°26S 36°31W **96** G9
Pago Pago *Amer. Samoa* 14°16S 170°43W **59** b
Pagosa Springs *U.S.A.* 37°16N 107°1W **77** H10
Pagri *China* 27°45N 89°10E **30** F6
Pagwa River *Canada* 50°2N 85°14W **72** B2
Pähala *U.S.A.* 19°12N 155°29W **75** M8
Pahang □ *Malaysia* 3°30N 102°45E **39** L4
Pahang → *Malaysia* 3°30N 103°9E **39** L4
Pahiatua *N.Z.* 40°27S 175°50E **59** D5
Pahokee *U.S.A.* 26°50N 80°40W **85** H14
Pahrump *U.S.A.* 36°12N 115°59W **79** J11
Pahute Mesa *U.S.A.* 37°20N 116°45W **78** H10
Pai *Thailand* 19°19N 98°27E **38** C2
Paicines *U.S.A.* 36°44N 121°17W **78** J5
Paide *Estonia* 58°53N 25°33E **9** G21
Paignton *U.K.* 50°26N 3°35W **13** G4
Paiho *Taiwan* 23°21N 120°25E **35** F13
Päijänne *Finland* 61°30N 25°30E **8** F21
Pailin *Cambodia* 12°46N 102°36E **38** F4
Painan *Indonesia* 1°21S 100°34E **36** E2
Painesville *U.S.A.* 41°43N 81°15W **82** E3
Paint Hills = Wemindji
  Canada 53°0N 78°49W **72** B4
Paint L. *Canada* 55°28N 97°57W **71** B9
Painted Desert *U.S.A.* 36°0N 111°0W **77** H8
Paintsville *U.S.A.* 37°49N 82°48W **81** G12
País Vasco □ *Spain* 42°50N 2°45W **21** A4
Paisley *Canada* 44°18N 81°16W **82** B3
Paisley *U.K.* 55°50N 4°25W **11** F4
Paisley *U.S.A.* 42°42N 120°32W **76** E3
Paita *Peru* 5°11S 81°9W **92** E2
Paithan *India* 19°29N 75°23E **44** E2
Paizhou *China* 30°12N 113°55E **35** B9
Pajares, Puerto de *Spain* 42°58N 5°46W **21** A3
Pak Lay *Laos* 18°15N 101°27E **38** C3
Pak Ou *Laos* 20°3N 102°12E **38** B4
Pak Phanang *Thailand* 8°21N 100°12E **39** H3
Pak Sane *Laos* 18°22N 103°39E **38** C4
Pak Song *Laos* 15°11N 106°14E **38** E6
Pak Suang *Laos* 19°58N 102°15E **34** H4
Pak Tam Chung *China* 22°24N 114°19E **31** a
Pak Thong Chai *Thailand* 14°43N 102°1E **38** E4
Pakala *India* 13°29N 79°8E **45** N11
Pakaur *India* 24°38N 87°51E **43** G12
Pakch'ŏn *N. Korea* 39°44N 125°35E **33** E13
Pakenham *Canada* 45°18N 76°18W **83** A8
Pakhuis *S. Africa* 32°9S 19°5E **56** E2
Pakistan ■ *Asia* 30°0N 70°0E **42** E4
Pakkading *Laos* 18°19N 103°59E **38** C4
Pakokku *Burma* 21°20N 95°0E **41** J19
Pakowki L. *Canada* 49°20N 111°0W **71** D6
Pakpattan *Pakistan* 30°25N 73°27E **42** D5
Paktīā □ *Afghan.* 33°30N 69°15E **40** C6
Paktīkā □ *Afghan.* 32°30N 69°0E **40** C6
Pakwach *Uganda* 2°28N 31°27E **54** D6
Pakxe *Laos* 15°5N 105°52E **38** E5
Pal Lahara *India* 21°27N 85°11E **43** J11
Pala *Chad* 9°25N 15°5E **53** G9
Pala *U.S.A.* 33°22N 117°5W **79** M9
Palacios *U.S.A.* 28°42N 96°13W **84** G6
Palagruža *Croatia* 42°24N 16°15E **22** C7
Palakkad *India* 10°46N 76°42E **45** J3
Palakol *India* 16°31N 81°46E **45** F5
Palalankwe *India* 10°52N 92°29E **45** J11
Palam *India* 19°0N 77°0E **44** E3
Palampur *India* 32°10N 76°30E **42** C7
Palana *Australia* 39°45S 147°55E **63** F4
Palana *Russia* 59°10N 159°59E **27** D16
Palanan *Phil.* 17°8N 122°29E **37** A6
Palanan Pt. *Phil.* 17°17N 122°30E **37** A6
Palandri *Pakistan* 33°42N 73°40E **43** C5
Palanga *Lithuania* 55°58N 21°3E **9** J19
Palangkaraya *Indonesia* 2°16S 113°56E **36** E4
Palani *India* 10°30N 77°30E **45** J3
Palani Hills *India* 10°14N 77°33E **45** J3
Palanpur *India* 24°10N 72°25E **42** G5
Palapye *Botswana* 22°30S 27°7E **56** B4
Palar → *India* 12°27N 80°13E **45** H5
Palas *Pakistan* 35°4N 73°14E **43** B5
Palasponga *India* 21°47N 85°34E **43** J11
Palatka *Russia* 60°6N 150°54E **27** C16
Palatka *U.S.A.* 29°39N 81°38W **85** G14
Palau ■ *Palau* 7°30N 134°30E **64** G5
Palauk *Burma* 13°10N 98°40E **38** F2
Palaw *Burma* 12°58N 98°39E **38** F2
Palawan *Phil.* 9°30N 118°30E **36** C5
Palayankottai *India* 8°45N 77°45E **45** K3
Paldiski *Estonia* 59°23N 24°9E **9** G21
Paleleh *Indonesia* 1°10N 121°50E **37** D6
Palembang *Indonesia* 3°0S 104°50E **36** E2
Palencia *Spain* 42°1N 4°34W **21** A3
Palenque *Mexico* 17°39N 91°58W **87** D6
Palermo *Italy* 38°7N 13°22E **22** E5
Palermo *U.S.A.* 39°26N 121°33W **78** F5

Palestina *Chile* 23°50S 69°47W **94** A2
Palestina *Chile* 23°50S 69°47W **96** A3
Palestine *Asia* 32°0N 35°0E **48** D4
Palestine *U.S.A.* 31°46N 95°38W **84** F7
Paletwa *Burma* 21°10N 92°50E **41** J18
Palghat = Palakkad *India* 10°46N 76°42E **45** J3
Palgrave, Mt. *Australia* 23°22S 115°58E **60** D2
Palhoça *Brazil* 27°38S 48°40W **95** B6
Pali *India* 25°50N 73°20E **42** G5
Palikir *Micronesia* 6°55N 158°9E **64** G7
Paliouri, Akra *Greece* 39°57N 23°45E **23** E10
Palisades Res. *U.S.A.* 43°20N 111°12W **76** E8
Paliseul *Belgium* 49°54N 5°8E **15** E5
Palitana *India* 21°32N 71°49E **42** J4
Palizada *Mexico* 18°15N 92°5W **87** D6
Palk Bay *Asia* 9°30N 79°15E **45** K4
Palk Strait *Asia* 10°0N 79°45E **45** K4
Palkānah *Iraq* 35°49N 44°26E **46** C5
Palkonda *India* 18°36N 83°48E **44** E6
Palkonda Ra. *India* 13°50N 79°20E **45** H4
Palkot *India* 22°53N 84°39E **43** H11
Pallanza = Verbánia *Italy* 45°56N 8°33E **20** D8
Pallarenda *Australia* 19°12S 146°46E **62** B4
Pallas-Yllästunturi △
  Finland 68°8N 24°15E **8** B21
Palleru → *India* 16°45N 80°2E **44** F5
Pallinup → *Australia* 34°27S 118°50E **61** F2
Pallu *India* 28°59N 74°14E **42** E6
Palm Bay *U.S.A.* 28°2N 80°35W **85** G14
Palm Beach *U.S.A.* 26°43N 80°2W **85** H14
Palm Coast *U.S.A.* 29°35N 81°12W **85** G14
Palm Desert *U.S.A.* 33°43N 116°22W **79** M10
Palm-Grove △ *Australia* 24°50S 149°21E **62** C4
Palm Is. *Australia* 18°45S 146°35E **62** B4
Palm Springs *U.S.A.* 33°50N 116°33W **79** M10
Palma, B. de *Spain* 39°30N 2°39E **21** C7
Palma de Mallorca *Spain* 39°35N 2°39E **21** C7
Palma Soriano *Cuba* 20°15N 76°0W **88** B4
Palmaner *India* 13°12N 78°45E **45** H4
Palmares *Brazil* 8°41S 35°28W **93** E11
Palmas *Brazil* 26°29S 52°0W **95** B5
Palmas, C. *Liberia* 4°27N 7°46W **52** H4
Pálmas, G. di *Italy* 39°0N 8°30E **22** E3
Palmdale *U.S.A.* 34°35N 118°7W **79** L8
Palmeira das Missões
  Brazil 27°55S 53°17W **95** B5
Palmeira dos Índios
  Brazil 9°25S 36°37W **93** E11
Palmer *Antarctica* 64°35S 65°0W **5** C17
Palmer *U.S.A.* 61°36N 149°7W **68** E2
Palmer → *Australia* 16°0S 142°26E **62** B3
Palmer Arch. *Antarctica* 64°15S 65°0W **5** C17
Palmer Lake *U.S.A.* 39°7N 104°55W **76** G11
Palmer Land *Antarctica* 73°0S 63°0W **5** D18
Palmerston *Australia* 12°31S 130°59E **60** B5
Palmerston *Canada* 43°50N 80°51W **82** C4
Palmerston *N.Z.* 45°29S 170°43E **59** F3
Palmerston North *N.Z.* 40°21S 175°39E **59** D5
Palmerton *U.S.A.* 40°48N 75°37W **83** F9
Palmetto *U.S.A.* 27°31N 82°34W **85** H13
Palmi *Italy* 38°21N 15°51E **22** E6
Palmira *Argentina* 32°59S 68°34W **94** C2
Palmira *Colombia* 3°32N 76°16W **92** C3
Palmyra = Tudmur *Syria* 34°36N 38°15E **46** C3
Palmyra *Mo., U.S.A.* 39°48N 91°32W **80** F8
Palmyra *N.J., U.S.A.* 40°0N 75°1W **83** F9
Palmyra *N.Y., U.S.A.* 43°5N 77°18W **82** C7
Palmyra *Pa., U.S.A.* 40°18N 76°36W **83** F8
Palmyra Is. *Pac. Oc.* 5°52N 162°5W **65** G11
Palmyras Pt. *India* 20°46N 87°1E **44** D8
Palo Alto *U.S.A.* 37°27N 122°10W **78** H4
Palo Seco *Trin. & Tob.* 10°4N 61°36W **93** K15
Palo Verde *U.S.A.* 33°26N 114°44W **79** M12
Palo Verde △ *Costa Rica* 10°21N 85°21W **88** D2
Palomar Mt. *U.S.A.* 33°22N 116°50W **79** M10
Palopo *Indonesia* 3°0S 120°16E **37** E6
Palos, C. de *Spain* 37°38N 0°40W **21** D5
Palos Verdes, Pt. *U.S.A.* 33°46N 118°25W **79** M8
Palos Verdes Estates
  U.S.A. 33°48N 118°23W **79** M8
Palu *Indonesia* 1°0S 119°52E **37** E5
Palu *Turkey* 38°45N 40°0E **46** B3
Paluma Ra. *Australia* 19°9S 146°22E **62** B4
Palwal *India* 28°8N 77°19E **42** E7
Pamanukan *Indonesia* 6°16S 107°49E **37** G12
Pamban I. *India* 9°15N 79°20E **45** K4
Pamekasan *Indonesia* 7°10S 113°28E **37** G15
Pamenang *Indonesia* 8°24S 116°6E **37** J19
Pamiers *France* 43°7N 1°39E **20** E4
Pamir *Tajikistan* 37°40N 73°0E **26** F8
Pamlico → *U.S.A.* 35°20N 76°28W **85** D16
Pamlico Sd. *U.S.A.* 35°20N 76°0W **85** D17
Pampa *U.S.A.* 35°32N 100°58W **84** D4
Pampa de las Salinas
  Argentina 32°1S 66°58W **94** C2
Pampanua *Indonesia* 4°16S 120°8E **37** E6
Pampas *Argentina* 35°0S 63°0W **94** D3
Pampas *Peru* 12°20S 74°50W **92** F4
Pamplona *Colombia* 7°23N 72°39W **92** B4
Pamplona-Iruña *Spain* 42°48N 1°38W **21** A5
Pampoenpoort *S. Africa* 31°3S 22°40E **56** D3
Pan de Azúcar *Chile* 23°35S 68°10W **94** A2
Pan de Azúcar △ *Chile* 26°0S 70°40W **94** B1
Pan Xian *China* 25°46N 104°38E **34** E5
Pana *U.S.A.* 39°23N 89°5W **80** F9
Panaca *U.S.A.* 37°47N 114°23W **77** H6
Panadura *Sri Lanka* 6°35N 79°55W **45** L4
Panaitan *Indonesia* 6°36S 105°12E **37** G11
Panaji *India* 15°25N 73°50E **45** G1
Panamá *Panama* 9°0N 79°25W **88** E4
Panama ■ *Cent. Amer.* 8°48N 79°55W **88** E4
Panamá, G. de *Panama* 8°4N 79°20W **88** E4
Panama, Isthmus of
  Cent. Amer. 9°0N 79°0W **88** E4
Panama Basin *Pac. Oc.* 5°0N 83°30W **65** G19
Panama Canal *Panama* 9°10N 79°37W **88** E4
Panama City *U.S.A.* 30°10N 85°40W **85** F12
Panamint Range *U.S.A.* 36°20N 117°20W **79** J9
Panamint Springs
  U.S.A. 36°20N 117°28W **79** J9

Panão *Peru* 9°55S 75°55W **92** E3
Panare *Thailand* 6°51N 101°30E **39** J3
Panay *Phil.* 11°10N 122°30E **37** B6
Panay, G. *Phil.* 11°0N 122°30E **37** B6
Pančevo *Serbia* 44°52N 20°41E **23** B9
Panda *Mozam.* 24°2S 34°45E **57** C5
Pandan *Malaysia* 1°32N 103°46E **39** d
Pandan *Phil.* 11°45N 122°10E **37** B6
Pandan Tampoi = Tampoi
  Malaysia 1°30N 103°39E **39** d
Pandegelang *Indonesia* 6°25S 106°5E **37** G12
Pandhana *India* 21°42N 76°13E **42** J7
Pandharkawada *India* 20°1N 78°32E **44** D4
Pandharpur *India* 17°41N 75°20E **44** F2
Pandhurna *India* 21°36N 78°35E **44** D4
Pando *Uruguay* 34°44S 56°0W **95** C4
Pando, L. = Hope, L.
  Australia 28°24S 139°18E **63** D2
Pandora *Costa Rica* 9°43N 83°3W **88** E3
Panevėžys *Lithuania* 55°42N 24°25E **9** J21
Pang Sida △ *Thailand* 14°5N 102°17E **38** E4
Pangandaran *Indonesia* 7°40S 108°39E **37** G13
Pangandaran △
  Indonesia 7°43S 108°42E **37** G13
Pangani *Tanzania* 5°25S 38°58E **54** F7
Pangfou = Bengbu
  China 32°58N 117°20E **33** H9
Pangga, Tanjung
  Indonesia 8°54S 116°2E **37** K19
Panghsang = Bangkang
  Burma 22°4N 99°1E **34** F2
Pangjiabu *China* 40°38N 115°26E **32** D8
Pangkah, Tanjung
  Indonesia 6°51S 112°33E **37** G15
Pangkai *Burma* 22°49N 98°39E **34** F2
Pangkajene *Indonesia* 4°46S 119°34E **37** E5
Pangkalanbrandan
  Indonesia 4°1N 98°20E **36** D1
Pangkalanbuun *Indonesia* 2°41S 111°37E **36** E4
Pangkalpinang *Indonesia* 2°10S 106°10E **36** E3
Pangkor, Pulau *Malaysia* 4°13N 100°34E **39** K3
Pangniqtuuq = Pangnirtung
  Canada 66°8N 65°43W **69** D18
Pangnirtung *Canada* 66°8N 65°43W **69** D18
Pangody *Russia* 65°52N 74°27E **26** C8
Pangong Tso = Bangong Co
  China 35°40N 78°43E **43** C8
Panguitch *U.S.A.* 37°50N 112°26W **77** H7
Pangutaran Group *Phil.* 6°18N 120°34E **37** C6
Panhala *India* 16°49N 74°7E **44** F2
Panhandle *U.S.A.* 35°21N 101°23W **84** D4
Pani Mines *India* 22°29N 73°50E **42** H5
Panikota I. *India* 20°46N 71°21E **42** J4
Panipat *India* 29°25N 77°2E **42** E7
Panjal Range = Pir Panjal Range
  India 32°30N 76°50E **42** C7
Panjgur *Pakistan* 27°0N 64°5E **40** F4
Panjhra → *India* 21°13N 74°57E **44** D2
Panjim = Panaji *India* 15°25N 73°50E **45** G1
Panjin *China* 41°3N 122°2E **33** D12
Panjnad → *Pakistan* 28°57N 70°30E **42** E4
Panjnad Barrage *Pakistan* 29°22N 71°15E **42** E4
Panjwai *Afghan.* 31°26N 65°27E **42** D1
Panmunjŏm *N. Korea* 37°59N 126°38E **33** F14
Panna *India* 24°40N 80°15E **43** G8
Panna △ *India* 24°40N 80°0E **43** G8
Panna Hills *India* 24°40N 81°15E **43** G9
Pannawonica *Australia* 21°39S 116°19E **60** D2
Pano Akil *Pakistan* 27°51N 69°7E **42** F3
Panorama *Brazil* 21°21S 51°51W **95** A5
Panruti *India* 11°46N 79°35E **45** J4
Pansemal *India* 21°39N 74°42E **42** J6
Panshan = Panjin *China* 41°3N 122°2E **33** D12
Panshi *China* 42°58N 126°5E **33** C14
Pantanal *Brazil* 17°30S 57°40W **92** H7
Pantanos de Centla △
  Mexico 18°25N 92°30E **87** D6
Pantar *Indonesia* 8°28S 124°10E **37** F6
Pante Macassar *E. Timor* 9°30S 123°58E **37** F6
Pantelleria *Italy* 36°50N 11°57E **22** F4
Pánuco *Mexico* 22°3N 98°10W **87** C5
Panvel *India* 18°59N 73°4E **44** E1
Panzhihua *China* 26°33N 101°44E **34** D3
Paola *U.S.A.* 38°35N 94°53W **80** F6
Paonia *U.S.A.* 38°52N 107°36W **76** G10
Paopao *Moorea* 17°30S 149°49W **59** d
Paoting = Baoding
  China 38°50N 115°28E **32** E8
Paot'ou = Baotou *China* 40°32N 110°2E **32** D6
Paoua *C.A.R.* 7°9N 16°20E **54** C3
Pápa *Hungary* 47°22N 17°30E **17** E9
Papa Stour *U.K.* 60°20N 1°42W **11** A7
Papa Westray *U.K.* 59°20N 2°55W **11** B6
Papagayo → *Mexico* 16°46N 99°43W **87** D5
Papagayo, G. de
  Costa Rica 10°30N 85°50W **88** D2
Papagni → *India* 15°35N 77°45E **45** G3
Papakura *N.Z.* 37°4S 174°59E **59** B5
Papantla *Mexico* 20°27N 97°19W **87** C5
Papar *Malaysia* 5°45N 116°0E **36** C5
Papara *Tahiti* 17°43S 149°31W **59** d
Paparoa △ *N.Z.* 42°7S 171°26E **59** E3
Papeete *Tahiti* 17°32S 149°34W **59** d
Papenoo *Tahiti* 17°30S 149°32W **59** d
Papetoai *Moorea* 17°29S 149°52W **59** d
Paposo *Chile* 25°0S 70°30W **94** B1
Papua □ *Indonesia* 4°0S 137°0E **37** E9
Papua, G. of *Papua N. G.* 9°0S 144°50E **58** B7
Papua New Guinea ■
  Oceania 8°0S 145°0E **58** B7
Papudo *Chile* 32°29S 71°27W **94** C1
Papun *Burma* 18°2N 97°30E **41** K20
Papunya *Australia* 23°15S 131°54E **60** D5
Pará = Belém *Brazil* 1°20S 48°30W **93** D9
Pará □ *Brazil* 3°20S 52°0W **93** D8
Paraburdoo *Australia* 23°14S 117°32E **60** D2
Paracatu *Brazil* 17°10S 46°50W **93** G9
Paracel Is. *S. China Sea* 15°50N 112°0E **36** A4

Parachilna *Australia* 31°10S 138°21E **63** E2
Parachinar *Pakistan* 33°55N 70°5E **42** C4
Paradip *India* 20°15N 86°35E **44** D8
Paradise *Calif., U.S.A.* 39°46N 121°37W **78** F5
Paradise *Nev., U.S.A.* 36°9N 115°10W **79** J11
Paradise → *Canada* 53°27N 57°19W **73** B8
Paradise Hill *Canada* 53°32N 109°28W **71** C7
Paradise River *Canada* 53°27N 57°17W **73** B8
Paradise Valley *U.S.A.* 41°30N 117°32W **76** F5
Paragould *U.S.A.* 36°3N 90°29W **85** C9
Paragua → *Venezuela* 6°55N 62°55W **92** B6
Paraguaçú → *Brazil* 12°45S 38°54W **93** F11
Paraguaçú Paulista
  Brazil 22°22S 50°35W **95** A5
Paraguaná, Pen. de
  Venezuela 12°0N 70°0W **92** A5
Paraguarí *Paraguay* 25°36S 57°0W **94** B4
Paraguarí □ *Paraguay* 26°0S 57°10W **94** B4
Paraguay ■ *S. Amer.* 23°0S 57°0W **94** A4
Paraguay → *Paraguay* 27°18S 58°38W **94** B4
Paraíba = João Pessoa
  Brazil 7°10S 34°52W **93** E12
Paraíba □ *Brazil* 7°0S 36°0W **93** E11
Paraíba do Sul → *Brazil* 21°37S 41°3W **95** A7
Paraíso *Mexico* 18°24N 93°14W **87** D6
Parak *Iran* 27°38N 52°25E **47** E7
Parakou *Benin* 9°25N 2°40E **52** G6
Paralkote *India* 19°47N 80°41E **44** E5
Paramaribo *Suriname* 5°50N 55°10W **93** B7
Páramos del Batallón y La Negra △
  Venezuela 8°2N 71°55W **89** E5
Paramushir, Ostrov
  Russia 50°24N 156°0E **27** D16
Paran → *Israel* 30°20N 35°10E **48** E4
Paraná *Argentina* 31°45S 60°30W **94** C3
Paraná *Brazil* 12°30S 47°48W **93** F9
Paraná □ *Brazil* 24°30S 51°0W **95** A5
Paraná → *Argentina* 33°43S 59°15W **94** C4
Paranaguá *Brazil* 25°30S 48°30W **95** B6
Paranaíba *Brazil* 19°40S 51°11W **93** G8
Paranaíba → *Brazil* 20°6S 51°4W **93** H8
Paranal, Cerro *Chile* 24°38S 70°24W **94** A1
Paranapanema → *Brazil* 22°40S 53°9W **95** A5
Paranapiacaba, Serra do
  Brazil 24°31S 48°35W **95** A6
Paranavaí *Brazil* 23°4S 52°56W **95** A5
Parang *Maguindanao, Phil.* 7°23N 124°16E **37** C6
Parang *Sulu, Phil.* 5°55N 120°54E **37** C6
Parangippettai *India* 11°30N 79°38E **45** J4
Parângul Mare, Vf.
  Romania 45°20N 23°37E **17** F12
Paranthan *Sri Lanka* 9°26N 80°24E **45** K5
Paraparaumu *N.Z.* 40°57S 175°3E **59** D5
Parauapebas *Brazil* 6°4S 49°54W **93** E9
Parbati → *Mad. P., India* 25°50N 76°30E **42** G7
Parbati → *Raj., India* 26°54N 77°53E **42** F7
Parbhani *India* 19°8N 76°52E **44** E3
Parchim *Germany* 53°26N 11°52E **16** B6
Pardes Hanna-Karkur
  Israel 32°28N 34°57E **48** C3
Pardo → *Bahia, Brazil* 15°40S 39°0W **93** G11
Pardo → *Mato Grosso,*
  Brazil 21°46S 52°9W **95** A5
Pardoo Roadhouse
  Australia 20°6S 119°3E **60** D2
Pardubice *Czech Rep.* 50°3N 15°45E **16** C8
Pare *Tanzania* 7°43S 112°12E **37** G15
Parecis, Serra dos *Brazil* 13°0S 60°0W **92** F7
Paren *Russia* 62°30N 163°15E **27** C17
Parenda *India* 18°16N 75°28E **44** E2
Parent *Canada* 47°55N 74°35W **72** C5
Parent, L. *Canada* 48°31N 77°1W **72** C4
Parepare *Indonesia* 4°0S 119°40E **37** E5
Parga *Greece* 39°15N 20°29E **23** E9
Pargas = Länsi-Turunmaa
  Finland 60°18N 22°18E **9** F20
Pargi *India* 17°11N 77°53E **44** E3
Parham *Canada* 44°39N 76°43W **83** B8
Paria → *U.S.A.* 36°52N 111°36W **77** H8
Paria, G. de *Venezuela* 10°30N 61°40W **93** K14
Pariaguán *Venezuela* 8°51N 64°34W **92** B6
Paricutín, Cerro *Mexico* 19°28N 102°15W **86** D4
Parigi *Indonesia* 0°50S 120°5E **37** E6
Parika *Guyana* 6°50N 58°20W **92** B7
Parikkala *Finland* 61°33N 29°31E **8** F23
Parima, Serra *Brazil* 2°30N 64°0W **92** C6
Parināri *Peru* 4°35S 74°25W **92** D4
Pariñas, Pta. *Peru* 4°30S 82°0W **90** D2
Parintins *Brazil* 2°40S 56°50W **93** D7
Paripariri Kyun *Burma* 14°52S 93°41E **45** G11
Paris *Canada* 43°12N 80°25W **82** C4
Paris *France* 48°53N 2°20E **20** B5
Paris *Idaho, U.S.A.* 42°14N 111°24W **76** E8
Paris *Ky., U.S.A.* 38°13N 84°15W **81** F11
Paris *Tenn., U.S.A.* 36°18N 88°19W **85** C10
Paris *Tex., U.S.A.* 33°40N 95°33W **84** E7
Parish *U.S.A.* 43°25N 76°8W **83** C8
Parishville *U.S.A.* 44°38N 74°49W **83** B10
Pariti *Indonesia* 10°1S 123°45E **60** B3
Park *U.S.A.* 48°45N 122°18W **78** B4
Park City *U.S.A.* 37°48N 97°20W **80** G5
Park Falls *U.S.A.* 45°56N 90°27W **80** C8
Park Head *Canada* 44°36N 81°9W **82** B3
Park Hills *U.S.A.* 33°9S 148°11E **63** E4
Park Range *U.S.A.* 40°41N 106°41W **76** F10
Park Rapids *U.S.A.* 46°55N 95°4W **80** B6
Park River *U.S.A.* 48°24N 97°45W **80** A5
Park Rynie *S. Africa* 30°25S 30°45E **57** E5
Parkā Bandar *Iran* 25°55N 59°35E **47** E8
Parkano *Finland* 62°1N 23°0E **8** E20
Parker *Ariz., U.S.A.* 34°9N 114°17W **79** L12
Parker *Pa., U.S.A.* 41°5N 79°41W **82** E5
Parker Dam *U.S.A.* 34°18N 114°8W **79** L12
Parkersburg *U.S.A.* 39°16N 81°34W **81** F13
Parkes *Australia* 33°9S 148°11E **63** E4
Parkfield *U.S.A.* 35°54N 120°26W **78** K6
Parkland *Canada* 43°15N 81°38W **82** C3
Parkland *U.S.A.* 47°9N 122°26W **78** C4
Parkston *U.S.A.* 43°24N 97°59W **80** D5
Parksville *Canada* 49°20N 124°21W **70** D4
Parkway *U.S.A.* 38°32N 121°29W **78** G5
Parla *Spain* 40°14N 3°46W **21** B4

Parlakimidi *India* 18°45N 84°5E **44** E7
Parli *India* 18°50N 76°35E **44** E3
Parma *Italy* 44°48N 10°20E **20** D9
Parma *Idaho, U.S.A.* 43°47N 116°57W **76** E5
Parma *Ohio, U.S.A.* 41°24N 81°43W **82** E3
Parnaguá *Brazil* 10°10S 44°38W **93** F10
Parnaíba *Brazil* 2°54S 41°47W **93** D10
Parnaíba → *Brazil* 3°0S 41°50W **93** D10
Parnassos *Greece* 38°35N 22°30E **23** E10
Parner *India* 19°0N 74°26E **44** E2
Pärnu *Estonia* 58°28N 24°33E **9** G21
Paro Dzong *Bhutan* 27°32N 89°53E **43** F13
Parola *India* 20°47N 75°7E **44** D2
Paroo → *Australia* 31°28S 143°32E **63** E3
Paros *Greece* 37°5N 25°12E **23** F11
Parowan *U.S.A.* 37°51N 112°50W **77** H7
Parral *Chile* 36°10S 71°52W **94** D1
Parramatta *Australia* 33°48S 151°1E **63** B5
Parras *Mexico* 25°25N 102°11W **86** B4
Parrett → *U.K.* 51°12N 3°1W **13** F4
Parris I. *U.S.A.* 32°20N 80°41W **85** E14
Parrsboro *Canada* 45°30N 64°25W **73** C7
Parry Channel *Canada* 74°15N 94°0W **69** C13
Parry I. *Canada* 45°18N 80°10W **82** A4
Parry Is. *Canada* 77°0N 110°0W **69** B10
Parry Sound *Canada* 45°20N 80°0W **82** A5
Parsnip → *Canada* 55°10N 123°2W **70** B4
Parsons *U.S.A.* 37°20N 95°16W **80** G7
Parsons Ra. *Australia* 13°30S 135°15E **62** A2
Partabpur *India* 20°0N 80°42E **44** E5
Partinico *Italy* 38°3N 13°7E **22** E5
Partizansk *Russia* 43°8N 133°9E **27** E14
Partridge I. *Canada* 55°59N 87°37W **72** A2
Partry Mts. *Ireland* 53°40N 9°28W **10** C2
Partur *India* 19°40N 76°14E **44** E3
Paru → *Brazil* 1°33S 52°38W **93** D8
Parur = North Paravar
   India 10°13N 76°14E **45** J3
Parván □ *Afghan.* 35°0N 69°0E **40** B6
Parvatipuram *India* 18°50N 83°25E **44** E6
Parvatsar *India* 26°52N 74°49E **42** F6
Parys *S. Africa* 26°52S 27°29E **56** C4
Pas, The *Canada* 53°45N 101°15W **71** C8
Pasadena *Canada* 49°1N 57°36W **73** C8
Pasadena *U.S.A.* 29°43N 95°13W **84** G7
Pasaje → *Argentina* 25°39S 63°56W **94** B3
Pasar *Indonesia* 8°27S 114°54E **37** J17
Pasargadae *Iran* 30°11N 53°10E **47** D7
Pascagoula *U.S.A.* 30°21N 88°33W **85** F10
Pascagoula → *U.S.A.* 30°23N 88°37W **85** F10
Paşcani *Romania* 47°14N 26°45E **17** E14
Paschimbanga □ *India* 23°0N 88°0E **43** H13
Pasco *U.S.A.* 46°14N 119°6W **76** C4
Pasco I. *Australia* 20°57S 115°20E **60** D2
Pascoag *U.S.A.* 41°57N 71°42W **83** E13
Pascua, I. de *Chile* 27°7S 109°23W **65** K17
Pasfield L. *Canada* 58°24N 105°20W **71** B7
Pasir Mas *Malaysia* 6°2N 102°8E **39** J4
Pasir Putih *Malaysia* 5°50N 102°24E **39** K4
Paskūh *Iran* 27°34N 61°39E **47** E9
Pasley, C. *Australia* 33°52S 123°35E **61** F3
Pašman *Croatia* 43°58N 15°20E **16** G8
Pasni *Pakistan* 25°15N 63°27E **40** G3
Paso Bravo △ *Paraguay* 22°32S 57°5W **94** A4
Paso Cantinela *Mexico* 32°33N 115°47W **79** N11
Paso de Indios *Argentina* 43°55S 69°0W **96** E3
Paso de los Libres
   Argentina 29°44S 57°10W **94** B4
Paso de los Toros
   Uruguay 32°45S 56°30W **94** C4
Paso Robles *U.S.A.* 35°38N 120°41W **78** K6
Paspébiac *Canada* 48°3N 65°17W **73** C6
Pasrur *Pakistan* 32°16N 74°43E **42** C6
Passage East *Ireland* 52°14N 7°0W **10** D5
Passage West *Ireland* 51°52N 8°21W **10** E3
Passau *Germany* 48°34N 13°28E **16** D7
Passero, C. *Italy* 36°41N 15°10E **22** F6
Passo Fundo *Brazil* 28°10S 52°20W **95** B5
Passos *Brazil* 20°45S 46°37W **93** H9
Pastavy *Belarus* 55°4N 26°50E **9** J22
Pastaza → *Peru* 4°50S 76°52W **92** D3
Pasto *Colombia* 1°13N 77°17W **92** C3
Pasuruan *Indonesia* 7°40S 112°44E **37** G15
Patag I. = Flat I.
   S. China Sea 10°49N 115°49E **36** B5
Patagonia *Argentina* 45°0S 69°0W **96** F3
Patagonia *U.S.A.* 31°33N 110°45W **77** L8
Patambar *Iran* 29°45N 60°17E **47** D9
Patan = Lalitpur *Nepal* 27°40N 85°20E **43** F11
Patan → Somnath *India* 20°53N 70°22E **42** J4
Patan *Gujarat, India* 23°54N 72°14E **42** H5
Patan *Maharashtra, India* 17°22N 73°57E **44** F1
Patani *Indonesia* 0°20N 128°50E **37** D7
Pataudi *India* 28°18N 76°48E **42** E7
Patchewollock *Australia* 35°22S 142°12E **63** F3
Patchogue *U.S.A.* 40°46N 73°1W **83** F11
Patea *N.Z.* 39°45S 174°30E **59** C5
Patensie *S. Africa* 33°46S 24°49E **56** D3
Paternò *Italy* 37°34N 14°54E **22** F6
Pateros *U.S.A.* 48°3N 119°54W **76** B4
Paterson *U.S.A.* 40°54N 74°9W **83** F10
Paterson Ra. *Australia* 21°45S 122°10E **60** D3
Pathankot *India* 32°18N 75°45E **42** C6
Pathein *Burma* 16°45N 94°30E **41** L19
Pathfinder Res. *U.S.A.* 42°28N 106°51W **76** E10
Pathiu *Thailand* 10°42N 99°19E **39** G2
Pathri *India* 19°13N 76°27E **44** E3
Pathum Thani *Thailand* 14°1N 100°32E **38** E3
Pati *Indonesia* 6°45S 111°1E **37** G14
Patía → *Colombia* 2°13N 78°40W **92** C3
Patiala *Punjab, India* 30°23N 76°26E **42** D7
Patiala *Ut. P., India* 27°43N 79°1E **43** F8
Patkai Bum *India* 27°0N 95°30E **41** F19
Patmos *Greece* 37°21N 26°36E **23** F12
Patna *India* 25°35N 85°12E **43** G11
Patnagarh *India* 20°43N 83°9E **44** D6
Pato Branco *Brazil* 26°13S 52°40W **95** B5
Patong, Ao *Thailand* 7°54N 98°17E **39** a
Patos *Brazil* 6°55S 37°16W **93** E11

Patos, L. dos *Brazil* 31°20S 51°0W **95** C5
Patos, Río de los →
   Argentina 31°18S 69°25W **94** C2
Patos de Minas *Brazil* 18°35S 46°32W **93** G9
Patquía *Argentina* 30°2S 66°55W **94** C2
Patra *Greece* 38°14N 21°47E **23** E9
Patraikos Kolpos *Greece* 38°17N 21°30E **23** E9
Patras = Patra *Greece* 38°14N 21°47E **23** E9
Patriot Hills *Antarctica* 82°20S 81°25W **5** E16
Patrocínio *Brazil* 18°57S 47°0W **93** G9
Pattadakal *India* 16°1N 75°42E **45** F2
Pattani *Thailand* 6°48N 101°15E **39** J3
Pattaya *Thailand* 12°52N 100°55E **38** F3
Patten *U.S.A.* 46°0N 68°38W **81** B19
Patterson *Calif., U.S.A.* 37°28N 121°8W **78** H5
Patterson *La., U.S.A.* 29°42N 91°18W **84** G9
Patterson, Mt. *U.S.A.* 38°29N 119°20W **78** G7
Patti *Punjab, India* 31°17N 74°54E **42** D6
Patti *Ut. P., India* 25°55N 82°12E **43** G10
Pattoki *Pakistan* 31°5N 73°52E **42** D5
Patton *U.S.A.* 40°38N 78°39W **82** F6
Patuakhali *Bangla.* 22°20N 90°25E **41** H17
Patuanak *Canada* 55°55N 107°43W **71** B7
Patuca → *Honduras* 15°50N 84°18W **88** C3
Patuca, Punta *Honduras* 15°49N 84°14W **88** C3
Patuca △ *Honduras* 14°30N 85°30W **88** D2
Patur *India* 20°27N 76°56E **44** D3
Patvinsuo △ *Finland* 63°7N 30°45E **8** E24
Pátzcuaro *Mexico* 19°31N 101°38W **86** D4
Pau *France* 43°19N 0°25W **20** E3
Paudash *Canada* 44°59N 77°58W **82** B7
Pauk *Burma* 21°27N 94°30E **41** J19
Paul I. *Canada* 56°30N 61°20W **73** A7
Paul Smiths *U.S.A.* 44°26N 74°15W **83** B10
Paulatuk *Canada* 69°25N 124°0W **68** D7
Paulding Bay *S. Ocean* 66°0S 118°0E **5** C8
Paulistana *Brazil* 8°9S 41°9W **93** E10
Paulo Afonso *Brazil* 9°21S 38°15W **93** E11
Paulpietersburg *S. Africa* 27°23S 30°50E **57** C5
Pauls Valley *U.S.A.* 34°44N 97°13W **84** D6
Pauma Valley *U.S.A.* 33°16N 116°58W **79** M10
Pauni *India* 20°48N 79°40E **44** D4
Pauri *India* 30°9N 78°47E **43** D8
Pavagada *India* 14°6N 77°16E **45** G3
Pāveh *Iran* 35°3N 46°22E **46** C5
Pavia *Italy* 45°7N 9°8E **20** D8
Pavilion *U.S.A.* 42°52N 78°1W **82** D6
Pāvilosta *Latvia* 56°53N 21°14E **9** H19
Pavlodar *Kazakhstan* 52°33N 77°0E **26** D8
Pavlograd = Pavlohrad
   Ukraine 48°30N 35°52E **19** E6
Pavlohrad *Ukraine* 48°30N 35°52E **19** E6
Pavlovo *Russia* 55°58N 43°5E **18** C7
Pavlovsk *Russia* 50°26N 40°5E **19** D7
Pavlovskaya *Russia* 46°17N 39°47E **19** E6
Pawai, Pulau *Singapore* 1°11N 103°44E **39** d
Pawayan *India* 28°4N 80°6E **43** E9
Pawhuska *U.S.A.* 36°40N 96°20W **84** C6
Pawling *U.S.A.* 41°34N 73°36W **83** E11
Pawnee *U.S.A.* 36°20N 96°48W **84** C6
Pawnee City *U.S.A.* 40°7N 96°9W **80** E6
Pawtucket *U.S.A.* 41°53N 71°23W **83** E13
Paxi *Greece* 39°14N 20°12E **23** E9
Paxton *U.S.A.* 40°27N 88°6W **80** E9
Payakumbuh *Indonesia* 0°20S 100°35E **36** E2
Payette *U.S.A.* 44°5N 116°56W **76** D5
Payne Bay = Kangirsuk
   Canada 60°0N 70°0W **69** F18
Payne L. *Canada* 59°30N 74°30W **69** F17
Paynes Find *Australia* 29°15S 117°42E **61** E2
Paynesville *U.S.A.* 45°23N 94°43W **80** C6
Paysandú *Uruguay* 32°19S 58°8W **94** C4
Payson *Ariz., U.S.A.* 34°14N 111°20W **77** J8
Payson *Utah, U.S.A.* 40°3N 111°44W **76** F8
Paz → *Guatemala* 13°44N 90°10W **88** D1
Paz, B. de la *Mexico* 24°9N 110°25W **86** C2
Pāzanān *Iran* 30°35N 49°59E **47** D6
Pazardzhik *Bulgaria* 42°12N 24°20E **23** C11
Pe Ell *U.S.A.* 46°34N 123°18W **78** D3
Peabody *U.S.A.* 42°31N 70°56W **83** D14
Peace → *Canada* 59°0N 111°25W **70** B6
Peace Point *Canada* 59°7N 112°27W **70** B6
Peace River *Canada* 56°15N 117°18W **70** B5
Peach Springs *U.S.A.* 35°32N 113°25W **77** J7
Peachland *Canada* 49°47N 119°45W **70** D5
Peachtree City *U.S.A.* 33°25N 84°35W **85** E12
Peak, The = Kinder Scout
   U.K. 53°24N 1°52W **12** D6
Peak Charles △ *Australia* 32°42S 121°10E **61** F3
Peak District △ *U.K.* 53°24N 1°46W **12** D6
Peak Hill *Australia* 32°47S 148°11E **63** E4
Peak Ra. *Australia* 22°50S 148°20E **62** C4
Peake Cr. → *Australia* 28°2S 136°7E **63** D2
Peale, Mt. *U.S.A.* 38°26N 109°14W **76** G9
Pearblossom *U.S.A.* 34°30N 117°55W **79** L9
Pearl → *U.S.A.* 30°11N 89°32W **85** F10
Pearl and Hermes Reef
   U.S.A. 27°55N 175°45W **75** K4
Pearl Banks *Sri Lanka* 8°45N 79°45E **45** K4
Pearl River = Zhu Jiang →
   China 22°15N 113°37E **35** F9
Pearl River *U.S.A.* 41°4N 74°2W **83** E10
Pearl River Bridge *China* 22°15N 113°48E **31** a
Pearsall *U.S.A.* 28°54N 99°6W **84** G5
Peary Chan. *Canada* 79°40N 101°30W **69** B11
Peary Land *Greenland* 82°40N 33°0W **4** A6
Pease → *U.S.A.* 34°12N 99°2W **84** D5
Peawanuck *Canada* 55°15N 85°12W **72** A2
Pebane *Mozam.* 17°10S 38°8E **55** H7
Pebas *Peru* 3°10S 71°46W **92** D4
Pebble Beach *U.S.A.* 36°34N 121°57W **78** J5
Peć = Pejë *Kosovo* 42°40N 20°17E **23** C9
Pechenga *Russia* 69°29N 31°4E **8** B24
Pechenizhyn *Ukraine* 48°30N 24°48E **17** D13
Pechora *Russia* 65°10N 57°11E **18** A10
Pechora → *Russia* 68°13N 54°15E **18** A9
Pechorskaya Guba *Russia* 68°40N 54°0E **18** A9
Pechory *Russia* 57°48N 27°40E **9** H22
Pecos *N. Mex., U.S.A.* 35°35N 105°41W **77** J11

Pecos *Tex., U.S.A.* 31°26N 103°30W **84** F3
Pecos → *U.S.A.* 29°42N 101°22W **84** G4
Pécs *Hungary* 46°5N 18°15E **17** E10
Pedasi *Panama* 7°32N 80°2W **88** E3
Pedda Bellala *India* 19°4N 78°9E **44** E4
Peddapalli *India* 18°40N 79°24E **44** E4
Peddapuram *India* 17°6N 82°8E **44** F6
Pedder, L. *Australia* 42°55S 146°10E **63** G4
Peddie *S. Africa* 33°14S 27°7E **57** D4
Pedernales *Dom. Rep.* 18°2N 71°44W **89** C5
Pedirka Desert *Australia* 26°47S 134°11E **63** A1
Pedra Azul *Brazil* 16°2S 41°17W **93** G10
Pedra Lume *C. Verde Is.* 16°40N 22°52W **52** b
Pedreiras *Brazil* 4°32S 44°40W **93** D10
Pedro Afonso *Brazil* 9°0S 48°10W **93** E9
Pedro Cays *Jamaica* 17°5N 77°48W **88** C4
Pedro de Valdivia *Chile* 22°55S 69°38W **94** A2
Pedro Juan Caballero
   Paraguay 22°30S 55°40W **95** A4
Pee Dee = Great Pee Dee →
   U.S.A. 33°21N 79°10W **85** E15
Peebinga *Australia* 34°52S 140°57E **63** E3
Peebles *U.K.* 55°40N 3°11W **11** F5
Peekskill *U.S.A.* 41°17N 73°55W **83** E11
Peel *I. of Man* 54°13N 4°40W **12** C3
Peel → *Australia* 30°50S 150°29E **63** E5
Peel → *Canada* 67°0N 135°0W **68** D5
Peel Sd. *Canada* 73°0N 96°0W **68** C12
Peera Peera Poolanna L.
   Australia 26°30S 138°0E **63** D2
Peerless Lake *Canada* 56°37N 114°40W **70** B6
Peers *Canada* 53°40N 116°0W **70** C5
Pegasus Bay *N.Z.* 43°20S 173°10E **59** E4
Pegu = Bago *Burma* 17°20N 96°29E **41** L20
Pegu Yoma *Burma* 19°0N 96°0E **41** K20
Pehuajó *Argentina* 35°45S 62°0W **94** D3
Pei Xian *China* 34°44N 116°55E **32** G9
Peikang *Taiwan* 23°34N 120°18E **35** F13
Peine *Chile* 23°45S 68°8W **94** A2
Peine *Germany* 52°19N 10°14E **16** B6
Peipus, L. = Chudskoye, Ozero
   Russia 58°13N 27°30E **9** G22
Peixe *Brazil* 12°0S 48°40W **93** F9
Peixe → *Brazil* 21°31S 51°58W **93** H8
Pejë *Kosovo* 42°40N 20°17E **23** C9
Pekalongan *Indonesia* 6°53S 109°40E **37** G13
Pekan *Malaysia* 3°30N 103°25E **39** L4
Pekan Nenas *Malaysia* 1°31N 103°31E **39** d
Pekanbaru *Indonesia* 0°30N 101°15E **36** D2
Pekin *U.S.A.* 40°35N 89°40W **80** E9
Pekutatan *Indonesia* 8°25S 114°49E **37** J17
Pelabuhan Ratu, Teluk
   Indonesia 7°5S 106°30E **37** G12
Pelagie, Is. *Italy* 35°39N 12°33E **22** G5
Pelaihari *Indonesia* 3°55S 114°45E **36** E4
Peleaga, Vf. *Romania* 45°22N 22°55E **17** F12
Pelée, Mt. *Martinique* 14°48N 61°10W **88** c
Pelee, Pt. *Canada* 41°54N 82°31W **72** D3
Pelee I. *Canada* 41°47N 82°40W **82** D2
Peleng *Indonesia* 1°20S 123°30E **37** E6
Pelentong *Malaysia* 1°32N 103°49E **39** d
Pelican *U.S.A.* 57°58N 136°14W **70** B1
Pelican L. *Canada* 52°28N 100°20W **71** C8
Pelican Narrows
   Canada 55°10N 102°56W **71** B8
Peljesac *Croatia* 42°55N 17°25E **22** C7
Pelkosenniemi *Finland* 67°6N 27°28E **8** C22
Pella *S. Africa* 29°1S 19°6E **56** C2
Pella *U.S.A.* 41°25N 92°55W **80** E7
Pello *Finland* 66°47N 23°59E **8** C20
Pelly → *Canada* 62°47N 137°19W **70** A1
Pelly Bay *Canada* 68°38N 89°50W **69** D14
Pelorus Sd. *N.Z.* 40°59S 173°59E **59** D4
Pelotas *Brazil* 31°42S 52°23W **95** C5
Pelotas → *Brazil* 27°28S 51°55W **95** B5
Pelvoux, Massif du *France* 44°52N 6°20E **20** D7
Pemalang *Indonesia* 6°53S 109°23E **37** G13
Pemanggil, Pulau
   Malaysia 2°37N 104°21E **39** L5
Pematangsiantar *Indonesia* 2°57N 99°5E **36** D1
Pemba *Mozam.* 12°58S 40°30E **55** G8
Pemba I. *Tanzania* 5°0S 39°45E **54** F7
Pemberton *Australia* 34°30S 116°0E **61** F2
Pemberton *Canada* 50°25N 122°50W **70** C4
Pembina → *Canada* 54°45N 114°17W **70** C6
Pembroke *Canada* 45°50N 77°7W **72** C4
Pembroke *U.K.* 51°41N 4°55W **13** F3
Pembrokeshire □ *U.K.* 51°52N 4°56W **13** F3
Pembrokeshire Coast △
   U.K. 51°50N 5°2W **13** F2
Pen *India* 18°45N 73°5E **44** E1
Pen-y-bont ar Ogwr = Bridgend
   U.K. 51°30N 3°34W **13** F4
Pen-y-Ghent *U.K.* 54°10N 2°14W **12** C5
Penal *Trin. & Tob.* 10°9N 61°29W **93** K15
Penang = Pinang *Malaysia* 5°25N 100°15E **39** c
Penápolis *Brazil* 21°30S 50°0W **95** A6
Peñarroya-Pueblonuevo
   Spain 38°19N 5°16W **21** C3
Penarth *U.K.* 51°26N 3°11W **13** F4
Peñas, C. de *Spain* 43°42N 5°52W **21** A3
Peñas, G. de *Chile* 47°0S 75°0W **96** F2
Pench → *India* 21°17N 79°10E **44** D4
Pench △ *India* 21°45N 79°20E **43** J8
Pench'i = Benxi *China* 41°20N 123°48E **33** D12
Pend Oreille → *U.S.A.* 49°4N 117°37W **76** B5
Pend Oreille, L. *U.S.A.* 48°10N 116°21W **76** B5
Pendembu *S. Leone* 9°7N 11°14W **52** G3
Pender B. *Australia* 16°45S 122°42E **60** C3
Pendleton *U.S.A.* 45°40N 118°47W **76** D4
Pendra *India* 22°46N 81°57E **43** H9
Penedo *Brazil* 10°15S 36°36W **93** F11
Penelokan *Indonesia* 8°17S 115°22E **37** J18
Penetanguishene *Canada* 44°50N 79°55W **82** B5
Penfield *U.S.A.* 41°13N 78°35W **82** E6
Penfro = Pembroke *U.K.* 51°41N 4°55W **13** F3
Peng'an *China* 31°2N 106°22E **34** B6
Pengana → *China* 19°53N 79°9E **44** E4
P'enghu Ch'üntou
   Taiwan 23°34N 119°30E **35** F12
Pecos *N. Mex., U.S.A.* 35°35N 105°41W **77** J11

Penglai *China* 37°48N 120°42E **33** F11
Pengshan *China* 30°14N 103°58E **34** B4
Pengshui *China* 29°17N 108°12E **34** C7
Pengxi *China* 30°44N 105°45E **34** B5
Pengze *China* 29°52N 116°32E **35** C11
Pengzhou *China* 31°4N 103°32E **34** B4
Peniche *Portugal* 39°19N 9°22W **21** C1
Penida, Nusa *Indonesia* 8°45S 115°30E **37** K18
Peninsular Malaysia □
   Malaysia 4°0N 102°0E **39** L4
Penitente, Serra do *Brazil* 8°45S 46°20W **93** E9
Penmarch, Pte. de *France* 47°48N 4°22W **20** C1
Penn Hills *U.S.A.* 40°28N 79°52W **82** F5
Penn Yan *U.S.A.* 42°40N 77°3W **82** D7
Pennant *Canada* 50°32N 108°14W **71** C7
Penner → *India* 14°35N 80°10E **45** G5
Pennines *U.K.* 54°45N 2°27W **12** C5
Pennington *U.S.A.* 39°15N 121°47W **78** F5
Pennsburg *U.S.A.* 40°23N 75°29W **83** F9
Pennsylvania □ *U.S.A.* 40°45N 77°30W **81** E15
Penny *U.S.A.* 53°51N 121°20W **70** C4
Penobscot → *U.S.A.* 44°30N 68°48W **81** C19
Penobscot B. *U.S.A.* 44°35N 68°50W **81** C19
Penola *Australia* 37°25S 140°48E **63** F3
Penong *Australia* 31°56S 133°1E **61** F5
Penonomé *Panama* 8°31N 80°21W **88** E3
Penrhyn *Cook Is.* 9°0S 158°0W **65** H12
Penrith *Australia* 33°43S 150°38E **63** E5
Penrith *U.K.* 54°40N 2°45W **12** C5
Penryn *U.K.* 50°9N 5°7W **13** G2
Pensacola *U.S.A.* 30°25N 87°13W **85** F11
Pensacola Mts. *Antarctica* 84°0S 40°0W **5** E1
Pense *Canada* 50°25N 104°59W **71** C8
Penshurst *Australia* 37°49S 142°20E **63** F3
Penticton *Canada* 49°30N 119°38W **70** D5
Pentland *Australia* 20°32S 145°25E **62** C4
Pentland Firth *U.K.* 58°43N 3°10W **11** C5
Pentland Hills *U.K.* 55°48N 3°25W **11** F5
Penukonda *India* 14°5N 77°38E **45** G3
Penza *Russia* 53°15N 45°5E **18** D8
Penzance *U.K.* 50°7N 5°33W **13** G2
Penzhino *Russia* 63°30N 167°55E **27** C17
Penzhinskaya Guba
   Russia 61°30N 163°0E **27** C17
Peoria *Ariz., U.S.A.* 33°43N 112°14W **77** K7
Peoria *Ill., U.S.A.* 40°42N 89°36W **80** E9
Pepani → *S. Africa* 25°49S 22°47E **56** D3
Pera Hd. *Australia* 12°55S 141°37E **62** A3
Perabumulih *Indonesia* 3°27S 104°15E **36** E2
Perak □ *Malaysia* 5°0N 101°0E **39** K3
Perak → *Malaysia* 4°0N 100°50E **39** K3
Perämeri △ *Finland* 65°35N 24°22E **8** D21
Perancak *Indonesia* 8°24S 114°37E **37** J17
Peräpohjola *Finland* 66°16N 26°10E **8** C22
Percé *Canada* 48°31N 64°13W **73** C7
Perche, Collines du *France* 48°30N 0°40E **20** B4
Percival Lakes *Australia* 21°25S 125°0E **60** D4
Percy Is. *Australia* 21°39S 150°16E **62** C5
Perdido, Mte. *Spain* 42°40N 0°5E **21** A6
Perdu, Mt. = Perdido, Mte.
   Spain 42°40N 0°5E **21** A6
Pereira *Colombia* 4°49N 75°43W **92** C3
Peremul Par *India* 11°10N 72°4E **45** J1
Perenjori *Australia* 29°26S 116°16E **61** E2
Pereyaslav-Khmelnytskyy
   Ukraine 50°3N 31°28E **19** D5
Pérez, I. *Mexico* 22°24N 89°42W **87** C7
Pergamino *Argentina* 33°52S 60°30W **94** C3
Pergau → *Malaysia* 5°23N 102°2E **39** K3
Perham *U.S.A.* 46°36N 95°34W **80** B6
Perhentian, Kepulauan
   Malaysia 5°54N 102°42E **39** K4
Péribonka → *Canada* 48°45N 72°5W **73** C5
Péribonka, L. *Canada* 50°1N 71°10W **73** B5
Péribonka, La Centrale de
   Canada 49°30N 71°10W **73** C5
Perico *Argentina* 24°20S 65°5W **94** A2
Pericos *Mexico* 25°3N 107°42W **86** B3
Périgueux *France* 45°10N 0°42E **20** D4
Perijá, Sierra de *Colombia* 9°30N 73°3W **92** B4
Perijá □ *Venezuela* 9°30N 72°55W **89** E5
Peringat *Malaysia* 6°2N 102°17E **39** J4
Perito Moreno *Argentina* 46°36S 70°56W **96** F2
Periyakulam *India* 10°5N 77°30E **45** J3
Periyar → *India* 10°15N 76°10E **45** J3
Periyar, L. *India* 9°25N 77°10E **45** K3
Periyar □ *India* 9°25N 77°10E **45** K3
Perkasie *U.S.A.* 40°22N 75°18W **83** F9
Perlas, Arch. de las
   Panama 8°41N 79°7W **88** E4
Perlas, Punta de Nic. *Nic.* 12°30N 83°30W **88** D3
Perlis □ *Malaysia* 6°30N 100°15E **39** J2
Perm *Russia* 58°0N 56°10E **18** C10
Pernambuco = Recife
   Brazil 8°0S 35°0W **93** E12
Pernambuco □ *Brazil* 8°0S 37°0W **93** E11
Pernatty Lagoon
   Australia 31°30S 137°12E **63** E2
Pernik *Bulgaria* 42°35N 23°2E **23** C10
Peron Is. *Australia* 13°9S 130°4E **60** B5
Peron Pen. *Australia* 26°0S 113°10E **61** E1
Perow *Canada* 54°35N 126°10W **70** C3
Perpignan *France* 42°42N 2°53E **20** E5
Perris *U.S.A.* 33°47N 117°14W **79** M9
Perry *Fla., U.S.A.* 30°7N 83°35W **85** F13
Perry *Ga., U.S.A.* 32°28N 83°44W **85** E13
Perry *Iowa, U.S.A.* 41°51N 94°6W **80** E6
Perry *N.Y., U.S.A.* 42°42N 78°0W **82** D7
Perry *Okla., U.S.A.* 36°17N 97°14W **84** C6
Perryville *U.S.A.* 37°43N 89°52W **80** G9
Persepolis *Iran* 29°55N 52°50E **47** D7
Pershotravensk *Ukraine* 50°13N 27°40E **17** C14
Persia = Iran ■ *Asia* 33°0N 53°0E **47** C7
Persian Gulf *Asia* 27°0N 50°0E **47** E6
Perth *Canada* 44°55N 76°15W **83** B8
Perth *Australia* 31°57S 115°52E **61** F2

Perth *U.K.* 56°24N 3°26W **11** E5
Perth & Kinross □ *U.K.* 56°45N 3°55W **11** E5
Perth Amboy *U.S.A.* 40°30N 74°15W **83** F10
Perth-Andover *Canada* 46°44N 67°42W **73** C6
Perth Basin *Ind. Oc.* 30°0S 108°0E **64** L2
Peru *Ind., U.S.A.* 40°45N 86°4W **80** E10
Peru *N.Y., U.S.A.* 44°35N 73°32W **83** B11
Peru ■ *S. Amer.* 4°0S 75°0W **92** D4
Peru Basin *Pac. Oc.* 20°0S 95°0W **65** J18
Peru-Chile Trench *Pac. Oc.* 20°0S 72°0W **92** G3
Perúgia *Italy* 43°7N 12°23E **22** C5
Pervomaysk *Ukraine* 48°10N 30°46E **19** E5
Pervouralsk *Russia* 56°59N 59°59E **18** C10
Pésaro *Italy* 43°54N 12°55E **22** C5
Pescadores = P'enghu Ch'üntou
   Taiwan 23°34N 119°30E **35** F12
Pescara *Italy* 42°28N 14°13E **22** C6
Peshawar *Pakistan* 34°2N 71°37E **42** B4
Peshkopi *Albania* 41°41N 20°25E **23** D9
Peshtigo *U.S.A.* 45°3N 87°45W **80** C10
Pesqueira *Brazil* 8°20S 36°42W **93** E11
Petah Tiqwa *Israel* 32°6N 34°53E **48** C3
Petaling Jaya *Malaysia* 3°4N 101°42E **39** L3
Petaluma *U.S.A.* 38°14N 122°39W **78** G4
Pétange *Lux.* 49°33N 5°55E **15** E5
Petaro *Pakistan* 25°31N 68°18E **42** G3
Petatlán *Mexico* 17°31N 101°16W **86** D4
Petauke *Zambia* 14°14S 31°20E **55** G6
Petawawa *Canada* 45°54N 77°17W **72** C4
Petén Itzá, L. *Guatemala* 16°58N 89°50W **88** C2
Peter I., Br. Virgin Is. *Br. Virgin Is.* 18°22N 64°35W **89** e
Peter I. Øy *Antarctica* 69°0S 91°0W **5** C16
Peter Pond L. *Canada* 55°55N 108°44W **71** B7
Peterbell *Canada* 48°36N 83°21W **72** C3
Peterborough *Australia* 32°58S 138°51E **63** E2
Peterborough *Canada* 44°20N 78°20W **82** B6
Peterborough *U.K.* 52°35N 0°15E **13** E7
Peterborough *U.S.A.* 42°53N 71°57W **83** D13
Peterborough □ *U.K.* 52°35N 0°15W **13** E7
Peterculter *U.K.* 57°6N 2°16W **11** D6
Peterhead *U.K.* 57°31N 1°48W **11** D7
Peterlee *U.K.* 54°46N 1°20W **12** C6
Petermann ◎ *Australia* 24°58S 130°0E **61** E4
Petermann Gletscher
   Greenland 80°30N 60°0W **69** A20
Petermann Ranges
   Australia 26°0S 130°30E **61** E5
Petersburg *Alaska,*
   U.S.A. 56°48N 132°58W **68** F5
Petersburg *Pa., U.S.A.* 40°34N 78°3W **82** F6
Petersburg *Va., U.S.A.* 37°14N 77°24W **81** G15
Petersburg *W. Va., U.S.A.* 39°1N 79°5W **81** F14
Petersfield *U.K.* 51°1N 0°56W **13** F7
Petit-Canal *Guadeloupe* 16°25N 61°31W **88** b
Petit-Goâve *Haiti* 18°27N 72°51W **89** C5
Petit Lac Manicouagan
   Canada 51°25N 67°40W **73** B6
Petit-Mécatina →
   Canada 50°40N 59°30W **73** B8
Petit-Mécatina, Î. du
   Canada 50°30N 59°25W **73** B8
Petit Piton *St. Lucia* 13°51N 61°5W **89** f
Petit-Saguenay *Canada* 48°15N 70°4W **73** C5
Petitcodiac *Canada* 45°57N 65°11W **73** C6
Petite Terre, Îles de la
   Guadeloupe 16°13N 61°9W **88** b
Petitot → *Canada* 60°14N 123°29W **70** A4
Petitsikapau L. *Canada* 54°37N 66°25W **73** B6
Petlad *India* 22°30N 72°45E **42** H5
Peto *Mexico* 20°8N 88°55W **87** C7
Petone *N.Z.* 41°13S 174°53E **59** D5
Petorca *Chile* 32°15S 70°56W **94** C1
Petoskey *U.S.A.* 45°22N 84°57W **81** C11
Petra *Jordan* 30°20N 35°22E **48** E4
Petra, Ostrov *Russia* 76°15N 118°30E **27** B12
Petra Velikogo, Zaliv
   Russia 42°40N 132°0E **28** C6
Petre, Pt. *Canada* 43°50N 77°9W **82** C7
Petrich *Bulgaria* 41°24N 23°13E **23** D10
Petrified Forest △ *U.S.A.* 35°0N 109°30W **77** J9
Petrikov = Pyetrikaw
   Belarus 52°11N 28°29E **17** B15
Petrolândia *Brazil* 9°5S 38°20W **93** E11
Petrolia *Canada* 42°54N 82°9W **82** D2
Petrolina *Brazil* 9°24S 40°30W **93** E10
Petropavl *Kazakhstan* 54°53N 69°13E **26** D7
Petropavlovsk = Petropavl
   Kazakhstan 54°53N 69°13E **26** D7
Petropavlovsk-Kamchatskiy
   Russia 53°3N 158°43E **27** D16
Petrópolis *Brazil* 22°33S 43°9W **95** A7
Petroşani *Romania* 45°28N 23°20E **17** F12
Petrovaradin *Serbia* 45°16N 19°55E **23** B8
Petrovsk *Russia* 52°22N 45°19E **18** D8
Petrovsk-Zabaykalskiy
   Russia 51°20N 108°55E **27** D11
Petrozavodsk *Russia* 61°41N 34°20E **18** B5
Petrus Steyn *S. Africa* 27°38S 28°8E **57** C4
Petrusburg *S. Africa* 29°4S 25°26E **56** D4
Peumo *Chile* 34°21S 71°12W **94** C1
Peureulak *Indonesia* 4°48N 97°45E **36** D1
Pevek *Russia* 69°41N 171°19E **27** C18
Pforzheim *Germany* 48°52N 8°41E **16** D5
Pha Taem △ *Thailand* 15°32N 105°30E **38** E5
Phagwara *India* 31°10N 75°40E **42** D6
Phala *Botswana* 23°45S 26°50E **56** B4
Phalaborwa *S. Africa* 23°57S 31°7E **57** B5
Phalera = Phulera *India* 26°52N 75°16E **42** F6
Phalodi *India* 27°12N 72°24E **42** F5
Phaltan *India* 17°59N 74°26E **44** F2
Phaluai, Ko *Thailand* 9°32N 99°41E **39** b
Phan *Thailand* 19°28N 99°43E **38** C2
Phan Rang -Thap Cham
   Vietnam 11°34N 109°0E **39** G7
Phan Ri Cua *Vietnam* 11°16N 108°40E **39** G7
Phan Si Pan *Vietnam* 22°18N 103°55E **38** A4
Phan Thiet *Vietnam* 11°1N 108°9E **39** G7
Phan Thiet, Vinh
   Vietnam 10°53N 108°5E **39** G7
Phan Wa, Laem *Thailand* 7°47N 98°25E **39** a

Phanat Nikhom
  Thailand   13°27N 101°11E 38 F3
Phangan, Ko Thailand   9°45N 100°00E 39 H3
Phangnga Thailand   8°28N 98°30E 39 H2
Phangnga, Ao Thailand   8°16N 98°33E 39 a
Phanom Sarakham
  Thailand   13°45N 101°21E 38 E3
Phaphund India   26°36N 79°28E 43 F8
Pharenda India   27°5N 83°17E 43 F10
Pharr U.S.A.   26°12N 98°11W 84 H5
Phatthalung Thailand   7°39N 100°6E 39 J3
Phayam, Ko Thailand   9°44N 98°25E 39 H2
Phayao Thailand   19°11N 99°55E 38 C2
Phelps U.S.A.   42°58N 77°3W 82 D7
Phelps L. Canada   59°15N 103°15W 71 B8
Phenix City U.S.A.   32°28N 85°1W 85 E12
Phet Buri = Phetchaburi
  Thailand   13°1N 99°55E 38 F2
Phetchabun Thailand   16°25N 101°8E 38 D3
Phetchabun, Thiu Khao
  Thailand   16°0N 101°20E 38 E3
Phetchaburi Thailand   13°1N 99°55E 38 F2
Phi Phi, Ko Thailand   7°45N 98°46E 39 J2
Phiafay Laos   14°48N 106°0E 38 E6
Phibun Mangsahan
  Thailand   15°14N 105°14E 38 E5
Phichai Thailand   17°22N 100°10E 38 D3
Phichit Thailand   16°26N 100°22E 38 D3
Philadelphia Miss.,
  U.S.A.   32°46N 89°7W 85 E10
Philadelphia N.Y., U.S.A. 44°9N 75°43W 83 C10
Philadelphia Pa., U.S.A. 39°57N 75°9W 83 G9
Philadelphia Int. ✈ (PHL)
  U.S.A.   39°51N 75°18W 83 G9
Philip U.S.A.   44°2N 101°40W 80 C3
Philip Smith Mts. U.S.A. 68°0N 148°0W 74 B10
Philippeville Belgium   50°12N 4°33E 15 D4
Philippi U.S.A.   39°9N 80°3W 81 F13
Philippi L. Australia   24°20S 138°55E 62 C2
Philippine Basin Pac. Oc. 17°0N 132°0E 64 F5
Philippine Sea Pac. Oc.   18°0N 125°0E 64 F4
Philippine Trench = Mindanao
  Trench Pac. Oc.   12°0N 126°6E 37 B7
Philippines ■ Asia   12°0N 123°0E 37 B6
Philippolis S. Africa   30°15S 25°16E 56 D4
Philippopolis = Plovdiv
  Bulgaria   42°8N 24°44E 23 C11
Philipsburg Canada   46°20N 73°5W 83 A11
Philipsburg Mont.,
  U.S.A.   46°20N 113°18W 76 C7
Philipsburg Pa., U.S.A.   40°54N 78°13W 82 F6
Philipstown = Daingean
  Ireland   53°18N 7°17W 10 C4
Philipstown S. Africa   30°28S 24°30E 56 D3
Phillip I. Australia   38°30S 145°12E 63 F4
Phillips U.S.A.   45°42N 90°24W 80 C8
Phillipsburg Kans., U.S.A. 39°45N 99°19W 80 F4
Phillipsburg N.J., U.S.A. 40°42N 75°12W 83 F9
Philmont U.S.A.   42°15N 73°39W 83 D11
Philomath U.S.A.   44°32N 123°22W 76 D2
Phimai Thailand   15°13N 102°30E 38 E4
Phitsanulok Thailand   16°50N 100°12E 38 D3
Phnom Kulen △
  Cambodia   13°38N 104°15E 38 F5
Phnom Penh Cambodia   11°33N 104°55E 39 G5
Phnom Penh = Phnom Penh
  Cambodia   11°33N 104°55E 39 G5
Pho, Laem Thailand   6°55N 101°19E 39 J3
Phoenicia U.S.A.   42°5N 74°14W 83 D10
Phoenix Mauritius   20°17S 57°30E 55 d
Phoenix Ariz., U.S.A.   33°26N 112°4W 77 K7
Phoenix N.Y., U.S.A.   43°14N 76°18W 83 C8
Phoenix Is. Kiribati   3°30S 172°0W 64 H10
Phoenix Sky Harbour Int. ✈ (PHX)
  U.S.A.   33°26N 112°5W 77 K7
Phoenixville U.S.A.   40°8N 75°31W 83 F9
Phon Thailand   15°49N 102°36E 38 E4
Phong ⇀ Thailand   16°23N 102°56E 38 D4
Phong Nha -Ke Bang △
  Vietnam   17°30N 106°10E 38 D6
Phong Saly Laos   21°42N 102°9E 34 G4
Phong Tho Vietnam   22°32N 103°21E 34 A4
Phonsavan Laos   19°27N 103°10E 38 C4
Phonum Thailand   8°49N 98°48E 39 H2
Phosphate Hill Australia 21°53S 139°58E 62 C2
Photharam Thailand   13°41N 99°51E 38 F2
Phra Nakhon Si Ayutthaya
  Thailand   14°25N 100°30E 38 E3
Phra Thong, Ko Thailand   9°5N 98°17E 39 H2
Phrae Thailand   18°7N 100°9E 38 C3
Phrom Phiram Thailand   17°2N 100°12E 38 D3
Phrom Thep, Laem Thailand 7°45N 98°19E 39 a
Phu Bia Laos   19°10N 103°0E 38 C4
Phu Chong -Na Yoi △
  Thailand   14°25N 105°30E 38 E5
Phu Hin Rong Kla △
  Thailand   17°0N 100°59E 38 D3
Phu Kao -Phu Phan Kham △
  Thailand   16°53N 102°31E 38 D4
Phu Kradung △ Thailand   17°2N 101°44E 38 D3
Phu Loi Laos   20°14N 103°14E 38 B4
Phu Luang △ Thailand   17°15N 101°29E 38 D3
Phu Ly Vietnam   20°35N 105°50E 34 G5
Phu My Vietnam   14°15N 109°5E 38 E7
Phu Pha Man △
  Thailand   16°44N 101°50E 38 D3
Phu Phan △ Thailand   17°0N 103°56E 38 D4
Phu Quoc, Dao Vietnam   10°20N 104°0E 39 G4
Phu Sa Dok Bua △
  Thailand   16°11N 104°45E 38 D5
Phu Sang △ Thailand   19°35N 100°19E 38 C3
Phu Tho Vietnam   21°24N 105°13E 34 G5
Phu Wiang △ Thailand   16°39N 102°20E 38 D4
Phuc Yen Vietnam   21°16N 105°45E 34 G5
Phuket Thailand   7°53N 98°24E 39 a
Phuket, Ko Thailand   8°0N 98°22E 39 a
Phul India   30°19N 75°14E 42 D6
Phulad India   25°38N 73°49E 42 G5
Phulbani India   20°28N 84°14E 44 D7

Phulera India   26°52N 75°16E 42 F6
Phulpur India   25°31N 82°49E 43 G10
Phunphin Thailand   9°7N 99°12E 39 H2
Phuntsholing Bhutan   26°51N 89°23E 43 F13
Phuphrabat Thailand   17°40N 102°45E 38 D4
Phuthaditjhaba S. Africa 28°29S 28°48E 57 C4
Phyu = Pyu Burma   18°30N 96°28E 41 K20
Pia ✦ Australia   27°7S 116°23E 61 E2
Piacenza Italy   45°1N 9°40E 20 D8
Piai, Tanjung Malaysia   1°17N 103°30E 39 d
Pian Cr. ⇀ Australia   30°2S 148°12E 63 E4
Pianosa Italy   42°35N 10°5E 22 C4
Piao'ertun China   41°50N 123°47E 33 D12
Piapot Canada   49°59N 109°8W 71 D7
Piatra Neamţ Romania   46°56N 26°21E 17 E14
Piauí □ Brazil   7°0S 43°0W 93 E10
Piauí ⇀ Brazil   6°38S 42°42W 93 E10
Piave ⇀ Italy   45°32N 12°44E 22 B5
Pibor Post South Sudan   6°47N 33°3E 53 G12
Picardie □ France   49°50N 3°0E 20 B5
Picardy = Picardie □
  France   49°50N 3°0E 20 B5
Picayune U.S.A.   30°32N 89°41W 85 F10
Pichhor India   25°58N 78°20E 43 G8
Pichilemu Chile   34°22S 72°0W 94 C1
Pichor India   25°11N 78°11E 42 G8
Pickerel L. Canada   48°40N 91°25W 72 C1
Pickering U.K.   54°15N 0°46W 12 C7
Pickering, Vale of U.K.   54°14N 0°45W 12 C7
Pickle Lake Canada   51°30N 90°12W 72 B1
Pickwick L. U.S.A.   35°4N 88°15W 85 D10
Pico Azores   38°28N 28°20W 52 a
Pico Bonito △ Honduras   15°34N 86°48W 88 C2
Pico Truncado Argentina   46°40S 68°0W 96 F3
Picos Brazil   7°5S 41°28W 93 E10
Picton Canada   44°1N 77°9W 82 B7
Picton N.Z.   41°18S 174°3E 59 D5
Pictou Canada   45°41N 62°42W 73 C7
Picture Butte Canada   49°55N 112°45W 70 D6
Pictured Rocks △
  U.S.A.   46°30N 86°30W 80 B10
Picún Leufú Argentina   39°30S 69°5W 96 D3
Pidurutalagala Sri Lanka 7°10N 80°50E 45 L5
Piedmont = Piemonte □
  Italy   45°0N 8°0E 20 D7
Piedmont Ala., U.S.A.   33°55N 85°37W 85 E12
Piedmont S.C., U.S.A.   34°42N 82°28W 66 F11
Piedras Negras Mexico   28°42N 100°31W 86 B4
Pieksämäki Finland   62°18N 27°10E 8 E22
Pielinen Finland   63°15N 29°40E 8 E23
Pieljekaise △ Sweden   66°20N 16°45E 8 C17
Piemonte □ Italy   45°0N 8°0E 20 D7
Pienaarsrivier S. Africa 25°15S 28°18E 57 C4
Piercefield U.S.A.   44°13N 74°35W 83 B10
Pierceland Canada   54°20N 109°46W 71 C7
Pierpont U.S.A.   41°45N 80°34W 82 E4
Pierre U.S.A.   44°22N 100°21W 80 C3
Pierrefonds Canada   45°29N 73°51W 83 A11
Piet Retief S. Africa   27°1S 30°50E 57 D5
Pietarsaari Finland   63°40N 22°43E 8 E20
Pietermaritzburg S. Africa 29°35S 30°25E 57 D5
Pietersburg = Polokwane
  S. Africa   23°54S 29°25E 57 B4
Pietrosul, Vf. Maramureş,
  Romania   47°35N 24°43E 17 E13
Pietrosul, Vf. Suceava,
  Romania   47°12N 25°18E 17 E13
Pigeon I. India   14°2N 74°20E 45 G2
Pigeon L. Canada   44°27N 78°30W 82 B6
Piggott U.S.A.   36°23N 90°11W 85 C9
Pigüe Argentina   37°36S 62°25W 94 D3
Pihani India   27°36N 80°15E 43 F9
Pihlajavesi Finland   61°45N 28°45E 8 F23
Pijijiapan Mexico   15°42N 93°14W 87 D6
Pikangikum Canada   51°49N 94°0W 71 C10
Pikes Peak U.S.A.   38°50N 105°3W 76 G11
Piketberg S. Africa   32°55S 18°40E 56 D2
Pikeville U.S.A.   37°29N 82°31W 81 G12
Pikou China   39°18N 122°22E 33 E12
Pikwitonei Canada   55°35N 97°9W 71 B9
Piła Poland   53°10N 16°48E 17 B9
Pilanesberg △ S. Africa   25°15S 27°4E 56 C4
Pilani India   28°22N 75°33E 42 E6
Pilar Paraguay   26°50S 58°20W 94 B4
Pilaya ⇀ Bolivia   20°55S 64°4W 92 H6
Pilbara Australia   21°15S 118°16E 60 D2
Pilcomayo ⇀ Paraguay   25°21S 57°42W 94 B4
Pilgrim's Rest S. Africa 24°55S 30°44E 57 B5
Pilibhit India   28°40N 79°50E 43 E8
Pilica ⇀ Poland   51°52N 21°17E 17 C11
Pilipinas = Philippines ■
  Asia   12°0N 123°0E 37 B6
Pilkhawa India   28°43N 77°42E 42 E7
Pilliga Australia   30°21S 148°54E 63 E4
Pilos Greece   36°55N 21°42E 23 F9
Pilot Mound Canada   49°15N 98°54W 71 D9
Pilot Point U.S.A.   33°24N 96°58W 84 E6
Pilot Rock U.S.A.   45°29N 118°50W 76 D4
Pima U.S.A.   32°54N 109°50W 77 K9
Pimba Australia   31°18S 136°46E 63 E2
Pimenta Bueno Brazil   11°35S 61°10W 92 F6
Pimentel Peru   6°45S 79°55W 92 E3
Pimpri Chinchwad India   18°37N 73°47E 44 E1
Pin Valley △ India   31°50N 77°50E 42 D7
Pinang Malaysia   5°25N 100°15E 39 c
Pinang Malaysia   5°20N 100°20E 39 K3
Pinar del Río Cuba   22°26N 83°40W 88 B3
Pınarhisar Turkey   41°37N 27°30E 23 D12
Pinatubo, Mt. Phil.   15°8N 120°21E 37 A6
Pinawa Canada   50°9N 95°50W 71 C9
Pinchang China   31°36N 107°3E 34 B6
Pincher Creek Canada   49°30N 113°57W 70 D6
Pinchi L. Canada   54°38N 124°30W 70 C4
Pinckneyville U.S.A.   38°5N 89°23W 80 F9
Pińczów Poland   50°32N 20°32E 17 C11
Pindar Australia   28°30S 115°47E 61 E2
Pindera Downs ✦
  Australia   29°24S 142°37E 63 A3
Pindi Gheb Pakistan   33°14N 72°21E 42 C5
Pindos Oros Greece   40°0N 21°0E 23 E9

Pindus Mts. = Pindos Oros
  Greece   40°0N 21°0E 23 E9
Pine ⇀ B.C., Canada   56°8N 120°43W 70 B4
Pine ⇀ Sask., Canada   58°50N 105°38W 71 B7
Pine Bluff U.S.A.   34°13N 92°1W 84 D8
Pine Bluffs U.S.A.   41°11N 104°4W 76 F11
Pine City U.S.A.   45°50N 92°59W 80 C7
Pine Cr. ⇀ U.S.A.   41°10N 77°16W 82 E7
Pine Creek Australia   13°50S 131°50E 60 B5
Pine Falls Canada   50°34N 96°11W 71 C9
Pine Flat L. U.S.A.   36°50N 119°20W 78 J7
Pine Grove U.S.A.   40°33N 76°23W 83 F8
Pine Hill Australia   23°38S 146°57E 62 C4
Pine Island Glacier
  Antarctica   76°0S 100°0W 5 D15
Pine Pass Canada   55°25N 122°42W 70 B4
Pine Ridge U.S.A.   43°2N 102°33W 80 D2
Pine River Canada   51°45N 100°30W 71 C8
Pine River U.S.A.   46°43N 94°24W 80 B6
Pine Valley U.S.A.   32°50N 116°32W 79 N10
Pinecrest U.S.A.   38°12N 120°1W 78 G6
Pinedale Calif., U.S.A.   36°50N 119°48W 78 J7
Pinedale Wyo., U.S.A.   42°52N 109°52W 76 E9
Pinega ⇀ Russia   64°30N 44°19E 18 B8
Pinehouse L. Canada   55°32N 106°35W 71 B7
Pineimuta ⇀ Canada   52°8N 88°33W 72 B1
Pinerolo Italy   44°53N 7°21E 20 D7
Pines, Akra Greece   40°5N 24°20E 23 D11
Pinetop-Lakeside U.S.A.   34°9N 109°58W 77 J9
Pineville U.S.A.   31°19N 92°26W 84 F8
Ping ⇀ Thailand   15°42N 100°9E 38 E3
Pingaring Australia   32°40S 118°32E 61 F2
Pingba China   26°33N 106°1E 34 D6
Pingbian China   23°0N 103°45E 34 F4
Pingchuan China   25°31N 101°55E 34 D3
Pingding China   37°47N 113°38E 32 F7
Pingdingshan China   33°43N 113°27E 32 H7
Pingdu China   36°42N 119°59E 33 F10
Pingelly Australia   32°32S 117°5E 61 F2
Pinghe China   24°17N 117°21E 35 E11
Pinghu China   30°40N 121°2E 35 B13
Pingjiang China   28°45S 113°36E 35 C9
Pingle China   24°40N 110°40E 35 E8
Pingli China   32°27N 109°22E 34 A7
Pingliang China   35°35N 106°31E 32 G4
Pingluo China   39°31N 106°30E 32 E4
Pingluo China   38°52N 106°30E 32 E4
Pingnan Fujian, China   26°35N 119°0E 35 D12
Pingnan Guangxi Zhuangzu,
  China   23°33N 110°22E 35 F8
Pingquan China   41°1N 118°37E 33 D10
Pingrup Australia   33°32S 118°29E 61 F2
Pingshan China   28°39N 104°3E 34 C5
Pingtan China   25°31N 119°47E 35 E12
Pingtang China   25°49N 107°17E 34 E6
P'ingtung Taiwan   22°38N 120°30E 35 F13
Pingwu China   32°25N 104°30E 32 H3
Pingxiang Guangxi Zhuangzu,
  China   22°6N 106°46E 34 F6
Pingxiang Jiangxi. China 27°43N 113°48E 35 D9
Pingyao China   37°12N 112°10E 32 F7
Pingyi China   35°30N 117°35E 33 G9
Pingyin China   36°20N 116°25E 32 F9
Pingyuan Guangdong,
  China   24°37N 115°57E 35 E10
Pingyuan Shandong,
  China   37°10N 116°22E 32 F9
Pingyuanjie China   23°45N 103°48E 34 F4
Pinheiro Brazil   2°31S 45°5W 93 D9
Pinheiro Machado Brazil   31°34S 53°23W 95 C5
Pinhel Portugal   40°50N 7°1W 21 B2
Pini Indonesia   0°10N 98°40E 36 D1
Pinios ⇀ Greece   39°55N 22°41E 23 E10
Pinjarra Australia   32°37S 115°52E 61 F2
Pink Mountain Canada   57°3N 122°52W 70 B4
Pinnacle Is. = Senkaku-Shotō
  E. China Sea   25°45N 123°30E 29 M1
Pinnacles △ U.S.A.   36°25N 121°12W 78 J5
Pinnaroo Australia   35°17S 140°53E 63 F3
Pinon Hills U.S.A.   34°26N 117°39W 79 L9
Pinos Mexico   22°18N 101°34W 86 C4
Pinos, Mt. U.S.A.   34°49N 119°8W 79 L7
Pinos Pt. U.S.A.   36°38N 121°57W 77 H3
Pinrang Indonesia   3°46S 119°41E 37 E5
Pins, Pte. aux Canada   42°15N 81°51W 82 D3
Pinsk Belarus   52°10N 26°1E 17 B14
Pintados Chile   20°35S 69°40W 92 H5
Pinyang China   27°42N 120°31E 35 D13
Pinyug Russia   60°5N 48°0E 18 B8
Pioche U.S.A.   37°56N 114°27W 77 H6
Piombino Italy   42°55N 10°32E 22 C4
Pioner, Ostrov Russia   79°50N 92°0E 27 B10
Piopiotaki = Milford Sd.
  N.Z.   44°41S 167°47E 59 F1
Piorini, L. Brazil   3°15S 62°35W 92 D6
Piotrków Trybunalski
  Poland   51°23N 19°43E 17 C10
Pip Iran   26°45N 60°10E 45 E9
Pipar India   26°25N 73°31E 42 F5
Pipar Road India   26°27N 73°27E 42 F5
Piparia Mad. P., India   21°49N 78°23E 42 J8
Piparia Mad. P., India   22°45N 78°23E 43 H8
Pipestone U.S.A.   44°0N 96°19W 80 D5
Pipestone ⇀ Canada   52°53N 89°23W 72 B2
Pipestone Cr. ⇀
  Canada   49°38N 100°15W 71 D8
Piplan Pakistan   32°17N 71°21E 42 C4
Pipmuacan, Rés. Canada   49°45N 70°30W 73 C5
Pippingarra Australia   20°27S 118°42E 60 D2
Piqua U.S.A.   40°9N 84°15W 81 E11
Piquiri ⇀ Brazil   24°3S 54°14W 95 A5
Pir Panjal Range India   32°30N 76°50E 42 C7
Pir Sohrab Iran   25°44N 60°54E 47 E9
Piracicaba Brazil   22°45S 47°40W 95 A6
Piracuruca Brazil   3°50S 41°50W 93 D10
Pirae Tahiti   17°33S 149°32W 59 d
Pirajuí Brazil   21°59S 49°29W 95 A6

Piram I. India   21°36N 72°21E 42 J5
Pirané Argentina   25°42S 59°6W 94 B4
Pirapora Brazil   17°20S 44°56W 93 G10
Pirawa India   24°10N 76°2E 42 G7
Pirgos Greece   37°40N 21°27E 23 F9
Piribebuy Paraguay   25°26S 57°2W 94 B4
Pirimapun Indonesia   6°20S 138°24E 37 F9
Pirin Planina Bulgaria   41°40N 23°30E 23 D10
Pírineos = Pyrénées
  Europe   42°45N 0°18E 20 E4
Piripiri Brazil   4°15S 41°46W 93 D10
Pirlangimpi Australia   11°24S 130°26E 60 B5
Pirmasens Germany   49°12N 7°36E 16 D4
Pirot Serbia   43°9N 22°33E 23 C10
Piru Indonesia   3°4S 128°12E 37 E7
Piru U.S.A.   34°25N 118°48W 79 L8
Pisa Italy   43°43N 10°23E 22 C4
Pisagua Chile   19°40S 70°15W 92 G4
Pisco Peru   13°50S 76°12W 92 F3
Pisek Czech Rep.   49°19N 14°10E 16 D8
Pishan China   37°30N 78°33E 30 D4
Pishin Iran   26°6N 61°47E 47 E9
Pishin Pakistan   30°35N 67°0E 42 D2
Pishin Lora ⇀ Pakistan   29°9N 64°5E 42 E1
Pising Indonesia   5°8S 121°53E 37 F6
Pismo Beach U.S.A.   35°9N 120°38W 79 K6
Pissis, Cerro Argentina   27°45S 68°48W 94 B2
Pistóia Italy   43°55N 10°54E 22 C4
Pistol B. Canada   62°25N 92°37W 71 A10
Pisuerga ⇀ Spain   41°33N 4°52W 21 B3
Pit ⇀ U.S.A.   40°47N 122°6W 76 F2
Pitarpunga L. Australia   34°24S 143°30E 63 E3
Pitcairn I. Pac. Oc.   25°5S 130°5W 65 K14
Pitch L. Trin. & Tob.   10°14N 61°39W 93 K15
Piteå Sweden   65°20N 21°25E 8 D19
Piteälven ⇀ Sweden   65°20N 21°25E 8 D19
Piteşti Romania   44°52N 24°54E 17 F13
Pithapuram India   17°10N 82°15E 44 F6
Pithara Australia   30°20S 116°35E 61 F2
Pithora India   21°16N 82°31E 44 D6
Pithoragarh India   29°35N 80°13E 43 E9
Pithoro Pakistan   25°31N 69°23E 42 G3
Pitlochry U.K.   56°42N 3°44W 11 E5
Pitt I. Canada   53°30N 129°50W 70 C3
Pitt I. India   10°50N 72°38E 45 J1
Pittsburg Calif., U.S.A. 38°2N 121°53W 78 G5
Pittsburg Kans., U.S.A.   37°25N 94°42W 80 G6
Pittsburg Tex., U.S.A.   33°0N 94°59W 84 E7
Pittsburgh U.S.A.   40°26N 79°58W 82 F5
Pittsfield Ill., U.S.A.   39°36N 90°49W 80 F8
Pittsfield Maine, U.S.A. 44°47N 69°23W 81 C19
Pittsfield Mass., U.S.A. 42°27N 73°15W 83 D11
Pittsfield N.H., U.S.A.   43°18N 71°20W 83 C13
Pittston U.S.A.   41°19N 75°47W 83 E9
Pittsworth Australia   27°41S 151°37E 63 D5
Pituri ⇀ Australia   22°35S 138°30E 62 C2
Piura Peru   5°15S 80°38W 92 E2
Piuthan Nepal   28°7N 82°56E 43 E10
Pixian China   30°48N 103°52E 34 B4
Pixley U.S.A.   35°58N 119°18W 78 K7
Pizhou = Pei Xian China   34°44N 116°55E 32 G9
Pizhou China   34°18N 117°57E 33 G9
Placentia Canada   47°20N 54°0W 73 C9
Placentia B. Canada   47°0N 54°40W 73 C9
Placerville U.S.A.   38°44N 120°48W 78 G6
Placetas Cuba   22°15N 79°44W 88 B4
Plaine des Jarres Laos   19°27N 103°10E 38 C4
Plainfield N.J., U.S.A.   40°37N 74°25W 83 F10
Plainfield Ohio, U.S.A.   40°13N 81°43W 82 F3
Plainfield Vt., U.S.A.   44°17N 72°26W 83 B12
Plains Mont., U.S.A.   47°28N 114°53W 76 C6
Plains Tex., U.S.A.   33°11N 102°50W 84 E3
Plainview Nebr., U.S.A.   42°21N 97°47W 80 D5
Plainwell U.S.A.   42°27N 85°38W 81 D11
Plaistow U.S.A.   42°50N 71°6W 83 D13
Plaka, Akra Greece   35°11N 26°19E 23 G12
Plana Cays Bahamas   22°38N 73°30W 89 B5
Planada U.S.A.   37°16N 120°19W 78 H6
Plano U.S.A.   33°1N 96°42W 84 E6
Plant City U.S.A.   28°1N 82°7W 85 G13
Plasencia Spain   40°3N 6°8W 21 B2
Plaquemine U.S.A.   30°17N 91°14W 84 F9
Plasencia Spain   40°3N 6°8W 21 B2
Plaster City U.S.A.   32°47N 115°51W 79 N11
Plaster Rock Canada   46°53N 67°22W 73 C6
Plastun Russia   44°45N 136°19E 28 B8
Plata, Río de la ⇀
  S. Amer.   34°45S 57°30W 94 C4
Plátani ⇀ Italy   37°23N 13°16E 22 F5
Platte U.S.A.   43°23N 98°51W 80 D4
Platte ⇀ Mo., U.S.A.   39°16N 94°50W 80 F6
Platte ⇀ Nebr., U.S.A.   41°4N 95°53W 80 E6
Platteville U.S.A.   42°44N 90°29W 80 D8
Plattsburgh U.S.A.   44°42N 73°28W 83 B11
Plattsmouth U.S.A.   41°1N 95°53W 80 E6
Plauen Germany   50°30N 12°8E 16 C7
Plavinas Latvia   56°35N 25°46E 9 H21
Playa del Carmen Mexico   20°37N 87°4W 87 C7
Playgreen L. Canada   54°0N 98°15W 71 C9
Pleasant Bay Canada   46°51N 60°48W 73 C7
Pleasant Hill U.S.A.   38°47N 94°16W 80 F7
Pleasant Mount U.S.A.   41°44N 75°26W 83 E9
Pleasanton Calif., U.S.A. 37°39N 121°52W 78 H5
Pleasanton Tex., U.S.A.   28°58N 98°29W 84 G5
Pleasantville N.J.,
  U.S.A.   39°24N 74°32W 81 F16
Pleasantville Pa., U.S.A. 41°35N 79°34W 82 E5
Plei Ku Vietnam   13°57N 108°0E 38 F7
Plenty ⇀ Australia   23°25S 136°31E 62 C2
Plenty, B. of N.Z.   37°45S 177°0E 59 B6
Plentywood U.S.A.   48°47N 104°34W 76 B11
Plesetsk Russia   62°43N 40°20E 18 B7
Plessisville Canada   46°14N 71°47W 73 C5
Plétipi, L. Canada   51°44N 70°6W 73 B5
Pleven Bulgaria   43°26N 24°37E 23 C11
Plevna Canada   44°58N 76°59W 82 B8
Pljevlja Montenegro   43°21N 19°21E 23 C8
Plock Poland   52°32N 19°40E 17 B10
Plöckenstein Germany   48°46N 13°51E 16 D7

Ploieşti Romania   44°57N 26°5E 17 F1
Plonge, Lac la Canada   55°8N 107°20W 71 B7
Plovdiv Bulgaria   42°8N 24°44E 23 C1
Plover Cove Res. China   22°28N 114°15E 31
Plum U.S.A.   40°29N 79°47W 82 F
Plum I. U.S.A.   41°11N 72°12W 83 E1
Plumas U.S.A.   39°45N 120°4W 78 F
Plummer U.S.A.   47°20N 116°53W 76 C
Plumridge Lakes
  Australia   29°26S 125°16E 61 E
Plumtree Zimbabwe   20°27S 27°55E 55 J
Plungė Lithuania   55°53N 21°59E 9 J1
Plymouth Trin. & Tob.   11°14N 60°48W 93 J1
Plymouth U.K.   50°22N 4°10W 13 G
Plymouth Calif., U.S.A.   38°29N 120°51W 78 G
Plymouth Ind., U.S.A.   41°21N 86°19W 80 E1
Plymouth Mass., U.S.A.   41°57N 70°40W 83 E1
Plymouth N.C., U.S.A.   35°52N 76°43W 85 D1
Plymouth N.H., U.S.A.   43°46N 71°41W 83 C1
Plymouth Pa., U.S.A.   41°14N 75°57W 83 E
Plymouth Wis., U.S.A.   43°45N 87°59W 80 D1
Plympton-Wyoming = Wyoming
  Canada   42°57N 82°7W 82 D2
Plynlimon = Pumlumon Fawr
  U.K.   52°28N 3°46W 13 E
Plyusa Russia   58°28N 29°27E 9 G2
Plzeň Czech Rep.   49°45N 13°22E 16 D7
Pmere Nyente ✦
  Australia   24°15S 136°10E 62 C
Po ⇀ Italy   44°57N 12°4E 22 B
Po Hai = Bo Hai China   39°0N 119°0E 33 E
Po Toi China   22°10N 114°16E 31 d
Pobeda Russia   65°12N 146°12E 27 C14
Pobedy, Pik Asia   42°0N 79°58E 30 C
Pocahontas Ark., U.S.A.   36°16N 90°58W 85 C
Pocahontas Iowa, U.S.A.   42°44N 94°40W 80 D7
Pocatello U.S.A.   42°52N 112°27W 76 E7
Pocomoke City U.S.A.   38°5N 75°34W 81 F1
Poços de Caldas Brazil   21°50S 46°33W 95 A6
Podgorica Montenegro   42°30N 19°19E 23 C8
Podile India   15°37N 79°37E 45 G
Podilska Vysochyna
  Ukraine   49°0N 28°0E 17 D14
Podolsk Russia   55°25N 37°30E 18 C6
Podporozhye Russia   60°55N 34°2E 18 B5
Pofadder S. Africa   29°10S 19°22E 56 C2
Pogranichnyy Russia   44°25N 131°24E 28 B5
Poh Indonesia   0°46S 122°51E 37 E6
Pohang S. Korea   36°1N 129°23E 33 F1
Pohjanmaa ⇀ Finland   62°58N 22°50E 8 E2
Pohnpei Micronesia   6°55N 158°10E 64 G7
Pohri India   25°32N 77°22E 42 G6
Poinsett, C. Antarctica   65°42S 113°18E 5 C
Point Arena U.S.A.   38°55N 123°41W 78 G3
Point Baker U.S.A.   56°21N 133°37W 70 B2
Point Calimere India   10°17N 79°49E 45 J4
Point Fortin Trin. & Tob. 10°10N 61°42W 93 K15
Point Hope U.S.A.   68°21N 166°47W 74 B6
Point L. Canada   65°15N 113°4W 68 D5
Point Lisas Trin. & Tob. 10°24N 61°29W 93 K15
Point Pedro Sri Lanka   9°50N 80°15E 45 K5
Point Pelee △ Canada   41°57N 82°31W 82 E2
Point Pleasant N.J., U.S.A. 40°5N 74°4W 83 F10
Point Pleasant W. Va.,
  U.S.A.   38°51N 82°8W 81 F12
Point Reyes △ U.S.A.   38°10N 122°55W 78 G2
Pointe-à-Pitre Guadeloupe 16°15N 61°32W 88 b
Pointe-au-Pic = La Malbaie
  Canada   47°40N 70°10W 73 C5
Pointe-Claire Canada   45°26N 73°50W 83 A11
Pointe-Gatineau Canada   45°27N 75°41W 83 A9
Pointe-Noire Congo   4°48S 11°53E 54 E2
Pointe-Noire Guadeloupe   16°14N 61°47W 88 b
Poipet Cambodia   13°39N 102°33E 38 F4
Poisonbush Ra.
  Australia   22°30S 121°30E 60 D3
Poissonnier Pt. Australia 19°57S 119°10E 60 C2
Poitiers France   46°35N 0°20E 20 C4
Poitou France   46°40N 0°10W 20 C3
Pojoaque U.S.A.   35°54N 106°1W 77 J10
Pokaran India   27°0N 71°50E 42 F4
Pokataroo Australia   29°30S 148°36E 63 D4
Pokhara Nepal   28°14N 83°58E 43 E10
Poko Dem. Rep. of the Congo 3°7N 26°52E 54 D5
Pokrovsk Russia   61°29N 129°0E 27 C13
Pola = Pula Croatia   44°54N 13°57E 16 F7
Polacca U.S.A.   35°50N 110°23W 77 J8
Polan Iran   25°30N 61°10E 47 E9
Poland Europe   52°0N 20°0E 17 C10
Poland ■ Europe   52°0N 20°0E 17 C10
Polar Bear △ Canada   55°0N 83°45W 72 A2
Polatsk Belarus   55°30N 28°50E 9 J23
Polavaram India   17°15N 81°38E 44 F5
Polcura Chile   37°17S 71°43W 94 D1
Polesye = Pripet Marshes
  Europe   52°10N 27°10E 17 B15
Polevskoy Russia   56°26N 60°11E 18 C11
Police Poland   53°33N 14°33E 16 B8
Police, Pte. Seychelles   4°51S 55°32E 55 b
Poligiros Greece   40°23N 23°25E 23 D10
Polillo Is. Phil.   14°56N 122°0E 37 B6
Polk U.S.A.   41°22N 79°56W 82 E5
Pollachi India   10°35N 77°0E 45 J3
Polnovat Russia   63°50N 65°54E 26 C7
Polokwane S. Africa   23°54S 29°25E 57 B4
Polokwane ⇀ S. Africa   22°25S 30°5E 57 B5
Polonnaruwa Sri Lanka   7°56N 81°0E 45 L5
Polonne Ukraine   50°6N 27°30E 17 C14
Polonnoye = Polonne
  Ukraine   50°6N 27°30E 17 C14
Polson U.S.A.   47°41N 114°9W 76 C6
Poltava Ukraine   49°35N 34°35E 19 E5
Põltsamaa Estonia   58°39N 25°58E 9 G21
Polunochnoye Russia   60°52N 60°25E 26 C7
Polur India   12°32N 79°11E 45 H4
Põlva Estonia   58°3N 27°3E 9 G22
Polyarny Russia   69°8N 33°20E 8 B25
Polyarnyye Zori Russia   67°22N 32°30E 8 C25
Polynesia Pac. Oc.   10°0S 162°0W 65 F11
Polynésie française = French
  Polynesia ☑ Pac. Oc.   20°0S 145°0W 65 J13

Pombal *Portugal* 39°55N 8°40W **21** C1
Pomene *Mozam.* 22°53S 35°33E **57** B6
Pomeroy *Ohio, U.S.A.* 39°2N 82°2W **81** F12
Pomeroy *Wash., U.S.A.* 46°28N 117°36W **76** C5
Pomézia *Italy* 41°40N 12°30E **22** D5
Pomona *Australia* 26°22S 152°52E **63** D5
Pomona *U.S.A.* 34°4N 117°45W **79** L9
Pomorskie, Pojezierze
  Poland 53°40N 16°37E **17** B9
Pompeys Pillar *U.S.A.* 45°59N 107°57W **76** D10
Pompeys Pillar △ *U.S.A.* 46°0N 108°0W **76** D10
Pompton Lakes *U.S.A.* 41°0N 74°17W **83** F10
Ponape = Pohnpei
  Micronesia 6°55N 158°10E **64** G7
Ponask L. *Canada* 54°0N 92°41W **72** B1
Ponca *U.S.A.* 42°34N 96°43W **80** D5
Ponca City *U.S.A.* 36°42N 97°5W **84** C6
Ponce *Puerto Rico* 18°1N 66°37W **89** d
Ponchatoula *U.S.A.* 30°26N 90°26W **85** F9
Poncheville, L. *Canada* 50°10N 76°55W **72** B4
Pond *U.S.A.* 35°43N 119°20W **79** K7
Pond Inlet *Canada* 72°40N 77°0W **69** C16
Pondicherry = Puducherry
  India 11°59N 79°50E **45** J4
Ponds, I. of *Canada* 53°27N 55°52W **73** B8
Ponferrada *Spain* 42°32N 6°35W **21** A2
Ponnaiyar → *India* 11°50N 79°45E **45** J4
Ponnani *India* 10°45N 75°59E **45** J2
Ponneri *India* 13°20N 80°15E **45** H5
Ponnuru *India* 16°5N 80°34E **45** F5
Ponoka *Canada* 52°42N 113°40W **70** C6
Ponorogo *Indonesia* 7°52S 111°27E **37** G14
Ponoy *Russia* 67°0N 41°13E **18** A7
Ponoy → *Russia* 66°59N 41°17E **18** A7
Ponta Delgada *Azores* 37°44N 25°40W **52** a
Ponta Grossa *Brazil* 25°7S 50°10W **95** B5
Ponta Porã *Brazil* 22°20S 55°35W **95** A4
Pontardawe *U.K.* 51°43N 3°51W **13** F3
Pontarlier *France* 46°54N 6°20E **20** C7
Ponteix *Canada* 49°46N 107°29W **71** D7
Pontevedra *Spain* 42°26N 8°40W **21** A1
Pontiac *Ill., U.S.A.* 40°53N 88°38W **80** E9
Pontiac *Mich., U.S.A.* 42°38N 83°18W **81** D12
Pontian Kechil *Malaysia* 1°29N 103°23E **39** d
Pontianak *Indonesia* 0°3S 109°15E **36** E3
Pontine Is. = Ponziane, Ísole
  Italy 40°55N 12°57E **22** D5
Pontine Mts. = Kuzey Anadolu
  Dağları *Turkey* 41°0N 36°45E **19** F6
Pontivy *France* 48°5N 2°58W **20** B2
Pontoise *France* 49°3N 2°5E **20** B5
Ponton → *Canada* 58°27N 116°11W **70** B5
Pontypool *Canada* 44°6N 78°38W **82** B6
Pontypool *U.K.* 51°42N 3°2W **13** F4
Pontypridd *U.K.* 51°36N 3°20W **13** F4
Ponziane, Ísole *Italy* 40°55N 12°57E **22** D5
Poochera *Australia* 32°43S 134°51E **63** E1
Poole *U.K.* 50°43N 1°59W **13** G6
Poole □ *U.K.* 50°43N 1°59W **13** G6
Poona = Pune *India* 18°29N 73°57E **44** E1
Poonamallee *India* 13°3N 80°10E **45** H5
Pooncarie *Australia* 33°22S 142°31E **63** E3
Poopelloe L. *Australia* 31°40S 144°0E **63** E3
Poopó, L. de *Bolivia* 18°30S 67°35W **92** G5
Popayán *Colombia* 2°27N 76°36W **92** C3
Poperinge *Belgium* 50°51N 2°42E **15** D2
Popiltah L. *Australia* 33°10S 141°42E **63** E3
Popio L. *Australia* 33°10S 141°52E **63** E3
Poplar *U.S.A.* 48°7N 105°12W **76** B11
Poplar → *Canada* 53°0N 97°19W **71** C9
Poplar Bluff *U.S.A.* 36°46N 90°24W **80** G8
Poplarville *U.S.A.* 30°51N 89°32W **85** F10
Popocatépetl, Volcán
  Mexico 19°2N 98°38W **87** D5
Popokabaka
  Dem. Rep. of the Congo 5°41S 16°40E **54** F3
Poprad *Slovak Rep.* 49°3N 20°18E **17** D11
Porali → *Pakistan* 25°58N 66°26E **42** G2
Porbandar *India* 21°44N 69°43E **42** J3
Porcher I. *Canada* 53°50N 130°30W **70** C2
Porcupine → *Canada* 59°11N 104°46W **71** B8
Porcupine → *U.S.A.* 66°34N 145°19W **68** D2
Porcupine Gorge △
  Australia 20°22S 144°26E **62** C3
Pordenone *Italy* 45°57N 12°39E **22** B5
Pori *Finland* 61°29N 21°48E **8** F19
Porkhov *Russia* 57°45N 29°38E **9** H23
Porlamar *Venezuela* 10°57N 63°51W **92** A6
Pormpuraaw *Australia* 14°59S 141°26E **62** A3
Pormpuraaw ◇
  Australia 14°55S 141°47E **62** A3
Poronaysk *Russia* 49°13N 143°0E **31** B17
Poroshiri-Dake *Japan* 42°41N 142°52E **28** C11
Porpoise B. *Antarctica* 66°0S 127°0E **5** C9
Porsangerfjorden *Norway* 70°40N 25°40E **8** A21
Porsgrunn *Norway* 59°10N 9°40E **9** G13
Port Alberni *Canada* 49°14N 124°50W **70** D4
Port Alfred *S. Africa* 33°36S 26°55E **56** D4
Port Alice *Canada* 50°20N 127°25W **70** C3
Port Allegany *U.S.A.* 41°48N 78°17W **82** E6
Port Allen *U.S.A.* 30°27N 91°12W **84** F9
Port Alma *Australia* 23°38S 150°53E **62** C5
Port Alma *Canada* 42°10N 82°14W **82** D2
Port Angeles *U.S.A.* 48°7N 123°27W **78** B3
Port Antonio *Jamaica* 18°10N 76°26W **88** a
Port Aransas *U.S.A.* 27°50N 97°4W **84** H6
Port Arthur *Australia* 43°7S 147°50E **63** G4
Port Arthur *U.S.A.* 29°54N 93°56W **84** G8
Port au Choix *Canada* 50°43N 57°22W **73** B8
Port au Port B. *Canada* 48°40N 58°50W **73** C8
Port-au-Prince *Haiti* 18°40N 72°20W **89** C5
Port Augusta *Australia* 32°30S 137°50E **63** E2
Port Austin *U.S.A.* 44°3N 83°1W **82** B2
Port Blair *India* 11°40N 92°45E **45** J11
Port Blandford *Canada* 48°20N 54°10W **73** C9
Port Bradshaw *Australia* 12°30S 137°20E **62** A2
Port Broughton
  Australia 33°37S 137°56E **63** E2

Port Bruce *Canada* 42°39N 81°0W **82** D4
Port Burwell *Canada* 42°40N 80°48W **82** D4
Port Campbell *India* 11°56N 92°37E **45** J11
Port Canning *India* 22°23N 88°40E **43** H13
Port Carling *Canada* 45°7N 79°35W **82** A5
Port Chalmers *N.Z.* 45°49S 170°30E **59** F3
Port Charlotte *U.S.A.* 26°59N 82°6W **85** H13
Port Chester *U.S.A.* 41°0N 73°40W **83** F11
Port Clements *Canada* 53°40N 132°10W **70** C2
Port Clinton *U.S.A.* 41°31N 82°56W **81** E12
Port Colborne *Canada* 42°50N 79°10W **82** D5
Port Coquitlam *Canada* 49°15N 122°45W **78** A4
Port Cornwallis *India* 13°17N 93°5E **45** H11
Port Credit *Canada* 43°33N 79°35W **82** C5
Port Curtis *Australia* 23°57S 151°20E **62** C5
Port Dalhousie *Canada* 43°13N 79°16W **82** C5
Port Darwin *Australia* 12°24S 130°45E **60** B5
Port Darwin *Falk. Is.* 51°50S 59°0W **96** G5
Port Davey *Australia* 43°16S 145°55E **63** G4
Port-de-Paix *Haiti* 19°50N 72°50W **89** C5
Port Dickson *Malaysia* 2°30N 101°49E **39** L3
Port Douglas *Australia* 16°30S 145°30E **62** B4
Port Dover *Canada* 42°47N 80°12W **82** D4
Port Edward *Canada* 54°12N 130°10W **70** C2
Port Elgin *Canada* 44°25N 81°25W **82** B3
Port Elizabeth *S. Africa* 33°58S 25°40E **56** D4
Port Ellen *U.K.* 55°38N 6°11W **11** F2
Port Erin *I. of Man* 54°5N 4°45W **12** C3
Port Essington *Australia* 11°15S 132°10E **60** B5
Port Ewen *U.S.A.* 41°54N 73°59W **83** E11
Port Fairy *Australia* 38°22S 142°12E **63** F3
Port Gamble *U.S.A.* 47°51N 122°34W **78** C4
Port-Gentil *Gabon* 0°40S 8°50E **54** E1
Port Germein *Australia* 33°1S 138°1E **63** E2
Port Ghalib *Egypt* 25°20N 34°50E **46** E2
Port Gibson *U.S.A.* 31°58N 90°59W **84** F9
Port Glasgow *U.K.* 55°56N 4°41W **11** F4
Port Harcourt *Nigeria* 4°40N 7°10E **52** H7
Port Hardy *Canada* 50°41N 127°30W **70** C3
Port Harrison = Inukjuak
  Canada 58°25N 78°15W **69** F16
Port Hawkesbury
  Canada 45°36N 61°22W **73** C7
Port Hedland *Australia* 20°25S 118°35E **60** D2
Port Henry *U.S.A.* 44°3N 73°28W **83** B11
Port Hood *Canada* 46°0N 61°32W **73** C7
Port Hope *Canada* 43°56N 78°20W **82** C6
Port Hope *U.S.A.* 43°57N 82°43W **82** C2
Port Hope Simpson
  Canada 52°33N 56°18W **73** B8
Port Hueneme *U.S.A.* 34°7N 119°12W **79** L7
Port Huron *U.S.A.* 42°58N 82°26W **82** D2
Port Jefferson *U.S.A.* 40°57N 73°3W **83** F11
Port Jervis *U.S.A.* 41°22N 74°41W **83** E10
Port Kenny *Australia* 33°10S 134°41E **63** E1
Port Klang *Malaysia* 3°0N 101°35E **39** L3
Port Láirge = Waterford
  Ireland 52°15N 7°8W **10** D4
Port Lavaca *U.S.A.* 28°37N 96°38W **84** G6
Port Leyden *U.S.A.* 43°35N 75°21W **83** C9
Port Lincoln *Australia* 34°42S 135°52E **63** E2
Port Loko *S. Leone* 8°48N 12°46W **52** G3
Port-Louis *Guadeloupe* 16°28N 61°32W **88** b
Port Louis *Mauritius* 20°10S 57°30E **55** d
Port MacDonnell
  Australia 38°5S 140°48E **63** F3
Port McNeill *Canada* 50°35N 127°6W **70** C3
Port Macquarie
  Australia 31°25S 152°25E **63** E5
Port Maria *Jamaica* 18°22N 76°54W **88** a
Port Matilda *U.S.A.* 40°48N 78°3W **82** F6
Port McNicoll *Canada* 44°44N 79°48W **82** B5
Port Mellon *Canada* 49°32N 123°31W **70** D4
Port-Menier *Canada* 49°51N 64°15W **73** C7
Port Moody *Canada* 49°17N 122°51W **78** A4
Port Morant *Jamaica* 17°54N 76°19W **88** a
Port Moresby *Papua N. G.* 9°24S 147°8E **58** B7
Port Muhammed Bin Qasim = Port
  Qasim *Pakistan* 24°46N 67°20E **42** G2
Port Musgrave *Australia* 11°55S 141°50E **62** A3
Port Neches *U.S.A.* 29°59N 93°59W **84** G8
Port Nolloth *S. Africa* 29°17S 16°52E **56** C2
Port Nouveau-Québec =
  Kangiqsualujjuaq
  Canada 58°30N 65°59W **69** F18
Port of Climax *Canada* 49°10N 108°20W **71** D7
Port of Coronach *Canada* 49°7N 105°31W **71** D7
Port of Spain
  Trin. & Tob. 10°40N 61°31W **93** K15
Port Orange *U.S.A.* 29°9N 80°59W **85** G14
Port Orchard *U.S.A.* 47°32N 122°38W **78** C4
Port Orford *U.S.A.* 42°45N 124°30W **76** E1
Port Pegasus *N.Z.* 47°12S 167°41E **59** G1
Port Perry *Canada* 44°6N 78°56W **82** B6
Port Phillip B. *Australia* 38°10S 144°50E **63** F3
Port Pirie *Australia* 33°10S 138°1E **63** E2
Port Qasim *Pakistan* 24°46N 67°20E **42** G2
Port Renfrew *Canada* 48°30N 124°20W **78** B2
Port Roper *Australia* 14°45S 135°25E **62** A2
Port Rowan *Canada* 42°40N 80°30W **82** D4
Port Safaga = Bûr Safâga
  Egypt 26°43N 33°57E **46** E2
Port Said = Bûr Sa'îd
  Egypt 31°16N 32°18E **53** B12
Port St. Joe *U.S.A.* 29°49N 85°18W **85** G12
Port St. Johns = Umzimvubu
  S. Africa 31°38S 29°33E **57** D4
Port St. Lucie *U.S.A.* 27°18N 80°21W **85** H14
Port Sanilac *U.S.A.* 43°26N 82°33W **82** C2
Port Severn *Canada* 44°48N 79°43W **82** B5
Port Shepstone *S. Africa* 30°44S 30°28E **57** D5
Port Simpson *Canada* 54°30N 130°20W **70** C2
Port Stanley = Stanley
  Falk. Is. 51°40S 59°51W **96** G5
Port Stanley *Canada* 42°40N 81°10W **82** D3
Port Sudan = Bûr Sûdân
  Sudan 19°32N 37°9E **53** E13
Port Sulphur *U.S.A.* 29°29N 89°42W **85** G10
Port Talbot *U.K.* 51°35N 3°47W **13** F4

Port Townsend *U.S.A.* 48°7N 122°45W **78** B4
Port-Vendres *France* 42°32N 3°8E **20** E5
Port Vila *Vanuatu* 17°45S 168°18E **58** C9
Port Vladimir *Russia* 69°25N 33°6E **8** B25
Port Wakefield *Australia* 34°12S 138°10E **63** E2
Port Washington
  U.S.A. 43°23N 87°53W **80** D10
Porta Orientalis *Romania* 45°6N 22°18E **17** F12
Portacloy *Ireland* 54°20N 9°46W **10** B2
Portadown *U.K.* 54°25N 6°27W **10** B5
Portaferry *U.K.* 54°23N 5°33W **10** B6
Portage *Pa., U.S.A.* 40°23N 78°41W **82** F6
Portage *Wis., U.S.A.* 43°33N 89°28W **80** D9
Portage la Prairie
  Canada 49°58N 98°18W **71** D9
Portageville *U.S.A.* 36°26N 89°42W **80** G10
Portalegre *Portugal* 39°19N 7°25W **21** C2
Portales *U.S.A.* 34°11N 103°20W **77** J12
Portarlington *Ireland* 53°9N 7°14W **10** C4
Portbou *Spain* 42°25N 3°9E **21** A7
Porter L. *N.W.T., Canada* 61°41N 108°5W **71** A7
Porter L. *Sask., Canada* 56°20N 107°20W **71** B7
Porterville *S. Africa* 33°0S 19°0E **56** D2
Porterville *U.S.A.* 36°4N 119°1W **78** J8
Porth Tywyn = Burry Port
  U.K. 51°41N 4°15W **13** F3
Porthcawl *U.K.* 51°29N 3°42W **13** F4
Porthill *U.S.A.* 48°59N 116°30W **76** B5
Porthmadog *U.K.* 52°55N 4°8W **12** E3
Portile de Fier *Europe* 44°44N 22°30E **17** F12
Portimão *Portugal* 37°8N 8°32W **21** D1
Portishead *U.K.* 51°29N 2°46W **13** F5
Portknockie *U.K.* 57°42N 2°51W **11** D6
Portland *N.S.W., Australia* 33°20S 150°0E **63** E5
Portland *Vic., Australia* 38°20S 141°35E **63** F3
Portland *Canada* 44°42N 76°12W **83** B8
Portland *Conn., U.S.A.* 41°34N 72°38W **83** E12
Portland *Maine, U.S.A.* 43°39N 70°16W **81** D18
Portland *Mich., U.S.A.* 42°52N 84°54W **81** D11
Portland *Oreg., U.S.A.* 45°32N 122°37W **78** E4
Portland *Pa., U.S.A.* 40°55N 75°6W **83** F9
Portland *Tex., U.S.A.* 27°53N 97°20W **84** H6
Portland, I. of *U.K.* 50°33N 2°26W **13** G5
Portland B. *Australia* 38°15S 141°45E **63** F3
Portland Bight *Jamaica* 17°52N 77°5W **88** a
Portland Bill *U.K.* 50°31N 2°28W **13** G5
Portland Canal *U.S.A.* 55°56N 130°0W **70** B2
Portland Int. ✈ (PDX)
  U.S.A. 45°35N 122°36W **78** E4
Portland Pt. *Jamaica* 17°42N 77°11W **88** a
Portlaoise *Ireland* 53°2N 7°18W **10** C4
Portmadoc = Porthmadog
  U.K. 52°55N 4°8W **12** E3
Portmore *Jamaica* 17°53N 76°53W **88** a
Porto *France* 42°16N 8°42E **20** E8
Porto *Portugal* 41°8N 8°40W **21** B1
Pôrto Alegre *Brazil* 30°5S 51°10W **95** C5
Porto de Moz *Brazil* 1°41S 52°13W **93** D8
Porto Empédocle *Italy* 37°17N 13°32E **22** F5
Porto Esperança *Brazil* 19°37S 57°29W **92** G7
Porto Franco *Brazil* 6°20S 47°24W **93** E9
Porto Inglês = Vila do Maio
  C. Verde Is. 15°21N 23°10W **52** b
Porto Mendes *Brazil* 24°30S 54°15W **95** A5
Porto Murtinho *Brazil* 21°45S 57°55W **92** H7
Porto Nacional *Brazil* 10°40S 48°30W **93** F9
Porto-Novo *Benin* 6°23N 2°42E **52** G6
Porto Primavera, Represa
  Brazil 22°10S 52°45W **95** A5
Porto Santo, I. de
  Madeira 33°45N 16°25W **52** B2
Porto São José *Brazil* 22°43S 53°10W **95** A5
Porto Seguro *Brazil* 16°26S 39°5W **93** G11
Porto Tórres *Italy* 40°50N 8°24E **22** D3
Porto União *Brazil* 26°10S 51°10W **95** B5
Porto-Vecchio *France* 41°35N 9°16E **20** F8
Porto Velho *Brazil* 8°46S 63°54W **92** E6
Porto Walter *Brazil* 8°15S 72°40W **92** E4
Portobelo *Panama* 9°35N 79°42W **88** E4
Portoferráio *Italy* 42°48N 10°20E **22** C4
Portola *U.S.A.* 39°49N 120°28W **78** F6
Portoscuso *Italy* 39°12N 8°24E **22** E3
Portoviejo *Ecuador* 1°7S 80°28W **92** D2
Portpatrick *U.K.* 54°51N 5°7W **11** G3
Portree *U.K.* 57°25N 6°12W **11** D2
Portrush *U.K.* 55°12N 6°40W **10** A5
Portsmouth *Dominica* 15°34N 61°27W **89** C7
Portsmouth *U.K.* 50°48N 1°6W **13** G6
Portsmouth *N.H., U.S.A.* 43°5N 70°45W **83** C14
Portsmouth *Ohio, U.S.A.* 38°44N 82°57W **81** F12
Portsmouth *R.I., U.S.A.* 41°36N 71°15W **83** E13
Portsmouth *Va., U.S.A.* 36°58N 76°23W **81** G15
Portsmouth □ *U.K.* 50°48N 1°6W **13** G6
Portsoy *U.K.* 57°41N 2°41W **11** D6
Portstewart *U.K.* 55°11N 6°43W **10** A5
Porttipahdan tekojärvi
  Finland 68°5N 26°40E **8** B22
Portugal ■ *Europe* 40°0N 8°0W **21** C1
Portumna *Ireland* 53°6N 8°14W **10** C3
Portville *U.S.A.* 42°3N 78°20W **82** D6
Poruma *Australia* 10°2S 143°4E **62** a
Porvenir *Chile* 53°10S 70°16W **96** G2
Posadas *Argentina* 27°30S 55°50W **95** B4
Posht-e Badam *Iran* 33°2N 55°23E **47** C7
Poso *Indonesia* 1°20S 120°55E **37** E6
Poso, Danau *Indonesia* 1°52S 120°35E **37** E6
Posse *Brazil* 14°4S 46°18W **93** F9
Possession I. *Antarctica* 72°4S 172°0E **5** D11
Possum Kingdom L.
  U.S.A. 32°52N 98°26W **84** E5
Post *U.S.A.* 33°12N 101°23W **84** E4
Post Falls *U.S.A.* 47°43N 116°57W **76** C5
Postavy = Pastavy *Belarus* 55°4N 26°50E **9** J22
Poste-de-la-Baleine =
  Kuujjuarapik *Canada* 55°20N 77°35W **72** A4
Postmasburg *S. Africa* 28°18S 23°5E **56** D3
Postojna *Slovenia* 45°46N 14°12E **16** F8
Poston *U.S.A.* 34°0N 114°24W **79** M12
Postville *Canada* 54°54N 59°47W **73** B8
Posyet *Russia* 42°39N 130°48E **28** C5

Potchefstroom *S. Africa* 26°41S 27°7E **56** C4
Poteau *U.S.A.* 35°3N 94°37W **84** D7
Poteet *U.S.A.* 29°2N 98°35W **84** G5
Potenza *Italy* 40°38N 15°48E **22** D6
Poteriteri, L. *N.Z.* 46°5S 167°10E **59** G1
Potgietersrus = Mokopane
  S. Africa 24°10S 28°55E **57** B4
Poti *Georgia* 42°10N 41°38E **19** F7
Potiskum *Nigeria* 11°39N 11°2E **53** F8
Potomac → *U.S.A.* 38°0N 76°23W **81** F15
Potosí *Bolivia* 19°38S 65°50W **92** G5
Potosi Mt. *U.S.A.* 35°57N 115°29W **79** K11
Pototan *Phil.* 10°54N 122°38E **37** B6
Potrerillos *Chile* 26°30S 69°30W **94** B2
Potsdam *Germany* 52°23N 13°3E **16** B7
Potsdam *U.S.A.* 44°40N 74°59W **83** B10
Pottersville *U.S.A.* 43°43N 73°50W **83** C11
Pottstown *U.S.A.* 40°15N 75°39W **83** F9
Pottsville *U.S.A.* 40°41N 76°12W **83** F8
Pottuvil *Sri Lanka* 6°55N 81°50E **45** L5
P'otzu *Taiwan* 23°28N 120°15E **35** F13
Pouce Coupé *Canada* 55°40N 120°10W **70** B4
Poughkeepsie *U.S.A.* 41°42N 73°56W **83** E11
Poulaphouca Res. *Ireland* 53°8N 6°30W **10** C5
Poulsbo *U.S.A.* 47°44N 122°38W **78** C4
Poultney *U.S.A.* 43°31N 73°14W **83** C11
Poulton-le-Fylde *U.K.* 53°51N 2°58W **12** D5
Pouso Alegre *Brazil* 22°14S 45°57W **95** A6
Pouthisat *Cambodia* 12°34N 103°50E **38** F4
Považská Bystrica
  Slovak Rep. 49°8N 18°27E **17** D10
Povenets *Russia* 62°50N 34°50E **18** B5
Poverty B. *N.Z.* 38°43S 178°2E **59** C7
Poverty Point Nat. Monument △
  U.S.A. 32°39N 91°24W **84** E9
Póvoa de Varzim *Portugal* 41°25N 8°46W **21** B1
Povorotnyy, Mys *Russia* 42°40N 133°2E **28** C6
Povungnituk = Puvirnituq
  Canada 60°2N 77°10W **69** E16
Powassan *Canada* 46°5N 79°25W **72** C4
Poway *U.S.A.* 32°58N 117°2W **79** N9
Powder → *U.S.A.* 46°45N 105°26W **76** C11
Powder River *U.S.A.* 43°2N 106°59W **76** E10
Powell *U.S.A.* 44°45N 108°46W **76** D9
Powell, L. *U.S.A.* 36°57N 111°29W **77** H8
Powell River *Canada* 49°50N 124°35W **70** D4
Powers *U.S.A.* 45°41N 87°32W **80** C10
Pownal *U.S.A.* 42°45N 73°14W **83** D11
Powys □ *U.K.* 52°20N 3°20W **13** E4
Poyang Hu *China* 29°5N 116°20E **35** C11
Poyarkovo *Russia* 49°36N 128°41E **27** E13
Poza Rica *Mexico* 20°33N 97°27W **87** C5
Požarevac *Serbia* 44°35N 21°18E **23** B9
Poznań *Poland* 52°25N 16°55E **17** B9
Pozo *U.S.A.* 35°20N 120°24W **79** K6
Pozo Almonte *Chile* 20°10S 69°50W **92** H5
Pozo Colorado *Paraguay* 23°30S 58°45W **94** A4
Pozoblanco *Spain* 38°23N 4°51W **21** C3
Pozzuoli *Italy* 40°49N 14°7E **22** D6
Prachin Buri *Thailand* 14°0N 101°25E **38** F3
Prachuap Khirikhan
  Thailand 11°49N 99°48E **39** G2
Prado *Brazil* 17°20S 39°13W **93** G11
Prahita → *India* 19°0N 79°55E **44** E4
Praia *C. Verde Is.* 15°2N 23°34W **52** b
Prainha *Brazil* 1°45S 53°30W **93** D8
Prainha Nova *Brazil* 7°10S 60°30W **92** E6
Prairie *Australia* 20°50S 144°35E **62** C3
Prairie City *U.S.A.* 44°28N 118°43W **76** D4
Prairie Dog Town Fork Red →
  U.S.A. 34°34N 99°58W **84** D5
Prairie du Chien *U.S.A.* 43°3N 91°9W **80** D8
Prairies, L. of the
  Canada 51°16N 101°32W **71** C8
Prambanan △ *Indonesia* 7°45S 110°28E **37** G14
Pran Buri *Thailand* 12°23N 99°55E **38** F2
Prapat *Indonesia* 2°41N 98°58E **36** D1
Praslin *Seychelles* 4°18S 55°45E **55** b
Prata *Brazil* 19°25S 48°54W **93** G9
Pratabpur *India* 23°28N 83°15E **43** H10
Pratapgarh *Raj., India* 24°2N 74°40E **42** G6
Pratapgarh *Ut. P., India* 25°56N 81°59E **43** G9
Pratas I. = Dongsha Dao
  S. China Sea 20°45N 116°43E **35** G11
Prato *Italy* 43°53N 11°6E **22** C4
Pratt *U.S.A.* 37°39N 98°44W **80** G4
Prattville *U.S.A.* 32°28N 86°29W **85** E11
Pravara → *India* 19°35N 74°45E **44** E2
Pravia *Spain* 43°30N 6°12W **21** A2
Praya *Indonesia* 8°39S 116°17E **36** F5
Prayag = Allahabad
  India 25°25N 81°58E **43** G9
Pre-delta △ *Argentina* 32°10S 60°40W **94** C3
Preah Seihanu = Kampong Saom
  Cambodia 10°38N 103°30E **39** G4
Preah Vihear *Cambodia* 14°23N 104°41E **38** E5
Preble *U.S.A.* 42°44N 76°8W **83** D8
Precipice △ *Australia* 25°18S 150°5E **63** D5
Precordillera *Argentina* 30°0S 69°1W **94** C2
Preeceville *Canada* 51°57N 102°40W **71** C8
Preiļi *Latvia* 56°18N 26°43E **9** H22
Premont *U.S.A.* 27°22N 98°7W **84** H5
Prentice *U.S.A.* 45°33N 90°17W **80** C8
Preobrazheniye *Russia* 42°54N 133°54E **28** C6
Preparis I. = Pariparit Kyun
  Burma 14°52N 93°41E **45** G11
Preparis North Channel
  Ind. Oc. 15°27N 94°5E **45** G11
Preparis South Channel
  Ind. Oc. 14°33N 93°30E **45** G11
Přerov *Czech Rep.* 49°28N 17°27E **17** D9
Prescott *Canada* 44°45N 75°30W **83** B9
Prescott *Ariz., U.S.A.* 34°33N 112°28W **77** J7
Prescott *Ark., U.S.A.* 33°48N 93°23W **84** E8
Prescott Valley *U.S.A.* 34°40N 112°18W **77** J7
Preservation Inlet *N.Z.* 46°8S 166°35E **59** G1
Presho *U.S.A.* 43°54N 100°3W **80** D3
Presidencia de la Plaza
  Argentina 27°0S 59°50W **94** B4
Presidencia Roque Saenz Peña
  Argentina 26°45S 60°30W **94** B3

Presidente Epitácio *Brazil* 21°56S 52°6W **93** H8
Presidente Hayes □
  Paraguay 24°0S 59°0W **94** A4
Presidente Prudente
  Brazil 22°5S 51°25W **95** A5
Presidio *U.S.A.* 29°34N 104°22W **84** G2
Prešov *Slovak Rep.* 49°0N 21°15E **17** D11
Prespa, L. = Prespansko Jezero
  Macedonia 40°55N 21°0E **23** D9
Prespansko Jezero
  Macedonia 40°55N 21°0E **23** D9
Presque I. *U.S.A.* 42°10N 80°6W **82** D4
Presque Isle *U.S.A.* 46°41N 68°1W **81** B19
Prestatyn *U.K.* 53°20N 3°24W **12** D4
Presteigne *U.K.* 52°17N 3°0W **13** E5
Preston *Canada* 43°23N 80°21W **82** C4
Preston *U.K.* 53°46N 2°42W **12** D5
Preston *Idaho, U.S.A.* 42°6N 111°53W **76** E8
Preston *Minn., U.S.A.* 43°40N 92°5W **80** D7
Preston, C. *Australia* 20°51S 116°12E **60** D2
Prestonsburg *U.S.A.* 37°40N 82°47W **81** G12
Prestwick *U.K.* 55°29N 4°37W **11** F4
Pretoria *S. Africa* 25°44S 28°12E **57** C4
Preveza *Greece* 38°57N 20°45E **23** E9
Prey Veng *Cambodia* 11°35N 105°29E **39** G5
Pribilof Is. *U.S.A.* 57°0N 170°0W **74** D6
Pribram *Czech Rep.* 49°41N 14°2E **16** D8
Price *U.S.A.* 39°36N 110°49W **76** G8
Price, C. *India* 13°34N 93°3E **45** H11
Price I. *Canada* 52°23N 128°41W **70** C3
Prichard *U.S.A.* 30°44N 88°5W **85** F10
Priekule *Latvia* 56°26N 21°35E **9** H19
Prienai *Lithuania* 54°38N 23°57E **9** J20
Prieska *S. Africa* 29°40S 22°42E **56** C3
Priest L. *U.S.A.* 48°35N 116°52W **76** B5
Priest River *U.S.A.* 48°11N 116°55W **76** B5
Priest Valley *U.S.A.* 36°10N 120°39W **78** J6
Prievidza *Slovak Rep.* 48°46N 18°36E **17** D10
Prikaspiyskaya Nizmennost =
  Caspian Depression
  Eurasia 47°0N 48°0E **19** E8
Prilep *Macedonia* 41°21N 21°32E **23** D9
Priluki = Pryluky
  Ukraine 50°30N 32°24E **19** D5
Prime Hd. *Antarctica* 63°12S 48°57W **5** C18
Prime Seal I. *Australia* 40°3S 147°43E **63** G4
Primo Tapia *Mexico* 32°16N 116°54W **79** N10
Primorskiy Kray □ *Russia* 45°0N 135°0E **28** B7
Primrose L. *Canada* 54°55N 109°45W **71** C7
Prince Albert *Canada* 53°15N 105°50W **71** C7
Prince Albert *S. Africa* 33°12S 22°2E **56** D3
Prince Albert △ *Canada* 54°0N 106°25W **71** C7
Prince Albert Mts.
  Antarctica 76°0S 161°30E **5** D11
Prince Albert Pen.
  Canada 72°30N 116°0W **68** C8
Prince Albert Sd. *Canada* 70°25N 115°0W **68** C8
Prince Alfred, C. *Canada* 74°20N 124°40W **4** B1
Prince Charles I.
  Canada 67°47N 76°12W **69** D16
Prince Charles Mts.
  Antarctica 72°0S 67°0E **5** D6
Prince Edward Fracture Zone
  Ind. Oc. 46°0S 35°0E **5** A4
Prince Edward I. □
  Canada 46°20N 63°20W **73** C7
Prince Edward Is. *Ind. Oc.* 46°35S 38°0E **3** G11
Prince George *Canada* 53°55N 122°50W **70** C4
Prince of Wales, C.
  U.S.A. 65°36N 168°5W **74** B6
Prince of Wales I.
  Australia 10°40S 142°10E **62** A3
Prince of Wales I. *Canada* 73°0N 99°0W **68** C12
Prince of Wales I.
  U.S.A. 55°47N 132°50W **68** F5
Prince of Wales Icefield
  Canada 78°15N 79°0W **69** B16
Prince of Wales Str.
  Canada 73°0N 117°0W **68** C8
Prince Patrick I. *Canada* 77°0N 120°0W **68** B8
Prince Regent Inlet
  Canada 73°0N 90°0W **69** C14
Prince Rupert *Canada* 54°20N 130°20W **70** C2
Prince William Sd.
  U.S.A. 60°40N 147°0W **68** E2
Princes Town
  Trin. & Tob. 10°16N 61°23W **93** K15
Princess Charlotte B.
  Australia 14°25S 144°0E **62** A3
Princess Elizabeth Trough
  S. Ocean 64°10S 83°0E **5** C7
Princess May Ranges
  Australia 15°30S 125°30E **60** C4
Princess Royal I. *Canada* 53°0N 128°40W **70** C3
Princeton *Canada* 49°27N 120°30W **70** D4
Princeton *Calif., U.S.A.* 39°24N 122°1W **78** F4
Princeton *Ill., U.S.A.* 41°23N 89°28W **80** E9
Princeton *Ind., U.S.A.* 38°21N 87°34W **80** F10
Princeton *Ky., U.S.A.* 37°7N 87°53W **80** G10
Princeton *Mo., U.S.A.* 40°24N 93°35W **80** E7
Princeton *N.J., U.S.A.* 40°21N 74°39W **83** F10
Princeton *W. Va., U.S.A.* 37°22N 81°6W **81** G13
Principe *São Tomé & Príncipe* 1°37N 7°25E **50** F4
Principe da Beira *Brazil* 12°20S 64°30W **92** F6
Prineville *U.S.A.* 44°18N 120°51W **76** D3
Prins Harald Kyst *Antarctica* 70°0S 35°1E **5** D4
Prinsesse Astrid Kyst
  Antarctica 70°45S 12°30E **5** D3
Prinsesse Ragnhild Kyst
  Antarctica 70°15S 27°30E **5** D4
Prinzapolca *Nic.* 13°20N 83°35W **88** D3
Priozersk *Russia* 61°2N 30°7E **8** F24
Pripet = Prypyat →
  Europe 51°20N 30°15E **17** C16
Pripet Marshes = Pripet Marshes
  Europe 52°10N 27°10E **17** B15
Pripyat Marshes = Pripet Marshes
  Europe 52°10N 27°10E **17** B15
Pripyats = Prypyat →
  Europe 51°20N 30°15E **17** C16

Prishtinë *Kosovo* 42°40N 21°13E **23** C9
Priština = Prishtinë *Kosovo* 42°40N 21°13E **23** C9
Privas *France* 44°45N 4°37E **20** D6
Privolzhskaya Vozvyshennost *Russia* 51°0N 46°0E **19** D8
Privolzhskiy □ *Russia* 56°0N 50°0E **26** D6
Prizren *Kosovo* 42°13N 20°45E **23** C9
Probolinggo *Indonesia* 7°46S 113°13E **37** G15
Proctor *U.S.A.* 43°40N 73°2W **83** C11
Proddatur *India* 14°45N 78°30E **45** G4
Profondeville *Belgium* 50°23N 4°52E **15** D4
Progreso *Coahuila, Mexico* 27°28N 100°59W **86** B4
Progreso *Yucatán, Mexico* 21°20N 89°40W **87** C7
Progress *Antarctica* 66°22S 76°22E **5** C12
Progress *Russia* 49°45N 129°37E **27** E13
Prokopyevsk *Russia* 54°0N 86°45E **26** D9
Prokuplje *Serbia* 43°16N 21°36E **23** C9
Prome = Pye *Burma* 18°49N 95°13E **41** K19
Prophet → *Canada* 58°48N 122°40W **70** B4
Prophet River *Canada* 58°6N 122°43W **70** B4
Propriá *Brazil* 10°13S 36°51W **93** F11
Propriano *France* 41°41N 8°52E **20** F8
Proserpine *Australia* 20°21S 148°36E **62** b
Prosna → *Poland* 52°6N 17°44E **17** B9
Prospect *U.S.A.* 43°18N 75°9W **83** C9
Prosser *U.S.A.* 46°12N 119°46W **76** C4
Prostějov *Czech Rep.* 49°30N 17°9E **17** D9
Proston *Australia* 26°8S 151°32E **63** D5
Provence *France* 43°40N 5°46E **20** E6
Providence *Ky., U.S.A.* 37°24N 87°46W **80** G10
Providence *R.I., U.S.A.* 41°49N 71°24W **83** E13
Providence Bay *Canada* 45°41N 82°15W **72** C3
Providence Mts. *U.S.A.* 35°10N 115°15W **79** K11
Providencia, I. de *Caribbean* 13°25N 81°26W **88** D3
Provideniya *Russia* 64°23N 173°18W **27** C19
Provincetown *U.S.A.* 42°3N 70°11W **81** D18
Provins *France* 48°33N 3°15E **20** B5
Provo *U.S.A.* 40°14N 111°39W **76** F8
Provost *Canada* 52°25N 110°20W **71** C6
Prudhoe Bay *U.S.A.* 70°18N 148°22W **74** A10
Prudhoe I. *Australia* 21°19S 149°41E **62** C4
Prud'homme *Canada* 52°20N 105°54W **71** C7
Pruszków *Poland* 52°9N 20°49E **17** B11
Prut → *Romania* 45°28N 28°10E **17** F15
Pruzhany *Belarus* 52°33N 24°28E **17** B13
Prydz B. *Antarctica* 69°0S 74°0E **5** C6
Pryluky *Ukraine* 50°30N 32°24E **19** D5
Pryor *U.S.A.* 36°19N 95°19W **84** C7
Prypyat → *Europe* 51°20N 30°15E **17** C16
Prypyatsky △ *Belarus* 52°0N 28°0E **17** C14
Przemyśl *Poland* 49°50N 22°45E **17** D12
Przhevalsk = Karakol *Kyrgyzstan* 42°30N 78°20E **30** C4
Psara *Greece* 38°37N 25°38E **23** E11
Psiloritis, Oros *Greece* 35°15N 24°45E **23** G11
Pskov *Russia* 57°50N 28°25E **9** H23
Ptich = Ptsich → *Belarus* 52°9N 28°52E **17** B15
Ptolemaida *Greece* 40°30N 21°43E **23** D9
Ptsich → *Belarus* 52°9N 28°52E **17** B15
Pu Xian *China* 36°24N 111°6E **32** F6
Pua *Thailand* 19°11N 100°55E **38** C3
Puán *Argentina* 37°30S 62°45W **94** D3
Pu'an *China* 25°46N 104°57E **34** E5
Pu'apu'a *Samoa* 13°34S 172°9W **59** b
Pubei *China* 22°16N 109°31E **34** F7
Pucallpa *Peru* 8°25S 74°30W **92** E4
Pucheng *China* 27°59N 118°31E **35** D12
Puch'on = Bucheon *S. Korea* 37°28N 126°45E **33** F14
Pudasjärvi *Finland* 65°23N 26°53E **8** D22
Puding *China* 26°18N 105°44E **34** D5
Pudozh *Russia* 61°48N 36°32E **18** B6
Pudu = Suizhou *China* 31°42N 113°24E **35** B9
Puducherry *India* 11°59N 79°50E **45** J4
Pudukkottai *India* 10°28N 78°47E **45** J4
Puebla *Mexico* 19°3N 98°12W **87** D5
Puebla □ *Mexico* 18°50N 98°0W **87** D5
Pueblo *U.S.A.* 38°16N 104°37W **76** G11
Puelches *Argentina* 38°5S 65°51W **94** D2
Puelén *Argentina* 37°32S 67°38W **94** D2
Puente Alto *Chile* 33°32S 70°35W **94** C1
Puente-Genil *Spain* 37°22N 4°47W **21** D3
Pu'er *China* 23°0N 101°15E **34** F3
Puerca, Pta. *Puerto Rico* 18°13N 65°36W **89** d
Puerco → *U.S.A.* 34°22N 107°50W **77** J10
Puerto Aisén *Chile* 45°27S 73°0W **96** F2
Puerto Ángel *Mexico* 15°40N 96°29W **87** D5
Puerto Arista *Mexico* 15°56N 93°48W **87** D6
Puerto Armuelles *Panama* 8°20N 82°51W **88** E3
Puerto Ayacucho *Venezuela* 5°40N 67°35W **92** B5
Puerto Barrios *Guatemala* 15°40N 88°32W **88** C2
Puerto Bermejo *Argentina* 26°55S 58°34W **94** B4
Puerto Bermúdez *Peru* 10°20S 74°58W **92** F4
Puerto Bolívar *Ecuador* 3°19S 79°55W **92** D3
Puerto Cabello *Venezuela* 10°28N 68°1W **92** A5
Puerto Cabezas *Nic.* 14°0N 83°30W **88** D3
Puerto Cabo Gracias á Dios *Nic.* 15°0N 83°10W **88** D3
Puerto Carreño *Colombia* 6°12N 67°22W **92** B5
Puerto Castilla *Honduras* 16°0N 86°0W **88** C2
Puerto Chicama *Peru* 7°45S 79°20W **92** E3
Puerto Coig *Argentina* 50°54S 69°15W **96** G3
Puerto Cortés *Honduras* 15°51N 88°0W **88** C2
Puerto Cumarebo *Venezuela* 11°29N 69°30W **92** A5
Puerto de los Angeles ⌂ *Mexico* 23°39N 105°45W **86** C3
Puerto del Rosario *Canary Is.* 28°30N 13°52W **52** C3
Puerto Deseado *Argentina* 47°55S 66°0W **96** F3
Puerto Escondido *Mexico* 15°50N 97°3W **87** D5
Puerto Heath *Bolivia* 12°34S 68°39W **92** F5
Puerto Inírida *Colombia* 3°53N 67°52W **92** C5
Puerto Juárez *Mexico* 21°11N 86°49W **87** C7
Puerto La Cruz *Venezuela* 10°13N 64°38W **92** A6
Puerto Leguízamo *Colombia* 0°12S 74°46W **92** D4
Puerto Lempira *Honduras* 15°16N 83°46W **88** C3
Puerto Libertad *Mexico* 29°55N 112°43W **86** B2
Puerto Limón *Colombia* 3°23N 73°30W **92** C4
Puerto Lobos *Argentina* 42°0S 65°3W **96** E3
Puerto Madryn *Argentina* 42°48S 65°4W **96** E3
Puerto Maldonado *Peru* 12°30S 69°10W **92** F5
Puerto Manatí *Cuba* 21°22N 76°50W **88** B4
Puerto Montt *Chile* 41°28S 73°0W **96** E2
Puerto Morazán *Nic.* 12°51N 87°11W **88** D2
Puerto Morelos *Mexico* 20°50N 86°52W **87** C7
Puerto Natales *Chile* 51°45S 72°15W **96** G2
Puerto Oscuro *Chile* 31°24S 71°35W **94** C1
Puerto Padre *Cuba* 21°13N 76°35W **88** B4
Puerto Páez *Venezuela* 6°13N 67°28W **92** B5
Puerto Peñasco *Mexico* 31°20N 113°33W **86** A2
Puerto Pinasco *Paraguay* 22°36S 57°50W **94** A4
Puerto Plata *Dom. Rep.* 19°48N 70°45W **89** C5
Puerto Princesa *Phil.* 9°46N 118°45E **37** C5
Puerto Quepos *Costa Rica* 9°29N 84°6W **88** E3
Puerto Rico ⊠ *W. Indies* 18°15N 66°45W **89** d
Puerto Rico Trench *Atl. Oc.* 19°50N 66°0W **89** C6
Puerto San Julián *Argentina* 49°18S 67°43W **96** F3
Puerto Santa Cruz *Argentina* 50°0S 68°32W **96** G3
Puerto Sastre *Paraguay* 22°2S 57°55W **94** A4
Puerto Suárez *Bolivia* 18°58S 57°52W **92** G7
Puerto Vallarta *Mexico* 20°37N 105°15W **86** C3
Puerto Varas *Chile* 41°19S 72°59W **96** E2
Puerto Wilches *Colombia* 7°21N 73°54W **92** B4
Puertollano *Spain* 38°43N 4°7W **21** C3
Pueu *Tahiti* 17°44S 149°13W **59** d
Pueyrredón, L. *Argentina* 47°20S 72°0W **96** F2
Puffin I. *Ireland* 51°50N 10°24W **10** E1
Pugachev *Russia* 52°0N 48°49E **18** D8
Pugal *India* 28°30N 72°48E **42** E5
Puge *China* 27°20N 102°31E **34** D4
Puget Sound *U.S.A.* 47°50N 122°30W **78** C4
Pugŏdong *N. Korea* 42°5N 130°0E **33** C16
Pūgūnzī *Iran* 25°49N 59°10E **47** E8
Puigcerdà *Spain* 42°24N 1°50E **21** A6
Puijiang *China* 30°14N 103°30E **34** B4
Pujiang *China* 29°29N 119°54E **35** C12
Pujon-ho *N. Korea* 40°35N 127°35E **33** D14
Pukaki, L. *N.Z.* 44°4S 170°1E **59** F3
Pukapuka *Cook Is.* 10°53S 165°49W **65** J11
Pukaskwa △ *Canada* 48°20N 86°0W **72** C2
Pukatawagan *Canada* 55°45N 101°20W **71** B8
Pukchin *N. Korea* 40°12N 125°45E **33** D13
Pukch'ŏng *N. Korea* 40°14N 128°19E **33** D15
Pukekohe *N.Z.* 37°12S 174°55E **59** B5
Pukhrayan *India* 26°14N 79°51E **43** F8
Puksubaek-san *N. Korea* 40°42N 127°45E **33** D14
Pula *Croatia* 44°54N 13°57E **16** F7
Pulacayo *Bolivia* 20°25S 66°41W **92** H5
Pulandian *China* 39°25N 121°58E **33** E11
Pulaski *N.Y., U.S.A.* 43°34N 76°8W **83** C8
Pulaski *Tenn., U.S.A.* 35°12N 87°2W **85** D11
Pulaski *Va., U.S.A.* 37°3N 80°47W **81** G13
Pulau → *Indonesia* 5°50S 138°15E **37** F9
Pulau Gili *Indonesia* 8°21S 116°1E **37** J19
Puławy *Poland* 51°23N 21°59E **17** C11
Pulga *U.S.A.* 39°48N 121°29W **78** F5
Pulgaon *India* 20°44N 78°21E **44** D4
Pulicat *India* 13°25N 80°19E **45** H5
Pulicat L. *India* 13°40N 80°15E **45** H5
Pulivendla *India* 14°25N 78°14E **45** G4
Puliyangudi *India* 9°11N 77°24E **45** K3
Pullman *U.S.A.* 46°44N 117°10W **76** C5
Pulog, Mt. *Phil.* 16°40N 120°50E **37** A6
Pułtusk *Poland* 52°43N 21°6E **17** B11
Pumlumon Fawr *U.K.* 52°28N 3°46W **13** E4
Puná, I. *Ecuador* 2°55S 80°5W **92** D2
Punaauia *Tahiti* 17°37S 149°34W **59** d
Punakaiki *N.Z.* 42°7S 171°20E **59** E3
Punakha Dzong *Bhutan* 27°42N 89°52E **41** F16
Punalur *India* 9°0N 76°56E **45** K3
Punasar *India* 27°6N 73°6E **42** F5
Punata *Bolivia* 17°32S 65°50W **92** G5
Punch *India* 33°48N 74°4E **43** C6
Punch → *Pakistan* 33°12N 73°40E **42** C5
Punda Maria *S. Africa* 22°40S 31°5E **57** B5
Pune *India* 18°29N 73°57E **44** E1
P'ungsan *N. Korea* 40°50N 128°9E **33** D15
Puning *China* 23°20N 116°12E **35** F11
Punjab □ *India* 31°0N 76°0E **42** D7
Punjab □ *Pakistan* 32°0N 72°30E **42** E6
Puno *Peru* 15°55S 70°3W **92** G4
Punpun → *India* 25°31N 85°18E **43** G11
Punta, Cerro de *Puerto Rico* 18°10N 66°37W **89** d
Punta Alta *Argentina* 38°53S 62°4W **96** D4
Punta Arenas *Chile* 53°10S 71°0W **96** G2
Punta del Díaz *Chile* 28°0S 70°45W **94** B1
Punta Gorda *Belize* 16°10N 88°45W **87** D7
Punta Gorda *U.S.A.* 26°56N 82°3W **85** H13
Punta Prieta *Mexico* 28°58N 114°17W **86** B2
Puntarenas *Costa Rica* 10°0N 84°50W **88** E3
Puntland *Somalia* 9°0N 50°0E **49** F4
Punto Fijo *Venezuela* 11°50N 70°13W **92** A4
Punxsutawney *U.S.A.* 40°57N 78°59W **82** F6
Pupuan *Indonesia* 8°19S 115°0E **37** J18
Puqi *China* 29°40N 113°50E **35** C9
Puquio *Peru* 14°45S 74°10W **92** F4
Pur → *Russia* 67°31N 77°55E **26** C8
Puracé, Vol. *Colombia* 2°21N 76°23W **92** C3
Puralia = Puruliya *India* 23°17N 86°24E **43** H12
Puranpur *India* 28°31N 80°9E **43** E9
Purbalingga *Indonesia* 7°23S 109°21E **37** G13
Purbeck, Isle of *U.K.* 50°39N 1°59W **13** G5
Purcell *U.S.A.* 35°1N 97°22W **84** D6
Purcell Mts. *Canada* 49°55N 116°15W **70** D5
Purdy *Canada* 45°19N 77°44W **82** A7
Puri *India* 19°50N 85°58E **44** E7
Purmerend *Neths.* 52°32N 4°58E **15** B4
Purna → *India* 19°6N 77°2E **44** E3
Purnia *India* 25°45N 87°31E **43** G12
Purnululu △ *Australia* 17°20S 128°20E **60** C4
Pursat = Pouthisat *Cambodia* 12°34N 103°50E **38** F4
Purukcahu *Indonesia* 0°35S 114°35E **36** E4
Puruliya *India* 23°17N 86°24E **43** H12
Purus → *Brazil* 3°42S 61°28W **92** D6
Puruvesi *Finland* 61°50N 29°30E **8** F23
Purvis *U.S.A.* 31°9N 89°25W **85** F10
Purwa *India* 26°28N 80°47E **43** F9
Purwakarta *Indonesia* 6°35S 107°29E **37** G12
Purwo, Tanjung *Indonesia* 8°44S 114°21E **37** K18
Purwodadi *Indonesia* 7°7S 110°55E **37** G14
Purwokerto *Indonesia* 7°25S 109°14E **37** G13
Puryŏng *N. Korea* 42°5N 129°43E **33** C15
Pus → *India* 19°55N 77°55E **44** E3
Pusa *India* 25°59N 85°41E **43** G11
Pusad *India* 19°56N 77°36E **44** E3
Pusan = Busan *S. Korea* 35°5N 129°0E **33** G15
Pushkin *Russia* 59°45N 30°25E **9** G24
Pushkino *Russia* 51°16N 47°0E **19** D8
Put-in-Bay *U.S.A.* 41°39N 82°49W **82** E2
Putahow L. *Canada* 59°54N 100°40W **71** B8
Putao *Burma* 27°28N 97°30E **41** F20
Putaruru *N.Z.* 38°2S 175°50E **59** C5
Puteran *Indonesia* 7°5S 114°0E **37** G15
Putian *China* 25°23N 119°0E **35** E12
Putignano *Italy* 40°51N 17°7E **22** D7
Puting, Tanjung *Indonesia* 3°31S 111°46E **36** E4
Putnam *U.S.A.* 41°55N 71°55W **83** E13
Putorana, Gory *Russia* 69°0N 95°0E **27** C10
Putrajaya *Malaysia* 2°55N 101°40E **39** L3
Puttalam *Sri Lanka* 8°1N 79°55E **45** K5
Puttalam Lagoon *Sri Lanka* 8°15N 79°45E **45** K4
Puttgarden *Germany* 54°30N 11°10E **16** A6
Puttur *Andhra Pradesh, India* 13°27N 79°33E **45** H4
Puttur *Karnataka, India* 12°46N 75°12E **45** H2
Putumayo → *S. Amer.* 3°7S 67°58W **92** D5
Putuo *China* 29°56N 122°20E **35** C14
Putussibau *Indonesia* 0°50N 112°56E **36** D4
Puvirnituq *Canada* 60°2N 77°10W **69** E16
Puy-de-Dôme *France* 45°46N 2°57E **20** D5
Puyallup *U.S.A.* 47°12N 122°18W **78** C4
Puyang *China* 35°40N 115°1E **32** G8
Pūzeh Rīg *Iran* 27°20N 58°40E **47** E8
Pweto *Dem. Rep. of the Congo* 8°25S 28°51E **54** F5
Pwllheli *U.K.* 52°53N 4°25W **12** E3
Pyaozero, Ozero *Russia* 66°5N 30°58E **8** C24
Pyapon *Burma* 16°20N 95°40E **41** L19
Pyasina → *Russia* 73°30N 87°0E **27** B9
Pyatigorsk *Russia* 44°2N 43°6E **19** F7
Pyay = Pye *Burma* 18°49N 95°13E **41** K19
Pye *Burma* 18°49N 95°13E **41** K19
Pyeongchang *S. Korea* 37°22N 128°23E **33** F15
Pyeongtaek *S. Korea* 37°1N 127°4E **33** F14
Pyetrikaw *Belarus* 52°11N 28°29E **17** B15
Pyhäjoki → *Finland* 64°28N 24°14E **8** D21
Pyhätunturi △ *Finland* 66°58N 27°5E **8** C22
Pyin-U-Lwin *Burma* 22°2N 96°28E **38** A1
Pyinmana *Burma* 19°45N 96°12E **41** K20
Pymatuning Res. *U.S.A.* 41°30N 80°28W **82** E4
Pyŏktong *N. Korea* 40°50N 125°50E **33** D13
P'yŏnggang *N. Korea* 38°24N 127°17E **33** E14
P'yŏngsong *N. Korea* 39°14N 125°52E **33** E13
P'yŏngyang *N. Korea* 39°0N 125°30E **33** E13
Pyote *U.S.A.* 31°32N 103°8W **84** F3
Pyramid L. *U.S.A.* 40°1N 119°35W **76** F4
Pyramid Pk. *U.S.A.* 36°25N 116°37W **79** J10
Pyrénées *Europe* 42°45N 0°18E **20** E4
Pyu *Burma* 18°30N 96°28E **41** K20

Q

Qaanaaq *Greenland* 77°30N 69°10W **69** B18
Qachasnek *S. Africa* 30°6S 28°42E **57** D4
Qa'el Jafr *Jordan* 30°20N 36°25E **48** E5
Qa'emābād *Iran* 31°44N 60°2E **47** D9
Qā'emshahr *Iran* 36°30N 52°53E **47** B7
Qagan Nur *Jilin, China* 45°15N 124°18E **33** B13
Qagan Nur *Nei Monggol Zizhiqu, China* 43°30N 114°55E **32** C8
Qahar Youyi Zhongqi *China* 41°12N 112°40E **32** D7
Qahremānshahr = Kermānshāh *Iran* 34°23N 47°0E **46** C5
Qaidam Pendi *China* 37°0N 95°0E **30** D8
Qajarīyeh *Iran* 31°1N 48°22E **47** D6
Qala-i-Jadid = Spīn Būldak *Afghan.* 31°1N 66°25E **42** D2
Qala Viala *Pakistan* 30°49N 67°17E **42** D2
Qala Yangi *Afghan.* 34°20N 66°30E **42** B2
Qal'at al Akhḍar *Si. Arabia* 28°4N 37°9E **46** E3
Qal'at Dīzah *Iraq* 36°11N 45°7E **46** B5
Qal'at Ṣāliḥ *Iraq* 31°31N 47°16E **46** D5
Qal'at Sukkar *Iraq* 31°51N 46°5E **46** D5
Qamani'tuaq = Baker Lake *Canada* 64°20N 96°3W **68** E12
Qamdo *China* 31°15N 97°6E **34** B1
Qamea *Fiji* 16°45S 179°45W **59** a
Qamruddin Karez *Pakistan* 31°45N 68°20E **42** D3
Qandahār = Kandahār *Afghan.* 31°32N 65°43E **40** D4
Qandahār = Kandahār □ *Afghan.* 31°0N 65°0E **40** D4
Qandyaghash *Kazakhstan* 49°28N 57°25E **19** E10
Qapān *Iran* 37°40N 55°47E **47** B7
Qapshaghay *Kazakhstan* 43°51N 77°14E **26** E8
Qaqortoq *Greenland* 60°43N 46°0W **4** C5
Qara Qash → *China* 35°0N 78°30E **43** B8
Qarabutaq *Kazakhstan* 50°0N 60°14E **26** E7
Qaraghandy *Kazakhstan* 49°50N 73°10E **30** B3
Qaraghayly *Kazakhstan* 49°26N 76°0E **26** E8
Qārah *Si. Arabia* 29°55N 40°3E **46** D4
Qarataū *Ongtüstik Qazaqstan, Kazakhstan* 43°30N 69°30E **26** E7
Qarataū *Zhambyl, Kazakhstan* 43°10N 70°28E **26** E8
Qarazhal *Kazakhstan* 48°2N 70°49E **26** E8
Qarchak *Iran* 35°25N 51°34E **47** C6
Qardho *Somalia* 9°30N 49°6E **49** F4
Qareh → *Iran* 39°25N 47°22E **46** B5
Qareh Tekān *Iran* 36°38N 49°29E **47** B6
Qarnein *U.A.E.* 24°56N 52°52E **47** E7
Qarqan He → *China* 39°30N 88°30E **30** D6
Qarqaraly *Kazakhstan* 49°26N 75°30E **30** B4
Qarshi *Uzbekistan* 38°53N 65°48E **26** F7
Qartabā *Lebanon* 34°4N 35°50E **48** A4
Qārūh *Kuwait* 28°49N 48°46E **47** D6
Qaryat al Gharab *Iraq* 31°27N 44°48E **46** D5
Qaryat al 'Ulyā *Si. Arabia* 27°33N 47°42E **46** E5
Qasr 'Amra *Jordan* 31°48N 36°35E **46** D3
Qaṣr-e Qand *Iran* 26°15N 60°45E **47** E9
Qaṣr-e Shīrīn *Iran* 34°31N 45°35E **46** C5
Qasr Farâfra *Egypt* 27°0N 28°1E **53** C11
Qasuittuq = Resolute *Canada* 74°42N 94°54W **69** C13
Qatanā *Syria* 33°26N 36°4E **48** B5
Qatar ■ *Asia* 25°30N 51°15E **47** E6
Qatlīsh *Iran* 37°50N 57°19E **47** B8
Qattâra, Munkhafed el *Egypt* 29°30N 27°30E **53** C11
Qattâra Depression = Qattâra, Munkhafed el *Egypt* 29°30N 27°30E **53** C11
Qawām al Ḥamzah = Al Ḥamzah *Iraq* 31°43N 44°58E **46** D5
Qāyen *Iran* 33°40N 59°10E **47** C8
Qazaqstan = Kazakhstan ■ *Asia* 50°0N 70°0E **26** E8
Qazımämmäd *Azerbaijan* 40°3N 49°0E **47** A6
Qazvīn *Iran* 36°15N 50°0E **47** B6
Qazvīn □ *Iran* 36°20N 50°0E **47** B6
Qena *Egypt* 26°10N 32°43E **53** C12
Qeqertarsuaq *Qaasuitsup, Greenland* 69°45N 53°30W **4** C5
Qeqertarsuaq *Qaasuitsup, Greenland* 69°15N 53°38W **4** C5
Qeshlāq *Iran* 34°55N 46°28E **46** C5
Qeshm *Iran* 26°55N 56°10E **47** E8
Qeys *Iran* 26°32N 53°58E **47** E7
Qezel Owzen → *Iran* 36°45N 49°22E **47** B6
Qezi'ot *Israel* 30°52N 34°26E **48** E3
Qi Xian *China* 34°40N 114°48E **32** G8
Qian Gorlos *China* 45°5N 124°42E **33** B13
Qian Hai *China* 22°32N 113°54E **31** a
Qian Xian *China* 34°31N 108°15E **32** G5
Qian'an *China* 40°0N 118°41E **33** E10
Qiancheng *China* 27°12N 109°50E **34** D7
Qianjiang *Guangxi Zhuangzu, China* 23°38N 108°58E **34** F7
Qianjiang *Hubei, China* 30°24N 112°55E **35** B9
Qianjiang *Sichuan, China* 29°33N 108°47E **34** C7
Qianjin *China* 47°34N 133°4E **31** B15
Qianshan *Anhui, China* 30°37N 116°35E **35** B11
Qianshan *Guangdong, China* 22°15N 113°31E **31** a
Qianwei *China* 29°13N 103°56E **34** C4
Qianxi *China* 27°3N 106°3E **34** D6
Qianyang *Hunan, China* 27°18N 110°10E **35** D8
Qianyang *Shaanxi, China* 34°40N 107°8E **32** G4
Qianyang *Zhejiang, China* 30°11N 119°25E **35** B12
Qi'ao *China* 22°25N 113°39E **31** a
Qi'ao Dao *China* 22°25N 113°38E **31** a
Qiaocun *China* 39°56N 112°55E **32** E7
Qiaojia *China* 26°56N 102°58E **34** D4
Qichun *China* 30°18N 115°25E **35** B10
Qidong *Hunan, China* 26°49N 112°7E **35** D9
Qidong *Jiangsu, China* 31°48N 121°38E **35** B13
Qiemo *China* 38°8N 85°32E **30** D6
Qijiang *China* 28°57N 106°35E **34** C6
Qijiaojing *China* 43°28N 91°36E **30** C7
Qikiqtaaluk = Baffin I. *Canada* 68°0N 75°0W **69** D17
Qikiqtarjuaq *Canada* 67°33N 63°0W **69** D19
Qila Saifullāh *Pakistan* 30°45N 68°17E **42** D3
Qilian Shan *China* 38°30N 96°0E **30** D8
Qimen *China* 29°50N 117°42E **35** C11
Qin He → *China* 35°1N 113°22E **32** G7
Qin Jiang → *Guangxi Zhuangzu, China* 21°53N 108°35E **34** F7
Qin Jiang → *Jiangxi, China* 26°15N 115°55E **35** D10
Qin Ling = Qinling Shandi *China* 33°50N 108°10E **32** H5
Qin'an *China* 34°48N 105°40E **32** G3
Qing Xian *China* 38°35N 116°45E **32** E9
Qingcheng *China* 37°15N 117°40E **33** F9
Qingcheng Shan *China* 30°58N 103°31E **34** B4
Qingchuan *China* 32°36N 105°9E **32** H3
Qingdao *China* 36°5N 120°20E **33** F11
Qingfeng *China* 35°52N 115°8E **32** G8
Qinghai □ *China* 36°0N 98°0E **30** D8
Qinghai Hu *China* 36°40N 100°10E **30** D9
Qinghecheng *China* 41°28N 124°15E **33** D13
Qinghemen *China* 41°48N 121°25E **33** D11
Qingjian *China* 37°8N 110°8E **32** F6
Qingjiang = Huaiyin *China* 33°30N 119°2E **33** H10
Qingliu *China* 26°11N 116°48E **35** D11
Qinglong *China* 25°49N 105°12E **34** E5
Qingping *China* 26°39N 107°47E **34** D6
Qingshui *China* 34°48N 106°8E **32** G4
Qingshuihe *China* 39°55N 111°35E **32** E6
Qingtian *China* 28°12N 120°15E **35** C13
Qingtongxia *China* 38°2N 106°3E **32** E4
Qingtongxia Shuiku *China* 37°50N 105°58E **32** F3
Qingxi *China* 27°8N 108°43E **34** D7
Qingxu *China* 37°34N 112°22E **32** F7
Qingyang *Anhui, China* 30°38N 117°50E **35** B11
Qingyang *Gansu, China* 36°2N 107°55E **32** F4
Qingyi Jiang → *China* 29°32N 103°44E **34** C4
Qingyuan *Guangdong, China* 23°40N 112°59E **35** F9
Qingyuan *Liaoning, China* 42°10N 124°55E **33** C13
Qingyuan *Zhejiang, China* 27°36N 119°3E **35** D12
Qingyun *China* 37°45N 117°20E **33** F9
Qingzhen *China* 26°31N 106°25E **34** D6
Qinhuangdao *China* 39°56N 119°30E **33** E10
Qinling Shandi *China* 33°50N 108°10E **32** H5
Qinshui *China* 35°40N 112°8E **32** G7
Qinyang = Jiyuan *China* 35°7N 112°57E **32** G7
Qinyang *China* 35°5N 112°56E **32** G7
Qinyuan *China* 36°29N 112°20E **32** F7
Qinzhou *China* 21°58N 108°38E **34** G7
Qionghai *China* 19°15N 110°26E **38** C8
Qionglai *China* 30°25N 103°31E **34** B4
Qionglai Shan *China* 31°0N 102°30E **34** B4
Qiongshan *China* 19°51N 110°26E **38** C8
Qiongzhou Haixia *China* 20°10N 110°15E **38** B8
Qiqihar *China* 47°26N 124°0E **31** B13
Qira *China* 37°0N 80°48E **30** D5
Qirāiya, W. → *Egypt* 30°27N 34°0E **48** E3
Qiryat Ata *Israel* 32°47N 35°6E **48** C4
Qiryat Gat *Israel* 31°32N 34°46E **48** D3
Qiryat Mal'akhi *Israel* 31°44N 34°44E **48** D3
Qiryat Shemona *Israel* 33°13N 35°35E **48** B4
Qiryat Yam *Israel* 32°51N 35°4E **48** C4
Qishan *China* 34°25N 107°38E **32** G4
Qitai *China* 44°2N 89°35E **30** C6
Qitaihe *China* 45°48N 130°51E **28** B5
Qiubei *China* 24°2N 104°12E **34** E5
Qixia *China* 37°17N 120°52E **33** F11
Qiyang *China* 26°35N 111°50E **35** D8
Qızılağac Körfäzi *Azerbaijan* 39°9N 49°0E **47** B6
Qods *Iran* 35°45N 51°15E **47** C6
Qojūr *Iran* 36°12N 47°55E **46** B5
Qom *Iran* 34°40N 51°0E **47** C6
Qom □ *Iran* 34°40N 51°0E **47** C6
Qomolangma Feng = Everest, Mt. *Nepal* 28°5N 86°58E **43** E12
Qomsheh *Iran* 32°0N 51°55E **47** D6
Qoqek = Tacheng *China* 46°40N 82°58E **30** B5
Qo'qon *Uzbekistan* 40°31N 70°56E **26** E8
Qoraqalpog'istan □ *Uzbekistan* 43°0N 58°0E **26** E6
Qorveh *Iran* 35°10N 47°48E **46** C5
Qosshaghyl *Kazakhstan* 46°40N 54°0E **19** E9
Qostanay *Kazakhstan* 53°10N 63°35E **26** D7
Qu Jiang → *China* 30°1N 106°24E **34** B6
Qu Xian *China* 30°48N 106°58E **34** B6
Quabbin Res. *U.S.A.* 42°20N 72°20W **83** D12
Quairading *Australia* 32°0S 117°21E **61** F2
Quakertown *U.S.A.* 40°26N 75°21W **83** F9
Qualicum Beach *Canada* 49°22N 124°26W **70** D4
Quambatook *Australia* 35°49S 143°34E **63** F3
Quambone *Australia* 30°57S 147°53E **63** E4
Quamby *Australia* 20°22S 140°17E **62** C3
Quan Long = Ca Mau *Vietnam* 9°7N 105°8E **39** H5
Quanah *U.S.A.* 34°18N 99°44W **84** D5
Quang Ngai *Vietnam* 15°13N 108°58E **38** E7
Quang Tri *Vietnam* 16°45N 107°13E **38** D6
Quang Yen *Vietnam* 20°56N 106°52E **34** G6
Quannan *China* 24°45N 114°33E **35** E10
Quantock Hills *U.K.* 51°8N 3°10W **13** F4
Quanyang *China* 42°21N 127°32E **33** C14
Quanzhou *Fujian, China* 24°55N 118°34E **35** E12
Quanzhou *Guangxi Zhuangzu, China* 25°57N 111°5E **35** E8
Qu'Appelle → *Canada* 50°33N 103°53W **71** C8
Quaqtaq *Canada* 60°55N 69°40W **69** E18
Quaraí *Brazil* 30°15S 56°20W **94** C4
Quartu Sant'Élena *Italy* 39°15N 9°10E **22** E3
Quartzsite *U.S.A.* 33°40N 114°13W **79** M12
Quatre Bornes *Mauritius* 20°15S 57°28E **55** d
Quatsino Sd. *Canada* 50°25N 127°58W **70** C3
Quba *Azerbaijan* 41°21N 48°32E **19** F8
Qūchān *Iran* 37°10N 58°27E **47** B8
Queanbeyan *Australia* 35°17S 149°14E **63** F4
Québec *Canada* 46°52N 71°13W **73** C5
Québec □ *Canada* 48°0N 74°0W **72** B6
Quebrada del Condorito △ *Argentina* 31°49S 64°40W **94** C3
Queen Alexandra Ra. *Antarctica* 85°0S 170°0E **5** E11
Queen Charlotte City *Canada* 53°15N 132°2W **70** C2
Queen Charlotte Is. = Haida Gwaii *Canada* 53°20N 132°10W **70** C2
Queen Charlotte Sd. *Canada* 51°0N 128°0W **70** C3
Queen Charlotte Strait *Canada* 50°45N 127°10W **70** C3
Queen Elizabeth Is. *Canada* 76°0N 95°0W **69** B13
Queen Elizabeth Land *Antarctica* 85°0S 60°0W **5** E17
Queen Mary Land *Antarctica* 70°0S 95°0E **5** D7
Queen Maud G. *Canada* 68°15N 102°30W **68** D11
Queen Maud Land = Dronning Maud Land *Antarctica* 72°30S 12°0E **5** D3
Queen Maud Mts. *Antarctica* 86°0S 160°0W **5** E12
Queens Channel *Australia* 15°0S 129°30E **60** C4
Queenscliff *Australia* 38°16S 144°39E **63** F3
Queensland □ *Australia* 22°0S 142°0E **62** C3
Queenstown *Australia* 42°4S 145°35E **63** G4
Queenstown *N.Z.* 45°1S 168°40E **59** F2
Queenstown *S. Africa* 31°52S 26°52E **56** D4
Queets *U.S.A.* 47°32N 124°19W **78** C2
Queguay Grande → *Uruguay* 32°9S 58°9W **94** C4
Queimadas *Brazil* 11°0S 39°38W **93** F11
Quelimane *Mozam.* 17°53S 36°58E **55** H7
Quellón *Chile* 43°7S 73°37W **96** E2
Quelpart = Jeju-do *S. Korea* 33°29N 126°34E **33** H14

Quemado N. Mex., U.S.A. 34°20N 108°30W 77 J9
Quemado Tex., U.S.A. 28°56N 100°37W 84 G4
Quemoy = Chinmen Taiwan 24°26N 118°19E 35 E12
Quepem India 15°13N 74°3E 45 G2
Quequén Argentina 38°30S 58°30W 94 D4
Querétaro Mexico 20°36N 100°23W 86 C4
Querétaro □ Mexico 21°0N 99°55W 86 C5
Queshan China 32°55N 114°2E 35 A10
Quesnel Canada 53°0N 122°30W 70 C4
Quesnel → Canada 52°58N 122°29W 70 C4
Quesnel L. Canada 52°30N 121°20W 70 C4
Questa U.S.A. 36°42N 105°36W 77 H11
Quetico ○ Canada 48°30N 91°45W 72 C1
Quetta Pakistan 30°15N 66°55E 42 D2
Quetzaltenango Guatemala 14°50N 91°30W 88 D1
Qufār Si. Arabia 27°26N 41°37E 46 E4
Qufu China 35°36N 116°58E 32 G9
Qui Nhon Vietnam 13°40N 109°13E 38 F7
Quibala Angola 10°46S 14°59E 54 G2
Quibaxe Angola 8°24S 14°27E 54 F2
Quibdó Colombia 5°42N 76°40W 92 B3
Quiberon France 47°29N 3°9W 20 C2
Quiet L. Canada 61°5N 133°5W 70 A2
Quiindy Paraguay 25°58S 57°14W 94 B4
Quilá Mexico 24°23N 107°13W 86 C3
Quilán, C. Chile 43°15S 74°30W 96 E2
Quilcene U.S.A. 47°49N 122°53W 78 C4
Quilimarí Chile 32°5S 71°30W 94 C1
Quilino Argentina 30°14S 64°29W 94 C3
Quillabamba Peru 12°50S 72°50W 92 F4
Quillagua Chile 21°40S 69°40W 94 A2
Quillota Chile 32°54S 71°16W 94 C1
Quilmes Argentina 34°43S 58°15W 94 C4
Quilon = Kollam India 8°50N 76°38E 45 K3
Quilpie Australia 26°35S 144°11E 63 D3
Quilpué Chile 33°5S 71°33W 94 C1
Quimili Argentina 27°40S 62°30W 94 B3
Quimper France 48°0N 4°9W 20 B1
Quimperlé France 47°53N 3°33W 20 C2
Quinault → U.S.A. 47°21N 124°18W 78 C2
Quincy Calif., U.S.A. 39°56N 120°57W 78 F6
Quincy Fla., U.S.A. 30°35N 84°34W 85 F12
Quincy Ill., U.S.A. 39°56N 91°23W 80 F8
Quincy Wash., U.S.A. 47°14N 119°51W 76 C4
Quines Argentina 32°13S 65°48W 94 C2
Quintana Roo □ Mexico 19°40N 88°30W 87 D7
Quintana Roo △ Quintana Roo, Mexico 20°15N 87°45W 87 C7
Quintanar de la Orden Spain 39°36N 3°5W 21 C4
Quintero Chile 32°45S 71°30W 94 C1
Quirihue Chile 36°15S 72°35W 94 D1
Quirindi Australia 31°28S 150°40E 63 E5
Quirinópolis Brazil 18°32S 50°30W 93 G8
Quissanga Mozam. 12°24S 40°28E 55 G5
Quissico Mozam. 24°42S 34°44E 57 B5
Quitilipi Argentina 26°50S 60°13W 94 B3
Quitman U.S.A. 30°47N 83°34W 85 F13
Quito Ecuador 0°15S 78°35W 92 D3
Quixadá Brazil 4°55S 39°0W 93 D11
Qujing China 25°32N 103°41E 34 E4
Qulan Kazakhstan 42°55N 72°43E 26 E8
Qul'an, Jazā'ir Egypt 24°22N 35°31E 46 E2
Qulsary Kazakhstan 46°59N 54°1E 19 E9
Qumbu S. Africa 31°10S 28°48E 57 D4
Quneitra = Al Qunayţirah Syria 33°5N 35°45E 48 B4
Qŭnghirot Uzbekistan 43°2N 58°50E 26 E6
Qu'nyido China 31°15N 98°6E 34 B2
Quoin I. Australia 14°54S 129°32E 60 B4
Quoin Pt. S. Africa 34°46S 19°37E 56 D2
Quorn Australia 32°25S 138°5E 63 E2
Qurnat as Sawdā' Lebanon 34°18N 36°6E 48 A5
Qûşaybā' Si. Arabia 26°53N 43°35E 46 E4
Qusaybah Iraq 34°24N 40°59E 46 C4
Quseir Egypt 26°7N 34°16E 46 E2
Quseir Amra = Qasr 'Amra Jordan 31°48N 36°35E 46 D3
Qūshchī Iran 37°59N 45°3E 46 B5
Qutang Gorge = Qutang Xia China 31°0N 109°40E 34 B7
Qutang Xia China 31°0N 109°40E 34 B7
Quthing Lesotho 30°25S 27°36E 57 D4
Qūţīābād Iran 35°47N 48°30E 47 C6
Quttinirpaaq = Ellesmere I. Canada 79°30N 80°0W 69 B16
Quttinirpaaq △ Canada 82°13N 72°13W 69 A17
Quwo China 35°38N 111°25E 32 G6
Quyang China 38°35N 114°40E 32 E8
Quynh Nhai Vietnam 21°49N 103°33E 38 B4
Quyon Canada 45°31N 76°14W 83 A8
Quzhou China 28°57N 118°54E 35 C12
Quzi China 36°20N 107°20E 32 F4
Qyzylorda Kazakhstan 44°48N 65°28E 26 E7

R

Ra, Ko Thailand 9°13N 98°16E 39 H2
Raahe Finland 64°40N 24°28E 8 D21
Raalte Neths. 52°23N 6°16E 15 B6
Raas Indonesia 7°8S 114°33E 37 G16
Raasay U.K. 57°25N 6°4W 11 D2
Raasay, Sd. of U.K. 57°30N 6°8W 11 D2
Raasepori Finland 60°0N 23°26E 9 G20
Rába → Hungary 47°38N 17°38E 17 E9
Rabat Malta 35°53N 14°24E 22 G6
Rabat Morocco 34°2N 6°48W 52 B4
Rabaul Papua N. G. 4°24S 152°18E 58 B8
Rabbit Flat Australia 20°11S 130°1E 60 D5
Rabbit Lake Mine Canada 58°4N 104°5W 71 B8
Rabi Fiji 16°30S 179°59W 59 a
Rābigh Si. Arabia 22°50N 39°5E 49 C2
Rābniţa = Rîbniţa Moldova 47°45N 29°0E 17 E15
Rābor Iran 29°17N 56°55E 47 D8
Rabwah = Chenab Nagar Pakistan 31°45N 72°55E 42 D5

Race, C. Canada 46°40N 53°5W 73 C9
Rach Gia Vietnam 10°5N 105°5E 39 G5
Rach Soi Vietnam 9°57N 105°7E 39 H5
Racha Noi, Ko Thailand 7°30N 98°19E 39 J2
Racha Yai, Ko Thailand 7°30N 98°21E 39 J2
Rachid Mauritania 18°45N 11°35W 52 E3
Racibórz Poland 50°7N 18°18E 17 C10
Racine U.S.A. 42°44N 87°47W 80 D10
Rackerby U.S.A. 39°26N 121°22W 78 F5
Rădăuţi Romania 47°50N 25°59E 17 E13
Radcliff U.S.A. 37°51N 85°57W 81 G11
Radekhiv Ukraine 50°25N 24°32E 17 C13
Radekhov = Radekhiv Ukraine 50°25N 24°32E 17 C13
Radford U.S.A. 37°8N 80°34W 81 G13
Radhanpur India 23°50N 71°38E 42 H4
Radhwa, Jabal Si. Arabia 24°34N 38°18E 46 E3
Radisson Qué., Canada 53°47N 77°37W 72 B4
Radisson Sask., Canada 52°30N 107°20W 71 C7
Radium Hot Springs Canada 50°35N 116°2W 70 C5
Radnor Forest U.K. 52°17N 3°10W 13 E4
Radom Poland 51°23N 21°12E 17 C11
Radomsko Poland 51°5N 19°28E 17 C10
Radomyshl Ukraine 50°30N 29°12E 17 C15
Radstock, C. Australia 33°12S 134°20E 63 E1
Raduzhnyy Russia 62°5N 77°28E 26 C8
Radviliškis Lithuania 55°49N 23°33E 9 J20
Radville Canada 49°30N 104°15W 71 D8
Rae = Behchoko Canada 62°50N 116°3W 70 A5
Rae Bareli India 26°18N 81°20E 43 F9
Rae Isthmus Canada 66°40N 87°30W 69 D14
Raeren Belgium 50°41N 6°7E 15 D6
Raeside, L. Australia 29°20S 122°0E 61 E3
Raetihi N.Z. 39°25S 175°17E 59 C5
Rafaela Argentina 31°10S 61°30W 94 C3
Rafah Gaza Strip 31°18N 34°14E 48 D3
Rafḥā Si. Arabia 29°35N 43°35E 46 D4
Rafsanjān Iran 30°30N 56°5E 47 D8
Raft Pt. Australia 16°4S 124°26E 60 C3
Raga South Sudan 8°28N 25°41E 53 G11
Ragachow Belarus 53°8N 30°5E 17 B16
Ragama Sri Lanka 7°0N 79°50E 40 R11
Ragged, Mt. Australia 33°27S 123°25E 61 F3
Ragged Pt. Barbados 13°9N 59°26W 89 g
Raghunathpalli India 22°14N 84°48E 43 H11
Raghunathpur India 23°33N 86°40E 43 H12
Raglan N.Z. 37°55S 174°55E 59 B5
Ragusa Italy 36°55N 14°44E 22 F6
Raha Indonesia 4°55S 123°0E 37 E6
Rahaeng = Tak Thailand 16°52N 99°8E 38 D2
Rahat Israel 31°24N 34°45E 48 D3
Rahatgarh India 23°47N 78°22E 43 H8
Rahimyar Khan Pakistan 28°30N 70°25E 42 E4
Rāhjerd Iran 34°22N 50°22E 47 C6
Rahon India 31°3N 76°7E 42 D7
Rahuri India 19°23N 74°39E 44 E2
Rai, Hon Vietnam 9°48N 104°38E 39 H5
Raiatéa, Î. French Polynesia 16°50S 151°25W 65 J12
Raichur India 16°10N 77°20E 45 F3
Raiganj India 25°37N 88°10E 43 G13
Raigarh India 21°56N 83°25E 44 D6
Raighar India 19°51N 82°6E 44 K6
Raijua Indonesia 10°37S 121°36E 37 F6
Raikot India 30°41N 75°42E 42 D6
Railton Australia 41°25S 146°28E 63 G4
Rainbow Bridge △ U.S.A. 37°5N 110°58W 77 H8
Rainbow Lake Canada 58°30N 119°23W 70 B5
Rainier U.S.A. 46°53N 122°41W 78 D4
Rainier, Mt. U.S.A. 46°52N 121°46W 78 D5
Rainy L. Canada 48°42N 93°10W 71 D10
Rainy River Canada 48°43N 94°29W 71 D10
Raippaluoto Finland 63°13N 21°14E 8 E19
Raipur India 21°17N 81°45E 44 D5
Rairakhol India 21°4N 84°21E 44 D7
Raisen India 23°20N 77°48E 42 H8
Raisio Finland 60°28N 22°11E 9 F20
Raj Nandgaon India 21°5N 81°5E 44 D5
Raj Nilgiri India 21°28N 86°46E 43 J12
Raja, Ujung Indonesia 3°40N 96°25E 36 D1
Raja Ampat, Kepulauan Indonesia 0°30S 130°0E 37 E8
Rajahmundry India 17°1N 81°48E 44 F5
Rajampet India 14°11N 79°10E 45 G4
Rajang → Malaysia 2°30N 112°0E 36 D4
Rajanpur Pakistan 29°6N 70°19E 42 E4
Rajapalaiyam India 9°25N 77°35E 45 K3
Rajapur India 16°40N 73°31E 44 F1
Rajasthan □ India 26°45N 73°30E 42 F5
Rajasthan Canal = Indira Gandhi Canal India 28°0N 72°0E 42 F5
Rajauri India 33°25N 74°21E 43 C6
Rajendranagar India 17°18N 78°27E 44 F4
Rajgarh Mad. P., India 24°2N 76°45E 42 G7
Rajgarh Raj., India 27°14N 76°38E 42 F7
Rajgarh Raj., India 28°40N 75°25E 42 E6
Rajghat Dam India 24°45N 78°20E 44 E4
Rajgir India 25°2N 85°25E 43 G11
Rajim India 20°58N 81°53E 44 D5
Rajkot India 22°15N 70°56E 42 H4
Rajmahal Hills India 24°30N 87°30E 43 G12
Rajpipla India 21°50N 73°30E 44 D1
Rajpur India 22°18N 74°21E 42 H6
Rajpura India 30°25N 76°32E 42 D7
Rajsamand = Kankroli India 25°4N 73°53E 42 G5
Rajshahi Bangla. 24°22N 88°39E 41 G16
Rajshahi □ Bangla. 25°0N 89°0E 43 G13
Rajula India 21°3N 71°26E 42 J4
Rajur India 20°7N 78°55E 44 D4
Rajura India 19°47N 79°22E 44 E4
Rakaia N.Z. 43°45S 172°1E 59 E4
Rakaia → N.Z. 43°36S 172°15E 59 E4
Rakan, Ra's Qatar 26°10N 51°20E 47 E6
Rakaposhi Pakistan 36°10N 74°25E 43 A6
Rakata, Pulau Indonesia 6°10S 105°20E 37 G11
Rakhine □ Burma 19°0N 94°15E 41 K18

Rakhiv Ukraine 48°3N 24°12E 17 D13
Rakhni Pakistan 30°4N 69°56E 42 D3
Rakhni → Pakistan 29°31N 69°36E 42 E3
Rakiraki Fiji 17°22S 178°11E 59 a
Rakitnoye Russia 45°36N 134°17E 28 B7
Rakiura = Stewart I. N.Z. 46°58S 167°54E 59 G1
Rakiura △ N.Z. 47°0S 167°50E 59 G1
Rakops Botswana 21°1S 24°28E 56 B3
Rakvere Estonia 59°20N 26°25E 9 G22
Raleigh U.S.A. 35°47N 78°39W 85 D15
Ralik Chain Pac. Oc. 8°0N 168°0E 64 G8
Ralls U.S.A. 33°41N 101°24W 84 E4
Ralston U.S.A. 41°30N 76°57W 82 E8
Ram → Canada 62°1N 123°41W 70 A4
Rama Nic. 12°9N 84°15W 88 D3
Ramachandrapuram India 16°50N 82°4E 44 F6
Ramagiri Udayagiri India 19°5N 84°18E 44 E7
Ramagundam India 18°55N 79°15E 44 E4
Ramakona India 21°43N 78°50E 43 J8
Raman Thailand 6°29N 101°18E 39 J3
Ramanathapuram India 9°25N 78°55E 45 K4
Ramanujganj India 23°48N 83°42E 43 H10
Ramas C. India 15°5N 73°55E 45 G1
Ramat Gan Israel 32°4N 34°48E 48 C3
Ramatlhabama S. Africa 25°37S 25°33E 56 C4
Ramban India 33°14N 75°12E 43 C6
Rambi = Rabi Fiji 16°30S 179°59W 59 a
Rambipuji Indonesia 8°12S 113°37E 37 H15
Ramdurg India 15°58N 75°22E 45 G2
Rame Hd. Australia 37°47S 149°30E 63 F4
Ramechhap Nepal 27°25N 86°10E 43 F12
Rameswaram India 9°17N 79°18E 45 K4
Ramganga → India 27°5N 79°58E 43 F8
Ramgarh Jharkhand, India 23°40N 85°35E 43 H11
Ramgarh Raj., India 27°16N 75°14E 42 F6
Ramgarh Raj., India 27°30N 70°36E 42 F4
Rāmhormoz Iran 31°15N 49°35E 47 D6
Ramīān Iran 37°3N 55°16E 47 B7
Ramingining Australia 12°19S 135°3E 62 A2
Ramla Israel 31°55N 34°52E 48 D3
Ramm = Rum Jordan 29°39N 35°26E 48 F4
Ramm, Jabal Jordan 29°35N 35°24E 48 F4
Ramnad = Ramanathapuram India 9°25N 78°55E 45 K4
Ramnagar Jammu & Kashmir, India 32°47N 75°18E 43 C6
Ramnagar Uttarakhand, India 29°24N 79°7E 43 E8
Râmnicu Sărat Romania 45°26N 27°3E 17 F14
Râmnicu Vâlcea Romania 45°9N 24°21E 17 F13
Ramona U.S.A. 33°2N 116°52W 79 M10
Ramore Canada 48°30N 80°25W 72 C3
Ramotswa Botswana 24°50S 25°52E 56 B4
Rampur H.P., India 31°26N 77°43E 42 D7
Rampur Mad. P., India 23°25N 73°53E 42 H5
Rampur Odisha, India 21°48N 83°58E 44 D6
Rampur Ut. P., India 28°50N 79°5E 43 E8
Rampur Hat India 24°10N 87°50E 43 G12
Rampura India 24°30N 75°27E 42 G6
Ramrama Tola India 21°52N 79°55E 43 J8
Ramree I. Burma 19°0N 93°40E 41 K19
Rāmsar Iran 36°53N 50°41E 47 B6
Ramsey I. of Man 54°20N 4°22W 12 C3
Ramsey U.S.A. 41°4N 74°9W 83 E10
Ramsey L. Canada 47°13N 82°15W 72 C3
Ramsgate U.K. 51°20N 1°25E 13 F9
Ramtek India 21°20N 79°15E 44 D4
Rana Pratap Sagar Dam India 24°58N 75°38E 42 G6
Ranaghat India 23°15N 88°35E 43 H13
Ranahu Pakistan 25°55N 69°45E 42 G3
Ranau Malaysia 6°2N 116°40E 36 C5
Rancagua Chile 34°10S 70°50W 94 C1
Rancheria → Canada 60°13N 129°7W 70 A3
Ranchester U.S.A. 44°54N 107°10W 76 D10
Ranchi India 23°19N 85°27E 43 H11
Rancho Cordova U.S.A. 38°36N 121°18W 78 G5
Rancho Cucamonga U.S.A. 34°10N 117°30W 79 L9
Randalstown U.K. 54°45N 6°19W 10 B5
Rander India 21°14N 72°47E 44 D1
Randers Denmark 56°29N 10°1E 9 H14
Randfontein S. Africa 26°8S 27°45E 57 C4
Randle U.S.A. 46°32N 121°57W 78 D5
Randolph Mass., U.S.A. 42°10N 71°2W 83 D13
Randolph N.Y., U.S.A. 42°10N 78°59W 82 D6
Randolph Utah, U.S.A. 41°40N 111°11W 76 F8
Randolph Vt., U.S.A. 43°55N 72°40W 83 C12
Randsburg U.S.A. 35°22N 117°39W 79 K9
Råneälven → Sweden 65°50N 22°20E 8 D20
Rangae Thailand 6°19N 101°44E 39 J3
Rangaunu B. N.Z. 34°51S 173°15E 59 A4
Rangeley U.S.A. 44°58N 70°39W 83 B14
Rangeley L. U.S.A. 44°55N 70°43W 83 B14
Rangely U.S.A. 40°5N 108°48W 76 F9
Ranger U.S.A. 32°28N 98°41W 84 E5
Rangia India 26°28N 91°38E 41 F17
Rangiora N.Z. 43°19S 172°36E 59 E4
Rangitaiki → N.Z. 37°54S 176°49E 59 B6
Rangitata → N.Z. 43°45S 171°15E 59 E3
Rangitoto ke te tonga = D'Urville I. N.Z. 40°50S 173°55E 59 D4
Rangkasbitung Indonesia 6°21S 106°15E 37 G12
Rangoon = Yangôn Burma 16°45N 96°20E 41 L20
Rangpur Bangla. 25°42N 89°22E 41 G16
Rangsang Indonesia 1°20N 103°5E 39 M4
Rani-ki-Vav India 23°38N 72°6E 42 H4
Ranibennur India 14°35N 75°30E 45 G2
Raniganj Paschimbanga, India 23°40N 87°5E 41 H15
Raniganj Ut. P., India 27°3N 82°13E 43 F9
Ranikhet India 29°39N 79°25E 43 E8
Ranippettai India 12°56N 79°23E 45 N6
Raniwara India 24°50N 72°10E 42 G5
Rāniyah Iraq 36°15N 44°53E 46 B5
Ranka India 23°59N 83°47E 43 H10

Ranken → Australia 20°31S 137°36E 62 C2
Rankin U.S.A. 31°13N 101°56W 84 F4
Rankin Inlet Canada 62°30N 93°0W 68 E13
Rankins Springs Australia 33°49S 146°14E 63 E4
Rannoch, L. U.K. 56°41N 4°20W 11 E4
Rannoch Moor U.K. 56°38N 4°48W 11 E4
Ranohira Madag. 22°29S 45°24E 55 J9
Ranong Thailand 9°56N 98°40E 39 H2
Ranpur India 20°5N 85°20E 44 D7
Rānsa Iran 33°39N 48°18E 47 C6
Ransiki Indonesia 1°30S 134°10E 37 E8
Rantau Abang Malaysia 4°52N 103°24E 39 K4
Rantauprapat Indonesia 2°15N 99°50E 36 D1
Rantemario Indonesia 3°15S 119°57E 37 E5
Ranthambore △ India 26°10N 76°42E 42 F7
Rantoul U.S.A. 40°19N 88°9W 80 E9
Raohe China 46°47N 134°0E 28 B7
Raoping China 23°42N 117°1E 35 F11
Raoyang China 38°15N 115°45E 32 E8
Rap, Ko Thailand 9°19N 99°58E 39 b
Rapa French Polynesia 27°35S 144°20W 65 K13
Rapa Nui = Pascua, I. de Chile 27°7S 109°23W 65 K17
Rapallo Italy 44°21N 9°14E 20 D8
Rapar India 23°34N 70°38E 42 H4
Rāpch Iran 25°40N 59°15E 47 E8
Rapel, Lago Chile 34°20S 71°14W 94 C1
Raper, C. Canada 69°44N 67°6W 69 D18
Rapid City U.S.A. 44°5N 103°14W 80 C2
Rapid River U.S.A. 45°55N 86°58W 80 C10
Rapla Estonia 59°1N 24°52E 9 G21
Rapti → India 26°18N 83°41E 43 F10
Raquette → U.S.A. 45°0N 74°42W 83 B10
Raquette Lake U.S.A. 43°49N 74°40W 83 C10
Rara △ Nepal 29°30N 82°10E 43 E10
Rarotonga Cook Is. 21°30S 160°0W 65 K12
Ra's al 'Ayn Syria 36°45N 40°12E 46 B4
Ra's Al Khair Si. Arabia 27°27N 49°18E 47 E6
Ra's al Khaymah U.A.E. 25°50N 55°59E 47 E7
Ra's aţ Ţib Tunisia 37°1N 11°2E 22 F4
Rasa, Pta. Argentina 36°20S 56°41W 94 D4
Raseiniai Lithuania 55°25N 23°5E 9 J20
Rashmi India 25°4N 74°22E 42 G6
Rasht Iran 37°20N 49°40E 47 B6
Rasi Salai Thailand 15°20N 104°9E 38 E5
Rasipuram India 11°30N 78°15E 45 J4
Raskot Nepal 29°14N 81°39E 43 E9
Rason L. Australia 28°45S 124°25E 61 E3
Rasra India 25°50N 83°50E 43 G10
Rasua Garhi Nepal 28°17N 85°23E 43 E11
Rasul Pakistan 32°42N 73°34E 42 C5
Rat → Canada 49°35N 97°10W 71 D9
Rat Buri = Ratchaburi Thailand 13°30N 99°54E 38 F2
Rat Islands U.S.A. 52°0N 178°0E 74 E3
Rat L. Canada 56°10N 99°40W 71 B9
Ratak Chain Pac. Oc. 1°0N 170°0E 64 G8
Ratangarh India 28°5N 74°35E 42 E6
Raţāwī Iraq 30°38N 47°13E 46 D5
Ratchaburi Thailand 13°30N 99°54E 38 F2
Rath India 25°36N 79°37E 43 G8
Rath Luirc = Charleville Ireland 52°21N 8°40W 10 D3
Rathangan Ireland 53°14N 7°0W 10 C4
Rathdrum Ireland 52°56N 6°14W 10 D5
Rathenow Germany 52°37N 12°19E 16 B7
Rathkeale Ireland 52°32N 8°56W 10 D3
Rathlin I. U.K. 55°18N 6°14W 10 A5
Rathmelton Ireland 55°2N 7°39W 10 A4
Ratibor = Racibórz Poland 50°7N 18°18E 17 C10
Ratlam India 23°20N 75°0E 42 H6
Ratmanova, Ostrov Russia 65°46N 169°6W 74 B6
Ratnagiri India 16°57N 73°18E 44 F1
Ratnapura Sri Lanka 6°40N 80°20E 45 L5
Ratodero Pakistan 27°48N 68°18E 42 F3
Raton U.S.A. 36°54N 104°24W 77 H11
Rattaphum Thailand 7°8N 100°16E 39 J3
Rattray Hd. U.K. 57°38N 1°50W 11 D7
Ratz, Mt. Canada 57°23N 132°12W 70 B2
Raub Malaysia 3°47N 101°52E 39 L3
Rauch Argentina 36°45S 59°5W 94 D4
Raudales Mexico 17°27N 93°39W 87 D6
Raufarhöfn Iceland 66°27N 15°57W 8 C6
Raufoss Norway 60°44N 10°37E 8 F14
Raukumara Ra. N.Z. 38°5S 177°55E 59 C6
Rauma Finland 61°10N 21°30E 8 F19
Raumo = Rauma Finland 61°10N 21°30E 8 F19
Raung, Gunung Indonesia 8°8S 114°3E 37 J17
Raurkela India 22°14N 84°50E 43 H11
Rausu-Dake Japan 44°4N 145°7E 28 B12
Rava-Ruska Ukraine 50°15N 23°42E 17 C12
Rava Russkaya = Rava-Ruska Ukraine 50°15N 23°42E 17 C12
Ravalli U.S.A. 47°17N 114°11W 76 C6
Ravānsar Iran 34°43N 46°40E 46 C5
Rāvar Iran 31°20N 56°51E 47 D8
Ravena U.S.A. 42°28N 73°49W 83 D11
Ravenna Italy 44°25N 12°12E 22 B5
Ravenna Nebr., U.S.A. 41°1N 98°55W 80 E4
Ravenna Ohio, U.S.A. 41°9N 81°15W 82 E3
Ravensburg Germany 47°46N 9°36E 16 E5
Ravenshoe Australia 17°37S 145°29E 62 B4
Ravensthorpe Australia 33°35S 120°2E 61 F3
Ravenswood Australia 20°6S 146°54E 62 C4
Ravenswood U.S.A. 38°57N 81°46W 81 F13
Raver India 21°15N 76°2E 44 D3
Ravi → Pakistan 30°35N 71°49E 42 D4
Rawalpindi Pakistan 33°38N 73°8E 42 C5
Rawang Malaysia 3°20N 101°35E 39 L3
Rawene N.Z. 35°25S 173°32E 59 A4
Rawi, Ko Thailand 6°33N 99°14E 39 J2
Rawlinna Australia 30°58S 125°28E 61 F4
Rawlins U.S.A. 41°47N 107°14W 76 F10
Rawlinson Ra. Australia 24°40S 128°30E 61 D4
Rawson Argentina 43°15S 65°5W 96 E3
Raxaul India 26°59N 84°51E 43 F11
Ray C. Canada ... (see Ray, C. Canada)

Ray, C. Canada 47°33N 59°15W 73 C8
Ray Mts. U.S.A. 66°0N 152°0W 74 B8
Raya Ring, Ko Thailand 8°18N 98°29E 39 a
Rayachoti India 14°4N 78°50E 45 G4
Rayadurg India 14°40N 76°50E 45 G3
Rayagada India 19°15N 83°20E 44 E6
Raychikhinsk Russia 49°46N 129°25E 27 E13
Rāyen Iran 29°34N 57°26E 47 D8
Rayleigh U.K. 51°36N 0°37E 13 F8
Raymond Canada 49°30N 112°35W 70 D6
Raymond Calif., U.S.A. 37°13N 119°54W 78 H7
Raymond N.H., U.S.A. 43°2N 71°11W 83 C13
Raymond Wash., U.S.A. 46°41N 123°44W 78 D3
Raymondville U.S.A. 26°29N 97°47W 84 H6
Raymore Canada 51°25N 104°31W 71 C8
Rayón Mexico 29°43N 110°35W 86 B2
Rayong Thailand 12°40N 101°20E 38 F3
Raystown L. U.S.A. 40°25N 78°5W 82 F6
Rayville U.S.A. 32°29N 91°46W 84 E9
Raz, Pte. du France 48°2N 4°47W 20 C1
Razan Iran 35°23N 49°2E 47 C6
Razāzah, Buḩayrat ar Iraq 32°40N 43°35E 46 C4
Razdel'naya = Rozdilna Ukraine 46°50N 30°2E 17 E16
Razdolnoye Russia 43°30N 131°52E 28 C5
Razeh Iran 32°47N 48°9E 47 C6
Razgrad Bulgaria 43°33N 26°34E 23 C12
Razim, Lacul Romania 44°50N 29°0E 17 F15
Razmak Pakistan 32°45N 69°50E 42 C3
Razzaza, L. = Razāzah, Buḩayrat ar Iraq 32°40N 43°35E 46 C4
Re, Cu Lao Vietnam 15°22N 109°8E 38 E7
Ré, Î. de France 46°12N 1°30W 20 C3
Reading U.K. 51°27N 0°58W 13 F7
Reading U.S.A. 40°20N 75°56W 83 F9
Reading □ U.K. 51°27N 0°58W 13 F7
Realicó Argentina 35°0S 64°15W 94 D3
Ream Cambodia 10°34N 103°39E 39 G4
Ream △ Cambodia 10°30N 103°45E 39 G4
Reay Forest U.K. 58°22N 4°55W 11 C4
Rebecca, L. Australia 30°0S 122°15E 61 F3
Rebi Indonesia 6°23S 134°7E 37 F8
Rebiana, Sahrâ' Libya 24°30N 21°0E 53 D10
Reboly Russia 63°49N 30°47E 8 E24
Rebun-Tō Japan 45°23N 141°2E 28 B10
Recherche, Arch. of the Australia 34°15S 122°50E 61 F3
Rechna Doab Pakistan 31°35N 73°30E 42 D5
Rechytsa Belarus 52°21N 30°24E 17 B16
Recife Brazil 8°0S 35°0W 93 E12
Recife Seychelles 4°36S 55°42E 55 b
Reckong Peo India 31°32N 78°16E 42 D8
Reconquista Argentina 29°10S 59°45W 94 B4
Recreo Argentina 29°25S 65°10W 94 B2
Red = Hong → Asia 20°16N 106°34E 38 B5
Red → U.S.A. 31°1N 91°45W 84 F9
Red Bank U.S.A. 40°21N 74°5W 83 F10
Red Bay Canada 51°44N 56°25W 73 B8
Red Bluff U.S.A. 40°11N 122°15W 76 F2
Red Bluff Res. U.S.A. 31°54N 103°55W 84 F3
Red Cliffs Australia 34°19S 142°11E 63 E3
Red Cloud U.S.A. 40°5N 98°32W 80 E4
Red Creek U.S.A. 43°14N 76°45W 83 C8
Red Deer Canada 52°20N 113°50W 70 C6
Red Deer → Alta., Canada 50°58N 110°0W 71 C7
Red Deer → Man., Canada 52°53N 101°1W 71 C8
Red Deer L. Canada 52°55N 101°20W 71 C8
Red Hook U.S.A. 41°55N 73°53W 83 E11
Red Indian L. Canada 48°35N 57°0W 73 C8
Red L. Canada 51°3N 93°49W 71 C10
Red Lake Canada 51°3N 93°49W 71 C10
Red Lake Falls U.S.A. 47°53N 96°16W 80 B5
Red Lake Road Canada 49°59N 93°25W 71 C10
Red Lodge U.S.A. 45°11N 109°15W 76 D9
Red Mountain U.S.A. 35°37N 117°38W 79 K9
Red Oak U.S.A. 41°1N 95°14W 80 E6
Red River of the North → N. Amer. 49°0N 97°15W 80 A5
Red Rock Canada 48°55N 88°15W 72 C2
Red Rock, L. U.S.A. 41°22N 92°59W 80 E7
Red Rocks Pt. Australia 32°13S 127°32E 61 F4
Red Sea Asia 25°0N 36°0E 49 C2
Red Slate Mt. U.S.A. 37°31N 118°52W 78 H8
Red Sucker L. Canada 54°9N 93°40W 72 B1
Red Tower Pass = Turnu Roşu, P. Romania 45°33N 24°17E 17 F13
Red Wing U.S.A. 44°34N 92°31W 80 C7
Redang, Pulau Malaysia 5°49N 103°2E 39 K4
Redange Lux. 49°46N 5°52E 15 E5
Redcar U.K. 54°37N 1°4W 12 C6
Redcar & Cleveland □ U.K. 54°29N 1°0W 12 C7
Redcliff Canada 50°10N 110°50W 70 A8
Redcliffe S. Australia 27°12S 153°6E 63 D5
Redcliffe, Mt. Australia 28°30S 121°30E 61 E3
Reddersburg S. Africa 29°41S 26°10E 56 D4
Redding U.S.A. 40°35N 122°24W 76 F2
Redditch U.K. 52°18N 1°55W 13 E6
Redfield U.S.A. 44°53N 98°31W 80 C4
Redford U.S.A. 44°38N 73°48W 83 B11
Redhead Trin. & Tob. 10°44N 60°58W 93 K16
Redlands U.S.A. 34°4N 117°11W 79 M9
Redmond Oreg., U.S.A. 44°17N 121°11W 76 D3
Redmond Wash., U.S.A. 47°40N 122°7W 78 C4
Redon France 47°40N 2°6W 20 C2
Redonda Antigua & B. 16°58N 62°19W 89 C7
Redondela Spain 42°15N 8°38W 21 A1
Redondo Beach U.S.A. 33°50N 118°23W 79 M8
Redoubt Volcano U.S.A. 60°29N 152°45W 74 C8
Redruth U.K. 50°14N 5°14W 13 G2
Redvers Canada 49°35N 101°40W 71 D8
Redwater Canada 53°55N 113°6W 70 C6
Redwood U.S.A. 44°18N 75°48W 83 B9
Redwood △ U.S.A. 41°40N 124°5W 76 F1
Redwood City U.S.A. 37°30N 122°15W 78 H4
Redwood Falls U.S.A. 44°32N 95°7W 80 C6

Ree, L. *Ireland* 53°35N 8°0W **10** C3
Reed City *U.S.A.* 43°53N 85°31W **81** D11
Reed L. *Canada* 54°38N 100°30W **71** C8
Reedley *U.S.A.* 36°36N 119°27W **78** J7
Reedsburg *U.S.A.* 43°32N 90°0W **80** D8
Reedsport *U.S.A.* 43°42N 124°6W **76** E1
Reedsville *U.S.A.* 40°39N 77°35W **82** F7
Reefton *N.Z.* 42°6S 171°51E **59** E3
Refugio *U.S.A.* 28°18N 97°17W **84** G6
Regensburg *Germany* 49°1N 12°6E **16** D7
Reggâne = Zaouiet Reggâne
  Algeria 26°32N 0°3E **52** C6
Réggio di Calábria *Italy* 38°6N 15°39E **22** E6
Réggio nell'Emília *Italy* 44°43N 10°36E **22** B4
Reghin *Romania* 46°46N 24°42E **17** E13
Regina *Canada* 50°27N 104°35W **71** C8
Regina Beach *Canada* 50°47N 105°0W **71** C8
Registro *Brazil* 24°29S 47°49W **95** A6
Rehar → *India* 23°55N 82°40E **43** H10
Rehli *India* 23°38N 79°5E **43** H8
Rehoboth *Namibia* 23°15S 17°4E **56** B2
Rehovot *Israel* 31°54N 34°48E **48** D3
Reichenbach *Germany* 50°37N 12°17E **16** C7
Reid *Australia* 30°49S 128°26E **61** F4
Reidsville *U.S.A.* 36°21N 79°40W **85** C15
Reigate *U.K.* 51°14N 0°12W **13** F7
Reims *France* 49°15N 4°1E **20** B6
Reina Adelaida, Arch.
  Chile 52°20S 74°0W **96** G2
Reindeer → *Canada* 55°36N 103°11W **71** B8
Reindeer I. *Canada* 52°30N 98°0W **71** C9
Reindeer L. *Canada* 57°15N 102°15W **71** B8
Reinga, C. *N.Z.* 34°25S 172°43E **59** A4
Reinheimen △ *Norway* 62°10N 7°45E **8** E12
Reinosa *Spain* 43°2N 4°15W **21** A3
Reitz *S. Africa* 27°48S 28°29E **57** C4
Reivilo *S. Africa* 27°36S 24°8E **56** D3
Reliance *Canada* 63°0N 109°20W **71** A7
Remanso *Brazil* 9°41S 42°4W **93** E10
Remarkable, Mt.
  Australia 32°48S 138°10E **63** E2
Rembang *Indonesia* 6°42S 111°21E **37** G14
Remedios *Panama* 8°15N 81°50W **88** E3
Remeshk *Iran* 26°55N 58°50E **47** E8
Remich *Lux.* 49°32N 6°22E **15** E6
Ren Xian *China* 37°8N 114°40E **32** F8
Rendang *Indonesia* 8°26S 115°25E **37** J18
Rendsburg *Germany* 54°17N 9°39E **16** A5
René-Levasseur, Î.
  Canada 51°20N 68°40W **73** B6
Renfrew *Canada* 45°30N 76°40W **83** A8
Renfrewshire □ *U.K.* 55°49N 4°38W **11** F4
Rengat *Indonesia* 0°30S 102°45E **36** E2
Rengo *Chile* 34°24S 70°50W **94** C1
Renhua *China* 25°5N 113°40E **35** E9
Renhuai *China* 27°48N 106°24E **34** D6
Reni → Taranagar *India* 28°43N 74°50E **43** H4
Reni *Ukraine* 45°28N 28°15E **17** F15
Renigunta *India* 13°38N 79°30E **45** H4
Renmark *Australia* 34°11S 140°43E **63** E3
Renner Springs *Australia* 18°20S 133°47E **62** B1
Rennes *France* 48°7N 1°41W **20** B3
Rennick Glacier
  Antarctica 70°30S 161°45E **5** D11
Rennie L. *Canada* 61°32N 105°35W **71** A7
Reno *U.S.A.* 39°31N 119°48W **78** F7
Reno → *Italy* 44°38N 12°16E **22** B5
Renqiu *China* 38°43N 116°5E **32** E9
Renshou *China* 29°59N 104°9E **34** C5
Rensselaer *Ind., U.S.A.* 40°57N 87°9W **80** E10
Rensselaer *N.Y., U.S.A.* 42°38N 73°45W **83** D11
Renton *U.S.A.* 47°28N 122°12W **78** C4
Renukoot *India* 24°12N 83°2E **43** G10
Reotipur *India* 25°33N 83°45E **43** G10
Repalle *India* 16°2N 80°45E **45** F5
Republic *Mo., U.S.A.* 37°7N 93°29W **80** G7
Republic *Wash., U.S.A.* 48°39N 118°44W **76** B4
Republican → *U.S.A.* 39°4N 96°48W **80** F5
Repulse B. *Australia* 20°35S 148°46E **62** b
Repulse Bay *Canada* 66°30N 86°30W **69** D14
Requena *Peru* 5°5S 73°52W **92** E4
Requena *Spain* 39°30N 1°4W **21** C5
Reserve *U.S.A.* 33°43N 108°45W **77** K9
Resht = Rasht *Iran* 37°20N 49°40E **47** B6
Resistencia *Argentina* 27°30S 59°0W **94** B4
Reşiţa *Romania* 45°18N 21°53E **17** F11
Reso = Raisio *Finland* 60°28N 22°11E **9** F20
Resolute *Canada* 74°42N 94°54W **69** C13
Resolution I. *Canada* 61°30N 65°0W **69** E19
Resolution I. *N.Z.* 45°40S 166°40E **59** F1
Ressano Garcia *Mozam.* 25°25S 32°0E **57** C5
Reston *Canada* 49°33N 101°6W **71** D8
Retalhuleu *Guatemala* 14°33N 91°46W **88** D1
Retford *U.K.* 53°19N 0°56W **12** D7
Rethimno *Greece* 35°18N 24°30E **23** G11
Reti *Pakistan* 28°5N 69°48E **42** E3
Réunion ☑ *Ind. Oc.* 21°0S 56°0E **55** c
Reus *Spain* 41°10N 1°5E **21** B6
Reutlingen *Germany* 48°29N 9°12E **16** D5
Reval = Tallinn *Estonia* 59°22N 24°48E **9** G21
Revda *Russia* 56°48N 59°57E **18** C10
Revelganj *India* 25°50N 84°40E **43** G11
Revelstoke *Canada* 51°0N 118°10W **70** C5
Reventazón *Peru* 6°10S 80°58W **92** E2
Revillagigedo, Is. de
  Pac. Oc. 18°40N 112°0W **86** D2
Rewa *India* 24°33N 81°25E **43** G9
Rewari *India* 28°15N 76°40E **42** E7
Rexburg *U.S.A.* 43°49N 111°47W **76** E8
Rey, I. del *Panama* 8°20N 78°30W **88** E4
Rey, L. del *Mexico* 27°1N 103°26W **86** B4
Rey Malabo *Eq. Guin.* 3°45N 8°50E **54** D1
Reyðarfjörður *Iceland* 65°2N 14°13W **8** D6
Reyes, Pt. *U.S.A.* 38°0N 123°0W **78** H3
Reykjahlíð *Iceland* 65°40N 16°55W **8** D5
Reykjanes *Iceland* 63°48N 22°40W **8** E2
Reykjavík *Iceland* 64°10N 21°57W **8** D3

Reynolds Ra. *Australia* 22°30S 133°0E **60** D5
Reynoldsville *U.S.A.* 41°6N 78°53W **82** E6
Reynosa *Mexico* 26°7N 98°18W **87** B5
Rēzekne *Latvia* 56°30N 27°17E **9** H22
Rezvān *Iran* 27°34N 56°6E **47** E8
Rhayader *U.K.* 52°18N 3°29W **13** E4
Rhein → *Europe* 51°52N 6°2E **15** C6
Rhein-Main-Donau-Kanal
  Germany 49°1N 11°27E **16** D6
Rheine *Germany* 52°17N 7°26E **16** B4
Rheinland-Pfalz □ *Germany* 50°0N 7°0E **16** C4
Rhin = Rhein → *Europe* 51°52N 6°2E **15** C6
Rhine = Rhein → *Europe* 51°52N 6°2E **15** C6
Rhinebeck *U.S.A.* 41°56N 73°55W **83** E11
Rhineland-Palatinate =
  Rheinland-Pfalz □
  Germany 50°0N 7°0E **16** C4
Rhinelander *U.S.A.* 45°38N 89°25W **80** C9
Rhinns Pt. *U.K.* 55°40N 6°29W **11** F2
Rhir, Cap *Morocco* 30°38N 9°54W **52** B4
Rhode Island □ *U.S.A.* 41°40N 71°30W **83** E13
Rhodes *Greece* 36°15N 28°10E **23** F13
Rhodope Mts. = Rodopi Planina
  Bulgaria 41°40N 24°20E **23** D11
Rhön *Germany* 50°24N 9°58E **16** C5
Rhondda *U.K.* 51°39N 3°31W **13** F4
Rhondda Cynon Taff □
  U.K. 51°42N 3°27W **13** F4
Rhône → *France* 43°28N 4°42E **20** E6
Rhum = Rùm *U.K.* 57°0N 6°20W **11** E2
Rhydaman = Ammanford
  U.K. 51°48N 3°59W **13** F4
Rhyl *U.K.* 53°20N 3°29W **12** D4
Riachão *Brazil* 7°20S 46°37W **93** E9
Riang, Laem *Thailand* 8°7N 98°27E **39** a
Riasi *India* 33°10N 74°50E **43** C6
Riau □ *Indonesia* 0°0 102°35E **36** E2
Riau, Kepulauan □
  Indonesia 0°30N 104°20E **36** D2
Riau Arch. = Riau, Kepulauan □
  Indonesia 0°30N 104°20E **36** D2
Ribadeo *Spain* 43°35N 7°5W **21** A2
Ribas do Rio Pardo
  Brazil 20°27S 53°46W **93** H8
Ribble → *U.K.* 53°52N 2°25W **12** D5
Ribe *Denmark* 55°19N 8°44E **9** J13
Ribeira Grande *C. Verde Is.* 17°0N 25°4W **52** b
Ribeirão Prêto *Brazil* 21°10S 47°50W **95** A6
Riberalta *Bolivia* 11°0S 66°0W **92** F5
Ribniţa *Moldova* 47°45N 29°0E **17** E15
Riccarton *N.Z.* 43°32S 172°37E **59** E4
Rice *U.S.A.* 34°5N 114°51W **79** L12
Rice L. *Canada* 44°12N 78°10W **82** B6
Rice Lake *U.S.A.* 45°30N 91°44W **80** C8
Rich, C. *Canada* 44°43N 80°38W **82** B4
Richards Bay *S. Africa* 28°48S 32°6E **57** C5
Richardson → *Canada* 58°25N 111°14W **71** B6
Richardson Lakes
  U.S.A. 44°46N 70°58W **81** C18
Richardson Springs
  U.S.A. 39°51N 121°46W **78** F5
Riche, C. *Australia* 34°36S 118°47E **61** F2
Richey *U.S.A.* 47°39N 105°4W **76** C11
Richfield *U.S.A.* 38°46N 112°5W **76** G7
Richfield Springs *U.S.A.* 42°51N 74°59W **83** D10
Richford *U.S.A.* 45°0N 72°40W **83** B12
Richibucto *Canada* 46°42N 64°54W **73** C7
Richland *Ga., U.S.A.* 32°5N 84°40W **85** E12
Richland *Wash., U.S.A.* 46°17N 119°18W **76** C4
Richland Center *U.S.A.* 43°21N 90°23W **80** D8
Richlands *U.S.A.* 37°6N 81°48W **81** G13
Richmond *Australia* 20°43S 143°8E **62** C3
Richmond *N.Z.* 41°20S 173°12E **59** D4
Richmond *U.K.* 54°25N 1°43W **12** C6
Richmond *Calif., U.S.A.* 37°56N 122°21W **78** H4
Richmond *Ind., U.S.A.* 39°50N 84°53W **81** F11
Richmond *Ky., U.S.A.* 37°45N 84°18W **81** G11
Richmond *Mich., U.S.A.* 42°49N 82°45W **82** D2
Richmond *Mo., U.S.A.* 39°17N 93°58W **80** F7
Richmond *Tex., U.S.A.* 29°35N 95°46W **84** G7
Richmond *Utah, U.S.A.* 41°56N 111°48W **76** F8
Richmond *Va., U.S.A.* 37°33N 77°27W **81** G15
Richmond *Vt., U.S.A.* 44°24N 72°59W **83** B12
Richmond Hill *Canada* 43°52N 79°27W **82** C5
Richmond Ra. *Australia* 29°0S 152°45E **63** D5
Richmondville *U.S.A.* 42°38N 74°33W **83** D10
Richtersveld △ *S. Africa* 28°15S 17°10E **56** C2
Richville *U.S.A.* 44°25N 75°23W **83** B9
Richwood *U.S.A.* 38°14N 80°32W **81** F13
Ridder *Kazakhstan* 50°20N 83°30E **26** D9
Rideau → *Canada* 45°27N 75°42W **83** A9
Ridgecrest *U.S.A.* 35°38N 117°40W **79** K9
Ridgefield *Conn., U.S.A.* 41°17N 73°30W **83** E11
Ridgeland *Wash., U.S.A.* 45°49N 122°45W **78** E4
Ridgeland *Miss., U.S.A.* 32°26N 90°8W **85** E9
Ridgeland *S.C., U.S.A.* 32°29N 80°59W **85** E14
Ridgetown *Canada* 42°26N 81°52W **82** D3
Ridgewood *U.S.A.* 40°59N 74°7W **83** F10
Ridgway *U.S.A.* 41°25N 78°44W **82** E6
Riding Mountain △
  Canada 50°50N 100°0W **71** C9
Ridley, Mt. *Australia* 33°12S 122°7E **61** F3
Riebeek-Oos *S. Africa* 33°10S 26°10E **56** D4
Ried *Austria* 48°14N 13°30E **16** D7
Riesa *Germany* 51°17N 13°17E **16** C7
Riet → *S. Africa* 29°0S 23°54E **56** C3
Rietbron *S. Africa* 32°54S 23°10E **56** E3
Rietfontein *Namibia* 21°58S 20°58E **56** B3
Rieti *Italy* 42°24N 12°51E **22** C5
Rif = Er Rif *Morocco* 35°1N 4°1W **52** A5
Riffe L. *U.S.A.* 46°32N 122°26W **78** D4
Rifle *U.S.A.* 39°32N 107°47W **76** G10
Riga *Latvia* 56°53N 24°8E **9** H21
Riga, G. of *Latvia* 57°40N 23°45E **9** H20
Rīgān *Iran* 28°37N 58°58E **47** D8
Rīgas Jūras Līcis = Riga, G. of
  Latvia 57°40N 23°45E **9** H20
Rigaud *Canada* 45°29N 74°18W **83** A10

Rigby *U.S.A.* 43°40N 111°55W **76** E8
Rīgestān *Afghan.* 30°15N 65°0E **40** D4
Riggins *U.S.A.* 45°25N 116°19W **76** D5
Rigolet *Canada* 54°10N 58°23W **73** B8
Rihand Dam *India* 24°9N 83°2E **43** G10
Riihimäki *Finland* 60°45N 24°48E **8** F21
Riiser-Larsen-halvøya
  Antarctica 68°0S 35°0E **5** C4
Riiser-Larsen Ice Shelf
  S. Ocean 74°0S 19°0W **5** D2
Riiser-Larsen Sea *S. Ocean* 67°30S 22°0E **5** C4
Riisitunturi △ *Finland* 66°27N 28°27E **8** C23
Rijeka *Croatia* 45°20N 14°21E **16** F8
Rijssen *Neths.* 52°19N 6°31E **15** B6
Rikuchū-Kaigan △
  Japan 39°20N 142°0E **28** E11
Rikuzentakata *Japan* 39°0N 141°40E **28** E10
Riley *U.S.A.* 43°32N 119°28W **76** E4
Rima → *Nigeria* 13°4N 5°10E **52** F7
Rimah, Wadi ar →
  Si. Arabia 26°5N 41°30E **46** E4
Rimau, Pulau *Malaysia* 5°15N 100°16E **39** c
Rimbey *Canada* 52°35N 114°15W **70** C6
Rimersburg *U.S.A.* 41°3N 79°30W **82** E5
Rímini *Italy* 44°3N 12°33E **22** B5
Rimouski *Canada* 48°27N 68°30W **73** C6
Rimrock *U.S.A.* 46°40N 121°7W **78** D5
Rinca *Indonesia* 8°45S 119°35E **37** F5
Rincón de Romos
  Mexico 22°14N 102°18W **86** C4
Rinconada *Argentina* 22°26S 66°10W **94** A2
Rind → *India* 25°53N 80°33E **43** G9
Ringas *India* 27°21N 75°34E **42** F6
Ringgold Is. *Fiji* 16°15S 179°25W **59** a
Ringkøbing *Denmark* 56°5N 8°15E **9** H13
Ringvassøya *Norway* 69°56N 19°15E **8** B18
Ringwood *U.S.A.* 41°7N 74°15W **83** E10
Rinjani, Gunung
  Indonesia 8°24S 116°28E **36** F5
Rinyirru △ *Australia* 15°24S 144°26E **62** B3
Rio Branco *Brazil* 9°58S 67°49W **92** E5
Río Branco *Uruguay* 32°40S 53°40W **95** C5
Río Bravo *Mexico* 25°59N 98°6W **87** B5
Río Bravo → *N. Amer.* 25°57N 97°9W **87** B5
Río Bravo del Norte →
  Mexico 25°57N 97°9W **87** B5
Rio Brilhante *Brazil* 21°48S 54°33W **95** A5
Río Claro *Brazil* 22°19S 47°35W **95** A6
Río Claro *Trin. & Tob.* 10°20N 61°10W **93** K15
Río Colorado *Argentina* 39°0S 64°0W **96** D4
Río Cuarto *Argentina* 33°10S 64°25W **94** C3
Rio das Pedras *Mozam.* 23°8S 35°28E **57** B6
Rio de Janeiro □ *Brazil* 22°50S 43°0W **95** A7
Río do Sul *Brazil* 27°13S 49°37W **95** B6
Río Dulce △ *Guatemala* 15°43N 88°50W **88** C2
Río Gallegos *Argentina* 51°35S 69°15W **96** G3
Río Grande *Argentina* 53°50S 67°45W **96** G3
Río Grande *Brazil* 32°0S 52°20W **95** C5
Río Grande *Mexico* 23°50N 103°2W **86** C4
Río Grande *Puerto Rico* 18°23N 65°50W **89** d
Río Grande → *N. Amer.* 25°58N 97°9W **84** J6
Río Grande City *U.S.A.* 26°23N 98°49W **84** H5
Río Grande de Santiago →
  Mexico 21°36N 105°26W **86** C3
Rio Grande do Norte □
  Brazil 5°40S 36°0W **93** E11
Rio Grande do Sul □ *Brazil* 30°0S 53°0W **95** C5
Río Hato *Panama* 8°22N 80°10W **88** E3
Río Lagartos *Mexico* 21°36N 88°10W **87** C7
Río Largo *Brazil* 9°28S 35°50W **93** E11
Río Mulatos *Bolivia* 19°40S 66°50W **92** G5
Río Muni □ *Eq. Guin.* 1°30N 10°0E **54** D2
Río Negro *Brazil* 26°0S 49°55W **95** B6
Río Pardo *Brazil* 30°0S 52°30W **95** C5
Río Pilcomayo △ *Argentina* 25°5S 58°5W **94** B4
Río Plátano △ *Honduras* 15°45S 85°0W **88** C3
Río Rancho *U.S.A.* 35°14N 106°41W **77** J10
Río Segundo *Argentina* 31°40S 63°59W **94** C3
Río Tercero *Argentina* 32°15S 64°8W **94** C3
Río Verde *Brazil* 17°50S 51°0W **93** G8
Río Verde *Mexico* 21°56N 99°59W **87** C5
Rio Vista *U.S.A.* 38°10N 121°42W **78** G5
Ríobamba *Ecuador* 1°50S 78°45W **92** D3
Ríohacha *Colombia* 11°33N 72°55W **92** A4
Ríosucio *Colombia* 7°27N 77°7W **92** B3
Riou L. *Canada* 59°7N 106°25W **71** B7
Ripley *Calif., U.S.A.* 33°32N 114°39W **79** M12
Ripley *N.Y., U.S.A.* 42°16N 79°43W **82** D5
Ripley *Tenn., U.S.A.* 35°45N 89°32W **85** D10
Ripley *W. Va., U.S.A.* 38°49N 81°43W **81** F13
Ripon *U.K.* 54°9N 1°31W **12** C6
Ripon *Calif., U.S.A.* 37°44N 121°7W **78** H5
Ripon *Wis., U.S.A.* 43°51N 88°50W **80** D9
Rishā', W. ar → *Si. Arabia* 25°33N 44°5E **46** E5
Rishikesh *India* 30°7N 78°19E **42** D8
Rishiri-Rebun-Sarobetsu △
  Japan 45°26N 141°30E **28** B10
Rishiri-Tō *Japan* 45°11N 141°15E **28** B10
Rishon le Ziyyon *Israel* 31°58N 34°48E **48** D3
Rison *U.S.A.* 33°58N 92°11W **84** E8
Risør *Norway* 58°43N 9°13E **9** G13
Rita Blanca Cr. →
  U.S.A. 35°40N 102°29W **84** D3
Ritchie's Arch. *India* 12°1N 93°0E **45** H11
Ritter, Mt. *U.S.A.* 37°41N 119°12W **78** H7
Rittman *U.S.A.* 40°58N 81°47W **82** F3
Ritzville *U.S.A.* 47°8N 118°23W **76** C4
Riva del Garda *Italy* 45°53N 10°50E **22** B4
Rivadavia *B. Aires,
  Argentina* 35°29S 62°59W **94** D3
Rivadavia *Mendoza,
  Argentina* 33°13S 68°30W **94** C2
Rivadavia *Salta, Argentina* 24°5S 62°54W **94** A3
Rivadavia *Chile* 29°57S 70°35W **94** B1
Rivas *Nic.* 11°30N 85°50W **88** D2
Rivash *Iran* 35°28N 58°26E **47** C8
River Cess *Liberia* 5°30N 9°32W **52** G4
River Jordan *Canada* 48°26N 124°3W **78** B2
Rivera *Argentina* 37°12S 63°14W **94** D3

Rivera *Uruguay* 31°0S 55°50W **95** C4
Riverbank *U.S.A.* 37°44N 120°56W **78** H6
Riverdale *U.S.A.* 36°26N 119°52W **78** J7
Riverhead *U.S.A.* 40°55N 72°40W **83** F12
Riverhurst *Canada* 50°55N 106°50W **71** C7
Rivers *Canada* 50°2N 100°14W **71** C8
Rivers Inlet *Canada* 51°42N 127°15W **70** C3
Riversdale *Canada* 44°5N 81°20W **82** B3
Riversdale *S. Africa* 34°7S 21°15E **56** D3
Riverside *U.S.A.* 33°59N 117°22W **79** M9
Riversleigh *Australia* 19°5S 138°40E **62** B2
Riverton *Australia* 34°10S 138°46E **63** E2
Riverton *Canada* 51°1N 97°0W **71** C9
Riverton *N.Z.* 46°21S 168°0E **59** G2
Riverton *U.S.A.* 43°2N 108°23W **76** E9
Riviera = Azur, Côte d'
  France 43°25N 7°10E **20** E7
Riviera *U.S.A.* 35°4N 114°35W **79** K12
Riviera di Levante *Italy* 44°15N 9°30E **20** D8
Riviera di Ponente *Italy* 44°10N 8°20E **20** D8
Rivière-au-Renard
  Canada 48°59N 64°23W **73** C7
Rivière-du-Loup *Canada* 47°50N 69°30W **73** C6
Rivière-Pentecôte *Canada* 49°57N 67°1W **73** C6
Rivière-Pilote *Martinique* 14°26N 60°53W **88** c
Rivière St-Paul *Canada* 51°28N 57°45W **73** B8
Rivière-Salée *Martinique* 14°31N 61°0W **88** c
Rivne *Ukraine* 50°40N 26°10E **17** C14
Rivne □ *Ukraine* 51°15N 26°30E **17** C14
Rívoli *Italy* 45°3N 7°31E **20** D7
Rivoli B. *Australia* 37°32S 140°3E **63** F3
Riyadh = Ar Riyāḍ
  Si. Arabia 24°41N 46°42E **46** E5
Rize *Turkey* 41°0N 40°30E **19** F7
Rizhao *China* 35°25N 119°30E **33** G10
Rizzuto, C. *Italy* 38°53N 17°5E **22** E7
Rjukan *Norway* 59°54N 8°33E **9** G13
Road Town *Br. Virgin Is.* 18°27N 64°37W **89** e
Roan Plateau *U.S.A.* 39°20N 109°20W **76** G9
Roanne *France* 46°3N 4°4E **20** C6
Roanoke *Ala., U.S.A.* 33°9N 85°22W **85** E12
Roanoke *Va., U.S.A.* 37°16N 79°56W **81** G14
Roanoke → *U.S.A.* 35°57N 76°42W **85** D16
Roanoke I. *U.S.A.* 35°53N 75°39W **85** D17
Roanoke Rapids *U.S.A.* 36°28N 77°40W **85** C16
Roatán *Honduras* 16°18N 86°35W **88** C2
Robāt Sang *Iran* 35°35N 59°10E **47** C8
Robāţkarīm *Iran* 35°25N 50°59E **47** C6
Robben I. *S. Africa* 33°48S 18°22E **56** E2
Robbins I. *Australia* 40°42S 145°0E **63** G4
Robe → *Australia* 21°42S 116°15E **60** D2
Robe *Australia* 21°42S 116°15E **60** D2
Robert Bourassa, Rés.
  Canada 53°40N 76°55W **72** B4
Robert Lee *U.S.A.* 31°54N 100°29W **84** F4
Robertsdale *U.S.A.* 40°11N 78°6W **82** F6
Robertsganj *India* 24°44N 83°4E **43** G10
Robertson *S. Africa* 33°46S 19°50E **56** D2
Robertson I. *Antarctica* 65°15S 59°30E **5** C18
Robertson Ra. *Australia* 23°15S 121°0E **60** D3
Robertstown *Australia* 33°58S 139°5E **63** E2
Roberval *Canada* 48°32N 72°15W **73** C5
Robeson Chan. *N. Amer.* 82°0N 61°30W **69** A19
Robesonia *U.S.A.* 40°21N 76°8W **83** F8
Robinson *U.S.A.* 39°0N 87°44W **80** F10
Robinson → *Australia* 16°3S 137°16E **62** B2
Robinson Crusoe I.
  Pac. Oc. 33°38S 78°52W **90** F2
Robinson Ra. *Australia* 25°40S 119°0E **61** E2
Robinvale *Australia* 34°40S 142°45E **63** E3
Roblin *Canada* 51°14N 101°21W **71** C8
Roboré *Bolivia* 18°10S 59°45W **92** G7
Robson, Mt. *Canada* 53°10N 119°10W **70** C5
Robstown *U.S.A.* 27°47N 97°40W **84** H6
Roca, C. da *Portugal* 38°40N 9°31W **21** C1
Roca Partida, I. *Mexico* 19°1N 112°2W **86** D2
Rocas, Atol das *Brazil* 4°0S 34°1W **93** D12
Rocha *Uruguay* 34°30S 54°25W **95** C5
Rochdale *U.K.* 53°38N 2°9W **12** D5
Rochefort *Belgium* 50°9N 5°12E **15** D5
Rochefort *France* 45°56N 0°57W **20** D3
Rochelle *U.S.A.* 41°56N 89°4W **80** E9
Rocher River *Canada* 61°23N 112°44W **70** A6
Rochester *U.K.* 51°23N 0°31E **13** F8
Rochester *Ind., U.S.A.* 41°4N 86°13W **80** E10
Rochester *Minn., U.S.A.* 44°1N 92°28W **80** C7
Rochester *N.H., U.S.A.* 43°18N 70°59W **83** C14
Rochester *N.Y., U.S.A.* 43°10N 77°37W **82** C7
Rock → *Canada* 60°7N 127°7W **70** A3
Rock, The *Australia* 35°15S 147°2E **63** F4
Rock Creek *U.S.A.* 41°40N 80°52W **82** E4
Rock Falls *U.S.A.* 41°47N 89°41W **80** E9
Rock Hill *U.S.A.* 34°56N 81°1W **85** D14
Rock Island *U.S.A.* 41°30N 90°34W **80** E8
Rock Port *U.S.A.* 40°25N 95°31W **80** E6
Rock Rapids *U.S.A.* 43°26N 96°10W **80** D5
Rock Sound *Bahamas* 24°54N 76°12W **88** B4
Rock Springs *Mont.,
  U.S.A.* 46°49N 106°15W **76** C10
Rock Springs *Wyo.,
  U.S.A.* 41°35N 109°14W **76** F9
Rock Valley *U.S.A.* 43°12N 96°18W **80** D5
Rockall *Atl. Oc.* 57°37N 13°42W **6** D3
Rockdale *Tex., U.S.A.* 30°39N 97°0W **84** F6
Rockdale *Wash., U.S.A.* 47°22N 121°28W **78** C5
Rockeby = Mungkan Kandju △
  Australia 13°35S 142°52E **62** A3
Rockefeller Plateau
  Antarctica 80°0S 130°0W **5** E14
Rockford *U.S.A.* 42°16N 89°6W **80** D9
Rockglen *Canada* 49°11N 105°57W **71** D7
Rockhampton *Australia* 23°22S 150°32E **62** C5
Rockingham *Australia* 32°15S 115°38E **61** F2
Rockingham *N.C.,
  U.S.A.* 34°57N 79°46W **85** D15
Rockingham *Vt., U.S.A.* 43°11N 72°29W **83** C12
Rockingham B. *Australia* 18°5S 146°10E **62** B4
Rocklake *U.S.A.* 48°47N 99°15W **80** A4
Rockland *Canada* 45°33N 75°17W **83** A9
Rockland *Idaho, U.S.A.* 42°34N 112°53W **76** E7
Rockland *Maine, U.S.A.* 44°6N 69°7W **81** C19

Rockland *Mich., U.S.A.* 46°44N 89°11W **80** B9
Rocklin *U.S.A.* 38°48N 121°14W **78** G5
Rockly B. *Trin. & Tob.* 11°9N 60°46W **93** J16
Rockmart *U.S.A.* 34°1N 85°3W **85** D12
Rockport *Mass., U.S.A.* 42°39N 70°37W **83** D14
Rockport *Tex., U.S.A.* 28°2N 97°3W **84** G6
Rocksprings *U.S.A.* 30°1N 100°13W **84** F4
Rockville *Conn., U.S.A.* 41°52N 72°28W **83** E12
Rockville *Md., U.S.A.* 39°5N 77°9W **81** F15
Rockwall *U.S.A.* 32°56N 96°28W **84** E6
Rockwood *Canada* 43°37N 80°8W **82** C4
Rockwood *Maine,
  U.S.A.* 45°41N 69°45W **81** C19
Rockwood *Tenn., U.S.A.* 35°52N 84°41W **85** D12
Rocky Ford *U.S.A.* 38°3N 103°43W **76** G12
Rocky Gully *Australia* 34°30S 116°57E **61** F2
Rocky Harbour *Canada* 49°36N 57°55W **73** C8
Rocky Island L. *Canada* 46°55N 83°0W **72** C3
Rocky Lane *Canada* 58°31N 116°22W **70** B5
Rocky Mount *U.S.A.* 35°57N 77°48W **85** D16
Rocky Mountain △
  U.S.A. 40°25N 105°45W **76** F11
Rocky Mountain House
  Canada 52°22N 114°55W **70** C6
Rocky Mts. *N. Amer.* 49°0N 115°0W **76** B6
Rocky Point *Namibia* 19°3S 12°30E **56** A2
Rødbyhavn *Denmark* 54°39N 11°22E **9** J14
Roddickton *Canada* 50°51N 56°8W **73** B8
Rodez *France* 44°21N 2°33E **20** D5
Ródhos = Rhodes *Greece* 36°15N 28°10E **23** F13
Rodna ○ *Australia* 23°45S 132°4E **60** D5
Rodney *Canada* 42°34N 81°41W **82** D3
Rodney, C. *N.Z.* 36°17S 174°50E **59** B5
Rodopi Planina *Bulgaria* 41°40N 24°20E **23** D11
Rodrigues *Ind. Oc.* 19°45S 63°20E **3** E13
Roe → *U.K.* 55°6N 6°59W **10** A5
Roebling *U.S.A.* 40°7N 74°47W **83** F10
Roebourne *Australia* 20°44S 117°9E **60** D2
Roebuck B. *Australia* 18°5S 122°20E **60** C3
Roebuck Roadhouse
  Australia 17°59S 122°36E **60** C3
Roermond *Neths.* 51°12N 6°0E **15** C6
Roes Welcome Sd. *Canada* 65°0N 87°0W **69** E14
Roeselare *Belgium* 50°57N 3°7E **15** D3
Rogachev = Ragachow
  Belarus 53°8N 30°5E **17** B16
Rogagua, L. *Bolivia* 13°43S 66°50W **92** F5
Rogatyn *Ukraine* 49°24N 24°36E **17** D13
Rogers *U.S.A.* 36°20N 94°7W **84** C7
Rogers City *U.S.A.* 45°25N 83°49W **81** C12
Rogersville *Canada* 46°44N 65°26W **73** C6
Roggan → *Canada* 54°24N 79°25W **72** B4
Roggan L. *Canada* 54°8N 77°50W **72** B4
Roggeveen Basin
  Pac. Oc. 31°30S 95°30W **65** L18
Roggeveldberge *S. Africa* 32°10S 20°10E **56** D3
Rogoaguado, L. *Bolivia* 13°0S 65°30W **92** F5
Rogojampi *Indonesia* 8°19S 114°17E **37** J17
Rogue → *U.S.A.* 42°26N 124°26W **76** E1
Roha *India* 18°26N 73°7E **44** E1
Rohnert Park *U.S.A.* 38°16N 122°40W **78** G4
Rohri *Pakistan* 27°45N 68°51E **42** F3
Rohri Canal *Pakistan* 26°15N 68°27E **42** F3
Rohtak *India* 28°55N 76°43E **42** E7
Roi Et *Thailand* 16°4N 103°40E **38** D4
Roja *Latvia* 57°29N 22°43E **9** H20
Rojas *Argentina* 34°10S 60°45W **94** C3
Rojo, C. *Mexico* 21°33N 97°20W **87** C5
Rokan → *Indonesia* 2°0N 100°50E **36** D2
Rokiškis *Lithuania* 55°55N 25°35E **9** J21
Rokua △ *Finland* 64°30N 26°15E **8** D22
Rolândia *Brazil* 23°18S 51°23W **95** A5
Rolla *Mo., U.S.A.* 37°57N 91°46W **80** G8
Rolla *N. Dak., U.S.A.* 48°52N 99°37W **80** A4
Rolleston *Australia* 24°28S 148°35E **62** C4
Rollingstone *Australia* 19°2S 146°24E **62** B4
Roma *Australia* 26°32S 148°49E **63** D4
Roma *Sweden* 57°32N 18°26E **9** H18
Roma-Los Saenz *U.S.A.* 26°24N 99°1W **84** H5
Romain, C. *U.S.A.* 33°0N 79°22W **85** E15
Romaine → *Canada* 50°18N 63°47W **73** B7
Roman *Romania* 46°57N 26°55E **17** E14
Romang *Indonesia* 7°30S 127°20E **37** F7
Români *Egypt* 30°59N 32°38E **48** E1
Romania ■ *Europe* 46°0N 25°0E **17** F12
Romano, Cayo *Cuba* 22°0N 77°30W **88** B4
Romans-sur-Isère *France* 45°3N 5°3E **20** D6
Romanzof C. *U.S.A.* 61°49N 166°6W **74** C6
Romblon *Phil.* 12°33N 122°17E **37** B6
Rome *Ga., U.S.A.* 34°15N 85°10W **85** D12
Rome *N.Y., U.S.A.* 43°13N 75°27W **83** C9
Rome *Pa., U.S.A.* 41°51N 76°21W **83** E8
Romney *U.S.A.* 39°21N 78°45W **81** F14
Romney Marsh *U.K.* 51°2N 0°54E **13** F8
Romny *Ukraine* 50°48N 33°28E **19** D5
Romorantin-Lanthenay
  France 47°21N 1°45E **20** C4
Rompin → *Malaysia* 2°49N 103°29E **39** L4
Romsdalen *Norway* 62°25N 7°52E **8** E12
Romsey *U.K.* 51°0N 1°29W **13** G6
Ron *Vietnam* 17°53N 106°27E **38** D6
Ron *U.K.* 57°34N 5°59W **11** D3
Ronan *U.S.A.* 47°32N 114°6W **76** C6
Roncador, Cayos
  Caribbean 13°32N 80°4W **88** D3
Ronda *Spain* 36°46N 5°12W **21** D3
Roncador, Serra do
  Brazil 12°30S 52°30W **93** F8
Rondane *Norway* 61°57N 9°50E **8** F13
Rondônia □ *Brazil* 11°0S 63°0W **92** F6
Rondonópolis *Brazil* 16°28S 54°38W **93** G8
Rondu *Pakistan* 35°32N 75°10E **43** B6
Rong, Koh *Cambodia* 10°45N 103°15E **39** G4
Rong Jiang → *China* 24°35N 109°28E **34** E7
Rong Xian *China* 22°50N 110°31E **35** F8
Rong'an *China* 25°14N 109°22E **34** E7
Rongchang *China* 29°20N 105°32E **34** C5

Rongcheng *China* 37°9N 122°23E **33** F12
Ronge, L. la *Canada* 55°6N 105°17W **71** B7
Rongjiang *China* 25°57N 108°28E **34** E7
Rongxian *China* 29°23N 104°22E **34** D5
Rønne *Denmark* 55°6N 14°43E **9** J16
Ronne Ice Shelf *Antarctica* 77°30S 60°0W **5** D18
Ronsard, C. *Australia* 24°46S 113°10E **61** D1
Ronse *Belgium* 50°45N 3°35E **15** D3
Roodepoort *S. Africa* 26°11S 27°54E **57** D4
Rooiboklaagte → *Namibia* 20°50S 21°0E **56** B3
Roof Butte *U.S.A.* 36°28N 109°5W **77** H9
Rooniu, Mt. *Tahiti* 17°49S 149°12W **59** d2
Roorkee *India* 29°52N 77°59E **42** E7
Roosendaal *Neths.* 51°32N 4°29E **15** C4
Roosevelt *U.S.A.* 40°18N 109°59W **76** F9
Roosevelt → *Brazil* 7°35S 60°20W **92** E6
Roosevelt, Mt. *Canada* 58°26N 125°20W **70** B3
Roosevelt I. *Antarctica* 79°30S 162°0W **5** D12
Roper → *Australia* 14°43S 135°27E **62** A2
Roper Bar *Australia* 14°44S 134°44E **62** A1
Roper River = St. Vidgeon's ☼
  Australia 14°47S 134°53E **62** A1
Roque Pérez *Argentina* 35°25S 59°24W **94** D4
Roquetas de Mar *Spain* 36°46N 2°36W **21** D4
Roraima □ *Brazil* 2°0N 61°30W **92** C6
Roraima, Mt. *Venezuela* 5°10N 60°40W **92** B6
Røros *Norway* 62°35N 11°23E **8** E14
Ros Comáin = Roscommon
  Ireland 53°38N 8°11W **10** C3
Ros Mhic Thriúin = New Ross
  Ireland 52°23N 6°57W **10** D5
Rosa, Monte *Europe* 45°57N 7°53E **20** D7
Rosalia *U.S.A.* 47°14N 117°22W **76** C5
Rosamond *U.S.A.* 34°52N 118°10W **79** L8
Rosario *Argentina* 33°0S 60°40W **94** C3
Rosário *Brazil* 3°0S 44°15W **93** D10
Rosario *Mexico* 22°58N 105°53W **86** C3
Rosario *Paraguay* 24°30S 57°35W **94** A4
Rosario de la Frontera
  Argentina 25°50S 65°0W **94** B3
Rosario de Lerma
  Argentina 24°59S 65°35W **94** A2
Rosario del Tala
  Argentina 32°20S 59°10W **94** C4
Rosário Baja Calif.,
  Mexico 32°20N 117°2W **79** N9
Rosario Baja Calif.,
  Mexico 28°38N 114°1W **86** B2
Roscoe *U.S.A.* 41°56N 74°55W **83** E10
Roscommon *Ireland* 53°38N 8°11W **10** C3
Roscommon □ *Ireland* 53°49N 8°23W **10** C3
Roscrea *Ireland* 52°57N 7°49W **10** D4
Rose → *Australia* 14°16S 135°27E **62** A2
Rose, L. *Bahamas* 21°0N 73°30W **89** B5
Rose Belle *Mauritius* 20°24S 57°36E **55** d
Rose Blanche *Canada* 47°38N 58°45W **73** C8
Rose Hill *Mauritius* 20°14S 57°27E **55** d
Rose Pt. *Canada* 54°11N 131°39W **70** C2
Rose Valley *Canada* 52°19N 103°49W **71** C8
Roseau *Dominica* 15°17N 61°24W **89** C7
Roseau *U.S.A.* 48°51N 96°46W **80** A6
Rosebery *Australia* 41°46S 145°33E **63** G4
Rosebud S. Dak., *U.S.A.* 43°14N 100°51W **80** D3
Rosebud Tex., *U.S.A.* 31°4N 96°59W **84** F6
Roseburg *U.S.A.* 43°13N 123°20W **76** E2
Rosedale *U.S.A.* 33°51N 91°2W **85** E9
Rosehearty *U.K.* 57°42N 2°7W **11** D6
Roseires Res. *Sudan* 11°51N 34°23E **53** F12
Roseland *U.S.A.* 38°25N 122°43W **78** G4
Rosemary *Canada* 50°46N 112°5W **70** C6
Rosenberg *U.S.A.* 29°34N 95°49W **84** G7
Rosenheim *Germany* 47°51N 12°7E **16** E7
Roses, G. de *Spain* 42°10N 3°15E **21** A7
Rosetown *Canada* 51°35N 107°59W **71** C7
Roseville Calif., *U.S.A.* 38°45N 121°17W **78** G5
Roseville Mich., *U.S.A.* 42°30N 82°56W **82** D2
Roseville Pa., *U.S.A.* 41°51N 76°57W **83** E8
Rosewood *Australia* 27°38S 152°36E **63** D5
Roshkhvār *Iran* 34°58N 59°37E **47** C8
Rosignano Maríttimo
  Italy 43°24N 10°28E **22** C4
Rosignol *Guyana* 6°15N 57°30W **92** B7
Roşiori de Vede *Romania* 44°9N 25°0E **17** F13
Roskilde *Denmark* 55°38N 12°3E **9** J15
Roslavl *Russia* 53°57N 32°55E **18** D5
Rosmead *S. Africa* 31°29S 25°8E **56** D4
Ross *Australia* 42°2S 147°30E **63** G4
Ross *N.Z.* 42°53S 170°49E **59** E3
Ross Dependency
  Antarctica 76°0S 170°0W **5** D12
Ross I. *Antarctica* 77°30S 168°0E **5** D11
Ross Ice Shelf *Antarctica* 80°0S 180°0E **5** E12
Ross L. *U.S.A.* 48°44N 121°4W **76** B3
Ross-on-Wye *U.K.* 51°54N 2°34W **13** F5
Ross River *Australia* 23°44S 134°30E **62** C1
Ross River *Canada* 62°30N 131°30W **70** A2
Ross Sea *Antarctica* 74°0S 178°0E **5** D11
Rossall Pt. *U.K.* 53°55N 3°3W **12** D4
Rossan Pt. *Ireland* 54°42N 8°47W **10** B3
Rossano *Italy* 39°36N 16°39E **22** E7
Rossburn *Canada* 50°40N 100°49W **71** C8
Rosseau *Canada* 45°16N 79°39W **82** A5
Rosseau, L. *Canada* 45°10N 79°35W **82** A5
Rosses, The *Ireland* 55°2N 8°20W **10** A3
Rossignol, L. *Canada* 52°43N 73°40W **72** B5
Rossignol L. *Canada* 44°12N 65°10W **73** D6
Rossiya = Russia ■
  Eurasia 62°0N 105°0E **27** C11
Rossland *Canada* 49°6N 117°50W **70** D5
Rosslare *Ireland* 52°17N 6°24W **10** D5
Rosslare Europort = Rosslare
  Harbour *Ireland* 52°15N 6°20W **10** D5
Rosslare Harbour *Ireland* 52°15N 6°20W **10** D5
Rossmore *Canada* 44°8N 77°23W **82** B7
Rosso *Mauritania* 16°40N 15°45W **52** E2
Rossosh *Russia* 50°15N 39°28E **19** D6
Røssvatnet *Norway* 65°45N 14°5E **8** D16
Røst *Norway* 67°32N 12°10E **8** C15

Rosthern *Canada* 52°40N 106°20W **71** C7
Rostock *Germany* 54°5N 12°8E **16** A7
Rostov Don, *Russia* 47°15N 39°45E **19** E6
Rostov Yaroslavl, *Russia* 57°14N 39°25E **18** C6
Roswell Ga., *U.S.A.* 34°2N 84°22W **85** D12
Roswell N. Mex., *U.S.A.* 33°24N 104°32W **77** K11
Rotan *U.S.A.* 32°51N 100°28W **84** E4
Rote *Indonesia* 10°50S 123°0E **37** F6
Rother → *U.K.* 50°59N 0°45E **13** G8
Rothera *Antarctica* 67°34S 68°8W **5** C17
Rotherham *U.K.* 53°26N 1°20W **12** D6
Rothes *U.K.* 57°32N 3°13W **11** D5
Rothesay *Canada* 45°23N 66°0W **73** C6
Rothesay *U.K.* 55°50N 5°3W **11** F3
Roti = Rote *Indonesia* 10°50S 123°0E **37** F6
Roto *Australia* 33°0S 145°30E **63** E4
Rotondo, Mte. *France* 42°14N 9°8E **20** E8
Rotorua *N.Z.* 41°55S 176°18E **59** C6
Rotorua, L. *N.Z.* 38°9S 176°16E **59** C6
Rotterdam *Neths.* 51°55N 4°30E **15** C4
Rotterdam *U.S.A.* 42°48N 74°1W **83** D10
Rottnest I. *Australia* 32°0S 115°27E **61** F2
Rottumeroog *Neths.* 53°33N 6°34E **15** A6
Rottweil *Germany* 48°9N 8°37E **16** D5
Rotuma *Fiji* 12°25S 177°5E **58** C10
Roubaix *France* 50°40N 3°10E **20** A5
Rouen *France* 49°27N 1°4E **20** B4
Rouleau *Canada* 50°10N 104°56W **71** C8
Roulpmaulpma ☼
  Australia 23°52S 133°0E **60** D5
Round I. *Mauritius* 19°51S 57°45E **55** d
Round Mountain *U.S.A.* 38°43N 117°4W **76** G5
Round Mt. *Australia* 30°26S 152°16E **63** E5
Round Rock *U.S.A.* 30°31N 97°41W **84** F6
Roundup *U.S.A.* 46°27N 108°33W **76** C9
Rousay *U.K.* 59°10N 3°2W **11** B5
Rouses Point *U.S.A.* 44°59N 73°22W **83** B11
Rouseville *U.S.A.* 41°28N 79°42W **82** E5
Rousse = Ruse *Bulgaria* 43°48N 25°59E **23** C12
Roussillon *France* 42°30N 2°35E **20** E5
Rouxville *S. Africa* 30°25S 26°50E **56** D4
Rouyn-Noranda *Canada* 48°20N 79°0W **72** C4
Rovaniemi *Finland* 66°29N 25°41E **8** C21
Rovereto *Italy* 45°53N 11°3E **22** B4
Rovigo *Italy* 45°4N 11°47E **22** B4
Rovinj *Croatia* 45°5N 13°40E **16** F7
Rovno = Rivne *Ukraine* 50°40N 26°10E **17** C14
Rovuma = Ruvuma →
  Tanzania 10°29S 40°28E **54** G8
Row'ān *Iran* 35°8N 48°51E **47** C6
Rowena *Australia* 29°48S 148°55E **63** D4
Rowley I. *Canada* 69°6N 77°52W **69** D16
Rowley Shoals *Australia* 17°30S 119°0E **60** C2
Roxas *Phil.* 11°36N 122°49E **37** B6
Roxboro *U.S.A.* 36°24N 78°59W **85** C15
Roxborough *Trin. & Tob.* 11°15N 60°35W **93** J16
Roxburgh *N.Z.* 45°33S 169°19E **59** F2
Roxbury N.Y., *U.S.A.* 42°17N 74°33W **83** D10
Roxbury Pa., *U.S.A.* 40°6N 77°39W **82** F7
Roxby Downs *Australia* 30°43S 136°46E **63** E2
Roy Mont., *U.S.A.* 47°20N 108°58W **76** C9
Roy N. Mex., *U.S.A.* 35°57N 104°12W **77** J11
Roy Utah, *U.S.A.* 41°10N 112°2W **76** F7
Roy Hill *Australia* 22°41S 119°57E **60** D3
Royal Bardia △ *Nepal* 28°20N 81°20E **43** E9
Royal Canal *Ireland* 53°30N 7°13W **10** C4
Royal Chitawan △
  Nepal 26°30N 84°30E **43** F11
Royal Geographical Society Is.
  Canada 68°56N 100°15W **68** D11
Royal Leamington Spa
  U.K. 52°18N 1°31W **13** E6
Royal Natal △ *S. Africa* 28°43S 28°51E **57** C4
Royal Tunbridge Wells
  U.K. 51°7N 0°16E **13** F8
Royale, Isle *U.S.A.* 48°0N 88°54W **80** B9
Royan *France* 45°37N 1°2W **20** D3
Royston *U.K.* 52°3N 0°0 **13** E7
Rozdilna *Ukraine* 46°50N 30°2E **17** E16
Rozhyshche *Ukraine* 50°54N 25°15E **17** C13
Rtishchevo *Russia* 52°18N 43°46E **18** D7
Ruacaná *Namibia* 17°27S 14°21E **56** A1
Ruahine Ra. *N.Z.* 39°55S 176°2E **59** C6
Ruapehu *N.Z.* 39°17S 175°35E **59** C5
Ruapuke I. *N.Z.* 46°46S 168°31E **59** G2
Ruâq, W. → *Egypt* 30°0N 33°49E **48** F2
Rub' al Khālī *Si. Arabia* 19°0N 48°0E **49** D4
Rubh a' Mhail *U.K.* 55°56N 6°8W **11** F2
Rubha Hunish *U.K.* 57°42N 6°20W **11** D2
Rubha Robhanais = Lewis, Butt of
  U.K. 58°31N 6°16W **11** C2
Rubicon → *U.S.A.* 38°53N 121°4W **78** G5
Rubio *Venezuela* 7°43N 72°22W **92** B4
Rubtsovsk *Russia* 51°30N 81°10E **30** A5
Ruby L. *U.S.A.* 40°10N 115°28W **76** F6
Ruby Mts. *U.S.A.* 40°30N 115°20W **76** F6
Rubyvale *Australia* 23°25S 147°42E **62** C4
Rucheng *China* 25°33N 113°38E **35** E9
Rūd Sar *Iran* 37°8N 50°18E **47** B6
Rudall *Australia* 33°43S 136°17E **63** E2
Rudall River △ *Australia* 22°38S 122°13E **60** D3
Rudbar *Iran* 36°48N 49°23E **47** B6
Rudnyy *Kazakhstan* 52°57N 63°7E **26** D7
Rudolfa, Ostrov *Russia* 81°45N 58°30E **26** A6
Rudong *China* 32°20N 121°12E **35** A13
Rudrapur *India* 28°59N 79°24E **43** E8
Rudyard *U.S.A.* 46°14N 84°36W **81** B11
Ruffling Pt. *Br. Virgin Is.* 18°44N 64°27W **89** e
Rufiji → *Tanzania* 7°50S 39°15E **54** F7
Rufino *Argentina* 34°20S 62°50W **94** C3
Rugao *China* 32°23N 120°31E **35** A13
Rugby *U.K.* 52°23N 1°16W **13** E6
Rugby *U.S.A.* 48°22N 100°0W **80** A4
Rügen *Germany* 54°22N 13°24E **16** A7
Ruhnu *Estonia* 57°48N 23°15E **9** H20
Ruhr → *Germany* 51°27N 6°43E **16** C4
Rui'an *China* 27°47N 120°40E **35** D13
Ruichang *China* 29°40N 115°40E **35** C10

Ruidoso *U.S.A.* 33°20N 105°41W **77** K11
Ruijin *China* 25°48N 116°0E **35** D10
Ruili *China* 24°6N 97°46E **34** E1
Rujm Tal'at al Jamā'ah
  Jordan 30°24N 35°30E **48** E4
Ruk *Pakistan* 27°50N 68°42E **42** F3
Rukhla *Pakistan* 32°27N 71°57E **42** C4
Ruki →
  Dem. Rep. of the Congo 0°5N 18°17E **54** E3
Rukumkot *Nepal* 28°37N 82°37E **43** E10
Rukwa, L. *Tanzania* 8°0S 32°20E **54** F6
Rulhieres, C. *Australia* 13°56S 127°22E **60** B4
Rum *Jordan* 29°39N 35°26E **48** F4
Rùm *U.K.* 57°0N 6°20W **11** E2
Rum Cay *Bahamas* 23°40N 74°58W **89** B5
Rum Jungle *Australia* 13°0S 130°59E **60** B5
Rumāḥ *Si. Arabia* 25°29N 47°10E **46** E5
Rumania = Romania ■
  Europe 46°0N 25°0E **17** F12
Rumaylah *Iraq* 30°47N 47°37E **46** D5
Rumaylah, 'Urūq ar
  Si. Arabia 22°0N 48°30E **49** C4
Rumbek *South Sudan* 6°54N 29°37E **53** G11
Rumford *U.S.A.* 44°33N 70°33W **83** B14
Rumia *Poland* 54°37N 18°25E **17** A10
Rumoi *Japan* 43°56N 141°39E **28** C10
Rumson *U.S.A.* 40°23N 74°0W **83** F11
Runan *China* 33°0N 114°30E **32** H8
Runanga *N.Z.* 42°25S 171°15E **59** E3
Runaway, C. *N.Z.* 37°32S 177°59E **59** B6
Runaway Bay *Jamaica* 18°27N 77°20W **88** a
Runcorn *U.K.* 53°21N 2°44W **12** D5
Rundu *Namibia* 17°52S 19°43E **56** A2
Rungwe *Tanzania* 9°11S 33°32E **50** G7
Rungwe, Mt. *Tanzania* 9°8S 33°40E **54** F6
Runton Ra. *Australia* 23°31S 123°6E **60** D3
Ruo Shui → *China* 41°0N 100°16E **30** C9
Ruokolahti *Finland* 61°17N 28°50E **8** F23
Ruoqiang *China* 38°55N 88°10E **30** D6
Rupa *India* 27°15N 92°21E **41** F18
Rupar *India* 31°2N 76°38E **42** D7
Rupat *Indonesia* 1°45N 101°40E **36** D2
Rupen → *India* 23°28N 71°31E **42** H4
Rupert *U.S.A.* 42°37N 113°41W **76** E7
Rupert → *Canada* 51°29N 78°45W **72** B4
Rupert B. *Canada* 51°35N 79°0W **72** B4
Rupert House = Waskaganish
  Canada 51°30N 78°40W **72** B4
Rupnagar = Rupar *India* 31°2N 76°38E **42** D7
Rupsa *India* 21°37N 87°1E **43** J12
Rurrenabaque *Bolivia* 14°30S 67°32W **92** F5
Ruschuk = Ruse
  Bulgaria 43°48N 25°59E **23** C12
Ruse *Bulgaria* 43°48N 25°59E **23** C12
Rush *Ireland* 53°31N 6°6W **10** C5
Rushan *China* 36°56N 121°30E **33** F11
Rushden *U.K.* . 52°18N 0°35W **13** E7
Rushikulya → *India* 19°23N 85°5E **44** E7
Rushmore, Mt. *U.S.A.* 43°53N 103°28W **80** D2
Rushville Ill., *U.S.A.* 40°7N 90°34W **80** E8
Rushville Ind., *U.S.A.* 39°37N 85°27W **81** F11
Rushville Nebr., *U.S.A.* 42°43N 102°28W **80** D2
Russas *Brazil* 4°55S 37°50W **93** D11
Russell *Canada* 50°50N 101°20W **71** C8
Russell *Kans., U.S.A.* 38°54N 98°52W **80** F4
Russell *N.Y., U.S.A.* 44°27N 75°9W **83** B9
Russell *Pa., U.S.A.* 41°56N 79°8W **82** E5
Russell Cave ○ *U.S.A.* 34°59N 85°49W **85** D12
Russell L. *Man., Canada* 56°15N 101°30W **71** B8
Russell L. *N.W.T., Canada* 63°5N 115°44W **70** A5
Russellkonda *India* 19°57N 84°42E **44** E7
Russellville Ala., *U.S.A.* 34°30N 87°44W **85** D11
Russellville Ark., *U.S.A.* 35°17N 93°8W **84** D8
Russellville Ky., *U.S.A.* 36°51N 86°53W **80** G10
Russia ■ *Eurasia* 62°0N 105°0E **27** C11
Russian → *U.S.A.* 38°27N 123°8W **78** G3
Russkaya Arktika △
  Russia 73°40N 55°55E **26** B6
Russkiy, Ostrov *Russia* 43°0N 131°50E **28** C5
Rustam Shahr *Pakistan* 26°58N 66°6E **42** F2
Rustavi *Georgia* 41°30N 45°0E **19** F8
Rustenburg *S. Africa* 25°41S 27°14E **56** C4
Ruston *U.S.A.* 32°32N 92°38W **84** E8
Ruteng *Indonesia* 8°35S 120°30E **37** F6
Rutenga *Zimbabwe* 21°15S 30°44E **57** B5
Ruth *U.S.A.* 43°42N 82°45W **82** C2
Rutherford *U.S.A.* 38°26N 122°24W **78** G4
Rutland *U.S.A.* 43°37N 72°58W **83** C12
Rutland □ *U.K.* 52°38N 0°40W **13** E7
Rutland I. *India* 11°25N 92°10E **45** J11
Rutland Water □ *U.K.* 52°39N 0°38W **13** E7
Rutledge → *Canada* 61°4N 112°0W **71** A6
Rutledge L. *Canada* 61°33N 110°47W **71** A6
Rutog *China* 33°27N 79°42E **30** E4
Rutshuru
  Dem. Rep. of the Congo 1°13S 29°25E **54** E5
Ruvuma → *Tanzania* 10°29S 40°28E **54** G8
Ruwais *U.A.E.* 24°5N 52°50E **47** E7
Ruwenzori *Africa* 0°30N 29°55E **54** D5
Ruya → *Zimbabwe* 16°27S 32°5E **57** A5
Ruyang *China* 34°9N 112°27E **32** G7
Ruyuan *China* 24°46N 113°16E **35** E9
Ruzhou *China* 34°11N 112°52E **32** G7
Ružomberok *Slovak Rep.* 49°3N 19°17E **17** D10
Rwanda ■ *Africa* 2°0S 30°0E **54** E5
Ryan, L. *U.K.* 55°0N 5°2W **11** G3
Ryazan *Russia* 54°40N 39°40E **18** D6
Ryazhsk *Russia* 53°45N 40°3E **18** D7
Rybachiy Poluostrov
  Russia 69°43N 32°0E **8** B25
Rybache = Balykchy
  Kyrgyzstan 42°26N 76°12E **30** C4
Rybinsk *Russia* 58°5N 38°50E **18** C6
Rybinskoye Vdkhr.
  Russia 58°30N 38°25E **18** C6
Rybnitsa = Rîbniţa
  Moldova 47°45N 29°0E **17** E15
Rycroft *Canada* 55°45N 118°40W **70** B5
Ryde *U.K.* 50°43N 1°9W **13** G6
Ryderwood *U.S.A.* 46°23N 123°3W **78** D3

Rye *U.K.* 50°57N 0°45E **13** G8
Rye → *U.K.* 54°11N 0°44W **12** C7
Rye Bay *U.K.* 50°52N 0°49E **13** G8
Rye Patch Res. *U.S.A.* 40°28N 118°19W **76** F4
Ryegate *U.S.A.* 46°18N 109°15W **76** C9
Ryley *Canada* 53°17N 112°26W **70** C6
Rylstone *Australia* 32°46S 149°58E **63** E4
Ryn Peski = Naryn Qum
  Kazakhstan 47°30N 49°0E **26** E5
Ryōtsu *Japan* 38°5N 138°26E **28** E9
Rypin *Poland* 53°3N 19°25E **17** B10
Ryūgasaki *Japan* 35°54N 140°11E **29** G10
Ryukyu Is. = Ryūkyū-Rettō
  Japan 26°0N 126°0E **29** M3
Ryūkyū-Rettō *Japan* 26°0N 126°0E **29** M3
Rzeszów *Poland* 50°5N 21°58E **17** C11
Rzhev *Russia* 56°20N 34°20E **18** C5

S

Sa Dec *Vietnam* 10°20N 105°46E **39** G5
Sa Kaeo *Thailand* 13°49N 102°4E **38** F4
Sa Pa *Vietnam* 22°20N 103°47E **38** A4
Sa'ādat Shahr *Iran* 30°10N 53°5E **47** D7
Sa'ādatābād Hormozgan,
  Iran 28°3N 55°53E **47** D7
Sa'ādatābād Kermān, *Iran* 29°40N 55°51E **47** D7
Saale → *Germany* 51°56N 11°54E **16** C6
Saalfeld *Germany* 50°38N 11°21E **16** C6
Saanich *Canada* 48°29N 123°26W **78** B3
Saar → *Europe* 49°41N 6°32E **15** E6
Saarbrücken *Germany* 49°14N 6°59E **16** D4
Saaremaa *Estonia* 58°30N 22°30E **9** G20
Saarijärvi *Finland* 62°43N 25°16E **8** E21
Sab 'Ābar *Syria* 33°46N 37°41E **46** C3
Saba *W. Indies* 17°38N 63°14W **89** C7
Šabac *Serbia* 44°48N 19°42E **23** B8
Sabadell *Spain* 41°28N 2°7E **21** B7
Sabah □ *Malaysia* 6°0N 117°0E **36** C5
Sabak Bernam *Malaysia* 3°46N 100°58E **39** L3
Sabalān, Kūhhā-ye *Iran* 38°15N 47°45E **46** B5
Sabalana, Kepulauan
  Indonesia 6°45S 118°50E **37** F5
Sabana de la Mar
  Dom. Rep. 19°7N 69°24W **89** C6
Sábanalarga *Colombia* 10°38N 74°55W **92** A4
Sabang *Indonesia* 5°50N 95°15E **36** C1
Sabari → *India* 17°35N 81°16E **44** E5
Sabarmati → *India* 22°18N 72°22E **42** H5
Sabattis *U.S.A.* 44°6N 74°40W **83** B10
Saberania *Indonesia* 2°5S 138°18E **37** E9
Sabhā *Libya* 27°9N 14°29E **53** C8
Sabi → *India* 28°29N 76°44E **42** E7
Sabie *S. Africa* 25°10S 30°48E **57** C5
Sabinal *U.S.A.* 29°19N 99°28W **84** G5
Sabinas *Mexico* 27°51N 101°7W **86** B4
Sabinas → *Mexico* 27°37N 100°42W **86** B4
Sabinas Hidalgo *Mexico* 26°30N 100°10W **86** B4
Sabine → *U.S.A.* 29°59N 93°47W **84** G8
Sabine L. *U.S.A.* 29°53N 93°51W **84** G8
Sabine Pass *U.S.A.* 29°44N 93°54W **84** G8
Sablayan *Phil.* 12°50N 120°50E **37** B6
Sable *Canada* 55°30N 68°21W **73** A6
Sable, C. *Canada* 43°29N 65°38W **73** D6
Sable, C. *U.S.A.* 25°9N 81°8W **88** A3
Sable I. *Canada* 44°0N 60°0W **73** D8
Sabrina Coast *Antarctica* 68°0S 120°0E **5** C9
Sabulubek *Indonesia* 1°36S 98°40E **36** E1
Sabzevār *Iran* 36°15N 57°40E **47** B8
Sabzvārān = Jiroft *Iran* 28°45N 57°50E **47** D8
Sac City *U.S.A.* 42°25N 95°0W **80** D6
Săcele *Romania* 45°37N 25°41E **17** F13
Sacheon *S. Korea* 35°0N 128°6E **33** G15
Sachigo → *Canada* 55°6N 88°58W **72** A2
Sachigo, L. *Canada* 53°50N 92°12W **72** B1
Sachimbo *Angola* 9°14S 20°16E **54** F4
Sachin *India* 21°5N 72°53E **44** D1
Sachsen □ *Germany* 50°55N 13°10E **16** C7
Sachsen-Anhalt □
  Germany 52°0N 12°0E **16** C7
Sackets Harbor *U.S.A.* 43°57N 76°7W **83** C8
Sackville *Canada* 45°54N 64°22W **73** C7
Saco Maine, *U.S.A.* 43°30N 70°27W **83** C14
Saco Mont., *U.S.A.* 48°28N 107°21W **76** B10
Sacramento *U.S.A.* 38°35N 121°29W **78** G5
Sacramento → *U.S.A.* 38°3N 121°56W **78** G5
Sacramento Mts.
  U.S.A. 32°30N 105°30W **77** K11
Sacramento Valley
  U.S.A. 39°30N 122°0W **78** G5
Sada-Misaki *Japan* 33°20N 132°5E **29** H6
Sadabad *India* 27°27N 78°3E **42** F8
Şa'dah *Yemen* 16°15N 43°37E **49** D3
Sadao *Thailand* 6°38N 100°26E **39** J3
Sadaseopet *India* 17°38N 77°59E **44** F3
Sadd el Aali *Egypt* 23°54N 32°54E **53** D12
Saddle Mt., *U.S.A.* 45°58N 123°41W **78** E3
Saddle Pk. *India* 13°9N 93°1E **45** H11
Sado *Japan* 38°0N 138°25E **28** E9
Sadra *India* 23°21N 72°43E **42** H5
Sadri *India* 25°11N 73°26E **42** G5
Sæby *Denmark* 57°21N 10°30E **9** H14
Saegertown *U.S.A.* 41°43N 80°9W **82** E4
Şafājah *Si. Arabia* 26°25N 39°0E **46** E3
Safata B. *Samoa* 14°0S 171°50W **59** b
Säffle *Sweden* 59°8N 12°55E **9** G15
Safford *U.S.A.* 32°50N 109°43W **77** K9
Saffron Walden *U.K.* 52°1N 0°16E **13** E8
Safi *Morocco* 32°18N 9°20W **52** B4
Şafiābād *Iran* 36°45N 57°58E **47** B8
Safid Dasht *Iran* 33°27N 48°11E **47** C6
Safid Kūh *Afghan.* 34°45N 63°0E **40** B3
Safid Rūd → *Iran* 37°23N 50°11E **47** B6
Safipur *India* 26°44N 80°21E **43** F9
Şāfītā *Syria* 34°48N 36°5E **46** C3
Safune *Samoa* 13°25S 172°21W **59** b
Sag Harbor *U.S.A.* 41°0N 72°18W **83** E12
Saga *Japan* 33°15N 130°20E **29** H5
Saga □ *Japan* 33°15N 130°20E **29** H5

Sagae *Japan* 38°22N 140°17E **28** E10
Sagaing *Burma* 21°52N 95°59E **41** J19
Sagamore *U.S.A.* 40°46N 79°14W **82** F5
Saganthit Kyun *Burma* 14°0N 98°0E **39** F2
Sagar *Karnataka, India* 16°38N 76°48E **44** F3
Sagar *Karnataka, India* 14°14N 75°6E **45** G2
Sagar *Mad. P., India* 23°50N 78°44E **43** H8
Sagarmatha = Everest, Mt.
  Nepal 28°5N 86°58E **43** E12
Sagarmatha △ *Nepal* 27°55N 86°45E **43** F12
Saginaw *U.S.A.* 43°26N 83°56W **81** D12
Saginaw B. *U.S.A.* 43°50N 83°40W **81** D12
Saglouc = Salluit
  Canada 62°14N 75°38W **69** E16
Sagone *France* 42°7N 8°42E **20** E8
Sagua la Grande *Cuba* 22°50N 80°10W **88** B3
Saguache *U.S.A.* 38°5N 106°8W **76** G10
Saguaro △ *U.S.A.* 32°12N 110°38W **77** K8
Saguenay → *Canada* 48°22N 71°0W **73** C5
Sagunt *Spain* 39°42N 0°18W **21** C5
Sagunto = Sagunt *Spain* 39°42N 0°18W **21** C5
Sagwara *India* 23°41N 74°1E **42** H6
Sahagún *Spain* 42°18N 5°2W **21** A3
Sahand, Kūh-e *Iran* 37°44N 46°27E **46** B5
Sahara *Africa* 23°0N 5°0E **52** D6
Saharan Atlas = Saharien, Atlas
  Algeria 33°30N 1°0E **52** B6
Saharanpur *India* 29°58N 77°33E **42** E7
Saharien, Atlas *Algeria* 33°30N 1°0E **52** B6
Saharsa *India* 25°53N 86°36E **43** G12
Sahaswan *India* 28°5N 78°45E **43** E8
Saheira, W. el → *Egypt* 30°5N 33°25E **48** E2
Sahel *Africa* 16°0N 5°0E **52** E5
Sahibganj *India* 25°12N 87°40E **43** G12
Sāhilīyah *Iraq* 33°43N 42°42E **46** C4
Sahiwal *Pakistan* 30°45N 73°8E **42** D5
Şahneh *Iran* 34°29N 47°41E **46** C5
Sahrawi = Western Sahara ■
  Africa 25°0N 13°0W **52** D3
Sahuaripa *Mexico* 29°3N 109°14W **86** B3
Sahuarita *U.S.A.* 31°57N 110°58W **77** L8
Sahuayo de Díaz *Mexico* 20°4N 102°43W **86** C4
Sai → *India* 25°39N 82°47E **43** G10
Sai Buri *Thailand* 6°43N 101°45E **39** J3
Sai Thong △ *Thailand* 15°56N 101°10E **38** E3
Sai Yok △ *Thailand* 14°25N 98°40E **38** E2
Saibai I. *Australia* 9°25S 142°40E **62** a
Sa'id Bundas *South Sudan* 8°24N 24°48E **53** G10
Sa'īdābād = Sīrjan *Iran* 29°30N 55°45E **47** D7
Sa'īdābād *Iran* 36°8N 54°11E **47** B7
Saidpur *Bangla.* 25°48N 89°0E **41** G16
Saidpur *India* 25°33N 83°11E **43** G10
Saidu Sharif *Pakistan* 34°43N 72°24E **43** B5
Saigō *Japan* 36°12N 133°20E **29** F6
Saigon = Thanh Pho Ho Chi Minh
  Vietnam 10°58N 106°40E **39** G6
Saijō *Japan* 33°55N 133°11E **29** H6
Saikai △ *Japan* 33°12N 129°36E **29** H4
Saikhoa Ghat *India* 27°50N 95°40E **41** F19
Saiki *Japan* 32°58N 131°51E **29** H5
Sailana *India* 23°28N 74°55E **42** H6
Sailolof *Indonesia* 1°15S 130°46E **37** E8
Sailu *India* 19°28N 76°28E **44** E3
Saimaa *Finland* 61°15N 28°15E **8** F23
Saimen = Saimaa *Finland* 61°15N 28°15E **8** F23
Şa'in Dezh *Iran* 36°40N 46°25E **46** B5
St. Abb's Head *U.K.* 55°55N 2°8W **11** F6
St. Alban's *Canada* 47°51N 55°50W **73** C8
St. Albans *U.K.* 51°45N 0°19W **13** F7
St. Albans *Vt., U.S.A.* 44°49N 73°5W **83** B11
St. Albans *W. Va.,
  U.S.A.* 38°23N 81°50W **81** F13
St. Alban's Head *U.K.* 50°34N 2°4W **13** G5
St. Albert *Canada* 53°37N 113°32W **70** C6
St. Andrew's *Canada* 47°45N 59°15W **73** C8
St. Andrews *U.K.* 56°20N 2°47W **11** E6
St-Anicet *Canada* 45°8N 74°22W **83** A10
St. Annes *Canada* 49°40N 96°39W **71** D9
St. Anns B. *Canada* 46°22N 60°25W **73** C7
St. Ann's Bay *Jamaica* 18°26N 77°12W **88** a
St. Anthony *Canada* 51°22N 55°35W **73** B8
St. Anthony *U.S.A.* 43°58N 111°41W **76** E8
St-Antoine *Canada* 46°22N 64°45W **73** C7
St-Augustin *Canada* 51°13N 58°38W **73** B8
St-Augustin → *Canada* 51°16N 58°40W **73** B8
St. Augustine *U.S.A.* 29°54N 81°19W **85** G14
St. Austell *U.K.* 50°20N 4°47W **13** G3
St. Barbe *Canada* 51°12N 56°46W **73** B8
St-Barthélemy ☑
  W. Indies 17°50N 62°50W **89** C7
St. Barts = St-Barthélemy ☑
  W. Indies 17°50N 62°50W **89** C7
St. Bees Hd. *U.K.* 54°31N 3°38E **12** C4
St. Bees I. *Australia* 20°56S 149°26E **62** b
St-Benoît *Réunion* 21°2S 55°43E **55** c
St. Bride's *Canada* 46°56N 54°10W **73** C9
St. Brides B. *U.K.* 51°49N 5°9W **13** F2
St-Brieuc *France* 48°30N 2°46W **20** B2
St. Catharines *Canada* 43°10N 79°15W **82** C5
St. Catherines I. *U.S.A.* 31°40N 81°10W **85** F14
St. Catherine's Pt. *U.K.* 50°34N 1°18W **13** G6
St-Chamond *France* 45°28N 4°31E **20** D6
St. Charles Ill., *U.S.A.* 41°54N 88°19W **80** E9
St. Charles Md., *U.S.A.* 38°36N 76°56W **81** F15
St. Charles Mo., *U.S.A.* 38°47N 90°29W **80** F8
St. Christopher-Nevis = St. Kitts &
  Nevis ■ *W. Indies* 17°20N 62°40W **89** C7
St. Clair Mich., *U.S.A.* 42°50N 82°30W **82** D2
St. Clair Pa., *U.S.A.* 40°43N 76°12W **83** F8
St. Clair → *U.S.A.* 42°38N 82°31W **82** D2
St. Clair, L. *N. Amer.* 42°27N 82°39W **82** D2
St. Clairsville *U.S.A.* 40°5N 80°54W **82** F4
St. Claude *Canada* 49°40N 98°20W **71** D9
St. Clears *U.K.* 51°49N 4°31W **13** F3
St-Clet *Canada* 45°21N 74°13W **83** A10

St. Cloud *Fla., U.S.A.* 28°15N 81°17W **85** G14
St. Cloud *Minn., U.S.A.* 45°34N 94°10W **80** C6
St. Cricq, C. *Australia* 25°17S 113°6E **61** E1
St. Croix *U.S. Virgin Is.* 17°45N 64°45W **89** C7
St. Croix *U.S.A.* 44°45N 92°48W **80** C7
St. Croix Falls *U.S.A.* 45°24N 92°38W **80** C7
St. David's *Canada* 48°12N 58°52W **73** C8
St. David's *U.K.* 51°53N 5°16W **13** F2
St. David's Head *U.K.* 51°54N 5°19W **13** F2
St-Denis *Réunion* 20°52S 55°27E **55** c
St-Denis ✈ (RUN) *Réunion* 20°53S 55°32E **55** c
St-Dizier *France* 48°38N 4°56E **20** B6
St. Elias, Mt. *U.S.A.* 60°18N 140°56W **68** E3
St. Elias Mts. *N. Amer.* 60°33N 139°28W **70** A1
St-Étienne *France* 45°27N 4°22E **20** D6
St. Eugène *Canada* 45°30N 74°28W **83** A10
St. Eustatius *W. Indies* 17°20N 63°0W **89** C7
St-Félicien *Canada* 48°40N 72°25W **72** C5
St-Flour *France* 45°2N 3°6E **20** D5
St. Francis *U.S.A.* 39°47N 101°48W **80** F3
St. Francis → *U.S.A.* 34°38N 90°36W **85** D9
St. Francis, C. *S. Africa* 34°14S 24°49E **56** E3
St. Francisville *U.S.A.* 30°47N 91°23W **84** F9
St-François, L. *Canada* 45°10N 74°22W **83** A10
St-Gabriel *Canada* 46°17N 73°24W **72** C5
St. Gallen = Sankt Gallen
   Switz. 47°26N 9°22E **20** C8
St-Gaudens *France* 43°6N 0°44E **20** E4
St. George *Australia* 28°1S 148°30E **63** D4
St. George *N.B., Canada* 45°11N 66°50W **73** C6
St. George *Ont., Canada* 43°15N 80°15W **82** C4
St. George *S.C., U.S.A.* 33°11N 80°35W **85** E14
St. George *Utah, U.S.A.* 37°6N 113°35W **77** H7
St. George, C. *Canada* 48°30N 59°16W **73** C8
St. George, C. *U.S.A.* 29°40N 85°5W **85** G12
St. George I. *U.S.A.* 56°35N 169°35W **74** D6
St. George Ra. *Australia* 18°40S 125°0E **60** C4
St. George's *Canada* 48°26N 58°31W **73** C8
St-Georges *Canada* 46°8N 70°40W **73** C5
St. George's *Grenada* 12°5N 61°43W **89** D7
St. George's B. *Canada* 48°24N 58°53W **73** C8
St. Georges Basin *N.S.W.,*
   Australia 35°7S 150°36E **63** F5
St. Georges Basin *W. Austral.,*
   Australia 15°23S 125°2E **60** C4
St. George's Channel *Europe* 52°0N 6°0W **10** E6
St. George's Channel
   India 7°15N 93°43E **45** L11
St. Georges Hd. *Australia* 35°12S 150°42E **63** F5
St. Gotthard P. = San Gottardo, P.
   del *Switz.* 46°33N 8°33E **20** C8
St. Helena *Atl. Oc.* 15°58S 5°42W **50** H3
St. Helena, *U.S.A.* 38°30N 122°28W **78** G4
St. Helena, Mt. *U.S.A.* 38°40N 122°36W **78** G4
St. Helena B. *S. Africa* 32°40S 18°10E **56** D2
St. Helens *Australia* 41°20S 148°15E **63** G4
St. Helens *U.K.* 53°27N 2°44W **12** D5
St. Helens *U.S.A.* 45°52N 122°48W **78** E4
St. Helens, Mt. *U.S.A.* 46°12N 122°12W **78** D4
St. Helier *U.K.* 49°10N 2°7W **13** H5
St-Hyacinthe *Canada* 45°40N 72°58W **72** C5
St. Ignace *U.S.A.* 45°52N 84°44W **81** C11
St. Ignace I. *Canada* 48°45N 88°0W **72** C2
St. Ignatius *U.S.A.* 47°19N 114°6W **76** C6
St. Ives *Cambs., U.K.* 52°20N 0°4W **13** E7
St. Ives *Corn., U.K.* 50°12N 5°30W **13** G2
St. James *U.S.A.* 43°59N 94°38W **80** D6
St-Jean → *Canada* 50°17N 64°20W **73** B7
St-Jean, L. *Canada* 48°40N 72°0W **73** C5
St-Jean-Port-Joli *Canada* 47°15N 70°13W **73** C5
St-Jean-sur-Richelieu
   Canada 45°20N 73°20W **83** A11
St-Jérôme *Canada* 45°47N 74°0W **72** C5
St. John *Canada* 45°20N 66°8W **73** C6
St. John *U.S.A.* 38°0N 98°46W **80** F4
St. John → *N. Amer.* 45°12N 66°5W **81** C20
St. John, C. *Canada* 50°0N 55°32W **73** C8
St. John I. *U.S. Virgin Is.* 18°20N 64°42W **89** e
St. John's *Antigua & B.* 17°6N 61°51W **89** C7
St. John's *Canada* 47°35N 52°40W **73** C9
St. Johns *Ariz., U.S.A.* 34°30N 109°22W **77** J9
St. Johns *Mich., U.S.A.* 43°0N 84°33W **81** D11
St. Johns → *U.S.A.* 30°24N 81°24W **85** F14
St. John's Pt. *Ireland* 54°34N 8°27W **10** B3
St. Johnsbury *U.S.A.* 44°25N 72°1W **83** B12
St. Johnsville *U.S.A.* 43°0N 74°43W **83** C10
St. Joseph *Canada* 43°24N 81°42W **82** C3
St-Joseph *Martinique* 14°39N 61°4W **88** c
St-Joseph *Réunion* 21°22S 55°37E **55** c
St. Joseph *La., U.S.A.* 31°55N 91°14W **84** F9
St. Joseph *Mo., U.S.A.* 39°46N 94°50W **80** F6
St. Joseph → *U.S.A.* 42°7N 86°29W **80** D10
St. Joseph, I. *Canada* 46°12N 83°58W **72** C3
St. Joseph, L. *Canada* 51°10N 90°35W **72** B1
St. Kilda *U.K.* 57°49N 8°34W **14** C2
St. Kitts & Nevis ■
   W. Indies 17°20N 62°40W **89** C7
St. Laurent *Canada* 50°25N 97°58W **71** C9
St. Lawrence *Australia* 22°16S 149°31E **62** C4
St. Lawrence *Canada* 46°54N 55°23W **73** C8
St. Lawrence → *Canada* 49°30N 66°0W **73** C6
St. Lawrence, Gulf of
   Canada 48°25N 62°0W **73** C7
St. Lawrence I. *U.S.A.* 63°30N 170°30W **74** C5
St. Lawrence Islands △
   Canada 44°27N 75°52W **83** B9
St. Léonard *Canada* 47°12N 67°58W **73** C6
St-Leu *Réunion* 21°9S 55°18E **55** c
St. Lewis → *Canada* 52°26N 56°11W **73** B8
St-Lô *France* 49°7N 1°5W **20** B3
St-Louis *Guadeloupe* 15°56N 61°19W **88** b
St-Louis *Réunion* 21°16S 55°25E **55** c
St-Louis *Senegal* 16°8N 16°27W **52** E2
St. Louis *U.S.A.* 38°37N 90°11W **80** F8
St. Louis → *U.S.A.* 46°44N 92°9W **80** B7
St-Luc *Canada* 45°22N 73°18W **83** A11
St. Lucia ■ *W. Indies* 14°0N 60°57W **89** f
St. Lucia, L. *S. Africa* 28°5S 32°30E **57** D5
St. Lucia ✈ *S. Africa* 28°6S 32°27E **57** C5
St. Lucia Channel
   W. Indies 14°15N 61°0W **89** D7

St. Maarten ☑ *W. Indies* 18°2N 63°5W **89** C7
St. Magnus B. *U.K.* 60°25N 1°35W **11** A7
St-Malo *France* 48°39N 2°1W **20** B2
St-Marc *Haiti* 19°10N 72°41W **89** C5
St. Maries *U.S.A.* 47°19N 116°35W **76** C5
St-Martin ☑ *W. Indies* 18°5N 63°5W **89** C7
St-Martin, C. *Martinique* 14°52N 61°14W **88** c
St. Martin, L. *Canada* 51°40N 98°30W **71** C9
St. Martins *Barbados* 13°5N 59°28W **89** g
St. Mary Is. *India* 13°20N 74°35E **44** N9
St. Mary Pk. *Australia* 31°32S 138°34E **63** E2
St. Marys *Australia* 41°35S 148°11E **63** G4
St. Marys *Canada* 43°20N 81°10W **82** C3
St. Mary's *Corn., U.K.* 49°55N 6°18W **13** H1
St. Mary's *Orkney, U.K.* 58°54N 2°54W **11** C6
St. Marys *Ga., U.S.A.* 30°44N 81°33W **85** F14
St. Marys *Pa., U.S.A.* 41°26N 78°34W **82** E6
St. Mary's, C. *Canada* 46°50N 54°12W **73** C9
St. Mary's B. *Canada* 46°50N 53°50W **73** C9
St. Mary's Bay *Canada* 44°25N 66°10W **73** D6
St-Mathieu, Pte. *France* 48°20N 4°45W **20** B1
St. Matthew I. *U.S.A.* 60°24N 172°42W **74** C5
St-Maurice → *Canada* 46°21N 72°31W **72** C5
St. Mawes *U.K.* 50°10N 5°2W **13** G2
St-Nazaire *France* 47°17N 2°12W **20** C2
St. Neots *U.K.* 52°14N 0°15W **13** E7
St-Omer *France* 50°45N 2°15E **20** A5
St-Pamphile *Canada* 46°58N 69°48W **73** C6
St-Pascal *Canada* 47°32N 69°48W **73** C6
St. Paul *Canada* 54°0N 111°17W **70** C6
St-Paul *Réunion* 20°59S 55°17E **55** c
St. Paul *Minn., U.S.A.* 44°56N 93°5W **80** C7
St. Paul *Nebr., U.S.A.* 41°13N 98°27W **80** E4
St-Paul → *Canada* 51°27N 57°42W **73** B8
St. Paul, Î. *Ind. Oc.* 38°55S 77°34E **3** F13
St. Paul I. *Canada* 47°12N 60°9W **73** C7
St. Paul I. *U.S.A.* 57°10N 170°15W **74** D5
St. Peter *U.S.A.* 44°20N 93°57W **80** C7
St. Peter Port *U.K.* 49°26N 2°33W **13** H5
St. Peters *N.S., Canada* 45°40N 60°53W **73** C7
St. Peters *P.E.I., Canada* 46°25N 62°35W **73** C7
St. Petersburg *U.S.A.* 27°46N 82°40W **85** H13
St-Phillippe *Réunion* 21°21S 55°44E **55** c
St-Pie *Canada* 45°30N 72°54W **83** A12
St-Pierre *Martinique* 14°45N 61°10W **88** c
St-Pierre *Réunion* 21°19S 55°28E **55** c
St-Pierre *St-P. & M.* 46°46N 56°12W **73** C8
St-Pierre, L. *Canada* 46°12N 72°52W **72** C5
St-Pierre-et-Miquelon ☑
   N. Amer. 46°55N 56°10W **73** C8
St-Quentin *Canada* 47°30N 67°23W **73** C6
St-Quentin *France* 49°50N 3°16E **20** B5
St. Regis *U.S.A.* 47°18N 115°6W **76** C6
St. Regis Falls *U.S.A.* 44°40N 74°32W **83** B10
St-Siméon *Canada* 47°51N 69°54W **73** C6
St. Simons I. *U.S.A.* 31°12N 81°15W **85** F14
St. Simons Island *U.S.A.* 31°9N 81°22W **85** F14
St. Stephen *Canada* 45°16N 67°17W **73** C6
St. Thomas *Canada* 42°45N 81°10W **82** D3
St. Thomas I.
   U.S. Virgin Is. 18°20N 64°55W **89** e
St-Tite *Canada* 46°45N 72°34W **72** C5
St-Trond = Sint-Truiden
   Belgium 50°48N 5°10E **15** D5
St-Tropez *France* 43°17N 6°38E **20** E7
St. Vidgeon's ۞ *Australia* 14°47S 134°53E **62** A1
St. Vincent = São Vicente
   C. Verde Is. 17°0N 25°0W **52** b
St. Vincent, G. *Australia* 35°0S 138°0E **63** F2
St. Vincent & the Grenadines ■
   W. Indies 13°0N 61°10W **89** D7
St. Vincent Passage
   W. Indies 13°30N 61°0W **89** D7
St-Vith *Belgium* 50°17N 6°9E **15** D6
St. Walburg *Canada* 53°39N 109°12W **71** C7
Saintala *India* 20°26N 83°20E **44** D6
Ste-Agathe-des-Monts
   Canada 46°3N 74°17W **72** C5
Ste-Anne *Guadeloupe* 16°13N 61°24W **88** b
Ste-Anne *Seychelles* 4°36S 55°31E **55** b
Ste-Anne, L. *Canada* 50°0N 67°42W **73** B6
Ste-Anne-des-Monts
   Canada 49°8N 66°30W **73** C6
Ste. Genevieve *U.S.A.* 37°59N 90°2W **80** G8
Ste-Marguerite →
   Canada 50°9N 66°36W **73** B6
Ste-Marie *Canada* 46°26N 71°0W **73** C5
Ste-Marie *Martinique* 14°48N 61°1W **88** c
Ste-Marie *Réunion* 20°53S 55°33E **55** c
Ste-Marie, Ile = Boraha, Nosy
   Madag. 16°50S 49°55E **55** H9
Ste-Rose *Guadeloupe* 16°20N 61°45W **88** b
Ste-Rose *Réunion* 21°8S 55°45E **55** c
Ste. Rose du Lac *Canada* 51°4N 99°30W **71** C9
Saintes *France* 45°45N 0°37W **20** D3
Saintes, Îs. des *Guadeloupe* 15°50N 61°35W **88** b
Saintfield *U.K.* 54°28N 5°49W **10** B6
Saintonge *France* 45°40N 0°50W **20** D3
Saipal *Nepal* 29°50N 81°40E **43** E9
Saipan *N. Marianas* 15°12N 145°45E **64** F6
Sairang *India* 23°50N 92°45E **41** H18
Sairecábur, Cerro *Bolivia* 22°43S 67°54W **94** A2
Saïtah *Si. Arabia* 16°36N 42°56E **49** D3
Saitama *Japan* 35°54N 139°38E **29** G9
Saitama □ *Japan* 36°25N 139°30E **29** F9
Saiyid *Pakistan* 33°7N 73°2E **42** C5
Sajama *Bolivia* 18°7S 69°0W **92** G5
Sajószentpéter *Hungary* 48°12N 20°44E **17** D11
Sajum *India* 33°20N 79°0E **43** C8
Sak → *S. Africa* 30°52S 20°25E **56** E3
Sakai *Japan* 34°19N 135°50E **29** G6
Sakaide *Japan* 34°19N 133°50E **29** G6
Sakaiminato *Japan* 35°38N 133°11E **29** G6
Sakākah *Si. Arabia* 30°0N 40°8E **46** D4
Sakakawea, L. *U.S.A.* 47°30N 101°25W **80** B3
Sakami → *Canada* 53°40N 76°40W **72** B4
Sakami, L. *Canada* 53°15N 77°0W **72** B4
Sakartvelo = Georgia ■
   Asia 42°0N 43°0E **19** F7
Sakarya *Turkey* 40°48N 30°25E **19** F5
Sakashima-Guntō *Japan* 24°46N 124°0E **29** M2

Sakata *Japan* 38°55N 139°50E **28** E9
Sakchu *N. Korea* 40°23N 125°2E **33** D13
Sakha □ *Russia* 66°0N 130°0E **27** C14
Sakhalin *Russia* 51°0N 143°0E **27** D15
Sakhalinskiy Zaliv
   Russia 54°0N 141°0E **27** D15
Sakhi Gopal *India* 19°58N 85°50E **44** E7
Sakiai *Lithuania* 54°59N 23°2E **9** J20
Sakoli *India* 21°5N 79°59E **44** D4
Sakon Nakhon *Thailand* 17°10N 104°9E **38** D5
Sakrand *Pakistan* 26°10N 68°15E **42** F3
Sakri *Maharashtra, India* 26°13N 86°5E **43** F12
Sakri *Maharashtra, India* 21°2N 74°20E **44** D2
Sakrivier *S. Africa* 30°54S 20°28E **56** E3
Sakti *India* 22°2N 82°58E **43** H10
Sakuma *Japan* 35°3N 137°49E **29** G8
Sakurai *Japan* 34°30N 135°51E **29** G7
Sakurai *Japan* 34°30N 135°51E **29** G7
Sal → *Russia* 47°33N 43°5E **19** E7
Sal *C. Verde Is.* 16°45N 22°55W **52** b
Sal Rei *C. Verde Is.* 16°11N 22°53W **52** b
Sala *Sweden* 59°58N 16°35E **9** G17
Sala Consilina *Italy* 40°23N 15°36E **22** D6
Sala-y-Gómez *Pac. Oc.* 26°28S 105°28W **65** K17
Sala-y-Gómez Ridge
   Pac. Oc. 25°0S 98°0W **65** K18
Salaberry-de-Valleyfield
   Canada 45°15N 74°8W **83** A10
Salada, L. *Mexico* 32°20N 115°40W **77** K6
Saladas *Argentina* 28°15S 58°40W **94** B4
Saladillo *Argentina* 35°40S 59°55W **94** D4
Salado → *B. Aires,*
   Argentina 35°44S 57°22W **94** D4
Salado → *La Pampa,*
   Argentina 37°30S 67°0W **96** D3
Salado → *Santa Fe,*
   Argentina 31°40S 60°41W **94** C3
Salado → *Mexico* 26°52N 99°19W **84** H5
Salaga *Ghana* 8°31N 0°31W **52** G5
Sālah *Syria* 32°40N 36°45E **48** C5
Şalāḩ ad Dīn □ *Iraq* 34°35N 43°35E **46** C4
Salālah *Oman* 16°56N 53°59E **49** D5
Salamajärvi △ *Finland* 63°12N 24°50E **8** E21
Salamanca *Chile* 31°46S 70°59W **94** C1
Salamanca *Spain* 40°58N 5°39W **21** B3
Salamanca *U.S.A.* 42°10N 78°43W **82** D6
Salāmatābād *Iran* 35°39N 47°50E **46** C5
Salamina *Greece* 37°56N 23°30E **23** F10
Salar de Atacama *Chile* 23°30S 68°25W **94** A2
Salar de Uyuni *Bolivia* 20°30S 67°45W **92** H5
Salatiga *Indonesia* 7°19S 110°30E **37** G14
Salavat *Russia* 53°21N 55°55E **18** D10
Salaverry *Peru* 8°15S 79°0W **92** E3
Salawati *Indonesia* 1°7S 130°52E **37** E8
Salawin △ *Thailand* 18°18N 97°40E **38** C1
Salaya *India* 22°19N 69°35E **42** H3
Salayar *Indonesia* 6°7S 120°30E **37** F6
Salcombe *U.K.* 50°14N 3°47W **13** G4
Saldanha *S. Africa* 33°0S 17°58E **56** D2
Saldanha B. *S. Africa* 33°6S 18°0E **56** D2
Saldus *Latvia* 56°38N 22°30E **9** H20
Sale *Australia* 38°6S 147°6E **63** F4
Salé *Morocco* 34°3N 6°48W **52** B4
Sale *U.K.* 53°26N 2°19W **12** D5
Salekhard *Russia* 66°30N 66°35E **26** C7
Salem *India* 11°40N 78°11E **45** J4
Salem *Ill., U.S.A.* 38°38N 88°57W **80** F9
Salem *Ind., U.S.A.* 38°36N 86°6W **80** F10
Salem *Mass., U.S.A.* 42°31N 70°53W **83** D14
Salem *Mo., U.S.A.* 37°39N 91°32W **80** G8
Salem *N.H., U.S.A.* 42°45N 71°12W **83** D13
Salem *N.J., U.S.A.* 39°34N 75°28W **81** F16
Salem *N.Y., U.S.A.* 43°10N 73°20W **83** C11
Salem *Ohio, U.S.A.* 40°54N 80°52W **82** F4
Salem *Oreg., U.S.A.* 44°56N 123°2W **76** D2
Salem *S. Dak., U.S.A.* 43°44N 97°23W **80** D5
Salem *Va., U.S.A.* 37°18N 80°3W **81** G13
Salerno *Italy* 40°41N 14°47E **22** D6
Salford *U.K.* 53°30N 2°18W **12** D5
Salgótarján *Hungary* 48°5N 19°47E **17** D10
Salgueiro *Brazil* 8°4S 39°6W **93** E11
Salher *India* 20°40N 73°55E **44** D1
Salibabu *Indonesia* 3°51N 126°40E **37** D7
Salibea = Salybia
   Trin. & Tob. 10°43N 61°2W **93** K15
Salida *U.S.A.* 38°32N 106°0W **76** G11
Salihli *Turkey* 38°28N 28°8E **23** E13
Salihorsk *Belarus* 52°51N 27°27E **17** B14
Salima *Malawi* 13°47S 34°28E **55** G6
Salina *Italy* 38°34N 14°50E **22** E6
Salina *Kans., U.S.A.* 38°50N 97°37W **80** F5
Salina *Utah, U.S.A.* 38°58N 111°51W **76** G8
Salina Cruz *Mexico* 16°10N 95°12W **87** D5
Salinas *Brazil* 16°10S 42°10W **93** G10
Salinas *Ecuador* 2°10S 80°58W **92** D2
Salinas *U.S.A.* 36°40N 121°39W **78** J5
Salinas → *Guatemala* 16°28N 90°31W **87** D6
Salinas → *U.S.A.* 36°45N 121°48W **78** J5
Salinas, B. de *Nic.* 11°4N 85°45W **88** D2
Salinas, Pampa de las
   Argentina 31°58S 66°42W **94** C2
Salinas Ambargasta
   Argentina 29°0S 65°0W **94** B3
Salinas de Hidalgo
   Mexico 22°38N 101°43W **86** C4
Salinas Grandes *Argentina* 30°0S 65°0W **94** C3
Salinas Pueblo Missions ◠
   U.S.A. 34°6N 106°4W **77** J10
Salinas Valley *U.S.A.* 36°15N 121°15W **78** J5
Saline → *Ark., U.S.A.* 33°10N 92°8W **84** E8
Saline → *Kans., U.S.A.* 38°52N 97°30W **80** F5
Salinópolis *Brazil* 0°40S 47°20W **93** D9
Salisbury *Australia* 34°46S 138°38E **63** E2
Salisbury *U.K.* 51°4N 1°47W **13** F6
Salisbury *Md., U.S.A.* 38°22N 75°36W **81** F16
Salisbury *N.C., U.S.A.* 35°40N 80°29W **85** D14
Salisbury I. *Canada* 63°30N 77°0W **69** E16
Salisbury Plain *U.K.* 51°14N 1°55W **13** F6
Şalkhad *Syria* 32°29N 36°43E **48** C5
Salla *Finland* 66°50N 28°49E **8** C23
Salliq = Coral Harbour
   Canada 64°8N 83°10W **69** E15

Sallisaw *U.S.A.* 35°28N 94°47W **84** D7
Salluit *Canada* 62°14N 75°38W **69** E16
Sallyana *Nepal* 28°22N 82°10E **43** E10
Salmās *Iran* 38°11N 44°47E **46** B5
Salmo *Canada* 49°10N 117°20W **70** D5
Salmon *U.S.A.* 45°11N 113°54W **76** D7
Salmon → *Canada* 54°3N 122°40W **70** C4
Salmon → *U.S.A.* 45°51N 116°47W **76** D5
Salmon Arm *Canada* 50°40N 119°15W **70** C5
Salmon Gums *Australia* 32°59S 121°38E **61** F3
Salmon Pt. *Canada* 43°52N 77°15W **82** C7
Salmon River Mts.
   U.S.A. 44°50N 115°30W **76** D6
Salmon River Res.
   U.S.A. 43°32N 75°55W **83** C9
Salo *Finland* 60°22N 23°10E **9** F20
Salome *U.S.A.* 33°47N 113°37W **79** M13
Salon *India* 26°2N 81°27E **43** F9
Salon-de-Provence *France* 43°39N 5°6E **20** E6
Salonica = Thessaloniki
   Greece 40°38N 22°58E **23** D10
Salonta *Romania* 46°49N 21°42E **17** E11
Salpausselkä *Finland* 61°3N 26°15E **8** F22
Salsacate *Argentina* 31°20S 65°5W **94** C2
Salsk *Russia* 46°28N 41°30E **19** E7
Salso → *Italy* 37°6N 13°57E **22** F5
Salt → *Canada* 60°0N 112°25W **70** B6
Salt → *U.S.A.* 33°23N 112°19W **77** K7
Salt Fork Red → *U.S.A.* 34°27N 99°21W **84** D5
Salt L. *Australia* 30°6S 142°8E **63** E3
Salt Lake City *U.S.A.* 40°45N 111°53W **76** F8
Salt Lake City Int. ✈ (SLC)
   U.S.A. 40°47N 111°58W **76** F7
Salt Range *Pakistan* 32°30N 72°25E **42** C5
Salta *Argentina* 24°57S 65°25W **94** A2
Salta □ *Argentina* 24°48S 65°30W **94** A2
Saltash *U.K.* 50°24N 4°14W **13** G3
Saltburn-by-the-Sea *U.K.* 54°35N 0°58W **12** C7
Saltcoats □ *U.K.* 55°38N 4°47W **11** F4
Saltee Is. *Ireland* 52°7N 6°37W **10** D5
Saltfjellet *Norway* 66°40N 15°15E **8** C16
Saltfjellet-Svartisen △
   Norway 66°45N 15°10E **8** C16
Saltfjorden *Norway* 67°15N 14°10E **8** C16
Saltillo *Mexico* 25°25N 101°0W **86** B4
Salto *Argentina* 34°20S 60°15W **94** C3
Salto *Uruguay* 31°27S 57°50W **94** C4
Salto → *Italy* 42°26N 12°25E **22** C5
Salto del Guairá *Paraguay* 24°3S 54°17W **95** A5
Salton City *U.S.A.* 33°18N 115°57W **79** M11
Salton Sea *U.S.A.* 33°15N 115°45W **79** M11
Saltsburg *U.S.A.* 40°29N 79°27W **82** F5
Saluda → *U.S.A.* 34°1N 81°4W **85** D14
Salue Timpaus, Selat
   Indonesia 1°50S 123°50E **37** E6
Salūm *Egypt* 31°31N 25°7E **53** B11
Salur *India* 18°27N 83°18E **44** E6
Salvador *Brazil* 13°0S 38°30W **93** F11
Salvador *Canada* 52°10N 109°32W **71** C7
Salvador, El *Cent. Amer.* 13°50N 89°0W **88** D2
Salvador, L. *U.S.A.* 29°43N 90°15W **85** G9
Salween → *Burma* 16°31N 97°37E **41** L20
Salyan *Azerbaijan* 39°33N 48°59E **47** B6
Salybia *Trin. & Tob.* 10°43N 61°2W **93** K15
Salzach → *Austria* 48°12N 12°56E **16** D7
Salzburg *Austria* 47°48N 13°2E **16** E7
Salzgitter *Germany* 52°9N 10°19E **16** B6
Salzwedel *Germany* 52°52N 11°10E **16** B6
Sam *India* 26°50N 70°31E **42** F4
Sam Neua *Laos* 20°29N 104°5E **34** G5
Sam Ngao *Thailand* 17°18N 99°0E **38** D2
Sam Rayburn Res. *U.S.A.* 31°4N 94°5W **84** F7
Sam Rong, Laem *Thailand* 9°30S 100°4E **39** b
Sam Son *Vietnam* 19°44N 105°54E **38** C5
Sama de Langreo = Langreo
   Spain 43°18N 5°40W **21** A3
Samagaltay *Russia* 50°36N 95°3E **27** D10
Samales Group *Phil.* 6°0N 122°0E **37** C6
Samalga Pass *U.S.A.* 52°50N 169°0W **74** E6
Samalkot *India* 17°3N 82°13E **44** F6
Samana *India* 30°10N 76°13E **42** D7
Samana Cays *Bahamas* 23°3N 73°45W **89** B5
Samangān □ *Afghan.* 36°15N 68°3E **40** B5
Samani *Japan* 42°7N 142°56E **28** C11
Samar *Phil.* 12°0N 125°0E **37** B7
Samara *Russia* 53°8N 50°6E **18** D9
Samarinda *Indonesia* 0°30S 117°9E **36** E5
Samarkand = Samarqand
   Uzbekistan 39°40N 66°55E **26** F7
Samarqand *Uzbekistan* 39°40N 66°55E **26** F7
Sāmarrā' *Iraq* 34°12N 43°52E **46** C4
Samastipur *India* 25°50N 85°50E **43** G11
Samba *India* 32°32N 75°10E **43** C6
Sambalpur *India* 21°28N 84°4E **44** D7
Sambar, Tanjung
   Indonesia 2°59S 110°19E **36** E4
Sambas *Indonesia* 1°20N 109°20E **36** D3
Sambhajinagar = Aurangabad
   India 19°50N 75°23E **44** E2
Sambhal *India* 28°35N 78°37E **43** E8
Sambhar *India* 26°52N 75°6E **42** F6
Sambhar L. *India* 26°55N 75°12E **42** F6
Sambir *Ukraine* 49°30N 23°10E **17** D12
Sambor *Cambodia* 12°46N 106°0E **38** F6
Sambor Prei Kuk
   Cambodia 12°46N 105°58E **38** F5
Samborombón, B.
   Argentina 36°5S 57°20W **94** D4
Samcheok *S. Korea* 37°30N 129°10E **33** F15
Samet, No *Thailand* 25°10N 101°27E **38** F3
Sammanturai *Sri Lanka* 7°36N 81°39E **45** L5
Samnah *Si. Arabia* 25°10N 37°15E **46** E3
Samo Alto *Chile* 30°22S 71°0W **94** C1
Samoa ■ *Pac. Oc.* 14°0S 172°0W **59** b
Samoan Is. *Pac. Oc.* 14°0S 171°0W **59** b
Samokov *Bulgaria* 42°18N 23°35E **23** C10
Samos *Greece* 37°45N 26°50E **23** F12
Samothráki = Mathraki
   Greece 39°48N 19°31E **23** E8
Samothraki *Greece* 40°28N 25°28E **23** D11

Sampacho *Argentina* 33°20S 64°50W **94** C3
Sampang *Indonesia* 8°41S 113°24E **37** K18
Sampang *Indonesia* 7°11S 113°13E **37** G15
Sampit *Indonesia* 2°34S 113°0E **36** E4
Sampit, Teluk *Indonesia* 3°5S 113°3E **36** E4
Samrong *Cambodia* 14°15N 103°30E **38** E4
Samsø *Denmark* 55°50N 10°35E **9** J14
Samsun *Turkey* 41°15N 36°22E **19** F6
Samui, Ko *Thailand* 9°30N 100°0E **39** b
Samut Sakhon *Thailand* 13°32N 100°17E **38** F3
Samut Songkhram
   Thailand 13°24N 100°1E **38** F3
Samwari *Pakistan* 28°30N 66°46E **42** E2
San *Mali* 13°15N 4°57W **52** F5
San → *Cambodia* 13°32N 105°57E **38** F5
San → *Poland* 50°45N 21°51E **17** C11
San Agustín, C. *Phil.* 6°20N 126°13E **37** C7
San Agustín de Valle Fértil
   Argentina 30°35S 67°30W **94** C2
San Ambrosio *Pac. Oc.* 26°28S 79°53W **90** F3
San Andreas *U.S.A.* 38°12N 120°41W **78** G6
San Andrés, I. de
   Caribbean 12°42N 81°46W **88** D3
San Andres Mts. *U.S.A.* 33°0N 106°30W **77** K10
San Andrés Tuxtla
   Mexico 18°27N 95°13W **87** D5
San Angelo *U.S.A.* 31°28N 100°26W **84** F4
San Anselmo *U.S.A.* 37°59N 122°34W **78** H4
San Antonio *Belize* 16°15N 89°2W **87** D7
San Antonio *Chile* 33°40S 71°40W **94** C1
San Antonio *N. Mex.,*
   U.S.A. 33°55N 106°52W **77** K10
San Antonio *Tex., U.S.A.* 29°25N 98°29W **84** G5
San Antonio → *U.S.A.* 28°30N 96°54W **84** G6
San Antonio, C.
   Argentina 36°15S 56°40W **94** D4
San Antonio, C. de *Cuba* 21°50N 84°57W **88** B3
San Antonio, Mt.
   U.S.A. 34°17N 117°38W **79** L9
San Antonio de los Baños
   Cuba 22°54N 82°31W **88** B3
San Antonio de los Cobres
   Argentina 24°10S 66°17W **94** A2
San Antonio Oeste
   Argentina 40°40S 65°0W **96** E4
San Ardo *U.S.A.* 36°1N 120°54W **78** J6
San Augustine *U.S.A.* 31°32N 94°7W **84** F7
San Benedetto del Tronto
   Italy 42°57N 13°53E **22** C5
San Benedicto, I.
   Mexico 19°18N 110°49W **86** D2
San Benito *U.S.A.* 26°8N 97°38W **84** H6
San Benito → *U.S.A.* 36°53N 121°34W **78** J5
San Benito Mt. *U.S.A.* 36°22N 120°37W **78** J6
San Bernardino *U.S.A.* 34°7N 117°19W **79** L9
San Bernardino Mts.
   U.S.A. 34°10N 116°45W **79** L10
San Bernardino Str.
   Phil. 12°37N 124°12E **37** B7
San Bernardo *Chile* 33°40S 70°50W **94** C1
San Bernardo, I. de
   Colombia 9°45N 75°50W **92** B3
San Blas *Mexico* 26°5N 108°46W **86** B3
San Blas, Arch. de
   Panama 9°50N 78°31W **88** E4
San Blas, C. *U.S.A.* 29°40N 85°21W **85** G12
San Borja *Bolivia* 14°50S 66°52W **92** F5
San Buenaventura = Ventura
   U.S.A. 34°17N 119°18W **79** L7
San Buenaventura
   Mexico 27°5N 101°32W **86** B4
San Carlos *Argentina* 33°50S 69°0W **94** C2
San Carlos *Chile* 36°10S 72°0W **94** D1
San Carlos *Baja Calif. S.,*
   Mexico 24°47N 112°7W **86** C2
San Carlos *Coahuila,*
   Mexico 29°1N 100°51W **86** B4
San Carlos *Nic.* 11°12N 84°50W **88** D3
San Carlos *Phil.* 10°29N 123°25E **37** B6
San Carlos *Uruguay* 34°46S 54°58W **95** C5
San Carlos *Venezuela* 9°40N 68°36W **92** B5
San Carlos de Bariloche
   Argentina 41°10S 71°25W **96** E2
San Carlos de Bolívar
   Argentina 36°15S 61°6W **94** D3
San Carlos del Zulia
   Venezuela 9°1N 71°55W **92** B4
San Carlos L. *U.S.A.* 33°11N 110°32W **77** K8
San Clemente *Chile* 35°30S 71°29W **94** D1
San Clemente *U.S.A.* 33°26N 117°37W **79** M9
San Clemente I. *U.S.A.* 32°53N 118°29W **79** N8
San Cristóbal *Argentina* 30°20S 61°10W **94** C3
San Cristóbal *Dom. Rep.* 18°25N 70°6W **89** C5
San Cristóbal *Solomon Is.* 10°30S 161°0E **58** C9
San Cristóbal *Venezuela* 7°46N 72°14W **92** B4
San Cristóbal de las Casas
   Mexico 16°45N 92°38W **87** D6
San Diego *Calif., U.S.A.* 32°42N 117°9W **79** N9
San Diego *Tex., U.S.A.* 27°46N 98°14W **84** H5
San Diego, C.
   Argentina 54°40S 65°10W **96** G3
San Diego de la Unión
   Mexico 21°28N 100°52W **86** C4
San Diego Int. ✈ (SAN)
   U.S.A. 32°44N 117°11W **79** N9
San Estanislao *Paraguay* 24°39S 56°26W **94** A4
San Felipe *Chile* 32°43S 70°42W **94** C1
San Felipe *Mexico* 31°1N 114°52W **86** A2
San Felipe *Venezuela* 10°20N 68°44W **92** A5
San Felipe → *U.S.A.* 33°10N 115°49W **79** M11
San Félix *Chile* 28°56S 70°28W **94** B1
San Félix *Pac. Oc.* 26°23S 80°0W **90** F2
San Fernando *Chile* 34°30S 71°0W **94** C1
San Fernando *Mexico* 24°51N 98°10W **87** C5
San Fernando *La Union,*
   Phil. 16°40N 120°23E **37** A6
San Fernando *Pampanga,*
   Phil. 15°5N 120°37E **37** A6
San Fernando *Spain* 36°28N 6°17W **21** D2
San Fernando
   Trin. & Tob. 10°16N 61°28W **93** K15

San Fernando *U.S.A.* 34°17N 118°26W **79** L8
San Fernando de Apure
  Venezuela 7°54N 67°15W **92** B5
San Fernando de Atabapo
  Venezuela 4°3N 67°42W **92** C5
San Francisco *Argentina* 31°30S 62°5W **94** C3
San Francisco →
  U.S.A. 32°59N 109°22W **77** K9
San Francisco, C. de
  Colombia 6°18N 77°29W **90** C3
San Francisco, Paso de
  S. Amer. 27°0S 68°0W **94** B2
San Francisco de Macorís
  Dom. Rep. 19°19N 70°15W **89** C5
San Francisco del Monte de Oro
  Argentina 32°36S 66°8W **94** C2
San Francisco del Oro
  Mexico 26°52N 105°51W **86** B3
San Francisco Int. ✈ (SFO)
  U.S.A. 37°37N 122°22W **78** H4
San Gabriel *Chile* 33°47S 70°15W **94** C1
San Gabriel Chilac
  Mexico 18°19N 97°21W **87** D5
San Gabriel Mts. *U.S.A.* 34°17N 117°38W **79** L9
San Gavino Monreale
  Italy 39°33N 8°47E **22** E3
San German *Puerto Rico* 18°4N 67°4W **89** d
San Gorgonio Mt.
  U.S.A. 34°6N 116°50W **79** L10
San Gottardo, P. del *Switz.* 46°33N 8°33E **20** C8
San Gregorio *Uruguay* 32°37S 55°40W **95** C4
San Gregorio *U.S.A.* 37°20N 122°23W **78** H4
San Guillermo △
  Argentina 27°50S 69°45W **94** B2
San Ignacio *Belize* 17°10N 89°5W **87** D7
San Ignacio *Bolivia* 16°20S 60°55W **92** G6
San Ignacio *Mexico* 27°27N 112°51W **86** B2
San Ignacio *Paraguay* 26°52S 57°3W **94** B4
San Ignacio, L. *Mexico* 26°54N 113°13W **86** B2
San Ildefonso, C. *Phil.* 16°0N 122°1E **37** A6
San Isidro *Argentina* 34°29S 58°31W **94** C4
San Jacinto *U.S.A.* 33°47N 116°57W **79** M10
San Javier *Misiones,*
  Argentina 27°55S 55°5W **95** B4
San Javier *Santa Fe,*
  Argentina 30°40S 59°55W **94** C4
San Javier *Bolivia* 16°18S 62°30W **92** G6
San Javier *Chile* 35°40S 71°45W **94** D1
San Jerónimo Taviche
  Mexico 16°44N 96°35W **87** D5
San Joaquin *U.S.A.* 36°36N 120°11W **78** J6
San Joaquin → *U.S.A.* 38°4N 121°51W **78** G5
San Joaquin Valley
  U.S.A. 37°20N 121°0W **78** J6
San Jon *U.S.A.* 35°6N 103°20W **77** J12
San Jorge *Argentina* 31°54S 61°50W **94** C3
San Jorge, B. *Mexico* 31°20N 113°20W **86** A2
San Jorge, G. *Argentina* 46°0S 66°0W **96** F3
San José *Argentina* 32°12S 58°15W **94** C4
San José *Costa Rica* 9°55N 84°2W **88** E3
San José *Guatemala* 14°0N 90°50W **88** D1
San José *Mind. Occ., Phil.* 12°27N 121°4E **37** B6
San Jose *Nueva Ecija,*
  Phil. 15°45N 120°55E **37** A6
San Jose *U.S.A.* 37°20N 121°53W **78** H5
San Jose → *U.S.A.* 34°25N 106°45W **77** J10
San José, I. *Mexico* 25°0N 110°38W **86** C2
San Jose de Buenavista
  Phil. 10°45N 121°56E **37** B6
San José de Chiquitos
  Bolivia 17°53S 60°50W **92** G6
San José de Feliciano
  Argentina 30°26S 58°46W **94** C4
San José de Jáchal
  Argentina 30°15S 68°46W **94** C2
San José de Mayo
  Uruguay 34°27S 56°40W **94** C4
San José del Cabo *Mexico* 23°3N 109°41W **86** C3
San José del Guaviare
  Colombia 2°35N 72°38W **92** C4
San Juan *Argentina* 31°30S 68°30W **94** C2
San Juan *Puerto Rico* 18°28N 66°7W **89** d
San Juan *Trin. & Tob.* 10°39N 61°29W **93** K15
San Juan □ *Argentina* 31°9S 69°0W **94** C2
San Juan → *Argentina* 32°20S 67°25W **94** C2
San Juan → *Nic.* 10°56N 83°42W **88** D3
San Juan → *U.S.A.* 37°16N 110°26W **77** H8
San Juan Bautista
  Paraguay 26°37S 57°6W **94** B4
San Juan Bautista
  U.S.A. 36°51N 121°32W **78** J5
San Juan Capistrano
  U.S.A. 33°30N 117°40W **79** M9
San Juan Cr. → *U.S.A.* 35°40N 120°22W **78** J5
San Juan de Guadelupe
  Mexico 24°38N 102°44W **86** C4
San Juan de la Costa
  Mexico 24°20N 110°41W **86** C2
San Juan de los Lagos
  Mexico 21°15N 102°18W **86** C4
San Juan de los Morros
  Venezuela 9°55N 67°21W **92** B5
San Juan del Norte *Nic.* 10°58N 83°40W **88** D3
San Juan del Norte, B. de
  Nic. 11°0N 83°40W **88** D3
San Juan del Río *Mexico* 20°23N 100°0W **87** C5
San Juan del Sur *Nic.* 11°20N 85°51W **88** D2
San Juan I. *U.S.A.* 48°32N 123°5W **78** B3
San Juan Island △
  U.S.A. 48°35N 123°8W **78** B4
San Juan Mts. *U.S.A.* 37°30N 107°0W **77** H10
San Justo *Argentina* 30°47S 60°30W **94** C3
San Kamphaeng *Thailand* 18°45N 99°8E **38** C2
San Lázaro, C. *Mexico* 24°50N 112°18W **86** C2
San Leandro *U.S.A.* 37°42N 122°9W **78** H4
San Leonardo *Argentina* 32°45S 60°45W **94** C3
San Lorenzo *Argentina* 27°20S 57°32W **94** B4
San Lorenzo *Ecuador* 1°15N 78°50W **92** C3
San Lorenzo *Paraguay* 25°20S 57°32W **94** B4
San Lorenzo → *Mexico* 24°15N 107°24W **86** C3
San Lorenzo, I. *Mexico* 28°38N 112°51W **86** B2

San Lorenzo, Mte.
  Argentina 47°40S 72°20W **96** F2
San Lucas = Cabo San Lucas
  Mexico 22°53N 109°54W **86** C3
San Lucas *Bolivia* 20°5S 65°7W **92** H5
San Lucas *Mexico* 27°10N 112°14W **86** B2
San Lucas, C. *Mexico* 22°52N 109°53W **86** C3
San Lucas, C. *Mexico* 36°8N 121°1W **78** J5
San Luis *Argentina* 33°20S 66°20W **94** C2
San Luis *Cuba* 22°17N 83°46W **88** B3
San Luis *Guatemala* 16°14N 89°27W **88** C2
San Luis *Ariz., U.S.A.* 32°29N 114°47W **77** K6
San Luis *Colo., U.S.A.* 37°12N 105°25W **77** H11
San Luis □ *Argentina* 34°0S 66°0W **94** C2
San Luis, I. *Mexico* 29°58N 114°26W **86** B2
San Luis, Sierra de
  Argentina 32°30S 66°10W **94** C2
San Luis de la Paz
  Mexico 21°18N 100°31W **86** C4
San Luis Obispo *U.S.A.* 35°17N 120°40W **79** K6
San Luis Potosí *Mexico* 22°9N 100°59W **86** C4
San Luis Potosí □ *Mexico* 23°0N 101°0W **86** C4
San Luis Res. *U.S.A.* 37°4N 121°5W **78** H5
San Luis Río Colorado
  Mexico 32°29N 114°58W **86** A2
San Manuel *U.S.A.* 32°36N 110°38W **77** K8
San Marcos *Calif., U.S.A.* 33°9N 117°10W **79** M9
San Marcos *Tex., U.S.A.* 29°53N 97°56W **84** G6
San Marcos, I. *Mexico* 27°13N 112°6W **86** B2
San Marino *San Marino* 43°55N 12°30E **16** G7
San Marino ■ *Europe* 43°56N 12°25E **22** C5
San Martín *Antarctica* 68°11S 67°0W **5** C17
San Martín *Argentina* 33°5S 68°28W **94** C2
San Martín → *Bolivia* 13°8S 63°43W **92** F6
San Martín, L. *Argentina* 48°50S 72°50W **96** F2
San Martín de los Andes
  Argentina 40°10S 71°20W **96** E2
San Mateo *U.S.A.* 37°34N 122°19W **78** H4
San Matías *Bolivia* 16°25S 58°20W **92** G7
San Matías, G. *Argentina* 41°30S 64°0W **96** E4
San Miguel *Bolivia* 28°35S 54°33W **94** B4
San Miguel *El Salv.* 13°30N 88°12W **88** D2
San Miguel *Panama* 8°27N 78°55W **88** E4
San Miguel *U.S.A.* 35°45N 120°42W **78** J5
San Miguel → *Bolivia* 13°52S 63°56W **92** F6
San Miguel de Tucumán
  Argentina 26°50S 65°20W **94** B2
San Miguel del Monte
  Argentina 35°23S 58°50W **94** D4
San Miguel I. *U.S.A.* 34°2N 120°23W **79** L6
San Nicandro Gargánico
  Italy 41°50N 15°34E **22** D6
San Nicolás de los Arroyos
  Argentina 33°25S 60°10W **94** C3
San Nicolas I. *U.S.A.* 33°15N 119°30W **79** M7
San Onofre *U.S.A.* 33°22N 117°34W **79** M9
San Pablo *Bolivia* 21°43S 66°38W **94** A2
San Pablo *U.S.A.* 37°58N 122°21W **78** H4
San Pedro *B. Aires,*
  Argentina 33°40S 59°40W **94** C4
San Pedro *Misiones,*
  Argentina 26°30S 54°10W **95** B5
San Pedro *Chile* 33°54S 71°28W **94** C1
San Pedro *Ivory C.* 4°50N 6°33W **52** H4
San Pedro *Mexico* 23°55N 110°17W **86** C2
San Pedro □ *Paraguay* 24°0S 57°0W **94** A4
San Pedro → *Chihuahua,*
  Mexico 28°21N 105°25W **86** B3
San Pedro → *Nayarit,*
  Mexico 21°45N 105°30W **86** C3
San Pedro → *U.S.A.* 32°59N 110°47W **77** K8
San Pedro, Pta. *Chile* 25°30S 70°38W **94** B1
San Pedro Channel
  U.S.A. 33°30N 118°25W **79** M8
San Pedro de Atacama
  Chile 22°55S 68°15W **94** A2
San Pedro de Jujuy
  Argentina 24°12S 64°55W **94** A3
San Pedro de las Colonias
  Mexico 25°45N 102°59W **86** B4
San Pedro de Macorís
  Dom. Rep. 18°30N 69°18W **89** C6
San Pedro del Norte *Nic.* 13°4N 84°33W **88** D3
San Pedro del Paraná
  Paraguay 26°43S 56°13W **94** B4
San Pedro Mártir, Sa. de
  Mexico 30°45N 115°13W **86** A1
San Pedro Ocampo = Melchor
  Ocampo *Mexico* 24°51N 101°39W **86** C4
San Pedro Pochutla
  Mexico 15°44N 96°28W **87** D5
San Pedro Sula *Honduras* 15°30N 88°0W **88** C2
San Pedro Tututepec
  Mexico 16°9N 97°38W **87** D5
San Pietro *Italy* 39°8N 8°17E **22** E3
San Rafael *Argentina* 34°40S 68°21W **94** C2
San Rafael *Calif., U.S.A.* 37°58N 122°32W **78** H4
San Rafael *N. Mex.,*
  U.S.A. 35°7N 107°53W **77** J10
San Rafael Mt. *U.S.A.* 34°41N 119°52W **79** L7
San Rafael Mts. *U.S.A.* 34°40N 119°50W **79** L7
San Ramón de la Nueva Orán
  Argentina 23°10S 64°20W **94** A3
San Remo *Italy* 43°49N 7°46E **20** E7
San Roque *Argentina* 28°25S 58°45W **94** B4
San Roque *Spain* 36°17N 5°21W **21** D3
San Rosendo *Chile* 37°16S 72°43W **94** D1
San Saba *U.S.A.* 31°12N 98°43W **84** F5
San Salvador *El Salv.* 13°40N 89°10W **88** D2
San Salvador de Jujuy
  Argentina 24°10S 64°48W **94** A3
San Salvador I. *Bahamas* 24°0N 74°30W **89** B5
San Sebastián = Donostia-San
  Sebastián *Spain* 43°17N 1°58W **21** A5
San Sebastián *Argentina* 53°10S 68°30W **96** G3
San Sebastián *Puerto Rico* 18°20N 66°59W **89** d
San Severo *Italy* 41°41N 15°23E **22** D6
San Simeon *U.S.A.* 35°39N 121°11W **78** K5
San Simon *U.S.A.* 32°16N 109°14W **77** K9
San Telmo *Mexico* 30°58N 116°6W **86** A1

San Tiburcio *Mexico* 24°8N 101°32W **86** C4
San Valentin, Mte. *Chile* 46°30S 73°30W **96** F2
San Vicente de Cañete
  Peru 13°8S 76°30W **92** F3
San Vicente de la Barquera
  Spain 43°23N 4°29W **21** A3
San Vito *Costa Rica* 8°50N 82°58W **88** E3
Sana' = San'ā' *Yemen* 15°27N 44°12E **49** D3
San'ā' *Yemen* 15°27N 44°12E **49** D3
Sana → *Bos.-H.* 45°3N 16°23E **16** F9
Sanaa = San'ā' *Yemen* 15°27N 44°12E **49** D3
Sanae IV *Antarctica* 70°20S 9°0W **5** D2
Sanaga → *Cameroon* 3°35N 9°38E **54** D1
Sanak I. *U.S.A.* 54°25N 162°40W **74** E7
Sanalona, Presa *Mexico* 24°49N 107°7W **86** C3
Sanana *Indonesia* 2°4S 125°58E **37** E7
Sanand *India* 22°59N 72°25E **42** H5
Sanandaj *Iran* 35°18N 47°1E **46** C5
Sanandita *Bolivia* 21°40S 63°45W **94** A3
Sanawad *India* 22°11N 76°5E **42** H7
Sancha He → *China* 26°48N 106°7E **34** D6
Sanchahe *China* 44°50N 126°2E **33** B14
Sánchez *Dom. Rep.* 19°15N 69°36W **89** C6
Sanchi *India* 23°28N 77°44E **42** H7
Sanchor *India* 24°45N 71°55E **42** G4
Sancti Spíritus *Cuba* 21°52N 79°33W **88** B4
Sancy, Puy de *France* 45°32N 2°50E **20** D5
Sand → *S. Africa* 22°25S 30°5E **57** B5
Sand Hills *U.S.A.* 42°10N 101°30W **80** D3
Sand Lakes △ *Canada* 57°51N 98°32W **71** B9
Sand Springs *U.S.A.* 36°9N 96°7W **84** C6
Sanda *Japan* 34°53N 135°14E **29** G7
Sandakan *Malaysia* 5°53N 118°4E **36** C5
Sandan = Sambor
  Cambodia 12°46N 106°0E **38** F6
Sandanski *Bulgaria* 41°35N 23°16E **23** D10
Sandaré *Norway* 59°10N 10°15E **9** G14
Sanders *U.S.A.* 35°13N 109°20W **77** J9
Sanderson *U.S.A.* 30°9N 102°24W **84** F3
Sandersville *U.S.A.* 32°59N 82°48W **85** E13
Sandfire Roadhouse
  Australia 19°45S 121°15E **60** C3
Sandfly L. *Canada* 55°43N 106°6W **71** B7
Sandfontein *Namibia* 23°48S 19°1E **56** B2
Sandheads, The *India* 21°10N 88°20E **43** J13
Sandía *Peru* 14°10S 69°30W **92** F5
Sandila *India* 27°5N 80°31E **43** F9
Sandnes *Norway* 58°50N 5°45E **9** G11
Sandnessjøen *Norway* 66°2N 12°38E **8** C15
Sandoa
  Dem. Rep. of the Congo 9°41S 23°0E **54** F4
Sandomierz *Poland* 50°40N 21°43E **17** C11
Sandover → *Australia* 21°43S 136°32E **62** C2
Sandoway = Thandwe
  Burma 18°20N 94°30E **41** K19
Sandoy *Færoe Is.* 61°52N 6°46W **8** F9
Sandpoint *U.S.A.* 48°17N 116°33W **76** B5
Sandray *U.K.* 56°53N 7°31W **11** E1
Sandringham *U.K.* 52°51N 0°31E **12** E8
Sandstone *Australia* 27°59S 119°16E **61** E2
Sandu *China* 26°0N 107°52E **34** E6
Sandur *India* 15°6N 76°33E **45** F3
Sandusky *Mich., U.S.A.* 43°25N 82°50W **82** C2
Sandusky *Ohio, U.S.A.* 41°27N 82°42W **82** E2
Sandveld *Namibia* 21°25S 20°0E **56** B3
Sandviken *Sweden* 18°36N 16°46E **8** F17
Sandwich, C. *Australia* 18°14S 146°18E **62** B4
Sandwich B. *Canada* 53°40N 57°15W **73** B8
Sandwich B. *Namibia* 23°25S 14°20E **56** B1
Sandy *Oreg., U.S.A.* 45°24N 122°16W **78** E4
Sandy *Pa., U.S.A.* 41°6N 78°46W **82** E6
Sandy *Utah, U.S.A.* 40°32N 111°50W **76** F8
Sandy Bay *Canada* 55°31N 102°19W **71** B8
Sandy Bight *Australia* 33°50S 123°20E **61** F3
Sandy C. *Queens.,*
  Australia 24°42S 153°15E **62** C5
Sandy C. *Tas., Australia* 41°25S 144°45E **63** G3
Sandy Cay *Bahamas* 23°13N 75°18W **89** B4
Sandy Cr. → *Australia* 13°45S 145°18E **63** B4
Sandy Cr. → *U.S.A.* 41°51N 109°47W **76** F9
Sandy Creek *U.S.A.* 43°38N 76°5W **83** C8
Sandy L. *Canada* 53°2N 93°0W **72** B1
Sandy Lake *Canada* 53°0N 93°15W **72** B1
Sandy Point *U.S.A.* 10°32N 92°22E **45** J11
Sandy Valley *U.S.A.* 35°49N 115°38W **79** K11
Sånfjället △ *Sweden* 62°17N 13°35E **8** E15
Sanford *Fla., U.S.A.* 28°48N 81°16W **85** G14
Sanford *Maine, U.S.A.* 43°27N 70°47W **83** C14
Sanford *N.C., U.S.A.* 35°29N 79°10W **85** D15
Sanford → *Australia* 27°22S 115°53E **61** E2
Sanford, Mt. *U.S.A.* 62°13N 144°8W **68** E3
Sang-i-Masha *Afghan.* 33°8N 67°27E **42** C2
Sanga → *Congo* 1°5S 17°0E **54** E3
Sanga *Congo* 2°0S 78°20W **92** D3
Sangamner *India* 19°37N 74°15E **44** E2
Sangān *Iran* 34°23N 60°15E **47** C9
Sangar *Afghan.* 32°56N 65°30E **42** C1
Sangar *Russia* 64°2N 127°31E **27** C13
Sangar Sarai *Afghan.* 34°27N 70°35E **42** B4
Sangareddi *India* 17°38N 78°7E **44** F4
Sangarh → *Pakistan* 30°43N 70°44E **42** D4
Sangay *Ecuador* 2°0S 78°20W **92** D3
Sangeang *Indonesia* 8°12S 119°6E **37** F5
Sanger *U.S.A.* 36°42N 119°33W **78** J7
Sangerhausen *Germany* 51°28N 11°18E **16** C6
Sanggan He → *China* 38°12N 117°15E **32** E9
Sanggau *Indonesia* 0°5N 110°30E **36** D4
Sanghar *Pakistan* 26°2N 68°57E **42** F3
Sangihe, Kepulauan
  Indonesia 3°0N 125°30E **37** D7
Sangihe, Pulau *Indonesia* 3°35N 125°30E **37** D7
Sangīran *S. Korea* 7°27S 110°50E **37** G14
Sangju *S. Korea* 36°25N 128°10E **33** F15
Sangkapura *Indonesia* 5°52S 112°40E **36** F4
Sangkha *Thailand* 14°37N 103°52E **38** E4
Sangkhla Buri *Thailand* 14°57N 98°28E **38** E2
Sangkulirang *Indonesia* 0°59N 117°58E **36** D5
Sangla *Pakistan* 31°43N 73°23E **42** D5
Sangli *India* 16°55N 74°33E **44** F2

Sangmélima *Cameroon* 2°57N 12°1E **54** D2
Sango *Zimbabwe* 18°44S 31°44E **57** A5
Sangod *India* 24°55N 76°17E **42** G7
Sangole *India* 17°26N 75°12E **44** F2
Sangre de Cristo Mts.
  U.S.A. 37°30N 105°20W **77** H11
Sangre Grande
  Trin. & Tob. 10°35N 61°8W **93** K15
Sangudo *Canada* 53°50N 114°54W **70** C6
Sangue → *Brazil* 11°1S 58°39W **92** F7
Sangzhi *China* 29°25N 110°12E **35** C8
Sanibel *U.S.A.* 26°27N 82°1W **85** H13
Sanirajak = Hall Beach
  Canada 68°46N 81°12W **69** D15
Sanjawi *Pakistan* 30°17N 68°21E **42** D3
Sanjiang *China* 25°48N 109°37E **34** E7
Sanjo *Japan* 37°37N 138°57E **28** F9
Sankarankovil *India* 9°10N 77°35E **45** K3
Sankeshwar *India* 16°23N 74°32E **45** F2
Sankh → *India* 22°15N 84°48E **43** H11
Sankt Gallen *Switz.* 47°26N 9°22E **20** C8
Sankt Michel = Mikkeli
  Finland 61°43N 27°15E **8** F22
Sankt Moritz *Switz.* 46°30N 9°51E **20** C8
Sankt Pölten *Austria* 48°12N 15°38E **16** D8
Sankuru →
  Dem. Rep. of the Congo 4°17S 20°25E **54** E4
Sanliurfa *Turkey* 37°12N 38°50E **46** B3
Sanlúcar de Barrameda
  Spain 36°46N 6°21W **21** D2
Sanmen *China* 29°5N 121°35E **35** C13
Sanmenxia *China* 34°47N 111°12E **32** G6
Sanming *China* 26°15N 117°40E **35** D11
Sanmu *Japan* 34°11N 134°37E **29** G7
Sanndraigh = Sandray
  U.K. 56°53N 7°31W **11** E1
Sannicandro *Italy* 43°49N 7°46E **20** E7
Sanshi *China* 26°58N 120°12E **35** D13
Sanshui *China* 23°10N 112°56E **35** F9
Sansui *China* 26°58N 108°39E **34** D7
Sant Antoni de Portmany
  Spain 38°59N 1°19E **21** C6
Sant Jordi, G. de *Spain* 41°45N 1°1E **21** B7
Sant Jordi, G. de *Spain* 40°53N 1°2E **21** B6
Santa Ana *Bolivia* 13°50S 65°40W **92** F5
Santa Ana *El Salv.* 14°0N 89°31W **88** D2
Santa Ana *Mexico* 30°33N 111°7W **86** A2
Santa Ana *U.S.A.* 33°46N 117°52W **79** M9
Santa Ana de los Ríos de Cuenca =
  Cuenca *Ecuador* 2°50S 79°9W **92** D3
Santa Bárbara *Chile* 37°40S 72°1W **94** D1
Santa Bárbara *Honduras* 14°53N 88°14W **88** D2
Santa Bárbara *Mexico* 26°48N 105°49W **86** B3
Santa Barbara *U.S.A.* 34°25N 119°42W **79** L7
Santa Barbara Channel
  U.S.A. 34°15N 120°0W **79** L7
Santa Barbara I. *U.S.A.* 33°29N 119°2W **79** M7
Santa Catalina, Gulf of
  U.S.A. 33°10N 117°50W **79** N9
Santa Catalina, I.
  Mexico 25°40N 110°47W **86** B2
Santa Catalina I.
  U.S.A. 33°23N 118°25W **79** M8
Santa Catarina □ *Brazil* 27°25S 48°30W **95** B6
Santa Catarina, I. de
  Brazil 27°30S 48°40W **95** B6
Santa Cecília *Brazil* 26°56S 50°18W **95** B5
Santa Clara *Cuba* 22°20N 80°0W **88** B4
Santa Clara *Calif.,*
  U.S.A. 37°21N 121°57W **78** H5
Santa Clara *N.Y., U.S.A.* 44°38N 74°27W **83** B10
Santa Clara *Utah, U.S.A.* 37°8N 113°39W **77** H7
Santa Clara → *Mexico* 29°51N 107°6W **86** A3
Santa Clara de Olimar
  Uruguay 32°50S 54°54W **95** C5
Santa Clara Valley
  U.S.A. 36°50N 121°30W **78** J5
Santa Clarita *U.S.A.* 34°24N 118°32W **79** L8
Santa Clotilde *Peru* 2°33S 73°45W **92** D4
Santa Cruz *Bolivia* 17°43S 63°10W **92** G6
Santa Cruz *Chile* 34°38S 71°27W **94** C1
Santa Cruz *Costa Rica* 10°15N 85°35W **88** D2
Santa Cruz *Phil.* 14°20N 121°24E **37** B6
Santa Cruz *U.S.A.* 36°58N 122°1W **78** J4
Santa Cruz → *Argentina* 50°10S 68°20W **96** G3
Santa Cruz de Mompox = Mompós
  Colombia 9°14N 74°26W **92** B4
Santa Cruz de Tenerife
  Canary Is. 28°28N 16°15W **52** C2
Santa Cruz del Norte
  Cuba 23°9N 81°55W **88** B3
Santa Cruz del Sur *Cuba* 20°44N 78°0W **88** B4
Santa Cruz do Rio Pardo
  Brazil 22°54S 49°37W **95** A6
Santa Cruz do Sul *Brazil* 29°42S 52°25W **95** B5
Santa Cruz Is. *Solomon Is.* 10°30S 166°0E **58** C9
Santa Cruz Mts. *Jamaica* 17°58N 77°43W **88** a
Santa Elena *Argentina* 30°58S 59°47W **94** C4
Santa Elena, C.
  Costa Rica 10°54N 85°56W **88** D2
Santa Fé *Argentina* 31°35S 60°41W **94** C3
Santa Fe *U.S.A.* 35°41N 105°57W **77** J11
Santa Fé □ *Argentina* 31°50S 60°55W **94** C3
Santa Fé do Sul *Brazil* 20°13S 50°56W **93** H8
Santa Filomena *Brazil* 9°6S 45°50W **93** E9

Santa Inês *Brazil* 13°17S 39°48W **93** F11
Santa Inês, I. *Chile* 54°0S 73°0W **96** G2
Santa Isabel *Argentina* 36°10S 66°54W **94** D2
Santa Isabel do Morro
  Brazil 11°34S 50°40W **93** F8
Santa Lucía *Corrientes,*
  Argentina 28°58S 59°5W **94** B4
Santa Lucía *San Juan,*
  Argentina 31°30S 68°30W **94** C2
Santa Lucia *Uruguay* 34°27S 56°24W **94** C4
Santa Lucia Range
  U.S.A. 36°0N 121°20W **78** K5
Santa Luzia *C. Verde Is.* 16°50N 24°35W **52** b
Santa Margarita
  Argentina 38°28S 61°35W **94** D3
Santa Margarita *U.S.A.* 35°23N 120°37W **78** K6
Santa Margarita →
  U.S.A. 33°13N 117°23W **79** M9
Santa Margarita, I.
  Mexico 24°27N 111°50W **86** C2
Santa María *Argentina* 26°40S 66°0W **94** B2
Santa Maria *Azores* 36°58N 25°6W **52** a
Santa Maria *Brazil* 29°40S 53°48W **95** B5
Santa Maria *C. Verde Is.* 16°31N 22°53W **52** b
Santa Maria *U.S.A.* 34°57N 120°26W **79** L6
Santa María → *Mexico* 31°0N 107°14W **86** A3
Santa María, B. de *Mexico* 25°4N 108°6W **86** B3
Santa María, Vol.
  Guatemala 14°45N 91°33W **88** D1
Santa Maria da Vitória
  Brazil 13°24S 44°12W **93** F10
Santa Maria di Léuca, C.
  Italy 39°47N 18°22E **23** E8
Santa Marta *Colombia* 11°15N 74°13W **92** A4
Santa Marta, Sierra Nevada de
  Colombia 10°55N 73°50W **92** A4
Santa Marta Grande, C.
  Brazil 28°43S 48°50W **95** B6
Santa Maura = Lefkada
  Greece 38°40N 20°43E **23** E9
Santa Monica Mts. △
  U.S.A. 34°4N 118°44W **79** L8
Santa Paula *U.S.A.* 34°21N 119°4W **79** L7
Santa Rosa *La Pampa,*
  Argentina 36°40S 64°17W **94** D3
Santa Rosa *San Luis,*
  Argentina 32°21S 65°10W **94** C2
Santa Rosa *Brazil* 27°52S 54°29W **95** B5
Santa Rosa *Calif., U.S.A.* 38°26N 122°43W **78** G4
Santa Rosa *N. Mex.,*
  U.S.A. 34°57N 104°41W **77** J11
Santa Rosa and San Jacinto Mts. △
  U.S.A. 33°28N 116°20W **79** M10
Santa Rosa de Copán
  Honduras 14°47N 88°46W **88** D2
Santa Rosa de Río Primero
  Argentina 31°8S 63°20W **94** C3
Santa Rosa del Sara
  Bolivia 17°7S 63°35W **92** G6
Santa Rosa I. *Calif.,*
  U.S.A. 33°58N 120°6W **79** M6
Santa Rosa I. *Fla.,*
  U.S.A. 30°20N 86°50W **85** F11
Santa Rosa Range
  U.S.A. 41°45N 117°40W **76** F5
Santa Rosalía *Mexico* 27°19N 112°17W **86** B2
Santa Sylvina *Argentina* 27°50S 61°10W **94** B3
Santa Tecla = Nueva San Salvador
  El Salv. 13°40N 89°18W **88** D2
Santa Teresa *Australia* 24°8S 134°22E **62** C1
Santa Teresa *Mexico* 25°17N 97°51W **87** B5
Santa Teresa △ *Uruguay* 33°57S 53°31W **95** C5
Santa Teresita *Argentina* 36°32S 56°41W **94** D4
Santa Vitória do Palmar
  Brazil 33°32S 53°25W **95** C5
Santa Ynez → *U.S.A.* 34°41N 120°36W **79** L6
Santa Ynez Mts. *U.S.A.* 34°30N 120°0W **79** L6
Santa Ysabel *U.S.A.* 33°7N 116°40W **79** M10
Santai *China* 31°5N 104°58E **34** B5
Santana, Coxilha de
  Brazil 30°50S 55°35W **95** C4
Santana do Livramento
  Brazil 30°55S 55°30W **95** C4
Santander *Spain* 43°27N 3°51W **21** A4
Santander Jiménez
  Mexico 24°13N 98°28W **87** C5
Santanilla, Is. *Honduras* 17°22N 83°57W **88** C3
Santaquin *U.S.A.* 39°59N 111°47W **76** G8
Santarém *Brazil* 2°25S 54°42W **93** D8
Santarém *Portugal* 39°12N 8°42W **21** C1
Santaren Channel
  W. Indies 24°0N 79°30W **88** B4
Santee → *U.S.A.* 32°50N 116°58W **79** N10
Santee → *U.S.A.* 33°7N 79°17W **85** E15
Santiago = Rio Grande de
  Santiago → *Mexico* 21°36N 105°26W **86** C3
Santiago = São Tiago
  C. Verde Is. 15°0N 23°40W **52** b
Santiago *Brazil* 29°11S 54°52W **95** B5
Santiago *Panama* 8°0N 81°0W **88** E3
Santiago *Phil.* 16°41N 121°33E **37** A6
Santiago → *Peru* 4°27S 77°38W **92** D3
Santiago de Compostela
  Spain 42°52N 8°37W **21** A1
Santiago de Cuba *Cuba* 20°0N 75°49W **88** C4
Santiago de los Caballeros
  Dom. Rep. 19°30N 70°40W **89** C5
Santiago del Estero
  Argentina 27°50S 64°15W **94** B3
Santiago del Estero □
  Argentina 27°40S 63°15W **94** B3
Santiago Ixcuintla
  Mexico 21°49N 105°13W **86** C3
Santiago Jamiltepec
  Mexico 16°17N 97°49W **87** D5
Santiago Papasquiaro
  Mexico 25°3N 105°25W **86** C3
Santiago Pinotepa Nacional
  Mexico 16°19N 98°1W **87** D5

Santiaguillo, L. de
  Mexico 24°48N 104°48W **86 C4**
Santo Amaro Brazil 12°30S 38°43W **93 F11**
Santo Anastácio Brazil 21°58S 51°39W **95 A5**
Santo André Brazil 23°39S 46°29W **95 A6**
Santo Ângelo Brazil 28°15S 54°15W **95 B5**
Santo Antão C. Verde Is. 16°52N 25°10W **52 b**
Sant' Antíoco Italy 39°4N 8°27E **22 E3**
Santo Antônio do Içá
  Brazil 3°5S 67°57W **92 D5**
Santo Antônio do Leverger
  Brazil 15°52S 56°5W **93 G7**
Santo Domingo
  Dom. Rep. 18°30N 69°59W **89 C6**
Santo Domingo Mexico 25°29N 111°55W **86 B2**
Santo Domingo Nic. 12°14N 84°59W **88 D3**
Santo Domingo, Cay
  Bahamas 21°25N 75°45W **88 B4**
Santo Domingo de los Colorados
  Ecuador 0°15S 79°9W **92 D3**
Santo Domingo Pueblo
  U.S.A. 35°31N 106°22W **77 J10**
Santo Domingo Tehuantepec =
  Tehuantepec Mexico 16°21N 95°13W **87 D5**
Santo Tomás Mexico 31°33N 116°24W **86 A1**
Santo Tomás Peru 14°26S 72°8W **92 F4**
Santo Tomé Argentina 28°40S 56°5W **95 B4**
Santo Tomé de Guayana = Ciudad
  Guayana Venezuela 8°0N 62°30W **92 B6**
Santoña Spain 43°29N 3°27W **21 A4**
Santorini Greece 36°23N 25°27E **23 F11**
Santos Brazil 24°0S 46°20W **95 A6**
Santos Dumont Brazil 22°55S 43°10W **95 A7**
Santuario de Aves Laguna
  Colorada △ Bolivia 22°10S 67°45W **94 A2**
Sanuki Japan 34°19N 134°10E **29 G7**
Sanur Indonesia 8°41S 115°15E **37 K18**
Sanwer India 22°59N 75°50E **42 H6**
Sanxia Shuiku China 30°30N 107°58E **34 B6**
Sanxiang China 22°21N 113°25E **31 a**
Sanya China 18°14N 109°29E **38 C7**
Sanyuan China 34°35N 108°58E **32 G5**
São Bernardo do Campo
  Brazil 23°45S 46°34W **95 A6**
São Borja Brazil 28°39S 56°0W **95 B4**
São Carlos Brazil 22°0S 47°50W **95 A6**
São Cristóvão Brazil 11°1S 37°15W **93 F11**
São Domingos Brazil 13°25S 46°19W **93 F9**
São Filipe C. Verde Is. 15°2N 24°30W **52 b**
São Francisco Brazil 16°0S 44°50W **93 G10**
São Francisco → Brazil 10°30S 36°24W **93 F11**
São Francisco do Sul
  Brazil 26°15S 48°36W **95 B6**
São Gabriel Brazil 30°20S 54°20W **95 C5**
São Gonçalo Brazil 22°48S 43°5W **95 A7**
São João da Boa Vista
  Brazil 22°0S 46°52W **95 A6**
São João da Madeira
  Portugal 40°54N 8°30W **21 B1**
São João del Rei Brazil 21°8S 44°15W **95 A7**
São João do Araguaia
  Brazil 5°23S 48°46W **93 E9**
São João do Piauí Brazil 8°21S 42°15W **93 E10**
São Joaquim Brazil 28°18S 49°56W **95 B6**
São Joaquim △ Brazil 28°12S 49°37W **95 B6**
São Jorge Azores 38°38N 28°3W **52 a**
São José Brazil 27°38S 48°39W **95 B5**
São José do Norte Brazil 32°1S 52°3W **95 C5**
São José do Rio Preto
  Brazil 20°50S 49°20W **95 A6**
São José dos Campos
  Brazil 23°7S 45°52W **95 A6**
São Leopoldo Brazil 29°50S 51°10W **95 B5**
São Lourenço Brazil 22°7S 45°3W **95 A6**
São Lourenço → Brazil 17°53S 57°27W **93 G7**
São Lourenço do Sul
  Brazil 31°22S 51°58W **95 C5**
São Luís Brazil 2°39S 44°15W **93 D10**
São Luís Gonzaga Brazil 28°25S 55°0W **95 B5**
São Marcos → Brazil 18°15S 47°37W **93 G9**
São Marcos, B. de Brazil 2°0S 44°0W **93 D10**
São Mateus Brazil 18°44S 39°50W **93 G11**
São Mateus do Sul Brazil 25°52S 50°23W **95 B5**
São Miguel Azores 37°47N 25°30W **52 a**
São Miguel do Oeste
  Brazil 26°45S 53°34W **95 B5**
São Nicolau C. Verde Is. 16°20N 24°20W **52 b**
São Paulo □ Brazil 22°0S 49°0W **95 A6**
São Paulo de Olivença
  Brazil 3°27S 68°48W **92 D5**
São Roque, C. de Brazil 5°30S 35°16W **93 E11**
São Sebastião, I. de
  Brazil 23°50S 45°18W **95 A6**
São Sebastião do Paraíso
  Brazil 20°54S 46°59W **95 A6**
São Tiago C. Verde Is. 15°0N 23°40W **52 b**
São Tomé
  São Tomé & Príncipe 0°10N 6°39E **50 F4**
São Tomé, C. de Brazil 22°0S 40°59W **95 A7**
São Tomé & Príncipe ■
  Africa 0°12N 6°39E **51 F4**
São Vicente Brazil 23°57S 46°23W **95 A6**
São Vicente C. Verde Is. 17°0N 25°0W **52 b**
São Vicente, C. de Portugal 37°0N 9°0W **21 D1**
Saona, I. Dom. Rep. 18°10N 68°40W **89 C6**
Saône → France 45°44N 4°50E **20 D6**
Saonek Indonesia 0°22S 130°55E **37 E8**
Sapam, Ao Thailand 8°0N 98°26E **39 a**
Saparua Indonesia 3°33S 128°40E **37 E7**
Sape Indonesia 8°34S 118°59E **37 F5**
Sapele Nigeria 5°50N 5°40E **52 G7**
Sapelo I. U.S.A. 31°25N 81°12W **85 F14**
Saposoa Peru 6°55S 76°45W **92 E3**
Sapphire Australia 23°28S 147°43E **62 C4**
Sappho U.S.A. 48°4N 124°16W **78 B2**
Sapporo Japan 43°0N 141°21E **28 C10**
Sapporo New Chitose ✈ (CTS)
  Japan 42°41N 141°41E **28 C10**
Sapt Kosi → Nepal 26°32N 86°56E **43 F12**
Sapudi Indonesia 7°6S 114°20E **37 G16**

Sapulpa U.S.A. 35°59N 96°5W **84 D6**
Saqqez Iran 36°15N 46°20E **46 B5**
Sar Dasht Āzarbāyjān-e Gharbī,
  Iran 36°9N 45°28E **46 B5**
Sar Dasht Khuzestān, Iran 32°32N 48°52E **47 C6**
Sar-e Pol □ Afghan. 36°20N 65°50E **40 B4**
Sar Gachīneh = Yāsūj
  Iran 30°31N 51°31E **47 D6**
Sar Planina Macedonia 42°0N 21°0E **23 C9**
Sara Buri = Saraburi
  Thailand 14°30N 100°55E **38 E3**
Sarāb Iran 37°55N 47°40E **46 B5**
Sarābādī Iraq 33°1N 44°48E **46 C5**
Saraburi Thailand 14°30N 100°55E **38 E3**
Saradiya India 21°34N 70°2E **42 J4**
Saragossa = Zaragoza
  Spain 41°39N 0°53W **21 B5**
Saraguro Ecuador 3°35S 79°16W **92 D3**
Sarahs Turkmenistan 36°32N 61°13E **47 B9**
Sarai Naurang Pakistan 32°50N 70°47E **42 C4**
Saraikela India 22°42N 85°56E **43 H11**
Saraipali India 21°20N 82°59E **44 D6**
Sarajevo Bos.-H. 43°52N 18°26E **23 C8**
Sarakhs = Sarahs
  Turkmenistan 36°32N 61°13E **47 B9**
Saran, Gunung Indonesia 0°30S 111°25E **36 E4**
Saranac Lake U.S.A. 44°20N 74°10W **83 B10**
Saranac Lakes U.S.A. 44°20N 74°28W **83 B10**
Sarandí del Yí Uruguay 33°18S 55°38W **95 C4**
Sarandí Grande Uruguay 33°44S 56°20W **94 C4**
Sarangani B. Phil. 6°0N 125°13E **37 C7**
Sarangani Is. Phil. 5°25N 125°25E **37 C7**
Sarangarh India 21°30N 83°5E **44 D6**
Saransk Russia 54°10N 45°10E **18 D8**
Sarapul Russia 56°28N 53°48E **18 C9**
Sarasota U.S.A. 27°20N 82°32W **85 H13**
Saratoga Calif., U.S.A. 37°16N 122°2W **78 H4**
Saratoga Wyo., U.S.A. 41°27N 106°49W **76 F10**
Saratoga □ U.S.A. 43°0N 73°38W **83 C11**
Saratoga L. U.S.A. 43°1N 73°44W **83 C11**
Saratoga Springs U.S.A. 43°5N 73°47W **83 C11**
Saratok Malaysia 1°55N 111°17E **36 D4**
Saratov Russia 51°30N 46°2E **19 D8**
Sarāvān Iran 27°25N 62°15E **47 E9**
Saravane Laos 15°43N 106°25E **38 E6**
Sarawak □ Malaysia 2°0N 113°0E **36 D4**
Saray Turkey 41°26N 27°55E **23 D12**
Saraykoy Turkey 37°55N 28°54E **23 F13**
Sarbāz Iran 26°38N 61°19E **47 E9**
Sarbīsheh Iran 32°30N 59°40E **47 C8**
Sarda → India 27°21N 81°23E **43 F9**
Sardar Sarovar Dam
  India 21°50N 73°50E **44 D1**
Sardarshahr India 28°30N 74°29E **42 E6**
Sardegna □ Italy 40°0N 9°0E **22 D3**
Sardhana India 29°9N 77°39E **42 E7**
Sardinia = Sardegna □ Italy 40°0N 9°0E **22 D3**
Sardis Turkey 38°28N 27°58E **23 E12**
Sārdūīyeh = Dar Mazār
  Iran 29°14N 57°20E **47 D8**
Sarek △ Sweden 67°22N 17°35E **8 C17**
Saren Indonesia 8°26S 115°34E **37 J18**
Sarera, G. of Indonesia 2°0S 135°0E **58 B6**
Sargasso Sea Atl. Oc. 27°0N 72°0W **66 G13**
Sargodha Pakistan 32°10N 72°40E **42 C5**
Sarh Chad 9°5N 18°23E **53 G9**
Sārī Iran 36°30N 53°4E **47 B7**
Saria India 21°38N 83°22E **43 J10**
Sariab Pakistan 30°6N 66°59E **42 D2**
Sargöl Turkey 38°14N 28°41E **23 E13**
Sarikei Malaysia 2°8N 111°30E **36 D4**
Sarila India 25°46N 79°41E **43 G8**
Sarina Australia 21°22S 149°13E **62 C4**
Sarita U.S.A. 27°13N 97°47W **84 H6**
Sariwŏn N. Korea 38°31N 125°46E **33 E13**
Sarju → India 27°21N 81°23E **43 F9**
Sark U.K. 49°25N 2°22W **13 H5**
Sarkari Tala India 27°39N 70°52E **42 F4**
Sarlat-la-Canéda France 44°54N 1°13E **20 D4**
Sarmi Indonesia 1°49S 138°44E **37 E9**
Sarmiento Argentina 45°35S 69°5W **96 F3**
Sārna Sweden 61°41N 13°8E **8 F15**
Sarnia Canada 42°58N 82°23W **82 D2**
Sarolangun Indonesia 2°19S 102°42E **36 E2**
Saronikos Kolpos Greece 37°45N 23°45E **23 F10**
Saros Körfezi Turkey 40°30N 26°15E **23 D12**
Sarpsborg Norway 59°16N 11°7E **9 G14**
Sarqan Kazakhstan 45°24N 79°55E **30 B4**
Sarre = Saar → Europe 49°41N 6°32E **15 E6**
Sarreguemines France 49°5N 7°4E **20 D7**
Sartell U.S.A. 45°37N 94°12W **80 C6**
Sarthe → France 47°33N 0°31W **20 C3**
Saruna → Pakistan 26°31N 67°7E **42 F2**
Sarvar India 26°4N 75°0E **42 F6**
Sarvestān Iran 29°20N 53°10E **47 D7**
Sary-Tash Kyrgyzstan 39°44N 73°15E **28 F8**
Saryshaghan Kazakhstan 46°12N 73°38E **26 E8**
Sasan Gir India 21°10N 70°36E **42 J4**
Sasaram India 24°57N 84°5E **43 G11**
Sasebo Japan 33°10N 129°43E **29 H4**
Saser Kangri India 34°50N 77°50E **43 B7**
Saskatchewan □ Canada 54°40N 106°0W **71 C7**
Saskatchewan →
  Canada 53°37N 100°40W **71 C8**
Saskatoon Canada 52°10N 106°38W **71 C7**
Saskylakh Russia 71°55N 114°1E **27 B12**
Saslaya △ Nic. 13°45N 85°4W **88 D2**
Sasolburg S. Africa 26°46S 27°49E **57 C4**
Sasovo Russia 54°25N 41°55E **18 D7**
Sassandra Ivory C. 4°55N 6°8W **52 H4**
Sassandra → Ivory C. 4°58N 6°5W **52 H4**
Sássari Italy 40°43N 8°34E **22 D3**
Sassie Australia 10°2S 142°51E **62 a**
Sassnitz Germany 54°29N 13°39E **16 A7**
Sassuolo Italy 44°33N 10°47E **22 B4**
Sastamala Finland 61°20N 22°54E **8 F20**
Sasvad India 18°20N 74°2E **44 E2**
Sasyk, Ozero Ukraine 45°45N 29°4E **17 F15**
Sata-Misaki Japan 31°0N 130°40E **29 J5**

Satadougou Mali 12°25N 11°25W **52 F3**
Satakunta □ Finland 61°45N 23°0E **8 F20**
Satara India 17°44N 73°58E **44 F1**
Satara S. Africa 24°29S 31°47E **57 B5**
Satbarwa India 23°55N 84°16E **43 H11**
Satevó Mexico 27°57N 106°7W **86 B3**
Satilla → U.S.A. 30°59N 81°29W **85 F14**
Satka Russia 55°3N 59°1E **18 C10**
Satluj = Sutlej → Pakistan 29°23N 71°3E **42 E4**
Satmala Hills Maharashtra,
  India 20°15N 74°40E **44 D2**
Satmala Hills Telangana,
  India 19°45N 78°45E **44 E4**
Satna India 24°35N 80°50E **43 G9**
Sátoraljaújhely Hungary 48°25N 21°41E **17 D11**
Satpura △ India 22°40N 78°15E **42 H8**
Satpura Ra. India 21°25N 76°10E **44 D3**
Satsuma-Sendai Japan 31°50N 130°20E **29 J5**
Satsunan-Shotō Japan 30°0N 130°0E **29 K5**
Sattahip Thailand 12°41N 100°54E **38 F3**
Sattenapalle India 16°25N 80°6E **45 F5**
Satu Mare Romania 47°46N 22°55E **17 E12**
Satui Indonesia 3°50S 115°27E **36 E5**
Satun Thailand 6°43N 100°2E **39 J3**
Satupa'itea Samoa 13°45S 172°18W **59 b**
Saturnina → Brazil 12°15S 58°10W **92 F7**
Sauce Argentina 30°5S 58°46W **94 C4**
Sauceda Mexico 25°46N 101°19W **86 B4**
Saucillo Mexico 28°1N 105°17W **86 B3**
Sauda Norway 59°40N 6°20E **9 G12**
Sauðarkrókur Iceland 65°45N 19°40W **8 D4**
Saudi Arabia ■ Asia 26°0N 44°0E **46 B3**
Sauerland Germany 51°12N 7°59E **16 C4**
Saugeen → Canada 44°30N 81°22W **82 B3**
Saugerties U.S.A. 42°5N 73°57W **83 D11**
Saugus U.S.A. 34°25N 118°32W **79 L8**
Sauk Centre U.S.A. 45°44N 94°57W **80 C6**
Sauk Rapids U.S.A. 45°35N 94°10W **80 C6**
Sault Ste. Marie Canada 46°30N 84°20W **72 C3**
Sault Ste. Marie U.S.A. 46°30N 84°21W **81 B11**
Saumlaki Indonesia 7°55S 131°20E **37 F8**
Saumur France 47°15N 0°5W **20 C3**
Saundatti India 15°47N 75°7E **45 G2**
Saunders, C. N.Z. 45°53S 170°38E **59 L3**
Saunders I. Antarctica 57°48S 26°28W **5 B1**
Saunders Pt. Australia 27°52S 125°38E **61 E4**
Saurimo Angola 9°40S 20°12E **54 F4**
Savá Honduras 15°32N 86°15W **88 C2**
Sava → Serbia 44°50N 20°26E **23 B9**
Savage U.S.A. 47°27N 104°21W **76 C11**
Savage I. = Niue ✷
  Pac. Oc. 19°2S 169°54W **65 J11**
Savage River Australia 41°31S 145°14E **63 G4**
Savai'i Samoa 13°28S 172°24W **59 b**
Savalou Benin 7°57N 1°58E **52 G6**
Savanna U.S.A. 42°5N 90°8W **80 D8**
Savanna-la-Mar Jamaica 18°10N 78°10W **88 a**
Savannah Ga., U.S.A. 32°5N 81°6W **85 E14**
Savannah Mo., U.S.A. 39°56N 94°50W **80 F6**
Savannah Tenn., U.S.A. 35°14N 88°15W **85 D10**
Savannah → U.S.A. 32°2N 80°53W **85 E14**
Savannakhet Laos 16°30N 104°49E **38 D5**
Savant L. Canada 50°16N 90°44W **72 B1**
Savant Lake Canada 50°14N 90°40W **72 B1**
Savantvadi India 15°55N 73°54E **45 G1**
Savanur India 14°59N 75°21E **45 G2**
Savarkundla = Kundla
  India 21°21N 71°25E **42 J4**
Savda India 21°9N 75°56E **44 D2**
Save → Mozam. 21°16S 34°0E **57 B5**
Sāveh Iran 35°2N 50°20E **47 C6**
Savelugu Ghana 9°38N 0°54W **52 G5**
Savo Finland 62°45N 27°30E **8 E22**
Savoie □ France 45°26N 6°25E **20 D7**
Savolax = Savo Finland 62°45N 27°30E **8 E22**
Savona Italy 44°17N 8°30E **20 D8**
Savonlinna Finland 61°52N 28°53E **8 F23**
Savoy = Savoie □ France 45°26N 6°25E **20 D7**
Savur Turkey 37°34N 40°53E **46 B4**
Savusavu Fiji 16°34S 179°15E **59 a**
Savusavu B. Fiji 16°45S 179°15E **59 a**
Savuti Botswana 18°37S 24°5E **56 A3**
Sawa Sawa Madhopur India 26°0N 76°25E **42 G7**
Sawai Indonesia 3°0S 129°5E **37 E7**
Sawai Madhopur India 26°0N 76°25E **42 G7**
Sawaleke Fiji 17°59S 179°18E **59 a**
Sawang Daen Din
  Thailand 17°28N 103°28E **38 D4**
Sawankhalok Thailand 17°19N 99°50E **38 D2**
Sawara Japan 35°55N 140°30E **29 G10**
Sawatch Range U.S.A. 39°0N 106°30W **76 G10**
Sawel Mt. U.K. 54°50N 7°2W **10 B4**
Sawi Thailand 10°14N 99°5E **39 G2**
Sawtooth △ U.S.A. 44°0N 114°50W **76 D6**
Sawtooth Range U.S.A. 44°3N 114°58W **76 D6**
Sawu Indonesia 10°35S 121°50E **37 F6**
Sawu Sea Indonesia 9°30S 121°50E **37 F6**
Saxby → Australia 18°25S 140°53E **62 B3**
Saxmundham U.K. 52°13N 1°30E **13 E9**
Saxony = Sachsen □
  Germany 50°55N 13°10E **16 C7**
Saxony, Lower = Niedersachsen □
  Germany 52°50N 9°0E **16 B5**
Saxton U.S.A. 40°13N 78°15W **82 F6**
Sayabec Canada 48°35N 67°41W **73 C6**
Sayaboury Laos 19°15N 101°45E **38 C3**
Sayán Peru 11°8S 77°12W **92 F3**
Sayan, Vostochnyy Russia 54°0N 96°0E **27 D10**
Sayan, Zapadnyy Russia 52°30N 94°0E **27 D10**
Sayanogorsk Russia 53°5N 91°23E **27 D10**
Saydā Lebanon 33°35N 35°25E **48 B4**
Sayhandulaan = Öldziyt
  Mongolia 44°40N 109°1E **32 B5**
Sayhūt Yemen 15°12N 51°10E **49 D5**
Saylac Somalia 11°21N 43°30E **49 E3**
Saynshand = Buyant-Uhaa
  Mongolia 44°55N 110°11E **32 B6**
Sayre Okla., U.S.A. 35°18N 99°38W **84 D5**
Sayre Pa., U.S.A. 41°59N 76°32W **83 E8**

Sayreville U.S.A. 40°28N 74°22W **83 F10**
Sayula Mexico 19°52N 103°36W **86 D4**
Say'ūn Yemen 15°56N 48°47E **49 D4**
Sayward Canada 50°21N 125°55W **70 C3**
Sazanit Albania 40°30N 19°20E **23 D8**
Sázava → Czech Rep. 49°53N 14°24E **16 D8**
Sazin Pakistan 35°35N 73°30E **43 B5**
Scafell Pike U.K. 54°27N 3°14W **12 C4**
Scalloway U.K. 60°9N 1°17W **11 A7**
Scalpay U.K. 57°18N 6°0W **11 D3**
Scandia Canada 50°20N 112°2W **70 C6**
Scandicci Italy 43°45N 11°11E **22 C4**
Scandinavia Europe 64°0N 12°0E **8 E15**
Scapa Flow U.K. 58°53N 3°3W **11 C5**
Scappoose U.S.A. 45°45N 122°53W **78 E4**
Scarba U.K. 56°11N 5°43W **11 E3**
Scarborough
  Trin. & Tob. 11°11N 60°42W **93 J16**
Scarborough U.K. 54°17N 0°24W **12 C7**
Scariff I. Ireland 51°44N 10°15W **10 E1**
Scarp U.K. 58°1N 7°8W **11 C1**
Scebeli = Shabeelle →
  Somalia 2°0N 44°0E **49 G3**
Schaffhausen Switz. 47°42N 8°39E **20 C8**
Schagen Neths. 52°49N 4°48E **15 B4**
Schaghticoke U.S.A. 42°54N 73°35W **83 D11**
Schefferville Canada 54°48N 66°50W **73 B6**
Schelde → Belgium 51°15N 4°16E **15 C4**
Schell Creek Ra. U.S.A. 39°25N 114°40W **76 G6**
Schellsburg U.S.A. 40°3N 78°39W **82 F6**
Schenectady U.S.A. 42°49N 73°57W **83 D11**
Schenevus U.S.A. 42°33N 74°50W **83 D10**
Schiedam Neths. 51°55N 4°25E **15 C4**
Schiermonnikoog Neths. 53°30N 6°15E **15 A6**
Schiermonnikoog △
  Neths. 53°30N 6°15E **15 A6**
Schio Italy 45°43N 11°21E **22 B4**
Schleiden Germany 50°32N 6°27E **15 C6**
Schleswig U.S.A. 42°9N 95°3W **80 D6**
Schleswig Germany 54°31N 9°34E **16 A5**
Schleswig-Holstein □
  Germany 54°30N 9°30E **16 A5**
Schœlcher Martinique 14°36N 61°7W **88 c**
Schoharie U.S.A. 42°40N 74°19W **83 D10**
Schoharie Cr. →
  U.S.A. 42°57N 74°18W **83 D10**
Schokland Neths. 52°38N 5°46E **15 B5**
Scholls U.S.A. 45°24N 122°56W **78 E4**
Schouten I. Australia 42°20S 148°20E **63 G4**
Schouten Is. = Supiori
  Indonesia 1°0S 136°0E **37 E9**
Schouwen Neths. 51°43N 3°45E **15 C3**
Schreiber Canada 48°45N 87°20W **72 C2**
Schroffenstein Namibia 27°11S 18°42E **56 C2**
Schroon Lake U.S.A. 43°50N 73°46W **83 C11**
Schuler Canada 50°20N 110°6W **71 C6**
Schumacher Canada 48°30N 81°16W **72 C3**
Schurz U.S.A. 38°57N 118°49W **76 G4**
Schuyler U.S.A. 41°27N 97°4W **80 E5**
Schuylerville U.S.A. 43°6N 73°35W **83 C11**
Schuylkill → U.S.A. 39°53N 75°12W **83 G9**
Schuylkill Haven U.S.A. 40°37N 76°11W **83 F8**
Schwäbische Alb Germany 48°20N 9°30E **16 D5**
Schwaner, Pegunungan
  Indonesia 1°0S 112°30E **36 E4**
Schwarzrand Namibia 25°37S 16°50E **56 C2**
Schwarzwald Germany 48°30N 8°20E **16 D5**
Schwatka Mts. U.S.A. 67°20N 156°30W **74 B8**
Schwedt Germany 53°3N 14°16E **16 B8**
Schweinfurt Germany 50°3N 10°14E **16 C6**
Schweizer-Reneke
  S. Africa 27°11S 25°18E **56 C4**
Schweiz = Switzerland ■
  Europe 46°30N 8°0E **20 C8**
Schwenningen = Villingen-
  Schwenningen Germany 48°3N 8°26E **16 D5**
Schwerin Germany 53°36N 11°22E **16 B6**
Schwyz Switz. 47°2N 8°39E **20 C8**
Sciacca Italy 37°31N 13°3E **22 F5**
Scilla Italy 38°15N 15°43E **22 E6**
Scilly, Isles of U.K. 49°56N 6°22W **13 H1**
Scioto → U.S.A. 38°44N 83°1W **81 F12**
Scituate U.S.A. 42°12N 70°44W **83 D14**
Scobey U.S.A. 48°47N 105°25W **76 B11**
Scone Australia 32°5S 150°52E **63 E5**
Scone U.K. 56°25N 3°24W **11 E5**
Scoresbysund = Ittoqqortoormiit
  Greenland 70°20N 23°0W **4 B6**
Scotia Calif., U.S.A. 40°29N 124°6W **76 F1**
Scotia N.Y., U.S.A. 42°50N 73°58W **83 D11**
Scotia Sea Antarctica 56°5S 56°0W **5 B18**
Scotland Canada 43°1N 80°22W **82 C4**
Scotland □ U.K. 57°0N 4°0W **11 E5**
Scott Antarctica 77°0S 166°45E **5 D11**
Scott, C. Australia 13°30S 129°49E **60 B4**
Scott City U.S.A. 38°29N 100°54W **80 F3**
Scott Glacier Antarctica 66°15S 100°5E **5 C8**
Scott I. Antarctica 67°0S 179°0E **5 C11**
Scott Is. Canada 50°48N 128°40W **70 C3**
Scott L. Canada 59°55N 106°18W **71 B7**
Scott Reef Australia 14°0S 121°50E **60 B3**
Scottburgh S. Africa 30°15S 30°47E **57 D5**
Scottdale U.S.A. 40°6N 79°35W **82 F5**
Scottish Borders □ U.K. 55°35N 2°50W **11 F6**
Scotts Valley U.S.A. 37°3N 122°1W **78 H4**
Scottsbluff U.S.A. 41°52N 103°40E **80 E2**
Scottsboro U.S.A. 34°40N 86°2W **85 D11**
Scottsdale Australia 41°9S 147°31E **63 G4**
Scottsdale U.S.A. 33°40N 111°53W **77 K8**
Scottsville Ky., U.S.A. 36°45N 86°11W **80 G10**
Scottsville N.Y., U.S.A. 43°2N 77°47W **82 C7**
Scottville U.S.A. 43°58N 86°17W **80 D10**
Scranton U.S.A. 41°25N 75°40W **83 E9**
Scugog, L. Canada 44°10N 78°55W **82 B6**
Scunthorpe U.K. 53°36N 0°39W **12 D7**
Scutari = Shkodër Albania 42°4N 19°32E **23 C8**
Sea Is. U.S.A. 31°15N 81°10W **85 F14**
Seabrook, L. Australia 30°55S 119°40E **61 F2**
Seaford U.K. 50°47N 0°7E **13 G8**
Seaford U.S.A. 38°39N 75°37W **81 F16**
Seaforth Australia 20°55S 148°57E **62 b**

Seaforth Canada 43°35N 81°25W **82 C3**
Seaforth, L. U.K. 57°52N 6°36W **11 D2**
Seagraves U.S.A. 32°57N 102°34W **84 E3**
Seaham U.K. 54°50N 1°20W **12 C6**
Seal → Canada 59°4N 94°48W **71 B10**
Seal L. Canada 54°20N 61°30W **73 B7**
Sealy U.S.A. 29°47N 96°9W **84 G6**
Searchlight U.S.A. 35°28N 114°55W **79 K12**
Searcy U.S.A. 35°15N 91°44W **84 D9**
Searles L. U.S.A. 35°44N 117°21W **79 K9**
Seascale U.K. 54°24N 3°29W **12 C4**
Seaside Calif., U.S.A. 36°37N 121°50W **78 J5**
Seaside Oreg., U.S.A. 46°0N 123°56W **78 E3**
Seaspray Australia 38°25S 147°15E **63 F4**
Seattle U.S.A. 47°36N 122°19W **78 C4**
Seattle-Tacoma Int. ✈ (SEA)
  U.S.A. 47°27N 122°18W **78 C4**
Seba Indonesia 10°29S 121°50E **37 F6**
Sebago L. U.S.A. 43°52N 70°34W **83 C14**
Sebago Lake U.S.A. 43°51N 70°34W **83 C14**
Sebastián Vizcaíno, B.
  Mexico 28°0N 114°30W **86 B2**
Sebastopol = Sevastopol
  Ukraine 44°35N 33°30E **19 F5**
Sebastopol U.S.A. 38°24N 122°49W **78 G4**
Sebewaing U.S.A. 43°44N 83°27W **81 D12**
Sebha = Sabhā Libya 27°9N 14°29E **53 C8**
Şebinkarahisar Turkey 40°22N 38°28E **46 B3**
Sebring Fla., U.S.A. 27°30N 81°27W **85 H14**
Sebring Ohio, U.S.A. 40°55N 81°2W **82 F3**
Sebringville Canada 43°24N 81°4W **82 C3**
Sebta = Ceuta N. Afr. 35°52N 5°18W **21 E3**
Sebuku Indonesia 3°30S 116°25E **36 E5**
Sechelt Canada 49°25N 123°42W **70 D4**
Sechura, Desierto de Peru 6°0S 80°30W **92 E2**
Secretary I. N.Z. 45°15S 166°56E **59 F1**
Secunderabad India 17°28N 78°30E **44 F4**
Security U.S.A. 38°45N 104°45W **76 G11**
Sedalia U.S.A. 38°42N 93°14W **80 F7**
Sedam India 17°11N 77°17E **44 F4**
Sedan France 49°43N 4°57E **20 B6**
Sedan U.S.A. 37°8N 96°11W **80 G5**
Sedbergh U.K. 54°20N 2°31W **12 C5**
Seddon N.Z. 41°40S 174°7E **59 D5**
Seddonville N.Z. 41°33S 172°1E **59 D4**
Sedé Boqér Israel 30°52N 34°47E **48 E3**
Sedeh Fārs, Iran 30°45N 52°11E **47 D7**
Sedeh Khorāsān, Iran 33°20N 59°14E **47 C8**
Sederot Israel 31°32N 34°37E **48 D3**
Sédhiou Senegal 12°44N 15°30W **52 F2**
Sedley Canada 50°10N 104°0W **71 C8**
Sedona U.S.A. 34°52N 111°46W **77 J8**
Sedova, Pik Russia 73°29N 54°58E **26 B6**
Sedro-Woolley U.S.A. 48°30N 122°14W **78 B4**
Seeheim Namibia 26°50S 17°45E **56 C2**
Seeis Namibia 22°29S 17°39E **56 B2**
Seekoei → S. Africa 30°18S 25°1E **56 E4**
Seeley's Bay Canada 44°29N 76°14W **83 B8**
Seemandhra = Andhra Pradesh □
  India 18°0N 79°0E **44 F4**
Seferihisar Turkey 38°10N 26°50E **23 E12**
Sefophe Botswana 22°11S 27°58E **57 B4**
Seg-ozero Russia 63°20N 33°46E **18 B5**
Segamat Malaysia 2°30N 102°50E **39 L4**
Segamat Indonesia 1°24S 130°58E **37 E8**
Segezha Russia 63°44N 34°19E **18 B5**
Ségou Mali 13°30N 6°16W **52 F4**
Segovia = Coco →
  Cent. Amer. 15°0N 83°8W **88 D3**
Segovia Spain 40°57N 4°10W **21 B3**
Segre → Spain 41°40N 0°43E **21 B6**
Seguam I. U.S.A. 52°19N 172°30W **74 E5**
Séguéla Ivory C. 7°55N 6°40W **52 G4**
Seguin U.S.A. 29°34N 97°58W **84 G6**
Segundo → Argentina 30°53S 62°44W **94 C3**
Segura → Spain 38°3N 0°44W **21 C5**
Seh Konj, Kūh-e Iran 30°6N 57°30E **47 D8**
Seh Qal'eh Iran 33°40N 58°24E **47 C8**
Sehitwa Botswana 20°30S 22°30E **56 B3**
Sehlabathebe △ Lesotho 29°53S 29°7E **57 C4**
Sehore India 23°10N 77°5E **42 H7**
Sehwan Pakistan 26°28N 67°53E **42 F2**
Seikan Tunnel Japan 41°28N 140°10E **28 D10**
Seil U.K. 56°18N 5°38W **11 E3**
Seiland Norway 70°25N 23°15E **8 A20**
Seiling U.S.A. 36°9N 98°56W **84 C5**
Seinäjoki Finland 62°40N 22°51E **8 E20**
Seine → France 49°26N 0°26E **20 B4**
Seistan = Sīstān Asia 30°50N 61°0E **47 D9**
Seistan, Daryācheh-ye = Sīstān,
  Daryācheh-ye Iran 31°0N 61°0E **47 D9**
Seitseminen △ Finland 61°55N 23°30E **8 F20**
Sejong S. Korea 36°35N 127°15E **33 F14**
Sekayu Indonesia 2°51S 103°51E **36 E2**
Sekondi-Takoradi Ghana 4°58N 1°45W **52 H5**
Sekudai Malaysia 1°32N 103°39E **39 d**
Sekuma Botswana 24°36S 23°50E **56 C3**
Selah U.S.A. 46°39N 120°32W **76 C3**
Selama Malaysia 5°12N 100°42E **39 K3**
Selangor □ Malaysia 3°20N 101°30E **39 L3**
Selaru Indonesia 8°9S 131°0E **37 F8**
Selatan, Selat Malaysia 5°15N 100°20E **39 c**
Selawik U.S.A. 66°30N 160°45W **74 B7**
Selby U.K. 53°47N 1°5W **12 D6**
Selby U.S.A. 45°31N 100°2W **80 C3**
Selçuk Turkey 37°56N 27°22E **23 F12**
Selden U.S.A. 39°33N 100°34W **80 F3**
Sele → Italy 40°29N 14°56E **22 D6**
Selebi-Phikwe Botswana 21°58S 27°48E **57 B4**
Selemdzha → Russia 51°42N 128°53E **27 D13**
Selenga = Selenge Mörön →
  Asia 52°16N 106°16E **30 A10**
Selenge Mörön → Asia 52°16N 106°16E **30 A10**
Seletan, Tanjung
  Indonesia 4°10S 114°40E **36 E4**
Seletin Sudan 15°10N 32°15E **53 E12**
Selibabi Mauritania 15°10N 12°15W **52 E3**
Seligman U.S.A. 35°20N 112°53W **77 J7**
Selinda Spillway
  Botswana 18°35S 23°10E **56 A3**

Selinsgrove *U.S.A.* 40°48N 76°52W **82** F8
Selkirk *Man., Canada* 50°10N 96°55W **71** C9
Selkirk *Ont., Canada* 42°49N 79°56W **82** D5
Selkirk *U.K.* 55°33N 2°50W **11** F6
Selkirk I. = Horse I.
　Canada 53°20N 99°6W **71** C9
Selkirk Mts. *Canada* 51°15N 117°40W **68** G8
Sellafield *U.K.* 54°25N 3°29W **12** C4
Sells *U.S.A.* 31°55N 111°53W **77** L8
Selma *Ala., U.S.A.* 32°25N 87°1W **85** E11
Selma *Calif., U.S.A.* 36°34N 119°37W **78** J7
Selma *N.C., U.S.A.* 35°32N 78°17W **85** D15
Selmer *U.S.A.* 35°10N 88°36W **85** D10
Selpele *Indonesia* 0°1S 130°5E **37** E8
Selsey Bill *U.K.* 50°43N 0°47W **13** G7
Seltso *Russia* 53°22N 34°4E **18** D5
Selu *Indonesia* 7°32S 130°55E **37** F8
Selva *Argentina* 29°50S 62°0W **94** B3
Selva Lancandona = Montes
　Azules △ *Mexico* 16°21N 91°3W **87** D6
Selvagens, Ilhas *Madeira* 30°5N 15°55W **52** B2
Selvas *Brazil* 6°30S 67°0W **92** E5
Selwyn L. *Canada* 60°0N 104°30W **71** B8
Selwyn Mts. *Canada* 63°0N 130°0W **68** E5
Selwyn Ra. *Australia* 21°10S 140°0E **62** C3
Seman → *Albania* 40°47N 19°30E **23** D8
Semarang *Indonesia* 7°0S 110°26E **37** G14
Semarapura = Klungkung
　Indonesia 8°32S 115°24E **37** K18
Sembung *Indonesia* 8°28S 115°11E **37** J18
Semeru *Indonesia* 8°4S 112°55E **37** H15
Semitau *Indonesia* 0°29N 111°57E **36** D4
Semmering P. *Austria* 47°41N 15°45E **16** E8
Semnán *Iran* 35°40N 53°23E **47** C7
Semnán □ *Iran* 36°0N 54°0E **47** C7
Semporna *Malaysia* 4°30N 118°33E **37** D5
Semuda *Indonesia* 2°51S 112°58E **36** E4
Sen → *Cambodia* 12°32N 104°28E **38** F5
Sená *Iran* 31°40N 47°0E **47** D6
Sena Madureira *Brazil* 9°5S 68°45W **92** E5
Senador Pompeu *Brazil* 5°40S 39°20W **93** E11
Senang, Pulau *Singapore* 1°11N 103°52E **39** d
Senanga *Zambia* 16°7S 23°16E **55** H4
Senatobia *U.S.A.* 34°37N 89°58W **85** D10
Sendai = Satsuma-Sendai
　Japan 31°50N 130°20E **29** J5
Sendai *Japan* 38°15N 140°53E **28** E10
Sendai-Wan *Japan* 38°15N 141°0E **28** E10
Sendhwa *India* 21°41N 75°6E **42** J6
Sendurjana *India* 21°32N 78°17E **44** D4
Seneca *U.S.A.* 34°41N 82°57W **85** D13
Seneca Falls *U.S.A.* 42°55N 76°48W **83** D8
Seneca L. *U.S.A.* 42°40N 76°54W **82** D8
Senecaville L. *U.S.A.* 39°55N 81°25W **82** G3
Senegal ■ *W. Afr.* 14°30N 14°30W **52** F2
Senegal → *W. Afr.* 15°48N 16°32W **52** E2
Senegambia *Africa* 12°45N 12°0W **50** E2
Senekal *S. Africa* 28°20S 27°36E **57** C4
Senge Khambab = Indus →
　Pakistan 24°20N 67°47E **42** G2
Senggigi *Indonesia* 8°29S 116°2E **37** J19
Senhor-do-Bonfim
　Brazil 10°30S 40°10W **93** F10
Senigállia *Italy* 43°43N 13°13E **22** C5
Senj *Croatia* 45°0N 14°58E **16** F8
Senja *Norway* 69°25N 17°30E **8** B17
Senkaku-Shotō
　E. China Sea 25°45N 123°30E **29** M1
Senlis *France* 49°13N 2°35E **20** B5
Senmonorom *Cambodia* 12°27N 107°12E **38** F6
Senneterre *Canada* 48°25N 77°15W **72** C4
Seno *Laos* 16°35N 104°50E **38** D5
Senqu = Orange →
　S. Africa 28°41S 16°28E **56** C2
Sens *France* 48°11N 3°15E **20** B5
Senta *Serbia* 45°55N 20°3E **23** B9
Sentinel *U.S.A.* 32°52N 113°13W **77** K7
Senwabarana *S. Africa* 23°17S 29°7E **57** B4
Seo de Urgel = La Seu d'Urgell
　Spain 42°22N 1°23E **21** A6
Seogwipo *S. Korea* 33°13N 126°34E **33** H14
Seohara *India* 29°15N 78°33E **43** E8
Seonath → *India* 21°44N 82°28E **43** J10
Seondha *India* 26°9N 78°48E **43** F8
Seongnam *S. Korea* 37°26N 127°8E **33** F14
Seoni *India* 22°5N 79°30E **43** H8
Seoni Malwa *India* 22°27N 77°28E **42** H8
Seonsan *S. Korea* 36°14N 128°17E **33** F15
Seoriuarayan *India* 21°45N 82°34E **44** D6
Seosan *S. Korea* 36°47N 126°27E **33** F14
Sepang *Malaysia* 2°49N 101°44E **39** L3
Sepīdān *Iran* 30°20N 52°5E **47** D7
Sepo-ri *N. Korea* 38°57N 127°25E **33** E14
Sepone *Laos* 16°45N 106°13E **38** D6
Sept-Îles *Canada* 50°13N 66°22W **73** B6
Sequim *U.S.A.* 48°5N 123°6W **78** B3
Sequoia △ *U.S.A.* 36°30N 118°30W **78** J8
Seraing *Belgium* 50°35N 5°32E **15** D5
Seram *Indonesia* 3°10S 129°0E **37** E7
Seram Sea *Indonesia* 2°30S 128°30E **37** E7
Serampore = Shrirampur
　India 22°44N 88°21E **43** H13
Serang *Indonesia* 6°8S 106°10E **37** G12
Serasan *Indonesia* 2°29N 109°4E **36** D3
Serbia ■ *Europe* 43°20N 20°0E **23** B9
Serbia ■ *Europe* 43°20N 20°0E **23** B9
Serdar *Turkmenistan* 39°4N 56°23E **47** B8
Serdobsk *Russia* 52°28N 44°10E **18** D7
Seremban *Malaysia* 2°43N 101°53E **39** L3
Sereth = Siret →
　Romania 45°24N 28°1E **17** F14

Sergeya Kirova, Ostrova
　Russia 77°30N 89°0E **27** B10
Sergino *Russia* 62°25N 65°12E **26** C7
Sergipe □ *Brazil* 10°30S 37°30W **93** F11
Sergiyev Posad *Russia* 56°20N 38°10E **18** C6
Serhetabat *Turkmenistan* 35°20N 62°18E **47** C9
Seria *Brunei* 4°37N 114°23E **36** D4
Serian *Malaysia* 1°10N 110°31E **36** D4
Sérigny → *Canada* 56°47N 66°0W **73** A6
Seringapatam Reef
　Australia 13°38S 122°5E **60** B3
Seririt *Indonesia* 8°12S 114°56E **37** J17
Serkout *Algeria* 23°56N 6°47E **52** D7
Sermata *Indonesia* 8°15S 128°50E **37** F7
Sermersuaq *Greenland* 79°30N 62°0W **69** B19
Serov *Russia* 59°29N 60°35E **18** C11
Serowe *Botswana* 22°25S 26°43E **56** B4
Serpentine Lakes
　Australia 28°30S 129°10E **61** E4
Serpent's Mouth = Sierpe, Bocas de
　la *Venezuela* 10°0N 61°30W **93** L15
Serpukhov *Russia* 54°55N 37°28E **18** D6
Serra do Navio *Brazil* 0°59N 52°3W **93** C8
Serranía San Luís △
　Paraguay 23°35S 57°22W **94** A4
Serranía San Rafael △
　Paraguay 26°30S 56°0W **95** B4
Serres *Greece* 41°5N 23°31E **23** D10
Serrezuela *Argentina* 30°40S 65°20W **94** C2
Serrinha *Brazil* 11°39S 39°0W **93** F11
Sertanópolis *Brazil* 23°4S 51°2W **95** A5
Sertar *China* 32°20N 100°41E **34** A3
Serua *Indonesia* 6°18S 130°1E **37** F8
Serui *Indonesia* 1°53S 136°10E **37** E9
Serule *Botswana* 21°57S 27°20E **56** B4
Sesepe *Indonesia* 1°30S 127°59E **37** E7
Sesfontein *Namibia* 19°7S 13°39E **56** A1
Sesheke *Zambia* 17°29S 24°13E **56** A3
Setana *Japan* 42°26N 139°51E **28** C9
Sète *France* 43°25N 3°42E **20** E5
Sete Lagoas *Brazil* 19°27S 44°16W **93** G10
Seti → *Nepal* 28°59N 81°8E **43** E9
Sétif *Algeria* 36°9N 5°26E **52** A7
Seto *Japan* 35°14N 137°6E **29** G8
Setonaikai *Japan* 34°20N 133°30E **29** G6
Setonaikai △ *Japan* 34°15N 133°15E **29** G6
Settat *Morocco* 33°0N 7°40W **52** B4
Setting L. *Canada* 55°0N 98°38W **71** C9
Settle *U.K.* 54°5N 2°16W **12** C5
Settlement, The
　Br. Virgin Is. 18°43N 64°22W **89** e
Settlers *S. Africa* 25°2S 28°30E **57** C4
Setúbal *Portugal* 38°30N 8°58W **21** C1
Setúbal, B. de *Portugal* 38°40N 8°56W **21** C1
Seul, Lac *Canada* 50°20N 92°30W **72** B1
Sevan, Ozero = Sevana Lich
　Armenia 40°30N 45°20E **46** A5
Sevana Lich *Armenia* 40°30N 45°20E **46** A5
Sevastopol *Ukraine* 44°35N 33°30E **19** F5
Seven Sisters *Canada* 54°56N 128°10W **70** C3
Severn → *Canada* 56°2N 87°36W **72** A2
Severn → *U.K.* 51°35N 2°40W **13** F5
Severnaya Zemlya *Russia* 79°0N 100°0E **27** B11
Severnyye Uvaly *Russia* 60°0N 50°0E **18** C8
Severo-Kurilsk *Russia* 50°40N 156°8E **27** D16
Severo-Yeniseyskiy
　Russia 60°22N 93°1E **27** C10
Severo-Zapadnyy □ *Russia* 65°0N 40°0E **26** C4
Severobaykalsk *Russia* 55°39N 109°19E **27** D11
Severodvinsk *Russia* 64°27N 39°58E **18** B6
Severomorsk *Russia* 69°5N 33°27E **8** B25
Severouralsk *Russia* 60°9N 59°57E **18** B10
Seversk *Russia* 56°36N 84°49E **26** D9
Sevier → *U.S.A.* 39°4N 113°6W **76** G7
Sevier Desert *U.S.A.* 39°40N 112°45W **76** G7
Sevier L. *U.S.A.* 38°54N 113°9W **76** G7
Sevilla *Spain* 37°23N 5°58W **21** D2
Seville = Sevilla *Spain* 37°23N 5°58W **21** D2
Sevlievo *Bulgaria* 43°2N 25°6E **23** C11
Sewani *India* 28°58N 75°39E **42** E6
Seward *Alaska, U.S.A.* 60°7N 149°27W **68** E2
Seward *Nebr., U.S.A.* 40°55N 97°6W **80** E5
Seward *Pa., U.S.A.* 40°25N 79°1W **82** F5
Seward Peninsula *U.S.A.* 65°30N 166°0W **74** B6
Sewell *Chile* 34°10S 70°23W **94** C1
Sewer *Indonesia* 5°53S 134°40E **37** F8
Sewickley *U.S.A.* 40°32N 80°12W **82** F4
Sexsmith *Canada* 55°21N 118°47W **70** B5
Seychelles ■ *Ind. Oc.* 5°0S 56°0E **55** b
Seyðisfjörður *Iceland* 65°16N 13°57W **8** D7
Seydişehir *Turkey* 37°25N 31°51E **19** G5
Seydvān *Iran* 38°34N 45°2E **46** B5
Seyhan → *Turkey* 36°43N 34°53E **46** B2
Seym → *Ukraine* 51°27N 32°34E **19** D5
Seymour *Australia* 37°2S 145°10E **63** F4
Seymour *S. Africa* 32°33S 26°46E **57** D4
Seymour *Conn., U.S.A.* 41°24N 73°4W **83** E11
Seymour *Ind., U.S.A.* 38°58N 85°53W **81** F11
Seymour *Tex., U.S.A.* 33°35N 99°16W **84** E5
Sfântu Gheorghe
　Romania 45°52N 25°48E **17** F13
Sfax *Tunisia* 34°49N 10°48E **53** B8
Sha Tau Kok *China* 22°33N 114°13E **31** a
Sha Xi → *China* 26°35N 118°0E **35** D11
Sha Xian *China* 26°23N 117°45E **35** D11
Shaanxi □ *China* 35°0N 109°0E **32** G5
Shaba = Katanga □
　Dem. Rep. of the Congo 8°0S 25°0E **54** F5
Shabeelle → *Somalia* 2°0N 44°0E **49** G3
Shabogamo L. *Canada* 53°15N 66°30W **73** B6
Shabunda
　Dem. Rep. of the Congo 2°40S 27°16E **54** E5
Shache *China* 38°20N 77°10E **30** D4
Shackleton Fracture Zone
　S. Ocean 60°0S 60°0W **5** B18
Shackleton Ice Shelf
　Antarctica 66°0S 100°0E **5** C8
Shackleton Inlet *Antarctica* 83°0S 160°0E **5** E11
Shādegān *Iran* 30°40N 48°38E **47** D6

Shadi *China* 26°7N 114°47E **35** D10
Shadi *India* 33°24N 77°14E **43** C7
Shadrinsk *Russia* 56°5N 63°32E **26** D7
Shadyside *U.S.A.* 39°58N 80°45W **82** G4
Shafter *U.S.A.* 35°30N 119°16W **79** K7
Shaftesbury *U.K.* 51°0N 2°11W **13** F5
Shaftsbury *U.S.A.* 43°0N 73°11W **83** D11
Shagram *Pakistan* 36°24N 72°20E **43** A5
Shah Alam *Malaysia* 3°5N 101°32E **39** L3
Shah Alizai *Pakistan* 29°25N 66°33E **42** E2
Shah Bunder *Pakistan* 24°13N 67°56E **42** G2
Shahabad *Karnataka, India* 17°10N 76°54E **44** F3
Shahabad *Punjab, India* 30°10N 76°55E **42** D7
Shahabad *Raj., India* 25°15N 77°11E **42** G7
Shahabad *Ut. P., India* 27°36N 79°56E **43** F8
Shahada *India* 21°33N 74°30E **44** D2
Shahadpur *Pakistan* 25°55N 68°35E **42** G3
Shahapur *India* 15°50N 74°34E **45** G2
Shahbā' *Syria* 32°52N 36°38E **48** C5
Shahdād *Iran* 30°30N 57°40E **47** D8
Shahdād, Namakzār-e
　Iran 30°20N 58°20E **47** D8
Shahdadkot *Pakistan* 27°50N 67°55E **42** F2
Shahdol *India* 23°19N 81°26E **43** H9
Shahe *China* 37°0N 114°32E **32** F8
Shahganj *India* 26°3N 82°44E **43** F10
Shahgarh *India* 27°15N 69°50E **42** F3
Shahid Rajaee Port = Bandar
　Shahid Rajaee *Iran* 27°7N 56°4E **47** E8
Shāhīn Shahr *Iran* 32°49N 51°32E **47** C6
Shahjahanpur *India* 27°54N 79°57E **43** F8
Shahpur = Salmās *Iran* 38°11N 44°47E **46** B5
Shahpur *Karnataka, India* 16°40N 76°48E **44** F3
Shahpur *Mad. P., India* 22°12N 77°58E **42** H7
Shahpur *Baluchistan,
　Pakistan* 28°46N 68°27E **42** E3
Shahpur *Punjab, Pakistan* 32°17N 72°26E **42** C5
Shahpur Chakar *Pakistan* 26°9N 68°39E **42** F3
Shahpura *Mad. P., India* 23°10N 80°45E **43** H9
Shahpura *Raj., India* 25°38N 74°56E **42** G6
Shahr-e Bābak *Iran* 30°7N 55°9E **47** D7
Shahr-e Kord *Iran* 32°15N 50°55E **47** C6
Shahr-I Sokhta *Iran* 30°34N 61°21E **47** D9
Shāhrakht *Iran* 33°38N 60°16E **47** C9
Shāhrezā = Qomsheh *Iran* 32°0N 51°55E **47** D6
Shahrig *Pakistan* 30°15N 67°40E **42** D2
Shāhrūd = Emāmrūd *Iran* 36°30N 55°0E **47** B7
Shahukou = China 40°20N 112°18E **32** D7
Shaikhabad *Afghan.* 34°2N 68°45E **42** B3
Shajapur *India* 23°27N 76°21E **42** H7
Shajing *China* 22°44N 113°48E **31** a
Shakargarh *Pakistan* 32°17N 75°10E **42** C6
Shakawe *Botswana* 18°28S 21°49E **56** A3
Shaker Heights *U.S.A.* 41°28N 81°32W **82** E3
Shakhtërsk *Russia* 49°10N 142°8E **27** E15
Shakhty *Russia* 47°40N 40°16E **19** E7
Shakhunya *Russia* 57°40N 46°46E **18** C8
Shaki *Nigeria* 8°41N 3°21E **52** G6
Shakotan-Hantō *Japan* 43°10N 140°30E **28** C10
Shaksam Valley *Asia* 36°0N 76°20E **43** A7
Shallow Lake *Canada* 44°36N 81°5W **82** B3
Shalqar *Kazakhstan* 47°48N 59°39E **26** E6
Shaluli Shan *China* 30°40N 99°55E **34** B2
Shām *Iran* 26°39N 57°21E **47** E8
Shām, Bādiyat ash *Asia* 32°0N 40°0E **46** C3
Shamāl Sīnī □ *Egypt* 30°30N 33°30E **48** E2
Shamattawa *Canada* 55°51N 92°5W **72** A1
Shamattawa → *Canada* 55°1N 85°23W **72** A2
Shamil *Iran* 27°30N 56°55E **47** E8
Shāmkūh *Iran* 35°47N 57°50E **47** C8
Shamli *India* 29°32N 77°18E **42** E7
Shammar, Jabal *Si. Arabia* 27°40N 41°0E **46** E4
Shamo = Gobi *Asia* 44°0N 110°0E **32** C6
Shamo, L. *Ethiopia* 5°45N 37°30E **49** F2
Shamokin *U.S.A.* 40°47N 76°34W **83** F8
Shamrock *Canada* 45°23N 76°50W **83** A8
Shamrock *U.S.A.* 35°13N 100°15W **84** D4
Shan □ *Burma* 21°30N 98°30E **41** J21
Shan Xian *China* 34°50N 116°5E **32** G9
Shanchengzhen *China* 42°20N 125°20E **33** C13
Shandak *Iran* 28°28N 60°27E **47** D9
Shandan *China* 38°45N 101°15E **30** D9
Shandon *U.S.A.* 35°39N 120°23W **78** K6
Shandong □ *China* 36°0N 118°0E **33** G10
Shandong Bandao *China* 37°0N 121°0E **33** F11
Shandur Pass *Pakistan* 36°4N 72°31E **43** A5
Shang Xian = Shangzhou
　China 33°50N 109°58E **32** H5
Shangani *Zimbabwe* 19°41S 29°20E **57** A4
Shangani → *Zimbabwe* 18°41S 27°10E **55** H5
Shangbancheng *China* 40°50N 118°1E **33** D10
Shangcheng *China* 31°47N 115°26E **35** H10
Shangchuan Dao *China* 21°40N 112°50E **35** G9
Shangdu *China* 41°30N 113°30E **32** D7
Shanggao *China* 28°17N 114°55E **35** C10
Shanghai Shi □ *China* 31°0N 121°0E **35** B13
Shanghang *China* 25°2N 116°23E **35** E11
Shanghe *China* 37°20N 117°10E **33** F9
Shanglin *China* 23°27N 108°33E **34** F7
Shangnan *China* 33°32N 110°50E **32** H6
Shangqiu *China* 34°26N 115°36E **32** G8
Shangrao *China* 28°25N 117°59E **35** C11
Shangri-La = Zhongdian
　China 27°48N 99°42E **34** D2
Shangshui *China* 33°42N 114°35E **32** H8
Shangsi *China* 22°8N 107°58E **34** F6
Shangyi *China* 41°4N 113°57E **32** D7
Shangyou *China* 25°48N 114°32E **35** E10
Shangyu *China* 30°0N 120°35E **35** B13
Shangzhou *China* 33°50N 109°58E **32** H5
Shanhetun *China* 44°33N 127°15E **33** B14
Shanklin *U.K.* 50°38N 1°11W **13** G6
Shannon *N.Z.* 40°33S 175°25E **59** D5
Shannon → *Ireland* 52°35N 9°30W **10** D2
Shannon → (SNN) *Ireland* 52°42N 8°57W **10** D3
Shannon, Mouth of the
　Ireland 52°30N 9°55W **10** D2
Shannon △ *Australia* 34°35S 116°25E **61** F2
Shannonbridge *Ireland* 53°17N 8°3W **10** C3

Shansi = Shanxi □ *China* 37°0N 112°0E **32** F7
Shantar, Ostrov Bolshoy
　Russia 55°9N 137°40E **27** D14
Shantipur *India* 23°17N 88°25E **43** H13
Shantou *China* 23°18N 116°40E **35** F11
Shantung = Shandong □
　China 36°0N 118°0E **33** G10
Shanwei *China* 22°48N 115°22E **35** F10
Shanxi □ *China* 37°0N 112°0E **32** F7
Shanyang *China* 33°31N 109°55E **32** H5
Shanyin *China* 39°25N 112°56E **32** E7
Shaodong *China* 27°15N 111°43E **35** D8
Shaoguan *China* 24°48N 113°35E **35** E9
Shaoshan *China* 27°55N 112°33E **35** D9
Shaowu *China* 27°22N 117°28E **35** D11
Shaoxing *China* 30°0N 120°35E **35** C13
Shaoyang *China* 27°14N 111°25E **35** D8
Shap *U.K.* 54°32N 2°40W **12** C5
Shapinsay *U.K.* 59°3N 2°51W **11** B6
Shaqra' *Si. Arabia* 25°15N 45°16E **46** E5
Sharafkhāneh *Iran* 38°11N 45°29E **46** B5
Sharavati → *India* 14°20N 74°25E **45** G2
Sharbot Lake *Canada* 44°46N 76°41W **83** B8
Shari *Japan* 43°55N 144°40E **28** C12
Sharjah = Ash Shāriqah
　U.A.E. 25°23N 55°26E **47** E7
Shark B. *Australia* 25°30S 113°32E **61** E1
Shark Bay △ *Australia* 25°30S 113°30E **61** E1
Sharm el Sheikh *Egypt* 27°53N 34°18E **53** C12
Sharon *Canada* 44°6N 79°26W **82** B5
Sharon *Mass., U.S.A.* 42°7N 71°11W **83** D13
Sharon *Pa., U.S.A.* 41°14N 80°31W **82** E4
Sharon Springs *Kans.,
　U.S.A.* 38°54N 101°45W **80** F3
Sharon Springs *N.Y.,
　U.S.A.* 42°48N 74°37W **83** D10
Sharp Pt. *Australia* 10°58S 142°43E **62** A3
Sharpe L. *Canada* 54°24N 93°40W **72** B1
Sharpsville *U.S.A.* 41°15N 80°29W **82** E4
Sharqi, Al Jabal ash
　Lebanon 33°40N 36°10E **48** B5
Sharqīya, Es Sahrâ esh
　Egypt 27°30N 32°30E **53** C12
Sharya *Russia* 58°22N 45°20E **18** C8
Shashemene *Ethiopia* 7°13N 38°33E **49** F2
Shashi *Botswana* 21°15S 27°27E **57** B4
Shasta, Mt. *U.S.A.* 41°25N 122°12W **76** F2
Shasta L. *U.S.A.* 40°43N 122°25W **76** F2
Shatsky Rise *Pac. Oc.* 34°0N 157°0E **64** D7
Shatt al ʻArab *Asia* 29°57N 48°34E **47** D6
Shaunavon *Canada* 49°35N 108°25W **71** D7
Shaver L. *U.S.A.* 37°9N 119°18W **78** H7
Shaw → *Australia* 20°21S 119°17E **60** D2
Shaw I. *Australia* 20°30S 149°2E **62** b
Shawanaga *Canada* 45°31N 80°17W **82** A4
Shawangunk Mts.
　U.S.A. 41°35N 74°30W **83** E10
Shawano *U.S.A.* 44°47N 88°36W **80** C9
Shawinigan *Canada* 46°35N 72°50W **72** C5
Shawmari, J. ash *Jordan* 30°35N 36°35E **48** E5
Shawnee *U.S.A.* 35°20N 96°55W **84** D6
Shay Gap *Australia* 20°30S 120°10E **60** D3
Shayang *China* 30°42N 112°29E **35** B9
Shaybārā *Si. Arabia* 25°26N 36°47E **46** E3
Shaykh, J. ash *Lebanon* 33°25N 35°50E **48** B4
Shaykh Miskīn *Syria* 32°49N 36°9E **48** C5
Shaykh Saʻd *Iraq* 32°34N 46°17E **46** C5
Shaykh 'Uthmān *Yemen* 12°52N 44°59E **49** E3
Shāzand *Iran* 33°56N 49°24E **47** C6
Shchūchīnsk *Kazakhstan* 52°56N 70°12E **26** D8
She Xian *Anhui, China* 29°50N 118°25E **35** C12
She Xian *Hebei, China* 36°30N 113°40E **32** F7
Shebele = Shabeelle →
　Somalia 2°0N 44°0E **49** G3
Sheboygan *U.S.A.* 43°46N 87°45W **80** D10
Shediac *Canada* 46°14N 64°32W **73** C7
Sheelin, L. *Ireland* 53°48N 7°20W **10** C4
Sheenjek → *U.S.A.* 66°45N 144°33W **74** B11
Sheep Haven *Ireland* 55°11N 7°52W **10** A4
Sheep Range *U.S.A.* 36°35N 115°15W **79** J11
Sheerness *U.K.* 51°26N 0°47E **13** F8
Sheet Harbour *Canada* 44°56N 62°31W **73** D7
Sheffield *U.K.* 53°23N 1°28W **12** D6
Sheffield *Ala., U.S.A.* 34°46N 87°41W **85** D11
Sheffield *Mass., U.S.A.* 42°5N 73°21W **83** D11
Sheffield *Pa., U.S.A.* 41°42N 79°3W **82** E5
Shegaon *India* 20°48N 76°47E **44** D3
Sheikhpura *India* 25°9N 85°53E **43** G11
Shekhupura *Pakistan* 31°42N 73°58E **42** D5
Shekou *China* 22°30N 113°55E **31** a
Shelburne *N.S., Canada* 43°47N 65°20W **73** D6
Shelburne *Ont., Canada* 44°4N 80°15W **82** B4
Shelburne *Vt., U.S.A.* 44°23N 73°14W **83** B11
Shelburne B. *Australia* 11°50S 142°50E **62** A3
Shelburne Falls *U.S.A.* 42°36N 72°45W **83** D12
Shelby *Mich., U.S.A.* 43°37N 86°22W **80** D10
Shelby *Miss., U.S.A.* 33°57N 90°46W **85** E9
Shelby *Mont., U.S.A.* 48°30N 111°51W **76** B8
Shelby *N.C., U.S.A.* 35°17N 81°32W **85** D14
Shelby *Ohio, U.S.A.* 40°53N 82°40W **82** F2
Shelbyville *Ill., U.S.A.* 39°24N 88°48W **80** F9
Shelbyville *Ind., U.S.A.* 39°31N 85°47W **81** F11
Shelbyville *Ky., U.S.A.* 38°13N 85°14W **81** F11
Shelbyville *Tenn., U.S.A.* 35°29N 86°28W **85** D11
Sheldon *U.S.A.* 43°11N 95°51W **80** D6
Sheldrake *Canada* 50°20N 64°51W **73** B7
Shelikhova, Zaliv *Russia* 59°30N 157°0E **27** D16
Shelikof Strait *U.S.A.* 57°30N 155°0W **74** D9
Shell Lakes *Australia* 29°20S 127°30E **61** E4
Shellbrook *Canada* 53°13N 106°24W **71** C7
Shellharbour *Australia* 34°31S 150°51E **63** E5
Shelter I. *U.S.A.* 41°4N 72°20W **83** E12
Shelton *Conn., U.S.A.* 41°19N 73°5W **83** E11
Shelton *Wash., U.S.A.* 47°13N 123°6W **78** C3
Shen Xian *China* 36°15N 115°40E **32** F8
Shenandoah *Iowa, U.S.A.* 40°46N 95°22W **80** E6
Shenandoah *Pa., U.S.A.* 40°49N 76°12W **83** F8
Shenandoah *Va., U.S.A.* 38°29N 78°37W **81** F14
Shenandoah → *U.S.A.* 39°19N 77°44W **81** F15

Shenandoah △ *U.S.A.* 38°35N 78°22W **81** F14
Shenchi *China* 39°8N 112°10E **32** E7
Shencottah *India* 8°59N 77°18E **45** K3
Shendam *Nigeria* 8°49N 9°30E **52** G7
Shendi *Sudan* 16°46N 33°22E **53** E12
Shendurni *India* 20°39N 75°36E **44** D2
Shengfang *China* 39°3N 116°42E **32** E9
Shengzhou *China* 29°35N 120°50E **35** C13
Shenjingzi *China* 44°40N 124°30E **33** B13
Shenmu *China* 38°50N 110°29E **32** E6
Shennongjia *China* 31°43N 110°44E **35** B8
Shenqiu *China* 33°25N 115°5E **32** H8
Shensi = Shaanxi □ *China* 35°0N 109°0E **32** G5
Shenyang *China* 41°48N 123°27E **33** C12
Shenzhen *China* 22°32N 114°5E **35** F10
Shenzhen Bao'an Int. ✈ (SZX)
　China 22°41N 113°49E **31** a
Shenzhen Shuiku *China* 22°34N 114°8E **31** a
Shenzhen Wan *China* 22°27N 113°55E **31** a
Sheo *India* 26°11N 71°15E **42** F4
Sheopur Kalan *India* 25°40N 76°40E **42** G7
Shepetivka *Ukraine* 50°10N 27°10E **17** C14
Shepparton *Australia* 36°23S 145°26E **63** F4
Sheppey, I. of *U.K.* 51°25N 0°48E **13** F8
Shepton Mallet *U.K.* 51°11N 2°33W **13** F5
Sheqi *China* 33°12N 112°57E **32** H7
Sher Qila *Pakistan* 36°7N 74°2E **43** A6
Sherborne *U.K.* 50°57N 2°31W **13** G5
Sherbro I. *S. Leone* 7°30N 12°40W **52** G3
Sherbrooke *N.S., Canada* 45°8N 61°59W **73** C7
Sherbrooke *Qué.,
　Canada* 45°28N 71°57W **83** A13
Sherburne *U.S.A.* 42°41N 75°30W **83** D9
Shergarh *India* 26°20N 72°18E **42** F5
Sherghati *India* 24°34N 84°47E **43** G11
Sheridan *Ark., U.S.A.* 34°19N 92°24W **84** D8
Sheridan *Wyo., U.S.A.* 44°48N 106°58W **76** D10
Sheringham *U.K.* 52°56N 1°13E **12** E9
Sherkin I. *Ireland* 51°28N 9°26W **10** E2
Sherkot *India* 29°22N 78°35E **43** E8
Sherlovaya Gora
　Russia 50°34N 116°15E **27** D12
Sherman *N.Y., U.S.A.* 42°9N 79°35W **82** D5
Sherman *Tex., U.S.A.* 33°38N 96°36W **84** E6
Sherpur *India* 25°34N 83°47E **43** G10
Sherridon *Canada* 55°8N 101°5W **71** B8
Shertallai = Cherthala
　India 9°42N 76°20E **45** K3
Sherwood Forest *U.K.* 53°6N 1°7W **12** D6
Sherwood Park *Canada* 53°31N 113°19W **70** C6
Sheslay → *Canada* 58°48N 132°5W **70** B2
Shethanei L. *Canada* 58°48N 97°50W **71** B9
Shetland □ *U.K.* 60°30N 1°30W **11** A7
Shetland Is. *U.K.* 60°30N 1°30W **11** A7
Shetrunji → *India* 21°19N 72°7E **42** J5
Sheung Shui *China* 22°31N 114°7E **31** a
Shevaroy Hills *India* 11°58N 78°12E **45** J4
Shevgaon *India* 19°21N 75°14E **44** E2
Shey-Phoksundo △
　Nepal 29°30N 82°45E **43** E10
Sheyang *China* 33°48N 120°29E **33** H11
Sheyenne → *U.S.A.* 47°2N 96°50W **80** B5
Shiashkotan, Ostrov
　Russia 48°49N 154°6E **27** E16
Shibām *Yemen* 15°59N 48°36E **49** D4
Shibata *Japan* 37°57N 139°20E **28** E9
Shibecha *Japan* 43°17N 144°36E **28** C12
Shibetsu *Hokkaidō,
　Japan* 43°30N 145°10E **28** C12
Shibetsu *Hokkaidō,
　Japan* 44°10N 142°23E **28** B11
Shibing *China* 27°2N 108°7E **34** D7
Shibogama L. *Canada* 53°35N 88°15W **72** B2
Shibushi *Japan* 31°25N 131°8E **29** J5
Shicheng *China* 26°22N 116°20E **35** D11
Shickshinny *U.S.A.* 41°9N 76°9W **83** E8
Shickshock Mts. = Chic-Chocs,
　Mts. *Canada* 48°55N 66°0W **73** C6
Shidao *China* 36°50N 122°25E **33** F12
Shidian *China* 24°40N 99°5E **34** E2
Shido = Sanuki *Japan* 34°19N 134°10E **29** G7
Shiel, L. *U.K.* 56°48N 5°34W **11** E3
Shield, C. *Australia* 13°20S 136°20E **62** A2
Shieli *Kazakhstan* 44°20N 66°15E **26** E7
Shifang *China* 31°8N 104°10E **34** B5
Shiga □ *Japan* 35°20N 136°0E **29** G8
Shigu *China* 26°51N 99°56E **34** D2
Shiguaigou *China* 40°52N 110°15E **32** D6
Shihchiachuang = Shijiazhuang
　China 38°2N 114°28E **32** E8
Shihezi *China* 44°15N 86°2E **30** C6
Shijiazhuang *China* 38°2N 114°28E **32** E8
Shijiu Hu *China* 31°25N 118°50E **35** B12
Shikarpur *India* 28°17N 78°7E **42** E8
Shikarpur *Pakistan* 27°57N 68°39E **42** F3
Shikohabad *India* 27°6N 78°36E **43** F8
Shikokuchō *Japan* 33°58N 133°33E **29** G6
Shikoku □ *Japan* 33°30N 133°30E **29** H6
Shikoku-Sanchi *Japan* 33°30N 133°30E **29** H6
Shikotan, Ostrov *Asia* 43°47N 146°44E **27** E15
Shikotsu-Ko *Japan* 42°45N 141°25E **28** C10
Shiliguri = Siliguri *India* 26°45N 88°25E **41** F16
Shiliu = Changjiang
　China 19°20N 108°55E **38** C7
Shilka *Russia* 52°0N 115°55E **27** D12
Shilka → *Russia* 53°20N 121°26E **27** D13
Shillelagh *Ireland* 52°45N 6°32W **10** D5
Shillington *U.S.A.* 40°18N 75°58W **83** F9
Shillong *India* 25°35N 91°53E **41** G17
Shilo *West Bank* 32°4N 35°18E **48** C4
Shilong *China* 23°5N 113°52E **35** F9
Shilou *China* 37°0N 110°48E **32** F6
Shimabara *Japan* 32°48N 130°20E **29** H5
Shimada *Japan* 34°49N 138°10E **29** G9
Shimane □ *Japan* 35°0N 132°30E **29** G6
Shimanovsk *Russia* 52°15N 127°30E **27** D13
Shimanto → *Kōchi, Japan* 33°12N 133°0E **29** H6
Shimanto → *Kōchi, Japan* 32°56N 132°56E **29** H6
Shimbiris *Somalia* 10°44N 47°14E **49** E4

Shimen China 29°35N 111°20E 35 C8
Shimenjie China 29°29N 116°48E 35 C11
Shimian China 29°17N 102°23E 34 C4
Shimizu Japan 35°0N 138°30E 29 G9
Shimla India 31°2N 77°9E 42 D7
Shimodate Japan 36°20N 139°55E 29 F9
Shimokita-Hantō Japan 41°20N 141°0E 28 D10
Shimonoseki Japan 33°58N 130°55E 29 H5
Shimpuru Rapids Namibia 17°45S 19°55E 56 A2
Shimsha → India 13°15N 77°10E 45 H3
Shin, L. U.K. 58°5N 4°30W 11 C4
Shinan China 22°44N 109°53E 34 F7
Shinano-Gawa → Japan 36°50N 138°30E 29 F9
Shinās Oman 24°46N 56°28E 47 E8
Shīndand Afghan. 33°12N 62°8E 40 C3
Shinglehouse U.S.A. 41°58N 78°12W 82 E6
Shingū Japan 33°40N 135°55E 29 H7
Shingwidzi S. Africa 23°5S 31°25E 57 C5
Shinjō Japan 38°46N 140°18E 28 E10
Shinkolobwe Dem. Rep. of the Congo 11°10S 26°40E 54 G5
Shinshār Syria 34°36N 36°43E 48 A5
Shinyanga Tanzania 3°45S 33°27E 54 E6
Shio-no-Misaki Japan 33°25N 135°45E 29 H7
Shiogama Japan 38°19N 141°1E 28 E10
Shiojiri Japan 36°6N 137°58E 29 F8
Shipchenski Prokhod Bulgaria 42°45N 25°15E 23 C11
Shiphoirt, L. = Seaforth, L. U.K. 57°52N 6°36W 11 D2
Shiping China 23°45N 102°23E 34 F4
Shippagan Canada 47°45N 64°45W 73 C7
Shippensburg U.S.A. 40°3N 77°31W 82 F7
Shippenville U.S.A. 41°15N 79°28W 82 E5
Shiprock U.S.A. 36°47N 108°41W 77 H9
Shiqian China 27°32N 108°13E 34 D7
Shiqma, N. → Israel 31°37N 34°30E 48 D3
Shiquan China 33°5N 108°15E 34 A7
Shiquan He = Indus → Pakistan 24°20N 67°47E 42 G2
Shīr Kūh Iran 31°39N 54°3E 47 D7
Shira'awh Qatar 25°2N 52°14E 47 E7
Shiragami-Misaki Japan 41°24N 140°12E 28 D10
Shirakawa Fukushima, Japan 37°7N 140°13E 29 F10
Shirakawa Gifu, Japan 36°17N 136°56E 29 F8
Shirane-San Gumma, Japan 36°48N 139°22E 29 F9
Shirane-San Yamanashi, Japan 35°42N 138°9E 29 G9
Shiraoi Japan 42°33N 141°21E 28 C10
Shīrāz Iran 29°42N 52°30E 47 D7
Shire → Africa 17°42S 35°19E 55 H7
Shiren China 41°57N 126°34E 33 D14
Shiretoko △ Japan 44°15N 145°15E 28 B12
Shiretoko-Misaki Japan 44°21N 145°20E 28 B12
Shirinab → Pakistan 30°15N 66°28E 42 D2
Shiriya-Zaki Japan 41°25N 141°30E 28 D10
Shiroishi Japan 38°0N 140°37E 28 E10
Shirol India 16°47N 74°41E 44 F2
Shirpur India 21°21N 74°57E 44 D2
Shirshov Ridge Pac. Oc. 58°0N 170°0E 64 B8
Shīrvān Iran 37°30N 57°50E 47 B8
Shirwa, L. = Chilwa, L. Malawi 15°15S 35°40E 55 H7
Shishaldin Volcano U.S.A. 54°45N 163°58W 74 E7
Shishi China 24°44N 118°37E 35 E12
Shishou China 29°38N 112°22E 35 C9
Shitai China 30°12N 117°25E 35 B11
Shivamogga India 13°57N 75°32E 45 H2
Shivpuri India 25°26N 77°42E 42 G7
Shixian China 43°4S 129°50E 33 C15
Shixing China 24°46N 114°5E 35 E10
Shiyan Guangdong, China 22°42N 113°56E 31 a
Shiyan Hubei, China 32°35N 110°45E 35 A8
Shiyan Shuiku China 22°42N 113°54E 31 a
Shizhu China 29°58N 108°7E 34 C7
Shizuishan China 39°15N 106°50E 34 E4
Shizuoka Japan 34°57N 138°24E 29 G9
Shizuoka □ Japan 35°15N 138°40E 29 G9
Shklov = Shklow Belarus 54°16N 30°15E 17 A16
Shklow Belarus 54°16N 30°15E 17 A16
Shkodër Albania 42°4N 19°32E 23 C8
Shkumbini → Albania 41°2N 19°31E 23 D8
Shmidta, Ostrov Russia 81°0N 91°0E 27 A10
Shō-Gawa → Japan 36°47N 137°4E 29 F8
Shoal L. Canada 49°33N 95°1W 71 D9
Shoal Lake Canada 50°30N 100°35W 71 C8
Shōdo-Shima Japan 34°30N 134°15E 29 G7
Sholapur = Solapur India 17°43N 75°56E 44 F2
Shōmrōn West Bank 32°15N 35°13E 48 C4
Shoranur India 10°46N 76°19E 45 J3
Shorapur India 16°31N 76°48E 45 F3
Shoreham U.S.A. 43°53N 73°18W 83 C11
Shoreham-by-Sea U.K. 50°50N 0°16W 13 G7
Shori → Pakistan 28°29N 69°44E 42 E3
Shorkot Pakistan 30°50N 72°0E 42 D4
Shorkot Road Pakistan 30°47N 72°15E 42 D5
Shortt's I. India 20°47N 87°4E 44 D8
Shoshone Calif., U.S.A. 35°58N 116°16W 79 K10
Shoshone Idaho, U.S.A. 43°14N 114°25W 76 E6
Shoshone L. U.S.A. 44°22N 110°43W 76 D8
Shoshone Mts. U.S.A. 39°20N 117°25W 76 G5
Shoshong Botswana 22°56S 26°31E 56 B4
Shoshoni U.S.A. 43°14N 108°7W 76 E9
Shou Xian China 32°37N 116°42E 35 A11
Shouchang China 29°18N 119°12E 35 C12
Shouguang China 37°52N 118°45E 33 F10
Shouning China 27°27N 119°31E 35 D12
Shouyang China 37°54N 113°8E 32 F7
Show Low U.S.A. 34°15N 110°2W 77 J8
Shqipëria = Albania ■ Europe 41°0N 20°0E 23 D9

Shreveport U.S.A. 32°31N 93°45W 84 E8
Shrewsbury U.K. 52°43N 2°45W 13 E5
Shri Mohangarh India 27°17N 71°18E 42 F4
Shrigonda India 18°37N 74°41E 44 E2
Shrirampur India 22°44N 88°21E 43 H13
Shropshire □ U.K. 52°36N 2°45W 13 E5
Shū Kazakhstan 43°36N 73°42E 26 E8
Shuangbai China 24°42N 101°38E 34 E3
Shuangcheng China 45°20N 126°15E 33 B14
Shuangfeng China 27°29N 112°11E 35 D9
Shuanggou China 34°2N 117°30E 33 G9
Shuangjiang China 23°26N 99°58E 34 F2
Shuangliao China 43°29N 123°30E 33 C12
Shuangshanzi China 40°20N 119°8E 33 D10
Shuangyang China 43°28N 125°40E 33 C13
Shuangyashan China 46°28N 131°5E 31 B15
Shucheng China 31°28N 116°57E 35 B11
Shuiji China 27°13N 118°20E 35 D12
Shujalpur India 23°18N 76°46E 42 H7
Shukpa Kunzang India 34°22N 78°22E 43 B8
Shule China 44°28N 127°0E 33 B14
Shule He → China 39°25N 76°3E 30 D4
Shumagin Is. U.S.A. 55°7N 160°30W 74 D7
Shumen Bulgaria 43°18N 26°55E 23 C12
Shumikha Russia 55°10N 63°15E 26 D7
Shunān Japan 34°3N 131°50E 29 G5
Shunchang China 26°54N 117°48E 35 D11
Shunde China 22°42N 113°14E 35 F9
Shungnak U.S.A. 66°52N 157°9W 74 B8
Shuo Xian = Shuozhou China 39°20N 112°33E 32 E7
Shuozhou China 39°20N 112°33E 32 E7
Shuqrā' Yemen 13°22N 45°44E 49 E4
Shūr → Fārs, Iran 28°30N 55°0E 47 D7
Shūr → Kermān, Iran 30°52N 57°37E 47 D8
Shūr → Yazd, Iran 31°45N 55°15E 47 D7
Shūr Āb Iran 34°23N 51°11E 47 C6
Shūr Gaz Iran 29°10N 59°20E 47 D8
Shūrāb Iran 33°43N 56°29E 47 C8
Shūrjestān Iran 31°24N 52°25E 47 D7
Shurugwi Zimbabwe 19°40S 30°0E 55 H6
Shūsf Iran 31°50N 60°5E 47 D9
Shūshtar Iran 32°0N 48°50E 47 D6
Shuswap L. Canada 50°55N 119°3W 70 C5
Shute Harbour △ Australia 20°17S 148°47E 62 b
Shuyang China 34°10N 118°42E 33 G10
Shūzū Iran 29°52N 54°30E 47 D7
Shwebo Burma 22°30N 95°45E 41 H19
Shwegu Burma 24°15N 96°26E 41 G20
Shweli → Burma 23°45N 96°45E 41 H20
Shyamnagar India 13°21N 92°57E 45 H11
Shymkent Kazakhstan 42°18N 69°36E 26 E7
Shyok India 34°13N 78°12E 43 B8
Shyok → Pakistan 35°13N 75°53E 43 B6
Si Kiang = Xi Jiang → China 22°5N 113°20E 35 F9
Si Lanna △ Thailand 19°17N 99°12E 38 C2
Si Nakarin Res. Thailand 14°35N 99°0E 38 E2
Si-ngan = Xi'an China 34°15N 109°0E 32 G5
Si Phangnga Thailand 9°8N 98°29E 39 H2
Si Prachan Thailand 14°37N 100°9E 38 E3
Si Racha Thailand 13°10N 100°48E 38 F3
Si Sa Ket Thailand 15°8N 104°23E 38 E5
Siachen Glacier Asia 35°20N 77°30E 43 B7
Siahaf → Pakistan 29°3N 68°57E 42 E3
Siahan Range Pakistan 27°30N 64°40E 40 F4
Siak Sri Indrapura Indonesia 0°51N 102°0E 36 D2
Sialkot Pakistan 32°32N 74°30E 42 C6
Siam = Thailand ■ Asia 16°0N 102°0E 38 E4
Sian = Xi'an China 34°15N 109°0E 32 G5
Sian Ka'an ○ Mexico 19°35N 87°40W 87 D7
Siantan Indonesia 3°10N 106°15E 36 D3
Siäreh Iran 28°5N 60°14E 47 D9
Siargao I. Phil. 9°52N 126°3E 37 C7
Siasi Phil. 5°34N 120°50E 37 C6
Siau Indonesia 2°50N 125°25E 37 D7
Šiauliai Lithuania 55°56N 23°15E 9 J20
Siavonga Zambia 16°33S 28°42E 57 A4
Sibâi, Gebel el Egypt 25°45N 34°10E 46 E2
Sibang Indonesia 8°34S 115°13E 37 K18
Sibay Russia 52°42N 58°39E 18 D10
Sibayi, L. S. Africa 27°20S 32°45E 57 C5
Šibenik Croatia 43°48N 15°54E 22 C6
Siberia = Sibirskiy □ Russia 58°0N 90°0E 27 D10
Siberut Indonesia 1°30S 99°0E 36 E1
Sibi Pakistan 29°30N 67°54E 42 E2
Sibirskiy □ Russia 58°0N 90°0E 27 D10
Sibirtsevo Russia 44°12N 132°26E 28 B5
Sibiti Congo 3°38S 13°19E 54 E2
Sibiu Romania 45°45N 24°9E 17 F13
Sibolga Indonesia 1°42N 98°45E 36 D1
Siborongborong Indonesia 2°13N 98°58E 39 L2
Sibsagar = Sivasagar India 27°0N 94°36E 41 F19
Sibu Malaysia 2°18N 111°49E 36 D4
Sibuco Phil. 7°50N 122°45E 37 C6
Sibuguey B. Phil. 7°50N 122°45E 37 C6
Sibut C.A.R. 5°46N 19°10E 54 C3
Sibutu Phil. 4°45N 119°30E 37 D5
Sibutu Passage E. Indies 4°50N 120°0E 37 D6
Sibuyan I. Phil. 12°25N 122°40E 37 B6
Sibuyan Sea Phil. 12°30N 122°20E 37 B6
Sicamous Canada 50°49N 119°0W 70 C5
Siccus → Australia 31°55S 139°17E 63 E2
Sichon Thailand 9°0N 99°54E 39 H2
Sichuan □ China 30°30N 103°0E 34 B5
Sichuan Pendi China 31°0N 105°0E 34 B5
Sicilia Italy 37°30N 14°30E 22 F6
Sicily = Sicilia Italy 37°30N 14°30E 22 F6
Sicily, Str. of Medit. S. 37°35N 11°56E 22 F5
Sico → Honduras 15°58N 84°58W 88 C3
Sicuani Peru 14°21S 71°10W 92 F4
Siddapur India 14°20N 74°53E 45 G2
Siddhapur India 23°56N 72°25E 42 H5

Siddipet India 18°5N 78°51E 44 E4
Sidhauli India 27°17N 80°50E 43 F9
Sidhi India 24°25N 81°53E 43 G9
Sidi-bel-Abbès Algeria 35°13N 0°39W 52 A5
Sidi Ifni Morocco 29°29N 10°12W 52 C3
Sidikalang Indonesia 2°45N 98°19E 39 L2
Sidlaw Hills U.K. 56°32N 3°2W 11 E5
Sidley, Mt. Antarctica 77°2S 126°2W 5 D14
Sidmouth U.K. 50°40N 3°15W 13 G4
Sidmouth, C. Australia 13°25S 143°36E 62 A3
Sidney Canada 48°39N 123°24W 78 B3
Sidney Mont., U.S.A. 47°43N 104°9W 76 C11
Sidney N.Y., U.S.A. 42°19N 75°24W 83 D9
Sidney Nebr., U.S.A. 41°8N 102°59W 80 E2
Sidney Ohio, U.S.A. 40°17N 84°9W 81 E11
Sidney Lanier, L. U.S.A. 34°10N 84°4W 85 D12
Sidoarjo Indonesia 7°27S 112°43E 37 G15
Sidon = Saydā Lebanon 33°35N 35°25E 48 B4
Sidra = Surt Libya 31°11N 16°39E 53 B9
Sidra, G. of = Surt, Khalīj Libya 31°40N 18°30E 53 B9
Siedlce Poland 52°10N 22°20E 17 B12
Sieg → Germany 50°46N 7°6E 16 C4
Siegen Germany 50°51N 8°0E 16 C5
Siem Pang Cambodia 14°7N 106°23E 38 E6
Siem Reap = Siemreab Cambodia 13°20N 103°52E 38 F4
Siemreab Cambodia 13°20N 103°52E 38 F4
Siena Italy 43°19N 11°21E 22 C4
Sieradz Poland 51°37N 18°41E 17 C10
Sierpe, Bocas de la Venezuela 10°0N 61°30W 93 L15
Sierra Blanca U.S.A. 31°11N 105°22W 84 F2
Sierra Blanca Peak U.S.A. 33°23N 105°49W 77 K11
Sierra City U.S.A. 39°34N 120°38W 78 F6
Sierra Colorada Argentina 40°35S 67°50W 96 E3
Sierra de Agalta △ Honduras 15°1N 85°48W 88 C2
Sierra de Bahoruco △ Dom. Rep. 18°10N 71°25W 89 C5
Sierra de La Culata △ Venezuela 8°45N 71°10W 89 E5
Sierra de Lancandón △ Guatemala 16°59N 90°23W 88 C1
Sierra de las Quijadas △ Argentina 32°29S 67°5W 94 C2
Sierra de San Luis △ Venezuela 11°20N 69°43W 89 D6
Sierra de San Pedro Mártir △ Mexico 31°0N 115°30W 86 A1
Sierra Gorda Chile 22°50S 69°15W 94 A2
Sierra Leone ■ W. Afr. 9°0N 12°0E 52 G3
Sierra Madre Mexico 16°0N 93°0W 87 D6
Sierra Madre Occidental Mexico 27°0N 107°0W 86 B3
Sierra Madre Oriental Mexico 25°0N 100°0W 86 C5
Sierra Mojada Mexico 27°18N 103°41W 86 B4
Sierra Nevada Spain 37°3N 3°15W 21 D4
Sierra Nevada U.S.A. 39°0N 120°30W 78 H8
Sierra Nevada △ Venezuela 8°35N 70°45W 89 E5
Sierra Nevada de Santa Marta △ Colombia 10°56N 73°36W 89 D5
Sierra Vista U.S.A. 31°33N 110°18W 77 L8
Sierraville U.S.A. 39°36N 120°22W 78 F6
Sifnos Greece 37°0N 24°45E 23 F11
Sifton Canada 51°21N 100°8W 71 C8
Sifton Pass Canada 57°52N 126°15W 70 B3
Sig Algeria 35°32N 0°12W 52 A5
Sigatoka Fiji 18°8S 177°32E 59 a
Sighetu-Marmaţiei Romania 47°57N 23°52E 17 E12
Sighişoara Romania 46°12N 24°50E 17 E13
Sigiriya Sri Lanka 7°57N 80°45E 45 L5
Sigli Indonesia 5°25N 96°0E 36 C1
Siglufjörður Iceland 66°12N 18°55W 8 C4
Signal Pk. U.S.A. 33°20N 114°2W 79 M12
Signy I. Antarctica 60°43S 45°36W 5 C18
Sigsig Ecuador 3°0S 78°50W 92 D3
Sigüenza Spain 41°3N 2°40W 21 B4
Sigüiri Guinea 11°31N 9°10W 52 F4
Sigulda Latvia 57°10N 24°55E 9 H21
Siguniangshan China 31°15N 103°0E 34 B4
Sihawa India 20°19N 81°55E 44 D5
Sihong China 33°27N 118°16E 33 H10
Sihora India 23°29N 80°6E 43 H9
Sihui China 23°20N 112°40E 35 F9
Siikajoki → Finland 64°50N 24°43E 8 D21
Siilinjärvi Finland 63°4N 27°39E 8 E22
Sika India 22°26N 69°47E 42 H3
Sikanni Chief → Canada 57°47N 122°15W 70 B4
Sikao Thailand 7°34N 99°21E 39 J2
Sikar India 27°33N 75°10E 42 F6
Sikasso Mali 11°18N 5°35W 52 F4
Sikeston U.S.A. 36°53N 89°35W 80 G9
Sikhote Alin, Khrebet Russia 45°0N 136°0E 28 B8
Sikhote Alin Ra. = Sikhote Alin, Khrebet Russia 45°0N 136°0E 28 B8
Sikinos Greece 36°40N 25°8E 23 F11
Sikkim □ India 27°50N 88°30E 41 F16
Sil → Spain 42°27N 7°43W 21 A2
Silacayoapan Mexico 17°30N 98°9W 87 D5
Silawad India 21°54N 74°54E 44 D2
Silchar India 24°49N 92°48E 41 G18
Silent Valley △ India 11°9N 76°28E 45 J3
Siler City U.S.A. 35°44N 79°28W 85 D15
Sileru → India 17°49N 81°24E 44 F5
Silesia = Śląsk Poland 51°0N 16°30E 16 C9
Silgarhi Doti Nepal 29°15N 81°0E 43 E9
Silghat India 26°35N 93°0E 41 F18
Silhouette Seychelles 4°29S 55°12E 55 b
Siliguri = Shiliguri India 26°45N 88°25E 41 F16

Siling Co China 31°50N 89°20E 30 E6
Silistra Bulgaria 44°6N 27°19E 23 B12
Silivri Turkey 41°4N 28°14E 23 D13
Siljan Sweden 60°55N 14°45E 8 F16
Silkeborg Denmark 56°10N 9°32E 9 H13
Silkwood Australia 17°45S 146°2E 62 B4
Sillajhuay, Cordillera Chile 19°46S 68°40W 92 G5
Sillamäe Estonia 59°24N 27°45E 9 G22
Sillod India 20°18N 75°39E 44 D2
Silloth U.K. 54°52N 3°23W 12 C4
Siloam Springs U.S.A. 36°11N 94°32W 84 C7
Silopi Turkey 37°15N 42°27E 46 B4
Silvan Turkey 38°7N 41°2E 46 B4
Silvani India 23°18N 78°25E 43 H8
Silvassa India 20°16N 73°1E 44 D1
Silver City U.S.A. 32°46N 108°17W 77 K9
Silver Cr. → U.S.A. 43°16N 119°13W 76 E4
Silver Creek U.S.A. 42°33N 79°10W 82 D5
Silver L. U.S.A. 38°39N 120°6W 78 G6
Silver Lake Calif., U.S.A. 35°21N 116°7W 79 K10
Silver Lake Oreg., U.S.A. 43°8N 121°3W 76 E3
Silvermine Mts. Ireland 52°47N 8°15W 10 D3
Silverton Colo., U.S.A. 37°49N 107°40W 77 H10
Silverton Tex., U.S.A. 34°28N 101°19W 84 D4
Silvies → U.S.A. 43°34N 119°2W 76 E4
Simaltala India 24°43N 86°33E 43 G12
Simanggang = Bandar Sri Aman Malaysia 1°15N 111°32E 36 D4
Simao China 22°47N 101°5E 34 F3
Simard, L. Canada 47°40N 78°40W 72 C4
Simav Turkey 39°4N 28°58E 23 E13
Simbirsk = Ulyanovsk Russia 54°20N 48°25E 18 D8
Simcoe Canada 42°50N 80°20W 82 D4
Simcoe, L. Canada 44°25N 79°20W 82 B5
Simdega India 22°37N 84°31E 43 H11
Simeria Romania 45°51N 23°1E 17 F12
Simeulue Indonesia 2°45N 95°45E 36 D1
Simferopol Ukraine 44°55N 34°3E 19 F5
Simi Greece 36°35N 27°50E 23 F12
Simi Valley U.S.A. 34°16N 118°47W 79 L8
Simikot Nepal 30°0N 81°50E 43 E9
Simla = Shimla India 31°2N 77°9E 42 D7
Simlipal △ India 21°45N 86°30E 43 J12
Simmie Canada 49°56N 108°6W 71 D7
Simmler U.S.A. 35°21N 119°59W 79 K7
Simo älv = Simojoki → Finland 65°35N 25°1E 8 D21
Simojoki → Finland 65°35N 25°1E 8 D21
Simojovel Mexico 17°12N 92°38W 87 D6
Simonette → Canada 55°9N 118°15W 70 B5
Simonstown S. Africa 34°14S 18°26E 56 D2
Simpang Empat Malaysia 5°27N 100°29E 39 c
Simplonpass Switz. 46°15N 8°3E 20 C8
Simpson Desert Australia 25°0S 137°0E 62 D2
Simpson Pen. Canada 68°34N 88°45W 69 D14
Simrishamn Sweden 55°33N 14°22E 9 J16
Simsbury U.S.A. 41°53N 72°48W 83 E12
Simushir, Ostrov Russia 46°50N 152°30E 27 E16
Sina → India 17°30N 75°55E 44 F2
Sina Dhago Somalia 5°50N 47°0E 49 F4
Sinabang Indonesia 2°30N 96°24E 36 D1
Sinai = Es Sînâ' Egypt 29°0N 34°0E 48 F2
Sinai, Mt. = Mûsa, Gebel Egypt 28°33N 33°59E 46 D2
Sinaloa □ Mexico 25°0N 107°30W 86 C3
Sinaloa de Leyva Mexico 25°50N 108°14W 86 B3
Sinan China 27°56N 108°13E 34 D7
Sincelejo Colombia 9°18N 75°24W 92 B3
Sinch'ang N. Korea 40°7N 128°28E 33 D15
Sinch'ŏn N. Korea 38°17N 125°21E 33 E13
Sinclair U.S.A. 41°47N 107°7W 76 F10
Sinclair Mills Canada 54°5N 121°40W 70 C4
Sinclair's B. U.K. 58°31N 3°5W 11 C5
Sinclairville U.S.A. 42°16N 79°16W 82 D5
Sincorá, Serra do Brazil 13°10S 41°20W 93 F10
Sind = Sindh □ Pakistan 26°0N 69°0E 42 G3
Sind → Jammu & Kashmir, India 34°18N 74°45E 43 B6
Sind → Mad. P., India 26°26N 79°13E 43 F8
Sind Sagar Doab Pakistan 32°0N 71°30E 42 D4
Sindangan Phil. 8°10N 123°5E 37 C6
Sindangbarang Indonesia 7°27S 107°1E 37 G12
Sindewahi India 20°17N 79°39E 44 D4
Sindgi India 16°55N 76°14E 44 F3
Sindh □ Pakistan 26°0N 69°0E 42 G3
Sindh → = Indus → Pakistan 24°20N 67°47E 42 G2
Sindhnur India 15°47N 76°46E 45 F3
Sindhuli Garhi Nepal 27°16N 85°58E 43 F11
Sindi India 20°48N 78°52E 44 D4
Sindri India 23°45N 86°42E 43 H12
Sines Portugal 37°56N 8°51W 21 D1
Sines, C. de Portugal 37°58N 8°53W 21 D1
Sing Buri Thailand 14°53N 100°25E 38 E3
Singa Sudan 13°10N 33°57E 53 F12
Singalila △ India 27°10N 88°5E 43 F13
Singanallur India 11°2N 77°4E 45 J3
Singapore ■ Asia 1°17N 103°51E 39 d
Singapore, Straits of Asia 1°15N 104°0E 39 d
Singaraja Indonesia 8°7S 115°6E 37 J18
Singatoka = Sigatoka Fiji 18°8S 177°32E 59 a
Singida Tanzania 4°49S 34°48E 54 E6
Singkaki → India 4°8S 104°0E 36 E2
Singkang Indonesia 4°8S 120°1E 37 E6
Singkawang Indonesia 1°0N 108°57E 36 D3
Singkep Indonesia 0°30S 104°25E 36 E2
Singkil Indonesia 2°17N 97°49E 39 L1
Singkuang Indonesia 1°3N 98°55E 39 L2
Singleton Australia 32°33S 151°0E 63 E5
Singleton, Mt. N. Terr., Australia 22°0S 130°46E 60 D5
Singleton, Mt. W. Austral., Australia 29°27S 117°15E 61 E2
Singoli India 25°0N 75°22E 42 G6

Singora = Songkhla Thailand 7°13N 100°37E 39 J3
Singrauli India 24°7N 82°23E 43 G10
Sinh Ton, Dao = Sin Cowe I. S. China Sea 9°53N 114°19E 36 C4
Sinharaja Sri Lanka 6°25N 80°30E 45 L5
Sinhgarh India 18°22N 73°45E 44 E1
Sinhŭng N. Korea 40°11N 127°34E 33 D14
Siniscóla Italy 40°34N 9°41E 22 D3
Sinjai Indonesia 5°7S 120°20E 37 F6
Sinjār Iraq 36°19N 41°52E 46 B4
Sinkat Sudan 18°55N 36°49E 53 E13
Sinkiang = Xinjiang Uygur Zizhiqu □ China 42°0N 86°0E 30 C6
Sinmak N. Korea 38°25N 126°14E 33 E14
Sinmi-do N. Korea 39°33N 124°53E 33 E13
Sinnamary Fr. Guiana 5°25N 53°0W 93 B8
Sinnar India 19°48N 74°0E 44 E2
Sinni → Italy 40°8N 16°41E 22 D7
Sinop Turkey 42°1N 35°11E 19 F6
Sinor India 21°55N 73°20E 42 J5
Sinp'o N. Korea 40°0N 128°13E 33 E14
Sinsk Russia 61°8N 126°48E 27 C13
Sint-Hubert Belgium 50°2N 5°23E 15 D5
Sint-Niklaas Belgium 51°10N 4°8E 15 C4
Sint-Truiden Belgium 50°48N 5°10E 15 D5
Sintang Indonesia 0°5N 111°35E 36 D4
Sinton U.S.A. 28°2N 97°31W 84 G6
Sintra Portugal 38°47N 9°25W 21 C1
Sinŭiju N. Korea 40°5N 124°24E 33 D13
Siocon Phil. 7°40N 122°10E 37 C6
Siófok Hungary 46°54N 18°3E 17 E10
Sion Switz. 46°14N 7°20E 20 C7
Sion Mills U.K. 54°48N 7°29W 10 B4
tSionainn, An = Shannon → Ireland 52°35N 9°30W 10 D2
Sioux Center U.S.A. 43°5N 96°11W 80 D5
Sioux City U.S.A. 42°30N 96°24W 80 D5
Sioux Falls U.S.A. 43°33N 96°44W 80 D5
Sioux Lookout Canada 50°10N 91°50W 72 B1
Sioux Narrows Canada 49°25N 94°10W 71 D10
Sipadan Malaysia 4°6N 118°38E 37 D5
Siparia Trin. & Tob. 10°8N 61°31W 93 K15
Sipicua China 43°8N 124°21E 33 C13
Sipiwesk L. Canada 55°5N 97°35W 71 B9
Siple I. Antarctica 73°40S 125°10W 5 D14
Sipra → India 23°55N 75°28E 42 H6
Sipsongpanna = Xishuangbanna China 22°5N 101°0E 34 F3
Sipur India 21°11N 85°9E 44 D7
Sipura Indonesia 2°18S 99°40E 36 E1
Siquia → Nic. 12°10N 84°20W 88 D3
Siquijor Phil. 9°12N 123°35E 37 C6
Siquirres Costa Rica 10°6N 83°30W 88 D3
Şır Abu Nu'ayr U.A.E. 25°20N 54°20E 47 E7
Şır Banī Yās U.A.E. 24°19N 52°37E 47 E7
Sir Edward Pellew Group Australia 15°40S 137°10E 62 B2
Sir Graham Moore Is. Australia 13°53S 126°34E 60 B4
Sir James MacBrien, Mt. Canada 62°7N 127°41W 68 E6
Sira India 13°41N 76°49E 45 H3
Sira → Norway 58°23N 6°34E 9 G12
Siracusa Italy 37°4N 15°17E 22 F6
Sirajganj Bangla. 24°25N 89°47E 43 G13
Sirathu India 25°39N 81°19E 43 G9
Sirdān Iran 36°39N 49°12E 47 B6
Sirdaryo → Kazakhstan 45°47N 92°24W 80 C7
Siret → Romania 45°24N 28°1E 17 F14
Sirghāyā Syria 33°51N 36°8E 48 B5
Sirhān, Wadi Saudi Arabia 17°45N 100°38E 38 C3
Sirinat △ Thailand 8°6N 98°17E 39 a
Sirjan Iran 29°30N 55°45E 47 D7
Sirkali = Sirkazhi India 11°15N 79°41E 45 J4
Sirkazhi India 11°15N 79°41E 45 J4
Sirmaur India 24°51N 81°23E 43 G9
Sirmilik △ Canada 72°50N 80°35W 69 C15
Sirohi India 24°52N 72°53E 42 G5
Sironj India 24°5N 77°39E 42 G7
Síros = Ermoupoli Greece 37°28N 24°57E 23 F11
Sirpur India 19°29N 79°36E 44 E4
Sirr, Nafud as Si. Arabia 25°33N 44°35E 46 E5
Sirretta Pk. U.S.A. 35°56N 118°19W 79 K8
Sirrī Iran 25°55N 54°32E 47 E7
Sirsa India 29°33N 75°4E 42 E6
Sirsa → India 26°51N 79°4E 43 F8
Sirsi Karnataka, India 14°40N 74°49E 45 G2
Sirsi Ut. P., India 18°23N 78°50E 44 E4
Sirsilla India 18°23N 78°50E 44 E4
Sirte = Surt Libya 31°11N 16°39E 53 B9
Siruguppa India 15°35N 76°54E 45 G3
Sirur India 18°50N 74°23E 44 E2
Şırvan Azerbaijan 39°59N 48°52E 47 B6
Sisak Croatia 45°30N 16°21E 16 F9
Sishen S. Africa 27°47S 22°59E 56 D3
Sishui China 35°42N 117°18E 33 G9
Sisipuk L. Canada 55°45N 101°50W 71 B8
Sisophon Cambodia 13°38N 102°59E 38 F4
Sisseton U.S.A. 45°40N 97°3W 80 C5
Sīstān Asia 30°50N 61°0E 47 D9
Sīstān va Balūchestān □ Iran 27°0N 62°0E 47 E9
Sisters U.S.A. 44°18N 121°33W 76 D3
Siswa Bazar India 27°9N 83°46E 43 F10
Sitamarhi India 26°37N 85°30E 43 F11
Sitapur India 27°38N 80°45E 43 F9
Siteki Swaziland 26°32S 31°58E 57 D5
Sitges Spain 41°17N 1°47E 21 B6
Sitia Greece 35°13N 26°6E 23 G12
Sitito-Ozima Ridge Pac. Oc. 23°0N 143°0E 64 E6
Sitka U.S.A. 57°3N 135°20W 70 B1
Sitoti Botswana 23°15S 23°40E 56 B3
Sittang Myit → Burma 17°20N 96°45E 41 L20
Sittard Neths. 51°0N 5°52E 15 C5
Sittingbourne U.K. 51°21N 0°45E 13 F8

Sittoung = Sittang Myit →
 Burma 17°20N 96°45E **41** L20
Sittwe Burma 20°18N 92°45E **41** J18
Situbondo Indonesia 7°42S 113°56E **37** G16
Si'umu Samoa 14°1S 171°48W **59** b
Siuna Nic. 13°37N 84°45W **88** D3
Siuri India 23°50N 87°34E **43** H12
Sivaganga India 9°50N 78°28E **45** K4
Sivagiri India 9°16N 77°26E **45** K3
Sivakasi India 9°24N 77°47E **45** K3
Sivand Iran 30°5N 52°55E **47** D7
Sivas Turkey 39°43N 36°58E **46** B3
Sivasagar India 27°0N 94°36E **41** F19
Sivasamudram India 12°16N 77°10E **45** H3
Siverek Turkey 37°50N 39°19E **46** B3
Sivomaskinskiy Russia 66°40N 62°35E **18** A11
Sivrihisar Turkey 39°30N 31°35E **19** G5
Siwa Egypt 29°11N 25°31E **53** C11
Siwa, El Wâhât es Egypt 29°10N 25°30E **50** D6
Siwa Oasis = Sîwa, El Wâhât es
 Egypt 29°10N 25°30E **50** D6
Siwalik Range Nepal 28°0N 83°0E **43** F10
Siwan India 26°13N 84°21E **43** F11
Siwana India 25°38N 72°25E **42** G5
Six Cross Roads Barbados 13°7N 59°28W **89** g
Sixian China 33°30N 117°50E **33** H9
Sixmilebridge Ireland 52°44N 8°46W **10** D3
Sixth Cataract Sudan 16°20N 32°42E **53** E12
Siyabuswa S. Africa 25°7S 29°3E **57** C4
Siyah Kuh, Kavīr-e Iran 32°55N 53°55E **47** C7
Siyang China 33°42N 118°40E **33** H10
Siziwang Qi China 41°25N 111°40E **32** D6
Sjælland Denmark 55°30N 11°30E **9** J14
Sjumen = Shumen
 Bulgaria 43°18N 26°55E **23** C12
Skadarsko Jezero Europe 42°10N 19°20E **23** C8
Skaftafell Iceland 64°1N 17°0W **8** D5
Skaftafell △ Iceland 64°9N 16°50W **8** D5
Skagafjörður Iceland 65°54N 19°35W **8** D4
Skagastølstindane Norway 61°28N 7°52E **8** F12
Skagaströnd Iceland 65°50N 20°19W **8** D3
Skagen Denmark 57°43N 10°35E **9** H14
Skagerrak Denmark 57°30N 9°0E **9** H13
Skagit → U.S.A. 48°23N 122°22W **78** B4
Skagway U.S.A. 59°28N 135°19W **70** B1
Skala-Podilska Ukraine 48°50N 26°15E **17** D14
Skalat Ukraine 49°23N 25°55E **17** D13
Skåne Sweden 55°59N 13°30E **9** J15
Skaneateles U.S.A. 42°57N 76°26W **83** D8
Skaneateles L. U.S.A. 42°51N 76°22W **83** D8
Skardu Pakistan 35°20N 75°44E **43** B6
Skarvan og Roltdalen △
 Norway 63°16N 11°31E **8** E14
Skarżysko-Kamienna
 Poland 51°7N 20°52E **17** C11
Skeena → Canada 54°9N 130°5W **70** C2
Skeena Mts. Canada 56°40N 128°30W **70** B3
Skegness U.K. 53°9N 0°20E **12** D8
Skeleton Coast Namibia 20°0S 13°0E **55** J2
Skeleton Coast △ Namibia 20°0S 13°0E **56** B1
Skellefteå Sweden 64°45N 20°50E **8** D19
Skellefteälven → Sweden 64°45N 21°10E **8** D19
Skellefteå Sweden 64°40N 21°9E **8** D19
Skellig Michael = Great Skellig
 Ireland 51°47N 10°33W **10** E1
Skerries Ireland 53°35N 6°8W **10** C5
Skerries, The U.K. 53°25N 4°36W **12** D3
Ski Norway 59°43N 10°52E **9** G14
Skiathos Greece 39°12N 23°30E **23** E10
Skibbereen Ireland 51°33N 9°16W **10** E2
Skiddaw U.K. 54°39N 3°9W **12** C4
Skidegate Canada 53°15N 132°1W **70** C2
Skien Norway 59°12N 9°35E **9** G13
Skierniewice Poland 51°58N 20°10E **17** C11
Skihist, Mt. Canada 50°12N 121°54W **70** C4
Skikda Algeria 36°50N 6°58E **52** A7
Skipton U.K. 53°58N 2°3W **12** D5
Skirmish Pt. Australia 11°59S 134°17E **62** A1
Skíros = Skyros Greece 38°55N 24°34E **23** E11
Skive Denmark 56°33N 9°2E **9** H13
Skjálfandafljót → Iceland 65°59N 17°25W **8** D5
Skjálfandi Iceland 66°5N 17°30W **8** C5
Skole Ukraine 49°3N 23°30E **17** D12
Skopelos Greece 39°9N 23°47E **23** E10
Skopje Macedonia 42°1N 21°26E **23** C9
Skövde Sweden 58°24N 13°50E **9** G15
Skovorodino Russia 54°0N 125°0E **31** D13
Skowhegan U.S.A. 44°46N 69°43W **81** C19
Skull Ireland 51°32N 9°34W **10** E2
Skunk → U.S.A. 40°42N 91°7W **80** E8
Skuodas Lithuania 56°16N 21°33E **9** H19
Skvyra Ukraine 49°44N 29°40E **17** D15
Sky Harbour Int., Phoenix ✈
 (PHX) U.S.A. 33°26N 112°5W **77** K7
Skye U.K. 57°15N 6°10W **11** D2
Skykomish U.S.A. 47°42N 121°22W **76** C3
Skyros Greece 38°55N 24°34E **23** E11
Slade Point Australia 21°4S 149°13E **62** b
Slade Pt. Australia 21°5S 149°13E **62** b
Slættaratindur Færoe Is. 62°18N 7°1W **8** E9
Slagelse Denmark 55°23N 11°19E **9** J14
Slamet Indonesia 7°16S 109°8E **37** G13
Slane Ireland 53°42N 6°33W **10** C5
Slaney → Ireland 52°26N 6°33W **10** D5
Slangberge S. Africa 31°32S 24°8E **56** D3
Śląsk Poland 51°0N 16°30E **16** C9
Slate Is. Canada 48°40N 87°0W **72** C2
Slatina Romania 44°28N 24°22E **17** F13
Slatington U.S.A. 40°45N 75°37W **83** F9
Slaton U.S.A. 33°26N 101°39W **84** E4
Slave → Canada 61°18N 113°39W **70** A6
Slave Coast W. Afr. 6°0N 2°30E **52** G6
Slave Lake Canada 55°17N 114°43W **70** B6
Slave Pt. Canada 61°11N 115°56W **70** A5
Slavgorod Russia 53°1N 78°37E **26** D8
Slavonski Brod Croatia 45°11N 18°1E **23** B8
Slavuta Ukraine 50°15N 27°2E **17** C14
Slavyanka Russia 42°53N 131°21E **28** C5
Slavyansk = Slovyansk
 Ukraine 48°55N 37°36E **19** E6

Slawharad Belarus 53°27N 31°0E **17** B16
Slea Hd. Ireland 52°6N 10°27W **10** D1
Sleaford U.K. 53°0N 0°24W **12** D7
Sleaford B. Australia 34°55S 135°45E **63** E2
Sleat, Sd. of U.K. 57°5N 5°47W **11** D3
Sleeper Is. Canada 58°30N 81°0W **69** F15
Sleeping Bear Dunes △
 U.S.A. 44°50N 86°5W **80** C10
Sleepy Eye U.S.A. 44°18N 94°43W **80** C6
Slemon L. Canada 63°13N 116°4W **70** A5
Slide Mt. U.S.A. 42°0N 74°25W **83** E10
Slidell U.S.A. 30°17N 89°47W **85** F10
Slieve Aughty Ireland 53°4N 8°30W **10** C3
Slieve Bloom Ireland 53°4N 7°40W **10** C4
Slieve Donard U.K. 54°11N 5°55W **10** B6
Slieve Gamph Ireland 54°6N 9°0W **10** B3
Slieve Gullion U.K. 54°7N 6°26W **10** B5
Slieve League Ireland 54°40N 8°42W **10** B3
Slieve Mish Ireland 52°12N 9°50W **10** D2
Slievenamon Ireland 52°25N 7°34W **10** D4
Sligeach = Sligo Ireland 54°16N 8°28W **10** B3
Sligo Ireland 54°16N 8°28W **10** B3
Sligo U.S.A. 41°6N 79°29W **82** E5
Sligo □ Ireland 54°8N 8°42W **10** B3
Sligo B. Ireland 54°18N 8°40W **10** B3
Slippery Rock U.S.A. 41°4N 80°3W **82** E4
Slite Sweden 57°42N 18°48E **9** H18
Sliven Bulgaria 42°42N 26°19E **23** C12
Sloan U.S.A. 35°57N 115°13W **79** K11
Sloansville U.S.A. 42°45N 74°22W **83** D10
Slobodskoy Russia 58°40N 50°6E **18** C9
Slobozia Romania 44°34N 27°23E **17** F14
Slocan Canada 49°48N 117°28W **70** D5
Slonim Belarus 53°4N 25°19E **17** B13
Slough U.K. 51°30N 0°36W **13** F7
Slough □ U.K. 51°30N 0°36W **13** F7
Sloughhouse U.S.A. 38°26N 121°12W **78** G5
Slovak Rep. ■ Europe 48°30N 20°0E **17** D10
Slovakia = Slovak Rep. ■
 Europe 48°30N 20°0E **17** D10
Slovakian Ore Mts. = Slovenské
 Rudohorie Slovak Rep. 48°45N 20°0E **17** D10
Slovenia ■ Europe 45°58N 14°30E **16** F8
Slovenija = Slovenia ■
 Europe 45°58N 14°30E **16** F8
Slovenska = Slovak Rep. ■
 Europe 48°30N 20°0E **17** D10
Slovenské Rudohorie
 Slovak Rep. 48°45N 20°0E **17** D10
Slovyansk Ukraine 48°55N 37°36E **19** E6
Sluch → Ukraine 51°37N 26°38E **17** C14
Sluis Neths. 51°18N 3°23E **15** C3
Słupsk Poland 54°30N 17°3E **17** A9
Slurry S. Africa 25°49S 25°42E **56** C4
Slutsk Belarus 53°2N 27°31E **17** B14
Slyne Hd. Ireland 53°25N 10°10W **10** C1
Slyudyanka Russia 51°40N 103°40E **27** D11
Småland Sweden 57°15N 15°25E **9** H16
Smalltree L. Canada 61°0N 105°0W **71** A8
Smallwood Res. Canada 54°5N 64°30W **73** B7
Smarhon Belarus 54°20N 26°24E **17** A14
Smartt Syndicate Dam
 S. Africa 30°45S 23°10E **56** D3
Smartville U.S.A. 39°13N 121°18W **78** F5
Smeaton Canada 53°30N 104°49W **71** C8
Smederevo Serbia 44°40N 20°57E **23** B9
Smeralda, Costa Italy 41°5N 9°35E **22** D3
Smerwick Harbour
 Ireland 52°12N 10°23W **10** D1
Smethport U.S.A. 41°49N 78°27W **82** E6
Smidovich Russia 48°36N 133°49E **27** E14
Smith Canada 55°10N 114°0W **70** B6
Smith Center U.S.A. 39°47N 98°47W **80** F4
Smith I. Canada 60°45N 78°25W **69** E16
Smith I. India 13°20N 93°4E **45** H11
Smith Islands △ Australia 20°40S 149°9E **62** b
Smith River △ U.S.A. 41°55N 124°0W **76** F2
Smith Sd. N. Amer. 78°25N 74°0W **69** B17
Smithburne → Australia 17°3S 140°57E **62** B3
Smithers Canada 54°45N 127°10W **70** C3
Smithfield S. Africa 30°9S 26°30E **57** E4
Smithfield N.C., U.S.A. 35°31N 78°21W **85** D15
Smithfield Utah, U.S.A. 41°50N 111°50W **76** F8
Smiths Falls Canada 44°55N 76°0W **83** B9
Smithton Australia 40°53S 145°6E **63** G4
Smithville Canada 43°6N 79°33W **82** C5
Smithville U.S.A. 30°1N 97°10W **84** F6
Smoke Creek Desert
 U.S.A. 40°30N 119°40W **76** F4
Smoky → Canada 56°10N 117°21W **70** B5
Smoky Bay Australia 32°22S 134°13E **63** E1
Smoky Hill → U.S.A. 39°4N 96°48W **80** F5
Smoky Hills U.S.A. 39°15N 99°30W **80** F4
Smoky Lake Canada 54°10N 112°30W **70** C6
Smøla Norway 63°23N 8°3E **8** E13
Smolensk Russia 54°45N 32°5E **18** D5
Smolikas, Oros Greece 40°9N 20°58E **23** D9
Smolyan Bulgaria 41°36N 24°38E **23** D11
Smooth Rock Falls
 Canada 49°17N 81°37W **72** C3
Smoothstone L. Canada 54°40N 106°50W **71** C7
Smorgon = Smarhon
 Belarus 54°20N 26°24E **17** A14
Smyley I. Antarctica 72°55S 78°0W **5** D17
Smyrna = İzmir Turkey 38°25N 27°8E **23** E12
Smyrna U.S.A. 39°18N 75°36W **81** F16
Snæfell Iceland 64°48N 15°34W **8** D6
Snaefell I. of Man 54°16N 4°27W **12** C3
Snæfellsjökull Iceland 64°49N 23°46W **8** D2
Snake → U.S.A. 46°12N 119°2W **76** C4
Snake I. Australia 38°47S 146°33E **63** F4
Snake Range U.S.A. 39°0N 114°20W **76** G6
Snake River Plain U.S.A. 42°50N 114°0W **76** E7
Snåsavatnet Norway 64°12N 12°0E **8** D15
Sneek Neths. 53°2N 5°40E **15** A5
Sneem Ireland 51°50N 9°54W **10** E2
Sneeuberge S. Africa 31°46S 24°20E **56** D3
Snelling U.S.A. 37°31N 120°26W **78** H6
Snežka Europe 50°41N 15°50E **16** C8
Snizort, L. U.K. 57°33N 6°28W **11** D2

Snøhetta Norway 62°19N 9°16E **8** E13
Snohomish U.S.A. 47°55N 122°6W **78** C4
Snoqualmie U.S.A. 47°31N 121°49W **78** C5
Snoqualmie Pass U.S.A. 47°25N 121°25W **78** C5
Snoul Cambodia 12°4N 106°26E **39** F6
Snover U.S.A. 43°27N 82°58W **82** C2
Snow Hill U.S.A. 38°11N 75°24W **81** F16
Snow Lake Canada 54°52N 100°3W **71** C8
Snow Mt. Calif., U.S.A. 39°23N 122°45W **78** F4
Snow Mt. Maine, U.S.A. 45°18N 70°48W **83** A14
Snow Shoe U.S.A. 41°2N 77°57W **82** E7
Snowbird L. Canada 60°45N 103°0W **71** A8
Snowdon U.K. 53°4N 4°5W **12** D3
Snowdonia △ U.K. 53°7N 3°59W **12** D4
Snowdrift = Łutsel K'e
 Canada 62°24N 110°44W **71** A6
Snowdrift → Canada 62°24N 110°44W **71** A6
Snowflake U.S.A. 34°30N 110°5W **77** J8
Snowshoe Pk. U.S.A. 48°13N 115°41W **76** B6
Snowtown Australia 33°46S 138°14E **63** E2
Snowville U.S.A. 41°58N 112°43W **76** F7
Snowy → Australia 37°46S 148°30E **63** F4
Snowy Mt. U.S.A. 43°42N 74°23W **83** C10
Snowy Mts. Australia 36°30S 148°20E **63** F4
Snug Corner Bahamas 22°33N 73°52W **89** B5
Snug Harbour Canada 45°22N 80°17W **82** A4
Snyatyn Ukraine 48°27N 25°38E **17** D13
Snyder Okla., U.S.A. 34°40N 98°57W **84** D5
Snyder Tex., U.S.A. 32°44N 100°55W **84** E4
Soalala Madag. 16°6S 45°20E **55** H9
Soan → Pakistan 33°1N 71°44E **42** C4
Sobat → South Sudan 9°22N 31°33E **53** G12
Sobhapur India 22°47N 78°17E **42** H8
Sobradinho, Represa de
 Brazil 9°30S 42°0W **93** E10
Sobral Brazil 3°50S 40°20W **93** D10
Soc Giang Vietnam 22°54N 106°1E **34** F6
Soc Trang Vietnam 9°37N 105°50E **39** H5
Socastee U.S.A. 33°41N 78°59W **85** E15
Soch'e = Shache China 38°20N 77°10E **30** D4
Sochi Russia 43°35N 39°40E **19** F6
Société, Îs. de la
 French Polynesia 17°0S 151°0W **65** J12
Society Is. = Société, Îs. de la
 French Polynesia 17°0S 151°0W **65** J12
Socompa, Portezuelo de
 Chile 24°27S 68°18W **94** A2
Socorro N. Mex., U.S.A. 34°4N 106°54W **77** J10
Socorro Tex., U.S.A. 31°39N 106°18W **84** F1
Socorro I. Mexico 18°45N 110°58W **86** D2
Socotra Yemen 12°30N 54°0E **49** E5
Soda L. U.S.A. 35°10N 116°4W **79** K10
Soda Plains India 35°30N 79°0E **43** B8
Soda Springs U.S.A. 42°39N 111°36W **76** E8
Sodankylä Finland 67°29N 26°40E **8** C22
Soddy-Daisy U.S.A. 35°17N 85°10W **85** D12
Söderhamn Sweden 61°18N 17°10E **8** F17
Söderköping Sweden 58°31N 16°20E **9** G17
Södermanland Sweden 58°56N 16°55E **9** G17
Södertälje Sweden 59°12N 17°39E **9** G17
Sodiri Sudan 14°27N 29°0E **53** F11
Sodus U.S.A. 43°14N 77°4W **82** C7
Sodwana Bay △ S. Africa 27°35S 32°43E **57** C5
Soe Indonesia 9°52S 124°17E **60** A3
Soekmekaar = Morebeng
 S. Africa 23°30S 29°55E **57** B4
Soest Neths. 52°9N 5°19E **15** B5
Sofala □ Mozam. 19°30S 34°30E **57** A5
Sofia = Sofiya Bulgaria 42°45N 23°20E **23** C10
Sofia → Madag. 15°27S 47°23E **55** H9
Sofiya Bulgaria 42°45N 23°20E **23** C10
Sōfu-Gan Japan 29°49N 140°21E **29** K10
Sogamoso Colombia 5°43N 72°56W **92** B4
Sogār Iran 25°53N 58°6E **47** E8
Sogndalsfjøra Norway 61°14N 7°5E **8** F12
Søgne Norway 58°5N 7°48E **9** G12
Sognefjorden Norway 61°10N 5°50E **8** F11
Soh Iran 33°26N 51°27E **47** C6
Sohâg Egypt 26°33N 31°43E **53** C12
Sohagpur India 22°42N 78°12E **42** H8
Sohar = Şuḩār Oman 24°20N 56°40E **47** E8
Sohela India 21°18N 83°24E **44** D6
Soheuksando S. Korea 34°4N 125°7E **33** H13
Soignies Belgium 50°35N 4°5E **15** D4
Soissons France 49°25N 3°19E **20** B5
Sōja Japan 34°40N 133°45E **29** G6
Sojat India 25°55N 73°45E **42** G5
Sokal Ukraine 50°31N 24°15E **17** C13
Sokcho S. Korea 38°12N 128°36E **33** E15
Söke Turkey 37°48N 27°28E **23** F12
Sokodé Togo 9°0N 1°11E **52** G6
Sokol Russia 59°30N 40°5E **18** C7
Sokółka Poland 53°25N 23°30E **17** B12
Sokołów Podlaski
 Poland 52°25N 22°15E **17** B12
Sokoto Nigeria 13°2N 5°16E **52** F7
Sol, Costa del Spain 36°30N 4°30W **21** D3
Sol Iletsk Russia 51°10N 55°0E **18** D10
Solan India 30°55N 77°7E **42** D7
Solana Beach U.S.A. 32°58N 117°16W **79** N9
Solander I. N.Z. 46°34S 166°54E **59** G1
Solapur India 17°43N 75°56E **44** E2
Soldotna U.S.A. 60°29N 151°3W **68** E1
Soledad Colombia 10°55N 74°46W **92** A4
Soledad U.S.A. 36°26N 121°20W **78** J5
Soledad Venezuela 8°10N 63°34W **92** B6

Solo → Indonesia 6°47S 112°22E **37** G15
Sologne France 47°40N 1°45E **20** C4
Solok Indonesia 0°45S 100°40E **36** E2
Solola Guatemala 14°49N 91°10W **88** D1
Solomon, N. Fork →
 U.S.A. 39°29N 98°26W **80** F4
Solomon, S. Fork →
 U.S.A. 39°25N 99°12W **80** F4
Solomon Is. ■ Pac. Oc. 6°0S 155°0E **58** B8
Solomon Rise Pac. Oc. 1°0N 157°0E **64** G7
Solon China 46°32N 121°0E **31** B13
Solon Springs U.S.A. 46°22N 91°49W **80** B8
Solor Indonesia 8°27S 123°0E **37** F6
Solothurn Switz. 47°13N 7°32E **20** C7
Solovetskiye Ostrova
 Russia 65°5N 35°40E **18** B6
Šolta Croatia 43°24N 16°15E **22** C7
Solṭānābād Khorāsān, Iran 34°13N 59°58E **47** C8
Solṭānābād Khorāsān, Iran 36°29N 58°5E **47** B8
Solṭāniyeh Iran 36°26N 48°47E **47** B6
Solunska Glava
 Macedonia 41°44N 21°31E **23** D9
Solvang U.S.A. 34°36N 120°8W **79** L6
Solvay U.S.A. 43°3N 76°13W **83** D8
Sölvesborg Sweden 56°5N 14°35E **9** H16
Solvychegodsk Russia 61°21N 46°56E **18** B8
Solway Firth U.K. 54°49N 3°35W **12** C4
Solwezi Zambia 12°11S 26°21E **55** G5
Sōma Japan 37°40N 140°50E **28** F10
Soma Turkey 39°10N 27°35E **23** E12
Somabhula Zimbabwe 19°42S 29°40E **57** A4
Somali Pen. Africa 7°0N 46°0E **50** F8
Somalia ■ Africa 7°0N 47°0E **49** F4
Somaliland □ Somalia 10°0N 46°0E **49** F4
Sombor Serbia 45°46N 19°9E **23** B8
Sombra Canada 42°43N 82°29W **82** D2
Sombrerete Mexico 23°38N 103°39W **86** C4
Sombrero Anguilla 18°37N 63°30W **89** C7
Sombrero Channel India 7°41N 93°35E **45** L11
Somdari India 25°47N 72°38E **42** G5
Somers U.S.A. 48°5N 114°13W **76** B6
Somerset Ky., U.S.A. 37°5N 84°36W **81** G11
Somerset Mass., U.S.A. 41°47N 71°8W **83** E13
Somerset Pa., U.S.A. 40°1N 79°5W **82** F5
Somerset □ U.K. 51°9N 3°0W **13** F5
Somerset East S. Africa 32°42S 25°35E **56** D4
Somerset I. Canada 73°30N 93°0W **68** C13
Somerset West S. Africa 34°8S 18°50E **56** D2
Somersworth U.S.A. 43°16N 70°52W **83** C14
Somerton U.S.A. 32°36N 114°43W **77** K6
Somerville U.S.A. 40°35N 74°38W **83** F10
Someş → Romania 47°49N 22°43E **17** D12
Somme → France 50°11N 1°38E **20** A4
Somnath India 20°53N 70°22E **42** J4
Somosomo Fiji 16°47S 179°58W **59** a
Somoto Nic. 13°28N 86°37W **88** D2
Somport, Túnel de Spain 42°48N 0°31W **20** E3
Somvarpet India 12°36N 75°52E **45** H2
Son → India 25°42N 84°52E **43** G11
Son Ha Vietnam 15°3N 108°34E **38** E7
Son La Vietnam 21°20N 103°50E **34** G4
Son Tay Vietnam 21°8N 105°30E **34** G5
Son Tinh Vietnam 15°10N 108°40E **38** E7
Soná Panama 8°0N 81°20W **88** E3
Sonamarg India 34°18N 75°21E **43** B6
Sonamukhi India 23°18N 87°27E **43** H12
Sonar → India 24°24N 79°56E **43** G8
Sondags → S. Africa 33°44S 25°51E **56** D4
Sønderborg Denmark 54°55N 9°49E **9** J13
Sóndrio Italy 46°10N 9°52E **20** C8
Sone Mozam. 17°23S 34°55E **55** H6
Sonepur India 20°55N 83°50E **44** D6
Song Thailand 18°28N 100°11E **38** C3
Song Cau Vietnam 13°27N 109°18E **38** F7
Song Ma Vietnam 20°56N 103°53E **34** G4
Song Xian China 34°12N 112°8E **32** G7
Songadh India 21°9N 73°33E **44** D1
Songan Indonesia 8°13S 115°24E **37** J18
Songea Tanzania 10°40S 35°40E **54** G7
Songgang China 22°46N 113°50E **31** a
Songhua Hu China 43°35N 126°50E **33** C14
Songhua Jiang →
 China 47°45N 132°30E **31** B15
Songimvelo △ S. Africa 25°50S 31°2E **57** C5
Songjiang China 31°1N 121°12E **35** B13
Songjianghe China 42°10N 127°29E **33** C14
Sŏngjin = Kimch'aek
 N. Korea 40°40N 129°10E **33** D15
Songkan China 28°35N 106°52E **34** C6
Songkhla Thailand 7°13N 100°37E **39** J3
Songming China 25°12N 103°2E **34** E4
Songnim N. Korea 38°45N 125°39E **33** E13
Songo Mozam. 15°34S 32°38E **57** A4
Songpan China 32°40N 103°30E **34** A4
Songxi China 27°31N 118°44E **35** D12
Songzi China 30°12N 111°45E **35** B8
Sonid Youqi China 42°45N 112°48E **32** C7
Sonid Zuoqi China 43°50N 113°42E **32** C7
Sonipat India 29°0N 77°5E **42** E7
Sonkach India 22°59N 76°21E **42** H7
Sonkovo Russia 57°50N 37°5E **18** C6
Sonmiani Pakistan 25°25N 66°40E **42** G2
Sonmiani B. Pakistan 25°15N 66°30E **42** G2
Sono → Brazil 9°58S 48°11W **93** E9
Sonora Calif., U.S.A. 37°59N 120°23W **78** H6
Sonora Tex., U.S.A. 30°34N 100°39W **84** F4
Sonora □ Mexico 29°0N 111°0W **86** B2
Sonora → Mexico 28°50N 111°33W **86** B2
Sonora Desert U.S.A. 33°40N 113°30W **79** L12
Sonoyta Mexico 31°51N 112°50W **86** A2
Sonsonate El Salv. 13°43N 89°44W **88** D2
Soochow = Suzhou
 China 31°19N 120°38E **35** B13

Sooke Canada 48°13N 123°43W **78** B3
Soomaaliya = Somalia ■
 Africa 7°0N 47°0E **49** F4
Sop Hao Laos 20°33N 104°27E **34** G5
Sop Prap Thailand 17°53N 99°20E **38** D2
Sopi Indonesia 2°34N 128°28E **37** D7
Sopot Poland 54°27N 18°31E **17** A10
Sopron Hungary 47°45N 16°32E **17** E9
Sopur India 34°18N 74°27E **43** B6
Sør-Rondane Antarctica 72°0S 25°0E **5** D4
Sorab India 14°23N 75°6E **45** G2
Sorada India 19°45N 84°26E **44** E7
Sorah Pakistan 27°13N 68°56E **42** F3
Soraon India 25°37N 81°51E **43** G9
Sorel-Tracy Canada 46°0N 73°10W **72** C5
Sórgono Italy 40°1N 9°6E **22** D3
Soria Spain 41°43N 2°32W **21** B4
Soriano Uruguay 33°24S 58°19W **94** C4
Sorkh, Kuh-e Iran 35°40N 58°30E **47** C8
Soroca Moldova 48°8N 28°12E **17** D15
Sorocaba Brazil 23°31S 47°27W **95** A6
Sorochinsk Russia 52°26N 53°10E **18** D9
Soroki = Soroca Moldova 48°8N 28°12E **17** D15
Sorong Indonesia 0°55S 131°15E **37** E8
Soroti Uganda 1°43N 33°35E **54** D6
Sørøya Norway 70°40N 22°30E **8** A20
Sørøysundet Norway 70°25N 23°0E **8** A20
Sorrell Australia 42°47S 147°34E **63** G4
Sorrento Italy 40°37N 14°22E **22** D6
Sorsele Sweden 65°31N 17°30E **8** D17
Sorsogon Phil. 13°0N 124°0E **37** B6
Sortavala Russia 61°42N 30°41E **8** F24
Sortland Norway 68°42N 15°25E **8** B16
Sørvågen Norway 67°53N 13°1E **8** C15
Soscumica, L. Canada 50°15N 77°27W **72** B4
Sosnogorsk Russia 63°37N 53°51E **18** B9
Sosnowiec Poland 50°20N 19°10E **17** C10
Sossus Vlei Namibia 24°40S 15°23E **56** B2
Sŏsura N. Korea 42°16N 130°36E **33** C16
Sot → India 27°27N 79°37E **43** F8
Sotavento C. Verde Is. 15°0N 24°0W **52** b
Sotkamo Finland 64°8N 28°23E **8** D23
Soto la Marina Mexico 23°46N 98°13W **87** C5
Soto la Marina →
 Mexico 23°45N 97°45W **87** C5
Sotuta Mexico 20°36N 89°1W **87** C7
Souanké Congo 2°10N 14°3E **54** D2
Soudas, Ormos Greece 35°25N 24°10E **23** G11
Souderton U.S.A. 40°19N 75°19W **83** F9
Soufrière Guadeloupe 16°5N 61°40W **88** b
Soufrière St. Lucia 13°51N 61°3W **89** f
Soufrière Bay Dominica 15°13N 61°22W **89** f
Soukhouma Laos 14°38N 105°48E **38** E5
Sound, The U.K. 50°20N 4°10W **13** G3
Sound I. India 12°58N 92°59E **45** H11
Sources, Mt. aux Lesotho 28°45S 28°50E **57** C4
Soure Brazil 0°35S 48°30W **93** D9
Souris Man., Canada 49°40N 100°20W **71** D8
Souris P.E.I., Canada 46°21N 62°15W **73** C7
Souris → N. Amer. 49°40N 99°34W **80** A4
Sousa Brazil 6°45S 38°10W **93** E11
Sousse Tunisia 35°50N 10°38E **53** A8
Sout → S. Africa 31°35S 18°24E **56** D2
South Africa ■ Africa 32°0S 23°0E **56** D3
South America 10°0S 60°0W **90** E5
South Andaman India 11°45N 92°10E **45** J11
South Aulatsivik I.
 Canada 56°45N 61°30W **73** A7
South Australia □
 Australia 32°0S 139°0E **63** E2
South Australian Basin
 Ind. Oc. 38°0S 126°0E **64** L4
South Ayrshire □ U.K. 55°18N 4°41W **11** F4
South Baldy Pk. U.S.A. 34°6N 107°11W **77** J10
South Bass I. U.S.A. 41°38N 82°49W **82** E2
South Bend Ind., U.S.A. 41°41N 86°15W **80** E10
South Bend Wash.,
 U.S.A. 46°40N 123°48W **78** D3
South Boston U.S.A. 36°42N 78°54W **81** G14
South Branch Canada 47°55N 59°2W **73** C8
South Brook Canada 49°26N 56°5W **73** C8
South Brother I. India 10°56N 92°37E **45** J11
South Bruny I. Australia 43°20S 147°15E **63** G4
South Carolina □ U.S.A. 34°0N 81°0W **85** E14
South Charleston
 U.S.A. 38°22N 81°44W **81** F13
South China Sea Asia 10°0N 113°0E **36** C4
South Cumberland Is. △
 Australia 20°42S 149°11E **62** b
South Dakota □ U.S.A. 44°15N 100°0W **80** C3
South Dayton U.S.A. 42°21N 79°3W **82** D5
South Deerfield U.S.A. 42°29N 72°37W **83** D12
South Downs U.K. 50°52N 0°25W **13** G7
South Downs △ U.K. 50°50N 0°50W **13** G7
South Dublin □ Ireland 53°16N 6°24W **10** C5
South East □ Botswana 25°0S 25°40E **56** C4
South East C. Australia 43°40S 146°50E **63** G4
South East Is. Australia 34°17S 123°30E **61** F3
South Esk → U.K. 56°43N 2°31W **11** E6
South Fiji Basin Pac. Oc. 26°0S 175°0E **64** K9
South Foreland U.K. 51°8N 1°24E **13** F9
South Fork American →
 U.S.A. 38°57N 120°59W **78** G5
South Fork Feather →
 U.S.A. 39°17N 121°36W **78** F5
South Fork Grand →
 U.S.A. 45°43N 102°17W **80** C2
South Fork Milk →
 U.S.A. 48°4N 106°19W **76** B10
South Fork Republican →
 U.S.A. 40°3N 101°31W **80** E3
South Georgia Antarctica 54°30S 37°0W **96** G9
South Gloucestershire □
 U.K. 51°32N 2°28W **13** F5
South Hadley U.S.A. 42°16N 72°35W **83** D12
South Haven U.S.A. 42°24N 86°16W **80** D10
South Henik L. Canada 61°30N 97°20W **71** A9
South I. India 10°3N 72°17E **45** J1
South I. N.Z. 44°0S 170°0E **59** F3

South Indian Lake
  Canada 56°47N 98°56W **71** B9
South Invercargill N.Z. 46°26S 168°23E **59** G2
South Knife → Canada 58°55N 94°37W **71** B10
South Koel → India 22°32N 85°14E **43** H11
South Korea ■ Asia 36°0N 128°0E **33** G15
South Lake Tahoe
  U.S.A. 38°57N 119°59W **78** G6
South Lanarkshire □
  U.K. 55°37N 3°53W **11** F5
South Loup → U.S.A. 41°4N 98°39W **80** E4
South Magnetic Pole
  Antarctica 64°8S 138°8E **5** C9
South Milwaukee
  U.S.A. 42°55N 87°52W **80** D10
South Molton U.K. 51°1N 3°51W **13** F4
South Moose L. Canada 53°49N 100°1W **71** C8
South Nahanni →
  Canada 61°3N 123°21W **70** A4
South Nation → Canada 45°34N 75°6W **83** A9
South Natuna Is. = Natuna
  Selatan, Kepulauan
  Indonesia 2°45N 109°0E **36** D3
South Negril Pt. Jamaica 18°16N 78°22W **88** a
South Orkney Is. Antarctica 63°0S 45°0W **5** C18
South Ossetia □ Georgia 42°21N 44°2E **19** F7
South Otselic U.S.A. 42°38N 75°46W **83** D9
South Pagai, I. = Pagai Selatan,
  Pulau Indonesia 3°0S 100°15E **36** E2
South Paris U.S.A. 44°14N 70°31W **83** B14
South Pittsburg U.S.A. 35°1N 85°42W **85** D12
South Platte → U.S.A. 41°7N 100°42W **80** E3
South Pole Antarctica 90°0S 0°0 **5** E
South Porcupine Canada 48°30N 81°12W **72** C3
South Portland U.S.A. 43°38N 70°15W **81** D18
South Pt. Barbados 13°2N 59°32W **89** g
South Pt. U.S.A. 44°52N 83°19W **82** B1
South River Canada 45°52N 79°23W **72** C4
South River U.S.A. 40°27N 74°23W **83** F10
South Ronaldsay U.K. 58°48N 2°58W **11** C6
South Sandwich Is.
  Antarctica 57°0S 27°0W **5** B1
South Sandwich Trench
  Atl. Oc. 56°0S 24°0W **5** B1
South Saskatchewan →
  Canada 53°15N 105°5W **71** C7
South Seal → Canada 58°48N 98°8W **71** B9
South Sentinel I. India 10°59N 92°14E **45** J11
South Shetland Is.
  Antarctica 62°0S 59°0W **5** C18
South Shields U.K. 55°0N 1°25W **12** C6
South Sioux City U.S.A. 42°28N 96°24W **80** D5
South Sister U.S.A. 44°4N 121°51W **76** D3
South Sudan ■ Africa 8°0N 30°0E **53** G11
South Taranaki Bight
  N.Z. 39°40S 174°5E **59** C5
South Tasman Rise
  S. Ocean 48°0S 146°0E **5** A10
South Thompson →
  Canada 50°40N 120°20W **70** C4
South Twin I. Canada 53°7N 79°52W **72** B4
South Tyne → U.K. 54°59N 2°8W **12** C5
South Uist U.K. 57°20N 7°15W **11** D1
South Valley U.S.A. 35°1N 106°41W **77** J10
South Wellesley Is.
  Australia 16°58S 139°17E **62** B2
South West C. Australia 43°34S 146°3E **63** G4
South West C. N.Z. 47°17S 167°28E **59** G1
South Williamson
  U.S.A. 41°13N 77°0W **82** E8
South Yorkshire □ U.K. 53°27N 1°36W **12** D6
Southampton Canada 44°30N 81°25W **82** B3
Southampton U.K. 50°54N 1°23W **13** G6
Southampton U.S.A. 40°53N 72°23W **83** F12
Southampton □ U.K. 50°54N 1°23W **13** G6
Southampton I. Canada 64°30N 84°0W **69** E15
Southaven U.S.A. 34°59N 90°0W **85** D9
Southbank Canada 54°2N 125°46W **70** C3
Southbridge N.Z. 43°48S 172°16E **59** E4
Southbridge U.S.A. 42°5N 72°2W **83** D12
Southend Canada 56°19N 103°22W **71** B8
Southend-on-Sea U.K. 51°32N 0°44E **13** F8
Southend-on-Sea □ U.K. 51°32N 0°44E **13** F8
Southern = Yuzhnyy □
  Russia 44°0N 40°0E **26** E5
Southern Alps N.Z. 43°41S 170°11E **59** E3
Southern Cross Australia 31°12S 119°15E **61** F2
Southern Indian L.
  Canada 57°10N 98°30W **71** B9
Southern Lau Group Fiji 18°40S 178°40W **59** a
Southern Ocean 62°0S 60°0E **5** C6
Southern Pines U.S.A. 35°11N 79°24W **85** D15
Southern Uplands U.K. 55°28N 3°52W **11** F5
Southington U.S.A. 41°36N 72°53W **83** E12
Southland □ N.Z. 45°51S 168°0E **59** F1
Southold U.S.A. 41°4N 72°26W **83** E12
Southport Australia 27°58S 153°25E **63** D5
Southport U.K. 53°39N 3°0W **12** D4
Southport U.S.A. 42°3N 76°49W **82** D8
Southwest △ Australia 43°8S 146°5E **63** G4
Southwest Pacific Basin
  Pac. Oc. 40°0S 140°0W **5** A12
Southwold U.K. 52°20N 1°41E **13** E9
Southwood △ Australia 27°48S 150°8E **63** D5
Soutpansberg S. Africa 23°0S 29°30E **57** B4
Sovetsk Kaliningrad, Russia 55°6N 21°50E **9** J19
Sovetsk Kirov, Russia 57°38N 48°53E **18** C8
Sovetskaya Gavan
  Russia 48°58N 140°18E **27** E15
Sowma'eh Sarā Iran 37°17N 49°18E **47** B6
Sōya-Kaikyō = La Perouse Str.
  Asia 45°40N 142°0E **28** B11
Sōya-Misaki Japan 45°30N 141°55E **28** B10
Soyo Angola 6°13S 12°20E **54** F2
Sozh → Belarus 51°57N 30°48E **17** B16
Spa Belgium 50°29N 5°53E **15** D5
Spaatz I. Antarctica 73°10S 75°0W **5** D17
Spain ■ Europe 39°0N 4°0W **21** B4
Spalding Australia 33°30S 138°37E **63** E2
Spalding U.K. 52°48N 0°9W **12** E7

Spanaway U.S.A. 47°6N 122°26W **78** C4
Spangler U.S.A. 40°39N 78°48W **82** F6
Spanish Canada 46°12N 82°20W **72** C3
Spanish Fork U.S.A. 40°7N 111°39W **76** F8
Spanish Town
  Br. Virgin Is. 18°26N 64°26W **89** e
Spanish Town Jamaica 18°0N 76°57W **88** a
Sparks U.S.A. 39°32N 119°45W **78** F7
Sparta = Sparti Greece 37°5N 22°25E **23** F10
Sparta Mich., U.S.A. 43°10N 85°42W **81** D11
Sparta N.J., U.S.A. 41°2N 74°38W **83** E10
Sparta Wis., U.S.A. 43°56N 90°49W **80** D8
Spartanburg U.S.A. 34°56N 81°57W **85** D14
Sparti Greece 37°5N 22°25E **23** F10
Spartivento, C. Calabria,
  Italy 37°55N 16°4E **22** F7
Spartivento, C. Sard., Italy 38°53N 8°50E **22** E3
Sparwood Canada 49°44N 114°53W **70** D6
Spassk-Dalniy Russia 44°40N 132°48E **28** B6
Spatha, Akra Greece 35°42N 23°43E **23** G10
Spatsizi → Canada 57°42N 128°7W **70** B3
Spatsizi Plateau Wilderness △
  Canada 57°40N 128°0W **70** B3
Spean → U.K. 56°55N 4°59W **11** E4
Spearfish U.S.A. 44°30N 103°52W **80** C2
Spearman U.S.A. 36°12N 101°12W **84** C4
Speculator U.S.A. 43°30N 74°22W **83** C10
Speightstown Barbados 13°15N 59°39W **89** g
Spence Bay = Taloyoak
  Canada 69°32N 93°32W **68** D13
Spencer Idaho, U.S.A. 44°22N 112°11W **76** D7
Spencer Iowa, U.S.A. 43°9N 95°9W **80** D6
Spencer N.Y., U.S.A. 42°13N 76°30W **83** D8
Spencer Nebr., U.S.A. 42°53N 98°42W **80** D4
Spencer, C. Australia 35°20S 136°53E **63** F2
Spencer B. Namibia 25°30S 14°47E **56** C1
Spencer G. Australia 34°0S 137°20E **63** E2
Spencerville Canada 44°51N 75°33W **83** B9
Spences Bridge Canada 50°25N 121°20W **70** C4
Spennymoor U.K. 54°42N 1°36W **12** C6
Spenser Mts. N.Z. 42°15S 172°45E **59** E4
Sperrgebiet △ Namibia 27°38S 15°56E **56** C2
Sperrin Mts. U.K. 54°50N 7°0W **10** B5
Spey → U.K. 57°40N 3°6W **11** D5
Speyer Germany 49°29N 8°25E **16** D5
Spezand Pakistan 29°59N 67°0E **42** E2
Spiddle Ireland 53°15N 9°18W **10** C2
Spin Būldak Afghan. 31°1N 66°25E **42** D2
Spirit Lake U.S.A. 46°15N 122°9W **78** D4
Spirit River Canada 55°45N 118°50W **70** B5
Spiritwood Canada 53°24N 107°33W **71** C7
Spithead U.K. 50°45N 1°10W **13** G6
Spitsbergen = Svalbard
  Arctic 78°0N 17°0E **4** B8
Spjelkavik Norway 62°28N 6°22E **8** E12
Split Croatia 43°31N 16°26E **22** C7
Split L. Canada 56°8N 96°15W **71** B9
Split Lake Canada 56°8N 96°15W **71** B9
Spofford U.S.A. 29°10N 100°25W **84** G4
Spokane U.S.A. 47°40N 117°24W **76** C5
Spoleto Italy 42°44N 12°44E **22** C5
Spooner U.S.A. 45°50N 91°53W **80** C8
Sporyy Navolok, Mys
  Russia 75°50N 68°40E **26** B7
Sprague U.S.A. 47°18N 117°59W **76** C5
Spratly I. S. China Sea 8°38N 111°55E **36** C4
Spratly Is. S. China Sea 8°20N 112°0E **36** C4
Spray U.S.A. 44°50N 119°48W **76** D4
Spree → Germany 52°32N 13°12E **16** B7
Sprengisandur Iceland 64°52N 18°7W **8** D4
Spring City U.S.A. 40°11N 75°33W **83** F9
Spring Creek U.S.A. 40°44N 115°35W **76** F6
Spring Garden U.S.A. 39°52N 120°47W **78** F6
Spring Hall Barbados 13°18N 59°36W **89** g
Spring Hill U.S.A. 28°27N 82°41W **85** G13
Spring Mts. U.S.A. 36°0N 115°45W **79** J11
Spring Temple Buddha
  China 33°46N 112°27E **32** H7
Spring Valley U.S.A. 32°44N 116°59W **79** N10
Springbok S. Africa 29°42S 17°54E **56** C2
Springboro U.S.A. 41°48N 80°22W **82** E4
Springdale Canada 49°30N 56°6W **73** C8
Springdale U.S.A. 36°11N 94°8W **84** C7
Springer U.S.A. 36°22N 104°36W **77** H11
Springerville U.S.A. 34°8N 109°17W **77** J9
Springfield Canada 42°50N 80°56W **82** D4
Springfield N.Z. 43°19S 171°56E **59** E3
Springfield Colo.,
  U.S.A. 37°24N 102°37W **77** H12
Springfield Ill., U.S.A. 39°48N 89°39W **80** F9
Springfield Mass., U.S.A. 42°6N 72°35W **83** D12
Springfield Mo., U.S.A. 37°13N 93°17W **80** G7
Springfield Ohio, U.S.A. 39°55N 83°49W **81** F4
Springfield Oreg., U.S.A. 44°3N 123°1W **76** D2
Springfield Tenn., U.S.A. 36°31N 86°53W **85** C11
Springfield Vt., U.S.A. 43°18N 72°29W **83** C12
Springfontein S. Africa 30°15S 25°40E **56** D4
Springhill Canada 45°40N 64°4W **73** C7
Springhill U.S.A. 33°0N 93°28W **84** E8
Springhouse Canada 51°56N 122°7W **70** C4
Springlands = Corriverton
  Guyana 5°55N 57°20W **92** B7
Springs S. Africa 26°13S 28°25E **57** C4
Springsure Australia 24°8S 148°6E **62** C4
Springvale Australia 43°28N 70°48W **83** C14
Springville Calif., U.S.A. 36°8N 118°49W **78** J8
Springville N.Y., U.S.A. 42°31N 78°40W **82** D6
Springville Utah, U.S.A. 40°10N 111°37W **76** F8
Springwater U.S.A. 42°38N 77°35W **82** D7
Spruce-Creek U.S.A. 40°36N 78°9W **82** F6
Spruce Knob-Seneca Rocks △
  U.S.A. 38°50N 79°30W **81** F14
Spruce Mt. U.S.A. 44°12N 72°19W **83** B12
Sprucedale Canada 45°29N 79°28W **82** A5
Spur U.S.A. 33°28N 100°52W **84** J4
Spurn Hd. U.K. 53°35N 0°8E **12** D8
Spuzzum Canada 49°37N 121°23W **70** D4
Squam L. U.S.A. 43°45N 71°32W **83** C13
Squamish Canada 49°45N 123°10W **70** D4

Square Islands Canada 52°47N 55°47W **73** B8
Squires, Mt. Australia 26°14S 127°28E **61** E4
Srbija = Serbia ■ Europe 43°20N 20°0E **23** B9
Sre Ambel Cambodia 11°8N 103°46E **39** G4
Sre Khtum Cambodia 12°10N 106°52E **39** F6
Sre Umbell = Sre Ambel
  Cambodia 11°8N 103°46E **39** G4
Srebrenica Bos.-H. 44°6N 19°18E **23** B8
Sredinnyy Khrebet
  Russia 57°0N 160°0E **27** D17
Sredinnyy Ra. = Sredinnyy
  Khrebet Russia 57°0N 160°0E **27** D17
Srednekolymsk Russia 67°27N 153°40E **27** C16
Śrem Poland 52°6N 17°2E **17** B9
Sremska Mitrovica Serbia 44°59N 19°38E **23** B8
Srepok → Cambodia 13°33N 106°16E **38** F6
Sretensk Russia 52°10N 117°40E **27** D12
Sri Aman = Bandar Sri Aman
  Malaysia 1°15N 111°32E **36** D4
Sri Kalahasti India 13°45N 79°44E **45** H4
Sri Lanka ■ Asia 7°30N 80°50E **45** L5
Sri Pada = Adam's Peak
  Sri Lanka 6°48N 80°30E **45** L5
Sriharikota I. India 13°40N 80°20E **45** H5
Srikakulam India 18°14N 83°58E **44** E6
Srinagar India 34°5N 74°50E **43** B6
Srivardhan India 18°4N 73°3E **44** E1
Srivilliputtur India 9°31N 77°40E **45** K3
Srono Indonesia 8°24S 114°16E **37** J17
Srungavarapukota India 18°7N 83°10E **44** E6
Staaten → Australia 16°24S 141°17E **62** B3
Staaten River △
  Australia 16°15S 142°40E **62** B3
Stabbursdalen △ Norway 70°5N 24°15E **8** A21
Stade Germany 53°35N 9°29E **16** B5
Stadskanaal Neths. 53°4N 6°55E **15** A6
Staffa U.K. 56°27N 6°21W **11** E2
Stafford U.K. 52°49N 2°7W **12** E5
Stafford U.S.A. 37°58N 98°36W **80** G4
Stafford Springs U.S.A. 41°57N 72°18W **83** E12
Staffordshire □ U.K. 52°53N 2°10W **12** E5
Staines-upon-Thames
  U.K. 51°26N 0°29W **13** F7
Stakhanov Ukraine 48°35N 38°40E **19** E6
Stalowa Wola Poland 50°34N 22°3E **17** C12
Stalybridge U.K. 53°28N 2°3W **12** D5
Stamford Australia 21°15S 143°46E **62** C3
Stamford U.K. 52°39N 0°29W **13** E7
Stamford Conn., U.S.A. 41°3N 73°32W **83** E11
Stamford N.Y., U.S.A. 42°25N 74°38W **83** D10
Stamford Tex., U.S.A. 32°57N 99°48W **84** E5
Stamps U.S.A. 33°22N 93°30W **84** E8
Standerton S. Africa 26°55S 29°7E **57** C4
Standish U.S.A. 43°59N 83°57W **81** D12
Stanford S. Africa 34°26S 19°29E **56** D2
Stanford U.S.A. 47°9N 110°13W **76** C8
Stanger S. Africa 29°27S 31°14E **57** D5
Stanislaus → U.S.A. 37°40N 121°14W **78** H5
Stanke Dimitrov Bulgaria 42°17N 23°9E **23** C10
Stanley Australia 40°46S 145°19E **63** G4
Stanley Falk. Is. 51°40S 59°51W **96** G5
Stanley U.K. 54°53N 1°41W **12** C6
Stanley Idaho, U.S.A. 44°13N 114°56W **76** D6
Stanley N. Dak., U.S.A. 48°19N 102°23W **80** A2
Stanley Wis., U.S.A. 44°58N 90°56W **80** C8
Stanley Mission Canada 55°25N 104°33W **71** B8
Stanley Res. India 11°50N 77°40E **45** J3
Stanovoy Khrebet Russia 55°0N 130°0E **27** D14
Stanovoy Ra. = Stanovoy Khrebet
  Russia 55°0N 130°0E **27** D14
Stansmore Ra. Australia 21°23S 128°33E **60** D4
Stansted, London ✈ (STN)
  U.K. 51°54N 0°14E **13** F8
Stanthorpe Australia 28°36S 151°59E **63** D5
Stanton U.S.A. 32°8N 101°48W **84** E4
Stanwood U.S.A. 48°15N 122°23W **78** B4
Staples Canada 42°10N 82°35W **82** D2
Staples U.S.A. 46°21N 94°48W **80** B6
Stapleton U.S.A. 41°29N 100°31W **80** E3
Star City Canada 52°50N 104°20W **71** C8
Star Lake U.S.A. 44°10N 75°2W **83** B9
Stara Planina Bulgaria 43°15N 23°0E **23** C10
Stara Zagora Bulgaria 42°26N 25°39E **23** C11
Starachowice Poland 51°3N 21°2E **17** C11
Staraya Russa Russia 57°58N 31°23E **18** C5
Starbuck I. Kiribati 5°37S 155°55W **65** H12
Starcke △ Australia 14°56S 145°2E **62** A4
Stargard Szczeciński
  Poland 53°20N 15°0E **16** B8
Staritsa Russia 56°33N 34°55E **18** C5
Starke U.S.A. 29°57N 82°7W **85** G13
Starkville U.S.A. 33°28N 88°49W **85** E10
Starogard Gdański
  Poland 53°59N 18°30E **17** B10
Starokonstantinov =
  Starokonstantyniv
  Ukraine 49°48N 27°10E **17** D14
Starokonstantyniv
  Ukraine 49°48N 27°10E **17** D14
Start Pt. U.K. 50°13N 3°39W **13** G4
Staryy Chartoriysk
  Ukraine 51°15N 25°54E **17** C13
Staryy Oskol Russia 51°19N 37°55E **19** D6
State College U.S.A. 40°48N 77°52W **82** F7
Stateline U.S.A. 38°57N 119°56W **78** G7
Staten, I. = Estados, I. de Los
  Argentina 54°40S 64°30W **96** G4
Staten I. U.S.A. 40°35N 74°9W **83** F10
Statesboro U.S.A. 32°27N 81°47W **85** E14
Statesville U.S.A. 35°47N 80°53W **85** D14
Statia = St. Eustatius
  W. Indies 17°20N 63°0W **89** C7
Stauffer U.S.A. 34°45N 119°3W **79** L7
Staunton Ill., U.S.A. 39°1N 89°47W **80** F9
Staunton Va., U.S.A. 38°9N 79°4W **81** F14
Stavanger Norway 58°57N 5°40E **9** G11

Staveley N.Z. 43°40S 171°32E **59** E3
Stavelot Belgium 50°23N 5°55E **15** D5
Stavern Norway 59°0N 10°1E **9** G14
Stavoren Neths. 52°53N 5°22E **15** B5
Stavropol Russia 45°5N 42°0E **19** E7
Stawell Australia 37°5S 142°47E **63** F3
Stawell → Australia 20°20S 142°55E **62** C3
Stayner Canada 44°25N 80°5W **82** B4
Stayton U.S.A. 44°48N 122°48W **76** D2
Steamboat Springs
  U.S.A. 40°29N 106°50W **76** F10
Steele U.S.A. 46°51N 99°55W **80** B4
Steelton U.S.A. 40°14N 76°50W **82** F8
Steen River Canada 59°40N 117°12W **70** B5
Steens Mt. U.S.A. 42°35N 118°40W **76** E4
Steenwijk Neths. 52°47N 6°7E **15** B6
Steep Pt. Australia 26°8S 113°8E **61** E1
Steep Rock Canada 51°30N 98°48W **71** C9
Stefanie L. = Chew Bahir
  Ethiopia 4°40N 36°50E **49** G2
Stefansson Bay Antarctica 67°20S 59°8E **5** C5
Stefansson I. Canada 73°20N 105°45W **69** C10
Steiermark □ Austria 47°26N 15°0E **16** E8
Steilacoom U.S.A. 47°10N 122°36W **78** C4
Steilrandberge Namibia 17°45S 13°20E **56** A1
Steinbach Canada 49°32N 96°40W **71** D9
Steinhausen Namibia 21°49S 18°20E **56** B2
Steinkjer Norway 64°1N 11°31E **8** D14
Steinkopf S. Africa 29°18S 17°43E **56** C2
Stellarton Canada 45°32N 62°30W **73** C7
Stellenbosch S. Africa 33°58S 18°50E **56** E2
Stendal Germany 52°36N 11°53E **16** B6
Steornabhaigh = Stornoway
  U.K. 58°13N 6°23W **11** C2
Stepanakert = Xankändi
  Azerbaijan 39°52N 46°49E **46** B5
Stephens Creek Australia 31°50S 141°30E **63** E3
Stephens I. Canada 54°10N 130°45W **70** C2
Stephens L. Canada 56°32N 95°0W **71** B9
Stephenville Canada 48°31N 58°35W **73** C8
Stephenville U.S.A. 32°13N 98°12W **84** E5
Steppe Asia 50°0N 50°0E **24** C7
Sterkstroom S. Africa 31°32S 26°32E **56** E4
Sterling Colo., U.S.A. 40°37N 103°13W **76** F12
Sterling Ill., U.S.A. 41°48N 89°42W **80** E9
Sterling Kans., U.S.A. 38°13N 98°12W **80** F4
Sterling City U.S.A. 31°51N 101°0W **84** F4
Sterling Heights U.S.A. 42°35N 83°2W **81** D12
Sterling Run U.S.A. 41°25N 78°12W **82** E6
Sterlitamak Russia 53°40N 56°0E **18** D10
Stettin = Szczecin Poland 53°27N 14°27E **16** B8
Stettiner Haff Germany 53°47N 14°15E **16** B8
Stettler Canada 52°19N 112°40W **70** C6
Steubenville U.S.A. 40°22N 80°37W **82** F4
Stevenage U.K. 51°55N 0°13W **13** F7
Stevens Point U.S.A. 44°31N 89°34W **80** C9
Stevenson U.S.A. 45°42N 121°53W **78** E5
Stevenson → Australia 27°6S 135°33E **63** D2
Stevenson L. Canada 53°55N 96°0W **71** C9
Stevensville U.S.A. 46°30N 114°5W **76** C6
Stewart Canada 55°56N 129°57W **70** B3
Stewart U.S.A. 39°5N 119°46W **78** F7
Stewart → Canada 63°19N 139°26W **68** E4
Stewart, C. Australia 11°57S 134°56E **62** A1
Stewart, I. Chile 54°50S 71°15W **96** G2
Stewart I. N.Z. 46°58S 167°54E **59** G1
Stewarts Point U.S.A. 38°39N 123°24W **78** G3
Stewartville U.S.A. 43°51N 92°29W **80** D7
Stewiacke Canada 45°9N 63°22W **73** C7
Steynsburg S. Africa 31°15S 25°49E **56** E4
Steyr Austria 48°3N 14°25E **16** D8
Steytlerville S. Africa 33°17S 24°19E **56** E3
Stigler U.S.A. 35°15N 95°8W **84** D7
Stikine → Canada 56°40N 132°30W **70** B2
Stilfontein S. Africa 26°51S 26°50E **56** D4
Stillwater N.Z. 42°27S 171°20E **59** E3
Stillwater N.Y., U.S.A. 42°55N 73°41W **83** D11
Stillwater Okla., U.S.A. 36°7N 97°4W **84** C6
Stillwater Range U.S.A. 39°50N 118°5W **76** G4
Stillwater Res. U.S.A. 43°54N 75°3W **83** C9
Stilwell U.S.A. 35°49N 94°38W **84** D7
Stînga Nistrului = Transnistria □
  Moldova 47°20N 29°15E **17** E15
Ştip Macedonia 41°42N 22°10E **23** D10
Stirling Canada 44°18N 77°33W **82** B7
Stirling U.K. 56°8N 3°57W **11** E5
Stirling □ U.K. 56°12N 4°18W **11** E4
Stirling Ra. Australia 34°23S 118°0E **61** F2
Stirling Range △
  Australia 34°26S 118°20E **61** F2
Stittsville Canada 45°15N 75°55W **83** A9
Stjernøya Norway 70°20N 22°40E **8** A20
Stjørdalshalsen Norway 63°29N 10°51E **8** E14
Stockerau Austria 48°24N 16°12E **16** D9
Stockport U.K. 53°25N 2°9W **12** D5
Stocksbridge U.K. 53°29N 1°35W **12** D6
Stockton Calif., U.S.A. 37°58N 121°17W **78** H5
Stockton Kans., U.S.A. 39°26N 99°16W **80** F4
Stockton Mo., U.S.A. 37°42N 93°48W **80** G7
Stockton-on-Tees U.K. 54°35N 1°19W **12** C6
Stockton-on-Tees □ U.K. 54°35N 1°19W **12** C6
Stockton Plateau
  U.S.A. 30°30N 102°30W **84** F3
Stoeng Treng Cambodia 13°31N 105°58E **38** F5
Stoer, Pt. of U.K. 58°16N 5°23W **11** C3
Stoke-on-Trent U.K. 53°1N 2°11W **12** D5
Stoke-on-Trent □ U.K. 53°1N 2°11W **12** D5
Stokes □ Australia 33°45S 121°11E **61** F3
Stokes Bay Canada 45°0N 81°28W **82** B3
Stokes Pt. Australia 40°10S 143°56E **63** G3
Stokes Ra. Australia 15°50S 130°48E **60** C5
Stokksnes Iceland 64°14N 14°58W **8** D6
Stokmarknes Norway 68°34N 14°54E **8** B16
Stolac Bos.-H. 43°5N 17°59E **23** C7
Stolbovoy, Ostrov
  Russia 74°44N 135°14E **27** B14
Stolbtsy = Stowbtsy
  Belarus 53°30N 26°43E **17** B14
Stolin Belarus 51°53N 26°50E **17** C14
Stone U.K. 52°55N 2°9W **12** E5

Stoneboro U.S.A. 41°20N 80°7W **82** E4
Stonehaven U.K. 56°59N 2°12W **11** E6
Stonehenge Australia 24°22S 143°17E **62** C3
Stonehenge U.K. 51°9N 1°45W **13** F6
Stonewall Canada 50°10N 97°19W **71** C9
Stony I. U.S.A. 43°53N 76°19W **83** C8
Stony L. Man., Canada 58°51N 98°40W **71** B9
Stony L. Ont., Canada 44°30N 78°5W **82** B6
Stony Point U.S.A. 41°14N 73°59W **83** E11
Stony Pt. U.S.A. 43°50N 76°18W **83** C8
Stony Rapids Canada 59°16N 105°50W **71** B7
Stony Tunguska = Tunguska,
  Podkamennaya →
  Russia 61°50N 90°13E **27** C10
Stonyford U.S.A. 39°23N 122°33W **78** F4
Stora Lulevatten Sweden 67°10N 19°30E **8** C18
Stora Sjöfallet △ Sweden 67°36N 17°45E **8** C17
Storavan Sweden 65°45N 18°10E **8** D18
Stord Norway 59°52N 5°23E **9** G11
Store Bælt Denmark 55°20N 11°0E **9** J14
Storkerson Pen.
  Canada 72°30N 106°30W **68** C10
Storm B. Australia 43°10S 147°30E **63** G4
Storm Lake U.S.A. 42°39N 95°13W **80** D6
Stormberge S. Africa 31°16S 26°17E **56** E4
Stormsrivier S. Africa 33°59S 23°52E **56** E3
Stornoway U.K. 58°13N 6°23W **11** C2
Storozhinets = Storozhynets
  Ukraine 48°14N 25°45E **17** D13
Storozhynets Ukraine 48°14N 25°45E **17** D13
Storrs U.S.A. 41°49N 72°15W **83** E12
Storsjön Sweden 63°9N 14°30E **8** E16
Storuman Sweden 65°5N 17°10E **8** D17
Storuman, L. Sweden 65°13N 16°50E **8** D17
Stouffville Canada 43°58N 79°15W **82** C5
Stoughton Canada 49°40N 103°0W **71** D8
Stour → Dorset, U.K. 50°43N 1°47W **13** G6
Stour → Kent, U.K. 51°18N 1°22E **13** F9
Stour → Suffolk, U.K. 51°57N 1°4E **13** F9
Stourbridge U.K. 52°28N 2°8W **13** E5
Stout L. Canada 52°0N 94°40W **71** C10
Stove Pipe Wells Village
  U.S.A. 36°35N 117°11W **79** J9
Stow U.S.A. 41°10N 81°27W **82** E3
Stowbtsy Belarus 53°30N 26°43E **17** B14
Stowmarket U.K. 52°12N 1°0E **13** E9
Strabane U.K. 54°50N 7°27W **10** B4
Strahan Australia 42°9S 145°20E **63** G4
Stralsund Germany 54°18N 13°4E **16** A7
Strand S. Africa 34°9S 18°48E **56** E2
Stranda Møre og Romsdal,
  Norway 62°19N 6°58E **8** E12
Stranda Nord-Trøndelag,
  Norway 63°33N 10°14E **8** E14
Strangford L. U.K. 54°30N 5°37W **10** B6
Stranorlar Ireland 54°48N 7°46W **10** B4
Stranraer U.K. 54°54N 5°1W **11** G3
Strasbourg Canada 51°4N 104°55W **71** C8
Strasbourg France 48°35N 7°42E **20** B7
Stratford Canada 43°23N 81°0W **82** C3
Stratford N.Z. 39°20S 174°19E **59** C5
Stratford Calif., U.S.A. 36°11N 119°49W **78** J7
Stratford Conn., U.S.A. 41°12N 73°8W **83** E11
Stratford Tex., U.S.A. 36°20N 102°4W **84** C3
Stratford-upon-Avon
  U.K. 52°12N 1°42W **13** E6
Strath Spey U.K. 57°9N 3°49W **11** D5
Strathalbyn Australia 35°13S 138°53E **63** F2
Strathaven U.K. 55°40N 4°5W **11** F4
Strathcona △ Canada 49°38N 125°40W **70** D3
Strathmore Canada 51°5N 113°18W **70** C6
Strathmore U.K. 56°37N 3°7W **11** E5
Strathmore U.S.A. 36°9N 119°4W **78** J7
Strathnaver Canada 53°20N 122°33W **70** C4
Strathpeffer U.K. 57°35N 4°32W **11** D4
Strathroy Canada 42°58N 81°38W **82** D3
Strathy Pt. U.K. 58°36N 4°1W **11** C4
Strattanville U.S.A. 41°12N 79°19W **82** E5
Stratton U.S.A. 45°8N 70°26W **83** A14
Stratton Mt. U.S.A. 43°4N 72°55W **83** C12
Straubing Germany 48°52N 12°34E **16** D7
Straumnes Iceland 66°26N 23°8W **8** C2
Strawberry → U.S.A. 40°10N 110°24W **76** F8
Streaky B. Australia 32°48S 134°13E **63** E1
Streaky Bay Australia 32°51S 134°18E **63** E1
Streator U.S.A. 41°8N 88°50W **80** E9
Streetsboro U.S.A. 41°14N 81°21W **82** E3
Streetsville Canada 43°35N 79°42W **82** C5
Streng → Cambodia 13°12N 103°37E **38** F4
Strezhevoy Russia 60°42N 77°34E **26** C8
Strimonas → Greece 40°46N 23°51E **23** D10
Strokestown Ireland 53°47N 8°5W **10** C3
Stroma U.K. 58°41N 3°7W **11** C5
Strómboli Italy 38°47N 15°13E **22** E6
Stromeferry U.K. 57°21N 5°33W **11** D3
Stromness U.K. 58°58N 3°17W **11** C5
Stromsburg U.S.A. 41°7N 97°36W **80** E5
Strömstad Sweden 58°56N 11°10E **9** G14
Strömsund Sweden 63°51N 15°33E **8** E16
Strongsville U.S.A. 41°19N 81°50W **82** E3
Stronsay U.K. 59°7N 2°35W **11** B6
Stroud U.K. 51°45N 2°13W **13** F5
Stroud Road Australia 32°18S 151°57E **63** E5
Stroudsburg U.S.A. 40°59N 75°12W **83** F9
Struer Denmark 56°30N 8°35E **9** H13
Strugi Krasnyye Russia 58°21N 29°1E **9** G23
Strumica Macedonia 41°28N 22°41E **23** D10
Struthers Canada 48°41N 85°51W **72** C2
Struthers U.S.A. 41°4N 80°39W **82** E4
Stryker U.S.A. 48°41N 114°46W **76** B6
Stryy Ukraine 49°16N 23°48E **17** D12
Strzelecki Cr. → Australia 29°37S 139°59E **63** D2
Strzelecki Desert
  Australia 29°30S 140°0E **63** D3
Stuart Fla., U.S.A. 27°12N 80°15W **85** H14
Stuart Nebr., U.S.A. 42°36N 99°8W **80** D4
Stuart → Canada 54°0N 123°35W **70** C4
Stuart Bluff Ra. Australia 22°50S 131°52E **60** D5
Stuart I. U.S.A. 63°35N 162°30W **74** C7

Stuart L. *Canada* 54°30N 124°30W **70** C4
Stuart Ra. *Australia* 29°10S 134°56E **63** D1
Stull L. *Canada* 54°24N 92°34W **72** B1
Stung Treng = Stoeng Treng
Cambodia 13°31N 105°58E **38** F5
Stupart ➤ *Canada* 56°0N 93°25W **72** A1
Sturge I. *Antarctica* 67°26S 164°47E **5** C11
Sturgeon B. *Canada* 52°0N 97°50W **71** C9
Sturgeon Bay *U.S.A.* 44°50N 87°23W **80** C10
Sturgeon Falls *Canada* 46°25N 79°57W **72** C4
Sturgeon L. *Alta., Canada* 55°6N 117°32W **70** B5
Sturgeon L. *Ont., Canada* 50°0N 90°45W **72** C1
Sturgeon L. *Ont., Canada* 44°28N 78°43W **82** B6
Sturgis *Canada* 51°56N 102°36W **71** C8
Sturgis *Mich., U.S.A.* 41°48N 85°25W **81** E11
Sturgis *S. Dak., U.S.A.* 44°25N 103°31W **80** C2
Sturt △ *Australia* 27°1S 141°37E **63** D3
Sturt Cr. ➤ *Australia* 19°8S 127°50E **60** C4
Sturt Stony Desert
Australia 28°30S 141°0E **63** D3
Stutterheim *S. Africa* 32°33S 27°28E **56** D4
Stuttgart *Germany* 48°48N 9°11E **16** D5
Stuttgart *U.S.A.* 34°30N 91°33W **84** D9
Stuyvesant *U.S.A.* 42°23N 73°45W **83** D11
Stykkishólmur *Iceland* 65°2N 22°40W **8** D2
Styria = Steiermark □
Austria 47°26N 15°0E **16** E8
Su Xian = Suzhou *China* 33°41N 116°59E **32** H9
Suakin *Sudan* 19°8N 37°20E **53** E13
Suamico *U.S.A.* 44°38N 88°2W **80** C9
Suan *N. Korea* 38°42N 126°22E **33** E14
Suana *Indonesia* 8°44S 115°36E **37** K18
Suar *India* 29°2N 79°3E **43** E8
Subang *Indonesia* 6°34S 107°45E **37** G12
Subansiri ➤ *India* 26°48N 93°50E **41** F18
Subarnagiri *India* 19°50N 83°51E **44** E6
Subarnarekha ➤ *India* 22°34N 87°24E **43** H12
Subayhah *Si. Arabia* 30°2N 38°50E **46** D3
Subi *Indonesia* 2°58N 108°50E **36** D3
Subotica *Serbia* 46°6N 19°39E **23** A8
Suceava *Romania* 47°38N 26°16E **17** E14
Suchan = Partizansk
Russia 43°8N 133°9E **27** E14
Suchil *Mexico* 23°39N 103°54W **86** C4
Suchou = Suzhou
China 31°19N 120°38E **35** B13
Süchow = Xuzhou
China 34°18N 117°10E **33** G9
Suck ➤ *Ireland* 53°17N 8°3W **10** C3
Sucre *Bolivia* 19°0S 65°15W **92** G5
Sucuriú ➤ *Brazil* 20°47S 51°38W **93** H8
Sud, Pte. du *Canada* 49°3N 62°14W **73** C7
Sud-Ouest, Pte. *Canada* 49°23N 63°36W **73** C7
Sud Ouest, Pte. *Mauritius* 20°28S 57°18E **55** d
Sudan *U.S.A.* 34°4N 102°31W **84** D3
Sudan ■ *Africa* 15°0N 30°0E **53** E11
Sudbury *Canada* 46°30N 81°0W **72** C3
Sudbury *U.K.* 52°2N 0°45E **13** E8
Sudd *South Sudan* 8°20N 30°0E **53** G12
Sudeten Mts. = Sudety
Europe 50°20N 16°45E **17** C9
Sudety *Europe* 50°20N 16°45E **17** C9
Suðuroy *Færoe Is.* 61°32N 6°50W **8** F9
Sudirman, Pegunungan
Indonesia 4°30S 137°0E **37** E9
Sudong, Pulau *Singapore* 1°13N 103°44E **39** d
Sueca *Spain* 39°12N 0°21W **21** C5
Suemez I. *U.S.A.* 55°15N 133°20W **70** B2
Suez = El Suweis *Egypt* 29°58N 32°31E **53** C12
Suez, G. of = Suweis, Khalîg el
Egypt 28°40N 33°0E **53** C12
Suez Canal = Suweis, Qanâ es
Egypt 31°0N 32°20E **53** B12
Suffield *Canada* 50°12N 111°10W **70** C6
Suffolk *U.S.A.* 36°44N 76°35W **81** G15
Suffolk □ *U.K.* 52°16N 1°0E **13** E9
Sugaing = Sagaing
Burma 21°52N 95°59E **41** J19
Sugar Grove *U.S.A.* 41°59N 79°20W **82** E5
Sugarcreek *U.S.A.* 41°25N 79°52W **82** E5
Sugarive ➤ *India* 26°16N 86°24E **43** F12
Sugluk = Salluit *Canada* 62°14N 75°38W **69** E16
Şuḩār *Oman* 24°20N 56°40E **47** E8
Sühbaatar *Mongolia* 50°17N 106°10E **30** A10
Sühbaatar □ *Mongolia* 45°30N 114°0E **32** B8
Suheli Par *India* 10°5N 72°17E **45** J1
Suhl *Germany* 50°36N 10°42E **16** C6
Sui *Pakistan* 28°37N 69°19E **42** E3
Sui Xian *China* 34°25N 115°2E **32** G8
Suichang *China* 28°29N 119°15E **35** C12
Suichuan *China* 26°20N 114°32E **35** D10
Suide *China* 37°30N 110°12E **32** F6
Suifenhe *China* 44°25N 131°10E **33** B16
Suihua *China* 46°32N 126°55E **31** B14
Suijiang *China* 28°40N 103°59E **34** C4
Suining *Hunan, China* 26°35N 110°10E **35** D8
Suining *Jiangsu, China* 33°56N 117°58E **33** H9
Suining *Sichuan, China* 30°26N 105°35E **34** B5
Suiping *China* 33°10N 113°59E **32** H7
Suir ➤ *Ireland* 52°16N 7°9W **10** D4
Suisse = Switzerland ■
Europe 46°30N 8°0E **20** C8
Suisun City *U.S.A.* 38°15N 122°2W **78** G4
Suixi *China* 21°19N 110°18E **35** G8
Suiyang *Guizhou, China* 27°58N 107°29E **34** D6
Suiyang *Heilongjiang,
China* 44°30N 130°56E **33** B16
Suizhong *China* 40°21N 120°20E **33** D11
Suizhou *China* 31°42N 113°24E **35** B9
Sujangarh *India* 27°42N 74°31E **42** F6
Sujiatun *China* 41°39N 123°20E **33** D12
Sukabumi *Indonesia* 6°56S 106°50E **37** G12
Sukadana *Indonesia* 1°10S 110°0E **36** E4
Sukagawa *Japan* 37°17N 140°23E **29** F10
Sukamade *Indonesia* 8°30S 113°52E **37** H15
Sukaraja *Indonesia* 2°28S 110°25E **36** E4
Sukarno-Hatta Int., Jakarta ✈
(CGK) *Indonesia* 6°7S 106°40E **37** G12
Sukawati *Indonesia* 8°35S 115°17E **37** K18
Sukch'ŏn *N. Korea* 39°22N 125°35E **33** E13

Sukhona ➤ *Russia* 61°15N 46°39E **18** C6
Sukhothai *Thailand* 17°1N 99°49E **38** D2
Sukhumi = Sokhumi
Georgia 43°0N 41°0E **19** F7
Sukkur *Pakistan* 27°42N 68°54E **42** F3
Sukkur Barrage *Pakistan* 27°40N 68°50E **42** F3
Sukma *India* 18°24N 81°45E **44** E5
Sukri ➤ *India* 25°4N 71°43E **42** G4
Sukumo *Japan* 32°56N 132°44E **29** H6
Sukunka ➤ *Canada* 55°45N 121°15W **70** B4
Sula *Honduras* 15°2N 87°44W **88** C2
Sula, Kepulauan *Indonesia* 1°45S 125°0E **37** E7
Sulaco ➤ *Honduras* 15°2N 87°44W **88** C2
Sulaiman Range *Pakistan* 30°30N 69°50E **42** D3
Sūlār *Iran* 31°53N 51°54E **47** D6
Sulawesi *Indonesia* 2°0S 120°0E **37** E6
Sulawesi Barat □ *Indonesia* 3°0S 119°0E **37** E5
Sulawesi Sea = Celebes Sea
Indonesia 3°0N 123°0E **37** D6
Sulawesi Selatan □
Indonesia 2°30S 120°0E **37** E6
Sulawesi Tengah □
Indonesia 1°30S 121°0E **37** E6
Sulawesi Tenggara □
Indonesia 3°50S 122°0E **37** E6
Sulawesi Utara □ *Indonesia* 1°0N 124°0E **37** D6
Sulima *S. Leone* 6°58N 11°32W **52** G3
Sulina *Romania* 45°10N 29°40E **17** F15
Sulitjelma *Norway* 67°9N 16°3E **8** C17
Sullana *Peru* 4°52S 80°39W **92** D2
Sullivan *Ill., U.S.A.* 39°36N 88°37W **80** F9
Sullivan *Ind., U.S.A.* 39°6N 87°24W **80** F10
Sullivan *Mo., U.S.A.* 38°13N 91°10W **80** F8
Sullivan Bay *Canada* 50°55N 126°50W **70** C3
Sullivan I. = Lanbi Kyun
Burma 10°50N 98°20E **39** G2
Sullom Voe *U.K.* 60°27N 1°20W **11** A7
Sulphur *La., U.S.A.* 30°14N 93°23W **84** F8
Sulphur *Okla., U.S.A.* 34°31N 96°58W **84** D6
Sulphur Pt. *Canada* 60°56N 114°48W **70** A6
Sulphur Springs *U.S.A.* 33°8N 95°36W **84** E7
Sultan *Canada* 47°36N 82°47W **72** C3
Sultan *U.S.A.* 47°36N 121°49W **78** C5
Sultanābād = Arāk *Iran* 34°0N 49°40E **47** C6
Sultanpur *Mad. P., India* 23°9N 77°56E **42** H7
Sultanpur *Punjab, India* 31°13N 75°11E **42** D6
Sultanpur *Ut. P., India* 26°18N 82°4E **43** F10
Sulu Arch. *Phil.* 6°0N 121°0E **37** C6
Sulu Sea *E. Indies* 8°0N 120°0E **37** C6
Suluq *Libya* 31°44N 20°14E **53** B10
Suluru *India* 13°42N 80°1E **45** H5
Sulzberger Ice Shelf
Antarctica 78°0S 150°0W **5** E13
Sumalata *Indonesia* 1°0N 122°31E **37** D6
Sumampa *Argentina* 29°25S 63°29W **94** B3
Sumatera □ *Indonesia* 0°40N 100°20E **36** D2
Sumatera Barat □ *Indonesia* 1°0S 101°0E **36** E2
Sumatera Selatan □
Indonesia 3°0S 104°0E **36** E2
Sumatera Utara □
Indonesia 2°30N 98°0E **36** D1
Sumatra = Sumatera
Indonesia 0°40N 100°20E **36** D2
Sumba *Indonesia* 9°45S 119°35E **37** F5
Sumba, Selat *Indonesia* 9°0S 118°40E **37** F5
Sumbawa *Indonesia* 8°26S 117°30E **36** F5
Sumbawa Besar *Indonesia* 8°30S 117°26E **36** F5
Sumbawanga □ *Tanzania* 8°0S 31°30E **54** F6
Sumbe *Angola* 11°10S 13°48E **54** G2
Sumburgh Hd. *U.K.* 59°52N 1°17W **11** B7
Sumdeo *India* 31°26N 78°44E **43** D8
Sumdo *China* 35°6N 78°41E **43** B8
Sumedang *Indonesia* 6°52S 107°55E **37** G12
Sumen = Shumen
Bulgaria 43°18N 26°55E **23** C12
Sumenep *Indonesia* 7°1S 113°52E **37** G15
Sumgait = Sumqayıt
Azerbaijan 40°34N 49°38E **19** F8
Summer L. *U.S.A.* 42°50N 120°45W **76** E3
Summerland *Canada* 49°32N 119°41W **70** D5
Summerside *Canada* 46°24N 63°47W **73** C7
Summersville *U.S.A.* 38°17N 80°51W **81** F13
Summerville *Ga., U.S.A.* 34°29N 85°21W **85** D12
Summerville *S.C., U.S.A.* 33°1N 80°11W **85** E14
Summit Lake *Canada* 54°20N 122°40W **70** C4
Summit Peak *U.S.A.* 37°21N 106°42W **77** H10
Sumner *Iowa, U.S.A.* 42°51N 92°6W **80** D7
Sumner *Wash., U.S.A.* 47°12N 122°14W **78** C4
Sumoto *Japan* 34°21N 134°54E **29** G7
Šumperk *Czech Rep.* 49°59N 16°59E **17** D9
Sumqayıt *Azerbaijan* 40°34N 49°38E **19** F8
Sumter *U.S.A.* 33°55N 80°21W **85** E14
Sumy *Ukraine* 50°57N 34°50E **19** D5
Sun City *S. Africa* 25°17S 27°3E **56** C4
Sun City Center *U.S.A.* 27°43N 82°21W **85** H13
Sun Kosi ➤ *Nepal* 26°59N 87°8E **43** F12
Sun Lakes *U.S.A.* 33°10N 111°52W **77** K8
Sun Valley *U.S.A.* 43°42N 114°21W **76** E6
Sunagawa *Japan* 43°29N 141°55E **28** C10
Sunan *N. Korea* 39°15N 125°40E **33** E13
Sunart, L. *U.K.* 56°42N 5°43W **11** E3
Sunburst *U.S.A.* 48°53N 111°55W **76** B8
Sunbury *Australia* 37°35S 144°44E **63** F3
Sunbury *U.S.A.* 40°52N 76°48W **83** F8
Sunchales *Argentina* 30°58S 61°35W **94** C3
Suncheon *S. Korea* 34°52N 127°31E **33** G14
Sunch'ŏn *N. Korea* 39°25N 125°56E **33** E13
Suncook *U.S.A.* 43°8N 71°27W **83** C13
Sunda, Selat *Indonesia* 6°20S 105°30E **36** F3
Sunda Is. *Indonesia* 5°0S 105°0E **64** H2
Sunda Str. = Sunda, Selat
Indonesia 6°20S 105°30E **36** F3
Sunda Trench = Java Trench
Ind. Oc. 9°0S 105°0E **36** F3
Sundance *Canada* 56°32N 94°4W **71** B10
Sundance *U.S.A.* 44°24N 104°23W **76** D11
Sundar Nagar *India* 31°32N 76°53E **42** D7
Sundarbans *India* 22°0N 89°0E **41** J16
Sundarbans △ *India* 22°0N 88°54E **43** J13
Sundargarh *India* 22°4N 84°5E **44** C7

Sundays = Sondags ➤
S. Africa 33°44S 25°51E **56** D4
Sunderland *Canada* 44°16N 79°4W **82** B5
Sunderland *U.K.* 54°55N 1°23W **12** C6
Sundown △ *Australia* 28°49S 151°38E **63** D5
Sundre *Canada* 51°49N 114°38W **70** C6
Sundsvall *Sweden* 62°23N 17°17E **8** E17
Sungai Acheh *Malaysia* 5°8N 100°30E **39** c
Sungai Kolok *Thailand* 6°2N 101°58E **39** J3
Sungai Lembing *Malaysia* 3°55N 103°3E **39** L4
Sungai Petani *Malaysia* 5°37N 100°30E **39** K3
Sungaigerong *Indonesia* 2°59S 104°52E **36** E2
Sungailiat *Indonesia* 1°51S 106°8E **36** E3
Sungaipenuh *Indonesia* 2°1S 101°20E **36** E2
Sungari = Songhua Jiang ➤
China 47°45N 132°30E **31** B15
Sunghua Chiang = Songhua
Jiang ➤ *China* 47°45N 132°30E **31** B15
Sunland Park *U.S.A.* 31°50N 106°40W **77** L10
Sunndalsøra *Norway* 62°40N 8°33E **8** E13
Sunnyside *U.S.A.* 46°20N 120°0W **76** C4
Sunnyvale *U.S.A.* 37°23N 122°2W **78** H4
Suntar *Russia* 62°15N 117°30E **27** C12
Suomenselkä *Finland* 62°52N 24°0E **8** E21
Suomi = Finland ■ *Europe* 63°0N 27°0E **8** E22
Suomussalmi *Finland* 64°54N 29°10E **8** D23
Suoyarvi *Russia* 62°3N 32°20E **18** B5
Supai *U.S.A.* 36°15N 112°41W **77** H7
Supaul *India* 26°10N 86°40E **43** F12
Superior *Ariz., U.S.A.* 33°18N 111°6W **77** K8
Superior *Mont., U.S.A.* 47°12N 114°53W **76** C6
Superior *Nebr., U.S.A.* 40°1N 98°4W **80** E4
Superior *Wis., U.S.A.* 46°44N 92°6W **80** B7
Superior, L. *N. Amer.* 47°0N 87°0W **72** C2
Suphan Buri *Thailand* 14°14N 100°10E **38** E3
Suphan Dağı *Turkey* 38°54N 42°48E **46** B4
Supiori *Indonesia* 1°0S 136°0E **37** E9
Supung Shuiku *China* 40°35N 124°50E **33** D13
Sūq ash Shuyūkh *Iraq* 30°53N 46°28E **46** D5
Sūq Suwayq *Si. Arabia* 24°23N 38°27E **46** E3
Suqian *China* 33°54N 118°8E **33** H10
Suqutrā = Socotra *Yemen* 12°30N 54°0E **49** E5
Sūr *Lebanon* 33°19N 35°16E **48** B4
Şūr *Oman* 22°34N 59°32E **47** C6
Sur, Pt. *U.S.A.* 36°18N 121°54W **78** J5
Sura ➤ *Russia* 56°6N 46°0E **18** C8
Surab *Pakistan* 28°25N 66°15E **42** E2
Surabaja = Surabaya
Indonesia 7°17S 112°45E **37** G15
Surabaya *Indonesia* 7°17S 112°45E **37** G15
Surakarta *Indonesia* 7°35S 110°48E **37** G14
Surat *Australia* 27°10S 149°6E **63** D4
Surat *India* 21°12N 72°55E **44** D1
Surat Thani *Thailand* 9°6N 99°20E **39** H2
Suratgarh *India* 29°18N 73°55E **42** E5
Surathkal *India* 12°58N 74°46E **45** H2
Şūraymilā *Si. Arabia* 25°7N 46°7E **46** E5
Surendranagar *India* 22°45N 71°40E **42** H4
Surf *U.S.A.* 34°41N 120°36W **79** L6
Surfers Paradise *Australia* 28°0S 153°25E **63** D5
Surgana *India* 20°34N 73°37E **44** D1
Surgut *Russia* 61°14N 73°20E **26** C8
Suriapet *India* 17°10N 79°40E **44** F4
Surigao *Phil.* 9°47N 125°29E **37** C7
Surin *Thailand* 14°50N 103°34E **38** E4
Surinam ■ = Suriname ■
S. Amer. 4°0N 56°0W **93** C7
Suriname ■ *S. Amer.* 4°0N 56°0W **93** C7
Suriname ➤ *Suriname* 5°50N 55°15W **93** B7
Surjagarh *India* 19°36N 80°25E **44** E5
Surprise *U.S.A.* 33°38N 112°19W **77** K7
Surrey *Canada* 49°7N 122°45W **78** A4
Surrey □ *U.K.* 51°15N 0°31W **13** F7
Sursand *India* 26°39N 85°43E **43** F11
Sursar ➤ *India* 26°14N 87°3E **43** F12
Surt *Libya* 31°11N 16°39E **53** B9
Surt, Khalīj *Libya* 31°40N 18°30E **53** B9
Surtanah *Pakistan* 26°22N 70°0E **42** F4
Surtsey *Iceland* 63°20N 20°30W **8** E3
Suruga-Wan *Japan* 34°45N 138°30E **29** G9
Sūsah *Libya* 32°52N 21°59E **53** B10
Susaki *Japan* 33°22N 133°17E **29** H6
Susangerd *Iran* 31°35N 48°6E **47** D6
Susanville *U.S.A.* 40°25N 120°39W **76** F3
Susner *India* 23°57N 76°5E **42** H7
Susong *China* 30°10N 116°5E **35** B11
Susquehanna *U.S.A.* 41°57N 75°36W **83** E9
Susquehanna ➤ *U.S.A.* 39°33N 76°5W **83** G8
Susques *Argentina* 23°35S 66°25W **94** A2
Sussex *Canada* 45°45N 65°37W **73** C6
Sussex *U.S.A.* 41°13N 74°37W **83** E10
Sussex, East □ *U.K.* 51°0N 0°20E **13** G8
Sussex, West □ *U.K.* 51°0N 0°30W **13** G7
Sustut ➤ *Canada* 56°20N 127°30W **70** B3
Susuman *Russia* 62°47N 148°10E **27** C15
Susunu *Indonesia* 3°7S 133°39E **37** E8
Susurluk *Turkey* 39°54N 28°8E **23** E13
Sutay Uul *Asia* 46°35N 93°38E **30** B7
Sutherland *S. Africa* 32°24S 20°40E **56** D3
Sutherland *U.K.* 58°12N 4°50W **11** C4
Sutherland *U.S.A.* 41°10N 101°8W **80** E3
Sutherland Falls *N.Z.* 44°48S 167°46E **59** F1
Sutherlin *U.S.A.* 43°23N 123°19W **76** E2
Suthri *India* 23°3N 68°55E **42** H3
Sutlej ➤ *Pakistan* 29°23N 71°3E **42** E4
Sutter *U.S.A.* 39°10N 121°45W **78** F5
Sutter Buttes *U.S.A.* 39°12N 121°49W **78** F5
Sutter Creek *U.S.A.* 38°24N 120°48W **78** G6
Sutton *Canada* 45°6N 72°37W **83** A12
Sutton *Nebr., U.S.A.* 40°36N 97°52W **80** E5
Sutton *W. Va., U.S.A.* 38°40N 80°43W **81** F13
Sutton ➤ *Canada* 55°15N 83°45W **72** A3
Sutton Coldfield *U.K.* 52°35N 1°49W **13** E6
Sutton in Ashfield *U.K.* 53°8N 1°16W **12** D6
Sutton L. *Canada* 54°15N 84°42W **72** B3
Suttor ➤ *Australia* 21°36S 147°2E **62** C4
Suttsu *Japan* 42°48N 140°14E **28** C10
Sutwik I. *U.S.A.* 56°34N 157°12W **74** D8
Suva *Fiji* 18°6S 178°30E **59** a

Suva Planina *Serbia* 43°10N 22°5E **23** C10
Suvorov Is. = Suwarrow Is.
Cook Is. 13°15S 163°5W **65** J11
Suwałki *Poland* 54°8N 22°59E **17** A12
Suwannaphum *Thailand* 15°33N 103°47E **38** E4
Suwannee ➤ *U.S.A.* 29°17N 83°10W **85** G13
Suwanose-Jima *Japan* 29°38N 129°43E **29** K4
Suwarrow Is. *Cook Is.* 13°15S 163°5W **65** J11
Suweis, Khalîg el *Egypt* 28°40N 33°0E **53** C12
Suweis, Qanâ es *Egypt* 31°0N 32°20E **53** B12
Suwon *S. Korea* 37°17N 127°1E **33** F14
Suzdal *Russia* 56°29N 40°26E **18** C7
Suzhou *Anhui, China* 33°41N 116°59E **32** H9
Suzhou *Jiangsu, China* 31°19N 120°38E **35** B13
Suzu *Japan* 37°25N 137°17E **29** F8
Suzu-Misaki *Japan* 37°31N 137°21E **29** F8
Suzuka *Japan* 34°55N 136°36E **29** G8
Svalbard *Arctic* 78°0N 17°0E **4** B8
Svalbard Radio = Longyearbyen
Svalbard 78°13N 15°40E **4** B8
Svappavaara *Sweden* 67°40N 21°3E **8** C19
Svartisen *Norway* 66°40N 13°59E **8** C15
Svay Chek *Cambodia* 13°48N 102°58E **38** F4
Svay Rieng *Cambodia* 11°9N 105°45E **39** G5
Svealand *Sweden* 60°20N 15°0E **9** F16
Sveg *Sweden* 62°2N 14°21E **8** E16
Svendborg *Denmark* 55°4N 10°35E **9** J14
Sverdlovsk = Yekaterinburg
Russia 56°50N 60°30E **26** D7
Sverdrup Chan. *Canada* 79°56N 96°25W **69** B12
Sverdrup Is. *Canada* 79°0N 97°0W **66** B10
Sverige = Sweden ■ *Europe* 57°0N 15°0E **9** H16
Svetlana *Russia* 33°43N 138°18E **28** A9
Svetlogorsk = Svyetlahorsk
Belarus 52°38N 29°46E **17** B15
Svir ➤ *Russia* 60°30N 32°48E **18** B5
Svishtov *Bulgaria* 43°36N 25°23E **23** C11
Svislach *Belarus* 53°3N 24°2E **17** B13
Svizzera = Switzerland ■
Europe 46°30N 8°0E **20** C8
Svobodnyy *Russia* 51°20N 128°0E **27** D13
Svolvær *Norway* 68°15N 14°34E **8** B16
Svyetlahorsk *Belarus* 52°38N 29°46E **17** B15
Swabian Alps = Schwäbische Alb
Germany 48°20N 9°30E **16** D5
Swaffham *U.K.* 52°39N 0°42E **13** E8
Swains I. *Amer. Samoa* 11°11S 171°4W **65** J11
Swainsboro *U.S.A.* 32°36N 82°20W **85** E13
Swakop ➤ *Namibia* 22°38S 14°36E **56** C2
Swakopmund *Namibia* 22°37S 14°30E **56** C1
Swale ➤ *U.K.* 54°5N 1°20W **12** C6
Swamihalli *India* 14°52N 76°38E **45** G3
Swan ➤ *Australia* 32°3S 115°45E **61** F2
Swan ➤ *Canada* 52°30N 100°45W **71** C8
Swan Hill *Australia* 35°20S 143°33E **63** F3
Swan Hills *Canada* 54°43N 115°24W **70** C5
Swan Is. = Santanilla, Is.
Honduras 17°22N 83°57W **88** C3
Swan L. *Man., Canada* 52°30N 100°40W **71** C8
Swan L. *Ont., Canada* 54°16N 91°11W **72** B1
Swan Ra. *U.S.A.* 48°0N 113°45W **76** C7
Swan River *Canada* 52°10N 101°16W **71** C8
Swanage *U.K.* 50°36N 1°58W **13** G6
Swansea *Australia* 42°8S 148°4E **63** G4
Swansea *Canada* 43°37N 79°27W **82** c1
Swansea *U.K.* 51°37N 3°57W **13** F4
Swansea □ *U.K.* 51°38N 4°3W **13** F3
Swartberge *S. Africa* 33°20S 22°0E **56** D3
Swartmodder *S. Africa* 28°1S 20°32E **56** D3
Swartnossob ➤ *Namibia* 23°8S 18°42E **56** B2
Swartruggens *S. Africa* 25°39S 26°42E **56** D4
Swastika *Canada* 48°7N 80°6W **72** C3
Swat ➤ *Pakistan* 34°40N 72°5E **43** B5
Swatow = Shantou
China 23°18N 116°40E **35** F11
Swaziland ■ *Africa* 26°30S 31°30E **57** C5
Sweden ■ *Europe* 57°0N 15°0E **9** H16
Sweet Grass *U.S.A.* 48°59N 111°58W **76** B8
Sweet Home *U.S.A.* 44°24N 122°44W **76** D2
Sweetwater *Nev., U.S.A.* 38°27N 119°9W **78** G7
Sweetwater *Tenn.,
U.S.A.* 35°36N 84°28W **85** D12
Sweetwater *Tex., U.S.A.* 32°28N 100°25W **84** E4
Sweetwater ➤ *U.S.A.* 42°31N 107°2W **76** E10
Swellendam *S. Africa* 34°1S 20°26E **56** D3
Świdnica *Poland* 50°50N 16°30E **17** C9
Świdnik *Poland* 51°13N 22°39E **17** C12
Świebodzin *Poland* 52°15N 15°31E **16** B8
Świecie *Poland* 53°25N 18°30E **17** B10
Swift Current *Canada* 50°20N 107°45W **71** C7
Swift Current ➤
Canada 50°38N 107°44W **71** C7
Swilly, L. *Ireland* 55°12N 7°33W **10** A4
Swindon *U.S.A.* 51°34N 1°46W **13** F6
Swindon □ *U.K.* 51°34N 1°46W **13** F6
Swinemünde = Świnoujście
Poland 53°54N 14°16E **16** B8
Swinford *Ireland* 53°57N 8°58W **10** C3
Świnoujście *Poland* 53°54N 14°16E **16** B8
Switzerland ■ *Europe* 46°30N 8°0E **20** C8
Swoyerville *U.S.A.* 41°18N 75°53W **83** E9
Sydenham ➤ *Canada* 42°33N 82°25W **82** D2
Sydney *Australia* 33°53S 151°10E **63** E5
Sydney *Canada* 46°7N 60°7W **73** C7
Sydney L. *Canada* 50°41N 94°25W **71** C10
Sydney Mines *Canada* 46°18N 60°15W **73** C7
Sydprøven = Alluitsup Paa
Greenland 60°30N 45°35W **4** C5
Sydra, G. of = Surt, Khalīj
Libya 31°40N 18°30E **53** B9
Sykesville *U.S.A.* 41°3N 78°50W **82** E6
Syktyvkar *Russia* 61°45N 50°40E **18** B9
Sylacauga *U.S.A.* 33°10N 86°15W **85** E11
Sylarna *Sweden* 63°2N 12°13E **8** E15
Sylhet *Bangla.* 24°54N 91°52E **41** G17
Sylhet □ *Bangla.* 24°50N 91°50E **41** G17
Sylt *Germany* 54°54N 8°22E **16** A5
Sylvan Beach *U.S.A.* 43°12N 75°44W **83** C9
Sylvan Lake *Canada* 52°20N 114°3W **70** C6
Sylvania *Ohio, U.S.A.* 41°43N 83°42W **81** E12
Sylvania *Ga., U.S.A.* 32°45N 81°38W **85** E14
Sym *Russia* 60°20N 88°18E **26** C9
Synnot Ra. *Australia* 16°30S 125°20E **60** C4

Syöte △ *Finland* 65°44N 27°58E **8** D22
Syowa *Antarctica* 68°50S 12°0E **5** C5
Syracuse *Kans., U.S.A.* 37°59N 101°45W **80** G3
Syracuse *N.Y., U.S.A.* 43°3N 76°9W **83** C8
Syracuse *Nebr., U.S.A.* 40°39N 96°11W **80** E5
Syrdarya ➤ *Kazakhstan* 46°3N 61°0E **26** E7
Syria ■ *Asia* 35°0N 38°0E **46** C3
Syrian Desert = Shām, Bādiyat ash
Asia 32°0N 40°0E **46** C3
Syros = Ermoupoli
Greece 37°28N 24°57E **23** F11
Syzran *Russia* 53°12N 48°30E **18** D8
Szczecin *Poland* 53°27N 14°27E **16** B8
Szczecinek *Poland* 53°43N 16°41E **17** B9
Szczeciński, Zalew = Stettiner Haff
Germany 53°47N 14°15E **16** B8
Szczytno *Poland* 53°33N 21°0E **17** B11
Szechuan = Sichuan □
China 30°30N 103°0E **34** B5
Szechuan Basin = Sichuan Pendi
China 30°45N 105°0E **34** B5
Szeged *Hungary* 46°16N 20°10E **17** E11
Székesfehérvár *Hungary* 47°15N 18°25E **17** E10
Szekszárd *Hungary* 46°22N 18°42E **17** E10
Szentes *Hungary* 46°39N 20°21E **17** E11
Szolnok *Hungary* 47°10N 20°15E **17** E11
Szombathely *Hungary* 47°14N 16°38E **17** E9

T

Ta Khli *Thailand* 15°15N 100°21E **38** E3
Ta Lai *Vietnam* 11°24N 107°23E **39** G6
Ta Phraya △ *Thailand* 14°11N 102°49E **38** E4
Taal Volcano *Phil.* 14°7N 120°59E **37** B6
Taamisaari = Raasepori
Finland 60°0N 23°26E **9** G20
Tabacal *Argentina* 23°15S 64°15W **94** A3
Tabaco *Phil.* 13°22N 123°44E **37** B6
Ṭābah *Si. Arabia* 26°55N 42°38E **46** E4
Tabanan *Indonesia* 8°32S 115°8E **37** K18
TabarDará, Serranía de
Panama 8°35N 81°40W **88** E3
Tabasco □ *Mexico* 18°0N 92°40W **87** D6
Tabāsīn *Iran* 31°12N 57°54E **47** D8
Tabatinga *Brazil* 4°6S 69°56W **92** D5
Tabatinga, Serra da
Brazil 10°30S 44°0W **93** F10
Taber *Canada* 49°47N 112°8W **70** D6
Tablas I. *Phil.* 12°25N 122°2E **37** B6
Table, Pte. de la *Réunion* 21°14S 55°48E **55** c
Table B. *Canada* 53°40N 56°25W **73** B8
Table I. *Burma* 14°12N 93°22E **45** G11
Table Rock L. *U.S.A.* 36°36N 93°19W **80** G7
Tabletop, Mt. *Australia* 23°24S 147°11E **62** C4
Tábor *Czech Rep.* 49°25N 14°39E **16** D8
Tabora *Tanzania* 5°2S 32°50E **54** F6
Tabou *Ivory C.* 4°30N 7°20W **52** H4
Tabrīz *Iran* 38°7N 46°20E **46** B5
Tabuaeran *Kiribati* 3°51N 159°22W **65** G12
Tabūk *Si. Arabia* 28°23N 36°36E **46** D3
Tabūk □ *Si. Arabia* 27°40N 36°50E **46** E3
Tacámbaro de Codallos
Mexico 19°14N 101°28W **86** D4
Tacheng *China* 46°40N 82°58E **30** B5
Tach'i *Taiwan* 24°53N 121°17E **35** E13
Tachia *Taiwan* 24°25N 120°28E **35** E13
Tachilek *Burma* 20°26N 99°52E **38** B2
Tach'ing Shan = Daqing Shan
China 40°40N 111°0E **32** D6
Tacloban *Phil.* 11°15N 124°58E **37** B6
Tacna *Peru* 18°0S 70°20W **92** G4
Tacoma *U.S.A.* 47°14N 122°26W **78** C4
Tacuarembó *Uruguay* 31°45S 56°0W **95** C4
Tademaït, Plateau du
Algeria 28°30N 2°30E **52** C6
Tādepallegudem *India* 16°50N 81°30E **44** F5
Tadjourah *Djibouti* 11°50N 42°55E **49** E3
Tadmor *N.Z.* 41°27S 172°45E **59** D4
Tadoba □ *India* 20°30N 78°40E **44** D4
Tadoule L. *Canada* 58°36N 98°20W **71** B9
Tadoussac *Canada* 48°11N 69°42W **73** C6
Tadpatri *India* 14°55N 78°1E **45** G4
Tadzhikistan = Tajikistan ■
Asia 38°30N 70°0E **26** F8
Taegu = Daegu
S. Korea 35°50N 128°37E **33** G15
Taegwan *N. Korea* 40°13N 125°12E **33** D13
Taejŏn = Daejeon
S. Korea 36°20N 127°28E **33** F14
Taen, Ko *Thailand* 9°22N 99°57E **39** b
Tafalla *Spain* 42°30N 1°41W **21** A5
Tafermaar *Indonesia* 6°47S 134°10E **37** F8
Tafí Viejo *Argentina* 26°43S 65°17W **94** B2
Tafīhān *Iran* 29°25N 52°39E **47** D7
Tafresh *Iran* 34°45N 49°57E **47** C6
Taft *Iran* 31°45N 54°14E **47** D7
Taft *Phil.* 11°57N 125°30E **37** B7
Taft *U.S.A.* 35°8N 119°28W **79** K7
Taftān, Kūh-e *Iran* 28°40N 61°0E **47** D9
Tafwap *India* 7°23N 93°43E **45** L11
Taga *Samoa* 13°46S 172°28W **59** b
Taga Dzong *Bhutan* 27°5N 89°55E **41** F16
Taganrog *Russia* 47°12N 38°50E **19** E6
Tagbilaran *Phil.* 9°39N 123°51E **37** C6
Tagish *Canada* 60°19N 134°16W **70** A2
Tagish L. *Canada* 60°10N 134°20W **70** A2
Tagliamento ➤ *Italy* 45°38N 13°6E **22** B5
Taguatinga *Brazil* 12°27S 46°22W **93** F10
Tagum *Phil.* 7°33N 125°53E **37** C7
Tagus = Tejo ➤ *Europe* 38°40N 9°24W **21** C1
Tahakopa *N.Z.* 46°30S 169°23E **59** G2
Tahan, Gunung *Malaysia* 4°34N 102°17E **39** K4
Tahat *Algeria* 23°18N 5°33E **52** D7
Tāherī *Iran* 27°43N 52°20E **47** E7
Tahiti *French Polynesia* 17°37S 149°27W **59** d
Tahiti, I. *Tahiti* 17°37S 149°27W **59** d
Tahlequah *U.S.A.* 35°55N 94°58W **84** D7

166 Tahoe, L. INDEX TO WORLD MAPS

Tahoe, L. U.S.A. 39°6N 120°2W 78 G6
Tahoe City U.S.A. 39°10N 120°9W 78 F6
Tahoka U.S.A. 33°10N 101°48W 84 E4
Taholah U.S.A. 47°21N 124°17W 78 C2
Tahoua Niger 14°57N 5°16E 52 F7
Tahrūd Iran 29°26N 57°49E 47 D8
Tahsis Canada 49°55N 126°40W 70 D3
Tahta Egypt 26°44N 31°32E 53 C12
Tahulandang Indonesia 2°27N 125°23E 37 D7
Tahuna Indonesia 3°38N 125°30E 37 D7
Tai Hu China 31°5N 120°10E 35 B13
Tai Pang Wan China 22°33N 114°24E 31 a
Tai Po China 22°27N 114°10E 31 a
Tai Rom Yen △ Thailand 8°45N 99°30E 39 H2
Tai Shan China 36°25N 117°20E 33 F9
Tai'an China 36°12N 117°8E 33 F9
Taiarapu, Presqu'île de Tahiti 17°47S 149°14W 59 d
Taibai Shan China 33°57N 107°45E 32 H4
Taibus Qi China 41°54N 115°22E 32 D8
Taicang China 31°30N 121°5E 35 B13
T'aichung Taiwan 24°9N 120°37E 35 E13
Taieri → N.Z. 46°3S 170°12E 59 G3
Taigu China 37°28N 112°30E 32 F7
Taihang Shan China 36°0N 113°30E 32 G7
Taihape N.Z. 39°41S 175°48E 59 C5
Taihe Anhui, China 33°20N 115°42E 32 H8
Taihe Jiangxi, China 26°47N 114°52E 35 D10
Taihu China 30°22N 116°20E 35 B11
Taijiang China 26°39N 108°21E 34 D7
Taikang China 34°5N 114°50E 32 G8
Tailem Bend Australia 35°12S 139°29E 63 F2
T'ailuko Taiwan 24°9N 121°37E 35 E13
Taimyr Peninsula = Taymyr, Poluostrov Russia 75°0N 100°0E 27 B11
Tain U.K. 57°49N 4°4W 11 D4
T'ainan Taiwan 23°0N 120°10E 35 F13
Taining China 26°54N 117°9E 35 D11
Taipa China 22°10N 113°35E 31 a
T'aipei Taiwan 25°4N 121°29E 35 E13
Taiping China 30°15N 118°6E 35 B12
Taiping Malaysia 4°51N 100°44E 39 K3
Taiping Dao = Itu Aba I. S. China Sea 10°23N 114°21E 36 B4
Taipingchuan China 44°23N 123°11E 33 B12
Taipingzhen China 33°35N 111°42E 32 H6
Taishan China 22°14N 112°41E 35 F9
Taishun China 27°30N 119°42E 35 D12
Taitao, Pen. de Chile 46°30S 75°0W 96 F2
T'aitung Taiwan 22°43N 121°4E 35 F13
Taivalkoski Finland 65°33N 28°12E 8 D23
Taiwan ■ Asia 23°30N 121°0E 35 F13
Taiwan Strait Asia 24°40N 120°0E 35 E12
Taixing China 32°11N 120°0E 35 A13
Taiyiba Israel 32°36N 35°27E 48 C4
Taiyuan China 37°52N 112°33E 32 F7
Taizhou Jiangsu, China 32°28N 119°55E 35 A12
Taizhou Zhejiang, China 28°40N 121°24E 35 C13
Taizhou Liedao China 28°30N 121°55E 35 C13
Ta'izz Yemen 13°35N 44°2E 49 E3
Taj Mahal India 27°10N 78°2E 42 F8
Tājābād Iran 30°2N 54°24E 47 D7
Tajikistan ■ Asia 38°30N 70°0E 26 F8
Tajima = Minamiaizu Japan 37°12N 139°46E 29 F9
Tajo = Tejo → Europe 38°40N 9°24W 21 C1
Tak Thailand 16°52N 99°8E 38 D2
Takāb Iran 36°24N 47°7E 46 B5
Takachiho Japan 32°42N 131°18E 29 H5
Takachu Botswana 22°37S 21°58E 56 B3
Takada Japan 37°7N 138°15E 29 F9
Takahagi Japan 36°43N 140°45E 29 F10
Takaka N.Z. 40°51S 172°50E 59 D4
Takamaka Seychelles 4°50S 55°30E 55 b
Takamatsu Japan 34°20N 134°5E 29 G7
Takaoka Japan 36°47N 137°0E 29 F8
Takapuna N.Z. 36°47S 174°47E 59 B5
Takasaki Japan 36°20N 139°0E 29 F9
Takatsuki Japan 34°51N 135°37E 29 G7
Takayama Japan 36°18N 137°11E 29 F8
Take-Shima Japan 30°49N 130°26E 29 J5
Takefu = Echizen Japan 35°50N 136°10E 29 G8
Takengon Indonesia 4°45N 96°50E 36 D1
Takeo Cambodia 10°59N 104°47E 39 G5
Takeo Japan 33°12N 130°1E 29 H5
Takeshima = Liancourt Rocks Asia 37°15N 131°52E 29 F5
Tākestān Iran 36°0N 49°40E 47 C6
Taketa Japan 32°58N 131°24E 29 H5
Takh India 33°6N 77°32E 43 C7
Takhmau Cambodia 11°29N 104°57E 39 G5
Takht-e Soleyman Iran 36°36N 47°14E 46 B5
Takht-Sulaiman Pakistan 31°40N 69°58E 42 D3
Takikawa Japan 43°33N 141°54E 28 C10
Takla L. Canada 55°15N 125°45W 70 B3
Takla Landing Canada 55°30N 125°50W 70 B3
Taklamakan China 38°0N 83°0E 30 D5
Taklamakan Shamo = Taklamakan China 38°0N 83°0E 30 D5
Taksimo Russia 56°20N 114°52E 27 D12
Taku → Canada 58°30N 133°50W 70 B2
Takua Thung Thailand 8°24N 98°27E 39 a
Tal Halāl Iran 28°54N 55°1E 47 D7
Tala Uruguay 34°21S 55°46W 95 C4
Talagang Pakistan 32°55N 72°25E 42 C5
Talagante Chile 33°40S 70°50W 94 C1
Talaimannar Sri Lanka 9°6N 79°43E 45 K4
Talamanca, Cordillera de Cent. Amer. 9°20N 83°20W 88 E3
Talampaya △ Argentina 29°43S 67°42W 94 B2
Talara Peru 4°38S 81°18W 92 D2
Talas Kyrgyzstan 42°30N 72°13E 26 E8
Talāta Egypt 30°36N 32°20E 48 E1
Talaud, Kepulauan Indonesia 4°30N 126°50E 37 D7
Talaud Is. = Talaud, Kepulauan Indonesia 4°30N 126°50E 37 D7
Talavera de la Reina Spain 39°55N 4°46W 21 C3
Talayan Phil. 6°52N 124°24E 37 C6
Talbandh India 22°3N 86°20E 43 H12
Talbot, C. Australia 13°48S 126°43E 60 B4
Talbragar → Australia 32°12S 148°37E 63 E4
Talca Chile 35°28S 71°40W 94 D1
Talcahuano Chile 36°40S 73°10W 94 D1
Talcher India 21°0N 85°18E 44 D7
Taldy Kurgan = Taldyqorghan Kazakhstan 45°10N 78°45E 30 B4
Taldyqorghan Kazakhstan 45°10N 78°45E 30 B4
Tālesh Iran 37°58N 48°58E 47 B6
Tālesh, Kūhhā-ye Iran 37°42N 48°55E 47 B6
Talguppa India 14°13N 74°56E 45 G2
Tali Post South Sudan 5°55N 30°44E 53 G12
Taliabu Indonesia 1°50S 125°0E 37 E6
Talibon Phil. 10°9N 124°20E 37 B6
Talihina U.S.A. 34°45N 95°3W 84 D7
Talikota India 16°29N 76°17E 45 F3
Talipparamba India 12°3N 75°21E 45 H2
Taliwang Indonesia 8°50S 116°55E 36 F5
Talkot Nepal 29°37N 81°19E 43 E9
Tall 'Afar Iraq 36°22N 42°27E 46 B4
Tall Kalakh Syria 34°41N 36°15E 48 A5
Talladega U.S.A. 33°26N 86°6W 85 E11
Tallahassee U.S.A. 30°27N 84°17W 85 F12
Tallangatta Australia 36°15S 147°19E 63 F4
Tallering Pk. Australia 28°6S 115°37E 61 E2
Talli Pakistan 29°32N 68°8E 42 E3
Tallinn Estonia 59°22N 24°48E 9 G21
Tallmadge U.S.A. 41°6N 81°27W 82 E3
Tallulah U.S.A. 32°25N 91°11W 84 E9
Talnakh Russia 69°29N 88°22E 27 C9
Taloda India 21°34N 74°11E 44 D2
Taloyoak Canada 69°32N 93°32W 68 D13
Talpa de Allende Mexico 20°23N 104°51W 86 C4
Talparo Trin. & Tob. 10°30N 61°17W 93 K15
Talsi Latvia 57°10N 22°30E 9 H20
Taltal Chile 25°23S 70°33W 94 B1
Taltson → Canada 61°24N 112°46W 70 A6
Talwood Australia 28°29S 149°29E 63 D4
Talyawalka Cr. → Australia 32°28S 142°22E 63 E3
Tam Dao △ Vietnam 21°45N 105°45E 38 B5
Tam Ky Vietnam 15°34N 108°29E 38 E7
Tam Quan Vietnam 14°35N 109°3E 38 E7
Tama U.S.A. 41°58N 92°35W 80 E7
Tama Abu, Banjaran Malaysia 3°50N 115°5E 36 D5
Tamale Ghana 9°22N 0°50W 52 G5
Taman Negara △ Malaysia 4°38N 102°26E 39 K4
Tamano Japan 34°29N 133°59E 29 G6
Tamanrasset Algeria 22°50N 5°30E 52 D7
Tamaqua U.S.A. 40°48N 75°58W 83 F9
Tamar → U.K. 50°27N 4°15W 13 G3
Tamarin Mauritius 20°19S 57°20E 55 d
Tamashima Japan 34°32N 133°40E 29 G6
Tamatave = Toamasina Madag. 18°10S 49°25E 55 H9
Tamaulipas ☐ Mexico 24°0N 98°45W 87 C5
Tamaulipas, Sierra de Mexico 23°30N 98°20W 87 C5
Tamazula Mexico 24°57N 106°57W 86 C3
Tamazunchale Mexico 21°16N 98°47W 87 C5
Tambacounda Senegal 13°45N 13°40W 52 F3
Tambaram India 12°55N 80°7E 45 H5
Tambelan, Kepulauan Indonesia 1°0N 107°30E 36 D3
Tambellup Australia 34°4S 117°37E 61 F2
Tambo Australia 24°54S 146°14E 62 C4
Tambo de Mora Peru 13°30S 76°8W 92 F3
Tambora Indonesia 8°12S 118°5E 36 F5
Tambov Russia 52°45N 41°28E 18 D7
Tambuku Indonesia 7°8S 113°40E 37 G15
Tâmega → Portugal 41°5N 8°21W 21 B1
Tamenglong India 25°0N 93°35E 41 G18
Tamiahua, L. de Mexico 21°35N 97°35W 87 C5
Tamil Nadu ☐ India 11°0N 77°0E 45 J3
Tamluk India 22°18N 87°58E 43 H12
Tammerfors = Tampere Finland 61°30N 23°50E 8 F20
Tampa U.S.A. 27°56N 82°27W 85 H13
Tampa, Tanjung Indonesia 8°55S 116°12E 37 K19
Tampa B. U.S.A. 27°50N 82°30W 85 H13
Tampere Finland 61°30N 23°50E 8 F20
Tampico Mexico 22°13N 97°51W 87 C5
Tampin Malaysia 2°28N 102°13E 39 L4
Tampoi Malaysia 1°30N 103°39E 39 d
Tamsagbulag Mongolia 47°14N 117°21E 31 B12
Tamu Burma 24°13N 94°12E 41 G19
Tamworth Australia 31°7S 150°58E 63 E5
Tamworth Canada 44°29N 77°0W 82 B8
Tamworth U.K. 52°39N 1°41W 13 E6
Tan An Vietnam 10°32N 106°25E 39 G6
Tan Chau Vietnam 10°48N 105°12E 39 G5
Tan Hiep Vietnam 10°27N 106°21E 39 G6
Tan-Tan Morocco 28°29N 11°1W 52 C3
Tan Yen Vietnam 22°4N 105°3E 38 A5
Tana → Kenya 2°32S 40°31E 54 E8
Tana → Norway 70°30N 28°14E 8 A23
Tana, L. Ethiopia 13°5N 37°30E 49 E2
Tanabe Japan 33°44N 135°22E 29 H7
Tanafjorden Norway 70°45N 28°25E 8 A23
Tanaga I. U.S.A. 51°48N 177°53W 74 E4
Tanah Merah Malaysia 5°48N 102°9E 39 K4
Tanahbala Indonesia 0°30S 98°30E 36 E1
Tanahgrogot Indonesia 1°55S 116°15E 36 E5
Tanahjampea Indonesia 7°10S 120°35E 37 F6
Tanahmasa Indonesia 0°12S 98°39E 36 E1
Tanahmerah Indonesia 6°5S 140°16E 37 F10
Tanakpur India 29°5N 80°7E 43 E9
Tanamalwila Sri Lanka 6°26N 81°8E 45 L5
Tanami Desert Australia 18°50S 132°0E 60 C5
Tanana U.S.A. 65°10N 152°4W 74 B9
Tanana → U.S.A. 65°10N 151°58W 68 D1
Tananarive = Antananarivo Madag. 18°55S 47°31E 55 H9
Tânaro → Italy 44°55N 8°40E 20 D8
Tancheng China 34°25N 118°20E 33 G10
Tanch'ŏn N. Korea 40°27N 128°54E 33 D15
Tanda Ut. P., India 26°33N 82°35E 43 F10
Tanda Ut. P., India 28°57N 78°56E 43 E8
Tandag Phil. 9°4N 126°9E 37 C7
Tandaué Angola 16°58S 18°5E 56 A2
Tandil Argentina 37°15S 59°6W 94 D4
Tandil, Sa. del Argentina 37°30S 59°0W 94 D4
Tandlianwala Pakistan 31°3N 73°9E 42 D5
Tando Adam Pakistan 25°45N 68°40E 42 G3
Tando Allahyar Pakistan 25°28N 68°43E 42 G3
Tando Bago Pakistan 24°47N 68°58E 42 G3
Tando Mohommed Khan Pakistan 25°8N 68°32E 42 G3
Tandou L. Australia 32°40S 142°5E 63 E3
Tandoureh △ Iran 37°50N 59°0E 47 B8
Tandragee U.K. 54°21N 6°24W 10 B5
Tandula → India 21°6N 81°14E 44 D5
Tandula Tank India 20°40N 81°12E 44 D5
Tandur Telangana, India 19°11N 79°30E 44 E4
Tandur Telangana, India 17°14N 77°35E 44 F3
Tane-ga-Shima Japan 30°30N 131°0E 29 J5
Taneatua N.Z. 38°4S 177°1E 59 C6
Tanen Tong Dan = Dawna Ra. Burma 16°30N 98°30E 38 D2
Tanezrouft Algeria 23°9N 0°11E 52 D6
Tang, Koh Cambodia 10°16N 103°7E 39 G4
Tang, Ra's-e Iran 25°21N 59°52E 47 E8
Tang Krasang Cambodia 12°34N 105°3E 38 F5
Tanga Tanzania 5°5S 39°2E 54 F7
Tangalla Sri Lanka 6°1N 80°48E 45 L5
Tanganyika, L. Africa 6°40S 30°0E 54 F6
Tangasseri India 8°53N 76°35E 45 K3
Tanger Morocco 35°50N 5°49W 52 A4
Tangerang Indonesia 6°11S 106°37E 37 G12
Tanggu China 39°2N 117°40E 33 E9
Tanggula Shan China 32°40N 92°10E 30 E7
Tanggula Shankou China 32°42N 92°27E 30 E7
Tanghe China 32°47N 112°50E 32 H7
Tanghla Range = Tanggula Shan China 32°40N 92°10E 30 E7
Tangi India 19°56N 85°24E 44 E7
Tangier = Tanger Morocco 35°50N 5°49W 52 A4
Tangjia China 22°22N 113°35E 31 a
Tangjia Wan China 22°21N 113°36E 31 a
Tangorin Australia 21°47S 144°12E 62 C3
Tangra Yumco China 31°0N 86°38E 30 E6
Tangshan China 39°38N 118°10E 33 E10
Tangtou China 35°28N 118°30E 33 G10
Tangxi China 29°3N 119°25E 35 C12
Tangyan He → China 28°54N 108°19E 34 C7
Tangyin China 35°54N 114°21E 32 G8
Taniantaweng Shan China 31°20N 98°0E 34 B2
Tanimbar, Kepulauan Indonesia 7°30S 131°30E 37 F8
Tanimbar Is. = Tanimbar, Kepulauan Indonesia 7°30S 131°30E 37 F8
Tanintharyi = Taninthayi Burma 12°6N 99°3E 39 F2
Taninthayi Burma 12°6N 99°3E 39 F2
Tanjay Phil. 9°30N 123°5E 37 C6
Tanjore = Thanjavur India 10°48N 79°12E 45 J4
Tanjung Kalimantan Selatan, Indonesia 2°10S 115°25E 36 E5
Tanjung Nusa Tenggara Barat, Indonesia 8°21S 116°9E 37 J19
Tanjung Malim Malaysia 3°42N 101°31E 39 L3
Tanjung Pelepas Malaysia 1°21N 103°33E 39 d
Tanjung Tokong Malaysia 5°28N 100°18E 39 c
Tanjungbalai Indonesia 2°55N 99°44E 36 D1
Tanjungbatu Indonesia 2°23N 118°3E 36 D5
Tanjungkarang Telukbetung = Bandar Lampung Indonesia 5°20S 105°10E 36 F3
Tanjungpandan Indonesia 2°43S 107°38E 36 E3
Tanjungpinang Indonesia 1°5N 104°30E 36 D2
Tanjungredeb Indonesia 2°9N 117°29E 36 D5
Tanjungselor Indonesia 2°55N 117°25E 36 D5
Tank Pakistan 32°14N 70°25E 42 C4
Tankhala India 21°58N 73°47E 42 J5
Tankwa-Karoo △ S. Africa 32°14S 19°50E 56 D2
Tannersville U.S.A. 41°3N 75°18W 83 E9
Tannu Ola Asia 51°0N 94°0E 27 D10
Tannum Sands Australia 23°57S 151°22E 62 C5
Tanout Niger 14°50N 8°55E 52 F7
Tanshui Taiwan 25°10N 121°28E 35 E13
Tansing Nepal 27°52N 83°33E 43 F10
Tanta Egypt 30°45N 30°57E 53 B12
Tantoyuca Mexico 21°21N 98°14W 87 C5
Tantung = Dandong China 40°10N 124°20E 33 D13
Tanuku India 16°45N 81°44E 44 F5
Tanunda Australia 34°30S 139°0E 63 E2
Tanur India 11°1N 75°52E 45 J2
Tanzania ■ Africa 6°0S 34°0E 54 F6
Tanzhou China 22°16N 113°28E 31 a
Tanzilla → Canada 58°8N 130°43W 70 B2
Tao, Ko Thailand 10°5N 99°52E 39 G2
Tao'an = Taonan China 45°22N 122°40E 33 B12
Tao'er He → China 45°45N 124°5E 33 B13
Taohua Dao China 29°50N 122°20E 35 C14
Taolanaro Madag. 25°2S 47°0E 55 K9
Taole China 38°48N 106°40E 32 E4
Taonan China 45°22N 122°40E 33 B12
Taos U.S.A. 36°24N 105°35W 77 H11
Taoudenni Mali 22°40N 3°55W 52 D5
Taoyuan China 28°55N 111°16E 35 C8
T'aoyüan Taiwan 25°0N 121°4E 35 E13
Tapa Estonia 59°15N 25°50E 9 G21
Tapa Shan = Daba Shan China 32°0N 109°0E 34 B7
Tapachula Mexico 14°54N 92°17W 87 E6
Tapah Malaysia 4°12N 101°15E 39 K3
Tapajós → Brazil 2°24S 54°41W 93 D8
Tapaktuan Indonesia 3°15N 97°10E 36 D1
Tapanahoni → Suriname 4°20N 54°25W 93 C8
Tapanui N.Z. 45°56S 169°18E 59 F2
Tapauá → Brazil 5°40S 64°21W 92 E6
Tapes Brazil 30°40S 51°23W 95 C5
Tapeta Liberia 6°29N 8°52W 52 G4
Taphan Hin Thailand 16°13N 100°26E 38 D3
Tapirapecó, Serra Venezuela 1°10N 65°0W 92 C6
Taplejung Nepal 27°1N 86°16E 43 F12
Tapo-Capara △ Venezuela 7°55N 71°15W 89 E5
Tapti → India 21°8N 72°41E 44 D1
Tapuae-o-Uenuku N.Z. 42°0S 173°39E 59 E4
Tapul Group Phil. 5°35N 120°50E 37 C6
Tapurucuará Brazil 0°24S 65°2W 92 D5
Ţaqţaq Iraq 35°53N 44°35E 46 C5
Taquara Brazil 29°36S 50°46W 95 B5
Taquari → Brazil 19°15S 57°17W 92 G7
Tara Australia 27°17S 150°31E 63 D5
Tara Canada 44°28N 81°9W 82 B3
Tara Russia 56°55N 74°24E 26 D8
Tara → Montenegro 43°21N 18°51E 23 C8
Tarābulus Lebanon 34°31N 35°50E 48 A4
Tarābulus Libya 32°49N 13°7E 53 B8
Tarābulus Libya 31°0N 13°0E 53 B8
Taradehi India 23°18N 79°21E 43 H8
Tarakan Indonesia 3°20N 117°35E 36 D5
Tarama-Jima Japan 24°39N 124°42E 29 M2
Taran, Mys Russia 54°56N 19°59E 9 J18
Taranagar India 28°43N 74°50E 42 E6
Taranaki ☐ N.Z. 39°25S 174°30E 59 C5
Taranaki, Mt. N.Z. 39°17S 174°5E 59 C5
Tarancón Spain 40°1N 3°1W 21 B4
Taransay U.K. 57°54N 7°0W 11 D1
Táranto Italy 40°28N 17°14E 22 D7
Táranto, G. di Italy 40°8N 17°20E 22 D7
Tarapacá Colombia 2°56S 69°46W 92 D5
Tarapacá ☐ Chile 20°45S 69°30W 94 A2
Tarapoto Peru 6°30S 76°20W 92 E3
Tararua Ra. N.Z. 40°45S 175°25E 59 D5
Tarasaigh = Taransay U.K. 57°54N 7°0W 11 D1
Tarashcha Ukraine 49°30N 30°31E 17 D16
Tarauacá Brazil 8°6S 70°48W 92 E4
Tarauacá → Brazil 6°42S 69°48W 92 E5
Taravao Tahiti 17°43S 149°18W 59 d
Taravao, Isthme de Tahiti 17°43S 149°19W 59 d
Tarawa Kiribati 1°30N 173°0E 64 G9
Tarawera N.Z. 39°2S 176°36E 59 C6
Tarawera, L. N.Z. 38°13S 176°27E 59 C6
Taraz Kazakhstan 42°54N 71°22E 30 C3
Tarazona Spain 41°55N 1°43W 21 B5
Tarbagatay, Khrebet Kazakhstan 48°0N 83°0E 30 B5
Tarbat Ness U.K. 57°52N 3°47W 11 D5
Tarbela Dam Pakistan 34°8N 72°52E 42 B5
Tarbert Ireland 52°34N 9°22W 10 D2
Tarbert Argyll & Bute, U.K. 55°52N 5°25W 11 F3
Tarbert W. Isles, U.K. 57°54N 6°49W 11 D2
Tarbes France 43°15N 0°3E 20 E4
Tarboro U.S.A. 35°54N 77°32W 85 D16
Tarcoola Australia 30°44S 134°36E 63 E1
Tarcoon Australia 30°15S 146°43E 63 E4
Taree Australia 31°50S 152°30E 63 E5
Tarfaya Morocco 27°55N 12°55W 52 C3
Târgovişte Romania 44°55N 25°27E 17 F13
Târgu Jiu Romania 45°5N 23°19E 17 F12
Târgu Mureş Romania 46°31N 24°38E 17 E13
Ţarif U.A.E. 24°3N 53°46E 47 E7
Tarifa Spain 36°1N 5°36W 21 D3
Tarija Bolivia 21°30S 64°40W 94 A3
Tarija ☐ Bolivia 21°30S 63°30W 94 A3
Tariku → Indonesia 2°55S 138°26E 37 E9
Tarīm Yemen 16°3N 49°0E 49 D4
Tarim Basin = Tarim Pendi China 40°0N 84°0E 30 C5
Tarim He → China 39°30N 88°30E 30 D6
Tarim Pendi China 40°0N 84°0E 30 C5
Taritatu → Indonesia 2°54S 138°27E 37 E9
Tarka → S. Africa 32°10S 26°0E 56 D4
Tarka La Bhutan 27°12N 89°44E 43 F13
Tarkastad S. Africa 32°0S 26°16E 56 D4
Tarkhankut, Mys Ukraine 45°25N 32°30E 19 E5
Tarko Sale Russia 64°55N 77°50E 26 C8
Tarkwa Ghana 5°20N 2°0W 52 G5
Tarlac Phil. 15°29N 120°35E 37 A6
Tarma Peru 11°25S 75°45W 92 F3
Tarn → France 44°5N 1°6E 20 E4
Târnăveni Romania 46°19N 24°13E 17 E13
Tarnobrzeg Poland 50°35N 21°41E 17 C11
Tarnów Poland 50°3N 21°0E 17 C11
Tarnowskie Góry Poland 50°27N 18°54E 17 C10
Ţārom Iran 28°11N 55°46E 47 D7
Taroom Australia 25°36S 149°48E 63 D4
Taroudannt Morocco 30°30N 8°52W 52 B4
Tarpon Springs U.S.A. 28°9N 82°45W 85 G13
Tarrafal C. Verde Is. 15°18N 23°39W 52 b
Tarragona Spain 41°5N 1°17E 21 B6
Tarraleah Australia 42°17S 146°26E 63 G4
Tarrasa = Terrassa Spain 41°34N 2°1E 21 B7
Tarrytown U.S.A. 41°4N 73°52W 83 E11
Tarsus Turkey 36°58N 34°55E 46 B2
Tartagal Argentina 22°30S 63°50W 94 A3
Tartu Estonia 58°20N 26°44E 9 G22
Ţarţūs Syria 34°55N 35°55E 46 C2
Tarumizu Japan 31°29N 130°42E 29 J5
Tarutao = Ko Tarutao △ Thailand 6°31N 99°26E 39 J2
Tarutao, Ko Thailand 6°33N 99°40E 39 J2
Tarutung Indonesia 2°0N 98°54E 36 D1
Taseko → Canada 52°8N 123°45W 70 C4
Tasgaon India 17°2N 74°39E 44 F2
Tash-Kömür Kyrgyzstan 41°40N 72°10E 26 E8
Tashauz = Daşoguz Turkmenistan 41°49N 59°58E 26 E6
Tashi Chho Dzong = Thimphu Bhutan 27°31N 89°45E 41 F16
Ţashk, Daryācheh-ye Iran 29°45N 53°35E 47 D7
Tashkent = Toshkent Uzbekistan 41°20N 69°10E 26 E7
Tashtagol Russia 52°47N 87°53E 26 D9
Tasiilaq Greenland 65°40N 37°20W 4 C6
Tasikmalaya Indonesia 7°18S 108°12E 37 G13
Tåsjön Sweden 64°15N 15°40E 8 D16
Taskan Russia 62°59N 150°20E 27 C16
Tasman B. N.Z. 40°59S 173°25E 59 D4
Tasman Basin Pac. Oc. 46°0S 158°0E 64 M7
Tasman Mts. N.Z. 41°3S 172°25E 59 D4
Tasman Pen. Australia 43°10S 148°0E 63 G4
Tasman Sea Pac. Oc. 36°0S 160°0E 58 E9
Tasmania ☐ Australia 42°0S 146°30E 63 G4
Tasmanian Wilderness World Heritage Area △ Australia 43°0S 146°0E 63 G4
Tassili n'Ajjer Algeria 25°47N 8°1E 52 C7
Tassili-oua-n-Ahaggar Algeria 20°41N 5°30E 52 D7
Tat Ton △ Thailand 15°57N 102°2E 38 E4
Tata Morocco 29°46N 7°56W 52 C4
Tatabánya Hungary 47°32N 18°25E 17 E10
Tataouine Tunisia 32°57N 10°29E 53 B8
Tatar Republic = Tatarstan ☐ Russia 55°30N 51°30E 18 C9
Tatarbunary Ukraine 45°50N 29°39E 17 F15
Tatarsk Russia 55°14N 76°0E 26 D8
Tatarskiy Proliv Russia 50°0N 141°0E 27 E15
Tatarstan ☐ Russia 55°30N 51°30E 18 C9
Tatatua, Pte. Tahiti 17°44S 149°8W 59 d
Tateyama Japan 35°0N 139°50E 29 G9
Tathlina L. Canada 60°33N 117°39W 70 A5
Tathra Australia 36°44S 149°59E 63 F4
Tatinnai L. Canada 60°55N 97°40W 71 A9
Tatla Lake Canada 52°0N 124°20W 70 C4
Tatnam, C. Canada 57°16N 91°0W 71 B10
Tatra = Tatry Slovak Rep. 49°20N 20°0E 17 D11
Tatry Slovak Rep. 49°20N 20°0E 17 D11
Tatshenshini → Canada 59°28N 137°45W 70 B1
Tatshenshini-Alsek ⌂ Canada 59°55N 137°45W 70 B1
Tatsuno Japan 34°52N 134°33E 29 G7
Tatta = Thatta Pakistan 24°42N 67°55E 42 G2
Tatuī Brazil 23°25S 47°53W 95 A6
Tatum U.S.A. 33°16N 103°19W 77 K12
Tat'ung = Datong China 40°6N 113°18E 32 D7
Tatvan Turkey 38°31N 42°15E 46 B4
Ta'ū Amer. Samoa 14°15S 169°30W 59 b
Taubaté Brazil 23°0S 45°36W 95 A6
Tauern Austria 47°15N 12°40E 16 E7
Taumarunui N.Z. 38°53S 175°15E 59 C5
Taumaturgo Brazil 8°54S 72°51W 92 E4
Taung S. Africa 27°33S 24°47E 56 C3
Taungdwingyi Burma 20°1N 95°40E 41 J19
Taunggyi Burma 20°50N 97°0E 41 J20
Taungoo = Tounggoo Burma 19°0N 96°30E 41 K20
Taungup Burma 18°51N 94°14E 41 K19
Taunsa Pakistan 30°42N 70°39E 42 D4
Taunsa Barrage Pakistan 30°42N 70°50E 42 D4
Taunton U.K. 51°1N 3°5W 13 F4
Taunton U.S.A. 41°54N 71°6W 83 E13
Taunus Germany 50°13N 8°34E 16 C5
Taupo N.Z. 38°41S 176°7E 59 C6
Taupo, L. N.Z. 38°46S 175°55E 59 C5
Tauragė Lithuania 55°14N 22°16E 9 J20
Tauranga N.Z. 37°42S 176°11E 59 B6
Tauranga Harb. N.Z. 37°30S 176°5E 59 B6
Taureau, Rés. Canada 46°46N 73°50W 72 C5
Taurianova Italy 38°21N 16°1E 22 E7
Taurus Mts. = Toros Dağları Turkey 37°0N 32°30E 46 B2
Tautira Tahiti 17°44S 149°9W 59 d
Tauyskaya Guba Russia 59°20N 150°20E 27 D16
Tavan Bogd Uul Mongolia 49°10N 87°49E 30 B6
Tavastehus = Hämeenlinna Finland 61°0N 24°28E 8 F21
Tavda Russia 58°7N 65°8E 26 D7
Tavda → Russia 57°47N 67°18E 26 D7
Taverner B. Canada 67°12N 72°25W 69 D17
Taveuni Fiji 16°51S 179°58W 59 a
Tavira Portugal 37°8N 7°40W 21 D2
Tavistock Canada 43°19N 80°50W 82 C4
Tavistock U.K. 50°33N 4°9W 13 G3
Tavoy = Dawei Burma 14°2N 98°12E 38 E2
Tavoy Pt. Burma 13°32N 98°10E 38 F2
Tavrichanka Russia 43°18N 131°59E 28 C5
Tavua Fiji 17°37S 177°5E 59 a
Tavuki Fiji 19°7S 178°8E 59 a
Taw → U.K. 51°4N 4°4W 13 F3
Tawa → India 22°48N 77°48E 42 H8
Tawa Res. India 22°35N 78°5E 44 C4
Tawas City U.S.A. 44°16N 83°31W 81 C12
Tawau Malaysia 4°20N 117°55E 36 D5
Tawi-tawi I. Phil. 5°10N 120°15E 37 C6
Tawu Taiwan 22°22N 120°54E 35 F13
Taxco Mexico 18°33N 99°36W 87 D5
Taxila Pakistan 33°42N 72°52E 42 C5
Taxkorgan Tajik Zizhixian China 37°49N 75°14E 30 D4
Tay → U.K. 56°37N 3°38W 11 E5
Tay, Firth of U.K. 56°25N 3°8W 11 E5
Tay, L. Australia 32°55S 120°48E 61 F3
Tay, L. U.K. 56°32N 4°8W 11 E4
Tay ⌂ U.K. 56°43N 3°59W 11 E5
Tay Ninh Vietnam 11°20N 106°5E 39 G6
Tayabamba Peru 8°15S 77°16W 92 E3
Taygetos Oros Greece 37°0N 22°23E 23 F10
Taylakova Russia 59°13N 74°0E 26 D8
Taylor Canada 56°13N 120°40W 70 B4
Taylor Nebr., U.S.A. 41°46N 99°23W 80 E4
Taylor Pa., U.S.A. 41°23N 75°43W 83 E9
Taylor Tex., U.S.A. 30°34N 97°25W 84 F6
Taylor, Mt. U.S.A. 35°14N 107°37W 77 J10
Taylorville U.S.A. 39°33N 89°18W 80 F9
Taymā Si. Arabia 27°35N 38°45E 46 E3
Taymyr, Oz. Russia 74°20N 102°0E 27 B11
Taymyr, Poluostrov Russia 75°0N 100°0E 27 B11
Taypaq Kazakhstan 49°0N 51°47E 19 E9

Tayport U.K. 56°27N 2°52W 11 E6
Tayrona △ Colombia 11°20N 74°2W 89 D5
Tayshet Russia 55°58N 98°1E 27 D10
Taytay Phil. 10°45N 119°30E 37 B5
Tāyyebād Iran 34°45N 60°45E 47 C9
Tāyyebād □ Iran 34°44N 60°44E 47 C9
Taz → Russia 67°32N 78°40E 26 C8
Taza Morocco 34°16N 4°6W 52 B5
Tāza Khurmātū Iraq 35°18N 44°20E 46 C5
Tazawa-Ko Japan 39°43N 140°40E 28 E10
Tazerbo Libya 25°45N 21°0E 53 C10
Tazin → Canada 59°48N 109°55W 71 B7
Tazin L. Canada 59°44N 108°42W 71 B7
Tazovskiy Russia 67°30N 78°44E 26 C8
Tbilisi Georgia 41°43N 44°50E 19 F7
Tchad = Chad ■ Africa 15°0N 17°15E 53 F8
Tchad, L. Chad 13°30N 14°30E 53 F8
Tch'eng-tou = Chengdu China 30°38N 104°2E 34 B5
Tchentlo L. Canada 55°15N 125°0W 70 B4
Tchibanga Gabon 2°45S 11°0E 54 E2
Tchogha Zanbil = Choghā Zanbīl Iran 32°1N 48°32E 47 C6
Tch'ong-k'ing = Chongqing China 29°35N 106°25E 34 C6
Tczew Poland 54°8N 18°50E 17 A10
Te Anau, L. N.Z. 45°15S 167°45E 59 F1
Te Aroha N.Z. 37°32S 175°44E 59 B5
Te Awamutu N.Z. 38°1S 175°20E 59 C5
Te Ika a Maui = North I. N.Z. 38°0S 175°0E 59 C5
Te Kuiti N.Z. 38°20S 175°11E 59 C5
Te Puke N.Z. 37°46S 176°22E 59 B6
Te Waewae B. N.Z. 46°13S 167°33E 59 G1
Te Wai Pounamu = South I. N.Z. 44°0S 170°0E 59 F3
Teague U.S.A. 31°38N 96°17W 84 F6
Teahupoo Tahiti 17°50S 149°16W 59 d
Teapa Mexico 17°33N 92°57W 87 D6
Tebakang Malaysia 1°6N 110°30E 36 D4
Teberau → Malaysia 1°30N 103°42E 39 d
Tébessa Algeria 35°22N 8°8E 52 A7
Tebicuary → Paraguay 26°36S 58°16W 94 B4
Tebingtinggi Riau, Indonesia 1°0N 102°45E 36 E2
Tebingtinggi Sumatera Utara, Indonesia 3°20N 99°9E 36 D1
Tecate Mexico 32°34N 116°38W 79 N10
Tecka Argentina 43°29S 70°48W 96 E2
Tecomán Mexico 18°55N 103°53W 86 D4
Tecopa U.S.A. 35°51N 116°13W 79 K10
Tecoripa Mexico 28°37N 109°57W 86 B3
Tecuala Mexico 22°23N 105°27W 86 C3
Tecuci Romania 45°51N 27°27E 17 F14
Tecumseh Canada 42°19N 82°54W 82 D2
Tecumseh Mich., U.S.A. 42°0N 83°57W 81 D12
Tecumseh Okla., U.S.A. 35°15N 96°56W 84 D6
Tedzhen = Tejen Turkmenistan 37°23N 60°31E 26 F7
Tees → U.K. 54°37N 1°10W 12 C6
Tees B. U.K. 54°40N 1°9W 12 C6
Teeswater Canada 43°59N 81°17W 82 C3
Tefé Brazil 3°25S 64°50W 92 D6
Tegal Indonesia 6°52S 109°8E 37 G13
Tegallalang Indonesia 8°27S 115°17E 37 J18
Tegalsari Indonesia 8°25S 114°8E 37 J17
Tegid, L. = Bala, L. U.K. 52°53N 3°37W 12 E4
Tegucigalpa Honduras 14°5N 87°14W 88 D2
Tehachapi U.S.A. 35°8N 118°27W 79 K8
Tehachapi Mts. U.S.A. 35°0N 118°30W 79 L8
Tehoru Indonesia 3°23S 129°30E 37 E7
Tehrān Iran 35°30N 51°30E 47 C6
Tehri India 30°23N 78°29E 43 D8
Tehuacán Mexico 18°27N 97°23W 87 D5
Tehuantepec Mexico 16°21N 95°13W 87 D5
Tehuantepec, G. de Mexico 15°50N 95°12W 87 D5
Tehuantepec, Istmo de Mexico 17°15N 94°30W 87 D6
Teifi → U.K. 52°5N 4°41W 13 E3
Teign → U.K. 50°32N 3°32W 13 G4
Teignmouth U.K. 50°33N 3°31W 13 G4
Teinainano = Tarawa Kiribati 1°30N 173°0E 64 G9
Tejakula Indonesia 8°8S 115°20E 37 J18
Tejen Turkmenistan 37°23N 60°31E 26 F7
Tejen → Turkmenistan 37°24N 60°38E 47 B9
Tejo → Europe 38°40N 9°24W 21 C1
Tejon Pass U.S.A. 34°49N 118°53W 79 L8
Tekamah U.S.A. 41°47N 96°13W 80 E5
Tekapo, L. N.Z. 43°53S 170°33E 59 E3
Tekax Mexico 20°12N 89°17W 87 C7
Tekeli Kazakhstan 44°50N 79°0E 26 E8
Tekeze → Ethiopia 13°10N 38°45E 47 E2
Tekirdağ Turkey 40°58N 27°30E 23 D12
Tekkali India 18°37N 84°15E 44 E7
Tekoa U.S.A. 47°14N 117°4W 76 C5
Tekong Besar, Pulau Singapore 1°25N 104°3E 39 d
Tel → India 20°50N 83°54E 44 D6
Tel Aviv ✈ (TLV) Israel 32°5N 34°49E 48 C3
Tel Aviv-Yafo Israel 32°4N 34°48E 48 C3
Tel Lakhish Israel 31°34N 34°51E 48 D3
Tel Megiddo Israel 32°35N 35°11E 48 C4
Tela Honduras 15°40N 87°28W 88 C2
Telanaipura = Jambi Indonesia 1°38S 103°30E 36 E2
Telangana □ India 17°30N 78°30E 44 F4
Telavi Georgia 42°0N 45°30E 19 F8
Telegraph Creek Canada 58°0N 131°10W 70 B2
Telekhany = Tsyelyakhany Belarus 52°30N 25°46E 17 B13
Telemark Norway 59°15N 7°40E 9 G12
Telén Argentina 36°15S 65°31W 94 D2
Teleng Iran 25°47N 61°3E 47 E9
Teles Pires → Brazil 7°21S 58°3W 92 E7
Telescope Pk. U.S.A. 36°10N 117°5W 79 J9
Telford U.K. 52°40N 2°27W 13 E5
Telford and Wrekin □ U.K. 52°45N 2°27W 12 E5

Telkwa Canada 54°41N 127°5W 70 C3
Tell City U.S.A. 37°57N 86°46W 80 G10
Teller U.S.A. 65°16N 166°22W 74 B6
Tellicherry = Thalassery India 11°45N 75°30E 45 J2
Telluride U.S.A. 37°56N 107°49W 77 H10
Teloloapán Mexico 18°21N 99°51W 87 D5
Telpos Iz Russia 63°16N 59°13E 18 B10
Telsen Argentina 42°30S 66°50W 96 E3
Telšiai Lithuania 55°59N 22°14E 9 J20
Teluk Anson = Teluk Intan Malaysia 4°3N 101°0E 39 K3
Teluk Bahang Malaysia 5°28N 100°13E 39 c
Teluk Betung = Bandar Lampung Indonesia 5°20S 105°10E 36 F3
Teluk Intan Malaysia 4°3N 101°0E 39 K3
Teluk Kumbar Malaysia 5°18N 100°14E 39 c
Telukbutun Indonesia 4°13N 108°12E 36 D3
Telukdalam Indonesia 0°33N 97°50E 36 D1
Tema Ghana 5°41N 0°0 52 G5
Temagami, L. Canada 47°0N 80°10W 72 C3
Temax Mexico 21°9N 88°56W 87 C7
Temba S. Africa 25°20S 28°17E 57 C4
Tembagapura Indonesia 4°20S 137°0E 37 E9
Tembe S. Africa 26°51S 32°24E 57 C5
Temblor Range U.S.A. 35°20N 119°50W 79 K7
Teme → U.K. 52°11N 2°13W 13 E5
Temecula U.S.A. 33°30N 117°9W 79 M9
Temengor, Tasik Malaysia 5°24N 101°18E 39 K3
Temerloh Malaysia 3°27N 102°25E 39 L4
Teminabuan Indonesia 1°26S 132°1E 37 E8
Temir Kazakhstan 49°1N 57°14E 19 E10
Temirtau Kazakhstan 50°5N 72°56E 30 A3
Témiscamie → Canada 50°59N 73°5W 73 B5
Témiscaming Canada 46°44N 79°5W 72 C4
Témiscamingue, L. Canada 47°10N 79°25W 72 C4
Temosachic Mexico 28°57N 107°51W 86 B3
Tempe U.S.A. 33°24N 111°54W 77 K8
Tempiute U.S.A. 37°39N 115°38W 78 H11
Temple U.S.A. 31°6N 97°21W 84 F6
Temple B. Australia 12°15S 143°3E 62 A3
Templemore Ireland 52°47N 7°51W 10 D4
Templeton U.S.A. 35°33N 120°42W 78 K6
Templeton → Australia 21°0S 138°40E 62 C2
Tempoal de Sánchez Mexico 21°31N 98°23W 87 C5
Temuco Chile 38°45S 72°40W 96 D2
Temuka N.Z. 44°14S 171°17E 59 F3
Ten Degree Channel India 10°0N 92°30E 45 K11
Tenabo Mexico 20°3N 90°14W 87 C6
Tenaha U.S.A. 31°57N 94°15W 84 F7
Tenakee Springs U.S.A. 57°47N 135°13W 70 B1
Tenali India 16°15N 80°35E 45 F5
Tenancingo Mexico 18°58N 99°38W 87 D5
Tenango del Valle Mexico 19°7N 99°33W 87 D5
Tenaro, Akra Greece 36°22N 22°27E 23 F10
Tenasserim = Taninthayi Burma 12°6N 99°3E 39 F2
Tenasserim □ Burma 14°0N 98°30E 38 F2
Tenasserim → Burma 12°24N 98°37E 38 F2
Tenby U.K. 51°40N 4°42W 13 F3
Tenda, Colle di France 44°7N 7°36E 20 D7
Tendaho Ethiopia 11°48N 40°54E 49 E3
Tendō Japan 38°20N 140°30E 28 E10
Tendukhera India 23°24N 79°33E 43 H8
Ténéré, Erg du Niger 17°35N 10°55E 53 E8
Tenerife Canary Is. 28°15N 16°35W 52 C2
Teng Xian Guangxi Zhuangzu, China 23°21N 110°56E 35 F8
Teng Xian Shandong, China 35°5N 117°10E 33 G9
Tengah, Kepulauan Indonesia 7°5S 118°15E 36 F5
Tengchong China 25°0N 98°28E 34 E2
Tengchowfu = Penglai China 37°48N 120°42E 33 F11
Tenggarong Indonesia 0°24S 116°58E 36 E5
Tengger Shamo China 38°0N 104°10E 32 F3
Tenggol, Pulau Malaysia 4°48N 103°41E 39 K4
Tengiz Köli Kazakhstan 50°30N 69°0E 30 A2
Tengzhou China 35°4N 117°9E 33 G9
Teniente Enciso △ Paraguay 21°5S 61°8W 94 A3
Tenino U.S.A. 46°51N 122°51W 78 D4
Tenkasi India 8°55N 77°20E 45 K3
Tennant Creek Australia 19°30S 134°15E 62 B1
Tennessee □ U.S.A. 36°0N 86°30W 85 D11
Tennessee → U.S.A. 37°4N 88°34W 85 C10
Tenojoki = Tana → Norway 70°30N 28°14E 8 A23
Tenom Malaysia 5°4N 115°57E 36 C5
Tenosique Mexico 17°29N 91°26W 87 D6
Tenryū-Gawa → Japan 35°39N 137°48E 29 G8
Tenterden U.K. 51°4N 0°42E 13 F8
Tenterfield Australia 29°0S 152°0E 63 D5
Teófilo Otoni Brazil 17°50S 41°30W 93 G10
Tepa Indonesia 7°52S 129°31E 37 F7
Tepalcatepec → Mexico 18°35N 101°59W 86 D4
Tepehuanes Mexico 25°21N 105°44W 86 B3
Tepetongo Mexico 22°28N 103°9W 86 C4
Tepic Mexico 21°30N 104°54W 86 C4
Teplice Czech Rep. 50°40N 13°48E 16 C7
Tequila Mexico 20°54N 103°47W 86 C4
Ter → Spain 42°2N 3°12E 21 A7
Ter Apel Neths. 52°53N 7°5E 15 B7
Téra Niger 14°0N 0°45E 52 F6
Teraina Kiribati 4°43N 160°25W 65 G12
Téramo Italy 42°39N 13°42E 22 C5
Terang Australia 38°15S 142°55E 63 F3
Terang, Teluk Indonesia 8°44S 116°0E 37 K19
Terceira Azores 38°43N 27°13W 52 a
Tercero → Argentina 32°58S 61°47W 94 C3
Terdal India 16°33N 75°3E 44 F2
Terebovlya Ukraine 49°18N 25°44E 17 D13
Terek → Russia 44°0N 47°30E 19 F8
Terengganu □ Malaysia 4°55N 103°0E 39 K4
Terepaima △ Venezuela 9°58N 69°17W 89 E6

Teresina Brazil 5°9S 42°45W 93 E10
Teressa India 8°15N 93°10E 45 K11
Terewah, L. Australia 29°52S 147°35E 63 D4
Teridgerie Cr. → Australia 30°25S 148°50E 63 E4
Termas de Río Hondo Argentina 27°29S 64°52W 94 B3
Términi Imerese Italy 37°59N 13°42E 22 F5
Términos, L. de Mexico 18°37N 91°33W 87 D6
Termiz Uzbekistan 37°15N 67°15E 26 F7
Térmoli Italy 42°0N 15°0E 22 C6
Ternate Indonesia 0°45N 127°25E 37 D7
Terneuzen Neths. 51°20N 3°50E 15 C3
Terney Russia 45°3N 136°37E 28 B8
Terni Italy 42°34N 12°37E 22 C5
Ternopil Ukraine 49°30N 25°40E 17 D13
Ternopol □ Ukraine 48°10N 25°10E 17 D13
Ternopol = Ternopil Ukraine 49°30N 25°40E 17 D13
Terowie Australia 33°8S 138°55E 63 E2
Terra Bella U.S.A. 35°58N 119°3W 79 K7
Terra Nova △ Canada 48°33S 53°55W 73 C9
Terrace Canada 54°30N 128°35W 70 C3
Terrace Bay Canada 48°47N 87°5W 72 C2
Terracina Italy 41°17N 13°15E 22 D5
Terralba Italy 39°43N 8°39E 22 E3
Terrassa Spain 41°34N 2°1E 21 B7
Terre Haute U.S.A. 39°28N 87°25W 80 F10
Terrebonne B. U.S.A. 29°5N 90°35W 85 G9
Terrenceville Canada 47°40N 54°44W 73 C9
Terry U.S.A. 46°47N 105°19W 76 C11
Terryville U.S.A. 41°41N 73°3W 83 E11
Terschelling Neths. 53°25N 5°20E 15 A5
Teruel Spain 40°22N 1°8W 21 B5
Tervola Finland 66°6N 24°49E 8 C21
Teryaweynya L. Australia 32°18S 143°22E 63 E3
Teshio Japan 44°53N 141°44E 28 B10
Teshio-Gawa → Japan 44°53N 141°45E 28 B10
Tesiyn Gol → Mongolia 50°40N 93°20E 30 A7
Teslin Canada 60°10N 132°43W 70 A2
Teslin → Canada 61°34N 134°35W 70 A2
Teslin L. Canada 60°15N 132°57W 70 A2
Tessalit Mali 20°12N 1°0E 52 D6
Tessaoua Niger 13°47N 7°56E 52 F7
Test → U.K. 50°56N 1°29W 13 G6
Testigos, Is. Los Venezuela 11°23N 63°7W 89 D7
Tetachuck L. Canada 53°18N 125°55W 70 C3
Tetas, Pta. Chile 23°31S 70°38W 94 A1
Tete Mozam. 16°13S 33°33E 55 H6
Teteven Bulgaria 42°58N 24°17E 23 C11
Tethul → Canada 60°35N 112°12W 70 A6
Tetiyev Ukraine 49°22N 29°38E 17 D15
Tetlit Zheh = Fort McPherson Canada 67°30N 134°55W 68 D5
Teton → U.S.A. 47°56N 110°31W 76 C8
Tétouan Morocco 35°35N 5°21W 52 A4
Tetovo Macedonia 42°1N 20°59E 23 C9
Tetufera, Mt. Tahiti 17°40S 149°26W 59 d
Teuco → Argentina 25°35S 60°11W 94 B3
Teulon Canada 50°23N 97°16W 71 C9
Teun Indonesia 6°59S 129°8E 37 F7
Teuri-Tō Japan 44°26N 141°19E 28 B10
Teutoburger Wald Germany 52°5N 8°22E 16 B5
Tevere → Italy 41°44N 12°14E 22 D5
Teverya Israel 32°47N 35°32E 48 C4
Teviot → U.K. 55°29N 2°38W 11 F6
Tewantin Australia 26°27S 153°3E 63 D5
Tewkesbury U.K. 51°59N 2°9W 13 F5
Texada I. Canada 49°40N 124°25W 70 D4
Texarkana Ark., U.S.A. 33°26N 94°2W 84 E7
Texarkana Tex., U.S.A. 33°26N 94°3W 84 E7
Texas Australia 28°49S 151°9E 63 D5
Texas □ U.S.A. 31°40N 98°30W 84 F5
Texas City U.S.A. 29°24N 94°54W 84 G7
Texel Neths. 53°5N 4°50E 15 A4
Texoma, L. U.S.A. 33°50N 96°34W 84 E6
Teyateyaneng Lesotho 29°7S 27°34E 56 D4
Tezin Afghan. 34°24N 69°30E 42 B3
Teziutlán Mexico 19°49N 97°21W 87 D5
Tezpur India 26°40N 92°45E 41 F18
Tezzeron L. Canada 54°43N 124°30W 70 C4
Tha-anne → Canada 60°31N 94°37W 71 A10
Tha Deua Laos 17°57N 102°53E 38 D4
Tha Deua Laos 19°26N 101°50E 38 C3
Tha Li Thailand 17°37N 101°25E 38 D3
Tha Pla Thailand 17°48N 100°32E 38 D3
Tha Rua Thailand 14°34N 100°44E 38 E3
Tha Sala Thailand 8°40N 99°56E 39 H2
Tha Song Yang Thailand 17°34N 97°55E 38 D1
Thaba Putsoa Lesotho 29°45S 28°0E 57 C4
Thaba-Tseka Lesotho 29°32S 28°36E 57 C4
Thabana Ntlenyana Lesotho 29°30S 29°16E 57 D4
Thabazimbi S. Africa 24°40S 27°21E 57 B4
Thādiq Si. Arabia 25°18N 45°52E 46 E5
Thai Binh Vietnam 20°35N 106°1E 34 G6
Thai Muang Thailand 8°24N 98°16E 39 H2
Thai Nguyen Vietnam 21°35N 105°55E 34 G5
Thailand ■ Asia 16°0N 102°0E 38 E4
Thailand, G. of Asia 11°30N 101°0E 39 G3
Thakhek Laos 17°25N 104°45E 38 D5
Thal Pakistan 33°28N 70°33E 42 C4
Thal Desert Pakistan 31°10N 71°30E 42 D4
Thala La = Hkakabo Razi Burma 28°25N 97°23E 34 C1
Thalabarivat Cambodia 13°33N 105°57E 38 F5
Thalang = Amphoe Thalang Thailand 8°1N 98°20E 39 a
Thalara Nepal 29°29N 80°59E 43 E9
Thalassery India 11°45N 75°30E 45 J2
Thale Sap Songkhla Thailand 7°12N 100°28E 39 J3
Thallon Australia 28°39S 148°49E 63 D4
Thalu, Ko Thailand 9°26N 99°54E 39 b
Tham Lot Thailand 19°34N 98°16E 38 C2
Thamarīt Oman 17°39N 54°2E 49 D5
Thames N.Z. 37°7S 175°34E 59 B5

Thames → Canada 42°20N 82°25W 82 D2
Thames → U.K. 51°29N 0°34E 13 F8
Thames → U.S.A. 41°18N 72°5W 83 E12
Thames Estuary U.K. 51°29N 0°52E 13 F8
Thamesford Canada 43°4N 81°0W 82 C4
Thamesville Canada 42°33N 81°59W 82 D3
Than India 22°34N 71°11E 42 H4
Than Kyun Burma 9°49N 98°4E 39 H1
Than Uyen Vietnam 22°0N 103°54E 34 G4
Thana Gazi India 27°25N 76°19E 42 F7
Thandla India 23°0N 74°34E 42 H6
Thandwe Burma 18°20N 94°30E 41 K19
Thane India 19°12N 72°59E 44 K1
Thanesar India 30°1N 76°52E 42 D7
Thanet, I. of U.K. 51°21N 1°20E 13 F9
Thangool Australia 24°38S 150°42E 62 C5
Thanh Hoa Vietnam 19°48N 105°46E 38 C5
Thanh Hung Vietnam 9°55N 105°43E 39 H5
Thanh Pho Ho Chi Minh Vietnam 10°58N 106°40E 39 G6
Thanh Thuy Vietnam 22°55N 104°51E 38 A5
Thanjavur India 10°48N 79°12E 45 J4
Thanlwin = Salween → Burma 16°31N 97°37E 41 L20
Thano Bula Khan Pakistan 25°22N 67°50E 42 G2
Thanya Buri Thailand 14°1N 100°45E 38 E3
Thaoge → Botswana 20°27S 22°56E 56 B3
Thaolintoa L. Canada 61°30N 96°25W 71 A9
Thap Lan △ Thailand 14°15N 102°16E 38 E4
Thap Sakae Thailand 11°30N 99°37E 39 G2
Thap Than Thailand 15°27N 99°54E 38 E2
Thar Desert India 28°0N 72°0E 42 F5
Tharad India 24°30N 71°44E 42 G4
Thargomindah Australia 27°58S 143°46E 63 D3
Tharp Fracture Zone S. Ocean 54°0S 135°0W 5 B14
Tharrawaddy Burma 17°38N 95°48E 41 L19
Tharthār, Buḩayrat ath Iraq 34°0N 43°15E 46 C4
Tharthar, L. = Tharthār, Buḩayrat ath Iraq 34°0N 43°15E 46 C4
Tharthār, W. ath → Iraq 34°32N 43°4E 46 C4
Thasos Greece 40°40N 24°40E 23 D11
That Khe Vietnam 22°16N 106°28E 34 F6
Thatcher Ariz., U.S.A. 32°51N 109°46W 77 K9
Thatcher Colo., U.S.A. 37°33N 104°7W 77 H11
Thaton Burma 16°55N 97°22E 41 L20
Thatta Pakistan 24°42N 67°55E 42 G2
Thaungdut Burma 24°30N 94°40E 41 G19
Thayawthadangy Kyun Burma 12°19N 98°0E 38 F1
Thayer U.S.A. 36°31N 91°33W 80 G8
Thayetmyo Burma 19°20N 95°10E 41 K19
Thazi Burma 21°0N 96°5E 41 J20
Thbeng Meanchey Cambodia 13°49N 104°58E 38 F5
The Bahamas ■ N. Amer. 24°0N 75°0W 89 B5
The Broads U.K. 52°45N 1°30E 12 E9
The Everglades U.S.A. 25°50N 81°0W 85 J14
The Gambia ■ W. Afr. 13°25N 16°0W 52 F2
The Gulf = Persian Gulf Asia 27°0N 50°0E 47 E6
The Hague = 's-Gravenhage Neths. 52°7N 4°17E 15 B4
The Pas Canada 53°45N 101°15W 71 C8
The Wash U.K. 52°58N 0°20E 12 E8
The Weald U.K. 51°4N 0°20E 13 F8
Thebes = Thíva Greece 38°19N 23°19E 23 E10
Thebes Egypt 25°40N 32°35E 53 C12
Thedford Australia 41°59N 100°35W 80 E3
Theebine Australia 25°57S 152°34E 63 D5
Thekulthili L. Canada 61°3N 110°0W 71 A7
Thelon → Canada 64°16N 96°4W 71 A8
Theodore Australia 24°55S 150°3E 62 C5
Theodore Canada 51°26N 102°55W 71 C8
Theodore U.S.A. 30°33N 88°10W 85 F10
Theodore Roosevelt △ U.S.A. 47°0N 103°25W 80 B2
Theodore Roosevelt L. U.S.A. 33°40N 111°10W 77 K8
Thepha Thailand 6°52N 100°58E 39 J3
Theresa U.S.A. 44°13N 75°48W 83 B9
Thermaïkos Kolpos Greece 40°15N 22°45E 23 D10
Thermopolis U.S.A. 43°39N 108°13W 76 E9
Thermopylæ Greece 38°48N 22°35E 23 E10
Thessalon Canada 46°20N 83°30W 72 C3
Thessalonica, Gulf of = Thermaïkos Kolpos Greece 40°15N 22°45E 23 D10
Thessaloniki Greece 40°38N 22°58E 23 D10
Thetford U.K. 52°25N 0°45E 13 E8
Thetford Mines Canada 46°8N 71°18W 73 C5
Theun → Laos 18°19N 104°0E 38 C5
Theunissen S. Africa 28°26S 26°43E 56 C4
Thevenard Australia 32°9S 133°38E 63 E1
Thibodaux U.S.A. 29°48N 90°49W 85 G9
Thicket Portage Canada 55°19N 97°42W 71 B9
Thief River Falls U.S.A. 48°7N 96°10W 80 A5
Thiel Mts. Antarctica 85°15S 91°0W 5 E16
Thiers France 45°52N 3°33E 20 D5
Thiès Senegal 14°50N 16°51W 52 F2
Thika Kenya 1°1S 37°5E 54 E7
Thimphu Bhutan 27°31N 89°45E 41 F16
Thina → S. Africa 31°18S 29°13E 57 D4
Þingvallavatn Iceland 64°11N 21°9W 8 D3
Thionville France 49°20N 6°10E 20 B7
Thira = Santorini Greece 36°23N 25°27E 23 F11
Third Cataract Sudan 19°42N 30°20E 53 D12
Thirsk U.K. 54°14N 1°19W 12 C6
Thiruvananthapuram India 8°41N 77°0E 45 K3
Thiruvarur India 10°46N 79°38E 45 J4
Thisted Denmark 56°58N 8°40E 9 H13
Thistle I. Australia 35°0S 136°8E 63 F2
Thithia = Cicia Fiji 17°45S 179°18W 59 a
Thíva Greece 38°19N 23°19E 23 E10
Þjórsá → Iceland 63°47N 20°48W 8 E3

Thlewiaza → Canada 60°29N 94°40W 71 A10
Thmar Puok Cambodia 13°57N 103°4E 38 F4
Tho Chu, Dao Vietnam 9°20N 103°28E 39 H4
Tho Vinh Vietnam 19°16N 105°42E 38 C5
Thoa → Canada 60°31N 109°47W 71 A7
Thoen Thailand 17°43N 99°12E 38 D2
Thoeng Thailand 19°41N 100°12E 38 C3
Thohoyandou S. Africa 22°58S 30°29E 55 J6
Thomas U.S.A. 35°45N 98°45W 84 D5
Thomas, L. Australia 26°4S 137°58E 63 D2
Thomas Hubbard, C. Canada 82°0N 94°25W 69 A13
Thomaston U.S.A. 32°53N 84°20W 85 E12
Thomasville Ala., U.S.A. 31°55N 87°44W 85 F11
Thomasville Ga., U.S.A. 30°50N 83°59W 85 F13
Thomasville N.C., U.S.A. 35°53N 80°5W 85 D14
Thompson Canada 55°45N 97°52W 71 B9
Thompson U.S.A. 41°52N 75°31W 83 E9
Thompson → Canada 50°15N 121°24W 70 C4
Thompson → U.S.A. 39°46N 93°37W 80 F7
Thompson Falls U.S.A. 47°36N 115°21W 76 C6
Thompson Pk. U.S.A. 41°0N 123°2W 76 F2
Thompson Springs U.S.A. 38°58N 109°43W 76 G9
Thompsontown U.S.A. 40°33N 77°14W 82 F7
Thomson U.S.A. 33°28N 82°30W 85 E13
Thomson → Australia 25°11S 142°53E 62 C3
Thong Yang Thailand 9°28N 99°56E 39 b
Thoothukudi = Tuticorin India 8°50N 78°12E 45 K4
Þórisvatn Iceland 64°20N 18°55W 8 D4
Thornaby on Tees U.K. 54°33N 1°18W 12 C6
Thornbury Canada 44°34N 80°26W 82 B4
Thorne U.K. 53°37N 0°57W 12 D7
Thornton Canada 44°16N 79°43W 82 B5
Thornton U.S.A. 39°52N 104°58W 76 G11
Thorold Canada 43°7N 79°12W 82 C5
Þórshöfn Iceland 66°12N 15°20W 8 C6
Thouin, C. Australia 20°20S 118°10E 60 D2
Thousand Islands U.S.A. 44°20N 76°0W 83 B9
Thousand Oaks U.S.A. 34°10N 118°50W 79 L8
Thrace Europe 41°0N 27°0E 23 D12
Three Forks U.S.A. 45°54N 111°33W 76 D8
Three Gorges Dam China 30°45N 111°15E 35 B8
Three Gorges Res. = Sanxia Shuiku China 30°3N 107°58E 34 B6
Three Hills Canada 51°43N 113°15W 70 C6
Three Hummock I. Australia 40°25S 144°55E 63 G3
Three Pagodas Pass Asia 15°20N 98°30E 38 E2
Three Points, C. Ghana 4°42N 2°6W 52 H5
Three Rivers Calif., U.S.A. 36°26N 118°54W 78 J8
Three Rivers Tex., U.S.A. 28°28N 98°11W 84 G5
Three Springs Australia 29°32S 115°45E 61 E2
Thrissur India 10°30N 76°18E 45 J3
Throssell, L. Australia 27°33S 124°10E 61 E3
Throssell Ra. Australia 22°3S 121°43E 60 D3
Thrushton △ Australia 27°47S 147°40E 63 D4
Thu Dau Mot Vietnam 10°58N 106°39E 39 G6
Thua → Kenya 1°31S 39°30E 54 E7
Thuamal Rampur India 19°23N 82°56E 44 E6
Thuan Hoa Vietnam 8°58N 105°30E 39 H5
Thubun Lakes Canada 61°30N 112°0W 71 A6
Thuin Belgium 50°20N 4°17E 15 D4
Thule = Qaanaaq Greenland 77°30N 69°10W 69 B18
Thule Air Base = Uummannaq Greenland 77°33N 68°52W 69 B18
Thun Switz. 46°45N 7°38E 20 C7
Thunder B. U.S.A. 45°0N 83°20W 82 B1
Thunder Bay Canada 48°20N 89°15W 72 C2
Thung Salaeng Luang △ Thailand 16°43N 100°50E 38 D3
Thung Song Thailand 8°10N 99°40E 39 H2
Thungyai △ Thailand 15°20N 98°55E 38 E2
Thunkar Bhutan 27°55N 91°0E 41 F17
Thuong Tra Vietnam 16°2N 107°42E 38 D6
Thüringer Wald Germany 50°35N 11°0E 16 C6
Thuringowa △ Australia 19°18S 146°43E 62 B4
Thurles Ireland 52°41N 7°49W 10 D4
Thurrock □ U.K. 51°31N 0°23E 13 F8
Thursday I. Australia 10°30S 142°3E 62 A3
Thurso Canada 45°36N 75°15W 72 C4
Thurso U.K. 58°36N 3°32W 11 C5
Thurso → U.K. 58°36N 3°32W 11 C5
Thurston I. Antarctica 72°0S 100°0W 5 D16
Thutade L. Canada 57°0N 126°55W 70 B3
Ti-Tree Australia 22°5S 133°22E 62 C1
Tian Shan Asia 40°30N 76°0E 30 C4
Tianchang China 32°40N 119°0E 35 A12
Tiandeng China 23°6N 107°7E 34 F6
Tiandong China 23°36N 107°8E 34 F6
Tian'e China 25°1N 107°9E 34 E6
Tianhe China 24°48N 108°40E 34 E7
Tianjin China 39°7N 117°12E 33 E9
Tianjin Shi □ China 39°8N 117°12E 33 E9
Tianjun China 37°3N 99°8E 32 D8
Tianlin China 24°21N 106°12E 34 E6
Tianmen China 30°39N 113°9E 35 B9
Tianquan China 30°2N 102°10E 34 B4
Tianshifu China 41°17N 124°22E 33 D13
Tianshui China 34°32N 105°40E 34 A5
Tiantai China 29°8N 121°2E 35 C13
Tianya China 18°18N 109°20E 38 C7
Tianyang China 23°42N 106°53E 34 F6
Tianyar Indonesia 8°12S 115°30E 37 J18
Tianzhen China 40°24N 114°5E 32 D8
Tianzhu China 24°25N 109°8E 34 D7
Tianzhuangtai China 40°43N 122°5E 33 D12
Tiarei Tahiti 17°32S 149°20W 59 d
Tiaret Algeria 35°20N 1°21E 52 A6
Tibagi Brazil 24°30S 50°24W 95 A5
Tibagi → Brazil 22°47S 51°1W 95 A5
Tībastī, Sarīr Libya 22°50N 18°30E 53 D9
Tibati Cameroon 6°22N 12°30E 54 C2
Tiber = Tevere → Italy 41°44N 12°14E 22 D5
Tiber Res. U.S.A. 48°19N 111°6W 76 B8
Tiberias = Teverya Israel 32°47N 35°32E 48 C4

Tiberias, L. = Yam Kinneret Israel 32°45N 35°35E 48 C4
Tibesti Chad 21°0N 17°30E 53 D9
Tibet = Xizang Zizhiqu □ China 32°0N 88°0E 30 E6
Tibet, Plateau of Asia 32°0N 86°0E 24 E10
Tibnī Syria 35°36N 39°50E 46 C3
Tibooburra Australia 29°26S 142°1E 63 D3
Tibrikot Nepal 29°3N 82°48E 43 E10
Tiburón, I. Mexico 29°0N 112°25W 86 B2
Ticino → Italy 45°9N 9°14E 20 D8
Ticonderoga U.S.A. 43°51N 73°26W 83 C11
Ticul Mexico 20°24N 89°32W 87 C7
Tidaholm Sweden 58°12N 13°58E 9 G15
Tiddim Burma 23°28N 93°45E 41 H18
Tiden India 7°15N 93°33E 45 L11
Tidioute U.S.A. 41°41N 79°24W 82 E5
Tidjikja Mauritania 18°29N 11°35W 52 E3
Tidore Indonesia 0°40N 127°25E 37 D7
Tiefa China 42°28N 123°26E 33 C12
Tiegang Shuiku China 22°37N 113°53E 31 a
Tiel Neths. 51°53N 5°26E 15 C5
Tieli China 46°57N 128°3E 31 B14
Tieling China 42°20N 123°55E 33 C12
Tielt Belgium 51°0N 3°20E 15 C3
Tien Shan = Tian Shan Asia 40°30N 76°0E 30 C4
Tien-tsin = Tianjin China 39°7N 117°12E 33 E9
Tien Yen Vietnam 21°20N 107°24E 38 B6
T'ienching = Tianjin China 39°7N 117°12E 33 E9
Tienen Belgium 50°48N 4°57E 15 D4
Tientsin = Tianjin China 39°7N 117°12E 33 E9
Tieri Australia 23°2S 148°21E 62 C4
Tierra Amarilla Chile 27°28S 70°18W 94 B1
Tierra Amarilla U.S.A. 36°42N 106°33W 77 H10
Tierra Colorada Mexico 17°11N 99°32W 87 D5
Tierra de Campos Spain 42°10N 4°50W 21 A3
Tierra del Fuego, I. Grande de Argentina 54°0S 69°0W 96 G3
Tiétar → Spain 39°50N 6°1W 21 C3
Tieté → Brazil 20°40S 51°35W 95 A5
Tiffin U.S.A. 41°7N 83°11W 81 E12
Tifton U.S.A. 31°27N 83°31W 85 F13
Tifu Indonesia 3°39S 126°24E 37 E7
Tiger Leaping Gorge = Hutiao Xia China 27°13N 100°9E 34 D3
Tighina = Bendery Moldova 46°50N 29°30E 17 E15
Tigil Russia 57°49N 158°40E 27 D16
Tigiria India 20°29N 85°31E 44 D7
Tignish Canada 46°58N 64°2W 73 C7
Tigre → Peru 4°30S 74°10W 92 D4
Tigre → Venezuela 9°20N 62°30W 92 B6
Tigris = Dijlah, Nahr → Asia 31°0N 47°25E 46 D5
Tigyaing Burma 23°45N 96°10E 41 H20
Tihāmah Asia 15°3N 41°55E 49 D3
Tiilikka △ Finland 63°40N 28°15E 8 E23
Tijara India 27°56N 76°31E 42 F7
Tijuana Mexico 32°32N 117°1W 79 N9
Tikal Guatemala 17°13N 89°24W 88 C2
Tikal △ Guatemala 17°23N 89°34W 88 C2
Tikamgarh India 24°44N 78°50E 43 G8
Tikchik Lakes U.S.A. 60°0N 159°0W 74 D8
Tikhoretsk Russia 45°56N 40°5E 19 E7
Tikhvin Russia 59°35N 33°30E 18 C5
Tikirarjuaq = Whale Cove Canada 62°10N 92°34W 71 A10
Tikrīt Iraq 34°35N 43°37E 46 C4
Tiksi Russia 71°40N 128°45E 27 B13
Tilā' al 'Alī Jordan 32°0N 35°52E 48 D4
Tilamuta Indonesia 0°32N 122°23E 37 D6
Tilburg Neths. 51°31N 5°6E 15 C5
Tilbury Canada 42°17N 82°23W 82 D2
Tilbury U.K. 51°27N 0°22E 13 F8
Tilcara Argentina 23°36S 65°23W 94 A2
Tilden U.S.A. 42°3N 97°50W 80 D5
Tilhar India 28°0N 79°45E 43 F8
Tilichiki Russia 60°27N 166°5E 27 C17
Till → U.K. 55°41N 2°13W 12 B5
Tillamook U.S.A. 45°27N 123°51W 76 D2
Tillanchong I. India 8°30N 93°37E 45 K11
Tillsonburg Canada 42°53N 80°44W 82 D4
Tilos Greece 36°27N 27°27E 23 F12
Tilpa Australia 30°57S 144°24E 63 E3
Tilt → U.K. 56°46N 3°51W 11 E5
Tilton U.S.A. 43°27N 71°36W 83 C13
Tiltonsville U.S.A. 40°10N 80°41W 82 F4
Timanskiy Kryazh Russia 65°58N 50°5E 18 A9
Timaru N.Z. 44°23S 171°14E 59 F3
Timber Creek Australia 15°40S 130°29E 60 C5
Timber Lake U.S.A. 45°26N 101°5W 80 C3
Timber Mt. U.S.A. 37°6N 116°28W 78 H10
Timbué, Ponta Mozam. 18°47S 36°22E 57 A6
Timbuktu = Tombouctou Mali 16°50N 3°0W 52 E5
Timika Indonesia 4°47S 136°32E 37 E9
Timimoun Algeria 29°14N 0°16E 52 C6
Timiris, Râs Mauritania 19°21N 16°30W 52 E2
Timiskaming, L. = Témiscamingue, L. Canada 47°10N 79°25W 72 C4
Timişoara Romania 45°43N 21°15E 17 F11
Timmins Canada 48°28N 81°25W 72 C3
Timok → Serbia 44°10N 22°40E 23 B10
Timoleague Ireland 51°39N 8°46W 10 E3
Timor Asia 9°0S 125°0E 37 F7
Timor Leste = East Timor ■ Asia 8°50S 126°0E 37 F7
Timor Sea Ind. Oc. 12°0S 127°0E 60 B4
Tin Can Bay Australia 25°56S 153°0E 63 D5
Tin Mt. U.S.A. 36°50N 117°10W 78 J9
Tin Shui Wai China 22°28N 114°0E 31 a
Tina = Thina → S. Africa 31°18S 29°13E 57 D4
Tina, Khalîg el Egypt 31°10N 32°40E 48 D1
Tinaca Pt. Phil. 5°30N 125°25E 37 C7
Tindal Australia 14°31S 132°22E 60 B5
Tindivanam India 12°15N 79°41E 45 H4
Tindouf Algeria 27°42N 8°10W 52 C4
Tinfunque △ Paraguay 23°55S 60°17W 94 A3
Ting Jiang → China 24°45N 116°35E 35 E11
Tinggi, Pulau Malaysia 2°18N 104°7E 39 L5
Tingo María Peru 9°10S 75°54W 92 E3
Tingrela Ivory C. 10°27N 6°25W 52 F4
Tingri China 28°34N 86°38E 30 F6
Tinh Bien Vietnam 10°36N 104°57E 39 G5
Tinian N. Marianas 15°0N 145°38E 64 F6
Tinnevelly = Tirunelveli India 8°45N 77°45E 45 K3
Tinogasta Argentina 28°5S 67°32W 94 B2
Tinos Greece 37°33N 25°8E 23 F11
Tinpahar India 24°59N 87°44E 43 G12
Tintina Argentina 27°2S 62°45W 94 B3
Tintinara Australia 35°48S 140°2E 63 F3
Tiobraid Árann = Tipperary Ireland 52°28N 8°10W 10 D3
Tioga N. Dak., U.S.A. 48°24N 102°56W 80 A2
Tioga Pa., U.S.A. 41°55N 77°8W 82 E7
Tioman, Pulau Malaysia 2°50N 104°10E 39 L5
Tionesta U.S.A. 41°30N 79°28W 82 E5
Tipperary Ireland 52°28N 8°10W 10 D3
Tipperary □ Ireland 52°37N 7°55W 10 D4
Tipton Calif., U.S.A. 36°4N 119°19W 78 J7
Tipton Iowa, U.S.A. 41°46N 91°8W 80 E8
Tipton Mt. U.S.A. 35°32N 114°12W 79 K12
Tiptonville U.S.A. 36°23N 89°29W 85 C10
Tiptur India 13°15N 76°26E 45 H3
Tīrān Iran 32°45N 51°8E 47 C6
Tiranë Albania 41°18N 19°49E 23 D8
Tirari Desert Australia 28°22S 138°7E 63 D2
Tiraspol Moldova 46°55N 29°35E 17 E15
Tire Turkey 38°5N 27°45E 23 E12
Tirebolu Turkey 40°58N 38°45E 19 F6
Tiree U.K. 56°31N 6°55W 11 E2
Tiree, Passage of U.K. 56°30N 6°30W 11 E2
Tîrgovişte = Târgovişte Romania 44°55N 25°27E 17 F13
Tîrgu Jiu = Târgu Jiu Romania 45°5N 23°19E 17 F12
Tîrgu Mureş = Târgu Mureş Romania 46°31N 24°38E 17 E13
Tirich Mir Pakistan 36°15N 71°55E 40 A7
Tiritiri o te Moana = Southern Alps N.Z. 43°41S 170°11E 59 E3
Tirna → India 18°4N 76°57E 44 E3
Tirnavos Greece 39°45N 22°18E 23 E10
Tirodi India 21°40N 79°44E 44 D4
Tirol □ Austria 47°3N 10°43E 16 E6
Tirrukkovil Sri Lanka 7°7N 81°51E 45 L5
Tirso → Italy 39°53N 8°32E 22 E3
Tirtagangga Indonesia 8°24S 115°35E 37 J18
Tirthahalli India 13°42N 75°14E 45 H2
Tiruchchendur India 8°30N 78°11E 45 K4
Tiruchchirappalli India 10°45N 78°45E 45 J4
Tirukkoyilur India 11°57N 79°12E 45 J4
Tirumangalam India 9°49N 77°58E 45 K3
Tirumayam India 10°14N 78°45E 45 J4
Tirunelveli India 8°45N 77°45E 45 K3
Tirupati India 13°39N 79°25E 45 H4
Tiruppattur Tamil Nadu, India 10°8N 78°37E 45 J4
Tiruppattur Tamil Nadu, India 12°30N 78°30E 45 H4
Tiruppur India 11°5N 77°22E 45 J3
Tirur India 10°54N 75°55E 45 J2
Tiruttani India 13°11N 79°58E 45 H4
Tirutturaippundi India 10°32N 79°41E 45 J4
Tiruvadaimarudur India 11°2N 79°27E 45 J4
Tiruvalla India 9°23N 76°34E 45 K3
Tiruvallar India 13°9N 79°57E 45 H4
Tiruvannamalai India 12°15N 79°5E 45 H4
Tiruvettipuram India 12°39N 79°33E 45 H4
Tiruvottiyur India 13°10N 80°22E 45 H5
Tisa India 32°50N 76°9E 42 C7
Tisa → Serbia 45°15N 20°17E 23 B9
Tisdale Canada 52°50N 104°0W 71 C8
Tishomingo U.S.A. 34°14N 96°41W 84 D6
Tissamaharama Sri Lanka 6°17N 81°17E 45 L5
Tisza = Tisa → Serbia 45°15N 20°17E 23 B9
Tit-Ary Russia 71°55N 127°2E 27 B13
Tithwal Pakistan 34°21N 73°50E 43 B5
Titicaca, L. S. Amer. 15°30S 69°30W 92 G5
Titiwa Nigeria 12°14N 12°53E 53 F8
Titlagarh India 20°15N 83°11E 44 D6
Titule Dem. Rep. of the Congo 3°15N 25°31E 54 D5
Titusville Fla., U.S.A. 28°37N 80°49W 85 G14
Titusville Pa., U.S.A. 41°38N 79°41W 82 E5
Tivaouane Senegal 14°56N 16°45W 52 F2
Tiverton Canada 44°16N 81°32W 82 B3
Tiverton U.K. 50°54N 3°29W 13 G4
Tivoli Italy 41°58N 12°45E 22 D5
Tiwi ☼ Australia 11°33S 130°42E 60 B5
Tizi-Ouzou Algeria 36°42N 4°3E 52 A6
Tizimín Mexico 21°9N 88°9W 87 C7
Tiznit Morocco 29°48N 9°45W 52 C4
Tjeggelvas Sweden 66°37N 17°45E 8 C17
Tjieggelvas = Tjeggelvas Sweden 66°37N 17°45E 8 C17
Tjirebon = Cirebon Indonesia 6°45S 108°32E 37 G13
Tjirrkarli ☼ Australia 26°0S 125°28E 61 E4
Tjluring Indonesia 8°25S 114°13E 37 J17
Tjörn Sweden 58°0N 11°35E 9 H14
Tjukayirla Roadhouse Australia 27°9S 124°34E 61 E3
Tjurabalan ☼ Australia 19°50S 128°0E 60 C4
Tlacotalpan Mexico 18°37N 95°40W 87 D5
Tlahualilo de Zaragoza Mexico 26°7N 103°27W 86 B4
Tlaquepaque Mexico 20°39N 103°19W 86 C4
Tlaxcala Mexico 19°19N 98°14W 87 D5
Tlaxcala □ Mexico 19°25N 98°10W 87 D5
Tlaxiaco Mexico 17°25N 97°35W 87 D5
Tlemcen Algeria 34°52N 1°21W 52 B5
Tlokweng Botswana 24°40S 25°58E 56 B4
To Bong Vietnam 12°45N 109°16E 38 F7
Toad → Canada 59°25N 124°57W 70 B4
Toad River Canada 58°51N 125°14W 70 B3
Toamasina Madag. 18°10S 49°25E 55 H9
Toay Argentina 36°43S 64°38W 94 D3
Toba China 31°19N 97°42E 34 B1
Toba Japan 34°30N 136°51E 29 G8
Toba, Danau Indonesia 2°30N 98°30E 36 D1
Toba Kakar Pakistan 31°30N 69°0E 42 D3
Toba Tek Singh Pakistan 30°55N 72°25E 42 D5
Tobago Trin. & Tob. 11°10N 60°30W 93 J16
Tobelo Indonesia 1°45N 127°56E 37 D7
Tobercurry Ireland 54°3N 8°44W 10 B3
Tobermory Canada 45°12N 81°40W 82 A3
Tobermory U.K. 56°38N 6°5W 11 E2
Tobi Palau 2°40N 131°10E 37 D8
Tobi-Shima Japan 41°12N 139°34E 28 D9
Tobin, L. Australia 21°45S 125°49E 60 D4
Tobin L. Canada 53°35N 103°30W 71 C8
Toboali Indonesia 3°0S 106°25E 36 E3
Tobol → Russia 58°10N 68°12E 26 D7
Toboli Indonesia 0°38S 120°5E 37 E6
Tobolsk Russia 58°15N 68°10E 26 D7
Tobruk = Tubruq Libya 32°7N 23°55E 53 B10
Tobyhanna U.S.A. 41°11N 75°25W 83 E9
Tobyl = Tobol → Russia 58°10N 68°12E 26 D7
Tocantinópolis Brazil 6°20S 47°25W 93 E9
Tocantins □ Brazil 10°0S 48°0W 93 F9
Tocantins → Brazil 1°45S 49°10W 93 D9
Toccoa U.S.A. 34°35N 83°19W 85 D13
Tochi → Pakistan 32°49N 70°41E 42 C4
Tochigi Japan 36°25N 139°45E 29 F9
Tochigi □ Japan 36°45N 139°45E 29 F9
Toco Trin. & Tob. 10°49N 60°57W 93 K16
Toconao Chile 23°11S 68°1W 94 A2
Tocopilla Chile 22°5S 70°10W 94 A1
Tocumwal Australia 35°51S 145°31E 63 F4
Tocuyo → Venezuela 11°3N 68°23W 92 A5
Todd → Australia 24°52S 135°48E 62 C2
Todeli Indonesia 1°40S 124°29E 37 E6
Todgarh India 25°42N 73°58E 42 G5
Todos os Santos, B. de Brazil 12°48S 38°38W 93 F11
Todos Santos Mexico 23°26N 110°13W 86 C2
Toe Hd. U.K. 57°50N 7°8W 11 D1
Tofield Canada 53°25N 112°40W 70 C6
Tofino Canada 49°11N 125°55W 70 D3
Tôfsingdalen △ Sweden 62°10N 12°28E 8 E15
Tofua Tonga 19°45S 175°5W 59 c
Tōgane Japan 35°33N 140°22E 29 G10
Togian, Kepulauan Indonesia 0°20S 121°50E 37 E6
Togliatti Russia 53°32N 49°24E 18 D8
Togo ■ W. Afr. 8°30N 1°35E 52 G6
Togtoh China 40°15N 111°10E 32 D6
Tohiea, Mt. Moorea 17°33S 149°49W 59 d
Tōhoku □ Japan 39°50N 141°45E 28 E10
Töhöm Mongolia 44°27N 108°2E 32 B5
Toibalewe India 10°32N 92°30E 45 J11
Toinya South Sudan 6°17N 29°46E 53 G11
Toiyabe Range U.S.A. 39°30N 117°0W 76 G5
Tojikiston = Tajikistan ■ Asia 38°30N 70°0E 26 F8
Tōjō Japan 34°53N 133°16E 29 G6
Tok U.S.A. 63°20N 142°59W 68 E3
Tokachi-Dake Japan 43°17N 142°5E 28 C11
Tokachi-Gawa → Japan 42°44N 143°42E 28 C11
Tokala Indonesia 1°30S 121°40E 37 E6
Tōkamachi Japan 37°8N 138°43E 29 F9
Tokanui N.Z. 46°34S 168°56E 59 G2
Tokara-Rettō Japan 29°37N 129°43E 29 K4
Tokarahi N.Z. 44°56S 170°39E 59 F3
Tokashiki-Shima Japan 26°11N 127°21E 29 L3
Tokat Turkey 40°22N 36°35E 19 F6
Tŏkch'ŏn N. Korea 39°45N 126°18E 33 E14
Tokdo = Liancourt Rocks Asia 37°15N 131°52E 29 F5
Tokeland U.S.A. 46°42N 123°59W 78 D3
Tokelau Is. ☒ Pac. Oc. 9°0S 171°45W 64 H10
Tokmak Kyrgyzstan 42°49N 75°15E 26 E8
Toko Ra. Australia 23°5S 138°20E 62 C2
Tokoro-Gawa → Japan 44°7N 144°5E 28 B12
Toku Tonga 18°10S 174°11W 59 c
Tokuno-Shima Japan 27°56N 128°55E 29 L4
Tokushima Japan 34°4N 134°34E 29 G7
Tokushima □ Japan 33°55N 134°0E 29 H7
Tokuyama = Shūnān Japan 34°3N 131°50E 29 G5
Tolaga Bay N.Z. 38°21S 178°20E 59 C7
Tolbukhin = Dobrich Bulgaria 43°37N 27°49E 23 C12
Toledo Brazil 24°44S 53°45W 95 A5
Toledo Spain 39°50N 4°2W 21 C3
Toledo Ohio, U.S.A. 41°39N 83°33W 81 E12
Toledo Oreg., U.S.A. 44°37N 123°56W 76 D2
Toledo Wash., U.S.A. 46°26N 122°51W 78 D4
Toledo, Montes de Spain 39°33N 4°20W 21 C3
Toledo Bend Res. U.S.A. 31°11N 93°34W 84 F8
Tolga Australia 17°15S 145°29E 62 B4
Toliara Madag. 23°21S 43°40E 55 J8
Tolima Colombia 4°40N 75°19W 92 C3
Tolitoli Indonesia 1°5N 120°50E 37 D6
Tollhouse U.S.A. 37°1N 119°24W 78 H7
Tolmachevo Russia 58°56N 29°51E 9 G23
Tolo, Teluk Indonesia 2°20S 122°10E 37 E6
Toluca Mexico 19°17N 99°40W 87 D5
Tolyatti = Togliatti Russia 53°32N 49°24E 18 D8
Tom Burke S. Africa 23°5S 28°0E 57 B4
Tom Price Australia 22°40S 117°48E 60 D2
Tomah U.S.A. 43°59N 90°30W 80 D8
Tomahawk U.S.A. 45°28N 89°44W 80 C9
Tomakomai Japan 42°38N 141°36E 28 C10
Tomales U.S.A. 38°15N 122°53W 78 G4
Tomales B. U.S.A. 38°15N 123°58W 78 G3
Tomanivi Fiji 17°37S 178°1E 59 a
Tomar Portugal 39°36N 8°25W 21 C1
Tomaszów Mazowiecki Poland 51°30N 20°2E 17 C10
Tomatlán Mexico 19°56N 105°15W 86 D3
Tombador, Serra do Brazil 12°0S 58°0W 92 F7
Tombigbee → U.S.A. 31°8N 87°57W 85 F11
Tombouctou Mali 16°50N 3°0W 52 E5
Tombstone U.S.A. 31°43N 110°4W 77 L8
Tombua Angola 15°55S 11°55E 56 A1
Tomé Chile 36°36S 72°57W 94 D1
Tome Japan 38°40N 141°20E 28 E10
Tomelloso Spain 39°10N 3°2W 21 C4
Tomini Indonesia 0°30N 120°30E 37 D6
Tomini, Teluk Indonesia 0°10S 121°0E 37 E6
Tomintoul U.K. 57°15N 3°23W 11 D5
Tomkinson Ranges Australia 26°11S 129°5E 61 E4
Tommot Russia 59°4N 126°20E 27 D13
Tomnop Ta Suos Cambodia 11°20N 104°15E 39 G5
Tomo → Colombia 5°20N 67°48W 92 B5
Toms Place U.S.A. 37°34N 118°41W 78 H8
Toms River U.S.A. 39°58N 74°12W 83 G10
Tomsk Russia 56°30N 85°5E 26 D9
Tomür Feng = Pobedy, Pik Asia 42°0N 79°58E 30 C4
Tonalá Chiapas, Mexico 16°4N 93°45W 87 D6
Tonalá Jalisco, Mexico 20°37N 103°14W 86 C4
Tonantins Brazil 2°45S 67°45W 92 D5
Tonasket U.S.A. 48°42N 119°26W 76 B4
Tonawanda U.S.A. 43°1N 78°53W 82 D6
Tonb U.A.E. 26°15N 55°15E 47 E7
Tonbridge U.K. 51°11N 0°17E 13 F8
Tondano Indonesia 1°35N 124°54E 37 D6
Tondi India 9°45N 79°4E 45 K4
Tondoro Namibia 17°45S 18°50E 56 A2
Tone → Australia 34°25S 116°25E 61 F2
Tone-Gawa → Japan 35°44N 140°51E 29 F9
Tonekābon Iran 36°45N 51°12E 47 B6
Tong Xian China 39°55N 116°35E 32 E9
Tong-yeong S. Korea 34°50N 128°20E 33 G15
Tonga ■ Pac. Oc. 19°50S 174°30W 59 c
Tonga Trench Pac. Oc. 18°0S 173°0W 64 J10
Tongaat S. Africa 29°33S 31°9E 57 C5
Tong'an China 24°37N 118°8E 35 E12
Tongareva = Penrhyn Cook Is. 9°0S 158°0W 65 H12
Tongariro △ N.Z. 39°8S 175°33E 59 C5
Tongatapu Tonga 21°10S 175°10W 59 c
Tongatapu Group Tonga 21°0S 175°0W 59 c
Tongbai China 32°20N 113°23E 35 A9
Tongcheng Anhui, China 31°4N 116°56E 35 B11
Tongcheng Hubei, China 29°15N 113°50E 35 C9
Tongchuan China 35°6N 109°3E 32 G5
Tongdao China 26°10N 109°42E 34 D7
Tongeren Belgium 50°47N 5°28E 15 D5
Tonggu China 28°31N 114°20E 35 C10
Tonggu Jiao China 22°22N 113°37E 31 a
Tongguan China 34°40N 110°25E 32 G6
Tonghai China 24°10N 102°53E 34 E4
Tonghua China 41°42N 125°58E 33 D13
Tongjiang Heilongjiang, China 47°40N 132°27E 31 B15
Tongjiang Sichuan, China 31°58N 107°11E 34 B6
Tongjosŏn-man N. Korea 39°30N 128°0E 33 E15
Tongking, G. of = Tonkin, G. of Asia 20°0N 108°0E 38 C7
Tongliang China 29°50N 106°3E 34 C6
Tongliao China 43°38N 122°18E 33 C12
Tongling China 30°55N 117°48E 35 B11
Tonglu China 29°45N 119°37E 35 C12
Tongnan = Anyue China 30°9N 105°50E 34 B5
Tongoy Chile 30°16S 71°31W 94 C1
Tongren Guizhou, China 27°43N 109°11E 34 D7
Tongren Qinghai, China 35°25N 102°5E 30 D9
Tongres = Tongeren Belgium 50°47N 5°28E 15 D5
Tongsa Dzong Bhutan 27°31N 90°31E 41 F17
Tongshi China 18°50N 109°20E 38 C7
Tongue U.K. 58°29N 4°25W 11 C4
Tongue → U.S.A. 46°25N 105°52W 76 C11
Tongwei China 35°0N 105°5E 32 G3
Tongxiang China 30°39N 120°34E 35 B13
Tongxin China 36°59N 105°58E 32 F3
Tongyang N. Korea 39°9N 126°53E 33 E14
Tongyu China 44°45N 123°4E 33 B12
Tongzhou China 32°12N 121°2E 35 A13
Tongzi China 28°9N 106°49E 34 C6
Tonj South Sudan 7°20N 28°44E 53 G11
Tonk India 26°6N 75°54E 42 F6
Tonkawa U.S.A. 36°41N 97°18W 84 C6
Tonkin = Bac Phan Vietnam 22°0N 105°0E 34 G5
Tonkin, G. of Asia 20°0N 108°0E 38 C7
Tonlé Sap Cambodia 13°0N 104°0E 38 F5
Tono Japan 39°19N 141°32E 28 E10
Tonopah U.S.A. 38°4N 117°14W 77 G5
Tonosí Panama 7°20N 80°20W 88 E3
Tons → Haryana, India 30°30N 77°39E 42 D7
Tons → Ut. P., India 26°1N 83°33E 43 F10
Tønsberg Norway 59°19N 10°25E 9 G14
Tonto ☼ U.S.A. 33°39N 111°7W 77 K8
Tonumea Tonga 20°30S 174°30W 59 c
Toobanna Australia 18°42S 146°9E 62 B4
Toodyay Australia 31°34S 116°28E 61 F2
Tooele U.S.A. 40°32N 112°18W 76 F7
Toompine Australia 27°15S 144°19E 63 D3
Toora Australia 38°39S 146°23E 63 F4
Toora-Khem Russia 52°28N 96°17E 27 D10
Toowoomba Australia 27°32S 151°56E 63 D5
Top Springs Australia 16°37S 131°51E 60 C5
Topaz U.S.A. 38°41N 119°30W 78 G7
Topeka U.S.A. 39°3N 95°40W 80 F6
Topley Canada 54°49N 126°18W 70 C3
Topocalma, Pta. Chile 34°10S 72°2W 94 C1
Topock U.S.A. 34°46N 114°29W 79 L12
Topoľčany Slovak Rep. 48°35N 18°12E 17 D10
Topolobampo Mexico 25°36N 109°3W 86 B3
Topozero, Ozero Russia 65°35N 32°0E 8 D25
Toppenish U.S.A. 46°23N 120°19W 76 C3
Torata Peru 17°23S 70°1W 92 G4
Torbalı Turkey 38°10N 27°21E 23 E12
Torbat-e Heydārīyeh Iran 35°15N 59°12E 47 C8
Torbat-e Jām Iran 35°16N 60°35E 47 C9
Torbay Canada 47°40N 52°42W 73 C9
Torbay □ U.K. 50°26N 3°31W 13 G4
Tordesillas Spain 41°30N 5°0W 21 B3
Torfaen □ U.K. 51°43N 3°3W 13 F4
Torgau Germany 51°34N 13°0E 16 C7
Torhout Belgium 51°5N 3°7E 15 C3
Tori-Shima Japan 30°29N 140°19E 29 J10
Torilla Pen. Australia 22°29S 150°5E 62 C5
Torino Italy 45°3N 7°40E 20 D7
Torit South Sudan 4°27N 32°31E 53 H12
Torkamān Iran 37°35N 47°23E 46 B5
Tormes → Spain 41°18N 6°29W 21 B2
Tornado Mt. Canada 49°55N 114°40W 70 D6
Torneå = Tornio Finland 65°50N 24°12E 8 D21
Torneälven → Europe 65°50N 24°12E 8 D21
Torneträsk Sweden 68°24N 19°15E 8 B18
Torngat Mountains Nat. Park △ Canada 59°0N 63°40W 69 F19
Torngat Mts. Canada 59°0N 63°40W 69 F19
Tornio Finland 65°50N 24°12E 8 D21
Tornionjoki = Torneälven → Europe 65°50N 24°12E 8 D21
Tornquist Argentina 38°8S 62°15W 94 D3
Toro, Cerro del Chile 29°10S 69°50W 94 B2
Toro Pk. U.S.A. 33°34N 116°24W 79 M10
Toronto U.S.A. 40°28N 80°36W 82 F4
Toropets Russia 56°30N 31°40E 18 C5
Tororo Uganda 0°45N 34°12E 54 D6
Toros Dağları Turkey 37°0N 32°30E 46 B2
Torpa India 22°57N 85°6E 43 H11
Torquay U.K. 50°27N 3°32W 13 G4
Torrance U.S.A. 33°50N 118°20W 79 M8
Torre de Moncorvo Portugal 41°12N 7°8W 21 B2
Torre del Greco Italy 40°47N 14°22E 22 D6
Torrejón de Ardoz Spain 40°27N 3°29W 21 B4
Torrelavega Spain 43°20N 4°5W 21 A3
Torremolinos Spain 36°38N 4°30W 21 D3
Torrens, L. Australia 31°0S 137°50E 63 E2
Torrens Cr. → Australia 22°23S 145°9E 62 C4
Torrens Creek Australia 20°48S 145°3E 62 C4
Torrent Spain 39°27N 0°28W 21 C5
Torreón Mexico 25°33N 103°26W 86 B4
Torres Brazil 29°21S 49°44W 95 B5
Torres Mexico 28°46N 110°47W 86 B2
Torres Strait Australia 9°50S 142°20E 62 a
Torres Vedras Portugal 39°5N 9°15W 21 C1
Torrevieja Spain 37°59N 0°42W 21 D5
Torrey U.S.A. 38°18N 111°25W 76 G8
Torridge → U.K. 51°0N 4°13W 13 G3
Torridon, L. U.K. 57°35N 5°50W 11 D3
Torrington Conn., U.S.A. 41°48N 73°7W 83 E11
Torrington Wyo., U.S.A. 42°4N 104°11W 76 E11
Tórshavn Færoe Is. 62°5N 6°56W 8 E9
Tortola Br. Virgin Is. 18°19N 64°45W 89 e
Tortosa Spain 40°49N 0°31E 21 B6
Tortosa, C. Spain 40°41N 0°52E 21 B6
Tortue, Î. de la Haiti 20°5N 72°57W 89 B5
Tortuguero △ Costa Rica 10°31N 83°29W 88 D3
Torūd Iran 35°25N 55°5E 47 C7
Toruń Poland 53°2N 18°39E 17 B10
Tory Hill Canada 44°58N 78°16W 82 B6
Tory I. Ireland 55°16N 8°13W 10 A3
Tosa Japan 33°24N 133°23E 29 H6
Tosa-Shimizu Japan 32°52N 132°58E 29 H6
Tosa-Wan Japan 33°15N 133°30E 29 H6
Toscana □ Italy 43°25N 11°0E 22 C4
Toshka, Buheirat en Egypt 22°50N 31°0E 53 D12
Toshkent Uzbekistan 41°20N 69°10E 26 E7
Tostado Argentina 29°15S 61°50W 94 B3
Tosu Japan 33°22N 130°31E 29 H5
Toteng Botswana 20°22S 22°58E 56 B3
Totma Russia 60°0N 42°40E 18 C7
Totnes U.K. 50°26N 3°42W 13 G4
Totness Suriname 5°53N 56°19W 93 B7
Totonicapán Guatemala 14°58N 91°12W 88 D1
Totoya, I. Fiji 18°57S 179°50W 59 a
Totten Glacier Antarctica 66°45S 116°10E 5 C8
Tottenham Australia 32°14S 147°21E 63 E4
Tottenham Canada 44°1N 79°49W 82 B5
Tottori Japan 35°30N 134°15E 29 G7
Tottori □ Japan 35°30N 134°12E 29 G7
Toubkal, Djebel Morocco 31°0N 8°0W 52 B4
Tougan Burkina Faso 13°11N 2°58W 52 F5
Touggourt Algeria 33°6N 6°4E 52 B7
Toul France 48°40N 5°53E 20 B6
Touliu Taiwan 23°42N 120°31E 35 F13
Toulon France 43°10N 5°55E 20 E6
Toulouse France 43°37N 1°27E 20 E4
Toummo Niger 22°45N 14°8E 53 D8
Tounan Taiwan 23°41N 120°28E 35 F13
Tounggoo Burma 19°0N 96°30E 41 K20
Touraine France 47°20N 0°30E 20 C4
Touran = Tūrān △ Iran 35°45N 56°30E 47 C8
Tourcoing France 50°42N 3°10E 20 A5
Touriñán, C. Spain 43°3N 9°18W 21 A1
Tournai Belgium 50°35N 3°25E 15 D3
Tournon-sur-Rhône France 45°4N 4°50E 20 D6
Tours France 47°22N 0°40E 20 C4
Toussoro, Mt. C.A.R. 9°7N 23°14E 54 C4
Touws → S. Africa 33°45S 21°11E 56 D3
Touwsrivier S. Africa 33°20S 20°2E 56 D3
Towada Japan 40°37N 141°13E 28 D10
Towada-Hachimantai △ Japan 40°20N 140°55E 28 D10
Towada-Ko Japan 40°28N 140°55E 28 D10
Towanda U.S.A. 41°46N 76°27W 83 E8
Tower U.S.A. 47°48N 92°17W 80 B7
Towerhill Cr. → Australia 22°28S 144°35E 62 C3
Towner U.S.A. 48°21N 100°25W 80 A3
Townsend U.S.A. 46°19N 111°31W 76 C8
Townshend I. Australia 22°10S 150°31E 62 C5
Townsville Australia 19°15S 146°45E 62 B4
Towraghondī Afghan. 35°13N 62°16E 40 B3
Towson U.S.A. 39°24N 76°36W 81 F15
Towuti, Danau Indonesia 2°45S 121°32E 37 E6
Tōya-Ko Japan 42°35N 140°51E 28 C10
Toyama Japan 36°40N 137°15E 29 F8
Toyama □ Japan 36°45N 137°30E 29 F8
Toyama-Wan Japan 37°0N 137°30E 29 F8

Toyapakeh *Indonesia* 8°41S 115°29E **37** K18
Toyohashi *Japan* 34°45N 137°25E **29** G8
Toyokawa *Japan* 34°48N 137°27E **29** G8
Toyooka *Japan* 35°35N 134°48E **29** G7
Toyota *Japan* 35°3N 137°7E **29** G8
Tozeur *Tunisia* 33°56N 8°8E **52** B7
Trá Lí = Tralee *Ireland* 52°16N 9°42W **10** D2
Trá Mhór = Tramore
Ireland 52°10N 7°10W **10** D4
Tra On *Vietnam* 9°58N 105°55E **39** H5
Tra Vinh *Vietnam* 9°50N 106°15E **39** H6
Trabzon *Turkey* 41°0N 39°45E **19** F6
Tracadie *Canada* 47°30N 64°55W **73** C7
Tracy *Canada* 46°1N 73°9W **72** C5
Tracy Calif., U.S.A. 37°44N 121°26W **78** H5
Tracy Minn., U.S.A. 44°14N 95°37W **80** C6
Trafalgar, C. *Spain* 36°10N 6°2W **21** D2
Trail *Canada* 49°5N 117°40W **70** D5
Trainor L. *Canada* 60°24N 120°17W **70** A4
Trakai △ *Lithuania* 54°30N 25°10E **9** J21
Tralee *Ireland* 52°16N 9°42W **10** D2
Tralee B. *Ireland* 52°17N 9°55W **10** D2
Tram Chim △ *Vietnam* 10°43N 105°31E **39** G5
Tramore *Ireland* 52°10N 7°10W **10** D4
Tramore B. *Ireland* 52°9N 7°10W **10** D4
Tran Ninh, Cao Nguyen
Laos 19°30N 103°10E **38** C4
Tranås *Sweden* 58°3N 14°59E **9** G16
Trancas *Argentina* 26°11S 65°20W **94** B2
Trang *Thailand* 7°33N 99°38E **39** J2
Trangan *Indonesia* 6°40S 134°20E **37** F8
Trangie *Australia* 32°4S 148°0E **63** E4
Trani *Italy* 41°17N 16°25E **22** D7
Tranoroa *Madag.* 24°42S 45°4E **55** J9
Tranqueras *Uruguay* 31°13S 55°45W **95** C4
Transantarctic Mts.
Antarctica 85°0S 170°0W **5** E12
Transilvania *Romania* 46°30N 24°0E **17** E12
Transilvanian Alps = Carpații
Meridionali *Romania* 45°30N 25°0E **17** F13
Transnistria □ *Moldova* 47°20N 29°15E **17** E15
Transylvania = Transilvania
Romania 46°30N 24°0E **17** E12
Trápani *Italy* 38°1N 12°29E **22** E5
Trapper Pk. U.S.A. 45°54N 114°18W **76** D6
Traralgon *Australia* 38°12S 146°34E **63** F4
Trasimeno, L. *Italy* 43°8N 12°6E **22** C5
Trat *Thailand* 12°14N 102°33E **39** F4
Tratani → *Pakistan* 29°19N 68°20E **42** E3
Traun *Austria* 48°14N 14°15E **16** D8
Travellers L. *Australia* 33°20S 142°0E **63** E3
Travemünde *Germany* 53°57N 10°52E **16** B6
Travers, Mt. N.Z. 42°1S 172°45E **59** E4
Traverse City U.S.A. 44°46N 85°38W **81** C11
Travis, L. U.S.A. 30°24N 97°55W **84** F6
Travnik *Bos.-H.* 44°17N 17°39E **23** B7
Trawbreaga B. *Ireland* 55°20N 7°25W **10** A4
Trébbia → *Italy* 45°4N 9°41E **20** D8
Třebíč *Czech Rep.* 49°14N 15°55E **16** D8
Trebinje *Bos.-H.* 42°44N 18°22E **23** C8
Trebonne *Australia* 18°37S 146°5E **62** B4
Trefaldwyn = Montgomery
U.K. 52°34N 3°8W **13** E4
Trefynwy = Monmouth
U.K. 51°48N 2°42W **13** F5
Tregaron U.K. 52°14N 3°56W **13** E4
Tregrosse Is. *Australia* 17°41S 150°43E **62** B5
Treherne *Canada* 49°38N 98°42W **71** D9
Treinta y Tres *Uruguay* 33°16S 54°17W **95** C5
Trelawney *Zimbabwe* 17°30S 30°30E **57** A5
Trelew *Argentina* 43°10S 65°20W **96** E3
Trelleborg *Sweden* 55°20N 13°10E **9** J15
Tremadog Bay U.K. 52°51N 4°18W **12** E3
Tremonton U.S.A. 41°43N 112°10W **76** F7
Tremp *Spain* 42°10N 0°52E **21** A6
Trenche → *Canada* 47°46N 72°53W **72** C5
Trenčín *Slovak Rep.* 48°52N 18°4E **17** D10
Trenggalek *Indonesia* 8°3S 111°43E **37** H14
Trenque Lauquen
Argentina 36°5S 62°45W **94** D3
Trent → *Canada* 44°6N 77°34W **82** B7
Trent → U.K. 53°41N 0°42W **12** D7
Trento *Italy* 46°4N 11°8E **22** A4
Trenton *Canada* 44°10N 77°34W **82** B7
Trenton Mo., U.S.A. 40°5N 93°37W **80** E7
Trenton N.J., U.S.A. 40°14N 74°46W **83** F10
Trenton Nebr., U.S.A. 40°11N 101°1W **80** E3
Trepassey *Canada* 46°43N 53°25W **73** C9
Tres Arroyos *Argentina* 38°26S 60°20W **94** D3
Três Corações *Brazil* 21°44S 45°15W **95** A6
Três Lagoas *Brazil* 20°50S 51°43W **93** H8
Tres Lomas *Argentina* 36°27S 62°51W **94** D3
Tres Montes, C. *Chile* 46°50S 75°30W **96** F1
Três Pinos *Brazil* 36°48N 121°19W **78** J5
Três Pontas *Brazil* 21°23S 45°29W **95** A6
Tres Puentes *Chile* 27°50S 70°15W **94** B1
Três Puntas, C. *Argentina* 47°0S 66°0W **96** F3
Três Valles *Mexico* 18°15N 96°8W **87** D5
Tresco U.K. 49°57N 6°20W **13** H1
Treviso *Italy* 45°40N 12°15E **22** B5
Triabunna *Australia* 42°30S 147°55E **63** G4
Triangle *Zimbabwe* 21°2S 31°28E **57** C5
Tribal Areas □ *Pakistan* 33°0N 70°0E **42** C4
Tribulation, C. *Australia* 16°5S 145°29E **62** B4
Tribune U.S.A. 38°28N 101°45W **80** F3
Trichinopoly = Tiruchchirappalli
India 10°45N 78°45E **45** J4
Trichur = Thrissur *India* 10°30N 76°18E **45** J3
Trichy = Tiruchchirappalli
India 10°45N 78°45E **45** J4
Trida *Australia* 33°1S 145°1E **63** E4
Trier *Germany* 49°45N 6°38E **16** D4
Trieste *Italy* 45°40N 13°46E **22** B5
Triglav *Slovenia* 46°21N 13°50E **16** E7
Trikala *Greece* 39°34N 21°47E **23** E9
Trikora, Puncak
Indonesia 4°15S 138°45E **37** E9
Trim *Ireland* 53°33N 6°48W **10** C5
Trimbak *India* 19°56N 73°33E **44** E1
Trimmu Dam *Pakistan* 31°10N 72°8E **42** D5

Trincomalee *Sri Lanka* 8°38N 81°15E **45** K5
Trindade *Atl. Oc.* 20°20S 29°50W **2** F8
Trindade *Brazil* 16°40S 49°30W **93** G9
Trinidad *Bolivia* 14°46S 64°50W **92** F6
Trinidad *Cuba* 21°48N 80°0W **88** B4
Trinidad *Paraguay* 27°7S 55°47W **95** B4
Trinidad *Uruguay* 33°30S 56°50W **94** C4
Trinidad Trin. & Tob. 37°10N 104°31W **77** H11
Trinidad & Tobago ■
W. Indies 10°30N 61°20W **93** K15
Trinity *Canada* 48°59N 53°55W **73** C9
Trinity U.S.A. 30°57N 95°22W **84** F7
Trinity → Calif., U.S.A. 41°11N 123°42W **76** F2
Trinity → Tex., U.S.A. 29°45N 94°43W **84** G7
Trinity B. *Canada* 48°20N 53°10W **73** C9
Trinity Hills Trin. & Tob. 10°7N 61°7W **93** K15
Trinity Is. U.S.A. 56°33N 154°25W **74** D9
Trinity Range U.S.A. 40°10N 118°40W **76** F4
Trinkat *India* 8°5N 93°30E **45** K11
Trinkitat *Sudan* 18°45N 37°51E **53** E13
Trinway U.S.A. 40°9N 82°1W **82** F2
Triolet *Mauritius* 20°4S 57°32E **55** d
Tripoli = Tarābulus
Lebanon 34°31N 35°50E **48** A4
Tripoli = Tarābulus *Libya* 32°49N 13°7E **53** B8
Tripoli *Greece* 37°31N 22°25E **23** F10
Tripolitania = Tarābulus
Libya 31°0N 13°0E **53** B8
Tripura □ *India* 24°0N 92°0E **41** H18
Tristan da Cunha *Atl. Oc.* 37°6S 12°20W **51** K2
Trisul *India* 30°19N 79°47E **43** D8
Triton I. *S. China Sea* 15°47N 111°12E **36** A4
Trivandrum =
Thiruvananthapuram
India 8°41N 77°0E **45** K3
Trnava *Slovak Rep.* 48°23N 17°35E **17** D9
Trochu *Canada* 51°50N 113°13W **70** C6
Trodely I. *Canada* 52°15N 79°26W **72** B4
Troglav *Croatia* 43°56N 16°36E **22** C7
Troilus, L. *Canada* 50°50N 74°35W **72** B5
Trois-Pistoles *Canada* 48°5N 69°10W **73** C6
Trois-Rivières *Canada* 46°25N 72°34W **72** C5
Trois-Rivières *Guadeloupe* 15°57N 61°40W **88** b
Troitsk *Russia* 54°10N 61°35E **26** D7
Troitsko Pechorsk
Russia 62°40N 56°10E **18** B10
Troll *Antarctica* 72°0S 2°30E **5** D3
Trölladyngja *Iceland* 64°54N 17°16W **8** D5
Trollhättan *Sweden* 58°17N 12°20E **9** G15
Trollheimen *Norway* 62°46N 9°1E **8** E13
Trombetas → *Brazil* 1°55S 55°35W **93** D7
Tromsø *Norway* 69°40N 18°56E **8** B18
Tron *Thailand* 17°28N 100°7E **38** D3
Trøndelag *Norway* 64°17N 11°50E **8** D14
Trondheim *Norway* 63°36N 10°25E **8** E14
Trondheimsfjorden
Norway 63°35N 10°30E **8** E14
Troon U.K. 55°33N 4°39W **11** F4
Tropic U.S.A. 37°37N 112°5W **77** H7
Trostan U.K. 55°3N 6°10W **10** A5
Trou Gras Pt. St. Lucia 13°51N 60°53W **89** f
Trout → *Canada* 61°19N 119°51W **70** A5
Trout L. N.W.T., Canada 60°40N 121°14W **70** A4
Trout L. Ont., Canada 51°20N 93°15W **71** C10
Trout Lake *Canada* 56°30N 114°32W **70** B6
Trout Lake U.S.A. 46°0N 121°32W **78** E5
Trout River *Canada* 49°29N 58°8W **73** C8
Trout Run U.S.A. 41°23N 77°3W **82** E7
Trouville-sur-Mer *France* 49°21N 0°5E **20** B4
Trowbridge U.K. 51°18N 2°12W **13** F5
Troy *Turkey* 39°57N 26°12E **23** E12
Troy Ala., U.S.A. 31°48N 85°58W **85** F12
Troy Kans., U.S.A. 39°47N 95°5W **80** F6
Troy Mo., U.S.A. 38°59N 90°59W **80** F8
Troy Mont., U.S.A. 48°28N 115°53W **76** B6
Troy N.Y., U.S.A. 42°44N 73°41W **83** D11
Troy Ohio, U.S.A. 40°2N 84°12W **81** E11
Troy Pa., U.S.A. 41°47N 76°47W **83** E8
Troyes *France* 48°19N 4°3E **20** B6
Truchas Pk. U.S.A. 35°58N 105°39W **77** J11
Trucial States = United Arab
Emirates ■ *Asia* 23°50N 54°0E **47** F7
Truckee U.S.A. 39°20N 120°11W **78** F6
Trudovoye *Russia* 43°17N 132°5E **28** C6
Trujillo *Honduras* 16°0N 86°0W **88** C2
Trujillo *Peru* 8°6S 79°0W **92** E3
Trujillo *Spain* 39°28N 5°55W **21** C3
Trujillo U.S.A. 35°32N 104°42W **77** J11
Trujillo *Venezuela* 9°22N 70°38W **92** B4
Truk *Micronesia* 7°25N 151°46E **64** G7
Trumann U.S.A. 35°41N 90°31W **85** D9
Trumansburg U.S.A. 42°33N 76°40W **83** D8
Trumbull, Mt. U.S.A. 36°25N 113°19W **77** H7
Trung Lon, Hon *Vietnam* 8°36N 106°8E **39** H6
Trung Phan *Vietnam* 17°0N 109°0E **38** D6
Truong Sa, Dao = Spratly I.
S. China Sea 8°38N 111°55E **36** C4
Truro *Canada* 45°21N 63°14W **73** C7
Truro U.K. 50°16N 5°4W **13** G2
Truskavets *Ukraine* 49°17N 23°30E **17** D12
Trutch *Canada* 57°44N 122°57W **70** B4
Truth or Consequences
U.S.A. 33°8N 107°15W **77** K10
Trutnov *Czech Rep.* 50°37N 15°54E **16** C8
Tryonville U.S.A. 41°42N 79°48W **82** E5
Tsandi *Namibia* 17°42S 14°50E **56** A1
Tsaratanana *Madag.* 16°47S 47°39E **55** G9
Tsau *Botswana* 20°8S 22°22E **56** C3
Tsavo *Kenya* 2°59S 38°28E **54** E7
Tsentralnyy □ *Russia* 52°0N 40°0E **26** D4
Tses *Namibia* 25°58S 18°8E **56** C2
Tsetserleg *Mongolia* 47°36N 101°32E **30** B9
Tsévié *Togo* 6°25N 1°20E **52** G6
Tshabong *Botswana* 26°2S 22°29E **56** C3
Tshane *Botswana* 24°5S 21°54E **56** C3
Tshela Dem. Rep. of the Congo 4°57S 13°4E **54** E2
Tshesebe *Botswana* 21°51S 27°32E **57** B4

Tshikapa
Dem. Rep. of the Congo 6°28S 20°48E **54** F4
Tshwane = Pretoria
S. Africa 25°44S 28°12E **57** C4
Tshwane *Botswana* 22°24S 22°1E **56** B3
Tsigara *Botswana* 20°22S 25°54E **56** B4
Tsihombe *Madag.* 25°10S 45°41E **55** K9
Tsiigehtchic *Canada* 67°15N 134°0W **68** D5
Ts'il-os △ *Canada* 51°9N 123°59W **70** C4
Tsimlyansk Res. = Tsimlyanskoye
Vdkhr. *Russia* 48°0N 43°0E **19** E7
Tsimlyanskoye Vdkhr.
Russia 48°0N 43°0E **19** E7
Tsinan = Jinan *China* 36°38N 117°1E **32** F9
Tsineng S. Africa 27°5S 23°5E **56** C3
Tsinghai = Qinghai □
China 36°0N 98°0E **30** D8
Tsingtao = Qingdao
China 36°5N 120°20E **33** F11
Tsirigo = Kythira *Greece* 36°8N 23°0E **23** F10
Tsitsikamma △ S. Africa 34°3S 23°40E **56** D3
Tskhinvali *Georgia* 42°14N 44°1E **19** F7
Tsna → *Russia* 54°55N 41°58E **18** D7
Tso Moriri, L. *India* 32°50N 78°20E **43** C8
Tsodilo Hills *Botswana* 18°49S 21°43E **56** A3
Tsogttsetsiy = Baruunsuu
Mongolia 43°43N 105°35E **32** C3
Tsolo S. Africa 31°18S 28°37E **57** D4
Tsomo S. Africa 32°0S 27°42E **57** D4
Tsu *Japan* 34°45N 136°25E **29** G8
Tsu L. *Canada* 60°40N 111°52W **70** A6
Tsuchiura *Japan* 36°5N 140°15E **29** F10
Tsugaru-Hantō *Japan* 41°0N 140°30E **28** D10
Tsugaru-Kaikyō *Japan* 41°35N 141°0E **28** D10
Tsumeb *Namibia* 19°9S 17°44E **56** A2
Tsumis *Namibia* 23°39S 17°29E **56** B2
Tsuruga *Japan* 35°45N 136°2E **29** G8
Tsurugi-San *Japan* 33°51N 134°6E **29** H7
Tsuruoka *Japan* 38°44N 139°50E **28** E9
Tsushima Gifu, Japan 35°10N 136°43E **29** G8
Tsushima Nagasaki,
Japan 34°20N 129°20E **29** G4
Tsuyama *Japan* 35°3N 134°0E **29** G7
Tsyelyakhany *Belarus* 52°30N 25°46E **17** B13
Tuam = Tuam *Ireland* 53°31N 8°51W **10** C3
Tual *Indonesia* 5°38S 132°44E **37** F8
Tualatin U.S.A. 45°23N 122°45W **78** E4
Tuam *Ireland* 53°31N 8°51W **10** C3
Tuamotu, Îs.
French Polynesia 17°0S 144°0W **65** J13
Tuamotu Arch. = Tuamotu, Îs.
French Polynesia 17°0S 144°0W **65** J13
Tuamotu Ridge Pac. Oc. 20°0S 138°0W **65** K14
Tuan Giao *Vietnam* 21°35N 103°25E **38** B4
Tuanfeng *China* 30°38N 114°52E **35** B10
Tuanxi *China* 27°28N 107°8E **34** D6
Tuao Phil. 17°45N 121°22E **37** A6
Tuapse *Russia* 44°5N 39°10E **19** F6
Tuatapere N.Z. 46°8S 167°41E **59** G1
Tuba City U.S.A. 36°8N 111°14W **77** H8
Tuban *Indonesia* 6°54S 112°3E **37** G15
Tubani *Botswana* 24°46S 24°18E **56** B3
Tubarão *Brazil* 28°30S 49°0W **95** B6
Tûbâs West Bank 32°20N 35°22E **48** C4
Tubas → *Namibia* 22°54S 14°35E **56** B2
Tübingen *Germany* 48°31N 9°4E **16** D5
Tubou *Fiji* 18°13S 178°48W **59** a
Tubruq *Libya* 32°7N 23°55E **53** B10
Tubuaï, Îs.
French Polynesia 25°0S 150°0W **65** K13
Tuc Trung *Vietnam* 11°1N 107°12E **39** G6
Tucacas *Venezuela* 10°48N 68°19W **92** A5
T'uch'ang *Taiwan* 24°35N 121°29E **35** E13
Tuchitua *Canada* 60°55N 129°13W **70** A3
Tuchodi → *Canada* 58°17N 123°42W **70** B4
Tuckanarra *Australia* 27°7S 118°5E **61** E2
Tucson U.S.A. 32°13N 110°58W **77** K8
Tucumán □ *Argentina* 26°48S 66°2W **94** B2
Tucumcari U.S.A. 35°10N 103°44W **77** J12
Tucupita *Venezuela* 9°2N 62°3W **92** B6
Tucuruí *Brazil* 3°42S 49°44W **93** D9
Tucuruí, Represa de *Brazil* 4°0S 49°30W **93** D9
Tudela *Spain* 42°4N 1°39W **21** A5
Tudmur *Syria* 34°36N 38°15E **46** C3
Tudor, L. *Canada* 55°50N 65°25W **73** A6
Tug Hill Plateau U.S.A. 43°45N 75°50W **83** C9
Tugela → S. Africa 29°14S 31°30E **57** C5
Tugela Falls S. Africa 28°42S 29°51E **57** C4
Tuguegarao Phil. 17°35N 121°42E **37** A6
Tugur *Russia* 53°44N 136°45E **27** D14
Tui *Spain* 42°3N 8°39W **21** A1
Tukangbesi, Kepulauan
Indonesia 6°0S 124°0E **37** F6
Tukarak I. *Canada* 56°15N 78°45W **72** A4
Tukayyid *Iraq* 29°47N 45°36E **46** D5
Tuktoyaktuk *Canada* 69°27N 133°2W **68** D5
Tuktut Nogait △ *Canada* 69°15N 122°0W **68** D7
Tukums *Latvia* 56°58N 23°10E **9** H20
Tukuyu *Tanzania* 9°17S 33°35E **54** F6
Tula Hidalgo, Mexico 20°3N 99°21W **87** C5
Tula Tamaulipas, Mexico 23°0N 99°41W **87** C5
Tula *Russia* 54°13N 37°38E **18** D6
Tulach Mhór = Tullamore
Ireland 53°16N 7°31W **10** C4
Tulancingo *Mexico* 20°5N 98°22W **87** C5
Tulare U.S.A. 36°13N 119°21W **78** J7
Tulare Lake Bed U.S.A. 36°0N 119°48W **78** K7
Tularosa U.S.A. 33°5N 106°1W **77** K10
Tulbagh S. Africa 33°16S 19°6E **56** D2
Tulcán *Ecuador* 0°48N 77°43W **92** C3
Tulcea *Romania* 45°13N 28°46E **17** F15
Tulchyn *Ukraine* 48°41N 28°49E **17** D15
Tüleh *Iran* 34°35N 51°9E **47** C6
Tulemalu L. *Canada* 62°58N 99°25W **71** A9
Tulia U.S.A. 34°32N 101°46W **84** D4
Tulita *Canada* 64°57N 125°30W **68** E6
Ţūlkarm West Bank 32°19N 35°2E **48** C4
Tulla *Ireland* 52°53N 8°46W **10** D3
Tullahoma U.S.A. 35°22N 86°13W **85** D11
Tullamore *Australia* 32°39S 147°36E **63** E4
Türkistan *Kazakhstan* 43°17N 68°16E **26** E7

Tullamore *Ireland* 53°16N 7°31W **10** C4
Tullow *Ireland* 52°49N 6°45W **10** D5
Tully *Australia* 17°56S 145°55E **62** B4
Tully U.S.A. 42°48N 76°7W **83** D8
Tulsa U.S.A. 36°10N 95°55W **84** C7
Tulsequah *Canada* 58°39N 133°35W **70** B2
Tuluá *Colombia* 4°6N 76°11W **92** C3
Tulum *Mexico* 20°13N 87°28W **87** C7
Tulun *Russia* 54°32N 100°35E **27** D11
Tulungagung *Indonesia* 8°5S 111°54E **37** H14
Tuma → Nic. 13°6N 84°35E **88** D3
Tumacacori △ U.S.A. 31°35N 111°6W **77** L8
Tumaco *Colombia* 1°50N 78°45W **92** C3
Tumakuru *India* 13°18N 77°6E **45** H3
Tumatumari *Guyana* 5°20N 58°55W **92** B7
Tumba *Sweden* 59°12N 17°48E **9** G17
Tumba, L.
Dem. Rep. of the Congo 0°50S 18°0E **54** E3
Tumbarumba *Australia* 35°44S 148°0E **63** F4
Tumbaya *Argentina* 23°50S 65°26W **94** A2
Tumbes *Peru* 3°37S 80°27W **92** D2
Tumbler Ridge *Canada* 55°8N 121°0W **70** B4
Tumby Bay *Australia* 34°21S 136°8E **63** E2
Tumd Youqi *China* 40°30N 110°30E **32** D6
Tumen *China* 43°0N 129°50E **33** C15
Tumen Jiang → China 42°20N 130°35E **33** C16
Tumeremo *Venezuela* 7°18N 61°30W **92** B6
Tumkur = Tumakuru
India 13°18N 77°6E **45** H3
Tump *Pakistan* 26°7N 62°16E **40** F3
Tumpat *Malaysia* 6°11N 102°10E **39** J4
Tumsar *India* 21°26N 79°45E **44** D4
Tumu *Ghana* 10°56N 1°56W **52** F5
Tumucumaque, Serra
Brazil 2°0N 55°0W **93** C8
Tumut *Australia* 35°16S 148°13E **63** F4
Tumwater U.S.A. 47°1N 122°54W **78** C4
Tuna *India* 22°59N 70°5E **42** H4
Tunapuna Trin. & Tob. 10°38N 61°24W **93** K15
Tunas de Zaza *Cuba* 21°39N 79°34W **88** B4
Tunbridge Wells = Royal
Tunbridge Wells U.K. 51°7N 0°16E **13** F8
Tunceli *Turkey* 39°6N 39°31E **46** B3
Tunchang *China* 19°21N 110°5E **38** C8
Tuncurry *Australia* 32°17S 152°29E **63** E5
Tundla *India* 27°12N 78°17E **42** F8
Tundzha → *Bulgaria* 41°40N 26°35E **23** C11
Tunga → *India* 15°0N 75°50E **45** G2
Tungabhadra → *India* 15°57N 78°15E **45** G4
Tungabhadra Dam *India* 15°0N 76°0E **45** G2
Tungla *Nic.* 13°24N 84°21W **88** D3
Tungsha Tao = Dongsha Dao
S. China Sea 20°45N 116°43E **35** G11
Tungshih *Taiwan* 24°12N 120°43E **35** E13
Tungsten *Canada* 61°57N 128°16W **70** A3
Tunguska, Nizhnyaya →
Russia 65°48N 88°4E **27** C9
Tunguska, Podkamennaya →
Russia 61°50N 90°13E **27** C10
Tuni *India* 17°22N 82°36E **44** F6
Tunica U.S.A. 34°41N 90°23W **85** D9
Tunis *Tunisia* 36°50N 10°11E **53** A8
Tunisia ■ *Africa* 33°30N 9°10E **53** A7
Tunja *Colombia* 5°33N 73°25W **92** B4
Tunkhannock U.S.A. 41°32N 75°57W **83** E9
Tunkinsky △ *Russia* 51°30N 102°0E **27** D11
Tunliu *China* 36°13N 112°52E **32** F7
Tunnel Creek △
Australia 17°41S 125°18E **60** C4
Tunnsjøen *Norway* 64°45N 13°25E **8** D15
Tunungayualok I. Canada 56°0N 61°0W **73** A7
Tunuyán *Argentina* 33°35S 69°0W **94** C2
Tunuyán → *Argentina* 33°33S 67°30W **94** C2
Tunxi = Huangshan
China 29°42N 118°25E **35** C12
Tuo Jiang → China 28°50N 105°35E **34** C5
Tuolumne U.S.A. 37°58N 120°15W **78** H6
Tuolumne → U.S.A. 37°36N 121°13W **78** H5
Tüp Äghäj *Iran* 36°3N 47°50E **46** B5
Tupã *Brazil* 21°57S 50°28W **95** A5
Tupelo U.S.A. 34°16N 88°43W **85** D10
Tupinambarana, I. *Brazil* 3°0S 58°0W **92** D7
Tupiza *Bolivia* 21°30S 65°40W **94** A2
Tupman U.S.A. 35°18N 119°21W **79** K7
Tupper *Canada* 55°32N 120°1W **70** B4
Tupper L. U.S.A. 44°10N 74°32W **83** B10
Tupper Lake U.S.A. 44°14N 74°28W **83** B10
Tupungato, Cerro
S. Amer. 33°15S 69°50W **94** C2
Tuquan *China* 45°18N 121°38E **33** B11
Túquerres *Colombia* 1°5N 77°37W **92** C3
Tura *Russia* 64°20N 100°17E **27** C11
Turabah Si. Arabia 28°20N 43°15E **46** D4
Türän *Iran* 35°39N 56°42E **47** C8
Turan *Russia* 51°55N 94°0E **27** D10
Türän □ *Iran* 35°45N 56°40E **47** C8
Turayf Si. Arabia 31°41N 38°39E **46** D3
Turda *Romania* 46°34N 23°47E **17** E12
Turek *Poland* 52°3N 18°30E **17** B10
Turen *Venezuela* 9°17N 69°6W **92** B5
Turfan = Turpan *China* 43°58N 89°10E **30** C6
Turfan Basin = Turpan Pendi
China 42°40N 89°25E **30** C6
Turfan Depression = Turpan Pendi
China 42°40N 89°25E **30** C6
Turgeon → *Canada* 50°0N 78°56W **72** C4
Türgovishte *Bulgaria* 43°17N 26°38E **23** C12
Turgutlu *Turkey* 38°30N 27°43E **23** E12
Turgwe → *Zimbabwe* 21°31S 32°15E **57** B5
Turia → *Spain* 39°27N 0°19W **21** C5
Turiaçu *Brazil* 1°40S 45°19W **93** D9
Turiaçu → *Brazil* 1°36S 45°19W **93** D9
Turin = Torino *Italy* 45°3N 7°40E **20** D7
Turkana, L. *Africa* 3°30N 36°5E **54** D7
Turkestan = Türkistan
Kazakhstan 43°17N 68°16E **26** E7
Turkey ■ *Eurasia* 39°0N 36°0E **19** G6
Turkey Creek = Warmun
Australia 17°2S 128°12E **60** C4
Türkistan *Kazakhstan* 43°17N 68°16E **26** E7

Türkmenabat
Turkmenistan 39°6N 63°34E **47** B9
Türkmenbashi
Turkmenistan 40°5N 53°5E **47** A7
Turkmenistan ■ *Asia* 39°0N 59°0E **26** F6
Turks & Caicos Is. ☑
W. Indies 21°20N 71°20W **89** B5
Turks Island Passage
Turks & Caicos 21°25N 71°19W **89** B5
Turku *Finland* 60°30N 22°19E **9** F20
Turkwel → *Kenya* 3°6N 36°6E **54** D7
Turlock U.S.A. 37°30N 120°51W **78** H6
Turnagain *Australia* 9°34S 142°17E **62** a
Turnagain → *Canada* 59°12N 127°35W **70** B3
Turnagain, C. N.Z. 40°28S 176°38E **59** D6
Turneffe Is. *Belize* 17°20N 87°50W **87** D7
Turner U.S.A. 48°51N 108°24W **76** B9
Turner Pt. *Australia* 11°47S 133°32E **62** A1
Turner Valley *Canada* 50°40N 114°17W **70** C6
Turners Falls U.S.A. 42°36N 72°33E **83** D12
Turnhout *Belgium* 51°19N 4°57E **15** C4
Turnor L. *Canada* 56°35N 108°35W **71** B7
Tŭrnovo = Veliko Tŭrnovo
Bulgaria 43°5N 25°41E **23** C11
Turnu Măgurele
Romania 43°46N 24°56E **17** G13
Turnu Roşu, P. Romania 45°33N 24°17E **17** F13
Turpan *China* 43°58N 89°10E **30** C6
Turpan Pendi *China* 42°40N 89°25E **30** C6
Turriff U.K. 57°32N 2°27W **11** D6
Tursāq *Iraq* 33°27N 45°47E **46** C5
Turtle Head I. *Australia* 10°56S 142°37E **62** A3
Turtle L. *Canada* 53°36N 108°38W **71** C7
Turtle Lake U.S.A. 47°31N 100°53W **80** B3
Turtleford *Canada* 53°23N 108°57W **71** C7
Turuépano ○ *Venezuela* 10°34N 62°43W **89** D7
Turukhansk *Russia* 65°21N 88°5E **27** C9
Tuscaloosa U.S.A. 33°12N 87°34W **85** E11
Tuscany = Toscana □
Italy 43°25N 11°0E **22** C4
Tuscarawas → U.S.A. 40°24N 81°25W **82** F3
Tuscarora Mt. U.S.A. 40°55N 77°55W **82** F7
Tuscola Ill., U.S.A. 39°48N 88°17W **80** F9
Tuscola Tex., U.S.A. 32°12N 99°48W **84** E5
Tuscumbia U.S.A. 34°44N 87°42W **85** D11
Tuskegee U.S.A. 32°25N 85°42W **85** E12
Tuticorin *India* 8°50N 78°12E **45** K4
Tutóia *Brazil* 2°45S 42°20W **93** D10
Tutong *Brunei* 4°47N 114°40E **36** D4
Tutrakan *Bulgaria* 44°2N 26°40E **23** B12
Tuttle Creek L. U.S.A. 39°15N 96°36W **80** F5
Tuttlingen *Germany* 47°58N 8°48E **16** E5
Tutuala E. Timor 8°25S 127°15E **37** F7
Tutuila Amer. Samoa 14°19S 170°50W **59** b
Tutume *Botswana* 20°30S 27°5E **55** J5
Tuul Gol → *Mongolia* 48°30N 104°25E **30** B9
Tuva □ *Russia* 51°30N 95°0E **27** D10
Tuvalu ■ *Pac. Oc.* 8°0S 178°0E **58** B10
Tuvuca *Fiji* 17°40S 178°48W **59** a
Tuxpan *Mexico* 20°57N 97°24W **87** C5
Tuxtla Gutiérrez *Mexico* 16°45N 93°7W **87** D6
Tuy = Tui *Spain* 42°3N 8°39W **21** A1
Tuy Duc *Vietnam* 12°15N 107°27E **39** G6
Tuy Phong *Vietnam* 11°14N 108°43E **39** G7
Tuya L. *Canada* 59°7N 130°35W **70** B2
Tuyen Hoa *Vietnam* 17°50N 106°10E **38** D6
Tuyen Quang *Vietnam* 21°50N 105°10E **34** G5
Tüysarkän *Iran* 34°33N 48°27E **47** C6
Tuz Gölü *Turkey* 38°42N 33°18E **19** G5
Ṭūz Khurmātū *Iraq* 34°56N 44°38E **46** C5
Tuzigoot △ U.S.A. 34°46N 112°2W **77** J7
Tuzla *Bos.-H.* 44°34N 18°41E **23** B8
Tver *Russia* 56°55N 35°59E **18** C6
Twain U.S.A. 40°1N 121°3W **78** E5
Twain Harte U.S.A. 38°2N 120°14W **78** G6
Twee River *Namibia* 25°27S 19°27E **56** C2
Tweed *Canada* 44°29N 77°19W **82** B7
Tweed → U.K. 55°45N 2°0W **11** F6
Tweed Heads *Australia* 28°10S 153°31E **63** D5
Tweedsmuir △ *Canada* 53°0N 126°20W **70** C3
Twentynine Palms
U.S.A. 34°8N 116°3W **79** L10
Twillingate *Canada* 49°42N 54°45W **73** C9
Twin Bridges U.S.A. 45°33N 112°20W **76** D7
Twin Falls *Canada* 53°30N 64°32W **73** B7
Twin Falls U.S.A. 42°34N 114°28W **76** E6
Twin Valley U.S.A. 47°16N 96°16W **80** B5
Twinsburg U.S.A. 41°19N 81°26W **82** E3
Twitchell Res. U.S.A. 34°59N 120°19W **79** L6
Two Harbors U.S.A. 47°2N 91°40W **80** B8
Two Hills *Canada* 53°43N 111°52W **70** C6
Two Rivers U.S.A. 44°9N 87°34W **80** C10
Two Rocks *Australia* 31°30S 115°35E **61** F2
Twofold B. *Australia* 37°8S 149°59E **63** F4
Twyfelfontein *Namibia* 20°34S 14°22E **56** B1
Tyachiv *Ukraine* 48°1N 23°35E **17** D12
Tychy *Poland* 50°9N 18°59E **17** C10
Tyler Minn., U.S.A. 44°17N 96°8W **80** C5
Tyler Tex., U.S.A. 32°21N 95°18W **84** E7
Tynda *Russia* 55°10N 124°43E **27** D13
Tyndall U.S.A. 43°0N 97°50W **80** D5
Tyne → U.K. 54°59N 1°32W **12** C6
Tyne & Wear □ U.K. 55°6N 1°17W **12** B6
Tynemouth U.K. 55°1N 1°26W **12** B6
Tyre = Şūr *Lebanon* 33°19N 35°16E **48** B4
Tyrifjorden *Norway* 60°2N 10°8E **9** F14
Tyrol = Tirol □ *Austria* 47°3N 10°43E **16** E6
Tyrone U.S.A. 40°40N 78°14W **82** F6
Tyrone □ U.K. 54°38N 7°11W **10** B4
Tyrrell → *Australia* 35°26S 142°51E **63** F3
Tyrrell, L. *Australia* 35°20S 142°50E **63** F3
Tyrrell L. *Canada* 63°7N 105°27W **71** A7
Tyrrhenian Sea *Medit. S.* 40°0N 12°30E **22** E5
Tysfjorden *Norway* 68°7N 16°25E **8** B17
Tyulgan *Russia* 52°22N 56°12E **18** D10
Tyumen *Russia* 57°11N 65°29E **26** D7
Tywi → U.K. 51°48N 4°21W **13** F3
Tywyn U.K. 52°35N 4°5W **13** E3
Tzaneen S. Africa 23°47S 30°9E **57** B5
Tzukong = Zigong
China 29°15N 104°48E **34** C5

U

U.S.A. = United States of America ■ *N. Amer.* 37°0N 96°0W **75** H20
U.S. Virgin Is. ◇ *W. Indies* 18°20N 65°0W **89** e
Uaimh, An = Navan *Ireland* 53°39N 6°41W **10** C5
Uanle Uen = Wanleweyne *Somalia* 2°37N 44°54E **49** G3
Uatumã → *Brazil* 2°26S 57°37W **92** D7
Uaupés *Brazil* 0°8S 67°5W **92** D5
Uaupés → *Brazil* 0°2N 67°16W **92** C5
Uaxactún *Guatemala* 17°25N 89°29W **88** C2
Ubá *Brazil* 21°8S 43°0W **95** A7
Ubaitaba *Brazil* 14°18S 39°20W **93** F11
Ubangi = Oubangi → *Dem. Rep. of the Congo* 0°30S 17°50E **54** E3
Ubauro *Pakistan* 28°15N 69°45E **42** E3
Ubayyiḍ, W. al → *Iraq* 32°34N 43°48E **46** C4
Ube *Japan* 33°56N 131°15E **29** H5
Úbeda *Spain* 38°3N 3°23W **21** C4
Uberaba *Brazil* 19°50S 47°55W **93** G9
Uberlândia *Brazil* 19°0S 48°20W **93** G9
Ubly *U.S.A.* 43°42N 82°55W **82** C2
Ubolratna Res. *Thailand* 16°45N 102°30E **38** D4
Ubombo *S. Africa* 27°31S 32°4E **57** C5
Ubon Ratchathani *Thailand* 15°15N 104°50E **38** E5
Ubort → *Belarus* 52°6N 28°30E **17** B15
Ubud *Indonesia* 8°30S 115°16E **37** J18
Ubundu *Dem. Rep. of the Congo* 0°22S 25°30E **54** E5
Ucayali → *Peru* 4°30S 73°30W **92** D4
Uchab *Namibia* 19°47S 17°42E **56** A2
Uchiura-Wan *Japan* 42°25N 140°40E **28** C10
Uchquduq *Uzbekistan* 41°50N 62°50E **26** E7
Uchur → *Russia* 58°48N 130°35E **27** D14
Ucluelet *Canada* 48°57N 125°32W **70** D3
Uda → *Russia* 54°42N 135°14E **27** D14
Uda Walawe △ *Sri Lanka* 6°20N 81°0E **45** L5
Udachnyy *Russia* 66°25N 112°24E **27** C12
Udagamandalam *India* 11°30N 76°44E **45** J3
Udainagar *India* 22°33N 76°13E **42** H7
Udaipur *India* 24°36N 73°44E **42** G5
Udaipur Garhi *Nepal* 27°0N 86°35E **43** F12
Udala *India* 21°35N 86°34E **43** J12
Udayagiri *Andhra Pradesh, India* 14°52N 79°19E **45** G4
Udayagiri *Odisha, India* 20°8N 84°23E **44** D7
Uddevalla *Sweden* 58°21N 11°55E **9** G14
Uddjaure *Sweden* 65°56N 17°49E **8** D17
Udegeyskaya Legenda △ *Russia* 45°45N 135°30E **28** B7
Uden *Neths.* 51°40N 5°37E **15** C5
Udgir *India* 18°25N 77°5E **44** E3
Udhampur *India* 33°0N 75°5E **43** C6
Údine *Italy* 46°3N 13°14E **22** A5
Udintsev Fracture Zone *S. Ocean* 57°0S 145°0W **5** B13
Udmurtia □ *Russia* 57°30N 52°30E **18** C9
Udon Thani *Thailand* 17°29N 102°46E **38** D4
Udong *Cambodia* 11°48N 104°45E **39** G5
Udskaya Guba *Russia* 54°50N 135°45E **27** D14
Udu Pt. *Fiji* 16°9S 179°57W **59** a
Udumalaippettai *India* 10°35N 77°15E **45** J3
Udupi *India* 13°25N 74°42E **45** H2
Udva *India* 20°5N 73°0E **44** D1
Udzungwa Range *Tanzania* 9°30S 35°10E **54** F7
Ueda *Japan* 36°24N 138°16E **29** F9
Uedineniya, Os. *Russia* 78°0N 85°0E **4** B12
Uele → *Dem. Rep. of the Congo* 3°45N 24°45E **54** D4
Uelen *Russia* 66°10N 170°0W **27** C19
Uelzen *Germany* 52°57N 10°32E **16** B6
Ufa *Russia* 54°45N 55°55E **18** D10
Ufa → *Russia* 54°40N 56°0E **18** D10
Ugab → *Namibia* 20°55S 13°30E **56** B1
Ugalla → *Tanzania* 5°8S 30°42E **54** F6
Uganda ■ *Africa* 2°0N 32°0E **54** D6
Ugie *S. Africa* 31°10S 28°13E **57** D4
Uglegorsk *Russia* 49°5N 142°2E **27** E15
Ugljan *Croatia* 44°12N 15°10E **16** F8
Ugolnye Kopi *Russia* 64°44N 177°42E **27** C18
Uhlenhorst *Namibia* 23°45S 17°55E **56** B2
Uhrichsville *U.S.A.* 40°24N 81°21W **82** F3
Uibhist a Deas = South Uist *U.K.* 57°20N 7°15W **11** D1
Uibhist a Tuath = North Uist *U.K.* 57°40N 7°15W **11** D1
Uig *U.K.* 57°35N 6°21W **11** D2
Uíge *Angola* 7°30S 14°40E **54** F2
Uiha *Tonga* 19°54S 174°25W **59** c
Uijeongbu *S. Korea* 37°44N 127°2E **33** F14
Ŭiju *N. Korea* 40°15N 124°35E **33** D13
Uinta Mts. *U.S.A.* 40°45N 110°30W **76** F8
Uis *Namibia* 21°8S 14°49E **56** B1
Uiseong *S. Korea* 36°21N 128°45E **33** F15
Uitenhage *S. Africa* 33°40S 25°28E **56** D4
Uithuizen *Neths.* 53°24N 6°41E **15** A6
Ujh → *India* 32°10N 75°18E **42** C6
Ujhani *India* 28°0N 79°6E **43** F8
Uji-guntō *Japan* 31°15N 129°25E **29** J4
Ujjain *India* 23°9N 75°43E **42** H6
Ujung Kulon △ *Indonesia* 6°46S 105°19E **37** G11
Ujung Pandang = Makassar *Indonesia* 5°10S 119°20E **37** F5
Uka *Russia* 57°50N 162°0E **27** D17
Ukai Sagar *India* 21°20N 73°43E **44** D1
Uke-Shima *Japan* 28°2N 129°14E **29** K4
uKhahlamba Drakensberg ⌓ *S. Africa* 29°27S 29°30E **57** C4
Ukhrul *India* 25°10N 94°25E **41** G19
Ukhta *Russia* 63°34N 53°41E **18** B9
Ukiah *U.S.A.* 39°9N 123°13W **78** F3
Ukkusiksalik △ *Canada* 65°20N 89°30W **68** D14
Ukmergė *Lithuania* 55°15N 24°45E **9** J21
Ukraine ■ *Europe* 49°0N 32°0E **19** E5
Ukwi *Botswana* 23°29S 20°30E **56** B3
Ulaan Nuur *Mongolia* 44°30N 103°40E **32** B2
Ulaan-Uul *Mongolia* 46°4N 100°49E **30** B9
Ulaanbaatar *Mongolia* 47°55N 106°53E **30** B10
Ulaangom *Mongolia* 50°5N 92°10E **30** A7
Ulaanjirem *Mongolia* 45°5N 105°30E **32** B3
Ulak I. *U.S.A.* 51°22N 178°57W **74** E4
Ulan Bator = Ulaanbaatar *Mongolia* 47°55N 106°53E **30** B10
Ulan Ude *Russia* 51°45N 107°40E **31** A10
Ulanhad = Chifeng *China* 42°18N 118°58E **33** C10
Ulanhot = Horqin Youyi Qianqi *China* 46°5N 122°3E **33** A12
Ulansuhai Nur *China* 40°53N 108°51E **32** D5
Ulcinj *Montenegro* 41°58N 19°10E **23** D8
Ulco *S. Africa* 28°21S 24°15E **56** C3
Ule älv = Oulujoki → *Finland* 65°1N 25°30E **8** D21
Ule träsk = Oulujärvi *Finland* 64°25N 27°15E **8** D22
Uleåborg = Oulu *Finland* 65°1N 25°29E **8** D21
Ulefoss *Norway* 59°17N 9°16E **9** G13
Ulhasnagar *India* 19°15N 73°10E **44** E1
Uliastay *Mongolia* 47°56N 97°28E **30** B8
Uljin *S. Korea* 36°59N 129°24E **33** F15
Ulladulla *Australia* 35°21S 150°29E **63** F5
Ullal *India* 12°48N 74°51E **45** H2
Ullapool *U.K.* 57°54N 5°9W **11** D3
Ulleungdo *S. Korea* 37°30N 130°30E **29** F5
Ullswater *Canada* 45°12N 79°29W **82** A5
Ullswater *U.K.* 54°34N 2°52W **12** C5
Ulm *Germany* 48°23N 9°58E **16** D5
Ulmarra *Australia* 29°37S 153°4E **63** D5
Ulricehamn *Sweden* 57°46N 13°26E **9** H15
Ulsan *S. Korea* 35°20N 129°15E **33** G15
Ulsta *U.K.* 60°30N 1°9W **11** A7
Ulster □ *U.K.* 54°35N 6°30W **10** B5
Ulubat Gölü *Turkey* 40°9N 28°35E **23** D13
Uludağ *Turkey* 40°4N 29°13E **23** D13
Ulukhaktok *Canada* 70°44N 117°44W **68** C8
Ulundi *S. Africa* 28°20S 31°25E **57** C5
Ulungur He → *China* 47°1N 87°24E **30** B6
Ulungur Hu *China* 47°20N 87°10E **30** B6
Uluru *Australia* 25°23S 131°5E **61** E5
Uluru-Kata Tjuta △ *Australia* 25°19S 131°1E **61** E5
Uluwatu *Indonesia* 8°50S 115°5E **37** K18
Ulva *U.K.* 56°29N 6°13W **11** E2
Ulverston *U.K.* 54°13N 3°5W **12** C4
Ulverstone *Australia* 41°11S 146°11E **63** G4
Ulya *Russia* 59°10N 142°0E **27** D15
Ulyanovsk *Russia* 54°20N 48°25E **18** D8
Ulyasutay = Uliastay *Mongolia* 47°56N 97°28E **30** B8
Ulysses *Kans., U.S.A.* 37°35N 101°22W **80** G3
Ulysses *Pa., U.S.A.* 41°54N 77°46W **82** E7
Ulysses, Mt. *Canada* 57°20N 124°5W **70** B4
Ulytau *Kazakhstan* 48°39N 67°1E **26** E7
Umala *Bolivia* 17°25S 68°5W **92** G5
'Umān = Oman ■ *Asia* 23°0N 58°0E **49** C6
Uman *Ukraine* 48°40N 30°12E **17** D16
Umaria *India* 23°35N 80°50E **43** H9
Umarkhed *India* 19°37N 77°46E **44** E3
Umarkot *Pakistan* 25°15N 69°40E **42** G3
Umarpada *India* 21°27N 73°30E **42** J5
Umatilla *U.S.A.* 45°55N 119°21W **76** D4
Umba *Russia* 66°42N 34°11E **18** A5
Umbagog L. *U.S.A.* 44°46N 71°3W **83** B13
Umbakumba *Australia* 13°47S 136°50E **62** A2
Umbrella Mts. *N.Z.* 45°35S 169°5E **59** F2
Umeå *Sweden* 63°45N 20°20E **8** E19
Umeälven → *Sweden* 63°45N 20°20E **8** E19
Umera *Indonesia* 0°12S 129°37E **37** E7
Umgwenya → *Mozam.* 25°14S 32°18E **57** C5
Umiujaq *Canada* 56°33N 76°33W **72** A4
Umkomaas *S. Africa* 30°13S 30°48E **57** D5
Umlazi *S. Africa* 29°59S 30°54E **55** L6
Umm ad Daraj, J. *Jordan* 32°18N 35°48E **48** C4
Umm al Qaywayn *U.A.E.* 25°30N 55°35E **47** E7
Umm al Qittayn *Jordan* 32°18N 36°40E **48** C5
Umm al Rasas *Jordan* 31°30N 35°55E **48** D4
Umm Bāb *Qatar* 25°12N 50°48E **47** E6
Umm Durman = Omdurmân *Sudan* 15°40N 32°28E **53** E12
Umm el Fahm *Israel* 32°31N 35°9E **48** C4
Umm el Ketef, Khalîg *Egypt* 23°40N 35°35E **46** F2
Umm Keddada *Sudan* 13°33N 26°35E **53** F11
Umm Lajj *Si. Arabia* 25°0N 37°23E **46** E3
Umm Qasr *Iraq* 30°1N 47°58E **46** D5
Umm Ruwaba *Sudan* 12°50N 31°20E **53** F12
Umm Sa'id *Qatar* 25°0N 51°33E **47** E6
Umm Tais △ *Qatar* 26°7N 51°15E **47** E6
Umnak I. *U.S.A.* 53°15N 168°20W **74** E6
Umniati → *Zimbabwe* 16°49S 28°45E **55** H5
Umpqua → *U.S.A.* 43°40N 124°12W **76** E1
Umred *India* 20°51N 79°18E **44** D4
Umreth *India* 22°41N 73°4E **42** H5
Umri *India* 19°2N 77°39E **44** E3
Umtata = Mthatha *S. Africa* 31°36S 28°49E **57** D4
Umuarama *Brazil* 23°45S 53°20W **95** A5
Umvukwe Ra. *Zimbabwe* 16°45S 30°45E **55** H6
Umzimvubu *S. Africa* 31°38S 29°33E **57** D4
Umzinto = eMuziwezinto *S. Africa* 30°15S 30°45E **57** D5
Una *India* 20°46N 71°8E **42** J4
Una → *Bos.-H.* 45°0N 16°20E **16** F9
Unadilla *U.S.A.* 42°20N 75°19W **83** D9
Unalakleet *U.S.A.* 63°52N 160°47W **74** C7
Unalaska *U.S.A.* 53°53N 166°32W **74** E6
Unalaska I. *U.S.A.* 53°35N 166°50W **74** E6
'Unayzah *Si. Arabia* 26°6N 43°58E **46** E4
'Unayzah, J. *Asia* 32°12N 39°18E **46** C3
Uncía *Bolivia* 18°25S 66°40W **92** G5
Uncompahgre Peak *U.S.A.* 38°4N 107°28W **76** G10
Uncompahgre Plateau *U.S.A.* 38°20N 108°15W **76** G9
Undara Volcanic △ *Australia* 18°14S 144°41E **62** B3
Underbool *Australia* 35°10S 141°51E **63** F3
Underwood *Canada* 44°18N 81°29W **82** B3
Ungarie *Australia* 33°38S 146°56E **63** E4
Ungarra *Australia* 34°12S 136°2E **63** E2
Ungava, Pén. d' *Canada* 60°0N 74°0W **69** F17
Ungava B. *Canada* 59°30N 67°30W **69** F18
Ungeny = Ungheni *Moldova* 47°11N 27°51E **17** E14
Unggi *N. Korea* 42°16N 130°28E **33** C16
Ungheni *Moldova* 47°11N 27°51E **17** E14
Unguja = Zanzibar *Tanzania* 6°12S 39°12E **54** F7
União da Vitória *Brazil* 26°13S 51°5W **95** B5
Unimak I. *U.S.A.* 54°45N 164°0W **74** E7
Unimak Pass. *U.S.A.* 54°15N 164°30W **74** E7
Union *Miss., U.S.A.* 32°34N 89°7W **85** E10
Union *Mo., U.S.A.* 38°27N 91°0W **80** F8
Union *S.C., U.S.A.* 34°43N 81°37W **85** D14
Union City *Calif., U.S.A.* 37°36N 122°1W **78** H4
Union City *Pa., U.S.A.* 41°54N 79°51W **82** E5
Union City *Tenn., U.S.A.* 36°26N 89°3W **85** C10
Union Dale *U.S.A.* 41°43N 75°29W **83** E9
Union Gap *U.S.A.* 46°33N 120°28W **76** C3
Union Springs *Ala., U.S.A.* 32°9N 85°43W **85** E12
Union Springs *N.Y., U.S.A.* 42°50N 76°41W **83** D8
Uniondale *S. Africa* 33°39S 23°7E **56** D3
Uniontown *U.S.A.* 39°54N 79°44W **81** F14
Unionville *U.S.A.* 40°29N 93°1W **80** E7
United Arab Emirates ■ *Asia* 23°50N 54°0E **47** F7
United Kingdom ■ *Europe* 53°0N 2°0W **14** E6
United States of America ■ *N. Amer.* 37°0N 96°0W **75** H20
Unity *Canada* 52°30N 109°5W **71** C7
University Park *U.S.A.* 32°17N 106°45W **77** K10
University Place *U.S.A.* 47°14N 122°33W **78** C4
Unjha *India* 23°46N 72°24E **42** H5
Unnao *India* 26°35N 80°30E **43** F9
Unst *U.K.* 60°44N 0°53W **11** A8
Unuk → *Canada* 56°5N 131°3W **70** B2
Unzen-Amakusa △ *Japan* 32°15N 130°10E **29** H5
Uong Bi *Vietnam* 21°2N 106°47E **38** B6
Uotsuri-Shima *E. China Sea* 25°45N 123°29E **29** M1
Uozu *Japan* 36°48N 137°24E **29** F8
Upata *Venezuela* 8°1N 62°24W **92** B6
Upemba, L. *Dem. Rep. of the Congo* 8°30S 26°20E **54** F5
Upernavik *Greenland* 72°49N 56°20W **4** B5
Upington *S. Africa* 28°25S 21°15E **56** C3
Upleta *India* 21°46N 70°16E **42** J4
'Upolu *Samoa* 13°58S 172°0W **59** b
Upper Alkali L. *U.S.A.* 41°47N 120°8W **76** F3
Upper Arrow L. *Canada* 50°30N 117°50W **70** C5
Upper Daly ☼ *Australia* 14°26S 131°3E **60** B5
Upper Darby *U.S.A.* 39°55N 75°16W **81** F16
Upper Foster L. *Canada* 56°47N 105°20W **71** B7
Upper Hutt *N.Z.* 41°8S 175°5E **59** D5
Upper Klamath L. *U.S.A.* 42°25N 121°55W **76** E3
Upper Lake *U.S.A.* 39°10N 122°54W **78** F4
Upper Liard *Canada* 60°3N 128°54W **70** A3
Upper Manzanilla *Trin. & Tob.* 10°31N 61°4W **93** K15
Upper Missouri Breaks ⌓ *U.S.A.* 47°50N 109°55W **76** C9
Upper Musquodoboit *Canada* 45°10N 62°58W **73** C7
Upper Red L. *U.S.A.* 48°8N 94°45W **80** A6
Upper Sandusky *U.S.A.* 40°50N 83°17W **81** E12
Upper Volta = Burkina Faso ■ *Africa* 12°0N 1°0W **52** F5
Uppland *Sweden* 59°59N 17°48E **9** G17
Uppsala *Sweden* 59°53N 17°38E **9** G17
Upshi *India* 33°48N 77°52E **43** C7
Upton *U.S.A.* 44°6N 104°38W **76** D11
Uqsuqtuuq = Gjoa Haven *Canada* 68°38N 95°53W **68** D12
Ur *Iraq* 30°55N 46°25E **46** D5
Urad Qianqi *China* 40°40N 108°30E **32** D5
Urahoro *Japan* 42°50N 143°40E **28** C11
Urakawa *Japan* 42°9N 142°47E **28** C11
Ural = Uralskiy □ *Russia* 64°0N 70°0E **26** C7
Ural = Zhayyq → *Kazakhstan* 47°0N 51°48E **19** E9
Ural *Australia* 33°21S 146°12E **63** E4
Ural Mts. = Uralskie Gory *Eurasia* 60°0N 59°0E **18** C10
Uralla *Australia* 30°37S 151°29E **63** E5
Uralsk = Oral *Kazakhstan* 51°20N 51°20E **19** D9
Uralskie Gory *Eurasia* 60°0N 59°0E **18** C10
Uralskiy □ *Russia* 64°0N 70°0E **26** C7
Urambo *Tanzania* 5°4S 32°0E **54** F6
Urandangi *Australia* 21°32S 138°14E **62** C2
Uranium City *Canada* 59°34N 108°37W **71** B7
Urapuntja = Utopia *Australia* 22°14S 134°33E **62** C1
Uraricoera → *Brazil* 3°2N 60°30W **92** C6
Urasoe *Japan* 26°15N 127°43E **29** L3
Uravakonda *India* 14°57N 77°12E **45** G3
Urawa = Saitama *Japan* 35°54N 139°38E **29** G9
Uray *Russia* 60°5N 65°15E **26** C7
'Uray'irah *Si. Arabia* 25°57N 48°53E **47** E6
Urbana *Ill., U.S.A.* 40°7N 88°12W **80** E9
Urbana *Ohio, U.S.A.* 40°7N 83°45W **81** E12
Urbandale *U.S.A.* 41°38N 93°43W **80** E7
Urbino *Italy* 43°43N 12°38E **22** C5
Urbión, Picos de *Spain* 42°1N 2°52W **21** A4
Urcos *Peru* 13°40S 71°38W **92** F4
Urdinarrain *Argentina* 32°37S 58°52W **94** C4
Ure → *U.K.* 54°5N 1°20W **12** C6
Urengoy *Russia* 65°58N 78°22E **26** C8
Ures *Mexico* 29°26N 110°24W **86** B2
Urewera △ *N.Z.* 38°29S 177°7E **59** C6
Urfa = Sanliurfa *Turkey* 37°12N 38°50E **46** B3
Urganch *Uzbekistan* 41°40N 60°41E **26** E7
Urgench = Urganch *Uzbekistan* 41°40N 60°41E **26** E7
Ürgüp *Turkey* 38°38N 34°56E **46** B2
Urho Kekkonen △ *Finland* 68°20N 27°40E **8** B22
Uri *India* 34°8N 74°2E **43** B6
Uribia *Colombia* 11°43N 72°16W **92** A4
Uriondo *Bolivia* 21°41S 64°41W **94** A3
Urique *Mexico* 27°13N 107°55W **86** B3
Urique → *Mexico* 26°29N 107°58W **86** B3
Urk *Neths.* 52°39N 5°36E **15** B5
Urla *Turkey* 38°20N 26°47E **23** E12
Urmia = Orūmīyeh *Iran* 37°40N 45°0E **46** B5
Uroševac = Ferizaj *Kosovo* 42°23N 21°10E **23** C9
Uroyan, Montanas de *Puerto Rico* 18°12N 66°50W **89** d
Urrampinyi Iltjiltarri ☼ *Australia* 24°20S 132°10E **60** D5
Uruaçu *Brazil* 14°30S 49°10W **93** F9
Uruapan *Mexico* 19°24N 102°3W **86** D4
Urubamba → *Peru* 10°43S 73°48W **92** F4
Urucará *Brazil* 2°32S 57°45W **92** D7
Uruçuí *Brazil* 7°20S 44°28W **93** E10
Uruguai → *Brazil* 26°0S 53°30W **95** B5
Uruguaiana *Brazil* 29°50S 57°0W **94** B4
Uruguay ■ *S. Amer.* 32°30S 56°30W **94** C4
Uruguay → *S. Amer.* 34°12S 58°18W **94** C4
Urumchi = Ürümqi *China* 43°45N 87°45E **30** C6
Ürümqi *China* 43°45N 87°45E **30** C6
Uruna ☼ *Australia* 24°3S 133°1E **60** D5
Urup, Ostrov *Russia* 46°0N 151°0E **27** E16
Ürzhar *Kazakhstan* 47°5N 81°38E **26** E9
Usa → *Russia* 66°16N 59°49E **18** A10
Uşak *Turkey* 38°43N 29°28E **19** G4
Usakos *Namibia* 21°54S 15°31E **56** B2
Usedom *Germany* 53°55N 14°2E **16** B8
Useless Loop *Australia* 26°8S 113°23E **61** E1
Ushakova, Ostrov *Russia* 82°0N 80°0E **27** A8
Ushant = Ouessant, Î. d' *France* 48°28N 5°6W **20** B1
'Ushayrah *Si. Arabia* 25°35N 45°47E **46** E5
Ushibuka *Japan* 32°11N 130°1E **29** H5
Üshtöbe *Kazakhstan* 45°16N 78°0E **26** E8
Ushuaia *Argentina* 54°50S 68°23W **96** G3
Ushumun *Russia* 52°47N 126°32E **27** D13
Usinsk *Russia* 65°57N 57°27E **18** A10
Usk *Canada* 54°38N 128°26W **70** C3
Usk → *U.K.* 51°33N 2°58W **13** F5
Uska *India* 27°12N 83°7E **43** F10
Usman *Russia* 52°5N 39°48E **18** D6
Usolye-Sibirskoye *Russia* 52°48N 103°40E **27** D11
Uspallata, P. de *Argentina* 32°37S 69°22W **94** C2
Ussuriysk *Russia* 43°48N 131°59E **28** C5
Ussurka *Russia* 45°12N 133°31E **28** B6
Ust-Chaun *Russia* 68°47N 170°30E **27** C18
Ust-Ilimsk *Russia* 58°3N 102°39E **27** D11
Ust-Ishim *Russia* 57°45N 71°10E **26** D8
Ust-Kamchatsk *Russia* 56°10N 162°28E **27** D17
Ust-Kamenogorsk = Öskemen *Kazakhstan* 50°0N 82°36E **26** D9
Ust-Khayryuzovo *Russia* 57°15N 156°45E **27** D16
Ust-Kut *Russia* 56°50N 105°42E **27** D11
Ust-Kuyga *Russia* 70°1N 135°43E **27** B14
Ust-Maya *Russia* 60°30N 134°28E **27** C14
Ust-Mil *Russia* 59°40N 133°11E **27** D14
Ust-Nera *Russia* 64°35N 143°15E **27** C15
Ust-Nyukzha *Russia* 56°34N 121°37E **27** D13
Ust-Olenek *Russia* 73°0N 120°5E **27** B12
Ust-Omchug *Russia* 61°9N 149°38E **27** C15
Ust-Port *Russia* 69°40N 84°26E **26** C9
Ust' Shchugor *Russia* 64°16N 57°36E **18** B10
Ust-Tsilma *Russia* 65°28N 52°11E **18** A9
Ust-Urt = Ustyurt Plateau *Asia* 44°0N 55°0E **26** E6
Ust-Usa *Russia* 66°2N 56°57E **18** A10
Ust-Vorkuta *Russia* 67°24N 64°0E **18** A11
Ústí nad Labem *Czech Rep.* 50°41N 14°3E **16** C8
Ústica *Italy* 38°42N 13°11E **22** E5
Ustinov = Izhevsk *Russia* 56°51N 53°14E **18** C9
Ustyurt Plateau *Asia* 44°0N 55°0E **26** E6
Usu *China* 44°27N 84°40E **30** C5
Usuki *Japan* 33°8N 131°49E **29** H5
Usulután *El Salv.* 13°25N 88°28W **88** D2
Usumacinta → *Mexico* 18°24N 92°38W **87** D6
Usumbura = Bujumbura *Burundi* 3°16S 29°18E **54** E5
Usutuo → *Mozam.* 26°48S 32°7E **57** C5
Uta *Indonesia* 4°33S 136°0E **37** E9
Utah □ *U.S.A.* 39°20N 111°30W **76** G8
Utah L. *U.S.A.* 40°12N 111°48W **76** F8
Utara, Selat *Malaysia* 5°28N 100°20E **39** c
Utarni *India* 26°5N 71°58E **42** F4
Utatlan *Guatemala* 15°2N 91°11W **88** C1
Ute Creek → *U.S.A.* 35°21N 103°50W **77** J12
Utena *Lithuania* 55°27N 25°40E **9** J21
Uthai Thani *Thailand* 15°22N 100°3E **38** E3
Uthal *Pakistan* 25°44N 66°40E **42** G2
Utiariti *Brazil* 13°0S 58°10W **92** F7
Utica *N.Y., U.S.A.* 43°6N 75°14W **83** C9
Utica *Ohio, U.S.A.* 40°14N 82°27W **82** F2
Utikuma L. *Canada* 55°50N 115°30W **70** B5
Utila *Honduras* 16°6N 86°56W **88** C2
Utkela *India* 20°6N 83°10E **44** D6
Utnur *India* 19°22N 78°46E **44** E4
Utopia *Australia* 22°14S 134°33E **62** C1
Utraula *India* 27°19N 82°25E **43** F10
Utrecht *Neths.* 52°5N 5°8E **15** B5
Utrecht *S. Africa* 27°38S 30°20E **57** C5
Utrecht □ *Neths.* 52°6N 5°7E **15** B5
Utrera *Spain* 37°12N 5°48W **21** D3
Utsjoki → *Finland* 69°51N 26°59E **8** B22
Utsunomiya *Japan* 36°30N 139°50E **29** F9
Uttar Pradesh □ *India* 27°0N 80°0E **43** F9
Uttaradit *Thailand* 17°36N 100°5E **38** D3
Uttarakhand □ *India* 30°0N 79°30E **43** D8
Utterson *Canada* 45°12N 79°19W **82** A5
Uttoxeter *U.K.* 52°54N 1°52W **12** E6
Utuado *Puerto Rico* 18°16N 66°42W **89** d
Uummannaq *Qaasuitsup, Greenland* 70°58N 52°17W **4** B5
Uummannaq *Qaasuitsup, Greenland* 77°33N 68°52W **69** B18
Uummannarsuaq = Nunap Isua *Greenland* 59°48N 43°55W **66** D15
Uusikaarlepyy *Finland* 63°32N 22°31E **8** E20
Uusikaupunki *Finland* 60°47N 21°25E **8** F19
Uva *Russia* 56°59N 52°13E **18** C9
Uvalde *U.S.A.* 29°13N 99°47W **84** G5
Uvat *Russia* 59°5N 68°50E **26** D7
Uvinza *Tanzania* 5°5S 30°24E **54** F6
Uvira *Dem. Rep. of the Congo* 3°22S 29°3E **54** E5
Uvs Nuur *Mongolia* 50°20N 92°30E **30** A7
'Uwairidh, Ḥarrat al *Si. Arabia* 26°50N 38°0E **46** E3
Uwajima *Japan* 33°10N 132°35E **29** H6
Uweinat, Jebel *Sudan* 21°54N 24°58E **53** D10
Uxbridge *Canada* 44°6N 79°7W **82** B5
Uxin Qi *China* 38°50N 109°5E **32** E5
Uxmal *Mexico* 20°22N 89°46W **87** C7
Üydzin *Mongolia* 44°9N 107°0E **32** B4
Uyo *Nigeria* 5°1N 7°53E **52** G7
Uyûn Mûsa *Egypt* 29°53N 32°40E **48** F1
Uyuni *Bolivia* 20°28S 66°47W **92** H5
Uzbekistan ■ *Asia* 41°30N 65°0E **26** E7
Uzboy → *Turkmenistan* 39°30N 55°0E **47** B7
Uzen, Mal → *Kazakhstan* 49°4N 49°44E **19** E8
Uzerche *France* 45°25N 1°34E **20** D4
Uzh → *Ukraine* 51°15N 30°12E **17** C16
Uzhgorod = Uzhhorod *Ukraine* 48°36N 22°18E **17** D12
Uzhhorod *Ukraine* 48°36N 22°18E **17** D12
Užice *Serbia* 43°55N 19°50E **23** C8
Uzunköprü *Turkey* 41°16N 26°43E **23** D12

V

Vaal → *S. Africa* 29°4S 23°38E **56** C3
Vaal Dam *S. Africa* 27°0S 28°14E **57** C4
Vaalwater *S. Africa* 24°15S 28°8E **57** B4
Vaasa *Finland* 63°6N 21°38E **8** E19
Vác *Hungary* 47°49N 19°10E **17** E10
Vacaria *Brazil* 28°31S 50°52W **95** B5
Vacaville *U.S.A.* 38°21N 121°59W **78** G5
Vach = Vakh → *Russia* 60°45N 76°45E **26** C8
Vache, Î. à *Haiti* 18°2N 73°35W **89** C5
Vacoas *Mauritius* 20°18S 57°29E **55** d
Vada *India* 19°39N 73°8E **44** E1
Vadakara *India* 11°35N 75°40E **45** J2
Vadnagar *India* 23°47N 72°40E **42** H5
Vadodara *India* 22°20N 73°10E **42** H5
Vadsø *Norway* 70°3N 29°50E **8** A23
Vaduj *India* 17°36N 74°27E **44** F2
Vaduz *Liech.* 47°8N 9°31E **20** C8
Vadvetjåkka △ *Sweden* 68°30N 18°28E **8** B18
Værøy *Norway* 67°40N 12°40E **8** C15
Vágar *Færoe Is.* 62°5N 7°15W **8** E9
Vågsfjorden *Norway* 68°50N 16°50E **8** B17
Váh → *Slovak Rep.* 47°43N 18°7E **17** D9
Vahsel B. *Antarctica* 75°0S 35°0W **5** D1
Váhtjer = Gällivare *Sweden* 67°9N 20°40E **8** C19
Vaiaku = Fongafale *Tuvalu* 8°31S 179°13E **58** B10
Vaigai → *India* 9°15N 79°10E **45** K4
Vaihiria, L. *Tahiti* 17°40S 149°25W **59** d
Vaijapur *India* 19°58N 74°45E **44** E2
Vaikam *India* 9°45N 76°25E **45** K3
Vail *U.S.A.* 39°40N 106°20W **76** G10
Vaippar → *India* 9°0N 78°25E **45** K4
Vairao *Tahiti* 17°47S 149°17W **59** d
Vaisali → *India* 26°28N 78°53E **43** F8
Vaitogi *Amer. Samoa* 14°24S 170°44W **59** b
Vajpur *India* 21°24N 73°17E **44** D1
Vakarai *Sri Lanka* 8°8N 81°26E **45** K5
Vakh → *Russia* 60°45N 76°45E **26** C8
Val-d'Or *Canada* 48°7N 77°47W **72** C4
Val Marie *Canada* 49°15N 107°45W **71** D7
Valaam *Russia* 61°22N 30°57E **8** F24
Valahia *Romania* 44°35N 25°0E **17** F13
Valaichenai *Sri Lanka* 7°54N 81°32E **45** L5
Valandovo *Macedonia* 41°19N 22°34E **23** D10
Valatie *U.S.A.* 42°24N 73°40W **83** D11
Valcheta *Argentina* 40°40S 66°8W **96** E3
Valdai Hills = Valdayskaya Vozvyshennost *Russia* 57°0N 33°30E **18** C5
Valdayskaya Vozvyshennost *Russia* 57°0N 33°30E **18** C5
Valdepeñas *Spain* 38°43N 3°25W **21** C4
Valdés, Pen. *Argentina* 42°30S 63°45W **96** E4
Valdez *U.S.A.* 61°7N 146°16W **68** E2
Valdivia *Chile* 39°50S 73°14W **96** D2
Valdivia Abyssal Plain *S. Ocean* 62°30S 70°0E **5** C6
Valdosta *U.S.A.* 30°50N 83°17W **85** F13
Valdres *Norway* 61°5N 9°5E **8** F13
Vale *U.S.A.* 43°59N 117°15W **76** E5
Vale of Glamorgan □ *U.K.* 51°28N 3°25W **13** F4
Valemount *Canada* 52°50N 119°15W **70** C5
Valença *Brazil* 13°20S 39°5W **93** F11
Valença do Piauí *Brazil* 6°20S 41°45W **93** E10
Valence *France* 44°57N 4°54E **20** D6
Valencia *Spain* 39°27N 0°23W **21** C5
Valencia *Trin. & Tob.* 10°39N 61°11W **93** K15
Valencia *U.S.A.* 34°48N 106°43W **77** J10
Valencia *Venezuela* 10°11N 68°0W **92** A5
Valencia □ *Spain* 39°20N 0°40W **21** C5
Valencia, G. de *Spain* 39°30N 0°20E **21** C6
Valencia de Alcántara *Spain* 39°25N 7°14W **21** C2
Valencia I. *Ireland* 51°54N 10°22W **10** E1
Valenciennes *France* 50°20N 3°34E **20** A5
Valentim, Sa. do *Brazil* 6°0S 43°30W **93** E10
Valentin *Russia* 43°8N 134°17E **28** C7
Valentine *Nebr., U.S.A.* 42°52N 100°33W **80** D3
Valentine *Tex., U.S.A.* 30°35N 104°30W **84** F2
Valera *Venezuela* 9°19N 70°37W **92** B4
Valga *Estonia* 57°47N 26°2E **9** H22
Valier *U.S.A.* 48°18N 112°16W **76** B7
Valjevo *Serbia* 44°18N 19°53E **23** B8

Walka *Latvia*	57°46N 26°3E	**9** H22
Walkeakoski *Finland*	61°16N 24°2E	**8** F21
Walkenswaard *Neths.*	51°21N 5°29E	**15** C5
Wall de Uxó = La Vall d'Uixó		
Spain	39°49N 0°15W	**21** C5
Walladolid *Mexico*	20°41N 88°12W	**87** C7
Walladolid *Spain*	41°38N 4°43W	**21** B3
Walle de la Pascua		
Venezuela	9°13N 66°0W	**92** B5
Walle de las Palmas		
Mexico	32°20N 116°43W	**79** N10
Walle de Santiago		
Mexico	20°23N 101°12W	**86** C4
Walle de Zaragoza		
Mexico	27°25N 105°50W	**86** B3
Walle Fértil, Sierra del		
Argentina	30°20S 68°0W	**94** C2
Walle Hermoso *Mexico*	25°35N 97°40W	**87** B5
Walle Nacional *Mexico*	17°47N 96°18W	**87** D5
Walledupar *Colombia*	10°29N 73°15W	**92** A4
Wallejo *U.S.A.*	38°7N 122°14W	**78** G4
Wallenar *Chile*	28°30S 70°50W	**94** B1
Walletta *Malta*	35°54N 14°31E	**22** G6
Walley Center *U.S.A.*	33°13N 117°2W	**79** M9
Walley City *U.S.A.*	46°55N 98°0W	**80** B5
Walley Falls *Oreg., U.S.A.*	42°29N 120°17W	**78** E3
Walley Falls *R.I., U.S.A.*	41°54N 71°24W	**83** E13
Walley of Flowers △ *India*	30°50N 79°40E	**43** D8
Walley Springs *U.S.A.*	38°12N 120°50W	**78** G6
Walley View *U.S.A.*	40°39N 76°33W	**83** F8
Walley Wells *U.S.A.*	35°27N 115°46W	**79** K11
Walleyview *Canada*	55°5N 117°17W	**70** B5
Wallimanca, Arroyo		
Argentina	35°40S 59°10W	**94** D4
Walmiera *Latvia*	57°37N 25°29E	**9** H21
Walognes *France*	49°30N 1°28W	**20** B3
Walona = Vlorë *Albania*	40°32N 19°28E	**23** D8
Walozhyn *Belarus*	54°3N 26°30E	**17** A14
Walparai *India*	10°22N 76°58E	**45** J3
Walparaíso *Chile*	33°2S 71°40W	**94** C1
Walparaiso *Mexico*	22°46N 103°34W	**86** C4
Walparaiso *U.S.A.*	41°28N 87°4W	**80** E10
Walparaiso □ *Chile*	33°2S 71°40W	**94** C1
Walpoy *India*	15°32N 74°8E	**45** G2
Wals *S. Africa*	27°23S 26°30E	**56** C4
Wals, Tanjung *Indonesia*	8°26S 137°25E	**37** F9
Walsad *India*	20°40N 72°58E	**44** J1
Walverde del Camino		
Spain	37°35N 6°47W	**21** D2
Wambori *India*	19°17N 74°44E	**44** E2
Wammala = Sastamala		
Finland	61°20N 22°54E	**8** F20
Wamsadhara → *India*	18°21N 84°8E	**44** E7
Wan, L. = Van Gölü *Turkey*	38°30N 43°0E	**46** B4
Wan Alstyne *U.S.A.*	33°25N 96°35W	**84** E6
Wan Blommestein Meer		
Suriname	4°45N 55°5W	**93** C7
Wan Buren *Canada*	47°10N 67°58W	**73** C6
Wan Buren *Ark., U.S.A.*	35°26N 94°21W	**84** D7
Wan Buren *Maine,*		
U.S.A.	47°10N 67°58W	**81** B20
Wan Buren *Mo., U.S.A.*	37°0N 91°1W	**80** G8
Wan Canh *Vietnam*	13°37N 109°0E	**38** F7
Wan Diemen, C. *N. Terr.,*		
Australia	11°9S 130°24E	**60** B5
Wan Diemen, C. *Queens.,*		
Australia	16°30S 139°46E	**62** B2
Wan Diemen G. *Australia*	11°45S 132°0E	**60** B5
Wan Gölü *Turkey*	38°30N 43°0E	**46** B4
Wan Horn *U.S.A.*	31°3N 104°50W	**84** F2
Wan Tivu *India*	12°42N 109°14E	**38** F7
Wan Rees, Pegunungan		
Indonesia	2°35S 138°15E	**37** E9
Wan Tivu *India*	8°51N 78°15E	**45** K4
Wan Wert *U.S.A.*	40°52N 84°35W	**81** E11
Wan Yen *Vietnam*	21°4N 104°42E	**34** G5
Wan Zylsrus *S. Africa*	26°52S 22°4E	**56** C3
Wanadzor *Armenia*	40°48N 44°30E	**19** F7
Wanavara *Russia*	60°22N 102°16E	**27** C11
Wancouver *Canada*	49°15N 123°7W	**78** A3
Wancouver *U.S.A.*	45°38N 122°40W	**78** E4
Wancouver, C. *Australia*	35°2S 118°11E	**61** G2
Wancouver I. *Canada*	49°50N 126°0W	**78** B2
Wancouver Int. ✈ (YVR)		
Canada	49°10N 123°10W	**78** A3
Wandalia *Ill., U.S.A.*	38°58N 89°6W	**80** F9
Wandalia *Mo., U.S.A.*	39°19N 91°29W	**80** F8
Wandavasi *India*	12°30N 79°30E	**45** H4
Wandeloos B. *Sri Lanka*	8°0N 81°45E	**45** L5
Wandenberg Village		
U.S.A.	34°43N 120°28W	**79** L6
Wanderbijlpark *S. Africa*	26°42S 27°54E	**57** C4
Wandergrift *U.S.A.*	40°36N 79°34W	**82** F5
Wanderhoof *Canada*	54°0N 124°0W	**70** C4
Wanderkloof Dam *S. Africa*	30°4S 24°40E	**56** E3
Wanderlin I. *Australia*	15°44S 137°2E	**62** B2
Wänern *Sweden*	58°47N 13°30E	**9** G15
Wänersborg *Sweden*	58°26N 12°19E	**9** G15
Wang Vieng *Laos*	18°58N 102°32E	**38** C4
Wangaindrano *Madag.*	23°21S 47°36E	**55** J9
Wanguard *U.S.A.*	49°55N 107°20W	**71** D7
Wanino *Russia*	48°50N 140°5E	**27** E15
Wanivilasa Sagara *India*	13°45N 77°30E	**45** H3
Waniyambadi *India*	12°46N 78°44E	**45** H4
Wankleek Hill *Canada*	45°32N 74°40W	**83** A10
Wännäs *Sweden*	63°58N 19°48E	**8** E18
Wannes *France*	47°40N 2°47W	**20** C2
Wannøya *Norway*	70°6N 19°50E	**8** A18
Wanrhynsdorp *S. Africa*	31°36S 18°17E	**56** E2
Wansada *India*	20°47N 73°25E	**44** D1
Wansbro *Sweden*	60°32N 14°15E	**9** F16
Wansittart B. *Australia*	14°3S 126°17E	**60** B4
Wansittart I. *Canada*	65°50N 84°0W	**69** D15
Wanua Balavu *Fiji*	17°12S 178°59W	**59** a
Wanua Levu *Fiji*	16°33S 179°15E	**59** a
Wanua Vatu *Fiji*	18°22S 179°15W	**59** a
Wanuatu ■ *Pac. Oc.*	15°0S 168°0E	**58** C9
Wanwyksvlei *S. Africa*	30°18S 21°49E	**56** D3

Vapi *India*	20°22N 72°54E	**44** D1
Vapnyarka *Ukraine*	48°32N 28°45E	**17** D15
Var → *France*	43°39N 7°12E	**20** E7
Varada → *India*	15°0N 75°40E	**45** G2
Varämïn *Iran*	35°20N 51°39E	**47** C6
Varämïn □ *Iran*	35°18N 51°35E	**47** B6
Varanasi *India*	25°22N 83°0E	**43** G10
Varangerfjorden *Norway*	70°3N 29°25E	**8** A23
Varangerhalvøya		
Norway	70°25N 29°30E	**8** A23
Varaždin *Croatia*	46°20N 16°20E	**16** E9
Varberg *Sweden*	57°6N 12°20E	**9** H15
Vardak □ *Afghan.*	34°0N 68°0E	**40** B6
Vardar = Axios →		
Greece	40°57N 22°35E	**23** D10
Varde *Denmark*	55°38N 8°29E	**9** J13
Vardø *Norway*	70°23N 31°5E	**8** A24
Varella, Mui = Nay, Mui		
Vietnam	12°54N 109°26E	**38** F7
Varéna *Lithuania*	54°12N 24°30E	**9** J21
Varese *Italy*	45°48N 8°50E	**20** D8
Varginha *Brazil*	21°33S 45°25W	**95** A6
Varillas *Chile*	24°0S 70°10W	**94** A1
Varkaus *Finland*	62°19N 27°50E	**8** E22
Värmland *Sweden*	59°45N 13°0E	**9** G15
Varna *Bulgaria*	43°13N 27°56E	**23** C12
Varna → *India*	16°48N 74°32E	**44** F2
Värnamo *Sweden*	57°10N 14°3E	**9** H16
Várnjárga = Varangerhalvøya		
Norway	70°25N 29°30E	**8** A23
Vars *Canada*	45°21N 75°21W	**83** A9
Varysburg *U.S.A.*	42°46N 78°19W	**82** D6
Varzaneh *Iran*	32°25N 52°40E	**47** C7
Vasa = Vaasa *Finland*	63°6N 21°38E	**8** E19
Vasa Barris → *Brazil*	11°10S 37°10W	**93** F11
Vasai-Virar *India*	19°28N 72°48E	**44** E1
Vascongadas = País Vasco □		
Spain	42°50N 2°45W	**21** A4
Vasht = Khäsh *Iran*	28°15N 61°15E	**47** D9
Vasilevichi *Belarus*	52°15N 29°50E	**17** B16
Vasilkov = Vasylkiv		
Ukraine	50°7N 30°15E	**17** C16
Vaslui *Romania*	46°38N 27°42E	**17** E14
Vassar *Canada*	49°10N 95°55W	**71** D9
Vassar *U.S.A.*	43°22N 83°35W	**81** D12
Västerås *Sweden*	59°37N 16°38E	**9** G17
Västerbotten *Sweden*	64°36N 20°4E	**8** D19
Västerdalälven → *Sweden*	60°30N 15°7E	**8** F16
Västervik *Sweden*	57°43N 16°33E	**9** H17
Västmanland *Sweden*	59°45N 16°20E	**9** G17
Vasto *Italy*	42°8N 14°40E	**22** C6
Vasylkiv *Ukraine*	50°7N 30°15E	**17** C16
Vat Phou *Laos*	14°51N 105°49E	**38** E5
Vatersay *U.K.*	56°55N 7°32W	**11** E1
Vatiu = Atiu *Cook Is.*	20°0S 158°10W	**65** J12
Vatnajökull *Iceland*	64°30N 16°48W	**8** D5
Vatnajökull △ *Iceland*	64°24N 16°48W	**8** D5
Vatra-Dornei *Romania*	47°22N 25°22E	**17** E13
Vatrak → *India*	23°9N 73°2E	**42** H5
Vättern *Sweden*	58°25N 14°30E	**9** G16
Vatu Vara *Fiji*	17°26S 179°31W	**59** a
Vatulele *Fiji*	18°33S 177°37E	**59** a
Vaudreuil-Dorion		
Canada	45°23N 74°3W	**83** A10
Vaughn *Mont., U.S.A.*	47°33N 111°33W	**76** C8
Vaughn *N. Mex.,*		
U.S.A.	34°36N 105°13W	**77** J11
Vaujours L. *Canada*	55°27N 74°15W	**72** A5
Vaupés → *Uaupés →*		
Brazil	0°2N 67°16W	**92** C5
Vaupés □ *Colombia*	1°0N 71°0W	**92** C4
Vauxhall *Canada*	50°5N 112°9W	**70** C6
Vav *India*	24°22N 71°31E	**42** G4
Vava'u *Tonga*	18°36S 174°0W	**59** c
Vava'u Group *Tonga*	18°40S 174°0W	**59** c
Vavuniya *Sri Lanka*	8°45N 80°30E	**45** K5
Vawkavysk *Belarus*	53°9N 24°30E	**17** B13
Växjö *Sweden*	56°52N 14°50E	**9** H16
Vaygach, Ostrov *Russia*	70°0N 60°0E	**26** C7
Veaikevárri = Svappavaara		
Sweden	67°40N 21°3E	**8** C19
Vechte → *Neths.*	52°34N 6°6E	**15** B6
Vedaranniyam *India*	10°25N 79°50E	**45** J4
Vedea → *Romania*	43°42N 25°41E	**17** G13
Vedia *Argentina*	34°30S 61°31W	**94** C3
Veendam *Neths.*	53°5N 6°52E	**15** A6
Veenendaal *Neths.*	52°2N 5°34E	**15** B5
Vefsna → *Norway*	65°48N 13°10E	**8** D15
Vega *Norway*	65°40N 11°55E	**8** D14
Vega *U.S.A.*	35°15N 102°26W	**84** D3
Vega Baja *Puerto Rico*	18°27N 66°23W	**89** d
Vegreville *Canada*	53°30N 112°5W	**70** C6
Vejer de la Frontera *Spain*	36°15N 5°59W	**21** D3
Vejle *Denmark*	55°43N 9°30E	**9** J13
Velachha *India*	21°26N 73°1E	**44** D1
Velanai I. *Sri Lanka*	9°45N 79°45E	**45** K4
Velas, C. *Costa Rica*	10°21N 85°52W	**88** D2
Velasco, Sierra de		
Argentina	29°20S 67°10W	**94** B2
Velddrif *S. Africa*	32°42S 18°11E	**56** D2
Velebit Planina *Croatia*	44°50N 15°20E	**16** F8
Veles *Macedonia*	41°46N 21°47E	**23** D9
Vélez-Málaga *Spain*	36°48N 4°5W	**21** D3
Vélez Rubio *Spain*	37°41N 2°5W	**21** D4
Velhas → *Brazil*	17°13S 44°49W	**93** G10
Velika Kapela *Croatia*	45°10N 15°5E	**16** F8
Velikaya → *Russia*	57°48N 28°10E	**18** C4
Velikaya Kema *Russia*	45°30N 137°12E	**28** B8
Veliki Ustyug *Russia*	60°47N 46°20E	**18** B8
Velikiy Novgorod *Russia*	58°30N 31°25E	**18** C5
Velikiye Luki *Russia*	56°25N 30°32E	**18** C5
Veliko Türnovo *Bulgaria*	43°5N 25°41E	**23** C11
Velikonda Range *India*	14°45N 79°10E	**45** G4
Vellar → *India*	11°30N 79°36E	**45** J4
Velletri *Italy*	41°41N 12°47E	**22** D5
Vellore *India*	12°57N 79°10E	**45** H4
Velsk *Russia*	61°10N 42°0E	**18** B7
Veluwezoom △ *Neths.*	52°5N 6°0E	**15** B6
Velva *U.S.A.*	48°4N 100°56W	**80** A3
Vembanad L. *India*	9°36N 76°15E	**45** K3

Venado *Mexico*	22°56N 101°6W	**86** C4
Venado Tuerto *Argentina*	33°50S 62°0W	**94** C3
Vendée □ *France*	46°50N 1°35W	**20** C3
Vendôme *France*	47°47N 1°3E	**20** C4
Venézia *Italy*	45°27N 12°21E	**22** B5
Venézia, G. di *Italy*	45°15N 13°0E	**22** B5
Venezuela ■ *S. Amer.*	8°0N 66°0W	**92** B5
Venezuela, G. de		
Venezuela	11°30N 71°0W	**92** A4
Vengurla *India*	15°53N 73°45E	**45** G1
Vengurla Rocks *India*	15°55N 73°22E	**45** G1
Venice = Venézia *Italy*	45°27N 12°21E	**22** B5
Venice *U.S.A.*	27°6N 82°27W	**85** H13
Venkatagiri *India*	14°0N 79°35E	**45** H4
Venkatapuram *India*	18°20N 80°30E	**44** E5
Venlo *Neths.*	51°22N 6°11E	**15** C6
Vennachar Junction		
Canada	45°5N 77°14W	**82** A7
Vennesla *Norway*	58°15N 7°59E	**9** G12
Venray *Neths.*	51°31N 6°0E	**15** C6
Ventana, Sa. de la		
Argentina	38°0S 62°30W	**94** D3
Ventersburg *S. Africa*	28°7S 27°9E	**56** C4
Venterstad *S. Africa*	30°47S 25°48E	**56** D4
Ventnor *U.K.*	50°36N 1°12W	**13** G6
Ventotène *Italy*	40°47N 13°25E	**22** D5
Ventoux, Mt. *France*	44°10N 5°17E	**20** D6
Ventspils *Latvia*	57°25N 21°32E	**9** H19
Ventuari → *Venezuela*	3°58N 67°2W	**92** C5
Ventucopa *U.S.A.*	34°50N 119°29W	**79** L7
Ventura *U.S.A.*	34°17N 119°18W	**79** L7
Vénus, Pte. *Tahiti*	17°29S 149°29W	**59** d
Venus B. *Australia*	38°40S 145°42E	**63** F4
Venustiano Carranza		
Mexico	30°25N 115°53W	**86** A1
Venustiano Carranza, Presa		
Mexico	28°20N 100°37W	**86** B4
Vera *Argentina*	29°30S 60°20W	**94** B3
Vera *Spain*	37°15N 1°51W	**21** D5
Veracruz *Mexico*	19°11N 96°8W	**87** D5
Veracruz □ *Mexico*	19°0N 96°15W	**87** D5
Veraval *India*	20°53N 70°27E	**42** J4
Verbánia *Italy*	45°56N 8°33E	**20** D8
Verbano, L. di = Maggiore, L.		
Italy	45°57N 8°39E	**20** D8
Vercelli *Italy*	45°19N 8°25E	**20** D8
Verdalsøra *Norway*	63°48N 11°30E	**8** E14
Verde → *Argentina*	41°56S 65°5W	**96** E3
Verde → *Goiás, Brazil*	18°1S 50°14W	**93** G8
Verde → *Mato Grosso do Sul,*		
Brazil	21°25S 52°20W	**93** H8
Verde → *Chihuahua,*		
Mexico	26°39N 107°11W	**86** B3
Verde → *Jalisco, Mexico*	20°42N 103°14W	**86** C4
Verde → *Oaxaca, Mexico*	15°59N 97°50W	**87** D5
Verde → *Paraguay*	23°9S 57°37W	**94** A4
Verde → *U.S.A.*	33°33N 111°40W	**77** K8
Verde, Cay *Bahamas*	23°0N 75°5W	**88** B4
Verden *Germany*	52°55N 9°14E	**16** B5
Verdi *U.S.A.*	39°31N 119°59W	**78** F7
Verdun *France*	49°9N 5°24E	**20** B6
Vereeniging *S. Africa*	26°38S 27°57E	**57** C4
Verga, C. *Guinea*	10°30N 14°10W	**52** F3
Vergara *Uruguay*	32°56S 53°57W	**95** C5
Vergemont Cr. →		
Australia	24°16S 143°16E	**62** C3
Vergennes *U.S.A.*	44°10N 73°15W	**83** B11
Veria *Greece*	40°34N 22°12E	**23** D10
Verín *Spain*	41°57N 7°27W	**21** B2
Verkhnetulomskoye Vdkhr.		
Russia	68°36N 31°12E	**8** B24
Verkhnevilyuysk		
Russia	63°27N 120°18E	**27** C13
Verkhniy Baskunchak		
Russia	48°14N 46°44E	**19** E8
Verkhoyansk *Russia*	67°35N 133°25E	**27** C14
Verkhoyansk Ra. =		
Verkhoyanskiy Khrebet		
Russia	66°0N 129°0E	**27** C13
Verkhoyanskiy Khrebet		
Russia	66°0N 129°0E	**27** C13
Vermilion *Canada*	53°20N 110°50W	**71** C6
Vermilion *U.S.A.*	41°25N 82°22W	**82** E2
Vermilion → *Canada*	53°22N 110°51W	**71** C6
Vermilion B. *U.S.A.*	29°42N 92°0W	**84** G9
Vermilion Bay *Canada*	49°51N 93°34W	**71** D10
Vermilion Cliffs Nat. Monument △		
U.S.A.	36°54N 112°5W	**77** H8
Vermilion L. *U.S.A.*	47°53N 92°26W	**80** B7
Vermillion *U.S.A.*	42°47N 96°56W	**80** D5
Vermillion → *Canada*	47°38N 72°56W	**72** C5
Vermont □ *U.S.A.*	44°0N 73°0W	**83** C12
Vernadsky *Antarctica*	65°0S 64°0W	**5** C17
Vernal *U.S.A.*	40°27N 109°32W	**76** F9
Vernalis *U.S.A.*	37°36N 121°17W	**78** H5
Verner *Canada*	46°25N 80°8W	**72** C3
Verneukpan *S. Africa*	30°0S 21°0E	**56** E3
Vernon *Canada*	50°20N 119°15W	**70** C5
Vernon *U.S.A.*	34°9N 99°17W	**84** D5
Vernonia *U.S.A.*	45°52N 123°11W	**78** E3
Vero Beach *U.S.A.*	27°38N 80°24W	**85** H14
Véroia = Veria *Greece*	40°34N 22°12E	**23** D10
Verona *Canada*	44°29N 76°42W	**83** B8
Verona *Italy*	45°27N 10°59E	**22** B4
Vert, C. *Senegal*	14°45N 17°30W	**52** F2
Verulam *S. Africa*	29°38S 31°2E	**57** C5
Verviers *Belgium*	50°37N 5°52E	**15** D5
Vesoul *France*	47°40N 6°11E	**20** C7
Vesterålen *Norway*	68°45N 15°0E	**8** B16
Vestfjorden *Norway*	67°55N 14°0E	**8** C15
Vestmannaeyjar *Iceland*	63°27N 20°15W	**8** E3
Vestvågøy *Norway*	68°18N 13°50E	**8** B15
Vesuvio *Italy*	40°49N 14°26E	**22** D6
Vesuvius, Mt. = Vesuvio		
Italy	40°49N 14°26E	**22** D6
Veszprém *Hungary*	47°8N 17°57E	**17** E9
Vetapalem *India*	15°47N 80°18E	**45** G5
Vetlanda *Sweden*	57°24N 15°3E	**9** H16

Vetlugu → *Russia*	56°36N 46°4E	**18** C8
Vettore, Mte. *Italy*	42°49N 13°16E	**22** C5
Veurne *Belgium*	51°5N 2°40E	**15** C2
Veys *Iran*	31°30N 49°0E	**47** D6
Vezhen *Bulgaria*	42°50N 24°20E	**23** C11
Vi Thanh *Vietnam*	9°42N 105°26E	**39** H5
Viacha *Bolivia*	16°39S 68°18W	**92** G5
Viamão *Brazil*	30°5S 51°0W	**95** C5
Viana *Brazil*	3°13S 44°55W	**93** D10
Viana do Alentejo		
Portugal	38°17N 7°59W	**21** C2
Viana do Castelo *Portugal*	41°42N 8°50W	**21** B1
Viangchan = Vientiane		
Laos	17°58N 102°36E	**38** D4
Vianópolis *Brazil*	16°40S 48°35W	**93** G9
Viaréggio *Italy*	43°52N 10°14E	**22** C4
Vibo Valéntia *Italy*	38°40N 16°5E	**22** E7
Viborg *Denmark*	56°27N 9°23E	**9** H13
Vic *Spain*	41°58N 2°19E	**21** B7
Vicenza *Italy*	45°33N 11°33E	**22** B4
Vich = Vic *Spain*	41°58N 2°19E	**21** B7
Vichada → *Colombia*	4°55N 67°50W	**92** C5
Vichy *France*	46°9N 3°26E	**20** C5
Vicksburg *Ariz.,*		
U.S.A.	33°45N 113°45W	**79** M13
Vicksburg *Miss., U.S.A.*	32°21N 90°53W	**85** E9
Victor *India*	21°0N 71°30E	**42** J4
Victor Harbor *Australia*	35°30S 138°37E	**63** F2
Victoria *Argentina*	32°40S 60°10W	**94** C3
Victoria *Canada*	48°30N 123°25W	**78** B3
Victoria *Chile*	38°13S 72°20W	**96** D2
Victoria *Seychelles*	4°38S 55°28E	**55** b
Victoria *Kans., U.S.A.*	38°52N 99°9W	**80** F4
Victoria *Tex., U.S.A.*	28°48N 97°0W	**84** G6
Victoria □ *Australia*	37°0S 144°0E	**63** F3
Victoria → *Australia*	15°10S 129°40E	**60** C4
Victoria, Grand L.		
Canada	47°31N 77°30W	**72** C4
Victoria, L. *Africa*	1°0S 33°0E	**54** E6
Victoria, L. *Australia*	33°57S 141°15E	**63** E3
Victoria, Mt. *Burma*	21°14N 93°55E	**41** J18
Victoria Beach *Canada*	50°40N 96°35W	**71** C9
Victoria de Durango = Durango		
Mexico	24°3N 104°39W	**86** C4
Victoria de las Tunas = Las Tunas		
Cuba	20°58N 76°59W	**88** B4
Victoria Falls *Zimbabwe*	17°58S 25°52E	**55** H5
Victoria Harbour *Canada*	44°45N 79°45W	**82** B5
Victoria I. *Canada*	71°0N 111°0W	**68** C9
Victoria L. *Canada*	48°20N 57°27W	**73** C8
Victoria Ld. *Antarctica*	75°0S 160°0E	**5** D11
Victoria Pk. *Belize*	16°48N 88°37W	**87** D7
Victoria River *Australia*	16°25S 131°0E	**60** C5
Victoria Str. *Canada*	69°31N 100°30W	**68** D11
Victoria West *S. Africa*	31°25S 23°4E	**56** D3
Victoriaville *Canada*	46°4N 71°56W	**73** C5
Victorica *Argentina*	36°20S 65°30W	**94** D2
Victorville *U.S.A.*	34°32N 117°18W	**79** L9
Vicuña *Chile*	30°0S 70°50W	**94** C1
Vicuña Mackenna		
Argentina	33°53S 64°25W	**94** C3
Vidal *U.S.A.*	34°7N 114°31W	**79** L12
Vidalia *U.S.A.*	32°13N 82°25W	**85** E13
Viddolatno = Vindelälven →		
Sweden	63°55N 19°50E	**8** E18
Vidin *Bulgaria*	43°59N 22°50E	**23** C10
Vidisha *India*	23°28N 77°53E	**42** H7
Vidzy *Belarus*	55°23N 26°37E	**9** J22
Viedma *Argentina*	40°50S 63°0W	**96** E4
Viedma, L. *Argentina*	49°30S 72°30W	**96** F2
Vielsalm *Belgium*	50°17N 5°54E	**15** D5
Vieng Pou Kha *Laos*	20°41N 101°4E	**34** G3
Vienna *Canada*	42°41N 80°48W	**82** D4
Vienna *Ill., U.S.A.*	37°25N 88°54W	**80** G9
Vienna *Mo., U.S.A.*	38°11N 91°57W	**80** F8
Vienne *France*	45°31N 4°53E	**20** D6
Vienne □ *France*	47°13N 0°5E	**20** C4
Vienne → *France*	47°13N 0°5E	**20** C4
Vientiane *Laos*	17°58N 102°36E	**38** D4
Vientos, Paso de los		
Caribbean	20°0N 74°0W	**89** C5
Vieques *Puerto Rico*	18°8N 65°25W	**89** d
Vierge Pt. *St. Lucia*	13°49N 60°53W	**89** f
Vierzon *France*	47°13N 2°5E	**20** C5
Viet Quang *Vietnam*	22°30N 104°48E	**34** F5
Viet Tri *Vietnam*	21°18N 105°25E	**38** B5
Vietnam ■ *Asia*	19°0N 106°0E	**38** C6
Vieux Fort *St. Lucia*	13°46N 60°58W	**89** f
Vigan *Phil.*	17°35N 120°28E	**37** A6
Vigévano *Italy*	45°19N 8°51E	**20** D8
Vigia *Brazil*	0°50S 48°5W	**93** D9
Vigo *Spain*	42°12N 8°41W	**21** A1
Vihowa *Pakistan*	31°8N 70°30E	**42** D4
Vihowa → *Pakistan*	31°8N 70°41E	**42** D4
Vijayadurg *India*	16°30N 73°25E	**44** F1
Vijayapura *India*	16°50N 75°55E	**44** F2
Vijayawada *India*	16°31N 80°39E	**44** F5
Vijosë → *Albania*	40°37N 19°24E	**23** D8
Vík *Iceland*	63°25N 19°1W	**8** E4
Vikarabad *India*	17°20N 77°54E	**44** E3
Vikeke = Viqueque		
E. Timor	8°52S 126°23E	**37** F7
Viking *Canada*	53°7N 111°50W	**70** C6
Vikna *Norway*	64°55N 10°58E	**8** D14
Vila Bela da Santissima Trindade		
Brazil	15°0S 59°57W	**92** G7
Vila da Ribeira Brava		
C. Verde Is.	16°32N 24°25W	**52** b
Vila do Bispo *Portugal*	37°5N 8°53W	**21** D1
Vila do Maio *C. Verde Is.*	15°21N 23°10W	**52** b
Vila Franca de Xira		
Portugal	38°57N 8°59W	**21** C1
Vila Gomes da Costa		
Mozam.	24°20S 33°37E	**57** B5
Vila Nova de Gaia *Portugal*	41°8N 8°37W	**21** B1
Vila Real *Portugal*	41°17N 7°48W	**21** B2
Vila-Real *Spain*	39°55N 0°3W	**21** C5
Vila Real de Santo António		
Portugal	37°10N 7°28W	**21** D2
Vila Velha *Brazil*	20°20S 40°17W	**95** A7

Vilagarcía de Arousa		
Spain	42°34N 8°46W	**21** A1
Vilaine → *France*	47°30N 2°27W	**20** C2
Vilanandro, Tanjona		
Madag.	16°11S 44°27E	**55** H8
Vilanculos *Mozam.*	22°1S 35°17E	**57** B6
Vilanova i la Geltrú *Spain*	41°13N 1°40E	**21** B6
Vilcheka, Ostrov *Russia*	80°0N 58°31E	**26** B6
Vilcheka, Zemlya *Russia*	80°30N 60°30E	**4** A11
Vileyka *Belarus*	54°30N 26°53E	**17** A14
Vilhelmina *Sweden*	64°35N 16°39E	**8** D17
Vilhena *Brazil*	12°40S 60°5W	**92** F6
Viliya = Neris → *Lithuania*	55°8N 24°16E	**9** J21
Viljandi *Estonia*	58°28N 25°30E	**9** G21
Vilkitskogo, Proliv		
Russia	78°0N 103°0E	**27** B11
Vilkovo = Vylkove		
Ukraine	45°28N 29°32E	**17** F15
Villa Abecia *Bolivia*	21°0S 68°18W	**94** A2
Villa Ana *Argentina*	28°28S 59°40W	**94** B4
Villa Angela *Argentina*	27°34S 60°45W	**94** B3
Villa Bella *Bolivia*	10°25S 65°22W	**92** F5
Villa Cañás *Argentina*	34°0S 61°35W	**94** C3
Villa Constitución		
Argentina	33°15S 60°20W	**94** C3
Villa de Arriaga *Mexico*	21°56N 101°20W	**86** C4
Villa de María *Argentina*	29°55S 63°43W	**94** B3
Villa de Méndez *Mexico*	25°7N 98°34W	**87** B5
Villa Dolores *Argentina*	31°58S 65°15W	**94** C2
Villa Gesell *Argentina*	37°15S 56°55W	**94** D4
Villa Guillermina		
Argentina	28°15S 59°29W	**94** B4
Villa Hayes *Paraguay*	25°5S 57°20W	**94** B4
Villa Hidalgo *Mexico*	24°15N 99°26E	**87** C5
Villa Iris *Argentina*	38°12S 63°12W	**94** D3
Villa Las Estrellas = Frei		
Antarctica	62°30S 58°0W	**5** C18
Villa María *Argentina*	32°20S 63°10W	**94** C3
Villa Mazán *Argentina*	28°40S 66°30W	**94** B2
Villa Montes *Bolivia*	21°10S 63°30W	**94** A3
Villa Ocampo *Argentina*	28°30S 59°20W	**94** B4
Villa Ocampo *Mexico*	26°27N 105°31W	**86** B3
Villa Ojo de Agua		
Argentina	29°30S 63°44W	**94** B3
Villa San Martín		
Argentina	28°15S 64°9W	**94** B3
Villa Unión *Mexico*	23°12N 106°14W	**86** C3
Villacarrillo *Spain*	38°7N 3°3W	**21** C4
Villach *Austria*	46°37N 13°51E	**16** E7
Villagrán *Mexico*	24°29N 99°29W	**87** C5
Villaguay *Argentina*	32°0S 59°0W	**94** C4
Villahermosa *Mexico*	17°59N 92°55W	**87** D6
Villajoyosa *Spain*	38°30N 0°12W	**21** C5
Villalba *Spain*	43°22N 7°40W	**21** A2
Villanueva *U.S.A.*	35°16N 105°22W	**77** J11
Villanueva de la Serena		
Spain	38°59N 5°50W	**21** C3
Villanueva y Geltrú = Vilanova i la		
Geltrú *Spain*	41°13N 1°40E	**21** B6
Villarreal = Vila-Real		
Spain	39°55N 0°3W	**21** C5
Villarrica *Chile*	39°15S 72°15W	**96** D2
Villarrica *Paraguay*	25°40S 56°30W	**94** B4
Villarrobledo *Spain*	39°18N 2°36W	**21** C4
Villavicencio *Argentina*	32°28S 69°0W	**94** C2
Villavicencio *Colombia*	4°9N 73°37W	**92** C4
Villaviciosa *Spain*	43°32N 5°27W	**21** A3
Villazón *Bolivia*	22°0S 65°35W	**94** A2
Ville-Marie *Canada*	47°20N 79°30W	**72** C4
Ville Platte *U.S.A.*	30°41N 92°17W	**84** F8
Villena *Spain*	38°39N 0°52W	**21** C5
Villeneuve-d'Ascq *France*	50°38N 3°9E	**20** A5
Villeneuve-sur-Lot *France*	44°24N 0°42E	**20** D4
Villiers *S. Africa*	27°2S 28°36E	**57** C4
Villingen-Schwenningen		
Germany	48°3N 8°26E	**16** D5
Villmanstrand = Lappeenranta		
Finland	61°3N 28°12E	**8** F23
Villupuram *India*	11°59N 79°31E	**45** J4
Vilna *Canada*	54°7N 111°55W	**70** C6
Vilnius *Lithuania*	54°38N 25°19E	**9** J21
Vilyuchinsk *Russia*	52°55N 158°24E	**27** D16
Vilyuy → *Russia*	64°24N 126°26E	**27** C13
Vilyuysk *Russia*	63°40N 121°35E	**27** C13
Vilyuyskoye Vdkhr.		
Russia	63°0N 112°0E	**27** C12
Viña del Mar *Chile*	33°0S 71°30W	**94** C1
Vinarós *Spain*	40°30N 0°27E	**21** B6
Vincennes *U.S.A.*	38°41N 87°32W	**80** F10
Vincennes Bay *S. Ocean*	66°0S 109°0E	**5** C8
Vincent *U.S.A.*	34°33N 118°11W	**79** L8
Vinchina *Argentina*	28°45S 68°15W	**94** B2
Vindelälven → *Sweden*	63°55N 19°50E	**8** E18
Vindeln *Sweden*	64°12N 19°43E	**8** D18
Vindhya Ra. *India*	22°50N 77°0E	**42** H7
Vineland *U.S.A.*	39°29N 75°2W	**81** F16
Vinh *Vietnam*	18°45N 105°38E	**38** C5
Vinh Long *Vietnam*	10°16N 105°57E	**39** G5
Vinh Moc *Vietnam*	21°18N 105°1E	**38** B5
Vinh Yen *Vietnam*	21°21N 105°35E	**34** G5
Vinita *U.S.A.*	36°39N 95°9W	**84** C7
Vinkovci *Croatia*	45°19N 18°48E	**23** B8
Vinnitsa = Vinnytsya		
Ukraine	49°15N 28°30E	**17** D15
Vinnytsya *Ukraine*	49°15N 28°30E	**17** D15
Vinnytsya □ *Ukraine*	49°20N 28°15E	**17** D15
Vinson Massif *Antarctica*	78°35S 85°25W	**5** D16
Vinton *Calif., U.S.A.*	39°48N 120°10W	**78** F6
Vinton *Iowa, U.S.A.*	42°10N 92°1W	**80** D7
Vinton *La., U.S.A.*	30°11N 93°35W	**84** F8
Vinukonda *India*	16°4N 79°45E	**45** F4
Violet Valley ⓘ *Australia*	17°10S 127°55E	**60** C4
Viðoslodrif *S. Africa*	28°6S 16°56E	**56** D2
Viqueque *E. Timor*	8°52S 126°23E	**37** F7
Virac *Phil.*	13°59N 106°49E	**38** D5
Virachey *Cambodia*	13°59N 106°49E	**38** E6
Virachey △ *Cambodia*	14°14N 106°55E	**38** E6
Virago Sd. *Canada*	54°0N 132°30W	**70** C2
Virajpet = Virarajendrapet		
India	12°10N 75°50E	**45** H2

Viramgam India 23°5N 72°0E **42 H5**
Virananşehir Turkey 37°13N 39°45E **46 B3**
Virarajendrapet India 12°10N 75°50E **45 H2**
Virawah Pakistan 24°31N 70°46E **42 G4**
Virden Canada 49°50N 100°56W **71 D8**
Vire France 48°50N 0°53W **20 B3**
Vírgenes, C. Argentina 52°19S 68°21W **96 G3**
Virgin → U.S.A. 36°28N 114°21W **77 H6**
Virgin Gorda Br. Virgin Is. 18°30N 64°26W **89 e**
Virgin Is. (British) ☑ W. Indies 18°30N 64°30W **89 e**
Virgin Is. (U.S.) ☑ W. Indies 18°20N 65°0W **89 e**
Virgin Islands △ U.S. Virgin Is. 18°21N 64°43W **89 C7**
Virginia S. Africa 28°8S 26°55E **56 C4**
Virginia U.S.A. 47°31N 92°32W **80 B7**
Virginia □ U.S.A. 37°30N 78°45W **81 G14**
Virginia Beach U.S.A. 36°49N 76°9W **81 F16**
Virginia City Mont., U.S.A. 45°18N 111°56W **76 D8**
Virginia City Nev., U.S.A. 39°19N 119°39W **78 F7**
Virginia Falls Canada 61°38N 125°42W **70 A3**
Virginiatown Canada 48°9N 79°36W **72 C4**
Viroqua U.S.A. 43°34N 90°53W **80 D8**
Virovitica Croatia 45°51N 17°21E **22 B7**
Virpur India 21°51N 70°42E **42 J4**
Virton Belgium 49°35N 5°32E **15 E5**
Virudhunagar India 9°30N 77°58E **45 K3**
Vis Croatia 43°4N 16°10E **22 C7**
Visalia U.S.A. 36°20N 119°18W **78 J7**
Visayan Sea Phil. 11°30N 123°30E **37 B6**
Visby Sweden 57°37N 18°18E **9 H18**
Viscount Melville Sd. Canada 74°10N 108°0W **69 C10**
Visé Belgium 50°44N 5°41E **15 D5**
Vise, Ostrov Russia 79°33N 76°50E **26 B8**
Višegrad Bos.-H. 43°47N 19°17E **23 C8**
Viseu Brazil 1°10S 46°5W **93 D9**
Viseu Portugal 40°40N 7°55W **21 B2**
Vishakhapatnam India 17°45N 83°20E **44 F6**
Visnagar India 23°45N 72°32E **42 H5**
Viso, Mte. Italy 44°38N 7°5E **20 D7**
Visokoi I. Antarctica 56°43S 27°15W **5 B1**
Vista U.S.A. 33°12N 117°14W **79 M9**
Vistula = Wisła → Poland 54°22N 18°55E **17 A10**
Vita India 17°17N 74°33E **44 F2**
Vitebsk = Vitsyebsk Belarus 55°10N 30°15E **18 C5**
Viterbo Italy 42°25N 12°6E **22 C5**
Viti Levu Fiji 17°30S 177°30E **59 a**
Vitigudino Spain 41°1N 6°26W **21 B2**
Vitim Russia 59°28N 112°35E **27 D12**
Vitim → Russia 59°26N 112°34E **27 D12**
Vitória Brazil 20°20S 40°22W **93 H10**
Vitória da Conquista Brazil 14°51S 40°51W **93 F10**
Vitória de Santo Antão Brazil 8°10S 35°20W **93 E11**
Vitoria-Gasteiz Spain 42°50N 2°41W **21 A4**
Vitsyebsk Belarus 55°10N 30°15E **18 C5**
Vittória Italy 36°57N 14°32E **22 F6**
Vittório Véneto Italy 45°59N 12°18E **22 B5**
Viveiro Spain 43°39N 7°38W **21 A2**
Vivian U.S.A. 32°53N 93°59W **84 E8**
Viwa Fiji 17°10S 177°58E **59 a**
Vizcaíno, Desierto de Mexico 27°30N 113°45W **86 B2**
Vizcaíno, Sierra Mexico 27°30N 114°0W **86 B2**
Vize Turkey 41°34N 27°45E **23 D12**
Vizianagaram India 18°6N 83°30E **44 E6**
Vlaardingen Neths. 51°55N 4°21E **15 C4**
Vladikavkaz Russia 43°0N 44°35E **19 F7**
Vladimir Russia 56°15N 40°30E **18 C7**
Vladimir Volynskiy = Volodymyr-Volynskyy Ukraine 50°50N 24°18E **17 C13**
Vladivostok Russia 43°10N 131°53E **28 C5**
Vlieland Neths. 53°16N 4°55E **15 A4**
Vlissingen Neths. 51°26N 3°34E **15 C3**
Vlorë Albania 40°32N 19°28E **23 D8**
Vltava → Czech Rep. 50°21N 14°30E **16 D8**
Vo Dat Vietnam 11°9N 107°31E **39 G6**
Vodlozersky △ Russia 62°15N 37°5E **26 C1**
Voe U.K. 60°21N 1°16W **11 A7**
Vogelkop = Doberai, Jazirah Indonesia 1°25S 133°0E **37 E8**
Vogelsberg Germany 50°31N 9°12E **16 C5**
Voghera Italy 44°59N 9°1E **20 D8**
Vohibinany Madag. 18°49S 49°4E **55 H9**
Vohimarina = Iharana Madag. 13°25S 50°0E **55 G10**
Vohimena, Tanjon' i Madag. 25°36S 45°8E **55 K9**
Vohipeno Madag. 22°22S 47°51E **55 J9**
Voi Kenya 3°25S 38°32E **54 E7**
Voiron France 45°22N 5°35E **20 D6**
Voisey B. Canada 56°15N 61°50W **73 A7**
Vojmsjön Sweden 65°0N 16°24E **8 D17**
Vojvodina □ Serbia 45°20N 20°0E **23 B9**
Volborg U.S.A. 45°51N 105°41W **76 D11**
Volcán de Colima △ Mexico 19°30N 103°40W **86 D4**
Volcano Is. = Kazan-Rettō Pac. Oc. 25°0N 141°0E **64 E6**
Volda Norway 62°9N 6°5E **8 E12**
Volga = Privolzhskiy □ Russia 56°0N 50°0E **26 D6**
Volga → Russia 46°0N 48°30E **19 E8**
Volga Hts. = Privolzhskaya Vozvyshennost Russia 51°0N 46°0E **19 D8**
Volgodonsk Russia 47°33N 42°5E **19 E7**
Volgograd Russia 48°40N 44°25E **19 E7**
Volgogradskoye Vdkhr. Russia 50°0N 45°20E **19 D8**
Volkhov → Russia 60°8N 32°20E **18 B5**
Volkovysk = Vawkavysk Belarus 53°9N 24°30E **17 B13**
Volksrust S. Africa 27°24S 29°53E **57 C4**
Volochanka Russia 71°0N 94°28E **27 B10**

Volodymyr-Volynskyy Ukraine 50°50N 24°18E **17 C13**
Vologda Russia 59°10N 39°45E **18 C6**
Volos Greece 39°24N 22°59E **23 E10**
Volosovo Russia 59°27N 29°32E **9 G23**
Volovets Ukraine 48°43N 23°11E **17 D12**
Volozhin = Valozhyn Belarus 54°3N 26°30E **17 A14**
Volsk Russia 52°5N 47°22E **18 D8**
Volta → Ghana 5°46N 0°41E **50 F4**
Volta, L. Ghana 7°30N 0°0 **52 G6**
Volta Redonda Brazil 22°31S 44°5W **95 A7**
Voltaire, C. Australia 14°16S 125°35E **60 B4**
Volterra Italy 43°24N 10°51E **22 C4**
Volturno → Italy 41°1N 13°55E **22 D5**
Volyn □ Ukraine 51°15N 24°30E **17 C13**
Volzhskiy Russia 48°56N 44°46E **19 E7**
Vomo Fiji 17°30S 177°15E **59 a**
Voreios Sporades Greece 39°15N 23°30E **23 E10**
Vorkuta Russia 67°48N 64°20E **18 A11**
Vormsi Estonia 59°1N 23°13E **9 G20**
Voronezh Russia 51°40N 39°10E **19 D6**
Voronezh → Russia 49°40N 42°1E **19 D6**
Võrts järv Estonia 58°16N 26°3E **9 G22**
Võru Estonia 57°48N 26°54E **9 H22**
Vosges France 48°20N 7°10E **20 B7**
Voss Norway 60°38N 6°26E **8 F12**
Vostochnyy Port Russia 42°44N 133°4E **28 C6**
Vostok Antarctica 78°30S 106°50E **5 D8**
Vostok I. Kiribati 10°5S 152°23W **65 J12**
Votkinsk Russia 57°0N 53°55E **18 C9**
Votkinskoye Vdkhr. Russia 57°22N 55°12E **18 C10**
Vouga → Portugal 40°41N 8°40W **21 B1**
Voyageurs △ U.S.A. 48°32N 93°0W **80 A7**
Voynitsa Russia 65°10N 30°20E **8 D24**
Voyvozh Russia 62°56N 54°56E **18 B9**
Vozhe, Ozero Russia 60°45N 39°0E **18 B6**
Voznesensk Ukraine 47°35N 31°21E **19 E5**
Voznesenye Russia 61°0N 35°28E **18 B6**
Vrangel Russia 42°43N 133°5E **28 C6**
Vrangelya, Ostrov Russia 71°0N 180°0E **27 B18**
Vranje Serbia 42°34N 21°54E **23 C9**
Vratsa Bulgaria 43°15N 23°30E **23 C10**
Vrbas → Bos.-H. 45°8N 17°29E **22 B7**
Vrede S. Africa 27°24S 29°6E **57 C4**
Vredefort S. Africa 27°0S 27°22E **56 C4**
Vredenburg S. Africa 32°56S 18°0E **56 D2**
Vredendal S. Africa 31°41S 18°35E **56 D2**
Vriddhachalam India 11°30N 79°20E **45 J4**
Vrindavan India 27°37N 77°40E **42 F7**
Vršac Serbia 45°8N 21°0E **23 B9**
Vryburg S. Africa 26°55S 24°45E **56 C3**
Vryheid S. Africa 27°45S 30°47E **57 C5**
Vu Liet Vietnam 18°43N 105°23E **38 C5**
Vukovar Croatia 45°21N 18°59E **23 B8**
Vulcan Canada 50°25N 113°15W **70 C6**
Vulcan Romania 45°23N 23°17E **17 F12**
Vulcănești Moldova 45°41N 28°18E **17 F15**
Vulcano Italy 38°24N 14°58E **22 E6**
Vulkaneshty = Vulcănești Moldova 45°41N 28°18E **17 F15**
Vung Tau Vietnam 10°21N 107°4E **39 G6**
Vunidawa Fiji 17°50S 178°21E **59 a**
Vunisea Fiji 19°3S 178°10E **59 a**
Vuntut △ Canada 68°25N 139°41W **68 D4**
Vyara India 21°8N 73°28E **44 D1**
Vyartsilya Russia 62°8N 30°45E **8 E24**
Vyatka = Kirov Russia 58°35N 49°40E **18 C8**
Vyatka → Russia 55°37N 51°28E **18 C9**
Vyatskiye Polyany Russia 56°14N 51°5E **18 C9**
Vyazemskiy Russia 47°32N 134°45E **27 E14**
Vyazma Russia 55°10N 34°15E **18 C5**
Vyborg Russia 60°43N 28°47E **8 F23**
Vychegda → Russia 61°18N 46°36E **18 B8**
Vychodné Beskydy Europe 49°20N 22°0E **17 D11**
Vyg-ozero Russia 63°47N 34°29E **18 B5**
Vylkove Ukraine 45°28N 29°32E **17 F15**
Vynohradiv Ukraine 48°9N 23°2E **17 D12**
Vypin India 10°10N 76°15E **45 J3**
Vyrnwy, L. U.K. 52°48N 3°31W **12 E4**
Vyshniy Volochek Russia 57°30N 34°30E **18 C5**
Vyshzha = imeni 26 Bakinskikh Komissarov Turkmenistan 39°22N 54°10E **47 B7**
Vyškov Czech Rep. 49°17N 17°0E **17 D9**
Vytegra Russia 61°0N 36°27E **18 B6**

W

W.A.C. Bennett Dam Canada 56°2N 122°6W **70 B4**
Wa Ghana 10°7N 2°25W **52 F5**
Waal → Neths. 51°37N 5°0E **15 C5**
Waalwijk Neths. 51°42N 5°4E **15 C5**
Waanyi-Garawa ۞ Australia 18°2S 137°33E **62 B2**
Wabakimi △ Canada 50°43N 89°29W **72 B2**
Wabana Canada 47°40N 53°0W **73 C9**
Wabasca-Desmarais Canada 55°57N 113°56W **70 B6**
Wabash U.S.A. 40°48N 85°49W **81 E11**
Wabash → U.S.A. 37°48N 88°2W **80 G9**
Wabigoon L. Canada 49°44N 92°44W **71 D10**
Wabowden Canada 54°55N 98°38W **71 C9**
Wabu Hu China 32°20N 116°50E **35 A11**
Wabush Canada 52°55N 66°52W **73 B6**
Waco U.S.A. 31°33N 97°9W **84 F6**
Waconichi, L. Canada 50°8N 74°0W **72 B5**
Wad Hamid Sudan 16°30N 32°45E **53 E12**
Wad Medanī Sudan 14°28N 33°30E **53 F12**
Wad Thana Pakistan 27°22N 66°23E **42 F2**
Wadayama Japan 35°19N 134°52E **29 G7**
Waddeneilanden Neths. 53°25N 5°10E **15 A5**
Waddenzee Neths. 53°6N 5°10E **15 A5**
Waddington U.S.A. 44°52N 75°12W **83 B9**

Waddington, Mt. Canada 51°23N 125°15W **70 C3**
Waddy Pt. Australia 24°58S 153°21E **63 C5**
Wadebridge U.K. 50°31N 4°51W **13 G3**
Wadena Canada 51°57N 103°47W **71 C8**
Wadena U.S.A. 46°26N 95°8W **80 B6**
Wadeye Australia 14°28S 129°52E **60 B4**
Wadgaon India 18°44N 73°39E **44 E1**
Wadhams Canada 51°30N 127°30W **70 C3**
Wadhwan India 22°42N 71°41E **42 H4**
Wadi India 17°4N 76°59E **44 F3**
Wādī as Sīr Jordan 31°56N 35°49E **48 D4**
Wadi Halfa Sudan 21°53N 31°19E **53 D12**
Wadian China 32°42N 112°29E **35 A9**
Wadsworth Nev., U.S.A. 39°38N 119°17W **76 G4**
Wadsworth Ohio, U.S.A. 41°2N 81°44W **82 E3**
Waegwan S. Korea 35°59N 128°23E **33 G15**
Wafangdian China 39°38N 121°58E **33 E11**
Wafrah Kuwait 28°33N 47°56E **46 D5**
Wagait ۞ Australia 13°1S 130°5E **60 B5**
Wageningen Neths. 51°58N 5°40E **15 C5**
Wager B. Canada 65°26N 88°40W **69 D14**
Wagga Wagga Australia 35°7S 147°24E **63 F4**
Waghai India 20°46N 73°29E **44 D1**
Waghete Indonesia 4°10S 135°50E **37 E9**
Wagin Australia 33°17S 117°25E **61 F2**
Wagner U.S.A. 43°5N 98°18W **80 D4**
Wagon Mound U.S.A. 36°1N 104°42W **77 H11**
Wagoner U.S.A. 35°58N 95°22W **84 D7**
Wah Pakistan 33°45N 72°40E **42 C5**
Wahai Indonesia 2°48S 129°35E **37 E7**
Wāhid Egypt 30°48N 32°21E **48 E1**
Wahnai Afghan. 32°40N 65°50E **42 C1**
Wahoo U.S.A. 41°13N 96°37W **80 E5**
Wahpeton U.S.A. 46°16N 96°36W **80 B5**
Wai India 17°56N 73°57E **44 F1**
Waialua U.S.A. 21°34N 158°8W **75 L8**
Waiau → N.Z. 42°47S 173°22E **59 E4**
Waiawe Ganga → Sri Lanka 6°15N 81°0E **45 L5**
Waibeem Indonesia 0°30S 132°59E **37 E8**
Waigeo Indonesia 0°20S 130°40E **37 E8**
Waihi N.Z. 37°23S 175°52E **59 B5**
Waihou → N.Z. 37°15S 175°40E **59 B5**
Waikabubak Indonesia 9°45S 119°25E **37 F5**
Waikaremoana, L. N.Z. 38°49S 177°9E **59 C6**
Waikari N.Z. 42°58S 172°41E **59 E4**
Waikato → N.Z. 37°23S 174°43E **59 B5**
Waikelo Indonesia 9°24S 119°19E **60 A2**
Waikerie Australia 34°9S 140°0E **63 E3**
Waikokopu N.Z. 39°3S 177°52E **59 C6**
Waikouaiti N.Z. 45°36S 170°41E **59 F3**
Waimakariri → N.Z. 43°24S 172°42E **59 E4**
Waimate N.Z. 44°45S 171°3E **59 F3**
Wainganga → India 18°50N 79°55E **44 E4**
Waingapu Indonesia 9°35S 120°11E **37 F6**
Waini → Guyana 8°20N 59°50W **92 B7**
Wainwright Canada 52°50N 110°50W **71 C6**
Wainwright U.S.A. 70°38N 160°2W **74 A7**
Waiouru N.Z. 39°28S 175°41E **59 C5**
Waipara N.Z. 43°3S 172°46E **59 E4**
Waipawa N.Z. 39°56S 176°38E **59 C6**
Waipiro N.Z. 38°2S 178°22E **59 C7**
Waipoua Forest N.Z. 35°39S 173°33E **59 A4**
Waipu N.Z. 35°59S 174°29E **59 A5**
Waipukurau N.Z. 40°1S 176°33E **59 D6**
Wairakei N.Z. 38°37S 176°6E **59 C6**
Wairarapa, L. N.Z. 41°14S 175°15E **59 D5**
Wairoa N.Z. 39°3S 177°25E **59 C6**
Waitaki → N.Z. 44°56S 171°7E **59 F3**
Waitangi N.Z. 35°16S 174°5E **59 A5**
Waitara N.Z. 38°59S 174°15E **59 C5**
Waitomo Caves N.Z. 38°16S 175°7E **59 C5**
Waitsburg U.S.A. 46°16N 118°9W **76 C4**
Waiuku N.Z. 37°15S 174°45E **59 B5**
Wajima Japan 37°30N 137°0E **29 F8**
Wajir Kenya 1°42N 40°5E **54 B5**
Wakasa Japan 35°20N 134°24E **29 G7**
Wakasa-Wan Japan 35°40N 135°30E **29 G7**
Wakatipu, L. N.Z. 45°5S 168°33E **59 F2**
Wakaw Canada 52°39N 105°44W **71 C7**
Wakaya Fiji 17°37S 179°0E **59 a**
Wakayama Japan 34°15N 135°15E **29 G7**
Wakayama □ Japan 33°50N 135°30E **29 H7**
Wake Forest U.S.A. 35°59N 78°30W **85 D15**
Wake I. Pac. Oc. 19°18N 166°36E **64 F8**
Wakefield Jamaica 18°26N 77°42W **88 a**
Wakefield N.Z. 41°24S 173°5E **59 D4**
Wakefield U.K. 53°41N 1°29W **12 D6**
Wakefield U.S.A. 46°29N 89°56W **80 B9**
Wakkanai Japan 45°28N 141°35E **28 B10**
Wakkerstroom S. Africa 27°24S 30°10E **57 C5**
Wakool Australia 35°28S 144°23E **63 F3**
Wakool → Australia 35°5S 143°33E **63 F3**
Wakre Indonesia 0°19S 131°5E **37 E8**
Wakuach, L. Canada 55°34N 67°32W **73 A6**
Walagunya ۞ Australia 23°10S 120°50E **60 D3**
Wałbrzych Poland 50°45N 16°18E **16 C9**
Walbury Hill U.K. 51°21N 1°28W **13 F6**
Walcha Australia 30°55S 151°31E **63 E5**
Walcheren Neths. 51°30N 3°35E **15 C3**
Walcott U.S.A. 41°46N 106°51W **76 F10**
Wałcz Poland 53°17N 16°27E **16 B9**
Walden Colo., U.S.A. 40°44N 106°17W **76 F10**
Walden N.Y., U.S.A. 41°34N 74°11W **83 E10**
Waldport U.S.A. 44°26N 124°4W **76 D1**
Waldron U.S.A. 34°54N 94°5W **84 D7**
Walebing Australia 30°41S 116°13E **61 F2**
Wales □ U.K. 52°19N 4°43W **13 E3**
Wales I. Canada 68°1N 86°40W **69 D14**
Walgett Australia 30°0S 148°5E **63 E4**
Walgreen Coast Antarctica 75°15S 105°0W **5 D15**
Walker U.S.A. 47°6N 94°35W **80 B6**
Walker, L. Canada 50°20N 67°11W **73 B6**
Walker L. Canada 54°42N 95°57W **71 C9**
Walker L. U.S.A. 38°42N 118°43W **76 G4**

Walkerston Australia 21°11S 149°8E **62 b**
Walkerton Canada 44°10N 81°10W **82 B3**
Wall U.S.A. 44°0N 102°8W **80 C2**
Walla Walla U.S.A. 46°4N 118°20W **76 C4**
Wallace Idaho, U.S.A. 47°28N 115°56W **76 C6**
Wallace N.C., U.S.A. 34°44N 77°59W **85 D16**
Wallaceburg Canada 42°34N 82°23W **82 D2**
Wallachia = Valahia Romania 44°35N 25°0E **17 F13**
Wallal Australia 26°32S 146°7E **63 D4**
Wallam Cr. → Australia 28°40S 147°20E **63 D4**
Wallambin, L. Australia 30°57S 117°35E **61 F2**
Wallangarra Australia 28°56S 151°58E **63 D5**
Wallaroo Australia 33°56S 137°39E **63 E2**
Wallasey U.K. 53°25N 3°2W **12 D4**
Wallenpaupack, L. U.S.A. 41°25N 75°15W **83 E9**
Wallingford Conn., U.S.A. 41°27N 72°50W **83 E12**
Wallingford Vt., U.S.A. 43°28N 72°58W **83 C12**
Wallis & Futuna, Îs. ☑ Pac. Oc. 13°18S 176°10W **58 C11**
Wallowa U.S.A. 45°34N 117°32W **76 D5**
Wallowa Mts. U.S.A. 45°20N 117°30W **76 D5**
Walls U.K. 60°14N 1°33W **11 A7**
Walls of Jerusalem △ Australia 41°56S 146°15E **63 G4**
Wallula U.S.A. 46°5N 118°54W **76 C4**
Wallumbilla Australia 26°33S 149°9E **63 D4**
Walmsley L. Canada 63°25N 108°36W **71 A7**
Walney, I. of U.K. 54°6N 3°15W **12 C4**
Walnut Canyon △ U.S.A. 35°15N 111°20W **77 J8**
Walnut Creek U.S.A. 37°54N 122°4W **78 H4**
Walnut Ridge U.S.A. 36°4N 90°57W **85 C9**
Walpole Australia 34°58S 116°44E **61 F2**
Walpole U.S.A. 42°9N 71°15W **83 D13**
Walpole-Nornalup △ Australia 35°0S 116°45E **61 G2**
Walsall U.K. 52°35N 1°58W **13 E6**
Walsenburg U.S.A. 37°38N 104°47W **77 H11**
Walsh U.S.A. 37°23N 102°17W **77 H12**
Walsh → Australia 16°31S 143°42E **62 B3**
Walsingham Canada 42°40N 80°31W **82 D4**
Waltair India 17°44N 83°23E **44 F6**
Walter F. George Res. U.S.A. 31°38N 85°4W **85 F12**
Walterboro U.S.A. 32°55N 80°40W **85 E14**
Walters U.S.A. 34°22N 98°19W **84 D5**
Waltman U.S.A. 43°4N 107°12W **76 E10**
Walton U.S.A. 42°10N 75°8W **83 D9**
Walton-on-the-Naze U.K. 51°51N 1°17E **13 F9**
Walvis Bay Namibia 23°0S 14°28E **56 B1**
Walvisbaai = Walvis Bay Namibia 23°0S 14°28E **56 B1**
Wamba Dem. Rep. of the Congo 2°10N 27°57E **54 D5**
Wambardi ۞ Australia 16°2S 130°55E **60 C5**
Wamego U.S.A. 39°12N 96°18W **80 F5**
Wamena Indonesia 4°4S 138°57E **37 E9**
Wampana Karlantijpa ۞ Australia 17°45S 132°10E **60 C5**
Wampaya ۞ Australia 17°20S 135°50E **62 B2**
Wampsville U.S.A. 43°4N 75°42W **83 C9**
Wamsutter U.S.A. 41°40N 107°58W **76 F10**
Wamulan Indonesia 3°27S 126°7E **37 E7**
Wan Tup Burma 21°13N 98°42E **34 G2**
Wan Xian China 38°47N 115°7E **32 E8**
Wana Pakistan 32°20N 69°32E **42 C3**
Wanaaring Australia 29°38S 144°9E **63 D3**
Wanaka N.Z. 44°42S 169°9E **59 F2**
Wanaka, L. N.Z. 44°33S 169°7E **59 F2**
Wan'an China 26°26N 114°49E **35 D10**
Wanapitei L. Canada 46°45N 80°40W **72 C3**
Wandel Sea = McKinley Sea Arctic 82°0N 0°0 **4 A7**
Wandhari Pakistan 27°42N 66°48E **42 F2**
Wanding China 24°5N 98°4E **34 E2**
Wandoan Australia 26°5S 149°55E **63 D4**
Wandur Marine △ India 11°30N 92°30E **45 J11**
Wanfu China 40°8N 122°38E **33 D12**
Wang → Thailand 17°8N 99°2E **38 D2**
Wang Noi Thailand 14°13N 100°44E **38 E3**
Wang Saphung Thailand 17°18N 101°46E **38 D3**
Wang Thong Thailand 16°50N 100°26E **38 D3**
Wanganella Australia 35°6S 144°49E **63 F3**
Wanganui N.Z. 39°56S 175°3E **59 C5**
Wangaratta Australia 36°21S 146°19E **63 F4**
Wangary Australia 34°35S 135°29E **63 E2**
Wangcang China 32°18N 106°20E **34 A6**
Wangcheng China 28°22N 112°49E **35 C9**
Wangdu China 38°40N 115°7E **32 E8**
Wangerooge Germany 53°47N 7°54E **16 B4**
Wangiwangi Indonesia 5°22S 123°37E **37 F6**
Wangjiang China 30°10N 116°42E **35 B11**
Wangmo China 25°11N 106°5E **34 E6**
Wangqing China 43°12N 129°42E **33 C15**
Wani India 20°5N 78°55E **44 E4**
Wanimiyn ۞ Australia 15°30S 130°49E **60 C5**
Wanjina Wunggurr Wilinggin ۞ Australia 16°0S 127°0E **60 C4**
Wankaner India 22°35N 71°0E **42 H4**
Wanless Canada 54°11N 101°21W **71 C8**
Wanleweyne Somalia 2°37N 44°54E **47 G3**
Wanneroo Australia 31°42S 115°46E **61 F2**
Wannian China 28°42N 117°4E **35 C11**
Wanning China 18°48N 110°22E **38 C8**
Wannoo Billabong Roadhouse Australia 27°25S 114°45E **61 E1**
Wanon Niwat Thailand 17°38N 103°46E **38 D4**
Wanqinsha China 22°43N 113°33E **31 a**
Wanquan China 40°50N 114°40E **32 D8**
Wanrong China 35°25N 110°50E **32 G6**
Wanshan China 27°30N 109°12E **34 D7**
Wanshan Qundao China 21°57N 113°45E **31 a**
Wantage U.K. 51°35N 1°25W **13 F6**
Wanxian China 30°42N 108°20E **34 B7**
Wanyuan China 32°4N 108°3E **34 A7**

Wanzai Guangdong, China 22°12N 113°31E **31 a**
Wanzai Jiangxi, China 28°7N 114°30E **35 C10**
Wapakoneta U.S.A. 40°34N 84°12W **81 E11**
Wapato U.S.A. 46°27N 120°25W **76 C3**
Wapawekka L. Canada 54°55N 104°40W **71 C8**
Wapikopa L. Canada 52°56N 87°53W **72 B2**
Wapiti → Canada 55°5N 118°18W **70 B5**
Wappingers Falls U.S.A. 41°36N 73°55W **83 E11**
Wapsipinicon → U.S.A. 41°44N 90°19W **80 E8**
Wapusk △ Canada 57°46N 93°22W **71 B10**
Warakurna Australia 24°59S 128°17E **61 D4**
Warangal India 17°58N 79°35E **44 F4**
Waraseoni India 21°45N 80°2E **43 J9**
Waratah Australia 41°30S 145°30E **63 G4**
Waratah B. Australia 38°54S 146°5E **63 F4**
Warburton Vic., Australia 37°47S 145°42E **63 F4**
Warburton W. Austral., Australia 26°8S 126°35E **61 E4**
Warburton ۞ Australia 26°7S 126°34E **61 E4**
Warburton → Australia 28°4S 137°28E **63 D2**
Warburton Groove Australia 28°18S 137°8E **63 A2**
Warburton Ra. Australia 25°55S 126°28E **61 E4**
Ward N.Z. 41°49S 174°11E **59 D5**
Ward → Australia 26°28S 146°6E **63 D4**
Ward Mt. U.S.A. 37°12N 118°54W **78 H8**
Warden S. Africa 27°50S 29°0E **57 D4**
Wardha India 20°45N 78°39E **44 D4**
Wardha → India 19°57N 79°11E **44 E4**
Wardsville Canada 42°39N 81°45W **82 D3**
Ware U.K. 51°49N 0°0 **13 F8**
Ware U.S.A. 42°16N 72°14W **83 D12**
Waregem Belgium 50°53N 3°27E **15 D3**
Wareham U.S.A. 41°46N 70°43W **83 E14**
Waremme Belgium 50°43N 5°15E **15 D5**
Warialda Australia 29°29S 150°33E **63 D5**
Warin Chamrap Thailand 15°12N 104°53E **38 E5**
Warkopi Indonesia 1°12S 134°9E **37 E8**
Warm Springs U.S.A. 38°10N 116°20W **77 G5**
Warman Canada 52°19N 106°30W **71 C7**
Warmbad = Bela Bela S. Africa 24°51S 28°19E **57 B4**
Warmbad Namibia 28°25S 18°42E **56 C2**
Warminster U.K. 51°12N 2°10W **13 F5**
Warmun Australia 17°2S 128°12E **60 C4**
Warner Mts. U.S.A. 41°40N 120°15W **76 F3**
Warner Robins U.S.A. 32°37N 83°36W **85 E13**
Waroona Australia 32°50S 115°58E **61 F2**
Warora India 20°14N 79°1E **44 D4**
Warrabri ۞ Australia 21°1S 134°19E **62 C1**
Warracknabeal Australia 36°9S 142°26E **63 F3**
Warragul Australia 38°10S 145°58E **63 F4**
Warrego → Australia 30°24S 145°21E **63 E4**
Warrego Ra. Australia 24°58S 146°0E **62 C4**
Warren Australia 31°42S 147°51E **63 E4**
Warren Ark., U.S.A. 33°37N 92°4W **84 E8**
Warren Mich., U.S.A. 42°28N 83°1W **81 D12**
Warren Minn., U.S.A. 48°12N 96°46W **80 A5**
Warren Ohio, U.S.A. 41°14N 80°49W **82 E4**
Warren Pa., U.S.A. 41°51N 79°9W **82 E5**
Warrenpoint U.K. 54°6N 6°15W **10 B5**
Warrensburg Mo., U.S.A. 38°46N 93°44W **80 F7**
Warrensburg N.Y., U.S.A. 43°29N 73°46W **83 C11**
Warrenton S. Africa 28°9S 24°47E **56 C3**
Warrenton U.S.A. 46°10N 123°56W **78 D3**
Warri Nigeria 5°30N 5°41E **52 G7**
Warrington U.K. 53°24N 2°35W **12 D5**
Warrington U.S.A. 30°23N 87°17W **85 F11**
Warrington □ U.K. 53°24N 2°35W **12 D5**
Warrnambool Australia 38°25S 142°30E **63 F3**
Warroad U.S.A. 48°54N 95°19W **80 A6**
Warruwi Australia 11°36S 133°20E **62 A1**
Warsak Dam Pakistan 34°11N 71°19E **42 B4**
Warsaw = Warszawa Poland 52°14N 21°0E **17 B11**
Warsaw N.Y., U.S.A. 42°45N 78°8W **82 D6**
Warsaw Ohio, U.S.A. 40°20N 82°0W **82 F3**
Warta → Poland 52°35N 14°39E **16 B8**
Warthe = Warta → Poland 52°35N 14°39E **16 B8**
Waru Indonesia 3°30S 130°36E **37 E8**
Warud India 21°30N 78°16E **44 D4**
Warumungu ۞ Australia 19°15S 134°44E **62 B1**
Warwick Australia 28°10S 152°1E **63 D5**
Warwick U.K. 52°18N 1°35W **13 E6**
Warwick N.Y., U.S.A. 41°16N 74°22W **83 E10**
Warwick R.I., U.S.A. 41°42N 71°28W **83 E13**
Warwickshire □ U.K. 52°14N 1°38W **13 E6**
Wasaga Beach Canada 44°31N 80°1W **82 B4**
Wasagaming Canada 50°39N 99°58W **71 C9**
Wasatch Ra. U.S.A. 40°0N 111°30W **76 F8**
Wasbank S. Africa 28°15S 30°9E **57 D5**
Wasco Calif., U.S.A. 35°36N 119°20W **79 K7**
Wasco Oreg., U.S.A. 45°36N 120°42W **76 D3**
Waseca U.S.A. 44°5N 93°30W **80 C7**
Wasekamio L. Canada 56°45N 108°45W **71 B7**
Wasgomuwa △ Sri Lanka 7°45N 81°0E **45 L5**
Wash, The U.K. 52°58N 0°20E **12 E8**
Washago Canada 44°45N 79°20W **82 B5**
Washburn N. Dak., U.S.A. 47°17N 101°2W **80 B3**
Washburn Wis., U.S.A. 46°40N 90°54W **80 B8**
Washim India 20°3N 77°0E **44 D3**
Washington U.K. 54°55N 1°30W **12 C6**
Washington Ga., U.S.A. 33°44N 82°44W **85 E13**
Washington Ind., U.S.A. 38°40N 87°10W **80 F10**
Washington Iowa, U.S.A. 41°18N 91°42W **80 E8**
Washington Mo., U.S.A. 38°33N 91°1W **80 F8**
Washington N.C., U.S.A. 35°33N 77°3W **85 D16**
Washington N.J., U.S.A. 40°46N 74°59W **83 F10**
Washington Pa., U.S.A. 40°10N 80°15W **82 F4**
Washington Utah, U.S.A. 37°8N 113°31W **77 H7**
Washington □ U.S.A. 47°30N 120°30W **76 C3**
Washington, Mt. U.S.A. 44°16N 71°18W **83 B13**

Washington Court House U.S.A. 39°32N 83°26W **81 F12**
Washington Dulles Int. ✈ (IAD) U.S.A. 38°57N 77°27W **81 F15**
Washington I. U.S.A. 45°23N 86°54W **80 C10**
Washougal U.S.A. 45°35N 122°21W **78 E4**
Washpool △ Australia 29°22S 152°20E **63 D5**
Wasian Indonesia 1°47S 133°19E **37 E8**
Wasilla U.S.A. 61°35N 149°26W **68 E2**
Wasior Indonesia 2°43S 134°30E **37 E8**
Wasiri Indonesia 7°30S 126°30E **37 F7**
Wāsiṭ □ Iraq 32°50N 45°50E **46 C5**
Waskaganish Canada 51°30N 78°40W **72 B4**
Waskaiowaka L. Canada 56°33N 96°23W **71 B9**
Waskesiu Lake Canada 53°55N 106°5W **71 C7**
Wasserkuppe Germany 50°29N 9°55E **16 C5**
Wasur △ Indonesia 8°41S 140°44E **37 F10**
Waswanipi Canada 49°40N 76°29W **72 C4**
Waswanipi, L. Canada 49°35N 76°40W **72 C4**
Watampone Indonesia 4°29S 120°25E **37 E6**
Watarrka △ Australia 24°20S 131°30E **60 D5**
Water Park Pt. Australia 22°56S 150°47E **62 C5**
Water Valley U.S.A. 34°10N 89°38W **85 D10**
Waterberg Plateau △ Namibia 20°25S 17°18E **56 B2**
Waterberge S. Africa 24°10S 28°0E **57 B4**
Waterbury Conn., U.S.A. 41°33N 73°3W **83 E11**
Waterbury Vt., U.S.A. 44°20N 72°46W **83 B12**
Waterbury L. Canada 58°10N 104°22W **71 B8**
Waterdown Canada 43°20N 79°53W **82 C5**
Waterford Canada 42°56N 80°17W **82 D4**
Waterford Ireland 52°15N 7°8W **10 D4**
Waterford Calif., U.S.A. 37°38N 120°46W **78 H6**
Waterford Pa., U.S.A. 41°57N 79°59W **82 E5**
Waterford □ Ireland 52°10N 7°40W **10 D4**
Waterford Harbour Ireland 52°8N 6°58W **10 D5**
Waterhen L. Canada 52°10N 99°40W **71 C9**
Waterloo Ont., Canada 43°30N 80°32W **82 C4**
Waterloo Qué., Canada 45°22N 72°32W **83 A12**
Waterloo Ill., U.S.A. 38°20N 90°9W **80 F8**
Waterloo Iowa, U.S.A. 42°30N 92°21W **80 D7**
Waterloo N.Y., U.S.A. 42°54N 76°52W **82 D8**
Watersmeet U.S.A. 46°16N 89°11W **80 B9**
Waterton Lakes △ Canada 48°45N 115°0W **70 D6**
Watertown Conn., U.S.A. 41°36N 73°7W **83 E11**
Watertown N.Y., U.S.A. 43°59N 75°55W **83 C9**
Watertown S. Dak., U.S.A. 44°54N 97°7W **80 C5**
Watertown Wis., U.S.A. 43°12N 88°43W **80 D9**
Waterval-Boven = Emgwenya S. Africa 25°40S 30°18E **57 C5**
Waterville Canada 45°16N 71°54W **83 A13**
Waterville Maine, U.S.A. 44°33N 69°38W **81 C19**
Waterville N.Y., U.S.A. 42°56N 75°23W **83 D9**
Waterville Pa., U.S.A. 41°19N 77°21W **82 E7**
Waterville Wash., U.S.A. 47°39N 120°4W **76 C3**
Watervliet U.S.A. 42°44N 73°42W **83 D11**
Wates Indonesia 7°51S 110°10E **37 G14**
Watford Canada 42°57N 81°53W **82 D3**
Watford U.K. 51°40N 0°24W **13 F7**
Watford City U.S.A. 47°48N 103°17W **80 B2**
Wathaman → Canada 57°16N 102°59W **71 B8**
Wathaman L. Canada 56°58N 103°44W **71 B8**
Watheroo Australia 30°15S 116°5E **61 F2**
Watheroo △ Australia 30°19S 115°48E **61 F2**
Wating China 35°40N 106°38E **32 G4**
Watkins Glen U.S.A. 42°23N 76°52W **82 D8**
Watling I. = San Salvador I. Bahamas 24°0N 74°30W **89 B5**
Watonga U.S.A. 35°51N 98°25W **84 D5**
Watrous Canada 51°40N 105°25W **71 C7**
Watrous U.S.A. 35°48N 104°59W **77 J11**
Watsa Dem. Rep. of the Congo 3°4N 29°30E **54 D5**
Watseka U.S.A. 40°47N 87°44W **80 E10**
Watson Canada 52°10N 104°30W **71 C8**
Watson Lake Canada 60°6N 128°49W **70 A3**
Watsontown U.S.A. 41°5N 76°52W **82 E8**
Watsonville U.S.A. 36°55N 121°45W **78 J5**
Wattiwarriganna Cr. → Australia 28°57S 136°10E **63 D2**
Watuata = Batuata Indonesia 6°12S 122°42E **37 F6**
Watubela, Kepulauan Indonesia 4°28S 131°35E **37 E8**
Watubela Is. = Watubela, Kepulauan Indonesia 4°28S 131°35E **37 E8**
Wau South Sudan 7°45N 28°1E **53 G11**
Waubamik Canada 45°27N 80°1W **82 A4**
Waubay U.S.A. 45°20N 97°18W **80 C5**
Wauchope N.S.W., Australia 31°28S 152°45E **63 E5**
Wauchope N. Terr., Australia 20°36S 134°15E **62 C1**
Wauchula U.S.A. 27°33N 81°49W **85 H14**
Waukarlycarly, L. Australia 21°18S 121°56E **60 D3**
Waukegan U.S.A. 42°22N 87°50W **80 D2**
Waukesha U.S.A. 43°1N 88°14W **80 D9**
Waukon U.S.A. 43°16N 91°29W **80 D8**
Waupaca U.S.A. 44°21N 89°5W **80 C9**
Waupun U.S.A. 43°38N 88°44W **80 D9**
Waurika U.S.A. 34°10N 98°0W **84 D6**
Wausau U.S.A. 44°58N 89°38W **80 C9**
Wautoma U.S.A. 44°4N 89°18W **80 C9**
Wauwatosa U.S.A. 43°2N 88°0W **80 D9**
Wave Hill = Kalkarindji Australia 17°30S 130°47E **60 C5**
Wave Rock △ Australia 32°26S 118°53E **61 F2**
Waveney → U.K. 52°35N 1°39E **13 E9**
Waverley N.Z. 39°46S 174°37E **59 C5**
Waverly Iowa, U.S.A. 42°44N 92°29W **80 D7**
Waverly N.Y., U.S.A. 42°1N 76°32W **83 D8**
Wavre Belgium 50°43N 4°38E **15 D4**
Wāw = Wau South Sudan 7°45N 28°1E **53 G11**
Wāw al Kabīr Libya 25°20N 16°43E **53 C9**
Wawa Canada 47°59N 84°47W **72 C3**
Wawanesa Canada 49°36N 99°40W **71 D9**
Wawona U.S.A. 37°32N 119°39W **78 H7**
Waxahachie U.S.A. 32°24N 96°51W **84 E6**
Way, L. Australia 26°45S 120°16E **61 E3**

Waya Fiji 17°19S 177°10E **59 a**
Waycross U.S.A. 31°13N 82°21W **85 F13**
Wayland U.S.A. 42°34N 77°35W **82 D7**
Wayne Nebr., U.S.A. 42°14N 97°1W **80 D5**
Wayne W. Va., U.S.A. 38°13N 82°27W **81 F12**
Waynesboro Ga., U.S.A. 33°6N 82°1W **85 E13**
Waynesboro Miss., U.S.A. 31°40N 88°39W **85 F10**
Waynesboro Pa., U.S.A. 39°45N 77°35W **81 F15**
Waynesboro Va., U.S.A. 38°4N 78°53W **81 F14**
Waynesburg U.S.A. 39°54N 80°11W **81 F13**
Waynesville U.S.A. 35°28N 82°58W **85 D13**
Waynoka U.S.A. 36°35N 98°53W **84 C5**
Wazirabad Pakistan 32°30N 74°8E **42 C6**
Waziristan Pakistan 33°0N 70°0E **42 C4**
We Indonesia 5°51N 95°18E **36 C1**
Weald, The U.K. 51°4N 0°20E **13 F8**
Wear → U.K. 54°55N 1°23W **12 C6**
Weatherford Okla., U.S.A. 35°32N 98°43W **84 D5**
Weatherford Tex., U.S.A. 32°46N 97°48W **84 E6**
Weaverville U.S.A. 40°44N 122°56W **76 F2**
Webb City U.S.A. 37°9N 94°28W **80 G6**
Webequie Canada 52°59N 87°21W **72 B2**
Webster Mass., U.S.A. 42°3N 71°53W **83 D13**
Webster N.Y., U.S.A. 43°13N 77°26W **82 C7**
Webster S. Dak., U.S.A. 45°20N 97°31W **80 C5**
Webster City U.S.A. 42°28N 93°49W **80 D7**
Webster Springs U.S.A. 38°29N 80°25W **81 F13**
Weda Indonesia 0°21N 127°50E **37 D7**
Weda, Teluk Indonesia 0°20N 128°0E **37 D7**
Weddell Abyssal Plain S. Ocean 65°0S 20°0W **5 C2**
Weddell I. Falk. Is. 51°50S 61°0W **96 G4**
Weddell Sea Antarctica 72°30S 40°0W **5 D1**
Wedderburn Australia 36°26S 143°33E **63 F3**
Wedgeport Canada 43°44N 65°59W **73 D6**
Wee Waa Australia 30°11S 149°26E **63 E4**
Weed U.S.A. 41°25N 122°23W **76 F2**
Weed Heights U.S.A. 38°59N 119°13W **78 G7**
Weedsport U.S.A. 43°2N 76°33W **83 C8**
Weedville U.S.A. 41°17N 78°30W **82 E6**
Weenen S. Africa 28°48S 30°7E **57 C5**
Weerribben △ Neths. 52°47N 5°58E **15 B5**
Weert Neths. 51°15N 5°43E **15 C5**
Wei He → Hebei, China 36°10N 115°45E **32 F8**
Wei He → Shaanxi, China 34°38N 110°15E **32 G6**
Weichang China 41°58N 117°49E **33 D9**
Weichuan China 34°20N 113°59E **32 G7**
Weiden Germany 49°41N 12°10E **16 D7**
Weifang China 36°44N 119°7E **33 F10**
Weihai China 37°30N 122°6E **33 F12**
Weihui China 35°25N 114°3E **32 G8**
Weinan China 34°31N 109°29E **32 G5**
Weining China 26°50N 104°17E **34 D5**
Weipa Australia 12°40S 141°50E **62 A3**
Weir → Australia 28°20S 149°50E **63 D4**
Weir → Canada 56°54N 93°21W **71 B10**
Weir River Canada 56°49N 94°6W **71 B10**
Weirton U.S.A. 40°24N 80°35W **82 F4**
Weiser U.S.A. 44°15N 116°58W **76 D5**
Weishan Shandong, China 34°47N 117°5E **33 G9**
Weishan Yunnan, China 25°12N 100°20E **34 E3**
Weishan Hu China 34°35N 117°14E **33 G9**
Weixi China 27°10N 99°1E **34 D2**
Weixin China 27°48N 105°3E **34 D5**
Weiyuan Gansu, China 35°7N 104°10E **32 G3**
Weiyuan Sichuan, China 29°35N 104°36E **34 C5**
Weizhou Dao China 21°0N 109°5E **34 G7**
Wejherowo Poland 54°35N 18°12E **17 A10**
Wekusko L. Canada 54°40N 99°50W **71 C9**
Welch U.S.A. 37°26N 81°35W **81 G13**
Welford △ Australia 25°5S 143°16E **62 D3**
Weligama Sri Lanka 5°58N 80°25E **45 M5**
Welkom S. Africa 28°0S 26°46E **56 C4**
Welland Canada 43°0N 79°15W **82 D5**
Welland → U.K. 52°51N 0°5W **13 E7**
Wellawaya Sri Lanka 6°44N 81°6E **45 L5**
Wellesley Is. Australia 16°42S 139°30E **62 B2**
Wellesley Islands ◇ Australia 16°32S 139°23E **62 B2**
Wellingborough U.K. 52°19N 0°41W **13 E7**
Wellington Australia 32°35S 148°59E **63 E4**
Wellington Canada 43°57N 77°20W **82 C7**
Wellington N.Z. 41°19S 174°46E **59 D5**
Wellington S. Africa 33°38S 19°1E **56 D2**
Wellington Somst., U.K. 50°58N 3°13W **13 G4**
Wellington Telford & Wrekin, U.K. 52°42N 2°30W **13 E5**
Wellington Colo., U.S.A. 40°42N 105°0W **76 F11**
Wellington Kans., U.S.A. 37°16N 97°24W **80 G5**
Wellington Nev., U.S.A. 38°45N 119°23W **78 G7**
Wellington Ohio, U.S.A. 41°10N 82°13W **82 E2**
Wellington Tex., U.S.A. 34°51N 100°13W **84 D4**
Wellington, I. Chile 49°30S 75°0W **96 F2**
Wellington, L. Australia 38°6S 147°20E **63 F4**
Wellington Chan. Canada 75°0N 93°0W **69 C13**
Wells U.K. 51°13N 2°39W **13 F5**
Wells Maine, U.S.A. 43°20N 70°35W **83 C14**
Wells N.Y., U.S.A. 43°24N 74°17W **83 C10**
Wells Nev., U.S.A. 41°7N 114°58W **76 F6**
Wells, L. Australia 26°44S 123°15E **61 E3**
Wells, Mt. Australia 17°25S 127°8E **60 C4**
Wells Gray Canada 52°30N 120°15W **70 C4**
Wells-next-the-Sea U.K. 52°57N 0°51E **12 E8**
Wells River U.S.A. 44°9N 72°4W **83 B12**
Wellsboro U.S.A. 41°45N 77°18W **82 E7**
Wellsburg U.S.A. 40°16N 80°37W **82 F4**
Wellsville N.Y., U.S.A. 42°7N 77°57W **82 D7**
Wellsville Ohio, U.S.A. 40°36N 80°39W **82 F4**
Wellsville Utah, U.S.A. 41°38N 111°56W **76 F8**
Wellton U.S.A. 32°40N 114°8W **77 K6**
Wels Austria 48°9N 14°1E **16 D8**
Welshpool U.K. 52°39N 3°8W **13 E4**
Welwyn Garden City U.K. 51°48N 0°12W **13 F7**
Wem U.K. 52°52N 2°44W **12 E5**
Wemindji Canada 53°0N 78°49W **72 B4**
Wemyss Canada 44°52N 76°23W **83 B8**
Wen Xian Gansu, China 32°43N 104°36E **32 H3**

Wen Xian Henan, China 34°55N 113°5E **32 G7**
Wenatchee U.S.A. 47°25N 120°19W **76 C3**
Wenchang China 19°38N 110°42E **38 C8**
Wencheng China 27°46N 120°4E **35 D13**
Wenchi Ghana 7°46N 2°8W **52 G5**
Wenchow = Wenzhou China 28°0N 120°38E **35 D13**
Wenchuan China 31°22N 103°35E **32 H3**
Wenden U.S.A. 33°49N 113°33W **79 M13**
Wendeng China 37°15N 122°5E **33 F12**
Wendesi Indonesia 2°30S 134°17E **37 E8**
Wendover U.S.A. 40°44N 114°2W **76 F6**
Weng'an China 27°5N 107°25E **34 D6**
Wengcheng China 24°22N 113°50E **35 E9**
Wengyuan China 24°20N 114°9E **35 E10**
Wenling China 28°21N 121°20E **35 C13**
Wenlock → Australia 12°2S 141°55E **62 A3**
Wenshan China 23°20N 104°18E **34 F5**
Wenshang China 35°45N 116°30E **32 G9**
Wenshui China 37°26N 112°1E **32 F7**
Wensleydale U.K. 54°17N 2°0W **12 C6**
Wensu China 41°15N 80°10E **30 C5**
Wensum → U.K. 52°40N 1°15E **12 E8**
Wentworth Australia 34°2S 141°54E **63 E3**
Wentzel L. Canada 59°2N 114°28W **70 B6**
Wenut Indonesia 3°11S 133°19E **37 E8**
Wenxi China 35°20N 111°10E **32 G6**
Wenzhou China 28°0N 120°38E **35 D13**
Weott U.S.A. 40°20N 123°55W **76 F2**
Wepener S. Africa 29°42S 27°3E **56 C4**
Werda Botswana 25°24S 23°15E **56 C3**
Weri Indonesia 3°10S 132°38E **37 E8**
Werra → Germany 51°24N 9°39E **16 C5**
Werrimull Australia 34°25S 141°38E **63 E3**
Werris Creek Australia 31°18S 150°38E **63 E5**
Weser → Germany 53°36N 8°28E **16 B5**
Weslaco U.S.A. 26°10N 97°58W **84 H6**
Weslemkoon L. Canada 45°2N 77°25W **82 A7**
Wesleyville Canada 49°9N 53°33W **73 C9**
Wesleyville U.S.A. 42°9N 80°1W **82 D4**
Wessel, C. Australia 10°59S 136°46E **62 A2**
Wessel Is. Australia 11°10S 136°45E **62 A2**
Wessex U.K. 51°0N 2°0W **13 F5**
Wessington Springs U.S.A. 44°5N 98°34W **80 C4**
West U.S.A. 31°48N 97°6W **84 F6**
West → U.S.A. 42°52N 72°33W **83 D12**
West Allis U.S.A. 43°1N 88°0W **80 D9**
West Antarctica Antarctica 80°0S 90°0W **5 D15**
West Baines → Australia 15°38S 129°59E **60 C4**
West Bank ■ Asia 32°6N 35°13E **48 C4**
West Bend U.S.A. 43°25N 88°11W **80 D9**
West Bengal = Paschimbanga □ India 23°0N 88°0E **43 H13**
West Berkshire □ U.K. 51°25N 1°17W **13 F6**
West Beskids = Západné Beskydy Europe 49°30N 19°0E **17 D10**
West Branch U.S.A. 44°17N 84°14W **81 C11**
West Branch Susquehanna → U.S.A. 40°53N 76°48W **83 F8**
West Bromwich U.K. 52°32N 1°59W **13 E6**
West Burra U.K. 60°5N 1°21W **11 A7**
West Canada Cr. → U.S.A. 43°1N 74°58W **83 C10**
West Caroline Basin Pac. Oc. 4°0N 138°0E **64 G5**
West Chazy U.S.A. 44°49N 73°28W **83 B11**
West Chester U.S.A. 39°58N 75°36W **83 G9**
West Coast □ Namibia 21°53S 14°14E **56 B1**
West Coast □ S. Africa 33°13S 18°0E **56 D2**
West Columbia U.S.A. 29°9N 95°39W **84 G7**
West Covina U.S.A. 34°4N 117°54W **79 L9**
West Des Moines U.S.A. 41°35N 93°43W **80 E7**
West Dunbartonshire □ U.K. 55°59N 4°30W **11 F4**
West End Bahamas 26°41N 78°58W **88 A4**
West Falkland Falk. Is. 51°40S 60°0W **96 G4**
West Fargo U.S.A. 46°52N 96°54W **80 B5**
West Fiji Basin Pac. Oc. 17°0S 173°0E **64 J9**
West Fjord = Vestfjorden Norway 67°55N 14°0E **8 C16**
West Fork Trinity → U.S.A. 32°48N 96°54W **84 E6**
West Frankfort U.S.A. 37°54N 88°55W **80 G9**
West Grand L. U.S.A. 45°14N 67°51W **81 C20**
West Hartford U.S.A. 41°45N 72°44W **83 E12**
West Haven U.S.A. 41°17N 72°57W **83 E12**
West Hazleton U.S.A. 40°58N 76°0W **83 F9**
West Hurley U.S.A. 41°59N 74°7W **83 E10**
West, I. India 13°35N 92°54E **45 H11**
West Ice Shelf Antarctica 67°0S 85°0E **5 C7**
West Indies Cent. Amer. 15°0N 65°0W **89 D7**
West Jordan U.S.A. 40°36N 111°56W **76 F8**
West Kavango □ Namibia 18°0S 18°30E **56 A2**
West Linn U.S.A. 45°21N 122°36W **78 E4**
West Lorne Canada 42°36N 81°36W **82 D3**
West Lothian □ U.K. 55°54N 3°36W **11 F5**
West MacDonnell △ Australia 23°38S 132°59E **60 D5**
West Mariana Basin Pac. Oc. 15°0N 137°0E **64 F5**
West Memphis U.S.A. 35°8N 90°10W **85 D9**
West Midlands □ U.K. 52°26N 2°0W **13 E6**
West Mifflin U.S.A. 40°21N 79°52W **82 F5**
West Milford U.S.A. 41°8N 74°22W **83 E10**
West Milton U.S.A. 41°1N 76°50W **82 E8**
West Monroe U.S.A. 32°31N 92°9W **84 E8**
West Newton U.S.A. 40°14N 79°46W **82 F5**
West Odessa U.S.A. 31°50N 102°30W **84 F3**
West Palm Beach U.S.A. 26°43N 80°3W **85 H14**
West Plains U.S.A. 36°44N 91°51W **80 G8**
West Point Miss., U.S.A. 33°36N 88°39W **85 E10**
West Point N.Y., U.S.A. 41°24N 73°58W **83 E11**
West Point Nebr., U.S.A. 41°51N 96°43W **80 E5**
West Point Va., U.S.A. 37°32N 76°48W **81 G15**
West Pt. = Ouest, Pte. de l' Canada 49°52N 64°40W **73 C7**
West Pt. Australia 35°1S 135°56E **63 F2**
West Road → Canada 53°18N 122°53W **70 C4**

West Rutland U.S.A. 43°36N 73°3W **83 C11**
West Schelde = Westerschelde → Neths. 51°25N 3°25E **15 C3**
West Seneca U.S.A. 42°51N 78°48W **82 D6**
West Siberian Plain Russia 62°0N 75°0E **24 B9**
West Sussex □ U.K. 50°55N 0°30W **13 G7**
West-Terschelling Neths. 53°22N 5°13E **15 A5**
West Valley City U.S.A. 40°42N 111°58W **76 F8**
West Virginia □ U.S.A. 38°45N 80°30W **81 F13**
West-Vlaanderen □ Belgium 51°0N 3°0E **15 D2**
West Walker → U.S.A. 38°54N 119°9W **78 G7**
West Wyalong Australia 33°56S 147°10E **63 E4**
West Yellowstone U.S.A. 44°40N 111°6W **76 D8**
West Yorkshire □ U.K. 53°45N 1°40W **12 D6**
Westall, Pt. Australia 32°55S 134°4E **63 E1**
Westbrook U.S.A. 43°41N 70°22W **81 D18**
Westbury Australia 41°30S 146°51E **63 G4**
Westby U.S.A. 48°52N 104°3W **76 B2**
Westend U.S.A. 35°42N 117°24W **79 K9**
Westerland Germany 54°54N 8°17E **16 A5**
Westerly U.S.A. 41°22N 71°50W **83 E13**
Western Australia □ Australia 25°0S 118°0E **61 E2**
Western Cape □ S. Africa 34°0S 20°0E **56 D3**
Western Dvina = Daugava → Latvia 57°4N 24°3E **9 H21**
Western Ghats India 14°0N 75°0E **45 H2**
Western Isles = Eilean Siar □ U.K. 57°30N 7°10W **11 D1**
Western Sahara ■ Africa 25°0N 13°0W **52 D3**
Western Samoa = Samoa ■ Pac. Oc. 14°0S 172°0W **59 b**
Western Sierra Madre = Madre Occidental, Sierra Mexico 27°0N 107°0W **86 B3**
Westernport U.S.A. 39°29N 79°3W **81 F14**
Westerschelde → Neths. 51°25N 3°25E **15 C3**
Westerwald Germany 50°38N 7°56E **16 C4**
Westfield Mass., U.S.A. 42°7N 72°45W **83 D12**
Westfield N.Y., U.S.A. 42°20N 79°35W **82 D5**
Westfield Pa., U.S.A. 41°55N 77°32W **82 E7**
Westhill U.K. 57°9N 2°19W **11 D6**
Westhope U.S.A. 48°55N 101°1W **80 A3**
Westland □ N.Z. 43°16S 170°16E **59 E2**
Westland Bight N.Z. 42°55S 170°5E **59 E3**
Westlock Canada 54°9N 113°55W **70 C6**
Westmar Australia 27°55S 149°44E **63 D4**
Westmeath □ Ireland 53°33N 7°34W **10 C4**
Westminster Calif., U.S.A. 33°45N 118°0W **79 M8**
Westminster Colo., U.S.A. 39°50N 105°2W **76 G11**
Westminster Md., U.S.A. 39°34N 76°59W **81 F15**
Westmont U.S.A. 40°19N 78°58W **82 F6**
Westmoreland Barbados 13°13N 59°37W **89 g**
Westmorland U.S.A. 33°2N 115°37W **79 M11**
Weston Oreg., U.S.A. 45°49N 118°26W **76 D4**
Weston W. Va., U.S.A. 39°2N 80°28W **81 F13**
Weston I. Canada 52°33N 79°36W **72 B4**
Weston-super-Mare U.K. 51°21N 2°58W **13 F5**
Westover U.S.A. 40°45N 78°40W **82 F6**
Westport Canada 44°40N 76°25W **83 B8**
Westport Ireland 53°48N 9°31W **10 C2**
Westport N.Z. 41°46S 171°37E **59 D3**
Westport N.Y., U.S.A. 44°11N 73°26W **83 B11**
Westport Oreg., U.S.A. 46°8N 123°23W **78 D3**
Westport Wash., U.S.A. 46°53N 124°6W **78 D2**
Westray Canada 53°36N 101°24W **71 C8**
Westray U.K. 59°18N 3°0W **11 B5**
Westree Canada 47°26N 81°34W **72 C3**
Westville U.S.A. 39°8N 120°42W **78 F6**
Westwood U.S.A. 40°18N 121°0W **76 F3**
Wetar Indonesia 7°48S 126°30E **37 F7**
Wetaskiwin Canada 52°55N 113°24W **70 C6**
Wete Tanzania 5°4S 39°43E **54 F7**
Wetherby U.K. 53°56N 1°23W **12 D6**
Wethersfield U.S.A. 41°42N 72°40W **83 E12**
Wetteren Belgium 51°0N 3°53E **15 D3**
Wetzlar Germany 50°32N 8°31E **16 C5**
Wewoka U.S.A. 35°9N 96°30W **84 D6**
Wexford Ireland 52°20N 6°28W **10 D5**
Wexford □ Ireland 52°20N 6°25W **10 D5**
Wexford Harbour Ireland 52°20N 6°25W **10 D5**
Weyburn Canada 49°40N 103°50W **71 D8**
Weymouth Canada 44°30N 66°1W **73 D6**
Weymouth U.K. 50°37N 2°28W **13 G5**
Weymouth U.S.A. 42°13N 70°58W **83 D14**
Weymouth, C. Australia 12°37S 143°27E **62 A3**
Wha Ti Canada 63°8N 117°16W **68 E8**
Whakaari N.Z. 37°30S 177°13E **59 B6**
Whakatane N.Z. 37°57S 177°1E **59 B6**
Whale = Baleine → Canada 58°15N 67°40W **73 A6**
Whale B. Burma 11°37N 98°38E **39 G2**
Whale Cove Canada 62°10N 92°34W **71 A10**
Whales, B. of Antarctica 78°0S 160°0W **5 D12**
Whalsay U.K. 60°22N 0°59W **11 A8**
Whangamata N.Z. 37°12S 175°53E **59 B6**
Whangamomona N.Z. 39°8S 174°44E **59 C5**
Whanganui □ N.Z. 39°17S 174°53E **59 C5**
Whangarei N.Z. 35°43S 174°21E **59 A5**
Whangarei Harb. N.Z. 35°45S 174°28E **59 A5**
Wharekauri = Chatham Is. Pac. Oc. 44°0S 176°40W **64 M10**
Wharfe → U.K. 53°51N 1°9W **12 D6**
Wharfedale U.K. 54°6N 2°1W **12 C5**
Wharton N.J., U.S.A. 40°54N 74°35W **83 F10**
Wharton Pa., U.S.A. 41°31N 78°1W **82 E6**
Wharton Tex., U.S.A. 29°19N 96°6W **84 G6**
Wharton Basin Ind. Oc. 22°0S 99°0E **64 K1**
Wheatland Calif., U.S.A. 39°1N 121°25W **78 F5**
Wheatland Wyo., U.S.A. 42°3N 104°58W **76 E11**
Wheatley Canada 42°6N 82°27W **82 D2**
Wheaton Md., U.S.A. 39°3N 77°3W **81 F15**
Wheaton Minn., U.S.A. 45°48N 96°30W **80 C5**
Wheelbarrow Pk. U.S.A. 37°26N 116°5W **78 H10**
Wheeler Oreg., U.S.A. 45°41N 123°53W **76 D2**
Wheeler Tex., U.S.A. 35°27N 100°16W **84 D4**
Wheeler → Canada 57°2N 67°13W **73 A6**

Wheeler L. U.S.A. 34°48N 87°23W **85 D11**
Wheeler Pk. N. Mex., U.S.A. 36°34N 105°25W **77 H11**
Wheeler Pk. Nev., U.S.A. 38°57N 114°15W **76 G6**
Wheeler Ridge U.S.A. 35°0N 118°57W **79 L8**
Wheelersburg U.S.A. 38°44N 82°51W **81 F12**
Wheeling U.S.A. 40°4N 80°43W **82 F4**
Whernside U.K. 54°14N 2°24W **12 C5**
Whiddy I. Ireland 51°41N 9°31W **10 E2**
Whim Creek Australia 20°50S 117°49E **60 D2**
Whiskey Jack L. Canada 58°23N 101°55W **71 B8**
Whiskeytown-Shasta-Trinity △ U.S.A. 40°45N 122°15W **76 F2**
Whistleduck Cr. → Australia 20°15S 135°18E **62 C2**
Whistler Canada 50°7N 122°58W **70 C4**
Whitby Canada 43°52N 78°56W **82 C6**
Whitby U.K. 54°29N 0°37W **12 C7**
White → Ark., U.S.A. 33°57N 91°5W **84 E9**
White → Ind., U.S.A. 38°25N 87°45W **80 F10**
White → S. Dak., U.S.A. 43°42N 99°27W **80 D4**
White → Tex., U.S.A. 33°14N 100°56W **84 E4**
White → Utah, U.S.A. 40°4N 109°41W **76 F9**
White → Vt., U.S.A. 43°37N 72°20W **83 C12**
White → Wash., U.S.A. 47°12N 122°15W **78 C4**
White, L. Australia 21°9S 128°56E **60 D4**
White B. Canada 50°0N 56°35W **73 C8**
White Bird U.S.A. 45°46N 116°18W **76 D5**
White Butte U.S.A. 46°23N 103°18W **80 B2**
White City U.S.A. 42°26N 122°51W **76 E2**
White Cliffs Australia 30°50S 143°10E **63 E3**
White Hall U.S.A. 39°26N 90°24W **80 F8**
White Haven U.S.A. 41°4N 75°47W **83 E9**
White Horse, Vale of U.K. 51°37N 1°30W **13 F6**
White I. = Whakaari N.Z. 37°30S 177°13E **59 B6**
White L. Canada 45°18N 76°31W **83 A8**
White L. U.S.A. 29°44N 92°30W **84 G8**
White Lake Canada 45°21N 76°29W **83 A8**
White Mountain Peak U.S.A. 37°38N 118°15W **78 H8**
White Mts. Calif., U.S.A. 37°30N 118°15W **78 H8**
White Mts. N.H., U.S.A. 44°15N 71°15W **83 B13**
White Mts. △ Australia 20°43S 145°12E **62 C4**
White Nile = Nil el Abyad → Sudan 15°38N 32°31E **53 E12**
White Otter L. Canada 49°5N 91°55W **72 C1**
White Pass U.S.A. 46°38N 121°24W **78 D5**
White Plains U.S.A. 41°2N 73°46W **83 E11**
White River Canada 48°35N 85°20W **72 C2**
White River U.S.A. 43°34N 100°45W **80 D4**
White Rock Canada 49°2N 122°48W **78 A4**
White Rock U.S.A. 35°50N 106°12W **77 J10**
White Rocks Nat. Recr. Area △ U.S.A. 43°22N 72°55W **83 C12**
White Russia = Belarus ■ Europe 53°30N 27°0E **17 B13**
White Sands △ U.S.A. 32°46N 106°20W **77 K10**
White Sea = Beloye More Russia 66°30N 38°0E **18 A6**
White Sulphur Springs Mont., U.S.A. 46°33N 110°54W **76 C8**
White Sulphur Springs W. Va., U.S.A. 37°48N 80°18W **81 G13**
White Swan U.S.A. 46°23N 120°44W **78 D6**
Whitecliffs N.Z. 43°26S 171°55E **59 E3**
Whitecourt Canada 54°10N 115°45W **70 C5**
Whiteface Mt. U.S.A. 44°22N 73°54W **83 B11**
Whitefield U.S.A. 44°23N 71°37W **83 B13**
Whitefish U.S.A. 48°25N 114°20W **76 B6**
Whitefish B. U.S.A. 46°40N 84°55W **72 C3**
Whitefish L. Canada 62°41N 106°48W **71 A7**
Whitefish Pt. U.S.A. 46°45N 84°59W **81 B11**
Whitegull, L. = Goélands, L. aux Canada 55°27N 64°17W **73 A7**
Whitehall Mich., U.S.A. 43°24N 86°21W **80 D10**
Whitehall Mont., U.S.A. 45°52N 112°6W **76 C7**
Whitehall N.Y., U.S.A. 43°33N 73°24W **83 C11**
Whitehall Wis., U.S.A. 44°22N 91°19W **80 C8**
Whitehaven U.K. 54°33N 3°35W **12 C4**
Whitehorse Canada 60°43N 135°3W **70 A1**
Whitemark Australia 40°7S 148°3E **63 G4**
Whiteriver U.S.A. 33°50N 109°58W **77 K9**
Whitesand → Canada 60°9N 115°45W **70 A5**
Whitesands S. Africa 34°23S 20°50E **56 D3**
Whitesboro N.Y., U.S.A. 43°7N 75°18W **83 C9**
Whitesboro Tex., U.S.A. 33°39N 96°54W **84 E6**
Whiteshell △ Canada 50°0N 95°40W **71 D10**
Whiteville U.S.A. 34°20N 78°42W **85 D15**
Whitewater U.S.A. 42°50N 88°44W **80 D9**
Whitewater Baldy U.S.A. 33°20N 108°39W **77 K9**
Whitewater L. Canada 50°50N 89°10W **72 B2**
Whitewood Australia 21°28S 143°30E **62 C3**
Whitewood Canada 50°20N 102°20W **71 C8**
Whithorn U.K. 54°44N 4°26W **11 G4**
Whitianga N.Z. 36°47S 175°41E **59 B5**
Whitman U.S.A. 42°5N 70°56W **83 D14**
Whitney Canada 45°31N 78°14W **82 A6**
Whitney, Mt. U.S.A. 36°35N 118°18W **78 J8**
Whitney Point U.S.A. 42°20N 75°58W **83 D9**
Whitstable U.K. 51°21N 1°3E **13 F9**
Whitsunday I. Australia 20°15S 149°4E **62 b**
Whitsunday Islands △ Australia 20°15S 149°0E **62 b**
Whittier U.S.A. 60°47N 148°41W **74 C10**
Whittlesea Australia 37°27S 145°9E **63 F4**
Wholdaia L. Canada 60°43N 104°20W **71 A8**
Whyalla Australia 33°2S 137°30E **63 E2**
Wiang Kosai △ Thailand 17°54N 99°29E **38 D2**
Wiang Sa Thailand 18°34N 100°46E **38 C3**
Wiarton Canada 44°40N 81°10W **82 B3**
Wiay U.K. 57°24N 7°13W **11 D1**
Wibaux U.S.A. 46°59N 104°11W **76 B2**
Wichian Buri Thailand 15°39N 101°7E **38 E3**
Wichita U.S.A. 37°42N 97°20W **80 G5**
Wichita Falls U.S.A. 33°54N 98°30W **84 E5**
Wick U.K. 58°26N 3°5W **11 C5**

Wickenburg U.S.A. 33°58N 112°44W **77 K7**
Wickepin Australia 32°50S 117°30E **61 F2**
Wickham Australia 20°42S 117°11E **60 D2**
Wickham, C. Australia 39°35S 143°57E **63 F3**
Wickliffe U.S.A. 41°36N 81°28W **82 E3**
Wicklow Ireland 52°59N 6°3W **10 D5**
Wicklow □ Ireland 52°57N 6°25W **10 D5**
Wicklow Hd. Ireland 52°58N 6°0W **10 D6**
Wicklow Mts. Ireland 52°58N 6°26W **10 D5**
Wicklow Mts. △ Ireland 53°6N 6°21W **10 C5**
Widgeegoara Cr. ➔
  Australia 28°51S 146°34E **63 D4**
Widgiemooltha Australia 31°30S 121°34E **61 F3**
Widnes U.K. 53°23N 2°45W **12 D5**
Wieluń Poland 51°15N 18°34E **17 C10**
Wiener Neustadt Austria 47°49N 16°16E **16 E9**
Wiesbaden Germany 50°4N 8°14E **16 C5**
Wigan U.K. 53°33N 2°38W **12 D5**
Wiggins Colo., U.S.A. 40°14N 104°4W **76 F11**
Wiggins Miss., U.S.A. 30°51N 89°8W **85 F10**
Wight, I. of U.K. 50°41N 1°17W **13 G6**
Wigston U.K. 52°35N 1°6W **13 E6**
Wigtown U.K. 54°53N 4°27W **11 G4**
Wigtown B. U.K. 54°46N 4°15W **11 G4**
Wik and Wikway People ◇
  Australia 13°55S 142°28E **62 A3**
Wilber U.S.A. 40°29N 96°58W **80 E5**
Wilberforce Canada 45°2N 78°13W **82 A6**
Wilberforce, C. Australia 11°54S 136°35E **62 A2**
Wilburton U.S.A. 34°55N 95°19W **84 D7**
Wilcannia Australia 31°30S 143°26E **63 E3**
Wilcox U.S.A. 41°35N 78°41W **82 E6**
Wildomar U.S.A. 33°36N 117°16W **79 M9**
Wildrose U.S.A. 36°14N 117°11W **79 J9**
Wildspitze Austria 46°53N 10°53E **16 E6**
Wilge ➔ S. Africa 27°3S 28°20E **57 C4**
Wilhelm II Coast Antarctica 68°0S 90°0E **5 C7**
Wilhelmshaven Germany 53°31N 8°7E **16 B5**
Wilhelmstal Namibia 21°58S 16°21E **56 B2**
Wilis Indonesia 7°51S 111°48E **37 G15**
Wilkes-Barre U.S.A. 41°15N 75°53W **83 E9**
Wilkes Land Antarctica 69°0S 120°0E **5 D9**
Wilkie Canada 52°27N 108°42W **71 C7**
Wilkins Ice Shelf
  Antarctica 70°30S 72°0W **5 C17**
Wilkinsburg U.S.A. 40°26N 79°52W **82 F5**
Wilkinson Lakes
  Australia 29°40S 132°39E **61 E5**
Willandra Creek ➔
  Australia 33°22S 145°52E **63 E4**
Willapa B. U.S.A. 46°40N 124°0W **78 D3**
Willapa Hills U.S.A. 46°35N 123°25W **78 D3**
Willard U.S.A. 41°3N 82°44W **82 E2**
Willare Bridge Roadhouse
  Australia 17°43S 123°38E **60 C3**
Willcox U.S.A. 32°15N 109°50W **77 K9**
Willemstad Curaçao 12°5N 68°55W **89 D6**
William ➔ Canada 59°8N 109°19W **71 B7**
William 'Bill' Dannelly Res.
  U.S.A. 32°6N 87°24W **85 E11**
William Creek Australia 28°58S 136°22E **63 D2**
Williams Australia 33°2S 116°52E **61 F2**
Williams Ariz., U.S.A. 35°15N 112°11W **77 J7**
Williams Calif., U.S.A. 39°9N 122°9W **78 F4**
Williams Harbour
  Canada 52°33N 55°47W **73 B8**
Williams Lake Canada 52°10N 122°10W **70 C4**
Williamsburg Ky.,
  U.S.A. 36°44N 84°10W **81 G11**
Williamsburg Pa., U.S.A. 40°28N 78°12W **82 F6**
Williamsburg Va.,
  U.S.A. 37°16N 76°43W **81 G15**
Williamson N.Y., U.S.A. 43°14N 77°11W **82 C7**
Williamson W. Va.,
  U.S.A. 37°41N 82°17W **81 G12**
Williamsport U.S.A. 41°15N 77°1W **82 E7**
Williamston U.S.A. 35°51N 77°4W **85 D16**
Williamstown Ky.,
  U.S.A. 38°38N 84°34W **81 F11**
Williamstown Mass.,
  U.S.A. 42°43N 73°12W **83 D11**
Williamstown N.Y.,
  U.S.A. 43°26N 75°53W **83 C9**
Willimantic U.S.A. 41°43N 72°13W **83 E12**
Willingboro U.S.A. 40°3N 74°54W **81 E16**
Williston S. Africa 31°20S 20°53E **56 D3**
Williston Fla., U.S.A. 29°23N 82°27W **85 G13**
Williston N. Dak., U.S.A. 48°9N 103°37W **80 A2**
Williston L. Canada 56°0N 124°0W **70 B4**
Willits U.S.A. 39°25N 123°21W **76 G2**
Willmar U.S.A. 45°7N 95°3W **80 C6**
Willmore Wilderness ○
  Canada 53°45N 119°30W **70 C5**
Willoughby U.S.A. 41°39N 81°24W **82 E3**
Willow Bunch Canada 49°20N 105°35W **71 D7**
Willow L. ➔ Canada 62°10N 119°8W **70 A5**
Willow Wall, The China 42°10N 122°0E **33 C12**
Willowick U.S.A. 41°38N 81°28W **82 E3**
Willowlake ➔ Canada 62°42N 123°8W **70 A4**
Willowmore S. Africa 33°15S 23°30E **56 D3**
Willows U.S.A. 39°31N 122°12W **78 F4**
Willowvale = Gatyana
  S. Africa 32°16S 28°31E **57 D4**
Wills, L. Australia 21°25S 128°51E **60 D4**
Wills Cr. ➔ Australia 22°43S 140°2E **62 C3**
Willsboro U.S.A. 44°21N 73°24W **83 B11**
Willunga Australia 35°15S 138°30E **63 F2**
Wilmington Australia 32°39S 138°7E **63 E2**
Wilmington Del., U.S.A. 39°45N 75°33W **81 F16**
Wilmington N.C.,
  U.S.A. 34°14N 77°55W **85 D16**
Wilmington Ohio,
  U.S.A. 39°27N 83°50W **81 F12**
Wilmington Vt., U.S.A. 42°52N 72°52W **83 D12**
Wilmslow U.K. 53°19N 2°13W **12 D5**
Wilpattu △ Sri Lanka 8°20N 79°50E **45 K4**
Wilpena Cr. ➔ Australia 31°25S 139°29E **63 E2**
Wilsall U.S.A. 45°59N 110°38W **76 D8**
Wilson N.C., U.S.A. 35°44N 77°55W **85 D16**
Wilson N.Y., U.S.A. 43°19N 78°50W **82 C6**

Wilson Pa., U.S.A. 40°41N 75°15W **83 F9**
Wilson ➔ Australia 16°48S 128°16E **60 C4**
Wilson Bluff Australia 31°41S 129°0E **61 F4**
Wilson Inlet Australia 35°0S 117°22E **61 G2**
Wilsons Promontory
  Australia 38°59S 146°23E **63 F4**
Wilton U.S.A. 47°10N 100°47W **80 B3**
Wilton ➔ Australia 14°45S 134°33E **62 A1**
Wiltshire □ U.K. 51°18N 1°53W **13 F6**
Wiltz Lux. 49°57N 5°55E **15 E5**
Wiluna Australia 26°36S 120°14E **61 E3**
Wimborne Minster U.K. 50°48N 1°59W **13 G6**
Wimmera ➔ Australia 36°8S 141°58E **63 F3**
Winburg S. Africa 28°30S 27°2E **56 C4**
Winchendon U.S.A. 42°41N 72°3W **83 D12**
Winchester U.K. 51°4N 1°18W **13 F6**
Winchester Idaho,
  U.S.A. 46°14N 116°38W **76 C5**
Winchester Ind., U.S.A. 40°10N 84°59W **81 E11**
Winchester Ky., U.S.A. 37°59N 84°11W **81 G11**
Winchester N.H., U.S.A. 42°46N 72°23W **83 D12**
Winchester Tenn., U.S.A. 35°11N 86°7W **85 D11**
Winchester Va., U.S.A. 39°11N 78°10W **81 F14**
Wind ➔ U.S.A. 43°12N 108°12W **76 E9**
Wind Cave △ U.S.A. 43°32N 103°17W **80 D2**
Wind River Range
  U.S.A. 43°0N 109°30W **76 E9**
Windamere, L. Australia 32°48S 149°51E **63 B4**
Windau = Ventspils
  Latvia 57°25N 21°32E **9 H19**
Windber U.S.A. 40°14N 78°50W **82 F6**
Winder U.S.A. 34°0N 83°45W **85 D13**
Windermere U.K. 54°23N 2°55W **12 C5**
Windhoek Namibia 22°35S 17°4E **56 B2**
Windidda ◇ Australia 26°23S 122°12E **61 E3**
Windjana Gorge △
  Australia 17°51S 125°0E **60 C3**
Windom U.S.A. 43°52N 95°7W **80 D6**
Windorah Australia 25°24S 142°36E **62 D3**
Windrush ➔ U.K. 51°43N 1°24W **13 F6**
Windsor Australia 33°37S 150°50E **63 E5**
Windsor N.S., Canada 44°59N 64°5W **73 D7**
Windsor Ont., Canada 42°18N 83°0W **82 D2**
Windsor U.K. 51°29N 0°36W **13 F7**
Windsor Calif., U.S.A. 38°33N 122°49W **78 G4**
Windsor Colo., U.S.A. 40°29N 104°54W **76 F11**
Windsor Conn., U.S.A. 41°50N 72°39W **83 E12**
Windsor Mo., U.S.A. 38°32N 93°31W **80 F7**
Windsor N.Y., U.S.A. 42°5N 75°37W **83 D9**
Windsor Vt., U.S.A. 43°29N 72°24W **83 C12**
Windsor & Maidenhead □
  U.K. 51°29N 0°40W **13 F7**
Windsorton S. Africa 28°16S 24°44E **56 C3**
Windward Is. W. Indies 13°0N 61°0W **89 D7**
Windward Passage = Vientos,
  Paso de los Caribbean 20°0N 74°0W **89 C5**
Winefred L. Canada 55°30N 110°30W **71 B6**
Winfield U.S.A. 37°15N 96°59W **80 G5**
Wingate Mts. Australia 14°25S 130°40E **60 B5**
Wingellina = Irrunytju
  Australia 26°3S 128°56E **61 E4**
Wingham Australia 31°48S 152°22E **63 E5**
Wingham Canada 43°55N 81°20W **82 C3**
Winisk ➔ Canada 55°17N 85°5W **72 A2**
Winisk L. Canada 52°55N 87°22W **72 B2**
Wink U.S.A. 31°45N 103°9W **84 F3**
Winkler Canada 49°10N 97°56W **71 D9**
Winlock U.S.A. 46°30N 122°56W **78 D4**
Winneba Ghana 5°25N 0°36W **52 G5**
Winnebago, L. U.S.A. 44°0N 88°26W **80 D9**
Winnecke Cr. ➔
  Australia 18°35S 131°34E **60 C5**
Winnemucca U.S.A. 40°58N 117°44W **76 F5**
Winnemucca L. U.S.A. 40°7N 119°21W **76 F4**
Winner U.S.A. 43°22N 99°52W **80 D4**
Winnett U.S.A. 47°0N 108°21W **76 C9**
Winnfield U.S.A. 31°56N 92°38W **84 F8**
Winnibigoshish, L.
  U.S.A. 47°27N 94°13W **80 B6**
Winnipeg Canada 49°54N 97°9W **71 D9**
Winnipeg ➔ Canada 50°38N 96°19W **71 C9**
Winnipeg, L. Canada 52°0N 97°0W **71 C9**
Winnipeg Beach Canada 50°30N 96°58W **71 C9**
Winnipegosis Canada 51°39N 99°55W **71 C9**
Winnipegosis L. Canada 52°30N 100°0W **71 C9**
Winnipesaukee, L.
  U.S.A. 43°38N 71°21W **83 C13**
Winnisquam L. U.S.A. 43°33N 71°31W **83 C13**
Winnsboro La., U.S.A. 32°10N 91°43W **84 E9**
Winnsboro S.C., U.S.A. 34°23N 81°5W **85 D14**
Winnsboro Tex., U.S.A. 32°58N 95°17W **84 E7**
Winokapau, L. Canada 53°15N 62°50W **73 B7**
Winona Minn., U.S.A. 44°3N 91°39W **80 C8**
Winona Miss., U.S.A. 33°29N 89°44W **85 E10**
Winooski U.S.A. 44°29N 73°11W **83 B11**
Winooski ➔ U.S.A. 44°32N 73°17W **83 B11**
Winschoten Neths. 53°9N 7°3E **15 A7**
Winsford U.K. 53°12N 2°31W **12 D5**
Winslow = Bainbridge Island
  U.S.A. 47°38N 122°32W **78 C4**
Winslow U.S.A. 35°2N 110°42W **77 J8**
Winsted U.S.A. 41°55N 73°4W **83 E11**
Winston-Salem U.S.A. 36°6N 80°15W **85 C14**
Winter Garden U.S.A. 28°34N 81°35W **85 G14**
Winter Haven U.S.A. 28°1N 81°44W **85 G14**
Winter Park U.S.A. 28°36N 81°20W **85 G14**
Winterhaven U.S.A. 32°44N 114°38W **79 N12**
Winters U.S.A. 38°32N 121°58W **78 G5**
Winterset U.S.A. 41°20N 94°1W **80 E7**
Wintersville U.S.A. 40°23N 80°42W **82 F4**
Winterswijk Neths. 51°58N 6°43E **15 C6**
Winterthur Switz. 47°30N 8°44E **20 C8**
Winthrop U.S.A. 48°28N 120°10W **76 B3**
Winton Australia 22°24S 143°3E **62 C3**
Winton N.Z. 46°8S 168°20E **59 G2**
Wirlyajarrayi ◇
  Australia 21°45S 132°35E **60 D5**
Wirrulla Australia 32°24S 134°31E **63 E1**
Wisbech U.K. 52°41N 0°9E **13 E8**

Wisconsin □ U.S.A. 44°45N 89°30W **80 C9**
Wisconsin ➔ U.S.A. 43°0N 91°15W **80 D8**
Wisconsin Rapids U.S.A. 44°23N 89°49W **80 C9**
Wisdom U.S.A. 45°37N 113°27W **76 D7**
Wiseman U.S.A. 67°25N 150°6W **74 B9**
Wishaw U.K. 55°46N 3°54W **11 F5**
Wishek U.S.A. 46°16N 99°33W **80 B4**
Wisła Poland 52°24N 18°55E **17 A10**
Wisłany, Zalew Poland 54°20N 19°50E **17 A10**
Wismar Germany 53°54N 11°29E **16 B6**
Wisner U.S.A. 41°59N 96°55W **80 E5**
Witbank = eMalahleni
  S. Africa 25°51S 29°14E **57 C4**
Witches Gorge = Wu Xia
  China 31°2N 110°10E **35 B8**
Witdraai S. Africa 26°58S 20°48E **56 C3**
Witham U.K. 51°48N 0°40E **13 F8**
Witham ➔ U.K. 52°59N 0°2W **12 E7**
Withernsea U.K. 53°44N 0°1E **12 D8**
Witjira △ Australia 26°22S 135°37E **63 D2**
Witless Bay Canada 47°17N 52°50W **73 C9**
Witney U.K. 51°48N 1°28W **13 F6**
Witnossob ➔ Namibia 23°55S 18°45E **56 C3**
Witriver S. Africa 25°0S 31°0E **57 C5**
Wittenberge Germany 53°0N 11°45E **16 B6**
Wittenoom Australia 22°15S 118°20E **60 D2**
Witvlei Namibia 22°23S 18°32E **56 B2**
Wiwon N. Korea 40°54N 126°3E **33 D14**
Wkra ➔ Poland 52°27N 20°44E **17 B11**
Wlingi Indonesia 8°5S 112°25E **37 H15**
Włocławek Poland 52°40N 19°3E **17 B10**
Włodawa Poland 51°33N 23°31E **17 C12**
Wodian China 32°50N 112°35E **32 H7**
Wodonga Australia 36°5S 146°50E **63 F4**
Woinbogoin China 32°51N 98°39E **34 A2**
Wokam Indonesia 5°45S 134°28E **37 F8**
Woking U.K. 51°19N 0°34W **13 F7**
Wokingham U.K. 51°24N 0°49W **13 F7**
Wokingham □ U.K. 51°25N 0°51W **13 F7**
Wolf ➔ Canada 60°17N 132°33W **70 A2**
Wolf Creek U.S.A. 47°0N 112°4W **76 C7**
Wolf L. Canada 60°24N 131°40W **70 A2**
Wolf Point U.S.A. 48°5N 105°39W **76 B11**
Wolfe Creek Crater △
  Australia 19°10S 127°47E **60 C4**
Wolfe I. Canada 44°7N 76°20W **83 B8**
Wolfeboro U.S.A. 43°35N 71°13W **83 C13**
Wolfsberg Austria 46°50N 14°52E **16 E8**
Wolfsburg Germany 52°25N 10°48E **16 B6**
Wolin Poland 53°50N 14°37E **16 B8**
Wollaston, Is. Chile 55°40S 67°30W **96 H3**
Wollaston L. Canada 58°7N 103°10W **71 B8**
Wollaston Lake Canada 58°3N 103°33W **71 B8**
Wollaston Pen. Canada 69°30N 115°0W **68 D9**
Wollongong Australia 34°25S 150°54E **63 E5**
Wolmaransstad S. Africa 27°12S 25°59E **56 C4**
Wolseley S. Africa 33°26S 19°7E **56 D2**
Wolsey U.S.A. 44°25N 98°28W **80 C4**
Wolstenholme, C.
  Canada 62°35N 77°30W **66 C12**
Wolvega Neths. 52°52N 6°0E **15 B6**
Wolverhampton U.K. 52°35N 2°7W **13 E5**
Wondai Australia 26°20S 151°49E **63 D5**
Wongalarroo L. Australia 31°32S 144°0E **63 E3**
Wongan Hills Australia 30°51S 116°37E **61 F2**
Wonju S. Korea 37°22N 127°58E **33 F14**
Wonosari Indonesia 7°58S 110°36E **37 G14**
Wonosobo Indonesia 7°22S 109°54E **37 G13**
Wonowon Canada 56°44N 121°48W **70 B4**
Wŏnsan N. Korea 39°11N 127°27E **33 E14**
Wonthaggi Australia 38°37S 145°37E **63 F4**
Wood Buffalo △ Canada 59°0N 113°41W **70 B6**
Wood Is. Australia 16°24S 123°19E **60 C3**
Wood L. Canada 55°17N 103°17W **71 B8**
Woodah, I. Australia 13°27S 136°10E **62 A2**
Woodbourne U.S.A. 41°46N 74°36W **83 E10**
Woodbridge U.S.A. 52°6N 1°20E **13 E9**
Woodburn Australia 29°6S 153°23E **63 A5**
Woodburn U.S.A. 45°9N 122°51W **76 D2**
Woodenbong Australia 28°24S 152°39E **63 D5**
Woodend Australia 37°20S 144°33E **63 F3**
Woodford Australia 26°58S 152°47E **63 D5**
Woodfords U.S.A. 38°47N 119°50W **78 G7**
Woodlake U.S.A. 36°25N 119°6W **78 J7**
Woodland Calif., U.S.A. 38°41N 121°46W **78 G5**
Woodland Maine, U.S.A. 45°9N 67°25W **81 C20**
Woodland Pa., U.S.A. 41°0N 78°21W **82 F6**
Woodland Wash., U.S.A. 45°54N 122°45W **78 E4**
Woodland Caribou ○
  Canada 51°0N 94°45W **71 C10**
Woodlands, The U.S.A. 30°9N 95°29W **84 F7**
Woodonga Australia 36°10S 146°50E **63 F4**
Woodridge Canada 49°20N 96°9W **71 D9**
Woodroffe, Mt. Australia 26°20S 131°45E **61 E5**
Woods, L. Australia 17°50S 133°30E **62 B1**
Woods, L. of the
  N. Amer. 49°15N 94°45W **71 D10**
Woods Bay Canada 45°8N 79°59W **82 A5**
Woodstock Australia 19°35S 146°50E **62 B4**
Woodstock N.B., Canada 46°11N 67°37W **73 C6**
Woodstock Ont., Canada 43°10N 80°45W **82 C4**
Woodstock U.K. 51°51N 1°20W **13 F6**
Woodstock Ill., U.S.A. 42°19N 88°27W **80 D9**
Woodstock N.Y., U.S.A. 42°4N 74°7W **83 D10**
Woodstock Vt., U.S.A. 43°37N 72°31W **83 C12**
Woodsville U.S.A. 44°9N 72°2W **83 B13**
Woodview Canada 44°35N 78°8W **82 B6**
Woodville N.Z. 40°20S 175°53E **59 D5**
Woodville Miss., U.S.A. 31°6N 91°18W **84 F9**
Woodville Tex., U.S.A. 30°47N 94°25W **84 F7**
Woodward U.S.A. 36°26N 99°24W **84 C5**
Woody ➔ Canada 52°31N 100°51W **71 C8**
Woody I. S. China Sea 16°50N 112°20E **36 A4**
Woolacombe U.K. 51°10N 4°13W **13 F3**
Woolamai, C. Australia 38°30S 145°23E **63 F4**
Wooler U.K. 55°33N 2°1W **12 B5**
Woolgoolga Australia 30°6S 153°11E **63 E5**
Woomera Australia 31°5S 136°56E **63 E2**
Woonsocket R.I., U.S.A. 42°0N 71°31W **83 E13**

Woonsocket S. Dak.,
  U.S.A. 44°3N 98°17W **80 C4**
Wooramel ➔ Australia 25°47S 114°10E **61 E1**
Wooramel Roadhouse
  Australia 25°45S 114°17E **61 E1**
Wooroonooran △
  Australia 16°25S 146°1E **62 B4**
Wooster U.S.A. 40°48N 81°56W **82 F3**
Worcester S. Africa 33°39S 19°27E **56 D2**
Worcester U.K. 52°11N 2°12W **13 E5**
Worcester Mass., U.S.A. 42°16N 71°48W **83 D13**
Worcester N.Y., U.S.A. 42°36N 74°45W **83 D10**
Worcestershire □ U.K. 52°13N 2°10W **13 E5**
Workington U.K. 54°39N 3°33W **12 C4**
Worksop U.K. 53°18N 1°7W **12 D6**
Workum Neths. 52°59N 5°26E **15 B5**
Worland U.S.A. 44°1N 107°57W **76 D10**
Worms Germany 49°37N 8°21E **16 D5**
Worsley Canada 56°31N 119°8W **70 B5**
Wortham U.S.A. 31°47N 96°28W **84 F6**
Worthing Barbados 13°5N 59°35W **89 g**
Worthing U.K. 50°49N 0°21W **13 G7**
Worthington Minn.,
  U.S.A. 43°37N 95°36W **80 D6**
Worthington Pa., U.S.A. 40°50N 79°38W **82 F5**
Wosi Indonesia 0°15S 128°0E **37 E7**
Wotjalum ◇ Australia 16°30S 123°45E **60 C3**
Wotjobaluk ◇ Australia 37°0S 142°0E **63 C3**
Wou-han = Wuhan
  China 30°31N 114°18E **35 B10**
Wousi = Wuxi China 31°33N 120°18E **35 B13**
Wowoni Indonesia 4°5S 123°5E **37 E6**
Wrangel I. = Vrangelya, Ostrov
  Russia 71°0N 180°0E **27 B18**
Wrangell U.S.A. 56°28N 132°23W **70 B2**
Wrangell Mts. U.S.A. 61°30N 142°0W **68 E3**
Wrath, C. U.K. 58°38N 5°1W **11 C3**
Wray U.S.A. 40°5N 102°13W **76 F12**
Wrekin, The U.K. 52°41N 2°32W **13 E5**
Wrens U.S.A. 33°12N 82°23W **85 E13**
Wrexham U.K. 53°3N 3°0W **12 D4**
Wrexham □ U.K. 53°1N 2°58W **12 D5**
Wright Fla., U.S.A. 30°27N 86°38W **85 F11**
Wright Wyo., U.S.A. 43°45N 105°28W **76 E11**
Wright Pt. Canada 43°48N 81°44W **82 C3**
Wrightmyo India 11°47N 92°43E **45 J11**
Wrightson, Mt. U.S.A. 31°42N 110°51W **77 L8**
Wrightwood U.S.A. 34°22N 117°38W **79 L9**
Wrigley Canada 63°16N 123°37W **68 E7**
Wrocław Poland 51°5N 17°5E **17 C9**
Września Poland 52°21N 17°36E **17 B9**
Wu Jiang ➔ China 29°40N 107°20E **34 C6**
Wu Kau Tang China 22°30N 114°14E **31 a**
Wu Xia China 31°2N 110°10E **35 B8**
Wu'an China 36°40N 114°5E **32 F8**
Wubalawun ◇ Australia 15°28S 133°1E **60 C5**
Wubin Australia 30°6S 116°37E **61 F2**
Wubu China 37°28N 110°42E **32 F6**
Wuchang China 44°55N 127°5E **33 B14**
Wucheng China 37°12N 116°20E **32 F9**
Wuchuan Guangdong,
  China 21°33N 110°43E **35 G8**
Wuchuan Guizhou, China 28°25N 108°3E **34 C7**
Wuchuan Nei Monggol Zizhiqu,
  China 41°5N 111°28E **32 D6**
Wuda China 39°29N 106°42E **32 E4**
Wudang Shan China 32°23N 111°2E **35 A8**
Wudi China 37°40N 117°35E **32 F9**
Wuding China 25°24N 102°12E **34 E4**
Wuding He ➔ China 37°2N 110°23E **32 F6**
Wudinna Australia 33°0S 135°22E **63 E2**
Wudongde Dam China 26°20N 102°15E **34 D4**
Wudu China 33°22N 104°54E **32 H3**
Wufeng China 30°12N 110°42E **35 B8**
Wugang China 26°44N 110°35E **35 D8**
Wugong China 34°40N 108°15E **32 G5**
Wuguishan China 22°25N 113°25E **31 a**
Wugullar = Beswick
  Australia 14°34S 132°53E **60 B5**
Wuhai China 39°39N 106°48E **32 E4**
Wuhan China 30°31N 114°18E **35 B10**
Wuhe China 33°10N 117°50E **33 H9**
Wuhsi = Wuxi China 31°33N 120°18E **35 B13**
Wuhu China 31°22N 118°21E **35 B12**
Wujiang China 31°10N 120°38E **35 B13**
Wukari Nigeria 7°51N 9°42E **52 G7**
Wulajie China 44°6N 126°33E **33 B14**
Wulanbulang China 41°5N 110°55E **32 D6**
Wular L. India 34°20N 74°30E **43 B6**
Wulian China 35°40N 119°12E **33 G10**
Wulian Feng China 27°48N 103°36E **34 D4**
Wuliang Shan China 24°30N 100°40E **34 E3**
Wuliaru Indonesia 7°27S 131°0E **37 F8**
Wuling Shan China 29°20N 110°30E **35 C8**
Wulong China 29°22N 107°43E **34 C6**
Wulong △ China 31°8N 103°52E **34 B4**
Wulumuchi = Ürümqi
  China 43°45N 87°45E **30 C6**
Wumeng Shan China 26°48N 104°0E **34 D5**
Wuming China 23°12N 108°18E **34 F7**
Wuning China 29°17N 115°5E **35 C10**
Wunna ➔ India 20°18N 78°48E **44 D4**
Wunnummin L. Canada 52°55N 89°10W **72 B2**
Wuntho Burma 23°55N 95°45E **41 H19**
Wupatki ○ U.S.A. 35°35N 111°20W **77 J8**
Wuping China 25°5N 116°5E **35 E11**
Wuppertal Germany 51°16N 7°12E **16 C4**
Wuppertal S. Africa 32°13S 19°12E **56 D2**
Wuqing China 39°23N 117°4E **32 E9**
Wurralibi ◇ Australia 15°43S 137°1E **62 B2**
Wurtsboro U.S.A. 41°35N 74°29W **83 E10**
Würzburg Germany 49°46N 9°55E **16 D5**
Wushan China 34°43N 104°53E **32 G3**
Wushi China 41°9N 79°13E **30 C4**
Wutai China 38°40N 113°12E **32 E7**
Wutai Shan China 39°3N 113°32E **32 E7**
Wuting = Huimin China 37°27N 117°28E **33 F9**
Wutong China 22°55N 109°5E **34 F7**
Wutonghaolai China 42°50N 120°5E **33 C11**
Wutongqiao China 29°22N 103°50E **34 C4**

Wuwei Anhui, China 31°18N 117°54E **35 B11**
Wuwei Gansu, China 37°57N 102°34E **30 D9**
Wuxi Jiangsu, China 31°33N 120°18E **35 B13**
Wuxi Sichuan, China 31°23N 109°35E **34 B7**
Wuxiang China 36°49N 112°50E **32 F7**
Wuxuan China 23°34N 109°38E **34 F7**
Wuxue China 29°52N 115°30E **35 C10**
Wuyang China 33°25N 113°35E **32 H7**
Wuyi Hebei, China 37°46N 115°56E **32 F8**
Wuyi Zhejiang, China 28°52N 119°50E **35 C12**
Wuyi Shan China 27°0N 117°0E **35 D11**
Wuyishan China 27°45N 118°0E **35 D11**
Wuyishan China 27°55N 117°54E **35 D11**
Wuyuan Jiangxi, China 29°15N 117°50E **35 C11**
Wuyuan Nei Monggol Zizhiqu,
  China 41°2N 108°20E **32 D5**
Wuzhai China 38°54N 111°48E **32 E6**
Wuzhi Shan China 18°45N 109°45E **38 C7**
Wuzhong China 38°2N 106°12E **32 E4**
Wuzhou China 23°30N 111°18E **35 F8**
Wyaaba Cr. ➔ Australia 16°27S 141°35E **62 B3**
Wyalkatchem Australia 31°8S 117°22E **61 F2**
Wyalusing U.S.A. 41°40N 76°16W **83 E8**
Wyandotte U.S.A. 42°12N 83°9W **81 D12**
Wyandra Australia 27°12S 145°56E **63 D4**
Wyangala, L. Australia 33°54S 149°0E **63 E4**
Wyara, L. Australia 28°42S 144°14E **63 D3**
Wycheproof Australia 36°5S 143°17E **63 F3**
Wycliffe Well Australia 20°48S 134°14E **62 C1**
Wye ➔ U.K. 51°38N 2°40W **13 F5**
Wyemandoo Australia 28°28S 118°29E **61 E2**
Wymondham U.K. 52°35N 1°7E **13 E9**
Wymore U.S.A. 40°7N 96°40W **80 E6**
Wyndham Australia 15°33S 128°3E **60 C4**
Wyndham N.Z. 46°20S 168°51E **59 G2**
Wynne U.S.A. 35°14N 90°47W **85 D9**
Wynyard Australia 41°5S 145°44E **63 G4**
Wynyard Canada 51°45N 104°10W **71 C8**
Wyola L. Australia 29°8S 130°17E **61 E5**
Wyoming Canada 42°57N 82°7W **82 D2**
Wyoming □ U.S.A. 43°0N 107°30W **76 E10**
Wyomissing U.S.A. 40°20N 75°59W **83 F9**
Wynong Australia 33°14S 151°24E **63 E5**
Wytheville U.S.A. 36°57N 81°5W **81 G13**

X

Xaafuun Somalia 10°25N 51°16E **49 E5**
Xaafuun, Ras Somalia 10°27N 51°24E **49 E5**
Xaçmaz Azerbaijan 41°31N 48°42E **19 F8**
Xai-Xai Mozam. 25°6S 33°31E **57 C5**
Xaignabouri = Sayaboury
  Laos 19°15N 101°45E **38 C3**
Xainza China 30°58N 88°35E **30 E6**
Xalapa Mexico 19°32N 96°55W **87 D5**
Xangongo Angola 16°45S 15°5E **56 A2**
Xankändi Azerbaijan 39°52N 46°49E **46 B5**
Xanthi Greece 41°10N 24°58E **23 D11**
Xanxerê Brazil 26°53S 52°23W **95 B5**
Xapuri Brazil 10°35S 68°35W **92 F5**
Xar Moron He ➔
  China 43°25N 120°35E **33 C11**
Xàtiva Spain 38°59N 0°32W **21 C5**
Xau, L. Botswana 21°15S 24°44E **56 B3**
Xavantina Brazil 21°15S 52°48W **95 A5**
Xebert China 44°2N 122°0E **33 B12**
Xenia U.S.A. 39°41N 83°56W **81 F12**
Xhora S. Africa 31°55S 28°38E **57 D4**
Xhumo Botswana 21°7S 24°35E **56 B3**
Xi Jiang ➔ China 22°5N 113°20E **35 F9**
Xi Ujimqin Qi China 44°32N 117°40E **33 B9**
Xi Xian Henan, China 32°20N 114°43E **35 A10**
Xi Xian Shanxi, China 36°41N 110°58E **32 F6**
Xia Xian China 35°8N 111°12E **32 G6**
Xiachengzi China 44°40N 130°18E **33 B16**
Xiachuan Dao China 21°40N 112°40E **35 G9**
Xiaguan China 25°32N 100°16E **34 E3**
Xiajiang China 27°30N 115°10E **35 D10**
Xiajin China 36°56N 116°0E **32 F9**
Xiamen China 24°25N 118°4E **35 E12**
Xi'an China 34°15N 109°0E **32 G5**
Xian Xian China 38°12N 116°6E **32 E9**
Xian Xianyang Int. ✈ (XIY)
  China 34°27N 108°45E **32 G5**
Xianfeng China 29°40N 109°8E **34 C7**
Xiang Jiang ➔ China 28°55N 112°50E **35 C9**
Xiang Khouang Laos 19°17N 103°25E **38 C4**
Xiangcheng Henan,
  China 33°50N 113°27E **32 H7**
Xiangcheng Sichuan,
  China 28°53N 99°47E **34 C2**
Xiangdu China 23°13N 106°58E **34 F6**
Xiangfan China 32°2N 112°8E **35 A9**
Xianggang = Hong Kong □
  China 22°11N 114°14E **31 a**
Xianghuang Qi China 42°2N 113°50E **32 C7**
Xiangjiaba Dam China 28°37N 104°17E **34 C5**
Xiangning China 35°58N 110°50E **32 G6**
Xiangquan China 36°30N 113°1E **32 F7**
Xiangquan He = Sutlej ➔
  Pakistan 29°23N 71°3E **42 E4**
Xiangshan China 29°12N 121°51E **35 C13**
Xiangshui China 34°12N 119°33E **33 G10**
Xiangtan China 27°51N 112°54E **35 D9**
Xiangxiang China 27°43N 112°28E **35 D9**
Xiangyin China 28°38N 112°54E **35 C9**
Xiangyun China 25°34N 100°35E **34 E3**
Xianju China 28°51N 120°44E **35 C13**
Xianshui He ➔ China 30°10N 100°59E **34 B3**
Xiantao China 30°25N 113°25E **35 B9**
Xianxia China 30°25N 120°38E **35 B13**
Xianyou China 25°22N 118°33E **35 E12**
Xiao Hinggan Ling China 49°0N 127°0E **31 B14**
Xiao Xian China 34°15N 116°55E **32 G9**
Xiaofeng China 30°35N 119°32E **35 B12**
Xiaogan China 30°52N 113°55E **35 B9**
Xiaojin China 30°59N 102°21E **34 B4**

Xiaolan China 22°38N 113°13E 35 F9
Xiaoshan China 30°12N 120°18E 35 B13
Xiaowan Dam China 24°42N 100°5E 34 E3
Xiaowutai Shan China 39°51N 114°59E 32 E8
Xiaoyi China 37°8N 111°48E 32 F6
Xiapu China 26°54N 119°59E 35 D12
Xiashan = Zhanjiang China 21°15N 110°20E 35 G8
Xiawa China 42°35N 120°38E 33 C11
Xiayi China 34°15N 116°10E 32 G9
Xichang China 27°51N 102°19E 34 D4
Xichong China 30°57N 105°54E 34 B5
Xichou China 23°25N 104°42E 34 E5
Xichuan China 33°0N 111°30E 32 H6
Xide China 28°8N 102°19E 34 C4
Xiemahe China 31°38N 111°12E 35 B8
Xifei He → China 32°45N 116°40E 32 H9
Xifeng Gansu, China 35°40N 107°40E 32 G4
Xifeng Guizhou, China 27°7N 106°42E 34 D6
Xifeng Liaoning, China 42°42N 124°45E 33 C13
Xifengzhen = Xifeng China 35°40N 107°40E 32 G4
Xigazê China 29°5N 88°45E 30 F6
Xihe China 34°2N 105°20E 32 G3
Xihua China 33°45N 114°30E 32 H8
Xili Shuiku China 22°36N 113°57E 31 a
Xiliao He → China 43°32N 123°35E 33 C12
Xilin China 24°30N 105°6E 34 E5
Xiling Gorge = Xiling Xia China 30°54N 110°48E 35 B8
Xiling Xia China 30°54N 110°48E 35 B8
Xilinhot China 43°52N 116°2E 32 C9
Xiluodu Dam China 28°12N 103°34E 34 C4
Ximeng China 22°50N 99°27E 34 F2
Ximiao China 40°59N 100°12E 30 C9
Xin Jiang → China 28°45N 116°35E 35 C11
Xin Xian = Xinzhou China 38°22N 112°46E 32 E7
Xin'anjiang Shuiku China 29°33N 118°56E 35 C12
Xinavane Mozam. 25°2S 32°47E 57 C5
Xinbin China 41°40N 125°2E 33 D13
Xincai China 32°43N 114°58E 35 A10
Xinchang China 29°28N 120°52E 35 C13
Xincheng Guangxi Zhuangzu, China 24°5N 108°39E 34 E7
Xincheng Jiangxi, China 26°48N 114°6E 35 D10
Xinfeng Guangdong, China 24°5N 114°16E 35 E10
Xinfeng Jiangxi, China 27°7N 116°11E 35 D11
Xinfeng Jiangxi, China 25°27N 114°58E 35 E10
Xinfengjiang Shuiku China 23°52N 114°30E 35 F10
Xing Xian China 38°27N 111°7E 32 E6
Xing'an Guangxi Zhuangzu, China 25°38N 110°40E 35 E8
Xingan Jiangxi, China 27°46N 115°20E 35 D10
Xingcheng China 40°40N 120°45E 33 D11
Xingguo China 26°21N 115°21E 35 D10
Xinghe China 40°55N 113°55E 32 D7
Xinghua China 32°58N 119°48E 33 H10
Xinghua Wan China 25°15N 119°20E 35 E12
Xinglong China 40°25N 117°30E 33 D9
Xingning China 24°3N 115°42E 35 E10
Xingping China 34°20N 108°28E 32 G5
Xingren China 25°24N 105°11E 34 E5
Xingshan China 31°15N 110°45E 35 B8
Xingtai China 37°3N 114°32E 32 F8
Xingu → Brazil 1°30S 51°53W 93 D8
Xingwen China 28°22N 104°50E 34 C5
Xingxingxia China 41°47N 95°0E 30 C7
Xingyang China 34°45N 112°52E 32 G7
Xingyi China 25°3N 104°59E 34 E5
Xinhe China 37°30N 115°15E 32 F8
Xinhua China 27°42N 111°13E 35 D8
Xinhuang China 27°21N 109°12E 34 D7
Xinhui China 22°25N 113°0E 35 F9
Xining China 36°34N 101°40E 30 D9
Xinji China 37°55N 115°13E 32 F8
Xinjian China 28°37N 115°46E 35 C10
Xinjiang China 35°34N 111°11E 32 G6
Xinjiang Uygur Zizhiqu □ China 42°0N 86°0E 30 C6
Xinjin = Pulandian China 39°25N 121°58E 33 E11
Xinjin China 30°24N 103°47E 34 B4
Xinkai He → China 43°32N 123°35E 33 C12
Xinken China 22°39N 113°36E 31 a
Xinle China 38°25N 114°40E 32 E8
Xinlitun China 42°0N 122°8E 33 D12
Xinlong China 30°57N 100°12E 34 B3
Xinmi China 34°30N 113°25E 32 G7
Xinmin China 41°59N 122°50E 33 D12
Xinning China 26°28N 110°50E 35 D8
Xinping China 24°5N 101°59E 34 E3
Xinshao China 27°21N 111°26E 35 D8
Xintai China 35°55N 117°45E 33 G9
Xintian China 25°55N 112°13E 35 E9
Xinwan China 22°47N 113°40E 31 a
Xinxiang China 35°18N 113°50E 32 G7
Xinxing China 22°35N 112°15E 35 F9
Xinyang China 32°6N 114°3E 35 A10
Xinye China 32°30N 112°21E 35 A9
Xinyi Guangdong, China 22°25N 111°0E 35 F8
Xinyi Nei Monggol Zizhiqu, China 34°23N 118°21E 33 G10
Xinyu China 27°49N 114°58E 35 D10
Xinzhan China 43°50N 127°18E 33 C14
Xinzheng China 34°20N 113°45E 32 G7
Xinzhou Hainan, China 19°43N 109°17E 38 C7
Xinzhou Hubei, China 30°50N 114°48E 35 B10
Xinzhou Shanxi, China 38°22N 112°46E 32 E7
Xiongyuecheng China 40°12N 122°5E 33 D12
Xiping Henan, China 33°22N 114°5E 32 H8
Xiping Henan, China 33°25N 111°8E 32 H6
Xiping Zhejiang, China 28°16N 119°29E 35 C12
Xique-Xique Brazil 10°50S 42°40W 93 F10
Xisha Qundao = Paracel Is. S. China Sea 15°50N 112°0E 36 A4
Xishuangbanna China 22°5N 101°1E 34 F3
Xishui Guizhou, China 28°19N 106°9E 34 C6
Xishui Hubei, China 30°30N 115°15E 35 B10
Xiu Shui → China 29°13N 116°0E 35 C10
Xiuning China 29°45N 118°10E 35 C12
Xiuren China 24°27N 110°12E 35 E8
Xiushan China 28°25N 108°57E 34 C7
Xiushui China 29°2N 114°33E 35 C10
Xiuwen China 26°49N 106°32E 34 D6
Xiuyan China 40°18N 123°11E 33 D12
Xiva Uzbekistan 41°30N 60°18E 26 E7
Xixabangma Feng China 28°20N 85°40E 43 E11
Xixia China 33°25N 111°29E 32 H6
Xixiang Guangdong, China 22°34N 113°52E 31 a
Xixiang Shaanxi, China 33°0N 107°44E 32 H4
Xixón = Gijón Spain 43°32N 5°42W 21 A3
Xiyang China 37°38N 113°38E 32 F7
Xizang Zizhiqu □ China 32°0N 88°0E 30 E6
Xochob Mexico 19°21N 89°48W 87 D7
Xu Jiang → China 28°0N 116°25E 35 D11
Xuan Loc Vietnam 10°56N 107°14E 39 G6
Xuan'en China 30°0N 109°30E 34 C7
Xuanhan China 31°18N 107°38E 34 B6
Xuanhua China 40°40N 115°2E 32 D8
Xuanwei China 26°15N 103°59E 34 C5
Xuanzhou China 30°56N 118°43E 35 B12
Xuchang China 34°2N 113°48E 32 G7
Xuefeng Shan China 27°5N 110°35E 35 D8
Xuejiaping China 31°39N 110°16E 35 B8
Xun Jiang → China 23°35N 111°30E 35 F8
Xun Xian China 35°42N 114°33E 32 G8
Xundian China 25°36N 103°15E 34 E4
Xunwu China 24°54N 115°37E 35 E10
Xunyang China 32°48N 109°22E 32 H5
Xunyi China 35°8N 108°20E 32 G5
Xupu China 27°53N 110°32E 35 D8
Xúquer → Spain 39°5N 0°10W 21 C5
Xushui China 39°2N 115°40E 32 E8
Xuwen China 20°20N 110°10E 35 G8
Xuyi China 32°55N 118°32E 35 A12
Xuyong China 28°10N 105°22E 34 C5
Xuzhou China 34°18N 117°10E 33 G9

Y

Y Drenewydd = Newtown U.K. 52°31N 3°19W 13 E4
Y Fenni = Abergavenny U.K. 51°49N 3°1W 13 F4
Y Gelli Gandryll = Hay-on-Wye U.K. 52°5N 3°8W 13 E4
Y Trallwng = Welshpool U.K. 52°39N 3°8W 13 E4
Ya Xian = Sanya China 18°14N 109°29E 38 C7
Yaamba Australia 23°8S 150°22E 62 C5
Ya'an China 29°58N 103°5E 34 C4
Yaapeet Australia 35°45S 142°3E 63 F3
Yablonovyy Khrebet Russia 53°0N 114°0E 27 D12
Yablonovyy Ra. = Yablonovyy Khrebet Russia 53°0N 114°0E 27 D12
Yabrai Shan China 39°40N 103°0E 32 E2
Yabrūd Syria 33°58N 36°39E 48 B5
Yabucoa Puerto Rico 18°3N 65°53W 89 d
Yacambú △ Venezuela 9°42N 69°27W 89 E6
Yacata Fiji 17°15S 179°31W 59 a
Yacheng China 18°22N 109°6E 38 C7
Yacuiba Bolivia 22°0S 63°43W 94 A3
Yacuma → Bolivia 13°38S 65°23W 92 F5
Yadgir India 16°45N 77°5E 44 F3
Yadkin → U.S.A. 35°23N 80°4W 85 D14
Yadua Fiji 16°49S 178°18E 59 a
Yaeyama-Rettō Japan 24°30N 123°40E 29 M1
Yagasa Cluster Fiji 18°57S 178°28W 59 a
Yagodnoye Russia 62°33N 149°40E 27 C15
Yahk Canada 49°6N 116°10W 70 D5
Yahuma Dem. Rep. of the Congo 1°0N 23°10E 54 D4
Yaita Japan 36°48N 139°56E 29 F9
Yajiang China 30°2N 100°57E 34 B3
Yakeshi China 49°17N 120°44E 31 B13
Yakima U.S.A. 46°36N 120°31W 76 C3
Yakima → U.S.A. 46°15N 119°14W 76 C4
Yakishiri-Jima Japan 44°26N 141°25E 28 B10
Yakobi I. U.S.A. 58°0N 136°30W 70 B1
Yakovlevka Russia 44°26N 133°28E 28 B6
Yaku-Shima Japan 30°20N 130°30E 29 J5
Yakumo Japan 42°15N 140°16E 28 C10
Yakutat U.S.A. 59°33N 139°44W 68 F4
Yakutat B. U.S.A. 59°45N 140°45W 74 D11
Yakutia = Sakha □ Russia 66°0N 130°0E 27 C14
Yakutsk Russia 62°5N 129°50E 27 C13
Yala Thailand 6°33N 101°18E 39 J3
Yala △ Sri Lanka 6°20N 81°30E 45 L5
Yalata Australia 31°59S 132°26E 61 F5
Yalata ✪ Australia 31°35S 132°7E 61 F5
Yalboroo Australia 20°50S 148°40E 62 b
Yale U.S.A. 43°8N 82°48W 82 C2
Yalgorup △ Australia 32°39S 115°38E 61 F2
Yalinga C.A.R. 6°33N 23°10E 54 C4
Yalkabul, Pta. Mexico 21°32N 88°37W 87 C7
Yalleroi Australia 24°3S 145°42E 62 C4
Yalobusha → U.S.A. 33°33N 90°10W 85 E9
Yalong China 18°12N 109°42E 38 C7
Yalong Jiang → China 26°40N 101°55E 34 D3
Yalova Turkey 40°41N 29°15E 23 D13
Yalpirakinu ✪ Australia 22°24S 132°15E 60 D5
Yalta Ukraine 44°30N 34°10E 19 F5
Yalu Jiang → China 39°55N 124°19E 33 E13
Yam Australia 9°54S 142°46E 62 a
Yam Ha Melaḥ = Dead Sea Asia 31°30N 35°30E 48 D4
Yam Kinneret Israel 32°45N 35°35E 48 C4
Yamada = Kama Japan 33°33N 130°49E 29 H5
Yamagata Japan 38°15N 140°15E 28 E10
Yamagata □ Japan 38°30N 140°0E 28 E10
Yamaguchi Japan 34°10N 131°32E 29 G5
Yamaguchi □ Japan 34°20N 131°40E 29 G5
Yamal, Poluostrov Russia 71°0N 70°0E 26 B8
Yamal Pen. = Yamal, Poluostrov Russia 71°0N 70°0E 26 B8
Yamanashi □ Japan 35°40N 138°40E 29 G9
Yamantau, Gora Russia 54°15N 58°6E 18 D10
Yamato Ridge Sea of Japan 39°20N 135°0E 28 E7
Yamba Australia 29°26S 153°23E 63 D5
Yambarran Ra. Australia 15°10S 130°25E 60 C5
Yambio South Sudan 4°35N 28°16E 53 H11
Yambol Bulgaria 42°30N 26°30E 23 C12
Yamburg Russia 68°21N 77°8E 26 C8
Yamdena Indonesia 7°45S 131°20E 37 F8
Yame Japan 33°13N 130°35E 29 H5
Yamethin Burma 20°29N 96°18E 41 J20
Yamma Yamma, L. Australia 26°16S 141°20E 63 D3
Yamoussoukro Ivory C. 6°49N 5°17W 52 G4
Yampa → U.S.A. 40°32N 108°59W 76 F9
Yampi Sd. Australia 16°8S 123°38E 60 C3
Yampil Moldova 48°15N 28°15E 17 D15
Yampol = Yampil Moldova 48°15N 28°15E 17 D15
Yamu, Laem Thailand 7°59N 98°26E 39 a
Yamuna → India 25°30N 81°53E 43 G9
Yamunanagar India 30°7N 77°17E 42 D7
Yamzho Yumco China 28°48N 90°35E 30 F7
Yan Oya → Sri Lanka 9°0N 81°10E 45 K5
Yana → Russia 71°30N 136°0E 27 B14
Yanagawa Japan 33°10N 130°24E 29 H5
Yanai Japan 33°58N 132°7E 29 H6
Yan'an China 36°35N 109°26E 32 F5
Yanaul Russia 56°25N 55°0E 18 C10
Yanbian China 26°47N 101°31E 34 D3
Yanbu 'al Baḥr Si. Arabia 24°5N 38°5E 46 E3
Yanchang China 36°43N 110°1E 32 F6
Yancheng Henan, China 33°35N 114°0E 32 H8
Yancheng Jiangsu, China 33°23N 120°8E 33 H11
Yanchep Australia 31°33S 115°37E 61 F2
Yanchi China 37°48N 107°20E 32 F4
Yanchuan China 36°51N 110°10E 32 F6
Yanco Cr. → Australia 35°14S 145°35E 63 F4
Yandang Shan China 28°0N 120°25E 35 D13
Yandeyarra ✪ Australia 21°17S 118°24E 60 D2
Yandicoogina Australia 22°49S 119°12E 60 D2
Yandoon Burma 17°0N 95°40E 41 L19
Yanfeng China 25°52N 101°8E 34 E3
Yang Xian China 33°15N 107°30E 34 A6
Yang-yang S. Korea 38°4N 128°38E 33 E15
Yangambi Dem. Rep. of the Congo 0°47N 24°24E 54 D4
Yangbi China 25°41N 99°58E 34 E2
Yangcheng China 35°28N 112°22E 32 G7
Yangch'ü = Taiyuan China 37°52N 112°33E 32 F7
Yangchun China 22°11N 111°48E 35 F8
Yanggao China 40°21N 113°55E 32 D7
Yanggu China 36°8N 115°43E 32 F8
Yangjiang China 21°50N 111°59E 35 G8
Yangliuqing China 39°2N 117°5E 33 E9
Yangôn Burma 16°45N 96°20E 41 L20
Yangping China 31°12N 111°25E 35 B8
Yangpingguan China 32°58N 106°5E 34 A6
Yangquan China 37°58N 113°31E 32 F7
Yangshan Guangdong, China 24°30N 112°40E 35 E9
Yangshan Shanghai, China 30°37N 122°4E 35 B14
Yangshuo China 24°48N 110°29E 35 E8
Yangtse = Chang Jiang → China 31°48N 121°10E 35 B13
Yangtze Kiang = Chang Jiang → China 31°48N 121°10E 35 B13
Yangxin China 29°50N 115°12E 35 C10
Yangyuan China 40°1N 114°10E 32 D8
Yangzhong China 32°22N 119°22E 35 A12
Yangzhou China 32°21N 119°26E 35 A12
Yanhe China 28°31N 108°29E 34 C7
Yanji China 42°59N 129°30E 33 C15
Yanjin China 28°5N 104°18E 34 C5
Yanjing China 29°7N 98°33E 34 C2
Yankton U.S.A. 42°53N 97°23W 80 D5
Yankunytjatjara-Antakirinja ✪ Australia 27°20S 134°30E 63 A1
Yanqi China 42°5N 86°35E 30 C6
Yanqing China 40°30N 115°58E 32 D8
Yanshan Hebei, China 38°4N 117°22E 33 E9
Yanshan Jiangxi, China 28°15N 117°41E 35 C11
Yanshan Yunnan, China 23°35N 104°20E 34 F5
Yanshou China 45°28N 128°22E 33 B15
Yantabulla Australia 29°21S 145°0E 63 D4
Yantai China 37°34N 121°22E 33 F11
Yantian China 22°35N 114°16E 31 a
Yanting China 31°11N 105°24E 34 B5
Yantongshan China 43°17N 126°0E 33 C14
Yanuca Fiji 18°24S 178°0E 59 a
Yanwa China 27°35N 98°55E 34 D2
Yanyuan China 27°25N 101°30E 34 D3
Yanzhou China 35°35N 116°49E 32 G9
Yao Xian China 34°55N 108°59E 32 G5
Yao Yai, Ko Thailand 8°7N 98°37E 39 a
Yao'an China 25°31N 101°18E 34 E3
Yaoundé Cameroon 3°50N 11°35E 54 D2
Yaowan China 34°15N 118°3E 33 G10
Yap Pac. Oc. 9°30N 138°10E 64 G5
Yapen Indonesia 1°50S 136°0E 37 E9
Yapen, Selat Indonesia 1°20S 136°10E 37 E9
Yapero Indonesia 4°59S 137°11E 37 E9
Yappar → Australia 18°22S 141°16E 62 B3
Yapuparra ✪ Australia 27°15S 126°20E 61 E4
Yaqaga Fiji 16°35S 178°36E 59 a
Yaqui → Mexico 27°37N 110°39W 86 B2
Yar Çalli = Naberezhnyye Chelny Russia 55°42N 52°19E 18 C9
Yar-Sale Russia 66°50N 70°50E 26 C8
Yaraka Australia 24°53S 144°3E 62 C3
Yaransk Russia 57°22N 47°49E 18 C8
Yare → U.K. 52°35N 1°38E 13 E9
Yaremcha Ukraine 48°27N 24°33E 17 D13
Yarensk Russia 62°11N 49°15E 18 B8
Yarí → Colombia 0°20S 72°20W 92 D4
Yarkand = Shache China 38°20N 77°10E 30 D4
Yarkant He → China 40°26N 80°59E 30 C5
Yarker Canada 44°23N 76°46W 83 B8
Yarkhun → Pakistan 36°17N 72°30E 43 A5
Yarlung Ziangbo Jiang = Brahmaputra → Asia 23°40N 90°35E 43 H13
Yarmouth Canada 43°50N 66°7W 73 D6
Yarmūk → Syria 32°42N 35°40E 48 C4
Yaroslavl Russia 57°35N 39°55E 18 C6
Yarqa, W. → Egypt 30°0N 33°49E 48 F2
Yarra Yarra Lakes Australia 29°40S 115°45E 61 E2
Yarram Australia 38°29S 146°39E 63 F4
Yarraman Australia 26°50S 152°0E 63 D5
Yarras Australia 31°25S 152°20E 63 E5
Yarrie Australia 20°40S 120°12E 60 D3
Yartsevo Russia 60°20N 90°0E 27 C10
Yarumal Colombia 6°58N 75°24W 92 B3
Yasawa Fiji 16°47S 177°31E 59 a
Yasawa Group Fiji 17°0S 177°23E 59 a
Yaselda Belarus 52°7N 26°28E 17 B14
Yasin Pakistan 36°24N 73°23E 43 A5
Yasinski, L. Canada 53°16N 77°35W 72 B4
Yasinya Ukraine 48°16N 24°21E 17 D13
Yasothon Thailand 15°50N 104°10E 38 E5
Yass Australia 34°49S 148°54E 63 E4
Yāsūj Iran 30°31N 51°31E 47 D6
Yatağan Turkey 37°20N 28°10E 23 F13
Yates Center U.S.A. 37°53N 95°44W 80 G6
Yathkyed L. Canada 62°40N 98°0W 71 A9
Yatsushiro Japan 32°30N 130°40E 29 H5
Yauco Puerto Rico 18°2N 66°51W 89 d
Yaval India 21°10N 75°42E 44 D2
Yavarí → Peru 4°21S 70°2W 92 D4
Yávaros Mexico 26°42N 109°31W 86 B3
Yavatmal India 20°20N 78°15E 44 D4
Yavne Israel 31°52N 34°45E 48 D3
Yavoriv Ukraine 49°55N 23°20E 17 D12
Yavorov = Yavoriv Ukraine 49°55N 23°20E 17 D12
Yawatahama Japan 33°27N 132°24E 29 H6
Yawri B. S. Leone 8°22N 13°0W 52 G3
Yaxi China 27°33N 106°41E 34 D6
Yaxian = Sanya China 18°14N 109°29E 38 C7
Yazd Iran 31°55N 54°27E 47 D7
Yazd □ Iran 32°0N 55°0E 47 D7
Yazd-e Khvāst Iran 31°31N 52°7E 47 D7
Yazman Pakistan 29°8N 71°45E 42 E4
Yazoo → U.S.A. 32°22N 90°54W 85 E9
Yazoo City U.S.A. 32°51N 90°25W 85 E9
Ybycuí △ Paraguay 26°5S 56°46W 94 B4
Ybytyruzú △ Paraguay 25°51S 56°11W 95 B4
Ye Burma 15°15N 97°15E 38 E1
Ye Xian China 33°35N 113°25E 32 H7
Yebyu Burma 14°15N 98°13E 38 E2
Yecheng China 37°54N 77°26E 30 D4
Yecheon S. Korea 36°39N 128°27E 33 F15
Yecla Spain 38°35N 1°5W 21 C5
Yécora Mexico 28°20N 108°58W 86 B3
Yedintsy = Edineţ Moldova 48°9N 27°18E 17 D14
Yegros Paraguay 26°20S 56°25W 94 B4
Yehbuah Indonesia 8°23S 114°45E 37 J17
Yehuda, Midbar Israel 31°35N 35°15E 48 D4
Yei South Sudan 4°9N 30°40E 53 H12
Yekaterinburg Russia 56°50N 60°30E 26 D7
Yekateriny, Proliv Russia 44°30N 146°30E 27 E15
Yelandur India 12°6N 77°0E 45 H3
Yelarbon Australia 28°33S 150°38E 63 D5
Yelets Russia 52°40N 38°30E 18 D6
Yelin = Lingshui China 18°27N 110°0E 38 C8
Yelizavetgrad = Kirovohrad Ukraine 48°35N 32°20E 19 E5
Yelizovo Russia 53°11N 158°23E 27 D16
Yell U.K. 60°35N 1°5W 11 A7
Yell Sd. U.K. 60°33N 1°15W 11 A7
Yellamanchilli = Elamanchili India 17°33N 82°50E 44 F6
Yellandu India 17°39N 80°23E 44 F5
Yellapur India 14°58N 74°43E 45 G2
Yellareddi India 18°12N 78°2E 44 E4
Yellow = Huang He → China 37°55N 118°50E 33 F10
Yellow Sea China 35°0N 123°0E 33 G12
Yellowhead Pass Canada 52°53N 118°25W 70 C5
Yellowknife Canada 62°27N 114°29W 70 A6
Yellowknife → Canada 62°31N 114°19W 70 A6
Yellowstone → U.S.A. 47°59N 103°59W 76 C12
Yellowstone △ U.S.A. 44°40N 110°30W 76 D8
Yellowstone L. U.S.A. 44°27N 110°22W 76 D8
Yelsk Belarus 51°50N 29°10E 17 C15
Yemen ■ Asia 15°0N 44°0E 49 E3
Yemmiganur India 15°44N 77°29E 45 G3
Yen Bai Vietnam 21°42N 104°52E 34 G5
Yenangyaung Burma 20°30N 95°0E 41 J19
Yenbo = Yanbu 'al Baḥr Si. Arabia 24°5N 38°5E 46 E3
Yenda Australia 34°13S 146°14E 63 E4
Yenice Turkey 39°55N 27°17E 23 E12
Yenisey → Russia 71°50N 82°40E 26 B9
Yeniseysk Russia 58°27N 92°13E 27 D10
Yeniseyskiy Zaliv Russia 72°20N 81°0E 26 B9
Yenyuka Russia 57°57N 121°15E 27 D13
Yeo → U.K. 51°2N 2°49W 13 G5
Yeo, L. Australia 28°0S 124°30E 61 E3
Yeo I. Canada 45°24N 81°48W 82 A3
Yeola India 20°2N 74°30E 44 D2
Yeon-gi = Sejong S. Korea 36°35N 127°15E 33 F14
Yeong-wol S. Korea 37°11N 128°28E 33 F15
Yeongcheon S. Korea 35°58N 128°56E 33 G15
Yeongdeok S. Korea 36°24N 129°22E 33 F15
Yeongdong S. Korea 36°10N 127°46E 33 F14
Yeongju S. Korea 36°50N 128°40E 33 F15
Yeosu S. Korea 34°47N 127°45E 33 G14
Yeotmal = Yavatmal India 20°20N 78°15E 44 D4
Yeovil U.K. 50°57N 2°38W 13 G5
Yeppoon Australia 23°5S 150°47E 62 C5
Yerbent Turkmenistan 39°19N 58°36E 47 B8
Yerbogachen Russia 61°16N 108°0E 27 C11
Yerevan Armenia 40°10N 44°31E 46 A5
Yerington U.S.A. 38°59N 119°10W 76 G4
Yerla → India 16°50N 74°30E 44 F2
Yermo U.S.A. 34°54N 116°50W 79 L10
Yeropol Russia 65°15N 168°40E 27 C17
Yershov Russia 51°23N 48°27E 19 D8
Yes Tor U.K. 50°41N 4°0W 13 G4
Yesan S. Korea 36°41N 126°51E 33 F14
Yeso U.S.A. 34°26N 104°37W 77 J11
Yessey Russia 68°29N 102°10E 27 C11
Yetman Australia 28°56S 150°48E 63 D5
Yeu, Î. d' France 46°42N 2°20W 20 C2
Yevpatoriya Ukraine 45°15N 33°20E 19 E5
Yeysk Russia 46°40N 38°12E 19 E6
Yezd = Yazd Iran 31°55N 54°27E 47 D7
Ygatimi Paraguay 24°5S 55°40W 95 A4
Yhati Paraguay 25°45S 56°35W 94 B4
Yhú Paraguay 25°0S 56°0W 95 B4
Yí → Uruguay 33°7S 57°8W 94 C4
Yi 'Allaq, G. Egypt 30°21N 33°31E 48 E2
Yi He → China 34°10N 118°8E 33 G10
Yi Xian Anhui, China 29°55N 117°57E 35 C11
Yi Xian Hebei, China 39°20N 115°30E 32 E8
Yi Xian Liaoning, China 41°30N 121°22E 33 D11
Yibin China 28°45N 104°32E 34 C5
Yichang China 30°40N 111°20E 35 B8
Yicheng Henan, China 31°41N 112°12E 35 B9
Yicheng Shanxi, China 35°42N 111°40E 32 G6
Yichuan China 36°2N 110°10E 32 F6
Yichun Heilongjiang, China 47°44N 128°52E 31 B14
Yichun Jiangxi, China 27°48N 114°22E 35 D10
Yidu China 36°43N 118°28E 33 F10
Yidun China 30°22N 99°21E 34 B2
Yifeng China 28°22N 114°45E 35 C10
Yihuang China 27°30N 116°12E 35 D11
Yijun China 35°28N 109°8E 32 G5
Yıldız Dağları Turkey 41°48N 27°36E 23 D12
Yilehuli Shan China 51°20N 124°20E 31 A13
Yiliang Yunnan, China 27°38N 104°2E 34 D5
Yiliang Yunnan, China 24°56N 103°11E 34 E4
Yilong China 31°34N 106°23E 34 B6
Yima China 34°44N 111°53E 32 G6
Yimen China 24°40N 102°10E 34 E4
Yimianpo China 45°7N 128°2E 33 B15
Yin Xu China 36°7N 114°18E 32 F8
Yi'nan China 35°31N 118°24E 33 G10
Yinchuan China 38°30N 106°15E 32 E4
Yindarlgooda, L. Australia 30°40S 121°52E 61 F3
Yindjibarndi ✪ Australia 22°0S 118°35E 60 D2
Ying He → China 32°30N 116°30E 32 H9
Ying Xian China 39°32N 113°10E 32 E7
Yingcheng China 30°56N 113°35E 35 B9
Yingde China 24°10N 113°25E 35 E9
Yingjiang China 24°41N 97°55E 34 E1
Yingjing China 29°41N 102°52E 34 C4
Yingkou China 40°37N 122°18E 33 D12
Yingpanshui China 37°26N 104°18E 32 F3
Yingshan Hubei, China 30°41N 115°32E 35 B10
Yingshan Sichuan, China 31°4N 106°35E 34 B6
Yingshang China 32°38N 116°12E 35 A11
Yingtan China 28°12N 117°0E 35 C11
Yingualyalya ✪ Australia 18°49S 129°12E 60 C4
Yining China 43°58N 81°10E 30 C5
Yiningarra ✪ Australia 20°53S 129°27E 60 D4
Yinjiang China 28°1N 108°21E 34 C7
Yinmabin Burma 22°10N 94°55E 41 H19
Yipinglang China 25°10N 101°52E 34 E3
Yirga Alem Ethiopia 6°48N 38°22E 49 F2
Yirrkala Australia 12°14S 136°56E 62 A2
Yishan China 24°28N 108°38E 34 E7
Yishui China 35°47N 118°30E 33 G10
Yitong China 43°13N 125°20E 33 C13
Yiwu China 29°20N 120°3E 35 C13
Yixing China 31°21N 119°48E 35 B12
Yiyang Henan, China 34°27N 112°10E 32 G7
Yiyang Hunan, China 28°35N 112°18E 35 C9
Yiyang Jiangxi, China 28°22N 117°20E 35 C11
Yizhang China 25°27N 112°57E 35 E9
Yizheng China 32°18N 119°10E 35 A12
Yli-Kitka Finland 66°8N 28°30E 8 C23
Ylitornio Finland 66°19N 23°39E 8 C20
Ylivieska Finland 64°4N 24°28E 8 D21
Yoakum U.S.A. 29°17N 97°9W 84 G6
Yog Pt. Phil. 14°6N 124°12E 37 B6
Yogyakarta Indonesia 7°49S 110°22E 37 G14
Yogyakarta □ Indonesia 7°48S 110°22E 37 G14
Yoho △ Canada 51°25N 116°30W 70 C5
Yojoa, L. de Honduras 14°53N 88°0W 88 D2
Yok Don △ Vietnam 12°50N 107°40E 38 F6
Yokadouma Cameroon 3°26N 14°55E 54 D2
Yokkaichi Japan 34°55N 136°38E 29 G8
Yoko Cameroon 5°32N 12°20E 54 C2
Yokohama Japan 35°27N 139°28E 29 G9
Yokosuka Japan 35°20N 139°40E 29 G9
Yokote Japan 39°20N 140°30E 28 E10
Yola Nigeria 9°10N 12°29E 53 G8
Yolaina, Cordillera de Nic. 11°30N 84°0W 88 D3
Yölöten Turkmenistan 37°18N 62°21E 47 B9
Yom → Thailand 15°35N 100°1E 38 E3
Yonago Japan 35°25N 133°19E 29 G6
Yonaguni-Jima Japan 24°27N 123°0E 29 M1
Yŏnan N. Korea 37°55N 126°11E 33 F14
Yonezawa Japan 37°57N 140°4E 28 F10
Yong-in S. Korea 37°14N 127°12E 33 F14
Yong Peng Malaysia 2°0N 103°3E 39 M4
Yong Sata Thailand 7°8N 99°41E 39 J2
Yongamp'o N. Korea 39°56N 124°23E 33 E13
Yong'an China 25°59N 117°25E 35 E11
Yongchang China 38°17N 102°7E 30 D9
Yongcheng China 33°55N 116°20E 32 H9
Yongchuan China 29°17N 105°55E 34 C5
Yongchun China 25°16N 118°20E 35 E12
Yongde China 24°5N 99°25E 34 E2
Yongdeng China 36°38N 103°25E 32 F2
Yongding China 24°43N 116°45E 35 E11
Yongfeng China 27°20N 115°22E 35 D10
Yongfu China 24°59N 109°59E 34 E7
Yonghe China 36°46N 110°38E 32 F6
Yŏnghŭng N. Korea 39°31N 127°18E 33 E14

Yongji *Jilin, China* 43°33N 126°13E **33 C14**
Yongji *Shanxi, China* 34°52N 110°28E **32 G6**
Yongjia *China* 28°10N 120°45E **35 C13**
Yongkang *Yunnan, China* 24°9N 99°20E **34 E2**
Yongkang *Zhejiang,*
  China 28°55N 120°2E **35 C13**
Yongnian *China* 36°47N 114°29E **32 F8**
Yongning *Guangxi Zhuangzu,*
  China 22°44N 108°28E **34 F7**
Yongning *Ningxia Huizu,*
  China 38°15N 106°14E **32 E4**
Yongping *China* 25°27N 99°38E **34 E2**
Yongren *China* 26°4N 101°40E **34 D3**
Yongshan *China* 28°11N 103°35E **34 C4**
Yongsheng *China* 26°38N 100°40E **34 D3**
Yongshun *China* 29°2N 109°51E **34 C7**
Yongtai *China* 25°49N 118°58E **35 E12**
Yongxing = Jinggangshan
Yongxing Dao = Woody I.
  S. China Sea 16°50N 112°20E **36 A4**
Yongxiu *China* 29°2N 115°42E **35 C10**
Yongzhou *China* 26°17N 111°37E **35 D8**
Yonibana *S. Leone* 8°30N 12°19W **52 G3**
Yonne □ *France* 48°23N 2°58E **20 B5**
Yonne → *France* 48°23N 2°58E **20 B5**
Yos Sudarso, Pulau = Dolak,
  Pulau *Indonesia* 8°0S 138°30E **37 F9**
Yosemite △ *U.S.A.* 37°45N 119°40W **78 H7**
Yosemite Village *U.S.A.* 37°45N 119°35W **78 H7**
Yoshino-Kumano △
  Japan 34°12N 135°55E **29 H8**
Yoshkar Ola *Russia* 56°38N 47°55E **18 C8**
Yotvata *Israel* 29°55N 35°2E **48 F4**
You Jiang → *China* 22°50N 108°6E **34 F7**
You Xian *China* 27°1N 113°17E **35 D9**
Youbou *Canada* 48°53N 124°13W **78 B2**
Youghal *Ireland* 51°56N 7°52W **10 E4**
Youghal B. *Ireland* 51°55N 7°49W **10 E4**
Young *Australia* 34°19S 148°18E **63 E4**
Young *Canada* 51°47N 105°45W **71 C7**
Young *Uruguay* 32°44S 57°36W **94 C4**
Young I. *Antarctica* 66°25S 162°24E **5 C11**
Younghusband, L.
  Australia 30°50S 136°5E **63 E2**
Younghusband Pen.
  Australia 36°0S 139°25E **63 F2**
Youngstown *Canada* 51°35N 111°10W **71 C6**
Youngstown *N.Y., U.S.A.* 43°15N 79°3W **82 C5**
Youngstown *Ohio, U.S.A.* 41°6N 80°39W **82 E4**
Youngsville *U.S.A.* 41°51N 79°19W **82 E5**
Youngwood *U.S.A.* 40°14N 79°34W **82 F5**
Youxi *China* 26°10N 118°13E **35 D12**
Youyang *China* 28°47N 108°42E **34 C7**
Youyu *China* 40°10N 112°20E **32 D7**
Yozgat *Turkey* 39°51N 34°47E **19 G5**
Ypacaraí △ *Paraguay* 25°18S 57°19W **94 B4**
Ypané → *Paraguay* 23°29S 57°19W **94 B4**
Ypres = Ieper *Belgium* 50°51N 2°53E **15 D2**
Yr Wyddgrug = Mold *U.K.* 53°9N 3°8W **12 D4**
Yreka *U.S.A.* 41°44N 122°38W **76 F2**
Ystad *Sweden* 55°26N 13°50E **9 J15**
Ystradgynlais *U.K.* 51°47N 3°46W **13 F4**
Ysyk-Köl = Balykchy
  Kyrgyzstan 42°26N 76°12E **30 C4**
Ysyk-Köl *Kyrgyzstan* 42°25N 77°15E **26 E8**
Ythan → *U.K.* 57°19N 1°59W **11 D7**
Ytyk-Kyuyel *Russia* 62°30N 133°45E **27 C14**
Yu Jiang → *China* 23°22N 110°3E **34 F7**
Yü Shan *Taiwan* 23°25N 120°52E **35 F13**
Yu Xian = Yuzhou
  China 34°10N 113°28E **32 G7**
Yu Xian *Hebei, China* 39°50N 114°35E **32 E8**
Yu Xian *Shanxi, China* 38°5N 113°20E **32 E7**
Yuan Jiang = Hong →
  Asia 20°16N 106°34E **38 B5**
Yuan Jiang → *Hunan,*
  China 28°55N 111°50E **35 C8**
Yuan Jiang → *Yunnan,*
  China 22°20N 103°59E **34 F4**
Yuan'an *China* 31°3N 111°34E **35 B8**
Yuanjiang *Hunan, China* 28°47N 112°21E **35 C9**
Yuanjiang *Yunnan, China* 23°32N 102°0E **34 F4**
Yüanli *Taiwan* 24°27N 120°39E **35 E13**
Yüanlin *Taiwan* 23°58N 120°30E **35 F13**
Yuanling *China* 28°29N 110°22E **35 C8**
Yuanmou *China* 25°42N 101°53E **34 E3**
Yuanping *China* 38°42N 112°46E **32 E7**
Yuanqu *China* 35°18N 111°40E **32 G6**
Yuanyang *Henan, China* 35°3N 113°58E **32 G7**
Yuanyang *Yunnan, China* 23°10N 102°43E **34 F4**
Yuba → *U.S.A.* 39°8N 121°36W **78 F5**
Yuba City *U.S.A.* 39°8N 121°37W **78 F5**
Yübetsu *Japan* 43°4N 141°59E **28 C10**
Yūbari *Japan* 43°13N 141°50E **28 C10**
Yūbetsu *Japan* 44°13N 143°50E **28 B11**
Yucatán □ *Mexico* 20°50N 89°0W **87 C7**
Yucatán, Canal de
  Caribbean 22°0N 86°30W **88 B2**
Yucatán, Península de
  Mexico 19°30N 89°0W **66 H11**
Yucatan Basin *Cent. Amer.* 19°0N 86°0W **87 D7**
Yucatan Channel = Yucatán,
  Canal de *Caribbean* 22°0N 86°30W **88 B2**
Yucca *U.S.A.* 34°52N 114°9W **79 L12**

Yucca Valley *U.S.A.* 34°8N 116°27W **79 L10**
Yucheng *China* 36°55N 116°32E **32 F9**
Yuci = Jinzhong *China* 37°42N 112°46E **32 F7**
Yudu *China* 25°59N 115°30E **35 E10**
Yuechi *China* 30°34N 106°25E **34 B6**
Yuen Long *China* 22°26N 114°2E **31 a**
Yuendumu *Australia* 22°16S 131°49E **60 D5**
Yuendumu ✪ *Australia* 22°21S 131°40E **60 D5**
Yueqing *China* 28°9N 120°59E **35 C13**
Yueqing Wan *China* 28°5N 121°20E **35 C13**
Yuexi *Anhui, China* 30°50N 116°20E **35 B11**
Yuexi *Sichuan, China* 28°37N 102°26E **34 C4**
Yueyang *China* 29°21N 113°5E **35 C9**
Yugan *China* 28°43N 116°37E **35 C11**
Yugorenok *Russia* 59°47N 137°40E **27 D14**
Yugyd Va △ *Russia* 62°25N 58°45E **26 C6**
Yuhuan *China* 28°9N 121°12E **35 C13**
Yühuan Dao *China* 28°5N 121°15E **35 C13**
Yujiang *China* 28°10N 116°43E **35 C11**
Yukon *U.S.A.* 35°31N 97°45W **84 D6**
Yukon → *U.S.A.* 62°32N 163°54W **74 C7**
Yukon Flats *U.S.A.* 66°40N 145°45W **74 B10**
Yukon Territory □
  Canada 63°0N 135°0W **68 E5**
Yukta *Russia* 63°26N 105°42E **27 C11**
Yukuhashi *Japan* 33°44N 130°59E **29 H5**
Yulara *Australia* 25°10S 130°55E **61 E5**
Yule → *Australia* 20°41S 118°17E **60 D2**
Yuleba *Australia* 26°37S 149°24E **63 D4**
Yüli *Taiwan* 23°20N 121°18E **35 F13**
Yulin *Guangxi Zhuangzu,*
  China 22°40N 110°8E **35 F8**
Yulin *Hainan, China* 18°10N 109°31E **38 C7**
Yulin *Shaanxi, China* 38°20N 109°30E **32 E5**
Yulong Xueshan *China* 27°6N 100°10E **34 D3**
Yuma *Ariz., U.S.A.* 32°43N 114°37W **79 N12**
Yuma *Colo., U.S.A.* 40°8N 102°43W **76 F12**
Yuma, B. de *Dom. Rep.* 18°20N 68°35W **89 C6**
Yumen *China* 39°50N 97°30E **30 D8**
Yun Gui Gaoyuan *China* 26°0N 104°0E **34 D5**
Yun Ling Shan *China* 27°0N 99°20E **34 D2**
Yun Xian *Hubei, China* 32°50N 110°46E **32 H6**
Yun Xian *Yunnan, China* 24°27N 100°8E **34 E3**
Yuna *Australia* 28°20S 115°0E **61 E2**
Yunan *China* 23°12N 111°30E **35 F8**
Yuncheng *Henan, China* 35°36N 115°57E **32 G8**
Yuncheng *Shanxi, China* 35°2N 111°0E **32 G6**
Yunfu *China* 22°5N 112°5E **35 F9**
Yungang Shiku *China* 40°6N 113°7E **32 D7**
Yungas *Bolivia* 17°0S 66°0W **92 G5**
Yungay *Chile* 37°10S 72°5W **94 D1**
Yunkai Dashan *China* 22°0N 111°0E **35 F8**
Yunkanjini ✪ *Australia* 22°33S 131°0E **60 D5**
Yunling Shan *China* 28°30N 98°50E **30 F8**
Yunlong *China* 25°57N 99°13E **34 E2**
Yunmeng *China* 31°2N 113°43E **35 B9**
Yunnan □ *China* 25°0N 102°0E **34 E4**
Yunta *Australia* 32°34S 139°36E **63 E2**
Yunxi *China* 33°0N 110°22E **32 H6**
Yunxiao *China* 23°59N 117°18E **35 F11**
Yunyang *Chongqing,*
  China 31°2N 108°51E **34 B7**
Yunyang *Henan, China* 33°26N 112°42E **35 A9**
Yupanqui Basin *Pac. Oc.* 19°0S 101°0W **65 J17**
Yuping *China* 27°13N 107°53E **34 D6**
Yuqing *China* 27°13N 107°53E **34 D6**
Yuraygir △ *Australia* 29°45S 153°15E **63 D5**
Yurga *Russia* 55°42N 84°51E **26 D9**
Yurihonjō *Japan* 39°23N 140°3E **28 E10**
Yurimaguas *Peru* 5°55S 76°7W **92 E3**
Yurubí △ *Venezuela* 10°26N 68°42W **89 D6**
Yuscarán *Honduras* 13°58N 86°45W **88 D2**
Yushan *China* 28°42N 118°10E **35 C12**
Yushanzhen *China* 29°28N 108°22E **34 C7**
Yushe *China* 37°4N 112°58E **32 F7**
Yushu *Jilin, China* 44°43N 126°38E **33 B14**
Yushu *Qinghai, China* 33°5N 96°55E **30 E8**
Yutai *China* 35°0N 116°45E **32 G9**
Yutian *Hebei, China* 39°53N 117°45E **33 E9**
Yutian *Sinkiang-Uigur,*
  China 36°52N 81°42E **30 D5**
Yuxarı Qarabağ = Nagorno-
  Karabakh □ *Azerbaijan* 39°55N 46°45E **46 B5**
Yuxi *China* 24°30N 102°35E **34 E4**
Yuyao *China* 30°3N 121°10E **35 B13**
Yuzawa *Japan* 39°10N 140°30E **28 E10**
Yuzhno-Kurilsk *Russia* 44°1N 145°51E **27 E15**
Yuzhno-Sakhalinsk
  Russia 46°58N 142°45E **31 B17**
Yuzhnyy □ *Russia* 44°0N 40°0E **26 E5**
Yuzhou *China* 34°10N 113°28E **32 G7**
Yvetot *France* 49°37N 0°44E **20 B4**

Z

Zāb al Kabīr → *Iraq* 36°1N 43°24E **46 B4**
Zāb aş Şaghīr → *Iraq* 35°17N 43°29E **46 C4**
Zabaykalsk *Russia* 49°40N 117°25E **27 E12**
Zabaykalsky △ *Russia* 53°40N 109°0E **27 D11**
Zābol *Iran* 31°0N 61°32E **47 D9**
Zābol □ *Afghan.* 32°0N 67°0E **40 D5**
Zābolī *Iran* 27°10N 61°35E **47 E9**
Zabrze *Poland* 50°18N 18°50E **17 C10**
Zacapa *Guatemala* 14°59N 89°31W **88 D2**
Zacapu *Mexico* 19°50N 101°43W **86 D4**
Zacatecas *Mexico* 22°47N 102°35W **86 C4**
Zacatecas □ *Mexico* 23°0N 103°0W **86 C4**
Zacatecoluca *El Salv.* 13°29N 88°51W **88 D2**
Zachary *U.S.A.* 30°39N 91°9W **84 F9**
Zacoalco de Torres
  Mexico 20°14N 103°35W **86 C4**
Zacualtipán *Mexico* 20°39N 98°36W **87 C5**
Zadar *Croatia* 44°8N 15°14E **16 F8**
Zadetkyi Kyun *Burma* 10°0N 98°25E **39 H2**
Zafarqand *Iran* 33°11N 52°29E **47 C7**
Zafra *Spain* 38°26N 6°30W **21 C2**
Żagań *Poland* 51°39N 15°22E **16 C8**
Zagaoua *Chad* 15°30N 22°24E **53 E10**
Zagazig *Egypt* 30°40N 31°30E **53 B12**
Zāgheh *Iran* 33°30N 48°42E **47 C6**

Zagreb *Croatia* 45°50N 15°58E **16 F9**
Zāgros, Kūhhā-ye *Iran* 33°45N 48°5E **47 C6**
Zagros Mts. = Zāgros, Kūhhā-ye
  Iran 33°45N 48°5E **47 C6**
Zāhedān *Fārs, Iran* 28°46N 53°52E **47 D7**
Zāhedān *Sīstān va Balūchestān,*
  Iran 29°30N 60°50E **47 D9**
Zahirabad *India* 17°43N 77°37E **44 F3**
Zahlah *Lebanon* 33°52N 35°50E **48 B4**
Zahrān al Janub
  Si. Arabia 17°40N 43°30E **49 D3**
Zaïre = Congo → *Africa* 6°4S 12°24E **54 F2**
Zaječar *Serbia* 43°53N 22°18E **23 C10**
Zaka *Zimbabwe* 20°20S 31°29E **57 B5**
Zakopane *Poland* 49°18N 19°57E **17 D10**
Zákynthos *Greece* 37°47N 20°54E **23 F9**
Zakynthos = Zakynthos
  Greece 37°47N 20°54E **23 F9**
Zalaegerszeg *Hungary* 46°53N 16°47E **17 E9**
Zalantun *China* 48°0N 122°43E **31 B13**
Zalari *Russia* 53°33N 102°30E **27 D11**
Zalău *Romania* 47°12N 23°3E **17 E12**
Zaleshchiki = Zalishchyky
  Ukraine 48°45N 25°45E **17 D13**
Zalingei *Sudan* 12°51N 23°29E **53 F10**
Zalishchyky *Ukraine* 48°45N 25°45E **17 D13**
Zama L. *Canada* 58°45N 119°5W **70 B5**
Zambeze = Zambezi →
  Africa 18°35S 36°20E **55 H7**
Zambezi = Zambeze →
  Africa 18°35S 36°20E **55 H7**
Zambezi *Zambia* 13°30S 23°15E **55 G4**
Zambezi □ *Namibia* 18°0S 23°30E **56 B3**
Zambia ■ *Africa* 15°0S 28°0E **55 H5**
Zamboanga *Phil.* 6°59N 122°3E **37 C6**
Zamora *Mexico* 19°59N 102°16W **86 D4**
Zamora *Spain* 41°30N 5°45W **21 B3**
Zamość *Poland* 50°43N 23°15E **17 C12**
Zamtang *China* 32°26N 101°6E **34 A3**
Zanda *China* 31°32N 79°50E **30 E4**
Zandvoort *Neths.* 52°22N 4°32E **15 B4**
Zanesville *U.S.A.* 39°56N 82°1W **82 G2**
Zangābād *Iran* 38°26N 46°44E **46 B5**
Zanjān *Iran* 36°40N 48°35E **47 B6**
Zanjān □ *Iran* 37°20N 49°30E **47 B6**
Zanjān → *Iran* 37°8N 47°47E **47 B6**
Zante = Zakynthos
  Greece 37°47N 20°54E **23 F9**
Zanthus *Australia* 31°2S 123°34E **61 F3**
Zanzibar *Tanzania* 6°12S 39°12E **54 F7**
Zaouiet El-Kala = Bordj Omar
  Driss *Algeria* 28°10N 6°40E **52 C7**
Zaouiet Reggâne *Algeria* 26°32N 0°3E **52 C6**
Zaoyang *China* 32°10N 112°45E **35 A9**
Zaozhuang *China* 34°50N 117°35E **33 G9**
Zap Suyu = Zāb al Kabīr →
  Iraq 36°1N 43°24E **46 B4**
Zapadnaya Dvina = Daugava →
  Latvia 57°4N 24°3E **9 H21**
Zapala *Argentina* 39°0S 70°5W **96 D2**
Zapaleri, Cerro *Bolivia* 22°49S 67°11W **94 A2**
Zapata *U.S.A.* 26°55N 99°16W **84 H5**
Zapolyarnyy *Russia* 69°26N 30°51E **8 B24**
Zapopan *Mexico* 20°43N 103°24W **86 C4**
Zaporizhzhya *Ukraine* 47°50N 35°10E **19 E6**
Zaporozhye = Zaporizhzhya
  Ukraine 47°50N 35°10E **19 E6**
Zara *Turkey* 39°58N 37°43E **46 B3**
Zaragoza *Coahuila,*
  Mexico 28°29N 100°55W **86 B4**
Zaragoza *Nuevo León,*
  Mexico 23°58N 99°46W **87 C5**
Zaragoza *Spain* 41°39N 0°53W **21 B5**
Zarand *Kermān, Iran* 30°46N 56°34E **47 D8**
Zarand *Markazī, Iran* 35°18N 50°25E **47 C6**
Zaranj *Afghan.* 30°55N 61°55E **40 D2**
Zarasai *Lithuania* 55°40N 26°20E **9 J22**
Zárate *Argentina* 34°7S 59°0W **94 C4**
Zard, Kūh-e *Iran* 32°22N 50°4E **47 C6**
Zāreh *Iran* 35°7N 49°9E **47 C6**
Zaria *Nigeria* 11°0N 7°40E **52 F7**
Zarneh *Iran* 33°55N 46°10E **46 C5**
Zarqā', Nahr az → *Jordan* 32°10N 35°37E **48 C4**
Zarrīn *Iran* 32°46N 54°37E **47 C7**
Zaruma *Ecuador* 3°40S 79°38W **92 D3**
Żary *Poland* 51°37N 15°10E **16 C8**
Zarzis *Tunisia* 33°31N 11°2E **53 B8**
Zaskar → *India* 34°13N 77°20E **43 B7**
Zaskar Mts. = Zanskar →
  India 33°15N 77°30E **43 C7**
Zastron *S. Africa* 30°18S 27°7E **56 E4**
Zavāreh *Iran* 33°29N 52°28E **47 C7**
Zave *Zimbabwe* 17°6S 30°1E **57 A5**
Zavitinsk *Russia* 50°10N 129°20E **27 D13**
Zavodovski I. *Antarctica* 56°0S 27°45W **5 B1**
Zawiercie *Poland* 50°30N 19°24E **17 C10**
Zāwiyat al Bayḍā = Al Bayḍā
  Libya 32°50N 21°44E **53 B10**
Zāwiyah *Iraq* 33°33N 44°13E **46 C5**
Zāyandeh → *Iran* 32°35N 52°0E **47 C7**
Zaysan *Kazakhstan* 47°28N 84°52E **26 E9**
Zaysan Köli *Kazakhstan* 48°0N 83°0E **26 E9**
Zayü *China* 28°48N 97°27E **41 E14**
Zbarazh *Ukraine* 49°43N 25°44E **17 D13**
Zdolbuniv *Ukraine* 50°30N 25°15E **17 C14**
Zduńska Wola *Poland* 51°37N 18°59E **17 C10**
Zeballos *Canada* 49°59N 126°50W **70 D3**
Zebediela *S. Africa* 24°20S 29°17E **57 B4**
Zeebrugge *Belgium* 51°19N 3°12E **15 C3**
Zeehan *Australia* 41°52S 145°25E **63 G4**
Zeeland □ *Neths.* 51°30N 3°50E **15 C3**
Zeerust *S. Africa* 25°31S 26°4E **56 D4**
Zefat *Israel* 32°58N 35°29E **48 C4**
Zehak *Iran* 30°31N 61°42E **47 D9**
Zeil, Mt. *Australia* 23°30S 132°23E **60 D5**
Zeila = Saylac *Somalia* 11°21N 43°30E **49 E3**
Zeist *Neths.* 52°5N 5°15E **15 B5**
Zeitz *Germany* 51°2N 12°7E **16 C7**

Zelenogorsk *Russia* 60°12N 29°43E **8 F23**
Zelenograd *Russia* 56°1N 37°12E **18 C6**
Zelienople *U.S.A.* 40°48N 80°8W **82 F4**
Zempoala *Mexico* 19°27N 96°23W **87 D5**
Zemun *Serbia* 44°51N 20°25E **23 B9**
Zengcheng *China* 23°13N 113°52E **35 F9**
Zenica *Bos.-H.* 44°10N 17°57E **23 B7**
Žepče *Bos.-H.* 44°28N 18°2E **23 B8**
Zevenaar *Neths.* 51°56N 6°5E **15 C6**
Zeya *Russia* 53°48N 127°14E **27 D13**
Zeya → *Russia* 51°42N 128°53E **27 D13**
Zêzere → *Portugal* 39°28N 8°20W **21 C1**
Zghartā *Lebanon* 34°21N 35°53E **48 A4**
Zgorzelec *Poland* 51°10N 15°0E **16 C8**
Zhabinka *Belarus* 52°13N 24°2E **17 B13**
Zhailma *Kazakhstan* 51°37N 61°33E **26 D7**
Zhambyl = Taraz
  Kazakhstan 42°54N 71°22E **30 C3**
Zhangaözen *Kazakhstan* 43°18N 52°48E **19 F9**
Zhangbei *China* 41°10N 114°45E **32 D8**
Zhangguangcai Ling
  China 45°0N 129°0E **33 B15**
Zhangjiabian *China* 22°33N 113°28E **31 a**
Zhangjiagang *China* 31°55N 120°30E **35 B13**
Zhangjiajie *China* 29°11N 110°30E **35 C8**
Zhangjiakou *China* 40°48N 114°55E **32 D8**
Zhangping *China* 25°17N 117°23E **35 E11**
Zhangpu *China* 24°8N 117°35E **35 E11**
Zhangshu *China* 28°4N 115°29E **35 C10**
Zhangye *China* 38°50N 100°23E **30 D9**
Zhangzhou *China* 24°30N 117°35E **35 E11**
Zhanhua *China* 37°40N 118°8E **33 F10**
Zhanjiang *China* 21°15N 110°20E **35 G8**
Zhannetty, Ostrov
  Russia 76°43N 158°0E **27 B16**
Zhanyi *China* 25°38N 103°48E **34 E4**
Zhanyu *China* 44°30N 122°30E **33 B12**
Zhao Xian *China* 37°43N 114°45E **32 F8**
Zhao'an *China* 23°41N 117°10E **35 F11**
Zhaocheng *China* 36°22N 111°38E **32 F6**
Zhaodong *China* 46°4N 125°59E **31 B13**
Zhaojue *China* 28°1N 102°49E **34 C4**
Zhaoping *China* 24°11N 110°48E **35 E8**
Zhaoqing *China* 23°0N 112°20E **35 F9**
Zhaotong *China* 27°20N 103°44E **34 D4**
Zhaoyuan *Heilongjiang,*
  China 45°27N 125°0E **33 B13**
Zhaoyuan *Shandong,*
  China 37°20N 120°23E **33 F11**
Zhari Namco *China* 31°6N 85°36E **30 E6**
Zhashkiv *Ukraine* 49°15N 30°5E **17 D16**
Zhashui *China* 33°40N 109°8E **32 H5**
Zhayylma *Kazakhstan* 51°37N 61°33E **26 D7**
Zhayyq → *Kazakhstan* 47°0N 51°48E **19 E9**
Zhdanov = Mariupol
  Ukraine 47°5N 37°31E **19 E6**
Zhecheng *China* 34°7N 115°20E **32 G8**
Zhegao *China* 31°46N 117°45E **35 B11**
Zhejiang □ *China* 29°0N 120°0E **35 C13**
Zheleznodorozhnyy
  Russia 62°35N 50°55E **18 B9**
Zheleznogorsk-Ilimskiy
  Russia 56°34N 104°8E **27 D11**
Zhen'an *China* 33°27N 109°9E **34 A7**
Zhenba *China* 32°34N 107°58E **34 A6**
Zhenfeng *China* 25°22N 105°40E **34 E5**
Zheng'an *China* 28°32N 107°27E **34 C6**
Zhengding *China* 38°8N 114°32E **32 E8**
Zhenghe *China* 27°20N 118°50E **35 D12**
Zhengyang *China* 32°37N 114°22E **35 A10**
Zhengyangguan *China* 32°30N 116°29E **35 A11**
Zhengzhou *China* 34°45N 113°34E **32 G7**
Zhenhai *China* 29°59N 121°42E **35 C13**
Zhenjiang *China* 32°11N 119°2E **35 A12**
Zhenkang *China* 23°58N 99°0E **34 F2**
Zhenlai *China* 45°50N 123°5E **33 B12**
Zhenning *China* 26°4N 105°45E **34 D5**
Zhenping *Henan, China* 33°10N 112°16E **32 H7**
Zhenping *Shaanxi, China* 31°50N 109°13E **34 A7**
Zhenxiong *China* 27°27N 104°50E **34 D5**
Zhenyuan *Gansu, China* 35°35N 107°30E **32 G4**
Zhenyuan *Guizhou, China* 27°4N 108°21E **34 D6**
Zhenyuan *Yunnan, China* 23°51N 100°58E **34 E3**
Zherong *China* 27°15N 119°52E **35 D12**
Zhetiqara *Kazakhstan* 52°11N 61°12E **26 D7**
Zhezqazghan *Kazakhstan* 47°44N 67°40E **26 E7**
Zhicheng *China* 30°25N 111°27E **35 B8**
Zhidan *China* 36°48N 108°48E **32 F5**
Zhigansk *Russia* 66°48N 123°27E **27 C13**
Zhijiang *Hubei, China* 30°28N 111°45E **35 B8**
Zhijiang *Hunan, China* 27°27N 109°42E **34 D7**
Zhijin *China* 26°37N 105°45E **34 D5**
Zhilinda *Russia* 70°0N 114°20E **27 C12**
Zhitomir = Zhytomyr
  Ukraine 50°20N 28°40E **17 C15**
Zhlobin *Belarus* 52°55N 30°0E **17 B16**
Zhmerynka *Ukraine* 49°2N 28°2E **17 D15**
Zhob *Pakistan* 31°20N 69°31E **42 D3**
Zhob → *Pakistan* 32°4N 69°50E **42 C3**
Zhodzina *Belarus* 54°5N 28°17E **17 A15**
Zhokhova, Ostrov
  Russia 76°4N 152°0E **27 B16**
Zhongba *China* 29°39N 84°10E **30 F5**
Zhongdong *China* 24°48N 107°47E **34 F6**
Zhongdu *China* 24°0N 109°40E **34 E7**
Zhongjian Dao = Triton I.
  S. China Sea 15°47N 111°12E **36 A4**
Zhongjiang *China* 30°53N 104°45E **34 B5**
Zhongning *China* 37°18N 105°40E **32 F3**
Zhongsha Qundao = Macclesfield
  Bank *S. China Sea* 16°0N 114°30E **36 A4**
Zhongshan *Antarctica* 69°0S 39°50E **5 C6**
Zhongshan *Guangdong,*
  China 22°26N 113°20E **35 F9**
Zhongshan *Guangxi Zhuangzu,*
  China 24°29N 111°18E **35 E8**
Zhongshankong *China* 22°35N 113°29E **31 a**
Zhongtiao Shan *China* 35°0N 111°10E **32 G6**

Zhongwei *China* 37°30N 105°12E **32 F3**
Zhongxian *China* 30°18N 107°58E **34 B6**
Zhongxiang *China* 31°12N 112°34E **35 B9**
Zhongyang *China* 37°20N 111°11E **32 F6**
Zhosaly *Kazakhstan* 45°29N 64°4E **26 E7**
Zhoucun *China* 36°47N 117°48E **33 F9**
Zhoukou *China* 33°38N 114°38E **32 H8**
Zhoukoudian *China* 39°41N 115°56E **32 E8**
Zhouning *China* 27°12N 119°20E **35 D12**
Zhoushan *China* 30°1N 122°6E **35 B14**
Zhoushan Dao *China* 30°5N 122°10E **35 B14**
Zhouzhi *China* 34°10N 108°12E **32 G5**
Zhovkva *Ukraine* 50°4N 23°58E **17 C12**
Zhu Jiang → *China* 22°45N 113°37E **35 F9**
Zhuanghe *China* 39°40N 123°0E **33 E13**
Zhucheng *China* 36°0N 119°27E **33 G10**
Zhugqu *China* 33°40N 104°30E **34 A5**
Zhuji *China* 29°40N 120°10E **35 C13**
Zhujiang Kou *China* 22°13N 113°45E **31 a**
Zhumadian *China* 32°59N 114°2E **35 A10**
Zhuo Xian = Zhuozhou
  China 39°28N 115°58E **32 E8**
Zhuolu *China* 40°20N 115°12E **32 D8**
Zhuozhou *China* 39°28N 115°58E **32 E8**
Zhuozi *China* 41°0N 112°25E **32 D7**
Zhushan *China* 32°15N 110°13E **35 A8**
Zhuxi *China* 32°25N 109°40E **34 A7**
Zhuzhou *China* 27°49N 113°12E **35 D9**
Zhytomyr *Ukraine* 50°20N 28°40E **17 C15**
Zhytomyr □ *Ukraine* 50°50N 28°10E **17 C15**
Zi Shui → *China* 28°40N 112°40E **35 C9**
Ziarat *Pakistan* 30°25N 67°49E **42 D2**
Zibo *China* 36°47N 118°3E **33 F10**
Zichang *China* 37°18N 109°40E **32 F5**
Zidi = Wandhari *Pakistan* 27°20N 66°25E **42 F2**
Zielona Góra *Poland* 51°57N 15°31E **16 C8**
Zierikzee *Neths.* 51°40N 3°55E **15 C3**
Zigong *China* 29°15N 104°48E **34 C5**
Ziguéy *Chad* 14°43N 15°50E **53 F9**
Ziguinchor *Senegal* 12°35N 16°20W **52 F2**
Zihuatanejo *Mexico* 17°39N 101°33W **86 D4**
Zijin *China* 23°33N 115°8E **35 F10**
Žilina *Slovak Rep.* 49°12N 18°42E **17 D10**
Zillah *Libya* 28°30N 17°33E **53 C9**
Zima *Russia* 54°0N 102°5E **27 D11**
Zimapán *Mexico* 20°45N 99°21W **87 C5**
Zimbabwe ■ *Africa* 19°0S 30°0E **55 H6**
Zimnicea *Romania* 43°40N 25°22E **17 G13**
Zinave △ *Mozam.* 21°35S 33°40E **57 B5**
Zinder *Niger* 13°48N 9°0E **52 F7**
Zion □ *U.S.A.* 37°15N 113°5W **77 H7**
Zirreh, Gowd-e *Afghan.* 29°45N 62°0E **40 E3**
Zitácuaro *Mexico* 19°24N 100°22W **86 D4**
Zitong *China* 31°37N 105°10E **34 B5**
Ziway, L. *Ethiopia* 8°0N 38°50E **47 F2**
Zixi *China* 27°45N 117°4E **35 D11**
Zixing *China* 25°59N 113°21E **35 D9**
Ziyang *Shaanxi, China* 32°30N 108°31E **34 A6**
Ziyang *Sichuan, China* 30°6N 104°49E **34 B5**
Ziyun *China* 25°45N 106°5E **34 E5**
Zizhong *China* 29°48N 104°47E **34 C5**
Zlatograd *Bulgaria* 41°22N 25°7E **23 D11**
Zlatoust *Russia* 55°10N 59°40E **18 C6**
Zlín *Czech Rep.* 49°14N 17°40E **17 D9**
Zmeinogorsk *Kazakhstan* 51°10N 82°13E **26 D9**
Znojmo *Czech Rep.* 48°50N 16°2E **16 D9**
Zobeyrī *Iran* 34°10N 46°40E **46 C5**
Zoetermeer *Neths.* 52°3N 4°30E **15 B4**
Zohreh → *Iran* 30°16N 51°15E **47 D6**
Zolochiv *Ukraine* 49°45N 24°51E **17 D13**
Zomba *Malawi* 15°22S 35°19E **55 H7**
Zongo
  Dem. Rep. of the Congo 4°20N 18°35E **54 D3**
Zonguldak *Turkey* 41°28N 31°50E **19 F5**
Zorritos *Peru* 3°43S 80°40W **92 D2**
Zou Xiang *China* 35°30N 116°58E **32 G9**
Zouar *Chad* 20°30N 16°32E **53 D8**
Zouérate = Zouîrât
  Mauritania 22°44N 12°21W **52 D3**
Zouîrât *Mauritania* 22°44N 12°21W **52 D3**
Zoutkamp *Neths.* 53°20N 6°18E **15 A6**
Zov Tigra △ *Russia* 43°25N 134°10E **28 C7**
Zrenjanin *Serbia* 45°22N 20°23E **23 B9**
Zufar *Oman* 17°40N 54°0E **49 D5**
Zug *Switz.* 47°10N 8°31E **20 C8**
Zugspitze *Germany* 47°25N 10°59E **16 E6**
Zuid-Holland □ *Neths.* 52°0N 4°35E **15 C4**
Zuidbeveland *Neths.* 51°30N 3°50E **15 C3**
Zuidhorn *Neths.* 53°15N 6°23E **15 A6**
Zula *Eritrea* 15°17N 39°40E **49 D2**
Zumbo *Mozam.* 15°35S 30°26E **55 H6**
Zumpango *Mexico* 19°48N 99°6W **87 D5**
Zunhua *China* 40°18N 117°58E **33 D9**
Zuni Pueblo *U.S.A.* 35°4N 108°51W **77 J9**
Zunyi *China* 27°42N 106°53E **34 D6**
Zuo Jiang → *China* 22°50N 108°6E **34 F7**
Zuoquan *China* 37°1N 113°27E **32 F7**
Zuozhou *China* 22°42N 107°27E **34 F6**
Zurbāţīyah *Iraq* 33°9N 46°3E **46 C5**
Zürich *Switz.* 47°22N 8°32E **20 C8**
Zutphen *Neths.* 52°9N 6°12E **15 B6**
Zuurberg △ *S. Africa* 33°15S 25°32E **56 D4**
Zuwārah *Libya* 32°58N 12°1E **53 B8**
Zūzan *Iran* 34°22N 59°53E **47 C8**
Zvishavane *Zimbabwe* 20°17S 30°2E **55 H6**
Zvolen *Slovak Rep.* 48°33N 19°10E **17 D10**
Zwettl *Austria* 48°35N 15°9E **16 D8**
Zwickau *Germany* 50°44N 12°30E **16 C7**
Zwolle *U.S.A.* 31°38N 93°39W **84 F8**
Żyrardów *Poland* 52°3N 20°28E **17 B11**
Żyryan *Kazakhstan* 49°43N 84°20E **26 E9**
Zyryanka *Russia* 65°45N 150°51E **27 C16**
Zyryanovsk = Zyryan
  Kazakhstan 49°43N 84°20E **26 E9**
Żywiec *Poland* 49°42N 19°10E **17 D10**